The Rāmāyaṇa of Vālmīki

The Rāmāyaṇa of Vālmīki

AN EPIC OF ANCIENT INDIA

Volume VI *Yuddhakāṇḍa*

Translation and Annotation by
Robert P. Goldman, Sally J. Sutherland Goldman, and
Barend A. van Nooten

Introduction by
Robert P. Goldman and Sally J. Sutherland Goldman

PRINCETON UNIVERSITY PRESS • PRINCETON AND OXFORD

In Memory of
Professor Murray Barnson Emeneau
1904–2005
Mentor, Colleague, and Friend

Published by Princeton University Press, 41 William Street,
Princeton, New Jersey 08540

In the United Kingdom: Princeton University Press, 6 Oxford Street, Woodstock,
Oxfordshire OX20 1TW

Library of Congress Cataloging-in-Publication Data
Vālmīki.
[Rāmāyaṇa. Yuddhakanda. English]
The Rāmāyana of Vālmīki : an epic of ancient India; volume VI, Yuddhakāṇḍa / translation and annotation by Robert P. Goldman, Sally J. Sutherland Goldman, and Barend A. van Nooten ; introduction by Robert P. Goldman and Sally J. Sutherland Goldman.
p. cm.—(Princeton Library of Asian translations)
Includes bibliographical references and index.
ISBN 978-0-691-17398-6 (softcover : alk. paper) 1. Vālmīki. Rāmāyaṇa. Yuddhakāṇḍa. I. Goldman, Robert P., 1942– II. Sutherland Goldman, Sally J. III. Nooten, Barend A. van, 1932– IV. Title.
BL1139.242.Y84E5 2009
294.5'92204521—dc22 2008032292

British Library Cataloging-in-Publication Data is available

This book has been composed in Baskerville
Printed on acid-free paper. ∞
press.princeton.edu

Printed in the United States of America

10 9 8 7 6 5 4 3 2 1

Frontispiece: The final battle between Rāma and Rāvaṇa. From the "Jagat Singh Rāmāyaṇa," Sahib Din 1653. British Library Add. 15297-166. By permission of the British Library.

The Rāmāyaṇa of Vālmīki: An Epic of Ancient India

Robert P. Goldman, *General Editor*

Sally J. Sutherland Goldman, *Associate Editor*

Kristi L. Wiley, *Editorial Assistant*

Translators: Robert P. Goldman, Rosalind Lefeber, Sheldon I. Pollock, Sally J. Sutherland Goldman, Barend A. van Nooten

PRINCETON LIBRARY OF ASIAN TRANSLATIONS

adya karma kariṣyāmi yal lokāḥ sacarācarāḥ
sadevāḥ kathayiṣyanti yāvad bhūmir dhariṣyati

Today, I shall perform such a feat that all the worlds, with their moving and fixed contents and including the gods themselves, will talk about as long as the earth shall endure.
—*Rām* 6.88.53

ātmānaṃ mānuṣaṃ manye rāmaṃ daśarathātmajam
yo 'haṃ yasya yataś cāhaṃ bhagavāṃs tad bravītu me

I think of myself only as a man, Rāma, the son of Daśaratha. May the Blessed Lord please tell me who I really am, to whom I belong, and why I am here.
—*Rām* 6.105.10

Contents

List of Abbreviations

Manuscripts, Commentaries, and Editions Used in Volume VI, Following the Conventions Established in the Critical Edition of the Yuddhakāṇḍa (see pp. ix–xi)

I. MANUSCRIPTS

Northern Manuscripts (N) forming the Northern Recension (NR) (18 MSS, including 7 Devanāgarī)

NW Northwestern Manuscripts
- i. Śāradā
  - Ś1 undated
  - Ś2 A.D. 1885

NE Northeastern Manuscripts
- i. Ñ Nepālī
  - Ñ1 A.D. 1020
  - Ñ2 A.D. 1675
- ii. V Maithilī
  - V1 A.D. 1748
  - V2 A.D. 1841
  - V3 undated
- iii. B Bengali
  - B1 A.D. 1671
  - B2 A.D. 1798
  - B3 undated
  - B4 undated
- iv. D Devanāgarī manuscripts allied with N, including Western (W)
  - D1 A.D. 1773 NW
  - D2 A.D. 1660 NW
  - D3 A.D. 1731 W
  - D4 A.D. 1732 W
  - D8 A.D. 1779 NW
  - D12 undated NW
  - D13 undated NE

Southern Manuscripts (S) forming the Southern Recension (SR) (16 MSS, including 6 Devanāgarī)

- i. T Telugu
  - T1 undated
  - T2 undated
  - T3 A.D. 1808
- ii. G Grantha
  - G1 A.D. 1818
  - G2 undated
  - G3 undated
- iii. Malayālam
  - M1 A.D. 1690
  - M2 A.D. 1642
  - M3 undated
  - M5 undated
- iv. D Devanāgarī manuscripts allied with S
  - D5 A.D. 1767 S
  - D6 A.D. 1776 S (Contains the commentary of Cg)
  - D7 A.D. 1776 S (Contains the commentary of Cm)
  - D9 A.D. 1686 S
  - D10 A.D. 1831 S
  - D11 A.D. 1715 S (Contains the commentary of Ct)

II. COMMENTARIES

(Note: Spelling follows the conventions established by the critical edition; see vol. 7, pp. 655–56.)

Cg	the commentary called *Bhūṣaṇa* of Govindarāja
Ck	the commentary called the *Amṛtakataka* of Mādhava Yogīndra
Cl	the commentary called *Manoharā* of Lokanātha Cakravartī
Cm	the commentary called *Tattvadīpikā* of Maheśvaratīrtha
Cnā	the commentary of Sarvajña Nārāyaṇa (as cited by Lokanātha Cakravartī)
Cr	the commentary called *Śiromaṇi* of Vaṃśīdhara (Bansidhara) Śivasahāya*
Crā	the commentary called *Ṭīkā* of Rāmānuja*
Cs	the commentary of Satyatīrtha
Ct	the commentary called *Tilaka* of Nāgeśa (Nāgoji) Bhaṭṭa, composed in the name of Rāmavarmā
Ctr	the commentary called *Dharmākūtam* of Tryambaka Yajvan
Ctś	the commentary called *Taniślokī* of Ātreya Ahobala
Cv	the commentary called *Vivekatilaka* of Varadarāja Uḍāli (Uḍāri)

III. EDITIONS

Gita Press	*Śrīmad Vālmīki-Rāmāyaṇa*. (1969). 3 vols. Gorakhpur: Gita Press.
Gorresio	*Ramayana, poema indiano di Valmici*. (1843–1867). Paris: Stamperia Reale. Edited by Gaspare Gorresio.
GPP	Gujarati Printing Press (also called the vulgate). *Rāmāyan of Vālmīki*. (1914–1920). 7 vols. Bombay: Gujarati Printing Press. With three commentaries called *Tilaka*, *Shiromani*, and *Bhooshana*. Edited by Shastri Shrinivas Katti Mudholkar.
KK	*Śrimadvālmīkirāmāyaṇam*. (1911–1913). 7 vols. Bombay: Nirṇayasāgar Press. Also called the Kumbakonam Edition. Edited by T. R. Krishnacharya and T. R. Vyasacharya.
Lahore	*Rāmāyaṇa*. (1928–1947). 7 vols. Lahore: D.A.V. College. Northwestern recension critically edited for the first time from original manuscripts by Vishva Bandhu. D.A.V. College Sanskrit Series, nos. 7, 12, 14, 17–20.
NSP	*The Rāmāyaṇa of Vālmīki*. (1930). 4th rev. ed. Bombay: Nirṇayasāgar Press. With the commentary (*Tilaka*) of Rāma. Edited by Wāsudeva Laxmaṇ Śāstrī Paṇaśīkar.

* The critical edition uses the abbreviation Cr for the commentary of Rāmānuja and gives no abbreviation for the commentary of Vaṃśīdhara (Bansidhara) Śivasahāya.

VSP	Veṅkaṭeśvara Steam Press. *Śrīmadvālmīkirāmāyaṇa*. 3 vols. Bombay: Lakṣmīveṅkaṭeśvara Mudraṇālaya, 1935. With the commentaries of Govindarāja, Rāmānuja, and Maheśvaratīrtha and the commentary known as *Taniślokī*. Edited by Gaṅgāviṣṇu Śrīkṛṣṇadāsa.

Journals

ABORI	*Annals of the Bhandarkar Oriental Research Institute*
AJP	*American Journal of Philology*
AOR	*Annals of Oriental Research (University of Madras)*
IHQ	*Indian Historical Quarterly*
JA	*Journal asiatique*
JAOS	*Journal of the American Oriental Society*
JAS	*Journal of Asian Studies*
JIP	*Journal of Indian Philosophy*
JOIB	*Journal of the Oriental Institute, Baroda*
JORM	*Journal of Oriental Research, Madras*
JRAS	*Journal of the Royal Asiatic Society*
PO	*Poona Orientalist*
ZDMG	*Zeitschrift der deutschen morgenländischen Gesellschaft*

Commonly Quoted Sanskrit Texts

AdhyāRā	*Adhyātmarāmāyaṇa*
AgniP	*Agnipurāṇa*
AitBr	*Aitareyabrāhmaṇa*
AmaK	*Amarakośa (-koṣa)*
ArthŚā	*Arthaśāstra*
AV	*Atharvavedasaṃhitā*
Avimā	*Avimāraka*
BhagGī	*Bhagavadgītā*
BhāgP	*Bhāgavatapurāṇa*
BrahmāṇḍP	*Brahmāṇḍapurāṇa*
BrahmP	*Brahmapurāṇa*
DevīBhāP	*Devībhāgavatapurāṇa*
GaruḍaP	*Garuḍapurāṇa*
HariVaṃ	*Harivaṃśa*
JaimiBr	*Jaiminīyabrāhmaṇa*
KāvyaPra	*Kāvyaprakāśa*
KumāSaṃ	*Kumārasaṃbhava*
KūrmaP	*Kūrmapurāṇa*
ManuSm	*Manusmṛti*
MatsyaP	*Matsyapurāṇa*

MBh	*Mahābhārata*
Meghdū	*Meghadūta*
Mṛcch	*Mṛcchakaṭika*
Pā	*Pāṇini's Aṣṭādhyāyī*
PadmaP	*Padmapurāṇa*
RaghuVa	*Raghuvaṃśa*
Rām	*Rāmāyaṇa*
ṚV	*Ṛgvedasaṃhitā*
SāhiDa	*Sāhityadarpaṇa*
ŚatBr	*Śatapathabrāhmaṇa*
ŚiśuVa	*Śiśupālavadha*
ŚivaP	*Śivapurāṇa*
TaiBr	*Taittirīyabrāhmaṇa*
TaiS	*Taittirīyasaṃhitā*
UttaRāC	*Uttararāmacarita*
VāmaP	*Vāmanapurāṇa*
VāyuP	*Vāyupurāṇa*
ViṣṇuP	*Viṣṇupurāṇa*
YājñaSm	*Yājñavalkyasmṛti*

Other Important Abbreviations

App.	Appendices to the critical edition of the *Rāmāyaṇa*
MW	Monier-Williams, Monier. (1899). *A Sanskrit-English Dictionary*. Oxford: Oxford University Press. Reprint 1964.
PW	Petersburg Wörterbuch: Böhtlingk, Otto, and Rudolph Roth. *Sanskrit-Wörterbuch*. St. Petersburg: Kaiserliche Akademie der Wissenschaften, 1855–1875. Reprint in seven volumes, Osnabrück/Wiesbaden, 1966.
v.l.	varia(e) lectio (nes)

Preface

THE TRANSLATION and annotation of so massive and complex a work as the *Yuddhakāṇḍa*, a work with a profound and intricate web of intertextuality throughout the religious, literary, artistic, and performative traditions of South and Southeast Asia, has required the intellectual and physical energies of many people over a very long period of time. This work could not have been carried forward without the support and assistance of several scholars and institutions whose help must be acknowledged here.

Before doing so, however, it would be appropriate, because of the collaborative nature of the work, to provide a brief history of the project and of how, and through whose efforts, it took its present shape. At the time of the first convening of the Sanskrit scholars who would form the *Rāmāyaṇa* Translation Consortium in the late 1970s, the daunting task of tackling the ponderous *Yuddhakāṇḍa* was heroically accepted by Professor Barend van Nooten of the University of California at Berkeley.

Professor van Nooten undertook this work with characteristic seriousness and energy and, working single-handedly, completed a draft translation of the text and a provisional annotation by the early 1990s. At that time the general and associate editors were deeply engrossed in work on the translation, annotation, and introduction of the *Sundarakāṇḍa*, which appeared in print in 1996. Thus the editing, revision, and expansion of Professor van Nooten's original draft did not begin in earnest until the mid-1990s. This work proceeded slowly as is invariably the case when university scholars are heavily burdened with instructional and administrative duties, which take precious time from their research and writing.

During this period Professors Robert and Sally Goldman reread the text closely, along with Professor van Nooten's draft translation, and significantly revised it in keeping with the protocols, styles, and conventions of the Consortium. They also significantly revised and expanded the original annotation, drawing on a number of additional translations, editions, and commentaries, as well as secondary sources not consulted by Professor van Nooten. In addition, they prepared the extensive Introduction to the *Yuddhakāṇḍa* that precedes the translation. The resulting volume is therefore a genuinely collaborative effort to which all three scholars have contributed significantly.

In addition to the principals mentioned above, the work has benefited from the scholarship, generosity, and assistance of a number of experts in Sanskrit and *Rāmāyaṇa* studies, and it would be highly remiss of us to fail to acknowledge them here.

First and foremost, we must express our gratitude to our friend, colleague, and guru, Dr. Ram Karan Sharma, the founder and former *kulapati* of the Rashtriya Sanskrit Sansthan. During his many protracted visits to Berkeley, Dr. Sharma ungrudgingly spent many hours with us reading over difficult passages in the text and the commentaries, and sharing with us his profound reservoir of knowledge of a vast spectrum of the Sanskrit literary and śāstraic corpora. Time and again his knowledge and insight clarified a problem that had left us utterly at a loss. We gratefully acknowledge his learned and unstinting assistance, mindful always of the vedic injunction, "*gurudevo bhava*."

We should also like to acknowledge the advice and help of Dr. V. Kutumba Sastry, Vice-Chancellor of the Rashtriya Sanskrit Sansthan, who, on a visit to Berkeley and in Delhi, helped us shed light on some problematic issues in the text. Professor Sheldon Pollock of Columbia University, one of the principal contributors to the translation project, was also unstinting in his excellent advice, while Professor Philip Lutgendorf of the University of Iowa, a great *Rāmāyaṇi* and *Hanumānbhakta*, was generous, as always, with his vast store of knowledge of variant versions of the *Rāmakathā* and especially the many tales of the monkey divinity.

Several of our Sanskrit students, past and present, have lent their labors to the production of this volume. Without their efforts the volume would never have seen the light of day. Among these we express our debt of gratitude to our Editorial Assistant, Dr. Kristi Wiley, whose meticulous scholarship, unstinting devotion of her energies, and careful reading of our drafts caught and corrected numerous errors and infelicities. Gratitude is similarly owed to Dr. Deven Patel of the University of Pennsylvania, who, as our research assistant, brought his careful and informed reading to the translation and annotation.

We also extend our thanks to a number of research assistants whose work has made the project possible. These include Geeta Pai, Siyonn Sophearith, Samir Shah, Dr. Chandan Narayan, Dr. Adheesh

Sathaye, Luther Obrock, Elisabeth Andersson Raddock, Lauren Bausch, and Robert Raddock. Special mention must be made of Michael Slouber, who, as our research assistant during the past year, meticulously read through the huge and challenging manuscript, checking for the accuracy and consistency of the textual apparatus and transliterations and making many valuable suggestions.

Support for the work has come, directly and indirectly, from a number of institutional sources. We thank the *Rāmāyaṇa* Department of the Oriental Institute of Baroda for generously making available to us copies of the transcripts of the commentaries of Mādhava Yogin and Uḍāli Varadarāja. The Committee on Research of the Academic Senate of the University of California at Berkeley has been consistently generous over the years in providing funding for the project, especially in supporting the work of the many research assistants mentioned above.

Special thanks are also due to the University of California's Dwinelle Computer Research Facility and its director, Mark Kaiser, for providing and maintaining a workstation dedicated to the *Rāmāyaṇa* Translation Project. The ability of our research assistants to have access to this invaluable facility around the clock has greatly expedited the complex and labor-intensive work they contributed to the project.

We must also express our thanks to Ms. Rita Bernhard, Copyeditor of Princeton University Press, who cheerfully took on the Herculean task of working through a complex manuscript of some twenty-six hundred pages filled with unfamiliar Sanskrit text and terms. Her innumerable suggestions for the improvement of the grammar, syntax, and general readability of the introduction, translation, and, above all, the dense and difficult annotation enabled us to make countless improvements in the finished work.

Finally, and with a profound sense of loss, we note the passing, during the past year, of two friends and scholars who played critical roles in the development of Translation Consortium.

Mr. K. Venugopalan (1922–2007), Sub-Editor Emeritus of the Dictionary Department of the Deccan College, Pune, was involved with the project from its inception in the mid-1970s through the publication of the *Sundarakāṇḍa* in 1996. Together with his colleague and mentor Pt. T. Śrīnivāsaśāstrī, "Venu" read closely through the text and several commentaries of the epic with the General and Associate Editors and helped clarify many difficult issues. He will be missed by many Sanskrit scholars to whom he extended his generosity.

The noted poet Leonard E. Nathan (1924–2007), Professor Emeritus of Rhetoric at the University of California at Berkeley, served the project as its Editorial Consultant. His extraordinary gifts as a poet and rhetoritician were placed at the disposal of the translators and helped to save the translation from many, if not all, of its infelicities. Both of these friends will be sorely missed.

Robert P. Goldman and
Sally J. Sutherland Goldman
Vālmīkijayantī, 2007

Guide to Sanskrit Pronunciation*

The pronunciation of Sanskrit is not very difficult for English speakers. A few guidelines will serve to clarify the basic pronunciation of the sounds. English examples are based on hypothetical "dictionary" pronunciation.

Vowels

a	like the u in "but"
ā	like the o in "mom"
i	like the i in "bit"
ī	like the ee in "beet"
u	like the first u in "suture"
ū	like the oo in "pool"
ṛ	somewhat like the ri in "rig"
e	like the a in "gate"
ai	somewhat like the i in "high"; this sound becomes a diphthong to glide slightly into the "i" vowel
o	like the o in "rote"
au	somewhat like the ou of "loud" with a similar lip-rounding glide

Consonants

k	like the k in "skate"
kh	like the k in "Kate"
g	like the g in "gate"
gh	somewhat like the gh in "doghouse"
n̄	like the n in "sing"
c	like the ch in "eschew"
ch	like the ch in "chew"
j	like the j in "jewel"
jh	like the dgeh in "hedgehog"
ñ	like the n in "cinch"
ṭ	like the t in "stop"
ṭh	like the t in "top"
ḍ	like the d in "dart"
ḍh	like the dh in "adhere"
ṇ	like the n in "tint"

*adapted from Goldman and Sutherland Goldman 2004

t th d dh n	like the five preceding sounds, respectively, but with the tip of the tongue touching or extending slightly between the teeth
p	like the p in "spin"
ph	like the p in "pin"
b	like the b in "bin"
bh	like the bh in "abhor"
m	like the m in "monk"
y	like the y in "yellow"
r	like the r in "drama"
l	like the l in "lug"
v	produced generally with just the slightest contact between the upper teeth and the lower lip; slightly greater than that used for English w (as in "wile") but less than that used for English v (as in "vile")
ś	like the sh in "shove"
ṣ	produced with the tip of the tongue farther back than for ś but giving a similar sound
s	like the s in "so"
h	like the h in "hope"
ṃ	a nasalization of the preceding vowel
ḥ	an aspiration of a preceding vowel pronounced, almost like an echo, as an "h" followed by the short form of the preceding vowel. For example: *devaḥ*, pronounced *deva(ha)*

INTRODUCTION

1. The Significance of the *Yuddhakāṇḍa*

IF, AS WE HAVE ARGUED, the *Sundarakāṇḍa* is the heart of the *Rāmāyaṇa*,[1] the *Yuddhakāṇḍa*, or "the Battle Book," may be seen as the guts, as it were, of the poem. This is so not simply in the sense that the wrought emotionality of the fifth Book is here replaced with the many, long, and pervasive renderings of battle replete with graphic descriptions of the gushing blood, mangled limbs, and spilling entrails of the slain. For the massive sixth Book, nearly twice the length of the next-longest *kāṇḍa*, concerns itself with what, from an important perspective, may be considered to be the real business of the *Rāmāvatāra*.

Clearly the two most significant roles of the towering figure of Rāma are his elaborate portrayal as the ideal man, the paragon of self-control and exemplar of social *dharma*, who calmly gives up his rightful succession to the throne to preserve the truth of his father's word, and his critical function as a major *avatāra*, or "incarnation," of the great Lord Viṣṇu, who takes on a human birth to rid the world of the oppression of the monstrous and otherwise invincible *rākṣasa* monarch, Rāvaṇa. In a rather mechanical fashion we can, perhaps, judge the cultural significance of these two aspects of the hero by the amount of energy—in the form of the sheer number of verses—the poet and later redactors have devoted to them.

The enactment of the former of these roles forms the subject of the second longest of the poem's seven *kāṇḍas*, the *Ayodhyākāṇḍa*.[2] The fulfillment of Rāma's mission in the latter constitutes the grand subject of the massive *Yuddhakāṇḍa*, which, at nearly forty-five hundred verses in the critical edition, dwarfs even the *Ayodhyākāṇḍa*.[3] By this fairly crude calculation we can infer that the central events of the

[1] See Goldman and Goldman 1996, pp. 13, 79–86.

[2] For a discussion of Rāma as an exemplar of idealized social behavior, see R. Goldman 1984, pp. 49–59 and Pollock 1986, pp. 64–73.

[3] The critical editors of the volume have admitted 4,435 verses as belonging to their best reconstruction of the text based on the manuscripts collated for the edition. The critical edition of the *Ayodhyākāṇḍa* has 3,170. Thus the *Yuddhakāṇḍa* is some 40 percent longer than the *Ayodhyākāṇḍa*. Other versions of the poem, notably the popular and widely published versions of the so-called vulgate text, are considerably longer. Vaidya states that the "traditional extent of *Yuddhakāṇḍa* has only 5,710 stanzas" (Vaidya 1971, p. xxxi).

Yuddhakāṇḍa, comprising the bridging of the ocean, the siege of Laṅkā, the prodigious battles fought before the city walls, the slaying of Rāvaṇa, the installation of the righteous *rākṣasa* prince Vibhīṣaṇa on the Laṅkan throne, and the long-delayed consecration of Rāma as the divine, universal monarch,[4] together form the principal theme of the epic. This observation is amply confirmed by the receptive history of the poem and by the majority of the innumerable versions in which it has been rendered over the course of the last two to three millennia in all regions and virtually all languages of southern Asia.

For what, after all, is the "point" of the Rāma story, especially in its many influential Vaiṣṇava versions, if not to narrate the edifying tale of the earthly incarnation of the Lord, who, at the behest of the gods, compassionately consents to take on the role of a vulnerable and suffering mortal to save the world from the depredations of the evil and powerful Rāvaṇa and his minions and to restore a golden age of righteousness to a universe on the point of rupture? As the framing of the narrative in the *Bālakāṇḍa*[5] makes abundantly clear, if the *Rāmakathā* is about any one thing, it is the history of God's descent to destroy the very avatar of evil in the world in keeping with the principle so famously stated by Rāma's successor incarnation Kṛṣṇa at *Bhagavadgītā* 4.7–8.

With this in mind, then, it is only natural that the poet should devote the greatest portion of his narrative in this Book to a detailed, extensive, and often repetitive account of the many battles—both chaotic mass encounters and richly described single combats—that prefigure and set the stage for the culminating duel between the hero Rāma and the classic anti-hero Rāvaṇa.[6] Just as in the poem's

[4] For a discussion of this matter, see Pollock 1971, pp. 15–54.

[5] 1.14–16.

[6] The intensity of this final struggle is popularly regarded as so great that it has given rise to the formulaic verse in *MBh* and *Rām* to the effect that, although even the vast ocean and sky can find objects of comparison in each other, the battle between these two mighty antagonists beggars comparison itself. For a discussion of the textual history of these verses, see notes to 6.96.19 below. Despite this, the final duel comes off as a bit anticlimactic after the description of the extraordinary fight put up by Rāvaṇa's incomparable son Indrajit. Indeed, many later versions of the Rāma story indicate that Rāvaṇa is, after all, not that formidable an adversary and that he is far exceeded in martial skill and power by such later creations as the much mightier subterranean demons Mahīrāvaṇa and/or his brother Ahirāvaṇa from whose clutches

sister epic, the *Mahābhārata*, with its five central "battle books,"[7] it is clear that the mythic heart of the tale and the culmination of its theological message lies precisely where its intended audience would no doubt find the greatest excitement and pleasure, that is, in its grand narrative of heroism and violence. It is in this sense, then, that the *Yuddhakāṇḍa*, although it may seem overly long, tiresome, and repetitive to audiences schooled on the "rapid, plain and direct" style of the Homeric epics,[8] comes into its own as in many ways the core and culmination of the epic narrative.[9] It is this, together with the at-long-last permissible epiphany of Rāma as the supreme divinity without need for his sustained representation of himself and his self-understanding as a mere man, that no doubt account for much of the impact of the Book.

But the *Yuddhakāṇḍa* is not entirely given over to gory combat. Its capacious *sargas* offer plenty of room for much other material, including some of the literature's finest discourses on *dharma*- and *nītiśāstra*, colorful renderings of fabulous and much larger than life characters, such as Indrajit and Kumbhakarṇa, and some of the tradition's best-known and deeply loved scenes, such as the building of the bridge to Laṅkā (*setubandha*), Rāma's emotional reunion with Bharata, and, of course, the highly iconic missions of Hanumān to bring back the mountain of healing herbs from the Himalayas to

Rāma and Lakṣmaṇa must be rescued by Hanumān. On the legends involving these figures, see Smith 1988, pp. 145–53 and Lutgendorf 2007, pp. 211–16, passim. Vālmīki himself can be somewhat ambivalent in his representation of Rāvaṇa's military prowess. Early on in the war, for example, Rāma is depicted as easily besting the demon king but then sparing his life and letting him withdraw in humiliation from the field of battle (6.47). Then, too, in the epic's closing chapters, we learn that a *rākṣasa*, Lavaṇa, even more powerful than the slain Rāvaṇa, is harassing the sages living along the Yamunā River, and Rāma must send his brother Śatrughna to defeat him with an immensely powerful divine lance (7.59–61). On this story, see R. Goldman 1986, pp. 471–83.

7 These are the *Bhīṣmaparvan* through the *Sauptikaparvan* (Books 6–10).

8 Arnold 1905, pp. 41ff.

9 Because of the centrality of the battle to the mission of the *avatāra* and its role as the centerpiece of this Book, the section is generally entitled the *Yuddhakāṇḍa*, or "Battle Book," although it is also called the *Laṅkākāṇḍa*, or "Book of Laṅkā," in many, mainly northern, manuscripts.

Lañkā. It also contains some of the most interesting and controversial scenes in the epic, most notably Rāma's harsh treatment of his recovered wife and her unforgettable fire ordeal. These are discussed in greater detail below.

Let us begin with a brief synopsis of the *kāṇḍa*.

2. Synopsis of the *Yuddhakāṇḍa*

THE ACTION of the *Yuddhakāṇḍa* takes place over a time frame the duration of which forms the object of considerable discussion and controversy among the commentators.[1] It is continuous with the closing scenes of the *Sundarakāṇḍa*, where Hanumān, having returned from his mission in Laṅkā, reports to Rāma on Sītā's condition and his own adventures in the *rākṣasa* capital.[2]

The Book then opens with Rāma commending Hanumān for the success of his mission and for his exploits in Laṅkā. The hero, however, then succumbs to despair at the thought of the formidable obstacle in the form of the ocean that lies between him and the island citadel. The monkey king Sugrīva, however, exhorts Rāma to be resolute and urges him to have a bridge built whereby he and his army can cross the ocean and lay siege to Laṅkā. Rāma, his resolve now restored, interrogates Hanumān as to the defenses of the citadel and receives a full briefing. Then, with the exuberant monkeys, the hero leads a march across the Sahyādri hills to the shore of the mighty ocean, observing many auspicious omens. Once encamped on the seashore, however, Rāma gives way once again to a moving lamentation for his lost love. This and the preceding action occupy the first five *sargas* of the Book.

One interesting feature of the *Yuddhakāṇḍa*'s narrative that is more prominent in this Book than in any of the others is the almost cinematic way in which the action jumps back and forth between the worlds of the hero and of his enemy. After these opening five chapters, the poet leaves the hero encamped on the shore and, for the next five, takes us to Laṅkā, where we join Rāvaṇa as he takes counsel with his ministers and military advisers. Most of the demon-king's courtiers and generals are mere sycophants ready to support their master in his evil ways and in his intransigence. His advisers

[1] See note to 6.4.12 and p. 17, note 1, for more detailed discussions of this issue, which occupies a good deal of the commentators' attention, energy, and ingenuity.

[2] In fact, there is no clear break in the action between the two Books, and the formal break between them is generally not made in the northern recension until after the construction of the causeway and the crossing of the ocean in *sarga* 15 of the critical edition.

urge him to fight and destroy the impudent human Rāma, reminding the king of his vast military resources and his own mighty exploits in subduing the gods themselves in battle. The *rākṣasa* generals then boast, in turn, of their own martial prowess, each vowing to slaughter Rāma and his monkey hosts single-handedly.

Rāvaṇa's younger brother Vibhīṣaṇa, alone willing to speak truth to power, restrains the impetuous generals and warns the king for his own good that he is facing an irresistibly mighty foe and that he should repent of his wrongful deed in abducting Sītā and return her to Rāma. In his arrogance and folly, however, Rāvaṇa harshly rejects his brother's sage counsel, accusing him of treachery motivated by envy. He launches into a meditation on the danger inherent in one's kinsmen, citing the example of the song of the wild elephants who lament the fact that it is their (domesticated) kin that bring them into captivity. Wounded and incensed by his brother's vituperative rejection of his well-meant advice, Vibhīṣaṇa flies up into the air accompanied by his own four retainers and announces that he is abandoning Rāvaṇa (*sargas* 6–10).

After this set of five *sargas*, the scene shifts for the next five once more to the northern shore of the sea, where we learn that Vibhīṣaṇa has not only abandoned his brother but has actually defected to Rāma's side. He announces himself to the monkey chiefs, promising to aid Rāma in his campaign against Rāvaṇa, all the while carefully hovering in the air so as to remain out of immediate reach. All the monkey leaders, except Hanumān, express grave suspicion of the *rākṣasa* and urge that he be killed or at least captured. Hanumān, however, perceives that Vibhīṣaṇa is as good as his word and advises that he be accepted as an ally. Rāma concurs, arguing that, in any case, he would never turn away someone who comes to him seeking refuge, regardless of his motives. Indeed, in advance of even confronting his enemy, Rāma has Lakṣmaṇa consecrate Vibhīṣaṇa as king of the *rākṣasas* in Rāvaṇa's place.

The newly crowned, but not yet enthroned, monarch seconds Sugrīva's earlier suggestion that Rāma, after first propitiating Sāgara, the god of the sea, somehow contrive to bridge the ocean. Rāma duly worships Sāgara for three days, but the divinity remains obdurate and will not calm his waters. At length Rāma loses patience and begins to pierce the waters with his fearsome and fiery arrows, throwing the sea and its creatures into turmoil. Chastened, Sāgara emerges from the deep and humbly consents to being bridged. He informs Rāma that one of the monkey chiefs, Nala, is the son of Viśvakarman, the architect-builder of the gods, and is capable of designing and constructing a causeway whereby the army may safely cross over to Laṅkā. Under Nala's direction, the monkeys gather trees and great boulders and hurl them into the sea to form a smooth and level causeway, a hundred leagues in length and ten in width. With Rāma and Sugrīva at their head, the vast army of monkeys crosses the ocean and encamps on the southern shore (*sargas* 11–15).

At the end of these five *sargas*, the poet returns once more to Rāvaṇa's council chamber from which the king dispatches two spies in order to discover the strength and disposition of Rāma's forces. Despite assuming the appearance of monkeys, the spies' disguise is quickly penetrated by Vibhīṣaṇa, who seizes them and brings them to Rāma. The latter, in keeping with his compassionate nature, frees them and sends them back with a message to Rāvaṇa, warning of the *rākṣasa* monarch's impending defeat. Rāvaṇa, taking the spies up to an observation tower, has them point out and identify the principal heroes besieging his city and enumerate the vast hordes of their monkey troops. Contemptuously dismissing the failed agents, Rāvaṇa sends out yet another spy, who meets with a similar fate. The monkeys handle this spy roughly before Rāma releases him to tell his tale to the *rākṣasa* king.

After further consultation with his counselors, Rāvaṇa decides that he can break Sītā's will and force her to bend to his by convincing her that Rāma has, in fact, been slain and his monkey army massacred during a night raid on the sleeping camp by the *rākṣasa* forces. To this end he has one of his more skilled illusionists, a *rāksasa* named Vidyujjihva, create a simulacrum of Rāma's severed head and one of his great bow. At the sight of the grisly simulacra, Sītā succumbs to despair and bitterly laments Rāma's and her own wretched fate. But when her tormentor is called away to attend to the looming military threat, the apparitions disappear and a friendly *rākṣasī* (*rākṣasa* woman) named Saramā privately reassures her that Rāvaṇa's tale was as false as the simulated head. Sītā is comforted and sends Saramā to eavesdrop on Rāvaṇa's consultations with his ministers.

During these consultations, a *rākṣasa* elder, Rāvaṇa's maternal great-uncle Mālyavān, sternly lectures the king on the folly of his ways and points out the many inauspicious omens that have appeared, presaging the destruction of the *rākṣasas*. But in his arrogance,

Rāvaṇa rebukes him and begins to make preparations for the defense of the city (*sargas* 16–27).

Rāma similarly prepares for the siege of Laṅkā and leads his forces to the summit of Mount Suvela where he is able to secure a good view of the citadel, which is described in rich detail. Rāma, who has also observed the various omens, disposes his troops at the four gates of Laṅkā and then sends Aṅgada to Rāvaṇa as an emissary to warn him of his impending doom. After Aṅgada returns, foiling Rāvaṇa's attempt to capture him, the *rākṣasa* king sends out his troops on their first sortie. This leads to a long and chaotic battle between the *rākṣasa* and the monkey armies. The fierce fighting continues into the night, with both sides lashing out blindly and indiscriminately against friend and foe alike. In the thick of the battle, Aṅgada attacks Rāvaṇa's mighty son Indrajit and succeeds in destroying his horses and chariot. In his rage, Indrajit takes recourse to a boon he had received from Brahmā whereby he can make himself invisible. Using this as a cloak, he employs his dreadful serpent-weapons to pierce and bind both Rāma and Lakṣmaṇa, rendering them hors de combat. Seeing the great Rāghava heroes felled, Sugrīva and his forces give way to despair but are reassured by Vibhīṣaṇa that this is but a temporary setback and that the heroes will ultimately regain consciousness (*sargas* 28–36).

Meanwhile, Indrajit, believing he has ended the threat posed by Rāma, returns to the city to report his victory to his father. The latter, attempting to press his advantage and break the will of Sītā, has her flown over the battlefield so that she can see with her own eyes the fall of her mighty husband. When she sees Rāma and Lakṣmaṇa struck down and comatose, she thinks that they are dead and gives way to despair and lamentation. But, as in the *Sundarakāṇḍa*, the kindly *rākṣasī* Trijaṭā consoles Sītā and points out that her husband still shows signs of life. Meanwhile, on the battlefield itself, Rāma, still bound fast by Indrajit's powerful serpent-weapons, regains consciousness. Seeing that his beloved brother has been similarly struck down and believing him to be dead, Rāma gives way to grief and despondency, stating, famously, that seeing Lakṣmaṇa dead, he no longer cares for Sītā nor even for life itself.

Sugrīva, perceiving that the brothers are merely injured and bound but not dead, consults with his wise father-in-law, Suṣeṇa, who informs him that there are two mountains—Candra and Droṇa—situated in the midst of the ocean of milk on which grow powerful healing herbs that can restore the heroes to health and vigor. Suṣeṇa urges the monkey king to dispatch swift monkey heroes, including Saṃpāti, Panasa, and Hanumān, to fetch the herbs. But, in what appears to be a strange narrative discontinuity, before Sugrīva can act on Suṣeṇa's advice, the great divine bird Garuḍa, the legendary enemy of all snakes, appears on the scene, causing the dreadful serpent arrows to flee and, with his touch, restoring Rāma and Lakṣmaṇa to health and vitality, their wounds completely healed (*sargas* 37–41).

Then follows a series of single combats between *rākṣasa* warriors and monkey heroes. In these battles Hanumān slays the *rākṣasas* Dhūmrākṣa and Akampana, while Nīla kills Prahasta. Enraged at the loss of these generals, Rāvaṇa himself comes forth to battle. He wreaks havoc among the monkey forces and engages in hard-fought duels with Sugrīva, Hanumān, and Lakṣmaṇa, wounding the latter with a powerful lance. Finally, he is confronted by Rāma. They fight until Rāma, seeing that Rāvaṇa has been dazed by his arrows and is weakening, refrains from killing him. Rāma then dismisses the *rākṣasa* king from the battlefield, humbling his pride (*sargas* 42–47).

Once back in Laṅkā, the *rākṣasa* lord, at last realizing Rāma's power and recalling his vulnerability to human foes, instructs his attendants to waken the most formidable of all the demons, his gargantuan brother Kumbhakarṇa. This monster is so powerful and voracious that Brahmā had placed him under a spell of nearly perpetual sleep to prevent him from devouring the whole world. The *rākṣasas* proceed to Kumbhakarṇa's cavelike sleeping chamber and engage in protracted, violent, and amusing efforts to wake the sleeping giant—beating him, sounding drums and trumpets, goading him with weapons, and having elephants trample him. At length the monster awakens and, after a truly gluttonous feast washed down with a thousand jars of liquor, reports to his brother.

Seeing the giant towering over the ramparts of the city, Rāma asks Vibhīṣaṇa who this giant might be, and the *rākṣasa* responds by giving one of the poem's several accounts of the career and curse of Kumbhakarṇa. The monkey hosts are terrified at the sight of the monstrous creature, and Vibhīṣaṇa urges Rāma to calm them by telling them that he is just a mechanical contraption.

Meanwhile, Kumbhakarṇa attends upon Rāvaṇa in his throne room, where he is informed of what has transpired during his sleep and of the grave threat now facing Laṅkā. Kumbhakarṇa lectures his brother on the folly of his ways, offering a number of arguments based on a sound reading of *nītiśāstra*, or the rules of proper governance. Rāvaṇa, now desperate, acknowledges for the first time how foolish he was to have abducted Sītā. Nonetheless, he calls upon his brother's loyalty in his time of need, and Kumbhakarṇa dutifully goes off to battle on his behalf. His arrival on the battlefield produces a rout of the monkeys, and he crushes and devours thousands of them. Finally, Rāma himself engages the giant and cuts him to pieces with his sharp arrows (*sargas* 48–55).

Rāvaṇa laments his fallen brother and then sends forth a series of other champions—Narāntaka, Devāntaka, Triśiras, Mahodara, Mahāpārśva, and Atikāya—all of whom are ultimately slain by one or another of the monkey warriors or by Lakṣmaṇa (*sargas* 56–59).

At this point, mighty Indrajit returns to the battlefield and, relying on his power of invisibility, annihilates or disables virtually the entire host of the monkeys, as well as Rāma and Lakṣmaṇa themselves. Only Hanumān and Vibhīṣaṇa appear to remain unscathed. Wandering the grisly battlefield at night, they come upon the gravely wounded Jāmbavān, who directs Hanumān to fly to the Himalayas, where there is a mountain covered in powerful healing herbs, and to bring back the herbs to heal and restore the fallen heroes. Hanumān makes this heroic journey. But, upon finding that the herbs have concealed themselves, he tears up the entire mountain and carries it back to the shores of Laṅkā, thus bringing the slain and wounded back to life and health. The revivified monkeys then launch a night raid on Laṅkā and set the citadel ablaze (*sargas* 60–61).

Following this, Rāvaṇa sends forth still more champions—Kumbha, Nikumbha, and Makarākṣa—all of whom make valiant sorties but are ultimately slain in combat. Distraught at the death of Makarākṣa, Rāvaṇa once again sends forth Indrajit, who performs a black magical sacrifice. Then, hiding behind his magically created cloak of fog, darkness, and invisibility, he rains down death and destruction on Rāma, Lakṣmaṇa, and their forces. In his frustration, Lakṣmaṇa proposes using the dreaded *brahmāstra*, which, he claims, could instantly annihilate all the *rākṣasas*, Indrajit included; but Rāma rebukes him, arguing that it would be wrong to punish an entire race for the transgressions of one of their number.

Unable to kill the two heroes with his weapons, Indrajit withdraws and decides to resort to deception and psychological warfare to demoralize his foes. Using his powers of *māyā*, or magical illusion, he creates an illusory double of Sītā, which he proceeds apparently to slaughter in his chariot right before the eyes of the horrified monkeys. This has its desired effect, and the monkeys flee in horror and dejection. But the rout is stopped by Hanumān, who rallies the troops once more (*sargas* 62–69).

Vibhīṣaṇa then manages to console Rāma and the monkeys, who are stricken with grief at the apparent murder of Sītā, explaining that Rāvaṇa would never countenance such an act and that this must have been one of Indrajit's feats of illusion. Indrajit, meanwhile, has withdrawn to the Nikumbhilā grove to perform yet another of his black magic rituals that seem to be the basis for his extraordinary powers. Lakṣmaṇa follows him there and challenges him to a duel before the rite can be concluded. A protracted and dramatic battle ensues between the two heroes, and, in the end, Lakṣmaṇa manages to kill the formidable warrior. The exhausted and wounded Lakṣmaṇa is then healed of his wounds by Suṣeṇa through the use of his powerful healing herbs (*sargas* 70–79).

Rāvaṇa grieves sorely for the loss of his son and, in his blind rage, seizes a sword with which to kill Sītā, but he is dissuaded from this gross iniquity by a righteous *rākṣasa*, Supārśva. He then orders his remaining troops into combat in one last desperate assault, and a grand, final clash begins in which Rāma cuts down the demonic troops by the thousand with his powerful weapons, leaving the *rākṣasīs* to bitterly lament their slain sons and husbands, and to decry the folly and wickedness of Rāvaṇa. At long last, his troops decimated and his last great champion slain, Rāvaṇa himself sallies forth with his remaining warriors for the final battle in the face of many evil omens presaging his doom. Before the final duel, however, yet a few more battles ensue between monkey and *rākṣasa* heroes during which Sugrīva kills Virūpākṣa and Mahodara, while Aṅgada dispatches Mahāpārśva (*sargas* 80–86).

The final duel now begins in earnest, with Rāma and Rāvaṇa assaulting each other with all kinds of powerful supernatural weapons. At one point Lakṣmaṇa joins the fray, only to be struck down by Rāvaṇa's mighty javelin. Rāma drives his enemy from the field but then succumbs to grief for his brother, whom he thinks has been killed. He is comforted, however, by the monkey physician Suṣeṇa, who once more dispatches Hanumān on a flight to the Himalayas to bring back healing herbs. In a reprise of his earlier feat, the great monkey brings back the whole mountain, and Suṣeṇa skillfully employs the herbs to effect Lakṣmaṇa's recovery.

Rāma and Rāvaṇa then resume their duel, but this time on more equal terms, as the god Indra sends the former his own divine chariot and his charioteer, Mātali, so that the battle now becomes a chariot duel. Rāma begins to get the better of his foe, and, to save him, Rāvaṇa's charioteer drives the *rākṣasa* king to safety. This enrages Rāvaṇa, who orders his charioteer to return to the field. The battle continues for some time with both heroes scoring hits and suffering blows. Rāma finally gains the advantage and begins to sever Rāvaṇa's heads, only to find that they grow back instantly when cut off. Mātali then advises Rāma that he will be unable to dispatch his foe unless he uses the all-powerful *brahmāstra*, the divine missile of the god Brahmā. Accordingly, Rāma selects a magnificent arrow and invests it with the power of the *astra*. He looses it, and it finds its mark, killing Rāvaṇa instantly (*sargas* 98–100).

The many women of Rāvaṇa's harem now come out to the battlefield and utter their lamentations for their fallen lord, after which the dead king's chief queen, Mandodarī, also laments piteously. The somewhat reluctant Vibhīṣaṇa, acting on Rāma's instructions, performs the funeral rites for his fallen brother and is then formally consecrated as king of the *rākṣasas* (*sargas* 98–100).

Hostilities now concluded, Rāma sends Hanumān as a messenger to Sītā to inform her of his victory and her liberation. Hanumān greets the queen and begs that she permit him to slaughter the fierce *rākṣasīs* who have tormented her during her captivity. But Sītā forbids such violence, arguing that the women were only following Rāvaṇa's orders, and that, in any case, it is the nature of *rākṣasas* to speak and act injuriously.

Urged by Hanumān to see Sītā, Rāma sends Vibhīṣaṇa to fetch her. But when she arrives to greet her beloved lord, he shocks the assembled monkeys and *rākṣasas* by harshly repudiating her. He tells her that he slew Rāvaṇa merely for the sake of his honor and that he has no further use for a woman who has dwelt in the house of another man. In her grief and desolation Sītā offers to prove her fidelity by entering the fire. A pyre is constructed and lit, and she mounts it only to be brought out unharmed by Agni, the fire god himself, who testifies to her faithfulness and purity. Rāma announces that he had never doubted her but treated her as he had to avoid any hint of scandal (*sargas* 101–106).

At this point the gods assemble and praise Rāma as the Supreme Lord, a circumstance that amazes him, since the prince had always thought of himself merely as an ordinary man, Daśaratha's son, because of the force of the boon of Rāvaṇa, which immunized the demon against the power of any god. Sītā and Rāma are at last happily reunited, and the shade of Daśaratha himself arrives to greet his sons and daughter-in-law.

The king of the gods, Indra, then offers boons to Rāma, who chooses the restoration to life and health of all the monkeys who fell in his cause. Vibhīṣaṇa then places the magical flying palace Puṣpaka at Rāma's disposal for his return journey to Ayodhyā, the fourteen years of his exile having been completed. Rāma takes Sītā and all the monkeys, along with Vibhīṣaṇa and his advisers, and sets out on the homeward flight, describing to his wife the various scenes of their struggle and exile as they pass over them. The party then proceeds to the ashram of the sage Bharadvāja. From there, Rāma dispatches his faithful messenger, Hanumān, to Nandigrāma to inform Bharata of his victory and his return to claim his rightful place as the king of Kosala. Hanumān takes on a human form and arrives just in time to prevent Bharata from carrying out his vow to immolate himself should Rāma not return before completing the fourteen-year period of exile that Kaikeyī had stipulated.

After hearing Hanumān's account of the trials and triumphs of Rāma and Sītā during their long absence from Ayodhyā, Bharata, together with the dowager queens and notables of Ayodhyā, goes forth to welcome his brother. Meanwhile, Vasiṣṭha and the other religious functionaries under the direction of Bharata and Śatrughna make preparations for a lavish royal consecration ceremony for Rāma, which is then carried out with great pomp and circumstance.

The Book concludes with a glowing description of the paradisiacal conditions that prevailed during the glorious ten-thousand-year reign of Rāma (*sargas* 107–116).

3. Statecraft and Violence: The Themes of the *Yuddhakāṇḍa*

THE *Yuddhakāṇḍa* is primarily a book of narrative action. Its considerable body of text appears to pack more dramatic events into a relatively short time frame[1] than any other Book of the epic. The action is generally linear, carrying the tale from Rāma's discussions with Sugrīva and Hanumān upon the latter's return from his mission to Laṅkā through the great military campaign, the fluctuations of battle, and Rāma's eventual triumph, to the hero's return to Ayodhyā and his long-deferred consecration as king.

The narrative sustains its dramatic interest by repeatedly switching its focus back and forth between the activities of Rāma and his allies, on the one hand, and those of Rāvaṇa, his advisers, and Sītā and her wardresses, on the other. Thus the scene of the action alternates periodically in an almost cinematic fashion between its principal locations, the encampment of the monkey army, and the council chamber and women's quarters of the *rākṣasa* king, frequently bringing the two streams of narration together in the intermediate no-man's-land of the grisly battlefield outside the city gates. This central pattern is broken only by occasional brief excursions to other Laṅkan locales, such as the sleeping chamber of the gargantuan *rākṣasa* Kumbhakarṇa, the fearsome Nikumbhilā

[1] The actual time frame of the events narrated in the critical edition of the text (and in the southern recension in general) is not unambiguously clear and forms the basis for considerable disagreement among those commentators who concern themselves closely with the chronology of the epic in general and of the Book in particular. The commentators either understand the duration of the battle to be approximately two weeks and the action of the entire Book to take somewhat longer than that (Cg, Cv, Cm, Ck), although Cg provides an alternative chronology that has the battle last only seven days (see notes to 6.80.55 and 6.96.30), or they understand the duration of the Book to include the sleep of Kumbhakarṇa, extending the duration of the events to just over six months (Ct). Cs, depending on the *Padmapurāṇa*'s account, seems to understand the battle to take some forty-eight days (see note to 6.50.12). See R. Goldman 2003 and 2006b. In any case, it appears that, for most of the commentators, the duration of the actual battle is about two weeks. See note to 6.4.4.

grove frequented by the sorcerer-warrior Indrajit, and, of course, the remote high country of the Himalayas to which Hanumān makes two visits to procure the powerful healing herbs that grow there. Although the action of the Book is thus framed almost entirely within the confines of the island kingdom of Laṅkā, that action is itself framed by locales on the mainland. For the Book begins with Rāma's march to and encampment on the northern shore of the ocean[2] and ends with his triumphal return to Ayodhyā, the starting point of the entire epic tale. In this way the Book, like the *Sundarakāṇḍa* and the epic as a whole, has a sort of annular structure of the "there and back again" type that characterizes many folk and epic quest tales.

As the title of the Book indicates, its major theme is the great *yuddha*, or war, between two formidable armies.[3] Rāma's host consists of himself, his brother Lakṣmaṇa, the *rākṣasa* defector Vibhīṣaṇa and his four loyal ministers, and the vast host of monkey troops under the command of the *vānara* monarch Sugrīva and the wise and sagacious king of the apes, the *ṛkṣarāja*, Jāmbavān. Rāvaṇa's forces are made up of himself, his powerful kinsmen and generals, and the hordes of *rākṣasa* soldiery.

For this reason, a great proportion of the Book is given over to discussions of the preparations for war and lengthy descriptions of the combatants, along with their weaponry and other military paraphernalia, and, above all, protracted, detailed, and often repetitive accounts of both large-scale clashes between the opposing armies and heroic single combat involving pairs of powerful rival warriors.

[2] Northern versions of the epic, including the printed editions of Lahore and Gorresio, place the break between the *Sundara-* and *Yuddhakāṇḍas* later in the narrative than do the southern texts. Thus northern versions of the poem generally begin the *kāṇḍa* only at a point after the army has built and crossed the bridge to Laṅkā. For this reason, for example, the Book's opening chapter in the editions of Lahore and Gorresio corresponds to the sixteenth *sarga* of the critical edition. On structural grounds, it would seem that the southern ordering of the *sargas* is to be preferred. For a discussion of the structure of the *Sundarakāṇḍa*, see Goldman and Goldman 1996, pp. 14–16.

[3] It should be noted that in some, mainly northern, manuscripts the Book is called the *Laṅkākāṇḍa*, perhaps in an effort to maintain consistency with the poem's other central four *kāṇḍas*, which, with the possible exception of the *Sundarakāṇḍa*, are named for the places where their principal plots unfold. For a discussion of the names of the *kāṇḍas*, especially the obscurely named *Sundarakāṇḍa*, see Goldman and Goldman 1996, pp. 75–78.

The encounters described are in some ways similar to those narrated in the "battle books" of the *Mahābhārata*, most especially when the poet focuses on the duels between the most prominent *rākṣasa* champions, such as Indrajit and Rāvaṇa himself, and the two heroic Rāghavas, Rāma and Lakṣmaṇa. Here, as in the longer epic, there are elaborate descriptions of the *astras*, or supernaturally powerful divine missiles, control of which the warriors have obtained through various boons, penances, sacrifices, and the like. However, because of the particular demands of the *Rāmāyaṇa*'s narrative, the only battle that truly approximates the typical *Bhāratayuddha* duel is the epic's culminating and most significant duel, the one between Rāma and Rāvaṇa. For it is only in this encounter that we see the classical epic duel between two powerful warriors, both mounted in chariots, launching, parrying, and receiving divinely empowered shafts while their drivers execute the various military movements for which they are trained.

It must be kept in mind that whereas both the Pāṇḍava and Kaurava combatants go to war with the full panoply of military mounts, vehicles, weaponry, and tactics, in the *Rāmāyaṇa* these things are, for the most part, available only to the *rākṣasas*. Rāma and his brother have gone into exile in the guise of wandering forest ascetics stripped of most of the accoutrements and resources of the warrior class of their day. They have only their powerful bows and arrows, and lack the armor, mounts, chariots, and arsenals of diverse weapons normally associated with epic warfare. Unlike Rāvaṇa, they are without the support of the classical army of the *śāstras*, the *caturaṅgabala* with its four divisions of chariots, cavalry, elephant corps, and infantry.

It is only in Rāma's final, magnificent duel with the *rākṣasa* lord that, in order to level the playing field, as it were, Indra lends him his own celestial chariot and his heavenly charioteer, Mātali, to drive it. This divine intervention lends the duel its more classical form, enabling both combatants to maneuver and wheel freely across the field of battle so that the great clash can earn its reputation as truly incomparable.[4]

The troops Rāma does have at his command and with which he must confront the heavily armed *rākṣasa* forces consist largely of a

[4] See notes to 6.96.19.

vast host of powerful, but often poorly disciplined,[5] forest-dwelling monkeys. Now it is true that these monkeys are the partial incarnations of the various vedic divinities[6] and are therefore gifted with extraordinary size, strength, and supernatural abilities, which make them formidable fighters. However, despite the fact that they are said in the *Bālakāṇḍa* to be as skilled in the use of divine missiles as the gods themselves,[7] nowhere are they represented in the *Yuddhakāṇḍa* as equipped with any sort of specific military weapon. Instead, almost invariably they are depicted as fighting with their hands, feet, and fangs and with a motley assortment of boulders and trees, which they uproot and use to smash their enemies, together with their vehicles. In the few cases where one of the monkey warriors is shown using a purpose-made weapon, it is one of those dropped on the battlefield by slain, wounded, or routed *rākṣasas*.

This significant difference lends many of the battle scenes in the *kāṇḍa* a kind of raw, even savage quality in which the chaos of violent conflict and the general "fog of war" is starkly rendered by the poet as he describes the frenzied armies of monkeys and demons flailing at one another almost indiscriminately. Consider, for example, the chilling passage in *sarga* 34, where the violent encounter continues unabated far into the night, when, in the dust and darkness, the combatants can no longer distinguish friend from foe.

> In that terrible darkness they slaughtered one another in battle: the tawny monkeys crying, "Are you a *rākṣasa*?" and the *rākṣasas* crying, "Are you a monkey?"
>
> "Kill!" "Rend" "Come on!" "What, running away?" Such were the tumultuous cries that were heard in that darkness.
>
> With their golden armor, in the darkness, the swarthy *rākṣasas* looked like great mountains with thickets of luminescent herbs.
>
> Beside themselves with fury, the swift *rākṣasas* raced about in that impenetrable darkness, devouring the monkeys.

[5] As witness the various occasions at which the *vānara* forces panic, break ranks, and flee in disarray only to be rallied by one figure or another.

[6] See 1.16, where the incarnation of the gods as allies of Rāma is described. The divine parentage of the principal monkey warriors is also frequently alluded to throughout the text.

[7] *sarvāstraguṇasampannān amṛtaprāśanān iva* (1.16.4).

> But the monkeys hurled themselves upon the *rākṣasas'* golden-plumed horses and their banners that resembled flames of fire and, in a terrifying rage, tore them to pieces with their sharp fangs.
>
> Beside themselves with fury, they dragged about elephants with their riders and chariots bedecked with flags and banners, slashing at them with their fangs.
>
> Meanwhile, with arrows that resembled venomous serpents, Lakṣmaṇa and Rāma cut down the foremost among the *rākṣasas*, whom they could make out but dimly in the darkness.
>
> The thick dust raised by the horses' hooves and chariot wheels blocked up the eyes and ears of the warriors.
>
> And there, as that terrible, hair-raising battle proceeded in this fashion, swift rivers with blood for water began to flow.[8]

Vālmīki's descriptions of the realities, the technologies, and the consequences of war are numerous, vivid, and interesting. On the one hand, he can be brutally direct and graphic, giving almost Homeric accounts of the devastating effects of the violence. Compare, for example, such passages as the following:

> His head shattered by the crushing blow of that fist, Devāntaka, son of the *rākṣasa* king, all at once fell lifeless to the ground, his teeth and eyes knocked out, his tongue lolling.[9]

or

> Then, spying an opening, the monkey, in his rage, brought his huge palm down upon Virūpākṣa's temple.
>
> Struck by that palm, which was like the thunderbolt of great Indra, he fell to the ground drenched in gore and vomiting blood.

[8] 6.34.3–11. One is all but inevitably reminded of Matthew Arnold's "Dover Beach":

> And we are here on a darkling plain
> Swept with confused alarms of struggle and flight,
> Where ignorant armies clash by night.

[9] 6.58.24.

> Drenched with foaming blood, his eyes rolling with rage, Virūpākṣa appeared to the monkeys to have his eyes still more disfigured than before.
>
> The monkeys watched their enemy as, drenched in blood, he rolled in convulsions from side to side, moaning piteously.[10]

On the other hand, the poet is fond of bringing out what one may call the aesthetics of violence by glossing the ugliness of the carnage with various poetic figures. Thus, for example, he will often describe stricken warriors gushing blood from their many wounds as resembling *kiṃśuka* or other red-flowering trees in full bloom.[11] Or, as in the following example, a hemorrhaging giant may be compared to a pleasant mountainside with its sparkling waterfalls.

> Stripped of his ears and nose and gushing blood, mighty Kumbhakarṇa looked like a mountain covered with waterfalls.[12]

In some cases the poet carries the juxtaposition of the emetic and the aesthetic to great lengths as in the following extended metaphor, where the horrific details of battlefield carnage are mapped onto a conventional description of a charming or romantic riverside scene.

> Indeed, the battleground resembled a river. Masses of slain heroes formed its banks, and shattered weapons, its great trees. Torrents of blood made up its broad waters, and the ocean to which it flowed was Yama. Livers and spleens made up its deep mud, scattered entrails its waterweeds. Severed heads and trunks made up its fish, pieces of limbs, its grass. It was crowded with vultures in place of flocks of *haṃsas*, and it was swarming with adjutant storks instead of *sārasa* cranes. It was covered with fat in place of foam, and the cries of the wounded took the place of its gurgling. It was not to be forded by the faint of heart. Truly, it resembled a river at the end of the rains, swarming with *haṃsas* and *sārasa* cranes.[13]

In some cases he is content merely to catalog in long lists the weaponry used.

[10] 6.84.28–31.

[11] For example, at 6.35.9; 6.55.22; 6.60.34; 6.67.33; and 6.76.28.

[12] 6.55.70.

[13] 6.46.25–28. Cf. notes to 6.7.15. Cf. 6.42.23, where the ghastly sounds of the battlefield are compared to a musical recital.

> As the *rākṣasas*, eager for victory, hurled themselves upon the monkeys, the swords, javelins, broadswords, arrows, lances, cudgels, maces, iron clubs, darts, various battle-axes, and splendid bows they had taken up glittered.[14]

Elsewhere, when the gravity of the occasion demands it, Vālmīki can lavish great attention on a single weapon, describing it thickly in terms of its appearance and sound as well as its history and the powers that invest it. The following is the poet's twelve-verse description of the ultimate weapon, the arrow with which Rāma finally succeeds in killing the mighty Rāvaṇa.

> Reminded by Mātali's words, Rāma took up a blazing arrow that, as he did so, made a hissing sound like that of a snake. Presented to him earlier by the powerful and blessed seer Agastya, it was a gift of Brahmā. It was a mighty arrow, unfailing in battle. Brahmā, whose power is immeasurable, had fashioned it long ago for the sake of Indra and had presented it to that lord of the gods, who was eager to conquer the three worlds. Pavana resided in its feathers. Agni, the purifier, and Sūrya, bringer of light, were in its arrowhead. Its shaft was made of all of space, and the mountains Meru and Mandara lent it their weight. Radiant with its splendor, beautifully fletched, and adorned with gold, it was fashioned with the blazing energy of all the elements, and it was as brilliant as Sūrya, bringer of light. It looked like the smoking fire at the end of a cosmic age and glistened like a venomous snake. It could instantaneously shatter hosts of chariots, elephants, and horses. It could shatter gateways, together with their iron beams, and even mountains. With its shaft drenched with the blood of many different creatures and smeared with their marrow, it was truly frightful. Hard as adamant and roaring deafeningly, it was terrifying in every sort of battle. Dreadful, hissing like a serpent, it inspired terror in all beings. It was fearsome and looked like Yama. In battle, it provided a never-ending supply of food to flocks of vultures and adjutant storks as well as *rākṣasas* and packs of jackals. Fletched with the various feathers of Garuḍa—beautiful and variegated—it brought joy to the monkey chiefs and despair to the *rākṣasas*. That ultimate arrow, which robbed one's

[14] 6.46.3–4.

> enemies of their glory but brought joy to oneself, was to encompass the destruction of that menace to the Ikṣvākus and indeed to all the worlds.
>
> Then immensely powerful and mighty Rāma consecrated that arrow with *mantras* and placed it on his bow in the manner prescribed by the science of archery.[15]

In these ways, the author deploys some of the tradition's repertory of poetic techniques of "ornamentation" (*alaṃkāra*) in order to soften and aestheticize the graphic violence that forms so central a theme of the Book.

Yet another rhetorical technique the poet uses to distance himself and his audience somewhat from the grim realities of the killing fields of Laṅkā is that of a kind of grand hyperbole (*atiśayokti*) that serves to leaven somewhat the sanguinary tone of the battle scenes while inspiring in the audience a sense of wonder. His most consistent and effective use of this technique is undoubtedly seen in his treatment of the almost comically gargantuan figure of Rāvaṇa's monstrous brother, the giant, narcoleptic Kumbhakarṇa. The magnificent excess of Vālmīki's treatment of this wonderfully drawn character is discussed in detail below when we examine the Book's various prominent characters. However, in the present context, we may consider the poet's dramatic rendering of the fall of the monster's head when it is severed from his body by Rāma's swift arrow.

> With it, Rāma severed the *rākṣasa* lord's head—huge as a mountain peak, its fangs bared, and its gorgeous earrings swinging wildly—just as, long ago, Indra, smasher of citadels, severed the head of Vṛtra.
>
> Struck off by Rāma's arrow, the *rākṣasa*'s head, which resembled a mountain, fell. It smashed the gates of the buildings on the main thoroughfares and knocked down the lofty rampart.
>
> Finally, the enormous *rākṣasa*, who looked like Himalaya, fell into the sea, abode of waters. There he crushed crocodiles, shoals of huge fish, and serpents before he entered the earth.[16]

[15] 6.97.3–14. Compare the shorter description of the arrow with which Rāma dispatches the giant Kumbhakarṇa at 6.55.120–23.
[16] 6.55.123–25.

Thus the frightful images that inspire the sentiments of fear, horror, or disgust (*bhayānaka, bibhatsā*, and *jugupsā rasas*) are often skillfully crafted by the poet to rouse other sentiments critical to the aesthetic appreciation of the piece, such as the sentiments of valor and wonder (*vīra* and *adbhuta rasas*).[17]

Aside from these graphic, figurative, and hyperbolic descriptions of conventional warfare as it was represented in the Indian epics with both ordinary and divinely empowered weapons, the *Yuddhakāṇḍa* contains some interesting passages that involve the use of unconventional methods of fighting, including the deployment of *abhicāra*, or black magic, and the application of what can only be thought of as a form of psychological warfare.

All the principal nonhuman characters in the epic drama, *vānaras* and *rākṣasas* alike, are represented as creatures endowed with certain supranormal powers. Specifically they are said to be *kāmarūpins*, beings capable of changing their appearance at will, and are beings possessed of *māyā*, or the power of creating magical illusions or simulacra of real people or objects.[18] These capacities are ascribed to the monkeys, in general, and also to the *rākṣasas*.[19]

Among the monkeys, the demonstration of the power to change form and size is most frequently associated with the figure of Hanumān, who changes both several times in the *Kiṣkindhā-*, *Sundara-*, and *Yuddhakāṇḍas*.[20]

Although the *rākṣasas*, too, seem to possess these powers as a class, only relatively few of them actually demonstrate them during the course of the epic narrative. Rāvaṇa, of course, as the most powerful of the *rākṣasas* and their master, possesses them and demonstrates them most notably and most infamously earlier in the poem when

[17] For a discussion of Vālmīki's use of the spectrum of *rasas* as cataloged in the *Nāṭyaśāstra*, see Goldman and Goldman 1996, pp. 36–37.

[18] For a discussion of *māyā* in the *Rāmāyaṇa*, see S. Goldman 2006b.

[19] On the monkeys, see 1.16.2–3; and for the *rākṣasas*, 1.25.11. At 4.3.3 Hanumān assumes the form of a mendicant on the instructions of Sugrīva in order to find out Rāma's intentions. At 6.28.33–34 Rāma orders Vibhīṣaṇa and his four ministers to assume human form for the battle.

[20] For a discussion of Hanumān's frequent changes of size in the *Sundarakāṇḍa*, see Goldman and Goldman 1996, pp. 45–47. Hanumān again takes on a human form when deputed by Rāma to serve as his messenger to Bharata at 6.113.18. At the end of the *Yuddhakāṇḍa* all the monkeys are said to assume human form when they accompany Rāma to Ayodhyā to participate in his consecration (6.115.35; 6.116.29).

he assumes the form of a pious forest ascetic in order to deceive and abduct Sītā.[21]

Nonetheless, in order to carry out his most nefarious plots, Rāvaṇa several times has recourse to *rāksasas* who appear to specialize, as it were, in this kind of deception. He does this most famously in forcing the reluctant Mārīca to assume the form of a golden deer in order to infatuate Sītā and lure Rāma away from his ashram, so he, Rāvaṇa, can carry out her abduction.[22] But perhaps the cruelest use of the *rākṣasas'* powers of illusion must be here in the *Yuddhakāṇḍa*, where Rāvaṇa instructs the *rākṣasa* Vidyujjihva, a master of illusion (*māyāvit*), to magically produce simulacra of Rāma's severed head, bow, and arrows in order delude Sītā and break down her spirited resistance to his threats and blandishments.[23] This ruse, accompanied by Rāvaṇa's fraudulent account of how his troops have slaughtered Rāma, Lakṣmaṇa, and all the monkeys, fails in its purpose, but it does succeed in reducing Sītā to a state of grief and despair, since she is forced to believe the testimony of her eyes. The illusion vanishes the moment Rāvaṇa, called away by urgent business, leaves the scene.[24]

Some fifteen *sargas* farther on, Rāvaṇa again tries to break Sītā's resistance to his advances by attempting to convince her that her husband has been slain, and that therefore she has no further hope of rescue. Convinced that Indrajit has, in fact, killed the Rāghava brothers, Rāvaṇa has Sītā's wardresses take her on a flight in the Puṣpaka flying palace over the battlefield where Rāma and

[21] 3.44.8. Aside from this, Rāvaṇa appears to have at least two basic forms: his fierce ten-headed and twenty-armed form, which he assumes in battle, and a less fearsome, one-headed and two-armed guise, which he takes on for his calmer and gentler moments. On this point, see notes to 5.8.13,19; 6.90.31.

[22] 3.38.15ff.

[23] 6.22.6ff.

[24] 6.23.38. This somewhat abortive episode does not exhaust the poet's fondness for having his characters devise deceptive and underhanded ways of attempting to demoralize either Rāma or Sītā. In *sarga* 52, the *rākṣasa* counselor Mahodara proposes that the *rākṣasas* stage an elaborate hoax, fabricating, and publicly celebrating, a false report that Rāma has been slain in battle. This, he argues, will break Sītā's will so that she will yield to Rāvaṇa. In this way, Mahodara reasons, Rāvaṇa will achieve his goal without having to risk battle. It is worth noting that this elaborate ruse is similarly never carried through, as both Kumbhakarṇa and Rāvaṇa dismiss it as the product of a coward's mind (6.52.24–35; 6.53.1–10).

Lakṣmaṇa lie gravely wounded.[25] Sītā is once more thrown into a paroxysm of sorrow and lamentation only to be consoled again, this time by the sympathetic *rākṣasī* Trijaṭā.[26]

The potential of psychological warfare through the demoralization of the enemy is a theme that seems to fascinate Vālmīki, especially when it is combined with the *rākṣasas'* powers of *māyā*, or illusion. This is demonstrated most dramatically, and most effectively, at the point where Indrajit, anticipating that Rāma may be able to defeat him despite his recourse to his deceptive battle tactics, stages his most horrific and elaborate deception. Employing his power of illusion, the *rākṣasa* prince conjures up an apparently living, breathing image of Sītā in his battle chariot and appears to brutally murder her before the very eyes of the monkey troops.[27] This heinous act shocks and demoralizes the monkeys and even the normally imperturbable Hanumān, who orders his troops to withdraw from the battlefield since, he now believes, the princess they have been sacrificing their lives to rescue has now been slain.[28]

Worse still, when Hanumān reports the apparent murder to Rāma, the hero is so demoralized and incapacitated with grief that he is unable to return to the battle for some time, even after Vibhīṣaṇa, well aware of his nephew's deceptive powers, reassures him that Rāvaṇa would never have countenanced Sītā's death.[29] Indeed, Rāma is so shocked by the report that he is temporarily unable to fight and must follow Vibhīṣaṇa's advice and send Lakṣmaṇa out for the final confrontation with the wily and formidable Indrajit.[30]

Another of the most prominent of the *rākṣasa* champions, Kumbhakarṇa, also avails himself of supranormal powers of this kind when, as he sets out for battle, he magically increases his already gargantuan body to truly colossal proportions.[31] Similarly, it would seem, Vibhīṣaṇa, although he never employs his powers of illusion to deceive anyone, is also able to use them to see through the

[25] 6.37.6ff.
[26] 6.38.
[27] 6.68.4–31.
[28] 6.69.19–22.
[29] 6.70.7–6.71.17.
[30] 6.72.14ff.
[31] At a height of six hundred bow lengths, Kumbhakarṇa is represented as making himself approximately one kilometer tall (6.53.33–35).

illusions of others as, for example, when he, alone among Rāma's allies, is able to clearly see the otherwise invisible Indrajit.[32]

But the *Yuddhakāṇḍa* is not entirely devoted to the strategies and conduct of war. In addition to its colorful and often harrowing descriptions of bloody conflict, the Book's narrative offers many opportunities for discussions of statecraft, moral and ethical debates, reflections on social and political relations, and moving lamentations for those who have been or are believed to have been slain during the course of the war. The poet makes ample use of these opportunities.

Thus the Book contains a number of striking passages that, in a way reminiscent of parts of the *Ayodhyākāṇḍa*, lend it something of the quality of *nītiśāstra* and *dharmaśāstra*. Notably, in many cases, the exponents of moral conduct and ethical statecraft are figures from whom one might least expect this kind of discourse, that is, some of the epic's greatest violators of the moral and ethical norms of brahmanical civilization, figures like the voracious monster Kumbhakarṇa and even the archenemy of the vedic order, that "thorn in the side of the world," Rāvaṇa himself.

The principal junctures for the exposition and discussion of ethical and expedient conduct are the councils and debates that take place frequently on both sides of the conflict when the leaders, Rāma and Rāvaṇa, are confronted with crises and calamities and are forced to make critical decisions.

The first of these occasions occurs quite early in the *Yuddhakāṇḍa*, even before Rāma has crossed the sea to begin the siege of Laṅkā. Rāvaṇa, after inspecting the destruction wrought in his city by Hanumān's rampage in the *Sundarakāṇḍa*, shows the first signs of doubt as to his invulnerability and summons his counselors to advise him on what course to take in response to the threat now confronting him. In so doing, he lectures them on the importance of sound counsel to a monarch and discourses learnedly on the different types of counsel and counselors that are described in the texts on *artha* and *nīti*.

[32] 6.36.8–10. The invisibility of Indrajit actually appears to be somewhat overdetermined. Although here it seems to be a function of the *rākṣasa*'s innate *māyā*, or power of illusion, at other points in the Book it is said to derive from specific *abhicāra*, or black magic, sacrifices that Indrajit performs at the Nikumbhilā shrine. Cf. 6.60.18–28; 6.71.13–22. The question of Indrajit's magical powers is discussed further below in connection with an analysis of his character. See pp. 78–80 and S. Goldman 2006a.

"Those who are venerable and wise say that counsel is the cornerstone of victory. Therefore, I seek your counsel, mighty warriors, with regard to Rāma.

"There are three types of men in this world: the highest, the lowest, and those in between. I will now set forth the merits and demerits of each of them.

"The highest type of man, they say, is he who first takes counsel with those counselors intent upon his welfare and competent in counsel, with those friends who share his goals, or with those kinsmen who wish him well, and only then initiates undertakings such that his efforts are in harmony with the will of the gods.

"The man who stands in between, they say, is he who reflects upon a matter by himself, who by himself directs his thoughts to righteous action, and then carries through those actions by himself.

"And the lowest type of man is he who, after saying, 'I will do this,' undertakes an action—regardless of its merits and demerits and without relying on the will of the gods—and then fails to carry it through.

"Just as men are invariably of three types: the highest, the lowest, and those in between, so also must counsel, itself, be of the same three types: the highest, the lowest, and that which is in between.

"The highest type of counsel, they say, is when counselors are consistently of one mind through insight informed by the *śāstras*.

"The counsel that is known as that which is in between, they say, is when counselors, having adopted many different opinions, subsequently reach unanimity as to how to decide a matter.

"The lowest type of counsel is when counselors go on debating, one after another, each defending his own position, and no conclusive argument can bring about unanimity.

"Therefore, you eminent counselors should agree on some excellent and appropriate counsel for me to follow. I will follow it faithfully.[33]

[33] 6.6.5–15.

The king's sycophantic counselors and generals predictably boast about how easily they will annihilate Rāma and his forces, and only his younger brother Vibhīṣaṇa has the good sense and moral courage to warn Rāvaṇa of the grave danger in which his evil behavior has placed him and to urge him to save himself and his people by returning Sītā to Rāma forthwith. His argument presents another example of śāstraic reasoning:

> But Vibhīṣaṇa stopped them as they all stood there, weapons in hand, and bade them be seated once again. Then, cupping his hands in reverence, he said these words:
>
> "The learned have prescribed as appropriate the use of force only on those occasions where one's object cannot be achieved by means of the other three stratagems, dear brother.
>
> "And, dear brother, the use of force, even when made judiciously and in accordance with the proper injunctions, succeeds only against those who are off guard, preoccupied, or stricken by misfortune.
>
> "How then can you all hope to assail someone who is vigilant, intent upon victory, firm in his strength, the master of his anger, and utterly unassailable?
>
> "Who could have imagined the impossible feat that Hanumān accomplished, leaping across the fearsome ocean, the lord of rivers and streams?
>
> "By no means, night-roaming *rākṣasas*, should we rashly underestimate our foes; for their forces and valor are immeasurable.
>
> "And what offense had Rāma previously committed against the king of the *rākṣasas* that the latter should have abducted that illustrious man's wife from Janasthāna?
>
> "Even if Rāma did kill Khara, who was attacking him, in battle, still, all living creatures must strive to the limit of their strength to save their own lives.
>
> "For this reason Vaidehī constitutes a grave danger to us. She who has been abducted must be surrendered. There is no point in acting merely to provoke a quarrel.

"It would therefore not be appropriate for us to engage in pointless hostility with this powerful and righteous man. You must give Maithilī back to him.

"You must give Maithilī back to him before, with his arrows, he lays waste to our city together with its elephants, its horses, and its myriad precious things.

"You must give back Sītā before this vast, dreadful, and unassailable army of tawny monkeys storms our Laṅkā.

"If you do not of your own free will give back Rāma's beloved wife, the city of Laṅkā and all its valiant *rākṣasas* will surely perish.

"As your kinsman, I beseech you. Do as I say. What I am telling you is both salutary and beneficial. You must give Maithilī back to him.

"You must give Maithilī back to Dāśaratha before he unleashes for your destruction his massive and unfailing arrows, newly tipped and fletched and resembling the rays of the autumnal sun.

"Give up your wrath, so destructive of both happiness and righteousness. Practice righteousness, which is conducive to pleasure and fame. Calm yourself that we may survive together with our sons and kinsmen. You must give Maithilī back to Dāśaratha."[34]

That Rāvaṇa's response to his brother's well-meaning words is harsh and bitter and that it drives the latter to defect to the side of Rāvaṇa's enemies is well known. Less well known, perhaps, is that this response, too, is couched in the form of an interesting bit of cynical worldly wisdom of the type associated with the *nīti* literature in both its aphoristic and fable genres. Arguing that one's own false friends and treacherous kinsmen are more dangerous than one's open enemies, and that the fraternal relationship is vitiated by sibling rivalry, the *rākṣasa* lord quotes a series of verses that he characterizes as "well known" and that he attributes to a group of wild elephants. The burden of this "song of the elephants" is that the greatest danger in this world arises from one's own jealous, ambitious kinfolk. He says,

[34] 6.9.7–22.

"One can live with one's enemy, or even with an enraged venomous serpent, but never with a false friend in the service of one's foes.

"I know very well the nature of kinsmen all the world over, *rākṣasa*. Kinsmen always take pleasure in one another's hardships.

"If a man is a leader, competent, learned, righteous in his conduct, and valiant, *rākṣasa*, then his kinsmen will malign him and bring him down.

"Always affecting pleasure in one's company, they turn on one in times of trouble. Concealing their true feelings, vicious kinsmen are a source of danger.

"There are these well-known verses that were sung once upon a time in the Padmavana by some elephants who had seen some men carrying ropes to snare them. Listen to them, as I recite them.

" 'It is not the fire, the other weapons, or the ropes that put us in danger; it is our own vicious kin intent on their own self-interest that are the real danger to us.

" 'For no doubt, it is they who point out the means of capturing us; therefore, we know that the danger presented by one's kin is the most severe of all.'

"In cattle there is wealth; in a brahman, self-restraint. In women, there is fickleness; from kinsmen, danger.

"And that is why, dear brother, you cannot bear it, that I am respected throughout the worlds, that I have attained universal sovereignty, and that I have set my foot on the heads of my enemies.[35]

In fact, despite the expectedly prevailing tone of warlike bravado that characterizes the advice of most of Rāvaṇa's more conventional *rākṣasa* advisers, several of his intimates, other than Vibhīṣaṇa, are noteworthy for their grounding in *nīti-* and *dharmaśāstra*. One noteworthy example of this is the sage advice given to the *rākṣasa*

[35] 6.10.2–10.

king during one of his first war councils by his maternal great-uncle Mālyavān. The *rākṣasa* elder rebukes Rāvaṇa, basing his arguments not only on the pragmatic issues of *nīti* and his interpretation of the unfavorable omens that have appeared but in terms of the broader universe of moral discourse. Indeed, his reference to the eternal conflict between *dharma* and *adharma* is reminiscent of Vaiṣṇava framings of the theology of the *avatāra* as put forth in such texts as the *Bhagavadgītā*. Mālyavān states, in part,

> "Therefore, Rāvaṇa, I would recommend making peace with Rāma. You should give him back Sītā on whose account we are so heavily besieged.
>
> "All the gods, seers, and *gandharvas* desire Rāma's victory. Therefore, you should not oppose him. You should choose to make peace with him.
>
> "The blessed Grandfather Brahmā created two races: that of the gods and that of the *asuras*, who had recourse to righteousness and unrighteousness, respectively.
>
> "For righteousness is said to be the way of the great gods, Rāvaṇa, while unrighteousness is the way of the *asuras* and the *rākṣasas*.
>
> "For they say that when righteousness eclipses unrighteousness, that ushers in the golden age, known as the Kṛta. But when unrighteousness eclipses righteousness, that brings on the degenerate Tiṣya Age.
>
> "In rampaging through the worlds, you trampled glorious righteousness and embraced unrighteousness instead. It is for that reason that your enemies have grown more powerful than we.
>
> "Grown strong through your reckless actions, the serpent of unrighteousness is devouring us; while righteousness, which the deities revere, strengthens the forces of the gods."[36]

Mālyavān then goes on to castigate Rāvaṇa for oppressing the holy and righteous *vaidika* sages[37] before, surprisingly, concluding that:

[36] 6.26.9–15.
[37] 6.26.16–20.

> "We truly believe that Rāma is none other than Viṣṇu, who has taken the body of a man. For this Rāghava, so firm in his valor, is surely no ordinary human."[38]

This theme of the "righteous *rākṣasa*" is clearly an important one to Vālmīki and, along with the major figure of Vibhīṣaṇa, such characters, both male and female, emerge at a number of critical points in the narrative of the *Sundara*- and *Yuddhakāṇḍas*.[39]

Nonetheless, it is particularly striking when one of the Book's most articulate exponents of the canons of morality and sound polity turns out to be the almost comically monstrous *rākṣasa* champion Kumbhakarṇa, a figure so grotesquely exemplary of his race's vice of bloodthirsty voracity that he makes the ordinary, run-of-the-mill demons seem almost civilized by comparison.[40]

When, after Rāvaṇa's first humiliating defeat at Rāma's hands, he has his attendants undertake the heroic task of waking the sleeping giant, Kumbhakarṇa reports to him for his instructions. But, upon hearing about the siege of Laṅkā, the monstrous warrior, who has trampled on all norms of righteous conduct, rather than taking his brother's part, first lectures him sternly on the śāstraic norms for the righteous exercise of royal power.

> "Since you paid no heed to those who had your welfare at heart, you have now met with that very calamity that we foresaw earlier, at the council of ministers.
>
> "You are suffering the immediate consequences of your wicked deed, just as evildoers suffer an instant descent into their respective hells.
>
> "You carried out this action, your majesty, without first reflecting upon it. In the sheer arrogance of your strength, you did not consider the consequences.
>
> "A person who, relying upon his royal authority, does later what ought to be done first, and first what ought to be done later, has

[38] 6.26.31.

[39] Goldman and Goldman 1996, pp. 65–68.

[40] Recall that the reason Kumbhakarṇa is being subjected to the curse (or "boon") of near-perpetual sleep is the gods' well-grounded fear that in his insatiable hunger he might devour the entire world. See 6.49.19–23; 7.10.31–42. See R. Goldman 2006b.

no comprehension of the distinction between sound and unsound policy.

"Actions that are performed in inverted order, without reference to the proper time and place, are harmful, just as are offerings of food to impious persons.

"A king who perceives the fivefold application of the three types of action after coming to a decision with his ministers remains on the proper path.

"So does a king who desires to reach a decision in conformance with the texts on polity, who pays heed to his ministers, and who recognizes his true friends by virtue of his own intelligence.

"A man should pursue all three human ends—righteousness, profit, and pleasure—at their proper times, lord of the *rākṣasas*, either all at once or two at a time.

"And a king or one exercising royal power who learns which among these three is foremost and yet does not take it to heart finds all his great learning to be in vain.

"But, foremost among *rākṣasas*, the self-possessed monarch should consult with his ministers concerning the timely use of bribery, conciliation, sowing dissension, coercive force, or any combination of these means, as well as the proper and improper ways of applying them. He who does so and practices righteousness, profit, and pleasure at their appropriate times never comes to grief in this world.

"And the king who, together with ministers who understand the true nature of things and have his interests at heart, deliberates over what he ought and ought not do in this world in order to achieve a beneficial result thrives.

"There are some men—dumb brutes, in fact—utterly ignorant of the import of the *śāstras*, who, once they are brought into discussions of policy, wish to speak out of sheer arrogance.

"One should not follow the pernicious advice of those who are ignorant of the *śāstras*, and unfamiliar with the treatises on statecraft, and simply eager to enhance their own positions.

"And those men who undermine all undertakings by foolishly uttering in their insolence pernicious advice that only seems beneficial should, after careful examination, be excluded from discussions of policy.

"For in this world some counselors, acting in concert with cunning enemies, persuade their master to engage in self-destructive actions, thus bringing him to ruin.

"When it comes to evaluating counsel, a master must, through a full investigation, determine which of his ministers are, in fact, enemies who are posing as friends although they have actually been suborned.

"For his enemies find the weak points of a rash king who suddenly rushes into undertakings, just as birds plunge into the gap in the Krauñca mountain.

"And so a king who underestimates his enemy and fails to protect himself meets with calamities and falls from his lofty state."[41]

Only when Rāvaṇa, in his anger and self-pity, rebukes Kumbhakarṇa and then begs him to offer his brotherly assistance does the latter vow to destroy the invading army.[42]

The last, most extensively argued, and in many ways the most interesting sustained discourse on the subjects of *dharma*, *artha*, and *nīti* is that delivered by Lakṣmaṇa at one of the Book's most emotionally wrought moments.

After Indrajit, as mentioned above, has deluded and demoralized the monkey army with his apparent murder of a simulacrum of Sītā, Hanumān sorrowfully reports the horrific event to Rāma. The latter, who must maintain his status as an "ordinary man" until the completion of his divine mission, collapses with grief at this news and will remain unfit for combat until after Indrajit is defeated and dies.

At this juncture Lakṣmaṇa, in what is represented as an attempt to console his brother,[43] delivers himself of a lengthy critique of *dharma*, truth, and the entire edifice of morality of which Rāma is the tradition's greatest exemplar and upon which his entire career is based.

[41] 6.51.2–20.
[42] 6.51.27ff.
[43] 6.71.1.

Essentially Lakṣmaṇa takes a cynical and worldly view, arguing that the fact that terrible things (such as the apparent murder of Sītā) happen to such virtuous people as Rāma, whereas those like Rāvaṇa, who flout every rule of *dharma*, prosper is proof that the practice of righteousness is in vain. Lakṣmaṇa revives his old argument that Rāma should never have agreed to accept banishment in deference to some abstract notion of truth but should, in fact, have imprisoned Daśaratha, who had treated him so wrongfully and cruelly.[44] Refuting the entire concept of *dharma* as an independent force, Lakṣmaṇa resorts to a more Machiavellian *realpolitik*, deriving its logic from the principles of *arthaśāstra*. He argues that the ability to perform righteous action is made possible only through wealth and power, both of which Rāma has foolishly forfeited by relinquishing the kingship that was rightfully his. Lakṣmaṇa then utters a virtual paean of praise to wealth and power from which, he argues, all blessings flow, concluding his peroration with a vow to avenge the killing of Sītā by destroying Rāvaṇa and Laṅkā along with him.[45]

What is particularly striking about Lakṣmaṇa's sustained critique of the fundamental principles of *dharmaśāstra* here is not so much its content as the fact that Rāma makes no effort to refute it. In a number of places in the epic, characters question or criticize actions that Rāma has taken or proposes to take.[46] In most of these episodes, the characters debating Rāma argue from the perspective of some aspect of *dharma* as it is encoded in the *śāstra* or in the oral tradition. Nonetheless, in each of his rebuttals, Rāma trumps these arguments with those derived from a higher, more comprehensive, or more correct reading of dharmic conduct.

In a few of these cases, however, a character will take a position directly contrary to the normal dharmic rules of filial deference and obedience to legitimate royal authority or even one that denies the

[44] See 2.18.

[45] 6.70.13–42.

[46] Examples are Kausalyā's arguments that Rāma should obey her maternal command to stay in Ayodhyā rather than Daśaratha's paternal order of banishment or at least allow her to accompany him into exile (2.18.18–24; 2.21.5–6), Sītā's argument that she should be permitted to accompany Rāma into exile (2.24.2–18; 2.26.2–21), Sītā's critique of Rāma's carrying weapons during his sojourn in the guise of a forest ascetic (3.8), and Vālin's denunciation of Rāma for his having shot him while he was engaged in single combat with his brother, Sugrīva (4.17.12–45). For a discussion of these and other *dharma* debates in the poem, see R. Goldman 2003a.

foundational ontological and eschatological principles of mainstream vedic and Hindu ideology. These positions proceed from a pragmatic and distinctly materialistic worldview that rejects such core concepts as rebirth and an afterlife whose conditions are governed by a karmic system of moral rewards and punishments. In denying—explicitly or implicitly—the existence of the *adṛśya*, or invisible, worlds of the gods, heavens, and hells, such arguments speak to a hedonistic and materialistic philosophy according to which one should take what one can get in this world in terms of pleasure, wealth, and power.

One example of this kind of argument in the *Rāmāyaṇa* can be found in Lakṣmaṇa's angry outbursts in the *Ayodhyākāṇḍa*, where he urges Rāma to resist his father's tacit compliance with Kaikeyī's demand that he be banished and instead depose the old king and seize the throne by force.[47] Another is the well-known and highly explicit critique of *dharma*, deference, and religion advanced by the brahman Jābāli in an effort to persuade the exiled prince to give up his adherence to the orders of the now deceased king and return to claim the Kosalan throne.[48]

But all these arguments, whether offering an incorrect interpretation of *dharma* or seeking to deny it altogether, have a single purpose. All serve as *pūrvapakṣas*, incomplete or utterly incorrect arguments, that provide opportunities for their proponents' interlocutor, Rāma himself, to correct them[49] and, in so doing, carry out his role as the narrative literature's most prominent exponent and exemplar of *dharma*.

Given this background, Lakṣmaṇa's attempt to "console" his grief-stricken and prostrated brother is curious. First, it seems odd that Lakṣmaṇa should seek to comfort Rāma by bringing up the same kind of arguments that the prince had so soundly refuted in the past and that had earned him, Lakṣmaṇa, his brother's rebuke on those

[47] 2.18.1–15; 2.20.1–35.

[48] 2.100.

[49] In the one case in which Rāma "loses" an argument, the one where he debates with Sītā the propriety of her accompanying him to the forest, it is made clear that it is he himself who is putting forward the *pūrvapakṣa* in an effort to test Sītā and thus assure himself that she truly understands and is able to articulate the correct dharmic position (2.27.26–31).

earlier occasions. Most striking is that this, the last of the epic's anti-*dharma* speeches, is the only one to go unanswered by Rāma. For instead of the anticipated correction on Rāma's part, the poet brings in Vibhīṣaṇa, who brusquely cuts off Lakṣmaṇa, assures Rāma that Sītā could not, in fact, have been killed, and instructs Rāma to send Lakṣmaṇa out to fight Indrajit before the latter has had a chance to complete his latest *abhicāra*, or black magical, rite.[50]

It is not clear why Rāma fails to respond to Lakṣmaṇa's radical deconstruction of *dharma* and morality in favor of a virtual hymn to *artha* and political expediency. His silence here goes against the otherwise uniform practice of the poet and appears to let stand an argument that runs counter to the most fundamental theme of the *Rāmāyaṇa* and the culture of which it is one of the principal handbooks. The explanation may lie, perhaps, in what one may consider Vālmīki's penchant for a certain kind of "realism" that is in keeping with his meticulous portrayal of the *avatāra* as faithfully acting out the role of an "ordinary" man in maintaining Viṣṇu's strict adherence to the terms of the boon given to Rāvaṇa by Brahmā.[51] In the present context, on the very eve of the final battle in which Rāma must at long last carry out his divine mission, it may well be that the poet is especially eager to remind us one last time of Rāma's mortality and of the vulnerabilities that are its hallmarks. It would appear that he does this by carrying through his portrayal of Rāma as truly prostrated by the news of Sītā's apparent death and so unable to take in, much less respond to, his brother's provocative and subversive statements. This idea gains strong support from the fact that Rāma not only fails to react to Lakṣmaṇa's diatribe but also apparently fails to comprehend Vibhīṣaṇa's subsequent assurance that Sītā is not dead and his advice that he needs to send Lakṣmaṇa out at once to confront Indrajit. Vālmīki confirms the hero's dazed state by noting that Vibhīṣaṇa is forced to repeat his speech, the import of which Rāma has been utterly unable to grasp.

> Although Rāghava had heard those words of Vibhīṣaṇa, he could not, racked with grief as he was, clearly understand what the *rākṣasa* had said.

[50] 6.71.5–22.

[51] 1.14.6–1.15.6. On this critical issue, see Pollock 1991, pp. 15–54.

> But then, in the presence of the monkeys, Rāma, the conqueror of enemy citadels, regaining his composure, spoke to Vibhīṣaṇa, who sat beside him.
>
> "Vibhīṣaṇa! Lord of the *rākṣasas*, sons of chaos, I would like to hear once more what you just said. Please repeat what you intended to say."
>
> When he had heard those words of Rāghava, Vibhīṣaṇa, skilled in speech, repeated what he had said.[52]

It is difficult to understand why the poet would include this otherwise pointless passage if not to demonstrate forcibly his hero's humanity. Given that Rāma has not been able to grasp the import of Vibhīṣaṇa's encouraging and exhortative words, clearly we are meant to understand that Lakṣmaṇa's words, which were framed precisely to provoke the hero's normal spirited defense of *dharma*, have gone utterly unheard and unheeded. Few things could more dramatically highlight Rāma's all-too-human, grief-induced stupor than his failure to respond to Lakṣmaṇa's challenge to all that Rāma stands for.

That Rāma, on the eve of the fulfillment of the mission he has undertaken on behalf of the gods and sages, must be clearly seen to be a man is again unmistakably signaled by the passage immediately after his final triumph over Rāvaṇa, where he is felicitated by the gods, who hail him as the omniscient and eternal creator of the universe.[53] In response to the gods' virtual hymn of praise, the seemingly bewildered prince replies,

> I think of myself only as a man, Rāma, the son of Daśaratha. May the Blessed Lord please tell me who I really am, to whom I belong, and why I am here.[54]

This seemingly naïve question, which elicits from Brahmā a full-fledged, seventeen-verse *stotra* in which Rāma is at last unambiguously revealed as the lord of the universe, Viṣṇu, and Sītā as his divine consort, Lakṣmī, puts the final seal, as it were, on this most critical point of the epic, namely, that in order to accomplish his

[52] 6.72.1–4.
[53] 6.105.1–8.
[54] 6.105.10.

purpose Rāma not only must act like a mere man, he must in some meaningful sense be one and must himself actually believe in his own humanity. For Vālmīki, unlike many of the influential *Rāmāyaṇa* authors who followed him, Rāma's humanity is taken both literally and seriously. This means that his hero, unlike those, say, of the *Adhyātmarāmāyaṇa* and the *Rāmcaritmānas*, must actually suffer the physical, mental, and emotional pains common to ordinary mortals and must be unaware of his own divinity.[55] Brahmā's revelation and Rāma's recognition of his divinity is therefore appropriate only now in the closing sections of the *Yuddhakāṇḍa* since the divine purpose that required the hero to live with full confidence in his own humanity has now, with the death of Rāvaṇa, been accomplished.

In making possible the revelation of Rāma's true nature, the death of Rāvaṇa thus marks, in a sense, the culmination of the *kāṇḍa* and, indeed, of the life mission of the epic hero. Yet there remain some important matters to be dealt with in the eleven, mostly short, chapters that follow Brahmā's hymn of praise to Rāma as the Lord Viṣṇu incarnate. Some of these are more or less formal, conventional, or ritual necessities, such as the funeral of Rāvaṇa, the lamentations of his widows, and the royal consecration ceremony of Vibhīṣaṇa.[56] Others are more or less narrative necessities, including the appearance of the shade of Daśaratha to greet Rāma and absolve Kaikeyī, the miraculous revival of Rāma's virtuous monkey allies who had been killed during the war, and, most important, the completion of the circle of the story that began with the banishment of Rāma in the *Ayodhyākāṇḍa* by bringing him safely back to his

[55] In this respect, it is illuminating to compare Vālmīki's representation of the *Rāmāvatāra* not only to those of the other authors but to the characterization of the *Kṛṣṇāvatāra* as it is found in the *Mahābhārata*, the *Harivaṃśa*, and the *Bhāgavata* literature in general. Bound as he is by nothing like the conditions of Rāvaṇa's boon, Kṛṣṇa can never experience any sort of suffering nor can there be any limitation on his omniscience. Thus, for example, Duryodhana's attempt to capture Kṛṣṇa when the latter comes to him as an emissary of the Pāṇḍavas is easily countered by the *avatāra*'s display of his divine nature as all the vedic gods and Pāṇḍava heroes are seen to issue from his body (*MBh* 5.129.1–16). Similarly, Kṛṣṇa repeatedly identifies himself as the supreme divinity in the great epic, most famously to Arjuna to whom he reveals, respectively, both his *vibhūtis* and his awesome universal form in the tenth and eleventh *adhyāyas* of the *Bhagavadgītā*.

[56] 6.99–100.

ancestral capital, reuniting him with his faithful and devoted brother Bharata, and, of course, describing his lavish and long-deferred consecration.[57] Aspects of several of these events and episodes are discussed in the following sections.

Undoubtedly the most strikingly dramatic, unexpected, and noteworthy episode to be found in the closing chapters of the Book is the complex narrative describing the reunion of Rāma with his beloved and long-suffering wife, Sītā, which occupies the four *sargas* from 101 through 104. The significance of this passage, its relevance to the political and social impact of the epic, and its reworking in several influential later versions of the *Rāmakathā* are such that the episode is dealt with at length separately in connection with the examination of the Book's portrayal of Sītā in the following section on the principal characters of the *Yuddhakāṇḍa*.

[57] 6.107–16.

4. The Major Characters of the *Yuddhakāṇḍa*

A BOOK AS lengthy and narratively complex as the *Yuddhakāṇḍa* would be expected to have a rather sizable cast of characters, and this expectation has not been left unfulfilled by the poet. Moreover, the nature of the narrative in which the principal antagonists, Rāma and Rāvaṇa, are each advised and assisted by a substantial number of counselors and warriors, many of whom are given significant "speaking parts," as it were, and/or accorded one or more whole chapters detailing their martial exploits, victories, or deaths, adds significantly to the bulk of the text. Indeed, the theme of this Book, in which the hosts of *vānaras* and *rākṣasas* clash by night and by day, affords the author the opportunity to back up the main champions on both sides with vast numbers of troops that make the proverbial cinematic "cast of thousands" seem more like Jones's "thin red line."[1] Thus not only are many warriors shown in action but many more are mentioned and described.[2] This tendency reaches its logical limit in the way that the text and some, notably southern, manuscripts describe truly astronomical numbers of monkeys.[3]

With this in mind, and because of space constraints, it is appropriate, we feel, to focus on only the most prominent and interesting of the many characters—humans, monkeys, and *rākṣasas*—that people the lengthy narrative of this *kāṇḍa*.

THE HUMANS

As is the case in the three *kāṇḍas* that precede it, the *Yuddhakāṇḍa*, because of its principal setting in regions outside the boundaries of significant human habitation, for most of its narrative contains a very small cast of human characters. Indeed, until the Book's final four *sargas*, when Rāma returns first to the ashram of the sage Bharadvāja and subsequently to Nandigrāma and Ayodhyā for his

[1] Jones 1962.
[2] Compare the elaborate enumeration and descriptions of the monkey troop leaders delivered to Rāvaṇa by his hapless spies Śuka and Sāraṇa in *sargas* 17–19.
[3] On this, see the notes to 6.19.4 and 6.19.32,33.

reunion with his patient brother Bharata and his long-delayed consecration as king of Kosala, its multitude of characters contains only the same three humans, Rāma, Sītā, and Lakṣmaṇa, who represent their species in the *Kiṣkindha-* and *Sundarakāṇḍas*.

These three are, of course, the central players in the entire drama of the *Rāmāyaṇa*, and, as such, their characterization has been discussed at length in the Introductions to the preceding volumes. Therefore, here we need only discuss briefly those aspects of their characters that may not have been brought fully into the foreground in the earlier portions of the epic.

Rāma

In the *Yuddhakāṇḍa*, as in all Books of the epic save only the *Sundarakāṇḍa*,[4] Rāma, the poem's eponymous hero, is the principal object of the poet's attention. However, because of the grand scope of the narrative, the very large number of characters who engage in debate, battle, or both with one another when Rāma is not present, and the frequent shifting of the scene from Rāma's command post to other parts of the battlefield, the council chambers, residences, and parapets of Laṅkā, and even to the far-off Himalayas, the hero's percentage of time "on camera," as it were, is, in terms relative to most of the other Books, often limited. There are, however, several groups of *sargas* distributed throughout the poem that place the hero squarely in the poet's field of vision.

Vālmīki's portrayal of the great hero is, for the most part, much the same as it is in the other Books. Rāma remains the stalwart, charismatic, valorous yet compassionate model of ideal human virtue that he is generally shown to be in the earlier sections of the poem.

On the other hand, the *Yuddhakāṇḍa* is the Book in which the *avatāra*'s human form will finally be thrown off and his true identity as the Supreme Lord of the universe at long last revealed. Because of the terms of Rāvaṇa's boon and the constraints it places on even Rāma's understanding of his divine nature, however, the hero is prevented from achieving full self-realization until he has fulfilled

[4] On Rāma's representation in the *Sundarakāṇḍa*, see Goldman and Goldman 1996, pp. 18–19.

the purpose for which he has taken human birth, the slaying of the arch demon. This, however, does not take place until the ninety-seventh *sarga* of the Book. Only after this, in *sarga* 105, can the gods "remind" Rāma of who he really is.

Perhaps for this reason, the poet introduces a number of scenes where the hero's humanity is highlighted most poignantly by showing him as prey to the human emotions of anger and grief and to be critically, even mortally, wounded and in need of urgent ministrations from the mighty bird Garuḍa or the monkey physician, Suṣeṇa, to save his life. Thus, at *sarga* 14, Rāma, confronted by the obduracy of the ocean god, Samudra, who will not permit him and his army to cross over to Laṅkā, abandons his habitual equanimity and vaunted forbearance to rage against the sea and even against those very virtues, forbearance and forgiveness, of which he is the great exemplar.

> Then Rāma, the corners of his eyes red in his rage at Samudra, said these words to Lakṣmaṇa of auspicious marks, who stood nearby.
>
> "Lakṣmaṇa, just see the arrogance of this ignoble Samudra, who will not manifest himself, even though I have worshiped him.
>
> "The virtues of the good—calmness, forbearance, straightforwardness, and kind words—are always taken for signs of weakness by those who lack them.
>
> "People only respect an evil, insolent person who runs about praising himself and unleashing violence on everyone.
>
> "Peaceful means can no more lead to fame or glory in this world, Lakṣmaṇa, than they can to victory in the vanguard of battle.
>
> "Now, Saumitri, you shall see the ocean, abode of sea monsters, with its waters choked with the dead bodies of those very creatures pierced by my arrows and floating everywhere.
>
> "Here and now, Lakṣmaṇa, you shall see me cut to pieces the bodies of gigantic fish, the trunks of sea elephants, and the coils of great serpents.
>
> "Now, launching a powerful assault, I shall with my arrows dry up the ocean together with its fish and sea monsters and its masses of conch and oyster shells.

> "This lord of the ocean, abode of sea monsters, thinks that because I am endowed with forbearance I am weak. To hell with forbearance for people like this!"[5]

Rāma's legendary equanimity also fails him several times in the Book when he is confronted with what appears to be the death of those most dear to him, notably his brother and inseparable companion, Lakṣmaṇa, and his beloved wife, Sītā.

The narrative presents the hero with several occasions to give way to unbearable sorrow and bitter despair when it appears that Lakṣmaṇa has been slain or mortally wounded. In *sarga* 39, Rāma, while still bound in the toils of Indrajit's fearsome serpent-arrows, regains consciousness to find that his brother has apparently died from his injuries. He laments bitterly, declaring that he himself cannot go on living without his brother. Notably, Rāma observes, in his profound sorrow, that the loss of Lakṣmaṇa is more grievous to him than that of Sītā herself, arguing that he can always find a woman to equal her, whereas a devoted brother like Lakṣmaṇa is irreplaceable.[6] Indeed, since Rāma now feels he must follow his brother in death, he regards the expedition to Laṅkā essentially as a failure. Warning the monkeys that in any case they cannot hope to defeat Rāvaṇa without Lakṣmaṇa, he thanks his allies and urges them to return home.[7]

Later, near the end of the battle, there is a striking reprise of this scene when Rāma, seeing Lakṣmaṇa struck down by Rāvaṇa's deadly javelin and assuming that he is dead, once more gives way to despair. He loses the will to continue fighting and once again claims he has no further interest in battle, kingship, or even Sītā herself.[8] In each case, Rāma recovers his composure and martial valor only when Lakṣmaṇa is cured of his injuries.

[5] 6.14.3–11. This episode, in its rendition by Tulsī Dās, is the setting for his famous verse about how certain things and creatures, including *śūdras* and women, only perform when beaten. This verse has been the subject of critique and controversy among members of the women's movement and Dalit advocacy groups in contemporary India. See *Rāmcaritmānas* 5.58.3: *ḍhola gavara sūdra pasu nārī / sakala tāḍanā ke adhikārī //*. On the towering rage of which Rāma is capable, see Pollock 1991, pp. 55–67.

[6] On this point, see R. Goldman 1980.

[7] 6.39.3–29.

[8] 6.89.1–8.

Despite Rāma's repeated lamentations for Lakṣmaṇa in which he twice appears to prize his brother more highly than his wife, the hero's greatest emotional crisis comes only when he is informed, falsely, as it turns out, that Sītā herself has been murdered at the hands of Indrajit, who has deployed his great powers of illusion to make it appear that he has committed this heinous deed. For now Rāma not only laments his loss poignantly, he actually loses, for a time, the physical and mental capacity to continue to fight or even understand fully what is going on around him. When Rāma hears of the report of Sītā's death from the trustworthy Hanumān, who has witnessed Indrajit's apparent murder of the princess, he at once loses consciousness without uttering a word.

> Upon hearing those words of his, Rāghava, fainting from grief, fell to the ground like a tree cut off at the roots.[9]

Even when Rāma is consoled by Vibhīṣaṇa, who reassures him that Rāvaṇa would have never permitted the murder of Sītā, the hero remains dazed and confused. Recognizing this, the *rākṣasa* urges that he rest awhile to compose himself and recoup his strength while Lakṣmaṇa takes up the battle against Indrajit.[10] Rāma listens to this sage advice, but, still too dazed and emotionally distraught to take it in, he is compelled to ask Vibhīṣaṇa to repeat it.[11] Even though Rāma has at last regained his composure, he still seems unable to plunge back into battle and so passively follows the *rākṣasa*'s advice, sending his brother off to deal with the powerful Indrajit.[12] Prior to these passages in the *Yuddhakāṇḍa*, Rāma, the literature's greatest exemplar of self-control, has rarely been shown to lose his composure in this fashion.[13]

Perhaps the most striking and deeply affecting insight into the inner emotional life of Vālmīki's hero comes neither through the poet's portrayal of a man in near total control of his emotions nor through the occasional lapses in his prodigious self-control that we see from time to time. Instead, it is gained through the poet's exploration of the profound emotional turmoil Rāma must go through

[9] 6.70.10.
[10] 6.71.17–20.
[11] 6.72.1–4; see, too, pp. 39–40.
[12] 6.72.19–20.
[13] See Pollock 1991, pp. 55–67; and 3.58–62. See, too, R. Goldman 1980.

at what should be his moment of greatest happiness, his reunion with his beloved and long-suffering wife.

This reunion, much as Rāma has longed for it and suffered to achieve it, presents him with one of those painful dilemmas that the epic poets like to thrust upon their exemplary heroes—crises where they are confronted with a seemingly irresoluble conflict between public duty, or *dharma*, and personal loyalty.[14] In this case Rāma, determined not to compromise his reputation as a dharmic monarch, must place the political over the personal, although doing so will cause him and his innocent wife terrible anguish.[15] Here, as elsewhere in the epic, Rāma, in his effort to elicit or prove the dharmic nature of another character, will turn out to be merely testing Sītā so as to prove her virtue publicly.[16]

For the first time in the epic, the hero, so rightly admired for his emotional stability and moral certitude, is shown to be prey to seriously conflicting emotions. When Hanumān reports to him that Sītā is eager to see him, Rāma, far from responding with joy, exhibits signs of distress.

> Addressed in this fashion by Hanumān, Rāma, foremost among upholders of righteousness, was suddenly plunged into gloomy thought, and he became somewhat tearful.
>
> Heaving long, hot sighs and staring at the ground, he spoke to Vibhīṣaṇa, who stood beside him, looking like a great storm cloud.[17]

Then, when Vibhīṣaṇa informs Rāma that he has brought Sītā to him, we see the hero struggling with feelings that pull him in different directions.

[14] The classic epic example of this kind of conflict is, of course, the one that faces Arjuna in the sixth *parvan* of the *Mahābhārata* (including the *Bhagavadgītā*), where he must choose between his *svadharma* as a warrior and his love of, and loyalty to, his kinsmen.

[15] In this episode, as in the later and more controversial one in the *Uttarakāṇḍa* where Rāma actually banishes Sītā, the hero is, as elsewhere, striving to serve as an exemplary monarch unlike his father, Daśaratha, who allows his infatuation for a woman to compromise his performance as a dharmic ruler. See 2.10. See, too, R. Goldman 1997 and 2004; and Pollock 1986, pp. 58–73.

[16] On this issue, see Sutherland 1989; S. Goldman 2004a; and R. Goldman 2004 and 2006b.

[17] 6.102.5–6.

> But when Rāghava heard that she who had dwelt so long in the *rākṣasa*'s house had come, three emotions—joy, sorrow, and anger—took hold of him.[18]

Only when Sītā has been publicly subjected to the humiliation of Rāma's cruel words of rejection and has undergone an ordeal by fire, and only after Rāma himself has been criticized for his actions by the god of fire, does he declare that he had, in fact, no doubts as to the princess's chastity but had acted so cruelly only to demonstrate it to the assembled multitudes. He tells Agni,

> "Unquestionably Sītā needed to be proven innocent before the three worlds, since this auspicious woman had long dwelt in Rāvaṇa's inner apartments.
>
> "For surely had I not put Jānakī to the test, the virtuous would have said of me, 'Daśaratha's son Rāma is a lustful fool.'
>
> "I know full well that Janaka's daughter Maithilī could give her heart to no other, since she is devoted to me and obeys my every thought.
>
> "But in order that the three worlds, too, should have faith in her, I, whose ultimate recourse is truth, simply stood by as Vaidehī entered the fire, eater of oblations."[19]

In this way, at the closing moments of Rāma's self-induced nescience regarding his own true nature as the Supreme Being, the poet is able to reaffirm once more that his hero's assumption of humanity is, in fact, genuine[20] while also giving a striking, if disturbing, demonstration of Rāma's unwavering adherence to the principles of *rājadharma* even when such adherence entails the price of immense suffering to himself and his beloved.

The focus on the vulnerability of Rāma and Lakṣmaṇa in the Book, however, should not blind us to the fact that, for Vālmīki, here

[18] 6.102.16. See the note to this verse for a discussion of how the commentators explain the three emotions and the reasons for them.

[19] 6.106.11–14.

[20] This is made unambiguously clear in Rāma's famous statement to the gods who are lauding him as the lord of the universe, "I think of myself only as a man, Rāma, the son of Daśaratha. May the Blessed Lord please tell me who I really am, to whom I belong, and why I am here" (6.105.10).

as throughout the poem, the heroes are always understood to be *aṃśāvatāras* of Lord Viṣṇu. This point has been thoroughly argued in the Introduction to the *Araṇyakāṇḍa*[21] and so need not be argued again here at any length. Nonetheless, the notion that the divinity of Rāma is essentially a feature only of the epic's first and last Books, which provide a Vaiṣṇava theological frame for an otherwise originally secular tale, has long been a favorite subject of *Rāmāyaṇa* scholarship[22] and continues to be put forward even to this day.[23] Whatever may have been the textual history of the five so-called core Books of the poem, it is clear that no version of the received text is unaware of Rāma's divinity even though, in keeping with the boon of Brahmā, this particular *avatāra* has to function, for the most part, as if he were a mere mortal. As elsewhere, the *Yuddhakāṇḍa* offers a number of strong hints that even if Rāma himself declares his ignorance of his divine nature until he is reminded of it by the gods after the completion of his divine mission,[24] we, the poet's audience, must never forget this central fact.

The Vaiṣṇava nature of Rāma and Lakṣmaṇa is indicated in a number of passages that strongly hint at the truth without making it clear to the heroes themselves. Thus when they are struck down by the powerful serpent-weapons of Indrajit, they are freed and restored to health and vitality by the sudden and unheralded appearance of the mighty Garuḍa.[25] The great bird is a figure intimately associated with Lord Viṣṇu as his emblem and his *vāhana*, and, although no explanation for his intervention is offered, the association cannot be lost on any South Asian audience. Again, when Mālyavān attempts to dissuade Rāvaṇa from his self-destructive obduracy in the face of Rāma's demands, the advice of some of his counselors, and the numerous ominous portents that confront him, the venerable *rākṣasa* explicitly states that several of the wiser demons are convinced that Rāma is, indeed, a manifestation of Viṣṇu, the ancient foe of the *rākṣasas*.[26] Then, too, when Lakṣmaṇa is struck down by Rāvaṇa, who attempts to carry his fallen foe from the

[21] See Pollock 1984b; 1991, pp. 15–67.
[22] See Brockington 1984, pp. 218–25; 1998, pp. 466–72, passim.
[23] González-Reimann 2006, pp. 203–20.
[24] See 6.105.10 and notes.
[25] See 6.40.36–59.
[26] See 6.26.31 and notes. Cf. 7.6–8.

battlefield, he proves far too heavy for even the immensely powerful *rākṣasa* lord to lift. Yet Hanumān, well known in the Vaiṣṇava tradition as a supreme devotee of Lord Rāma, easily carries him to safety.[27]

Through episodes and allusions such as these,[28] the poet manages to allude cleverly at strategic moments in the Book to the central theological message of the poem while demonstrating time and again the emotional and physical vulnerability and abjection to which the *avatāra* has willingly subjected himself in the service of the gods and of *dharma* itself.

Sītā

More than any other figure in the epic, Sītā is rendered with extraordinary skill by the poet as a character capable of the expression of a full and finely drawn range of emotions. Although she is commonly held up as the model of the perfectly passive and subservient wife, she can be independent minded, strong-willed, and, when the situation demands it, sharp tongued.[29] Thus we have seen in the *Ayodhyākāṇḍa* her powerful and even cutting critique of Rāma's attempt to persuade her to stay behind in the capital when he is sent into exile.[30] In the *Araṇyakāṇḍa* one sees her willfulness in wheedling Rāma to pursue the illusory deer to gratify her childish whim and her somewhat darker side when, in her fear for her husband, she harshly impugns faithful Lakṣmaṇa's motives.[31] Then, too, in that Book and in the *Sundarakāṇḍa* she is given some fine and forceful speeches in which, despite her terror, she contemptuously lectures mighty Rāvaṇa on the error of his ways and the fearful retribution that awaits him.[32] Her emotional range, too, is shown in

[27] See 6.47.104 and notes. Compare *BhāgP* 10.7.18–30, where the child Kṛṣṇa makes himself heavy and then bears down with his weight the whirlwind demon, Tṛṇāvarta, after which he permits himself to be picked up by the *gopīs* and returned to his foster mother, Yaśodhā.

[28] Compare, too, Mandodarī's lament, where, in her expression of grief, she wonders how so great a being as Rāvaṇa could have been defeated by a mere mortal (6.99.5–10).

[29] See Sutherland 1989 and S. Goldman 2001; 2003a; and 2004a.

[30] 2.24–27.

[31] 3.41,43.

[32] 3.45.28–44; 3.54.1–19; 5.19; and 5.20.12–22.

the latter Book as she oscillates from near suicidal despondency[33] to the heights of joy.[34]

The highly dramatic events of the *Yuddhakāṇḍa* present the poet with several opportunities to further expand upon Sītā's emotional repertoire, as it were.[35] Our first encounter with the heroine in the *Yuddhakāṇḍa* occurs in the twenty-second *sarga*, where Rāvaṇa, having failed through his earlier threats and blandishments to make the princess waver in her devotion to Rāma, resorts to sorcery and psychological torture in an attempt to accomplish his goal. In order to demoralize her, he has his courtier Vidyujjihva, apparently a specialist in magical illusion, create simulacra of Rāma's bow and severed head, which he then shows to Sītā as he tells her a completely fictitious account of how the *rākṣasas* have staged a successful night attack on the hero's troops. He informs her that most of the principal monkey warriors have been slain, wounded, or put to flight and that Rāma himself has been slain in his sleep by the *rākṣasa* champion Prahasta.[36] Taken in by this cruel deception, Sītā delivers a forceful and moving *vilāpa* in which she expresses her desolation and her anger, castigating first Kaikeyī as the ultimate cause for Rāma's death and the destruction of the family, Rāma for having allowed himself to be taken unawares, and, finally, herself, whom, as a surviving widow and the proximate cause of her husband's death, she likens to Kālarātri, the dark night of universal destruction. In the midst of Sītā's lamentation, however, Rāvaṇa is suddenly called away. The moment he leaves, the illusion vanishes.[37]

As elsewhere in the poem, Sītā is consoled and reassured by a friendly *rākṣasī*, in this case Saramā.[38] When the *rākṣasī* offers to carry a message to Rāma, Sītā shows that she, too, is capable of placing her excellent political instincts ahead of her emotional needs by telling Saramā that she should instead spy on Rāvaṇa's council and report back to her on his deliberations and intentions.[39]

[33] 5.24.36–49; 5.27.5–18.
[34] 5.34.3–4.
[35] See S. Goldman 2003b.
[36] 6.22.12–43.
[37] 6.23.1–38.
[38] Cf. Trijaṭā's consoling report to Sītā and her *rākṣasī* wardresses of her dream at 5.25.
[39] 6.25.5–11.

Shortly after this, Sītā is once more subjected to the most severe emotional shock. When Indrajit, cloaked in the invisibility his magical powers enable him to achieve, has managed to gravely wound both Rāma and Lakṣmaṇa in battle, Rāvaṇa, mistakenly believing his enemy to be dead, orders the *rākṣasīs* to take Sītā by force in the flying palace Puṣpaka over the battlefield so that she may see for herself that her husband has been slain and that she now has no choice but to marry him.[40] This situation affords the princess the opportunity to show yet another aspect of her personality. Although the text indicates that, as before, she laments piteously,[41] the tenor of her lamentation here is rather different from what we have seen at *sarga* 23.

For where she abandoned herself to her grief, anger, and self-condemnation on the earlier occasion, the poet takes this second opportunity to showcase her familiarity with elements in the śāstraic corpus. She remarks that all the astrologers and soothsayers in her father's court had been mistaken in foretelling that she would be a queen and she learnedly critiques the tenets of the *sāmudrikaśāstra*, the science of bodily signs, by noting that, although she is possessed of a significant catalog of auspicious physical characteristics, the whole science must now be shown to be false since she has, or so she thinks, been reduced to early widowhood.[42]

But not even these two incidents, in which Sītā must confront what she believes to be the death of her beloved husband and her only savior, can prepare her, or, for that matter, the audience, for the bitter blow she receives when Rāma, at the moment of their longed-for reunion, repudiates her with cutting and humiliating words before Lakṣmaṇa and the assembled monkeys and *rākṣasas*.

Deeply wounded and shamed by Rāma's harsh reception, Sītā gives way to tears, but not for long. Wiping her tear-stained face, she replies to her husband with calm and reasoned dignity, defending her honor, asserting her loyalty, and criticizing him for harboring feelings of misogyny. She accuses him of giving way to anger like some common man and faults him for failing to consider her own virtue and lofty birth, as well as for his disloyalty to the woman he

[40] 6.37.5–21.
[41] 6.37.20–21; 6.38.1.
[42] 6.38.2–14.

married when she was still a child. At length, she turns to Lakṣmaṇa and instructs him to build her a pyre, since, as she says, she cannot live under the shadow of Rāma's false allegations.[43] Lakṣmaṇa sees that Rāma will not interfere and so complies with Sītā's request. She reverently circumambulates the fire and, to the horror of the onlookers, calmly enters it.[44]

Brahmā now arrives along with the other gods to proclaim Rāma's divinity and to announce that Sītā is, in fact, the goddess Lakṣmī.[45] The fire god, Agni, then emerges from the blazing pyre holding Sītā and testifies at length to her purity.[46] Only then does Rāma indicate that he has never actually doubted the fidelity and chastity of his beloved but only acted as he had to prove her purity to the world. He then takes her back, noting that she "is as inseparable from me as is its radiance from Sūrya, bringer of light," a statement laden with irony considering that he will banish her in the *Uttarakāṇḍa*.[47] Sītā is thus reunited with her lord who, it is noted, experiences happiness at the reunion.[48] Her own reaction is left to be inferred by the audience.

There is yet one more passage in the *Yuddhakāṇḍa* in which Sītā's character is portrayed in an interesting and positive light as that of a woman of independent mind and uncommon compassion. In *sarga* 101, when Hanumān has been sent to Sītā to tell her that her husband has been victorious and that her captivity is over, he begs of her only one boon. He asks her permission to avenge the torment and threats she has suffered at the hands of her *rākṣasī* wardresses by killing them in brutally violent ways.[49] Sītā's response is striking and illuminating in its humane, almost modernist tenor. She curtly refuses the monkey's request, arguing that the *rākṣasīs* were mere functionaries, following the orders of their master, and so do not

[43] 6.104.1–19. These are the last words Sītā will say in the *Yuddhakāṇḍa*. Although she will appear "on camera," as it were, several more times in its closing *sargas*, she will either listen silently to her husband's words or act wordlessly. See S. Goldman 2001.

[44] 6.104.2–27.

[45] 6.105.25.

[46] 6.106.1–9.

[47] 6.106.11–18. See S. Goldman 2004a.

[48] 6.106.20.

[49] 6.101.23–28.

deserve punishment. In keeping with the norms of the metaphysic of *karma*, she attributes her suffering to her own past misdeeds and tells Hanumān that refined people do not requite evil with evil. She concludes by observing that no one is entirely innocent, and therefore one should not mete out harsh punishment even to creatures like the *rākṣasas*, who take pleasure in harming people.[50]

Lakṣmaṇa

Rāma's devoted younger brother and constant companion is foregrounded in the *Yuddhakāṇḍa* in a number of significant passages. He is, of course, an active participant in the battle and serves, as elsewhere in the poem, as Rāma's principal, if sometimes unwilling, agent. Thus he follows Rāma's instructions to consecrate Vibhīṣaṇa as de jure king of Laṅkā prior to the onset of hostilities[51] and, as noted above, assures himself of his brother's consent before obeying Sītā's command to build her a pyre.[52]

But by far, Lakṣmaṇa's most important act in the *Yuddhakāṇḍa* comes at a critical juncture in the battle when Rāma, shattered by the report that Indrajit has murdered Sītā, becomes, for a time, unfit for combat. Thus it falls to Lakṣmaṇa, acting on the advice of Vibhīṣaṇa, to stand in for his brother and confront that all-but-invincible sorcerer-warrior, who is in many ways the most formidable of Rāma's demonic foes. Lakṣmaṇa's struggle with Indrajit is protracted and elaborate and occupies seven full *sargas* (72–78) of the Book.

One of the more noteworthy aspects of this episode is the situation that makes Lakṣmaṇa's intervention necessary, that is, Sītā's apparent murder. Shattered by the news, Rāma is unable to focus on the battle at hand. Seeing his virtuous brother's pitiable state, Lakṣmaṇa is moved to deliver a bitter and interesting diatribe against *dharma* itself, since, as Rāma's fate seems to show, the practice of righteousness and restraint yields no benefits. Lakṣmaṇa concludes from Rāma's despair and Rāvaṇa's apparent triumph that all that matters in this world is wealth and power, both of which his brother has

[50] 6.101.29–37.
[51] 6.13.7–9.
[52] 6.104.17–21.

foolishly abandoned in the interests of the futile practice of *dharma*. His speech adds another line of materialist and hedonistic discourse to the better-known critique of *dharma* and piety delivered by the brahman Jābāli in the *Ayodhyākāṇḍa*.[53] The treatment of these two speeches differ, however, in an important way. Jābāli's speech is characterized, even before it is quoted, as at variance with *dharma* (*dharmāpetam*).[54] Moreover, Rāma roundly refutes it as soon as it is uttered.[55] Lakṣmaṇa's denunciation of *dharma*, on the other hand, at its very inception, is described as both rational and meaningful (*hetvarthasaṃhitam*).[56] Then, too, unlike in the encounter with Jābāli, Rāma is in no condition to refute Lakṣmaṇa's case for materialism, and so it remains the only argument against righteousness in this most dharmic of texts that the poet lets stand without rebuttal by his righteous hero.[57]

Aside from these significant words and deeds, Lakṣmaṇa's role in the *Yuddhakāṇḍa* is largely a passive one. He serves as a focus for the articulation of Rāma's grief, a grief that several times is diverted from its normal concentration on the abducted and seemingly murdered Sītā to expend itself on his inseparable brother and companion.

When, early on in the battle, Rāma and Lakṣmaṇa have been struck down and immobilized by Indrajit's deadly serpent-arrows, the former, the hardier of the two, recovers his senses first and, thinking that his brother is dead, gives way to a famous outpouring of grief[58] in which he claims to value him above even Sītā and vows to commit suicide in his sorrow at his apparent loss.

> "What do I care for Sītā or even for my life itself now that I see my brother lying defeated in battle?
>
> "Were I to search the world, I could find another woman like Sītā, but never a brother, a companion, or a warrior to equal Lakṣmaṇa.

[53] 2.100. For a detailed discussion of this passage, see pp. 36–41, and cf. Pollock 1986, pp. 34, 68.
[54] 2.100.1.
[55] 2.101.
[56] 6.70.13.
[57] On this issue, see R. Goldman 2003a.
[58] 6.39.4–21.

"If Lakṣmaṇa, the increaser of Sumitrā's joy, has indeed returned to the elements, then I shall abandon my life right before the eyes of the monkeys."[59]

This sentiment regarding Lakṣmaṇa is expressed by Rāma a second time, later in the Book, when the former, pierced by Rāvaṇa's terrible javelin, once more appears to Rāma to be dead.

"Here is heroic Lakṣmaṇa, fallen to the ground through the power of Rāvaṇa. He is writhing like a snake, filling me with sorrow.

"When I see that hero, dearer to me than life itself, drenched with blood, my mind is in such turmoil that I wonder what power I have left to fight.

"For if my brother, so praiseworthy in battle and marked with auspicious signs, has truly returned to the elements, then of what use to me is pleasure or indeed life itself?

"For my valor itself seems to hang its head in shame, while my bow seems to slip from my grasp. My arrows drop away, and my sight is dimmed with tears. Dreadful thoughts grow in my mind, and I wish now only for death.

"...Seeing my brother Lakṣmaṇa struck down in the dust of the battlefield, I have no further use for battle, for my life, or even for Sītā herself.

"Now that Lakṣmaṇa lies slain in the forefront of battle, what use have I for kingship or for life itself? There is now no longer any purpose to this war."[60]

After Rāvaṇa's death, Lakṣmaṇa plays a distinctly secondary, and largely ceremonial, role in the remainder of the *Yuddhakāṇḍa*. He

[59] 6.39.5–7.

[60] 6.89.2–5,7–8. On this theme of Rāma's relative valuation of Lakṣmaṇa and other male associates, on the one hand, and Sītā, on the other, see R. Goldman 1980. The passage is significant in that, as indicated above, it tends to foreground one last time the human frailty and emotional vulnerability of the epic hero on the eve of the fulfillment of his avatāric mission. This is further emphasized in the description of the wounding of Lakṣmaṇa. As Rāma sees Rāvaṇa's deadly spear hurtling toward his brother, he attempts to thwart it by deploying what one assumes is a kind of supernatural power. He actually addresses the javelin:

carries out, of course, a supporting role in Rāma's consecration, but his only other significant independent act is his refusal to accept his own consecration as *yuvarāja* to rule jointly with Rāma, an honor which, with his usual deference to his elders, he declines and which Rāma then confers upon Bharata.[61] Here, in the Book's closing *sarga*, Lakṣmaṇa's words, like Sītā's, are not recorded by the poet.

Bharata

The logic of the epic narrative has, of course, driven Bharata to the margins or frame of the central story. After his active role in chastising Kaikeyī, performing the funerary rites for Daśaratha, and seeking out and arguing with Rāma over who is to serve as king, he returns to Nandigrāma, where he establishes Rāma's sandals on the throne and serves as a reluctant regent while patiently waiting for the fourteen years of his beloved brother's exile to pass.[62] All this is described in the second half of the *Ayodhyākāṇḍa*. Following that Book, the epic action moves away from the capital into the forest groves of Pañcavatī, the wilderness of the Daṇḍakas, the monkey kingdom of Kiṣkindhā, and finally through the regions of the far south to Laṅkā, the island stronghold of the *rākṣasas*. Thus the backgrounded figure of Bharata does not return to the epic stage, as it were, until the final four chapters of the *Yuddhakāṇḍa*. Bharata reenters the story in *sarga* 113 when Rāma, pausing on his return journey in the ashram of the sage Bharadvāja, sends Hanumān on

---

> But even as that javelin was hurtling toward Lakṣmaṇa, Rāma Rāghava addressed it, saying, "May Lakṣmaṇa be spared! And may you, your energy thwarted, be foiled!" (6.88.33)

But Rāma's intervention appears to have no effect, for,

> Nonetheless, that immensely brilliant weapon, flashing like the flickering tongue of a serpent king, fell with tremendous force on Lakṣmaṇa's broad chest.
>
> Then Lakṣmaṇa, his heart pierced by that javelin, so deeply embedded through Rāvaṇa's strength, fell to the ground. (6.88.34–35)

Perhaps we are to understand that, without Rāma's adjuration, the weapon would indeed have killed Lakṣmaṇa, but it is highly unusual in this text for the word of the hero or heroine to be uttered in vain.

[61] 6.116.78–79.
[62] 2.107.12–22.

ahead to convey the news of the victory in Laṅkā and the impending return of the exiles.

Rāma's instructions to the monkey hero are interesting in that they remind us one final time of the deflected political tensions that lie at the heart of the abortive succession struggle that forms the subject of the *Ayodhyākāṇḍa*. The first hint that Rāma may anticipate some hesitation on his brother's part to relinquish his power as regent appears in the first verse of the chapter where we learn that the hero's reaction to the sight of his home is not one of unmingled joy.

> "But once Rāghava had caught sight of Ayodhyā, he was plunged into thought. Then, after some reflection, he cast his glance upon the monkeys."[63]

The reason for Rāma's hesitation, and, indeed, for sending a messenger ahead of him, soon becomes clear. In keeping with his well-established character as someone who places family harmony above political power, Rāma wants to determine whether, as one might expect in the case of lesser men, Bharata will resent or even resist having to cede sovereignty to his older brother who has now fulfilled the terms of Kaikeyī's boon and has returned at long last to ascend his ancestral throne. These are his instructions to Hanumān:

> "Tell him: 'Having conquered the hosts of his enemies, attained unsurpassed glory, and accomplished his purpose, immensely powerful Rāma has returned with his allies.'
>
> "And whatever facial expression Bharata may adopt upon hearing this, you must report that to me fully.
>
> "Through the color of his face, his glance, and his manner of speaking, you should accurately determine everything about Bharata's state of mind and his intentions.
>
> "For whose head would not be turned by an ancestral kingdom rich in every object of desire and filled with elephants, horses, and chariots?
>
> "And should majestic Bharata, being long accustomed to it, desire the kingship for himself, then let that delight of the Raghus rule the entire earth without exception.

[63] 6.113.1.

> "Once you have determined his state of mind and his intentions, monkey, you must return quickly before we have gone very far."[64]

Surely we have here the poet's final effort to establish the renunciant and selfless character of his hero before the latter at last assumes his rightful role as the god-king.[65]

In order to finally defuse any residual hint of the kind of power struggle that forms the central theme of the *Mahābhārata*, it seems necessary that the self-denying and ascetic character of Bharata, too, must be fully emphasized. Any lingering doubts one might entertain on this score are dramatically put to rest by the spectacular, even hyperbolic, representation of Bharata's abjection engendered by his brother's absence. The poet describes him as he appears to Hanumān:

> A quarter of a league from Ayodhyā he spied Bharata, who was living in an ashram. Dejected and emaciated, he was clad in garments of barkcloth and black antelope skin. Wearing matted locks, his body was smeared with dirt. Tormented by the catastrophe that had befallen his brother and practicing righteousness, he engaged in asceticism, restrained and subsisting on fruits and roots. He had a mass of matted hair piled high and was clad in barkcloth and animal skins. Self-controlled and with focused mind, he was equal in blazing energy to a brahman-seer. Having placed Rāma's sandals in a position of honor, he ruled the earth, protecting the people of all four social classes from every danger. He was attended by incorruptible ministers, household priests, and attentive army chiefs, all clad in ochre garments.[66]

With the two heroic princes, both in the barkcloth and matted locks of the forest renunciant, once more acting out their respective desires to defer to the other, the audience can have no doubt as to the final quashing of any latent competition.

Bharata's meeting with Hanumān also serves another purpose. Throughout the poem, the poet has not missed one opportunity to recapitulate the events of Rāma's career. Often he uses the intro-

[64] 6.113.12–17.

[65] On Vālmīki's characterization of Rāma as a figure who integrates the royal and the brahmanical functions, see Pollock 1986, pp. 64–73.

[66] 6.113.26–30.

duction of a new character or the reappearance of one who has been removed from the main narrative for some time to have one figure or another rehearse the major events of the epic story up to whatever point in the narrative the author has reached.[67]

The reappearance of Bharata, who has missed all his brothers' trials and adventures in the forest and in Laṅkā, affords the poet one final occasion to present yet another synopsis of the epic story. Thus Hanumān, in response to Bharata's question as to how Rāma had come to be associated with monkeys, takes the opportunity to recapitulate at some length the events of the full fourteen years from Rāma's banishment to his arrival at the hermitage of Bharadvāja.[68]

Bharata then goes forth with his entourage to meet Rāma in a kind of reprise of his elaborately described journey to Citrakūṭa in the *Ayodhyākāṇḍa*,[69] and an emotional reunion takes place. He then formally returns the reins of power to Rāma and only then can the two brothers, along with Lakṣmaṇa, put off their ascetic garb, bathe, and resume the trappings of royalty.[70] Following this, Bharata assumes the role of the master of ceremonies at Rāma's consecration.

After the consecration, there is an interesting, but barely noticed, episode in which Rāma, now ruling his kingdom in supreme felicity, offers to share governance with Lakṣmaṇa whom he proposes to consecrate as *yuvarāja*. Lakṣmaṇa declines this honor, without giving a reason, and Rāma then confers the appointment upon Bharata.[71] Neither Bharata nor the author makes any comment on this development. However, at the very end of the poem, when Rāma, in his desolation at having had to banish Lakṣmaṇa, attempts to consecrate Bharata as king, the latter once again refuses to accept sovereignty. He proposes that Rāma divide the kingdom between his sons, Lava and Kuśa, and, once this has been done, he follows his brother into the Sarayū River and thence to heaven.[72]

[67] For a brief discussion of this aspect of the poem, see Goldman and Goldman 1996, pp. 18–20.
[68] 6.114.4–45.
[69] 2.74–105.
[70] 6.116.1–17.
[71] 6.116.77–79.
[72] 7.97.2ff.

THE MONKEYS

The number of monkeys that participate in the siege and battle at Lañkā is, of course, staggering. The poet seems to delight in recording the vast numbers of the simian divisions that form Sugrīva's mighty host.[73] However, as in the case of the *rākṣasas*, only a few are given "speaking parts," as it were, and, of those, still fewer emerge as figures of consequence.

Hanumān

As elsewhere in the poem and the larger narrative and devotional traditions of which it forms a part, Hanumān, despite his formal status as merely one of Sugrīva's advisers, is unquestionably the most important of the *vānaras*, who play so prominent a role in the epic story. Although his role in the huge and complex narrative of the *Yuddhakāṇḍa* is, of necessity, less central than the one which he plays in the *Sundarakāṇḍa*,[74] it is clear at a number of points in the Book that he is as indispensable to the effort to defeat Rāvaṇa as he was in the search for Sītā.[75]

As a consequence of his heroic feats in the *Sundarakāṇḍa*, Hanumān is naturally the first *vānara* to be mentioned in the *Yuddhakāṇḍa*. Indeed, the opening twelve verses of the Book record Rāma's fulsome praise of the great monkey for his having flown across the mighty ocean, penetrated the fortress of Lañkā, and found the abducted princess.[76] Then, too, as a result of his exploits in Lañkā, Hanumān is uniquely able to provide Rāma with detailed and vital

[73] On the astronomical numbers used in this connection, see the translation and notes to 6.17.16–19,27,30,34,39; 6.19.4,32; and notes.
[74] On the characterization and role of Hanumān in the *Sundarakāṇḍa*, see Goldman and Goldman 1994 and 1996, pp. 39–56.
[75] The significance of Hanumān to the *Rāmāyaṇa*, and, indeed, to the entire Hindu tradition, can be judged from the number of times the story of his childhood is repeated in the poem. It is first narrated by Jāmbavān at 4.65.8–25 and is retold at great length by the seer Agastya at 7.35–36. The *Yuddhakāṇḍa* also finds a place for this well-known tale when, at 6.19.9–17, the *rākṣasa* spy Śuka pauses, while pointing out the monkey generals to Rāvaṇa, to give a concise version. For a discussion of this narrative in the *Rāmāyaṇa*, see S. Goldman 1999.
[76] 6.1.1–12.

intelligence as to the layout, troop strength, and defensive fortifications of the *rākṣasa* capital.[77]

Shortly afterward, when Vibhīṣaṇa, having defected from his brother's side, presents himself as a valuable ally to Rāma, Hanumān, as usual, allows the other monkeys to give their various opinions before concluding the debate with a lengthy, pointed, and carefully reasoned discussion as to why it would be best to accept the *rākṣasa* at face value. It is his view that Rāma will act upon.[78]

It is also Hanumān who is most often called upon by Rāma to undertake special or delicate missions. Thus, later in the Book, when the war is over and Rāvaṇa has been slain, it is Hanumān who is deputed to go to the palace to bring the good news to Sītā.[79] Similarly, when Rāma has returned to the hermitage of the sage Bharadvāja, he selects Hanumān to carry the potentially disturbing news of his return to Bharata.[80]

Like several of the other monkey champions, Hanumān does his part in the great battle. He is placed in command of the forces stationed at the western gate of the citadel, where he opposes the *rākṣasa* defensive troops under the command of the most formidable of their warriors, Indrajit.[81] In single combat the great monkey kills such doughty opponents as Akampana[82] and Nikumbha.[83]

Hanumān's extraordinary martial power and, indeed, his superiority to all the other *vānaras* in this respect can, however, be clearly discerned from the account of his encounters with Rāvaṇa himself during the course of the elaborate set of confrontations detailed in *sarga* 47 in which the *rākṣasa* monarch sequentially fights with the monkeys Sugrīva, Gavākṣa, Gavaya, Sudaṃṣṭra, Ṛṣabha, Jyotimukha, Nala, and Nīla, before engaging with Rāma, Lakṣmaṇa, and Hanumān. Although Lakṣmaṇa and some of the monkey warriors are able momentarily to discomfit Rāvaṇa, all of them, save Hanumān, are put out of action by the demon. Hanumān, alone, is able to hold his own, and even when stunned by a blow of the *rākṣasa*'s fist,

77 6.3.
78 6.11.41–59.
79 6.101.
80 6.113–14.
81 6.28.11–12,27.
82 6.44.11–29.
83 6.64.11–23.

manages to recover quickly.[84] When mighty Lakṣmaṇa himself is finally rendered unconscious by Rāvaṇa's javelin, the mighty demon is unable to carry him, a portion of Lord Viṣṇu, from the field.[85] Hanumān, in turn, rushes in and knocks Rāvaṇa unconscious. He then carries Lakṣmaṇa to safety and bears Rāma into battle on his back.[86]

The *Yuddhakāṇḍa* also contains, in full or nascent form, the episodes that, in their endlessly repeated literary and plastic representation, have given rise to the three perhaps best-known and most widely recognized iconic images of the great monkey hero.

One widely disseminated and immediately recognizable image is that of Hanumān carrying Rāma and Lakṣmaṇa, each seated on one of his broad shoulders. This precise scenario does not actually occur anywhere in Vālmīki's poem. However, in the *Yuddhakāṇḍa*, Hanumān does carry one or the other of the heroic brothers on a few occasions. As Rāma's forces set out on their march to the sea, the prince announces that he will ride mounted on Hanumān and Lakṣmaṇa will be carried by Aṅgada.[87] Also, as noted above, Hanumān, in another context, carries the stunned Lakṣmaṇa from the battlefield when the latter is wounded by Rāvaṇa.[88]

One episode at the very end of the *Yuddhakāṇḍa* has provided the germ of yet another popular story and art motif centering on Hanumān. In the Book's closing *sarga*, in the passage where Rāma distributes rewards to those who have served him in his quest for Sītā and in the battle in Laṅkā, he gives a splendid pearl necklace to Sītā with the evident intention that she give it in turn to the one with whom she is most pleased. She gives it, naturally enough, to Hanumān, and he is described as looking resplendent as he wears it.[89] Nothing further is said about the necklace here, but the episode no doubt forms the kernel of the popular episode, widely depicted in texts, painting, performance, and poster art, in which the monkey begins to crack the pearls with his teeth in an effort to see if Sītā and

[84] 6.47.65–70.
[85] 6.47.104–5.
[86] 6.47.108–18; *37–38.
[87] 6.4.15–16.
[88] 6.47.104–5. Cf. 1016* (following note to 6.47.124). Cf. 314* (at note to 6.15.27).
[89] 6.116.68–73.

Rāma are inside. For without this the jewels are meaningless to him. When this seeming ingratitude evokes indignation among the assembly, Hanumān responds by tearing open his own chest to reveal the image of the divine couple in his heart.[90]

Of all the mighty deeds of Hanumān in the *Yuddhakāṇḍa* and, indeed, in the entire vast corpus of *Rāmāyaṇa* literature, surely none is more dramatic, better known, or more widely depicted than his extraordinary feat of fetching the mountain of healing herbs from the heights of the Himalayas to the shores of Laṅkā in order to heal and revive the heroes, human and simian, felled in battle by Indrajit or Rāvaṇa. This motif of the fetching of a mountain covered with curative plants obviously exerted a powerful fascination on the author or authors of the Book as it is brought into the narrative no fewer than three times.

The first reference to this motif occurs when the monkey hosts are in despair over the fact that both Rāma and Lakṣmaṇa have been struck down and immobilized by the potent serpent-weapons of Indrajit. The monkey physician, Suṣeṇa, recalling that Bṛhaspati had used healing herbs along with magical spells to restore the gods, who had been struck down in their battle with the *asuras*, recommends that a party of monkeys, including Saṃpāti, Panasa, and Hanumān, among others, be dispatched at once to the ocean of milk, where they will find the great healing herbs growing on two mountains called Candra and Droṇa.[91] This mission, oddly enough, is never carried out, however, since, before the monkeys can depart, a sudden gust of wind heralds the arrival of the divine bird Garuḍa and the serpent-arrows flee in terror. Garuḍa's mere touch restores the wounded princes to health and vigor, thus obviating the need for the healing herbs.[92]

The next and principal occurrence of the motif is found toward the middle of the *Yuddhakāṇḍa* when the formidable Indrajit has once

[90] For a learned and entertaining discussion of this episode in popular retellings of the *Rāmāyaṇa* story, see Lutgendorf 2007, pp. 218–20.

[91] 6.40.26–32.

[92] 6.40.33–40. This abortive episode is confused and confusing. It seems to be a kind of pastiche of elements from various epic-purāṇic myths that may have been inserted here at some point in emulation of the later versions of the story of the fetching of the mountain of herbs. See the notes to this passage for further discussion.

more employed the weapons he had received from Lord Brahmā to strike down Rāma, Lakṣmaṇa, and no fewer than 670 million monkeys, including most of their great champions. Among the principal monkey heroes, Hanumān alone is uninjured, and he and Vibhīṣaṇa search the gory battlefield by night to seek out and comfort any survivors of the massacre. At length they come upon the gravely wounded and nearly blind Jāmbavān. Vibhīṣaṇa questions him about his condition, but the *ṛkṣarāja*, cutting straight to the heart of the matter, responds as follows:

> "O *rākṣasa*, son of chaos, does the foremost of the monkeys Hanumān, in whom Añjanā and Vāyu Mātariśvan have an excellent son, still live?"
>
> When Vibhīṣaṇa heard these words of Jāmbavān, he said this: "Why do you ignore the king's sons Rāma and Lakṣmaṇa and ask only about Māruti?
>
> "Noble sir, you have not shown the same extraordinary concern for King Sugrīva, Añgada, or even Rāghava himself, as you have for the son of Vāyu."
>
> Upon hearing the words of Vibhīṣaṇa, Jāmbavān spoke these words: "Now hear, tiger among *rākṣasas*, sons of chaos, why I inquired only about Māruti.
>
> "So long as Hanumān is alive, then our army will survive, even if it should be massacred. But if that hero has lost his life, then, even though we survive, we are as good as dead.
>
> "For, dear boy, if Māruti, the equal of Māruta and the rival in power of Agni Vaiśvānara still lives, only then do we have any hope of survival."[93]

This is surely the epic's most direct statement of the significance of Hanumān to the success of the mission of the *Rāmāvatāra*. Its specific reference soon becomes clear, however, as Jāmbavān tells Hanumān that he must fly to the Himalayas to find and fetch the great healing herbs that grow there on a certain mountain. In a kind of reprise of the monkey hero's epic leaps across the ocean in the *Sundarakāṇḍa*,

[93] 6.61.18–23.

the poet then gives a lengthy account of his flight, replete with a description of the crushing of the mountain from which he leaps and the many geographic and sacred landscapes over which he flies. Reaching the mountain, Hanumān is unable to find the herbs, which have rendered themselves invisible. In his impatience, he rips off the entire mountain peak and flies back with it to Laṅkā, where the aroma of its healing herbs restores the wounded and slain warriors to health and life.[94]

The fondness the poet and his audiences had for this particular episode is betrayed not only by the long and detailed treatment it is given in the poem but by the fact that it is brought back yet a third time as if "by popular demand" twenty-eight *sargas* farther on. When Lakṣmaṇa is again gravely wounded, this time by Rāvaṇa's javelin, Suṣeṇa instructs Hanumān to return once more to the mountain he had earlier visited on the orders of Jāmbavān to gather the potent medicinal herbs. Hanumān does so, and this time, although the herbs do not conceal themselves, he is, nonetheless, unable to identify them and so is compelled to bring back the entire peak once again. Suṣeṇa can then pluck the appropriate herb, hold it to Lakṣmaṇa's nose, and thus heal him.

Sugrīva

Sugrīva, who, as king of the monkeys and at least the nominal leader of the forces marshaled to assist Rāma in his campaign to defeat Rāvaṇa and recover Sītā, plays so significant a role in the events leading up to the discovery of Sītā and the war at Laṅkā, seems to recede somewhat into the background in the *Yuddhakāṇḍa*. This in no way, however, means that he is reduced to a mere "extra" or a figurehead serving as leader in name only.

In the opening *sarga* of the *Yuddhakāṇḍa*, when Rāma praises and congratulates Hanumān on his superhuman feats in crossing the ocean, finding Sītā, and wreaking havoc among the *rākṣasa* forces, he is careful to state several times that the great monkey hero has accomplished these wonders in the service of Sugrīva.[95] Then, too, the monkey king is given pride of place in being recognized as the first

[94] 6.61.26–68.
[95] 6.1.6–9.

monkey, indeed, the first character, to address Rāma in the Book, when its entire second chapter is dedicated to his elaborate speech of reassurance and exhortation to the despondent prince who, confronted by the seemingly impassable ocean, has once more given way to despair.[96]

Sugrīva is also moderately active in combat. He personally dispatches many powerful *rākṣasas*, including the formidable Virūpākṣa and Mahodara,[97] and Rāma places him, along with Jāmbavān and Vibhīṣaṇa, in command of the central encampment of the *vānara* forces.[98] Nonetheless, he is, despite his confident exhortation of Rāma, himself prone to despair, requiring the comforting words of Vibhīṣaṇa to keep him from utter panic and despondency.[99] Certainly it is worth noting that, despite his divine ancestry, godlike power, and prominent position, he is unable to withstand the sorcery and magical weaponry of Indrajit, a capacity that only Hanumān and Vibhīṣaṇa seem to possess.[100]

In the so-called vulgate text of the southern commentators, Sugrīva makes an unauthorized solo attack on Rāvaṇa, knocking off the king's crown and fighting him to the point of exhaustion. This rash deed earns him only a rebuke from Rāma.[101]

Aṅgada

Aṅgada, the son of the incomparably powerful Vālin and the monkey chosen by Rāma to serve as *yuvarāja*, or heir apparent, under Sugrīva, is given special mention a number of times in the *Yuddhakāṇḍa*. He is assigned command of the *vānara* attack force posted at the southern gate of Laṅkā.[102] He rallies the monkeys when they are on the point of fleeing in terror at the sight of Kumbhakarṇa.[103]

[96] 6.1.11–16; 6.2.1–21.
[97] 6.84,85.
[98] 6.28.31.
[99] 6.36.24–37.
[100] 6.60.37–40; 6.61.1–11.
[101] See notes to 6.30.26 and 6.31.1.
[102] 6.28.26.
[103] 6.54.3–7.

He, too, kills his share of noteworthy *rākṣasa* champions, such as Narāntaka[104] and Mahāpārśva,[105] and manages to kill Indrajit's horses and charioteer.[106]

Aṅgada also is given, or takes upon himself, one special mission of note. He is chosen by Rāma to enter Laṅkā in the role of a messenger and to present himself before Rāvaṇa to demand that he return Sītā or suffer defeat and destruction. Rāvaṇa is, predictably, enraged and orders that the monkey be captured and killed. Aṅgada, however, leaps to the pinnacle of the palace and, with his would-be captors clinging to him like insects until they fall, crushes the structure under his great weight before leaping back to his own lines.[107] The episode is strongly reminiscent of the more elaborate passage in the *Sundarakāṇḍa* where Hanumān allows himself to be captured and dragged before Rāvaṇa, scolds and warns the demon king, and then sets fire to Laṅkā with his flaming tail.[108]

Nala and Suṣeṇa

Among the numerous other monkeys mentioned as having played some role in the siege and war at Laṅkā, two deserve individual mention because of the special skills that set them apart from their warrior companions. The first of these is Nala, the son of the divine architect and builder, Viśvakarman. Having inherited his father's skills, he serves in the indispensable role of chief engineer of the monkey forces. Thus it is he who designs and supervises the construction of the great bridge that enables Rāma and his troops to cross the otherwise impassable sea.[109]

Suṣeṇa, as noted above, is particularly skilled as an herbalist and physician, and is the father-in-law of Sugrīva.[110] His skills are, like those of Nala, essential to the success of Rāma's mission, for it is he

[104] 6.57.77–88.
[105] 6.86.5–27.
[106] 6.34.27.
[107] 6.31.48–78.
[108] 5.46–52.
[109] 6.15.8–26.
[110] 6.40.23.

who is able to identify and utilize the healing herbs that restore the dead and wounded men and monkeys to life and health.[111]

THE *RĀKṢASAS*

Rāvaṇa

As in the preceding Book, the great lord of the *rākṣasas* remains a fascinating and commanding presence here in the *Yuddhakāṇḍa*. Whereas in the *Sundarakāṇḍa* Rāvaṇa is viewed either directly through the eyes of Hanumān as a magnificent creature of almost godlike power[112] or indirectly through those of Sītā as a besotted, lecherous suitor,[113] in the *Yuddhakāṇḍa* an even more nuanced portrait emerges. He is still, of course, the domineering tyrant and formidable warrior of the earlier Books, but here, under the pressure of the siege and the continual flow of ominous news from the battlefield, cracks in his facade of arrogance and invincibility begin to appear. Sensing, it seems, that, despite his mighty army, his seemingly impregnable fortress, and his own invincibility derived from his well-known boon, the threat to his reign and his life is real, he is shown as querulous, paranoid, depressive, and self-pitying, even admitting at one point the foolishness of having carried off Sītā. Nonetheless, despite the evil portents that attend his and his champions' sorties, the successive deaths of his most powerful and cherished kinsmen and allies, and the fact that he is bested by Rāma early on in the conflict, he persists in his pride and vainglory,

[111] Suṣeṇa's medical skills are mentioned twice in the *Yuddhakāṇḍa*, although they are actually put into practice only once. At 6.89.9–25, he sends Hanumān on his second mission to fetch the healing herbs from the Himalayas and uses them to cure the mortally wounded Lakṣmaṇa. At 6.40.26–32, he describes the history and uses of the herbs and prepares to send a party of monkeys to the ocean of milk to collect them. However, as noted above, this mission is aborted and rendered otiose by the unexpected arrival of Garuḍa. In 6.61, Hanumān fetches the mountain of healing herbs on Jāmbavān's instructions, and the aroma of the plants revives and restores the dead and wounded men and monkeys with no further intervention on Suṣeṇa's part. Note, too, that at the end of the *kāṇḍa*, rather than depend on Suṣeṇa's intervention to resurrect the monkeys slain in battle, Rāma solicits a boon from Indra, who revives them through his divine power (6.108.5–11).

[112] Cf. 5.8.5–9 and 5.47.2–20.

[113] 5.16.5–28; 5.18,20. See S. Goldman 2001.

stubbornly refusing to surrender his captive and beg forgiveness for his crimes. His arrogance thus drives him inexorably onward to his own impending doom. In this, he seems to be cast by the poet as more nearly a tragic figure than any other in the vast epic and narrative literature with the possible exception of the *Mahābhārata*'s Karṇa.

Evidence of Rāvaṇa's progressive mental and emotional disintegration abounds in the *Yuddhakāṇḍa*. At first the *rākṣasa* appears to take a rational approach to his predicament. After surveying the damage wrought in his capital by Hanumān,[114] and even before Rāma and his forces have managed to cross the sea to besiege Laṅkā, the king consults sensibly with his advisers as to how he should proceed.[115]

His generals and courtiers—flatterers, braggarts, and sycophants for the most part—reassure him that he is invincible and boast that they will easily dispatch the upstart Rāma and his band of mere monkeys.[116] Theirs is the advice, of course, that Rāvaṇa, in his vanity and folly, will follow. His weak grasp of reality and his emotional instability are immediately signaled, however, by his exchange with his righteous brother, Vibhīṣaṇa, who scoffs at the generals' advice and counsels Rāvaṇa to return Sītā both because it is the right thing to do and as an act of self-preservation.[117]

Rāvaṇa's reaction to his brother's sound advice is telling. He takes Vibhīṣaṇa's well-intentioned words as a personal attack and launches into a diatribe against kinsmen whom he sees as envious and eager for the downfall of their successful relatives.[118] His abusive words toward his brother drive the latter into his enemies' camp and only hasten and assure his own destruction.

Rāvaṇa's inability to benefit from sound counsel is demonstrated time and again in the Book. When his two hapless spies Śuka and Sāraṇa return and describe to their master the overwhelming strength of the forces opposing him after having been unmasked in their failed attempt to infiltrate the monkey army, their report definitely shakes his confidence. But at the same time, it sends him

[114] See 5.52, where the destruction of Laṅkā is described.
[115] 6.6.
[116] 6.7–8.
[117] 6.9.
[118] 6.10.1–11.

into one of his periodic rages. He reviles and dismisses them after threatening them with death for what he takes as praise of his enemies.[119]

The demon king is given yet another opportunity to reflect on the error of his ways when the venerable *rākṣasa* Mālyavān, his great-uncle, urges him to make peace and reminds him of the terrible portents that have arisen presaging the destruction of the *rākṣasa* race. He even openly states the *rākṣasas*' dread that Rāma is, in fact, none other than Viṣṇu.[120] But here again, Rāvaṇa remains obdurate and boastful. Flying into a rage, he reviles Mālyavān who withdraws.[121]

After the death of many of his most valorous champions, Rāvaṇa, in increasing desperation, has his troops arouse the fearsome sleeping giant, his gargantuan brother Kumbhakarṇa. The latter, after hearing of his plight first laughs at him and then, in terms similar to those used by Vibhīṣaṇa and Mālyavān, lectures him at length on the folly of his ways.[122] Rāvaṇa's response to Kumbhakarṇa's scolding is significant in that here, for the first time, the demon king acknowledges his folly and deficient policy. Although he is predictably angry with his insubordinate younger brother and rebukes him for lecturing him like some venerable elder, he continues in the following striking fashion:

> "It is useless now to keep on repeating what I failed to do then, whether from error, mental confusion, or reliance on my strength and valor.
>
> "If you truly love me, if you truly understand what it means to be a brother, or if you believe in your heart that this mission is of the utmost urgency, then you must immediately do what suits the present situation. Please remedy through your valor this catastrophic result of my unsound policy.
>
> "A true friend is one who stands by a poor wretch who has lost everything. A true kinsman is one who renders assistance to those who have gone astray."[123]

[119] 6.20.1–13.
[120] 6.26.5–33.
[121] 6.27.1–15.
[122] 6.51.1–20.
[123] 6.51.23–26.

Rāvaṇa's self-pitying tone and confession of helplessness achieve his purpose, and Kumbhakarṇa agrees to fight, adopting the same tone of braggadocio as the other *rākṣasa* warriors before their destruction.[124]

Aside from his alternating outbursts of fury and fits of despair, Rāvaṇa is also prone to bouts of grief over the deaths of his kinsmen who give their lives fighting in his doomed cause. Although his reaction to the deaths of many of his generals is rage,[125] this anger is often mingled with grief.[126] However, when the casualties involve those closest to him, the outpourings of sorrow are profound and moving. Thus he loses consciousness upon hearing of the death of Kumbhakarṇa, lamenting loud and long over his brother and reflecting on his foolishness in failing to heed Vibhīṣaṇa's advice.[127]

In one of the most dramatic scenes in the poem, Rāvaṇa learns of the death of his beloved son and heir, the all-but-invincible Indrajit, at the hands of Lakṣmaṇa. His wild grief and lamentation soon turn to a terrifying access of mad rage. In his desolation and frustration, he turns his fury upon poor Sītā and, in spite of the *rākṣasas,* who try to hold him back, rushes toward her with an upraised sword intending to kill her on the spot. At the last moment he is dissuaded from this ultimate depravity by the *rākṣasa* Supārśva.[128]

Finally, it should be noted that, in his pride and obdurate refusal to give up Sītā, Rāvaṇa ignores not only the sage advice of his wisest counselors and the slaughter, one by one, of his foremost warriors but also the clear evidence of his own inferiority to Rāma on the field of battle. When, in his fury at the death of Prahasta, Rāvaṇa enters the battlefield himself for the first time, his valor and martial skill are such that he wreaks havoc among the monkey troops and puts out of action such doughty warriors as Sugrīva, Nīla, and even Hanumān and Lakṣmaṇa.[129] Nonetheless, when he finally encounters Rāma

[124] 6.51.29–47.

[125] Cf., for example, his response to the news of Akampana's death at 6.45.1.

[126] As at the death of Prahasta at 6.47.3.

[127] 6.56.1–19.

[128] 6.80. It is telling that, in his final despair, Rāvaṇa should turn his frustration and rage against his victim, his passion for whom is the cause of all his woes. It is also somewhat ironic that he should intend to kill Sītā in an effort to make real her illusory slaying at Indrajit's hands at 6.68.4–30. For in consoling Rāma after this apparent murder, Vibhīṣaṇa assures him that the murder of his beloved Sītā is the one act that Rāvaṇa would never countenance (6.71.9–12).

[129] 6.47.34–107.

for the first time, it becomes clear that he has met his match. Without being so much as touched by Rāvaṇa's weapons, Rāma easily pierces his foe through the chest with an arrow and, with a second, knocks the demon king's crown from his head. He then magnanimously spares and dismisses Rāvaṇa on the grounds of the latter's exhaustion, leaving the humiliated *rākṣasa* to slink back to his citadel.[130]

Despite this humiliating setback, Rāvaṇa remains a formidable presence both on and off the battlefield. And, although he seems to have been so easily and rapidly bested and then dismissed by Rāma in this episode, their final battle rages furiously for several days[131] and occupies a full eight *sargas* (90–97) of the Book. It has thus come to be regarded in the epic and literary imagination as the unrivaled and finally incomparable standard for a heroic duel.

The outcome of the battle is, of course, predetermined, as the representative of virtue, restraint, order, and, in a word, *dharma* must triumph over and eliminate the incarnation of everything that is antithetical to the norms of brahmanical civilization. Nonetheless, in death, the monstrous *rākṣasa* monarch and "thorn in the side of the world (*lokakaṇṭaka*)," is given the full honors appropriate to a noble adversary and a member of brahmanical society.

Although Rāvaṇa is sometimes represented as having abducted his womenfolk by force from their homes,[132] his death is greeted with an outpouring of grief and lamentation on the part of his wives and consorts[133] as well as by his chief queen, Mandodarī.[134]

The ambivalent attitude toward Rāvaṇa, as both ruthless tyrant and reckless criminal, on the one hand, and noble warrior and exalted monarch, on the other, is, perhaps, nowhere more clearly illustrated than in the debate between Rāma and Vibhīṣaṇa over the propriety of giving the fallen king a proper vedic funeral. At the conclusion of Mandodarī's lamentation, Rāma instructs Vibhīṣaṇa to perform his brother's funeral rites in accordance with custom and

[130] 6.47.127,135; 6.48.1–7.

[131] See note to 6.96.30 for a discussion of varying understandings of the length of the battle.

[132] The poem as a whole has no consistent stance on whether the women of Rāvaṇa's harem have been abducted or have come of their own free will out of their love for him. For a discussion of this issue, see notes to 5.7.65 and 66.

[133] 6.98.

[134] 6.99.1–29.

propriety. The latter at first declines to do so, citing Rāvaṇa's cruel nature, his unrighteousness, and his crimes of abducting the wives of others.[135] Rāma, however, gently rebukes Vibhīṣaṇa for his attitude, noting Rāvaṇa's valor, power, and conquest even of the gods as virtues to be set against his evil nature. He notes enigmatically that Rāvaṇa stood in the same (fraternal) relation to him (Rāma) as he (Rāvaṇa) did to his brother (Vibhīṣaṇa)[136] and that, in any case, all hostilities end with death. Vibhīṣaṇa accordingly, if grudgingly, then performs the funeral ceremony.[137]

In retrospect, a careful reading of the text of the *Yuddhakāṇḍa* reveals a Rāvaṇa who, if unquestionably one of world literature's grand villains, is by no means the mono-dimensional bogeyman that later and more popular versions of the epic story depict. In his towering stature, megalomania, pride, and power, vitiated only by his mad and self-destructive passion for the one thing in the universe he cannot possess, he comes as close as any figure in the epic to an approximation of a classic tragic hero.

Kumbhakarṇa

If the *Yuddhakāṇḍa* contains any sustained elements associated with the *adbhuta* and *hāsya rasas*, the aesthetic moods of sheer wonder and humor, then they are no doubt to be found in the remarkable nine-*sarga* minisaga of the awakening, the exploits, and the fall of Rāvaṇa's gargantuan younger brother, the voracious but somnolent giant Kumbhakarṇa.[138]

The elaborate account of the strenuous efforts of the *rākṣasas* to awaken the sleeping giant—shouting, beating drums, pounding him with all sorts of weapons and driving horses, camels, donkeys, and even elephants over his sleeping form[139]—and the fantastic account of his breakfast—vast mountains of deer, buffalo, and boar washed down with draughts of blood and a thousand jars of strong drink[140]—has an effect that is both astonishing and comical in a way

[135] 6.99.31,35.
[136] On this point, see note to 6.99.39.
[137] 6.99.3–42.
[138] 6.48–56.
[139] 6.48.20–47.
[140] 6.48.24–26,81–82.

reminiscent of the orgy of gorging and drunkenness in which the southern search party of monkeys indulges when it ravages Sugrīva's *madhuvana* in the *Sundarakāṇḍa*.[141]

If Rāvaṇa, in all his spectacular excess,[142] represents vedic civilization's vision of the radical "other" contrasted with the ideal of restraint, self-control, and deference represented by Rāma, then Kumbhakarṇa, in his vast corporeality, voracity, and violence, takes the characterization of the *rākṣasa* to still more hyperbolic heights. This is a figure so monstrous that his very snoring literally blows mighty warriors out of his cave.[143] His footsteps cause the earth itself to tremble as he strides along, towering above the battlements of Laṅkā.[144] As he marches forth to war, he expands his already colossal frame to the truly ridiculous dimensions of some thirty-six hundred feet in height and six hundred feet in breadth.[145] The very sight of this grotesque figure is enough to sow terror among the monkey troops, who can be kept from breaking ranks and fleeing only by virtue of Vibhīṣaṇa's spreading the false report that he is only some large mechanical man or animated scarecrow.[146] Kumbhakarṇa wreaks enormous destruction among the monkeys until he is finally slain by Rāma. But even in death the hyperbole continues as, for example, in the poet's description of the fall of the *rākṣasa*'s severed head and body.[147]

Kumbhakarṇa's excesses of stature, appetite, and violence are matched only by the extent and profundity of his sleep, the feature for which he is perhaps best known in the popular imagination. The epic gives four accounts of the circumstances that lead to his near-permanent state of somnolence. The two in the *Yuddhakāṇḍa* ascribe it to a curse pronounced by Brahmā to prevent the demon from literally devouring the world,[148] while the two in the *Uttarakāṇḍa* attribute it to a boon the demon had received as a result of his

[141] 5.59–60.
[142] See R. Goldman 2000 and S. Goldman 2004b and 2006b.
[143] 6.48.18–19.
[144] 6.48.84–87.
[145] 6.53.33–34.
[146] 6.49.31; 6.54.4–5.
[147] See pp. 24–25 and 92–94, and 6.55.124–25.
[148] 6.48.9–12; 6.49.23–27.

austerities but which, through a stratagem of the gods, he is tricked out of using to his advantage.[149]

Yet despite the utterly unrestrained hyperbole with which the poet renders the brutishness of this figure, Kumbhakarṇa, too, like his brother Rāvaṇa, is not quite monolithic in his characterization. For although he appears to be the very personification of sensual excess and mindless violence, he is, interestingly, also portrayed as deeply grounded in *dharmaśāstra* and *nītiśāstra* since, as noted above, he has the good moral sense, learning, and courage to lecture Rāvaṇa at length on the evil and error of his ways.[150]

Indrajit

Although he is not given the elaborate speeches and hence the richer characterization afforded to some of the other prominent *rākṣasas*, Rāvaṇa's most formidable son, Meghanāda[151] Rāvaṇi—best known in the *Yuddhakāṇḍa*, perhaps, by his epithet Indrajit, earned in battle with the king of the gods—is, in some ways, the most fearsome of Rāma's demonic foes.

He has already made an impressive appearance in the *Sundarakāṇḍa*, where he is the only one of the *rākṣasa* warriors able to withstand mighty Hanumān in battle and indeed to take him captive.[152] In the *Yuddhakāṇḍa*, too, it is clear that Indrajit is by far the most dangerous and formidable of all the *rākṣasas*, wreaking injury, death, and destruction upon many of the principal champions in the besieging army, including Rāma and Lakṣmaṇa themselves.

Indrajit first appears in the Book during the initial battle between the opposing armies when he engages Aṅgada in single combat. The encounter does not seem at first to be particularly unusual as, in keeping with the almost formulaic sequence of such combats, the monkey warrior succeeds in destroying the horses and chariot of his *rākṣasa* foe.[153] The situation soon proves to be anything but normal

[149] 7.10.31–41; 7.13.1–7.

[150] See pp. 34–36 above and 6.51.1–20.

[151] The name Meghanāda is not known to the *Yuddhakāṇḍa*; it apparently is first used in the *Uttarakāṇḍa* (7.25.4). See note to 6.35.22.

[152] 5.46.1–40. It should be noted that Hanumān allows himself to be taken prisoner in deference to the weapons of Lord Brahmā that Indrajit is able to deploy.

[153] 6.33.6,18–19; 6.34.

as Indrajit, his vehicle destroyed, has recourse to his unique command of the power of magical illusion, or *māyā*, to render himself invisible. Shooting now under the protection of his invisibility, he is able with impunity to riddle both Rāma and Lakṣmaṇa with his dreadful and disabling serpent-arrows.[154]

Thus we see at the very outset of the war that Indrajit possesses the power to do what not even his monstrous uncle Kumbhakarṇa nor his seemingly invincible father can accomplish, the near-mortal wounding of both epic heroes. Rāma and Lakṣmaṇa are immobilized and pierced to the quick and, to all appearances, near death.[155] The heroes are rendered hors de combat for five *sargas* until they are at last liberated by the unheralded appearance of Garuḍa.[156]

But this is not the only time that Indrajit is able to defeat Rāma and Lakṣmaṇa in battle. Some twenty chapters farther on he is sent forth once more by his father and, again cloaking himself through his unique power of invisibility, he lays low virtually the entire monkey host as well as the two Rāghavas.[157] Indrajit emerges for battle yet again after the fall of the *rākṣasa* warrior Makarākṣa and once more creates a cloak of invisibility from which he can safely rain hails of deadly arrows down upon Rāma, Lakṣmaṇa, and their allies. For some reason, however, this time he is unable to wound the heroes and, when he perceives that Rāma intends to shoot him down, he withdraws momentarily from the battlefield.[158]

Returning to the front lines almost immediately, Indrajit, perhaps feeling that his skill at arms has failed to achieve his purpose, tries his hand at a sinister form of psychological warfare. Employing his unparalleled command of the power of illusion, he conjures up a simulacrum of Sītā, which he proceeds to hack to death right before the eyes of Hanumān and his forces.[159] This bold and horrendous deception very nearly succeeds in completely demoralizing his father's foes. For, after a brief skirmish, Hanumān pulls his troops out

[154] 6.34.28–30.

[155] 6.36.4–7. Indeed, Indrajit believes that he has, in fact, slain the heroic brothers and reports this to Rāvaṇa, who praises him for this feat (6.36.39–43).

[156] 6.40.33–42.

[157] 6.60.3–49.

[158] 6.67; 6.68.1.

[159] 6.68.5–30.

of action, arguing that with the apparent death of Sītā, whom they were fighting to recover, there is no longer any point to the war.[160] The news of Indrajit's apparent murder of Sītā also has a devastating effect on Rāma himself. Upon hearing Hanumān's report, Rāma faints from grief and, even after his return to consciousness, remains so stunned that he cannot return to battle for some time or even fully comprehend what is being said to him.[161] At this point Vibhīṣaṇa once more intervenes and instructs Rāma that he must send Lakṣmaṇa forth to confront and destroy Indrajit before the latter can complete the sacrifice in which he is engaged and which, we now come to fully understand, is the source of his devastating power of invisibility.[162]

For at last we are given to know the two reasons for Indrajit's power and invincibility, a deadly combination of asceticism and sacrifice, the two most empowering practices of the epic tradition. Through his austerities, Indrajit has received, as a boon from Brahmā, the knowledge and mastery over the powerful *brāhma* weapons, and through his repeated performances of a kind of black-magical version of the vedic *yajña*, he has mastered the power of making himself invisible.[163] These two assets, coupled with his native mastery of the power of illusion, a power seemingly common to many prominent *rākṣasas*, make him all but invincible in battle.

It is clear that, given his lethal combination of these supernatural powers, Indrajit himself is the most critical figure in the ranks of the *rākṣasas* defending Laṅkā, just as it emerged that Hanumān is the key figure among those besieging the city.[164] Moreover, although his powers of illusion and his mastery of the weapons of Brahmā are always with him, it appears that the magical power of invisibility, his most fearsome attribute, is acquired through, and must be constantly refreshed by, repeated performances of a peculiar sacrifice in the grove of the dark goddess Nikumbhilā.[165] This fact is heavily stressed by the poet, as we see Indrajit perform the rite fully twice in the Book—becoming invisible as the oblation is completed—and

[160] 6.69.19–22.
[161] 6.70.10–6.72.3.
[162] 6.72.10–18.
[163] 6.72.12–17.
[164] 6.61.18–23.
[165] See S. Goldman 2006b.

undertake it yet a third time only to be interrupted by Lakṣmaṇa and his detachment of monkeys.[166]

Thus, in fulfilling a prophecy that Indrajit would fall to an enemy only at such time as he would be unable to complete one of his magical rites in the Nikumbhilā grove, Lakṣmaṇa eliminates, in a single stroke, the most dangerous of the *rākṣasa* warriors and the last major champion to stand between Rāvaṇa and his doom. The significance of this battle as well as the enormous difficulty of subduing so formidable a foe as Indrajit, even without his power of invisibility, is signaled by the poet in drawing out the account of the encounter for seven full *sargas*.[167] Unlike many of his elders, Indrajit is a figure almost exclusively of action. Thus his speeches are largely confined to vows of victory and battlefield taunts and boasts rather than the sometimes lengthy lectures on *dharma*, *nīti*, and strategy in which his uncles and their peers indulge. Therefore his character is more monolithic and less complex than that of many of the other *rākṣasas* who play prominent roles in the epic drama. Nonetheless, because of his unparalleled martial skills, he is a figure who has captured the popular imagination every bit as much as characters such as Kumbhakarṇa and Vibhīṣaṇa.[168]

Vibhīṣaṇa

Another of Rāvaṇa's younger brothers, Vibhīṣaṇa, plays an essential role in the *Yuddhakāṇḍa*. This role, however, is radically different from that played by any other principal *rākṣasa* of Rāvaṇa's court. For whereas his other kinsmen and counselors encourage him in his evil ways and haughty disdain of Rāma's power, as most do, or, like Mālyavān and even Kumbhakarṇa, attempt to preach to him on righteousness and proper statecraft or warn him of his folly and his peril, all the while remaining loyal to their elder and master and laying down their lives in battle for his sake, Vibhīṣaṇa alone does not. Adhering firmly to the dictates of *dharma* and unable to abide the abuse his brother reserves for those who attempt to

[166] 6.60.18–28; 6.67.4–15; 6.69.23–26; 6.73.13.

[167] 6.72–78.

[168] Most notably in a revisionist nineteenth-century literary reworking of the *Rāmāyaṇa*, the Bengali poet Michael Madhusudan Datta makes him the tragic hero of his long narrative poem, the *Meghnādbadhakābya*. See Seely 2004.

counsel him for his own good, Vibhīṣaṇa defects early on in the Book to the side of his brother's mortal enemies. There, as one gifted with intimate knowledge of Rāvaṇa's allies and military arrangements as well as the defenses of Laṅkā and as a powerful warrior in his own right, he contributes as much as, if not more than, anyone to the triumph of Rāma and the downfall and death of his brother.

Although Vibhīṣaṇa holds a secure and revered place in the minds of Vaiṣṇavas as one of the most exemplary of Rāmabhaktas, appearing in all kinds of courtly and popular plastic representations of *Paṭṭābhiṣekarāma*, his characterization in the poem is somewhat more complex than is often recognized.

No doubt Vibhīṣaṇa fits the mold of one of the most striking and theologically significant character types in the Vaiṣṇava literature, that of the virtuous, or dharmic, demon. This role is perhaps best and most famously exemplified by the *asura* prince Prahlāda of the epic-purāṇic myth of the *Narasiṃhāvatāra*, the pious demon who rejects the evil ways of his race to devote himself to the worship of the Lord.[169] But Vibhīṣaṇa is surely a close second in illustrating the possibility of salvation through devotion for even the most lowly or sinful by nature. His defection, moreover, provides an ideal opportunity for Rāma to expound eloquently his doctrine of compassion for all refugees, whether virtuous or sinful, and thus to declare that he would accept and shelter even Rāvaṇa himself should he come to him seeking refuge.[170] This speech is perhaps the earliest statement of the role of the *Rāmāvatāra* as above all *śaraṇya*, or the refuge of all beings, a doctrine that, held in common with other *bhakti* traditions, will become particularly central to the *viśiṣṭādvaita*, or Śrīvaiṣṇava school associated with Rāmānuja.[171]

Vibhīṣaṇa's role in the *Yuddhakāṇḍa* is, in fact, extremely significant. For at several critical junctures he assists, advises, or rallies the forces of his new friends when they are at an impasse or on the point of despair. It is he who explains to Rāma and his allies that the god of the ocean, Samudra, must be propitiated if he is to permit the army to cross his vast expanse.[172] Vibhīṣaṇa is the only one who is able to

[169] Pollock 1991, pp. 37–38, especially note 71.
[170] 6.12.9–21.
[171] See notes to 5.7.68 and 5.16.5; and Mumme 1991.
[172] 6.13.13–15.

see through the illusions of Indrajit,[173] and he is able to reassure the despairing monkeys that, although Rāma and Lakṣmaṇa are bound by Indrajit's serpent-arrows, they are not, in fact, dead and will recover.[174] It is he who easily sees through the simian disguises of Rāvaṇa's spies, Śuka and Sāraṇa,[175] and captures them and their replacements.[176] Again, when the heroic brothers are struck down a second time by Indrajit, Vibhīṣaṇa alone understands that they have submitted to the power of his weapons out of their deference to Lord Brahmā.[177] He is the one who narrates the history of Kumbhakarṇa to Rāma when the giant first looms above the ramparts of Laṅkā and who, in order to calm and rally the terrified monkeys, devises the strategic falsehood that the monstrous *rākṣasa* is merely some large mechanical device.[178]

When Indrajit has managed to put Rāma, Lakṣmaṇa, and virtually all the monkey heroes out of action, only Vibhīṣaṇa and Hanumān have the power to resist the demon's sorcery and powerful weapons and are thus able to save the day by locating the wounded Jāmbavān on the gory battlefield.[179] Perhaps most critical of all, it is Vibhīṣaṇa alone who is able to end the despair of the monkeys and of Rāma himself by explaining that Indrajit's apparent murder of Sītā is a mere illusion, and by advising Lakṣmaṇa of the need to engage and kill the otherwise invincible *rākṣasa* warrior before he has time to complete yet another of his dark *yajñas*.[180] In these ways, when the situation is, or appears to be, hopeless, he saves the day time and again.

Finally, it is Vibhīṣaṇa to whom Rāma entrusts the very sensitive mission of bringing Sītā to him publicly for their wrought reunion, and it is he who lends Rāma the flying palace Puṣpaka to enable him to return to Ayodhyā by the end of his fourteen-year exile, thus saving Bharata from having to fulfill his vow and end his life.[181]

173 6.36.9–10.
174 6.36.26–38.
175 6.16.13.
176 6.20.22.
177 6.49.8–27; 6.49.31; 6.61.2–5.
178 6.49.8–27; 6.49.31.
179 6.61.5–20.
180 6.71.
181 6.102.6–33; 6.109.8–27.

Through both his actions and words, then, Vibhīṣaṇa emerges as one of the most important figures in the Book if not the entire epic.

He is also held up as the paragon of virtue and devotion to Rāma, thus acquiring a reputation he no doubt deserves. Nonetheless, one should note here that there is a certain degree of complexity, even ambiguity, in Vālmīki's portrayal of this important and intriguing figure. In the first place, even though Vibhīṣaṇa's actions are uniformly dharmic and therefore fully in keeping with the boon of perpetual righteousness he received from Brahmā,[182] it cannot be said that they are devoid of self-interest. For in exchange for his defection and aid, Rāma immediately confers the kingship of Laṅkā upon his new ally, thus making him the de jure ruler of the *rākṣasas* even before the war with Rāvaṇa has begun.[183] The more serious and controversial aspect of the characterization of Vibhīṣaṇa is, of course, his treacherous betrayal of his elder brother, his kinsmen, and his race. This is especially striking in the context of an epic that is one of the principal instruments in upholding its culture's absolute imperative of deference to one's elders.[184] The critique of Vibhīṣaṇa as a traitor to his family and his race is eloquently made by Indrajit,[185] and, although his uncle has the final word, defending himself on the grounds of Rāvaṇa's incorrigibly evil nature and his own commitment to *dharma*, something of a cloud continues to hover over Vibhīṣaṇa as witnessed by such popular proverbs on the subject of treachery as that found in Bengali, and quoted when someone wishes to denigrate someone as disloyal or a traitor to one's own, "*ghore śotru bibhīṣon* (a traitor in one's own house, a Vibhīṣaṇa)."

[182] 7.10.26–30.

[183] 6.13.7–9. This "field promotion" of the exiled *rākṣasa* is apparently somewhat provisional as Rāma ordains a formal and elaborate consecration ceremony once the war is concluded and Rāvaṇa is dead (6.100). In installing Vibhīṣaṇa on the throne in place of his deposed and slain brother, Rāma appears to be following an oft-repeated motif of both epics, that of the displaced elder. On this, see R. Goldman 1978.

[184] Rāma is, of course, the greatest exemplar of filial deference, unquestioningly obeying his father's unjust order of banishment and disinheritance at enormous personal cost. On this, see R. Goldman 1985 and Pollock 1986, pp. 54–73. Similarly Lakṣmaṇa and Rāma's other brothers unquestioningly obey him even when they find his orders disturbing. On this, see 6.104.20–22, where Lakṣmaṇa reluctantly builds a pyre for Sītā, or 7.44–46, where the brothers silently hear Rāma's command that Sītā be banished and Lakṣmaṇa unwillingly carries out the order.

[185] 6.74.11–16.

Mālyavān, Vidyujjihva, Śuka, Sāraṇa, and Śārdūla

As in the case of the *vānaras*, there are a number of *rākṣasas* who, although much less prominent than the principals discussed above, nonetheless stand in importance somewhere between them and the various demon champions whose stereotypical duels and deaths punctuate the narrative, not to mention the various "walk-ons" and innumerable "extras" who serve at Rāvaṇa's court and in his vast army. These figures are of note either because of their unusual or courageous speeches or because of some specialized function they serve.

One of those who falls into the former category is Rāvaṇa's great-uncle, the wise and venerable *rākṣasa* Mālyavān. Aside from his brothers, the banished defector Vibhīṣaṇa and the formidable giant Kumbhakarṇa, few of the courtiers and sycophants who surround the *rākṣasa* king have the temerity to speak with the frankness of Mālyavān, who, risking, and indeed provoking, his master's wrath, argues forcefully for Sītā's return and Rāma's conciliation, pointing out the obvious portents of doom that have attended every one of Rāvaṇa's moves.[186] One of the most interesting aspects of Mālyavān's speech is that he reveals that he and some like-minded *rākṣasas* have concluded on the basis of the signs that Rāma is, in fact, none other than the mighty Lord Viṣṇu, who has taken on the body of a man.[187] This is particularly striking in the context of the occluded nature of the *Rāmāvatāra*, which prevents Rāma's closest friends and allies, and even Rāma himself, from realizing his divine nature until he has accomplished his purpose in killing Rāvaṇa.[188]

In the case of the *rākṣasa* specialists, a few are worthy of note. One is Vidyujjihva, who appears to be particularly adept in the art of magical illusion, or *māyā*. The control of *māyā* appears to be a gift that is common to most of the major *rākṣasas*, including Rāvaṇa himself.[189] In the *Araṇyakāṇḍa*, for example, Rāvaṇa enlists the aid of the demon-ascetic Mārīca, who, apparently especially skilled in the magical arts, reluctantly turns himself into the famous golden deer

[186] 6.26.5–6.27.14.
[187] 6.26.31.
[188] On this point, see Pollock 1991, pp. 13–54.
[189] However, few of the *rākṣasas* said to possess this power actually employ it. See S. Goldman 2006a.

to enchant Sītā and draw Rāma away from their hermitage.[190] Rāvaṇa, too, transforms himself into a holy mendicant in order to gain Sītā's confidence.[191] It is not clear, however, to what extent we are meant to distinguish this power of shape-shifting (*kāmarūpitva*), common to most supernatural beings in the epic and purāṇic literature, including the *vānaras* of the *Rāmāyaṇa*, from the power of illusion that enables one to actually conjure up illusory figures from thin air.[192]

This latter power is evidenced only rarely in the epic. One example, mentioned above, is seen when Indrajit, a true master of the art of illusion, conjures up and appears to murder a simulacrum of Sītā.[193] Thus, when Rāvaṇa wishes to employ this type of illusion, he apparently requires the assistance of a specialist. One of his more sinister efforts to demoralize Sītā so as to break her spirit and bend her to his will involves his false claim that Rāma has been beheaded during the course of a night raid on his camp led by the *rākṣasa* general Prahasta. To convince the princess of the truth of this fiction, Rāvaṇa, who is himself described here as possessed of great powers of illusion (*mahāmāya*), commissions another *rākṣasa*, Vidyujjihva, said to be expert in the magical arts (*māyāvit*), to conjure up illusions of Rāma's severed head and his bow. Vidyujjihva complies and is rewarded for his skill. The grisly apparition is utterly convincing and causes Sītā to lament piteously for both her lord and her fate. Although the illusion has been created by Vidyujjihva, it seems to be sustained only by the efforts or presence of Rāvaṇa. For as soon as he is summoned away to an urgent meeting, it vanishes.[194]

One remaining specialization with which several *rākṣasas* are associated is that of espionage. Rāvaṇa has a number of counselors to whom he entrusts the sensitive tasks of infiltrating, undetected, the ranks of his enemies and reporting back to him on their strength and disposition.

Once Rāma and his forces have crossed the ocean and encamped on the Laṅkan shore, Rāvaṇa deputes two trusted courtiers, Śuka and Sāraṇa, to penetrate the enemy lines and bring back a thorough

[190] 3.34–40.
[191] 3.44.2–3.
[192] See pp. 25–28.
[193] 6.68.4–29.
[194] 6.22.6–6.23.38.

enumeration of their troops. The two take on the appearance of monkeys and attempt to do as they have been ordered. The vastness of the monkey hosts, however, is beyond their reckoning, and they are, in any case, immediately recognized, despite their disguise, by Vibhīṣaṇa, who seizes them and brings them before Rāma. Their capture, however, proves to be yet another opportunity for the poet to demonstrate the kindness and compassion of his hero. For Rāma, "devoted to the welfare of all beings," receives them kindly and sends them back unharmed with a message for their master.[195]

The hapless secret agents dutifully report to Rāvaṇa to tell him what happened, and they give him an elaborate description of Rāma and the monkey forces.[196] Their master, however, finding their account to be excessively laudatory, flies into a rage and dismisses them as a pair of duffers.[197] He then instructs his minister Mahodara to find him some spies who are competent in their profession.[198] Others are found and sent out, but they suffer a fate even worse than that of their discredited predecessors. Not only are they, too, immediately spotted and captured by Vibhīṣaṇa, they are badly beaten by the monkeys before they are released. Upon interrogation by Rāvaṇa, one of their number, Śārdūla, reports on their misadventures and informs his master that it is impossible, in fact, to spy on the monkeys, as they are too powerful and are under Rāma's protection.[199]

THE *RĀKṢASĪS*

Although the *Yuddhakāṇḍa* contains a few references to the fearsome *rākṣasī* wardresses who guard and torment Sītā in her captivity,[200] and who are so graphically described in the *Sundarakāṇḍa*,[201] no further scenes portray the threats, cajoling, and torment of the princess at their hands. On the other hand, it does extend and

[195] 6.16.1–22.
[196] 6.17–19.
[197] 6.20.1–13.
[198] 6.20.14.
[199] 6.20.21–6.21.13.
[200] 6.25.9; 6.101.23–37.
[201] 5.20.30–35; 5.21–23; 5.25.1–3. For a discussion on why this is the case, see S. Goldman 2006b.

elaborate on a theme found in the previous Book, that of the aid and comfort extended to the long-suffering princess by a few sympathetic *rākṣasīs* who act against the wishes and interests of their master in order to help her.

Noteworthy among these friendly *rākṣasīs* is Saramā. Although she is said to have been deputed by Rāvaṇa to guard Sītā, she is described as a dear friend of the princess. When the *rākṣasa* king, who had been tormenting Sītā with a false account of Rāma's death and the apparition of his severed head, is called away, Saramā comforts her with assurances that Rāma and his allies could never be defeated by the *rākṣasas*. After informing Sītā that she has been the victim of an illusion, she predicts Rāma's victory and his happy reunion with Sītā. She even places herself at Sītā's service, offering to carry a message in secret to Rāma and agreeing to spy on her master at Sītā's behest.[202] In this way, Saramā, a figure not mentioned in the *Sundarakāṇḍa*, serves as a kind of female counterpart to Vibhīṣaṇa,[203] the virtuous *rākṣasa*, who, despite his evil birth, stands resolutely on the side of righteousness. These figures, as noted above, come to serve an important theological function as metaphors for the human sinner who can attain salvation through devotion and service to the Lord or the Goddess. They also fit in with one of the epic's overarching themes of Rāma's and Sītā's refusal to hold all the *rākṣasas* or the *rākṣasīs* collectively guilty for the sins of some among them.[204]

Saramā, moreover, is not the only *rākṣasī* to befriend and comfort Sītā in her affliction. Early in the war, when it appears that Indrajit has slain Rāma and Lakṣmaṇa with his powerful serpent-arrows, Rāvaṇa orders a party of Sītā's wardresses to take her on an aerial survey of the battlefield in the flying palace Puṣpaka so she can see for herself that her hopes of rescue and reunion with her husband are in vain.[205] Among those sent on this mission is one Trijaṭā. This is doubtless the same elderly *rākṣasī* who is introduced in the *Sundarakāṇḍa*, where she defends Sītā from the other *rākṣasa* women

[202] 6.24–25.

[203] This is perhaps why a number of the commentators identify Saramā as Vibhīṣaṇa's wife. See note to 6.24.1.

[204] Cf. 6.67.36–39; 6.101.29–36. On this important theme in the *Rāmāyaṇa*, see R. Goldman 2006a.

[205] 6.37.

who are tormenting her and relates her prophetic dream foretelling Rāma's victory, his reunion with Sītā, and the destruction of Rāvaṇa and his allies. Trijaṭā concludes her speech by pointing out omens favorable to the princess and warning the *rākṣasīs* that they must cease their abuse of Sītā and propitiate her.[206]

Here, too, Trijaṭā intervenes to comfort the despairing Sītā, reassuring her that Rāma and Lakṣmaṇa are not dead and pointing out various signs indicating that they are still alive. She notes, among other things, that the auspicious flying palace in which they are traveling would never carry a widow and declares that Sītā's conduct and demeanor have won her over as a friend.[207]

These interventions on the part of Saramā and Trijaṭā serve not only to sustain Sītā's faith through her long ordeal but also somewhat humanize the *rākṣasas*, an important element in Vālmīki's construction of the epic tale and his characterization of its hero and heroine. This is made particularly clear near the end of the Book when Sītā, in response to Hanumān's request for permission to slaughter the *rākṣasīs* who have been tormenting her, refuses on the grounds that they were only following the order of their perverse master and that, in any case, one ought not to punish creatures for being what they are.[208]

A few other *rākṣasīs* and women of Rāvaṇa's court appear in the Book in fairly sympathetic roles. Thus, for example, the poet gives voice to both Mandodarī, Rāvaṇa's chief queen, and his other—unnamed and unidentified—consorts whose moving lamentations for their slain lord are quoted at length.[209]

[206] 5.25.4–38.
[207] 6.38.22–33.
[208] 6.101.29–37.
[209] 6.98–99. See Goldman and Goldman 1996, pp. 65–67.

5. Style and Structure of the *Yuddhakāṇḍa*

THE CENTRAL THEME of the *Yuddhakāṇḍa*, the climactic battle between the forces of *dharma* and those of *adharma*, a battle against an antagonist so powerful that it requires no less a figure than the Supreme Lord of the universe and the gods incarnate to defeat him, lends itself particularly well to the spectacular. The poet has not been slow to take advantage of the visual opportunities that the narrative presents in abundance.

This is evident early on in the Book where Vālmīki provides visually compelling back-to-back descriptions of the convulsive turbulence of the ocean, when Rāma, furious at the sea-god's obduracy in refusing to appear before him and grant him and his army passage, fires his blazing arrows into its depths. The poet follows this with a dramatic rendering of the construction of the bridge and the passage of the monkey hosts.[1]

> Blazing with energy, those swift and excellent arrows plunged into the waters of the sea, terrifying its great serpents.
>
> Then, along with a howling gale, there arose a huge and terrifying surge of the ocean, carrying with it sharks and sea monsters.
>
> All at once the ocean was covered with garlands of towering waves and filled with conch and oyster shells, its waves shrouded in a vaporous haze.
>
> Great serpents and the immensely powerful *dānavas*, who dwell in the underworld known as Pātāla, were in agony, flames shooting from their mouths and eyes.
>
> Suddenly from the ocean, king of rivers, there arose thousands of waves as tall as the Vindhya or Mandara mountains and filled with sharks and sea monsters.

[1] For a discussion of the Indo-European versions of the motif of the hero on the beach, see Slatin 2006.

> Such was the state of the ocean, the repository of all waters: its masses of waves were swirling, its *rākṣasas* and great serpents were terrified, and its huge crocodiles were tossed about...[2]
>
> There those monkeys, bulls among the hosts of tree-dwelling monkeys, resembling mountains, broke down trees and dragged them to the sea.
>
> The monkeys filled the sea with bamboo and *sāla*, *aśvakarṇa*, *dhava*, *kuṭaja*, *arjuna*, palmyra, *tilaka*, *timiśa*, *bilvaka*, *saptaparṇa*, flowering *karṇikāra*, mango, and *aśoka* trees.
>
> Holding aloft those tree trunks, with and without their roots, like so many flagstaffs of Indra, the foremost among the tawny monkeys carried off the trees.
>
> Heaved up violently by the boulders hurled into it, the water rose into the sky and cascaded down on all sides.
>
> Nala constructed a great bridge, ten leagues in width and one hundred in length, right through the middle of the ocean, lord of rivers and streams.
>
> Then, in the ocean, the great receptacle of waters, there arose a tumultuous sound from the boulders being hurled into it and the mountains being cast down.
>
> The bridge that Nala constructed over the ocean, abode of sea monsters, was as majestic and splendid as the path of the constellation Svātī through the heavens.
>
> Then the gods, *gandharvas*, perfected beings, and supreme seers gathered and hovered in the sky, eager to witness that marvel.
>
> The leaping monkeys were bounding, bellowing, and leaping. All beings gazed upon that inconceivable, seemingly impossible, and hair-raising marvel: the building of a bridge over the ocean.[3]

For a modern audience, these descriptions call to mind the increasingly sophisticated special effects of Hollywood films on classical and

[2] 6.14.16–21.
[3] 6.15.15–24.

biblical themes and natural disasters.[4] Similarly the highly visual, grotesquely comic account of the rousing of Kumbhakarṇa and his rampage among the monkey troops is reminiscent of any number of modern monster films.[5]

The astute reader will have noted here and in much of the above a number of allusions to the cinematic in connection with our analysis of the *Yuddhakāṇḍa*. This reflects our observation that this Book, perhaps more than any other section of the *Rāmāyaṇa* or its sister epic, the *Mahābhārata*, seems to lend itself to a cinematic type of structure and framing.[6] In this respect, referring anachronistically to this modern medium may be a useful window through which to view and better appreciate the art of Vālmīki.

For the *Yuddhakāṇḍa* has a number of features in common with modern cinematic technique, features that have been studied by scholars in the field of film studies. Aside from the "special effects" in the highly spectacular scenes noted above, scenes that by no means are restricted to the Book or the poem, there are a number of features here that seem to call out for comparison with cinematic techniques.

One of these, discussed to some extent above, is the foregrounding and aestheticization of violence. As noted earlier, Vālmīki appears to delight in graphic descriptions of massive and sanguinary violence. This is, of course, quite appropriate to the central and defining theme of the Book, warfare. But what is noteworthy is the poet's constant effort to beautify the grisly details of the carnage that takes place on the killing fields of Laṅkā.

In so doing, Vālmīki manages to create a poetry of violence that, even as it details the horrific effects of weaponry on the bodies of men, monkeys, *rākṣasas*, and their mounts, and so gratifies the voyeuristic appetites of its audiences, frequently diverts the reader/auditor's eye from the sanguinary to the charming through the exploitation of an elaborate and highly conventionalized set of tropes of

[4] One might cite, for example, deMille's 1956 epic, *The Ten Commandments*, with its massive crowd scenes and its representation of the parting of the Red Sea.

[5] These range from B movies such as Nathan Juran's 1958 *The Attack of the 50 Foot Woman* to films such as Merian C. Cooper and Ernest B. Schoedsack's *King Kong* (1933) (also Peter Jackson's 2005 remake) and Ang Lee's *The Hulk* (2003).

[6] See R. Dwyer 2006. See, too, S. Goldman 2003a; 2003b; and 2004a.

comparison. Thus, on the one hand, one finds many passages like the following:

> His head shattered by the crushing blow of that fist, Devāntaka, son of the *rākṣasa* king, all at once fell lifeless to the ground, his teeth and eyes knocked out, his tongue lolling.[7]

or

> Struck by that palm, which was like the thunderbolt of great Indra, he fell to the ground, drenched in gore and vomiting blood.[8]

On the other hand, passages such as the following are still more numerous:

> Covered with wounds, the bodies of those two great warriors were as resplendent as a *śālmali* and a *kiṃśuka* tree in full bloom in the forest before their leaves appear.[9]

> Stripped of his ears and nose and gushing blood, mighty Kumbhakarṇa looked like a mountain covered with waterfalls.[10]

> or

> The ground, covered with torrents of blood, looked as if it were covered with blossoming *palāśa* trees in the month of Mādhava.[11]

The poet's most elaborate and striking use of this technique of rhetorically superimposing the aesthetic upon the emetic may be seen in his extended metaphor at 6.46.25–28 in which the hideous gore of the battlefield is overlaid with the conventional description of a charming riparian landscape.[12]

The rendering of extreme violence into spectacle that so characterizes the Book's numerous battle scenes reaches its most dramatic and most "cinematic," as it were, representation in the prolonged narration of the maiming, dismemberment, and death of the giant

[7] 6.58.24.
[8] 6.84.29.
[9] 6.76.28.
[10] 6.55.70.
[11] 6.46.24.
[12] See chapter 3, above.

Kumbhakarṇa in *sarga* 55. The sequence[13] begins when the monkey king Sugrīva, who had been knocked unconscious and carried off by the monstrous *rākṣasa*, comes to his senses and rips off his adversary's ears and nose with his sharp claws and fangs. Maddened by his wounds and streaming blood "like a mountain covered with waterfalls," Kumbhakarṇa throws off Sugrīva and begins a violent rampage among the monkey troops, devouring them in huge numbers so that his body is drenched in their blood and fat. At length, Kumbhakarṇa encounters Rāma himself, and, after some inconclusive exchanges, the latter uses his divine missiles to sever, one by one, the *rākṣasa*'s arms and feet. Despite these disabling injuries, he still manages to hurl himself upon Rāma with gaping jaws only to have his cavernous mouth filled with arrows and, at last, his huge head severed.

The complex battle with and final destruction of Kumbhakarṇa is clearly one of the most spectacular scenes in the epic. At 129 verses in the critical edition, it is by a mere six *ślokas* the second longest chapter in the Book and one of the longest in the entire poem. Its length and its detailed and graphic description of violence make it apparent that it was a favorite of the author and, in all likelihood, his audience as well. In its striking visual images and slow progression to the monster's final fall, it is strongly reminiscent of the detailed and highly stylized depiction of bloody violence that characterize the films of Akira Kurosawa and, after him, the post-1966 films of such American cinematic *auteurs* as Arthur Penn, Sam Peckinpah, Quentin Tarantino, and others.[14] In the grotesquely comical depiction of Kumbhakarṇa continuing to fight despite his gradual dismemberment, one is reminded of the parodic scene of the Black Knight in Gilliam and Jones's 1975 mock epic film, *Monty Python and the Holy Grail.*

[13] See pp. 24–25 and 75–77 and 6.55.65–125.

[14] The substitution of the Motion Picture Association of America's rating system in 1966 for the older Production Code, which was much more restrictive in the way violence could be represented in Hollywood films, allowed these directors and their successors to use various special effects (slow motion, squibs, latex flesh, etc.) to render bloodshed, violence, and mutilation in graphic ways that echo the poetic imagery of Vālmīki. These techniques enable the filmmaker to aestheticize visually what Penn, in a discussion of his highly influential 1967 film *Bonnie and Clyde*, calls the "spastic and balletic" qualities of violent death. For a discussion of these issues in the realm of film studies, see Prince 1998; 2000a; 2000b; and 2003; and Sobchack 2000.

That scenes such as these were imbibed and experienced visually as well as through oral performance is suggested by the multiplicity of their graphic representations in sculptural friezes and manuscript illustrations in premodern India. One should keep in mind the precinematic method of Indian court painters of rendering motion by depicting the same figures multiple times in the same frame at progressive stages of movement. Thus, for example, the painter of the scene of Kumbhakarṇa's death in the copiously illustrated seventeenth-century Mewar idiom, "Jagat Singh *Rāmāyaṇa*," depicts the progressive mutilation, dismemberment, and fall of the giant in a memorable sequence of illustrations of this type.[15]

One other quasi-cinematic aspect of the Book deserves mention. More than any of the preceding Books, which tend mainly to follow the adventures and fortunes of one central character,[16] the *Yuddhakāṇḍa*, by virtue of its theme, frequently shifts its perspective back and forth between the camps and councils of Rāma and Rāvaṇa, detailing the deliberations, strategies, and sorties of the opposing sides as they plan and execute their war strategies, meeting only on the field of battle. This shift of perspective is measured, regular, and evidently well thought out. Thus the Book's first five *sargas* place the omniscient authorial eye with Rāma and his forces, following them in their southward march from Kiṣkindhā to the northern shore of the sea. The next five take us to the council chambers of Laṅkā, where we witness the discussions between Rāvaṇa and his military and political advisers as to how to respond to the threat posed by Rāma's appearance across the water. In the next group of five *sargas* the poet follows Vibhīṣaṇa from Laṅkā to Rāma's encampment,

[15] British Library Add. 15297, Book 6, folios 85–89.

[16] In the first four Books, the poet's eye tends to stay very closely on Rāma and his associates, following them in their adventures and trials and only departing occasionally to narrate a story or, when necessary, briefly following a secondary character or theme. In the first case, the stories, like those told by Viśvāmitra and others in the *Bālakāṇḍa* or by Sugrīva in the *Kiṣkindhākāṇḍa*, are narrated in Rāma's presence. In the second, the authorial eye will briefly follow a figure like Bharata during his sojourn in and travel from Rājagṛha, or revert episodically to the action in Ayodhyā after Rāma's departure, or in Laṅkā immediately before and after the abduction of Sītā. In the *Sundarakāṇḍa* the action is set mainly in Laṅkā, where the poet mostly follows the adventures of Hanumān and Sītā, albeit peppering his narrative with numerous retellings of the main epic story. For a discussion of this phenomenon, see Goldman and Goldman 1996, pp. 18–20.

where the monkeys debate whether to trust him, Rāma takes him in and consecrates him as king of the *rākṣasas*, and the monkeys, acting on the *rākṣasa*'s advice, build a bridge and cross the ocean. This section, in turn, is followed by a passage of twelve *sargas* in which we return to Laṅkā to watch as Rāvaṇa sends out agents to spy on Rāma's forces, attempts to demoralize Sītā with the illusion of Rāma's head and bow, consults further with his advisers, and makes his preparations for the defense of the city. At this point we return once again, for four *sargas*, to Rāma's camp, where we see the hero make his preparations for the assault on Laṅkā and begin the siege.

After this the battle is joined, and much of the action takes place on and around the battlefield between the city and Rāma's main encampment, where it whipsaws rapidly and violently between the two sides and their various dueling champions. This back-and-forth pattern basically dominates the central two-thirds of the Book, until, near the very end, Rāma finally kills Rāvaṇa. Following this, the Book's culminating moment, the poet's eye remains on Rāma, with only brief departures.[17]

This stately and majestic sweep of the authorial eye back and forth between the councils and camps of the opposing warriors, although not unknown to other ancient epics,[18] is strongly reminiscent of the techniques used by the makers of modern major cinematic war epics such as Annikin, Martin, and Wicki's 1962 filmic tale of the D Day landings, *The Longest Day*, or Fleischer, Fukasaku, and Masuda's 1970 film depicting the events leading up to the Japanese attack on Pearl Harbor, *Tora! Tora! Tora!* In these films, as in the *Yuddhakāṇḍa*, the spectator, reader, or auditor is carefully and artfully shifted from the intimacy of the war councils on each side to the chaotic and spectacular violence of the battleground.[19]

[17] As, for example, when it follows Hanumān once more to the *aśoka* grove to bring the good news to Sītā (*sarga* 101) or to Ayodhyā to report to Bharata (*sargas* 113–14).

[18] Compare the *Iliad*'s shifting between the siege encampment of Agamemnon and Priam's court in Troy or the *Odyssey*'s occasional shifting from the wanderings of Odysseus to the trials of Penelope in Ithaca.

[19] It is perhaps worth noting here that, just as Vālmīki strives to convey with his descriptions of the grotesqueness of figures such as Kumbhakarṇa or the uncanny black magic of Indrajit the otherness of the *rākṣasa* camp in contrast to that of Rāma, these films were among the first American war epics to insist on having the German and Japanese characters speak in their own respective languages, adding subtitles for the benefit of their audiences.

THE SHAPE OF THE *YUDDHAKĀṆḌA*

Like the preceding *Sundarakāṇḍa*, the *Yuddhakāṇḍa* has a distinctly annular structure.[20] Both Books can be described as more or less self-contained pieces of quest literature in which a hero sets out on a dangerous mission, accomplishes it despite obstacles and trials, and returns triumphant. In the *Sundarakāṇḍa*, we witness Hanumān's prodigious leap across the ocean, his daunting search for Sītā, his battles with the *rākṣasas*, his brief captivity, and his return leap.[21]

Although the *Yuddhakāṇḍa* constitutes the final movement in the larger quest-saga of the *Rāmāyaṇa* from the hero's exile and the loss of his wife to his recovery of Sītā and his consecration, it can also be seen as a symmetrical miniepic in its own right within the larger narrative of exile and return in which the hero crosses the seemingly impassable barrier of the ocean by miraculous means (a bridge sanctioned by the ocean god and built by monkeys), defeats his archenemy, recovers his lost wife, and once more crosses the sea by a miraculous device (the fabulous flying palace Puṣpaka).

The Book marks the completion of the central tale of Prince Rāma, taking him to the culmination of his long-deferred consecration and, perhaps more important, the fulfillment of the mission of the *Rāmāvatāra*. This no doubt made its ending a highly attractive and appropriate place for the addition of a traditional *phalaśruti*, or statement of the benefits, spiritual and material, that accrue to those who recite or hear the text. Indeed, such statements are to be found at the conclusion of the final *sarga* of the Book in virtually all known versions. Since *phalaśrutis* mark the conclusion of many of the religious texts of Hinduism, some scholars have taken this to suggest that the "original *Rāmāyaṇa*" must have ended with the *Yuddhakāṇḍa*.[22] It is a commonly held view among epic scholars that the *Uttarakāṇḍa*, like the *Bālakāṇḍa* but perhaps more so, belongs to the latest stratum of the formation of the poem.[23] This may well be

[20] See S. Goldman 2003b, for a discussion of gender as a structural determinant in the *Yuddhakāṇḍa*.
[21] On this, see Goldman and Goldman 1996, pp. 14–17.
[22] See, for example, Bulcke 1960, pp. 40–41 and Vaidya 1971, p. xxxi. Vaidya refers to the *Yuddhakāṇḍa* as "the last Kāṇḍa of the real and original Rāmāyaṇa."
[23] For a discussion of this issue, see Brockington 1998, pp. 379, 391–94.

entirely or partly true, but we do not believe that the presence across the manuscript traditions of the various versions of the *phalaśruti* in any way demonstrates this.

For, in addition to the issues noted above, it must be observed that the manuscript evidence for the *phalaśruti* is so complicated as to suggest that, whatever the relative date of the *Yuddhakāṇḍa*, the *phalaśrutis* must have been still later additions, appended to the Book for reasons of piety.[24]

[24] For a discussion of the extraordinary textual complexity of the *phalaśruti* passages, see notes to 6.116.90.

6. Text, Translation, and Commentaries[1]

In general, the constitution of the critical edition of the *Yuddhakāṇḍa* follows the principles established for the other Books.[2] A discussion of these principles with special reference to the present translation is included in our Introduction to the *Bālakāṇḍa*[3] and so requires no further elaboration here.

It should be noted, however, that, because of the unusual length of the volume and perhaps as a consequence of some of the difficulties in its preparation alluded to by its editor,[4] the text contains a few more problematic readings and occasional typographical errors than are found in the earlier volumes. We have accordingly felt compelled to propose emendations to the critical text but have done so sparingly and only where we felt that it was absolutely necessary for comprehensibility. These have been marked with an asterisk (*) in the translation as has been our practice elsewhere. We have provided a glossary of these emendations. Our notes, however, point out numerous additional places where we have questioned the choices made by the critical editors.[5]

THE COMMENTATORS[6]

Our observations on the dating, relationships, sectarian affiliations, and so forth, of the major medieval and early modern commentators on the Vālmīki *Rāmāyaṇa* have been discussed in previous volumes.[7] Nonetheless, the *Yuddhakāṇḍa*, because of its theme,

[1] Portions of the following section are adapted from our Introduction to the *Sundarakāṇḍa* (Goldman and Goldman 1996, pp. 87–98), with changes and additions relevant to the present volume.
[2] Bhatt 1960, pp. xxix-xxxiv and Jhala 1966, p. xxxv.
[3] Pollock 1984a, pp. 82, 93.
[4] Vaidya 1971, pp. xxxvi–xxxvii.
[5] See, for example, notes to 6.28.37; 6.40.21; 6.41.10; 6.42.3; and passim.
[6] For a useful summary of the somewhat confused state of knowledge about the Sanskrit commentaries on the Vālmīki *Rāmāyaṇa* and a brief bibliography on the subject, see Lefeber 1994, pp. 17–28.
[7] R. Goldman 1984, pp. 114–17; Pollock 1986, pp. 75–76; Lefeber 1994, pp. 17–28; and Goldman and Goldman 1996, pp. 91–93.

presents the commentators with an unusually large number of theologically challenging situations that call on them to offer some of their most detailed exegeses and their most sharply worded critiques of one another's interpretations of these critical matters. It also allows us an opportunity to reevaluate our understanding of the commentators' relationships to one another. The most critical aspect of the Book, from the perspective of the commentators, is no doubt the type and degree of the suffering to which Rāma, Lakṣmaṇa, and, to some extent, Sītā are subjected.

The heroic brothers have, of course, been depicted as experiencing various degrees of mental and emotional pain in the course of their adventures from the moment of Rāma's banishment through his excruciating grief and longing brought about by the abduction of Sītā. But in none of the various violent confrontations with the powerful *rākṣasas* they have faced—from their first encounters as boys with Tāṭakā, Mārīca, Subāhu, and the like,[8] in the *Bālakāṇḍa* to their encounter with Virādha[9] and their fierce battles with the powerful demon warriors Khara, Dūṣaṇa, Triśiras, and their legions in the *Araṇyakāṇḍa*[10]—do the heroes seem to suffer much physically. Even when, in his encounters with the powerful and valorous *rākṣasas* of Janasthāna, Rāma's body is actually pierced by the hail of the demons' weapons, it appears to cause him little if any discomfort.[11]

But this is far from the case in some of the major battles of the *Yuddhakāṇḍa*, especially when the heroes engage with the mighty and elusive Indrajit or with Rāvaṇa himself. For, in these battles, the normal epic theme of the hero, riddled with arrows or struck with the mighty blows of fists or weapons, shaking off his seemingly devastating injuries, does not universally apply.

Thus Rāma and Lakṣmaṇa are both laid low twice by Indrajit, once when they are bound and nearly slain by his serpent-arrows,[12] and then again when they and their entire army are knocked out of action during the *rākṣasa*'s second sortie.[13] In both cases they are

[8] 1.25.8–15; 1.29.10–21.
[9] 3.3.
[10] 3.19–29.
[11] 3.24.12–13; 3.27.16–17.
[12] 6.35–40.
[13] 6.60.32–49. The brothers are also riddled with arrows and bloodied by Indrajit at 6.67.32–33 although they do not lose consciousness on this occasion.

unable to recover on their own, requiring, in the first instance, the sudden appearance of Garuḍa and, in the second, the intervention of Hanumān with the mountain of healing herbs to save them.[14] Later on in the battle Lakṣmaṇa is pierced through the chest by Rāvaṇa's mighty javelin, despite Rāma's effort to divert it, and falls unconscious, drenched in blood.[15] Once again he can be saved only through the intervention of Hanumān, who is obliged to fetch the mountain of healing herbs a second time.[16]

Although passages such as these lend drama to Vālmīki's narrative and, above all, reinforce the portrayal of the *avatāra* as, in some meaningful sense, a real man who suffers pain, bleeds, and faints like an ordinary mortal, several of the commentators, steeped in the devotional traditions of medieval Vaiṣṇavism, have difficulty in squaring the portrayal of a figure who shares human frailty and physical vulnerability with their understanding of the *avatāra* as an omnipotent, omniscient, and invulnerable manifestation of the Supreme Lord. For them, incidents such as these call out for explanation, and they tend to adopt one of two possible interpretive strategies. In the first, the *avatāra* merely *plays* at being mortal, acting out the emotional and physical signs of distress so as either not to appear to transgress the terms of Brahmā's boon that make Rāvaṇa invulnerable to gods and other supernatural beings or to serve as a shining example of stoicism.

This matter is of particular concern to Govindarāja (Cg) and Śivasahāya (Cr), who, on occasion, go to considerable exegetical lengths to argue, in cases where the text shows Rāma and Lakṣmaṇa wounded and bleeding, that, as gods, they do not really have the kind of flesh and blood that mortals have. Therefore, for them, their bleeding is a product of their *māyā*, or illusive power, manifested like the devices of an actor in order to appear to conform to Brahmā's boon or to serve as an example of stoic endurance of suffering or of human dharmic conduct.[17] Or, as an alternative, when one of the

[14] 6.40.33–42; 6.61.67.
[15] 6.88.30–39.
[16] 6.89.17–24.
[17] For a more detailed illustration of this important theological point, see note to 6.35.9, where the response of these two commentators to the description of Rāma's and Lakṣmaṇa's bleeding is discussed. See also notes to 6.35.9,17,19,20; 6.36.4–7; 6.37.19; and 6.38.7.

heroes is depicted as covered with blood, a commentator may instruct us to understand that the blood is, in fact, that of his enemy.[18]

The second interpretive strategy that some commentators resorted to is to manipulate the language in an effort to show that, in passages where violence appears to be directed against or inflicted upon the heroes, the text can or should be read in a way that modifies, or even negates, its apparent meaning. The simplest way to do this is to exploit the ambiguity that is often built into a Sanskrit utterance by resolving the *sandhi*, or euphonic combination, in different possible ways, breaking up nominal compounds differently, adding words, or reading words in unusual senses that are sanctioned by the *kośas*, or lexicons. Deploying these linguistic techniques, commentators who want to deny that Rāma or Lakṣmaṇa or both have actually been struck or injured may read a word such as "wounded" to mean "not wounded," "nearly wounded," and the like.

An example of this technique may be seen in Cr's commentary to 6.88.39. There the text appears to describe Lakṣmaṇa as "pierced by that javelin . . . and drenched in blood (*śaktyā bhinnam . . . rudhirādigdham*)." In keeping with his usual denial that Lakṣmaṇa is injured, Cr reads these two sequences as "not pierced by the javelin (*śaktyā abhinnam*)" and "not drenched with blood (*rudhira-adigdham*)."[19]

Maheśvaratīrtha (Cm) is particularly adept at this strategy, often suggesting that a word be added to modify the sense of a sentence, as when, for example, Rāvaṇa is shown to anticipate that Kumbhakarṇa will slaughter the two heroic princes along with the monkey army. Cm, in his gloss, adds the adverb *vinā*, "excluding," to reflect his interpretation that only the monkeys will be slain and not Rāma and Lakṣmaṇa.[20] Similarly Cr, whose text at one point describes Lakṣmaṇa as "defeated (*nirjita-*)," glosses, "nearly defeated (*nirjitaprāya-*)."[21]

One particular strategy Cm uses extensively is to take the Sanskrit verbal root √*han*, "to strike, injure, kill," in the sense of "to go,

[18] See, for example, Cr's comment at 6.35.9 and 6.79.1.

[19] See note to 6.88.39.

[20] See note to 6.48.13.

[21] See note to 6.47.113. This kind of analysis is sometimes extended to Rāma's principal allies. Thus Cr rejects the apparent sense of the adjective *kṛtavraṇa*, "wounded," when it is applied to Hanumān at 6.47.126, glossing, "upon whom an attempt was made to inflict a wound (*vraṇāya kṛtaḥ prayatno yasmiṃs tam*)." He does this

approach," on the authority of *Naighaṇṭuka* 2.14 (*hanahiṃsāgatyoḥ*). This device affords him fertile ground (since the root √*han* is naturally so common in the text) to reinterpret passages in which Rāma or Lakṣmaṇa or both are struck not only to show that they have not, in fact, been wounded but to exploit the sense of "approach" in the theological sense that so colors his reading of the poem.[22]

In utilizing these linguistic devices, several commentators have created—explicitly or implicitly—a powerful tool for the exegesis of the *Rāmāyaṇa* as both a martial epic and a religious text. For what is proposed here, most unequivocally and consistently by Maheśvaratīrtha, is a technique for reading the poem on two distinct levels of meaning—a surface, literal reading (*prakaṭitārtha*) of the tale of abduction and war and a deeper reading (*vāstavārtha*) that is both theologically and metaphysically significant.

In the first reading, Rāvaṇa, a supernaturally empowered and utterly evil demon king, in his uncontrollable passion, abducts the beautiful wife of a virtuous warrior prince only to be slain in the end after a prolonged and grueling war between the two antagonists and their vast armies. In the second, Rāvaṇa, in all his mad passion and virulent antagonism, is revealed in many ways as the ultimate *bhakta*, or devotee, of the Supreme Lord (Bhagavān) and his consort, the Goddess Śrī.[23]

The commentators' deep grounding in the medieval devotional *Rāmāyaṇa* texts and traditions can also color their understanding and exposition of other critical moments in the epic story. One of the most significant of these for our understanding of the receptive history of the text down to the present day has to do with the emotionally charged account of Rāma's cruel reception of Sītā when she is first brought into his presence after her release, and of the

no doubt because of the legend, referred to several times in the poem, that Hanumān had received a boon so that no weapon could harm him. See note to 6.47.126. But Cr is not necessarily consistent in this respect, because at other points in the text the monkey hero is said to be wounded, and the commentator is silent.

22 See, for example, note to 6.27.9. Compare notes to 6.37.9; 6.80.29; 6.81.4; and 6.91.19.

23 See, for example, note to 6.47.91. This is a theme Cm introduced and elaborated on in his commentary to the earlier Books of the poem. Compare, for example, his efforts to bring out the *vāstavārtha* in his exegesis on 5.18, where he interprets Rāvaṇa's lustful advances to the captive Sītā as expressions of his deep religious devotion.

famous *agniparīkṣā*, or fire ordeal, she submits to in response so as to demonstrate her fidelity publicly.[24] Vālmīki's description of the anguish this event produces in the actors and spectators is one of the most intensely emotional and affecting passages in the poem, and the poet gives no hint that the sequence of events is anything other than what it appears to be.

The situation is quite different in some of the most influential and popular medieval and early modern versions of the Rāmakathā. In most popular contemporary understandings of the story there is a motif that is at least as old as the *Kūrmapurāṇa* and the *Adhyātmarāmāyaṇa*[25] and that was popularized by Tulsī Dās's immensely influential *Rāmcaritmānas*,[26] that Sītā herself, the great Goddess, must never be sullied by the touch of the monstrous demon king and so is never actually abducted. Instead, on the advice of the omniscient Lord Rāma, she enters the sacred fire after producing, through her divine powers of illusion, a simulacrum of herself, which is known traditionally as either *Māyā* (Illusion) or *Chāyā* (Shadow) Sītā. It is this simulacrum that is carried off and held in captivity by Rāvaṇa, while the real Sītā remains hidden in the fire until Rāvaṇa's death. In this version of the story, then, the wrenching scene of the fire ordeal is merely a convenient device that allows the false Sītā to enter the fire and the real one to emerge unscathed, thus shielding this divine secret from the public. This episode is utterly unknown to Vālmīki,[27] but several of the commentators attempt to read it back, as it were, into his poem.[28]

[24] 6.102–106.

[25] *KūrmaP* 2.33.112ff. and *AdhyāRā* 3.7; see 6.104.27; 6.106.4; and notes.

[26] *Rāmcaritmānas Araṇyakāṇḍ* 23.1–2; *Laṅkākāṇḍ* 108.1–2 [between *dohas* 108 and 109].

[27] Although, as indicated above, the possibility of such an illusion is well known to the poet, who shows Indrajit creating and killing just such a simulacrum of Sītā at 6.68. Indeed, scholars have argued that Vālmīki's episode provided the inspiration for the traditions of *chāyāsītā*. See 6.102.5; 6.104.27; and 6.106.4 and notes. See, too, note to 5.51.24. See *AdhyāRā* 3.7.1ff. Also see note to 3.43.34 for a discussion of Ct's treatment of the story of *chāyāsītā* derived from *Kūrmapurāṇa* 2.33.112ff. See Brockington 1984, pp. 237, 253, 282, and passim.

[28] Compare, for example, Ct's comments at 6.102.5, where the poet describes Rāma as becoming plunged in thought at Hanumān's report that Sītā, who has now been freed from captivity, wishes to see him. Ct argues that, in reality, Rāma is thinking about how he can recover the principal or real Sītā from the fire [where she was supposed to have been hiding] (*vastuto mukhyasītālābho 'gneḥ kathaṃ syād iti cintātra*).

One interesting bit of information to come out of the commentators' close reading of the *Yuddhakāṇḍa* bears on the vexed issue of the relative dating of these scholars. The question at hand is the chronological relation of Kataka Mādhavayogin (Ck), the author of the *Amṛtakataka*, and Maheśvaratīrtha (Cm), the author of the *Tattvadīpikā*. As noted by Rosalind Lefeber in her Introduction to her translation of the *Kiṣkindhākāṇḍa* in this series, among the widely divergent opinions about the dates of the various *Rāmāyaṇa* commentators, two of the most generally agreed upon are those of these particular authors. She notes that "For commentator Cm there is fortunately unanimity of opinion that he wrote in the mid-sixteenth century," and "For Kataka Mādhavayogin, all editors of the critical edition agree on mid-seventeenth century; yet his dates are given as 1675–1750 by Varadacharya, who edited the complete text of his commentary for the University of Mysore edition."[29] Thus the conventional scholarly wisdom has tended to place Kataka at least one hundred years later than Maheśvaratīrtha, and the translators and editors of the present series have tended to accept this dating. However, our reading of the commentaries on the *Yuddhakāṇḍa* shows that this relative chronology cannot be correct. For in his commentary to the Book, Maheśvaratīrtha quotes or paraphrases Kataka by name on several occasions, just as does Nāgojibhaṭṭa, the author of the widely published *Rāmāyaṇatilakaṭīkā*, which virtually all authorities date to the early eighteenth century.[30]

Since either or both dates may thus be uncertain, the whole issue of the exact dating of these two commentators requires further research. Nonetheless, it is now clear that the conventional wisdom that places Maheśvaratīrtha in the mid-sixteenth century cannot possibly be correct, unless we place Kataka still earlier, which, on the basis of the evidence, seems improbable.[31]

This discussion, in turn, brings up the issue of what one might term the "lineages" of the commentators. As noted before in this series, there has been a fair amount of discussion of the sectarian and

[29] Lefeber 1994, p. 18.

[30] Lefeber 1994, p. 18. For passages where Cm quotes Ck, see notes to 6.78.19 and the note immediately preceding the notes to 6.96.1.

[31] Cf. notes to 6.24.2,4–5, where the evidence suggests that Kataka was, in fact, familiar with, or actually consulting, the commentary of Rāmānuja.

philosophical affiliations of the various scholiasts.[32] For various reasons, assigning specific schools of thought to individual commentators is difficult. What clearly appears to be the case, however, is that the major commentators seem to fall into commentarial schools or lineages even if the relative chronology of the individual commentators within a given lineage is difficult to determine. The most basic and obvious division among the major commentators on the southern recensions reflects the fundamental split that characterizes their texts.[33] Thus the commentators who work basically with one version of this text tend naturally to rely on their predecessors who have shared the same text. In this way Kataka is quoted or paraphrased frequently by Nāgojibhaṭṭa, who, in turn, is often quoted or imitated by Śivasahāya, while a similar succession characterizes the commentaries of Varadarāja, Rāmānuja, Maheśvaratīrtha, and Govindarāja. Cross-lineage comment is often harshly critical.

But the lines are not unambiguous, and the affiliations are not uniformly clear. As we saw above, Maheśvaratīrtha occasionally quotes or paraphrases Kataka and aligns himself with the latter's view. Similarly Nāgoji not infrequently offers the same explanations as Maheśvaratīrtha suggests, often in the same words.

On the other hand, some commentators might be termed "independents," notably Satyatīrtha (Cs). This late commentator appears basically to follow the textual tradition of Varadarāja et al., but he does not blindly follow the interpretive tradition of either "school." Satyatīrtha is, in fact, something of a contrarian and seems not to belong to any clearly identifiable philosophical or sectarian tradition. He particularly likes to provide idiosyncratic glosses, which he arrives at by breaking up words or compounds in ways the other scholiasts have not considered or by selecting highly unusual lexical meanings for words.[34]

Although Satyatīrtha sometimes follows the interpretation of one or more of the earlier scholiasts, he is often highly critical of them. This is especially so when Nāgojibhaṭṭa follows the interpretation of Maheśvaratīrtha. In many of these cases, Satyatīrtha quotes the two "Bhaṭṭa and Tīrtha" at length and dismisses their interpretations

[32] See R. Goldman 1984, pp. 114–16 and Lefeber 1994, pp.18–19.

[33] See W. Rubin 1936 and Goldman and Goldman 1996, pp. 90–93.

[34] Examples abound in his commentary. For a typical example, see note to 6.13.5.

contemptuously, noting that it is "to be ignored (*upekṣyam*)." Sometimes he waxes ironic, likening an interpretation of Nāgojibhaṭṭa or Maheśvaratīrtha or both to that of a person who has heard the *Rāmāyaṇa* twelve times and yet still wants to know the relationship between Rāma and Sītā.[35]

THE ANNOTATION

A number of factors, some generic to the *Rāmāyaṇa* and some specific to the *Yuddhakāṇḍa*, have combined to require a particularly dense and extensive annotation of this Book.

First and foremost of these, of course, is the inordinate size of the text, which necessitates proportionally extensive annotation. The much greater length of the *Yuddhakāṇḍa* when compared to that of the other *kāṇḍas* also brings with it, not unexpectedly, longer and more numerous appendix passages in the critical apparatus. As in the previous volumes in this series, we have elected to provide in the annotation the translation or summary of all passages from the popular, widely known, and extensively published *devanāgarī* recensions of the text aligned with its southern recension. According to the editor of the critical edition of the Book, the "traditional extent" of the *Yuddhakāṇḍa* is a bit less than thirteen hundred verses longer than that of the critically established text.[36] Our notes, therefore, contain many hundreds of translated and annotated verses that are excised from the critical edition. In general, we have translated the reconstructed star passages given in the critical apparatus, ignoring most of the variants. However, when the variant coincides with the text of a printed edition, we have provided it. Only in cases where an individual passage of this kind runs to one hundred lines or more have we given a summary rather than a full translation.

Three other factors have contributed to the great extent of the notes. One is that, as mentioned above, the Book, in depicting the fulfillment of the mission of the *Rāmāvatāra* and in permitting its central hero to finally recognize his own divinity after suffering the emotional and physical ills proper to mere mortals, offers the

[35] See, for example, notes to 6.71.12 and 6.96.12.

[36] Vaidya 1971, p. xxxi. Vaidya is, no doubt, referring to the so-called vulgate or popular version of the southern text.

commentators fertile ground for the theological exegesis so critical to our understanding of the poem's unparalleled significance in the religious thought of Hindu India. It was important, we felt, to place their discussions and debates before our readers to make as widely known as possible the critical early thinking associated with the religious movements that have centered their attention and devotion on the figures of Rāma and Sītā.

Another factor is the Book's many passages dealing with often obscure technical information in areas such as military science, omens, traditional physiognomy, and the like. For example, numerous weapons are listed, the exact nature of which was no longer clear even by the time of the earliest commentators. This requires some discussion. As with the previous volumes, we hope that the density of the annotation, offering as it does a complete discussion of virtually every one of the poem's numerous textual, exegetical, cultural, and rhetorical difficulties, and at least a summary of the commentarial discussions and debates these difficulties have provoked, will provide all those interested in this culminating section of the *Rāmāyaṇa* story an apparatus for achieving the fullest possible appreciation of it.

The third factor is that, in order to fulfill the terms of Rāma's exile to the exact date, the commentators, more than in any of the other Books, spend a great deal of time and energy rationalizing and establishing the precise chronology of the events of the *kāṇḍa* and of the epic as a whole. To defend their respective views, they quote *in extenso* passages from other versions of the *Rāmāyaṇa*, from well-known versions of the Rāma story, such as those found in the *Padmapurāṇa*, *Mahābhārata*, *Kūrmapurāṇa*, and Mādhva version of Āgniveśya. The subject is fraught with much disagreement and vituperativeness among the commentators, and so we have attempted to present all the various opinions.[37]

One final note in this connection is appropriate. Readers of the annotation will notice that in the present volume we provide the full Sanskrit text for all the comments of the commentators we quote. We apologize to those who do not read Sanskrit and may find the quotations distracting. Nonetheless, we include them in this volume because many of the sources for the commentators' texts are either

[37] See note to 6.4.4 for a list of notes that discuss the Book's chronology.

unpublished or, if published, are now out of print, making it extremely difficult for Sanskrit scholars who wish to verify or challenge our understanding of these important texts to gain access to the originals.

THE TRANSLATION

In this volume, as with the other Books of the *Rāmāyaṇa*, our twin goals of accuracy and readability have often coexisted uneasily. In our efforts to render every word and nuance of the text as closely as possible in an alien idiom and to map the architecture of Vālmīki's verses into readable English prose, we were often forced by the highly compacted style of the epic Sanskrit to resort to a prose style less felicitous than we would have liked. The style of the original is characterized by a profusion of embedded adjectives, epithets, vocatives, participles, and gerunds that can be accurately rendered only with a plethora of relative and dependent clauses. Whereas the original poem was composed to be aesthetically pleasing and culturally syntonic for an intended audience who would imbibe it mainly aurally as it was chanted by a performer, it may become tiresome to contemporary western readers who consume the text visually from the printed page.[38] If, in our efforts to balance the desideratum of readability against our commitment to leave no element of the original untranslated, we have sometimes been driven toward an inelegant prose style, we beg the readers' indulgence. If, on the other hand, we have in some small way captured the flavor and feel of this powerful narrative, offered a glimpse of the pleasure we experienced in immersing ourselves in its depths, or provided some new insight into its power and significance, our labors will have been amply rewarded.

One of our concerns here, as in the earlier volumes, was to convey, within the limits of contemporary English diction and usage, something of the staggering lexical profusion of epic Sanskrit. The latter is far richer in synonyms, kennings, epithets, and patronymics than modern literary English. To capture at least something of the

[38] For a detailed discussion of the conventions, stylistics, and difficulties of Sanskrit epic poetry and a statement on how we attempted to cope with them in rendering the Sanskrit verse into English prose, see Goldman 1984, pp. 96–117 and Pollock 1986, pp. 74–76.

flavor these features impart to the text while avoiding excessive repetitiveness or distracting footnotes, we adopted a number of conventions. When, for example, the poet deploys the extraordinary richness of his idiom in synonyms and kennings for monkeys, we translated the sense of the term by subordinating it adjectivally to the word "monkey" or another term synonymous with "monkey."

Thus terms like *hari*, "tawny one," *plava(ṃ)ga(ma)*, "going by leaps," *śākhāmṛga*, "branch animal," *piṅgākṣa*, "yellow-eyed," *valīmukha*, "wrinkle-faced," and so on, are rendered, respectively, as "tawny monkey," "leaping monkey," "tree-dwelling monkey," "yellow-eyed monkey," and "wrinkle-faced monkey." The basic terms *vānara* and *kapi* are translated simply as "monkey," whereas terms that seem to refer to specific species of primates, such as *golāṅgūla*, "cow-tailed," and *ṛkṣa*, "injurious," are translated as "langur" and "ape," respectively.[39]

Similarly, regarding the innumerable epithets and patronymics used for the various animals, gods, humans, and demons mentioned in the text, we have generally translated them and subordinated them to the proper names that an Anglophone audience is most likely to recognize. Thus epithets like Śatakratu, "having a hundred sacrifices," Antaka, "Ender," and Daśagrīva, "Ten-necked," are rendered as "Indra of the hundred sacrifices," "Yama, the ender of all things," and "Ten-necked Rāvaṇa." Patronymics of most characters are supplemented with more familiar names or epithets. Thus Rāvaṇi, "son of Rāvaṇa," is translated as "Indrajit Rāvaṇi." But patronymics of the most major figures are generally not supplemented as the reader will easily recognize their referents. Thus names deriving from lineage or country of origin, such as Rāghava, "descendent of Raghu," or Dāśarathi, "son of Daśaratha," for Rāma and Lakṣmaṇa, Māruti, "son of Māruta," or Jānakī, " daughter of Janaka," and Vaidehī, "woman of Videha," for Sītā, when applied to the most central figures of the epic, are left untranslated and without supplement.

Some epithets, when rendered literally, may strike the English ear as odd or awkward. Nowhere, perhaps, is this more so than when they contain the names of animals that serve as metaphors for the

[39] For a discussion of the latter term in the sense of a primate rather than (as it later came to be understood) a bear, see R. Goldman 1989.

virtues of strength, valor, and virility so critical to the masculine and martial culture of the epics. The creatures that most exemplify these qualities in the Indian literary imagination are the lion, the tiger, the elephant, and, perhaps most characteristically, the bull.

For this reason, characters whose virtues of this kind the poet wishes to emphasize are frequently referred to with compound epithets in which they are identified metaphorically with one or another of these animals. Thus compounds such as *munipuṃgava*, "bull among sages," *naravyāghra*, "tiger among men," *rākṣasarṣabha*, "bull among *rākṣasas*," and *kapikuñjara*, "elephant among monkeys," abound in the text.

One could easily "flatten" these expressions by replacing the animal names with adjectives such as "mighty," "powerful," "valorous," "heroic," and so on. Indeed, one reviewer of an earlier volume criticized us precisely for not doing so. Nonetheless, given the powerful cultural value placed on these creatures and their ascribed natures, we believe it would be a disservice to the text and its readers to reduce these colorful expressions to the relative banality of such adjectives, which, in any case, themselves permeate the text. It is our hope that any jarring effect these expressions may have for readers will be more than compensated for by the sense they may conjure up of a different cultural universe.

Given the subject matter of the *Yuddhakāṇḍa*, the text refers to numerous weapons and war regalia.[40] The exact weapon to which any given term refers is often difficult to determine. Not only do many terms refer to multiple weapons, but a number of terms refer to weapons of which we know little or nothing. We have tried to assign each term an equivalent English rendering of the weapon mentioned in the text. Thus, for example, we translate *śūla* as "lance," *prāsa* as "dart," and *śakti* as "javelin." Some of these terms can be rendered in English differently, and a number of the Sanskrit terms can be translated with the same English word. The word *śakti*, for example, when used to designate a weapon, can be rendered by such terms as "missile," "spear," "dart," "pike," or "lance," and a term like *śūla*, which we render as "lance," can equally well be translated as "pike," "dart," "spear," or "lance." Then again, the term *prāsa* can be rendered as "dart" or "barbed missile."

[40] Cf. Brockington 2006.

Of all the terms for weapons mentioned in the text, perhaps the most semantically complex is *astra*. We understand this term to reflect three different semantic fields in its usage in Vālmīki's *Rāmāyaṇa*. It can, in some instances, refer merely to a weapon that is thrown or shot, and in this case we translate it as "missile."[41] More commonly, however, the term does not refer specifically to a weapon but to a *mantra*, or magical formula, given to one of the principal characters by one of the gods or powerful sages. This *mantra* is invoked and then infused into a weapon or weapons that are already in the warrior's possession. In such cases we have translated the term *astra* as "divine weapon-spell."[42] Finally, in a number of situations the term *astra* refers not to the spell itself but to the weapon that has been infused with the *mantra*, and here we render the term as "divinely charged weapon."[43]

PREVIOUS TRANSLATIONS

Although ours is the first translation into any language of the critical edition of the *Vālmīki Rāmāyaṇa* as it has been reconstructed by the scholars of the Oriental Institute, Baroda, and so offers the reader a rendition of the only scientific reconstruction of the poem based on a critical analysis of all its major recensions and subrecensions, it is by no means the first translation of the poem. In a sense, the oral-performative nature of the work and the unparalleled popularity and pervasiveness of its theme have ensured that the poem has been subject to "translation" in one form or another from the moment of its earliest performances far back in the first millennium BCE. Indeed, viewed from this perspective, the vast and ever-growing body of *Rāmāyaṇas* that have, in many literary, plastic, and performative media, so long dominated the cultural, aesthetic, and religious life of South and Southeast Asia can be regarded as a great and unbounded essay in translation.[44] But only in quite modern times has the *Vālmīki Rāmāyaṇa* been subjected to that particular kind of mapping of a text from one language to another that we think of as true translation.

[41] E.g., 6.3.25; 6.47.127; etc.
[42] See, for example, 6.59.82,86.
[43] See, for example, 6.59.61.
[44] For an insightful discussion on this phenomenon, see Ramanujan 1992, pp. 22–49.

Since the early nineteenth century the *Vālmīki Rāmāyaṇa*, in whole or significant part, has been translated in this sense perhaps several dozen times into a number of the languages of India and Europe. Although, for historical reasons, the greatest number of such translations produced by both European and Indian scholars have been in English, a number of accurate and scholarly translations have also been produced in other languages, including Latin, French, German, Italian, and most, if not all, of the literary languages of India.

According to a maxim quoted by *Ādiśaṅkarācārya*, "Not even a well-trained acrobat can climb onto his own shoulders,"[45] we carefully read through several translations of the *Yuddhakāṇḍa* that we regard as the most accurate and scholarly and provide in our notes numerous examples of their renditions of difficult or disputed passages. Here a few words are in order about the translations we found to be the most reliable renditions of their respective versions of the poem.

All prior translations, one should recall, represent the rendition of one or another of the major recensions of the epic. In the case of the translations of the southern recension, all earlier translations, as noted above, render either the vulgate, that is, the text associated with Ct and Ck, or that associated with Cg, Cm, and Crā.

The oldest complete English translations of the *Vālmīki Rāmāyaṇa* in current use are those of Griffith (1870–1873) and Dutt (1892). The former is a verse rendering, now difficult to read and, because of the constraints imposed by the choice of rhymed verse, less literal than many others. We have therefore not used it. Dutt's prose translation employs a deliberately archaic diction, delighting in such terms as "welkin" for "sky," and is thus difficult to read. It relies heavily not only on the text but on the commentary of Ct, which, as noted above, has proved to be textually inferior to the parallel text of Cg et al. It is a work of considerable scholarship but is erratic, and its renderings often appear to be wide of the mark. The prose is flowing but not quite literal, and the diction in places is archaic. The translations of Shastri (1957) and the Gita Press (1969) are slightly more modern in diction than the preceding ones. Both appear to rely largely on the text and commentary of Ct, and Shastri occasionally is

[45] *Brahmasūtrabhāṣya* 3.3.54: *na hi naṭaḥ śikṣitaḥ san svaskandham adhirokṣyati.* Cf. also Jacob 1907, vol. 2, p. 44.

influenced by Dutt's translation. The Gita Press rendering incorporates many of Ct's interpretations and glosses into the translation itself. In our opinion, the most accurate and useful modern English translation of the popular southern recension is that of Raghunathan (1982). It is based on the superior southern text of Cg and is in the main accurate and readable. It is provided with at least a modest annotation.

Of the translations into European languages other than English, we have used three in particular. The first of these is Gorresio's elegant Italian translation of his own edition of the Bengal recension produced by Stamperia Reale di Francia from 1847–1870.[46] This work is of special importance for it is virtually the only translation available of a text other than the two versions of the southern commentators' text. It also includes an apparatus in the form of a modest annotation. This latter, moreover, is perhaps the only annotation to make extensive use of the northern commentator Lokanātha (Cl). Gorresio's notes served as our source for the observations of this commentator.

We have also consulted the somewhat stilted French translation of Roussel (1903), which rather routinely follows the text of Ct and, so far as we can determine, that scholiast's interpretations. One troubling feature of Roussel's translation is his tendency to leave most Sanskrit terms for classes of beings, realia, and so forth, untranslated and thereby avoid certain difficult interpretive decisions. Thus, for example, where it is important to know whether the term *nāga* refers to an elephant or one of the mythical dragonlike serpents of Indian myth and legend, Roussel simply keeps the Sanskrit term in his translation.

We have also paid careful attention to the contemporary French translation of the *Yuddhakāṇḍa* prepared and annotated by Brigitte Pagani (1999) under the direction of Madeleine Biardeau and Marie-Claude Porcher. This work appeared in print after the publication of our *Sundarakāṇḍa*, and therefore we were able to consult it only for the present volume. The work is based explicitly, and, we believe, unfortunately, on the so-called vulgate text associated with

[46] Or so the press is identified in the translation of the *Bāla-* and *Ayodhyākāṇḍas* (1847). It is referred to variously in subsequent volumes as the Stamperia Imperiale (*Araṇya-*, *Kiṣkindhā-*, *Sundara-*, and *Yuddhakāṇḍas*) and the Stamperia Nazionale (*Uttarakāṇḍa*).

the Tilaka commentary of Nāgojibhaṭṭa (Ct) as it is published—albeit with the variant readings of the texts of the commentators Govindarāja (Cg) and Śivasahāya (Cr)—by the Gujarati Printing Press. As noted above, the apparatus of the critical edition (a version rejected by Biardeau et al.) as well as a careful reading of the poem clearly show the text of Ct to be inferior to that of Cg.[47] The translation is generally lucid and readable although, as suggested below, it sometimes appears overly indebted to Roussel. The translation is accompanied by a certain degree of annotation much of which is useful. It has considerably less density, however, than a text of this significance and complexity should perhaps provoke. Some of the notes also seem to wander into undocumented and occasionally less than germane cultural issues.

Our reading of the translations of the Book into European languages has brought to the fore a number of apparent connections that link several of them. Gorresio's great mid-nineteenth-century edition, translation, and annotation of the Bengal recension no doubt made a significant impression on subsequent scholarship on and translations of the *Rāmāyaṇa*. The work would surely have been known to Roussel. Although Roussel's early-twentieth-century translation is based on the rather different southern text of Ct, the French work in a number of places appears to have been influenced by the Italian, and not always to the benefit of the former. In fact, Roussel's translation occasionally diverges from the southern text and appears to follow a northern variant or, at any rate, Gorresio's rendition of the passage, and it is difficult to find an explanation for this other than that Roussel was influenced by Gorresio.[48]

Whereas Roussel's translation thus displays what appears to be the influence of his Italian predecessor, it has itself exerted considerable influence on some of its successors. Nowhere is this more apparent than in the 1959 translation of Hari Prasad Shastri. Shastri was a renowned Sanskrit scholar well versed in a number of European and Asian languages, and his version of the southern recension (basically Ct's), published in London in 1929 by Shanti Sadan, the Yoga and Vedanta center founded by Shastri, has long been the

[47] For Biardeau's justification of the selection of the GPP text, see Biardeau 1999, pp. lii–lvi.

[48] For examples of this phenomenon, see notes to 6.9313; 6.98.2,21,23; 6.116.11.

most accessible and readable complete English translations of the poem.

However, a careful reading of the various translations cited above makes it abundantly clear that Shastri, for some reason, relied heavily on the work of Roussel, and to a lesser extent that of Dutt.[49] This is frequently evident in the choice and order of words Shastri employs, which often replicate those of Roussel's French. Moreover, it becomes painfully obvious in those cases where Roussel is clearly in error, having misread or misunderstood the text, and Shastri's translation replicates the mistake. Examples of this, alas, are far too numerous either to ascribe to coincidence or to fully list here. A few examples will have to suffice.

At 6.78.24–26, the text refers to "another arrow, the greatest of all (*anyaṃ mārgaṇaśreṣṭham*)." Literally this would be translated as "another excellent arrow." Roussel,[50] evidently misreading the *devanāgarī* character "*n* (न)" of *anya*, "another," for a "v (व)," mistakenly understands the missile in question to be called "the Avya." This unfortunate error is replicated by Shastri,[51] who translates this as "the Avya Weapon." The critical apparatus records no such variant.[52]

Again, at 6.3.15, Roussel appears to have misread the term *paṅktibhiḥ*, "with rows *or* lines," as if it were *pañcabhiḥ*, "with five." He therefore translates it as "*D'énormes constructions, disposées par cinq*."[53] Shastri follows this erroneous reading with the even more extraordinary translation "and five great cannons" (1959, vol. 3, p. 7).[54]

Roussel's influence, not surprisingly, is also apparent in Pagani's translation. Although such cases are rather less common than in Shastri, by no means are they rare, and in several cases where Shastri has followed Roussel's questionable, even erroneous, renderings, Pagani has done so as well.

[49] For Shastri's reliance on Dutt, see, for example, notes to 6.23.19,22; 6.26.16,24, passim.

[50] Roussel 1903, vol. 3, p. 300.

[51] Shastri 1959, vol. 3, p. 265. See note to 6.78.24–26.

[52] For another particularly clear and striking example of this, see notes to 6.109.17–19. See also notes to 6.2.13; 6.3.15,20; note 2 to 177* following note to 6.11.16; 6.15.24; 6.17.16–19; 6.18.16–17; 6.20.6; 6.23.19,22; 6.26.16,24, passim.

[53] Roussel 1903, vol. 3, p. 6.

[54] Shastri 1959, vol. 3, p. 7. See, too, notes to 6.33.20; 6.34.8; 6.35.10; etc.

One example is the rendering of the vulgate passage numbered 2082* in the critical edition, which occurs after verse 6.90.4. There Roussel appears to misunderstand the appositional *karmadhāraya* compound *vacomṛtam*, "nectarlike words," literally, "speech-nectar." He renders, "*cette parole des Immortels.*" In this he is followed both by Shastri, who translates "the words of the Immortals"[55] and by Pagani, who offers "*la remarque des Immortels.*"[56] Once again, such frequent similarities cannot be the result of coincidence.[57]

A final word on translations into Indian languages is in order. In meeting dozens of Indian *Rāmāyaṇa* scholars from every part of India and examining collections in research libraries in various centers of learning, we were deeply impressed, even awed, by the enormous scholarship and energy that has gone into translations of the epic into most of the major regional languages of the country. We often had the opportunity to meet with such scholars and discuss with them difficult points of *Rāmāyaṇa* interpretation only to learn that they themselves had translated the great epic into Hindi, Kannada, Telugu, Marathi, or other Indian languages. Although we have read through some portions of those translations in the Indian languages we can read, we have been closed off from others by our own ignorance of the languages into which they have been rendered.

We found, moreover, that it was difficult to use Indian-language translations to resolve many of the really difficult or disputed portions of the *Rāmāyaṇa* text because of the enormous degree to which Sanskrit has permeated the lexica of Indian languages, both Indo-Aryan and Dravidian, especially at the level of the literary discourse typically used to translate epic Sanskrit. We soon discovered that when the interpretation of a term is difficult or is hard to isolate with precision from a cluster of possible meanings, each of which may have its partisans among the commentators, the tendency of scholars translating into Indian languages is simply to replicate the Sanskrit word in the translation. Without a dense annotation, such a procedure left us no further along in our effort to hone in on the

[55] Shastri 1959, vol. 3, p. 297.

[56] Pagani 1999, p. 1148. Cf. note to 6.90.5–7.

[57] See, too, for example, notes to 6.14.11; 6.15.24; 6.20.6; 6.23.19; 6.31.61; 6.31.75; 6.31.85; 6.32.2; 6.33.2; 6.35.5; 6.38.30; 6.40.34; 6.41.35; 6.43.24; 6.44.22; 6.45.23; 6.51.22; 6.52.14; 6.55.40; 6.55.87; 6.55.127.

poet's probable intention. Nonetheless, although we did not rely heavily on such translations, we often availed ourselves of the generosity of their authors and the many other scholars learned in the *Rāmāyaṇa* whom we have been fortunate enough to meet during our years of research in India.

YUDDHAKĀṆḌA

Sarga 1

1. When Rāma had heard Hanumān's report, so faithfully rendered, he was delighted and responded in these words:

2. "Hanumān has performed an enormous feat, difficult to accomplish in this world, which no one else on the face of the earth would be able to do, even in his imagination.

3. "For apart from Garuḍa and Vāyu I know of no one other than Hanumān who could cross the vast ocean.

4–5. "The citadel of Laṅkā is well guarded by Rāvaṇa and so is unassailable by gods, *dānavas*, *yakṣas*, *gandharvas*, great serpents, and *rākṣasas*. Who, relying on his own strength, could possibly enter it and emerge alive? Who, indeed, could enter that unassailable citadel, well guarded by the *rākṣasas*, unless he were so endowed with might and valor as to be the equal of Hanumān?

6. "In thus putting forth his own power, which is commensurate with his valor, Hanumān has performed a truly great service for Sugrīva.

7. "A servant who, assigned a difficult task by his master, loyally carries it out is considered to be the best type of servant.

8. "A servant, given an assignment, who, even though fit and competent, fails to carry out the business of the king single-mindedly is considered to be the worst type of servant.

9. "Given this assignment, Hanumān did what he had to do without disgracing himself. What is more, Sugrīva is satisfied.

10. "The discovery of Vaidehī has preserved powerful Lakṣmaṇa, the House of Raghu, and myself from unrighteousness.

11. "But wretched as I am, it pains my heart still more that I cannot, here and now, return a commensurate favor to this bearer of good news.

12. "Yet let me give to great Hanumān this embrace, which is all the wealth I have at this time.

13. "Thus far, the search for Sītā has gone well in every regard, but now that we confront the ocean, my mind once again gives way to despair.

14. "The ocean, with its vast waters, is impossible to cross. How in the world are all the tawny monkeys going to reach its southern shore?

15. "Even though this news about Vaidehī has been reported to me, what on earth are we to do next to get the tawny monkeys to the farther shore of the ocean?"

16. When great-armed Rāma, the slayer of his foes, had spoken in this fashion to Hanumān, he was distracted by sorrow and fell to brooding.

The end of the first *sarga* of the *Yuddhakāṇḍa* of the *Śrī Rāmāyaṇa*.

Sarga 2

1. Then majestic Sugrīva spoke these words to Rāma, Daśaratha's son, who was stricken with grief, dispelling his sorrow.

2. "Why do you grieve, hero, like some other, ordinary man? Don't be like that! Abandon your grief, as an ingrate does friendship.

3. "I see no grounds for your sorrow, Rāghava, since we have received news, and we know the enemy's lair.

4. "You are resolute, learned in the *śāstras*, wise, and erudite. Give up this reprehensible attitude, Rāghava, as a man of resolute mind does a thought that undermines his purpose.

5. "We shall leap across the ocean infested with huge sharks, scale the battlements of Laṅkā, and slay your enemy!

6. "All the undertakings of a person who lacks resolve, who is despondent, and whose mind is overwhelmed by sorrow fail utterly; and so, he comes to grief.

7. "All the leaders of my troops of tawny monkeys are valorous and powerful. In order to please you, they are determined even to enter fire.

8–9. "I am absolutely certain of this; I can tell by their excitement. Rāghava, you must arrange it so that a bridge is constructed such that we may reach the city of the *rākṣasa* king, and that, through my valor, I may slay the enemy and bring back Sītā.

10. "From the very moment that we see the city of Laṅkā, set on the peak of Mount Trikūṭa, you may consider Rāvaṇa to be as good as slain in battle.

11. "As soon as a bridge to Laṅkā has been built over the ocean and the whole army has crossed over, you may claim victory.

12. "For these tawny monkeys are valorous in battle and can take on any form at will. So, your majesty, enough of this craven attitude, so destructive to all endeavors.

13. "In this world, grief saps a man's valor. But, wise Rāma, now is the time for you to resort energetically to strength, which is the proper recourse of a man who relies on valor.

14. "For surely, in the case of death or disappearance, grief vitiates all the efforts of great and valorous men like you.

15. "You are foremost among the wise and expert in the essence of all the *śāstras*. And, together with comrades like me, you must now defeat your enemy.

16. "For I cannot think of anyone in all the three worlds, Rāghava, who can stand before you in battle once you take your bow in hand.

17. "Entrusted to the monkeys, your mission shall not fail. Soon you shall cross the inexhaustible ocean and find Sītā.

18. "So enough of giving way to grief, lord of the earth. Unleash your anger! Passive kshatriyas fare badly; but everyone fears the impetuous.

19. "It is in order to cross the dreadful ocean, lord of rivers, that you have come here with us. You have a subtle mind, you should consider how to accomplish this.

20. "For these tawny monkeys are valorous in battle and can take on any form at will. They will smash their enemies with volleys of boulders and trees.

*21. "In one way or another, we shall reach Rāvaṇa's abode. And then, what more is to be said? You shall be completely victorious."

The end of the second *sarga* of the *Yuddhakāṇḍa* of the *Śrī Rāmāyaṇa*.

* An asterisk (*) in the translation indicates that the verse contains a proposed emendation. See Introduction, p. 99.

Sarga 3

1. When Kākutstha had heard Sugrīva's reasonable speech and grasped its essential meaning, he concurred and then spoke to Hanumān:

2. "Whether by building a bridge or even drying up the ocean, in one way or another, I will be able to cross the sea quickly.

3–4. "Tell me, monkey, how many defenses does the fortress of Laṅkā have? The size of the army, the fortification of the gates, the defensive works of Laṅkā, and the residences of the *rākṣasas*: I wish to know about all of this as if I had seen it for myself.

5. "In Laṅkā you were able to reconnoiter carefully and at will. Now you must tell me everything exactly as it is, for you are in every way well qualified to do so."

6. Upon hearing Rāma's words, Hanumān, son of Māruta and foremost among the eloquent, spoke to him once more in these words:

7. "Listen, and I will tell you everything about the arrangement of the defensive works—how the city of Laṅkā is protected and how it is defended by its troops."

8–39*. When he had spoken in this fashion, the foremost of monkeys began accurately to describe the fearsome nature of the sea, the extraordinary wealth of Laṅkā, the disposition of its massive numbers of troops, and a detailed description of its mounts and vehicles.

9. "The vast city of Laṅkā is joyous and filled with crowds of happy *rākṣasas*. It is full of chariots and rutting elephants.

10. "It has four gateways, lofty and broad, whose gates are firmly fastened with massive iron bars.

11. "On its ramparts, there are huge and powerful devices for hurling stones. Any enemy force approaching there would be driven back by them.

12. "Around the gateways, the hosts of valorous *rākṣasas* have constructed hundreds of sharp, fearsome hundred-slayers made of black iron and fully deployed.

13. "Its rampart is made of gold. It is immense and impossible to scale. Its interior is studded with gemstones, coral, lapis, and pearls.

14. "All around it there are moats—deep, fearsome, and menacing—their icy waters full of crocodiles and teeming with fish.

15. "At their gates, there are four extremely long bridges equipped with many huge instruments of war crowded one upon the other.

16. "Those bridges protect the city at those points. For should hostile troops approach, they would be cast into the moats on every side by the instruments of war emplaced upon them.

17. "One bridge, in particular, is solid, strong, and extremely stable. It is adorned with many pilings and watchtowers, all made of gold.

18. "Rāvaṇa is always in full command of himself, Rāma. Always ready for battle, he is both energetic and vigilant in inspecting his troops.

19. "The citadel of Laṅkā is not to be scaled. It is inaccessible even to the gods. It is fearsome with its fourfold defenses: its rivers, mountains, forests, and defensive constructions.

20. "It is situated far off, on the other side of the vast ocean. Yet, Rāghava, the sea has no navigable passage there, for the way is all uncharted.

21. "Built on a mountaintop, the city is as inaccessible as the city of the gods. Filled with war-horses and elephants, Laṅkā is supremely difficult to conquer.

22. "Iron clubs, hundred-slayers, and various other instruments of war adorn Laṅkā, the city of evil-minded Rāvaṇa.

23. "On one side, at the western gate, ten thousand unassailable *rākṣasas* are stationed. They all bear lances and fight with their swords in the vanguard.

24. "On the next side, at the southern gate, a hundred thousand *rākṣasas* are stationed along with an army, complete with all four divisions. They, too, are unsurpassed fighters.

25. "Next, at the eastern gate, are stationed a million *rākṣasas*. Bearing shields and swords, they are all adept in the use of every missile.

26. "Finally, at the northern gate, ten million *rākṣasas*—chariot-warriors and cavalry—are stationed. They are the sons of noble families and are treated with great respect.

27. "The central encampment is garrisoned by ten million unassailable *yātudhānas* and an even greater number of *rākṣasas*.

28. "I have smashed those bridges and filled in the moats. I have burned the city of Laṅkā and leveled its ramparts.

29. "By one means or another, we shall cross the ocean, the abode of Varuṇa. Then you may regard the city of Laṅkā as destroyed by the monkeys.

30. "Here are Aṅgada, Dvivida, Mainda, Jāmbavān, Panasa, Nala, and General Nīla. What need have you for the rest of the army?

31. "For once, leaping through the air, those monkeys reach Rāvaṇa's great city with its ramparts and palaces, they will bring back Maithilī.

32. "You must at once command the entire army to that effect. You must select a propitious moment to set forth."

The end of the third *sarga* of the *Yuddhakāṇḍa* of the *Śrī Rāmāyaṇa*.

Sarga 4

1. When truly valorous Rāma of immense blazing energy had duly listened to Hanumān's speech from beginning to end, he said:

2. "I can immediately destroy Laṅkā, the city of the fearsome *rākṣasa*, which you have had described. This is the truth I am telling you.

3. "I wish to set forth this very moment, Sugrīva, for the sun, maker of day, has reached its zenith, and the propitious juncture called Vijaya is at hand.

4."Moreover, today is the day of the lunar asterism Uttarāphalgunī. Tomorrow the moon will enter the asterism Hasta. So let us set forth, Sugrīva, surrounded by the entire army.

5. "The omens that appear to me are auspicious. I shall slay Rāvaṇa and bring back Sītā Jānakī.

6. "For the upper lid of my eye is throbbing, foretelling, it seems, victory, the fulfillment of my desire.

7. "Let Nīla, accompanied by one hundred thousand swift monkeys, go in advance of the army to scout the way.

8. "General Nīla, you must at once lead your army by a route rich in fruit, roots, and honey and furnished with cool groves and waters.

9. "But you must be constantly vigilant and guard the roots, fruit, and water along the way against the evil *rākṣasas*, who might poison them.

10. "As your forest-dwelling monkeys leap all around, let them be on the lookout for enemy forces that may be hidden in hollows, swamps, and thickets.

11. "Let the mighty lions among monkeys in their hundreds and thousands lead the fearsome vanguard of the army, which resembles the surge of the sea.

12. "Let mountainlike Gaja, powerful Gavaya, and Gavākṣa march before them, like haughty bulls before their cows.

13. "Let the monkey Ṛṣabha, a bull among monkeys and a lord of the leaping monkeys, march guarding the right flank of the monkey army.

14. "And let swift Gandhamādana, as irresistible as an unrivaled war-elephant, march forth commanding the left flank of the monkey army.

15. "I myself shall go forth at the center of the army, mounted on Hanumān, like lord Indra on Airāvata, urging on the vast host.

16. "And let Lakṣmaṇa here, who resembles Yama, ender of all things, go forth on Aṅgada, like Kubera, the ruler of the *yakṣas* and lord of wealth, on Sārvabhauma.

17. "Let these three, Jāmbavān the mighty king of the apes, Suṣeṇa, and the monkey Vegadarśin, guard the rear."

18. When he had heard Rāghava's words, Sugrīva, that bull among monkeys and the commander of the army, gave those orders to the powerful monkeys.

19. Then all the troops of monkeys, eager for battle, leaping up, came bounding swiftly from their caves and mountaintops.

20. Thus honored by the monkey king and Lakṣmaṇa, righteous Rāma, together with his army, set out toward the south.

21. He set out surrounded by tawny monkeys resembling elephants. They numbered in the hundreds, the tens of thousands, the hundreds of thousands, and the tens of millions.

22. The vast host of tawny monkeys followed him as he set forth.

23–24. Excited and filled with joy, all the leaping monkeys, leaping outward and onward, bellowing, roaring, and howling, marched toward the south under Sugrīva's command, eating fruit and fragrant honey and carrying huge trees laden with masses of blossoms.

25. In their wild exuberance, they would carry one another about. Then they would suddenly throw down those being carried. Some would fall down, then leap up and knock the others down.

26. In the presence of Rāghava, the tawny monkeys bellowed, "We shall surely kill Rāvaṇa and all the night-roaming *rākṣasas*."

27. Mighty Ṛṣabha, Nīla, and Kumuda, along with many monkeys, scouted the path ahead of them.

28. In the center marched King Sugrīva, Rāma, and Lakṣmaṇa, those crushers of their foes, surrounded by many powerful and fearsome monkeys.

29. The heroic, tawny monkey Śatabali, surrounded by one hundred million troops, took over the sole supervision and protection of the entire army of tawny monkeys.

30. With their retinues of billions of monkeys, Kesarin, Panasa, Gaja, and mighty Arka each guarded one of the army's flanks.

31. Then, placing Sugrīva at their head, Suṣeṇa and Jāmbavān, surrounded by many apes, guarded the tail end of the army.

32. And that bull among monkeys, Nīla, their heroic general, foremost in leaping, moving swiftly about, guarded the army on every side.

33. The heroes Darīmukha, Prajaṅgha, Jambha, and the monkey Rabhasa moved about everywhere, urging the leaping monkeys onward.

34. As they were proceeding in this fashion, those tigers among monkeys, proud of their strength, beheld the magnificent Sahya mountains covered with trees and creepers.

35. That fearsome army of monkeys, vast as the ocean's flood, streamed onward with a mighty roar, like the ocean in its dreadful rush.

36. All those heroic elephants among monkeys who flanked Dāśarathi leapt swiftly onward, like excellent steeds spurred on.

*37. As they were being carried along by the two monkeys, the two bulls among men resembled the sun and moon in conjunction with two great planets.

38. Mounted on Aṅgada, Lakṣmaṇa, bold and learned in the traditional texts, his quest certain of success, addressed Rāma in a sweet voice:

39. "You will swiftly slay Rāvaṇa and recover Vaidehī, whom he has abducted. Then, your goals accomplished, you will return to prosperous Ayodhyā.

40. "For I perceive significant and auspicious omens in the sky and on earth, Rāghava, all of which presage the success of your quest.

41. "An auspicious breeze, favorable and pleasant, is blowing in the direction of the army's march, and birds and wild animals are calling continually with sweet voices.

42. "It is clear in all directions, and the sun, maker of day, is bright. The Bhārgava Uśanas is shining with bright rays behind you.

43. "The constellation Brahmarāśi is clear as are the Great Seers, which, shining brightly, all encircle and illuminate Dhruva, the North Star.

44. "The royal sage Triśaṅku, the foremost among the forefathers of our great Ikṣvāku lineage, is shining brightly together with his preceptor.

45. "The twin stars, the two Viśākhās, most significant of constellations for our great Ikṣvāku lineage, shine brightly, boding no ill.

46. "But the constellation of those *rākṣasas*, sons of chaos, Mūla, whose regent is Nirṛti, is occluded. Crossed by a nearby comet, it is eclipsed.

47. "All of this presages the destruction of the *rākṣasas*. For the constellations of those who are in the grip of death are always occluded by inimical planets at the hour of their doom.

48. "The water is clear and sweet; the forest is laden with fruit. Fragrant breezes blow briskly, and the trees are filled with the blossoms of the season.

49. "Arrayed in battle formations, my lord, the monkey armies are as resplendent as were the armies of the gods during the battle in which Tāraka was slain.

50. "Considering these things, noble brother, you should be pleased." Thus did Saumitri in his delight speak, reassuring his brother.

51. Then that vast host filled with those tigers among the apes and monkeys—whose weapons were their fangs and claws—advanced, covering all the land.

52. And the dust raised by the monkeys with their fore and hind feet covered the earthly world blocking out the light of the sun.

53. Day and night the vast host of tawny monkeys marched. Under the protection of Sugrīva, the army was excited and jubilant.

54. Eager for battle, all the monkeys marched swiftly. Anxious to rescue Sītā, they did not rest anywhere, not even for a moment.

55. At length they reached the Sahya and then the Malaya mountains, dense with trees and abounding in all sorts of wild creatures.

56. Viewing the variegated woodlands and the streams and waterfalls, Rāma passed through the Sahya and Malaya ranges.

57. And the leaping monkeys broke down many trees—*campakas*, *tilakas*, mangos, *aśokas*, *sinduvārakas*, *karavīras*, and *timiśas*.

58. Intoxicated with their strength, the monkeys ate the fruits, fragrant as nectar, roots, and the blossoms of the trees.

59. The monkeys, as tawny as honey, went along happily drinking from the honeycombs, which hung down as big as bushels.

60. And so those bulls among leaping monkeys went on their way, smashing trees and trailing creepers, devastating the lofty hills.

61. Some of the monkeys, exhilarated with the honey-wine, bellowed from the trees. Others climbed up trees while still others threw themselves down.

62. Covered with those bulls among the tawny monkeys, the earth looked as if it were covered with fields of ripened winter rice.

63. Then, when great-armed Rāma, his eyes resembling blue lotuses, reached Mount Mahendra, he climbed to its summit, which was adorned with trees.

64. And when Rāma, son of Daśaratha, had climbed to the summit, he saw the ocean, the abode of waters, full of turtles and fish.

65. And so at last, having traversed the Sahya range and the great Malaya mountains, they reached the dreadful-sounding sea in good order.

66. Then, descending, Rāma, foremost of those who inspire delight, moved swiftly to a lovely grove near the shore accompanied by Sugrīva and Lakṣmaṇa.

67. Reaching the broad shore, whose stony surface was washed by the surging waves, Rāma spoke these words:

*68. "Sugrīva, we have reached the ocean, Varuṇa's abode. Here and now our earlier concern arises once again.

69. "Beyond this point lies only the boundless ocean, lord of rivers. Without some extraordinary measure, it is impossible to cross it.

70. "Therefore, we should camp here and begin now to deliberate as to how the monkey army might reach the farther shore."

71. Thus, upon reaching the sea, did great-armed Rāma, in his torment over the abduction of Sītā, give the order to make camp.

72. "The time has come for us to deliberate about crossing the ocean. No one is to leave his unit for any reason whatsoever, but let some of the monkey heroes go on patrol, for we must find out what hidden dangers lie before us."

73. When Sugrīva, who was accompanied by Lakṣmaṇa, had heard those words of Rāma, he had the army make camp on the densely wooded seashore.

74. Spread out along the seashore, the army seemed almost to be a second magnificent ocean, its waters tawny as honey.

75. Anxious to reach the farther shore of the great ocean, those bulls among tawny monkeys entered a grove near the shore and made camp.

76. Having reached the great ocean, the monkey army, watching it churned up by the force of the wind, was thrilled.

77. But as they gazed upon the vast and featureless ocean, abode of Varuṇa, the lair of hosts of *rākṣasas*, the leaders of the troops of tawny monkeys gave way to despair.

78–80. For it was dreadful with its fierce sharks and crocodiles. And now, as the day waned and the night came on, the ocean, Varuṇa's lair, agitated at the rising of the moon, was covered with reflections of its orb. It was swarming with huge crocodiles as powerful as fierce gales and with whales and whale sharks. It was teeming, it appeared, with serpents, their coils flashing. It swarmed with huge creatures and was studded with all sorts of rocks. The abode of *asuras*, it was fathomless, unapproachable, and impossible to cross.

81. Teeming with crocodiles and the coils of great serpents, huge waves rose and fell, churned by the winds.

82. With its great sea serpents glittering, the fearsome ocean, realm of the enemies of the gods, ever as unapproachable as the underworld known as Pātāla, resembled a scattered shower of sparks.

83. The ocean looked just like the sky, the sky just like the ocean. Ocean and sky appeared indistinguishable.

84. For the waters merged into the sky and the sky into the waters. Filled with stars and gems, respectively, they both looked exactly alike.

85. Between the sky with its scudding clouds and the ocean covered with waves passing in succession, not the slightest distinction could be found.

86. Crashing ceaselessly against one another, with a terrifying roar, the waves of the ocean, lord of rivers, sounded like mighty *bherī* drums in battle.

87–88. And so the great monkeys gazed upon the wind-whipped sea, the abode of waters. With the roaring of its waters and of its masses of precious stones, it was as if one with the raging gale. Whipped by the wind and swarming with hordes of huge sea creatures, the ocean with its waves appeared to be leaping into the sky in fury. With its surging waves and the roar of its waters, the ocean seemed to have gone mad.

The end of the fourth *sarga* of the *Yuddhakāṇḍa* of the *Śrī Rāmāyaṇa*.

Sarga 5

1. Then Nīla had the army make camp on the northern shore of the ocean, in proper fashion and according to precept, in such a way that it was well ordered and secure on every side.

2. Mainda and Dvivida, those two bulls among monkeys, themselves stood picket duty to protect the army on all sides.

3. Once the army had made camp on the shore of the ocean, lord of rivers and streams, Rāma, seeing Lakṣmaṇa beside him, said these words:

4. "They say that grief diminishes with the passage of time. But bereft as I am of the sight of my beloved, mine only increases day by day.

5. "I do not suffer because my beloved is so far away, nor even because she has been abducted. This alone is the source of all my grief: her youth is slipping away.

6. "Blow, breeze, where my beloved stays. Touch her and then touch me. For the touching of our limbs now depends on you, as on the moon depends the meeting of our glances.

7. "And this, too, lodged in my heart, brings torment to my every limb, like poison once swallowed, that, as my darling was being carried off, she must have cried out to me, 'Alas, my protector!'

8. "Night and day my body is consumed by the fire of love, whose fuel is my separation from her and whose towering flames are my constant brooding on her.

9. "I shall plunge into the ocean without you, Saumitri, and rest there. For it would be hard for the flame of desire to burn me were I to sleep in its waters.

10. "And yet, even though I long for her so much, I can survive just knowing that that lady of the lovely thighs and I still share the same earth.

11. "And like a parched rice paddy drawing water from a flooded one, I live on through knowing that she lives.

12. "Oh, when shall I defeat my enemies and gaze once more upon fair-hipped Sītā, her eyes as wide as hundred-petaled lotuses, as if upon splendid Śrī herself?

13. "And when shall I once more gently raise and kiss her lotuslike face with its full and lovely lips, as a sickly person might drink a powerful tonic?

14. "And when will her full and close-set breasts, so like the ripe palmyra fruit, be once more pressed against me, shaking as she laughs?

15. "I am the protector of that dark-eyed woman. But now, in the clutches of the *rākṣasas*, like a woman without a protector, she will surely find no one to rescue her.

16. "When will she outwit the *rākṣasas*, evade them, and escape, like the crescent of the hare-marked autumn moon emerging from the midst of dark storm clouds?

17. "Although Sītā is naturally slender, she must surely now be truly emaciated what with the grief and fasting attendant upon the reversal of her fortunes.

18. "When shall I bury my arrows in the breast of the lord of the *rākṣasas*, so that I may bring Sītā back and thus dispel the anguish of my heart?

19. "When will virtuous Sītā, who is like a daughter of the immortal gods, clasp her arms eagerly about my neck, shedding tears of joy?

20. "When shall I instantaneously cast off this dreadful sorrow over my separation from Maithilī, as one might a soiled garment?"

21. As wise Rāma was lamenting in this fashion, the sun, the bringer of light, set, its radiance fading at the close of day.

22. Consoled by Lakṣmaṇa, Rāma performed the evening *sandhyā* rite, still preoccupied with lotus-eyed Sītā and overwhelmed with sorrow.

The end of the fifth *sarga* of the *Yuddhakāṇḍa* of the *Śrī Rāmāyaṇa*.

Sarga 6

1. Meanwhile, when the lord of the *rākṣasas* had inspected the dreadful and terrifying havoc that great Hanumān, the equal of Śakra, had wrought in Laṅkā, he addressed all the *rākṣasas*, his face downcast in humiliation.

2. "Not only has this mere monkey breached and laid waste the impregnable citadel of Laṅkā, he has found Sītā Jānakī as well.

3. "This Hanumān has smashed the domed palace, slaughtered the leading *rākṣasas*, and reduced the city of Laṅkā to chaos.

4. "What, pray, am I to do? Or what would be an appropriate next step? Please tell me what would be best for us to do and what would be most effective?

5. "Those who are venerable and wise say that counsel is the cornerstone of victory. Therefore, I seek your counsel, mighty warriors, with regard to Rāma.

6. "There are three types of men in this world: the highest, the lowest, and those in between. I will now set forth the merits and demerits of each of them.

7–8. "The highest type of man, they say, is he who first takes counsel with those counselors intent upon his welfare and competent in counsel, with those friends who share his goals, or with those kinsmen who wish him well, and only then initiates undertakings such that his efforts are in harmony with the will of the gods.

9. "The man who stands in between, they say, is he who reflects upon a matter by himself, who by himself directs his thoughts to righteous action, and then carries through those actions by himself.

10. "And the lowest type of man is he who, after saying, 'I will do this,' undertakes an action—regardless of its merits and demerits and without relying on the will of the gods—and then fails to carry it through.

11. "Just as men are invariably of three types: the highest, the lowest, and those in between, so also must counsel itself be of the same three types: the highest, the lowest, and that which is in between.

12. "The highest type of counsel, they say, is when counselors are consistently of one mind through insight informed by the *śāstras*.

13. "The counsel that is known as that which is in between, they say, is when counselors, having adopted many different opinions, subsequently reach unanimity as to how to decide a matter.

14. "The lowest type of counsel is when counselors go on debating, one after another, each defending his own position, and no conclusive argument can bring about unanimity.

15. "Therefore, you eminent counselors should agree on some excellent and appropriate counsel for me to follow. I will follow it faithfully.

16. "For Rāma will soon march on the city of Laṅkā accompanied by thousands of heroic monkeys in order to blockade us.

17. "It is quite clear that by virtue of his power, which is equal to the task, Rāghava will easily cross the ocean together with his younger brother, his troops, and his allies.

18. "This being the case and hostilities with the monkeys being imminent, you must counsel me fully concerning the well-being of the city and the army.

The end of the sixth *sarga* of the *Yuddhakāṇḍa* of the *Śrī Rāmāyaṇa*.

Sarga 7

1. Addressed in this fashion by Rāvaṇa, lord of the *rākṣasas*, all those mighty *rākṣasas* cupped their hands in reverence and replied to him:

2. "Your majesty, we have a vast army, equipped with iron clubs, javelins, broadswords, lances, and spears. Why then do you give way to despair?

3. "Inflicting massive slaughter, you subjugated Kubera, bestower of wealth, who lives on the summit of Mount Kailāsa, surrounded by many *yakṣas*.

4. "Despite his boasting of his alliance with Maheśvara, you defeated, in your fury, that powerful world guardian in battle, lord.

5. "Slaughtering, baffling, or capturing the *yakṣa* hosts, you took this flying palace from the summit of Mount Kailāsa.

6. "Seeking an alliance in fear of you, the *dānava* lord Maya gave you his daughter to be your wife, bull among *rākṣasas*.

7. "And you subdued and brought under your sway the unassailable *dānava* lord Madhu, arrogant in his might, the bringer of joy to Kumbhīnasī.

8. "You went to the underworld known as Rasātala, great-armed hero, where you conquered the great serpents and brought Vāsuki, Takṣaka, Śaṅkha, and Jaṭin under your sway.

9–10. "Then again, lord, you waged war for a year against those powerful and indestructible *dānava* heroes, with their powerful boons, and relying solely on your own might, brought them under your sway, tamer of your foes. And there you also acquired many magical powers, lord of the *rākṣasas*.

11. "Moreover, great-armed warrior, you defeated in battle the heroic and mighty sons of Varuṇa, who were accompanied by the four divisions of their army.

12–13. "And, your majesty, you plunged into Yama's host, a veritable ocean—with the rod of Death as its great crocodile and all studded with islands in the form of *śālmali* trees—and you gained a great victory, warding off Death himself. All the worlds were pleased with your brilliant fighting there.

14. "This treasure-laden earth was once filled with as many heroic kshatriyas, Śakra's equal in valor, as it is with mighty trees.

15. "This Rāghava is no match for them in battle, whether in courage, virtues, or power, and yet, your majesty, you violently assaulted and slew them, virtually invincible though they were.

16. "Your majesty, it is unimaginable that any harm could come to you from such vulgar folk. You ought not entertain any such thought in your heart. You will certainly kill Rāghava."

The end of the seventh *sarga* of the *Yuddhakāṇḍa* of the *Śrī Rāmāyaṇa*.

Sarga 8

1. Then the heroic *rākṣasa* general Prahasta, who looked like a dark storm cloud, cupped his hands in reverence and spoke these words:

2. "Even the gods, *dānavas*, *gandharvas*, *piśācas*, great birds, and mighty serpents are unable to withstand you in battle. What then of mere monkeys?

3. "All of us were negligent and overconfident, and thus Hanumān got the better of us. But that forest-ranging monkey will not escape with his life again so long as I live.

4. "I shall rid the entire ocean-girdled earth—its mountains, woods, and forests included—of monkeys. Just command me, sir.

5. "And, night-roaming *rākṣasa*, I shall set a guard against that monkey, so that you shall suffer no harm whatever as a result of your transgression."

6. Next a *rākṣasa* named Durmukha, in a towering rage, said, "This cannot be tolerated, for it is an attack upon us all!

7. "Moreover, this attack on the part of the monkey lord constituted an outrage against the city, the inner apartments, and the majestic lord of the *rākṣasas* himself.

8. "This very instant I shall single-handedly repulse the monkeys, slaying them, even if they should seek refuge in the fearsome ocean, the sky, or the underworld known as Rasātala."

9. Then, in a towering rage, powerful Vajradaṃṣṭra spoke, seizing his dreadful iron club all smeared with flesh and blood.

10. "Why do you concern yourself with this contemptible and miserable Hanumān, while the formidable Rāma, Sugrīva, and Lakṣmaṇa are close at hand?

11. "This very day, with my iron club, I shall single-handedly kill Rāma, together with Sugrīva and Lakṣmaṇa, and then return after routing the host of tawny monkeys."

12. Then, in a towering rage, the mighty and heroic Nikumbha Kaumbhakarṇi addressed Rāvaṇa, who makes the worlds cry out.

13. "All of you gentlemen can remain here in the company of our great king. I shall single-handedly kill Rāma as well as Lakṣmaṇa."

14. Next a *rākṣasa* named Vajrahanu, who was like a mountain, licking his chops with his tongue, said these words in anger:

15. "You gentlemen may go about your business as you like, free from care. I shall devour all those leaders of the troops of tawny monkeys by myself.

16. "You can amuse yourselves at your leisure, without a care, and drink honey-wine. I shall single-handedly kill Sugrīva as well as Lakṣmaṇa, Aṅgada, Hanumān, and Rāma, their leader in battle."

The end of the eighth *sarga* of the *Yuddhakāṇḍa* of the *Śrī Rāmāyaṇa*.

Sarga 9

1–5. Then the *rākṣasas* Nikumbha, Rabhasa, mighty Sūryaśatru, Suptaghna, Yajñakopa, Mahāpārśva, Mahodara, unassailable Agniketu, the *rākṣasa* Raśmiketu, Indrajit—the mighty and immensely powerful son of Rāvaṇa—Prahasta, Virūpākṣa, the mighty Vajradaṃṣṭra, Dhūmrākṣa, Atikāya, and the *rākṣasa* Durmukha, seizing iron clubs, spears, darts, javelins, lances, battle-axes, bows and arrows, and broad, sharp swords, all leapt to their feet in a towering rage and, as if blazing with their fierce energy, addressed Rāvaṇa:

6. "This very day we shall kill Rāma, as well as Sugrīva and Lakṣmaṇa, and that contemptible Hanumān, who dared to assault Laṅkā."

7. But Vibhīṣaṇa stopped them as they all stood there, weapons in hand, and bade them be seated once again. Then, cupping his hands in reverence, he said these words:

8. "The learned have prescribed as appropriate the use of force only on those occasions where one's object cannot be achieved by means of the other three stratagems, dear brother.

9. "And, dear brother, the use of force, even when made judiciously and in accordance with the proper injunctions, succeeds only against those who are off guard, preoccupied, or stricken by misfortune.

10. "How then can you all hope to assail someone who is vigilant, intent upon victory, firm in his strength, the master of his anger, and utterly unassailable?

11. "Who could have imagined the impossible feat that Hanumān accomplished, leaping across the fearsome ocean, the lord of rivers and streams?

12. "By no means, night-roaming *rākṣasas*, should we rashly underestimate our foes; for their forces and valor are immeasurable.

13. "And what offense had Rāma previously committed against the king of the *rākṣasas* that the latter should have abducted that illustrious man's wife from Janasthāna?

14. "Even if Rāma did kill Khara, who was attacking him, in battle, still, all living creatures must strive to the limit of their strength to save their own lives.

*15. "For this reason Vaidehī constitutes a grave danger to us. She who has been abducted must be surrendered. There is no point in acting merely to provoke a quarrel.

16. "It would therefore not be appropriate for us to engage in pointless hostility with this powerful and righteous man. You must give Maithilī back to him.

17. "You must give Maithilī back to him before, with his arrows, he lays waste to our city together with its elephants, its horses, and its myriad precious things.

18. "You must give back Sītā before this vast, dreadful, and unassailable army of tawny monkeys storms our Laṅkā.

19. "If you do not of your own free will give back Rāma's beloved wife, the city of Laṅkā and all its valiant *rākṣasas* will surely perish.

20. "As your kinsman, I beseech you. Do as I say. What I am telling you is both salutary and beneficial. You must give Maithilī back to him.

21. "You must give Maithilī back to Dāśaratha before he unleashes for your destruction his massive and unfailing arrows, newly tipped and fletched and resembling the rays of the autumnal sun.

22. "Give up your wrath, so destructive of both happiness and righteousness. Practice righteousness, which is conducive to pleasure and fame. Calm yourself, that we may survive together with our sons and kinsmen. You must give Maithilī back to Dāśaratha."

The end of the ninth *sarga* of the *Yuddhakāṇḍa* of the *Śrī Rāmāyaṇa*.

Sarga 10

1. Although Vibhīṣaṇa had uttered these sound and beneficial words, Rāvaṇa, impelled as he was by his own impending doom, replied with harsh words:

2. "One can live with one's enemy, or even with an enraged venomous serpent, but never with a false friend in the service of one's foes.

3. "I know very well the nature of kinsmen all the world over, *rākṣasa*. Kinsmen always take pleasure in one another's hardships.

4. "If a man is a leader, competent, learned, righteous in his conduct, and valiant, *rākṣasa*, then his kinsmen will malign him and bring him down.

5. "Always affecting pleasure in one's company, they turn on one in times of trouble. Concealing their true feelings, vicious kinsmen are a source of danger.

6. "There are these well-known verses that were sung once upon a time in the Padmavana by some elephants who had seen some men carrying ropes to snare them. Listen to them, as I recite them.

7. "'It is not the fire, the other weapons, or the ropes that put us in danger; it is our own vicious kin intent on their own self-interest that are the real danger to us.

8. "'For no doubt, it is they who point out the means of capturing us; therefore, we know that the danger presented by one's kin is the most severe of all.'

9. "In cattle there is wealth; in a brahman, self-restraint. In women, there is fickleness; from kinsmen, danger.

10. "And that is why, dear brother, you cannot bear it, that I am respected throughout the worlds, that I have attained universal sovereignty, and that I have set my foot on the heads of my enemies.

11. "Anyone else, night-roaming *rākṣasa*, who had spoken such words as these, would have died that very moment. To hell with you, you disgrace to our family."

12. Addressed in this fashion with harsh words, Vibhīṣaṇa, who had spoken justly, flew up, mace in hand, along with four other *rākṣasas*.

13. Then, hovering in midair, majestic Vibhīṣaṇa, roused to anger, spoke these words to his brother, the lord of the *rākṣasas*.

14. "You are my brother, your majesty. You can say whatever you like to me, but I will not stand for these false and abusive words of yours.

15. "Those who have lost all self-control and are already under the power of death never accept judicious advice uttered by one who wishes them well, ten-headed Rāvaṇa.

16. "It is always easy enough, your majesty, to find men who will say what will please you, but it is hard to find someone who will say or listen to what is unpleasant yet beneficial.

17. "But I could not ignore one who, like a burning house on the verge of destruction, was caught in the noose of death, which carries off all creatures.

18. "I would not like to see you slain by Rāma with his sharp arrows, ornamented with gold and resembling blazing fires.

19. "For like dikes of sand, even mighty heroes, skilled in weapons, are destroyed in battle once they fall under the power of doom.

20. "So, by all means, take care of yourself and this city with all its *rākṣasas*. Farewell, I am leaving. May you be happy without me.

21. "Although I have tried to dissuade you, night-roaming *rākṣasa*, in my desire for your well-being, my words have not found favor with you. For men whose time is at hand, whose lives are at an end, never accept the beneficial advice offered by their friends."

The end of the tenth *sarga* of the *Yuddhakāṇḍa* of the *Śrī Rāmāyaṇa*.

Sarga 11

1. The moment Rāvaṇa's younger brother had finished speaking these harsh words to Rāvaṇa, he went to where Rāma and Lakṣmaṇa were.

2. The monkey lords standing on the ground saw him there in the sky, resembling the peak of Mount Meru and blazing like lightning.

3. When Sugrīva, the wise and unassailable lord of the monkeys, had seen him and his four companions, he deliberated with the monkeys.

4. Then, when they had deliberated for a while, he spoke these excellent words to all the monkeys, Hanumān and the rest:

5. "Look! There can be no doubt that this *rākṣasa* armed with every weapon and accompanied by four *rākṣasas* is approaching in order to kill us."

6. When they had heard Sugrīva's words, all those great monkeys picked up *sāla* trees and boulders, and said these words:

7. "Command us at once, your majesty, to kill these evil-minded creatures. Let them fall to the ground slain, their lives cut short."

8. Now, as they were conversing with one another, Vibhīṣaṇa reached the northern shore and hovered there in the sky.

9. Seeing Sugrīva and the other monkeys, great and wise Vibhīṣaṇa, still hovering in the sky, addressed them in resounding tones.

10. "The evil *rākṣasa* named Rāvaṇa is lord of the *rākṣasas*. I am his younger brother, and I am known as Vibhīṣaṇa.

11. "He abducted Sītā from Janasthāna after killing Jaṭāyus. Now helpless and miserable, she is imprisoned and closely guarded by *rākṣasa* women.

12. "With various sound arguments, I repeatedly advised him, 'You must return Sītā to Rāma straightaway.'

13. "But although he was given good advice, Rāvaṇa, impelled by his own impending doom, would not accept it, any more than a dying man will take his medicine.

14. "He spoke bitter words to me and treated me contemptuously, as if I were a servant. Therefore, I have abandoned my wife and my sons, and I have come seeking refuge with Rāghava.

15. "Please inform great Rāghava, the refuge of all the worlds, at once that I, Vibhīṣaṇa, have come to him for shelter."

16. When he had heard these words, swift-striding Sugrīva in the presence of Lakṣmaṇa addressed Rāma with great agitation.

17. "The younger brother of Rāvaṇa, known as Vibhīṣaṇa, along with four other *rākṣasas*, has come seeking refuge with you, sir.

18. "You must realize that Rāvaṇa has sent Vibhīṣaṇa as a spy. You always know what is appropriate, but I think it would be appropriate to take him prisoner.

19. "Cloaking himself in deception, this *rākṣasa* comes seeking refuge with deceitful intent and with instructions to kill you, once he has gained your trust, Rāghava.

20. "He should be put to death with harsh torture together with his ministers. For he is Vibhīṣaṇa, the brother of cruel Rāvaṇa."

21. When, in his agitation, he had spoken in this fashion to eloquent Rāma, the leader of the troops, himself skilled in speech, fell silent.

22. Upon hearing these words of Sugrīva, powerful Rāma said this to Hanumān and the rest of the tawny monkeys who stood near him.

23. "What the king of the monkeys has said regarding Rāvaṇa's younger brother is quite reasonable. You, sirs, have also heard it.

24. "When it comes to difficult matters, it is appropriate that one be advised by a friend who is intelligent, virtuous, capable, and eager for one's long-term good fortune."

25. Questioned in this fashion and desiring to act for the best, each of them gave Rāma his own opinion diligently and courteously.

26. "There is nothing in the three worlds that you do not know, Rāghava. But Rāma, out of friendship, you are questioning us in order to show us honor.

27. "You are faithful to your vows, heroic, righteous, and firm in valor. You act judiciously, are learned in traditional texts, and trust your friends wholeheartedly.

28. "Therefore, let your advisers, who are wise and capable, speak in turn on this matter giving various sound arguments."

29. When they had spoken in this fashion, the tawny monkey wise Aṅgada was the first to speak to Rāghava concerning the interrogation of Vibhīṣaṇa.

30. "Since Vibhīṣaṇa has come to us from the enemy, he must be considered suspect in every way. By no means should we too hastily regard him as worthy of our trust.

31. "For treacherous people go about concealing their true intentions, only to strike when they find an opportunity. To trust him would be a great calamity.

32. "Only after reflecting on the advantages and disadvantages should one come to a decision. One should accept a person if he is virtuous, but if he is evil one should cast him out.

33. "If we find there to be a preponderance of evil in him, we should turn him away without hesitation. But if we should find a preponderance of virtue, then we ought to accept him, your majesty."

34. But then Śarabha, having reflected, said these sensible words: "You must send a spy to him at once, tiger among men.

35. "Only after we have dispatched a spy of subtle intellect, and he has conducted an investigation, would it be appropriate to accept Vibhīṣaṇa."

36. But then wise Jāmbavān, after reflecting on the matter with an intellect steeped in the *śāstras*, communicated his view, which was filled with virtues and free from defects:

37. "Vibhīṣaṇa has come at the wrong time and to the wrong place from the wicked lord of the *rākṣasas*, who is resolute in his hostility. Therefore, he is, by all means, to be viewed with suspicion."

38. Next, Mainda, who was eloquent and adept in discerning good and bad policy, spoke, upon reflection, these exceedingly reasonable words:

39. "This Vibhīṣaṇa ought to be interrogated gently and gradually regarding what Rāvaṇa has to say, lord of kings."

40. "Once you have accurately determined his intentions, then, upon reflection, you can act according to whether he is good or evil, bull among men."

41. Then the highly cultivated Hanumān, foremost of ministers, spoke the following speech, which was polished, meaningful, mellifluous, and concise:

42. "Even Bṛhaspati himself is incapable of besting you in argument, sir, for you are superior in intellect, capable, and eloquent.

43. "Rāma, it is not in order to demonstrate my skill in disputation, my desire to outshine the others, nor out of a wish to prove myself the best, or fondness for the sound of my own voice that I shall say the following truthful words. Rather, your majesty, it is because of the gravity of the situation.

44. "I see a serious problem in what your ministers have said regarding the advantages and disadvantages here: it is impossible to put it into practice.

45. "For, on the one hand, we cannot determine whether he is trustworthy unless we employ him, but, on the other hand, it seems to me that it would be a mistake to employ him too hastily.

46. "Now as to what your ministers said about the propriety of sending out spies, that strategy is unsuitable in this case, as it lacks any purpose.

47. "It has also been argued that 'Vibhīṣaṇa has come at the wrong time and to the wrong place.' Now there is something I would like to say about this as well. Consider it from my perspective.

48–49. "This is precisely the right time and place. For him to have left an evil person to come over to a virtuous one, in light of their vices and virtues, respectively, that is, having perceived the wickedness in Rāvaṇa and the heroism in you, is perfectly appropriate and in keeping with his excellent judgment.

50. "Furthermore, it has been argued that he should be interrogated by undercover agents, your majesty. Here, too, I can offer my considered opinion.

51. "Any intelligent person who is interrogated would immediately become suspicious of the questions. Thus a welcome ally, if interrogated deceitfully, would be alienated.

52. "Moreover, your majesty, even for someone who is confident in his own ability, it is impossible immediately to determine the inner feelings of a stranger simply on the basis of what he says about himself.

53. "Still, at no time while he was speaking could one observe any signs of a wicked nature. His facial expression, moreover, was composed. For these reasons, I harbor no doubts about him.

54. "A deceitful person would not approach so confidently and without hesitation. Moreover, he is well spoken. For these reasons, one should harbor no doubts about him.

55. "It is impossible to conceal one's facial expression completely, even if one tries. And it is this that inexorably betrays the hidden intentions of men.

56. "Moreover, foremost of those who know what action should be taken, an action that is undertaken promptly and energetically and that is appropriate to the time and place quickly brings success.

57–58. "He has witnessed your mighty undertaking and the vainglory of Rāvaṇa. He has also heard about the killing of Vālin and the royal consecration of Sugrīva. He seeks the kingship for himself, and, with this in mind, he has come here. Keeping all this foremost in mind, it would be appropriate to accept him.

59. "I have argued to the best of my ability that the *rākṣasa* is trustworthy. Having heard this, foremost among the wise, you must be the judge of what is to follow."

The end of the eleventh *sarga* of the *Yuddhakāṇḍa* of the *Śrī Rāmāyaṇa*.

Sarga 12

1. Now, when Rāma, his mind composed, had heard this speech of Hanumān, son of Vāyu, that unassailable and learned man responded with his own thoughts.

2. "I, too, have something to say with regard to Vibhīṣaṇa that I would like you, devoted as you are to my welfare, to hear in its entirety.

3. "Under no circumstances would I turn away someone who had come to me in friendship, even if he had some flaw. For the virtuous would condemn such conduct."

4. When Sugrīva, lord of the leaping monkeys, had heard Rāma Kākutstha's words, he replied to him, motivated by friendship.

5. "Knower of righteousness! Crest-jewel among kings! You are mighty and firmly established in the path of virtue. What wonder is it then that you should speak so nobly!

6. "Moreover, my heart knows that Vibhīṣaṇa is virtuous, for he has been thoroughly investigated through inference and on the basis of his probable intentions.

7. "Therefore, Rāghava, let the extremely wise Vibhīṣaṇa at once become your ally on an equal basis with us."

8. When Rāma had heard these words of Sugrīva and had considered them, he replied to that bull among the tawny monkeys in exceedingly beautiful words.

9. "Whether this night-roaming *rākṣasa* be thoroughly evil or virtuous, is he not utterly incapable of causing me even the slightest harm?

10. "For, lord of the hosts of tawny monkeys, if I so desired, I could slaughter the *piśācas*, the *dānavas*, the *yakṣas*, and all the *rākṣasas* on earth with the tip of my finger.

11. "There is a well-known story about a dove that showed great hospitality to an enemy who had come seeking shelter. He even offered him his own flesh.

12. "And so, best of monkeys, even a dove took in his wife's abductor who had come to him. How much more so should a person such as I?

13. "Now listen to these verses, conducive to righteousness, which were chanted long ago by the great and truthful seer Kaṇḍu, son of the seer Kaṇva.

14. " 'For the sake of compassion, scorcher of your foes, one ought never slay a poor wretch who has come for refuge, begging for protection with his hands cupped in reverence, even should he be one's enemy.

15. " 'Even at the cost of his own life, a magnanimous person should save an enemy who has come for refuge from his enemies, whether he be abject or arrogant.

16. " 'Should one fail to offer this protection to the best of one's ability and the limits of one's strength, whether through fear, confusion, or greed, that would be a sin condemned by all the world.

17. " 'Moreover, if a man who has come seeking refuge should die for want of protection while the person who could have saved him merely looks on, then the former would depart from this world taking with him the latter's good works.'

18. "Thus, it is a serious transgression to fail to protect those who come seeking shelter, for it blocks the path to heaven, destroys one's reputation, and undermines one's strength and valor.

19. "So I shall fully carry out Kaṇḍu's excellent advice, for it is righteous, beneficial to one's reputation, and, at the time of one's final reward, it leads one to heaven.

20. "I always grant protection to all beings who come to me for shelter, imploring me with the words, 'I place myself in your hands.' Such is my vow.

21. "So bring him here, Sugrīva, best of tawny monkeys, for I will grant him protection whether he be Vibhīṣaṇa or Rāvaṇa himself."

22. Then, having listened to the words of Sugrīva, the lord of men quickly welcomed Vibhīṣaṇa as he had been advised by the lord of the tawny monkeys, just as Indra, smasher of citadels, might welcome Garuḍa, the king of birds.

The end of the twelfth *sarga* of the *Yuddhakāṇḍa* of the *Śrī Rāmāyaṇa*.

Sarga 13

1. Once Rāghava had granted him protection, Rāvaṇa's younger brother, bowing humbly, descended from the sky to the earth in great delight accompanied by his devoted followers.

2. Seeking refuge, righteous Vibhīṣaṇa prostrated himself at Rāma's feet along with his four *rākṣasa* companions.

3. Then Vibhīṣaṇa addressed Rāma with words that were righteous, fitting, timely, and delightful.

4. "I am the younger brother of Rāvaṇa, but he has humiliated me. Thus I have come for refuge to you, sir, the refuge of all beings.

5. "I have abandoned Laṅkā, my friends, and everything I own. Now, my homeland, my life, and my happiness depend on you, sir.

6. "I shall help you kill the *rākṣasas* and assault Laṅkā so long as breath remains in my body, and I shall penetrate their forces."

7–8. As Vibhīṣaṇa was speaking in this fashion, Rāma embraced him and, in great delight, said to Lakṣmaṇa, "Bring some water from the ocean and, with it, anoint wise Vibhīṣaṇa as king of the *rākṣasas* at once, since I am so pleased with him, bestower of honor."

9. Addressed in this fashion, Saumitri, acting on Rāma's instructions, anointed Vibhīṣaṇa as king there in the midst of the monkey leaders.

10. When the leaping monkeys witnessed Rāma's graciousness, they suddenly began chattering loudly, crying, "Excellent! Excellent!"

11. Then Hanumān and Sugrīva addressed Vibhīṣaṇa, saying, "How are we to cross the ocean, the imperturbable abode of Varuṇa?"

12. "Please tell us the means whereby all of us might approach the ocean, lord of streams and rivers, the abode of Varuṇa, so that we might quickly cross over together with our troops."

13. When Vibhīṣaṇa, who knew what was right, had been addressed in this fashion, he replied, saying, "King Rāghava must solicit the help of Samudra.

14. "For it was Sagara who caused the great and immeasurable ocean to be dug; therefore, the great ocean ought to carry forward the mission of his kinsman Rāma."

15. When the wise *rākṣasa* Vibhīṣaṇa had spoken in this fashion, Rāghava, righteous by nature, found what he said to be agreeable.

16. And immensely powerful and skillful Rāma smiled and, in order to honor them, said this to Lakṣmaṇa and Sugrīva, the lord of the tawny monkeys:

17. "This counsel of Vibhīṣaṇa pleases me, Lakṣmaṇa. Now, you, together with Sugrīva, should tell me if it pleases you as well.

18. "Sugrīva is always wise, and you yourself are skilled in counsel. The two of you should consider this matter and tell me what pleases you."

19. Addressed in this fashion, the two heroes, Sugrīva and Lakṣmaṇa, responded with these courteous words:

20. "Why, tiger among men, would the advice of Vibhīṣaṇa not please us? For, at this moment, it seems the most feasible plan, Rāghava.

21. "Without constructing a bridge across the fearsome ocean, the abode of Varuṇa, even the gods and *asuras* themselves, accompanied by Indra, would be incapable of reaching Laṅkā.

22. "We should properly carry out the advice of the heroic Vibhīṣaṇa. Enough of this delay. You should petition Samudra.

23. When Rāma had been addressed in this fashion, he sat down on a bed of *kuśa* grass that had been spread on the shore of the ocean, lord of streams and rivers, like fire, eater of oblations, installed upon an altar.

The end of the thirteenth *sarga* of the *Yuddhakāṇḍa* of the *Śrī Rāmāyaṇa*.

Sarga 14

1. Three nights passed and still Rāma, keeping strictly to his vow, lay there on a bed of *kuśa* grass spread on the ground.

2. But although Rāma had worshiped him attentively and properly, Sāgara, being obdurate, would not manifest himself.

3. Then Rāma, the corners of his eyes red in his rage at Samudra, said these words to Lakṣmaṇa of auspicious marks, who stood nearby.

4. "Lakṣmaṇa, just see the arrogance of this ignoble Samudra, who will not manifest himself, even though I have worshiped him.

5. "The virtues of the good—calmness, forbearance, straightforwardness, and kind words—are always taken for signs of weakness by those who lack them.

6. "People only respect an evil, insolent person who runs about praising himself and unleashing violence on everyone.

7. "Peaceful means can no more lead to fame or glory in this world, Lakṣmaṇa, than they can to victory in the vanguard of battle.

8. "Now, Saumitri, you shall see the ocean, abode of sea monsters, with its waters choked with the dead bodies of those very creatures pierced by my arrows and floating everywhere.

9. "Here and now, Lakṣmaṇa, you shall see me cut to pieces the bodies of gigantic fish, the trunks of sea elephants, and the coils of great serpents.

10. "Now, launching a powerful assault, I shall with my arrows dry up the ocean together with its fish and sea monsters and its masses of conch and oyster shells.

11. "This lord of the ocean, abode of sea monsters, thinks that, because I am endowed with forbearance, I am weak. To hell with forbearance for people like this!

12. "Fetch my bow, Saumitri, and my arrows, which are like venomous serpents, for now in my fury I shall convulse the imperturbable ocean.

13. "With my arrows, I shall cause the wave-crested ocean, the abode of Varuṇa, which always keeps within its bounds, to overflow them violently."

14. When he had spoken in this fashion, unassailable Rāma, bow in hand and eyes flashing with anger, resembled the blazing fire at the end of a cosmic age.

15. Bending his fearsome bow, he made the world quake with his arrows. He let fly his dreadful shafts as does Indra of the hundred sacrifices, his thunderbolts.

16. Blazing with energy, those swift and excellent arrows plunged into the waters of the sea, terrifying its great serpents.

17. Then, along with a howling gale, there arose a huge and terrifying surge of the ocean, carrying with it sharks and sea monsters.

18. All at once the ocean was covered with garlands of towering waves and filled with conch and oyster shells, its waves shrouded in a vaporous haze.

19. Great serpents and the immensely powerful *dānavas*, who dwell in the underworld known as Pātāla, were in agony, flames shooting from their mouths and eyes.

20. Suddenly from the ocean, king of rivers, there arose thousands of waves as tall as the Vindhya or Mandara mountains and filled with sharks and sea monsters.

21. Such was the state of the ocean, the repository of all waters: its masses of waves were swirling, its *rākṣasas* and great serpents were terrified, and its huge crocodiles were tossed about.

The end of the fourteenth *sarga* of the *Yuddhakāṇḍa* of the *Śrī Rāmāyaṇa*.

Sarga 15

1. Then Samudra Sāgara himself arose from the midst of the sea. Rising together with great serpents, flames shooting from their mouths, he resembled the sun, bringer of day, rising from the great mountain Meru.

2. His complexion was that of polished lapis and he was adorned with *jāmbūnada* gold. His garlands and robes were red and his eyes were like lotus petals.

3. Mighty Sāgara first hailed Rāghava, who stood arrow in hand. Then, cupping his hands in reverence, he approached and said:

4. "All the elements, gentle Rāghava—earth, air, ether, water, and fire—must abide by their respective natures. They must follow the eternal path.

5. "It is thus my inherent nature to be fathomless and impossible to cross. I tell you that it would violate that nature for me to become shallow.

6. "Nor would I for any reason, prince, whether desire, greed, or fear, make solid my waters, abounding with crocodiles and sharks.

7. "I shall, however, devise some means that I can tolerate whereby the sea monsters will not attack while the army is crossing, Rāma.

8. "Here, gentle Rāma, is the majestic son of Viśvakarman, Nala by name. He is the equal of Viśvakarman and has been granted a boon by his father.

9. "This highly energetic monkey must construct a bridge over me. I shall support it, for he is just like his father."

10. When the ocean, that receptacle of waters, had spoken in this fashion, he vanished. Then the mighty Nala, foremost among the monkeys, stood up and said these words to Rāma:

11. "The ocean, that great receptacle of waters, has told you the truth. Relying upon my father's skill, I shall build a bridge across the wide ocean, abode of Varuṇa.

12. "Once, on Mount Mandara, Viśvakarman granted my mother a boon. I am the equal of Viśvakarman, for I am his legitimate son.

13. "But I could not proclaim my own virtues without being called upon. Very well, let the bulls among monkeys construct a bridge this very day."

14. Then, with Rāma's permission, all the leaders of the troops of tawny monkeys rushed excitedly into the great forest by the hundreds and the thousands.

15. There those monkeys, bulls among the hosts of tree-dwelling monkeys, resembling mountains, broke down trees and dragged them to the sea.

16–17. The monkeys filled the sea with bamboo and *sāla*, *aśvakarṇa*, *dhava*, *kuṭaja*, *arjuna*, palmyra, *tilaka*, *timiśa*, *bilvaka*, *saptaparṇa*, flowering *karṇikāra*, mango, and *aśoka* trees.

18. Holding aloft those tree trunks, with and without their roots, like so many flagstaffs of Indra, the foremost among the tawny monkeys carried off the trees.

19. Heaved up violently by the boulders hurled into it, the water rose into the sky and cascaded down on all sides.

20. Nala constructed a great bridge, ten leagues in width and one hundred in length, right through the middle of the ocean, lord of rivers and streams.

21. Then, in the ocean, the great receptacle of waters, there arose a tumultuous sound from the boulders being hurled into it and the mountains being cast down.

22. The bridge that Nala constructed over the ocean, abode of sea monsters, was as majestic and splendid as the path of the constellation Svātī through the heavens.

23. Then the gods, *gandharvas*, perfected beings, and supreme seers gathered and hovered in the sky, eager to witness that marvel.

24. The leaping monkeys were bounding, bellowing, and leaping. All beings gazed upon that inconceivable, seemingly impossible, and hair-raising marvel: the building of a bridge over the ocean.

25. And so, constructing that bridge over the sea, those hundreds of billions of immensely powerful monkeys reached the farther shore of the ocean, the great receptacle of the waters.

26. Broad, well-built, majestic, smooth-surfaced, and beautifully proportioned, the great bridge resembled a dividing line in the midst of the ocean.

27. Then, mace in hand, Vibhīṣaṇa, together with his ministers, took up his position on the farther shore of the sea in order to ward off the enemy.

28. Carrying his bow, righteous and majestic Rāma marched at the head of the army, accompanied by Sugrīva.

29. Some of the leaping monkeys marched down the center of the bridge, while others moved along the edges; some dove into the water, while others could find no space in which to march. Still others, moving through the sky, flew like great birds.

30. As it crossed, the terrifying army of tawny monkeys drowned out with its loud roar the terrifying roar rising from the ocean.

31. Once the army of monkeys had crossed by means of Nala's bridge, it made camp, together with its king, on the shore in a spot well provided with roots, fruits, and fresh water.

32. When the gods, along with the perfected beings and celestial bards, had witnessed that marvelous and seemingly impossible feat of Rāma Rāghava, they approached him in the company of the great seers and anointed him, one after the other, with holy water.

33. "May you conquer your enemies, lord of men, and long may you rule the earth and the seas." With various auspicious blessings such as this, they did homage to Rāma, who was honored by gods and men.

The end of the fifteenth *sarga* of the *Yuddhakāṇḍa* of the *Śrī Rāmāyaṇa*.

Sarga 16

1. When Rāma, the son of Daśaratha, had crossed the ocean with his army, majestic Rāvaṇa addressed two of his ministers, Śuka and Sāraṇa:

2. "A whole host of monkeys has crossed the impassable ocean, and Rāma has done something unprecedented in building a bridge across the sea.

3. "I would never have believed that a bridge could be built over the ocean. Nonetheless, I must now obtain an accurate count of the monkey army.

4–7. "You two gentlemen must infiltrate the monkey army undetected. There you must accurately determine its size and strength, who the leaders of the leaping monkeys are, which counselors are most highly regarded by Rāma and Sugrīva, which ones lead the way, and which of the leaping monkeys are truly heroic. You must also find out how the bridge was constructed over the ocean, that great body of water, and how the great monkeys are bivouacked. In addition, you must determine the resolve, strength, and weaponry of Rāma and heroic Lakṣmaṇa.

8. "Who is the commander of these immensely powerful monkeys? When you have accurately determined all of this, you must return swiftly."

9. When Śuka and Sāraṇa had been instructed in this fashion, those two heroic *rākṣasas* took on the form of tawny monkeys and infiltrated the monkey army.

10. But Śuka and Sāraṇa were unable to count that hair-raising and inconceivably vast host of monkeys.

11. For it filled the mountaintops, caverns, and caves, as well as the shores of the sea, the forests, and the parklands.

12. On every side that vast army was raising a terrifying din. Part of it was crossing the ocean, part had already crossed, while yet another part remained anxious to do so. Part had already made camp, while another was in the process of doing so.

13. Then immensely powerful Vibhīṣaṇa recognized Śuka and Sāraṇa, even though they were disguised. He seized them and then reported to Rāma, saying, "Conqueror of enemy citadels, two spies have come from Lañkā."

14. When they saw Rāma, they began to tremble and despaired of their lives. Terrified, cupping their hands in supplication, they addressed him with these words:

15. "The two of us have come here, kind sir, delight of the Raghus, because we were dispatched by Rāvaṇa in order to gather intelligence about your entire army."

16. When Daśaratha's son Rāma, who was devoted to the welfare of all beings, had heard this speech of theirs, he smiled and said these words:

17. "If you have finished inspecting the entire army and have carefully examined us, and if you have carried out your mission as you were instructed, then you may return as you please.

18. "And you two must enter the city of Laṅkā and there address these words of mine exactly as I tell you to the king of the *rākṣasas,* younger brother of Kubera, the bestower of wealth.

19. " 'Now, together with your army and your kinsmen, you may demonstrate as you please the valor on which you relied when you carried off my Sītā.

20. " 'But tomorrow at the proper moment you shall see the city of Laṅkā, along with its gates and ramparts as well as the *rākṣasa* army, destroyed by me with my arrows.

21. " 'Muster your forces, Rāvaṇa! For tomorrow at the proper moment I shall unleash my dreadful wrath upon you, just as Vāsava, the wielder of the *vajra,* did upon the *dānavas.*' "

22. When Śuka and Sāraṇa had been instructed in this fashion, the two *rākṣasas* returned to the city of Laṅkā and addressed the lord of the *rākṣasas*:

23. "Lord of the *rākṣasas,* we were captured by Vibhīṣaṇa, and, although we deserved to die, righteous Rāma of immeasurable power released us the moment he saw us.

24–26. "Those four bulls among warriors—majestic Rāma Dāśarathi, Lakṣmaṇa, Vibhīṣaṇa, and the powerful Sugrīva, whose valor equals that of great Indra—are as heroic, skilled in weaponry, and firm in their valor as the divine guardians of the worlds. Since they are assembled in one place, they themselves are capable of uprooting the city of Laṅkā with its ramparts and gates and hurling it far away, even without all these monkeys.

27. "Rāma's appearance and weapons are such that he will be able to lay waste the city of Laṅkā all by himself, even without those other three.

28. "And the army, protected by Rāma, Lakṣmaṇa, and Sugrīva, seemed as if it were completely unassailable even by all the gods and *asuras*.

29. "Moreover, this army consists of great forest-dwelling monkeys, who are wildly excited and eager for battle. So enough of this hostility! You must make peace. You must return Maithilī to Daśaratha's son."

The end of the sixteenth *sarga* of the *Yuddhakāṇḍa* of the *Śrī Rāmāyaṇa*.

Sarga 17

1. When King Rāvaṇa had heard the sound words that Sāraṇa had courageously uttered, he replied to him:

2. "Even if the gods, *gandharvas*, and *dānavas* should assault me, I would not give up Sītā, not for fear of all the worlds.

3. "Now you, my good man, are terrified because the tawny monkeys got the better of you. So now you think it would be best to give back Sītā. But what rival can possibly get the better of me in battle?"

4. When majestic Rāvaṇa, lord of the *rākṣasas*, had uttered these harsh words, he ascended to the top of his snow-white palace, many *tālas* in height, in his desire to see for himself.

5. Accompanied by his two spies, Rāvaṇa, beside himself with rage, gazed about him at the ocean, the mountains, and the forests and saw that the land was completely covered with leaping monkeys.

6. As King Rāvaṇa gazed upon that vast army of monkeys, boundless and innumerable, he questioned Sāraṇa:

7. "Which among these monkey leaders are heroic? Which are very powerful? Which ones, filled with great energy, always lead the way in battle?"

8. "Which ones' advice does Sugrīva heed? And who are the leaders of the troop leaders? You must tell me all of this, Sāraṇa. Who are the leaders of the leaping monkeys?"

9. Upon hearing these words of the *rākṣasa* lord, who was questioning him, Sāraṇa, familiar with the leaders of the forest-dwelling monkeys, began to describe them.

10–12. "That monkey who stands bellowing before Laṅkā, surrounded by a hundred thousand troop leaders, and whose mighty roaring makes all of Laṅkā with its ramparts and gateways, its mountains, forests, and groves tremble, is the heroic troop leader named Nīla. He stands at the head of the army of great Sugrīva, lord of all the tree-dwelling monkeys.

13–15. "That powerful one, stretching out his forelegs and stalking the earth on his hind legs, ever showing his fangs toward Laṅkā in his rage, the one who resembles a mountain peak, who is the color of lotus filaments, and who, furious, lashes his tail repeatedly, the sound of which makes, so it seems, the ten directions resound, he is known as Aṅgada, and he has been consecrated heir apparent by the monkey king Sugrīva. He is summoning you to battle.

16–19. "And those bulls among tawny monkeys who are bracing their limbs, roaring and bellowing, leaping up and showing their fangs in rage are dreadful, fierce, of fierce valor, and impossible to withstand. Their number is ten billion eight hundred thousand. They are the heroic denizens of the sandalwood forest. The one whom they follow is the powerful silver-hued Śveta. Dreadful in his valor, he is eager for battle and expects to crush Laṅkā with his own forces. This wise and heroic monkey is famed throughout the three worlds.

20. "After reporting to Sugrīva, that monkey is now moving swiftly to marshal the monkey army, urging his troops onward.

21–22ab. "And that monkey, who used to roam the charming mountain on the banks of the Gomatī, Mount Saṃkocana, covered with every sort of tree, is the troop leader called Kumuda. He once ruled a kingdom there.

22cd–24. "And that one, over there, commanding one hundred million troops, the fur on whose long tail—red, yellow, black, and white—sticks out so far in all directions, is the mettlesome and furious Caṇḍa, dreadful in his actions. He is eager for battle and expects to crush Laṅkā with his own forces.

25–26. "And the tawny one with the long mane over there, your majesty, who looks like a lion and glares fixedly at Laṅkā as if to scorch it with his gaze is the troop leader named Rambha, who always haunts the Vindhya, Kṛṣṇagiri, and the beautiful Sahya mountains.

27. "Three billion leaders of the troops of tawny monkeys follow him as his entourage in order to crush Laṅkā with their tremendous power.

28–29. "And that one, pricking up his ears and showing his fangs again and again, is the fearless and immensely powerful troop leader Śarabha. He has no fear of death and never flees an opposing host. He, your majesty, haunts the charming Sālveya mountains.

30. "He commands a full four million powerful troop leaders, known as the Vihāras, your majesty.

31–33. "Now, that huge one standing in the midst of monkey heroes, like Vāsava in the midst of the gods, who seems to block out the sky like a storm cloud, is Panasa, the terrifying troop leader of the tree-dwelling monkey lords, who are eager for battle. One can hear his mighty bellowing like the roaring of *bherī* drums, and none can withstand him in battle. He dwells on that splendid mountain Pāriyātra.

34. "Five million troop leaders, each with his separate troop, form the entourage of that leader among troop leaders.

35–37ab. "The one who stands there like a second Sāgara as an ornament to the fearsome and surging army encamped upon the seashore and who resembles Mount Dardara is the troop leader Vinata. He roams about drinking from the river Parṇāśā, foremost of rivers. His army consists of six million leaping monkeys.

37cd. "The one challenging you to battle is the troop leader Krathana.

38. "The one who is the color of red clay is the powerful monkey known as Gavaya. Expanding his body, he advances toward you in a rage.

39. "His entourage consists of seven million, and he expects to crush Lañkā with his own forces.

40. "These, then, are the dreadful and powerful troop leaders and leaders of troop leaders whom none can withstand. They are numberless and can take on any form at will."

The end of the seventeenth *sarga* of the *Yuddhakāṇḍa* of the *Śrī Rāmāyaṇa*.

Sarga 18

1. "And now, as you survey them, I shall describe to you those troop leaders, who will engage in acts of valor, risking their lives for Rāghava's sake.

2–3. "The one on whose tail the glossy, bristling fur—red, yellow, black, and white, glistening like the rays of the sun—sticks out so far in all directions as it drags across the ground, is the troop leader called Hara, dreadful in his actions.

4. "Hundreds and thousands follow in his train, wielding trees. Banding together, they are intent upon scaling the ramparts of Lañkā.

5. "Together with his ten billion immensely powerful monkeys, he is eager to defeat you in battle, conqueror of enemy citadels.

6–8. "The heroes you see standing before you, like great black clouds, dark as collyrium, of true valor in battle, and, with claws and fangs for weapons, are terrifying and fierce in their anger. As numberless and indistinguishable as grains of sand on the far shore of the sea, they are utterly savage apes, denizens of the mountains, hill country, and rivers, your majesty. They are advancing toward you.

9–10. "That one, with the dreadful eyes and fearsome looks, your majesty, is the lord of all the apes, the troop leader Dhūmra. Standing in their midst, he looks like Parjanya surrounded on all sides by storm clouds. He dwells on that foremost of mountains Ṛkṣavant, where he drinks the waters of the Narmadā.

11–12. "And there, as huge as a mountain, is his younger brother, the great troop leader among troop leaders, Jāmbavān. He looks just like his brother but surpasses him in valor. Although peaceful by nature and obedient to his superiors, he is unyielding in battle.

13. "Wise Jāmbavān rendered great assistance to Śakra during the wars of the gods and *asuras* and has thus received many boons.

14–15. "In his army there are many enormous, shaggy apes of fiery energy, who resemble *rākṣasas* and *piśācas* and have no fear of death. They scale the mountain peaks and hurl down boulders as vast as huge clouds.

16–17. "And standing there, watched by all the monkeys, is that troop leader among troop leaders, your majesty, the mighty lord of the tawny monkeys, Rambha, who with his troops serves thousand-eyed Indra. Although he is standing still, in his eagerness that troop leader appears to be leaping about.

18–19. "And that one who, when he moves, rubs his flanks against a mountain standing a league away and who, when he stretches his body upward, reaches a league in height, is known as Saṃnādana, the grandfather of the monkeys. His form is unsurpassed among creatures that move on four feet.

20a–d. "This wise troop leader among troop leaders once fought a battle with Śakra himself and yet was not defeated.

20ef–23. "Now that one, whose valor when he goes forth in battle is the equal of Śakra's, is the troop leader Krathana, who never boasts on the battlefield. He was fathered long ago by Agni of the black path on a *gandharva* maiden in order to assist the gods, the inhabitants of heaven, in their wars with the *asuras*. This majestic and powerful bull among monkeys dwells on the king of lordly mountains—frequented by many *kinnaras*—which always serves as the delightful pleasure garden of your brother, King Vaiśravaṇa Kubera, and on which he disports himself among *jambū* trees, O lord of the *rākṣasas*.

24. "He has come here surrounded by ten billion monkeys. He is eager for battle and expects to crush Laṅkā with his own forces.

25–28. "And the one upon whom ten million attend is the troop leader Pramāthin, your majesty, impossible to withstand. Keeping in mind the ancient hostility between the elephants and monkeys, he haunts the banks of the Ganges, terrifying the leaders of the elephant herds. As troop leader, commander, and general of the tawny monkeys, he moves along the Ganges River, the daughter of the Himalaya, sleeping in mountain caves. Resorting to Mount Uśīrabīja, the equal of Mount Mandara, that foremost of monkeys takes his pleasure, as does Śakra himself in heaven.

29–30ab. "And what you see there, like a cloud raised by the wind, where that great column of dust is swirling copiously, are the dreadful and immensely powerful black-faced langurs.

30cd–31. "Having witnessed the construction of the bridge, ten million of them follow their troop leader, the swift langur Gavākṣa, as his entourage in order to crush Laṅkā with their tremendous power.

32–34. "And there, your majesty, is the foremost among the foremost monkeys, the troop leader Kesarin, who disports himself on the lovely golden mountain whose peaks the great seers never abandon. It is there where the trees, swarming with bees, bear fruit to gratify every desire. He roams about that mountain, the color of which is equal to that of the sun and through the radiance of which the beasts and birds take on that color.

35. "Of the sixty thousand mountains, the most beautiful are the golden mountains. This foremost of mountains stands among them, as do you, blameless one, among the *rākṣasas*.

36. "These monkeys—tawny, white, red-faced, honey-yellow—with sharp fangs and claws for weapons, dwell on that highest of mountains.

37. "Like lions with their four great fangs, as unassailable as tigers, they are all as fierce as Agni Vaiśvānara or like venomous serpents inflamed with anger.

38. "With their long tails arching upward, they resemble rutting elephants. They look like huge mountains, and their roar is like that of mighty storm clouds.

39. "Their mighty commander, standing there in their midst, is renowned throughout the earth, your majesty, by the name Śatabalin. He is eager for battle and expects to crush Laṅkā with his own forces.

40. "And there are Gaja, Gavākṣa, Gavaya, Nala, and the monkey Nīla, each of them surrounded by one hundred million troops.

41. "And there are yet other swift and formidable monkeys, inhabitants of the Vindhya mountains, who because of their vast numbers are impossible to count.

42. "All of them, your majesty, are enormously powerful. All of them possess bodies that resemble huge mountains. All of them are capable of instantly covering the earth with the mountains they have shattered."

The end of the eighteenth *sarga* of the *Yuddhakāṇḍa* of the *Śrī Rāmāyaṇa*.

Sarga 19

1. Then, after Śuka had listened to Sāraṇa's speech, he looked out over the whole army and addressed these words to Rāvaṇa, lord of the *rākṣasas*:

2–3. "Those monkeys—resembling great rutting elephants, banyan trees along the Ganges, or *sāla* trees in the Himalayas—whom you see taking up their positions are powerful and impossible to withstand, your majesty. They can take on any form at will, and they are like the *daityas* and the *dānavas*. Their valor is that of the gods in battle.

4. "There are tens of billions of them—times nine, times five, and times seven, and there are quadrillions and septillions more.

5. "They are Sugrīva's followers and Kiṣkindhā is their home. They are tawny monkeys born of the gods and *gandharvas*, and they are able to take on any form at will.

6. "Those two youthful monkeys whom you see standing there looking like gods are Mainda and Dvivida. No one is their equal in battle.

7. "With Brahmā's blessing they have partaken of the nectar of immortality, and they thus expect to crush Laṅkā with their tremendous power in battle.

8. "And those two whom you see standing beside them, looking like mountains, are Sumukha and Vimukha. They are the sons of Mṛtyu, and they are just like their father.

9–10. "Now the monkey you see standing over there, like an elephant in rut, is the same one who has already come to Laṅkā and sought out Vaidehī and yourself, lord. Look at him! You have seen this monkey before and he has now returned. If angered, he could make the ocean itself tremble with his strength.

11. "He is the eldest son of Kesarin, but he is called the son of the wind god. He is known as Hanumān, and it is he who leapt over the ocean.

12. "Foremost among tawny monkeys, he is endowed with strength and beauty and can take on any form at will. His advance can no more be checked than that of the ever-moving lord, the wind god.

13–15. "They say that once, when he was a child, he grew hungry and, seeing the sun rising, he swooped down a distance of three thousand leagues, thinking in the arrogance of his strength, 'I shall devour the sun, so that my hunger shall not return.' But, failing to reach that divinity, who is beyond the reach of even the gods, seers, and *dānavas*, he fell upon the mountain from behind which the sun rises.

16. "One of that monkey's jaws was slightly broken as he fell on the stone surface. And since this toughened his jaw [*hanu*], he came to be known as Hanumān, he of the powerful jaw.

17. "I can accurately identify this tawny monkey on the basis of this authoritative account. His strength, beauty, and power are impossible to describe. With his tremendous power, he expects to crush Laṅkā all by himself.

18–21. "And the dark, lotus-eyed hero next to him is Rāma, the great chariot-warrior of the Ikṣvākus, famed for his valor throughout the world. His righteousness never wavers, nor does he ever transgress it. Foremost among those who know the *vedas*, he knows the *vedas* and Brahmā's divine weapon-spell as well. With his arrows he might rend the heavens and shatter the mountains. His wrath is like that of Mṛtyu, and his valor like that of Śakra. Sītā, whom you abducted from Janasthāna, is his wife; and so, your majesty, he is advancing upon you in order to give battle.

22–23. "And standing to his right—the one with a complexion as radiant as pure *jāmbūnada* gold, a broad chest, reddened eyes, and dark, curling hair—is his brother Lakṣmaṇa, as dear to him as life itself. He is skillful in statecraft and in battle, and he is adept in all the *śāstras*.

24. "Implacable, invincible, victorious, valorous, intelligent, and powerful, he is Rāma's right arm, like another life breath constantly moving outside his body.

25. "He would give his own life for Rāghava's sake, and he expects to slaughter all the *rākṣasas* in battle.

26. "And the one standing on Rāma's left, surrounded by a group of *rākṣasas*, is none other than King Vibhīṣaṇa.

27. "He was consecrated as king of Laṅkā by the majestic king of kings. And, in his rage, he, too, is advancing toward you for battle.

28. "The one whom you see standing in their midst, as unshakeable as a mountain, is Sugrīva, the unconquered lord of all the leaders of the tree-dwelling monkeys.

29. "In power, glory, intelligence, knowledge, and lineage, he outshines the other monkeys, as does Himalaya all other mountains.

30. "With his principal troop leaders, he dwells in the densely forested and inaccessible cavern Kiṣkindhā, which is hidden in a mountain fastness.

31. "He is the one whose necklace of a hundred golden lotuses shines so brightly; for Lakṣmī herself, coveted by gods and men, resides in it.

32. "Sugrīva acquired that necklace along with Tārā and the everlasting kingship of the monkeys through Rāma, who had slain Vālin.

33. "And thus Sugrīva, the lord of the monkeys, is advancing upon you for battle accompanied by one hundred trillion, ten billion troops.

34. "Now that you have seen this army that has come here like some baleful planet, your majesty, you must exert yourself to the utmost so that you may be victorious and not suffer defeat at the hands of your enemies."

The end of the nineteenth *sarga* of the *Yuddhakāṇḍa* of the *Śrī Rāmāyaṇa*.

Sarga 20

1–3. Rāvaṇa looked out upon the leaders of the troops of tawny monkeys. He saw Vibhīṣaṇa—his own brother—standing at Rāma's side, immensely powerful Lakṣmaṇa, the right arm of Rāma, and Sugrīva of terrifying valor, the king of all the monkeys, just as they had been described by Śuka. He was somewhat shaken at heart, yet, flaring up with anger, he reviled the heroic Śuka and Sāraṇa when they had finished their report.

4. Enraged, his voice choked with anger, he spoke harsh words to Śuka and Sāraṇa, who stood there humbly, hanging their heads.

5. "It is utterly inappropriate for a king's ministers, dependents after all, to utter words that are displeasing to him when he is able to punish or imprison them.

6. "How fitting it is that the two of you should at so inopportune a moment heap praises upon my enemies who have approached in such a menacing fashion to make war upon me!

7. "Clearly your attendance upon your teachers, parents, and elders was to no purpose, since you have failed to learn the essence of the science of politics, which should govern your conduct.

8. "Or even if you had once learned it, you failed to fully comprehend it. You carry your education as mere mental baggage. With imbeciles such as you for ministers, it is only through sheer luck that I have retained my hold on the kingdom.

9. "Have you no fear of death that you say such harsh words to me, your sovereign, whose tongue metes out rewards and punishments.

10. "Trees touched by a forest fire may survive, but those whose offences have incurred the wrath of the king cannot.

11. "I would have slain you two wretches, who dare to praise my enemies, had not my rage been softened by your previous acts of service.

12. "Go! Get out of my sight! Remembering your past acts of service, I do not wish to kill you. Nevertheless, you two ingrates, who have turned away from my affections, are as good as dead to me."

13. When Śuka and Sāraṇa had been addressed in this fashion, they were humiliated. Then, saluting Rāvaṇa with invocations of victory, they withdrew.

14. Next, ten-necked Rāvaṇa spoke to Mahodara, who stood near him, saying, "Hurry up and get me some spies who really understand the science of politics."

15. Then spies, hastening at the king's command, approached him. They attended upon him with hands cupped in reverence, glorifying him with blessings of victory.

16. Rāvaṇa, lord of the *rākṣasas,* then addressed these words to those spies, who were reliable, heroic, devoted, and utterly fearless.

17. "Go forth from here and find out Rāma's plans. Find out also who have allied themselves with him out of affection and are privy to his counsel.

18. "When does he sleep? When does he wake? What else is he planning to do? Come back when you have ascertained all of this accurately and completely.

19. "For an enemy whose intentions are discovered by a spy is easily attacked and destroyed in battle by clever kings."

20. Enthusiastically saying, "So be it," to the lord of the *rākṣasas,* the spies reverently circumambulated him and went off to where Rāma and Lakṣmaṇa were.

21. Departing, they concealed themselves near Mount Suvela, where they spied upon Rāma and Lakṣmaṇa, who were in the company of Sugrīva and Vibhīṣaṇa.

22. But, as it happened, the *rākṣasas* who were there were spotted by Vibhīṣaṇa, the righteous lord of the *rākṣasas,* and captured.

23. Beaten by swift and valorous monkeys, they returned to Laṅkā, dazed and breathing hard.

24. Then, approaching ten-necked Rāvaṇa, those mighty night-roaming *rākṣasas*, spies accustomed to serving in foreign lands, reported to him regarding the terrifying army encamped near Mount Suvela.

The end of the twentieth *sarga* of the *Yuddhakāṇḍa* of the *Śrī Rāmāyaṇa*.

Sarga 21

1. Then the spies informed the lord of Laṅkā that Rāghava, along with an unassailable army, was encamped near Mount Suvela.

2. When Rāvaṇa had heard from his spies that Rāma had come with a vast army, he became somewhat agitated, and he spoke these words to Śārdūla:

3. "You look pale, night-roaming *rākṣasa*, and you seem despondent. You haven't by any chance fallen into the clutches of our enraged enemies?"

4. Questioned in this fashion, Śārdūla, stupefied with fear, faintly spoke these words to that tiger among *rākṣasas*:

5. "It is impossible to spy upon those bulls among monkeys, your majesty. For they are valiant, powerful, and under the protection of Rāghava.

6. "It is impossible even to speak with them. There is no question of interrogating them. For the paths on every side are guarded by monkeys the size of mountains.

7. "The moment I entered, I was recognized. Before I even had a chance to observe the army, I was violently seized by many monkeys and badly wounded.

8. "Fiercely pummeled with knees, fists, teeth, and palms, I was paraded about by those tawny monkeys, who are both powerful and relentless.

9. "When I had been paraded all around, I was taken to Rāma's headquarters, stupefied, my senses reeling, my entire body covered with blood.

10. "Belabored by the tawny monkeys and pleading with my hands cupped in supplication, I was spared by Rāghava. Truly, I am lucky to be alive.

11. "Rāma has filled in the vast ocean with mountains and boulders and now stands at the very gates of Laṅkā, heavily armed.

12. "After releasing me, that immensely powerful warrior arranged his troops in the *garuḍa* formation, and now, completely surrounded by tawny monkeys, he is advancing on Laṅkā.

13. "Soon he will reach the outer walls, and so you must quickly do one of two things: you must either return Sītā to him at once or offer fierce battle."

14. When Rāvaṇa, lord of the *rākṣasas*, had heard those grave words of Śārdūla, he was stricken at heart, but he replied:

15. "Even if the gods, *gandharvas*, and *dānavas* should assault me, I would not give up Sītā, not for fear of all the worlds."

16. Having spoken in this fashion, the immensely powerful Rāvaṇa continued speaking: "You, sir, have spied upon this army. Which of the leaping monkeys in it are truly heroes?

17. "What are they like? What are the powers of these unassailable monkeys? Whose sons and grandsons are they? Tell me truthfully, *rākṣasa*.

18. "Once I know their strengths and weaknesses, I shall take appropriate action. A person wishing to engage in battle must first take account of the opposing forces."

19. When the chief spy, Śārdūla, had been addressed in this fashion by Rāvaṇa, he began to speak the following words in Rāvaṇa's presence:

20. "To begin with, your majesty, there is the son—utterly invincible in battle—of Ṛkṣarajas. Then there is Jāmbavān the renowned son of Gadgada.

21. "There is also the other son of Gadgada. And, in addition, there is the son of the *guru* of Indra of the hundred sacrifices. It is his son who single-handedly slaughtered the *rākṣasas*.

22. "Then there is righteous and powerful Suṣeṇa, the son of Dharma, and, your majesty, the gracious monkey Dadhimukha, the son of Soma.

23. "Then there are Sumukha, Durmukha, and the monkey Vegadarśin. Surely self-existent Brahmā created death in the form of these monkeys.

24. "General Nīla over there is himself the son of Agni, bearer of oblations, and the son of Anila, over here, is famed as Hanumān.

25. "That young, powerful, and unassailable Aṅgada is the grandson of Śakra, while powerful Mainda and Dvivida are both sons of the Aśvins.

26. "Those five sons of Vaivasvata, who themselves are like Kāla, the ender of all things, are Gaja, Gavākṣa, Gavaya, Śarabha, and Gandhamādana.

27. "Śveta and Jyotirmukha are both the sons of Sūrya, bringer of light, while the leaping monkey Hemakūṭa is the son of Varuṇa.

28. "That foremost among leaping monkeys is heroic Nala, son of Viśvakarman, while swift and valorous Sudurdhara is the son of the Vasus.

29. "There are one hundred million of these majestic and heroic monkeys, who are all the sons of gods and are lusting for battle. I am unable to describe the rest.

30. "And that youth whose build is that of a lion is the son of Daśaratha. He is the one who slew Dūṣaṇa, Khara, and Triśiras.

31. "There is no one on earth who is equal to Rāma in valor; for he slew Virādha and Kabandha, who was like Yama, the ender of all things.

32. "No man on earth is able to recount the virtues of Rāma, who slew all the *rākṣasas* in Janasthāna.

33. "And there also is righteous Lakṣmaṇa, resembling a bull elephant. Once having come into the range of his arrows, not even Vāsava himself could survive.

34. "And there is your brother Vibhīṣaṇa, foremost among the *rākṣasas*, who, having received the city of Laṅkā, is devoted to Rāghava's cause.

35. "In this way I have described to you the entire monkey army, which is encamped upon Mount Suvela. You, sir, must now decide what is to be done next."

The end of the twenty-first *sarga* of the *Yuddhakāṇḍa* of the *Śrī Rāmāyaṇa*.

Sarga 22

1. Meanwhile, in Laṅkā, the spies reported to the king that Rāghava, along with an unassailable army, was encamped near Mount Suvela.

2. When Rāvaṇa had heard from his spies that Rāma had come with a vast army, he became somewhat agitated, and he spoke these words to his ministers:

3. "*Rākṣasas*! Let all my counselors assemble, focusing their thoughts. The time has come for us to take counsel."

4. Upon hearing that command of his, the counselors hurriedly approached. Then he took counsel with his *rākṣasa* ministers.

5. After taking counsel with them as to what was appropriate for them to do next, the unassailable Rāvaṇa dismissed his ministers and entered his own residence.

6. Then, summoning an immensely powerful *rākṣasa* named Vidyujjihva, a master of illusion, Rāvaṇa, himself a great master of illusion, went to where Maithilī was.

7. The lord of the *rākṣasas* addressed Vidyujjihva, master of illusion, saying, "Let us delude Sītā, Janaka's daughter, with an illusion.

8. "Night-roaming *rākṣasa*, you must come to me bearing Rāghava's head along with his great bow and arrows—all fashioned through the power of illusion."

9. When he had been addressed in this fashion, the night-roaming *rākṣasa* Vidyujjihva responded, "So be it." The king was pleased with him and presented him with a piece of jewelry.

10. Entering the *aśoka* grove, the immensely powerful younger brother of Kubera, bestower of wealth, saw Sītā seated on the bare earth, her face lowered, overcome with sorrow, although she did not deserve it.

11. Seated there in the *aśoka* grove, thinking only of her lord, she was closely surrounded by horrible *rākṣasa* women.

12. Approaching Sītā and calling out to her in feigned delight, he arrogantly addressed these words to the daughter of Janaka.

13. "I have just now slain in battle your husband, Rāghava, the slayer of Khara, about whom you are wont to speak so boastfully.

14. "I have completely undermined your grounds for refusing me and have crushed your pride. As a result of your catastrophic loss, Sītā, you will have to become my wife.

15. "Your merit is exhausted and your purpose has failed, you foolish woman, who think yourself so clever. Now you shall hear about your husband's death, Sītā, which was as dreadful as the slaying of Vṛtra.

16. "Rāghava had come to our shores surrounded by a vast army led by the lord of the monkeys in a futile effort to kill me.

17. "When he reached the southern shore of the sea, Rāma made camp with his vast army just as the sun was going down.

18. "Then, in the middle of the night, my spies approached that army as it slept peacefully, exhausted from its long march, and spied upon it.

19. "Then, in the night, on that very spot where Rāma and Lakṣmaṇa lay, Rāma's army was slaughtered by my own vast army led by Prahasta.

20–21. "Over and over again, the *rākṣasas* raised their weapons—spears, iron clubs, swords, small discuses, staves heavy with iron, streams of arrows, lances, shining mallets and war hammers, clubs, iron cudgels, darts, large discuses, and cudgels—and let them fall upon the monkeys.

22. "Then murderous, deft-handed Prahasta with his huge sword completely severed the head of Rāma, who lay sleeping.

23. "Vibhīṣaṇa tried to flee, but, as it happened, he was captured. Then Lakṣmaṇa and all the leaping monkeys were driven off in all directions.

24. "Sugrīva, lord of the leaping monkeys, lies there with a broken neck. Hanumān, too, lies there, slain by the *rākṣasas*, his jaw smashed.

25. "Then Jāmbavān, as he leapt up in battle, was stricken at the knees. Pierced by many spears, he was cut down like a tree.

26. "Those two bulls among monkeys, Mainda and Dvivida, were also cut down, gasping and wailing, drenched in their own blood.

27. "Cut through the middle with a sword, Panasa, destroyer of his enemies, fell thunderously to the ground like a jackfruit.

28. "Pierced by many iron arrows, Darīmukha lies in a pit, while the hugely powerful Kumuda, struck by arrows, is moaning.

29. "Aṅgada has been attacked and felled by the *rākṣasas*, who pierced him with many arrows. Adorned with his armlets, he lies on the ground vomiting blood.

30. "Some of the tawny monkeys, scattered like clouds driven by the force of the wind, are lying about, trampled by elephants, while others have been crushed by row upon row of chariots.

31. "Others have fled in terror, being harried from the rear, pursued by the *rākṣasas*, like great elephants by lions.

32. "Some have thrown themselves into the ocean, others have taken refuge in the sky. Apes and monkeys, all mixed together, have scampered up trees.

33. "On the shores of the sea, in the mountains, and in the forests, many of the yellow-eyed monkeys have been slaughtered by innumerable evil-eyed *rākṣasas*.

34. "In this way your husband, along with his army, was killed by my forces. Here, I have had them bring you his head, dripping with blood and covered with dust."

35. Then unassailable Rāvaṇa, lord of the *rākṣasas*, addressed a *rākṣasa* woman, so that Sītā could hear him.

36. "Go and fetch Vidyujjihva, that *rākṣasa* of cruel deeds, the very one who has brought the head of Rāghava from the battlefield."

37. Then Vidyujjihva, grasping the head along with the bow, presented himself before Rāvaṇa, bowing his head in reverence.

38. Then King Rāvaṇa addressed the long-tongued *rākṣasa*, Vidyujjihva, who stood close beside him.

39. "Place the head of Dāśarathi before Sītā at once. Let the wretched woman clearly see her husband's final state."

40. Addressed in this fashion, the *rākṣasa* placed that beautiful head before Sītā and swiftly withdrew.

41. But Rāvaṇa threw down the great and shining bow that was famed throughout the three worlds and said this to Sītā:

42. "Here is the bow of your precious Rāma, complete with its bowstring. It was brought here by Prahasta after he slew that human during the night.

43. When he and Vidyujjihva had flung that head and bow upon the ground, Rāvaṇa said to the glorious daughter of the king of Videha, "You must obey me."

The end of the twenty-second *sarga* of the *Yuddhakāṇḍa* of the *Śrī Rāmāyaṇa*.

Sarga 23

1–3. Sītā stared at the head and at that magnificent bow. Recalling the alliance with Sugrīva that had been mentioned by Hanumān and seeing those eyes and that facial complexion that were so like those of her husband—his hair, his forehead, and his splendid crest-jewel—she recognized all those familiar things and was stricken with grief. Shrieking like an osprey, she reviled Kaikeyī:

4. "I hope you are satisfied now, Kaikeyī! The delight of our family has been slain. You malicious creature! You have destroyed our entire family.

5. "In what way did noble Rāma offend Kaikeyī such that she had him exiled from his home to the forest in the barkcloth garments of an ascetic?"

6. When Vaidehī, trembling, had spoken in this fashion, that wretched young woman fell to the ground like a plantain tree that has been cut down.

7. After a moment, she heaved a sigh and regained consciousness. Then the large-eyed woman kissed that head and broke into lamentation.

8. "Alas, great-armed hero, I am undone! For I have pledged myself to one who followed the code of the warrior. I have now been made a widow and so must share this, your final state.

9. "When a husband dies first, they say it is because of the wife's lack of virtue. But even though my conduct has been exemplary, you, who were so virtuous, departed before me.

10. "While I, having gone from one sorrow to another, am sunk in an ocean of grief, you, who were trying to rescue me, have now been slain.

11. "And, Rāghava, my mother-in-law Kausalyā, bereft of you, her son, is now like a loving cow bereft of her calf.

12. "Your valor was beyond imagination, Rāghava! And yet, the words of those who foretold a long life for you have proven false, for your life has been cut short.

13. "Or did your wisdom fail you, even though you were so wise? For Kāla, who creates all beings, leads them inevitably to destruction.

14. "How could you, so learned in the science of politics, so knowledgeable about and skillful at strategies for averting disaster, have fallen prey to an unforeseen death?

15. "Having fallen into my clutches—I who am the fierce and pitiless Kālarātri, the dark night of universal destruction—you, a lotus-eyed hero, have been thus cut down and carried off.

16. "Abandoning me to my misery, great-armed bull among men, you lie in the embrace of the earth, as if she were a beautiful and beloved woman.

17. "And this, hero, is your gold-inlaid bow, so dear to me, which you and I always worshiped so assiduously with fragrances and garlands.

18. "Surely, blameless hero, you have now been reunited in heaven with my father-in-law, your father, Daśaratha, and with your other ancestors as well.

19. "You have become a shining star in the heavens through the great and pleasing deed that you performed, but thus you now ignore your own lineage, the holy race of royal seers.

20. "Why do you not look at me, your majesty? Why will you not speak to me? It is I, your lifelong companion, whom you took as your wife when I was but a girl and you yourself a mere boy.

21. "'I will be with you forever.' That is what you promised when you took my hand in marriage, Kākutstha. So please recall that to mind and take me, full of sorrow, with you.

22. "Why have you abandoned me and gone away, resourceful hero? You have departed from this world to the next, leaving me here, full of sorrow.

23. "Your body was once accustomed to only the finest things and embraced by me alone. Now, surely, it is being dragged and torn apart by beasts of prey.

24. "You performed the vedic rites—the Agniṣṭoma and the rest—with ample fees for the officiants. How is it then that you will be denied the purificatory rite of cremation in the sacred fire?

25. "Kausalyā, sorrowfully longing, will now have to question only Lakṣmaṇa, who, alone among the three of us who set out in exile, will return.

26. "And since she will ask him, he will surely have to tell her about the slaughter of the forces of your ally and your own murder in the night by the *rākṣasas*.

27. "When she hears that you have been murdered in your sleep and that I am living in the *rākṣasa*'s household, she will die of a broken heart, Rāghava.

28. "But enough of this! Please, Rāvaṇa, let me throw myself upon Rāma's body at once. Do this one truly fine thing: reunite a husband and wife.

29. "Join my head with his head, and my body with his body, Rāvaṇa, and I shall follow the path of my great husband. I do not wish to live for even another moment, wicked woman that I am.

30. "Once, in my father's house, I heard from some brahmans learned in the *vedas* that women to whom their husbands are dear gain auspicious worlds.

31. "What recourse is left for me without him who was possessed of forbearance, self-restraint, renunciation, truth, righteousness, gratitude, and nonviolence toward all creatures?"

32. Thus did that large-eyed lady, the daughter of Janaka, burning with sorrow, lament as she gazed there upon her husband's head and bow.

33. As Sītā was lamenting bitterly in this fashion, a *rākṣasa* sentry approached his master, hands cupped in reverence.

34. After saluting and propitiating Rāvaṇa with the words, "May my lord be victorious," he reported that General Prahasta had arrived.

35. "Prahasta has presented himself with all your ministers. The matter appears to be rather urgent. Therefore, kindly grant them an audience."

36. When ten-necked Rāvaṇa had heard the *rākṣasa*'s message, he left the *aśoka* grove to grant an audience to his counselors.

37. Deliberating with his counselors as to how he should proceed, he entered his council hall and there, knowing full well the martial valor of Rāma, laid his plans.

38. But no sooner had Rāvaṇa departed than that head and splendid bow vanished.

39. Nonetheless, the lord of the *rākṣasas* went on deliberating with his counselors, fearsome in their valor, as to what action he should take with regard to Rāma.

40. Then Rāvaṇa, lord of the *rākṣasas*, who looked like Kāla himself, addressed all the commanders of his troops assembled before him, eager to act on his behalf.

41. "Assemble the troops at once with the loud beating of *bherī* drums sharply struck with drumsticks, but do not tell them why."

42. Then the commanders of the troops, receiving those instructions, said, "So be it." Assembling each his own vast host, they reported to their lord, who was so eager for battle, that they were assembled.

The end of the twenty-third *sarga* of the *Yuddhakāṇḍa* of the *Śrī Rāmāyaṇa*.

Sarga 24

1. Meanwhile, a certain *rākṣasa* woman named Saramā, a dear friend of her beloved Sītā Vaidehī, seeing that she was utterly confused, came quickly to her side.

2. For, as she had been instructed by Rāvaṇa to protect Sītā, who was under guard, and because she was compassionate and firm in her vows, she had become Sītā's friend.

3. Saramā saw that her friend, who had now arisen covered with dirt, like a mare that had been rolling in the dust, was completely bewildered.

4–5. Firm in her vows, she consoled Sītā out of love for her friend. "Timorous lady, in my love for you, my friend, I overcame my fear of Rāvaṇa, and, concealing myself in a deserted thicket, I overheard everything Rāvaṇa said to you and what you said to him in return. For, wide-eyed lady, I would gladly die for your sake.

6. "Then, when the overlord of the *rākṣasas* had departed, Maithilī, I followed after him and learned the whole reason for his agitation.

7. "It would be impossible to slay the ever-vigilant Rāma in his sleep. Indeed, no one can kill that tiger among men.

8. "Nor would it be possible to kill the monkeys, who use trees as weapons. For they are as fully protected by Rāma as are the divinities by Indra, bull among the gods.

9–11. "Majestic Rāghava, destroyer of his foes, could not have been slain, Sītā. For his arms are long and muscular and his chest is massive. He is majestic and fierce in valor. He is righteous and powerfully built, a bowman famed throughout the world. Along with his brother Lakṣmaṇa, that courageous hero always protects himself and others. Skillful, deeply learned in the science of statecraft, and of inconceivable strength and valor, he slaughters the hosts of enemy soldiers.

12. "This was just an illusion, perpetrated upon you by that savage master of illusion, whose every thought and deed is reprehensible and who is inimical to all creatures.

13. "Put all your grieving behind you. Happiness awaits you. Surely Lakṣmī herself is smiling upon you. Now hear the good news, which will delight you.

14. "Rāma has crossed the ocean with an army of monkeys. And now, having reached the southern shore, he is encamped.

15. "I myself have seen Kākutstha, who has practically accomplished his mission. Right now, he is standing with Lakṣmaṇa on the seashore guarded by his massed forces.

16. "And those swift-footed *rākṣasas* whom Rāvaṇa had dispatched brought back the news that Rāghava has crossed the ocean.

17. "Hearing that news, wide-eyed lady, Rāvaṇa, the overlord of the *rākṣasas*, took counsel with all his ministers."

18. Now, while the *rākṣasa* woman Saramā was speaking in this fashion, she and Sītā heard the dreadful sound of the troops fully preparing themselves for war.

19. When Saramā heard the deafening sound of the *bherī* drums resounding with the strokes of the drumsticks, she spoke to Sītā in a sweet voice.

20. "That, timid woman, is the terrifying sound of the *bherī* drum, a call to arms. Listen to its deep sound so like the rumble of storm clouds.

21. "Rutting war-elephants are being made ready, while chariot-horses are being yoked. Everywhere armed foot soldiers are forming their ranks.

22. "The royal highways are filled with rushing, roaring soldiers, amazing in their appearance, just as the ocean is filled with rushing, roaring torrents of water.

23–24. "Just look at the multicolored radiance arising from the *rākṣasas'* shining weapons, shields, armor, chariots, horses, elephants, and ornaments as they glitter. It looks like a blazing forest fire in the hot season.

25. "Listen to the clanging of the bells and the rumbling of the chariots. Listen to the neighing of the war-horses, like the blaring of trumpets.

26. "These are the frenzied preparations—tumultuous and hair-raising—of the followers of the *rākṣasa* lord, their weapons held aloft.

27. "Good fortune will favor you, dispelling your sorrow. But fear of Rāma has come upon the *rākṣasas*, lotus-petal-eyed woman, as fear of Vāsava overcame the *daityas*.

28. "When your inconceivably valorous husband, who has subdued his anger, has defeated and slain Rāvaṇa in battle, he will surely take you back.

29. "Together with Lakṣmaṇa, your husband will defeat the *rākṣasas*, just as that slayer of his foes, Vāsava, together with Viṣṇu, did his enemies.

30. "Soon Rāma will come, and I shall see you seated upon his lap, your enemy slain and all your wishes fulfilled.

31. "Lovely lady, once you are reunited and in his tight embrace, you will shed tears of joy on the chest of that broad-chested hero.

32. "Soon, Sītā, my lady, mighty Rāma will unbind the braid—falling to your waist—that you have worn these many months.

33. "Once you see his face, my lady, which is like the full moon newly risen, you will abandon these tears born of your sorrow, as a female serpent sheds her skin.

34. "Very soon, Maithilī, Rāma will slay Rāvaṇa in battle. Then he, who deserves happiness, will enjoy complete happiness together with you, his beloved.

35. "Once you are reunited with Rāma, you will rejoice with that great man, just as the earth does with its ample crops when watered with copious rains.

36. "My lady, you must take refuge with Sūrya, bringer of day and sustainer of all creatures, who, like a horse, moves swiftly in his orbit, circumambulating the foremost of mountains."

The end of the twenty-fourth *sarga* of the *Yuddhakāṇḍa* of the *Śrī Rāmāyaṇa*.

Sarga 25

1. Thus, with her words, did Saramā bring new life to the confused and suffering Sītā, as do the heavens to the earth with their rains.

2. Then, as a friend desiring what was best for her friend and, with a good sense of timing, she smiled and spoke these timely words:

3. "Dark-eyed lady, I can go and return unseen in order to give Rāma a message from you, informing him that you are safe.

4. "For when I traverse the unsupported sky, neither Pavana nor even Garuḍa himself is able to follow my path."

5. As Saramā was speaking in this fashion, Sītā replied to her in a voice that was sweet, soft, and tinged with her recent sorrow.

6. "You are capable of going to the heavens or even to the underworld known as Rasātala. I know that for my sake you could accomplish even the impossible.

7. "But if your mind is set on doing me a favor, you should go to Rāvaṇa as I wish to know what he is doing now.

8. "For that cruel and wicked Rāvaṇa, who makes his enemies cry out, is a master of illusion. He robbed me of my senses, as does wine the moment you drink it.

9. "He has the terrifying *rākṣasa* women, who constantly stand guard over me, menace and threaten me incessantly.

10. "I am fearful and apprehensive and have no peace of mind. I tremble in fear of him, here in the *aśoka* grove.

11. "If you can report to me everything that he may have discussed or decided, then that would be the greatest favor you could do for me."

12. As Sītā was speaking in this fashion, the soft-spoken Saramā, caressing her, replied in words choked with tears.

13. "If that is what you wish, Jānakī, I shall go, and you shall see me when I return after learning your enemy's plans."

14. When she had spoken in this fashion, she proceeded from there to the presence of the *rākṣasa* Rāvaṇa and eavesdropped on his deliberations with his counselors.

15. Once she had heard and familiarized herself with the evil-minded *rākṣasa*'s decisions, she then swiftly returned once more to the *aśoka* grove.

16. She reentered the grove, where she saw Janaka's daughter waiting for her and looking like the goddess Śrī, robbed of her lotus.

17. When soft-spoken Saramā had returned, Sītā embraced her affectionately and offered her a seat.

18. "Once you are comfortably seated, please report to me accurately everything that the cruel and wicked Rāvaṇa has decided."

19. Addressed in this fashion by the tremulous Sītā, Saramā reported to her all of Rāvaṇa's deliberations with his counselors.

20. "The *rākṣasa* lord was given earnest advice to release you by his own mother and his elder counselor Aviddha, who said:

21. " 'You must give back Maithilī to the lord of men with full honor. His amazing deeds in Janasthāna should be sufficient evidence for you.

22. " 'Then, too, there was Hanumān's leaping of the ocean, his finding Sītā, and his slaughter of the *rākṣasas* in battle. What mere human on earth could have brought all this about?'

23. "Although his aged counselors and his mother argued with him in this vein at length, he can no more bear to give you up than can a miser his money.

24. "He will not give you up, Maithilī, unless he dies in battle. For such is the fixed resolve of that cruel *rākṣasa* and his ministers.

25. "That, indeed, is the unwavering resolve he has formed, befuddled as he is by his impending doom. He will have to be completely crushed in battle through the slaughter of the *rākṣasas* and himself. Intimidation alone cannot force him to release you.

26. "But, with his sharp arrows, Rāma will completely destroy Rāvaṇa in battle, and then, dark-eyed lady, he will take you back to Ayodhyā."

27. At that very moment, the din of the *bherī* drums and conches of the entire army was heard, causing the ground to shake.

28. And when, there in Laṅkā, the servants of the *rākṣasa* king heard the din of the monkey army, their spirits failed them. Their energies were sapped by despair, and they foresaw no good arising from the crimes of their king.

The end of the twenty-fifth *sarga* of the *Yuddhakāṇḍa* of the *Śrī Rāmāyaṇa*.

Sarga 26

1. Thus, to the mingled sound of conches and *bherī* drums, did great-armed Rāma Rāghava, the conqueror of enemy citadels, draw near.

2. Now, when Rāvaṇa, lord of the *rākṣasas*, heard that tumultuous sound, he fell to brooding for a while, before turning to his ministers.

3. Then mighty Rāvaṇa, addressing all his ministers, spoke so that the entire assembly hall resounded:

4. "Gentlemen, I have listened to what you have said concerning Rāma's crossing of the ocean, his valor, and the size of his army. But I know that you, sirs, are also truly valorous in battle."

5. Then, after listening to his words, a very wise *rākṣasa* named Mālyavān, the paternal uncle of Rāvaṇa's mother, began to speak:

6. "Your majesty, a king who is well versed in the traditional branches of learning and who acts in accordance with sound policy will long exercise sovereignty and bring his foes under his power.

7. "And if he makes peace or war with his enemies at the appropriate times and strengthens his own side, he will thus enjoy broader sovereignty.

8. "A king who is weaker than his rival or equal to him in strength should sue for peace. Only one who is stronger should make war, but even he must never underestimate his enemy.

9. "Therefore, Rāvaṇa, I would recommend making peace with Rāma. You should give him back Sītā on whose account we are so heavily besieged.

10. "All the gods, seers, and *gandharvas* desire Rāma's victory. Therefore, you should not oppose him. You should choose to make peace with him.

11. "The blessed Grandfather Brahmā created two races: that of the gods and that of the *asuras*, who had recourse to righteousness and unrighteousness, respectively.

12. "For righteousness is said to be the way of the great gods, Rāvaṇa, while unrighteousness is the way of the *asuras* and the *rākṣasas*.

13. "For they say that when righteousness eclipses unrighteousness, that ushers in the golden age, known as the Kṛta. But when unrighteousness eclipses righteousness, that brings on the degenerate Tiṣya Age.

14. "In rampaging through the worlds, you trampled glorious righteousness and embraced unrighteousness instead. It is for that reason that your enemies have grown more powerful than we.

15. "Grown strong through your reckless actions, the serpent of unrighteousness is devouring us; while righteousness, which the deities revere, strengthens the forces of the gods.

16. "Doing whatever you pleased in your addiction to sensuality, you have caused great suffering to the firelike seers. Their power is as irresistible as a blazing fire.

17. "Their minds are purified through their austerities, and they are devoted to the furtherance of righteousness. These twice-born brahmans constantly perform all the different principal sacrificial rites.

18. "Reciting the *vedas* aloud, they pour oblations into the sacrificial fire according to the ritual injunctions. Thwarting the *rākṣasas*, they chant the vedic *mantras* because of which all the *rākṣasas* scatter in all directions like thunderclouds in the hot season.

19. "And, spreading in all ten directions, the smoke arising from the Agnihotra rites of those firelike seers saps the energy of the *rākṣasas*.

20. "Moreover the fierce austerities that those sages, firm in their vows, practiced in their various holy places torment the *rākṣasas*.

21. "And, observing many different, dreadful omens, I foresee the destruction of all the *rākṣasas*.

22. "Thundering deafeningly, dreadful and terrifying storm clouds drench all of Laṅkā with hot blood.

23. "Teardrops fall from our weeping mounts, while our battle flags, dusty and discolored, do not shine as brightly as once they did.

24. "Beasts of prey, jackals, and vultures keep pouring into Laṅkā, shrieking horrendously as they form into packs.

25. "Dark women with deathly white teeth appear before us in dreams laughing wildly, speaking menacingly, and looting houses.

26. "Dogs are devouring the *bali* offerings in house after house. Cows are giving birth to donkeys, while rats are mating with mongooses.

27. "Cats are mating with tigers, pigs with dogs, *kinnaras* are mating with *rākṣasas* and even with humans.

28. "White doves with red feet flutter through the sky impelled by doom and presaging the destruction of the *rākṣasas*.

29. "Screeching, '*cīcīkūcī*,' domesticated *śārikas* are flying about, even though they are tethered. Although once tamed, they have become aggressive.

30. "Death himself, in the form of a terrifying and hideous bald man, all yellow and black, peers into everyone's houses at all hours. These and other evil omens continue to appear.

31. "We truly believe that Rāma is none other than Viṣṇu, who has taken the body of a man. For this Rāghava, so firm in his valor, is surely no ordinary human.

32. "Therefore, Rāvaṇa, you should make peace with Rāma, the king of men, who built that utterly extraordinary bridge across the ocean."

33. When mighty and supremely valorous Mālyavān had spoken these words there among those foremost counselors and had judged the intentions of the *rākṣasa* overlord, he fell silent, watching Rāvaṇa closely.

The end of the twenty-sixth *sarga* of the *Yuddhakāṇḍa* of the *Śrī Rāmāyaṇa*.

Sarga 27

1. But ten-faced Rāvaṇa, evil-minded as he was and driven by his doom, could not abide the words of Mālyavān, although they had been uttered for his own good.

2. Overwhelmed with anger, he replied to Mālyavān, knitting his brows on his forehead and rolling his eyes in rage:

3. "I shall not listen to these harmful words you have so harshly uttered, thinking them to be beneficial. For you are, in effect, siding with my enemies.

4. "What makes you think that this wretched human Rāma, who lives alone in the wilderness, abandoned by his own father, and has been forced to rely on monkeys, is so formidable?

5. "And what makes you think that I, the lord of the *rākṣasas* and the terror of the gods, who am in no way lacking in valor, am so weak?

6. "I suspect that you have addressed me so harshly out of resentment of my prowess, sympathy for my enemies, or at the prompting of my foes.

7. "For, unless he were prompted by an enemy, what wise man learned in the *śāstras* would dare speak so harshly to a powerful man of high station?

8. "Besides, after taking Sītā—who, but for the lotus, resembles the goddess Śrī—from the forest, why would I give her back for fear of Rāghava?

9. "In a few short days, you will see me slay Rāghava along with Sugrīva, Lakṣmaṇa, and their tens of millions of monkeys.

10. "Even the gods themselves dare not stand before Rāvaṇa in single combat. Whom, then, should he fear in battle?

11. "I might be cut in two, but never would I bow down to anyone. This is an innate fault of mine; and it is impossible to overcome one's nature.

12. "Even if, somehow or other, Rāma actually built a bridge over the ocean, what is so miraculous about this that it should fill you with fear?

13. "And I swear to you truthfully that now that Rāma has crossed the ocean with his army of monkeys, he shall not return alive."

14. Now, when Mālyavān saw that Rāvaṇa was speaking with such agitation and was so angry, he was humiliated and made no reply.

15. Then, after praising the king in the customary fashion with prayers for victory, Mālyavān took his leave and returned to his own dwelling.

16. But as for the *rākṣasa* Rāvaṇa, he went on taking counsel and deliberating with his counselors before ordering an unparalleled defense of Laṅkā.

17. He assigned the *rākṣasa* Prahasta to the eastern gate, and immensely powerful Mahāpārśva and Mahodara to the southern gate.

18. He assigned his son Indrajit, the great master of illusion, to the western gate, in the company of many *rākṣasas*.

19. Then, after assigning Śuka and Sāraṇa to the northern gate, he told his counselors, "I shall be there myself."

20. He then stationed the immensely powerful and valorous *rākṣasa* Virūpākṣa in the central encampment along with many *rākṣasas*.

21. Thus did that bull among *rākṣasas* complete his arrangements in Laṅkā. Then, being under the power of fate, he considered himself to have accomplished his objective.

22. After he had ordered these elaborate arrangements for the city and dismissed his counselors, he entered his vast and luxurious inner apartments, honored by his hosts of counselors with prayers for victory.

The end of the twenty-seventh *sarga* of the *Yuddhakāṇḍa* of the *Śrī Rāmāyaṇa*.

Sarga 28

1–3. Meanwhile, having entered enemy territory, Rāma the king of men, Sugrīva the king of the monkeys, the monkey Hanumān son of Vāyu, Jāmbavān the king of the apes, the *rākṣasa* Vibhīṣaṇa, Aṅgada son of Vālin, Saumitri, the monkey Śarabha, Suṣeṇa and his sons, as well as Mainda, Dvivida, Gaja, Gavākṣa, Kumuda, Nala, and Panasa took counsel together, saying:

4. "There lies the citadel of Laṅkā, ruled by Rāvaṇa. It is not to be conquered even by the immortal gods along with the *asuras*, great serpents, and *gandharvas*.

5. "It is time to take counsel and formulate a plan, keeping the success of our mission foremost in mind. For this is the principal stronghold of Rāvaṇa, lord of the *rākṣasas*."

6. As they were speaking in this fashion, Vibhīṣaṇa, Rāvaṇa's younger brother, addressed to them a speech rich in meaning and free from all vulgarity.

7. "My counselors, Anala, Śarabha, Saṃpāti, and Praghasa, have gone to the city of Laṅkā and returned.

8. "Turning themselves into birds, they infiltrated the enemy's army. Then, once they had observed the defensive preparations that have been put in place, they all reported back.

9. "Now listen to me, Rāma, as I describe to you faithfully the entire defensive preparations of evil-minded Rāvaṇa, just as they have reported it.

10. "Prahasta with his army is stationed at the eastern gate, while the immensely powerful Mahāpārśva and Mahodara are at the southern gate.

11–12. "Rāvaṇa's son Indrajit—accompanied by heroes armed with various weapons and by many *rākṣasas* bearing spears, swords, and bows, and wielding lances and war hammers—is stationed at the western gate. He has with him many thousands of *rākṣasas* with weapons in hand.

13. "Rāvaṇa himself, focused and supremely confident and accompanied by many *rākṣasas*, has taken up his position at the northern gate of the city.

14. "And Virūpākṣa, along with still more *rākṣasas* and a force armed with lances, swords, and bows, is stationed in the central encampment.

15. "Once they had surveyed those garrisons, arranged in that fashion, all my ministers returned as quickly as possible.

16. "In the city there are one thousand elephants, ten thousand chariots, twenty thousand horses, and more than ten million *rākṣasas*.

17. "Those night-roaming *rākṣasas*—valorous, powerful, and fierce in battle—are at all times the handpicked guard of the *rākṣasa* king.

18. "And, in order to give battle, an entourage of one million attends upon each one of those *rākṣasas* here, lord of the people."

19. After Vibhīṣaṇa had delivered his account of the activities in Laṅkā as they had been reported by his counselors, he made these concluding comments to Rāma, whose eyes were like lotus petals:

20–21. "When Rāvaṇa went to war against Kubera, Rāma, six million *rākṣasas*—the equals of evil-minded Rāvaṇa in valor, strength, energy, power, dignity, and pride—marched forth.

22. "Please do not be angry with me over this. I am trying to rouse your fury for battle, not alarm you. For, with your valor, you are able to defeat even the gods.

23. "Once you have arrayed the monkey forces for battle, you, sir, surrounded by this great host with its four divisions, will utterly destroy Rāvaṇa."

24. When Vibhīṣaṇa, the younger brother of Rāvaṇa, had spoken in this fashion, Rāghava uttered these words in order to repulse his enemies:

25. "Let that bull among monkeys, Nīla, surrounded by many monkeys, confront Prahasta at Laṅkā's eastern gate.

26. "And let Vālin's son, Aṅgada, accompanied by a large force, attack Mahāpārśva and Mahodara at the southern gate.

27. "Meanwhile, let the son of Pavana, Hanumān, of boundless vitality, accompanied by many monkeys, force and breach the western gate.

28–29. "I am determined to kill the lord of the *rākṣasas* myself. For that lowly wretch, whose power derives from the gift of a boon, takes delight in harming the hosts of *daityas* and *dānavas* as well as the great seers, as he rampages through all the worlds oppressing all creatures.

30. "Thus, together with Saumitri, I shall force and breach the northern gate of the city, where Rāvaṇa is stationed with his forces.

31. "Let the powerful king of the monkeys, Sugrīva, Jāmbavān, king of the apes, and Vibhīṣaṇa, the younger brother of the *rākṣasa* lord, take up their positions at the central encampment.

32. "Let none of the monkeys take on human form in battle. For this shall be our mark of recognition for the monkey army in battle.

33–34. "The monkey form itself will be the sign of recognition for our own forces. Only the seven of us—my friend Vibhīṣaṇa with his four companions, and I myself, together with my immensely powerful brother Lakṣmaṇa—will, in human form, confront our enemies."

35. When resolute Rāma had spoken in this fashion to Vibhīṣaṇa in order to secure the success of their mission, he resolved purposefully to ascend Mount Suvela.

36. Then, covering the land with his vast army, wise and great Rāma marched on Laṅkā in great excitement, determined to slay his enemy.

The end of the twenty-eighth *sarga* of the *Yuddhakāṇḍa* of the *Śrī Rāmāyaṇa*.

Sarga 29

1–2. Once Rāma, who was accompanied by Lakṣmaṇa, had made up his mind to climb Mount Suvela, he spoke in sweet and polished tones to Sugrīva and to the devoted and righteous Vibhīṣaṇa, the night-roaming *rākṣasa*, who was skillful both in counsel and in action:

3. "Let us all straightaway climb this great mountain Suvela, abounding in hundreds of minerals. For we shall camp there tonight.

4–5. "There we shall survey Laṅkā, the abode of that *rākṣasa*, the evil-minded wretch who stole away my wife to his own undoing. He has no regard for righteousness, proper conduct, or his own high lineage. And so, in his vile *rākṣasa* nature, he has done this contemptible thing.

6. "For at the mere mention of that vilest of *rākṣasas*, my anger blazes up, and, because of the transgression of that lowly wretch, I shall have to witness the slaughter of the *rākṣasas*.

7. "A single person acting under the power of the noose of Kāla has committed this crime; and because of this despicable offense an entire race must perish."

8. Speaking in this fashion, Rāma, filled with rage toward Rāvaṇa, ascended Mount Suvela with its lovely slopes to make camp there.

9. Behind him came Lakṣmaṇa, ever vigilant, holding his bow and arrows, intent on deeds of great valor.

10–11. Behind him climbed Sugrīva with his counselors and Vibhīṣaṇa as well as Hanumān, Aṅgada, Nīla, Mainda, Dvivida, Gaja, Gavākṣa, Gavaya, Śarabha, Gandhamādana, Panasa, Kumuda, Hara, and the troop leader Rambha.

12. These and many other swift monkeys, denizens of the mountains, swarmed up Mount Suvela by the hundred, leaping with the speed of the wind to where Rāghava was.

13. When, after a short time, they had scaled the mountain from all sides, they saw, perched as they were on its summit, a city that seemed to be suspended in the sky.

14. And the leaders of the monkey troops gazed upon splendid Laṅkā, adorned with magnificent gates and ramparts and filled with *rākṣasas*.

15. There the foremost monkeys saw what appeared to be a second rampart made up of those dark night-roaming *rākṣasas* who were stationed at the base of the city wall.

16. When the monkeys saw those *rākṣasas*, so eager for battle, they all bellowed loudly, as Rāma stood watching.

17. Then, reddened at twilight, the sun set and night came on, illumined by the full moon.

18. Then Rāma, the commander of the forces of the tawny monkeys, received and honored by Vibhīṣaṇa, settled in at his leisure on the summit of Mount Suvela. He was accompanied by Lakṣmaṇa and surrounded by the hosts of the monkey troop leaders.

The end of the twenty-ninth *sarga* of the *Yuddhakāṇḍa* of the *Śrī Rāmāyaṇa*.

Sarga 30

1–2. After passing the night on Mount Suvela, those heroic bulls among the tawny monkeys gazed upon the parks and woodlands of Laṅkā. They were level, hospitable, pleasant, broad, long, and charming to look upon. Gazing upon them, the monkeys were wonderstruck.

3–5. The city of Lañkā was filled with trees: *campaka*, *aśoka*, *puṃnāga*, *sāla*, and palmyra. It was screened by groves of *tamāla* trees and surrounded by rows of *nāga* trees. Indeed, with its celestial trees of every kind entwined with creepers and bursting with blossoms on every side—*hintālas*, *arjunas*, *nīpas*, flowering *saptaparṇas*, *tilakas*, *karṇikāras*, and *pāṭalas*—it was as lovely as Indra's city of Amarāvatī.

6–7. Replete with varicolored blossoms, red and tender leaf-buds, dark lawns, and variegated groves, those trees wore their fragrant and enticing flowers and fruit, as people do their jewelry.

8. They looked just like the Caitraratha gardens. Delightful and resembling the Nandana groves, those parklands—charming in every season and filled with bees—were ravishing.

9. It was filled with birds—*natyūhas*, *koyaṣṭibhakas*, and dancing peacocks. The sweet notes of the cuckoo could be heard across the rushing woodland streams.

10–12. In great excitement and delight, the heroic tawny monkeys, who could take on any form at will, entered those parks and woodlands. These were swarming with bees and filled with birds, constantly enflamed with passion. Cuckoos flocked in their groves, which resounded with the songs of birds. They were filled with the song of drongos and were swarming with bees. They echoed with the song of *koṇālakas* and resounded with the cries of *sārasa* cranes.

13. And as those immensely powerful monkeys entered, a breeze, fragrant from its contact with the blossoms, began to blow.

14–15. But with the permission of Sugrīva, some of the troop leaders, notable for their deafening roars, separated themselves from the troops of heroic tawny monkeys and marched toward many-bannered Lañkā, terrifying birds, frightening deer and elephants, and shaking Lañkā itself with their roaring.

16. Those immensely swift monkeys crushed the earth under their feet, while clouds of dust rose up suddenly, kicked up by their feet.

17. Frightened by the noise, bears, lions, boar, buffalo, elephants, and deer fled in all ten directions, terrified.

18–20. There, reaching into the sky, stood one of the lofty summits of Mount Trikūṭa. Covered on all sides with flowers, it seemed to be made of gold. It was bright and lovely to behold, and its breadth was a hundred leagues. It was beautiful, grand, and majestic and impossible for even the birds to reach. It was impossible for men to scale, even in their imagination, let alone in reality. And there, on that peak, stood Laṅkā, under the protection of Rāvaṇa.

21. The citadel was adorned with ramparts of gold and silver and with lofty gateway towers resembling white clouds.

22. Indeed, Laṅkā was as magnificently adorned by its palaces and mansions as are the heavens, Viṣṇu's middle step, with clouds at summer's end.

23. In the city could be seen a palace adorned with a thousand columns, which, seeming to scrape the sky, resembled the peak of Mount Kailāsa.

24. It was the domed palace of the *rākṣasa* lord, and it was the ornament of the city. It was constantly guarded by a full complement of a hundred *rākṣasas*.

25. Thus did Lakṣmaṇa's fortunate elder brother, Rāma, whose objective had been thus far achieved, first gaze, together with the monkeys, upon Rāvaṇa's opulent citadel.

26. Rāma and his vast army looked out upon the city. It was glittering with gems, abounding with defensive works, and adorned with rows of palaces. Its mighty gates were studded with great defensive engines.

The end of the thirtieth *sarga* of the *Yuddhakāṇḍa* of the *Śrī Rāmāyaṇa*.

Sarga 31

1. Now, at this juncture, observing various portents, Lakṣmaṇa's elder brother addressed these words to fortunate Lakṣmaṇa:

2. "Lakṣmaṇa, let us secure these cool lakes and woodlands abounding in fruit. We shall make camp here, dividing this massive army into companies and marshaling it in formation.

3. "I see signs of a horrendous universal catastrophe near at hand, presaging the annihilation of the heroic apes, monkeys, and *rākṣasas*.

4. "Winds blow fiercely and the earth trembles. The hilltops shake, and the mountains crumble.

5. "Frightful and terrible clouds, resembling beasts of prey and thundering ominously, pour down fierce torrents mingled with drops of blood.

6. "The evening sky, the color of red sandalpaste, is deeply ominous. A blazing ball of fire plummets from the sun.

7. "Dreadful beasts and birds of ill omen, mournful and with mournful voices, howl at the sun, engendering intense fear.

8. "At night the moon glows dully, emitting a dark and reddish glare, just as it might at the end of the world.

9. "A faint but menacing corona, crimson and inauspicious, encircles the orb of the sun, while a dark spot is visible on its surface, Lakṣmaṇa.

10. "And look, Lakṣmaṇa! The constellations themselves look strange. All of this that appears to us seems to presage the destruction of the world.

11. "Crows, kites, and vultures are spiraling downward, while jackals emit loud and inauspicious howls.

12. "Therefore, surrounded on all sides by tawny monkeys, we should, this very day, swiftly and without delay attack that citadel, which is protected by Rāvaṇa."

13. As that mighty hero, Lakṣmaṇa's elder brother, was speaking in this fashion to Lakṣmaṇa, he swiftly descended from the mountain peak.

14. And when righteous Rāghava had descended from the mountain, he inspected his troops, who were not to be vanquished by their enemies.

15. Together with Sugrīva, Rāghava, who was a master of timing, prepared the vast army of the monkey king and, at the proper moment, sent them into battle.

16. Then, when the time was right, that great-armed hero, armed with his bow and surrounded by his vast army, led the march toward the citadel of Laṅkā.

17. Vibhīṣaṇa, Sugrīva, Hanumān, Jāmbavān, Nala, the king of the apes, Nīla, and Lakṣmaṇa all followed him.

18. Behind them, a vast army of apes and forest-dwelling monkeys, covering a huge swath of land, followed Rāghava.

19. By the hundred, those monkeys, resembling elephants and able to drive off their foes, seized mountain peaks and full-grown trees.

20. In a short time, the two brothers, Rāma and Lakṣmaṇa, subduers of their foes, reached Laṅkā, the citadel of Rāvaṇa.

21. Garlanded with pennants, adorned with parks and groves, it was lovely with its splendid ramparts. But with its lofty walls and gateways, it seemed impregnable.

22. Urged on by Rāma's words, the forest-dwelling monkeys, following orders, closely besieged the city, which was unassailable even by the gods.

23. Armed with his bow and accompanied by his younger brother, Rāma both guarded and blockaded Laṅkā's northern gate, which was as lofty as a mountain peak.

24–25. Thus did Rāma, the heroic son of Daśaratha, followed by Lakṣmaṇa, approach the northern gate, where Rāvaṇa was stationed, and begin his siege of the city of Laṅkā, which was guarded by Rāvaṇa. For none other than Rāma was capable of guarding that gate.

26. For, with Rāvaṇa stationed there, it was as fearsome as the ocean guarded by Varuṇa. It struck terror into the hearts of the weak. It was guarded on every side by terrifying and well-armed *rākṣasas*, just as is the underworld known as Pātāla by the *dānavas*.

27. And Rāma saw arrayed there many and various stores of weapons and armor belonging to the warriors.

28. Meanwhile, the powerful general Nīla of the army of tawny monkeys approached the eastern gate and took up his position there together with Mainda and Dvivida.

29. The very powerful Aṅgada took up his post at the southern gate, along with Ṛṣabha, Gavākṣa, Gaja, and Gavaya.

30. The mighty monkey Hanumān, accompanied by Pramāthin, Praghasa, and other heroes, guarded the western gate.

31. Meanwhile, Sugrīva stationed himself in the central encampment along with all the foremost among the tawny monkeys, who were as swift as Suparṇa or the wind.

32. And thus, at the place where Sugrīva had stationed himself, three hundred and sixty million illustrious leaders of the monkey troops were encamped, pressing their siege.

33. Acting on Rāma's orders, Lakṣmaṇa and Vibhīṣaṇa posted the tawny monkeys by the tens of millions at each of the gates.

34. Meanwhile, Sugrīva and Jāmbavān, accompanied by many troops, took up their position in the central encampment, a little to the west of Rāma's post.

35. Seizing trees and mountaintops, those tigers among monkeys, whose fangs were like those of tigers, held their positions, eager for battle.

36. All of them held their tails erect. All were armed with fangs and claws. All were flexing their variegated limbs. And all their faces were contorted.

37. Some of them were as powerful as ten elephants, and others yet ten times stronger than that, while some were equal in strength to a thousand elephants.

38. Some of them were as powerful as an *ogha* of elephants, others were a hundred times as powerful as that. Some of the troop leaders of the tawny monkeys had strength beyond measure.

39. The host of those monkey warriors was as variegated and awe inspiring as a swarm of locusts.

40. The ground seemed to be completely filled with the monkeys who were encamped before Laṅkā, while the sky was as if covered with those who were still converging on the city.

41. A hundred divisions each of one hundred thousand apes and forest-dwelling monkeys stationed themselves at the gates

of Laṅkā, while still more of them swarmed in from every side to fight.

42. The mountain was completely covered on every side by all those leaping monkeys. Meanwhile, an additional ten million marched upon the city.

43. And thus Laṅkā was blockaded on every side by powerful, tree-wielding monkeys, so that not even the wind could enter.

44. Suddenly besieged by monkeys who resembled great clouds and who were equal to Śakra in valor, the *rākṣasas* were dumbfounded.

45. From that huge mass of troops as it marched forth, a deafening roar arose, which was like the sound that might arise from the waters if the ocean itself were to be shattered.

46. That deafening sound shook all of Laṅkā together with its ramparts, gateways, hills, parks, and woodlands.

47. Under the protection of Rāma and Lakṣmaṇa along with Sugrīva, the army was completely unassailable even by all the gods and *asuras*.

48–49. When Rāghava had deployed his army in this fashion for the destruction of the *rākṣasas*, he once again took counsel with his counselors and arrived at a decision. Fully conversant with the sequential application of the various stratagems and of their consequences, he was eager to move on to the next stage. Abiding by the advice of Vibhīṣaṇa, he called to mind the protocol of kings. Summoning Vālin's son, Aṅgada, he said this:

50. "Abandoning fear and free from anxiety, my good monkey, you must leap into the city of Laṅkā. Approaching ten-necked Rāvaṇa, you are to address him in my words as follows:

51–53. "'You have lost your royal majesty, your lordship is at an end. You have lost your wits and doomed yourself. Since, night-roaming *rākṣasa*, in your delusion and pride you have committed crimes against the seers, gods, *gandharvas*, *apsarases*, great serpents, *yakṣas*, and kings, surely your arrogance, born of the boon of self-existent Brahmā, will today be humbled. For, tormented by the abduction of my wife and bearing the rod of punishment against you, I have encamped at the gates of Lañkā to inflict that punishment upon you.

54. "'Once I have killed you, *rākṣasa*, you shall attain the realm of the gods, the great seers, and all the royal seers.

55. "'Now show me the strength, wretched *rākṣasa*, with which you carried Sītā off after first luring me away with an illusion.

56. "'Unless you hand Maithilī over to me and come to me for refuge, I shall rid the earth of *rākṣasas* with my keen arrows.

57. "'The foremost of *rākṣasas*, righteous-minded Vibhīṣaṇa, has come over to me. Endowed with majesty, he shall obtain the secure and unchallenged lordship of Lañkā.

58. "'For since you are unrighteous, unrestrained, wicked, and surround yourself with fools, you cannot possibly continue to enjoy your kingship for even another moment.

59. "'So gather up your fortitude and, relying on your valor, fight, *rākṣasa*! Then, slain by my arrows in battle, you shall be purified.

60. "'Even if you were to take the form of a bird, swift as thought, and fly through the three worlds, once you came within the range of my sight, you would not escape alive.

61. "'Let me tell you something for your own good: prepare yourself for the next world. Take a good long look at Lañkā. Your life is in my hands.'"

62. When Tārā's son, Añgada, had been addressed in this fashion by Rāma, tireless in action, he leapt into the sky and sped on his way, like Agni, bearer of oblations, incarnate.

63. Reaching Rāvaṇa's palace in an instant, the majestic monkey spied Rāvaṇa, calmly seated with his ministers.

64. Landing a short distance from him, that bull among tawny monkeys, Añgada, with his golden armlets, stood there like a blazing fire.

65. After first identifying himself in his own words, he then repeated that entire excellent speech of Rāma to Rāvaṇa and his ministers, neither adding nor omitting anything.

66. "I am a messenger of Rāma, the Lord of Kosala, tireless in action. I am called Aṅgada, son of Vālin, perhaps you have heard of me.

67. "Rāma Rāghava, the bringer of joy to Kausalyā, says this to you: 'Savage, lowest of men, come out and fight.

68. " 'I am going to kill you along with your counselors, sons, friends, and all your kinsmen. Once you have been slain, the three worlds will be free of your menace.

69. " 'This very day I shall pluck you out, thorn that you are in the side of the seers and foe of the gods, *dānavas*, *yakṣas*, *gandharvas*, great serpents, and *rākṣasas*.

70. " 'If you do not give back Vaidehī, after first begging her forgiveness and falling at my feet, then, once you have been killed, the kingship shall be Vibhīṣaṇa's.' "

71. As that bull among tawny monkeys was uttering these harsh words, the lord of the host of night-roaming *rākṣasas* was transported with rage.

72. His eyes red with rage, he then repeatedly commanded his ministers, "Seize this fool and kill him!"

73. Upon hearing Rāvaṇa's words, four dreadful night-roaming *rākṣasas*, whose energy was like that of a blazing fire, seized Aṅgada.

74. Tārā's heroic son freely allowed himself to be captured in order to demonstrate his power before the hosts of the *yātudhānas*.

75. Then Aṅgada leapt to the top of the palace, which resembled a mountain peak, carrying with him those *rākṣasas* who clung to his arms like locusts.

76. Shaken loose by his speed, all four *rākṣasas* fell from the sky to the ground right before the eyes of the *rākṣasa* lord.

77. And then, as he landed upon the pinnacle of the palace, lofty as a mountain peak, it crumbled right before the eyes of ten-necked Rāvaṇa.

78. When he had smashed the pinnacle of the palace, he loudly proclaimed his own name, and then, letting out a great roar, he flew off through the sky.

79. Rāvaṇa flew into a towering rage at the assault on his palace. But, foreseeing his own destruction, he fell to sighing.

80. But as for Rāma—eager to slay his enemy—he advanced for battle in the company of many leaping monkeys, who roared in their excitement.

81–82. At Sugrīva's command the tawny monkey Suṣeṇa—immensely powerful, unassailable, and resembling a mountain peak—surrounded by many monkeys, who could take on any form at will, made a tour of all four city gates, much as the moon passes through the lunar mansions.

83–84. When the *rākṣasas* saw those hundreds of battalions of forest-dwelling monkeys laying siege to Laṅkā and stretching all the way to the sea, some of them were amazed, some were terrified, while others were filled with excitement because of their fervor for battle.

85. Since the entire area between the ramparts and the moat was covered with monkeys, the disheartened *rākṣasas* gazed upon what appeared to be a wall of monkeys.

86. In the midst of that terrifying and tumultuous uproar in the *rākṣasa* capital, the *rākṣasas* took up their mighty weapons and raced about, like the fierce winds at the end of a cosmic age.

The end of the thirty-first *sarga* of the *Yuddhakāṇḍa* of the *Śrī Rāmāyaṇa*.

Sarga 32

1. Then the *rākṣasas* went straightaway to Rāvaṇa's palace and reported to him that Rāma and the monkeys had laid siege to the city.

2. When the night-roaming *rākṣasa* heard that the city was besieged, he grew furious. After first doubling his defensive arrangements, he climbed up to the terrace of the palace.

3. He saw that Laṅkā, together with its hills, parks, and woodlands, was surrounded on all sides by countless troops of tawny monkeys, eager for battle.

4. Seeing the entire land swallowed up by monkeys, he fell to brooding, thinking, "How can they be destroyed?"

5. After brooding for a long time, Rāvaṇa drew upon his fortitude and gazed wide-eyed at Rāghava and the troops of tawny monkeys.

6. As the *rākṣasa* lord stood watching, the armies, division after division, began to scale the walls of Laṅkā in order to accomplish Rāghava's most cherished desire.

7. Willing to lay down their lives for Rāma's sake, the red-faced monkeys, shimmering like gold, advanced upon Laṅkā armed with *sāla* and palmyra trees as well as boulders.

8. Those leaping monkeys smashed the lofty tops of palaces and gateway arches with trees, mountaintops, and even their fists.

9. With earth, mountaintops, grass, and timber, the monkeys filled in the moats, which had held clear water.

10. Then other troop leaders with their troops that numbered in the thousands, tens of millions, and billions scaled the walls of Laṅkā.

11–12. Like great bull elephants, the leaping monkeys advanced upon Laṅkā, jumping back and forth, roaring, crushing golden archways, and smashing towers that resembled the peaks of Mount Kailāsa.

13–14. Those leaping monkeys, who could take on any form at will, hurled themselves upon the ramparts of Laṅkā, roaring and shouting, "Victory to supremely powerful Rāma and mighty Lakṣmaṇa! Victory to King Sugrīva, who is protected by Rāghava!"

15. Vīrabāhu, Subāhu, and the forest-ranging Nala, leaders of the troops of tawny monkeys, made a breach in the rampart and stationed themselves there.

16. At that juncture, they established a bridgehead.

17. Accompanied by a hundred million tawny monkeys, all with a victorious air, mighty Kumuda stationed himself at the eastern gate, blockading it.

18. The powerful and valorous monkey Śatabali proceeded with two hundred million troops to the southern gate and took up his post there, blockading it.

19. Tārā's father, the powerful tawny monkey Suṣeṇa, proceeded to the western gate with six hundred million troops and took up his post there, blockading it.

20. Together with Saumitri, mighty Rāma himself and Sugrīva, lord of the tawny monkeys, approached the northern gate and took up their posts, blockading it.

21. At Rāma's side stood the huge langur Gavākṣa. Enormously powerful, mighty, and dreadful to look upon, he was accompanied by ten million troops.

22. Also at Rāma's side stood valorous Dhūmra, crusher of his foes, accompanied by ten million apes of terrifying speed.

23. There, too, accompanied by his ministers, stood immensely powerful and valorous Vibhīṣaṇa, girded for war, his mace in hand.

24. Gaja, Gavākṣa, Gavaya, Śarabha, and Gandhamādana patrolled swiftly on all sides, guarding the army of tawny monkeys.

25. Then Rāvaṇa, lord of the *rākṣasas*, his mind suffused with rage, ordered all of his forces to make an immediate sortie.

26. Urged on by Rāvaṇa, his troops rushed forth in great excitement, like the waves of the great ocean when, at the appointed time, it is filled to overflowing.

27. At that juncture, a horrific battle ensued between the *rākṣasas* and the monkeys, just like the one long ago between the gods and the *asuras*.

28. The dreadful *rākṣasas* slaughtered the monkeys with blazing maces, lances, javelins, and battle-axes, boasting of their valorous deeds.

29. Similarly, the huge and swift monkeys slaughtered the *rākṣasas* with trees, mountaintops, claws, and teeth.

30. Meanwhile, other dreadful *rākṣasas* positioned on the rampart hewed the monkeys on the ground with short javelins, swords, and lances.

31. But the leaping monkeys on the ground were enraged and, leaping up, hurled down the *rākṣasas* stationed on the ramparts.

32. That tumultuous conflict of the *rākṣasas* and monkeys, in which the ground grew thick with flesh and blood, was something unimaginable.

The end of the thirty-second *sarga* of the *Yuddhakāṇḍa* of the *Śrī Rāmāyaṇa*.

Sarga 33

1. As those great monkeys continued to fight, a terrible rage against their army arose among the *rākṣasas*.

2–3. Those tigers among *rākṣasas* sallied forth, causing the ten directions to resound. They were *rākṣasas* of dreadful deeds, eager for Rāvaṇa's victory. They had golden-plumed horses, banners that resembled flames of fire, chariots resplendent as the sun, and exquisite armor.

4. And the vast host of monkeys, who also desired victory, hurled itself upon the army of the *rākṣasas*, who could take on any form at will.

5. At this juncture, as they hurled themselves at one another, the monkeys and the *rākṣasas* engaged in single combat.

6. The *rākṣasa* Indrajit fought with Aṅgada, Vālin's son, just as long ago the immensely powerful *asura* Andhaka fought with three-eyed Śiva.

7. Saṃpāti, ever irresistible in battle, fought with Prajaṅgha, while the monkey Hanumān engaged Jambumālin.

8. In a towering rage, Rāvaṇa's younger brother, the *rākṣasa* Vibhīṣaṇa, closed in combat with Mitraghna, of blazing speed.

9. Mighty Gaja fought with the *rākṣasa* Tapana, and powerful Nīla with Nikumbha.

10. The lord of the monkeys, Sugrīva, engaged with Praghasa, while majestic Lakṣmaṇa closed in battle with Virūpākṣa.

11. Rāma engaged with the irresistible Agniketu, the *rākṣasa* Raśmiketu, Suptaghna, and Yajñakopa.

12. Two of the leading monkeys engaged with a pair of particularly dreadful *rākṣasas*: Mainda with Vajramuṣṭi and Dvivida with Aśaniprabha.

13. The heroic and dreadful *rākṣasa* Pratapana, irresistible in battle, engaged in combat with Nala, of blazing speed.

14. The son of Dharma, the great and powerful monkey known as Suṣeṇa, fought with Vidyunmālin.

15. And many other fearsome monkeys engaged in single combat in various ways with many other *rākṣasas*.

16. The great battle that took place there between the heroic *rākṣasas* and monkeys, both desirous of victory, was tumultuous and hair-raising.

17. From the bodies of the tawny monkeys and *rākṣasas* flowed gushing rivers of blood, with hair in place of weeds and carrying logjams of corpses.

18. In a rage, Indrajit struck the heroic Aṅgada, breaker of enemy ranks, with his mace, just as Indra of the hundred sacrifices might with his thunderbolt.

19. And in that combat, the swift monkey, majestic Aṅgada, smashed Indrajit's gilded chariot together with its horses and charioteer.

20. Prajaṅgha shot Saṃpāti with three arrows; but he, in turn, struck Prajaṅgha with an *aśvakarṇa* tree in the vanguard of battle.

21. In that battle, immensely powerful Jambumālin, furious, mounted his chariot and, with a javelin he kept there, struck Hanumān in the middle of the chest.

22. But Hanumān, the son of Māruta, leapt upon Jambumālin's chariot and, with a blow of his hand, swiftly destroyed it together with that *rākṣasa*.

23. Then Gaja, his body pierced by the sharp arrows of the dexterous *rākṣasa* Tapana, smashed him with a mountain peak held in his fist.

24. Sugrīva, overlord of the monkeys, then killed Praghasa, who seemed almost to be devouring the troops, smashing him to pieces with a *saptaparṇa* tree.

25. After tormenting the fearsome-looking *rākṣasa* Virūpākṣa with a hail of arrows, Lakṣmaṇa killed him with a single shaft.

26. The irresistible Agniketu, the *rākṣasa* Raśmiketu, Suptaghna, and Yajñakopa all pierced Rāma with their arrows.

27. But, with four fearsome arrows resembling tongues of flame, Rāma, enraged, lopped off the heads of all four of them in battle.

28. In combat Mainda smashed Vajramuṣṭi with his fist so that, along with his chariot and horses, he crashed down to the earth, like the lofty tower of a citadel.

29. Then Dvivida, whose blows were like that of Indra's *vajra* or thunderbolt, struck Aśaniprabha with a mountain peak right before the eyes of all the *rākṣasas*.

30. But, in the battle, with arrows that resembled thunderbolts, Aśaniprabha, in turn, riddled the monkey lord Dvivida, who used trees as weapons.

31. And, in turn, with a *sāla* tree, Dvivida, his body bristling with arrows and beside himself with rage, crushed Aśaniprabha, along with his horses and chariot.

32. Then, in battle, Nikumbha pierced Nīla, whose dark luster was like that of a mass of collyrium, with sharp arrows, just as the bright-rayed sun pierces a dark cloud with its beams.

33. Next, that dexterous night-roaming *rākṣasa* Nikumbha once again riddled Nīla in combat with a hundred arrows and laughed.

34. But Nīla, like Viṣṇu in battle, cut off the heads of Nikumbha and his charioteer in combat with a discus taken from their chariot.

35. Mounted in his chariot, Vidyunmālin struck Suṣeṇa with gold-inlaid arrows and roared repeatedly.

36. Then, seeing him mounted in his chariot, that foremost among monkeys Suṣeṇa quickly smashed the chariot with a huge mountain peak.

37. But the night-roaming *rākṣasa* Vidyunmālin, who was endowed with great speed, swiftly leapt from his chariot and, mace in hand, made a stand on the ground.

38. Then, suffused with rage, Suṣeṇa, that bull among the tawny monkeys, seized an enormous boulder and charged at the night-roaming *rākṣasa*.

39. With his mace, the night-roaming *rākṣasa* Vidyunmālin swiftly struck Suṣeṇa, foremost of tawny monkeys, who was rushing toward him, in the chest.

40. But that best of leaping monkeys paid no heed to that terrible blow of the mace, and in that great battle, he hurled the boulder down upon Vidyunmālin's chest.

41. Struck by the blow of that boulder, the night-roaming *rākṣasa* Vidyunmālin fell lifeless to the earth, his chest crushed.

42. In this fashion, the valorous monkeys slaughtered the valorous night-roaming *rākṣasas* in single combat, just as the gods, dwellers in heaven, slaughtered the *daityas*.

43–44. With its crescent-headed arrows, swords, maces, javelins, iron cudgels, spears, broken chariots, butchered war-horses, slaughtered rutting elephants, monkeys, and *rākṣasas*, and shattered wheels, axles, and yokes lying on the ground, the battlefield, haunted by packs of jackals, was a place of horror.

45. And in that tumultuous conflict, which was comparable to the battle of the gods and the *asuras*, headless corpses of monkeys and *rākṣasas* leapt about in every direction.

46. As they were being torn to pieces by the bulls among the tawny monkeys, the night-roaming *rākṣasas*, their limbs smeared with blood, swiftly hurled themselves into battle once again, anxious now for the sun, maker of day, to set.

The end of the thirty-third *sarga* of the *Yuddhakāṇḍa* of the *Śrī Rāmāyaṇa*.

Sarga 34

1. As the monkeys and *rākṣasas* continued to fight, the sun set and a deadly night came on.

2. Then ensued a clash by night between those terrifying monkeys and *rākṣasas*, locked in their mutual hostility, all of them eager for victory.

3. In that terrible darkness they slaughtered one another in battle: the tawny monkeys crying, "Are you a *rākṣasa*?" and the *rākṣasas* crying, "Are you a monkey?"

4. "Kill!" "Rend" "Come on!" "What, running away?" Such were the tumultuous cries that were heard in that darkness.

5. With their golden armor, in the darkness, the swarthy *rākṣasas* looked like great mountains with thickets of luminescent herbs.

6. Beside themselves with fury, the swift *rākṣasas* raced about in that impenetrable darkness, devouring the monkeys.

7. But the monkeys hurled themselves upon the *rākṣasas'* golden-plumed horses and their banners that resembled flames of fire and, in a terrifying rage, tore them to pieces with their sharp fangs.

8. Beside themselves with fury, they dragged about elephants with their riders and chariots bedecked with flags and banners, slashing at them with their fangs.

9. Meanwhile, with arrows that resembled venomous serpents, Lakṣmaṇa and Rāma cut down the foremost among the *rākṣasas*, whom they could make out but dimly in the darkness.

10. The thick dust raised by the horses' hooves and chariot wheels blocked up the eyes and ears of the warriors.

11. And there, as that terrible, hair-raising battle proceeded in this fashion, swift rivers with blood for water began to flow.

12. And there arose an astonishing sound of battle drums—*bherīs*, *mṛdaṅgas*, and *paṇavas*—mingled with sounds of conch and flute.

13. A very horrifying clamor arose from the clash of arms and from the *rākṣasas* and monkeys, screaming as they were struck down.

14. Strewn with weapons, as if with floral offerings, and thick with mud that oozed blood, the battleground was impassable, transformed beyond all recognition.

15. Like Kālarātrī, the dark night of universal destruction, which no living thing can escape, that dreadful night was devastating to both the *rākṣasas* and the tawny monkeys.

16. Then, in that terrible darkness, the frenzied *rākṣasas* attacked Rāma with hails of arrows.

17. And the uproar that they made as they rushed upon him, roaring in fury, was like the sound of the upheaval of the seven seas at the time of universal destruction.

18–19. But in the blink of an eye, with six sharp arrows, like flames of fire, Rāma struck six of those night-roaming *rākṣasas*: unassailable Yajñaśatru, Mahāpārśva, Mahodara, the giant Vajradaṃṣṭra, and both Śuka and Sāraṇa.

20. Pierced in every vital point by Rāma with his hail of arrows, they crawled away from the battle, barely clinging to life.

21. Then mighty Rāma illuminated all directions with his arrows, which, with their shafts adorned with gold, resembled flames of fire.

22. As for the remaining *rākṣasa* heroes who stood their ground before Rāma, they, too, were destroyed, like moths entering a flame.

23. With thousands of arrows flying, their feathers fletched with gold, the night was as lovely as an autumnal evening sparkling with fireflies.

24. The bellowing of the *rākṣasas* and the roaring of the tawny monkeys made that dreadful night more dreadful still.

25. As that deafening sound increased on every side, Mount Trikūṭa, with its many echoing caverns, seemed almost to shout in reply.

26. Huge langurs, as black as the darkness itself, crushed night-roaming *rākṣasas* in their arms, rending them with their fangs.

27. At this point Aṅgada threw himself into the battle in order to destroy his enemy. He swiftly slew the charioteer and horses of Indrajit Rāvaṇi.

28. His horses and charioteer slain by Aṅgada, Indrajit, who possessed great powers of illusion, vanished on the spot.

29. The evil Indrajit Rāvaṇi, a hero ruthless in battle, possessed a boon from Brahmā. Seething with rage, he concealed himself; and, unseen, he loosed sharp arrows, blazing like lightning bolts.

30. In a rage, the *rākṣasa* pierced Rāma and Lakṣmaṇa in every part of their bodies with dreadful arrows in the form of great serpents.

The end of the thirty-fourth *sarga* of the *Yuddhakāṇḍa* of the *Śrī Rāmāyaṇa*.

Sarga 35

1. Eager to find out where Indrajit had gone, the valorous and exceedingly mighty Prince Rāma ordered ten leaders of the monkey troops to search for him.

2–3. That scorcher of his foes gave his command to the two sons of Suṣeṇa, that bull among monkeys Nīla, Aṅgada, son of Vālin, swift Śarabha, Vinata, Jāmbavān, mighty Sānuprastha, Ṛṣabha, and Ṛṣabhaskandha.

4. In great excitement, those tawny monkeys ripped up fearsome trees as they all flung themselves into the sky, searching the ten directions.

5. But Indrajit Rāvaṇi, expert in divine weapon-spells, used the greatest of such weapon-spells to halt the swift movement of those swift monkeys with arrows that were swifter still.

6. Pierced and mutilated by his iron arrows, those tawny monkeys of terrifying speed could not discern him, obscured as he was by darkness, as is the sun by clouds.

7. Indrajit Rāvaṇi, victorious in battle, completely overwhelmed Rāma and Lakṣmaṇa with arrows that pierced every vital point.

8. In his fury Indrajit riddled the heroic brothers, Rāma and Lakṣmaṇa, with great serpents that had turned into arrows. Their bodies were thus thickly covered with arrows that had not a hair's breadth between them.

9. From their wounds, the pathways of blood, the blood flowed copiously so that they both resembled *kiṃśuka* trees covered with their bright red blossoms.

10. Then, as hard to discern as a scattered mass of collyrium, Indrajit Rāvaṇi, his eyes rimmed with red, addressed the two brothers in these words:

11. "Not even Śakra himself, the lord of the thirty gods, can see me or attack me when I fight unseen. How much less could the two of you?

12. "Rāghavas! In my towering rage, I shall send you both—tightly bound in my web of heron-fletched arrows—to the abode of Yama."

13. When he had spoken in this fashion to the brothers Rāma and Lakṣmaṇa, who understood righteousness, he pierced them with sharp arrows, as he exulted and roared.

14. As obscure as a scattered mass of collyrium, he drew his great bow and again and again let fly terrifying arrows in that great conflict.

15. Roaring repeatedly, that hero, who knew the vital points, sank sharp arrows into the vitals of Rāma and Lakṣmaṇa.

16. In the blink of an eye, the two of them were so tightly bound in the bonds of those arrows there in the forefront of the battle that they could not even see.

17. Then, pierced with arrows and darts and wounded in every limb, the two of them trembled, like two of great Indra's banners cut loose from their sustaining cords.

18. Weakened by the piercing of their vitals, those two great archers, heroic lords of the earth, staggered and fell to the earth.

19. Their every limb constricted by arrows, suffering and in great agony, the two heroes lay upon the battlefield, a hero's bed, spattered with blood.

*20. There was not a finger's breadth between the wounds that covered their bodies. There was no part of their bodies down to their very fingertips that had not been wounded and immobilized by straight-flying arrows.

21. Struck down by that fierce *rākṣasa*, who could take on any form at will, they both poured forth their blood copiously, as two fountains might their water.

22. Rāma fell first, pierced to the vitals with arrows by the raging Indrajit, who had once defeated Śakra.

23. He riddled him with iron arrows, half-iron arrows, crescent-headed arrows, and arrows with heads like folded palms, calves' teeth, lions' fangs, and razors.

24. Rāma lay there on the battlefield, a hero's bed, clutching his gilded, thrice-curved bow, now unstrung, its grip shattered.

25. Seeing Rāma, that bull among men, fallen there in the midst of that hail of arrows, Lakṣmaṇa despaired of his own life.

26. And the monkeys, headed by Hanumān, the son of Vāyu gathered and stood surrounding the two fallen heroes, who lay in bondage. In their affliction, they, too, became deeply despondent.

The end of the thirty-fifth *sarga* of the *Yuddhakāṇḍa* of the *Śrī Rāmāyaṇa*.

Sarga 36

1. Then the forest-dwelling monkeys, glancing nervously at the earth and the sky, gazed upon the two brothers Rāma and Lakṣmaṇa, who were riddled with arrows.

2. When the *rākṣasa* had accomplished his task and ceased his onslaught, like the god Indra after pouring down the rains, Vibhīṣaṇa arrived at that spot together with Sugrīva.

3. Nīla, Dvivida, Mainda, Suṣeṇa, Sumukha, and Aṅgada, together with Hanumān, began at once to mourn the two Rāghavas.

4–7. As the monkeys, along with Vibhīṣaṇa, gazed upon the two fallen Rāghavas, ensnared in a web of arrows, they were all shaken to their depths. For both heroes were motionless, barely breathing, and drenched in gouts of blood. Lying on beds of arrows, they were immobilized, tightly bound with webs of arrows. Their labored breathing was like the hissing of snakes; they barely moved for their strength had all but left them. Their bodies drenched in streams of blood, they resembled flagstaffs of burnished gold. Surrounded by the troop leaders, whose eyes were filled with tears, the two heroes lay there on the battlefield, a hero's bed, barely moving.

8. Although the monkeys scanned the sky and all directions, they could not see Indrajit Rāvaṇi, who had concealed himself in the battle with his powers of illusion.

9. But Vibhīṣaṇa, in looking about, was able, through his own magical powers, to discern his brother's son, who stood there, concealed by his powers of illusion.

10. Vibhīṣaṇa was thus able to see that hero, unequaled in his feats and unrivaled in battle, who had concealed himself through the gift of a boon.

11. But Indrajit, as he observed his handiwork and the two heroes lying there, was supremely pleased with himself, and he spoke as follows to the delight of all the *rākṣasas*, sons of chaos:

12. "The two mighty brothers, Rāma and Lakṣmaṇa, slayers of Khara and Dūṣaṇa, have been struck down by my arrows.

13. "Not even all the gods and *asuras* together, along with the hosts of seers, can free these two from the bonds of my arrows.

14–15. "I have put an end to the menace they posed, which could have destroyed us all. It is because of them that the three watches of the night now pass without my father—consumed as he was by anxiety—so much as touching his bed. And it is because of them that the whole city of Laṅkā has become as turbulent as a river in the rainy season.

16. "All the valorous deeds of Rāma, Lakṣmaṇa, and all the forest-dwelling monkeys have proven to be as fruitless as rain clouds in autumn."

17. When he had spoken in this fashion to all the *rākṣasas* who stood beside him, Rāvaṇi began once more to assail all the monkey troop leaders.

18. Once he had afflicted them with torrents of arrows and terrified the monkeys, the great-armed hero laughed and said this:

19. "Look, *rākṣasas*, at those two brothers, whom I have bound with the terrible bonds of my arrows right in front of their troops!"

20. Addressed in this fashion, the *rākṣasas*, treacherous fighters all, were greatly amazed and gratified by that feat.

21. Thinking, "Rāma has been slain!" those *rākṣasas*, who resembled storm clouds, uttered a great roar and honored Rāvaṇi.

22. Seeing both Rāma and Lakṣmaṇa motionless on the ground and scarcely breathing, he assumed that they had been killed.

23. Filled with delight, Indrajit, victorious in battle, entered the citadel of Laṅkā to the delight of all the *rākṣasas*, sons of chaos.

24. When Sugrīva saw that the bodies of Rāma and Lakṣmaṇa were riddled with arrows in each and every limb, terror seized him.

25. Then Vibhīṣaṇa addressed the monkey king, who was terrified and dejected, his face covered with tears and his eyes suffused with sorrow.

26. "Enough of this faintheartedness, Sugrīva! Hold back this flood of tears! Battles are often like this. Victory is far from certain.

27. "If there is any remnant of good fortune left to us, hero, the brothers Rāma and Lakṣmaṇa will regain consciousness.

28. "So pull yourself together, monkey, and thus encourage me, who am without any recourse. Those who are devoted to the true path of righteousness have no fear of death."

29. When he had spoken in this fashion, Vibhīṣaṇa dipped his hand in water and, with it, wiped Sugrīva's lovely eyes.

30. Once he had wiped the wise monkey king's face, he calmly spoke these timely words:

31. "This is not the time to give way to despair, greatest of monkey kings. Moreover, at this inopportune moment, excessive tenderness could prove fatal.

32. "Therefore, you must abandon despair, which undermines all endeavors. You must think about what would be best for these troops under Rāma's leadership.

33. "Rather, you should stand guard over Rāma until he regains consciousness. Once the two Kākutsthas have regained consciousness, they will dispel our fear.

34. "This is nothing to Rāma; nor is he about to die. For that vital glow, which is never found in the dead, is not deserting him.

35. "So you must console yourself and rally your forces, while I regroup all the troops.

36. "For, bull among tawny monkeys, these tawny monkeys, filled with alarm, their eyes wide with terror, are spreading rumors from ear to ear.

37. "But once the tawny monkeys see me rushing about to encourage the army, they will cast aside their fear, as one would a used garland."

38. Once that foremost of *rākṣasas* Vibhīṣaṇa had reassured Sugrīva, he set about rallying the terrified monkey army.

39. But as for Indrajit, that great master of illusion, he entered the city of Laṅkā, surrounded by all his troops, and presented himself before his father.

40. Hands cupped in reverence, he respectfully greeted his father, Rāvaṇa, who was seated there, and told him the good news that Rāma and Lakṣmaṇa had been slain.

41. When Rāvaṇa heard that his two enemies had been felled, he leapt up in great delight and embraced his son, right in the midst of the *rākṣasas*.

42. Delighted at heart, he kissed him on the head before questioning him. Indrajit then reported everything, just as it had happened, to his father, who was questioning him.

43. His heart flooded with a great access of joy upon hearing the words of that great chariot-warrior, he cast aside the anxiety that Dāśarathi had caused and, in great delight, praised his son.

The end of the thirty-sixth *sarga* of the *Yuddhakāṇḍa* of the *Śrī Rāmāyaṇa*.

Sarga 37

1. Once Indrajit, the son of Rāvaṇa, had returned to Laṅkā, his mission accomplished, the bulls among monkeys, in great distress, surrounded Rāghava to protect him.

2–4. Then those monkeys—Hanumān, Aṅgada, Nīla, Suṣeṇa, Kumuda, Nala, Gaja, Gavākṣa, Gavaya, Śarabha, Gandhamādana, Jāmbavān, Ṛṣabha, Sunda, Rambha, Śatabali, and Pṛthu—put their troops in battle formation and, maintaining a watch on all sides, armed themselves with trees. Scanning all directions, above as well as on every side, they thought at the mere stirring of the grass that the *rākṣasas* had come.

5. Meanwhile, in great delight, Rāvaṇa, having dismissed his son Indrajit, summoned the *rākṣasa* women who were guarding Sītā.

6. Those *rākṣasa* women, together with Trijaṭā, attended upon him at his command. Then, in great delight, the lord of the *rākṣasas* addressed those *rākṣasa* women.

7. "You are to tell Vaidehī that Rāma and Lakṣmaṇa have been slain by Indrajit. Then take her in the flying palace Puṣpaka and show her the two of them, slain on the battlefield.

8. "That husband of hers, relying on whom she stubbornly spurned me, has been destroyed, along with his brother, in the vanguard of battle.

9. "Now Sītā Maithilī, free from anxiety, longing, and hope, and adorned with all manner of jewelry, will surely come to me.

*10. "Seeing that Rāma, along with Lakṣmaṇa, has succumbed to the power of Kāla in battle and finding no alternative, she will have her hopes finally dashed this very day."

11. Upon hearing those words of evil-minded Rāvaṇa, the *rākṣasa* women said, "So be it," and went off to where the flying palace Puṣpaka was.

12. Then, in compliance with Rāvaṇa's command, the *rākṣasa* women took the flying palace Puṣpaka and fetched Maithilī, who was in the *aśoka* grove.

13. The *rākṣasa* women seized Sītā, who was lost in sorrow for her husband, and forced her into the flying palace Puṣpaka.

14. Once Rāvaṇa had seen to it that Sītā had been taken aboard the flying palace Puṣpaka along with Trijaṭā, he had Laṅkā festooned with flags and banners.

15. And, in great delight, the lord of the *rākṣasas* had the following proclamation made throughout Laṅkā: "Indrajit has slain Rāghava and Lakṣmaṇa in battle!"

16. Meanwhile, Sītā, traveling with Trijaṭā in the flying palace, saw that practically the entire monkey army had been annihilated.

17. And she saw that the flesh-eating *rākṣasas* were delighted at heart, while the monkeys standing beside Rāma and Lakṣmaṇa were afflicted with sorrow.

18. Then Sītā spied both Lakṣmaṇa and Rāma lying unconscious on their beds of arrows, riddled with arrows.

19. Their armor was shattered and their bows had slipped from their grasp. Their every limb riddled with arrows, the two heroes looked like two pillars of arrows fallen to the ground.

20. When Sītā saw the two heroic brothers, those bulls among men, she was overwhelmed with terrible grief, and she lamented piteously.

21. Seeing those two brothers, who were equal in power to the gods, Sītā, overwhelmed with tears and sorrow, assumed that they were dead. Stricken with grief, she uttered these words.

The end of the thirty-seventh *sarga* of the *Yuddhakāṇḍa* of the *Śrī Rāmāyaṇa*.

Sarga 38

1. When Sītā, drawn with grief, saw that her husband as well as mighty Lakṣmaṇa had been struck down, she lamented piteously and profusely:

*2. "Those scholars who know the science of bodily signs said that I would bear sons and never be a widow. Now that Rāma has been slain, it is clear that all those wise men spoke falsely.

*3. "And they said that I would be the chief queen of a king who performed the rites of royalty, the wife of a great patron of sacrifices. Now that Rāma has been slain, it is clear that all those wise men spoke falsely.

*4. "And although they told me, 'You shall be the wife of a heroic king and very fortunate,' now that Rāma has been slain, it is clear that all those wise men spoke falsely.

*5. "And as for those astrologers who foretold in my presence that I should enjoy good fortune, now that Rāma has been slain, it is clear that all those wise men spoke falsely.

6. "And here, on my feet, are those lotus marks, whereby it is said women come to be consecrated for sovereignty together with their royal husbands.

7. "Nor, though I search for them, do I find on my body those inauspicious signs whereby unfortunate women become widows. Indeed, the signs on my body are meaningless.

8. "In the science of bodily signs, the lotus marks of women are said to be infallible. But now that Rāma has been slain, they have proven false for me.

9. "My hair is fine, even, and dark. My eyebrows do not meet. My legs are smooth and tapering, and my teeth are closely set.

10. "And my temples, eyes, hands, feet, ankles, and thighs are nicely developed. My nails are rounded and glossy. My fingers and toes are well proportioned.

11. "My breasts, their nipples sunken, are full and closely set. My navel is deep with sloping sides. My chest and sides are nicely developed.

12. "My complexion has the radiance of a jewel. My body hair is fine. Since I stand so firmly on my feet—all twelve points making contact—they said that I was possessed of auspicious signs.

13. "My hands and feet are of excellent color, without gaps, and marked with the auspicious sign of a whole barleycorn. Those who know the science of the bodily signs of girls said of me, 'She has that faint smile.'

14. "The brahman astrologers foretold that I should be consecrated for sovereignty together with my husband. Now that has all proven false.

15. "After scouring Janasthāna and finding out what had become of me, the two brothers crossed the imperturbable ocean only to be slain in a petty skirmish.

16. "Didn't the two Rāghavas obtain the divine weapon-spells of Varuṇa, Agni, Indra, and Vāyu, as well as the divine Brahmaśiras weapon-spell?

17. "My two protectors, Rāma and Lakṣmaṇa, who are comparable to Vāsava himself, have been slain in battle by an invisible foe through the power of illusion. Now there is no one to protect me.

18. "For in battle no enemy whom Rāghava could see would have escaped with his life, even were he as swift as thought itself.

19. "Since Rāma and his brother lie slain in battle, I see that nothing is beyond the power of Kāla and that it is impossible to avert one's destiny.

20. "I do not grieve for my slain husband and Lakṣmaṇa, nor for myself and my mother, as much as for my poor mother-in-law.

21. "For she must be constantly thinking, 'Oh, when will I see Rāma, his vow completed, return together with Sītā and Lakṣmaṇa?' "

22. But as Sītā was lamenting in this fashion, the *rākṣasa* woman Trijaṭā said to her, "Do not despair, my lady, for your husband still lives.

23. "And I shall give you powerful and convincing reasons, my lady, why the brothers Rāma and Lakṣmaṇa must be alive.

24. "For if their leader had been slain in battle, his troops' faces would not be so suffused with anger and animated with excitement.

25. "Moreover, Vaidehī, if those two heroes had really lost their lives, this celestial flying palace, which goes by the name of Puṣpaka, would not be carrying you.

26. "Then, too, when its heroic leader is slain, an army, dispirited and irresolute, drifts aimlessly across the battlefield, like a rudderless vessel on the water.

27. "But this army is neither confused nor despondent. On the contrary, it is moving swiftly to protect the two Kākutsthas, who have been defeated in battle by the power of illusion.

28. "You should be reassured by these signs, which presage happiness. You must realize that the Kākutsthas have not been slain. I tell you this out of affection.

29. "I have never uttered a falsehood, nor will I ever. Through your virtuous conduct and pleasant demeanor, you have found a place in my heart.

30. "These two could never be defeated in battle even by the gods and *asuras* together with Indra. I have told you this on the basis of my observation of their faces.

31. "And observe carefully, Maithilī, the most important sign of all: although they are both unconscious, their vital glow has not left them.

32. "For, invariably, when men have lost their vital spark and breath of life, a terrible change is apparent in their faces.

33. "So, daughter of Janaka, you must give up your grief, pain, and delusion on account of Rāma and Lakṣmaṇa. For it is not possible that they could have been killed this day."

34. When Sītā Maithilī, who was like a daughter of the gods, had heard these words of Trijaṭā, she cupped her hands in reverence and said this: "May it be so."

35. Trijaṭā then turned around the flying palace Puṣpaka, swift as thought, and took the despondent Sītā back to Laṅkā.

36. When Sītā, together with Trijaṭā, had descended from the flying palace Puṣpaka, the *rākṣasa* women took her straight back to the *aśoka* grove.

37. Sītā entered the *rākṣasa* lord's pleasure ground with its many groves of trees. And there, brooding about the king's sons whom she had just seen, she sank into the most profound despair.

The end of the thirty-eighth *sarga* of the *Yuddhakāṇḍa* of the *Śrī Rāmāyaṇa*.

Sarga 39

1–2. Meanwhile, overcome with grief, all the mighty monkey leaders, including Sugrīva, stood surrounding the two great sons of Daśaratha. As the two of them lay there drenched in blood, bound with the terrible bonds of arrows, their labored breathing was like the hissing of great serpents.

3. At that moment, because he was so hardy and through the exertion of his strength, powerful Rāma regained consciousness, though he remained bound by the arrows.

4. But then, when he saw that his brother was stricken—deeply wounded, covered with blood, his face deathly—he began to lament in his desolation.

5. "What do I care for Sītā or even for my life itself now that I see my brother lying defeated in battle?

6. "Were I to search the world, I could find another woman like Sītā, but never a brother, a companion, or a warrior to equal Lakṣmaṇa.

7. "If Lakṣmaṇa, the increaser of Sumitrā's joy, has indeed returned to the elements, then I shall abandon my life right before the eyes of the monkeys.

8. "Whatever shall I tell Kausalyā, and what shall I tell mother Kaikeyī? And how shall I tell mother Sumitrā, longing for the sight of her son?

9. "And how shall I console Sumitrā, trembling and shrieking like an osprey at the loss of her darling son, if I should return without him?

10. "And how shall I tell Śatrughna and the illustrious Bharata, if I were to go back again without him with whom I went to the forest?

11. "Alas! I shall not be able to endure the reproaches of Sumitrā. I shall abandon my body right here, for I cannot bear to go on living.

12. "Damn me, an ignoble evildoer, on whose account Lakṣmaṇa lies fallen on a bed of arrows, his life breaths ebbing.

13. "You always used to comfort me, Lakṣmaṇa, when I was downcast. But now, your life breaths ebbing, you can no longer even speak to me in my pain.

14. "That hero, who struck down so many *rākṣasas* in combat on the field of battle, now lies on the very same field, struck down by his foes.

15. "Lying on this bed of arrows, covered with his own blood, and bound in a web of arrows, he looks like the sun, bringer of light, as it sets.

16. "His vitals pierced with arrows, he can no longer see. And, although he cannot speak, the expression of his eyes betrays his torment.

17. "Just as that glorious hero followed me as I went to the forest, so will I now follow him to the abode of Yama.

18. "He always cherished his family, and he was ever devoted to me. But now through my failed tactics—ignoble as I am—he has been reduced to this state.

19. "I cannot recall heroic Lakṣmaṇa ever uttering a harsh or unpleasant word, even when he was enraged.

20. "Lakṣmaṇa, who could loose five hundred arrows in one swift motion, thus surpassed even Kārtavīrya himself in archery.

21. "He who, with his divine weapon-spells, could destroy the divine weapon-spells of even great Śakra and who deserves the most costly bed now lies stricken on the bare earth.

22. "In that I have failed to make Vibhīṣaṇa the king of the *rākṣasas*, there is no doubt that what has proven to be my idle boast will torment me.

23. "And you, King Sugrīva, should return home this very instant, for once mighty Rāvaṇa realizes that you no longer have me to assist you, he will attack.

24. "Placing Aṅgada in the lead, you, together with your troops and allies, must once again cross the ocean by that very same bridge.

25. "Hanumān accomplished feats in battle impossible for others to accomplish. I am also well pleased with the king of the apes and the overlord of the langurs.

26. "Aṅgada accomplished great deeds as did Mainda and Dvivida, while Kesarin and Saṃpāti fought fearsome battles in the war.

27. "Gavaya, Gavākṣa, Śarabha, Gaja, and the other tawny monkeys fought on my behalf, heedless of their lives.

28. "Truly, Sugrīva, it is impossible for men to evade their fate. Nonetheless, Sugrīva, scorcher of your foes, in your anxiety lest you transgress righteousness, you did everything that was possible for a friend or ally to do.

29. "Bulls among monkeys! You have discharged the obligations of friendship. I therefore give you all leave. You may depart as you please."

30. As those tawny-eyed monkeys listened to Rāma's lament, they began to weep.

31. Meanwhile, Vibhīṣaṇa, having prevented all the troops from fleeing, rushed back, mace in hand, to where Rāghava lay.

32. But when the monkeys saw him rushing toward them, like a mass of black collyrium, they all fled, thinking that he was Indrajit Rāvaṇi.

The end of the thirty-ninth *sarga* of the *Yuddhakāṇḍa* of the *Śrī Rāmāyaṇa*.

Sarga 40

1. Then the mighty and powerful king of the tawny monkeys asked: "Why is the army fleeing wildly, like a ship driven to and fro by contrary winds at sea?"

2–3. Hearing Sugrīva's words, Vālin's son, Aṅgada, replied: "Can't you see that the two great heroes, the sons of Daśaratha, Rāma and mighty Lakṣmaṇa, are lying on beds of arrows, drenched with blood and tightly bound with webs of arrows?"

4. Then Sugrīva, lord of the monkeys, responded to his son, Aṅgada: "I do not doubt that that is one reason. Still, there must be some other cause for their alarm.

5. "For the tawny monkeys, their faces downcast, have dropped their weapons and are fleeing in all directions, their eyes wide with terror.

6. "They have no sense of shame before one another; nor do they look back. They drag one another out of their way and leap over the fallen."

7. At that very moment, the hero Vibhīṣaṇa, mace in hand, hailed Sugrīva and then stared at Rāghava.

8. Perceiving that it was Vibhīṣaṇa, who was the cause of the monkeys' terror, Sugrīva said to Jāmbavān, the king of the apes, who was close at hand:

9. "It is Vibhīṣaṇa who has come. Upon seeing him, these bulls among monkeys are fleeing in terror, fearing that it was Rāvaṇa's son.

10. "You must stop them, for, in their terror, they are running off in all directions as fast as they can. Tell them that it is only Vibhīṣaṇa who has come."

11. Addressed in this fashion by Sugrīva, Jāmbavān, the king of the apes, turned back the monkeys from their flight and reassured them.

12. When the monkeys heard the words of the king of the apes and saw that it was indeed Vibhīṣaṇa, they all abandoned their fear and returned.

13. But as for righteous Vibhīṣaṇa, when he saw the bodies of Rāma and Lakṣmaṇa riddled with arrows, he became deeply distraught.

14. Wiping their eyes with a hand moistened with water, he wept and lamented, his heart overwhelmed with sorrow.

15. "These two powerful and brave warriors, delighting in battle, have been reduced to this condition by those treacherous warriors, the *rākṣasas*.

16. "With his crooked *rākṣasa* mind, my brother's evil and unworthy son has tricked these two whose valor was untainted by guile.

17. "Drenched with blood, they lie sleeping on the ground. Completely riddled with arrows, they look like two hedgehogs.

18. "These bulls among men, upon whose might I had pinned my hopes for royal consecration, now both lie sleeping on the point of death.

19. "Though still living, I am now as good as dead, my hopes of kingship dashed. Meanwhile, my enemy, Rāvaṇa, has accomplished his vow and has had his wish fulfilled."

20. As Vibhīṣaṇa was lamenting in this fashion, powerful Sugrīva, king of the tawny monkeys, embraced him and said this:

21. "Knower of righteousness, you shall obtain kingship over Laṅkā. Of this there can be no doubt. Rāvaṇa and his son will not retain the kingship here.

22. "Rāghava and Lakṣmaṇa are both merely pinioned by arrows. Once they shake off their stupor, they will surely kill Rāvaṇa and all his troops in battle."

23. When he had consoled and reassured the *rākṣasa* in this fashion, he spoke to his father-in-law, Suṣeṇa, who stood at his side.

24. "Take the brothers Rāma and Lakṣmaṇa, tamers of their foes, once they have regained consciousness, and, together with the heroic troops of tawny monkeys, go back to Kiṣkindhā.

25. "But as for me, I shall slay Rāvaṇa along with his son and his kinsmen and bring back Maithilī, just as Śakra did Śrī when she was lost."

26–27. When Suṣeṇa had heard this speech of the lord of the monkeys, he spoke these words: "I have heard about a great and terrible battle between the gods and the *asuras*. At that time, the *dānavas*, who were expert in the use of arrows, concealed themselves and thus repeatedly struck down the gods although they, too, were skilled in weaponry.

28. "Then although they were afflicted, unconscious, or dead, Bṛhaspati restored them with healing herbs and with magical spells replete with *mantras*.

29. "Therefore, let Saṃpāti, Panasa, and the other monkeys go with all possible speed to the ocean of milk to bring back those healing herbs.

30. "Those tawny monkeys will recognize the two powerful healing herbs that grow on the mountains there, the divine *saṃjīvakaraṇī*, restorer of life, and the *viśalyā*, healer of arrow wounds, which was created by the gods.

31. "In that great ocean, there are two mountains called Candra and Droṇa. There, where the nectar of immortality was churned forth, is where those two supreme herbs of healing are to be found.

32. "Those two supreme herbs of healing were planted on the mountains there by the gods. So, king, let Hanumān, son of Vāyu, go there."

33. Just at that moment there arose a wind hurling up the water in the ocean, driving away the lightning-streaked clouds, and seeming almost to shake the very mountains.

34. That powerful wind, driven by a pair of wings, snapped the branches of all the island's great trees and sent them flying, roots and all, into the salt sea.

35. The hooded serpents who dwelt there were terrified and the great sea serpents swiftly plunged deep into the salt sea.

36. Then, a moment later, all the monkeys spied immensely powerful Garuḍa Vainateya as radiant as fire.

37. And when those great serpents, who had assumed the form of arrows and who had bound fast those two virtuous and immensely powerful men, saw him coming, they fled in all directions.

38. Then Suparṇa, spying the Kākutsthas, greeted them and stroked their faces, as lustrous as the moon, with both his hands.

39. No sooner had Vainateya touched them than their wounds healed over and their bodies immediately became smooth and lustrous once more.

40. And their cardinal virtues—courage, prowess, strength, vigor, and fortitude, as well as their insight, intelligence, and memory—returned to them with redoubled force.

41. Helping the two delighted heroes, equals of Vāsava, to their feet, Garuḍa embraced them. Rāma then said this:

42. "Through your grace, sir, we have overcome the great calamity wrought here by Rāvaṇi and have been swiftly restored to our full strength.

43. "On meeting you, my heart is as soothed as if I had met my father, Daśaratha, or my grandfather, Aja.

44. "You are endowed with beauty and adorned with heavenly garlands and unguents. You wear spotless garments and are adorned with heavenly ornaments. Who are you, sir?"

45. Then mighty and powerful Vainateya, king of the birds, delighted at heart, his eyes lighting up with joy, said to him:

46. "I am Garutmān, Kākutstha, your dear comrade, your second life breath outside your body. I have come here to the aid of you both.

47–48. "Neither the powerful *asuras* nor the mighty *dānavas*, not even the gods and *gandharvas* with Indra of the hundred sacrifices at their head, would have been able to loose this terrible bondage of arrows effected by cruel Indrajit through the power of illusion.

49. "Through the *rākṣasa*'s power of illusion, those great serpents, the sons of Kadrū, sharp fanged and fiercely venomous, had become arrows and fastened themselves upon you.

50. "Along with your brother Lakṣmaṇa, a slayer of enemies in battle, you have been fortunate, righteous Rāma, true in your valor.

51. "For as soon as I heard what had happened, I came at once, in great haste, out of my affection for you both and to honor my friendship.

52. "Now that you have been freed from the very dreadful bondage of those arrows, you must both be constantly on your guard.

53. "By their very nature all *rākṣasas* are treacherous fighters in battle. On the other hand, the strength of pure-hearted heroes, such as yourselves, lies in the fact that they are honorable.

54. "Therefore, you two should not trust *rākṣasas* on the battlefield. This very example serves to show that *rākṣasas* are always treacherous."

55. When mighty Suparṇa had addressed Rāma in this fashion, he embraced him with the affection befitting a friend and began to take his leave.

56. "Rāghava, my righteous friend, compassionate even to your enemies, I should like to take leave of you, for I shall now depart just as I came.

57. "Once you have slaughtered the male population of Laṅkā with your waves of arrows, sparing only the children and the aged, and have slain your enemy Rāvaṇa, you shall surely recover Sītā."

58–59. When mighty Suparṇa, swift in flight, had spoken these words in this fashion and had healed Rāma of his wounds there in the midst of the forest-dwelling monkeys, he reverently circled and embraced him. Then, hurling himself into the sky like Pavana, Suparṇa departed.

60. Seeing that the two Rāghavas were healed of their wounds, the leaders of the monkey troops unleashed lionlike roars and lashed their tails.

61. They beat the *bherī* drums and made the *mṛdaṅgas* resound. They blew their conches and frolicked about happily just as before.

62. The valiant monkeys, who used trees as their weapons, clapped their upper arms again and again. Ripping up trees of various kinds, they took their stand there by the hundreds of thousands.

63. Emitting mighty roars and terrifying the night-roaming *rākṣasas*, the leaping monkeys advanced upon the gates of Laṅkā, eager for battle.

64. The terrifying and tumultuous roar that arose from those leaders of the troops of the tree-dwelling monkeys was like the frightful rumbling of the thundering storm clouds in the dead of night at summer's end.

The end of the fortieth *sarga* of the *Yuddhakāṇḍa* of the *Śrī Rāmāyaṇa*.

Sarga 41

1. Then Rāvaṇa and the *rākṣasas* heard the tumultuous sound of the swift monkeys as they roared.

2. Upon hearing that mighty uproar with its deep and joyous resonance, he spoke these words in the midst of his ministers:

3–4. "From this tremendous uproar, arising from these many excited monkeys, roaring like thunderclouds, it is clear beyond a doubt that they are experiencing tremendous joy. Indeed, the ocean itself, abode of Varuṇa, is agitated by their loud cries.

5. "Granted, the two brothers, Rāma and Lakṣmaṇa, have been bound fast with sharp arrows; nonetheless, this great uproar causes me concern."

6. Having addressed these words to his counselors, the lord of the *rākṣasas* then spoke to the *rākṣasas*, sons of chaos, who stood at their posts all around him.

7. "Find out at once why all these forest-dwelling monkeys are rejoicing at a time when they ought to be grieving."

8. Addressed by him in this fashion, they climbed the ramparts in great agitation and surveyed the army that was under the protection of great Sugrīva.

9. When those *rākṣasas* saw the two illustrious Rāghavas standing there, freed from the terrible bondage of arrows, their hearts sank.

10. Terrified at heart and with faces downcast, they all descended from the ramparts and presented themselves before the *rākṣasa* lord.

11. Their dismay evident in their faces, the night-roaming *rākṣasas*, skilled in speech, broke the bad news to Rāvaṇa faithfully and accurately.

12–13. "Indrajit had bound the two brothers, Rāma and Lakṣmaṇa, with bonds of arrows so that their arms were immobilized. But just now, on the battlefield, we saw those two, powerful as lordly elephants, freed from the bondage of arrows, like two elephants who have broken their chains."

14. When the mighty lord of the *rākṣasas* had heard those words of theirs, he was overwhelmed with anxiety and grief. With downcast face, he said:

15–16. "In combat, Indrajit had struck down and bound those two with fearsome and unfailing arrows. Resembling venomous serpents and brilliant as the sun, they were given to him as a boon. If, having once been subject to such bondage by weapons, my two enemies are now free, then I see that my entire army is in peril.

17. "Those arrows, as powerful as the great serpent Vāsuki, which used to steal away the lives of my enemies in battle, have now been rendered useless."

18. Having spoken in this fashion, Rāvaṇa, hissing like a serpent in his rage, addressed a *rākṣasa* called Dhūmrākṣa there in the midst of the *rākṣasas*.

19. "Take a large force of *rākṣasas*, fearsome in their deeds, and go forth to slaughter Rāma together with the monkeys."

20. Addressed in this fashion by the wise lord of the *rākṣasas*, Dhūmrākṣa made his obeisance and, in great excitement, left the king's residence.

21. As he passed through the palace gates, he ordered the officer in charge of the garrison, "Mobilize the troops at once! What use is delay to one eager to fight?"

22. When the officer in charge of the garrison, the leader of his troops, had heard Dhūmrākṣa's words, he quickly mobilized his troops following the command of Rāvaṇa.

23. Those mighty and terrifying night-roaming *rākṣasas* fastened on their war bells and, roaring loudly in their great excitement, surrounded Dhūmrākṣa.

24–25. They wielded various weapons. In their hands they held lances and war hammers. Roaring like thunderclouds, those terrible *rākṣasas* marched forth vigorously armed with maces, spears, staves, iron cudgels, iron clubs, short javelins, crescent-headed arrows, darts, and battle-axes.

26–27. Unassailable as tigers, those tigers among *rākṣasas* sallied forth. Some wore armor and rode in chariots adorned with banners, inlaid with fretworks of gold, and drawn by donkeys with faces of many different kinds. Others rode extremely swift horses and lordly elephants intoxicated with rut.

28. With harsh cries, Dhūmrākṣa then mounted a heavenly chariot yoked to donkeys, which had the faces of wolves and lions and were adorned with gold.

29. Laughing, the mighty Dhūmrākṣa, surrounded by *rākṣasas*, proceeded to the western gate, where the troop leader Hanumān was stationed.

30. But as that very terrible and fearsome looking *rākṣasa* proceeded, savage birds of ill omen appeared in the sky, blocking his path.

31. A very fearsome vulture alighted on the top of his chariot, while long lines of carrion birds perched on the edge of his battle standard.

32. A huge, headless corpse, ghastly pale and drenched with blood, lay on the earth in Dhūmrākṣa's path, emitting discordant sounds.

33. It rained blood and the earth shook. The wind blew in an unfavorable direction with a thunderous roar. Shrouded in a flood of darkness, the directions were no longer visible.

34. Seeing those very gruesome portents that had appeared, bringing terror to the *rākṣasas*, Dhūmrākṣa himself was shaken.

35. As that mighty and very fearsome *rākṣasa*, eager for battle, marched forth, surrounded by many night-roaming *rākṣasas*, he gazed upon the army under the protection of Rāghava's arms, which, with its many monkeys, resembled an ocean.

The end of the forty-first *sarga* of the *Yuddhakāṇḍa* of the *Śrī Rāmāyaṇa*.

Sarga 42

1. When the monkeys saw the *rākṣasa* Dhūmrākṣa marching forth with his fearsome cries, they all roared in their excitement, eager for battle.

2. Then a frenzied battle broke out between the tawny monkeys and the *rākṣasas*, who slaughtered one another—the former with terrifying trees, the latter with lances and war hammers.

3. The *rākṣasas* cut down the fearsome monkeys on all sides, while the monkeys smashed the *rākṣasas* to the ground with trees.

4. And the *rākṣasas*, in their fury, pierced the monkeys with sharp and fearsome-looking arrows, fletched with heron feathers and flying true.

5–6. Although they were wounded by the *rākṣasas* with fearsome maces, spears, mallets, and war hammers, various and dreadful iron clubs, and sharp tridents, the very powerful monkeys, their fervor aroused by their indignation, fearlessly accomplished great feats.

7. Their limbs pierced with arrows and their bodies pierced with lances, the leaders of the troops of tawny monkeys seized trees and boulders.

8. Bellowing and calling out their names, the tawny monkeys, fearsome in their speed, annihilated the fearsome *rākṣasas* on every side.

9–10. It was an amazing and horrific battle that took place between the monkeys and the *rākṣasas*. With a victorious air, the monkeys annihilated some of the *rākṣasas* with various boulders and trees with many branches. Other *rākṣasas*, accustomed to drinking blood, now spewed it from their mouths.

11. Some had their flanks ripped open, others were beaten to a shapeless mass with trees; still others were pulverized by boulders, while some were rent with fangs.

12–860. The ground was littered with torn and broken banners, slain donkeys, shattered chariots, fallen night-roaming *rākṣasas*, lordly elephants that resembled mountains, and, together with their riders, war-horses that had been crushed with mountain peaks by the forest-dwelling monkeys.

13. The *rākṣasas* had their faces ripped open by the sharp claws of the swift monkeys, who leapt at them again and again, fearsome in their valor.

14. Their faces pale, their hair flying wildly about, the *rākṣasas* fell to the ground again and again, fainting from the smell of blood.

15. But some of the *rākṣasas*, fearsome in their valor, attacked the tawny monkeys with their open hands, which struck like thunderbolts.

16. But as they rushed swiftly onward, they were struck down by the monkeys—who were swifter still—with fists, feet, fangs, and trees.

17. Seeing his forces put to flight, that bull among *rākṣasas*, Dhūmrākṣa, in a rage, began to slaughter those monkeys, who were eager for battle.

18. Some of the monkeys, wounded with darts, gushed blood, while others, smashed by war hammers, fell to the ground.

19. Some were wounded with iron clubs, others were slashed with short javelins. Still others, struck down by spears, staggered and breathed their last.

20. Some of the forest-dwelling monkeys were knocked to the ground, drenched in blood; still others, fleeing the battle, were slaughtered by the furious *rākṣasas*.

21. Some of them lay on one side, their chests ripped open; still others were ripped open by tridents so that their entrails spilled forth.

22. With its hosts of tawny monkeys and *rākṣasas*, its abundance of weapons, and masses of boulders and trees, that great battle looked truly frightening.

23. With the twanging of bowstrings in place of the sweet sound of the lute, the gasps of the dying for the beating of time, and the faint cries of the wounded in place of singing, the battle resembled a musical recital.

24. And as for Dhūmrākṣa, he stood laughing in the forefront of the battle, bow in hand, as he scattered the monkeys in all directions with showers of arrows.

25. When Māruti saw that the army was being harassed and tormented by Dhūmrākṣa, he seized an enormous boulder and rushed at him in a rage.

26. Equal in might to his father, his eyes now doubly red with rage, he hurled that boulder at Dhūmrākṣa's chariot.

27. When Dhūmrākṣa saw that boulder hurtling toward him, he grabbed his mace in great agitation and, quickly leaping from his chariot, took his stand on the ground.

28. As it fell to the ground, the boulder smashed his chariot along with its wheels, poles, horses, flagstaffs, and bows.

29. After smashing his chariot, Hanumān, son of Māruta, began to slaughter the *rākṣasas* with trees—trunks, branches, and all.

30. Some of the *rākṣasas*, crushed by trees, their heads smashed, lay on the ground, drenched in blood.

31. When he had put the *rākṣasa* army to flight, Hanumān, son of Māruta, seized a mountain peak and charged straight at Dhūmrākṣa.

32. With a roar, mighty Dhūmrākṣa seized his mace and charged violently toward Hanumān as the latter ran toward him.

33. Then, in a fury, Dhūmrākṣa forcefully brought his mace, with its numerous spikes, down upon Hanumān's skull.

34. Struck with that fearsome-looking mace, the monkey, who had the strength of Māruta, shrugged off that blow and brought the mountain peak down on the middle of Dhūmrākṣa's head.

35. Struck by that mountain peak, his every limb buckling, he fell violently to the ground, like a shattered mountain.

36. When the surviving night-roaming *rākṣasas* saw that Dhūmrākṣa had been slain, they were terrified. They fled back to Laṅkā with the leaping monkeys still slaughtering them.

37. When the great son of Pavana had slain his enemy and sent rivers of blood flowing in all directions, he succumbed to the fatigue born from slaughtering his enemies. Then, honored by the monkeys, he experienced great joy.

The end of the forty-second *sarga* of the *Yuddhakāṇḍa* of the *Śrī Rāmāyaṇa*.

Sarga 43

1. When Rāvaṇa, lord of the *rākṣasas*, heard that Dhūmrākṣa had been slain, he said this to the officer in charge of the garrison, who stood before him with his hands cupped in reverence:

2. "Let unassailable *rākṣasas* of fearsome valor go forth led by Akampana, skilled in the use of every weapon."

3. Then, at the urging of the officer in charge of the garrison, fearsome-looking *rākṣasa* leaders, with fearsome eyes and bearing all kinds of weapons, marched forth.

4. Wearing earrings of burnished gold, Akampana mounted a huge chariot and set forth, surrounded by fearsome *rākṣasas*.

5. He was incapable of being shaken in a great battle, even by the gods themselves. Thus he was called Akampana, the unshakeable, and, in their midst, he was like the sun in blazing energy.

6. But as he raced forth filled with fury in his eagerness to fight, the horses drawing his chariot were seized with a lethargy that had no apparent cause.

7. Though normally he delighted in battle, his left eye now began to twitch, his face took on a sickly hue, and his voice began to crack.

8. Although the weather had been clear, the sky grew dark and a harsh wind blew. Fierce birds and beasts all uttered fearsome cries.

9. But, ignoring these ominous signs, Akampana, whose shoulders were as massive as a lion's and whose stride was that of a tiger, proceeded toward the battleground.

10. And as the *rākṣasa* marched forth with his *rākṣasas*, he uttered a roar so mighty that it seemed to make the ocean itself tremble.

11. Terrified by that sound, the vast army of monkeys, armed with trees and boulders, arrayed itself for battle.

12. Then an extremely violent battle broke out between the monkeys and the *rākṣasas*, who were prepared to lay down their lives for the sake of Rāma and Rāvaṇa, respectively.

13. The tawny monkeys and the *rākṣasas* were all exceedingly powerful heroes, all as huge as mountains. And they were eager to slaughter one another.

14. As those swift warriors roared in battle and bellowed at one another in their fury, a tremendous din arose.

15. The red dust, thick and terrible, kicked up by the *rākṣasas* and tawny monkeys, obscured the ten directions.

16. Enveloped in that dust, as pale as floating silk, the opposing forces could not see one another on the battlefield.

17. Because of that dust, neither flag nor banner, armor nor horse, weapon nor chariot was visible.

18. A tremendous din could be heard as they roared and raced about in that tumultuous battle, though nothing at all could be seen.

19. In their towering fury, tawny monkeys killed tawny monkeys in battle, while *rākṣasas* slaughtered *rākṣasas* in the darkness.

20. And as the monkeys and *rākṣasas* slaughtered friend and foe alike, they drenched the earth with blood, making it slick with mud.

21. The gouts of blood that were spattered all around settled the dust, and the ground was littered with dead bodies.

22. With speed and power, the tawny monkeys and the *rākṣasas* slaughtered one another with trees, javelins, boulders, darts, maces, iron clubs, and cudgels of iron.

23. Fighting with their arms, which resembled iron clubs, the tawny monkeys, fearsome in their deeds and huge as mountains, slaughtered the *rākṣasas* in battle.

24. For their part, the furious *rākṣasas*, with darts and iron cudgels in hand, slaughtered the monkeys there with their pitiless weapons.

25. But, counterattacking, the tawny monkeys bravely seized those weapons from them and smashed the *rākṣasas* with huge trees and enormous boulders.

26. At that juncture, the heroic tawny monkeys Kumuda, Nala, and Mainda, in a towering rage, charged with unparalleled speed.

27. And, as if in play, those immensely swift leaders of the troops of tawny monkeys wrought tremendous slaughter with their trees in the front ranks of the *rākṣasa* army.

The end of the forty-third *sarga* of the *Yuddhakāṇḍa* of the *Śrī Rāmāyaṇa*.

Sarga 44

1. When he witnessed the immense feat accomplished by the foremost among the monkeys, Akampana gave vent to a savage fury in the midst of the battle.

2. Seeing that feat of his enemies, he was beside himself with rage. Brandishing his mighty bow, he said these words to his charioteer:

3. "Charioteer! Drive the chariot at once to where so many monkeys are slaughtering so many *rākṣasas* in battle.

4. "For there, armed with trees and boulders, mighty monkeys with fearsome bodies stand facing me.

5. "It appears that they have crushed the entire *rākṣasa* army, and therefore I wish to exterminate these boastful warriors."

6. Then, in his chariot, whose horses were whipped to a gallop, Akampana, foremost of chariot-warriors, in his fury, assailed the tawny monkeys with a hail of arrows.

7. The monkeys were unable to stand before him in battle, much less to fight. Routed by Akampana's arrows, every last one of them fled.

8. Now, when mighty Hanumān saw that his kin had come under the power of Akampana and, indeed, the power of death, he rushed over.

9. When the heroic leaders of the troops of leaping monkeys saw that great leaping monkey, they all gathered together around him in the battle.

10. When the leaders of the troops of tawny monkeys saw Hanumān take his stand there, they recovered their strength, placing their trust in that powerful warrior.

11. But as Hanumān, who looked like a mountain, took his stand there, Akampana pelted him with arrows, just as great Indra might with torrents of rain.

12. Paying no heed to the hail of sharp arrows falling on his body, the mighty monkey set his mind on killing Akampana.

13. Laughing, Hanumān, the immensely powerful son of Māruta, charged that *rākṣasa*. As he did so, he shook the very earth, or so it seemed.

14. Roaring and blazing with energy, he took on a form that was as irresistible as a blazing fire.

15. Realizing that he had no weapon, that bull among tawny monkeys, in a transport of rage, swiftly ripped up a mountain by its roots.

16. Grasping that huge mountain in one hand, mighty Māruti swung it about, uttering a tremendous roar.

17. With it, he rushed upon the *rākṣasa* lord Akampana, just as Indra, smasher of citadels, with his *vajra*, rushed upon Namuci in battle.

18. But when Akampana saw that mountain peak held aloft, he smashed it to pieces from afar with huge half-moon-headed arrows.

19. Seeing the mountaintop shattered in midair by the *rākṣasa*'s arrows and fallen in pieces, Hanumān was beside himself with rage.

20. Filled with rage and pride, the tawny monkey raced over to an *aśvakarṇa* tree, as tall as a mighty mountain, and swiftly tore it up by the roots.

21. Seizing that *aśvakarṇa* tree with its vast trunk, Hanumān, blazing with splendor, swung it about in battle, laughing in supreme delight.

22. Racing onward with tremendous speed and breaking down trees in his haste, Hanumān, in a towering rage, tore up the earth with the pounding of his feet.

23. Wise Hanumān then smashed elephants along with their riders, chariot-warriors together with their chariots, and the *rākṣasa* foot soldiers as well.

24. When the *rākṣasas* spied Hanumān, enraged and wreaking slaughter on the battlefield like Yama himself, the ender of all things, they fled in all directions.

25. Seeing the enraged Hanumān rushing onward and terrifying the *rākṣasas*, heroic Akampana flew into a rage and roared.

26. Akampana then pierced immensely powerful Hanumān with fourteen sharp arrows that tore through his body.

27. Riddled in this fashion with many volleys of arrows, heroic Hanumān resembled a densely forested mountain.

28. Then, ripping up yet another tree and exerting unsurpassed force, he quickly struck the *rākṣasa* lord Akampana on the head.

29. Struck with that tree by the wise monkey lord in his wrath, the *rākṣasa* fell and died.

30. When the *rākṣasas* saw the *rākṣasa* lord Akampana lying on the ground slain, they all trembled, like trees in an earthquake.

31. Terrified and defeated, the *rākṣasas* all dropped their weapons and fled to Laṅkā, pursued by the monkeys.

32. Their hair flying, their pride shattered, their limbs running with sweat, they fled panicked in defeat, gasping for breath.

33. Trampling one another and glancing behind them again and again in their terror, they entered the city in total disarray.

34. Once the *rākṣasas* had entered Laṅkā, all the immensely powerful tawny monkeys gathered and honored Hanumān.

35. And, for his part, Hanumān, endowed with strength, in great delight graciously honored all the tawny monkeys according to their merit.

36. With a victorious air the tawny monkeys roared at the top of their lungs and dragged about those *rākṣasas* who were still alive.

37. In encountering and slaughtering the *rākṣasas*, the great monkey Māruti achieved as much heroic glory as did Viṣṇu in slaying the great, terrible, and mighty *asura*, destroyer of his foes, in the vanguard of the hosts.

38. Then the hosts of the gods, Rāma himself, and the exceedingly powerful Lakṣmaṇa, as well as mighty Vibhīṣaṇa, and the leaping monkeys, headed by Sugrīva, honored that monkey.

The end of the forty-fourth *sarga* of the *Yuddhakāṇḍa* of the *Śrī Rāmāyaṇa*.

Sarga 45

1. When the lord of the *rākṣasas* heard about the slaying of Akampana, he was enraged. His face somewhat downcast, he looked at his ministers.

2. He brooded for a while, and then, after taking counsel with his counselors, he made a tour of the city of Laṅkā in order to inspect all its military encampments.

3. He saw that the city of Laṅkā was protected by hosts of *rākṣasas*, surrounded by military encampments, and garlanded with flags and banners.

4. Perceiving that the city was besieged, Rāvaṇa, lord of the *rākṣasas*, angrily spoke at that critical moment to Prahasta, who was skilled in warfare.

5. "You are skilled in warfare. I can see no means other than war to free this city, which is hard-pressed and closely besieged.

6. "Only Kumbhakarṇa, you—the general of my army—Indrajit, Nikumbha, or I would be capable of bearing such a burden.

7. "So you must take the troops from here and, placing them under your command, march forth swiftly for victory, to where all the forest-dwelling monkeys are.

8. "In the face of your sortie, the irresolute army of tawny monkeys, hearing the roar of the roaring lords of the *rākṣasas*, will surely flee.

9. "For monkeys are irresolute, undisciplined, and fickle-minded. They will no more be able to withstand your roaring than are elephants the roaring of lions.

10. "Once the army has fled, Rāma, along with Saumitri, powerless and lacking support, will fall into your hands, Prahasta.

11. "We risk a great calamity, and victory is far from certain in this matter. So tell me what you think is best for us, whether I find it agreeable or not."

12. Addressed in this fashion by Rāvaṇa, Prahasta, the general of the army, said this to the lord of the *rākṣasas*, just as Uśanas might to the lord of the *asuras*:

13. "We discussed this earlier, your majesty, together with your able counselors. We debated the matter with due consideration for one another.

14. "I concluded that our well-being could be assured only through the return of Sītā. I foresaw that, if she were not returned, it would mean war, and that is exactly what has come upon us.

15. "You have always honored me with gifts, tokens of respect, and all manner of kind words. Would I not now, at such a critical moment, do what pleases you?

16. "For I do not care for my life, my sons, my wives, or my wealth. Just watch me as I strive to sacrifice my life for your sake in battle."

17. When Prahasta, the general of the army, had addressed his master, Rāvaṇa, in this fashion, he said this to the troop commanders who stood before him: "Assemble a large force of *rākṣasas* for me at once.

18. "Once I have slain the forest-dwelling monkeys on the battlefield today with the crushing force of those thunderbolts that are my arrows, the carrion birds may eat of their flesh to their heart's content."

19. Addressed in this fashion by Prahasta, the troop commanders, making haste, mustered their forces at the *rākṣasa*'s palace.

20. Within the hour Laṅkā was filled with *rākṣasa* heroes who, armed with every sort of sharp weapon, resembled elephants.

21. As they gratified the sacred fire, eater of oblations, and made obeisance to the brahmans, a fragrant breeze began to blow, bearing the aroma of clarified butter.

22. Prepared for battle and in great excitement, they took garlands of various kinds that had been consecrated with sacred spells and adorned themselves with them.

23. When they saw their king, Rāvaṇa, the *rākṣasas*, clad in armor and armed with their bows, leapt up swiftly and encircled Prahasta.

24. Then, taking leave of the king, Prahasta bid them beat the fearsome *bherī* drum as he mounted a celestial chariot well equipped for war.

25. Yoked to the swiftest of horses and driven by a skilled charioteer, it rumbled like a great storm cloud and blazed with the brilliance of the moon and sun.

26. With its serpent banners it was irresistible. It had a splendid fender and was beautiful in every part. It was covered with a fretwork of gold and seemed almost to be laughing with its splendor.

27. Then, once he had received his orders from Rāvaṇa, Prahasta mounted that chariot and, surrounded by his vast army, drove swiftly out of Laṅkā.

28. As the general of the armies sallied forth, the rumble of war drums, like that of thunderclouds, and the sound of conches could be heard.

29. In the vanguard, preceding Prahasta, marched huge *rākṣasas* with terrifying forms, uttering dreadful cries.

30. And so, surrounded by that vast and dreadful army in military array and resembling a herd of elephants, he sallied forth from the eastern gate.

31. As Prahasta went forth swiftly in anger, surrounded by that army whose vast multitude was like the ocean, he resembled Kāla, the ender of all things.

32. As he and the roaring *rākṣasas* set forth, their clamor caused all the creatures of Laṅkā to utter unnatural cries.

33. Rising into the cloudless sky, birds that feed on flesh and blood wheeled in clockwise circles around his chariot.

34. Dreadful jackals howled, belching forth flames of fire.

35. A blazing meteor fell from the sky, and a harsh wind blew. The heavenly bodies, occluding one another, were no longer visible.

926*–36. And over the *rākṣasa*'s chariot, harshly thundering clouds poured down blood, drenching his followers. Meanwhile, a vulture, facing to the south, perched on the top of his flagstaff.

37. Although his charioteer was of the *sūta* caste and was a skilled driver of horses, his whip repeatedly slipped from his hand as he plunged into battle.

38. And the extraordinary and radiant splendor that he displayed as he set forth vanished in an instant, while his horses stumbled on the level ground.

39. As Prahasta, famed for his strength and valor, marched forth, the monkey army advanced upon him for battle, armed with various weapons.

40. Then a tumultuous sound arose from the tawny monkeys as they broke off trees and seized heavy boulders.

41. Both armies—that of the hosts of *rākṣasas* and that of the forest-dwelling monkeys—were in a frenzy of excitement. They were swift, capable, and intent upon slaughtering one another. As they hurled their challenges at one another, one could hear a tremendous din.

42. Then the evil-minded Prahasta hurled himself upon the army of the monkey king. He plunged into that fast-moving host, as a moth, intent upon death, plunges into the fire.

The end of the forty-fifth *sarga* of the *Yuddhakāṇḍa* of the *Śrī Rāmāyaṇa*.

Sarga 46

1–2. The vast army of roaring monkeys, powerful and infuriated, watched as Prahasta—huge, terrifying, of terrifying valor, and surrounded by *rākṣasas*—marched forth, bellowing.

3–4. As the *rākṣasas*, eager for victory, hurled themselves upon the monkeys, the swords, javelins, broadswords, arrows, lances, cudgels, maces, iron clubs, darts, various battle-axes, and splendid bows they had taken up glittered.

5. Bounding toward them, the bulls among monkeys, eager for battle, seized flowering trees and boulders that were long and broad.

6. As the two vast forces clashed with each other, the one side raining stones, the other arrows, a huge battle broke out between them.

7. Numerous *rākṣasas* slaughtered numerous leaders of the monkey troops in battle, while numerous monkeys slaughtered numerous *rākṣasas*.

8. Some of the monkeys were rent with lances, others by discuses. Some were struck with iron clubs, while others were hacked with battle-axes.

9. Still others fell to the ground, robbed of their life breaths, while some, ensnared in the continuous volley of arrows, were pierced to the heart.

10. Some, cut in two with swords, fell to the ground, twitching. Still other monkeys were pierced by *rākṣasas* through their flanks with lances.

11. But as for the monkeys, in their fury, they crushed hordes of *rākṣasas* to the ground on every side with trees and mountain peaks.

12. Struck violently with fists and open hands, whose palms had the force of thunderbolts, the *rākṣasas*, their teeth and eyes knocked out, vomited blood from their mouths.

13. A tumultuous sound—the cries of those screaming in their affliction and the lionlike roars of those who were bellowing—arose from the tawny monkeys and the *rākṣasas* in battle.

14. Rolling their eyes in rage, the pitiless monkeys and *rākṣasas*, following the path of heroes, fearlessly performed great feats.

15. Prahasta's companions, Narāntaka, Kumbhahanu, Mahānāda, and Samunnata, all slaughtered forest-dwelling monkeys.

16. But as they launched their swift attack, slaughtering the monkeys, Dvivida killed one of them, Narāntaka, with a mountain peak.

17. Then the nimble-handed monkey Durmukha ripped up a huge tree by the roots and, with it, killed the *rākṣasa* Samunnata.

18. Next, powerful Jāmbavān, in a towering rage, seized a huge boulder and brought it down upon Mahānāda's chest.

19. Then the mighty *rākṣasa* Kumbhahanu, confronted by Tāra, was struck on the head with a tree and so died.

20. Unable to endure this deed, Prahasta, mounted in his chariot, bow in hand, began a fearsome slaughter of the forest-dwelling monkeys.

21. Then both armies swirled about like a maelstrom, and from them arose a sound like that of the immeasurable ocean when it is agitated.

22. Skilled in combat, the furious Prahasta massacred the monkeys in that great battle with an immense torrent of arrows.

23. Heaped up with the corpses of monkeys and *rākṣasas*, as if covered with fallen mountains, the earth looked ghastly.

24. The ground, covered with torrents of blood, looked as if it were covered with blossoming *palāśa* trees in the month of Mādhava.

25–28. Indeed, the battleground resembled a river. Masses of slain heroes formed its banks, and shattered weapons, its great trees. Torrents of blood made up its broad waters, and the ocean to which it flowed was Yama. Livers and spleens made up its deep mud, scattered entrails its waterweeds. Severed heads and trunks made up its fish, pieces of limbs, its grass. It was crowded with vultures in place of flocks of *haṃsas*, and it was swarming with adjutant storks instead of *sārasa* cranes. It was covered with fat in place of foam, and the cries of the wounded took the place of its gurgling. It was not to be forded by the faint of heart. Truly, it resembled a river at the end of the rains, swarming with *haṃsas* and *sārasa* cranes.

29. Such was the river, all but impossible to cross, that the *rākṣasas* and the foremost of the monkeys forded, as might the leaders of elephant herds, a lotus pond covered with lotus pollen.

30. Then Nīla spied Prahasta, who, mounted in his chariot and loosing torrents of arrows, was rapidly slaughtering the leaping monkeys.

31. Ripping up a tree by its roots, the great monkey struck the supremely unassailable Prahasta, who was attacking him.

32. Struck by that tree, that bull among *rākṣasas* was enraged, and, roaring, he loosed hails of arrows upon the lord of the army of the leaping monkeys.

33–34. Unable to deflect it, he shut his eyes and withstood it. Just as a prize bull might withstand a sudden autumnal squall, so did Nīla, his eyes tightly closed, endure with fortitude Prahasta's dreadful hail of arrows, so difficult to withstand.

35. Enraged by that hail of arrows, Nīla killed Prahasta's horses, swift as thought, with a huge *sāla* tree.

36. Stripped of his bow by him, Prahasta, the general of the army, seized a dreadful cudgel and leapt down from his chariot.

37. Enraged, the two swift leaders of their armies, their bodies smeared with blood, stood there, like two bull elephants in rut.

38. Slashing at each other with their razor-sharp fangs, they looked like a lion and a tiger and, indeed, moved just like them.

39. Seeing victory within their grasp, those two heroes, who never turned back from battle, were as eager to gain glory as were Vṛtra and Vāsava.

40. Then, making a supreme effort, Prahasta struck Nīla on the forehead with his cudgel, so that his blood gushed forth.

41. His body smeared with blood, the great monkey seized an enormous tree and, in a rage, hurled it at Prahasta's chest.

42. Disregarding that blow, the mighty *rākṣasa* seized his huge cudgel and charged at the mighty leaping monkey Nīla.

43. Seeing Prahasta rushing furiously toward him with terrifying force, the swift and great monkey seized a huge boulder.

44. In that battle, Nīla then swiftly brought the boulder down upon the head of the cudgel-warrior Prahasta, who was eager for combat.

45. Hurled by that foremost of monkeys, that huge and terrible boulder shattered Prahasta's head into many pieces.

46. Prahasta fell suddenly to the ground, like a tree cut off at the roots—stripped of life, stripped of splendor, stripped of strength, and stripped of his senses.

47. Blood gushed copiously from his shattered head, as well as from his body, like a cataract from a mountain.

48. When Prahasta had been slain by Nīla, his great and unshakeable army of *rākṣasas*, who were now despondent, returned to Laṅkā.

49. Once their general had been slain, they were no more able to hold their lines than would water upon reaching a shattered dam.

50. With the leader of their army slain, the *rākṣasas* became dispirited. Proceeding to the palace of the *rākṣasa* lord, they stood silently, brooding.

51. Then the immensely powerful and victorious troop leader Nīla joined Rāma and Lakṣmaṇa. Being praised for the feat he had accomplished, he was greatly delighted.

The end of the forty-sixth *sarga* of the *Yuddhakāṇḍa* of the *Śrī Rāmāyaṇa*.

Sarga 47

1. When Prahasta, the protector of the *rākṣasa* forces, was slain in battle by Nīla, bull among leaping monkeys, the army of the *rākṣasa* king, equal in force to the ocean and armed with fearsome weapons, fled.

2. They went and reported to the lord of the *rākṣasas* that his general had been slain by Nīla, the son of Agni, the purifier. No sooner had the lord of the *rākṣasas* heard their words than he gave way to anger.

3. Upon hearing that Prahasta had been slain in battle, he was grief stricken, and his mind was suffused with rage. He addressed the principal warriors of the *rākṣasas*, sons of chaos, just as Indra might the principal warriors of the immortal gods.

4. "One ought not underestimate an enemy who has destroyed the guardian of my army—the destroyer of the army of Indra—along with his followers and elephants.

5. "Therefore, without further deliberation, I myself will proceed to that extraordinary battlefront for the sake of victory and for the destruction of my enemies.

6. "I shall this very day with a hail of arrows consume that army of monkeys, Rāma and Lakṣmaṇa included, as with blazing fires one might a forest."

7. When he had spoken in this fashion, the enemy of the king of the immortal gods mounted a chariot yoked to a team of superb horses. It was as luminous as fire, and it glowed, blazing with splendor.

8. Then, to the sounds of conches and *bherī* and *paṭaha* drums and to the clapping of arms, war shouts, and lionlike roars, the foremost of *rākṣasa* lords went forth, honored with auspicious hymns of praise.

9. Surrounded by the foremost of the *rākṣasa* lords, flesh-eaters whose bodies resembled mountains or clouds and whose eyes blazed like fire, he resembled Rudra, lord of the immortal gods, surrounded by his malignant spirits.

10. Then, racing swiftly forth from the city, the immensely powerful *rākṣasa* spied the formidable army of monkeys. It was well prepared, armed with trees and boulders, and was roaring like the mighty ocean or a thundercloud.

11. Closely followed by his army, Rāma, whose arms resembled serpent lords and whose majesty was immense, spied the exceedingly wrathful *rākṣasa* host and addressed Vibhīṣaṇa, foremost among those who bear weapons:

12. "Who is in command of this unassailable army with its various flags, banners, and weapons, its darts, swords, lances, bows, and discuses, its war-elephants as huge as Himalaya, lord of mountains, and its fearless warriors?"

13. And when Vibhīṣaṇa, who was equal in valor to Śakra, had heard those words of Rāma, he described for him the splendid army of those great bulls among the *rākṣasas*.

14. "Your majesty, know that that huge *rākṣasa*, whose face is as red as the newly risen sun and who approaches mounted on an elephant's back, making its head tremble, is Akampana.

15. "The one who is mounted in a chariot and whose banner bears the king of beasts, he who brandishes a bow that resembles the bow of Śakra, and who, with his fierce and protuberant fangs, resembles an elephant, is called Indrajit, preeminent by virtue of a boon.

16. "And that immensely powerful bowman and superb chariot-warrior, who, with his gigantic body, resembles the Vindhya mountain, Western mountain, or Mount Mahendra, and who is twanging a bow of unparalleled size, is called Atikāya.

17. "And that huge hero, his eyes as red as the newly risen sun, who bellows harshly as he sits astride an elephant, its bells clanging, is called Mahodara.

18. "And the one mounted on a horse, which, with its trappings bright with gold, resembles a mountain shrouded in evening clouds, and who holds aloft a dart haloed with light, is Piśāca, equal in power to a thunderbolt.

19. "And mounted upon a lordly and mountainous bull, he who comes grasping a keen lance that flashes like lightning, its power surpassing that of the thunderbolt, is the illustrious Triśiras.

20. "And there we see Kumbha, his form like that of a storm cloud, his chest broad, muscular, and splendid. His banner bears the king of serpents, and he is utterly intent, brandishing and twanging his bow.

21. "And the one who comes holding a blazing, smoking iron club, studded with diamonds and *jāmbūnada* gold, is the standard-bearer of the *rākṣasa* hosts, Nikumbha, of wondrous and fearsome deeds.

22. "And that huge warrior who appears mounted on a chariot—equipped with masses of bows, swords, and arrows, decked with banners, and blazing like fire—is Narāntaka, who can battle even mountain peaks.

23–24. "And over there, where that fine white umbrella with its slender ribs is gleaming like the moon, that is where the great overlord of the *rākṣasas*, he who crushes the pride of even the gods, has appeared. Surrounded by his servants, whose faces are those of tigers, camels, elephant lords, and the king of beasts—all rolling their eyes—he resembles Rudra, surrounded by his malignant spirits.

25. "He wears a crown, and, with his face adorned with swinging earrings and his body as fearsome as that of an elephant lord or the Vindhya mountain, that overlord of the *rākṣasas*, who crushes the pride of great Indra and Vaivasvata, shines like the sun."

26. Then Rāma replied to Vibhīṣaṇa, subduer of his foes, "Ah! How resplendent is Rāvaṇa, lord of the *rākṣasas*, with his tremendous blazing energy!

27. "Rāvaṇa is as hard to gaze upon as is the sun with its shining rays. Yet I can clearly make out his form, haloed with blazing energy.

28. "Not even the heroes among the gods and *dānavas* could possess a brightly shining form like that of the lord of the *rākṣasas*.

29. "And all the warriors of that immensely powerful *rākṣasa* bear blazing weapons. They all look like mountains, and they can all give battle even to mountains.

30. "Surrounded by those blazing warriors, fearsome in their valor, the king of the *rākṣasas* looks like Yama, the ender of all things, surrounded by fierce malignant spirits in bodily form."

31. When he had spoken in this fashion, mighty Rāma took up his bow, drew forth a splendid arrow, and, accompanied by Lakṣmaṇa, took his stand.

32. Meanwhile, the great overlord of the *rākṣasas* addressed his powerful *rākṣasas*: "You are to remain calm and free from care at the city gates and the gates of the buildings on the main thoroughfares."

33. Then, when he had summarily dismissed them and they had departed according to their orders, he clove through the flood of that ocean of monkeys, as might a great fish cleave the brimming waters of the sea.

34. When Sugrīva, lord of the tawny monkeys, spied the *rākṣasa* lord racing suddenly toward him in battle with blazing bow and arrows, he tore off a huge mountain peak and charged at him.

35. Seizing that mountain peak, whose slopes were thick with trees, he hurled it at the night-roaming *rākṣasa*. But the latter, seeing it hurtling suddenly toward him, shattered it with arrows fletched with burnished gold.

36. Once that mountain peak, with huge and splendid trees on its slopes, had fallen, shattered, to the ground, the lord of the *rākṣasa* folk took up an arrow that resembled a huge serpent. It looked like Yama, the ender of all things.

37. In a rage he grasped that arrow, whose force was equal to that of the wind or great Indra's thunderbolt and whose brilliance was that of a fire shooting out sparks. Then he loosed it in order to kill Sugrīva.

38. Loosed by Rāvaṇa's arm, the sharp-tipped arrow, whose appearance was like that of Śakra's thunderbolt, struck Sugrīva with full force, piercing him, just as the fearsome javelin hurled by Guha once pierced Mount Krauñca.

39. Agonized by that arrow, his mind reeling, the hero fell to the earth groaning. But when the *yātudhānas* saw him fallen senseless to the ground in battle, they roared with delight.

40. But then the immense monkeys Gavākṣa, Gavaya, Sudaṃṣṭra, Ṛṣabha, Jyotimukha, and Nala took up boulders and charged the lord of the *rākṣasas*.

41. But the overlord of the *rākṣasas* warded off their blows with swarms of sharp-tipped arrows. He then pierced the monkey lords with masses of arrows, whose feathers were adorned with *jāmbūnada* gold.

42. Pierced by the arrows of that enemy of the thirty gods, the fearsome monkey lords fell to the ground. Then he completely covered the fierce monkey army with masses of arrows.

43. Afflicted by Rāvaṇa's arrows, their heroic leaders fallen, and riven by the dart of fear, the tree-dwelling monkeys, wailing loudly, sought refuge with Rāma, the refuge of all.

44. At once, the mighty bowman, great Rāma, took up his bow and came running, but Lakṣmaṇa accosted him and, his hands cupped in reverence, spoke these deeply significant words:

*45. "Granted, my noble lord, you are perfectly capable of killing this evil-minded *rākṣasa*. Nonetheless, I should kill this despicable creature. Just grant me permission, my lord."

46. Rāma of true valor and tremendous power replied to him: "Go, Lakṣmaṇa. You must exert yourself to the fullest in battle.

47. "For Rāvaṇa is enormously powerful and astonishingly valorous in battle. There is no doubt that, once his fury is aroused, it is impossible even for all the three worlds together to withstand him.

48. "You must seek out his weak points and defend your own. Stay focused and strive to protect yourself with your eye as well as your bow."

49. Upon hearing those words of Rāma Rāghava, Saumitri embraced him. Then, after doing him honor and respectfully saluting him, he went off to battle.

50. He whose arms resembled the trunks of elephants gazed upon Rāvaṇa, who, with his blazing, fearsome bow held high, was covering the monkeys—their bodies torn and scattered—with a massive hail of arrows.

51. But when the immensely powerful Hanumān, son of Māruta, spied Rāvaṇa, he charged toward him, evading those masses of arrows.

52. Reaching his chariot, wise Hanumān raised his right arm and, menacing Rāvaṇa, spoke these words:

53. "Because of your invulnerability, you vanquished the gods, *dānavas*, *gandharvas*, and *yakṣas*, along with the *rākṣasas*. But you should fear the monkeys.

54. "This upraised right hand of mine, with its five fingers, will drive the living spirit from your body where it has long dwelt."

55. When Rāvaṇa, of fearsome valor, heard those words of Hanumān, he spoke these words, his eyes red with rage:

56. "Then strike quickly and without hesitation and so acquire eternal fame. Once I have thus determined your prowess, I will destroy you, monkey."

57. When the son of Vāyu heard those words of Rāvaṇa, he said these words: "Please keep in mind that, on an earlier occasion, I struck down your son Akṣa."

58. Addressed in this fashion, the immensely powerful Rāvaṇa, mighty lord of the *rākṣasas*, struck the son of Anila on the chest with the palm of his hand.

59. Struck by him with the palm of his hand, he staggered back and forth. Then, infuriated, he struck that enemy of the immortal gods with the palm of his own hand.

60. When that great monkey had struck him with the palm of his hand, ten-necked Rāvaṇa shook like a mountain during an earthquake.

61. Seeing Rāvaṇa slapped down in this fashion in battle, the seers, monkeys, perfected beings, gods, and *asuras* cheered.

62. Steadying himself, the immensely powerful Rāvaṇa spoke these words: "Well done, monkey! Your strength makes you a praiseworthy opponent for me."

63. But when Māruti was addressed in this fashion by Rāvaṇa, he said these words: "Since you are still alive, Rāvaṇa, then I say to hell with my strength!

64. "But why bother praising me? Now strike once again, fool! Then my fist shall lead you to the abode of Yama." At these words of Māruti, Rāvaṇa's anger blazed up once more.

65. His eyes reddened, the mighty *rākṣasa* energetically raised his right fist and brought it down with force on the monkey's chest. Struck once again on his broad chest, Hanumān staggered.

66. Seeing that mighty Hanumān was stunned, the great chariot-warrior raced swiftly in his chariot toward Nīla.

67. With his fearsome arrows that resembled serpents and pierced the vitals of his foes, he tormented Nīla, lord of the army of tawny monkeys.

68. Hard-pressed by that stream of arrows, Nīla, lord of the monkey army, with one hand, hurled a mountain peak at the overlord of the *rākṣasas*.

69–70. Meanwhile, wise and powerful Hanumān, now recovered and eager for battle, saw that Rāvaṇa, the lord of the *rākṣasas*, was engaged in battle with Nīla. Angrily he said, "It is not appropriate to attack someone who is locked in battle with another."

71. Meanwhile, powerful Rāvaṇa smashed that peak with seven sharp-tipped arrows so that it fell, shattered.

72. Seeing the mountain peak shattered, Nīla, the lord of the army of tawny monkeys, slayer of enemy heroes, flared up with anger, like the fire at the end of time.

73. In that battle, Nīla then hurled *aśvakarṇas*, *dhavas*, *sālas*, mangos in full bloom, and various other trees as well.

74. But Rāvaṇa splintered those trees as they came toward him. He then deluged Nīla, the son of Agni, the purifier, with a very fearsome hail of arrows.

75. But, inundated by that hail of arrows, like a great mountain by a storm cloud, he shrunk his body and alighted on the tip of Rāvaṇa's flagstaff.

76. Seeing the son of Agni, the purifier, perched on the tip of his flagstaff, Rāvaṇa flared up in anger. Nīla then roared.

77. When Lakṣmaṇa, Hanumān, and Rāma saw that tawny monkey first on the tip of Rāvaṇa's flagstaff, next on the point of his bow, and then on the top of his crown, they were amazed.

78. Even the immensely powerful Rāvaṇa himself was astonished at the monkey's swiftness. He then invoked the wondrous and blazing divine weapon-spell of Agni.

79. Then the leaping monkeys, observing that Rāvaṇa was baffled in combat by Nīla's swiftness, chattered in delight as they watched intently.

80. Enraged by the screeching of the monkeys, his mind utterly confused, Rāvaṇa could do nothing.

81. Taking up an arrow charged with the divine weapon-spell of Agni, the night-roaming *rākṣasa* Rāvaṇa fixed his glance on Nīla, who was perched on the head of his flagstaff.

82. Then Rāvaṇa, the powerful lord of the *rākṣasas*, spoke: "Your swiftness derives from this extraordinary trickery of yours, monkey.

83–84. "Now try to save your life, if you can, monkey. You seem to appear in many different forms. Nonetheless, this arrow, loosed by me and charged with a divine weapon-spell, will rob you of your life, even as you seek to save it."

85. When he had spoken in this fashion, great-armed Rāvaṇa, lord of the *rākṣasas*, nocked the arrow and, with that divinely charged weapon, struck the lord of the army.

86. Struck in the chest and burnt by that arrow charged with the divine weapon-spell, Nīla fell at once to the ground.

87. Although he had fallen to the ground on his knees, nonetheless, because he was endowed with his father's divine power as well as his own blazing energy, he was not killed.

88. Seeing that the monkey had lost consciousness, ten-necked Rāvaṇa, still eager for battle, raced toward Saumitri in his chariot that thundered like a storm cloud.

89. His spirit undaunted, Saumitri addressed Rāvaṇa, who was twanging his immeasurable bow: "Come after me, lord of the night-roaming *rākṣasas*! You shouldn't be fighting with monkeys."

90. Hearing his words and the fearsome resonant twanging of his bowstring, the *rākṣasa* king confronted Saumitri where he stood and spoke these wrathful words:

91. "How fortunate for me, Rāghava, that you, headed for destruction, your wits disordered, have come into my sight. This very moment, stricken by my streams of arrows, you shall depart for the land of death."

92. As Rāvaṇa was bellowing in this fashion, exposing the white tips of his fangs, Lakṣmaṇa, undaunted, replied: "The truly powerful do not bellow, your majesty. Foremost of evildoers, you are merely boasting.

93. "I know all about your courage, lord of the *rākṣasas*, your strength, your valor, and your prowess. Here I stand bow and arrows in hand. Come on! What is the use of this vain boasting?"

94. The overlord of the *rākṣasas* was furious at being spoken to in this fashion, and he loosed seven beautifully fletched arrows. But Lakṣmaṇa cut them to pieces with arrows whose tips and edges were honed and whose fletching was adorned with gold.

95. When the lord of Laṅkā saw them suddenly cut to pieces, like serpent lords whose coils are cloven, he gave way to anger and loosed still other sharp arrows.

96. But Rāma's younger brother released from his bow a fierce shower of arrows. With these arrows—razor-tipped, half-moon-headed, finely barbed, and crescent-headed—he calmly cut Rāvaṇa's arrows to pieces.

97. Then, swiftly fitting to his bow sharp-tipped arrows, whose luster was that of blazing fire and whose impact was equal to that of great Indra's *vajra* or the thunderbolt, Lakṣmaṇa released them in an effort to kill the overlord of the *rākṣasas*.

98. But the lord of the *rākṣasas* cut them to pieces. Then, when he had done so, he struck Lakṣmaṇa in the forehead with an arrow given to him by self-existent Brahmā—its luster equal to that of the fire at the end of time.

99. Tormented by Rāvaṇa's arrow, Lakṣmaṇa staggered and slackened his grip on his bow. Then, regaining consciousness with difficulty, he cut to pieces the bow of that enemy of Indra, lord of the thirty gods.

100. Then, with three sharp-tipped arrows, Dāśarathi struck him whose bow was shattered. Tormented by those arrows, the king staggered but with difficulty regained consciousness.

101. Tormented by arrows, his limbs bathed in sweat, drenched in blood, his bow shattered, the immensely powerful enemy of the gods then, in that battle, seized a javelin he had been given by self-existent Brahmā.

102. The lord of the *rākṣasa* kingdom then swiftly hurled that blazing lance at Saumitri. Terrifying the monkey armies, it resembled a smokeless fire.

103. As it flew toward him, the younger brother of Bharata struck it with divinely charged weapons and with arrows that blazed like

sacrificial fires. Nonetheless, the javelin plunged deep into Dāśarathi's broad chest.

104. Wounded in the breast by the javelin of Brahmā, Saumitri recalled that he himself was an inconceivable portion of Viṣṇu.

105. Then, although he grasped Saumitri, humbler of the *dānavas'* pride, with both his arms, that thorn in the side of the gods was unable to budge him.

106. With his two arms, he was able to lift the Himalayas, Mount Mandara, Mount Meru, or even the three worlds along with the immortal gods; yet, in that battle, he could not lift Bharata's younger brother.

107. When Rāvaṇa saw that Lakṣmaṇa, who was a portion of Viṣṇu in a human body, was unconscious, he was astonished.

108. At this juncture, Hanumān, son of Vāyu, enraged, rushed at Rāvaṇa. In his rage, he struck him on the chest with a fist like adamant.

109. The blow of that fist made Rāvaṇa, lord of the *rākṣasas*, slump to his knees on the floor of his chariot. He swayed for a moment and collapsed.

110. Seeing Rāvaṇa of fearsome valor unconscious in battle, the seers, monkeys, and gods, together with Vāsava, cheered.

111. But powerful Hanumān picked up Lakṣmaṇa, who had been wounded by Rāvaṇa, in both his arms and carried him to Rāghava.

112. For, on account of the affection and supreme devotion of the son of Vāyu, Lakṣmaṇa became light for that monkey, even though he could not be budged by his enemies.

113. Meanwhile, the javelin extracted itself from Saumitri, who was unconquerable in battle, and returned to its place in Rāvaṇa's chariot.

114. But powerful Rāvaṇa, regaining consciousness in that great battle, took up sharp arrows and grasped a great bow.

115. And Lakṣmaṇa, destroyer of his foes, recalling that he himself was an inconceivable portion of Viṣṇu, was freed of that dart and restored to health.

116. Meanwhile, when Rāghava saw that the great heroes of that vast host of monkeys had been struck down in battle, he raced toward Rāvaṇa.

117. But Hanumān, intercepting him, spoke these words: "You should climb on my back and punish this *rākṣasa*."

118. When Rāghava heard the words uttered by Hanumān, son of Vāyu, that hero immediately climbed up on the great monkey. Then the overlord of men gazed upon Rāvaṇa mounted on his chariot in battle.

119. Keeping him in sight, immensely powerful Rāghava raced toward him, as did the wrathful Viṣṇu, his weapon raised, toward Vairocana.

120. He made his bowstring resound sharply with a sound like the crash of a thunderbolt. Then, in a deep voice, he addressed the lord of the *rākṣasas*:

121. "Stay where you are! For after doing me such an injury, tiger among *rākṣasas*, where can you go to escape me?

122. "If you were to fly for refuge to Indra, Vaivasvata, Sūrya, bringer of light, self-existent Brahmā, Agni Vaiśvānara, or even Śiva, bringer of auspiciousness—even if you were to flee to the ten directions—still, no matter where you might go, you would not escape me now.

123. "And he whom you struck with your javelin this day will soon return in his desire to cause you sorrow. This very day he will bring death to you in battle, king of the *rākṣasa* hosts, and to your sons and wives as well."

124. Upon hearing Rāghava's words, the *rākṣasa* lord struck the great monkey with sharp arrows that were like the flames of the fire at the end of time.

125. But since he was endowed with innate blazing energy, that blazing energy only increased as he was struck with those arrows by the *rākṣasa* in battle.

126. But immensely powerful Rāma, seeing that that tiger among leaping monkeys had been wounded by Rāvaṇa, was overwhelmed with rage.

127. Advancing toward Rāvaṇa's chariot, Rāma cut it to pieces with his well-fletched arrows along with its wheels, horses, banners, umbrella, and great flagstaff, as well as its charioteer, missiles, lances, and swords.

128. Then he swiftly struck that enemy of Indra on his broad and beautiful chest with an arrow that resembled Indra's *vajra* or a thunderbolt, just as Lord Indra himself might strike Mount Meru with his *vajra*.

129. That heroic king, who had neither trembled nor staggered at the blows of Indra's *vajra* or of thunderbolts, now, struck by Rāma's arrow, was sorely afflicted. He staggered and dropped his bow.

130. Perceiving that the overlord of the *rākṣasas* was dazed, magnanimous Rāma took up a blazing, half-moon-headed arrow and, with it, swiftly cut off his crown, which shone like the sun.

131. Then, in the midst of the battle, Rāma addressed the lord of the *rākṣasas*, who, with the top of his crown severed, had lost his royal splendor and resembled a serpent robbed of its venom or a darkened sun, its rays extinguished.

132. "You have performed great and fearsome deeds and struck down my heroic warriors. Still, recognizing that you are exhausted from all that, I shall not bring you under the sway of death with my arrows."

133. Addressed in this fashion, the king, wounded with arrows, his pride and excitement crushed, his bow cut to pieces, his horses and charioteer slain, and his great crown cut off, quickly entered Laṅkā.

134. Once the mighty lord of the night-roaming *rākṣasas*, the enemy of the *dānavas* and the gods, had returned to Laṅkā, Rāma, along with Lakṣmaṇa, removed those darts from the tawny monkeys in the forefront of the great battle.

135. When the enemy of Indra, lord of the thirty gods, had been humbled, the gods and the *asuras*, the hosts of creatures, the guardians of the directions, and the denizens of the deep, along with the seers, the great serpents, and the creatures of land and water, rejoiced.

The end of the forty-seventh *sarga* of the *Yuddhakāṇḍa* of the *Śrī Rāmāyaṇa*.

Sarga 48

1. Now, when the king, afflicted by the fear of Rāma's arrows, his pride humbled, reentered the citadel of Laṅkā, he was nearly insensible with agitation.

2. For great Rāghava had vanquished the king, as might a lion, an elephant or Garuḍa, a serpent.

3. Remembering Rāghava's arrows that, like the staff of Brahmā, blazed with the brilliance of lightning, the lord of the *rākṣasas* shuddered.

4. Seated on his magnificent heavenly golden throne, Rāvaṇa gazed at the *rākṣasas* and said these words:

5. "Since I, who am the equal of great Indra, have been defeated by a mere human, it is clear that the supreme austerities I performed have all been in vain.

6. "And those frightening words of Brahmā, 'Know that you still must fear humans,' have now come back to haunt me, for they have proven true.

7. "For although I obtained invulnerability with respect to the gods, *dānavas*, *gandharvas*, *yakṣas*, *rākṣasas*, and great serpents, I did not request it with respect to humans.

8. "Bearing this in mind, you must exert yourselves. Let *rākṣasas* be stationed on top of the gateways at the main thoroughfares.

9. "And you must awaken the incomparably profound Kumbhakarṇa, crusher of the pride of the gods and *dānavas*, who has been overcome by Brahmā's curse."

10. Realizing that Prahasta had been slain and he himself defeated, mighty Rāvaṇa dispatched a fearsome army of *rākṣasas*.

11. "Exert yourselves at the gateways! Ascend the ramparts! Kumbhakarṇa, who is overwhelmed by sleep, must be awakened!

12. "That *rākṣasa* sleeps for six, seven, eight, even nine months at a time. Nonetheless, you must awaken mighty Kumbhakarṇa immediately.

13. "For that great-armed warrior, greatest of all the *rākṣasas*, will quickly slaughter the monkeys and the two princes in battle.

14. "Addicted to this vulgar pleasure, Kumbhakarṇa sleeps all the time in a stupor. But once Kumbhakarṇa is awakened, my grief at being humiliated by Rāma in that terrible battle will be banished.

15. "For of what use to me is that hero, whose strength is equal to that of Śakra, if he can be of no assistance to me when I am in such trouble?"

16. Upon hearing those words of the *rākṣasa* lord, the *rākṣasas* proceeded in great agitation to the residence of Kumbhakarṇa.

17. As instructed by Rāvaṇa, those eaters of flesh and blood gathered perfumes, garlands, and food and went on their way hurriedly.

18–19. As they passed through the huge gates into Kumbhakarṇa's lovely cavern, which extended a league on every side and was redolent with every fragrance, the immensely powerful *rākṣasas* were driven back by the force of his breath. Nonetheless, retaining their footing with difficulty, they managed to enter the cavern with effort.

20. Once they had entered that charming and splendid cavern, its floors inlaid with gold, they spied that tiger among *rākṣasas*, sons of chaos, sleeping. He was fearsome to behold.

21. All together they began to rouse grotesque Kumbhakarṇa, who lay sleeping in the midst of his long sleep, like some crumbled mountain.

22–23. They stared at the immensely powerful Kumbhakarṇa, tiger among *rākṣasas*, sons of chaos, as he lay there, his body hairs bristling, hissing like a great serpent, and terrifying them with his stertorous breathing. With his fearsome nostrils and his huge mouth as wide as the underworld Pātāla, he was fearsome to behold.

24. Then those mighty *rākṣasas* placed before Kumbhakarṇa a supremely gratifying heap of meats as huge as Mount Meru.

25. Those tigers among *rākṣasas*, sons of chaos, set down massive quantities of deer, buffalo, and boar—an astonishing heap of food.

26. Then those foes of the thirty gods placed before Kumbhakarṇa pots of blood and strong drink of various kinds.

27. And they smeared that scorcher of his foes with costly sandal-paste and covered him with heavenly garlands and fragrant perfumes.

28. The *yātudhānas* released fragrant incense and sang the praises of that scorcher of his foes, roaring loudly in their thousands, like storm clouds.

29. They sounded conches, whose luster was like that of the hare-marked moon, and they roared tumultuously all together in their impatience.

30. Those night-roaming *rākṣasas* roared, clapped their upper arms, and shook him. Thus they made a huge commotion in order to awaken Kumbhakarṇa.

31. Upon hearing that din—the sound of conches and *bherī* and *paṭaha* drums, along with the clapping of the upper arms, the shouting, and the lionlike roars—the birds, who were flying in all directions and soaring into the heavens, suddenly came crashing down.

32. When the huge, sleeping Kumbhakarṇa was still not awakened by those cacophonous sounds, all the *rākṣasa* troops took up bludgeons, cudgels, and maces.

33. Then, with mountain peaks, cudgels, maces, trees, war hammers, and their palms and fists, those huge *rākṣasas* began to belabor Kumbhakarṇa as he slept there comfortably on the ground.

34. However, because of the wind caused by the *rākṣasa* Kumbhakarṇa's stertorous breathing, the *rākṣasas*, although powerful, were unable to remain standing before him.

35. Then those *rākṣasas* of fearsome valor, ten thousand strong, all together loudly sounded their *mṛdaṅga*, *paṇava*, and *bherī* drums, along with many conches and jugs, right in front of him.

36. Roaring and beating him, they tried to rouse him as he lay there, like a mass of collyrium. But he was oblivious to it all.

37. When they were still unable to wake him, they resorted to more drastic and more violent efforts.

38. With staves, whips, and goads, they drove horses, camels, donkeys, and elephants over him, and they sounded conches and *bherī* and *mṛdaṅga* drums with all their might.

39. They struck his limbs with great bundles of sticks, war hammers, and cudgels, wielded with all their might.

40. That tremendous din filled all of Laṅkā together with its surrounding woods and mountains. But still he did not awaken.

41. Next, they incessantly and simultaneously beat a thousand *bherī* drums with drumsticks of refined gold, all around him.

42. But when in that profound slumber brought about by the power of the curse he still did not awaken, the night-roaming *rākṣasas* became furious.

43. All those *rākṣasas* of fearsome valor were in a towering rage. Some of them, in their effort to awaken the *rākṣasa*, actually assaulted him.

44. Some beat *bherī* drums, while others raised a tremendous racket. Some of them tore out his hair, while others bit his ears. Nonetheless, Kumbhakarṇa, plunged in his profound slumber, did not stir.

45. Other powerful *rākṣasas*, armed with mallets and war hammers, brought them down on his head, chest, and limbs.

46. Even though that huge *rākṣasa* was hammered all over with hundred-slayers tied to ropes and straps, he still did not awaken.

47. But, finally, when they made a thousand elephants trample across his body, Kumbhakarṇa, aware of a slight sensation, at last awoke.

48. Ignoring the tremendous blows of mountaintops and trees that were being hurled down upon him, he suddenly leapt up at the violent interruption of his sleep, yawning and oppressed by fear and hunger.

49. Stretching wide his arms, which were as strong as mountain peaks and resembled two mountain peaks or great serpents, that night-roaming *rākṣasa* yawned grotesquely, opening his mouth, which was like the gaping mare's head fire that lies beneath the sea.

50. And as he yawned prodigiously, his mouth, as wide as the underworld Pātāla, resembled the sun, maker of day, risen over the summit of Mount Meru.

51. Yawning, the enormously powerful night-roaming *rākṣasa* was at last fully awake. His breath was like a gale from the mountains.

52. As Kumbhakarṇa arose, his appearance was like that of a drenching storm cloud crossed by cranes at summer's end.

53. His enormous eyes, which resembled blazing fires and whose luster was like that of lightning, looked like two great blazing planets.

54. Since he was hungry, he ate the meat. And since he was thirsty, he drank the blood. Then that foe of Śakra drank wine and a pot of marrow.

55. At last, when the night-roaming *rākṣasas* reckoned that he was sated, they approached him and surrounded him on every side with their heads bowed.

56. First that bull among *rākṣasas*, sons of chaos, reassured the *rākṣasas*, sons of chaos. Then, astonished at having been awakened, he said this to the *rākṣasas*:

*57. "Why have you gentlemen put so much effort into waking me? I trust that all is well with the king and that no danger of any kind presents itself.

58. "On the other hand, some great danger from enemies must surely have presented itself, on account of which you gentlemen have so urgently awakened me.

59. "I shall this very day eliminate the danger to the king of the *rākṣasas*. I shall cast down great Indra or smash Anala, god of fire.

60. "For no one would have awakened me so violently from my slumber for some trivial reason. So now tell me truthfully the reason for awakening me."

61. Then Yūpākṣa, a minister of the king, cupping his hands in reverence, replied to that tamer of his foes, Kumbhakarṇa, who was speaking so agitatedly in this fashion.

62. “The gods have never presented us with any danger, nor have we been presented with any danger from the *daityas* or *dānavas* such as now presents itself to us from a man, your highness.

63. “Laṅkā is surrounded by monkeys who look like mountains. A catastrophic danger from Rāma, inflamed at the abduction of Sītā, now confronts us.

64. “Earlier, a single monkey burned down the great citadel and slaughtered Prince Akṣa along with his troops and elephants.

65. “Even the lord of the *rākṣasas* himself, Rāvaṇa Paulastya, the thorn in the side of the gods, was dismissed in battle by Rāma, whose splendor is that of the sun, with the words, ‘You are as good as dead.’

66. “What neither the gods nor the *daityas* and *dānavas* could do to the king has been done to him by Rāma, who then released him, sparing his life.”

67. When Kumbhakarṇa had heard these words of Yūpākṣa and had learned of his brother’s defeat in battle, he opened his eyes wide and said this to him:

68. “This very day, Yūpākṣa, I shall slaughter in battle the entire army of tawny monkeys along with Lakṣmaṇa and Rāghava. Only then will I go to see Rāvaṇa.

69. “I shall sate the *rākṣasas* with the flesh and blood of the tawny monkeys, and then I shall drink the blood of Rāma and Lakṣmaṇa all by myself.”

70. Upon hearing those arrogant words of which the defects were magnified by anger, Mahodara, one of the principal warriors of the *rākṣasas*, sons of chaos, cupped his hands in reverence and said these words:

71. “Only after you have heard Rāvaṇa’s words and carefully considered the advantages and disadvantages of any action should you attempt to conquer our enemies in battle, great-armed warrior.”

72. Upon hearing these words of Mahodara, the mighty and enormously powerful Kumbhakarṇa prepared to set forth, surrounded by *rākṣasas*.

73. Once they had awakened Kumbhakarṇa, fearsome in eye, form, and valor, the *rākṣasas* went in haste to the palace of ten-necked Rāvaṇa.

74. When they arrived there, all those night-roaming *rākṣasas*, joining their cupped palms in reverence, addressed ten-necked Rāvaṇa as he sat on his splendid throne.

75. "Your brother Kumbhakarṇa is awake, bull among *rākṣasas*. How should he proceed? Should he sally forth directly or will you first see him here?"

76. Delighted, Rāvaṇa replied to those *rākṣasas* who had come there, "I wish to see him here, duly honored."

77. Saying, "So be it," all those *rākṣasas* went back again and, as instructed by Rāvaṇa, said these words to Kumbhakarṇa:

78. "The king, that bull among all the *rākṣasas*, wishes to see you. So set your mind on going and bring delight to your brother."

79. Upon receiving his brother's command, mighty and unassailable Kumbhakarṇa said, "So be it," and leapt up from his bed.

80. In high spirits, he rinsed his mouth, bathed, and adorned himself splendidly. As he was thirsty, he urgently sent for invigorating drink.

81. Then, hastening on his account, the *rākṣasas*, at Rāvaṇa's command, quickly brought intoxicating drink and various kinds of food.

82. After first drinking a thousand jars, he made ready to go.

83. Filled with energy and strength, exhilarated, and slightly intoxicated, Kumbhakarṇa, in his frenzy, resembled Yama, who brings time itself to an end.

84. As Kumbhakarṇa made his way toward his brother's palace, accompanied by an army of *rākṣasas*, his footsteps shook the very earth.

85. As he went on his way, Kumbhakarṇa flooded the royal highway with light through his own bodily radiance, as does the thousand-rayed sun the earth with its beams. Encircled with a garland of hands cupped in reverence, he resembled Indra of the hundred sacrifices on his way to the abode of self-existent Brahmā.

86–87. Seeing him, so huge and extraordinary, diademed and tall as a mountain peak, as if matching the sun itself with his innate splendor, the forest-dwelling monkeys were stricken with fear and fled in all directions. Some ran for refuge to Rāma, the refuge of all, while others, in their panic, fell down. Some, in their panic, fled in all directions, while others, stricken with fear, simply lay on the ground.

The end of the forty-eighth *sarga* of the *Yuddhakāṇḍa* of the *Śrī Rāmāyaṇa*.

Sarga 49

1–2. Huge, diademed Kumbhakarṇa looked like a mountain. Seeing him striding along as did Lord Nārāyaṇa long ago through the heavens, mighty and immensely powerful Rāma took up his bow and stared at him.

3. But when the great army of monkeys spied Kumbhakarṇa, who, adorned with his golden armlets, looked like a storm cloud charged with rain, it broke and ran once more.

4. When he saw his army on the run and the *rākṣasa* looming above him, Rāma, in his amazement, said this to Vibhīṣaṇa:

5. "Who is that tawny-eyed, diademed hero, who looks like a mountain and looms over Laṅkā, like a storm cloud laced with lightning?

6. "From here he looks like some great and solitary banner raised high above the earth. At the sight of him all the monkeys are scattering every which way.

7. "Tell me, who is this enormous creature? Is he a *rākṣasa* or an *asura*? I have never seen a creature like him before."

8. Thus questioned by Prince Rāma Kākutstha, tireless in action, wise Vibhīṣaṇa said this to him:

9. "That is Kumbhakarṇa, the valorous son of Viśravas, who defeated both Vaivasvata and Vāsava in battle.

10. "In battle, Rāghava, he has crushed thousands of gods, *dānavas*, *yakṣas*, great serpents, flesh-eating demons, *gandharvas*, *vidyādharas*, and *kinnaras*.

11. "The thirty gods themselves were unable to kill him, mistakenly thinking that mighty Kumbhakarṇa with his dreadful eyes and lance in hand was, in fact, Kāla himself.

12. "For mighty Kumbhakarṇa is powerful by nature, while the power of the other *rākṣasa* lords derives from the gift of boons.

13. "No sooner had this huge *rākṣasa* been born than, tormented by hunger, he devoured many thousands of living beings.

14. "As they were being devoured, the creatures, stricken with terror, ran for refuge to Śakra and reported the matter to him.

15. "In a rage, great Indra, the wielder of the sharp *vajra*, struck Kumbhakarṇa with it. Struck by Śakra's *vajra*, the huge *rākṣasa* staggered and roared loudly in his rage.

16. "Upon hearing the roars of wise Kumbhakarṇa, who was roaring loudly, the earth, already terrified, became still more so.

17. "And, in his rage at great Indra, mighty Kumbhakarṇa tore out one of Airāvata's tusks and, with it, struck Vāsava on the chest.

18. "Wounded by Kumbhakarṇa's blow, Vāsava staggered. Then all at once the gods, brahman-seers, and *dānavas* despaired.

19. "Śakra then proceeded with all creatures to the abode of self-existent Brahmā, lord of creatures, where they told him about Kumbhakarṇa's vicious nature, his devouring of creatures, and his assaulting the gods.

20. " 'If he continues to devour creatures in this fashion, the whole world will be empty within no time.'

21. "When Brahmā, grandfather of all the worlds, had heard those words of Vāsava, he sent for the *rākṣasas* and fixed his gaze on Kumbhakarṇa.

22. "When Brahmā, lord of creatures, saw Kumbhakarṇa, he was frightened. Fixing him with his glance, self-existent Brahmā took a deep breath and said this:

23. " 'Undoubtedly, you were created by Paulastya for the destruction of the world. Therefore, you shall sleep from this day forward as if you were dead.' That very instant, overcome by Brahmā's curse, he collapsed right in front of the Lord.

24. "Then, profoundly agitated, Rāvaṇa spoke these words, 'You are cutting down a full-grown golden tree, just as it is about to bear fruit.

25. " 'It is not right, lord of creatures, to curse one's own grandson in this fashion. Since your words may never prove false, there is no doubt but that he will sleep. Still, you should set some time limit to his sleeping and waking.'

26. "Upon hearing Rāvaṇa's words, self-existent Brahmā said this: 'He shall sleep for six months and wake for but a single day.

27. " 'But on that one day, this ravening hero will roam the earth with gaping mouth, devouring all creatures, like a raging conflagration.'

28. "But now, King Rāvaṇa, in a desperate situation and terrified of your valor, has had Kumbhakarṇa awakened.

29. "That hero of terrifying valor has emerged from his lair. Soon, in a towering rage, he will race about, devouring the monkeys.

30. "At the mere sight of Kumbhakarṇa, the tawny monkeys have fled. How then will the monkeys stand up to him when he is in the fury of battle?

31. "Let's tell all the monkeys that he is just some giant mechanical man. Once they accept that, they will lose their fear of him."

32. Upon hearing Vibhīṣaṇa's reasonable and encouraging words, Rāghava addressed Nīla, the general of the army.

33. "Go, Nīla Pāvaki! Put all the troops into battle formation and take up your post. Seize control of the gateways, thoroughfares, and bridges of Laṅkā.

34. "Let all the monkeys collect mountain peaks, trees, and boulders and take up their posts, well armed and boulders in hand."

35. Thus instructed by Rāghava, Nīla, that elephant among monkeys and general of the hosts of tawny monkeys, gave his orders accordingly to the monkey troops.

36. Then, Gavākṣa, Śarabha, Hanumān, Aṅgada, and Nala, who themselves resembled mountains, seized mountain peaks and approached the gateways.

37. With boulders held aloft and trees in their hands, the formidable army of monkeys resembled a vast and formidable mass of huge storm clouds, looming up against a mountain.

The end of the forty-ninth *sarga* of the *Yuddhakāṇḍa* of the *Śrī Rāmāyaṇa*.

Sarga 50

1. Meanwhile, that tiger among the *rākṣasas*, whose valor was tremendous, proceeded along the majestic royal highway, groggy with sleep and drink.

2. As that supremely invincible warrior continued on his way, he was surrounded by thousands of *rākṣasas* and strewn with showers of blossoms raining from the houses along his route.

3. At length he spied the vast and beautiful mansion of the *rākṣasa* lord, which, covered with a fretwork of gold, blazed with the radiance of the sun.

4. Then he entered the dwelling of the *rākṣasa* lord, as might the sun a mass of clouds. There, just as Śakra might behold the self-existent Brahmā seated on his throne, he beheld from afar his elder brother seated on his.

5. Now that he had arrived at his brother's house and had entered its innermost chamber, he spied his elder seated dejectedly in the flying palace Puṣpaka.

6. But when ten-necked Rāvaṇa saw that Kumbhakarṇa had arrived, he quickly sat up in great excitement and had him ushered into his presence.

7. Immensely powerful Kumbhakarṇa made his obeisance at the feet of his brother, who sat upon his throne, and said, "What task must I perform?" Then, springing up in great delight, Rāvaṇa embraced him.

8. When he had been embraced by his brother and duly welcomed, Kumbhakarṇa took a superb, splendid, and heavenly seat.

9. Immensely powerful Kumbhakarṇa settled himself on his seat. Then, his eyes red with rage, he said these words to Rāvaṇa:

10. "Why have you put such effort into waking me, your majesty? Tell me. Who are you afraid of? Who will become a ghost this very day?"

11. His eyes rolling slightly, Rāvaṇa spoke these words to his angry brother Kumbhakarṇa, who sat beside him:

12. "As of today, you have been asleep for a very long time, mighty warrior. Since you were resting comfortably, you do not know of the danger Rāma poses to me.

13. "This powerful Rāma Dāśarathi has crossed the ocean with Sugrīva and an army and is cutting us off at the roots.

14. "Just look at the woods and parklands of Laṅkā! He has turned them all into one big sea of monkeys after easily coming here via a causeway.

15. "The very foremost among the *rākṣasas* have been slaughtered in battle by the monkeys. But never do I see the destruction of the monkeys in battle.

16. "You must understand that I have exhausted all my resources. You must save the city of Laṅkā in which only the children and the aged remain.

17. "Great-armed warrior, you must accomplish this most formidable task for your brother's sake. I have never before spoken in this fashion to anyone, scorcher of your foes. For, my brother, I have placed my love and my fullest confidence in you.

18. "Many times, bull among *rākṣasas*, in our wars with the gods and *asuras*, you faced off against them and defeated them in battle. For there is not to be found among all living beings any one as mighty as you.

19. "You must do me this supreme favor and service. You, who love battle and love your kinsmen, must, according to your pleasure, scatter the army of our enemies with your own blazing energy, just as a strong gale might spring up to scatter the clouds of autumn."

The end of the fiftieth *sarga* of the *Yuddhakāṇḍa* of the *Śrī Rāmāyaṇa*.

Sarga 51

1. When Kumbhakarṇa had heard the lamentation of the king of the *rākṣasas*, he laughed and then said these words:

2. "Since you paid no heed to those who had your welfare at heart, you have now met with that very calamity that we foresaw earlier, at the council of ministers.

3. "You are suffering the immediate consequences of your wicked deed, just as evildoers suffer an instant descent into their respective hells.

4. "You carried out this action, your majesty, without first reflecting upon it. In the sheer arrogance of your strength, you did not consider the consequences.

5. "A person who, relying upon his royal authority, does later what ought to be done first, and first what ought to be done later, has no comprehension of the distinction between sound and unsound policy.

6. "Actions that are performed in inverted order, without reference to the proper time and place, are harmful, just as are offerings of food to impious persons.

7. "A king who perceives the fivefold application of the three types of action after coming to a decision with his ministers remains on the proper path.

8. "So does a king who desires to reach a decision in conformance with the texts on polity, who pays heed to his ministers, and who recognizes his true friends by virtue of his own intelligence.

9. "A man should pursue all three human ends—righteousness, profit, and pleasure—at their proper times, lord of the *rākṣasas*, either all at once or two at a time.

10. "And a king or one exercising royal power who learns which among these three is foremost and yet does not take it to heart finds all his great learning to be in vain.

11–12. "But, foremost among *rākṣasas*, the self-possessed monarch should consult with his ministers concerning the timely use of bribery, conciliation, sowing dissension, coercive force, or any combination of these means, as well as the proper and improper ways of applying them. He who does so and practices righteousness, profit, and pleasure at their appropriate times never comes to grief in this world.

13. "And the king who, together with ministers who understand the true nature of things and have his interests at heart, deliberates over what he ought and ought not do in this world in order to achieve a beneficial result thrives.

14. "There are some men—dumb brutes, in fact—utterly ignorant of the import of the *śāstras*, who, once they are brought into discussions of policy, wish to speak out of sheer arrogance.

15. "One should not follow the pernicious advice of those who are ignorant of the *śāstras*, and unfamiliar with the treatises on statecraft, and simply eager to enhance their own positions.

16. "And those men who undermine all undertakings by foolishly uttering in their insolence pernicious advice that only seems beneficial should, after careful examination, be excluded from discussions of policy.

17. "For in this world some counselors, acting in concert with cunning enemies, persuade their master to engage in self-destructive actions, thus bringing him to ruin.

18. "When it comes to evaluating counsel, a master must, through a full investigation, determine which of his ministers are, in fact, enemies who are posing as friends although they have actually been suborned.

19. "For his enemies find the weak points of a rash king who suddenly rushes into undertakings, just as birds plunge into the gap in the Krauñca mountain.

20. "And so a king who underestimates his enemy and fails to protect himself meets with calamities and falls from his lofty state."

21. But when ten-necked Rāvaṇa had heard Kumbhakarṇa's speech, he knit his brows in anger and said this to him in a rage:

22. "How dare you lecture me like some venerable elder or preceptor? Why waste your effort on words like this? You must do what suits the present situation.

23. "It is useless now to keep on repeating what I failed to do then, whether from error, mental confusion, or reliance on my strength and valor.

24–25. "If you truly love me, if you truly understand what it means to be a brother, or if you believe in your heart that this mission is of the utmost urgency, then you must immediately do what suits the present situation. Please remedy through your valor this catastrophic result of my unsound policy.

26. "A true friend is one who stands by a poor wretch who has lost everything. A true kinsman is one who renders assistance to those who have gone astray."

27. As Rāvaṇa was speaking these firm and harsh words in this fashion, Kumbhakarṇa, thinking, "He is angry!" addressed him softly and soothingly.

28. Recognizing that his brother was extremely agitated, Kumbhakarṇa now spoke softly, soothing him.

29. "Enough of this agonizing, foremost king of the *rākṣasas*! You must put aside your anger and regain your composure.

30. "You need not give way to despondency as long as I am alive, your majesty. I will destroy him on whose account you are so anguished.

31. "Regardless of your mood, my bond of kinship and brotherly affection forced me to offer beneficial advice, your majesty.

32. "What is appropriate for a loving kinsman to do in the present circumstances is to slaughter your enemies. Now watch, as I do just that in battle.

33. "This very day, great-armed warrior, you shall see the hosts of tawny monkeys fleeing, once I have slain Rāma and his brother in the forefront of battle.

34. "This very day, you shall be happy, great-armed warrior, while Sītā will be desolated upon seeing me bring Rāma's head back from the battle.

35. "This very day, all the *rākṣasas* in Laṅkā whose kinsmen have been slain shall witness the most welcome death of Rāma.

36. "This very day, through the destruction of the enemy in battle, I shall wipe away the tears of those afflicted with grief on account of the slaughter of their kinsmen.

37. "This very day, you shall see the lord of the leaping monkeys, Sugrīva—huge as a mountain—torn to pieces in battle, like a storm cloud when the sun breaks through.

38. "You should not send out anyone else to fight, warrior of unequaled valor. I myself will slaughter your enemies, mighty king.

39. "I shall fight them, whether they be Śakra, Yama, Agni the purifier, Māruta, or even Varuṇa and Kubera.

40. "For even Indra himself, the smasher of citadels, would be terrified of me—with my sharp fangs and my body the size of a mountain—when I roar, holding aloft my keen lance.

41. "Or even were I to cast my weapon aside and swiftly trample our enemies, not one of them, if he valued his life, would be able to stand and face me.

42. "Not with a javelin, not with a mace, not with a sword, nor with keen arrows, but with my own two hands I shall, in my fury, slay even Indra himself, the wielder of the *vajra*.

43. "Even should Rāghava withstand the impact of my fist this day, then a hail of arrows will drink his blood.

44. "Why are you oppressed by anxiety while I am here, your majesty? I stand poised to sally forth for the destruction of your foes.

45. "Give up this fear of Rāma, your majesty. I shall slay Rāghava in battle as well as Lakṣmaṇa and mighty Sugrīva. For I wish to confer upon you great and extraordinary renown.

46. "I am off to bring you pleasure, the greatest of all pleasures, through the slaughter of Dāśarathi. Once I have slain Rāma along with Lakṣmaṇa, I shall devour all the leaders of the troops of tawny monkeys.

47. "So enjoy yourself to your heart's content. Drink fine wines. Attend to your duties and banish all cares. Once I have, this very day, sent Rāma to the abode of Yama, Sītā will at long last submit to your will."

The end of the fifty-first *sarga* of the *Yuddhakāṇḍa* of the *Śrī Rāmāyaṇa*.

Sarga 52

1. Now when Mahodara had heard those words uttered by huge, powerful Kumbhakarṇa with his immense arms, he said this:

2. "Although you were born in a noble family, Kumbhakarṇa, you are presumptuous and have a vulgar mind. You are arrogant and incapable of understanding what is to be done in any situation.

3. "It is not the case that the king does not understand sound and unsound policy, Kumbhakarṇa. But you, presumptuous in your childishness, just like to prattle.

4. "He is quite familiar with the distinctions of place and time; and he knows all about stasis, increase, and diminution both of himself and his enemies, bull among *rākṣasas*.

5. "For what wise man would engage in an action such as could only be performed by a vulgar-minded man of brute strength who does not honor his elders?

6. "And as for righteousness, profit, and pleasure, which you claim can be practiced separately, you lack the capacity to understand them as they truly are.

7. "For action alone is the motivating force behind all things. And in this world, even the most wicked actions may bear excellent fruit.

8. "Righteousness and sound policy may yield excellent results, but so may their opposites. Still, unrighteousness and unsound policy may also yield results that are calamitous.

9. "Men engage in actions with reference to this world and the next. So a person who indulges in pleasure may still attain excellent consequences.

10. "The king set his heart on this deed, and we all approved it. And besides, what is wrong with the use of violence against an enemy?

11. "Furthermore, as to your rationale for going forth to battle on your own, I shall explain to you why that is both inappropriate and harmful.

12. "How can you single-handedly defeat that very same Rāghava who earlier slaughtered so many immensely powerful *rākṣasas* in Janasthāna?

13. "You can see throughout the city all those mighty *rākṣasas* whom he earlier defeated in Janasthāna. They are still terrified to this day.

14. "In your ignorance you wish to rouse Daśaratha's son Rāma, who is like a raging lion, as one might rouse a sleeping serpent.

15. "For who can possibly assail him who is as irresistible as death, unassailable in his wrath, and ever blazing with energy?

16. "Our whole army would be in danger if it faced this enemy. Therefore, I do not approve of your going there alone.

17. "Who, moreover, lacking all resources, could hope, like some common fool, to subdue an enemy who possesses a wealth of resources and is determined to lay down his life?

18. "How, best of *rākṣasas*, can you possibly hope to fight someone who has no peer among men, but is equal to Indra or Vivasvant?"

19. Having spoken in this fashion to the enraged Kumbhakarṇa, Mahodara then, in the midst of the *rākṣasas*, addressed Rāvaṇa, who caused the world to cry out.

20. "Since you already have Vaidehī, why do you go on talking? Sītā will submit to your wishes whenever you desire.

21. "I have devised a ruse whereby Sītā will come to you. If it appeals to your way of thinking, lord of the *rākṣasas*, then hear me out.

22. "Have it proclaimed that these five—Dvijihva, Saṃhrādin, Kumbhakarṇa, Vitardana, and I—are going forth to kill Rāma.

23. "Then we will go out and engage Rāma in fierce battle. If we should defeat your enemies, then we shall have no further need of such a ruse.

24. "If, on the other hand, when we have finished the battle, our enemy should survive, then we shall adopt the ruse that I have devised in my mind.

25. "Our bodies rent by sharp arrows marked with Rāma's name, we shall return from the battle, covered with blood.

26. "Announcing, 'We have devoured Rāghava and Lakṣmaṇa,' we shall reverently clasp your feet. You must then reward us to our heart's content.

27. "Then, your majesty, you must have the following proclaimed throughout the city from elephant-back: 'Rāma has been slain along with his brother and his troops!'

28–29. "Then, feigning the greatest delight, subduer of your foes, you must cause your attendants to be given delicacies, servants, various desirable things, and wealth. Also have your heroic warriors given garlands, garments, and unguents. Your soldiers should be given copious drink, and you yourself must drink, feigning delight.

30ab–1138–30cdef. "Once this vicious rumor, 'The *rākṣasas* have devoured Rāma along with his companions!' has been heard and spread everywhere, you must go to Sītā privately and comfort her with consoling words. Then you should seduce her with wealth, grain, jewels, and various desirable things.

31. "By means of this deception, your majesty, which will give rise to fear and grief, Sītā, believing her husband dead, will come under your sway, unwilling though she may be.

32. "For once she grasps that her beloved husband is dead, she will come under your sway in her despair and feminine frailty.

33. "Previously she was raised in comfort, and though that is what she deserves, she has been racked with suffering. Once she realizes that her comfort is dependent upon you, she will, by all means, come to you.

34. "In my view this is the best policy. It would be catastrophic for you to confront Rāma. Don't be so anxious. If you remain here without fighting, you will surely gain great happiness.

35. "And so, conquering one's enemies without a fight, without the loss of one's army, and without placing oneself in danger, lord of the

people, one can long enjoy fame, great merit, majesty, and glory, lord of the earth!"

The end of the fifty-second *sarga* of the *Yuddhakāṇḍa* of the *Śrī Rāmāyaṇa*.

Sarga 53

1. When Kumbhakarṇa had been addressed in this fashion, he first reviled Mahodara and then addressed his brother Rāvaṇa, foremost of the *rākṣasas*.

2. "In killing that evil-minded Rāma this very day, I shall remove a terrible danger to you. With your enemy out of the way, may you be content.

3. "True heroes do not boast in vain, like empty clouds thundering. Watch now as my boasts are proven true by my feats in battle.

4. "True heroes do not tolerate insult, nor do they indulge in self-praise. But, without swaggering, they perform seemingly impossible feats.

*5. "It was through heeding the advice of cowards like you, Mahodara, ignorant fools, who think that they are wise, that the king has been brought to such a sorry state.

6. "It is people like you—cowards in battle and sycophants of the king, saying only what he wants to hear—that have constantly subverted this undertaking.

7. "Moreover, in counseling the king in the guise of friendship, you have acted, in fact, like an enemy. For Laṅkā has been virtually emptied save for the king, the treasury has been drained, and the army decimated.

8. "In order to remedy your unsound policy, I shall this very day go forth to war, fully prepared to defeat the enemy in battle."

9. When wise Kumbhakarṇa had spoken these words in this fashion, the lord of the *rākṣasas*, laughing, replied in these words:

10. "There is no doubt that Mahodara is terrified of Rāma. That's why the idea of battle does not appeal to him, dear boy so skillful in battle.

11. "I have no one who can equal you in loyalty and in strength. So go forth, Kumbhakarṇa, for the slaughter of our enemy and for victory!"

12. That slayer of his enemies swiftly seized his sharp lance. It was made entirely of black iron, but it glittered with ornaments of burnished gold.

13. The equal of Indra's thunderbolt, it was fearsome and as heavy as the *vajra*. It was a killer of gods, *dānavas*, *gandharvas*, *yakṣas*, and *kinnaras*.

14. It was adorned with massive garlands of red blossoms and stained red with the blood of his enemies. It spewed forth its inner fire. Seizing that sharp lance, the immensely powerful Kumbhakarṇa spoke these words to Rāvaṇa:

15. "Let your vast army stay here. I shall go forth alone. This very day, in my rage and ravenous hunger, I shall devour the monkeys!"

16. Upon hearing Kumbhakarṇa's speech, Rāvaṇa uttered these words: "You had best go forth accompanied by soldiers armed with lances and war hammers.

17. "For those great monkeys are swift and determined. They would surely kill you with their fangs should you be alone or caught off guard.

18. "Therefore you had best go forth accompanied by unassailable soldiers. You must annihilate the entire enemy force, which is such a menace to the *rākṣasas*."

19. Then, rising from his throne, immensely powerful Rāvaṇa bound upon Kumbhakarṇa's head a chaplet with a jewel at its center.

20. And he fastened upon great Kumbhakarṇa armlets, rings, a necklace of pearls that shone like the hare-marked moon, and other fine ornaments.

21. And Rāvaṇa hung upon him fragrant and celestial garlands of blossoms and placed magnificent earrings on his ears.

22. Wearing his golden bracelets and armlets and adorned with golden necklaces and other ornaments, huge-eared Kumbhakarṇa resembled a fire blazing up with oblations.

23. With his great black sword belt, he was as resplendent as Mount Mandara girded with the great serpent when the nectar of immortality was churned forth.

24. Girding on his impenetrable golden armor, which could withstand any blow and, blazing with its own luster, glittered like lightning, he resembled the king of the mountains, shrouded in clouds at sunset.

25. His body adorned with every ornament and lance in his hand, the *rākṣasa* resembled Nārāyaṇa when he had resolved to take his three strides.

26. He embraced his brother and reverently circumambulated him. Then, bowing his head to him, the immensely powerful warrior set forth. Rāvaṇa sent him off with auspicious blessings.

27. Chariot-warriors accompanied that great hero, himself the foremost of chariot-warriors, to the blare of conches and the beating of war drums. They were accompanied in turn by well-armed soldiers, elephants, horses, and chariots that rumbled like storm clouds.

28. They followed the fearsome and immensely powerful Kumbhakarṇa on serpents, camels, donkeys, horses, lions, elephants, and various other beasts and birds.

29. Strewn with showers of blossoms, a parasol held above him, and his sharp lance in hand, that foe of gods and *dānavas* went forth, intoxicated with strong drink and frenzied with the smell of blood.

30. Behind him, making a huge uproar, came many fearsome and immensely powerful *rākṣasa* foot soldiers. They had fearsome eyes and held weapons in their hands.

31–32. With their red eyes and their huge bodies, they looked like masses of black collyrium. They brandished lances, swords, keen battle-axes, iron clubs many fathoms long, maces, cudgels, huge trunks of palmyra trees, and slings that were not to be withstood.

33. Then taking on a different form—horrific and hair-raising—the highly energetic and immensely powerful Kumbhakarṇa marched forth.

34. He was now a hundred bow lengths wide and six hundred tall. Terrifying, his eyes as big as cartwheels, he looked like a huge mountain.

35. Resembling a scorched mountain, the huge Kumbhakarṇa, with his enormous mouth, arranged the *rākṣasas* in battle order. Then, laughing, he said this:

36. "This very day in my wrath I shall burn up the troops of the monkey leaders, one after another, just as a fire would so many moths.

37. "Granted, these forest-ranging monkeys have done me no harm. In fact, their kind is an ornament to the city parks of folks like us.

38. "However, it is Rāghava, along with Lakṣmaṇa, who is the root cause of the blockade of our city. Once he is killed, all of them will be destroyed, and I am going to kill him in battle."

39. As Kumbhakarṇa was speaking in this fashion, the *rākṣasas* sent up an extremely dreadful roar that seemed to make the very ocean tremble.

40. But as wise Kumbhakarṇa marched swiftly forth, dreadful omens appeared on every side.

41. Extremely dreadful clouds thundered, shedding meteors and lightning bolts, while the earth, together with its seas and forests, trembled.

42. Dreadful looking jackals howled, their mouths emitting flames, while birds wheeled in clockwise circles.

43. As he marched along the road, a vulture perched upon his lance. His left eye throbbed and his left arm trembled.

44. A blazing meteor crashed down with a horrific sound. The sun grew dim, and an ill wind began to blow.

45. But driven by the power of fate, Kumbhakarṇa marched on, heedless of the great and hair-raising portents that had appeared.

46. Stepping over the ramparts, that hero, who resembled a mountain, gazed upon the extraordinary monkey army, which looked like a mass of clouds.

47. And like clouds driven by the wind, the monkeys fled in all directions when they saw the foremost of the *rākṣasas*, who looked like a mountain.

48. Seeing that immensely fierce monkey army fleeing in all directions, like a scattered mass of clouds, Kumbhakarṇa, who resembled a cloud, in his joy roared thunderously like a cloud.

49. Upon hearing his dreadful roaring, which was like the rumbling of a rain-charged cloud in the sky, many of the leaping monkeys fell to the ground, like *sāla* trees cut off at the roots.

50. Great Kumbhakarṇa marched forth wielding a huge iron club for the destruction of his enemies. He looked like Lord Yama, with his servants and his rod, at the end of a cosmic age. Thus he inspired a paralyzing fear in the ranks of the monkeys.

The end of the fifty-third *sarga* of the *Yuddhakāṇḍa* of the *Śrī Rāmāyaṇa*.

Sarga 54

1. Kumbhakarṇa let loose a mighty roar that caused the ocean to resound, producing, as it were, thunderclaps and shattering, so it seemed, the very mountains.

2. When the monkeys saw him approaching, with his terrible eyes—he whom not even magnanimous Indra, Yama, or Varuṇa could kill—they scattered.

3. Seeing them scatter, Aṅgada, Vālin's son, addressed Nala, Nīla, Gavākṣa, and the immensely powerful Kumuda.

4. "Where are you going in such an access of panic, like vulgar tawny monkeys, forgetting who you are, your heroic deeds, and your noble lineage?

5. "Enough of this, gentle friends! Turn back! Why are you trying to save yourselves? This is no *rākṣasa* capable of fighting. It is just some huge scarecrow.

6. "With our valor we shall smash this huge scarecrow towering amid the *rākṣasas*. Turn back, leaping monkeys!"

7. When the tawny monkeys, with some difficulty, had been reassured, they regrouped here and there. Then, with trees and boulders in hand, they advanced toward the battlefield.

8. Turning back in a rage, the immensely powerful forest-dwelling monkeys, like wildly enraged bull elephants in rut, struck Kumbhakarṇa with lofty mountain peaks and boulders.

9. Although he was struck with trees, their branches in blossom, he was not shaken. Falling on his limbs, the boulders shattered into hundreds of pieces, while the trees, their branches in blossom, fell to the ground, splintered.

10. In a towering rage, he exerted himself mightily and wrought havoc upon the armies of the immensely powerful monkeys, just as a fire that has flared up might wreak havoc in a forest.

11. Hurled down, many of the bulls among monkeys lay there, drenched with blood, like crimson-blossomed trees that have fallen.

12. Leaping and running, the monkeys did not watch where they were going. Some fell into the sea, while others took to the sky.

13. As they were being slaughtered by the immensely powerful *rākṣasa*, those heroes fled along the same path by which they had crossed the ocean.

14. Some, their faces dejected through fear, fled down to the shore. Some apes climbed trees, while others fled to the mountain.

15. Some of them plunged into the sea, while others took refuge in caves. Some of the leaping monkeys sank down; none of them stood their ground.

16. Seeing that the monkeys had broken ranks, Aṅgada said this: "Turn back, leaping monkeys! Stand fast! Let us fight!

17. "If you break ranks, I can see no safe place for you, even should you circle the earth itself. Turn back, all of you! Why are you trying to save yourselves?

18. "Nothing can hinder your progress and your valor. But if you flee weaponless, your wives will mock you. But though you will have survived, that will be like death to you.

19. "Surely you were all born in long and great lineages. If, abandoning your valor, you flee in fear, you will certainly become contemptible.

20. "Where have they gone now, your great and lofty boasts that we heard before in the public assembly?

21. "When someone survives but is subject to censure, tales of his cowardice are bandied about. So follow the path that is fit for honorable men; abandon your fear.

22. "If, our life spans being short, we should lie slain upon the earth, then, since we would have died in battle, we would attain the world of Brahmā, so difficult to reach. But if we should slay the enemy in battle, we would attain glory.

23. "In any case, once Kumbhakarṇa sees Kākutstha, he will no more escape with his life than would a moth that flies into a blazing fire.

24. "If we who are so renowned should save our lives by fleeing, our reputations would be destroyed, since we, who are so many, would have been routed by a single warrior."

25. As heroic Aṅgada of the golden armlets was speaking in this fashion, the monkeys, still fleeing, responded to him in words that are to be condemned by the brave.

26. "The *rākṣasa* Kumbhakarṇa has wrought terrible slaughter among us. This is no time to stand our ground. We value our lives; so we're getting out of here."

27. Having said this much, all the monkey troop leaders, keeping their eyes on the advancing *rākṣasa*, so terrible with his terrible eyes, fled in all directions.

28. But, with soothing and respectful words, Aṅgada managed to get those heroic, wrinkle-faced monkeys to turn back, even as they fled.

29. Then Ṛṣabha, Śarabha, Mainda, Dhūmra, Nīla, Kumuda, Suṣeṇa, Gavākṣa, Rambha, and Tāra, led by Dvivida, Panasa, and Hanumān, the son of Vāyu, swiftly turned and headed back to the battlefield.

The end of the fifty-fourth *sarga* of the *Yuddhakāṇḍa* of the *Śrī Rāmāyaṇa*.

Sarga 55

1. And so, when those gigantic monkeys had heard Aṅgada's words, they turned back, eager for battle, resigning themselves to death.

2. At the words of Aṅgada, the wrinkle-faced monkeys were calmed, infused with courage, and incited to valor.

3. Then, marching forward in great excitement and resigned to death, the monkeys fought furiously, heedless of their lives.

4. Holding aloft trees and huge mountain peaks, those gigantic monkeys charged swiftly at Kumbhakarṇa.

5. But the valiant and colossal Kumbhakarṇa raised his mace and, in a towering rage, struck at his enemies, sending them flying in all directions.

6. Struck down by Kumbhakarṇa, the monkeys lay sprawled on the ground in groups of seven and eight hundred, and even in groups of thousands.

7. He raced about sweeping up groups of monkeys—sixteen, eight, ten, twenty, and thirty at a time—in his two arms and devouring them, just as Garuḍa, in his towering rage, devours the great serpents.

8. Hovering in the sky, Hanumān rained down mountain peaks and many different kinds of trees on Kumbhakarṇa's head.

9. But, with his lance, mighty Kumbhakarṇa shattered the mountain peaks and deflected the cascade of trees.

10. Then, grasping his keen lance, he raced toward the fearsome army of tawny monkeys. But Hanumān, seizing a mountain, stood directly in the path of the charging Kumbhakarṇa.

11. With it, the enraged monkey forcefully struck Kumbhakarṇa, whose body was as fearsome as a great mountain. Overwhelmed by that blow, the blood-splattered *rākṣasa* staggered, his limbs moistened with fat.

12. Brandishing his lance, which glittered like lightning and resembled a mountain, its highest peak in flames, he struck Māruti full in the chest, just as Guha struck Mount Krauñca with his fearsome javelin.

13. His mighty chest pierced by the lance, Hanumān was dazed and vomited blood from his mouth. There, in that great battle, he loosed a horrendous cry that was like the thundering of the clouds at the end of a cosmic age.

14. Then the *rākṣasa* hosts, seeing him afflicted, were suddenly delighted and sent up a cheer. But the monkeys themselves were afflicted, and, overwhelmed with fear of Kumbhakarṇa, they fled in the midst of battle.

15. Nīla then hurled a mountaintop at wise Kumbhakarṇa; but the latter, seeing it rushing toward him, struck it with his fist.

16. Struck by his fist, the mountaintop shattered and fell to the earth, shooting forth sparks and flames.

17. Then five tigers among monkeys—Ṛṣabha, Śarabha, Nīla, Gavākṣa, and Gandhamadana—rushed Kumbhakarṇa.

18. Those immensely powerful monkeys battered gigantic Kumbhakarṇa on all sides with mountains and trees and with their palms, feet, and fists.

19. But those blows felt like mere caresses to him, and he was not shaken in the least. He crushed swift Ṛṣabha with both arms.

20. Crushed in Kumbhakarṇa's arms, the fearsome Ṛṣabha, bull among monkeys, collapsed, blood oozing from his mouth.

21. Then, in battle, Kumbhakarṇa, Indra's foe, struck Śarabha with his fist, Nīla with his knee, and Gavākṣa with the palm of his hand.

22. Shaken by the blows they had been dealt, dazed, and spattered with blood, they fell to the ground, like *kiṃśuka* trees that have been cut down.

23. When those great monkey leaders had fallen, thousands of monkeys rushed Kumbhakarṇa.

24. And all those mighty bulls among leaping monkeys, who resembled mountains, began to bite him as they jumped and climbed up upon him, as if he were a mountain.

25. Those bulls among leaping monkeys struck at the gigantic Kumbhakarṇa with their claws, fangs, fists, and knees.

26. Covered with those thousands of monkeys, that tiger among *rākṣasas*, who already resembled a mountain, now looked like one overgrown with trees.

27. Then the mighty *rākṣasa* seized all those monkeys in his arms and devoured them, just as Garuḍa, in his rage, devours the great serpents.

28. Kumbhakarṇa crammed the monkeys into his mouth—as wide as the underworld Pātāla—until they came out of his nose and ears.

29. As he devoured those tawny monkeys in his towering rage, the furious *rākṣasa* chief, who looked like a mountain, routed the entire monkey host.

30. Drenching the earth with blood and flesh, the frenzied *rākṣasa* rampaged through the ranks of the tawny monkeys like the fire at the end of time.

31. In that battle, with his lance in hand, powerful Kumbhakarṇa resembled Śakra, *vajra* in hand, or Yama, ender of all things, with his noose in hand.

32. Kumbhakarṇa raged through the monkey ranks like Agni, the purifier, blazing through the dry woodlands in the summer.

33. Then, their troops decimated and their leaders slain, the monkeys, trembling with fear, cried out loudly and discordantly as they were slaughtered.

34. With so many of them being slaughtered by Kumbhakarṇa, the monkeys fled to Rāghava for refuge, shaken and despairing.

35. But the heroic lord of the monkeys, Sugrīva, seeing mighty Kumbhakarṇa rushing toward him, sprang up.

36. The great monkey tore off a mountain peak and, brandishing it, charged swiftly at mighty Kumbhakarṇa.

37. When Kumbhakarṇa, his every limb unscathed, saw that leaping monkey rushing toward him, he stopped and faced the monkey lord.

38. Seeing Kumbhakarṇa standing there devouring huge monkeys, his body smeared with their blood, Sugrīva said these words:

39. "You have struck down heroes; you have performed an impossibly difficult feat. You have devoured our troops and have gained the highest renown.

40. "But you should leave the monkey army alone. What have you to do with common soldiers? Now try to withstand a single blow of this mountain of mine, *rākṣasa*."

41. When the tiger among *rākṣasas*, Kumbhakarṇa, had heard that speech of the king of the tawny monkeys—a speech that showed his strength and fortitude—he uttered these words:

42. "You are the grandson of Prajāpati and the son of Ṛkṣarajas, and you are endowed with learning and valor. That is why you boast so, monkey."

43. When Sugrīva had heard these words of Kumbhakarṇa, he hefted the mountain and hurled it violently. He struck Kumbhakarṇa in the chest with that mountain, which was like Indra's *vajra* or a thunderbolt.

44. But the mountain peak shattered violently against his broad chest. At that, the leaping monkeys immediately grew despondent, while the hosts of *rākṣasas* roared with delight.

45. Kumbhakarṇa was furious at being struck by that mountain peak. He opened his mouth and bellowed with rage. Hefting his

lance, which glittered like lightning, he hurled it in order to kill the lord of the apes and tawny monkeys.

46. But Hanumān, son of Anila, swiftly leaping up, caught in both hands the sharp gold-corded lance, hurled by Kumbhakarṇa's arm, and quickly broke it.

47. Placing that immense lance, made of black iron and weighing many tons, across his knee, that bull among leaping monkeys snapped it in great excitement.

48. When the great *rākṣasa* lord saw that his lance was broken, he was enraged. Tearing off the summit of Laṅkā's Mount Malaya, he closed with Sugrīva and struck him with it.

49. Struck with that mountain peak in battle, the lord of the monkeys fell senseless to the ground. Seeing him fallen senseless to the ground in battle, the *yātudhānas* roared in delight.

50. Then Kumbhakarṇa rushed upon the lord of the monkeys, whose valor was fierce and wondrous. Seizing Sugrīva, he carried him off, as a violent wind might a cloud.

51. Moving through the battle, holding aloft Sugrīva, who resembled a huge cloud, Kumbhakarṇa, whose form rivaled that of Mount Meru, now resembled Mount Meru with a new, fearsome peak soaring above it.

52. The hero Kumbhakarṇa, holding Sugrīva aloft, proceeded on his way, as the *rākṣasa* lords sang his praises in the battle. He heard the cries of those who dwelt in heaven, home of the thirty gods, who were astonished at the capture of the king of the leaping monkeys.

53. Then, as Indra's foe, whose valor was that of Indra, was carrying off the lord of tawny monkeys, the equal of Indra himself, he reflected, "With this one out of the way, the entire army, Rāghava included, is as good as gone."

54–55. When wise Hanumān, son of Māruta, saw that the monkey army had fled in all directions and that the monkey Sugrīva had been taken by Kumbhakarṇa, he reflected, "What am I to do now that Sugrīva has been captured in this way?

56. "By all means, I shall do what is proper for me to do. I shall become like a mountain and crush the *rākṣasa*.

57. "Once I have slain mighty Kumbhakarṇa in battle, smashing his body with my fists, and freed the king of the monkeys, all the leaping monkeys shall rejoice.

58. "On the other hand, the king will surely free himself as he would even were he to be captured by the thirty gods together with the *asuras* and great serpents.

59. "I believe that because he was struck down in battle by Kumbhakarṇa with the blow of a mountain, the lord of the monkeys must not yet have regained consciousness.

60. "After a while, when he has regained consciousness, he will do what is best for himself and the monkeys in this great battle.

61. "On the other hand, if I were to free great Sugrīva, it would incur his most severe displeasure, as his reputation would be forever tarnished.

62. "Therefore, I shall wait awhile until our king's valor is recouped. Meanwhile, I shall rally the scattered army of the monkeys."

63. After reflecting in this fashion, Hanumān, son of Māruta, once more halted the flight of the vast monkey army.

64. Meanwhile, Kumbhakarṇa entered Laṅkā carrying the huge tawny monkey, who was still twitching. As he did so, he was strewn with showers of splendid blossoms by those standing on the palaces and at the gates of the buildings on the main thoroughfares.

65. Then, still held in the arms of the much stronger *rākṣasa*, the great monkey somehow regained consciousness. Gazing about him again and again at the city's royal highway, he fell to thinking.

*66. "Since I have been captured in this fashion, how in the world can I now strike back? I must perform such a feat as will be both desirable and beneficial for the tawny monkeys."

67. Suddenly grasping the foe of Indra, lord of the immortal gods, with his fingertips, the king of the tawny monkeys rent his ears with his claws and his nose with his fangs. Then he slashed Kumbhakarṇa along his flanks.

68. Bruised and wounded by him, robbed of his ears and nose, his body drenched in blood, Kumbhakarṇa was in a towering rage. Flinging Sugrīva off, he smashed him to the ground.

69. Smashed to the ground with terrible force and beaten all the while by the *rākṣasas*, the foes of the gods, Sugrīva, jumping up, flew swiftly into the sky and once more joined Rāma.

70. Stripped of his ears and nose and gushing blood, mighty Kumbhakarṇa looked like a mountain covered with waterfalls.

71. Then the great *rākṣasa* Kumbhakarṇa, rushing swiftly from the city, began to devour that fierce monkey army, as the blazing fire at the end of a cosmic age devours all creatures.

72. Ravenous and craving blood and flesh, Kumbhakarṇa plunged into the fierce monkey army and, in his madness, began to devour *rākṣasas*, tawny monkeys, *piśācas*, and apes in battle.

73. With one hand he seized monkeys in his rage—one, two, three, or more—and swiftly hurled them into his mouth, together with *rākṣasas*.

74. Streaming with blood and fat and pounded with the peaks of lordly mountains, the mighty *rākṣasa* devoured the monkeys. As they were being devoured, the tawny monkeys ran to Rāma for shelter.

75. At that moment, Sumitrā's son Lakṣmaṇa, destroyer of enemy armies and conqueror of enemy citadels, entered the fight in a rage.

76. Valiant Lakṣmaṇa sunk seven arrows into Kumbhakarṇa's body. Then he took up some more and let them fly.

77. But mighty Kumbhakarṇa bypassed Saumitri and raced directly toward Rāma, seeming as he did so to tear up the very earth.

78. Then Rāma Dāśarathi, invoking the divine weapon-spell of Rudra, loosed sharp arrows at Kumbhakarṇa's breast.

79. As he ran about violently in a rage, wounded by Rāma, flames mixed with blazing coals poured from his mouth.

80. As those arrows, fletched with peacock feathers, sank into his chest, his massive mace slipped from his hand and fell to the ground.

81. When the immensely powerful *rākṣasa* realized that he had no weapons left, he wrought tremendous slaughter with his fists and his feet.

82. Drenched with blood, his body pierced all over with arrows, he poured forth blood, as a mountain does its waterfalls.

83. Suffused with fierce rage and covered with blood, he raced about devouring monkeys, *rākṣasas*, and apes.

84. At this point, righteous Lakṣmaṇa, who was intent upon killing Kumbhakarṇa and who had been weighing many methods of doing so, spoke to Rāma.

85. "He cannot distinguish between monkeys and *rākṣasas*. Intoxicated with the smell of blood, he is devouring his allies and his enemies alike.

86. "Very well, let the bulls among monkeys swarm all over him so that the principal troop leaders may take their stand all around him.

87. "Then, after some time, that evil-minded *rākṣasa*, falling to the ground, crushed by that heavy burden, will not kill any more of the leaping monkeys."

88. When the leaping monkeys had heard those words of the wise prince, they swarmed upon Kumbhakarṇa in great excitement.

89. But Kumbhakarṇa was enraged at being swarmed all over by the leaping monkeys, and he shook them off violently, as a vicious elephant might riders mounted on his back.

90. Seeing them shaken off, Rāma, thinking, "This *rākṣasa* is infuriated," took up his splendid bow and sprang toward him.

91. Rāma, his splendid quiver of arrows fastened on him, took up his fearsome, tautly strung bow, variegated with burnished gold and resembling a serpent. He sprang forward, rallying the tawny monkeys.

92. Accompanied by Lakṣmaṇa and surrounded by the monkey troops, invincible and mighty Rāma continued to advance.

93–96. He gazed upon great and mighty Kumbhakarṇa, the diademed tamer of his foes, whose every limb was drenched with blood. Rushing upon them all in a mad fury, that *rākṣasa* was like one of the great elephants that support the earth. Furious and surrounded by *rākṣasas*, he was hunting down the tawny monkeys. Adorned with golden armlets, he resembled the Vindhya mountain or Mount Mandara. He spewed blood from his mouth, like a towering storm cloud pouring rain. Drenched with blood, he lapped it up with his tongue. Crushing the monkey hosts, he resembled Yama, who brings time itself to an end.

97. As he gazed upon that foremost of the *rākṣasas*, whose splendor was that of a blazing fire, the bull among men twanged his bowstring.

98. Enraged at the sound of his bow and unable to endure it, that bull among *rākṣasas*, sons of chaos, charged at Rāghava.

99. Then, as the mountainous Kumbhakarṇa, his arms like the splendid coils of the king of great serpents, rushed toward him in battle, like a storm cloud driven by the wind, Rāma addressed him.

100. "Don't lose heart now, lord of the *rākṣasas*! Know, foe of Śakra, that it is I, Rāma, who stand before you, wielding my bow. You are about to die."

101. When Kumbhakarṇa realized, "It's Rāma!" he laughed with a hideous sound that caused the hearts of all the forest-dwelling monkeys to sink.

102. With a fearsome and hideous laugh that was like the thundering of storm clouds, immensely powerful Kumbhakarṇa said these words to Rāghava:

103. "You should know that I am no Virādha, Kabandha, Khara, Vālin, or Mārīca. It is I, Kumbhakarṇa, who have come.

104. "Gaze upon my huge and fearsome war hammer, all made of black iron. In the past, I defeated the gods and *dānavas* with it.

105. "Nor should you treat me contemptuously, thinking, 'He has lost his ears and nose!' For the loss of my ears and nose causes me not the slightest discomfort.

106. "Now, tiger among the Ikṣvākus, you should demonstrate your puny strength against my limbs. Then, once I have witnessed your manliness and valor, I will devour you."

107. Upon hearing these words of Kumbhakarṇa, Rāma let fly beautifully fletched arrows. Though they struck him with the impact of a thunderbolt, that enemy of the gods was neither shaken nor harmed.

108. Those same arrows—like thunderbolts—that had pierced the great *sāla* trees and slain Vālin, bull among monkeys, could not wound Kumbhakarṇa's body.

109. That foe of great Indra, however, absorbed those arrows with his body, as one might drink a trickle of water. For, in whirling his war hammer with its fierce impact, he had blunted the impact of Rāma's arrows.

110. Then, covered with blood, the *rākṣasa*, a terror to the vast hosts of the gods, whirling his war hammer with its fierce impact, put the army of tawny monkeys to flight.

111. Then, taking up the excellent divine weapon-spell of Vāyu, Rāma loosed it at that night-roaming *rākṣasa* and, with it, took off his arm that held the war hammer. His arm severed, Kumbhakarṇa roared deafeningly.

112. Severed by Rāghava's arrow, that arm of his, which was like a mountain peak and was still holding the war hammer, fell upon the army of the king of the tawny monkeys, wreaking carnage among the monkey troops.

113. The monkeys who had survived that carnage were routed and fled in despair to the edge of the battlefield. From there, their bodies trembling, they watched the fearsome duel between the *rākṣasa* lord and the lord of men.

114. His arm severed by the divinely charged weapon, Kumbhakarṇa tore up a tree with his hand and rushed in battle at the lord of men, like some huge and lordly mountain whose peak had been severed.

115. But, with an arrow variegated with *jāmbūnada* gold and charged with the divine weapon-spell of Indra, Rāma cut off Kumbhakarṇa's upraised arm, which resembled the coils of a great serpent and held the *sāla* tree.

116. Kumbhakarṇa's severed arm, resembling a mountain, fell to the ground, where, thrashing about, it crushed trees, mountains, rocks, monkeys, and *rākṣasas*.

117. Seeing Kumbhakarṇa, his arms severed, rushing suddenly upon him and roaring, Rāma took up two sharp half-moon-headed arrows and, with them, cut off the *rākṣasa*'s feet in battle.

118. His arms and feet severed, Kumbhakarṇa opened wide his mouth, which was like the mare's head fire that lies beneath the sea. Bellowing, he hurled himself suddenly upon Rāma, like Rāhu, demon of the eclipse, upon the moon in the heavens.

119. But Rāma filled Kumbhakarṇa's mouth with sharp arrows, their fletching bound with gold. His mouth full, Kumbhakarṇa was unable to speak. With great effort, he moaned and lost consciousness.

120. Then Rāma took up the arrow of Indra, sharp, beautifully fletched and perfect. It shone like the rays of the sun. It had the speed of Māruta, and it resembled the staff of Brahmā or Kāla, the ender of all things.

121. Its fletching was gorgeous with diamonds and *jāmbūnada* gold, and it shone like the blazing sun or fire. It had the striking power of great Indra's *vajra* or a thunderbolt; and Rāma loosed it at the night-roaming *rākṣasa*.

122. Set in motion by Rāghava's arm, the arrow sped on its way, lighting up the ten directions with its inherent splendor. Its appearance was as brilliant as that of Agni Vaiśvānara, undimmed by smoke, and its power was equal to that of mighty Śakra's thunderbolt.

123. With it, Rāma severed the *rākṣasa* lord's head—huge as a mountain peak, its fangs bared, and its gorgeous earrings swinging wildly—just as, long ago, Indra, smasher of citadels, severed the head of Vṛtra.

124. Struck off by Rāma's arrow, the *rākṣasa*'s head, which resembled a mountain, fell. It smashed the gates of the buildings on the main thoroughfares and knocked down the lofty rampart.

125. Finally, the enormous *rākṣasa*, who looked like Himalaya, fell into the sea, abode of waters. There he crushed crocodiles, shoals of huge fish, and serpents before he entered the earth.

126. When Kumbhakarṇa, that mighty foe of brahmans and gods, was slain in battle, the earth shook and all the mountains trembled, while the gods in delight raised a tumultuous cheer.

127. The divine seers, great seers, great serpents, gods, the spirits of the departed, the great birds, and *guhyakas*, together with the troops of *yakṣas* and *gandharvas*, hovering in the sky, were delighted by Rāma's valor.

128. Those countless monkeys, their faces like blooming lotuses, were overjoyed, and they paid honor to Rāghava, who had achieved his objective in having slain an unassailable enemy of such fearsome power.

129. Once Bharata's older brother had slain in combat Kumbhakarṇa, crusher of the hosts of the gods, whose efforts had never before been thwarted in great battles, he rejoiced, as did Indra, the lord of the immortal gods, when he had slain the great *asura* Vṛtra.

The end of the fifty-fifth *sarga* of the *Yuddhakāṇḍa* of the *Śrī Rāmāyaṇa*.

Sarga 56

1. When the *rākṣasas* saw that Kumbhakarṇa had been slain by great Rāghava, they reported it to Rāvaṇa, lord of the *rākṣasas*.

2. Upon hearing that the immensely powerful Kumbhakarṇa had been slain in battle, Rāvaṇa was stricken with grief. He lost consciousness and collapsed.

3. Hearing that their paternal uncle had been slain, Devāntaka, Narāntaka, Triśiras, and Atikāya were stricken with grief and wept.

4. When Mahodara and Mahāpārśva heard that their brother had been slain by Rāma, tireless in action, they were overwhelmed with grief.

5. Then Rāvaṇa, bull among *rākṣasas*, regained consciousness with difficulty. Despondent at the slaying of Kumbhakarṇa, he began to lament.

6. "Alas, Kumbhakarṇa, mighty and valorous crusher of your enemies' pride! After single-handedly scorching the army of our foe, where have you gone, abandoning me?

7. "Now I am truly lost, since my right arm, relying on which I feared neither the gods nor the *asuras*, has now fallen.

8. "How could such a hero, a crusher of the pride of the gods and *dānavas*, who was like the fire at the end of time, have been slain today in battle by Rāghava?

9. "How can it be that you, whom the blow of even Indra's *vajra* could never harm, now sleep on the ground, mangled by Rāma's arrows.

10. "Seeing you struck down in battle, the hosts of gods, hovering in the sky together with the seers, are shouting in delight.

11. "Undoubtedly, the leaping monkeys, in their excitement, will seize the opportunity and scale the unbreachable gates of Laṅkā from every side.

12. "I have no further use for kingship, and what good is Sītā to me now? Without Kumbhakarṇa, I can take no pleasure in life.

13. "If I should fail to kill in battle Rāghava, my brother's killer, then, surely death would be better for me than this pointless existence.

14. "I shall go this very day to the place where my younger brother has gone. For I cannot bear to live a single moment without my brothers.

15. "The gods will surely laugh when they see me, who have done them great injury. But how, Kumbhakarṇa, shall I vanquish Indra now that you have been slain?

16. "This has befallen me, because, in my folly, I failed to heed the beneficial advice of great Vibhīṣaṇa.

17. "Since Kumbhakarṇa and Prahasta suffered such cruel deaths, the words of Vibhīṣaṇa have put me to shame.

18. "Now, I have experienced the grievous fruit of my action in that I drove out majestic and righteous Vibhīṣaṇa."

19. Thus piteously lamenting for Kumbhakarṇa in many ways, ten-faced Rāvaṇa was shaken to his innermost core. Realizing that his younger brother, the foe of Indra, had been slain, he collapsed in profound distress.

The end of the fifty-sixth *sarga* of the *Yuddhakāṇḍa* of the *Śrī Rāmāyaṇa*.

Sarga 57

1. After listening to the lamentations of evil-minded Rāvaṇa, who was lamenting in his burning grief, Triśiras spoke these words:

2. "True enough, our dear and immensely valorous uncle, middlemost among you three brothers, has been slain. Nonetheless, your majesty, true men do not lament as you have done.

3. "Surely you are a match for all the three worlds, lord. Why then do you feel sorry for yourself in this fashion, like some ordinary person?

4. "Brahmā has given you a javelin, armor, a bow and arrow, and a chariot rumbling like a thundercloud and yoked to a thousand donkeys.

5. "Time and again, even when unarmed, you have slain the gods and the *dānavas*. Now, equipped with all your weapons, you must slay Rāghava.

6. "Or rather remain here, great king. I myself shall go forth to battle. I shall exterminate your enemies, just as does Garuḍa the great serpents.

7. "Struck down by me this very day in battle, Rāma shall be laid low, just as was Śambara by Indra, king of the gods, and Naraka by Viṣṇu."

8. When Rāvaṇa, lord of the *rākṣasas*, had heard those words of Triśiras, he felt—impelled as he was by his own impending doom—that he had obtained a new lease on life.

9. And when Devāntaka, Narāntaka, and powerful Atikāya had heard the words of Triśiras, they were filled with eagerness for battle.

10. Then those heroic sons of Rāvaṇa, bulls among *rākṣasas*, sons of chaos, equal in valor to mighty Śakra himself, cried out, "I'll go! I'll go!"

11. All of them could fly through the air. All of them were skilled in magical illusion. All of them had crushed the pride of the thirty gods. All of them were ferocious in battle.

12. All were provided with troops and divinely charged weapons. All had gained wide renown. None had ever been known to suffer defeat in battle.

13. All those heroes were expert in the use of divine weapon-spells. All were adept in combat. All were endowed with higher knowledge. All had obtained boons.

14. Surrounded by his sons, whose brilliance equaled that of the sun and who had crushed the strength of their enemies, the king resembled magnanimous Indra surrounded by the immortal gods, destroyers of the pride of the great *dānavas*.

15. He embraced his sons and adorned them with ornaments. Then, invoking the highest blessings, he sent them off to battle.

16. Rāvaṇa also dispatched his two brothers Mahodara and Mahāpārśva to guard the princes in battle.

17. Taking respectful leave of great Rāvaṇa, who made his enemies cry out, and reverently circling him, those gigantic warriors set forth.

18. Those six immensely powerful and prominent *rākṣasas*, sons of chaos, anointed themselves with all protective herbs and fragrances and then set forth, eager for battle.

19. Mahodara mounted an elephant named Sudarśana, born in the lineage of Airāvata and resembling a black storm cloud.

20. Mounted upon that elephant, which was equipped with every weapon and adorned with quivers, he was as splendid as Sūrya,

impeller of all creatures, perched on the summit of the western mountain.

21. Triśiras, Rāvaṇa's son, mounted a splendid chariot, which was yoked to magnificent horses and laden with every sort of weapon.

22. Mounted in his chariot, bow in hand, Triśiras was as resplendent as a storm cloud charged with lightning and meteors, flashing fire, and traversed by a rainbow.

23. Mounted on that splendid chariot, Triśiras, with his three diadems, was as splendid as Himalaya, lord of mountains, with his three golden peaks.

24. Next, Atikāya, foremost of all bowmen and a powerful son of the *rākṣasa* lord, mounted his splendid chariot.

25. It had a magnificent axle and wheels and was splendidly yoked. It had a fine frame and yoke pole. It glittered with quivers and bows, and it was laden with darts, swords, and iron clubs.

26. With his glittering diadem, variegated with gold, and his ornaments, Atikāya was as resplendent as Mount Meru illuminated by the rays of the shining sun.

27. Standing in that chariot, surrounded by those tigers among the *rākṣasas*, sons of chaos, the mighty son of the king was as resplendent as Indra, *vajra* in hand, surrounded by the immortal gods.

28. Narāntaka then mounted a huge white horse. Swift as thought and adorned with gold, it resembled Uccaiḥśravas himself.

29. Taking up a dart that was like a meteor, Narāntaka was as resplendent as powerful Guha when he has taken up his javelin amid his enemies in battle.

30. Taking up an iron club studded with diamonds, Devāntaka looked like the very image of Viṣṇu when he had seized the mountain with both arms.

31. Taking up his mace, powerful and heroic Mahāpārśva resembled Kubera himself in battle, mace in hand,

32. As they set forth surrounded by incomparable troops, those great warriors were like the gods in Amarāvatī, surrounded by incomparable troops.

33. They were followed by great *rākṣasas* with splendid weapons, mounted on elephants and horses and riding on chariots that rumbled like storm clouds.

34. Endowed with splendor, those great princes, diademed and radiant as the sun, looked like blazing planets in the sky.

35. The white row of parasols held above them, resembling a bank of autumnal clouds, looked like a line of *haṃsas* in the sky.

36. Eager for battle, the heroes marched forth, grimly resolved, for they had determined either to conquer their enemies or die.

37. As those great warriors, ferocious in battle, marched forth, they bellowed, roared, and loosed arrows in their frenzy.

38. The earth itself seemed to shake from the sounds of their roaring and the slapping of their arms, while the lion roars of the *rākṣasas* seemed almost to shatter the sky.

39. As they marched forth, in great delight, the mighty *rākṣasa* lords spied the monkey army with its upraised boulders and trees.

40. The great tawny monkeys, too, spied the army of the *rākṣasas*, sons of chaos. It was crowded with elephants, horses, and chariots, and it resounded with the jingling of hundreds of little bells.

41. It looked like a black storm cloud, and it bristled with huge weapons. It was filled on every side with *rākṣasas*, sons of chaos, resplendent as blazing fires or the sun.

42. Watching the approaching army, the leaping monkeys, perceiving their opportunity, raised huge mountains and roared again and again.

43. Hearing the resounding cries of the monkey troop leaders, the mighty hosts of *rākṣasas*, unable to endure the fierce enthusiasm of their enemies, roared more frightfully still.

44. As they plunged into the fearsome *rākṣasa* army, the troop leaders of the tawny monkeys, resembling mountains with lofty summits, stormed about with upraised boulders.

45. Armed with trees and boulders, the leaping monkeys stormed through the *rākṣasa* troops in a rage, some leaping into the air, others remaining on the ground.

46. Then, though they were kept at bay by torrents of arrows, the tawny monkeys, fearsome in their valor, unleashed a stupendous hail of trees, rocks, and mountains.

47. Both the *rākṣasas* and the monkeys uttered leonine roars in the battle. And the leaping monkeys crushed the *yātudhānas* with boulders.

48–49. In a rage some of the leaping monkeys slew in battle heroes, clad in armor and adornments and mounted on chariots, elephants, and horses, while others, leaping up violently, slaughtered the *yātudhānas*. Those bulls among *rākṣasas*, their eyes knocked out by fists and falling mountain peaks, fled, fell, and shrieked.

50. In a short while, the ground was covered with boulders and swords dropped by the tawny monkeys and *rākṣasas*, and it was drenched with blood.

51. Crushers of their foes, the *rākṣasas*, who looked like shattered mountains, hurled their broken lances; but these were repulsed by the monkeys.

52. Night-roaming *rākṣasas* slaughtered monkeys with monkeys, while monkeys slaughtered *rākṣasas* with *rākṣasas*.

53. Snatching away the tawny monkeys' boulders, the *rākṣasas* slaughtered them, while the monkeys, stripping away the *rākṣasas*' weapons, slaughtered them.

54. Smashing one another with boulders, lances, and missiles, the monkeys and *rākṣasas* roared like lions in battle as they slaughtered one another.

55. Struck down by the monkeys, their mail and armor pierced, the *rākṣasas* oozed blood, as trees do their vital sap.

56. In that battle, some of the monkeys smashed chariot with chariot, elephant with elephant, and horse with horse.

57. But the *rākṣasas* cut down the trees and boulders of the monkey lords with sharp arrows—horseshoe-headed, half-moon-headed, and crescent-headed.

58. With the monkeys and *rākṣasas* slain in battle, and with all the shattered mountaintops and splintered trees, the ground became impassable.

59. When the wrinkle-faced monkeys showed their excitement in that tumultuous battle and the *rākṣasas* were being struck down, the great seers and the hosts of gods cheered.

60. But then Narāntaka, mounting a horse as swift as Māruta, and seizing a sharp javelin, plunged into the army of the monkey king, as might a fish into the vast ocean.

61. That hero pierced seven hundred monkeys with his glittering dart. In an instant, that great foe of Indra single-handedly decimated the army of those bulls among tawny monkeys.

62. The *vidyādharas* and great seers watched that great warrior as, mounted on horseback, he rampaged through the troops of tawny monkeys.

63. One could mark his path, mired in flesh and blood and littered with the monkeys—huge as mountains—who had fallen.

64. No sooner would the bulls among leaping monkeys resolve to attack him than Narāntaka would attack and pierce them.

65. Raising his blazing dart in the midst of the battle, Narāntaka consumed the troops of tawny monkeys, as fire might the forests.

66. No sooner would the forest-dwelling monkeys uproot trees and boulders than they would fall, struck down by that dart, like mountains riven by a thunderbolt.

67. In that battle, mighty Narāntaka rampaged in all directions, like the wind in the rainy season, leveling everything in his path.

68. Those heroes were unable to flee, or stand their ground, or even stir in any direction. For that mighty warrior pierced them all, whether they leapt, ran, or stood still.

69. Pierced by that lone warrior, who, with his dart as brilliant as the sun, was like Yama, the ender of all things, the monkey troops fell to the ground.

70. Unable to withstand the blows of that dart, which had the crushing force of a thunderbolt, the monkeys wailed loudly.

71. As they fell, the bodies of the heroes among the tawny monkeys resembled mountains falling as their tall summits were shattered by thunderbolts.

*72. Meanwhile, those great monkey leaders who had earlier been struck down by Kumbhakarṇa, now fully recovered, approached Sugrīva.

73. Gazing about him, Sugrīva saw the army of tawny monkeys fleeing in all directions, terrified in their fear of Narāntaka.

74. As he watched the fleeing army, he spied Narāntaka, mounted on horseback and heading toward him, holding his dart.

75. Then immensely powerful Sugrīva, overlord of the monkeys, addressed heroic Prince Aṅgada, who was equal in valor to Śakra.

76. "Hero, you must advance against that *rākṣasa,* the one mounted on horseback, who has been terrorizing the army of tawny monkeys. And you must swiftly kill him."

77. Upon hearing these words of his lord, Aṅgada burst forth from that host—so like a cloud—as does the many-rayed sun from a host of clouds.

78. Adorned with his golden armlets and resembling a dense mass of stone, Aṅgada, foremost of the tawny monkeys, was as resplendent as a mountain laced with shining ore.

79. Armed only with his claws and fangs and lacking any other weapon, Vālin's immensely powerful son confronted Narāntaka and spoke these words:

80. "Stop! Why bother with such common tawny monkeys? Hurl your dart swiftly against this chest of mine, as hard to the touch as adamant."

81. Upon hearing Aṅgada's words, Narāntaka, biting his lips with his teeth and hissing like a serpent, flew into a rage.

82. Then he brandished his blazing dart and suddenly loosed it against Aṅgada. But it shattered against the adamantine chest of Vālin's son and fell to the ground.

83. Then, glancing at that shattered dart, which now resembled the coils of a serpent torn to pieces by Suparṇa, Vālin's son raised his palm and, with it, struck Narāntaka's horse on the head.

84. At that blow of his palm, the horse, which looked like a mountain, collapsed to the ground, its head shattered, its feet driven into the earth, the pupils of its eyes burst, and its tongue lolling out.

85. When immensely powerful Narāntaka saw that his horse had fallen, slain, he was beside himself with rage. He raised his fist and, with it, struck Vālin's son on the head in battle.

86. His head split open by that fist, Aṅgada poured forth great gouts of scalding blood. For a moment he flared up in anger, then fainted. Regaining consciousness, he was astonished.

87. Then Vālin's great son Aṅgada clenched his fist, which resembled a mountain peak and the impact of which was equal to that of a thunderbolt, and brought it down upon Narāntaka's chest.

88. His chest shattered by the impact of that fist and his body drenched with blood, Narāntaka, like a mountain shattered by the force of a thunderbolt, fell to the ground vomiting flames.

89. When that most eminent of heroes, Narāntaka, had thus been slain in battle by Vālin's son, the foremost among the thirty gods, hovering in the sky, along with the forest-dwelling monkeys gave a mighty cheer.

90. When Aṅgada, that warrior of extraordinary might and valor, had performed this nearly impossible feat of valor—cheering the heart of Rāma—he was somewhat astonished, but was filled once more with energy for battle.

The end of the fifty-seventh *sarga* of the *Yuddhakāṇḍa* of the *Śrī Rāmāyaṇa*.

Sarga 58

1. When those bulls among the *rākṣasas*, sons of chaos—Devāntaka, Trimūrdhan Paulastya, and Mahodara—saw that Narāntaka had been slain, they began to wail.

2. Then mighty Mahodara, mounted upon a magnificent bull elephant as huge as a cloud, charged at Añgada, Vālin's immensely powerful son.

3. And mighty Devāntaka, too, anguished at the slaughter of his brother, took up a blazing iron club and rushed toward Añgada.

4. The heroic Triśiras, mounted on a chariot as radiant as the sun and yoked to splendid horses, also raced toward Vālin's son.

5. Attacked by those three lords of the *rākṣasas*, sons of chaos, crushers of the pride of the gods, Añgada tore up a tree with huge branches.

6. Just as Śakra hurls his blazing thunderbolt, so did heroic Añgada violently hurl that huge tree with its huge branches at Devāntaka.

7. But Triśiras cut it to pieces with arrows like venomous serpents. Then Añgada, seeing the tree splintered, leapt up into the sky.

8. From there, that elephant among monkeys rained down trees and boulders. But Triśiras, in a towering rage, cut them to pieces with his sharp arrows.

9. And Surāntaka as well smashed those trees with the tip of his iron club, while Triśiras assaulted heroic Añgada with arrows.

10. Mahodara, too, in a towering rage, charged at Vālin's son on his elephant and hit him on the chest with iron cudgels that struck with the force of thunderbolts.

11. Meanwhile, in a towering rage, swift Devāntaka confronted Añgada and, after striking him with an iron club, swiftly withdrew.

12. But although the son of Vālin was assaulted simultaneously by those three formidable *rākṣasas*, sons of chaos, that immensely powerful and valorous warrior remained unshaken.

13. Leaping up, he struck Mahodara's great elephant violently with his open hand. Its eyes knocked out, the bull elephant trumpeted loudly.

14. Then, ripping out one of its tusks, the immensely powerful son of Vālin rushed upon Devāntaka in battle and struck him with it.

15. Swaying with every limb like a tree buffeted by the wind, Devāntaka spewed blood the color of lac from his mouth.

16. Then, recovering with difficulty, powerful and mighty Devāntaka brandished his dreadful iron club and once more struck Aṅgada.

17. Struck with that iron club, the son of the lord of the monkeys sank to his knees on the ground but then leapt up once more.

18. But as the son of the lord of the tawny monkeys sprang up, Triśiras struck him in the forehead with three dreadful arrows that resembled venomous serpents.

19. When Hanumān and Nīla realized that Aṅgada had been surrounded by three of the bulls among *rākṣasas*, sons of chaos, they ran to his aid.

20. Then Nīla hurled a mountaintop at Triśiras. But that wise son of Rāvaṇa shattered it with sharp arrows.

21. Pierced by hundreds of arrows, its stony surface shredded, the mountaintop fell, shooting forth sparks and flames.

22. Then, upon witnessing that explosion with delight, Devāntaka, with his iron club, rushed toward Hanumān, son of Māruta, in battle.

23. But Hanumān, son of Māruta, leapt upon the charging Devāntaka and struck him on the head with his fist, which had the force of a thunderbolt.

24. His head shattered by the crushing blow of that fist, Devāntaka, son of the *rākṣasa* king, all at once fell lifeless to the ground, his teeth and eyes knocked out, his tongue lolling.

25. When mighty Devāntaka, foremost of *rākṣasa* warriors and foe of the gods, had been slain in battle, Trimūrdhan, enraged, loosed a fierce shower of sharp-tipped arrows at Nīla's chest.

26. Deluged by those torrents of arrows and pierced in every limb, Nīla, the guardian of the monkey troops, was slack limbed and immobilized by mighty Triśiras.

27. But then, regaining consciousness, Nīla ripped up a mountain along with its masses of trees, and, springing up with huge and terrible speed, he struck Mahodara on the head with it.

28. Crushed together with his elephant by the mountain as it fell, Mahodara was mortally wounded and fell lifeless to the ground, like a mountain struck by a thunderbolt.

29. When Triśiras saw that his paternal uncle had been slain, he took up his bow and, in a towering rage, riddled Hanumān with sharp arrows.

30. But, in a rage, Hanumān sprang up and tore the horses of Triśiras to pieces with his claws, just as a lion, king of beasts, might a mighty elephant.

31. Then, seizing his javelin, Triśiras, son of Rāvaṇa, hurled it at the son of Anila, just as Yama, ender of all things, unleashes Kālarātri, the dark night of universal destruction.

32. But the tiger among tawny monkeys caught that javelin, which had been hurled, as it flew unimpeded, like a blazing meteor hurtling through the sky. He broke it and roared.

33. When the hosts of monkeys saw that Hanumān had broken that fearsome-looking javelin, they were delighted, and they roared thunderously like storm clouds.

34. Then Triśiras, foremost among the *rākṣasas*, raised his sword and, in his rage, buried it in the chest of the monkey lord.

35. Although he was injured by that sword stroke, mighty Hanumān, son of Māruta, struck Trimūrdhan on the chest with his open hand.

36. When Hanumān struck him with his open hand, immensely powerful Triśiras let his garments slip from his hands, and he fell to the ground unconscious.

37. And as Triśiras fell, the great monkey, who looked like a mountain, grabbed his sword and roared, terrifying all the *rākṣasas*, sons of chaos.

38. Then that night-roaming *rākṣasa*, unable to bear that sound, sprang up and struck Hanumān with his fist.

39. The great monkey was angered by the blow of that fist, and, in a rage, he seized that bull among *rākṣasas* by the crown.

40. Then, with Triśiras's own sharp sword, the furious son of Anila cut off his heads—with their diadems and earrings—just as did Śakra the heads of Tvaṣṭṛ's son.

41. Like so many stars fallen from the path of the sun, those heads of Indra's foe, huge as mountains, with their gaping orifices and their eyes blazing like Agni Vaiśvānara, fell to the ground.

42. When Hanumān, whose valor was equal to that of Śakra, had slain Triśiras, foe of the gods, the leaping monkeys cheered, the earth trembled, and the *rākṣasas* fled in all directions.

43–44. Once the extremely irascible and mighty Mahāpārśva saw that Triśiras had been slain as well as Mahodara and the unassailable warriors Devāntaka and Narāntaka, he flew into a rage and seized his splendid, blazing mace made of solid iron.

45–46. It was encircled with bands of gold and smeared with flesh and blood. Reddened with the blood of his enemies, it shone with splendor. Adorned with red garlands, its tip blazing with energy, it could terrify even the mighty elephants Airāvata, Mahāpadma, and Sārvabhauma.

47. Grasping that mace in a towering rage, mighty Mahāpārśva hurled himself upon the tawny monkeys, like the blazing fire at the end of a cosmic age.

48. But the mighty monkey Ṛṣabha sprang up and, confronting Mahāpārśva, Rāvaṇa's younger brother, took a stand before him.

49. Seeing that monkey, huge as a mountain, standing before him, Mahāpārśva, in a rage, struck him on the chest with that mace, which was like a thunderbolt.

50. Struck by him with that mace, the bull among monkeys was rocked. His chest split open, he gushed forth gouts of blood.

51. Regaining consciousness after a long time, Ṛṣabha, bull among monkeys, his lips quivering in his rage, glared at Mahāpārśva.

52. Seizing that fearsome mace and whirling it round and round, he struck Mahāpārśva Mattānīka with it in the forefront of the battle.

53. Mangled by his own mace, his teeth and eyes knocked loose, Mahāpārśva collapsed, like a mountain struck by a thunderbolt.

54. Once Rāvaṇa's brother had been slain, the army of the *rākṣasas*, sons of chaos, which resembled an ocean, dropped its weapons and ran for its life, like an ocean scattering in all directions.

The end of the fifty-eighth *sarga* of the *Yuddhakāṇḍa* of the *Śrī Rāmāyaṇa*.

Sarga 59

1–3. Immensely powerful Atikāya, that mountainous crusher of the pride of gods and *dānavas*, saw that his thunderous and hair-raising army had been devastated. And, seeing that his brothers, whose valor was equal to that of Śakra, had been slain in battle together with his two paternal uncles, the brothers Mahodara and Mahāpārśva, bulls among *rākṣasas*, that warrior, who had been granted boons by Brahmā, flew into a rage in the midst of battle.

4. Mounting his chariot, which blazed with the brilliance of a thousand suns, that foe of Śakra hurtled toward the monkeys.

5. Loudly twanging his great bow, Atikāya, adorned with a diadem and burnished earrings, proclaimed his name and roared loudly.

6. With his leonine roar, the proclamation of his name, and the fearsome sound of his bowstring, he terrified the monkeys.

7. Gazing upon his gigantic form, which was like that of Viṣṇu when he traversed the three worlds, all the monkeys were stricken with terror and fled in the ten directions.

8. Confronted by Atikāya, their wits addled, the monkeys sought refuge in battle with Lakṣmaṇa's older brother, the refuge of all.

9. Then Kākutstha gazed from afar at Atikāya, huge as a mountain, who stood mounted in his chariot, bow in hand, roaring like a black storm cloud.

10. Observing that gigantic warrior, Rāghava was astonished. After reassuring the monkeys, he said to Vibhīṣaṇa:

11. "Who is that mountainous warrior—armed with a bow and with the gaze of a lion—mounted in that huge chariot yoked to a thousand horses?

12. "Surrounded with his sharp lances and his formidable and glittering darts and iron cudgels, he resembles Maheśvara surrounded by his malignant spirits.

13. "Surrounded with his glittering chariot-javelins, which resemble the tongues of Kāla, he looks like a storm cloud surrounded by streaks of lightning.

14. "His well-strung bows with their golden facing illuminate his splendid chariot on every side, as does the rainbow, Śakra's bow, the heavens.

15. "Who is this tiger among *rākṣasas*, the foremost among chariot-warriors, who approaches on a chariot as radiant as the sun, illuminating the battlefield?

16. "Illuminating the ten directions with arrows that have the brilliance of the sun's rays and, with the emblem of Rāhu, demon of the eclipse, waving from his flagstaff, he looks resplendent.

17. "And his thrice-curved bow with golden facing, ornamented and reverberating like a thundercloud, is as resplendent as the rainbow, the bow of Indra of the hundred sacrifices.

18. "His great chariot is furnished with flags and banners and has a fine frame. It is manned by four grooms and rumbles with the thunder of a storm cloud.

19. "There are thirty-eight quivers mounted on his chariot, along with fearsome bows, their bowstrings yellow with gold.

20. "And in his chariot there are two swords, one on each side. Clearly visible, their blades are fifteen feet in length and their hilts, six. They beautify both sides.

21. "With a red garland hung about his neck and his huge mouth like that of Kāla, that dark warrior, steadfast and huge as a great mountain, looks like the sun rising above a storm cloud.

22. "His arms girded with golden armlets, he is as resplendent as Himalaya, greatest of mountains, with its tall twin peaks.

23. "With its two earrings, that radiant face of his resembles the orb of the full moon passing between the twin stars of the constellation Punarvasu.

24. "Tell me, great-armed hero, about that outstanding *rākṣasa* at the sight of whom all the monkeys have fled in all directions, overcome with fear."

25. When immensely powerful Vibhīṣaṇa had been questioned in this fashion by Prince Rāma Rāghava of immeasurable power, he said to him:

26. "The immensely powerful and enormously energetic king, ten-necked Rāvaṇa of fearsome deeds, is the younger brother of Kubera Vaiśravaṇa and is the overlord of the *rākṣasas*.

27. "He had a mighty son, the equal in battle of Rāvaṇa himself, respectful of his elders, deeply learned, and foremost of those who know all the divine weapon-spells.

28. "He is highly regarded for his skill on horseback, chariot, and elephant, with the sword, the bow, and the noose, in the arts of sowing dissension, conciliation, and bribery, as well as in statecraft and counsel.

29. "He is known as Atikāya, Dhānyamālinī's son. Relying on his arm, Laṅkā remains secure.

30. "His mind focused, he propitiated Brahmā by means of his austerities. Thus he acquired divine weapon-spells and conquered his enemies.

31. "And self-existent Brahmā granted him that suit of armor and that chariot, radiant as the sun, as well as invulnerability to the gods and *asuras*.

32. "He has defeated hundreds of gods and *dānavas*, protected the *rākṣasas*, and slaughtered the *yakṣas*.

33–34. "For he is Atikāya, the wise and mighty son of Rāvaṇa. He is a bull among *rākṣasas* and the crusher of the pride of the gods and *dānavas*. With his arrows he stopped wise Indra's *vajra* in its course and repelled in battle the noose of Varuṇa, monarch of the waters.

35. "Therefore, bull among men, you must quickly exert yourself against him before he annihilates the monkey troops with his arrows."

36. Then mighty Atikāya, plunging into the hosts of tawny monkeys, twanged his bow and roared again and again.

37. Seeing that foremost of chariot-warriors, fearsome to behold, mounted on his chariot, the great and preeminent leaping monkeys hurled themselves upon him.

38. Armed with trees and mountain peaks, Kumuda, Dvivida, Mainda, Nīla, and Śarabha, acting as one, hurled themselves upon him.

39. But immensely powerful Atikāya, foremost among those skilled in the use of divine weapon-spells, cut their trees and rocks to pieces with his gold-ornamented arrows.

40. Then that mighty night-roaming *rākṣasa* with his fearsome body, facing those tawny monkeys, pierced them all in battle with arrows made of solid iron.

41. Wounded by that hail of arrows, pierced in every limb, the leaping monkeys were unable to fight back against Atikāya in that great battle.

42. The *rākṣasa* terrified the army of heroic tawny monkeys, just as a raging lion in the full flush of youth might a herd of deer.

43. But there in the midst of the army of tawny monkeys, that *rākṣasa* lord would not strike any that did not resist. Then, armed with bow and quiver, he approached Rāma and arrogantly spoke these words:

44. "Here I stand, mounted in my chariot, bow and arrow in hand; but I will not fight any ordinary foe. Let whomever has the ability coupled with resolve quickly give me battle here and now."

45. Now Saumitri, slayer of his foes, overheard those words of Atikāya as he was speaking. He could not abide them, and he flew into a rage. Leaping up, he seized his bow with a contemptuous smile.

46. Leaping up in a rage, Saumitri drew an arrow from his quiver and bent his great bow right in front of Atikāya.

47. The fearsome sound of Lakṣmaṇa's bowstring could be heard, filling the earth, the mountains, the sky, and the ocean and terrifying the night-roaming *rākṣasas*.

48. Upon hearing the terrifying sound of Saumitri's bow, the mighty and immensely powerful son of the *rākṣasa* lord was astonished.

49. Seeing that Lakṣmaṇa had leapt up, Atikāya, enraged, took up a sharp arrow and spoke these words:

50. "You are a mere child, Saumitri, unskilled in deeds of valor. Get out of my way! Do you really want to provoke me to fight, I who am like Kāla himself?

51. "Not even Himalaya, the sky, or the earth itself is able to withstand the force of the divinely charged weapons released by my arm.

52. "Would you want to stir up the fire at the end of a cosmic age when it is sleeping peacefully? Put down your bow and go back. Don't sacrifice your life by confronting me.

53. "Or if you are obstinate and do not wish to go back, then stay, and, losing your life, you shall go to the abode of Yama.

54. "Just look at these sharp arrows of mine, adorned with burnished gold. Resembling the weapon of Lord Śiva, they crush the pride of my enemies.

55. "This arrow, resembling a serpent, will drink your blood, just as a raging lion, king of beasts, would the blood of a king among elephants."

56. When Prince Lakṣmaṇa had heard those angry and arrogant words of Atikāya in the midst of the battle, the exceedingly powerful and enormously majestic hero spoke these highly sensible words:

57. "You cannot attain excellence by mere words; nor are true heroes produced by boasting. As long as I am standing here, armed with a bow, arrow in hand, you should demonstrate your prowess, evil-minded wretch!

58. "Show what you are made of through your deeds. You oughtn't boast. Only he who is truly endowed with manly valor is accounted a hero.

59. "You are armed with a bow, mounted in a chariot, and equipped with every kind of weapon. So demonstrate your prowess with arrows or divinely charged weapons.

60. "Then, with my sharp arrows, I shall cause your head to fall, just as the wind does a ripened palmyra fruit from its stalk.

61. "This very day my arrows, adorned with burnished gold, will drink the blood spurting from the gaping holes made in your body by my arrowheads.

62. "You should not underestimate me, thinking, 'He is only a child.' Whether I be young or old, you must know me to be your death in battle."

63. When Atikāya had heard those words of Lakṣmaṇa, reasonable and supremely sensible though they were, he was enraged and took up a splendid arrow.

64. Then *vidyādharas*, spirits of the departed, gods, *daityas*, great seers, and the great *guhyakas* watched that fight.

65. In a rage, Atikāya fitted an arrow to his bow and shot it at Lakṣmaṇa, shrinking, as it were, the space between them.

66. But as that sharp arrow, like a venomous serpent, hurtled toward him, Lakṣmaṇa, slayer of enemy heroes, cut it to pieces with a half-moon-headed arrow.

67. When he saw his arrow cut to pieces, like a serpent whose coils have been slashed, Atikāya was beside himself with rage. He took up five more arrows.

68. Then that night-roaming *rākṣasa* shot those arrows at Lakṣmaṇa. But, before they could reach him, Bharata's younger brother cut them to pieces with his own sharp arrows.

69. Once he had cut them to pieces with his sharp arrows, Lakṣmaṇa, slayer of enemy heroes, took up another sharp arrow that seemed to blaze with energy.

70. Taking it up, Lakṣmaṇa fitted it to his splendid bow. Then, drawing the bow, he released the arrow with tremendous force.

71. And that mighty man struck that foremost of *rākṣasas* in the forehead with that straight arrow that had been drawn to the full.

72. Buried in the forehead of that fearsome *rākṣasa*, the arrow, smeared with blood, resembled a serpent lord in battle.

73. Rocked by Lakṣmaṇa's arrow, the *rākṣasa* was shaken, just as was the fearsome gateway of Tripura when it was struck by Rudra's arrow.

74. Regaining his composure and reflecting, the immensely powerful *rākṣasa* thought, "Well done! The impact of your arrow proves you to be a praiseworthy opponent for me."

75. Reflecting in this fashion, he lowered his face and both his arms. He advanced in his chariot, settling into its seat.

76. That bull among *rākṣasas* took up one, three, five, or seven arrows at a time, nocked them, and then drew and released them.

77. Loosed from the bow of the *rākṣasa* lord, those arrows, which were like Kāla himself and, with their golden fletching, were as radiant as the sun, seemed to light up the heavens.

78. But, not the least bit perturbed, Rāghava's younger brother cut those torrents of arrows loosed by the *rākṣasa* to pieces with many sharp arrows of his own.

79. When Rāvaṇa's son, the enemy of the thirty gods, saw his arrows cut to pieces in battle, he was enraged and seized yet another sharp arrow.

80. The immensely powerful warrior nocked that arrow and released it with tremendous force. It then struck Saumitri in the center of his chest as he advanced.

81. Wounded in the chest by Atikāya in battle, Saumitri gushed forth great gouts of blood as does a rutting elephant rut fluid.

82. But then that mighty man swiftly removed that dart from his body. Then, taking up a sharp arrow and invoking a divine weapon-spell, he nocked it.

83. He charged that arrow with the divine weapon-spell of Agni. The arrow of that great warrior then blazed brightly, as did his bow.

84. The immensely powerful Atikāya, in turn, invoked the divine weapon-spell of Sūrya, and, with it, he charged a gold-fletched arrow that resembled a serpent.

85. Meanwhile, Lakṣmaṇa loosed at Atikāya the fearsome and blazing arrow that he had fitted to his bow, just as Kāla, the ender of all things, might his staff of doom.

86. When he saw that arrow charged with the divine weapon-spell of Agni, the night-roaming *rākṣasa* released his blazing arrow, charged with the divine weapon-spell of Sūrya.

87. Like angry serpents, the two arrows struck each other as they flew through the sky, their tips blazing with energy.

88. Consuming each other, they fell to the ground. Reduced to ashes, their flames extinguished, those two splendid arrows blazed no more.

89. Then Atikāya, in a towering rage, released the divinely charged *aiṣīka* missile. But mighty Saumitri cut that divinely charged missile to pieces with the divinely charged missile of Indra.

90. Seeing that the divinely charged *aiṣīka* missile had been destroyed, the prince, son of Rāvaṇa, in a towering rage, charged an arrow with the divine weapon-spell of Yama.

91. Then the night-roaming *rākṣasa* shot that divinely charged missile at Lakṣmaṇa. But Lakṣmaṇa knocked it down with the divinely charged missile of Vāyu.

92. Then, in a towering rage, Lakṣmaṇa showered the son of Rāvaṇa with volleys of arrows, as might a storm cloud with torrents of rain.

93. As those arrows struck Atikāya, their arrowheads shattered against his diamond-studded armor, and they fell with tremendous force to the ground.

94. Perceiving that they had been ineffectual, glorious Lakṣmaṇa, slayer of enemy heroes, showered him with a thousand arrows.

95. Although he was pelted with torrents of arrows, the mighty *rākṣasa* Atikāya, with his impenetrable armor, was not the least bit discomfited in that battle.

96. Indeed, that foremost of men was unable to wound him in battle. But then Vāyu approached him and said:

97. "Granted a boon from Brahmā, this *rākṣasa* is encased in impenetrable armor. You must pierce him with the divinely charged missile of Brahmā; for there is no other way that he can be killed."

98. Then, upon hearing the words of Vāyu, Saumitri, who equaled Indra in valor, took up an arrow of irresistible force and swiftly charged it with the divine weapon-spell of Brahmā.

99. As that splendid, sharp-tipped arrow was being charged by Saumitri with that supreme, divine weapon-spell, all the directions, as well as the moon, the sun, the great planets, and the heavens, shook with fear, and the earth groaned.

100. Once he had charged that beautifully fletched arrow, which resembled the messenger of Yama, with the divine weapon-spell of Brahmā, Saumitri fitted it to his bow. Then, in that battle, he shot that arrow, which was like Indra's *vajra*, at the son of Indra's foe.

101. Atikāya saw it hurtling toward him, loosed by Lakṣmaṇa in battle. Its force was irresistible, and, with its fletching bright with gold and splendid diamonds, it shone like fire.

102. Sighting it, Atikāya struck it violently with many sharp arrows. But that arrow, swift as Suparna, continued to hurtle toward him with tremendous speed.

103. Watching that arrow, which was like fiercely blazing Kāla, the ender of all things, Atikāya never slackened his efforts but continued to strike at it with javelins, broadswords, maces, hatchets, lances, and ploughshares.

104. But that arrow, blazing with fire, was impervious to those wondrously formed weapons, and it violently struck off Atikāya's head, crowned with its diadem.

105. Battered by Lakṣmaṇa's arrow, his head, along with its headdress, fell violently to the ground, as might the summit of Himalaya.

106. Now that their unassailable enemy of fearsome strength had been slain, the multitude of monkeys, filled with joy, their faces like blooming lotuses, honored Lakṣmaṇa, who had accomplished their cherished goal.

The end of the fifty-ninth *sarga* of the *Yuddhakāṇḍa* of the *Śrī Rāmāyaṇa*.

Sarga 60

1. Then the hosts of *rākṣasas* who had survived the slaughter immediately reported to Rāvaṇa that those bulls among *rākṣasas*, Triśiras, Atikāya, Devāntaka, and the rest, had been slain.

2. When the king heard in this sudden fashion that they had been slain, he was stunned and his eyes filled with tears. Reflecting upon the destruction of his sons and the horrific slaughter of his brothers, the king began to brood deeply.

3. Now, when that bull-like warrior Indrajit, son of the *rākṣasa* king, saw that the king was despondent and floundering in a sea of grief, he said these words:

4. "Father, lord of the *rākṣasas*, you must not give way to despondency so long as Indrajit remains alive. For no one who is struck in battle by the arrows of Indra's foe can escape with his life.

5. "This very day you will surely see Rāma along with Lakṣmaṇa lying lifeless on the ground, his body pierced and dismembered by my arrows, his every limb bristling with sharp shafts.

6. "Now hear the vow of Śakra's foe, which is well founded and infused with both human and divine power: 'Today, with my unfailing arrows, I shall consume Rāma along with Lakṣmaṇa.'

7. "This very day Indra, Vaivasvata, Viṣṇu, Mitra, the *sādhyas*, the Aśvins, Agni Vaiśvānara, Candra, and Sūrya shall witness my immeasurable valor, which is like the fearsome valor of Viṣṇu in Bali's sacrificial enclosure."

8. When he had spoken in this fashion, Indrajit, the enemy of the lord of the thirty gods, took his leave of the king and, in high spirits,

mounted a chariot as swift as the wind. It was yoked to splendid donkeys and equipped with the implements of war.

9. Mounted in that chariot, the equal of the chariot of Indra himself, that immensely powerful tamer of his foes drove swiftly to where the battle raged.

10. As great Indrajit set forth, many immensely powerful warriors followed him in great delight, their splendid bows in hand.

11. Some were mounted on elephant-back, while others rode splendid chargers. They were armed with darts, war hammers, swords, battle-axes, and maces.

12. Praised by the night-roaming *rākṣasas*, the foe of the lord of the thirty gods went forth to the fearsome blaring of conches and the thunderous sound of *bherī* drums.

13. With his parasol of the hue of conch shell or the hare-marked moon, that crusher of his enemies was as resplendent as the sky illuminated by the full moon.

14. That hero, foremost of all bowmen, was fanned with the most splendid, golden yak-tail fly whisks, all adorned with gold.

15. Then, illuminated by Indrajit, who was unmatched in valor and equal in blazing splendor to the sun, the city of Laṅkā was as resplendent as the heavens illuminated by the radiant sun.

16. When Rāvaṇa, the majestic overlord of the *rākṣasas*, saw his son marching forth surrounded by a vast host, he said to him:

17. "You are a peerless warrior, my son. You have conquered even Vāsava in battle. How then would you not more easily slay Rāghava, a vulnerable mortal."

18. Addressed in this fashion by the *rākṣasa* lord and having received his fulsome blessings, the hero proceeded swiftly to the shrine of Nikumbhilā in his horse-drawn chariot.

19. Upon reaching the battleground, that immensely powerful tamer of his foes stationed the *rākṣasas* all around his chariot.

20. Then, to the accompaniment of sacred *mantras* and in accordance with the ritual prescriptions, the foremost of *rākṣasas*, whose

splendor was like that of Agni, eater of oblations, offered oblations to Agni, eater of oblations.

21. The valorous *rākṣasa* lord offered oblations to Agni, the purifier, along with ritual offerings of parched grain accompanied by flowers and sandalwood paste.

22. Weapons served as the *śarapatra* grass, myrobalan wood was the kindling. His garments were red and his ladle was of black iron.

23. Having strewn the fire altar there with weapons, including iron cudgels, in place of *śarapatra* grass, he seized the throat of a live, pure black goat.

24. Once kindled, the smokeless fire with its huge flames displayed signs that betokened victory.

25. Glowing like burnished gold, his flames swirling in an auspicious clockwise direction, Agni, the purifier, himself rose up and received that oblation.

26. Foremost among those familiar with divine weapon-spells, Indrajit invoked the divine weapon-spell of Brahmā. And there with that spell, he infused his bow, his chariot, and all of his weaponry.

27. And as that divine weapon-spell was being invoked and Agni, the purifier, was being gratified with oblations, the heavens shook along with the sun, the planets, the moon, and the constellations.

28. Once Indrajit, whose blazing energy was like that of Agni, the purifier, and whose power was equal to that of great Indra, had made oblation to Agni, the purifier, he vanished into thin air along with his bow, arrows, sword, chariot, horses, and charioteer, his form no longer perceptible.

29. Emerging from his own army, Indrajit swiftly plunged in among the monkey ranks, and there, in that great battle, invisible, he rained down a fearsome torrent of arrows, just as a black storm cloud does torrents of rain.

30. Baffled by his magical illusion, their bodies rent by the arrows of Śakra's conqueror, the tawny monkeys, huge as mountains, fell in battle uttering discordant cries, like lordly mountains smashed down by Indra's *vajra*.

31. All they could see in the battle were the sharp-tipped arrows raining on the monkey troops. For they could not see the *rākṣasa*, the foe of the lord of the gods, concealed as he was by magical illusion.

32. Then the great *rākṣasa* lord filled all the directions with volleys of arrows as radiant as the sun, further disheartening the monkey lords.

33. Brandishing lances, swords, and battle-axes, which were like shining fires and emitted blazing flames along with sparks, he fiercely rained them down upon the army of the lord of the leaping monkeys.

34. Then, struck by the sharp arrows—blazing like fire—of the conqueror of Śakra, the leaders of the monkey troops resembled red-blossoming *kiṃśuka* trees.

35. Pierced by the divinely charged weapons of the *rākṣasa* lord, those bulls among monkeys fell, crawling over one another and uttering discordant cries.

36. Some of them, peering into the sky, were struck in the eyes with arrows so that they fell to the ground and clung to one another.

37–40. Then, with darts, lances, and sharp arrows charged with *mantras*, Indrajit, foremost of *rākṣasas*, pierced all those tigers among the monkeys: Hanumān, Sugrīva, Aṅgada, Gandhamādana, Jāmbavān, Suṣeṇa, Vegadarśin, Mainda, Dvivida, Nīla, Gavākṣa, Gaja, Gomukha, Kesari, Hariloman, the monkey Vidyuddaṃṣṭra, Sūryānana, Jyotimukha, the tawny monkey Dadhimukha, Pāvakākṣa, Nala, and the monkey Kumuda.

41. Then, once he had torn apart the troop leaders of the tawny monkeys with maces and with arrows fletched with burnished gold, he pelted Rāma and Lakṣmaṇa with massive torrents of arrows that shone like the rays of the sun.

42. Pelted by those showers of arrows, Rāma regarded them no more seriously than showers of rain. Supremely wondrous in his majesty, he turned his gaze to Lakṣmaṇa and said this:

43. "Here is that *rākṣasa* lord again, Lakṣmaṇa, the enemy of the lord of the gods. Relying upon the divine weapon-spell of Brahmā, he has

laid low the fierce army of tawny monkeys and is now constantly harassing us with arrows.

44. "The great warrior, having been granted a boon by self-existent Brahmā, is hovering in the sky, his fearsome body hidden. How is it possible to kill Indrajit in battle today, when he is invisible and is wielding his divinely charged weapon?

45. "I know that the self-existent lord Brahmā, who is the creator of all things, is inconceivable. And this divine weapon-spell belongs to him. Therefore, wise Lakṣmaṇa, with a calm mind you must endure with me the blows of these arrows here and now.

46. "The *rākṣasa* lord is filling all directions with massive torrents of arrows. And the whole army of the monkey king, its foremost heroes fallen, presents a sorry sight.

47. "Once he sees that we have fallen unconscious and have ceased to fight or show signs either of anger or excitement, he will surely return to Laṅkā, the abode of the foes of the immortal gods, having achieved the greatest glory in battle."

48. At that point, the two brothers were cut down on the spot by the mass of Indrajit's divinely charged weapons. Having laid them low there, the *rākṣasa* lord roared with delight in battle.

49. Having thus laid low in battle the army of the monkey king, as well as Rāma and Lakṣmaṇa, he swiftly reentered the city of Laṅkā, which lay under the protection of the arms of ten-necked Rāvaṇa.

The end of the sixtieth *sarga* of the *Yuddhakāṇḍa* of the *Śrī Rāmāyaṇa*.

Sarga 61

1. Then, when the two heroes, Rāma and Lakṣmaṇa, had been struck down in the forefront of battle, the army of the leaders of the troops of tawny monkeys was stunned. Even Sugrīva, Nīla, Aṅgada, and Jāmbavān could do nothing.

2. But then Vibhīṣaṇa, foremost among the wise, seeing that the army was despondent, addressed the king of the tree-dwelling monkeys and his heroic warriors, comforting them with inimitable words:

3. "Have no fear! Just because the two sons of the king are lying helpless, this is no time for despondency. For, in being struck down by the mass of Indrajit's divinely charged weapons, they are merely observing the command of self-existent Brahmā.

4. "Brahmā's supreme divine weapon-spell of unfailing force was given to Indrajit by the self-existent one himself. If, in order to show their reverence for it, the king's two sons have fallen down, why is that an occasion for despondency?"

5. When wise Hanumān Māruti, who had already once shown his reverence to Brahmā's divine weapon-spell, heard those words of Vibhīṣaṇa, he said this to him:

6. "Let us comfort any of those in the decimated army of the swift monkeys who may still be alive."

7. Then, torches in hand, those two heroes, Hanumān and that foremost of the *rākṣasas* Vibhīṣaṇa, together roamed the battlefront during that night.

8–9. They saw the ground heaped up on every side with shining weapons that had been dropped and with fallen monkeys, huge as mountains, oozing blood from their limbs and dribbling urine, their tails, hands, thighs, feet, fingers, and necks severed.

10–11. And there Vibhīṣaṇa and Hanumān saw that Sugrīva, Aṅgada, Nīla, Śarabha, Gandhamādana, Jāmbavān, Suṣeṇa, Vegadarśin, Āhuka, Mainda, Nala, Jyotimukha, Dvivida, and Panasa had been struck down in battle.

12. For, within the fifth part of a day, Indrajit, self-existent Brahmā's favorite, had struck down six hundred and seventy million swift monkeys.

13. Seeing that that fearsome host, which was like the vast flood of the ocean, had been decimated by arrows, Hanumān and Vibhīṣaṇa sought out Jāmbavān.

14–15. Observing the wise and heroic son of Prajāpati, who, riddled with hundreds of arrows and showing the signs of advanced age, resembled a dying flame, Vibhīṣaṇa Paulastya approached him and spoke these words: "I trust, noble sir, that you have not been mortally wounded by these sharp arrows."

16. Upon hearing the words of Vibhīṣaṇa, Jāmbavān, bull among apes, uttered this speech, articulating the words only with great difficulty:

17. "Mighty hero, lord of the *rākṣasas*, sons of chaos, wounded as I am by these sharp arrows, I cannot see you, but I recognize you by your voice.

18. "O *rākṣasa*, son of chaos, does the foremost of the monkeys Hanumān, in whom Añjanā and Vāyu Mātariśvan have an excellent son, still live?"

19. When Vibhīṣaṇa heard these words of Jāmbavān, he said this: "Why do you ignore the king's sons Rāma and Lakṣmaṇa and ask only about Māruti?

20. "Noble sir, you have not shown the same extraordinary concern for King Sugrīva, Aṅgada, or even Rāghava himself as you have for the son of Vāyu."

21. Upon hearing the words of Vibhīṣaṇa, Jāmbavān spoke these words: "Now hear, tiger among *rākṣasas*, sons of chaos, why I inquired only about Māruti.

22. "So long as Hanumān is alive, then our army will survive, even if it should be massacred. But if that hero has lost his life, then, even though we survive, we are as good as dead.

23. "For, dear boy, if Māruti, the equal of Māruta and the rival in power of Agni Vaiśvānara, still lives, only then do we have any hope of survival."

24. Then Hanumān, son of Māruta, approached wise Jāmbavān. Devotedly clasping his feet, he respectfully greeted him.

25. Although his every organ was in agony, when Jāmbavān, bull among apes, heard Hanumān's words, he felt as if he had been born again.

26. Then the immensely powerful Jāmbavān said to Hanumān, "Come, tiger among the tawny monkeys, you must save the monkeys.

27. "For no one else possesses valor equal to the task. You are the monkeys' greatest friend. Now is the moment for you to show your prowess; for I can see no one else who can accomplish this.

28. "You must heal the arrow wounds of Rāma and Lakṣmaṇa, who have been struck down, and thus restore the spirits of the hosts of heroic apes and monkey.

29. "Taking the highest path, far above the ocean, you must go, Hanumān, to Himalaya, greatest of mountains.

30. "Then, slayer of your foes, you will see the great and forbidding Mount Ṛṣabha, all made of gold, and the peak of Mount Kailāsa.

31. "Between those two peaks, hero, you will see the mountain of healing herbs, which, covered with every sort of healing herb, glows with unequaled radiance.

32–33. "And growing on its peak, tiger among monkeys, you will find four healing herbs, glowing so as to illuminate the ten directions. They are *mṛtasaṃjīvaṇī*, 'the restorer of life to the dead,' *viśalya-karaṇī*, 'the healer of arrow wounds,' *sauvarṇakaraṇī*, 'the restorer of a golden glow,' and the great healing herb *saṃdhānī*, 'the joiner of limbs.'

34. "You must gather them all, Hanumān, and swiftly return. For you must restore the tawny monkeys to life and rally them, son of Vāyu, bearer of scents."

35. When Hanumān, bull among tawny monkeys, had heard those words of Jāmbavān, he was filled with a great upsurge of strength, as is the ocean with its mighty currents.

36. Perching on the top of the mountain slope and crushing that foremost of mountains, the hero Hanumān looked like a second mountain himself.

37. Then, crumbling under the feet of that tawny monkey, the mountain caved in. For, crushed so severely, it was unable to bear its own weight.

38. The tremendous force of that tawny monkey caused the mountain's trees to fall to the ground and burst into flame. And as it was being crushed by Hanumān, its peaks shattered.

39. As that great mountain, its trees and rock faces smashed, was being crushed, it shook so that the monkeys could not keep their footing.

40. With her great gateways shaking and the gates of her buildings crumbling, Laṅkā, overcome with panic in the night, seemed almost to be dancing.

41. Crushing that mountain, the mountainous Hanumān, son of Māruta, made the earth together with the ocean tremble.

42. As he crushed the mountain with his feet, he opened his mouth, which was as fearsome as the gaping mare's head fire that lies beneath the sea, and he roared loudly, terrifying the *rākṣasas*.

43. When they heard that extraordinary roar of fiercely roaring Hanumān, all the *rākṣasas* in Laṅkā were paralyzed with fear.

44. Then, after first offering obeisance to Rāma, Māruti, that scorcher of his foes, so fearsome in his valor, turned his thoughts to that vital mission on behalf of Rāghava.

45. Extending his tail, which resembled a serpent, crouching down, laying back his ears, and opening his mouth, which was like the gaping mare's head fire that lies beneath the sea, Hanumān leapt into the sky with terrifying force.

46. With his great speed he carried along with him stands of trees, mountains, boulders, and lesser monkeys. Drawn upward and swept along by the force of his arms and thighs, they fell into the ocean as their speed slackened.

47. Stretching out his arms, which resembled the coils of serpents, the son of Vāyu, his power like that of Garuḍa, foe of serpents, headed toward Mount Meru, the prominent king of the mountains, drawing, so it seemed, the directions in his wake.

48. Then, as he flew swiftly along, like the discus loosed by Viṣṇu's fingers, he looked down upon the ocean with its roiling garland of waves and all its creatures tossed violently about.

49. Observing mountains, forests, lakes, rivers, ponds, splendid cities, and prosperous lands, Hanumān, whose swiftness equaled that of his father, flew swiftly onward.

50. Reaching the path of the sun, he flew on tirelessly. Then that foremost of tawny monkeys spied Himalaya, greatest of mountains.

51. It had various kinds of waterfalls and many caves and rushing streams. It was endowed with beautiful peaks that resembled white clouds.

52. As he approached that great lord of the mountains, with its huge, splendid, and formidable peaks, he spied vast and holy ashrams frequented by the hosts of the foremost gods and seers.

53. He saw the abode of Brahmā, the abode of Hiraṇyagarbha in his silver-naveled form, the abode of Śakra, the place where Rudra loosed his arrows, the abode of Hayānana the horse-faced god, and the luminous place where Brahmā's head fell. And he saw the servants of Vaivasvata.

54. He saw the place where the *vajra* was presented as well as the abode of Kubera Vaiśravaṇa. He also saw the abode of the sun—resplendent as the sun itself—the throne of Brahmā, the place of Śaṅkara's bow, and the very navel of the earth.

55. Then he saw the prominent Mount Kailāsa, the rock face of the Himalayas, and the prominent golden mountain Ṛṣabha. And, at last, he spied the lordly mountain of all herbs, which was illuminated by all its glowing herbs of healing.

56. When Hanumān, son of Vāsava's messenger, the wind god, saw that lordly mountain of healing herbs, glowing as if with flames of fire, he was astonished. Alighting on it, he began to search there for the healing herbs.

57. The great monkey, son of Māruta, roamed that mountain bearing divine herbs of healing for thousands of leagues.

58. However, recognizing the purpose for which he had come, all the powerful healing herbs on that foremost of mountains made themselves invisible.

59. Unable to find them, great Hanumān was furious and bellowed loudly in his rage. Losing patience, his eyes blazing like fire, he said these words to that lordly mountain:

60. "What is this that you have thus resolved upon, in your lack of compassion toward Rāghava? This very day, lord of mountains,

overwhelmed by the strength of my arms, you shall see yourself smashed to pieces."

61. Then, forcibly seizing hold of its peak, filled with thousands of minerals, together with its trees, elephants, and gold, he violently tore it off so that its summit crumbled and the tops of its slopes began to slide.

62. Tearing it off, that hero, whose fearsome power was like that of Garuḍa, flew up into the sky, terrifying the worlds, together with the gods and the lords of the gods. Then, praised by innumerable creatures of the air, he proceeded swiftly on his way.

63. Grasping that peak, which shone like the sun, he followed the sun's path. Then, when he whose radiance was like that of the sun drew near the sun, he appeared to be a rival sun.

64. Holding that mountain, the mountainous son of Vāyu, bearer of scents, shone as brightly in the sky as Viṣṇu holding aloft his flaming, thousand-bladed discus.

65. Then, when the monkeys caught sight of him, they roared, and he, too, spotting them, roared back in delight. But when the *rākṣasas* in Laṅkā heard their resounding cries, they roared more fearsomely still.

66. Then great Hanumān alighted on splendid Mount Trikūṭa in the midst of the monkey army. After bowing his head in respectful salutation to the foremost among the tawny monkeys, he embraced Vibhīṣaṇa there.

67. No sooner had the two human princes smelled the fragrance of those powerful healing herbs than they were freed on the spot from their arrow wounds. The others, too, the heroic tawny monkeys, stood up as well.

68. Then that immensely powerful tawny monkey, the son of Vāyu, bearer of scents, swiftly took the mountain of healing herbs back to the Himalayas and then rejoined Rāma.

The end of the sixty-first *sarga* of the *Yuddhakāṇḍa* of the *Śrī Rāmāyaṇa*.

Sarga 62

1. Then Sugrīva, the immensely powerful overlord of the monkeys, spoke sensibly, instructing mighty Hanumān as to what should be done next:

2. "Since Kumbhakarṇa has been slain and the *rākṣasa* princes slaughtered, Rāvaṇa will now no longer be able to launch a sortie against us.

3. "Bulls among leaping monkeys! Those leaping monkeys who are powerful and agile are to take torches and leap into Laṅkā at once."

4. Then, when the sun had set and the dread onset of night had come, the leaping monkeys marched toward Laṅkā, holding torches.

5. Overrun on every side by swarms of tawny monkeys holding torches, the sentries at the gates, with their hideous eyes, abruptly fled.

6. In a frenzy, the monkeys unleashed fire, the eater of oblations, on gateways, towers, highways, various streets, and mansions.

7. And the fire, eater of oblations, consumed thousands of houses and the residences of all the *rākṣasas*, including those who performed the household rites.

8–11. Fire, the purifier of all things, consumed thousands of the houses of the residents of Laṅkā. Some of those residents wore armor, beautified with gold, while others wore garlands of flowers and costly garments. Some, their eyes rolling from drinking rum, staggered in their intoxication. The garments of some were clutched at by their lovers. Some held maces, lances, or swords in their hands, as they raged at the enemy, while others went on eating and drinking. Some were asleep with their beloveds in costly beds, while others, terrified, grabbed their sons and fled swiftly in all directions. As the fire burned their homes, it flared up again and again.

12–14. And the fire consumed mansions that looked like mountains. They were firmly built and costly, beautiful with their grand upper stories. They were shaped like full- and half-moons made of gold, soaring aloft with their penthouses. Their round windows were adorned with jewels. They were richly furnished throughout.

Adorned with gems and coral, they seemed almost to touch the sun, bringer of light, and they echoed with the cries of *krauñcas* and peacocks, the strains of lutes, and the tinkling of ornaments.

15. Wreathed in flames, their gates looked like masses of clouds encircled with lightning at summer's end.

16. As they were being burned alive, the exquisite women, who had been sleeping in their lofty mansions, cast off all their ornaments and loudly shrieked, "Ah! Ah!"

17. The dwellings there, engulfed in fire, collapsed, like the peaks of a huge mountain smashed by the *vajra* of Indra, the *vajra* wielder.

18. As those mansions burned, they looked from afar like the peaks of the Himalayas with their thickets of glowing herbs.

19. With the rooftops of its mansions burning and brightly illuminated with flames, Laṅkā looked that night as if it were filled with red-blossoming *kiṃśuka* trees.

20. With its elephants and horses turned loose by their keepers, Laṅkā resembled the ocean with its huge creatures thrashing about at the end of a cosmic age.

21. Whenever a terrified elephant would encounter a horse roaming free, it would run away, and when a terrified horse would encounter a terrified elephant, it, too, would shy away.

22. Set ablaze by the tawny monkeys, the city in an instant came to resemble the blazing earth, bearer of wealth, at the dreadful destruction of the world.

23. The cries of the womenfolk, who shrieked loudly as they were enveloped in smoke and scorched by the flames, could be heard for a distance of ten leagues.

24. Meanwhile, the tawny monkeys, eager for battle, violently pounced upon any of the *rākṣasas* who rushed forth, their bodies ablaze.

25. The shouts of the monkeys and the wailing of the *rākṣasas* made the ten directions, the ocean, and the earth itself resound.

26. Then the great warriors, Rāma and Lakṣmaṇa, now healed of their arrow wounds, calmly took up their splendid bows.

27. Twanging his splendid bow, Rāma produced a thunderous sound that sowed terror among the *rākṣasas*.

28. As he twanged his great bow, Rāma looked as splendid as Lord Bhava, when, in his rage, he twangs his bow that consists of the *vedas*.

29. Those three sounds—the clamor of the monkeys' shouts, the wailing of the *rākṣasas*, and the twanging of Rāma's bowstring—filled the ten directions.

30. Shattered by the arrows loosed from Rāma's bow, the citadel's gateway, which was like the peak of Mount Kailāsa, crashed to the ground.

31. Then, when the *rākṣasa* lords saw Rāma's arrows in their houses and mansions, they began frantic preparations for war.

32. And as the *rākṣasa* lords, roaring like lions, girded themselves for battle, the night took on the aspect of the dark night of universal destruction.

33–34. Then great Sugrīva commanded the monkey lords as follows: "Creeping near, you must assault the gate and give battle, bulls among leaping monkeys. And if any one of you, no matter where he may be posted, should disobey, he is to be pounced upon and slain as a violator of the king's command."

35. When the monkey leaders, their hands illuminated by their flaming torches, had approached the gate and taken up their positions there, rage seized hold of Rāvaṇa.

36. The violent force of the expansion of his body threw the ten directions into confusion, for he looked like an incarnation of the wrath that fills the body of Rudra.

37. In a rage, he sent forth Nikumbha and Kumbha, the two sons of Kumbhakarṇa, accompanied by many *rākṣasas*.

38. Roaring like a lion, the lord of the *rākṣasas* commanded all of those *rākṣasas*, "*Rākṣasas*! Depart at once."

39. Then, at his command, the heroic *rākṣasas*, roaring again and again, marched forth from Laṅkā, their weapons glittering.

40–41. With its terrifying horses, chariots, and elephants, and crowded with various types of foot soldiers, the fearsome *rākṣasa* army emerged into view, its lances, maces, swords, darts, iron cudgels, and bows glittering. Its valor and prowess were terrifying. Its darts were flashing and it resounded with hundreds of little bells.

42–44. The soldiers, their arms covered with golden ornaments, swung their battle-axes about and whirled their mighty weapons. They had fixed their arrows to their bows. They perfumed the strong breeze with their fragrances, floral wreaths, and the honey-wine of their stirrup-cups. Filled with mighty warriors and rumbling like a great storm cloud, the army was truly fearsome. Seeing that truly terrifying army of the *rākṣasas* approaching, the army of leaping monkeys leapt forward, roaring loudly.

45. Springing swiftly forward, the great *rākṣasa* army hurled itself at the enemy host, as a moth might hurl itself into a flame.

46. With its iron clubs—like bolts of lightning—burnished from the rubbing of their arms, the *rākṣasas'* magnificent army shone more brightly still.

47. Then some of the fearsome-looking night-roaming *rākṣasas* began to cut down the monkey heroes on all sides with their sharp swords.

48. The warriors on both sides cursed, bit, struck down, and killed one another.

49. One cried, "Attack!" "He's attacking!" said another, while still a third cried, "I'll attack!" "Did you wound him?" "Stand!" thus did they shout there to one another.

50. With huge darts held on high amid a welter of fists, lances, and swords, the immensely fierce battle between the monkeys and the *rākṣasas* raged on.

51. The *rākṣasas* cut down the monkeys ten and seven at a time, while the monkeys slaughtered the *rākṣasas* in battle ten and seven at a time.

52. Then the monkeys cut off and surrounded the *rākṣasa* troops, whose hair and drawstrings were flying loose, their armor and weapons lost.

The end of the sixty-second *sarga* of the *Yuddhakāṇḍa* of the *Śrī Rāmāyaṇa*.

Sarga 63

1. In the thick of that fearsome slaughter of heroes, Añgada, thirsting for battle, encountered the heroic *rākṣasa* Kampana.

2. After challenging Añgada, Kampana, in a rage, swiftly struck first, hitting him with his mace. Struck with such violence, Añgada staggered.

3. But, coming to his senses, powerful Añgada hurled the peak of a mountain. Kampana then fell to the ground, slain by that blow.

4. Now that their champions were slain, the *rākṣasa* troops, deeply shaken, ran headlong to Kumbha, Kumbhakarṇa's son. When Kumbha saw them approaching so swiftly, he calmed them.

5. Then, in deep concentration, that foremost of bowmen took up his bow and loosed arrows that looked like venomous snakes and could rend bodies.

6. With the arrows fixed to it, his splendid bow shone more brightly still as if it were a second bow of Indra, illumined by the splendor of lightning and a great rainbow.

7. Then, with a beautifully feathered, gold-fletched arrow that he had drawn back as far as his ear before releasing it, he struck Dvivida.

8. Struck violently by that arrow, that best of leaping monkeys, who resembled a mountain peak, lost his footing and collapsed, dazed and twitching.

9. Seeing his brother wounded in that great battle, Mainda seized a huge boulder and came running at full speed.

10. The immensely powerful Mainda flung that boulder at the *rākṣasa*. But Kumbha shattered it with five blazing arrows.

11. Then, nocking another arrow, tipped with a splendid arrowhead and resembling a venomous serpent, the immensely powerful *rākṣasa* struck Dvivida's elder brother in the chest with it.

12. Struck by him in the vitals with such a blow, Mainda, leader of the monkey troops, fell to the ground, stunned.

13. When Añgada saw that his two immensely powerful maternal uncles had fallen, he charged swiftly at Kumbha, who stood with bow drawn.

14. As Añgada rushed upon him, Kumbha pierced him—first with five iron shafts and then with three more sharp arrows—as one might an elephant with javelins.

15. Mighty Kumbha pierced Añgada with various arrows adorned with gold, their tips honed to razor sharpness, their cutting edges keen.

16. Although his body was pierced all over, Vālin's son, Añgada, was not shaken. He rained hails of trees and boulders upon Kumbha's head.

17. But Kumbhakarṇa's majestic son cut down all those trees and smashed the boulders—everything that was thrown by Vālin's son.

18. Seeing the leader of monkey troops rushing upon him, Kumbha struck him in the brow with two arrows, as one might an elephant with two flaming brands.

19. Covering his eyes, which were bathed in blood, with one hand, Añgada seized a nearby *sāla* tree with the other.

20–21. But even as he was about to swiftly hurl that tree, which looked like the flagstaff of Indra and was as huge as Mount Mandara, Kumbha cut him down with seven sharp arrows, rending his body, while all the *rākṣasas* looked on. In great agony, Añgada collapsed and lost consciousness.

22. Seeing the unassailable Añgada in agony, drowning as it were in the ocean, the foremost among the tawny monkeys reported it to Rāghava.

23. When Rāma heard that Vālin's son had been gravely wounded in the great battle, he sent forth the foremost among tawny monkeys, led by Jāmbavān.

24. As soon as they heard Rāma's orders, those tigers among monkeys hurled themselves in a towering rage upon Kumbha, who stood with bow drawn.

25. In their desire to rescue Aṅgada, those bulls among monkeys raced onward with trees and boulders in their hands, their eyes red with rage.

26. In a rage, Jāmbavān, Suṣeṇa, and the monkey Vegadarśin rushed toward Kumbhakarṇa's heroic son.

27. But when Kumbha saw those immensely powerful monkey lords rushing toward him, he stopped them in their tracks with a torrent of arrows, as a barrage of trees might stop a rushing stream.

28. For when they ran into that mass of arrows, the great monkey lords could no more get past it than can the ocean, the great reservoir of the waters, its shore.

29–30. But when Sugrīva, lord of the leaping monkeys, saw that the troops of tawny monkeys had been overwhelmed by those hails of arrows, he stepped in front of Aṅgada, his brother's son, and rushed swiftly upon Kumbha in battle, just as a swift lion might upon an elephant roaming the mountain slopes.

31. The immensely powerful Sugrīva tore up huge mountains as well as many *aśvakarṇas*, *dhavas*, and various other trees, and let fly with them.

32. But with his sharp arrows, Kumbhakarṇa's majestic son cut down that hail of trees—so difficult to withstand—that covered the sky.

33. Completely riddled with sharp arrows by that fierce and celebrated marksman Kumbha, those trees resembled fearsome hundred-slayers.

34. But the majestic, fearless, and immensely powerful overlord of the monkeys was not in the least disturbed when he saw his hail of trees cut to pieces by Kumbha.

35. Although he was himself grievously wounded, Sugrīva withstood those arrows. Then, snatching away Kumbha's bow, as lustrous as the bow of Indra, he broke it.

36. Then, when Sugrīva had accomplished this all-but-impossible feat, he swiftly bore down upon Kumbha, who now resembled an elephant with broken tusks, and, in a rage, said to him:

37. "Elder brother of Nikumbha, your power and the force of your arrows are truly extraordinary. Your chivalry and your majesty are shared only by Rāvaṇa himself.

38. "Peer of Prahrāda, Bali, Indra the slayer of Vṛtra, Kubera, and Varuṇa, you alone take after your father, though you are mightier still.

39. "The thirty gods can no more get the better of you—a single-handed great-armed tamer of foes, lance in hand—than can worldly cares, one who has vanquished his senses.

40. "Your paternal uncle Rāvaṇa conquered the gods and *dānavas* through the gift of a boon, while Kumbhakarṇa did so through his own enormous strength.

41. "You are Indrajit's equal in archery and Rāvaṇa's in valor. In strength and prowess you are the foremost among *rākṣasas* in the world today.

42. "Let all beings witness this day the great and extraordinary clash in battle between you and me, like that between Śakra and Śambara.

43. "You have performed an unparalleled feat and demonstrated your mastery of missiles; for you have felled all these heroes among the tawny monkeys, fearsome in their valor.

44. "It is only out of fear of incurring censure that I have not killed you thus far, hero. For you must be exhausted after performing this feat. Once you are rested, you shall witness my strength."

45. Kumbha had first been flattered, but now, at the contemptuous words of Sugrīva, his blazing energy flared up, like that of a sacrificial fire into which an oblation of melted butter has been poured.

46. Then, leaping up, Kumbha hurled himself upon Sugrīva and, in a rage, struck him on the chest with a fist that had the force of a thunderbolt.

47. His skin was torn open and his blood poured out; for that fist, with its tremendous force, had penetrated to the bone.

48. Then, from that impact, there briefly sprang forth a blazing flame, like the flame that arises on Mount Meru when it is struck by lightning.

49. Although Sugrīva, the immensely powerful bull among monkeys, had been struck there by him, he clenched his fist, as hard as adamant.

50. Then the mighty monkey brought that fist, which, radiant with a thousand rays of light, was as brilliant as the sun's orb, down upon Kumbha's chest.

51. Struck by that fist, the *rākṣasa* fell swiftly, like the red planet Mars, with its glowing rays, somehow fallen from the heavens.

52. As Kumbha's body fell, its chest caved in by that fist, it looked like the body of Sūrya, lord of cows, when he was vanquished by Rudra.

53. When Kumbha had been slain in battle by that bull among leaping monkeys, so fearsome in his valor, the earth trembled together with its mountains and forests, while tremendous fear filled the *rākṣasas*.

The end of the sixty-third *sarga* of the *Yuddhakāṇḍa* of the *Śrī Rāmāyaṇa*.

Sarga 64

1. When Nikumbha saw that his brother had been struck down by Sugrīva, he glared at the lord of the monkeys, as if to burn him up with his rage.

2–3. That hero then took up a splendid iron club. It was bound with garlands of flowers, stamped with the sign of five fingers, and it was as huge as the peak of a lordly mountain. It was bound with plates of gold and adorned with diamonds and coral. That fearsome dispeller of the *rākṣasas'* fear was like the staff of Yama.

4. It was like the flagstaff of Śakra. Brandishing it in battle, immensely powerful Nikumbha, fearsome in his valor, opened wide his mouth and roared.

5–6. With his iron club and his ornaments—the golden necklace hanging across his chest, the armlets on his arms, his burnished earrings, and his variegated garland—Nikumbha resembled a storm cloud replete with thunder, lightning, and rainbow.

7. The tip of that huge warrior's iron club could smash the lair of the winds in the sky. It blazed like a roaring, smokeless fire, purifier of all things.

8–9. The whirling of Nikumbha's iron club seemed to set the very sky spinning, along with the heavenly city of Viṭapāvatī with its splendid mansions of the *gandharvas*, the celestial city of Amarāvatī with all its mansions, and with its constellations, its hosts of stars, the moon, and the great planets.

10. With his iron club and ornaments for his flames and his rage for kindling, the fire that was Nikumbha was as unapproachable as the fire at the end of a cosmic age when it blazes forth.

11. The *rākṣasas* and the monkeys were frozen with fear. But mighty Hanumān, thrusting out his chest, took a stand before him.

12. Then mighty Nikumbha, whose arms resembled iron clubs, brought that iron club, radiant as the sun, bringer of light, down upon the chest of mighty Hanumān.

13. But that iron club shattered violently into a hundred pieces against his broad and adamantine chest, so that it resembled a hundred flaming meteors in the heavens.

14. And shaken by that iron club, the great monkey staggered under the blow, as would a mountain during an earthquake.

15. Struck by that iron club in this fashion, the immensely powerful Hanumān, foremost among the leaping monkeys, tightly clenched his fist.

16. Raising it, the forceful, immensely powerful, and mighty monkey, whose power was that of Vāyu, drove it forcefully into Nikumbha's chest.

17. His skin was torn open and the blood gushed forth. That fist sparked flames that resembled lightning bursting forth.

18. Nikumbha staggered under that blow, but, recovering, he seized the immensely powerful Hanumān.

19. Seeing immensely powerful Hanumān swept up by Nikumbha, the inhabitants of Laṅkā roared frighteningly in the midst of battle.

20. But even as he was being carried off in this fashion by Kumbhakarṇa's son, the son of Anila struck him with a fist that had the force of a thunderbolt.

21. Then, freeing himself, Hanumān, son of Māruta, leapt to the ground and swiftly began to belabor Nikumbha.

22. Exerting all his strength, he threw Nikumbha down and pummeled him. Then, leaping up, that powerful monkey landed on his chest with tremendous force.

23. Locking Nikumbha's neck in both his arms, Hanumān twisted it until he tore off the huge head of the *rākṣasa*, who was shrieking horribly.

24. Once Nikumbha had been slain in battle by Pavana's son, an intense and terrifying battle broke out between the enraged armies of Daśaratha's son and the *rākṣasa* lord.

The end of the sixty-fourth *sarga* of the *Yuddhakāṇḍa* of the *Śrī Rāmāyaṇa*.

Sarga 65

1. Upon hearing that Nikumbha had been slain and Kumbha struck down as well, Rāvaṇa, in a towering rage, flared up like fire.

2. Beside himself with grief and rage, the *rākṣasa*, son of chaos, exhorted large-eyed Makarākṣa, Khara's son:

3. "Go, son, at my command, with an army. You must kill Rāma and Lakṣmaṇa along with the forest-dwelling monkeys."

4. Upon hearing these words of Rāvaṇa, the proud night-roaming *rākṣasa* hero Makarākṣa, Khara's courageous son, replied, "Very well."

5. Then, after respectfully saluting and reverentially circumambulating ten-necked Rāvaṇa, the mighty *rākṣasa* went forth from that splendid mansion at Rāvaṇa's command.

6. He then said this to the officer who was standing by: "Let my chariot be brought at once and have the army brought up quickly."

7. Upon hearing those words of his, that night-roaming *rākṣasa* officer had the chariot and army brought up.

8. After reverentially circumambulating the chariot, the night-roaming *rākṣasa* mounted it and urged on his charioteer, crying, "Drive my chariot swiftly."

9. Then Makarākṣa said this to all those *rākṣasas*: "*Rākṣasas*! You must all fight as my vanguard.

10. "I have been commanded by Rāvaṇa, the great king of the *rākṣasas*, to kill both Rāma and Lakṣmaṇa in battle.

11. "This very day, night-roaming *rākṣasas*, with my splendid arrows I shall slay Rāma, Lakṣmaṇa, the tree-dwelling monkey Sugrīva, and his monkeys.

12. "And this very day, hurling my lance, I shall consume the vast host of the monkeys that has assembled here, just as fire does dry kindling."

13. Upon hearing that speech of Makarākṣa, all of those mighty night-roaming *rākṣasas*, armed with various weapons, formed themselves into a column.

14–15. Terrifying with their great fangs, yellow eyes, and bristling hair, those heroes, who could take on any form at will, roared like bull elephants trumpeting. Surrounding the huge son of Khara, those huge *rākṣasas* then marched forth in great excitement, shaking the earth.

16. A deafening roar arose on every side as they sounded thousands of battle conches and *bherī* drums, clapped their upper arms, and roared out their battle cries.

17. But suddenly the whip slipped from the hand of Makarākṣas's charioteer, and the *rākṣasa*'s battle standard fell.

18. The horses yoked to his chariot were robbed of their strength. Moving along with halting steps, despondent, they proceeded with tearful faces.

19. As fierce and evil-minded Makarākṣa marched forth, a harsh and fearsome wind filled with dust began to blow.

20. Although they saw those omens, all those immensely powerful *rākṣasas* paid them no heed and proceeded to where Rāma and Lakṣmaṇa stood.

21. Their bodies as dark in hue as clouds, elephants, or buffalos, the night-roaming *rākṣasas*, having been wounded many times with sword and mace in the forefront of battle, were seasoned in combat. They raced onward, roaring and crying out, "Here I am!" "Here I am!"

The end of the sixty-fifth *sarga* of the *Yuddhakāṇḍa* of the *Śrī Rāmāyaṇa*.

Sarga 66

1. When the bulls among monkeys saw that Makarākṣa had marched forth, they all immediately leapt up and arrayed themselves, eager for battle.

2. Then there ensued a tremendous, hair-raising battle between the night-roaming *rākṣasas* and the leaping monkeys, just like that between the gods and the *dānavas*.

3. The monkeys and the night-roaming *rākṣasas* belabored each other, the former with blows of trees and hails of boulders, the latter with volleys of lances and blows of iron clubs.

4–5. From every side the night-roaming *rākṣasas*, who prowl in the darkness, slaughtered those lions among monkeys with javelins, lances, maces, swords, iron cudgels, spears, short javelins, volleys of arrows, nooses, war hammers, staves, *nirghātas*, and other weapons as well.

6. Tormented by Khara's son with his hails of arrows, the monkeys panicked. Stricken with terror, they all fled.

7. When the *rākṣasas* saw that the forest-dwelling monkeys were fleeing, they roared like lions in their excitement. The *rākṣasas* then took on an air of victory.

8. But even as the monkeys fled in all directions, Rāma stopped the *rākṣasas* in their tracks with a hail of arrows.

9. When the night-roaming *rākṣasa* Makarākṣa saw that his *rākṣasas* had been stopped in their tracks, he was consumed with the fire of anger, and he said these words:

10. "Stay where you are, Rāma! I challenge you to single combat. With sharp arrows loosed from my bow, I shall rob you of your life.

11. "You are the one who killed my father back then in the Daṇḍaka Forest. Therefore, when I think that the author of that foul deed is standing right before me, my rage redoubles.

12. "My whole body is burning fiercely in that I did not catch sight of you, you evil-minded Rāghava, back then in the great forest.

13. "But now, Rāma, as luck would have it, I find you here right before my eyes. I have been as desperate to catch you as a famished lion is a deer.

14. "This very day, dispatched to the realm of Yama, king of the dead, by the impact of my arrows, you shall meet the heroes you have slain.

15. "But what is the use of endless talking? Hear my words, Rāma. Let all the worlds behold the two of us on the battlefield.

16. "So now, in the midst of this great conflict, give battle, Rāma, with any weapon in which you are skilled—a missile, a mace, or even your bare hands."

17. When Rāma, the son of Daśaratha, had heard this speech of the endlessly talkative Makarākṣa, he laughed and spoke these words:

18. "In the Daṇḍaka Forest, I slaughtered fourteen thousand *rākṣasas*, including Triśiras, Dūṣaṇa, and the one who was your father.

19. "Today, evil wretch, the vultures, jackals, and crows with their sharp beaks and fangs and their hooked claws will gorge themselves on your flesh."

20. When Rāma had addressed him in this fashion, Khara's son, the night-roaming *rākṣasa*, loosed a torrent of arrows at Rāghava on the battlefield.

21. But Rāma cut those arrows into myriad pieces with a hail of his own arrows. Cut to pieces, the golden-fletched arrows fell to the ground by the thousand.

22. Then the battle between them commenced as the son of the *rākṣasa* Khara and Daśaratha's son rushed violently toward each other.

23. The sound of their bowstrings striking their armguards was like that of two thunderclouds clashing in the sky. The deafening sound of their bows could then be heard throughout the battlefield.

24. Eager to witness that awesome sight, all the gods, *dānavas*, *gandharvas*, *kinnaras*, and great serpents assembled in the sky.

25. As they pierced each other's bodies, their strength only redoubled. They both engaged in thrusts and counterthrusts with each other on the battlefield.

26. In that battle, the *rākṣasa* cut down the swarms of arrows loosed by Rāma, while Rāma, for his part, with his arrows cut the arrows loosed by the *rākṣasa* into myriad pieces.

27. All the cardinal and intermediate directions were filled with torrents of arrows. The earth, covered as well on every side, was no longer visible.

28. In a rage, great-armed Rāghava shattered the *rākṣasa*'s bow. With eight iron arrows he slew the charioteer. Then, after smashing the chariot with his arrows, Rāma cut down the chariot-horses.

29. Robbed of his chariot, the night-roaming *rākṣasa* Makarākṣa took his stand on the ground. In his hand, the *rākṣasa* held his lance, which, equal in radiance to the fire that ends a cosmic age, struck terror into all beings.

30. Brandishing that huge and blazing lance, the night-roaming *rakṣasa* hurled it furiously at Rāghava in that great battle.

31. But even as the blazing lance, released from the hand of Khara's son, flew toward him, Rāghava cut it to pieces in the sky with three arrows.

32. Struck by Rāma's arrows, the lance, adorned with heavenly gold, was cut into myriad pieces so that it shattered on the ground, like some great meteor.

33. When the great beings stationed in the sky saw that the lance had been destroyed by Rāma of wondrous deeds, they cried out, "Excellent! Excellent!"

34. When the night-roaming *rākṣasa* Makarākṣa saw that his lance had been destroyed, he raised his fist and cried out to Kākutstha, "Halt! Stay right where you are!"

35. Seeing Makarākṣa rushing toward him, Rāma, the delight of the Raghus, laughed and fitted to his bow the divinely charged weapon of Agni, the purifier.

36. When he was struck by Kākutstha with that divinely charged weapon in battle, the *rākṣasa*, pierced to the heart, collapsed and died.

37. Then, when the *rākṣasas* had witnessed Makarākṣa's fall, they all fled back to Laṅkā, harried by Rāma's arrows.

38. Seeing Khara's son, the night-roaming *rākṣasa*, struck down by the force of the arrows of King Daśaratha's son, like a mountain struck by a thunderbolt and shattered, the gods were delighted.

The end of the sixty-sixth *sarga* of the *Yuddhakāṇḍa* of the *Śrī Rāmāyaṇa*.

Sarga 67

1. When Rāvaṇa, victorious in battle, heard that Makarākṣa had been slain, he was furious, and he ordered his son Indrajit into battle.

2. "Hero, you must slay those two heroic brothers, Rāma and Lakṣmaṇa. For, whether visible or invisible, you are mightier still in every way.

3. "In battle you defeated Indra, whose feats are unmatched. How much more easily will you slay two men when you encounter them in battle?"

4. Addressed in this fashion by the *rākṣasa* lord, Indrajit accepted his father's instructions. Then, in the sacrificial ground, he offered oblations into the purifying sacrificial fire according to the ritual prescriptions.

5. As Rāvaṇi began his oblation into the sacrificial fire, *rākṣasa* women, bearing red turbans, came in haste to where he stood.

6. Weapons served as the *śarapatra* grass, myrobalan wood was the kindling. His garments were red and his ladle of black iron.

7. Having strewn the fire altar all around on every side with weapons in place of *śarapatra* grass, he seized the throat of a live, pure black goat.

8. When kindled and fed the oblation of rice-gruel, the smokeless fire with its huge flames displayed signs betokening victory.

9. Glowing like burnished gold, his flames swirling in an auspicious clockwise direction, Agni, the purifier, himself rose up and received that oblation.

10. Once he had made his oblations into the sacrificial fire and thus gratified the gods, *dānavas*, and *rākṣasas*, Indrajit mounted his excellent and radiant chariot, which could be rendered invisible.

*11. Complete with its four horses, its sharp arrows, and a mighty bow fastened in place, that magnificent chariot looked splendid.

12. Blazing with splendor and covered with burnished gold, the chariot was decorated with motifs of arrows, moons, and half-moons.

13. With its device of a great conch of *jāmbūnada* gold, Indrajit's battle standard, adorned with lapis, looked like a blazing fire, purifier of all things.

14. And, protected as he was by the divine weapon-spell of Brahmā, as brilliant as the sun, the immensely powerful Rāvaṇi was unassailable.

15. Once he had completed his oblation into the sacrificial fire to the accompaniment of *mantras* peculiar to the *rākṣasas*, Indrajit, victorious in battle and able to render himself invisible, marched forth from the city and said:

16. "This very day I shall slay in combat those two false forest ascetics and thus give my father a great victory in battle.

17. "Once I have cleared the earth of monkeys and slain Rāma along with Lakṣmaṇa, I will have given my father the greatest delight." When he had spoken in this fashion, he became invisible.

18. Acting on ten-necked Rāvaṇa's orders, Indrajit, the fierce foe of Indra, in a rage drove swiftly into battle armed with his pitiless bow and iron arrows.

19. He spied the two immensely powerful heroes in the midst of the monkeys. As they prepared to unleash volleys of arrows, they resembled three-headed cobras.

20. With the thought, "There they are!" he strung his bow and inundated them with torrents of arrows, as, with a downpour, might a storm cloud charged with rain.

21. In his chariot, he flew up into the sky, and, stationing himself there out of the range of sight, he riddled Rāma and Lakṣmaṇa with sharp arrows.

22. Beset on every side by the force of his arrows, Rāma and Lakṣmaṇa placed arrows on their bows and invoked a divine weapon-spell.

23. Those very mighty warriors, who resembled gods, covered the sky with their volleys of arrows. But their divinely charged weapons did not so much as graze Indrajit.

24. For he had created dense darkness so as to obscure the heavens. Thus did that majestic warrior, shrouded in a murky fog, make it impossible to see in any direction.

25. Not even the sound of his bowstring striking his armguard could be heard or the noise of his chariot wheels and horses' hooves as he darted to and fro. Nor could one discern his form.

26. With his torrent of iron arrows, the great-armed warrior, in that dense and blinding darkness, let loose a veritable and prodigious downpour of arrows.

27. In that battle, the angry Rāvaṇi, who had been granted a boon, completely riddled Rāma in every limb with arrows as radiant as the sun.

28. Although those two tigers among men were pelted with iron arrows like two mountains inundated by torrential rains, they continued to shoot their own sharp gold-fletched arrows.

29. Soaring into the sky, those heron-feathered arrows wounded Rāvaṇi and then fell back to earth, smeared with blood.

30. Although those two splendid men were sorely afflicted by that torrent of arrows, they cut down those shafts as they rained down, with many crescent-headed arrows.

31. The two sons of Daśaratha would loose a splendid divinely charged weapon in any direction from which they saw those sharp arrows raining down.

32. But the great chariot-warrior Rāvaṇi, whose divinely charged weapons flew swiftly, darted in all directions in his chariot and continued to riddle the two sons of Daśaratha with his sharp arrows.

33. Thoroughly riddled by him with those finely made, gold-fletched arrows, the two heroic sons of Daśaratha looked like twin *kiṃśuka* trees covered with crimson blossoms.

34. No one could follow Indrajit's movements, nor could anyone discern his form, his bow, or his arrows. Nothing whatever of his could be discerned, as if he were the sun hidden behind a dense mass of clouds.

35. Pierced through by him, the tawny monkeys were struck down by the hundred and lay fallen on the ground, robbed of their life breaths.

36. Then, in a towering rage, Lakṣmaṇa said these words to his brother: "I shall use the divine weapon-spell of Brahmā in order to exterminate all the *rākṣasas*."

37. But Rāma said this in reply to Lakṣmaṇa of auspicious marks: "You must not slaughter all the *rākṣasas* of the earth on account of a single one.

38. "A foe who does not resist, is in hiding, cups his hands in supplication, approaches seeking refuge, is fleeing, or is caught off guard—you must not slay any of these.

39. "Therefore, mighty warrior, let us strive to slay him alone. Let us summon our divine weapon-spells, which strike with tremendous force and resemble venomous serpents.

40. "For if the monkey troop leaders could but see that vile master of illusion with his invisible chariot, they could then overpower and slay that *rākṣasa*.

41. "Whether he enters the earth, the heavens, the underworld Rasātala, or the sky—no matter where he may hide—he shall fall to earth consumed by my divinely charged weapons and robbed of his life breaths."

42. Thus did the great hero of the Raghus speak, surrounded by those bulls among leaping monkeys. Then, the great man urgently began to contemplate how to kill that fierce *rākṣasa* of cruel deeds.

The end of the sixty-seventh *sarga* of the *Yuddhakāṇḍa* of the *Śrī Rāmāyaṇa*.

Sarga 68

1. Now, when Indrajit realized what great Rāghava had in mind, he withdrew from the battle and reentered the city.

2. But as that immensely lustrous hero recalled the slaughter of those courageous *rākṣasas*, his eyes grew red with rage and he sallied forth once more.

3. Surrounded by *rākṣasas*, the immensely powerful Indrajit Paulastya, that thorn in the side of the gods, marched forth through the western gate.

4. But then, perceiving that the two heroic brothers, Rāma and Lakṣmaṇa, were prepared for battle, Indrajit displayed his power of magical illusion.

5. Placing an illusory Sītā on his chariot in the midst of his vast host, he made as if to kill her.

6. Determined to deceive all of them, that very evil-minded *rākṣasa* marched out right in front of the monkeys, displaying every intention of killing Sītā.

7. When the forest-dwelling monkeys saw him marching forth from the city, they leapt up in a towering rage, with boulders in their hands, eager for battle.

8. Before them strode Hanumān, elephant among monkeys, holding an immense mountain peak that was impossible to withstand.

9–10. There, in Indrajit's chariot, he saw Sītā. She was sorrowful, wearing a single braid, dejected, her face gaunt with fasting. That splendid woman, Rāghava's beloved, wore only a single garment, now much worn. She was unwashed so that all her limbs were covered with dust and dirt.

11. After observing her closely for a moment and concluding that she was indeed Maithilī, Hanumān became deeply agitated, his face awash in tears.

12–13. Seeing poor Sītā there in the chariot, sorrowful and afflicted with grief, in the clutches of the *rākṣasa* lord's son, the great monkey thought, "What does he mean to do?" Then, after voicing this concern, he rushed upon Rāvaṇi together with those excellent monkeys.

14. But when Rāvaṇi spied the monkey host, he was beside himself with rage. Unsheathing his sword, he seized Sītā by the head.

15. Then, right before their eyes, Rāvaṇi struck that woman, whom he had conjured up in his chariot through his power of magical illusion, as she cried out, "Rāma! Rāma!"

16. When Hanumān saw Sītā seized by her hair, that son of Māruta shed tears born of grief from his eyes. In anger, he spoke harsh words to the son of the *rākṣasa* lord:

17. "Evil wretch! You have seized her braid to your own destruction. Though born in a lineage of brahman-seers you dwelt in a *rākṣasa* woman's womb. Damn you, you creature of foul deeds, whose mind has sunk to this!

18. "Savage! Ignoble! Evildoer! Lowest of the low! Criminal! Such is the act of an ignoble creature! You are without pity, pitiless *rākṣasa*!

19. "Taken from her home, her country, and the arms of Rāma, what offense has Maithilī done you that you should want to kill her?

20. "If you kill Sītā, you will certainly die soon. For through this deed, for which you would deserve to die, you would fall into my clutches.

21. "And then, once you have lost your life and passed on to the next world, you will surely obtain those worlds reserved for those who kill women, worlds that are despised even by others who deserve death at the hands of all men."

22. Even as he was speaking in this fashion, Hanumān, surrounded by tawny monkeys wielding weapons, rushed in a rage at the son of the *rākṣasa* lord.

23. But Indrajit, with his army of fearsomely swift *rākṣasas*, drove back the immensely powerful army of forest-dwelling monkeys as it rushed onward.

24. Once he had routed the army of tawny monkeys with a thousand arrows, Indrajit replied to Hanumān, foremost among the tawny monkeys:

25. "This very day, right before your very eyes, I shall kill Vaidehī, on whose account Sugrīva, you, and Rāma have come here.

26. "And after I kill her, monkey, I shall then kill Rāma, Lakṣmaṇa, you, Sugrīva, and that ignoble Vibhīṣaṇa.

27. "Now, as to what you said, leaping monkey, 'Women are not to be killed,' I would respond that one must do whatever causes pain to one's enemies."

28. When he had addressed him in this fashion, Indrajit himself slew the wailing, illusory Sītā with his sharp-edged sword.

29. Hacked in two from her shoulder to her hip, the poor woman, so beautiful and broad-hipped, fell to the ground.

30. After he had killed that woman, Indrajit said to Hanumān: "Now behold Rāma's woman, whom I have slaughtered in my wrath."

31. Then, having slain her himself with his huge sword, Indrajit mounted his chariot in great delight and unleashed a deafening roar.

32. As he withdrew to the safety of his own forces, roaring loudly, his mouth opened wide, the monkeys standing nearby could hear the din.

33. When evil-minded Rāvaṇi had slain Sītā in this fashion, he was delighted at heart. But when the monkeys saw how thoroughly delighted he was, they fled every which way in profound dejection.

The end of the sixty-eighth *sarga* of the *Yuddhakāṇḍa* of the *Śrī Rāmāyaṇa*.

Sarga 69

1. When those bulls among monkeys heard that terrifying sound, they fled in all directions, glancing back toward Indrajit, whose roar was like the sound of Śakra's thunderbolt.

2. But as they all scattered, terrified and dejected, their faces downcast, Hanumān, son of Māruta, called out to them:

3. "Leaping monkeys! Why are you fleeing with downcast faces, abandoning your enthusiasm for battle? Where now are all your heroics?

4. "Follow close behind me as I advance before you into battle. It ill befits heroes endowed with noble birth to run away."

5. Addressed in this fashion by the wise son of Vāyu, the monkeys were highly indignant. Their minds filled with excitement, they seized mountain peaks and trees.

6. Those bulls among monkeys rushed, roaring, toward the *rākṣasas*. Surrounding Hanumān, they followed him into the great battle.

7. Like fire, eater of oblations, wreathed in flames, Hanumān, surrounded on every side by the principal monkeys, consumed the army of his foes.

8. Surrounded by the monkey host, the great monkey—like Yama, who brings time itself to an end—wrought destruction among the *rākṣasas*.

9. Consumed with grief and rage, the great monkey Hanumān hurled an enormous boulder at Rāvaṇi's chariot.

10. But when the charioteer saw it hurtling toward him, he drove the chariot, drawn by obedient horses, well out of range.

11. Failing in its purpose, the boulder fell short of Indrajit, who remained in his chariot with his charioteer. It split open the earth and buried itself.

12. But in falling, it wrought havoc among the *rākṣasa* host. Then, roaring, the forest-dwelling monkeys hurled themselves by the hundred upon Indrajit.

13. Arming themselves, those huge monkeys, fearsome in their valor, hurled trees and mountain peaks into the midst of their enemies.

14. Struck down powerfully with trees by the immensely powerful monkeys, the grotesque night-roaming *rākṣasas* writhed on the battleground.

15. But when Indrajit saw his army being harried by the monkeys, he seized his weapons in a towering rage and rushed at his foes.

16–17. Surrounded by his own troops, he displayed his valor, releasing torrents of arrows. And he slaughtered many of those tigers among monkeys with lances, darts, swords, spears, mallets, and war hammers. The monkeys, in turn, slew his followers in battle.

18. With *sāla* trees, complete with trunks and branches, and with boulders, immensely powerful Hanumān slaughtered the *rākṣasas* of fearsome deeds.

19. Once he had driven back the enemy army, Hanumān said to the forest-dwelling monkeys: "Withdraw! There is no point in defeating this army.

20. "For Janaka's daughter, on whose account we have been fighting, struggling, and sacrificing our lives to please Rāma, has been slain.

21. "Let us first report this matter to Rāma and Sugrīva. Then, we shall do whatever they may ordain."

22. When he had spoken in this fashion, that foremost of monkeys turned back all the monkeys and, calmly and deliberately, withdrew.

23. Now, when Indrajit saw that Hanumān was heading back to where Rāghava waited, he retired to the Nikumbhilā shrine, eager to make oblation to the sacred fire, purifier of all things.

24. The sacred fire, purifier of all things, blazed up fiercely, as, in accordance with the sacrificial injunctions, the *rākṣasa* poured oblations of blood into it there on the sacrificial ground.

25. Glutted with the oblations of blood and swathed in flames, that fierce fire blazed up like the sun at twilight.

26. Then Indrajit, in accordance with the sacrificial injunctions, made oblations according to those injunctions for the success of the *rākṣasas*. And the *rākṣasas*, who knew what was and was not proper conduct, stood around in their vast troops, watching.

The end of the sixty-ninth *sarga* of the *Yuddhakāṇḍa* of the *Śrī Rāmāyaṇa*.

Sarga 70

1. Now, when Rāghava heard the deafening noise of the battle between the *rākṣasas* and the forest-dwelling monkeys, he said to Jāmbavān:

2. "My friend, surely Hanumān must have accomplished an all-but-impossible feat, since we hear such a mighty and terrifying clash of arms.

3. "Therefore you should go quickly, lord of the apes, surrounded by your own forces, and render assistance to that foremost of monkeys, who is engaged in battle."

4. With the words, 'So be it,' the king of the apes, surrounded by his own army, proceeded toward the western gate, where the monkey Hanumān was.

5. But then, on the road, the lord of apes encountered Hanumān returning, surrounded by his monkeys, who were fresh from battle and breathing hard.

6. Encountering on the road that fearsome army of apes all ready for battle and resembling a black storm cloud, Hanumān halted it and turned it back.

7. With his army of tawny monkeys, the illustrious Hanumān quickly approached Rāma and, in great sorrow, said these words to him:

8. "While we were engaged in battle, Indrajit, the son of Rāvaṇa, slew the wailing Sītā right before our eyes.

9. "When I saw her like that, I was devastated and despondent, tamer of your foes. Then I came straightaway to report this news to you, sir."

10. Upon hearing those words of his, Rāghava, fainting from grief, fell to the ground, like a tree cut off at the roots.

11. Seeing the godlike Rāghava fallen to the ground, those excellent monkeys leapt up and rushed to him from every side.

12. They doused him with water fragrant with red and blue lotuses, as if he were an unbearable blazing fire that had sprung up.

13. Then Lakṣmaṇa, deeply grieving himself, took the stricken Rāma in his arms and addressed him in words that were both rational and meaningful:

14. "Since the practice of righteousness has been unable to protect you, noble brother—you, who have always trodden the path of virtue and controlled your senses—from calamities, it is truly pointless.

15. "For since we cannot directly perceive the force of righteousness in the same way that we perceive moving and fixed objects, it is my opinion that it does not exist.

16. "This thing called 'righteousness' is not demonstrable in the same way that moving and fixed objects are. Otherwise, a person like you would not experience such suffering.

17. "By the same token, if the force of unrighteousness were real, Rāvaṇa would go to hell, while you, sir, who are devoted to righteousness, would not thus suffer calamity.

18. "Since he has suffered no calamity, while you are immersed in one, can it be true that one obtains felicity through the practice of righteousness and that suffering arises from the practice of unrighteousness?

19. "Now, if those people who were averse to unrighteousness would thereby experience the felicity arising from the practice of righteousness, that is, if those who conducted themselves

righteously would experience happiness, then they would receive their just deserts.

20. "Therefore, since the fortunes of those among whom unrighteousness is practiced increase, while those who always practice righteousness suffer torments, these two concepts are meaningless.

21. "And if, Rāghava, it were true that evildoers perish through the force of unrighteousness, then the force of righteousness would also be destroyed by the very act of destruction. Then, once it is destroyed, whom could it harm?

22. "Or if we are to understand that it is because of fate that a person is either killed by or kills another, then it is fate alone that would be tainted by that evil act and not the person himself.

23. "Since the results of righteousness are imperceptible and it itself is unmanifest and, in fact, unreal, how, tormentor of your foes, would it be possible to attain the highest good by means of it?

24. "If there were really such a thing as the power of virtue, then you, foremost among the virtuous, would never have suffered any evil. But since such a calamity has befallen you, it must follow that the power of virtue does not exist.

25. "On the other hand, it may be that the force of righteousness is weak and impotent and is merely auxiliary to manly effort. And since it is weak and blurs all distinctions, it should, in my opinion, be ignored.

26. "And if the force of righteousness is merely auxiliary to manly effort when it comes to effective action, then you should abandon it and devote yourself to manly effort, just as you now do to righteousness.

27. "Or should it be argued that righteousness consists, as they say, in speaking the truth, scorcher of your foes, then why is it that you would not imprison our father, who acted both untruthfully and cruelly toward you?

28. "Moreover, scorcher of your foes, if either righteousness or human effort were to be practiced exclusively, then the wielder of the *vajra*, Indra of the hundred sacrifices, would not first have slain a sage and then performed a sacrifice.

29. "When either human effort or righteousness is practiced exclusively, it destroys a person, Rāghava. Therefore, Kākutstha, a man should act as he pleases in all such matters.

30. "Such is righteousness according to my way of thinking, Rāghava, my poor brother. Besides, when you relinquished the kingship, you cut off righteousness at its root.

31. "For all righteous actions flow from wealth that is drawn and amassed from different sources, just as rivers flow from the mountains.

32. "But when a man is stripped of his wealth and so becomes powerless, all his righteous actions cease to flow like rivulets in the hot season.

33. "And such a man who has been raised to enjoy pleasures will come to crave them. If he should lose his wealth, he will resort to evil deeds. In this way dire consequences will ensue.

34. "A rich man has friends. A rich man has kinsmen. A rich man is an important person in this world. A rich man is considered learned.

35. "A rich man is powerful. A rich man is wise. A rich man is highly fortunate. A rich man is endowed with the finest qualities.

36. "I have thus laid out for you the disadvantages inherent in relinquishing wealth. I cannot imagine, heroic brother, what led you to such a decision when you abandoned your kingship.

37. "A rich man gains righteousness, pleasure, and profit—everything is propitious for him. But a poor man, though he may desire wealth and seek it, can never acquire it.

38. "Joy, desire, pride, righteousness, anger, tranquility, and self-restraint: all of these proceed from wealth, lord of men.

39. "Those who wander about practicing righteousness lose everything of value in this world. Those things of value are no more to be seen in you than are the heavenly bodies on stormy days.

40. "For, hero, it was when you were living in exile, adhering to your father's word, that the *rākṣasa* stole away your wife, dearer to you than life itself.

41. "But this very day, with feats of valor, hero, I shall dispel the great suffering wrought by Indrajit. Therefore, arise Rāghava!

42. "For I have arisen to aid you, sinless brother. In my rage at learning of the murder of Janaka's daughter, I shall, with my arrows, completely level Laṅkā, along with its horses, elephants, and chariots, as well as the lord of the *rākṣasas* himself."

The end of the seventieth *sarga* of the *Yuddhakāṇḍa* of the *Śrī Rāmāyaṇa*.

Sarga 71

1. Now, while Lakṣmaṇa, so fond of his brother, was consoling Rāma, Vibhīṣaṇa returned after having stationed the troops at their proper posts.

2. Surrounded by his four valiant ministers, all armed with various weapons and resembling masses of collyrium, he resembled the leader of a herd surrounded by bull elephants.

3. As he drew near, he saw that the great Rāghava was immersed in grief and that the monkeys' eyes were awash with tears.

4. Then he saw the great Rāma Rāghava, delight of the House of Ikṣvāku, who lay dazed in Lakṣmaṇa's lap.

5. Upon seeing Rāma tormented by grief and deeply chagrined, Vibhīṣaṇa, his heart sinking with an inner sorrow, said, "What's wrong?"

6. Looking first at Vibhīṣaṇa's face, then at Sugrīva and the monkeys, Lakṣmaṇa, overwhelmed with tears, said these words:

7. "Upon hearing Hanumān report that Indrajit had slain Sītā, Rāghava fainted on the spot, dear friend."

8. But Vibhīṣaṇa cut Saumitri off even as he was speaking and said these deeply meaningful words to the barely conscious Rāma:

9. "Lord of men, I think that what Hanumān told you in his despair is as preposterous as would be the drying up of the ocean.

10. "For I know full well the plans that the evil-minded Rāvaṇa has for Sītā, great-armed warrior. He would never countenance her murder.

11. "Desiring what was best for him, I begged him over and over again, 'You must give up Vaidehī!' But he would not heed that advice.

12. "But no one can so much as get a glimpse of her, whether through conciliation, sowing dissension, bribery, or any other means, much less through violence.

13. "After deluding the monkeys, the *rākṣasa* Indrajit has returned to the shrine known as Nikumbhilā, where he will perform a sacrifice.

14. "And should that son of Rāvaṇa return after having completed his oblation, he will be unassailable in battle, even by the gods, Vāsava included.

15. "He must surely have employed this illusion, dear boy, in his desire to undermine the monkeys' valor. We must go there with our troops before he completes his sacrifice.

16. "So cease this baseless grieving that has overcome you, tiger among men, for when they see you racked with grief, the whole army becomes despondent.

17. "You must remain here to compose yourself and recoup your strength. Send Lakṣmaṇa, along with us and the leaders of the troops.

18. "For that tiger among men with his sharp arrows will force Rāvaṇi to abandon his sacrifice. Then that *rākṣasa* can be killed.

19. "Then his sharp and pitiless feathered shafts, made swift by the feathers of birds, will, like birds of prey themselves, drink Indrajit's blood.

20. "Thus, great-armed warrior, you must send forth Lakṣmaṇa of auspicious marks for the destruction of this *rākṣasa,* just as might Indra, the wielder of the *vajra*, send forth that weapon.

21. "Nor, best of men, must there be any delay in regard to killing our enemy. So issue your orders for the destruction of our foe, as does great Indra for the smashing of the citadels of the *asuras*.

22. "For if the *rākṣasa* lord should complete his sacrifice, he would become invisible in battle to the gods and *asuras* alike. Then, having completed his sacrifice, should he wish to fight, even the gods themselves would be in grave peril."

The end of the seventy-first *sarga* of the *Yuddhakāṇḍa* of the *Śrī Rāmāyaṇa*.

Sarga 72

1. Although Rāghava had heard those words of Vibhīṣaṇa, he could not, racked with grief as he was, clearly understand what the *rākṣasa* had said.

2. But then, in the presence of the monkeys, Rāma, the conqueror of enemy citadels, regaining his composure, spoke to Vibhīṣaṇa, who sat beside him.

3. "Vibhīṣaṇa! Lord of the *rākṣasas*, sons of chaos, I would like to hear once more what you just said. Please repeat what you intended to say."

4. When he had heard those words of Rāghava, Vibhīṣaṇa, skilled in speech, repeated what he had said.

5. "No sooner had you ordered me to station the troops at their proper posts than I executed your command, great-armed hero, just as you said.

6. "All the forces have been disposed separately on every side, while the troop leaders have been duly posted with their respective divisions.

7. "But please, illustrious hero, listen to my request once more. When you were grieving baselessly, our hearts were filled with grief.

8. "So abandon this sorrow, your majesty, this baseless grief that has overcome you. You must give up your brooding, which serves only to delight your enemies.

9. "If you are to recover Sītā and slay the night-roaming *rākṣasas*, you must bestir yourself, hero, and lift your spirits.

10. "Listen, delight of the Raghus, to the beneficial advice that I will now give you. Let Saumitri set out directly, accompanied by a large army, in order to confront Rāvaṇi in the Nikumbhilā shrine and kill him in battle.

11. "There with arrows—like the venom of venomous serpents—loosed from his full-drawn bow, that mighty bowman, victorious in battle, shall slay Rāvaṇi.

12. "Through the boon of self-existent Brahmā, acquired by virtue of his asceticism, that hero will obtain the divine Brahmaśiras weapon-spell and chariot-horses that can take him wherever he desires.

13. "But this is the way in which the death of that cunning warrior was foreordained, your majesty: 'Should an enemy ever strike you, enemy of Indra, before you can reach the Nikumbhilā grove and there complete your oblation into the fire, he shall compass your death even as you draw your bow to slay him.'

14. "Therefore, Rāma, you must depute mighty Lakṣmaṇa to kill Indrajit. For once he is slain, you can consider Rāvaṇa and all his companions to be as good as dead."

15. When Rāma had heard these words of Vibhīṣaṇa, he replied: "Well do I know, truly valorous hero, the illusory power of that fierce warrior.

16. "For he is cunning and has mastered the divine weapon-spell of Brahmā. He is mighty and mighty is the power of his illusion. Indeed, he can render even the gods themselves, including Varuṇa, unconscious in battle.

17. "And when, illustrious hero, mounted in his chariot, he travels through the sky, his movements can no more be discerned than those of the sun behind a dense mass of clouds."

18. Then Rāghava, who knew well the illusory power of his evil-minded foe, said these words to illustrious Lakṣmaṇa:

19–20. "Lakṣmaṇa! Accompanied by the entire army of the monkey lords and the troop leaders led by Hanumān as well as Jāmbavān, lord of the apes, and his army, you must slay the son of that *rākṣasa*, skilled though he may be in the power of illusion.

21. "And Vibhīṣaṇa, the great night-roaming *rākṣasa*, who knows this country intimately, will bring up the rear together with his ministers."

22. When Lakṣmaṇa, of fearsome valor, who was accompanied by Vibhīṣaṇa, heard these words of Rāghava, he took up a superb and extraordinary bow.

23. Girt for battle with his armor, sword, arrows, and golden bow, Saumitri touched Rāma's feet and spoke in great excitement:

24. "This very day, arrows loosed from my bow will pierce Rāvaṇi and then plunge into Laṅkā, as do *haṃsas* into a lotus pond.

25. "Indeed, this very day, my arrows, flying from the bowstring of my mighty bow, will strike that fierce warrior and tear his body to pieces."

26. When he had spoken in this fashion in the presence of his brother, glorious Lakṣmaṇa departed in haste, eager to slay Rāvaṇi.

27. Then, having made his obeisance to his elder brother's feet and having circled him reverentially, he set out for Nikumbhilā, the shrine guarded by Rāvaṇi.

28. His mission blessed by his brother, the valorous prince hastened on his way, accompanied by Vibhīṣaṇa.

29. Then Hanumān, surrounded by many thousands of monkeys, and Vibhīṣaṇa, together with his ministers, followed Lakṣmaṇa.

30. Accompanied by a vast army of tawny monkeys, Lakṣmaṇa quickly encountered the army of Jāmbavān, king of the apes, which was stationed along the way.

31. After he had traveled a long way, Saumitri, delight of his friends, spied in the distance the army of the *rākṣasa* lord, which was drawn up in battle array.

32. When the delight of the Raghus, tamer of his foes, had thus encountered that master of illusion Indrajit, he took his stand, bow in hand, in order to triumph according to the decree of Brahmā.

33. Then he plunged into the army of his enemies as into a vast darkness. It was diverse and gleamed with shining weapons. It was thick with battle standards and abounded in great chariot-warriors. In the immeasurable force of its onset, it was utterly terrifying.

The end of the seventy-second *sarga* of the *Yuddhakāṇḍa* of the *Śrī Rāmāyaṇa*.

Sarga 73

1. Now, at this critical juncture, Rāvaṇa's younger brother Vibhīṣaṇa addressed Lakṣmaṇa in words that were inimical to their enemies and instrumental to the achievement of their own ends:
2. "Lakṣmaṇa, you must make every effort to annihilate this vast army. For once it has been annihilated, the son of the *rākṣasa* lord will become visible.

3. "Showering your enemies with arrows like Indra's thunderbolt, you must attack at once while his sacrifice is not yet completed.

4. "Hero, you must slay evil-minded Rāvaṇi, so unrighteous and adept in magical illusion, for he is cruel in his actions and a terror to all the worlds."

5. Upon hearing these words of Vibhīṣaṇa, Lakṣmaṇa of auspicious marks unleashed a hail of arrows in the direction of the *rākṣasa* lord's son.

6. Meanwhile, the apes and tree-dwelling monkeys, armed with huge trees and mountains, together hurled themselves upon the army that stood before them.

7. The *rākṣasas* for their part, eager to annihilate the monkey host, fought back with sharp arrows, swords, and with upraised javelins and iron cudgels.

8. And thus a tumultuous clash of arms took place between the monkeys and the *rākṣasas*, which, with its colossal din, caused Laṅkā to reverberate on every side.

9. The very sky itself was hidden from view by weapons of many different kinds: sharp arrows, trees, and fearsome, upraised mountain peaks.

10. Hurling their weapons at the monkeys, the *rākṣasas*, with their deformed faces and arms, sowed immense panic among them.

11. By the same token, the monkeys struck and slaughtered the bulls among *rākṣasas* in battle with whole trees and mountain peaks.

12. Immense panic broke out among the *rākṣasas* as they were being slaughtered by the huge and immensely powerful leaders of the apes and monkeys.

13. When unassailable Indrajit learned that his army was demoralized and afflicted by the enemy, he rose up, his sacrifice still incomplete.

14. Emerging from the shadow of the trees, the *rākṣasa* Rāvaṇi, in a rage, mounted his chariot, which stood fully equipped and already yoked.

15. Resembling a mass of black collyrium, his eyes and face an angry red, that cruel *rākṣasa* with his fearsome bow and arrows looked like Death himself, the ender of all things.

16. As soon as the army of the *rākṣasas*—fearsome in their onslaught and eager to fight with Lakṣmaṇa—saw Indrajit mounted in his chariot, they surrounded him.

17–18. But at that moment, Hanumān, that tamer of his foes, who resembled a mountain, took up a huge and unstoppable tree and, with it, tore through the *rākṣasa* ranks like the fire at the end of a cosmic age. And, in that battle, the monkey knocked them unconscious with many trees.

19–20. When they saw that Hanumān, son of Pavana, was wreaking swift destruction upon them, thousands of *rākṣasas* unleashed a hail of weapons toward him—bearers of sharp lances assailed him with their lances, swordsmen with their swords, javelin-wielders with their javelins, and spearmen with their spears.

21–23. Besetting the mountainous monkey on every side, the *rākṣasas* belabored him with iron clubs, maces, splendid-looking barbed darts, hundreds of hundred-slayers, iron war hammers, fearsome battle-axes, short javelins, fists with the force of the *vajra*, and palms like thunderbolts. Meanwhile, Hanumān, in a towering rage, wrought great slaughter among them.

24. Indrajit saw that Pavana's mountainous son, the foremost of monkeys, Hanumān, destroyer of his enemies, was slaughtering his enemies.

25. He then said to his charioteer, "Drive to where that monkey is, for if we do not deal with him, he will surely destroy us *rākṣasas*."

26. When he had been addressed by him in this fashion, the charioteer drove to where Māruti was, conveying the utterly invincible Indrajit, mounted in the chariot.

27. Closing in, the invincible *rākṣasa* unleashed upon the monkey's head a hail of arrows, swords, spears, scimitars, and battle-axes.

28. But Māruti, parrying those fearsome weapons, was seized with a towering rage and spoke these words:

29. "Come and fight if you are such a hero, evil-minded son of Rāvaṇa! Having now encountered Vāyu's son, you will not escape with your life.

30. "If you want to engage me in single combat in this battle, then fight me with your bare hands. If you can sustain my crushing force, evil-minded wretch, then you will prove to be the best of the *rākṣasas*."

31. But just then Vibhīṣaṇa informed Lakṣmaṇa that Indrajit, the son of Rāvaṇa, intent on killing Hanumān, had taken up his bow:

32. "Rāvaṇa's son, the conqueror of Vāsava, intent on killing Hanumān, has now mounted his chariot.

33. "Saumitri, you must slay Rāvaṇi with your fearsome, foe-piercing arrows, incomparable in their workmanship and utterly lethal."

34. Addressed in this fashion by that terror to his foes, Vibhīṣaṇa, great Lakṣmaṇa spied the unassailable Indrajit of fearsome power, resembling a mountain and mounted in his chariot.

The end of the seventy-third *sarga* of the *Yuddhakāṇḍa* of the *Śrī Rāmāyaṇa*.

Sarga 74

1. After addressing Saumitri in this fashion, Vibhīṣaṇa, in great excitement, took him, still armed with his bow, and swiftly advanced.

2. Proceeding for a short distance, Vibhīṣaṇa entered a vast grove and there pointed out to Lakṣmaṇa the sacrificial ground.

3. There Rāvaṇa's powerful brother pointed out to Lakṣmaṇa a fearsome-looking banyan tree that resembled a black storm cloud.

4. "It is only after offering oblations to malignant spirits at this spot that the mighty son of Rāvaṇa goes forth to battle.

5. "Then the *rākṣasa* becomes invisible to all creatures and is able to bind and slay his enemies in battle with his splendid arrows.

6. "Therefore, with your keen arrows, you must destroy the mighty son of Rāvaṇa, together with his chariot, horses, and charioteer, before he returns to that banyan tree."

7. With the words, "So be it," immensely powerful Saumitri, delight of his friends, took up his stand there, twanging his splendid bow.

8. At that, Indrajit, Rāvaṇa's mighty son, appeared in his flame-colored chariot with his armor, sword, and battle standard.

9. Then immensely powerful Lakṣmaṇa addressed the invincible Paulastya: "I challenge you to a duel. Give me a fair fight."

10. Although the resolute and immensely powerful son of Rāvaṇa had been challenged in this fashion, he turned his gaze to Vibhīṣaṇa and spoke these bitter words:

11. "Born and bred in our House, you are the very brother of my father. How then, *rākṣasa*, can you, my own uncle, betray me, your son?

12. "You evil-minded defiler of righteousness! You have no sense of kinship, affection, loyalty to your kind, sound judgment, fraternal feeling, or righteousness.

13. "You are truly pathetic, you evil-minded wretch, and an object of contempt to the virtuous since, abandoning your own kind, you have chosen to serve our enemies.

14. "With your feeble wits you do not perceive this glaring difference. How can one even compare life with one's own kinfolk to despicable servitude to one's enemy?

15. "Even if one's enemy is virtuous and one's kinfolk devoid of every virtue, still one's kinfolk, devoid of virtue though they be, are to be preferred. An enemy is always an enemy.

16. "No kinsman other than you, night-roaming *rākṣasa*, could demonstrate such pitilessness and callousness as you have, younger brother of Rāvaṇa."

17. When Vibhīṣaṇa had been addressed in this fashion by his brother's son, he replied, "Why do you disparage me, *rākṣasa*, as if you knew nothing of my character?

18. "Vicious son of the *rākṣasa* lord, cease your impudent speech out of respect for me. Although I was born in the race of savage *rākṣasas*, my nature is not that of the *rākṣasas*. Instead, I share the better nature of virtuous men.

19. "I take delight in neither cruelty nor unrighteousness. Otherwise, how could a brother, even one of radically different character, reject his brother?

20. "There are three faults that lead one to ruin: theft of another's property, raping another man's wife, and excessive distrust of one's friends.

21–22. "My brother's horrific murder of the great seers, his warring with all the gods, his arrogance, his wrathfulness, his unremitting hostility, and his perversity—these crimes and defects of his, so threatening to his life and his rule, obscure his virtues, as do storm clouds a mountain.

23. "It is because of these crimes and defects that I have forsaken my brother, your father. Neither you nor your father nor the city of Laṅkā shall long endure.

24. "You are an arrogant and ill-disciplined whelp, *rākṣasa*! Say what you will about me; you are bound by the noose of Kāla.

25. "Your death is at hand this very day. What can you say to me now? Lowest of the *rākṣasas*, you will never make it back to that banyan tree.

26. "If you confront the two Kākutsthas in battle, you will not escape with your life. And now you must do battle with Prince Lakṣmaṇa. Once you are slain, you will accomplish the purpose of the gods in the abode of Yama.

27. "So demonstrate all the power you can muster. Discharge all your weapons and arrows. But once you come within the range of Lakṣmaṇa's shafts, you and your army will not escape with your lives."

The end of the seventy-fourth *sarga* of the *Yuddhakāṇḍa* of the *Śrī Rāmāyaṇa*.

Sarga 75

1. When Rāvaṇi had heard these words of Vibhīṣaṇa, he was beside himself with rage. He replied in harsh words and swiftly rushed forward.

2. Standing in his huge and ornate chariot yoked to black steeds, with his sword and other weapons raised, he resembled Kāla, the ender of all things.

3–4. Taking up his broad and thick bow, so firm, fearsome, and powerful, and fingering his foe-destroying arrows, he spoke in his fury to Saumitri, Vibhīṣaṇa, and the tigers among monkeys, saying, "Behold my valor!

5. "Now try to ward off in battle the irresistible hail of arrows loosed from my bow, like a torrential downpour from the sky.

6. "This very day my arrows, loosed from my immense bow, will scatter your limbs, as the wind might a heap of straw.

7. "I shall send you all this very day to the abode of Yama, your bodies mangled by sharp arrows, lances, javelins, broadswords, and iron cudgels.

8. "For who can stand before me in battle when, like a thundering storm cloud, I release a hail of arrows with my deft hands?"

9. When Lakṣmaṇa heard the boasting of the *rākṣasa* lord, his face displayed not the slightest sign of fear. But he was enraged, and he said these words to Rāvaṇi:

10. "The fulfillment of the goals of which you boast is not so easy to accomplish, *rākṣasa*. He alone is truly wise who fulfills his goals through action.

11. "You are utterly incapable of accomplishing this feat. In fact, no one can accomplish it. Yet after merely boasting about it, fool, you think, 'I have accomplished my purpose!'

12. "As for what you accomplished in battle on that other occasion by making yourself invisible, that is the way of thieves. It is not to be followed by heroes.

13. "So now that I am standing here, *rākṣasa*, within range of your arrows, go ahead and show us your martial prowess. Why boast with mere words?"

14. Addressed in this fashion, immensely powerful Indrajit, victorious in battle, drew his fearsome bow and let fly sharp arrows.

15. Once launched, those arrows, venomous as serpents, reached Lakṣmaṇa and cascaded upon him with their tremendous striking force, like hissing serpents.

16. With those arrows, exceedingly powerful in their striking force, Rāvaṇa's son Indrajit, whose own striking force was great, pierced Saumitri of auspicious marks in battle.

17. Drenched in blood, his body riddled with arrows, majestic Lakṣmaṇa resembled a smokeless fire.

18. When Indrajit saw what he had done, he drew near and, letting out a tremendous roar, uttered these words:

19. "Now, Saumitri, lethal arrows—sharp edged and well fletched—loosed from my bow will rob you of your life.

20. "Soon, Lakṣmaṇa, packs of jackals, vultures, and flocks of kites will descend upon you as you lie lifeless, slain by me.

21. "This very day, the supremely evil-minded and ever ignoble Rāma, a warrior in name only, will see you, his brother and devotee, slain by me.

22. "Yes, he will soon see you sprawled on the ground, Saumitri, slain by me, your armor cut to pieces, your bow smashed, and your head severed."

23. But as Rāvaṇa's son was speaking these harsh words in such a frenzy, Lakṣmaṇa responded to him with words that were perfectly reasonable.

24. "Why do you boast, *rākṣasa*, when you have accomplished no feat? You must perform some feat through which I may come to believe your boasting.

25. "Observe, man-eater! Without uttering any harsh speech, any word of censure, and without boasting, I am going to kill you."

26. When he had spoken in this fashion, Lakṣmaṇa sank five arrows of tremendous striking force—iron arrows drawn fully back to his ear—into the *rākṣasa*'s chest.

27. Enraged at being struck by Lakṣmaṇa with those arrows, Rāvaṇa's son pierced him in return with three well-aimed arrows.

28. And thus ensued an immensely fearsome and tumultuous clash in battle between those two lions—man and *rākṣasa*—each eager to kill the other.

29. For both were endowed with might, both were valorous, both were extremely heroic, and both were skilled in every weapon and divine weapon-spell.

30. Both were supremely invincible and unequaled in their power and blazing energy. The two great heroes clashed like two planets in the heavens.

31. For then the two great warriors, as unassailable as Bala and Vṛtra, fought like a pair of lions.

32. Discharging many torrents of arrows, the two lions—man and *rākṣasa*—continued fighting in great excitement.

33. Like two great storm clouds, the two champions—man and *rākṣasa*—bows and arrows in hand and both eager for victory, inundated each other in high excitement with torrents and hails of arrows.

The end of the seventy-fifth *sarga* of the *Yuddhakāṇḍa* of the *Śrī Rāmāyaṇa*.

Sarga 76

1. Then, hissing like an angry serpent, Dāśarathi, tormentor of his foes, fitted an arrow to his bow and released it toward the *rākṣasa* lord.

2. When the son of Rāvaṇa heard the slapping of the bowstring against Lakṣmaṇa's armguard, his face went pale, and he stared at him.

3. Meanwhile, Vibhīṣaṇa, observing the downcast face of the *rākṣasa*, son of Rāvaṇa, addressed Saumitri, who was absorbed in battle.

4. "I perceive unpropitious signs on the person of this son of Rāvaṇa. Therefore, you must make haste, great-armed warrior, for he is doubtless broken."

5. Then Saumitri nocked sharp arrows, like flames of fire or serpents engorged with venom, and let them fly.

6. Struck by Lakṣmaṇa with those arrows, whose impact was like that of Śakra's thunderbolt, Indrajit was momentarily stunned, all his senses wildly disordered.

7. But he regained consciousness after a moment. And, his senses fully restored, that hero stared at Daśaratha's heroic son who stood before him.

8. His eyes red with rage, Indrajit advanced upon Saumitri, and, as he drew near, he once again addressed him in harsh words:

9. "Have you completely forgotten my prowess in our first encounter, when, in battle, you and your brother writhed in bondage?

10. "That first time, during the great battle, the two of you and your followers were struck to the ground unconscious by my arrows, which are like the thunderbolts of Śakra.

11. "So since you dare to attack me, I think that you either must have forgotten that or else, clearly, you desire to depart for the abode of Yama.

12. "If you failed to observe my prowess in that first encounter, I will demonstrate it for you today. Now stand your ground!"

13. And so saying, he pierced Lakṣmaṇa with seven arrows and Hanumān with ten splendid, sharp-edged shafts.

14. Then, his frenzy redoubled in his fury, that powerful warrior pierced Vibhīṣaṇa with one hundred well-aimed arrows.

15–16. But when Rāma's younger brother had witnessed this feat performed by Indrajit, he dismissed it with a laugh, saying, "That's nothing!" Then Lakṣmaṇa, bull among men, his face betraying not the slightest sign of fear, took up fearsome arrows and, in battle, loosed them angrily at Indrajit Rāvaṇi, saying:

17. "This is not the way heroes engaged in battle strike their blows, night-roaming *rākṣasa*. These arrows of yours are inconsequential and have little force. Indeed, they feel quite pleasant.

18. "No, this is not the way heroes fight if they desire victory in battle." And, speaking in this fashion, he showered him with hails of arrows.

19. Smashed by his arrows, Indrajit's armor, all adorned with gold, shattered across the chariot floor, like a constellation falling from the sky.

20. His armor torn away, heroic Indrajit was wounded with iron arrows, so that he resembled a mountain bristling with trees.

21. Breathing hard, they fought incessantly and savagely in that battle, pierced with arrows in every limb and completely drenched with blood.

22. Deploying their divine weapon-spells again and again, those two, foremost among those expert in divine weapon-spells, filled the sky with arrows of every size and shape.

23. Both man and *rākṣasa*, shooting flawlessly, swiftly, marvelously, and accurately, continued their fearsome and tumultuous conflict.

24. Each terrifying crash of their bowstrings against their armguards was like that of two fearsome storm clouds thundering in the heavens.

25. The golden-fletched arrows struck their bodies only to emerge smeared with blood and plunge into the ground.

26. Meanwhile, some of their arrows were intercepted in the air by other well-honed weapons. They smashed and splintered one another by the thousand.

27. During the struggle, a ghastly carpet of arrows formed around them, so that it looked like a carpet of *kuśa* grass around two blazing fires at a sacrificial session.

28. Covered with wounds, the bodies of those two great warriors were as resplendent as a *śālmali* and a *kiṃśuka* tree in full bloom in the forest before their leaves appear.

29. Tumultuously and gruesomely the two of them—Indrajit and Lakṣmaṇa—clashed again and again, each eager to vanquish the other.

30. Although they continued to strike at each other—Lakṣmaṇa, Rāvaṇi and Rāvaṇi, Lakṣmaṇa—neither of them grew weary in that battle.

31. With the masses of arrows deeply rooted, yet protruding from their bodies, the two powerful and mighty heroes looked like twin mountains bristling with trees.

32. Drenched with blood and completely covered with arrows, all their limbs resembled blazing fires.

33. A long time elapsed while they were thus engaged in combat, but neither of them turned his face from combat or felt any weariness.

34. At that moment, immensely powerful Vibhīṣaṇa joined the fray and took his stand in order to aid and comfort Lakṣmaṇa, unconquered in the forefront of battle, and to give him respite from the fatigue of combat.

The end of the seventy-sixth *sarga* of the *Yuddhakāṇḍa* of the *Śrī Rāmāyaṇa*.

Sarga 77

1. Rāvaṇa's brother, the heroic Vibhīṣaṇa, then took up his position in the front line of battle, watching the two of them—man and *rākṣasa*—who were locked in combat.

2. He twanged his great bow as he took up his stance and then shot huge, keen-tipped arrows at the *rākṣasas*.

3. Those arrows, glowing like fire, fell thick and fast. They tore the *rākṣasas* to pieces, as thunderbolts might great mountains.

4. Vibhīṣaṇa's followers as well, those outstanding *rākṣasas*, cut down the heroic *rākṣasas* in combat with lances, swords, and spears.

5. Surrounded by those *rākṣasas*, Vibhīṣaṇa then resembled a great bull elephant in the midst of its excited calves.

6. Then, at the appropriate time, that foremost of *rākṣasas*, who well understood timing, said these words, urging on the tawny monkeys, who took pleasure in battling the *rākṣasas*:

7. "Indrajit alone is, as it were, the last hope of the *rākṣasa* lord, and this is the mere remnant of his forces. What are you waiting for, lords of the tawny monkeys?

8. "Once this evil *rākṣasa* is slain in the forefront of battle, then, with the exception of Rāvaṇa himself, the enemy forces will have been destroyed.

9–11. "In slaying so many mighty *rākṣasa* chiefs—the loyal hero Prahasta, immensely powerful Nikumbha, Kumbhakarṇa, Kumbha, the night-roaming *rākṣasa* Dhūmrākṣa, Akampana, Supārśva, the *rākṣasa* Cakramālin, Kampana, Devāntaka, Narāntaka, and other mighty foes—you have crossed the ocean with your bare hands. You need now only hop across a small puddle.

12. "He is the only one left here for you to conquer, monkeys. All the other *rākṣasas* who joined battle here, arrogant in their strength, have been slain.

13. "True, it is not right for someone like me, who is like a father to him, to kill one who is like my own son. Still, for Rāma's sake, I must put all pity aside and compass the death of my brother's son.

14. "But although I would like to kill him, tears cloud my vision. Therefore, it is great-armed Lakṣmaṇa who will have to finish him off. Now let the monkeys form up their ranks and slaughter his retainers, who have clustered around him."

15. Urged on in this fashion by the very illustrious *rākṣasa*, the monkey lords were roused to a frenzy and beat their tails against the ground.

16. Then, roaring again and again, those tigers among monkeys unleashed various screeches, as peacocks do when they see storm clouds.

17. Then Jāmbavān, surrounded by all his troops, assailed the *rākṣasas* with boulders, claws, and teeth.

18. But those immensely powerful *rākṣasas*, casting aside their fear and wielding all kinds of weapons, surrounded the lord of the apes even as he attacked them.

19. They belabored Jāmbavān in battle with arrows, keen battle-axes, spears, and iron cudgels even as he was slaughtering the *rākṣasa* army.

20. A tumultuous clash then ensued between the monkeys and the *rākṣasas*. It was as fearsome and deafening as the clash between the gods and *asuras* in their fury.

21. And Hanumān, too, in a rage, ripped up a *sāla* tree from the mountain and, advancing to the attack, slaughtered the *rākṣasas* by the thousand.

22. Then, after having engaged in a tumultuous struggle with his paternal uncle Vibhīṣaṇa in that battle, Indrajit charged once again at Lakṣmaṇa, slayer of enemy heroes.

23. Then those two heroes, Lakṣmaṇa and the *rākṣasa*, violently engaged in battle, struck at each other, raining torrents of arrows.

24. The two swift and immensely powerful archers were concealed from view, again and again, by swarms of arrows, just as are the sun and moon by storm clouds at summer's end.

25–26. Such was the dexterity of their hands as they fought that one could not perceive them taking up their arrows, nocking them, grasping their bows, releasing their arrows, drawing back the bow-strings, taking up their stances, tightly gripping their weapons, or striking their marks.

27. Since the sky was completely covered in every direction with swarms of arrows sent flying by the force of their bows, nothing could be seen. A great and utterly terrifying darkness engulfed everything.

28. The wind ceased to blow and fire to burn. The great seers muttered, "Heaven help us!" while the *gandharvas* and the celestial bards came and gathered at that place.

29. With four arrows Saumitri pierced the four black, gold-ornamented horses of that lion among *rākṣasas*.

30. Then, with yet another shaft, a crescent-headed arrow, the majestic Rāghava deftly severed the head from the body of the charioteer as he drove back and forth.

31. Now when the son of Rāvaṇa saw that his charioteer had been slain in combat, he lost his enthusiasm for battle and became dejected.

32. And when the troop leaders of the tawny monkeys saw the *rākṣasa* with his dejected face, they were supremely delighted, and they honored Lakṣmaṇa.

33. Then four lords of the tawny monkeys—Pramāthin, Śarabha, Rabhasa, and Gandhamādana—unable to hold themselves back, launched a violent assault.

34. Leaping swiftly upward, the four immensely powerful monkeys, terrifying in their valor, landed on Indrajit's splendid horses.

35. Blood gushed visibly from the mouths of the horses as those monkeys, huge as mountains, came crashing down upon them.

36. Having slain his horses, they smashed his great chariot. Then, swiftly leaping back, they stood once more at Lakṣmaṇa's side.

37. But Rāvaṇi, leaping down from his chariot—its horses slain, its charioteer slaughtered—assailed Saumitri with a hail of arrows.

*38. Then, with masses of arrows—and sharp and splendid arrows they were—Lakṣmaṇa, the equal of great Indra, forcefully warded him off, who was now on foot and was releasing sharp and splendid arrows in battle.

The end of the seventy-seventh *sarga* of the *Yuddhakāṇḍa* of the *Śrī Rāmāyaṇa*.

Sarga 78

1. His horses slain, the enormously powerful night-roaming *rākṣasa* Indrajit now stood on the ground. In his towering rage, he blazed with energy.

2. Wholly intent on killing each other with their arrows for the sake of victory, the two bowmen charged at each other like two bull elephants in the forest.

3. Meanwhile, the *rākṣasas* and the forest-dwelling monkeys raced back and forth in battle, slaughtering one another. Yet they never abandoned their respective masters.

4. Then, taking aim at Lakṣmaṇa and relying on his unsurpassed dexterity, Indrajit unleashed torrents of arrows, as does Indra, smasher of citadels, torrents of rain.

5. But Lakṣmaṇa calmly parried that all-but-unstoppable torrent of arrows unleashed by Indrajit.

6. Realizing that Lakṣmaṇa's armor was impenetrable, Indrajit, son of Rāvaṇa, in a towering rage, shot him in the forehead with three well-fletched arrows, thus demonstrating his extraordinary swiftness in releasing divinely charged weapons.

7. With those arrows planted in his forehead, there in the forefront of battle, the delight of the Raghus, who delighted in battle, looked as splendid as a mountain with three summits.

8. Although the *rākṣasa* had thus pierced him with arrows in the great battle, Lakṣmaṇa nonetheless swiftly pierced him in turn with five arrows.

9. And thus did the two heroes, Lakṣmaṇa and Indrajit, armed with their immensely powerful bows and fearsome in their valor, strike each other with sharp arrows.

10. Charging toward each other, the two bowmen, their hearts set on victory, pierced each other in every limb with fearsome arrows.

11. But Vibhīṣaṇa, still further enraged at Indrajit, whose horses had been slain, shot him through the chest with five arrows that struck with the force of thunderbolts.

12. Flying straight to their mark, those gold-fletched arrows pierced his body. Smeared with his blood, they resembled huge red serpents.

13. Then immensely powerful Indrajit, enraged at his uncle there in the midst of the *rākṣasas*, took up a splendid arrow that had been given to him by Yama.

14–15. But when immensely powerful Lakṣmaṇa, fearsome in his valor, saw him nock that great arrow, he took up another arrow. It had been granted to him in a dream by immeasurable Kubera himself. It was invincible and impossible to withstand even for the gods and *asuras*, Indra included.

16. Fixed to their splendid bows and drawn back by those heroes, the two magnificent arrows blazed brightly in their splendor.

17. Released from their bows, the two arrows lit up the heavens. They struck each other head on, colliding with tremendous force.

18. Colliding with each other in battle like two great planets, the arrows fell to the ground, shattered into a hundred pieces.

19. Seeing their arrows thwarted there in the forefront of battle, both Lakṣmaṇa and Indrajit were filled with shame and rage.

20. Then, in a towering rage, Saumitri took up the divinely charged weapon of Varuṇa, while the conqueror of great Indra, standing firm in battle, loosed the divinely charged weapon of Rudra.

21. Then a tumultuous and wondrous battle took place between the two of them. Hovering in the sky, the supernatural beings surrounded Lakṣmaṇa.

22. As that fearsome battle, with its terrifying roar, raged on between the monkeys and the *rākṣasas*, the sky was completely filled with numerous supernatural beings, all wonderstruck.

23. The seers, the ancestors, the gods, and the *gandharvas* along with the great birds and the great serpents, placing Indra of the hundred sacrifices at their head, watched over Lakṣmaṇa in battle.

24–26. And now, Rāghava's heroic younger brother nocked yet another arrow, the greatest of all. It struck with the burning force of fire, eater of oblations, and was capable of piercing Rāvaṇa's son. It was beautifully fletched and its shaft was tapered with smooth joints. Finely crafted and adorned with gold, it was a lethal arrow, impossible either to ward off or to withstand. The terror of the *rākṣasas*, it was like the venom of venomous serpents, and it was worshiped by the hosts of gods.

27. This was the very arrow with which, long ago, the immensely powerful and heroic lord Śakra of the tawny steeds had defeated the *dānavas* during the war of the gods and *asuras*.

28. Then Saumitri, foremost of men, placed upon his foremost of bows that foremost of arrows, the divinely charged weapon of Indra, which had never known defeat in battle.

29. Nocking that foe-destroying, divinely charged weapon, the unassailable Lakṣmaṇa drew his well-strung bow, stretching it to its limit, like Kāla himself at the destruction of the world.

30. Once he had placed the arrow on his splendid bow, fortunate Lakṣmaṇa, drawing it back, uttered these words in order to accomplish his purpose:

31. "If Rāma, the son of Daśaratha, be righteous, true to his word, and unrivaled in manly valor, then may you slay Rāvaṇi."

32. When he had spoken in this fashion, fortunate Lakṣmaṇa, heroic slayer of enemy heroes, drew that straight-flying arrow back to his ear. Then, charging it with the weapon-spell of Indra, he shot it at Indrajit in battle.

33. It severed Indrajit's majestic head—with its helmet and blazing earrings—from his body, before falling to the ground.

34. Lying on the ground, drenched with blood, severed from his shoulders, the huge head of the *rākṣasa*'s son looked like burnished gold.

35. Slain in this fashion, the son of Rāvaṇa collapsed instantly, sprawling on the ground, along with his armor, helmet, and bow.

36. Then, once Indrajit was slain, all the monkeys along with Vibhīṣaṇa raised a shout, rejoicing, as did the gods at the death of Vṛtra.

37. Then in the heavens there arose a mighty shout on the part of the great seers and all beings, including the *gandharvas* and *apsarases*.

38. Realizing that their champion had fallen, the vast *rākṣasa* host fled in all directions, being slaughtered by the tawny monkeys, who now had a victorious air.

39. Being slaughtered by the monkeys, all the *rākṣasas* dropped their weapons and ran, dazed, toward Laṅkā.

40. In their panic, all the *rākṣasas* fled by the hundreds in many directions, abandoning their weapons—spears, swords, and battle-axes.

41. Some, harried by the monkeys and terrified, entered Laṅkā. Some threw themselves into the sea, while others took refuge on the mountain.

42. Of the thousands of *rākṣasas* who had seen Indrajit slain and lying on the battlefield, not a single one was to be found.

43. Once Indrajit had fallen, the *rākṣasas* vanished in all directions, just as do the solar rays when the sun has set behind the western mountain.

44. Like the sun when its rays grow faint or fire, the purifier, when it dies out, that warrior of immense blazing energy lay there, stripped of life, his limbs sprawling.

45. Then, once the son of the *rākṣasa* lord had fallen, the world—its enemy destroyed, its oppression nearly at an end—was filled with joy.

46. And Lord Śakra himself, along with all the bulls among the gods, was delighted when that *rākṣasa* of evil deeds was slain.

47. The waters and the heavens became limpid and the *daityas* and *dānavas* assembled and rejoiced when that terror to all the worlds had fallen.

48. And all the gods, *gandharvas*, and *dānavas* together cried, "May the brahmans now move about free from anxiety, their impurities removed."

49. Then, seeing that warrior of unrivaled strength, a bull among *rākṣasas*, sons of chaos, slain in battle, the delighted leaders of the troops of tawny monkeys rejoiced.

50. And Vibhīṣaṇa, Hanumān, and Jāmbavān, the troop leader of the apes, praising Lakṣmaṇa, rejoiced as well in his victory.

51. Their goal obtained, the leaping monkeys pressed close around that scion of the Raghus and stood there, roaring, howling, and bellowing.

52. Beating their tails on the ground and clapping their upper arms, the monkeys raised a shout, "Lakṣmaṇa has triumphed!"

53. Their hearts delighted, the monkeys, great and small, embraced one another as they chattered about Rāghava's exploits.

54. When his dear friends had witnessed Lakṣmaṇa's all-but-impossible feat in battle, they were delighted. And the gods, seeing that Indra's foe had been slain, felt in their hearts the greatest delight.

The end of the seventy-eighth *sarga* of the *Yuddhakāṇḍa* of the *Śrī Rāmāyaṇa*.

Sarga 79

1. When Lakṣmaṇa of auspicious marks, his body drenched with blood, had slain in battle the conqueror of Śakra, he was delighted.

2–3. Then mighty and immensely powerful Lakṣmaṇa, taking Jāmbavān, Hanumān, and all the forest-dwelling monkeys with him, went straightaway, leaning on Vibhīṣaṇa and Hanumān, to where Sugrīva and Rāghava waited.

4. Approaching Rāma, Saumitri greeted him respectfully and stood there at his brother's side, as might Viṣṇu, Indra's younger brother, at the side of his brother, Śakra. That hero then reported to him the horrific slaughter of Indrajit.

5. Then Vibhīṣaṇa, in delight, told Rāma that great Lakṣmaṇa had cut off Rāvaṇi's head.

6. The bull among men, Rāma, took Lakṣmaṇa on his lap and embraced him tightly. He kissed him on the head and, swiftly

stroking him again and again, he spoke these words, comforting him:

7. "You, who can accomplish all-but-impossible deeds, have performed a supremely auspicious feat. Today, I have been freed from my enemy. Surely Rāvaṇa himself will now come forth with a vast array of troops, once he learns that his son has been struck down.

8. "And then, surrounded by my own vast army, I shall kill the lord of the *rākṣasas*, so difficult to defeat, as he marches forth, burning with grief at the slaying of his son.

9. "Lakṣmaṇa, now that you, my guardian, have slain the conqueror of Śakra, both Sītā and the earth itself have been placed within my grasp."

10. Having thus embraced and comforted his brother, Rāma Rāghava, delighted, spoke these words, addressing Suṣeṇa:

11. "Wise Saumitri, so loving of his friends, is still riddled with darts. You must act in such a way that he is restored to health. You must immediately rid Saumitri and Vibhīṣaṇa of these darts.

12. "And you must assiduously heal the others among the heroic ape and monkey troops—who fight with trees—who were wounded and pierced with darts as they fought."

13. Addressed in this fashion by Rāma, Suṣena, the great troop leader of the tawny monkeys, held a powerful medicinal herb to Lakṣmaṇa's nose.

14. The moment he smelled its fragrance, the darts fell away from him, his pain subsided, and his wounds healed over.

15. At Rāghava's command, Suṣeṇa treated his comrades, starting with Vibhīṣaṇa, as well as all the monkey leaders.

16. Saumitri was instantly restored to his normal state. The darts were removed, his fever had subsided, and he was free of pain and in good spirits.

17. Then, when they saw Saumitri rise up restored to health and in good spirits, Rāma, along with Sugrīva, the lord of the leaping monkeys, Vibhīṣaṇa, and Jāmbavān, lord of the apes, rejoiced together with their troops for a long time.

18. Great Dāśarathi praised Lakṣmaṇa's all-but-impossible feat, while the foremost of the troop leaders were delighted upon hearing that the conqueror of Śakra had fallen in battle.

The end of the seventy-ninth *sarga* of the *Yuddhakāṇḍa* of the *Śrī Rāmāyaṇa*.

Sarga 80

1. Upon hearing that Indrajit had been slain, the ministers of ten-necked Paulastya confirmed the news for themselves and then, in great distress, reported it to him.

2. "Great and glorious king! With Vibhīṣaṇa's help, Lakṣmaṇa has slain your son in battle right before our eyes.

3. "Encountering another heroic warrior, that heroic warrior who was unvanquished in battle, your heroic son, the conqueror of the lord of the all-wise gods, has been slain by Lakṣmaṇa."

4. When he heard about the grievous, terrible, and horrifying death of his son Indrajit in battle, he fell into a profound stupor.

5. Regaining his wits after a long time, the king, that bull among *rākṣasas*, was overwhelmed with grief for his son. Despondent, his senses reeling, he gave way to lamentation.

6. "Alas, my dear child! Leader of the *rākṣasa* host! Great chariot-warrior! How could you, who had conquered Indra, have succumbed this day to the power of Lakṣmaṇa?

7. "When roused to anger in battle, you could surely, with your arrows, have cut to pieces even Kāla or Yama, the ender of all things, or even the peaks of Mount Mandara. What then to speak of Lakṣmaṇa?

8. "Today King Vaivasvata has risen greatly in my estimation. For he has now brought you, great-armed warrior, under the power of time.

9. "This is the way of brave warriors, even among all the hosts of the immortal gods. A man who gives up his life for his lord attains heaven.

10. "This night all the hosts of the gods along with the guardians of the world and the seers, having seen Indrajit slain, will sleep soundly, freed from fear.

11. "Today, through the loss of Indrajit alone, all the three worlds and the forest-covered earth seem as if empty to me.

12. "Today, in the inner apartments, I shall hear the cries of the daughters of the *rākṣasas*, sons of chaos, like the shrill trumpeting of a herd of elephant cows in a mountain cavern.

13. "Where have you gone, scorcher of your foes, giving up your succession to the throne and abandoning Laṅkā and all of us—the *rākṣasas*, your mother, your wife, and me?

14. "Surely, it was for you, hero, to have performed the rites for the departed when I had gone to the realm of Yama. But now you have reversed this.

15. "Since Sugrīva, Rāghava, and Lakṣmaṇa yet live, where have you gone, abandoning us without first removing this source of all my torment?"

16. But even as Rāvaṇa, lord of the *rākṣasas*, was afflicted with lamentations such as these, an immense anger, born of the loss of his son, took hold of him.

17. His appearance, which was dreadful by nature, was now transfigured with the fire of his wrath, so that it was as unbearable as that of Rudra when he is filled with wrath.

18. And from the furious *rākṣasa*'s eyes fell teardrops, like flaming drops of oil from two blazing lamps.

19. And as he gnashed his teeth, a grinding sound was heard, as if from some vast engine being turned by the *dānavas*.

20. In whichever direction he cast his glance, the *rākṣasas*, petrified with terror, hid themselves. For in his rage, he was like the fire at the end of a cosmic age.

21. The *rākṣasas* did not dare come near him as he glared in all directions in his rage, like Yama, the ender of all things, intent upon devouring everything in the world.

22. Then, in a towering rage, Rāvaṇa, lord of the *rākṣasas*, spoke in their midst, anxious to steady them in battle:

23. "Over the course of thousands of years I practiced all-but-impossible austerities whereby, time after time, self-existent Brahmā was fully gratified.

24. "As a result of these austerities, through the grace of self-existent Brahmā, I have nothing to fear from either the *asuras* or the gods.

25. "And the armor, as resplendent as the sun, that Brahmā gave me was never pierced by *vajra* or javelin in any of my battles with the gods and *asuras*.

26. "Who then, even Indra, smasher of citadels himself, can approach me, when, this very day, equipped with that armor and mounted in my chariot, I take my stand in combat on the battlefield.

27–28. "Now, for the slaughter of Rāma and Lakṣmaṇa in the ultimate battle, bring forth to the blare of hundreds of trumpets the great and terrible bow and arrows that were given to me during my battles with the gods and *asuras* by self-existent Brahmā, who was pleased with me."

29. Tormented by the killing of his son and in the grip of his rage, heroic Rāvaṇa, reflecting in his mind, resolved to kill Sītā.

30. The fearsome *rākṣasa*, his eyes red, gazed in his dejection at all the fearsome-looking night-roaming *rākṣasas*, who were murmuring dejectedly, and said:

31. "A short time ago, in order to deceive the forest-dwelling monkeys, my beloved son, employing his power of illusion, showed them an apparition of a murdered woman, saying, 'Here is your Sītā!'

32. "Now I will make that a reality, just to please myself. I shall murder Vaidehī, so devoted to that false kshatriya!" When he had addressed his ministers in this fashion, he quickly took up his sword.

33–34. In his rage, Rāvaṇa hurriedly seized his magnificent sword, which shone like a cloudless sky, and drew it. Then, surrounded by his ministers, his mind reeling with grief for his son, he swiftly rushed forth from the assembly hall to where Maithilī was.

35. Seeing that *rākṣasa* rushing forth, the *rākṣasas* roared like lions. Perceiving that he was enraged, they huddled together and said:

36. "When the two brothers see Rāvaṇa today they will tremble. For in his wrath he conquered the four guardians of the world and laid low many another foe in battle."

37. As they were conversing together, Rāvaṇa, beside himself with rage, went storming toward Vaidehī, who was in the *aśoka* grove.

38. Although his friends, concerned for his welfare, tried to restrain him, he rushed on in his towering rage, like the angry planet racing toward Rohiṇī in the heavens.

39. Blameless Maithilī, who was guarded by the *rākṣasa* women, spied the furious *rākṣasa* brandishing his magnificent sword.

40. Seeing him armed with a sword and not turning back, though his friends tried many times to restrain him, Janaka's daughter was terrified.

41. "From the way he is racing toward me, suffused with rage, it is clear that this evil-minded wretch is going to kill me, as if I had no one to protect me, although, in fact, I do.

42. "For no matter how many times he pressed me, saying, 'Be my wife, enjoy yourself!' I rejected him, devoted as I am to my husband.

43. "It is clear that because I rejected him as a suitor, he has given up all hope of winning me. Overwhelmed with anger and mad passion, he is now on the point of murdering me.

44. "Or perhaps just now, on my account, the ignoble creature has slain in battle the brothers Rāma and Lakṣmaṇa, tigers among men. Ah! What an evil fate that I should be the cause of the princes' death.

45. "For, foolish wretch that I am, I did not heed the advice of Hanumān. If only I had returned, mounted on his back, then, seated blamelessly in my husband's lap, I should not now be grieving in this fashion.

46. "I think that when Kausalyā, who has but one son, hears that her son has been slain in battle, her heart will surely break.

47. "For, weeping, she will surely call fondly to mind that great man's birth, childhood, youth, righteous deeds, and beauty.

48. "Losing all hope upon the slaughter of her son, she will perform his funerary rites. Then, in her distraction, she will surely mount the funeral pyre or hurl herself into the water.

49. "Damn that hunchbacked slut Mantharā and her wicked scheming! It is on her account that Kausalyā must endure such suffering."

50–51. Now, when the wise *rākṣasa* Supārśva saw poor Maithilī lamenting in this fashion, like the constellation Rohiṇī occluded by a hostile planet and so cut off from the moon, her lord, he spoke these words to Rāvaṇa, lord of the *rākṣasas*, whose ministers were attempting to restrain him:

52. "How can you, ten-necked Rāvaṇa, the younger brother of Kubera Vaiśravaṇa himself, even think of killing Vaidehī, abandoning righteousness in your anger?

53. "You have completed your discipleship in vedic knowledge, and you are ever devoted to the proper duties of your rank. How then, heroic lord of the *rākṣasas*, can you possibly think of killing a woman?

54. "You should spare Maithilī, your majesty, endowed as she is with such beauty, and instead, together with us, unleash your wrath upon Rāghava himself.

55. "So you must make your preparations this very day, the fourteenth of the dark fortnight. Then, surrounded by your troops, you shall march forth to victory tomorrow on the new-moon day.

56. "A wise and heroic warrior, armed with a sword and equipped with a chariot, you, sir, mounted in your splendid chariot, will slay Rāma Dāśarathi and win Maithilī."

57. Mighty and evil-minded Rāvaṇa paid heed to that advice that was offered by his friend, in keeping as it was with righteousness. Then, returning to his residence, he went once more to his assembly hall surrounded by his friends.

The end of the eightieth *sarga* of the *Yuddhakāṇḍa* of the *Śrī Rāmāyaṇa*.

Sarga 81

1. Upon entering his assembly hall, the king sat down on his splendid throne, despondent and deeply pained, snarling like an angry lion.

2. Tormented by the loss of his son, immensely powerful Rāvaṇa then addressed the leaders of his army, who stood with their hands cupped in reverence:

3. "All of you gentlemen are to march forth surrounded by the entire cavalry and elephant corps and accompanied by the chariot divisions and infantry.

4. "Exerting yourselves, you must isolate Rāma, surround him, and then slay him in battle with a hail of arrows, like storm clouds in the rainy seasons.

5. "Otherwise tomorrow, in a great battle, as the whole world watches, I shall kill Rāma, whose limbs you gentlemen will have pierced with your sharp arrows."

6. When the *rākṣasas* had received these instructions from the lord of the *rākṣasas*, they set forth swiftly, surrounded by chariots and columns of elephants.

7. And so at sunrise a fearsome and tumultuous battle broke out between the *rākṣasas* and the monkeys.

8. Then the monkeys and the *rākṣasas* assaulted one another with various types of clubs, darts, swords, and battle-axes.

9. Rivers of blood began to flow, carrying logjams of corpses. They had elephants and chariots for their banks, war-horses for their fish, and flagstaffs for their trees.

10. Springing up again and again in battle, those splendid monkeys smashed flagstaffs, armor, chariots, horses, and all kinds of weapons.

11. With their sharp fangs and their claws, the leaping monkeys rent the hair, ears, foreheads, and noses of the *rākṣasas*.

12. A hundred of those bulls among monkeys swarmed about each *rākṣasa* in battle, as birds might a tree laden with fruit.

13. Similarly, the *rākṣasas*, huge as mountains, belabored the fearsome monkeys with darts, swords, battle-axes, and heavy maces.

14. Then the vast host of monkeys, being slaughtered by the *rākṣasas*, sought refuge with Daśaratha's son Rāma, the refuge of all.

15. Then mighty Rāma of enormous blazing energy took up his bow and, plunging into the *rākṣasa* host, unleashed a hail of arrows.

16. Once Rāma had plunged in, fearsome and blazing with the fire of his arrows, the *rākṣasas* could no more approach him than can clouds approach the sun in the heavens.

17. The night-roaming *rākṣasas* could witness the very fearsome and all-but-impossible feats of Rāma in battle only after he had accomplished them.

18. Although he was shaking their vast host and crushing their great chariot-warriors, they could no more see Rāma than can one a gale tearing through a forest.

19. Although they saw that through the skill of Rāma their forces had been cut to pieces, shattered, scorched with arrows, broken, and afflicted by weapons, they could not catch sight of him, so swiftly did he move.

20. Although Rāghava was striking their very bodies, they could no more see him than can creatures see the inner spirit that resides among the objects of sense.

21–22. "He is slaughtering the elephant corps!" "He is slaughtering the great chariot-warriors!" "With his sharp arrows he is slaughtering the infantry along with the cavalry!" So thinking, because of their seeming similarity to Rāma, all the *rākṣasas* began in their fury to slaughter one another in battle, slaying those *rākṣasas* who resembled Rāghava.

23. And since great Rāma had befuddled them with the mighty, divine weapon-spell of the *gandharvas*, they could not see him, even though he was burning up the army of his foes.

24. Sometimes the *rākṣasas* saw a thousand Rāmas in battle, while at other times they saw but a single Kākutstha in that great conflict.

25. Sometimes they would see only the golden tip of the great warrior's bow, whirling about like a circle of blazing fire, but not Rāghava himself.

26–27. As he massacred the *rākṣasas* in battle, Rāma appeared to them like a spinning wheel, as does the wheel of time to all creatures. It had his body for its hub, his power for its flames, his arrows for its spokes, his bow for its rim, the sound of his bowstring striking his armguard for its rumbling, his qualities of blazing energy and mental brilliance for its radiance, and the power of his divine weapon-spell for its sharp edge.

28–30. Thus, in the eighth part of a day, did Rāma with his arrows like flames of fire single-handedly annihilate the forces of the *rākṣasas*, who could take on any form at will: a host of ten thousand chariots as swift as the wind, eighteen thousand mighty war-elephants, fourteen thousand battle-steeds along with their riders, and a full two hundred thousand *rākṣasa* foot soldiers.

31. Their horses slaughtered, their chariots smashed, and their battle standards shattered, the remnants of the night-roaming *rākṣasas* fled back to the citadel of Laṅkā, exhausted.

32. With its slaughtered elephants, foot soldiers, and horses, the battlefield resembled the playground of wrathful Rudra, wielder of the Pināka.

33. The gods, along with the *gandharvas*, perfected beings, and supreme seers, praised that feat of Rāma, crying, "Well done! Well done!"

34. Then Rāma addressed Sugrīva, who stood nearby, saying, "The power of this divine weapon-spell belongs only to me and three-eyed Śiva."

35. When he had slaughtered the *rākṣasa* host, great Rāma, who had conquered all fatigue and who was the equal of Śakra in the use of weapons and divine weapon-spells, was praised by the delighted hosts of the gods.

The end of the eighty-first *sarga* of the *Yuddhakāṇḍa* of the *Śrī Rāmāyaṇa*.

Sarga 82

1–3. Thousands of war-elephants and battle-steeds with their riders, thousands of chariots, blazing like fire and flying their battle flags, thousands of valiant *rākṣasas*, who could take on any form at will, were armed with maces and iron clubs, and were resplendent with their golden battle standards—all of these sent forth by Rāvaṇa, Rāma, tireless in action, had now slaughtered with his sharp arrows adorned with burnished gold.

4. When the remnants of the night-roaming *rākṣasa* troops had seen what had happened and the *rākṣasa* women had heard about it, they huddled together in panic, despondent and overwhelmed with gloomy thought.

5. The *rākṣasa* women—widows, those who had lost their sons, and those who had lost their kinsmen—were grief stricken. Wailing, they huddled together and lamented thus:

6. "How could that potbellied, snaggletoothed hag Śūrpaṇakhā have possibly made advances in the forest to Rāma, who is as handsome as Kandarpa, the god of love?

7–8. "Rāma is delicate, yet immensely powerful. He is devoted to the welfare of all beings. He is mighty, fair of face, and replete with every virtue. This *rākṣasa* woman, on the other hand, with her ugly face, is hideous and lacking in every virtue. Really, someone ought to kill her. How, after seeing him, could that lustful creature have possibly hoped to win him?

9–10. "It is just the bad luck of our race that this white-haired crone, so ill-suited to Rāghava, should have made advances to him. For this was an impermissible and ludicrous act, condemned by everyone, and it has led to the destruction of Dūṣaṇa, Khara, and the *rākṣasas* in general.

11. "It was on her account that Rāvaṇa incurred this tremendous enmity. And so the ten-necked *rākṣasa* abducted Sītā to his own destruction.

12. "Yet although he has not won over Sītā, Janaka's daughter, Rāvaṇa has forged an undying enmity with mighty Rāghava.

13. "When he heard that the *rākṣasa* Virādha, who was assaulting Vaidehī, had been killed by Rāma single-handedly, that should have been a sufficient warning.

14. "Then, too, in Janasthāna, Rāma slaughtered fourteen thousand *rākṣasas* of fearsome deeds with his arrows, which were like flames of fire.

15. "And he slew Khara, Dūṣaṇa, and Triśiras in battle with arrows that blazed like the sun. That, too, should have been a sufficient warning.

16. "Next he slew the blood-guzzling Kabandha, whose arms were a league in length and who bellowed in a transport of rage. That, too, should have been a sufficient warning.

17. "Rāma also slew thousand-eyed Indra's mighty son Vālin, who resembled a storm cloud. That, too, should have been a sufficient warning.

18. "Sugrīva, his dreams shattered, had been dwelling despondently on Mount Ṛśyamūka. Rāma established him in royal sovereignty. That, too, should have been a sufficient warning.

19. "In his delusion, Rāvaṇa paid no heed to the fitting words spoken by Vibhīṣaṇa, though they were fully in accord with righteousness and polity and were beneficial for all the *rākṣasas*.

20. "If only Rāvaṇa, the younger brother of Kubera, bestower of wealth, had acted upon Vibhīṣaṇa's advice, this city of Laṅkā would not have become a cremation ground, overwhelmed by sorrow.

21. "Even when he heard that immensely powerful Kumbhakarṇa had been slain by Rāghava and that his own beloved son Indrajit had been slain as well, Rāvaṇa still did not understand.

22. " 'My son has been slain in battle! My brother has been slain! My husband has been slain!' Such are the cries that are heard in household after household of the *rākṣasas*.

23. "For in battle valiant Rāma has destroyed chariots, horses, elephants, and *rākṣasa* foot soldiers by the hundreds of thousands.

24. "It must be Rudra, Viṣṇu, great Indra of the hundred sacrifices, or even Yama himself, the ender of all things, who, in the guise of Rāma, is slaughtering us.

25. "With our heroes slain by Rāma, we have lost all hope of life. Foreseeing no end to this terror and bereft of our protectors, we lament.

26. "Having been granted his boon, the valiant ten-necked Rāvaṇa does not realize the terrible danger he faces at Rāma's hands in battle.

27. "For not even the gods, the *gandharvas*, the *piśācas*, or the *rākṣasas* can save one who is assailed by Rāma in battle.

28. "Moreover, portents regularly appear to Rāvaṇa in battle after battle, foretelling his death at Rāma's hands.

29. "For Grandfather Brahmā, being gratified, granted Rāvaṇa invulnerability to the gods, *dānavas*, and *rākṣasas*. But Rāvaṇa never requested invulnerability to men.

30. "I believe that this is undoubtedly that very same dangerous vulnerability to men that has now presented itself. It is sure to prove fatal to both Rāvaṇa and the *rākṣasas*.

31. "Oppressed by the mighty *rākṣasa* through the gift of his boon, the wise gods worshiped Grandfather Brahmā with fierce austerities.

32. "Gratified, the Grandfather, great Brahmā, spoke these grave words to all the divinities for their benefit:

33. " 'From this day hence, all the *dānavas* and *rākṣasas* will eternally wander the three worlds constantly beset by danger.'

34. "Then all the gods, led by Indra, came together and propitiated the great god, bull-bannered Śiva, destroyer of Tripura.

35. "Gratified, the great god Śiva spoke these words to the gods: 'For your sake, a woman shall be born who will bring about the destruction of the *rākṣasas*.'

36. "Employed by the gods, this destroyer of the *rākṣasas*, Sītā, will devour us along with Rāvaṇa, just as, long ago, famine was used to devour the *dānavas*.

37. "This dreadful lamentation suffused with sorrow is the direct result of the misconduct of this evil-minded criminal Rāvaṇa.

38. "Afflicted as we are by Rāghava, we can see no one in the world who can afford us refuge, any more than one could afford refuge to creatures afflicted by Kāla himself at the end of a cosmic age."

39. Thus did all the women of the night-roaming *rākṣasas* loudly and grievously lament. Afflicted and tormented by a terrible fear, they grew despondent, holding one another in their arms.

The end of the eighty-second *sarga* of the *Yuddhakāṇḍa* of the *Śrī Rāmāyaṇa*.

Sarga 83

1. Rāvaṇa heard that piteous sound, the lamentation of the grief-stricken *rākṣasa* women, in household after household throughout Laṅkā.

2. Heaving a deep sigh, he remained for a moment lost in thought. Then, seized with a towering rage, Rāvaṇa became fearsome to look upon.

3. Gnawing at his lip, his eyes red with rage, flaring up like the fire at the end of a cosmic age, he was unbearable to look upon, even for the *rākṣasas*.

4. The lord of the *rākṣasas* then addressed the *rākṣasas* who stood near him, their speech slurred with fear, as if to scorch them with his gaze:

5. "Quickly! On my authority, tell Mahodara, Mahāpārśva, and the *rākṣasa* Virūpākṣa, 'Send forth the troops!' "

6. Hearing the king's words and acting on his orders, the *rākṣasas*, although stricken with fear, exhorted the *rākṣasa* warriors, who retained their composure.

7. Then all those *rākṣasas* of fearsome aspect said, "So be it!" After performing benedictory rites, they all presented themselves before Rāvaṇa.

8. Honoring Rāvaṇa in the prescribed fashion, all of those great chariot-warriors stood with their hands cupped in reverence, eager for the victory of their lord.

9. Then, laughing but beside himself with rage, Rāvaṇa addressed Mahodara, Mahāpārśva, and the *rākṣasa* Virūpākṣa.

10. "This very day, with arrows loosed from my bow and blazing like the sun at the end of a cosmic age, I shall lead Rāghava and Lakṣmaṇa to the abode of Yama.

11. "This very day, through the slaughter of my enemies, I shall avenge Khara, Kumbhakarṇa, Prahasta, and Indrajit.

12. "Obscured by the clouds of my arrows, the atmosphere, directions, rivers, and even the ocean itself shall disappear from view.

13. "This very day, with waves in the form of arrows springing from the ocean that is my bow, I shall annihilate the masses of monkey troops, one division after another.

14. "This very day, like a bull elephant, I shall wreak havoc upon the lotus ponds that are the monkey troops, their faces like full-blown lotuses, their color that of lotus filaments.

15. "This very day in battle the leaders of the monkey troops, their faces riddled with arrows, shall adorn the earth, like lotuses with their protruding stalks.

16. "With each of the arrows I let fly this day in battle, I shall pierce hundreds and hundreds of the tawny monkeys, so ferocious in combat and armed with trees.

17. "Through the slaughter of the enemy, I shall, this very day, wipe away the tears of these women whose husbands, brothers, and sons have been slain.

18. "This very day, with the monkeys strewn about pierced by my arrows and robbed of life, I shall make it so that one will have to strain to see the surface of the earth.

19. "I shall, this very day, let all the jackals, vultures, and other carnivorous beasts gorge on the flesh of my enemies rent by my arrows.

20. "Quickly! Get my chariot ready. Bring my bow at once! Let those night-roaming *rākṣasas* who remain follow me into battle."

21. When Mahāpārśva heard those words of his, he addressed these words to the commanders of the army, who stood nearby, "Assemble the troops at once!"

22. And the commanders of the army then, in great agitation, raced about Laṅkā with rapid strides, rousting the *rākṣasas* from house after house.

23–25. In a short time, fearsome-faced *rākṣasas* of fearsome valor issued forth, roaring. They had mighty arms and bore all manner of weapons: swords, spears, lances, maces, cudgels, ploughshares, sharp-edged javelins, huge mallets and war hammers, clubs, shining discuses, sharp battle-axes, short javelins, hundred-slayers, and other splendid weapons.

26. Then, acting on Rāvaṇa's orders, four commanders of the army swiftly brought up a chariot yoked with eight horses and driven by a charioteer.

27. Rāvaṇa then mounted that celestial chariot, which blazed with its own splendor. In the excess of his power, it seemed as if he would tear up the earth itself.

28. With Rāvaṇa's consent, Mahāpārśva, Mahodara, and the unassailable Virūpākṣa then mounted their chariots.

29. Bellowing in their excitement, as if to rend the earth itself, they marched forth, eager for victory, releasing fearsome roars.

30. And thus, endowed with blazing energy and surrounded by the hosts of *rākṣasa* troops, Rāvaṇa marched forth. Holding his bow aloft, he resembled Yama, who brings time itself to an end.

31. Then, in his chariot drawn by swift horses, that great chariot-warrior issued forth through the gate to where Rāma and Lakṣmaṇa stood.

32. Suddenly the sun grew dim and the directions were shrouded in darkness. Fierce birds screeched and the earth shook.

33. It rained blood and the horses stumbled. A vulture alighted on the tip of his flagstaff and jackals howled inauspiciously.

34. His left eye throbbed and his left arm trembled. His face grew pale; his voice grew faint.

35. And so, as the *rākṣasa* ten-necked Rāvaṇa raced forth to war, these manifestations appeared, presaging his death in battle.

36. A blazing meteor fell from the sky with a sound like that of a thunderclap. Vultures screeched inauspiciously, their cries echoed by the crows.

37. But, heedless of these terrible portents that appeared before him, Rāvaṇa, in his delusion, marched forth, impelled by his own impending doom, to seek his own destruction.

38. Hearing the rumbling of the great *rākṣasas*' chariots, the monkey army hurled itself into battle.

39. A hugely tumultuous battle then broke out between the monkeys and the *rākṣasas* as they challenged one another in their fury, eager for victory.

40. Then, with arrows adorned with gold, ten-necked Rāvaṇa, in his rage, wrought a tremendous slaughter among the monkey hosts.

41. Some of the wrinkle-faced monkeys were beheaded by Rāvaṇa, while others were struck dead, their breathing stopped forever. Still others had their flanks ripped open. Some had their heads shattered, while others had their eyes torn out.

42. Wherever ten-faced Rāvaṇa moved through the battle in his chariot, his eyes wide with fury, the troop leaders of the tawny monkeys could not withstand the crushing force of his arrows.

The end of the eighty-third *sarga* of the *Yuddhakāṇḍa* of the *Śrī Rāmāyaṇa*.

Sarga 84

1. Thus did Rāvaṇa litter the ground, covering it with tawny monkeys, their limbs severed by his arrows.

2. The leaping monkeys could no more withstand Rāvaṇa's single-handed and irresistible barrage of arrows than can moths a blazing fire.

3. Tormented by those sharp arrows, they ran shrieking in all directions, as might elephants burned by the flames of a forest fire that surrounds them.

4. Rāvaṇa careened through the battle, scattering with his arrows the hosts of leaping monkeys, as would a mighty wind great banks of clouds.

5. Having swiftly wrought his slaughter of the forest-dwelling monkeys, the *rākṣasa* lord then immediately approached Rāghava in battle.

6. When Sugrīva saw his monkeys broken in battle and fleeing in all directions, he placed Suṣeṇa in charge of the encampment and resolved to enter the fight at once.

7. Having placed that heroic monkey, his equal, in charge, Sugrīva turned his face toward the enemy and set forth armed with a tree.

8. All the troop leaders, whether at his side or in his train, voluntarily followed him, wielding huge boulders and various gigantic trees.

9. Roaring with a mighty voice in battle, great Sugrīva began to slaughter the principal *rākṣasas*, felling various others as well.

10. The gigantic lord of the monkeys knocked down the *rākṣasas*, as the mighty gale at the end of a cosmic age does full-grown trees.

11. He showered hails of stones upon the *rākṣasa* hosts, just as a storm cloud might a shower of hailstones on flocks of birds in the forest.

12. Their heads shattered by the hails of boulders released by the king of the monkeys, the *rākṣasas* crumpled like mountains cut to pieces.

13–14. As the *rākṣasas* were being annihilated on every side by Sugrīva, routed, falling, and crying out, the unassailable *rākṣasa* Virūpākṣa, calling out his own name, took up his bow and, leaping from his chariot, mounted the back of a war-elephant.

15. Once the great chariot-warrior Virūpākṣa had mounted the elephant, he charged at the monkeys, unleashing a terrifying roar.

16. He loosed fearsome arrows at Sugrīva in the vanguard of the army and, rallying the frightened *rākṣasas*, he made them hold their lines.

17. Completely riddled with sharp arrows by that *rākṣasa*, the irascible lord of the monkeys flew into a rage and resolved to kill him.

18. Then, uprooting a tree, the heroic tawny monkey leapt forward and, in battle, struck Virūpākṣa's great war-elephant in the face.

19. Stricken with that blow by Sugrīva, the great elephant staggered back a bow length and collapsed, bellowing.

20–21. Jumping clear of the wounded elephant, the mighty *rākṣasa* turned to face the monkey, who stood his ground. Seizing his sword and oxhide shield, he advanced upon Sugrīva with swift strides, reviling him.

22. In his rage at Virūpākṣa, Sugrīva seized a boulder as huge as a storm cloud and hurled it at him.

23. Seeing that boulder hurtling toward him, the immensely valiant bull among *rākṣasas* dodged it and then struck Sugrīva with his sword.

24. In a towering rage, he cut away Sugrīva's armor with his sword there in the forefront of battle. Struck with that sword, the monkey fell.

25. But the fallen monkey sprang up and unleashed a blow with the palm of his hand, which, with its terrifying sound, was like a thunderbolt.

26. The *rākṣasa*, however, skillfully dodged the blow that Sugrīva had dealt and in return struck him on the chest with his fist.

27. Now, when Sugrīva, lord of the monkeys, saw that the *rākṣasa* had dodged his blow, he grew even more enraged.

28. Then, spying an opening, the monkey, in his rage, brought his huge palm down upon Virūpākṣa's temple.

29. Struck by that palm, which was like the thunderbolt of great Indra, he fell to the ground, drenched in gore and vomiting blood.

30. Drenched with foaming blood, his eyes rolling with rage, Virūpākṣa appeared to the monkeys to have his eyes still more disfigured than before.

31. The monkeys watched their enemy as, drenched in blood, he rolled in convulsions from side to side, moaning piteously.

32. Then those vast and powerful armies—that of the monkeys and that of the *rākṣasas*—who were engaged in battle, roared fearsomely, like two great oceans that have crashed beyond their shorelines.

33. When the combined host of the monkeys and the *rākṣasas* saw the immensely powerful *rākṣasa* Virūpākṣa, his eyes disfigured, slain by the king of the tawny monkeys, it became as agitated as the Ganges in raging flood.

The end of the eighty-fourth *sarga* of the *Yuddhakāṇḍa* of the *Śrī Rāmāyaṇa*.

Sarga 85

1. As the two armies were being rapidly slaughtered by each other in that tremendous battle, they both were vastly diminished, like two lakes in the scorching heat of summer.

2. At the slaughter of his troops and the slaying of Virūpākṣa, Rāvaṇa, lord of the *rākṣasas*, grew doubly furious.

3. Seeing his army decimated by the wrinkle-faced monkeys and thus diminished, he realized that the fortunes of war had turned against him and he grew agitated.

4. He said to Mahodara, tamer of his foes, who stood beside him, "At this point, great-armed warrior, you are my only hope of victory.

5. "Annihilate the army of our enemies, hero! Demonstrate this day your valor! Now is the time to repay your obligation to your master. Fight bravely!"

6. Addressed in this fashion, Mahodara replied, "So be it," to the *rākṣasa* lord and then plunged into the enemy army, like a moth into a fire.

7. Then, urged on by his master's words and his own valor, that immensely powerful *rākṣasa*, filled with blazing energy, sowed destruction among the monkeys.

8. Then Sugrīva, seeing the vast monkey army routed, ran toward Mahodara, who happened to be nearby.

9. Seizing a huge and fearsome boulder as big as a mountain, the immensely powerful lord of the tawny monkeys hurled it in order to kill Mahodara.

10. When Mahodara saw that unstoppable boulder hurtling violently toward him, he was not in the least agitated, and he cut it to pieces with his arrows.

11. Shattered into a thousand fragments by the *rākṣasa* with his torrents of arrows, the boulder fell to earth, like a frenzied flock of vultures descending.

12. When Sugrīva saw that his boulder had been shattered, he was beside himself with rage. Uprooting a *sāla* tree, he hurled it at the *rākṣasa* in the forefront of battle. But that heroic conqueror of enemy citadels cut it to pieces with his arrows.

13. In his rage, Sugrīva then spied an iron club that had fallen to the ground. He brandished that blazing iron club and made a display of it before his foe. Then, with its tip, he violently struck down Mahodara's splendid horses.

14. Jumping down from his huge chariot, now that its horses had been slain, the heroic *rākṣasa* Mahodara, in his rage, seized a mace.

15. Like two bellowing bulls, the two heroes closed with each other in combat. With one holding a mace and the other an iron club, they resembled two storm clouds streaked with lightning.

16. The lord of the tawny monkeys struck the *rākṣasa*'s mace with his iron club; but, shattered by that mace, his iron club fell to the ground.

17. Then Sugrīva, filled with blazing energy, snatched up from the ground a fearsome iron cudgel, fully ornamented with gold.

18. Raising it aloft, he threw it, just as Mahodara hurled a second mace. The two collided and fell, shattered, to the earth.

19. Their weapons shattered, the two warriors closed in combat with their fists. Filled with strength and blazing energy, they resembled two blazing fires, eaters of oblations.

20. They struck at each other and roared again and again. Slapping each other with their open hands, they both fell to the ground.

21. Jumping swiftly to their feet, they struck each other once again. The two heroes flailed at each other with their arms, yet neither could get the better of the other.

22. Then the immensely swift *rākṣasa* Mahodara seized a sword and a shield that were lying nearby.

23. But, swifter still, Sugrīva, foremost of monkeys, also seized a huge sword and shield that had fallen.

24. Their very bodies suffused with rage, the two warriors, skilled in the use of weapons, hurled themselves at each other on the battlefield, swords raised, roaring in the fury of battle.

25. Raging at each other and intent on victory, the two quickly circled each other to the right and to the left.

26. Then the immensely swift hero, evil-minded Mahodara, praiseworthy for his valor, brought his sword down upon Sugrīva's great shield.

27. The sword lodged in the shield; and, as Mahodara struggled to free it, that elephant among monkeys, with his sword, cut off the *rākṣasa*'s head, along with its helmet and earrings.

28. When they saw that, the army of the *rākṣasa* lord—who had fallen to the ground with his head cut off—fled.

29. Having slain Mahodara, the tawny monkey was overjoyed, and he and his monkeys roared in unison. Ten-necked Rāvaṇa was enraged, while Rāghava appeared delighted.

The end of the eighty-fifth *sarga* of the *Yuddhakāṇḍa* of the *Śrī Rāmāyaṇa*.

Sarga 86

1. Once Mahodara had been struck down, the immensely powerful Mahāpārśva wrought havoc with his arrows upon Aṅgada's fearsome army.

2. On every side, he struck off the heads from the bodies of the principal monkeys, just as the wind might fruit from its stalk.

3. In a towering rage, the *rākṣasa*, with his arrows, cut off the arms and shoulders of some of the monkeys and tore open the sides of others.

4. Afflicted by Mahāpārśva with his hail of arrows, the monkeys, their faces cast down in despair, were stunned.

5. Now, when great-armed Aṅgada saw that his army was cowed and afflicted by the *rākṣasa*, he surged powerfully forward, like the ocean on the new- or full-moon day.

6. Seizing an iron club, whose radiance was like that of the sun's rays, the foremost of monkeys brought it down in combat upon Mahāpārśva.

7. Stunned by that blow, Mahāpārśva fell senseless from his chariot to the ground along with his charioteer.

8. At this point, the extraordinarily powerful Gavākṣa, filled with blazing energy and resembling a mass of black collyrium, accompanied by Jāmbavān, the king of the apes, burst forth from his own troop, which resembled a great storm cloud.

9. In his rage, he seized a huge boulder that resembled a mountain peak, swiftly killed Mahāpārśva's horses, and smashed his chariot.

10. But regaining consciousness after a short while, immensely powerful Mahāpārśva once again riddled Aṅgada with numerous arrows.

11. He struck Jāmbavān, king of the apes, in the center of his chest with three arrows and hit Gavākṣa with many more.

12. Now, when Aṅgada saw Gavākṣa and Jāmbavān tormented by arrows, he was beside himself with rage, and he seized a fearsome iron club.

13–14. Enraged at that *rākṣasa*, who stood at a distance, Vālin's powerful son, Aṅgada, grasped with both hands that iron club, whose radiance was like that of the sun's rays, and, whirling it about, he hurled it at Mahāpārśva in an effort to kill him.

15. Hurled by the powerful monkey, the iron club struck the bow and arrows from the *rākṣasa*'s hand and knocked off his helmet.

16. Rushing violently upon him in his rage, the valorous son of Vālin struck him with his palm just below the ear, where his earring hung.

17. But the immensely powerful Mahāpārśva of blazing splendor was enraged in turn and seized an immense battle-axe with one hand.

18. In a towering rage, the *rākṣasa* brought down that weapon—honed with oil, spotless, solid, and made of the essence of the mountains—upon Vālin's son.

19. He swung the battle-axe powerfully at Aṅgada's left shoulder blade, but, in his fury, Aṅgada dodged it.

20. In a towering rage, heroic Aṅgada, equal in valor to his own father, clenched his adamantine fist.

21. Knowing all the body's vital points, he brought that fist, whose impact was equal to that of Indra's thunderbolt, down upon the *rākṣasa*'s chest, just over his heart.

22. By virtue of that blow delivered in that great battle, the *rākṣasa*'s heart burst, and he fell at once to the ground, dead.

23. When he had fallen to the ground, his army was deeply shaken there in that battle, but Rāvaṇa flew into a tremendous rage.

The end of the eighty-sixth *sarga* of the *Yuddhakāṇḍa* of the *Śrī Rāmāyaṇa*.

Sarga 87

1–2. When Rāvaṇa saw that the *rākṣasas* Mahodara and Mahāpārśva had been slain and that the immensely powerful hero Virūpākṣa had been slain before them, a tremendous rage seized hold of him there in that great battle. He urged on his charioteer, saying these words:

3. "In killing those two, Rāma and Lakṣmaṇa, I shall allay my grief for my slaughtered ministers and my besieged city.

4. "I shall destroy in battle the tree that is Rāma, which dispenses fruit and has Sītā for its blossom, and whose branches are Sugrīva, Jāmbavān, Kumuda, and Nala."

5. Causing the ten directions to resound with the rumbling of his chariot, that great and splendid chariot-warrior raced swiftly onward and charged directly at Rāghava.

6. Filled with that sound, the entire earth, along with its rivers, mountains, and forests, its boar, deer, and elephants, shook.

7. Rāvaṇa then produced the extremely horrifying and fearsome divine weapon-spell, the Tāmasa, bringer of darkness, and, with it, he scorched all the monkeys. They fled on every side.

8. When Rāghava saw that those numerous hosts had been routed in their hundreds by Rāvaṇa's splendid arrows, he took up his battle stance.

9–10. Rāvaṇa then spied the unconquerable Rāma, who stood there with his brother Lakṣmaṇa like Vāsava with Viṣṇu. Holding aloft his great bow, the long-armed, lotus-eyed tamer of his foes seemed as if to scrape the very sky.

11. Meanwhile, Rāghava, for his part, seeing the monkeys routed in battle and Rāvaṇa rushing toward him, was delighted. He grasped his bow in the middle.

12. Then he began to twang that magnificent bow powerfully and loudly, as if to shatter the earth itself.

13. As Rāvaṇa came within the range of the princes' arrows, he looked like Rāhu, the demon of the eclipse, as he bears down upon the sun and the hare-marked moon.

14. The streams of Rāvaṇa's arrows and the sound of Rāma twanging his bow knocked the *rākṣasas* down by the hundred.

15. Eager to be the first to fight Rāvaṇa with his own sharp arrows, Lakṣmaṇa drew his bow and released arrows that were like flames of fire.

16. But no sooner had those arrows been released by the bowman Lakṣmaṇa than the immensely powerful Rāvaṇa intercepted them in the air with his own arrows.

17. He cut down one of Lakṣmaṇa's arrows with one of his own, three with three, and ten with ten, thus displaying his deftness of hand.

18. Then, leaving Saumitri aside, Rāvaṇa, victorious in battle, advanced upon Rāma, who stood there as immovable as a mountain.

19. And as he advanced upon Rāma Rāghava in battle, Rāvaṇa, his eyes red with rage, unleashed hails of arrows upon him.

20. But Rāma, seeing those torrents of arrows hurtling swiftly toward him as they were loosed from Rāvaṇa's bow, quickly took up his crescent-headed arrows.

21. Then, with his sharp, crescent-headed arrows, Rāghava cut down those torrents of immensely powerful arrows, which blazed like angry, venomous serpents.

22. In this way, they swiftly showered each other—Rāghava, Rāvaṇa and Rāvaṇa, Rāghava—with all manner of sharp arrows.

23. Never yet defeated in battle, the two of them circled each other for a long time to the left and to the right in an astonishing way, each of them keeping his eyes on the trajectory of the other's arrows.

24. All creatures were terrified as those two fierce warriors, like Yama and Death himself, ender of all things, fought each other, unleashing their arrows.

25. At that time the sky was completely covered with their various arrows, just as it is at the end of the hot season by storm clouds laced with streaks of lightning.

26. The streams of their arrows—arrows that were immensely powerful, keenly honed, fletched with vulture feathers, and extremely swift—made the sky appear to be densely covered with latticework.

27. With their arrows, the two heroes then created a massive and fearsome darkness, as might two vast storm clouds arising at sunset.

28. A tumultuous battle—like that between Vṛtra and Vāsava—unequaled and unimaginable, then raged between the two warriors, each intent on killing the other.

29. Both were armed with splendid bows, both were skilled in the use of weapons, both were preeminent among those familiar with divine weapon-spells, and they hurled themselves at each other in battle.

30. As they maneuvered, waves of arrows preceded them, as might the waves of two oceans driven by the wind.

31. Then Rāvaṇa, who makes the world cry out, his hands working swiftly, unleashed a chain of iron arrows upon Rāma's forehead.

32. Although he bore that chain of iron arrows—shot from that fearsome bow and shining like the petals of a blue lotus—on his head, Rāma took no harm.

33–34. Rāma, suffused with rage, muttered sacred *mantras* and invoked the divine weapon-spell of Rudra. Then, taking up his arrows once again, that mighty warrior of immense blazing energy bent his bow and let them fly. Allowing no interruption in the stream of his arrows, he loosed them toward the lord of the *rākṣasas*.

35. But those arrows fell harmlessly on the *rākṣasa* lord's impenetrable armor, which resembled a huge storm cloud.

36. But then, with a splendid, divinely charged weapon, Rāma, skilled in all divine weapon-spells, pierced the *rākṣasa* lord through the forehead, as the latter stood in his chariot.

37. But those arrows, after shattering the splendid arrows of Rāvaṇa, were deflected by him and so entered the earth, hissing like five-headed serpents.

38. Having thus thwarted Rāghava's divinely charged weapons, Rāvaṇa, beside himself with rage, invoked yet another divine weapon-spell, the truly dreadful one belonging to the *asuras*.

39–40. He then released sharp arrows. The heads of some were like those of lions and tigers, while others had the heads of adjutant storks and crows. Some had the heads of vultures and falcons, while others had the heads of jackals. Some had the heads of wolves, their jaws gaping and terrifying. Still others were like five-headed serpents with flickering tongues.

41–42. Hissing like an angry serpent, the immensely powerful *rākṣasa*, employing his powers of illusion, then loosed still more sharp arrows at Rāma. Some of these arrows had the heads of donkeys, while others were shaped like the heads of boars. Some had the heads of dogs and cocks, while others had the heads of sea monsters and venomous serpents.

43. Assaulted by that divine weapon-spell of the *asuras*, the immensely energetic delight of the Raghus invoked the divine weapon-spell of Agni, the purifier, a weapon-spell that was like fire itself.

44–45. Rāma then released sharp arrows. Some of these arrows had heads blazing with fire, while some had heads like the sun. Some had heads like the moon or half-moon, while others had heads like comets. Some resembled planets and constellations, while others had heads shaped like huge meteors. Still others were like streaks of lightning.

46. Intercepted in the air by Rāghava's divinely charged weapons, Rāvaṇa's fearsome arrows disappeared, shattering into thousands of fragments.

47. When the monkeys, who could take on any form at will, saw that Rāma, tireless in action, had struck down Rāvaṇa's divinely charged weapons, they roared in delight.

The end of the eighty-seventh *sarga* of the *Yuddhakāṇḍa* of the *Śrī Rāmāyaṇa*.

Sarga 88

1. Now, when that divine weapon-spell of his had been thwarted, Rāvaṇa, lord of the *rākṣasas*, redoubled his fury and, in his rage, invoked yet another divine weapon-spell.

2. Immensely lustrous Rāvaṇa then prepared to invoke against Rāghava that other fierce and fearsome divine weapon-spell devised by Maya, the craftsman of the *asuras*.

3. Then, from his bow, lances, maces, and cudgels flew forth—all of them blazing and as hard as adamant.

4. Like the mighty gales at the end of a cosmic age, there flew forth various mallets, war hammers, nooses, and blazing darts, as well as various other sharp weapons.

5. But immensely lustrous Rāghava, foremost of those familiar with the great divine weapon-spells, thwarted that divine weapon-spell with the supreme divine weapon-spell of the *gandharvas*.

6. But when that divine weapon-spell of his had been thwarted by great Rāghava, Rāvaṇa, his eyes red with rage, invoked the divine weapon-spell of Sūrya.

7. Then huge and blazing discuses flew forth from the bow of wise ten-necked Rāvaṇa of fearsome power.

8. As they descended on every side, they lit up the sky, as the blazing moon, sun, and planets might light up the directions, if they were to fall.

9. But, with torrents of arrows, Rāghava cut down the discuses and various other weapons of Rāvaṇa there in the vanguard of the army.

10. When Rāvaṇa, lord of the *rākṣasas*, saw that that divine weapon-spell had been thwarted, he riddled Rāma in all his vital points with ten arrows.

11. Nonetheless, although Rāvaṇa had riddled him with ten arrows loosed from his mighty bow, immensely powerful Rāghava was not shaken in the least.

12. And then Rāghava, victorious in battle, in a towering rage, riddled Rāvaṇa in every limb with numerous arrows.

13. At this juncture, Rāghava's younger brother, mighty Lakṣmaṇa, slayer of enemy heroes, took up seven arrows in a rage.

14. And, with those seven immensely powerful arrows, that immensely lustrous hero shredded Rāvaṇa's battle flag with its image of a human head.

15. With a single arrow, majestic and immensely powerful Lakṣmaṇa took off the head of the charioteer of the *rākṣasa*, son of chaos, along with its glittering earrings.

16. And with five sharp arrows Lakṣmaṇa cut to pieces the *rākṣasa* lord's bow, so like an elephant's trunk, along with his arrows.

17. Meanwhile, Vibhīṣaṇa leapt forward and, with his mace, slew Rāvaṇa's splendid horses, as huge as mountains and resembling black storm clouds.

18. Jumping swiftly down from his great chariot, now that its horses had been slain, powerful Rāvaṇa conceived a burning rage toward his brother.

19. Then the valorous and immensely powerful *rākṣasa* lord hurled at Vibhīṣaṇa a blazing javelin that was like a blazing bolt of lightning.

20. But Lakṣmaṇa cut it to pieces with three arrows before it reached Vibhīṣaṇa. At that, a mighty roar went up in the battle from the monkeys.

21. Encircled with gold, the javelin fell to earth cut into four pieces, like a huge glowing meteor falling from the sky in a shower of blazing sparks.

22. Then Rāvaṇa took up a huge javelin, which he prized greatly. It glowed with its own blazing energy, and even Kāla himself could not withstand it.

23. Brandished violently by the mighty but evil-minded Rāvaṇa, that supremely terrifying weapon blazed with a splendor equal to that of Śakra's thunderbolt.

24. At that very moment, heroic Lakṣmaṇa ran quickly to Vibhīṣaṇa, who was now in mortal danger.

25. In order to save him, heroic Lakṣmaṇa drew back his bow and, with a hail of arrows, showered Rāvaṇa, who stood there, javelin in hand.

26. Pelted by that torrent of arrows let loose by great Lakṣmaṇa, Rāvaṇa, his martial ardor now diverted, decided not to strike his brother.

27. Seeing that Lakṣmaṇa had saved his brother, Rāvaṇa positioned himself so that he faced Lakṣmaṇa and said these words:

28. "Since you, so proud of your strength, have saved Vibhīṣaṇa in this fashion, this javelin, sparing the *rākṣasa*, will now fall upon you.

29. "After piercing your heart, this blood-stained javelin, flung by the iron club that is my arm, will fly on its way, taking with it your life breaths."

30–31. When he had spoken in this fashion, Rāvaṇa, taking aim at Lakṣmaṇa, roared and, in a towering rage, hurled that javelin. With its eight bells it made a terrific sound. Maya, the craftsman of the *asuras*, had forged it with his magical powers so that it was infallible in slaying one's enemies. It glowed with blazing energy.

32. Hurled with terrifying force and emitting a roar like that of Śakra's thunderbolt, the javelin struck Lakṣmaṇa with tremendous impact there in the forefront of battle.

33. But even as that javelin was hurtling toward Lakṣmaṇa, Rāma Rāghava addressed it, saying, "May Lakṣmaṇa be spared! And may you, your energy thwarted, be foiled!"

34. Nonetheless, that immensely brilliant weapon, flashing like the flickering tongue of a serpent king, fell with tremendous force on Lakṣmaṇa's broad chest.

35. Then Lakṣmaṇa, his heart pierced by that javelin, so deeply embedded through Rāvaṇa's strength, fell to the ground.

36. When Rāghava of enormous blazing energy, who was nearby, saw Lakṣmaṇa in that condition, his heart sank out of love for his brother.

37. He remained lost for a moment in thought, his eyes filled with tears. Then he flared up in anger, like the fire at the end of a cosmic age.

38. Reflecting, "This is no time for despondency," Rāghava began a tumultuous battle, intent upon slaying Rāvaṇa.

39. Rāma then gazed at Lakṣmaṇa, who, pierced by that javelin in the great battle and drenched in blood, resembled a mountain with a mighty serpent.

40. Try as they might, the foremost among the tawny monkeys, harried as they were by the swift-handed *rākṣasa* with his torrents of arrows, were unable to extract the javelin that had been flung by mighty Rāvaṇa.

41. But Rāma, in the rage of battle, seized with both hands that terrifying javelin, which, having transfixed Saumitri, was embedded in the earth. Wrenching it out violently, he broke it in two.

42. But even as Rāma was wrenching out the javelin, mighty Rāvaṇa pelted his every limb with arrows that pierced his vitals.

43. Heedless of those arrows, Rāghava embraced Lakṣmaṇa and then said this to Hanumān and Sugrīva: "Foremost of monkeys, you must stay here and care for Lakṣmaṇa.

44. "The moment to display my valor is now at hand, a moment I have long awaited, as does a thirsty *cātaka* the sight of rain clouds at the end of the hot season. Now the evil-minded ten-necked Rāvaṇa of evil intent must die.

45. "I give you my solemn word here and now, monkeys, that very soon you shall see a world that is either without Rāvaṇa or without Rāma.

46–47. "For once I have slain Rāvaṇa in battle today, I will put behind me all the terrible suffering and hellish torment that I endured: the loss of my kingdom, the sojourn in the wilderness, the wandering in the Daṇḍaka, the assault on Vaidehī, and the clashes with the *rākṣasas*.

48–49. "For that evil wretch—on whose account I bridged and crossed the ocean and brought the monkey army here after slaying Vālin in combat and placing Sugrīva on the throne—has now come within my sight here in battle.

50. "Indeed, once he comes within the range of my sight, Rāvaṇa can no more survive than can a person seen by a serpent whose mere glance is deadly venom.

51. "So, unassailable bulls among monkeys, you should seat yourselves comfortably on the mountaintops and watch the battle between Rāvaṇa and me.

52. "This very day let the three worlds, along with the *gandharvas*, the gods, the seers, and the celestial bards, witness in battle what makes Rāma Rāma.

53. "Today, I shall perform such a feat that all the worlds, with their moving and fixed contents and including the gods themselves, will talk about as long as the earth shall endure."

54. When he had spoken in this fashion, Rāma, with great concentration, struck ten-necked Rāvaṇa in battle with sharp arrows adorned with burnished gold.

55. And Rāvaṇa, in turn, then showered Rāma with blazing iron arrows and cudgels, as might a storm cloud with its torrential rains.

56. And a tumultuous sound arose as the various arrows loosed by Rāma and Rāvaṇa crashed into one another.

57. Broken and scattered, the arrows of Rāma and Rāvaṇa fell from the sky to the ground, their arrowheads blazing.

58. The deafening sound of the bowstrings of Rāma and Rāvaṇa striking against their armguards was almost miraculous, and it terrified all beings.

59. Rāvaṇa was covered with dense hails of arrows and thus tormented by the great wielder of the blazing bow. Having first joined battle, he now fled in terror, like a great storm cloud driven before the wind.

The end of the eighty-eighth *sarga* of the *Yuddhakāṇḍa* of the *Śrī Rāmāyaṇa*.

Sarga 89

1. When Rāma had thus given tumultuous battle to evil-minded Rāvaṇa, he spoke these words to Suṣeṇa, even as he continued to discharge his torrents of arrows:

2. "Here is heroic Lakṣmaṇa, fallen to the ground through the power of Rāvaṇa. He is writhing like a snake, filling me with sorrow.

3. "When I see that hero, dearer to me than life itself, drenched with blood, my mind is in such turmoil that I wonder what power I have left to fight.

4. "For if my brother, so praiseworthy in battle and marked with auspicious signs, has truly returned to the elements, then of what use to me is pleasure or indeed life itself?

5. "For my valor itself seems to hang its head in shame, while my bow seems to slip from my grasp. My arrows drop away, and my sight is dimmed with tears. Dreadful thoughts grow in my mind, and I wish now only for death."

6. Thus did Rāma, his senses overwhelmed, lament in the greatest despair when he saw his brother struck down by evil-minded Rāvaṇa.

7. "Seeing my brother Lakṣmaṇa struck down in the dust of the battlefield, I have no further use for battle, for my life, or even for Sītā herself.

8. "Now that Lakṣmaṇa lies slain in the forefront of battle, what use have I for kingship or for life itself? There is now no longer any purpose to this war."

9. Then, consoling Rāma, heroic Suṣeṇa spoke these words: "Great-armed Lakṣmaṇa, increaser of prosperity, is not dead.

10. "For his face has not altered, nor has it darkened or lost its radiance. Indeed, his countenance looks quite radiant and clear.

11. "The palms of his hands are as red as the lotus, and his eyes are clear. This is not the way people look, lord of the peoples, when their life breaths have left them. So do not despair, heroic tamer of your foes. He is still alive.

12. "As he lies here unconscious, his limbs sprawling on the ground, the rhythmic movement of his chest proclaims that he still lives, hero."

13. Once Suṣeṇa, skilled in speech, had uttered these words to Rāghava, he immediately said this to Hanumān, who stood nearby:

14–15. "Go swiftly hence, gentle friend, to the splendid mountain known as the mountain of healing herbs, which Jāmbavān told you about earlier. Then bring back the splendid healing herb known as *viśalyakaraṇī*, the healer of arrow wounds, which grows on its southernmost peak.

16. "Go swiftly and, in order to revive the great hero Lakṣmaṇa, you must also bring the *sauvarṇakaraṇī*, the restorer of a golden glow, the *saṃjīvanī*, the restorer of life, and the *saṃdhānakaraṇī*, the joiner of limbs."

17. Addressed in this fashion, Hanumān proceeded to the mountain of healing herbs. But, unable to identify those potent herbs, the majestic monkey fell to brooding.

18. But then Māruti of immeasurable blazing energy had this idea: "I will take this mountain peak and go back!

19. "For if I were to return without bringing the *viśalyakaraṇī*, the healer of arrow wounds, the loss of time would lead to dire consequences and there might be a serious calamity."

20. Reflecting thus, immensely powerful Hanumān immediately descended on the peak of that mountain and, seizing it, flew off.

21. "I could not identify those healing herbs, bull among tawny monkeys; so I brought the entire mountain peak."

22. Suṣeṇa, foremost of monkeys, praised the son of Pavana, who was speaking in this fashion. Then he plucked and gathered the healing herbs.

23. Then that foremost of monkeys, Suṣeṇa of immense luster, crushed one of the herbs and held it to Lakṣmaṇa's nose.

24. No sooner had that slayer of enemy heroes, Lakṣmaṇa, who had been pierced by that javelin, inhaled that aroma than he leapt up from the ground, free from the javelin and the pain it had caused.

25. When the tawny monkeys saw that Lakṣmaṇa had leapt up from the ground, they were delighted and, crying, "Excellent! Excellent!" they honored Suṣeṇa.

26. Then Rāma, slayer of enemy heroes, addressed Lakṣmaṇa, saying, "Come to me, come to me." His eyes clouded with tears, he embraced him tightly in his affection.

27. Embracing Saumitri, Rāghava then said to him, "Thank heavens, I see you, hero, risen from the dead.

28. "Sītā, victory, and life itself have no meaning for me. For if you had returned to the elements, what purpose, indeed, would I have had in living?"

29. As great Rāma was speaking in this fashion, Lakṣmaṇa, distressed at this fainthearted speech, said these words:

30. "Having first made that vow, truly valorous warrior, you must not now speak in this fashion, like some weak and insignificant person.

31. "For, blameless hero, the virtuous do not falsify their vows. Indeed, the keeping of one's vows is the sign of greatness.

32. "So enough of your giving way to despair on my account, blameless hero. You must keep your vow by slaying Rāvaṇa this very day.

33. "For once he comes within range of your arrows, your enemy will no more escape with his life than would a great bull elephant that comes within the clutches of a roaring, sharp-fanged lion.

34. "I long for the swift death of that evil-minded wretch before the sun, bringer of day, sets behind the western mountain, his day's work done."

The end of the eighty-ninth *sarga* of the *Yuddhakāṇḍa* of the *Śrī Rāmāyaṇa*.

Sarga 90

1. When Rāghava had heard those words uttered by Lakṣmaṇa, he loosed fearsome arrows at Rāvaṇa there in the vanguard of the army.

2. But ten-necked Rāvaṇa, mounted in his chariot, in turn pelted Rāma with enormously fearsome arrows that resembled thunderbolts, as might a storm cloud with torrents of rain.

3. Nonetheless, Rāma, with great concentration, pierced ten-necked Rāvaṇa in battle with arrows, which, adorned with gold, resembled blazing fires.

4. Then the gods, *gandharvas*, and *dānavas* declared, "This combat between Rāma, who is standing on the ground, and the *rākṣasa*, mounted in his chariot, is not fair."

5–7. Just then, shining like the rising sun, the majestic and splendid chariot of the king of the gods, ornamented with hundreds of bells, its body studded with gold, its yoke pole made of lapis, and its flagstaff made of gold, descended from Triviṣṭapa, Indra's heaven. It was yoked with splendid tawny horses, which, with their golden plumes, white tufts, and ornaments of gold fretwork, were as radiant as the sun. It drew near to Kākutstha.

8. Standing in the chariot and holding the whip, Mātali, the charioteer of thousand-eyed Indra, cupped his hands in reverence and spoke these words to Rāma:

9. "Thousand-eyed Indra has given you this majestic, foe-destroying chariot so that you may obtain victory, mighty Kākutstha.

10. "And here, too, are Indra's great bow, armor shining like fire, arrows as brilliant as the sun, and a sharp, glittering javelin.

11. "So mount this chariot, heroic Rāma, and, with me as your charioteer, slay the *rākṣasa* Rāvaṇa, just as did great Indra the *dānavas*."

12. Addressed in this fashion, Rāma respectfully circumambulated the chariot and, after reverentially saluting Mātali, mounted it, illuminating the worlds with his splendor as he did so.

13. Then there ensued an astonishing and hair-raising chariot duel between great-armed Rāma and the *rākṣasa* Rāvaṇa.

14. Rāghava, who had mastered the most powerful divine weapon-spells, thwarted each divine weapon-spell of the *rākṣasa* king with one of his own—a divine weapon-spell of the *gandharvas* with a divine weapon-spell of the *gandharvas*, a divine weapon-spell of the gods with a divine weapon-spell of the gods.

15. Then, in a towering rage, the lord of the night-roaming *rākṣasas* invoked the supremely fearsome divine weapon-spell of the *rākṣasas*.

16. Loosed from Rāvaṇa's bow, the arrows, adorned with gold, turned into venomous serpents and sped toward Kākutstha.

17. With gaping jaws and mouths aflame, those terrifying serpents hurtled toward Rāma, spewing blazing fire from their mouths.

18. All the cardinal directions were filled, and the intermediate ones covered, by those serpents with their blazing hoods and deadly venom. Their very touch was equal to that of the great serpent Vāsuki.

19. But when Rāma saw those serpents hurtling toward him in battle, he produced the dreadful and fear-inspiring divine weapon-spell of Garuḍa.

20. Loosed from Rāghava's bow, the gold-fletched arrows, blazing like fire, turned into golden eagles, the foes of the serpents, and intercepted them.

21. Rāma's arrows, which could take on any form at will, took the form of eagles and struck down all of those swift arrows, which had taken on the form of serpents.

22. Enraged at the thwarting of his divine weapon-spell, Rāvaṇa, lord of the *rākṣasas*, pelted Rāma with dreadful hails of arrows.

23. Then, after harassing Rāma, tireless in action, with a thousand arrows, he riddled Mātali with a veritable torrent of them.

24. After first knocking the golden battle standard to the floor of the chariot, Rāvaṇa struck down Indra's horses with a mass of arrows.

25. Then, seeing that Rāma was hard pressed, the gods, *gandharvas*, *dānavas*, celestial bards, perfected beings, and supreme seers became despondent

26. And the foremost of monkeys, together with Vibhīṣaṇa, seeing the moon in the form of Rāma swallowed up, as it were, by Rāhu, the demon of the eclipse in the form of Rāvaṇa, were similarly distressed.

27. Mercury, the planet baleful to all creatures, stood in occlusion of Rohiṇī, the constellation beloved of the hare-marked moon and presided over by Prajāpati, lord of creatures.

28. The sea seemed to be ablaze, its waves shrouded in smoke. Heaving upward in its fury, it seemed almost to touch the sun, bringer of day.

29. The sun, bringer of day, its rays dimmed, its color that of iron, looked ghastly. In conjunction with a smoke-bannered comet, it seemed to be crossed by a headless trunk.

30. And Mars stood in occlusion of Viśākhā, the constellation of the ruling House of Kosala. This constellation, whose presiding deities are Indra and Agni, was clearly visible in the sky.

31. With his ten faces and twenty arms, ten-necked Rāvaṇa, grasping his bow, looked like Mount Maināka.

32. Hard pressed by the *rākṣasa* ten-necked Rāvaṇa in the forefront of the battle, Rāma was unable even to nock his arrows.

33. Knitting his brows in anger, his eyes turning red with fury, Rāma flew into a towering rage, seeming almost to scorch his foe with his gaze.

The end of the ninetieth *sarga* of the *Yuddhakāṇḍa* of the *Śrī Rāmāyaṇa*.

Sarga 91

1. At the sight of the face of wise Rāma in his fury, all creatures were stricken with terror, and the earth itself trembled.

2. The mountain, with its lions and tigers and its deeply rooted trees, shook violently, while the ocean, lord of rivers, grew wildly agitated.

3. And, on every side, ominous birds with harsh cries, braying like donkeys, circled in the sky, screeching.

4. Seeing Rāma in such a towering rage and observing those extremely dire portents, all creatures were stricken with terror, and fear entered Rāvaṇa's heart.

5–6. The gods, standing in their aerial chariots, the *gandharvas*, the great serpents, seers, *dānavas*, *daityas*, and the great birds, who soar through the sky, then watched the battle between those two heroes as they engaged with their various fearsome weapons. It seemed like the destruction of the universe.

7. And as they watched that great duel, all the gods and *asuras*, hostile as always to each other, shouted words of support in their excitement.

8. Arrayed in their ranks, the *asuras* shouted, "Be victorious!" to ten-necked Rāvaṇa, while the gods cried out again and again to Rāma, "May you be victorious!"

9–12. At this juncture, evil-minded Rāvaṇa, in his rage at Rāghava, fingered his mighty weapons in his desire to strike him down. Then, blazing, as it were, with fury, he seized a lance. Hard as adamant and emitting a mighty clangor, it was lethal to all enemies. Fitted with barbs as huge as mountain peaks, it was fearsome to look upon. Sharp-tipped and belching smoke, as it were, it resembled the holocaust at the end of a cosmic era. It was so vastly terrifying and irresistible that even Kāla himself could not stand before it. Rending and cutting, it was a terror to all beings.

13. Surrounded in battle by many heroic *rākṣasas*, mighty Rāvaṇa, in a towering rage, grasped that lance in the middle.

14. His eyes red with rage, the gigantic warrior raised the lance on high and roared frighteningly in battle, encouraging his forces.

15. That terrifying roar of the *rākṣasa* lord caused the earth, the atmosphere, and the cardinal and intermediate directions to tremble.

16. At that roar of the extremely loudly roaring and evil-minded *rākṣasa*, all beings were filled with terror and the sea grew tumultuous.

17. Grasping his huge lance, the immensely powerful Rāvaṇa released a tremendous roar and spoke harshly to Rāma:

18. "Wielded by me in my wrath, Rāma, this lance, hard as adamant, will instantly steal away your life breaths though you have your brother as an ally.

19. "Arrogant in battle though you be, this very day, striking you down, I shall quickly reduce you to the state of the *rākṣasa* heroes who have been slain in the forefront of battle.

20. "Stand your ground, Rāghava, for I shall now kill you with my lance!" When the overlord of the *rākṣasas* had spoken in this fashion, he hurled his lance.

21. As it hurtled onward, Rāghava strove to stop it with hails of arrows, just as Vāsava might strive to suppress with torrents of rain the fire that blazes up at the end of a cosmic age.

22. But Rāvaṇa's great lance burned up the arrows loosed from Rāma's bow, as a blazing fire might so many moths.

23. When Rāghava saw his arrows shattered and reduced to ashes in the air by the impact of that lance, he was furious.

24. In a towering rage, Rāghava, the delight of the Raghus, then took up a javelin that had been crafted for Vāsava, and which Mātali had brought.

25. Hefted by that mighty warrior, the javelin, resounding with the sound of its bells, lit up the sky, like a blazing meteor at the end of a cosmic age.

26. Once hurled, it collided with the lance of the *rākṣasa* lord. Shattered by the javelin, the great lance fell, its blazing splendor dimmed.

27. Then Rāma riddled Rāvaṇa's swift horses with arrows, arrows that were powerful, swift, hard as adamant, and sharp.

28. Rāghava pierced Rāvaṇa in the chest with sharp arrows and again, concentrating his energies, through the forehead with three feathered shafts.

29. His entire body pierced with arrows, gushing blood from every limb, the *rākṣasa* lord in the midst of that host looked like an *aśoka* tree in full bloom.

30. His every limb riddled with Rāma's arrows and his body drenched with blood, the lord of the night-roaming *rākṣasas* grew weary there in the midst of his hosts, and he gave way to a towering rage.

The end of the ninety-first *sarga* of the *Yuddhakāṇḍa* of the *Śrī Rāmāyaṇa*.

Sarga 92

1. Stricken in battle by Rāma in his wrath, Rāvaṇa, arrogant in battle, gave way to a towering rage.

2. His eyes blazing with fury, that mighty warrior drew back his bow and, in his rage, assailed Rāghava in that ultimate battle.

3. Rāvaṇa filled Rāma with his arrows, just as a storm cloud fills a pond with its thousands of arrowlike torrents of rain from the sky.

4. Although riddled with a mass of arrows loosed from the bow in battle, Kākutstha, as unshakeable as a mighty mountain, did not so much as tremble.

5. Standing firm in battle, the mighty warrior slowed that mass of arrows with arrows of his own, so that he received them as if they were no more than rays of sunshine.

*6. Then, enraged, the nimble-handed night-roaming *rākṣasa* sank thousands of arrows into great Rāghava's chest.

7. Drenched with blood in battle, Lakṣmaṇa's elder brother looked like a great *kiṃśuka* tree in full bloom in the forest.

8. Enraged by the blows of those arrows, immensely powerful Kākutstha, in turn, took up arrows whose radiance was like that of the sun at the end of a cosmic age.

9. In their fury, neither Rāma nor Rāvaṇa could see the other in the midst of that battle, shrouded as it was in the darkness of their arrows.

10. Then, suffused with rage, heroic Rāma, son of Daśaratha, laughed and spoke these harsh words to Rāvaṇa:

11. "You are surely no hero, lowest of the *rākṣasas*, since you abducted my helpless wife from Janasthāna, behind my back.

12. "You forcibly abducted Vaidehī when she was alone in the vast forest, frightened without me to protect her. And now you think, 'Oh, what a great hero am I!'

13. "Great hero! Molester of other men's wives! You commit contemptible acts against defenseless women and then think, 'Oh, what a great hero am I!'

14. "Violator of all boundaries! Shameless wretch! You are utterly lacking in character! Having brought death upon yourself, in your arrogance, you think, 'Oh, what a great hero am I!'

15. "Indeed, you, the heroic brother of Kubera, bestower of wealth, accompanied by your troops, have accomplished a great, praiseworthy, and glorious deed.

16. "This very day, you shall receive the truly fitting reward for this evil and contemptible act that you committed in your arrogance.

17. " 'Oh, what a great hero am I,' that is how you think of yourself, evil-minded wretch, and yet you feel no shame for having carried off Sītā, as if you were a common thief.

18. "If you had dared to lay violent hands upon Sītā in my presence, you would have then and there joined your brother Khara, whom I had earlier slain with arrows.

19. "But now, evil-minded wretch, by my good fortune, you have come into my presence, and, this very day, with my sharp arrows, I shall convey you to the abode of Yama.

20. "This very day, carrion eaters will drag off your head, along with its glittering earrings, as it rolls in the dust of the battlefield, severed by my arrows.

21. "Let the vultures alight on your chest as you sprawl on the ground, Rāvaṇa, and thirstily drink the blood flowing from the wounds made by my arrowheads.

22. "This very day, as you lie dead riddled with my arrows, the carrion birds shall drag out your intestines, as eagles do serpents."

23. Speaking in this fashion, Rāma, annihilator of his foes, pelted the *rākṣasa* lord, who stood nearby, with hails of arrows.

24. Since he was so eager for the destruction of his enemy, Rāma's valor, strength, zeal for battle, and the power of his divine weapon-spells were all redoubled.

25. All the divine weapon-spells then manifested themselves before that celebrated warrior. And, in his excitement, that immensely powerful hero became still more nimble handed.

26. Perceiving those auspicious signs within himself, Rāma, exterminator of the *rākṣasas*, pressed Rāvaṇa harder still.

27. As ten-necked Rāvaṇa was being pelted by masses of stones from the tawny monkeys and by hails of arrows from Rāghava, his heart began to falter.

28. Then, his heart faltering, he could no longer deploy his weapons, draw his bow, or counter Rāma's valor in any way.

29. Even those arrows and various other weapons that he managed to deploy proved useless in battle—as he now approached the hour of his death.

30. Seeing his condition, Rāvaṇa's charioteer, who was controlling the chariot, kept his composure and slowly drove the chariot from the field of battle.

The end of the ninety-second *sarga* of the *Yuddhakāṇḍa* of the *Śrī Rāmāyaṇa*.

Sarga 93

1. Furious in his delusion, his eyes red with rage, Rāvaṇa, impelled by the power of destiny, now addressed his charioteer:

2–3. "Fool! Acting on your own authority, you treat me with contempt, as if I were weak, incompetent, devoid of manliness, cowardly, a person of no consequence, bereft of blazing energy, utterly lacking powers of illusion, and stripped of divine weapon-spells.

4. "Why have you driven off my chariot in full view of the enemy, disregarding my wishes and treating me with contempt?

5. "For now, ignoble wretch, you have utterly undermined my fame—built up over long years—as well as my valor, blazing energy, and reputation.

6. "Though I am eager for battle, you have made me look like a coward in the eyes of an enemy famed for his martial power, one who deserves to be gratified with valorous deeds.

7. "In that you stupidly failed to drive the chariot forward, fool, my conjecture that you have been bribed by the enemy must be true.

8. "This is not the action of a friend who wishes one well. Indeed, it is more typical of one's enemies. What you have done is wrong.

9. "If you are my longtime friend or if you recall my many favors, then you must quickly turn the chariot around, before my enemy departs."

10. Addressed harshly in this fashion by that fool, the charioteer, who wished his master well, addressed to Rāvaṇa these beneficial and conciliatory words:

11. "I am not afraid, nor am I a fool. I have not been suborned by your enemies, nor am I derelict in my duties. I am not lacking in my affection for you, nor have I forgotten the favors you have bestowed.

12. "My heart overflowing with love for you, I did you this favor, which has so displeased you, out of a desire for your well-being and to preserve your reputation.

13. "In this matter, great king, you should not, like some lowly and ignoble person, find fault with me, who am devoted only to your pleasure and well-being.

14. "Listen! I will tell you the reason that I turned the chariot back from the battle, as the current of a river is turned back by the rising tide.

15. "I perceived your exhaustion resulting from your mighty feats in battle. And, heroic warrior, I did not see your wonted enthusiasm and exuberance.

16. "Moreover, these chariot-horses, exhausted from drawing the chariot and overcome by the heat, are as dejected as cattle battered by torrential rain.

17. "And given all the many portents that have appeared before us, I foresee no good outcome for us.

18–20. "Moreover, a good charioteer when driving his chariot must be familiar with all of these things: the proper time and place, signs and gestures, and the despondency, exuberance, exhaustion, and relative strength and weakness of his master. He must also be familiar with the elevations and depressions of the terrain, where it is level and where it is uneven. He must know the proper time to fight and how to spot the weak points of the enemy. He must also know when to advance, when to pull back, when to stand his ground, and when to retreat.

21. "It was in order to alleviate this crushing fatigue and provide some respite for you as well as for the chariot-horses that I acted in this fitting manner.

22. "It was not on my own account, heroic warrior, that I drove the chariot off. I did this, my lord, since I was overwhelmed with love for you, my master.

23. "Command me as is proper. With my mind discharged of its obligations I shall do whatever you say, heroic slayer of your enemies,"

24. Satisfied with the charioteer's words, Rāvaṇa, lusting for battle, praised him profusely and said this:

25. "Charioteer, turn this chariot immediately toward Rāghava! Rāvaṇa shall never turn back without first killing his enemies in battle."

26. Then, having spoken in this fashion, Rāvaṇa, lord of the *rākṣasas*, pleased, gave him a splendid and unequaled ring.

27. Then, urged on by Rāvaṇa's words, the charioteer swiftly drove the horses so that, within an instant, the great chariot of the *rākṣasa* lord stood before Rāma on the battlefield.

The end of the ninety-third *sarga* of the *Yuddhakāṇḍa* of the *Śrī Rāmāyaṇa*.

Sarga 94

1–2. The king of men watched the chariot of the *rākṣasa* king as, with its great flagstaffs, it hurtled toward him with a tremendous din. It was yoked to black horses and glowed with a fearsome radiance. It was thick with banners resembling streaks of lightning, and it displayed weapons that were like the weapons of Indra himself. It was pouring forth streams of arrows as a storm cloud might a torrential downpour.

3. As he watched his enemy's chariot, which looked like a great storm cloud and rumbled with the sound of a mountain being

shattered by a lightning bolt, Rāma said to Mātali, the charioteer of thousand-eyed Indra:

4. "Mātali! Observe my enemy's chariot as it hurtles furiously toward us. Since he is rushing toward me once more so rapidly on our right flank, he must now have determined to kill me.

5. "Therefore, remain vigilant and head for my enemy's chariot for I wish to destroy him utterly, as a strong wind does a cloud that has newly formed.

6. "Now, keeping firm control of the reins, drive the chariot forward—swiftly, boldly, calmly, and with a steady heart and eye.

7. "Granted, as someone well familiar with this chariot of Indra, the smasher of citadels, you are not in need of instruction. But single-mindedly eager for battle as I am, I am merely reminding you, not giving you instruction."

8. Gratified with that speech of Rāma, Mātali, foremost of the charioteers of the gods, drove his chariot onward.

9. Then, keeping Rāvaṇa's great chariot on his right, Mātali discomfited him with the dust raised by his own wheels.

10. Then, with his arrows, ten-necked Rāvaṇa, infuriated, his eyes red and wide with rage, assailed Rāma, who faced him in his chariot.

11. Provoked by this assault, Rāma, endowed with great blazing energy, in his rage put patience aside, and there, in that battle, took up the enormously powerful bow of Indra, along with arrows and with a radiance equal to that of the sun's rays.

12. Then began the battle between the two of them, who, each intent on killing the other, resembled two proud lions face to face.

13. Anxious for the destruction of Rāvaṇa, the gods, together with the *gandharvas*, the perfected beings, and the great seers, assembled to watch that chariot duel.

14. Terrifying and hair-raising omens now appeared. They presaged destruction for Rāvaṇa and victory for Rāghava.

15. It rained blood over Rāvaṇa's chariot, and fierce whirlwinds arose, circling to the left.

16. A vast flock of vultures, wheeling in the sky, raced after his chariot whichever way it went.

17. Laṅkā was shrouded in an untimely twilight as crimson as a *japā* blossom, and, even in bright daylight, the very ground appeared to be ablaze.

18. Huge meteors flew past with a thunderous sound, accompanied by violent gusts of wind. Then, as they were clearly ominous for Rāvaṇa, they plunged the *rākṣasas* into despair.

19. The earth trembled wherever Rāvaṇa went, and, as the *rākṣasas* prepared to strike, it seemed as if something held back their arms.

20. As the rays of the sun—red and yellow, pallid and bright white—played across Rāvaṇa's body, they looked like veins of variegated ores on a mountainside.

21. Jackals, shadowed by vultures, howled angrily and inauspiciously, spewing flames from their mouths while staring him in the face.

22. The wind blew directly in the face of the *rākṣasa* king, whipping up dust across the battlefield and blinding him.

23. From every side, Indra's terrible thunderbolts fell upon his army with an unbearable sound. And yet, there was no rumbling of storm clouds.

24. All directions—both cardinal and intermediate—were shrouded in darkness. A huge dust storm made the sky itself impossible to see.

25. In a fearsome assault upon his chariot, dreadful *sārika* birds swooped down by the hundred with dreadful cries.

26. His horses incessantly shed blazing sparks from their hindquarters and tears from their eyes so that they poured forth both fire and water equally.

27. Indeed, many dreadful portents of this type appeared, foretelling great danger and presaging Rāvaṇa's destruction.

28. But, in the case of Rāma, favorable and auspicious portents arose on every side, presaging his victory.

29. Observing on the battlefield those portents that augured well for him, Rāghava, skilled in interpreting portents, was excited, and, supremely happy, he redoubled his valor in battle.

The end of the ninety-fourth *sarga* of the *Yuddhakāṇḍa* of the *Śrī Rāmāyaṇa*.

Sarga 95

1. Then the great battle between Rāma and Rāvaṇa commenced, a fierce chariot duel that terrified all the worlds.

2. Both the *rākṣasa* army and the vast host of tawny monkeys stood motionless, their weapons still in their hands.

3. As they watched those two mighty warriors—man and *rākṣasa*—engaged in battle, their attention was riveted and all of them were struck with the greatest amazement.

4. Although their hands were filled with all sorts of weapons, their minds were filled with astonishment. Thus, they stood there gazing at that battle and struck no blows at one another.

5. With the *rākṣasas* gazing at Rāvaṇa and the monkeys at Rāma, both armies, their eyes wide with astonishment, seemed frozen as if in a painting.

6. Observing those various portents, Rāghava and Rāvaṇa, grimly determined and fixed in their enmity, fought on, unafraid.

7. Kākutstha thought, "I will surely win," while Rāvaṇa realized, "I must surely die." Then those two resolute warriors displayed their utmost valor in battle.

8. Then, in anger, mighty ten-necked Rāvaṇa nocked his arrows and, taking aim at the flagstaff on Rāghava's chariot, let them fly.

9. But those arrows never reached the flagstaff on the chariot of Indra, smasher of citadels. Instead, merely brushing the chariot-javelin, they fell to the ground.

10. In turn, mighty Rāma drew his bow in anger and resolved to return blow for blow.

11. Taking aim at Rāvaṇa's flagstaff, he loosed a sharp arrow that, glowing with its own blazing energy, was as impossible to withstand as a mighty serpent.

12. After cutting down the flagstaff of ten-necked Rāvaṇa, the arrow came to rest on the ground. Cut down, Rāvaṇa's chariot standard likewise fell to the ground.

13. Upon witnessing the destruction of his flagstaff, immensely powerful Rāvaṇa seemed to blaze up on the battlefield with a fire born of anger.

14. In an uncontrollable rage, Rāvaṇa poured forth an immense hail of arrows and, with those arrows, riddled Rāma's celestial horses.

15. Riddled though they were, the tawny steeds never stumbled or swerved. They remained as serene at heart as if they had been stroked with lotus stalks.

16–17. Seeing that the horses had been utterly unaffected, Rāvaṇa, in a towering rage, once more loosed a hail of arrows. He also hurled maces, iron clubs, discuses, cudgels, mountain peaks, and trees, as well as lances and battle-axes.

18. His heart and energies unflagging, he continued to loose his arrows by the thousand, and that hail of weapons that he let fly was invested with the power of magical illusion.

19. It was tremendous and deafening, and consisted of innumerable weapons. It was fearsome and reverberated fearsomely in the midst of the battle. It was unendurable, and it sowed panic everywhere.

20. Missing Rāghava's chariot, it fell upon the monkey host from every side. But ten-necked Rāvaṇa, with unbroken concentration, continued to loose his arrows so that he quickly filled the entire atmosphere with his shafts.

21. But Kākutstha, watching Rāvaṇa exert himself with such concentration in battle, smiled faintly and nocked sharp arrows.

22. Then, in that battle, he loosed hundreds of thousands of arrows. Seeing them, Rāvaṇa filled the entire sky with arrows of his own.

23. By virtue of that blazing hail of arrows discharged by the two warriors, it looked as if there were a second shining sky composed entirely of arrows.

24. As long as Rāma and Rāvaṇa discharged their arrows in that battle, not one of those arrows failed to hit its precise mark, caused excessive damage, or failed to achieve its intended purpose.

25. The two heroes fought on without respite, shooting left and right. With their torrents of arrows, they seemed to leave no room even for air in the sky.

26. Rāma struck Rāvaṇa's horses, and Rāvaṇa struck Rāma's. Thus did the two of them strike at each other, trading blow and counter-blow.

The end of the ninety-fifth *sarga* of the *Yuddhakāṇḍa* of the *Śrī Rāmāyaṇa*.

Sarga 96

1. All beings watched with amazement in their hearts as Rāma and Rāvaṇa fought on in this fashion on the battleground.

2. Each pressing the other hard in battle and intent on slaying each other, the two splendid chariot-warriors assumed terrifying forms.

3. Their charioteers demonstrated the various movements exemplary of their skill as drivers—driving in circles and in straight lines, advancing and retreating.

4. Pressing each other hard—Rāma, Rāvaṇa and Rāvaṇa, Rāghava—the two of them advanced and retreated at tremendous speed.

5. And as the two of them loosed their hails of arrows, their splendid chariots moved across the battlefield like two storm clouds unleashing torrential rains.

6. Then, when they had demonstrated their various moves on the battlefield, they once again took up their positions facing each other.

7. And as the two chariots stood there, their yoke poles and battle standards brushed each other and their horses stood face to face.

8. But then, with four sharp arrows loosed from his bow, Rāma drove off Rāvaṇa's four fiery steeds.

9. The night-roaming *rākṣasa* flew into an uncontrollable rage over the flight of his horses and loosed sharp arrows at Rāghava.

10. Although he was completely riddled by powerful ten-necked Rāvaṇa, Rāghava seemed unaffected and showed no signs of pain.

11. So then the night-roaming *rākṣasa*, taking aim at the charioteer of Indra, wielder of the *vajra*, once again loosed arrows that roared with the crash of thunderbolts.

12. But although they fell upon Mātali's body in battle, those immensely powerful arrows caused neither the slightest distraction nor pain.

13. Enraged at that attack upon Mātali as he had never been at those upon himself, Rāghava made his enemy recoil with a mass of arrows.

14. Mighty Rāghava then loosed his arrows—twenty, thirty, sixty, and then by the hundred and by the thousand—upon his enemy's chariot.

15. The seven seas themselves were thrown into turmoil by the sounds of maces, cudgels, and iron clubs, and by the winds stirred up by the fletching of the arrows.

16. Since the seas were thrown into turmoil, all the thousands of great serpents and *dānavas* who dwelt in the underworld Pātāla were terrified.

17. The whole earth, together with its mountains, groves, and forests, shook. The sun grew dim and the winds ceased to blow.

18. Then all the gods, together with the *gandharvas*, perfected beings, great seers, *kinnaras*, and great serpents, were plunged into anxiety, praying:

19. "May all be well with cows and brahmans! May the worlds endure forever! May Rāghava be victorious in battle over Rāvaṇa, lord of the *rākṣasas*."

20. Then, in anger, great-armed Rāma, increaser of the glory of the Raghus, placed on his bow a razor-tipped arrow that was like a

venomous serpent. With it, he cut off Rāvaṇa's majestic head, together with its shining earrings.

21. As the three worlds looked on, that head fell to the ground. But a new head exactly like it emerged from Rāvaṇa.

22. Then, with his arrows, quick-handed Rāma, acting quickly, quickly cut off that second head of Rāvaṇa in battle.

23. But no sooner had that head been severed than yet another appeared in its place. And so, with arrows that were like thunderbolts, Rāma cut off that one as well.

24. And so in this way, a hundred heads—all exactly alike—were cut off. But still, there seemed to be no way to bring about the end of Rāvaṇa's life.

25. Therefore, although valorous Rāghava, increaser of Kausalyā's joy, was expert in the use of every divine weapon-spell and still had many arrows, he fell to brooding.

26–27. "These are all the very same arrows upon which I have always relied in battle and with which I killed Mārīca and Khara along with Dūṣaṇa. They are the very ones with which I killed Virādha in the Krauñca forest and Kabandha in the forest of the Daṇḍakas. Why then are they so ineffectual against Rāvaṇa?"

28. Although he was consumed with brooding in this fashion, Rāghava kept up his guard in battle and continued to rain hails of arrows upon Rāvaṇa's chest.

29. Meanwhile, Rāvaṇa, the lord of the *rākṣasas*, was in a rage, and, mounted in his chariot, he assailed Rāma in battle with a hail of maces and cudgels.

30. The great battle raged all night long as the gods, *dānavas*, *yakṣas*, *piśācas*, great serpents, and *rākṣasas* looked on.

31. Indeed, the duel between Rāma and Rāvaṇa continued night and day without stopping for an hour or even a moment.

The end of the ninety-sixth *sarga* of the *Yuddhakāṇḍa* of the *Śrī Rāmāyaṇa*.

Sarga 97

1. But then Mātali reminded Rāghava, "Why, hero, do you merely match him blow for blow, as if you knew no better?

2. "In order to kill him, my lord, you must unleash upon him the divinely charged weapon of Grandfather Brahmā. For the moment ordained by the gods for his destruction is now at hand."

3–13. Reminded by Mātali's words, Rāma took up a blazing arrow that, as he did so, made a hissing sound like that of a snake. Presented to him earlier by the powerful and blessed seer Agastya, it was a gift of Brahmā. It was a mighty arrow, unfailing in battle. Brahmā, whose power is immeasurable, had fashioned it long ago for the sake of Indra and had presented it to that lord of the gods, who was eager to conquer the three worlds. Pavana resided in its feathers. Agni, the purifier, and Sūrya, bringer of light, were in its arrowhead. Its shaft was made of all of space, and the mountains Meru and Mandara lent it their weight. Radiant with its splendor, beautifully fletched, and adorned with gold, it was fashioned with the blazing energy of all the elements, and it was as brilliant as Sūrya, bringer of light. It looked like the smoking fire at the end of a cosmic age and glistened like a venomous snake. It could instantaneously shatter hosts of chariots, elephants, and horses. It could shatter gateways, together with their iron beams, and even mountains. With its shaft drenched with the blood of many different creatures and smeared with their marrow, it was truly frightful. Hard as adamant and roaring deafeningly, it was terrifying in every sort of battle. Dreadful, hissing like a serpent, it inspired terror in all beings. It was fearsome and looked like Yama. In battle, it provided a never-ending supply of food to flocks of vultures and adjutant storks as well as *rākṣasas* and packs of jackals. Fletched with the various feathers of Garuḍa—beautiful and variegated—it brought joy to the monkey chiefs and despair to the *rākṣasas*. That ultimate arrow, which robbed one's enemies of their glory but brought joy to oneself, was to encompass the destruction of that menace to the Ikṣvākus and indeed to all the worlds.

14. Then immensely powerful and mighty Rāma consecrated that arrow with *mantras* and placed it on his bow in the manner prescribed by the science of archery.

15. Filled with fury toward Rāvaṇa and exerting himself to the utmost, he bent the bow fully and loosed that arrow, which struck at one's vital points.

16. As unstoppable as the *vajra* hurled by Indra, the *vajra* wielder, and as inescapable as fate, it fell upon Rāvaṇa's chest.

17. Loosed with tremendous force, that lethal arrow pierced evil-minded Rāvaṇa's heart.

18. Drenched with blood, the lethal arrow swiftly entered the earth, carrying off the life breaths of Rāvaṇa.

19. Once the arrow had accomplished its purpose in killing Rāvaṇa, it dutifully returned to its quiver, glistening with its still-wet blood.

20. Meanwhile, the bow and arrows of him who had been struck down so suddenly slipped from his grasp, along with his life breaths, as he lay dying.

21. Thus did the lord of the *rākṣasas*, sons of chaos, once so fearsome in his power and dazzling in his splendor, now tumble lifeless to the ground from his chariot, like Vṛtra struck down by Indra's *vajra*.

22. Seeing him fallen to the ground, the surviving night-roaming *rākṣasas*, their lord slain, fled, terrified, in all directions.

23. Meanwhile, the monkeys, armed with trees, seeing that Rāghava was victorious and that ten-necked Rāvaṇa had been slain, roared loudly and fell upon the *rākṣasas*.

24. Hard pressed by the jubilant monkeys, the *rākṣasas* fled in fear to Laṅkā, their piteous faces drenched with tears over the death of their protector.

25. Then the jubilant monkeys, with a victorious air, roared loudly, proclaiming Rāghava's victory and the death of Rāvaṇa.

26. The auspicious war drums of the thirty gods then resounded in the sky, and a pleasant breeze blew, wafting a divine fragrance.

27. An extraordinary and delightful shower of blossoms fell from the sky to the earth, covering Rāghava's chariot.

28. And from the great gods in heaven a magnificent shout, filled with the praise of Rāghava, was heard, "Excellent! Excellent!"

29. Now that fearsome Rāvaṇa, the terror of all the worlds, had been slain, great exultation filled the gods and celestial bards.

30. In slaying that bull among *rākṣasas*, Rāghava, delighted, had fulfilled the wishes of Sugrīva and immensely powerful Añgada.

31. The hosts of the Maruts regained tranquility. The directions were limpid, and the sky grew clear. The earth ceased its trembling, and the winds blew gently, while the sun, the bringer of day, shone with a steady light.

32. Then Rāghava's closest allies—Sugrīva, Vibhīṣaṇa, and the rest—together with Lakṣmaṇa, gathered around him, rejoicing in his victory and, with all due ceremony, paid homage to him who was so magnificent in battle.

33. Having thus slain his enemy, the immensely powerful hero, the delight of the king of the Raghu dynasty, proved true to his vow. Surrounded by his kinsman and his troops there on the field of battle, he looked as resplendent as Indra surrounded by the hosts of the thirty gods.

The end of the ninety-seventh *sarga* of the *Yuddhakāṇḍa* of the *Śrī Rāmāyaṇa*.

Sarga 98

1. Now, when the *rākṣasa* women heard that Rāvaṇa had been slain by great Rāghava, they rushed from the inner apartments, overwhelmed with grief.

2. Although many tried to restrain them, they rolled in the dust of the earth, their hair flying loose. They were as stricken with grief as cows whose calves have been butchered.

3. Together with the *rākṣasas* they poured out through the northern gate and entered the ghastly battlefield, searching for their slain lord.

4. Crying, "My husband!" "Alas, my lord!" on every side, they wandered about the battleground, which was strewn with headless trunks and thick with bloody mire.

5. Overcome with grief for their lord, their eyes filled with tears, they cried, shrieking like elephant cows when the leader of their herd is slain.

6. Then they saw Rāvaṇa lying slain on the ground. With his huge body, his tremendous strength, and his vast splendor, he resembled a mass of black collyrium.

7. When they suddenly spied their husband lying in the dust of the battlefield, they fell upon his limbs like forest creepers that have been cut down.

8. One of them embraced him in her devotion and wept. One clasped his feet, while yet another clung to his neck.

9. Raising her arms, one rolled on the ground. Seeing the face of her dead husband, yet another fainted.

10. One placed his head on her lap and, gazing on his face, wept, so that his face was bathed with tears, as is a lotus with dewdrops.

11. Thus anguished at seeing their lord Rāvaṇa lying slain on the ground, they keened in various ways in their grief and then began to lament once more.

12–13. "He who once terrorized Śakra and even Yama, he who robbed King Kubera Vaiśravaṇa of his flying palace Puṣpaka, and he who sowed tremendous fear among the *gandharvas*, seers, and the great gods, now lies slain in battle.

14. "He who knew no fear from the *asuras*, gods, or great serpents had much to fear from a mere human.

15. "He who was invulnerable to the gods, *dānavas*, and *rākṣasas* now lies on the battlefield, slain by a mere human fighting on foot.

16. "He whom neither the gods, the *yakṣas*, nor the *asuras* could kill has, like some feeble creature, been slain by a mere mortal."

17. Speaking in this fashion, Rāvaṇa's women wept copiously. Then, overcome by grief, they began once more to lament repeatedly.

18. "Since you consistently refused to heed the words of your friends, who advised you for your own good, all of us and you yourself have now been ruined all together.

19. "Although your dear brother Vibhīṣaṇa was speaking words that were beneficial to you, you, in your delusion, abused him cruelly, desiring, it appears, your own destruction.

20. "If only you had restored Sītā Maithilī to Rāma, this immense catastrophe, this total extermination, would not have befallen us.

21. "Your brother Vibhīṣaṇa would have had his wish fulfilled, and Rāma would have become an ally of our House. None of us would have been widowed, nor would your enemies have seen their wish fulfilled.

22. "But instead, in holding Sītā by force, cruel Rāvaṇa, you have destroyed the *rākṣasas*, us, and yourself, all three at the same time.

23. "Nonetheless, it is true, bull among *rākṣasas*, that this was not an action taken of your own free will. For it is fate that sets all things in motion. Whatever is destroyed, is destroyed by fate.

24. "And so the destruction in battle of the monkeys, the *rākṣasas*, and you yourself, great-armed warrior, occurred through the power of fate.

25. "For in this world the relentless march of fate cannot be stopped by wealth or act of will, by valor or by imperious command."

26. Thus did the wretched women of the *rākṣasa* lord lament, afflicted with grief, their eyes clouded with tears, shrieking like ospreys.

The end of the ninety-eighth *sarga* of the *Yuddhakāṇḍa* of the *Śrī Rāmāyaṇa*.

Sarga 99

1. Now even as the *rākṣasa* women were lamenting in this fashion, Rāvaṇa's beloved seniormost wife, Mandodarī, gazed on her husband in her sorrow.

2. And as pitiable Mandodarī gazed there upon her husband, ten-necked Rāvaṇa, who had been slain by Rāma of inconceivable deeds, she lamented.

3. "Surely, great-armed younger brother of Kubera Vaiśravaṇa, even Indra himself, the smasher of citadels, feared to stand before you when you were angry.

4. "And surely it was because of your power that the seers, the gods on earth, the illustrious *gandharvas*, and the celestial bards fled in all directions.

5. "Yet now you have been vanquished in battle by Rāma, a mere human. Are you not ashamed, your majesty? How could this be, bull among *rākṣasas*?

6. "How could a mere human, a wanderer in the wilderness, have slain you, who had conquered the three worlds, who was endowed with majesty and might, and whom no one could withstand?

7. "It makes no sense that Rāma could have slain you in battle—you who could wander in realms inaccessible to mere mortals and could take on any form at will.

8. "I do not believe that it was, in fact, Rāma who accomplished this feat in vanquishing you in the vanguard of the hosts when you were fully equipped for battle.

9. "Instead, it was your sensual appetites alone that vanquished you, since they recalled, as it were, your hostility when, long ago—before you conquered the three worlds—you subjugated your senses.

10. "Or perhaps it was Vāsava himself who came here in the form of Rāma, putting forth some unimaginable magical illusion in order to destroy you.

11. "For when in Janasthāna he killed your brother Khara, who was surrounded by many *rākṣasas*, it was clear right then that this was no mere human.

12. "And when, through his might, Hanumān entered the city of Laṅkā, which even the gods could not enter, we were all deeply shaken.

13. "When I told you, 'You should make peace with Rāghava,' you would not listen. And this is the result that has come of it.

14. "Unaccountably, bull among *rākṣasas*, you conceived this desire for Sītā, which has only led to the loss of your sovereignty, your kinsmen, and your life.

15. "You acted utterly improperly, you fool, when you assaulted Sītā, who is worthy of respect and who is superior even to Arundhatī and Rohiṇī.

16. "This Maithilī is in no way my superior or even my equal in breeding, beauty, or talent. But in your infatuation you did not realize this.

17. "No creature ever dies without a reason. In your case, then, your death has been brought about because of your treatment of Maithilī.

18. "Now Maithilī, free from all sorrow, will enjoy herself with Rāma, while I, a person of little merit that I am, have been plunged into a dreadful ocean of sorrow.

19–20. "I, who used to enjoy myself with you on Mount Kailāsa, Mount Mandara, Mount Meru, the Caitraratha Garden, and in all the gardens of the gods, traveling in unparalleled splendor in a flying chariot befitting our station, wearing marvelous garlands and garments, and gazing out upon the many different lands, have now, because of your death, hero, been robbed of the enjoyment of all pleasures.

21. "The destruction of the principal *rākṣasas*, which my illustrious brother-in-law Vibhīṣaṇa, a speaker of truth, foretold, has now come to pass.

22. "Through this catastrophe born of your lust and anger and characterized by your obsession, you have deprived the entire *rākṣasa* race of its protector.

23. "I really should not grieve for you, for you were a warrior famed for strength and manly valor. But still, because of the inherent nature of women, my heart is in a pitiable state.

24. "Taking with you both the good and the evil deeds you performed, you have gone to your proper destination. It is for myself that I grieve, miserable as I am, because of my separation from you.

25. "Resembling a black storm cloud, with your yellow garments and bright armlets, why do you lie here drenched in blood, splaying out all your limbs? I am overcome with sorrow. Why do you not answer me, as if you were asleep?

26. "Why do you not look at me, the granddaughter of an immensely powerful and skillful *yātudhāna* who never fled in battle.

27–28. "You always used to worship your iron club, adorned with a fretwork of gold and, with a radiance like that of the sun, as if it were the *vajra* of Indra, the wielder of the *vajra*. With it you used to slaughter your enemies in battle. But now that smasher of your foes in battle, shattered by arrows, lies scattered in a thousand pieces.

29. "Curse me whose heart, oppressed by sorrow, does not shatter into a thousand pieces now that you have returned to the five elements."

30. At this juncture, Rāma said to Vibhīṣaṇa, "Perform the funeral rites for your brother and send these women back."

31. When he had heard those words, Vibhīṣaṇa, who was deferential and understood righteousness, reflected and, in order to conform to Rāma's wishes, replied with words that were filled with righteousness and political sense.

32. "I cannot perform the funeral rites for someone who abandoned both righteousness and his vows, who was cruel, heartless, and untruthful, and who assaulted the wives of others.

33. "Ever intent on injuring all creatures, he was my enemy in the form of a brother. So, although he should be respected because of the deference one owes to one's elders, still Rāvaṇa does not merit respect.

34. "In this world, people will say I am heartless, Rāma, but once they hear about his qualities, they will all say that I acted properly."

35. Upon hearing that, Rāma, foremost of those who upheld righteousness, was greatly pleased, and, skilled in speech, he said this to Vibhīṣaṇa, who was similarly expert in speech:

36. "I really ought to do what pleases you, since it was through your might that I have been victorious. Nonetheless, I must address you with regard to what is proper, lord of the *rākṣasas*.

37. "Granted, the night-roaming *rākṣasa* was given to unrighteousness and untruthfulness. Nonetheless, he was always a powerful and energetic hero in battle.

38. "Rāvaṇa, who made the worlds cry out, was a great hero, endowed with might. One never heard that the gods, led by Indra of the hundred sacrifices, ever defeated him.

39. "But hostilities cease with death. Our purpose has been accomplished. You may now perform his funeral rites, for as he was to you, so he is to me.

40. "For he deserves a quick and proper funeral at your hands, great-armed knower of righteousness. Thus, you will reap glory."

41. Having heard Rāghava's words, Vibhīṣaṇa, hastening, provided Rāvaṇa with a fitting funeral.

42. Vibhīṣaṇa then cremated him according to the prescriptions of the ritual texts. Then, speaking soothing words again and again, he consoled the women.

43. And then, once all the *rākṣasa* women had gone back, Vibhīṣaṇa came to Rāma's side and stood there humbly.

44. Then, having slain his mortal enemy, Rāma, together with his army, Sugrīva, and Lakṣmaṇa, attained as much delight as did Indra of the hundred sacrifices after slaying Vṛtra.

The end of the ninety-ninth *sarga* of the *Yuddhakāṇḍa* of the *Śrī Rāmāyaṇa*.

Sarga 100

1. When the gods, *gandharvas*, and *dānavas* had witnessed the slaying of Rāvaṇa, they departed, each in his own flying chariot, proclaiming those auspicious events.

2–3. Proclaiming the frightful slaying of Rāvaṇa, the valor of Rāghava, the brave fighting of the monkeys, the counsel of Sugrīva, and the devotion and heroism of Lakṣmaṇa Saumitri, those noble beings, in great delight, departed as they had come.

4. But as for noble Rāghava, he released the celestial chariot, radiant as fire, that Indra had loaned him and paid homage to Mātali.

5. Granted leave by Rāghava, Mātali, the charioteer of Śakra, mounted that celestial chariot and ascended into the sky.

6. Once that foremost of the charioteers of the gods had ascended into the sky, Rāghava embraced Sugrīva with the greatest delight.

7. After embracing Sugrīva, he returned to the army's encampment, reverently saluted by Lakṣmaṇa and honored by the foremost of the tawny monkeys.

8. And then Rāma spoke to mighty Lakṣmaṇa Saumitri, of blazing energy, who stood beside him:

9. "Gentle brother, you must consecrate Vibhīṣaṇa in the kingship of Laṅkā, for he has been loyal and devoted and has rendered me great assistance.

10. "For this is my most cherished desire, gentle brother: that I should see Rāvaṇa's younger brother Vibhīṣaṇa consecrated in the kingship of Laṅkā."

11. Addressed in this fashion by great Rāghava, Saumitri replied, "So be it," and, greatly delighted, he brought a golden vessel.

12. Then, in the midst of the *rākṣasas*, at Rāma's command, Saumitri used that vessel to consecrate Vibhīṣaṇa as king in Laṅkā.

13. Thus did that righteous hero consecrate pure-minded Vibhīṣaṇa, while the latter's ministers and those *rākṣasas* who were devoted to him rejoiced.

14. Upon seeing the lord of the *rākṣasas*, Vibhīṣaṇa, consecrated in the kingship of Laṅkā, Rāghava, together with Lakṣmaṇa, experienced the greatest delight.

15. When he had received that great kingdom, which Rāma had conferred upon him, Vibhīṣaṇa comforted his people and then approached Rāma.

16. In great delight, the night-roaming *rākṣasas* of the city then brought unhusked rice, sweetmeats, parched grain, and celestial flowers for him.

17. When he had received all those auspicious offerings, the unassailable and mighty hero presented them in an auspicious fashion to Rāghava and Lakṣmaṇa.

18. And Rāma, seeing that Vibhīṣaṇa had accomplished his purpose and was now endowed with prosperity, accepted it all, merely out of a desire to please him.

19. Rāghava then spoke these words to the leaping monkey, mighty Hanumān, as huge as a mountain, who stood beside him, his hands cupped in reverence:

20–21. "My gentle friend, after obtaining permission of the great king Vibhīṣaṇa, you must enter Rāvaṇa's palace. Once there, foremost among the victorious, you are to humbly approach Vaidehī and inform her that Sugrīva, Lakṣmaṇa, and I are well, and that I have slain Rāvaṇa.

22. "Lord of the tawny monkeys, once you have related the good news to Maithilī, please take a message from her and return."

The end of the one hundredth *sarga* of the *Yuddhakāṇḍa* of the *Śrī Rāmāyaṇa*.

Sarga 101

1. Instructed in this fashion and honored by the night-roaming *rākṣasas,* Hanuman, son of Māruta, entered the city of Laṅkā.

2. Entering Rāvaṇa's palace, that hero of immense blazing energy spied Sītā, who resembled the constellation Rohiṇī cut off from her lord, the hare-marked moon, and occluded by a malevolent planet.

3. Modest, humble, and deferential, he approached her, greeted her respectfully, and began to tell her everything that Rāma had said:

4. "Rāma is quite well, Vaidehī, as are Sugrīva and Lakṣmaṇa. Having slain his foe and having thus accomplished his purpose, that tamer of his enemies inquires after your well-being.

5. "With Vibhīṣaṇa as his ally and together with the tawny monkeys, Rāma, through the wise counsel of Lakṣmaṇa, has slain Rāvaṇa, O queen.

6. "Inquiring as to your well-being, the mighty hero Rāma, delight of the Raghus, greatly delighted, his heart having achieved its purpose, now says this to you:

7. " 'I bring you this good news, my lady, and once again I offer you my respectful salutations. Thank god, O knower of righteousness, you have survived by virtue of my victory in battle.

8. " 'We have gained victory, Sītā. You may now be at ease and free from care. My enemy Rāvaṇa has been slain, and Laṅkā is under my control.

9. " 'With grim determination to win you back, without pause even for sleep, I built a bridge across the mighty ocean and thus fulfilled my vow.

10. " 'Nor should you have any further anxiety about staying in Rāvaṇa's palace, for the lordship of Laṅkā has now been made over to Vibhīṣaṇa.

11. " 'So, trusting in that, be comforted. For now you are living in your own home, as it were. Moreover, in great delight, he is on his way, eager to see you.' "

12. Addressed in this fashion, Sītā, whose face was like the hare-marked moon, sprang to her feet, speechless with joy.

13. Since Sītā did not reply, that foremost of the tawny monkeys said, "What are you worried about, O queen? Why do you not speak to me?"

14. Addressed in this fashion by Hanumān, Sītā, so firmly grounded in righteousness, replied in the greatest delight with a voice that was choked with joy.

15. "When I heard the wonderful news concerning my husband's victory, I was overwhelmed with joy and momentarily speechless.

16. "Even upon reflection, leaping monkey, I can think of no adequate response to you who have brought me this wonderful news.

17. "Nor, gentle monkey, can I think of anything on this earth to give you for reporting this news—so wonderful for me—that would be fitting and adequate.

18. "Neither gold nor silver, various gems, or even the kingship over the three worlds can be said to equal this."

19. Addressed in this fashion by Sītā Vaidehī, the leaping monkey cupped his hands in reverence and, standing before her, replied with these words:

20. "You alone are capable of speaking such affectionate words, you who are so devoted to your husband's welfare and have longed so for his victory.

21. "Indeed, these words of yours, gentle lady, so affectionate and full of meaning, are more precious to me than a heap of all kinds of jewels or even the kingship of the gods.

22. "In that I see Rāma still standing after having slain his enemy and gained victory, I have truly already attained those treasured things, such as the kingship of the gods, and the like.

23. "However, if you permit me, I should like to kill all these *rākṣasa* women who previously threatened you.

24–25. "Please grant me this wish. These cruel and horrible *rākṣasa* women with their dreadful rumors, their fierce glances, and terrifying threats, tormented you, who are so devoted to your husband, when you were suffering in the *aśoka* grove. I would really like to slaughter them with different types of blows.

*26–28. "Illustrious and lovely queen, these creatures have done you such injury. I would like to slaughter them with punches, slaps, kicks, fearsome blows of the knees, slashes of my fangs, biting off their ears and noses, tearing out their hair, violent clawing, dreadful flying kicks, and many more of these kinds of assaults."

29. Addressed in this fashion by Hanumān, the illustrious Vaidehī, daughter of Janaka, responded to him in words that were in keeping with righteousness.

30. "Who, foremost of monkeys, could be angry at servant women, for, as mere functionaries and dependent on the king, they are obedient and act only on the orders of another.

31. "It is as a consequence of my evil destiny and my own misdeeds in the past that I have suffered all of this. For one always experiences the fruits of one's actions.

32. "I have concluded that I had to suffer this as a consequence of my fate, and, being helpless, I had to endure all of this here at the hands of Rāvaṇa's servant women.

33. "These *rākṣasa* women tormented me only on the orders of Rāvaṇa. Now that he has been slain, foremost of monkeys, they will not torment me anymore.

34. "There is an ancient verse in keeping with righteousness that a bear once recited in the presence of a tiger. Hear it now from me, leaping monkey.

35. " 'A superior person never requites evil on the part of evildoers with evil.' This rule of conduct must always be adhered to. For good conduct is the ornament of the virtuous.

36. "A noble person must act compassionately whether people are wicked, virtuous, or even if deserving of death. For, leaping monkey, no one is entirely innocent.

37. "One should not harm the *rākṣasas*, who can take on any form at will and take pleasure in injuring people, even when they do evil."

38. When he was addressed in this fashion by Rāma's illustrious wife, Sītā, eloquent Hanumān replied to her:

39. "You are a fitting, illustrious, and righteous wife to Rāma. Please give me your return message, queen, and I shall go to where Rāghava is."

40. When Vaidehī, Janaka's daughter, had been addressed in this fashion, she said, "Foremost of monkeys, I wish to see my husband."

41. When Hanumān, son of Pavana, had heard those words of hers, that immensely splendid hero said these words, lifting Maithilī's spirits:

42. "Noble lady, just as the goddess Śacī gazes upon Indra, lord of the thirty gods, you shall gaze upon Rāma, whose face is like the full moon, whose allies are staunch, whose enemies have been slain, and who is accompanied by Lakṣmaṇa."

43. When he had spoken in this fashion to Sītā, who was as radiant as Śrī incarnate, the immensely swift Hanumān returned to where Rāghava waited.

The end of the one hundred first *sarga* of the *Yuddhakāṇḍa* of the *Śrī Rāmāyaṇa*.

Sarga 102

1. Approaching the exceedingly wise Rāma, foremost of all bowmen, the leaping monkey, who understood the matter at hand, addressed him with these words:

2. "Now you really must see Queen Maithilī, who has been tormented with grief, she on whose account we undertook this entire mission and achieved the culmination of our efforts.

3. "For Maithilī, who had been overwhelmed with grief, her eyes brimming with tears, was filled with joy upon hearing of your victory.

4. "Since she trusted me because of the confidence I had earlier inspired in her, she said to me, 'I desire to see my husband, who, together with Lakṣmaṇa, has accomplished his purpose.' "

*5. Addressed in this fashion by Hanumān, Rāma, foremost among upholders of righteousness, was suddenly plunged into gloomy thought and became somewhat tearful.

6. Heaving long, hot sighs and staring at the ground, he spoke to Vibhīṣaṇa, who stood beside him, looking like a great storm cloud:

*7. "Have Sītā Vaidehī come here anointed with celestial unguents, adorned with celestial ornaments, her hair freshly washed. Make haste!"

8. Addressed in this fashion by Rāma, Vibhīṣaṇa, hurrying, entered the inner apartments and there had his own wives instruct Sītā in these words:

9. "Vaidehī, anointed with celestial unguents and adorned with celestial ornaments, you are to mount a carriage. For, bless you, your husband desires to see you."

10. Addressed in this fashion, Vaidehī replied to Vibhīṣaṇa, "But I wish to see my husband without having bathed, lord of the *rākṣasas*."

11. When Vibhīṣaṇa heard those words of hers, he replied, "You should do exactly as your husband, Rāma, says."

12. Upon hearing those words of his, virtuous Maithilī, whose husband was her god and whose vow was devotion to him, responded, "So be it."

13–14. Young women then washed her hair and adorned her with costly garments and ornaments. Then Vibhīṣaṇa took Sītā with him, after having had her mount a shining palanquin that was draped in costly fabrics and guarded by many *rākṣasas*.

15. Approaching the great man and noting that he was lost in brooding thought, he bowed and, in great delight, announced that Sītā had come.

16. But when Rāghava heard that she who had dwelt so long in the *rākṣasa*'s house had come, three emotions—joy, sorrow, and anger—took hold of him.

17. Then, perceiving that Vibhīṣaṇa now stood beside him, Rāghava, miserable and debating inwardly, spoke to him:

18. "Gentle lord of the *rākṣasas*, ever dedicated to my victory, please bring Vaidehī to me at once."

19. Heeding those words of Rāghava, Vibhīṣaṇa quickly made an effort to have the area cleared on every side.

20. Guards, wearing mail and turbans and holding staves and drums in their hands, began to move about there, clearing the area on every side.

21. Then, being driven back on every side, the crowds of apes, monkeys, and *rākṣasas* withdrew to a distance.

22. And as they were all being driven back, there arose a sound like the roar of the ocean being whipped up by a gale.

23. But when Rāghava saw them being driven back in great agitation on all sides, he stopped it out of kindness and because he could not abide it.

24. Furious, Rāma spoke reproachful words to the immensely wise Vibhīṣaṇa, seeming almost to burn him up with his eyes:

25. "Why are you harassing these people with complete disregard for my wishes? Stop this business at once. These people are like my own kin.

26. "It is not houses, garments, high walls, curtains, or such royal treatment as this that shields a woman; it is her virtuous conduct alone.

27. "Moreover, there is nothing wrong with a woman being seen in public during emergencies, periods of hardship, in time of war, at a ceremony of choosing her husband, during a sacrifice, or at a wedding ceremony.

28. "She has been through a war and has been placed in tremendous hardship. Therefore, there would be nothing wrong in her being seen publicly, especially in my company.

29. "So bring her into my presence at once, Vibhīṣaṇa. Let Sītā see me surrounded by the hosts of my friends."

30. Addressed in this fashion by Rāma, Vibhīṣaṇa, reflecting on all of this, obediently led Sītā into his presence.

31. And as for Lakṣmaṇa, Sugrīva, and the leaping monkey Hanumān, they, too, became deeply troubled upon hearing Rāma's words.

32. Because of his demeanor that was so pitiless and seemed to show no regard for his wife, they inferred that Rāghava was displeased with Sītā.

33. Trying to make her body appear small in her shame, Maithilī, followed by Vibhīṣaṇa, approached her husband.

34. Covering her face with her garment in her shame there before the assembled people, she wept as she came near her husband, murmuring, "My noble husband."

35. She whose husband was her divinity and whose face was more radiant than the moon gazed upon the moonlike face of her husband with amazement, joy, and love.

36. Then, gazing upon her beloved's face, which she had not seen for so long and which was as lovely as the full moon rising, she shed her depression of spirit and her face became as radiant as the hare-marked moon.

The end of the one hundred second *sarga* of the *Yuddhakāṇḍa* of the *Śrī Rāmāyaṇa*.

Sarga 103

1. As he gazed upon Maithilī, who stood so meekly beside him, Rāma began to speak, as rage simmered in his heart:

2. "So here you are, my good woman. I have won you back after conquering my enemy in battle. Whatever there was to be done through manly valor, I have now accomplished.

3. "I have wiped clean the affront, and so my wrath is appeased. For I have eliminated both the insult and my enemy at the same time.

4. "Today my manly valor has been witnessed. Today my efforts have borne fruit. Today, having fulfilled my vow here, I am once more master of myself.

5. "You were carried off by that wanton *rākṣasa* when you were left alone, but now, through manly action, I have expunged that affront brought about by fate.

6. "What human purpose can man serve if his spirit is so feeble that he will not wipe clean through his own blazing energy an insult he has received?

7. "The leaping of the ocean and the razing of Laṅkā—today those praiseworthy deeds of Hanumān have borne fruit.

8. "Today, through their valor in battle and their beneficial counsel to me, the efforts of Sugrīva and his army have borne fruit as well.

9. "And the efforts of my devoted Vibhīṣaṇa, who abandoned his evil brother and came to me of his own accord, have likewise borne fruit."

10. As Rāma was saying these words in that fashion, Sītā, wide-eyed like a doe, was overcome with tears.

11. But as Rāma gazed upon her, his anger flared up once more, like the raging flame of a blazing fire drenched with melted butter.

12. Knitting his brows on his forehead and glancing at her from the corner of his eye, he spoke harshly to Sītā there in the midst of the monkeys and *rākṣasas*.

13–14. "In wiping away this affront, Sītā, I have accomplished all that a man could do. In my wrath, I have won you back from the hands of my enemy, just as, through his austerities, the contemplative sage Agastya won back the southern lands that had been inaccessible to all living beings.

15. "Bless you, but let it be understood that it was not on your account that I undertook the effort of this war, now brought to completion through the valor of my allies.

16. "Instead, I did all this in order to protect my reputation and in every way to wipe clean the insult and disgrace to my illustrious lineage.

17. "Since, however, your virtue is now in doubt, your presence has become as profoundly disagreeable to me as is a bright lamp to a man afflicted with a disease of the eye.

18. "Go, therefore, as you please, daughter of Janaka. You have my permission. Here are the ten directions. I have no further use for you, my good woman.

19. "For what powerful man born in a respectable family—his heart tinged with affection—would take back a woman who had lived in the house of another man?

20. "How could I who boast of my noble lineage possibly take you back—just risen from Rāvaṇa's lap and gazed upon by his lustful eye?

21. "I have recovered my reputation, and that is the purpose for which I won you back. I do not love you anymore. Go hence wherever you like.

22. "I have made up my mind in saying this, my good woman. Turn your thoughts toward Lakṣmaṇa or Bharata as you please.

23. "Or, Sītā, set your mind on Sugrīva, lord of the monkeys, or on the *rākṣasa* lord Vibhīṣaṇa, or on whomever you please.

24. "For surely, Sītā, once Rāvaṇa had seen you, so enchanting with your heavenly beauty, he would not long have left you unmolested while you were dwelling in his house."

25. When Maithilī, who deserved to hear only kind words, had heard those cruel words of her beloved after such a long time, she shed tears and trembled violently, like a *vallarī* creeper struck down by the trunk of an elephant lord.

The end of the one hundred third *sarga* of the *Yuddhakāṇḍa* of the *Śrī Rāmāyaṇa*.

Sarga 104

1. When Vaidehī was addressed in this cruel and horrifying manner by the furious Rāghava, she was deeply wounded.

2. Hearing those cutting words of her husband—words such as she had never heard before—in the presence of that great multitude, Maithilī was overcome with shame.

3. Pierced, as it were, by those verbal barbs, the daughter of Janaka seemed to shrink within herself and gave way to bitter tears.

4. Wiping her tear-stained face, she replied softly to her husband in a faltering voice:

5. "How can you, heroic prince, speak to me with such cutting and improper words, painful to the ears, as some vulgar man might speak to his vulgar wife?

6. "I am not as you think of me, great-armed prince. You must believe in me, for I swear to you by my own virtue.

7. "You harbor suspicion against all women because of the conduct of the vulgar ones. If you really knew me, you would abandon your suspicion.

8. "If I came into contact with another's body against my will, lord, I had no choice in this matter. It is fate that was to blame here.

9. "My heart, which I do control, was always devoted to you. But I could not control my body, which was in the power of another. What could I have done?

10. "If, my love, you do not truly know me despite our long-nurtured love and intimacy, then surely I am lost forever.

11. "When you dispatched the hero Hanumān to search for me, why, heroic prince, did you not repudiate me then, while I was still being held in Laṅkā?

12. "No sooner had I heard your words to that effect, heroic prince, than, abandoned by you, I would have abandoned my own life right before the eyes of that monkey lord.

13. "Then you would not have had to risk your life in a useless effort nor would your allies have had to suffer hardship to no purpose.

14. "But now, tiger among men, you have given way to anger like some lesser man, taking into account only that I am a woman.

15. "Since my name is derived from Janaka, you failed to take into account the fact that I was born from the earth itself, nor, though you are an expert judge of conduct, have you given due consideration to my virtuous conduct.

16. "Moreover, you do not weigh the fact that, as a boy, you firmly clasped my hand while I was but a child. My devotion, my virtuous conduct—you have turned your back on all of that."

17. As she was speaking in this fashion, Sītā turned, weeping, to Lakṣmaṇa, who stood there, despondent and brooding. Then she spoke, her voice choked with tears.

18. "Build me a pyre, Saumitri, the only remedy for this calamity. I cannot bear to live tainted by these false allegations.

19. "Rejected in this public gathering by my husband, who is not satisfied with my virtues, I shall enter the fire, bearer of oblations, so that I may follow the only path proper for me."

20. When Lakṣmaṇa, slayer of enemy heroes, had been addressed in this fashion by Vaidehī, he was overcome with anger and closely studied Rāghava's face.

21. But, sensing Rāma's intentions, which were betrayed by his facial expression, mighty Saumitri, obedient to Rāma's wishes, built the pyre.

22. Then Vaidehī slowly and reverently circumambulated Rāma, whose face was downcast, and approached the blazing fire, eater of oblations.

23. After making her obeisance to the gods and the brahmans, Maithilī cupped her hands in reverence and, in the presence of Agni, said this:

24. "Since my heart has never once strayed from Rāghava, so may Agni, the purifier, witness of all the world, protect me in every way."

25. When she had spoken in this fashion, Vaidehī reverently circumambulated the fire, eater of oblations. Then, with complete detachment, she entered the blazing flames.

26. The vast crowd assembled there, filled with children and the aged, watched as Maithilī entered the fire, eater of oblations.

27. As Sītā entered the fire, a deafening and prodigious cry of "Alas! Alas!" arose from the *rākṣasas* and monkeys.

The end of the one hundred fourth *sarga* of the *Yuddhakāṇḍa* of the *Śrī Rāmāyaṇa*.

Sarga 105

1–3. Then King Kubera Vaiśravaṇa; Yama, dragger of his foes; great Indra of the thousand eyes; Varuṇa, scorcher of his foes; the great god, majestic Śiva, with his half-six eyes and the bull on his banner; and Brahmā, foremost of those who know the *vedas*, the creator of the entire universe—all these assembled in their flying chariots as radiant as the sun, and, coming to the city of Laṅkā, they approached Rāghava.

4. Then, raising their broad arms covered with bracelets, the foremost of the thirty gods addressed Rāghava, who stood before them, his hands cupped in reverence.

5. "How can you, the creator of the entire universe, the most ancient one, and foremost among those possessing supreme knowledge,

stand by and watch as Sītā falls into the fire, eater of oblations? How can you not realize that you are the foremost among the hosts of the gods?

6. "Long ago, you were the Vasu Ṛtadhāman, the progenitor of the Vasus. You are the primal creator of the three worlds, the untrammeled lord.

7. "You are Rudra, the eighth among the Rudras, and you are fifth among the *sādhyas*. The twin Aśvins are your ears, the moon and the sun your eyes.

8. "You are present before the beginning and after the end of the worlds, scorcher of your foes. And yet, like some ordinary man, you ignore Vaidehī."

9. When Rāma Rāghava, the lord of the world, was addressed in this fashion by those guardians of the world, that foremost of those who uphold righteousness said to the foremost of the thirty gods:

10. "I think of myself only as a man, Rāma, the son of Daśaratha. May the Blessed Lord please tell me who I really am, to whom I belong, and why I am here."

11. As Kākutstha was speaking in this fashion, Brahmā, foremost among those who know the *vedas*, said to him: "Truly valorous Rāma, now hear the truth from me.

12. "You are a god, the majestic Lord Nārāyaṇa, wielder of the discus. You are the single-tusked boar and the conqueror of your enemies, past and future.

13. "You are the imperishable Brahman, existent in the beginning, the middle, and the end. You are the highest governing principal of all the worlds, the four-armed Viṣvaksena.

14. "You are the wielder of the horn bow, you are Hṛṣīkeśa, the primal person, the Supreme Spirit. You are Viṣṇu, the invincible wielder of the sword, and you are Kṛṣṇa of immense strength.

15. "You are the leader of the hosts. You are the leader of all beings. You are intelligence, strength, forbearance, and self-control. You are the origin and the dissolution. You are Upendra, Indra's younger brother, and Madhusūdana, slayer of the *asura* Madhu.

16. "You are the author of Indra's deeds. You are the lord of the great gods. You are the lotus-naveled god. You are the destroyer of your enemies in battle. The divine great seers call you fit for refuge and refuge itself.

17. "You are the great bull of a thousand horns and a hundred tongues that is the *veda* itself. You are the sacrifice, the sacred utterance *vaṣaṭ*, and the sacred syllable *oṃ*, scorcher of your foes.

18. "No one knows your origin or your end. People wonder, 'Who are you?' You are manifest in all creatures—especially brahmans and cows—and also in all the directions, the sky, the mountains, and the forests.

19. "You are the majestic Lord of a thousand feet, a thousand heads, and a thousand eyes. You support all beings as well as the earth with all its mountains.

20. "At the end of the world, you manifest yourself resting on the great serpent on the waters. You support the three worlds, Rāma, along with the gods, *gandharvas*, and *dānavas*.

21. "I am your heart, Rāma, your tongue is the goddess Sarasvatī. It is I, Brahmā, O Lord, who made the gods, who are the hairs on your limbs.

22. "When you close your eyes, it is night; when you open them, it is day. Your ritual practices are the ordinances of the *vedas*. Without you, there is nothing.

23. "Your body is this world; your steadfastness, the earth. Agni is your wrath; Soma, your gentleness, O bearer of the Śrīvatsa mark.

24. "In ancient times, you spanned the three worlds with as many strides. After confining the great *asura* Bali, you made great Indra king.

25. "Sītā is Lakṣmī; you are the god Viṣṇu. You are Kṛṣṇa. You are Prajāpati, the lord of creatures. It was in order to slay Rāvaṇa that you entered a human body here.

26. "Thus have you accomplished our purpose, foremost of upholders of righteousness. Rāvaṇa has been slain. Now, Rāma, in your delight, please return to heaven.

27. "Your strength and might have not been in vain, nor has your valor. Nor will men who are devoted to you ever fail of their purpose.

28. "You are the ancient god and Supreme Spirit. Those who are firmly devoted to you and those men who praise you will never fail in any way."

The end of the one hundred fifth *sarga* of the *Yuddhakāṇḍa* of the *Śrī Rāmāyaṇa*.

Sarga 106

1. Upon hearing that auspicious speech uttered by Grandfather Brahmā, Agni, the shining god of fire, arose, holding Vaidehī at his side.

2–3. Adorned with ornaments of burnished gold and clad in a red garment, the young woman was as radiant as the rising sun. Her hair was dark and curling and her garland and ornaments were unsinged. Her mind was calm and she looked unchanged. Holding Vaidehī at his side, Agni, the shining god of fire, gave her back to Rāma.

4. Then Agni, the purifier and witness of all the world, spoke to Rāma, saying, "Here is your Vaidehī, Rāma. She has committed no sin.

5. "She is of pure conduct and high moral character and has never betrayed you by word, thought, imagination, or glance.

6. "When you left her alone, she was carried off—helpless and sorrowful—from the deserted forest by the *rākṣasa* Rāvaṇa, arrogant in his power.

7. "Hidden and imprisoned in the inner apartments, thinking only of you and having you for her only recourse, she was guarded by hordes of hideous *rākṣasa* women, dreadful to behold.

8. "Although she was enticed and threatened in various ways, Maithilī would not even think of the *rākṣasa*, since her heart was utterly devoted to you.

9. "You must take her back, Rāghava, for her heart is pure and she is free from sin. I am giving you an order; there is nothing further to be said."

10. When Rāma, of immense blazing energy, steadfast and firm in his valor, had been addressed in this fashion, that foremost of those who maintain righteousness replied to that most eminent among the thirty gods:

11. "Unquestionably Sītā needed to be proven innocent before the three worlds, since this auspicious woman had long dwelt in Rāvaṇa's inner apartments.

12. "For surely had I not put Jānakī to the test, the virtuous would have said of me, 'Daśaratha's son Rāma is a lustful fool.'

13. "I know full well that Janaka's daughter Maithilī could give her heart to no other, since she is devoted to me and obeys my every thought.

14. "But in order that the three worlds, too, should have faith in her, I, whose ultimate recourse is truth, simply stood by as Vaidehī entered the fire, eater of oblations.

15. "Rāvaṇa could no more have violated that wide-eyed lady, protected by her own blazing energy, than could the mighty ocean violate its shore.

16. "That evil-minded wretch was incapable of assaulting Maithilī, even in his thoughts. For she is as unapproachable as a blazing flame of fire.

17. "This auspicious woman could never have ruled over Rāvaṇa's inner apartments. For she is as inseparable from me as is its radiance from the sun, bringer of light.

18. "Janaka's daughter Maithilī has been proven innocent before the three worlds, and I am no more able to give her up than is a self-controlled man, his good name.

19. "Moreover, I must follow the good advice that all of you affectionate friends, respected throughout the worlds, have uttered in this fashion for my own good."

20. When he had uttered these words, mighty Rāma, praised by his mighty companions for the feat he had accomplished, was reunited with his beloved. Then Rāghava experienced the happiness he so richly deserved.

The end of the one hundred sixth *sarga* of the *Yuddhakāṇḍa* of the *Śrī Rāmāyaṇa*.

Sarga 107

1. Upon hearing that auspicious speech so beautifully spoken by Rāghava, Maheśvara responded with these still more auspicious words:

2. "Lotus-eyed, great-armed, broad-chested scorcher of your foes! Foremost of weapon bearers! Thank heavens you have accomplished this feat.

3. "Thank heavens, Rāma, you have dispelled in battle the vast and terrible darkness in the form of the fear of Rāvaṇa that had engulfed the entire world.

4–6. "You must now console despondent Bharata and the illustrious Kausalyā and see Kaikeyī and Lakṣmaṇa's mother, Sumitrā. You must assume the kingship of Ayodhyā and reward all your allies. Then, mighty hero, you must establish a lineage in the House of the Ikṣvākus. At last, once you have offered the Horse Sacrifice and attained unsurpassed glory, you should give away your wealth to the brahmans and ascend to the triple heaven.

7. "And here, Kākutstha, in his flying chariot, is your father, King Daśaratha, who, in the world of men, was your illustrious elder.

8. "Saved by you, his son, the majestic king has attained the world of Indra. Together with Lakṣmaṇa, you must now respectfully salute him."

9. Upon hearing these words of the great god Śiva, Kākutstha, together with Lakṣmaṇa, made obeisance to his father, who stood atop his flying chariot.

10. Then the lord, together with his brother Lakṣmaṇa, gazed upon his father, who was clad in a spotless garment and was blazing with his own innate splendor.

11–12. Filled with the greatest joy, the lord of the earth, Daśaratha, mounted on his flying chariot, gazed upon his son, who was dearer to him than life itself. Then, seated on a splendid throne, the great-armed lord took him on his lap and, taking him in his arms, said these words:

13. "I swear to you truthfully, Rāma, that without you I care nothing for heaven and the esteem of the divine seers.

14. "And, most eloquent of men, those words that Kaikeyī uttered regarding your banishment were still rankling in my heart.

15. "But today, seeing that you are safe and sound and having embraced you and Lakṣmaṇa, I have been freed from my sorrow, like the sun, maker of day, emerging from a dense fog.

16. "My son, you, an excellent son and a great man, have saved me, just as a righteous brahman was saved by Aṣṭāvakra.

17. "I now realize, my gentle son, that you are the Supreme Spirit, who was enjoined by the lords of the gods to slay Rāvaṇa.

18. "Surely, Rāma, Kausalyā will have achieved her most cherished desire when, in delight, she sees that you, slayer of your enemies, have returned home from the wilderness.

19. "And just as surely, Rāma, will the people have achieved their most cherished desire when they see that you have returned to the city and, dripping with water, have been consecrated as lord of the earth, bearer of wealth.

20. "I only wish that I could see you reunited with devoted, powerful, honest, and righteous Bharata.

21. "My gentle son, you have spent fourteen years in the wilderness living with Sītā and wise Lakṣmaṇa.

22. "You have completed your sojourn in the forest and have thus fulfilled your vow. Moreover, having slain Rāvaṇa in battle, you have gratified the gods.

23. "You have performed a praiseworthy feat and gained renown, slayer of your foes. Now, established in the kingship, may you attain long life, together with your brothers."

24. As the king was speaking in this fashion, Rāma, cupping his hands in reverence, said this to him: "O you who understand righteousness, please extend your grace to Kaikeyī and Bharata.

25. "And may that terrible curse that you invoked when you told Kaikeyī, 'I renounce both you and your son,' not be visited upon Kaikeyī and her son, Lord."

26. The great king said, "So be it," to Rāma, who stood there with his hands cupped in reverence. Then, embracing Lakṣmaṇa, he now spoke to him in these words:

27. "In devotedly serving Rāma as well as Sītā Vaidehī, you have given me the greatest pleasure and attained the fruit of your righteousness.

28. "And since Rāma is pleased with you, O you who know righteousness, you will attain righteousness, great renown on earth, heaven, and everlasting glory.

29. "Bless you, increaser of Sumitrā's joy, you must serve Rāma. For Rāma is perpetually devoted to the welfare of all the world.

30. "All these gods, including Indra, along with the three worlds, the perfected beings, and the supreme seers, have approached him, the great Supreme Spirit, and are worshiping him.

31. "Rāma, scorcher of his foes, has been revealed by them, my gentle son, to be Brahman, the unmanifest and imperishable Supreme Spirit, the secret heart of the gods.

32. "Devotedly serving Rāma as well as Sītā Vaidehī, you have attained righteousness and immense glory."

33. When he had spoken in this fashion to Lakṣmaṇa, who stood with his hands cupped in reverence, the righteous and great-armed king then said these splendid words to Vaidehī:

34. "You should not be angry over this repudiation, Vaidehī. Wishing only what is best for you, Rāma did this to demonstrate your purity.

35. "Fair-browed woman, you do not need to be instructed with regard to your obedience to your husband. Nonetheless, it is necessary for me to tell you that he is your highest divinity."

36. When radiant Daśaratha had instructed his two sons and his daughter-in-law Sītā in this fashion, he proceeded in his flying chariot to Indra's world.

The end of the one hundred seventh *sarga* of the *Yuddhakāṇḍa* of the *Śrī Rāmāyaṇa*.

Sarga 108

1. When Daśaratha Kākutstha had departed, great Indra, the chastiser of Pāka, spoke in the greatest delight to Rāghava, who stood with his hands cupped in reverence:

2. "Rāma, scorcher of your foes! Your seeing us should not be without its reward. I am pleased, and therefore you must say what your heart desires."

3. Addressed in this fashion, Kākutstha, together with his brother Lakṣmaṇa and his wife, Sītā, cupped his hands in reverence and replied:

4. "If you are truly pleased with me, lord of all the gods, I will tell you. Please make my words prove true, foremost among the eloquent.

5. "May all those valorous monkeys who, for my sake, have gone to the abode of Yama rise up, restored to life.

6. "Let them, who were devoted to my service and heedless of death, be reunited through your grace. This is the boon I choose.

7. "Humbler of pride, I wish to see the langurs and apes free from their pain and their wounds and filled once more with strength and vigor.

8. "May there always be choice roots and fruits, even out of season, and may the rivers run clear wherever those monkeys may dwell."

9. When great Indra had heard those words of great Rāghava, he responded with these words, which manifested his pleasure:

10. "This is a major boon that you have requested, my son, delight of the Raghus. But these tawny monkeys shall arise, just like sleepers when their sleep is done.

11. "Filled with the greatest joy, they will all be reunited with their friends, their relatives, their kinsmen, and their own people.

12. "The trees shall be filled with fruit and varicolored with blossoms, even out of season, great bowman, and the rivers shall be filled with water."

13. Then all the monkeys—their bodies, which had been covered with wounds, now healed and free of wounds—were wonderstruck, crying, "What is this?"

14. When all the principal gods saw that Kākutstha had had his wish fulfilled, they first praised him, who was so praiseworthy and who was accompanied by Lakṣmaṇa, and then they said:

15. "Proceed from here to Ayodhyā, hero, and discharge the monkeys. You should also console your devoted and long-suffering Maithilī.

16. "You must see your brother Bharata, who is practicing austerities in his grief for you. Then, once you have gone there, have yourself consecrated, and so bring joy to the people of the city."

17. When they had spoken in this fashion, the gods took their leave of Rāma and Saumitri and, in great delight, they went off to heaven in their flying chariots, which were as radiant as the sun.

18. Then Kākutstha, along with his brother Lakṣmaṇa, after respectfully saluting all of the most eminent of the thirty gods, ordered the army to make camp.

19. Under the protection of Lakṣmaṇa and Rāma, that great and glorious army, radiant with splendor, its troops delighted, glowed on every side, as does the night illumined by the cool-rayed moon.

The end of the one hundred eighth *sarga* of the *Yuddhakāṇḍa* of the *Śrī Rāmāyaṇa*.

Sarga 109

1. When Rāma, tamer of his enemies, had passed the night and risen at his leisure, Vibhīṣaṇa, cupping his hands in reverence and wishing him victory, said to him:

2–3. "Here is water for your bath, ointments for your body, garments and ornaments, heavenly sandalpaste, and various kinds of garlands. These lotus-eyed women, skilled in the arts of grooming their like, are at your service. They will bathe you in the proper fashion, Rāghava."

4. Addressed in this fashion, Kākutstha replied to Vibhīṣaṇa, "You should instead invite the tawny monkeys, led by Sugrīva, to bathe.

5–6. "For the great-armed and righteous prince Bharata, Kaikeyī's son, who is delicate and accustomed to comforts, is nonetheless true to his vows and suffering hardship for my sake. Without him—so righteous in his conduct—I do not care for baths, garments, and ornaments.

7. "Moreover, we must return to the city immediately by this very road, for the path of one traveling to Ayodhyā is extremely difficult."

8. Addressed in this fashion, Vibhīṣaṇa replied to Kākutstha, "I shall see to it that you reach your city in a single day, prince.

9. "For, bless you, there is a flying palace, as radiant as the sun, called Puṣpaka, which Rāvaṇa took from my brother Kubera by force.

10. "That flying palace, which resembles a cloud, is kept nearby. By means of this conveyance you shall go to Ayodhyā free from anxiety.

11. "But if I am at all worthy of your favor, if you are cognizant of my virtues, and if you have any affection for me, my wise friend, then please stay here for a while.

12. "Then, Rāma, honored with all manner of desirable things, you can depart with your brother Lakṣmaṇa and your wife, Vaidehī.

13. "You are very dear to me, Rāma, as is your army and your host of friends. Therefore, please accept this appropriate hospitality that I am offering.

14. "But I am not trying to give you orders, Rāghava. I am your servant, and I am beseeching you out of my affection, esteem, and friendship."

15. Addressed in this fashion, Rāma replied to Vibhīṣaṇa in such a way that all the *rākṣasas* and monkeys could hear him:

16. "I have been greatly honored by you, heroic scorcher of your foes, through your counsel, your wholehearted assistance, and your unparalleled friendship.

17–19. "It is not that I would not heed your words, lord of the *rākṣasas*. But my heart is eager to see my brother Bharata. For he came out to Citrakūṭa to bring me back, and, though he beseeched me, bowing his head to my feet, I would not heed his words. And my heart is eager also to see Kausalyā, Sumitrā, and illustrious Kaikeyī, as well as my elders, my friends, and the citizens, together with their children.

20. "So please get that flying palace ready for me immediately, lord of the *rākṣasas*. For how indeed could I agree to stay here, now that my mission has been accomplished?

21. "Please grant me leave, Vibhīṣaṇa, my gentle friend. I have already been deeply honored. Please don't be angry, but since I am in haste, I beseech you."

22–27. Vibhīṣaṇa then stood waiting after announcing to Rāma that that unassailable flying palace, as swift as thought, had arrived. Each of its parts was variegated with gold, and its raised platforms were made of lapis. It was covered on every side with penthouses, and it shone like silver. It was adorned with white flags and banners. It was splendid with golden mansions and adorned with golden lotuses. It was covered with masses of tiny bells and had windows of pearl. It was covered with masses of bells on every side so that it made a sweet sound. Fashioned by Viśvakarman, it resembled the peak of Mount Meru. It was adorned with many mansions that shone with pearl and silver. It had floors whose sections were variegated with crystal, and its splendid and costly seats of lapis were spread with expensive coverlets.

The end of the one hundred ninth *sarga* of the *Yuddhakāṇḍa* of the *Śrī Rāmāyaṇa*.

Sarga 110

1. When Vibhīṣaṇa saw that the flying palace Puṣpaka, all adorned with flowers, had come, he spoke to Rāma, who stood nearby.

2. Cupping his hands in reverence, the humble and obedient lord of the *rākṣasas*, filled with a sense of urgency, said to Rāghava, "What should I do now?"

3. After some reflection, Rāghava of immense blazing energy said these affectionate words to him in such a way that Lakṣmaṇa could hear them:

4. "Vibhīṣaṇa, the forest-dwelling monkeys have performed arduous deeds. You must honor them with gems, various ornaments, and other valuables.

5. "O lord of the *rākṣasas*, Laṅkā was besieged and conquered with the assistance of these monkeys, who, filled with the excitement of battle, cast off their fear of death and never retreated in battle.

6. "Honored in this fashion by you, bestower of honor, in your gratitude, these leaders of the troops of tawny monkeys, who are deserving of honor, will be delighted.

7. "I am advising you to do this so that they may recognize that you know both how to acquire wealth and dispense it and that you are compassionate and illustrious."

8. Addressed in this fashion by Rāma, Vibhīṣaṇa honored all the monkeys, each according to his share, with gems and other valuables.

9–10. Then, having seen the troop leaders honored with gems and other valuables, Rāma, taking the glorious, but embarrassed, Vaidehī on his lap, ascended that magnificent flying palace, together with his valorous brother Lakṣmaṇa, who was armed with a bow.

11. Once he had ascended the flying palace, Kākutstha addressed the immensely powerful Sugrīva, the *rākṣasa* Vibhīṣaṇa, and all the monkeys:

12. "Foremost among the monkeys, you have done all that friends could be expected to do. I grant you leave. You may now all depart at your leisure.

*13. "And you, Sugrīva, scorcher of your foes, you who fear only unrighteousness, have accomplished all that a friend and ally could be expected to do. You may now quickly return to Kiṣkindhā accompanied by your army.

14. "And you, Vibhīṣaṇa, may dwell in Laṅkā, your own kingdom, which I have given you. Not even the heaven-dwelling gods along with Indra will be capable of assaulting you.

15. "I will now return to Ayodhyā, my father's capital. I wish to take my leave, and I bid you all farewell."

16. Addressed in this fashion by Rāma, the immensely powerful monkeys and the *rākṣasa* Vibhīṣaṇa cupped their hands in reverence and said to him, "We wish to go to Ayodhyā. Please, sir, take us all."

17. "Once we have seen you dripping from your consecration and have respectfully saluted Kausalyā, we will immediately return to our own homes, O son of the lord of men."

18. Addressed in this fashion by Vibhīṣaṇa and the monkeys, righteous and majestic Rāghava replied to them and to Sugrīva:

19. "All my friends and I would experience a pleasure greater than any other if I could share the joy of returning to the city together with all of you.

20. "So quickly ascend the flying palace, Sugrīva, together with your monkeys. And you too, Vibhīṣaṇa, lord of the *rākṣasas*, ascend along with your ministers."

21. Then, hastening, Sugrīva, together with his army, quickly ascended the heavenly flying palace Puṣpaka, as did Vibhīṣaṇa, together with his ministers.

22. Once they had all ascended the superb vehicle of Kubera, lord of wealth, it rose into the sky at Rāghava's command.

23. Then Rāma departed in that radiant flying palace yoked to *haṃsas*. Delighted in mind and body, he resembled Kubera himself.

The end of the one hundred tenth *sarga* of the *Yuddhakāṇḍa* of the *Śrī Rāmāyaṇa*.

Sarga 111

1. At Rāma's command that magnificent flying palace flew onward, like a great cloud driven before the wind.

2. Casting his gaze in all directions, Rāma, the delight of the Raghus, said to Sītā Maithilī, whose face was like the hare-marked moon:

3. "Vaidehī, behold Laṅkā, fashioned by Viśvakarman himself, situated there on the peak of Mount Trikūṭa, which resembles the peak of Mount Kailāsa.

4. "And look, Sītā, there, mired with flesh and blood, is the battlefield that was the scene of that huge slaughter of the tawny monkeys and the *rākṣasas*.

5. "It was here, on your account, wide-eyed lady, that I slew Rāvaṇa. Here, too, Kumbhakarṇa was slain as well as the night-roaming *rākṣasa* Prahasta.

6. "And it was here that Lakṣmaṇa slew Indrajit Rāvaṇi in battle, while Virūpākṣa, impossible to even look upon, as well as Mahāpārśva and Mahodara were also slain.

7. "Akampana was slain here as were those other powerful *rākṣasas*, Triśiras, Atikāya, Devāntaka, and Narāntaka.

8. "And here Rāvaṇa's wife Mandodarī, surrounded by a thousand of her co-wives all drenched with tears, mourned him.

9. "And there you can see the shore of the ocean, fair-faced woman, where we camped for the night after crossing the sea.

10. "And, wide-eyed lady, that bridge is Nala's bridge, all-but-impossible to build, which, for your sake, I had constructed across the ocean, the reservoir of waters.

11. "Observe the imperturbable ocean, Vaidehī, Varuṇa's abode, boundless and roaring, abounding in conch and mother of pearl.

12. "And look, Maithilī, at the golden lord of mountains, Mount Maināka, with its golden peak, which, parting the sea, rose up to provide a resting place for Hanumān.

13. "And here is where Vibhīṣaṇa, king of the *rākṣasas* came over to me.

14. "And there, Sītā, one can see Sugrīva's charming city, Kiṣkindhā, with its lovely woodlands. That is where I killed Vālin.

15. "There, Sītā, one can see Ṛśyamūka, foremost of mountains. Laced with golden minerals, it resembles a huge storm cloud laced with lightning.

16. "It was here that I met Sugrīva, lord of the monkeys, and where I forged a pact, Sītā, with the purpose of slaying Vālin.

17. "And there one can see the lotus pond Pampā, with its lovely woodlands where, bereft of you, I lamented in my profound grief.

18. "On its banks I met Śabarī, who practiced righteousness. And it was here that I killed Kabandha, his arms a league in length.

19. "And there, graceful Sītā, in Janasthāna, one can see that majestic tree, the lord of the forest, where, on your account, a great battle took place between cruel Rāvaṇa and great Jaṭāyus.

20. "And it was here, too, that, with my straight-flying arrows, I slew Khara and struck down Dūṣaṇa and immensely powerful Triśiras in battle.

21. "There one can see the charming and beautiful leaf hut from which you were forcibly abducted by Rāvaṇa, the lord of the *rākṣasas*.

22. "And there is the lovely and auspicious Godāvarī River with its limpid waters. Look, Maithilī, one can see the ashram of Agastya.

23. "And, Vaidehī, here one can see the vast ashram of Śarabhañga to which thousand-eyed Śakra, smasher of citadels, himself came.

24. "Over there, slender-waisted woman, one can see the dwellings of the ascetics, where Atri, the ashram elder, whose radiance is like that of Sūrya or Agni Vaiśvānara, dwells. It was here, Sītā, that you met the ascetic woman who practiced righteousness.

25. "It was in this region that I killed the giant Virādha.

26. "And here, slender woman, just coming into view, is Citrakūṭa, the lord of mountains, where Kaikeyī's son came to beseech me to return.

27. "Over there, in the distance, where Bharadvāja's majestic ashram is just coming into view, one can see the Yamunā with its lovely woodlands.

28. "And over there one can see the Ganges, which flows by three paths, lady of the fair complexion. And that is the city of Śṛṅgavera, where Guha met us.

29. "And there one can see Ayodhyā, my father's capital. Now that you have returned, Vaidehī, you should make obeisance to Ayodhyā."

30. Then all the monkeys and the *rākṣasa* Vibhīṣaṇa, jumping up again and again, gazed at that beautiful city.

31. Those leaping monkeys gazed upon the city of Ayodhyā, garlanded with white mansions. It had spacious courtyards and was crowded with elephants and horses, just like Amarāvatī, the city of great Indra.

The end of the one hundred eleventh *sarga* of the *Yuddhakāṇḍa* of the *Śrī Rāmāyaṇa*.

Sarga 112

1. And so, on the fifth day of the fortnight when the fourteenth year was just complete, Lakṣmaṇa's older brother reached Bharadvāja's ashram and, with complete self-possession, praised that sage.

2. When he had respectfully saluted that treasure trove of asceticism Bharadvāja, he inquired of him: "I trust, holy sage, that you hear that the people of the city are healthy and well fed. I trust that Bharata is intent on his duties and that my mothers are still living."

3. Addressed in this fashion by Rāma, the great sage Bharadvāja smiled and, in great delight, replied to that foremost of the Raghus.

4. "Smeared with mud and wearing matted locks, Bharata awaits you, having placed your sandals in a position of honor. And, yes, everything is fine in your household.

5–7. "When last I saw you, conqueror in battle, you were entering the deep forest on foot, clad in barkcloth garments, with but one lone companion and a woman. Desiring only righteousness, you had been driven from the kingdom, giving up everything to obey your father's instructions and intent on obeying those of Kaikeyī. Stripped of all objects of enjoyment and subsisting on wild roots and fruits, you were like an immortal god fallen from heaven. At that time, I was deeply saddened.

8. "But now, when I see that you have accomplished your mission and triumphed over your enemy in the company of your kinsmen and your hosts of friends, I feel unsurpassed delight.

9–14. "And I know, Rāghava, about all the many joys and sorrows you experienced, starting with the slaughter in Janasthāna. There was the encounter with Mārīca and the assault on Sītā while you were employed on behalf of the brahmans to protect all the ascetics. Then there was the encounter with Kabandha, your arrival at Lake Pampā, and your alliance with Sugrīva on account of which you slew Vālin. I know about the search for Vaidehī, the feats of the son of the wind god, and how Nala's bridge was built once Vaidehī had been found. I know, too, about how the excited troop leaders of the tawny monkeys set Laṅkā ablaze, and how Rāvaṇa, that thorn in the side of the gods, was destroyed, along with his sons, his kinsmen, his ministers, his army, and his vehicles. Finally, I know about your meeting with the thirty gods and how they granted you a boon. All of that is known to me, lover of righteousness, through the power of my asceticism.

15. "And I, too, will grant you a boon, foremost of those who bear weapons. So please accept my guest-offering. Tomorrow you shall go to Ayodhyā."

16. The majestic son of the king, bowing his head, accepted his instructions with the words, "Very well." Then, in great delight, he requested his boon.

17. "Holy sage, may all the trees along the road I take to Ayodhyā bear fruit out of season and drip with honey."

18. Then, suddenly, those trees that had no fruit were filled with fruit, those that had no blossoms were covered with them. Those that were bare were covered with leaves, and all of them dripped with honey.

The end of the one hundred twelfth *sarga* of the *Yuddhakāṇḍa* of the *Śrī Rāmāyaṇa*.

Sarga 113

1. But once Rāghava had caught sight of Ayodhyā, he was plunged into thought. Then, after some reflection, he cast his glance upon the monkeys.

2. Then wise Rāma of blazing energy, wishing to do a kindness, spoke kindly to the leaping monkey, swift-striding Hanumān:

3. "Go quickly, best of leaping monkeys. Hastening to Ayodhyā, you must find out if all is well with the people in the king's palace.

4. "When you reach the city of Śṛṅgavera, you must inform the chief of the Niṣādas, Guha, whose realm is the deep forest, in my words, that I am safe.

5. "For once my friend and equal Guha hears that I am safe, well, and free from anxiety, he will be delighted.

6. "And Guha, chief of the Niṣādas, in great delight, will show you the way to Ayodhyā and will inform you of Bharata's activities.

7. "You are to inform Bharata in my words that I am safe. Tell him that, together with my wife and Lakṣmaṇa, I have accomplished my purpose.

8–11. "Tell him about Vaidehī's abduction by powerful Rāvaṇa, my negotiations with Sugrīva, the slaying of Vālin in battle, the search for Maithilī, and how you found her after leaping across the great water, the imperishable lord of rivers. And tell him about the march to the sea and the encounter with Sāgara, god of the ocean, and how the bridge was built and Rāvaṇa slain. Tell him about the granting of the boon by great Indra, Brahmā, and Varuṇa, and about my reunion with our father through the grace of the great god Śiva.

12. "Tell him: 'Having conquered the hosts of his enemies, attained unsurpassed glory, and accomplished his purpose, immensely powerful Rāma has returned with his allies.'

13. "And whatever facial expression Bharata may adopt upon hearing this, you must report that to me fully.

14. "Through the color of his face, his glance, and his manner of speaking, you should accurately determine everything about Bharata's state of mind and his intentions.

15. "For whose head would not be turned by an ancestral kingdom rich in every object of desire and filled with elephants, horses, and chariots?

16. "And should majestic Bharata, being long accustomed to it, desire the kingship for himself, then let that delight of the Raghus rule the entire earth without exception.

17. "Once you have determined his state of mind and his intentions, monkey, you must return quickly before we have gone very far."

18. Instructed in this fashion, Hanumān, son of Māruta, took on a human form and hastened to Ayodhyā.

19–20. Leaping along the path of his father and crossing the fearsome confluence of the Ganges and the Yamunā rivers, the auspicious abode of the serpent lords, powerful Hanumān reached the city of Śṛṅgavera, and, approaching Guha, he delightedly addressed him with these auspicious words:

21. "Your truly valorous friend Rāma Kākutstha, who is accompanied by Sītā and Saumitri, informs you that he is safe.

22. "On the instructions of Bharadvāja, Rāghava spent last night, the night of the fifth, with him. Now, since he has taken his leave of the sage, you shall see him this very day."

23. When he had spoken in this fashion, swift Hanumān of immense blazing energy, without further hesitation, swiftly flew up once more, the hairs of his body bristling with excitement.

24. He saw the spot sacred to Rāma and the river Vālukinī. And he saw the Gomatī River and a fearsome forest of *sāla* trees.

25. When he had swiftly traveled a long way, that elephant among monkeys reached the blossoming trees that grew near Nandigrāma.

26–30. A quarter of a league from Ayodhyā he spied Bharata, who was living in an ashram. Dejected and emaciated, he was clad in garments of barkcloth and black antelope skin. Wearing matted locks, his body was smeared with dirt. Tormented by the catastrophe that had befallen his brother and practicing righteousness, he engaged in asceticism, restrained and subsisting on fruits and roots. He had a mass of matted hair piled high and was clad in barkcloth and animal skins. Self-controlled and with focused mind, he was equal in blazing energy to a brahman-seer. Having placed Rāma's sandals in a position of honor, he ruled the earth, protecting the people of all four social classes from every danger. He was attended by incorruptible ministers, household priests, and attentive army chiefs, all clad in ochre garments.

31. For the citizens, who loved righteousness, were determined never to abandon the prince, who was clad in barkcloth and black antelope skin.

32. Cupping his hands in reverence, Hanumān, son of Māruta, spoke these words to that knower of righteousness, who was like a second Dharma, god of righteousness, incarnate:

33. "Kākutstha, for whom you have been grieving and who had been living in the Daṇḍaka Forest wearing barkcloth garments and matted hair, informs you that he is safe.

34. "I bring you wonderful news, your majesty! Reunited with your brother Rāma within the very hour, you shall put aside your terrible sorrow.

35. "Having slain Rāvaṇa and recovered Maithilī, Rāma, who has accomplished his purpose, has come back with his immensely powerful allies.

36. "And so have Lakṣmaṇa of immense blazing energy and illustrious Sītā Vaidehī, who is united with Rāma, just as is Śacī with great Indra."

37. Addressed in this fashion by Hanumān, Bharata, Kaikeyī's son, in a sudden access of delight, fell and fainted dead away in his joy.

38. Regaining consciousness and getting up after a short while, Bharata Rāghava then said this to Hanumān, who had told him the good news.

39. Embracing the monkey in his excitement, majestic Bharata drenched him with copious teardrops of joy and delight.

40–42. "Whether you be a god or a man, you have come here out of compassion. My gentle friend, I shall give you, the bearer of this good news who reported it to me, a hundred thousand cows, a hundred prosperous villages, and sixteen maidens of excellent character, adorned with earrings, to be your wives. These are women of excellent caste and family, adorned with every ornament. Their complexions are like gold, their faces as lovely as the moon, and their noses and thighs perfect."

43. When the king's son had heard from the monkey hero about Rāma's seemingly miraculous return, he was delighted, and in his joy and eagerness to see Rāma, he once more spoke these words.

The end of the one hundred thirteenth *sarga* of the *Yuddhakāṇḍa* of the *Śrī Rāmāyaṇa*.

Sarga 114

1. "I am hearing such delightful news of my lord, who had gone to the deep forest for so many years.

2. "So it seems to me that the popular verse, 'Joy comes to a man even if he has to wait a hundred years,' is quite true.

3. "How and in what country and for what reason did Rāghava come to be associated with the tawny monkeys? Tell me truthfully, since I am asking you."

4. Questioned in this fashion by the prince, Hanumān, seated on an ascetic's seat, recounted all of Rāma's adventures in the forest:

5–9. "Great-armed prince, you already know all about how Rāma was exiled, about the two boons given to your mother, and about how King Daśaratha died from grief for his son. And you know how you yourself, lord, were hastily brought back from Rājagṛha by messengers, and how, when you entered Ayodhyā, you declined the kingship. You also know how, when you had gone to Mount Citrakūṭa, your brother, the tormentor of his foes, remained faithful to the king's vow and rejected the kingdom, even though you—following the righteous path of the virtuous—begged him to accept it. And you know, of course, how, taking your noble brother's sandals, you came back once again. Now learn from me what took place once you had gone back.

10. "Once you had departed, Rāma entered the vast and deserted Daṇḍaka Forest, whose beasts and birds were wildly agitated.

11. "And as they were making their way through that dense forest, the powerful Virādha appeared before them, roaring a mighty roar.

12. "Seizing him, they hurled him, face down with his arms raised, into a pit, as he roared a mighty roar like an elephant.

13. "After accomplishing that difficult feat, the brothers Rāma and Lakṣmaṇa came, that very evening, to Śarabhaṅga's lovely ashram.

14. "Once Śarabhaṅga had gone to heaven, truly valorous Rāma respectfully saluted all the sages and then proceeded to Janasthāna.

15. "While great Rāghava was living there, he slaughtered fourteen thousand *rākṣasas* of fearsome deeds.

16–17. "Then, a little later, Śūrpaṇakhā approached Rāma. Instructed by Rāma, immensely powerful Lakṣmaṇa suddenly sprang up, seized his sword, and hacked off her ears and nose. Mutilated by him, that foolish creature then approached Rāvaṇa.

18. "Next, a fearsome *rākṣasa*, a servant of Rāvaṇa named Mārīca, turned himself into a bejeweled deer and infatuated Vaidehī.

19. "When she caught sight of it, Vaidehī said to Rāma, 'You must catch it! Oh, how charming and beautiful it would be in our ashram!'

20. "Then Rāma chased him as he fled and, as he fled, killed him with a straight arrow.

21. "Then, gentle prince, when Rāghava had gone after the deer and Lakṣmaṇa, too, had gone out, ten-necked Rāvaṇa entered the ashram. He violently seized Sītā, just as a baleful planet might seize the constellation Rohiṇī in the heavens.

22. "Once he had killed the vulture Jaṭāyus, who tried to rescue her, Rāvaṇa seized Sītā violently and swiftly departed.

23. "However, some monkeys of extraordinary form, as huge as mountains, who were there on a mountaintop, were astonished to see Rāvaṇa, lord of the *rākṣasas*, going by, clutching Sītā.

24. "Rāvaṇa, who made the world cry out, then entered Laṅkā.

25. "There Rāvaṇa installed Maithilī in a vast and beautiful palace covered with gold and tried to calm her with soothing words.

26. "Finding the vulture upon his return, Kākutstha was distraught.

*27. "After cremating the slain vulture, a dear friend of his father, Rāma wandered along the Godāvarī River and through its forest regions all in blossom. Then the two princes encountered the *rākṣasa* Kabandha in the vast forest.

28. "On the advice of Kabandha, truly valorous Rāma went to Mount Ṛśyamūka and met with Sugrīva.

29. "Even before they had met, the two had formed an emotional bond through their mutual affection. Through their conversations with each other, it became a profound love.

30. "Once he had slain the gigantic and immensely powerful Vālin through the strength of his own arms in battle, Rāma bestowed upon Sugrīva a kingship of his own.

31. "Once Sugrīva had been established in the kingship, he promised Rāma that, together with all the monkeys, he would search for the princess.

32. "Under orders from Sugrīva, the great lord of the monkeys, a hundred million monkeys were sent out in all directions.

33. "And then, while we were lost in the great Vindhya mountain range and were sorely afflicted with sorrow, a great deal of time passed.

34. "But the mighty brother of the king of vultures, Saṃpāti by name, informed us about Sītā's dwelling in the abode of Rāvaṇa.

35. "Then, relying on my own strength, I leapt a hundred leagues, dispelling the sorrow of my kinsmen, who were overcome with sorrow.

36. "And there I found that woman, all alone, in an *aśoka* grove, clad in a silken garment, covered with dirt, miserable but firm in her vows.

37. "After meeting with that blameless woman and having thoroughly questioned her in the proper fashion, I took a jewel as a token of recognition and, having accomplished my mission, returned.

38. "When I returned, I presented that great and glittering gem to Rāma, tireless in action, as a token of recognition.

39. "Once he had heard about Maithilī, he was delighted and regained his will to live, as might a gravely ill man at the point of death after drinking the nectar of immortality.

40. "Putting in motion a great undertaking, he turned his thoughts to the destruction of Laṅkā, just as Agni, the shining god of fire, desires to destroy all the worlds at the end of a cosmic age.

41. "Then, when he reached the sea, he had Nala construct a bridge. It was by means of that bridge that the army of monkeys crossed over.

42. "Nīla slew Prahasta, and Rāghava killed Kumbhakarṇa. Lakṣmaṇa slew Rāvaṇa's son Indrajit, and Rāma himself killed Rāvaṇa.

43. "Then Kākutstha, that scorcher of his foes, having met with Śakra, Yama, and Varuṇa, along with the gods and seers, received boons.

44. "And when he had received those boons, he was reunited with the monkeys in great delight. He then proceeded to Kiṣkindhā in the flying palace Puṣpaka.

45. "Nothing can prevent you from seeing Rāma tomorrow on the auspicious day of the moon's conjunction with the constellation Puṣya. For, having once more reached the Ganges, he is staying there with the sage Bharadvāja."

46. Then, when Bharata had heard that great and truthful speech of Hanumān, he was delighted. Cupping his hands in reverence, he spoke these words that delighted one's heart, "At long last, indeed, my fondest wish has been fulfilled."

The end of the one hundred fourteenth *sarga* of the *Yuddhakāṇḍa* of the *Śrī Rāmāyaṇa*.

Sarga 115

1. When truly valorous Bharata, slayer of enemy heroes, had heard those words that filled him with joy, he gave instructions to Śatrughna, who was similarly delighted.

2. "Let pious men worship all the divinities and the shrines of the city with fragrant garlands and musical instruments.

3. "And let the king's wives and his ministers, the soldiers, the army troops and their womenfolk go out to see Rāma's face, which is like the hare-marked moon."

4. When powerful Śatrughna, slayer of enemy heroes, had heard those words of Bharata, he commanded his many thousands of conscripted laborers:

5. "Level the road—depressions, rough places, as well as smooth areas—from Nandigrāma onward, sparing only the roadside shrines.

6. "Have some men sprinkle the whole ground with ice-cold water, and then have others strew it everywhere with parched grain and flowers.

7. "Let them raise flags along the main road in our splendid city, and let them beautify their houses starting at daybreak.

8. "Let hundreds of men strew the broad royal highway with garlands, festoons, and loose blossoms and with fragrant powders in five colors."

9. Given their orders, great chariot-warriors went forth swiftly in their chariots along with thousands of rutting elephants adorned with gold, while others went forth with bull- and cow-elephants with golden girths.

10. Next, all of Daśaratha's wives went forth mounted in carriages, placing Kausalyā and Sumitrā at their head.

11. The thundering of the horses' hooves, the rumbling of the chariot wheels, and the din of conches and war drums seemed to shake the very earth.

12. Indeed, the entire city went forth to Nandigrāma.

13–16. Thus did great and righteous Bharata, together with his counselors, set forth to meet Rāma. He was surrounded by eminent brahmans, the leaders of the caste guilds, and merchants, as well as by his ministers, who held garlands and sweets in their hands. To the sounds of conches and *bherī* drums, he was lauded by panegyrists. Deeply learned in righteousness, he bore his noble brother's sandals on his head and carried with him a white umbrella festooned with white garlands, and a pair of white yak-tail fly whisks adorned with gold and fit for a king. He who had been earlier downcast and was still emaciated with fasting and clad in garments of barkcloth and black antelope skin was now filled with joy upon hearing of his brother's return.

17. Looking about him, Bharata said these words to the son of Pavana: "I hope you have not fallen prey to the typical flightiness of monkeys. For I do not see the noble Rāma Kākutstha, the scorcher of his foes."

18. When these words had been spoken, Hanumān said this to truly valorous Bharata, informing him of the reason:

19. "They have reached those trees that, through the grace of Bharadvāja, are always in fruit and flower, dripping honey, and resounding with intoxicated bees.

20. "For such, scorcher of your foes, was the boon granted to Rāma by Vāsava. And this was the hospitality, complete with every desirable thing, that was offered to him and his army.

21. "One can hear the fearsome racket of the excited forest-dwelling monkeys. I think the monkey army must be crossing the Gomatī River.

22. "Look at the cloud of dust that has been kicked up over toward the Vālukinī River. I think that the leaping monkeys must be crashing their way through the lovely forest of *sāla* trees.

23. "And there in the distance one can see the bright celestial flying palace Puṣpaka, which looks like the moon and was created by the mind of Brahmā.

24. "Through the grace of Kubera, bestower of wealth, great Rāma obtained this celestial flying palace, as swift as thought, after killing Rāvaṇa together with his kinsmen.

25. "In it are the two heroic Rāghava brothers, together with Vaidehī as well as Sugrīva of immense blazing energy and Vibhīṣaṇa, the lord of the *rākṣasas*."

26. Then a great clamor of joy arose reaching to the heavens, as the women, children, youths, and elderly cried out, "There's Rāma!"

27. The men got down from their chariots, elephants, and horses and, standing on the ground, gazed at Rāma, who, in his flying palace, resembled the moon in the sky.

28. Cupping his hands in reverence and facing Rāghava, Bharata joyfully honored Rāma with a fitting welcome.

29. In that flying palace, which Brahmā created with his mind, the elder brother of Lakṣmaṇa, with his long and wide eyes, looked as splendid as a second Indra, wielder of the *vajra*.

30. Then Bharata humbly praised his brother Rāma, who stood atop the flying palace, like the sun, maker of day, on the summit of Mount Meru.

31. Invited on board the flying palace, truly valorous Bharata approached Rāma in great delight and once more respectfully saluted him.

32. Then Kākutstha, raising up Bharata, whom he had not seen in such a long time, placed him on his lap and embraced him in great joy.

33. After warmly greeting Lakṣmaṇa, Bharata, scorcher of his foes, respectfully saluted Vaidehī and, in great delight, announced his name.

34. Next, the son of Kaikeyī embraced Sugrīva, Jāmbavān, Aṅgada, Mainda, Dvivida, Nīla, and Ṛṣabha.

35. Those monkeys, who could take on any form at will, took on human forms and, in great delight, inquired of Bharata about his welfare.

36. Then Bharata graciously spoke these words to Vibhīṣaṇa: "Thank heavens that through your assistance this all-but-impossible feat has been accomplished!"

37. Next, Śatrughna respectfully saluted Rāma and Lakṣmaṇa and, afterward, humbly worshiped Sītā's feet.

38. Then Rāma approached his mother, who was so disconsolate and drawn with grieving, and, bending, he clasped her feet, soothing her heart.

39. Then, after respectfully saluting Sumitrā and illustrious Kaikeyī, he approached all his other mothers and the household priest.

40. All the people of the city addressed him, their hands cupped in reverence, crying, "Welcome great-armed increaser of Kausalyā's joy!"

41. And Bharata's elder brother gazed upon those thousands of cupped hands that were extended by the people of the city and that were like so many full-blown lotuses.

42. Then, taking Rāma's sandals, Bharata, who knew righteousness, himself placed them on the feet of the lord of men.

43. Cupping his hands in reverence, Bharata said to Rāma, "Here, your majesty, is your well-guarded kingdom, which I have now given back.

44. "Today the purpose of my birth has been accomplished and my most cherished wish fulfilled, in that I see you returned to Ayodhyā once more as king.

45. "Sir, please inspect the treasury, the granary, the city, and the army. Through your blazing energy, I have increased all of them tenfold."

46. When the monkeys and the *rākṣasa* Vibhīṣaṇa saw Bharata speaking in this fashion, with such love for his brother, they shed tears.

47. Then, taking Bharata on his lap in great delight, Rāghava proceeded with his army in the flying palace to Bharata's ashram.

48. Once he reached Bharata's ashram, Rāghava, together with his army, descended from atop the flying palace and stood on the ground.

49. Rāma then addressed that unsurpassed flying palace, saying, "You must now carry the god Kubera Vaiśravaṇa. I give you leave. You may go."

50. Given leave by Rāma, that unsurpassed flying palace departed in a northerly direction to the abode of Kubera, bestower of wealth.

51. Just as Śakra, lord of the immortal gods, might grasp the feet of Bṛhaspati, mighty Rāghava clasped the feet of his household priest,

who was his equal. Then they sat down together, each on a separate, splendid seat.

The end of the one hundred fifteenth *sarga* of the *Yuddhakāṇḍa* of the *Śrī Rāmāyaṇa*.

Sarga 116

1. Cupping his hands to his forehead in reverence, Bharata, increaser of Kaikeyī's joy, addressed his elder brother, truly valorous Rāma:

2. "You showed my mother respect and gave over the kingdom to me. I now give it back to you, just as you once gave it to me.

3. "I am no more able to bear this heavy burden than could a young calf bear a yoke set down by a powerful but solitary bullock.

4. "I think that any threat facing the kingdom, if unaddressed, would be as difficult to remedy as it would be to repair a dike that, breached by a tremendous flood of water, has sprung a leak.

5. "Your majesty, tamer of your foes, I am no more able to follow the path you have blazed than is a donkey to match the speed of a horse, or a crow to match that of a *haṃsa*.

6–7. "A tree planted in one's inner court might grow to a great height, impossible to climb with its huge trunk and many branches. But after coming into blossom, it might wither and fail to bear fruit. And thus he for whose sake it was planted would reap no benefit from it.

8. "This is merely an analogy, great-armed lord of men. But if you do not rule us, your devoted servants, you will come to realize its significance.

9. "Let the whole world see you consecrated this very day, shining with radiant energy like the blazing sun at noon.

10. "You should fall asleep and waken to the sounds of musical ensembles, the jingling of women's anklets and girdles, and the sweet sounds of singing.

11. "As long as the wheel of heavenly bodies shall turn and as long as the earth, bearer of wealth, shall endure, so long may you exercise lordship over all in this world."

12. Upon hearing Bharata's words, Rāma, the conqueror of enemy citadels, accepted them, saying, "So be it," as he sat on his splendid seat.

13. Then, at the command of Śatrughna, skillful barbers with a gentle touch and quick at their work attended upon Rāghava.

14–15. Once Bharata, immensely powerful Lakṣmaṇa, the monkey lord Sugrīva, and the *rākṣasa* lord Vibhīṣaṇa had all bathed before him, Rāma gave up his matted locks and bathed. Then, wearing multicolored garlands and unguents and clad in costly garments, he stood there, blazing with splendor.

16. Thus did mighty and splendid Śatrughna, increaser of the House of Ikṣvāku, see to the adornment of Rāma and Lakṣmaṇa.

17. Then the virtuous wives of Daśaratha themselves saw to the ravishing adornment of Sītā.

18. Finally, with great care, Kausalyā, delighted and deeply fond of her son, beautified all the wives of the Rāghavas.

19. Then, at the command of Śatrughna, the charioteer named Sumantra yoked a chariot that was richly adorned throughout and brought it up.

20. When he saw that heavenly chariot standing before him and blazing like the orb of the sun, great-armed and truly valorous Rāma mounted it.

21. Meanwhile, those ministers of King Daśaratha who had remained in Ayodhyā, placing the household priest at their head, purposefully took counsel together.

22–23. They took counsel with regard to the prosperity of Rāma and the maintenance of the city. "Preceding all your actions with auspicious rites, you must do everything necessary for the consecration of great Rāma, so worthy of success." Having thus instructed the household priest, all the ministers quickly left the city, their minds intent on seeing Rāma.

24. Like blameless, thousand-eyed Indra mounting his chariot yoked to tawny steeds, Rāma mounted his chariot and proceeded toward the splendid city.

25. Bharata held the reins and Śatrughna the umbrella, while Lakṣmaṇa waved a fan over Rāma's head.

26. Sugrīva, the lord of the monkeys, held one white yak-tail fly whisk, while Vibhīṣaṇa, the lord of the *rākṣasas*, held another as bright as the moon.

27. In the heavens was heard the sweet sound made by the hosts of seers and gods, together with the Maruts, as they praised Rāma.

28. Then Sugrīva, the lord of the monkeys, filled with immense blazing energy, mounted an elephant named Śatruṃjaya, as huge as a mountain.

29. The other monkeys, too, who had taken on human form and were adorned with every ornament, mounted nine thousand elephants and set forth.

30. Thus, to the sound of conches, cheers, and the thundering of war drums, did the tiger among men proceed toward the mansion-garlanded city.

31. And as the great chariot-warrior Rāghava, radiant with splendor, passed in his chariot with his retinue, the people gazed upon him.

32. Congratulating Rāma Kākutstha and graciously acknowledged by him, they followed the great man, who was accompanied by his brothers.

33. Like the moon surrounded by the constellations, Rāma, surrounded by the brahmans, his ministers, and his subjects, shone with splendor.

34. As he proceeded, he was accompanied by musicians who went before him, holding cymbals and *svastikas* in their hands, and by delighted people shouting out blessings.

35. And, before Rāma, went cows, maidens, and brahmans, bearing unhusked, golden rice, and men with sweetmeats in their hands.

36. Rāma then told his counselors about his friendship with Sugrīva, the supernatural strength of Hanumān, the son of Anila, and the deeds of the monkeys. When the people of Ayodhyā heard this, they were wonderstruck.

37. After reporting all of this, Rāma, resplendent and surrounded by the monkeys, made his entrance into Ayodhyā, which was thronged with delighted and prosperous people.

38. Then, as the citizens raised flags on house after house, he reached his father's lovely residence, the ancestral home of the Ikṣvākus.

39. When he reached the palace of his great father, he entered it and respectfully saluted Kausalyā, Sumitrā, and Kaikeyī.

40. Then the prince, the delight of the Raghus, sweetly addressed Bharata, foremost among the righteous, with these significant words:

41. "Place at Sugrīva's disposal my vast and splendid palace, the one adjacent to the *aśoka* grove and covered with pearls and lapis."

42. When truly valorous Bharata had heard those words of his, he took Sugrīva by the hand and entered that dwelling.

43. Then, ordered by Śatrughna, servants entered at once holding oil lamps and bed coverings.

44. Rāghava's younger brother, of immense blazing energy, then said to Sugrīva, "Lord, you must dispatch emissaries in connection with Rāma's consecration."

45. At once, Sugrīva gave four golden vessels, adorned with every gem, to four of the monkey lords.

46. "Monkeys, you must act in such a way that you are waiting for me at daybreak with these four vessels filled, respectively, with water from each of the four oceans."

47. Addressed in this fashion, those great monkeys, as huge as elephants, swiftly flew up into the sky, like so many Garuḍas, swift in flight.

48. Jāmbavān, Hanumān, the monkey Vegadarśin, and Ṛṣabha then fetched pitchers full of water. And in urns they brought the waters of five hundred rivers.

49. From the eastern ocean, Suṣeṇa, endowed with might, fetched a pitcher adorned with every gem and filled with water.

50. Ṛṣabha swiftly brought water from the southern ocean.

51. Gavaya brought a golden vessel covered with camphor and red sandalwood paste. In it was water from the vast western ocean.

52. He whose power was that of Māruta and whose pace that of Garuḍa or the wind swiftly brought frigid water from the northern ocean in a great jeweled urn.

53. Then Śatrughna, together with his ministers, presented that water to the foremost of household priests and his assistants for the purpose of Rāma's consecration.

54. Then the aged and devout Vasiṣṭha, together with the brahmans, seated Rāma and Sītā on a jeweled throne.

55–56. Vasiṣṭha, Vāmadeva, Jābāli, Kāśyapa, Kātyāyana, Suyajña, Gautama, and Vijaya all consecrated that tiger among men with fragrant and pellucid water, just as the Vasus consecrated thousand-eyed Indra Vāsava.

57–58. And thus, in great delight, with that water and with the extracts of all the different herbs, did they perform the consecration, first with the officiating priests and brahmans, and then with maidens, counselors, soldiers, and merchants, as well as with the divinities, who were hovering in the sky, the four world guardians, and all the assembled gods.

59. Śatrughna held his splendid white umbrella. Sugrīva, the lord of the monkeys, held one white yak-tail fly whisk, while Vibhīṣaṇa, the lord of the *rākṣasas*, held another as bright as the moon.

60. Then, on the orders of Vāsava, Vāyu gave Rāghava a golden necklace with a hundred lotuses that glowed with splendor.

61. And, on the orders of Śakra, he also gave the lord of men a pearl necklace strung with every sort of jewel and adorned with an immense gem.

62. The gods and *gandharvas* sang and the troops of *apsarases* danced at the consecration of wise Rāma, who so richly deserved it.

63. And, on the festive occasion of Rāghava's consecration, the land grew rich in grain, the trees heavy with fruit, and the flowers redolent with fragrance.

64. First, that bull among men made gifts to the brahmans of a hundred bulls and a hundred thousand each of cows that had newly calved and horses.

65. Next, Rāghava gave the brahmans three hundred million gold pieces as well as costly jewels and garments of every kind.

66. Then that bull among men gave Sugrīva a heavenly diadem of gold encrusted with gems and shining like the rays of the sun.

67. And as he was greatly pleased with Aṅgada, the son of Vālin, Rāma gave him a pair of armlets adorned with diamonds and gems and variegated with lapis and jewels.

68. Rāma then presented Sītā with an unsurpassed pearl necklace set with the finest gems, its luster equal to that of moonbeams.

69. Then, keeping her eyes on her husband, Vaidehī gave the son of Vāyu two spotless and divine garments as well as splendid ornaments.

70. Unfastening the necklace from her neck, the delight of Janaka looked back and forth repeatedly from her husband to all the tawny monkeys.

71–72. Rāma, skillful at divining people's true intentions, looked closely at Janaka's daughter and said, "Beloved and charming lady, you should give the necklace to him with whom you are pleased, that is, to him in whom might, valor, and wisdom are ever present." Then that dark-eyed woman gave the necklace to the son of Vāyu.

73. Wearing that necklace, Hanumān, bull among monkeys, looked as resplendent as a mountain wreathed with a white cloud illuminated by a flood of moonlight.

74. Then the lord of the earth, that scorcher of his foes, after some thought, gave every desirable thing to Dvivida, Mainda, and Nīla.

75. And all the seniormost monkeys and the other monkey lords as well were honored according to their merit with garments and ornaments.

76. When each one of them had been honored according to his merit with many jewels and other desirable things, they all returned as they had come, delighted at heart.

77. Supremely magnanimous Rāghava then ruled in supreme felicity. And Rāma, who loved righteousness, said to Lakṣmaṇa, a knower of righteousness:

78. "Knower of righteousness, please govern with me this land of which those kings who came before us took possession with their forces. In the capacity of prince regent, you must, as my equal, bear this burden, which was borne by our forefathers."

79. But although Saumitri was being offered the position of prince regent of the land and was most earnestly entreated to accept this appointment, he would not do so. So great Rāma therefore consecrated Bharata.

80. Once righteous Rāghava had obtained that unsurpassed kingdom, he performed many different kinds of sacrifices, together with his friends, his brothers, and his kinsmen.

81. That bull among kings performed the Pauṇḍarīka, Aśvamedha, and Vājapeya sacrifices many times, as well as various other sacrifices.

82. Rāghava ruled his kingdom for ten thousand years and performed one hundred Aśvamedha sacrifices with splendid sacrificial horses and generous sacrificial fees.

83. With broad shoulders and his arms extending to his knees, valorous Rāma ruled the land with Lakṣmaṇa at his side.

84. While Rāma ruled the kingdom, no widows mourned, nor was there any fear of snakes or threat of disease.

85. The world was free from thieves, and misfortune afflicted no one. The elders never had to perform the funeral rites for their children.

86. Everyone was content. Everyone was devoted to righteousness. Looking constantly to Rāma alone, people did not harm one another.

87. While Rāma ruled the kingdom, people lived for thousands of years and had thousands of sons. They suffered no illness and were free from all sorrow.

88. The trees with their spreading boughs were always in flower and filled with fruit. Parjanya brought the rains at the proper time, and the breeze was pleasant to the touch.

89. While Rāma ruled, his subjects adhered to their own proper occupations and were satisfied with their own duties. Devoted to righteousness, they adhered always to the truth.

90. Everyone was endowed with auspicious marks. Everyone was devoted to righteousness. And so, for ten thousand years, Rāma ruled his kingdom.

The end of the one hundred sixteenth *sarga* of the *Yuddhakāṇḍa* of the *Śrī Rāmāyaṇa*.

The end of the *Yuddhakāṇḍa*.

NOTES

Sarga 1

In many N manuscripts (Ś1,Ñ,V1,B,D3,8,9,12), as well as the printed editions of Gorresio and Lahore, the first fifteen *sargas* of our *Yuddhakāṇḍa* form the last part of the *Sundarakāṇḍa*. In these manuscripts, the *Yuddhakāṇḍa* begins immediately after the bridge to Laṅkā has been built (*sarga* 16). Most of the other manuscripts begin with an invocation to one deity or another—Gaṇeśa, Rāma, Viṣṇu, etc. The previous *sarga* left off with the account of Hanumān reciting from memory to Rāma a fiery speech he had delivered to Sītā, whom he has just visited in her prison in Laṅkā. The beginning of the *Yuddhakāṇḍa* finds Hanumān and Rāma, two allies in a war against Rāvaṇa, on Mount Prasravaṇa, some distance away from the monkey capital, Kiṣkindhā. Hanumān has just told Rāma that Sītā's grief has somewhat abated.

1. According to Cg and Cm, the syllable "*ma*" in the name Hanumān (*hanumataḥ*) is the fifteenth syllable of the *Gāyatrīmantra*. See Goldman and Goldman 1996, p. 3 and note; and B. N. Bhatt 1976. See notes to 2.39.5; 2.65.22; 2.93.24; 3.45.10; 5.1.1; 5.12.48; and 5.25.14. See, too, notes to 6.19.26; 6.40.40; 6.56.1; 6.68.1; and 6.97.33, App. I, No. 67, n. 34.

"report, so faithfully rendered" *vākyaṃ yathāvad abhibhāṣitam*: Literally, "words accurately *or* properly spoken." Cs, apparently trying to avoid the repetition of words for speech (*vākyam . . . abhibhāṣitam*), understands *abhibhāṣitam*, "spoken, delivered," nominally in the sense of "speech" and reads *avākyam*, "without speech," for *vākyam*. He then takes *avākyam* adverbially with the gerund *śrutvā*, "having heard," in the sense of "having listened silently."

"he was delighted" *prītisamāyuktaḥ*: Literally, "[he was] joined *or* filled with delight."

"responded in these words" *vākyam uttaram abravīt*: Literally, "he spoke words [by way] of response." Several commentators, including Cg, Cm, Cs, and Ct, understand, "appropriate to the period after hearing good news (*uttaraṃ priyaśravaṇottarakālārham*—so Cg)."

2. Cg sees the verse as illustrative of the maxim: "One's elders are to be praised to their face, friends and relatives behind their backs, slaves and servants at the end of an assignment, and sons never (*pratyakṣe guravaḥ stutyāḥ parokṣe mitrabāndhavāḥ / karmānte dāsabhṛtyāś ca na kadācana putrakāḥ //*)." According to him, Rāma here praises his servant Hanumān upon the completion of his assignment.

"enormous feat, difficult to accomplish in this world" *sumahad bhuvi duṣkaram*: Cg understands the various words of praise in the verse to refer incrementally to the successive feats accomplished by Hanumān. He describes as great (*mahat*) the monkey's crossing of the ocean, and what is very great (*sumahat*) as his managing to enter Laṅkā. His assault on the city is well-nigh impossible (*durlabham* v.l. for *duṣkaram*), while what is not to be accomplished by others even in their imagination is Hanumān's return from his adventures. (*atra mahad ity anena sāgarataraṇam uycate. sumahad ity anena laṅkāpraveśaḥ. durlabham ity anena laṅkādharṣaṇam. manasāpi na śakyam ity anena punar nirgamaḥ.*) Cs, typically eccentric, reads the sequence *sumahad* + *bhuvi* as a compound in the sense of "in the realm of the great ones, i.e., the gods." He then understands the verse to say, "Hanumān has accomplished here on earth a feat, that is, the finding of Sītā, that would be impossible to accomplish even in heaven (*sumahatāṃ mahātmanāṃ devānāṃ yā bhūḥ svargādirūpaṃ sthānaṃ tasyām api durlabham asādhyaṃ yat kāryaṃ sītāsaṃdarśanarūpaṃ tad dharaṇītale hanumatā kṛtam*)."

"imagination" *manasā*: Literally, "by one's mind *or* thought."

3. "from Garuḍa and Vāyu" *garuḍād vāyoḥ*: Literally, "of Garuḍa and Vāyu." Cg understands the verse to suggest that Hanumān is not only equal to but superior to the great mythical eagle and the wind god. He paraphrases, "Garuḍa and Vāyu together might cross, [but he (Hanumān) has done it on his own] (*garuḍavāyū militvā taretām iti bhāvaḥ*)."

4–5. The repetitiveness of the two verses has not gone unnoticed by the commentators. Cv suggests that 5ab (*praviṣṭaḥ sattvam āśritya jīvan ko nāma niṣkramet*) has been added to the verse he sees as beginning with 4cd (*apradhṛṣyāṃ purīṃ laṅkāṃ rāvaṇena surakṣitām*). He further notes that 5cd (*ko viśet sudurādharṣāṃ rākṣasaiś ca surakṣitām*) has been added on and is, moreover, misplaced in some manuscripts due to scribal error (*apradhṛṣyām ity ādeḥ ślokasyoparitanam ardhaṃ praviṣṭaḥ sattvam āśritya jīvan ko nāma niṣkramed ity etat ko viśed ity ādeḥ ślokasyoparitanam ardhaṃ yo vīryabalasampanno na samaḥ syād dhanūmata etat keṣucit kośeṣu vyatyāsena dṛśyate tal lekhakadoṣakṛtam*).

"citadel of Laṅkā . . . unassailable . . . unassailable citadel" *apradhṛṣyāṃ purīṃ laṅkām . . . sudurādharṣām*: Literally, "unassailable citadel of Laṅkā . . . wholly impregnable one."

"unless he were so endowed with might and valor as to be the equal of Hanumān" *yo vīryabalasampanno na samaḥ syād dhanūmataḥ*: Literally, "who, endowed with might and valor, would not be the equal of Hanumān."

6. "his own power, which is commensurate with his valor" *svabalaṃ sadṛśaṃ vikramasya*: We follow the interpretation of all commentators and translators consulted in understanding that *sadṛśam*, "commensurate," modifies *svabalam*, "own power." One could also take *sadṛśam* to modify *bhṛtyakāryam*, "service," in *pāda* a, lending the line the sense of "a great service, commensurate with his valor." Cg appears to emphasize the prior member *sva-*, "his own," in *svabalam*, understanding the word to refer specifically to those actions performed on Hanumān's own initiative, without any authorization on the part of his master, Sugrīva. These actions, such as the destruction of the *aśoka* grove, etc., are thus contrasted to the service to Sugrīva mentioned in the first half of the verse and comprising those actions that were specifically enjoined upon Hanumān [that is, leaping the ocean, infiltrating Laṅkā, and finding Sītā] (*svabalam aśokavanikābhaṅgādikaṃ pauruṣaṃ svayam ātmanaḥ svāminiyogaṃ vinā vidhāya sugrīvasya bhṛtyakāryaṃ bhṛtyena kartavyaṃ mahad adhikaṃ kṛtam ity arthaḥ*—so Cg). Cm and Ct understand similarly. All three understand the adjective *mahat*, "[truly] great," to mean "exceeding his instructions (*mahad uktād adhikam*—so Ct)."

7. This verse and the one that follows seem to be quoted or paraphrased from a treatise on statecraft that has not been traced. Sternbach 1965–1967, vol. 2, pt. 2 cites a few aphorisms of the same import from the *Mahābhārata* and other works.

"loyally" *anurāgeṇa*: The translation follows the commentators who understand the word in its normal lexical sense of "devotion, affection, loyalty (*atiprītyā*—so Cr)."

"is considered to be" *tam āhuḥ*: Literally, "they call him."

"the best type of servant" *puruṣottamam*: Literally, "the best of men."

Following verse 7, D5–7,10,11,S, and the texts and printed editions of the southern commentators insert a passage of two lines. This verse is unnumbered in the critical apparatus, which understands the additional verse as a repetition with variants of verse 8. The verse as found in GPP 6.1.8; VSP 6.1.8; and KK 6.1.8 reads: "A servant who, although given an important assignment, does not carry it out to the satisfaction of the king, though he is fit and competent, is considered to be the middle type of servant."

8. "single-mindedly" *samāhitaḥ*: Literally, "focused, concentrated."

"is considered to be" *tam āhuḥ*: Literally, "they call him."

"the worst type of servant" *puruṣādhamam*: Literally, "the worst of men."

9. "assignment" *niyoge*: The commentators return to the theme of Hanumān's having exceeded his instructions. Cm, Ct, and Cr, for example, understand the term *niyoga*, "assignment," to refer exclusively to the search for Sītā (*sītānveṣaṇamātre*—so Ct). Ct then understands *kṛtyam*, "what he had to do," to refer to the additional deeds of Hanumān (*kṛtyam adhikam api kṛtyaṃ kṛtam ata uttamabhṛtyo 'yam iti bhāvaḥ*).

"without disgracing himself" *na cātmā laghutāṃ nītaḥ*: Literally, "nor was he himself brought to insignificance." The commentators agree that the reference here is to Hanumān's not being bested by the *rākṣasas* (*rakṣobhir aparājitatvāt*).

10. "preserved...from unrighteousness" *dharmataḥ parirakṣitāḥ*: Literally, "preserved in accordance with righteousness." The commentators offer a variety of interpretations of this vague phrase. The translation follows the majority of commentators, including Cg, Cm, and Cv, who understand that Hanumān's actions have established Rāma and his brothers in righteousness, reasoning that, "If Sītā had not been discovered by Hanumān, Rāma would have committed the sin of taking his own life. This, in turn, would have driven Lakṣmaṇa and the other members of the Raghu clan to suicide. (*dharmataḥ parirakṣitā dharme sthāpitā adharmān nirvartitā iti yāvat. yadi hanumān vaidehīṃ nādrākṣīt tadāhaṃ jīvitaṃ jahyāṃ madviyogāsahiṣṇavo lakṣmaṇādayaś ca tathā kuryuḥ. tathā cātmahananarūpādharmaḥ sarveṣāṃ saṃbhaved iti bhāvaḥ*—so Cm.)" Cf. Hanumān's contemplation of this scenario in 5.11.20ff. and 5.53.8ff. Ct also understands the term *parirakṣitāḥ* to refer to the saving of Rāma and his kinsmen from suicide. He and Cr, however, understand *dharmataḥ* to refer to the righteousness or propriety of Hanumān's execution of the duties of a servant in carrying out his master's orders (*bhṛtyadharmaṃ prāpya*—so Cr). Cg offers as an alternative yet a third explanation, glossing *dharma* with *upakāra*, "service, assistance, favor," in the form of finding Sītā, and notes that, through that service, he [Rāma] and his kinsmen have been rescued from infamy (*yadvā vaidehīdarśanarūpeṇa dharmeṇopakāreṇa sarve vayaṃ parirakṣitā nirapavādāḥ kṛtāḥ smeti bhāvaḥ*).

11. "here and now" *iha*: Literally, "here."

12. "all the wealth" *sarvasvabhūtaḥ*: The commentators explain this collocation in terms of Śrīvaiṣṇava theology. Ct, citing Rāmānuja's utterance in his commentaries on the *Bhagavadgītā* and *Viṣṇusahasranāmastotra* that "the essence of the Lord is pure bliss (*ānanda eva hi bhagavataḥ sarvasvam*)" and that this bliss is manifested through "illusion (*māyā*)," in the bodily forms of Rāma, etc., sees the expression as a reference to the supreme bliss of union with the Lord. He further cites the parallel of the bliss associated with Brahmā to have been communicated to Hanumān through the means of the god's embrace. (*bhagavaddehasya śuddhānandarūpatvāt svaliṅganasya sarvasvabhūtatvaṃ bodhyam. ānanda eva hi bhagavataḥ sarvasvaṃ. ānanda eva hi māyayā rāmādidehatvena bhāsata iti gītābhāṣyaviṣṇusahasranāmabhāṣyayor bhagavadpādaiḥ spaṣṭam evoktam*). Next, Ct makes reference to the *Brahmāṇḍapurāṇa* and similar texts (*brahmāṇḍapurāṇādiṣu caivaṃ pariṣvaṅgadvārā brahmānandārpaṇam eva hanūmate kṛtam iti bodhitam*).

Cr takes the phrase to suggest that Hanumān has no use for anything other than Rāma's embrace and that, through this embrace, one accomplishes the supreme goals of mankind (*etena pariṣvaṅgātiriktaṃ hanumadupayogivastvantaraṃ nāstīti sūcitaṃ tena rāmapariṣvaṅgaprāpteḥ paramapuruṣārthatvaṃ sūcitam*).

Cg suggests a much more elaborate theological and psychological analysis in which he interprets the inner workings of Rāma's mind that underlie the sentiments expressed in the verse. His analysis may be summarized as follows: Rāma's distress [at having no fitting reward for Hanumān's service] cannot be assuaged without compensation in the form of giving him [Hanumān] all his wealth. Rāma thinks that his embrace will serve as a substitute for giving all his wealth. The embrace is equivalent to all his wealth because of Rāma's embodiment in a large and desirable form and because of his limitless capacity to be enjoyed. Thus, in this world the Lord instructs those whom he loves regarding his own capacity to be enjoyed, because if the Lord were to give all he owned apart from that, the gift would be wanting, whereas in the gift of that capacity itself everything is given, since all things are dependent upon his body. That very embrace alone is to be given to Hanumān as one who is truly a lover of the Lord's form, for one should not give an eater of ambrosia a mouthful of straw. (*etad pradāne tu sarvaṃ dattam etad vigrahasya sarvāśrayatvāt pariṣvaṅgo hanūmataḥ. amṛtāśino hi tṛṇakavalādikaṃ na deyam.*)

Cs offers a somewhat forced alternative explanation: Rāma derives his wealth from the Goddess (reading *mayā* as the instrumental of *mā* = *lakṣmī*), and thus he was previously unable to pass it on to Hanumān in the form of an embrace, suggestive of perfect union with the Lord, as the time was not propitious (reading *mayākālam* as *mayā akālam*). He can, however, do so now. All of this, Cs concludes, illuminates [the Lord's] overmastering compassion. (*eṣa pariṣvaṅga āliṅganarūpaḥ. imaṃ kālam etādṛśaṃ samayaṃ prāpya. mahātmanaḥ tasya hanumato dattaḥ. mayā ramayā mahātmano mama ca sarvasvabhūta eṣo 'pīmam akālaṃ sāyujyasūcakasya tasyedānīm ayogyatvāt tatkālabhinnaṃ kālaṃ prāpyāpi mayā datta iti vā.*) According to Cs, by this we understand the Lord's utter devotion to compassion (*anena kṛpā pāravaśyaṃ dyotyate*).

"at this time" *kālam imaṃ prāpya*: Cr remarks that the time is suitable for giving gifts (*imaṃ dānayogyaṃ kālaṃ prāpya sarvasvabhūto mama sarvadhanatvaṃ prāptaḥ*). Cg continues (see above *sarvasvabhūtaḥ*) his representation of Rāma's thoughts, explaining, "He certainly merits a gift, since he is filled with love for this body [i.e., Rāma's form] as evidenced by his expression, 'I have the greatest love [for you], your majesty' (7.40.16 = GPP 7.39.15). I will give him something at this time. He [Hanumān] is not expecting anything from me, but I am filled with anxiety about when I will be able to give him something. Therefore, I will give him something right now because to do so is not prohibited at this time. (*sneho me paramo rājann ity etadvigrahe premavataḥ sa eva dātavyaḥ. mayā kālam imaṃ prāpya dattaḥ. ayaṃ kiṃcid api matto 'napekṣamāṇo vartate. kadā mayāsmai kiṃcid dattaṃ syād iti sotkaṇṭhena mayā sthitaṃ saṃpraty apratiṣedhasamayalābhād dattavān asmi.*)" Interestingly, Cg sees Rāma as concerned that even his cherished embrace may not be adequate compensation for Hanumān's extraordinary service. He explains Rāma's thinking as follows: "Is it proper to give a single body to one who has performed such service to two bodies, that is, to him who has given [i.e., saved] two bodies—Sītā's when she was about to hang herself by her hair (5.27.17) and Rāma's when he was on the point of throwing himself into the sea (6.5.9) by providing him with the message about Sītā? (*dehadvayam upakṛtavataḥ kim ekadehapradānam ucitam iti bhāvaḥ. veṇyudgrathanasamaye sītāṃ saṃrakṣya dattvāvagāhyārṇavaṃ svapsya iti daśāyāṃ rāmadehaṃ ca sītāsaṃdeśavacanenājīvayad dhi. evaṃ dehadvayaṃ dattavataḥ kim *ekadehadānam ucitam iti bhāvaḥ.*)" Evidently, Cg sees Rāma in his compassion and gratitude as thinking that even his embrace is insufficient compensation for Hanumān's feat.

Following verse 12, D5,7,11,S, and the texts and printed editions of the southern commentators insert a passage of four lines [9*]: "When Rāma had spoken in this fashion, his body bristling with delight, he embraced great Hanumān, who had returned after accomplishing his mission. Then, after pondering, the delight of the Raghus once more spoke these words as Sugrīva, lord of the tawny monkeys, stood listening."

13. "my mind once again gives way to despair" *punar naṣṭaṃ mano mama*: Literally, "once again my mind is destroyed." Most commentators understand that Rāma, having been cheered by the news of Sītā's discovery, is plunged once more into despondency when he sees how formidable an obstacle the ocean is (*punar naṣṭaṃ sītāvṛttāntaśravaṇena hṛṣṭam api punar viṣādaṃ prāptam*—so Ct).

14. "all" *samāhitāḥ*: Literally, "assembled, joined together."

15. "what on earth are we to do next" *kim ivottaram*: Literally, "what indeed [is] next?" The commentators generally supply the word "action (*karma*—Cr)" or "means, method (*sādhakam*—Cm, Cg)." Cg understands the question to be rhetorical, indicating that Rāma believes that there is no possible way of getting monkeys across (*kiṃ na kim apīty arthaḥ*).

16. "distracted by sorrow" *śokasaṃbhrāntaḥ*: Cr proposes reading *uktvāśoka-* (*uktvā + aśoka-*) instead of the critical *uktvā śoka-*. He interprets the compound to mean "Rāma who was devoid of any real sorrow (*vāstavaśokasaṃbhrāntirahitaḥ*)."

"fell to brooding" *dhyānam upāgamat*: Literally, "he went to meditation." The commentators generally understand the phrase to mean that Rāma is pondering the means of crossing the ocean (*sāgarataraṇopāyacintām akarod ity arthaḥ*—so Cg).

Sarga 2

1. "majestic" *śrīmān*: Cg takes the adjective as an opportunity to quote the *Kāmandaka* on the qualities of a friend of which we are to understand Sugrīva is exemplary. They are honesty, selflessness, heroism, stoicism, loyalty, courtesy, and truthfulness (*śucitā tyāgitā śauryaṃ samānasukhaduḥkhatā / anurāgaś ca dākṣiṇyaṃ satyatā ca suhṛdguṇāḥ //*). Cg also remarks on the slightly unusual fact that Sugrīva responds to a speech that was uttered in his presence but directed to Hanumān. See note to 6.4.1, where Rāma, in response to a speech of Hanumān, appears to reply to Sugrīva. See 9* at note to 6.1.12. Cg explains this departure from the epic convention by saying that Sugrīva is reflecting on the *nītiśāstra* rule that one who wishes someone well at a moment of crisis may speak helpful words, even though unasked (*āpady unmārgagamane kāryakālātyayeṣu cāpṛṣṭo 'py hitānveṣī brūyāt kalyāṇabhāṣitam*).

2. "other, ordinary man" *anyaḥ prākṛtaḥ*: Literally, "another, ordinary [one]." Cr understands the term to mean a person different from one who is independent, and so on (*anyaḥ svatantrādibhinnaḥ prākṛto janaḥ*).

4. "resolute, learned in the *śāstras*, wise, and erudite" *dhṛtimāñ śāstravit prājñaḥ paṇḍitaś ca*: D6,7,10,11,G3,M3,5, and the texts and printed editions of Cm, Cg, and Ct read *matimān*, "intelligent," for *dhṛtimān*, "resolute." This is one of the frequent epic

lists of near synonyms. The commentators offer similar, but by no means identical, explanations of the individual terms. Ct, Cg, and Cm understand *śāstravit* to mean "learned in the traditional texts on polity (*nītiśāstraḥ*), etc." Ct understands *prājñaḥ* to mean "skillful in deliberation (*vicārakuśalaḥ*)," while Cg and Cm understand this word to mean "learned in positive and negative argumentation (*ūhāpohajñaḥ*)." Ct understands *paṇḍitaḥ* to mean "capable of setting forth the proper conclusion after deliberation (*siddhāntapratiṣṭhāpanaḥ*)." Cg understands, "making accurate determinations (*paricchetā*)." Cm offers the same explanation as Cg plus an alternative: "understanding the essence of a matter (*arthatattvajñaḥ*)." Cv understands *paṇḍitaḥ* to mean "capable of positive and negative argumentation (*ūhāpohasamarthaḥ*)." See note to verse 14 below.

"reprehensible attitude" *pāpikāṃ buddhiṃ*: Literally, "sinful idea *or* thought." Cg explains, "tainted with sin, that it to say, inducing lethargy *or* torpor (*pāpayuktām anutsāhakāriṇīm iti yāvat*)." Cm glosses, "wholly inauspicious, wrongful (*aśubhātmikām, kaluṣitām*)." Ś1,Ñ1,D1,2,4,8,10–12, and the texts and printed editions of Ct read instead *prākṛtām*, "ordinary, vulgar."

5. "We shall . . . scale the battlements of Laṅkā" *laṅkām ārohayiṣyāmaḥ*: Literally, "we shall climb Laṅkā."

"huge sharks" *mahānakra-*: Cf. 5.7.6 and notes.

6. "fail utterly" *vyavasīdanti*: Literally, "they fail *or* come to grief."

8–9. "I am absolutely certain of this" *tarkaś cāsmin dṛḍho mama*: Literally, "my reasoned conclusion with respect to this is firm." The placement of this phrase lends a certain ambiguity to the referent, an ambiguity only heightened by the fact that some printed versions of the text take 8ab as a separately numbered and defective verse (KK and VSP = 6.3.8) or number it as *pādas* ef of verse 7 (GPP). The issue is whether Sugrīva's conclusion refers backward to the readiness of the monkeys for battle or forward to the necessity for crossing the ocean and assaulting Rāvaṇa. We have selected the former approach on the basis of the normal range of meanings of *tarka*, that is, "logical conclusion, conjecture, etc.," and see the phrase as a reiteration of Sugrīva's inference of the monkeys' state of mind based on their outward manifestation of excitement. We are joined in this interpretation by Cg and Cm. Ct and Ck, however, take the latter view.

"excitement" *harṣeṇa*: Ct understands that the excitement of the monkeys is brought about by the mention of crossing the ocean [and confronting] Rāvaṇa. He goes on to say that Sugrīva is able to infer the monkeys' enthusiasm from their excited facial expressions [at the thought] of the mission. (*harṣeṇa samudrataraṇarāvaṇaprasaṅge jāyamānena. tatkāryamukhavikāsādinānumitenety arthaḥ*.) (Cm similarly.) Cg understands the term to refer to Sugrīva's inference based on the tranquility (*prasāda*) of the monkeys' facial expressions (*harṣeṇa mukhaprasādānumānena*).

"we may reach" *paśyema*: Literally, "that we may see."

Following verse 8, D5–7,10,11,S insert, while D3 substitutes for 9cd, a passage of one line [16*]: "You must act in such a way that [having killed your enemy], the wicked Rāvaṇa . . ."

10. "From the very moment that we see" *dṛṣṭvā . . . darśanāt*: Literally, "having seen . . . from the sight." The reading *darśanāt*, "from the sight," is both awkward and ambiguous. The majority of commentators understand, as we do, that it is the sight of Laṅkā alone that will serve as a sign of the doom of Rāvaṇa (*trikūṭaśikharasthāṃ tāṃ*

laṅkāṃ dṛṣṭvā darśanāt taddarśanasamanantaram eva yuddhe rāvaṇaṃ hatam avadhāraya jānīhi—so Ct). The idea, which seems to follow from the preceding verses, is that the major obstacle is not Rāvaṇa himself but the crossing of the ocean. Cr, alone among the commentators, understands *darśanāt* to refer to the sight of Rāvaṇa, an interpretation that, though perhaps less appropriate to the context, has the advantage of avoiding the redundancy with *dṛṣṭvā* in *pāda* a (*purīṃ laṅkāṃ dṛṣṭvā rāvaṇadarśanād rāvaṇadarśanaṃ prāpya yuddhe rāvaṇaṃ hatam avadhāraya jānīhi*).

"on the peak of Mount Trikūṭa" *trikūṭaśikhare*: Literally, "on the peak of Trikūṭa." See 6.3.29; 6.30.18–20; 6.34.25; 6.61.66; and notes. See, too, notes to 6.29.13; 6.78.41; and 6.91.2. See also 5.1.183,189; 5.2.1,8,18; 5.3.1; 5.37.49; and 5.54.9 and notes.

Following verse 10, D5–7,10,11,S insert a passage of two lines [17*]: "For without building a bridge across the dreadful ocean, the abode of Varuṇa, not even the gods and *asuras* along with Indra could lay waste to Laṅkā."

11. "to Laṅkā" *laṅkāsamīpataḥ*: Literally, "near Laṅkā."

"you may claim victory" *jitam ity upadhāryatām*: Literally, "You may think, 'Conquered!'" See *MBh* 2.54.3–29 for a similar construction (*jitam ity eva*). The syntax of the participle *jitam* is somewhat unusual. Cg explains it as a *kartari niṣṭhā*, that is [normally] the passive participial ending *kta* used actively, while Cv explains it as an abstract use of the participle (*bhāve niṣṭhā*).

12. 12ab = 20ab.

"So . . . enough of this craven attitude, so destructive to all endeavors" *tad alaṃ viklavā buddhiḥ . . . sarvārthanāśinī*: The syntax is slightly opaque, although the meaning is unambiguous. Various manuscripts associated with the southern recension and the texts and printed editions of the southern commentators select alternately the accusative or the nominative of *buddhi* and its modifying adjectives. Neither case is normally governed by *alam* in the classical grammar, and we must therefore assume that these variants are particular to the epic language (Apte s.v. *alam*). Cg tries to avoid the difficulty by using the prohibitive force of *alam* to render it in the sense of the injunctive form *mā bhūt*. In order to support this use of *alam*, he quotes *Amarakośa* 3.3.882. (*alaṃ mā bhūt. alaṃ bhūṣaṇaparyāptiśaktivāraṇavācakam ity amaraḥ.*)

Following 12ab, M, VSP (6.2.15ab in brackets), and KK (6.12.14cd) insert a passage of one line [18*]: "They are capable of uprooting Laṅkā—*rākṣasas* included—and bringing it here." No translation consulted renders this line.

13. "But, wise Rāma, now is the time for you to resort energetically to strength, which is the proper recourse of a man who relies on valor." *yat tu kāryaṃ manuṣyeṇa śauṇḍīryam avalambatā / asmin kāle mahāprājña sattvam ātiṣṭha tejasā //*: *Pādas* c–f of the critical text are somewhat difficult to construe as they stand. The critical reading is well represented in a variety of southern manuscripts and is also the reading of Cg and the texts and printed editions that follow him (VSP; KK). The major problem with the critical reading is the poor resolution of the relative clause of *pādas* cd. Our translation assumes an implied correlative *tat* referring to *sattvam*, "strength," in *pāda* f. Even so, the verse is semantically, as well as syntactically, problematic. Different northern and southern texts attempt to avoid the difficulty in various ways. D10,11, and the texts and printed editions of Ct and Ck include an additional line [19*]. Reading 13cd with 19*, the verse would translate as "Whatever action must be taken by a man who relies on valor redounds to the credit [literally, "adorns"] of him who

does it with alacrity." Those translations based on the text of Ct (Dutt 1893, p. 1108; Shastri 1959, vol. 3, p. 5; Gita Press 1969, vol. 3, p. 74; and Roussel 1903, vol. 3, p. 4) follow this version. This reading leaves 13ef to be construed as a separate sentence: "At this time, wise Rāma, you must energetically resort to strength." As a result of these complications, few of the published editions number this passage as does the critical edition. Several northern manuscripts, including the text of Gorresio (5.71.6), avoid the problem by substituting *tat tvam* for *sattvam*. Thus, the text of Gorresio reads, "At this time, lord of men, you must have active recourse to that which is practiced by a man who cherishes valor."

"wise Rāma" *mahāprājña*: Literally, "O one of great wisdom!"

"energetically" *tejasā*: Literally, "with energy." Cg suggests, "with valor (*parākrameṇa*)."

"strength" *sattvam*: Cg, Cm, and Cr gloss, "fortitude *or* resolve (*dhairyam*)." Cg optionally understands, "strength (*balam*)." Ct takes the word in its other sense of "virtue (*guṇam*)." He is followed in this by Dutt (1893, p. 1108), who translates, "Do thou realize goodness through thy energy." Dutt explicitly acknowledges Ct in his footnote, where he remarks, "i.e., as I understand this rather obscure passage, *prove thou good through thy vigor—secure victory to the cause of goodness through thy might.*—T [= Ct]." Similarly Roussel (1903, vol. 3, p. 4) translates, "*unis l'énergie à la vertu*," followed by Shastri (1959, vol. 3, p. 5), who renders, "unite energy with virtue."

14. "in the case of death or disappearance" *vinaṣṭe vā pranaṣṭe vā*: Literally, "when [someone] has died or disappeared." Here, the commentators generally agree that one of these near synonyms means the disappearance of a living person, while the other means death. Ct understands *vinaṣṭa* to refer to someone who has been removed from one's sight, like Sītā, and *pranaṣṭa* to refer to someone who has been irrevocably removed from one's sight, i.e., dead, like Daśaratha (*vinaṣṭe sītāvad adarśanaṃ gate pranaṣṭe daśarathavat sarvathādarśaṇaṃ gate*). Cm and Cg concur with Ct. Cm understands *vinaṣṭa* to mean "disappeared," citing the form as a participle of the root √*naś* [√*ṇaś*] in the sense of invisibility. He offers no comment on the meaning of *pranaṣṭa*. Cr reverses the two meanings and understands *vinaṣṭa* to mean "destroyed (*vidhvastaḥ*)," i.e., dead, and *pranaṣṭa* to mean "removed from sight (*adarśanam*)." For another commentarial discussion on the range of meanings for these two terms, see note to 5.11.17.

The use of such synonyms is common in Vālmīki's epic as we have noted elsewhere. Cf. 5.1.33; 5.2.14–15; 5.7.12,40; 5.24.2,11; 5.31.9; 5.34.8; 5.35.63; 5.55.29; 5.60.12; and notes. Cf., too, 6.2.4; 6.4.17,41; 6.7.5; 6.8.10; 6.9.20; 6.12.18; 6.14.7; 6.20.5; 6.27.14,16; 6.28.20–21; 6.28.35; 6.35.6,19; 6.36.4–7; 6.37.9; 6.40.23,40; 6.48.31,83; 6.47.93; 6.55.106; 6.57.37; 6.63.15; 6.64.16; 6.80.4; 6.81.19; 6.93.2–3; 6.115.13–16; and notes.

15. "comrades" *sacivaiḥ*: The term can also mean counselors or ministers, and we generally translate it in the latter sense.

"now" *iha*: Literally, "here." The translation follows the interpretation of Cr (*asmin samaye*) and Cg (*idānīm*).

16. "I cannot think" *na . . . paśyāmy aham*: Literally, "I do not see."

"once you take your bow in hand" *grahītadhanuṣaḥ*: Literally, "of [you] who have grasped a bow."

18. "Unleash your anger!" *krodham ālambha*: Literally, "Have recourse to your anger!"

"Passive . . . fare badly" *niśceṣṭāḥ . . . mandāḥ*: Literally, "inactive ones [are] sluggish." Commentators differ somewhat as to the interpretation of these terms. Ct and Ck understand the latter term, *manda*, to refer to warriors who are lacking in rage toward their enemies and who therefore become *niśceṣṭa* (literally, "motionless") by virtue of their becoming imprisoned by their enemies. (*mandāḥ satruviṣaye krodhahīnāḥ kṣatriyāḥ niśceṣṭā bhavanti. śatrukṛtabandhanādineti śeṣaḥ.*) Similarly, Cr explains *niśceṣṭa* as "devoid of actions caused by appropriate anger (*ucitakrodhahetukavyāpārarahitāḥ mandā bhavanti*)." Cg and Cm, whom we follow, understand that warriors who are not aggressive (*nirudyogāḥ*) fare poorly (literally, "become unfortunate") (*mandabhāgyāḥ*).

"impetuous" *caṇḍasya*: The term commonly refers to violent or furious anger. It has been taken as such by commentators and translators alike. Despite Sugrīva's exhortation to anger in *pāda* b, however, we feel the sense of *caṇḍa* is contextually most apposite in the second half of the verse as "impetuous," where the issue appears to be that of aggressive action versus passivity.

19. The verse lends itself to a certain ambiguity of interpretation. As a result, the prepositional phrase *sahāsmābhiḥ*, "with us," can be read with any or all of the three verbal elements, "crossing (*laṅghana*)," "coming (*upeta*)," and "deliberating (*vicāraya*)." In addition, the participle *upetaḥ* is ambiguous and can mean either "together with" or "approached." Ct reads the prepositional phrase with both *laṅghana-* and *upetaḥ*, yielding the sense "you have come with us for the purpose of crossing with us." Cr reads *upetaḥ* in the first of the above-mentioned senses, glossing, "joined (*yukta-*)," which yields the sense "joined with us, you should consider the means to cross the ocean."

"you should consider how to accomplish this" *vicāraya*: Literally, "you must think *or* consider."

Following verse 19, D5–7,10,11,T,G,M3,5, and the texts and printed editions of Ct, Ck, and Cm insert a passage of two lines [25*], whereas the text of Cg inserts only line 2 of 25*: "Once they [the monkeys] have crossed it, consider [Rāvaṇa's] army as good as destroyed. Once my whole army has crossed, you may claim victory." Ct's reading, which many translators follow, has a slight variant: "Once my soldiers have crossed, you may claim victory. Once my whole army has crossed, you may claim victory."

20. 20ab = 12ab.

"smash" *vidhamiṣyanti*: Literally, "they will blow away *or* they will disperse." Cg glosses, "they will scorch *or* burn (*dhakṣyanti*)."

*21ab. "Rāvaṇa's abode" *rāvaṇālayam*: We have emended the critical text's reading, *varuṇālayam*, "Varuṇa's abode," i.e., "the ocean." The critical reading of *pāda* ab is not well attested, being derived mainly from a small number of northwest manuscripts. As it stands, the critical reading makes little sense. The whole thrust of the verse, and indeed of Sugrīva's argumentation, is that, once the monkeys have found a way to cross the ocean, victory over the *rākṣasas* is assured. Aside from the northwest manuscripts and the critical edition, no southern or northern manuscript makes *vāruṇālaya* the object of the verb *paripaśyāmaḥ*. D10,11, and the texts and printed editions aligned with Ct, Cr, and Ck avoid the problem by reading *laṅghitam*, "crossed over," in place of the critical text's *te vayam*, "we [who are] they," which would then modify *varuṇālayam*. The sense of this reading—"Somehow or other I [reading *paripaśyāmi*] will see that the abode of Varuṇa is crossed"—is, if awkward, at least in keeping with the tenor of this passage. This is rendered in the translations that follow

Ct. D6,7,T2,M3, and the texts and printed editions associated with Cm and Cg, which read *varuṇālayam*, read for *paśyāmaḥ*, "we shall see," *saṃtariṣyāmaḥ*, "we shall cross," yielding the meaning "One way or another we shall cross the abode of Varuṇa." This variant is rendered only in the translation of Raghunathan (1982, vol. 3, p. 3–4). The majority of the remaining manuscripts, northern and southern, including the text of Gorresio, read *rāvaṇālayam* instead of *varuṇālayam*, and we have therefore selected it as the most plausible reading. The Lahore edition excises this half verse, relegating it, roughly in the form found in the critical edition, to its critical apparatus.

"what more is to be said" *kim uktvā bahudhā*: Literally, "what is the use of speaking in so many ways?"

Following 21ab, D5–7,10,11,S insert a passage of one line [28*]: "Then I regard him [Rāvaṇa] as slain in battle, O you who delight in battle." After 21cd, these same manuscripts insert one additional line [30*]: "I see [auspicious] omens and my heart is filled with joy."

Sarga 3

1. "grasped its essential meaning" *paramārthavit*: The critical edition follows the text of Cg, who understands this epithet to be suggestive of Rāma's ability to grasp the essence of any matter (*sāragrāhitvam*). D7,10,11,T1,M1,2,5, and the texts and printed editions of Ct and Cs read instead *paramārthavat*, which is then an adjective with the sense "filled with profound meaning," modifying *vacaḥ*, "speech." Ct and Ck suggest that the ending *-vat* has no semantic value here (*paramārthavat paramārthabhūtaṃ svārthe vatiḥ*—so Ct). Cr understands the adjective to mean "awakening [Rāma] to his supreme purpose (*paramārthabodhakam*)." Cs understands "the supreme purpose" to be the principal purpose of the [Rāma] *avatāra*, that is, the destruction of Rāvaṇa, and so on," and then understands the adjective to mean "bringing that about." (*paramārtho 'vatāramukhyārtho rāvaṇamaraṇādis tadvat. tadghaṭakam iti yāvat.*)

2. "by building a bridge" *setubandhena*: Ct and Ck envisage Rāma doing so with his arrows in a manner similar to that employed by the young Bhīṣma in the *Mahābhārata* to dam the Ganges (*setubandhanena gaṅgāyāṃ gāṅgeyena śarair iva*). Compare *MBh* 1.94.24 (*divyam astraṃ vikurvāṇaṃ yathā devaṃ purandaram / kṛtsnāṃ gaṅgāṃ samāvṛtya śarais tīkṣṇair avasthitam*).

"by . . . drying up the ocean" *sāgarocchoṣaṇena*: Ct and Ck note that Rāma would be capable of so doing through the power of his divine *astras* (*divyāstrabalata iti śeṣaḥ*).

"quickly" *tarasā*: A wide variety of northern and southern manuscripts (Ś1,Ñ,V1,3,B3,D,T1,3,G1,3,M), virtually all the southern commentators, and all printed editions, with the exception of Gorresio (1856, vol. 9, p. 133), read *tapasā*, "through [the power of my] austerities." The critical reading is mentioned as a variant by Cg, who glosses it as *vegena*, "swiftly." On the reading *tapasā*, Ct and Ck remark that the power of Rāma's austerities can also be seen from his leading all the inhabitants of his own city [Ayodhyā] to the Brahmaloka at the end of the epic (Compare 1.1.76 and 7.100.1–4,23 [*devaloka*]). (*tapasā tapaḥkāryasaṃkalpasiddhyā. ata eva sakalasvapuravartiprāṇināṃ brahmalokanayanaṃ vakṣyamāṇaṃ saṃgacchate.*) Ck adds that this power is similar to that manifested by Svayaṃprabhā when she rescues the monkeys from the enchanted cavern in the *Kiṣkindhākāṇḍa* (4.52.1–12) (*svayaṃprabhayā bilād vānarottāraṇavad ity arthaḥ*).

3–4. "defenses" *durgāṇi*: The term here appears to apply broadly to both the natural and artificial defenses of the city. Ct and Ck understand the reference to be to the city's natural defenses, such as its bodies of water, mountains, forests, etc. (*jalagirivanādinānāprakāradurgeṣu*). Cg glosses the term as "defensive parapets (*durgaprākāraḥ*)" but goes on to enumerate the defensive works as consisting of bodies of water, mountains, earthworks, etc. (*jalagiristhalātmakāni durgāṇi*).

"the fortress of Laṅkā" *durgāyā laṅkāyāḥ*: Literally, "of the fortress Laṅkā." We read the term *durgā* here in its common nominal sense of "fortress, citadel, fortified place," against the majority of commentators and translators, who take it adjectivally in the sense of "difficult of access, inaccessible (*duṣprāpāyāḥ*—so Cg; *gantum aśakyāyāḥ*—so Ct)."

"the fortification of the gates" *dvāradurgakriyām*: Ct, Cr, Ck, Cg, and Cv explain that these are the arrangements to make entry at the gates difficult (*dvārāṇāṃ duṣpraveśatvasaṃpādanam*—Ct). Cr enumerates them as the construction of moats, etc. (*parikhādiviśeṣanirmitam*). Cg extends the list to include bolts, moats, devices for flooding, etc. (*kīlakhananajalaughaplavanakaraṇādibhir durgamatvakaraṇam*).

"the defensive works" *guptikarma*: Ct and Cr understand the reference to be to the emplacement of defensive devices (*yantras*) on the ramparts of the city (*prākārādiṣu yantrādisthāpanarūpam*—so Ct). These defensive devices (*yantras*) are frequently understood to be some kind of military machinery, but it is likely that the term *guptikarma* here is understood in the root sense of the word as a restraint or bolt. This notion is perhaps strengthened by Cg's explanation, which is "the fixing of bars, etc., on the ramparts (*prākāraparighādinirmāṇam*)." Cf. 5.40.31 and note. Cm understands, "the construction of watchtowers, and so on, on the ramparts (*prākārāṭṭālakādinirmāṇam*)." Ck (Ct as variant) reads *guptikrama*, "sequence of defenses." Cf. 6.30.26; 6.80.19; and notes.

5. "you were able to reconnoiter" *asi dṛṣṭavān*: Literally, "you saw."

"carefully" *yathāvat*: Literally, "duly, properly."

"at will" *yathāsukham*: Cg and Cm see this term as referring to the fearlessness (Cg—*niḥśaṅkam*; Cm—*visrabdham* [v.l. of *viśrabdham*]) of Hanumān.

"qualified to do so" *kuśalaḥ*: Literally, "skillful." Cg, Ct, Ck, and Cm indicate, in various ways, that the sense is that Hanumān is qualified both to reconnoiter and to explain what he has seen (*laṅkāyāṃ dṛṣṭavān kuśalaḥ tadvarṇanādau nipuṇaś ca*—so Cr).

7. Following verse 7, D5–7,10,11,S insert a passage of one line [38*], which can be, and has been, read in two ways by commentators and translators according to whether they construe the second *pāda* with the preceding or following verse. Thus it can be read with the preceding verse to mean "and how the *rākṣasas* are devoted because of Rāvaṇa's magnificent power," or construing the second *pāda* with verse 8, which reads "and how devoted the *rākṣasas* are. And how, because of Rāvaṇa's power . . ." See note to verse 8 below.

8–39*. The syntax of verse 8 is extremely awkward. No manuscript, northern or southern, reads as does the critical text. The problem with the text as constituted is that the string of accusatives that make up verse 8 is orphaned, as it were, with no verb in the surrounding syntax to govern it. Cr, who reads 8ab ["the fearsome nature of the sea, the extraordinary wealth of Laṅkā"] with 38* (see note to verse 7 above), tries to link it to *akhyāsye*, "I will tell you," in 7a, but this is difficult to accept, given the intervening nominatives of 7cd. For this reason, we have chosen to include the southern reading 39*, which provides at least a plausible verb in *kathayāmāsa*, "he reported." The problem does not arise in the northern recension, for there the critical edition's verse 8 does not occur until somewhat later, where its accusatives are clearly governed by the verb *ācacakṣe*, "he described," from a previous verse. Cf. Gorresio 5.73.3–4 and Lahore 5.70.23–24. See Sutherland 1992.

"of its mounts and vehicles" *vāhanasya*: Literally, "of its vehicle *or* mount." We follow Ct in taking the term here as a reference to the collectivity of the city's vehicles and mounts. He glosses, "characterized by elephants, horses, and chariots (*gajāśvarathalakṣaṇasya*)."

9–20. This appears to be one of the few extant literary descriptions of an ancient Indian fortress. See Singh 1965. Cf. the description of Laṅkā at 5.3 and also Kauṭilīya's *Arthaśāstra* 2.3.

9. "joyous and filled with crowds of happy *rākṣasas*" *prahṛṣṭā muditā... rakṣogaṇasamākulā*: Literally, "joyous and happy... filled with crowds of *rākṣasas*." We have followed the suggestion of Cr and Cm, who understand at least one of the adjectives, both of which modify the city, to refer to its inhabitants (*hṛṣṭaiḥ harṣaviśiṣṭai rākṣasaiḥ pramuditā prāptapramodā*—Cr). To avoid redundancy, we have connected the adjective "happy (*prahṛṣṭā*)" with the adjective "filled with crowds of *rākṣasas* (*rakṣogaṇasamākulā*)."

Following verse 9, D7,M3, and the texts and printed editions of Cg insert a passage of one line [40*]: "Filled with horses, that citadel is unapproachable by enemies."

10. "lofty and broad" *vipulāni... sumahānti ca*: Literally, "wide and very large." Cg and Cr attempt to avoid the redundancy of the two terms. Cg, whom we follow, understands the latter term to refer to the height of the gateways (*unnatāni*). Cr understands it as a value judgment rather than a measurement of size, glossing, "worthy of great praise (*atipraśaṃsanīyāni*)."

"massive iron bars" *mahāparigha-*: See note to 5.3.30.

11. "On its ramparts" *vapreṣu*: The reading is based on relatively sparse manuscript evidence (Ś2,V2,D13,T1,M1,2,5,G3). Subrecensions show some variation. D6,7,10, 11,T2,3,M3, as well as the texts and printed editions of all southern commentators, read *tatreṣūpalayantrāṇi*, which yields the translation, "there [on the gateways] are devices for hurling arrows and stones." Many northwestern and western manuscripts and the Lahore edition (5.70.8, p. 444) read *yantreṣūpari* (Ś1,D1,2,4,8,12), while the northeastern manuscripts (V1,3,B,D9) read *yantrāṇy upari*, which Gorresio (5.72.8) translates as "*macchine guerriere d'ogni sorta*" (1856, vol. 9, p. 133).

"devices for hurling stones" *upalayantrāṇi*: These weapons may have been large bows like the Roman *ballista* or single-armed catapults, like the Roman *onager*. Cf. Singh 1965, p. 113. Dikshitar (1944, p. 123) lists both *gospaṇāpāṣāṇa* (stones thrown by a rod) and *yantrapāṣāṇa* (stones thrown by a machine), which may reflect the same distinction. Sensarma (1979, p. 93) quotes Chakravarti (1941, p. 161) to this effect: "We are inclined to believe that these were of the nature of catapults and ballistae used by the ancient Hebrews, Greeks and Romans in their warfare. Like them, these engines were enormous in size, and were used for propelling large arrows and stones." Cf. 6.15.15; 6.30.26; 6.49.11; 6.80.19; and notes.

12. "hundred-slayers" *śataghnyaḥ*: Here, as in 1.5.11 and 5.3.30, the *śataghnī* appears to be a weapon placed along the ramparts. See Dikshitar (1944, p. 105). Cf. Singh (1965, pp. 114–15), who distinguishes fixed, movable, or portable *śataghnīs*, some even rolling on wheels. According to the commentators, this term is used principally of a club or a mace studded with spikes four *hastas* (the length between the elbow and the tip of the middle finger, about 18 inches), or approximately two meters. Dutt (1893, p. 1109) notes, "a kind of fire-arms, or ancient Hindu rocket; or a stone set round with sharp iron spikes—according to Râmânuya, a sort of mace about two yards in length with spikes." See notes to 1.5.11; 5.2.22; 5.3.30; and 5.41.14 and notes. See, too, 6.48.46; 6.60.12; 6.73.20–23 and notes.

"black iron" *kālāyasa-*: The meaning of the term is uncertain. Ct, Cg, and Cm gloss *āyaḥsāra-*, which we take to mean "steel." Secondary sources vary in their interpretation. Thus Vyas (1967, p. 244) understands *kālāyasa* to refer to blue steel but renders the apparently synonymous *kārṣṇāyasa* as "wrought iron." But Guruge (1960, p. 113) understands "black iron" for *kālāyasa*. Apte understands *kālāyasa* (s.v. *kāla-*) as "iron" but renders *kṛṣṇāyasa* (s.v.) as "iron, crude or black iron." PW (s.v.) understands "*Eisen*," as does MW (s.v.), who renders, "iron, made of iron." Cf. 5.39.11; 5.51.38; and notes, where the term is used. See, too, 6.53.12; 6.55.47; 6.63.14; and notes.

"fully deployed" *saṃskṛtāḥ*: We follow Cg, Ct, and Cm, who interpret the term as "ready *or* made ready (*sajjāḥ*)." Cr explains, "distinguished by appropriate *saṃskāras* (*ucitasaṃskāraviśiṣṭāḥ*)." This could mean either "adequately prepared" or "consecrated with appropriate *mantras*."

13. "impossible to scale" *duṣpradharṣaṇaḥ*: We follow Cg, who glosses, "hard to climb (*durārohaḥ*)." As Ct points out, the adjective could also mean "difficult to assault (*dharṣayitum aśakyaḥ*)."

"Its interior is studded with" *-viracitāntaraḥ*: Cr understands the compound as a *bahuvrīhi samāsa* and glosses *antarāṇi* as "middle, central [portions] (*madhyāni*)." This could either be interpreted as in the translation or in the sense of "its central portion studded with."

"gemstones" *maṇi-*: Cg glosses, "rubies (*padmarāgāḥ*)."

"coral, lapis" *vidrumavaidūrya-*: See note to 5.52.12. For *vaidūrya*, see note to 6.67.13; and notes to 3.30.9 and 4.13.5–8. See also 5.2.50; 5.3.8; and notes.

14. "deep" *āgādhāḥ*: Cr explains this to mean that it is impossible to touch the bottom (*talasparśarahitāḥ*).

"menacing" *mahāśubhāḥ*: The term is ambiguous and the reading uncertain. The compound may mean either "highly auspicious (*mahā* + *śubhāḥ*)" or "highly inauspicious (*mahā* + *aśubhāḥ*)." Aside from those northeastern and eastern manuscripts (Ñ2,V3,B1,2,4,D9) that replace the term with *bhayāvahāḥ* (redundant with *mahābhīmāḥ*), a wide range of southern and northern manuscripts (Ś1,Ñ1,V1,B3,D1–4,6,8,12, T3,G2,3,M), as well as the texts and printed editions of Cg, have readings that oblige us to read *śubhāḥ* as "auspicious" or "beautiful." For example, for *mahāśubhāḥ*, Cg reads [*śītatoya*]*vahāḥ śubhāḥ*, lending the line the meaning "auspicious [moats] having streams of cold water." This variant is rendered in the translation of Raghunathan (1982, vol. 3, p. 5), who, however, appears mistakenly to read the adjective *śubhāḥ* to modify the waters, rendering, "filled with pure cold water." Other translators render variously. Cr, alone among the commentators, takes up the term *mahāśubhāḥ*, explaining it to mean "inauspicious for enemies, that is, fatal (*mahānty aśubhāni ripūṇām amaṅgalāni vināśā ity arthaḥ*)." Given the tenor of this verse, with its emphasis on the fearsome and formidable quality of the defenses, we have translated according to this interpretation.

"icy waters" *śītatoyāḥ*: The term *śīta-*, too, can be ambiguous, meaning either "pleasantly cool" or "unpleasantly cold." Once again, in keeping with the context, we have chosen the latter in agreement with Cg, who remarks that "by the mention of the water's coldness is suggested the impossibility of entering it (*śītatoyatvena duṣpraveśatvam uktam*)."

"full of crocodiles" *grāhavatyaḥ*: Literally, "possessed of crocodiles." Cf. note to 5.7.6. See, too, notes to 6.4.78; 6.14.21; 6.15.6,7; 6.62.20 and notes.

See Singh (1965, pp. 127ff.) for a discussion on walls and moats.

15. "bridges" *saṃkramāḥ*: Literally, "passageways." There is some disagreement among the commentators as to the precise nature of these structures. Ct, Cr, and Cv understand them to be constructed in the manner of platforms (*mañcarūpeṇa baddhāḥ*), by which we think they are referring to pierlike structures raised on pilings above the moats. This seems to accord well with verse 17 below, where the pilings (*stambhaiḥ*) of one such structure are mentioned. Cm seems to concur, explaining the structures as "a type of pathway constructed in the form of a platform in the vicinity of the gates of a walled city for the purpose of traversing a moat (*puradvārapradeśeṣu parikhopari saṃcaraṇārthaṃ mañcarūpeṇa baddho mārgaviśeṣaḥ*)," but see the note below, where he offers an alternative opinion. Cg describes these as "passageways made out of wooden planks (*dāruphalakanirmitasaṃcāramārgāḥ*)" that are arranged over moats. As it becomes clear from his commentary on the following verse, he understands these to be a type of drawbridge (see note to verse 16 below). Cg supports his interpretation by citing the *Viśvakośa* (also cited by Cm), which defines *saṃkrama* as "a gateway mechanism good for crossing (*saṃkramaḥ kramaṇe samyag dvārasaṃcārayantraka iti viśvaḥ*)."

"with... instruments of war" *yantraiḥ*: Literally, "with devices *or* machines." In keeping with his understanding of *saṃkrama* as "drawbridge," Cg understands these to be "devices for extending the bridges (*yantraiḥ saṃkramāvakīryakaiḥ*)." We follow Cr, who understands the *yantras* to be military devices, such as the *śataghnīs* mentioned in verse 12 above.

"crowded one upon the other" *dṛḍhasaṃdhibhiḥ*: This could also mean "firmly fastened." The reading is highly dubious, since it is found in only two southern (T2,3) and three *devanāgarī* (D3,4,13) manuscripts collated for the critical edition. A majority of the southern manuscripts, including the texts and printed editions of all the southern commentators, read instead *gṛhapaṅktibhiḥ*, literally, "with rows of houses." This is explained by Ct and Ck as meaning "lined with rows of turrets on the ramparts (*prākāraśirogṛhapaṅktibhiḥ*)." Cg explains that the bridges are lined with rows of the houses or barracks of its guards (*rakṣijanāvāsasthānapaṅktibhir upetāḥ*). Roussel appears to have misread the term *paṅktibhiḥ*, "with rows *or* lines," as if it were *pañcabhiḥ*, "with five." He therefore translates, "*D'énormes constructions, disposées par cinq*" (1903, vol. 3, p. 6). In this erroneous reading he has been followed by Shastri, who has the even more extraordinary reading, "and five great cannons" (1959, vol. 3, p. 7).

16. "at those points" *tatra*: Literally, "there." We agree with Cm and Cg, who gloss, "in the areas of the gates (*dvārapradeśeṣu*—so Cg)."

"cast into the moats on every side" *avakīryante parikhāsu samantataḥ*: Commentators differ as to who or what is cast into the moats, depending on their views as to the nature of the bridges (*saṃkramas*) and their associated machinery (*yantras*) (see note to verse 15 above). Our translation follows Cr, who understands that, upon the approach of hostile forces, the weaponry mounted on the bridges drives them into the moats, and it is in this way that the bridges can be said to protect the city. (*taiḥ saṃkramasthair yantraiḥ samantataḥ parikhāsv avakīryante prakṣipyante parasainyānīti śeṣaḥ. ata eva parasainyāgame sati saṃkramās trāyante puraṃ rakṣante.*) Ct and Ck have a similar interpretation differing only in that they see the weapons as placed on the ramparts of the city rather than on the bridges themselves (*prākāropari pratiṣṭhāpitaiḥ*). Cm offers two variants on this interpretation. The first is quite similar to that of Cr. In the second, however, he interprets the verb *avakīryante*, "are hurled *or* scattered," to have as its object not the enemy troops but the missiles fired by the military devices. He says, "alternatively, they are hurled into the moats on every side by those instruments; that is to say, stones, etc., are fired when enemies approach the moat to prevent them from reaching the ramparts of the city (*yadvā . . . pareṣāṃ parikhāmukhena prākārasamīpaprāptinivāraṇārthaṃ śilādayo vikṣipyante 'tas tatra dvāreṣu saṃkramās trāyante purīṃ rakṣantīty arthaḥ*)." Cg, in keeping with his understanding that the *saṃkramas* are drawbridges, appears to understand that the *yantras* are the mechanisms for lifting and lowering the bridges. He says:

> He [Vālmīki] now explains the function of the drawbridges with the verse beginning, "They . . . protect (*trāyante*)." "There" means in the areas around the gateways. When hostile forces approach, the drawbridges protect the city. And we must supply the word[s] "the city." He [Vālmīki] explains how, with the half verse beginning, "by the instruments (*yantraiḥ*)." The instruments are the mechanisms for lowering the planks of the bridges. "Into the moats" means "over the moat." "Extended on all sides" means "laid down." Normally, the planks are laid down across the waters of the moats. They are, however, drawn up at the approach of hostile troops. Because of the impassable waters of the moats, it is impossible [for them] to approach the ramparts. That is the point of the verse. (*saṃkramāṇām upayogam āha trāyanta iti. tatra dvārapradeśeṣu parasainyāgame sati saṃkramās trāyante purīm iti śeṣaḥ katham ity atrāha. yantraiḥ saṃkramaphalakavikṣepayantraiḥ. parikhāsu parikhopari. samantato 'vakīryante kṣipyante. sarvathā parikhājalopari phalakā nikṣipyante. śatrusainyāgame tu tā utkṣipyante tena durgaparikhājalena prākārasamīpagamanaṃ na śakyata iti ślokatātparyam.*)

Although the translators understand the *yantras* to be instruments of war rather than mechanical devices for lifting the bridges, the majority of them appear to follow Cg in translating *saṃkramas* as "drawbridges" (Raghunathan 1982, vol. 3, p. 5; Shastri 1959, vol. 3, p. 7; and Gita Press 1969, vol. 3, p. 1377). Dutt (1893, p. 1110) renders, "bridges." Pagani (1999, p. 877) understands similarly, translating, "*ponts*." Gorresio (1856, vol. 9, p. 133) seems to prefer another sense of *saṃkrama-*, that of "a long *or* narrow passage," rendering, "*angusti passi*." Roussel (1903, vol. 3, p. 6), possibly influenced by Gorresio, offers, "*galeries*." See notes to 6.93.13; 6.98.2; and 6.116.11 for other examples of Gorresio's apparent influence on Roussel.

"emplaced upon them": Following the suggestion of Cr and Cm (first interpretation), we have added these words for the sake of clarity (*saṃkramasthair* [*yantraiḥ*])."

17. "One" *ekaḥ*: Ct and Ck gloss, "principal (*mukhyaḥ*)."

"solid" *akampyaḥ*: Literally, "unshakeable." Ct interprets, "impossible to break (*durbhedaḥ*)." Cr understands, "incapable of being shaken by enemies (*paraiḥ kampayitum aśakyaḥ*)." Cg sees the bridge's unshakeability to be a consequence of its extremely strong construction (*atyantavṛddhasaṃghaṭano 'ta evākampyaḥ*).

"strong" *balavān*: Ct, Cr, and Ck understand the term *bala-* in its sense of "army, troops." Thus, they see the adjective *balavān* here as meaning "characterized by its many troops (*bahusenāviśiṣṭaḥ*)." Cg, whom we have followed, takes *bala-* in its sense of "strength." He thus takes the term to mean "strong" and attributes the strength to its massiveness of construction. He glosses, "possessed of massiveness (*sthaulyavān*)."

"extremely stable" *sumahādṛḍhaḥ*: Literally, "very firm." Ct and Ck gloss, "having a firm foundation (*dṛḍhapratiṣṭhānaḥ*)."

"pilings" *stambhaiḥ*: We agree with Cg in taking these as the posts or pilings upon which the bridge itself is supported. He explains, "posts set in the moats to support the bridges (*saṃkramādhārārthaṃ parikhāsu sthāpitaiḥ stambhaiḥ*)."

"watchtowers" *vedikābhiḥ*: Literally, "raised platforms, seats." Here this polysemic term appears to refer to raised seats, which, as Cg suggests, are raised platforms *or* balconies for the guards (*rakṣijanādhārārthābhīr vitardikābhiḥ*). See notes to 5.3.8–11 and 5.7.14–15. See Sharma 1971, p. 262.

Various commentators provide additional bits of information about this bridge. Ct and Ck indicate that it is the main means of entrance to the city and passes through the middle of the rampart (*mukhyaḥ saṃkramaḥ prākāramadhyavartī sākṣāt purapraveśasādhanabhūtaḥ*). Cr takes the reference to the bridge's golden accoutrements to suggest that it is by this bridge that Rāvaṇa leaves and enters the city (*etena tenaiva rāvaṇo nirgacchatīti praviśati ceti sūcitam*). Cg notes that this bridge leads to the northern gate of Laṅkā (*uttaradvārasthaḥ*). The northern gate is, of course, the one at which Rāma stations himself (see 6.27.19).

18. "in full command of himself" *svayaṃ prakṛtisampannaḥ*: Literally, "inherently endowed with [his own] nature" or "naturally well-endowed." Cg, the only one among the southern commentators to have this precise reading, takes it to mean "devoid of any distractions in the form of addiction to gambling, etc. (*dyūtādivyasanarūpavicārarahitaḥ*)." B2,D1,4,5,7,10,11,T1,M3, and the texts and printed editions of Ct, Cm, Ck, and Cr read instead the well-attested variant *prakṛtim āpannaḥ*, which appears to be roughly synonymous. Ct and Cm take the phrase to mean that Rāvaṇa's spirit never falters. Cr explains that he is grounded in his own inherent nature, which is to say that he does not undergo any transformation even when engaged in drinking, and so on (*prakṛtiṃ svasvabhāvam āpanno madyapānādāv api svabhāvapariṇāmarahita ity arthaḥ*). The thrust of all these interpretations, and indeed of the entire verse, is that Rāvaṇa is always a formidable foe and that Rāma cannot expect to catch him off guard or when he is incapacitated.

"Always ready for battle" *yuyutsuḥ*: We feel the context supports Cg's gloss, "always prepared (*sarvadā yuddhodyataḥ*)," against the more straightforward interpretation of the desiderative, such as Cr's, "always desirous of battle (*nityaṃ yoddhum icchuḥ*)." Cf. 6.4.19 and note.

"energetic and vigilant in inspecting his troops" *utthitaś cāpramattaś ca balānām anudarśane*: Cg and Cm claim that this means that Rāvaṇa is wakeful for the purpose of inspecting his troops daily (*bālānāṃ sainyānām anudarśane pratidinam avalokananimittam utthito jāgarūkaḥ*). Cm glosses "vigilant (*apramattaḥ*)" as "devoid of carelessness (*pramattarahitaḥ*)." Cm, perhaps disturbed by the abrupt change of subject, from the bridges to Rāvaṇa, remarks, "Whenever Rāvaṇa is desirous of battle, he stands on this bridge to review his troops (*yadā rāvaṇo yuyutsur bhavati tadā tasmin saṃkrame senādarśanārthaṃ tiṣṭhatīti bhāvaḥ*)."

19. "not to be scaled" *nirālambā*: Literally, "without dependency *or* self-sufficient." This adjective could suggest that Laṅkā is self-sufficient and therefore all the more able to withstand a siege. However, in the present context, with its virtually exclusive focus on the city's natural and constructed defenses, we feel it best to follow the unanimous commentarial tradition whereby *ālambana-* is taken to refer to the climbing [lit., clinging] to the walls of the lofty citadel. The commentators argue that the fortress is not to be climbed because of its situation on the peak of a high and sheer mountain (*nirālambātiślakṣṇamahoccagiriśikharapratiṣṭhitatvenārohaṇālambanarahitā*—so Ct). Cg embellishes this interpretation by suggesting that the sheerness of the slope of Mount Trikūṭa is not purely natural but has been enhanced through the work of a stonecutter's chisel (*ṭaṅkacchedamasṛṇīkṛtatrikūṭaśikharasthitatvād ārohaṇālambanarahitā*—so, too, Cv and Cm). Cs, alone among the commentators, understands *ālambā* in its sense of support, explaining the term to mean "lacking any support; that is, seeming to hang in the sky because of having very firm support in the form of a mountain peak, etc. (*nirālambāmbaralambinīti nirālambeva nirālambā nitarāṃ dṛḍheti yāvat. ālambaḥ parvataśikharādirūpa āśrayo yasyāḥ sā.*)" Many northern manuscripts and Gorresio's edition substitute *durālambā*, literally, "difficult to cling to," which appears to be an example of the northern tendency to gloss. See Pollock 1984a, pp. 85–86. Translators generally render the commentators' interpretation as "impregnable" (Shastri 1959, vol. 3, p. 7) and "*emprenable*" (Roussel 1903, vol. 3, p. 6). Gita Press (1969, vol. 3, p. 1377) attempts to provide a literal meaning of *ālambā*, rendering, "no base for invasion." Dutt (1893, p. 1110) gives a literal rendition of Ct, "[Lankā] cannot be ascended by means of any support." On Mount Trikūṭa, see note to 6.2.10.

"inaccessible even to the gods" *devadurgā*: The translation follows Cr, Cg, Cm, and Cs (first alternative), who understand, "unattainable even by the gods (*devair api duṣprāpā*—so Cg)." Ct and Ck understand, "having the appearance of a fortress built by the gods (*devanirmitadurgarūpiṇī*—so Ck)." Cv offers both alternatives.

"defensive constructions" *kṛtrimam*: Literally, "artificial, man-made." The term contrasts the constructed defenses of the city with the other, natural defenses mentioned in the verse. Commentators point out that this refers to the rampart surrounding the city of Laṅkā (*kṛtimaṃ prākārarūpaṃ catuṣprākāravattvena prākārarūpam*—so Ct).

20. "far off, on the other side of the vast ocean" *pāre samudrasya dūrapārasya*: Literally, "on the far shore of the ocean whose far shore is distant."

"navigable passage" *naupathaḥ*: Literally, "path for ships."

"the way is all uncharted" *nirādeśaś ca sarvataḥ*: Literally, "completely lacking information." The translation follows the suggestion of Cg and Cm, who explain, "the meaning is 'this region is devoid of the transmission of [any] information' (*sarvato nirādeśaś cādeśo vartāsaṃcāras tadrahito 'yaṃ deśa ity arthaḥ*)." Cm adds that this suggests the impassability of the waters (*anena jaladurgavattvaṃ sūcitam*). Ś1,Ñ,D1–4,8–12, and the texts and printed editions of Ct and Ck read instead *niruddeśaḥ*, literally, "devoid of regions," for the critical reading *nirādeśaḥ*. Ct and Ck explain, "devoid of regional subdivisions (*pradeśavibhāgarahitaḥ*—so Ct)." This interpretation is followed by Gita Press (1969, vol. 3, p. 1377) and Dutt (1893, p. 1110). Roussel (1903, vol. 3, p. 6), followed by Shastri (1959, vol. 3, p. 7), offers "*car elle n'offre de port nulle part.*"

"there" *atra*: Literally, "here." The commentators are unanimous in understanding this to refer to the ocean (*atra samudre*—so Cr).

22. "hundred-slayers" *śataghnyaḥ*: See note to verse 12 above.

"instruments of war" *yantrāṇi*: See note to verse 15 above.

23. "On one side" *atra*: Literally, "here." Cg and Cr understand "in Laṅkā." The use of the adverb in this and the following three verses may suggest that Hanumān is pointing to places on a drawing or sketch of the layout of the city, perhaps scratched in the dirt or sand.

"They . . . bear lances" *śūlahastāḥ*: Literally, "lances in hand."

"fight . . . in the vanguard" *-agrayodhinaḥ*: We follow Cg, who glosses, "at the front of the army (*senāgre*)." Ct understands similarly. This could also mean "they fight with the tips of their swords," as Ck suggests.

24. "On the next side" *atra*: Literally, "here." Cg and Cr understand, "in Laṅkā (*laṅkāyām*)."

"an army, complete with all four divisions" *caturaṅgeṇa sainyena*: Literally, "a four-limbed army." This is the classic army of four divisions, mentioned throughout the literature. It consists of specific numbers of infantry, cavalry, chariot, and elephant corps. See *BrahmāṇḍP* 3.26.7, 45.1, 46.18; *MatsyaP* 240.19–21; and *BhāgP* 1.10.32 for technical definitions of *caturaṅga*. See, too, *ArthŚā* 2.33.9 and 9.2.29. See 6.7.11; 6.28.23; 6.31.41,83–84; 6.46.931*; 6.53.27; 6.81.3; 6.84.6; and notes.

"fighters" *yodhāḥ*: Cg, who wishes to see the four divisions of the traditional army represented among the forces stationed at the four city gates, glosses, "infantrymen (*padātayaḥ*)." See note to verse 26 below.

25. "Next" *atra*: Literally, "here." See notes to verses 23 and 24 above.

"adept in the use of every missile" *sarvāstrakovidāḥ*: Literally, "skilled in all missiles."

26. "Finally" *atra*: Literally, "here."

"ten million" *arbudam*: This could also mean one hundred million. The commentators are silent. D6,10,11,M3, and the texts and printed editions of the southern commentators read instead *nyarbudam*, which generally means "one hundred million" and is seen, for example, in the translation of Gita Press (1969, vol. 3, p. 1377), which translates accordingly.

"and cavalry" *aśvavāhāś ca*: Literally, "horsemen." Cg argues that the conjunction *ca*, "and," is intended to include the forces mounted on elephants who are the fourth standard division of the army (*cakāreṇa gajavāhāḥ samucīyante*).

"sons of noble families" *kulaputrāḥ*: The commentators waver between understanding this term in its usual sense, as we have done, and taking it as a kind of proper noun used of the *kiṃkaras*, an elite group of Rāvaṇa's troops with whom Hanumān fights at 5.40. See notes to 5.40.23ff. Thus, Ct remarks, "the *kulaputras* are the *kiṃkaras*, or they are those born in noble warrior families. (*kulaputrāḥ kiṃkarāḥ. yadvā yoddhṛsatkule prasūtāḥ*.)" Cm gives similar alternatives. Cr and Ck see them only as the *kiṃkaras*. Crā sees them only as the sons of noble families. Cg similarly offers only the latter sense but interprets it to mean that these warriors are therefore trustworthy (*satkulaprasūtā viśvasanīyā iti yāvat*).

"treated with great respect" *supūjitāḥ*: Literally, "well-honored." Cg understands that the warriors are the *kiṃkaras* held in high esteem by Rāvaṇa (*rāvaṇena bahumatāḥ kiṃkarā iti śeṣaḥ*).

27. "central encampment" *madhyamaṃ gulmam*: D6,7,10,11,T2,G1,3,M3,5, and the texts and printed editions of the southern commentators read instead *skandham* for *gulmam*, "encampment." This is explained by most commentators as "army camp in the middle of the city (*puramadhyasenāniveśasthānam*—so Ct)," and by Cg as "the place in the middle of the city (*nagaramadhyamasthānam*)." Cf. 5.3.27; 6.27.20; 6.28.31; 6.31.31; 6.45.2; 6.62.5; 6.71.1; 6.72.5; 6.84.6; and notes.

"ten million" *śataṃ śatasahasrāṇām*: Literally, "a hundred hundred-thousands." D5,7,10,11,T1,G,M3,5, and the texts and printed editions of the southern commentators read instead *śataśo 'tha sahasrāṇi*, "hundreds of thousands."

"*yātudhānas*" *yātudhānāḥ*: *Yātudhānas* are said to be a type of *rākṣasa*. See 6.31.74; 6.47.39; 6.48.28; 6.55.49; 6.57.47–48; 6.99.26; and notes. Cf. 5.3.26 and 5.4.12 and notes, where the term refers to the more virtuous of the *rākṣasas*. See also the discussion of *rākṣasas* in Goldman and Goldman 1996, pp. 65–68 and note 246. See, too, *MBh* 18.5.19.

"and an even greater number" *sāgrakoṭiś ca*: Literally, "and ten million with a surplus." Ct and Cr are quite specific and understand that the phrase *sāgrakoṭi* means "one and one-quarter crore, *or* 12.5 million," a number that turns up in the translations of Raghunathan (1982, vol. 3, p. 6) and Gita Press (1969, vol. 3, p. 1377). Raghunathan, however, understands this to be a cumulative total of all the *rākṣasas* in the city. Ck, with whom we agree, is less specific, explaining, "somewhat more [than a crore] (*sāgrā kiṃcid abhyadhikā*)." Roussel (1903, vol. 3, p. 6) translates, "*une Koti et plus*." Cg understands, "a full crore (*pūrṇakoṭiḥ*)."

Following verse 27, D7,G2,3,T2,M3, and Ct (after 28); G1 (after 29ab); and the texts and printed editions of Cg and Cr (unnumbered in GPP in brackets between 6.3.29–30; Gita Press 6.3.29cd; VSP 6.3.30; and KK 6.3.30) insert a passage of one line [49*]: "But I annihilated a part of that army[1] of great[2] *rākṣasas*."

[1]"but I annihilated a part of that army" *balaikadeśaḥ kṣapitaḥ*: Literally, "a part of the army was destroyed." The reference is, of course, to Hanumān's slaughter of the *rākṣasas* in the *Sundarakāṇḍa* (40–45). See, too, 5.52.3.

Cg says that it means that Hanumān destroyed one-quarter of the army (*senācaturthāṃśa ity arthaḥ*). Cr notes that Ct, who does not accept this passage, nonetheless understands its sense to be conveyed by the conjunction *ca* in 28c. Cr's commentary to GPP 6.3.29 does indeed indicate that the conjunction *ca* of 28c should be read as implying the destruction of a portion of the army (*etad arthapāṭho na bhaṭṭasaṃmato 'ta eva cena balaikadeśakṣayo 'pi kṛta iti tair uktam*).

[2]"of great" *mahātmanām*: Cg, taking the term *ātman* in its sense of "body," glosses, "of huge bodies (*mahākāyānām*)."

28. Hanumān burns the city of Laṅkā at 5.52.7–17. Although there is no explicit mention of the destruction of the bridges or moats, the towers, ramparts, and archways are said to have been destroyed at 5.53.26.

29. "you may regard . . . as destroyed by the monkeys" *hateti . . . vānarair avadhāryatām*: We follow Ct and Cr in taking *vānaraiḥ*, "by the monkeys," to be the subject of the participle *hatā*, "[Laṅkā] is destroyed," rather than, as do some translators

(Roussel 1903, vol. 3, p. 6 and Shastri 1959, vol. 3, p. 7), understanding it to be the subject of the verb *avadhāryatām*, "let it be considered." To us, the interpretation of Ct and Cr seems clearly more harmonious with the context; it also parallels the similar construction used twice in the preceding *sarga* (cf. 6.2.10,19). Note, too, the northern reading, which seems to gloss by dropping the confusing *iti* in *pāda* c and substituting the second person singular imperative (*upadhāraya*) for the ambiguous passive imperative of the critical text. See Pollock 1984a, pp. 85–86.

30. Cm explains the sense of the verse as follows: "What is the use of worrying over a means to get the whole army across? If a few of the troop leaders get across the ocean, they will uproot Laṅkā, along with its mountains, forest, etc. [52*], and bring it back. (*sarvasainyataraṇopayacintayā kiṃ? katipayayūthapā eva samudraṃ laṅghayitvā parvatavanādiviśiṣṭāṃ laṅkām utpāṭyāneṣyantīty āha*.)"

31. "leaping through the air, those monkeys" *plavamānāḥ*: Literally, "[those] leaping [ones]." We understand, with the commentators and most translators, that the subject is the group of monkey troop leaders, Aṅgada, etc., mentioned in the previous verse.

"will bring back Maithilī" *ānayiṣyanti maithilīm*: Ś1,Ñ,V1,3,B,D1–4,6–12,T2,3, G1,3,M3, and the printed editions of Gorresio 5.72.19 and Lahore 5.70.19, as well as the texts and printed editions of the southern commentators, substitute the vocative singular *rāghava*, "O Rāghava," for the accusative singular *maithilīm*, "Maithilī." It should be noted, however, that for the southern commentators who do not read *maithilīm*, *ānayiṣyanti* lacks an explicit object. This deficit is remedied by Ct and Ck, who supply the proper noun *sītām*, "Sītā." Alternatively Cg and Cm understand the city of Laṅkā to be the object of both the gerund and the finite verb. They understand that the monkeys will bring back the entire city of Laṅkā with its palaces, ramparts, etc. This interpretation is represented in the translation of Raghunathan (1982, vol. 3, p. 6).

Following 31ab, D5–7,10,11,S, and the texts and printed editions of the southern commentators insert a passage of one line [52*]: "Having smashed [Laṅkā] along with its mountains and forests, its moats, and its gateway arches."

32. "to that effect" *evam*: Literally, "thus, in this fashion." Cg specifies that this refers to the mode of action proposed in the preceding verse (*evaṃ plavamānā ityādy uktarītyā*). Ct and Ck see Hanumān as presenting Rāma with two options in this verse. The first, signaled by the adverb *evam*, is for the principal monkeys to carry out the mission as proposed in verses 30–31 above. If Rāma wishes that option, he should so order immediately. If, however, he selects the second option, that is, leading the entire monkey army to the opposite shore, [then he should select an auspicious juncture to set out]. (*evaṃ pradhānair eva kāryasādhanam iṣṭaṃ cet kṣipram idānīm evānayatety ājñāpaya. yadi balānāṃ sarvasaṃgrahaṃ balasaṃmelanam uddiśya balānām api pāranayanam iṣṭaṃ tadā*—so Ct.)

"entire army" *balānāṃ sarvasaṃgraham*: As noted above, this is the interpretation of Ct and Ck. Cg and Cm, however, understand the term in the sense of "the elite forces in the midst of the army," and see it as a reference to the elite monkey warriors mentioned in verse 30 above. (*sarvasaṃgrahaṃ saṃgṛhyata iti saṃgrahaḥ. balānāṃ madhye sarvasārabhūtaṃ balam aṅgadādikam ājñāpaya*.)

"You must select a propitious moment to set forth" *muhūrtena tu yuktena prasthānam abhirocaya*: Literally, "choose a departure at a suitable moment." The commentators understand the meaning here as "choose the moment of your own departure at an hour suitable for a journey or expedition (*tadā yuktena yātrocitena muhūrtena prasthānaṃ svayātrām abhirocaya*—so Ct)." See note to 6.4.3.

Sarga 4

1. "said" *abravīt*: Cg claims that Rāma addresses Sugrīva (*sugrīvam iti śeṣaḥ*), although, in the following verse, he appears to be addressing Hanumān. Cg's explanation is that the reference in verse 2 to the description of Laṅkā is "caused to be related [by Sugrīva] through the mouth of Hanumān (*hanumanmukhena nivedayasi*)." The issue of the person to whom Rāma addresses his remarks hinges on whether the word "Sugrīva" in verse 3 is to be taken as a vocative or a prior member of a compound. Gorresio's text (5.73.13) specifies Sugrīva as Rāma's interlocutor. See note to verse 3 below. Cf. note to 6.2.1 above.

2. "Laṅkā, the city . . . which you have had described . . . This is the truth I am telling you" *yāṃ nivedayase laṅkāṃ purīm . . . satyam etad bravīmi*: Literally, "you have described which city, Laṅkā . . . I speak this truth *or* I speak this truly." Given the critical reading of the vocative *sugrīva*, "Sugrīva," in verse 3 below, we concur with Cg's reading of the verb as a causative whose subject is Sugrīva and whose simplex subject is Hanumān. See notes to verse 1 above and notes to verse 3 below.

D10,11, and the texts and printed editions of Ct and Ck read instead *yan nivedayase*, "what you have been telling me." They then understand the thrust of this verse rather differently. In their reading, the neuter pronoun *yat*, "what," refers specifically to Hanumān's statement, that he can see to the destruction of Laṅkā. Ct and Ck then understand *etat*, "this," in *pāda* d as the correlative pronoun, which is modified by the word *satyam*, "true." In their view, Rāma, realizing that the proposed mission to be undertaken by an advance party consisting of Aṅgada, etc., is not feasible, is diplomatically rejecting the plan enunciated at 6.3.30–31 above, whereby only a few of the great monkey warriors would assault Laṅkā, leaving the bulk of the army and Rāma behind. According to them, Rāma thinks the plan unworkable but diplomatically endorses it before putting forth his own plan, which will involve the use of the entire monkey army. A translation of the verse according to this interpretation would read: "What you have said—that I could quickly destroy Laṅkā, this city of the *rākṣasa*—is quite true. Nonetheless I will tell you [my own plan]. (*tatrāṅgadādimukhena kāryanirvahaṇam aśakyaṃ matvā tatprarocanāya tad aṅgīkurvann iva svamatam āha—yad iti. rakṣasa enāṃ purīṃ kṣipram eva vadhiṣyāmīti yan nivedayase tat satyam eva tathā te śaktir asty eva tathāpi te tubhyaṃ svamataṃ bravīmīty arthaḥ.*)" Cm, who reads *yām* in *pāda* a, also sees a reference to the plan involving Aṅgada, etc. as enunciated by Hanumān, but sees Rāma as accepting it (*hanumatoktam aṅgadādimukhena kāryanirvahaṇam aṅgīkurvann āha*).

3. "I wish to set forth this very moment, Sugrīva" *sugrīva prayāṇam abhirocaye*: Manuscript traditions vary here in two respects that bear on the murky issue of whom Rāma is addressing in the opening verses of this *sarga*. The questions here are whether Rāma is addressing Sugrīva or Hanumān and whether he is discussing his own or Sugrīva's proposed expedition. The first issue is whether the sequence *sugrīvaprayāṇam* should be read as separate words, thus making the former a vocative; the second is whether the verbal form is the second person imperative *abhirocaya* or the

first person indicative *abhirocaye*. This yields four possible permutations. The first of these is largely indeterminate, as manuscripts typically do not separate words. Thus, it becomes a matter of interpretation as to whether we are to understand the sequence as a compound. Printed editions of the northern recensions, i.e., Gorresio and Lahore, separate the words and use the first person form of the verb. The sense yielded thereby is the one we have rendered in our translation. Some printed versions of the southern recension, e.g., KK, VSP, and NSP, read with the critical edition and northern recension. Gita Press has the vocative but reads the second person; GPP, which normally represents the text of Ct, reads the compound and the second person imperative, noting, however, that Cg reads the first person. Ct is unambiguous in identifying *sugrīvaprayāṇam* as a *ṣaṣṭhitatpuruṣasamāsa*, while Ck concurs by providing the *vigraha*. Cr prefaces his discussion of this verse by remarking, "having first addressed Hanumān, he now addresses Sugrīva (*hanumantaṃ pratyuktvā sugrīvaṃ pratyāha*)." He thus understands *sugrīva* to be a vocative and sees Rāma as asking Sugrīva to approve of his [Rāma's] setting forth. Cg reads the vocative and the first person as in the critical edition and makes no specific comment on either point. However, see note to verse 1 above. Cm reads the second person imperative and appears, in reading *prayāṇam abhirocaya*, to understand the vocative, although he does not indicate this explicitly. Cs is the only commentator to explicitly acknowledge the alternate readings. His own preference appears to be the vocative and the first person, that is, the reading of the critical text. He then goes on to state: "The alternate reading *abhirocaya* has the meaning 'please sanction *or* permit (*anumodasva*).' By reading *sugrīvaprayāṇam* as a single word and in accepting [Rāma's] utterance [to Sugrīva] to be delivered while facing Hanumān, it is clear that the text is consistent with the following verse, which contains the words *abhiprayāma sugrīva sarvānīkasamāvṛtāḥ*, 'let us set forth, Sugrīva, surrounded by the entire army.' (*abhirocayeti pāṭhe 'numodasvety arthaḥ. sugrīvaprayāṇam ity aikapadyena hanumadābhimukhyena vacanam ity aṅgīkāre "abhiprayāma sugrīva sarvānīkasamāvṛtāḥ" ity agrimagranthānānuguṇyaṃ sphuṭam.*)" In other words, Cs understands the compound to be consistent with the vocative in the following verse (verse 4) if we understand that Rāma is speaking to Sugrīva in this verse through the mediation of Hanumān. Cs remarks that Rāma delivers this speech while glancing indirectly at Sugrīva because of the latter's kingship (*rājatvāt sugrīvaṃ kaṭākṣīkṛtyāha*). Shastri (1959, vol. 3, p. 8), Roussel (1903, vol. 3, p. 8), and Gita Press (1969, vol. 3, p. 1378) all understand Rāma to be asking Sugrīva to approve his [Rāma's] departure. Raghunathan (1982, vol. 3, p. 6) and Gorresio (1856, vol. 9, p. 135) translate as we do. Dutt (1893, p. 1111) understands Rāma to be asking Hanumān to arrange for Sugrīva's march (following Ct and Ck; cf. Cs's alternative reading).

"propitious" *yuktaḥ*: We follow Cg's explanation, "propitious for a journey (*yukto yātrārthaḥ*)." D3,8,10,11, and the texts and printed editions of Ct, Ck, and Cr read *muhūrte* for the critical reading *muhūrtaḥ*. Ct, Ck, and Cr take the adjective *yuktaḥ* to refer to Rāma's departure, the words for which must be supplied (*me nirgama iti śeṣaḥ*—Ct). See Gita Press 1969, vol. 3, p. 1378.

"juncture called Vijaya" *muhūrto vijayaḥ*: Vijaya ("victory") is mentioned earlier in the *Rāmāyaṇa* (see 1.72.8) as a propitious moment for undertaking a journey. It is a forty-eight-minute period—11:36 AM through 12:24 PM—and is, as the commentators suggest, called by this name because it is conducive to success or triumph. In fact, as several commentators point out, the more common and, perhaps, more technically correct name for this *muhūrta* is Abhijit (cf. Ct, Ck, Cs, Cm, Cg). Cg then quotes the *Vidyāmādhavīya*, which provides a list of the daytime *muhūrtas*, among which Abhijit is the eighth. See Hopkins 1903, passim. Cg uses the identification of this *muhūrta* as a starting point for a geographical discussion, which bears on his notion of the location of Laṅkā relative to Kiṣkindhā. He quotes an unnamed *śāstra* that prohibits the starting of a journey to the south during the Abhijit *muhūrta*, for to undertake such a journey will be fatal, like several other actions taken at that time. Cg claims, however, that this is not a problem in the present case, since Laṅkā is to the southeast of Kiṣkindhā so that the prohibited southward journey does not occur. See note to verse 42 below. (*tad uktaṃ vidyāmādhavīye "ārdroragamitramakhāvasujalaviśvābhijid viriñcendrāḥ / aindrāgnimūlavaruṇāryamabhagatārā divā muhūrtāḥ syur iti //" nanv abhijid muhūrtā dakṣiṇayātrāsu niṣiddhā yathā jyautiṣaratnākare "bhuktau dakṣiṇayātrāyāṃ pratiṣṭhāyāṃ dvijanmani / ādhāne ca dhvajārohe mṛtyudaḥ syāt sadābhijit" ity ucyate. laṅkā hi dakṣiṇapūrvasyāṃ kiṣkindhāyāḥ. ato neyaṃ dakṣiṇayātreti noktadoṣaḥ.*) See Kane for which activities are appropriate for particular *muhūrtas* (1974, vol. 5, p. 537) and also see note to 6.81.28 below.

Following verse 3, D5–7,10,11,S, and the texts and printed editions of the southern commentators insert a passage of four lines [56*]. D5,6,10,11,T1,G1,2, and the texts of Ct and Ck omit, in whole or in part, line 1: "For if I set forth at this auspicious juncture known as Vijaya, when the sun has reached its zenith,[1] where in the world will that fellow [Rāvaṇa], having taken Sītā, flee?[2] When Sītā hears of my expedition, life will once more hold hope for her[3], just as one grievously ill and at death's door from drinking poison might [gain hope] at the taste of the nectar of immortality.[4]"

4. "Moreover, today is the day of the lunar asterism Uttarāphalgunī" *uttarāphalgunī hy adya*: Literally, "for today is Uttarāphalgunī." This is the name of the tenth (Kane 1974, vol. 5, p. 502) or twelfth (Apte s.v.) lunar asterism. According to Ct, this is Sītā's natal asterism. He goes on to state that, in order to liberate a person held in captivity, it is necessary to set out for that purpose on the day in which the moon enters that person's natal asterism. In keeping with his own chronology of the *Rāmāyaṇa* story, Ct uses the mention of this asterism to note that the events taking place in this *sarga* occur on either the seventh or the eighth of the dark half of Mārgaśīrṣa [November–December], calculating from the end of the new-moon day. (*uttarā ca sītāyā janmatārā baddhasya janmatārāyāṃ tanmocanārthayātrāyām avaśyaṃ tanmuktir iti bhāvaḥ. adyāmāntamānena mārgaśīrṣakṛṣṇāṣṭamyāṃ kṛṣṇasaptamyāṃ vā mārgaśīrṣapūrṇimottaraṃ tadanyattarasminn uttarālābhāt.*)

Cg and Cm remark that this asterism is particularly favorable for Rāma.

And it is this, coupled with the fatal quality of the following asterism, Hasta, that, for them, accounts for Rāma's urgency to begin his march. (*hasto rāmasya nidhanatārā. uttarāphalgunī tu sādhanatārā. ato 'dyaiva sarvānīkasamāvṛtāḥ santo 'bhiprayāma gacchema*—so Cg.) See note below. Cg, who characteristically disagrees with Ct's understanding of the chronology of the *Rāmāyaṇa*, takes the reference to the asterism to demonstrate that the events described here take place on the full-moon day of the month Phālguna (February–March), i.e., Holi. (*atrottarāphalgunīty anena sa divasaḥ phālgunapaurṇamāsīty avagamyate. idam uttaratra pratipādayiṣyate.*) He claims that this position will be substantiated later in the text. On epic chronology, see Hopkins 1903. On the chronology of epic events in the *Yuddhakāṇḍa*, see notes to 6.29.17; 6.32; 6.34.2; 6.36.43; 6.42.37; 6.43.1; 6.44.38; 6.46.51; 6.47.135; 6.48.12; 6.50.12; 6.55.129; 6.59.106;

6.61.68; 6.62.4; 6.65.1; 6.66.38; 6.69.23; 6.73.14; 6.78.54; 6.79.7; 6.80.55; 6.81.7, 28–31; 6.88.59; 6.97.31,33; 6.99.41,43; 6.100.7; and 6.112.1. See, too, 5.2.54 and note.

"Tomorrow the moon will enter the asterism Hasta." *śvas tu hastena yokṣyate*: Literally, "Tomorrow it will be conjoined with Hasta." We follow Ct, Ck, and Cm in adding the word *candra*, "moon." Hasta is the eleventh (Kane 1974, vol. 5, p. 502) or thirteenth (Apte s.v.) lunar asterism. Cg notes that this asterism is particularly inauspicious for Rāma. Ct, Ck, and Cm all elaborate, noting that it is inauspicious for anyone like Rāma who is under the asterism Punarvasū (*punarvasau jātasya mama śvas tu naidhanatārā*). In astrology, *naidhana* refers to the eighth house, or "the House of Death." This accounts for his urgency to set out immediately. See note to 6.59.23.

For a thorough discussion of Rāma's horoscope based on the data furnished by the southern recension, see Pillai 1922, pp. 112–22.

5. "Jānakī" *jānakīm*: According to Cg, the use of the epithet here indicates that Rāma needs to bring Sītā back in order to please Janaka (*jānakīm iti viśeṣaṇena janakaprītyartham cāvaśyaṃ sā netavyeti vyajyate*). Perhaps Cg is anticipating the important scene of the late *Yuddhakāṇḍa*, where Rāma claims that he has not recovered Sītā for her sake or to keep her. See 6.103.13–24, esp., verses 15–16.

6. "For the upper lid of my eye is throbbing" *upariṣṭāt... nayanaṃ sphuramāṇam idaṃ mama*: Literally, "from above, this eye of mine is throbbing." Cm, no doubt keeping in mind the general tradition that throbbing on the right side of the body is auspicious for men, proposes adding the word "right" (*nayanaṃ dakṣiṇam iti śeṣaḥ*). Cg, however, disputes this view, quoting a verse from an unnamed astrological text, which, although supporting the view that throbbing above the eye is an auspicious sign, appears to interpret the throbbing of the right eye as negative. From this verse he calls into question the explanation [no doubt Cm's] that the eye referred to in the verse is the right one. (*tathoktaṃ jyotiḥśāstre netrasyādhaḥ sphuraṇam asakṛt saṅgare bhaṅgahetur netropānte harati nayanaṃ netramūle ca mṛtyuḥ / netrasyordhvaṃ harati sakalaṃ mānasaṃ duḥkhajātaṃ vāme caivaṃ phalam avikalaṃ dakṣiṇe vaiparītyam // ity evaṃ vacane vidyamāne dakṣiṇanayanam iti vyākhyānaṃ cintyam.*) However, Cm's view is consistent with the general understanding that throbbing of the right part of the body is auspicious for men and inauspicious for women, and vice versa. See 6.43.7; 6.53.43; 6.83.34; and notes. For a discussion of omens in the *Rāmāyaṇa*, see Sharma 1971, pp. 177–79; Vyas 1967, pp. 145–51, esp. pp. 148–49; and Guruge 1960, pp. 227–32. Cf. Kapadia 1967, p. 255. See also Dange 1986, pp. 445–51. See, too, *AgniP* 230–31. See also 5. 25.35–37; 5.27.4; and notes. Cf. 6.26.21–30; 6.31.7; 6.41.30–33; 6.43.6–8; 6.45.32–38; 6.49.6; 6.53.40–44; 6.60.22; 6.76.4; 6.94.14; 6.96.1; and notes.

Following verse 6, D5–7,10,11,S (except G1,M5) insert a passage of two lines [58*]: "Then honored by Lakṣmaṇa and the monkey king, righteous Rāma, who was expert in worldly affairs, spoke once more."

8. "honey" *madhu-*: The term is used in the sense of honey-wine, or mead, in connection with the monkey army's refreshment at the end of the *Sundarakāṇḍa*. See note to 5.59.8.

"furnished with cool groves and waters" *śītakānanavāriṇā*: Cr reads the *bahuvrīhi* compound *kānanavāriṇā* as a *madhyamapadalopī* rather than as a *dvandva* as we have done. His interpretation would then be "furnished with cool forest-waters (*śītāni kānanavārīṇi vanasaṃbandhijālāni yasmin*)."

9. "you must... guard... against [them]" *parirakṣethās tebhyaḥ*: We follow the interpretation of Cr, who makes it clear that Nīla is to secure the provisions against the depredations of the *rākṣasas*. A number of manuscripts, both northern and southern (V1,B1,3,D6,10,11,T2,3,M1,2), and the texts and printed editions of Ct, Cr, and Ck redundantly read *pathi*, "on the path *or* road," for the critical *pari*.

"might poison" *dūṣayeyuḥ*: Literally, "they might spoil *or* taint." Ct, Cg, and Cm add "with poison, etc. (*viṣādineti śeṣaḥ*—so Ct)."

10. "hidden" *nihitam*: Ct, Cg, and Cm add, "placed in hiding in order to strike secretly (*guptaprahārārthaṃ līnatayā sthāpitam*—Ct) *or* at an unguarded moment (*randhre prāhārārthaṃ sthāpitam*—Cg, Cm)." Cr understands, "stationed in order to destroy their enemies (*svaripuvināśāya saṃsthāpitam*)."

"in hollows, swamps, and thickets" *nimneṣu vanadurgeṣu vaneṣu ca*: The three terms are subject to a certain amount of ambiguity in interpretation, which is accentuated by the poet's repetition of the word *vana-*, "forests," to resonate with the *vana* in *vanaukasaḥ*, "forest dwellers." Ct and Cg understand *nimneṣu* to refer to depressed or low-lying land (*nimneṣu gartapradeśeṣu*—so Cg), and we agree that this best suits the context. Cr appears to take *nimna* as an adjective modifying *vanadurgeṣu*, which would then have the sense of "characterized by excavations, etc. (*khātādiviśiṣṭeṣu*)." The commentators differ somewhat in their interpretations of *vanadurgeṣu*, "forest fastnesses." Ct and Ck understand, "inaccessible places consisting of forests (*vanātmakeṣu durgeṣu*)." They contrast this to the following word *vana-*, which they then take to refer to "forest areas that are not inaccessible (*vaneṣv adurgavaneṣu ca*)." Cr distinguishes the excavated or entrenched forest fastnesses from the *vanas*, which he sees as "areas near water (*jalasamīpadeśeṣu*)." Cg, whom we follow, has the opposite interpretation. On the basis of a lexical citation from *Amarakośa* 1.10.3, whereby *vanam* may have the sense of water, he interprets *vanadurga* to mean "places made inaccessible by waters (*vanair jalair durgeṣu durgamapradeśeṣu*)." He then gives the following word *vana-* its more common sense of "forest *or* woodlands."

Following verse 10, Ñ2,V1,3,B,D5–11,S insert a passage of two lines [59*]: "Any part of the force that is not fit[1] should be employed here.[2] For our mission is a formidable one and must be undertaken through valor."

[1]"is not fit" *phalgu*: Literally, "weak *or* defective."

[2]"should be employed here" *prayujyatām*: D10,11, and the texts and printed editions of Ct and Ck read instead *upapadyatām*, literally, "let it approach *or* go near." Ct glosses, "let it stay *or* remain (*tiṣṭhatu*)."

11. "resembles the surge of the sea" *sāgaraughanibham*: Cr remarks that the army's resemblance to the sea derives from the tumultuous noise that both make (*atighoṣavattayā sāgarapravāhaughasadṛśam*).

12. "Let... march... like haughty bulls" *yāntu... dṛptā ivarṣabhāḥ*: Literally, "let them go like haughty bulls." V1,B3,D10,11,M3, and the texts and printed editions of Ct read instead the singular, *yātu... dṛpta ivarṣabhaḥ*. This can be taken collectively, as Cr does, or to refer only to Gavākṣa, as does Dutt (1893, p. 1112).

13. "right flank" *dakṣiṇaṃ pārśvam*: Citing a passage claimed to be from *Kāmandaka*[*nītiśāstra*], which specifies how the different wings of an army are to be arranged,

Cg notes that this refers to the western flank of the force. (*dakṣiṇaṃ paścimapārśvam ity arthaḥ. yataś ca bhayam āśaṅki tāṃ prācīṃ parikalpayed iti kāmandakaḥ.*)

14. "Gandhamādana... as an unrivaled war-elephant" *gandhahastīva... gandhamādanaḥ*: Literally, "like a scent-elephant... Gandhamādana." The *upamāna* here is no doubt chosen because of the resonance of the term with the name Gandhamādana, literally, "intoxicating by scent." Cg glosses, "rutting elephant (*mattagajaḥ*)." Although his interpretation appears in most translations, it is not quite accurate. As Ct and Cm explain, the reference is to a special and superior kind of elephant, the smell of whose rut fluid causes other elephants to flee (*yasya madagandhād itare hastino dravanti sa*—Cm). See Apte (s.v.). See notes to 6.97.33, App. I, No. 67, line 52 and n. 15; and notes to 6.15.33, App. I, No. 16, lines 57–69.

15. "lord Indra" *īśvaraḥ*: Literally, "the lord."

"urging on" *abhiharṣayan*: Cg takes the verse to be consonant with the military dictum, "having put them in formation [a leader] should exhort the troops (*praharṣayed balaṃ vyūhyety ukteḥ*)."

"the vast host" *balaugham*: Literally, "the flood *or* throng of troops."

16. Cg argues that, by these instructions, Rāma is implicitly suggesting to Sugrīva that he mount a palanquin and march in company with him and Lakṣmaṇa (*atra tvaṃ ca śibikām ārūhyāvābhyām āgaccheti siddham*).

"Yama, ender of all things" *antaka-*: Literally, "the ender."

"on Aṅgada" *aṅgadena*: Literally, "with Aṅgada." We agree with Ct, Cr, and Cg, who understand that Lakṣmaṇa is to ride on Aṅgada (*aṅgadam ārūhya saṃyātv ity arthaḥ*).

"Kubera, the ruler of the *yakṣas*" *bhūteśaḥ*: Literally, "the lord of *bhūtas*." This term is most commonly an epithet of Śiva or Skanda in the sense of "lord of ghosts *or* spirits." These figures are said to form Śiva's entourage. The term *bhūteśa* is sometimes also used as an epithet of Brahmā or Viṣṇu with the broader sense of "lord of [all] creatures." Here, however, the appositional epithet, "*draviṇādhipatiḥ* (lord of wealth)," and the association with the elephant Sārvabhauma make it clear that Kubera is intended and that *bhūta* is to be read as "supernatural being," with the particular sense of *yakṣa*. Kubera is the *lokapāla* of the north. See *MatsyaP* 67.15 and *ViṣṇuP* 5.36.12. See, too, 6.7.3; 6.22.10; 6.69.26; 6.80.52; 6.82.2; 6.92.15; 6.98.12–13; 6.110.23; 6.115.24,49; and notes. Cf. 6.47.9, where *bhūtas* are understood as malignant spirits; and 6.55.127 and note, where the term refers to spirits of the departed.

"Sārvabhauma" *sārvabhaumena*: The majority of commentators agree that this is the name of one of the earth-supporting elephants and the one that serves as Kubera's mount. See *BrahmāṇḍP* 2.22.47,51; *VāyuP* 51.43–45; and *MatsyaP* 1.1.125.17–21. Cg, Cm, and Cv add that this is the elephant stationed in the northern quarter. This is the name found in the standard lists of the *diggajas* (*AmaK* 1.3.4), but note that earlier in the *Rāmāyaṇa* the *diggaja* of the north is named Bhadra. See 1.39.12,21 and notes. Bhadrā is also named as Kubera's wife in *Mahābhārata* 1.191.6. See, too, 6.31.4 and 6.58.45–46.

17. "the... king of the apes" *ṛkṣarājaḥ*: There is some disagreement among the commentators and translators as to the actual number of monkeys mentioned here and regarding which one is called "king of the apes." Cv, Cm, and Ct, whom we follow, hold that only three monkeys are named and that Jāmbavān is the *ṛkṣarāja*. This latter identification is in keeping with a well-established tradition in Vālmīki (6.28.1; 6.40.11; etc.), as well as in the *Mahābhārata* (3.264.23) and later texts (*Tulsīdās*

Rāmāyaṇa caupai 4 following *dohā* 28 of the *Kiṣkindhākāṇḍa*), that identifies Jāmbavān as the king of the *ṛkṣas*, creatures most commonly understood in the later tradition to be bears instead of apes (see 1.16.10 and note). The difficulty here arises from the fact that the names of the other two monkeys intervene between "Jāmbavān" and the title. Normal epic usage in such cases would be to attach the title to the last-named monkey, in this case Vegadarśin, and that is precisely how Roussel has translated it (1903, vol. 3, p. 9). Cg, evidently disturbed by the disjunction, takes *ṛkṣarāja* here to be a proper noun, the name of a brother of Jāmbavān, and thus finds four monkeys named in the verse, "these three" viz., Jāmbavān, Suṣeṇa, and Vegadarśin, and Ṛkṣarāja. See R. Goldman 1989. See 6.28.31; 6.31.17; 6.39.25; 6.40.11; 6.72.30; 6.86.8; and notes, where Jāmbavān is identified as "king of the *ṛkṣas*." Cf. 6.61.16,26; 6.70.3; and notes. On the term *ṛkṣa* as "ape," see 6.28.1–3; 6.22.32; 6.54.14; 6.55.45; 6.102.21; etc. Compare, however, below verse 57, 7*, lines 24–25 and n. 12, as well as 6.12.12; 6.30.17; 6.101.34; and notes, where the term is translated as "bear."

"rear" *kukṣim*: In the context, we are inclined to agree with Ck, Ct, Cr, and Cg that this term, whose normal meaning is "belly *or* interior," is used as a technical military term, in the sense of "the rear guard of an army (*paścādbhāgam*—so Ct)," the one portion of the force that has not thus far been mentioned. Ck, Ct, and Cr elaborate, saying that the rear part of the army is characterized as being its belly (*kukṣyupalakṣitaṃ senāpucchabhāgam*). See verse 30 below and note.

18. "gave those orders" *vyādideśa*: Literally, "he commanded." The idea is, as Cg notes, that Sugrīva instructs the monkeys to do as Rāma has just said (*rāmoktaṃ sarvaṃ kurutety ājñāpayāmāsa*).

19. "eager for battle" *yuyutsavaḥ*: D7,10,11, and the texts and printed editions of Ct and Cr read instead *mahaujasaḥ*, "of immense strength."

21. "They numbered in the hundreds" *śataiḥ*: Literally, "by the hundreds."

22. "The vast host of tawny monkeys" *mahatī harivāhinī*: Cg claims that these are different from the monkeys belonging to the previously mentioned army (*pūrvoktabalavānarabhinnā*). See verse 6.4.18.

23–24. "Excited and filled with joy" *hṛṣṭāḥ pramuditāḥ*: This is another of the epic poet's frequent groups of near synonyms, the nuances of whose meanings are difficult to ascertain. Ct argues that the distinction between the two is that the former represents the outward manifestations of delight, whereas the latter refers to inner feelings (*harṣapramodayor bāhyābhyantarakṛto bhedaḥ*). Cr sees a causal relation between the two, arguing that the former means that the monkeys are "satisfied *or* content (*hṛṣṭa*)" and are therefore "pleased *or* delighted (*pramudita*)" (*hṛṣṭāḥ prāptasaṃtoṣā ata eva pramuditāḥ*). See note to 6.2.14.

"leaping outward and onward" *āplavantaḥ plavantaś ca*: Here, too, the terms are nearly synonymous. The commentators distinguish them by taking the former to refer to the monkey's leaping around in all directions (Ct, Ck, Cr, Cm, Cg). Ct, Ck, and Cr add that this is by way of patrolling to protect the army (*samantād rakṣaṇārthaṃ plavamānāḥ*—so Ct). The second term is taken to mean bounding in a forward direction either to lead the troops (*senām ākarṣayantaś ca santaḥ*—Cr) or clearing *or* investigating [the path] (*agre śodhanārthaṃ gacchantaḥ*—Ct, Ck). The two participles have been used, no doubt, to create a resonance with the term *plavaṅgamāḥ*, "leaping monkeys." See note to 6.2.14.

"bellowing, roaring, and howling" *garjantaḥ . . . kṣvelanto ninadantaś ca*: This is yet another set of near synonyms. See note to 6.2.14. Cf. 5.55.29; 5.60.12; and notes. Commentators offer various explanations for the sounds the monkeys make. Ct explains *garja* as the sound similar to that of thunderclouds, etc., and, citing the *Nighaṇṭu*, understands that *kṣvelā* is a leonine roar. He then understands *ninād*a as the ordinary sound [that monkeys make]. (*kṣvelā tu siṃhanādaḥ syād iti nighaṇṭuḥ. garjo meghādisadṛśaḥ śabdaḥ. ninādaḥ sāmānyaśabdaḥ.*) Cg agrees on the first two, adding, "it is well known that [clouds] bellow deeply *or* growl (*ghanagarjitam iti prasiddhiḥ*)." He defines the third noise as an indistinct sound (*ninandato 'vyaktaṃ śabdāyamānāḥ*). Cm comments only on the second sound. He agrees with the other two commentators, and, like them, cites the definition in the *Nighaṇṭu* (Cg cites *AmaK* 2.8.107) of *kṣvelā* as "a lion's roar." See, too, 6.17.16–19; 6.47.8; 6.48.31; 6.77.16; 6.78.5; and notes.

"carrying huge trees laden with masses of blossoms" *udvahanto mahāvṛkṣān mañjarīpuñjadhāriṇaḥ*: The syntax is somewhat ambiguous. We agree with the interpretation of Cr, who glosses "laden with masses of blossoms (*mañjarīpuñjadhāriṇaḥ*)" as "possessing many masses of blossoms (*mañjarīsamūhavataḥ*)." Following Ct, who takes both adjectives to refer to the monkeys, the phrase could also be rendered as "bearing clusters of blossoms (*or* blossoming shrubs), they [the monkeys] carried huge trees." This second, and, to our mind, less plausible interpretation, has been adopted by several translators (Shastri 1959, vol. 3, p. 9; Roussel 1903, vol. 3, p. 9; Dutt 1893, p. 1113; and Raghunathan 1982, vol. 3, p. 8). Virtually all commentators agree that the monkeys are carrying the trees [and blossoms] for sport (*līlārtham*—Ct, Cr). The commentators are thus indicating their understanding that the trees in question are not the ones that serve as one of the monkeys' principal weapons in combat. Note that most northern manuscripts substitute for *mañjarīpuñjadhāriṇaḥ* words meaning large rocks, boulders, mountain peaks, etc. These texts thus see the monkeys as armed for battle with their characteristic weapons rather than simply frolicking along with trees as playthings.

25. "In their wild exuberance" *dṛptāḥ*: Normally, "proud, haughty." The context, however, supports the term's less common meaning, "wild, frenetic."

"they would carry one another about. Then they would suddenly throw down those being carried." *nirvahanti kṣipanti ca*: Literally, "they carry and they throw." The idea here, as Ct and Ck suggest, is that the monkeys' horseplay is for the sake of amusement (*vinodārtham*—Ct, Ck). Compare the still more violent clowning of the inebriated monkeys at 5.59.11–22 and 5.60. Following Ct, who understands, "they threw to the ground those mounted on them (*svamārūḍhaṃ bhūmau pātayanti*), the words "those being carried" have been added.

"Some would fall down then leap up" *patantaś cotpatanty anye*: Literally, "others, falling, leap up." We take the root $\sqrt{}$*pat* in its sense of "to fall down," and *ut* $\sqrt{}$*pat* in its sense of "to jump *or* leap up" [in order to knock down those who had caused them to fall]; this seems to us the central point of the verse. Commentators, however, interpret differently. Thus Ct and Ck interpret: "Some simply proceeded, while others fly up, that is, go on a path through the sky. (*patantaś ca bhavanti kevalaṃ gacchantīty arthaḥ. anye utpatanty ākāśamārge gacchanti.*)" Cr has a similar explanation. M3 and the texts and printed editions of Cg read *ākṣipanti* for *utpatanti*. Cg explains this sequence as follows: "Some, falling down (*patantaḥ*), reviled (*ākṣipanti*) those who made them fall. The meaning is 'those who were unable to retaliate, merely talked back, while those who were capable of it, knocked down (*pātayanti*) those who had made them fall.' (*pratikārakaraṇāsāmarthyena paribhāṣaṇaṃ kurvantīty arthaḥ. apare śaktāḥ parān pātayitṝn pātayanti.*)" For the use of √*kṣip* in the sense of "to verbally abuse," in a similar context, see 5.60.11.

27. "Ṛṣabha" *ṛṣabhaḥ*: Commentators differ as to whether this monkey is the same individual that was appointed to the guardianship of the right flank in verse 13 above. Ct, Cm, and Ck argue that this is another monkey, a companion of Nīla (*ayam ṛṣabho dakṣiṇapārśvaviniyuktād anyo nīlasahakārī*—so Ct). See verses 7 and 8 above. Cg, however, argues that, "although Kumuda and the rest are different from Nīla and so forth—who were appointed earlier by Rāma to guard the army's route [verses 7–9 above]—they present themselves for this service because of their devotion to Rāma. The Ṛṣabha mentioned here," Cg claims, "is the same as the one earlier [verse 13 above] appointed to the right flank. We are," he goes on, "to understand that he volunteers for this additional duty because of his devotion as well as his tremendous valor (*ṛṣabho dakṣiṇapārśvarakṣaṇāya niyukto bhaktyā parākramātiśayena cātrāpi rakṣaṇaṃ kṛtavān iti jñeyam*)."

"scouted the path ahead of them" *panthānaṃ śodhayanti sma*: Here, too, the causative of the verb √*śudh*, "to purify," can mean either "to clear" or "to investigate."

28. "In the center marched" *madhye*: Literally, "in the center [were]." The verse provides no explicit finite verb. We have added one for the sake of clarity.

"powerful and fearsome monkeys" *balibhir bhīmaiḥ*: Literally, "with powerful, fearsome [ones]."

29. "one hundred million troops" *koṭībhir daśabhiḥ*: Literally, "by ten *koṭis or* crore." A crore or a *koṭi* is ten million.

"sole" *ekaḥ*: Literally, "one, alone."

"took over the . . . supervision and protection of" *avaṣṭabhya rarakṣa*: Literally, "having taken charge, he protected." Cr and Cg understand the gerund *avaṣṭabhya* in the sense of "having taken charge *or* control of (*adhiṣṭhāya*)," whereas Ct and Ck explain the phrase to mean "patrolling on all sides, he guarded (*samantato bhraman rakṣati smety arthaḥ*)."

30. "Kesarin" *kesarī*: For a discussion of the name of this monkey in the *Rāmāyaṇa* and his identification as Hanumān's father, see Bulcke 1959–1960 and S. Goldman 1999.

"Gaja" *gajaḥ*: Cm (also quoted by Ct) argues that this is not the same monkey who was assigned to march in the vanguard of the army (*eṣa gajaḥ pūrvabhāganiyuktād anya iti tīrthaḥ*—so Ct). Cg feels, however, that it is the same monkey who, in his great devotion, takes on both assignments (*gajasyāgrabhāganiyuktasyāpi pārśvarakṣaṇaṃ bhaktyatiśayāt*). Compare notes to verse 27 above, where similar arguments are made about Ṛṣabha.

"mighty" *atibalaḥ*: D10,11, and the texts and printed editions of Ct and Ck read instead *bahubhiḥ*, "with many [monkeys]."

"each guarded one of the army's flanks" *pārśvam ekaṃ tasyābhirakṣati*: Literally, "he guarded one of its flanks." The commentators differ as to the flanks that are guarded by the various monkeys. Ck, also quoted by Ct, sees the four monkeys as assigned in pairs to the left and right flanks, respectively (*kesaryādīnāṃ caturṇāṃ dvau dvau tasya balasya dakṣiṇaṃ vāmaṃ caikaikaṃ pārśvam abhirakṣata ity artha iti katakaḥ*—so Ck, as quoted by Ct). Cr agrees and specifically assigns Kesarin and Panasa to the right flank and Gaja and Arka to the left (*keśarī panasaś ca tasya balasyaikaṃ dakṣiṇam ity arthaḥ ... gajo 'rkaś caikaṃ vāmam ity arthaḥ*). Cg understands only one wing to be mentioned here and that is the left (*ekaṃ pārśvaṃ savyaṃ pārśvam*). Cm understands the reference to be to the rear guard of the army on the grounds that the right and left flanks had already been assigned in verses 13 and 14 above to Ṛṣabha and Gandhamādana, respectively (*pārśvam ekaṃ paścād bhāgam ṛṣabhagandamādanayoḥ pūrvam eva dakṣiṇasavyapārśvayor viniyogāt*). Since he does not appear to object to a similar redundancy with regard to the rear guard from verse 17, it is likely that he, against the other commentators, understands the term *kukṣi* there to mean "interior" rather than "rear guard."

31. "the tail end of the army" *jaghanam*: Literally, "the hindmost part." This conforms with the assignment of Jāmbavān and Suṣeṇa to protect the rear guard (*kukṣi*). See note to verse 17 above. Cv, apparently anticipating a redundancy between the two verses, notes that *jaghana* here refers to the tail end of the *kukṣi*, the rear guard (*sugrīvasya pṛṣṭhataḥ kukṣeḥ paścimabhāgam*). Cm, also noting the previous assignment of Jāmbavān and Suṣeṇa to the rear, sees this verse as referring specifically to the portion of the army following behind Sugrīva (*sugrīvasya pṛṣṭhataḥ kukṣiṃ paścimabhāgam*).

32. "moving swiftly about, guarded the army on every side" *saṃpatan patatāṃ śreṣṭhas tad balaṃ paryapālayat*: Cg and Cm, the only commentators to comment on this reading, understand that Nīla is moving in advance of the army in order to clear or scout the way. Cg states that he protects the army on all sides because he is the general (*senapatitvāt*). Cm argues that he is able to do this because of his extraordinary speed in leaping (*nīlaḥ puromārgaśodhanakaḥ sann api plavanavegātiśayavattayā paritaḥ sarvato rarakṣety arthaḥ*). D10,11, and the texts and printed editions of Ct, Ck, and Cr read instead *saṃyataś caratāṃ śreṣṭhas tad balaṃ paryavārayat*, "self-controlled, that best of marchers restrained the army on every side." Ct, Cr, and Ck all interpret this to mean that General Nīla led his troops in such a way as to prevent them from harassing cities, etc., along their route (*paryavārayan nagarādipīḍārāhityaṃ yathā bhavati tathā parivāryānayat*).

33. "urging ... onward" *tvarayantaḥ*: Literally, "hastening, hurrying up."

34. "the ... Sahya mountains" *sahyam*: One of the seven major mountain ranges of Bhāratadvīpa understood to be the northern part of the Western Ghats (Law 1944, p. 1). Cg notes that we must understand that the monkeys saw the mountains "from a distance (*apaśyan dūrād iti śeṣaḥ*)." Ct observes that the reference to the mountains is to be understood to indicate that this is where the monkeys will make camp after their first day of marching (*atra prathamadinavāsa iti jñāyate*). See note to verse 4 above.

Following verse 34, D5–7,10,11,S insert a passage of three lines [72*]: "[They saw] large ponds and lakes covered with blossoms.[1] Heeding in their fear the orders of Rāma, whose wrath was dreadful, they avoided the settled countryside and the vicinity of towns.[2–3]"

35. "mighty roar ... dreadful rush" *mahāghoṣaṃ bhīmavegaḥ*: D6,7,10,11, and the texts and printed editions of Ct and Cr read instead *mahāghoraṃ bhīmaghoṣam*, "[the ocean] very dreadful, having a fearsome roar." D5,T1,2,G1,2,M, and the texts and printed editions of Cg read *mahāghoṣaḥ*, "having a tremendous roar," for *bhīmavegaḥ*, "dreadful rush."

36. "leapt swiftly onward" *tūrṇam āpupluvuḥ*: Cg understands the sense of the verse to be that the monkeys act in this fashion in order to cheer up or divert Rāma (*tanmukhollāsāyeti bhāvaḥ*).

37. "by the two monkeys" *kapibhyām*: The reference is to Aṅgada and Hanumān, who carry Lakṣmaṇa and Rāma, respectively. See verses 15 and 16 above.

*"two great planets" *grāhābhyām* [*sic*]: Literally, "by two crocodiles." The critical reading as it stands is absurd. The word must be a misprint for *grahābhyām*, for it is attested in no available printed edition of any recension. The form *grahābhyām*, moreover, is not given as a variant in the critical apparatus. All commentators who gloss the word use *grahābhyām*, including the critical edition's own quotation of Crā. It is not listed under the errata and corrigenda (critical edition, p. 1103). No translation consulted understands *grāhābhyām*.

The commentators are divided as to the identity of the planets in question. Ct, Ck, and Cm identify them as Rāhu and Ketu, or the ascending and descending nodes of the moon (sometimes considered the ninth planet). Cg and Cs, however, understand the reference to be to Śukra (Venus) and Bṛhaspati (Jupiter). Cg sees the reference in the simile to the conjunction of four heavenly bodies to suggest the destruction of a great army [Rāvaṇa's] through the conjunction of Hanumān and Aṅgada with Rāma and Lakṣmaṇa on the grounds that such a planetary event portends the death of large numbers of people. Thus he sees the figure as effecting a suggestion of the plot (*vastudhvani*). (*atropamāne caturgrahasaṃyogasya bahujanavināśahetutvād dhanumadaṅgadābhyāṃ rāmalakṣmaṇayogasya mahāsenāvināśakatvaṃ gamyata ity alaṃkāreṇa vastudhvaniḥ*.) Cs understands the reference to these planets quite differently. He indicates that Lakṣmaṇa is compared to the moon and Rāma to the sun, and understands that just as the splendor of those two planets (Śukra and Bṛhaspati) is outshone by the radiance of the sun, so the splendor of the two monkey *vāhanas* is outshone by the splendor of Rāma. (*śukrabṛhaspatibhyāṃ kavikāvyayutajyotsnākāntavat sa vyarocata ity ukter lakṣmaṇapakṣe candro nidarśanam. rāmapakṣe bhāskaraḥ tataś ca kavikāvyābhyāṃ sakāntiś candra iva vāhanasāhityena sa kāntir lakṣmaṇaḥ. sūryaprakāśābhibhūtaprakāśas tayor iva rāmaprakāśābhibhavo vāhanarūcor iti nidarśanaviveko draṣṭavyaḥ*.) On Bṛhaspati, cf. 6.7.9–10; 6.11.42; 6.40.28; 6.115.51; and notes.

Following verse 37, D5–7,10,11,S repeat verse 20.

38. "bold" *pratibhānavān*: We have departed from the reading favored by most commentators and translators, which takes *pratibhāna* in its more common sense of "intellect." In this way we agree with Gorresio, who renders *animoso* (1856, vol. 9, p. 137). Thus, Cg glosses, "his intellect [focused] on the moment (*tātkālikabuddhimān*)"; Cm reads similarly (*tatkālocitaprajñaḥ*).

"learned in the traditional texts" *smṛtimān*: Cr, whom we follow, understands, "distinguished in the foremost scientific texts (*praśastasmṛtiviśiṣṭaḥ*)." Cg understands the reference to be more specific, glossing, "recalling the meaning of the texts on omens (*nimittaśāstrārthasmaraṇavān*)." Cm understands the adjective to refer not to traditional texts but to Lakṣmaṇa's lived experience, glossing, "whose nature is not to forget past experiences (*anubhūtārthāvismaraṇaśīlaḥ*)."

D10,11, and the texts and printed editions of Ct read instead *pūrṇārtha-*. This reading yields the compound *pūrṇārthapratibhānavān*, literally, "possessing intelligence with respect to the completed matter." Ct explains, "possessing intelligence, that is, knowledge of the completed matter, that is undertaken by means of omens. The meaning is 'possessing knowledge of the completion of the mission that is going to be undertaken' (*pūrṇasyārthasya kāryasya śakunaiḥ pratibhānavāñ jñānavān kariṣyamāṇasya kāryasya pūrṇatvajñānavān ity arthaḥ*)."

"his quest certain of success" *pratipūrṇārthaḥ*: The term presents ambiguities for both semantic and textual reasons. Northern manuscripts, many *devanāgarī* manuscripts (D1–4,8–12), southern manuscripts (G,M5), and the texts and printed editions of Ct read *paripūrṇārtham* and simply render the compound as an adjective modifying Rāma. Gorresio (5.73.49), who reads *vacanam* in place of the critical edition's *smṛtimān*, translates, "*con liete parole*" (1856, vol. 9, p. 137).

Our interpretation is similar to that of Cg, who glosses, "whose desire was fulfilled (*paripūrṇārthamanorathaḥ*)," and Ct, who understands the term to refer specifically to the fulfillment of Rāma's mission (see above).

39. "whom he has abducted" *hṛtām*: Literally, "[she who was] abducted."

"your goals accomplished . . . prosperous" *samṛddhārthaḥ . . . samṛddhārthām*: Literally, "having goals that were accomplished . . . having an abundance of wealth." Note the poet's play on the two meanings of the compound. The commentators are silent. Translators consulted understand both occurrences of the term in the same sense, that is, "whose purpose has been accomplished." The majority of these translators also understand the second occurrence to refer to the city of Ayodhyā, as do we. Raghunathan (1982, vol. 3, p. 9), however, takes the second term to refer to Vaidehī in *pāda* a, translating, "whose dearest wish had been fulfilled."

41. "auspicious . . . favorable and pleasant" *śubho . . . mṛduhitaḥ sukhaḥ*: The list of the wind's qualities presents yet another series of near synonyms of which Vālmīki is so fond. Commentators offer slightly different interpretations of the individual adjectives and, in some cases, disagree as to their number. Cg and Cm explain *śubhaḥ* as "foretelling future auspiciousness (*bhāviśubhasūcakaḥ*)." Cr reads the synonymous variant *śivaḥ*, "conveying auspiciousness (*maṅgalapradaḥ*)." Cm, who also reads *śivaḥ*, glosses, "foretelling auspiciousness (*śubhasūcakaḥ*)." Ct and Ck read the compound *mṛduhitaḥ* as a *dvandva* and so see the wind as qualified by four adjectives: *śiva*, "auspicious"; *mṛdu*, "gentle"; *hita*, "beneficial"; and *sukha*, "pleasant." They explain that the adjectives *mṛdu*, *hita*, and *sukha*, respectively, express the coolness, gentleness, and fragrance of the wind (*mṛduhitasukhapadaiḥ krameṇa māndyaśaityasaurabhāṇy uktāni*—so Ct). Cm explains the sequence of modifiers similarly but takes *mṛdu* adverbially, i.e., "gently (*mṛdu mandaṃ yathā tathā*)." He thus takes *hitaḥ* separately to mean "beneficial in that it allays the weariness of the journey (*adhvaśrāntiharaṇād dhitaś ca*)." Cr reads the compound as a *tatpuruṣa*, understanding, "beneficial by virtue of its gentleness (*mṛdutvena hitakārī*)." He further explains *sukhaḥ* as "producing pleasure through coolness and fragrance (*śaityasaugandhyābhyāṃ sukhapradaḥ*)." (Note that Cg's text as represented in GPP [6.4.46] is incorrect.) Cg, whom we follow, understands the compound as a *dvandva* and glosses, "joined with gentleness (*mṛdur mārdavayuktaḥ*)" and "favorable (*anukūlaḥ*)." (Note that Cg's text as represented in GPP [6.4.46] is incorrect.) See note to 6.2.14.

"in the direction of the army's march" *anu . . . senām*: Literally, "following the army." As several commentators explain, the wind is blowing at the army's back (*senāpṛṣṭhabhāgena vāti*—so Ct). This is significant because it is considered an auspicious omen. See note to 5.25.10 for references on auspicious omens. See 6.41.33; 6.43.8; 6.45.35; 6.53.44; 6.65.19; and notes. Cf. 6.94.22, where the wind blowing into Rāvaṇa's face is a bad omen.

"continually" *pūrṇa-*: Literally, "full." We follow Ct, Cr, and Ck, who understand the term to mean "without interruption, continuously (*vicchedarahitāḥ*—so Ct)."

42. "the Bhārgava Uśanas" *uśanā . . . bhārgavaḥ*: The sage Uśanas, also known as Śukrācārya, is a scion of the Bhārgava *gotra* and is identified with the planet Venus. See Sutherland 1979. See 6.40.28; 6.45.12; and notes.

"behind you" *anu tvāṃ . . . gataḥ*: Literally, "has gone after you." Cg offers two explanations of this phrase. In the first, he understands *anu* in the sense of *anukūla*, "favorable," and renders, "is positioned in a region favorable to you (*tavānukūladiśi sthitaḥ*)." The second, which we have followed, Cg bases upon an astrological injunction against undertaking a journey or expedition in a direction facing the planet Venus. He quotes an astrological text to the effect that a king who sets forth on a campaign in the face of Venus, Mercury, or Mars will suffer calamity on the battlefield, even if he is Indra's equal. (*yadvānugataḥ paścād bhāgaṃ gataḥ. puraḥ śukrasya yātrāsu pratiṣedhād iti bhāvaḥ. tathoktaṃ jyautiṣe pratiśukraṃ pratibudhaṃ pratibhaumaṃ gato nṛpaḥ / api śakreṇa sadṛṣo hatasainyo nivartate // iti*.) Ct and Ck disagree with Cg's second interpretation. They argue that it is never possible for people either traveling north or south to be facing Venus (*dakṣiṇottaragantṝṇāṃ kadāpi puraḥ śukraprasakter abhāvāt*). (Venus normally appears in roughly the same direction as the sun because it is closer to the sun than the earth.) It should be kept in mind, however, that Cg understands that Laṅkā is not to the south but to the southeast of Kiṣkindhā, and therefore, for him, Rāma would not be traveling due south. See notes to verse 3 above.

Cg then offers a lengthy discussion of the astrological positions of various planets and other heavenly bodies at the time of Rāma's birth and other significant moments in his career. The general thrust of his discussion is to show that, like the planets described in this and the following verses, these astrological signs are favorable to Rāma and unfavorable to his *rākṣasa* foes. It is of some interest here to note that in the course of this discussion he indicates that it is now the thirty-eighth year of the *Rāmāvatāra* (*aṣṭātriṃśadvarṣe yuddhayātrakālaḥ*). This point conforms to the general chronology of the epic according to which Rāma was twenty-five years old at the time of his exile. See notes to 2.17.26 and 5.14.5.

43. "The constellation Brahmarāśi is clear" *brahmarāśir viśuddhaś ca*: The commentators are divided in their opinion as to the significance of this term. Cv, Cg, and Cm (first alternate) take the word *brahma* in its sense of "*vedas*," reading the compound as an epithet of Uśanas in verse 42 above in the sense of "master of the entire *veda* (*adhītasarvavedaḥ*)." They then read the following adjective, "clear (*viśuddha*)," with Uśanas as well. Cg takes it to mean "free from conjunction with inimical planets (*pāpagrahāsaṃyuktaḥ*)," and Cm takes *viśuddha* in its sense of "pure," a quality that he sees deriving from Uśanas's vedic learning. (*brahmarāśir vedānāṃ rāśibhūtaḥ. adhītasarvaveda ity arthaḥ. ata eva viśuddha uśanāś ca tvām anugataḥ*.) Ct, Ck, and Cr understand the reference to be to the constellation known as the Saptarṣis, here called the Great Seers (Paramarṣis), or Ursa Major. Cr understands the word *brahmarāśiḥ* as a *bahuvrīhi*, referring to Dhruva, in the sense of "that in which there is a collection of the stars known as the Seven Seers (*brahmaṇāṃ saptarṣīṇāṃ rāśiḥ samūho yatra saḥ*)." Ck and Ct understand, similarly, "that which has for its tail the Seven Seers (*pucchabhāgo yasmin sa tathā*—so Ck)." They thus take it as a kind of kenning for Dhruva, the North Star (*brahmarāśir dhruvaḥ*—so Ct). In the second alternate, only Cm—whom we follow—appears to read it as a *tatpuruṣa* in the sense of "the collection of seers (*teṣāṃ rāśiḥ saṅgaḥ*)." Thus, he refers not to the North Star or Saptarṣis but to a different group of stars situated in the southern sky along the path of the *pitṛs*, which he claims are described in a verse of

the *Viṣṇupurāṇa* (*tatrāsate mahātmāna ṛṣayo yo 'gnihotriṇaḥ / bhūtārambhakṛtaṃ brahma śaṃsanto ṛtvigudyatāḥ // prārabhante lokakāmās teṣāṃ panthāḥ sa dakṣiṇaḥ*).

"illuminate" *prakāśante*: Literally, "they shine." We agree with Cr in reading the verb in the sense of the causative (*prakāśayante*).

44. "Triśaṅku" *triśaṅkuḥ*: The story of Triśaṅku and how, under the tutelage of Viśvāmitra, he was transformed into the constellation of the Southern Cross is narrated at length at 1.56–59 (see ad loc. and notes). See 2.36.10 and note. See, too, 6.23.19; 6.60.24; and notes.

"the foremost among the forefathers of our great Ikṣvāku lineage" *pitāmahavaro 'smākam ikṣvākūṇāṃ mahātmanām*: Literally, "the best grandfather of us, the great Ikṣvākus." Cg interprets the word *-varaḥ* to mean that Triśaṅku was the most eminent among the most prominent of the Ikṣvāku dynasts (*ikṣvākūṇāṃ pradhānakūṭasthaḥ*). Ś1,Ñ1,B3,D3,4,8,10–12,T3, and the texts and printed editions of Ct, Ck, and Cr read *puraḥ* [*asmākam*], for *-varaḥ*, yielding the sense "[is shining] before [us]." Ct and Ck take this interpretation to be in accordance with the constellation Triśaṅku's position in the southern sky (*dakṣiṇadiksthatvāt*). Ck insists that this is the authentic reading (*iti pāṅktaḥ*).

"with his preceptor" *sapurohitaḥ*: The commentators are also divided as to whether the sage referred to here is the traditional preceptor of the Ikṣvāku dynasty, Vasiṣṭha, or his archenemy, the Kauśika sage Viśvāmitra, who serves as a *guru* to both Triśaṅku and Rāma. Thus, Ct, Ck, Cm, and Cg (as an alternative) see the term as a reference to Vasiṣṭha, who is situated near him in the midst of the alternate set of seven seers that was created in anger by Viśvāmitra (1.59.20–21) (*bhagavadviśvāmitrasṛṣṭasvasamīpavartisaptarṣimaṇḍalamadhyavartivasiṣṭhasahita ity arthaḥ*—so Ct). Cv, Cg, and Cr see Triśaṅku's preceptor as Viśvāmitra himself.

45. "the two Viśākhās" *viśākhe*: These twin stars constitute the fourteenth or sixteenth lunar mansion and form part of the constellation Libra. See 6.90.30 and note; and 6.63.3, App. I, No. 43, lines 23–24 and n. 13. According to Kirfel (1920, p. 36), the four stars constitute Libra. See, too, 2.36.11 and note. Cf. 6.46.24.

"most significant of constellations for our... Ikṣvāku lineage" *nakṣatraṃ param asmākam ikṣvākūṇām*: Cg, alone among the commentators, addresses the association of this particular constellation with the Ikṣvāku dynasty, citing a passage from the *Jyotiṣadarpaṇa* (*aśvinyāṃ yadi ketuḥ... ikṣvākukūlanāthas tu hy anyato yadi bhaved viśākhāsthas tu*). See, too, note to 2.36.11.

46. "those *rākṣasas*, sons of chaos... whose regent is Nirṛti" *nairṛtam... nairṛtānām*: Literally, "that which belongs to Nirṛti... of those who descend from Nirṛti." The poet plays here on the epithet of the constellation Mūla and an occasional epithet of the *rākṣasas*. The commentators are in general agreement that the former indicates that Nirṛti, the personification of destruction or chaos and regent of the southwestern quarter, is the presiding divinity of the constellation. See 5.43.7; 5.45.3; 5.50.15; and notes. See, too, 6.36.11 and note.

"Mūla" *mūlam*: Mūla is generally regarded as the nineteenth *nakṣatra*, or lunar mansion (Jacobi 1888, p. 37; Apte s.v.). It is associated with two stars in the tail of Scorpio (Macdonell and Keith 1967, s.v. *nakṣatra*). According to Apte (s.v. *mūla*), it contains eleven stars (in its tail). See note to 6.97.33, App. I, No. 67, n. 17.

"nearby" *mūlavatā*: Our translation follows the interpretation of Cm, Cg, and Cv, who justify it by citing the lexicon *Vaijayantī*, which gives *antika*, "proximity," as one of the meanings of the word *mūla*. Other commentators, however, offer differing interpretations. Ct and Ck understand, "rising on high in the form of a staff (*uccair daṇḍākāratayotthitena*)." Cr interprets, "governing *or* constraining Mūla *mūlaniyāmakena*)." Cs, alone among the commentators, sees the presence of the ominous comet as a direct result of Rāvaṇa's transgression. He appears to understand *mūla* here in its sense of "root, ground, basis," glossing, "[a comet] the very embodiment [lit., taking its origin from the form] of the sin produced by the abduction of Sītā (*sītāharaṇajanyapāpaparūpakāraṇavatā*)." Differences among those translators who directly engage this term can be traced to the disagreements among these various commentators. Thus, Dutt (1893, p. 1115) renders, "rod-bearing," and Gita Press (1969, vol. 3, p. 1382), "risen with a tail of light," both appearing to follow Ct and Ck, whereas Raghunathan (1982, vol. 3, p. 9) translates, "proximity," like us, following Cm, Cg, and Cv.

"by a . . . comet" *dhūmaketunā*: Cm glosses, "a planet foreboding calamity (*utpātagraheṇa*)."

47. "All of this" *sarvaṃ caitat*: As the commentators indicate, the reference is a collective one to all the omens presaging the destruction of the *rākṣasas* (*rākṣasavināśasūcakānekanimittajātam*—so Cm).

"inimical planets" *graha-*: Literally, "planets." We have added the word "inimical" in keeping with the interpretation of Ct and Ck, who gloss, "occluded by planets, such as Saturn, Mars, Rāhu, etc. (*śanyaṅgārakarāhvādigrahapīḍitam*)." The astronomical bodies referred to are thought to have a baleful influence. See note to 5.46.20.

"at the hour of their doom" *kāle*: Literally, "at the time." The translation reflects our agreement with Ct, Cg, Ck, and Cm, who gloss, *antakāle*, "at the time of death [end]." Cr alone understands, "at this time (*asmin samaye*)."

48. Ct remarks that Lakṣmaṇa's observations concerning the astrological phenomena starting at verse 42 up to this verse have been delivered while the army rested for a while in the Sahya mountains and refreshed itself with fruits and roots. The following observations, he feels, are made by Lakṣmaṇa when the army sets out again that same night. He justifies this with reference to verse 53 below, where it is stated that the monkey army marches both day and night. (*uśanā cetyādy etad antaṃ sahye kiṃcit kālaṃ viśramya phalamūlādi bhuktvā punā rātrau gamanakāle lakṣmaṇena pradarśyate. ata eva vakṣyati sā sma yāti divārātram iti.*)

"Fragrant breezes" *gandhāḥ*: Literally, "fragrances." Like most commentators and all translators, we add the word "breezes."

"briskly" *abhyadhikam*: Literally, "strongly, excessively." There seems to be no way around this somewhat unusual description of a favorable breeze. The convention is that favorable breezes blow gently, and, indeed, D10,11, and the texts and printed editions of Ct, Ck, and Cr read the poorly attested *nādhikāḥ*, "not excessive, gentle," which yields the conventional sense. Virtually all translators consulted render this variant reading.

"of the season" *yathartu-*: For some reason, Shastri (1959, vol. 3, p. 11) translates, "out of season," although no printed text or commentator supports such a reading. Quoting a verse from *Varāhamihira* (*Bṛhatsaṃhitā*), Cg notes that the blossoming and fruiting of trees out of season is considered a portent of calamity; however, Cg believes that this is not the case in the present instance. (*akālakusumotpattir hy utpātaḥ sa idānīṃ nāstīty arthaḥ. tathoktaṃ varāhamihireṇa śītoṣṇānāṃ viparyāsaḥ phalapuṣpam akālajam aśoṣyāṇāṃ viśoṣaś ca phalaṃ ṣāṇmāsikaṃ bhaved iti.*) Nevertheless, the blossoming of trees out of season or in all seasons is often taken as a sign of extraordinary natural beauty or of some miraculous or auspicious events. Compare the description of the *aśokavanikā* at 5.12.2–39 and 5.13.2–14, as well as 6.108.12 (and note), where Indra gives the monkeys such a miraculous boon. Similarly, see the miraculous boon of Bharadvāja at 6.112.17 and note. See, too, 6.115.19 and Kālidāsa's description of the splendid transformation wrought by Kāma in Śiva's penance grove (*KumāSaṃ* 3.24–42). See, too, 6.18.32–34.

49. "Tāraka was slain" *tārakāmaye*: The commentators generally agree that the reference here is to the well-known purāṇic episode in which the *asura* Tāraka is destroyed by the armies of the gods, who are under the leadership of Śiva's son Skanda. Dikshitar (1951–1955, pp. 19–20) understands that that particular battle between the gods and *asuras* took place during the Kṛtayuga, citing some purāṇic references (*BhāgP* 9.14.4–7; *BrahmāṇḍP* 3.5.32; *MatsyaP* 129.16, 172.10). If we understand this battle to be the one referred to here, the word *āmaya*, which normally means "illness *or* affliction," must be read in a secondary sense to mean "death *or* destruction." Cg and Cm claim that it takes this sense because of its suggestion of misery (*duḥkhatvāt*—Cg) or oppression (*baddhatvāt*—Cm). These two commentators, however, also offer an alternative reading of the phrase, which retains the primary sense of *āmaya*. According to this interpretation, the reference here is not to the battle with the *asura* Tāraka at all but to a battle fought for the sake of Bṛhaspati's wife, Tārakā. This latter battle takes its name from the mental affliction suffered by this woman. (*yadvā tārakā nāma bṛhaspatipatnī. tannimittatvāt saṃgrāmasya tārakāmaya iti saṃjñā.*) In support of this interpretation they cite a verse from the *Viṣṇupurāṇa* (4.6.16): "And thus did an extremely fierce battle take place between those two on account of Tārakā. And so it came to be known as [the battle of] Tārakā's affliction (*tathāha śrīviṣṇupurāṇa evaṃ ca tayor atīvograḥ saṃgrāmas tārakānimittas tārakāmayo nāmābhavat*)."

50. "Considering these things" *samīkṣyaitān*: Literally, "having considered these." Neither this phrase nor the vulgate variant *samīkṣyaitat* has a clear antecedent. Nevertheless, the context leads us to agree with the commentators in taking the reference to be to the various omens mentioned by Lakṣmaṇa (*etat phalakaṃ nimittaṃ samīkṣya*—so Cr). This is further supported by a northern insertion [74*]: "Observing those omens, Rāma was delighted."

"noble brother" *ārya*: Literally, "O noble one."

51. "apes and monkeys" *ṛkṣavānara-*: See note to 6.4.17.

52. "fore and hind feet" *kārāgraiś caraṇāgraiś ca*: Literally, "with the tips of their hands and the tips of their feet." We have used these terms particularly when the context refers to the locomotion of the monkeys as opposed to their handling of objects or use of their limbs in combat. See note to 5.1.10.

"earthly world" *bhaumam* . . . *lokam*: Ś1,Ñ1,B1,3,4,D1–5,7–12,T1,G,M3,5, and the texts and printed editions of the southern commentators read *bhīmam*, "frightful, fearsome," for *bhaumam*, "earthly," which then must modify *rajaḥ*, "dust," in *pāda* d.

Following 52, D5–7,10,11,S insert a passage of twenty-two lines [75*]: "The fearsome host of tawny monkeys advanced, covering the southern lands with their vast expanses of mountains and forests,[1] just as a vast canopy of clouds[2] might cover the sky.[1–2] And as the army crossed over in a continuous column for many leagues in length,[3] all the currents of the rivers seemed to flow upstream.[4] [3–4] Plunging through lakes with their cool waters, skirting mountains covered with trees, swarming across the level tracts of land, and moving under forests laden with fruit,[5] the great host advanced, covering the land.[5–8] All the tawny monkeys, swift as Māruta,[6] marched forward, their hearts delighted[7] and their valor high for Rāghava's sake.[9–10] Showing off to one another the excess of their excitement, valor, and strength,[8] along the way they performed all manner of prideful feats out of the abundance of their youthful exuberance.[9] [11–12] Some of the forest-ranging monkeys ran, while others leapt, and still others chattered.[10] [13–14] They lashed their tails against the ground,[11] and they stamped their feet. Some flung out their arms and broke off rocks and trees.[15–16] Scaling the peaks of the mountains, the mountain-ranging monkeys loosed great roars while others roared like lions.[12] [17–18] With the force of their thighs they crushed many thickets of creepers. Expanding themselves, those valorous monkeys played with boulders and trees.[19–20] And so the earth was covered with troops[13] of very fearsome monkeys in their hundreds, hundreds of thousands, and tens of billions.[21–22]"

[1]"southern lands with their vast expanses of mountains and forests" *saparvata-vanākāśāṃ dakṣiṇām*: Literally, "the southern [direction], together with mountains, forests, and space." Some translators take *ākāśa* in its sense of "sky."

[2]"vast canopy of clouds" *ambudasaṃtatiḥ*: Literally, "a line of clouds."

[3]"in a continuous column for many leagues" *satataṃ bahuyojanam*: Literally, "continuously for many *yojanas*." Some translators understand this phrase to refer to the distance to which the waters back up.

[4]"seemed to flow upstream" *sasyandur viparītavat*: Literally, "they flowed as if in reverse *or* backward." According to Ct and Cr, the force of the army crossing the rivers causes them to flow backward (*vānarādibhir atyantam āhatatvāt pravāhābhimukhaṃ celur ity arthaḥ*).

[5]We follow Cg in taking the monkeys' different movements respectively with the different kinds of terrain they traverse. According to Ct (and quoted by Cr), lines 6 and 7 of this insert mark the second night's encampment (*ayaṃ dvitīyo vāsa iti pratīyate*). See note to verse 53 below.

[6]"swift as Māruta" *mārutaraṃhasaḥ*: Literally, "with the speed of Māruta."

[7]"their hearts delighted" *hṛṣṭamanasaḥ*: D7,10,11, and the texts and printed editions of Ct and Cr read instead *hṛṣṭavadanāḥ*, "their faces delighted."

[8]"the excess of their excitement, valor, and strength" *harṣavīryabalodrekān*: D5,7,10,11, and the texts and printed editions of Ct and Ck read instead *harṣaṃ vīryaṃ balodrekān*, yielding the sense "[demonstrating their] excitement and valor and [feats] of excessive strength."

[9]"they performed all manner of prideful feats out of the abundance of their youthful exuberance" *yauvanotsekajān darpān vividhāṃś cakruḥ*: Printed editions of Ct read for the accusative plural the ablative singular, *-jād darpād*, yielding the sense "out of the pride born from the exuberance of youth." This variant is unnoted in the critical edition.

[10]"chattered" *kilakilāṃ cakruḥ*: We understand with Cg and Cr that the term here refers to the unique sound that monkeys make. See 5.55.22 and note.

[11]"lashed their tails against the ground" *prāsphoṭayaṃś ca pucchāni*: Literally, "they clapped [their] tails." Like all translators consulted, we understand *pucchāni*, "tails," to construe with the verb *prāsphoṭayan*, "they clapped," even though this verb is normally intransitive and refers to the action of clapping one's arms as one enters into battle. Cf. 5.55.30 and note.

[12]"while others roared like lions" *kṣvelām anye pracakrire*: See note to 5.55.29.

[13]"with troops" *yūthaiḥ*: D10,11,G1,M3, and the texts and printed editions of the southern commentators read instead *śrīmat*. Construing this word in the syntax of the sentence is most difficult. The commentators offer various solutions. Ct, Ck, and Cs understand the term to be an instrumental plural that has lost its case ending. Thus, in their opinion, the term stands for *śrīmadbhiḥ*, "by those majestic [ones, i.e., hosts]" (*śrīmal luptatṛtīyāntaṃ śrīmadbhir ity arthaḥ*—so Ct). Cs understands that the term refers to the most majestic among the monkeys (*śrīmadbhiḥ . . . vānarāṇāṃ madhye*). Cg understands the term adverbially in the sense of "majestically [covered]" (*śrīmad yathā bhavati tathā parivṛtāsīd iti saṃbandhaḥ*).

53. "Day and night" *divārātram*: Ct and Cs note that this means the army rested for one brief period of three hours only (*yāma*) (in the middle of the night [*madhyarātre*]—so Ct). According to Ct, this marks the third night's encampment (*ayaṃ tṛtīyo vāsaḥ*). See note to 52 above 75*, line 6.

"army" *senā*: Cg, Crā, and Cm, perhaps disturbed by the redundancy of this term with *vāhinī* in *pāda* b, read *senā* etymologically as an adjective in the sense of "accompanied by its leader (*senā inena svāminā sahitā*)."

54. "not even for a moment" *muhūrtam . . . nāsata*: Literally, "they did not sit for a *muhūrta*." Ct and Cs, who understood the phrase "day and night" in the previous verse to allow for a brief rest during the night, take note, in different ways, of the seeming contradiction. Ct, commenting on his variant reading, *nāvasan*, "they did not camp," remarks that the expression "by day (*divasā*)" should be supplied, thus remaining consistent to his notion that the monkeys do take a short rest at night. Cs, in his comment on verse 53, notes this suggestion of Ct but takes exception to it, remarking that the natural sentiment of the verse requires us to understand that the monkeys marched the whole night and that this interpretation is further supported by the fact that the syntax of the verse can be easily construed without the ellipsis seen by Ct. (*ahorātraṃ yāmamātravāsa ity āśayaḥ. uttaratra diveti śeṣa iti ca nāgojibhaṭṭo 'khaṇḍāhorātram ity arthaḥ svarasaḥ. muhūrtaṃ kvāpi nāvasann ity uttaragranthasvārasyāt. śeṣaṃ vinā 'nvayasambhavāc ca.*) Evidently, Cs believes that the monkeys did rest briefly on the previous night, but now, in their eagerness for action, they march without rest.

55. "Sahya and then the Malaya mountains" *sahyaparvatam . . . malayaṃ ca mahīdharam*: Literally, "the Sahya Mountain and the upholder of the earth Malaya." These two ranges of the southern portion of the Western Ghats lie, as Cg notes, along the line of the monkeys' march. According to Dey (1927, pp. 123, 171), Sahya is that portion of the mountain range that lies to the north of the Kāverī River, while the Malaya range lies to the south of the river. See note to verse 34 above.

Ñ2,V1,3,B,D6,9,11,12,T2,3,G2,3,M1,2,5, and the texts and printed editions of Ct read instead *sahyaparvatam āsādya . . . vānarās te samāruhan*, "having reached the Sahya Mountain, those monkeys climbed [it]." Ct notes the variant of Cm (shared by Cg, Crā), which is the reading accepted by the critical edition.

"abounding in all sorts of wild creatures" *nānāmṛgasamāyutam*: Ñ2,D10,11, and the texts and printed editions of Ct read instead *nānāvanasamāyutam*, "covered with all types of forests."

56. "passed through" *atiyayau*: (Printed incorrectly, we believe, in the critical text as *ati yayau*.) We read the form as governing the objective genitives *malayasya* and *sahyasya*, as we feel this best captures the force of the *upasarga ati*. Ś1,Ñ, V1,B3,D2,7,10–12, and the texts and printed editions of Ct and Cr read *api* for *ati*, yielding the sense "even as he gazed, Rāma marched."

57. "many trees": The phrase has been added.

"*aśokas*" *aśokān*: B4,D10,11, and the texts and printed editions of Ct read instead *prasekān*, "flowering (*sinduvārakas*)."

Following this verse, D5–7,10,11,S insert a passage of thirty lines [78*]: "And those leaping monkeys broke down other trees:[1] *aṅkolas*,[2] *karañjas*, *plakṣas*, banyans, *tindukas*,[3] *jambukas*, *āmalakas*, and *nāgas*.[4] [1–2] On the lovely tablelands, the various kinds of forest trees shaken by the force of the wind strewed the earth[5] with their blossoms.[3–4] In those honey-scented woodlands, loud with the buzzing of bees, a wind cooled by sandalwood blew pleasantly to the touch.[5–6] That king of mountains was richly adorned with minerals.[7] And the dust that streamed from those minerals, whipped up by the force of the wind, completely covered that vast host of monkeys.[8–9] On the lovely slopes of the mountain, beautiful blossoming *ketakīs*, *sinduvāras*, and charming *vāsantīs* were everywhere.[10–11] And there were also fragrant spring creepers (*mādhavīs*) and flowering clusters of jasmine[12] as well as *ciribilvas*, *madhūkas*, *bakulas*, *vañjulas*, *sphūrjakas*,[6] *tilakas*, and flowering *nāga* trees, mangos, *pāṭalis*,[7] and flowering *kovidāras*.[13–15] And there were also *muculindas*, *arjunas*, *śiṃśapas*, *kuṭajas*, *dhavas*, *śālmalis*, red *kurabakas*,[8] *hintālas*, *timiśas*, *cūrṇakas*, *nīpakas*, blue *aśokas*, *varaṇas*,[9] *aṅkolas*, and *padmakas*.[16–19] All of them were thrown into disarray by the leaping monkeys as they leapt about.[10] [20] And on that mountain there were charming lakes and cool[11] ponds, which were thronged with *cakravākas* and frequented by *kāraṇḍavas*. They were crowded with *plavas* and *krauñcas*, and frequented by boar and deer.[21–23] They were frequented on every side by bears,[12] hyenas, lions, and fearsome tigers, as well as many terrifying serpents.[24–25] And those pools were lovely with different kinds of flowers that grew in their water: red lotuses, full-blown, white water lilies, night-blooming lotuses, and blue lotuses.[26–27] And on its slopes, flocks of different birds were warbling.[28] The monkeys bathed there, drank the water, and played in it.[29] Having scaled the mountain, the monkeys threw one another into the water.[30]"

[1]"broke down other trees" *bhañjanti sma*: Literally, "they broke." D11,G2,3,M5, and the texts and printed editions of Ct read instead *bhajanti sma*, "they partook of *or* enjoyed."

[2]"*aṅkolas*" *aṅkolān*: D10,11,M5, and the texts and printed editions of Ct read instead *aśokān*, "*aśokas*." See Brockington 1984, p. 106.

[3]"*tindukas*" *tindukān*: D10,11, and the texts and printed editions of Ct read instead *-pādapān*, "[banyan] trees." See Brockington 1984, p. 105.

[4]"*nāgas*" *nāgān*: M3 and the texts and printed editions of Cg read instead *nīpān*, "*nīpas*."

[5]"earth" *gām*: Literally, "the cow [i.e., the earth]." D6,10,11,T2,M3, and the texts and printed editions of the southern commentators read instead *tān*, "them," i.e., the monkeys.

[6]"*sphūrjakas*" *sphūrjakāḥ*: D7,10,11, and the texts and printed editions of Ct and Cr read instead *rañjakāḥ*, "*rañjakas*." According to Brockington (1984, p. 107), this plant is relegated to the "fourth stage" in the northern recension.

[7]"*pāṭalis*" *pāṭalayaḥ*: D7,10,11,G2,3,M5, and the texts and printed editions of Ct read instead *pāṭalikāḥ*, "*pāṭalikas*."

[8]"*dhavas*, *śālmalis*, red *kurabakas*" *dhavāḥ śālmalayaś caiva raktāḥ kurabakāḥ*: D10,11,G2, and the texts and printed editions of Ct omit this line. GPP reads the line in brackets as 6.4.80ef.

[9]"*varaṇas*" *varaṇāḥ*: D10,11, and the texts and printed editions of Ct read instead *saralāḥ*, "*saralas*." See Brockington 1984, p. 106.

[10]"as they leapt about" *plavamānaiḥ*: D10,11, and the texts and printed editions of Ct read instead *prīyamāṇaiḥ*, "delighted."

[11]"cool" *śītāḥ*: D10,11, and the texts and printed editions of Ct read instead *ramyāḥ*, "lovely *or* charming."

[12]"bears" *ṛkṣaiḥ*: Given the context in which carnivorous beasts are being listed, it is unlikely that we are to take the term *ṛkṣa* in its common Vālmīkian sense of "ape *or* monkey." See note to verse 17 above.

58. "Intoxicated with their strength" *balotkaṭāḥ*: Ś1,Ñ1,D1,7,10–12,T1,G2,M3, and the texts and printed editions of the southern commentators read instead *madotkaṭāḥ*, "elated with intoxication." Thus, all translations consulted, with the exception of Gorresio, indicate that the monkeys are inebriated. The idea, no doubt, is the same as that elaborately depicted at 5.59.11–22 and 60, where the monkeys gorge themselves on the intoxicating honey-wine of Sugrīva's *madhuvana*.

"ate" *bubhujuḥ*: Ś1,Ñ,V1,3,B,D,T2,3,G2,3,M1,2,5, and the texts and printed editions of Ct read instead *babhañjuḥ*, "they broke," which several translators render as "they plucked" (Shastri 1959, vol. 3, p. 12; Roussel 1903, vol. 3, p. 12—*arrachaient*) or "crumbled" (Dutt 1893, p. 1117). Gorresio (1856, vol. 9, p. 139) translates, "*schiantavano*."

According to Ct, this verse marks the fourth night's encampment (*ayaṃ caturtho vāsaḥ*).

59. "drinking from" *pibantaḥ*: Literally, "[they] drinking."

"honeycombs" *madhūni*: Literally, "honeys." We follow Cg and Cm, who gloss, "masses of honey *or* a beehive (*madhupaṭalāni*)." See note to 5.60.8. See verse 61 and note below.

"as big as bushels " *droṇamātra-*: We take *droṇa* in the sense of "a tub *or* bucket," as at note to 5.60.8. Cg defines the measure here as equal to two "*śivas*," a term we are unable to trace in the sense of a measure.

60. "devastating" *vidhamantaḥ*: We believe that the use of the root $\sqrt{}$*dhmā*, "to blow," suggests that the monkey armies have stripped the hills of their vegetation in the manner of a strong wind. Cg, taking the root in its sense of "fanning a fire," thinks that the monkeys actually burned the hilltops (*vidhamantaḥ dahantaḥ*).

61. "exhilarated with the honey-wine" *madhudarpitāḥ*: Literally, "exalted by honey." Given the intoxicated or exalted state of the monkeys, we take *madhu* here in its sense

of "fermented honey *or* honey-wine." This seems confirmed by the monkeys' boisterous behavior here, which is strongly reminiscent of the much more elaborate passage at 5.59–60, where the wild behavior of the inebriated monkeys is described in great detail. See 5.8.21–22; 5.59.8; 5.60.6; 5.61.5; 5.62.4; and notes. See note to verse 59 above.

62. "the earth looked as if it were covered with fields of ripened winter rice" *yathā kalamakedāraiḥ pakvair iva vasuṃdharā*: Literally, "like the bearer of treasure with ripened paddies of winter rice as it were." The commentators seem confused and indecisive as to the precise sense of the simile. This is largely owing to the poet's use of two words of comparison, *yathā* and *iva*. Commentators struggle to avoid the seeming redundancy. One option proposed by Ct and Ck, whom we more or less follow, is to take *iva* in the sense of *tathā* and understand a similarity in which the earth, covered with tawny monkeys, appears to be covered with rice paddies of [golden] grain. (*pakvaiḥ pakvaphalaiḥ kalamakedārair vrīhikṣetrair yathā bhāti. ivaśabdas tathārthe. tathā taiḥ pūrṇā vasudhā babhūva.*) Cr understands the earth to be as full of tawny monkeys as it is with rice standing in the fields (*pakvaiḥ kalamakedāraiḥ kṣetrāropitaśālibhir yathāvat sampūrṇā vasuṃdhareva haripuṅgavaiḥ sampūrṇā vasudhā babhūva*). Cg offers a variety of explanations, some of which he attributes to other commentators. His first explanation involves reading *iva* as merely ornamental (*vākyālaṃkāra*), thus stripping it of any semantic value that might duplicate that of *yathā*. This would appear to yield a meaning similar to that given by Cr. Cg goes on to note that some commentators (probably Cv, see below) construe the verse to mean: "The earth was as full of tawny monkeys as it was with fields of ripened rice." To others, he attributes the construction: "Filled with tawny monkeys, who resembled ripened rice, the earth was like a field of ripened rice." In this interpretation, Cg continues, the use of both words *iva* and *yathā* is intentional on the part of the poet who wishes to make clear the duality of the object of comparison (*upamāna*), i.e., that the earth resembles a field, while the monkeys resemble the rice within the field. He gives another example of what he sees as such a usage in a verse involving a *samastavasturūpaka*. (*anye tu. tatra tadānīm. pakvaiḥ kalamakedāraiḥ pakvaśālikṣetraiḥ saṃpūrṇā vasuṃdhareva yathā bhavet tathā tair haripuṅgavaiḥ saṃpūrṇā vasudhā babhūveti yojayanti. apare tu kalamakedārair yathā kalamakedārasadṛśair haripuṅgavaiḥ saṃpūrṇā vasudhā vasuṃdhareva kalamakedārabhūr iva babhūvety āhuḥ. upamānadvitvaṃ vyañjayitum upamāvācikadvayaṃ prayuñjate kavayaḥ. yathā "uddhṛtya meghais tata eva toyam arthaṃ munīndrair iva saṃpraṇītāḥ / ālokayamāsa hariḥ patantīr nadīḥ smṛtīr vedam ivāmburāśim" iti //.*) Cm similarly offers three interpretations. His first is the same as Cg's first. The second explanation is the same as Cg's last interpretation. Cm's third interpretation, reading *iva* in the sense of *tathā*, understands: "The earth was as full of tawny monkeys as it was of ripened rice." This rendering is similar to the first interpretation of Cg and that of Cr. Cv understands: "That just as the earth might be filled with fields of rice, in the same way it was filled with them [the monkeys] (*kalamakedāraiḥ śālikṣetrair yuktā vasuṃdhareva bhaved yathā tathā taiḥ saṃpūrṇā vā vasudhā vā*)." Compare 6.5.11 and note.

63. "Then" *atha*: Cg understands the adverb to indicate that the army has crossed the Sahya and Malaya ranges (*atha sahyamalayātikramaṇānantaram*).

"his eyes resembling blue lotuses" *rājīvalocanaḥ*: Cg takes this stock epithet to indicate here that Rāma is eager [presumably manifested by his wide eyes] to climb the mountain peak in order to glimpse the sea (*rājīvalocana iti samudradarśanāya mahendraśikhārarohaṇakutūhalitvam uktam*).

Ct and Cm note that, although it is not explicitly stated here, we are to understand that the army encamps itself for three nights at the seashore. They tell us that we are to infer this interpretation from other passages, notably the text of one Āgniveśya, a disciple of Madhva. (*tatrānuktam api vāsatrayam anyasmād bodhyam. āgniveśyokteḥ.*) See notes to 6.40.64 and 6.97.33.

65. "at last": The phrase is added to provide a transition.

"in good order" *ānupūrvyeṇa*: Ct, Ck, and Cm explain, "in the order of the army's formations (*ānupūrvyeṇa senāsaṃniveśakrameṇa*)." Cr says merely, "in appropriate order (*ucitakrameṇa*)."

66. "descending" *avaruhya*: As Ct, Cr, and Cm note, Rāma is descending from Mount Mahendra, which he climbed in verse 64 above (*mahendrād ity arthaḥ*—so Ct). Cg, however, appears to have a somewhat different conception of Rāma's movements, indicating that the gerund is used because of the elevation of the seaside grove. He appears to envisage Rāma as climbing down from the grove to the shore, although the syntax of the verse hardly supports this interpretation (*velāvanasyonnatatvād avaruhyety uktam*).

"Rāma, foremost of those who inspire delight" *rāmo ramayatāṃ śreṣṭhaḥ*: Cg notes this etymological epithet of Rāma, explaining that it is used here to show how Rāma delights Lakṣmaṇa and the others by showing them the tumult of the ocean (*samudrasaṃbhramapradarśanena lakṣmaṇādirañjakatvaṃ vyañjitam*). Cf. 6.5.3; 6.8.12; 6.14.13; and notes. See Slatin 2006.

67. "surging waves" *toyaugaiḥ sahasotthitaiḥ*: Literally, "by violently rising floods of water."

*68. "Here and now our earlier concern arises once again." *ihedānīṃ vicintā sā yā na* [*sic*] *pūrvaṃ samutthitā*: Literally, "here and now [is] that concern of ours which arose previously." As Ct, Cr, Cg, and Cm point out, the concern to which Rāma alludes is the problem of how to cross the ocean, which he and the monkeys have discussed at length at 6.1.13–16 and 6.2.5–11,19–21 above. The critical edition's reading *na* (for *naḥ*) must surely be an erratum although it is not indicated in the errata. The critical apparatus fails to show the almost universal southern reading *naḥ*, which suggests that this is the reading the editor intends. Moreover, the meaning that the critical text yields, "this concern, which has not arisen previously," stands in glaring contradiction to the passages mentioned above.

69. "Beyond this point lies only the boundless ocean" *ataḥ param atīro 'yaṃ sāgaraḥ*: The phrase is ambiguous and can be read in two ways: either as *ataḥ param atīraḥ* or *ataḥ parama-tīraḥ*. The sequence in the manuscripts would appear the same.

We follow Ct, Cg, Cm, and Ck in breaking up the phrase as indicated and translating as we do. Commentators explain the adjective *atīraḥ*, "shoreless, boundless," as "having an unreachable farther shore (*alabhyaparatīraḥ*—so Ct)"; "whose farther shore cannot be seen (*adṛśyaparapāraḥ*—so Ck)"; and "having no shore, i.e., consisting entirely of water (*avidyamānatīraḥ. jalapraya iti yāvat*—so Cg)." Cr reads the phrase as *ataḥ parama-tīraḥ*, which he explains in two ways: 1) "having a delightful shore (*paramaṃ ramaṇīyaṃ tīraṃ yasya saḥ*)" and 2) "possessing a shore rendered extraordinary by the grandeur of the eminent *rākṣasa* (*utkṛṣṭarākṣasasampattiviśiṣṭatīravān*)."

"ocean . . . it" *sāgaraḥ . . . arṇavaḥ*: Literally, "ocean . . . ocean."

"Without some extraordinary measure" *na . . . anupāyena*: Literally, "not with a non-stratagem." We follow the commentators, who generally understand the term *anupāyena* to mean "without a stratagem (*upāyaṃ vinā*—so Cg)." Clearly the magnitude of the task calls for a stronger reading of the term.

71. "Thus" *itīva*: Cg believes that the collocation of the two particles *iti*, marking the end of quote, and *iva*, "as it were," suggests that the consultation about the means for crossing the ocean is not the central reason for Rāma's instructing the army to make camp. Rather, he argues, the real reason is Rāma's torment over the abduction of Sītā (*itīvety anena senāniveśaniyoge sāgarataraṇopāyavicāro 'hṛdayo hetur vastutas tu sītāharaṇakleśa eva hetur iti vyajyate*).

Following verse 71, Ñ,V3,B,D5–7,9–11,S insert a passage of one line [86*]: "Let all the troops camp upon the shore, bull among tawny monkeys."

72. "his unit" *svāṃ svāṃ senām*: Literally, "his own, his own army." Cm and Cv envisage the monkey army as divided into troops by species. Thus, they see Rāma as ordering the *vānaras* to remain with the *vānaras* and the *ṛkṣas* with the *ṛkṣas*. Cv adds *golāṅgūlas* to the list. See note on verse 17 above. (*svāṃ svāṃ senāṃ vānaro vānarasenām ṛkṣa ṛkṣasenāṃ samutsṛjya kaścid api kuto 'pi mā vrajet*—so Cm.)

"let . . . go on patrol" *gacchantu*: Literally, "let them go." We follow Ct, Cr, and Cg, who see the instruction for the monkeys to go as connected with the warning about hidden dangers expressed in the last line of the verse. Thus, they argue, the pickets are to be dispatched on all sides of the encampment to watch for danger. (*senāraksārthaṃ gacchantu. senāyāś caturdikṣu gatvā tatra sthitvā tāṃ rakṣāntv ity arthaḥ*—so Ct.) Cm and Ck take the verb in a general sense and understand that the monkeys are simply being told to go and make camp (*balaniveśanārtham*—so Cm).

"hidden dangers" *channaṃ bhayam*: Literally, "hidden danger." Ct, Cr, and Ck understand the dangers to be invisible because of the magical powers of the *rākṣasas* (*channaṃ rakṣomāyākṛtatvād gūḍhaṃ bhayam astīti jñeyam*). Cg and Cm see the reference as a warning against the possibility of attack from a hidden enemy (*tatra tatra līnaiḥ śatrubhiḥ prāyaśaḥ praharaṇasaṃbhavād iti bhāvaḥ*—so Cm).

73. "on the densely wooded seashore" *tīre sāgarasya drumāyute*: Literally, "on the tree-covered shore of the sea."

74. "Spread out along the seashore" *samīpasthaṃ sāgarasya*: Literally, "near the sea."

"seemed almost" *virarāja . . . iva*: Literally, "it shone like." Our translation follows Cg and Cm, who take the figure here to be *utprekṣā*, "fanciful ascription."

"its waters tawny as honey" *madhupāṇḍujalaḥ*: Literally, "its waters pale as honey." Either because of the force of the word *madhu*, "honey" (Ct, Ck), or because of lexical citation (Cv, Cm), several commentators note that the word *pāṇḍu*, "pale," should be understood in the sense of "yellow" (*piṅgalavarṇavācī*—so Ct). Cg agrees but provides no reason. Cm and Crā note a variant reading, otherwise unattested in the critical apparatus, namely, *madhupānotkaṭaṃ śrīmān*, "the majestic [army] drunk with honey-wine resembled a second ocean" (so—Crā).

75. Following verse 75, D5–7,10,11,S (in full),Ñ2,V1,3,B1–4,D9 (in part) insert a passage of four lines [89*] further describing the mode of encampment: "The sound of the army as it pitched camp drowned out the roar of the ocean. Under the direction of Sugrīva, the great army of monkeys encamped themselves in three groups[1] intent on Rāma's quest."

[1]"encamped themselves in three groups" *tridhā niviṣṭā*: Most commentators offer two alternative explanations: 1) The monkeys divide themselves into their three subspecies: *ṛkṣas*, *golāṅgūlas* [or *gopucchas*], and *vānaras* (compare note to verse 72 above); 2) The monkeys divide themselves into three separate circular encampments (*valaya*).

76. "the great ocean . . . it" *mahārṇavam . . . mahārṇavam*: Literally, "the great ocean . . . great ocean."

77. "vast" *dūrapāram*: Literally, "having a distant [farther] shore." Here we follow Cg, who glosses, "vast (*viśālam*)."

"abode of Varuṇa" *varuṇāvāsam*: See note to verse 78 below.

"featureless" *asaṃbādham*: Literally, "without obstruction." We follow the interpretation of Ct and Ck, who understand the reference to be to the ocean: "devoid in the middle of a place to rest, such as a mountain, etc. (*madhye giryādyāśrāyarahitam*—so Ct)." Cg, Cm, and Cr, on the other hand, understand, "imperturbable (*akṣobhyam*—so Cg)." Although such a characterization of the ocean is common in Sanskrit literature, we feel that the present context, with its emphasis on the turbulence of the waters, makes it a less probable interpretation. Of the translators consulted, only Raghunathan (1982, vol. 3, p. 12) appears to follow Cg's interpretation, translating, "inviolable."

"lair of hosts of *rākṣasas*" *rakṣogaṇaniṣevitam*: Literally, "frequented by hosts of *rākṣasas*." The reading is slightly puzzling. Although some *rākṣasas*, such as Siṃhikā (see Goldman and Goldman 1996, pp. 8, 43, 45, 70; and 5.1.166–78; 5.56.36–43; and notes; also see 4.40.26), dwell in the ocean, and despite Cg's assertion that it is well known that they dwell there, the *rākṣasas* of the *Rāmāyaṇa* are not generally thought of as creatures of the deep. In the *Uttarakāṇḍa*, however, the *rākṣasas*, defeated by Viṣṇu, fall into the ocean (7.7.48–50). Later the *rākṣasas* are said to abandon Laṅkā and retreat to the underworld known as Pātāla (7.8.21). A variety of northern manuscripts (Ś1,Ñ,V1,3,B,D1–4,8,9,12, and the printed editions of Gorresio and Lahore read *yādo-*, "aquatic creatures," perhaps a *facilior* for the critical *rakṣo-*, "*rākṣasas*." Shastri (1959, vol. 3, p. 14) and Dutt (1893, p. 1118) attempt to get around the problem by seeing *rakṣogaṇaniṣevita* as a reference to Laṅkā and forcibly subordinating it to *dūrapāram*, translating, "whose distant shore was inhabited by titans (Shastri)" and "having its distant shore inhabited by the demons (Dutt)."

"gave way to despair" *niṣeduḥ*: This can also be read as "they sat" or "they settled down," and all translators consulted have understood it in this way. We feel, however, that, in light of the shock that the exuberant monkey hosts have experienced in seeing the terrifying ocean, such an interpretation is far too weak.

78–80. "For it was dreadful with its fierce sharks and crocodiles." *caṇḍanakragraham*: The *bahuvrīhi* compound is somewhat ambiguous. We understand the sequence *-nakragraha-* to be a *dvandvasamāsa* meaning "sharks and crocodiles." Cg and Cm, the only commentators to read with the critical text, on the other hand, take *graha* in its etymological sense of "seizing" and understand the underlying compound as a kind of *tatpuruṣa*, so that the whole compound yields the sense of "snaring [creatures] through the agency of its great sharks (*caṇḍanakraiḥ karaṇair graho grahaṇaṃ yasya sa tathoktas tam*)." Ct, Cr, and Ck read the less ambiguous *-grāha-*, "crocodile, large fish." Ct reads the compound as an appositional *karmadhāraya* in the sense of "very dreadful because of its great marine creatures in the form of fierce sharks (*caṇḍanakrarūpair grāhair mahāghoram*)." See note on *caṇḍānilagrāhaiḥ* below.

"the night came on" *kṣapādau*: Literally, "at the beginning of night." We follow all available commentaries with the exception of Cs. Cs idiosyncratically understands *ādi*, "first, beginning," in the sense of "lord," thus rendering the compound "lord of the night" as a kenning for the moon. He takes the locative as a *sati saptamī* in the sense of "the moon being present [i.e., having risen]." This, however, seems redundant in the light of the phrase *candrodaye* in *pāda* c.

"Varuṇa's lair" *varuṇālayam*: Cg and Cm, noting the seeming redundancy of the synonymous kennings for ocean in verses 77 ("abode of Varuṇa") and 78, argue that the first is "more etymological (*yoga*)," in other words, that it refers specifically to the waters being the abode of the god Varuṇa, whereas the second is merely a conventional usage (*rūḍhi*) in the sense of "ocean." Ct and Ck attempt, it seems, to avoid the perceived redundancy by understanding *varuṇālayam* as a kenning for Pātāla, the lowest of the seven subterranean worlds. They then read the half verse as an *upamā*, deriving its force from the tradition that Pātāla is inhabited by great serpents (*bhujagair ākīrṇaṃ varuṇālayaṃ pātālam iva*—so Ct).

"covered with reflections of its orb" *praticandrasamākulam*: Literally, "crowded with counter-moons." Cr reads *samākulam*, "crowded," simply as *saṃyuktam*, "joined," and thus understands that the ocean reflects but one image of the moon. Ct, Cg, and Ck, whom we follow, all understand that the agitation of the waves causes multiple reflections (*ūrmisthapraticandraiḥ samākulaṃ vyāptam*—so Ct).

"It was swarming with huge crocodiles... and with whales and whale sharks" *-mahāgrāhaiḥ kīrṇaṃ timitimiṃgilaiḥ*: See notes to 5.7.6 and 5.35.47 for a discussion of *nakras*, *makaras*, *timis*, and *timiṅgilas*; for *grāha*, see notes to 6.3.14; 6.14.21; 6.15.6,7; and 6.62.20. Most commentators cite a verse from an unidentified source, which states that *timi* is the name of a fish one hundred *yojanas* in length and that *timiṅgila* is the name of a fish capable of swallowing a *timi*. There is, the verse continues, an even more monstrous creature, the *timiṅgilagila*, which can swallow a *timiṅgila*." (*timayaḥ śatayojanāyatā mahāmatsyāḥ. tān api bhakṣayituṃ kṣamās timiṅgilāḥ ... tad uktaṃ purāṇe "asti matsyas timir nāma śatayojanam āyataḥ / timiṅgilagilo 'py asti tad gilo 'py asti sāgare" iti*—Cg.)

"as powerful as fierce gales" *caṇḍānilamahāgrāhaiḥ*: Cg, Cm, Cv, and Ct, whom we follow, understand the compound as a *samastopamā* in the sense of "great sea creatures equal in strength to fierce winds (*caṇḍānilatulyavegair jalacarair mahāgrāhaiḥ*—so Ct)." Ck and Cr differ slightly in taking the compound as subordinate to *timitimiṅgilaiḥ* in the sense of "violently seizing hold [of creatures] like a fierce wind for the purpose of harming them (*caṇḍānilavan mahāgrāhair hiṃsārtham atyantaṃ grāhakaiḥ*—so Cr)." They thus take *grāha* in its etymological sense of "grasping, seizing." See note on *caṇḍanakragraham* above.

"with ... their coils flashing" *dīptabhogaiḥ*: It appears likely that the poet is referring to the moonlight reflected off the glistening scales of the serpents. Ct, Cr, and Ck understand, "with ... their shining bodies (*ujjvaladehair*—so Ct)." Cm understands, "with ... their bodies shining with extraordinary brilliance (*tejotiśayenojjvaladehaiḥ*)." However, they do not specify the source of the light. Cg alone falls back on the convention that serpents hold luminous jewels in their heads, remarking that "the serpents' hoods are illuminated, as it were, by the brilliance of the jewels in their heads (*śiroratnakāntyā prakāśitaphaṇair iva sthitaiḥ*)." See note 82 below.

"unapproachable, and impossible to cross" *durgaṃ durgamamārgam*: We, along with Cg and Cr, understand the ocean to be "unapproachable" because of the fearsome marine creatures mentioned earlier in the passage. Cg explains "impossible to cross" as "unnavigable (*naupathasaṃcārāyogyam*)." Ct and Ck gloss, "it was impossible to find a means of reaching the farther shore (*duṣprāpaparapārapräptyupāyam*)." Dutt (1893, p. 1119) and Gita Press (1969, vol. 3, p. 1387) oddly understand *durga* in its sense of "fortress," translating, respectively, "it had picturesque fortresses on its marge" and "which had excellent fastnesses (like Laṅkā) on its shore."

Following verse 78ab, D5–7,10,11,S insert a passage of one line [90*]: "With its masses of foam and its waves, the sea appeared to be laughing[1] and dancing."

[1]"appeared to be laughing" *hasantam iva*: The simile depends on the Sanskrit poetic convention associating whiteness with laughter. See Ingalls 1965, p. 166, vs. 389; p. 226, vs. 684, etc.

Following verse 78, D7,G3,M3, and VSP (in brackets between verses 6.4.114 and 115) include a passage of two lines [91*]: "With the tips of its waves, the ocean seemed to be grinding a sandalpaste of foam, which the moon, taking up with its rays, seemed to be smearing on the women who were the directions." No translation consulted renders this verse.

81. Cg remarks that the description of the ocean, which continues here, is the product of poetic fancy (*utprekṣā*).

"crocodiles" *makaraiḥ*: See note to 5.7.6 and notes to 78–80 above.

"waves" *jalarāśayaḥ*: Literally, "masses of water."

82. "great sea serpents glittering" *bhāsvarāmbumahoragam*: The commentators are divided as to whether to analyze the *bahuvrīhi* compound as a *dvandva*, "with its shining water and great serpents (*bhāsvarāmbu-mahoragam*)" or as a *tatpuruṣa*, as we have done. Cg and Cm choose the former option, Cg remarking that it is well known that the droplets of water resemble sparks at night (*rātrau sāgarasya salilaśīkarā agnicūrṇā iva dṛśyanta iti prasiddhiḥ*). Cm explicitly attributes the luminescence of the ocean spray to the rays of the moon. (*bhāsvarāmbu candrakiraṇasamparkāt. bhāsvarāṇi śīkararūpāmbūni yasya tat.*) Ck, Ct, and Cr, who see the luminescence as a property of the water snakes (*jalasarpāḥ*—Ct, Ck), attribute it to the glowing gemstones in their hoods (*jalarāśaya ūrmirūpā bhāsvarāḥ phaṇāmaṇibhir bhāsamānā ambumahoragā jalasarpā yasmiṃs tam*—so Ct). See note to verses 78–80 above.

"enemies of the gods" *surāri-*: These are, of course, the *asuras* and *rākṣasas*, as Cg and Cm point out.

"unapproachable" *-viṣamam*: Literally, "uneven, rough." V1,3,D1,5,7,9–11,T1,2,G1, and the texts and printed editions of Ct, Ck, and Cr read instead *-viṣayam*, yielding "extending as far as Pātāla (*pātālaparyantasthāpinam*—Cr)" or "ranging to Pātāla (*pātālagocaram*—Ct, Ck)."

"resembled a scattered shower of sparks" *agnicūrṇam ivāviddham*: Literally, "like scattered fire particles." We believe that the reference is to sparks of a fire scattering into the air. However, given Cg's comment above (see note 81) that the whole description partakes of *utprekṣā*, one might well, like Raghunathan ("powdered fire"; 1982, vol. 3, p. 13), take the compound literally.

Cg, Cm, and Cv regard this verse as the beginning of the elaborate comparison of the sky and the ocean that extends to verse 86 below. Cg, Cv, and Cm seek at this point to demonstrate that each of the attributes of the ocean has its corresponding attribute in the atmosphere. Thus, they argue, the shining droplets of ocean spray described in this verse have their celestial parallel in the stars. (*ambaraṃ ca kīrṇair nakṣatrais tathā dṛśyante. bhāsvarāmbu vimalatuhinaṃ ca*—so Cg.) The shining water is paralleled by the bright moonlight (*tuhina*). The great serpents are common to both realms, Cg continues, as the *nāgas*, or great serpents, are said to roam the heavens just like the *gandharvas* and other celestial beings or because of the presence in the skies of serpents, such as Rāhu. (*ākāśe gandharvādīnām iva nāgānām api saṃcārasaṃbhavāt. rāhvādirūporagasaṃbhavād vā.*) Both the heavens and the oceans are inhabited by the enemies of the gods (*surārayo 'surā rākṣasāś ca teṣāṃ viṣayam āvāsabhūtam idam apy ubhayatra tulyam*—so Cg, Cm, Cv). Cg, Cv, and Cm state that both are as deep as Pātāla, and Cg and Cv say that both are dreadful (*pātālaviṣamaṃ pātālavad gambhīram idam apy ubhayatra tulyaṃ ghoraṃ bhayaṅkaram idam apy ubhayatra tulyam*—so Cg). Cg and Cm conclude this analysis by stating that the enumeration of these shared properties sets the stage, as it were, for the following rhetorical exposition of the impossibility of differentiating between the ocean and the sky (*evam uktaviśeṣaṇaviśiṣṭaṃ sāgaraṃ sāgaro 'mbaraprakhyam ambarābham uktaviśeṣaṇaviśiṣṭam ambaraṃ ca sāgaropamam adṛśyatety ākṛṣya yojanā*—so Cg). Cf. note to 6.96.16, 3064*, n. 1.

83. Ct and Ck see the basis for this comparison in the shared features of expansiveness and unfathomableness (*ambaraprakhyaṃ vaipulyātalatvaiḥ*—so Ct), and (Ck) blueness (*nailya-*). Cr, evidently anticipating the next verse, understands it to be the similarity between the ocean's many gems and the stars in the sky (*sāgaram ambaraprakhyaṃ tārāgaṇasadṛśamaṇyādimatvenākāśasadṛśam*). Cg remarks that the point of this verse is not merely similarity between the sky and the ocean but their absolute similarity in every possible respect (*na kevalaṃ sāmyaṃ sarvathā sāmyaṃ cety āha*). Ct notes that the rhetorical figure is *upameyopamā alaṃkāra*. This figure, also called *anyonyopamā*, is a simile in which the comparison between the *upameya* and the *upamāna* is reciprocal. Cf. note to 6.96.16, 3064*, n. 1.

85. "waves passing in succession" *vīcimālā*: Literally, "garland *or* series of waves." We have added the participle to enhance the parallelism.

86. "ceaselessly" *saktāḥ*: Literally, "clinging, attached [to one another]." We agree with Ct, Cr, and Cm, who understand "without intervals (*nirantarāḥ*)" and thus read the adjective adverbially as "ceaselessly." Cg appears to prefer the more usual meaning of the participle, remarking, "[they] first approach [cling to] one another and then strike (*prathamaṃ saktā athāhatā ity anvayaḥ*)."

"of the ocean, lord of rivers" *sindhurājasya*: Literally, "lord of rivers."

"in battle" *āhave*: D10,11, and printed editions of Ct read instead *ambare*, "in the sky."

87–88. "the great monkeys" *mahātmānah*: Literally, "the great ones."

"the . . . sea," *jalāśayam*: Literally, "the abode of waters."

"the wind-whipped sea, the abode of waters, as if one with the raging gale. Whipped by the wind" *viṣaktam iva vāyunā . . . vātāhatajalāśayam . . . aniloddhūtam*: Literally, "as if attached by the wind . . . the abode of waters struck by the wind . . . tossed up by the wind." The poet's repetitive allusion to the force of the wind in this passage has attracted the attention of Cg, who attriibutes the redundancy to the requirements of this particular description (*etan nirūpaṇārtham evāniloddhatam iti punaruktih*). The second of these expressions, *viṣaktam iva vāyunā*, "as if one with the raging gale," is slightly obscure in its meaning. Ct, Cr, and Ck gloss *viṣaktam*, normally, "attached, clinging to," as *saṃbaddham*, "connected with," by which they appear to understand something like "driven by the wind." We prefer the interpretation of Cg, Cm, and Cv. Cm understands, "mingled with, that is to say, at one with (*miśrībhūtam iva ekībhūtam iti yāvat*)" (Cg, Cv "at one with [*ekībhūtam iva*]"). This interpretation seems to us to better reflect the poet's vision of the wildly agitated mix of wind and water and to be in keeping with the tenor of the previous verses where sea and sky are merged.

"With the roaring of its waters and of its masses of precious stones" *ratnaughajalasaṃnādam*: Literally, "possessing a roar of masses of gems and waters." We follow Cg and Cm, who understand that since the waters are whipped up by the wind, they are making a sound as a result of their masses of gems and torrents of water. They go on to say that, by this, we are to understand that because of the excessive agitation produced by the violent winds, the gems that lie within the ocean are being hurled up. (*aniloddhūtam ata eva ratnaughajalasaṃnādaṃ ratnaughajalaughayoḥ saṃnādo yasmiṃs tam. anena vegavad vāyujanitakṣobhātiśayāt tadantargataratnānām udgamanam avagamyate*—so Cm.)

"in fury" *kruddham*: Literally, "angry." Cm sees the apparent rage of the ocean to derive from the fierce sea creatures swarming in its waves (*kruddhaṃ yādogaṇasamākulam ity anena krūrayādogaṇasamākulatvāt kruddham iva sthitam*).

"seemed to have gone mad" *pralolam iva*: We prefer the interpretation of Cg and Cm, who gloss, "as if wildly agitated *or* mad (*udbhrāntam iva*)," to that of Ct and Ck, who gloss, "shaken *or* moving on (*pracalad iva*—Ct; *pracalam iva*—Ck)."

Following 88cd, Ñ2,V3,B,D5–7,9–11,S insert a passage of one line [98*]: "Then the tawny monkeys, filled with amazement, gazed upon [the ocean]."

Sarga 5

2. "stood picket duty to protect the army on all sides" *viceratuś ca tāṃ senāṃ rakṣārthaṃ sarvato diśam*: Literally, "the two walked about the army in every direction for the sake of protection."

3. "the ocean, lord of rivers and streams" *nadanadīpateḥ*: Literally, "the lord of *nadas* and *nadīs*." It is difficult to distinguish absolutely between these differently gendered synonyms for river (*nadaḥ*—masculine; *nadī*—feminine). Apte (s.v. *nadaḥ*) gives as one meaning "great river" (such as the Indus), so the issue may be one of size. On the other hand, there is a tradition that the feminine is used for rivers flowing to the east (except the Narmadā) and the masculine for those flowing to the west. See Mallinātha on *ŚiśuVa* 4.66 (*prāksrotaso nadyaḥ pratyaksrotaso nadāḥ narmadā vinety āhuḥ*). See also note to 1.31.8. Probably the compound is employed here for its metrical and alliterative effect. Compare 5.1.33; 5.2.14–15; 5.24.2,11; 5.31.9; 5.34.8; 5.35.63; and notes. See, too, 6.2.4; 6.4.41; 6.7.5; 6.8.10; 6.9.20; 6.41.28; 6.47.16; 6.54.25; 6.110.1; and notes; and note to 6.13.15, 223*, n. 2.

4. "But... mine" *mama ca*: Ct, Cr, Cg, and Cm see Rāma as making a distinction between the grief engendered by the loss of ordinary objects, grief that passes with time, and his sorrow for his beloved, which to the contrary only increases. (*gacchatā*

kāleneṣṭāntaraviyogajaḥ śoko 'pi gacchatīti prasiddhiḥ. mama priyāvirahaje śoke tu viparītam ity āha—so Ct.)

5. Cg feels that Rāma's relative lack of concern for Sītā's abduction and her absence are to be explained by the fact that he sees them as remediable, the first by Sugrīva's expedition and the second through his own killing of Rāvaṇa. He grieves for Sītā's passing youth, however, precisely because it can never be recovered. (*duḥkham iti priyā dūre sthiteti me na duḥkhaṃ sugrīveṇa prasthānena tasya nivartyatvāt. prabalarakṣasā hṛteti me duḥkhaṃ nāsti tasya tacchiraḥ kṛntanāpanodyatvāt. etad evānuśocāmīdam ekam eva śokanimittaṃ vayo 'syā hy ativartate gataṃ yauvanaṃ na pratyāhartuṃ śakyam iti bhāvaḥ.*) Ct and Ck feel that Rāma is able to distance himself emotionally from Sītā's absence as he would during her menstrual period and her abduction, through the rationalization that it must be the result of some overpoweringly evil *karma*. (*priyā dūre sthiteti duḥkhaṃ me nāsti strīdharma-divasavat. tathā hṛtety api na duḥkhaṃ prabaladuṣkarmavaśaṃ prāptatvāt*—so Ct.)

"youth" *vayaḥ*: Cm alone unambiguously understands this term to refer to Sītā's period of youthful sexual attractiveness. He glosses the term as "the means of my [Rāma's] enjoyment (*madbhogasādhanam*)." Cg understands similarly but qualifies his understanding in light of the theological context of the story. He argues that, although Rāma is indeed lamenting the fruitless passing of Sītā's period of sexual attractiveness, we are not to understand the verb *ativartate*, "it passes *or* goes by," literally, since Sītā [as a divinity] is forever young; rather, he feels Rāma is merely regretting the fact that time [that he could have spent with her] is passing fruitlessly. He does, however, note that Rāma may well be speaking here in conformity with his human nature. (*atra yauvanam ativartata iti nārtho nityayauvanatvāt tasyāḥ kiṃ vayo 'tivartate vyarthatayaiva yātīti bhāvaḥ. mānuṣabhāvānusāreṇa cedaṃ vacanam.*) On this point, see Pollock 1984b. Ct, Cr, and Ck prefer to see no hint of sexuality in this passage and instead interpret the reference to be to the period of two months remaining for Sītā to live before the end of the grim deadline set by Rāvaṇa (see 5.20.8–9 and notes). Ct and Ck, however, propose an alternative: the possibility that Rāma may be speaking here like a common man and therefore referring to Sītā's youth. (*api tv asyā vayaḥ prāṇāvasthitikālo 'tivartate. māsa-dvayamātraṃ jīvanam ity ukteḥ. tatrāpi bahudivasātyayāt. yadvā vayo yauvanam iti prākṛtavad vādaḥ.*) Cf. Rāvaṇa's words at 5.18.12, where the reference to the passing of Sītā's youth is unambiguous. Among the translators consulted, only Dutt (1893, p. 1120) and Gita Press (1969, vol. 3, p. 1389) follow the interpretation of Ct, Ck, and Cr.

6. "For the touching of our limbs now depends on you, as on the moon depends the meeting of our glances." *tvayi me gātrasaṃsparśaś candre dṛṣṭisamāgamaḥ*: Literally, "the touching of my limbs [is] on you, on the moon, the meeting of glances." Following the commentators, especially Cg and Cm, our translation fleshes out the elliptical original. The verse plays on the conventional capacities of the breeze and moonlight to soothe, literally cool, the anguish of separated lovers. As Cg and Cm explain here, Rāma implicitly refutes the conventional wisdom in stating that neither the touch of the wind nor the moonlight has the capacity to allay his torment unless the former has actually first touched her body and the latter been gazed upon by her eyes. (*dṛṣṭi-samāgamaś candre yathā candrādhīnas tathā me tadgātrasaṃsparśo 'pi tvayi tvadadhīnaḥ. yathā tadavalokitaṃ candraṃ paśyaṃs tat praṇālikayā tāṃ dṛṣṭavān asmi tadvat tadaṅgaspṛṣṭaṃ tvāṃ spṛśaṃs tām eva spṛṣṭavān bhaveyam ity arthaḥ*—so Cg.) In this way, Rāma hopes to use the wind and the moon as intermediaries through whose intercession he can experience the pleasure of Sītā's touch and glance. Ct regards the figure implicit in

the second half of the verse to be an example of the poetic figure *nidarśanā*, a type of negative illustration. See Gerow 1971 s.v. *nidarśanā* (II.2), p. 202. Cf. *KāvyaPra* 10.97 (the example given is from *RaghuVa* 1.2). Cr remarks that it is out of the excess of his grief that Rāma addresses the breeze (*atyantaśokāveśād vātaṃ pratyāha*). Compare the elaborate description of Rāma's madness where he addresses all manner of animate and inanimate beings. See Pollock 1991, pp. 8, 55–67 and 3.60.18–61.4. These passages may be the earliest example of, and indeed the inspiration for, the familiar literary trope of the lovelorn appeal to an inanimate object to serve as a messenger to the beloved, a trope made famous by Kālidāsa in his *Meghadūta*.

7. "lodged in my heart" *āśaye*: Literally, "in the receptacle." We follow the commentators, who generally gloss some term meaning "heart (*hṛdaye*)," "mind (*citte* or *buddhau*)," or "seat of emotions (*antaḥkaraṇe*)." In addition to the interpretations of the other commentators, Cm alone offers an alternative, "in the stomach (*udare*)," reading the term as the locus (*adhikaraṇa*) of the poison rather than of Sītā's imagined cry. Following the commentators' suggestion, we have added the word "lodged (*sthitaḥ*)."

"must have cried out... 'Alas, my protector!' " *hā nātheti... yad abravīt*: Literally, "that she said, 'Alas, protector!' " Ct and Ck note that Rāma is merely inferring what Sītā must have said, since obviously he was not present at her abduction. In fact, the word *nātha*, "protector," which Rāma finds so poignant here, is never attributed to Sītā at the moment of her abduction. At the four instances in the text where reference is made to the words Sītā says during her abduction (3.50.3–5,8,12,40cd; 4.6.8; 4.57.16; 4.58.22), Sītā only cries out the names of Rāma and Lakṣmaṇa (at 3.5.50, *kākutstha*). The poignancy of the term *nātha* here derives from its connotation of guardian or protector, a role in which Rāma feels himself, in this case, to have been singularly deficient. Cg highlights this issue by quoting Sītā's words to Rāvaṇa in the *Sundarakāṇḍa* (5.20.20; see, too, 3.35.64 and 3.37.29) to the effect that she could have defended herself through the power of her chastity but did not do so, because it would have been more fitting for Rāma, as her husband, to protect and rescue her from the *rākṣasa*. He concludes that we are to understand that Rāma's grief consists precisely in his compassionate feeling for Sītā's pain (*etena rāmaśokaḥ sītāviṣayakāruṇyam ity avagamyate*).

8. "towering" *-vipula-*: Literally, "large, expansive." B1,D10,11,T1,2, and the texts and printed editions of Ct, Cr, and Ck substitute *-vimala-*, "bright."

"my constant brooding on her" *taccintā-*: Literally, "thinking *or* brooding about her." The compound is somewhat ambiguous. It can be understood as we have done or as her [Sītā's] brooding. Several translators choose this second, and to our mind much less plausible, alternative (Dutt 1893, p. 1120, "her thoughts for its flame"; Roussel 1903, vol. 3, p. 15, "*sa pensée pour flammes*"). As suggested by Cg, we have added the word "constant" to flesh out the meaning (*saṃtatatvena cintāyāḥ*).

9. "without you" *bhavatā vinā*: Ct, Ck, and Cr understand Rāma to be instructing Lakṣmaṇa to stay while he goes off to the ocean (*saumitre tvam atraiva tiṣṭheti śeṣaḥ*—so Ct). Cr expands on this, claiming that the words suggest that Lakṣmaṇa is to remain awake to keep others away from Rāma, who has no desire to see anyone other than Sītā. (*bhavatā vinety uktyā jāgrad eva tvaṃ tiṣṭheti sūcitam. tena tvadbhinno mannikaṭe nāgacchatv iti hetuḥ sūcitas tena sītātiriktaviṣaye tadānīṃ didṛkṣābhāvaḥ sūcitaḥ.*) Cg understands that Rāma wishes to exclude Lakṣmaṇa because he reminds him of Sītā. Cg goes on to argue that, in telling Lakṣmaṇa that he will take his repose in the ocean, Rāma is alluding to the fact that Lakṣmaṇa is an incarnation of the cosmic serpent

Śeṣa, upon whom Viṣṇu reposes during the intervals between creations. For, he argues, it is only Viṣṇu who takes his rest upon the ocean. (*saumitre kāntāsmarakeṇa bhavatā vinārṇavam avagāhya svapsye. anena lakṣmaṇasya śeṣāvatāratvam uktam. arṇava-śayanaṃ hi śeṣiṇaiva.*) Cs, typically original, understands Rāma to be telling Lakṣmaṇa to stay back because he would suffer from the cold [of the water] (*tava śītabādhā bhavet*).

"For it would be hard for the flame of desire to burn me were I to sleep in its waters." *kathaṃcit prajvalan kāmaḥ samāsuptaṃ jale dahet*: Literally, "blazing desire would only with difficulty burn [me] asleep in water." The idea, as expressed by Cg, Cv, and Cm, is that Rāma wishes to enter the waters in the hope that they will at least dampen the fires of love that afflict him. (*kṛcchrād dahet. mandībhaved ity arthaḥ*—so Cg.) B1,D10,11, and the texts and printed editions of Ct (*pace* critical apparatus) read *evaṃ ca*, "in this way," for *kathaṃcit*, "with difficulty." The reading *samāsuptam* is marked as doubtful. Cg, Cv, Cm, and Crā break up the critical reading as *sa mā suptam*. This reading and that of the critical edition result in no great difference of meaning. Ś1,Ñ, V1,B1,2,D6,10–12,T2,3, and the texts and printed editions of Ct, Cr, and Ck read instead *na māṃ suptam*. With these two variants, the line in Ct's text yields the sense "and in this way blazing desire would not burn me asleep in the water."

10. "long for her so much" *bahv etatkāmayānasya*: Literally, "of [me] longing so much for her." We agree with Ct, Ck, and Cr in understanding *bahu* as an adverb governing the participle *kāmayānasya*. Cg, Cm, and Cv read *bahu* as an adjective modifying the pronoun *yat*, for which they gloss *jīvanasādhanam*. The sense is thus "a major means of survival."

"that lady ... and I still share the same earth" *yad ahaṃ sā ca ... ekāṃ dharaṇim āśritau*: Literally, "that I and she rest on one earth." Cg notes that, by the maxim of "sleeping on a single bed," we are to understand the intention here to be that the sharing of a single resting place, in this case, the earth, is the means by which the two lovers can survive (*ekaśayyāśrayaṇanyāyena kāminor ekadharaṇyāśrayaṇam api jīvanasādhanaṃ bhavatīty abhiprāyaḥ*).

11. "And like a parched rice paddy, drawing water from a flooded one, I live on through knowing that she lives." *kedārasyeva kedāraḥ sodakasya nirūdakaḥ / upasnehena jīvāmi jīvantīṃ yac chṛṇomi tām*: The verse is based on a slightly elliptical and somewhat awkward agricultural metaphor. A literal translation would be: "Hearing that she is living, I live as does a field without water through the moisture of a field with water." The idea apparently is that Rāma, cut off from the source of his existence, Sītā, manages to survive on the trickle of hope engendered by the news [brought by Hanumān] that she lives, just as a dry paddy field might remain fruitful through the trickling runoff of a neighboring, flooded one. A critical term here is *upasnehena*, which we read, with Cg, Cm, and Cv, in the sense of "secondary moistening (*upa-kledena*)." The term also strongly suggests the emotional realm since *sneha* can mean either "moistening *or* love," thus suggesting that, like the field, Rāma lives on through some derivative connection with the source of his longing. Ct and Cr simply gloss, "contact (*saṃbandhaḥ*—Ct; *saṃsargaḥ*—Cr)." Compare 6.4.42 and notes.

12. "as if upon splendid Śrī herself" *sphītām iva śriyam*: Literally, "like the bounteous Śrī." Ct glosses *sphīta*, literally, "abundant, prosperous, fat," as "the prosperous [goddess of] royal splendor (*samṛddhāṃ rājyalakṣmīm iva*)." Cr understands similarly.

13. "when shall I ... kiss ... might drink" *kadā nu ... pāsyāmi*: Literally, "When will I drink?" Ñ,V3,D6,10,11,T3, and the texts and printed editions of Ct, Cr, and Ck read

for the emphatic particle *nu*, "indeed," *su-*, "very," which is in compound with their variant *cārudantoṣṭham*. See below.

"full and lovely lips" *cārubimboṣṭham*: Literally, "lips like lovely *bimba* fruit." Ś1,Ñ,V3,B,D2,8–11,G1, and the texts and printed editions of Ct, Cr, and Ck, read instead *-cārudantoṣṭham*, "with its lovely teeth and lips." This, combined with the variant *su-*, "very," mentioned above, yields the compound *sucārudantoṣṭham*, "with its exquisite teeth and lips."

"powerful tonic" *rasāyanam*: A tantric and medicinal term for the universal tonic generally consisting of, or compounded with, mercury. See White 1996. Ct glosses, "[compounds] such as mercury, etc. (*pāradādi*)." Cr is more specific, explaining, "appropriate medicinal compound of mercury (*yuktasiddhapāradam*)." Cg and Cm, on the other hand, understand, "herbal medication effective for healing the body (*śarīrasiddhikaram auṣadhaviśeṣam*)."

14. "pressed against me" *māṃ bhajiṣyataḥ*: Literally, "those two will have recourse to *or* resort to."

"as she laughs" *hasantyāḥ*: D6,M3, and the texts and printed editions of Cg, Cm, and Crā read instead *śliṣyantyāḥ*, "as she embraces [me]."

15. "I am the protector of that dark-eyed woman." *asitāpāṅgī ... mannāthā*: Literally, "[that woman] of the dark eye-corners has a protector in me." Reference to corners of a woman's eyes is usually made to stress their length, considered a sign of beauty. Therefore, a possible translation of this compound could be "with her long, dark eyes."

"in the clutches of the *rākṣasas*" *rakṣomadhyagatā satī*: Literally, "[she] being situated in the midst of *rākṣasas*."

Following verse 15, D5–7,10,11,S insert a passage of two lines [101*]: "How can my beloved, the daughter of King Janaka and daughter-in-law of Daśaratha, find any repose in the midst of the *rākṣasa* women."

16. "When will she outwit the *rākṣasas*, evade them" *kadā vikṣobhya rakṣāṃsi sā vidhūya*: Literally, "she, having shaken off the *rākṣasas* [and] having spurned *or* evaded." The syntax of the two gerunds seems slightly strange, especially since the ranges of meaning of the two verbal roots overlap and the second gerund is repeated in *pāda* c. An additional problem here is that the text lends itself to ambiguity as the same syllables can be and are broken up differently by the critical editors and some of the commentators. Thus, Cg and Cm break the sequence *kadāvikṣobhyarakṣāṃsi* into two words *kadā avikṣobhyarakṣāṃsi* and understand *avikṣobhya-* as an adjective modifying *rakṣāṃsi* in the sense of "unshakeable *or* unassailable *rākṣasas*." They would thus read the first half of the verse as follows: "When, having evaded those unassailable *rākṣasas*, will she escape?" As most manuscripts run all the words together, it is not clear on what basis the critical editors have decided to divide them. D10,11, and the texts and printed editions of Ct and Cr read instead *avikṣobhyāṇi rakṣāṃsi sā vidhūya*, which has the same meaning as that of Cg and Cm. Ct comments on this reading, noting, "defeating the unassailable *rākṣasas* by means of me (*maddvārā teṣāṃ vidhūnanaṃ kṛtvā*)." Many northern manuscripts (Ś1,Ñ1,V1,3,B,D1–4,8,9,12) avoid the sequence of gerunds by substituting *sā vadhūḥ*, "she, that daughter-in-law," for *sā vidhūya*.

"crescent of the hare-marked ... moon" *śaśilekhā*: Literally, "line *or* digit of the one with the hare."

17. "naturally slender... truly emaciated" *svabhāvatanukā... bhūyas tanutarā*: Literally, "naturally slender, even more slender."

"reversal of her fortunes" *deśakālaviparyayāt*: Literally, "through the inversion of place and time." We understand with Cg, Cm, Cv, and Crā that the reference is to Sītā's loss of her former joyful circumstances and to her current wretched state (*sukhāvahayor deśakālayor apagamāt tadviruddhayor upagamāc cety arthaḥ*—so Cg). Ct and Ck understand Sītā's wretchedness as having been brought about as a result of her evil past *karma* (*prācīnaduṣkarmavaśaprāptaduḥkhasādhanadeśakālasaṃbandhāt*—so Ct).

18. "I may bring Sītā back... anguish" *sītāṃ pratyāhariṣyāmi śokam*: Literally, "I will bring back Sītā... sorrow." B4,D10,11, and the texts and printed editions of Ct read *śokam*, "grief," for *sītām*, resulting in the repetition of the word *śokam*, "sorrow." This awkward reading yields a translation something like "when shall I dispel [Sītā's] sorrow [and thus dispel] the sorrow [of my heart]." This is the reading followed by those translators who follow the text of Ct, except for Dutt (1893, p. 1121), who fails to render the phrase.

19. "immortal gods" *amara-*: Literally, "immortal ones."

"clasp her arms... about my neck, shedding tears of joy" *kaṇṭham ālambya mokṣyaty ānandajaṃ jalam*: Literally, "having hung on the neck, will she release water born of joy."

20. "as one might a soiled garment" *vāsaḥ śukletaraṃ yathā*: Literally, "like a garment that is other than white." We follow the commentators, who gloss, "dirty (*malinam*)."

21. "its radiance fading" *mandavapuḥ*: Literally, "its form diminished." Cr, alone among the commentators, notes, "its brilliance occluded (*tirohitatejāḥ*)."

22. Cg, evidently disturbed that Rāma should have spoken so freely in front of another, especially his brother, argues that there is no real impropriety here because of the latter's performing every kind of service for Rāma (*bhrātur api lakṣmaṇasya purato raghunāthasyaivaṃvidhavacanaprayogas tasya sarvavidhasevakatvād ato nānaucityam*).

"evening *sandhyā* rite" *sandhyām*: See note to 5.12.48.

Sarga 6

1. "meanwhile" *tu*: Literally, "but." The commentators generally note that the poet, who had been describing Rāma's adventures [up until his arrival at the seashore], now reverts to Rāvaṇa's activities from the moment of Hanumān's departure [from Laṅkā] (*evaṃ rāmavṛttāntam uktvā hanumannirgamakālānantarakālikaṃ rāvaṇavṛttāntaṃ vaktum upakramate*—so Cg).

"havoc... had wrought" *kṛtaṃ karma*: Literally, "act *or* feat performed *or* accomplished."

"great Hanumān, the equal of Śakra" *hanumatā śakreṇeva mahātmanā*: The phrase lends itself to two interpretations. It can be read as a simile, yielding the sense "[wrought by] Hanumān, as if by great Śakra" or, as we have done following Cg, in the sense of "who was equal to Śakra (*śakreṇeva śakratulyena*—Cg)." Cs, appearing to expand on this understanding, argues that the epithet *mahātmanā* is applied to Hanumān to suggest that his feat, although potentially accomplishable by Indra, is beyond the power of Rāvaṇa's son, whom he calls Jitendra [= Indrajit]. He sees the epithet as being applied in the manner of the vedic verse "*indro vṛtraṃ hatvā mahān āsa* (Having slain Vṛtra, Indra became great)" (*mahātmanā śakreṇevety anena hanumatkṛtakarmaṇaḥ "indro vṛtraṃ hatvā mahān āsa" ity uktarītyā mahendrakṛtisādhyatve 'pi rāvaṇasutajitendraprayatnāviṣayatvaṃ sūcayati*).

2. "this mere monkey" *tena vānaramātreṇa*: We are inclined to agree more or less with Cg, who takes the word *-mātreṇa* in its usual sense of "merely *or* only." However, we do not agree with Cg's further explanation that the expression amounts to saying "one of the smaller monkeys (*vānareṣv alpena*)," since Hanumān wrought the destruction of Laṅkā and its champions in a colossal body, a form he abandons momentarily after his interview with Rāvaṇa only to escape from his bonds, resuming it immediately (5.51.36–37) to set fire to the citadel. Ct, Cm, and Cr understand the word to suggest that the monkey is alone and unarmed or (Cr) unassisted. Ck seems to offer both explanations, glossing, "alone unarmed, a mere animal (*ekena nirāyudhena mṛgamātreṇa*)."

3. "domed palace" *prāsādaḥ... caityaḥ*: On the identification and destruction of Rāvaṇa's domed and pillared palace, see 5.13.15–17; 5.41.1; and notes. The commentators differ in their identification of this structure and also differ from their identification of it in their commentaries on the *Sundarakāṇḍa*. Here Cr calls the building "a palace inhabited by some form of divinity (*devaviśeṣāviṣṭaḥ prāsādaḥ*)," i.e., a shrine or a temple. At 5.13.16 (=GPP 5.15.16), he had understood the building to be, "a kind of rounded *or* domed structure (*vartulākāraprāsādaviśeṣam*)." Cg here calls the structure "the principal palace *or* edifice in the city (*nagarapradhānabhūtaḥ prāsādaḥ*)," whereas at 5.13.16 (=GPP 5.15.16) he had called it "a palace *or* building in the form of a Buddhist temple *or stūpa* because of its height and length. (*caityaprāsādaṃ caityaṃ buddhamandiraṃ tadākāraṃ prāsādaṃ. prāṃśubhāvatvād dīrghasvabhāvatvāt.*)" Furthermore, at 5.56.99 (=GPP 5.58.118) he understands it to be a palace in the middle of the city rather than the principal palace of the city. Ct, who at 5.13.16 had defined the building as "a palace resembling a Buddhist *stūpa* because of its roundness (*vartulākāratvād buddhāyatanam iva prāsādam*)," is silent. Ck understands, "round like a shrine (*caityavartī*)." See 6.30.24 and note; cf. 6.7.13; 6.115.2; and notes.

"reduced... to chaos" *āvilā... kṛtā*: Literally, "made turbid *or* soiled." Ct, Cr, and Ck gloss *āvilā* as "shaken, agitated, *or* disturbed (*kṣubhitā*)." Cg understands it to mean "devastated through burning (*dāhenākulā*)."

4. "pray... Or" *bhadraṃ vaḥ... vā*: Literally, "bless you... or." The formulaic phrase *bhadraṃ vaḥ* or *te*, literally, "auspiciousness *or* blessing to you [plural or singular, respectively]," is a commonly used epic phrase indicating politeness. See 6.102.9; 6.103.5; 6.107.29; and 6.109.9. It can serve as a blessing, a marker of polite imperative, or, as in this case, simply a marker indicating respect or attention. For a discussion of this formula and its various meanings, see Tubb 2006. D10,11, and the texts and printed editions of Ck, Ct, and Cr read instead *vaḥ... vaḥ*, "you... for you," yielding the meaning "[bless] you... [what would be an appropriate next step] for you?" Dutt (1893, p. 1122), Gita Press (1969, vol. 3, p. 1391), Shastri (1959, vol. 3, p. 16), and Roussel (1903, vol. 3, p. 17) all follow this reading.

5. "Those who are venerable and wise say" *prāhur āryā manasvinaḥ*: Literally, "the noble [and] wise say." V1,D7,10, and the texts and printed editions of Ct and Cr read *pravadanti*, "they say," for *prāhur āryāḥ*, "the venerable ones say." Ck, in rare agreement with the reading of Cg's text (as opposed to Ct's), understands the term a bit unusually as "learned in *nīti or* polity (*nītividaḥ*)." He glosses *manasvinaḥ* as "heroes

(*śūrāḥ*)." The texts of Ct and Crā have only the second term, which Ct glosses as "heroes (*śūrāḥ*)."

"cornerstone" *-mūlam*: Literally, "root, basis, *or* foundation."

"mighty warriors" *mahābalāḥ*: Literally, "ones of great strength."

6. "the highest, the lowest, and those in between" *uttamādhamamadhyamāḥ*: Ct, Cg, Cm, and Ck understand that the highest type of man possesses only virtues (*guṇas*), the lowest only defects (*doṣas*), and the man in between both (*guṇadoṣau*—so Ct). Compare *MBh* 5.33.56. See Sternbach 1965–1967, vol. 2, p. 429, no. 137.

"each of them" *teṣāṃ* . . . *samavetānām*: Literally, "of them grouped together." Ct, Cg, and Cm understand this as "intermingled with one another (*saṃkīrṇarūpāṇām*)," and they, along with Cr, explain that, without a clear knowledge of their individual characteristics, it is impossible to distinguish their respective strengths and weaknesses (*lakṣaṇajñānaṃ vinā vivektum aśakyānāṃ guṇadoṣau*—so Ct). This interpretation is interpolated into the translation of Dutt (1893, p. 1122), who translates, "This distinction cannot be perceived without a knowledge of the signs."

7–8. "with those counselors intent upon his welfare" *mantribhir hitasaṃyuktaiḥ*: D10,11, and the texts and printed editions of Ct, Ck, and Cr read instead *mantras tribhir hi saṃyuktaḥ*, "counsel connected with those three."

"or . . . who wish him well" *vā hitaiḥ*: D10,11, and the texts and printed editions of Ct read instead *vādhikaiḥ*, "or with superior [kinsmen]."

"such that his efforts are in harmony with the will of the gods" *daive . . . yatnam*: Literally, "effort with respect to fate *or* the divine." Ct understands, "with the assistance of fate *or* with divine assistance (*daivasahāye*)," while Ck glosses, "with the assistance of the gods (*devasahāyena*)." Cr glosses, "with respect to the purpose of the gods (*devakārye*)," and Cg understands, "relying on fate *or* the gods (*daivasamāśrayeṇa*)." The context makes it difficult to decide whether to understand *daiva* in its sense of "fate, destiny," or "that which pertains to the gods." Although the latter seems more appropriate to this particular context, the discussion does call to mind the recurrent epic concern with the dichotomy of *daiva*, "fate," and *puruṣakāra*, "individual effort." The peculiarity of having Rāvaṇa, the archenemy of the gods, discourse in this fashion can perhaps be explained by the gnomic quality of the passage. See 6.98.23; 6.103.5; and notes.

9. "The man who stands in between" *madhyamaṃ naram*: Literally, "the middle man."

"directs his thoughts to righteous action" *dharme prakurute manaḥ*: Literally, "places [his] mind in righteousness." Cg here understands *manaḥ*, "mind," to mean "thoughtful action (*manaḥpūrvaṃ yatnam*)." Cg further understands the reference to righteousness to be to the reliance upon divine will (*daiva*), alluded to in the preceding verse. In keeping with the notion he expressed earlier that the intermediate type of man combines both virtues and defects, Ct notes here that his merit (*guṇa*) consists of deliberation and his demerit (*doṣa*) consists of disregard for [the advice of] others. (*vicāro 'sya guṇaḥ. itaranirapekṣatā doṣaḥ.*)

10. "undertakes an action . . . and then fails to carry it through" *kāryam upekṣet*: Literally, "he would neglect the action." Here we follow the interpretation of Ct, Ck, Cg, and Cm, who understand that the inferior person's defect lies in his failure to complete the actions he begins. In order to do this, they understand that the person, having first undertaken an action, saying, "I will do it," fails to complete it, that is, follow through (*kariṣyāmīty upakramya yaḥ kāryam upekṣed upekṣeta na samāpnuyāt*—so

Cg). A simpler reading of the verse, and the one proposed by Cr and found in many translations, would be to take the word *kāryam*, "action," as somehow implicitly part of the quote "I will do," that is, "I will undertake an action." He suggests adding the phrase "having said." According to this reading, the person fails even to undertake the action he has said he would do (*kāryaṃ kariṣyāmīty utkveti śeṣaḥ. upekṣet tyajet*). The problem here is that such an interpretation accords poorly with the subordinate clauses in the verse, which seem to presuppose the undertaking of some kind of action. B,D9, and the printed edition of Gorresio (5.77.10) avoid this problem by substituting the reading *kurute*, "he carries out," for *upekṣet*, "he would neglect," and substituting *vyaktam*, "certainly," for *tyaktvā*, "having abandoned [without regard to]." Thus Gorresio (1856, vol. 9, p. 147) understands that the defect referred to consists in a man's carrying out an action without regard for its merits or demerits, relying entirely on fate (*daiva*), and translates, "*Colui che senza considerare i pregi e i difette d'un' impresa e tutto commettendosi al destino e dicendo: 'Or pur farò!' pon mano all 'opra.*"

"without relying on the will of the gods" *daivavyapāśrayam*: See note to verses 7–8 above. M3 and the texts and printed editions of Cg and Cm read *dharma-* for *daiva-* lending the phrase the sense "without relying on *dharma or* righteousness."

11. "of three types... of the same three types": The verse parallels verse 6 above, and we have added the phrases to reflect this.

12. "consistently" *niratāḥ*: Literally, "devoted, dedicated." We agree with Ct and Ck, who understand, "fixed *or* firm [in their counsel] (*pratiṣṭhitāḥ*)."

"are... of one mind" *ekamatyam upāgamya*: Literally, "having reached unanimity." Despite the gerund's suggestion of a process, we believe the next verse makes it clear that the best counselors are always unanimous in their advice.

"through insight informed by the *śāstras*" *śāstradṛṣṭena cakṣuṣā*: Literally, "with a vision found in *or* through the *śāstras*." Cg reads the compound as *paranipāta*, and glosses, "through properly studied *śāstra* (*svabhyastaśāstreṇa*)." As Ct and Ck note, the *śāstras* in question are undoubtedly the texts on polity (*nītiśāstra*).

13. "The counsel that is known as that which is in between, they say, is when counselors, having adopted many different opinions, subsequently reach unanimity as to how to decide a matter." *bahvyo 'pi matayo gatvā mantriṇo hy arthanirṇaye / punar yatraikatāṃ prāptaḥ sa mantro madhyamaḥ smṛtaḥ //*: Although the meaning of this verse in its several variations is not in doubt, the text as it appears in the critical edition is impossible to construe grammatically. The textual evidence for the verse is complicated and confusing, although the critical reading does find support among a number of southern manuscripts. The major grammatical problem is that no clear syntactic relation can be established between the nominative plural *matayaḥ*, "opinions," and the nominative plural *mantriṇaḥ*, "counselors." The texts of the southern commentators present several variant readings that are, if not perfectly lucid, at least somewhat easier to construe. B,D10,11, and the texts and printed editions of Cr, Ct, and Gorresio 5.77.13 read the accusative plural *bahvīr api matīḥ* for the critical text's *bahvyo 'pi matayaḥ* with the gerund *gatvā*, "having gone" (Gorresio—*dattvā*, "having given"), and, in addition, D10,11, and the texts and printed editions of Ct and Cr read the genitive plural *mantriṇām*, "of counselors," for the nominative plural *mantriṇaḥ*, and read the nominative singular *arthanirṇayaḥ*, "resolution of a matter," in place of the critical edition's locative singular. These variants would lend the verse the following sense: "When the resolution of a matter on the part of the counselors, after first

having been divided among many opinions, subsequently comes to the point of unanimity, that counsel is known as the one in between."

M3 and the texts and printed editions of Cm and Cg substitute the gerund *bhūtvā*, "having become," for *gatvā*, "having gone"; the genitive plural *mantriṇām*, "of counselors," for the nominative singular of the critical edition; and the nominative plural *prāptāḥ*, "[they] have reached," for the nominative singular *prāptaḥ*. This sequence yields the sense: "When, with regard to the resolution of a matter, the counselors have many opinions but subsequently reach unanimity, their counsel is known as in between." This variant is more or less rendered in the translation of Raghunathan (1982, vol. 3, p. 16).

Cm, the only commentator to acknowledge the reading that appears in the critical text, notes it as a variant and analyzes it by suggesting that one effectively has to read the nominative plurals (*bahvyaḥ* and *matayaḥ*) in *pāda* a as accusatives. Ct remarks that these quarreling counselors are brought to agreement only through such devices as fear of the king, etc. (*rājabhītyādyupādhitaḥ*).

14. "when counselors go on debating" *saṃpratibhāṣyate*: Literally, "it is spoken in turn." The verb *saṃpratibhāṣyate*, like other words and phrases in this elliptical verse, is somewhat ambiguous. We understand the passive in its general sense of the root "to speak in turn." The idea, which we believe is supported by the sense of the northern variant (*bruvate sadā*, "they speak incessantly"), is that the counselors debate endlessly without reaching any collective decision. Ck, Ct, Cm, and Cr place greater emphasis on the *upasarga prati*, "against." Thus, Ct understands, "it is spoken in rivalry (*pratispardhayā bhāṣyate*)." Cm glosses, "contradictory speech is made (*viruddhabhāṣaṇaṃ kriyate*)." Cg, in the same vein, glosses *vyavahriyate*, by which we understand him to mean "to engage in disputation."

"no conclusive argument can bring about unanimity" *na caikamatye śreyo 'sti*: Literally, "with respect to unanimity there is no good." This phrase is particularly enigmatic, and commentators as well as translators differ as to how to understand it. Ct, Cr, and Ck understand that, even though agreement may be achieved with difficulty, no good or benefit comes of it (*kathaṃcit kaṣṭenaikamatye 'pi śreyaś ca nāsti*—so Ct). In this opinion they are followed by Dutt (1893, p. 1122) and Gita Press (1969, vol. 3, p. 1391). We find this interpretation dubious, for if the counselors are able to reach agreement after their debate, the situation would be no different from that described in the preceding verse. Cg understands *śreyaḥ* to mean "pleasure (*prītiḥ*)" and thus explains, "when the counselors take no pleasure in agreement (*ekamatye teṣāṃ mantriṇāṃ śreyaś ca prītiś ca nāsti*)." Our translation follows the explanation of Cm, who understands *śreyaḥ* as "that good which has as its object unanimity (*aikamatyaviṣayaṃ śreyaḥ*)," explaining that the phrase means, therefore, "that there is no conclusive argument capable of producing consensus (*aikamatyajanakapratipādanaṃ nāsti*)."

15. "eminent counselors" *mantrisattamāḥ*: V1,D10,11,T1,3,G2,M5, and the texts and printed editions of Ck and Ct read *matisattamāḥ*, "eminent in wisdom." Printed editions based on the text of Cg (VSP and KK) read the similar *matimattamāḥ*, "most sagacious."

"some excellent and appropriate counsel for me to follow" *sumantritaṃ sādhu* ... *kāryam*: These words lend themselves to a variety of readings. We read *sumantritam*, "well advised *or* good advice," nominally and *sādhu*, "excellent," as well as *kāryam*, "[what is] to be done *or* deed," adjectivally. Ct, Ck, and Cr tend to reverse this, explaining, instead, "well advised (*sumantritam*) and therefore excellent (*sādhu*) course of action (*kāryam*)."

"I will follow it faithfully." *kṛtyatamaṃ mama*: Literally, "is to be done by me to a great extent." D6,10,11,T2,M, and the texts and printed editions of the southern commentators read instead *kṛtyaṃ mataṃ mama*, "I will accept that [i.e., approve that] action."

16. "will soon march on" *abhyeti*: Literally, "he is approaching." Several of the commentators, no doubt recalling that this is a flashback (see note to verse 1 above), remark that we are to read the present here as an immediate future (*vartamānasamīpe laṭ*), glossing, "he will soon arrive (*acirād āgamiṣyati*—Ct)."

"heroic" *vīrāṇām*: D10,11, and the texts and printed editions of Ct and Cr read instead *dhīrāṇām*, "steadfast *or* wise."

17. "power, which is equal to the task" *tarasā yuktarūpeṇa*: Literally, "appropriate power." Ct and Ck see the power (*tarasā*) referred to here as distinct from that which Rāma possesses by virtue of his austerities, that which he possesses innately, and from the power of his divine weaponry (*astras*) (*tapobalasahajabaladivyāstrāṇām anyatamenety arthaḥ*). Cr understands that this power is suitable to Rāma's inherent nature (*svasvarūpayogena*), while Ck regards it as appropriate to the time and place (*kāladeśocitena*). Cm merely says that it is "highly appropriate (*atyantam ucitena*)."

"his troops, and his allies" *sabalānugaḥ*: Literally, "with troops and followers." We agree with Ct that *bala*, "troops, army," refers to the monkey hosts, and *-anuga-*, "followers," to their leaders, such as Sugrīva, etc. Cm understands similarly. For some reason, most translators who follow this reading render the *dvandva* as though it were a single collective term for the monkey troops.

Following verse 17, D5–7,10,11,S insert a passage of one line [112*]: "He [Rāghava] will dry up the ocean with his might, or employ some alternative.[1]"

[1]"employ some alternative" *anyat karoti vā*: Literally, "or do something else." Cg, Ct, and Ck see this as a reference to the construction of a causeway (*anyatsetubandhanam*—so Ct).

18. "This being the case and hostilities with the monkeys being imminent" *asminn evaṃgate kārye viruddhe vānaraiḥ saha*: Literally, "since the matter has come to such [a pass] and hostility with the monkeys [is at hand]." Ñ2,V1,3,B1–3,D9–11, and the texts and printed editions of Ct, Cr, and Ck read instead *tasminn evaṃvidhe kārye*, "since the matter [is] of such a sort." Ct, Cr, and Ck flesh out this phrase variously. Ct and Ck take the pronoun *tasmin*, "in that [one]," to refer elliptically to "in reference to that single monkey," i.e., Hanumān, and the adjective *evaṃvidhe*, "of such a sort," to refer to the kind of havoc he had wrought upon Laṅkā. They then render the first half of the verse to mean "that single monkey, having accomplished such a deed, and Rāma prepared to carry out hostilities along with many monkeys (*tasminn ekasmin vānara evaṃvidhavyāpāre sati bahubhir vānaraiḥ saha rāme viruddha kārye viruddhaṃ kartum udyate sati*)." Cr, on the other hand, takes *evaṃvidhe* to refer to Rāma himself and renders, "Rāghava, who is of such a nature, that is, whose power is such as I have described, is standing in opposition to us with the monkeys in order to accomplish his own objective [*kārye*] (*evaṃvidha uktapratāpavati tasmin rāghave kārye svakāryārthaṃ vānaraiḥ saha viruddhe sati*)." Our translation follows the explanation of Cg and Cm, who read with the critical edition. As

Cg explains, the reference is to the matter of the blockade of Laṅkā in the manner described and the impending conflict with the monkeys (*asmiṃl laṅkānirodhanarūpe kārya evaṃgata uktarītyā pravṛtte vānaraiḥ saha viruddhe virodhe ca prāpte*).

"of the city" *pure*: Literally, "in regard to the city." Curiously enough, Cr appears to read *purā*, which he glosses as *ādau*, "at the outset." Neither the critical apparatus nor any printed edition or variant shows this reading.

Sarga 7

1. Following verse 1, D5,T1,G2,3,M2,3,5 insert a passage of two lines [117*], while D6,7,10,11,T2,3,G1,M1, and the texts and printed editions of the southern commentators read the first line only: "Those foolish [*rākṣasas*] ignorant of sound policy, and underestimating the forces opposing them."

"lord of the *rākṣasas* ... him" *rākṣasendreṇa* ... *rākṣaseśvaram*: Literally, "by the lord [Indra] of the *rākṣasas* ... [to] the lord of the *rākṣasas*."

2. "iron clubs, javelins, broadswords, lances, and spears" *parighaśaktyṛṣṭiśūlapaṭṭasa-*: For a discussion of these and other weapons, see notes to 5.3.30,32. A *ṛṣṭi* is a broad, double-edged sword (see 6.46.3–4). We understand *paṭṭasa*, unattested in the dictionaries consulted, as a variant of *paṭṭiśa*, "spear." Cg claims that his variant *paṭṭiśa* is "a kind of sword (*khaḍgaviśeṣa*)."

Following verse 2, D5–7,10,11,S insert a passage of one line [118*]: "Entering Bhogavatī, you defeated the great serpents in battle."

3. "Inflicting massive slaughter" *sumahat kadanaṃ kṛtvā*: We agree with most translators in taking *kadanam* in its normal sense of "slaughter, havoc." The commentators understand the term in its other sense of "war (*yuddham*)."

"Kubera, bestower of wealth" *dhanadaḥ*: Literally, "giver of wealth." See note to 6.4.16.

4. "Despite his boasting of his alliance with Maheśvara" *maheśvarasakhyena ślāghamānaḥ*: Literally, "[he] praising because of a friendship with Maheśvara." Ct and Ck understand the verb to be used reflexively in the sense of "praising himself by reason of his alliance (*maheśvarasakhyena hetunā svayaṃ ślāghamāno 'pi*—Ct)."

5. The episode referred to here is described in detail at *Uttarakāṇḍa* 15. Rāvaṇa takes Kubera's Puṣpakavimāna at 7.15.29. See 6.28.21 and notes. Cf. 6.109.22–27 and 6.110.23 and notes.

"Slaughtering, baffling, or capturing" *vinihatya ca* ... *vikṣobhya ca vigṛhya ca*: Literally, "having slaughtered, having agitated, and having captured." Actually these three terms overlap considerably in their meanings, thus constituting one of those sets of near synonyms of which the poet is so fond. (See note to 6.2.14.) Any or all of them can mean "to overcome *or* defeat." We read the gerunds distributively with the understanding that the various actions are inflicted upon different sections of the *yakṣa* forces, and thus translate the conjunction *ca*, "and," here as "or."

D5–7,10,11,T1,G, and the texts and printed editions of Ct, Ck, and Cr read *vinipātya*, "having thrown down, having overthrown," for *vinihatya*, "having slaughtered."

"this flying palace" *vimānam idam*: The reference here is, of course, to Rāvaṇa's magical flying palace Puṣpaka. See 5.6.5–14; 5.7.9–15; and notes. See, too, 6.109.22–27; 6.110.23; and notes.

6. The episode in which Maya gives his daughter Mandodarī to Rāvaṇa in marriage is described at *Uttarakāṇḍa* 12. Notably that episode portrays the *dānava* lord as quite willing, even eager, to marry his daughter to the *rākṣasa* lord. There is no mention of his doing so out of fear. Cg, the only commentator to note the seeming contradiction, remarks that, "although the poet will later state in the *Uttarakāṇḍa* that Maya gave the girl away with the composure born of his noble breeding, the ministers refer to fear here as part of their panegyric on Rāvaṇa's valor (*yady api mayenābhijātyabhramād dattety uttare vakṣyati tathāpy atra praśaṃsāyāṃ bhayād dattety uktam*)." Curiously, at the later passage (GPP 7.12.21), Ct mentions Maya's fear of capture at the hands of the cruel Rāvaṇa as one of his motives for giving him Mandodarī. See, too, notes to 6.99.25, where Mandodarī's lineage is discussed.

7. The reference here is to an episode narrated at *Uttarakāṇḍa* 25 in which the *rākṣasa* or *dānava* lord Madhu, in Rāvaṇa's absence, carries off the *rākṣasī* princess Kumbhīnasī to be his bride. Rāvaṇa mounts a punitive expedition to crush Madhu but is dissuaded by the entreaties of Kumbhīnasī. Rāvaṇa then makes Madhu his ally in his ongoing war against the gods.

"Madhu" *madhur nāma*: Literally, "Madhu, by name." Ś1,Ñ,V1,3,B,D1–5,7–12,T1,G1,3,M5, the texts and printed editions of Ct and Cr, and the edition of Gorresio read instead the vocative *mahābāho*, "O great-armed one."

"the bringer of joy to Kumbhīnasī" *kumbhīnasyāḥ sukhāvahaḥ*: Kumbhīnasī's precise relationship to Rāvaṇa is somewhat ambiguous. Cr, Cg, Cm, and Cv call her his sister here, although Ct is content to attribute this identification to Cm. Ck alone understands Kumbhīnasī to be Rāvaṇa's daughter (*rāvaṇasutā*). In the *Uttarakāṇḍa* account of the episode, Vibhīṣaṇa describes her to Rāvaṇa at 7.25.25 as "the daughter of our mother's sister and so by law [*dharmataḥ*] our sister." The commentators generally agree that "bringer of joy" is a kenning for husband (*sukham āvahatīti sukhāvahaḥ bhartā*—so Cg).

8. "great-armed hero" *mahābāho*: Literally, "O great-armed one."

"Vāsuki" *vāsukiḥ*: This episode is described at 7.23.2–4.

"Takṣaka" *takṣakaḥ*: The abduction of Takṣaka's wife is also mentioned in the epic (3.30.13). See note ad loc.

"Śaṅkha" *śaṅkhaḥ*: A *nāga* of this name is mentioned at *MBh* 1.31.8; 5.101.12; and 16.5.14.

"Jaṭin" *jaṭī*: The name does not appear to occur elsewhere in connection with *nāgas*. We tentatively follow the practice of the translators in seeing this as the proper name of a *nāga* lord. The commentators who address this name—Ct, Ck, Cg, and Cm—are unanimous in understanding it to be that of a type or species of snake (*sarpaviśeṣasya*—Cg).

9–10. The incident is mentioned by Śūrpaṇakhā at 7.24.21, where it emerges that her husband was among her brother's victims.

"you waged war" *yuddhvā samare*: Literally, "having fought in battle."

"indestructible" *akṣayāḥ*: Cg remarks that the indestructibility of the *dānavas* is evidenced by their capacity for regenerating themselves even after being ground to a powder (*cūrṇīkaraṇe 'pi punar utpattimattvena kṣayarahitā ity arthaḥ*). It is not clear whether Cg is alluding to a specific incident or thinking of the often-mentioned ability of the *dānavas' purohita* Uśanas Kāvya, or Śukrācārya, to bring them back to life when they are slain by the gods in battle (*MBh* 1.71 and *MatsyaP* 47). In the former passage

Uśanas does revive Kaca, the son of Bṛhaspati, who has been killed and ground to a powder by the *dānavas*. See 6.11.42; 6.40.28; 6.115.51; and notes.

"with their powerful boons" *labdhavarāḥ*: Literally, "having obtained boons." Cg notes that their boons were acquired from Brahmā (*brahmaṇā iti śeṣaḥ*). Cf. note to 6.28.28–29.

"*dānava* heroes" *śūrāḥ . . . dānavāḥ*: Ct, Ck, Cv, Cg, and Cm identify these particular *dānavas* as the Kālakeyas. Vidyujjīhva, husband of Śūrpaṇakhā, is the leader of this group of demons (7.12.2). Rāvaṇa is said to travel to the capital city of the Kālakeyas, Aśmanagara, and defeat its inhabitants (7.23.15; see also Shukla 2003, p. 139). Their extermination is again mentioned by Śūrpaṇakhā at 7.24.21. According to the *Uttarakāṇḍa* passage (7.24.21), Rāvaṇa is said to have slaughtered them in battle (see also Shukla 2003, p. 139). Arjuna is said to have fought them in battle (*MBh* 5.155.27).

"there . . . many magical powers" *māyāḥ . . . tatra bahavaḥ*: Literally, "many *māyās* [were acquired] there." Ct, Cr, and Cm understand that Rāvaṇa acquired these powers during a period when he lived among the *dānavas* (*tatra taiḥ* [*dānavaiḥ*] *saha vāsān māyāś cādhigatā prāptāḥ*—so Ct). These are the illusory powers that will be employed by Rāvaṇa and other *rākṣasas* at various points in the epic (see, for example, 6.22.6–43). At 7.23.12–14, we are told that Rāvaṇa learns illusory powers from the Nivātakavacas. See S. Goldman 2006a and 2006b.

Following verse 10, M3 and the texts and printed editions of Cg (VSP 6.7.10, in brackets; KK 6.7.11, in brackets) insert a passage of two lines [123*]: "In [your] fury, [you] conquered in battle the immensely powerful world guardians. Then, having gone from here to the world of the gods, [you] conquered even Śakra."

11. The episode of the defeat of the sons of Varuṇa referred to here is told at *Uttarakāṇḍa* 23.

"great-armed warrior" *mahābāho*: Literally, "O great-armed one." D10,11, and the texts and printed editions of Ct read instead *mahābhāga*, "O fortunate one."

"four divisions of their army" *caturvidhabala-*: See note to 6.3.24.

12–13. Rāvaṇa's battle with Yama's army is detailed at *Uttarakāṇḍa* 21 and his battle with Yama at *Uttarakāṇḍa* 22.

"Yama's host, a veritable ocean" *yamasya balasāgaram*: Literally, "the army-ocean of Yama." Those translators who render the term, with the exception of Raghunathan, understand *bala* here in its sense of "strength *or* power," although many seem to extend this meaning to the sense of "realm *or* domain," and translate variously: Dutt (1893, p. 1124), "dominion"; Gita Press (1969, vol. 3, p. 1393), "realm"; Roussel (1903, vol. 3, p. 20), "*le monde*"; and Gorresio (1856, vol. 9, p. 149), "*possanza*." Raghunathan (1982, vol. 3, p. 17), like us, reads the term in its sense of "army." We believe that this word is more appropriate both rhetorically, as the ocean is commonly used as a metaphor for an army in epic poetry, and in the context of Rāvaṇa's elaborately described destruction of Yama's army at *Uttarakāṇḍa* 21. Cg and Cm implicitly understand "army." See below note to verse 15, 127*, where the metaphor is repeated.

"islands in the form of *śālmali* trees" *śālmalidvīpamaṇḍitam*: Literally, "ornamented with *śālmali*-islands." The reading here appears to be suspect. The great majority of manuscripts (Ś,Ñ,V3,B,D1–4,6–12,T2,3,G,M3) collated for the critical edition, including the texts of all the commentators, read instead *druma-*, "tree," for *dvīpa*, "island." Given the principles upon which the critical edition has been based, one would think that the reading should, at least, be marked as uncertain. The substitution of *druma-* would yield the meaning "set about with *śālmali* trees."

Ct, who reads the variant *śālmalī*, explains that this means that the ocean is adorned on its islands (*dvipeṣu*) by *śālmalī* trees, the trees of "hellish torment (*yātanāvṛkṣa*)." Cr glosses similarly. (*śālmalīdrumair yātanāvṛkṣair maṇḍitaṃ sāgaro 'pi dvipeṣu vṛkṣamaṇḍito bhavati.*) Cg and Cm understand *śālmalī* to refer to a weapon so named because of its resemblance to the thorny *śālmalī* tree, and thus read the compound as part of the compound metaphor, i.e., "having *śālmalī* weapons for its trees." This interpretation is represented in the translation of Raghunathan (1982, vol. 3, p. 17), who renders, "which had... spiked racks fashioned like the silk-cotton tree for ornamental park trees of death."

The *śālmali*, or silk-cotton tree (*Salmalia malabarica*), has sharp thorns growing from its trunk, which are apparently used to torture the denizens of hell. It is also the name of a river in Pātāla (Apte s.v.). Shukla notes that the *śālmalī* tree, according to the *Araṇyakāṇḍa*, has "iron thorns" and is "covered under golden flowers and leaves of excellent cat's eye gem" (Shukla 2003, p. 211; see 3.51.18–19). Interestingly, *śālmalidvīpa*, the reading adopted by the critical edition, is the name of one of the seven principal continents, or *dvīpas*, of traditional Indian geography (Bhattacharyya 1991, pp. 7, 265; Narayan 1980, p. 10). See note to 6.76.28, where the red flowers of the *śālmali* tree are compared to blood.

"warding off" *pratiṣedhitaḥ*: Cr glosses, "made to flee (*palāyanaṃ prāpitaḥ*)," while Cg glosses, "made to withdraw from battle (*yuddhād apakrāmitaḥ*)." Ct understands, "made to turn away (*parāṅmukhaḥ kṛtaḥ*)." The reference is to Yama's withdrawal from the battlefield when forbidden by Brahmā to kill Rāvaṇa (7.22.32–38).

"All the worlds were pleased with your brilliant fighting there" *suyuddhena ca te sarve lokās tatra sutoṣitāḥ*: The reference is most likely to the epic convention that gods and other celestial beings assemble to watch great feats of combat. See, for example, 6.91.5–6. At 7.22.15, in fact, the celestials do so gather to watch the battle between Rāvaṇa and Yama. Ct, evidently concerned at the thought that the worlds would be gratified by the victory of the monstrous Rāvaṇa, takes *lokāḥ* in its other sense of "people," explaining, "by you all these people, that is all the *rākṣasas*, were delighted (*te tvayā sarve lokāḥ sarve rākṣasāḥ sutoṣitāḥ prīṇitāḥ*)."

D6,M3, and the texts and printed editions of Cg read *vilolitāḥ*, "were shaken *or* agitated," for *sutoṣitāḥ*, "were pleased." This variant is rendered only in the translations of Raghunathan (1982, vol. 3, p. 17), who translates, "With but a brief fight, you put whole worlds in a state of turmoil."

Following12ab, D5,7,10,11,T1,G2,3,M3, and the texts and printed editions of the southern commentators insert a passage of two lines [124*] (D5,T1,G3,M3, and the texts and printed editions of Cg—KK, in brackets 6.7.14ab—omit line 2) continuing the compound metaphor of Yama's forces as an ocean: "... with the noose of Kāla for its great waves,[1] and the servants of Yama for its great serpents, the mighty ocean of Yama's realm, unendurable because of its many torments.[2]"

[1]"great waves" *mahāvīcim*: Raghunathan (1982, vol. 3, p. 17) inexplicably renders, "[the noose of death] was the shark."

[2]"unendurable because of its many torments" *mahājvareṇa durdharṣam*: Literally, "unapproachable because of its great fever *or* affliction." The exact meaning of the

phrase is unclear. Gita Press (1969, vol. 3, p. 1393) renders, "difficult to overcome on account of the mighty Jwara (the spirit presiding over fevers)." The commentators are silent.

14. According to Cg, the warriors referred to here are those such as Anaraṇya, the Ikṣvāku dynast slain by Rāvaṇa at *Uttarakāṇḍa* 19.

15. Following verse 15, B,D5–7,10,11,S insert a passage of fourteen lines [127*]: "Better yet, stay here, mighty king. Why exert yourself? Great-armed[1] Indrajit will destroy the monkeys by himself.[1–2] For, mighty king, having performed a sacrifice to the unsurpassed Maheśvara, he has received a boon all but impossible to obtain in this world.[3–4] And he, encountering that great[2] ocean of the army of the gods—with its javelins and iron cudgels for its fish, its scattered missiles for its seaweed, filled with elephants for its turtles, and horses for its frogs, with the Rudras and Ādityas for its great crocodiles, and the Maruts and Vasus for its great serpents, with the chariot, cavalry, and elephant corps for its surging waters, and infantry for its great sandbanks—captured Indra, lord of the gods,[3] and brought him back to Laṅkā.[4][5–10] That slayer of Śambara and Vṛtra was released on the order of Grandfather Brahmā[5] and then returned to the triple heaven, your majesty, honored by all the gods.[11–12] He is the one, mighty king, your son Indrajit—the conqueror of Indra—whom you must dispatch so that he may lead the army of the monkeys along with Rāma to destruction.[13–14]"

[1]"Great-armed" *mahābāhuḥ*: D5–7,10,11,T,G2,3, and the texts and printed editions of Ct and Cr read instead *mahārāja*, "O great king" (with hiatus).

[2]"great" *mahat*: We follow Cm, Ck, and Ct, who gloss the masculine *mahāntam* to modify *sāgaram*, "ocean," for the text's neuter *mahat*.

[3]"Indra, lord of the gods" *daivatapatiḥ*: Literally, "lord of the gods." Cs thinks that the use of the neuter *daivata* instead of the more usual masculine "*deva*" in this epithet of Indra is to suggest the emasculation of the divinities [at Rāvaṇa's hands] (*daivataśabdagrahaṇena teṣāṃ napuṃsakatvaṃ dhvanyate*).

[4]For a similar comparison of the battlefield with a river, see 6.46.25–28 and note.

[5]"Grandfather Brahmā" *pitāmaha-*: Literally, "grandfather." Ck and Ct, who quotes him, are at pains to insist that the reference here is to the four faced Rudra, whom they regard as the grandfather of all worlds. See note to 4.42.56, where Ck, while attacking Cg, says that Brahmā is Rudra. See also note to 4.50.15, where Ck brands Cm as a Brahmā-hater and the "lowest of brahmans."

16. "it is unimaginable that any harm" *āpad ayukteyam āgatā*: Literally, "an inappropriate calamity has arrived." We agree with the commentators that the thought of a calamity that could proceed from these ignoble enemies is improper for Rāvaṇa, not the calamity itself. Cg, whom we follow, glosses *asaṃbhāvitā*, "impossible *or* inconceivable," for *ayuktā*, "inappropriate." The syntax is rather unclear.

"such vulgar folk" *prākṛtāj janāt*: Whereas Ct and Ck understand *jana*, "person *or* people," as a plural and take the compound to refer to the men and monkeys [poised to assault Laṅkā], Cg takes it as a singular and sees the compound as a reference to "the insignificant Hanumān (*kṣudrād dhanumatah*)."

"You ought not entertain any such thought in your heart." *hṛdi naiva tvayā kāryā*: Literally, "It should not at all be done by you in the heart." We agree with Ct and Ck, who add the substantive *cintā*, "worry, concern, *or* thought."

Sarga 8

1. "Prahasta" *prahasto nāma*: Literally, "Prahasta by name." This is the same *rākṣasa* whose mansion is mentioned at 5.48.2 and whose son, Jambumālin, was slain by Hanumān at 5.42.15–17.

2. "are unable to withstand you in battle. What then of mere monkeys?" *na tvāṃ dharṣayituṃ śaktāḥ kiṃ punar vānarā raṇe*: D10,11, and the texts and printed editions of Ct, Ck, and Cr read instead *sarve dharṣayituṃ śakyāḥ kiṃ punar mānavau raṇe*, "All of them are capable of being overcome [by us] in battle. What then of two mere men?"

3. "negligent and overconfident" *pramattā viśvastāḥ*: Cm, Ct, Ck, Cr, Cg, and Cv understand that the negligence of the *rākṣasas* is a result of their abandoning themselves to sensual pleasures and that they were overconfident in their belief that they were immune to attack. (*pramattā bhogādiparavaśāḥ. viśvastāḥ śatrudharṣaṇāsaṃbhavabuddhyā niḥśaṅkatayā sthitāḥ*—so Ct.) Crā understands their overconfidence in a more restricted sense, saying that it derived from the contemptuous thought, "What can a single monkey do?" (*viśvastā eko vānaraḥ kiṃ kariṣyatīty avajñayā visrabdhāḥ*). Ct, Cm, and Cg note that the thrust of the counselors' argument is that to be bested when off guard does not mean that one is inferior to one's adversary (*prāmādikaśatruparibhavo na nyūnatām āpādayatīti bhāvaḥ*). See note to 6.9.9.

"will not escape with his life again so long as I live" *na hi me jīvato gacchej jīvan sa*: Literally, "while I am living, he will not go, living."

5. "night-roaming *rākṣasa*" *rajanīcara*: Literally, "O night-ranger." This particular kenning for "*rākṣasa*" seems to have a somewhat pejorative or contemptuous connotation. Sītā appears to use it in this way in the *Sundarakāṇḍa* (5.19.7), whereas here, Cs argues that it is only through his intoxication with his own valor that Prahasta dares to address his monarch in this fashion (*śauryamadena rajanīcarety uktiḥ*). Cf. the more common variant, *niśācara*.

"transgression" *-aparādha-*: As several commentators point out, this refers to the abduction of Sītā.

6. "Next... in a towering rage" *ca susaṃkruddhaḥ*: D10,11, and the texts and printed editions of Ct (GPP, NSP) read instead *tam asaṃkruddhaḥ*, "not angry [said] to him."

7. "outrage against the city, the inner apartments, and the majestic lord of the *rākṣasas* himself" *paribhavaḥ... purasyāntaḥpurasya / ca śrīmato rākṣasendrasya*: According to Ct and Cr, the outrage to the city and the inner apartments consists in Hanumān's having set them on fire (5.52.6–14) (*purasyāntaḥpurasya cāyaṃ paribhavo dāharūpaḥ*—Ct). According to Cm, the outrage against Rāvaṇa consists in his slaying of Akṣa, and so forth (5.45.32–39) (*rākṣasendrapradharṣaṇam akṣavadhādirūpam*). Although we read the verse as an independent sentence, Ct, Cr, Ck, and Cm think that it should be subordinated syntactically to the gerundive *na kṣamaṇīyam* in verse 6 above, thus understanding, "this attack... this outrage... must not be tolerated." A number of translators follow this interpretation.

8. "I shall... repulse" *nivartiṣyāmi*: We read the form as a causative with the sense of "I shall drive back, I shall repulse," as do Roussel (1903, vol. 3, p. 21), "*relancer les Vānaras*"; Gorresio (1856, vol. 9, pp. 150–51), "*li forzerò ben io a retrocedere*"; and Gita Press (1969, vol. 3, pp. 1395), "I shall repulse the monkeys." Other translators understand the verb to mean "kill, destroy": Dutt (1893, p. 1125) and Shastri (1959, vol. 3, p. 20), "exterminate"; and Raghunathan (1982, vol. 3, p. 18), "destroy." Ct and Ck understand the verb to mean something like "expunge, wipe out," and see its object as the unexpressed injury caused by (Hanumān's) attack (*pradharṣaṇaduḥkham*). This interpretation forces Ct to supply the gerund *hatvā*, "having killed," which is absent from his text. See note below. The verbal sequence in the critical edition could also be interpreted to mean "having slain the monkeys... I shall return," as does Crā, who clearly reads the form as a simplex and corrects it (*nivartiṣye*, "I will come back").

"slaying them" *hatvā*: D10,11,M3, and the texts and printed editions of Ct and Ck read instead *gatvā*, "having gone."

"even if they should seek refuge" *praviṣṭān*: Literally, "entered into." Ct and Ck indicate that the monkeys would have done so out of fear (*bhītyā*) [of Durmukha].

9. "all smeared" *rūṣitam*: B3,D7,10,11, and the texts and printed editions of Ct read instead *dūṣitam*, "stained, fouled."

10. "contemptible and miserable" *kṛpaṇena tapasvinā*: This is yet another of those sets of near synonyms of which the poet is very fond. The commentators attempt variously to differentiate them. Most (Ct, Ck, Cm, Cg, Cv) agree that Hanumān is contemptible (*kṛpaṇa*) in that he is afraid of moving about openly and thus had to carry out his mission at night (5.2.31–33; 5.3.46) (*prakāśasaṃcāre bhayād rātrau kṛtakāryeṇa*—Ct). They differ somewhat on the interpretation of *tapasvin*. Ct, Cg, and Cm simply gloss, "pitiable (*śocyena*)." Cr believes that the term refers to the pains that Hanumān (as a monkey) must endure to seek out his food (*tapasvināhārādyanveṣaṇārthaṃ saṃtāpayuktena hanūmatā*). Crā says the term is used because he eats the same fruits that are the normal fare of ascetics (*tapasvinā tapasvyāhārabhūtaphalāśinety arthaḥ*). Cv believes that the reference is to Hanumān's possessing the deceptive power of taking on various forms (*tapasvinā rūpavaividhyakaraṇakuhakaśaktiyuktena*). Ct and Ck, indicating that their usage is like that of vile pejoratives, such as "one who sleeps with his mother (*mātṛgāmin*)," note that these terms are purely abusive and not substantive (*kṛpaṇādiśabdānāṃ pāruṣyamātre tātpāryaṃ na tv arthe mātṛgāmyādigālidānavat*). See notes to 5.7.12 and 10. See note to 6.2.14.

11. Following verse 11, D5–7,10,11,S insert a passage of fourteen lines [131*]: "And if it please your majesty, hear now my further words. For he who is skilled in strategy and ever vigilant will defeat his enemies.[1–2] Lord of the *rākṣasas*, you have thousands of heroic and resolute *rākṣasas*, terrifying, terrible to look upon, and able to take on any form at will.[3–4] Let them all take on[1] human form and, betraying no agitation, approach Kākutstha and speak as follows to that foremost of the Raghus:[5–6] 'We have been dispatched by your younger brother, Bharata.' For his part, he [Rāma] will mobilize his army[2] and come here at once.[3][7–8] Then we will set out swiftly from here and proceed there in haste, bearing lances, javelins, and maces and with bows, arrows, and swords in hand.[9–10] Stationing ourselves in the sky, troop upon troop, we will crush the host of tawny monkeys with a great hail of stones and weapons and send them to the house of Yama.[11–12] If Rāma and Lakṣmaṇa should fall

for this trick,[4] then through their mistaken policy they will surely lose their lives. [13–14]"

[1]"take on" *bibhrataḥ*: Literally, "bearing." D10,11, and the texts and printed editions of Ct read instead *vivṛtam*, "clear, manifest." Ct glosses, "clear *or* evident (*spaṣṭam*)," and adds the gerund *dhṛtvā*, "having taken on a body (*vapur dhṛtveti śeṣaḥ*)."

[2]"will mobilize his army" *senāṃ samutthāpya*: Literally, "having caused the army to rise." We believe that the sense here is that, according to Vajradaṃṣṭra's stratagem, Rāma, thinking he has received reinforcements from Bharata, will break camp and march immediately upon Laṅkā. Similarly, Ct explains that Rāma will combine this new army with his own army of monkeys under the mistaken impression that they are loyal to him, and then begin to march. (*senāṃ vānarasenāṃ samutthāpya yuṅktvā svīyabuddhyā kṣipram evopayāsyati. asmān iti śeṣaḥ.*) Cr, however, glosses, "having abandoned (*saṃtyajya*)," and seems to think that Rāma, upon hearing Bharata's [spurious] message, will abandon his monkey allies in favor of the army of disguised *rākṣasas* (*sa śrutabharatasaṃdeśo rāmaḥ senāṃ samutthāpya saṃtyajyety arthaḥ kṣipram evopayāsyati*).

[3]Following line 7, M3 and the printed editions of VSP and KK (following 6.8.15ab, in brackets) insert a passage of one line [131(A)*]: "There are things to be done urgently requiring your return."

[4]"If... fall for this trick" *evaṃ ced upasarpetām anayam*: Literally, "if those two should approach this deceit in this fashion."

12. "Nikumbha Kaumbhakarṇi" *kaumbhakarṇiḥ ... nikumbhaḥ*: The counselor Nikumbha, here identified as one of the sons of Kumbhakarṇa, is mentioned at 5.47.11. He engages in battle with Hanumān and is killed at 6.64.1–23. See, too, notes to 6.10.1; 6.33.34; 6.45.6; 6.47.21; and notes.

"Rāvaṇa, who makes the worlds cry out" *rāvaṇaṃ lokarāvaṇam*: This is one of the common etymological epithets that Vālmīki likes to apply to his central characters. For a discussion of this term, see notes to 3.30.20 and 6.10.1. See, too, 6.17.4; 6.25.8; 6.53.19; 6.57.17; 6.87.31; 6.99.38; 6.114.24; and notes. See also R. Goldman 1984, pp.105–6.

13. Following verse 13, D5–7,10,11,S insert a passage of one line [134*]: "as well as Sugrīva, Hanumān, and all the monkeys here."

14. "chops" *vaktram*: Literally, "mouth." D10,11, and the texts and printed editions of Ct read instead *sṛkkām*, "corner of the mouth." Licking the corners of the mouth is normally a sign of fear in the epic. See *MBh* 3.124.23 (*lelihañ jihvayā vaktraṃ vidyuccapalalolayā / vyāttānano ghoradṛṣṭir grasann iva jagad balāt*), where it is a sign of appetite, as appears to be intended here. But see R. Goldman 1977, p. 58.

15. The critical edition marks *pāda* d as uncertain. Ś1,Ñ1,D1–4,6–8,10–12,T2, 3,G1,2,M1,2,5, and the texts and printed editions of Cr and Ct read instead *tāṃ sarvāṃ harivāhinīm*, "the whole army of tawny monkeys."

16. "their leader in battle" *raṇakuñjaram*: Literally, "an elephant in battle." The term *kuñjara* is frequently used to refer to anything that is the most outstanding in its class, and we have taken it in this sense here. One might also translate, "a war-elephant in battle." Raghunathan, for example, translates, "who fights like an elephant (1982,

vol. 3, p. 10). D10,11, and the texts and printed editions of Ct substitute instead *sarvāṃś caivātra vānarān*, "and all the monkeys here."

Sarga 9

1–5. Like many of the epic lists, this one is subject to variation in the different subrecensions.

"Indrajit—the mighty and immensely powerful son of Rāvaṇa" *indrajic ca mahātejā balavān rāvaṇātmajaḥ*: D10,11, and the texts and printed editions of Ct read instead *indraśatruś ca balavāṃs tato vai rāvaṇātmajaḥ*, "and Rāvaṇa's mighty son, the foe of Indra."

"Nikumbha... Atikāya" *nikumbhaḥ... atikāyaś ca*: Cg notes that the list begins with Nikumbha in order to suggest that the other *rākṣasas* all agree with him (i.e., Nikumbha) in the matter (*ādau nikumbhopādānaṃ nikumbhamatānusaraṇasūcanārtham*). D7,10,11,G, and the texts and printed editions of Cr and Ct repeat the name Nikumbha in *pāda* 3c in place of the critical edition's Atikāya. This redundancy has not escaped Cr's attention. He rationalizes this repetition by noting that there are many *rākṣasas* with the same name (*nikumbhādināmatvena bahūnāṃ sattvān na paunaruktyam*). See, too, note to 6.8.12.

"leapt to their feet" *samutpatya*: Literally, "having leapt up." Cg glosses, "having risen from [their] seats (*āsanebhyaḥ samutthāya*)."

6. "who dared to assault Laṅkā" *laṅkā yena pradharṣitā*: Literally, "by whom Laṅkā was assaulted."

7. "as they all stood there, weapons in hand" *tān gṛhītāyudhān sarvān*: Literally, "all of them by whom weapons had been seized."

"bade them be seated once again" *punaḥ pratyupaveśya tān*: Literally, "having once more made them sit."

8. "The learned have prescribed as appropriate the use of force only on those occasions where one's object cannot be achieved by means of the other three stratagems, dear brother." *apy upāyais tribhis tāta yo 'rthaḥ prāptuṃ na śakyate / tasya vikramakālāṃs tān yuktān āhur manīṣiṇaḥ //*: A literal translation would be: "For that end, dear [brother], which is incapable of being achieved by the three stratagems, the learned have specified the appropriate occasions for force."

"Use of force" *vikramakālān*: Literally, "occasions for valor." The term *vikrama*, "valor, strength," is used as a synonym for the more conventional term *daṇḍa*. See notes to verse 9 below.

"the other three stratagems" *upāyais tribhiḥ*: As the commentators note, these are the standard three nonviolent means specified in the *nītiśāstra* by which kings achieve their objectives: viz., conciliation (*sāma*), gifts or bribery (*dāna*), and the sowing of discord (*bheda*). See notes to 5.2.27 and 5.34.16; cf. 5.39.2,3. The set of four *upāyas*, "strategic means," of *sāma, dāna, bheda*, and *daṇḍa* (violence or coercion) is a commonplace of the *nīti* literature and the *Arthaśāstra* (9.6.56–61 and 9.7.68–80). Cg here, as well as in the following verses, quotes the appropriate verses from the *Kāmandaka* treatise (*tad uktaṃ kāmandakena—sāmādīnām upāyānāṃ trayāṇāṃ viphale naye / vinayen nayasaṃpanno daṇḍaṃ daṇḍyeṣu daṇḍabhṛd iti*) (*Kāmandaka* 10.14 or 18.1). See Sternbach 1965–1967, vol., 2, pp.171–72. See 6.51.11–13; 6.59.28; 6.71.12; and notes. Cf. notes to 6.31.48–49.

9. "the use of force" *vikramāḥ*: Literally, "prowess, strength, valor." Cg glosses, "acts of war (*vigrahāḥ*)." This constitutes the fourth stratagem set forth in the *śāstras* that is to be used when the three peaceful means (*sandhi*) fail. This is, of course, the equivalent of the stratagem of *daṇḍa*, "coercive force." See notes to verse 8 above.

"those who are off guard" *pramatteṣu*: Literally, "negligent." The commentators agree that this term means "unvigilant (*anavadhāneṣu*—so Cg)." Cg further suggests that it refers to those who are addicted to sensuality (*viṣayasakteṣu*). Cf. 6.8.3 and note.

"preoccupied" *abhiyukteṣu*: The commentators generally agree (Cg as second alternative) that this refers to kings who are engaged in hostilities with third parties (*śatrvantarākrānteṣu*). As his first alternative, Cg curiously suggests that the reference is to renunciant sages or scholars (*jñāniṣu virakteṣv iti yāvat*).

"stricken by misfortune" *daivena prahateṣu*: Ct and Cr, who read with the critical edition, understand this phrase to refer to those who are afflicted with serious illnesses, etc., (*mahārogādineti śeṣaḥ*—Ct). D7,T3,G2,M3, and the texts and printed editions of Crā, Cg, and Cm read *prahṛteṣu*, "carried away," for *prahateṣu*, "struck *or* seized." Cm gives the critical edition's reading as his gloss. Cg interprets, "those whose prosperity has been carried away, i.e., diminished by fate (*daivena bhāgyena prahṛteṣu kṣīyamāṇasampatsv ity arthaḥ*)." Cg understands Vibhīṣaṇa's list here to be merely a *pratīka* for the longer catalogue of opponents against whom the use of force, as opposed to peaceful means, is appropriate. Thus, he sees the conjunction *ca*, "and," as a kind of ellipsis here and quotes a passage from *Kāmandaka* in which twenty such opponents are enumerated. They include a child, an old man, one who is chronically ill, one who has been expelled by a kinsmen, a cowardly person, one whose citizens are cowardly, one who is avaricious, one whose citizens are avaricious, one whose subjects are disaffected, one who is excessively addicted to sensual pleasures, one whose advisers are not of one mind, one who reviles gods and brahmans, one who is stricken by misfortune, one who is fatalistic (an astrologer?—*daivacintaka*), one whose country has been afflicted by famine, one whose army has suffered a crushing defeat, one who is away from his homeland, one who is beset by many enemies, one who is doomed, and one who is devoid of truth and righteousness (*yathāha kāmandakaḥ—bālo vṛddho dīrgharogī tathā jñātibahiṣkṛtaḥ / bhīruko bhīrukajano lubdho lubdhajanas tathā // viraktaprakṛtiś caiva viṣayeṣv atisaktimān / anekacittamantraś ca devabrāhmaṇanindakaḥ // daivopahatakaś caiva daivacintaka eva ca / durbhikṣavyasanopeto balavyasanasaṃyutaḥ // adeśastho bahuripur yukto 'kālena yaś ca saḥ / satyadharmavyapetaś ca viṃśatiḥ puruṣā amī // etaiḥ sandhiṃ na kurvīta vigṛhṇīyāt tu kevalam iti*).

10. "can you all hope to assail" *pradharṣayitum icchatha*: Literally, "you desire to assail." The word "all" has been added to clarify the change in the text to the plural. As Cg and Cm note, Vibhīṣaṇa, who had previously been addressing Rāvaṇa, is now addressing the entire [assembly]. (*pūrvaṃ rāvaṇaṃ prativacanam. atra sarvān pratīti bahuvacanam.*) This interpretation, according to Cm, is supported by the use of the plural vocative *niśācarāḥ*, "O night-roaming *rākṣasas*," in verse 12 below.

"intent upon victory" *vijigīṣum*: According to Ct, this suggests Rāma's lack of any other enemies [than Rāvaṇa] (*anena śatrvantararāhityam*).

"firm in his strength" *bale sthitam*: Ct and Ck gloss, "firm in power of divinity *or* fate (*daivabale sthitam*)." Cg suggests, "of unwavering strength (*sthirabalam*)."

"master of his anger" *jitaroṣam*: Literally, "who has conquered anger." Ct and Ck understand this to mean that Rāma is "free from any foolishness (*maurkhyarāhityam*)."

Cg understands that he is "free from anger at inappropriate times (*akāle roṣarahitam*)." Cm suggests that the term refers to Rāma, who, being utterly without sin, is therefore free from the vagaries of fate. He goes on to remark that the other three adjectives suggest that Rāma is not to be stopped by anyone. (*anena pāpābhāvād daivopahatatvābhāva uktaḥ. itaraviśeṣaṇatrayeṇānyoparuddhatvābhāvaḥ.*)

"utterly unassailable" *durādharṣam*: Ct and Ck see the adjective as suggesting Rāma's possession of divine missiles (*durādharṣatvena divyāstrasampad uktā*).

11. "feat that Hanumān accomplished, leaping" *laṅghayitvā...kṛtaṃ hanumatā karma*: The syntax of the verse is slightly ambiguous. Normal Sanskrit syntax would lead one to take the gerund and the participle as referring to separate actions occurring sequentially. By this reading, "the impossible feat accomplished by Hanumān" should be the destruction of Laṅkā, etc., after his crossing of the ocean. Nevertheless, the context here and the sense of the unimaginable lead us to feel that the impossible feat is the monkey's uncanny flight over the ocean. This interpretation is perhaps supported by a widely distributed variant for *pāda* cd. For *pāda* 11cd, Ś1,Ñ,V1,3,B,D1–4,6–12,T2,3,M1,2,5 substitute, while G2 inserts after 11, a passage of one line [139*]: "Who in the world could have imagined (*cintayitum arhati*) Hanumān's path?" Given the textual evidence, 11cd should probably be considered doubtful. See Bhatt 1960, p. xxxiv. D7,10,11,M1,2, and the texts and printed editions of Cr and Ct read a variant of 139*: "Who in this world could have known or even imagined Hanumān's path *or* flight (*gatiṃ hanūmato loke ko* [*na*—D7] *vidyāt tarkayeta vā*)?" 139* and its variant strike us as an example of the glossing tendency of some, particularly northern, manuscripts, focusing, as it does, explicitly on Hanumān's mode of travel (*gati*). See Pollock 1984a, pp. 85–86. The translation of Raghunathan (1982, vol. 3, p. 20), the only other translator to read with the critical text (i.e., Cg), is similar to ours.

"the lord of rivers and streams" *nadanadīpatim*: See note to 6.5.3.

14. On the episode of Khara's death, see *Araṇyakāṇḍa* 29.

"who was attacking him" *ativṛttaḥ*: Literally, "transgressive, offensive." The commentators are at pains to show that Khara (and Dūṣaṇa) were the aggressors in their conflict with Rāma, who thus killed them in self-defense. Ct and Ck explain, "[who] having transgressed the boundaries of his own territory and having proceeded into Rāma's, began (*pravṛttaḥ*) to assault him (*svasthānam atikramya taddeśaṃ gatvā tatpīḍāyai pravṛtta iti tena sa hataḥ*)." Cr simply explains, "having come to kill (*hantum āgataḥ*)."

Following this verse, D5–7,T1,2,G,M, and the texts and printed editions of Cg (KK 6.9.15; VSP 6.9.15; GPP, in brackets between 6.9.14 and 6.9.15) insert a passage of two lines [140*]: "The violation of another man's wife is a terrible thing, for it leads to the loss of one's reputation, one's wealth, and one's life. It is simply another form of sin.[1]"

[1]"another form of sin" *pāpasya ca punarbhavam*: Literally, "a reincarnation of sin." Our translation follows Cg, who glosses, "another birth, that is to say, another form (*janmāntaraṃ mūrtyantaram iti yāvat*)." Cm understands, "the source of sin (*pāpasya ca bhavam utpattisthānam*)."

15. "For this reason" *etan nimittam*: Ct, Cr, and Ck understand this to be a reference to the *casus belli* mentioned in the preceding verse: "Vaidehī, who was abducted for this reason, i.e., because of the slaying of Khara, etc. (*kharādivadhanimittam āhṛtā*

vaidehī—so Ct)." Cg and Cm consider the phrase to be a reference to the general rule concerning abduction posited in 140* (see above). Although various commentators take up the issue of whether Khara or Rāma began the hostilities, none of them makes any mention of the disfigurement of Śūrpaṇakhā (see 3.17.20–22), which leads Khara to attack Rāma in the first place.

*"Vaidehī . . . danger" *vaidehībhayam*: The critical edition prints the two words as if they constituted a compound. This would literally yield the awkward sense "the danger posed by *or* from Vaidehī." D6,7,G2,3,M1,2, and Cg, Cm, as well as VSP (6.9.16), read *vaidehyā bhayam*, "the danger from Vaidehī." Ct, Ck, and Cm [variant], as well as KK (6.9.16), GPP (6.9.15), NSP, and Gita Press, read *vaidehī bhayam*, "Vaidehī, [who is] the danger," which strikes us as most probable, and is, in any case, indistinguishable in manuscripts from the critical reading. We have translated accordingly.

*"There is no point in acting" *kṛte na kim*: The critical reading, as printed, appears awkward and elliptical at best. D10,11, and the texts and printed editions of Ct, Cr, and Cv substitute the particle *nu* for the negative *na*, which Ct explains by supplying the word *phalam*, "benefit," thus yielding the sense "What benefit would there be in some action [*kṛte*] merely for the sake of a quarrel? (*kalahārthe kalahaphalake kasmiṃś cit karmaṇi kṛte kiṃ nu phalam iti śeṣaḥ. anartha evety arthaḥ*—Ct.)" The texts and printed editions of Cg and Cm read the same as the critical edition, but do not separate *kṛte* and *na*, understanding instead the instrumental *kṛtena*, and explain the passage to mean "what is the point in an action merely for the sake of a quarrel? (*kalahārthe kṛtena kim iti. kalahārthe viṣaye kṛtena karmaṇā kim ity arthaḥ*.)" We feel that this is an appropriate reading. No printed edition other than the critical one reads *kṛte na*, and we feel that once again, as in the case of *vaidehī bhayam*, the critical editors have broken up the words incorrectly. We have translated the sequence as *kṛtena kim*.

16. "for us" *naḥ*: D10,11,T1,M5, and the texts and printed editions of Ct, Ck, and Cr read instead the particle *tu*. This reading leaves the subject of the infinitive ambiguous. Translators such as Dutt (1893, p. 1128) and Shastri (1959, vol. 3, p. 22) understand that it is Rāma who would never engage in pointless hostility.

17. "its myriad precious things" *bahuratnasamākulām*: Literally, "filled with many jewels." We take *ratna*, "jewel," here, in its sense of "excellent *or* precious thing."

18. "storms" *avaskandati*: The commentators understand the sense of this verb variously. Thus, Cr glosses, "it destroys (*vināśayati*)"; Cg, "it blockades (*ruṇaddhi*)"; and Cm, "it scales *or* overwhelms (*ārokṣyati*)."

20. "salutary and beneficial" *hitaṃ pathyam*: This is yet another pair of near synonyms of which the poet is so fond. See note to 6.2.14.

21. The meter is *vaṃśasthavila*.

22. The meter is *vaṃśasthavila*.

Following verse 22, D5–7,10,11,S insert a passage of two lines [151*]: "When Rāvaṇa, lord of the *rākṣasas*, had heard that speech of Vibhīṣaṇa, he dismissed all those present and withdrew into his own residence."

Following *sarga* 9, D5–7,10,11,S and all printed editions of the southern text insert a passage of four hundred seventeen lines [App. I, No. 3, 417 lines] (= GPP, VSP, KK, Gita Press, and NSP 6.10–15). Some N manuscripts also insert segments of this passage (see critical edition, p. 905). Following is a summary of the passage (see Introduction, p. 107): [Lines 1–65 = GPP 6.10]: On the dawn of the next day, Vibhīṣaṇa, having come to a decision as to what was in the interest of righteousness and policy, enters Rāvaṇa's palace, which is densely described as being like a great mountain peak, with splendid rooms, and filled with wise and devoted ministers and capable *rāksasas*. It is replete with elephants, and resounding with the sound of conches and musical instruments. Crowded with beautiful women and covered with gold and precious gems, it resembles a palace of the *gandharvas* or a mansion of the great serpents.[1–14] There he hears the holy sounds of the recitation of the *vedas* and hymns invoking victory for Rāvaṇa, and sees many brahmans.[15–18] Honored by the *rākṣasas* and shining with his own blazing energy, he makes his obeisance to his mighty brother, who is seated on the throne.[19–20] Knowing proper etiquette, he takes a seat that his brother, with his glance, indicates for him.[21–22] Then, in that chamber containing only the two brothers and Rāvaṇa's ministers, he offers his wholesome advice to the king.[23–24] He ingratiates himself with Rāvaṇa and then delivers a speech that is appropriate to the time and place.[25–26] He tells Rāvaṇa that, ever since the time of Sītā's arrival, evil omens have been seen.[27–28] The sacrificial fires are smoky and throw out sparks, even though they are properly fed; lizards have appeared in the fire shrines, and the oblations are swarming with ants.[29–32] Milk trickles out from the udders of the cows, while the war-elephants seem listless. The horses neigh disconsolately and take no pleasure in their fodder. Donkeys, camels, and mules have their hair bristling, and weep, and, despite being looked after solicitously, they do not recover their normal state.[33–36] Savage crows flock on every side, cawing continually. They are seen gathering on the roofs of palaces.[37–38] Flocks of vultures descend upon the city, and jackals howl ominously at dawn and dusk.[39–40] Beasts of prey mass at the city gates, and their loud and harsh cries are heard continually.[41–42] This being the case, Vibhīṣaṇa argues, it would be appropriate to make some expiation. Rāvaṇa should resolve to return Sītā to Rāma.[43–44] He begs Rāvaṇa not to be angry with him, even if he feels that he is speaking out of delusion or personal interest, since these calamitous portents have been noted by all the male and female *rākṣasas* of the town and inner apartments.[45–48] Vibhīṣaṇa tells Rāvaṇa that all the counselors are hesitant to give him this counsel, but he himself is obligated to report what he has seen and heard. Vibhīṣaṇa advises Rāvaṇa that he must act in the proper fashion after due consideration.[49–51] Upon receiving this beneficial and cogent advice, Rāvaṇa becomes annoyed and replies.[52–57] He says that he sees no danger from any quarter and vows that Rāghava shall never recover Sītā. He boasts that Rāma cannot withstand him even were he to be accompanied by the gods, including Indra.[58–61]. Having spoken in this fashion, mighty Rāvaṇa, who had destroyed the armies of the gods, dismisses Vibhīṣaṇa.[62–65]

[Lines 66–141 = GPP 6.11]: Having become emaciated in his unfulfilled desire for Sītā, and because of the disdain in which he has come to be held by his friends because of his sinful actions, Rāvaṇa, obsessed with Sītā for a long time, at last summons his council of ministers and friends.[66–70] He mounts a great bejeweled and gilded chariot that rumbles like a great storm cloud and proceeds to his assembly hall accompanied by armed soldiers.[71–74] He is accompanied by well-dressed and richly adorned *rākṣasas* on every side, along with great chariot-warriors mounted in chariots and those mounted on rutting elephants and swift horses.[75–80] His retinue is armed with all manner of weapons, and his passage is heralded by thousands of musical instruments and conches which make a mighty sound.[81–84] His great chariot rolls splendidly along, making the royal highway resound with the rumbling of its wheels.[85–86] His royal umbrella is as bright as the full moon, while to his right and left, yak-tail flywhisks are adorned with gold and crystal. As he passes, Rāvaṇa is rendered obeisance by the *rākṣasas*, who cup their hands in reverence and bow their heads to him, praising him with hymns of victory.[87–93] Mighty Rāvaṇa reaches his splendid assembly hall, all covered with gold, silver, and crystal. Blazing with its own splendor and covered with gold and fine fabrics, it is guarded by six hundred *piśācas*.[94–97] He enters his council hall, which was built by Viśvakarman, and there takes his seat on a great, splendid lapis throne, covered with costly deerskins and cushions.[98–100] He then orders swift messengers to assemble quickly all the *rākṣasas* at that place, telling them that some very important matter is at hand.[101–103] On hearing his commands, those *rākṣasas* move about Laṅkā, through all the houses, gardens, and parks, fearlessly mustering the other *rākṣasas*.[104–106] The *rākṣasas* come by horses, elephants, and chariots, and by foot. Filled with their speeding chariots, elephants, and horses, the city resembles the sky filled with birds.[107–110] Parking their various mounts and vehicles, the *rākṣasas* enter the assembly hall on foot, like lions entering a mountain cave.[111–112] After touching the king's feet and being honored by him, they sit, some on seats, some on mats, and some on the bare ground.[113–114] Assembled at the king's command in the assembly hall, the *rākṣasas* attend upon their lord in due order.[115–116] All the king's ministers and counselors, who are endowed with every virtue and learned in all matters, assemble by the hundreds as do many warrior-heroes, gathering in the gilded assembly hall for the well-being and happiness of all.[117–121] At this point, the illustrious Vibhīṣaṇa arrives mounted in a splendid chariot.[122–125] Vibhīṣaṇa praises his elder brother and bows at his feet.[126–127] Śuka and Prahasta arrive and are given seats according to their rank. The fragrance of the garlands, aloe, and sandalpaste, worn by those exquisitely dressed and richly ornamented *rākṣasas* in the assembly hall, wafts on all sides.[129–133] They do not chatter idly, and none of them tells a falsehood; they do not speak loudly. All those champions of fierce valor, who had accomplished their goals, gaze at the face of their lord.[134–136] In that assembly of armed, haughty, and powerful warriors, haughty Rāvaṇa shines with his own splendor as does Indra, wielder of the *vajra* in the midst of the Vasus.[137–141]

[Lines 142–229 = GPP 6.12]: Gazing at the assembly, Rāvaṇa, conqueror in battle, commands the general of his army, Prahasta.[142–143] He tells him that he is to order the troops of all the fourfold divisions under his command to defend the city.[144–145] Prahasta, obedient and wishing to carry out his orders, disposes his troops both inside and outside the palace.[146–147] Then, having disposed his troops for the protection of the city, Prahasta returns and takes his seat, telling the king that his forces have been disposed both inside and outside so that Rāvaṇa can, without any concern, do as he pleases.[148–152] Upon hearing the reassuring words of Prahasta, Rāvaṇa, eager for happiness, speaks in the midst of all his friends, telling them that they are the authorities with respect to what is pleasurable and what is not pleasurable, pleasure and pain, gain and loss, what is beneficial and harmful, in all difficult matters of righteousness, pleasure, and polity.[153–155] He reminds them that all of his undertakings performed with them and assisted by their counsel and actions have always proven successful. He expresses confidence that together with them he will attain glory, just as did Vāsava together with the moon, the planets, the constellations, and the gods.[156–159] He announces that he was prepared to inform them fully but that he could not fully discuss the matter because Kumbhakarṇa had been asleep.[160–161] He notes, however, that mighty Kumbhakarṇa, who has been asleep for six months[1] and is the foremost of all those who bear arms, is now present.[162–163] Rāvaṇa then tells the assembly how he had abducted Sītā from the Daṇḍaka Forest but that she refuses to come to his bed.[164–165] He goes on at some length about how he regards her as the most beautiful woman in the three worlds, listing her many charms, including her slender waist, her broad hips, her moonlike face, her golden complexion, and so on. He confesses that the sight of her beautiful red-soled feet kindled a blazing passion within him and that he has become a slave of love where she is concerned.[166–173] He describes his pangs of passion for the beautiful woman and tells his counselors that she begged a year's grace period[2] from him in the hopes that her husband might come. He remarks that he has granted this request but is now exhausted from his constant desire, like a horse that has traveled a long road.[174–181] He expresses doubts as to whether Rāma, Lakṣmaṇa, and the monkeys can possibly cross the vast ocean filled with great creatures but acknowledges that, on the other hand, a single monkey was able to wreak great havoc in his city. He confesses that the outcomes of affairs are difficult to know and urges each of his counselors to speak his mind.[182–185] He notes that he has no fear of men but, nonetheless, urges his counselors to reflect. He reminds them that with their help he has achieved victory in his wars with the gods and the *asuras*.[186–187] He notes that Sugrīva and his monkeys have reached the farther shore of the sea with Rāma and Lakṣmaṇa and that, having discovered Sītā's whereabouts, they are camped by the sea.[188–190] He urges his counselors to devise some strategy in keeping with good policy such that Sītā will not have to be given up and the two sons of Daśaratha can be slain.[191–192] Rāvaṇa notes that he can conceive of nobody in the world as having the ability to cross the ocean with monkeys and so he is sure of victory.[193–194] At this point, Kumbhakarṇa, having listened to the complaints of Rāvaṇa, who was overwhelmed with lust, grows angry and addresses him.[195–196] He tells Rāvaṇa that he should have taken the advice of his ministers before so rashly abducting Sītā.[197–200] Kumbhakarṇa lectures Rāvaṇa on the proper behavior of kings, reminding him that he should have consulted with his ministers earlier and telling him that a king who carries out his royal duties according to proper policy will not have reason to regret them afterward.[201–204] He reminds Rāvaṇa that actions taken without recourse to proper means are as fruitless as oblations made in an impure sacrifice.[205–206] He argues that someone who does later what he should have done first, and vice versa, is unable to distinguish good from bad policy.[207–208] He notes that an unstable person who acts only on the basis of his superior strength is taken advantage of by others, as is the gap in the Krauñca mountain by the birds [who fly through it].[3] [209–210] He adds that, in having thoughtlessly undertaken this action, Rāvaṇa is lucky that Rāma did not kill him on the spot as would poisoned meat.[211–212] Then, despite this critique, Kumbhakarṇa vows to rectify the situation by slaying Rāvaṇa's enemies,[213–214] promising to root them out, even should they be Śakra, Vivasvān, Agni, the purifier, Māruta, Kubera, or Varuṇa.[215–217] For he claims that even Indra himself, smasher of citadels, would fear him, with his mountainous body, his great iron club, and his sharp fangs as he roars in battle.[218–219] He reassures Rāvaṇa that even if Rāma should strike him with a second arrow, he, Kumbhakarṇa, will still drink his blood.[220–221] He promises that he will make every effort to bring victory to Rāvaṇa by killing Rāma and that, once he has slain him and Lakṣmaṇa, he will devour all the leaders of the monkey troops.[222–225] Kumbhakarṇa concludes his speech by telling Rāvaṇa to enjoy himself and do as he pleases, for once he, Kumbhakarṇa, has sent Rāma to the abode of Yama, Sītā will be under Rāvaṇa's control forever.[226–229]

[Lines 230–273 = GPP 6.13] Now the powerful *rākṣasa* Mahāpārśva, seeing how angry Rāvaṇa is, thinks for a moment and then addresses him.[230–231] He asks Rāvaṇa why, since he has nothing and no one to fear, he does not force himself upon Sītā, arguing that a person who does not, for example, avail himself of the honey he finds in the woods is a fool, and then advising Rāvaṇa that he should force himself upon Sītā in the manner of a rooster, placing his foot, as it were, on his enemies' head.[232–237] He reassures Rāvaṇa that after taking his pleasure with Sītā, if he still faces danger, the *rākṣasas*, including Kumbhakarṇa, Indrajit, etc., who are capable of driving off even the *vajra*-wielding Indra, will come to his aid.[239–241] He urges Rāvaṇa to reject the nonviolent means of dealing with one's rivals and to accomplish his ends through force.[242–243] He reassures him that he and the other *rākṣasas* will deal with any enemies that come.[244–245] Upon hearing the words of Mahāpārśva, Rāvaṇa praises him but then relates by way of explanation a secret tale.[246–248] He tells of how long ago he spied the woman Puñjikasthalā[4], who was on her way to the abode of Brahmā. Rāvaṇa stripped and raped her so that she arrived at Brahmā's abode in a disheveled state.[249–253] As a result of this transgression, Brahmā cursed Rāvaṇa to the effect that should he ever from that day forward take a woman by force, his head would shatter into one hundred pieces.[254–257] It is in fear of this curse, Rāvaṇa continues, that he does not force Sītā to his bed.[5] [258–259] Rāvaṇa then begins to boast about his own enormous strength and prowess, vowing to slay Rāma in battle with his immensely powerful arrows and claiming that his forces will annihilate the host of his enemies. He boasts that not even the gods can defeat him and remarks that he had earlier conquered the city of Laṅkā, which had been ruled by Kubera Vaiśravaṇa.[260–273]

[Lines 274–361 = GPP 6.14. This section is composed entirely in *upajāti* meter.] Upon hearing the speech of Rāvaṇa and the blustering of Kumbhakarṇa, Vibhīṣaṇa once more addresses the *rākṣasa* king with beneficial and sensible words.[274–277] He asks why Rāvaṇa has chosen to abduct Sītā, whom he likens metaphorically to a venomous serpent.[278–281] He urges Rāvaṇa once more to return Sītā to Rāma before the monkeys overrun Laṅkā [282–285] and before Rāma's swift and powerful arrows behead the *rākṣasa* champions.[286–289] He argues that none of the great *rākṣasa* warriors, Kumbhakarṇa, Indrajit, and so forth, are able to withstand Rāma in battle.[290–293] He warns Rāvaṇa that he will not be able to escape Rāma alive, even should he be protected by Savitṛ, or the Maruts, or even should he seek shelter with Indra or the god of death himself, or even should he flee into the sky or the underworld.[294–297] Prahasta then replies to Vibhīṣaṇa's words by noting that the *rākṣasas* have never been afraid of anyone, not even the gods, *dānavas*, *yakṣas*, *gandharvas*, great serpents, or mighty birds.[298–303] How then, he continues, should they ever fear in battle Rāma, the son of a mere lord of men.[304–305] Vibhīṣaṇa, whose mind was fixed in righteousness, polity, and pleasure, however, desiring only what is good for the king, responds to Prahasta's pernicious speech with very meaningful words.[306–309] He chides Prahasta, saying that the things that he and the other *rākṣasas* are saying in regard to Rāma are as impossible as it would be for an evil person to obtain heaven.[310–313] He claims that he himself or Prahasta or indeed all the *rākṣasas* could no more compass the death of the supremely competent Rāma than can a person cross the mighty ocean without a boat.[314–317] He notes that even the gods would be baffled by the great chariot-warrior Rāma, a king born in the race of the Ikṣvākus and competent in all actions.[318–321] He tells Prahasta that he is only able to boast because Rāma's sharp and irresistible arrows fletched with heron feathers have not yet ripped through his body.[322–329] Vibhīṣaṇa states once again that none of the powerful *rākṣasas*, such as Kumbhakarṇa, Indrajit, and the others, are able to withstand Rāma, the equal of Śakra, in battle.[330–337] He argues further that the king, who is by nature impetuous, given to acting without reflection, and a victim of addictions, is being counseled by friends who are, in effect, acting as enemies.[338–341] He argues that the counselors should, instead, be striving to free, by force if necessary, Rāvaṇa from his disastrous situation, which he likens to the coils of a mighty, terrifying thousand-headed serpent.[342–345] He tells the *rākṣasas* that, as his friends, they should all collectively save their king, even to the point of dragging him by the hair, as one might a person possessed by powerful spirits.[346–349] He goes on to advise them that it is fitting that they should join forces to rescue their master, who is drowning in the deep waters of the ocean that is Rāghava and on the point of falling into the pit of Pātāla, that underworld that is Kākutstha.[350–353] Vibhīṣaṇa then offers his own opinion, which he believes to be highly beneficial to the king, his friends, as well as the city and its *rākṣasas*. He argues that they should give the prince back his wife.[354–357] He concludes by stating that a counselor should always give suitable and beneficial advice to his master after duly taking into consideration the strength of one's enemy, one's own strength, and the advisability on behalf of one's own party of advancing, retreating, or maintaining the status quo.[358–361]

[Lines 362–417 = GPP 6.15; This section is composed entirely in *upajāti* meter.] Indrajit, foremost general of the *rākṣasas*, having barely controlled himself while listening to the words of Vibhīṣaṇa, who was the equal in wisdom of Bṛhaspati, now responds,[362–365] asking how dare his dear junior uncle utter such senseless and timid words, when even a person not born in their great lineage would not do so.[366–369] He tells his father that Vibhīṣaṇa is the only one in the family that lacks the virtues of strength, valor, courage, fortitude, heroism, and blazing energy.[370–373] He asks why Vibhīṣaṇa is so fearful as to try to frighten them, when these two princes could be easily killed by any ordinary *rākṣasa*.[374–377] He boasts that he himself had dragged Śakra, king of the gods and lord of the three worlds, down to earth while all the hosts of the gods had fled in all directions in fear of him,[378–381] that he had thrown down Indra's mighty war-elephant, Airāvata, who trumpeted discordantly as his tusks were ripped out, and that he had thus terrified all the hosts of the gods.[382–385] He concludes by asking how he, who was so powerful as to crush the pride of the gods and bring grief to the foremost among the *daityas*, would not be able to deal with these two ordinary human princes.[386–389] But Vibhīṣaṇa, foremost among those who bear weapons, gives a sensible reply to that irresistible warrior, the equal of Indra.[390–393] He chides Indrajit as an immature child, unskilled in counsel, who is prattling senseless words to his own destruction.[394–397] He tells him that in speaking as Rāvaṇa's son he is really an enemy in the guise of a friend, since he is encouraging his father even after hearing about the destruction that awaits him at the hands of Rāma.[398–401] He claims that Indrajit is a fool who deserves to be put to death, as does whoever brought him, rash child that he is, into the assembly of counselors.[402–405] He reviles Indrajit as an undisciplined, hot-headed, and ignorant fool, who speaks only childish nonsense.[406–409] He asks who can withstand the blazing arrows loosed in battle by Rāghava, which glow like the staff of Brahmā, resemble the staff of Yama, and look like death itself.[410–413] Vibhīṣaṇa concludes by telling Rāvaṇa that they should give back queen Sītā, along with gifts of wealth, jewels, ornaments, divine garments, etc., so that the *rākṣasas* can live happily.[414–417]

[1]"who has been asleep for six months" *suptaḥ ṣaṇmāsān*: The wakefulness of Kumbhakarṇa and his participation in the council accords poorly with the latter passages where Kumbhakarṇa must be awakened from his long slumber and shows no awareness of his having been involved in prior deliberations about Rāvaṇa holding Sītā captive. This only serves to confirm that this passage cannot be part of the oldest stratum of the text. See 6.49.26 and notes. See R. Goldman 2003b and 2006b.

[2]"year's grace period" *saṃvatsaraṃ kālam*: In the *Sundarakāṇḍa* we are told of the two months [remaining of the year]. See 5.20.8–9 and notes.

[3]"gap in the Krauñca mountain" *krauñcasya kham iva*: Literally, "the space in the Krauñca." See 6.51.19 and notes.

[4]"Puñjikasthalā" *puñjikasthalām*: See notes to 1026*, following notes to 6.48.7, where Cm identifies Puñjikasthalā as Varuṇa's daughter. See, too, 4.65.8–9, where an *apsaras* named Puñjikasthalā is identified with Hanumān's mother. Cf. S. Goldman 1999.

[5]This episode is parallel to, but seems to contradict, the better-known story found at *Uttarakāṇḍa* 26, where it is the *apsaras* Rambhā, whom Rāvaṇa assaults, and Nalakūbara who issues the curse. Cs is greatly concerned by the discrepancy and discusses it at length, citing passages from the *Uttarakāṇḍa* and the *Rāmopākhyāna* of the *Mahābhārata* (*MBh* 3.275.32: *nalakūbaraśāpena*); *MBh* 3.275.33: *yadi hy akāmām āsevet striyam anyām api dhruvam / śatadhāsya phaled dehe ity uktaḥ so 'bhavat purā*). He rationalizes the contradiction on the grounds that the two events must have taken place in different *kalpas* (*kalpe kalpe*). See notes to 1026*, following notes to 6.48.7.

Sarga 10

1. "sound" *suniviṣṭam*: Literally, "concentrated, fixed, settled." We generally follow the interpretation of Ct and Ck, who gloss, "valid (*arthatattvam*)." Cm explains the term as "properly grounded in good conduct (*suṣṭhu vinītiniṣṭham*)." Cg expends considerable effort explaining why Rāvaṇa should react so harshly to such excellent and well-intended advice. This explanation leads Cg into a brief discussion of the etymology of Rāvaṇa's name, a favorite topic of the commentators. He explains that it can be understood in two ways, that is, "he who causes others to weep (*rodayati*) since he is known throughout the world as engaging in injury to others (*parahiṃsāyāṃ jagadviditaḥ*), and he who roars or bellows (*rauti*)." See, too, notes to 6.8.12.

"impelled as he was by his own impending doom" *kālacoditaḥ*: Literally, impelled by Kāla. See note to 6.57.8.

2. "with one's enemy" *sapatnena*: The idea, as articulated by Cg, for example, is that living with an internal enemy is even more to be avoided than living with an [avowed] enemy or a serpent (*śatrusarpasahavāsād api sahajaśatrusahavāsaḥ sudūraṃ parihartavya iti bhāvaḥ*). Cg understands the implication of this remark to be that Vibhīṣaṇa should leave the city at once (*atas tvayāsmān nagarāt sadyo gantavyam iti dyotyate*).

"false friend" *mitrapravādena*: Literally, "one who declares himself as a friend."

"in the service of one's foes" *śatrusevinā*: Ct understands this term to suggest Vibhīṣaṇa's devotion to the Lord [Rāma] (*anenāsya bhagavadbhaktatvaṃ sūcitam*). Cr takes the term to suggest that Rāvaṇa has already determined that Vibhīṣaṇa is an ally of Rāma (*etena vibhīṣaṇo rāmasaṃsargīti rāvaṇasya niścayo dhvanitaḥ*).

3. "Kinsmen . . . in one another's" *jñātīnāṃ jñātayaḥ*: Literally, "Kinsmen . . . in kinsmen's."

4. "leader" *pradhānam*: Literally, "first, foremost." Ct and Ck understand this to be a reference to Rāvaṇa, who holds the kingship because he is the eldest (*jyeṣṭhatvādīnāṃ prāptarājyam*). Cr understands similarly. Cg explains, "the most outstanding in his family (*svajātiśreṣṭham*)." This interpretation is reflected in the translation of Raghunathan (1982, vol. 3, p. 33).

"competent" *sādhakam*: Literally, "effective, efficient." Ct, Ck, and Cr see this as a reference to Rāvaṇa's discharging the functions of the king (*rājakāryanirvāhakam*—so Cr). Cg, Crā, Cv, and Cm, who read the variant *sādhanam*, explain similarly.

5. "affecting pleasure in one's company" *anyonyasaṃhṛṣṭāḥ*: Our translation follows the interpretation of Cg, who glosses, "outwardly manifesting affection (*bahiḥsnehavanta iva sthitāḥ*)." Ct, Cr, and Ck, and the translators who follow them construe the adjective with the locative *vyasaneṣu* in *pāda* b, yielding the sense "delighting in one another's calamities."

"they turn on one in times of trouble" *vyasaneṣu ātatāyinaḥ*: Literally, "inimical *or* murderous in calamities." As a consequence of their reading of the previous phrase, the two "schools" of southern commentators must read this phrase differently as well. As noted above, Cg, whom we have followed, construes *vyasaneṣu* with *ātatāyinaḥ*, yielding "they are hostile in [times of] trouble." Ct, Ck, and Cr construe *vyasaneṣu* with the previous phrase, as noted above. This reading leaves *ātatāyinaḥ* as a separate modifier in its basic sense of "malicious, inimical, hostile." Ct and Ck quote a verse in which the six *ātatāyins* are catalogued as "the arsonist, the poisoner, an armed person, the thief of property, one who steals land, and a wife-stealer—these are the six inimical ones (*agnido garadaś caiva śastrapāṇir dhanāpahaḥ, kṣetradāraharaś caiva ṣaḍ ete ātatāyinaḥ*)." Apte (s.v. *ātatāyin*) cites a similar verse from the *Śukranītiśāstra*.

"Concealing their true feelings" *pracchannahṛdayāḥ*: Literally, "whose hearts are hidden."

6. "There are these well-known verses" *śrūyante . . . ślokāḥ*: Literally, "verses *or ślokas* are heard." Cr suggests that Rāvaṇa heard these verses from the lips of his elders (*vṛddhānāṃ mukhato 'śrauṣam ity arthaḥ*), while Cg understands that they have been passed down by word of mouth (*vaktṛparaṃparayā*).

"in the Padmavana by some elephants" *hastibhiḥ . . . padmavane*: Literally, "by elephants . . . in the lotus forest." Ct and Ck explain that these are elephants of the heavenly forest, dwelling in the Padmavana, which we may then assume to be a heavenly forest (*padmavanavartidivyavanagajaiḥ*).

"ropes to snare them" *pāśa-*: Literally, "snare, noose." Cg glosses, "ropes to capture elephants (*pāśāḥ gajagrahaṇarajjavaḥ*)."

7. In our opinion, all the dangers alluded to are parts of the process of capturing wild elephants for domestication. Since the process relies on the use of previously domesticated elephants to corral their wild cousins, the verse focuses on this perceived betrayal as more perilous than the mere tools of men.

"intent on their own self-interest" *svārthaprayuktāḥ*: Literally, "focused on their own goals." The idea, of course, as indicated by Cr and Ct, is that the tame elephants betray their wild kin in order to obtain the excellent food, etc. [doled out by their keepers] (*uttamabhojanalābhādisvārthaparāḥ*—so Ct).

8. "they who point out" *ete vakṣyanti*: Literally, "they will declare."

9. D6,10,11,T2,3,G, and the texts and printed editions of Ct transpose *pādas* 9b and 9d.

"wealth" *sampannam*: Literally, "arrived at, possessed of." Cg and Cm gloss, "prosperity, wealth (*saṃpattiḥ*)." Cattle are, of course, a major index of wealth in traditional India. Ct, Cr, and Ck understand the reference here to be the wealth that enables the performance of sacrificial rites to the gods and deceased ancestors (*havyakavyasādhanasaṃpat*—so Ct).

"self-restraint" *damaḥ*: D10,11,T3, and the texts and printed editions of Ct and Cr substitute *tapaḥ*, "asceticism."

10. "dear brother" *saumya*: Literally, "dear *or* gentle one." Crā, noting what seems apparent in this context, suggests that this term of endearment here is an example of the figure of speech called *ākṣepokti*, "indirect," or, in this case, "ironic." See Gerow (1971, pp. 124–25) for a full discussion of the rhetorical device *ākṣepa*.

"that I have attained universal sovereignty" *aiśvāryam abhijātaḥ*: Literally, "[that] I was born to lordship." We follow Cg and Cm, who gloss *abhijātaḥ* as "obtained, attained (*prāptaḥ*)."

"I have set my foot on the heads of my enemies" *ripūṇāṃ mūrdhni ca sthitaḥ*: Literally, "[I] stand on the head of my enemies."

D5–7,10,11,S insert a passage of ten lines [156*]: "Just as drops of water that have fallen on lotus leaves do not adhere, so is it with affection lavished upon the unworthy.[1–2] As it is with the honeybee, which in its thirst sips at the *kāśa* flower but finds no nectar there, so is it with affection lavished upon the unworthy.[3–4] As it is with the elephant who having first bathed then takes up dust with his trunk to soil his own body, so it is with affection lavished upon the unworthy.[5–6] As it is with the honeybee who in its thirst finds nectar and then departs—and you are just the same—so it is with affection lavished upon the unworthy.[7–8] As it is with clouds in autumn, which sprinkle and rumble but fail to produce any heavy rain,[1] so it is with affection lavished upon the unworthy.[9–10]"

[1]"heavy rain" *ambusaṃkledaḥ*: Literally, "wetting *or* soaking with water."

Various manuscripts and the printed editions of the southern commentators transpose several of the lines of this passage.

11. "would have died" *na bhavet*: Literally, "he would not exist." As Cr and Cg note, Rāvaṇa is saying that he would have had anyone else killed on the spot (*vinaśyeta nāśayeyam iti yāvat*).

"To hell with you" *tvāṃ tu dhik*: Cg explains this common curse here to mean, "I renounce you (*tyakṣyāmīty arthaḥ*)." Ct notes that, since Vibhīṣaṇa cannot be executed because he is Rāvaṇa's brother, this curse is to be considered his punishment (*sodaratvena vadhānarhatvād dhikkṛtir eva te daṇḍa iti bhāvaḥ*).

12. "four other *rākṣasas*" *caturbhiḥ saha rākṣasaiḥ*: According to Ct and Ck, these are Vibhīṣaṇa's counselors. They are named below at 6.28.7 (see ad loc. and notes). See, too, 6.11.3 and notes.

13. "hovering in midair" *antarikṣagataḥ*: Literally, "gone into the atmosphere." It is not uncommon for supernatural beings, when wronged, to prophesy their oppressors' doom from a position in the sky. Compare *BhāgP* 10.4.9–12, where Yogamāyā rises into the sky to foretell the destruction of Kaṃsa.

"to his brother" *bhrātaram*: B1,D10,11,M2, and the texts and printed editions of Ct read instead *bhrātā vai*, "his brother [Vibhīsaṇa spoke]."

14. "brother" *bhrātā*: T1 and the texts and printed editions of Ct read instead *bhrāntaḥ*, "in error *or* deluded."

Following 14ab, D5–7,10,11,S insert a passage of one line [158*]: "An elder is to be respected just as is one's father, but [you] have not followed the path of righteousness."

15. "ten-headed Rāvaṇa" *daśānana*: Literally, "O ten-faced one."

17. "burning house" *pradīptaṃ śaraṇam*: Here the word *śaraṇam*, which normally means "refuge, resort," is used in its less common meaning, "dwelling, house, abode." See 6.12.11 and note. Cf. note to 6.13.13.

19. D5–7,10,11,S insert one line [163*]: "So, as my elder, please excuse what I said, in my desire for your welfare."

21. "in my desire for your well-being" *mayā hitaiṣiṇā*: Literally, "by me desiring well-being [for you]."

"whose time is at hand" *parītakālāḥ*: Literally, "whose time has lapsed." Ñ1,D10,11, and the texts and printed editions of Ct read instead *parāntakāle*, "in [their] final moments."

The meter is *vaṃśasthavila*.

Sarga 11

1. Cg is greatly concerned about what could be argued to be Vibhīṣaṇa's betrayal of Rāvaṇa. He takes this verse as a starting point for a lengthy disquisition on the Śrīvaiṣṇava doctrine of taking refuge with the Lord, even though it may involve the betrayal of other venerable but flawed figures, such as Daśaratha, in the case of Lakṣmaṇa, and Rāvaṇa, in the case of Vibhīṣaṇa. He describes the loyalty to elders as the general, or *sāmānya, dharma* over which the special, or *viśeṣa, dharma*, or worship of the Lord, must take precedence. Cm, much more concisely, expresses the same points.

"The moment . . . had finished speaking . . . he went" *ity uktvā . . . ājagāma muhūrtena*: Literally, "having spoken, he came in a moment."

2. "standing on the ground" *mahīsthāḥ*: Ctś offers two explanations. The first is that the monkeys are on guard duty all around the encampment, and their looking into the sky is a sign of their extraordinary watchfulness. The second is that the monkeys, who had been resting in trees, etc., come to earth to surround Rāma [protectively]

when they see Vibhīṣaṇa approaching. (*mahīsthā bhūmau parito rakṣaṇaniyuktā ākāśa-stham api dadṛśur iti jāgarūkatvātirekaḥ. yadvā mahīsthās tatra tatra vṛkṣādiṣu sthitāḥ sarve tadātva eva gaganastham dṛṣṭvā rāmam paryavārayan.*)

"there in the sky" *gaganastham*: Cg notes that this suggests that the monkeys were able to see Vibhīṣaṇa from a considerable distance and indicates that Vibhīṣaṇa may have been hesitating to "land" out of anxiety that the monkeys, who were devoted to Rāma, would not admit him (*rāmabhaktā vānarā nāsmāt praveśayiṣyantīti kampaḥ*).

"resembling the peak of Mount Meru and blazing like lightning" *meruśikharākāraṃ dīptām iva śatahradām*: The various commentators point out that the basis for the first simile is Vibhīṣaṇa's height, breadth, and abundance of jewels, and the second, his radiance and location in the sky (*unnatatvapīvaratvaratnabahulatvādibhir meruśikhara-tulyam . . . tejiṣṭhatvagaganasaṃcārābhyāṃ vidyuddṛṣṭāntaḥ*).

Following verse 2, Ñ2,V1,3,B,D7,9–11,G2,3,M (D6 inserts after 6.10.20), and the texts and printed editions of the southern commentators (NSP and GPP 6.17.3–4, and the verses are inverted; VSP, bracketed unnumbered verses between 6.17.2 and 3; KK 6.17.3–4, in brackets) insert a passage of four lines [167*]: "Black, with the shape of a man, and resembling a cloud or a mountain, that majestic *rākṣasa*[1] was flying through the air carrying a noose, the weapon of Dharma.[2] [1–2] And those four followers of his, fearsome in their valor, were similarly equipped with armor and weapons and glittered with their ornaments.[3] [3–4]"

[1]"majestic *rākṣasa*" *śrīmān*: Literally, "the majestic one."

[2]"carrying a noose, the weapon of Dharma" *dharmāyudhadharaḥ*: Literally, "bearing the weapon of Dharma." The reading is awkward. Variants include "bearing excellent weapons (*varāyudhadharaḥ*)" and "bearing every weapon (*sarvāyudhadharaḥ*)."

The texts and translations of the southern commentators read a substantially different version of lines 1 and 2. D7,10,11, and the texts and printed editions of Ct and Cr read instead *sa ca* [*hi*—D7] *meghācalaprakhyo vajrāyudhasamaprabhaḥ / varāyudhadharo vīro divyābharaṇabhūṣitaḥ*, "Resembling a cloud or a mountain, and as lustrous as the *vajra* weapon, holding an excellent weapon, that hero adorned with divine ornaments." M3 and the texts and printed editions of Cg read *mahendrasamavikramaḥ*, "equal in valor to great Indra," for *vajrāyudhasamaprabhaḥ*, "as lustrous as the *vajra* weapon," and *sarvāyudhadharaḥ*, "holding every [sort of] weapon," for *varāyudha-dharaḥ*, "holding an excellent weapon."

[3]"glittered with their ornaments" *bhūṣaṇaiś ca babhāsire*: D7,10,11, and the texts and printed editions of Cr and Ct read instead *bhūṣaṇottamabhūṣitāḥ*, "adorned with the finest ornaments."

3. "his four companions" *tam ātmapañcamam*: Literally, "him, who had himself for a fifth." The reference is to Vibhīṣaṇa's four *rākṣasa* companions mentioned at 6.10.12. According to Cg, the names of the companions are Anala, Śarabha, Saṃpāti, and Praghasa. See, too, 6.10.12; 6.13.2; 6.28.7,32; 6.71.2; and notes.

6. "*sāla* trees" *sālān*: *Shorea robusta* or *Vatica robusta*. These are stout trees with hard wood about a hundred feet tall. In the remainder of the battle the monkeys often use them as weapons.

7. "evil-minded creatures" *durātmanām*: Literally, "of evil-minded ones."

"Let them fall... slain" *nipatantu hatāś caite*: D3,10,11,M1,T3, and the texts and printed editions of Ct read instead *nipatanti hatā yāvat*, "so that they fall, slain."

"their lives cut short" *alpajīvitāḥ*: Literally, "who have little life [remaining]." The latter element of the compound, *-jīvitāḥ*, is marked as uncertain in the critical edition. Ś,Ñ1,D1–5,8,12,T1,M1,2 read *-cetasaḥ*, "mind," while D10,11, and the texts and printed editions of Ct read *-cetanāḥ*, "mind," both of which lend the compound the sense of "stupid." D6,7,T3,G1,3,M3,5, and the texts and printed editions of Cg read *-tejasaḥ*, "energy, power," giving the compound the sense of "weak, feeble." Ñ2,V1,3,B1,3,4,D9 read *rudhirokṣitāḥ*, "splattered with blood." The various translators follow different readings here: Dutt (1893, p. 1145), "limited as is the tenure of their life"; Shastri (1959, vol. 3, p. 37), "weaklings"; Raghunathan (1982, vol. 3, p. 35), "puny creatures"; Roussel (1903, vol. 3, p. 42), "*peu de sens*"; Gita Press (1969, vol. 3, p. 1419), "endowed as they are with poor vitality"; and Gorresio (1856, vol. 9, p. 176), "*bagnati del loro sangue.*"

8. "Now, as they were conversing with one another" *teṣāṃ saṃbhāṣamāṇānām anyonyam*: Ct, Cm, and Cg read the absolute as the genitive of disrespect (*anādare ṣaṣṭhī*), arguing that, in his profound faith in Rāma's compassion, Vibhīṣaṇa pays no attention to the monkeys despite their words and actions (*tān anyonyaṃ saṃbhāṣamāṇān anādṛtya rāmasya bhagavataḥ paramadayālutvabhāvanayā teṣām anādaraḥ*—so Ct). Crā understands this as a *vyatyayena ṣaṣṭhī*, or a genitive of opposition. Ck understands it as a *bhāvalakṣaṇe ṣaṣṭhī* and reads it as equivalent to a locative absolute, *sati saptamī*.

"hovered there in the sky" *khastha eva vyatiṣṭhata*: Ct, Cg, and Cm argue that the repetition of the forms derived from $\sqrt{}$*sthā* suggests the calm and fearless way in which Vibhīṣaṇa waits, facing the hostile monkeys (*khastha eva vyatiṣṭhateti tiṣṭhater dviḥprayogo nirbhayatvenāvasthānasūcanāya*—so Ct).

9. "and the other monkeys" *tāṃś ca*: Literally, "and them."

10. Ct, Cg, and Cm are eager to demonstrate that each of the terms used by Vibhīṣaṇa here has a specific connotation and that, in making this declaration, Vibhīṣaṇa is opening with a statement of his own flaws (*doṣas*) and is not to be construed as boasting of his relationship with Rāvaṇa. According to Ct and Cg, Rāvaṇa's name suggests its bearer's oppression of all the worlds, while the term "evil (*durvṛttaḥ*)" indicates his commission of wrongful acts. The generic term *rākṣasa* shows that he is cruel by nature, while the designation "lord of the *rākṣasas*" indicates that he has evil followers as well. The commentators further feel that Vibhīṣaṇa's self-identification as the younger brother of Rāvaṇa is an admission of his implication in his brother's crimes and his abjection in abandoning his pride. (*rāvaṇatvena sarvalokapīḍakatvam. durvṛttatvenākṛtyakartṛtvam. rākṣasatvena jātikrauryam. rākṣaseśvara ity anena bhṛtyakrauryam. tadbhrātṛtvena svasyāpi doṣavattvakathanād garvahānirūpakārpaṇyam uktam.*)

11. "closely guarded by *rākṣasa* women" *rākṣasībhiḥ surakṣitā*: Ct advances a curious notion that this phrase suggests the preservation of Sītā's fidelity to her husband. For, he argues, if her chastity had been compromised, what purpose would have been served by guarding her (*anena sītāpātivratyāhāniḥ sūcitā tad dhānau hi tābhī rakṣaṇānupayoga iti bhāvaḥ*).

Cg notes that Sītā is so well guarded that even someone learned in the nine systems of grammar would not have been able to gain access to her (*āśvāsakanavavyākaraṇapaṇḍitasyāpi yathā na praveśas tathā rakṣitā*). The term "knowing substance of the nine systems of grammar"(*navavyākaraṇārthavettṛ*) can also be found as a qualification of Hanumān, in praise of his wisdom, at *Uttarakāṇḍa* 36.41 (in an interpolation found in a southern manuscript, M3 [730*]).

12. Ctś attempts to fill what he sees as a gap in Vibhīṣaṇa's statement, saying that Vibhīṣaṇa is anticipating and accepting that he should have come to Rāma the moment Rāvaṇa abducted Sītā and that it was wrong of him to stay and argue with his brother (*sītāharaṇasamakālam evāgamanaṃ mamocitaṃ tathā kṛtvā tasya hitaṃ vaktuṃ vilambito 'ham eva pāpīyān iti*).

13. "dying man" *viparītaḥ*: The term almost invariably means "perverse, inverted." Nonetheless, given the context, we have accepted the universal interpretation of the commentators, who gloss, "about to die (*mumūrṣuḥ*)."

15. "great" *mahātmane*: In keeping with their strongly theological reading of this verse, Śrīvaiṣṇava commentators are inclined to read this common epithet in a vedāntic sense. Thus Cm glosses, "Supreme Spirit (*paramātmane*)."

"the refuge of all the worlds" *sarvalokaśaraṇyāya*: Ct, Cg, Cm, and Ck indicate that Vibhīṣaṇa is aware of Rāma's salvific power as a result of the boon given by Brahmā's son Viśravas to his wife, Vibhīṣaṇa's mother, Kaikasī, that her son would be supremely righteous. See *Uttarakāṇḍa* 9.

"have come to him for shelter" *upasthitam*: Literally, "has come *or* is waiting upon." Given the tenor of the verse with its prior reference to Rāma as "the refuge of all the worlds," Vibhīṣaṇa's statement in verse 14 above ("I have come seeking refuge with Rāghava—*rāghavaṃ śaraṇaṃ gataḥ*"), and following the commentators, we feel that the reference to shelter here is amply justified.

16. Following verse 16, all southern manuscripts and the texts and printed editions of all southern commentators insert, in whole or in part, a passage of fourteen lines [177*]. The passage, however, is located somewhat differently in the two commentarial traditions of the southern texts. The texts and printed editions of Ct and Cr place the passage immediately after verse 16 (= GPP 6.17.19–25), while the texts and printed editions of Crā, Cm, and Cg insert lines 1–2 following verse 19 and lines 3–14 following verse 16 (177* lines 1–2 = VSP 6.17.26; 177* lines 3–14 = VSP 6.17.18–23; 177* lines 1–2 = KK 6.17.28; 177* lines 3–14 = KK 6.17.20–25). "Having previously entered the forces of the enemy, he has now come[1] here as an unrecognized foe, who, finding an opportunity, will slay us as an owl would crows.[1–2] Bless you, scorcher of your foes, you must therefore be vigilant with respect to counsel, the disposition of your forces, leading your troops, and the dispatching of spies both in regard to the monkeys and to your enemy.[3–4] For these *rākṣasas* can take on any form at will and even make themselves invisible. They are bold and skilled in deception. One must never trust them.[5–6] He must be a spy of Rāvaṇa, the lord of the *rākṣasas*. Once he joins us, he will, without doubt, sow discord among us.[7–8] On the other hand, this clever fellow, having entered our midst and found an opportunity, might kill us himself, once we had come to trust him.[9–10]. Troops from one's allies, from the forest,[2] hereditary retainers, or mercenaries—all of these one may accept, but one must avoid forces that come from one's enemy.[11–12] He is a *rākṣasa* by nature and the brother of your enemy to boot, lord. He comes straight from the opposing side; how can one possibly trust him?[13–14]"

[1]"has . . . come" *prāptaḥ*: D6,M3, and the texts and printed editions of Cg, Cm, Cr, and the translators who follow their texts read instead *prājñaḥ*, "clever, wise."

[2]"Troops from one's allies, from the forest" *mitrāṭavibalam*: The sense of the compound and its slight variant *mitrāṭavībalam* is not perfectly clear, and commentators as well as translators differ on its interpretation. Ct and Ck understand the compound *mitrāṭavi-* as a kind of *pūrvanipāta* compound and read it as "sent by a forest ally (*mitreṇāṭavikenāraṇyakena preṣitam*) (Ck—*āṭavikapreṣitabalam*)." Cr reads the compound *mitrāṭavi* as a *dvandva* and explains *aṭavi* as meaning "those who dwell in the forest (*aṭavīnivāsīnām*)," which he then glosses as *udāsīnānām*, "neutrals." Cg and Cm understand *aṭavi* to mean "consisting of forest people (*āṭavika* [*āraṇya*—Cm] *janarūpam*)." Dutt (1893, p. 1146) sees Sugrīva's advice not as a general maxim but as relevant to the moment, understanding, "we should now collect the forest rangers." Raghunathan (1982, vol. 3, p. 36) has "one should utilize the resources... of the forest belt round one's kingdom." Roussel (1903, vol. 3, p. 43), followed by Shastri (1959, vol. 3, p. 38), understands the reference to be to the monkeys themselves, translating, "*d'un habitant des bois* (*comme nous*)" (Shastri: "an inhabitant of the woods like ourselves"). Gita Press (1969, vol. 3, p. 1420) translates merely "foresters."

17. Following verse 17, D5,T1,G2,M3,5, and the texts and printed editions of Crā, Cm, and Cg insert 177*, lines 3–14. See note 16 above.

18. Verse 18 = App. I, No. 8, lines 28–29. See notes to 6.12.3.

"sent... as a spy" *praṇihitam*: D10,11, and the texts and printed editions of Ct, Ck, and Cr read instead *praṇītaṃ hi*, "sent, dispatched."

"You always know what is appropriate... appropriate" *kṣamaṃ kṣamavatāṃ vara*: The formulaic epithet is actually a vocative here, "O you who know what is appropriate," and is probably used largely for the alliterative effect with *kṣamam*. Cs proposes two other alternative readings. One is to take *kṣama* in the sense of "powerful beings (*śaktāḥ*)" and thus understand the suggestion to be that Rāma's powerful generals can easily capture Vibhīṣaṇa and that Rāma, himself, can do so even more easily. The other alternative is to take *kṣama* with an irregular shortening of its final vowel in the sense of *kṣamā*, "patience, forbearance." (*kṣamāḥ śaktā eṣāṃ santīti kṣamavantas teṣu vara. etena tvatsenānayakair asmābhir api tannigrahaḥ susādhyaḥ kim u tvayeti sūcayati. "kṣamaṃ yukte kṣamānvite / vācyavac chaktahitayoḥ kṣamā bhūmititīkṣayoḥ" iti viśvaḥ. etena titīkṣārthaṃ kṣamaśabdam aṅgīkṛtya hrasvatvasyārṣatvavarṇanaṃ parāstam.*) Some translators follow this reading: Dutt 1893, p. 1146, "foremost of forgiving persons"; Gita Press 1969, vol. 3, p. 1420, "foremost of the indulgent", and Gorresio 1856, vol. 9, p. 177, "*o uom di gran pazienza.*" In the context, such a reading could be construed as ironic, as if Sugrīva is alluding to Rāma's reputation for forbearance, a virtue he would find misplaced here. Note the parallel usage at *sarga* 12.3, App. I, No. 8, lines 28–29.

"take him prisoner" *tasya... nigraham*: Literally, "his imprisonment." The term *nigraha*, "imprisonment," can also be taken, as suggested by Cr, to mean physical punishment including execution (*daṇḍam*). This interpretation has been followed by Dutt (1893, p. 1146, "worthy of being slain") and Raghunathan (1982, vol. 3, p. 36, "he should be put to death").

19. Verse 19ab = App. I, No. 8, line 30 (cd variant of 31). See notes to 6.12.3.

"comes seeking refuge" *upasthitaḥ*: See note to verse 15 above.

"with instructions to kill you" *saṃdiṣṭaḥ... prahartum*: We follow the suggestion of Cg, who construes the participle in *pāda* b with the infinitive in *pāda* c. Ct, Cg, and Cm supply the phrase "by Rāvaṇa" after the participle "instructed (*saṃdiṣṭaḥ*)."

20. Verse 20ab is a variant of App. I, No. 8, line 32. See notes to 6.12.3.

Verse 20cd = App. I, No. 8, line 33. See notes to 6.12.3.

"harsh torture" *tīvreṇa daṇḍena*: Literally, "with severe punishment." Cg rises to the occasion by suggesting the specific tortures that should be applied. He interprets Sugrīva's general advice to mean that, "since it would not serve the purpose either to drive Vibhīṣaṇa off, as was done with Mārīca (1.29.14–15), or kill him humanely with a single arrow, as was done in the case of Vālin (4.16.34), they should set a wick or oily cloth on Vibhīṣaṇa's head and then set him alight, like a lamp, having first severed the heads of his retainers and placed them in his hands. (*vadhyatāṃ kevalanirasane kṛte mārīcavad anarthakārī syād iti bhāvaḥ. tīvreṇa daṇḍena vālivad ekena bāṇena na hantavyaḥ. kiṃtu śirasi vartiṃ kṛtvā dīpāropaṇaṃ kāryam. sacīvaiḥ saha prathamaṃ teṣāṃ śirāṃsi chittvā vibhīṣaṇahaste dattvā tato 'yam vadhyatām.*)

21. 21ab is a variant of App. I, No. 8, line 34. See notes to 6.12.3.

21cd = App. I, No. 8, line 35. See notes to 6.12.3.

22. "powerful Rāma" *rāmo mahābalaḥ*: D5,6,T1,3,M3,5, and the texts and printed editions of Cg read instead *mahāyaśāḥ*, "of great renown, illustrious."

24. "by a friend" *suhṛdā*: D6,10,11,M1,2, and the texts and printed editions of Ct and Cr read instead *suhṛdām*, "among friends, of [one's] friends." The sense then would be "[wishing the lasting well-being] of his friends."

"by . . . who is . . . virtuous" *satā*: We read this word adjectivally rather than simply as a participle. D5,6,10,11,T1,3,G2,M1,2, and the texts and printed editions of Ct read instead *sadā*, "always."

26. "Rāma, out of friendship . . . in order to show us honor" *ātmānaṃ pūjayan rāma . . . suhṛttayā*: Literally, "Rāma, honoring the self with friendship." One would normally expect the reflexive construction here to refer to Rāma's own self, but the context seems clearly to preclude such an interpretation. The commentators suggest a variety of interpretations of this slightly enigmatic expression. Ct offers two interpretations. In the first, which he shares with Ck, he reads the instrumental *suhṛttayā* with the participle *pūjayan*, "honoring," and takes it in the sense of "demonstrating your [i.e., Rāma's] friendly nature." For him, then, the expression means "you honor us by manifesting your friendly nature (*asmākam ātmānaṃ suhṛttayā suhṛdbhāvaprakāśanena pūjayann ity arthaḥ*)." According to Ct's second interpretation, the word *ātmānam* refers to Rāma, and the expression *suhṛtayā*, "out of friendship," refers specifically to Sugrīva, the lord of the monkeys. Thus the phrase would mean "spreading his own fame *or* glory by regarding the lord of the monkeys as his friend *or* ally (*yadvaivaṃ vānareśvaro 'py ayaṃ suhṛd ity ātmanaḥ kīrtiṃ prathayann ity arthaḥ*)."

Cr understands the phrase simultaneously in two different ways such that the term *ātmānam* refers both to the monkeys and to Rāma himself. He explains that Rāma, in asking as a friend, honors himself in that the monkeys have become his own body. In this case, the singular has to be taken in the sense of an entire class. Moreover, he is praising [himself] since, in asking the monkeys, he builds his reputation as someone who observes all the rules of propriety in that he does nothing without being counseled (*suhṛttayātmānaṃ svaśarīrabhūtavānaram ity arthaḥ pūjayann asmān pṛcchasy ātmānam ity atra jātyabhiprāyeṇaikavacanam. kiṃcātmānaṃ svaṃ pūjayann ayam atīvamaryādāpālako yad amantritaṃ kiṃcin na karotīti praśaṃsayan pṛcchasi*).

Cg and Cm, for whom *pūjayan* is a variant reading, see the singular as an indicator that Rāma is asking each monkey individually (*pratyekaṃ pūjayan mānayann asmān prcchasi*). Their second interpretation takes *ātmānam* in the sense of *ātmasvabhāvam*, "one's true nature," which they see as a reference to Rāma's instinctive grasp of the conduct of statecraft (*rājanīti*). They then gloss *pūjayan* as "observing, keeping (*pālayan*)," so that the phrase would mean "observing the rules of statecraft." Cg offers a third interpretation according to which Rāma is using his friendliness to demonstrate his own superior powers of judgment. According to this interpretation, Rāma solicits the monkeys' opinions only to supersede them with his own superior judgment (*asmanmatāni pūrvapakṣīkṛtya svamatam eva siddhāntayitum iti bhāvaḥ*).

M3 and the texts and printed editions of Cm and Cg read *sūcayañ jānan*, "indicating [and] knowing," for *pūjayan rāma*, "honoring, O Rāma." According to this reading, the line would mean "even though you know, you ask us out of friendship in order to point out your true nature." This is explained by Cg and Cm as "Your question is [asked] in order to spread throughout the world your fame as a friend to the monkeys (*ayaṃ vānarāṇāṃ suhṛd itīmāṃ kīrtiṃ loke khyāpayituṃ tavāyaṃ praśna ity arthaḥ*)."

27. "faithful to your vows" *satyavrataḥ*: Ct, Cg, and Cm understand this conventional epithet here to refer to Rāma's adherence to a vow of providing refuge to all who seek it, even *rākṣasas* (*rakṣaḥsv api śaraṇāgatarakṣaṇavratapālakaḥ*—Ct).

"act judiciously" *parīkṣyakārī*: Literally, "acting only after examination."

"trust your friends wholeheartedly" *nisṛṣṭātmā suhṛtsu*: Literally, "who has consigned one's self to one's friends." Ct and Ck understand, "[you] who trust your friends (*suhṛtsu kṛtaviśvāsaḥ*)." Cr, Cg, and Cm interpret more strongly in the sense of "[you] who make yourself dependent upon your friends (*suhṛdaparatantrīkṛtātmasvarūpaḥ*—so Cg)."

28. "your advisers" *sacivās tava*: Normally, we render the word *saciva* as "minister." However, since the monkey counselors here are not, strictly speaking, Rāma's ministers but rather those of Sugrīva, we have used the more general term.

"speak . . . on this matter" *bruvantu*: Literally, "let them speak."

"giving . . . sound arguments" *hetutaḥ*: Literally, "reasonably, logically."

"various" *punaḥ . . . punaḥ*: Literally, "over and over again."

29. "When they had spoken in this fashion" *ity ukte*: Literally, "when it had been spoken in this fashion." As noted by Ct, Cr, and Ck, the unexpressed subjects are the monkey ministers, Hanumān, etc.

"was the first to speak" *agrataḥ . . . uvāca*: Literally. "he spoke from the beginning." According to Ct, Cg, and Ck, Aṅgada has the right to speak first (after Sugrīva—Cg) because of his position as heir apparent to the monkey kingdom (4.25.35) (*aṅgado yuvarājatvād agrata uvāca*—Ct, Ck). See note to 6.51.10.

"concerning the interrogation of Vibhīṣaṇa" *vibhīṣaṇaparīkṣārtham . . . vacanam*: Literally, "speech for the purpose of the test *or* trial of Vibhīṣaṇa."

31. "To trust him" *saḥ*: Literally, "that." We have provided the phrase for the sake of clarity, following Cr, who glosses, "trusting one's enemies (*ripujanaviśvāsaḥ*)."

32. "advantages and disadvantages" *arthānarthau*: The compound occurs in *ManuSm* 8.24, where Bühler's translation (1886, p. 256) reads, "what is expedient or inexpedient." Doniger (1991, p. 154) renders, "what is intrinsically just and unjust." Cf. *ArthŚā* 1.1.11; 1.2.11; and 9.7.37–57. See, too, verse 44 and note below.

"if he is virtuous . . . if he is evil" *guṇataḥ . . . doṣataḥ*: Literally, "on the basis of good qualities . . . on the basis of bad qualities."

33. "preponderance of evil . . . preponderance of virtue" *doṣo mahān . . . guṇān . . . bahūn*: Literally, " a great defect . . . many virtues." As Cg makes clear, it is a question of

weighing the relative good and evil since it is difficult to find someone who is either wholly good or wholly bad (*nanu sarvātmanā guṇī doṣī vā durlabhaḥ*).

34. "But" *tu*: Cg and Cm claim that this particle *tu* indicates that Śarabha's advice is offered in contradiction to that of Aṅgada (*tuśabdaḥ pūrvasmād vailakṣaṇyaparaḥ*).

"sensible" *sārtham*: Literally, "meaningful." The critical edition here follows the texts of Ct, Ck, and Cr. D7,T2,3,G1,M3, and the texts and printed editions of Cg, Cm, and Cv read instead *sādhyam*, "practicable."

"spy" *cāraḥ*: See *ArthŚā* 1.11–12 and Dikshitar 1944, pp. 353–63. See 6.17.5 and note, and note to 5.3.27.

35. "would it be appropriate to accept Vibhīṣaṇa" *kāryo yathānyāyaṃ parigrahaḥ*: Literally, "an acceptance should be made [by one] according to the proper policy."

37. "at the wrong time and to the wrong place" *adeśakāle*: The commentators offer various explanations. Ct (so, too, Ck) says it is the wrong place because Vibhīṣaṇa has come to enemy territory without any message from his master (leaving his master's country—Ck), and it is the wrong time because one should not abandon one's lord at a time of trouble. (*svāmisaṃdeśaṃ* [*deśam*—Ck] *vihāya ripudeśa āgamanenānucitadeśaprāptatvam. svāminaḥ saṃkaṭakāle tatprahāṇānaucityād anucitakālaprāptaḥ.*) Cg says it is the wrong place in that there is no purpose in Vibhīṣaṇa's coming because he has come from afar when there is no imminent danger, and it is the wrong time for him to abandon his lord. (*dūratayā sāṃpratikabhayābhāvenāgamanaprayojanarahite. akāle svāmiparityāgānarhakāle.*) Cm believes that it is the wrong place because it is near one's enemies (*śatrusamīpadeśe*). Cv believes that it is the wrong place because the proper place would be the seashore near his own country (*apadeśe svadeśe pratyāsannasamudratīre*). Both Cm and Cv agree with Ct that the time is wrong because it is nighttime (*rātrau*), but Cm offers as an alternative the same explanation given by Cg. See verse 47 and note below.

38. At *Kiṣkindhākāṇḍa* 38.23, Mainda and Dvivida are said to be the sons of the Aśvins. In the *Sundarakāṇḍa* they are also said to have been granted invulnerability by Brahmā. See 5.58.12–16 and notes.

39. "interrogated" *pṛcchyatām*: Ct, Cg, and Cm, evidently influenced by verse 50 below, indicate that Mainda intends this questioning to be carried out by undercover agents (*gūḍhadūtamukhena*—Ct, Cm; *ajñātapuruṣamukhena*—Cg). Although Mainda himself makes no such specification of this condition, Cg believes that this is in keeping with Hanumān's suggestion, articulated at verse 50 below (*tathaiva hanumatānuvādāt*). See note to verse 50 below.

"regarding what Rāvaṇa has to say" *vacanaṃ nāma tasya ... rāvaṇasya*: Literally, "the very words of Rāvaṇa." D10,11,M1,2, and the texts and printed editions of Ct read *anujaḥ*, "younger brother," for *vacanam*, "words," yielding the sense "the younger brother of Rāvaṇa ought to be interrogated."

40. "accurately ... then" *tatas tattvam*: We read this adverbially with Cg and Cm, who gloss, "truly (*tattvataḥ*)." V1,D5,10,11,T1,G,M1,2,5, and the texts and printed editions of Ct, Cr, Cv, and Ck read instead *tattvatas tvam*, "accurately ... you."

41. "highly cultivated" *saṃskārasampannaḥ*: The commentators are in general agreement that this term refers to the cultivation that arises from knowledge of all the *śāstras* (*sakalaśāstrajñānajasaṃskārasaṃyuktaḥ*—so Ct).

42. "Bṛhaspati" *bṛhaspatiḥ*: Bṛhaspati, the legendary *purohita* of the gods, is held up here as an example of extraordinary learning. See App. I, No. 3, lines 362–65 (fol-

lowing notes to 6.9.22), where the name is employed similarly. See 6.7.9–10; 6.40.28; 6.115.51; and notes.

"besting you in argument" *bhavantam . . . atiśāyayitum . . . bruvan*: Literally, "surpassing you while [he is] speaking."

"capable" *samartham*: According to Ct and Ck, this term refers to Rāma's ability to ascertain the essence of all *śāstras* (*sakalaśāstrārthatattvanirūpaṇasamartham*—so Ct).

43. "Rāma, it is not in order to demonstrate my skill in disputation, my desire to outshine the others, a wish to prove myself the best, or fondness for the sound of my own voice that I shall say the following truthful words. Rather, your majesty, it is because of the gravity of the situation." *na vādān nāpi saṃgharṣān nādhikyān na ca kāmataḥ / vakṣyāmi vacanaṃ rājan yathārthaṃ rāma gauravāt //*: Literally, "Not from debate, or from rivalry, or from superiority, or from desire will I speak [this] truthful speech, O king, but from gravity." The verse is somewhat elliptical, and we have had to flesh it out a bit for the sake of intelligibility, in keeping with the fairly unanimous opinions of the commentators.

"in order to demonstrate my skill in disputation" *vādāt*: Literally, "because of debate." Ct explains, "in order to demonstrate my skill in debate (*tarkakuśalatvaprakaṭanād dhetoḥ*)." Other commentators explain similarly.

"my desire to outshine the others" *saṃgharṣāt*: Literally, "from *or* out of rivalry." Ct explains, "in the grip of rivalry with the other ministers (*sacivāntaraspardhāvaśāt*)." Other commentators explain similarly.

"a wish to prove myself the best" *ādhikyāt*: Literally, "from *or* out of superiority." Cm explains, "out of pride in [my own] superiority, which takes the form of the thought, 'I am the most intelligent, I am the most skilled in policy, I am the most eloquent, etc.' (*'ahaṃ dhīmān nītimān vāgmī ca' ity ādhikyābhimānāt*)." The quote, which is similar to Cg's, appears to be a paraphrase of the description Nārada gives of Rāma at 1.1.9. The idea, for these commentators, seems to be that Hanumān does not want to claim that he is superior to Rāma.

"fondness for the sound of my own voice" *kāmataḥ*: Literally, "out of desire." Ct explains, "out of a desire to speak (*vacanecchātaḥ*)." Cg and Cm gloss, "out of a desire to speak freely (*svairabhāṣaṇecchātaḥ*)." Cr offers "out of a desire whose focus is simply to say something (*kiṃcidgrahaṇādiviṣayakecchātaḥ*)." Cg provides an alternative explanation: "or it could mean 'out of favoritism for Vibhīṣaṇa' (*vibhīṣaṇapakṣapātād vā*)."

"gravity of the situation" *gauravāt*: Literally, "because of seriousness." We follow the commentators, who offer different ways of expressing "because of the gravity of the thing to be done (*kāryagauravād dhetoḥ*—Cm)." Cm offers, as an alternative, "or it could mean 'for the sake of [gaining] your respect' (*yadvā tvatkṛtāt sammānāt*)."

44. "ministers" *sacivaiḥ*: According to Ct, Cg, and Cm, Hanumān is specifically criticizing Aṅgada's advice offered above in verses 30–33. Cg comments that Hanumān avoids mentioning Aṅgada's name and uses the plural in order to avoid any transient animosity [on Aṅgada's part] (*sacivair aṅgadena tādātvikasaṃrambhaparihārāya nāmānuktir bahuvacanaṃ ca*).

"advantages and disadvantages" *-arthānartha-*: See notes to verse 32 above.

"impossible to put it into practice" *kriyā na hy upapadyate*: Literally, "action is not possible." Ct explains that the proposal of Aṅgada and the others to regard Vibhīṣaṇa as suspect until interrogated is fine as far as it goes, but it lacks any effective follow-up (so, too, Ck). (*śaṅkitavyaḥ parīkṣaṇīyaś ceti yad uktaṃ tad yuktam eva kiṃ tv evaṃ niścaya ity anukter idam anuttaram. tad evāha kriyā na hy upapadyate kriyottararūpā*—Ct.) He suggests, as an alternative, that even the action of investigation is not feasible (*yadvā parīkṣaṇarūpā kriyedānīṃ nopapadyata ity arthaḥ*). This alternative is reflected in the opinions of Cr, Cg, and Cm.

45. "whether he is trustworthy" *sāmarthyam*: Literally, "[his] capacity." Ct and Ck understand, "the propriety of either rejecting or accepting him (*hānopādānaucityam*)." Cr understands, "the power to do good or cause harm (*hitāhitasaṃpādakasamarthatvam*)." Cg and Cm, whom we have more closely followed, offer, "honesty (*sādhutvam*)" and "virtue (*sadguṇavattvam*)," respectively.

46. "your ministers" *sacivais tava*: The reference is to the advice of Śarabha in verses 34–35 above. See note to verse 44 above on the issue of Hanumān's diplomatic use of the generic plural when criticizing the advice of a particular individual.

"strategy" *kāraṇam*: Literally, "cause, valid reason." Ct, Ck, and Cr understand the term in its usual, literal sense, but we view this as somewhat redundant in light of the term *artha*, "purpose," in *pāda* c. Cv avoids this problem by arguing for the propriety of the variant reading *cāraṇam*, in the sense of "the dispatching *or* the movement of spies." Cg and Cm, whom we follow, acknowledge the variant but prefer the critical reading, understanding *kāraṇam* in its most basic sense of "action," which they take as a reference to strategy (*upāyaḥ*).

47. "Vibhīṣaṇa has come at the wrong time and to the wrong place" *adeśakāle saṃprāpta ity ayaṃ yad vibhīṣaṇaḥ*: Hanumān is paraphrasing Jāmbavān's words in verse 37 above. See, too, notes to verse 37 above.

"Consider it from my perspective." *tāṃ nibodha yathāmati*: Literally, "know *or* consider that in accordance with opinion." The phrase is slightly ambiguous in that one might also take the sequence to mean "Consider it according to your own way of thinking."

48–49. "For him to have left an evil person to come over to a virtuous one, in light of their vices and virtues, respectively" *puruṣāt puruṣaṃ prāpya tathā doṣaguṇāv api*: Literally, "having reached a man from a man and vice and virtue as well." Following the commentators, our translation fleshes out the elliptical clause. Thus, for example, Ct notes, "Having come to you, an excellent person, from an evil person, Rāvaṇa, and considering in his mind, that is, having considered in his mind the vices and virtues, respectively, of the two (*pāpāt puruṣād rāvaṇād uttamaṃ puruṣaṃ tvāṃ prāpya buddhyā niścitya tathā dvayos tayor doṣaguṇāv api prāpya buddhyā niścitya*—so Ct)."

"that is, having perceived the wickedness" *daurātmyam . . . dṛṣṭvā*: Literally, "having seen the wickedness." As the various commentators note, the reference is to Rāvaṇa's abduction of another man's wife (*paradārāpaharaṇād rāvaṇe daurātmyam*—so Ct) and his refusal to return her (*-tatpratyarpaṇāpekṣitvāt*—so Cg).

"heroism" *vikramam*: Cg sees this term as a reference to Rāma's having killed the foremost among the *rākṣasas*, having given the kingdom to Sugrīva, having first slain Vālin, and having made the effort to cross the ocean, so difficult to cross (*tvayi vikramaṃ kharadūṣaṇapramukharākṣasavadhādikaṃ vālivadhapūrvakasugrīvarājyapradānam atidustarasamudrataraṇodyogaṃ ca*). Ct understands that Rāma slew Vālin—who himself, having first put Rāvaṇa under his armpit, made a circumambulation of the four oceans (*Uttarakāṇḍa* 34)—with one arrow (*tvayi vikramaṃ ca kakṣapuṭe rāvaṇaṃ kṛtvā catuḥsāgarīṃ pradakṣiṇaṃ kṛtavato vālina ekenaiva bāṇena tvayā hananāt*). Cr understands similarly.

"in keeping with his excellent judgment" *tasya buddhitaḥ*: Literally, "according to intellect."

50. "undercover agents" *ajñātarūpaiḥ puruṣaiḥ*: Literally, "men whose [true] appearances are unknown." Ct, Cr, Cg, Cm, Cv, and Ck, keeping to the order of the speakers who preceded Hanumān, understand him to be refuting Mainda's suggestion here, although Mainda had made no explicit reference to the use of undercover agents (see verse 39 and note above). In fact, it was Śarabha who suggested the use of spies (see verses 34–35 and notes above). According to Ct and Ck, the reference is to "spies whose families, activities, and purposes are unknown (*ajñātakulaśīlaprayojanaiḥ puruṣaiḥ*)." According to Cg and Cm, these are "people whose appearance and true nature are unfamiliar [to Vibhīṣaṇa] (*aparicitasvarūpasvabhāvaiḥ*)." Cv observes that these are "monkeys whose appearance would be unfamiliar (*anabhyastarūpair vānaraiḥ*)."

51. "questions" *vacaḥ*: Literally, "word, speech."

"alienated" *praduṣyeta*: Literally, "he would be spoiled, corrupted."

52. "confident in his own ability" *naipuṇyaṃ paśyatā bhṛśam*: Literally, "by one who clearly sees cleverness." The phrase is somewhat obscure. Cg and Cm understand the reference to be to the deceitful interrogator who perceives his own skill or cleverness (*bhṛśam atyarthaṃ svasmin naipuṇyāṃ paśyatāpi mithyā praṣṭrā*). This is plausible, and our own translation is not very different. Raghunathan (1982, vol. 3, p. 39), the only other translator rendering the critical reading, offers, "however clever he might fancy himself." One could also reasonably understand, "who clearly sees through the cleverness [of the suspected enemy]." D10 and the texts and printed editions of Ct read *paśyatām*, "you, sir, must see," for *paśyatā*, yielding such translations as "determine... his secret motive" (Dutt 1893, p. 1148) and "you should fully discover the good intentions" (Gita Press 1969, vol. 3, p. 1423). Shastri (1959, vol. 3, p. 40), following Roussel (1903, vol. 3, p. 45), translates in such a way as to make it unclear how the phrase is read.

"on the basis of what he says about himself" *antaḥsvabhāvair gītais taiḥ*: Literally, "through those inner feelings, which are sung out." Cg, Cv, and Cm read with the critical text but understand the phrase differently. Cg understands, "inner intentions of a stranger that are expressed in words (*antarhitasvābhiprāyaiḥ . . . parasya gītair bhāṣitaiḥ*)." Cm and Cv understand these to be "the inner intentions [of the interrogator] expressed in the form of questions (*gūḍhābhiprāyaiḥ tair gītaiḥ praśnarūpabhāṣitaiḥ*—Cm)." Texts and printed editions of Ct, Cr, and Ck read instead *antareṇa svarair bhinnaiḥ*, "by different sounds in the midst [of questioning]." According to Ct and Ck, what Hanumān is saying is "In the midst of the interrogation you, sir, should find out, that is, determine, the cleverness, that is, the virtue or vice, [of the subject] on the basis of different sounds, i.e., distorted sounds, such as hemming and hawing. You, sir, should determine the truthfulness or dishonesty of a person by such verbal manifestations as a tearful voice and stammering through fear. (*antareṇa vyavahāramadhye bhinnaiḥ svarair vilakṣaṇasvaraiḥ kaṇṭhadhvanibhir naipuṇyaṃ sadasadanyataratvaniścayaṃ paśyatāṃ kurutāṃ bhavān iti śeṣas tatra bāṣpakaṇṭhatve bhītyā pūrvāparāsaṃgatakathane cāsann anyathā sann iti niścīyatām*—so Ct.)" Ct and Ck insist that this is the correct reading. Cr understands that the stranger placed in the midst (*antareṇa*) of one's own forces may speak variously, sometimes favoring one's own side and sometimes that of one's enemies, and from this one could determine his intentions on the basis of these various utterances. (*svasainyamadhye sthāpaneneti śeṣaḥ. bhinnair asmatpriyaviṣayatayā ripupriyaviṣayatayā ca bhedaviśiṣṭaiḥ svarair vāgvyāpāraiḥ.*)

53. "signs of a wicked nature" *duṣṭabhāvatā*: Literally, "the state of having evil feelings." As Ct notes, a person's inner feelings can be determined by outward physical manifestations. He glosses, "the state of having an evil heart [as manifested] by speech, gestures, etc. (*vacanaceṣṭādibhir duṣṭāntaḥkaraṇatā*)."

"facial expression" *vadanam*: Literally, "face."

"composed" *prasannam*: This could also mean "open, clear, *or* kindly."

54. "A deceitful person" *śaṭhaḥ*: Literally, "rogue, villain." Cr, against the other commentators, glosses, "knavery (*śaṭhatvam*)" and takes this as the subject of the verb *parisarpati*, understanding, "therefore, knavery does not approach him (*śaṭhatvaṃ na parisarpati asmin prāpnoti*)." Cg, Ck, and Ct understand, "a person whose hostile actions [intentions—Ct, Ck] are concealed (*gūḍhavipriyakārī*—so Ct; *-dhī*—so Ck)."

"without hesitation" *aśaṅkitamatiḥ*: Literally, "whose mind is without doubt *or* fear." Ct and Ck offer a Śrīvaiṣṇava interpretation of the term, explaining that it should be understood to indicate that Vibhīṣaṇa has firmly resolved that the best path of action for him is to seek refuge with Rāma (*niścitaśaraṇagamanamatī rāmaśaraṇagamanam eva mameṣṭasādhanam iti supratiṣṭhitacittaḥ*—so Ct).

"Moreover, he is well spoken" *na cāsya duṣṭā vāk*: Literally, "and his speech is not corrupt." Ct and Ck read the compound *duṣṭavāk*, "corrupt speech," and gloss, "speech containing defects of both sound and sense (*śabdārthadoṣavatī vāk*)." See notes to 6.14.5.

"one should harbor no doubts about him" *nāstīha saṃśayaḥ*: Literally, "there is no doubt here." D7,10,11,G2,3,M5, and the texts and printed editions of Ct and Cr read *me nāsti* for *nāstīha*, which is a repetition of the closing phrase of the preceding verse and yields the sense "I have no doubt."

55. "facial expression" *ākāraḥ*: We follow Cg in taking this term in its common sense of facial expression, particularly as betraying inner emotions (Apte s.v.). Compare *RaghuVa* 1.20. Ct, Cr, and Ck take the term to mean "the inner emotions (*āntaro bhāvaḥ*—Ct, Ck)" or "one's own intentions (*svābhiprāyaḥ*—Cr)." Cr then takes the term *ākāra* to function as the object of *pādas* ab and the subject of *pādas* cd. He thus understands the verse to mean "that the *ākāras*, i.e., inner emotions, are impossible to conceal and these same *ākāras*, i.e., inner emotions, betray one's intentions (*ākāraḥ svābhiprāyaḥ . . . sarvathā chādayituṃ na śakyo 'ta eva nṛṇām antargataṃ bhāvam abhiprāyam . . . vivṛṇoti*)." Otherwise, like Ct and Ck, we are obliged to provide a deus ex machina, as it were, in the form of one's inner presiding divinity (*antaryāmidevatā*—Ct).

56. "foremost of those who know what action should be taken" *kāryavidāṃ vara*: Literally, "O best among those who know what is to be done." This epithet echoes the word *kārya*, "action," which immediately precedes it. See below.

"action" *kāryam*: We, like Cg, understand this verse to embody an exhortation to Rāma based on the rules of *nītiśāstra*. It appears to us that in adducing this general principle, Hanumān is implicitly urging Rāma to act expeditiously to accept Vibhīṣaṇa as an ally, as he will urge explicitly in verse 58 below. Ct, Ck, and Cr, however, understand the verse to be a comment on the propriety of Vibhīṣaṇa's action in having come over to Rāma at this particular time and place (*asyedam atrāgamanaṃ rūpaṃ kāryaṃ deśakālopapannam eva*).

57–58. "mighty undertaking" *udyogam*: Literally, "effort." As several commentators (Ct, Ck, Cs) point out, this word refers to Rāma's campaign to destroy Rāvaṇa (*rāvaṇavadhaviṣayam*—Ck, Ct).

"vainglory of Rāvaṇa" *mithyāvṛttaṃ ca rāvaṇam*: Literally, "that Rāvaṇa acts in vain *or* falsely." Commentators are divided as to how to interpret the adjective. Ct and Ck suggest that it encompasses both Rāvaṇa's false pride in his power as well as his evil conduct (*mithyābalagarvitaṃ pāpavṛttaṃ ca*). Cr takes it to refer only to the vanity of Rāvaṇa's undertakings, while Cs sees it as a reference only to his evil ways.

"seeks the kingship for himself" *rājyaṃ prārthayamānaḥ*: As Ct, Ck, Cr, and Cs suggest, Vibhīṣaṇa, seeing the parallels between the political situations in Laṅkā and Kiṣkindhā, assumes that Rāma will kill the wicked older brother and consecrate the virtuous younger brother in his place (*rāvaṇād apy adhikabalaṃ vālinaṃ hataṃ śrutvā buddhipūrvaṃ vālivad eva rāvaṇaṃ haniṣyati sugrīvavad eva mahyaṃ rājyaṃ dāsyati*—so Ct).

"Keeping all this foremost in mind" *etāvat tu puraskṛtya*: Literally, "putting this much forward."

59. "that the *rākṣasa* is trustworthy" *rākṣasasyārjavaṃ prati*: Literally, "with reference to the honesty of the *rākṣasa*."

"of what is to follow" *śeṣasya*: Literally, "of the remainder." Cr glosses, "the decision as to what ought to be done (*kṛtyanirṇayasya*)."

Sarga 12

1. "his mind composed" *prasannātmā*: Literally, "whose mind was calm." Cm and Cg argue, not implausibly, that we should understand that Rāma's thoughts, which had been confused by the differing opinions of the monkeys who spoke before Hanumān, have now been clarified by the latter monkey's advice (*sugrīvādivākyaiḥ kaluṣīkṛte manasi sati hanumadvākye prasannamanāḥ*—so Cg).

"speech of Hanumān, son of Vāyu" *vāyusutasya*: Literally, "of the son of Vāyu." We have supplied, as do the commentators, the missing word for speech (*vāyusutasya vacanam iti śeṣaḥ*—so Ct) and have added the name Hanumān.

"unassailable" *durdharṣaḥ*: Cg suggests that this more or less standard epithet refers here to Rāma's inability to be shaken "by the imperfect arguments of his advisers (*pūrvapakṣair akṣobhyaḥ*)."

"learned" *śrutavān*: Ct and Cr give the normal interpretation, "learned in all the *śāstras* (*sakalaśāstraśravaṇavān*—so Ct)." Cg, however, understands this term to be a reference to parables such as those of the dove and of the sage Kaṇḍu (verses 11–18 below), which he would have heard from Vasiṣṭha and others (*vasiṣṭhādibhyaḥ śruta-kapotakaṇḍūpākhyānādimān*).

"with his own thoughts" *ātmani sthitam*: Literally, "what was situated in his mind." This apparently refers to Rāma's decision and is glossed by Cg as "what was firmly fixed in his thoughts (*cittāvasthitam*)."

2. "that I would like you... to hear in its entirety" *śrutam icchāmi tat sarvaṃ bhavadbhiḥ*: Literally, "I want all that heard by you." B4,D6,7,9–11,T,G2,3,M, and the texts and printed editions of Ct, Cr, Cg, and Cm read the slightly syntactically awk-

ward infinitive *śrotum*, "to hear." Commentators who share the variant reading come up with various paraphrases to express the desired meaning.

3. Not surprisingly, Cg takes Rāma's pledge as the inspiration for an extensive and close analysis of the verse in terms of its Śrīvaiṣṇava significance. He is particularly eager to stress the idea, often encountered in the devotional literature, that it makes no difference to the Lord if those who seek refuge with him have faults and that, moreover, it is more virtuous for him to take in the wicked than the virtuous.

"Under no circumstances would I turn away... For the virtuous would condemn such conduct." *na tyajeyaṃ kathaṃcana / ... satām etad agarhitam*: Literally, "I would by no means abandon... that is not condemned by [of] the virtuous." The double negative construction makes a literal rendering in English somewhat opaque. What Rāma means is that turning away a suppliant would be condemned by the virtuous. We have therefore rendered *agarhitam*, "not condemned," as "condemned." See note to 6.37.10 for other examples of double negatives in the text.

Following verse 3, D5–7,10,11,S insert a passage of thirty-five lines [App. I, No. 8 = GPP, NSP, KK, VSP 6.18.4–20]: "Then Sugrīva, bull among the tawny monkeys, repeating those words to himself and reflecting on them, spoke these excellent words:[1–2] 'What do we care for this night-roaming *rākṣasa*, whether he is good or evil, a person who would abandon his own brother who is confronting such a calamity?[3–4] Who would he then not abandon no matter what their relationship might be?'[1] Upon hearing those words of the lord of the monkeys, truly valorous Kākutstha gazed at them all and, with a faint smile, addressed these words to Lakṣmaṇa of auspicious marks:[5–8] 'Unless someone has deeply studied the *śāstras* and attended upon his elders, he could not possibly speak the way the lord of the tawny monkeys has spoken.[9–10] But there is, it seems to me, a practical[2] but subtle matter that is openly known to all kings.[11–12] In times of crisis, one's kinsmen and one's neighbors become known as enemies and strike at one. He must have come here for that reason.[13–14] Virtuous rulers of good family hold their kinsmen who wish them well in high esteem. Yet it often happens that kings come to view a virtuous man with suspicion.[15–16] Now as to the error of which you spoke, that is, accepting one of the enemy's forces, I will tell you something on that subject that is in keeping with the *śāstras*. Please listen.[17–18] We are not of his lineage, and this *rākṣasa* covets the kingship. Some *rākṣasas*, moreover, are shrewd; therefore we should accept Vibhīṣaṇa.[19–20] They may assemble[3] calmly and happily, but still some great disagreement[4] may erupt and, for that reason, fear has arisen in him.[5] In this way, dissension arises among them. Therefore we should accept Vibhīṣaṇa.[21–23] Not all brothers, dear brother, are similar to Bharata. Not all sons act toward their fathers as I have done. Not all friends are like you, sir.'[24–25] Addressed in this fashion by Rāma, wise Sugrīva, along with Lakṣmaṇa, rose and humbly spoke these words:[26–27] 'You must realize that Rāvaṇa has sent Vibhīṣaṇa as a spy. You always know what is appropriate, but I think it would be appropriate to take him prisoner.[28–29] Cloaking himself in deception,[6] this *rākṣasa* has come seeking refuge with deceitful intent and with instructions to kill you once he has gained your trust or mine, or Lakṣmaṇa's, blameless and great-armed one. [30–31] He should be put to death together with his ministers. For he is Vibhīṣaṇa, the brother of cruel Rāvaṇa.'[32–33] When Sugrīva had spoken in this fashion to the foremost of the Raghus, himself skilled in speech, that eloquent leader of the troops fell silent.[34–35]"

[1]"no matter what their relationship might be" *ko nāma sa bhavet tasya*: Literally, "indeed who would he be to him."

[2]"practical" *laukikam*: Literally, "pertaining to this world."

[3]"They may assemble" *te bhaviṣyanti saṃgatāḥ*: D6,T1,2,G,M, and the texts and printed editions of Cg and Cm read the negative particle *na*, "not," for the nominative plural pronoun *te*, "they." This lends the line the sense "they [the *rākṣasas*] will not assemble happily and peacefully."

[4]"disagreement" *pravādaḥ*: D6,7,10,11,T3,G3,M1,2, and the texts and printed editions (VSP reads with the critical) of Cm, Cg, Ct, Ck, and Cr read instead *praṇādaḥ*, "uproar." All translators consulted render this variant as either referring to the loud outcry of Vibhīṣaṇa (so Cg) or the loud cry of conflict (so Ct).

[5]"for that reason . . . in him" *tato 'sya*: D10,11, and the texts and printed editions of Ct read instead *anyonyasya*, "of one another."

[6]"Cloaking himself in deception . . . once he has gained your trust or mine" *viśvaste pracchannaḥ*: Literally, "[once you and I] trust [him] . . . [he,] concealed." D7,10,11, and the texts and printed editions of Ct repeat the participle *viśvaste*, yielding the sense "once [you] trust [him] . . . [and I] trust [him]."

Lines 28–35 closely parallel or duplicate verses 6.11.18–21 above.

4. = GPP 6.18.35.

D5–7,10,11,S read verses 4–7 after verse 21 (= GPP, KK = 6.18.35–38; VSP = 6.18.37–40).

5. = GPP 6.18.36; see note to verse 4 above.

6. = GPP 6.18.37; see note to verse 4 above.

Cg and Cm note, perhaps not without some irony, that this is the same Sugrīva who moments before suggested that Vibhīṣaṇa be tortured to death (see 6.11.20 above) (*mama vadhyatām eṣa tīvreṇa daṇḍenety uktavato 'pi*—Cg). As Ct notes, Sugrīva's change of heart is attributable to the opinion expressed by Rāma (*tvadvākyaśravaṇāt*).

"on the basis of his probable intentions" *bhāvāt*: The word has a broad range of meanings, two of which are perhaps relevant here: "emotion *or* intention" and "condition *or* state of being." We follow Cg's first of two alternatives. In the first, he glosses, "from signs such as the calmness of his face, which betray his true feelings (*bhāvabodhakān mukhaprasādādiliṅgāt*)." The second alternative understands *bhāvāt* as "because of that state of being *or* nature," that is, "through his gentle nature, which is illuminated by his piteous tone (*ārtadhvaniprakāśitamṛdusvabhāvāt*)."

7. = GPP 6.18.38; see note to verse 4 above.

8. = GPP 6.18.21; see note to verse 4 above.

9. "is . . . not . . . incapable . . . ?" *kim . . . aśaktaḥ*: Northern and some southern manuscripts (D9,10,11,G,M1), as well as the printed editions of Lahore, Gorresio, GPP, and NSP, read *śaktaḥ*, "capable," for *aśaktaḥ*. This reading yields the sense of "what harm . . . is he capable of causing me." Cr regards the question to be ironic (*kākuḥ*), with the sense of "he cannot cause me any harm." The interrogative *kim* in the critical reading, if it is to have any sense at all, must be taken—as we have done—as an

indeclinable, which makes the entire sentence a question, rather than pronominally with *ahitam*, "harm," as in the variant reading.

10. Ct and Ck, anticipating the question as to why Rāma does not, in fact, destroy Rāvaṇa and the *rākṣasas* himself since he is so powerful, allude to the conditions of the boon of Rāvaṇa, noting that Rāma himself, i.e., Viṣṇu, has granted the *rākṣasa* his invulnerability to the powers of the divinities. He also notes that Rāma wishes to remain within the limits of the human birth he has chosen, as illustrated by his weeping over his separation from Sītā, his alliance with the monkeys, etc. (*svadivyabhāvaṃ svaśaktyaivāntardhāya mānuṣamaryādāyāṃ sthityā tadbhāvaprakaṭanāyaiva sītāviyogaprayuktarodanavadbhavādṛśasahāyamelanam*). On Rāvaṇa's boon, see note to 6.28.28–29. Ck, citing "Yadvābhaṭṭa"—apparently paraphrasing Cg's comment ("from an absence of desire, not from an absence of ability, is there an absence of killing him [*icchābhāvād eva tadvadhābhāvo na tv aśaktyeti bhāvaḥ*])"—remarks that the reason Rāma does not kill all the *rākṣasas* of Laṅkā is not because of his lack of power but because he does not wish to do so (*yadvābhaṭṭas tu kimartham aṅgulyagreṇa tān sarvān rākṣasān ity atrāha—icchann iti mama tathāhanana icchā nāsti na tu śaktyabhāvād ity arthaḥ*). Compare 6.67.37, where Rāma expressly forbids the killing of all the *rākṣasas*. On the relationship among the commentators, see Introduction, pp. 99–107. See, too, Lefeber 1994, p. 24 and footnote 77; and notes to 3.2.56 and 3.33.15,44. Cf. note to 5.1.77. See, too, notes to 6.52.10 and 6.80.1.

11. = *MBh* 12.141.4 [*pūjitaḥ* for *arcitaḥ*]: The story of the virtuous and self-sacrificing dove is narrated at length at *MBh* 12.141–145. (The story is also known to the *Hitopadeśa* 1.41; *Pañcatantra* III.140,141; and *MBh* 3.130.19–20; 3.131ff.). Since the story is alluded to so elliptically here, the commentators flesh it out. According to the tale, a hunter, suffering from cold and hunger, cages a dove hen that has gone out to seek food for its mate. Eventually the starving hunter, seeking shelter, arrives at the tree where the waiting male resides. The virtuous dove, urged by his wife and seeing the suffering of the hunter, manages to build him a fire for warmth and, at length, hurls himself into it to offer the hunter a cooked meal of his own flesh. The hunter is overwhelmed by the bird's extraordinarily righteous behavior, which is followed by the bird's mate promptly hurling herself into the fire as the world's first, and perhaps only, avian *satī*. The birds ascend to heaven lauded by gods and sages. Upon seeing their celestial bliss, the hunter resolves to give up his evil way of life and adopt the life of a religious mendicant. After some time, he hurls himself into a forest fire and is thus able to rejoin his feathered friends in heaven. Cg sees in this story a parallel to the tale in the *Rāmāyaṇa* of the sage Śarabhaṅga, who immolates himself after receiving the *darśan* of Rāma and so ascends to the highest heaven (3.4.31–36).

"There is a well-known story" *śrūyate*: Literally, "it is heard."

"about a dove" *kapotena*: Dave (1985, pp. 24–27, 250–64) notes that the term *kapota* may refer to pigeons (*pārāvata*) and doves, as well as nuthatches. He notes, too, that many varieties of doves and pigeons are mentioned in Sanskrit literature.

"showed great hospitality" *arcitaś ca yathānyāyam*: Literally, "[the hunter] was honored according to custom."

"enemy" *śatruḥ*: As the commentators note, it is the capture of the dove's wife that has made the hunter his enemy (*bhāryāhartṛtvāt kapotaśatrur vyādhaḥ*).

"had come seeking shelter" *śaraṇam āgataḥ*: Cm, Ct, Cr, Ck, and, as a second alternative, Cg take the term in its sense of "home, abode," which they explain as the tree in which the male dove was dwelling (*vanaspatirūpagṛham*). See 6.10.17 and note. Cf. 6.13.13 and note. These commentators are apparently uncomfortable with the idea of a man seeking refuge with a bird. Cg's first interpretation is that the hunter is actually not seeking refuge with the bird but rather addressing himself to the tree divinity that presides over the doves' nesting spot (*svāvāsavanaspatidevatāṃ pratyuktavān na tu kapotam*). This interpretation is in keeping with the *Mahābhārata* story, where the hunter takes shelter for the night under the tree and seeks refuge from the divinities that inhabit it. To this end, Cg quotes a variant of *MBh* 12.141.26.

"He even offered him his own flesh" *svaiś ca māṃsair nimantritaḥ*: Literally, " He [the hunter] was invited with his [the bird's] own flesh."

12. "best of monkeys" *vānaraśreṣṭha*: Cg understands that the story is to remind Sugrīva that, since he is the overlord of the monkeys, he, too, should adhere to the *dharma* of protection of those who come to him for refuge (*bhavān vānarādhipatye sthitaḥ san svajātidharma iti śaraṇāgatarakṣaṇam*). Cg illustrates this theme of animals' adherence to the *dharma* of protection by narrating a story about a monkey (*vānara*) who saved a tribal hunter from a tiger by granting him shelter in his tree. Even after the evil-minded hunter had obliged the tiger by trying to throw down his sleeping protector, the monkey refused to yield up his refugee. This story is alluded to later in the critical edition (6.101.34–35 = GPP 6.113.4), where several of the commentators repeat a variant of the story of the virtuous monkey/bear (*ṛkṣa*).

"wife's abductor" *bhāryāhartāram*: Cg sees the reference as an indication that Rāma's intention is to suggest that, even if Rāvaṇa himself were to come seeking refuge, Rāma would grant it (*evam eva rāvaṇa āgataś ced asmābhiḥ kārya ity abhiprāyaḥ*).

"person such as I" *madvidho janaḥ*: Various commentaries take this as an allusion to Rāma's noble birth (*uttamakulaprasūtaḥ*—Cr), his knowing the secret of all *dharma* (*sakaladharmarahasyavettā*—so Ct), his being an authority on all *śāstras* (*sakalaśāstrādhikārī*—so Cm), and his belonging to the dynasty of the Raghus, who are noted for their devotion to the protection of all (*śaraṇāgatarakṣaṇāya samucchritadhvaje raghuvaṃśe jātaḥ*—so Cg).

13. Cg, Ct, Cr, and Cs argue that Rāma repeats the verses of the sage Kaṇḍu in anticipation of an objection that the virtues of a mere animal, a dove in this case, cannot be regarded as exemplary. Cs goes so far as to regard the virtuous bird's "conduct as purely accidental, like 'the scribbling of an ant' (*pipīlikālipivad yādṛcchikatvān na taccceṣṭā dharme pramāṇī syāt*)."

"verses ... chanted long ago" *gāthāṃ pūrā gītām*: Literally, *gāthā* means "chant, stanza." The term normally refers to metrical verses of a religious or moral nature that are not found in the *vedas*. Cg notes that "because of the musical quality of the stanza[s] that was present long ago, they are capable of being sung even now (*ṛca eva sāmatvāt pūrā vidyamānām evedānīṃ gīyamānāṃ gītām*)." He further comments that, because the verses were sung long ago, we should not imagine that they were composed by Kaṇḍu (*purā gītāṃ kaṇḍukalpiteyam iti na mantavyam*).

"by ... Kaṇḍu" *kaṇḍunā*: A sage of this name is mentioned at 4.47.10–12 (see ad loc. and note), where he is said to have cursed the forest where his young son died.

"great ... seer" *paramarṣiṇā*: Cs observes that this epithet, which indicates that Kaṇḍu is a greater seer than his father, suggests that one should give great respect to the verses being chanted (*pitur ṛṣitvam etasya paramarṣitvam iti tadgītā kathādartavyety anena sūcayati*). He notes that the epithet is specifically added in keeping with the maxim that "a son does not become learned through the learning of his father (*na hi pituḥ pāṇḍityena putraḥ paṇḍito bhavati*)."

14. "scorcher of your foes" *paraṃtapa*: Cg and Cm remind us that this vocative refers to whomever (a king—according to Cg) Kaṇḍu was addressing. Cg adds that the sense is that Kaṇḍu was saying to his auditor, "What is the use of your valor in the case of a person who has come to you for refuge? You should save that for your enemies." (*kaṇḍur api kaṃcid rājānaṃ pratyuktavān iti gamyate. paraṃtapa śaraṇāgate kiṃ pauruṣaprakaṭanena pratyarthiṣu khalu tat kartavyam iti bhāvaḥ.*)

"begging for protection" *yācantam*: Literally, "begging." Ck, Ct, and Cr supply an object, such as "his own protection (*svarakṣaṇam*—Cr)" or "refuge (*śaraṇam*—Ck, Ct)."

15. "Even at the cost of his own life" *prāṇān parityajya*: Literally, "having abandoned life breaths."

"magnanimous" *kṛtātmanā*: Cf. 5.6.17 and 5.34.47 and notes.

16. "and the limits of one's strength" *yathāsattvam*: Ś,Ñ1,D1,2,8,10–12,T3,G1,M1,2, and the texts and printed editions of Cm, Cr, and Ct read instead *yathānyāyam*, "properly."

"greed" *kāmāt*: Literally, "out of desire." We interpret according to Cm, who glosses, "out of expectation of some reward from one's enemies (*śatroḥ sakāśāt kiñcitphalāpekṣaṇāt*)."

17. As the commentators point out, this verse shows that someone who fails to offer protection to a refugee suffers for his inaction not only in this world, as indicated in verse 16 above, but in the next as well by losing all his previously accumulated merit. The verse is somewhat elliptical, and we have had to paraphrase to make it intelligible.

"should die for want of protection" *vinaṣṭaḥ . . . arakṣitaḥ*: Literally, "is destroyed unprotected."

"while the person who could have saved him merely looks on" *paśyatas tasya rakṣiṇaḥ*: Literally, "of a protector looking on *or* watching [i.e., without doing anything to save the supplicant]."

"the former would depart from this world" *gacchet*: Literally, "he would go."

"the latter's" *tasya*: Literally, "his."

18. Ct and Ck understand this verse to be Rāma's speech, the *gāthās* of Kaṇḍu having ended with verse 17. Cg explicitly states that, in this verse, the speaker, i.e., Rāma, is summing up the essence of the four-verse speech of Kaṇḍu (verses 14–17 above). Cm seems ambiguous on this point.

"it blocks the path to heaven" *asvargyam*: Literally, "unheavenly."

"destroys one's reputation" *ayaśasyam*: Literally, "inglorious."

"strength and valor" *balavīrya-*: This is another of those pairs of close synonyms of which Vālmīki is so fond (see notes on 5.7.12 and 5.7.40). The commentators explain the terms variously. Thus, Ck and Ct read this pair as a *karmadhāraya* rather than a *dvandva* in the sense of "that power, i.e., the capacity to punish or reward that is produced through the power of asceticism (*tapobalajaṃ yad vīryaṃ nigrahānugrahasāmarthyam*)." Cr, reading a *dvandva*, understands, "physical strength and sensory acuity (*śarīrendriyabalayoḥ*)." Cg reads the compound as we do, glossing, "physical strength and valor (*śarīrabalavīryayoḥ*)." See note to 6.2.14.

19. "at the time of one's final reward" *phalodaye*: Literally, "at the arising of fruit *or* reward."

20. Cg, Ct, and Ck naturally take this verse as an occasion for a discussion of the Lord's compassionate nature.

"always" *sakṛd eva*: Literally, "one time, always, at once." Cr, Cg, and Cm all take the adverb in its sense of "once *or* one time (*ekavāram eva*)," which they then construe with the adjective *prapanna*, "seeking shelter," yielding the sense "who come for shelter even once." Ct understands similarly. One could also take the adverb in its sense of "at once, immediately," thus yielding the sense "I grant protection at once."

"to all beings" *sarvabhūtebhyaḥ*: Cg, Ck, and Ct want to read this as an ablative (*pañcamī*) as well as a dative (*caturthī*), that is, "from all beings," as well as "to all beings."

"protection" *abhayam*: Literally, "freedom from fear *or* security." Ck and Ct argue that Rāma's protection is twofold. It is both eternal, as it grants one freedom from the fear of rebirth, and temporal, in that it grants freedom from the fear of death arising from such creatures as Rāvaṇa. The latter, they argue, is a synecdoche for all dangers in this world, such as the depredations of thieves, enemies, etc. (*atra tātkālikam ātyantikaṃ cety ubhayavidham apy abhayadānaṃ pratijñāyate. tatrātyantikaṃ saṃsārabhayoparatirūpam. dvitīyaṃ tu rāvaṇād ita utthitamṛtyubhayanivṛttirūpam idaṃ corārigrahanimittakābhayadānasyāpy upalakṣaṇam.*)

"I place myself in your hands." *tavāsmi*: Literally, "I am yours." Ct and Ck interpret this as a statement of total worshipful submission to the Lord, fleshing the phrase out with terms indicative of various critical relationships of inequality, such as "I am the servant, you are the master; I am the disciple, you are the *guru*; I am the seeker of protection, you are the protector, etc. (*ahaṃ sevakas tvaṃ me svāmī, ahaṃ śiṣyas tvaṃ guruḥ, ahaṃ rakṣyas tvaṃ rakṣakaḥ, ity evam upāsanāṃ kurvate*)."

21. "I will grant" *dattam* ... *mayā*: Literally, "I have given."

"Vibhīṣaṇa or Rāvaṇa himself" *vibhīṣaṇo vā* ... *rāvaṇaḥ svayam*: Ct, Ck, and Cm understand that Rāma is entertaining the possibility that Rāvaṇa, through his power of taking on forms at will (or in disguise [*vibhīṣaṇaveṣadhārī*—Cm], may have assumed the appearance of Vibhīṣaṇa (*kāmarūpatayākārāntarāvaṣṭambhavān iti śeṣaḥ*). Cg gives this as one of his alternative explanations. His others are:

1) Rāma would like to grant refuge to Rāvaṇa because to grant refuge to such a cruel creature as he is would demonstrate his [Rāma's] superior powers to a far greater extent than the protection of virtuous Vibhīṣaṇa and, moreover, would have the desirable consequence of saving all the inhabitants of Laṅkā rather than only the four ministers who have accompanied Vibhīṣaṇa. (*vibhīṣaṇas tu dharmātmeti vibhīṣaṇasvīkāro karmavatsvīkāratayā notkarṣāya. rāvaṇasya nṛśaṃsasyeti rāvaṇasvīkāra evotkarṣaḥ syād iti. vibhīṣaṇasvīkāre tatparikarāś catvāra eva rakṣitāḥ syuḥ. rāvaṇasvīkāre tu laṅkāsthāḥ sarve 'pi rakṣitāḥ syur iti mahān lābhaḥ.*)
2) Because of Vibhīṣaṇa's close relationship to Rāvaṇa, he himself is still seriously suspect (*yadi vā rāvaṇaḥ svayaṃ yatsaṃbandhena vibhīṣaṇe 'py atiśaṅkā sa evāstu*).
3) He may be Rāvaṇa himself who has come here without bringing Sītā (*svayaṃ sītām apuraskṛtya svayam āgato rāvaṇo vā vāstu*).

Cg concludes this discussion by suggesting that what Rāma means to say to Sugrīva is that he is simply to fetch their visitor without announcing "You are really Rāvaṇa and not Vibhīṣaṇa. (*tvam api rāvaṇo 'yaṃ na tu vibhīṣaṇa iti vijñāpanāyāpi punar nāgaccheḥ. kiṃ tv ānayaivety arthaḥ.*)"

On the order of the verses in the vulgate, see notes to verse 4 above.

22. The meter is *vaṃśasthavila*.

The placement of this verse in the critical edition and/or the placement of Sugrīva's speech appear to be highly suspect both on contextual and textual grounds. The longer meter is, of course, normally found at the end of a *sarga*, and the placement of this verse seems reasonable in the southern recension and the *devanāgarī* manuscripts aligned with it. In those manuscripts and editions, the arrangement of verses (see notes to verses 3 and 4 above) places the speech of Sugrīva (= critical edition verses 5–7) immediately before this longer-metered verse (critical edition verse 22), thus making the narrative sequence plausible. Ś1,Ñ,B,V1–3,D1–4,8,9,12 read this after verse 7 (Ś2 omits). The Lahore edition substitutes a completely different verse (213* = Lahore 5.92.56 [vol. 5, p. 588]). Gorresio omits this verse entirely. No manuscript or printed edition appears to have the sequence found in the critical edition. One can only think that the critical editors have either improperly located verses 3–8 or have placed this verse at the end on the basis of its metrical and rhetorical features. See Sutherland 1992.

"welcomed" *jagāma saṃgamam*: Literally, "went to union *or* meeting [with]." Cg suggests that, by mentioning "meeting" as grammatically "the most desired object of the agent [i.e., Rāma]," we are to understand that the phrasing suggests that the meeting is to be regarded as Rāma's gain (*saṃgamo 'pi kartur īpsitatamatvakathanena rāmasyāyaṃ lābha iti gamyate*) (see *Pā* 1.4.49). Cg offers two alternative interpretations in which we are to take the verb *jagāma*, "went," literally, and thus understand that Rāma physically rushed off to meet Vibhīṣaṇa. Cg's explanations for this unusual violation of protocol is that Rāma is so intent on fulfilling his vow of never abandoning a suppliant and so unwilling to brook any delay by further argumentation on the part of Sugrīva and the other monkeys that he simply rushes off to meet the *rākṣasa* (*na tyajeyaṃ kathaṃcanety ādibhiḥ sugrīvādivākyarūpavirodhinirasanapūrvakaṃ śrīvibhīṣaṇasvīkāraṃ pratiśrutya kathaṃcit sugrīvādivākyajanitaṃ vilambam aviṣahya tvarayā rakṣituṃ svayam eva tena saṃgata ity āha vibhīṣaṇenāśu jagāma saṃgamam iti*).

"had been advised" *abhihitam*: We are following the interpretation of Cm, who takes this as a reference to Sugrīva's final support of the idea of an alliance with Vibhīṣaṇa as expressed in verses 6 and 7 above. Ct understands the term to be a reference to Sugrīva's speech to Rāma, who, having brought the *rākṣasa*, announces, "This is Vibhīṣaṇa (*tam ānīyāyaṃ vibhīṣaṇa iti bodhitam*)." Cg takes it as a reference to Sugrīva's speech to Vibhīṣaṇa: "Vibhīṣaṇa, Rāghava has granted you protection, you must approach Rāghava (*he vibhīṣaṇa rāghavas tavābhayaṃ dattavān rāghavam upayāhy evaṃ sugrīvoktam*)."

"just as Indra, smasher of citadels, might welcome Garuḍa, the king of birds" *patattrirājena yathā puraṃdaraḥ*: Literally, "just as the smasher of citadels, the king of the birds." The precise mythological reference is unclear, since Indra has little direct involvement with Garuḍa, who is the mount and associate of Viṣṇu. Cs understands the simile to allude to Indra's having formed an alliance with Garuḍa at the time of the theft of the *amṛta* in the story of the churning of the ocean (see *MBh* 1.29.22–33; 1.30.7) (*patattrirājena garuḍena puraṃdaro yathāmṛtaharaṇakāle sakhyaṃ jagāma tadvat*). Ct, Cr, and Ck understand the term *patattrirājena* to refer elliptically or, perhaps, by *lakṣaṇā*, to Indra's younger brother (Upendra) Viṣṇu, who was brought to him by Garuḍa, although no specific episode is mentioned (*patattrirājena garuḍānitenopen-*

dreṇa saṃgamam puraṃdaro yathā—so Cr). Cg comments that the intention of the illustration is to show that Rāma regarded his union with Vibhīṣaṇa to be his own gain, just as Indra did in the case of Garuḍa (*puraṃdaro yathā patattrirājena saṃgamaṃ svalābham amanyata tathāyam apīti dṛṣṭāntābhiprāyaḥ*). Alternatively, Cg sees the illustration as showing that Rāma rushes off to meet Vibhīṣaṇa fearing that if Sugrīva's mind is still opposed to Vibhīṣaṇa's acceptance, he might undermine his [Rāma's] purpose (*yadvā sugrīvasya buddhiḥ punar viparītā cet kāryahānir iti śīghraṃ jagāma*). Cs offers a rather different interpretation: he understands *harīśvareṇa*, "by the lord of the tawny monkeys," to refer not to Sugrīva but to Hanumān, and then interprets "he formed an alliance in his mind as had been advised by Hanumān (*harīśvareṇa hanumatābhihitaṃ vibhīṣaṇena saṃgamaṃ sakhyaṃ jagāma manaseti śeṣaḥ*)." On the story of the churning of the ocean, see 6.40.29; 6.41.17; 6.53.23; 6.80.19; 6.105.19; and notes.

Sarga 13

1. "devoted" *bhaktaiḥ*: Cg argues that, through their devotion to their master, Vibhīṣaṇa's attendants now have devotion for Rāma equal to his own (*vibhīṣaṇasyaikasyaivopāyānuṣṭhānaśravaṇe 'pi tadanubandhināṃ tadbhaktivaśād eva rāmaparicaraṇaṃ samānam ity ucyate*).

Following 1ab, D5–7,10,11,S insert a passage of one line [215*]: "[Rāvaṇa's younger brother] wise Vibhīṣaṇa, fixing his eyes on the ground, [descended]."

2. "Seeking refuge" *śaraṇānveṣī*: D10,11, and the texts and printed editions of Ct read instead *nipapātātha*, "then he descended *or* fell."

"four *rākṣasa* companions" *caturbhiḥ saha rākṣasaiḥ*: Literally, "with four *rākṣasas*." The names of Vibhīṣaṇa's attendants as given by Cg are listed in the note to 6.11.3 above. Cs offers an idiosyncratic interpretation in which Vibhīṣaṇa alone bows at Rāma's feet, after which Rāvaṇa, accompanied by the four *rākṣasas* Kumbhakarṇa, Mahāpārśva, Indrajit, and Prahasta, bows down. (*atha vibhīṣaṇasya rāmapādanipatanānantaram. sa rāvaṇaś caturbhī rākṣasaiḥ kumbhakarṇamahāpārśvendrajitprahastaiḥ saha nipapāta.*) See, too, 6.10.12; 6.28.7,32; 6.71.2; and notes.

3. "fitting" *yuktam*: Ct and Cm explain, "replete with reasonable argument (*yuktiyuktam*)." Cg interprets, "fitting by virtue of their falling within the scope of what is suitable to a situation requiring effective and compassionate refuge (*samarthakāruṇikaśaraṇyaviṣayatayā yogyam*)." We follow Cr in taking the term in its basic sense. He glosses, "proper to say (*vaktuṃ yogyam*)."

"timely" *sāmpratam*: Cr, Cm, Ck, and Ct take this word adverbially with *saṃpraharṣaṇam*, "delightful," to mean, "bringing instant gratification (*tatkālaṃ saṃtoṣakaraṇam*)." Cg appears to understand it in the adverbial sense of "now," explaining that previously the announcement that Vibhīṣaṇa was seeking refuge with Rāghava was bitter to the ears of Sugrīva and the other monkeys but that now, [after the speeches of Hanumān and Rāma], it was delightful to them all (*pūrvaṃ rāghavaṃ śaraṇaṃ gata ity uktidāśāyāṃ sugrīvādīnāṃ śrutikaṭukaṃ jātam idānīṃ sarvasampraharṣaṇam*). We, however, understand it in the sense of "suitable to the moment *or* occasion."

4. Cg and Cm are concerned that Vibhīṣaṇa is repeating himself here, having already stated his situation and his purpose to the monkeys at 6.11.14 above. Cg argues that there is no impropriety in this repetition, as his previous announcement

was to Rāma's monkey subordinates and this report is directly to Rāma himself, who is the direct source of refuge (*pūrvaṃ nivedayatety atra puruṣakārabhūtān pratyuktam idānīṃ sākṣāccharaṇyaṃ pratīti na punaruktiḥ*). Cm thinks that he repeats himself in order to increase Rāma's pleasure (*tyaktvā putrāṃś ca dārāṃś ca rāghavaṃ śaraṇaṃ gataḥ* [6.11.14] *ityādisugrīvādisarvavānarasannidhau kṛtaṃ pralapanaṃ śaraṇyarāmaprītivardhanāya punar apy anusaṃdhatte*).

"refuge of all beings" *sarvabhūtānāṃ śaraṇyam*: Ct, Ck, and Cs argue, not implausibly, that Vibhīṣaṇa's use of the epithet demonstrates that he, Vibhīṣaṇa, is aware of Rāma's status as an *avatāra* of the Lord (*sarvabhūtānāṃ śaraṇyam ity anena tasya rāme bhagavadavatāratvāvagamaḥ sūcitaḥ*). Cg comments that the epithet derives from Rāma's resolution to offer refuge even to Rāvaṇa (6.12.21), but he does not indicate how he thinks Vibhīṣaṇa could have become aware of this (*sarvabhūtānāṃ śaraṇyaṃ rāvaṇasyāpi śaraṇaṃ bhavāmīti kṛtasaṃkalpaṃ bhavantam*). See 5.36.26–29 and notes. See, too, 6.31.56; 6.47.43; 6.59.8; 6.81.14; 6.105.15; and notes.

5. "everything I own" *dhanāni*: Literally, "properties, wealth."

"homeland" *rājyam*: Literally, "kingdom, country." Given the immediate context, we believe that Vibhīṣaṇa here is alluding to his exile from his native land rather than to any hopes he may have of succeeding his brother on the throne of Laṅkā. Ck and Ct, however, understand that by virtue of his omniscience, Vibhīṣaṇa has determined that Rāma will kill Rāvaṇa [and place Vibhīṣaṇa on the throne] (*sarvajñatvena rāmo rāvaṇavadhaṃ kariṣyaty eveti niścitam iti gamyate*). Cg avoids the touchy political question here by explaining *rājyam* as a synecdoche (*upalakṣaṇam*) for all of Vibhīṣaṇa's possessions. Translators have generally rendered the term as "kingdom" (Dutt 1893, p. 1152; Shastri 1959, vol. 3, p. 43); as "empire"(Roussel 1903, vol. 3, p. 50); as "sovereignty" (Gita Press 1969, vol. 3, p. 1428); or, to avoid the problem raised by the fact that Vibhīṣaṇa is not currently a king, as "hopes of kingdom" (Raghunathan 1982, vol. 3, p. 43) or "*speranza di regno*" (Gorresio 1856, vol. 9, p. 183).

Cs reverts to his fondness for breaking up Vālmīki's words peculiarly, reading the phrase "*parityaktā mayā laṅkā* (Laṅkā is abandoned by me)" as *parityaktāmayā laṅkā*, explaining the *bahuvrīhi* compound as follows: "Laṅkā, which has fought off (*parityaktaḥ*) its illness (*āmayaḥ*), that is, Rāvaṇa in the form of a disease (*rāvaṇo rogarūpī*), who had brought about the destruction of the various parts of the city, its ramparts, etc. (*prākārādyaṅgabhaṅgakāritvāt*)."

Following verse 5, D5–7,10,11,S insert a passage of thirty-three lines [App. I, No. 9]: "Upon hearing those words of his, Rāma replied, comforting him with his words and drinking him in, as it were, with his eyes[1–2]: 'Describe to me accurately the strengths and weaknesses of the *rākṣasas*.' Addressed in this fashion by Rāma, tireless in action, the *rākṣasa* began to describe all the forces of Rāvaṇa [3–5]: 'Prince, as a result of a boon from self-existent Brahmā, ten-necked Rāvaṇa is not to be killed by any of the powerful beings, such as *gandharvas*, great serpents, and *rākṣasas*.[1] [6–7] The next younger brother of Rāvaṇa is my elder brother, the valorous and immensely powerful Kumbhakarṇa, whose strength in battle rivals that of Śakra.[8–9] And, Rāma, Rāvaṇa's[2] field marshal is well known as Prahasta. It was he who defeated Māṇibhadra[3] at the battle of Kailāsa.[10–11] When his wrist and finger guards are strapped on,[4] when he is wearing his impenetrable armor, and when he takes up his bow to stand in battle, Indrajit becomes invisible.[12–13] Once his forces are arrayed at the time of battle,[5] he makes an offering to the fire, eater of oblations; then, having become invisible, Indrajit slaughters his enemies,[6] Rāghava.[14–15] Then there are his generals:[7] Mahodara, Mahāpārśva, and the *rākṣasa* Akampana, who are the equals of the world guardians in battle.[16–17] In the city of Laṅkā dwell ten billion *rākṣasas*, who feed on flesh and blood and can take on any form at will.[18–19] Together with them, the king made war upon the world guardians, who, along with the gods, were crushed by evil-minded[8] Rāvaṇa.'[20–21] When Rāma, firm in his valor,[9] had heard Vibhīṣaṇa's words, he considered all of this in his mind and then said these words: [22–23] 'I know all about those magnificent deeds of Rāvaṇa, which have been narrated fully, Vibhīṣaṇa.[24–25] Still, I shall slay ten-necked Rāvaṇa along with his son and Prahasta, and then I shall make you king; this is the truth I am telling you.[10][26–27] Rāvaṇa may enter the underworlds known as Rasātala or Pātāla or even the presence of Grandfather Brahmā himself; still, he will not escape me alive.[28–29] I swear by my three brothers that I shall not reenter Ayodhyā until I have slain Rāvaṇa in battle along with his sons, his troops,[11] and his kinsmen.[30–31]' When he had heard this speech of Rāma, tireless in action, righteous Vibhīṣaṇa[12] bowed his head and began to speak.[32–33]"

1"any of the powerful beings, such as *gandharvas*, great serpents, and *rākṣasas*" *sarvabhūtānāṃ gandharvoragarakṣasām*: Literally, "of all beings, *gandharvas*, *uragas*, and *rākṣasas*." Given the terms of Rāvaṇa's boon, we must understand that the reference is to superhuman beings. D7,10,11, and the texts and printed editions of Cr and Ct read *-pakṣiṇām*, "[great] birds," for *-rakṣasām*, "*rākṣasas*." D5,T1,G2,M5, and the texts and printed editions of Cg read instead *-[a]sura-*, "*asuras*," for *-[u]raga-*, "[great] serpents." This variant is rendered only in the translation of Raghunathan (1982, vol. 3, p. 43). See note to 6.28.28–29.

2"Rāvaṇa's" *tasya*: Literally,"his."

3"Māṇibhadra" *māṇibhadraḥ* (v.l. *maṇibhadraḥ*): Cg identifies this character as a general of Kubera (*kuberasenāpatiḥ*). Cr identifies him as a [*yakṣa*] defeated by Prahasta (*yena māṇibhadraḥ parājitaḥ sa prahastas tasya rāvaṇasya senāpatiḥ*). Shastri has two separate entries: Manibadra [*sic*], whom he identifies as "one of Kuvera's warriors who was slain by Prahasta," and Manibhadra, whom he identifies as "a Yaksha defeated by Dashagriva" (Shastri 1959, vol. 3, p. 662). He cross-references this latter figure to a figure called "Parshva mauli," a name he takes as an epithet of Maṇibhadra. A story is told in the *Uttarakāṇḍa* (7.15.6–10) of a fight between Rāvaṇa and a *yakṣa* named Māṇibhadra (v.l. Maṇibhadra). Māṇibhadra first bests Prahasta in battle. But Rāvaṇa, seeing this, attacks him and knocks his diadem askew. As a result, the *yakṣa* receives the epithet Pārśvamauli, "he of the skewed diadem." See also Shastri 1959, vol. 3, p. 667.

4"his wrist and finger guards are strapped on" *baddhagodhāṅgulitrāṇaḥ*: See note to 1.21.8. See, too, note to 6.66.23; and 6.67.25; 6.76.2,24; 6.81.26–27; and notes. Also see 1701* at note to 6.77.30.

5"Once his forces are arrayed at the time of battle" *saṃgrāmasamayavyūhe*: D10,11, and the texts and printed editions of Ct read instead *saṃgrāme sumahadvyūhe*, "in the midst of a great array in battle."

6"enemies" *śatrūn*: D10,11, and the texts and printed editions of Ct read instead *śrīmān*, "majestic [Indrajit]."

[7]"generals" *anīkasthāḥ*: Literally, "standing in battle, warriors." We follow Cg, who glosses, "generals (*senāpatayaḥ*)." D10,11,M1,2, and the texts and printed editions of Ct read instead *anīkapāḥ*, "protectors of the army, generals."

[8]"evil-minded" *durātmanā*: D6,G1,M3,5, and the texts and printed editions of Cg read *mahātmanā*, "great, mighty." Raghunathan (1982, vol. 3, p. 44) alone renders this variant.

[9]"firm in his valor" *dṛḍhaparākramaḥ*: D7,10,11,G2,3,M1,2,5, and the texts and printed editions of Cr and Ct read [with other minor variants] *raghusattamaḥ*, "foremost of the Rāghus."

[10]"I am telling you" *bravīmi te*: D10,11, and the texts and printed editions of Ct read instead *śṛṇotu me*, "[let you, sir,] hear," misprinted in the critical apparatus as *śruṇotu me*.

[11]"his troops" *-bala-*: D7,10,11,G1, and the texts and printed editions of Cr and Ct read instead *-jana-*, "people."

[12]"righteous Vibhīṣaṇa" *dharmātmā*: Literally, "righteous one."

6. "so long as breath remains in my body" *yathāprāṇam*: Literally, "to the extent of my life breaths." Cg glosses *yathābalam*, "with all my strength."

"I shall penetrate their forces" *pravekṣyāmi ca vāhinīm*: We are following Ct, Cr, and Ck in seeing this as a reference to Rāvaṇa's army. The phrase is, however, ambiguous. It could also mean "enter, i.e., join, your army." Northern manuscripts and printed editions substitute *nayiṣyāmi* or *neṣyāmi tava*, "I shall lead *or* I shall lead your," which would then yield the sense of "I shall be the leader of your army" (*saro condottiero dell'esercito*—Gorresio 1856, vol. 9, p. 183).

7–8. "bestower of honor" *mānada*: Literally, "giver *or* destroyer of honor *or* pride." We follow Cg, who glosses, "bestower of honor," and indicates that the sense of the epithet here is that Lakṣmaṇa provides the [concrete] rewards when he, Rāma, is gratified or pleased (*mānada bahumānaprada matprasāde sati phalapradas tvam iti bhāvaḥ*). See note 1 to 3310* following 6.108.5. See, too, 6.110.6; cf. 6.104.10 and notes.

9. "anointed Vibhīṣaṇa" *abhyaṣiñcad vibhīṣaṇam*: This appears to be a sort of provisional consecration as the formal consecration of Vibhīṣaṇa will not take place until nearly the end of the *kāṇḍa* at *sarga* 100 (6.100.12–16). Nevertheless, Vibhīṣaṇa is referred to as king at 6.19.26–27 below. See notes to 6.19.26,27. See, too, notes to 6.100.9. Cf. 6.39.22 and App. I, No. 72, lines 3–5 and n. 2, at note to 6.111.114.

10. "suddenly" *sadyaḥ*: Several translators (Raghunathan 1982, vol. 3, p. 44; Gita Press 1969, vol. 3, p. 1430; and Gorresio 1856, vol. 9, p. 183) take the adverb adjectivally with *prasādam*, in the sense of "the quick grace of Rāma."

"began chattering loudly" *pracukruśur mahānādān*: Literally, "they cried great sounds." Ct and Ck understand, "they made a *kilakilā* in their satisfaction (*saṃtoṣāt kilakilām akurvan*)." For a discussion of the simian vocalization *kilakilā*, see notes on 5.55.22 and 5.62.34. Cr describes the sound as the noise made by their species to indicate joy. Cf. note 10 to 75* following 6.4.52.

D5–7,10,11,T,G2,3,M, and the texts and printed editions of the southern commentators read *mahātmānam* for *mahānādān*, yielding the sense "cried out to that great man [Rāma *or* Vibhīṣaṇa]." This reading is reflected in the translations of those who follow the text of Ct, for example, Dutt (1893, p. 1154), "eulogized the high-souled one"; Roussel (1903, vol. 3, p. 54), "*acclamèrent le magnanime* (*Rakshasa*)"; Shastri (1959, vol. 3, p. 45), "acclaimed that magnanimous titan"; and Gita Press (1969, vol. 3, p. 1430), "hailed Śrī Rāma in the words."

11. Cg argues that Hanumān and Sugrīva have taken Vibhīṣaṇa aside at a slightly different time to pose their questions as to how the monkey army is to cross over the ocean (*atha samayāntare kutracid ekānte pradeśe hanumatsugrīvau sthalajñaṃ vibhīṣaṇaṃ vānarasenātaraṇopāyam apṛcchatām iti*). This argument on Cg's part is necessary because the southern recension contains a passage [223*], which will be discussed in the notes to verse 15 below, in which, after his conversation with Vibhīṣaṇa, Sugrīva goes to report it to Rāma and Lakṣmaṇa, who are not, as in the critical text, present during their interview.

Following verse 11, D5–7,10,11,S insert a passage of one line [221*]: "[How are we] all of us, surrounded by the forces of the immensely powerful monkeys."

12. "Please tell us the means whereby all of us might approach" *upāyair abhigacchāmaḥ... sarve*: Literally, "through [what] means we might all approach." The critical reading is elliptical, providing no wording that indicates either that this phrase is a question or that the monkeys are explicitly requesting information. D10,11, and Ct and Ck read *abhigacchāma* (the imperative [*loṭ*]) for *abhigacchāmaḥ* (the present indicative [*laṭ*]). Cr, who reads with the critical edition, glosses, "we have reached (*abhyagacchāma*—the imperfect [*lañ*])." He understands the whole utterance to be indirect (*bhaṅgyantareṇa*), as well as elliptical, and explains, "We have reached [the ocean], please tell us the means whereby we may cross. Moreover, you should tell us not only the means whereby we may cross the ocean, but by which we might obtain (*abhigacchāma*) Sītā as well. (*varuṇālayam abhigacchāma abhyagacchāma prāpnuma te vayaṃ tarasā upāyair yathā tarāma tathā brūhīti śeṣaḥ. kiṃca varuṇālayaṃ yathā tarāma yathā copāyair abhigacchāma sītāṃ prāpnuyāṃ tathā brūhi.*)" Cm reads *adhigacchāmaḥ* (*laṭ*) and glosses it with the future (*lṛṭ*) *adhigamiṣyāmaḥ*, explaining, "We reach, that is, we shall reach, the lord of streams and rivers by some means or other. You must tell us the means whereby all [of us] may cross the abode of Varuṇa together with the troops. (*upāyaiḥ kaiścid upāyair nadanadīpatim adhigacchāmo 'dhigamiṣyāmaḥ. sasainyāḥ sarve tarasā varuṇālayaṃ yathā tarāma tādṛśopāyān vadeti śeṣaḥ.*)" Ñ2,D1–4,G3,M3, and the texts and printed editions of Cg (Cm and Crā as an alternative) read the variant *upāyaṃ nādhigacchāmaḥ*, which Cm explains as "We do not understand, that is, we do not know of a means such that we might cross the abode of Varuṇa (*varuṇālayaṃ yathā tarāma tādṛśam upāyaṃ nādhigacchāma na jānīma ity arthaḥ*)." Northern texts avoid the ellipsis and ambiguity but substitute various alternate readings. Thus, for example, Gorresio's edition (5.92.6–7) reads *upāyaṃ brūhi naḥ saumya yathā nadanadīpatim... uttarema* ("Please tell us, dear friend, a means whereby we may cross the lord of rivers and streams").

13. "who knew what was right" *dharmajñaḥ*: Ñ2,V1,3,B2–4,D5–7,9–11,T1,3,M5, and the texts and printed editions of Cr, Ct, and Ck read instead *dharmātmā*, "righteous."

"must solicit the help of" *śaraṇaṃ gantum arhati*: Literally, "he must go to for assistance *or* refuge." The most common usage of the term *śaraṇa*, especially in the present context in which Vibhīṣaṇa has sought *śaraṇa* with Rāma, the refuge of all the worlds, is, of course, "refuge *or* shelter." In this verse, however, we believe that the word must be taken in another of its meanings, that of "aid, succor, assistance." Cr, perhaps disturbed by the prospect of the refuge of all the world, Rāma, seeking refuge with such a minor deity as Samudra, takes *śaraṇa* in yet another of its meanings, that of "home," understanding that the ocean is practically Rāma's own home (*svagṛha-prāyam*), a notion he clarifies further in his comments to verse 14 in connection with the legend that the ocean was dug out under the orders of Rāma's ancestor King Sagara (see note to verse 14 below). See notes to 6.10.17 and 6.12.11. See, too, *MBh* 3.130.19–20 and 3.131ff.

14. The story of King Sagara and the circumstances under which his sons excavate the earth to create the cavity that will become the ocean when filled by the descent of the celestial Gaṅgā is narrated at great length in the *Bālakāṇḍa* (1.38–41). The idea underlying this verse is that, since the ocean divinity Sāgara can thus be regarded as the creation, or "child," of Sagara, one of Rāma's ancestors, he would look upon Rāma as his kinsman. For another expression of this idea, see 5.1.103.

"great... ocean" *mahodadhiḥ* ... *mahodadhiḥ*: Literally, "great ocean... great ocean." A few manuscripts (B2,3,D6,7) and the texts and printed editions of Cg substitute *mahāmatiḥ*, "highly intelligent," for *mahodadhiḥ* in *pāda* d, thus avoiding the repetition.

15. "When... Vibhīṣaṇa had spoken in this fashion, Rāghava... found what he said to be agreeable" *evaṃ vibhīṣaṇenokte* ... *rāghavasyāpy arocata*: Literally, "when it had been spoken thus by Vibhīṣaṇa, [it] was agreeable to Rāghava as well." The critical reading provides no clear grammatical subject for the verb *arocata*, "to be pleasing to," and we have therefore added the words "what he said." In his comments on 223.3*, Cm argues that it is the idea of propitiating the ocean that pleases Rāma (*sāgarasyopaveśanam upāsanaṃ rāghavasyāpy arocata*). Cg and Ct interpret similarly. Cr, however, understands the reference to be to Vibhīṣaṇa's speech as reported by Sugrīva (*rāmasamīpāgamanānantaraṃ sāgarasyopaveśanaṃ vibhīṣaṇavacaḥ sugrīva ākhyātum ārebhe*). Ś,Ñ,V1,3,B2–4,D1–4,7,8,10–12, and the texts and printed editions of Ct and Cr read instead the neuter nominative *uktam*, "what was said," for the locative *ukte*, which variant provides a grammatical subject for the verb *arocata*. D6,T2,3,G1,2,M3,5, and the texts and printed editions of Cg read the nominative masculine *uktaḥ*, "addressed," which construes with the proper noun *sugrīvaḥ* in the southern insert 223.1*.

D10,11, and the texts and printed editions of Ct read *rāmasyāsyāpi*, "of [to] that Rāma as well," for *rāghavasyāpi*.

"wise *rākṣasa*" *rākṣasena vipaścitā*: Cg claims that, by the term "wise," the poet suggests Vibhīṣaṇa's possession of timely knowledge, and by the term "*rākṣasa*," he suggests Vibhīṣaṇa's knowledge of the [*rākṣasas*'] territory. (*rākṣaseneti sthalajñatoktā. vipaściteti tātkālikabuddhimattā.*)

Following 15ab, D5–7,10,11,S insert a passage of three lines [223*]: "[When the wise *rākṣasa* Vibhīṣaṇa had spoken in this fashion (15ab)], Sugrīva came to[1] where Rāma and Lakṣmaṇa were.[1] Then broad-necked[2] Sugrīva began to report on Vibhīṣaṇa's excellent advice concerning the winning over of[3] Sāgara.[2–3]"

[1]"came to" *ājagāma*: Cg, repeating his remarks from verse 11 above, understands the verb to indicate that the questions directed by Sugrīva and the others were asked at a different time and place (*anena kālāntare deśāntare sugrīvādipraśna iti gamyate*). Cf. verse 11 above.

[2]"broad-necked" *vipulagrīvaḥ*: This is another of the epithets that echo the name of a character (see note on 5.7.12 and 5.7.40). Cg evidently understands it to mean

"having a long [i.e., extended] neck" and claims that the epithet is used to indicate the monkey king's eagerness (*kutūhalitvam*). Perhaps he has in mind the term *utkaṇṭha*, literally, "with upraised *or* extended neck," which is often used to express eagerness, anxiety, or anticipation.

[3]"concerning the winning over of" *upaveśanam*: Literally, "the winning over of." We understand the term here to be synonymous with *śaraṇam* in the sense that it was used in verse 13 above (i.e., "aid, succor, help"). The literal meaning of the word is "sitting near," but it often has the sense in Sanskrit of sitting near in order to cajole or coerce someone as in the usage *prayopaveśanam*, "to sit and fast against someone whom one wishes to coerce." Ct glosses, "seeking refuge with or the help of (*śaraṇagamanam*)," while Cg glosses, "sitting near, attending upon, worshiping (*upāsanam*)."

16. "skillful" *kriyādakṣaḥ*: Literally, "skilled *or* competent in action." Cg understands the compound to mean "even though he was capable of carrying out the undertaking by himself (*svayaṃ kāryakaraṇasamartho 'pi*). The compound is doubtless employed here for its echoing effect with the adverb *satkriyārtham* that precedes it. D1,10,11,T2, and the texts and printed editions of Ct, Ck, and Cr read instead the accusative *kriyādakṣam*, which then modifies Sugrīva in *pāda* b. See note below.

"Rāma . . . to Lakṣmaṇa and Sugrīva" *sa lakṣmaṇam . . . sugrīvaṃ ca*: Literally, "he . . . to Lakṣmaṇa and Sugrīva." The printed editions of Ct (NSP, GPP, and Gita Press [6.19.34]) read instead the opening words of the verse *sa lakṣmaṇam*, "he . . . to Lakṣmaṇa," as a compound adjective, *salakṣmaṇam*, "together with Lakṣmaṇa."

"in order to honor them" *satkriyārtham*: Literally, "for the sake of honor." The commentators differ as to whom or what Rāma wishes to honor in the speech that follows. Ct says it is to honor Vibhīṣaṇa; Cg says it is Vibhīṣaṇa's counsel; Cr understands that it is "Sugrīva, etc."; and Cm claims that it is Lakṣmaṇa and Sugrīva whom Rāma wishes to honor. We have followed Cm because, in the following verses, Rāma is clearly attempting to bolster the egos of Sugrīva and Lakṣmaṇa in asking for their opinions.

17. "Now, you, together with Sugrīva, should tell me if it pleases you as well." *brūhi tvaṃ sahasugrīvas tavāpi yadi rocate*: Ñ1,V3,D8,10,11,T1,3, and the texts and printed editions of Ct and Cr omit this line.

19. "courteous" *samudācārasaṃyuktam*: Literally, "joined with courtesy." The word can be read, as we have done, as an adjective modifying *vacanam*, "words," or, as suggested by Cg, as an adverb modifying the verb *ūcatuḥ*, "those two said *or* responded,"and having the sense "responded with every gesture of civility, such as cupping the hands in reverence, etc." (*añjalibandhādyupacāraḥ tatsaṃyuktam iti kriyāviśeṣaṇam*).

20. "advice" *uktam*: Literally, "what was said."

"at this moment" *asmin kāle*: Cg explains, "at [this] time of considering without any plan (*upāyam antarā darśanakāle*)."

"seems the most feasible plan" *sukhāvaham*: Literally, "bringing happiness *or* ease." Cg explains, "a means of accomplishing our purpose effortlessly (*ayatnena kāryasādhakam*)."

21. "reaching" *āsāditum*: This could also mean "attacking *or* assaulting" and has been so rendered by some translators.

22. "You should petition" *niyujyatām*: Literally, "let [the ocean] be enjoined *or* employed." We believe the context supports the interpretation of Cg and Cm, who gloss,

"should be petitioned [for the construction of a bridge—Cm] ([*setubandhāya*] *prārthyatām*)." Ck and Ct interpret,"you yourself should be enjoined to petition Sāgara. (*sāgaraprārthanārthaṃ niyujyatām. svātmā iti śeṣaḥ.*)"

Following verse 22, D5–7,10,11,S insert a passage of one line [227*]: "So that we may proceed with our army to the city guarded by Rāvaṇa."

23. "sat down" *saṃviveśa*: Cr notes that Rāma is practicing the rites appropriate to a pilgrimage spot [such as the seashore] (*rāmasya tīrthavidhikaraṇam*).

"on a bed of *kuśa* grass that had been spread on the shore" *kuśāstīrṇe tīre*: Literally, "on the *kuśa*-strewn shore."

"like fire, eater of oblations, installed upon an altar" *vedyām iva hutāśanaḥ*: Literally, "like the oblation eater on an altar." Cg notes that the simile suggests the imminent blazing splendor of Rāma (*anena jvaliṣyamāṇatvaṃ vyajyate*), while Cm, perhaps concerned at the notion of Rāma coming as a suppliant to the ocean, remarks that the simile suggests not only Rāma's blazing energy but his absence of abjection (*hutāśanadṛṣṭāntena tattejoyuktatayā kārpaṇyābhāvaḥ sūcitataḥ*).

Following *sarga* 13, D5–7,10,11,S insert a passage of one hundred three lines [App. I, No. 10; GPP; VSP; KK, NSP=*sargas* 20, 21.1–9]. In this *sarga* one of Rāvaṇa's *rākṣasa* spies, Śārdūla, observes Sugrīva's army encamped on the shore and, after reconnoitering, hastens back to Laṅkā to report to Rāvaṇa.[1–5] He informs the king that there is a vast host of apes and monkeys, ten leagues in extent, encamped on the opposite shore and, with them, are the two well-armed sons of Daśaratha who are on the trail of the missing Sītā.[6–11] He urges Rāvaṇa to send out messengers to spy on the army and recommends that he consider one of three strategies: the restoration of Sītā, conciliation, or an attempt to sow dissension in his enemies' ranks.[12–14] Hearing the words of Śārdūla, Rāvaṇa becomes agitated and decides to send a *rākṣasa* named Śuka to deliver a message to Sugrīva forthrightly but in soothing words.[15–19] Śuka is to flatter Sugrīva, saying that Sugrīva has nothing to gain or lose in this affair and that he is like a brother to Rāvaṇa. Rāvaṇa's message goes on to say that his abduction of Rāma's wife has nothing to do with Sugrīva and that the latter should therefore go back to Kiṣkindhā. Moreover, he argues that, if the gods and the *gandharvas* themselves are unable to conquer Laṅkā, how then would it be possible for mere men and monkeys?[20–27] Śuka turns himself into a bird and swiftly flies across the ocean, where, hovering in the sky, he conveys the message to Sugrīva as it had been given to him by wicked Rāvaṇa.[28–32] While Śuka is delivering his message, the monkeys leap up into the sky and begin to tear off his wings and pummel him with their fists. Violently seized by the monkeys, the messenger is hurled out of the sky to the earth.[33–36] Assaulted in this fashion, he addresses Rāma, arguing that it is wrong to kill a messenger and urging him to call off his monkeys. He notes that the only messenger who deserves death is he who departs from the instructions of his master and speaks on his own behalf.[37–40] Hearing the lamentation of Śuka, Rāma instructs the monkeys to spare him. Released by the monkeys, Śuka flies up once more into the sky and from there addresses Sugrīva, asking him what he is to report to Rāvaṇa.[41–46] Sugrīva responds, saying that Śuka is to report his [Sugrīva's] response as follows. Sugrīva sends the message to Rāvaṇa that he is no friend of his and that he deserves no mercy from him. He has not helped him in any way nor is he dear to him. Rāvaṇa, along with his kinsmen, on the other hand, is an enemy of Rāma and, like Vālin, deserves to die. He vows to slay Rāvaṇa and all his kinsmen and to reduce

Laṅkā to ashes.[47–58] Sugrīva goes on to vow that Rāvaṇa will not escape Rāghava even should he gain the protection of the gods along with Indra, or if he should hide himself in the path of the sun or in the underworld Pātāla, or if he were [to take refuge] at the lotus feet of Śiva himself.[59–64] Sugrīva goes on to say that he can see no being in all the three worlds, whether *piśāca*, *rākṣasa*, *gandharva*, or *asura*, that will be able to save Rāvaṇa. He then taunts Rāvaṇa for his cowardice in killing the aged vulture king Jaṭāyus and in abducting Sītā in the absence of Rāma and Lakṣmaṇa. He says that Rāvaṇa does not understand the enormous power of Rāma, who will kill him.[65–71] Next Aṅgada speaks up, saying that he thinks Śuka is not a messenger but a spy who has taken advantage of his presence there to evaluate the strength of Rāma's forces. He says that he feels that Śuka should be taken prisoner.[72–75] Thus, on the orders of their king, the monkeys spring up and once more bind the wailing Śuka. The *rākṣasa* cries out to Rāma, complaining that the monkeys are tearing out his wings and poking out his eyes. Śuka threatens that, if he should be killed, his tormentor will then have to bear the burden of all the evil deeds that he, Śuka, has performed during his lifetime. Hearing this lamentation, Rāma once again makes the monkeys desist from killing Śuka and tells them to release him since he has indeed come as a messenger.[76–85] [Colophon GPP 6.20]

[GPP 6.21.1–9] Rāma spreads *darbha* grass on the seashore and lies upon it after making reverential gestures toward the ocean. Resting his head on an arm of which the beauty, ornamentation, and romantic and martial associations are elaborately described [86–100], Rāma, controlling his senses, vows either to cross the ocean or die in the attempt.[101–103]

Sarga 14

Before verse 1, D5–7,10,11,S insert a passage of eighteen lines (App. I, No. 10, lines 86–103 = GPP, VSP, KK, and NSP *sarga* 21.1–9). See note to 6.13.23 for a summary of the passage.

1. "on a bed of *kuśa* grass spread on the ground" *kuśāstīrṇe mahītale*: Literally, "on the surface of the earth, which was spread with *kuśa* grass."

Following verse 1, D5–7,10,11,S insert a passage of two lines [230*]: "And, dwelling there for three nights, Rāma, who knew statecraft and was devoted to righteousness, attended upon Sāgara, lord of rivers."

2. Cg is evidently disturbed at the whole notion of Rāma, refuge of all worlds, seeking refuge with some minor divinity, let alone his being rebuffed by the latter. He entertains the objection that, although Rāma properly takes refuge with the ocean, he does not obtain the desired results, as he lacks the right to seek refuge, like a brahman attempting to perform the *rājasūya* rite. Cg refutes this objection, however, by saying that, although it is true in general that Rāma lacks the right to seek refuge, in his present state of destitution (*akiṃcanaḥ*) he has gained this right. (*nanu rāmeṇa samyakkṛtā śaraṇāgatiḥ kuto na phalitocyate 'nadhikāriṇā kṛtatvād brāhmaṇakṛtarājasūyavat. na ca śaraṇāgatāv adhikārī rāmo 'kiṃcano hi tatrādhikārī.*)

"being obdurate" *mandaḥ*: The term has two meanings that may be applicable here: 1) "sluggish, tardy, unresponsive"; and 2) "dull, foolish." We believe the context better supports the first of these. Ct, Ck, Cr, and Cg offer the second (*mandabuddhiḥ*—Ct, Ck, or *mandamatiḥ*—Cr, or *ajñaḥ*—Cg), although Cr proposes the alternative "characterized by excessive joy (*atipramodaviśiṣṭaḥ*)." Cr understands that Sāgara refuses to appear before Rāma, because he [Sāgara] is eager to have Rāma demonstrate his supernatural power (*sāgaro rūpaṃ svasvarūpaṃ rāmasya na darśayate 'darśayad etena tasya rāmaprabhāvadarśanākāṅkṣitvaṃ vyaktam*). Translators vary in their interpretation. Some, like us, see it as a reference to the ocean's stubbornness or sluggishness, interpreting it to mean indolent, etc. (Gita Press 1969, vol. 3, p. 1436; Shastri 1959, vol. 3, p. 49; Roussel 1903, vol. 3, p. 56; and Pagani 1999, p. 917). Raghunathan (1982, vol. 3, p. 48), following Cg, translates, "dull-witted." Only Dutt (1893, p. 1159) sees the term as a reference to moral turpitude, translating, "wicked," a possible but relatively rare meaning of the term.

"would not manifest himself" *na ca darśayate*: Literally, "does not show." Cv, Cg, and Cm supply the word *ātmānam* ("himself").

3. "Lakṣmaṇa of auspicious marks" *lakṣmaṇaṃ śubhalakṣaṇam*: This alliterative formulaic epithet of a type dear to Vālmīki is used frequently for Lakṣmaṇa. See 6.67.37; 6.71.20; 6.73.5; 6.75.16; 6.79.1; 6.89.4; and notes. Cf. 6.31.1 and note. See also R. Goldman 1984, p. 105. An epithet of this type used in conjunction with Lakṣmaṇa's matronymic Saumitri is *mitranandana* ("who delights his friends") as at 6.74.7 and 6.72.31 and notes.

4. "just see the arrogance of this ignoble Samudra . . . even though I have worshiped him" *paśya tāvad anāryasya pūjyamānasya lakṣmaṇa / avalepaṃ samudrasya*: D5–7,10,11,T,G1,2,M, and the texts and printed editions of the southern commentators omit 4ab. G3 is damaged for verse 4. Thus, the entire available southern recension omits this line. Therefore, the inclusion of 4ab in the critical edition is highly suspect. In addition, in 4c, these same manuscripts substitute the nominative *avalepaḥ* for the critical edition's accusative *avalepam*, yielding the sense, as suggested by the commentators, of "in that he will not show himself, that is the arrogance of Samudra."

5. "straightforwardness" *ārjavam*: Literally, "straightness." Cg gives the standard interpretation but also suggests an alternative, that is, "amenability to the wishes of others (*paracittānusāritvam*)." Cm defines it as "uniformity among the three faculties (*karaṇatrayaikarūpyam*)," presumably thought, speech, and external gestures. See notes on 6.11.54 above.

"taken for signs of weakness" *asāmarthyaṃ phalanty ete*: Literally, "These bear the fruit of incapacity." We follow Cg and Cm, the only commentators to read with the critical edition, who gloss, respectively, "produce an impression of weakness (*asamarthatvabuddhiṃ janayanti*)" and "evil people regard one who, though he may possess omnipotence, is devoted to calmness, etc., as weak (*duṣṭajanāḥ sarvaśaktiyukto 'pi praśamādiparaś cet tam asamarthaṃ manyanta ity arthaḥ*)." Cm goes on to say that the conclusion to be drawn from this interpretation is that the current situation calls for the use of force (*ato 'yaṃ daṇḍasyaiva viṣaya iti bhāvaḥ*). Ct, although he has a variant reading (*asāmarthyaphalā hy ete* for *asāmarthyaṃ phalanty ete*), repeats Cm's comments here.

"by those who lack them" *nirguṇeṣu*: Literally, "among those who lack virtues."

6. "People" *lokaḥ*: Cr and Cg appear unwilling to accept this word as a general comment on humanity and so add a pejorative adjective. Thus, Cr understands, "arrogant people (*garvavāñ janaḥ*)," and Cg, "ignorant people (*ajño janaḥ*)."

"insolent" *dhṛṣṭam*: Commentators differ as to the precise meaning of the adjective here. Ck and Ct gloss, "reckless in unrighteous conduct (*adharmapravṛttau sāhasikam*)."

Cr suggests, "devoid of a sense of shame arising from being the source of evil actions (*duṣkarmasādhanahetukalajjāhīnam*)." Cg suggests, "cruel, pitiless (*nirdayam*)."

"person" *naram*: Literally, "man." Cr glosses, "king (*rājānam*)."

"who runs about praising himself" *ātmapraśaṃsinam* ... *viparidhāvakam*: Literally, "self-praising ... running about." We follow Ct, Cr, and Ck, who explain this to mean "habitually running here and there in order to trumpet his own virtues (*itas tataḥ svaguṇakhyāpanāya paridhāvanaśīlam*—so Ct)." Cg appears to understand this as a derivative of the *ṇijanta* (causative) of the root √*dhāv*, "to run," and thus glosses, "causing everyone to run away (*sarvapalāyanakaram*)." Cm explains, "going on the wrong path (*amārgavartinam*)," while Cv understands, "going by his own special path (*viśeṣavartinam*)."

7. "Peaceful means can no more lead to fame or glory ... than they can to victory" *na sāmnā śakyate kīrtir na sāmnā śakyate yaśaḥ / prāptum ... jayo vā*: Literally, "it is not possible to obtain fame through peaceful means; it is not possible to obtain glory through peaceful means ... or victory."

The pair *kīrti*, "fame," and *yaśaḥ*, "glory," constitute another set of close synonyms that are so frequent in the *Rāmāyaṇa*. Commentators struggle to differentiate the terms, offering a variety of seemingly idiosyncratic distinctions. Thus, Ck and Ct define *kīrti* as "international fame (*deśāntarakhyātiḥ*)," and *yaśaḥ* as "national *or* local fame (*svadeśakhyātiḥ*)." Cr defines the two similarly as "widely spread (*digantarakhyātiḥ*)" and "minor *or* local (*alpakhyātiḥ*)," respectively. Cg glosses *yaśaḥ* with "fame gained through strength (*balakṛtā prathā*)," and *kīrti* with "fame gained through valor (*parākramakṛtā prathā*)." Cm takes *kīrti* to mean "fame won through the possession of virtues (*guṇavattāprathā*)," and *yaśaḥ* to mean "fame produced through generosity (*dānajanitā prathā*)." Cv defines *yaśaḥ* as "the causes of *kīrtiḥ*, such as pure conduct and so on (*kīrteḥ kāraṇam apadānādikam*)," and *kīrti* as "the praise of such actions on the part of their beneficiaries (*tasya* [*yaśasaḥ*] *jalpanaṃ bhoginām*)." See note to 6.2.14.

8. "abode of sea monsters ... with the dead bodies of those very creatures" *makarair makarālayam*: Literally, "the abode of sea monsters with sea monsters." We have added the words "with the dead bodies," following Ct, who explains, "fish and so on pierced by my arrows, and, therefore, having died, are floating everywhere (*madbāṇanirbhinnair ata eva mṛtvā sarvataḥ plavadbhiḥ matsyādibhiḥ*)." See notes on 5.7.6 and 5.34.7 for the term *makara*. Cf. notes to 6.4.78–80.

"choked" *niruddha* : Literally, "blocked, obstructed." Ct glosses, "covered (*pracchādita-*)," while Cg understands, "pervaded (*vyāpta-*)."

9. According to the apparatus on verse 9, only T1 appears to read as does the critical edition. D7,10,11,T2,G2,3, and the texts and printed editions of Ct transpose *pādas* ab and cd, which Cv notes in his commentary.

"Here and now" *iha*: Literally, "here."

"bodies of gigantic fish" *mahābhogāni matsyānām*: Literally, "the huge bodies of fish."

"trunks of sea elephants" *kariṇāṃ* ... *karān*: Literally, "the trunks of elephants." We use the term "sea elephant" here in a general sense and not to refer specifically to the elephant seal (either the northern elephant seal [*Mirounga angustirostris*] or the southern elephant seal [*Mirounga leonina*]), which is sometimes referred to by the term "sea elephant." Some commentators (e.g., Cr) and translators (Raghunathan 1982, vol. 3, p. 49 and Dutt 1893, p. 1159) seem content to see a reference to actual elephants here. Other commentaries (e.g., those of Ct, Ck) are more ambiguous as to what sort of creature is intended, glossing *jalakarin*, "water *or* sea elephant." This interpretation is followed by Gita Press (1969, vol. 3, p. 1436), which renders "(sea) elephants." Roussel (1903, vol. 3, p. 57) and Shastri (1959, vol. 3, p. 49) appear to depart somewhat from this reading, understanding an implicit simile, thus Roussel offers, "*Ces grandes articulations des poissons ainsi que la trompe des éléphants* (*de mer*)" and Shastri, "the limbs of the great fish like unto the trunks of elephants." Pagani (1999, p. 917) understands similarly. We are inclined to agree with Cg, who understands the reference to be to a fish that resembles an elephant (*gajākāramatsyānām*) and possesses some kind of trunklike protuberance (*śuṇḍādaṇḍa*). He supports this view with an observation from the lexicon of Halāyudha, which says, "the *makara* is a type of fish and the elephant *makara* is one of its subtypes (*matsyaviśeṣo makaraḥ karimakaro bhavati tadviśeṣaś ca*)." Perhaps something like the bottlenose dolphin (*Tursiops truncatus*) is intended or, less likely because of its range, the Gangetic dolphin (*Platanista gangetica*). Cf. notes to 6.4.78–80.

10. "launching a powerful assault" *yuddhena mahatā*: Literally, "with a great battle." Since no real battle is envisaged here, we are inclined to follow the suggestion of Ct and Cm, who gloss *yuddhena* as "the strikes *or* blows [of arrows] ([Cm *bāṇa-*]*prahāreṇa*)."

"with my arrows" *śaraiḥ*: D10,11, and the texts and printed editions of Ct read instead *tathā*, "and, as well as." See Slatin 2006.

"sea monsters" *-makaram*: This could also mean crocodiles. See note to 6.14.8 above.

11. "This lord of the ocean, abode of sea monsters, thinks" *makarālayaḥ . . . vijānāti*: Literally, "the abode of sea monsters thinks." Cg sees the use of the epithet here as a kind of sarcasm on the part of Rāma who, he argues, is suggesting that the lord of the ocean thinks to himself, "This is merely the lord of Ayodhyā, the overlord of the Kosalas," when, in fact, he [Sāgara] is nothing but a hole for catching some fish and therefore knows nothing. (*vijānāti makarālayaḥ. ayodhyādhipatiḥ kosalādhipatir itivat. svam ātmānaṃ manyate. katipayamīnagrahaṇagarttā iti na jānāti.*)

"To hell with forbearance" *dhik kṣamām*: See Introduction, p. 46, n. 5.

"for people like this" *īdṛśe jane*: Cg suggests that the ocean has become corrupted from living in such close proximity to the *rākṣasas* (*prāptarakṣaḥsahavāsadoṣe*).

Following verse 11, D5–7,10,11,S insert a passage of one line [236*]: "Sāgara will not manifest himself to me through peaceful means."

12. Here, as in the previous verses, Cg feels compelled to explain the most subtle nuances of each word. Thus, he offers some punning explanations of the phrase "fetch my bow," saying, "The inner intention is 'bring my bow with its bowstring (*saguṇam*) so I may subjugate that person lacking all virtues (*nirguṇam*); bring my bent (*namram*) bow so that I may remove his insolence (*anamratva*).' (*cāpam ānaya nirguṇaṃ vaśīkartuṃ saguṇam ānayety āśayaḥ. cāpam ānayāsyānamratvaṃ nivartayituṃ namraṃ cāpam ānaya.*)" Cg also, relying on the popular Vaiṣṇava, but post-Vālmīkian, representation of Lakṣmaṇa as an incarnation of the great serpent Śeṣa, claims, "He [Lakṣmaṇa] hesitates for a moment in carrying out Rāma's instructions out of his affection for the ocean, which is the resting place of the great serpent." It is because of this hesitation, Cg argues, that Rāma invokes the authority of Lakṣmaṇa's mother by choosing the matronymic epithet Saumitri. This is because Lakṣmaṇa would have to obey his mother's instructions if not those of his elder. (*samudrasya śeṣaśayyātvena tasmin kiṃcitsauhārdavatā lakṣmaṇena kṣaṇaṃ vilambaḥ kṛtaḥ. ata āha saumitra iti. sumitrāvacanam*

eva kartavyaṃ jyeṣṭhavacanaṃ tu na kartavyam iti niyamo 'sti.) Cg provides an alternative explanation, according to which Rāma's use of the matronymic suggests that Lakṣmaṇa must not forget his mother's instructions not to be neglectful of Rāma (*yadvā saumitre rāme pramādaṃ mā kārṣīr iti mātropadiṣṭaṃ mā vismārṣīḥ*).

Following 12ab, D5–7,10,11,S insert a passage of one line [238*]: "I shall dry up the ocean so that the leaping monkeys can proceed on foot."

13. "to overflow them violently" *sahasā...nirmaryādaṃ kariṣyāmi*: Literally, "I will violently render it without bounds."

Following verse 13, D5–7,10,11,T,G1,2,M, and the texts and printed editions of the southern commentators insert a passage of one line [239*]: "I shall convulse the mighty ocean filled with great sharks.[1]"

[1]D6,7,10,11,G1,2,M3,5, and the texts and printed editions of the southern commentators substitute *mahādānavasaṃkulaṃ*, "filled with great *dānavas*," for the second *pāda* of 239*, *mahānakrasamākulam*, "filled with great sharks."

14. "eyes flashing with anger" *krodhavisphāritekṣaṇaḥ*: The adjective *visphārita* can have three different meanings, each of which can be applied to the eyes. Thus, the compound can mean "his eyes wide *or* dilated with anger" (so Gita Press 1969, vol. 3, p. 1427; Dutt 1893, p. 1160; Raghunathan 1982, vol. 3, p. 49; Roussel 1903, vol. 3, p. 57; and Shastri 1959, vol. 3, p. 50); "eyes rolling *or* trembling with anger"—so Cg (see notes to 5.20.23); or "eyes blazing *or* flashing with anger" (Gorresio 1856, vol. 9, p. 186, "*corruscanti*"). We feel that the last of these definitions is most appropriate in view of the simile of fire.

15. "Bending" *saṃpīḍya*: Literally, "having pressed *or* having crushed." We follow Ct and Ck, who understand that Rāma is bending his bow in order to string it (*saṃpīḍanapūrvaṃ sajyaṃ kṛtvā*). We believe that this interpretation is supported by the apparent glossing of the reading in the northern recension, which generally offers various forms of the root $\sqrt{}$*nam*, "to bend." Cg, on the other hand, understands the gerund to refer to Rāma's firm grasp of the middle portion of his bow (*dṛḍhamuṣṭinā madhyam avalambya*). Among the translators consulted, Raghunathan (1982, vol. 3, p. 49), Roussel (1903, vol. 3, p. 57), Shastri (1959, vol. 3, p. 50), and Pagani (1999, p. 917) follow this interpretation.

"made the world quake" *kampayitvā...jagat*: Among the commentators, only Cg remarks on this phrase, understanding it to mean that Rāma caused the creatures inhabiting the world to tremble with fear. (*kampayitvā bhayakampitaṃ kṛtvā. jagaj jagatsthajantūn.*) Northern manuscripts and printed editions of the northern recension generally substitute a clearly geological term such as *talam*, "surface of the earth," (Lahore 5.95.15) or *medinīm*, "earth," (Gorresio 5.103.16) for the ambiguous *jagat*, "world."

"with his arrows" *śaraiḥ*: D1,5–7,10,11,T1,3,G2,3,M1,2,5, and the texts and printed editions of Ct and Cr read instead the adverb *śanaiḥ*, "slowly, gently," which they construe with the gerund *saṃpīḍya*. Among the translations we have consulted, this reading is followed by only Gita Press (1969, vol. 3, p. 1437, "gently stringing"). Roussel (1903, vol. 3, p. 57), followed by Shastri (1959, vol. 3, p. 50), understands, "*de plus en plus*." Pagani (1999, p. 917), alone among the translators consulted, appears to read the adverb with the gerund *kampayitvā*, paraphrasing the construction as "*semant une terreur croissante.*"

"his thunderbolts" *vajrāṇi*: Cg, who, like the other southern commentators, reads the masculine *vajrān* for the critical edition's neuter *vajrāṇi*, regards the figure here as an *abhūtopamā*, i.e., a simile with a nonexistent object of comparison, since, in mythology, Indra has only one *vajra*.

16. "plunged into the waters of the sea, terrifying its great serpents" *praviśanti samudrasya salilaṃ trastapannagam*: Literally, "entered the ocean's water in which the serpents were terrified." See Slatin 2006 for a discussion of the significance of this episode in Indo-European mythology.

17. "Then" *tataḥ*: A number of manuscripts (Ñ2,V3,D10,11,M3,5), as well as the texts and printed editions of Ct and Cg, read instead *toya*[*vegaḥ*], "[agitation] of the waters." Cg glosses this reading with "a series of waves (*taraṅgavitatiḥ*)."

"along with a howling gale" *samārutaravaḥ*: Literally, "accompanied by the sound of the wind." Ct and Cr note that the wind is whipped up by the passage of the arrows themselves (*bāṇavegahetukapravartitamārutaśabdasahitaḥ*—so Ct).

"carrying with it sharks and sea monsters" *sanakramakaraḥ*: Literally, "along with sharks and sea monsters." D7,10,11, and the texts and printed editions of Ck, Ct, and Cr substitute for *-nakra-*, "sharks," *-mīna-*, "fish."

18. "covered with garlands of towering waves" *mahormimālāvitataḥ*: Cg reads the participle *vitataḥ*, "covered," in another of its basic meanings, "stretched, extended," understanding that the ocean was extended onto the shore through the force of its waves. D6,10,11, and the texts and printed editions of Ct read *-jālacalitaḥ* for *-mālāvitataḥ*, lending the compound the sense of "agitated with masses of towering waves."

"filled with conch and oyster shells" *śaṅkhaśuktisamākulaḥ*: Cg (reading *āvṛtaḥ* for *samākulaḥ*) understands that the shells have been tossed up by the violence of the waves. Ñ2,V1,3,B2–4,D6,7,9–11,G,M5, and the texts and printed editions of Ct and Cr read instead *śaṅkhajālasamāvṛtaḥ*, "covered with masses of conch shells."

"vaporous haze" *sadhūma-*: Literally, "with smoke *or* mist." Cr and Cg understand the reference to be to the steam arising from the contact of Rāma's blazing arrows with the water (*sajvālaśarapraveśena sadhūmaḥ*—so Cg).

19. "who dwell in the underworld known as Pātāla" *pātālatalavāsinaḥ*: Literally, "inhabitants of Pātāla." Cg indicates that the intention of this verse is to show that Rāma's arrows can penetrate even into the underworld (*āpātālaṃ śarāḥ praviṣṭā iti bhāvaḥ*).

"were in agony, flames shooting from their mouths and eyes" *vyathitāḥ . . . āsan dīptāsyā dīptalocanāḥ*: Literally, "they were agitated, with flaming mouths and with flaming eyes." Although the context would appear to suggest that the condition of the serpents is a result of the conflagration caused by Rāma's blazing arrows, we should note that it is a characteristic mark of these supernatural cobras to emit flames from their mouths and eyes. Compare 6.15.1 below, where the serpents accompanying Sāgara are described in exactly these terms.

20. "sharks and sea monsters" *-nakramakarāḥ*: See note to 6.11.8 above.

21. "Such was the state of the ocean, the repository of all waters" *saṃvṛttaḥ salilāśayaḥ*: Literally, "[so] was the repository of waters." D7,10,11, and the texts and printed editions of Ct and Cr read *saghoṣo varuṇālayaḥ*, "[the ocean,] abode of Varuṇa, emitted a sound," for *pāda* cd.

"crocodiles" *-grāhaḥ*: Cf. note to 5.7.6. See, too, 6.3.14; 6.4.78; 6.15.6,7; 6.62.20; and notes.

Following verse 21, D5–7,10,11,S insert a passage of twelve lines in the *upajāti* meter [244*]: "Then, as Rāghava, breathing hard, was drawing his incomparable bow with enormous force, Saumitri sprang up crying, 'Don't! Don't!' and seized the bow.[1] [1–4] 'The purpose of so powerful a person as you will be achieved this very day even without this treatment[2] of the ocean. People of your caliber never give way to anger. Sir, you must consider the immemorial[3] behavior of virtuous people.'[5–8] Then brahman-seers and divine seers, who hovered invisibly in the sky, raised a great uproar in the sky, crying, 'Woe!' and crying loudly, 'Don't! Don't!' [9–12]"

[1]D5,6,T1,3,G1,M3, and the texts and printed editions of Cm and Cg omit lines 5–12. Among the translators of the southern recension consulted, only Raghunathan (1982, vol. 3, p. 50), who generally renders the text of Cg, omits these lines.

[2]"even without this treatment" *etad vinā*: Literally, "without this." Ct understands, "without this agitation (*etad vināpi kṣobhanam*)," while Cr glosses, "destruction (*etad vināśanam*)."

[3]"immemorial" *dīrgham*: Literally, "long."

Sarga 15

Before *sarga* 15, Ś,D1–8,10–12,S insert a passage of thirty-two lines [App. I, No. 11]: "Then, the foremost of the Raghus addressed harsh words to Sāgara, 'This very day, mighty ocean, I will dry you up[1] all the way to the underworld Pātāla.[2] [1–2] A great cloud of dust will arise from you, Sāgara, once I have dried you up, your waters burnt off, and your creatures desiccated.[3] [3–4] By virtue of the hail of arrows released from my bow, Sāgara, the leaping monkeys shall this very day reach your farther shore[4] on foot.[5–6] You do not know enough to recognize[5] my power or my valor, and so, abode of the *dānavas*, you will come to grief at my hands.'[6] [7–8] The immensely powerful hero invoked the divine weapon-spell of Brahmā and, with it, charged an arrow that resembled Brahmā's staff. Then, nocking his superb bow, he drew it.[9–10] When that bow had been forcefully drawn by Rāghava, heaven and earth seemed to shatter and the mountains shook.[11–12] Darkness engulfed the world, and the directions became obscured. Lakes and rivers immediately overflowed.[13–14] The sun and the moon together with the constellations moved obliquely. Though illuminated by the rays of the sun, bringer of light, the sky was shrouded[7] in darkness.[15–16] Ablaze with hundreds of comets, the heavens glowed, while thunderbolts fell from the sky with an incomparable sound.[17–18] Gusts of heavenly wind sprang up in the sky. They broke down trees and caused the storm clouds to pour forth their rain.[8] [19–20] They shattered[9] the mountaintops, smashing[10] their peaks; huge thunderclouds gathered, reaching up to the heavens and thundering loudly.[21–22] With great claps of thunder, they released fiery bolts of lightning. All creatures that could be seen cried out as loudly as the claps of thunder.[23–24] Those who were invisible unleashed terrifying cries. Overwhelmed and terrified, they trembled and cowered.[11] Deeply pained, they remained frozen in fear.[25–27] Then all at once the ocean became fearsomely agitated through this agitation. And together with its waves of water, its creatures, its great serpents, and its *rākṣasas*, it flooded and washed over its boundaries for a distance of a league.[28–30] But Rāma Rāghava, slayer of his enemies, did not give any ground even as the ocean, lord of rivers and streams, surged, swollen beyond its boundaries.[12] [31–32]"

[1]"mighty ocean, I will dry you up" *tvāṃ śoṣayiṣyāmi … mahārṇava*: D10,11, and the texts and printed editions of Ct read the nominative *aham*, "I," for *tvām*, "you," and the accusative singular *mahārṇavam*, "mighty ocean," for the vocative, yielding the sense "I will dry up the mighty ocean."

[2]"all the way to the underworld Pātāla" *sapātālam*: Literally, "along with Pātāla." Cr glosses, "together with Pātāla (*pātālasahitam*)." A number of translations render accordingly. We, however, prefer the interpretation of Cg, who glosses, "to the limit of Pātāla (*pātālaparyantam*)," since the underworld Pātāla is thought to lie underneath the sea and Rāma has no particular grievance with it or its inhabitants.

[3]"your creatures desiccated" *śoṣitasattvasya*: We follow Ct and Cr here in taking the polysemic term *sattva-* in the sense of "living being" or, here, "aquatic creature." D10,11,M1,2, and the texts and printed editions of Ct read *nihata-*, "slain," for *śoṣita-*, "desiccated, dried up."

[4]"this very day … farther shore" *pāraṃ te 'dya*: D10,11, and the texts and printed editions of Ct read instead *paraṃ tīram*, "the other shore."

[5]"You do not know enough to recognize" *vicinvan nābhijānāsi*: Literally, "reflecting, you do not understand." The construction is ambiguous, but we believe that Cg and Cm have understood the sense best. Cg glosses, "you do not know to reflect upon *or* investigate particularly (*vicinvan viśeṣeṇa paryālocayituṃ nābhijānāsi*)." Raghunathan (1982, vol. 3, p. 50) interprets accordingly. Ct and Cr understand the verb *vi* √*ci* in its other sense of "collect, gather" and take the phrase here to mean that the ocean, because of the great mass of water it has collected, [thinks itself immune to Rāma's power] (*vipulajalādiparigṛhṇaṃs tvam*—so Cr).

[6]"you will come to grief at my hands" *saṃtāpaṃ matto nāma gamiṣyasi*: Literally, "you will surely go to suffering from me." G2,3,M3, and the texts and printed editions of Crā and Cg read *nādhigamiṣyasi* (*nāvagamiṣyasi*—so Cm), "you do not understand [the suffering]," for *nāma gamiṣyasi*, "surely you will go."

[7]"Though illuminated … the sky was shrouded" *ādīptam … samāvṛtam*: Literally, "illuminated … shrouded." Following the suggestion of Ct and Cr, we have supplied the word "sky (*ākāśam*—Ct; *nabhaḥ*—Cr)."

[8]"Gusts of heavenly wind sprang up in the sky. They broke down trees and caused storm clouds to pour forth their rain." *pusphuruś ca punar divyā divi mārutapaṅktayaḥ / babhañja ca tadā vṛkṣāñ jaladān udvavarṣa ca //*: Literally, "Heavenly groups *or* rows of winds burst forth in the sky. It then broke trees and it made the clouds rain." The lines are both grammatically and contextually problematic. The construction of the verse is peculiar since the subject, *mārutapaṅktayaḥ*, "gusts [lines] of winds," appears to construe logically with the two singular verbs, *babhañja*, "broke down," and *udvavarṣa*, "made rain." Ct and Cr read *vapuḥprakarṣeṇa vavur divyamārutapaṅktayaḥ*, "gusts of heavenly wind blew because of the strength of their form," for the first line, and

udvahan muhuḥ, "driving forth repeatedly," for the critical edition's *udvavarṣa ca* in the second line. They understand that the second line has an unexpressed singular subject, *mārutapaṅktiḥ*, "a line or mass of clouds" (Ct), or *mahāvātaḥ*, "mighty wind" (Cr). Cg understands the compound *mārutapaṅktayaḥ* to refer to the seven winds or layers of air that are supposed to characterize the atmospheric realm between heaven and earth (*āvahodvahādivātaskandhāḥ*). He then takes the adjective *divyāḥ*, "heavenly," in the sense of "praiseworthy *or* venerable (*ślāghyāḥ*)."

[9]"They shattered" *ārujan*: The form is ambiguous. It can be interpreted either as a plural imperfect of the sixth *gaṇa* verb *ā* $\sqrt{}$*ruj*, or as the nominative singular masculine of its present participle. In keeping with the prevailing syntax of lines 20–21 where the other verbal and nominal forms are singular, we suppose that this form is also intended to be singular, although, given that the logical subject remains the plural noun *mārutapaṅktayaḥ* of line 19, we have rendered it as if it were plural. Cg reads the unambiguously plural imperfect *arujan*, which he then hastens to inform us is an irregular plural, i.e., that we should understand it as a singular (*bahuvacanam ārṣam*).

[10]"smashing" *prabhañjanaḥ*: Literally, "the breaker *or* smasher." The poet concludes this awkward sequence with a singular noun in place of the expected plural verbal element.

[11]"they . . . cowered" *śiśyire*: Literally, "they lay down."

[12]"did not give any ground . . . surged, swollen beyond its boundaries" *samatikrāntaṃ nāticakrāma . . . tam uddhatam*: Literally, "he [Rāghava] did not transgress *or* cross [the ocean], which, swollen, had transgressed." Like several translators, we understand the phrase *nāticakrāma*, as does Cr, to mean that, despite the dramatic surging of the ocean, Rāma stood his ground (*tatraiva tasthau*). Cg, however, understands the phrase to mean that Rāma did not attack the ocean by using his weapons (*śastraprayoga-rūpātikramaṃ na cakāra*). Ct understands simply, "he did not budge (*na cacāla*)."

1. "Samudra Sāgara . . . he" *sāgaraḥ . . . samudraḥ*: Cs identifies the ocean divinity as Varuṇa, a vedic divinity who presides over the waters and is often identified with Sāgara.

"flames shooting from their mouths" *dīptāsyaiḥ*: See note above on 6.14.19.

"from the great mountain Meru" *mahāśailān meroḥ*: Cs cites the lexicon *Viśvakośa*, whose listing of "bow" as one of the meanings of Meru inspires him to suggest as an alternative that Sāgara is rising because of his fear of Rāma's weapon. (*meror dhanuṣo bhayād utthita iti vā. "merur bhūdharadhanvanoḥ" iti viśvaḥ.*)

2. "His complexion was that of polished lapis" *snigdhavaidūryasaṃkāśaḥ*: Literally, "having the appearance of glistening *or* smooth lapis." The idea is that Sāgara's complexion is as dark and shining as polished lapis. A dark blue and/or black complexion is not uncommon among the Hindu divinities, such as Viṣṇu. Compare 1.1.11; 5.33.16; and *UttaRāC* I.15.5. See note to 6.73.13. On lapis, see note to 6.3.13.

"he was adorned with *jāmbūnada* gold" *jāmbūnadavibhūṣitaḥ*: Cg identifies *jāmbūnada* as gold produced in the Jambū River, one of the seven heavenly rivers (*jāmbūnadaṃ jambūnadīprabhavaṃ svarṇam*). See 6.19.22–23; 6.47.21,41; 6.55.115,121; 6.67.13. See Vyas 1967, p. 244; cf. p. 247. See, too, 5.2.53; 5.3.8–11; 35–37; 5.5.32–33,39; 5.6.13; 5.9.20–21; 5.45.3–4; and notes. Cf. note on 5.34.27.

"His garlands and robes were red" *raktamālyāmbaradharaḥ*: Literally, "wearing red garlands and clothing." See 6.67.5 and notes.

Following verse 2, D5–7,10,11,S insert a passage of four lines [247*] in which Sāgara is further described: "On his head he wore a celestial wreath consisting of every type of blossom, together with ornaments made of burnished gold. Adorned with the most exquisite ornaments made of gems produced within himself, he resembled the Himalaya mountain adorned with his various mineral ores.[1–4]" Various northern manuscripts (Ś,Ñ2,D1–4,8,9,12, while B4 continues after line 1 of 246*) insert 247* after verse 1.

Following this insert, some southern manuscripts (D7,G2,M3,5) and the texts and printed editions of Cg and the edition of Gita Press (6.22.21cd–22ab) add another passage of two lines [249*]: "On his broad chest he wore a glittering rose-colored gem, which lay at the center of his pearl necklace. It was the twin of the Kaustubha gem.[1]"

[1]"Kaustubha gem" *kausthubhasya*: The Kaustubha gem is one of the magnificent jewels produced at the time of the churning of the primal ocean. It is one of the accoutrements of Lord Viṣṇu.

Following this passage, all southern manuscripts except M4 insert a passage of three lines [250*]: "His masses of waves were swirling, his waters were agitated by the stormy winds.[1] He was accompanied by the rivers among whom the foremost were the Ganges and the Indus.[1] [2] His *rākṣasas* and great serpents were terrified, and his huge crocodiles were tossed about.[3]" Compare 6.14.21.

[1]"the Ganges and the Indus" *gaṅgāsindhu-* Literally, "the Gaṅgā and the Sindhu." We are, of course, to understand that it is the goddesses presiding over the rivers that are meant.

Following this, a few southern manuscripts (G2,M3,5,T2 [after 3ab]) and the texts and printed editions of Cm [VSP unnumbered in brackets between 6.22.23 and 24] and Gita Press (6.22.24ab) insert a passage of one line [251*] further describing the rivers: "[accompanied by the rivers] who had taken on the various forms of beautiful goddesses . . . that lord."

3. Cs notes an apparent contradiction between this version of Rāma's meeting with Sāgara and that found in the *Rāmopākhyāna* (*MBh* 3.267.32cd and 33), where the text indicates that Rāma has a vision of the ocean god in a dream as he lies sleeping on the shore. Citing a parallel passage from the *Bhāgavatapurāṇa* (9.10.13) and the different contexts of the three versions, Cs concludes that there is no real contradiction, for although Rāma may have slept, Sāgara and his sea creatures appear to him in the flesh in the *Mahābhārata* version as well as in our passage.

4. "All the elements . . . earth, air, ether, water, and fire" *pṛthivī vāyur ākāśam āpo jyotiś ca*: The reference is to the five irreducible elements [*pañcamahābhūtas*] of traditional Indian philosophy. We have added the phrase, "all the elements," to convey this idea. See notes to 6.15.4; 6.55.127; 6.81.20; and 6.97.7. Cf. 6.39.7; 6.89.4; and notes.

"gentle Rāghava" *rāghava . . . saumya*: Cg glosses, "propitiated *or* pacified (*prasanna*)" for *saumya*. He argues that the epithet shows that Rāma has been pacified by Sāgara's having cupped his hands in reverence (*anenāñjalikaraṇānantaram eva rāmaḥ prasanna iti gamyate*). It is more likely that Sāgara's use of the term here is intended to accomplish the propitiation of Rāma.

"must abide by their respective natures" *svabhāve . . . tiṣṭhanti*: Literally, "they stand in their own nature." The commentators give different explanations as to the inherent nature of water, which is relevant to the current passage. Ct, Ck, and Cr understand that it is "movement (*syandanam*)" and "contact (*śleṣaṇam*)." Cg and Cv, adhering to the context made clear in verse 5 below, stress the fathomless depth (*-agādha-*) of the ocean as one of its inherent qualities.

"eternal path" *śāśvataṃ mārgam*: Ck, Ct, and Cr explain that this refers to the rule of abiding by one's inherent nature, which was set down by the creator, Brahmā (*anādiṃ brahmasṛṣṭaṃ svarūpasthitiprakāram āsthitāḥ santaḥ sve sve bhāve tiṣṭhanti*).

5. "impossible to cross" *aplavaḥ*: Literally, "impossible to jump *or* swim."

"I tell you that" *etat te pravadāmy aham*: By the grammatical rule *vartamānasāmīpye laṭ*, the present indicative may indicate near past or near future time. All commentators understand the present (*laṭ*) here as either a reference to what Sāgara has already told Rāma or to what he is just about to tell him. Thus Cg, Cm, and Cv understand the verb to be a preterit (*laṅ*), seeing it as a reference to what Sāgara has already told Rāma about the natural qualities of the elements. Cg mentions a variant reading *pradadāmi*, "I give," unattested in the critical apparatus, which he claims would have the same meaning. Cm sees this as Sāgara's explanation as to why he did not previously appear before Rāma. Ct, Cr, and Ck understand it to be a near future and supply the word *upāyam*, "means [for crossing]," understanding, "I will now tell you the means."

"it would violate that nature" *vikāras tu bhavet*: Literally, "it would be a transformation."

6. "desire, greed" *kāmāt . . . lobhāt*: Ct, Cg, and Cm distinguish the two, defining the former as "the desire for objects (*arthecchayā*—Cg)" and the latter as "the inability to bear giving up one's own things (*svavastuparityāgāsahiṣṇutayā*—Cg)."

"make solid" *stambhayeyam*: The verb is slightly ambiguous. It can be understood either as we have understood it in our translation or in the sense of "to immobilize," that is, in the present context, to calm or still the ocean's turbulent waters. Both the commentators and the various northern readings more or less unanimously support the notion that it is the actual freezing or solidification of the water that is at issue here. Ct and Ck say that the ocean will not solidify his waters because that would be the occasion for doing violence to his inherent nature since that nature is to be watery, i.e., liquid (*jalarūpasya me svarūpapīḍāprasaṅgāt*). Cg is somewhat ambiguous, saying that the ocean refuses because to do so would do harm (*pīḍākaratvāt*). Cm and Cv are more explicit, claiming that the ocean refuses so as to avoid harming the aquatic creatures (*jalacarajantupīḍā*). Cm explicitly glosses the root √*stambh* with the term *ghanībhavanena*, "becoming solid *or* congealed." Northern variants are entirely unambiguous (see 258* and apparatus). Thus, the Lahore edition (5.96.28, vol. 5, p. 606) reads, "I will solidify my waters, Rāma, and thus create a footpath, whereby the tawny monkeys will be able to cross without obstruction (*stambhayeyaṃ jalaṃ rāma padbhyāṃ caiva tathā gatim / gaccheraṃs tena harayo na tu stambho bhaviṣyati //*)." Gorresio's edition (5.104.8) has a variant, which reads, "Solidify my waters, Rāma, and I will provide you an excellent path by which the tawny monkeys may proceed. There will be no [need of a] bridge (*stambhayaitaj jalaṃ rāma dadyāṃ te mārgam uttamam / gaccheyur yena harayo na ca setur bhaviṣyati //*)." Both go on to say that the appearance of dry land in the ocean would be a great miracle. In the end, however, as in our text, Sāgara declines to perform this miracle, not because of the violation of his inherent nature or the possible injury to marine life but because of his fear that other beings as powerful as Rāma, taking this as a precedent, might compel its repetition. Translators have disagreed as to how to understand the root √*stambh*. Some (Gita Press 1969, vol. 3, p. 1440; Roussel 1903, vol. 3 p. 60; and Shastri 1959, vol. 3, p. 52) understand as we have. Dutt (1893, p. 1163) understands, "deprive my waters . . . of their (perpetual) motion." Raghunathan (1982, vol. 3, p. 51) seems to straddle the issue slightly, rendering, "freeze into immobility my waters." This latter interpretation is not entirely unreasonable, as the commentators explain in reference to the preceding verse that one of the immutable characteristics of water is its constant motion (*syandanam*).

"crocodiles and sharks" *grāhanakra-*: Some southern manuscripts (D6,10,11,T2,3), including the texts and printed editions of Ct, Ck, and Cr, read *rāgāt* for *grāha-*, thus adding another inducement, "passion, affection," to those that Sāgara claims cannot influence him to still his waters. See note on verse 7 below.

7. "I shall . . . devise some means" *vidhāsye rāma yenāpi*: Literally, "I shall arrange . . . whereby . . . Rāma." Some southern manuscripts (D7,10,11,G2,3), including the texts of Ct, Cr, and Ck, read *yena gantāsi*, "whereby you will proceed," for *rāma yenāpi*.

"sea monsters" *grāhāḥ*: Here we interpret the term as generic for predatory sea creatures rather than as a specific type of animal. Cf. note on 5.7.6. See, too, 6.3.14; 6.4.78; 6.14.21; 6.15.6; 6.62.20; and notes.

"will not attack" *na prahariṣyanti*: D10,11,G2, and the texts and printed editions of Ct and Ck read *na . . . vidhamiṣyanti*, "they will not scatter, destroy."

Following verse 7, many northern manuscripts (Ś,Ñ2,D1–4,8,9,12) insert 261*, 263*, 265*, 266*, 267*, App. I, No. 12, and 268*, while all southern manuscripts (D5–7,10,11,S) insert 262*(missing in KK and VSP), 263*, 264*, 265*, and 269*. The southern insert appears in the published editions of GPP (6.22.26de–40), VSP (6.22.28–43), and KK (6.22.28–42).

In 262*, a passage of five lines, Sāgara continues his speech to Rāma: " 'In order that the tawny monkeys may cross, Rāma, I shall create some dry ground.'[1] Then Rāma said to him, 'Listen to me, O god of the ocean, abode of Varuṇa. This great arrow of mine can never be taken up in vain.[1] On which place shall I let it fall?'[2–3] When the mighty lord of the ocean, of immense blazing energy, had heard Rāma's words and seen that great arrow, he said these words to Rāghava.[4–5]"

[1]"taken up in vain" *amoghaḥ*: Literally, "in vain, unerring." See also 5.36.30, where the divine weapon-spell of Brahmā similarly may not be loosed in vain, and 1.75.8, where the divine arrow of Viṣṇu is said to never fly in vain." Cf. note to 6.88.22, where the javelin of Rāvaṇa is considered to be renowned for its infallibility.

In 263*, a passage of eleven lines, Sāgara responds: " 'Away to the north lies one of my most beautiful tracts. It is called Drumakulya[1] and is as famous throughout the world as you are, sir.[1–2] In that place, drinking up my waters, are many savage tribes, the Ābhīras, etc., whose practices are frightful to see.[3–4] I cannot bear the defiling touch of those evildoers. Please use your great and unfailing arrow against them, Rāma.'[5–6] When Rāghava had heard his words, he released that supreme, blazing arrow in keeping with the instructions of Sāgara.[2] [7–8] At the spot famed throughout the earth as Marukāntāra,[3] 'The Wasteland,' he caused his arrow, whose splendor was equal to that of a blazing lightning bolt, to fall to the earth, the bestower of treasures. Stricken by that shaft, the earth itself gave a loud roar.[9–11]"

[1]"Drumakulya" *drumakulyaḥ*: Literally, "associated with a group *or* family of trees." This name contrasts with the subsequent name of the place, Marukāntāra, and appears to suggest that Rāma's fiery arrow has deforested or defoliated the once densely forested region.

[2]"in keeping with the instructions of Sāgara" *sāgaradarśanāt*: Literally, "from the sight of Sāgara." The word *darśana* is polysemic and is used here in its sense of "mentioning, judgment, teaching" rather than in its more common sense of "sight, vision, *or* appearance."

[3]"Marukāntāra, 'The Wasteland' " *marukāntāram*: Literally, "desert-wilderness." A tract known as Marubhūmi is described as "a desert area around the Jodhpur region" (Narayan 1980, p. 145). See also *MBh* 5.19.29.

In 264*, a passage of six lines, the story continues: "From the opening of the resulting wound (*vraṇa*), water spurted up from the underworld known as Rasātala, and that became the well famed as "The Wound (*vraṇa*)." A geyser of water is seen constantly to rise there, as if from the ocean itself, accompanied by a terrifying sound of something being torn apart.[1–4] By virtue of the [destruction caused by the] impact of his arrow, [Rāma] dried up the standing waters in low-lying places, and that place became famous throughout the three worlds as Marukāntāra, 'The Wasteland.'[5–6]"

In 265*, a passage of six lines, the narrative continues: "Once Rāma, the son of Daśaratha, had drained the low-lying places, that wise man, whose valor was like that of the immortals, conferred a boon on that wasteland.[1–2] By virtue of Rāma's bestowal of his boon, that wasteland became a prosperous region, forever possessed of these many virtues: it had ample pasturage and was virtually free of disease, it was richly endowed with fruits and roots and honey,[1] rich in ghee[2] and milk, and fragrant with various aromatic herbs.[3–6]"

[1]"honey" *-rasa-*: The precise sense of the polysemic term *rasa* here, "juice, sap, essence, water, flavor," and the like, is difficult to determine. We follow the gloss of Cg, who understands *madhu*, "honey."

[2]"rich in ghee" *bahusnehaḥ*: Literally, "having much oil *or* grease." We follow Cg, who glosses *ghṛtam*, "ghee," for *snehaḥ*. Cr understands more literally, "things characterized by oil *or* grease (*snehaviśiṣṭavastūni*)."

269* is a passage of two lines: "When those low-lying places had been parched, Samudra, lord of rivers, said these words to Rāghava, who was expert in all the *śāstras*.[1–2]"

8. "equal of Viśvakarman" *pratimo viśvakarmaṇaḥ*: This reading is apparently found only in V2,B1,M3,G2,3. KK 6.22.43 and VSP 6.22.46 also read with the critical edition; KK notes, however, that six of its manuscripts read *prītimān*, "affectionate," while

two read *dhṛtimān*, "resolute," for *pratimaḥ*, "equal." The critical reading is an otherwise unattested masculine form of the expected feminine *pratimā*. The reading should be considered doubtful at best. A number of southern manuscripts (D6,7,10, 11,T2,3,M4), including the texts and printed editions of Ct, Cr, and Cs, substitute *prītimān*, "affectionate," for *pratimaḥ*. Ct, Cr, and those translators who follow this reading understand, "affectionate toward you [that is, Rāma]." We understand that the quality referred to here is Nala's ability to build things, a quality that he shares with his father, the divine architect.

"granted a boon" *dattavaraḥ*: Ct, Cr, and Ck understand that the boon confers the power to construct anything. Ck adds the quality of invulnerability to all beings. Cg understands that the boon consists in Viśvakarman's promise to his [son's] mother that his son will be his equal (*dattavaraḥ mattulyaḥ putras te bhaviṣyatīti mātre dattavaraḥ*) (Cv similarly). Cm amplifies upon this, saying that the son will have equal ability with his father, who is skillful enough to construct solid buildings on top of water and even in the sky (*pitrā viśvakarmaṇā dattavara ākāśajaloparisthāyigamanaśīlavimānādinirmāṇādisvakarmakuśalena sadṛśasāmarthyaḥ*). Most interesting in this context is that the former group of commentators accepts one additional line [276* = GPP 6.22.47cd], which specifies the terms of the boon as equality with Viśvakarman, whereas Cg, Cm, Cv, and the critical edition do not read this line. Cv, on the other hand, acknowledges that the substance of the line must be understood in order for the passage to make sense (*mama mātur varo datta iti mayā sadṛśaḥ putraḥ tava bhaviṣyatīty evaṃ rūpo 'yam arthaḥ*). See note to verse 12 below.

9. Cm, commenting upon 307(C)* (see notes to verse 11 below for the translation), raises the interesting question as to why, since the ocean was a kinsman of Rāma and had already provided assistance to Hanumān through the agency of Mount Maināka (5.1.75–120), he did not propose this solution when Rāma first came and had a pleasant frame of mind. Cm's response is that Sāgara has planned his delay deliberately in order to arouse Rāma's anger, which could then be used to destroy his, i.e., the ocean's, enemies [the *dasyus*]. He had planned all along to propitiate Rāma once the latter had accomplished this feat. Cm finds no fault with this strategy. (*nanu rāmasambandhitvamātreṇa hanumate maināakadvāreṇa kṛtopakāraḥ sāgaraḥ sākṣād rāme samāgatya prasanne saty amūm upāyaṃ prathamata evāvilambena kim arthaṃ nopadiṣṭavān iti cet? satyam. mayā ca vilambe kriyamāṇe vilambam asahamāno rāmo mayi kopād astraṃ sandhāsyaty etasminn antare taṃ prasādayitvā saṃhitenāstreṇa mama śatrūn mārayitvā paścād upakariṣyāmīti dhiyā sthita iti na doṣaḥ*.) Ct understands similarly.

10. "mighty" *mahābalaḥ*: D5,7,10,11,T,G3, and the texts and printed editions of Ct and Cr read instead the masculine singular accusative, *mahābalam*, which then modifies Rāma.

11. "abode of Varuṇa" *varuṇālaye*: A number of manuscripts, both northern and southern (Ś,Ñ,V1,3,B2–4,D1,4,8–12,G2,3), including the texts and printed editions of Ct and Cr, read *makara-*, "sea monster," for *varuṇa-*.

Virtually all the northern manuscripts (Ś,Ñ,V1,3,B2–4,D1–4,8,9,12) insert a passage of twenty lines [307*] following verse 23. A number of southern manuscripts (D6,7, 10,11,T2,3,G,M), including the texts and printed editions of the southern commentators, insert four of these lines following verse 11 [307* lines 5,6,307 (C) *,8]: "It seems to me that, in this world, force is the best thing to use upon the wicked.[1] [5] To hell with forbearance,[2] conciliation, and bribery when it comes to ingrates.[6] It was only out of eagerness to see[3] the construction of a bridge and his fear of force that this dreadful Sāgara, great receptacle of waters, granted shallow passage to Rāghava. [307(C)*, 8]"

[1]"use upon the wicked" *durjane pratibhāti naḥ*: The southern manuscripts and commentators (D6,7,10,11,T2,3,G,M) read instead *puruṣasyeti* (D6 *puruṣasyaiva*) *me matiḥ*, " '. . . against a man' is my opinion."

[2]"To hell with forbearance" *dhik kṣamām*: See 6.14.11 and note.

[3]"out of eagerness to see" *didṛkṣayā*: Literally, "with a desire to see." Ct argues that Sāgara's desire to see the bridge built is a product only of his fear of Rāma's use of force against him, since he is an ingrate in that he does not acknowledge the fact that he was made to grow by Rāma's ancestors, the sons of King Sagara (*yato 'yaṃ sāgaro rāmapūrvaiḥ sagaraputrair vardhito 'py akṛtajñatayā daṇḍabhayād eva saṃjātayā didṛkṣayā tajjanyadarśanena rāghavāya setuṃ kartuṃ gādhaṃ dadau*). See note to verse 9 above. He continues his argument in a fashion similar to Cm's discussion on verse 9 above.

12. "boon" *varaḥ*: The actual boon is not mentioned in the critical edition (see note to verse 8 above). This deficiency is made up in a passage of one line [276*], which is found in D7,10,11,G2,3, and Ct after 12ab: "Your son, my lady, shall be my equal."

"legitimate son" *aurasaḥ . . . putraḥ*: Literally, "born from the breast." The term is frequently used to indicate a biological or legitimate child as distinct from a stepchild or an adopted child. Ct is explicit in this regard, stating that the term here means "a son created through the emission of his [Viśvakarman's] semen while he was embracing (Nala's) mother (*mātur āliṅganapūrvaṃ svatejoniśekadvārānirmitaḥ putra ity arthaḥ*)." It is this genetic relationship, Ct argues, that explains the fact that Nala shares Viśvakarman's ability to create extraordinary constructions. See 5.49.14 and note.

13. "I could not proclaim . . . without being called upon" *na cāpy aham anukto vai prabrūyām*: Literally, "unaddressed I could not announce *or* speak out." As Ck and Ct explain, Nala has not spoken up previously because he would have been ashamed to indulge in self-praise (*ātmapraśaṃsālajjayeti*). See Goldman and Goldman 1996, pp. 27, 76, and 5.64.25 and note.

"Very well" *kāmam*: We have read the term here as an interjection. It could also be read adverbially in the sense of "at will." Two *devanāgarī* manuscripts (D10,11) and the texts and printed editions of Ct and Cr read instead *tasmāt*, "on account of that, therefore."

Following 13ab, D5–7,10,11,T2,3,G,M, and the texts and printed editions of Cg and Ct insert a passage of one line [278*]: "And I am certainly capable of building a bridge across the ocean, abode of Varuṇa." Following this D5 continues, while D7 and M3 insert following verse 12, a passage of one line [275* line 2]. The verse as it is found in the southern recension (the second *pāda* differs from the northern version) reads: "I was reminded of this by him. The ocean, that great receptacle of waters, has told you the truth (= 11d)." Printed editions that read this text are GPP 6.22.48cd; Gita Press 6.22.52ab; KK 6.22.50ab; and VSP 6.22.52ab.

15. "monkeys, bulls among the hosts of tree-dwelling monkeys" *śākhāmṛgagaṇarṣabhāḥ . . . vānarāḥ*: Literally, "monkeys . . . bulls among the hosts of branch-animals." The word *śākhāmṛga*, literally, "branch-deer, branch-animal," is a kenning for monkey. See note to 6.47.43. See, too, 6.17.32; 6.19.20; 6.40.64; 6.61.2; 6.65.11;

6.73.6; and notes. D7,10,11, and the texts and printed editions of Ct avoid the redundancy here by substituting *pādapān*, "trees," literally, "foot-drinkers." See the following note.

"resembling mountains... trees" *nagān nagasaṃkāśāḥ*: The first *pāda* exploits the repetition of the word *naga*. The term is ambiguous, however. A kenning meaning, "that which does not move," *naga* can refer equally to trees and mountains. We have chosen "resembling mountains" for the phrase *nagasaṃkāśāḥ*, both because it is the universal choice of the commentators and because mountains are a common *upamāna* for the giant *vānaras* throughout the poem. For *nagān*, the ambiguity is greater. We chose "trees" because, in the following two verses (16 and 17), there is a list of the names of the different kinds of trees the monkeys throw into the water. This idea is supported by Cg, who reads with the critical edition. The other southern commentators substitute *pādapān*, "trees," for *vānarāḥ*, "monkeys," in *pāda* c. This reading, found in D7,10,11, and Ct, Ck, and Cr, opens up yet another area of ambiguity. The verse can now be read to mean that the monkeys break up "mountains (*nagān*)" and "trees (*pādapān*)" and drag them to the sea. The southern commentators Ct, Ck, and Cr, however, propose to read the second "n" of *nagān* as the *sandhi* form of the final "t" of the ablative (*pañcamī*) singular *nagāt*. They would thus read, "broke down trees and dragged them from the mountain to the sea." Most translators who follow this reading (Roussel 1903, vol. 3, p. 62; Shastri 1959, vol. 3, pp. 53–54; Pagani 1999, p. 921; and Gita Press 1969, vol. 3, p. 1443) understand that the monkeys break up both rocks and timber. In any case, all recensions indicate that both trees and mountains are used in the construction of the bridge.

16–17. Cg claims that the poet enumerates all these trees in order to show that the ones named have achieved their purpose, which is to assist in the construction of the bridge (*setubandhanasāhyakṛtāṃ vṛkṣāṇāṃ kṛtārthatāṃ vyañjayituṃ tān parigaṇayati*).

"*sāla, aśvakarṇa*" *sālaiś cāśvakarṇaiś ca*: Both names normally refer to the tree *Vatica robusta*. According to Ck and Ct, they refer to subspecies of the same plant (*sālāśvakarṇayor avāntarajātikṛto bhedaḥ*). Ck understands that one, presumably the *sāla*, has white flowers, whereas the *aśvakarṇa* has red flowers (*śvetaraktapuṣpādibhedena*). Since the two terms usually appear in close proximity in the *Rāmāyaṇa*, Brockington argues that *aśvakarṇa* ("horse-eared") was at one time an adjective for *sāla* or that they are two different trees (1984, p. 102).

18. "tree trunks... trees" *pādapān... tarūn*: Literally, "trees... trees." We have translated the first as "tree trunks," in keeping with the simile of the flagstaffs as well as to avoid repetition. Cf. 6.30.26 and note.

"the foremost among the tawny monkeys" *harisattamāḥ... harayaḥ*: Literally, "the foremost among the tawny monkeys... the tawny monkeys. We have collapsed the two terms to avoid repetition.

Following verse 18, D5–7,10,11,S, and the texts and printed editions of Ct insert a passage of four lines [293*]: "They carried off from various places palmyras, clusters of pomegranate, coconut palms, *vibhītakas*, *bakulas*, *khadiras*, and neem trees. After smashing the mountains, those huge and powerful monkeys with the aid of various conveyances[1] carried off boulders the size of elephants."

[1]"with the aid of various conveyances" *yantraiḥ*: Literally, "with machines, devices." The commentators understand that these are devices that facilitate easy transport

(*sukhāharaṇasādhanaiḥ*—so Ct). Cg glosses, "with carts, etc. (*śakatādibhiḥ*)." Cf. 6.3.11; 6.30.26; 6.49.11; 6.80.19; and notes.

19. "boulders" *acalaiḥ*: Normally, "mountains." The context, however, supports the less common usage.

Following verse 19, D5–7,10,11,S insert a passage of two lines [295*]: "Hurling[1] them from every side, they whipped up the ocean. Meanwhile, others held lines[2] stretching one hundred leagues in length."

[1]"Hurling" *nipatantaḥ*: Literally, "falling." This would appear to refer to the boulders in verse 19. However, since the second half of the verse clearly refers to other monkeys, we follow Cr, who reads the simplex participle as a causative.

[2]"lines" *sūtrāṇi*: Commentators differ as to the purpose of the lines. Ck and Ct see them as used for hauling [the rocks and trees, etc.] (*ākarṣaṇārtham iti śeṣaḥ*). Cr, Cg, and Ct, as his second option, argue that they are stretched out to ensure that the bridge is straight (*setor avakratvāyeti vā śeṣaḥ*—Ct). Cm and Cs envision them as measuring tapes to ensure that the bridge is neither too long nor too short (*śatayojanadīrghaparyantasya nyūnātiriktaparihārārtham*—Cm) or to make the bridge exactly one hundred *yojanas* in length (*śatayojanam āyataṃ dīrghaṃ setuṃ kartum*—Cs).

20. "Nala constructed" *nalaś cakre*: Cr comments that in saying here that Nala built the bridge and elsewhere that the other monkeys built it, the poet intends us to understand that the monkeys gather the materials for the construction while Nala is responsible for putting them together to form the structure (*nalo mahāsetuṃ cakre sa setuḥ tadā vānarair itarakapibhir api kriyata etena pāṣāṇādisaṃghaṭṭanaṃ nalāyattaṃ sāmāgrīsaṃpādanaṃ tu tad itarāyatam iti sūcitam*). We believe we are to understand Nala to be the architect or chief engineer of the project while the monkeys are the laborers.

The textual history of this passage is complex and rather confusing. No known version reads with the reconstruction of the critical edition. *Pādas* ab of this verse correspond to GPP 6.22.72cd (VSP 6.22.77ab; KK 6.22.76ab) and *pādas* cd correspond to GPP 6.22.59ab (VSP 6.22.63ab; KK 6.22.61ab). The vulgate text of the southern recension (GPP 6.22.59–72; VSP 6.22.63–77; and KK 6.22.61–76) is represented in the critical text and apparatus by the following sequence: 6.15.20cd; 299*; 6.15.21; App. I, No. 13, lines 1–2; 303*; 6.15.22; 6.15.23; 6.15.20ab; and 296*. As a result of this, some events as rendered in our translation will occur in a different sequence than the same events represented in other editions and translations. See Sutherland 1992.

Following 20ab, V1,3,B2 (after 26),D5–7,10,11,S, and the texts and printed editions of the southern commentators insert a passage of one line [296*] (= GPP 6.22.72cd): "And the gods and the *gandharvas* gazed upon Nala's bridge, all but impossible to build."

Following 20cd, D5–7,10,11,S, and the texts and printed editions of the southern commentators insert a passage of seven lines [299*] (= GPP 6.22.59cd–62): "Thus was the bridge built by those monkeys of awesome deeds.[1] Some held rods,[1] while others gathered materials.[2] [2] Hundreds of monkeys, obedient to Rāma's command and resembling great clouds and mountains, built it with straw and logs.[3–4] The monkeys built the bridge out of trees with flowering tips. Monkeys resembling great elephants could be seen racing about, carrying boulders that were like mountains and even the peaks of the mountains themselves.[5–7]"

[1]"rods" *daṇḍān*: Cr understands these to be some kind of measuring or surveying rods. Cg offers two suggestions: that they are the rods to which the surveyors' lines [in 295* above] are attached or that they are used, as he delicately puts it, to speed up the monkeys [presumably by flogging them].

[2]"gathered materials" *vicinvanti*: Literally, "they gather."

21. = GPP 6.22.63.

Following verse 21, D5–7,10,11,S, and the texts and printed editions of the southern edition insert a passage of two lines [App. I, No. 13, lines 1–2] (= GPP 6.22.64): "On the first day, the monkeys, resembling mountains and engrossed in their work on the bridge,[1] completed fourteen leagues."

[1]"monkeys, resembling mountains and engrossed in their work on the bridge" *vānarair nagasaṃkāśaiḥ setukarmaṇi niṣṭhitaiḥ*: D5–7,10,11,S, and the texts and printed editions of the southern commentators read instead *prahṛṣṭair gajasaṃkāśais tvaramāṇaiḥ plavaṅgamaiḥ*, "the leaping monkeys resembling elephants, hastening in their great excitement."

Following this insertion and before verse 22, the same manuscripts insert a passage of ten lines [303*] (= GPP 6.22.65–69): "On the second day, the powerful leaping monkeys of terrifying forms swiftly completed twenty leagues.[1–2] On the third day, those huge monkeys, hastening, completed twenty-one leagues.[3–4] On the fourth day, the very swift monkeys, hastening, completed twenty-two leagues.[5–6] On the fifth day, the leaping monkeys, working swiftly, completed [the remaining] twenty-three leagues, reaching the splendid shore.[7–8] And thus did the foremost of monkeys, Viśvakarman's majestic and mighty son—who was just like his father—construct a bridge over the ocean. [9–10]"

Cs notes that the various versions of the story of the building of the bridge, found in the *Mahābhārata*, *Padmapurāṇa*, etc., give different numbers of days for its construction. Thus, according to him, the *Mahābhārata* says that the bridge was completed on the fourth day, a reference not known to the critical or the vulgate text of the *Mahābhārata* (*daśayojanavistaraṃ triṃśadyojanam āyatam / babandhur vānarāḥ setuṃ prathame divase tadā / sandhyām arvāg dvitīye tu triṃśadyojanavistaraḥ / evaṃ tribhir dinair viraiḥ setur navatiyojanam / caturthe tu dine sārdhe yāme te ca valīmukhāḥ / dṛṣṭā laṅketi rāmāya śaśaṃsuḥ*). Cf. *MBh* 3.267.40–45 (= Citraśāla edition 3.283.40–45) and apparatus. Cs quotes the *Padmapurāṇa*, which claims that the project was completed in three days (*PadmaP* I.38.63: *eṣa setur mayā baddhaḥ samudre vāruṇālaye / tribhir dinaiḥ samāptiṃ me nīto vānarasattamaiḥ*). Citing several other cases of variation in purāṇic legends, Cs concludes that this one, too, is best attributed to "*kalpabheda*," that is, the slight differences that occur in the same events as they recur in different *kalpas*.

22. = GPP 6.22.70.

"the path of the constellation Svātī" *svātīpathaḥ*: Svātī is the name of the thirteenth or fifteenth of the *nakṣatras*, or lunar mansions, and is identified with the star Arcturus. See *GaruḍaP* 1.59.2–9; *AgniP* 130.2–17; Dange 1986–1990, pp. 298–313; Kane 1941–1975, vol. 5, pp. 501–4; and Hopkins 1903. Cm (and to a lesser extent Cg and Cv), citing the *Vāyupurāṇa*, understands this to be one of the constellations that travel along the *madhyama*, or middle, path of the heavenly bodies (*sarvagrahāṇāṃ triṇy eva sthānāni dvijasattamāḥ ... tad evaṃ madhyamottaradakṣiṇamārgatrayaṃ pratyekaṃ vīthitrayeṇa tridhā bhidyate. aśvinī kṛttikā yāmyā nāgavīthīti śabditā ... hastaś citrā tathā svātī govīthīti tu śabditā*). This detail seems to provide a basis for the simile since Nala's bridge bisects the ocean, just as the path of Svātī does the heavens. The *Vāyupurāṇa* passage gives as a synonym for *svātī*, *govīthī*, which, according to Apte (s.v. *govīthī*), "is a name of that portion of the moon's path which contains the asterisms Bhādrapadā, Revatī, and Aśvinī or, according to some, '*hasta*, *citrā*, and *svātī*.'" Apte cites *Bṛhatsaṃhitā* 9.2 for this information. The commentators, however, are of two minds as to the exact meaning of this compound. Ct, Cm, and Cg, as their first alternative, gloss, "*chāyāpatha*," literally, "the path of radiance." Cg's second alternative, and the explanation of Cm and Cv, is the same as ours. The term *chāyāpatha* is somewhat obscure but has been taken by several translators to mean the Milky Way. Mallinātha explains the term *chāyāpatha* at *Raghuvaṃśa* 13.2—where Kālidāsa uses it again as an *upamāna* for Nala's bridge—as "a certain horizontal space located in the midst of the circle of heavenly bodies (*jyotiścakramadhyavartī kaścit tiraścīno 'vakāśaḥ*)." Cāritravardhana on the same passage equates this term with the *svātīpatha*. Lexical entries for *chāyāpatha* include "the galaxy, the atmosphere" (Apte s.v., citing *Raghuvaṃśa* 13.2); "the Milky Way" (Monier-Williams s.v.); "*der luftraum*" (PW s.v., citing *Trikāṇḍaśeṣa* 1.1.97 and Hemacandra's *Abhidhānacintāmaṇi*). Of the translators consulted, Gita Press (1969, vol. 3, p. 1444) and Dutt (1893, p. 1166) translate "Milky Way."

23. = GPP 6.22.71.

Following verse 23, D5,T1,M1,2 repeat 20ab, while following 23ab, D6,7,10,11,T2,3,G,M3,5 repeat 20ab ("ten leagues in width and one hundred in length"). Here many northern manuscripts insert a twenty-line interpolation [307*] in which the gods and sages praise Rāma for his justifiable violence against the ocean, which cowed the latter into complying with Rāma's wishes. D6,7,10,11,T2,3,G,M insert lines 5, 6, and 8, which follow the critical edition's verse 11 (see note to verse 11 above).

24. = GPP 6.22.73.

The syntax of this three-line verse is slightly ambiguous and has given rise to some disagreement among the commentators. The problem has three possible solutions: 1) take *plavaṃgamāḥ*, "leaping monkeys," (*pāda* a) and *sarvabhūtāni*, "all beings," (*pāda* e) as a joint subject of the verb *dadṛśuḥ*, "they gazed upon," in *pāda* e, as proposed by Ct, Cm, and Crā (first alternative); 2) read *plavaṃgamāḥ* and the participles in agreement with it (*āplavantaḥ*, *plavantaḥ*, and *garjantaḥ*) as the objects of *dadṛśuḥ*, despite their case forms, as Cr proposes, thus making the monkeys, as well as the bridge, part of the spectacle observed by the assembled celestials; or 3) provide a copula *abhuvan*, "were," making *pādas* ab an independent sentence, as Crā proposes as a second alternative. We have followed the last option.

"bounding ... and leaping" *āplavantaḥ plavantaś ca*: Cr, the only commentator who attempts to differentiate these two terms, explains, "Some monkeys made extraordinary leaps, while others made ordinary ones (*āplavanto 'dhikaplutiṃ kurvantaḥ ke cit sādhāraṇaplutim*)." The verbal root √*plu* can also refer to flying and/or swimming. Thus Roussel (1903, vol. 3, p. 63) renders, "*plongeaient, nageaient*" (followed by Pagani 1999, p. 922); and Shastri (1959, vol. 3, p. 55) translates, "dived, and swam." Raghunathan (1982, vol. 3, p. 54), however, prefers "flying and leaping over it."

"inconceivable" *acintyam*: Ct, Cm, and Ck explain, "the construction of which was inconceivable (*acintyam acintyaracanam*)." Cg glosses, "impossible to be conceived of, even mentally, before this [time] (*itaḥpūrvaṃ manasāpi cintayitum anarham*)." Cr understands, "the means to which were inconceivable (*acintanīyopāyam*)."

"seemingly impossible" *asahyam*: Ct, Cm, and Ck explain, "impossible for anyone without a relation to the Lord (*bhagavatsaṃbandhaṃ vinā kenāpy aśakyakaraṇam*)." Cg understands, "beyond the scope of anyone's effort (*kasyāpi yatnāviṣayam*)." Cr interprets, "bearing the form of the imagination of a construction that is impossible (*asahanīyanirmitisaṃkalparūpabharam*)." He sees this condition as a logical consequence of the inconceivability of the project and as the cause of its therefore being a miracle (*adbhutam*).

25. "those hundreds of billions" *koṭisahasrāṇī*: Literally "thousands of *koṭis*." A *koṭi* is a crore, or ten million.

26. "well-built" *sukṛtaḥ*: Cr and Cg gloss, "beautifully built (*śobhanaṃ kṛtaṃ kṛtir yasya*)" and "firmly built (*dṛḍhatayā kṛtaḥ*)," respectively. All translators consulted follow this interpretation. Cg, however, offers as an alternative the option of taking *sukṛtaḥ* in its nominal sense of "good fortune, auspiciousness" and glosses, *sukṛtakaro vā*, "bringing good fortune."

"smooth-surfaced" *subhūmiḥ*: Cr glosses, "whose surface (*bhūmiḥ*) was beautiful." Cg believes it means "devoid of high or low spots (*nimnonnatatvarahitaḥ*)," that is, level.

"beautifully proportioned" *susamāhitaḥ*: Cr explains, "well-paved (*samyagviyastaḥ*)." Cg glosses, "devoid of potholes (*nirvivaraḥ*)."

"resembled a dividing line" *aśobhata ... sīmanta iva*: Literally, "it shone *or* was as beautiful as a dividing line." The word *sīmanta* also commonly refers to the line made by parting a woman's hair. Among the commentators, only Cr addresses this term. He glosses, "like a tress of hair (*keśaveśa iva*)" (s.v. Apte, MW, PW), by which he appears to mean the parting-line of hair, normally *keśaveṣṭa*. This interpretation, as a partial metaphor for the head of the personified ocean or of a woman, has been adopted and fleshed out by several translators, including Gita Press (1969, vol. 3, p. 1445), Dutt (1893, p. 1166), Raghunathan (1982, vol. 3, p. 54), and Pagani (1999, p. 922). Only Roussel (1903, vol. 3, p. 63) and Gorresio (1856, vol. 9, p. 192) see the reference simply to a geographical feature. Shastri (1959, vol. 3, p. 55) tries to have it both ways, translating, "like unto a line traced on the waves, resembled the parting of a woman's hair." We are inclined to reject this metaphor as it is, at best, highly defective here. In any case, it does not accord well with the masculine ocean divinity.

27. Following verse 27, D5–7,10,11,S insert a passage of four lines [314*]: "But now Sugrīva addressed truly valorous Rāma saying, 'Please climb up on Hanumān's shoulders and let Lakṣmaṇa do the same with Aṅgada.[1] For the ocean, abode of sea monsters, is wide, hero, and these two flying monkeys will carry you across it.' "

[1]"Please climb up on Hanumān's shoulders and let Lakṣmaṇa do the same with Aṅgada" *hanūmantaṃ tvam āroha aṅgadaṃ cāpi lakṣmaṇaḥ*: Literally, "you must mount

Hanumān and Lakṣmana, Aṅgada." This passage is in all likelihood the origin of the popular tradition that depicts the heroes being carried on the shoulders of their monkey companions. See Introduction, p. 64.

28. "marched . . . accompanied by Sugrīva" *jagāma . . . sugrīveṇa samanvitaḥ*: The southern commentators, all of whom read 314* (see note to verse 27 above), naturally assume that Rāma and Lakṣmaṇa are flying ahead of the army. In this context, they note that we can infer from the verse that Sugrīva, too, is capable of flight.

29. "Some . . . marched down the center of the bridge, while others moved along the edges" *anye madhyena gacchanti pārśvato 'nye*: Literally, "some went by the center, others along the sides." We have fleshed out the elliptical sentence on the assumption that the reference is to the bridge. One could also, like many translators, take this to be a reference to a military formation, understanding that some marched in the main formation while others marched along the flanks.

"others could find no space in which to march" *mārgam anye na lebhire*: Literally, "some could find no road." We assume that the reference is to the enormous crowding of the monkeys during their passage via bridge, sea, and air. Cg, the only commentator to read with the critical edition, explains, "Because of the unavailability of passage, some remained on the shore for some time (*mārgālābhāt tīra eva kaścit kālaṃ sthitā ity arthaḥ*)." D6,10,11,T2,3, as well as Ck, Ct, and Cr, read *prapedire*, "they followed," for *na lebhire*.

31. "on the shore in a spot well provided with roots, fruits, and fresh water" *tīre . . . bahumūlaphalodake*: Literally, "on the shore, which had abundant roots, fruits, and water." We have added the word "fresh" to indicate that the reference is to drinking water rather than seawater.

32. "in the company of" *sahitāḥ*: D7,10,11,G1,M3,5, and the texts and printed editions of the southern commentators read instead *sahasā*, "all at once."

"anointed . . . with holy water" *samabhyaṣiñcan suśubhair jalaiḥ*: Ct and Cm claim that what is taking place here is, in fact, Rāma's royal consecration at the hands of the gods, like Vibhīṣaṇa's at the hands of Rāma. Ck sees only the latter. Ct and Ck argue that the waters used are those of such sacred bodies as the celestial Gaṅgā, etc., while Cr contends that it is seawater (*samudre setubandhanahṛṣṭair devais tadānīm eva rāmasya rājyābhiṣekaḥ kṛto rāmeṇa vibhīṣaṇasyaiva*—so Ct).

The meter is *vaṃśasthavila*.

33. "May you conquer" *jayasva*: Cg believes that the verbal form here is the *parasmaipada loṭ jaya*, and that the ending *-sva* of the *ātmanepada* should instead be prefixed to the following term, *śatrūn* ("enemies"), giving it the sense of "your own enemies," which he interprets to mean "those enemies who have taken refuge [with Rāma]."

"lord of men . . . gods and men" *naradeva . . . naradeva-*: The term is a typical kenning for "king." The literal meaning is, of course, "god among men." Here it may also have a particular resonance in that it can refer both to the humanity and divinity of Rāma. Commentators are divided as to how to read the second occurrence of the term. We have followed Cv, Cg, and Cm in reading it as a *dvandva*, literally, "men and gods." Ct reads it as a *tatpuruṣa*, in the sense of "gods among men," which he sees as a kenning for brahmans much in the spirit of more common expressions such as *bhūmyāṃ devāḥ*, "gods on earth."

"long" *śāśvatīḥ samāḥ*: Literally, "for eternal years." Compare 1.2.14.

The meter is *vaṃśasthavila*.

Following *sarga* 15, D5–7,10,11,S insert a passage of one hundred twenty-five lines [App. I, No. 16]. In lines 1–32 (=GPP 6.23; KK 6.23; VSP 6.23), Rāma, who is described as conversant with omens, embraces Lakṣmaṇa and begins to describe to him the numerous portents of impending destruction that he observes.[1–2] Rāma states his intention of marshaling his troops in a wooded area well provided with edible fruit and cool drinking water.[3–4] Then he details some evil portents. He foresees, he says, terrible destruction at hand and a great slaughter of the ape, monkey, and *rākṣasa* warriors.[5–6] Turbid winds are blowing and the earth trembles. The mountaintops tremble and mighty trees fall to the ground.[7–8] Ghastly thunderclouds, resembling beasts of prey, rumble ominously and shed drops of rain mixed with blood.[9–10] The twilight sky, the color of red sandalpaste, looks horrible, while fireballs fall from the blazing sun.[11–12] Wretched and fierce-sounding birds and beasts howl at the sun causing great fear.[13–14] At night, the moon glows faintly. Surrounded by a blackish red glow, it rises as if at the end of the world.[15–16] That glow is dim, harsh, unpleasant, and reddish. A dark spot appears on the spotless sun.[17–18] The heavenly bodies, obscured by a great dust cloud, presage the destruction of all worlds.[19–20] Crows, eagles, and vultures swoop down, while jackals howl inauspiciously and frightfully.[21–22] The ground, muddy with flesh and blood, will soon be covered with rocks, spears, and swords wielded by the monkeys and *rākṣasas*.[23–24] Rāma then exhorts Lakṣmaṇa, urging him that, surrounded on all sides by monkeys, they should proceed immediately and swiftly to Rāvaṇa's unassailable citadel.[25–26] So saying, righteous Rāma, armed with his bow and filled with the joy of battle, sets out toward Laṅkā at the head of his troops.[27–28] Accompanied by Vibhīṣaṇa and Sugrīva, the monkey warriors, resolved to kill their enemies, set out in his wake.[29–30] Rāma is delighted with the actions of the powerful and steadfast monkeys, which they have undertaken in order to please him.[31–32]

In lines 33–125 (=GPP 6.24; KK 6.24; VSP 6.24), the army of the monkeys is described. The assemblage of heroic monkeys, marshaled in ranks by their king, resembles the autumn sky on a full-moon night illuminated by the brilliant stars and the moon.[33–34] Pressed down by those hosts of warriors, which resembled an ocean, the earth trembled as if in fright.[35–36] The woodland creatures of Laṅkā heard the uproar and the hair-raising tumult of *bherī* and *mṛdaṅga* war drums.[37–38] But the leaders of the monkey troops were only roused by that sound and, not to be outdone by it, bellowed all the louder.[39–40] The *rākṣasas* then heard the bellowing of those leaping monkeys, which was like the thundering of storm clouds about to break.[41–42] When Rāma sets his eyes upon Laṅkā with its multicolored flags and banners, his thoughts travel painfully to Sītā.[43–44] "It is here that fawn-eyed Sītā is held captive by Rāvaṇa, like the constellation Rohiṇī crossed by Mars, the red planet."[45–46] Heaving long and hot sighs, Rāma turns to Lakṣmaṇa and addresses him with words that fit the occasion and suit his own purpose. He describes the beautiful city of Laṅkā, which he says is raised so high that it appears to scrape the sky, as if it had been constructed on a mountaintop through the mental effort of Viśvakarman.[47–50] It is very beautiful, filled with many mansions, and resembles the heavenly regions, covered by white clouds, where Viṣṇu set his foot. It is adorned with blossoming parklands, which resemble the heavenly garden Caitraratha and which are filled with all kinds of birds and flowering trees.[51–54] He calls Lakṣmaṇa's attention to the beauties of the park, mentioning the intoxicated birds, clinging bees, and the gentle breezes swaying the thickets filled with impassioned cuckoos.[55–56] Rāma then turns his attention to the ordering of his troops in accordance with military science. He issues his commands to the monkey army. His arrangements are as follows: Invincible Aṅgada along with Nīla should stand in the center of the monkey army. Ṛṣabha is to station himself on the right flank of the monkey army, surrounded by a large number of monkeys. Swift Gandhamādana, who is as unassailable as an indomitable elephant bull,[1] is to station himself at the left flank. Rāma himself, fully prepared, will stand at the head of the army together with Lakṣmaṇa. The three great apes Jāmbavān, Suṣeṇa, and Vegadarśin will guard the interior. The king of the monkeys, Sugrīva, is to guard the army's rear, just as Pracetas Varuṇa, swathed in splendor, guards the western quarter of the world.[57–69] Properly divided into formations and guarded by the foremost monkeys, the army resembles the sky filled with clouds. Seizing mountain peaks and huge trees, they march upon Laṅkā, eager to lay waste to it in battle.[70–73] The great monkeys then resolve that they will level the city of Laṅkā with mountain peaks and their own fists. Then powerful Rāma addresses Sugrīva, telling him that the troops are now properly marshaled and instructing him to release Śuka.[2] Hearing Rāma's words, the powerful king of the monkeys acts upon his instructions and frees Rāvaṇa's messenger Śuka.[74–79] Freed on Rāma's instructions and badly beaten by the monkeys, the terrified Śuka reports to the lord of the *rākṣasas*. Rāvaṇa laughs at him and asks him why, since he appears to have clipped wings, his wings are tied up, and asks if he has not perhaps fallen into the hands of those frivolous creatures.[80–84] Pressed by the king, the terrified Śuka responds, saying that, as instructed, he had proceeded to the northern shore of the ocean and attempted to deliver Rāvaṇa's message in a calm and soothing voice. However, the moment the monkeys spied him, they flew into a rage, leapt up, captured him, and set about tearing at him and beating him with their fists.[85–90] It was impossible to engage them in conversation, much less to question them. He tells Rāvaṇa that the monkeys are wrathful and savage by nature, and with them, following the trail of Sītā, is Rāma—the murderer of Virādha, Kabandha, and Khara—along with Sugrīva. Śuka reports that Rāma has built a bridge to cross the ocean and has already crossed.[91–95] He has now come, armed with his bow, disparaging the *rākṣasas*. He informs Rāvaṇa that a vast army of thousands upon thousands of apes and monkeys, resembling mountains or clouds, has covered the earth. He argues that there can be no more peace between the two opposing armies than there can be between the gods and *dānavas* [96–100]. He exhorts Rāvaṇa to act before the monkeys scale the city ramparts. He tells him that he should either return Sītā at once or offer battle.[101–102] Rāvaṇa is infuriated by Śuka's words and responds as if to scorch him with his gaze. He vows that he will never relinquish Sītā, even should the gods, *gandharvas*, and *dānavas* together assault him, and not even for fear of all the worlds.[103–106 (106 = 6.17.2cd)] He expresses his longing for the moment when his arrows shall rush toward Rāma, like intoxicated bees flying toward a blossoming tree in the springtime.[107–108] He wonders when, with showers of his flaming arrows which had lain in his quiver[3] and will soon be loosed from his bow, he will consume Rāma's body, as flaming meteors might an elephant. He vows that, with the assistance of his vast army, he will rob Rāma of his strength, just as the rising sun robs all other heavenly bodies of their light.[109–112] He boasts that his striking force is like that of the sea and his speed like that of the wind. It is only because Rāma is unaware of this that he dares to fight him. It is only, he says, because Rāma has never seen his, Rāvaṇa's, arrows, which had lain in his quiver and resemble venomous serpents, that he dares to fight him. He claims that, up until now, Rāma did not recognize Rāvaṇa's power in battle.[113–117] Rāvaṇa then delivers an elaborate musical metaphor. He boasts that he shall enter upon the concert stage, in the form of the opposing army, and there, in the battle, will play his dreaded lute, in the form of his bow, causing it to resound with the lute's bow, in the form of his arrow. The lute will have the twanging of the bowstring for its loud tone, the screams of the stricken for its high tones, and the striking of its iron arrows for its rhythmic accompaniment. Rāvaṇa concludes his vaunting by saying that not even the great divinities, thousand-eyed Indra, Varuṇa, Yama, or Kubera, could possibly assail him with their flaming arrows in battle.[118–125]

[1]"indomitable elephant bull" *gandhahastī*: Literally, "scent-elephant." See note to 5.8.12. This is a technical term for an elephant whose scent inspires fear in other elephants. See notes to 6.15.33, App. I, No. 16, lines 57–69; notes to 6.97.33, App. I, No. 67, line 52 and note 15; and 6.4.14 and notes.

[2]"Śuka": See *sarga* 13, App. I, No. 10, above, where Śuka was taken prisoner. Śuka had taken on the form of a bird, and the monkeys begin to tear off his wings (lines 28–36).

[3]"lain in his quiver" *tūṇīśayaiḥ*: D10,11, Ct, and Ck read *śoṇitadigdhāṅgam*, "his limbs smeared with blood."

Sarga 16

This is the opening *sarga* of the *Yuddhakāṇḍa* in the majority of northern manuscripts (all but B1,D2).

1. "son of Daśaratha" *daśarathātmaje*: Cg argues that the poet uses this particular epithet here to highlight Rāma's humanity (*manuṣyatvoktiḥ*). Perhaps the idea is to restore the ambiguity of Rāma's divinity, since his supernatural powers have been foregrounded in the encounter with Sāgara. See Pollock 1991, pp. 19–20. See notes on verse 16 below.

"majestic" *śrīmān*: Cg claims that this generally positive epithet is used as an allusion to Rāvaṇa's excessive and overweening pride (*madātiśayoktiḥ*).

"Śuka and Sāraṇa" *śukasāraṇau*: The southern commentators are concerned about the question of whether the former of these two ministers is the same as the spy Śuka who was captured and released by Rāma's forces and who has just reported to Rāvaṇa in the immediately preceding *sarga* (GPP 6.24.22–35 = App. I, No. 16, lines 74–103). See *sarga* 13, App. I, No. 10, lines 28–36; and *sarga* 15, App. I, No. 16, lines 74–103. The general consensus among the commentators is that the two are different, although the reasons given vary somewhat.

Crā and Cm argue that the two cannot be the same *rākṣasa* for two reasons: first, they argue that the individual named in this *sarga* had been sent out to report on the activities of the previously dispatched agent of the same name, and second, that the

Śuka mentioned in the present verse is described as a minister (*amātya*) [implying that the earlier mentioned Śuka is not] (*pūrvapreṣitaśukoktavṛttāntajñāpanapūrvakaṃ preṣaṇād amātyatvena viśeṣāc cātratyaśuko 'nya ity avagamyate*—so Crā and Cm). Ct cites the second of these reasons and adds that the first is put forward by Kataka (Ck), etc. (*katakādayaḥ*). According to Ct and the critical apparatus, the first position is shared by Ck, although Ck's discussion of this passage is absent from our version of his commentary. Moreover, the critical apparatus apparently ascribes both positions to Ck. Cg argues that the two are different because the one in this *sarga* is teamed with Sāraṇa [whereas the other was not] (*śukaḥ pūrvasmād anyaḥ sāraṇasāhityāt*). Cs is uncertain on this point and is willing to entertain both positions, that of identity and that of difference. He says, like Ct and others, that this Śuka may be thought of as different from the previously mentioned spy because he is referred to as a minister. On the other hand, he admits that the two may be the same. Since the individual in question is fully familiar with the enemy's army and is also completely trustworthy, it is proper to dispatch him in this way [as a spy]. Thus, Cs argues, it would be possible for him to take on the form of a bird and infiltrate the enemy forces. Cs further argues that if one were to claim that they are different since one of them is a minister and not a spy, that argument would fail because at 329* (see note at 13cd below = VSP, KK, GPP 6.25.14), Śuka and Sāraṇa are referred to as both counselors (*mantriṇau*) and spies (*carau*), thus leading to the conclusion that a minister may also serve as a spy. On the other hand, Cs suggests that this could be the same spy as originally mentioned who is merely referred to as a minister in the same way as one may conventionally say that people are carrying umbrellas, when, in fact, only some of them are. This is the well-known *chatrinyāya*, "the maxim of the people carrying umbrellas." Thus, the two may be different and the minister Sāraṇa might quite properly be sent out with someone who knows the numbers, disposition, and so forth, of the army, for example, a spy like Śuka.

2. "whole" *samagram*: The placement of this adjective at the beginning of the line, before *sāgaram*, "ocean," would seem to argue for the words being in agreement, thus yielding the sense of "a monkey army has crossed the entire ocean." Only Dutt (1893, p. 1172) among the translators renders in this way. Ct and all other translations consulted read the adjective as modifying *balam*, "host, army," as we have done. It would also appear that northern versions avoid the slight awkwardness by shifting the adjective to *pāda* b, where it unambiguously refers to the army. Cg's gloss, *viśālam*, "broad, spacious, large," is also, perhaps, ambiguous. The term could, of course, refer to a body of troops but would far more commonly be found as a description of the ocean.

"has done something unprecedented" *abhūtapūrvam*: Cm, Ct, and Cr all understand that the term "unprecedented" applies to both the building of the bridge and the crossing of the ocean (*vānaraṃ balaṃ dustaraṃ sāgaraṃ tīrṇam iti rāmeṇa sāgare setubandhanaṃ kṛtam iti caitad ubhayam api abhūtapūrvam iti sambandhaḥ*—so Cm).

3. "I would never have believed that a bridge could be built over the ocean" *sāgare setubandhaṃ tu na śraddadhyāṃ kathaṃcana*: Literally, "I would not in any way believe the building of a bridge on the ocean."

4–7. "you . . . must accurately determine . . . You must also find out . . . In addition, you must determine" *tattvato jñātum arhathaḥ*: In the original, all three verses constitute a single sentence. For the sake of style and readability, we have broken it into three English sentences and thus have had to repeat the verb in each one.

"highly regarded" *saṃmatāḥ*: D10,11, and the texts and printed editions of Ct read instead *saṃgatāḥ*, "allied with, associated with."

"over the ocean, that great body of water" *sāgare salilārṇave*: Literally, "on the ocean, on the ocean of water." Ct, Cg, and Cm gloss the expression as "the saltwater ocean (*lavaṇajale samudre*)."

8. "immensely powerful" *mahaujasām*: D9–11 and the texts and printed editions of Ct read instead *mahātmanām*, "great."

10. "inconceivably vast" *acintyam*: Literally, "unimaginable."

11. "filled" *sthitam*: Literally, "was situated in *or* on."

"as well as the shores of the sea, the forests, and the parklands" *samudrasya ca tīreṣu vaneṣūpavaneṣu ca*: D0,9–11, and the texts and printed editions of Ct omit this *pāda*.

12. "Part . . . part . . . another part . . . Part . . . another": We have broken the army into parts for the sake of readability. The original states that the entire army was engaged in all the various actions enumerated.

Following verse 12, D5–7,9–11,S insert a passage of one line [326*]: "The two night-roaming *rākṣasas* simply stared at that imperturbable ocean of an army."

13. "recognized" *dadarśa*: Literally, "he saw."

Following verse 13cd, D5–7,9 (continues after 326*),10,11,S insert a passage of one line [329*]: "These two, Śuka and Sāraṇa, are counselors of the lord of the *rākṣasas*."

15. "gather intelligence" *parijñātum*: Literally, "to find out about *or* to observe."

16. "Daśaratha's son" *daśarathātmajaḥ*: Cg, as in his commentary to verse 1 above, understands that the poet uses the patronymic pointedly. He suggests that, by highlighting that Rāma is the son of a great man, Vālmīki is alluding to his innate compassion (*daśarathātmajo mahāpuruṣaprasūtatvena sahajakāruṇyaḥ*).

"who was devoted to the welfare of all beings" *sarvabhūtahite rataḥ*: As Cg notes, the idea is that Rāma is affectionate even toward his enemies (*ripūṇām api vatsalaḥ*).

"he smiled" *prahasan*: Literally, "smiling." Ct and Ck claim that Rāma is smiling at the thought that Rāvaṇa, after having seen Rāma's power—demonstrated both in his building of the bridge and in his nonchalant slaughter of Khara, etc., in the forest of Janasthāna—still did not recognize Rāma's strength (*setubandhanena janasthāne nirapekṣaṃ kharādivadhena ca na madbalajñānaṃ vṛttam iti prahāsaḥ*). Cg simply says that Rāma's smile is provoked by his recollection of Rāvaṇa's stupidity (*rāvaṇabuddhimāndyasmaraṇāt prahāsaḥ*).

17. "carefully examined" *susamīkṣitāḥ*: D9,11, and the texts and printed editions of Ct read instead *susamāhitāḥ*, literally, "concentrated, focused, well ordered." Ct glosses his reading as *jñātabalāḥ*, "[our] strengths revealed." Cg reads the variant *suparīkṣitāḥ*, which differs little in meaning from the critical reading. Cr reads with the critical edition. Cs notes the variants *susamīkṣitāḥ* and *susamāhitāḥ*. He glosses the latter as *svasthacittāḥ*, "of calm minds," which he glosses as "free from fear of the enemy troops (*pratibhaṭabhītirahitā iti yāvat*)." Cs idiosyncratically proposes a third alternative, viz., to break the sequence *vā susamāhitāḥ* into *vā asusamāhitāḥ*, which he explains as "careless because of our disdain for Rāvaṇa and his troops (*vā asusamāhitā iti rāvaṇaṃ sagaṇaṃ tṛṇīkṛtyānavadhānenaiva sthitā iti vā*)."

Following verse 17, D5–7,9–11,S, as well as many northern manuscripts, insert a passage of six lines [330*] in which Rāma continues his speech to the *rākṣasa* spies:

"Or, if there is anything that you have not yet seen, please see it now. Vibhīṣaṇa, here, will surely show you everything.[1–2] Nor need you have any fear for your lives, even though you have been captured. For messengers who have either laid down their weapons or been captured should surely not be put to death. Vibhīṣaṇa,[3–4] please release these two disguised, night-roaming *rākṣasa* spies, who are ever destroying the forces of their enemies.[5–6]"

18. "the city of Laṅkā" *nagarīṃ laṅkām*: Several manuscripts, including the texts and printed editions of Ct, read *mahatīm*, "great," for *nagarīm*.

20. "tomorrow at the proper moment" *śvaḥ kāle*: Literally, "tomorrow at the time." D6,13,M3, and the texts and printed editions of Ct, Cg, and Cm read *kālye* for *kāle*, which the commentators explain as meaning "in the morning (*prātaḥkāle*—so Ct)." Cm notes the critical reading as a variant. He reads *kāle* as pleonastic and suggests that the phrase means simply "tomorrow (*śva ity arthaḥ*)."

21. "Muster your forces" *balaṃ dhāraya*: Virtually all northern manuscripts, all *devanāgarī* manuscripts, with the exception of D5, and some southern manuscripts (M1,2,G2,3), read *sasainye tvayi*, "[I shall unleash my wrath] on you and your army." This is probably a *lectio facilior* in that it provides an explicit object for Rāma's wrath, thus creating a more perfect parallelism in the simile. The critical reading, however, is the appropriate choice on textual grounds.

"tomorrow at the proper moment" *śvaḥ kāle*: See note to verse 20 above.

"I shall unleash my dreadful wrath upon you" *ghoraṃ roṣam ahaṃ mokṣye*: Literally, "I shall release dreadful wrath." We have provided an object for Rāma's wrath. See note above.

22. Following verse 22, D5–7,9–11,S insert a passage of one line [336*]: "The two of them then joyfully hailing Rāghava, who loved righteousness, [with the words], 'Be Victorious!' "

23. "although we deserved to die" *vadhārhau*: Literally, "[we two are] worthy of death." D6,9–11, and the texts and printed editions of Ct read instead *vadhārtham*, "in order to kill [us]."

24–26. "bulls among warriors" *puruṣarṣabhāḥ*: Literally, "bulls among men." The expression is slightly odd here since two of the heroes described, the monkey Sugrīva and the *rākṣasa* Vibhīṣaṇa, are not, in fact, men. The term *puruṣa*, "man," can refer to the male of any species, but the translation then becomes awkward, especially in light of the redundancy implicit in the common metaphorical usage of the term *ṛṣabha*, "bull." We have therefore substituted "warrior" for stylistic reasons.

"skilled in weaponry" *kṛtāstrāḥ*: Cg points out that since Sugrīva, the monkey, is not trained in the use of weapons, the adjective here should be understood through the *chatrinyāya*, or "the maxim of the people carrying umbrellas" (see note to verse 1 above). (*kṛtāstrāḥ śikṣitāstrāḥ. chatriṇo gacchantītivad ayaṃ nirdeśyaḥ sugrīvasyākṛtāstratvāt.*)

"Since" *yatra*: Literally, "where." We follow Ct and Cr in reading this normally locative adverb as the ablative (*yasmād dhetoḥ*). Cm, however, sees it as a locative, explaining, "in which, that is, in the action of destroying Laṅkā (*laṅkāmardanarūpakārye*)."

"assembled in one place" *ekasthānagatāḥ*: We follow Ct, who explains "gathered in one place (*ekatra militāḥ*)." Cm understands "are of one mind (*ekamatyaṃ prāptāḥ*)." Cg offers both alternatives.

"hurling it far away" *saṃkrāmayitum*: Literally "to transfer, to transport." Ct understands the action to be like that of digging out a column and erecting it elsewhere (*nikhātaśālāstambham ivopari kṛtvā punaḥ pratiṣṭhāpayitum ity arthaḥ*). We prefer the interpretation of Cg and Cm, who explain, "to throw it somewhere else (*anyatra kṣeptum*)."

"even without all these monkeys" *sarve tiṣṭhantu vānarāḥ*: Literally, "let all the monkeys stand." We follow the interpretation of Cr, who explains, "the meaning is that there is no need for the other monkeys (*anyavānarāṇāṃ na prayojanam ity arthaḥ*)."

27. "appearance" *rūpam*: None of the commentators remarks on this term, and we are inclined to take it in its basic sense of form or appearance. The idea, we believe, is that the spies have made their judgment as to Rāma's capacities on the basis of their direct observation of his awesome physique and armaments. The word *rūpam* can also refer to one's nature or character. Although this appears less plausible to us in the context, it has been adopted by Raghunathan (1982, vol. 3, p. 61), who renders, "personality," and Roussel (1903, vol. 3, p. 70), who translates, "*la nature.*" Other translators use or extend one or the other of these meanings; thus Gita Press (1969, vol. 3, p. 1454) renders, "charm"; Dutt (1893, p. 1174), "figure"; Shastri (1959, vol. 3, p. 62), "capacity"; and Gorresio (1856, vol. 9, p. 198), "*il suo aspetto.*"

"will be able to lay waste" *vadhiṣyati*: Literally, "he will destroy."

"even without those other three" *tiṣṭhantu te trayaḥ*: Literally, "let the other three stand." See note above to verses 24–26.

28. "seemed as if it were" *babhūva*: Literally, "it was."

29. "wildly excited" *prahṛṣṭarūpāḥ*: Literally, "of excited appearance." We follow Crā, who takes *rūpa* as an intensifying suffix. He understands, "extremely excited (*atyantaṃ prahṛṣṭāḥ*)," quoting *Pā* 5.3.66 (*praśaṃsāyāṃ rūpap*). Ś,Ñ,V1,2,B,D0,2,8–13, and the texts and printed editions of Ct, Ck, and Cr read instead *prahṛṣṭayodhāḥ*, "having excited warriors."

The meter is *vaṃśasthavila*.

Sarga 17

1. "sound" *pathyam*: Literally, "wholesome, fit, suitable." B3,D9–11, and the texts and printed editions of Ct and Cr read instead *satyam*, "truth," which has been translated as either "truthful" or "sincere" by those who translate these texts.

"Sāraṇa ... him" *sāraṇena ... sāraṇam*: Literally, "by Sāraṇa ... [to] Sāraṇa." Only Cr seems perturbed by the temporary disappearance of Śuka, who is not mentioned again until verse 5 and will not speak again in his own right until *sarga* 19. He remarks that "there is no lapse here in mentioning the name of only one, since Śuka and Sāraṇa are of one mind (*śukasāraṇayor aikamatyād ekatarasyaiva nāmagrahaṇe 'pi na nyūnatā*)."

"courageously" *aklībam*: Literally, "in a not unmanly fashion." We read the term adverbially here, as we believe it better suits the context. It can also be read adjectivally with *vacaḥ*, "words." All translations consulted—except Raghunathan (1982, vol. 3, p. 61, "boldly")—have chosen this second alternative.

2. *Pādas* cd = App. I, No. 16, line 106. This verse is a close variant of 6.21.15 (= App. I, No. 16, lines 105–6), where the verse is identical except for the verb *pratiyudhyeran*, "they should assault," which is substituted for, and is synonymous with, *abhiyuñjīran*.

3. "you... because the tawny monkeys got the better of you... what rival can possibly get the better of me" *tvaṃ... haribhir nirjito bhṛśam / ko... sapatno mām... jetum arhati*: Literally, "you, completely defeated by the monkeys... what rival can defeat me." D7,9–11, and the texts and printed editions of Ct, Cm, and Cr read *pīḍitaḥ*, "crushed, abused," for *nirjitaḥ*.

4. "Rāvaṇa... he" *rāvaṇaḥ... rāvaṇaḥ*: Only Cg among the commentators seems concerned by the repetition. He explains it by saying that the second occurrence of the name should be understood in its etymological sense of "he who makes [the world] cry out (*atra dvitīyo rāvaṇaśabdo rāvayatīti vyutpattyā kriyānimittakaḥ*)." See 6.8.12 and note.

"many *tālas* in height" *bahutālasamutsedham*: The word *tāla* is subject to the same ambiguity as its English equivalent, "palm," in that it may refer both to the palm of the hand and a palm tree. The term *tāla* has come to stand for a measure of distance in both of these senses in Sanskrit. As Cg notes, the term as used in this verse may refer either to the height of the *tāla*, or palmyra tree, or to the distance measured across the palm from the tips of the outstretched thumb and middle finger (*anekatālavṛkṣatulyaunnatyaṃ yadvā vitatāṅguṣṭhamadhyāmitas tālaḥ*). Because it is the poet's intention to indicate the loftiness of Rāvaṇa's palace, we presume that the former measure is intended.

"in his desire to see for himself" *didṛkṣayā*: Literally, "through the desire to see." The expression is elliptical here, and we are, of course, meant to understand, as Cg notes, that the reference is to Rāvaṇa's desire to observe the monkey army for himself (*vānarabaladidṛkṣayā*).

5. "two spies" *tābhyāṃ carābhyām*: As the commentators note, *cara* is an irregular form for *cāra*, "spy." The reference is, of course, to Śuka and Sāraṇa, although, as noted above, only the latter is specifically addressed in this *sarga*. See note to verse 1 above. Also see note to 6.11.24.

6. "innumerable" *asaṃkhyeyam*: D7,9–11, and the texts and printed editions of Ct and Cm read instead *asahyaṃ ca*, "and not to be withstood."

7. "always" *samantataḥ*: Normally, "on *or* from all sides," but we follow Cr here in interpreting the word as "all the time (*sarvakālam*)."

"lead the way in battle" *pūrvam abhivartante*: Literally, "they move on before."

8. "Which one's advice does Sugrīva heed?" *keṣāṃ śṛṇoti sugrīvaḥ*: Literally, "of [to] which ones does Sugrīva listen?" We concur with the commentators that some object, such as *vacanam*, "words, advice," has to be supplied, and we have translated accordingly (*vacanam iti śeṣaḥ*—so Ct).

"me all of this" *me sarvam*: D5,T1,M3, and the texts and printed editions of Cg read instead *tattvena*, "truthfully." This variant is rendered only in the translation of Raghunathan (1982, vol. 3, p. 62), who renders, "[give me] a full and correct picture."

9. "Upon hearing these words... Sāraṇa... began to describe" *sāraṇaḥ... vacanam ...ācacakṣe*: Literally, "words *or* speech... Sāraṇa spoke." The sentence is elliptical, and we agree with Cr and Cg, who state that one should supply a gerund with the sense of "having heard" of which *vacanam* would be the object (*vacanaṃ niśamyeti śeṣaḥ*). Ct and Ck disagree and argue that *vacanam*, which they gloss as "answer (*uttaram*)," is the object of the verb *ābabhāṣe*, "spoke," [v.l. for the critical edition's *ācacakṣe* of *pāda* c] (*vacanam uttaram ābabhāṣa ity anvayaḥ*—so Ct). Although this, by itself, yields an acceptable syntax, it creates problems for construing the accusatives *mukhyāṃs tāṃs tu vanaukasaḥ*, "those principal forest dwellers," of *pāda* d.

"familiar with the forest-dwelling monkeys . . . them" *mukhyajño mukhyāṃs tāṃs tu vanaukasaḥ*: Literally, "the knower of the leaders [began to describe] those forest-dwelling leaders."

10–12. "tremble" *pravepate*: D9–11 and the texts and printed editions of Ct read *pratihatā*, "smashed, stricken, shattered."

13–15. "showing his fangs" *vijṛmbhate*: Literally, "he gapes, yawns." See notes to 16–19 below.

"the color of lotus filaments" *padmakiñjalkasaṃnibhaḥ*: Literally, "resembling lotus filaments." As Cg points out, this is a reference to the monkey's tawny yellow color (*padmakesaravatpītavarṇa ity arthaḥ*).

"lashes his tail . . . the sound of which" *sphoṭayati . . . lāṅgūlam . . . yasya lāṅgūlaśabdena*: Literally, "he expands his tail . . . the sound of the tail of whom." The verb is probably used here in the sense of *āsphoṭayati*, "he waves about *or* slaps [the arms, for example]." Cg, the only commentator to discuss this term, glosses, "he strikes [it] on the earth (*bhumau tāḍayati*)." See notes to 6.40.62; 6.47.8; 6.48.30; 6.57.38; and 6.62.63.

"heir apparent" *yauvarājye*: See note to 6.51.10. Ś,Ñ,V,B2,3,D0–4,8–13,T2, and the texts and printed editions of Ct and Cr read instead *yuvarājaḥ*, "[he is] the heir apparent."

Following verse 15, D5–7,9–11,S insert a passage of eight lines [352*] in which the description of Aṅgada is extended: "He is the son of Vālin and is his equal. But he is always very dear to Sugrīva. He is as valorous on Rāghava's behalf as is Varuṇa on Śakra's.[1–2] It was entirely through his idea that Janaka's daughter was discovered by swift Hanumān, who desires what is best for Rāghava.[3–4] Powerful and invincible, he has gathered many troops of excellent monkeys and is advancing toward you with his own forces.[5–6] And, surrounded by a large army, the hero Nala, stalwart in battle and the builder of the bridge, is following Vālin's son.[7–8]"

16–19. "And those bulls among tawny monkeys . . . leaping up and showing their fangs in rage, are dreadful, fierce, of fierce valor, and impossible to withstand. Their number is ten billion eight hundred thousand." *utthāya ca vijṛmbhante krodhena haripuṃgavāḥ // ete duṣprasahā ghorāś caṇḍāś caṇḍaparākramāḥ / aṣṭau śatasahasrāṇi daśa koṭiśatāni ca //*. D9–11 and the texts and printed editions of Ct and Cr omit these lines (16cd–17).

"who are bracing their limbs" *viṣṭabhya gātrāṇi*: Literally, "having immobilized their limbs." Commentators and translators differ somewhat in their understanding of the gerund. Cr glosses, "propping (*saṃstabhya*)," an idea apparently shared by Gorresio (1856, vol. 9, p. 200), who translates, "*appoggiando le membra l'un soll'altro*." Cg glosses, "raising (*unnamya*)." Dutt (1893, p. 1176) understands the verb literally, translating, "with their limbs lying inactive." Raghunathan (1982, vol. 3, p. 62) translates, "who swing their arms," while Gita Press (1969, vol. 3, p. 1456) and Pagani (1999, p. 930) render, "having stiffened [their limbs]." Roussel (1903, vol. 3, p. 73) and Shastri (1959, vol. 3, p. 63) translate, "*qui s'étirent les membres*" and "stretching their limbs," respectively.

"showing their fangs in rage" *vijṛmbhante krodhena*: Cg understands here, "they distort their limbs in rage (*kopena gātravināmaṃ kurvanti*)," although he explains the virtually identical expression in verse 13 above as "he gapes (*jṛmbhaṇaṃ karoti*)." We see the reference here to be to the characteristic behavior of *rhesus macaques* and other primates of opening their jaws wide and revealing their impressive canine teeth as part of an aggressive display. See notes to 13–15 above and the note to 1.16.10 on monkeys in general.

"roaring . . . bellowing" *kṣveḍayanti . . . nadanti*: See notes on 5.55.29 and 6.17.13–15.

"denizens of the sandalwood forest" *candanavāsinaḥ*: Literally, "sandalwood dwellers." Commentators and translators are divided as to the meaning of the compound. Cr glosses, "their limbs smeared with sandalpaste (*candanaliptāṅgāḥ*)," a suggestion Pagani (1999, p. 930) apparently follows. Roussel (1903, vol. 3, p. 73) and Shastri (1959, vol. 3, p. 63) understand that the monkeys are clad in saffron-colored garments. Cg and Cm, whom we follow, explain, "dwelling in the sandal forest (*candanavanavāsinaḥ*)." Cv has a variant reading, *candanavānarāḥ*, which he and Cg, who notes it, gloss as *candanavāsinaḥ* and interpret as above. Cs offers two explanations. In the first, he takes *candana* as the proper name of a particular mountain. This idea is similar to that expressed by Dutt (1893, p. 1176), "dwelling in *Chandana*." Dutt footnotes the name, saying, "This may mean some *wood of sandals*; but the commentator [Ct] is silent over it." Cs's second interpretation is that the reference is to Mount Malaya because of the abundance of sandalwood trees there. Gorresio (1856, vol. 9, p. 200) follows this idea, translating, "*son venuti dal monte Malaya*."

"The one whom they follow . . . Śveta" *ya enam anugacchanti . . . śvetaḥ*: Here, too, the commentators are divided as to which leader is followed by the monkey warriors described in this passage. Cr and Cg believe the reference is to Nala, who was described in the verses immediately preceding this passage in the southern recension (see 352*, lines 7,8 above in notes to verses 13–15). Ct and Cm, whom we follow, see the pronoun *enam* in 18a as a prospective reference to Śveta in 19a (compare Dutt's footnote [1893, p. 1176]). If one were to read the pronoun retrospectively in the critical text, it would then be a reference to Aṅgada. We believe that Ct and Cm are correct because of the relative pronoun *yaḥ* in 18a. In this passage, the relative pronouns signal descriptions of new individuals.

"silver-hued" *rajatasaṃkāśaḥ*: Literally, "resembling silver." The description clearly mirrors the monkey's name, which means "white, bright."

"he . . . expects to crush Laṅkā with his own forces" *eṣa āśaṃsate laṅkāṃ svenānīkena marditum*: This phrase is repeated at 39cd below and occurs almost verbatim at 24cd below, as well as at 6.18.24cd and 6.18.39ef.

"expects" *āśaṃsate*: Literally, "he hopes, wishes." Cg and Cm gloss, "he begs, requests (*prārthayate*)."

20. "After reporting to Sugrīva" *sugrīvam āgamya*: Literally, "having approached Sugrīva."

"that monkey" *vānaraḥ*: Cr, perhaps concerned that the verse does not really specify which monkey is intended (Śveta or Nala, see notes on verses 16–19 above) and that the name Śveta can merely be a general adjective, "white," proposes to analyze the term *vānara* here as "he who advises [*rāti* = *bodhayati*] a particular military formation [*vānam* = *racanāviṣeśam*] (*vānaṃ racanā viśeṣaṃ rāti bodhayatīty arthaḥ*)."

"to marshal" *vibhajan*: Literally, "separating." We understand that Śveta is separating his forces into their various units. Cg explains, "splitting up the densely massed army (*nibiḍāṃ senāṃ bhittvā*)."

"urging . . . onward" *praharṣayan*: Literally, "exciting, inciting."

21–22ab. "used to roam . . . once ruled" *purā . . . paryeti . . . praśāsti*: Literally, "formerly roamed . . . he rules." Cg notes that by the use of the adverb *purā*, "formerly, long ago," we are to understand that Kumuda now resides in the company of Sugrīva (*purety anenādya sugrīvasamīpa eva vasatīti gamyate*).

"charming mountain" *ramyam . . . parvatam*: Ct believes that the word *ramya* is another name of Mount Saṃkocana (*ramyaṃ ramyākhyām*).

"Mount Saṃkocana" *saṃkocano nāma . . . giriḥ*: Literally, "the mountain, Saṃkocana by name." D7,10,11, and the texts and printed editions of Ct and Cr read the variant *saṃrocanaḥ*, "Saṃrocana," for *saṃkocanaḥ*.

22cd–24. "commanding one hundred million troops" *yo 'sau śatasahasrāṇāṃ sahasraṃ parikarṣati*: Literally, "he leads one thousand hundred thousands." We agree with all commentators and available translators in reading the relative clause prospectively to refer to Caṇḍa. The versification in the critical edition places the line so as to suggest that one might read it retrospectively in reference to Kumuda.

23ab is a close variant of 6.18.2ab.

23cd = 6.18.2cd.

"dreadful in his actions" *ghorakarmaṇaḥ*: D7,9–11, and the texts and printed editions of Ct and Cr read instead the nominative plural *ghoradarśanāḥ*, "of dreadful appearance," which must then modify *vālāḥ*, "hair, fur," in 23a.

"sticks out . . . in all directions" *prakīrṇāḥ*: Literally, "scattered."

"so far" *bahuvyāmāḥ*: Literally, "many *vyāmas* [in length]." According to Cg, who cites *Amarakośa* 2.6.87, a *vyāma* is the distance between the tips of the hands of a person whose arms are extended sideways (*vyāmo bāhvoḥ sakarayos tatayos tiryag antaram ity amaraḥ*). Cm describes it somewhat similarly as the measure of two long arms (*bahuvyāmā dīrghabāhudvayapramāṇāḥ*). We have chosen to follow Cr, who avoids the technical measurement, glossing merely, "very long (*atidīrghāḥ*)."

"He . . . expects to crush Laṅkā with his own forces." *eṣaivāśaṃsate laṅkāṃ svenānīkena marditum*: This phrase is repeated at 6.18.24cd and 6.18.39ef, and occurs almost verbatim at 18cd above and 39cd below.

25–26. "long mane" *dīrghakesaraḥ*: D5,T1,3,M3, and the texts and printed editions of Cg read instead *dīrghalocanaḥ*, "long- *or* wide-eyed." This variant is rendered only in the translation of Raghunathan (1982, vol. 3, p. 63).

"glares fixedly" *nibhṛtaḥ prekṣate*: Literally, "he, motionless, looks." We follow the suggestion of Ct, Cr, and Cm, who understand "with single-minded attention (*ekāgracittaḥ*—so Cr)," and read the adjective adverbially with the verb *prekṣate*, "he looks at."

"beautiful" *sudarśanam*: We agree with those translators (Shastri 1959, vol. 3, p. 64; Pagani 1999, p. 930; and Roussel 1903, vol. 3, p. 73) who understand the word as an adjective modifying the mountain Sahya. This interpretation appears to be supported by Gorresio's variant, *cārudarśanam*, which he translates as "*dilettoso*." Gorresio (1856, vol. 9, p. 201), incidentally, understands the other names to be additional adjectives, viz. "*kṛṣṇagiri* (black)" and "*sahya* (agreeable)." Dutt (1893, p. 1177) and Gita Press (1969, vol. 3, p. 1457) see the term as the name of yet another mountain, Sudarśana.

"Rambha" *rambhaḥ*: This monkey or another of the same name is described at 6.18.17 below. See note there.

27. "Three billion" *śataṃ śatasahasrāṇāṃ triṃśac ca*: Literally, "one hundred hundred thousands and thirty." The number is ambiguous. It can be read as one hundred hundred-thousands plus thirty hundred-thousands (i.e., 10,000,000 + 3,000,000 = 13,000,000) or, taking the numbers in the nominative as multiplication factors rather

than as addends, as thirty hundred, hundred thousands (=three billion). Roussel (1903, vol. 3, p. 73), Pagani (1999, p. 930), and Raghunathan (1982, vol. 3, p. 63) understand the former. Dutt (1893, p. 1177) and Shastri (1959, vol. 3, p. 64) understand, "three hundred kotis," or three billion. Gorresio's text is less ambiguous, compounding the numbers and reading *triṃśacchatasahasrāṇi*, or three million ("*trenta centinaia di mila*") (1856, vol. 9, p. 201). Gita Press (1969, vol. 3, p. 1457) uniquely comes up with "one crore and thirty," which adds up to ten million and thirty monkeys, a somewhat improbable number in this context. We have chosen to read *triṃśat* as factorial, despite the particle *ca*—which would seem to indicate a conjunction—in light of how the numbers are expressed in verse 30ff. In verses 30–39 below, the numbers are increased by one million each time, from four million to seven million. In each case, the decade number, for example, *catvāriṃśat*, "forty," at verse 30 below, is used as a multiplicand along with *śatasahasram*, "hundred thousand." This is entirely in keeping with the pattern of handling numbers that we have seen earlier in the epic, as, for example, when the monkeys, one after another, declare how far they can leap (4.64) or when Hanumān engages in the contest with the mock demoness Surasā (5.1.130–155). For this reason, we chose to ignore the conjunctions here and at verse 30 to preserve what we see as a pattern. This, of course, leaves unexplained the problem of the current verse, which, in order to fit the progression, should enumerate three million rather than three billion. Although the textual evidence supports the additional *śatam*, "hundred," in *pāda* a, the progression alluded to, and the likely glossative variants proposed by some manuscripts and the printed text of Gorresio, lend some support to the notion that the number was originally intended to be three million. Cr is the only commentator to grapple consistently with the question of the numbers. He reads the decade numbers, thirty, forty, etc., as addends, thus maintaining a more modest numeric progression of ten thousand per time from verse 30 on, where he understands there to be one hundred forty thousand monkeys. His progression is, of course, also thrown off by the extra *śatam* in *pāda* a, where, by Cr's reckoning, there are thirteen million monkeys. Compare, too, 4.37.30–32 and notes; and notes to 6.19.32, 411* (following notes to 19.32) and 416* (following notes to 19.33).

27cd is a close variant of 6.18.31cd.

Following 27ab, D5–7,9–11,S insert a passage of one line [357*], which expands on the description of the monkeys in Rambha's entourage. "whom these dreadful and fierce [monkeys], of fierce valor [follow]."

28–29. "pricking up his ears" *karṇau vivṛṇute*: Literally, "displays his ears." Several translators offer, "open *or* dilate his ears," but this makes little sense. Shastri (1959, vol. 3, p. 64) translates, "shaking his ears," but this forces the sense of the verb and, besides, is somewhat ludicrous.

"showing his fangs" *jṛmbhate*: See notes to verses 16–19 above.

"immensely powerful" *mahābalaḥ*: D10,11, and the texts and printed editions of Ct read instead the grammatically awkward instrumental *mahaujasā*, "[endowed] with great power *or* energy," while D6,T2,G1,M1,2,5, and the texts of VSP (6.26.36), KK (6.26.34), and Gita Press (6.26.35) read *mahājavaḥ*, "of great speed." Translations that follow the texts and printed editions of Ct render the former, while Raghunathan (1982, vol. 3, p. 63) renders, "of the immense strength and speed" and Gita Press (1969, vol. 3, p. 1457) translates, "with extraordinary might."

"never flees an opposing host" *na ca yūthād vidhāvati*: Literally, "and does not run from the troop." The expression is slightly ambiguous, as it could also mean "does not desert his [own] troop," but, in the context, this seems to us less likely, although Gorresio (1856, vol. 9, p. 201) translates his variant *na ca yūthān nivartate* in this sense, "*e non si discosta dalla sua schiera*." The critical reading is rare in the texts of the southern commentators. Ct and Cr read *na ca senāṃ paridhāvati*, "does not run to [his] army," which Ct explains as meaning "he prefers to fight alone (*kiṃtv eka eva yoddhum icchatīty arthaḥ*)." Cg has, instead, the *facilior yuddhāt* for *yūthāt*, yielding the sense "and does not flee from battle."

Following verse 28, D5–7,9–11,S insert a passage of two lines [358*]: "He shakes with fury and casts his glances sideways. Staring at his tail,[1] that immensely powerful monkey roars."

[1]"Staring at his tail" *paśyan lāṅgūlam api ca*: It is unclear why Śarabha is looking at his tail. The commentators are silent. This phrase is rendered only in the translation of Raghunathan (1982, vol. 3, p. 63). D7,9–11, and the texts and printed editions of Ct and Cr read instead *paśya lāṅgūlavikṣepam* [D7, *-vikṣepaiḥ*], "observe the lashing of his tail."

30. "He commands" *etasya*: Literally, "of him [there are]."

"a full four million" *sarve . . . śatasahasrāṇi catvariṃśat tathaiva ca*: Literally, "all the hundred thousand and forty." As in verse 27 above, the numbering of the monkeys leaves room for multiple interpretations. The number here lacks the additional mention of "hundred (*śatam*)," which is found in verse 27. Only Cr among the commentators mentions the number, reading it without explanation as "one hundred thousand and forty (*śatasahasrāṇi catvariṃśac ca*)." Like us, some translators, including Dutt (1893, p. 1177) and Shastri (1959, vol. 3, p. 64), understand *catvariṃśat* as a multiplicand rather than an addend, yielding a total of forty hundred thousand, or four million. Others (Raghunathan 1982, vol. 3, p. 63; Roussel 1903, vol. 3, p. 74; Pagani 1999, p. 931; and Gita Press 1969, vol. 3, p. 1457: "one lakh and forty") have totaled the number to yield one hundred forty thousand. A number of northern manuscripts as well as the text of Gorresio read *śatasahasrāṇi catvāriṃśac chatāni ca* (6.2.38). Gorresio (1856, vol. 9, p. 201) understands these numbers as addends and totals them as one hundred thousand plus forty hundreds (= 104,000).

"powerful" *balinaḥ*: The form is ambiguous. It can be read as a genitive singular referring to Śarabha and has been translated as such by Roussel (1903, vol. 3, p. 74), Pagani (1999, p. 931), Shastri (1959, vol. 3, p. 64), and Gorresio (1856, vol. 9, p. 201). We, however, agree with the other translators, who read it as a nominative plural referring to Śarabha's followers on the grounds that otherwise these monkeys would be left with no descriptive adjective concerning their strength, valor, and ferocity, which would be rather unusual in this context. It would also be somewhat redundant with the adjective *mahābalaḥ* used to describe Śarabha in the preceding verse.

"Vihāras" *vihārāḥ*: The name appears to refer to these monkeys' propensity to roam at will. The word can mean something like "wanderers *or* vagabonds."

31–33. "of *bherī* drums" *bherīṇām*: A *bherī* appears to be specifically a war drum. See Vyas 1967, p. 229; 5.8.36; and 5.46.27 and notes. See 6.23.41; 6.24.19; 6.25.27;

6.26.1; 6.27.14,16; 6.34.12; 6.40.23; 6.45.24; 6.47.8; 6.48.31; and 6.65.16 and notes. Cf. 6.53.28.

"none can withstand him in battle" *yuddhe duṣprasaho nityam*: Literally, "always irresistible in battle."

"that... mountain, Pāriyātra" *parvatam... pāriyātram*: It is unclear whether the reference here is to a mountain or to a mountain range. B. C. Law (1954, pp. 19–20) notes the discrepancy in his identification: "The earliest mention of the Pāripātra [v.l. Pāriyātra] is found in the *Dharmaśūtra* of Baudhāyana [1.1.25], who refers to it as being situated on the southern limit of Āryāvarta. The *Skanda Purāṇa* refers to it as the farthest limit of Kumārīkhaṇḍa, the centre of Bhāratavarṣa... [while] Pargiter identifies [it]... with that portion of the modern Vindhya range which is situated west of Bhopal in Central India together with the Aravalli mountains identified with the Apokopa by Ptolemy." Bhattacharyya (1991, p. 245) understands it to be one of the seven mountain ranges of India. He locates it in the western Vindhyas, as it is said to be where the Chembal, Betwa, and Śiprā rivers originate. The name is known from the Nāsik inscriptions of Gautamīputra Sākarṇī and is attested to in the *Mahābhāṣya* (Kielhorn 1.475 on *Pā* 2.4.10), where it is said to be on the southern boundary of Āryāvarta.

34. "Five million" *śatasahasrāṇāṃ śatārdham*: Literally, "half a hundred, hundred thousands." See note to verse 27 above. Cm, who has not heretofore commented on the numbers, understands the number to be half a hundred thousand, or fifty thousand (*śatārdhaṃ sahasrāṇi*). Cr understands one hundred fifty thousand (*śatādhikapañcāśasahasrasaṃkhyākā ity arthaḥ*), while Ct, whom we follow, understands fifty lakhs, or five million (*pañcāśallakṣasaṃkhyam*).

"each with his separate troop" *bhāgaśaḥ*: Literally, "by divisions." See note to 6.3.24.

"form the entourage of" *paryupāsate*: Literally, "they surround, accompany." Compare verse 39 below and note.

35–37ab. "surging" *pravalgantīm*: Literally, "leaping." Cr explains, "jumping with excitement (*utsāhena plavamānām*)." We have translated in such a way as to reinforce the oceanic simile (*dvitīya iva sāgaraḥ*) in 35cd and to avoid the somewhat comical notion of a jumping army.

"Mount Dardara" *dardara-*: According to Cg, this is the name of a mountain near the Ganges (*dardaro nāma gaṅgāsamīpasthaḥ parvataḥ*). Bhattacharyya (1991, p. 115) identifies Dardara as the name of a people who resided "in the Upper Kishenganga valley in Kashmir on the Upper Indus." Cf. 4.34.36–37. D5–7,D10,11,T, and the texts and printed editions of Ct and Cr read instead *dardura-*, which Cr explains as "[resembling] a cloud (*meghasadṛśaḥ*)."

"from the river Parṇāśā" *parṇāśām... nadīm*: According to the apparatus of the *MBh* (*Sabhāparvan* 103* [B1], p. 50), this is the name of a river in western India (*kiṃpunā... caiva parṇāśā ca mahānadī*). See Bhattacharyya (1991, p. 245), who identifies the Parṇāśā with either the Banas River in Rajasthan or the Rann River in Cutch. The word *parṇāśā* is subject to considerable variation among the various manuscript traditions. The texts and printed editions of Ct and Cr read instead *yo veṇām* (misprinted at GPP 6.26.41 as *yau veṇām*). The river watering Vinata's home territory is thus referred to as the Veṇā in translations that follow this text. Ck insists that the authentic reading here is *yo vedīm*, for *yo nadīm*, yielding the sense "[roams] the Vedī region."

"six million" *ṣaṣṭiḥ śatasahasrāṇi*: Literally, "sixty hundred thousands." See note to verse 27 above.

37cd. "Krathana" *krathanaḥ*: Ñ1,Ś,V1,B3,D4,7,8,12,M3, and the texts and printed editions of Cg and Cm substitute instead *krodhanaḥ*, which appears in several translations. Gita Press (1969, vol. 3, p. 1458) renders this as the name of a monkey, while Raghunathan (1982, vol. 3, p. 64) inexplicably understands the variant to be an alternate name of the river Parṇāśā.

Following verse 37, D5–7,9–11,S insert a passage of one line [364*]: "[His forces] are valorous, powerful, and marshaled in divisions troop by troop."

38. "Expanding his body" *vapuḥ puṣyati*: Literally, "he nourishes his body." Cr reads the phrase with the ablative *krodhāt*, "out of anger," in *pāda* d, but this seems somewhat forced. Cm and Cg suggest that Gavaya is expanding his body in the joy of battle (*yuddhaharṣād abhivardhayatīty arthaḥ*—Cg).

Following verse 38ab, D5–7,9–11,S insert a passage of one line [365*]: "[expanding his body, while] completely ignoring all the other monkeys, arrogant in their strength."[1]

[1]"arrogant in their strength" *baladarpitān*: The text of Cg reads instead the contextually superior nominative singular *baladarpitaḥ*, thus making Gavaya ignore the other monkeys in his own pride of power.

39. "His entourage consists of" *paryupāsate*: Literally, "they surround, accompany." Compare verse 34 and note.

"seven million" *śatasahasrāṇi saptatiḥ*: Literally, "seventy hundred thousands." See note to verse 27 above.

"he expects to crush Laṅkā with his own forces" *eṣa āśaṃsate laṅkāṃ svenānīkena marditum*: This phrase is repeated at 18cd above and occurs almost verbatim at 24cd above, as well as at 6.18.24cd and 6.18.39ef.

40. "dreadful" *ghorāḥ*: D7,9–11, and the texts and printed editions of Ct and Cr read instead *vīrāḥ*, "heroes."

"powerful . . . they . . . can take on any form at will" *balinaḥ kāmarūpiṇaḥ*: For *pāda* b, D10,11, and the texts and printed editions of Ct and Cr substitute the critical edition's *pāda* d, "*yeṣāṃ saṃkhyā na vidyate* (they are numberless)." In place of the critical edition's *pāda* d, these manuscripts read: "*teṣāṃ yūthāni bhāgaśaḥ* (each with his separate troop)" (a variant of the critical edition's 34d).

"troop leaders and leaders of troop leaders" *yūthapā yūthapaśreṣṭhāḥ*: Literally, "troop protectors [and] the foremost of troop protectors." Cg explains the difference in status by noting that the former are Aṅgada and his like, and the latter are Sugrīva and his equals. (*yūthapā aṅgadādayaḥ. yūthapaśreṣṭhāḥ sugrīvādayaḥ.*)

Ck (quoted by Ct and also quoted in parentheses after the colophon of Cm in VSP) claims that the division of *sargas* here is inauthentic (*apāṅktaḥ*) on the grounds that there is neither a break in the action nor a change in the subject (*atra sargacchedo 'pāṅkto vṛttabhedābhāvād ekaprakaraṇatvāc ceti katakaḥ*).

Sarga 18

1. "those troop leaders" *tān . . . yūthapān*: Several of the commentators attempt to distinguish the monkey leaders described in this *sarga* as a distinct class from those mentioned in the preceding *sarga*. Cr sees these monkeys as belonging to a different species, noting by way of introduction, "He [Vālmīki] now describes those monkeys, beginning with the species of langur (*lāṅgūlajātiprabhṛtīn āha*)." See note to 6.34.26. Cg feels that the monkeys described here are the principal troop leaders, who are superior to those mentioned previously (*punaruktebhyo 'py utkṛṣṭān pradhānayūthapatīn*). Cm, relying on the relative clause in *pāda* b, thinks that the reference is specifically to those monkeys who are willing to sacrifice their lives for Rāma (*teṣāṃ prasiddhānāṃ vānarāṇāṃ madhye ye rāghavārthe jīvitaṃ na rakṣanti tān*). As indicated in the note to 6.17.40 above, Ck believes that the narrative is continuous and that the *sarga* break here is spurious.

"risking their lives" *na rakṣanti jīvitam*: Literally, "they do not protect [their own] lives."

2–3. "on whose tail . . . fur" *vālā lāṅgūlam āśritāḥ*: Literally, "hair depending on the tail." D10,11, and the texts and printed editions of Ct read instead *dīrghalāṅgūlam āśritāḥ*, literally, "depending on his long tail." This reading provides no explicit substantive for the participle *āśritāḥ*, "depending on," leaving one to simply infer that the fur or hair of the monkey's tail is intended (*keśāḥ*—so Cr).

2ab is a close variant of 6.17.23ab.

2cd = 6.17.23cd.

"bristling" *pragṛhītāḥ*: Literally, "separated." The commentators generally explain this as meaning "standing up, erected (*utthitāḥ*—so Cr)."

"sticks out so far in all directions" *bahuvyāmāḥ . . . prakīrṇāḥ*: See notes to 6.17.23 above.

"the troop leader called Hara" *haro nāmaiṣa yūthapaḥ*: Ct suggests that Hara is not so much a proper name of a specific hero as a designation of a particular species of langur (*haro golāṅgūlajātiḥ*).

4. "Banding together" *sahitāḥ*: Literally, "united, grouped together." A large number of manuscripts from both recensions (Ś,V1,3,B1,D0–6,8–13,T1,M) and the texts and printed editions of the southern commentators read instead *sahasā*, "all at once."

"scaling the ramparts of Laṅkā" *laṅkārohaṇa-*: Literally, "climbing Laṅkā."

Following verse 4, D5–7,9–11,T,G,M1,2,5 [M3 after verse 5], and the texts and printed editions of the southern commentators insert a passage of one line [375*], which continues the description of Hara's troops: "These troop leaders who are present are servants of the king of the tawny monkeys."

5. V2,D5–7,9–11,T,G,M1,2,5 all omit this verse. According to the principles upon which the critical edition is based, it should have been relegated to the apparatus (Bhatt 1960, p. xxiv, no. 4). T. R. Krishnacharya, the editor of KK, includes this verse as 6.27.5 but notes in his apparatus that it is found only in very late manuscripts and is not seen in the older ones (*ayaṃ ślokaḥ prācīnakośeṣu na dṛśyate. auttarāhapāṭha eva dṛśyate*). The editor of the VSP edition places this verse within brackets, between 6.27.4 and 6.27.5. Gita Press, GPP, and NSP omit the verse entirely. Among the translators consulted, only Gorresio (1856, vol. 9, p. 203) renders it.

6–8. "The heroes . . . with claws and fangs for their weapons, are terrifying and fierce in their anger" *nakhadaṃṣṭrāyudhān vīrāṃs tīkṣṇakopān bhayāvahān*: This line (= 7ab) is omitted by D5–7,9–11,T,G1,M1,3. V2 omits verse 7 entirely. Like verse 5 above, it should have been relegated to the critical apparatus. This line is rendered only by Gorresio (1856, vol. 9, p. 203).

"As numberless and indistinguishable as grains of sand on the far shore of the sea" *asaṃkhyeyān anirdeśyān paraṃ pāram ivodadheḥ*: Literally, "as uncountable and indescribable as the farther shore of the sea." Ct explains, "impossible to enumerate by name (*anirdeśyā*)." Cg explains, "impossible to describe individually (*anirdeśyān pratyekaṃ nirdeṣṭum aśakyān*)." Cr, Ct, and Ck believe that the expression "far shore (*paraṃ pāram*)" by metonymy refers to dust, i.e., sand, located there, and we have followed their suggestion (*paraṃ pāram iva parapārasthareṇūn iva*).

"apes" *ṛkṣāḥ*: See note to 6.4.17. See, too, note to 1.16.10 and also R. Goldman 1989.

"denizens of the mountains, hill country, and rivers" *parvateṣu ca ye kecid viṣameṣu nadīṣu ca*: Literally, "those who [are] in the mountains, in the uneven places, and along the rivers." We have supplied the word "denizens," following the suggestion of Cr, who adds the phrase "they previously lived (*avasann iti śeṣaḥ*)."

9–10. "like Parjanya" *parjanya iva*: This is the vedic rain god, often associated, or even identified, with Indra (*parjanya indra iva*—so Cr). See translations and notes to 6.41.33; 6.67.20; 6.83.33; and 6.116.88.

"where he drinks the waters of the Narmadā" *narmadāṃ piban*: Literally, "drinking the Narmadā." Cr sees Dhūmra as drying up the waters of the river (*pibañ śoṣayan san*). See 4.40.8–10. The Narmadā River, one of few major rivers in India that flow from east to west, is considered holy and thought to mark the boundary between North and South India.

11–12. "his younger brother" *yavīyān asya tu bhrātā*: Cs argues that the description of Jāmbavān indicates that both he and Dhūmra are sons of Brahmā. He claims, however, that in the *Bālakāṇḍa*'s listing of the partial incarnations of the divinities (490* = GPP 1.17.7), only the former is mentioned because of his possessing superior qualities relative to those of his brother. (*etena jāmbavata iva dhūmrasyāpi brahmajātatvaṃ jñāyate. bālakāṇḍe 'ṃśāvataraṇaprastāve guṇajyeṣṭhatvāj jāmbavata evoktiḥ.*) As an alternative, Cs suggests that we might understand the word "brother" metaphorically so that the sense might be, "He is like a brother in his affection (*sauhardād bhrāteva vā*)."

"He looks just like his brother" *bhrātrā samāno rūpeṇa*: Literally, "equal to his brother in appearance." Cs understands this reference to be to the two brothers having the form of *ṛkṣas*, "apes." Cs, like many medieval and later authors, may understand the term *ṛkṣa* to refer to bears (*rūpeṇarkṣākāreṇa*). See notes to 6.4.17 and Goldman 1989.

"peaceful by nature" *praśāntaḥ*: Literally, "peaceful, calm." M3 and the texts and printed editions of Cg (GPP footnote, KK, VSP) substitute *prakrāntaḥ*, "valiant." This is reflected in the translation of Raghunathan (1982, vol. 3, p. 65).

"obedient to his superiors" *guruvartī*: Literally, "conformable to *or* following his gurus." Cg understands, "obedient to his elders (*guruśuśruṣakaḥ*)," while Ck and Ct understand, "serving his true *guru* (*sadgurūpāsakaḥ*)."

13. "the wars of the gods and *asuras*" *devāsure*: Literally, "with respect to the gods and *asuras*." Most commentators supplement this elliptical adjective with a word meaning either battle or rivalry, and we concur.

14–15. "there are" *vicaranti*: Literally, "they roam about."

"shaggy apes" *romaśāḥ*: Literally, "hairy." We have supplied the word "apes."

"who resemble *rākṣasas* and *piśācas*" *rākṣasānāṃ ca sadṛśāḥ piśācānām*: Cr construes this phrase with the immediately following adjective *romaśāḥ*, "hairy," yielding the sense "hairy as *rākṣasas* and *piśācas*." Ct and Ck, however, with whom we are inclined to agree, read these separately and add that the apes are similar to the demons in their ferocity (*rakṣaḥpiśācasādṛśyaṃ krauryeṇa*).

"They scale the mountain peaks and hurl down boulders" *ārūhya parvatāgrebhyo . . . śilāḥ / muñcanti*: Literally, "having climbed, they release stones from mountain peaks." For the sake of readability, we have adjusted the syntax slightly.

16–17. "standing there" *sthitam*: This participle, occurring at 16d, is replaced in D6,7,G1,M3, and the texts and printed editions of Cg by the plural *sthitāḥ*, which then modifies *sarve vānarāḥ*, "all the monkeys."

"Rambha" *rambho nāma*: A number of manuscripts show variants for the name, including Ḍaṃbha (D11,G1,3), Daṃbha (T3,G2,M3,5), and Jaṃbha (D9). Pagani (1999, p. 932 and note, p. 1656) and Raghunathan (1982, vol. 3, p. 65) read Daṃbha. This monkey or another of the same name is mentioned above at 6.17.26.

"with his troops serves thousand-eyed Indra" *sahasrākṣaṃ paryupāste . . . balena*: We follow the interpretation of Cr, who construes *balena* in *pāda* 17c with the verb *paryupāste*, "he honors, worships, waits upon," in *pāda* b, explaining, "He dispatched his own army in order to assist Indra (*indrasāhāyyārthaṃ svasainyaṃ preṣayāmāsety arthaḥ*)." Cg, although less explicit, expresses the same idea in glossing, "He pleases [Indra] with his army [*or* with his strength] (*balena prīṇayati*)." Translators offer various renderings, depending on how they understand the verb *paryupāste* and the epithet *sahasrākṣa*, "thousand-eyed." Thus Dutt (1893, p. 1179) renders, "dwelleth near the thousand-eyed Deity"; Gita Press (1969, vol. 3, p. 1460), "ministers to Indra (the thousand-eyed god) with his army"; Raghunathan (1982, vol. 3, p. 65), "he finds favor in the eyes of the Lord-of-the-thousand-eyes, whom he worships"; Roussel (1903, vol. 3, p. 76), "*habite le Sahasrāksha*"; Shastri (1959, vol. 3, p. 66), following Roussel, "dwells on the Sahasraksha Mountain"; and Pagani (1999, p. 932), "*et au service d'Indra aux mille yeux.*"

"Although he is standing still, in his eagerness he appears to be leaping about." *abhisaṃrabdhaṃ plavamānam iva sthitam*: Literally, "agitated, he is standing as if jumping." Like Cg, we understand the apparent motion of Rambha, while he is, in fact, standing still, to be some kind of extraordinary manifestation of his energy or agitation. Cg suggests supplying "in wonder (*āścaryeṇa*)," to be read adverbially with the verb *prekṣante*, "they watch." Cm appears to understand the phrase to indicate that Rambha is a creature "who jumps by nature (*plavamānatvena vartamānam*)." Many manuscripts (Ñ2,V3,D0–5,7,9–11,13,T2,G2,M1,2, and the texts and printed editions of Cv, Crā, Ck, Ct, and Cr) substitute *avasthitam* for the critical reading *iva sthitam*. Ct and Ck explain, "leaping about for sport and then standing still for sport. (*plavamānam. līlartham iti śeṣaḥ. sthitaṃ līlārtham eva punaḥ sthitam.*)" Translators, other than Raghunathan, have generally followed Ct's lead, and thus Dutt (1893, p. 1179) renders, "leaping and resting (by turns)"; Roussel (1903, vol. 3, p. 76), "(*tour à tour*) *bondit, retombe, se tient immobile*"; Shastri (1959, vol. 3, p. 66), "now leaps up . . . and then stands motionless"; Pagani (1999, p. 932), "*sans cesse bondit puis s'arrête sans un geste*"; and Gita Press (1969, vol. 3, p. 1460), "whether leaping . . . or standing."

18–19. "when he moves, rubs his flanks against a mountain standing a league away" *sthitaṃ yojane śailaṃ gacchan pārśvena sevate*: Literally, "in going, he attends with his side a mountain located *or* standing at a *yojana*." The commentators agree that the idea here is that Saṃnādana's body is one league in breadth. Most of them, like Cm, understand that, in moving, he touches a mountain one league away with his side (*yaḥ... gacchan yojane sthitaṃ śailaṃ pārśvena sevate spṛśati*). Cg places more emphasis on the participle *gacchan*, "going," explaining that, when Saṃnādana moves, his very first step places a one league distant mountain right at his side (*asya gamanakāla ekapada-prakṣepadaśāyām ekayojanaparimitaḥ parvataḥ pārśvastho bhavati*).

"league" *yojanam*: See notes to 1.5.7 and 5.1.69.

"who, when he stretches his body upward, reaches a league in height" *ūrdhvaṃ tathaiva kāyena gataḥ prāpnoti yojanam*: Literally, "and going upward with his body, reaches one *yojana*."

"His form is unsurpassed" *yasmān na paramaṃ rūpam... vidyate*: Literally, "than which no greater form is found."

"among creatures that move on four feet" *catuṣpādeṣu*: Literally, "among quadrupeds."

20a–d. The numbering of verses here in the critical edition is confusing and does not appear to conform to that of any printed edition or to any version known to the commentators. All commentators consulted (Ct, Cr, Crā, Cm, Ck, Cv), except Cg, understand the critical edition's 20ef (=GPP 6.27.20ab; VSP 6.27.20ab; KK 6.27.20ab) as beginning the description of the next monkey general, Krathana (v.l. Krodhana—Cr). Cg, on the other hand, sees lines 20ef–21cd as a continuation of the description of Saṃnādana, with the description of Krathana beginning only in verse 22. Printed editions of Cg's text (VSP, KK) have the critical edition's 21cd (=GPP 21ab) as an independently numbered half *śloka* (KK 21; VSP 21). The critical edition's division of the verses suggests that 20ef marks the end of the description of Saṃnādana, but this is not persuasive as the style of this and the previous *sarga* shows that relative pronouns generally mark the beginning of new descriptions. Moreover, none of the commentators, not even Cg, sees the description of Krathana beginning with the critical edition's 21ab.

"once fought a battle with Śakra himself" *yena yuddhaṃ tadā dattaṃ raṇe śakrasya*: Literally, "by whom combat was given in battle to Śakra (reading *śakrasya* as *sādhāraṇa-ṣaṣṭhī*)." Cg disagrees with the other commentators in seeing Saṃnādana as having fought not against Indra but rather successfully on his behalf in the god's war with the *asuras*. (*śakrasya raṇe śakrasyāsuraiḥ saha yuddhe. yenāsurebhyo yuddhaṃ dattaṃ tadā parājayaś cāsurebhyo na prāptaḥ so 'yaṃ saṃnādana iti śruto nāma.*) Cg does this, no doubt, in order to avoid a contradiction that would otherwise arise as a consequence of his belief that verses 20 and 21, where service as an ally of Indra is mentioned, constitute part of the description of Saṃnādana.

D3,6,7,T2,M3, and the texts and printed editions of Cg read *purā*, "long ago," for the critical edition's "*tadā*, "once [literally, "then"]. This variant is rendered in the translation of Raghunathan (1982, vol. 3, p. 65).

20ef–23. The syntax of verses 22–23cd is awkward, and we have adjusted it somewhat to achieve a more lucid translation. A literal translation of the two verses would be: "That majestic, powerful bull among monkeys lives there [23cd] on that king of the lords of mountains, which is frequented by many *kinnaras* [22cd], which always offers the pleasures of a pleasure garden to your brother, O lord of *rākṣasas*, [23ab] and whose *jambū* trees King Vaiśravaṇa enjoys [22ab]."

"never boasts on the battlefield" *yuddheṣv akatthano nityam*: Literally, "always not boasting in battles." Ct explains that Krathana demonstrates his valor by deeds alone (*akatthana ātmaślāghārahitaḥ kāryeṇaiva parākramapradarśakaḥ*). The adjective *akatthana* is no doubt used here because of its alliterative effect with the name Krathana.

"Agni of the black path" *kṛṣṇavartmanā*: Literally, "by him of the black path." This common kenning may refer to either a path blackened along the earth or, perhaps, to the black path of smoke that the fire builds to the heavens. Compare *RaghuVa* 11.42 and *ManuSm* 2.94.

"in their wars with the *asuras*" *devāsure yuddhe*: Literally, "in the war between the gods and the *asuras*."

"the king of lordly mountains" *yo rājā parvatendrāṇām*: Literally, "the king of the lords of mountains." Ct, no doubt correctly, identifies the unnamed mountain as Kailāsa, which is regularly identified as Kubera's abode (for example, see 4.42.19–20; see also notes to 5.19.30). Ck glosses, "in the fragrant groves of Kailāsa (*kailāsagandhamādane*)."

"which always serves as the delightful pleasure garden" *vihārasukhado nityam*: Literally, "always giving the pleasure of a pleasure garden."

"King Vaiśravaṇa Kubera" *vaiśravaṇo rājā*: Literally, "King Vaiśravaṇa."

"disports himself among *jambū* trees" *jambūm upaniṣevate*: Literally, "enjoys the *jambū* tree." Commentators differ as to how to understand this phrase. We follow Ct and Ck, who understand King Vaiśravaṇa to be the subject of *upaniṣevate*, that is, that Kubera enjoys the *jambū* tree or trees growing on the mountain. Cg and Cm, however, take the subject to be the mountain itself. They interpret the phrase, therefore, to mean "which (mountain) is covered with *jambū* trees (*jambūyuktaḥ*)." Translators generally offer variations on these two themes. Thus Dutt (1893, p. 1179) offers, "where king Vaiśravaṇa eateth rose apples"; Gita Press (1969, vol. 3, p. 1460), "takes his seat beneath a Jambū (a variety of rose-apple) tree"; Shastri (1959, vol. 3, p. 66), "sits beneath a Jambhu tree on that mountain"; Roussel (1903, vol. 3, p. 76), "*à cet endroit de la Jambû*"; and Raghunathan (1982, vol. 3, p. 65), "where rose-apple trees grow in abundance."

Pagani (1999, p. 932), on the other hand, renders, "*à côté de la Jambū*," making it clear in her footnote (p. 1656) that she understands the reference here to be to the legendary river of heaven by that name. This position, however, seems hard to maintain, as the *purāṇas* generally locate the Jambū River on Mount Meru and/or Mount Mandara (*BhāgP* 5.16.19–20) or around Mount Meru (*VāyuP* 35.26–30). V. Mani (1975, s.v.) understands the *jambū* tree to be "a mythical tree growing on the southern slope of Mt. Meru. It is watered every year by the subjects of King Kubera, or Vaiśravaṇa." The *jambū* is commonly identified as the rose apple tree or the black plum (*Syzygium cuminii* L., syn. *Eugenia jambos* Linn, Roxb., or *Eugenia Jambolana* syn. *Syzygium jambolanum* W.). See Brandis 1874, pp. 233–34 and 1906, pp. 317; and Brockington 1984, p. 105.

24. "He . . . expects to crush Laṅkā with his own forces." *eṣaivāśaṃsate laṅkāṃ svenānīkena marditum*: This phrase is repeated at 39ef below and at 6.17.24cd, and occurs almost verbatim at 6.17.18cd and 6.17.39cd.

25–28. "attend" *abhivartate*: Literally, "turns toward, approaches."

"the ancient hostility between the elephants and monkeys" *hastināṃ vānarāṇāṃ ca pūrvaṃ vairam*: Ck, Ct, Cr, Cg, Cm, and Cv refer with varying degrees of detail to the ancient, or purāṇic, story according to which, at the request of some sages, the monkey Kesarin, the father of Hanumān, killed the *asura* [*rākṣasa*—Cm] Śambasādana, who had taken the form of an elephant and was oppressing them. Cg and Cv add that in gratitude the sages granted Kesarin a boon whereby he received so mighty a son as Hanumān. The incident with the *asura* Śambasādana is mentioned in the *Sundarakāṇḍa* (5.33.74,80 and notes). There, however, the *asura* is not said to have taken the form of an elephant. The hostility referred to dates, according to the commentators, from this incident. See, too, *Prācīna Caritrakoṣa* (s.v. Kesarin). Pagani (1999, p. 1656) provides a note explaining only that Kesarin kills an *asura* who had taken on the form of an elephant.

"he haunts the banks of the Ganges" *gaṅgām anu paryeti*: Literally, "he moves around following the Ganges."

"moves along" *gacchan*: Literally, "[he] going." Ñ1,B2,3,D7,9–11,M5, and the texts and printed editions of Ct and Cr read instead *garjan*, "roaring."

"of the tawny monkeys . . . foremost of monkeys" *harīṇām . . . vānaraśreṣṭhaḥ*: Cg remarks that, even though Pramāthin is said to be the leader of the tawny monkeys (*harīṇām*), the poet also describes him as the foremost of monkeys (*vānaraśreṣṭhaḥ*) in order to dispel the erroneous notion that any difference of species is intended here (*harivāhinīmukhyatve 'pi bhinnajātīyatvabhramavyudāsārthaṃ vānaraśreṣṭha ity uktam*).

"Mount Uśīrabīja, the equal of Mount Mandara" *uśīrabījam . . . parvataṃ mandaropamam*: Mount Uśīrabīja is located in North India. See *MBh* 3.140.1 (*uśīrabījaṃ mainākaṃ giriṃ śvetam*). Ś1,V1,D9,10, and the texts and printed editions of Ct read instead *mandaraṃ parvatottamam*, "that best of mountains, Mount Mandara." This rather awkward reading forces translators who follow Ct's text either to see Uśīrabīja and Mandara in apposition (so Dutt 1893, p. 1180; Roussel 1903, vol. 3, p. 76; and Shastri 1959, vol. 3, p. 67) or as two different mountains (Gita Press 1969, vol. 3, p. 1461).

Following 26ab, D5–7,9–11,S insert a passage of one line [386*]: "Roaring, he [Pramāthin] attacks the forest deer and trees." There are numerous variants of this verse. The most common vulgate text, that of Ct, reads, "*gajān rodhayate vanyān ārujaṃś ca mahīruhān* (He [Pramāthin] harasses the forest elephants and smashes the trees)." Cg's variant, which is the most readable, substitutes the critical edition's *yodhayate*, "fights," for Ct's *rodhayati*, and reads, "He [Pramāthin] fights the forest elephants and smashes trees."

Following 28ab, D5–7,9–11,S insert a passage of two lines [387*]: "He [Pramāthin] is the leader of these great bellowing monkeys, who are so powerful[1] and so proud of their strength and valor."

[1]"powerful" *balaśālinām*: Literally, "endowed with strength." D7,9–11,G1,3,M1,2,5, and the texts and printed editions of Ct and Cr read instead *bāhuśālinām*, "having [powerful] arms."

29. This verse is somewhat elliptical and follows the northern reading more closely than the southern. In southern manuscripts and printed editions, *pādas* 29ab are separated by an entire *śloka* from 29cd. The southern commentators, in general, and some translators understand 29–30, including 387*, to refer to Pramāthin.

29–30ab. "column of dust" *rajaḥ*: Literally, "dust."

Following 29ab, D5–7,9–11,S insert a passage of two lines [388*]: "That frenzied army of swift monkeys [is like] red [dust] raised up on all sides by the wind." This verse, too, is elliptical, and the commentators struggle to construe it. Ct and Ck understand that the dust is raised by the army and then scattered by the wind. Cg and Cm think that the dust is raised by the wind but within the army. The southern commentators further understand an implicit relative pronoun *yasya*, "in whose [army]," so that the object of Rāvaṇa's vision, which resembles a great cloud, is not the army but the monkey leader, Pramāthin himself. This idea is accepted by virtually all translators who follow the text of the southern recension.

30cd–31. "Having witnessed the construction of the bridge" *dṛṣṭvā vai setubandhanam*: Ck, Cm, and Ct indicate that the langurs attended Nala, the architect of the bridge, as his assistants (*nalasamīpe tatsahāyatayā sthitvā*—so Ct). Cr argues that it was their leader Gavākṣa who aided in the construction (*nalakartṛkasetubandhanasahāyībhūtaṃ gavākṣaṃ nāma*).

"swift" *mahāvegam*: Ñ,B,D9–11,G1, and the texts and printed editions of Ct read instead the vocative *mahārāja*, "O great king, your majesty."

"with their tremendous power" *ojasā*: Cg argues that what is suggested here is that the members of this particular troop have still greater strength than their troop leader (*yūthapatyapekṣayā yūthānāṃ balotsāhādhikyaṃ vyajyate*).

31cd is a close variant of 6.17.27cd.

32–34. "Kesarin" *kesarī*: The *Vālmīki Rāmāyaṇa* apparently knows two Kesarins. For the one here, see 6.4.30; 6.39.26; and 6.60.38. The other Kesarin is, of course, Hanumān's father. See 4.38.17; 4.65.27; 4.66.27; 5.33.73–74; 6.19.11; and 7.35.19. See, too, *MBh* 3.147.27 and 8.686*. See also Bulcke 1959–1960 and S. Goldman 1999.

"lovely golden mountain" *ramye kāñcanaparvate*: Cr, Ck, and Ct identify the mountain as Meru or Mahāmeru, the *axis mundi*. Cm states further that this is the Mount Meru that is situated near the western, or sunset, mountain (*astādri*) and that is the residence of Manusāvarṇi, the eighth Manu (*astādrisamīpavartini sāvarṇinivāsamerau*). See 6.48.50; and 6.47.106 and notes.

"great seers" *mahātmānaḥ . . . maharṣayaḥ*: Literally, "the great, great seers."

"trees . . . bear fruit to gratify every desire" *sarvakāmaphaladrumāḥ*: Ñ1,B1,3,D5, 9–11,T2,3,G1,3,M, and the texts and printed editions of Ct substitute *-kāla-*, "time," for *-kāma-*, "desire." Translators who follow the text of Ct thus give the compound the sense "bearing fruit in all seasons." See 6.4.48, 6.108.12, 6.115.19, and notes.

"He roams about that mountain the color of which is equal to that of the sun" *yaṃ sūryatulyavarṇābham anuparyeti parvatam*: The reading of the critical edition is quite difficult, as it provides no apparent subject for the verb *anuparyeti*. Many manuscripts of both the north and the south (Ś1,Ñ2,V2,3,B3,D5,7,9–11,T1,M1–3), and the texts and printed editions of the southern commentators replace the first member of the compound, *sūrya-*, with the nominative singular *sūryaḥ*, thus yielding the sense "which mountain, the color of itself, the sun circles." This image is, of course, in keeping with the standard notion that Mount Meru is the axis around which the sun revolves. Manuscripts that read with the critical edition here generally supply the nominative singular *yaḥ* for the critical edition's *yam*, thus providing a grammatical subject, "who [Kesarin]," for the verb. Our translation has essentially followed this reading, supplying the referent "he [Kesarin]." Virtually no manuscript collated for the critical edition other than G1 seems to have the peculiar sequence of the critical text. Based on the divided nature of the readings, the critical reading probably should have been marked as uncertain. See Sutherland 1992.

"take on that color" *bhānti tadvarṇāḥ*: Literally, "possessing that color, they shine."

Following verse 33, D5–7,9–11,S insert a passage of two lines [391*]: "On which foremost of mountains, there are trees whose fruit gratifies every desire and that are constantly[1] in fruit. There are also honeys of great worth."

[1]"constantly" *sadā*: D9–11 and the texts and printed editions of Ct read instead *sarve*, "all, every," modifying *vṛkṣāḥ*, "trees."

35. "Of the sixty thousand mountains" *ṣaṣṭir girisahasrāṇām*: Many manuscripts, as well as the texts and printed editions of Ct, Ck, and Cr, read instead *ṣaṣṭir girisahasrāṇi*. This reading yields the sense "There are sixty thousand [beautiful golden] mountains."

"stands among them" *teṣāṃ madhye*: Literally, "in their midst."

36. "These monkeys—tawny, white, red-faced, honey-yellow—" *kapilāḥ śvetās tāmrāsyā madhupiṅgalāḥ*: Literally, "tawny, white, red-faced, honey-yellow." It is not entirely clear whether the poet intends us to understand that individual monkeys are multicolored or whether the various monkeys are colored differently from one another.

"on that highest of mountains" *uttamagirau*: This could also mean "on the most excellent of mountains." D9–11 and the texts and printed editions of Ct read instead *antimagirau*, "on the last *or* most distant mountain."

37. "four great fangs" *caturdaṃṣṭrāḥ*: Literally, "four-fanged."

"as fierce as Agni Vaiśvānara" *vaiśvānarasamāḥ*: Literally, "equal to Vaiśvānara." Vaiśvānara is a common kenning for Agni, the fire god. We follow Cg in understanding that the common quality underlying the simile is "fierceness (*tadvadugrāḥ*)." Cf. note to 6.61.23.

"like venomous serpents inflamed with anger" *jvalitāśīviṣopamāḥ*: Literally, "similar to flaming, venomous serpents." Again, we agree with Cg, who explains that the monkeys are "enraged like them [the serpents] (*tadvatkopanāḥ*)."

38. "arching upward" *-añcita-*: Literally, "curved, arching." We follow the suggestion of Cg, who glosses, "curved upward (*udañcita-*)." We believe, as Cg probably did, that the resemblance of the monkeys' thick, upraised tails to elephants' trunks is the basis for the simile.

"rutting elephants... huge mountains... mighty storm clouds" *mattamātaṅga- ... mahāparvata- ... mahājīmūta-*: Cg indicates that these three objects of comparison (*upamānas*) suggest the monkeys' great size (*mattetyādinā mahākāyatvam uktam*). Additionally, he notes that the second of the three *upamānas* suggests "unyieldingness (*dārḍhyam*)."

Following verse 38, D5–7,9–11,S insert a passage of two lines [394*]: "Terrifying, with terrifying gait and roars,[1] they stand there with their round eyes, yellow and red,[2] glaring at Laṅkā as if they were already smashing it."

[1]"Terrifying, with terrifying gait and roars" *bhīmā bhīmagatisvanāḥ*: D7,10,11, and the texts and printed editions of Ct and Cr read instead *mahābhīmagatisvanāḥ*, "with great and terrifying gait and roars."

[2]"with their round eyes, yellow and red" *vṛttapiṅgalaraktākṣāḥ*: D7,9–11, and the texts and printed editions of Ct and Cr read instead *vṛttapiṅgalanetrā hi*, "with round and yellow eyes."

39. "He ... expects to crush Laṅkā with his own forces." *eṣaivāśaṃsate laṅkāṃ svenānīkena marditum*: This phrase is repeated at 6.17.24cd and 24cd above, and occurs almost verbatim at 6.17.18cd and 6.17.39cd.

Following verse 39ab, D5–7,9–11,S insert a passage of one line [396*], expanding the description of Śatabalin: "That powerful [monkey] eager for victory constantly worships the sun."

Following verse 39, D5–7,9–11,S insert a passage of two lines [398*]: "Courageous and powerful, that heroic tawny monkey is firm in his valor. In his efforts to please Rāma, he would show no concern for his own life.[1]"

[1]"he would show no concern for his own life" *prāṇānāṃ dayāṃ na kurute*: Literally, "he makes [shows] no mercy for [of] his life breaths." Like most translators, we follow the idea expressed by Cg, who glosses, "with regard to [his own] life breaths (*prāṇeṣu*)." The phrase could also quite plausibly mean "be merciless to living beings," following Cr, who glosses, "toward living beings (*prāṇinām*)." Among the translators consulted, only Raghunathan (1982, vol. 3, p. 67) follows Cg's interpretation, translating, "could be pitiless." Compare 6.19.25 and note.

40. "troops" *yūthānām*: Ś,Ñ,V2,B,D2,3,8–12,M5, and the texts and printed editions of Ct and Cr read instead *yodhānām*, "warriors."

41. "formidable monkeys" *vānaraśreṣṭhāḥ*: Literally, "best of monkeys."

42. "covering the earth with the mountains they have shattered" *pṛthivīm ... kartuṃ pravidhvastavikīrṇaśailām*: Literally, "making the earth one that possesses smashed and scattered mountains."

The meter is *indravajrā*.

Sarga 19

1. "Then" *atha*: Cg, citing *Amarakośa* (3.3.246), suggests that the significance of this common polysemic particle here is that of "completeness." The idea is that Śuka is supplementing the account of Sāraṇa (*atha kārtsnyenābravīt*).

"he looked out over" *ālokayan*: Literally, "looking." A large number of southern manuscripts (D5–7,9–11,T,M), and the texts and printed editions of the southern commentators read instead *ādiśya tat*, "pointing out, indicating."

"lord of the *rākṣasas*" *rākṣasādhipam*: Cg argues that the epithet is used to illustrate the humility with which Sāraṇa addresses his master (*savinayoktidyotanāya rākṣasādhipam ity uktam*).

2–3. "Those monkeys ... whom" *yān ... ete*: Literally, "those whom."

"along the Ganges" *gāṅgeyān*: Literally, "belonging to or descended from the Gaṅgā." We follow the commentators, who explain that the reference is to banyan trees growing on the banks of the Ganges (*gāṅgeyān gaṅgātaṭotpannān*). Ct and Ck note that this usage of the normally *āpatyavācaka* suffix *ḍhak* is irregular (*anāpatye 'pi ḍhag-ārṣaḥ*).

"taking up their positions" *sthitān*: Literally, "standing."

4. "and there are quadrillions and septillions more" *tathā śaṅkusahasrāṇi tathā vṛndaśatāni ca*: Literally, "and there are thousands of *śaṅkus* and also hundreds of *vṛndas*." The precise meanings of the numerical terms *śaṅku* and *vṛnda* vary from one text to another and from lexicon to lexicon. Our reckoning of the numbers follows the definitions in the progressive series of numbers at 411* below (following verse 32). According to this passage, one accepted by all manuscripts, a *śaṅku* equals one trillion and a *vṛnda* is ten sextillion (10^{22}). The *Śabdakalpadruma*, citing the Līlāvatī section of Bhāskara's *Siddhāntaśiromaṇi*, defines a *śaṅku* as ten trillion (10^{13}). This is the same number as given in PW (s.v.). Monier-Williams (s.v.), perhaps misreading PW's long string of zeros, understands the term to indicate ten billion (10^{10}), and, in this, he is followed by Apte (s.v.). According to the *Śabdakalpadruma*, a *vṛnda* refers to one billion (10^{9}). (Compare Whitney 1889, p. 177). According to PW, a *vṛnda* is either one hundred billion (10^{11}) or one billion (10^{9}). Monier-Williams (s.v.) agrees, while Apte only cites one billion (10^{9}).

Ct and Ck remind us that the huge numbers mentioned in the verse apply only to the ministers of Sugrīva, as indicated in verse 5 below, while the full tally of the monkey troops will not be given until the end of the *sarga* (see notes to verse 33 below) (*eṣāṃ koṭīti sugrīvasacivasaṃkhyā sarvabalasaṃkhyāṃ tu sargānte vakṣyati*—Ct). See, too, notes to 411* following verse 32 below.

5. "followers" *-sacivāḥ*: Although normally we have translated this term as "ministers," here we follow Cg, who, citing *Amarakośa* 3.3.205, suggests taking the meaning "ally, follower (*sahāya*)" in preference to "minister (*mantrī*)," no doubt because the numbers mentioned here seem high for ministers.

6. "youthful" *kumārau*: D9–11 and the texts and printed editions of Ct read instead *samānau*, "identical, similar."

"looking like gods" *devarūpiṇau*: Cg does not read this as a compound but instead as the vocative *deva*, "your majesty," followed by the adjective *rūpiṇau*, which he interprets as "handsome," by understanding the possessive suffix *ini* in the sense of *matu[p]*, where that suffix indicates the possession of something to a praiseworthy extent (*rūpiṇau praśastarūpau praśaṃsāyāṃ matvarthīya ini pratyayaḥ*).

7. "With Brahmā's blessing they have partaken of the nectar of immortality" *brahmaṇā samanujñātāv amṛtaprāśināv ubhau*: Literally, "permitted by Brahmā, they are eaters of *amṛta*." The nectar of immortality was brought to the surface during the churning of the ocean. See notes to 6.12.22. We know of no incident of two monkeys drinking *amṛta* or involved in its churning in the Indian literature. However, on a bas-relief of Angkor Wat (twelfth century) in Cambodia, where the churning of the ocean is represented, one monkey, wearing a tiara of the gods, is shown supporting the snake's tail. Perhaps this is a representation of this scene. See Giteau 1951, p. 154.

Compare *pāda* d with 6.18.31d above.

8. This verse is not found in a variety of northern and southern manuscripts (V2,B3,4,D5–7,9–11,T,G,M1,2), including the *devanāgarī* manuscripts of the southern commentators. It is printed in brackets in VSP between verses 7 and 8 of *sarga* 28, and has no number of its own. KK also brackets the verse [KK 6.28.8] and notes (p. 116, n. 5), "This verse is not found in the older manuscripts but is found only as a

latter-day reading. (*ayaṃ ślokaḥ prācīnakośeṣu na dṛśyate. auttarāhapāṭha eva dṛśyate.*)" Based on the critical evidence, this verse should probably have been omitted following the principles on which the critical edition is based (Bhatt 1960, p. xxxiv), or at least marked as a suspicious reading.

9–10. "one who has already come to Laṅkā and sought out Vaidehī and yourself" *eṣo 'bhigantā laṅkāyā vaidehyās tava ca*: Literally, "this one who approaches Laṅkā, Vaidehī, and you." The agentive noun *abhigantā* governs the three genitives *laṅkāyāḥ*, *vaidehyāḥ*, and *tava*. But, as noted by Cg, it is used in a somewhat different sense in each case. Thus, Cg notes that, with reference to Sītā, the action referred to is "seeking (*anveṣaṇam*)," whereas, in the case of Rāvaṇa, it is "meeting [lit., seeing] (*darśanam*)." (*vaidehīpakṣe 'bhigamanam anveṣaṇam. rāvaṇapakṣe darśanam.*) B2,D5,7,10,11,T2,G,M5, and the texts and printed editions of Ct and Cr read, instead of the genitive *laṅkāyāḥ*, the locative *laṅkāyām*, "in Laṅkā." Ct understands the action to be that of seeking and approaching in all three cases. (*eṣa laṅkāyāṃ vaidehyās tava cābhigantānveṣī. samīpam āgataś cety arthaḥ.*)

11. "the eldest son of Kesarin" *jyeṣṭhaḥ kesariṇaḥ putraḥ*: Cs, alone among the commentators, notes that this phrase implies the existence of younger brothers of Hanumān (*jyeṣṭha ity anenānye 'py avarajāḥ santīti jñāyate*). For Hanumān's father, Kesarin, see *MBh* 3.147.23ff. See also note to 6.18.34; Bulcke 1959–60; and S. Goldman 1999.

12. "endowed with strength and beauty" *balarūpasamanvitaḥ*: Cg wants to take *-rūpa-*, here, "beauty," as a laudatory suffix (*praśaṃsāyāṃ rūpap pratyayaḥ*) and thus understands the compound to mean "endowed with praiseworthy strength (*praśastabalasamanvitaḥ*)."

"the ever-moving lord, the wind god" *satatagaḥ prabhuḥ*: Literally, "the ever-moving lord."

13–15. The childhood exploits of Hanumān are also recounted in the *Kiṣkindhākāṇḍa* (4.65.8–28) and in the *Uttarakāṇḍa* (*sarga* 35).

"he grew hungry" *pipāsitaḥ*: Literally, "thirsty." Cg notes that this means "yearning for the breast, which amounts to being hungry. (*pipāsitaḥ stanyāpekṣaḥ. kṣudhita iti yāvat.*)" D10,11,G1,2,M1,2, and the texts and printed editions of Ct read instead *bubhukṣitaḥ*, "hungry."

"once, when he . . . swooped down a distance of three thousand leagues" *triyojanasahasraṃ tu adhvānam avatīrya hi . . . puraiṣaḥ*: Literally, "he formerly . . . having descended a three thousand league path." The direction of Hanumān's leap is a matter of some dispute. In the poem's other versions of this story (4.65.8–28; 7.35), the infant leaps up, as one would expect, in his effort to grasp the sun, and, indeed, Cr, reading *pupluve* for the critical edition's *puraiṣaḥ*, explains, "*avatīrya* [lit., 'having descended'], that is, having leapt up; he leapt, that is, he went to a higher elevation by means of his upward leap (*avatīryotplutya pupluva utplavanenordhvadeśaṃ jagāma*)." Cg, however, offers two explanations. According to the first, we are to take the gerund *avatīrya*, "having descended," literally. For the child Hanumān, living in his father's home at the summit of the Golden Mountain (Mount Meru), around the middle elevation of which the sun revolves, would naturally have to swoop down to reach that luminous body. (*hanumatpituḥ kesariṇaḥ kanakācalavāsitvāt tasya cātyunattatvād ity asya tacchikharasya ca madhyamād vā trisahasrayojanaparimita ity uktam. ata evāvatīryety uktaṃ na tūtpatyeti.*) Cs simply understands that Hanumān got down from his mother's hip [where he would have been carried] (*avatīrya mātur utsaṅgāt*). Cg's alternative explanation, which is shared by Cm, implicitly accepts the idea of Hanumān's leaping upward, but only if we take the number three thousand to stand figuratively for many thousands of *yojanas*, since, as he argues, the sun is, in fact, a hundred thousand *yojanas* from the earth. The idea evidently is that, if we take the number three thousand literally, then it would not be appropriate to think of an upward leap, since the sun is so much more distant than that (*yadvādityasya bhūmer upari lakṣayojanāntaratvāt triyojanasahasram ity etad anekasahasropalakṣaṇam*). In the *Kiṣkindhākāṇḍa* version of the story, the distance to the sun is reckoned as three hundred leagues (*yojanas*), although the commentators Crā, Cm, and Cg also take this as a figurative illusion to a vastly greater distance. See 4.65.20 and note. At 7.35.29, Hanumān is said to have traversed "many thousand of *yojanas* (*bahuyojanasahasram*)." Cs similarly takes the number three thousand figuratively. (*triyojanasahasram. upalakṣaṇam etat.*)

"my hunger shall not return" *na me kṣut pratiyāsyati*: The idea here, as Ct explains, is that we should understand the words "for earthly fruits (*bhūlokavartiphalair iti śeṣaḥ*)," that is, having swallowed the heavenly fruit of the sun, Hanumān expects that he will no longer require earthly food. Cr has much the same idea.

"failing to reach" *anāsādya*: Cg feels that one should supply the words "because of its blazing energy" in order to explain Hanumān's failure actually to reach the sun, arguing on the basis of the *Kiṣkindhākāṇḍa* version where it explicitly states that the monkey was driven off by the sun's brilliance (4.65.20). (*anāsādyety atra tattejasety upaskāryam. tejasā tasya nirdhūta iti kiṣkindhākāṇḍokteḥ.*) He notes, however, that in the *Uttarakāṇḍa* version, it is a blow of Indra's *vajra* that causes Hanumān's fall (7.35.46–47) (*yady apy uttarakāṇḍa indravajreṇa patanam uktam*). See verse 12 below and notes. Cg sees no real contradiction here, noting that we should understand that Indra's attack is merely an additional reason for Hanumān's failure to reach the sun (*tathāpi tad api hetvantaram iti jñeyam*). Cs argues that we should supply the phrase "because of Indra's *vajra* (*anāsādya patita indravajrād iti śeṣaḥ*)."

"who is beyond the reach" *anādhṛṣyatamam*: Literally, "most unassailable."

"upon the mountain from behind which the sun rises" *bhāskarodayane girau*: The reference is to the easternmost mountain, which is often viewed as the point from which both the sun and the moon rise.

16. "One of... jaws" *hanur ekā*: Cg glosses *tālupradeśa*, "the region of the palate," by which we understand him to refer to the upper jaw. The *Uttarakāṇḍa* (7.35.47) and *Kiṣkindhākāṇḍa* (4.65.22) versions of this story further specify that the break is on the left side.

"slightly broken as he fell on the stone surface" *patitasya... śilātale... kiṃcid bhinnā*: This account of the breaking of Hanumān's jaw agrees more or less with those given in the *Kiṣkindhākāṇḍa* (4.65.21–22) and *Uttarakāṇḍa* (7.35.46–47), although in both of these other versions, Hanumān is knocked from the sky by Indra's *vajra*.

"toughened his jaw [*hanu*], he came to be known as Hanumān, he of the powerful jaw" *dṛḍhahanor hanūmān eṣa tena vai*: Literally, "[of that monkey] who has a firm jaw,... because of that, he is Hanumān." The idea here appears to be that, with the healing of the fracture, Hanumān's jawbone has become somewhat thickened or strengthened (*dṛḍha*). The resulting visible anatomical anomaly becomes the basis for the monkey's name, on the understanding, as Cr suggests, that we are to take the possessive suffix *-mant* as laudatory (*praśastārthako 'tra matup*), yielding the sense "he of the large *or* powerful jaw." Ś,Ñ1,V3,B4,D6,8–13,T2,M1, and the texts and printed editions of Ct read the nominative *dṛḍhahanuḥ* for the critical edition's genitive singular *dṛḍhahanoḥ*.

17. "on the basis of this authoritative account" *āgamayogena*: The phrase is obscure and ambiguous. The commentators have understood it in different ways, and these interpretations are reflected in the various translations we have consulted. Our translation is based largely on the first of Cg's two alternative explanations [= Cm], although we recognize that the interpretations offered by Ct, Ck, and Cr do not contradict this. What Cg and Cm argue is that we are to understand the term *āgama* in its sense of "authoritative discourse (*āptavākyam*)," the term *yoga* in its sense of "means *or* method (*upāyaḥ*)," and the compound *āgamayogena* as an appositional *karmadhāraya* in the sense of "by means of an authoritative account." The reference, it would appear, is to the narrative of Hanumān's childhood, which Sāraṇa has just repeated, and the implication, we imagine, is that he recognizes Hanumān by his large jaw. Cg's second interpretation is that one should read the compound as a *bahuvrīhi* modifying the instrumental pronoun *mayā*, "by me," which, he argues, we are to read in place of the text's *mama*. The sense of the verse would then become, "Even though I have heard an authoritative account (*āptavākyaśravaṇena mayā*), I am still unable to describe [him]." Ct and Ck take the compound as an instrumental of accompaniment, the sense of which is "along with the previous account, which provides the reason for Hanumān's name (*hanumannāmanimittabhūtapūrvavṛttāntena saha*)," by which they appear to mean "I know that monkey along with the previous account." Again, the idea is probably that Hanumān is recognizable by his jaw. Cr understands the compound quite differently. He takes *āgama-* in its root sense of "to come," seeing it as a reference to those monkeys, etc., who have come into the presence of Sāraṇa. He glosses *-yogaḥ* as *yojana*, which he takes somewhat idiosyncratically to mean *kathana*, "story, narrative." He thus understands, "I know this monkey on the basis of the story told to me by those monkeys who came into my presence (*āgaminām matsamīpe prāptānām*)." Gorresio, on the basis of his text, which reads, "*ity evāgamayuktena mayaiṣa vidito hariḥ*" (6.4.18), translates, "*Io ben conobbe quel scimio, allor ch'ei qui venne*" (Gorresio 1856, vol. 9, p. 208), evidently, like Cr, understanding *āgama-* in the sense of "to come *or* approach (*venne*)." Gorresio (1856, vol. 9, p. 365, n. 98) remarks that the commentator (Cl) offers three or four alternative explanations of the phrase, one of which is to take the adjective *āgamayuktena* as modifying an implicit *hanumatā*, "by Hanumān," the sense being, "by the fact of this Hanumān's having already come here to Laṅkā (*ihaiva laṅkāyām āgamayuktena hanumatāgamanayogena*)." Gorresio goes on to say that he was attracted to this interpretation as it seems the most reasonable to him. But he acknowledges that the passage is susceptible to other interpretations.

"With his tremendous power, he expects to crush Laṅkā all by himself." *eṣa āśaṃsate laṅkām eko marditum ojasā*: Compare 6.17.18cd; 6.17.24cd; 6.17.39ef; 6.18.24cd; and 6.18.39cd.

Following verse 17, D7,9–12, KK (in brackets), and the texts and printed editions of Ct and Cr insert a passage of two lines [405*]: "He is the one who recently set a blazing smoke-bannered fire to your Laṅkā. How could you have forgotten that monkey?"

18–21. "dark, lotus-eyed" *śyāmaḥ padmanibhekṣaṇaḥ*: Cg, waxing somewhat poetic here, glosses *śyāmaḥ*, "dark," as "possessing a body as desirable as a black cloud perched upon a mountain of gold (*kanakamayaśikharārūḍhakālāmbudakamanīyavigrahaḥ*)." This is evidently an allusion to Rāma's being seated, in Cg's view, on the shoulders of Hanumān. He glosses *padmanibhekṣaṇaḥ*, "lotus-eyed," as "possessing eyes as desirable as full-blown lotuses growing in the great lotus pond, which is his divine body (*divyavigrahamahātaṭākasthavikasitakamalalobhanīyavilocanaḥ*)."

"next to him" *yaś caiṣo 'nantaraḥ*: Literally, "the one who is next." A number of northern and southern manuscripts substitute a reading incorporating the genitive *asya* (*yas tv asya*) (Ś,V1,3,D0–4,8,12,13) or *yasya* (*yasyaiṣaḥ*) (B2,D10,11,G2,3, and the texts and printed editions of Cm, Ck, and Ct) for the *yaś caiṣo* of the critical edition (and Cg) referring to Hanumān. The notion that Rāma is next to Hanumān is, in any case, implicit. Ct, Ck, Cr, and Cm see Rāma as merely standing close to Hanumān, while Cg, evidently alluding to references at 315* and 6.4.15,28, understands that Rāma is actually seated on Hanumān's shoulders.

"the great chariot-warrior of the Ikṣvākus" *ikṣvākūṇām atirathaḥ*: Cg feels Sāraṇa is saying that Rāvaṇa should understand that Rāma is a truly invincible chariot-warrior, unlike his ancestor Anaraṇya [whom Rāvaṇa defeated]. (*anaraṇyādivad ayaṃ na mantavyaḥ. kiṃtu ikṣvākūṇāṃ madhye 'tiratho 'tiśayitarathaḥ. aparājitaratha ity arthaḥ.*) See *Uttarakāṇḍa* 19. Cf. 6.47.17.

"His righteousness never wavers" *yasmin na calate dharmaḥ*: Literally, "in whom *dharma* never moves." Cg sees this as an illustration that Rāma did not swerve from his duty, even when people such as Jābāli tried to confuse him (*jābāliprabhṛtibhir ākulito 'py aprakampitaḥ*). See *Ayodhyākāṇḍa* 100–101.

"nor does he ever transgress it" *yo dharmaṃ nātivartate*: Literally, "who does not exceed *dharma*." Cg illustrates this virtue by noting that Rāma did not deviate from his righteous adherence to his father's word and his own vow to live as a *muni* despite being pressed to do so by Bharata, Sītā, and so on (*bharatasītādibhiḥ kṛte 'pi pratibandhe pitṛvacanamunipratijñādharmaṃ nātivartate*). See *Ayodhyākāṇḍa* 96. Cg further attempts to demonstrate that Rāma does not depart from *kṣatriyadharma* by claiming that he gave ground in his battle with Khara only in order to find room for the flight of his arrows (3.27ff.) and that he killed Vālin from ambush only in order to carry out his vow to his suppliant [Sugrīva] (4.18.26–27). (*kharayuddhe 'pasarpaṇaṃ bāṇapātāvakāśalābhārtham. chadmanā vālivadhas tv anyathānupapattyāvaśyam āśritaviṣayapratijñāyā nirvoḍhavyatayā ca.*)

"Foremost among those who know the *vedas*" *vedavidāṃ varaḥ*: Cg explains this as "foremost among those who know the meaning of the *vedas*" and notes that Rāma is superior in this regard even to his own teachers, Vasiṣṭha, etc. (*vedārthavidāṃ vara upadeṣṭṛbhyo vasiṣṭhādibhyo 'py utkṛṣṭaḥ*).

"he knows . . . Brahmā's divine weapon-spell" *brāhmam astram . . . veda*: Literally, "he knows the *astra* of Brahmā." Cg observes that, even though knowledge of the *mantra* controlling the *brahmāstra* is included in the *vedas*, it is mentioned separately to indicate its importance in this context (*brahmāstramantrasya vedāntargatatve 'pi prādhānyāt pṛthaguktiḥ*). See notes to 5.36.26 and 6.35.5.

"might rend the heavens" *bhindyād gaganam*: Literally, "he might split the sky." Cg interprets this to mean that Rāma might destroy objects, such as flying chariots, etc., located in the sky (*gaganasthavimānādi*). Ct, Ck, and Cm see the point of this phrase as demonstrating that what is impossible [for others] is easily feasible for Rāma (*sarvaduṣkaram api tasya sukaram iti tātparyam*—so Ct).

"shatter the mountains" *parvatāṃś cāpi dārayet*: The word *parvatān*, "mountains," is marked as uncertain by the critical editors. Collated manuscripts, including the texts and printed editions of Ck, Ct, and Cr, as well as the printed editions of Gorresio

(6.4.22) and Lahore (6.4.21), show a variety of variant readings, many of which substitute a word for the earth, such as *vasudhām, medinīm,* or *pṛthivīm.*

"His wrath is like that of Mṛtyu" *yasya mṛtyor iva krodhaḥ*: Cr interprets this to mean that, "[but] when it comes to killing those enemies who have sought refuge with him, [Rāma's] unavoidable wrath is held in check (*śaraṇāgataripuvidhvaṃsane gṛhītānivāryakopa ity arthaḥ*)."

22–23. "standing to his right" *dakṣiṇe pārśve*: Literally, "on his right side." This is the position conventionally assigned to Lakṣmaṇa in painted and sculptural representations of Rāma and his court.

"the one with a complexion as radiant as pure *jāmbūnada* gold" *śuddhajāmbūnadaprabhaḥ*: Literally, "with the radiance of pure *jāmbūnada* gold." Note the often-stressed contrast between fair Lakṣmaṇa and dark Rāma. See Goldman 1980. On *jāmbūnada* gold, see also note to 6.15.2.

"reddened eyes" *tāmrākṣaḥ*: Cg suggests that Lakṣmaṇa's eyes are reddened "with anger toward you [i.e., Rāvaṇa] (*tvadviṣayakopena*)." See note to 6.31.72. See, too, 5.8.5–9; 5.8.25 and notes; 5.47.1; and 5.48.2.

"his brother... as dear to him as life itself" *bhrātā prāṇasamaḥ priyaḥ*: Compare the similar expression in verse 24 and note below. A few *devanāgarī* manuscripts (D7,9–11) and the texts and printed editions of Ct, Ck, and Cr read instead *bhrātuḥ priyahite rataḥ*, "devoted to his brother's welfare (*hita*) and service (*priya*)."

"adept in all the *śāstras*" *sarvaśāstraviśāradaḥ*: A few manuscripts, including the *devanāgarī* manuscripts and the printed editions of Ck, Ct, and Cr, read instead *sarvasastrabhṛtāṃ varaḥ*, "foremost among all who bear weapons." Cg thinks that the word *śāstra* here indicates scientific texts above and beyond the science of statecraft (*śāstraśabdo nītiśāstravyatiriktaparaḥ*).

24. "Implacable" *amarṣī*: Cr explains, "lacking forgiveness toward those who offend against Rāma (*rāmāparādhiṣu kṣamārahitaḥ*)."

"intelligent" *buddhimān*: D9–11,T3, and the texts and printed editions of Ct read instead *ca jayī*, "and victorious," which is redundant with the term *jetā*, "victor," in *pāda* a.

"like another life breath constantly moving outside his body" *nityaṃ prāṇo bahiścaraḥ*: Literally, "a breath constantly moving externally." Cg argues that the phrase is expressive of Lakṣmaṇa's role as the protector of [Rāma's] life (*prāṇasaṃrakṣakatvam ucyate*). A similar description of Lakṣmaṇa is found in the *Bālakāṇḍa* (1.17.17): "like another life breath outside [his body] (*bahiḥ prāṇa ivāparaḥ*)." The present verse is found also in the *Araṇyakāṇḍa*. See 3.32.13 and note ad loc.

25. "He would give his own life" *na... jīvitaṃ parirakṣati*: Literally, "he does not protect life." Compare the expression in 398* (see note above to 6.18.39).

26. "surrounded by a group of *rākṣasas*" *rakṣogaṇaparikṣiptaḥ*: Ck, Ct, Cg, and Cm, whom we follow, understand the verb *pari* √*kṣip* in one of its principal meanings, namely,"surround, encircle" and observe that we are to understand the term *gaṇa*, "host, troop," to refer to Vibhīṣaṇa's four *rākṣasa* companions mentioned at 6.10.12 above (see also note to 6.11.3). Cg, cognizant of the irony of referring to four individuals as a host, observes that the term is used here because the four are as mighty as a whole host (*caturṇām eva rakṣasāṃ gaṇatulyavikramatvāt tathoktam*). Cr and Cs take the participle in its other principal sense of "thrown out, rejected." Thus, Cr and Cs (second explanation) interpret, "abandoned *or* expelled by the *rākṣasa* hosts (*rakṣogaṇaiḥ parikṣiptas tyaktaḥ*)." Cs alternatively proposes reading *rakṣogaṇa-* as a *bahuvrīhi*

in the sense of "he who possesses hosts of *rākṣasas*" and thus as a kenning for Rāvaṇa. The sense, according to him, would then be "cast out by the lord of the *rākṣasa* hosts, i.e., you, Rāvaṇa." The ambiguity of *parikṣiptaḥ* is avoided, perhaps intentionally, in the north, where, for example, Gorresio's text substitutes *rakṣogaṇavṛto bhrātā*, "[your] brother surrounded by a group of *rākṣasas*" (6.4.27 = Lahore 6.4.27).

"none other than" *hi*: Cg and Cm observe that this emphatic particle, the eleventh syllable of the verse, serves as the sixteenth syllable of the *Gāyatrīmantra*, which is believed to be inscribed throughout the text of the poem. See note to 6.1.1.

"King" *rājā*: The question of Vibhīṣaṇa's kingship is a delicate one. Cs, reading ahead to verse 27, where it is indicated that Vibhīṣaṇa has already been consecrated to the throne of Laṅkā, observes that Sāraṇa, by using the word "king" in connection with Vibhīṣaṇa, is suggesting that Rāvaṇa has been deposed (*tucchīkṛtaḥ*, literally, "made void, diminished"). See note to verse 27 below. See 6.13.7–9 and notes. See, too, notes to 6.100.9.

27. "consecrated as king of Laṅkā" *laṅkāyām abhiṣecitaḥ*: Literally, "caused to be consecrated in Laṅkā." The issue of Vibhīṣaṇa's consecration is somewhat confusing here. Although Vibhīṣaṇa has been consecrated as king of Laṅkā in *sarga* 13, that consecration seems to be somewhat provisional. Vibhīṣaṇa's formal and uncontested installation on the throne can only take place after the death of his brother. Thus, the formal consecration will not take place until *sarga* 100. Cr, in an apparent effort to reconcile the seeming contradiction, describes Vibhīṣaṇa here as merely "desirous of the kingship of Laṅkā (*eṣa laṅkārājyaviṣayakecchāvān*)." Cg offers two readings: "[consecrated] at a ceremony in Laṅkā (*laṅkāyāṃ nimitte*)" (cf. *MBh* 12.61.6 for a similar use of *nimitta*) or "[consecrated] as king in Laṅkā (construing with *rājā* in verse 26 above) (*laṅkāyāṃ rājeti vānvayaḥ*)."

"by the majestic king of kings" *śrīmatā rājarājena*: The reference is, of course, to Rāma. Cg explains the adjective *śrīmatā* as meaning that "Rāma does not desire the kingship of Laṅkā for himself, as he already has accomplished all his desires (*avāptasamastakāmatvena laṅkārājyānabhilāṣiṇā*)." With regard to the title "king of kings," Cg explains, "Rāma realizes that unless he installs Vibhīṣaṇa and others [as lesser kings], he will not be able to attain the position of king of kings (*vibhīṣaṇādirājyatvānirvāhe svasya rājarājatvaṃ na nirvahed iti manvānena*)."

28. "in their midst" *madhye*: Cg understands this to mean that Sugrīva is standing between Rāma and Vibhīṣaṇa (*rāmavibhīṣaṇayor madhye*).

"The one whom . . . is Sugrīva" *yam*: Literally, "whom." The proper name Sugrīva has been added.

29. "In . . . intelligence" *buddhyā*: Literally, "with intelligence." Cg glosses, "knowledge that takes the form of thorough logical consideration (*ūhāpoharūpajñānena*)."

"In . . . knowledge" *jñānena*: Literally, "with knowledge." Cg glosses, "knowledge born of [the study of] the *śāstras* (*śāstrajanyajñānena*)." Ñ,V,B,D0–4,6,7,9–11,G2,3,M5, and the texts and printed editions of Ct and Cr read instead *balena*, "with strength, power."

"all other mountains" *parvatān*: Literally, "mountains."

30. "densely forested" *sagahanadrumām*: Literally, "with dense trees." Cr glosses, "with densely [planted] trees (*nibiḍadrumasahitām*)."

"the . . . cavern Kiṣkindhā" *kiṣkindhām . . . guhām*: See 4.25.7; 4.26.1–3; 4.32.4–8, etc., where Kiṣkindhā is described as a cave. D9–11 and the texts and printed editions of Ct read instead *durgām*, "inaccessible," which is redundant with the same term in *pāda* c.

"which is hidden in a mountain fastness" *parvatadurgasthām*: Literally, "situated in an inaccessible mountain location."

31. "necklace" *mālā*: This is the necklace that Vālin was given by his father, Indra, and that he puts on prior to his battle with Dundubhi (see 4.11.37ff. and notes). As is made clear at 4.17.4–8, the necklace functions as a kind of life index of its owner, so that Vālin cannot die so long as he wears it (see notes ad loc.). Just before his death, Vālin, mortally wounded by Rāma, confers the necklace upon Sugrīva, telling him that the Goddess Śrī, who abides in it, will depart from him upon his [Vālin's] death (4.22.16–19 and notes). The idea is that Vālin is transferring the splendor of royalty, *rājyaśrī*, to his brother as the new owner of the necklace.

Cg remarks that since Lakṣmī, who resides in the necklace, is the goddess of valor, *vīralakṣmī*, a person wearing it can never be defeated. He further notes that it is well known that Vālin always wore the necklace, and it is for that reason that Rāma had to shoot him from ambush. (*lakṣmīr vīralakṣmīḥ. taddhāraṇe kadācid api parājayo na bhavatīti sadā vālī tāṃ vahati smeti prasiddhiḥ. taddhāraṇād eva hi rāmas tad anabhimukha eva vālinaṃ hatavān.*) The reasoning, although not made explicit here, is that, according to Cg at 4.11.37, Indra had promised Vālin that, so long as he wore the necklace, he would acquire the strength of anyone who might approach him in battle. The implication is that, by not approaching Vālin face to face in equal combat, Rāma was able to negate the power of the necklace. See notes to 4.11.37. See R. Goldman 1997 and 2003a.

"Lakṣmī herself, coveted by gods and men" *kāntā devamanuṣyāṇām . . . lakṣmīḥ*: The reference here is probably to *rājyaśrī* or *rājyalakṣmī*, the incarnate goddess of royal splendor. However, Cg's gloss, *vīralakṣmī*, is also quite plausible. The syntax of the verse allows for a certain ambiguity. One could also interpret, "Lakṣmī herself resides in it [the necklace], and it is thus coveted by gods and men." In fact, some commentators and several translators construe the adjective *kāntā*, "desired, coveted," with *mālā*, "necklace." Cr, for example, does so but reads the compound *devamanuṣyāṇām* with *lakṣmī*, yielding the sense "Lakṣmī, the goddess of the fortunes of gods and men, resides in that coveted necklace." See Gita Press (1969, vol. 3, p. 1465), Dutt (1893, p. 1183), and Raghunathan (1982, vol. 3, p. 69), who all construe *kāntā* with *mālā*.

32. "Sugrīva acquired . . . through Rāma, who had slain Vālin" *sugrīvo vālinaṃ hatvā rāmeṇa pratipāditaḥ*: There is a difference of opinion as to how to construe the syntax here. According to Cg, whom we follow, the participle *pratipāditaḥ* should be understood as a causative with the sense of *prāpitaḥ*, "caused to obtain." In this reading, *rāmeṇa* is the subject both of the causative participle and the gerund *hatvā*, while Sugrīva is the subject of the simplex, *pra* $\sqrt{}$*āp*. According to Cr, however, we are to read the causative participle as the simplex in the sense of *prāptaḥ*, "acquired," and the simplex gerund *hatvā* as the causal *ghātayitvā*, "having caused to kill." According to this reading, the syntax would be "Sugrīva obtained . . . after having gotten Rāma to kill Vālin."

Following verse 32, all manuscripts and printed editions, southern and northern, read a passage of seven lines [411*], in which the astronomical numbers that are used to enumerate the monkeys are defined in sequence. Despite the abruptness of the narrative transition, it is not clear to us on what grounds this passage has been relegated to the critical apparatus: "Learned men refer to one hundred hundred thousands as a *koṭi* [ten million = 10^7]. One hundred thousand *koṭis* is called a *śaṅku* [one trillion = 10^{12}]. One hundred thousand *śaṅkus* is a *mahāśaṅku* [one hundred quadrillion = 10^{17}]. One hundred thousand *mahāśaṅkus* is said to be a *vṛnda* [ten sextillion = 10^{22}]. One hundred thousand *vṛndas* is known as a *mahāvṛnda* [one octillion = 10^{27}]. One hundred thousand *mahāvṛndas* is a *padma* [one hundred nonillion = 10^{32}]. One hundred thousand *padmas* is known as *mahāpadma* [ten undecillion = 10^{37}]." We are using the standard American terms for numbers over one million, as listed in *Merriam Webster's Collegiate Dictionary* (10th ed., 1993, p. 798). Note that these numbers do not correspond to the definitions given in Whitney (1889, pp. 177–78) and in the lexicons, nor do they necessarily reflect the numbers used in other passages.

Following 411*, many manuscripts (B2,3,D5–7,9–11,S except G1) insert an additional passage of three lines [412*] in which the sequence of astronomical numbers is continued: "One hundred thousand *mahāpadmas* is called a *kharva* [one tredecillion = 10^{42}]. One hundred thousand *kharvas* is called a *samudra* [one hundred quattuordecillion = 10^{47}]. And one hundred thousand *samudras* is known as a *mahaugha* [ten sexdecillion = 10^{52}]."

Compare, too, 4.37.30–32 and notes; 6.17.27; and 416* (at note to 6.19.33).

33. "accompanied by one hundred trillion, ten billion troops" *evaṃ koṭisahasreṇa śaṅkūnāṃ ca śatena ca*: Literally, "and with a thousand *koṭis* and a hundred *śaṅkus*." Our calculation of the number here is based on our understanding that a *śaṅku* is one trillion (see 411* above). Another possible way of construing the line would be "and with one hundred and one thousand *koṭis* of *śaṅkus*." This would yield a total of 10^{37}, that is, ten undecillion monkeys. This is the number referred to in 411* as a *mahāpadma*.

Following 33ab, D5–7,10,11,S insert a passage of six lines [416*], which is a description of the hosts accompanying Sugrīva: "He is surrounded by Vibhīṣaṇa and his *rākṣasa* companions, and by a *mahaugha* of *koṭis* [of monkeys] resembling the ocean, and there are, in addition, a thousand *mahāśaṅkus*, a hundred *vṛndas*, a thousand *mahāvṛndas*, a hundred *padmas*, a thousand *mahāpadmas*, and a hundred *kharvas*." The astronomical total can be calculated on the basis of the terms given in the preceding note. Compare, too, 4.37.30–32 and notes; 6.17.27; and 411* (at notes to 6.19.32) above.

Following verse 33, D5–7,9–11,S insert a passage of one line [418*] in which the description of Sugrīva is extended: "Possessing enormous strength and valor, he is always surrounded by a huge army."

34. "like some baleful planet" *prajvalitagrahopamām*: Literally, "like a blazing planet." Ct, Ck, and Cm explain, "resembling the glare of a blazing planet (*prajvalitagrahajvālopamām*)." Cg, whom we follow, glosses, "resembling a malign planet (*krūragrahopamām*)." Ck also offers the possibility of reading *graha*, "planet," as etymologically synonymous with *vigraha*, "strife, battle," in which case one might read the adjective to mean "like a blazing battle itself." Cf. 6.90.27; 6.114.21; and notes.

"so that you may be victorious and not suffer defeat at the hands of your enemies" *yathā jayaḥ syān na paraiḥ parājayaḥ*: Literally, "so that there would be victory not defeat by enemies." Cg, evidently regarding Sāraṇa's remarks to be somewhat ironic given the overwhelming host he has just described, comments, "What is suggested here is that 'you should make an effort such that you do not attain victory but rather suffer defeat at the hands of your enemies' (*yathā jayo na syāt pratyuta paraiḥ parājaya eva syāt tathā yatnaḥ kriyatām iti dhvanyate*)."

The meter is *vaṃśasthavila*.

Sarga 20

1–3. "Rāvaṇa looked out upon . . . He saw" *dṛṣṭvā* . . . *rāvaṇaḥ*: Literally, "having seen . . . Rāvaṇa."

"somewhat shaken at heart, yet flaring up with anger" *kiṃcid āvignahṛdayo jātakrodhaś ca*: Ct, Ck, and Cm feel that Rāvaṇa's display of anger toward his agents is intended to cover the visible signs of the fear he experiences when he sees the formidable enemy facing him (*svakīyabhītākāragopanārtho 'yaṃ vyāpāraḥ*—so Ct). Cg claims that Rāvaṇa's anger arises from his having heard his enemies praised (*parastavākarṇanena kupita ity arthaḥ*).

Following verse 2, D5,7,9–11,T1,2,G,M, and the texts and printed editions of the southern commentators insert a passage of four lines [419*] in which the list of Rāvaṇa's enemies is extended: "[He saw] Gaja, Gavākṣa, Śarabha, Mainda, Dvivida, mighty Aṅgada, the son of the son of Indra, wielder of the *vajra*, valorous Hanumān, invincible Jāmbavān, Suṣeṇa, Kumuda, Nīla, and that bull among monkeys, Nala."

4. "hanging their heads" *adhomukhau*: Literally, "with faces down *or* with lowered faces."

5. "utterly inappropriate" *na tāvat sadṛśaṃ nāma*: Literally, "not appropriate at all." Cr takes the emphatic adverb *nāma* to mean "it is well known that . . . (*nāma prasiddham etat*)." Cg amplifies this by saying that it indicates that this principle is well established in *nītiśāstra* (*nāmeti nītiśāstraprasiddhiḥ*). Cr reads the adverb *tāvat*, which we have treated as pleonastic, as part of an elliptical clausal structure with the sense "To the extent that it is [at all] unpleasant (*yāvad apriyam*), it is wholly unpleasant (*tāvat sakalam apriyam*)." Cg reads it adverbially, in the sense of "firstly (*prathamataḥ*)."

"when he is able" *vibhoḥ*: We agree with Cr and Cg [who gloss the synonymous variant *prabhoḥ*] in taking this term in its sense of "capable (*samarthasya*—Cr; *śaktasya*—Cg)," as opposed to reading it nominally in its sense of "lord, master," which would, in any case, make it more or less redundant with *nṛpateḥ*, "king's," in *pāda* c.

"punish or imprison" *nigrahapragrahe*: We follow the normal lexical meaning of this compound, which would be something like "arrest and imprison." Our understanding is that Rāvaṇa, as the context makes clear, intends to menace rather than cajole his ministers. And the *dvandva* (recorded as two words in the texts and printed editions of Ct and Ck) may be seen as yet another of those common epic pairs of synonyms or near synonyms that we have noted elsewhere. See note to 6.2.14. Our interpretation, however, is directly counter to the unanimous opinion of the southern commentators, who gloss *anugrahaḥ*, "grace, favor, reward," for *pragraha*. This gloss is similarly apparent in virtually all northern manuscripts, including the editions of Lahore (6.5.5) and Gorresio (6.5.5), which actually read *nigrahānugrahe*. Cf. note to verse 9 below.

6. "How fitting" *sadṛśaṃ nāma*: Literally, "fitting indeed." Commentators are divided as to how to read Rāvaṇa's seemingly anomalous declaration. Ct, Cs, and Ck, whom we are inclined to follow, see the statement as sarcastic or, more specifically, as an example of the rhetorical device *kāku*, in which a speaker uses a change in the inflection of the voice to suggest a meaning diametrically opposed to what is actually stated. Cr, Cg, and Cm read the emphatic *nāma* here as an interrogative marker, turning the statement into a rhetorical question, "Is it proper?"

"at so inopportune a moment" *aprastave*: We follow the interpretations of Cr (*prasaṅgarahitasamaye*), Cg (*anavasare*), and Cm (*stutyanarhakāle*). Ct, Ck, and Cs, on the other hand, interpret the expression to mean "without having been asked to do so (*praśnābhāve*—Ct, Ck; *tadviṣayakapraśnābhāve*—Cs)." Ck and Ct elaborate on this idea, explaining that here Rāvaṇa is saying that Śuka and Sāraṇa were sent out only to discover who the monkey troop leaders were and how many troops they had and should have confined their remarks to these subjects alone. Moreover, they remark that the meaning here is that it was inappropriate for the spies, without being asked about the [monkeys'] power, to have suggested, as they did, that each individual [monkey] was capable of destroying Laṅkā on his own. (*ke yūthapāḥ kiyad balam iti vicārya vaktavyam iti preṣite tāvanmātraṃ vācyam apṛṣṭaṃ tu teṣāṃ prābalyam ekaiko nāśayituṃ śakta ityādi vaktuṃ na yuktam ity arthaḥ*.)

"enemies...in such a menacing fashion" *ripūṇāṃ pratikūlānām*: Literally, "[my] hostile enemies." Cs and Cr explain this tautology by defining the adjective as "whose conduct [and character—so Cr] is so wrongful (*viruddhācaraṇaśīlānām*—Cr; *viruddhācaraṇavatām*—Cs)." Roussel (1903, vol. 3, p. 81), perhaps mistaking the element *kūla* in *pratikūla* for *kula*, "family, race," translates, "*des ennemis de race étrangère*." In this he is followed, as so often is the case, by Shastri (1959, vol. 3, p. 71), "the foe belonging to an alien race." Pagani (1999, p. 937) similarly renders, "*ces étrangers hostiles*."

"to make war upon me" *yuddhārtham*: Literally, "for the sake of battle."

7. "teachers, parents, and elders" *ācāryā guravo vṛddhāḥ*: The polysemic term *guru*, "teacher, spiritual guide, parent, elder, etc.," overlaps in meaning, on the one hand, with *ācārya*, "teacher," and, on the other, with *vṛddha*, "elder." The commentators are at pains to differentiate these potential synonyms. The most elaborate of these efforts is that of Cm, who defines *ācāryas* as "one's teachers of the *veda* and *vedāṅgas* up until the *upanayana* ceremony of initiation (*upanayanapūrvakaṃ sāṅgavedādhyāpakāḥ*)," *gurus* as "fathers, etc. (*pitrādayaḥ*)," and *vṛddhas* as "those who are advanced both in learning and in age (*jñānavayovṛddhāḥ*)." Ct agrees but with minor modifications. Cg, however, takes *ācāryas* to be "instructors in the science of politics (*nītiśāstropadeṣṭāraḥ*)," *gurus* to be "distinguished *or* eminent persons (*mahantaḥ*)," and *vṛddhas* to be "those endowed with knowledge, age, and virtue (*jñānavayaḥśīlasampannāḥ*)." Cs notes that, although one's principal *guru* is one's biological father (*niṣekakṛn mukhyaḥ*), the term can also be used, as he thinks it is here, to refer to one's "secondary fathers," as it were, that is, one's paternal uncles, etc. (*tadbhrātrādyā amukhyāḥ*).

Elsewhere in the literature, the titles *ācārya* and *guru*, along with a third common term for teacher, *upādhyāya*, are either differentiated as to the type of teacher or used interchangeably to refer to one's teacher. See, for example, *Vāsiṣṭhadharmaśāstra* 3.21–23 and *ManuSm* 2.141,142. See, too, S. K. Sharma 1996, pp. 24–47; and Kane 1941–1975, vol. 4, pp. 323, 361.

"which should govern your conduct" *anujīvyam*: Literally, "in accordance with which one should live."

8. "Or even if you had once learned it, you failed to fully comprehend it." *gṛhīto vā na vijñātaḥ*: The commentators are divided as to how to understand this and other portions of this somewhat ambiguous verse. Ct, Ck, and Cr understand the word *gṛhītaḥ* in the sense of "learned, understood (*jñātaḥ*)" and the phrase *na vijñātaḥ* to mean "completely forgotten (*atyantaṃ vismṛta ity arthaḥ*)." For them the sense would be "and even if you did learn it, you have completely forgotten it." Ck appears to see the two terms as synonymous, and he explains, "Either one of the words *gṛhīta* or *vijñāta* would be sufficient; the surplus word can be chucked into the sea. (*tatraikena paryāptaṃ*

gṛhītapadena vijñātapadena vā. adhikaṃ padaṃ tu samudre prakṣiptam.) The sense is that they did not reflect on [what they learned] (*tad vicaraṇaṃ na kṛtam*)." Cg interprets, "If you had grasped the meaning, you did not really understand it, that is, you have forgotten it. (*gṛhīto vārtho na vijñāto na viśeṣeṇa jñātaḥ. vismṛta ity arthaḥ.*)" Cm, whom we more or less follow, understands, "Even if you learned it by rote [*abhyastaḥ*], you did not reflect upon it properly, since you did not consider what was proper (*gṛhīto vābhyasto 'pi na vijñāta aucityaparyālocanayā samyañ na cintitaḥ*)."

"You carry your education as mere mental baggage." *bhāro jñānasya vohyate*: Literally, "A burden of knowledge is borne." The commentators belonging to the two vulgate subrecensions are divided as to how to understand this sequence. Ct and Cr read the variant *bhāro 'jñānasya vāhyate*, "A burden of ignorance is carried," [reading the causative *vāhyate* for the simplex *uhyate*] and interpret it to mean "You bear a great burden of ignorance, the sense being you have not one whit of knowledge (*ajñānabāhulyam eva vartate na jñānaleśo'pīti bhāvaḥ*—so Ct)." The remaining commentators (Cg, Crā, Cm, Cv) read with the critical edition (*bhāro jñānasya vohyate*). Crā, however, takes the phrase *jñānasya bhāraḥ* as the modificand of the participle *gṛhītaḥ* and explains the resulting clause as, "You did not properly take away (*gṛhītaḥ*) the burden of knowledge from the presence of your *guru*. (*jñānasya bhāro na gṛhītaḥ. guroḥ sakāśāt samyañ na gṛhītaḥ.*)" Cg offers two alternative explanations: 1) "Although this knowledge was produced, it did not result in any practical application (*jātam api jñānaṃ nānuṣṭhānaparyavasāyīty arthaḥ*)"; or 2) "Although you pride yourselves on the weightiness of your knowledge, it does not produce any results. (*yadvā jñānasya bhāra uhyate. jñānabhārabharaṇābhimāna eva kriyate na tu tatkāryam ity arthaḥ.*)" Cm understands *jñāna* to refer to the scientific texts, which are the means to acquire knowledge (*jñānasādhanasya śāstrasya*). Cv understands the expression to mean "The burden of action (*karma*) derived from knowledge is borne," and sees the expression as one of irony or sarcastic denial, *ākṣepoktiḥ*, perhaps in the sense of "Some learned advisers you two have turned out to be! (*karmabhāro jñānasya vohyata ity ākṣepoktiḥ*, literally, 'the burden of action derived from action is borne [by you two]')." Ck, alone among the commentators, indicates his awareness of the possibility of reading either *jñāna* or *ajñāna*. Reading first with Ct and Cr, he explains the phrase to mean "the great and excessive burden of inadequate familiarity with the substance of the *śāstras* (*ajñānasya śāstrārthāparijñānasyaivādhiko bhāro bharaṇaṃ vartate*)." He adds, "If one accepts the reading *jñānasya*, then the sense is '[you] have not grasped, that is, fully understood, the burden of the *śāstras* containing this knowledge' (*jñānasyeti padaṃ parigṛhya jñāna-śāstrabhāro na gṛhīto na vijñātaś cety āha*)."

"I have retained my hold on the kingdom" *dharāmy aham*: Literally, "I retain *or* bear up." Most of the commentators see Rāvaṇa's comment here as an allusion to his ability to retain control of his realm, despite his ministers' ineptitude. They therefore read the phrase as elliptical, supplying the word *rājyam*, "kingdom," as the object of the verb. Given the context, with its focus on the science of politics, we are inclined to follow this suggestion. Several of the commentators (Cg, Cv, and Cm [alternative]) take the verb in its common dramatic usage of "to live, sustain life (*dharāmi jīvāmīti vā*—so Cg)" and thus understand *pādas* cd to mean "With such imbeciles as you for ministers, I'm lucky to be still alive."

9. "your sovereign, whose tongue" *yasya me śāsato jihvā*: Literally, "of whom, that is me, while ruling . . . the tongue." One could also plausibly take the participle *śāsataḥ*, "ruling," to mean "issuing commands."

"rewards and punishments" *śubhāśubham*: Literally, "auspiciousness and inauspiciousness." We follow Ct and Cr, who gloss, "punishment *or* favor (*nigrahānugraham*)." Cg explains similarly, "death or well-being (*mṛtyuṃ śreyo vā*)." Cf. note to verse 5 above.

10. "touched by a forest fire may survive" *apy eva dahanaṃ spṛṣṭvā vane tiṣṭhanti*: Literally, "They stand even after having touched fire in the forest."

"those whose offences have incurred the wrath of the king cannot" *rājadoṣaparāmṛṣṭās tiṣṭhante nāparādhinaḥ*: Literally, "Those offenders touched by the injurious character (*doṣa*) of the king do not stand." We follow Cm and Cg, who respectively gloss *kopa* and *krodha*, "anger," for *doṣa*, "fault." This interpretation seems also to be supported by a northern variant (V2,B1,2,4 and Gorresio 6.5.10) *-roṣa-*, "anger." D9–11 and the texts and printed editions of Ct and Cm read *-daṇḍa-*, "punishment."

11. "you two wretches... by your previous acts of service" *imau pāpau... pūrvopakāraiḥ*: Literally, "these two evildoers... by previous services." Rāvaṇa apparently addresses his spies here in the third person to indicate his displeasure. Ct, Ck, and Cm understand *pūrvopakāraiḥ*, "previous services," to refer to acts of service in war, etc., on the part of Śuka and Sāraṇa (*yuddhādau kṛtaiḥ*).

"who dare to praise my enemies" *śatrupakṣapraśaṃsakau*: Literally, "who praise the enemy's side."

12. "Go! Get out of my sight!" *apadhvaṃsata gacchadhvaṃ saṃnikarṣād ito mama*: Literally, "Go away, go hence from my presence." The two commands appear to be somewhat redundant, and the commentators make efforts to distinguish more clearly the two actions that Rāvaṇa is enjoining. Ct and Ck understand *apadhvaṃsata* to mean "You are to be barred from entry into my assembly hall (*matsabhāpraveśyād bhraṣṭā bhavata*)." Cr forces the syntax to construe the verb *apadhvaṃsata* with *pāda* b, skipping over the intervening verb *naśyadhvam* (v.l. for *gacchadhvam*). Thus, for him, the phrase means "Get out of my presence (*mama sannikarṣāt sānnidhyād yūyam apadhvaṃsata nirgacchata*)." Cg and Cm understand Rāvaṇa to be dismissing the two spies from their posts (*sthānāt pracyavadhvam*—Cg; *adhikārād bhraśyata*—Cm).

Several manuscripts (B1,D10,11,G1,M1,2) and the texts and printed editions of Ct, Cr, and Ck read *naśyadhvam*, "vanish, perish," for *gacchadhvam*. Ct and Ck explain the phrase as, "Vanish from my sight (*adarśanaṃ gacchadhvam*)." They evidently see the sequence of commands here as being out of logical order but note that this is not a rhetorical flaw, given the force of Rāvaṇa's rage (*krodhavaśād vacanavyatyāso na doṣāya*—so Ct).

"you... are as good as dead to me" *hatāv eva*: Ck and Ct flesh out the phrase by adding, "Even without [my] cutting off your heads, you are [dead] merely through my utter contempt (*vināpi śiraśchedaṃ dhikkārād eveti śeṣaḥ*—so Ct)."

13. Ct and Cm indicate that the withdrawal and disgrace of Śuka and Sāraṇa mark the termination of a curse that caused them to become *rākṣasas*. This, they maintain, is made clear elsewhere (*ayam eva tayo rākṣasatvaprāpakaśāpasyānta ity anyatra spaṣṭam*). Śuka and Sāraṇa, along with Mahodara (see verse 14 below), are listed, at 6.34.18–19, among those who are wounded by Rāma and barely escape with their lives.

"they" *tāv ubhau*: Literally, "both of them." Some *devanāgarī* manuscripts (D9–11) and the texts and printed editions of Ct and Cr read instead *tau dṛṣṭvā*, "those two having seen." This reading is reflected in translations of Dutt (1893, p. 1185) and Gita Press (1969, vol. 3, p. 1468).

14. "Hurry up and get me" *upasthāpaya śīghraṃ me*: Literally, "Quickly cause to attend upon me."

"spies who really understand the science of politics" *cārān nītiviśāradān*: Ñ,V2,B3,D6,7,9–11,T2,3,M5, and the texts and printed editions of Ct read instead *cārān iti niśācaraḥ* or near variants. This variant lends the verse the sense of "Next, the night-roaming *rākṣasa*, ten-necked Rāvaṇa, spoke to Mahodara, who stood near him, saying, 'Hurry up and get me some spies.' "

Following verse 14, D5,7,10,T1,2,G,M3,5, and the texts and printed editions of Ct insert a passage of one line [425*]: "Addressed in this fashion, Mahodara quickly summoned spies."

16. "devoted" *bhaktān*: D9–11 and the texts and printed editions of Ct read instead *dhīrān*, "bold, steadfast."

17. "plans" *vyavasāyam*: Literally, "resolve, intention." Cg interprets the word to mean "resolution as to what to do (*kartavyaniścayam*)" and sees the idea underlying Rāvaṇa's instructions as his desire to have his spies discover how firm Rāma's resolve may be. For if Rāma's resolve seems weak, Rāvaṇa will be able, he thinks, to intimidate him (*śithilavyavasāyaś ced amuṃ bhīṣayāma iti bhāvaḥ*).

"find out... Find out" *parīkṣatha*: Literally, "you [plural] investigate." Ś,Ñ,V1,2,B1,3,D0,2–4,8–13,G1, and the texts and printed editions of Ct and Cr read instead the infinitive *parīkṣitum*, "in order to investigate." V3,D1,T1,G3, and the text of Crā read the plural imperative (*loṭ*), *parīkṣata*, "Investigate!" We follow Cg in taking the present indicative (*laṭ*) in the sense of the imperative (*loṭ*).

The second half of the verse is elliptical, consisting as it does of an unresolved relative clause. We follow Cg in supplying the correlative clause "*tān api parīkṣadhvam* (find out about them as well)." Both Cr and Cg further expand on the passage, explaining that the spies are also to determine the resolve of Rāma's allies. As above, Cg comments that if their resolution is weak, they will be subject to intimidation. Cs proposes reading the relative pronoun *ye* as the interrogative *ke*, yielding the sense "Who are those who have allied themselves with him out of affection and are privy to his counsel?"

18. "When does he sleep?" *kathaṃ svapiti*: Literally, "How does he sleep?" Cg understands the point of the question to be whether Rāma sleeps by himself or is surrounded by many [attendants] who are awake. Rāvaṇa's intention here, Cg argues, is to attack Rāma when he first falls asleep. (*kim ekaḥ svapity uta jāgradbhir anekair āvṛtaḥ svapiti. ādye supte yuddhaṃ pravartayiṣyāmi iti hṛdayam.*)

"When does he wake?" [*kathaṃ*] *jāgarti*: Literally, "[How does] he wake?" Cg understands the question to mean "Is he consumed with anxiety or not?" For him, Rāvaṇa's intention here is to strike at Rāma when he is distracted. (*kiṃ cintākula utānākula ity arthaḥ. ādye vyākṣiptaṃ prahariṣyāmīty ākūtam.*)

"What else is he planning to do?" *kiṃ anyac ca kariṣyati*: Literally, "What else will he do?" Cg explains, "Will he lay siege to the city after some time or do so immediately?" Cg understands the intent to be that Rāvaṇa will deceive Rāma from the very outset in due course. (*kiṃ kaṃcit kālaṃ vilambya nagaram uparotsyaty uta sadya iti. ādye krameṇa vañcayiṣyāmīti tātparyam.*)

"accurately" *nipuṇam*: Cg glosses, "covertly (*pracchannam*)," which is equally plausible.

"when you have ascertained... completely" *vijñāya ... aśeṣataḥ*: The somewhat unusual placement of the adverb at the end of the verse after the gerundive *āgantavyam* leads Cg to offer three alternatives to its most probable construction with the gerund *vijñāya*, "having ascertained." The first of these is to understand *aśeṣataḥ* to refer to the totality of the information that Rāvaṇa has requested (*sarvam uktaṃ svāpādikam aśeṣataḥ sarvaprakāreṇa vijñāyāgantavyam*). Cg's second interpretation understands the adverb to construe with an unexpressed noun, "with spies (*cāraiḥ*)," yielding "by all of the [literally, 'having no remaining'] spies (*aśeṣaiś cārair iti vārthaḥ*)." The third alternative is to understand *aśeṣataḥ* to refer to anything that remains to be done (*uttaraśeṣo vā*).

20. Following verse 20ab, Ś,Ñ2,B1,3,4,D2,3,5–13,S insert a passage of two lines [427*]: "Then, placing Śārdūla at their head, the spies reverently circumambulated the great leader of the *rākṣasas*." The southern commentators who read this verse identify Śārdūla as the chief of the spies dispatched here. Śārdūla is mentioned again at 431* following verse 22 below but is not named in the critical text until 6.21.2 below.

21. "concealed themselves" *pracchannāḥ*: This could also mean, as Cg suggests, "disguised (*veṣāntaradhāriṇaḥ*)."

"near Mount Suvela" *suvelasya śailasya samīpe*: Literally, "in the vicinity of the mountain Suvela." According to Apte (s.v.), Mount Suvela is another name for Mount Trikūṭa. Compare note to 5.1.189.

Following verse 21, D5–7,9–11,S insert a passage of one line [428*]: "And as they observed the army, they were overwhelmed with fear."

22. Following verse 22, D1,5–7,9–11,13,S insert a passage of three lines [431*]: "However, only the *rākṣasa* Śārdūla was taken prisoner[1] on the grounds that he was particularly wicked. But just as Śārdūla was on the point of being killed by the leaping monkeys, Rāma had him freed. Then merciful Rāma had the other *rākṣasas* released."

[1]"taken prisoner" *grāhitaḥ*: Literally, "caused to be captured." When read in the context of the southern recension and the vulgate, the passage presents some minor logical difficulties concerning the special treatment of Śārdūla. In verse 22, all the *rākṣasa* spies are said to have been taken into custody; but here it appears that only their leader, Śārdūla, is seized. However, both Śārdūla and his followers are separately said to be set free at Rāma's urging. Probably, the intention here is that the entire *rākṣasa* party is apprehended, but only Śārdūla, because of his wickedness, is subjected to severe punishment. Cg attempts to avoid the problem by glossing *nigṛhītāḥ* in verse 22 as *tarjitāḥ*, which would have the sense here of "denounced." He then reads *grāhitaḥ* as "taken into custody (*grāhaṇaṃ prāpitaḥ*)." He next takes *mocitaḥ*, from 431*, line 2 [=GPP 6.29.27ab (v.l. *mokṣitaḥ*)], to mean "released from beating (*mocitaḥ prahārād iti śeṣaḥ*)." The idea for him then is that Vibhīṣaṇa merely identifies the *rākṣasas*, and, although the entire party is, of course, temporarily detained, only Śārdūla is subjected to serious punishment until Rāma sets him free.

23. "dazed" *naṣṭacetasaḥ*: Literally, "their consciousness destroyed," i.e., unconscious.

24. "mighty" *mahābalāḥ*: Cs, evidently struck by the seeming incongruity of this epithet in the light of the spies' pathetic performance and humiliating return, argues that the adjective is intended to show that the *rākṣasas* had managed to survive the attack of the monkeys (*vānarair upadrutā api jīvantīti mahābalā ity uktam*).

"accustomed to serving in foreign lands" *bahirnityacarāḥ*: Literally, "constantly moving outside." Ck, Ct, Cg, and Cm variously explain the compound to mean that these spies habitually travel in hostile countries to gather intelligence (*pararāṣṭreṣu vṛttāntajñānāya sadā saṃcāraśīlāḥ*—so Cg).

"terrifying army" *bhīmabalam*: Cs reads the compound as a *bahuvrīhi* referring to Rāma and having the sense of "whose bodily strength *or* army is terrifying (*bhīmaṃ bhayaṅkaraṃ balaṃ śarīraṃ sainyaṃ vā yasya taṃ rāmam*)." D9–11 and the texts and printed editions of Ct read instead *rāmabalam*, "Rāma's army."

"near Mount Suvela" *gireḥ suvelasya samīpa-*: Literally, "the vicinity of the mountain Suvela." See note above at verse 21.

The meter appears to be a defective *vaṃśasthavila*, whose first *pāda* is hypometric.

Sarga 21

The place of this *sarga* in the narrative is somewhat confusing. Rāvaṇa has already heard in great detail the enumeration of the monkey hosts and the identity of its leaders through the report of Śuka and Sāraṇa (*sargas* 16–19). Therefore, Śārdūla's shorter account here seems redundant. Moreover, the following *sarga* (22) begins with virtually the same two verses as this one, as though Śārdūla's report had never been made. The commentators are aware of these problems and seek to rationalize them. Thus, Cr on verse 1 (= GPP 6.30.1) remarks, by way of introduction to the *sarga*, "The same report is now given from another perspective for the sake of narrative consistency (*saṃdarbhaśuddhaye nivedanam eva bhaṅgyantareṇāha*)." Similarly, Cg on 6.22.1 (= GPP 6.31.1) remarks, "He [the poet] repeats what was said in the previous *sarga* for the sake of narrative consistency (*kathāsaṃghaṭanāya pūrvasargoktam anuvadati*)."

1. "with an unassailable army" *akṣobhyabalam*: Literally, "an imperturbable army." We take the compound as a *bahuvrīhi* modifying *rāghavam*, in the sense of "whose army *or* whose strength is unassailable." Cr, on the other hand, takes the army as a separate object of *pratyavedayan*, i.e., "They informed . . . that Rāghava and an unassailable army were encamped (*niviṣṭam akṣobhyabalaṃ rāghavaṃ ca pratyavedayan*)."

"near Mount Suvela" *suvele . . . śaile*: Literally, "on the mountain Suvela." See 6.20.21 above.

The verse is a close variant of 6.22.1.

2. "vast army" *mahābalam*: See notes to 6.20.24 and 6.21.1 above.

The verse is a close variant of 6.22.2.

3. "You look pale" *ayathāvat . . . te varṇaḥ*: Literally, "Your color is not as it should be."

4. "Questioned" *anuśiṣṭaḥ*: Literally, "instructed." The context obliges us to agree with the universal gloss of the commentators "questioned (*pṛṣṭaḥ*)." The verb *anu* $\sqrt{}$*śās* is unusual in this sense, which is not recorded in either Monier-Williams (s.v.) or PW (s.v.). Apte (s.v.), however, gives the meaning "questioned," citing this verse.

"Śārdūla . . . tiger among *rākṣasas*" *rākṣasaśārdūlaṃ śārdūlaḥ*: Rāvaṇa's epithet here is clearly chosen to echo the chief spy's name, Śārdūla, which means "tiger." Cf. 6.52.2 and note; 6.4.66; 6.5.3; 6.8.12; 6.14.13; and notes.

"stupefied with fear" *bhayavihvalaḥ*: Cs offers two explanations for Śārdūla's disabling terror: 1) He is stupefied by fear of the monkeys, as were Śuka and Sāraṇa (*kapibhayavihvalaḥ śukasāraṇavat*); and 2) He is stupefied with fear, thinking, "What did he [Rāvaṇa] say to them [Śuka and Sāraṇa] and what will happen [to me] (*kim uktau kiṃ bhaviṣyatīti bhayavihvalo vā*)?"

7. "Before I even had a chance to observe the army" *bale tasminn acārite*: Literally, "while the army was still unspied upon." D7,10,11, and the texts and printed editions of Ck, Ct, and Cr read *vicārite*, "examined." This reading, as Ct explains, would mean "Just as I had begun to examine [the army] (*vicārayituṃ prakrāntaḥ*)."

"many monkeys" *bahubhiḥ*: Literally, "by many." A number of manuscripts (V2,D5–7,9–11,T2,3,M) and the texts and printed editions of the southern commentators read instead *rakṣobhiḥ*, "by *rākṣasas*." The *rākṣasas* in question, according to Cg, are the ministers of Vibhīṣaṇa (*vibhīṣaṇasacivaiḥ*). See 6.10.12 above and note to 6.11.3. This variant is rendered by all translators who follow the text of the southern commentators, except for Shastri (1959, vol. 3, p. 73). Ct and Ck understand similarly (*vibhīṣaṇaparivāraiḥ*). Cs offers two explanations: the first is similar to that of Cg; the second is to read *rakṣobhiḥ* as an instrumental of accompaniment (*sahāgataiḥ saheti vā*), thus giving the meaning "I was seized along with the *rākṣasas* who accompanied me." Cs further supplies the word *vānaraiḥ*, "by the monkeys," to serve as the subject of the participle *gṛhītaḥ*, "seized."

8. "paraded about" *pariṇītaḥ*: Ct and Ck understand that Śārdūla is led all around the monkey encampment by his captors in order to proclaim that he is a spy. They note that this is the same treatment that the *rākṣasas* afforded Hanumān earlier (5.51.5–34) (*hanumān iva ghoṣaṇārtham itas tato nīto 'smi*—so Ct).

"powerful" *balavadbhiḥ*: D9–11 and the texts and printed editions of Ct read instead *balamadhye*, "in the midst of the army."

9. "Rāma's headquarters" *rāmasaṃsadam*: Literally, "Rāma's court *or* assembly hall."

"my entire body covered with blood" *rudhirādigdhasarvāṅgaḥ*: D7,10,11, and the texts and printed editions of Ct and Cr read *rudhirasrāvidīnāṅgaḥ*. Ct and Cr understand this as a *karmadhāraya* compound with the sense "my body bleeding profusely and thus suffering miserably." This reading is rendered variously by the translators who follow the text of Ct: thus Dutt (1893, p. 1187) renders, "bleeding, with my limbs showing sorry work"; Shastri (1959, vol. 3, p. 73), "my limbs covered with blood and wounds"; Roussel (1903, vol. 3, p. 84), "*les membres couverts de sang, de meurtrissures*"; Pagani (1999, p. 939), "*mes membres étaient meurtris, ruisselaient de sang*"; and Gita Press (1969, vol. 3, p. 1470), "my limbs bleeding and afflicted."

10. "Truly, I am lucky to be alive." *jīvāmi ha yadṛcchayā*: Literally, "Indeed, I survive by sheer luck." D9–11 and the texts and printed editions of Ct substitute *mā meti ca*, "and saying, 'Don't! Don't!' " for *jīvāmi ha*, "I am alive," giving the second half of the verse the sense of "Fortunately, I was spared by Rāghava, who cried, 'Stop! Stop!' " Cm reads with Cg and the critical edition but construes the verse somewhat more in the fashion of Ct. He claims the syntax is as follows: "Beaten by the tawny monkeys, I managed to survive. Then, pleading, my hands cupped in supplication, I was fortunately spared by Rāghava (*haribhir vadhyamāno jīvāmīti kṛtāñjaliḥ san yācchamāno 'haṃ yadṛcchayā rāghaveṇa paritrāta iti sambandhaḥ*)."

12. "immensely powerful warrior" *mahātejāḥ*: Literally, "the immensely powerful one."

"arranged his troops in the *garuḍa* formation" *garuḍavyūham āsthāya*: Literally, "having recourse to the *garuḍa* formation." This particular military array is, no doubt, similar to the form of other constructions (such as altars, etc.) named for either the mythical bird Garuḍa or an eagle. The idea must be that the troops are spread on either side of their commander in two "wings." See *ManuSm* 7.187. Dikshitar (1944, p. 271) notes that Bhīṣma uses a *gāruḍavyūha* in the *Mahābhārata* (6.52.2). Ct, Cs, and Ck note that this formation is appropriate for marching or advancing (*prasthānārtham*—Ct, Ck). Ct further notes that earlier, when the army was encamped, it had adopted the *puruṣa*, or "man," formation. Cs, alone among the commentators, reads a covert theological message in Rāma's choice of this particular formation. He argues, "He [Rāma] has made this arrangement under the pretext of a military formation thinking, 'If Rāvaṇa, seeing me mounted on the real Garuḍa, were to recognize my godhead and take refuge with me, the purpose of my incarnation would not be accomplished.' That is the suggested meaning (*sākṣād garuḍārohe jñātabhagavattvo rāvaṇaḥ prapannaś ced avatāravyāpārāniṣpādanaṃ syād iti vyūhamiṣeṇa taṃ viracayya tatra sthita iti dhvaniḥ*)." The idea is that Rāma as Viṣṇu would normally enter battle against a demonic foe mounted upon the great bird Garuḍa. Were he to do so in this case, however, Rāvaṇa, recognizing his divinity, might throw himself upon the Lord's mercy, thus subverting the mission of the *avatāra*, viz., the destruction of Rāvaṇa. Rāma, one may presume, thus selects the *garuḍavyūha* both as a tribute to his great mount and perhaps as a cryptic message to his devotees.

13. "fierce battle" *suyuddham*: Literally, "good battle." A number of manuscripts (V2,B3,D5,10,11,G,M5) and texts and printed editions of Ct read *yuddhaṃ vāpi*, "or battle," for *suyuddhaṃ vā*.

14. "those grave words of Śārdūla" *śārdūlasya mahadvākyam*: Ś,Ñ2,V,D0–2,4,8–13,M3, and the texts and printed editions of Ct read instead *śārdūlaṃ sumahadvākyam*, "[spoke] these exceedingly grave words to Śārdūla."

"he was stricken at heart, but he replied" *manasā saṃtatāpa ... athovāca*: Literally, "He suffered in his heart *or* mind ... then said." The reading of *pāda* a varies widely and significantly among the various manuscripts collated for the critical edition. The critical reading has mixed southern and northern support (B4,D5,7,T1,G2,3,M4). No commentator or printed edition, however, shares this reading. The southern commentators have either *manasā tat tadā prekṣya* ("then having reflected upon that [speech] in his mind"—Ct, Cr, Ck) or the more problematic variant *manasā taṃ tadā prekṣya* ("then having reflected on him [Śārdūla]"—Cg, Cm, Crā). Since the critical reading and, we believe, the logic of the passage (supported by numerous variants) shows Rāvaṇa to be pained or frightened by Śārdūla's report, we have added the conjunction "but" to indicate that, despite his inner misgivings, Rāvaṇa speaks defiantly out of pride and in order to keep up a brave front. Compare text and notes to 6.20.1–3 above.

15. This verse equals 6.17.2 except for the substitution of the synonymous verb *abhiyuñjīran* for *pratyudhyeran*.

16. "spied upon this army" *cāritā ... senā*: Ct and Ck, evidently perceiving a contradiction here since Śārdūla had failed so miserably in his mission as a spy, explains that Rāvaṇa means to say here that the *rākṣasa* has had the opportunity to observe the army through the happenstance of his having been paraded in captivity and proclaimed a spy (see verses 8–9 above) (*daivagatyā ghoṣaṇārthaṃ praṇayaneneti bhāvaḥ*).

17. "What are they like? What are the powers ...?" *kīdṛśāḥ kiṃprabhāvāś ca*: There is considerable variation among the various recensions for the first *pāda*. D9–11 and the

texts and printed editions of Ct read *kiṃprabhāḥ kīdṛśāḥ saumya*, while D5,6,T,G1,3,M3, and Cg reverse the order, reading *kīdṛśāḥ kiṃprabhāḥ saumya*. The meaning of these variants would literally be "What are they like? What is their radiance, my good man?" Cg glosses the term *kiṃprabhāḥ* as *kiṃprabhāvāḥ*, "What are their powers?" the reading of the critical edition. D7 and Cr read instead *kiṃpramāṇāḥ*, "What is their size *or* measure?" This obscure variant is rendered only in the translation of Pagani (1999, p. 939) as "*Quelle est leur taille*...?"

"*rākṣasa*" *rākṣasa*: D9–11 and the texts and printed editions of Ct read instead *suvrata*, "virtuous one." This is rendered variously by the translators who follow Ct as "O thou of fair vows" (Dutt 1893, p. 1188); "O Faithful Friend" (Shastri 1959, vol. 3, p. 74); "*loyal ami*" (Roussel 1903, vol. 3, p. 85); and "*fidèle ami*" (Pagani 1999, p. 939). Cs notes this reading as a variant and explains it as expressive of Rāvaṇa's suggestion that he would be able to recognize it were Śārdūla to speak untruthfully (*suvratety anenānṛtabhāṣaṇe pratyaveyām iti parijñānam astīti sūcyate*).

18. "take account of the opposing forces" *balasaṃkhyānaṃ kartavyam*: Literally, "an accounting of the forces is to be made." D9–11 and the texts and printed editions of Ct substitute the emphatic particle *khalu* for *bala-*, "forces." This yields the sense "must indeed make a reckoning."

20. "To begin with...then" *atha*...*atha*: Literally, "now...now." Cg, noting the repetition, remarks that the first *atha* marks the beginning of Śārdūla's speech and the second, according to him, is *metri causa* (*athety uttaravacanārambhe dvitīyothaśabdaḥ pādapūraṇe*).

"your majesty" *rājan*: Literally, "O king." D5–7,G2,3,M3, and Cv, Crā, Cm, and Cg substitute the nominative *rājā* for the critical edition's vocative. This would yield the sense of "the king [of the monkeys] utterly invincible in battle."

"the son of Ṛkṣarajas" *ṛkṣarajasaḥ putraḥ*: The reference is, of course, to Sugrīva. For an account of Sugrīva's birth, see *Uttarakāṇḍa*, App. I, No. 3, lines 74–78.

"the son of Gadgada" *gadgadasya*...*putraḥ*: Ct, Ck, Cr, and Cm cite the passage from the *Bālakāṇḍa* (critical edition 490* = GPP 1.17.7) at which Jāmbavān is said to have been born directly from the mouth of Brahmā while the latter was yawning. They argue, however, that there is no contradiction, since it was actually a *śakti*, or "creative energy," that issued from the god's mouth and entered "the field (*kṣetra*)," i.e., the wife of Gadgada, thus entitling Jāmbāvan to be considered Gadgada's son. (*gadgado jāmbavataḥ kṣetradvārā pitā. yady api jāmbavato jṛmbhamāṇasya sahasā mama vaktrād ajāyateti brahmamukhād utpattir uktā, tathāpi jṛmbhaṇasamaya udgatāyā brahmaśakter gadgadakṣetram āviśya tadrūpeṇa pariṇāmād adoṣaḥ*—so Cm; Ct similarly.) Cg adds that, since Jāmbavān was raised by Gadgada, he can be considered his son, just as in the case of Pāñcālī (Draupadī), [who, although born directly from the sacrificial fire, is regarded as the daughter of Drupada] (*pāñcālīnyāyena gadgadena poṣitatvāt tatputro jāmbavān tasya brahmaṇo jṛmbhārambhasaṃbhūtatvāt*).

21. "the other son of Gadgada" *gadgadasyaiva putro 'nyaḥ*: The text provides no name for this individual. However, the commentators generally identify him as Dhūmra. See 6.18.9–10; 6.32.22; and 6.54.29. See also notes to 6.18.9–10,11–12; and 6.31.17. Cs's interpretation differs from those of the other commentators, which are discussed in the notes to the previous verse. He quotes Cm's and Ct's argument that Jāmbavān was actually the *kṣetraja*, "son," of Gadgada born from the *śakti* of Lord Brahmā, which had entered Gadgada's wife. However, he regards this as a less

plausible explanation for the seeming contradiction involving the two sons of Gadgada, suggesting that Gadgada fathered the two sons in two different births (*gadgadasya dvitīyajanmani*).

"the son of the *guru* of Indra of the hundred sacrifices" *guruputraḥ śatakratoḥ*: The reference, as noted by the commentators, is to Kesarin, a son of Bṛhaspati, the famous *purohita* of Indra and the gods (see note to 6.18.32–34 above).

"his son who single-handedly slaughtered the *rākṣasas*" *kadanaṃ yasya putreṇa kṛtam ekena rakṣasām*: The reference here, as pointed out by the commentators, is to Kesarin's son, Hanumān, and the latter's slaughter of the *rākṣasa* forces described in the *Sundarakāṇḍa* (*sargas* 40–45).

22. "the son of Dharma" *putro dharmasya*: Cg sees the possibility of a contradiction here in light of the *Bālakāṇḍa* passage (491*, line 11 = GPP 1.17.15), where Suṣeṇa is said to be the son not of Dharma but of Varuṇa. He explains the apparent contradiction by arguing that 1) in this passage Varuṇa is called by the name Dharma; 2) Śārdūla was so frightened that he misheard the genealogy of Suṣeṇa; or 3) the reference here is to a different Suṣeṇa than the one previously mentioned. (*nanu varuṇo janayāmāsa suṣeṇa nāma vānaram iti bālakāṇḍoktam. satyam uktaṃ sa evātra dharmaśabdenocyate. śārdūlo vā bhayākūlo 'nyathā śrutavān. anyo 'yaṃ suṣeṇa ity apy āhuḥ.*)

"Dadhimukha" *dadhimukhaḥ*: This would appear to be Sugrīva's uncle, who is the superintendent of the king's Madhuvana in the *Sundarakāṇḍa* (*sargas* 59–62).

23. "Vegadarśin" *vegadarśī*: Literally, "perceiving speed." Cr appears to understand this not as the name of a third monkey but as an epithet applying either to Durmukha or Durmukha and Sumukha. He explains the compound as meaning "having the nature of recognizing the respective speed [of the various monkeys] (*svasvavegadarśanaśīlaḥ*)." See 6.116.48 and note.

"created death in the form of these monkeys" *mṛtyur vānararūpeṇa . . . sṛṣṭaḥ*: Literally, "death was created in monkey form." The commentators differ as to whether this means that these previously named monkeys resemble Death itself (*mṛtyutulyāḥ*—Ct, Cm, Cg, first alternative) or that they are the sons of Mṛtyu, the god of death (*yadvā sumukhādayo mṛtyuputrā ity arthaḥ*—so Cg, second alternative; Cv, Crā similarly).

24. Several of the commentators note that, because of the distinction between biological fatherhood (*bījitva*) and legal fatherhood (*kṣetritva*), we see two fathers mentioned for several of the monkey heroes (*evaṃ tatra tatra pitṛdvayanirdeśo bījitvakṣetritvābhyām iti mantavyam*—so Cg).

25. "grandson" *naptā*: Although the term normally refers to the son of one's daughter, both Cr and Cg remark that, in this case, it refers to the son of one's son (*atra naptṛśabdo 'rthasāmarthyāt pautre vartate*—so Cg).

26. "like Kāla, the ender of all things" *kālāntakopamāḥ*: This expression and its variant, *kālāntakayamopama* (like Yama, who brings time [Kāla] itself to an end, see 6.55.93), is a commonplace in the *Yuddhakāṇḍa* (6.45.31; 6.48.83; 6.55.93–96; 6.69.8; 6.75.2; 6.83.30; 6.104.31; and notes) as well as in the *Mahābhārata* (see, for example, 3.23.30; 3.28.23; 3.138.12; 3.154.40; 3.175.15; 6.50.42; 6.51.38; 6.87.7; 7.95.19; 7.134.35; 8.35.18; 8.40.18; 10.13.20; 14.73.27). Professor Sharma has informed us, and we concur, that the compound should be read as a *karmadhāraya*, i.e., "Time itself is the Ender." See verse 31 below. See, too, R. K. Sharma 1964, p. 26. Cf. 6.80.7 and note.

27. Ñ1 (omits verse 28) and all southern manuscripts (D5–7,9–11,S) read verses 27–28 after verse 33. It is not clear on what basis the critical editors have chosen to follow

the northern sequence. Perhaps the northern redactors and the critical editors after them were disturbed by the inclusion of Lakṣmaṇa in the middle of a list of monkeys rather than after it with the description of Rāma.

28. "Sudurdhara" *sudurdharaḥ*: The critical edition follows the reading of Cg, Cv, Crā, and Cm. D6,7,10,T3,M5, and the texts and printed editions of Ct read instead *sa durdharaḥ*, giving Durdhara as the name of the monkey.

"son of the Vasus" *vasuputraḥ*: The term "Vasu" is generally used to indicate a group of eight vedic divinities, one of the classes of divinities that make up their traditional number of thirty-three. The individual members of this class vary from text to text. Less commonly, the term may be used in the singular to refer to a variety of individual vedic divinities, including Indra, Dyaus, etc. If the term is intended to be singular here, it is unclear which particular divinity is meant. The commentators are silent. See, too, note to 6.45.38.

29. "one hundred million of these . . . heroic monkeys" *daśa vānarakoṭyaḥ . . . śūrāṇām*: The commentators note the irregular loss of the expected genitive plural ending of the word *vānara-*, which would put it into agreement with the nouns and adjective with which it is in apposition. Cg cites *Pā* 7.1.39 (*supāṃ suluk*), which accounts for such elisions in vedic.

"I am unable to describe the rest." *śeṣān nākhyātum utsahe*: Literally, "I am unable to describe the remaining ones." We follow the interpretation of Ct, Cr, and Ck, who understand that Śārdūla is unable to enumerate all the remaining monkeys. Cg reads *śeṣam*, "the rest," for the plural *śeṣān* and understands the phrase to mean that the *rākṣasa* is unable to specify further details about the monkeys, such as their places of birth, and so on (*śeṣaṃ janmasthānādi*).

30. "whose build is that of a lion" *siṃhasaṃhananaḥ*: Cg, quoting *Amarakośa* (3.1.12) (*varāṅgarūpopeto yaḥ siṃhasaṃhananaḥ*), argues that this phrase means "possessing a pleasing arrangement of the limbs (*ramaṇīyāvayavasanniveśavān*)."

"the one who slew Dūṣaṇa, Khara, and Triśiras" *dūṣaṇo nihato yena kharaś ca triśirās tathā*: See *Araṇyakāṇḍa* 24–29.

31. "for he slew Virādha and Kabandha" *virādho nihato yena kabandhaś ca*: See *Araṇyakāṇḍa* 2–3, 65–69.

"who was like Yama, the ender of all things" *antakopamaḥ*: See verse 26 above.

32. "all" *tāvantaḥ*: Literally, "so many." We follow the reading of Cg, who quotes *Amarakośa* (3.3.245) to the effect that *yāvat* and *tāvat* may be used in the sense of "totality." (*ye janasthānagatās te yāvantas te sarve 'pi hatā ity arthaḥ. yāvat tāvac ca sākalya ity amaraḥ.*) Ck understands similarly.

"who slew all the *rākṣasas* in Janasthāna" *janasthānagatā yena . . . rākṣasā hatāḥ*: See *Araṇyakāṇḍa* 24–25.

33. "resembling a bull elephant" *mātaṅgānām ivarṣabhaḥ*: Literally, "like a bull of *or* among elephants." Despite the homology of this trope with the stereotypical metaphor of the bull as a symbol of power, etc., we are inclined to read this construction with Cr and Cg, who understand, "best of elephants (*gajaśreṣṭha iva*)."

34. "having received the city of Laṅkā" *parigṛhya purīṃ laṅkām*: We are inclined to agree with Cg and Cr, who supply the word *rāghavāt* or *rāmāt*, "from Rāghava *or* from Rāma," and see the phrase as a reference to Rāma's having transferred sovereignty from Rāvaṇa to Vibhīṣaṇa at 6.13.9. All translators consulted follow this interpretation, with the exception of Dutt (1893, p. 1189), who understands, "hath laid siege to

Lañkā." This is a plausible but less persuasive reading of the gerund *pratigṛhya* (v.l. for the critical edition's *parigṛhya*), which can also have the sense of "seize, attack."

35. "upon Mount Suvela" *suvele . . . śaile*: Literally, "on the mountain Suvela." See note to 6.20.21.

"You, sir, must now decide what is to be done next." *śeṣakārye bhavān gatiḥ*: Literally, "You, sir, are the highest recourse with respect to action that remains to be done."

Several of the commentators call our attention to discrepancies between the accounts of the ancestry of various monkeys as they are given in this *sarga* and at *Bālakāṇḍa* 16. Most of them, following Cm, note the discrepancies but deny any contradiction on the grounds that many monkeys may have the same names. (*nanv atra sarge dharmasya putraḥ suseṇaḥ. vaivasvataputrau śarabhagandhamādanāv ity ucyete. bālakaṇḍe tu "varuṇo janayāmāsa suṣeṇaṃ nāma vānaram. śarabhaṃ janayāmāsa parjanyas tu mahābalam. dhanadasya sutaḥ śrīmān vānaro gandhamādanaḥ" iti trayāṇām anyata utpattir uktā. satyam. suṣeṇādi saṃjñāvatām anekeṣām api sattvān na virodhaḥ.*) Cg, however, regards the entire *sarga* as suspect for two reasons—first, because of these very discrepancies, and, second, because he finds the chapter unnecessary to the sequence of the epic narrative, which, he claims, would remain intact even without this chapter (*atra vānarajanmokte prāyaśo bālakāṇḍoktavirodhād etat sargaṃ vināpi pūrvottarakathā saṃghaṭṭanāc ca sargo 'yaṃ kalpita ity āhuḥ*).

Sarga 22

1. "Meanwhile" *tatah*: Literally, "then." Crā and Cg take note of the apparent repetition here of the account given in the previous *sarga*. Cg, who had already noted the narrative superfluity of *sarga* 21 (see note to 6.21.35), claims here that the previous material is repeated in order to maintain the sequence of the narrative (*kathāsaṃghaṭanāya pūrvasargoktam anuvadati*). Crā also notes the repetition and, alluding to the type of inconsistencies in the tales of the origins of the monkey heroes noted above (at *sarga* 21), remarks, as Cg remarked earlier (6.21.35), that *sarga* 21 is unnecessary to the narrative sequence (*tatas tam akṣobhyabalam ity anuvādaḥ pūrvasargādau ca kṛtaḥ . . . pūrvasargam antareṇāpi kathā saṃgacchate*). Still, he concludes resignedly with the maxim, "one must take into consideration the existing situation (*tathāpi sthitasya gatiḥ cintanīyeti nyāyena pūrvasargo vyākhyataḥ*)," and therefore comments on the seemingly otiose *sarga*.

"near Mount Suvela" *suvele . . . śaile*: See notes to 6.20.21 and 6.21.1.

This verse is a close variant of 6.21.1.

2. "somewhat agitated" *jātodvego 'bhavat kiṃcit*: Cr is of two minds as to how to construe *kiṃcit*. He notes that it can be taken, as we do, with *jātodvegaḥ*, or as modifying *idam* in *pāda* d, thus yielding the sense "He said something to his ministers. (*sacivān kiṃcid abravīc ca. kiṃcid iti jātodvegānvayi vā.*)"

The verse is a close variant of 6.21.2.

3. "*Rākṣasas*! . . . counselors" *mantriṇaḥ . . . rākṣasāḥ*: Cg sees some ambiguity in the syntax of this verse and offers three alternative readings. The first is similar to our translation. The second, which he borrows from Cv, sees *rākṣasāḥ* not as a vocative but as a nominative plural and part of the subject of the following verse. His third alternative is to take *mantriṇaḥ* and *rākṣasāḥ* as vocatives in apposition and then to read

the third person imperative *samāyāntu* as a polite second person, thus giving the sense "O *rākṣasa* counselors, please assemble." Ct and Ck, who follow the first interpretation, supply the phrase "[Let them assemble] on your instructions (*yuṣmadvacanāt*)."

"focusing their thoughts" *susamāhitāḥ*: Literally, "well focused *or* fully intent." Cg glosses, "skilled in the science of politics (*nītikuśalāḥ*)."

5. "what was appropriate for them to do next" *kṣamaṃ yat samanantaram*: Ct and Ck supply the words "with respect to winning over Sītā (*sītāprāptāv iti śeṣaḥ*)." Cg explains, "What was to be done after the approach of Rāma. (*rāmasya samīpagamanānantaram. yat kṣamaṃ kartum ucitam.*)"

"unassailable Rāvaṇa" *durdharṣaḥ*: Literally, "unassailable one."

6. "summoning" *āhūya*: Literally, "having summoned." D7,10–11,T2,3,G2,M1,2,5, and the texts and printed editions of Ct and Cr read instead *ādāya*, "having taken [with him]."

"Rāvaṇa, himself a great master of illusion" *mahāmāyaḥ*: Literally, "having great powers of illusion." Ñ2,B2,D10,11,M5, and the texts and printed editions of Ck and Ct read instead *mahāmāyam*, thus making this a redundant epithet of Vidyujjihva.

"went to where . . . was" *prāviśad yatra*: Literally, "he entered where."

8. "Rāghava's head along with his great bow and arrows—all fashioned through the power of illusion" *śiro māyāmayam . . . rāghavasya . . . mahac ca saśaraṃ dhanuḥ*: Literally, "Rāghava's head made through illusion and a great bow with arrows."

9. Following 9ab, Ñ,V2,B1–3,D6,7,9–11,T2, and the texts and printed editions of Ct, Ck, and Cr insert a passage of one line [456*], evidently out of their concern that the king should reward his servant without the latter actually having done anything: "He then demonstrated the proper use of his powers of illusion to Rāvaṇa."

10. "Sītā seated" *upaviṣṭām*: Literally, "[her] seated."

Following 10a, D3–7,10,11,S, and the texts and printed editions of the southern commentators insert a passage of one line [458*], which extends the description of Rāvaṇa: "Eager to see Sītā, the lord of the *rākṣasas*, sons of chaos."

11. "surrounded by . . . *rāksasa* women" *upāsyamānām . . rākṣasībhiḥ*: Literally, "being waited *or* attended upon by *rākṣasīs*." Cg takes the participle in its sense of "worship, attend upon" and, understanding Sītā to be its subject rather than object, glosses, "devoted [wife] (*anuvratām*)."

For elaborate descriptions of Sītā's *rākṣasī* wardresses, see 5.15.4–17; 5.20.31–36. See, too, Sutherland 1989; and S. Goldman 2001, 2003a, 2003b.

12. "calling out . . . in feigned delight" *praharṣan nāma kīrtayan*: Literally, "falsely delighting [and] calling." Like Ck, Ct, and Cg, we take the particle *nāma* here in its sense as a marker of falsehood (*aparamārthe*). (See Mallinātha's comments on *KumāSaṃ* 5.32 for a similar usage.) The texts and printed editions of the southern commentators as well as a number of northern and southern manuscripts (Ś,V1–3,D0, 4–6,8–13,T1,2,M3, and Cv, Cm, Cg, and Ct) read the variant *praharṣaṃ nāma*, which would make *praharṣam* the object of the participle *kīrtayan*. Ct and Ck read *nāma* as we have done and explain that Rāvaṇa is proclaiming his joy, which is a result of his feigned victory over Rāma. (*nāma ity aparamārthe. aparamārthabhūtaṃ rāmajayajaṃ praharṣaṃ kīrtayan*—so Ct.) Cr reads the accusative *praharṣam* adverbially and takes *nāma* nominally in its sense of "name" as the object of the participle *kīrtayan*. He thus understands the clause to mean "joyfully proclaiming his name (*praharṣaṃ yathā syāt tathā nāma svābhidhāṃ kīrtayan san*)." Cg understands *praharṣam* metonymically for "as

if proclaiming the joyful news (*praharṣavarttāṃ kīrtayann iva*)." Cm understands, "joyfully calling out Sītā's name (*praharṣam kīrtayan 'he site!' iti sambandhaḥ*)."

13. "about whom you are wont to speak so boastfully" *yam upāśritya valgase*: Literally, "with reference to whom you boast." Cg, the only commentator who both reads and comments upon the verb *valgase*, glosses, "prattle, talk too much (*jalpasi*)," and understands, "You spoke harshly or cruelly (*niṣṭhuram avada ity arthaḥ*)." Our interpretation is based on an attested, if not common, sense of the root $\sqrt{}$*valg* [normally, "jump, leap"] as noted in the *Śabdakalpadruma* (s.v. *valganam*), which offers *bahubhāṣaṇam*, "talking too much," as one of the meanings of the term. The idea, no doubt, is that Rāvaṇa is referring to Sītā's harsh rebuke of his attempt to woo her at *Sundarakāṇḍa* 18–19, where she tells him of Rāma's great power and warns him of the destruction he faces at her husband's hands. D10–11 and the texts and printed editions of Ct and Cr read instead *yam āśritya vimanyase*, that is, "with reference to whom you spurn [me]."

14. "I have completely undermined your grounds for refusing me" *chinnaṃ te sarvato mūlam . . . mayā*: Literally, "By me your root is completely cut off." Ck and Ct explain, "The basis for your refusal to marry me is cut off in every way [v.l. *sarvathā* for *sarvataḥ*] (*te mūlam asmad aparigrahanidānaṃ sarvathā sarvaprakāreṇa chinnam*)." Cg glosses, "that which has been [your] basis (*ādhārabhūtam*)" for *mūlam*, "root."

"you will have to become" *bhaviṣyasi*: Literally, "You will be." We agree with Ck in understanding that Rāvaṇa feels that, in feigning the death of Rāma, he has left Sītā no alternative but to marry him of her own accord (*gatyantarābhāvāt svayam eveti śeṣaḥ*).

Following verse 14, Ñ2,D5–7,9–11,S insert a passage of two lines [462*]: "Foolish woman, give up this notion![1] Of what use is a dead man to you? My lady, you must become the foremost among all my wives."

[1]"notion" *matim*: Cr understands Rāvaṇa to be referring to Sītā's intention of following Rāma to the next world. He feels that Rāvaṇa is dissuading her on the grounds that she will not be able to obtain her husband in the afterlife (*enāṃ tallokagamanaviṣayāṃ matiṃ visṛja tyaja mṛtena lokāntaraṃ gatena patyā tvaṃ kiṃ kariṣyasi tatprāptir na bhaviṣyatīty arthaḥ*).

15. "Your merit is exhausted and your purpose has failed" *alpapūṇye nivṛttārthe*: Literally, "O woman of little merit, O woman whose purpose has been thwarted." Ct explains that Sītā's purpose or goal was nothing other than [the recovery of] Rāma himself (*nivṛttārthe nivṛtto rāmarūpo 'rtho yasyāḥ*).

Cr has a unique perspective on this whole passage. He reads it as indirect (*bhaṅgyantareṇa*) praise of Sītā on the part of Rāvaṇa (presumably as a devotee—see note to 5.18.6). Thus, he takes *alpapuṇyā* to mean that Sītā purifies even the lowliest, who attain purity through the recollection of her name, etc. (*alpapuṇye 'lpānāṃ kṣudrāṇām api puṇyaṃ pavitratvaṃ yayā yannāmasmaraṇādinā kṣudrā api pūtā bhavantīty arthaḥ*). He understands the vocative *nivṛttārthe* as the negative *anivṛttārthe*, which is plausible given the *sandhi* environment. The sense according to him would then be, "one who has accomplished all of her objectives (*na nivṛtto 'rtho yasyāḥ sarvārthasampannety arthaḥ*)."

"you foolish woman" *mūḍhe*: Cr takes the normally highly pejorative term *mūḍha*, "fool," in an opposite sense, adducing the terminology of the *Yogasūtra* (1.2) and glossing *prāptanirodhe*, "O you who have transcended the state of *mūḍhatva* and attained the cessation of random thoughts (*he prāptanirodhe*)." We are indebted to Professor R. K. Sharma for this interpretation.

"who think yourself so clever" *paṇḍitamānini*: Cr sees this normally pejorative term to mean "one whose habit is to honor *paṇḍits* (*paṇḍitān manyate satkaroti tacchīlā*)."

"the slaying of Vṛtra" *vṛtravadham*: This refers to the famous legend of Indra slaying the demon Vṛtra, which can be traced back to the earliest vedic literature. The event has become a common standard of comparison for the slaying of powerful warriors. See, for example, *ṚV* 1.32; *TaiS* 6.5.5; *ŚatBr* 1.6.3; *JaimiBr* 2.155; *MBh* 5.9–10; and *Rām* 1.23.17–19; 5.20.28.

16. "our shores" *samudrāntam*: Literally, "to the edge of the sea."

"in a futile effort to kill me" *māṃ hantuṃ kila*: Literally, "to kill me indeed." We interpret the adverbial particle *kila* here in its sense of indicating contempt or disdain.

17. "reached the southern shore" *tīram āsādya dakṣiṇam*: D6,7,9–11,T2,3,M3, and the texts and printed editions of all southern commentators read instead *pīḍya* (*tīrtvā*—D6,T2) *tīram athottaram*, "having devastated the northern shore." This reading thus places the action Rāvaṇa describes as having taken place before Rāma crosses the ocean rather than, as in the critical reading, on the shore of Laṅkā.

18. "exhausted from its long march" *adhvani pariśrāntam* . . . *sthitam*: Literally, "located on the road, exhausted."

19. "on that very spot where Rāma and Lakṣmaṇa lay" *yatra rāmaḥ salakṣmaṇaḥ*: Literally, "where Rāma [was] together with Lakṣmaṇa."

"Rāma's" *asya*: Literally, "his."

20–21. The list of weapons differs somewhat among the various manuscripts and printed editions. Similarly, the identification of the specific weapons varies among the different translations. See Glossary of Weapons.

"staves heavy with iron" *daṇḍān mahāyasān*: The term *mahāyasa* is poorly attested in the literature. It appears to be a compound consisting of the adjectives *mahant*, "great," and *āyasa*, "made of iron." We take it more or less in the sense given in PW and MW (s.v.). The term occurs in the Citraśāla Press edition of the *Mahābhārata* (4.65.7), where Nīlakaṇṭha glosses *mahāphalaka*, which seems to be a type of broad-headed spear. Cf. Apte s.v. *mahāphalam*. Cf. also note to 6.3.12.

"streams of arrows" *bāṇajālāni*: Literally, "masses of arrows."

22. "deft-handed" *kṛtahastena*: Literally, "of accomplished hand." We follow Ct and Cg, who gloss, "of trained hand (*śikṣitahastena*)." Cr, however, sees the compound not as a *bahuvrīhi* modifying *prahastena* but as a *pūrvanipāta tatpuruṣa* in the sense of "wielded in his hand (*haste kṛtena*)." The adjective is undoubtedly used for its echoing effect with the name Prahasta.

23. "Vibhīṣaṇa tried to flee, but, as it happened, he was captured" *vibhīṣaṇaḥ samutpatya nigṛhīto yadṛcchayā*: Literally, "Leaping up, Vibhīṣaṇa, as it happened, was captured." The syntax is somewhat ambiguous. We follow Ct, Ck, and Cg in reading Vibhīṣaṇa as the subject of the gerund *samutpatya*, literally, "having jumped up, having rushed forth," which they understand to mean "fled (*gataḥ*)." The verb *sam* + *ut* √*pat* can also mean "to attack," and so the phrase could also plausibly mean "[Prahasta—so Cr], as it happened, attacked and captured Vibhīṣaṇa."

"and all the leaping monkeys" *sarvaiḥ* . . . *plavagaiḥ saha*: Literally, "with all the leaping monkeys." D9–11 and the texts and printed editions of Ct read *sainyaiḥ*, "[along] with troops, soldiers," for *sarvaiḥ*, "with all."

24. "Sugrīva . . . with a broken neck . . . Hanumān . . . his jaw smashed" *sugrīvo grīvayā . . . bhagnayā . . . nirastahanukaḥ . . . hanūmān*: Here and in the following verses Rāvaṇa's description of the monkeys' injuries plays upon their names, many of which include references to body parts, etc. Thus, Sugrīva means, literally, "having a beautiful neck" and Hanumān, "having a [great] jaw." For the origin of Sugrīva and his name, see *Uttarakāṇḍa*, App. I, No. 3, line 75; for Hanumān's, see 7.35.47.

"lies there . . . lies there" *śete . . . śete*: Literally, "he lies . . . he lies." D9–11,M3, and the texts and printed editions of the southern commentators and Lahore read the vocative *sīte*, "O Sītā," for the first *śete*, "he lies [there]," in *pāda* a. D9–11,M5, and the texts and printed editions of Ct also read the vocative *sīte*, "O Sītā," for the second occurrence of the verb *śete* in *pāda* c.

25. "as he leapt up . . . stricken at the knees" *jānubhyām utpatan nihataḥ*: We follow Cg here, who reads the instrumental dual *jānubhyām* irregularly as a locative (*jānubhyām jānunoḥ*) as this seems to be in keeping with the tenor of the previous verse, where the monkeys are wounded on those parts of the body from which their names are derived or with which they resonate alliteratively. Cr and most available translators, except Gita Press (1969, vol. 3, p. 1475), understand that the monkey is rising to, or from, his knees or thighs when he is struck down (*jānubhyām utpatan*).

26. "two bulls among monkeys . . . cut down" *nihatau vānararṣabhau*: Ñ2,D9–11, and the texts and printed editions of Ct read instead *tau vānaravararṣabhau*, "those two bulls among the foremost monkeys." The texts and printed editions of Ct provide no verbal element in the verse to inform us of the fate of Mainda and Dvivida. This defect is remedied in these texts and editions in a variant to *pādas* 27ab. See note to verse 27 below.

27. "Cut through the middle with a sword . . . destroyer of his enemies" *asinābhyāhataś chinno madhye ripuniṣūdanaḥ*: D6,7,9–11,T2,3,G2,3,M3,5, and the texts and printed editions of the southern commentators read instead *asinā vyāyatau chinnau madhye hy ariniṣūdanau*, "those two powerful destroyers of their enemies [Mainda and Dvivida] were cut through the middle with a sword." As noted above, this syntax completes the vulgate variant of verse 26.

"fell thunderously" *abhiṣṭanati*: This unusual verb, *abhi* $\sqrt{stan}$, known primarily to the vedic corpus, means, literally, "to thunder" (Grassmann 1872 [1964 reprint] s.v.). Manuscripts show many variants. Ct, Cr, and Ck read *anusvanati*, "he resounds, makes a noise." Cg, Cm, and Cv read *anutiṣṭhati*, which Cg glosses as "he lies (*śete*)."

"Panasa . . . like a jackfruit" *panasaḥ panaso yathā*. Here, again, Rāvaṇa's choice of *upamāna* is derived from a play on a character's name. We understand with Cr, who glosses, "like a ripe *panasa* fruit that has split open (*vidīrṇapakvapanasaphalam iva*)," that the object of comparison here is the fruit of the jackfruit tree rather than the tree itself. The idea, we think, is that given the critical reading *abhiṣṭanati*, we are to understand Panasa has fallen with a thud like a ripe jackfruit. Dutt (1893, p. 1191), Roussel (1903, vol. 3, p. 88), Shastri (1959, vol. 3, p. 77), Pagani (1999, p. 942), and Raghunathan (1982, vol. 3, p. 75), however, all understand the reference to be to the jackfruit tree (*Artocarpus integrifolia*) itself, which is technically more correct, given the masculine gender of the word.

28. Darīmukha lies in a pit" *śete daryāṃ darīmukhaḥ*: Here, again, Rāvaṇa plays on a monkey's name. Darīmukha means "whose mouth is like a pit *or* cave."

"is moaning" *niṣkūjan*: Literally, "moaning." So we render the participle. Other translators, such as Gita Press (1969, vol. 3, p. 1475), Shastri (1959, vol. 3, p. 77), and

Roussel (1903, vol. 3, p. 88), similarly understand that the monkey is emitting a sound ("shrieking, *hurlant*"). Ck and Ct insist that the critical edition's reading is the authentic one (*pāñktaḥ*). Cm, Cg, and Crā, however, read *niṣkūjaḥ sāyakaiḥ kṛtaḥ*, which yields the meaning "silenced by arrows." This interpretation is followed by Dutt (1893, p. 1191), Pagani (1999, p. 942), and Raghunathan (1982, vol. 3, pp. 75–76).

29. "Añgada... Adorned with his armlets, he lies" *añgadaḥ ... nipatito 'ñgadaḥ*: The repetition of the name Añgada here is problematic. In keeping with the tenor of the passage (i.e., the repeated playing upon the names and attributes of the monkeys), we have cautiously accepted the reading of Cr, who explains the second occurrence of the name as "characterized by armlets (*añgadaviśiṣṭaḥ*)." Evidently, he is reading the term as a *taddhita* derivation of the name formed with the suffixation of the *ac pratyaya* (*Pā* 5.2.127). Cg attempts to finesse the problem by reading *nipatitāñgadaḥ* for the critical edition's *nipatito 'ñgadaḥ*, thus providing an easily intelligible *bahuvrīhi* with the sense "his armlets fallen."

"felled... he lies" *pātitaḥ ... nipatitaḥ*: The somewhat awkward repetition of *pātitaḥ* and *nipatitaḥ* is avoided by V3,D10–11, and the texts and printed editions of Ct, which read *paritaḥ*, "on all sides," for *pātitaḥ*, "felled." Ś,V1,B2,4,D0–3,5–9,12,13,T2,3, G2,M3,5, and the texts and printed editions of Cg read *patitaḥ*, "fallen," for *pātitaḥ*, "felled." Cg's reading avoids redundancy by making the substitution mentioned above, where he substitutes a *bahuvrīhi* compound. These variants are rendered only in the translation of Raghunathan (1982, vol. 3, p. 76).

30. "scattered" *mṛditāḥ*: Literally, "crushed."

"trampled... crushed" *mathitāḥ*: Literally, "crushed, destroyed." We have used two English verbs to reflect the different agents of the various monkeys' destruction.

"by row upon row of chariots" *rathajālaiḥ*: Literally, "by networks *or* masses of chariots."

31. "harried from the rear" *hanyamānā jaghanyataḥ*: Literally, "being struck from behind." The term *jaghanya*, normally, "hindquarters, buttocks," is used here in a technical military sense of "rear guard of an army" (Apte s.v. *jaghanam*). See *MBh* 3.267.16; 6.46.54; 6.104.9,15; 9.18.34; etc.

32. "Apes and monkeys, all mixed together" *ṛkṣāḥ ... vānarais tu vimiśritāḥ*: Literally, "apes intermingled with monkeys." The idea here is that, in their panic, the army has broken ranks so that the different troops and species have become mixed up. For a discussion of the difference between *ṛkṣas*, "apes" [commonly rendered as "bears"], and *vānaras*, see 6.4.17 and R. Goldman 1989.

33. "many of the yellow-eyed monkeys have been slaughtered by innumerable evil-eyed *rākṣasas*" *piñgākṣās te virūpākṣair bahubhir bahavo hatāḥ*: Literally, "many tawny- *or* yellow-eyed ones were killed by many squint-eyed ones." D5,9–11,T1,3,M1,3, and the texts and printed editions of the southern commentators read *piñgalāḥ*, "tawny *or* yellow [monkeys]," for *piñgākṣāḥ*, "yellow-eyed [monkeys]." The half verse is somewhat ambiguous as it fails to identify clearly the killers and the killed. The texts and printed editions of Ct, Ck, and Cr substitute *rākṣasaiḥ*, "by *rākṣasas*," for *bahubhiḥ*, "by many," and we believe the intention of the passage is to continue the description of the slaughter of the monkeys by the *rākṣasas*. Cg and Cm, who read *bahubhiḥ* with the critical edition, understand that what we see here is monkeys whose vision may be impaired (*virūpākṣa*) killing other tawny monkeys, perhaps in panic. (*piñgalāḥ vānarāḥ*.

virūpākṣair vānaraiḥ.) This is not implausible in light of the preceding verse, where the monkey troops are represented as having lost all sense of order and discipline in their flight.

34. "Here, I have had them bring you his head" *idaṃ cāsyāhṛtaṃ śiraḥ*: Literally, "This head of his has been brought." The head actually does not appear in the presence of Sītā until verse 37 below.

35. "so that Sītā could hear him" *sītāyām upaśṛṇvantyām*: Literally, "while Sītā was listening."

38. "the long-tongued *rākṣasa*, Vidyujjihva" *vidyujjihvaṃ mahājihvam*: The poet continues to play upon the names and physical attributes of his characters. Vidyujjihva means "lightning-tongued."

39. "wretched woman" *kṛpaṇā*: A number of manuscripts (V,B2,D0–4,9–11,T1) and the texts and printed editions of Ct read the accusative *kṛpaṇām* for the critical edition's *kṛpaṇā*. This reading is reflected in those translations that follow the text of Ct. For them, the adjective *kṛpaṇām* must modify *avasthām*, "state, condition," rather than *sītām*, "Sītā." The meaning would thus be "Let her clearly see the pitiful final state of her husband."

40. "beautiful" *priyadarśanam*: Despite the sorry condition of the head referred to in verse 34 above, the head, as Ct notes, is just as beautiful as Rāma's own (*rāmaśirovat priyadarśanam ity arthaḥ*).

"swiftly withdrew" *kṣipram antaradhīyata*: Literally, "disappeared quickly." Several of the commentators read something into Vidyujjihva's rapid departure. Ct thinks Vidyujjihva withdraws so quickly because he has realized the impropriety of remaining for any length of time in the women's quarters (*apāgacchat strīgoṣthyāṃ sthātum ayuktatvadhīyeti bhāvaḥ*). Cr attributes a still higher motive to Vidyujjihva, arguing that his rapid withdrawal suggests that his compassion has been aroused by the mere sight of Sītā (*sītādarśanamātreṇa tasya dayotpanneti sūcitam*).

41. "threw down" *cikṣepa*: Ct, Cg, and Cm gloss, "he snatched (*ācakarṣa*)," with Cg supplying the additional phrase, "from Vidyujjihva's hand (*vidyujjihvahastād ity arthaḥ*)."

"famed throughout the three worlds" *triṣu lokeṣu vikhyātam*: Cg explains that the bow is renowned because it is, in fact, Viṣṇu's bow (*vaiṣṇavatvād iti bhāvaḥ*). This is presumably the bow that Rāma took from the hand of Rāma Jāmadagnya in the *Bālakāṇḍa* (1.75.4).

"and said this to Sītā" *sītām idam uvāca ha*: Ś,Ñ,V,B,D1–4,8–13,M1,2, and the texts and printed editions of Cr and Ct read instead *rāmasyaitad iti bruvan*, "saying, 'this is Rāma's.'"

42. "your precious Rāma" *tava rāmasya*: Literally, "Of your Rāma." We have added the ironic adjective to convey the contemptuous tone Rāvaṇa would use.

43. "When he . . . had flung . . . Rāvaṇa" *vinikīrya rāvaṇaḥ*: Literally, "Rāvaṇa having flung." D9–11 and the texts and printed editions of Ct read instead *vini*(*ca vi*—D9) *kīryamāṇaḥ*, "flinging down."

"and Vidyujjihva" *vidyujihvena saha*: Literally "with Vidyujihva." Several of the commentators note the irregular loss of the first "j" of the name.

"You must obey me." *bhava me vaśānugā*: Literally, "you must be submissive to me." See 6.23.1–3 for a theological explication of this verse by Cr.

The meter is *vaṃśasthavila*.

Sarga 23

1–3. Cm subjects this passage to a close and elaborate theological reading in which he argues that the Sītā who is being fooled by Rāvaṇa's trickery is really fictive and is described here only in keeping with the demands and conventions of the divine narrative. He notes that Rāvaṇa fully recognizes the divinity of the goddess and desires only death at Rāma's hands. Cm further argues, as he has done previously, that Rāvaṇa's solicitation of Sītā's favors here is actually a cryptic appeal for the grace and favor of the goddess. He claims that the allegations that Rāma is dead, etc., are merely a ruse to deceive the other *rākṣasas*, and he concludes by resorting to the *ekākṣarakoṣa*, according to which the syllable *mā*, "mother," refers to the goddess Lakṣmī (i.e., Sītā) and the syllable "*a*" refers to Viṣṇu (i.e., Rāma). Thus, he argues that Rāvaṇa's apparent demand that Sītā submit herself to his will in verse 6.22.43 is actually an exhortation to Sītā to remain always devoted to her lord, Viṣṇu (in the form of Rāma). Thus, he reads *bhava me vaśānugā* ("You must obey me") as "O Mā (Lākṣmī), always follow the wishes of 'A' (Viṣṇu)." Here he reads "*me vaśānugā*" as "*me 'vaśānugā*." (*vāstavārthas tu me vaśānugety atrāvaśānugeti chedaḥ he me lakṣmīḥ! avaśānugā asya viṣṇo rāmasya vaśam anugacchatīty avaśānugā bhavety arthaḥ*.) See notes to 5.18.4ff. See, too, 6.22.43; 6.37.9; and 6.48.13 and notes.

"alliance with Sugrīva that had been mentioned by Hanumān" *sugrīvapratisaṃsargam ākhyātaṃ ca hanūmatā*: See 5.33.47. As Ct notes, Sītā's prior knowledge of the alliance with the monkeys lends credence to Rāvaṇa's report of the devastation of the monkey host in verse 6.22.24 above (*hanūmatākhyātaṃ sugrīvapratisaṃsargaṃ sugrīvarāmasambandhaṃ rāvaṇakalpitavānaravadhasyopapādakam*). Cg is uncertain as to whether Sītā has heard about the alliance from Rāvaṇa or observed it directly. (*rāvaṇamukhāc chrutveti śeṣaḥ. yadvā dṛṣṭvā jñātvety arthaḥ . . . anyatra sākṣātkāraḥ*.)

"forehead" *keśāntadeśam*: Literally, "the place where the hair ends." We follow Cg, Cm, and Ct in reading this as a kenning for "forehead (*lalāṭa*)."

"crest-jewel" *cūḍāmaṇim*: At 5.36.52, the term refers to Sītā's hair ornament.

"Shrieking like an osprey" *krośantī kurarī yathā*: The image is a commonplace in the literature to represent lamenting women. Cf. 6.30.10–12; 6.39.9; 6.98.26; and notes; and also *Pratijñāyaugandharāyaṇa* iv.24. The male osprey (*Pandion haliaetus haliaetus* [*kurara*]) is particularly known for its piercing screams during the bird's elaborate aerial display at the time of courting and early incubation. See Fitzgerald 1998. Hammer (unpublished) in a detailed study argues that the *kurarī* is not, in fact, an osprey (*Pandion haliaetus*) but rather a curlew (*Numenius arquata orientalis*).

"Kaikeyī" *kaikeyīm*: Cr takes the name as an adjectival derivative (*taddhita*) referring to Kaikeyī's maidservant, Mantharā (*kekayīdāsīṃ mantharām*).

4. "I hope you are satisfied now, Kaikeyī" *sakāmā bhava kaikeyi*: Literally, "May you be one whose wish has been fulfilled, Kaikeyī!" Cr understands that Sītā is speaking with an ironic tone of voice (*kāku*) and thus means to say to Kaikeyī (by which he understands, as before, Mantharā) that her dreams, too, have come to naught (*kākvā tavāpi manoratho bhraṣṭa iti sūcitam*).

"You malicious creature!" *kalahaśīlayā*: Literally, "by you, whose nature is quarrelsome." Cg understands the epithet to mean that Kaikeyī's very purpose was to bring about the destruction of Rāma through the pretext of his temporary exile, and, in so doing, she has inadvertently brought about the destruction of the entire *Raghuvaṃśa*, whose members are dependent on Rāma. Thus, Kaikeyī has occasioned a perverse fulfillment of her plans. (*tvayā sarvaṃ kulaṃ raghuvaṃśa utsāditaṃ bhavati. tathā kulanandano 'yaṃ rāmo hataḥ. pravrājanavyājena rāmahananam eva tvayā saṃkalpitaṃ tad idānīṃ viparītaphalaṃ te jātam. kulatantubhūtarāmahananena tad ekaparāḥ sarve bharatādayo hatā eva kalaha eva te prayojanaṃ phalitam iti bhāvaḥ.*) Cf. 5.11.23–36, where Hanumān describes the potential destruction of the lineage in the event of the failure to find Sītā.

5. "Kaikeyī . . . she " *kaikeyyāḥ . . . tayā*: Literally, "of Kaikeyī . . . by her." M3 and the texts and printed editions of Cg substitute instead the vocative *kaikeyi*, "O Kaikeyī," and the pronoun *tvayā*, "by you" (printed editions only), thus making this verse a continuation of Sītā's direct address to Kaikeyī. Raghunathan, alone among the translators, renders this variant (1982, vol. 3, p. 77).

"from his home" *gṛhāt*: D5–7,10,11,T,M3, and the texts and printed editions of Ct, Crā, Ck, and Cg read instead *mayā*, which must then be construed, following Ct, as *mayā saha*, "along with me."

"in the barkcloth garments of an ascetic" *cīravasanas tayā*: Literally, "wearing *cīra* . . . by her." The word *cīra* normally refers to rags or tattered garments but is attested elsewhere in the sense of the barkcloth garments of an ascetic (cf. *KumāSaṃ* 6.93 and *ManuSm* 11.101). Our choice of reading is, of course, informed by 3.33.6–13, where Rāma, Lakṣmaṇa, and Sītā put on barkcloth garments. See, too, Emeneau 1988. D7,10,11, and the texts and printed editions of Ct and Cm read instead *cīravasanaṃ dattvā*, "having given [him] barkcloth garments."

6. "young woman" *bālā*: Literally, "child, girl." Cg understands that the term suggests Sītā's tenderheartedness (*mṛdubuddhir ity arthaḥ*).

"fell to the ground" *jagāma jagatīm*: Literally, "went to the earth." The term *jagatī* is slightly unusual in the sense of the ground under one's feet. As is suggested by Cg, and made clear in the following verse, we are to understand that Sītā has fainted (*mūrcchitety arthaḥ*).

7. "she heaved a sigh and regained consciousness" *samāśvasya pratilabhya ca cetanām*: In normal usage, *sam* + *ā* $\sqrt{}$*śvas* means "to regain consciousness *or* to take comfort." Thus, for example, Bhavabhūti uses it regularly to indicate that a character has regained consciousness (see, for example, *UttaRāC* 3.6.7; 3.8.5,6; 3.9.3; etc.). Here, in agreement with Cg, who understands, "having taken a breath (*ucchvāsaṃ prāpya*)," and, given the context, we are forced to take the gerund in its root meaning, "to sigh *or* breathe deeply."

"large-eyed woman" *āyatekṣaṇā*: Cg reads this stereotyped description of a beautiful woman to mean that Sītā, her vision blurred by tears, has had to open her eyes wide in order to see the head (*āyatekṣaṇāśrumiśratvena śirovalokanārthaṃ vistṛtalocanety arthaḥ*).

"kissed" *samupāghrāya*: V2,B3,D9–11, and the texts and printed editions of Ct read instead *samupāsthāya*, "having brought near *or* having approached."

8. "one who followed the code of the warrior" *vīravratam anuvratā*: Literally, "vowed to one whose vow is that of a hero." Many northern and southern manuscripts (D0,1,3,5,7,9–11,T3,M1–3) and the texts and printed editions of the southern commentators read instead the masculine vocative *vīravratam anuvrata*, "O you who are devoted to the vow of a hero," which would then refer to Rāma. Ct interprets *vīravratam* as "the firm vow to keep his father's words (*sudṛḍhaṃ pitṛvākyapālanavratam*)." Cr interprets the phrase as "O one whose character is to adhere to the heroic way of life (*vīrarītipālanaśīla*)." Cg glosses, "O one who has made a vow never to turn back

without having slain his foe (*vīravratam̐ śatrum ahatvā na nivartiṣya iti saṃkalpam anuvrata anuprāpta*)."

"I have now been made a widow and so must share this, your final state." *imāṃ te paścimāvasthāṃ gatāsmi vidhavā kṛtā*: Literally, "Made a widow, I have gone to this final state of yours [i.e., died]." The syntax and the exact sense of this sentence are unclear. Ct proposes supplying the word *nāśāt*, "because of death *or* destruction," to be governed by the enclitic pronoun *te*, yielding the sense "Because of your death, I have come to this final condition, that is, I have been made a widow. (*te tava nāśād imāṃ paścimāvasthāṃ gatāsmi. tām avasthām āha vidhavā kṛteti.*)" Cr, Cm, and Cg, on the other hand, derive the sense of the participle *gatā* from the root $\sqrt{}$*gam* in its meaning of "to know *or* perceive." They thus understand Sītā to be saying, "I have seen your final state and thus have been made a widow. (*gatāsmi dṛṣṭavaty asmi. gatyārthā jñānārthā iti nyāyāt. ato vidhavā kṛtā*—so Cg.)" These commentators may have been influenced by the construction in verse 6.22.39 above, where Rāvaṇa orders Vidyujjihva to make Sītā witness her husband's final state. Our translation is influenced by the northern reading "*iyaṃ te paścimāvasthā hatāsmi vidhavā kṛtā* (Such is your final state; having been made a widow, I am destroyed)." The sense is that Sītā, witnessing the apparent death of Rāma, cannot continue to live and, as a *pativratā*, must follow him in death.

9. "because of the wife's lack of virtue: *nāryāḥ* . . . *vaiguṇyam*: We follow the interpretation of Cg, Cm, and Ck, who put forward the culturally sanctioned cliché that holds the wife accountable for her own widowhood (*prathamaṃ bhartur maraṇaṃ bhāryādoṣanimittakaṃ bhavati*). Ct and Cr gloss *vaiguṇyam*, "lack of virtue," as *anarthaḥ*, "calamity," understanding that the prior death of a husband is the greatest calamity that can befall a woman (*mukhyo 'narthaḥ*). Cg suggests that the verse can be read in two ways. The first of these, which we follow, has Sītā questioning the traditional wisdom in that, since she sees herself as having been an exemplary wife, she cannot understand how Rāma could have predeceased her. She thus may be seen as blaming Rāma. (*suvṛttas tvaṃ sādhuvṛttāyā mamāgrataḥ saṃvṛtto mṛtaḥ katham idaṃ saṃgacchata iti bhāvaḥ. asmin pakṣe na suvṛttapadasvārasyam.*) As an alternate reading, Cg suggests that Sītā is, in essence, accepting blame for her husband's death (*yadvā bhavanmaraṇasya maddoṣa eva hetur ity āha*).

"departed" *saṃvṛttaḥ*: Given the clear context, we must agree with the majority of the commentators in understanding this term in the unusual sense of "died." Cr reads *saṃvṛtaḥ*, "hidden, obscured," which he glosses as *tirohitaḥ*, "hidden," which here, also somewhat unusually, must mean "dead." This reading is unattested as a variant in the critical apparatus, or in any of the printed editions consulted, except for the 1930 edition of NSP (6.32.9); but compare the 1888 edition of NSP, which reads with the critical edition.

10. "While I . . . am sunk in an ocean of grief" *magnāyāḥ śokasāgare*: The syntax of the verse, with its unresolved genitive construction in *pādas* a and b, has puzzled the commentators. Cm and Ct propose adding the phrase *mama maraṇam eva varam*, that is, "for me [who am sunk] . . . death would be preferable." Cr proposes adding the phrase *mama duḥkham avalokya* in the sense of "[you, Rāma], having seen the distress of me [who am sunk]." Cg, whom we follow here, reads the first half of the verse as a genitive absolute in keeping with *Pā* 2.3.37, which he quotes, glossing it with the parallel locative absolute. One can perhaps read this as a kind of *anādaraṣaṣṭhī* (*Pā* 2.3.38) in which Sītā could be seen as blaming Rāma for allowing himself to be slain while attempting to rescue her.

"from one sorrow to another" *duḥkhād duḥkham*: Cg details the sequence of sorrows that Sītā has had to endure, including the exile to the forest, her abduction by Rāvaṇa, and, finally, the death of her husband. A few *devanāgarī* manuscripts and the texts and printed editions of Ct and Cr read instead *mahad duḥkham*, "great sorrow."

11. "now like a loving cow bereft of her calf" *vatseneva yathā dhenur vivatsā vatsalā kṛtā*: Literally, "like a loving cow made calf-less by her calf." The pathetic image of a cow bereft of its calf is used frequently to describe Kausalyā when bereft of Rāma, as well as to refer to other women in similar circumstances. See 2.34.4; 2.36.7; 2.38.16–17; 2.68.24–25; and notes. See, too, 6.39.9 and note. Apparently to avoid the awkwardness of *vatseneva . . . vivatsā*, "like [one] calf-less by a calf," D9,11, and the texts and printed editions of Ct replace the phrase *vatseneva*, "as if by a calf," with the phrase *vatsalā te*, "so loving toward you."

12. "Your valor was beyond imagination . . . who" *yair acintyaparākrama*: Literally, "O you of unimaginable valor! . . . by whom."

"who foretold a long life for you" *ādiṣṭaṃ dīrgham āyus te yair*: Literally, "by whom long life was foretold of you." Cg notes that those brahmans who had predicted a long life for Rāma did so only on the basis of their observation of his valor and not on the basis of their consultation of the *śāstras* (*acintyaparākramety anena te parākramaṃ dṛṣṭvā tair uktaṃ na tu śāstraṃ dṛṣṭveti gamyate*). By using the term *śāstras*, Cg is no doubt referring to the scientific texts on astrology (*jyotiḥśāstra*) and bodily signs (*sāmudrikaśāstra*). See 5.33.11–20 and notes.

D7,10,11, and the texts and printed editions of Ct and Cr substitute, for *pāda* a, *dai(de*—D11*)vajñair api rāghava*, "O Rāghava, even by the fortune tellers *or* astrologers."

"for your life has been cut short" *alpāyur asi*: Literally, "you are one of little life span."

13. The verse is slightly elliptical and somewhat ambiguous, and the commentators have proposed a variety of interpretations. We believe that the basic meaning is that Sītā, puzzled that so wise and clever a person as Rāma could have fallen into the *rākṣasas'* trap, thinks that he must have been befuddled by fate or doom. This is in keeping with the popular maxim *vināśakāle viparītabuddhiḥ*, "at the appointed hour of doom one's mind becomes befuddled." The verse also relies on the popular metaphor of Kāla (Time, Death) "cooking" all creatures, in the sense that Kāla leads all creatures to maturity and finally death. See *MBh* 1.1.188, 17.1.3, and *Maitrāyaṇī Upaniṣad* 6.15 (*kālaḥ pacatīti bhūtāni*).

"Or . . . ?" *atha vā*: We agree with the critical edition and the suggestion of several of the commentators (Ct, Ck, and Cs) that the common indeclinable *athavā*, "or," should be read as two words, *atha* and *vā*. These commentators understand *atha* as a question marker (*athaśabdaḥ praśne*) and take *vā* in the sense of *athavā* (*vā athavā*). The notion, as expressed by some of the commentators, is that Sītā, having raised the question of the inaccuracy of the astrologers' predictions in the previous verse, now rejects that notion and introduces the concept of an imponderable fate beyond the ability of wise men to predict.

"did your wisdom fail you, even though you were so wise" *naśyati prajñā prājñasyāpi sataḥ*: According to Ct and Ck, the idea here is that, owing to some lapse or failure of wits, Rāma fell asleep and so fell into the power of his enemies (*prajñādaurbalyāt supto 'rivaśaṃ prāpta iti śeṣaḥ*). Cg and Cs suggest that perhaps it is not Rāma who has lost his wits but the astrologers themselves, who, according to Cg, were no match for Rāma's evil destiny (*athavā teṣām anṛtavāditvaṃ nāsty eva kiṃ tu tavaiva bhāgyaviparyāsāt teṣām api prajñā naṣṭeti pakṣāntaram avalambate*).

"who creates all beings" *bhūtānāṃ prabhavaḥ*: Literally, "the source of beings." Most of the commentators whom we follow take *prabhavaḥ* in its common meaning of "source *or* origin." Thus, Cs explains, "Kāla is both the creator (*utpādakaḥ*) and destroyer (*saṃhārakaḥ*) of creatures."

"leads them inevitably to destruction" *pacaty enam*: Literally, "he cooks *or* ripens him."

14. "unforeseen death" *adṛṣṭaṃ mṛtyum*: Literally, "unseen death." Commentators generally take the adjective *adṛṣṭaṃ*, "unseen," in the sense of "unexpected (*ajñātam*—Ct, Cr, Ck)." Cg, however, understands it to mean "[unforeseen] because of [Rāma's] having been asleep (*sauptikatvāt*)."

15. "Having fallen into my clutches" *saṃpariṣvajya*: Literally, "having embraced."

"I who am... Kālarātri, the dark night of universal destruction" *kālaratryā mayā*: Literally, "by me, Kālarātri." Cg describes Kālarātri as "a certain female divinity (*śakti*) who carries off all creatures (*kālarātrir nāma sarvabhūtāpahāriṇī kācana śaktiḥ*)." Through the use of this metaphor (*vyastarūpaka*, or "uncompounded" metaphor, according to Cg [see Gerow 1971, s.v. *asamastarūpaka*, p. 245]), Sītā is blaming herself for her husband's death. Notably, in an earlier context, Hanumān has described her in exactly the same way when warning Rāvaṇa of the destruction Sītā will ultimately bring to the city of Laṅkā (see 5.49.33 and note). See Sutherland 1989. A few manuscripts and the texts and printed editions of Cg and Cv appear uncomfortable with the metaphor, substituting the genitive *mama* for the instrumental *mayā*. This, as Cg proposes, should be read as the ablative *mattaḥ*, "from me," yielding the sense "who has been taken away from me by Kālarātri." Among the translators consulted, only Raghunathan (1982, vol. 3, p. 77) and Gita Press (1969, vol. 3, p. 1478) follow Cg's reading. Cg notes the critical reading and its interpretation as a variant.

"you, a lotus-eyed hero" *tvam... kamalalocanaḥ*: Literally, "you, a lotus-eyed one." V3,D0,3,13,T1,2,G2,3,M, and the texts and printed editions of Cm and Cg read the vocative *kamalalocana*. Cg remarks on the propriety of the epithet here, noting that Rāma was taken away by Kālarātrī (v.l. Kālarātri), literally, "the night of Kāla," because of his lotus eyes. The allusion is to the well-known fact that lotus blossoms are closed at night. Cg identifies the figure here as a metaphor, *rūpaka*, supported by the figure *parikara*, in which each modifier of a noun lends a particular meaning (see Gerow 1971, s.v. *parikara*, p. 203).

"thus" *tathā*: Cg suggests that this phrase is used to avoid the inauspiciousness and sense of revulsion that would arise if Sītā had referred directly to the severing of Rāma's head (*śiraśchedāder aślīlatvena tathety uktam*).

16. "to my misery" *māṃ... tapasvinīm*: Literally, "miserable, *or* pitiable, me."

"bull among men" *puruṣarṣabha*: Cg argues that this term is used here to illuminate the impropriety of the treachery suggested in this verse on the part of so well-bred and noble a hero (*anena dakṣiṇasya śaṭhatvam anucitam iti dyotate*).

"lie in the embrace of the earth, as if she were a beautiful and beloved woman" *upaśeṣe... priyām iva śubhāṃ nārīṃ pṛthivīm*: Literally, "you lie [on] the earth, which is like a beloved, beautiful woman." The syntax seems elliptical, and we follow the suggestion of Cs, who supplies the gerund *āliṅgya*, "having embraced." D9–11,G2, and the texts and printed editions of Ct and Cr read *iha śeṣe*, "you lie here," for *upaśeṣe*. Cr understands the indeclinable *iha* to mean "at this time (*asmin samaye*)." Cs understands *iha* to refer to "the land protected by the *rākṣasas* (*rakṣorakṣitakṣitau*)."

M3 and the texts and printed editions of Cg correct the ellipsis by reading *samāśliṣya*, "having embraced," for *śubhāṃ nārīm*, "beautiful woman." This yields the sense "having embraced the earth, as if a beloved, [you lie]." This variant is rendered by the translation of Raghunathan (1982, vol. 3, p. 77).

D5,9–11,M5, and the texts and printed editions of Ct read *yathā*, "just as," for *śubhām*, "beautiful." This reading is redundant with the *iva* of *pāda* c.

Cg takes *priyām*, "beloved," as a comparative adjective, glossing, "beloved in comparison with me (*mattaḥ priyām*)." This idea is represented in a number of translations.

18. "blameless hero" *anagha*: Literally, "O one without sin." Cs notes that this epithet suggests the propriety of [Rāma's] attainment of a heavenly world accessible [only] through meritorious action (*anena puṇyalabhyasvargagatiyogyatāṃ sūcayati*).

"and with your other ancestors as well" *pūrvaiś ca pitṛbhiḥ*: Literally, "and with previous fathers." Cs, referring to a text he identifies as the *Aitareyabhāṣya*, quotes a passage to the effect that all one's male ancestors may be designated by the term *pitṛ* (*pitāmahādyāś ca pitaro nāma kīrtitāḥ*). D5–7,9–11,T1,G3,M, and the texts and printed editions of the southern commentators read *sarvaiḥ*, "with all [your forefathers]," for *pūrvaiḥ*, "with previous [fathers]."

19. The verse exhibits a number of variants across the numerous recensions, each of which presents problems of construction and interpretation. The situation is exacerbated in the critical edition, which collocates variants that appear to be found together in no printed edition or commentator's text. See Sutherland 1992.

"You have become a shining star" *nakṣatrabhūtas tvam*: The reading appears to be shared by the majority of southern manuscripts, with the exception of the textual tradition associated with Ct, Cr, and Ck, who, with most northern manuscripts (Ś, Ñ,V,B,D0–4,8,10–13), read "*nakṣatrabhūtaṃ ca* (Ñ,V1,B2–4—*tu*;V2,3—*tvam*)." In this latter variant, the distinction of becoming a star or constellation belongs not to Rāma but to his entire lineage (*rājarṣivaṃśam* in *pāda* c). Ct and Ck explain that the entire Ikṣvāku lineage is accorded this distinction by virtue of the accomplishment of their legendary ancestor Triśaṅku through the application of the "*chatrinyāya* (the 'maxim of the man with the umbrella,' where there is the ascription of a quality of a single member to an entire group) (*triśaṅkos tathātvāc chatrinyāyena vaṃśasya tathātvam*—so Ct)." It will be recalled that the Ikṣvāku dynast Triśaṅku attains the status of a *nakṣatra* at *Bālakāṇḍa* 59. It is a commonplace of epic and later Indian literature that individuals who acquire great merit in their lifetimes may become stars in the firmament until their good *karma* has been exhausted (see, for example, 5.15.20). See 6.4.44 and 6.60.24 and notes. Cr, on the other hand, understands the compound to modify the noun *karma*, "action," in *pāda* b. He thus explains, "you who have accomplished a great feat, which itself has become a shining star in heaven. That is, it shines brightly everywhere (*yena tvayā divi nakṣatrabhūtaṃ sarvatra prakāśamānam ity artho mahat karma kṛtam*)." This interpretation is followed by Gita Press (1969, vol. 3, p. 1478). Cs appears to be aware of this reading and, quoting Ct, offers it as an alternative, understanding the phrase to modify *rājarṣivaṃśam*, "the royal lineage of the Ikṣvākus." This interpretation of the reading *-bhūtam* is found in Gorresio (1856, vol. 9, p. 221) and among translators of the texts and printed editions of Ct, for example, Roussel (1903, vol. 3, p. 91) and Shastri (1959, vol. 3, p. 79). Cg, who reads with the critical edition, glosses "become a shining star in the sky" as "mounted in a celestial flying chariot (*vimānasthaḥ san*)." *Vimānas* are the typical vehicles from which the gods and other celestial beings survey events on earth. See notes to 5.6.4 and 5.7.18.

Cs takes this opportunity to offer one of his idiosyncratic alternative readings in which he separates the word *nakṣatra*, "constellation," into *na* and *kṣatra*, that is, "not belonging to the *kṣatriya-varṇa*, 'warrior class.'" He then argues that, although Rāma was born in a kshatriya lineage, he has transcended the status of a mere kshatriya because there are no kshatriyas to equal him even in heaven. This superiority to ordinary royalty is, Cs suggests, also applicable to Rāma's wider lineage in that its dynasts, such as Daśaratha, etc., regularly consort with Indra and the other divinities. It is this fact, indeed, that entitles the lineage to the qualifier *puṇyam*, "holy." (*yanmahatkarmakṛtaṃ bhuvi tadvaṃśasthātiriktakṣatrabhūtaṃ kṣatrajātyutpannasaṃbaddhaṃ kṣatrabhūsaṃbaddhaṃ neti kiṃ vaktavyam. divy api tādṛśaṃ tatrāpy etat sadṛśaḥ kṣatriyo nāsti tannakṣatrabhūtaṃ kṣatrabhūyiṣṭaṃ neti vā. daśarathādibhir indrādisāhitīkaraṇād iti bhāvaḥ. etādṛśaṃ puṇyaṃ rājarṣivaṃśam upekṣase.*)

"great and pleasing deed that you performed" *mahat karma kṛtaṃ priyam*: Given the reading of the critical edition and the way in which it separates the words, placing a space between *karma* and *kṛtam*, which follows the printed editions of Ct, Cr, and Ck, we are inclined to follow Cr's reading in regarding the clause as elliptical. Like Cr, we have supplied the words "that you [performed] (*yena tvayā*)." Cr, however, understands the adjective *priyam*, which we have translated as "pleasing," to modify not the deed performed by Rāma but rather his royal lineage. He thus gives the terms the sense "dear *or* beloved." Ct and Ck read the three words as a compound, *mahatkarmakṛtam*, which would then modify their reading *nakṣatrabhūtam*, "the state of being celestial bodies," which these commentators, as indicated above, ascribe to Rāma's entire lineage. Their interpretation is, then, "You have acquired the status of a shining star by means of that great feat." They understand the feat in question to be Rāma's famous adherence to his father's word (*mahatā pitṛvacaḥpālanarūpeṇa karmaṇā*). Cv and Cs understand *mahatkarma* to be a *tatpuruṣa* compound either in the sense of "performing the feats of the great (*mahatāṃ karmakāriṇam*—so Cv)" or "a feat of the great (*mahatām karma*—so Cs)."

Cg, Cm, and Crā have a different reading, *mahatkarmakṛtām*, which here is a genitive plural. Cg takes the compound in the sense of "[that merit] that belongs to those who have performed great deeds (*mahākarmakṛtām*)." Cg notes that the *karmadhāraya mahatkarma* is an epic irregularity for the Pāṇinian *mahākarma* (*ātvābhāva ārṣaḥ*).

Cm and Crā avoid the grammatical problem by reading *mahat* nominally in the sense of "great persons." Cm reads the compound as a *dvandva* to mean "of those great men and those who have performed [good] actions (*mahantaś ca te karmakṛtaś ca teṣām*)" and thus sees this as governing the adjective *priyam*, which he takes to mean "desirable" and which he sees as referring to the Ikṣvāku lineage.

"you . . . ignore" *samupekṣase*: Manuscripts and the southern commentators are divided as to whether to read as the critical edition does in the sense of "you neglect, ignore, disdain" (so Cm, Ct) or some variant of *samavekṣase* in the sense of "you see, survey, look down upon" (so Ś,Ñ,V,B,D0–5,8,12,13,G1,2,M1,2,5, and the texts and printed editions of Cg and Ck). Among the commentators consulted, Ct, Cr, Cm, and

Cs read with the critical edition, while Cg and Ck read the variant. The issue is whether Sītā is rebuking Rāma for having abandoned his lineage on earth by ascending to the heavens or whether he has ascended to the heavens for the purpose of seeing his departed ancestors there. Thus, Ct glosses, "having abandoned, you depart (*tyaktvā gacchasi*)." Cr sees an implicit critical question, adding the interrogative "why [do you neglect your own royal lineage]? (*kim artham*)." Cg glosses, simply, "you see (*paśyasi*)." Ck is similar. Cm, reading with the critical edition, offers no explanation. Cs, while reading with the critical edition, appears to offer both alternatives plus a third option of his own. Thus, he offers an interpretation similar to that of Ct, whose interpretation he also quotes in full. But he also raises the possibility that Rāma has gone to heaven in order to see his royal lineage, headed by his father, etc. Cs then adds yet another twist to this verse by offering the possibility of taking the term *rājarṣivaṃśam* as Sītā's reference to her own noble lineage, the Janakavaṃśa, which she accuses Rāma of insulting by his failure to take her along with him to the heavens. (*mahatkarmakṛtaṃ puṇyam rājarṣivaṃśaṃ pitrādikaṃ yathā rāma īkṣase paśyasi. tatra gataḥ. tathā puṇyam ātmano mama rājarṣivaṃśaṃ janakavaṃśam. kim upekṣase madanayaneneti vā.*)

Roussel (1903, vol. 3, p. 91) understands Sītā to be saying that Rāma disdains to rejoin his holy lineage of royal seers. In this interpretation, he is followed by Shastri (1959, vol. 3, p. 79) and Pagani (1999, p. 944). Pagani, who follows the text of the GPP with its three commentators (Ct, Cr, and Cg), amplifies this interpretation in a note (p. 1657) in which she claims that the commentators understand that Rāma neglects his lineage because he has died without an heir. We are unable to locate any commentary that says anything even remotely like this.

20. "I was but a girl and you yourself a mere boy" *bālāṃ bālena*: Literally, "a girl by a boy." Cr, alone among the commentators, understands the term *bālā* to mean "ignorance" and appears to suggest that it was through Sītā's ignorance [perhaps of the fact that she would be widowed so early] that she was acquired by Rāma (*bālāṃ samprāptāṃ māṃ bālena mamājñānena hetubhūtena kiṃ na prekṣase*). See notes to 2.17.26 and 3.45.10, dealing with the ages of Rāma and Sītā.

D6,T2,3,G2,3,M, and the texts and printed editions of Cg and Cm read *bālyena*, "by childhood." Raghunathan (1982, vol. 3, p. 78), the only translator consulted to render this, understands, "whom you wedded as a youth."

21. " 'I will be with you forever.' " *cariṣyāmīti*: Literally, "I will go *or* I will wander." We follow Cg and Cm, who supply the phrase "with you (*tvayā saha*)." Ct, Cr, and Ck do so as well but also add a direct object for the root √*car*, "to move," namely, "religious activities, etc. (*dharmādikam*)." They thus read √*car* in the sense of "to do *or* perform," having evidently in mind the common kenning for a spouse, *dharmasahacārin*; *-cāriṇī*. The ellipsis is easily understood in light of the final word of the preceding verse where Sītā describes herself as Rāma's "*sahacāriṇī* (lifelong companion)."

"you . . . took my hand in marriage" *gṛhatā pāṇim . . . tvayā*: Literally, "by you taking the hand." The reference is to the ancient custom in the Hindu wedding ceremony of *pāṇigrahaṇa*, in which the bride and groom grasp hands and circumambulate the ritual fire (see Kane 1974, vol. 2, pt. 1, p. 427).

22. "abandoned me . . . leaving me" *mām apahāya . . . tyaktvā mām*: Several of the commentators are disturbed by the redundancy and seek either to eliminate or explain it. Cr argues that the verbal root √*hā*, "to abandon," when preceded by the *upasarga apa* and having the sense of "motion" need not be interpreted to mean

"leave," its common meaning. Thus, Cr glosses the phrase *mām apahāya*, "having left me," as *vana ānīya*, "having brought me through the forest," thereby avoiding the redundancy. Cg reads the gerund *tyaktvā* to refer to Sītā and supplies as its object *tvām*, "you," thus yielding the sense "having left me who had left you." Cs offers a similar interpretation but reverses the referents of the two gerunds. He also suggests that the redundancy here reflects the excess of Sītā's grief, quoting a passage to the effect that speech uttered in jest or lamentation is meaningless. (*"duḥkhātiśayād vā punaruktiḥ. parihāse pralāpe ca vāg anarthāpi dṛśyate" anarthā nirarthā.*)

"resourceful hero" *gatimatāṃ vara*: Literally, "O best of those endowed with motion *or* alternatives." The precise sense of the epithet is not entirely clear here, and it is probable that it is used primarily to echo the participle *gataḥ*, "gone away," which immediately precedes it. Translators have offered a variety of explanations, such as Dutt's simple, but opaque, "best of goers" (1893, p. 1194); Raghunathan's "you who aim at the highest of goals" (1982, vol. 3, p. 78); Gita Press's "O jewel among the resourceful" (1969, vol. 3, p. 1478); and Roussel's "*le plus sensé*" (1903, vol. 3, p. 94), echoed by Shastri's "the wisest of Sages" (1959, vol. 3, p. 79) and Pagani's "*toi le plus avisé des hommes d'ici-bas*" (1999, p. 944). These last three reflect the sense found in the northern recension, *matimatāṃ vara*, "foremost among the wise," which itself is probably a gloss on the southern reading. Cf. Gorresio 1856, vol. 9, p. 222 and our Introduction, pp. 115–16.

23. "Your body" *śarīraṃ te*: Ck, wishing to be technically correct, notes that this is the headless trunk of Rāma (*kabandharūpam ity arthaḥ*).

"accustomed to" *ucitam*: D5–7,9–11,T3,G1,2,M1,2, and the texts and printed editions of Ct, Cr, and Ck read instead *ruciram*, "beautiful."

"only the finest things" *kalyāṇaiḥ*: Commentators differ as to what is being referred to here. Ct and Cm simply gloss, "auspicious things (*maṅgalaiḥ*)." Cr explains, "many auspicious ministrations (*anekamāṅgalikopacāraiḥ*)." Cg offers two alternatives: "excellent sandalpaste, etc., or golden ornaments (*śubhaiś candanādibhir vā suvarṇābharaṇair vā*)."

"embraced by me alone" *pariṣvaktaṃ mayaiva*: Cg notes that the phrase demonstrates Rāma's monogamy, adding the words "and by none other (*ananyayā*)." Even though this is a relatively unusual characteristic among the Indian epic heroes, it is rarely highlighted or mentioned in the commentaries.

"dragged and torn apart" *viparikṛṣyate*: Literally, "dragged apart and about." We have used the two verbs in an effort to render the sense of the two *upasargas*, *vi* and *pari*.

24. "You performed the vedic rites" *yajñair iṣṭavān*: Cg, striving to be technically correct, notes that Rāma would only properly perform the vedic rites after ending his period of life as a forest renunciant. He further notes that, in the *Ayodhyākāṇḍa*, Rāma did not offer vedic sacrifices before going into the forest. According to Cg, Sītā is lamenting that Rāma has been cut off in the midst of life and thus has been denied the opportunity to perform his ritual duties as a householder and so be eligible for the last rites of the vedic religion. (*atra vanavasāt pūrvam agnyādhānādyabhāvāt tannivṛttyanantaram ādhānāgniṣṭomādikam anuṣṭhāya paścātkramaprāptāyuravasāne yajñīyāgnibhiḥ saṃskāraṃ prāptuṃ yogyas tvaṃ katham evaṃ madhye maraṇaṃ prāpto 'sīti bhāvaḥ.*)

"Agniṣṭoma" *agniṣṭoma-*: This is the name of a *soma* sacrifice typically performed in the spring as part of the Jyotiṣṭoma sacrifice. See Kane 1974, vol. 2, pt. 2, pp. 1134–1203; and Renou 1954, p. 4.

"purificatory rite of cremation" *saṃskāram*: The term here can carry either or both the senses of 1) purification and 2) a vedic rite of passage, in this case specifically the *antyeṣṭi*, or funerary ritual.

"in the sacred fire" *agnihotreṇa*: Literally, "by means of the *agnihotra*." *Agnihotra* is the name of a particular oblation to the fire god, Agni, but is used frequently to refer to the sacrificial fire itself. See Kane 1974, vol. 2, pt. 2, pp. 998–1008; and Renou 1954, pp. 4–5.

25. "sorrowfully longing" *śokalālasā*: Literally, "[she] longing in grief." Cg glosses, "[she] stupefied with grief (*śokamandā*)."

"will now have to question" *paripraksya*(D7,11—*kṣa*)*ti*: Literally, "she will ask." Ś2,Ñ,V,B1–3,D7,9–11,13,T,G1,3, and the texts and printed editions of Ct, Ck, and Cr read instead *paripreksyati*, "she will see."

"who, alone . . . will return" *ekam āgatam*: Literally, "one [who has] come." Cs notes that Sītā's understanding is correct based on Rāvaṇa's statement at 6.22.23 above, where he tells her that Lakṣmaṇa has fled with the surviving monkeys (*"diśaṃ pravrājitaḥ sarvair lakṣmaṇaḥ plavagaiḥ saha" iti lakṣmaṇasya jīvatvokter īyam uktir yuktā*).

27. "and that I am living in the *rākṣasa*'s household" *māṃ ca rakṣogṛhaṃ gatām*: Literally, "and me, gone to the house of a *rākṣasa*."

"she will die of a broken heart" *hṛdayena vidīrṇena na bhaviṣyati*: Literally, "with a shattered heart, she will not exist."

Following verse 27, Ś,D1–3,5–13,S (G3 after verse 28) insert a passage of two lines [484*]: "For the sake of a worthless wretch like me,[1] the king's son Rāma, who did not deserve this,[2] has crossed the mighty ocean only to drown in a puddle.[3]"

[1]"For the sake of a worthless wretch like me" *mama hetor anāryāyāḥ*: Literally, "because of ignoble me."

[2]"who did not deserve this" *anarhaḥ*: Cg and Crā point out that Sītā means that Rāma did not deserve such a death, that is, in his sleep (*etādṛśasauptikavadhānarhaḥ*). D5,9–11,T1,G2,M5, and the texts and printed editions of Ct read instead *anaghaḥ*, "sinless, irreproachable."

[3]"has crossed the mighty ocean only to drown in a puddle" *sāgaram uttīrya . . . goṣpade hataḥ*: Literally, "having crossed the ocean was killed in a cow's hoofprint." As several of the commentators point out, this is a proverbial metaphorical expression. The sense is that Rāma, having slain formidable foes such as Khara, has been slain by an insignificant foe, Prahasta (*kharatarakharādīn hatvā kṣudreṇa prahastena hata ity arthaḥ*).

Following 484*, D1,2,5–7,9–11,S continue with a passage of four lines [485*]: "It was out of delusion that the son of Daśaratha married me, a disgrace to my own family. I was born to be the death of my noble lord, Rāma, in the guise of his wife.[1] Indeed, I think I must have once[2] prevented some great gift,[3] since now that I have become the wife of him for whom all the world is a guest,[4] I am left here to grieve."

[1]"I was born to be the death of . . . Rāma, in the guise of his wife" *rāmasya bhāryā mṛtyur ajāyata*: Literally, "a wife was born as Rāma's death *or* death was born as Rāma's wife."

[2]"Indeed, I think I must have once" *nūnaṃ manye mayā jātu*: D6,7,T2,3,G1,M3, and the texts and printed editions of the southern commentators read instead *nūnam anyāṃ mayā jātim*. According to this reading, which is followed by all the translators of the southern recension, the sense is "Surely, I must have prevented some great gift in a previous birth." According to the southern commentators, Sītā feels that she has failed to make some significant gift, presumably to the brahmans, in a previous life. The commentators understand the accusative *jātim* either as a locative (so Ct, Cr, Cg, second alternative) (*anyāṃ jātim anyasmiñ janmani*—so Cg) or as the object of an implicit gerund, "having obtained (*prāpya*—so Cg, first alternative)."

[3]"[I must have]... prevented some great gift" [*mayā*] ... *vāritaṃ dānam uttamam*: Cg notes that the reference would be to the gift of a girl in marriage (*kanyādānam*), while Ct adds to this the prized gifts of cattle, land, and gold (*kanyādānaṃ gobhūhiraṇyādi-dānaṃ ca*).

[4]"for whom all the world is a guest" *sarvātither iha*: Literally, "having everyone as a guest here." Commentators vary in their understanding of this obscure epithet. Ct and Ck understand it to mean "affectionate toward all guests" and construe it with the following adverb *iha*, "here," in the sense of "at the proper time and place (*sarvātithi-priyasyeha kāle deśe ca*)." Cr understands it to mean "for whom everyone is a guest, that is, a supplicant (*sarvo 'tithir yācako yasya*)." Cg offers two possible interpretations: 1) "he for whom all are guests, that is, the protector of all (*sarve 'tithayo yasya tasya sarvātitheḥ sarvarakṣitur ity arthaḥ*)," and 2) "he who reverences every guest (*sarvātithipūjakasyeti vārthaḥ*)." Cv and Cm agree with Cg's second interpretation.

28. "But enough of this!" *sādhu*: We take the term as an interjection. The idea is that Sītā has now finished the lamentation for her departed lord and turns her thoughts to actually joining him in death. Other translators have tended to take the term either in its other sense as an interjection, "very well" (Roussel 1903, vol. 3, p. 92; and Pagani 1999, p. 944), or adverbially in the sense of "done well *or* properly" (Gita Press 1969, vol. 3, p. 1479; Raghunathan 1982, vol. 3, p. 78; and Gorresio 1856, vol. 9, p. 222). Some translations, for example, those of Dutt and Shastri, appear to ignore the term completely.

"Please... let me throw myself upon" *pātaya mām* ... *upari*: Literally, "[you] make *or* let me fall upon *or* over." Virtually the entire northern recension, as well as all *devanāgarī* manuscripts collated for the critical edition and all printed editions consulted with the exception of some texts associated with Cg (D5–6, VSP, KK), reads instead *ghātaya*, "[you] have [me] slain." Cr explains the syntax as "Place me on top of Rāma and have me slain." In either case, it is clear from the succeeding verses that Sītā is expressing a wish to accompany her husband in death.

29. "Join my head with his head, and my body with his body" *śirasā me śiras cāsya kāyaṃ kāyena yojaya*: The separate mention of the head and the body perhaps reflects Sītā's understanding that Rāma has been beheaded. Cr, the only commentator to hint at this, glosses, "the remainder of [his] body (*śeṣaśarīram*)" for "body (*kāyam*)."

"I shall follow" *anugamiṣyāmi*: This appears to be a clear allusion to the practice of *anugamana*, by which a wife follows her husband shortly after his death. It is a variant of the more infamous practice of *sahagamana*, or so-called suttee. One also sees here a reference to the vedic funerary rite in which the wife lies down on or near the body of her deceased husband but arises before the actual cremation. Cf. *RV* 10.18.7.

"I do not wish to live for even another moment, wicked woman that I am." *muhūrtam api necchāmi jīvituṃ pāpajīvitā*: This line, *pādas* ef, and the following two verses belong mainly to the northern recension (being omitted in D5,7,9–11,T1,3,G,M1,2,5). The editor of the *Kumbakonam* edition includes these lines in his numbered running text (KK 6.32.33–34) but encloses them in brackets, noting that these verses are not found in older manuscripts, only in modern ones. (*idaṃ śloka-dvayaṃ prācīnakośeṣu na dṛśyate. auttarāhapāṭha eva dṛśyate*). The editor of VSP relegates the entire passage to a footnote after his verse 32 (VSP 6.32.32*, p. 254), noting that it is added in some manuscripts (*ity adhikaḥ pāṭhaḥ keṣucit pustakeṣu dṛśyate*). Given this textual history, the inclusion of these five lines in the critical text seems highly suspicious. The lines probably should have been relegated to the apparatus or, at the very least, marked as an uncertain reading. One wonders if the choice to include the lines was made because they express the normative and stereotypical portrayal of Indian wifehood.

30. See note to verse 29 above.

31. See note to verse 29 above.

32. "large-eyed lady" *āyatekṣaṇā*: See note to verse 7 above.

"daughter of Janaka" *janakātmajā*: M3 and the printed editions of Cg read instead *ca punaḥ punaḥ* for *janakātmajā*. This is rendered by Raghunathan (1982, vol. 3, p. 79) as "[as she looked] again and again."

"there" *tatra*: Cg glosses, "in the region before [her] (*purodeśe*)." Northern manuscripts, some southern manuscripts, and the texts and printed editions of Ct, Ck, and Cr read instead *caiva* [or *cāpi*], "and."

33. "lamenting bitterly" *lālapyamānāyām*: Cg takes the reference to Sītā's lamentation as a departure point for a brief theological excursus. He anticipates an objection to the effect that, since Sītā [although she is the goddess] weeps and laments at the sight of her husband's severed head, just like some ordinary mortal woman, she ought by rights to die of grief and shock in the same fashion. He explains that this is not the case because the divine couple share a common state of being (*parasparasattā*), which is keeping Sītā alive, since, in fact, there has been no injury to her husband. He notes that this shared state of existence does not necessarily translate into mutual consciousness. By this we understand him to see Sītā's lamentations as genuine, for she does not really know that her husband is alive. (*nanu laukikīṣu kācid iva sītā bhartṛśiraḥsākṣātkāro 'pi ciraṃ ruditvā vilapya kathaṃ jīvitaṃ dhārayati sma. ucyate. atra yayor divyadampatyoḥ parasparasattaiva jīvitadhāraṇe nimittaṃ na tu jñānājñāne. ato bhartṛjīvitavaikalyābhāvāt sā jīvati sma.*) See notes to verses 41 and 42 below, where Cm and Ct express a different view as to the nature of Sītā's knowledge of the truth.

"sentry" *anīkasthaḥ*: Literally, "one situated in the army." The term is often used for a guard or sentry. Cm, Ck, Ct, and Cg gloss, "guardian of the gate (*dvārarakṣī*)," while Cr glosses, "a type of spy *or* secret agent (*cāraviśeṣaḥ*)."

34. "May my lord be victorious" *vijayasvāryaputra*: Literally, "O son of the noble one, be victorious." Ct, Ck, and Cm note that although the term *āryaputra* is normally used as a wife's stereotypical mode of address to her husband, we are to understand it here as a generic term of respect [reading *ārya* in the sense of nobleman, master, etc.] (*āryaputraśabdo yady api strībhir bhartari prayujyate prāyeṇa tathāpi pūjāmātre sāmānyataḥ prayogo 'pi bodhyaḥ*). Cs breaks the *sandhi* of the sequence *vijayasvāryaputra* to read *vijayasva* + *aryaputra* and then glosses the latter term as *svāmiputra*, "son of my master,"

citing *Amarakośa* (3.3.106) for this sense of *arya*. With his typical ingenuity, he also offers a different separation of the compound as *ari* + *aputra*, which he then reads as a *bahuvrīhi* compound in the sense of "one who renders his enemies sonless." He concludes by saying that his reading and alternate explanations avoid the confusion engendered by the reading *āryaputra*, which, he insists, is invariably used in a marital context. (*aryaputra svāmiputra "syād aryaḥ svāmivaiśyayoḥ" ity amaraḥ. arayo 'putrā yeneti vā. tenāryaputreti patiṃ prati bhāryā saṃbodhanasyaiva sarvatra sattvena katham evam iti śaṅkānavakāśaḥ.*) See 6.102.35 and notes. Cf. 6.61.19 and note.

35. Following 35ab, D5–7,9–11,S insert a passage of two lines [490*]: "Desiring an audience, he [Prahasta] has sent us,[1] lord. Surely, your majesty, it must be a matter that demands the attention of the king.[2]"

[1]"has sent us" *vayaṃ prasthāpitāḥ*: Literally, "we have been sent." Cg suggests that since it is most improbable that a group of messengers would be admitted to the inner apartments, the sentry [erroneously] uses the plural out of fear. (*vayam iti. bhayena bahuvacanam. bahūnām antaḥpure samāgamāsambhavāt.*) D7,9–11,M1,2, and the texts and printed editions of Cr and Ct read instead *ahaṃ prasthāpitaḥ*, "I have been sent."

[2]"it must be a matter that demands the attention of the king" *rājabhāvāt kṣamānvitam*: Literally, "because of the nature of the king, [it] is accompanied by *or* associated with forbearance." The phrase is awkward and obscure, and our translation follows the somewhat labored explanation of Cv, Cg, and Cm, who share this reading. Cg explains, " 'because of the nature of the king' means 'because of the fact of being king.' 'Associated with forbearance' means 'that because of the urgency of action at that moment, there is an expectation of your command because you are the king.' (*rājabhāvād rājatvād dhetoḥ. kṣamānvitaṃ tadānīm eva kartavyatveti tava rājabhāvāt kṣamayā tvadājñāpratīkṣaṇenānvitam.*)" Ct, Ck, and Cr read the *facilior* vocative *kṣamānvita*, which they and those translators who follow them interpret as part of an interjection, "O you who are forbearing because of your kingly nature (*he kṣamānvita rājabhāvād rājadharmād dhetoḥ*—so Cr)."

36. "to grant an audience to his counselors" *mantriṇāṃ darśanaṃ yayau*: Literally, "he went to the sight of his counselors." Ct, Ck, and Cm suggest supplying the gerund *uddiśya*, "with reference to *or* for the purpose of," which would then govern the accusative *darśanam*, "sight *or* audience." Cr glosses, "[went] in order to see (*avalokanārtham*)."

37. "counselors" *mantribhiḥ*: Ct and Ck editorialize by supplying the adjective *duṣṭa-*, "corrupt, evil."

"knowing full well the martial valor of Rāma" *viditvā rāmavikramam*: Cr notes that he would have learned this from the mouths of his spies (*cāramukhād avagatya*).

40. "assembled before him" *avidūrasthitān*: Literally, "standing not far off."

"eager to act on his behalf" *hitaiṣiṇaḥ*: Literally, "desiring well-being."

41. "with the loud beating of *bherī* drums sharply struck with drumsticks" *bherīninādena sphuṭakoṇāhatena*: See 6.17.31–33; 6.24.19; and notes.

"but do not tell them why" *vaktavyaṃ ca na kāraṇam*: Literally, "and the reason is not to be stated." Ct explains, "say only that the king has issued a summons, but do not tell its purpose (*rājāhvayata ity etāvad eva vaktavyaṃ na tu etad artham itīti bhāvaḥ*)." Cv, Cg, and Cm understand Rāvaṇa's thinking here to be that if the commanders proclaim throughout the city that the troops are to go forth to battle, Sītā will inevitably hear this and understand that Rāvaṇa's story about the destruction of Rāma's army was a lie (*yuddhārthaṃ niryāteti pure pravadanti ced balādhyakṣās tadānīṃ devyāḥ sannidhau kathitaṃ svakīyaṃ rāmasainyavadhavṛttāntavākyam asatyam iti tasyā viditaṃ syād iti bhāvaḥ*—so Cg).

Cm goes on to observe that the real meaning of Sītā's lament in verses 1–32 above is that, even though she is fully aware that Rāma's head and bow are illusory, she engages in this elaborate feigned lamentation in order to deceive the *rākṣasas*. (*"sā sītā tacchiro dṛṣṭvā tac ca kārmukam uttamam" ity ārabhya "iti sā duḥkhasaṃtaptā vilalāpāyatekṣaṇā" ity antānāṃ sītāpralāpavākyānāṃ vāstavārthe 'yam āśayaḥ. sītāpi rāmaśiraādikaṃ māyākalpitaṃ jñātvāpi tat satyam iti matveva mithyāpralāpādinā rākṣasān vañcayituṃ bahuvidhaṃ pralapati.*) Note that this idea is at variance with the ideas Cg expresses about divinity and omniscience at verse 33. See, too, Ct's comments to verse 42 below.

42. "the commanders of the troops... each his own vast host" *balādhipās te mahad ātmano balam*: D7,9–11, and the texts and printed editions of Cr and Ct read instead *tadaiva dūtāḥ sahasā mahad balam*, "then [his] emissaries immediately [assembled] a vast host."

The meter is *vaṃśasthavila*.

Ct concludes his remarks on this *sarga* by noting that we are to understand that Sītā's lamentations here are simply for the purpose of demonstrating her human nature (*atra sītāpralāpaḥ svasya mānuṣadharmaprakaṭanāyeti bodhyam*). This, of course, bears on the whole question of the ambiguous nature of the *avatāra*, especially in the case of Rāma (see Pollock 1991, pp. 15–67; and Goldman and Goldman 1996, pp. 29–30, passim). Compare the comments of Cg on verse 33 and Cm on verse 41 above.

Sarga 24

1. "Saramā" *saramā*: The commentators are in general agreement that this is the wife of Vibhīṣaṇa and a woman deeply devoted to Sītā. (*vibhīṣaṇapatnīyaṃ saramā. sā tu sītāyāṃ bhaktimatī*—so Ct.) Ct, Cm, and Ck argue that we are to understand that Saramā has been deputed by Rāvaṇa to console Sītā since he fears that her delicate nature might succumb to the intense badgering to which he has subjected her (*sā hi rāvaṇena jñātasāttvikābhāvātībhartsanena nāśam āśaṅkya sītāśvāsanārthaṃ saṃdiṣṭeti bodhyam*—so Ct).

"dear friend" *praṇayinī sakhī*: D1,4,6,T1,G,M3,5, and the texts and printed editions of Cg, Cm, and Crā read the accusatives *praṇayinīṃ sakhīm*, which would then refer to Sītā rather than Saramā. This reading is rendered only in the translation of Raghunathan (1982, vol. 3, p. 79).

Following verse 1, D5–7,9–11,S insert a passage of two lines [496*]: "Then soft-spoken Saramā consoled Sītā, who had been deluded by the lord of the *rākṣasas* and therefore was afflicted with the deepest sorrow."

2. All the commentators consulted raise the question of how a *rākṣasa* woman could possibly offer friendship and consolation to Sītā. They find the rationale for this in the present verse. It should be noted, however, that Saramā is not the only *rākṣasa* woman to act protectively or to show sympathy toward Sītā during her captivity. Others

include Trijaṭā (5.25.4–7ff.), Saramā's own daughter, Analā (5.35.11), and Rāvaṇa's queens (5.20.10–12).

"instructed by Rāvaṇa" *rāvaṇādiṣṭā*: According to Cr, Rāvaṇa has instructed Saramā to protect Sītā from the vicious (*krūra*) *rākṣasa* women. The abuse and threats that these *rākṣasa* women direct toward Sītā is graphically described in the *Sundarakāṇḍa* (*sargas* 21–23) (*krūrarākṣasībhyo rakṣaṇāya rāvaṇenājñāpitā*). Ck is more specific, arguing that Rāvaṇa has instructed Saramā to protect Sītā at all times and by all means, fearing that she might otherwise die as a result of the abuse of the *rākṣasa* women (*sā hi saramā rāvaṇena rakṣārthaṃ sandiṣṭā sarvathā sarvadā bhartsanādau naśyatīti vicārya rāvaṇenaiva samāśvāsanārtham ādiṣṭā*). Cg, Cm, and Cv extend this idea somewhat by claiming that Rāvaṇa has ordered Saramā to look out for Sītā's general well-being (*yogakṣema*). Crā, however, is skeptical about the whole matter. He notes that, although we are clearly meant to understand from the passage that Rāvaṇa has assigned Saramā the task of protecting Sītā, it would also seem quite inappropriate for the demon king to have given orders to his brother's wife. Crā also sees a contradiction between the idea that, on the one hand, Saramā appears to be acting as an agent of Rāvaṇa, while on the other, she is represented below (verses 4–5) as eavesdropping on Rāvaṇa's conversation with Sītā. There she is said to have concealed herself out of fear of Rāvaṇa and appears to be assisting Sītā of her own volition and against Rāvaṇa's interests. Crā admits to being unable to resolve this contradiction and invites the learned to consider how to do so. (*upari sakhīsnehena tadbhīru mayā sarvaṃ pratiśrutam. līnayā gahane śūnye bhayam utsṛjya rāvaṇād iti rāvaṇabhayād gūḍhāvasthānena rāvaṇoktavākyaśravaṇaṃ ca pratīyate. vibhīṣaṇabhāryāyā rāvaṇena niyogo 'nucita iva pratibhāti. rāvaṇaniyuktatve tadbhayād gūḍhāvasthānam anupapannam iti pratīyate. atra parihāro vidvadbhiś ca cintanīyaḥ.*) See Ck's comments to verses 4–5 below, where he uses similar wording in the same connection. This would suggest that Ck was, in fact, reading, or familiar with, Crā.

"compassionate" *sānukrośā*: Cr sees Saramā's compassion for Sītā to be a direct consequence of Rāvaṇa's having instructed her to protect the latter (*sītāviṣayakadayāviśiṣṭā sā saramā rakṣamāṇayā sītayā mitraṃ kṛtā*).

"firm in her vows" *dṛḍhavratā*: Ct, Ck, and Cm take the adjective to mean that Saramā has firmly vowed to guard Sītā even with her life (*prāṇair api mameyaṃ rakṣaṇīyeti dṛḍhapratijñā*). Cg understands it to indicate that her friendship for Sītā was undying (*anena sakhyasyāpracyutir nirdarśitā*).

3. "her friend" *sakhīm*: Ś1,V,B1,D4,9–12, and Ct, Cr, and Ck read instead the nominative *sakhī*, which would then refer to Saramā instead of Sītā.

"covered with dirt" *dhvastām*: The commentators are divided as to how to understand this polysemic adjective. Ct, Cm, and Ck understand, "oppressed by grief [in the case of Sītā] and by the fatigue of a long journey [in the case of the mare to which Sītā is being compared] (*pīḍitām adhvaśrameṇa śokena* ca—so Ct)." Cv, Cr, and Cg, however, understand the term in its other sense of "covered with dust or dirt (*dhūlyupahatām*)." We prefer the latter interpretation because of the specific reference to Sītā's rolling in the dust in *pāda* d, an image reinforced by the closely similar description of Kausalyā at 2.17.18, where the queen is described as having rolled on the ground like a mare in her grief at learning of Rāma's exile.

"like a mare that had been rolling in the dust" *upāvṛtya . . . vaḍavām iva pāṃsuṣu*: Vālmīki is fond of equine similes to describe women, particularly when they are overwhelmed by sorrow. As noted above, Kausalyā is similarly described at 2.17.18; Sītā herself is compared to a filly rolling on the ground at 5.24.2. In other contexts, Kausalyā is compared to a mare approaching her colt in delight at 2.17.9, while the women of Rāvaṇa's harem are compared to fillies relieved of their heavy loads at 5.7.43. D6,T2,3,M3,5, and the texts and printed editions of Cg read *pāṃsulām*, "dusty," for the critical edition's *pāṃsuṣu*, "in the dust," despite its redundancy with Cg's interpretation of *dhvastām*. Ct and Ck understand that the mare would roll in the dust to relieve fatigue (*śramaṇanāśārthaṃ luṭhitvā*).

4–5. "Sītā" *tām*: Literally, "her."

Following 4ab, D5,T1,M3, and GPP, KK, and VSP insert a passage of one line [498*]: "Take heart, Vaidehī, do not despair!"

"Timorous lady, in my love for you, my friend... I overheard everything" *sakhīsnehena tad bhīru mayā sarvaṃ pratiśrutam*: The texts and printed editions of Ct either omit or bracket this line. This creates an awkward and defective reading. Dutt (1893, p. 1196) glosses over the issue by partially including the line, while Roussel (1903, vol. 3, p. 93), Shastri (1959, vol. 3, p. 81), and Pagani (1999, p. 945) omit the line entirely. Gita Press (1969, vol. 3, p. 1481) and Raghunathan (1982, vol. 3, p. 80) read and translate the line.

"I overcame my fear of Rāvaṇa" *bhayam utsṛjya rāvaṇāt*: Literally, "having abandoned my fear of Rāvaṇa." The commentators continue to exhibit concern over the apparent contradiction between Saramā's role, on the one hand, as a friend and confidant of Sītā, and, on the other, as an agent of the latter's tormentor, Rāvaṇa. Ct raises the question of how, after the banishment of Vibhīṣaṇa, his wife, Saramā, could have come close enough to Rāvaṇa to overhear his private conversations with Sītā. His explanation is that Saramā had previously overheard the history of the illusory head and bow (*māyākṛtavṛttāntam*) and had subsequently hidden herself in order to protect Sītā. Saramā claims that she never had any fear of Rāvaṇa, since he had appointed her to guard Sītā and because she was a member of his own race (*tava rakṣaṇe niyuktatvāt tajjātitvāc ca*). Because of the seeming contradictions here, Ct and Cg note that some authorities think there is a second Saramā (*tato anyaivaiṣā sarametу anye*). Ck certainly offers such a solution, and Ct's reference may well be to him. Cr raises another contradiction. If, he asks, Saramā had to conceal herself to overhear Rāvaṇa's words, how then could she claim to have overcome her fear of him? Cr proposes that what Saramā means to say is that, since she had no fear of Rāvaṇa when it came to aiding Sītā, she was able to discover the reason for Rāvaṇa's hasty departure. (*nanu līnaśravaṇe 'pi rāvaṇāt kuto na bhītir ity ata āha. tava hetoḥ tvatprayojanasiddhyarthaṃ rāvaṇān me bhayaṃ nāsti. ata eva yatkṛte yad arthaṃ sasaṃbhrānto rāvaṇo niṣkrāntas tat sarvam abhiniṣkramya bahir gatvā me mama viditam.*) See note to verse 6 below.

Ck's interpretation is similar to Ct's. However, he amplifies it somewhat by suggesting that what is meant is that someone other than Saramā was appointed to guard Sītā. Acknowledging the seeming insolubility of the conundrum, he suggests that it should be left to the learned to figure out the solution (*atra parihāro vidvadbhiś cintyaḥ*). See Crā's similar comment above on verse 2. Note that Ck is perhaps ridiculing Crā in that he actually offers a response to the rhetorical question. Ck offers his own idiosyncratic solution according to which someone other than Saramā, hidden in a thicket out of fear of Rāvaṇa, has blurted out the words quoted by Saramā (*saramāntaroktatve bhayān nilayajalpastutasya*). The authentic sense, according to Ck, is that the speaker had merely conquered the power of Rāvaṇa's illusion, not his or her fear of the demon king (*mohamātram utsṛjya rāvaṇād iti pāṅktatvāt*).

Cg raises a different question, asking how Saramā, if not present at the time of [Sītā's] encounter with Rāvaṇa, could have overheard their conversation. He suggests that she was concealed in the hollow of a tree [preferring the v.l. *gagane*, "in the sky," for the critical reading *gahane*, "in a thicket"]. He then raises the question of why, just because she was in a deserted spot, she would have lost her fear of Rāvaṇa. He explains, as does Cr, that she places Sītā's welfare above her own life. (*tadānīm asannihitayā tvayā katham śrutam ity atrāha līnayeti. līnāya cchannāya gagane kutra cit tarurandhre gahana iti pāṭha āvṛtta ity arthaḥ. śūnye nirjane katham ghorād rāvaṇād bhayaṃ tyaktaṃ tatrāha taveti. tava hetos tvannimittaṃ me jīvitam api na priyam.*) Cg now raises the same contradiction raised by Crā at verse 2 above, viz., that it would have been inappropriate for Rāvaṇa to employ his brother's wife, but that if she had been so employed, she could have hardly had to hide from him while discharging her duties. Cg's explanation relies on the change in circumstances between the time of Saramā's employment while her husband, Vibhīṣaṇa, was still in good standing in Rāvaṇa's court, and now, when he had been banished. Cg argues that, although Saramā was originally appointed to become an intimate friend of Sītā's to look after her well-being, now, after her husband's exile, she would have cause to fear her brother-in-law. Alluding to the issue of social propriety, Cg further notes that Saramā's appointment would have been conveyed to her through the mouth of a servant woman, and that Rāvaṇa, regarding her as his younger sister-in-law [*snuṣā*, literally, daughter-in-law], would not have spoken to her directly. Cg concludes by noting that some authorities understand that the reference is to another Saramā. (*nanu vibhīṣaṇabhāryā kathaṃ sītārakṣaṇe rāvaṇena niyogārhā niyoge vā kathaṃ tasyā rāvaṇabhayād gūḍhāvasthānam. ucyate. vibhīṣaṇāvasthānakāle sītāyogakṣemaparāmarṣāyāntaraṅgabhūtā saramā niyuktā. tannirgamanād idānīm antaraṅgavartāśravaṇe bhītāsīd iti na virodhaḥ. niyogaś ca dāsīmukhenādarśanaṃ ca snuṣātvād iti ca bodhyam. anyeyaṃ sarametу eke.*)

Cs raises the question of how the wife of Vibhīṣaṇa, who could not remain in Rāvaṇa's confidence, could have been in a position to overhear his private conversation. He explains that she would have had no fear of Rāvaṇa despite the fact that he was cruel and an enemy of her husband, since she would have thought, "What could he do to a woman?" Her concealment, however, Cs proposes, would not so much result from her fear, which she had overcome, but from her shame or modesty [which she felt toward her brother-in-law]. (*nanu vibhīṣaṇabhāryātvena tvaṃ tattvatas tena na viśvasanīyeti kathaṃ saṃkathanaṃ śrutaṃ bhavaty ety* [*sic*] *ata āha. līnayeti. śūnye janaiḥ. gahana itarāparijñātasthāne. rāvaṇabhayam utsṛjya krūro 'pi rāvaṇo ramaṇaripur api yoṣitaḥ kiṃ karotīti bhītiṃ tyaktvā nīlāyanaṃ tu bhāvatvād rāvaṇasya lajjayeti bhāvaḥ.*)

"For, wide-eyed lady, I would gladly die for your sake." *tava hetor viśālākṣi na hi me jīvitaṃ priyam*: Literally, "on your account, O you of wide eyes, life is not dear to me." Cg sees the epithet as highly meaningful here, explaining that the inner meaning of the passage is "Having seen the beauty of your eyes, how could I bear your suffering? (*tatra hetur viśālākṣīti tava nayanasaundaryaṃ paśyantyā me kathaṃ tvatpīḍā soḍhavyeti bhāvaḥ*)."

6. "Then, when the overlord of the *rākṣasas* had departed, Maithilī, I followed after him and learned the whole reason for his agitation." *sa saṃbhrāntaś ca niṣkrānto yatkṛte rākṣasādhipaḥ / tac ca me viditaṃ sarvam abhiniṣkramya maithili*: Literally, "Going out,

Maithilī, I learned the whole reason why the overlord of the *rākṣasas* had left in a state of agitation." Rāvaṇa departed at 6.23.36. See Cr's comments on verses 4–5 above.

7. Several of the commentators are evidently disturbed by the way in which this verse seems to break the narrative sequence of Saramā's report. The point is that where one expects Saramā to tell Sītā the reason for Rāvaṇa's sudden departure, she now appears to go back and reveal to her the nature of the deception he had attempted to perpetrate. Thus, Ck and Ct note the narrative disjuncture (*tasya paścād api kathane bādhakābhāvenādau rāmamohaṃ nivartayati*). Cs, reading Saramā's thoughts, renders them as: "Since it [the reason for Rāvaṇa's departure] is not really urgent, I will tell you about it later (*atyanāvaśyakatvād anantaraṃ vadiṣyāmi*)."

"It would be impossible to slay... in his sleep" *na śakyaṃ sauptikaṃ kartum*: The phrase is elliptical, and we have followed the commentators, who take the term *sauptika* either in its adjectival meaning, "pertaining to sleep," adding a noun such as "battle, slaying, etc." to complete the sense (*sauptikaṃ suptau maraṇam*—so Cg, Cv) or in its nominal meaning in the sense of "night raid *or* an attack on sleeping men (*suptikālayuddham*—so Ct)," the way in which it is used in the tenth *parvan* of the *Mahābhārata* (Ct, Ck, Cm, Cr). The reference here is to Rāvaṇa's false claim (6.22.22) that Prahasta had beheaded Rāma in his sleep.

"ever-vigilant" *viditātmanaḥ*: Ct and Ck explain, "having vanquished such mental defects as sleepiness, laziness, etc. (*jitanidrālasyādidoṣacittasyety arthaḥ*)"; Cr explains, "knowing the nature of the *rākṣasas* (*jñātarākṣasasvabhāvasya*)." Cs, who gives the critical reading as a variant, glosses, "whose effort will prove successful (*viditātmana iti pāṭhe vidito 'yaṃ phaliṣyatīti jñāta ātmā yatno yena sa tathety arthaḥ*)." See notes to 6.92.25 and 6.31.58.

"no one can kill" *vadhaś ca . . . naivopapadyate*: Literally, "and slaying is not possible." Ct, Cg, and Ck, whom we have followed, take the statement to be a general one in the sense that Rāma is invincible because of his superiority to all others in valor (*sarvātiśāyiśauryavati*—so Ct). Cm and Cs distinguish between the term *sauptika*, "[killing someone] asleep," and *vadhaḥ*, "slaying," which they take to mean killing someone who is awake. (*sauptikaṃ karma suptamaraṇam. vadho jāgradavasthāyāṃ hananam*—so Cm.) They thus understand Saramā to be saying that Rāma cannot be killed either while sleeping or while awake.

8. Saramā is referring to Rāvaṇa's false description of the slaughter of the monkey hosts at 6.22.19–31 above.

"Nor would it be possible to kill" *na . . . hantuṃ śakyāḥ*: Cr and Cs attribute the invulnerability of the *vānaras* solely to Rāma's protection (*rāmeṇa surakṣitāḥ*), while Cg sees it as a consequence both of Rāma's power and their own (*svabalād rāmabalāc ca*).

"who use trees as weapons" *pādapayodhinaḥ*: Literally, "tree warriors."

"by Indra, bull among the gods" *devarṣabheṇa*: Literally, "by the bull among the gods." According to the normal epic topos, one would take this as a reference to Indra, the king and chief warrior of the vedic gods. The only commentators who remark on the epithet (Cr, Cs) understand this, however, to be a reference to Viṣṇu.

9–11. For descriptions of Rāma's qualities and virtues, see translations and notes to 1.1.8–19; 2.1.15–26; and 5.33.12–20.

"muscular" *-vṛtta-*: Literally, "rounded, stout."

"fierce in valor" *pratāpavān*: Literally, "possessed of heat, splendor, *or* heroism."

"powerfully built" *saṃhananopetaḥ*: Literally, "endowed with [bodily] firmness."

12. "whose every thought and deed is reprehensible" *ayuktabuddhikṛtyena*: Literally, "by him of improper thought and deed." We follow the commentators in analyzing the compound as a *bahuvrīhi* whose final member is a *dvandva*.

13. "Put all your grieving behind you." *śokas te vigataḥ sarvaḥ*: Literally, "All your sorrow has departed." D5,6,11,M1, and the texts and printed editions of Ct and Cr read *sarva-[kalyāṇām]* for *sarvaḥ*, thus making the adjective "all" apply not to Sītā's grief but to her impending happiness.

"Lakṣmī herself is smiling upon you." *tvāṃ bhajate lakṣmīḥ*: Literally, "Lakṣmī favors *or* chooses you."

"which will delight you" *prītikaraṃ*: D7,9–11, and the texts and printed editions of Ct and Cr read instead *te bhavati*, "of you . . . my lady."

15. "I myself have seen" *dṛṣṭo me*: Ck proposes fleshing out the verse with a phrase explaining that Saramā has been able to observe Rāma by exploiting her power to fly through the air (*khacaritvād bahir nirgatyeti śeṣaḥ*). Ct accepts this as a possible explanation but suggests as an alternative that Saramā might have climbed to a turret on her housetop to observe Rāma (*svagṛhavartyūrdhvagṛham āruhya iti śeṣaḥ*).

"who has practically accomplished his mission" *paripūrṇārthaḥ*: Literally, "who has fulfilled his purpose." It is unclear what Saramā is referring to specifically. She may be alluding only to Rāma's success in crossing the formidable ocean with his forces or, as we have translated, to her certainty of Rāma's impending defeat of Rāvaṇa and rescue of Sītā. Only Cs among the commentators consulted addresses this term. He explains Rāma's success as inhering in his "having treated the lord of *rākṣasas* as insignificant (*alakṣyīkṛtarakṣodhyakṣatvāt*)."

"guarded" *rakṣitaḥ*: We follow Cr in understanding *balaiḥ*, "by the forces," as subjects of the root $\sqrt{}$*rakṣ*. Ct and Ck take a different view, understanding that Rāma is protected "by his own immense power (*svamahimnā*)," understanding *balaiḥ* as an instrumental of accompaniment.

"by his massed forces" *sahitaiḥ . . . balaiḥ*: We read the adjective *sahitaiḥ* with Ct, who glosses *saṃgataiḥ*, "gathered together." Cs accepts this, glossing *militaiḥ*, "assembled," but also proposes the alternative *sa-hitaiḥ*, in the sense of "well-wisher, benefactor."

16. "Rāvaṇa" *anena*: Literally, "by him."

"Rāghava has crossed the ocean" *rāghavas tīrṇaḥ*: Literally, "Rāghava has crossed."

17. "took counsel" *mantrayate*: According Ct, Ck, and Cm, one should supply a phrase such as "having gone out from here (*ito nirgatya*)."

18. "while the *rākṣasa* woman Saramā was speaking in this fashion, she and Sītā heard" *iti bruvāṇā saramā rākṣasī sītayā saha / . . . śuśrāva*: Literally, "As the *rākṣasī* Saramā was speaking thus, she, together with Sītā, heard." We follow Cg, who suggests that we are to read the phrase "with Sītā (*sītayā saha*)" from *pāda* b with the finite verb *śuśrāva*, "she heard," rather than with the more proximate present participle *bruvāṇā*, "was speaking" (as Cr suggests). Although this reading is metrically somewhat dislocated, it has some things to recommend it. For example, the formulaic use of the present participle *bruvāṇā*, which is common in Vālmīki, rarely governs this type of prepositional phrase. Moreover, the use of this phrase with *bruvāṇā* suggests a conversation or dialogue, whereas, up to this point, we have seen only a monologue on Saramā's part.

"dreadful sound" *śabdam . . . bhairavam*: Given the description of the beating of drums, the harnessing of battle animals, and the preparations of the armies in the following verses, we are inclined to understand the sound in question to be the clatter and commotion of a large body of soldiers arming for war. Ct and Cm, however, understand the sound to refer specifically to the leonine bellowing (*siṃhanādam*) of the troops. This interpretation has been followed by Dutt (1893, p. 1197), Shastri (1959, vol. 3, p. 82), and Roussel (1903, vol. 3, p. 94). Cf. 6.57.47; 6.62.38; and notes.

"fully preparing themselves for war" *sarvodyogena*: Literally, "by every effort."

19. "*bherī* drums" *bheryāḥ*: See 6.17.31–33; 6.23.41; and notes.

20. "timid woman . . . terrifying . . . sound of the *bherī* drum . . . its" *bhairavā bhīru bherikā / bherī-*: Literally, "terrifying, O timid [woman], *bherī* drum, of the *bherī* drum." The poet seems to attempt to echo the sound of the drumbeats with his extended alliteration (*anuprāsa*) of the consonant *bh* through *pādas* b and c. See note on verse19 above.

"call to arms" *saṃnāhajananī*: Literally, "bringing about preparations for battle."

21. "are being made ready" *kalpyante*: Cr explains that the elephants are being fitted with their various equipment so that they can proceed into battle (*gamanārthaṃ racanāviśeṣair yujyanta ity arthaḥ*). Cg understands *ākalpyante*, which he glosses in the sense of "being ornamented *or* being caparisoned (*alaṃkriyante*)."

"Everywhere" *tatra tatra*: Literally, "there [and] there." Cr explains, "in their assigned place (*niyojitapratiṣṭhāne*)."

"foot soldiers" *padātayaḥ*: D6,7,9–11,T2,3, and the texts and printed editions of Ct and Cr read instead *sahasraśaḥ*, "by the thousands." This substitution eliminates an explicit substantive so it is not clear to what the adverb *sahasraśaḥ* refers. Cr, the only commentator to address this issue, refers it back to the rutting elephants in *pāda* a, while most translations that follow the text of Ct see it as a reference to warriors.

"forming their ranks" *saṃpatanti*: Literally, "rushing together, gathering."

Following 21ab, D5–7,9–11,S insert a passage of one line [509*] in which the fourth division of the traditional fourfold army, the cavalry, is mentioned: "Thousands of swift horsemen, lances in hand,[1] are in a state of excitement.[2]"

[1]"horsemen, lances in hand" *turagārūḍhāḥ prāsahastāḥ*: Literally, "[men] mounted on horses, having *prāsas* in hand." We have translated *prāsa* elsewhere as "dart" (see, for example, 5.41.11; and 6.41.24–25 and note), but that does not seem to fit the context here.

[2]"in a state of excitement" *hṛṣyante*: Literally, "they are excited, rejoice." The texts and printed editions of Ct, Ck, and Cr read instead *dṛśyante*, "they are seen."

22. "rushing, roaring . . . rushing, roaring" *vegavadbhir nadadbhiś ca*: The participles clearly refer to both the soldiers and the torrents of water, and we have therefore repeated them.

23–24. "from the *rākṣasas'* . . . and ornaments" *bhūṣitānāṃ ca rakṣasām*: B1,D9,10, and the texts and printed editions of Ct read instead *rākṣasendrānuyāyinām*, "of the followers of the lord of the *rākṣasas*."

"shining" *prasannānām*: Literally, "bright." The idea here, according to Ct, is that the weapons are bright from having been sharpened on whetstones (*śāṇollekhananirmalānām*) and, according to Cr, polished (*saṃskṛtatvena nirmalānām*).

"Just look at the . . . radiance . . . as they glitter" *prabhāṃ visṛjatāṃ paśya*: The syntax is a bit awkward. We have followed the suggestion of Cg, Cm, Ck, and Ct in understanding *prabhām*, "radiance," to be the object of both the participle and the finite verb. Cg alternatively offers a way to avoid the awkward syntax by proposing to break the participle *visṛjatām*, "releasing, emitting," into the imperative *visṛja*, "release," and the demonstrative pronoun *tām*, and then to supply the word *śokam*, "grief," as the direct object of the imperative. This reading would yield something like "behold the radiance . . . and abandon your grief."

"It looks like a blazing forest fire in the hot season." *vanaṃ nirdahato gharme yathā rūpaṃ vibhāvasoḥ*: Literally, "like the appearance of a fire burning a forest in the hot season."

Following verse 23, D7,9–11, and the texts and printed editions of Ct and Cr insert a passage of one line [511*]: "It is the uproar of the swift and frenzied *rākṣasas*."

Published editions of Ct either omit (NSP) or bracket without numbering (GPP) verses 24cd–26ab. Gita Press, however, includes the passage (6.33.26cd–28ab). Ck notes that these two *ślokas* are interpolated into some manuscripts (*atra madhye kvacic chlokadvayaṃ prakṣiptam*). Ct agrees with this textual judgment and quotes Ck.

25. "of the bells" *ghaṇṭānām*: Cg thinks that these are the bells worn by war-elephants (*gajaghaṇṭānām*).

"the rumbling of the chariots" *rathānām . . . nisvanam*: Literally, "the sound of the chariots." Cg understands the reference to be to the sound made by the friction of the wheel rims (*nemisaṃghaṭṭanajam*).

"the neighing of the war-horses" *hayānāṃ heṣamāṇānām*: Literally, "of the neighing horses." The phrase is elliptical, omitting any clear direct object of the finite verb *śṛṇu*, "listen." Commentators resolve the ellipsis in one of two ways. Cr proposes reading *nirghoṣam*, "clanging, sound," from *pāda* a to refer to the noise of both the bells and the horses. In a similar vein, Cg proposes to employ *anuvṛtti*, "repetition," to read *nisvanam*, "sound," of *pāda* b with *hayānāṃ heṣamāṇānām*. Alternatively, Cg, somewhat more ingeniously, proposes breaking the participle into *heṣam*, "the neighing," and *āṇānām*, "making noise, sounding," which would yield "the neighing of the neighing [horses]."

"like the blaring of trumpets" *tūryadhvaniṃ yathā*: Literally, "like the sound of *tūryas*." Apte, PW, and Monier-Williams (s.v., respectively) all understand the term to refer only to a type of musical instrument. Dutt (1893, p. 1198) and Raghunathan (1982, vol. 3, p. 81) both take the term to mean a type of drum, while Gita Press (1969, vol. 3, p. 1482) understands the term, as we do, to refer to trumpets, which seems more appropriate given the simile. See, too, 6.90.27–28. Cf. 6.116.24.

26. "the frenzied preparations" *saṃbhramaḥ*: Cr glosses, "agitation, excitement, *or* alarm (*udvegaḥ*)." Cg glosses, "preparations (*saṃnāhaḥ*)."

27. "But fear of Rāma has come upon the *rākṣasas*, lotus-petal-eyed woman . . . as fear of Vāsava overcame the *daityas*" *rakṣasāṃ bhayam āgatam / rāmāt kamalapatrākṣi . . . daityānām iva vāsavāt*: D5–7,10,11,T,G1,M3,5, and the texts and printed editions of the southern commentators read *pādas* ab separately and take *pāda*s cd with 28ab, substituting the nominatives *rāmaḥ* and *vāsavaḥ* for the ablatives *rāmāt* and *vāsavāt*. In addition, D10,11,M3, and the texts and printed editions of the southern commentators read the nominative masculine *kamalapatrākṣaḥ* for the critical edition's feminine vocative *kamalapatrākṣi*. The sense thus derived is "Fear has come upon the *rākṣasas*.

Once lotus-petal-eyed Rāma has defeated (*avajitya* of 28ab) [Rāvaṇa], as Vāsava did the *daityas*, [he will surely take you back]." The commentators offer a variety of interpretations in an effort to flesh out the passage. Ct, Ck, and Cm appear to understand an unexpressed simile to the effect that Rāma, having defeated and slain Rāvaṇa, will recover Sītā, just as Vāsava recovered Lakṣmī when she was in the possession of the *daityas*. Among the commentators consulted, only Cr, who reads *tam avajitya* with the critical edition, understands the gerund *avajitya* to refer to Rāma's defeat of Rāvaṇa. Cg and Cm, who read *tvām avajitya*, understand "having won you back from his enemy's house (*vinijitya śatrugṛhād apanīya tvām abhigamiṣyatīti yojanā*)." Ct, whose reading is the same as Cr's, nevertheless understands *tvām avajitya* as Cg and Cm do.

The genitive plural *daityānām* presents syntactical difficulties in the vulgate reading. Cr and Cg propose reading the genitive as an accusative. As an alternative, Cg suggests reading *adaityānām*, which then permits the interpretation "like Vāsava [foremost] among the gods [i.e., the non-*daityas*]."

28. See note to verse 27 above.

30. "Soon Rāma will come, and I shall see you seated upon his lap" *āgatasya hi rāmasya kṣipram aṅkagatāṃ satīm / ahaṃ drakṣyāmi ... tvām*: Literally, "I shall soon see you, being one who has gone to the lap of Rāma, who has come." One could also interpret the participle *satīm* in its nominal sense of "chaste woman, devoted wife," as several of the translators do. For example, Gita Press (1969, vol. 3, p. 1483) translates, "a virtuous lady"; Dutt (1893, p. 1198), "devoted to thy lord"; and Raghunathan (1982, vol. 3, p. 81), "the chaste wife." The context of Saramā's speech, with its suggestion that Rāma will surely take Sītā back (verses 27 and 28 above), makes this interpretation equally plausible, despite the fact that the syntax would tend to support the participial reading. The commentators are silent. See S. Goldman 1992 and 1996.

31. "Lovely lady" *śobhane*: D7,9–11, and the texts and printed editions of Ct read instead the vocative, *jānaki*, "O Jānakī."

"broad-chested hero" *mahorasaḥ*: Literally, "of the broad-chested one."

32. "Sītā, my lady" *site devi*: Like Raghunathan (1982, vol. 3, p. 81), we understand the vocative *devi* in its common sense of "O my lady *or* queen." Several of the translations consulted, however, understand it in its sense of "O goddess, O divinity," which, in the present context, seems inappropriate.

"the braid—falling to your waist" *jaghanaṃ gatām ... veṇīm*: Literally, "the braid reaching to your buttocks." See 5.13.24 and note.

"many months" *bahūn māsān*: The time elapsed since Sītā was taken captive has to have been at least ten months. At 3.54.22, Rāvaṇa sets a time period of twelve months for Sītā either to come to his bed or be eaten. At 5.31.27, Sītā tells Hanumān that she has only two more months remaining before Rāvaṇa plans to kill and eat her. See, too, 5.20.6–9 and notes; and note to 6.112.1.

33. "you will abandon ... sheds" *mokṣyase*: Literally, "you will release."

34. "Rāma ... he, who deserves happiness" *sukhārhaḥ*: Literally, "one worthy of happiness."

"complete" *samagram*: Many manuscripts (Ñ1,B1,3,D6,9–11,T3,G2,3,M1–3) and the texts and printed editions of the southern commentators read the nominative *samagraḥ* instead, which the commentators treat variously. Ct and Ck gloss, "together with (*sahitaḥ*)." Cg and Cm gloss, "his every wish fulfilled (*saṃpūrṇamanorathaḥ*)." According to GPP (6.33.36), Cr appears to read instead *samagnaḥ*, which he explains as *tvayā saha magnaḥ*, "absorbed with you."

35. "reunited" *samāgatā*: D7,9–11, and the texts and printed editions of Ct and Cr read *sabhājitā*, which Ct glosses as "honored, respected (*satkṛtā*)." Translators who follow Ct translate in this vein. Thus Dutt (1893, p. 1198) renders, "loved," and Roussel (1903, vol. 3, p. 95), "*au milieu des caresses*." Shastri (1959, vol. 3, p. 83), following Roussel, renders, "embraced."

"with Rāma" *rāmeṇa*: M3 and the texts and printed editions of Cg substitute *vīryeṇa*, "with valor *or* strength."

"just as the earth does with its ample crops when watered with copious rains" *suvarṣeṇa samāyuktā yathā sasyena medinī*: The syntax allows for a certain amount of ambiguity. One could, for example, like Dutt (1893, p. 1198), take *suvarṣeṇa* as a *bahuvrīhi* modifying *sasyena*, thus yielding the sense "as does the earth with well-watered crops." We believe, however, that the basis for the simile is the notion of the parched and heated (= sorrowful) earth in the hot season being cooled, refreshed, and revivified by the onset of the monsoon. This interpretation clearly underlies the northern variant of 516*, "as does the earth previously parched by lack of rain with its new crops."

"earth" *medinī*: According to footnote 3 on page 2218 of GPP, Cg reads the variant *maithilī*, "Maithilī," for *medinī*. This reading, however, is unattested in printed editions of Cg (KK, VSP) and the critical apparatus.

36. "Sūrya, bringer of day" *divasakaram*: Literally, "the maker of day." Ct and Ck remind us that the sun is Sītā's [i.e., the Sūryavaṃśa's] clan divinity (*kuladaivatam*).

"sustainer of all creatures" *prabhavaḥ . . . prajānām*: Ct, Ck, and Cr see the reference as elliptical. They take *prabhavaḥ* in its sense of "source" and supply the phrase "[the source] of the happiness and [the source] of the destruction of unhappiness (*sukhaduḥkhahānyor iti śeṣaḥ*)." Cr understands, "the cause of people's happiness and unhappiness (*prajānāṃ sukhaduḥkhayor iti śeṣaḥ prabhavaḥ kāraṇam*)." Cg, whom we have followed, understands that the sun is actually the means of production and sustenance of all living creatures according to the well-known vedic belief that the sun receives the sacrificial offering and returns it in the form of rain, which produces the food that sustains all creatures. Cg further argues that this characterization of the sun does not duplicate that of the true source of all beings, i.e., the *ātman*. He argues that this is suggested by the use of the horse simile in *pāda* b and substantiates this identification by quoting *Taittirīya Upaniṣad* 2.8 (cf. *Kaṭha Upaniṣad* 6.3), where it is stated that the sun rises out of fear of the *ātman*. (*ayaṃ divasakaraḥ prajānāṃ devatiryañmanuṣyasthāvarāṇāṃ prabhavaḥ kāraṇam. hiḥ prasiddhau varṣādidvārā jagadāpyāyaka ity arthaḥ. agnau prāstāhutiḥ samyag ādityam upatiṣṭhate. ādityāj jāyate vṛṣṭir vṛṣṭer annaṃ tataḥ prājā ity ukteḥ. na punar atra jagatkāraṇatvoktiḥ. aśvopamānena svātiriktapuruṣapreryatvābhidhānāt. bhīṣāsmād vātaḥ pavate bhīṣodeti sūrya iti śruteḥ*.) Ck identifies the divinity with whom Sītā must seek refuge as the indwelling deity Brahmā, who is her only hope (*antargataṃ bhagavantaṃ brahmāṇaṃ śaraṇaṃ vrajeḥ*).

"foremost of mountains" *girivaram*: The reference, as all commentators agree, is to the axial mountain Meru, around which the sun was believed to revolve.

The meter is *vaṃśasthavila*.

Sarga 25

1. "with her words" *tena vākyena*: The commentators and the translators who follow them differ in their opinions as to whose words are intended here and with what to construe them. Ct, Cr, Ck, and Cg (alternate interpretation) believe the words to be those of Rāvaṇa at 6.22.13–34. These commentators understand that these words are the source of Sītā's distress. Cr, who, along with Cg (*pace* GPP 6.34.1) and the critical edition, reads *mohitām* for Ct's and Ck's *moditām*, explains, "deluded by those words that had been uttered by Rāvaṇa, Sītā was therefore suffering (*tena rāvaṇoktena vākyena mohitām ata eva jātasaṃtāpāṃ sītām*)." All translators who follow the text of Ct (Dutt 1893, p. 1199; Shastri 1959, vol. 3, p. 83; Roussel 1903, vol. 3, p. 96; Gita Press 1969, vol. 3, p. 1484; and Pagani 1999, p. 947) accept that the words referred to are Rāvaṇa's. We think that this interpretation is improbable, however, as it is unusual, to say the least, for Vālmīki to refer in this way to a speech that is separated from the moment he is describing by an intervening speech. We therefore find Cg's construction of the verse, in which the phrase refers to Saramā's immediately preceding speech as the source of Sītā's comfort, more persuasive. It should be noted, however, that Cg also admits the possibility that the words may be Rāvaṇa's. (*atheti prathamaślokena pūrvasargoktānuvādaḥ tena vākyena hrādayāmāsety anvayaḥ. yadvā tena vākyena rāvaṇavākyena.*) This interpretation is also followed by Raghunathan (1982, vol. 3, p. 82) and Gorresio (1856, vol. 9, p. 227).

"confused" *mohitām*: As indicated in the previous note, Cr understands the term to refer to Sītā's having been deluded by Rāvaṇa's speech [concerning his alleged slaying of Rāma]. D7,10,G1,3,M1,2, and the texts and printed editions of Ct and Ck read instead *moditām*, "cheered, made happy."

"as do the heavens to the earth" *pṛthivīṃ dyaur iva*: D10,11,G3,M1,2,5, and the texts and printed editions of Ct and Ck read instead *mahīṃ dagdhām iva*, "as to the parched earth." This reading, which all translators rendering the text of Ct follow, appears to be defective in that it omits a feminine *upamāna* corresponding to Saramā (the *upameya*). Ct and Ck attempt to remedy this deficiency by supplying the phrase "like a bank of clouds (*meghapaṅktir iva*)."

3. "unseen" *praticchannā*: Literally, "concealed."

"a message from you informing him that you are safe" *tvadvākyam . . . nivedya kuśalam*: Literally, "having informed him of your well-being through your words." The phrase is somewhat awkward and ambiguous, and has produced a variety of interpretations among the commentators and translators. Our translation basically follows the interpretation of Ct, who glosses the adjective *kuśalam* as "informing [him] of your well-being (*kuśalāvedakam*)." Given the context, this seems to be the most probable content of a potential message from Sītā. Cg glosses *kuśalam* as "inspiring *or* producing well-being [in Rāma] (*kuśalapratipādakam*)." Cm offers yet a third alternative, glossing, "[your words] in the form of an inquiry about [Rāma's] well-being (*kuśalapraśnarūpam*)." Cr, along with a few, mainly *devanāgarī*, manuscripts, reads *tadvākyam* for *tvadvākyam*. Thus, he understands the phrase to mean "his, that is Rāvaṇa's, words directed toward you and your well-being (*tad rāvaṇoktaṃ vākyaṃ tvāṃ prati vacanaṃ kuśalaṃ tava maṅgalaṃ ca*)."

5. "tinged with her recent sorrow" *pūrvaśokābhipannayā*: We follow the interpretation of Ct, Cr, and Cm, who understand that Sītā's speech still bears a trace of the grief

she was experiencing prior to being consoled by Saramā (*pūrvaśokābhipannayā śvāsanāt pūrvaṃ jātena śokeneṣadyuktayā*—so Ct). Cg, however, breaks the adjective *pūrva*- out of the compound, giving it the sense of "which had previously been tinged by sorrow but which was now cheerful (*pūrvaṃ śokābhipannayā samprati hṛṣṭayety arthaḥ*)." This interpretation is followed only by Raghunathan (1982, vol. 3, p. 82).

6. Ct, Ck, and Cg offer here, in advance, an explanation of why Sītā declines Saramā's offer to serve as a messenger to Rāma and instead instructs her in the following verses to spy on Rāvaṇa. These commentators agree that Sītā is concerned about the impropriety of dispatching a *rākṣasa* woman to her husband, Rāma. Ct and Ck even liken such a meeting to that between Śūrpaṇakhā and Rāma. Ct and Ck claim that by praising Saramā's abilities, as she does in this verse, Sītā is able gracefully to divert her to the more appropriate mission that she has in mind (*atha sītā śūrpaṇakhāyā ivāsyā api rāmasamīpagamanam anucitam iti vicārya tat sāmārthyaślāghāpūrvaṃ tām ucitakṛtye niyojayati*—so Ct). Cg further remarks that Sītā does not wish to ruin her friendship with the *rākṣasa* woman by simply refusing her offer, but skillfully uses a pretext to divert her (*saṃdeśam āhariṣyāmīti vadantīṃ saramāṃ prati na gantavyam ity ukte sakhyahāniḥ* . . . *ato vyājena nipuṇaṃ pariharati*).

"for my sake" *madantare*: Like most of the commentators, we take *antara* in its sense of "with reference to *or* for the sake of." Cs, with his usual eccentricity, takes the term in its sense of "innermost soul *or* essence," and thus reads the expression as a vocative addressed to Saramā, in the sense of "my heart of hearts, dearest friend," and so forth. (*he madantare! mayi antaram antarātmā manaḥ prāṇo vāyasyāḥ sā tat saṃbuddhiḥ*.)

"I know that . . . you could accomplish even the impossible" *avagacchāmy akartavyaṃ kartavyaṃ te*: Literally, "I understand that which is not to be done is to be done by you." Ñ1,B3,D10,11,13,G2,3,M5, and the texts and printed editions of Ck and Ct read instead *avagacchādya kartavyaṃ kartavyaṃ te*, "now learn the task that is to be done by you." Ck claims that this is the authentic reading (*iti pāñktaḥ*).

7. "you should go to Rāvaṇa as I wish to know what he is doing now." *jñātum icchāmi taṃ gatvā kiṃ karotīti rāvaṇaḥ*: Literally, "having gone to him, I wish to know, 'What is Rāvaṇa doing?'" The syntax of this line is extremely awkward, and the commentators struggle to make it yield its sense. The major difficulty here is the construction of the gerund *gatvā*, "having gone," of which Sītā would appear to be the grammatical subject, but Saramā is obviously the logical one. Cr, Cg, and Cm, with whom we agree, understand, despite the syntax, that Sītā is asking Saramā to go and spy on her master, Rāvaṇa. Ct, however, understands Rāvaṇa to be the subject of *gatvā* and interprets the line to mean "I wish to know about him, i.e., what Rāvaṇa has been doing since leaving this place (*ito gatvā rāvaṇaḥ kiṃ karotīti rāvaṇaṃ jñātum icchāmi*)." Of the translators consulted, only Dutt (1893, p. 1199) follows this interpretation. Our interpretation is perhaps supported by the seemingly glossing readings of the north (see Pollock 1984a, p. 85). Thus, Ś,V,D0–4,8,12,13 (=Lahore 6.10.8cd) read *tvatto 'haṃ jñātum icchāmi* (or close variants), "I wish to find out from you," for *pāda* c (*jñātum icchāmi taṃ gatvā*); Ñ and B1–3 (=Gorresio 6.10.8cd) read *jñātum arhasi gatvā tvam*, "having gone, you must find out."

8. "Rāvaṇa, who makes his enemies cry out" *rāvaṇaḥ śatrurāvaṇaḥ*: This is yet another example of the etymological epithets of which the poet is very fond. See note to 6.8.12.

"master of illusion" *māyābalaḥ*: Literally, "whose power is illusion."

9. "He has... menace and threaten me" *tarjāpayati... bhartsāpayati*: Several of the commentators note the irregular causative formations and distinguish the two terms as referring to nonverbal and verbal forms of intimidation, respectively (*avācikī bhīṣikā tarjanaṃ vācikī tu sā bhartsanam*—so Ct).

"who... stand guard over me" *yā māṃ rakṣanti*: Ś,Ñ1,V1,2,B1–3,D0–4,7–13,T3,G1,3, M5, and the texts and printed editions of Ct and Cr read instead *yo māṃ rakṣati*, "[he] who stands guard over me," thus placing Rāvaṇa, not the *rākṣasa* women, in the role of Sītā's warder.

10. "I am fearful... I tremble in fear of him" *udvignā... asmi... tadbhayāc cāham udvignā*: Literally, "I am fearful... I am fearful from fear of him." The term *udvigna*, "frightened, trembling," is repeated in *pādas* a and c. Although none of the commentators takes explicit objection to this example of *punarukti*, "repetition, redundancy," Cr and Cs make efforts to mitigate it. Cr takes advantage of the hiatus between *pādas* c and d to read *udvignā* as the *sandhi* form of the feminine plural *udvignāḥ*. He thus understands Sītā to be saying to Saramā, "And you [the *rākṣasa* women] are frightened of him as well (*udvignā yūyam apīti śeṣaḥ*)." Cs proposes, in his first interpretation, that we read the negative particle *na* with *pāda* a rather than b. This enables him to interpret the verse as follows: "Formerly, I was neither fearful nor apprehensive of anything whatsoever and my mind was at peace. But now, through fear of him, I, who am in the *aśoka* grove, have become frightened. (*yāhaṃ prāñ nodvignā na śaṅkitā ca kasmāccid api. mama manaḥ svastham. tādṛśy apy ahaṃ tadbhayād rāvaṇakartṛkabhītihetoḥ. aśokavanikāṃ gatā prāptā. ataś codvignety anvayaḥ.*)"

"here in the *aśoka* grove" *aśokavanikāṃ gatā*: Literally, "gone to *or* situated in the *aśoka* grove." Cr supplies the particle *api* after *gatā*, suggesting the sense "even though I am in the *aśoka* grove," apparently thinking that Sītā is commenting that she is fearful of Rāvaṇa, even though she is not in his presence. We do not find this interpretation persuasive, although it is followed in the translations of Gita Press (1969, vol. 3, p. 1484) and Raghunathan (1982, vol. 3, p. 82).

11. "that he may have discussed or decided" *kathā tasya niścitaṃ vāpi yad bhavet*: Literally, "what his conversations or decisions might be." Ct, Cr, and Ck understand that Rāvaṇa's deliberations concern whether he should release Sītā (*kathā madvimokṣaviṣayakathā*). Cs thinks that they refer either to Rāvaṇa's preparations for battle or to the further imprisonment of or clemency toward Sītā. (*kathā yuddhasaṃnāhakathā. madviṣayanigrahānugrahakathā vā.*) Cg and Cv do not specify the subject, taking the reference to be to the news of what Rāvaṇa is doing (*vartā*).

"that would be the greatest favor you could do for me" *paro me syād anugrahaḥ*: Literally, "[that] would be the highest grace *or* favor for me."

12. "caressing her, replied in words choked with tears" *uvāca vacanaṃ tasyāḥ spṛśantī bāṣpaviklavam*: Most of the commentators (Cv, Ct, Cr, Ck, and Cg) read, or appear to read, *vadanam*, "face," for *vacanam*, "words." This reading for them thus becomes the object of the participle *spṛśantī*, "touching," as well as the modificand of the adjective *bāṣpaviklavam*, "tearful." Their reading thus would mean: "Saramā replied, wiping her [Sītā's] tear-stained face." Printed texts of VSP and KK read *vadanam*, but NSP and GPP read *vacanam*, even though the commentaries they reproduce read *vadanam*. Crā notes that *vadanam* is a [variant] reading, while Cv does the same for *vacanam*. All translators of the vulgate translate "face." The textual evidence for *vadanam* is weak, however, confined only to a few southern manuscripts (D6,T1,M3, and Cg and Ct).

13. "you shall see me when I return" *upāvṛttāṃ ca paśya mām*: Literally, "see me returned." V1,3,D1,10,11, and the texts and printed editions of Ct and Cr read instead *upāvartāmi maithili*, "I shall return, Maithilī."

14. "she... eavesdropped on his deliberations with his counselors" *śuśrāva kathitaṃ tasya... samantriṇaḥ*: Literally, "she heard the conversation of him who was with his counselors."

15. "then" *tadā*: Ś,Ñ,V,B1–3,D0–4,7–13, and the texts and printed editions of Ct and Cr read instead *śubhām*, "lovely," which modifies *aśokavanikām*, "the *aśoka* grove."

16. "the grove" *tatra*: Literally, "there."

"robbed of her lotus" *bhraṣṭapadmām iva*: Literally, "whose lotus was lost or fallen." As Pagani (1999, p. 1658) comments in her note to this *sarga*, Śrī, the goddess of fortune and consort of Viṣṇu, is commonly represented in iconography as seated on an expanded lotus. Thus, Cg glosses, "deprived of her lotus seat (*padmāsanahīnām ity arthaḥ*)." Cs offers another explanation that calls to mind the common representation of Śrī as holding a lotus. According to him, the idea here is that, while playing, Lakṣmī has dropped from her hand the lotus she was using as a ball (*kamalaṃ kandukīkṛtya khelanasamaye hastavicyutalatādilīnanālīkām*).

17. "and offered her a seat" *dadau ca svayam āsanam*: Literally, "and she gave a seat of her own accord." The gesture indicates that Sītā regards Saramā as more or less her social equal.

19. "the tremulous Sītā" *sītayā vepamānayā*: Cg notes that Sītā trembles in anticipation of what dreadful news Saramā may bring (*kiṃ vā bhayaṃ vakṣyatīti kampamānayā*).

"Rāvaṇa's deliberations with his counselors" *kathitam... rāvaṇasya samantriṇaḥ*: Literally, "the conversation of Rāvaṇa, who was with his counselors."

20. "given earnest advice" *bṛhadvacaḥ... bodhitaḥ*: Literally, "advised *or* made aware [of] a great speech."

"his own mother" *jananyā*: As Cm and Cg remind us, Rāvaṇa's mother's name is Kaikasī (see 7.9.15–25).

"by... his elder counselor" *mantrivṛddhena*: Literally, "by the eldest among the counselors." The epithet is used largely for its echoing effect with the name *aviddhena*.

"Aviddha" *aviddhena*: The name Aviddha (v.l. Avidhya, Āviddha) is almost certainly one of the variations of the name of the character called Avindhya (v.l. Suvindhya, Avandhya) at 5.35.12–13 (D5,T1,3,G,M, and the texts and printed editions of Cg omit these two verses), a *rākṣasa* adviser to Rāvaṇa who is consistently supportive of Rāma and Sītā, and who advises Rāvaṇa to return Sītā to Rāma. A *rākṣasa* by the name of Avindhya (v.l. Avindya, Avandhya, Avidhya, etc.) is mentioned several times in the *Rāmopākhyāna* (*MBh* 2.273.28,32; 3.264.55; 3.266.64–65; and 3.275–276.39). D10,11,M1,2, and the texts and printed editions of Ct, Ck, and Cr read instead *atisnigdhena*, "most affectionate *or* devoted," in place of the counselor's name. Ck, who insists that this reading is authentic, identifies the unnamed counselor as Mālyavān. Cf. 6.80.50–51 and note.

"who said": The words have been added to provide a transition to the following speech.

21. "His amazing deeds in Janasthāna" *janasthāne yad adbhutam*: Literally, "the wonder in Janasthāna." As most of the commentators point out, the reference is to Rāma's slaying of Khara and the other *rākṣasas* at 3.24–29.

"sufficient evidence for you" *nidarśanaṃ te paryāptam*: Literally, "the illustration is enough for you." As the commentators indicate, the reference is to Rāma's valor (*tat parākramasyety arthaḥ*).

22. "his finding Sītā" *darśanam*: Literally, "finding *or* seeing." We agree with the commentators that the reference is to Hanumān's discovery of Sītā.

"What mere human . . . could have brought all this about?" *kaḥ kuryān mānuṣaḥ*: The verse is slightly confusing in that it speaks initially of Hanumān's exploits, and then refers to someone who is, at least apparently, a human, i.e., Rāma. Cg, Cm, and Ct understand that Rāma's power is such that even his mere servant, Hanumān, is capable of defeating all the *rākṣasas*. (*tiṣṭhatu raghunāthaḥ. tad anucaro hanumān eva sarvān rākṣasān jetuṃ samartha ity āśayena tat parākramaṃ varṇayati*—so Cm.) Several commentators note that the thrust of the rhetorical question here is to show that Rāma is indeed an incarnation of God (*svadūtamukhenānekakāryakārī rāmo deva eveti bhāvaḥ*—so Cg). Ct and Ck extend this idea by stating that Hanumān and Rāma, respectively, are not merely a monkey and a man but that they are incarnations of god. (*hanūmān rāmo vānaro manuṣyo vā na. api tu devāvatāra iti bhāvaḥ*.) Cr describes Rāma simply as "an extraordinary human being (*vilakṣaṇo mānuṣaḥ*)."

"on earth" *bhuvi*: D7,9–11, and the texts and printed editions of Ct and Cr read instead *yudhi*, "in battle," which is completely redundant with *yuddhe*, "in battle," in *pāda* c.

23. "aged counselors" *mantrivṛddhaiḥ*: Cg and Cs note the shift from the singular in verse 20 above to the plural here. The former ascribes it merely to the use of the respectful plural (*pūjāyāṃ bahuvacanam*). Cs offers three other explanations. According to the first, there were always multiple counselors, but, in verse 20, the reference in the singular to Aviddha (v.l. Avindhya) is to be taken as synecdoche (*upalakṣaṇa*) of the part for the whole (*pūrvamantrivṛddhenety ekavacanam upalakṣakam aparamantrivṛddhānām iti jñāpayitum atra mantrivṛddhair iti bahuvacanam*). According to his second interpretation, through the use of the singular we must understand that there is only one Avindhya. However, we must also understand that there is a collectivity (*itiḥ*) because of the different kinds of arguments [employed]. Cs's third interpretation again understands the use of the singular to represent the group. The idea here is that the word *avindhya* is derived from the employment of the Pāṇinian *taddhita* suffix "*ya*" as enjoined at *Pā* 4.2.49, which allows the singular to indicate a group, as in the case of the secondary derivate *pāśyā*, "a collection of nooses," from the noun *pāśaḥ*, "noose" (*tatraikavacanenaika evāvindhya upapādanaprakārabhedād itiḥ pāśānityādivad bahuvacanam iti vā*). Cs also notes the inversion of the order in which Rāvaṇa's mother and counselors are mentioned in the two verses (20 and 23). He argues, curiously enough, that, although she is mentioned first in verse 20 out of respect, she is put second here because she is merely reflecting [while presumably the counselors make their arguments]. (*tatra mānyatvān mātuḥ puraskaraṇam. tasyā ālocanakāryāniyuktatvenātra vṛddhamantripuraskaraṇam iti vivekaḥ*.)

24. "such" *iti*: The odd and ambiguous placement of this particle between the words *tvām*, "you," and *maithili*, "O Maithilī," in *pāda* b has caused consternation and debate among many of the commentators. Our interpretation follows that proposed by Cr, Cv, Crā, and Cm. This interpretation is also ascribed by Cg to "some commentators." The idea is that the *iti* marks the statement of Rāvaṇa's resolution as a kind of quo-

tation marker, despite the syntactic dislocation (*iti niścaya ity anvaya ity eke*). Cg's principal interpretation is that the particle should be read as indicating causality, i.e., "for (*iti hetau*)." He offers yet another interpretation, also ascribed to other commentators, in which we are to supply the word *manye*, "I think (*iti manya ity apare*)." Thus, he uses it to mark the end of Saramā's statement of Rāvaṇa's intentions. Finally, Cg notes that some manuscripts (in the critical apparatus V3,G,M5) read *iha*, "here," for *iti*, thus avoiding the problem entirely (*iha maithilīti keṣucit pāṭhaḥ*).

25. "That, indeed" *tad eṣā*: Literally, "this then." Printed editions of Ct (GPP, NSP, and KK—noted in a footnote—6.34.25) read instead *eṣām*, "of them, theirs." The variant is unnoted in the critical apparatus.

"unwavering" *susthirā*: Literally "firmly established." M1–3 and the texts and printed editions of Cg read instead *niścitā*, "resolved."

"befuddled as he is by his impending doom" *mṛtyulobhāt*: Literally, "because of the confusion of death." We follow Ct, Ck, and Cr in taking *lobha*, normally, "greed, lust, desire," in its less common sense of "confusion, delusion." The idea here is almost certainly the common notion that those who are about to die lose their rational faculties. Cg does not expand upon the term, and it is probably for this reason that Raghunathan (1982, vol. 3, p. 83), who generally follows him, translates, "he is courting death." Cs understands *lobha* in its more common sense of *gārdhya*, "desire," but explains the compound obscurely as "out of the desire among them [the *rākṣasas*?] for the goddess of death (*mṛtyudevyā eṣu vidyamānād gārdhyāt*)."

"He will have to be completely crushed in battle" *anirastas tu saṃyuge*: Literally, "not [i.e. unless he is] turned back in battle."

"Intimidation alone cannot force him to release you." *bhayān na śaktas tvāṃ moktum*: Literally, "he cannot release you out of fear."

27. "*bherī* drums" *bherī-*: See 6.17.31–33 and notes.

"the entire army" *sarvasainyānām*: Literally, "of all the troops, armies." As Cg notes, we are to understand that the reference here is also to the monkey hosts, whose employment of *bherī* drums, etc., is also mentioned in the *Kiṣkindhākāṇḍa* (*atra bheryādiśabdo bheryādiśabdaparo vānarasainyānām api bheryādikam astīti kiṣkindhākāṇḍe darśitam*) (4.37.13). This is confirmed in the next verse as well as in the first verse of *sarga* 26.

28. "their spirits failed them" *naṣṭaujasaḥ*: Literally, "their vitality destroyed."

"Their energies were sapped by despair" *dainyaparītaceṣṭāḥ*: Literally, "their exertions overcome by despondency."

The meter is *indravajrā*.

Sarga 26

1. "to the . . . sound of . . . *bherī* drums" *bherīśabdena*: See 6.17.31–33 and notes.

"Rāghava" *rāghavaḥ*: D9–11,G2, and the texts and printed editions of Ck, Ct, and Cr substitute the adjective *nādinā*, "resounding" (modifying *-śabdena*, "sound"). Cs notes this as a variant reading, explaining it first as "echoing, resounding" but then, in his typically eccentric fashion, as a *bahuvrīhi* modifying *-śabdena*, "sound," with the sense "whereby the *rākṣasas* were not eaters (*na vidyanta ādino rākṣasā yena tādṛśena*)." He bases this interpretation on an unattested passage that he claims is from the tenth *skandha* of the *Bhāgavatapurāṇa*, "*rākṣasas* are said to be those who eat (*ādino rākṣasāḥ proktā iti bhāgavatadaśamaskandhatātparyāt*)." The idea seems to be that the daunting sound of Rāma's approaching army has made the *rākṣasas* lose their appetite. Cs is perhaps trying to extend the thrust of 6.25.28 above, where the sound similarly makes the *rākṣasas* lose their will to live.

"the conqueror of enemy citadels" *parapurañjayaḥ*: Cs proposes, as an alternate reading, breaking the compound into *parapuram* and *jayaḥ*. This reading, with a little rhetorical supplementation, yields for him the meaning "Rāma... approached the enemy citadel as victory approached him. (*parapuraṃ vairinagaram. mahābāhū rāma upayāti. jayaś ca tam upayāti.*)"

"did... draw near" *upayāti*: Several commentators, including Ct, Ck, and Cr, supply the word "Lañkā."

3. Following verse 3, D5–7,9–11,T,G,M3,5, and the texts and printed editions of the southern commentators insert a passage of one line [534*]: "[Rāvaṇa]... that cruel lord of the *rākṣasas*, who brought so much suffering to the world, [spoke] without reproach.[1]"

[1]"without reproach" *agarhayan*: D5–7,9,T,G,M3,5, and Cv, Crā, and Cg read instead *garhayan*, "reproaching." Those translators who accept this latter reading differ as to the object of Rāvaṇa's reproach. Some, e.g., Dutt (1893, p. 1201) and Shastri (1959, vol. 3, p. 85), understand that Rāvaṇa is belittling Rāma's exploits listed in verse 4 below. Others, including Raghunathan (1982, vol. 3, p. 84), Pagani (1999, p. 949), and Roussel (1903, vol. 3, p. 98), see him as reproaching his ministers (presumably for their timidity). Gita Press (1969, vol. 3, p. 1484) reads with Ct and the critical edition.

4. "the size of his army" *balasaṃcayam*: Literally, "accumulation *or* mass of his forces." D7,9–11, and the texts and printed editions of Ct, Ck, and Cr read instead *balapauruṣam*, which those translators who follow this text read as a *samāhāradvandva* in the sense of "strength and valor."

Following verse 4, Ñ,V2,B1–4,D2,5–7,9–11,S insert a passage of two lines [539*]: "When the night-roaming *rākṣasas* heard those words of Rāvaṇa,[1] they looked at one another in silence, realizing Rāma's valor.[1][2]"

[1]"they looked at one another in silence, realizing Rāma's valor" *tūṣṇīm anyonyam aikṣanta viditvā rāmavikramam*: D5–7,9–11,S omit line 1 and substitute the accusative plural participle *īkṣataḥ*, "looking at," for the critical text's third person plural imperfect *aikṣanta*, "they looked at." This line is then an extension of the syntax of verse 4 with the sense "But I know that you, sirs, who, realizing Rāma's valor, are looking at one another in silence, are also truly valorous in battle."

5. "the paternal uncle of... mother" *mātuḥ paitāmahaḥ*: There is some disagreement among the commentators as to Mālyavān's precise relationship to Rāvaṇa. This disagreement is heightened by a variant in the reading that appears to be known to most of the commentators. The critical reading is shared by Cg, Cv, Crā, and Cm. They agree that the phrase works out to mean "the son of the grandfather of the mother," i.e., Kaikasī's father or paternal uncle. Cg relies on the *Uttarakāṇḍa*'s genealogy of the

rākṣasas to demonstrate, correctly in our opinion, that Mālyavān is Kaikasī's uncle and, thus, Rāvaṇa's maternal granduncle. The *Uttarakāṇḍa* (7.5.5) tells of the birth of the three sons of Sukeśa: Mālyavān, Sumāli, and Māli. At 7.5.34–36, the offspring of Sumāli, including Rāvaṇa's mother, Kaikasī, are mentioned. Despite this, as Cg notes, some commentators (Cv, Crā, Cm) understand Mālyavān to be Kaikasī's father. Ct, Ck, and Cr, along with a variety of northern and southern manuscripts, read *vṛddho mātāmahaḥ*, "aged maternal grandfather," for *mātuḥ paitāmahaḥ*. This inferior reading is rendered in the translations of Dutt (1893, p. 1201), Roussel (1903, vol. 3, p. 98), Shastri (1959, vol. 3, p. 85), Pagani (1999, p. 949), and Gita Press (1969, vol. 3, p. 1487).

6. "in the traditional branches of learning" *vidyāsu*: The commentators differ on the identification of the branches of learning referred to here. Ct and Ck claim that there are fourteen branches (see *Yajñavalkyasmṛti* 1.3) but neither enumerate them nor cite a source for such a list. Cg and Cm understand the reference to be to the four branches of learning, which they enumerate as metaphysics or logic (*ānvīkṣikī*), vedic studies (*trayī*), economics (*vārtā*), and political science (*daṇḍanīti*). Cg supports this identification with a quotation from *Kāmandaka* 2.1, where a monarch is advised to consider these four areas in consultation with those who are knowledgeable and practiced in them (*ānvīkṣikīṃ trayīṃ vārtāṃ daṇḍanītiṃ ca pārthivaḥ / tadvidbhis tatkriyopetaiś cintayed vinayānvitaḥ //*). *Arthaśāstra* 1.2–4 identifies the same four *vidyās*. These are vedic studies (*trayī*), economics (*vārtā*), political science (*daṇḍanīti*), and metaphysics (*ānvīkṣikī*) (1.2.1). *Arthaśāstra* 1.2.8 explicitly states that Kauṭilya understands that there are four *vidyās* (*catasra eva vidyā iti kauṭilyaḥ //*).

7. "peace or war" *saṃdadhānaḥ . . . vigṛhṇan*: Literally, "making peace [and] fomenting strife." The participles are derived from the verbal roots that are the source of the nouns *sandhi*, "peace," and *vigraha*, "war," that refer to two of the six *guṇas*, or modes of policy, as enumerated at *Arthaśāstra* 7.1.2, *Manusmṛti* 7.162, *Yajñavalkyasmṛti* 13.347, and *Śiśupālavadha* 2.26.

"at the appropriate times" *kālena*: Literally, "according to time." Cg and Cm are more specific, noting that one makes peace when one's own forces are weak and makes war when they are strong. (*kālena saṃdadhānaḥ svabalakṣayakālena saṃdhānaṃ kurvan. kālena vigṛhṇan svabalavṛddhikālena vigrahaṃ kurvan*—so Cm.)

8. "weaker than his rival" *hīyamānena*: Literally, "by one being diminished *or* a lesser one."

"he must never underestimate his enemy" *na śatrum avamanyeta*: Cv and Cm read *sa[ḥ]* for *na*, yielding the sense "he should despise his enemy." Cm notes our reading as a variant. Cg is apparently aware of the reading *sa[ḥ]*, simply correcting it to *na*. No attestation of this variant appears either in the critical apparatus of the critical edition or that of KK.

9. "I would recommend making peace" *mahyaṃ rocate saṃdhiḥ*: Literally, "I choose *or* prefer peace."

"so heavily besieged" *abhiyuktāḥ sma*: The particle *sma* here must be read as emphatic. B4,D7,10,11, and Ct, Cr, and Ck read instead *abhiyukto 'si*, "you are besieged *or* obsessed." This reading exploits the ambiguity of the verb *abhi* $\sqrt{yuj}$, which can mean, among other things, "to attack, besiege, invade," as well as "to be attached to, devoted to, obsessed with." Cr takes the word in the latter sense, while Ct offers the two as alternatives. All translations consulted take *abhiyukta*, either in the singular or plural, in some variation of the former sense, with the exception of Raghunathan. Although he normally follows Cg (who glosses here *viruddhāḥ*, "blockaded, besieged"), Raghunathan (1982, vol. 3, p. 84) translates, "Sita, who has been an obsession with you."

10. "the gods, seers" *devarṣayaḥ*: We agree with Cg, who understands the compound as a *dvandva*. Other commentators ignore the issue of how to read the compound. However, some translators, including Dutt (1893, p. 1202), Gita Press (1969, vol. 3, p. 1487), and Raghunathan (1982, vol. 3, p. 84), read the compound as a *karmadhāraya*, either leaving the word untranslated or rendering, "celestial sages."

"Rāma's" *tasya*: Literally, "his."

11. "two races" *pakṣau*: Normally, the term means "side *or* faction," as in verse 7 above. Here, however, although the term surely has a connotation of opposition, the context better supports the usage of *pakṣa* as "race, family, lineage" (s.v. Apte and cf. *MBh* 13.57.40 [*rūpānvitāṃ pakṣavatīṃ manojñāṃ bhāryām ayatnopagatāṃ labhet saḥ*]), where the term *pakṣavatīṃ* would appear to refer to a woman of good family.

"who had recourse to righteousness and unrighteousness, respectively" *dharmādharmau tadāśrayau*: Literally, "righteousness and unrighteousness were their recourses."

"respectively": Following several commentators, we add the term (*kramāt*—so Ct) for clarity.

12. "the way . . . the way" *pakṣaḥ . . . pakṣaḥ*: The poet continues to use this polysemic term in a variety of its meanings. Compare notes to verses 7 and 11 above. Here the term carries something of its sense of "side" or "faction."

"of the great" *mahātmanām*: Cg insists that this normally bland epithet must be read pregnantly here so as to emphasize the great difference in quality between the exalted gods and the lesser *asuras*. (*mahātmanām iti hetugarbhaviśeṣaṇam. mahāsvabhāvānām ity arthaḥ. samīcīnaprakṛtīnām iti yāvat.*)

"Rāvaṇa" *rāvaṇa*: D6,9–11,T2, and the texts and printed editions of Ct and Cr read instead *rākṣasa*, "O *rākṣasa*!"

"*asuras* and the *rākṣasas*" *rakṣasām . . . asurāṇām*: Ct notes, with reference to the *guṇa* theory of Sāṃkhya, that the *rākṣasas* are to be distinguished from the *asuras* in that the former are "*rājasic*," or passionate in nature, wheras the latter are "*tāmasic*," or turgid in nature (*rajastamaḥprakṛtitvāt*)

13. "when . . . when" *tataḥ . . . tataḥ*: Literally, "then . . . then." D10,11, and the texts and printed editions of Ck and Ct read instead *yadā*, "when," for the first *tatah*, while D10, GPP, and NSP read *tadā*, "then," (Gita Press reads *yadā . . . yadā*) for the second occurrence of *tataḥ*.

"eclipses" *grasate*: Literally, "it swallows, consumes." The verb is also used in the science of astronomy to describe the action of an eclipse, and the sense of "to overshadow *or* to dominate" seems to make that metaphor appropriate here.

"ushers in . . . brings on" *abhūt . . . pravartate*: Literally, "it was . . . it goes forward *or* occurs." The commentators differ among themselves as to the chain of causation intended here. Some, including Cv, Cg, Cr, and Cm, see, as we do, that it is the relative strength of *dharma* and *adharma* that lends to each cosmic age its particular character (*dharmo 'dharmaṃ yadā grasate 'bhibhavati tadā kṛtaṃ yugam abhūt . . . adharmo yadā dharmaṃ grasate tadā tiṣyaḥ kaliḥ pravartate*—so Cg). Others, such as Crā, Ct, and

Ck, seem to take a more mechanistic view, in which it is the immutable progression of the cosmic ages that determines the relationship between the two, *dharma* and *adharma*. (*yadā kṛtaṃ yugam abhūt tadā tasmād eva kālād dhetoḥ pravṛddho dharmo 'dharmaṃ grasate 'bhibhavati vai prasiddham. yadā tiṣyaḥ kaliḥ pravartate tadā tata eva hetor adharmo dharmaṃ grasate kalau pādena dharmasthiteḥ*—so Ct.) The translators reflect the two views. Dutt (1893, p. 1202) and Gita Press (1969, vol. 3, p. 1487) follow the position of Crā, Ct, and Ck; while Roussel (1903, vol. 3, p. 99), Pagani (1999, p. 950), Raghunathan (1982, vol. 3, p. 84), and Shastri (1959, vol. 3, p. 86) translate with Cv, Cg, Cr and Cm. Ct and Ck take the verse as a jumping-off point for similar and moderately lengthy discussions of the nature of *dharma* and types of *adharma* relative to the observed behavior of *rākṣasas* and *asuras*. Both note that the gods are exclusively devoted to *dharma*. The demons, on the other hand, although they may perform actions that are in keeping with *dharma* and thus may enjoy their fruits, are *tāmasic* and *rājasic* by nature, and must, in the end, at the exhaustion of the fruits of their righteous conduct, experience the fruits of their unrighteousness. (*devāḥ kevaladharmaparāḥ. rakṣosurāḥ kāmyarājasatāmasadharmamātraparāḥ. tādṛśadharmam anutiṣṭhato 'pi tān uktatriprakārādharmo na muñcaty eva. rajastamaḥprakṛtitvāt. ato dharmakaraṇena sukhino 'pi te kāmyatvena sāntatayā dharmaphalānte 'dharmaphalabhogabhāja iti na doṣaḥ*—so Ct.)

"in the golden age, known as the Kṛta" *kṛtam . . . yugam*: Literally. "The Kṛta Yuga."

"the degenerate Tiṣya Age" *tiṣyaḥ*: Literally, "Tiṣya." This is an alternate name for the last and most degenerate of the four *yugas*, or cosmic ages. It is more commonly known as the Kali Age. Cg quotes *Amarakośa* 3.3.148 to this effect (*tiṣyaḥ kalau ca puṣye ca*).

14. "In rampaging through the worlds" *caratā lokān*: Literally, "by [you] ranging *or* wandering the worlds." The commentators take the reference to be to Rāvaṇa's *digvijaya*, or "career of conquest of the worlds," described in the *Uttarakāṇḍa* (7.13–34).

"trampled . . . embraced" *vinihataḥ . . . pragṛhītaś ca*: Literally, "struck down . . . adopted." As various commentators point out, the references here are to Rāvaṇa's numerous acts of oppression of the brahmans, gods, divine sages, etc. (*anekadvijadevarṣyādipīḍaneneti śeṣaḥ*—so Ct). Note the typographical error in the critical edition, which reads *pragṛhatiś ca*. This is not noted in the errata.

15. "your reckless actions" *pramādāt . . . te*: Literally, "because of your heedlessness, recklessness."

"righteousness, which the deities revere" *surabhāvanaḥ*: Literally, "that which has the reverence of the gods." Following the suggestion of Ct, Cr, and Ck, we have added the word "righteousness (*dharma*)" to maintain the binary opposition between *dharma* and *adharma* that forms the backbone of Mālyavān's argument. We also accept these commentators' gloss on *bhāvanam*, "feeling of devotion *or* faith," as "constant worship *or* practice (*bhāvanaṃ nityānuṣṭhānam*—Ck, Ct)." Cr glosses, "it is revered (*bhāvyate*)." Cg and Cm, on the other hand, understand *adharma* to be the subject of both clauses. In keeping with this interpretation, they understand *surabhāvanam* to mean "favoring the gods (*surānukulaḥ*—Cg)" or "strengthening the gods (*surān bhāvayati vardhayati*—Cm)." This, however, seems redundant in the context.

16. "Doing whatever you pleased" *yat kiṃcit kāriṇā tvayā*: Literally, "by you doing whatever." Roussel (1903, vol. 3, p. 99) mistakenly translates, "*tout ce que tu fais*." In this he has been followed by Shastri (1959, vol. 3, p. 86) and Pagani (1999, p. 950).

"suffering" *udvegaḥ*: We agree with Cg, who glosses, "mental anguish (*manastāpaḥ*)," in taking this term in its usual sense of "pain, affliction, suffering." Ct and Cm understand the term somewhat unusually to mean "wrath, anger (*krodhaḥ*—Ct)." This interpretation has been followed by the majority of translators consulted, with the exception of Pagani ("*une profonde détresse*"; 1999, p. 950) and Gita Press ("great molestation"; 1969, vol. 3, p. 1488). Gorresio's text reads *saṃtrāsaḥ*, "fear." Cg and Cm understand that the seers' agitation is caused by such acts as the abduction of their daughters and wives [by Rāvaṇa] (*kanyāpatnīharaṇādikam*).

17. "all the different principal sacrificial rites" *mukhyair yajñaiḥ . . . tais taiḥ*: Literally, "those [and] those principal sacrifices."

18. "Reciting the *vedas* aloud . . . they chant the vedic *mantras*" *vedāṃś coccair adhīyate . . . brahmaghoṣān udairayan*: Here again, Cg attempts to eliminate the apparent redundancy, arguing that the second phrase is a kind of gloss or explanation (*vivaraṇam*) of the first.

"They pour oblations" *juhvati*: Cg tries to distinguish between the action described here and the seemingly identical action of sacrifice mentioned in the preceding verse. He argues that sacrifice (*yāga*) is the renunciation of some substance on behalf of a divinity, whereas oblation (*homa*) is the physical offering in the sacrificial fire of that which is renounced. (*devatoddeśena dravyatyāgo yāgaḥ. tyaktasyāgnau prakṣepo homa ity anayor bhedaḥ.*)

"Thwarting" *abhibhūya*: The most common sense of *abhi* √*bhū* is "to defeat, overcome, humiliate." All translations consulted interpret the gerund in this sense. Among the commentators, only Cg provides a gloss, *agaṇayitvā*, "paying no heed to." On the basis of their silence, we presume that the other commentators accept the more common meaning. Cg's interpretation seems to reflect the normal relationship between the vedic *ṛṣis* and the *rākṣasas* as it has been described earlier in the poem, where the brahmans required Rāma's services to protect them and their rituals from the depredations of the demons.

"all the *rākṣasas* scatter in all directions" *diśo vipradrutāḥ sarve*: Literally, "all run in [all] directions." We follow the commentators in adding the word *rākṣasas* to provide the subject. A variety of mainly northern manuscripts, but including the text of Cg and the printed editions of VSP, KK, Gorresio, Gita Press, and Lahore, read *sarvāḥ* instead of *sarve*, which yields the sense "they scatter in all directions." This reading is followed by all translations consulted regardless of the text on which they are based.

"thunderclouds in the hot season" *stanayitnur ivoṣṇage*: Literally, "like thunder in the hot season." We follow Cv, Cm, Cg, and Cr, who interpret *uṣṇage* in its common meaning of *grīṣme*, "hot season." Ck, Ct, and Cs interpret *uṣṇage* as a compound in which the prior member refers to the hot season, while the compound refers elliptically to the sun at that time of year. They thus read the phrase as a kind of locative absolute in the sense of "when the sun is in the hot season" (*uṣṇo grīṣmas tadgate ravāv iti śeṣaḥ*—so Ct).

19. "the Agnihotra rites" *agnihotra-*: See note to 6.23.24.

"saps" *ādatte*: Literally, "it takes away." The texts and printed editions of Ct, Ck, and Cr read instead the gerund *āvṛtya*, "enveloping, occluding." Because in this reading the gerund replaces the finite verb, Ct and Cr must provide a replacement. Ct offers *uttiṣṭhati*, "it rises up," while Cr suggests *atiṣṭhat*, "it stood."

20. Following verse 20, D5–7,9–11,S insert a passage of three lines [547*] in which Mālyavān continues his speech, stating, "You obtained a boon[1] against gods, *dānavas*, and *yakṣas*. But it is powerful and mighty men, monkeys, apes, and langurs, firm in their valor, who have come here and are roaring."

[1]"boon" *varaḥ*: The critical edition makes no mention of the boon of Rāvaṇa at this point. Cg and Cm specifically mention that the boon is that of "invulnerability (*avadhyatva*)." They understand Mālyavān's comment to be in anticipation of Rāvaṇa's possible objection based on his boon of invulnerability to the gods, etc. (*balino 'pi devā brahmadattavaramahimnā na prahartuṃ śaknuyur iti cet tatrāha devadānavetyādinā*). For Rāvaṇa's boon of invulnerability, see note to 6.28.28–29.

21. For similar passages listing inauspicious omens, see 6.31.3–12; 6.41.30–34; 6.45.31–37; 6.53.41–45; 6.65.17–19; 6.83.32–24; 6.94.14–27; and notes. Compare the similar evil omens that presage the destruction of Dvārakā at *Mahābhārata* 16.3. Cf. *AgniP* 529–33.

"And . . . many different" *vividhān . . . bahuvidhāṃs tathā*: Literally, "and . . . various . . . of many kinds." D0–3,7,9–11, and the texts and printed editions of Ct and Cr read *bahūn*, "many, " for *tathā*. The commentators are eager to avoid any redundancy. They distinguish the adjectives in slightly different ways. Cg and Cm, who follow the critical text, understand *vividhān* to mean "divided into different types: celestial, atmospheric, and terrestrial (*divyāntarikṣabhaumabhedabhinnān*)." Cg takes *bahuvidhān* to refer to differences within the types just mentioned (*bhaumādiṣu pratyekaṃ vividhān*). Cm and Cv understand similarly. Ct understands *bahuvidhān* in the same sense in which Cg understands *vividhān*, that is, "divided into different types: celestial, atmospheric, and terrestrial (*divyāntarikṣabhaumabhedabhinnān*)." He does not comment on *vividhān*. Cr takes *vividhān* to mean "producing many forbidden consequences (*anekaniṣiddhaphalavidhāyakān*)." Cr then explains *bahuvidhān* as "of many types (*anekaprakārān*)."

22. "thundering deafeningly" *kharābhistanitāḥ*: Literally, "harshly thundering." See 6.31.5; 6.41.33; 6.45.926*–36; and 6.53.41; and notes.

"with hot blood" *śoṇitena . . . uṣṇena*: For blood raining down, see 6.31.5; 6.41.33; 6.45.926*–36; 6.83.33; 6.94.15; and notes. Cf. note to 6.76.2, inserted passage 1674*, lines 5–7. For a discussion on evil omens, see 5.25.35–37 and note; see also 5.27.4 and note.

23. "weeping mounts" *rudatāṃ vāhanānām*: The crying or weeping of mounts is a commonly mentioned ill omen. See 6.65.18; 6.83.33; and 6.94.26 and notes.

"battle flags" *dhvajāḥ*: Ś,V2,3,D4,7–9,11–13,G2,3,M5, and the texts and printed editions of Ct, Ck, and Cr substitute *rajo-*, yielding the adjective *rajodhvastāḥ*, "covered with dust." This reading provides no explicit modificand for the adjective, leaving the commentators who share it to supply one. Ct and Cr supply *diśaḥ*, "quarters, directions," which is in accordance with the conventional evil omen of dust-occluded horizons. This interpretation has been followed by Dutt (1893, p. 1203), Gita Press (1969, vol. 3, p. 1489), Shastri (1959, vol. 3, p. 86), and Roussel (1903, vol. 3, p. 99). Ct also notes that "some [commentators]" propose supplying instead the word *vāhanāni*, "mounts" (despite the gender disagreement that this would cause). Of the translators consulted, only Pagani (1999, p. 950) follows this suggestion.

24. "Beasts of prey" *vyālāḥ*: The term has a number of meanings, several of which are possible in this context. We agree, however, with Ct and Ck, who gloss, "carnivorous beasts (*māṃsādāḥ paśavaḥ*)." Cg takes the term in its adjectival sense of "malicious, vicious (*duṣṭāḥ*)" and sees it as modifying the jackals and vultures. All translators consulted, with the exception Roussel (1903, vol. 3, p. 99) and Shastri (1959, vol. 3, p. 87), agree with Ct and Ck. Roussel, however, followed as usual by Shastri, understands *vyāla* in another of its senses, viz., "serpent." Cf. 6.31.5 and note.

The howling or shrieking of beasts of prey, especially jackals, is a common evil portent. See 6.31.7; 6.45.32,34; 6.53.42; 6.83.33; 6.94.21; and notes. Cf. 6.41.32 and note.

"keep pouring into" *praviśya . . . aniśam*: Literally, "constantly entering." D9–11 and the texts and printed editions of Ct, Ck, and Cr substitute the locative *ārāme*, "in the garden," for the adverb *aniśam*, "constantly." This inferior reading is reflected in all translations consulted, with the exception of Raghunathan (1982, vol. 3, p. 85), who follows Cg, and Gorresio, whose text reads *sahasā*, "all at once," in place of *aniśam*.

25. "Dark women" *kālikāḥ . . . striyaḥ*: Commentators differ as to the identity of these women. Ct and Ck understand them to be Mahākālīs, which are horrific forms of the goddess. Cs defines them similarly as "village divinities, such as Mahākālī, Bhadrakālī, and so forth (*grāmasthāḥ mahākālībhadrakālītyādayaḥ*)." Cm and Crā in a similar vein describe them as "*śaktis*," meaning supernatural females, such as Pūtanā, etc. (*pūtanāpramukhaśaktayaḥ*—Cm). Cg, whom we have followed, describes them as women of blue-black complexion, such as Pūtanā (*nīlavarṇāḥ striyaḥ pūtanāpramukhā iti yāvat*), while noting that some commentators (e.g., Cm, Crā) have called them "*śaktis*" (*śaktaya ity eke*)." Cr glosses *karālāḥ*, "deformed, hideous, *or* having protuberant teeth." Crā and Cm gloss *striyaḥ* with the accusative plural *strīḥ* and understand that the *kālikās* are speaking menacingly to the women [of Laṅkā]. For a discussion of the nature and history of malignant supernatural females in early India, see White (2003, pp. 27–66). See 6.34.15 and note. Cf. 5.22.41 and note; and 6.60.18; 6.69.23; 6.71.13; and notes.

"deathly white teeth" *pāṇḍurair dantaiḥ*: Literally, "with white teeth." Most commentators simply note that the women are characterized (*upalakṣitāḥ*) by white teeth but attribute no specific meaning to this feature. Our translation is influenced by the interpretation of Cs, who feels that the mention of the color of the teeth, along with the activities attributed to the women, indicates that death is inevitable after a short interval. (*dantānāṃ pāṇḍuratvoktyoktyā ca viruddhabhāṣaṇamoṣaṇahasanādīnāṃ niścitaṃ maraṇam. kiṃcid vyavadhānena bhaviṣyatīti sūcayati.*)

"laughing wildly" *prahasanti*: Literally, "they laugh." We have added the adverb in keeping with the tenor of the verse.

"speaking menacingly" *pratibhāṣya*: Ct, Ck, Cg, and Cm all understand the *upasarga prati* as *pratikūlam*, "adversely, threateningly, menacingly." Ck additionally notes, "speaking improperly (*asabhyabhāṣaṇaṃ kṛtvā* [lit., 'having made improper speech'])." Cs understands, "contrary speech (*viruddhabhāṣaṇa-*)," while Cv glosses, "shouting back (*pratikruśya*)." Cr simply glosses, "addressing (*saṃbodhya*)."

"looting houses" *muṣṇantyo gṛhāṇi*: Ct, Ck, Cr, Cg, and Cm all feel that the word *gṛhāṇi* here is a kind of metonymy for the contents of the houses (*gṛhāṇi tadvartidravyajātam*—so Ct, Ck). This interpretation is followed by Dutt (1893, p. 1203) and Raghunathan (1982, vol. 3, p. 85), who translate "furniture" and "household goods," respectively.

26. "the *bali* offerings in house after house" *gṛhāṇāṃ balikarmāṇi*: Literally, "the *bali* rites of houses." The term *bali* refers to a commonly practiced household ritual of offering or scattering various foods for spirits, divinities, birds, and so on. As Cg points out, the term is used here by metonymy for the offerings or oblations that are needed to perform the rite (*balikarmasādhanāni havīṃṣi*). Crā understands similarly.

"Cows are giving birth to donkeys" *kharā goṣu prajāyante*: Literally, "donkeys are being born to cows."

"while rats are mating with mongooses" *mūṣikā nakulaiḥ saha*: Literally, "rats with mongooses." To make sense of this reading, one has to supply a verb. Cg, who shares the reading, suggests the bland *vartante*, "they are." Given the context of what follows, we prefer to borrow the verb *sameyuḥ*, "they mate, have sex with," from verse 27 below. Most northern manuscripts and the texts and printed editions of Ck, Ct, and Cr read the locative *nakaleṣu* [v.l. *nakulīṣu*] *ca* for the critical reading. This then creates a parallel construction to that in *pāda* c, reading "mongooses are giving birth to rats."

27. "with tigers" *dvīpibhiḥ*: We follow Ck and Ct, who gloss, "with tigers (*śārdūlaiḥ*)." The word can also mean leopard, and some translators render accordingly.

"and even with humans" *mānuṣaiḥ saha*: Note the apparent contradiction here, since, with the exception of Sītā, there are no humans in Laṅkā. Cg explains that the humans must have been produced supernaturally as a result of the omens of which Mālyavān is speaking (*mānuṣāś cātrotpātajanitā eva*). Crā claims that *pādas* cd are found only in a few manuscripts and that they contain a clear contradiction because there are no humans in Laṅkā. (*kiṃnarā rākṣasaiś cāpi samīyur mānuṣaiḥ sahety ardhaṃ keṣucit kośeṣu na dṛśyate. tasmin virodho 'sti laṅkāyāṃ mānuṣābhāvāt.*)

28. "White doves with red feet" *pāṇḍurā raktapādāś ca . . . kapotāḥ*: The red color here signals inauspiciousness. Cf. 6.67.5 and note. Cf. *AgniP* 232.4–5.

"flutter through the sky" *vihagāḥ . . . vicaranti*: Literally, "sky-goers move about." The term *vihaga* is most commonly used as a kenning for "bird *or* other flying creature." Given the presence of the noun "dove *or* pigeon (*kapota*)," it must be taken as an adjective or even as a participle. Ct and Ck understand that the omen consists not so much in the fact that the birds are flying about but that they do so inside people's houses. They therefore suggest adding the phrase "inside the houses (*gṛheṣu madhya iti śeṣaḥ*)." For other references to birds as ill omens, see 6.31.8; 6.41.30; 6.43.8; 6.45.18,33,36; 6.53.43; 6.83.32; and notes. See, too, 6.94.25 and note.

29. "*śārikas*" *śārikāḥ*: Probably the common mynah (also called *sārika*), *Acridotheres tristis*. See Dave 1985, pp. 81–82, 85–86; Ali and Ripley 1968–1974, vol. 5, pp. 177–180; and Brockington 1984, p. 95. Monier-Williams (s.v.) offers "*Turdus salica*." See 6.94.25 and note.

"screeching, "*cīcīkūcī*" " *cīcīkūcīti vāśyantyaḥ*: Cg, reading the variant *vīcīkūcī*, remarks that these birds, nurtured in houses for their sweet singing, have now abandoned their dulcet tones and are screeching fiercely (*veṣmasu madhurasaṃlāpārthaṃ poṣitāḥ śārikā madhurabhāṣaṇāni vihāya vīcīkūcīti krūraṃ vāśyantīty arthaḥ*). Cr, on the other hand, understands that the birds are mimicking the cries of various species, cries such as *cīcī* and *kūcī* (*cīcīti kūcīti ca tattajjātīyaśabdānukaraṇaṃ vāśyantaḥ santaḥ*).

"tethered . . . once tamed, they have become aggressive" *grathitāś cāpi nirjitāḥ kalahaiṣiṇaḥ*: Literally, "even though tied and subdued, quarrelsome." It appears to us that the situation being described is that the pet birds have suddenly abandoned their docile demeanor and have become wild and savage. In this, our understanding is informed somewhat by that of Cg, who groups the mynahs together with the birds and beasts mentioned in the southern interpolated passage 558* (see below), arguing that the creatures are quarrelsome, even though they have been previously tamed and bound together in bunches (*pūrvaṃ nirjitā api punaḥ kalahaiṣiṇaḥ santo grathitāḥ puñjībhūtāḥ patanti dhāvanti*). Ct, Ck, and Cr, however, understand the situation to be that the birds have been worsted by other birds in fights and are tied to one another as they flutter about (*pakṣyantarair nirjitā grathitāḥ patanti parasparam ābadhya patanti*).

Following verse 29, D5–7,9–11,S insert a passage of one line [558*]: "All the birds and beasts are screeching at the sun."

30. "at all hours" *kāle kāle*: Literally, "in time, in time." Cr, Ct, and Ck understand, "at each of the *saṃdhya* times, that is, dawn and twilight (*saṃdhyākāleṣu*)." Cg similarly explains, "morning and evening (*sāyaṃ pratāś ca*)." Cf. 5.12.48.

31. This verse and the one that follows it are interesting from a textual point of view, and their inclusion in the critical edition bears upon the debate as to whether the oldest stratum of the text recognizes the divinity of Rāma and his identity with Viṣṇu. Both verses are omitted in D5,6,T, while D11 omits only verse 31. The verses are poorly attested in the texts and printed editions of the southern commentators, with only Cr and Cs accepting and commenting upon them. Ck mentions the verses and notes that the older, i.e., more authentic, textual authorities regard them as interpolated and, therefore, decline to comment upon them (*viṣṇuṃ manyāmahe rāmam ityādi saṃdhiṃ rāmeṇa rāvaṇa ity antaṃ ślokadvayaṃ prakṣiptam iti prācīnair na vyākhyātam*). Ct quotes his remarks approvingly. Cr explains verse 31, saying that Mālyavān, etc., think that Rāma must be Viṣṇu in human form because of his extraordinary valor. They reason, therefore, that he must be something other than an ordinary human and that he is indeed the Supreme Being (*parapuruṣa*) (*mānuṣaṃ rūpam āsthitaṃ rāmaṃ viṣṇuṃ svapratāpadvārā sarvatra pūrṇaṃ manyāmahe 'to 'yaṃ rāghavo mānuṣamātro 'smajjñānaviṣayībhūtamanuṣyaśarīravān na prākṛtavilakṣaṇaḥ parapuruṣa ity arthaḥ*).

The two verses are treated variously in the different printed editions of the southern texts. GPP brackets and places them between 6.35.34cd [=critical edition 30ef] and 6.35.34ef [=critical edition 565*]. The editors of KK bracket them but number them as verses 6.35.38–39, noting that the verses are absent from five of their manuscripts. VSP omits them from its running text, placing them in a footnote marked between its verses 6.35.36 and 6.35.37. It quotes Ck and Cs in that same note. Gita Press includes these verses as 6.36.35,36a–d. Because of the spotty representation of this passage in the printed editions of the south, it is rendered in only a few of the translations consulted. Thus only Dutt (1893, p. 1203), Shastri (1959, vol. 9, p. 87), and Gita Press (1969, vol. 3, p. 1489) translate the verses, while Pagani, Roussel, and Raghunathan omit them. A variant of the passage appears in Gorresio (1856, vol. 9, p. 232) and corresponds to his edition's 6.11.32cd–34ab [=Lahore edition 6.11.28–29]. That this passage has such strong textual support in what is generally acknowledged to be one of the "core books" of the epic speaks in favor of the position that the oldest strata of the text are fully aware of Rāma's divinity and of his identification as a Vaiṣṇava *avatāra* (see Pollock 1984b and 1991, pp. 15–67; *pace* Brockington 1984, chap. 7 and Gonzales-Reimann 2006). Cf. Hopkins 1902, p. 139. Compare 6.47.104 and note.

"We truly believe" *manyāmahe*: Literally, "we think."

32. Following verse 32, D5–7,9–11,S insert a passage of one line [565*]: "You should consider these events[1] and then do what will be beneficial for our future."

[1]"events" *karmāṇi*: Literally, "actions, deeds." Cr understands these actions to be the heroic deeds of Rāma. Ct agrees but adds the omens reported by Mālyavān. Ck refers only to the omens. VSP, KK, and GPP record Cg's reading as *kāryāṇi* (which is the reading of Cm), while the critical edition reports his reading as *karmāṇi*. In his commentary Cg appears to read *karmāṇi*. Both he and Cm gloss, "*kartavyāni*," which, Cg further explains, are the actions incumbent on Rāvaṇa, such as returning Sītā, etc.

33. "among those foremost counselors" *anuttameṣu*: Literally, "among the foremost." Following Cg, we have supplied the noun "counselors" for clarity. Commentators are divided as to how to read the adjective. We agree with Cg in taking it as a *bahuvrīhi* in the sense of "having no superior," as this seems to fit the context in which the virtues of Rāvaṇa's counselors have been described (6.9.1–5). Cr and Cm understand the term in the sense of "non-excellent" and take it as a reference to the lowly and vile *rākṣasas* who form Rāvaṇa's entourage. Cs offers both alternatives, glossing, "either incomparable or vile (*anuttameṣv asadṛśeṣu rākṣaseṣu yadvānuttameṣu nīceṣu*)." None of the translators consulted takes the term as pejorative, with the exception of Dutt (1893, p. 1202), who seems to take the plural term as a reference to Rāvaṇa himself, translating, "having said this unto that vile one."

"had judged the intentions" *parīkṣya* ... *manaḥ*: Literally, "having examined the mind." Ct and Ck explain, "having realized that 'my words do not please him' (*tasmai rāvaṇāyety artho manaḥ parīkṣya maduktam asmai na rocata iti jñātvety arthaḥ*—so Ct)." Cg, Cs, and Cm explain, "realizing that his mind was not to be changed (*manaḥ parīkṣyānivartyaṃ jñātvā*—so Cg)."

"watching Rāvaṇa closely" *samavekṣya rāvaṇam*: Cg explains, "having observed Rāvaṇa's appearance closely, that is, principally observing his gestures, etc. (*rāvaṇākāraṃ samavekṣyeṅgitādidarśanapuraḥsaraṃ dṛṣṭvā*)." He thus explicitly distinguishes this action from the action of examining Rāvaṇa's feelings expressed in the gerund *parīkṣya* above. Pagani (1999, p. 951) understands, "*devant la moue de Rāvaṇa*."

The meter is *vaṃśasthavila*.

Sarga 27

1. "could not abide" *na marṣayati*: Literally, "he does not tolerate."

"the words ... uttered for his own good" *vākyaṃ hitam uktam*: Literally, "speech spoken beneficially *or* beneficial speech spoken." All translators consulted, with the exception of Raghunathan (1982, vol. 3, p. 86) and Gorresio (1856, vol. 7, p. 232), understand the word *hitam* as an adjective meaning "beneficial," modifying *vākyam*, "speech." We, however, tend to agree with Cg, who reads the term *hitam* adverbially with the participle *uktam*, "spoken" (*uktaṃ hitaṃ yathā bhavati tathā*).

2. "rolling his eyes in rage" *amarṣāt parivṛttākṣaḥ*: On rolling one's eyes as a sign of rage, see 5.20.23; 6.46.14; 6.84.30; and notes. Cf. 6.47.55 and 6.50.9.

3. "I shall not listen to these" *naitac chrotragataṃ mama*: Literally, "this has not entered *or* gone to my ears."

"thinking them to be beneficial" *hitabuddhyā*: Literally, "with an idea of [being] beneficial."

"you are in effect siding with my enemies" *parapakṣaṃ praviśyaiva*: Literally, "having actually entered the enemies' camp *or* side." We interpret with the majority of the commentators. Ct and Ck, however, gloss, "having accepted their [the enemies'] superiority (*tatprābalyaṃ parigṛhyaiva*)." Among the translators consulted, only Dutt (1893, p. 1204) follows this interpretation.

4. Cg and Cm subject this verse to two interesting but very different close readings. Cg explains each of the terms in Rāvaṇa's description. Thus, *mānuṣam*, "human," means that Rāma is weak by reason of his very species (*jātyā hīnabalam*); *kṛpaṇam*, "wretched," means that he is deficient by nature (*prakṛtyā hīnam*); *ekam*, "alone," indicates that he has no (significant) allies (*asahāyam*); *śākhāmṛgāśrayam*, "has to rely on tree-dwelling monkeys," means that he has only inferior allies (*kṣudrasahāyam*); *tyaktaṃ pitrā*, "abandoned by his own father," means that he is impoverished (*nirdhanam*); and *vanālayam*, "lives in the forest," indicates that he is without a kingdom (*rājyahīnam*). Cm, in one of his intermittent bursts of devotional energy (see note to 5.20.3; cf. notes to 6.47.6; 6.53.38; 6.56.13; 6.57.7; 6.59.53; 6.60.6; 6.65.10; 6.68.26; 6.75.19–22; 6.80.15; and 6.81.4), reinterprets each of these terms to make Rāvaṇa deliver a virtual *stotra* in praise of the *Rāmāvatara*. He claims that in reality (*vastutas tu*) the inner meaning of the verse is as follows:

> *Vanālayam* means "he whose resting place (*ālaya*) is the water (*vanam*), i.e., the ocean (*udadhiḥ*)," in other words, "who sleeps on a banyan leaf (*vaṭapatraśayinam*) [in the ocean], or Nārāyaṇa." This divinity is abandoned by his father (*pitrā tyaktaṃ*) in the sense that he has no beginning, etc., for the Lord, lacking any birth, and so forth, has therefore no father. Thus, he is alone (*ekam*). That is, he is without a second. (*ata eva pitrā tyaktaṃ janmādirahitam ity arthaḥ. īśvarasya janmādyabhāvād eva pitrādyabhāvaḥ. ata evaikam advitīyam.*) He is *śākhāmṛgāśrayam* in the sense that he must be sought (*mṛgyate*) through the *śākhās*, or branches of the vedic corpus, that is, he is to be known through the *vedas* (*ata eva śākhāmṛgāśrayaṃ śākhābhir vedaśākhābhir mṛgyata iti śākhāmṛgo vedavedyaḥ*). Also, since he is the universal Lord (*sarveśvaraḥ*), he is thus the *āśrayaḥ*, or Universal recourse (*sarveśvaraḥ sa cāsāv āśrayaś ceti tam*). He is human (*mānuṣam*) in that he has incarnated himself in the form of a man and *kṛpaṇa* in the sense of compassionate (*kṛpālu*). Moreover, in regarding Rāma in these terms, Rāvaṇa is saying that Mālyavān is quite correct in seeing him as capable (*tathāpi kenāpi hetunā mānuṣaṃ manuṣyarūpeṇāvatīrṇam ata eva kṛpaṇaṃ kṛpāluṃ rāmaṃ samarthaṃ manyase kila tad yuktam eva*).

5. Cm continues his devotional interpretation in this verse, inverting the order of the adjectives *ahīnam*, "in no way lacking," and *hīnam*, "weak, deficient," to yield the sense "What makes you (Mālyavān) think that I, the lord of the *rākṣasas*, who am lacking in all valor, am so strong (*ahīnam*)? (*kena hetunā rakṣasām īśvaraṃ sarvaparākramair hīnaṃ māṃ ahīnaṃ manyasa ity arthaḥ*)." See verse 4 above.

6. "out of resentment of my prowess" *vīradveṣeṇa*: Literally, "through hatred of a hero." Cg explains, "through animus toward a hero of your own race (*svajātīyavīradveṣeṇa*)."

"the prompting of my foes" *paraprotsāhanena*: A few, mostly *devanāgarī*, manuscripts and the texts and printed editions of Ck, Ct, and Cr read *mama*, "my," for *para-*, "foe." This reading gives the phrase the sense of "[or] in order to provoke me." Ct and Ck explain that Mālyavān hopes to provoke Rāvaṇa to fight by praising his enemy (*śatrupraśaṃsāyāṃ krodhād yuddhāya pravartiṣyata iti*). This reading, both textually and contextually inferior, is reflected in the translations of Dutt (1893, p. 1204), Shastri (1959, vol. 3, p. 88), Pagani (1999, p. 951), and Roussel (1903, vol. 3, p. 101).

7. "unless he were prompted by an enemy" *vinā protsāhanād ripoḥ*: Some *devanāgarī* manuscripts (D7,9–11) and the texts and printed editions of Ck, Ct, and Cr read instead *vinā protsāhanena vā*, "unless through incitement." They interpret the phrase as they did in the previous verse and are followed by the same translators who are mentioned in the previous note.

8. "who, but for the lotus, resembles the goddess Śrī" *padmahīnām iva śriyam*: Literally, "like Śrī devoid of a lotus." Commentators are somewhat divided as to how to interpret the phrase. Ct takes it similarly to the parallel expression, *bhraṣṭapadmām iva śriyam* at 6.25.16, arguing that it suggests Sītā's loss of splendor and her vulnerability to abduction (*lakṣmītvābhāvabodhanam atyupādeyatvabodhanaṃ ca*). The context here, however, would seem to call for a reference to Sītā's beauty and desirability rather than her loss of radiance as at 6.25.16. We therefore follow Cs and Ck, who understand that it is only the lotus that distinguishes Sītā from the splendid Goddess of Fortune (*kevalaṃ padmenaivaitasyās tasyāś ca bheda iti bhāvaḥ*).

"for fear of Rāghava" *rāghavasya bhayāt*: We read the phrase with Cg, who glosses *rāghavāt* for *rāghavasya*. Cm and Cr agree. Some of the translators take the genitive *rāghavasya* (*sādharaṇaṣaṣṭhī*) as the indirect object of the verb *pratidāsyāmi*, "to give back." They thus understand, "why would I give . . . back to Rāghava?" Cm provides a devotional explanation, interpreting as follows: "Since I took Sītā from the forest only out of a desire to be slain at Rāma's hands, why then would I return her out of fear of him? (*rāmahastād vadhecchayaiva vanāt sītām ānīya rāghavasya bhayāt kim arthaṃ pratidāsyāmīty arthaḥ*)." See note to verse 4 above.

9. "In a few short days" *kaiścid ahobhiḥ*: Literally, "with *or* by some days."

"you will see me slay Rāghava" *paśya . . . rāghavaṃ nihataṃ mayā*: Literally, "Behold Rāghava slain by me." Cm, continuing his devotional reading of the passage, proposes taking the root $\sqrt{han}$, "slay," in the sense of "come ($\bar{a}\sqrt{gam}$)." He thus understands, "[behold Rāma] coming here on my account." (*mayā hetunā nihatam āgatam ity arthaḥ. "hanahiṃsāgatyoḥ"* [*Naighaṇṭuka* ii, 14] *iti dhātor evam arthaḥ.*) See note to verse 4 above. See, too, notes to 6.37.9; 6.80.29; 6.81.4; and 6.91.19. Cf. 6.67.17 and note.

"and their tens of millions of monkeys" *vṛtaṃ vānarakoṭībhiḥ*: Literally, "surrounded by tens of millions of monkeys."

11. Cg believes that Rāvaṇa utters this verse out of regret for having spoken so harshly to his venerable granduncle (see note to 6.25.5), who only wants what is good for him (*atyantahitaparaṃ vṛddhaṃ mātāmahaṃ katham evaṃ paruṣam uktavān asmīty anutāpenāha*).

"I might be cut in two" *dvidhā bhajyeyam*: Literally, "I might divide into two." Ct says that Rāvaṇa might break like bamboo but will not bend like a reed (*dvidhā bhajyeyam itaraveṇuvan na nameyaṃ vetasavat*). We prefer the interpretation of Cg, who glosses, "I might have my head cut off (*śiraśchedaṃ prāpnuyām*)." Cm supplies the word *śatruṇā*, "by an enemy."

"This is an innate fault of mine" *eṣa me sahajo doṣaḥ*: Cg, with whom Cm agrees, notes that Rāvaṇa makes this self-deprecatory comment in the knowledge that his position violates the maxim of political science that holds that an inferior party sues for peace (*tarhi hīyamānena sandhiḥ kārya iti nītiśāstravirodhaḥ syāt tatrāha eṣa me sahajo doṣa iti*). See 6.26.8 and *ArthŚā* 7.1.13 (*parasmād dhīyamānaḥ saṃdadhīta*).

12. "somehow or other... actually" *tāvat... yadṛcchayā*: Literally, "really... by chance." Ct and Ck understand Rāvaṇa to be attributing the feat of bridging the ocean to a lucky accident rather than to any great power on Rāma's part. They cite in this connection the maxim of the writing of the bark beetle (*ghuṇākṣaranyāya*) in which the burrowed tracks of the insect in wood or paper may chance to resemble letters of the alphabet. (*rāmeṇa samudre setur baddha iti vismayo yadi ko 'tra vismayaḥ. yataḥ sa yadṛcchayā daivagatyā ghuṇākṣaranyāyena na tu svasāmarthyenety arthaḥ.*) Cg, similarly, invokes the maxim of the crow and the palmyra fruit (*kākatālīyanyāya*) in which the alighting of the bird on the palmyra tree and the fall of its fruit are falsely thought to be causally connected (*atha setubandhena vismayase cet tad api kākatālīyam ato mā bhūt te bhayam ity āha*). The two maxims seem somewhat inapposite here, as it is difficult to see how anyone could accidentally build a bridge over the ocean. Cg attempts perhaps to minimize the incongruity by taking the polysemic indeclinable *tāvat* in its sense of "just a little" to indicate that it was only a small ocean that Rāma bridged (*tāvat samudre svalpasamudra ity arthaḥ*).

"what is so miraculous about this" *vismayaḥ ko 'tra*: Literally, "what miracle is there in this?" Cr says that Rāvaṇa means to say, "I am (lit., we are) capable of accomplishing many [such miracles] (*vayam evam anekaśaḥ kartuṃ samarthā ity arthaḥ*)."

13. "not" *na*: Continuing his devotional reading, Cm proposes taking the negative particle out of the syntax of the primary sentence and reading it separately, in the sense of "no doubt (*na sandehaḥ*)." He thus reads, "having crossed... Rāma will return alive, without a doubt, I promise you (*sa tv ity asya vāstavārthas rāmo vānarasenayā sahārṇavaṃ tīrtvā jīvan pratiyāsyatīti te satyaṃ pratijānāmi na sandehaḥ*)." See note to verse 4 above.

14. "with such agitation... angry" *saṃrabdhaṃ ruṣṭam*: We read the former term adverbially with the participle *bruvāṇam*, "speaking," and the second adjectivally with *rāvaṇam*, "Rāvaṇa." Ct, Cr, and Cg read the former adjectivally and thus are obligated to distinguish the near synonyms. Ct understands *saṃrabdham* to mean "worked up for battle (*saṃrabdhaṃ yuddhe saṃrambhavantam*)," while Cr glosses, "prepared for battle (*yuddhodyogavantam*)." Cg explains, "filled with egotism (*ahaṃkārayuktam*)." Ct glosses *ruṣṭam* as "angry (*kupitam*)." See note to 6.2.14.

"humiliated" *vrīḍitaḥ*: Cg suggests that Mālyavān is humiliated because of the futility of his advice (*svopadeśavaiphalyād iti bhāvaḥ*).

16. "he went on taking counsel and deliberating" *mantrayitvā vimṛśya ca*: Cg attempts to differentiate the near synonyms by arguing that the former refers to deliberating the course of action and the latter to the taking of decisions. (*mantrayitvā kartavyaṃ vicārya. vimṛśya niścitya.*)

"ordering" *kārayāmāsa*: Literally, "he caused to make."

"unparalleled defense of Laṅkā" *laṅkāyām atulāṃ guptim*: Literally, "an unequaled protection in Laṅkā." D7,9–11, and the texts and printed editions of Ct and Cr read instead *laṅkāyās tu tadā guptim*, "then... the defense of Laṅkā."

19. "after assigning Śuka and Sāraṇa" *vyādiśya śukasāraṇau*: Ct, apparently referring to the tense exchanges between Rāvaṇa and these two *rākṣasa* spies at 6.20.1–13 above,

notes that Rāvaṇa contemptuously relieves them of duty [at the northern gate] after hearing their reports [of their botched intelligence missions] (*tanmukhato vṛttānta-śravaṇottaraṃ tau tiraskṛtyety arthaḥ*). The idea is that Rāvaṇa intends to take that position himself. Ct's understanding is perhaps supported by the fact that, at 6.28.13 below, Rāvaṇa alone is said to be stationed at the northern gate, while no mention of Śuka and Sāraṇa is made. See 6.34.19 and notes.

"I shall be there" *atra bhaviṣyāmi*: As is made clear by 6.28.13, the sense is that Rāvaṇa plans to take up his position at the northern gate as well. B4,D5,7,10,11, and the texts and printed editions of Ct and Cr read instead *gamiṣyāmi*, "I shall go." Cr believes that Rāvaṇa is indicating a planned inspection of all the four positions to which he has ordered his ministers (*atrādiṣṭarākṣasasthitadikṣv ahaṃ gamiṣyāmi yathā-kālaṃ sarvaṃ drakṣyāmīty arthaḥ*).

20. "the central encampment" *madhyame... gulme*: Cg defines *gulma* here as "a shrine or domed structure in the center of the city (*nagaramadhyacaityasthānam*)." This contrasts somewhat with his explanation of the same term at 5.3.27, where he defines it as "a military assembly point in the center of the city (*nagaramadhyasthitasainyasamājaḥ*)." Ct and Ck gloss, "an army encampment in the center of the city (*puramadhyavartini senā-sanniveśe*)," while earlier Ct understands, "central courtyard (*madhyamakakṣyāpradeśaḥ*)." See 5.3.27 (= GPP 5.4.15) and note. Cf. 6.3.27; 6.28.31; 6.31.31; 6.45.2; 6.62.5; 6.71.1; 6.72.5; 6.84.6; and notes.

"Virūpākṣa" *virūpākṣam*: This *rākṣasa*'s name was used by Jacobi (1893) as part of his argument for the interpolated nature of much of the text of the *Sundarakāṇḍa*. See Goldman and Goldman 1996, p. 23. See, too, 6.28.31 and note.

21. "Thus did... complete... Then... he considered" *evam... kṛtvā... mene*: Literally, "Having made [arrangements] thus, he thought."

"Then, being under the power of fate, he considered himself to have accomplished his objective." *mene kṛtārtham ātmānaṃ kṛtāntavaśam āgataḥ*: D5–7,9–11,T,M, and the texts and printed editions of the southern commentators read instead the paraphrase *kṛtakṛtyam ivātmānaṃ manyate kālacoditaḥ*, "impelled by Kāla (i.e., his own impending doom), he thought himself to have, as it were, accomplished his purpose." Cf. 6.38.19 and note.

22. The meter is *vaṃśasthavila*.

Sarga 28

1–3. "Rāma the king of men, Sugrīva the king of the monkeys, the monkey Hanumān, son of Vāyu" *naravānararājau tau sa ca vāyusutaḥ kapiḥ*: Literally, "the two kings of men and monkeys [respectively] and the monkey, the son of Vāyu."

"apes" *ṛkṣa-*: On the identity of *ṛkṣas*, see note to 6.4.17. See, too, 1.16.10 and note and R. Goldman 1989.

"Suṣeṇa and his sons" *suṣeṇaḥ sahadāyādaḥ*: The term can refer specifically to a son, to any male heir, or, generically, to any male relative. Here, both Ct and Cg select the more generic meaning, "kinsmen," citing *Amarakośa* (3.3.89) (*dāyādau sutabāndhavāv ity amara*). However, at 6.35.2–3, the same term is used in connection with Suṣeṇa in a context in which the sense of "son[s]" is clearly preferable, and, for the sake of consistency, we have translated similarly here. Elsewhere in the *Rāmāyaṇa* the term generally is used in the sense of "heir" (1.59.5,6; 2.102.29; and 3.66.10).

"took counsel together, saying" *samavetāḥ samarthayan*: Literally, "assembled, they deliberated." Note the irregular absence of the preterit augment in the imperfect.

4. "It is not to be conquered even by the immortal gods" *amarair api durjayā*: B1,D7,9–11, and the texts and printed editions of Ct read instead *sarvair api sudurjayā*, "extremely difficult to conquer even by all." It is evident to the commentators and translators who share this reading that a word for "gods" must be understood or supplied.

5. "It is time to take counsel and formulate a plan" *mantrayadhvaṃ vinirṇaye*: Literally, "you [pl.] must take counsel in reference to a fixed plan."

"For this is the principal stronghold of Rāvaṇa" *nityaṃ saṃnihito hy atra rāvaṇaḥ*: Literally, "for Rāvaṇa is constantly present here."

6. "rich in meaning" *puṣkalārtham*: Ct explains, "having few words, but abundant meaning (*bahvarthālpaśabdam*)."

"free from all vulgarity" *agrāmyapadavat*: Literally, "having no vulgar words." Ct explains, "having no vulgar meanings or words and free from incorrect usages (*agrāmyārthapadavad apaśabdahīnaṃ ca*)." Cr and Ck understand only, "free from incorrect usages (*apaśabdahīnam*)," while Cm explains only, "having no vulgar meanings or words (*agrāmyārthapadavat*)." Cg understands the expression to refer explicitly to a dual linguistic code, including Sanskrit and a regional Laṅkān, or *rākṣasa*, language or dialect. He glosses the term as "possessing Sanskrit words" and explains that Vibhīṣaṇa speaks without the use of his regional language in order that all his listeners may understand him clearly. (*agrāmyapadavat saṃskṛtapadavat. sarveṣāṃ sphuṭapratipattaye svadeśabhāṣāpadarahitam uktavān ity arthaḥ.*) See note to 4.3.25 (App. I, No. 3) concerning Hanumān's proficiency in Sanskrit. See, too, 5.28.19 and note.

7. "Anala, Śarabha, Saṃpāti, and Praghasa": See note to 6.11.3, where Cg identifies the four by the same names. See, too, 6.10.12, where the four are first mentioned. Cf. 6.13.2; 6.28.7; and 6.71.2. See verses 32–34 and notes below. See also 7.5.39, where the four are said to be Anala, Anila, Hara, and Saṃpāti.

8. "Turning themselves into birds" *bhūtvā śakunayaḥ sarve*: Compare note to 6.13.23 (App. I, No. 10), where Śuka similarly turns himself into a bird for the purpose of espionage.

"the defensive preparations" *vidhānam*: Literally, "arrangements." We follow Ct, Ck, Cm, and Cr, and also the logic of the narrative in adding the word "defensive" (*pururakṣārtham iti śeṣaḥ*—so Ct).

11–12. "spears, swords, and bows, and wielding lances and war hammers" *paṭṭasāsidhanuṣmadbhiḥ śūlamudgarapāṇibhiḥ*: See Emeneau 1953, and cf. Brockington 2006. See Glossary of Weapons.

"is stationed": The two verses referring to Indrajit have no finite verb or nominal equivalent. We agree with Cg in borrowing the verbal phrase "is stationed (*āsādya tiṣṭhati*)" from verse 10 (*indrajit paścimadvāram āsādya tiṣṭhatīty anukṛṣyate*).

13. "supremely confident" *param asaṃvignaḥ*: Literally, "supremely unperturbed." We have followed the reading and interpretation of Cg and Cs, who read the sequence as two words, *param* plus *asaṃvignaḥ*, and then take *param* adverbially. Ct and Ck read the sequence as a *karmadhāraya* compound *parama-saṃvignaḥ*, which yields the meaning "extremely agitated." They explain that, despite Rāvaṇa's outward

demeanor, his heart is gripped by fear because of the report he has had from his spies, Śuka and Sāraṇa, concerning the enormous size of the forces opposing him (see *sargas* 17–19 above) (*śukasāraṇāveditamahābalasmaraṇād antaḥkaraṇe 'tibhītaḥ*—so Ct). This interpretation, which is followed by all translators who follow the text of Ct, is plausible in light of the reference at 6.22.2, where Rāvaṇa is shown as somewhat shaken by his spies' report. On the other hand, fear does not appear to be in keeping with Rāvaṇa's character, and this interpretation seems to accord poorly with the adjective *yukta*, "focused," that precedes it. Cs quotes the interpretation of Ck and Ct but claims that it is not in keeping with the tenor of praise of Rāvaṇa. He notes that, if the author had intended to express fear, he would have done so in the context of Rāvaṇa's witnessing the heroic deeds of Hanumān (see 5.44.1 and 5.46.1), since witnessing something directly is more powerful than merely hearing about it. (*śukasāraṇāveditamahābalasmaraṇād antaḥkaraṇe bhīta iti vyākhyā stutiprastāvānanuguṇā. yadi vaktavyā bhītis tarhi hanumataikalena kṛtasya karmaṇo dṛṣṭatvena vaktavyā. śravaṇāpekṣayā svasākṣiṇaḥ prābalyāt.*)

14. "Virūpākṣa" *virūpākṣaḥ*: See 6.27.20 and note; and note to verse 31 below.

"still more *rākṣasas*" *rākṣasaiḥ*: Literally, "with *rākṣasas*." Here, as in verse 12 above, there seems to be a distinction between notable *rākṣasa* warriors and the company of foot soldiers. In this case, Cg adds the word "principal *or* leading (*mukhyaiḥ*)" as a modifier of *rākṣasaiḥ*.

"swords" *-khaḍga-*: Although the reading is unattested in the critical apparatus, printed versions of the text of Ct and Cr read instead *mudga-* "war hammer *or* mace." This variant is reflected in the translations of Dutt (1893, p. 1206), Shastri (1959, vol. 3, p. 89), and Roussel (1903, vol. 3, p. 104).

15. "as quickly as possible" *śīghram*: Literally, "quickly."

16. "In the city" *pure*: A variety of manuscripts (Ś,V,B4,D0–4,7–13,G2,3,M5) and the texts and printed editions of Ct, Ck, and Cr read *tathā*, "and," in place of *pure*.

"one thousand . . . and" *ca sahasraṃ ca*: A few manuscripts (D10,11,M1,2) and the texts and printed editions of Ct, Ck, and Cr substitute *daśasāhasram*, "ten thousand." The larger number thus appears in translations that follow these commentators.

"elephants . . . chariots . . . horses . . . *rākṣasas*" *gajānām . . . rathānām . . . hayānām . . . rakṣasām*: If, as we suggested above in note 14, the term *rākṣasa* here refers specifically to foot soldiers, then the verse alludes to the classic four divisions of the ancient Indian army (see notes to 6.3.24). Several of the commentators, including Ct, Cm, and Cg (first alternative), clearly understand this to be the case. (*gajānāṃ gajayodhinām. rathānāṃ hayānām ity atrāpy evaṃ draṣṭavyam*—so Cg.) Thus, several translations refer to the warriors rather than the mounts. Cg's second interpretation, referring specifically to the elephants, etc., is the one we have followed (*yadvā gajānām ityādiśabdā gajādiparāḥ*). Cm proposes adding the phrase "ready for battle (*sannaddha*)" to each of these war vehicles as well as to the *rākṣasas* mentioned in the verse.

"more than ten million" *sāgrakoṭī*: The term is ambiguous, as *sāgra-* can mean either "full, entire" or "with a surplus, more than." Ct and Cr understand, "ten million increased by some hundreds of thousands (*kiṃciṃllakṣyasaṃkhyādhikā koṭir ity arthaḥ*—so Ct)." Ck, who reads the plural *koṭīḥ*, understands, "tens of millions increased by some thousands (*sāgrakoṭīḥ koṭibhyo 'dhikakiṃcitsahasrasaṃkhyā ity arthaḥ*)." Cg understands, "a full ten million (*pūrṇā koṭiḥ*)."

17. "the handpicked guard" *iṣṭāḥ*: Literally, "cherished *or* favored ones." We agree with the interpretation of Cg, who glosses, "belonging to the innermost circle (*antarañgāḥ*)" and explains, "his personal attendants (*svasevinaḥ*)."

19. "he made these concluding comments" *idam uttaram abravīt*: Normally, this would mean "he uttered this reply." Since, however, Vibhīṣaṇa is not responding to any prior speech on Rāma's part, we take *uttaram* adjectivally in the sense of "last, final, concluding," understanding an implicit word for speech. Cg suggests the equally plausible "the following speech (*anantaravaktavyam*)." Northern texts avoid the awkwardness by reading the more conventional "he spoke these further [words] (*idaṃ punar uvāca ha*).

Following 19ab, D5–7,9–11,S insert a passage of two lines [576*]: "Having spoken in this fashion, that great-armed [Vibhīṣaṇa] introduced those *rākṣasas* and had those ministers report to Rāma all that was going on[1] in Lañkā."

[1]"all that was going on" *sarvam*: Literally, "all."

Following verse 19, D7,9–11,M3, and the texts and printed editions of the southern commentators insert an additional line [577*]: "Rāvaṇa's majestic younger brother, in his desire to aid Rāma."

20–21. "Kubera" *kuberam*: This incident from Rāvaṇa's past is related in the *Uttarakāṇḍa* (*sargas* 14–15). See 6.7.3–5 and notes.

"six million" *ṣaṣṭiḥ śatasahasrāṇi*: Literally, "sixty hundred thousand." According to Cg, Vibhīṣaṇa's point here is that, as he has shown in the previous verses, the *rākṣasa* army Rāma is about to confront is many times larger than even the one that assisted Rāvaṇa in conquering the worlds in a previous era (*digvijayakālikabalād ādhunikabalam adhikam iti kathayituṃ pūrvabalaṃ parigaṇayati*).

"valor, strength, energy, power, dignity, and pride" *parākrameṇa vīryeṇa tejasā sattvagauravāt... darpeṇa*: Cg attempts to distinguish these semantically overlapping terms as follows: *parākrama* means "the power to conquer one's enemies (*parābhibhavasāmarthyena*)"; *vīrya*, "the quality of keeping oneself steadfast in battle (*svayam avikṛtatvena*)"; and *tejasā*, "courage, splendor (*pratāpena*)." Like Cm, he understands *sattvagauravāt* as a compound with the sense of "extreme steadfastness (*dhairyātiśayena*)." See note to 6.2.11.

22. According to Cg, Vibhīṣaṇa, anticipating [the objection] that it is improper to describe an enemy's army in the presence of one's lord, refutes [the objection] (*svāmisannidhau śatrubalavarṇanam ayuktam ity āśañkya pariharati*).

"Please do not be angry with me over this." *atra manyur na kartavyaḥ*: Literally, "Let there be no anger *or* despondency in this." Ct and Ck, who take *manyuḥ* in both its senses of anger and despair, here see Vibhīṣaṇa as urging Rāma not to give way like Rāvaṇa to these emotions upon hearing of his enemy's strength (*atra rāvaṇabalavarṇanaviṣaye manyuḥ svāntaḥkaraṇe dainyam api roṣaś ca na kāryo rāvaṇavat*—so Ct). See 6.17.5 and 6.20.1–12.

"I am trying to rouse your fury for battle" *roṣaye*: Literally, "I would make you angry." We have followed the interpretation of Ct, Cg, and Cm. The latter two understand that Rāma's ability to defeat even the gods, described in the second half of the verse, is a result of his being roused to fury in battle (*roṣaye śatrunirasanāya roṣam utpādaye na bhīṣaye śatrubalavarṇanena na bhītim utpādaye*). Cr understands the phrase somewhat differently. He applies the negative particle *na* to *kopaye* (his v.l. for *roṣaye*) as well as to *bhīṣaye* in *pāda* b. He thus explains, "Since you are capable of defeating even the gods, you should not get too angry in the current battle. For you will gain the victory even without excessive anger. Therefore, I will try to rouse neither your anger nor your fear (*yataḥ surāṇām api nigrahe tvaṃ samartho 'sy ato 'tra yuddhe manyur atikopo na kartavyo 'tikopanam antaraiva te vijayo bhaviṣyatīti tātparyam ata eva tvāṃ na kopaye nāpi bhīṣaye*)." Ck's understanding is similar to that of Cr.

23. "you, sir . . . will . . . destroy" *bhavān . . . nirmathiṣyasi*: Cr and Cg note the irregular use of the second person with the formal third person pronoun *bhavān*. Cg attributes this to an irregular epic usage (*madhyamapuruṣatvam ārṣam*), while Cr attributes it to carelessness (*vyatyayena madhyamaḥ puruṣaḥ*). Manuscript evidence supports the critical edition's reading.

"with its four divisions" *caturaṅgeṇa*: This term conventionally describes the classical Indian army with its four kinds of fighting forces: infantry, cavalry, chariots, and elephants. See note to 6.3.24. This description is entirely inapposite for the monkey forces marshaled by Sugrīva, as they use neither mounts nor vehicles. The problem does not arise for Ct nor for the translators who follow him, for his text [and that of Crā] reads *vṛtam* for *vṛtaḥ*, "surrounded," in which case the description is of Rāvaṇa's army and is perfectly appropriate. Cg, Cm, and Ck, however, who share the reading of the critical text, need to justify the usage. Cg explains, "the monkey army is divided into four sections on the analogy of Rāvaṇa's army (*rāvaṇasenāvac caturāvayavena vyūhya vibhajya*)." Presumably he understands that one segment of the monkey troops confronts a corresponding *aṅga* of the *rākṣasa* host. Cm, whose position Cg mentions and ascribes to others (*anye*), thinks that the monkey host is said to have four divisions because it is the instrument of accomplishing the mission that [normally] is to be effected by an army of four divisions (*caturaṅganirvāhyakāryakaraṇasadbhāvād vānarabalasya caturaṅgatvoktiḥ*). Ck believes that the reference is to the spatial division of the army of which one division is stationed at each of the four gateways of the city wall of Laṅkā in order to blockade it (*yasmāt tena caturdvāreṣu sarvāpi senā vibhajya pratiṣṭhāpitā tat tasmād bhavān apīḍaṃ vānarānīkaṃ caturaṅgena caturdvāropa*[*ro*]*dhārthaṃ caturavayavavibhāgena vyūhya tathā*).

24. "When Vibhīṣaṇa, the younger brother of Rāvaṇa, had spoken in this fashion" *rāvaṇāvaraje vākyam evaṃ bruvati*: Literally, "when Rāvaṇa's younger brother had thus spoken this speech."

27. "of boundless vitality" *aprameyātmā*: The precise sense of the term is hard to determine, principally because of the broad semantic range of the noun *ātman* in compounds of this type. The term can and does mean anything from "self, soul, mind, *and* spirit" to "body" in the epic literature. Given the context, we have chosen the sense of "vital spirit *or* energy." The epithet is used elsewhere of Śiva, usually in the sense "[he] of inscrutable spirit" (Apte s.v.). Cg understands the epithet to suggest that Hanumān is a worthy [foe] of that master of illusion Indrajit [whom Rāvaṇa has posted at the western gate (see verses 11 and 12 above)] (*aprameyātmeti māyāvina indrajito 'yam evārha iti bhāvaḥ*).

"let . . . force and breach" *nipīḍya . . . praviśatu*: Literally, "having pressed upon, let him enter."

28–29. "gift of a boon" *varadāna-*: For Rāvaṇa's qualified boon of invulnerability, see 1.14.12–15 and notes. Cf. 7.10.17–20. On the motif of Rāvaṇa's boon, see Pollock 1991, pp. 15–54. See, too, 6.47.53,104; 6.49.12; 6.59.82; 6.63.40; 6.82.26,29 and notes; and notes to 6.7.15; 6.12.10; 6.13.15; 6.26.20; 6.31.51–52; 6.40.56 (835*); 6.47.104; 6.49.56; 6.54.54; 6.59.82; and 6.99.9. Cf. 6.57.4; 6.59.31; and 6.67.27 and notes. See, too, 5.49.23–26 and 5.58.14 and notes.

31. "the . . . king of the monkeys, Sugrīva, Jāmbavān, king of the apes, and Vibhīṣaṇa, the younger brother of the *rākṣasa* lord" *vānarendraś ca . . . ṛkṣarājaś ca jāmbavān / rākṣasendrānujaś caiva*: Literally, "the king of the monkeys, Jāmbavān, king of the apes, and the younger brother of the *rākṣasa* lord." V2,3,D3,5,7,9–11,T1,M3, and the texts and printed editions of the southern commentators read *vīryavān*, "heroic," for *jāmbavān*, "Jāmbavān," See note to 6.4.17.

"Let . . . take up their positions at the central encampment" *gulme bhavatu madhyame*: Literally, "Let him be at the central encampment." The singular is used by attraction for the three warriors mentioned in the verse. The reference here is undoubtedly to the defensive position manned by Virūpākṣa, as mentioned above at verse 14. (On the *rākṣasa* Virūpākṣa, see 5.44.2–3,27; 6.27.20; 6.33.10; 6.83.5,28; 6.84.13–15,22,30,33; 6.82.5; 6.87.1,2; and notes.) A few manuscripts and the texts of Cg and Cm, as well as the printed editions of KK and VSP, read instead *gulmo bhavatu madhyamaḥ*, "Let them constitute a central force." Cg, the only commentator to note this reading, understands that the warriors mentioned in the verse should constitute an intermediate force posted between the northern and western [gates] occupied by powerful Rāvaṇa and Indrajit [respectively]. (*gulmo bhavatu madhyamo madhyamasenā bhavatv ity arthaḥ. balavadbhyāṃ rāvaṇendrajidbhyām adhiṣṭhitayor uttarapaścimayor madhyamagulmo bhavatv ity arthaḥ.*) Cf. 5.3.27; 6.3.27; 6.27.20; 6.31.31; 6.45.2; 6.62.5; 6.71.1; 6.72.5; 6.84.6; and notes.

32. "take on human form" *mānuṣaṃ rūpaṃ kāryam*: As the various commentators suggest, the idea here is that if the monkeys were to take on human [or *rākṣasa*] form, exploiting their power of "shape-shifting (*kāmarūpatā*)," they could not be distinguished from the enemy (*atha vānarāṇām api kāmarūpatayā rūpāntarakaraṇe yuddhe svīyaparakīyavivekāsaṃbhavād āha*—so Ct). Cg notes that if the monkeys were to fight by using their power to change their appearance, then, because of [their] similarity with the *rākṣasas*, it would be impossible to distinguish one's allies from one's enemies. Moreover, he understands that the *rākṣasas* would be unlikely to take on the form of monkeys since they would deem such a form inferior. (*yadi vānarā api kāmarūpadharaṇena yudhyeyū rākṣasānām api tādṛśatvād ātmaparaviveko na syāt. vānaratvaṃ tu jaghanyatayā na te bhajiṣyantīti bhāvaḥ.*) As will emerge in the following verses, only seven of the warriors on Rāma's side bear human forms in the conflict. As specified in verses 33–34 below and noted by Ct, those warriors would be Rāma and Lakṣmaṇa [who lack the power of changing their form at will], Vibhīṣaṇa, and his four *rākṣasa* companions, Anala, Śarabha, Saṃpāti, and Praghasa. Ct notes that, with the exception of those seven, anyone bearing a human form is to be killed without hesitation (*evaṃ cāsmān sapta hitvā manuṣyākāro niḥśaṅkaṃ vadhyaḥ*). See note to verse 7 above.

33–34. "The monkey form itself" *vānarā eva*: Literally, "monkeys alone." As the various commentators note, the reference here must be to the physical appearance of monkeys.

"our" *naḥ*: D10,11,G2,M1,2, and the texts and printed editions of Ct and Ck read instead *vaḥ*, "your."

"with his four companions" *ātmanā pañcamaḥ*: Literally, "with himself as the fifth." The reference is to Vibhīṣaṇa's four *rākṣasa* companions, Anala, Śarabha, Saṃpāti, and Praghasa. See note to verse 7 above.

35. "in order to secure the success of their mission" *kāryasiddhyartham*: Cm, alone among the commentators, reads the adverb as a *bahuvrīhi* compound modifying Vibhīṣaṇa, with the sense "whose purpose was the success of the mission." (*kṛtya-siddhyartham kṛtyaṃ kartavyam eva siddhiḥ prayojanaṃ yasya tam. vibhīṣaṇaviśeṣaṇam idam.*)

"resolute Rāma... resolved purposefully" *Rāmaḥ... buddhiṃ cakāra matimān matim*: The texts of the commentators and the corresponding printed editions show a certain amount of variation in their readings of the two nearly synonymous terms *buddhi* and *mati-*. In addition, the various commentators, most of whom are aware of the variants, offer multiple interpretations of the different readings. The central problem, the presence of the two terms in the accusative as apparent objects of the finite verb *cakāra*, is most difficult in the critical reading. The text of Ct, Ck, and Cr avoids the seeming redundancy by reading *prabhuḥ*, "lord [Rāma]," for *matim*. This permits the interpretation "resolute lord Rāma made up his mind [*buddhim*]." Ct notes the variant *matim*, reading it quasi-adjectivally with *buddhim*, in the sense of "discerning, selective (*arthanirdhāraṇātmikām*)." He cites Cm, who quotes "knowledgeable sources (*tajjñāḥ*)" for the sense of "discernment (*arthanirdhāraṇam*)," explaining that Rāma was taking a decision that was "appropriate to the moment (*tātkālikarūpāṃ matim*)." This is, however, Cm's alternate explanation of what is, for him, an alternate reading. Cm's first alternative is to take *matim* in the sense of "thoughtful (*mananātmikām*)," which he also takes as an adjective modifying *buddhim*. Cg also acknowledges *buddhim* as a variant reading but reads it as the final member of a compound, *suvelārohaṇabuddhim*, which would stand in apposition with *matim*, yielding the sense "he formed a notion—the exclusive intention to climb Mount Suvela and no other (*suvelārohaṇabuddhim eva matiṃ cakāra nānyam ity arthaḥ*)." Cg's and Cm's principal reading of the verse has, however, the nominative *buddhiḥ* for the critical edition's *buddhim*. This reading is also difficult to construe, and the two commentators, it seems to us, struggle to make sense of it. Cg's idea is to read *buddhiḥ* in the sense of the possessive adjective *buddhimān* "intelligent, wise," which has irregularly lost its possessive suffix (*matublopa ārṣaḥ*). He then glosses *matim* as *icchām*, "desire." Thus, his interpretation of the verse would be "wise and intelligent Rāma desired to climb." He makes no effort to address or clarify the resulting redundancy between *buddhiḥ* and *matimān*. Cm proposes yet another epic irregularity as an interpretive strategy, reading *suvelārohaṇe buddhiḥ* as an irregular *aluksamāsa* to be read as a *bahuvrīhi* modifying Rāma (*suvelārohaṇebuddhiḥ*). The sense of the compound would then be "[Rāma] whose thoughts were directed toward climbing Mount Suvela." Cm then explains *matimān* as "discerning with respect to future events (*āgāmigocarabuddhimān*)" and, like Cg, glosses *matim* as "the desire to climb Mount Suvela (*suvelārohaṇecchām*)." See note to 6.2.14.

"Mount Suvela": See note to 5.1.189. Only Cg among the commentators pays any attention to the purpose of Rāma's sudden jaunt into the mountains, which seems to have no relevance to his military objective. Taking his cue from 584*, translated below, he notes, "[Rāma's] climb was merely for the purpose of viewing the beauty [of the landscape] and not for getting to Laṅkā. Therefore," Cg continues, "the following verse [verse 36] describes the descent from the mountain in order to besiege Laṅkā. (*ārohaṇecchāhetum āha ramaṇīyataram iti. saundaryāvalokanam eva tadārohaṇahetur na tu laṅkāprāptiḥ. ata eva laṅkoparodhāyāvarohaṇaṃ vakṣyati tatas tv iti.*)" See 6.21.21 and 6.29.1 and notes.

Following verse 35, D5,7,10,11,S insert a passage of one line [584*]: "Seeing the supremely charming slopes of Mount Suvela... [Rāma]."

36. Ck, quoted in part and with some variation by Ct, argues, somewhat heatedly, that this verse has been pointlessly interpolated here in order to artificially and inappropriately break the text into two *sargas*. He regards this as reckless tampering with the text of the seer [Vālmīki] and argues that there should not be a *sarga* boundary here. (*tatas tu rāma ityādi vakṣyamāṇasaṃgrahaślokaś ca na. nāpi coktir anuvādaḥ. nāpīha pūrvāparaprakaraṇavicchedaḥ. ata imaṃ ślokaṃ vṛthā prakṣipyātra sargaṃ vicchindanti. evam evaṃ kusṛṣṭita ṛṣyuktasargasaṃkhyābhyadhikadarśanaṃ jāyate. ato nātra sargavicchedaḥ.*) His position finds little support in the critical apparatus.

"wise and great" *mahātmā* ... *mahātmā*: Cg and Cr are disturbed by the repetition and differentiate the meanings of the term in its two occurrences. Cr takes the first occurrence to mean "whose inherent form is worthy of worship (*pūjyasvarūpaḥ*)" and the second to mean "very active, energetic, *or* persevering (*atiprayatnavān*)." Cg takes the first to mean "highly intelligent (*mahābuddhiḥ*)" and the second to mean "of great fortitude (*mahādhṛtiḥ*)."

The meter is *upajāti*.

Sarga 29

1–2. "Mount Suvela" *suvelasya*: Cg notes that, as the *sarga* will bear out, the purpose of the ascent of Suvela is to permit surveillance of the citadel of Laṅkā (*laṅkādarśanārthaṃ suvelārohaṇam*). In this connection, he identifies Suvela as a mountain of similar elevation to Laṅkā itself (*suvelo nāma laṅkāsamatuṅgatāko giriviśeṣaḥ*). See note to 6.28.35, where reference is made to Cg's position that the first reason for the climb is to enjoy the scenery and only later on (i.e., in verse 36) does its military purpose come into play. See 6.20.21; 6.21.21; and notes. See, too, 6.22.1. Cf. 6.31.42.

"devoted and righteous... skillful both in counsel and in action" *dharmajñam anuraktam* ... *mantrajñaṃ ca vidhijñaṃ ca*. Although the placement of all these adjectives appears to make them apply exclusively to Vibhīṣaṇa, Cg, for some reason, understands that they are also meant to apply to Sugrīva (*dharmajñetyādi sugrīvasyāpi viśeṣaṇam*). Ct, Cg, and Cm, whom we follow, gloss *vidhijñam*, "knowing custom, precept, proper usage," with *kāryajñam*, "knowing duty, what is to be done."

3. Cg, alone among the commentators, is concerned about the seemingly nonlinear quality of the narrative, which appears here to be taking us back to the point in *sarga* 20 [verse 21] where Rāma is described as encamped on Mount Suvela. Cg's explanation is that the current passage is merely a more detailed account of the events of the day on which Rāma crossed the ocean. According to him, these events, until now, have been described in a more summary fashion. (*ayaṃ ca samudrataraṇadivasavṛttāntaḥ. pūrvaṃ saṃgraheṇokto 'dya saviśeṣam ucyate.*) See note to 6.15.33 (App. I, No. 16, lines 33–125), where Rāma's initial observation of Laṅkā is first described in the vulgate. See 6.20.21; 6.21.21; 6.22.1; 6.28.35; and note. See, too, notes to verses 1–2 above.

"straightaway" *sādhu*: Literally, "properly, correctly."

4–5. "proper conduct" *vṛttam*: Cs, as we and Cg have done, understands the term as "conduct of the virtuous (*vṛttaṃ sadācāraḥ*)." However, he proposes as an alternative taking the term in its other meaning of "news, report," and explains, "or, the report that 'we are more powerful than he (*asmadbaliṣṭhatāvārtā vā*).' "

"his own high lineage" *kulam*: Literally, "family, good family, high breeding." We agree with Cg in understanding the reference to be to the rules of conduct for one of noble lineage enjoined in the *dharmaśāstra* (*dharmaśāstravihitasvakulācāraḥ*). Cm construes the second half of verse 5 somewhat differently, taking the adjective *garhitam*, "contemptible," as a modifier of *kulam* rather than *kṛtam*, "action." He thus reads, "Rāvaṇa, who knows nothing of righteousness, has brought his own lineage into contempt (*yena rāvaṇena dharmādikaṃ na jñātaṃ tena tatkulaṃ garhitam iti saṃbandhaḥ*)."

"in his vile *rākṣasa* nature" *rākṣasyā nīcayā buddhyā*: Literally, "because of [his] low or vile *rākṣasa* nature." The term *buddhi* normally means "mind, thought, intellect." Here, however, the context demands the term's less common meaning of "nature." Cs, anticipating that this comment might injure Vibhīṣaṇa's feelings, explains as follows: "Because it belongs to a *rākṣasa*, [that is,] only because it is related to a *rākṣasa*, is it also low. Rāma says this in order not to offend Vibhīṣaṇa. (*rākṣasyā rākṣasasaṃbandhinyā. tatrāpi nīcayā. vibhīṣaṇaṃ sumukhīkartum iyam uktiḥ.*)" This is an early case of political correctness.

"this contemptible thing" *tad garhitaṃ kṛtam*: We agree with Cg that the reference is retrospective to the abduction of Sītā (3.47–52). Cr, however, interprets it as a generic allusion to all of Rāvaṇa's misdeeds, such as the harassment of the seers, etc. (*yena garhitaṃ ninditaṃ karmarṣipīḍanādi kṛtam*).

6. This and the following verse are omitted from D10,11, and the text of Ct. They are inserted in brackets, without verse numbers, between verses 5 and 6 in the GPP. Gita Press includes the verses as do KK and VSP. These verses are absent from NSP.

"at the mere mention of that vilest of *rākṣasas*" *yasmin . . . kīrtite rākṣasādhame*: We read the phrase as a *sati saptamī* (locative absolute), in the sense of "when that vilest of *rākṣasas* is mentioned." It is also possible to read *kīrtite* as a simple adjective in the sense of "infamous, notorious." But this seems less plausible here.

"my anger blazes up" *me vardhate roṣaḥ*: Literally, "my anger swells *or* grows." D1,2,M3, and the texts and printed editions of Cg read *vartate*, "it occurs, exists," for *vardhate*, "it grows."

7. See note to verse 6 above.

8. "Speaking" *saṃmantrayan*: Literally, "taking counsel *or* advising." We follow Cg, who glosses, simply, "speaking (*vadan*)." Ct and Ck suggest, "reflecting (*saṃcintayan*)."

"to make camp there" *vāsāya*: Literally, "for dwelling." D9–11 and the texts and printed editions of Ct read instead the gerund *āsādya*, "having approached."

10–11. The three lines from 10cd–11cd ("as well as Hanumān, Aṅgada, Nīla, Mainda, Dvivida, Gaja, Gavākṣa, Gavaya, Śarabha, Gandhamādana, Panasa, Kumuda, Hara, and the troop leader Rambha [*hanūmān aṅgado nīlo maindo dvivida eva ca / gajo gavākṣo gavayaḥ śarabho gandhamādanaḥ / panasaḥ kumudaś caiva haro rambhaś ca yūthapaḥ*])" are not found in the texts of Ct, Ck, and Cr and are placed in brackets without verse numbers in GPP after 6.38.8ab; NSP omits them entirely. Gita Press, VSP, and KK all include the verses.

"Hanumān" *hanūmān*: Cg notes that the separate mention of Hanumān suggests that Rāma and Lakṣmaṇa are proceeding on foot here [as opposed to riding on the shoulders of Hanumān and Aṅgada, respectively, as they did during the earlier march] (*hanumān iti pṛthaguktyā rāmalakṣmaṇau padbhyām evārūḍhāv iti gamyate*). See note to 15.27 (314*).

Following verse 11, Ñ,V,B1,2,3,D5–7,9,S, GPP in brackets, and the texts and printed editions of Cg and Cm insert a passage of two lines that extends the list of names [587*]: "Jāmbavān, Suṣeṇa, wise Praghasa, immensely powerful Durmukha, and the monkey Śatabali."

12. "These . . . swarmed up" *ete . . . adhyārohanta*: Literally, "these ascended *or* climbed up."

"leaping with the speed of the wind" *vāyuvegapravaṇāḥ*: Literally, "endowed with the speed of the wind."

13. "perched as they were on its summit" *śikhare tasya*: Literally, "on its summit." The commentators are divided as to whether to read the locative *śikhare* as referring to the placement of Rāma and the monkeys or to that of the city of Laṅkā itself. The former position, which we feel is somewhat more justified by the context, is held by Ct, Ck, and Cr, all of whom suggest supplying a form of the root √*sthā* (*sthityā* or *sthitvā*) to refer to the placement of the monkeys. Cg and Cm, however, take the genitive pronoun *tasya* to refer not to Mount Suvela, the monkeys' observation post, but instead to Mount Trikūṭa, upon whose peaks the fortress city of Laṅkā was built (see 5.2.1 and note) (*tasya prasiddhasya trikūṭasya khe viṣaktām ākāśe lambamānām iva sthitāṃ purīṃ laṅkām*).

"suspended in the sky" *viṣaktām iva khe*: Literally, "as if attached in the sky." Ct glosses the participle as "built (*racitām*)"; Cg, "suspended (*lambamānām*)"; and Cm, "as if floating (*carantīm iva sthitām*)." Cs offers the most charming metaphor, "that is to say, kissing the sky (*ambaracumbinīm iti yāvat*)."

15. "saw what appeared to be a second rampart" *dadṛśuḥ . . . prākāram aparam*: Literally, "they saw another rampart." We follow Cr, Ct, Cm, and Ck, who indicate in various ways that the host of huge *rākṣasas* was like a wall or was perceived as such by the monkeys (*aparaṃ prākāraṃ prākāratayā pratīyamānaṃ rākṣasasamūham ity arthaḥ*—so Cr).

"stationed at the base of the city wall" *prākāracayasaṃsthaiḥ*: Only the texts and printed editions of Cg and Cm read *-caya-* with the critical edition. Both of these commentators gloss, "earthen wall (*vapram*)," and thus appear, as we have done, to understand the reference to be to the earthen base or foundation of the defensive rampart of the city. Our visualization of the scene is that the city wall is surrounded by a dense formation of *rākṣasa* troops that gives rise to the perception that the city has two concentric walls. It is also possible to take *caya*, and even *vapra*, in the sense of "top *or* summit," in which case the image would be of a second wall of *rākṣasas* rising vertically from the top of the rampart. This idea may gain some support from the northern variant 590*, line 6, which reads *prākāravaḍabhīsaṃsthaiḥ*, "stationed at the turrets of the city wall." D10,11,M1,2, and the texts and printed editions of Ct, Ck, and Cr read *-vara-*, "best," for *-caya-*, yielding the sense "stationed on *or* at that splendid rampart."

16. "so eager for battle" *yuddhakāṅkṣiṇaḥ*: The modificand of this adjective is somewhat ambiguous. Since the form can be read either as a nominative or an ac-

cusative, the adjective could describe either the *rākṣasas* or the monkeys. We, along with Gita Press (1969, vol. 3, p. 1496) and Gorresio (1856, vol. 9, p. 239), take it with the former largely because of its placement in the verse. Cr, the only commentator to take note of the phrase, reads the adjective with the monkeys. In so doing, he is influenced by the reading of Ct's and Ck's texts, which have *tam*, "that," for the critical reading *te*, "they." Cr glosses the accusative pronoun with *rākṣasagaṇam*, "the host of *rākṣasas*," which thus becomes the direct object of *dṛṣṭvā*, "having seen." This reading, however, leaves hanging the accusative plural *rākṣasān* of *pāda* d. Translators other than the two mentioned above, however, appear to follow this reading and indicate that it is the monkeys who are eager for battle.

"loudly" *vipulān*: B2,3,D5–7,9–11,T1,M3, and the texts and printed editions of the southern commentators read instead *vividhān*, "various," yielding the meaning "[they all bellowed] variously."

17. "illumined by the full moon" *pūrṇacandrapradīpā*: Literally, "having the full moon for its lamp." Several of the commentators, including Cv, Cg, and Cm, note that the adjective tells us that the ascent of Mount Suvela took place on the full-moon night (*paurṇamāsyām*) and that the battle therefore commences on the next day, which is the first day of the succeeding dark half of the month (*tena pratipadi yuddhārambhaḥ*—so Cm). Ct, alone among the commentators, specifies that the month is Pauṣa and that the ascent takes place either on the fourteenth day of the bright half or on the full-moon night itself (*anena pauṣaśuklacaturdaśyāṃ pūrṇimāyāṃ vā suvelārohaṇam iti bodhyam*). Cg, however, perhaps uncomfortable with the chronology here, proposes an alternative explanation whereby the night is illuminated with lamps as bright as the full moon, which were placed in the monkeys' encampment to provide light (*yadvā pūrṇacandratulyapradīpavatīti vārthaḥ saṃbhavanti hi vānarasenāyām api prakāśārtham āropitā dīpāḥ*). Ct also suggests that the reference to the fullness of the moon is made [to indicate] the fulfillment of [Rāma's] resolve (*pūrṇacandratvoktiḥ pūrṇakalpatvād iti*). On the chronology of epic events, see note to 6.4.4.

18. The meter is *vaṃśasthavila*.

Sarga 30

1–2. "those bulls among the tawny monkeys" *haripuṅgavāḥ*: Ś,V,B3,D,T3,G,M5, and the texts and printed editions of Ct, Ck, and Cr read instead *hariyūthapāḥ*, "troop leaders of the tawny monkeys."

"parks and woodlands" *vanāny upavanāni ca*: Literally, "forests and cultivated groves." As Cg explains, *vanāni* refers to natural woodlands, while *upavanāni* refers to landscaped ones (*vanāny akṛtrimāṇy upavanāni kṛtrimāṇi*).

"level" *sama-*: Cg and Cr note that this means "free from elevations and depressions (*nimnonnatatvarahitāni*)." Cm glosses, "equal in length and breadth (*dairghyaviśālaiḥ samāni*)," an idea Ct echoes in different terms.

"hospitable" *-saumyāni*: Literally, "charming, gentle." We agree here with Ct, Cr, Cm, and Ck, who explain, "free from dangers, such as wild animals, etc. (*duṣṭamṛgādy-upadravarāhityena*—so Ct)." Cg glosses, "friendly, smooth (*snigdhāni*)."

"the monkeys were" *te . . . babhūvuḥ*: Literally, "they were."

8. "charming in every season" *sarvartukaṃ ramyam*: We read the two adjectives together in keeping with our understanding that the former refers to the fact that the groves are in full fruit and flower at all seasons. Cf. 5.2.9–13 and note. See, too, 6.108.12; 6.115.20; and notes. Cg, Ck, Ct, and Cm understand, "in which all seasons [are simultaneously present] (*sarva ṛtavo yasmiṃs tat*)."

9. "*natyūhas*" *natyūha-*: According to Monier-Williams (s.v.), this is probably a variant of *dātyūha*, which he identifies as *Cuculus melanoleucus*. The word *dātyūha* is itself a variant term for *cātaka*, also identified by Monier-Williams as *Cuculus melanoleucus*. According to Dave (1985, pp. 131–33), both terms commonly refer to the hawk-cuckoo. Ali and Ripley (1968–1974, vol. 3, pp. 200–202) identify the hawk-cuckoo as the *Cuculus varius varius*, the common hawk-cuckoo, or brainfever bird. This bird is famous for the sound of its call and is referred to commonly in Indian love poetry. Brockington (1984, p. 95) identifies this bird as the Indian moorhen (*Gallinula chloropus indica* Blyth). (On the Indian moorhen, see Ali and Ripley 1968–1974, vol. 2, pp. 174–76.) Dave (1985, pp. 293–94) identifies the *natyūha* of the *Rāmāyaṇa* as the white-breasted water-hen (*Amaurornis phoenicurus insularis*). See Ali and Ripley 1968–1974, vol. 2, pp. 171–72.

"*koyaṣṭibhakas*" *-koyaṣṭibhakaiḥ*: This is probably the night heron (*Nycticorax nycticorax*). See 5.1.42 and note. Cf. 2.48.36 and 3.71.11, where Pollock identifies the bird as a type of plover known as a lapwing. See Dave 1985, pp. 357–60.

"The sweet notes of the cuckoo" *rutaṃ parabhṛtānām*: Literally, "the cry of the *parabhṛtas*." The cry of the *parabhṛta* (literally, "raised by another [i.e., the crow]"), or *kokila*, that is, the Indian cuckoo (*Cuculus saturatus*), is considered one of the most romantic and charming sounds of nature and is referred to constantly in the poetic literature. See Dave 1985, pp. 127ff.

"rushing woodland streams" *vananirjhare*: Literally, "in *or* over a forest cascade."

10–12. "heroic" *vīrāḥ*: Cg suggests that this term is used because the monkeys have no fear, even when entering their enemies' woods (*śatruvanapraveśe 'pi nirbhayāḥ*).

"who could take on any form at will" *kāmarūpiṇaḥ*: Cg suggests that this stock epithet of the monkeys indicates that they possessed both small and large bodies suitable for entering small and large places (*sūkṣmavipulapradeśānuguṇasthūlasūkṣmaśarīravantaḥ*). Cf. Hanumān's many changes of size in the *Sundarakāṇḍa* (5.1.8; 5.1.186–87; 5.35.31–41; and notes).

"drongos" *bhṛṅgarāja-*: According to Apte (s.v.) and Monier-Williams (s.v.), the term refers both to a type of bird and to a variety of large bee. Raghunathan (1982, vol. 3, p. 91) appears to understand, "beetle." The bird in question is usually identified as the greater racket-tailed drongo (*Dicrurus paradiseus*), also called the fork-tailed shrike (Dave 1985, pp. 64–67).

"were swarming with bees" *bhramaraiḥ sevitāni*: Literally, "frequented by bees." A variety of southern and northern manuscripts substitute one or another of a number of variants in which a form of the word *kurara/kurarī*, "osprey/female osprey" (Dave 1985, p. 185) is found. Among these, D10,11, and the texts and printed editions of Ct, Ck, and Cr read *kurarasvanitāni ca*, "resounding with the cries of ospreys." See 6.23.1–3; 6.98.26; 6.39.9; and notes. See Fitzgerald 1998.

"*koṇālakas*" *koṇālaka-*: The name is not cited in PW, Monier-Williams, or Apte. Brockington (1984, p. 95) notes it as unidentified. Cv and Cg understand it to be a kind of wagtail (*khañjanaḥ* [*Motacilla indica* Gmelin]).

"They echoed with the song of *koṇālakas* and resounded with the cries of *sārasa* cranes." *koṇālakavighuṣṭāni sārasābhirutāni ca*: This half *śloka*, 11cd of the critical edition, is omitted by Ś1,B3,D3,9–11,G2,M1,2, and the texts and printed editions of Ct, Cr, and Ck. The half verse is bracketed between 6.39.11ab and cd in GPP. It is found in KK, Gita Press, and VSP (6.39.11cd).

13. "fragrant" *ghrāṇasukhaḥ*: Literally, "pleasant to the sense of smell." D7,9–11, and the texts and printed editions of Ct, Ck, and Cr read instead *prāṇasamaḥ*, "equal to the breath of life." Ct explains the simile by saying that the breeze is compared to a breath because of its gentleness (*mandatā*).

"began to blow" *vavau*: Literally, "it blew."

14–15. "notable for their deafening roars" *nadatāṃ varāḥ*: Literally, "foremost among those who roar." Recall that in the *Bālakāṇḍa* (1.16.16) the *vānaras* are said to be able to knock birds out of the sky with their roaring. Cf. also 4.14.20.

"many-bannered" *patākinīm*: Literally, "possessing banners."

16. "crushed the earth" *kurvantaḥ . . . mahīṃ caraṇapīḍitām*: Literally, "making the earth foot-crushed." This half verse lacks a finite verb and is, in fact, yet another participial clause of verses 14–15 above. As Cg points out, *pādas* cd need to be construed as a separate sentence (*rajaś cety ardham ekaṃ vākyam*).

17. "bears" *ṛkṣāḥ*: Although this term normally refers to a species of primate in the *Vālmīki Rāmāyaṇa* (see Goldman 1989 and 1.16.10 and note), in the present context in which the poet refers to the natural fauna of the region, he may well have bears in mind. This is even more likely, since the list of animals mentioned emphasizes the fiercer forms of wildlife. Compare 6.101.34 and note, where again it appears that the term is probably used in the sense of "bear." See also 6.12.12 and note.

18–20. "reaching into the sky" *divispṛśam*: Literally, "touching the sky." The commentators remark on the various irregularities of the formation. Thus, for example, Cm glosses, "*divaṃ spṛśatīti divispṛśam*."

"There . . . stood one of the lofty summits" *śikharam . . . prāṃśu caikam*: Literally, "and one lofty peak *or* summit." These verses lack an explicit finite verb. The term *ekam*, "one," is slightly problematic in this context because, as its name implies, Trikūṭa is a mountain with three peaks. Indeed, Cg notes that Mount Suvela, which has been described in the preceding *sarga* (6.29.1,3ff.), is the name of the first peak of Trikūṭa, and that the peak now under discussion is the well-known middlemost of the three. It is, he comments, lofty in comparison with the peaks on either side of it. He thus glosses the word *ekam* as "an incomparable middle peak." (*evaṃ trikūṭasya prathamaśikharaṃ suvelākhyam uktvā madhyamaśikharaṃ varṇayati . . . tat prasiddham. prāṃśu pārśvavartiśikharadvayāpekṣayonnatam. ekam advitīyaṃ madhyamam ity arthaḥ.*) Ck and Ct gloss, "unbroken, single (*akhaṇḍam*)." Cf. GPP 7.5.23cd–24ab, where the relationship between the two peaks is further clarified. See, too, note to 6.2.10.

"Mount Trikūṭa" *trikūṭasya*: Literally, "of Trikūṭa." See note to 6.2.10.

"it seemed to be made of gold" *mahārajatasaṃnibham*: Literally, "appearing to be gold." The word *mahārajata-*, literally, "great silver," we believe is explained correctly by Cr, Ct, Cm, and Cg (second interpretation) as "gold (*suvarṇasya*—so Cr)." Cg, however, offers, as his first explanation, "resembling abundant silver (*pṛthurajatasannibham*)."

"beautiful" *ślakṣṇam:* This term can mean "smooth" or "charming/beautiful." We have chosen the latter, although the former is also plausible in the context. Certainly, this is the reading of Ck and Ct, who gloss, "like a paved *or* inlaid floor (*kuṭṭimabhū-mivat*)."

"even in their imagination, let alone in reality" *manasāpi*... *kiṃ punaḥ karmaṇā*: Literally, "even by thought, much less by action."

Following verse 20, D5–7,9–11,S, and the texts and printed editions of Ct, Ck, and Cr insert a passage of one line [606*] describing the measurements of the city of Laṅkā: "It is ten leagues wide and twenty long (*daśayojanavistīrṇā viṃśadyojanam āyatā*)." The texts and printed editions of Cg, Crā and Cv, however, have a somewhat grander conception of the city's dimensions, reading instead, "It is a hundred leagues long and thirty wide (*śatayojanavistīrṇā triṃśadyojanam āyatā*)." The discrepancy between these two measurements has caught the attention of Ct, who attempts to reconcile his measurement with the latter as it is found in the vulgate text (GPP 7.5.25 [=CE 7.5.22a–83*, line1]). He claims that the smaller measurement refers to the inner citadel, which is Rāvaṇa's residence, whereas the greater one refers to the larger dimensions of the city as a whole. (*idaṃ ca laṅkārūpamahādurgāntarvartirāvaṇavāsa-sthānabhūtāntardurgaparam. śatayojanavistīrṇā triṃśadyojanam āyatety atraivānyatra sthala ukteḥ.*) See, too, Gita Press 1969, vol. 3, p. 1498, note.

22. "the heavens, Viṣṇu's middle step" *madhyamaṃ vaiṣṇavaṃ padam*: Literally, "the middle step of Viṣṇu." The reference is, of course, to the well-known story of Viṣṇu's *vāmanāvatāra* in which he traverses the universe in three strides. The midmost of these strides is, as the commentators point out, the sky. See 6.40.43; 6.47.119; 6.49.1–2; 6.53.26; 6.59.7; and notes. See, too, 1.28.2 and note.

"at summer's end" *ātapāpāye*: Literally, "at the passing of the hot season." The reference, as noted by Cm and Cg, is to the beginning of the monsoon (*varṣā-rambhasamaye*—so Cg). The simile thus compares the lofty buildings of the city to the towering clouds of the rainy season.

24. "the domed palace" *caityaḥ*: See 6.6.3 and note.

"a full complement" *samagreṇa*: Literally, "complete." Commentators differ somewhat on how to take this adjective, which modifies *śatena*, "a hundred." Ct and Ck gloss, "with full military equipment (*samagrasaṃnāhavatā*)." Cr glosses, "assembled, massed (*militena*)." Cg does not find the term problematic since his text reads *balena*, "force, army," for *śatena*, yielding the meaning "a whole army." This reading is reflected in the translation of Raghunathan (1982, vol. 3, p. 92), who renders, "a large... force."

Following verse 24, D5–7,9–11,S insert a passage of four lines [608*], summarizing the description of Laṅkā: "[Rāma saw that city], which was charming, wooded, adorned with mountains, abounding in parks and woodlands, variegated with all kinds of minerals, resounding with the songs of various birds, frequented by all kinds of animals, covered with all types of flowers, and frequented by all manner of *rākṣa-sas*."

25. "Lakṣmaṇa's fortunate elder brother" *lakṣmīvāṃl lakṣmaṇāgrajaḥ*: This is an example of the sort of alliterative epithet of which the poet is so fond.

"whose objective had been thus far achieved... opulent" *samṛddhāṃ samṛddhārthaḥ*: This is yet another example of alliteration. The more common meaning of the term *samṛddhārthaḥ*, "whose wealth was ample," would fit the context poorly here, as Rāma, during the years of his exile, is described as a penniless wanderer (see, for example, Rāvaṇa's description of Rāma at 5.20.29). We understand the term *artha* here to mean "goal *or* purpose" and understand the reference of the adjective to be to Rāma's having fulfilled the first, critical part of his quest, viz., to arrive with his forces at the gates of Laṅkā. A number of manuscripts, including Ś,V1,2,B2,D5,6,8,10–12,T1,M3, as well as the printed editions of all southern commentators read instead *samṛddhārthām*. This reading makes the adjective modify Laṅkā rather than Rāma and yields the sense "opulent, prosperous." The difficulty of this reading, which is followed by all translations based on the southern recension, is that it creates a redundancy with *samṛddhām*, which also means "opulent, prosperous." The commentators try to differentiate the two terms. Cr glosses, "grown to a great size (*atipravṛddhām*)" for *samṛddhām*, while Cg glosses, "lofty (*unnatām*)" to avoid the redundancy. Variations on the themes of size and opulence appear in the various translations of the southern text. The Lahore edition (6.15.25) reads with the critical text, while Gorresio (6.15.28) drops *samṛddhārtha* completely, using only the adjective *samṛddha*, "prosperous," to refer to Rāma.

Following verse 25, D5–7,9–11,S insert a passage of two lines [609*]: "As he gazed upon that city, crowded with great mansions, Lakṣmaṇa's godlike and powerful elder brother was wonderstruck."

26. "and his vast army" *mahatā balena*: Literally, "with a large army." Cr understands the vast army to be yet another of Laṅkā's attributes (*mahatā balenopalakṣitāṃ purīṃ laṅkām*).

"glittering with gems" *ratnapūrṇām*: Literally, "full of jewels." Cg proposes taking *ratna-*, "jewel," in its generic sense of "[any] excellent thing (*śreṣṭhavastūni*)."

"abounding with defensive works" *bahusaṃvidhānām*: Literally, "with many arrangements." On the basis of a similar usage at 6.3.10, we agree with Cg, who glosses, "defense, protection (*rakṣaṇam*)" for *saṃvidhānam*. Cr glosses, "types of constructions/arrangements (*racanāviśeṣāḥ*)," which is somewhat more ambiguous but probably means the same thing.

"Its mighty gates were studded with great defensive engines" *mahāyantrakavāṭamuhkyām*: Literally, "having principal gates with great engines." Although some translators (Roussel 1903, vol. 3, p. 109; Dutt 1893, p. 1211; and Shastri 1959, vol. 3, p. 93) interpret the underlying compound as a *dvandva* and thus understand the reference to be to great engines and gateways, we follow the suggestion of Cr, who glosses, "Laṅkā in which the principal gates were fitted with engines (*mahāyantrayuktāḥ kavāṭamukhyā yasyāṃ tām* [*laṅkām*])." Like the commentators on 6.3.15–16 above, modern translators differ in their opinion as to whether the *yantras* mentioned are military engines or mechanical devices connected with the operation of the gates. Thus, Raghunathan (1982, vol. 3, p. 93) translates, "huge gates operated by machines." Pagani (1999, p. 957) renders, "*ses portes aux puissantes serrures*." We share the view of Gita Press (1969, vol. 3, p. 1499), "fitted with huge engines of war." See 6.3.3–4,11 and notes. Cf. 6.15.18; 6.49.11; and 6.80.19 and notes.

The meter is *upajāti*.

Following *sarga* 30, D5–7,9–11,S insert an additional *sarga* of eighty lines [App. I, No. 18]: "Then Rāma, along with Sugrīva and the troop leaders of the tawny monkeys, climbed Mount Suvela, which was two leagues in breadth.[1–2] Standing there for a while and looking around in all ten directions, he spied the perfectly situated city of Laṅkā, ornamented with beautiful woodlands and built by Viśvakarman on the lovely summit of Mount Trikūṭa.[3–5] [And there he saw,] standing on the top of a tower, the unassailable lord of the *rākṣasas*. He was surrounded by white yak-tail fly whisks and adorned with the parasol of victory. He was smeared with red sandalwood paste and adorned with jeweled[1] ornaments.[6–8] He looked like a black storm cloud and was clad in golden garments. His chest was scarred by the tips of the tusks of Indra's war elephant, Airāvata. He was clad in garments as red as hare's blood, and he resembled a mass of storm clouds in the sky, suffused with the light of the setting sun.[9–12] The moment Sugrīva saw the *rākṣasa* lord, he leapt up, right before the eyes of Rāghava and the monkey lords.[13–14] Inflamed by an access of rage, he sprang up with strength and courage from the mountain peak to the gateway tower. He stood there for a moment watching, his mind utterly free from fear.[15–17] Regarding the *rākṣasa* as lightly as a piece of straw, he spoke these harsh words to him: 'I am the servant and ally of Rāma, lord of the world, *rākṣasa*. Through the blazing energy of that lord of kings, you shall not escape me this day.'[18–20] Having spoken in this fashion, he suddenly jumped up and leapt over him. Tearing off his splendid crown and casting it down, he landed on the ground.[21–22] Watching him as he swiftly advanced, the night-roaming *rākṣasa* said to him, 'Before you came into my sight, you were Sugrīva, "of the beautiful neck [*su-grīva*]," but now, you shall be Hīnagrīva, "the one with no neck at all [*hīna-grīvaḥ*]."'[23–24] Having spoken in this fashion, he swiftly sprang up and with both arms hurled him to the ground. But the tawny monkey, bouncing up like a ball, then threw him down with both arms.[25–26] Their limbs bathed in sweat, their bodies red with blood, they remained motionless, locked in each other's embrace, like a *śālmalī* and a *kiṃśuka* tree.[2] [27–30] The two of them, the immensely powerful *rākṣasa* and the monkey lord, engaged in a nearly unendurable battle with blows of their fists, palms, elbows, and fingertips.[31–34] The two of them, endowed with fearsome power, engaged in a terrific struggle for a long time on the terrace of the gateway tower. Throwing each other up and down, bending their bodies, they held their ground on the gateway tower with their footwork.[35–38] Grappling with each other, their bodies clinging fast, they both then fell into the moat of the rampart. But without touching the ground, they both flew up again and stood still for a moment, breathing hard.[39–42] Grasping each other repeatedly in the bonds of their arms, they engaged once more in battle. Thus did they then perform the various techniques of battle, engaging each other with anger, skill, and strength.[43–46] Like a lion and tiger filled with pride, like two young elephant bulls engaged in combat, striking and pressing each other with their chests, they both fell to the ground at once.[47–50] Dragging each other up and hurling each other down, they performed many techniques of battle. Endowed with strength and training in the martial arts, neither of those warriors soon tired.[51–54] Like two splendid bull-elephants, the two of them warded each other off with their mighty arms that were like elephant trunks. They fought each other fiercely for a long time, circling each other swiftly in the wheeling movements of combat.[3] [55–58] Confronting each other, bent on killing each other, they paused again and again, like two tomcats intent on food.[59–60] They wheeled in different circular movements and took up various postures. They advanced and retreated variously, like the flow of cow's urine. They moved sideways and crookedly. They parried blows, evaded, and ran about. They ran swiftly toward each other, crouching and posing, and grasping each other. They faced each other, turned their backs on each other, raced about and leapt. Both skilled in the techniques of battle, they approached each other and drew back.[4] [61–67] Thus did Rāvaṇa and the lord of the monkeys engage each other.[68] At that juncture, the *rākṣasa* attempted to employ his power of magic illusion. But the overlord of the monkeys, aware of this, then leapt into the sky with a victorious air, having conquered his fatigue.[69–71] And so Rāvaṇa stood there, cheated by the king of the tawny monkeys.[72] Then the lord of the best of the tawny monkeys, the son of the sun god, having gained fame in battle and having exhausted the lord of the night-roaming *rākṣasas* in battle, leapt up into the vast sky and went to Rāma's side in the midst of the army of the host of the tawny monkeys.[73–76] Thus, the lord of the tawny monkeys, son of Savitṛ, having accomplished this feat, flying like the wind, reentered the army in great excitement, honored by the foremost of the tree-dwelling monkeys and increasing the ardor for battle of the son of the king of the splendid Raghus.[5][77–80]"

[1]"jeweled" *ratna-*: D5–7,9–11, and the texts and printed editions of Ct and Cr read instead *rakta-*, "red."

[2]"like a *śālmalī* and a *kiṃśuka* tree" *śālmalikiṃśukāv iva*: See 6.76.28 and note. See, too, 6.35.9 and note.

[3]"circling each other swiftly in the wheeling movements of combat" *saṃceratur maṇḍalamārgam*: Literally, "they carried out the technique of the circle." The commentators discuss at great length the various type of military movements referred to here. See 6.87.23,25,30 and notes. Translators offer a variety of definitions based primarily on the commentators. Dutt (1893, pp. 1213–14) lists all the terms in Sanskrit and attempts to define them in a series of footnotes.

The meter of lines 27–58 is *upajāti*.

[4]Lines 61–67 provide a detailed technical account of the battle between Rāvaṇa and Sugrīva, alluding to a variety of technical terms for the different movements of hand-to-hand combat. Commentators and translators offer a variety of interpretations of these sometimes obscure terms. Our translation is basically informed by the analysis of Cg, who gives the most detailed discussion of this passage.

[5]The meter of lines 73–80 is *mālinī*.

Sarga 31

1. "at this juncture . . . various portents" *atha tasmin nimittāni*: Literally, "now, at *or* on that . . . portents." The phrase is elliptical but, in the context of the critical edition, is probably best read as we and Cr ("at this time [*tasmin samaye*]") have done. An alternative would be to understand "on that [mountain, i.e., Suvela]." The other southern commentators operate in the context of the southern recension in which the immediately preceding *sarga* (App. I, No. 18, translated at note to 6.30.26) describes Sugrīva's unauthorized struggle with Rāvaṇa. They understand *tasmin* here to refer to Sugrīva's body upon which Rāma sees signs (*nimittāni*). They interpret these as the signs of combat, such as blood, etc. (*tasmin sugrīve. nimittāni kṣatajādirūpāṇi yuddhacihnāni*—so Ct).

"Lakṣmaṇa's elder brother . . . fortunate Lakṣmaṇa" *lakṣmaṇapūrvajaḥ / . . . lakṣmaṇaṃ lakṣmisampannam*: This is another example of the poet's fondness for alliteration, especially involving his characters' names. According to Cg, however, the word *lakṣmī* (here, *lakṣmi-*), normally, "good fortune, the goddess of good fortune," refers to [Lakṣmaṇa's] gratification upon seeing favorable portents (*lakṣmīr atra nimittadarśanajaḥ santoṣaḥ*). Cf. 6.14.3 and note.

Following 1ab, D5–7,9–11,S insert a passage of eighteen lines [610*] in which Rāma addresses not Lakṣmaṇa but Sugrīva, rebuking him for his impulsive and unauthorized attack on Rāvaṇa: "Embracing Sugrīva, he [Rāma] then spoke these words, 'You did this rash act without consulting me. Lords of the people do not engage in such rash undertakings. Fond of reckless deeds, hero, you did this rash thing mischievously, placing me and the army along with Vibhīṣaṇa in peril.[1–5] From now on, hero, you must not engage in such thoughtless actions. If you had been killed somehow or other, what use would I have for Sītā, Bharata, my younger brother Lakṣmaṇa, Śatrughna, or even my own body, great-armed slayer of your foes?[6–9] Even though I knew your strength, you who are the equal of great Indra or Varuṇa, before you returned, I had made up my mind that, once I had destroyed Rāvaṇa in battle, together with his sons, troops, and mounts, and had consecrated Vibhīṣaṇa as king of Laṅkā, I would transfer my kingship to Bharata and abandon my body, mighty one.'[10–14] Sugrīva then replied to Rāma, who was speaking in this fashion, saying, 'How, heroic Rāghava, could I, knowing my own strength, have simply stood by once I saw Rāvaṇa, the abductor of your wife?' Rāghava, commending that hero, who had spoken in this fashion. . . . [15–18]"

2. "these cool lakes" *udakaṃ śītam*: Literally, "cool water." We follow Ct, who glosses, "bodies of water filled with that [water] (*tadvato jalāśāyān*)."

"dividing this massive army into companies and marshaling it in formation" *balaughaṃ saṃvibhajyemaṃ vyūhya*: Literally, "having divided and marshaled this flood of troops." We follow Cg in understanding two separate military actions here. The first, according to Cg, is the breaking up of the mass of troops into units under the command of their various troop leaders; the second is the marshaling of these forces into the defensive and offensive formations (*vyūhas*), such as the eagle formation, etc. (*saṃvibhajya tattadyūthapādhīnaṃ kṛtvā vyūhya garuḍādirūpeṇa sthāpayitvā*).

Verses 2–12 recur with minor variations at App. I, No. 16, lines 3–26 [=GPP 6.23.2–13]. See note to 6.15.33. Ct declines to comment on the passage here, noting that he has done so earlier (*vyākhātaprāyā ime ślokāḥ*).

3. For similar passages listing inauspicious omens, see 6.26.21–30; 6.41.30–34; 6.45.31–37; 6.53.11–15; 6.65.17–19, 6.83.32–34; 6.94.14–27; and notes.

"I see signs of a horrendous universal catastrophe" *lokakṣayakaraṃ bhīmaṃ bhayaṃ paśyāmi*: Literally, "I see a fearful danger, destructive of the world." We agree with Cg in understanding *bhayam*, "fear, danger," to refer here to "portents of danger (*bhayanimittam*), which indicate the impending universal destruction (*lokakṣayasūcakam*)."

"presaging the annihilation" *nibarhaṇam*: Literally, "destruction." We follow Cg, who glosses, "indicating destruction (*vināśasūcakam*)."

4. "the mountains crumble" *patanti dharaṇīdharāḥ*: Literally, "the upholders of the earth fall." Ś,Ñ2,V1–3,B2,3,D2–4,6,8,10–12,T2,3,G1,2,M5, and the texts and printed editions of Ct, Ck, and Cr read *nadanti*, "they roar, bellow," for *patanti*, "they fall." Based on this reading, Cr believes that the noun *dharaṇīdharāḥ* refers not to the mountains but to the elephants of the four quarters, who in Hindu cosmology are represented as supporting the earth on their foreheads. See 6.4.6 and 6.58.45–46 and notes. See, too, 1.39.12,16,17 and notes. Cr thinks that these elephants are trum-

peting (*diggajā nadanti*). Gita Press (1969, vol. 3, p. 1504), following Cr here, understands that the elephants are trumpeting. Roussel (1903, vol. 3, p. 113), Dutt (1893, p. 1213), and Pagani (1999, p. 960) understand that the mountains are emitting sounds. Raghunathan (1982, vol. 3, p. 96) and Shastri (1959, vol. 3, p. 97), following the variant *dharaṇīruhāḥ*, "[things that] grow on mountains, (i.e., trees)," found in a number of southern manuscripts (D5,T1,G3,M3; KK 6.41.13; VSP 6.41.13), understand that trees are falling.

5. "resembling beasts of prey" *kravyādasaṃkāśāḥ*: Most commentators list the kinds of beasts intended, including hawks, jackals, vultures, wolves, and so on, and understand the clouds' likeness to these creatures to consist in their dark color, or, as Cg puts it at his comments to the identical verse at GPP 6.23.5 (= CE App. I, No. 16, lines 9–10), "wolf colored (*vṛkavarṇāḥ*)." Cg offers an alternative, i.e., that the clouds may have the shape of birds of prey, such as hawks, etc. (*śyenādisaṃsthānā iti vā*). The latter is the only explanation he offers at the current verse (*śyenādisadṛśyasaṃsthānāḥ*). See 6.26.24 and note.

"mingled with drops of blood" *miśraṃ śoṇitabindubhiḥ*: At GPP 6.23.5, Cg quotes Varāhamihira, who gives a list of evil omens, including showers of blood (*divy ulkapatanaṃ caiva divānakṣatradarśanam / divā śanis tathā kāṣṭhatṛṇaraktapravarṣaṇam /*). Varāhamihira's quote does not appear to come from either his *Bṛhatsaṃhitā* or *Bṛhajjātaka*. Varāhamihira, however, does mention showers of blood as portents of wars between kings (46.40,43). For blood raining down from the heavens as a portent, see 6.26.22; 6.41.33; 6.45.926*–36; 6.83.33; 6.94.15; and notes. Cf. note to 6.76.2, inserted passage 1674*, lines 5–7.

6. "The evening sky, the color of red sandalpaste" *raktacandanasaṃkāśā saṃdhyā*: Literally, "twilight, the color of red sandalwood." At GPP 6.23.6, Cg explains, "filled with clouds like red sandalpaste (*raktacandanatulyameghavatīty arthaḥ*)." For red sandalwood, Cg glosses, "saffron (*kuṅkumam*)."

7. The howling or shrieking of beasts of prey, especially jackals, is a common portent of destruction. See 6.26.24; 6.45.32,34; 6.53.42; 6.83.33; 6.94.21; and notes. Cf. 6.41.32 and note.

"beasts and birds of ill omen" *apraśastā mṛgadvijāḥ*: Literally, "inauspicious beasts and birds." These, according to Cg and Cr, are forbidden (Cg, "lowly [*hīnāḥ*]") scavenger animals, such as jackals, vultures, etc. (*niṣiddhāḥ . . . śṛgālagṛdhraprabhṛtayaḥ*—so Cr). See notes to 6.4.6 and 6.26.28.

8. "glows dully" *aprakāśaś ca saṃtāpayati*: Literally, "and, devoid of light, [it] emits heat *or* burns." As Cg notes at GPP 6.23.8, the heating of something naturally cool [such as the moon] is an evil omen (*śītasya saṃtāpakaraṇaṃ hy utpāta iti bhāvaḥ*).

"emitting a dark and reddish glare" *kṛṣṇaraktāṃśuparyantaḥ*: Literally, "surrounded by black and red rays." Cg, in his comments on GPP 6.23.8, explains it exactly in this way. Here, however, Cg reads the variant *kṛṣṇaraktāntaparyantaḥ*, "having a dark interior and red borders" (D6,T3,G1,3,M5, VSP 6.41.17, and Cg—not noted in KK or GPP), which, he understands, is an adjective modifying not the moon but the halo around the sun in the following verse (see note above). This yields the sense "dark in its central orb but red at its circumference." This reading is reflected only in the translation of Raghunathan (1982, vol. 3, p. 96), who, however, unaccountably reverses Cg's interpretation, rendering, "black at the outer edge and red inside," and understanding it as a reference to the halo of the moon.

9. "faint" *hrasvaḥ*: Literally, "short, diminutive, diminished." Cg takes the term here to refer to a measure of one *vyāma* (*vyāmamātraḥ*), the distance between the tips of the fingers of the outstretched arms (about a fathom, or six feet). See Apte s.v.

"menacing" *rūkṣaḥ*: Literally, "harsh, rough." We follow Cg, who glosses, *bhayaṃkaraḥ*, "frightening," although at GPP 6.23.9, he glosses the more lexically supportable *krūraḥ*, "cruel."

"corona" *pariveṣaḥ*: Cg, who reads 8cd together with 9ab as describing the solar corona, thus understands that the corona is tricolored, namely, black (*kṛṣṇa*), red (*rakta*), and crimson (*sulohita*). Cg, in his comments to GPP 6.23.9, claims that the appearance of such a solar corona is an omen presaging the death of a king. He supports this claim by quoting Kāśyapa: "A double corona [presages] the destruction of an army, a triple corona that of a king (*dvimaṇḍalaś camūpaghno nṛpaghno yas trimaṇḍalaḥ*)." He also quotes a text, possibly Kāśyapa, to the effect that a solar corona presages different things at different times of the day. Thus, "[its appearance] in the first watch (*yāma*) of the day indicates affliction (*pīḍā*); in the second watch, it presages an intense battle (?) (*vṛṣṭiyuddha*); in the third watch of the day, such a corona foretells prosperity (*kṣema*), they say; and, in the fourth, universal destruction (*sarvanāśa*) (*dinakarapariveṣaḥ pūrvayāme tu pīḍā, dinakarapariveṣo vṛṣṭiyuddhaṃ dvitīye / dinakarapariveṣaṃ kṣemam āhus tṛtīye dinakarapariveṣaḥ sarvanāśaś caturthe //*)." According to this reckoning, Rāma's sighting of the corona in the evening, which should correspond to the fourth *yāma* of the day, would suggest the universal destruction of which he speaks in verses 8 and 10.

"inauspicious" *apraśastaḥ*: As at verse 7 above, we follow Cr and Cg, who gloss, *aśubhakaraḥ*. At GPP 6.23.9, Cg, on the other hand, glosses, "unfamiliar (*aprasiddhaḥ*)," which he explains as "unprecedented (*itaḥ purvam adṛṣṭa ity arthaḥ*)."

"dark spot . . . Lakṣmaṇa" *nīlaṃ lakṣma lakṣmaṇa*: Literally, "dark blue mark, Lakṣmaṇa." Cg describes this mark or sunspot as being like one of the dark spots on the moon (*candrakalaṅka iva*). He then cites a passage from the *Chāndogya Upaniṣad* (6.4.2) in which the dark manifestations of the sun are represented as food, one of the three constituents (fire, water, and food—*tejobanna*) of the material universe according to the *Chāndogya* cosmology. At GPP 6.23.9, however, Cg gives this explanation and citation only as his second alternative. For the first, he says that the mark is of the nature of a fissure (*chidrarūpam*) and quotes Varāhamihira to the effect that the appearance of such a fissure on the sun or the moon and the eclipse of these luminaries on a non-*parvan* day each presage the destruction of a kingdom (*aparvaṇi tathā rāhugrahaṇaṃ candrasūryayoś candrārkamaṇḍalacchidraṃ dṛṣṭvā janapadakṣaye*).

Note the alliteration in the sequence *lakṣma* and *lakṣmaṇa*.

10. "look strange" *dṛṣyante na yathāvat*: Literally, "they do not look as they should." Cg suggests that they are obscured (*malināni*).

"All of this that appears to us seems to presage" *abhivartate . . . iva . . . śaṃsati*: Literally, "it approaches . . . it seems to indicate." We agree with Cg and Cm, who understand the implicit subject of the predicate *abhivartate* to be the sum total of the previously described evil portents (*uktaṃ nimittajālam*). Ct, who reads the singular *dṛśyate* for the critical edition's plural *dṛśyante*, proposes an implied subject, which is "the Milky Way[?], etc. (*prakāśagatyādikam*)." This enables Ct to read the plural *nakṣatrāṇi*, "constellations," as an accusative. Thus, he understands the phrase to mean "the Milky Way, etc., which leads to the constellations, does not appear as it should."

Cr takes *abhivartate* as the dative of the irregular *parasmaipada* participle of the verb *abhi* √*vṛt* in the sense of "to advance, attack." He thus understands, "the appearance of the *nakṣatras* presages destruction for a person who is about to launch an attack in the world (*lokasya loke 'bhivartate 'bhivartamānāya janāya yugāntam iva śaṃsati bodhayati*)." Cf. note to verse 42 below.

11. "kites" *śyenāḥ*: Normally the term *śyena* refers to a hawk, eagle, or other type of bird of prey. In the present context, however, where the discussion is of flocking, downward-spiraling carrion birds, it is probable, we believe, that the poet was thinking of the common kite, despite the lack of lexical support. See notes to 6.75.20; cf. notes to 6.87.39–40. Cf. Dave 1985, pp. 242–43.

"spiraling downward" *nīcaiḥ paripatanti*: Literally, "they fall *or* swoop down." Several translators understand the reference to be to the diving or swooping of the birds, but we see it more as the slow descending spirals of birds that feed on carrion. Cg, on the other hand, understands that the birds are coming down to alight on low altars or platforms (*nīcair hrasvaṃ vedikāsthānaṃ paripatanti prāpnuvanti*). Cm reads *nīcaiḥ* adjectivally rather than adverbially, taking it to mean "together with [other] lowly creatures (*kṣudrajantubhiḥ saha*)."

"jackals" *śivāḥ*: Cg notes that, although a blanket mention has been made (verse 7 above) of the mournful and frightful cries of all the inauspicious birds and beasts, the repetition of the specific species here is owing to the extreme inauspiciousness of the animals mentioned (*apraśastamṛgajātyuktāv api punaruktir aśubhādhikyāt*).

Following verse 11, D7,10,11, and the texts and printed editions of Ct and Cr insert a passage of two lines [615*]: "Soon the earth, covered with a mire of flesh and blood, will be littered with stones, spears, and swords loosed by the monkeys and *rākṣasas*."

12. "this very day, swiftly and without delay" *kṣipram adya . . . javenaiva*: Literally, "quickly, right now, with great speed."

14. "he inspected" *dadarśa*: Literally, "he saw, viewed." Cg observes that Rāma's reviewing his troops at the foot of the mountain indicates that the entire army did not climb Mount Suvela (*anena sarvaṃ balaṃ na suvelam āruhad iti gamyate*).

15. "master of timing" *kālajñaḥ*: Literally, "knowing the [proper] time."

"prepared" *saṃnahya*: Normally, the verb *sam* √*nah* is used reflexively in the sense of " to prepare, equip, or arm oneself for battle." Here, however, it is used in a transitive sense. Thus, we read with Cg, "having incited *or* stimulated (*protsāhya*)."

"army of the monkey king" *kapirājabalam*: Cg understands *kapirāja* in the sense of "foremost monkeys," thus giving the meaning "the army of outstanding monkeys (*kapiśreṣṭhānāṃ balam*)."

"at the proper moment" *kāle*: Literally, "in time." We follow Cr, Cg, and Cm in understanding the reference to be to an appropriate time for battle (*saṃgrāmasamaye*—so Cr). Ct, however, sees an implicit reference to an auspicious moment as specified in the science of astrology (*jyotiḥśāstroktakāle*).

16. "when the time was right" *kāle*: Literally, "in time." This term, which is repeated from the previous verse, is treated somewhat differently here by the various commentators, perhaps in an attempt to absolve the poet of the flaw of redundancy. Thus, Ct, who in the earlier passage referred to the moment selected by astrology, here sees the time as chosen by the prognosticative science of [nasal] sounds (*svaraśāstra*) (Apte s.v.). Ct indicates that these would be used to select the proper moment to initiate the battle (*yuddhayogye kāle*). Cg, who earlier had interpreted, "the [proper time] for battle

(*kāle yuddhakāle saṃyugāya yuddhāya*)," here understands, "in the morning (*prātaḥkāle*)."

17. "the king of the apes" *ṛkṣarājaḥ*: This epithet is normally applied to Jāmbavān. The disjunction of the epithet here from the name "Jāmbavān" makes the identification difficult. Translators vary in their interpretations. Some, in keeping with tradition, assign the epithet to Jāmbavān, despite the disjunction (Gita Press 1969, vol. 3, p. 1505 and Shastri 1959, vol. 3, p. 97). Some take it as a reference to the monkey Nīla, whose name immediately follows it (Dutt 1893, p. 1216). Some read it as referring to Nala, whose name immediately precedes it (Raghunathan 1982, vol. 3, p. 97 and Gorresio 1856, vol. 9, p. 243). Still others (Pagani 1999, p. 961 and Roussel 1903, vol. 3, p. 114) understand, as do we, that the epithet stands alone and is not in apposition to any of the names in the verse. The commentators are largely silent on this, with the exception of Cs, who reads as we do, identifying the king of the *ṛkṣas* as Dhūmra. On the issue of the identification of *ṛkṣas*, see Goldman 1989 and 1.16.10 and notes. See, too, 6.4.17 and note.

18. "forest-dwelling monkeys" *-vanaukasām*: Literally, "forest dwellers."

21. The verse consists entirely of accusative feminine adjectives modifying Laṅkā. Technically, it should be construed with either the previous or the following verse. We have read it as if it were a separate descriptive sentence in order to avoid an excessively long construction.

"it seemed impregnable" *suduṣprāpām*: Literally, "exceedingly inaccessible *or* unattainable."

22. "following orders" *yathānideśam*: Literally, "according to instructions." Ś,Ñ, V1,B1,2,4,D1–4,6,8,12,T3,M3, and the texts and printed editions of Cg read instead *yathāniveśam*, "according to encampment," which, according to Cg, gives the sense that the monkeys each took up their assigned position. (*yathāsthānam. rāmavaco 'nyūnaṃ svaṃ svaṃ sthānam anatikramyety arthaḥ.*) Cm, however, interprets the critical reading in the sense in which we do, glossing, "not deviating from Rāma's instructions (*yathāniveśaṃ rāmanideśam anatikramya*)." In fact, the word *nideśa-* itself can also mean "place *or* station," and various translators have interpreted accordingly (e.g., Raghunathan 1982, vol. 3, p. 97).

"closely besieged" *saṃpīḍya nyaviśanta*: Literally, "having pressed closely together, they encamped." Compare note to verse 32 below.

23. "guarded and blockaded" *jugopa ca rurodha ca*: That Rāma is represented as simultaneously blockading and protecting the gate is troubling to many of the commentators, who see the sequence as contradictory. Ct, Ck, Cg, Cm, and Cs suggest supplying a separate object, "his army (*ātmīyabalam*)," for the verb *jugopa*, "he protected." Their idea is that Rāma is engaged in two separate activities, one offensive and the other defensive. Cs, however, suggests an additional explanation of a theological nature. He proposes that Rāma protects through his indwelling form that is internal to Rāvaṇa, etc. [i.e., all other beings], while at the same time he besieges [the city] in his exterior [human] form as Rāma. This, Cs continues, suggests that in the absence of an impulse from Rāma, Rāvaṇa is incapable of doing anything. (*jugopa anta[ḥ]sthitarāvaṇādyantaḥsthitena rūpeṇa jugopa. bahī rāmarūpeṇa rurodha ceti vā. antareṇa rāmapreraṇāṃ rāvaṇaḥ kim api kartuṃ na kṣama ity anena sūcyate.*) Cg argues that the use of the verb *rurodha*, "he blockaded," here enables us to infer from the context (*arthasiddham*) that [Rāma's forces] had also ascended to the peak of Mount Trikūṭa,

[where Lañkā is located], which was described at 6.30.18. Cg quotes this verse (*rurodhety anena śikharaṃ trikūṭasya prāṃśu caikaṃ divispṛśam ity uktatrikūṭaśikharārohaṇam arthasiddham*).

24–25. "capable of guarding" *samarthaḥ parirakṣitum*: Cs explains that only Rāma is able to guard the gate in such a way that Rāvaṇa and his allies will be unable to force their way out (*rāvaṇādayo yathā na bahir āgaccheyus tathā rakṣitum ity arthaḥ*). Cm, evidently unhappy with the use of the verb *pari* √*rakṣ*, "to protect," in regard to something one is attempting to assault, suggests that the phrase *tad dvāram*, "that gate," is a compound referring to the army [of Rāma] assigned to the blockade of that gate (*taddvāraṃ taddvārarodhikāṃ senām*).

26. "the ocean guarded by Varuṇa" *varuṇeneva sāgaram*: Literally, "as the ocean by Varuṇa." The word "guarded" has been borrowed here from the following syntactic unit for the sake of clarity.

"It struck terror into the hearts of the weak." *laghūnāṃ trāsajananam*: Literally, "generating fear in the weak." We follow Cg, Cm, Ck, and Cr, all of whom provide different glosses with the sense of "weak, cowardly, unsteady, etc." for *laghu*, "light, insignificant."

"just as is the underworld known as Pātāla" *pātālam iva*: Literally, "just as Pātāla."

27. "Rāma saw" *dadarśa*: Literally, "he saw."

"stores" *-jālāni*: Literally, "masses."

28. "Mainda and Dvivida" *maindena dvividena ca*: Although it is stated at 6.28.25 above that Nīla was assigned to the eastern gate with many other monkeys, Mainda and Dvivida are not specifically named there. Cg notes, however, that we should understand that Rāma had previously assigned them to this position (*maindena dvividena cetyādinā pratidvāram adhikayūthapatigamanasyātroktatvāt pūrvaṃ rāmeṇa te niyuktā iti jñeyam*).

29. See 6.28.26, where Rāma assigns Añgada to the southern gate.

30. "Pramāthin, Praghasa" *pramāthipraghasābhyāṃ ca*: D7,10,11, and the texts and printed editions of Ct and Cr read instead the names Prajañgha and Tarasa. Compare 6.28.27.

31. "central encampment" *madhyame . . . gulme*: The idea here, according to Ct, Ck, Cg, and Cm, is that in order to be able to swiftly lend support to Rāma or Hanumān, who are stationed, respectively, at the northern and western gates, where, again respectively, the most invincible of the *rākṣasas*, Rāvaṇa and Indrajit, are stationed, Sugrīva encamps with the main monkey force midway between those two gates. This would place Sugrīva, according to the commentators, in the direction guarded by the divinity Vāyu, i.e., the northwestern quarter. According to Cg, Ck, and Cm, that Sugrīva so positions himself is an illustration of the *kākākṣinyāya*, or maxim of the crow's eye, according to which a single element, e.g., a word in a sentence, can do double duty in different places. Ct, however, cites the *madhyamaṇinyāya*, or maxim of the central gemstone, which presumably refers to the stone's ability to illuminate articles on either side. (*atidurjayarāvaṇendrajidadhiṣṭhitayor uttarapaścimadvārayor madhye vāyudiśi. tadubhayadvāranirodhakānāṃ madhyamaṇinyāyena sāhāyyaṃ kartuṃ sugrīvaḥ samatiṣṭhatety arthaḥ*—so Ct.) Cf. 5.3.27; 6.3.27; 6.27.20; 6.28.31; 6.45.2; 6.62.5; 6.71.1; 6.72.5; 6.84.6; and notes.

"swift as Suparṇa or the wind" *suparṇaśvasanopamaiḥ*: Literally, "comparable to Suparṇa or the wind." Since both Suparṇa [Garuḍa] and the wind are stereotyped *upamānas* for the quality of speed, we have fleshed out the elliptical simile accordingly. The idea here, presumably, is to emphasize the swiftness with which Sugrīva's troops could respond to the aid of either Rāma or Hanumān as needed. V3,D5,10,11,G1, and the texts and printed editions of Ct read *suvarṇa-*, "gold," for *suparṇa-*, while V3,D7,9–11,G1,2 read *-pavana-*, "wind (lit., the purifier)," for *śvasana-*, "wind." Although the text of GPP (6.41.42; but not NSP [6.41.42]) reads the all-but-untranslatable *suvarṇa-*, no commentator mentions the variant, and no translator renders it.

32. "illustrious leaders of the monkey troops" *vānarāṇām* ... *prakhyātayūthapāḥ*: Literally, "the illustrious troop leaders of the monkeys." Ct and Cm, evidently disturbed by the relatively small number of monkeys mentioned here [compared to the astronomical numbers given at 6.15.25 and 6.19.4] as constituting Sugrīva's main force, emphasize the word *prakhyāta-*, "illustrious," to indicate that the less prominent monkeys, not mentioned here, are simply innumerable. Ct notes further that when the text mentions [in verse 31] that these are "all the foremost monkeys," we are to understand that this leaves out the monkeys already stationed at the four gates. (*sarvair hariśreṣṭhair dvāranirodhaniyuktebhyo 'vaśiṣṭaiḥ prakhyātayūthapāḥ ṣaṭtriṃśatkoṭyaḥ. aprakhyātayūthapānāṃ tatsenānāṃ ca gaṇanābhāva iti bhāvaḥ*—so Ct.)

"were encamped, pressing their siege" *nipīḍyopaniviṣṭāḥ*: Literally, "having pressed, were encamped." Cr fleshes out the phrase, explaining, "having pressed the *rākṣasas* who were stationed there, they were encamped (*tatstharākṣasān pīḍayitvopaniviṣṭā abhavann iti śeṣaḥ*)." Compare note to verse 23 above.

34. "Sugrīva" *sugrīvaḥ*: D5,7,10,11,T1,G1, and the texts and printed editions of Ct and Cr read instead *suṣeṇaḥ*, "Suṣeṇa."

"a little to the west of Rāma's post" *paścimena tu rāmasya* ... *adūrāt*: Literally, "not far off to the west of Rāma." Ct, Cr, and Cm explain that Sugrīva (or Suṣeṇa in Ct's and Cr's variant) is providing close support as a rear guard to Rāma (*āsannapṛṣṭhabhāgāvaṣṭambhena*—Ct, Cm).

36. "erect ... flexing ... contorted" *vikṛta-* ... *vikṛta-* ... *vikṛta-*: Like other translators, we have had to render this adjective, which normally means "transformed, distorted, hideous," in different ways in order to accommodate the contexts in which it is used. In the case of the monkeys' tails, we have followed Cg, who glosses, "extending their tails upward (*ūrdhvaṃ prasāritapucchāḥ*)." This is, as we understand it, an aggressive posture on the part of the monkeys. Ct and Cr understand the action to be a product of the monkeys' rage but do not describe it precisely (*atikrodhāveśavaśat*—so Cr). In the case of the monkeys' limbs, we understand them to be extended or flexed menacingly. Cg explains the compound *vikṛtacitrāṅgāḥ*, "flexing their variegated limbs," as follows: "The transformation (*vikṛtatvam*) of the limbs refers to the fact that the monkeys' faces and eyes are red with rage and therefore their limbs are of variegated colors [i.e., blotchy]. (*vikṛtatvaṃ koparaktamukhanetratvam. ata eva citraṃ citravarṇam aṅgaṃ yeṣāṃ te tathoktā iti vigrahaḥ*.)" As for the monkeys' faces, the contortion is also probably a product of their anger, as Cr suggests. Cg believes that they are twisting their features in imitative mockery of the *rākṣasas* (*rākṣasaviḍambanāya kūṭilitamukhāḥ*). See Maestripieri 1999a–f and Flack et al. 2000a–d.

38. "as powerful as an *ogha* of elephants" *oghabalāḥ*: Literally, "having the strength of an *ogha*." We provide the word "elephant" to retain the standard of measure established in the preceding verse. The term *ogha* here is somewhat problematic. Normally, it has the sense of "a flood, a host, a vast number." However, because the

verse specifically refers to a multiple of one hundred [*oghas*], it seems likely to us that the term is intended here in the spirit of the earlier passages where the monkeys are enumerated (see 6.19.32 and notes). Thus, it appears that the poet is referring to a specific astronomical number. One problem with this interpretation is that the term *ogha* appears to be citable in this meaning only in one passage in a few *Rāmāyaṇa* manuscripts, where it is said to equal one hundred thousand *samudras* (following 6.19.32 at 412[E]* in D5,T1,M1–3, and in the published editions of Cg; also found in KK 6.28.39 and VSP 6.28.38 and as a bracketed and unnumbered line between GPP 6.28.37 and 38, where it is stated to be an additional half verse belonging to the text of Cg [*śataṃ samudrasāhasram ogha ity abhidhīyate*]). On the other hand, the term *mahaugha*, or "great *ogha*," occurs at 412*, line 3 ([following 6.19.32] = GPP 6.28.37). See note to 6.19.32, where we are given the definition of a *mahaugha* as one hundred thousand *samudras* [ten sexdecillion = 10^{52}]. By this calculation, the terms *ogha* and *mahaugha* would be synonymous. If, however, one were to take the modifier *mahā-* in these numerical compounds in its usual sense of "one hundred thousand," then an *ogha* would be one one-hundred-thousandth of a *mahaugha* and thus equal to a *samudra*. For a discussion of this system of numeration used in connection with the numbering of the monkey troops, see notes to 6.19.32.

Ct, Cr, Cg, and Cm all understand the reference to be to a specific number, "having the strength of one count *or* number of *oghas* of elephants (*nāga*) (*oghasaṃkhyānāgabalāḥ*)."

Many northern manuscripts, as well as the edition of Gorresio (6.16.42), avoid the confusion regarding the exact number the term *ogha* represents by substituting *vāyubalopamāḥ*, "as powerful as the wind," for *śataguṇottarāḥ*, "a hundred times [as powerful as that]," of *pāda* b. This makes it possible to interpret *ogha* in the sense of a force of nature (the flood *or* ocean) similar to the massed monkey troops. Gorresio (1856, vol. 9, p. 245) translates accordingly, "*Alcuni han l'impeto de' flutti.*" This reading gains some credence, perhaps, from the fact that the term *ogha* is clearly used in its sense of "an ocean, flood, *or* mass" in verse 45 below to describe the massed armies whose sound is compared to that of the ocean. Other northern and *devanāgarī* manuscripts, as well as the Lahore edition (6.16.39), avoid the problem by reading *megha-*, "clouds," for *ogha-*, yielding the somewhat awkward sense of "as powerful as clouds." The monkeys themselves will be compared to clouds at verse 44 below.

39. "variegated" *vicitraḥ*: The idea, according to Cg, is that the army is of various colors, etc., because of its being made up of monkeys, langurs, and bears (*vicitraḥ vānaragopucchabhallūkajuṣṭatayā nānāvarṇaḥ*). Cs takes two minor lexical meanings of the word *citra* here as the basis for alternate explanations of the term. According to the first, in which *citra* is a synonym for *māyā*, it means that "the monkey host is devoid of magical or deceitful means [*māyika*], unlike the *rākṣasas*, etc. (*na ca rākṣasādīnām iva māyika ity āha. vicitra iti vigatamāya ity arthaḥ*)." According to the second, in which *citra* means "sky," the monkey host is "not going through the sky [that is entirely situated on the ground] (*vicitro 'gaganaga ity arthaḥ*)."

"swarm of locusts" *śalabhānām ivodgamaḥ*: Ct, Ck, and Cg (second alternative) understand the reference to be to the sudden calamitous swarming of these insects (*utpātakāle iti śeṣaḥ*—so Ct). Cg, however, for his first alternative, understands *śalabha-* to refer to the terrifying, mythical, eight-legged beast called *śarabha*, which is said to be stronger than a lion (Apte s.v.). He thus sees the point of the simile not to be so much the vast number of troops but their fearsomeness (*śalabhānāṃ śarabhāṇām aṣṭapādamṛgāṇām udyamaḥ samāgama āsīt tathā bhayaṅkaro 'bhūd ity arthaḥ*). For a description of the mythical creature called *śarabha*, see *Ṛtusaṃhāra* 1.23.

40. "seemed to be... filled... as if covered" *paripūrṇam iva... saṃchanneva*: We follow Ct, Cr, and Cg in reading the participles distributively. Cr and Cg are disturbed by the poet's repetition of the comparative particle *iva* in the verse. Cr argues that we should take one *iva* in the sense of *api*, "as well" (*eka ivaśabdo 'pyarthe*). Cg, on the other hand, writes the repetition off as the figure of speech *vākyālaṃkāra* (*atraivaśabdadvayam api vākyālaṃkāre*).

"converging on the city" *saṃpatadbhiḥ*: Literally, "[by those] flying *or* leaping together."

41. "A hundred divisions each of one hundred thousand" *śataṃ śatasahasrāṇāṃ pṛthak*: V3,D10,11,T3,M1,2, and the texts and printed editions of Ck, Ct, and Cr read *pṛtanā*, "an army *or* a division of an army [consisting of 243 elephants, 243 chariots, 729 cavalry, and 1,215 foot soldiers]," for *pṛthak*, yielding the sense of "armies of ten millions [of apes...]." Ct takes the term *sahasra*, "thousand," in the sense of *koṭi*, "ten million." He thus sees the monkeys here as numbering ten billion (*śatakoṭi*). Ct, Cg, Cm, and Ck inform us that the monkeys mentioned here are to be understood as over and above those who have been previously stationed at and around the gates of the city (*ete pūrvaniyuktādhikā iti bodhyam*—so Ct). See note to 6.3.24.

"stationed themselves at... swarmed in" *upājagmuḥ*: Literally, "they approached." The same verb does double duty for the two groups of monkeys, and we have translated it in two ways to reflect the warriors' different situations.

42. "mountain" *giriḥ*: According to Ct, Ck, Cv, Cg, and Cm, the mountain in question is Trikūṭa (see 5.2.1 and note). Cr specifies that the mountain includes [all three of its peaks] Suvela, etc. (*suvelaprabhṛtiḥ*). See 6.29.1–2 and notes.

"marched upon" *abhyavartata*: We understand the verb here in its sense of "to attack *or* approach with hostile intent." Ct, Cr, and Ck suggest that this additional force of monkeys is moving around the citadel in order to gather information as to what is happening with the troops stationed at the four gates (*sarvadvāravartisvasenāsarvavṛttāntagrahaṇārthaṃ saṃcaratām iti śeṣaḥ*). Cf. note to verse 10 above.

43. "tree-wielding" *drumapāṇibhiḥ*: Literally, "with trees in hand."

"so that not even the wind could enter" *duṣpraveśāpi vāyunā*: Literally, "hard to enter, even by the wind." We understand, with Cr and Cg, that it is the mass of monkeys surrounding the city that makes it impenetrable (*vānaraiḥ saṃvṛtā laṅkā vāyunāpi duṣpraveśā babhūva*—so Cr). It is also possible, as some translators have done, to understand the adjective to refer to the preexisting impenetrability of the city. (See, for example, Raghunathan 1982, vol. 3, p. 98.)

45. "like the sound that might arise from the waters if the ocean itself were to be shattered" *sāgarasyeva bhinnasya yathā syāt salilasvanaḥ*: Literally, "such as might be the sound of the water of the ocean being split." Ct, Ck, and Cr understand the figure to be an imaginary one (*abhūtopameyam*) in which the sound arises from the ocean's being divided by the causeway (see 6.15.15–24). (*bhinnasya sāgarasya kṛtasetuvibhedanasya. abhūtopameyam*—so Ct.) We agree that the simile is an imaginative one, but we are not persuaded that there is any reference here to the *setubandha*. Cg understands the adjective *bhinna*, "split, shattered," to refer to the ocean having broken its boundaries, and then understands the sound of the monkey hosts to be like that of the

ocean in that it was like the sound of water. Cg tells us that, with this reading, the problem of the apparent redundancy of the adverb *yathā* in *pāda* d and the particle *iva* in *pāda* c is eliminated. (*bhinnamaryādasya. sāgarasyevābhivartato 'bhivartamānasya balaughasya. salilasvano yathā syāt tathā mahāñ chabdo babhūveti yojanā. ato na yathāśabdavaiyyarthyam.*) Cm and Cv read similarly although their glosses are less detailed.

46. "parks, and woodlands" *-vanakānanā*: Literally, "woods and forests." We follow Cg, who avoids the redundancy by glossing *vana* with *udyāna*, "park." See 6.32.3.

48–49. "for the destruction of the *rākṣasas*" *rakṣasāṃ vadhe*: Literally, "with respect to the destruction of the *rākṣasas*." Cs reads this phrase as an indication that, despite Rāma's going through the motions of royal diplomacy, the slaying of the obdurate *rākṣasa* king has already been decided. (*etena lokānukṛtyā eva rājanītyanusaraṇam. na śṛṇoti rāvaṇo 'to māraṇam eva niścitam iti sūcayati.*)

"once again" *punaḥ punaḥ*: Literally, "again and again."

"Fully conversant with the sequential application of the various stratagems and of their consequences" *kramayogārthatattvavit*: Literally, "knowing the essence of the stratagems of sequential application." This ambiguous term is, evidently, a reference to the six stratagems (see 6.9.8 and notes) that a king may employ in regard to his enemies. The term *kramayoga*, "gradual *or* sequential application," does not appear to be used in the *Arthaśāstra* in a technical sense, although it is citable from the *Pañcatantra* (Hertel 1908, p. 122:9) and *Manusmṛti* 1.42 in the general sense of "gradually, successively." Our translation follows the interpretation of Cg, who explains the compound as follows: "*kramayoga* refers to the sequentially employed stratagems of statecraft, conciliation, and so forth. The *artha* of these stratagems is their consequences. One who understands (*vit*) the essence (*tattva*) of these consequences is a *kramayogārthatattvavit* (*kramayuktā yogāḥ sāmādyupāyāḥ teṣām arthaḥ phalaṃ tasya tattvaṃ yāthārthyaṃ vettīti tathoktaḥ*)." Cm has a similar interpretation, except that he glosses *krama* as *nīti*, "statecraft," itself. Ct and Ck also interpret similarly, taking *artha* to mean *sādhya*, "goal," rather than *phalam*, "consequence." Ct further understands *tattva*, "essence," in the sense of the application of the stratagems (*tattvaṃ tatprayojanam*).

"Abiding by the advice of Vibhīṣaṇa" *vibhīṣaṇasyānumate*: Literally, "in the agreement *or* permission of Vibhīṣaṇa." The commentators are divided as to how to interpret this elliptical phrase. Ct, Cr, Ck, and Cm (second alternative) supply the participle *sthitaḥ* (*sthitvā*—Cm) to indicate that Rāma is abiding by the advice of, or is in agreement with, Vibhīṣaṇa. Ct and Cm explain that Vibhīṣaṇa's advice to Rāma is that, were Rāvaṇa to seek refuge with him, Rāma should return the sovereignty of Laṅkā [which he had earlier conferred upon Vibhīṣaṇa (see 6.19.26–27 and notes; see, too, 6.13.9 and notes)] to him (*yadi rāvaṇo bhavantaṃ śaraṇam upeyāt tadā laṅkārājyaṃ tasyaiva deyam iti vibhīṣaṇamate sthita ity arthaḥ*). Cs offers a different perspective, noting that, since Rāma had already consecrated Vibhīṣaṇa as king, it would be impossible, in the event of reconciliation [with Rāvaṇa], to abrogate that prior arrangement. Under these conditions, it is only appropriate for Rāma to consult with Vibhīṣaṇa before taking any action. Cs goes on to state that the inner meaning of this expression is a reflection of Rāma's omniscience and not any duplicity on the part of Vibhīṣaṇa. (*vibhīṣaṇasya rājyābhiṣeko jāta iti sandhau ca na tadabhisandhisiddhir iti tatsammatīkaraṇam ucitam iti bhāvaḥ. sarvajñatvaṃ rāmasya virājata iti na duścittatā vibhīṣaṇasyeti paramārthaḥ.*)

"the protocol of kings" *rājadharmam*: Ct and Ck understand the reference to be to the *dharma*, or righteous behavior, of kings, according to which the stratagem of force, *daṇḍa*, ought not to be employed in the first instance, as it is injurious to the people (*sāmāditryupāyasādhye 'rthe daṇḍo na moktavyaḥ prajānāśahetur ity evaṃrūpaṃ rājadharmam anucintayan*). Ck sees this as a reference to Rāma's supremely compassionate nature. Cg and Cm, however, whom we follow, understand the reference to be to the proper protocol of a king who is about to attack an enemy city. According to this protocol, the king must first employ a messenger through whom he issues a challenge to his rival to come out and fight (*yuyutsayā śatrupuraṃ pratyāgatā rājāno yuddhārthaṃ dūtamukhena prathamam āhvayantīty evaṃrūpaṃ rājadharmam anusmaran*). This interpretation, we believe, provides a better explanation for Rāma's appointment of Aṅgada as his emissary. On the stratagem of force, see 6.9.8; 6.51.11–13; 6.59.28; 6.71.12; and notes.

50. "free from anxiety" *gatavyathaḥ*: Literally, "whose anxiety has gone." Cg and Cm, perhaps in an effort to avoid a perceived redundancy with the phrase "abandoning fear (*bhayaṃ tyaktvā*)," gloss, "having cast off fatigue (*gataśramaḥ san*)." Ct and Ck, in keeping with their rather different reading of this passage, understand the adjective to refer not to Aṅgada but to Rāma, and gloss "without incident, safely (*nirupadravaḥ*)." They take the adjective as a reference to Rāma's crossing of the ocean. See below.

"monkey" *kape*: Cg notes that the use of this particular term here is to illuminate Aṅgada's power to leap (*kape ity anena laṅghanasāmarthyaṃ dyotayati*).

"you must leap into the city of Laṅkā" *laṅghayitvā purīṃ laṅkām*: Normally, this phrase would mean "having leapt over the city of Laṅkā," just as it is used so commonly in the text to describe Hanumān's leap over the ocean (see *Sundarakāṇḍa* 1). In recognition of the slightly odd usage, Cr and Cg add some more immediate object of the gerund, the former glossing, "having leapt over, that is, having disregarded, the city of Laṅkā, that is, the *rākṣasas* stationed there (*laṅkāṃ purīṃ tatstharākṣasān laṅghayitvā anādṛtya*)." Cg glosses *purīm*, "city," as "its ramparts (*laṅkāṃ purīṃ tatprākāraṃ laṅghayitvā*)." Ct and Ck, as well as the translators who follow their texts, understand that *pādas* cd are not part of Rāma's instructions to Aṅgada but rather the beginning of Rāma's message to Rāvaṇa. They thus see Rāma himself as the subject of the gerunds *laṅghayitvā* and *tyaktvā* and understand the passage to be an elliptical reference to Rāma's having leapt, i.e., having crossed over, the ocean. In order to make this reading intelligible, Ct and Ck must supply not only the word "ocean" but an entire complex sentence, viz., "one must supply the words, 'having abandoned fear and having regarded your army as a mere straw, I have laid siege to Laṅkā.' " (*laṅghayitvā samudram . . . bhayaṃ tyaktvā tvadbalam tṛṇīkṛtya laṅkām upāruṇadham iti śeṣaḥ*.)

"ten-necked Rāvaṇa" *daśagrīvam*: Literally, "the ten-necked one."

"you are to address him in my words as follows" *brūhi madvacanāt*: Literally, "speak according to my speech."

51–53. "You have lost your royal majesty, your lordship is at an end. You have lost your wits and doomed yourself." *bhraṣṭaśrīka gataiśvarya mumūrṣo naṣṭacetana*: Literally, "O you whose majesty has lapsed, O you whose lordship has gone, O you who desire to die, O you whose wits are destroyed." A variety of manuscripts, including the texts of Ct and Ck, read these terms instead as singular accusatives, with the last two forming the compound *mumūrṣānaṣṭacetanam*, "whose wits are destroyed by the desire for death." Ct reads these accusatives as objects of the imperative *brūhi*, "[you, Aṅgada] speak *or* address," in 50b. Translators who follow the text of Ct therefore take 51ab as part of Rāma's instructions to Aṅgada, since the epithets become, in Ct's reading, adjectives modifying *daśagrīvam* in 50a. The notion that one's wits desert one at the point of impending death is a common one and is enshrined in such maxims as "*vināśakāle viparītā buddhiḥ* (at the time of destruction, one's wits become addled)."

"will... be humbled" *gataḥ*: Literally, "gone."

"born of the boon of self-existent Brahmā" *svayaṃbhūvaradānajaḥ*: Literally, "born of the gift of a boon of the self-existent one." The reference is, of course, to Rāvaṇa's boon of invulnerability to superhuman beings. See note to 6.28.28–29.

Following verse 52, D7,G2, and the text of Cr (found in GPP in brackets between 63bc and 64ab) insert a passage of one line [642*]: "Today the unbearable fruit of that evil act [will be] obtained [by you]."

54. "Once I have killed you" *mayā hataḥ*: D10,11,T3, and the texts and printed editions of Ct, Ck, and Cr read *yudhi sthiraḥ* (v.l. *yudhi sthitaḥ*—Ś,Ñ,V,B,D0–4,6–9,12,13,T2,G2,3,M5), "firm *or* steadfast in battle." Northern manuscripts generally read the first person, *gamiṣyāmi*, and thus the phrase *yudhi sthitaḥ* would refer to Rāma.

"realm" *padavīm*: This term can have a variety of meanings, chiefly, "way, path" and "state, condition." Ct and Ck take as their first meaning the idea that Rāvaṇa will follow the path of the seers, etc., in the sense that he will, like them, die. However, they note, since Rāvaṇa is, according to their reading, steadfast in battle and, moreover, a worshiper of self-existent Brahmā, he will, upon his death, attain a blessed world through the grace of that divinity. In support of this contention, Ct cites a verse from the *Kiṣkindhākāṇḍa* (4.18.30, which is also found at *Manusmṛti* 8.3.18) to the effect that "men who commit crimes are, when punished by kings, purified and thus attain heaven, just as do the virtuous." (*tadvat tavāpi maraṇaṃ bhaviṣyatīti bhāvaḥ. kiṃca yudhi sthiratve svayaṃbhūpāsakasya te tadanugrahān matto maraṇe puṇyalokaprāptis taveti bhāvaḥ. "rājabhir dhṛtadaṇḍās tu kṛtvā pāpāni mānavaḥ / nirmalāḥ svargam āyānti santaḥ sukṛtino yathā //" ity ukteḥ.*) Cr notes that, since Rāvaṇa is steadfast in battle, he will attain the highest station, that is, the next world. (*yudhi sthiras tvaṃ devaprabhṛtīnāṃ padavīṃ caramagatiṃ paralokam ity arthaḥ. gamiṣyasi prāpsyasi.*) Cg offers two alternate interpretations. In his first he takes *padavī* in its sense of "state *or* condition," which he sees as the condition of defeat (*paribhava*) to which Rāvaṇa had subjected the gods, etc., and sees Rāma as telling Rāvaṇa that he will suffer the same fate (*padavīṃ teṣu kṛtaṃ paribhavaṃ kamapi gamiṣyasīty arthaḥ*). Cg's second alternative is much the same as that of Ct and Ck. Even though Cg does not share the reading *yudhi sthiraḥ* of Ct and Ck, he notes that, since Rāvaṇa is steadfast in battle, he will go to the world of the gods, etc., because a person who is firm in battle is purified of all his sins (*yuddhe sthitvā sarvapāpaviśuddhaḥ san gatiṃ gamiṣyasi*). Cm similarly understands the reference to be to the blessed realms reserved for those who are steadfast in battle. He quotes the same verse as Ct, adding to it an additional half verse (a variant of *ManuSm* 8.3.16), to the effect that "a king who fails to punish a criminal shares that criminal's guilt (*rājā tv aśāsan pāpasya tad avāpnoti kilbiṣam*)." This latter is evidently cited as part of a justification of Rāma's killing Rāvaṇa.

55. "wretched *rākṣasa*" *rākṣasādhama*: Literally, "worst or lowest of *rākṣasas*." The epithet is no doubt intended to stand in pointed contrast with the descriptive phrase *rakṣasāṃ śreṣṭhaḥ*, "best *or* foremost of *rākṣasas*," applied to Vibhīṣaṇa in verse 57 below.

"with an illusion" *māyayā*: As Cg notes, the illusion referred to here is probably that employed by the *rākṣasa* Mārīca, who assumed the form of a magic deer to lure Rāma away (see 3.40.12ff.). Perhaps one could also understand the term more generally in the sense of "deceptively, deceitfully," as a reference to Rāvaṇa's own *māyā* in assuming the appearance of a wandering mendicant to gain Sītā's confidence (see 3.44.2–3).

56. "Unless you . . . come to me for refuge" *na cec charaṇam abhyeṣi*: Cg, no doubt keeping in mind the Śrīvaiṣṇava concept of *śaraṇāgati*, "seeking refuge with the Lord," remarks that, if Rāvaṇa were to take refuge with him, Rāma would forgive everything he had done. However, Cg continues, Rāvaṇa would not be allowed to seek refuge unless he first returns Sītā any more than a thief could obtain forgiveness without returning the gold he had stolen. Cg also argues that, if Rāvaṇa were actually to seek refuge with Rāma, the latter would then confer the kingship of Kosala upon Vibhīṣaṇa. (*śaraṇāgatau tu sarvaṃ kṣamiṣya iti bhāvaḥ. maithilīm upādāyety anena svarṇasteye svarṇapratyarpaṇam antareṇa prayaścittānadhikāravat sītāpratyarpaṇābhāve śaraṇāgatau tu nādhikāra ity uktam. rāvaṇena śaraṇāgatau kṛtāyāṃ vibhīṣaṇāya kosalarājyaṃ dāsyāmīty abhiprayaḥ.*) The idea here, no doubt, is that, if Rāma were to forgive Rāvaṇa and let him keep his throne, he would still have to honor his promise of a kingdom to Vibhīṣaṇa. This idea is in sharp contrast to a well-attested northern insertion [644*] in which Rāma enjoins Rāvaṇa to save his life by returning Sītā while forfeiting his throne.

57. Expanding on his comments to verse 56, Cg notes that in this verse Rāma outlines what he is going to do should Rāvaṇa not seek refuge with him. Even should Rāvaṇa take refuge, Rāma would spare only his life but would not permit him to retain his kingdom (*śaraṇāgatyakaraṇe svakartavyam āha* . . . [*dharmātmeti*] . . . *yadvā śaraṇāgatau prāṇatrāṇaṃ kariṣyāmi na tu rājyaṃ dāsyāmīty abhiprāyeṇāha*).

"The foremost of *rākṣasas*, righteous-minded . . . Endowed with majesty" *dharmātmā rakṣasāṃ śreṣṭhaḥ . . . śrīmān*: Ct and Ck argue that these generic modifiers have particular reference here to the propriety of Vibhīṣaṇa's succession. Thus, Ct argues that righteous-mindedness, or the quality of holding righteousness as foremost, is a prime prerequisite for kingship. Ct goes on to suggest that by the phrase *rakṣasāṃ śreṣṭhaḥ*, "foremost among the *rākṣasas*," it is suggested that the succession of the throne [to Vibhīṣaṇa] after you [Rāvaṇa] is legitimate. Ct finally suggests that *śrīmān*, "endowed with majesty," indicates that Vibhīṣaṇa possesses all the auspicious marks that indicate accession to kingship. (*dharmātmā dharmapradhāno nityaṃ dharmacittaś ca. idam aiśvaryasya sākṣān nidānam. rākṣasaśreṣṭha ity anena tvadanantaraṃ nyāyaprāptaṃ tasya rājyam iti darśitam. śrīmān ity anena tadaiśvaryaprāpakāśeṣalakṣaṇavattvam.*) Cg understands these terms similarly.

"come over to me" *samprāptaḥ*: Literally, "[he] has come." Following Ct, Cg, Ck, Cv, and Cm, we have supplied the pronoun *mām*, "to me." We thus read the adjective, as do Cm, Gorresio (1856, vol. 9, p. 247), Dutt (1893, p. 1219), Pagani (1999, p. 963), and Raghunathan (1982, vol. 3, p. 99), as a reference to Vibhīṣaṇa's defection to Rāma. Ct, Cg, Ck, and Cv interpret the adjective more strongly as a reference to Vibhīṣaṇa's having taken refuge (*śaraṇāgataḥ/prapannaḥ*) with Rāma. A few translators take the participle to refer simply to Vibhīṣaṇa's having arrived at the gates of Laṅkā. Thus, Gita Press (1969, vol. 3, p. 1509) renders, "has arrived here (with me)"; Roussel (1903, vol. 3, p. 116), "*que voici*"; and Shastri (1959, vol. 3, p. 100), "who is here." See note to verse 56 above.

"secure" *dhruvam*: We understand the term here as an adjective modifying *aiśvaryam*, "lordship." It can also be understood, as other translators have done (Gita Press 1969, vol. 3, p. 1509; Raghunathan 1982, vol. 3, p. 99; Dutt 1893, p. 1219; Pagani 1999, p. 963; Roussel 1903, vol. 3, p. 116; and Shastri 1959, vol. 3, p. 100), as an adverb modifying *prāpnoti*, "he shall obtain," and having the sense "surely *or* certainly." Ct and Cm understand the word adverbially as well.

"unchallenged" *akaṇṭakam*: Literally, "without thorns," i.e., "without obstacles *or* hindrances." Here we agree with Ct and Ck, who gloss, "devoid of an obstacle in the form of you [Rāvaṇa] (*tvadrūpakaṇṭakarahitam*).

58. "unrestrained" *avijitātmanā*: Literally, "[by you] not having conquered your mind." D5,7,9–11,T1–3,M3–5, and the texts and printed editions of Ck, Ct, and Cr read instead *aviditātmanā*. Cg, the only commentator to remark on this term, interprets it as if it were the critical reading, glossing, "[by one] whose mind is not under his own control (*asvādhīnamanaskena*)." The opposite of this term, *viditātman*, is often used of Rāma and normally means either "well-known, celebrated" or "knowing one's self." See 6.24.7 and note, where we have translated the term as "ever-vigilant." Translators who follow the texts of Ct and Cg tend to render the compound as "not knowing one's self." Pagani (1999, p. 963), understanding as Cg does, renders, "*qui ne se maîtrise pas*," as if reading *avijitātmanā*. In her note on the term, however, she translates, "*qui ne se connaît pas lui-même.*" She points out that this epithet corresponds to the one used of Rāma, "he who knows the self (*viditātman*)." If, Pagani continues, Rāma is the good king par excellence, then Rāvaṇa is his complete opposite (p. 1660). See notes to 6.24.7 and 6.92.25.

"surround yourself with fools" *mūrkhasahāyena*: Literally, "[by you] having fools for companions." Cr explains, "by you, who are characterized by undiscriminating companions (*avivekisahāyaviśiṣṭena tvayā*)," while Cs says, "by this term is suggested that 'the counselors [literally, speakers] in your presence are not great' (*mahānto na santi vaktāras tava samīpa iti sūcyate*)."

59. "So" *vā*: Literally, "or." The critical reading is shared by Cg, Cr, and Cm, who appear to understand the term as suggesting that, for Rāvaṇa, battle is an alternative to seeking refuge with Rāma. For example, Cg introduces his gloss by saying, "If you bring Sītā, seek refuge [with me], and hand the kingdom over to Vibhīṣaṇa, then I will spare your life; otherwise, you must fight (*sītām ādāya śaraṇam āgato 'si ced vibhīṣaṇāya rājyaṃ dattvā tvatprāṇān rakṣāmy anyathā yudhyasva*)." D10,11, and the texts and printed editions of Ct and Ck read instead the pronoun *mā*, "[fight] me." These two commentators insist that this poorly attested reading is the authentic one (*pāṅktaḥ pāṭhaḥ*).

"slain" *śāntaḥ*: Literally, "calmed, pacified." We follow the commentators who interpret the term as "finished off (*samāptaḥ*—so Ct, Ck)"; "dead (*mṛtaḥ*—so Cg, Cr)"; or "slain (*hataḥ*—so Cm)."

"purified" *pūtaḥ*: Cg, who shares the critical reading, understands the reference in the context of the ancient Indian code of the warrior, according to which death faced bravely in battle cleanses one of all sins (*yuddha aparavṛttyā mṛteḥ sarvapāpaprāyaścittatvād iti bhāvaḥ*). Cf. *BhagGī* 2.37 (*hato vā prāpsyasi svargaṃ jitvā vā bhokṣyase mahīm / tasmād uttiṣṭha kaunteya yuddhāya kṛtaniścayaḥ*). D9–11 and the texts and printed editions of Ct and Cr read a second *śāntaḥ* for *pūtaḥ*. They are, however, forced to read the second occurrence of the adjective in the sense of *pūtaḥ*, "purified of sins." Unlike Cg, however, Ct and Ck understand Rāvaṇa's purification to be the result not so much of his heroic death as his having been slain at the hands of the Vaiṣṇava *avatāra*. Ct, for example, glosses the second *śāntaḥ* as "[you will be] purified of the sins committed since birth (*ājanmakṛtāt pāpāt pūto [bhaviṣyasi]*)" and notes that we are to understand that the true purpose of the *avatāra* is purification of sin through the means of direct vision and the recollection of his name (*darśananāmasmaraṇaiḥ pāpaśodhanaphalaka evāyam avatāras tattvena jñāyate*). Ct further notes that, even should Rāvaṇa lack this understanding of the [saving power of the] *avatāra*, he would still, if killed by Rāma, be reborn after some interval in a noble kshatriya family (*tathā jñānābhāve 'pi matto maraṇe kiṃcit kālottaram uttamakṣatriyakule janmaprāptir iti bhāvaḥ*). Evidently, this is a reference to the Vaiṣṇava tradition that Rāvaṇa would one day be reborn as Śiśupāla. See note to 5.16.5. Cr similarly interprets the second *śāntaḥ* in the sense of "free from crime and sins (*aparādhapāparahitaḥ*)" but does not indicate why he believes that this purification will take place, noting merely that the statement is a hint to Rāvaṇa not to attempt to flee (*etena palāyanaṃ na kartavyam iti sūcitam*).

60. The image is not as fanciful as it may seem. For the situation described is identical to the one narrated at 5.36.16–32, where Rāma's divinely charged weapon pursues a mischievous crow throughout the three worlds.

"swift as thought" *manojavaḥ*: D7,9–11, and the texts and printed editions of Ct and Cr read instead *niśācara*, "O night-roaming [*rākṣasa*]!"

61. "prepare yourself for the next world" *kriyatām aurdhvadehikam*: The most literal interpretation of this phrase would be, "perform your funeral rites," and, indeed, this is the way most translators have rendered it. Of the commentators consulted, however, only Cg is content to take *aurdhvadehikam* in its usual sense of "funerary rites." Like us, however, he is concerned, perhaps, at the peculiarity of the notion of someone performing one's own funeral. He explains as follows: "Since, by my making the [world] free from *rākṣasas* (see verse 56 above), there will be no one to perform your commemorative rites (*śrāddha*), you had better perform 'a memorial for the living' yourself (*arākṣasakaraṇena śrāddhakartrabhāvāt svayam eva jīvacchrāddhaṃ kuru ity arthaḥ*)." The other commentators, however, understand the term here not so much as a technical term for a funeral but rather, on the basis of the literal meaning of *ūrdhvadeha* as "that which comes after the body," as a reference to the afterlife. They then interpret *aurdhvadehika*, the derivative of this term, as "that which prepares one for the afterlife, e.g., charity, etc." (*dehād ūrdhvaṃ prāpta ūrdhvadehaḥ. paralokas tatra hitaṃ dānādikam aurdhvadehikam* so Ct.)

"a good long look" *sudṛṣṭā kriyatām*: Literally, "make [Laṅkā] well looked upon." We share the view of the majority of the commentators that the idea here is that Rāvaṇa had best take a last look at his capital as he is about to die and hence will see it no more (*itaḥ paraṃ darśanābhāvāt*—so Ct). Cg interprets the phrase more specifically as a reference to the fact that, in their restlessness, people at the point of death gaze upon the faces of their sons, wives, etc. (*mriyamāṇā hi cāpalena putrakalatrādimukhadarśanaṃ kurvanti tadvad iti bhāvaḥ*)." Roussel (1903, vol. 3, p. 117) idiosyncratically renders, "*laisse Lankā retrouver sa splendeur*." In this he is followed word for word by Pagani (1999, p. 963). Shastri (1959, vol. 3, p. 100) similarly renders, "Let Lanka regain her splendour."

"Your life is in my hands." *jīvitaṃ te mayi sthitam*: Literally, "Your life rests on me."

62. "Tārā's son, Aṅgada" *tāreyaḥ*: Literally, "the son of Tārā."

"sped on his way" *jagāma*: Literally, "he went."

"incarnate" *mūrtimān*: Literally, "possessing bodily form." Ct and Ck understand, "in the guise of a monkey (*vānaraveṣaḥ*)." Cg explains, "possessing an arrangement of hands, feet, etc. (*karacaraṇādisaṃsthānavān*)."

63. "Reaching" *atipatya*: Literally, "having leapt *or* flown over." We follow Cr and Cg, who gloss, "having gone to (*gatvā*)" and "having reached (*prāpya*)," respectively. Ct, Ck, and Cm, also concerned about the unusual usage, supply, as an object of the gerund, *mārgam*, "way, path," thus giving the sense "traversing the way [to Rāvaṇa's palace.]"

"the majestic monkey" *saḥ* . . . *śrīmān*: Literally, "he, the majestic one." Cg argues that the use of the word "majestic (*śrīmān*)" here indicates that the monkey was very excited (*anena harṣavattvam ucyate*).

64. Aṅgada, with his golden armlets" *aṅgadaḥ kanakāṅgadaḥ*: Here the poet plays with the repetition of the word "*aṅgada*" as the monkey's name and as the term for an armlet.

65. "in his own words" *ātmanā*: Literally, "by himself."

"repeated" *śrāvayāmāsa*: Literally, "he caused [him] to hear."

"speech . . . neither adding nor omitting anything" *–vacanam* . . . *anyūnādhikam*: Literally, "speech that was neither reduced nor expanded."

"to Rāvaṇa and his ministers" *sāmātyam*: Literally, "[to him] along with his ministers."

66. "perhaps you have heard of me" *yadi te śrotram āgataḥ*: Literally, "if [I] have come to your hearing." Ct, Cm, and Ck are perhaps correct in taking this formulaic expression somewhat ironically to mean, in effect, "no doubt you must have heard of me." These commentators understand the conditional particle *yadi*, "if," to be an expression of doubt used in a situation that admits of no doubt as, for example, in the expression "if the *vedas* be authoritative." They thus explain that Aṅgada has no need of describing to Rāvaṇa his own powers and that of his allies, since these must already be known to the *rākṣasas*. (*yadīty asaṃdigdhe saṃdigdhavacanaṃ vedāḥ pramāṇaṃ ced itivat. śrotram āgata eva. etena svasya svīyānāṃ ca balādi tubhyaṃ na vācyam eva tvayā jñātatvād iti bhāvaḥ*—so Ct.) Cr and Cg, however, take the expression more literally. The former glosses, "Perhaps (*kadācit*) you have heard of me. The sense is 'You have heard.' (*yadi kadācit te śrotram āgataḥ. śruta ity arthaḥ.*)" The latter reads the expression as an interrogative, "Have you heard of me (*māṃ śrutavān asi kim*)?" This expression is seen elsewhere in Vālmīki in situations where strangers introduce themselves. Cf. 3.21.24 and GPP 3.17.21.

67. "lowest of men" *puruṣādhama*: This seems an odd epithet to use of a *rākṣasa*. V,B1,2,D0,1,3,4,6,7,10,11,M3, and the texts and printed editions of the southern commentators read instead *puruṣo bhava*, "be a man," which, according to some commentators, is used in much the same way as the English expression "Go ahead, be a hero." ("You will become a eunuch [*klībatvaṃ prāpsyasi*—so Cr]"; "Be a hero [*śūro bhava*—Ct, Cg].") Cg, the only commentator to acknowledge the critical reading as a variant, explains it as follows: "Since you do not come forth even when your city is besieged, surely you are the lowest of men (*puroparodhe 'py anirgamane nūnaṃ puruṣādhama evāsīti bhāvaḥ*)."

68. "all your kinsmen" *-jñātibāndhavam*: Either term, *jñāti* or *bāndhava*, may refer to kinsmen in general (cf. 5.1.43 and 6.10.3). When used together, as here, the former refers to paternal male kin and the latter to maternal male kin.

69. "thorn that you are in the side of" *tvām* ... *kaṇṭakam*: Literally, "you, a thorn."
"of the gods, *dānavas*, *yakṣas*, *gandharvas*, great serpents, and *rākṣasas*." *devadānavayakṣāṇāṃ gandharvoragarakṣasām*: This conventionalized list of supernatural beings has been used apparently without concern for the fact that Rāvaṇa would not normally be regarded as an enemy to his own kind.

70. "If you do not give back Vaidehī, after first begging her forgiveness and falling at my feet" *na cet satkṛtya vaidehīṃ praṇipatya pradāsyasi*: Literally, "if you do not give Vaidehī, after honoring and prostrating." Ct and Ck gloss the word *satkṛtya*, normally "having honored," as *kṣamāpanaṃ kṛtvā*, "having begged forgiveness." The syntax of this first line is ambiguous, as it does not specify the object or objects of the two gerunds. Commentators and translators, therefore, tend to differ somewhat in their reading of the line. Cm (similarly Dutt 1893, p. 1220 and Gorresio 1856, vol. 9, p. 248) understands the object of both gerunds to be "me (*mām*)," i.e., Rāma. Raghunathan (1982, vol. 3, p. 100) renders, "If you do not pray for my forgiveness and restore Vaidehī to me." Ct and Ck construe *satkṛtya* with the accusative *vaidehīm* and *praṇipatya* with a supplied *mām*, "me," i.e., Rāma. They are followed by Gita Press (1969, vol. 3, p. 1520), Pagani (1999, p. 964), Roussel (1903, vol. 3, p. 117), and Shastri (1959, vol. 3, p. 100).

71. "transported with rage" *amarṣavaśam āpannaḥ*: Literally, "went to the influence of anger."

72. "His eyes red with rage" *roṣatāmrākṣaḥ*: D9–11 and the texts and printed editions of Ct, Ck, and Cr read instead *roṣam āpannaḥ*, "enraged." See 6.19.22–23; 6.35.11; 6.42.26; and 6.50.9. Cf. 6.27.2; 6.46.14; 6.50.11; and notes.

"fool" *durmedhāḥ*: Cg understands the epithet to refer not to Aṅgada but to Rāvaṇa in the sense of "ignorant of the śāstraic ordinance that a messenger must not be slain. (*durmedhā durbuddhiḥ. na dūto vadhya iti śāstrānabhijña ity arthaḥ*.)" Cg does allow for the alternative reading, as in our translation (*yadvā durmedhā ity aṅgadam evāha*). (Cf. 5.50.1–11 and notes, where Rāvaṇa and Vibhīṣaṇa debate over the propriety of killing Hanumān, who is Rāma's messenger.)

73. "four" *catvāraḥ*: Cs claims that the four were able to act simultaneously by each seizing, respectively, one of Aṅgada's arms or shoulders. (*rākṣasāḥ vacaḥ śrutveva jagṛhuḥ. caturṣu aṅgeṣu skandhabhujeṣu pārśvadvayavartiṣu iti saṃbhavaty aikakaṇṭhyam*.) Cs quotes the parallel passage from the *Rāmopākhyāna* (*MBh* 3.268.18), where, acting on Rāvaṇa's gestures alone, four *rākṣasas* seize Aṅgada, as birds might seize a tiger. We see in verse 75 below that the *rākṣasas* have seized Aṅgada's arms.

"Aṅgada" *tam*: Literally, "him."

74. "freely" *svayam* ... *ātmanā*: Literally, "on his own ... by himself." This somewhat redundant expression is avoided in a number of manuscripts (B2,4,D5–7,9–11,T1,2,G1,M1–3) and in the texts and printed editions of Ck, Ct, Cg, and Crā, which replace *ātmanā* with the adjective *ātmavān*, "self-possessed, self-controlled." The critical apparatus, apparently in error, attributes the critical reading to Cg, despite the fact that his commentary and the printed editions of his text all read with the vulgate. According to the editorial principles laid out in the *Bālakāṇḍa* for the critical edition, this *pāda* should most likely be marked as uncertain. (See Bhatt 1960, p. xxxiv.)

"*yātudhānas*" *yātudhāna*-: A type of *rākṣasa*. See 6.3.27 and note.

75. "leapt to the top of the palace" *prāsādam* ... *utpapāta*: Literally, "he leapt up to the palace."

"those *rākṣasas*" *tān*: Literally, "them."

"locusts" *patagān*: The word normally refers principally to birds, and Raghunathan (1982, vol. 3, p. 100), Gita Press (1969, vol. 3, p. 1510), and Gorresio (1865, vol. 9, p. 248) have translated accordingly. We believe, however, that here the word can be used synonymously with *pataṃga*, "flying insect, moth, locust, bird, flying animal," which we think fits the context much better. This idea also seems to have occurred to Dutt (1893, p. 1221), who, alone among the translators, renders, "like insects." Roussel (1903, vol. 3, p. 117), followed by Shastri (1959, vol. 3, p. 101) and Pagani (1999, p. 964), inexplicably translates, "serpents." Perhaps he has mistakenly read *pannagān*, unattested in the critical apparatus and the texts and printed editions consulted. The commentators are silent on this point, and the manuscripts consulted are remarkably free from variants, except for D4, which reads *nāgān patagarāḍ iva*, "like [Garuḍa] the king of birds [carrying] serpents."

76. "Shaken loose by his speed, all four *rākṣasas* fell from the sky" *te 'ntarikṣād vinirdhūtās tasya vegena rākṣasāḥ / . . . sarve*: Literally, "shaken off by [his] speed, all the *rākṣasas* [fell] from the sky." D7,9–11, and the texts and printed editions of Ct, Ck, and Cr read *tasyotpatanavegena nirdhūtās tatra rākṣasāḥ . . .* [*nipatitāḥ*] "shaken off by the speed of his flight there . . . the *rākṣasas* [fell]" for *pādas* ab.

77. "as he landed on the pinnacle of the palace . . . it crumbled" *prāsādaśikharam . . . tat paphāla tadākrāntam*: Literally, "trodden by him, the pinnacle of that palace burst." A variety of northern and southern manuscripts (Ñ1,V1,3, D0,2,4,5,7,9,13,T2,3,G3,M3) as well as the printed editions of Cg (VSP and KK) read instead *padākrāntam*, "trodden *or* struck by his foot." Among the translators consulted, this reading is followed only by Raghunathan (1982, vol. 3, p. 100), who renders, "dislodged with a kick."

Following 77ab, D5–7,9–11,S insert a passage of one line [652*]: "The valorous son of Vālin saw[1] [the pinnacle of the palace] of the *rākṣasa* lord."

[1]"saw" *dadarśa*: Among the commentators who mention this passage, only Cg and Cm read with the critical edition. Ck, Ct, and Cr substitute *cakrāma*, "he trod upon." Cm mentions this as an alternative reading.

Following verse 77, D5–7,9–11,S insert a passage of one line [653*]: "Just as long ago the peak of the Himalayas was shattered by the thunderbolt (*vajra*)."

78. Following verse 78, D5–7,9–11,S insert a passage of two lines [663*]: "Distressing all the *rākṣasas* and delighting the monkeys, he returned to Rāma's side in the midst of the monkeys."

79. "foreseeing his own destruction" *vināśam . . . ātmanaḥ paśyan*: Cm, Ck, and Ct express Rāvaṇa's gloomy thought as follows: " 'This creature has single-handedly humiliated my entire army and escaped with impunity. With so many of his kind bent on my destruction, how can I possibly survive?' Thus did he reflect. (*paśyann eko 'pi samagraṃ mama balaṃ parābhūya nirbhayaṃ gacchati. evaṃvidheṣv anekeṣu mannāśodyateṣu kathaṃ jīvanam iti paryālocayann ity arthaḥ*—so Ct and Cm.)" Ck reads a slight variant of the above.

81–82. "the tawny monkey" *hariḥ . . . kapiḥ*: Literally, "the tawny [monkey] . . . monkey." The two verses naturally form a single syntactic unit. Two of the commentators, however, Cr and Cg, wish to take the two verses as independent sentences, supplying the copula "he was (*abhavat*—Cr; *babhūva*—Cg)." This would yield the sense "Suṣeṇa . . . was surrounded." Cg makes his reason for this awkward breaking of the verses explicit by noting, "if one construes the two verses as a single sentence, there is redundancy of the terms *hariḥ* and *kapiḥ* (*uttaraślokenaikavākyatve harikapiśabdayoḥ paunaruktyaṃ syāt*)." Because we believe that the syntax is more compelling than the issue of redundancy, we have resolved the problem by taking the term *hari* in its adjectival sense of "tawny."

"made a tour . . . passes" *paryākramata*: Literally, "he circumambulated." We have rendered this as two separate verbs, in keeping with the force of the simile. Ct and Ck note that Suṣeṇa makes his tour in order to see to the protection of the entire army, as well as to gather intelligence from all the gates of the citadel (*sarvabalarakṣārthaṃ sarvadvāravṛttāntagrahaṇārthaṃ ca*).

"of all four city gates" *caturdvārāṇi sarvāṇi*: D9–11 and the texts and printed editions of Ct read instead *sa tu dvārāṇi saṃyamya*, "but he, having controlled *or* blockaded the gates." Translators who share this reading render the gerund variously. Gita Press (1969, vol. 3, p. 1511) renders most literally, "having controlled," while Roussel (1903, vol. 3, p. 118), followed by Pagani (1999, p. 964), renders, "*surveillait*." Shastri (1959, vol. 3, p. 101) translates, "patrolled."

83–84. "hundreds of battalions" *akṣauhiṇīśatam*: Literally, "one hundred *akṣauhiṇīs*." The word *akṣauhiṇī* is a technical term from ancient Indian military texts, where it refers to a vast fourfold military force consisting of 21,870 chariots, an equal number of elephants, 65,610 cavalry, and 109,350 infantry. Clearly this term cannot be applied in its technical sense to an undifferentiated mass of weaponless monkey warriors. Ct and Cm explain that here the term merely indicates a number, i.e., the total number of warriors in an *akṣauhiṇī* (218,700). Since even a hundred such divisions would not nearly approximate the vast number of monkeys mentioned earlier in the *kāṇḍa* (6.15.25; 6.19.4; and notes), these same commentators explain the number *śatam*, "one hundred," here as expressing an endless number (*yāvanto 'kṣauhiṇyāṃ gajāśvarathipadātayas tat saṃkhyā vānarā ity arthaḥ śataśabdo 'nantavācī*—so Ct). We have compromised somewhat by translating *śatam* in the plural. See notes to 6.4.24.

"filled with excitement" *harṣam evopapedire*: Literally, "they went to excitement." Cr explains that some of the *rākṣasas*, remembering their joy in other battles, are once again filled with the thrill of combat (*anyasamaraharṣasmaraṇād dharṣam evopapedire*). Cg understands that these are the "steadfast *or* courageous (*dhīrāḥ*), while the others are less brave (*adhīrāḥ*)."

85 "gazed upon what appeared to be a wall of monkeys" *dadṛśuḥ . . . prakāraṃ vānarīkṛtam*: Literally, "they saw a rampart that had been turned into monkeys." The commentators are divided as to how to interpret this colorful expression. Ct, Cr, and Ck seem to feel that [because of the large numbers of monkeys swarming over the city walls, the rampart] itself appears to be made of monkeys (*vānararūpanirmitarūpam*—so Ct). Ck clarifies this with an example of a mountain of rocks, etc. (*śilādigirir iva vānaranirmitarūpam ivety arthaḥ*). Several translators have followed this interpretation. Thus Raghunathan (1982, vol. 3, p. 101) translates, "the ramparts one mass of monkeys," and Gita Press (1969, vol. 3, p. 1511), "the defensive wall converted (as it were) into monkeys (themselves)." Dutt (1893, p. 1222) translates, "the wall thronging with monkeys," and notes, "A translator cannot help a feeling of disappointment at the difference—to the disadvantage of English—between Sanskrit and English. The original for 'thronging with monkeys' is a verbal attributive—*vānarikrita*—lit. *monkeyed*." Cg, whom we have followed, understands that the huge mass of monkeys in the

space beyond the city walls gives rise to the impression on the part of the *rākṣasas* that there is, in fact, a second wall consisting of monkeys (*vānarapracuratayā kṛtam aparam iva prākāraṃ dadṛśur ity arthaḥ*). This interpretation is represented in the translation of Roussel (1903, vol. 3, p. 118), who has been followed by Shastri (1959, vol. 3, p. 101) and Pagani (1999, p. 965).

Following verse 85, D5–7,9–11,S insert a passage of one line [673*]: "Addled with fear,[1] the *rākṣasas* cried out, 'Alas! Alas.'" This line has been inserted by the southern redactors perhaps to provide a smoother transition to the following verse, which alludes to an uproar that is mentioned nowhere in either the critical or the northern text.

[1]"Addled with fear" *bhayamohitāḥ*: Literally, "bewildered by fear." D6,7,9–11, and the texts and printed editions of Ct and Cr read instead *bhayam āgatāḥ*, "became frightened."

86. "the fierce winds at the end of a cosmic age" *yugāntavātāḥ*: The mythical winds and fires that bring about universal destruction at the end of a cosmic age (*yuga*) are a favorite object of comparison for the poet (cf. 6.14.14).

"in the *rākṣasa* capital" *rākṣasarājadhānyām*: D10,11, and the texts and printed editions of Ct read instead *rākṣasarājayodhāḥ*, "the soldiers of the *rākṣasa* king."

The meter is *upajāti*.

Sarga 32

Cg tells us that this *sarga* marks the beginning of the battle (*yuddhārambhaḥ*). See note to 6.4.4.

2. "doubling his defensive arrangements" *vidhānaṃ dviguṇaṃ kṛtvā*: Literally, "having made the arrangements double." The commentators agree that the reference is to the defensive preparations of the city. Ct and Ck specify that the reference is to the defenses of the city gates (*dvārāṇāṃ rakṣāvidhānam ity arthaḥ*—so Ct). V1,3,B1,D8, and the texts and printed editions of Ct and Cr (NSP, GPP; unnoted by the critical edition) read, in *pāda* c, a second *śrutvā*, "having heard," for *kṛtvā*, "having made." Among the translators consulted, only Dutt (1893, p. 1222) appears to render this reading, translating, "hearing that double arrangements had been made (by Rāma) in guarding the gateways." Roussel (1903, vol. 3, p. 119), followed as is often the case by Shastri (1959, vol. 3, p. 102) and Pagani (1999, p. 965), translates, "*réitéra ses ordres précédents*."

"he climbed up to the terrace of the palace" *prāsādaṃ so 'dhyarohata*: Literally, "he climbed *or* ascended the palace." See 6.62.6 and notes.

3. "together with its hills, parks, and woodlands" *saśailavanakānanām*: See 6.31.46.

4. "entire" *sarvām*: Ś,Ñ2,V1,D7–12,T2,G1, and the texts and printed editions of Ct, Ck, and Cr read instead *sarvaiḥ*, yielding the sense "[swallowed up] . . . by all [the tawny monkeys]."

"swallowed up" *kavalīkṛtām*: Literally, "made into a mouthful." Cg, the only commentator to address this reading, glosses, "covered (*ācchāditām*—KK)." A number of southern manuscripts (D7,9–11, G1,M1,2) and the texts and printed editions of Cm,

Ck, Ct, and Cr read instead *kapilīkṛtām*, "made tawny." These commentators and Cg, who notes this as a variant, gloss, "turned tawny by the color of the monkeys (*vānaravarṇena kapilīkṛtām*—so Cg)." The critical editors have marked the syllable *-va-* of *kavalī-* as uncertain, despite the fact that the entire north, and all but four southern manuscripts and two *devanāgarī* manuscripts, read *kapilī-*. We feel that, given the textual evidence, the critical edition's reading should perhaps be emended to read *kapilī-*. Of the translators consulted, only Raghunathan (1982, vol. 3, p. 101), a staunch follower of Cg, renders the critical reading, translating, "gobbled up."

5. "wide-eyed" *āyatalocanaḥ*: This epithet is most frequently used to indicate the beauty of someone's eyes. Here, however, we are inclined to agree with Cg, who sees it as expressing Rāvaṇa's great astonishment (*anena vismayātiśaya ucyate*).

Following verse 5, D5–7,9–11,T1,3,G,M1,3,5 insert, while M2 inserts after 5ab, a passage of fourteen lines [676*]: "In great delight Rāma and his army advanced rapidly.[1] He gazed upon Laṅkā, which was surrounded by *rākṣasas* and defended on every side.[1–2] As Rāma Dāśarathi gazed upon Laṅkā with its various banners and flags, he turned his thoughts to Sītā with a grieving heart [3–4]: 'Here is where the fawn-eyed daughter of Janaka is tormented on my account, burning with sorrow, emaciated and lying on the bare ground.'[5–6] Brooding about Vaidehī in her torment, that righteous man quickly ordered the monkeys to slaughter his enemies.[7–8] As soon as Rāma, tireless in action, had issued his orders, the leaping monkeys roared out lionlike roars in great delight.[2] [9–10] All the leaders of the troops of tawny monkeys resolved, 'We must smash Laṅkā with mountain peaks or even with our fists!'[11–12] Hefting mountain peaks and huge boulders, and ripping up various trees, the leaders of the troops of tawny monkeys took up their positions.[13–14]"

[1]"advanced rapidly" *pupluve*: Literally, "he jumped, he bounded." The commentators are disturbed at the notion of Rāma leaping along and explain that this is a figurative usage, expressive of the fact that he is being carried by the leaping monkeys (*rāmādhirūḍhavānaraplavanaṃ rāme upacaryate*—so Ct).

[2]"the leaping monkeys roared out lionlike roars in great delight" *saṃharṣamāṇāḥ plavagāḥ siṃhanādair anādayan*: D6,7,9–11,M3 read *saṃgharṣamāṇāḥ*, "competing with *or* rivaling [one another]," for *saṃharṣamāṇāḥ*, "in great delight," while D7,9–11, and the texts and printed editions of Ct and Cr read *apūrayan*, "they filled," for *anādayan*, "they roared." This reading requires supplementation with a direct object, such as "the air, the atmosphere, Laṅkā, etc."

6. "As the *rākṣasa* lord stood watching" *prekṣato rākṣasendrasya*: Literally, "as the *rākṣasa* lord looked on." We agree with Ct, Ck, and Cg, who understand this to be a genitive of disrespect (*anādare ṣaṣṭhī*), glossing, "paying no heed to him who was watching (*prekṣamāṇam anādṛtya*—so Cg)."

"division after division" *bhāgaśaḥ*: Literally, "in sections *or* section by section." Cg explains, "each at its own assigned spot (*svasvaniyuktapradeśe*)."

"began to scale the walls of Laṅkā" *laṅkām āruruhuḥ*: Literally, "they climbed Laṅkā." As the commentators point out, the reference is to the ramparts of Laṅkā (*laṅkāṃ laṅkāprākāram*—so Cg).

7. "Willing to lay down their lives" *tyaktajīvitāḥ*: Literally, "who had given up their lives." Several of the commentators indicate in various ways that the past participle *tyakta-* is to be read with a sense of futurity (*āśaṃsāyāṃ bhūtavac ceti ktaḥ*). See *Pā* 3.3.132.

"armed with *sāla* and palmyra trees as well as boulders" *sālatālaśilāyudhāḥ*: Literally, "having *sāla* trees, palmyra trees, and stones for weapons." D10,11, and the texts and printed editions of Ct read instead *sālabhūdharayodhinaḥ*, "those fighters with *sāla* trees and mountains."

8. "the lofty tops of palaces and" *prāsādāgrāṇi coccāni*: There is considerable variation in the manuscript evidence here, which has led the critical editors to mark the *-sāda-* of the word *prāsāda-* and the *cocc*[*ā*]- of *coccāni* as uncertain. B1,D7–11, Gorresio, and the texts and printed editions of Ck, Ct, and Cr read instead *prākārāgrāṇy asaṃkhyāni*. This would then best be construed with *pāda* d and translated as, "the tops of ramparts and countless [gateway arches]." M3 and the texts and printed editions of Cg read instead *prākārāgrāṇy araṇyāni*, which would mean "the tops of the ramparts and the forest groves."

10. "troop leaders" *yūthapāḥ*: A number of manuscripts, both northern and southern, and the texts and printed editions of Cg read instead *vānarāḥ*, "monkeys." This has led the critical editors to mark the word as uncertain.

11–12. "the leaping monkeys" *plavaṅgamāḥ . . . plavaṅgamāḥ*: The noun occurs in both verses. However, as Cg also notes, because the two verses form a single syntactic unit (*kāñcanānītyādiślokadvayam*), we have translated accordingly, dropping one occurrence to avoid redundancy.

"jumping back and forth" *āplavantaḥ plavantaś ca*: We agree with Cg in taking the *upasarga* "*ā*" in its normal sense with a verb of motion as reversing the direction of that motion. Cg glosses, "going and coming (*gamanāgamane kurvantaḥ*)." The idea is perhaps that the monkeys rush forward with stones, etc., to attack the battlements and then rush back for more ammunition. Ct and Cm understand *āplavantaḥ* to mean "jumping about (*samantāt plavantaḥ*)" and *plavantaḥ* as "jumping toward the ramparts (*prākārābhimukhaṃ plavantaḥ*)." Cr's interpretation is similar, except that he glosses, "running all around (*āplavantaḥ sarvataḥ paridhāvantaḥ*)." Ck gives a slightly more expansive version, explaining that, after jumping all about, the monkeys gather at a single point and then leap toward the city walls (*āplavantaḥ āsamantāt plavantaḥ, ekatrasthitvā prākārābhimukhaṃ plavantaḥ*).

"resembled the peaks of Mount Kailāsa" *kailāsaśikharābhāni*: D7,10,11,13, and the texts and printed editions of Ct and Cr read instead *kailāsaśikharāgrāṇi*, "the tops of the peaks of Mount Kailāsa," forcing those commentators who have this reading to make explicit the now implicit, and somewhat different, simile, glossing, "towers as uneven in height as the peaks of Mount Kailāsa (*kailāsaśikharāgrāṇi tadvad uccāvacāni gopurāṇi*—so Ct)."

15. "forest-ranging" *vanagocaraḥ*: The word *-gocaraḥ*, "range," is marked as doubtful by the critical editors. A number of manuscripts (Ś1,Ñ2,V1,2,D2,8,12,13,G1) read instead the plural *-gocarāḥ*, which would extend the kenning to all three of the monkeys. D7,9–11, and the texts and printed editions of Ct, Ck, and Cr read instead the name of a fourth monkey, Panasa (*panasas tathā*). It is doubtful whether the entire word *-gocaraḥ* should be marked as uncertain. Given the lack of substantial variation, at most one would expect that only the final syllable, "*-aḥ*," would be so marked.

"made a breach in the rampart" *nipīḍya...prākāram*: Literally, "having injured *or* oppressed the rampart." We follow Ct and Ck, who gloss, "after breaching the outer rampart so that their army could enter, they stationed themselves there (*senāpraveśārthaṃ bahiḥ prākāraṃ bhaṅktvā sthitāḥ*)."

16. "At that juncture" *etasminn antare*: We agree with the commentators in interpreting this as a reference to the interval of time during or after which the wall has been breached (*bahiḥ prākāraṃ bhaṅktvā senā praveśasamaye*—so Ct, Ck). It could also conceivably refer spatially to the breach itself, in the sense of "in *or* near the breach."

"a bridgehead" *skandhāvāraniveśanam*: We agree with the majority of the commentators in understanding this term to refer to an encampment at which troops are put into battle formations (*skandhāvārasya senāniveśasya niveśanaṃ vyūhabhāvena sthāpanam*—so Ct). Cg offers this as his second interpretation, suggesting first that a *skandhāvāra* is instead a camp established for the rest and relaxation of troops during lulls or intervals of battle (*yuddhe 'ntarāntarā viśramārthaṃ vāsasthānaṃ skandhāvāraḥ*).

17. "all with a victorious air" *jitakāśibhiḥ*: Literally, "having the appearance *or* air of victors." Vālmīki is fond of this phrase; see 6.42.9–10; 6.44.36; 6.49.36; 6.78.38; and notes.

"the eastern gate" *pūrvadvāram*: The commentators are concerned by Kumuda's assignment here, since it was earlier stated (at 6.28.25 and 6.31.28) that the monkey general Nīla was the officer in charge at the eastern gate. They explain that we are to understand the directions in this passage to refer not directly to the cardinal compass points, which have already been assigned, but to the intermediate points, where the monkeys will reinforce and support the detachments mentioned at *sarga* 28 (*atra pūrvādiśabdā agnyādikoṇaparāḥ pūrvādiṣu nīlādīnāṃ sthāpanasya prāg uktatvāt*—so Cr). In the case of Kumuda, Cg states that, having been stationed at the northeast quarter (*aiśāna*), he advances toward the eastern gate and stations himself there (*īśānakoṇe sthitvā pūrvadvāram ākramya sthitavān ity arthaḥ*).

Following verse 17, D6,7,9–11,T,G1,2,M insert a passage of two lines [683*]: "In order to assist him, the tawny monkey Praghasa [D9–11 and the texts and printed editions of Ct, Cr read Prasabha] was posted there, as was great-armed Panasa surrounded by many monkeys."

18. "the southern gate" *dakṣiṇadvāram*: According to Cg, we are to understand that Śatabali, having been stationed in the southeast quarter, now proceeds toward the southern gate and stops (*āgneyakoṇe sthitvā dakṣiṇadvāram ākramya sthitavān ity arthaḥ*). This is similar to Cg's explanation of Kumuda's position in verse 17 above. Recall that, at 6.28.26 and 6.31.29, Aṅgada was assigned to the southern gate.

"two hundred million troops" *viṃśatyā koṭibhiḥ*: Literally, "with twenty *koṭis*."

19. According to Cg, Suṣeṇa had been in the *nairṛti*, or southwest quarter, and then proceeded to the west (*paścimadvāraṃ gata āvṛtya tasthau nairṛtakoṇe sthitvā paścimadvāram ākramya sthitavān ity arthaḥ*). Note that Hanumān had been assigned to the western gate at 6.28.27 and 6.31.30, while at 6.31.81–82 Suṣeṇa was said to have made a tour of all four city gates.

"the...tawny monkey" *hariḥ*: D7,9–11, and the texts and printed editions of Ct and Cr read instead *balī*, "powerful," which is redundant in light of the synonymous *balavān*, "powerful," in *pāda* c.

"six hundred million troops" *ṣaṣṭikoṭibhiḥ*: Literally, "with sixty *koṭis*." D7,9–11, and the texts and printed editions of Cr and Ct read instead *koṭikoṭibhiḥ*, "with a *koṭi* of *koṭis*." This minor variant yields the astronomical figure of 10^{14}, or one hundred trillion.

20. Ct and Cg understand that Sugrīva was assigned to the *vāyavya*, or northwest quarter, on the basis of 6.31.34, where it states that Sugrīva, along with others, was encamped a little to the west of where Rāma was stationed, i.e., in the north. Cg quotes 6.31.34 in full, commenting that, as in the case of Kumuda and the rest, Sugrīva's being posted in an intermediate position explains the reference to his blockading the gate stationed in the principal direction, here the north (*vāyavyakoṇe sthitasya sugrīvasya uttaradvāranirodhakatvābhidhānād etadanusāreṇa kumudādīnāṃ tattatkoṇāvasthitatvena tattaddvāranirodhakatvam iti vyākhyātam*—Cg).

21. "dreadful to look upon" *bhīmadarśanaḥ*: Literally, "of a fearful appearance." V3,G1,2,M1,2,5 read instead *bhīmavikramaḥ*, "of fearsome valor." On the basis of this evidence, the critical editors have marked *-darśanaḥ*, "appearance," as uncertain. However, it seems that, on the basis of the manuscript evidence, this was an inappropriate choice.

"by ten million troops" *koṭyā*: Literally, "with a *koṭi*."

22. "Dhūmra" *dhrūmraḥ* [*sic*]: The critical edition, no doubt as the result of a typographical error, not noted in the errata, prints *dhrūmraḥ* for *dhūmraḥ*. No printed edition attests such a form, and the critical apparatus makes no mention of such a variant.

"of terrifying speed" *bhīmavegānām*: V1,D9–11, and the texts and printed editions of Ct read instead *bhīmakopānām*, "of terrifying anger."

24. At 6.31.29, Gaja, Gavaya, and Gavākṣa are said to be assigned to guard the southern gate with Aṅgada. At 6.32.21, we see a langur named Gavākṣa standing at Rāma's side. Ct, Cg, and Cm are at pains to assure us that the Gavākṣa mentioned in this verse is different from the one named in verse 21 above (*rāmapārśvasthād gavākṣād anyo jñeyaḥ*—so Cg).

"patrolled swiftly" *paridhāvantaḥ*: Literally, "[they] running about."

25. "immediate" *drutam*: Literally, "swift." We read the term adjectivally with *niryāṇam*, "sortie." It can also be read, as some translators have done, adverbially with *ājñāpayat*, "he ordered."

Following verse 25, D5–7,9–11,S insert a passage of eight lines [690*]: "The instant they heard those words issue from Rāvaṇa's mouth, the night-roaming *rākṣasas* uttered dreadful shouts.[1–2] Then at his command[1] the dreadful *bherī* drums of the *rākṣasas*—their drum heads white as the moon—were beaten with golden drumsticks on all sides.[3–4] Deafening conches, filled with the breath of those terrible *rākṣasas*, sounded by the hundreds and thousands.[5–6] With their conches and their dark blue limbs, the color of parrots,[2] the night-roaming *rākṣasas* resembled storm clouds girt with streaks of lightning and crossed by lines of cranes.[7–8]"

[1]"at his command" *pracoditāḥ*: Literally, "urged on." D9–11 and the texts and printed editions of Ct read instead *prabodhitāḥ*, "awakened."

[2]"With . . . their dark blue limbs, the color of parrots" *śukanīlāṅgāḥ*: D6,T2,M3,5, and the texts and printed editions of Cg and Gita Press (6.42.36) read instead *śubhanīlāṅgāḥ*, "[having *or* with their] splendid, dark blue bodies."

26. "the waves" *vegāḥ*: Normally, in the context of water, *vegaḥ* means "stream *or* current." Ct, whom we have followed, glosses, "waves (*taraṅgāḥ*)." Cg glosses, "stream *or* flood in general, *or* the rising of a body of water (*pūrāḥ*)."

"at the appointed time" *samaye*: Literally, "at the time." All the commentators who gloss this elliptical term take it as a reference to the *pralaya*, or time of universal destruction. Cg alone also offers, as an alternative, "the time of moonrise (*candrodaye vā*)."

"filled to overflowing" *pūryamāṇasya*: Literally, "being filled." Ct suggests that we supply the words, "by great storm clouds (*mahāmeghaiḥ*)." Ck is a bit more explicit, offering, "by the seven great clouds (*saptamahāmeghaiḥ*)." The idea, of course, is that it is the torrential rains from these clouds that are causing the ocean to spill over its shore.

Following verse 26, D5–7,9–11,S insert a passage of six lines [692*]: "Then the monkey army let loose a roar on all sides, filling the Malaya mountain together with its slopes, peaks, and caves.[1–2] The sound of conches and war drums, as well as the leonine roars of the swift [monkeys], caused the earth, sky, and ocean to resound.[3–4] [These sounds were] accompanied by the trumpeting of elephants, the neighing of battle-steeds, the rumbling of chariot wheels, and the tramping of the *rākṣasas'* feet.[5–6]"

27. "between the gods and the *asuras*" *devāsure*: Literally, "in that pertaining to the *devas* and *asuras*." The expression is somewhat elliptical. Ct, Cm, Cr, and Cg (first alternative) understand this as a reference to the battle or conflict between the gods and the demons (*devāsurayuddhe*—Cr). Cg, attempting to establish grammatical parallelism, amplifies this by saying that the meaning is "just as in the case of the gods and the *asuras* at the time of the conflict between the gods and *asuras* (*yathā devāsuravirodhe devānām asurāṇām iva ity arthaḥ*)." Cg alternatively explains the expression as involving "the irregular substitution of the locative singular ending '*e*' for the genitive plural, referring to *Pā* 7.1.39 (*yadvā ṣaṣṭhībahuvacanasya supāṃ suluk* [*pūrvasavarṇāc*] *ityādinā śe-ādeśaḥ*)." The critical apparatus quotes Crā as advancing the same argument. (*devāsure devāsurāṇām iva. supāṃ suluk pūrvasavarṇāc cheyāsāsyā* [*ḍāḍyā?*]*yājāla ityāmaḥ śebhāvaḥ*.)

28. "the dreadful *rākṣasas*" *ghorāḥ*: Literally, "the dreadful ones." D7,9–11,G2, and the texts and printed editions of Ct and Cr read instead the accusative plural *sarvān*, "all," which would then refer to the monkeys.

29. D5,T1,G (after verse 28); D7,10,11,M1,2,5 (after verse 29); D6,T2,3,M3 (after 649*; see below); and the texts of the southern commentators and all printed editions insert a passage of two lines [693*]: "A great shout of 'Victory to King Sugrīva!' arose. Then, after shouting, 'Be victorious, O king, be victorious!'[1] each recited [literally, 'having recited'] his own name."

[1] " 'Be victorious, O king, be victorious!' " *rājañ jaya jaya*: Ct, Ck, and Cs, followed by many translators, are of the opinion that the cries of "Be victorious, O king, be victorious" are addressed by the *rākṣasa* warriors to Rāvaṇa (*rājan rāvaṇa jaya jayeti rakṣasām uktiḥ*—so Ct). Dutt (1893, p. 1225) believes that, rather than each soldier shouting his own name, the two sides cry out the names of their respective kings.

693*, line 1 [first half] = 6.32.13c.

Following 693*, a few southern manuscripts (D6,T2,3,M3) and VSP (unnumbered, in brackets, between verses 6.42.42 and 43) insert a passage of two lines [694*]: "The immensely powerful monkeys slaughtered the *rākṣasas* in battle [crying], 'Victory to supremely powerful Rāma and mighty Lakṣmaṇa!' " Of the translators consulted, only Raghunathan (1982, vol. 3, p. 104) renders this verse.

694*, line 2 = 6.32.13ab.

30. According to Ck, *pādas* ab are *prakṣipta*, "interpolated," i.e., spurious. Ct notes Ck's objection and appears to document it by noting that, according to the *Mahābhārata* version of the battle, several verses of which he quotes (*MBh* 3.268.40ab–3.269.1ab,3), Rāma orders a withdrawal of the monkey army after it has successfully breached the ramparts. Then a group of invisible *rākṣasas* harries the monkeys in their camp, until Vibhīṣaṇa destroys their invisibility. Cm and Cs similarly mention Ck's view and likewise quote from the same passage of the *Rāmopākhyāna*. They note that, even though the withdrawal is not mentioned in the present passage, we must infer it on the basis of the parallel passage from the *Mahābhārata*. See note to 6.33.2–3.

"short javelins" *bhiṇḍipālaiḥ*: According to Monier-Williams (s.v.) a *bhiṇḍipāla* [v.l. *bhindipāla, bhiṇḍimāla*] is either a short javelin or an arrow thrown from the hand or shot through a tube. Some think, however, that it is more like a slingshot, "a stone fastened to a string, a kind of sling for throwing stones" (Monier-Williams [s.v.]). Cg understands, "a type of mace (*gadābheda*)." On *bhiṇḍipālas*, see 6.42.19; 6.53.32; 6.73.20–23; 6.83.25; and notes. Oppert (1880, p. 13) identifies the weapon as "a crooked club" and includes it among the "*mukta*," or released weapons. Dikshitar (1944, pp. 106, 122) understands the *bhiṇḍipāla* to be "a heavy club which had a broad and bent tail end, measuring one cubit in length." According to him, it was used on the left foot of a warrior "for cutting, hitting, striking, and breaking." See, too, *AgniP* 251.15.

31. "leaping monkeys" *vānarāḥ . . . plavaṅgamāḥ*: Literally, "monkeys . . . going by leaps." Cg and Cm note that, in order to avoid redundancy, we are to read the standard synonym for monkey, *plavaṅgamāḥ*, with its full force as a descriptive adjective, i.e., "moving by leaps." (*plavanaṃ plutagatiṃ gacchantīti plavaṅgamāḥ. asaṃjñāyām api khaśārṣaḥ. anena plutagatimatvam uktam. ato na vānaraśabdena punaruktiḥ*—so Cg.)

32. "in which the ground grew thick with flesh and blood" *māṃsaśoṇitakardamaḥ*: Literally, "having flesh and blood for mud."

"was something unimaginable" *adbhutopamaḥ*: Literally, "was comparable to a miracle."

Sarga 33

1. "As those . . . monkeys continued to fight" *yudhyatāṃ tu tatas teṣāṃ vānarāṇām*: We follow the suggestion of Cr, Cg, and Cm, who read the first half of the verse as a genitive absolute construction (*vānarāṇāṃ yudhyatāṃ satām*—so Cr). According to this reading, it is the monkeys alone who are fighting, while the *rākṣasas*' fury for battle increases. On

the basis of Ck's and Ct's interpretation of *balaroṣaḥ* (Ct's v.l. for *balakopaḥ*) as, "the rage produced by the sight of each other's armies (*parasparabaladarśanajo roṣaḥ*)," it appears that Ck and Ct read the genitive plurals of *pādas* ab in parallel with the genitive plural, *rakṣasām*, of *pāda* c. This interpretation yields the following translation: "A terrible rage at each other's armies then arose among the *rākṣasas* and the great monkeys as they continued to fight." All translators consulted follow this reading of the verse.

"rage against their army" *balakopaḥ*: The compound is somewhat ambiguous in its meaning. Ct and Ck, who read the synonymous variant *balaroṣaḥ*, as noted above, interpret it as "the rage produced by the sight of each other's armies (*parasparabaladarśanajo roṣaḥ*)." Cr glosses, explicitly, "rage against the monkey army [on the part of the *rākṣasas*] (*vānarasenākopaḥ*)." Cg and Cm seem to agree with Cr and gloss, "anger of the army (*senāyāḥ kopaḥ*)." Cg further notes that the word *bala* here lacks any specification of the case ending (*balety avibhaktikanirdeśaḥ*). In other words, as Professor R. K. Sharma points out, the compound exhibits the grammatical defect of *asamarthadoṣa*, in that the word *rakṣasām*, "of the *rākṣasas*," construes with the prior member of the compound, *bala-*.

2–3. "Those tigers among *rākṣasas*... They were *rākṣasas*" *rākṣasavyāghrāḥ*... *rākṣasāḥ*: Cg, the only commentator to read *rākṣasavyāghrāḥ*, is concerned about the apparent redundancy. He explains that "tigers among *rākṣasas*" refers to an elite type of *rākṣasa* but that they still belong to the generic type, and so are referred to by the generic term *rākṣasa* as well. (*rākṣasavyāghrā rākṣasaśreṣṭhāḥ. rākṣasaśreṣṭhatve 'pi jātyantaratvaṃ saṃbhavatīti rākṣasā ity uktam.*) D7,9–11, and the texts and printed editions of Ct, Cr, and Ck make the redundancy still worse, reading *rākṣasā vīrāḥ*, "*rākṣasa* heroes," for *rākṣasavyāghrāḥ*. Cr attempts to deal with the problem by reading the first occurrence of the term *rākṣasa* as a kind of adjective with the sense "characterized *or* accompanied by many *rākṣasas* (*bahurākṣasaviśiṣṭāḥ*)."

"sallied forth" *niryayuḥ*: Ct thinks that, by using this verb, Vālmīki is suggesting that there has been a withdrawal of the combatants in the intervening period (*anena vālmīkināpi pratyavahāro dhvanitaḥ*). See note to 6.32.30, where the commentators infer a pause in the battle at this point. See, too, notes to 6.41.8; 6.49.33; and 6.62.2.

"golden-plumed" *kāñcanāpīḍaiḥ*: See 6.90.6 and note.

"banners" *dhvajaiḥ*: A few manuscripts (D9–11) and the texts and printed editions of Ct and Ck read *gajaiḥ*, "elephants," for *dhvajaiḥ*. Ct, no doubt aware of the awkwardness of the simile comparing elephants to the tongues of a flame, explains that the elephants are as unapproachable as flames (*agniśikhopamais tadvad durdharśaiḥ*). Raghunathan (1982, vol. 3, p. 104), who normally follows Cg, seems to have ignored the term entirely, ascribing the adjective *agniśikhopamaiḥ* to the golden plumes of the horses.

4. "who also desired victory" *jayam icchatām*: Cr sees this as a reference to the *rākṣasas* (*jayam icchatāṃ rakṣasām*).

"who could take on any form at will" *kāmarūpiṇām*: D7,9–11, and the texts and printed editions of Cr, Ck, and Ct read instead *ghorakarmaṇām*, "of dreadful deeds."

5. "as they hurled themselves at one another" *anyonyam abhidhāvatām*: Literally, "of them running toward one another." Cm, Ct, and Ck understand that the combatants approach one another for the specific purpose of single combat (*dvandvayuddhārtham*—so Ct).

"engaged in single combat" *dvandvayuddham avartata*: Literally, "a paired battle took place."

6. "just as long ago the . . . *asura* Andhaka fought with three-eyed Śiva" *tryambakeṇa yathāndhakaḥ*: Literally, "like Andhaka with Tryambaka." Andhaka is one of the great *asura* enemies of Śiva known from the epics, *purāṇas*, etc. Tryambaka, literally, "three-eyed one," is a common epithet of Śiva. Cf. 6.81.34.

7. "Saṃpāti . . . fought with Prajaṅgha" *prajaṅghena ca saṃpātiḥ*: Literally, "and Saṃpāti with Prajaṅgha." The half verse is elliptical, and the verb must be supplied. We carry the verb *ayudhyata*, "he fought," down from verse 6 above. The identity of these individuals is somewhat unclear. Saṃpāti is the name of one of Vibhīṣaṇa's four companions (6.28.7; cf. 6.11.3; and note to 6.10.12) and this could well be the same individual, as Cg asserts (*saṃpātir vibhīṣaṇasacivaḥ*). On the other hand, at verse 20 below, Saṃpāti uses an *aśvakarṇa* tree as a weapon. The use of trees and stones as weapons is characteristic of the monkeys, not the *rākṣasa* warriors.

Ct, Cr, Ck, and Cg are in agreement that Prajaṅgha is the name of a *rākṣasa*. Ct and Ck seek to confirm this by quoting verse 20ab below, where Prajaṅgha uses a bow and arrow, which would presumably distinguish him from the monkeys. But it should be noted that Prajaṅgha is elsewhere a name of a monkey officer (see 6.4.33; and note to 6.31.30).

"engaged" *ārabdhaḥ*: Literally, "began." Ct, Cg, and Cr all add some wording to complete the ellipsis, such as "to fight *or* strike (*yoddhum iti śeṣaḥ*—Cr; *yuddham ārabdhavān*—Ct; and *hantum iti śeṣaḥ*—Cg)."

8. "Mitraghna" *mitraghnena*: Literally, "slayer of friends," a peculiar name by any standard. A few *devanāgarī* manuscripts (D9–11) and the texts and printed editions of Ct and Cr read instead the more normative name Śatrughna (*śatrughena*), "slayer of enemies." Ct, however, notes the reading of the critical edition as a variant. See notes to verses 11 and 26 below.

10. "Virūpākṣa" *virūpākṣeṇa*: See note to verse 25 below; and Goldman and Goldman 1996, pp. 24–26. See 6.28.31 and note.

11. *pādas* abc = 26abc.

"Suptaghna" *suptaghnaḥ*: Literally, "killer of sleepers." A number of southern manuscripts (D9–11,T2,3,G3,M1,2) and the texts and printed editions of Ct read instead the unusual name seen above at verse 8, *mitraghnaḥ*, "slayer of friends." See, too, verse 26 below and note.

14. "The son of Dharma" *dharmasya putraḥ*: According to the southern recension of the *Bālakāṇḍa* (491*, line 11—after 1.16.8), the monkey hero Suṣeṇa's father is Varuṇa, not Dharma. However, because of the variations and duplications of the monkeys' names in the text, it is difficult to determine whether this is indeed a contradiction. See note to 1.16.8.

15. "engaged in single combat" *dvandvaṃ samīyuḥ . . . yuddhāya*: Literally, "they came together in pairs for battle." Ñ2,D9–11, and the texts and printed editions of Ct read instead *yuddhvā ca*, "and having fought" for *yuddhāya*.

"many other . . . many other" *bahubhiḥ*: As Cg notes, although the adjective is applied here only to the *rākṣasas*, we must supply it for the monkeys as well (*bahubhir iti rākṣasaviśeṣaṇād vānarāś cety atrāpi bahava iti viśeṣaṇaṃ vijñeyam*).

"in various ways" *bahudhā*: Cg specifies that this would include fighting with weapons, missiles, arms, feet, and so forth (*yuddhāya śastrāstrabāhucaraṇaprabhṛtibhir yuddhāya*). D7,9–11,T3, and the texts and printed editions of Ct and Cr read instead *sahasā*, "violently, suddenly."

17. "with hair in place of weeds" *keśaśāḍvalāḥ*: The word *śāḍvala* frequently means "grass" or "herbage," and some translators take the reference to be to the grass or moss on the banks of a river (Dutt 1893, p. 1226; Raghunathan 1982, vol. 3, p. 105; Roussel 1903, vol. 3, p. 123; Shastri 1959, vol. 3, p. 105; and Gorresio 1856, vol. 9, p. 254). We, however, see the reference to be to vegetation floating in a stream or water weeds, a view shared by Gita Press (1969, vol. 3, p. 1517) and Pagani (1999, p. 968).

"logjams" *-saṃghāṭa-*: Literally, "heaps, bunches, clusters." We follow the interpretation of all the commentators, who gloss, "a pile *or* clump of logs (*kāṣṭhasaṃcayaḥ*—so Cg)." Cf. 6.81.9 and note.

19. "in that combat... smashed" *jaghāna samare*: Literally, "he struck in battle." D10,11, and the texts and printed editions of Ct read *gadayā*, "with a mace," for *samare*, "in battle." This minor variant raises the question of why a monkey would be using a formal weapon. Ct, aware of the difficulty, proposes that Aṅgada is using Indrajit's mace, having snatched it from him (*tasyaiva gadayā svāpahṛtayā jaghāna*).

"Indrajit's" *tasya*: Literally, "his." The context supports Ct's and Cr's note that this must be Indrajit's chariot (*tasyendrajitaḥ*).

"gilded" *kāñcanacitrāṅgam*: Literally, "its body beautified *or* variegated with gold."

20. See note 7 above, where a number of the commentators cite this verse in support of their contention that Saṃpāti is a monkey and Prajaṅgha, a *rākṣasa*.

"he... struck" *nijaghāna*: The verb could also mean "he killed," and Gita Press (1969, vol. 3, p. 1518) and (Dutt 1893, p. 1227) translate accordingly. The problem, as with many of the combatants' names, is that it is not always clear when a figure who appears to have been killed subsequently seems to reappear in the narrative, whether, as has been argued, Vālmīki has nodded (Goldman and Goldman 1996, pp. 24–26) or whether another figure with the same name is intended. In this case, a *rākṣasa* named Prajaṅgha appears again in the battle in the southern recension and is finally killed off at GPP 6.76.27 (=critical edition *Yuddhakāṇḍa*, App. I, No. 43, lines 47–48), where he is beheaded by a blow of Aṅgada's fist.

"in the vanguard of battle" *raṇamūrdhani*: Literally, "at the head of the battle." Roussel (1903, vol. 3, p. 123) has apparently misread the expression, translating, "[*lui asséna un coup*]... *sur la tête*." He has been followed in this lapse by Shastri (1959, vol. 3, p. 105), who renders, "[struck him] over the head."

21. "mounted his chariot" *rathasthaḥ*: Literally, "standing in a chariot."

"javelin he kept there" *rathaśaktyā*: Literally, "with a chariot-javelin." This seemingly simple compound is actually rather ambiguous in its meaning, which has led translators to render it variously. Ct, Cr, Cm, and Ck understand the term to be a reference to a javelin (*śakti*) that is located in, or mounted on, a chariot. Cg amplifies somewhat, explaining, "a javelin that is always to be found in a chariot (*ratha eva sadā vartamānayā śaktyā*)." The term also occurs in the *Mahābhārata* (Citraśāla Press edition, 10.6.13) and *Harivaṃśa* (Citraśāla Press edition, *Viṣṇuparva* 106.5). In the former, the term describes a blazing missile, which Aśvatthāman hurls at Kṛṣṇa. At that occurrence, the commentator Nīlakaṇṭha glosses, simply, *cakram*, "discus." In the latter, it appears to refer to a structural element of the chariot, against which the wounded demon Śambara leans for support. Here Nīlakaṇṭha defines it as "a flagpole whose purpose is to stabilize or strengthen a chariot (*rathasyotsāhahetuṃ dhvajam*)." This latter definition is the one given by Apte, MW, and PW. Apte (s.v.) cites the *Mahābhārata* verse, which seems to support this definition poorly at best. Translators have treated this object variously. Raghunathan (1982, vol. 3, p. 105) and Gita Press (1969, vol. 3, p. 1518) take it as we and the commentators do. Pagani (1999, p. 969) evidently following the dictionaries, translates, "*la hampe de son étendard*." Roussel (1903, vol. 3, p. 123) avoids the issue by simply repeating the Sanskrit term. Gorresio (1856, vol. 9, p. 254) does not confront the issue since his text reads instead *tathā śaktyā*, "and with his javelin." Dutt (1893, p. 1227) and Shastri (1959, vol. 3, p. 105) apparently understand *śakti* in its other sense of "force, power, energy." The former renders, "with all the access of force derived from his car," and the latter, "with the force of his driving." Cf. verse 34 below. See notes to 6.59.13; 6.78.10; and 6.95.9.

"in the middle of the chest" *stanāntare*: Literally, "between the breasts."

22. "Jambumālin's" *tasya*: Literally, "his."

"together with that *rākṣasa*" *saha tenaiva rakṣasā*: We agree with the majority of commentators in seeing this as a reference to Jambumālin himself. Ct, in fact, feels that we are to understand by this reference that Jambumālin has been killed (*tena jambumālī mṛta iti gamyate*). Ck, however, understands the reference to be to another *rākṣasa*, an emissary of Jambumālin (*jambumālidūta iti gamyate*).

Following verse 22, D5 (after 30)–7,9–11,T (T1after 31),G,M1,2 (after 31),3,5 insert a passage of two lines [706*]: "Roaring, the terrible Pratapana pursued Nala, but Nala swiftly knocked out his eyes."

23. "his body pierced" *bhinnagātraḥ*: The texts and printed editions of the southern commentators as well as virtually all southern manuscripts read 23ab with 706* [translated above]. Thus, in these texts, Nala's body is pierced by Pratapana's arrows whereas, in the critical edition, Gaja is shot by Tapana.

"Then Gaja . . . smashed him [Tapana] with a mountain peak held in his fist." *prajaghānādriśṛṅgeṇa tapanaṃ muṣṭinā gajaḥ*: Literally, "Gaja struck Tapana with a fist, with a mountain peak." This half verse is omitted from D5–7,9–11,T,G3,M1–3, and the texts and printed editions of the southern commentators and therefore does not appear in any translation of the southern recension. Moreover, no northern manuscript appears to juxtapose a monkey, Gaja, with a *rākṣasa*, Tapana. The northern parallel to this passage in the critical apparatus, as well as in printed versions of the north, represents Tapana as being slain by Nala (Lahore 6.18.55 and Gorresio 6.18.31). It appears that only M4,5 read Gaja, while all other manuscripts either omit the half verse or give the name of the monkey as Nala. The inclusion of this half verse is doubtful at best and should be so indicated, while the name Nala would have been the stronger choice based on textual evidence.

The expression *adriśṛṅgeṇa . . . muṣṭinā* seems somewhat elliptical unless, as we have done, one reads the compound as a *bahuvrīhi*, yielding the sense "a fist in which there was the peak of a mountain." One could alternately and, to our mind, less plausibly supply either the conjunction "*ca*," yielding "with a mountain peak and his fist," or the comparative particle "*iva*," yielding "with a fist that was like a mountain peak." The northern variants avoid this collocation, while the southern commentators, as noted, do not share the reading.

24. "killed . . . smashing him to pieces" *nirbibheda jaghāna ca*: Literally, "he smashed and killed." A few *devanāgarī* manuscripts (D7,9,10) and the texts and printed editions of Ct, Ck, and Cr read instead *nijaghāna javena ca*, "and he swiftly killed."

25. "Virūpākṣa" *virūpākṣam*: See note to verse 10 above.

26. *pādas* abc = 11abc.

"Suptaghna" *suptaghnaḥ*: D5,10,11,T,M1,2, and the texts and printed editions of Ct, Ck, and Cr read instead *mitraghnaḥ*, "Mitraghna." See notes to verses 8 and 11 above.

"all pierced" *nirbibhiduḥ*: Literally, "they pierced." D10,11,G3,M5, and the texts and printed editions of Ct and Ck read instead *ādīpayat*, "he enflamed, scorched." Cr, who reads with the critical edition, glosses, "undertook activity favorable to piercing (*bhedanānukūlavyāpāraṃ cakruḥ*)." Evidently he is unwilling to accept the idea that Rāma could actually be wounded, especially by such relatively minor *rākṣasas*. See notes to 6.33.26; 6.35.9; 6.75.17; 6.76.25,32; and 6.79.1.

27. "with four" *caturbhiḥ*: Ct calls our attention to Rāma's marksmanship by noting that he needed no more than four arrows to behead the four *rākṣasas* (*nādhikair ity arthaḥ*).

28. "Vajramuṣṭi with his fist" *vajramuṣṭiḥ . . . muṣṭinā*: The name Vajramuṣṭi means "adamantine fisted," and here the poet exploits the name playfully for an ironic effect.

"the lofty tower of a citadel" *purāṭṭaḥ*: D10,11, and the texts and printed editions of Ct, Ck, and Cr read instead *surāṭṭaḥ*, or "an *aṭṭa* of the gods." Ck glosses the term *aṭṭaḥ* in the sense of *kṣaumam*, "a room at the top of a house *or* a fortified structure in front of a building." Ct quotes Ck and notes that other unspecified commentators understand the term to refer to a *vimāna*, "a flying chariot *or* a seven-storied mansion." This latter sense is given by Cr, who glosses, "an aerial chariot *or* mansion of the gods" (*devavimānam*)," and by Cs, who explains, "an aerial chariot *or* mansion of the demons given by the gods (*devadatto daiteyavimānaḥ*)." Cr's interpretation appears to be followed by Gita Press (1969, vol. 3, p. 1518) and Shastri (1959, vol. 3, p. 106), both of whom understand the reference to be to an aerial chariot. Roussel (1903, vol. 3, p. 123) and Pagani (1999, p. 969), respectively, understand *aṭṭaḥ* in the sense of "*un pavillon de Suras*" and "*le donjon des dieux*." Cg, with whom we agree, and the only commentator to deal with the critical reading, glosses, "turret *or* topmost part of the city *or* citadel (*puravalabhiḥ*)." Raghunathan (1982, vol. 3, p. 106), evidently following Cg, translates, "the attic of the citadel." See *RaghuVa* 6.67. See also notes to 6.62.6 and 6.86.23 [1961*].

Following verse 28, Ñ,B1,4,D6,7,9–11,T2,3,M3,5, and the texts and printed editions of the southern commentators read verses 32–34.

29. "whose blows were like that of Indra's *vajra* or thunderbolt" *vajrāśanisamasparśaḥ*: Literally, "contact with which is equal to that of the *vajra* and thunderbolt." Ct explains the compound as meaning "a savage blow of the fist equal to that (*tathā krūramuṣṭiprahāra ity arthaḥ*)." The use of the word *sparśa*, "contact," to refer to the devastating impact of a weapon or person is attested elsewhere, as at *Mahābhārata* 6.114.55, where it refers to arrows loosed in battle. As in verse 28, the poet plays with the name of the *rākṣasa* and the person or weapon that strikes him. In this case, the play is on *aśani*, "lightning bolt." The name Aśaniprabha means "having the radiance of lightning." See note to 6.55.43.

30. "that resembled thunderbolts, Aśaniprabha" *aśanisaṃkāśaiḥ . . . aśaniprabhaḥ*: As above, the poet plays with the name of the demon and the weapon employed.

32. Verses 32 and 34 occur after verse 28 in the texts and printed editions of the southern commentators.

"Nīla, whose dark luster was like that of a mass of collyrium" *nīlaṃ nīlāñjanacayaprabham*: Again the poet plays on the name of one of the combatants, repeating the monkey's name, Nīla ("Dark" *or* "Blue-Black"), in the descriptive adjective. Pagani

(1999, p. 1661) in her note argues that, since recipes for collyrium are given in medical and alchemical literature as part of the paraphernalia of a magician, the comparison of a warrior to a heap of this substance is a bad omen for his opponent. Here, as elsewhere, she may be extracting more levels of signification from the text than its author may have intended (see notes to verses 34 and 45 below).

34. "the heads of Nikumbha and his charioteer" *śiraḥ . . . nikumbhasya ca sāratheḥ*: Literally, "the head of Nikumbha and of the charioteer." Of all the commentators and translators consulted, Cs and Raghunathan (1982, vol. 3, p. 106), perhaps concerned at the singular *śiraḥ*, "head," understand the syntax to mean that Nīla cuts off the head only of Nikumbha's charioteer (*nikumbhasya sāratheḥ śiraś cicchedety anvayaḥ*). This is certainly a reasonable reading on syntactic grounds. However, given that no further mention is made of Nikumbha in this passage, we agree with the majority of commentators and translators in understanding that both he and his charioteer have been killed in this fashion (*nikumbhasya sāratheś ca śiraḥ*).

"with a discus taken from their chariot" *rathacakreṇa*: Literally, "with a chariot wheel *or* discus" All the commentators and translators consulted understand the reference to be to a wheel of Nikumbha's chariot. However, given the force of the simile involving Viṣṇu, whose principal weapon is a *cakra*, or "discus," and in light of what we see as a parallel usage in the case of *rathaśakti* (verse 21 above), we feel that the context better supports the sharp discus rather than a chariot wheel, which would not serve so well as a cutting tool. Pagani (1999, pp. 969, 1661), who translates, "*la roue de char*," claims, somewhat imaginatively, that a chariot wheel always refers to Viṣṇu's discus with its sharp edge, which is then, in turn, linked to the wheel of Time.

36. "smashed" *nyapātayat*: Literally, "he knocked down."

40. "upon Vidyunmālin's chest" *tasyorasi*: Literally, "on his chest."

43–44. "swords" *khaḍgaiḥ*: V3,D7,9–11, and the texts and printed editions of Ct and Cr read instead *cānyaiḥ*, "and with others."

"spears" *-paṭṭasaiḥ*: Ś,Ñ,V,B,D1–4,7–12,T3, and the texts and printed editions of Ct, Ck, and Cr read instead *-sāyakaiḥ*, "with arrows."

"broken chariots, butchered war-horses" *apaviddhaiś ca bhinnaiś ca rathaiḥ sāṃgrāmikair hayaiḥ*: Literally, "with broken and split chariots and war-horses." We have followed the suggestion of Cg and Cr in construing the first adjective with the first noun, and the second with the second. D9–11 and the texts and printed editions of Ct read *cāpi*, "as well as *or* and," for *bhinnaiḥ*, "broken."

"place of horror" *ghoram*: Literally, "horrible, dreadful."

45. "headless corpses" *kabandhāni*: Dutt (1893, p. 1229) envisages these in a note as ghostly apparitions, "Spectres having bodies without heads." Pagani (1999, p. 1661), who is fond of reading larger symbolism into the text, notes here, again somewhat imaginatively, that the headless trunks littering the battlefield symbolize sacrificial posts, thus lending the battlefield itself an air of sacrifice.

Pādas cd are repeated in brackets in printed versions of Cg (= KK and VSP 6.44.12ef).

46. "being torn to pieces" *vidāryamāṇāḥ*: D7,9–11, and the texts and printed editions of Ct, Ck, and Cr read instead *nihanyamānāḥ*, "being killed *or* slaughtered."

"their limbs smeared with blood" *śoṇitadigdhagātrāḥ*: B1,D9–11,G2,3,M5, and the texts and printed editions of Ct, Ck, and Cr read instead *śoṇitagandhamūrcchitāḥ*, "stupefied with the smell of blood." Although this interpretation is reflected in those translations that follow the texts and printed editions of Ct, Shastri (1959, vol. 3, p. 107) uniquely translates both variants, "maddened by the smell of blood . . . their limbs covered with blood."

"anxious now for the sun, maker of day, to set" *divākarasyāstamayābhikāṅkṣiṇaḥ*: The *rākṣasas'* eagerness for nightfall can be interpreted in either of two ways. On the one hand, it may be that, as they have been badly beaten in this first day of battle, they are eager simply for the respite that nightfall generally brings so that they can regroup. On the other hand, as several of the commentators and translators note, it is widely known that the power of the nocturnal *rākṣasas* increases after sundown, a fact alluded to throughout the literature (*rātrau rākṣasānāṃ balādhikyād iti bhāvaḥ*—so Cg). See note to 1.25.13; *Bālakāṇḍa*, App. I, No. 5, lines 14–16 = GPP 1.17.22–23.

The meter is *vaṃśasthavila*.

Sarga 34

1. "deadly" *prāṇahāriṇī:* Literally, "carrying off life breaths." Cr believes that the night is perilous for all beings other than *rākṣasas (niśācarātiriktānāṃ bhayāvahety arthaḥ)*. Cg believes we should supply the phrase "to the monkeys *(vānarāṇām iti śeṣaḥ)*." Cf. note to 6.33.46.

2. "a clash by night" *niśāyuddham*: Ct and Cs feel that they can more or less precisely date the onset of this night battle by referring to the events described previously. Ct reasons as follows: The ascent of Mount Suvela took place on the full-moon day of the month of Pauṣa [December–January]. Following this, the division of the monkey troops occupied the entire dark half of that month. The battle described in the preceding *sarga* commenced, then, on the first day of the month of Māgha [January–February] and continued for many days. This battle is generally described as "chaotic (*saṃkulam*)." It is on the last day of this protracted engagement that the night battle described here begins. (*pauṣapaurṇamāsyāṃ suvelarohaṇasya spaṣṭapratīteḥ. tenāvibhāgādinā pauṣakṛṣṇe 'tīte māghaśuklapratipadi yuddhārambhe bahudinaparyantaṃ saṃkulaṃ yuddhaṃ sāmānyenoktam. taduttaradine cedaṃ niśāyuddhaṃ pravṛttam.*) Ct substantiates his argument by quoting a verse, apparently from the *Padmapurāṇa*, in which it is stated that a great and "chaotic (*saṃkulaṃ*)" battle between the monkeys and *rākṣasas* began at noon on the first day of the month (*tato jajñe mahāyuddhaṃ saṃkulaṃ kapirakṣasām / madhyāhne prathamaṃ yuddhaṃ prārabdhaṃ pratipady abhūd iti pādmoktaḥ*). Cs, commenting on verse 1, quotes Ct by name more or less as he is represented in GPP (6.44.2–3). However, he disagrees with Ct's analysis, on the grounds that he cannot find the quoted verse in the *Padmapurāṇa*. Instead, he quotes another verse, which offers a different view, according to which the great battle took place on the fourteenth day of the bright half of the month of Caitra [March–April] and Rāvaṇa was killed on the forty-eighth day of the war. Cs thus argues that we should reckon the date of the battle here as forty-seven days prior to the fourteenth day of the bright half of Caitra (counting the fourteenth itself as one of the forty-eight days). Cf. note to 6.50.12. Cs concludes by mentioning yet a third position, which he ascribes to unnamed others: that the night battle took place in the dark half of the month of Phālguna [February–March]. (*padmapurāṇe pañcaṣeṣu pustakeṣv etat padyādarśanena "atra yuddhaṃ mahad vṛttaṃ caitraśuklacaturdaśīm / aṣṭacatvāriṃśaddinaṃ yatrāsau rāvaṇo*

hataḥ //" ity anyathādarśanena ca tac cintyam. caitraśuklacaturdaśītaḥ prāk saptacatvāriṃśaddinī grāhyā. caturdaśyā sahāṣṭacatvāriṃśaddinī bhavati. bhavati phālguṇakṛṣṇe rātriyuddham ity anye.) See Introduction, p. 17, note 1; and note to 6.4.4.

3. "tawny monkeys... monkey" *harayo hariḥ*: Literally, "tawny monkeys... tawny monkey." Although it is our convention to render the term *hari* in its etymological sense of "tawny, tawny monkey," we believe that the context of the verse argues for the use of the second term in its most generic sense. Ś,Ñ,V1,2,B,D1–4,8–13,T3,G2, and the texts and printed editions of Ct and Cr read *vānaraḥ*, "monkey," for *hariś cā[sīti]*, "and... a tawny monkey." See note to verse 6 below.

"'Are you...?' 'Are you...?'" *asīti... asīti*: Literally, "You are... You are." Since there is no interrogative particle in the verse, it is impossible to say for certain whether the utterances are declarative or interrogative. However, given the context in which the combatants are unable to see one another and are groping and striking blindly, we are inclined to share the view of Roussel (1903, vol. 3, p. 125), Shastri (1959, vol. 3, p. 107), and Gita Press (1969, vol. 3, p. 1520) in understanding the phrases to be questions. Other translators render these as exclamations. Cg argues that, because of the terrible darkness, even the *rākṣasas* (who are typically at home in the darkness, see note to 6.33.46) are themselves confused (*dāruṇatamaskatvena rakṣasām api moho 'bhūd iti bhāvaḥ*). Raghunathan extrapolates from this, it seems, the idea that both the *rākṣasas* and monkeys are attacking their own kind (1982, vol. 3, p. 107).

4. "in that darkness" *tamasi*: The editors of the critical edition have marked this reading as doubtful. V3,D5,7,9–11,T2,3, and the texts and printed editions of Ct, Ck, and Cr read instead *sainye tu*, "among the troops."

5. "with thickets of luminescent herbs" *dīptauṣadhivanāḥ*: We agree with Dutt (1893, p. 1229), Raghunathan (1982, vol. 3, p. 107), Shastri (1959, vol. 3, p. 107), and Gita Press (1969, vol. 3, p. 1521) in understanding the reference to be to the luminescent or phosphorescent herbs that are a commonplace in Sanskrit poetry (cf. 6.61.55 and *KumāSaṃ* 1.2, etc.). European translators (Roussel 1903, vol. 3, p. 125; Gorresio 1856, vol. 9, p. 257; and Pagani 1999, p. 970), however, have tended to read the compound *oṣadhivana* as a *dvandva* in the sense of "herbs and forests," which then leads them to understand the adjective *dīpta-*, "glowing," in the sense of "flaming *or* burning." Pagani (1999, p. 1661) has a rather forced interpretation, according to which the mountains in question are the Himalayas. In her view, because these mountains are by definition snow white, comparing them to the *rākṣasas* must be done on the basis of their great size and not their color. She further argues that the unusual representation of the Himalayas as being on fire, which is contrary to their nature, refers to the demonic and *adharmic* aspect of the *rākṣasas*, who disturb the order of the world.

6. "impenetrable" *duṣpāre*: Literally, "impossible to cross."

"monkeys" *plavaṅgamān*: Literally, "going by bounds." We normally translate the kenning as "leaping monkeys." In the context, however, this would appear restrictive. See note to verse 3 above.

7. "the monkeys" *te*: Literally, "they."

"the *rākṣasas*' golden-plumed horses and their banners that resembled flames of fire" *hayān kāñcanāpīḍān dhvajāṃś cāgniśikhopamān*: Literally, "the golden-plumed horses and the banners that were like flames of fire." Cf. 6.33.2ab, where horses and banners are described identically. D7,9–11, and the texts and printed editions of Ck and Ct read [*cā*]*śīviṣopamān*, "[and] like venomous serpents" for [*cā*]*gniśikhopamān*, "[and] that resembled flames of fire." Cr appears to have a reading that is unattested in the critical apparatus. He reads [*hayān*] *śikharopamān* [*dhvajāṃś ca*], "horses like mountain peaks and banners." The adjective *śikharopamān* is attested (but with *gajān* for *hayān*) in G2 and M5.

Following verse 7, D5–7,9–11,S insert a passage of one line [718*]: "Those mighty monkeys rocked the *rākṣasa* army."

8. "they dragged about" *cakarṣuḥ*: Roussel (1903, vol. 3, p. 125) prefers the less common sense of the root √*kṛṣ*, "to scratch" (Apte s.v.). In this he is followed, as is so often the case, by Shastri (1959, vol. 3, p. 108), who translates, "clawed."

"bedecked with flags and banners" *patākādhvajinaḥ*: Ct and Ck understand, "equipped with flagpoles complete with flying flags (*patākopetadhvajavantaḥ*)."

"slashing" *dadaṃśuś ca*: Literally, "and they bit [them]."

9. "whom they could make out but dimly in the darkness" *dṛśyādṛśyāni*: Literally, "both visible and invisible." Translators, with the exception of Raghunathan, who follows Cg, have understood the compound to refer distributively to those *rākṣasas* who were visible to Rāma and Lakṣmaṇa and those who were not. This interpretation is plausible in light of the ability of Indian epic archers to strike unseen targets by sound alone (*śabdavedha*). Compare, for example, the stories at 2.57.14ff. and 2.58.12–15, where this ability proves to be the undoing of King Daśaratha. The mastery of blind archery is also ascribed to Arjuna in the *Mahābhārata*. See *MBh* 1.123.1–6, where, through practice, Arjuna is said to learn to shoot at night. See, however, 6.35.13 and note, where Rāma and Lakṣmaṇa regard this practice as *adharmic*, "unrighteous." On the other hand, we agree with Cg, who understands the term to mean "barely visible (*īṣaddṛśyāni*)" in the sense of both visible and invisible at the same time. We have added the words "in the darkness" for the sake of clarity. See, too, Cg's comments at note to 6.35.13.

10. "The thick dust" *dharaṇīrajaḥ*: Literally, "the dust of the earth."

"of the warriors" *yudhyatām*: Literally, "of those who were fighting."

11. "swift" *mahāvegāḥ*: B3,D5–7,9–11,T,G3,M3, and the texts and printed editions of the southern commentators read instead *mahāghorāḥ*, "very terrible."

"with blood for water" *rudhirodāḥ*: B2,D6,7,9–11,T2,3,G1,3,M5, and the texts and printed editions of Ct, Ck, and Cr read instead *rudhiraughāḥ*, "with torrents of blood." Cg, who reads with the critical edition, notes the irregularity of the substitution of the word *uda* for the word *udaka*, "water," in this compound (*asaṃjñāyām apy udaka-śabdasyodādeśa ārṣaḥ*).

12. "of battle drums—*bherīs*, *mṛdaṅgas*, and *paṇavas*" *bherīmṛdaṅgānāṃ paṇavānāṃ ca*: For *bherīs*, see 6.17.31–33 and note; for *mṛdaṅgas*, see 5.8.38 and Vyas 1967, p. 229; and for *paṇavas*, see 5.8.39. Vyas (1967, p. 229) identifies the *paṇava* as a type of drum. But compare Apte (s.v.), who understands the term to refer either to a type of musical instrument or a small drum. Cf. 5.46.27.

"flute" *-veṇu-*: Ñ2,D10,11,G3, and the texts and printed editions of Cr and Ct read instead *-nemi-*, "chariot wheel."

Following verse 12, printed versions of Cg (=KK and VSP 6.44.12ef) repeat 6.33.45cd in brackets. The apparatus of KK indicates that these *pādas* are found in this location in five of the manuscripts on which the edition is based. The critical apparatus makes no mention of the inclusion of this passage here or at 6.33.45. The passage would be translated as follows: "And in that tumultuous conflict, which was comparable to the battle of the gods and the *asuras*."

13. "the clash of arms" *śastrāṇām*: Literally, "of weapons." D5,7,T1,G,M, and the texts and printed editions of Ct, Cg, Cm, and Ck read instead *śastānām*, "cut down, wounded," which can be taken to refer to the monkeys, the *rākṣasas*, or both. The reading is perhaps an emendation to enhance the parallelism of the verse. With this reading, one could understand that the *rākṣasas* are stricken, i.e., with the fists, feet, knees, boulders, etc., of the monkeys, while the monkeys, in turn, are cut and pierced by the sharp arrows and cutting weapons of the *rākṣasas*. The collocation of the adjectives *hatānām* and *śastānām*, as noted below, belongs mainly to the manuscript tradition of Cg, Cm, Crā, and Cv. This is followed in the translations of Gita Press (1969, vol. 3, p. 1521) and Raghunathan (1982, vol. 3, p. 107).

"screaming" *stanamānānām*: We construe this participle as well as the following one, (*hatānām*) *kākākṣigolikavat*, with both monkeys and *rākṣasas*.

"as they were struck down" *hatānām*: V,D1–3,6,10,11,T2,3, the texts and printed editions of Ct, and at least several of Cg's manuscripts (D6 and three manuscripts cited in the apparatus of KK) read instead *hayānām* "of horses." This variant is then to be construed with the adjective *stanamānānām*, in the sense of "neighing [horses]." This reading is represented in all translations consulted with the exception of Gita Press (1969, vol. 3, p. 1521) and Raghunathan (1982, vol. 3, p. 107).

Following verse 13 (or in a few cases, verse 14), virtually all manuscripts except Ś and D1–4,8,10 include a passage of two lines [724*], which construes grammatically with verse 14 below: "[Covered as it was] with the slaughtered monkey leaders, javelins, lances, and battle-axes, and the butchered *rākṣasas*, huge as mountains, who could take on any form at will, [the battlefield]..."

14. "Strewn with weapons, as if with floral offerings" *śastrapuṣpopahārā*: Literally, "with weapons for floral offerings."

"thick with mud that oozed blood" *śoṇitāsravakardamā*: Literally, "its mud [characterized by] flows of blood."

"transformed beyond all recognition" *durjñeyā*: Literally, "difficult to recognize."

15. "Kālarātrī, the dark night of universal destruction" *kālarātrī*: Literally, "Kālarātrī." As at 6.23.15 above, we understand, with Ct and Ck, that the reference is to the night of universal or cosmic dissolution or destruction (*saṃhārarātrī*). Cg, however, believes that the reference is to Bhīmarathi, the inauspicious and dangerous seventh night of the seventh month of a person's seventy-seventh year. This night is believed to be especially fraught with peril for the individual. (*kālarātrir bhīmarathirātriḥ. rātrir bhīmarathir nāma sarvaprāṇibhayāvahety ukteḥ.*) (See Apte s.v.) As an alternative, Cg proposes that the term could refer to the more horrific form of the goddess Śakti, the fearsome leader of the *gaṇas*, the demonic hosts of the Śaiva tradition. (*śaktir vā. satī ca kālarātriś ca bhairavī gaṇanāyikety ukteḥ.*) See, too, 6.58.31 and note. Cf. 6.26.25 and note.

16. "frenzied" *saṃhṛṣṭāḥ*: Literally, "excited, delighted." Ct and Cr share this reading with the critical edition. The translators who follow their texts tend to understand the adjective in its common sense of "happy, joyous," which seems ill suited to the context. T3,M1–3, and the texts and printed editions of Cg and Ck read instead *saṃsṛṣṭāḥ*, which Cg glosses as *saṃmilitāḥ* in the sense of "grouped together." Ck un-

derstands, *saṃyuktāḥ*, "united." This reading is reflected in the translation of Raghunathan (1982, vol. 3, p. 108), who renders, "made a united attack."

17. "roaring in fury" *kruddhānām abhigarjatām*: Literally, "of them who were angry [and] roaring."

"of the upheaval of the seven seas" *saptānāṃ samudrāṇām*: Literally, "of the seven seas." The reference here is to the purāṇic cosmology, according to which the earth consists of seven continents, or *dvīpas*, separated by seven concentric oceans. In place of *saptānām*, "seven," D9–11 and the texts and printed editions of Ct substitute *sattvānām*, "of living beings," which must then be construed with *udvarte* in the somewhat redundant sense of "the universal destruction of [all] creatures." See note to 6.40.29.

"universal destruction" *udvarte*: We follow Ct, Cr, and Cg (second alternative) in understanding this term, whose normal sense is "remainder, surplus, excess," to refer here to the *pralaya*, or "the universal destruction (*pralayakāle*—so Ct, Cr)." Cg, however, relying evidently on the more normal usage of the term, gives, as his first alternative explanation, "increase, augmentation (*abhivṛddhau*)," by which he no doubt refers to the rising or flooding of the oceans' waters. Cv glosses, "destruction, dissolution (*saṃvartaḥ*)."

18–19. "sharp arrows" *śaraiḥ . . . śitaiḥ*: V3,D4,7,10,11,13,T1,G,M5, and the texts and printed editions of Ct read the redundant *śaraiḥ*, "arrows," for *śitaiḥ*, "sharp," in *pāda* 18d. Translations that follow Ct tend to eliminate the redundancy by ignoring the term here. Cv and Crā note that, in their opinion, *śitaiḥ* is the [proper] reading (*iti pāṭhaḥ*).

"six . . . night-roaming *rākṣasas*" *ṣaṭ . . . niśācarān*: Literally, "six night-roaming ones." Ct and Ck indicate that we should understand that these are six prominent *rākṣasas* (*pradhānā iti śeṣaḥ*).

"Yajñaśatru" "*yajñaśatruḥ*": D3,6,T2,3,G,M, and the texts and printed editions of Cg and Ck read instead *yamaśatruḥ*, "enemy of Yama." Accordingly, the name Yamaśatru appears in the translation of Raghunathan (1982, vol. 3, p. 108).

"Mahāpārśva, Mahodara" *mahāpārśvamahodarau*: Two *rākṣasa* warriors of these names were mentioned previously among those guarding Laṅkā's southern gate (6.27.17). The ones mentioned previously, however, are probably the *rākṣasas* killed in *sargas* 85 and 86 by Sugrīva and Aṅgada, respectively, while the two mentioned here are apparently different *rākṣasas* of the same name.

"giant" *mahākāyaḥ*: Literally, "having a large body." We follow Ct, Cg, and Ck in taking this term as an adjective modifying Vajradaṃṣṭra (*atra mahākāya iti vajradaṃṣṭraviśeṣaṇam*).

"both Śuka and Sāraṇa" *śukasāraṇau*: These are the names of Rāvaṇa's hapless spies whose misadventures were recounted in *sargas* 16–20 above. Ct notes that there is some disagreement among scholars, however, as to whether the warriors mentioned here are the same as the spies mentioned earlier. He notes that many authorities believe that these two are different from the two figures mentioned earlier, whereas others understand that they are the same two, who, having first been sent out as spies, were later rebuked by the king and so left the royal presence and died in battle. (*imau śukasāraṇau cāratvena preṣitābhyām anyāv evety bahavaḥ. tāv iti padasvārasyāc cāratvena preṣitāv evemau rājñā dhikkṛtāv api rājasaṃnidhiṃ parityajya yuddhe mṛtāv ity anye.*) See 6.27.19 and notes. But compare 6.28.13 and notes.

Cg notes that Śuka and Sāraṇa were mentioned earlier as having been posted to guard the northern gate (6.27.19) (*tāv uttaradvārarakṣakatvena pūrvoktāv ubhau śuka-sāraṇau*).

20. "crawled away" *apasṛtāḥ*: Literally, "departed, withdrew." Cr glosses, "desisted [from battle] (*nivṛttāḥ*)," whereas Cg offers, "fled (*palāyitāḥ*)."

"barely clinging to life" *sāvaśeṣāyuṣaḥ*: Literally, "whose lives had but a remainder." We follow the interpretations of Cr and Cg, who understand the compound to indicate that the wounded *rākṣasas* have, in fact, only a short time to live (*kiṃcin mātrāvaśiṣṭāyurbalā āsannamaraṇā ity arthaḥ*—so Cr). This is consistent, we believe, with the information in the verse that they have been pierced to the vitals. All translations consulted that follow this reading, however, have interpreted the compound more or less in the sense of "having barely escaped with their lives." Thus, for example, Dutt (1893, p. 1230) renders, "having only their lives left to them"; Roussel (1903, vol. 3, p. 126), "*n'ayant plus du souffle*"; Shastri (1959, vol. 3, p. 108), "barely escaping with their lives"; Raghunathan (1982, vol. 3, p. 108), "managed to escape with their bare lives"; Pagani (1999, p. 971), "*ne leur laissant qu'un souffle de vie*"; and Gita Press (1969, vol. 3, p. 1522), "and their life was saved." All these translations, in our opinion, misinterpret the passage in suggesting that the wounded *rākṣasas* actually survive their encounter with Rāma. Cf. verse 22 below.

21. "mighty Rāma" *mahābalaḥ*: Literally, "one of great strength." Ñ1,D1,3,4,7,9–11,13,T1,3,G1,2, and the texts and printed editions of Ct, Ck, and Cr read instead *mahārathaḥ*, "great chariot-warrior."

"all directions" *diśaḥ . . . pradiśaś ca*: Literally, "the cardinal directions and the intermediate directions."

"Then . . . with their shafts adorned with gold" *tataḥ kāñcanacitrāṅgaiḥ*: Literally, "Then . . . with gold-adorned bodies." D7,9–11, and the texts and printed editions of Ct, Ck, Cr read instead *nimeṣāntaramātreṇa* (= 18c) "in the blink of an eye."

"arrows" *śaraiḥ*: D7,9–11, and the texts and printed editions of Ct, Ck, and Cr read instead the adjective *ghoraiḥ*, "terrible," leaving the audience to supply the term "arrows."

22. "remaining" *anye*: Literally, "other."

"entering" *samāsādya*: Literally, "having approached."

23. "thousands" *sahasraśaḥ*: Literally, "by the thousand." Ñ,B,D7,9–11,T3,G3, and the texts and printed editions of Ct and Cr read instead *samantataḥ*, "in all directions, on all sides."

"fletched with gold" *suvarṇapuṅkhaiḥ*: Literally, "with golden feathers."

"sparkling with fireflies" *khadyotaiḥ*: Literally, "with fireflies."

24. "of the tawny monkeys" *harīṇām*: D9–11,M5, and the texts and printed editions of Ct and Cr read instead *bherīṇām*, "of the *bherīs* [drums]."

25. "deafening" *mahatā*: Literally, "great."

"Mount Trikūṭa" *trikūṭaḥ*: Literally, Trikūṭa." See 6.2.10; 6.30.18–20; 6.34.25; 6.61.66; and notes. See, too, notes to 6.29.13 and 6.78.41. See also 5.1.183,189; 5.2.1,8,18; 5.3.1; 5.37.49; and 5.54.9 and notes. Cf. note to 6.3.19.

"with its many echoing caverns" *kandarākīrṇaḥ*: Literally, "scattered with caves." We have added the word "echoing" to bring out more fully the sense of the common poetic trope of sounds reverberating in mountain caves. The printed text of GPP (6.44.26) reads the awkward *kandaraḥ kīrṇaḥ*, for which the critical apparatus finds attestation only in its manuscript D7. It is not clear to us whether this is, in fact, a typographical error in GPP, as GPP's apparatus notes no variants, while NSP's text (6.44.26) of Ct reads with the critical edition. We are not certain as to how one would interpret this reading, although Pagani seems to read it in such a way that the caves (reading plural for singular) of Mount Trikūṭa become the subject of the verb *pravyāharat*, "he/it spoke." Thus, she translates, "*les innombrables caverns du mont Trikūṭa poussaient des cris* . . ." (Pagani 1999, p. 971).

"seemed almost to shout in reply" *pravyāharad iva*: We agree with Cg in interpreting the verb *pra* + *vi* + *ā* √*hṛ* in the sense of "to respond, reply (*prativyāharat*)." Roussel (1903, vol. 3, p. 126), Shastri (1959, vol. 3, p. 109) and Pagani (1999, p. 971) take the verb in its sense of "to utter confused *or* inarticulate sounds."

26. "langurs" *golāṅgūlāḥ*: Literally, "cow-tailed [monkeys]." Elsewhere these monkeys are called *gopuccha-*, which has the same meaning. See the note on the identification of these primates at 1.16.10 and Goldman 1989. This is the *Presbytis entellus*, i.e., the Hanuman, or common gray langur, known for its black face and long tail.

"crushed" *saṃpariṣvajya*: Literally, "having embraced." The idea, as suggested by Cr, is that the monkeys crushed the *rākṣasas* to death by hugging them tightly (*pariṣvaṅgena nihatya*).

"rending them with their fangs" *bhakṣayan*: The most common meaning of the root √*bhakṣ* is "to eat." All translations of the southern recension consulted, with the exception of Gita Press (1969, vol. 3, p. 1522), understand the verb in this sense, that is, that the monkeys are actually eating the bodies of the *rākṣasas* they have killed. We find this to be an unlikely scenario in the context of the *Rāmāyaṇa*, where the monkeys, however violent, are always shown as subsisting on fruits, roots, and other plant foods (for example, at 6.15.31), whereas the *rākṣasas* are reviled for their bloodthirsty, carnivorous behavior (for example, at 6.48.25; 6.97.11; etc.). We believe that the context requires us to understand the root √*bhakṣ* in its less common but attested sense of "to bite." We have strengthened the language somewhat by adding the phrase "with their fangs." Some northern manuscripts, as well as the text of Gorresio (6.19.31), substitute forms of the root √*daṃś*, "to bite," which we believe to be an example of the well-known glossing character of the northern recension (see Pollock 1984a). For the most part, the commentators avoid any discussion of the term other than to gloss the irregular *bhakṣayan* with the correctly augmented *abhakṣayan* (Ct, Cg). Cr alone indicates his disquiet at the notion that the monkeys would eat the *rākṣasas*. He reads the simplex *bhakṣayan* (corrected to *abhakṣayan*) as a causative, in the sense of "to allow to eat *or* to feed," explaining that the monkeys kill the *rākṣasas* by crushing them and then feed them to dogs and other scavengers (*śvādibhir akhādayan*). Of all the translators consulted, only the author of the Gita Press translation (1969, vol. 3, p. 1522) follows this line of thinking, rendering, "allowed them to be devoured (by jackals and vultures, etc.)."

27. "enemy" *śatrum*: As Cr points out, the enemy in question is Indrajit, with whom Aṅgada had initially engaged at 6.33.18–19. We are in agreement with Cg that the action described here is the continuation of the single combat that began in the previous *sarga* (*pūrvaprasaktasyāṅgadendrajitor dvandvayuddhasya śeṣaṃ vaktum upakramate*).

"He swiftly slew the charioteer and horses of Indrajit Rāvaṇi." *rāvaṇer nijaghānāśu sārathiṃ ca hayān api*: Literally, "He swiftly killed Rāvaṇi's charioteer and horses as well." D6,10,11,T2,3,G,M5, and the texts and printed editions of Ct omit this line (27cd). Only Gita Press (1969, vol. 3, p. 1522) and Raghunathan (1982, vol. 3, p. 108) among the translators consulted render this line. However, they follow the reading shown in the text of Cg, where the accusative *rāvaṇim* is substituted for the genitive *rāvaṇeḥ*. According to this reading, Aṅgada strikes Indrajit as well as his horses and charioteer. Compare 6.33.19 above, where Aṅgada smashes Indrajit's chariot along with its horses and driver.

It is not clear whether Indrajit's charioteer here is actually slain (to be replaced by another later) or merely struck down, since, at 6.77.30, there is a more elaborate and graphic description of the slaying of Indrajit's charioteer. See 6.77.30 and notes.

Following verse 27, or in place of it, a variety of manuscripts read, in whole or in part, a passage of eight lines [731*] in which the battle between Aṅgada and Indrajit is further described. Manuscripts and printed texts of Cg (M3, VSP, KK) include only the first line of this passage: "As that terrible and fearsome battle continued..." (KK 6.44.29ab and VSP 6.44.29ab read *ghore*, "terrible," and *bhṛśadāruṇe*, "fearsome," respectively, for the critical edition's synonymous *raudre* and *[a]tibhayaṅkare*). This line is a variant of the formulaic line found above at 6.34.11ab.

28. "who possessed great powers of illusion" *mahāmāyaḥ*: A variety of manuscripts and the texts of the commentators show variants for this term. Cg, Cm, and Crā read *mahākāyaḥ*, "with a huge body." Among the translators consulted, only Raghunathan (1982, vol. 3, p. 108), following Cg, renders this variant as "huge." Ct, Ck, and the Gita Press edition read *mahāyastaḥ*, "greatly fatigued *or* distressed," misprinted in NSP (6.44.28) as *mahāyas*. This reading is rendered by those translators who follow the text of Ct, with the exception of Pagani (1999, p. 972), who translates, "*s'aidant de sa grande connaissance de la magie*." Although she follows the text of GPP, she appears to select that text's footnoted variant of Cr, who reads *mahāmāyaḥ* with the critical edition.

Following verse 28, B1,2,4,D2,5–7,9–11,S insert a passage of eight lines [734*]: "All the gods together with the seers and both Rāma and Lakṣmaṇa praised that feat of Aṅgada, Vālin's praiseworthy son.[1][1–2] All beings were aware of Indrajit's prowess in battle. Therefore, they were pleased to see that great warrior discomfited.[3–4] Then the monkeys, together with Sugrīva and Vibhīṣaṇa, seeing their foe discomfited, were delighted and cried out, 'Well done! Well done!'[5–6] But Indrajit, having been bested in battle by Vālin's son of fearsome deeds, flew into a terrifying rage.[7–8]"

[1]"Aṅgada, Vālin's... son" *vāliputrasya*: Literally, "of Vālin's son."

Following 734*, line 3, D7,M3, KK and VSP (in brackets between 6.44.31ab and cd) insert a passage of one line [734 (A)*]: "He [Indrajit] who, having become invisible to all beings, was now unconquerable in battle..." A footnote in KK (vol. 6, p. 173) notes that this half verse is not to be found in the oldest manuscripts. No translations consulted render this line.

Following 734* or 734 (A)*, D6,7,T2,M3, and the texts and printed editions of Cg, Cm, and Crā insert a passage of five lines [735*]: "At that point, Rāma addressed these words to the monkeys, 'All of you must stay close to the monkey king.[1–2] Since he was granted a boon[1] by Brahmā, Indrajit cruelly oppresses the three worlds.[3] Through the force of Kāla,[2] he has come here to accomplish his purpose at your expense.[3] I must, however, spare him today.[4] Still you need have no concern.[4–5]"

[1]"boon" *-varaḥ*: The boon is the gift of the divine serpent-weapons with which Indrajit will shortly bind and temporarily disable Rāma and Lakṣmaṇa (6.34.30 and 6.35.8–26 below). See 6.36.10 and note; and 7.30.10–13.

[2]"Kāla" *kālena*: Literally, "by destiny *or* time." We follow Cm, who explains, "by the force of time *or* destiny (*kālabalena*)," and accept the explanation of Cs, "by time *or* destiny, which makes manifest the boon of Brahmā (*kālena brahmavarojjṛmbhakena samāgataḥ*)."

[3]"accomplish his purpose at your expense"*bhavatām arthasiddhyartham*: One would normally read this phrase to mean "to accomplish a purpose on your behalf." However, given the context, and in keeping with the explanations of Cm and Cs, we understand that the reference is to Indrajit's purpose with respect to the monkeys, i.e., his victory over them (*bhavatām arthasiddhyartham samāgataḥ kālabalena bhavato jetuṃ samāgata ity arthaḥ*—so Cm).

[4]"I must, however, spare him" *kṣamitavyaṃ me*: Literally, "It must be pardoned *or* permitted by me." Both Cm and Cs explain that Rāma is unable to defeat Indrajit because of the respect that he owes [to the boon of] Brahmā (*brahmaṇo mānyatvād iti bhāvaḥ*). This is quite plausible and is in keeping with the theme of a warrior accepting capture or defeat by an enemy out of respect for the divinity who has granted that enemy a boon. Compare 5.46.36–41, where Hanumān similarly subjects himself to the power of Brahmā's divine weapons in the hands of Indrajit.

The passage occurs in GPP as unnumbered and bracketed between verses 6.44.32 and 6.44.33.

29. Ś,Ñ1,V,B3,4,D1,3,4,8,12,13 all omit this verse. According to the principles of the critical editors, this would give reasonable cause to relegate the verse to the apparatus (see Bhatt 1960, p. xxxiv). According to the editors of GPP (6.44.33cd), *pādas* cd (*brahmadattavaro vīro rāvaṇiḥ krodhamūrcchitaḥ* "[Indrajit] Rāvaṇi, a hero... possessed a boon from Brahmā. Seething with rage...") are not known to the text of Cg; indeed, the half verse is omitted from VSP (see 6.44.37, where it would have occurred following *pādas* ab). KK includes the half verse in brackets following 6.44.37ab and notes that it is found in seven of the manuscripts collated for the edition. The critical edition notes that this half verse is omitted from D5,6,T1,2,M1–3.

"Indrajit Rāvaṇi" *rāvaṇiḥ... rāvaṇiḥ*: Literally, "Rāvaṇi [son of Rāvaṇa]... Rāvaṇi." We have substituted the name Indrajit for one of the repeated patronymics.

"ruthless in battle" *raṇakarkaśaḥ*: B1,D9–11, and the texts and printed editions of Ct read instead *raṇakarśitaḥ* (*-karṣitaḥ*—so critical apparatus), "worn out, fatigued, *or* harassed in battle."

"possessed a boon from Brahmā" *brahmadattavaraḥ*: See note to 6.36.10.

"Seething with rage" *krodhamūrchitaḥ*: Literally, "stupefied with rage."

30. "the *rākṣasa*" *rākṣasaḥ*: D9–11 and the texts and printed editions of Ct read instead the accusative dual *rāghavau*, "the two Rāghavas."

"in the form of great serpents" *nāgamayaiḥ*: Literally, "made *or* consisting of *nāgas*."

Following verse 30, D5–7,9–11,S (G2 omits) insert a passage of one line [737*]: "Shrouded there through the power of illusion, and deluding the two Rāghavas in battle . . ."

Following 737*, all the above manuscripts continue, while a number of other manuscripts include, in various locations, a passage of two lines [738*]: "Invisible to all beings and fighting deceitfully, the night-roaming *rākṣasa* bound the brothers, Rāma and Lakṣmaṇa, in bonds made of arrows."

Following 738*, D5–7,9–11,S continue with a passage of two lines [739*]: "The monkeys then saw those two heroes, tigers among men, suddenly struck down by that enraged *rākṣasa*[1] with his arrows in the form of venomous serpents."

[1]"by that . . . *rākṣasa*" *tena*: Literally, "by him."

Following 739*, all the above manuscripts continue, while a number of other manuscripts include in various locations, a passage of four lines [740*] in *upajāti* meter: "When the son of the *rākṣasa* king proved unable to harm those two as long as he remained visible, that evil *rākṣasa*[1] resorted to the power of illusion and thus bound the two princes."

[1]"evil *rākṣasa*" *durātmā*: D4,5,G,M3,5, and the texts and printed editions of Cg read instead *mahātmā*, "the great one," which Cg glosses as "very wise (*mahābuddhiḥ*)." Of the translators consulted, only Raghunathan (1982, vol. 3, p. 109) follows this reading, rendering, "the powerful one."

Sarga 35

1. "where Indrajit had gone" *tasya gatim*: Literally, "his place *or* path."

"ordered . . . to search for him" *dideśa*: Literally, "he instructed *or* ordered." We follow Cr in supplying the ellipsis (*anveṣayitum jñāpayāmāsa*).

2–3. "to the two sons of Suṣeṇa" *dvau suṣeṇasya dāyādau*: The term *dāyāda* can refer specifically to a son, to any male heir, or, generically, to any male relative. We agree here with Cg and Cr, who cite *Amarakośa* 3.3.88 in support of the first meaning (*dāyādau putrau dāyādau putrabāndhavāv ity amaraḥ*—Cr). The names of the two sons are not specified here nor apparently elsewhere. At 6.28.2 the same term, *dāyāda*, is used in connection with Suṣeṇa (*suṣeṇaḥ sahadāyādaḥ*). See 6.28.1–3 and note.

"that bull among monkeys" *plavagarṣabham*: V3,D7,9–11, and the texts and printed editions of Ct instead read *plavagādhipam*, "lord of the monkeys." This term normally refers to the monkey king, Sugrīva, but here it appears to be an epithet of Nīla, with the sense of "monkey leader, general."

"Vinata, Jāmbavān" *vinataṃ jāmbavantaṃ ca*: B2,D2,4,9–12,T3,M1,2, and the texts and printed editions of Ct and Cv read instead *dvividaṃ ca hanūmantam*, "Dvivida and Hanumān."

4. "they . . . flung themselves into the sky" *ākāśaṃ viviśuḥ*: Literally, "they entered the sky."

5. "Indrajit Rāvaṇi" *rāvaṇiḥ*: Literally, "Rāvaṇi."

"expert in divine weapon-spells... the greatest of such weapon-spells" *astravit paramāstreṇa*: Literally, "knowing the *astra*, with the supreme *astra*." We understand the term *astra* to refer to the divine esoteric spell, or *mantra*, infused into material weapons to lend them supernatural power. See note to 5.36.26. Ct and Cr understand the term to refer here to the fearsome *brahmāstra* and supply an adjective, *mantritaiḥ* (Ct) or *abhimantritaiḥ* (Cr), which links the term "with arrows (*iṣubhiḥ*)" with the instrumental *paramāstreṇa*, to yield the sense "arrows into which was invoked [the spell governing] the *brahmāstra*." Cg reads instead the plural *paramāstrais tu*, which obliges him to take the term in apposition with *iṣubhiḥ*, "with arrows." He thus glosses, "arrows in the form of supreme divine weapons (*paramāstrarūpair iṣubhiḥ*)." Of the translators consulted, only Raghunathan (1982, vol. 3, p. 109) follows Cg, translating, "arrows powered with mighty celestial missiles." Roussel (1903, vol. 3, p. 128), followed by Shastri (1959, vol. 3, p. 110) and Pagani (1999, p. 973), understands *paramāstra* here to refer to Indrajit's bow, an interpretation we do not find persuasive. Dutt (1893, p. 1232) understands the *paramāstra* and the arrows to be separate and unrelated, translating, "by means of a powerful weapon... as well as arms." Gita Press (1969, vol. 3, p. 1524) incorporates Ct's interpretation in his translation, rendering, "by means of his very swift arrows charged with the potency of the supreme mystic weapon (presided over by Brahmā)." Gorresio (1856, vol. 9, p. 263) interprets similarly to Dutt.

"the swift movement of those swift monkeys with arrows that were swifter still" *teṣāṃ vegavatāṃ vegam iṣubhir vegavattaraiḥ*: Literally, "the speed of those speeding ones with speedier arrows."

6. "Pierced and mutilated" *kṣatavikṣatāḥ*: Literally, "wounded and injured." It is difficult to determine any clear distinction between the two nearly synonymous terms. Only Cr among the commentators attempts to do so, glossing, "having minor and major injuries (*alpādhikavraṇayuktāḥ*)." In any case, the sense clearly is that the monkeys are covered with multiple wounds. See note to 6.2.14.

"those tawny monkeys... could not discern him, obscured as he was by darkness, as is the sun by clouds" *tam... harayaḥ... andhakāre na dadṛśur meghaiḥ sūryam ivāvṛtam*: Literally, "the tawny [ones] did not see him in the darkness as if [he were] the sun shrouded by clouds." Our translation follows the gloss of Cr (*harayo meghair āvṛtaṃ sūryam ivāndhakāra āvṛtaṃ rāvaṇiṃ taṃ na dadṛśuḥ*).

7 "completely overwhelmed... with arrows" *śarān... bhṛśam āveśayamasa*: Literally, "to a great degree he caused arrows to enter."

"that pierced every vital point" *sarvamarmabhidaḥ*: Only a handful of manuscripts consulted by the critical editors actually appear to contain this reading. A variety of northern and southern manuscripts (Ñ1,B3,D5–7,9–11,T,G2,3,M3,5), and the texts and printed editions of the commentators read *-deha-*, "body," for *-marma-*, "vital point." This yields the meaning "piercing their entire bodies." Cr, however, interprets the word *sarva-*, "every, all," here not to refer to the entire bodies of Rāma and Lakṣmaṇa but rather to all creatures, understanding, "arrows that pierced the bodies of all beings, the gods, etc. (*sarveṣāṃ devādīnāṃ dehaṃ bhindanti tāñ charān*)."

8. "Indrajit riddled... Rāma and Lakṣmaṇa, with great serpents that had turned into arrows. Their bodies were thus thickly covered with arrows that had not a hair's breadth between them." *nirantaraśarīrau... rāmalakṣmaṇau... indrajitā... pannagaiḥ śaratāṃ gataiḥ*: The verse is rather elliptical. A literal reading of the skeletal syntactic

structure would be "by Indrajit, Rāma and Lakṣmaṇa [were rendered] ones whose bodies had no intervals by means of serpents that had become arrows." The verse, in fact, contains no finite verb or verbal noun. Several of the commentators supply the participle *kṛtau*, "were made *or* rendered." We have added the word "riddled" to complete the syntax of the sentence. Cr explains the sense of the compound *nir-antaraśarīrau*, "the two whose bodies had no intervals," to be that the upper bodies of Rāma and Lakṣmaṇa were devoid of any open spaces (*uparibhāge 'ntararahitadehau kṛtau*). We have attempted to interpret the term idiomatically. The idea, of course, is not that the brothers' bodies are pressed closely together but rather that their bodies are completely covered with Indrajit's arrows.

Cv understands the phrase "with great serpents that had turned into arrows (*pannagaiḥ śaratāṃ gataiḥ*)," we believe correctly, to refer to arrows that strike and wound their victims before turning to serpents, which then bind them in their coils. He says, "Having first discharged the functions of piercing, cutting, etc., they subsequently carry out the functions of serpents, biting, constricting, etc. (*bhedacchedādi-kāryaṃ kṛtvā paścād daṃśanaveṣṭanādikaṃ pannagakāryaṃ kurvadbhiḥ*)." Crā also understands the missiles to carry out both functions: that of arrows, i.e., cutting, and that of serpents, i.e., constricting (*śarakāryaṃ bhedanaṃ pannagakāryaṃ saṃveṣṭanaṃ ca kurvadbhir ity arthaḥ*). Cg merely understands that the serpents now carry out the functions of arrows, such as cutting, etc. (*śarakāryaṃ bhedanādikaṃ kurvadbhir ity arthaḥ*). The dual function of the missiles thus accounts for the fact that the heroes are both wounded and immobilized. See below, verse 19 and note. See, too, 6.40.37,49 and notes. Compare 6.90.16 and note.

"the brothers" *bhrātarau*: D6,7,9–11,T2,3,G3,M1,2,5, the texts and printed editions of Ct, Ck, and Cr, and some manuscripts representing the text of Cg read instead *tāv ubhau*, "those two." Printed editions of Cg read with the critical edition, but KK (6.45.8) indicates in its apparatus that ten of the manuscripts consulted read *tāv ubhau* with the vulgate. Raghunathan (1982, vol. 3, p. 110) is thus the only translator consulted to render *bhrātarau*, "brothers."

9. "wounds, the pathways of blood" *kṣatajamārgeṇa*: The compound can be read in two ways. Ct, Cg, and Cm analyze the term *kṣataja-* as an instrumental *tatpuruṣa* compound in the sense of "born from *or* produced by a wound (*kṣatajamārgeṇa kṣatena vraṇena jāto yo mārgas tena*—so Ct)." The resulting compound then becomes the prior member of a *karmadhāraya*, the sense of which is "a path produced by a wound." We find this analysis to be somewhat forced and agree with Cr, who interprets *kṣataja*, "born from a wound," to refer to blood (*rudhira*). Vālmīki uses this kenning for blood elsewhere (cf., for example, 5.8.17; 6.42.37; etc.). The larger compound can then be taken as a genitive *tatpuruṣa* with the sense of "the path of blood." This, in turn, can be seen as a kenning for wound.

"blood" *rudhiram*: Cr and Cg are concerned about the potential theological implications of divinities such as Rāma and Lakṣmaṇa bleeding. Cr contents himself with noting that Rāma and Lakṣmaṇa make their blood appear to flow through their power of magical illusion (*māyayā*). He understands the verb "flow (*susrāva*)" as a simplex with a causal meaning. (*rudhiraviṣayakavicāreṇa rāmalakṣmaṇaśarīre bhītijanaka-rudhirapradarśanāyety arthaḥ. tayo rāmalakṣmaṇayor upari bahurudhiraṃ susrāva māyayā srāvayāmāsāntarbhāvitaṇijarthaḥ sravatiḥ.*) Cg takes the matter rather more seriously.

He anticipates the objection expressed in a verse he quotes to the effect that, since the supreme divinity does not have, like other creatures, an ordinary body of flesh and blood, how can he possibly bleed? Cg responds that, although it is true that Rāma and Lakṣmaṇa do not really have blood, they manifest it as an actor might, in keeping with their having taken on the condition of mortals. The objector counters by questioning the purpose of the divinity's obsessive demonstration of his human condition. Cg offers several explanations. First, he notes that, if Rāma did not exhibit such signs of mortality, the common people would think that he was a god, not a man, and, consequently, the dharmic behavior he has come to exemplify would be impossible for them to emulate. This, he suggests, is an esoteric explanation of Rāma's behavior. Second, Cg reminds us that Rāvaṇa can [by virtue of his boon] be destroyed only by a human being. Third, Cg observes that by first succumbing to, and then escaping from, the bondage of Indrajit's serpent-weapons, Rāma is providing an example for people that calamities may come and go swiftly. (*nanu na bhūtasaṅghasaṃsthāno deho 'sya paramātmanaḥ. na tasya prākṛtā mūrtir māṃsamedosthisaṃbhavetyādibhī rāmalakṣmaṇayor divyavigrahasyāprākṛtatvasmaraṇāt kathaṃ rudhirodgama iti ced atrāhuḥ. vastuto 'nayo rudhirābhāve 'pi manuṣyabhāvanānurodhena naṭa iva rudhirāṇi darśayataḥ sma. nanv evaṃ nirbandhena manuṣyabhāvaṃ bhāvayataḥ kiṃ prayojanam? śṛṇu. sarvātmanā manuṣyabhāvanānanurodhe jana evaṃ manyeta nāyaṃ martyaḥ kiṃ tu devas tena tadvad asmākaṃ na śakyam anuṣṭhātuṃ dharmān iti. sarvathā manuṣyabhāvanāyāṃ tu mahājanānuṣṭhānadarśanena svayam anuṣṭhāsyati loka iti rahasyam. rāvaṇasya manuṣyaikavadhyatvena tadbhāvanety apy āhuḥ. nāgapāśabaddhatayāvasthānaṃ tu dharmaniratānām api kadācid āpad upatiṣṭhati nivartate ca jhaṭitīti lokānāṃ pradarśanāyeti. evaṃ mohādiṣv api draṣṭavyam.*) See notes below to verses 17, 19, and 20. See, too, 6.36.4–7; 6.37.19; 6.39.4,6; 6.75.17; 6.76.25,32; 6.79.1; 6.88.33; 6.89.24; and notes. Cf. note to 6.38.7. See Leslie 1999.

"resembled *kiṃśuka* trees covered with their bright red blossoms" *puṣpitāv iva kiṃśukau*: Literally, "like two blossoming *kiṃśuka* trees." The *kiṃśuka*, or *palāśa* tree (*Butea frondosa*), is noted for its bright red, odorless blossoms and, in the epic, frequently serves as an *upamāna* for wounded and bleeding warriors. See 6.55.22; 6.60.34; 6.62.19; 6.76.28; and notes.

10. "as hard to discern as a scattered mass of collyrium" *bhinnāñjanacayopamaḥ . . . antardhānagataḥ*: Literally, "like a shattered heap of collyrium . . . invisible." The image is not entirely clear. Translators have rendered it in various ways. Our best understanding is that the poet refers to the obscurity with which Indrajit has shrouded himself by using the image of a diffuse cloud of black collyrium powder. Cg is silent on the term here, but when it is repeated below, at verse 14, he explains, "the term is used because of the likelihood of a grayish dusty area at the top of [a pile] of collyrium (*añjanoparipradeśasya dhūsara*-[misprinted as *dūra* in GPP]*tvasaṃbhavād bhinnety uktam*)." Cr glosses, "similar to a mass of compounded *or* prepared collyrium (*siddhāñjanasamūhasadṛśaḥ*)." Dutt (1893, p. 1233) and Raghunathan (1982, vol. 3, p. 110) take the participle *bhinna*- in two of its other related meanings. The former translates, "crushed," and the latter, "cloven." Roussel (1903, vol. 3, p. 128), perhaps following Cr, renders, "*mêlé d'huile*." In this interpretation, he is, as is so often the case, followed by Shastri (1959, vol. 3, p. 110). Pagani (1999, p. 973) and Gita Press (1969, vol. 3, p. 1524) simply omit the adjective. Many northern manuscripts and printed editions of Gorresio and Lahore substitute *nīla*-, "black." See verse 14 below.

"his eyes rimmed with red" *paryantaraktākṣaḥ*: According to Cg, this description [as opposed to a description of the full reddening of the eyes] is intended to suggest that Indrajit is now only slightly angry (*aneneṣatkopatvaṃ lakṣyate*). See 6.31.72 and note.

12. "Rāghavas! . . . you both" *rāghavau*: We agree with Cg in understanding this as a vocative. There is thus no real object in the verse for the verb *nayāmi*, "I lead" (see below). Cg instructs us that we are to supply the pronoun from the previous verse, making the appropriate transformation from nominative to accusative. (*rāghavāv iti saṃbodhanam. atrāpi yuvām iti dvitīyāntatayā vipariṇamyānuṣañjanīyam.*)

"In my towering rage" *roṣaparītātmā*: Literally, "whose mind is overcome with anger."

"I shall send" *eṣaḥ . . . nayāmi*: Literally, "he [i.e., I] shall lead." The use of the third person pronoun for the first person is not uncommon in Sanskrit [with or without the first or second personal pronoun]. Here Cg argues that the pronoun is used to show that Indrajit [although unseen] is quite close to the brothers (*eṣa ity avyavadhānadyotanāya*).

"tightly bound" *prāvṛtau*: Literally, "enclosed, encircled." D9–11 and the texts and printed editions of Ct read instead *prāpitau*, literally, "caused to attain." This reading is inferior and defective, and obligates Ct to supply the word *bandhanam*, "bondage." This yields a sense quite similar to that of the critical reading. Cm observes that, although the manifest meaning here is quite clear, we should understand, in fact, that Indrajit means merely to bind the two Rāghavas with his arrows. It is the monkeys, Cm continues, that Indrajit plans to send to Yama. (*prātītikārthaḥ spaṣṭaḥ. vastutas tu rāghavāv iṣujālena prāvṛtau kevalam. yamasādanaṃ nayāmi vānarān iti śeṣaḥ.*)

"heron-fletched" *kaṅkapatriṇā*: The term *kaṅka* is normally thought to refer to the gray heron (*Ardea cinera*) (see Dave 1985, p. 400). However, Fitzgerald has argued persuasively that, when the term refers to a carrion bird in the *Mahābhārata*, the bird in question is most likely one or another of the species of the adjutant stork, and this usage is seen in the *Yuddhakāṇḍa* as well. See notes to 6.46.25–28. When the reference is merely to the fletching of arrows, with no description of the bird or its habits, we have preferred to translate, "heron," although the identification of the actual bird remains unclear. It is possible that the poet is making a subtle play on words here, since the word *kaṅka* is also a synonym for Yama, who is mentioned later in the verse. See 6.42.4 and note. Cf. 6.46.28; 6.47.127; 6.55.80; 6.87.26; 6.97.1; and notes.

13. "who understood righteousness" *dharmajñau*: Cg understands that this stereotypical epithet of the epic heroes is used here to suggest that they cannot bear [the thought of] employing their skill in shooting an unseen object by sound alone (*śabdavedhaprayogāsahiṣṇū*). If we understand his reasoning correctly, he is trying to explain why Rāma and Lakṣmaṇa do not deploy this advanced skill in archery to shoot down Indrajit, whether he is visible or not. Cg evidently believes that this skill is unsportsmanlike and non-dharmic, and so the perfectly righteous brothers disdain it, even though this may cost them their lives. Cf. note to 6.34.9.

14. "As obscure as a scattered mass of collyrium" *bhinnāñjanacayaśyāmaḥ*: Literally, "dark *or* black as a shattered heap of collyrium." We have rendered *śyāmaḥ*, "dark," here as "obscure," in keeping with our reading of the similar epithet at verse 10 above. In both cases, we believe that the reference is to Indrajit's obscurity or invisibility. See note to verse 10 above for Cg's comments in this regard.

16. "they could not even see" *na śekatur udīkṣitum*: Ct understands the purpose of this phrase [with his synonymous v.l. *avekṣitum*] to indicate that Rāma and Lakṣmaṇa are merely feigning or acting out the condition of humans (*tādṛśāv iva sthitau manuṣyatvanāṭanāyeti bodhyam*). Cr, who shares Ct's variant reading, thinks that we should read the infinitive as an unmarked causative, giving the phrase the sense that the heroes were unable to manifest their true nature (*ātmānaṃ darśayituṃ na śekatuḥ*). His idea is that the heroes forego their true power and that this suggests their strict adherence to the bounds of morality. (*sāmārthyaṃ dadatur antarbhāvitaṇijarthaḥ. etena rāmasya maryādāpālakatvaṃ dhvanitam.*) The reference is, no doubt, to Rāma's unwillingness to transgress the boon of Brahmā by evading Indrajit's divine weapons. See note to 6.34.28, 734(A)*. See, too, note to 6.36.10.

17. "pierced with arrows and darts" *śaraśalyācitau*: Literally, "covered *or* heaped up with arrows and darts." Cr glosses, "covered, pervaded (*vyāptau*)." We are inclined to agree with Cg, who glosses, "rendered transfixed by arrowheads (*śarāgraprotau kṛtau*)." Cr understands the heroes to be injured with two different types of arrows (*śaras* and *śalyas*) (*śaraśalyābhyāṃ bāṇaviśeṣābhyāṃ*).

"trembled" *prakampitau*: Cr gives the participle a causative spin, in the sense of "causing their own army to tremble (*svasenāprakampanakartārau*)."

"cut loose from their sustaining cords" *rajjumuktau*: Literally, "freed from ropes." Cg, reading ahead to verse 18, and Cr understand the *upamāna* to be Indra's banners, which, freed from their cords, are now fluttering about [on the ground—see notes to verse 18 below]. (*rajjumuktau muktarajjū. ata eva prakampitau mahendrasya dhvajāv iva kṛtau*—so Cg.)

18. "Weakened by the piercing of their vitals" *marmabhedena karśitau*: Literally, "drawn *or* pained by the piercing of [their] vitals." Cr, unhappy with his heroes being weakened, adds the particle *iva* so that the phrase would mean "as if weakened." See note to verse 9 above.

"lords of the earth . . . fell to the earth" *nipetatuḥ . . . jagatyāṃ jagatīpatī*: The poet plays with the repetition of the word *jagatī*, "earth, world," to enhance the pathos of the heroes' situation. Cr, still unwilling to entertain the notion of Rāma's suffering, once again reads the simplex *nipetatuḥ*, "fell," as a causative. He thus explains, "the two of them caused the monkeys to fall down by displaying their condition (*tādṛksvāvasthādarśanena vānarān nipātayāmāsatuḥ*)."

"staggered" *sampracalitau*: Cr, who as elsewhere dislikes the idea of his divine heroes suffering, glosses, "who set the minds of all beings in motion (*sarveṣāṃ buddhicālakau*)." See note to verse 9 above. D1,5,7,10,11, and the texts and printed editions of Ct read instead *samprabalitau*, "mighty."

19. "Their every limb constricted by arrows" *śaraveṣṭitasarvāṅgau*: The idea here, as noted by Ct, Cv, Cg, and Cm, is that the heroes are constricted by the serpents that have taken the form of arrows (*śarabhūtasarpaveṣṭitasarvagātrau*—so Ct). See verse 8 above and note.

"suffering and in great agony" *ārtau paramapīḍitau*: Cr offers a grammatical explanation according to which the two participles are to be seen as derived from a denominative root formed from the *kvip* suffix, which, in accordance with the *vārttika* on *Pā* 3.1.11, is used to indicate imitative behavior. (*paramapīḍitāv iva ca babhūvatur iti śeṣaḥ. ārtaparamapīḍitaśabdāv ācārakvibantaprakṛtikakartṛkvibantau.*) This, of course, is in keeping with Cr's insistence that the heroes are merely miming suffering (see note to verse 9 above). Cg distinguishes the two near synonyms by characterizing the former as mental suffering and the latter as physical suffering (*ārtau manaḥpīḍāvantau paramapīḍitau śārīrakapīḍāvantau*). See notes to 6.39.5 and 6.47.126. See also note to 6.2.14.

"the battlefield, a hero's bed" *vīraśayane*: Literally, "a hero's bed." We have followed the interpretation of Ct, Cg, and Cm, who read the term as a kenning for battlefield (*vīrāḥ śerate 'sminn iti vīraśanayaṃ raṇabhūmiḥ*—Cg). Cv and Cg, as an alternative, offer "bed of arrows (*śaratalpaṃ vā*)," reminiscent of the famous *iṣuśayyā*, the "bed of arrows," upon which the dying Bhīṣma rests in the *Mahābhārata* (6.115.8ff.). See verse 24 below and 6.36.4–7 and note. See, too, 6.37.18; 6.38.27; 6.39.12; and notes.

"spattered with blood" *rudhirokṣitau*: Cr, of course, hastens to explain that the blood has been produced only through the power of illusion (*māyāpātitaraktenokṣitau siktau tau*). See note to verse 9 above.

*20. "There was not a finger's breadth between the wounds that covered their bodies." *na hy aviddhaṃ tayor gātraṃ babhūvāṅgulam antaram*: Literally, "there was not an unpierced limb, having a gap of [even] a finger, of those two." The text of the critical edition, particularly the collocation of the words *gātram, aṅgulam* [*āṅgulam*?], and *antaram*, is syntactically problematic and textually questionable. As far as one can reconstruct the situation from the critical apparatus, this particular collocation appears to be found only in B2 and D5,6. D6 is one of the manuscripts associated with the commentary of Cg. However, printed editions of Cg's text (VSP and KK = 6.46.20) have the *facilior* reading *gātre*, found also in the text of Ct, including GPP [6.46.20], which notes no variant for Cg. This variant is also found in the printed editions of the northern recension [= Lahore 6.21.22 and Gorresio 6.20.22]. The critical apparatus of KK notes the variant with *gātram* in seven of its manuscripts, but these then lack the critical edition's *aṅgulam antaram*, reading instead *aṅgulamātrakam*. The situation is further complicated in that the vowel *sandhi* makes it unclear whether the word in question is *aṅgulam* or *āṅgulam*. According to Cg's text in KK and Cs's reading, there is the option of reading the adjective *āṅgula* in the sense of "connected with *or* in the measure of a finger's breadth." Cg's commentary itself appears to indicate that he reads both *gātram* and *a*[or *ā*]*ṅgulam antaram*. Cg struggles with this awkward construction, offering two less than persuasive interpretations. In the first, after arguing that we should take the word *aṅgula*, on the basis of a citation from the *Amarakośa* (*Trikāṇḍī*), which we cannot locate, as signifying the space occupied by a finger, he states that the heroes' bodies were not uninjured even in the space of a finger's breadth. For his second interpretation, he takes *āṅgulam* [so KK and Cs, *contra* GPP and VSP] as an adjective modifying *antaram*, in the sense of a space "connected with the fingers (*aṅgulasaṃbandhi*)." (*aṅgulam aṅgulipramāṇam. athavāṅgulir aṅgulam iti trikāṇḍīsmaraṇād aṅgulipramāṇavācyaṅgulaśabdo 'kārānto 'py asti. tayor gātram aṅgulamātre 'py avakāśe 'viddhaṃ nābhūd iti bhāvaḥ. yadvā tayor gātram aṅgulam aṅgulasaṃbandhy apy antaram avakāśaḥ.*) Cs glosses *āṅgulam* as "the measure of a finger (*aṅgulipramāṇam*)." On the basis of the textual evidence and the syntactic impossibility of the critical reading, we propose emending—with the southern commentators as in the printed editions of their text (a reading also found in Ś,Ñ,V,B1–3,4,D1,3,8,10–13,M3)—*gātre* for *gātram* and reading *āṅgulam* as an adjective modifying *antaram*. The literal meaning thus becomes "on their bodies, there was not a space of the measure of a finger that was unpierced."

In keeping with his consistent effort to portray Rāma as invulnerable, Cr offers an idiosyncratic interpretation of the verse. He takes *antaram*, "space, interval," in the sense it frequently has at the end of compounds of "other, different." He then interprets this as a description of the heroes' bodies as being "different *or* distinct from ordinary bodies, and therefore perpetually uninjured. (*antaraṃ prākṛtavilakṣaṇam ity arthaḥ. ata evāviddhaṃ nityaṃ bhedasaṃsargarahitam.*)" See note to verse 9 above.

It is noteworthy that Dutt (1893, p. 1233) remarks, in a footnote, that "This *sloka* is rather obscure, and the Bengali translators have conveniently passed it by!"

"There was no part...that had not been wounded" *nānirbhinnam*: Literally, "not unwounded." This then construes with the negative particle *na* in *pāda* a governing the finite verb *babhūva* in *pāda* b. Ñ1,V1,B4,D10,11, and the texts and printed editions of Ct, Ck, and Cr read instead *nānirviṇṇam*, which would normally mean "not undejected." Ck, however, glosses, "without wounds (*avidāram*)." Translators who follow Ct's text offer a similar interpretation. Cr interprets the term idiosyncratically, explaining it as meaning "[whose bodies are] a constant source of passion *or* delight to their kinsmen (*nityaṃ svajanānurāgi* [*tayor gātram*])."

"immobilized" *na...astabdham*: Literally, "not unparalyzed." Ś1,Ñ2,V2,B1,2,D3, M1,2, and the texts and printed editions of Ct and Ck read instead *adhvastam*, "[not] undamaged *or* uninjured." Ct is aware of the critical reading as a variant, and he glosses it as "moving *or* writhing (*ceṣṭāvat*)." Cv provides a unique interpretation, understanding, "having skin rendered immobile because of having arrowheads not removed (*anirgataśarāgrasamuttambhicarmety arthaḥ*)."

21. "copiously" *tīvram*: We follow Cg in reading this adverbially in its sense of "intensely *or* violently (*atyantam*)." It is also possible, although not as convincing, to read the term as an adjective in the sense of "warm *or* hot," modifying "blood."

"two fountains" *prasravaṇau*: The term, which literally means "flowing forth," can refer to any source of water: a fountain, spring, waterfall, etc. It is also, of course, the name of a mountain near where Rāma, Sītā, and Lakṣmaṇa lived up until the time of Sītā's abduction at *Araṇyakāṇḍa* 47. The mountain is so named because of its copious streams. See, for example, 3.29.21; 3.47.30; and 3.60.14. Ct, Cg, and Cm all interpret in this latter sense, i.e., "like two Mount Prasravaṇas (*prasravaṇau prasravaṇākhyaparvatāv iva*—so Ct)." Translators are divided, some translating "spring," and others, "Mount Prasravaṇa."

22. "Rāma...pierced to the vitals" *rāmo viddho marmasu*: Cr takes advantage of the *visarga sandhi* between *rāmaḥ* and *viddhaḥ* (i.e., *rāmo 'viddho marmasu*) to provide an alternative reading, "[Rāma] not pierced to the vitals (*marmasv apy aviddho rāmaḥ*)."

"fell first" *papāta prathamam*: Cr, continuing with his theological reading, argues that Rāma falls in keeping with his role as the maintainer of the bounds of moral behavior. The reference is, no doubt, to his unwillingness to transgress the boon of Brahmā (see note to verse 16 above). He falls first, according to Cr, after reflecting that, unless Lakṣmaṇa sees him fall, he himself will not fall (*etena rāmasya maryādāpālakatvaṃ sūcitaṃ prathamam ity anena matkartṛkapatanadarśanam antarā lakṣmaṇo na patiṣyatīti hetur vyañjitaḥ*).

"raging" *krodhāt*: Literally, "out of anger."

"who had once defeated Śakra" *yena purā śakro vinirjitaḥ*: Ct and Cg note that this phrase explains how Rāvaṇa's son, whose given name is Meghanāda, "Thunderer," acquired his epithet Indrajit, literally, "conqueror of Indra." The story of his subjugation of the god is told at *Uttarakāṇḍa* 29–30.

Following verse 22, Ñ2,V,B1,2,4,D5–7,9,11,S insert, while Ñ1,B3,D13 insert following verse 23 (many northern manuscripts repeat it in various locations), a passage of one line [751*], which expands the description of Indrajit's arrows that follows in verse 23 below: "[with arrows] golden fletched, swift, with burnished heads, and having a straight flight.[1]"

[1]"having a straight flight" *añjogatibhiḥ*: Literally, "with straight gait *or* course." D7,9,11,G2,3, and the texts and printed editions of Ct, Cm, and Cr read instead *rajogatiḥ*, "moving like [a] dust [cloud]." Ct understands that the arrows fly like a dust cloud driven by the wind, that is, with no interval between them (*vāyunā vistīryamāṇarajovan nīrandhraṃ saṃpatadbhiḥ*). The texts and printed editions of Cg read instead *adhogatiḥ*, "moving downward." This variant is not noted in the critical apparatus. Cg explains, "moving downward because the shooter was in the sky (*prahartur ākāśasthatvena adhogatiḥ*).

23. "with iron arrows" *nārācaiḥ*: These are generally thought to be arrows that are either made of iron or iron-tipped. Cr defines them merely as a type of arrow (*bāṇaviśeṣaiḥ*), while Cg is more specific, characterizing them as arrows with straight and rounded heads (*ṛjuvṛttāgraiḥ*)."

"[with] half-iron arrows" *ardhanārācaiḥ*: According to the commentaries, these are arrows half of which are similar to *nārācas* (*ardhabhāge nārācatulyaiḥ* [*sadṛśaiḥ*—Cr] Ck, Ct). Cg believes that they are similar to *nārācas* cut or split in the middle (*madhye bhinnanārācatulyaiḥ*).

"[with] crescent-headed arrows" *bhallaiḥ*: Cg understands, "axe-headed arrows (*paraśvadhāgraiḥ*)."

"[with] arrows with heads like folded palms" *añjalikaiḥ*: The commentators agree that these are arrows with heads shaped like the cupped or folded hands of the familiar *añjali mudrā* (*añjalyākāramukhaiḥ*—so Ct).

"[with arrows with heads like] calves' teeth" *vatsadantaiḥ*: The commentators agree that these are arrows with heads shaped like calves' teeth (*vatsadantasadṛśāgraiḥ*—so Cg).

"[with arrows with heads like] lions' fangs" *siṃhadaṃṣṭraiḥ*: The commentators agree that these are arrows with heads shaped like lions' fangs (*siṃhadaṃṣṭrāsadṛśāgraiḥ*—so Cg).

"[with arrows with heads like] razors" *kṣuraiḥ*: Cg and Crā note that these arrows have razor or razorlike heads (*kṣurāgraiḥ*—Cg). Cv understands that they have heads shaped like the half-moon (*ardhacandraiḥ*). Cf. 6.57.57 and note; and 6.55.117 and note.

Excavations have shown evidence of iron-tipped arrows and arrowheads of different shapes, but no true iron arrows have been found (Singh 1965, p. 105). Arrows dating from Moghul times show many varieties of heads, including crescents, circles, narrow-tipped, and broad-tipped. See J. S. Lee 1961, pp. 19–22.

24. "Rāma lay there on the battlefield, a hero's bed" *vīraśayane śiśye*: Literally, "He lay on a hero's bed." Cg gives the same explanation of this term as he did above at verse 19, whereas Cr, silent above but eager as always to show that Rāma is not seriously incapacitated, explains, "he stood in a spot befitting a hero (*vīrocitadeśe śiśye tasthau*)." See verse 19 above.

"clutching" *ādāya*: Literally, "having taken, having held." We follow Cg, who glosses, "having clung to, having supported [himself] on (*avalambya*)." D9–11 and the texts and printed editions of Ct read instead *āvidhya*, literally, "having thrown away, having cast off." The commentators who follow this reading interpret it variously. Ct glosses, "having released, having abandoned (*tyaktvā*)." Cr, in keeping with his continuing interpretation of this passage, glosses, "having firmly grasped (*dṛḍhaṃ gṛhītvā*)."

"gilded" *rukmabhūṣitam*: Literally, "ornamented with gold." Cg glosses, "with gilded cloth binding (*rukmapaṭṭabandham*)." The two printed editions of Cg's text that were consulted [KK and VSP 6.45.24] both print the variant *ratnabhūṣitam*, "ornamented with jewels," a reading known to M. The apparatus of KK lists ten manuscripts that share the critical reading. Cg does not acknowledge the variant in his commentary. GPP, as a result of a typographical error, reads the meaningless *rukyabhūṣitam*.

"thrice-curved" *triṇatam*: Literally, "triply bent." The reference is to a recurved bow, which, as Cg mentions, is bent in the middle and at each end (*triṣu sthāneṣu pārśvayor madhye ca natam*). Ck glosses *śārṅgam*, a term referring to the composite type of bow made partly of horn, to a bow in general, or, as a proper noun, to Viṣṇu's great bow. See Emeneau 1953, pp. 77–87.

"now unstrung" *vijyam*: Literally, "devoid of a bowstring." Cg explains, "the string is removed because of the lack of any opportunity to fit an arrow to the bow (*vijyaṃ śarasaṃdhānaprasaṅgābhāvād vigatajyam*)." Cr, in keeping with his continuing denial that any harm has come to Rāma, exploits the vowel *sandhi* between *śiśye* and *vijyam* to read [*śiśye*] *avijyam* in the sense of "strung." See notes to verse 9 above. Gita Press (6.45.24) and GPP (6.45.24) both print an *avagraha* between the two words, indicating that their editors understand the elision of the negative prefix (*śiśye 'vijyam*). Among the translators, only Gita Press (1969, vol. 3, p. 1525) follows this reading, translating, "which was (still) strung." NSP (6.46.24), which gives the text of Ct, like the critical edition, shows no *avagraha*. KK and VSP (6.45.24), following Cg, both read with the critical edition.

"its grip shattered" *bhinnamuṣṭiparīṇāham*: Literally, "the place for the fist severed." Cg explains, "the fist binding slackened (*śithilamuṣṭibandham*)," the sense of which is that Rāma has slackened his own grip on the bow. Cr, in keeping with his idiosyncratic reading of the passage, takes *bhinna* in its sense of "different," glossing, "whose grip was quite different from [that of] an ordinary [bow] (*prākṛtavilakṣaṇamuṣṭiparīṇāho muṣṭigrahaṇadeśo yasya*)."

25. "in the midst of that hail of arrows" *bāṇapātāntare*: Literally, "within a fall of arrows." Ct, Cg, Cv, and Ck gloss, "on a bed of arrows (*śaratalpe*—so Ct)," an interpretation that Raghunathan (1982, vol. 3, p. 111) follows. Cr understands, "in the midst of the fallen arrows (*patitabāṇamadhye*)." Dutt (1893, p. 1234) and Gita Press (1969, vol. 3, p. 1526) understand the obscure expression to refer to the fact that Rāma has fallen within an arrow's range of his brother. Roussel (1903, vol. 3, p. 129), followed by Shastri (1959, vol. 3, p. 111) and Pagani (1999, p. 974), renders, "*jonchée de flèches*."

"despaired of his own life" *nirāśo jīvite 'bhavat*: Literally, "he became devoid of hope in respect to life." Cr glosses *jīvite* as "protecting the world (*lokapālane*)."

Following verse 25, D5–7,9–11,S insert a passage of three lines [754*]: "Seeing his brother Rāma, his eyes like lotus petals, fallen to the earth, afflicted by the bondage of those arrows,[1] he grieved. And the tawny monkeys, too, when they saw him, were moved to the greatest sorrow."

[1]"afflicted by the bondage of those arrows" *śarabandhaparikṣatam*: D7,10,11, and the texts and printed editions of Cr and Ct read instead *śaraṇyaṃ raṇatoṣiṇam*, "who was fit for refuge, and who delighted in battle."

Following 754*, D7,10,11,G3, and the texts and printed editions of Ct and Cr insert a passage of one line [755*]: "Afflicted with sorrow, they wailed dreadfully, their eyes overflowing with tears."

26. "two fallen heroes" *vīrau patitau*: D7,10,11, and the texts and printed editions of Cr and Ct read instead *tau vīraśaye*, "those two . . . on a hero's bed."

"who lay in bondage" *baddhau*: Literally, "bound." Cr provides a theological interpretation in line with his reading of this *sarga*. He explains, "those two who themselves bind the whole universe to their commands (*svājñāyāṃ nikhilajagadbandhakau*)." See, too, note to 6.39.1–2.

"In their affliction" *ārtāḥ*: Literally, "afflicted." Cr understands the term here to suggest that the monkeys actually remain apathetic because they are unable to discern the actual form of the *rākṣasa* [Indrajit] (*rākṣasasvarūpādarśanenodāsīnāḥ*).

The meter is *upajāti*.

Sarga 36

1. "glancing nervously" *vīkṣamāṇāḥ*: Literally, "looking." We have added the word "nervously" in keeping with Ct's comment, "in their great fear (*atibhayāt*) (so, too, Ck—*bhayād iti śeṣaḥ*)." Cr makes it explicit that they are looking around for Indrajit (*rākṣasoddeśenāvalokayantaḥ*).

"riddled" *saṃtatau*: Literally, "stretched, extended." We follow the commentators who gloss, "covered, pervaded (*vyāptau*)."

2. "When the *rākṣasa* had accomplished his task and ceased his onslaught like the god Indra after pouring down the rains" *vṛṣṭvevoparate deve kṛtakarmaṇi rākṣase*: Literally, "When the *rākṣasa* had accomplished [his] mission, like the god who desists after having rained." The reference is undoubtedly to the god Indra, who is universally recognized in Indian mythology as the divinity of the monsoon. The image is apposite because of Indrajit's having showered down arrows like rain. A number of manuscripts (Ñ2,B1,2,D6,7,9,11,T2,3,M5) and the texts and printed editions of Ck and Cr read *dṛṣṭvā*, "having seen," for *vṛṣṭvā*, "having poured down." Although the critical apparatus indicates that manuscripts associated with the texts of Ct (D11) and Cg (D6) read *dṛṣṭvā*, the apparatus later indicates that both of these commentators read with the critical edition, a situation borne out, in fact, by the printed editions of these commentators' texts. Left without a verb suggestive of the god's rain-making powers, Cr exploits the vowel *sandhi* between *uparate* and *deve* to read *uparate 'deve*, "when that anti-god (i.e., Indrajit) had desisted." Cr then understands Vibhīṣaṇa to be the subject of the gerund *dṛṣṭvā*, "having seen." Thus he takes the verse to mean "When that non-god, that is, that foe of the gods, the *rākṣasa* [Indrajit], had accomplished his feat and

desisted somewhat from shooting arrows, Vibhīṣaṇa, seeing Rāma, came to that place with Sugrīva (*adeve devavirodhini kṛtakarmaṇi rākṣasa uparate bāṇaprakṣepāt kiṃcin nivṛtte sati dṛṣṭvā rāmam iti śeṣas taṃ deśaṃ sasugrīvo vibhīṣaṇa ājagāma*)."

3. "Sumukha" *-sumukha-*: Ś,Ñ1,2,V,B1–4,D1–4, 7–13,T2,3,G1,M3 and the texts and printed editions of the southern commentators, Lahore, and Gorresio read instead *-kumuda-* or *kumudaḥ*, "Kumuda."

"began at once to mourn" *tūrṇam...anvaśocanta*: Literally, "they swiftly mourned." Several translators, apparently inspired by the unusual adverb in collocation with the verb "to grieve *or* mourn," have supplied some verb of motion, giving the passage the sense of "approaching in haste [they mourned]." Dutt (1893, p. 1235) translates, "came in all haste"; Roussel (1903, vol. 3, p. 130) and Pagani (1999, p. 974), "*accourus*"; and Shastri (1959, vol. 3, p. 112), "came to that place in haste." The lack of a verb of motion suggests to Cg that Nīla, etc., had, in fact, arrived on the spot before Sugrīva in verse 2 above (*nīlādayaḥ sugrīvāt pūrvam evāgatāḥ*). In this notion he is followed by Raghunathan (1982, vol. 3, p. 111), who translates, "he [Vibhīṣaṇa] found Nīla... [all grieving greatly]."

4–7. "motionless, barely breathing... immobilized... labored breathing... barely moved... barely moving" *niśceṣṭau mandaniḥśvāsau...stabdhau...niḥśvasantau...niśceṣṭau...mandaceṣṭitau*: Several of the commentators indicate disquiet with the apparent redundancy of these adjectives. Cg, who reads the synonymous *aceṣṭau* for *niśceṣṭau* in *pāda* 4a, offers two at least partial solutions to the problem. In the first, he understands that the condition of being *stabdhau*, "immobilized," is a direct result of the heroes' motionlessness. He then suggests that the different or repeated descriptions of the heroes' movements and respiration are to be understood as occurring sequentially over intervals (*madhye madhye*). He ascribes the repetitiveness to excessive grief (presumably on the part of the poet) (*atra punaruktayo duḥkhātirekāt*). Alternatively, Cg proposes to minimize the sense of repetition by construing verse 4 with verse 3 rather than with the following verses (*yadvāceṣṭāv iti ślokaḥ pūrvaślokenānvitaḥ*). See note to 6.2.14.

"Lying on beds of arrows" *śayānau śaratalpayoḥ*: Cr, in keeping with his interpretation of this entire episode (see notes to 6.35.9,17,19,20,22,23), regards virtually all the afflictions visited upon the heroes as merely illusory, as they are feigning their suffering. See, too, 6.37.19 and note.

"tightly bound with webs of arrows" *śarajālācitau*: Literally, "covered *or* heaped up with networks of arrows." Compare 6.35.17 above, where the context seems better to support the translation of "pierced." See below at 6.40.2–3, where the phrase is used again.

"Their labored breathing was like the hissing of snakes" *niḥśvasantau yathā sarpau*: Literally, "hissing like snakes." See 6.39.1–2 and note; cf. 6.41.18 and note.

"their strength had all but left them" *mandavikramau*: Literally, "with little strength *or* energy."

"on the battlefield, a hero's bed" *vīraśayane*: Literally "on a hero's bed." See 6.35.19,24 and notes above.

9. "through his own magical powers" *māyayaiva*: Literally, "by *māyā* alone." Cr and Cg regard this power as a special spell or esoteric knowledge (*vidyā*) that enables one to see invisible things (*antarhitavastudarśanahetubhūtayā vidyayety arthaḥ*—so Cg). Ck ascribes Vibhīṣaṇa's unique ability to discern his invisible nephew to his (avuncular) affection (*prītim āśrayeṇa rāvaṇiṃ dadarśa*).

10. "through the gift of a boon" *varadānāt*: Ck and Ct remark that Indrajit's gift consisted of a spell of invisibility that he had obtained through a boon that Brahmā had granted him (*brahmavaradānalabdhayāntardhānavidyayā*) in return for releasing Indra whom Indrajit had captured. The boon contained the following condition: Indrajit would be granted invulnerability if he were to perform a complete sacrifice to the Sun before entering battle (7.30.10–13). See 6.34.29; 6.40.30; 6.47.15; 6.67.27; 6.72.12,13,32; and notes. See, too, note to 6.34.28.

Following verse 10, D5–7,9–11,S insert a passage of one line [756*] expanding the description of Indrajit: "and who was endowed[1] with power, glory, and valor..."

[1]"endowed" *saṃyutam*: D9–11,T3,G1, and the texts and printed editions of Ct read the nominative *saṃyutaḥ* for the critical edition's accusative. According to this reading, the three attributes mentioned in this line are ascribed to Vibhīṣaṇa rather than to Indrajit.

11. "as he observed his handiwork and the two heroes lying there" *ātmanaḥ karma tau śayānau samīkṣya ca*: Literally, "having observed his own work and those two lying." Our interpretation follows that of Ct and Cg in taking both *karma*, "handiwork," and *tau*, "the two [heroes]," as the objects of the gerund *samīkṣya*, "as he observed." Cr, however, proposes a somewhat more difficult construction in which *karma*, "handiwork," is taken as the object of *uvāca*, "he spoke." The sense would then be the following: "observing the two heroes... he proclaimed his feat to the sons of chaos." Among the translations consulted, only Gita Press (1969, vol. 3, p. 1527) follows this interpretation.

"supremely pleased with himself" *paramaprītaḥ*: Literally, "greatly pleased."

"to the delight of" *harṣayan*: Literally, "gladdening, delighting."

"sons of chaos" *-nairṛtān*: Literally, "descendants of Nirṛti." Nirṛti is a goddess, the personification of "death, destruction, *or* chaos." She is the supervising deity of the southwestern quarter. See 6.4.46 and note. Ñ2,V,B1,2,4,D7,9–11,13,T3, and the texts and printed editions of Ct read instead *-rākṣasān*, "*rākṣasas*."

pāda d = 23d.

12. "slayers" *hantārau*: Cs, alone among the commentators, observes that, in fact, it was Rāma alone who slew Khara and Dūṣaṇa. However, he ascribes Indrajit's inclusion of Lakṣmaṇa here to the use of the *chatrinyāya*, "the maxim of the people with umbrellas (*dūṣaṇasya ca hantārāv ityādy uktiś chatrinyāyena rāmasyaiva taddhantṛtvāt*)." The idea is that just as we say that people are carrying umbrellas, when, in fact, only some of them are, we may include Lakṣmaṇa as a killer of Khara and Dūṣaṇa by association.

"Khara and Dūṣaṇa" *dūṣaṇasya ca... kharasya ca*: These are the *rākṣasa* chieftains whom Rāma killed in the Daṇḍaka Forest at *Araṇyakāṇḍa* 24–29. Cf. 6.21.32.

14–15. "put an end" *nihataḥ*: Literally, "killed, destroyed." D7,10,11, and the texts and printed editions of Ct and Cm read instead *śamitaḥ*, "quieted, extinguished, pacified."

"the menace they posed" *anarthaḥ*: Literally, "the calamity, danger."

"which could have destroyed us all" *mūlaharaḥ... sarveṣām*: Literally, "the root destroyer of all." Cf. 6.98.20 and note.

"three watches of the night" *triyāmā ... śarvarī*: Literally, "the night with its three watches." A *yāma* is a unit of time corresponding to three hours, or an eighth of a day.

"without ... so much as touching his bed" *aspṛṣṭvā śayanaṃ gātraiḥ*: Literally, "not having touched the bed with limbs." The commentators agree that the idea here is that Rāvaṇa is spending sleepless nights [worrying about Rāma] (*anidra eva niśāḥ kṣapayatīty arthaḥ*—so Ct). Cg notes that the sense is that he does not sleep through even one of the watches of the night (*śarvaryām ekasminn api yāme na nidrātīty arthaḥ*). Cs ingeniously wishes to break the sequence *gātrais triyāmā*, "by limbs, the three watches," as *gātrai[ḥ] striyā amā*, "by limbs, with the woman." This he takes to mean that Rāvaṇa has not been able to sleep with Mandodarī (*striyā mandodaryā amā saha śayanaṃ śayyāṃ gātrair aspṛṭvaiva cintayānasya mama pituḥ śarvarī yāti*).

"turbulent" *ākulā*: Literally, "agitated, overcome." It is difficult to find a single adjective that can apply equally to the city and river here. Cg notes that the term "city" actually refers to "the people of Laṅkā (*laṅkāsthajanaḥ*)." Cg takes the adjective to mean "turbid (*āvilā*)" in connection with the river and "alarmed (*vyagrā*)" for the citizens of the city. (*nadīpakṣa āvilety arthaḥ. lāṅkāpakṣe vyagrety arthaḥ.*)

16. "valorous deeds" *vikramāḥ*: Cg notes that these would be "the building of the causeway, etc. (*setubandhanādayaḥ*)."

"as fruitless as rain clouds in autumn" *niṣphalāḥ ... yathā śaradi toyadāḥ*: The reference is to the large, but unproductive, rain clouds that mark the autumn sky after the end of the monsoon.

17. "who stood beside him" *paripārśvagān*: D7,9–11,T3, and the texts and printed editions of Cr and Ct read instead the participle *paripaśyataḥ*, "who were looking on." Cr understands this participle to modify the monkey troop leaders (*paripaśyato yūthapān api*).

"monkey troop leaders" *yūthapān*: Literally, "troop leaders."

Following verse 17, D5–7,9–11,S insert a passage of ten lines [759*]: "That slayer of his enemies struck Nīla with nine excellent arrows and Mainda and Dvivida with three each.[1–2] That great archer pierced Jāmbavān in the chest with an arrow and loosed ten at swift Hanumān.[3–4] Then, in the battle, swift Rāvaṇi shot Gavākṣa and Śarabha of immeasurable power[1] with two arrows each.[5–6] Then swift Rāvaṇi pierced the lord of the langurs[2] and Aṅgada, Vālin's son, with many arrows.[7–8] Then, when he had pierced those foremost of monkeys with arrows that were like flames of fire, the strong and mighty Rāvaṇi roared.[9–10]"

[1]"of immeasurable power" *amitatejasau*: D7,10,11,G3,M5, and the texts and printed editions of Cr and Ct read instead *amitavikramau*, "of immeasurable valor."

[2]"lord of the langurs" *golāṅgūleśvaram*: According to Cg and Cm, this is an epithet of Gavākṣa. This interpretation is rendered in the translation of Gita Press (1969, vol. 3, p. 1528). This interpretation seems unlikely, however, as the epithet comes two lines away from Gavākṣa's name. Cr understands the epithet to refer to Aṅgada, with whose name it at least shares a line. We are uncertain and have taken the epithet as a reference to a separate, unnamed langur. See note to 6.34.26.

18. "them ... monkeys" *tān ... vānarān*: Cr and the translators consulted understand both terms to refer to a single group of monkeys who are the object of both the

gerunds *ardayitvā*, "having afflicted," and *trāsayitvā*, "having terrified." We feel, however, that *tān* refers specifically to the monkey troop leaders who are attacked in the preceding verse, whereas *vānarān* refers to the larger mass of monkey troops who are terrified to see their leaders wounded.

19. "right in front of their troops" *camūmukhe*: Literally, "in the face *or* in front of the army."

22. "both" *tāv ubhau*: Ñ,V,B,D7,9–11,T3,G1,2, and the texts and printed editions of Cr and Ct read instead *bhrātarau*, "the two brothers."

"he assumed" *anvamanyata*: Literally, "he thought." We follow Cr in bringing down "Rāvaṇi" as the subject from the preceding verse. Perhaps because the most immediately preceding subject is the plural *rākṣasāḥ* of verses 20 and 21 above, several of the translators consulted give the singular verb here a plural subject (Dutt 1893, p. 1236; Roussel 1903, vol. 3, p. 131; Shastri 1959, vol. 3, p. 113; and Pagani 1999, p. 976). Only Gorresio's text (6.21.23) reads the plural *viduḥ*, "they knew *or* thought."

23. *pāda* d = 11d. See note to verse 11 above.

"entered the citadel of Laṅkā" *praviveśa purīṃ laṅkām*: Indrajit appears to repeat his entrance to Laṅkā at verse 39. See verse 39 below and note.

24. "in each and every limb" *sarvāṇi cāṅgopāṅgāni*: Literally, "[as were] every limb and subsidiary limb." The commentators agree that one has to supply a second participle in the plural, "riddled (*citāni*)," to modify the compound. Cg alone specifies that the *aṅgas*, "limbs," are such things as "hands, etc. (*karādīni*)" whereas the *upāṅgas*, or subsidiary limbs, are "fingers, etc. (*aṅgulādīni*)." The awkward phrasing conveys an idea similar to that expressed above at 6.35.20, where the heroes were described as wounded "down to their very fingertips." See 6.35.20 and note.

25. "his eyes suffused with sorrow" *śokavyākulalocanam*: Ś,Ñ1,D3,4,6–13,T2,3,G1,3, and the texts and printed editions of Cr and Ct read *krodha*, "anger, wrath," for *śoka*, "sorrow." This reading is rendered in the translations that follow the text of Ct with two exceptions: Gita Press (1969, vol. 3, p. 1529) reads with Cg and the critical edition, and Shastri (1959, vol. 3, p. 114), unaccountably, translates, "his eyes wild with terror," a reading for which we find no textual support.

26. "Battles are often like this" *evaṃprāyāṇi yuddhāni*: Literally, "battles are generally this way." The idea, as clarified in *pāda* d, is that the course of battle is uncertain. Cr, however, understands the phrase to mean "battles may be largely illusory, and [potential] victory may be turned to defeat through a deceitful agent and therefore is uncertain. (*evaṃprāyāṇy etādṛśāni māyāmayānīty arthaḥ. yāni yuddhāni tatra vijayo māyikakartṛkaparābhavo naiṣṭhiko niścito na.*)" The point of this, Cr continues, is that "the sight of [Rāma and Lakṣmaṇa] in bondage may itself be illusory (*māyayāpīdṛśadarśanasaṃbhavād iti tātparyam*)."

27. "any remnant of good fortune left" *saśeṣabhāgyatā*: Literally, "the state of possessing good fortune with a remainder." D10,11, and the texts and printed editions of Ct read instead *sabhāgyaśeṣatā*, "the state of having a remainder that includes good fortune." The inversion of the word order, however, yields a similar meaning.

"the brothers Rāma and Lakṣmaṇa" *bhrātarau rāmalakṣmaṇau*: D5,7,9–11,T1,3, G3,M1–3, and the texts and printed editions of the southern commentators read instead *mahātmānau mahābalau*, "those two great and mighty [heroes]."

"will regain consciousness" *moham . . . prahāsyete*: Literally, "those two will abandon their swoon."

28. "So pull yourself together . . . and thus encourage me" *paryavasthāpayātmānam . . . māṃ ca*: Literally, "compose yourself and me." We follow Cg, who suggests that "in gaining control of himself, i.e., steadying his mind, Sugrīva will cause Vibhīṣaṇa, too, to be steady. (*paryavasthāpayātmānaṃ mano niścalaṃ kuru. svātmaparyavasthāpanena māṃ ca paryavasthāpaya. dhairyaṃ kārayety arthaḥ.*)"

"who am without any recourse" *anātham*: Literally, "without a lord *or* protector." Ct and Cs understand Vibhīṣaṇa to be saying that he requires bracing at the hands of Sugrīva because, unlike the latter, he has no independent kingdom to fall back upon [in the event of defeat]. (*tava tu svatantraṃ rājyam apy asti. ahaṃ tv agatir iti bhāvaḥ.*)

29. "dipped his hand in water and, with it" *jalaklinnena pāṇinā*: Literally, "with a hand wet with water."

Following verse 29, D5–7,9–11,S insert a passage of two lines [762*]: "Then righteous Vibhīṣaṇa took water that he had sanctified with a spell and wiped Sugrīva's eyes."

30. "calmly" *asaṃbhrāntam*: Literally, "without agitation." We agree with Cg, who reads the variant *asaṃbhramam*, found in D5,6,T1,2,G3,M3,5, adverbially. Cr reads the critical reading adjectivally, glossing, "dispelling agitation (*saṃbhrāntinivartakam*)."

31. "at this inopportune moment" *akāle 'smin*: D5,7,9,T1,3 read *kāle*, "in time, at the proper moment," for *akāle*. The sense then is "at this particular moment *or* juncture."

"could prove fatal" *maraṇāyopapadyate*: Literally, "it would lead to death."

32. "which undermines all endeavors" *sarvakāryavināśanam*: Literally, "destroying all undertakings."

33. "Rather, you should stand guard" *athavā* [printed as *atha vā* in the critical edition] *rakṣyatām*: Ct argues that Vibhīṣaṇa is saying that if Sugrīva lacks the fortitude to rally his own troops, then he himself will do so while Sugrīva stands guard over the fallen Rāma (*yadi tava senāsamāśvāsane dhairyaṃ nāsti tadā tad ahaṃ kariṣyāmi tvayā tu rāmo rakṣaṇīya ity āha*).

"until he regains consciousness" *yāvat saṃjñāviparyayaḥ*: Literally, "so long as there is loss *or* inversion of consciousness."

34. "This is nothing to Rāma" *naitat kiṃcana rāmasya*: As Cg points out, the reference is to Rāma's bondage, which Vibhīṣaṇa does not regard as life-threatening. (*etac chastrabandhanaṃ rāmasya na kiṃcana. idam asatprāyaṃ bādhakaṃ na bhavatīty arthaḥ. ato na mumūrṣati.*) Cr takes the reference to be to the temporary delusion [of the monkeys] in Rāma's presence. He regards this as nothing serious (*etad alpakālaṃ prati bhasamānaṃ mohādi rāmasya samīpe kiṃcana na tuccham ity arthaḥ*). Ct and Ck explain that Rāma has experienced nothing fatal (*rāmasya naitat kiṃcana. apāyakaraṇam ity arthaḥ*—so Ct).

"nor is he about to die" *na ca rāmo mumūrṣati*: Literally, "and Rāma does not wish to die." The desiderative here is used in an inceptive sense. This is the position of Cg, who here reads the desiderative (*sannanta*) form of the root $\sqrt{}$*mṛ*, "to die," in the sense of "anticipation," and cites *Siddhāntakaumudī vārttika* 2622 (= *Pā* 6.4.17) to that effect. (*mariṣyatīti śaṅkā na kartavyety arthaḥ. "āśaṅkāyām upasaṃkhyānam" iti mṛyateḥ san.*) Cr reads the desiderative as a causative, taking the sense of the form to be "he does not wish to cause us to die (*asmān mārayituṃ necchati*)." Roussel (1903, vol. 3 p. 132) and Pagani (1999, p. 976) take the desiderative in its primary sense of "wishing to die."

"that vital glow" *lakṣmīḥ*: We agree with Cg and Cr, who understand, each in his own way, that the reference is to the perceptible vital spark that differentiates the living, even when unconscious, from the dead. Cr glosses, "bodily splendor (*śarīraśobhā*)," an interpretation followed by Gita Press (1969, vol. 3, p. 1530). Cg glosses, "facial luster *or* brightness (*mukhakāntiḥ*)." He is followed by Raghunathan (1982, vol. 3, p. 113). Pagani (1999, p. 976) also understands the term in this sense, translating, "*éclat*." Dutt (1893, p. 1237), Shastri (1959, vol. 3, p. 114), and Gorresio (1856, vol. 9, p. 267) all understand the reference to be to Lakṣmī, the goddess of fortune. See 6.38.31 and note for the same idea. Roussel (1903, vol. 3, p. 132) leaves the term *lakṣmī* untranslated.

"is not deserting him" *na hy enaṃ hāsyate*: Literally, "it will not leave him." We agree with Ct, Cr, and Cg in understanding the future in the sense of the present (*na jahātīty arthaḥ*—so Cg). Ct additionally reads a future sense (*idānīṃ na jahāty evāgre 'pi na hāsyatīty arthaḥ*).

35. "you must console . . . rally" *āśvāsaya . . . āśvāsaya*: Literally, "[you] console . . . console."

"forces" *balam*: Ct and Ck understand the term in its other sense of "strength, vital force," glossing, "life force (*prāṇam*)." This interpretation has been followed by Gita Press (1969, vol. 3, p. 1530), Roussel (1903, vol. 3, p. 132), Pagani (1999, p. 976), and Shastri (1959, vol. 3, p. 114).

"regroup" *saṃsthāpayāmi*: Ct glosses, "[while] I steady [them] (*sthirāṇi karomi*)."

"all the troops" *sarvāṇi sainyāni*: D5–7,T1,2,M3, and the texts and printed editions of Cg and Cm read instead "all the things that need to be done," while D9,T3 read *sarvāṇi kāryāṇi*. With the verb *saṃsthāpayāmi*, Cg then interprets the phrase to mean "while I take care of everything that needs to be done." Cg also notes that some interpreters read the adverb *yāvat*, "while," adjectivally with *kāryāṇi* in the sense of "as many things as need to be done (*kecit tu yāvat kāryāṇi yāvanti kartavyāni tāni sarvāṇīty āhuḥ*)." The reading *kāryāṇi* is rendered only in the translation of Raghunathan (1982, vol. 3, p. 113).

36. "bull among tawny monkeys" *haripuṅgava*: D6,10,11,T2,G3,M, and the texts and printed editions of Ct, Ck, and Cg read instead *harisattama*, "best of tawny monkeys."

"spreading rumors from ear to ear" *karṇe karṇe prakathitāḥ*: Literally, "make announcements in ear after ear." Ct and Ck understand that the monkeys are spreading reports of Rāma's death (*rāmavipadviṣayaprakathanavanto bhavanti*—so Ct). Cr merely notes that they are talking about what has happened to Rāma (*rāmavṛttāntakathanavantaḥ santīti śeṣaḥ*), while Cg and Cm believe that they are encouraging one another to flee (*palāyanārthaṃ pravṛttakathā ity arthaḥ*).

37. "see me rushing about to encourage the army" *māṃ tu dṛṣṭvā pradhāvantam anīkaṃ saṃpraharṣitum*: D9–11 and the texts and printed editions of Ct, Cr, and Ck read the adjective *saṃpraharṣitam*, "cheered, encouraged," for the critical edition's infinitive *saṃpraharṣitum*. This reading introduces an ambiguity in that the adjective can modify either the accusative pronoun *mām*, "me," or the nominative noun *anīkam*, "army." Commentators who share this reading construe the adjective with *anīkam*, as do all translators who follow the text of Ct, with the exception of Shastri (1959, vol. 3, p. 114), who translates, "seeing me cheerfully going about."

38. "he set about rallying" *samāśvāsayat*: Literally, "he comforted, reassured." Cg understands Vibhīṣaṇa to be reassuring the troops that he is, in fact, Vibhīṣaṇa and not Indrajit (*nāham indrajit kiṃtu vibhīṣaṇa iti samāśvāsayad ity arthaḥ*). This is not an

unreasonable anticipation, as we see at 6.39.32 below that the monkeys actually do mistake Vibhīṣaṇa for Indrajit.

"terrified" *vidrutam*: We understand the participle in this sense rather than in its other sense of "fled." We do so against virtually all translators consulted on the grounds that there has been no indication up to this point that the monkeys have indeed been put to flight. Raghunathan (1982, vol. 3, p. 114) attempts to avoid the problem by understanding the action of the verbal root as incipient, translating, "army that was on the point of flight." Roussel (1903, vol. 3, p. 132), followed by Shastri (1959, vol. 3, p. 114), deals unconvincingly with the problem by taking *vidrutam* apparently adverbially with *samāśvāsayat*, translating, "*Vibhīshana, parcourut les rangs Vānara et y rétablit la confiance.*" Shastri renders, "Bibishana, passed through the monkey lines reviving their confidence." See 6.38.31 and note below, where Vibhīṣaṇa's success at preventing a rout is mentioned.

39. "entered the city of Laṅkā" *viveśa nagarīṃ laṅkām*: Cg notes the repetition of this action, which was first mentioned in verse 23 above, arguing that the repetition is employed for the sake of the narrative flow (*kathāsaṃghaṭṭanāya pūrvoktam anuvadati*).

40. "who was seated there" *āsīnam*: Ñ2,V1,2,B2,4,D5–7,9–11,T,G3, and the texts and printed editions of Ct and Ck read instead *āsādya*, "having approached."

42. "he kissed him on the head" *upāghrāya sa mūrdhny enam*: The verb *upa* + *ā* $\sqrt{}$*ghrā* means either "to smell" or, especially when its locus is the head, "to kiss."

"everything" *sarvam*: D1,2,7,10,11,13,T2,G3,M5, and the texts and printed editions of Ct, Cr, and Ck read instead *tasmai*, "to him."

Following verse 42, D5–7,9–11,S insert a passage of one line [766*]: "[and] how the two had been deprived of movement and luster by the bonds of his arrows."

43. "His heart flooded with a great access of joy" *harṣavegānugatāntarātmā*: Literally, "his inner self overtaken by a current of joy."

"that Dāśarathi had caused" *dāśaratheḥ samutthitam*: Literally, "arisen from Dāśarathi." Ś,Ñ,V,B,D2,3,7,8,13,G2, and the texts and printed editions of Ct, Ck, and Cr read *samuttham*, "sprung *or* produced from," for *samutthitam*, apparently to correct the hypermetric quality of *pāda* c as it stands in the critical edition.

"in great delight, praised" *prahṛṣya vācābhinananda*: Literally, "having experienced delight, he praised with words." Cm, noting the seeming pleonasm of the expression "praised with words," remarks, "for the pleasure of his son [Indrajit] he praised him with words alone but not in reality [i.e., with any material gifts] (*putraprītyai kevalaṃ taṃ vāṅmātreṇa nananda na tu paramārthataḥ*)." D6,7,10,11,T2,3,G1,3,M3, and the texts and printed editions of Ct, Cr, and Ck read instead *prahṛṣṭavācā*, "with joyous words."

The meter is *upajāti*; *pāda* c is hypermetric, with twelve syllables, unnoted in the critical apparatus.

Cg observes that some scholars understand that on the night [of the battle that has just ended], the first day of the lunar half month of the new moon has passed (*anayā rātryā pratipad gatety ūcuḥ*). Cm observes that the battle between the monkeys and the *rākṣasas* that took place on the night of the new moon and was described from 6.31.15 to 6.36.39 has now been concluded (*kālajño rāghavaḥ kāle saṃyugāyābhyacodayad ity ārabhyendrajit tu mahāmāyaḥ sarvasainyasamāvṛtaḥ / viveśa nagarīṃ laṅkām ity antena vānararakṣasāṃ pratipatpravṛttaṃ yuddham uktam*). See note to 6.4.4.

Sarga 37

1. "Indrajit, the son of Rāvaṇa" *rāvaṇātmaje*: Literally, "the son of Rāvaṇa."
"in great distress" *ārtāḥ*: Ñ2,V2,B2,D1,6,7,9–11,13,G2 read instead *atha*, "now."
"surrounded... to protect" *parivārya*... *rarakṣuḥ*: Literally, "having surrounded, they protected."

2–4. "Gavaya, Śarabha, Gandhamādana" *gavayaḥ śarabho gandhamādanaḥ*: As with many of the epic's lists of proper nouns, we see numerous variations among the manuscripts. The printed text of the vulgate associated with Ct and Cr (GPP) reads instead *panasaḥ sānuprastho mahāhariḥ*, "Panasa and the great tawny monkey Sānuprastha." Gita Press (6.47.2), which normally reads with the text of Ct, here reads with the critical edition.
"Sunda" *sundaḥ*: Printed editions associated with Cg (VSP and KK = 6.47.2) and Gita Press (6.47.3) read instead *skandhaḥ*, "Skandha."
"maintaining a watch on all sides" *yattāḥ*... *sarvataḥ*: Literally, "being watchful *or* attentive on all sides." The adverb *sarvataḥ*, "on all sides," is construed with other phrases by the various translators consulted.
"armed themselves with trees" *drumān ādāya*: Literally, "having taken up trees."
"they thought at the mere stirring of the grass that the *rākṣasas* had come" *tṛṇeṣv api ca ceṣṭatsu rākṣasā iti menire*: Literally, "whenever the blades of grass moved, they thought, '*Rākṣasas*!'"

5. "the *rākṣasa* women who were guarding Sītā" *sītārakṣaṇī rākṣasīḥ*: These are the women described in exuberant detail at *Sundarakāṇḍa* 15 and 20.30–33. They torment Sītā at *Sundarakāṇḍa* 21–22.

6. "together with Trijaṭā: *trijaṭā cāpi*: Literally, "and Trijaṭā." This would be the *rākṣasa* woman whose dream foretells Rāma's triumph and Sītā's rescue at *Sundarakāṇḍa* 25. Cs is the only commentator to note that Trijaṭā is mentioned separately from the other *rākṣasīs*. He feels that this suggests that Rāvaṇa suspects her of taking Sītā's side. (*rākṣasya itarāḥ. trijaṭeti tābhyaḥ pṛthakkṛte*[?]*tyoktir uttaratrasāmānyato rākṣasīr ity uktiś ca trijaṭā sītāpakṣe vartata iti rāvaṇamanasi sandeham sūcayataḥ.*)

7. "take her in the flying palace Puṣpaka" *puṣpakaṃ ca samāropya*: Literally, "having caused her to board Puṣpaka." The Puṣpakavimāna is described elaborately at 5.7.9–15.

8. "she stubbornly spurned me" *avaṣṭabdhā neyaṃ mām upatiṣṭhati*: Literally, "obdurate, she does not come to me." The commentators and translators generally interpret the participle *avaṣṭabdhā* in the sense of "proud, arrogant (*garvitā*—Ct, Cr, Cg)."

9. "free from anxiety, longing, and hope" *nirviśaṅkā nirudvignā nirapekṣā ca*: Literally, "free from fear, free from sorrow, and free from expectation." Each of these terms is ambiguous and subject to meanings that overlap with one another. Our understanding is that the first term refers to freedom from anxiety as to Rāma's fate, whereabouts, intentions, etc. The second, we feel, means freedom from the specific kind of distress associated with being separated from one's beloved. We understand the third term to refer to the loss of any hope or anticipation of rescue by, and reunion with, her husband. The commentators offer a number of similar interpretations. Thus, for *nirviśaṅkā*, Ct and Cr gloss, "devoid of fear *or* anxiety for Rāma (*rāmaśaṅkārahitā*)," while Cg glosses, "free from indecision *or* hesitation (*nirvicārā*)." For *nirudvignā*, Ct, Cm, and Cg gloss, "without grief (*niḥśokā*)." For *nirapekṣā*, Ct glosses,

"devoid of any hope that Rāma will meet [with her] (*rāmo milişyatīty āśārahitā*)." Cr glosses, "without expectation of returning to Ayodhyā (*ayodhyāprāptyapekṣārahitā*)." Cg and Cm understand as Ct does, "without hope that Rāma will meet [with her] (*rāmaḥ sameṣyatīty āśārahitā*)." See note to 6.2.14.

"adorned with all manner of jewelry" *sarvābharaṇabhūṣitā*: For a discussion on the importance of Sītā's jewelry, see S. Goldman 2000.

"will surely come to me" *mām upasthāsyate*: Cm, in keeping with his larger theological interpretation, understands the word *mām* here not as the accusative first person pronoun but rather as the accusative of the feminine *mā*, "mother," which he takes to be a reference to the goddess Lakṣmī. With this and his reading of the various forms of the root √*han*, "slay," in verses 7ff., to mean "come" (see note to 6.27.9), Cm creates a scenario in which Rāvaṇa is arguing that Sītā, having seen her husband come to the battlefield to fight with Indrajit, will realize, as a perfectly devoted wife, that she has no other interest than Rāma. She will then come to [merge with] the goddess Lakṣmī, who has been temporarily placed in the care of Rāvaṇa. (*māṃ lakṣmīṃ madīyām iti śeṣaḥ. nopatiṣṭhati nānubhavatīty arthaḥ. asyā bhartā raṇamūrdhani bhrātrā saha nihata āgataḥ khalu. taṃ dṛṣṭvetaḥ paraṃ nirviśaṅkā nirudvignaitāvat paryantaṃ nirapekṣāpi maithilī sarvābharaṇabhūṣitā satī māṃ madīyāṃ lakṣmīṃ niveditāṃ lakṣmīm ity arthaḥ. upasthāsyate 'nubhaviṣyatīty arthaḥ.*) See notes to 5.18.4ff. for Cm's theological reading of the text. See, too, notes to 6.23.1–3.

10. "succumbed to the power of Kāla" *kālavaśaṃ prāptam*: This phrase is one of several epic euphemisms for death.

*"and finding no alternative" *nānyāṃ gatim apaśyatī*: The critical text, apparently supported by a number of southern manuscripts (D5,9,M,T,G3), contains a difficult double negative, which would translate literally as "failing to see no alternative." This seems to be directly opposite to the expected meaning in the context. D6,7,10,11,G2, and the texts and printed editions of the commentators read *ca*, "and," for the negative particle *na*, and we have translated in accordance with this reading. Northern manuscripts avoid the problem entirely by substituting two lines [774*]. See 6.92.15 and 6.95.24 and notes. For additional examples of double negatives, see 6.12.3; 6.52.3; 6.67.36; 6.93.15; 6.95.24; 6.101.36; and notes. See, too, 6.99.24, 3132*, lines 7–8 and note 4. Cf. 6.38.33.

"her hopes finally dashed" *vinivṛttāśā*: D6,9–11,G,M1,2,5, and the texts and printed editions of Ct and Ck read instead *vinivṛttā sā*, "she [would] desist *or* turn back."

Following verse 10, D5–7,9–11,S insert a passage of one line [775*]: "Devoid of hope, the wide-eyed woman will come to me of her own accord."

12. "fetched" *samupānayan*: The verb *sam + upa* √*nī* has several meanings, such as "fetch, bring to, lead." Translators have interpreted variously to indicate that the *rākṣasa* women went together to Sītā, rejoined her, or conducted the flying palace to her. Cr, the only commentator to deal with this term, accepts the latter sense, glossing, "causing [Puṣpaka] to reach [her] (*prāpayan*)."

"*aśoka* grove" *aśokavanikā-*: This is, of course, the well-known site of Sītā's confinement. See *Sundarakāṇḍa* 12 for a description.

13. "seized" *ādāya*: Literally, "having taken." We follow Cr, who reads more strongly, glossing, "seizing with their hands (*karair gṛhītvā*)."

"who was lost in sorrow for her husband" *bhartṛśokaparāyaṇām*: The reference is probably to Sītā's ongoing grief over her separation from her husband as described so poignantly at 5.13.18ff., etc. Cr, however, appears to understand that Sītā is suffering from the fresh sorrow of learning of her husband's apparent death from the conversation of the *rākṣasa* women who have come to take her (*bhartṛśokena rākṣasīvacanaśravaṇajanitabhartṛviṣayakapaścāttāpena parājitām* [v.l. for *parāyaṇām*]).

Ś,Ñ2,V1,2,D2,4,5,7,8,10,12,13,T1,2,M1–3, and the texts and printed editions of the southern commentators read instead *bhartṛśokaparājitām*, "overwhelmed with sorrow for her husband."

"forced her into" *tām* ... *āropayāmāsuḥ*: Literally, "caused her to mount."

14. "Once Rāvaṇa had seen to it that Sītā had been taken aboard" *āropya sītām* ... *rāvaṇaḥ*: Literally, "Rāvaṇa having caused Sītā to mount." Following 14ab, D5,T1,M1–3, and the texts and printed editions of Cg and Cm (VSP, KK = 6.47.14cd; GPP bracketed after 6.47.14ab), as well as the text of Gita Press (6.47.15ab), insert a passage of one line [777*], which makes the *rākṣasa* women, and not Rāvaṇa, the subject of the gerund *āropya*, "having caused to mount." This would then yield the meaning: "And the *rākṣasa* women went off to show Rāma and Lakṣmaṇa to Sītā." Cg, the only commentator to discuss this line, observes that Rāvaṇa ordered both Sītā and Trijaṭā to mount the Puṣpakavimāna. He goes on to say that he gave this order to Trijaṭā specifically because of her cleverness and because she was his daughter. (*trijaṭayā saha sītām āropya. ubhayor eva vimānārohaṇam anujñāyety arthaḥ. putrītvān nipuṇatayā ca trijaṭāyā vimānarohaṇānujñā.*) Vālmīki nowhere mentions a filial relationship between Trijaṭā and Rāvaṇa (cf. verses 6 above and 16 below; and also 5.25.4,7,9; 5.28.1; and 6.38.22,35,36).

"had Laṅkā festooned with flags and banners" *akārayal laṅkāṃ patākādhvajamālinīm*: Literally, "he caused Laṅkā to have flags and banners as garlands." D10,11, and the texts and printed editions of Ct and Ck read *cārayāmāsa*, "caused to move about," for *akārayal laṅkāṃ*. The sense of the line then becomes: "He caused her to be taken around [Laṅkā], which was festooned with flags and banners." Translators who follow Ct are divided as to whether the causative here suggests that Rāvaṇa merely sent Sītā off with the *rākṣasa* women (Roussel 1903, vol. 3, p. 135; Pagani 1999, p. 978; and Gita Press 1969, vol. 3, p. 1522, which also reads 777*) or actually accompanies her on the flight (Dutt 1893, p. 1239 and Shastri 1959, vol. 3, p. 115).

16. "practically the entire ... army" *sarvaṃ sainyam*: Literally, "the entire army." We have added the word "practically" in keeping with Ct's eminently sensible gloss, "many (*bahv ity arthaḥ*)." It is contextually impossible, of course, to understand that the entire monkey army has been destroyed.

17. "while the monkeys ... were afflicted with sorrow" *vānarāṃś cāpi duḥkhārtān*: Literally, "and also the monkeys afflicted with sorrow." V2,D7,9–11,G1, and the texts and printed editions of Cr and Ct read *cātiduḥkhārtān*, "and [the monkeys] exceedingly afflicted with sorrow," for *cāpi duḥkhārtān*.

18. "lying ... on their beds of arrows" *śayānau śaratalpayoḥ*: Literally, "the two lying on two arrow-beds." Ñ2,D10,11, and the texts and printed editions of Ct read *śaratalpagau*, "gone to arrow-beds," for *śaratalpayoḥ*. See 6.35.19,24 and notes; and 6.36.4–7 and note.

"riddled with arrows" *śarapīḍitau*: Literally, "oppressed *or* afflicted by arrows."

19. "Their armor was shattered" *vidhvastakavacau*: Cr, as ever unwilling to admit injury or defeat in the case of his heroes, reads this and the following two compounds as *bahuvrīhis* in which Rāma and Lakṣmaṇa become the subjects of the participles that

form the first members. He thus understands the compounds as references to Rāma's and Lakṣmaṇa's heroic feats in their battle with the *rākṣasas* in Janasthāna, where, according to him, the two heroes inflicted the damage described in the verse upon their enemies (*Araṇyakāṇḍa* 24–29). Thus, Cr translates the compound as "those two [heroes] by whom the armor of the *rākṣasas* was destroyed in Janasthāna (*vidhvastā janasthāne vināśitāḥ kavacāḥ rākṣasavarmāṇi yābhyāṃ*)." See note to 6.35.9.

"their bows had slipped from their grasp" *vipraviddhaśarāsanau*: We follow Cg, Ct, and Cm, who gloss the participle *vipraviddha* with its common meaning of "fallen, cast aside (*bhraṣṭa*—so Ct, Cg)." In keeping with his interpretation, noted above, Cr understands the participle in its other common sense of "pierced, shattered." He would thus read: "the two by whom the bows [of the *rākṣasas*] were shattered (*vipraviddhāni śarāsanāni yābhyām*)." See note to 6.35.9.

"Their every limb riddled with arrows" *sāyakaiś chinnasarvāṅgau*: Cr continues to understand the adjectives as references to Rāma's and Lakṣmaṇa's heroic feats in the *Araṇyakāṇḍa* (*sargas* 24–29). He interprets, "by whom every limb [of the *rākṣasas*] had been severed with arrows (*śāyakaiś chinnāni sarvāṅgāni yābhyāṃ tau*)." See note to 6.35.9.

"looked like two pillars of arrows fallen to the ground" *śarastambhamayau kṣitau*: Literally, "the two on the ground [were] made of arrow-pillars." The visual image intended here is not entirely clear. Apparently, we are to understand that the bodies of the two heroes are so thickly riddled with arrows that they themselves resemble [fallen] columns made of arrows. So we understand Ck, the only commentator to read with the critical edition, who glosses, "having the form of [two] pillars made of arrows that were embedded in every limb (*sarvāṅgakhacitaśarakṛtasthūṇārūpau*)." The situation is further complicated by the scattered nature of the textual evidence. The critical reading is apparently shared by D5,9,M,G2,3,T1, and Ck. Several southern and northern manuscripts, and the texts and printed editions of the southern commentators other than Ck read *-stamba-*,"clump, cluster, thicket," for *-stambha-*, "pillar." This reading allows for an ambiguity in the meaning of the word *śara*, which can be read as either "arrow" or "grass, reeds." The image becomes either "a clump *or* thicket of reeds *or* a cluster of arrows." Cg thus explains, "made of thickets of reeds [arrows?] (*śaragulmamayau*)" but notes that others understand *-stamba-* to mean *-samūha-*, "collection" (*stambaḥ samūha ity eke*). He is evidently quoting Cm, who gives this same gloss, as does Ct. Compare the similar reference to Lakṣmaṇa's "having become [like] an arrow (*śarabhūtaḥ*)" in the text of Ct at note to 6.39.15.

20. Following 20ab, D5,6 (line 1 after 20ab; line 2 after 19),7,9–11,T,G1(adds after 19),2,3,M insert a passage of two lines [780*]: "The two lotus-eyed princes, those bulls among men, who were like sons of Agni, the purifier, were lying in that condition on beds of arrows."

Following verse 20, D5–7,9–11,S insert an additional passage of two lines [781*]: "When Janaka's dark-eyed daughter, whose limbs were flawless, spied her husband and Lakṣmaṇa, both writhing in the dust, she began to weep."

21. "who were equal in power to the gods" *devasamaprabhāvau*: D7,10,11, and the texts and printed editions of Ct read *-suta-*, "sons," for *-sama-*, "equal," yielding the sense "as powerful as the sons of the gods."

"assumed that they were dead" *vitarkayantī nidhanaṃ tayoḥ*: Literally, "presuming the death of those two."

The meter is *indravajrā* (with the first syllable of *pāda* c irregularly light).

Sarga 38

1. "had been struck down" *nihatam*: Literally, "had been slain." Cm and Ct add the comparative particle *iva*, "like," giving the sense "seemed to be slain."

"lamented" *vilalāpa*: Several of the commentators feel compelled to explain how the omniscient goddess Sītā could give way to lamentation when Rāma is not really dead. Cm argues that, although she knows the truth, she laments in order deceive the *rākṣasas* (*vāstavārthe 'yam āśāyaḥ sarveśvarā sarvajñā devī rāmalakṣmaṇayoḥ kāpi hānir nāstīti jñātvāpi rākṣasān vañcayitum bahuvidham pralapatīti*). Ct adds that she laments as an actress might in order to firmly establish in the *rākṣasas'* minds the notion of her humanity (*sarvajñāpi devī rākṣasānāṃ mānuṣabuddhisthairyāya naṭavad vilalāpety arthaḥ*).

2. "scholars who know the science of bodily signs" *lakṣaṇikāḥ*: Literally, "having to do with marks or signs." The form is not well attested and is apparently known only to six of the manuscripts collated for the critical edition (D6,11,12,T2,M4,5). The better-attested *lākṣaṇikāḥ* is found in Ñ2,V,B,D9–11,T2,M1,2, and the texts and printed editions of Ck, Ct, and Cr. Ct and Ck explain this as "those who know the signs in the *sāmudrikaśāstra* (*sāmudrikalakṣaṇajñāḥ*)," a reference to the science of prognostication by bodily characteristics (see 5.33.15–19 and notes to 5.31.9). Cr glosses, "knowing the signs that indicate auspiciousness and inauspiciousness (*śubhāśubhasūcakalakṣaṇajñāḥ*)." A number of manuscripts (Ś,D1–6,8,13,T1,G,M3), and the texts and printed editions of Cm and Cg read instead *lakṣaṇinaḥ* [*lākṣaṇinaḥ* Ñ1,D7,M5]. Cm glosses, "experts in the *sāmudrikaśāstra* (*sāmudrikāḥ*)." Cg understands that the term *lakṣaṇa*, "sign," here by secondary derivation refers to the knowledge of signs so that the term means those possessing such knowledge, which, Cg continues, consists of knowledge of the sixty-six bodily signs specific to women. (*lakṣaṇaśabdenātra lakṣaṇajñānam lakṣyate tad eṣām astīti lakṣaṇinaḥ. ṣaḍuttaraṣaṣṭilakṣaṇasāmudrikaśāstrajñā ity arthaḥ. ṣaṣṭiṣṣaḍuttarā yoṣidaṅgalakṣaṇam īritam ity ukteḥ.*)

"would bear sons and never be a widow" *putriṇy avidhavā*: Cg quotes relevant verses from the *sāmudrikaśāstra* that link specific bodily characteristics to the states of non-widowhood and motherhood. The first verse states:

A woman whose chest is hairless, smooth, and free from indentation will enjoy power, will never be a widow, and will gain the love of her beloved.

nirloma hṛdayaṃ yasyāḥ samaṃ nimnatvavarjitam /
aiśvaryam cāpy avaidhavyaṃ priyaprema ca sā labhet //

Cf. *GaruḍaP* 1.64.8 and 1.65.118, where hair on the breasts of women is considered inauspicious; and *Garuḍa P* 1.65.98, where the absence of such hair is considered auspicious.

The second says:

A woman with long fingers and long hair will have a long life and sons.

dīrghāṅguliś ca yā nārī dīrghakeśī ca yā bhavet /
dīrgham āyur avāpnoti putraiś ca saha vartate //

*"those wise men" [*a*]*jñāninaḥ*: The critical edition, supported only by Ck, reads *ajñāninaḥ*, literally, "ignorant ones." Given the phonological environment in the verse, in which the locative *rāme* precedes the term, and given that manuscripts generally omit the *avagraha*, it is difficult to determine on what basis the critical editors have decided on the negative here and in the following three verses. The critical apparatus provides no textual support for the reading and offers no explanation for their choice. All printed versions consulted of both northern and southern texts read *jñāninaḥ*, "wise men," which, we believe, makes better sense contextually. Sītā is, as we and other translators agree, arguing that the scholars have made an error, not that they are ignorant. Cg (quoted in the critical apparatus) glosses *jñāninaḥ* as "those who possess the knowledge of [bodily] signs (*lakṣaṇajñānavantaḥ*)." Ct and Cr both concur. Only Ck definitively reads *ajñāninaḥ* (*ajñānina iti padam*). All things considered, we have emended the critical text to read *jñāninaḥ*.

3. "of a king who performed the rites of royalty" *yajvanaḥ*: Literally, "of one who performs [vedic] sacrifices." This can refer to any sacrificer. However, in the context of the term *mahiṣī*, "chief queen," we agree with Ct, Cr, Cv, Cg, and Cm, who take the reference to be to the sacrifices associated with kingship, such as the *aśvamedha*, etc. Thus, for example, Cg, quoting the *Amarakośa* (2.7.8), comments, "*yajvanaḥ kṛtāśvamedhādikasya. yajvā tu vidhineṣṭavān ity amaraḥ*." Ck, who reads this verse following our verse 14 below, understands the sacrifices to be the *agniṣṭoma*, etc. (*yajvano mahiṣīm agniṣṭomādi yājirājamahiṣīm*).

"a great patron of sacrifices" *satriṇaḥ*: Literally, "a performer of *satras*." The term *satra* (v.l. *sattra*) can refer to any sacrifice. However, the term is frequently used, as the commentators indicate here, to refer to long sacrificial sessions presided over by many officiants (*satriṇo bahudinasādhyabahukartṛkayāgakartuḥ*—so Ct). Apparently the two terms (*yajvan* and *satrin*) are used to refer, respectively, to Rāma's kingly role as the chief officiant of the realm and as his role as a householder-sacrificer. See *Bālakāṇḍa* 11–13 and notes. See, too, 6.116.81 and note.

*"those wise men" [*a*]*jñāninaḥ*: See note to verse 2 above.

4. The order of verses 4 and 5 varies in different manuscript traditions. The texts of Cv, Crā, Cg, Cm, Ck, and Cr read verse 5 before verse 4. Printed editions of VSP and KK (6.48.4–5) read in this order as well. Among the commentators, only Ct reads with the critical text. Printed editions of GPP, NSP, and Gita Press read with the critical edition. Gorresio's edition reads with the critical edition but reverses the order of verses 3 and 4 (6.23.5–7). Raghunathan (1982, vol. 3, p. 116) is the only translator consulted who reads in the inverted order.

"they told" *viduḥ*: Literally, "they knew." The context obliges us to read the simplex as a causative. Cg glosses, "having known, they told (*viditvā ūcuḥ*)." Ct simply glosses, "they told (*prāhuḥ*)."

"And although they told me, 'You shall be the wife of a heroic king and very fortunate' " *vīrapārthivapatnī tvaṃ ye dhanyeti ca māṃ viduḥ*: D7,10,11, and the texts and printed editions of Cr, Ct, and Ck and the text of Gita Press read instead *vīrapārthivapatnīnāṃ ye vidur bhartṛpūjitām*, "And although they foretold that I would be honored among the wives of heroic kings and honored by my husband." The reading is awkward, and the word *pūjanīyām*, "to be honored," must be supplied according to Ct and Ck (*pūjanīyām iti śesaḥ*). Cv insists that the critical [=Cg] reading is the authentic one (*iti samyakpāṭhaḥ*), while Ck, equally emphatically, insists on the authenticity of the variant (*bhartṛpūjitām iti vai pāñktaḥ pāṭhaḥ*).

*"those wise men" [*a*]*jñāninaḥ*: See note to verse 2 above.

5. "in my presence" *saṃśravaṇe*: Literally, "within the range of hearing." We follow Ct, Ck, Cm, and Cr, who understand, "in my presence (*matsaṃnidhau*—Cr)." Cg offers

this as his second alternative, arguing, probably correctly, that the prophecy would have been made to Sītā's mother, etc. (*mātrādisamīpa iti śeṣaḥ*). For his first interpretation, he takes the term more literally to mean "directly within my range of hearing (*mama saṃyak śravaṇe*)," glossing, "while I was listening (*mayi śṛṇvantyām*)."

"that I should enjoy good fortune" *mām . . . śubhām*: Literally, "me . . . fortunate." The commentators generally agree that here "good fortune" means that she, Sītā, would never be widowed (*avidhavām*—so Ct). Cg glosses, "ever-auspicious [married woman] (*nityamaṅgalām*)" and gives a list of appropriate physical characteristics:

> For lovely ladies, the following [characteristics] betoken good fortune: a pleasant smile, unblinking eyes, and a nose with even and round sides (lit., coverings), with small nostrils.
> *smitaṃ praśastaṃ sudṛśāṃ animīlitalocanam /*
> *samavṛttapuṭā nāsā laghuchidrā śubhāvahā //*

*"those wise men" [*a*]*jñāninaḥ*: See note to verse 2 above.

6. "those lotus marks" *padmāni*: Literally, "lotuses." The commentators agree that the reference is to lines on the hands and/or feet in the shape of a lotus (*padmāni pāṇipādavartirekhārūpapadmāni*—so Ct, Ck). In a note, Gorresio (1856, vol. 9, pp. 370–71, note 119), quotes Cl as well, who glosses, "lotus signs (*padmacihnāni*)." These marks betoken royal sovereignty (see *GaruḍaP* 1.65.105–106).

"whereby it is said women" *kila striyaḥ*: Literally, "women, it is said." B1,D5,7,9–11,T1,G, and the texts and printed editions of Ct and Cr read *kula-*, "good family," for *kila*, yielding the compound *kulastriyaḥ*, "women of good family."

7. According to Ct, many authorities regard this verse as an interpolation (*idaṃ padyaṃ prakṣiptam iti bahavaḥ*). None of the other commentators consulted, however, makes this claim.

"though I search for them" *paśyantī*: Literally, "[I] looking." We follow the interpretation of Cg and Cr, who understand that Sītā is looking in vain for the signs [of widowhood to explain her ill fortune] (*vimṛśantī*). Ct, however, understands, "although I see auspicious signs [the signs on my body are meaningless] (*sulakṣaṇāni paśyanty api*)."

"inauspicious signs" *alakṣaṇaiḥ*: The reading of the critical edition is shared by a number of manuscripts, including the texts and printed editions of Ct, who indicates that this is his reading (*yair alakṣaṇaiḥ*). Printed texts of Cg and Cm read instead *lakṣaṇaiḥ*, "signs." Cm specifically notes that this is the correct dissolution of the *sandhi* (*lakṣaṇair iti chedaḥ*). Cs also reads *lakṣaṇaiḥ* and explains it as meaning either "those who know the science of signs or the signs themselves. (*lakṣayanti janān iti tajjñaiḥ kartṛbhiḥ. lakṣaṇaiḥ karaṇair vā.*)"

"Indeed, the signs on my body are meaningless." *hatalakṣaṇā*: Literally, " I, having worthless signs." We agree with Ct, Cg, and Cm in understanding that what Sītā is saying is that the presence of auspicious marks on her body (and the absence of inauspicious ones) has proven meaningless. Cr offers a rather idiosyncratic explanation, in keeping with his position that Sītā cannot even have imagined that Rāma had been killed. He does this by taking *hatalakṣaṇā* not as the compound *hata-lakṣaṇā* but rather as the emphatic particle *ha* plus the compound *tala-kṣaṇā,* which he takes as a *bahuvrīhi* in the sense of "one who has auspicious [literally, "festival-producing"] signs [literally, "moments"] on the palms of her hands and the soles of her feet (*talayoḥ pāṇipādatalayoḥ kṣaṇam utsavapradacihnaṃ yasyāḥ sāham*)." Cr understands, "I who have these auspicious signs on my palms and soles do not see any of the inauspicious signs that foretell widowhood." This, he suggests, indicates that Rāma's death could not possibly have occurred (*sāham ātmano naiva paśyāmy etena rāmanidhanaṃ na saṃbhavatīti sūcitam*). Cf. note to 6.35.9.

As before, Cg quotes the *sāmudrikaśāstra*'s listing of some of the physical signs that indicate auspiciousness and inauspiciousness for women:

> If her toes ride up on one another, then a woman, after killing many husbands, will become a servant. If the little toe of a woman fails to touch the ground while she is walking, it kills two husbands. If it is the first or second [toe], it kills three husbands. If a woman has a single hair growing out of each pore, she becomes the wife of a king; if she has two, she experiences supreme felicity, but if she has three, she suffers the miseries of widowhood.

parasparaṃ samārūḍhāḥ pādāṅgulyo bhavanti cet /
hatvā bahūn api patīn parapreṣyā tathā bhavet //
yasyāḥ kaniṣṭhikā bhūmiṃ na gacchantyāḥ parispṛśet /
patidvayaṃ nihanty ādyā dvitiyā ca patitrayam //
ekaromā rājapatnī dviromātisukhānvitā /
triromā romakūpeṣu bhaved vaidhavyaduḥkhabhāk //

Cf. *GaruḍaP* 1.64.11; 1.65.112; and 1.65.7,8.

8. "In the science of bodily signs" *lakṣaṇe*: Literally, "in the sign." We take this by secondary derivation to refer to the science of signs, following the lead of Cg on verse 2, who says, "by the word *lakṣaṇa*, the science of signs is indicated by secondary derivation (*lakṣaṇaśabdenātra lakṣaṇajñānaṃ lakṣyate*)." B1,D5–7,9–11,T,G,M3,5, and the texts and printed editions of Crā, Cm, Cg, Ct, and Cr read instead *lakṣaṇaiḥ*, which Ct and Cr take to mean "those knowledgeable in the bodily signs (*lakṣaṇa[abhi]jñaiḥ*)." Cg takes this to be an instrumental of accompaniment and thus understands, "lotus marks along with such marks as the 'banner,' etc. (*dhvajādilakṣaṇaiḥ saha padmāni*)."

"the . . . infallible" *satyānīmāni*: Literally, "these [are] true." D5–7,9–11,T,G1,3,M3, and the texts and printed editions of Crā, Cm, Cg, Ct, and Cr read instead *satyanāmāni*, "accurately named." Ct and Cr gloss, "having unfailing results (*amoghaphalāni*)." Cg struggles with the literal meaning, playing first with the name *padma* and then simply arguing that the marks are aptly named because they consist of lines that are said to represent a lotus (*yāni satyanāmāni padmāny uktāni tāni me*).

9. Ck claims that this and the following verse are interpolated in some manuscripts (*atra madhye dvau ślokau prakṣiptau kvacit*). This claim, however, finds no support in the critical apparatus of either the critical edition or KK.

"My eyebrows do not meet." *bhruvau cāsaṃgate*: Cf. *GaruḍaP* 1.65.102. Ś,Ñ1,V1,D1–3,8,10–12,M1,2, and the texts and printed editions of Ct read *asaṃhate*, "are not closely joined," for *asaṃgate*, "not meeting."

"My legs are smooth and tapering" *vṛtte cālomaśe jaṅghe*: Literally, "my legs are round and hairless." The word *jaṅgha* can refer either to the calf or the thigh. We have taken it to refer to the entire leg. Translations consulted vary from "leg" (Shastri 1959, vol. 3, p. 117; Roussel 1903, vol. 3, p. 136; and Pagani 1999, p. 979) to "shanks" (Gita Press 1969, vol. 3, p. 1534 and Raghunathan 1982, vol. 3, p. 116) to "hips" (Dutt 1893, p. 1240). Cg quotes a verse he attributes to the *Skandapurāṇa*:

She whose legs are hairless, beautiful, smooth, free from veins, and gently tapered will become the lovely wife of a king.

romahīne śubhe snigdhe yajjaṅghe kramavartule /
sā rājapatnī bhavati viśire sumanoharā //

Cf. *GaruḍaP* 1.64.25 and 1.65.94–96.

10. "And my . . . are nicely developed" *ca me citau*: Literally, "and my . . . [are] piled up." We follow Cv, Ck, Ct, and Cg, who gloss, "increased *or* full grown (*upacitau*)." Cr glosses, "fleshy (*māṃsalau*)." The texts and printed editions of Ct read *samau*, "equal *or* even," for *ca me*, "and my."

"temples" *śaṅkhe*: The commentators agree that this term, whose most common meaning is "conch shell," refers to the temporal bones at the outer corners of the eyes (*netropāntabhūtalalāṭapārśve*—so Cg). But see 6.84.28 and note.

"nails are rounded" *anuvṛttā nakhāḥ*: V3,D6,9–11,T2,3,M3, and the texts and printed editions of Cm, Cg, and Cr read instead the compound *anuvṛttanakhāḥ*, which thus becomes a *bahuvrīhi* compound subordinated to the noun *aṅgulayaḥ*, "toes and fingers," in *pāda* d. The sense would thus be "my toes and fingers have rounded nails." Several of the translators evidently follow this reading. If one accepts this reading, then one must construe the adjective *snigdhāḥ*, "glossy," with *aṅgulayaḥ*, "fingers and toes," in the sense of "soft *or* smooth."

"fingers and toes" *aṅgulayaḥ*: The term may refer equally to the fingers or the toes. We agree here with Cg, who understands that both are intended (*pādahastāṅgulayaḥ*).

"well proportioned" *samāḥ*: Literally, "equal, identical, *or* similar." We understand the term here to mean that the fingers and toes are even and regular in their shape. Cg, evidently puzzled by the term, offers three distinct alternative explanations. First, the digits are "equal" in the sense that they are roughly the length of the hand; that is, they are neither too long nor too short. (*hastaparimāṇasadṛśāḥ. nātidīrghā nātihrasvā ity arthaḥ.*) Second, the digits of one hand [or foot] are equal to the [corresponding] digits of the other (*yadvāikahastavad dhastāntare 'pi tulyaparimāṇā ity arthaḥ*). Third, the digits are neither deficient nor excessive in number (*anyūnādhikasaṃkhyākā iti vārthaḥ*).

11. "with sloping sides" *utsaṅginī*: Cg understands this to mean that the navel "has a protuberant *or* elevated area surrounding it (*unnataparyantapradeśaḥ*)." D5,10,11, and the texts and printed editions of Ct and Cr read instead *utsedhanī*, "possessing an elevation," for which Ct and Cr provide the same gloss as Cg does for *utsaṅginī*. Ck, who reads with the critical edition, glosses *utsedhavat*, "possessing an elevation." In other words, this latter reading suggests that the navel protrudes.

12. "Since I stand so firmly on my feet—all twelve points making contact—they said that I was possessed of auspicious signs." *pratiṣṭhitāṃ dvādaśabhir māṃ ūcuḥ śubhalakṣaṇām*: Literally, "they said that I was possessed of auspicious signs [and] was established with twelve." The phrase is both elliptical and enigmatic. The number twelve could refer to twelve auspicious marks, but none of the commentators suggests this, and the number twelve in this context does not provoke the commentators to refer to any specific set of signs with this number. The adjective *pratiṣṭhitām*, "fixed, established," can also mean, among other things, "celebrated *or* endowed." Apte (s.v. *pratiṣṭhita*) gives "endowed" as his meaning number eleven, a meaning he documents with this verse. Apte, however, evidently uncertain about this meaning, attempts to reinforce his interpretation by quoting Ct on the verse, although, as stated below, we

do not believe that Ct understands it in this sense. Ct, Cg, Cm, Cv, Cl, and Ck all understand that the reference is to Sītā's standing firmly [on the ground—so Ck, Cg, Cm, Cl] with twelve points of contact consisting of her ten toes and the two soles of her feet (*pādadvayavartyaṅgulidaśakaṃ dve pādatale ca*—so Ct). This appears to make some sense in light of the view of the *sāmudrikaśāstra*, namely, that toes that do not make contact with the ground are signs of inauspiciousness. (See notes to verse 7 above.) Our translation reflects this interpretation. Cr, the only commentator to dissent from this interpretation, understands the number twelve to refer to the ten senses plus the mental faculty and the higher intellectual faculty (*daśabhir indriyair manobuddhibhyām*). Cr does not make clear, however, how he then understands the adjective *pratiṣṭhitām* for which none of the normal meanings seems to make much sense, given his interpretation. Gorresio's text (6.23.15) reads *śubhalakṣaṇaiḥ* for *śubhalakṣaṇām*, providing, in effect, a *lectio facilior* in which the number twelve is directly linked to the auspicious signs. In his note 121 on this passage (1856, vol. 9, p. 371), Gorresio quotes Cl, whose explanation is identical to that of the southern commentators. Gorresio notes, however, that the verse has elicited a different interpretation on the part of Vimalabodha, although he fails to provide the interpretation. Gorresio declares that he is unable to determine which of the two interpretations is correct. He contents himself with merely noting that inadequate attention has been given to the ancient art of bodily features, an art, he claims, that was widely believed in and practiced in ancient India and one that had its followers even in his own day. Of the translators consulted, Gorresio (1856, vol. 9, p. 272), Raghunathan (1982, vol. 3, p. 116), and Gita Press (1969, vol. 3, p. 1534) base their translations, as do we, on the interpretation of the overwhelming majority of commentators. Roussel (1903, vol. 3, p. 137), Shastri (1959, vol. 3, p. 117), Pagani (1999, p. 979), and Dutt (1893, p. 1241) all understand the verse merely to be saying that Sītā was said to be endowed with twelve auspicious signs.

13. "of excellent color" *varṇavat*: Literally, "possessing color." We follow the interpretation of Ct, Cr, Ck, and Cm in reading the possessive suffix *-vant* in the sense of "having an excellent glow (*praśastakānti*)." Cg glosses, "of rosy *or* reddish hue (*aruṇavarṇam*)." Cg is followed by Raghunathan (1982, vol. 3, p. 116) and Gita Press (1969, vol. 3, p. 1534). Cs, citing the *Viśvakośa*, glosses, "beautiful (*rūpavat*)." See *GaruḍaP* 1.65.92.

"without gaps" *acchidram*: The commentators explain the term to mean that the fingers and toes lie close to one another without spaces in between (*śliṣṭāṅgulyantarālam*—so Cg). See *GaruḍaP* 1.65.92; cf. 1.65.46–47.

"marked with the auspicious sign of a whole barleycorn" *samagrayavam*: Literally, "possessing a whole *yava* [mark]." This is an auspicious mark on the thumb (of a man) mentioned in the *Garuḍapurāṇa* (1.65.45–46). It is described by Ct, Cr, and Ck as a mark the size and shape of a barleycorn formed by double lines in the middle of the joints of the digits (*aṅguliparvamadhyagasamagrayavapramāṇadvidvirekhāvat*—so Ct). Cg and Cm describe it merely as a line in the shape of a whole barleycorn (*sampūrṇayavākārarekham*). Shastri (1959, vol. 3, p. 117), in a note, explains the term as "a natural line crossing the thumb at the second joint resembling a barley corn, which is considered auspicious." Pagani (1999, p. 1662) includes a similar note. See *GaruḍaP* 1.65.104.

"Those who know the science of the bodily signs of girls said of me" *māṃ kanyālakṣaṇikā viduḥ*: Literally, "Those who interpret the marks of girls knew regarding me." M3 and the printed editions of Cg read *dvijāḥ*, "brahmans [literally, twice-born ones]," for *viduḥ*, "they knew." See notes to verse 2 above.

"She has that faint smile." *mandasmitety eva*: Evidently, this is a permanent feature of the countenance (*nityamandasmitā*—Cg) and not merely a transient sign of pleasure. It is also apparently considered to be auspicious. Cf. *GaruḍaP* 1.65.99–104, however, where no mention is made of such a sign.

14. "together with my husband" *patinā saha*: Literally, "with the lord." Cs reminds us that the proper instrumental for the noun *patiḥ* in the sense of "husband" is *patyā*. He thus understands the term *pati*, "lord," to mean "husband" by secondary derivation. (*patinā patyā. patir ity ākhyātaḥ patir iti lākṣaṇikaḥ.*)

Following verse 14, D5,T1,G2, and the text of Ck read or repeat verse 3. Cg and, according to the critical apparatus, Crā note this fact and attribute it to carelessness on the part of scribes. (*tataḥ paraṃ yajvano mahiṣīṃ ye mām ity adhastanaślokaḥ keṣucit kośeṣu dṛśyate. sa tu lekhakapramādakṛtaḥ*—so Crā.)

15. "After scouring Janasthāna" *śodhayitvā janasthānam*: Literally, "having purified Janasthāna." We agree with Cr that the reference is to cleansing Janasthāna of the evil *rākṣasas* as described at *Araṇyakāṇḍa* 24–29 (*duṣṭavadhena saṃśodhya*). Cg, however, glosses, "having searched (*anviṣya*)," while Cm glosses, "having destroyed (*nāśaṃ nītvā*)."

"finding out what had become of me" *pravṛttim upalabhya*: Literally, "having obtained news." We have supplied the phrase "of me," in agreement with Cr, who glosses, "having obtained news of me by means of sending out Hanumān, and so forth (*hanumatpreṣaṇādinā madvṛttāntam upalabhya*)."

"crossed the... ocean" *tīrtvā sāgaram*: Literally, "having crossed." The reference here is to the great feat of bridging and crossing the mighty ocean (*Yuddhakāṇḍa* 15). Ct understands the word *sāgaram*, "ocean," to refer both to the sea and, metaphorically, to the army of *rākṣasas* (*sāgaraṃ samudraṃ rākṣasasenāsāgaraṃ ca*). Dutt (1893, p. 1241) finds the second interpretation "hardly necessary."

"a petty skirmish" *goṣpade*: Literally, "in a cow's hoofprint." A cow's hoofprint or the small puddle formed therein is a common metaphor in Sanskrit for something trivial or insignificant. Compare, for example, the well-known invocatory stanza from the *Rāmāyaṇa Māhātmya* tradition in which Hanumān is represented as leaping over the ocean as if it were nothing more than a cow's hoofprint (*goṣpadīkṛtavārīśaṃ* [*maśakīkṛtarākṣasam / rāmāyaṇamahāmālāratnaṃ vande 'nilātmajam*]). The expression "battle in a cow's hoofprint (*goṣpade yuddham*)" is also used to refer to an insignificant squabble, or a "tempest in a teapot." The idea here is that Sītā is referring to the great irony that Rāma and Lakṣmaṇa should have accomplished the enormously heroic feats she enumerates, only to fall in this petty encounter with the solitary Indrajit. Ct, however, in keeping with his metaphor of the army as an ocean, thinks that the term *goṣpada* refers to the small remnant of the [monkey] army in which, as noted at verse 6.37.16 above, only a few of the troop leaders remain standing after many days of battle. It is in this small circle of survivors that Rāma and Lakṣmaṇa are bound by Indrajit's arrows. (*goṣpade 'lpāvaśiṣṭasainye hatāv ity arthaḥ. anena bahudinayuddhottaram alpāvaśiṣṭe sainye katipayayūthaparūpe 'yaṃ śarabandha iti labhyate.*) Cg understands the reference to be to the mere illusion of Indrajit (*indrajinmāyāmātra iti bhāvaḥ*).

16. "Didn't... obtain" *nanu... pratyapadyatām*: The particle *nanu* has a number of uses, including that of raising a question, especially of a rhetorical nature. Sītā is

wondering why Rāma and Lakṣmaṇa allowed themselves to be defeated when they controlled such powerful weapons. Ct argues that we should supply the phrase: "Since [they had obtained] them earlier, how is it that they did not remember [them] now (*nanu itaḥ pūrvam tatkim idānīṃ na smṛtam iti śeṣaḥ*)?" Cg, citing *Amarakośa* 3.4.10 on the various uses of the particle *nanu*, thinks that the two most appropriate meanings in this context are that of indicating that something is well known or as a marker of invocation (*nanv iti prasiddhāv āmantraṇe vā praśnāvadhāraṇānujñānunayāmantraṇe nanv ity amaraḥ*). Cg further suggests that invocation may occur for no particular reason in the case of lamentation (*pralāpe nirnimittam āmantraṇaṃ saṃbhavati*).

"divine weapon-spells . . . divine . . . weapon-spell" *astram*: The term here is used collectively. These *astras*, or divine weapon-spells, of the various divinities named in the verse are weapon-spells that generally employ the elements of which the divinities are the personifications or presiding deities. These and other divine weapon-spells were given to Rāma by Viśvāmitra at 1.26.2–24. See note to 6.35.5.

17. "My two protectors . . . Now there is no one to protect me." *mama nāthāv anāthāyāḥ*: Literally, "the two protectors of me, who am without a protector."

"by an invisible foe" *adṛśyamānena*: Literally, "by an invisible one."

18. "whom Rāghava could see" *dṛṣṭipathaṃ prāpya rāghavasya*: Literally, "having reached Rāghava's field of vision."

"with his life" *jīvan*: Literally, "living."

19. "I see that nothing is beyond the power of Kāla and that it is impossible to avert one's destiny" *na kālasyātibhāro 'sti kṛtāntaś ca sudurjayaḥ*: Literally, "No burden is too heavy for Kāla [Time], and destiny is completely unconquerable." The commentators differ considerably in the ways in which they read this verse. Our interpretation follows that of Cg and Cm. Ct reads the negative particle *na* with both phrases so that he understands, "Since there is no obstacle to Kāla's accomplishment of its good and evil ends, it is able to defeat even destiny. (*kālasya śubhāśubhaphalaprāpakasya tatprāpaṇe 'tibhāro nāsti. atas tad upasthāpitaphalanirvartako yaḥ kṛtānto daivaṃ sa na sudurjayaḥ.*)" He thus takes the second phrase as a substantiation of the first general principle (*samarthanarūpo 'rthāntaranyāsaḥ*). This interpretation, as far as we can determine, is followed only by Gita Press (1969, vol. 3, p. 1535). Cr offers a somewhat forced interpretation in which *kālaḥ* and *kṛtāntaḥ* are seen to be in apposition, and the negative particle *na* is read only with the compound *atibhāraḥ*, which he later glosses as *atibhītiḥ*, "great fear." His interpretation then is that "Kāla, that is, destiny, is, in fact, capable of being overcome by some individuals. Therefore one should not be overly fearful of Kāla. (*kṛtāntaḥ kālaḥ sudurjayaḥ kaiścid api jetuṃ śakyaḥ. ata eva kālasyātibhāro 'tibhītir nāsti.*)" This, Cr continues, is "intended to suggest that everyone will come to have no fear of Rāvaṇa (*rāvaṇam evāśritya sarve nirbhayā bhaviṣyantīti sūcitam*)." Cf. 6.27.21; 6.53.46; 6.97.16; and notes.

20. "my mother" *jananīm*: Literally, "mother." Cg glosses, "my mother (*manmātaram*)." Cs understands the reference to be to Janaka's wife (who, of course, would be Sītā's stepmother) and, by secondary denotation, to Janaka himself. (*janakabhāryām. janako 'py upalakṣyate.*) Sītā's actual mother is said to be the goddess Earth (see 1.65.14–16 and notes). See, too, 5.37.2 and note; and *Uttarakāṇḍa* 88.

"mother-in-law" *śvaśrūm*: The reference, as Cr notes, is to Rāma's mother, Kausalyā. Sītā, as the ideal daughter-in-law, thinks first of her mother-in-law. Cs offers an explanation as to why Kausalyā is the principal object of Sītā's grief. It is, he says, because of Kausalyā's advanced age, because her husband is deceased, and because she had only one son (*vārdhakād gatapatitvād ekaputratvāt tām eva śocāmīti bhāvaḥ*).

D5–7,9–11,T,G,M3,5, and the texts and printed editions of the southern commentators substitute a passage of one line for 20ab [789*]: "I do not grieve so much for Rāma and that great chariot-warrior[1] Lakṣmaṇa."

[1]"great chariot-warrior" *mahāratham*: D5,T1,M3, and the texts and printed editions of Cg read instead *mahābalam*, "mighty." Cf. 6.47.16 and note.

21. "Rāma... together with Sītā and Lakṣmaṇa" *sītāṃ ca rāmaṃ ca sahalakṣmaṇam*: Literally, "Sītā and Rāma together with Lakṣmaṇa." D9–11,T3,M3, and the texts and printed editions of the southern commentaries read instead *sītāṃ ca lakṣmaṇaṃ ca sarāghavam*, "Sītā and Lakṣmaṇa along with Rāghava."

22. "But as Sītā was lamenting in this fashion" *paridevayamānāṃ tām*: Literally. "to her who was lamenting."

23. "convincing" *sadṛśāni*: Literally, "suitable *or* conformable." Ct, Cg, and Cm gloss, "conformable to experience (*anubhūtatulyāni*)," and then explain, "expressive of what is observed (*dṛṣṭasaṃvādāni*)." Ck understands, "believable because of their propriety (*śraddheyāny aucityena*)," and Cr glosses, "suitable *or* appropriate (*yogyāni*)."

24. "would not be so suffused with anger and animated with excitement" *na... kopaparītāni harṣaparyutsukāni ca*: As Ck, Ct, and Cg note, Trijaṭā is arguing *ex silentio* (*vyatireka*) for the absence of the cause, i.e., Rāma's death, from the absence of the effect, i.e., the expected facial expressions of the monkey troops. For the first compound, Ct and Ck understand that, if their lord had actually been killed, then the faces of the monkey warriors would not display manifestations of eagerness and anger expressive of such thoughts as "Let us kill the enemy! Where has he gone?" (*tāny eva vyatirekamukhenāha. na hīti. patau patyau nihate sati yodhānāṃ mukhāni kṣaṇena śatruṃ haniṣyāmaḥ kva gacchatīty evaṃ kopena vyāptāni na bhavanti*—so Ct.) For the second compound, we follow Cg's simple gloss, "pleased, delighted (*prasannāni*)." Ct, Ck, and Cr have a somewhat more complex explanation. They understand that were Rāma actually dead, the monkeys would have no expectation of the cessation of Rāma's faint, which would bring them joy, but instead would simply be weeping. Since this is not the case, Sītā should understand that Rāma is indeed alive. (*harṣajanakamohaśāntidarśananotsukāni na bhavanti. api tu rudanti kevalam. naivaṃ prakṛte. ato jīvatīti niścinu.*)

25. "those two heroes" *etau*: Literally, "these two."

"had really lost their lives" *gatajīvitau*: Literally, "were those from whom life has departed."

"goes by the name of" *nāma nāmataḥ*: Literally, "namely by name." This redundant idiom is not uncommon in Vālmīki. See 1.24.6; 1.26.10,14,16; 1.37.3; 1.69.24; 1.70.5; 2.32.14; 4.40.9; 4.58.8; 7.9.3; 7.23.19; 7.32.26; and 7.67.3.

"this" *idam... idam*: Literally, "this... this." The critical text, which agrees with the text of Ct, Ck, and Cr, is redundant, although none of the commentators remarks on this. M3 and the texts and printed editions of Cg substitute *evam*, "in this fashion," for the second occurrence of the pronoun. Of the translators consulted, only Pagani (1999, p. 980) appears to follow this variant.

"would not be carrying you" *tvāṃ dhārayen na*: Only Cr among the commentators seeks to make explicit the reason for this statement. He says it is because the flying palace Puṣpaka will not transport a widow. See Cs's comments at App. I, No. 72, lines 26–28 (note 6) following notes to verse 6.111.14. Cf. 6.7.5; and 6.37.7 and notes.

26. "dispirited and irresolute" *hatotsāhā nirudyamā*: The nouns *utsāhaḥ* and *udyamaḥ* are nearly synonymous in the senses of "resolve, energy, *or* strenuous action." The commentators make no effort here to distinguish the two, while translators have rendered them variously.

"across the battlefield" *saṃkhyeṣu*: Literally, "in battles." All translators consulted, with the exception of Raghunathan, translate as we do. Raghunathan (1982, vol. 3, p. 117) reads the locative with the compound *hatavīrapradhānā* in *pāda* a, yielding the meaning "[an army] that has had its great chiefs slain in battle."

"rudderless" *hatakarṇā*: Literally, "whose rudder is destroyed." Cr, Cm, Cv, and Cg, and, as an alternate, Ct gloss, "whose helmsman has been slain (*hatakarṇadhārā*)." They do so, no doubt, to forge a parallelism between the death of a general and that of the helmsman. We, however, agree with Ck's and Ct's first explanation: "which has lost the board (i.e., rudder) under the control of the helmsman (*hatakarṇadhārādhiṣṭhitaphalakā*—so Ct)." Ck's gloss is for an apparent variant *hatakaṇṭhā* not noted in the critical apparatus. The translators are divided. Gita Press (1969, vol. 3, p. 1536), Dutt (1893, p. 1242), and Raghunathan (1982, vol. 3, p. 117) translate, "helmsman" for *karṇa*, while Roussel (1903, vol. 3, p. 137), Shastri (1959, vol. 3, p. 118), and Pagani (1999, p. 980) understand, "rudder." Gorresio (1856, vol. 9, p. 273), who shares the reading of the critical text, oddly appears to have ignored the nautical image entirely.

27. "But... On the contrary" *punaḥ*: Literally, "then again *or* on the other hand."

"nor despondent" *nirudvignā*: Literally, "devoid of despondency."

"it is moving swiftly" *tarasvinī*: Literally, "swift." D6,11,T2,3,G,M3,5, and the text of Cr read *tapasvinī*, "suffering." D7,9,10, and the texts and printed editions of Ct and Ck read the vocative, *tapasvini*, "poor, wretched," which would then refer to Sītā. Translators are divided. Gita Press (1969, vol. 3, p. 1536) and Dutt (1893, p. 1242) clearly read with Ct. Raghunathan (1982, vol. 3, p. 117) reads with Cg, who, in turn, reads with the critical edition. Pagani (1999, p. 980), rendering, "*pleine d'énergie*," appears to translate following Cg, even though Cg's variant is overlooked in the apparatus of GPP, the text she indicates she is translating. Perhaps she is taking *tapas* here in its sense of "ascetic energy." It is not clear to us exactly what Roussel (1903, vol. 3, p. 137), who renders "*brave*" (followed by Shastri [1959, vol. 3, p. 118], "intrepid"), is translating. Gorresio's text (6.23.31) reads here with the critical edition.

"who have been defeated in battle by the power of illusion" *māyayā nirjitau raṇe*: The reading of the critical edition appears to be attested in only three Malayalam manuscripts (M1,2,4). The north, including *devanāgarī* manuscripts associated with it, has three variant readings: 1) *śayānaṃ* [*or śayānau*] *raṇa*[*bala-*]*mūrdhani*, "lying in the forefront of the battle [*or* the army]"; 2) *śayānau śaratalpayoḥ*, "lying on two beds of arrows"; and 3) *śayānaṃ śaratalpagam*, "lying on a bed of arrows." With the exception of M1,2,3, the entire south, including *devanāgarī* manuscripts associated with it, and the texts and printed editions of all southern commentators read instead "*mayā prītyā niveditau*, "I have told [you] about [those two] out of affection." The commentators flesh out this phrase: "I have reported to you that those two are alive (*niveditajīvitau*—so Cg)." Given the manuscript evidence, we regard the critical reading as highly suspect. It should have, at the very least, been marked as doubtful. See note to 6.35.19. See Bhatt 1960, p. xxxiv.

28. "by these signs, which presage happiness" *anumānaiḥ sukhodayaiḥ*: Literally, "by inferences whose outcome is happiness." Cr and Cg understand *sukhodayaiḥ* to mean "easily made clear *or* understood (*sukhena pratibhāsamānaiḥ*—Cr; *sujñeyaiḥ*—Cg)."

29. "nor will I ever" *na ca vakṣye kadācana*: Literally, "nor will I speak [a falsehood] ever." Ś,Ñ,V,B,D1–4,6–13,T2,3,G3, and the texts and printed editions of Ct, Ck, and Cr read instead *na ca*[V3 *vaco*] *vakṣyāmi maithili*, "nor will I speak [a falsehood], Maithilī."

"virtuous conduct" *cāritra-*: Ct, Ck, Cg, and Cm gloss, "devotion to your husband (*pātivratyam*—Cg, Cm)." Cr glosses, "spotless conduct (*nirmalācāreṇa*)." Cg provides an alternative gloss: "because of your having a delightful nature (*āhlādakasvabhāvatvāt*)."

"you have found a place in my heart" *praviṣṭāsi mano mama*: Literally, "you have entered my heart *or* mind." Ct observes that the underlying meaning of Trijaṭā's comment is that, because of her affection for Sītā, she is telling her these things, even though they are opposed to the interests of her own lord, Rāvaṇa (*ata etat sarvaṃ svasvāmino rāvaṇasya viruddham api mayā tavoktam iti bhāvaḥ*).

30. "together with Indra" *sendraiḥ*: Roussel (1903, vol. 3, p. 138), followed by Shastri (1959, vol. 3, p. 118) and Pagani (1999, p. 980), understand *-indra* in its sense of "chief *or* best." They thus understand the compound to mean "[the gods and *asuras*] together with their leaders."

"on the basis of my observation of their faces" *etayor ānanaṃ dṛṣṭvā*: Literally, "having seen the face of those two." The critical reading has weak textual support. Ś,Ñ,V1,2,B,D1–8,10–13,T1,2,G3,M3, Cv, Crā, Cm, Cr, Cg, Ct, Ck, and Lahore all read instead *tādṛśaṃ darśanaṃ dṛṣṭvā*, "having seen such a sight." Gorresio (6.23.34) reads *tādṛśaṃ lakṣaṇaṃ dṛṣṭvā*, "having seen such a sign." Apparently only V3,D9,T3,G1,2,M1,2,4,5 read with the critical edition. Based on the principles articulated in the *Bālakāṇḍa* (Bhatt 1960, p. xxxiv), the reading should at least be marked as doubtful. The southern commentators vary somewhat in their understanding of the term *darśanam*. Ct understands it in the sense of "signs indicating life [on the part of Rāma and Lakṣmaṇa] and the appearance of the troops (*jīvanasūcakam anayoḥ sainikānāṃ cākāram*)." Cr, Cm, and Cg analyze the terms *tādṛśam*, "of such an appearance," and *darśanam*, "sight," separately. Cr understands the former to mean "indicative of the absence of defeat (*parābhāvābhāvasūcakam*)" and the latter to mean "a sign (*lakṣaṇam*)." Cg and Cm understand the former to mean "suggestive of life (*jīvanavyañjakam*)" and the latter to refer to "[the sight of] the happy faces of the soldiers, etc. (*sainyamukhaprasādādikam*)." Cv and Cg, as an alternative explanation, understand *darśana* to be a reference to the auspicious dream-vision foretelling Rāma's victory reported by Trijaṭā at 5.25.4–34 (*pūrvadṛṣṭaṃ svapnam iti vārthaḥ*).

31. A few manuscripts show a number of variants in this verse, most significantly involving the words *cihnam*, "sign," and *śanaiḥ*, "carefully," in *pāda* a, and *apy ubhāv etau*, "although they [are] both," in *pāda* c. The texts of Ct and Cr thus read *idaṃ tu sumahac citraṃ śaraiḥ paśyasva maithili / visaṃjñau patitāv etau naiva lakṣmīr vimuñcati //*, "And behold, Maithilī, this great marvel. Although the two of them are fallen and rendered unconscious by arrows, their vital glow does not abandon them."

"carefully" *śanaiḥ*: We follow Cg's suggestion in reading *śanaiḥ*, normally, "slowly, quietly," in the sense of "carefully (*sāvadhānena*)."

"vital glow" *lakṣmīḥ*: See 6.36.34 and note above.

"has not left them" *etau na*... *viyujyate*: Literally, "it is not separated [from] those two." The syntax here is rather awkward. Ct, whose text reads the *facilior*: *na* ... *vimuñcati*, "it does not abandon," acknowledges, as a variant, the reading of the critical edition. He notes, however, that this does not change the meaning (*lakṣmīr naiva viyujyata iti pāṭhe 'pi na muñcatīty evārthaḥ*).

32. "invariably" *prāyeṇa*: Literally, "for the most part, as a general rule." Given the force of Trijaṭā's logic, we feel that the term should be interpreted so as not to admit exceptions.

"a terrible change is apparent in their faces" *dṛśyamāneṣu vaktreṣu paraṃ bhavati vaikṛtam*: Literally, "on their faces, when they are observed, there is a great transformation."

33. "grief, pain, and delusion" *śokaṃ ca duḥkhaṃ ca mohaṃ ca*: Cg differentiates these terms. He understands *śoka*, "grief," to mean "the facial transformation produced by grief (*śokakṛtaṃ mukhavikāram*)"; *duḥkha*, "pain," to mean "mental anguish (*manovyathām*)"; and *moha*, "delusion," to mean "incorrect ideas *or* thoughts (*viparītabuddhim*)."

"For it is not possible that they could have been killed this day." *nādya śakyam ajīvitum*: Literally, "It is not possible not to live today." The infinitive construction is awkward here, and the commentators gloss and rephrase it in a number of ways. Ct and Ck explain: "Thus by virtue of their bright faces, it is not possible that they could be in a condition that is devoid of life. Therefore, you must conclude that he [Rāma] is alive. (*evaṃ prasannamukhābhyām ajīvituṃ jīvanarāhityenāvasthātum aśakyam. ato jīvatīti niścinu.*)" Cr explains: "It is not possible to snuff out the lives of Rāma and Lakṣmaṇa (*rāmalakṣmaṇayor jīvanaṃ nivartayituṃ na śakyam*)." Cg rephrases the expression in the positive, saying that it means: "They can be alive (*jīvituṃ śakyam eva*)." Cm, whom we most closely follow, reads the simplex infinitive as a causative, *ajīvayitum*, meaning: "It is impossible to make them not live." Dutt (1893, p. 1242), alone among the translators consulted, understands Sītā to be the subject of the infinitive construction, translating, "For the sake of Rāma and Lakṣmaṇa, thou canst not today put a period to thy existence." For other examples of double negatives in Vālmīki, cf. 6.12.3; 6.67.36; 6.93.15; 6.95.24; 6.101.36; and notes. See, too, 6.99.24, 3132*, lines 7–8, and note 4.

34. "these words of Trijaṭā" *vacanaṃ tasyāḥ*: Literally, "her speech."

"cupped her hands in reverence" *kṛtāñjaliḥ*: Cg, evidently concerned that Sītā should make a respectful gesture to a lowly *rākṣasī*, observes that anyone who provides instruction concerning the Lord is worthy of reverence regardless of who he or she may be (*anena bhagavadviṣayopadeṣṭā yo 'pi ko 'py ādaraṇīya ity uktam*)."

35. "Trijaṭā ... turned around ... Puṣapaka ... took ... Sītā back to Laṅkā" *puṣpakam* ... *saṃnivartya* ... *trijaṭayā sītā laṅkām eva praveśitā*: Literally, "having caused the Puṣpaka to turn around, Trijaṭā made Sītā enter Laṅkā." We agree with Cg in taking the instrumental *trijaṭayā* as the subject of the causative forms *saṃnivartya* and *praveśitā* (*sannivartane praveśane ca trijaṭaiva kartrī*). Most of the translators consulted, including Dutt (1893, p. 1242), Gorresio (1856, vol. 9, p. 274), Roussel (1903, vol. 3, p. 138), Shastri (1959, vol. 3, p. 119), and Pagani (1999, pp. 980–81), ignore the causative construction and take the instrumental as one of accompaniment, rendering variations on the idea: "Sītā reentered Laṅkā with Trijaṭā." Only the translator of the Gita Press (1969, vol. 3, pp. 1536–37) and Raghunathan (1982, vol. 3, p. 118) read the verse as we do.

36. "the *rākṣasa* women" *rākṣasībhiḥ*: Cg says, "We are to understand 'by the *rākṣasīs*' to mean that [Sītā] was taken out of the presence of Trijaṭā (*rākṣasībhir ity anena trijaṭādarśanāyānīteti gamyate*)."

37. "she had just seen" *saṃprekṣya*: Literally, "having seen." Commentators are divided as to how to understand the gerund. Cr thinks that Sītā is merely looking around her in the *aśoka* grove (*sarvatrāvalokya*). Cg understands either that she is gazing about as part of her brooding (*prekṣitaprakāreṇa saṃcintyety arthaḥ*) or that, through the extremity of her emotional state, she is actually visualizing [Rāma and Lakṣmaṇa] standing before her (*yadvā bhāvanāprakarṣāt puraḥsthitau saṃprekṣyety arthaḥ*).

The meter is *upajāti*.

Sarga 39

1–2. "bound" *baddhau*: As before, Cr understands the form to mean that Rāma and Lakṣmaṇa are merely acting as if they are bound (*baddhāv iva*). See 6.35.16,26 and notes.

"their labored breathing was like the hissing of great serpents" *niśvasantau yathā nāgau*: Literally, "hissing like *nāgas*." See 6.36.4–7 and note. Cf. 6.41.18 and note.

3. "because he was so hardy and through the exertion of his strength" *sthiratvāt sattvayogāc ca*: Literally, "because of his steadfastness and the exertion of his strength." Our translation of *sthiratvāt*, "from steadfastness," basically follows Ck and Ct, who understand both terms to refer to physical characteristics. They gloss *sthiratvāt* as "because of the extraordinary toughness of his body (*atidṛḍhagātratvāt*)" and *sattvayogāt* as "because of his possession of great strength (*mahābalayuktatvāt*)." Cr takes the first term to be a consequence of the second, glossing *sattvayogāt* as "because of his permanent possession of superiority that is utterly distinct from that of ordinary beings [i.e., because of his supernatural essence] (*nityaṃ prākṛtavilakṣaṇasattāsaṃbandhāt*)." Because of this capacity, Cr argues, Rāma possesses *sthiratva*, or "freedom from any contact with fear (*udvegasaṃsargarahitatvāt*)." Cg takes *sthiratvāt* as a moral quality, glossing, "courage, steadfastness (*dhīratvāt*)." Like Ct and Ck, he takes *sattvayogāt* as a reference to the possession of physical strength (*balayogāt*). Cs reads *sthiratvāt* in a fully theological fashion, glossing, "because of the unique stability of him [Rāma] even through such events as the end of the world, etc., that is, because of his being unqualifiedly eternal. (*pralayādāv apy ekasyaiva sthairyāt. nityanityatvād iti yāvat.*)" Cs glosses, "by means of his strength (*balopāyāt*)" for *sattvayogāt*.

"bound" *saṃdānitaḥ*: Cr and Cs do not accept the idea that Rāma could be bound against his will. The former argues that the verse suggests that Rāma has concealed his consciousness earlier in order to honor his observance of the limits of Brahmā, etc., that is, to maintain his voluntary submission to the power of the weapons that Brahmā had conferred upon Indrajit (*etena pūrvaṃ tādṛśaprabodhatirobhāvaḥ svaniyamyabrahmādimaryādāpālanāyaiveti sūcitam*—so Cr). Cs argues that we are to understand that Rāma has voluntarily submitted to the binding in order to delude the demons (*etenāsuramohanāya rāmaḥ svecchayaiva saṃdānita iti jñāyate*)." On Brahmā's boon, see note to 6.36.10. See, too, 7.30.10–13.

4. "stricken" *viṣaṇṇam*: Literally, "downcast, dejected."

"deeply wounded" *gāḍham arpitam*: We read the term *arpitam* in the sense of "pierced [with arrows]" as used by Vālmīki at 3.27.17. Ct glosses, "tightly bound by arrows (*śarair baddhaṃ gāḍham*)." Ck and Cg suggest adding the words "with an arrow *or* arrows (*śareṇeti śeṣaḥ*—so Ck; *śarair iti śeṣaḥ*—so Cg)," but offer no gloss of *arpitam*. Cr breaks the adjective "covered with blood (*sarudhiram*)" into the pronoun *sa[ḥ]* (he = Rāma) and *rudhiram* (blood). He then reads *arpitam* in the sense of "spattered (*prakṣiptam*)." According to him, then, we are to read the verse as follows: "when he saw the spattered blood and his brother." See note to 6.35.9.

"his face deathly" *dīnavadanam*: Literally, "with a downcast *or* wretched face."

"in his desolation" *āturaḥ*: Literally, "pained, distressed."

5. "What do I care for Sītā or even for my life itself" *kiṃ nu me sītayā kāryaṃ kiṃ kāryaṃ jīvitena vā*: Literally, "what of mine is to be accomplished by Sītā or what is to be accomplished by life?" Ñ1,D6,7,9–11,T2,3,G3, and the texts and printed editions of Ct and Cr substitute the feminine instrumental adjective *labdhayā*, "[by her] obtained," for the second occurrence of *kiṃ kāryam*. This yields the sense "Of what use would Sītā, even if recovered, be to me?" Compare 6.89.28 and note.

"defeated" *nirjitam*: Cr, continuing his denial that Rāma or Lakṣmaṇa could actually suffer defeat or injury, argues that we are to take this term in the sense of the emulation of defeat. He sees the participle as an example of the zero, or *kvip*, suffix in the sense of imitation or acting like something (*nirjitaśabda ācārakvibantaprakṛtikadvitīyāntaḥ*). See 6.35.9 and note.

6. This verse is well known and frequently quoted. It is one of a series of remarks that Rāma makes in which he appears to value his male relations and companions over Sītā. See R. Goldman 1980. Compare 6.89.28 and note.

"Were I to search the world, I could find" *śakyā . . . prāptuṃ loke vicinvatā*: Literally, "by one searching in the world, it would be possible to obtain." There is a considerable amount of variation among the manuscripts here. D5,7,9–11,T1,3,M3, and the texts and printed editions of Ct and Cr read *martyaloke*, "in the world of mortals," for *prāptuṃ loke*, "to obtain in the world." This reading is elliptical and lacks any verbal form meaning "to find." Consistent with his denial of any negative references to Rāma or Sītā, Cr insists on reading the negative particle *na* from *pāda* c with the word *śakyā* in *pāda* a to refer to both Sītā and Lakṣmaṇa. This yields the meaning: "Searching, that is, by gathering my army, I could not find a woman equal to Sītā in this world of mortals (*sītāsamā nārī vicinvatā senāsaṃcayaṃ kurvatā mayā martyaloke na śakyā labdhum iti śeṣaḥ*)."

"a companion" *sacivaḥ*: We agree with Ct, Ck, and Cg in taking this word in the sense of "friend, companion (*sahāyaḥ*—so Ct)." Cr prefers its other sense of "counselor, minister (*sācivyakartā*)." Cr concludes by saying that the point of this verse is "to indicate the absence of anyone to equal either of the two [Sītā or Lakṣmaṇa] (*etena tatsadṛśayor abhāvaḥ sūcitaḥ*)."

7. "returned to the elements" *pañcatvam āpannaḥ*: Literally, "attained fiveness." This expression, which refers to the dissolution of the body into the five fundamental elements of ancient Indian science, is a common literary euphemism for death. See 6.15.4; 6.89.4; and notes.

8. "Whatever shall I tell Kausalyā, and what shall I tell mother Kaikeyī? And how shall I tell mother Sumitrā" *kiṃ nu vakṣyāmi kausalyāṃ mātaraṃ kiṃ nu kaikeyīm / katham ambāṃ sumitrāṃ ca*: Literally, "What shall I tell Kausalyā and what mother Kaikeyī? And how mother Sumitrā?" We go against virtually all translators consulted, who

understand the term *mātaram*, "mother," of *pāda* b to refer specifically to *kausalyā* in *pāda* a rather than to *kaikeyī* in *pāda* b. We do so because of the *pāda* structure of the verse and because of the use of the term *ambā*, "mother," in connection with *sumitrā*, in *pāda* c, which suggests that the poet intended to differentiate Kausalyā from her two junior wives. The commentators are silent.

9. "And how shall I console Sumitrā, trembling . . . at the loss of her darling son" *vivatsāṃ vepamānām . . . katham āśvāsayiṣyāmi*: Literally, "How shall I console [her] who is trembling [and] bereft of her child." Like Cg, we understand the reference here to be specifically to Lakṣmaṇa's mother, Sumitrā. Cr, however, understands the reference to be to the collectivity of the heroes' mothers, Kausalyā, etc. (*kausalyāprabhṛtim*).

"shrieking like an osprey" *krośantīṃ kurarīm iva*: The crying of the hen osprey, *kurarī*, is a frequent *upamāna* for the lamentations of a woman in Vālmīki. Compare 6.23.1–3 and 6.98.26. D7,10,11, and the texts and printed editions of Ct read the redundant and inapposite *vepantīm*, "trembling," for *krośantīm*. Most translators, even those who follow the text of Ct, have, however, rendered some word such as mourning, moaning, crying, etc. Only Pagani (1999, p. 981) appears to follow Ct's reading exactly, rendering, "*secoué de sanglots*." Compare 6.98.26 and notes. See Fitzgerald 1998.

10. "illustrious" *yaśasvinam*: Cg believes the use of this term indicates that Rāma is despondent at the thought that he has not attained [his] Bharata's glory (*yaśasvinam ity anena tadyaśo mayā na labdham iti khidyati*). Perhaps he is thinking of Rāma's regret at his loss of the throne while Bharata governs as regent.

Compare note at 6.89.8 to 2029*, lines 13–14.

11. "Alas" *bata*: Ñ2,V2,B2,4,D9–11, and the texts and printed editions of Ct and Cr read *ambā-*, "mother." The resulting compound *ambāsumitrayā* would then have the meaning "by mother Sumitrā."

Compare note at 6.89.8, 2029*, line 11.

12. "evildoer" *duṣkṛtakarmāṇam*: Cg asserts that the wrongful deed referred to here is that of taking Lakṣmaṇa to the forest (*lakṣmaṇavanānayanam eva duṣkṛtaṃ karma*).

"on whose account" *yatkṛte*: Ñ1,V2,B,D6,7,9–12,T2,3, and the texts and printed editions of Ct and Cr read instead *matkṛte*, "for my sake." In this reading, the compound sentence of the critical edition is transformed into a pair of simple sentences.

"on a bed of arrows" *śaratalpe*: See note to 6.35.19.

"his life breaths ebbing" *gatāsuvat*: Literally, "like one whose life breaths have departed." Since the following verses indicate that Rāma understands that Lakṣmaṇa is not quite dead but is dying, we have avoided the literal translation. See note to verse 13 below.

13. "You always used to comfort me" *nityam . . . mām āśvāsayasi*: Literally, "you always comfort me."

"your life breaths ebbing" *gatāsuḥ*: Literally, "one whose life breaths have departed." Ct, Ck, and Cr gloss, "as if dead (*gatāsur iva*)." No doubt Ct and Ck understand, as we do, that Rāma sees Lakṣmaṇa as dying but not yet dead. Cr, however, in keeping with his reading of the text, notes, in addition, that we must take the term as a metonym, much in the way that one would call a king the "royal preceptor" (*purohito 'yaṃ rājetyādāv iva gatāsuśabdo lākṣaṇikaḥ*). See note to verse 12 above.

14. "who struck down so many . . . on the field of battle" *yena . . . bahavaḥ . . . nihatāḥ kṣitau*: The texts and printed editions of Cg reads *nihatāḥ*, "struck down, killed," for

bahavaḥ, and *vinipātitāḥ*, "felled," for *nihatāḥ kṣitau*. This yields the sense of "who struck down [and] slew." This reading is rendered only in the translation of Raghunathan (1982, vol. 3, p. 119), who adds the word "many" despite its omission from Cg's text.

"on the field of battle . . . on the very same field" *kṣitau . . . tasyām eva kṣitau*: Literally, "on the ground . . . on that very ground."

"That hero . . . now lies on the very same field struck down by his foes" *tasyām eva kṣitau vīraḥ sa śete nihataḥ paraiḥ*: There is considerable variation in the rendering of *pādas* cd. The texts and printed editions of Ct, Ck, and Cr read instead *tasyām evādya śūras tvaṃ śeṣe vinihataḥ śaraiḥ*, "On that very [field], you, a hero, now lie struck down by arrows."

15. "bound in a web of arrows, he looks like" *śarajālaiś cito bhāti*: The manuscripts show considerable variation in *pāda* c. The texts and printed editions of Cr, Ck, and Ct read instead *śarabhūtas tato bhāsi*, "you, having become an arrow, look like." Ct explains the peculiar phrase *śarabhūtaḥ* as "looking like an arrow because of his body being completely covered with arrows (*śarair vyāptaśarīratvāc chararūpaṃ prāptaḥ*)." Cr explains similarly. See note to 6.37.19, where Rāma and Lakṣmaṇa are said to resemble "fallen pillars made of arrows." See note to 6.35.19.

"like the sun, bringer of light, as it sets" *bhāskaro 'stam iva vrajan*: Literally, "like the light-bringer going to the setting mountain." Ct explains the image by noting that "the arrows covered with the blood flowing from their respective wounds take the place of the sun's rays (*tattadrandhraniḥsaradrudhiravyāptaśarāḥ kiraṇasthānīyāḥ*)." Cr and Cg agree with the comparison of the arrows to rays, while Cg additionally suggests that the setting mountain is in place of the bed of arrows and that the reddish color [of the sunset] is in place of the blood (*atra śaratalpasthānīyo 'stagiriḥ . . . śonitasthāne raktavarṇatvam*)." Cf. notes to 6.57.20; 6.47.16; and 6.78.43.

16. "he can no longer see" *na śaknoty abhivīkṣitum*: D7,9–11,T3, and the texts and printed editions of Ct read instead *na śaknoṣīha bhāṣitum*, "you can no longer speak here."

"the expression of his eyes" *dṛṣṭirāgeṇa*: Literally, "the feeling *or* emotion of his eyes." The term is ambiguous and lends itself to a variety of interpretations. We understand it here in the sense that it is used at *Abhijñānaśākuntalam* 2.10.6. Ct and Ck understand the expression to refer not only to the look in Lakṣmaṇa's eyes but also to the changed appearance of his face (*anyayā mukhaśobhayā*). Ct, who reads "cannot speak" for the critical edition's "cannot see," additionally notes that the use here of the word *dṛṣṭi*, "eye," suggests that Lakṣmaṇa is still able to see (*anena darśanaśaktimattvaṃ sūcyate*). Cr interprets the compound to mean "the redness of the eyes (*nayanāruṇyena*)." Cg takes *rāga* in yet a third of its meanings, that of "passion, love, affection," glossing, "by the love in his glance (*vīkṣaṇapremṇā*)."

17. "Just as . . . so" *yathaiva . . . tathaiva*: Ct, Cm, and Cg understand the adverbs to mean that just as Lakṣmaṇa disregarded his affection for his parents, etc., in order to follow Rāma, so now will Rāma do the same in following him (*yathāyaṃ mātrādiṣu sneham aparyālocyaiva mām anugatas tathāham api tatsnehaṃ tyaktvānuyāsyāmīti bhāvaḥ*—so Ct).

Verse 17 is virtually identical to 2029* lines 1,2 (see note to 6.89.8, 2029*).

18. "through my failed tactics—ignoble as I am" *mamānāryasya durnayaiḥ*: Literally, " through the bad policies of me who am ignoble." Cr, in keeping with his larger

project, is unwilling to associate Rāma with anything deficient or unworthy. He therefore understands *anāryasya* to refer to the *rākṣasa* [Indrajit] and *durnayaiḥ* to refer to Indrajit's powers of illusion. He then reads the pronoun *mama*, "mine," with a supplied word, *agre*, in the sense of "right before me." He understands the half verse then to mean: "But now through the evil tactics of that ignoble wretch [Indrajit], that is, his powers of illusion, you have been reduced to this condition right before me. (*anāryasya rākṣasasya durnayair māyābhir ity arthaḥ. mamāgra imām avasthāṃ gato 'si.*)" Many of the translators understand *durnayaiḥ* in the sense of "misdeeds," which we believe is not quite the meaning here.

19. "even when he was enraged" *suruṣṭenāpi*: Rāma seems not to recall Lakṣmaṇa's violent outbursts at *Ayodhyākāṇḍa* 20 and 90.

"a harsh or unpleasant word" *paruṣaṃ vipriyaṃ vāpi*: Literally, "harsh or even unpleasant." Ct, Cm, and Cg understand *ahitam*, "harmful," to mean *vipriyam*, "unpleasant."

20. "could loose" *visasarja*: Literally, "he released."

"in one swift motion" *ekavegena*: Literally, "with one impulse." Cg and Cm gloss, "with a single effort (*ekaprayatnena*)."

"surpassed even Kārtavīrya" *adhikas tasmāt kārtavīryāt*: Literally, "greater than Kārtavīrya." The reference is to the legendary Haiheya monarch Arjuna Kārtavīrya, often referred to by the epithet "thousand-armed (*sahasrabāhu*)." This figure appears in the *Mahābhārata* (3.116.19ff.), where he or his sons kill the Bhārgava sage Jamadagni, and at *Uttarakāṇḍa* 32, where he fights with and defeats Rāvaṇa. The idea here, as explained by Ct, Cm, and Cg, is that, whereas Kārtavīrya had a thousand arms and could thus presumably discharge five hundred arrows simultaneously, Lakṣmaṇa, with a mere two, is able to fire the same number of arrows in the same time. In this manner, he is said to surpass Kārtavīrya (*ekavegena pañcabāṇaśatāni visasarja kārtavīryas tasmāt kārtavīryāt sahasrabāhor ayaṃ dvibāhur ekena vegena tāvato bāṇān visṛjann adhika ity arthaḥ*—so Ct). See R. Goldman 1977.

"in archery" *iṣvastreṣu*: Literally, "in respect to bows (lit., arrow throwers)." Ck appears to read the compound as a *dvandva* referring to *iṣus*, ordinary arrows, and *astras*, "missiles *or* divine weapon-spells," in the use of both of which Lakṣmaṇa excels Kārtavīrya (*iṣvastre . . . bāṇaprayoge divyāstrayoge ca*).

21. "on the bare earth" *urvyām*: Literally, "on the earth."

22. "what has proven to be my idle boast" *mithyāpralaptam*: Literally, "false prattling." As the commentators remind us, the reference is to Rāma's earlier promise to consecrate Vibhīṣaṇa as king in place of his brother. This now seems to have been but an idle boast (*vibhīṣaṇo rājā na kṛta iti yad yataḥ tasmāt tad vibhīṣaṇam abhiṣekṣyāmīti mithyā pralaptaṃ pralapitam*—so Ct). See note to 6.13.9. The formal consecration of Vibhīṣaṇa occurs at 6.100.

"will torment me" *māṃ pradhakṣyati*: Literally, "it will burn me." The issue here is the epic aristocracy's fierce adherence to the truth of the given word. As Cg points out, the failure to deliver on a promise is regarded as equivalent to lying (*āśrutakāryanirvāhābhāvena mithyety ucyate*—so Cg).

23. "you should return home" *pratiyātum ito 'rhasi*: Literally, "you should return from here." Cg explains that we must add "to Kiṣkindhā." Printed editions of Ct (NSP and GPP 6.49.23) read the awkward *iva*, "as if, like," for *itaḥ*, "from here."

"for once mighty Rāvaṇa realizes that you no longer have me to assist you, he will attack" *matvā hīnaṃ mayā rājan rāvaṇo 'bhidraved balī*: Literally, "having realized [you] to be deprived of me, mighty Rāvaṇa may attack." D6,9–11, and the texts and printed editions of Ct and Cr read *sattva-*, "strength, power," for the gerund *matvā*, "having realized." D1,3,4,7,9–11, and the texts and printed editions of Ct and Cr read *abhibhaviṣyati*, "he will conquer," for *abhidraved balī*, "the mighty one might attack." The sense of the text of Ct, as found in GPP and NSP, is then: "O king, Rāvaṇa will overpower you, who are deprived of strength."

24. "once again... by that very same bridge" *punas tenaiva setunā*: D5–7,9,11,T,G3,M1–3, and the texts and printed editions of the southern commentators read instead *nīlena ca nalena ca*, "and with Nīla and Nala as well."

"together with your... allies" *sasuhṛjjanaḥ*: D7,9–11, and the texts and printed editions of Ct and Cr read instead *saparicchadam*, "together with [your] entourage."

25. "Hanumān accomplished feats" *kṛtaṃ hanumatā kāryam*: D9–11 and the texts and printed editions of Ct read instead *kṛtaṃ hi sumahat karma*, "a very great feat was accomplished." This reading fails to specify the agent of the feat, and translators differ in assigning it. Ct understands the referent to be to all the monkey heroes, starting with Hanumān (*hanumadādibhir*). Gita Press (1969, vol. 3, p. 1539) and Dutt (1893, p. 1244) take the reference to be to Sugrīva, whom Rāma is addressing. Shastri (1959, vol. 3, p. 120) and Pagani (1999, p. 982), who usually read with Ct, here appear to follow Cg and the critical edition in assigning the feat to Hanumān. Roussel (1903, vol. 3, p. 140) assigns the feat to the monkey troop leaders mentioned in the second half of the verse.

"the king of the apes" *ṛkṣarājena*: The reference here is to Jāmbavān. See Goldman 1989. See, too, 6.4.17 and 6.86.8 and notes.

"the overlord of the langurs" *golāṅgūlādhipena*: The reference here is to Gavākṣa. See 6.86.8 and note. Cf. 6.4.17.

26. "great deeds" *karma*: Literally, "deed, feat."

"Kesarin" *kesariṇā*: This is the name of Hanumān's earthly father, although, given the free use of names among monkeys and *rākṣasas*, it is by no means clear that this is the individual meant here. See Bulcke 1959 and S. Goldman 1999. See, too, 4.65.8; 6.4.30; and 7.35.20. Cf. 6.21.2.

"Saṃpāti" *saṃpātinā*: Cg reminds us that this is a monkey (i.e., not the vulture of the same name who informs the monkeys of Sītā's whereabouts at *Kiṣkindhākāṇḍa* 57.26ff.).

"fought fearsome battles in the war" *yuddham... saṃkhye ghoram... kṛtam*: Literally, "a terrible battle was made in the war."

27. "fought" *yuddham*: Literally, "battle." The verse is elliptical, and one must construe the noun with the adjective *kṛtam*, "was done," from the previous verse, as Ct suggests (*kṛtam iti pūrveṇa saṃbandhaḥ*).

"on my behalf" *madarthe*: D6,9–11, and the texts and printed editions of Ct and Cr read instead *durdharam*, "formidable, impossible to accomplish." The critical edition erroneously ascribes its reading to Ct instead of Cg. With the exception of Gita Press (1969, vol. 3, p. 1539), which reads with Cg and the critical edition, all printed editions of the text of Ct as well as all translators who follow that text render the variant.

"heedless of their lives" *tyaktajīvitaiḥ*: Literally, "by whom life has been abandoned."

28. "in your anxiety lest you transgress righteousness" *bhavatādharmabhīruṇā*: Literally, "by you, who fear unrighteousness." The commentators and printed editions differ as to how to break up the sequence. One can break it either as *bhavatā* + *adharmabhīruṇā* or as *bhavatā* + *dharmabhīruṇā* "by you who fear righteousness." The word division is, of course, a matter of interpretation, since manuscripts would show no break between the two words. The different readings are signaled in printed editions by the presence or absence of a space between the two words. Cm states unequivocally that the second word should be *adharma*, and Cg gives this as a second alternative. Ct takes strong exception to Cm's reading, denouncing it as "quite pointless" (*adharmabhīruṇeti cheda iti tīrthas tad viphalam eva*). He admits that, even with the reading he prefers, it is possible to interpret the sequence to mean "you who are fearful of abandoning righteousness (*dharmabhīruṇeti chede 'pi dharmatyāgād bhīruṇeti vyākhyātuṃ śakyatvāt*)." Cg explains this reading as meaning "fearful of the thought, 'righteousness will be destroyed' (*dharmo naśyatīti bhīruṇety arthaḥ*)." Translators render the expression variously, but, as with the commentators, both readings yield much the same sense. Dutt (1893, p. 1245), who follows the reading of Ct, observes, "*Dharma-bhiru—fearing righteousness*—is the epithet generally applied to persons fearing not in fact *righteousness*, but unrighteousness. This may be taken as an *idiotism* in Sanskrit."

29. "You have discharged the obligations of friendship." *mitrakāryaṃ kṛtam idam*: Literally, "This duty of a friend has been done."

30. "tawny-eyed" *kṛṣṇetarekṣaṇāḥ*: Literally, "whose eyes were other than black." The normal meaning of *kṛṣṇetara* would be "white," but this seems unlikely here. Commentators and, after them, translators differ in their understanding of the ambiguous compound. Ct and Cr, whom we have followed, gloss, "having yellow eyes *or* tawny-eyed (*piṅgākṣāḥ*—so Ct; *piṅgalanayanāḥ*—so Cr)." This kenning for monkeys is found elsewhere in the epic (see 6.22.33; 6.49.5; and notes). Cg and Cm, however, gloss, "red-eyed (*raktekṣaṇāḥ*)," presumably understanding that the monkeys' eyes are red because they are weeping.

"Rāma's" *tasya*: Literally, "his."

"began to weep" *vartayāṃcakrur aśrūṇi netraiḥ*: Literally, "they caused tears to flow through [their] eyes."

31. "having prevented all the troops from fleeing" *sarvāṇy anīkāni sthāpayitvā*: Literally, "having stabilized *or* immobilized all the troops." The reference is to Vibhīṣaṇa's efforts to prevent the flight of the terrified monkeys at 6.36.38 above. See note to 6.36.38.

32. "the monkeys" *vānarāḥ*: Ct and Ck indicate that these are the monkeys standing with Sugrīva [and so distinct from those whose flight Vibhīṣaṇa has just prevented] (*sugrīvasamīpasthā iti śeṣaḥ*).

"rushing toward them" *tvaritaṃ yāntam*: Literally, "going swiftly."

Following verse 32, Ś,Ñ1 [lines 1–2],V,B,D1–3,8,12,13,M3,D4 [after verse 31] insert a passage of six lines (two verses) [807*]. This passage is printed in brackets as verses 6.49.34–35 in KK with the notation that it does appear in the older manuscripts. VSP prints the passage as a footnote after verse 6.49.33: "Vibhīṣaṇa came up to find [the two heroes] lying on beds of arrows, motionless, unconscious, covered with the dust of the battlefield.[1–2] When the forest-dwelling monkeys, who had witnessed the might of the son of the *rākṣasa* king, saw the two princes struck down, they began to scatter from back to front, like clouds driven before the wind in autumn.[1] [3–6]"

[1]"the forest-dwelling monkeys... they began to scatter from back to front, like clouds driven before the wind in autumn" *jaghanyato vivyathire vanaukaso vāteritās te śaradīva meghāḥ*: The reading of M3, which is recorded in VSP and KK, substitutes a variant for lines 5 and 6, *vibhīṣaṇaṃ vivyathire ca dṛṣṭvā meghā yathā vāyuhatāḥ plavaṅgamāḥ*, "When the leaping monkeys saw Vibhīṣaṇa, they scattered like clouds whipped by the wind."

The meter is *upajāti* with a hypermetric *pāda* c.

Sarga 40

1. "Why is the army fleeing wildly, like a ship driven to and fro by contrary winds at sea" *kim iyaṃ vyathitā senā mūḍhavāteva naur jale*: Literally, "Why is the army agitated, like a ship [caught in] contrary winds on the water?" The image of a ship driven off course or foundering in a violent storm at sea is a popular one with the epic poets. Vālmīki has used this same phrase to describe the plight of Sītā at 5.26.8. Ct and Ck gloss, "possessing [i.e., caught in] winds blowing to and fro so as to cause confusion as to the [desired and undesired—so Ck] course ([*iṣṭāniṣṭa*]*digvyāmohakaravātyāvātavatī*)." Cg and Cm take the meaning to be "battered by winds blowing in the contrary direction, that is, driven off course by the wind. (*viruddhadigvāyvantarābhihata ity arthaḥ. vātyāhateti yāvat.*)"

2–3. "mighty" *mahābalam*: D7,9–11,T3, and the texts and printed editions of Ct and Cr read instead *mahāratham*, "great chariot-warrior."

"tightly bound with webs of arrows" *śarajālācitau*: The phrase occurs above at 6.36.4. See 6.36.4–7 and note above.

4. "son" *putram*: Either the term is used loosely for a relative of a younger generation or Sugrīva is now regarded as having effectively adopted his brother's son.

"I do not doubt that that is one reason." *nānimittam idaṃ manye*: Literally, "I do not think that this is not a reason" or "I do not think that this has no cause." The commentators are divided as to the reference of the pronoun *idam*, "this, that." Cs, Ck, and Cm (second alternative) understand the reference to be to the flight of the monkeys (*kapipalāyanam*). Thus, they and all translators of the southern recension understand the meaning of the phrase to be "I do not think that there is no reason for this [the flight of the monkeys]." This interpretation makes little sense to us, since there is no indication that Sugrīva does not think that there is no reason for the monkeys to flee. He has merely inquired as to that reason. We follow Ct, Cr, Cm (first alternative), and Cg in understanding the pronoun to refer to the reason proposed by Aṅgada for the flight, that is, the apparent death of Rāma and Lakṣmaṇa. What the commentators are saying in essence is that, while not denying the causal power of Rāma's apparent demise, Sugrīva feels that the sudden panic must be the result of some more immediate cause (*idaṃ raghusiṃhayoḥ śaratalpaśayanam animittaṃ na bhavatīti manye kiṃ tu bhayenānyabhayahetunātra bhavitavyam ity arthaḥ*—so Cm).

"Still, there must be some other cause for their alarm." *bhavitavyaṃ bhayena tu*: Literally, "But there must be a danger."

5. Ct and Ck argue that, although the monkeys (in their distress over Rāma's fall) have downcast faces and have dropped their weapons, they have hitherto stood their ground. Only now, however, do they run away. This, these commentators hold, is proof that there has been some new cause for alarm. (*viṣaṇṇavadanās tyaktapraharaṇāś ca santa etāvatparyantam ihaiva sthitāḥ. samprati tv ito diśaḥ pratipalāyante. tat tu trāsāt sāmpratikād eva nānyathety arthaḥ.*)

"dropped their weapons" *tyaktapraharaṇāḥ*: Literally, "by whom weapons were abandoned." Cg meticulously notes that this would refer to stones, etc. (*tyaktaśilādyāyudhāḥ*).

"terror" *trāsāt*: Cs, as well as Ct and Ck, as noted above, stresses that this is some new cause for alarm (*nūtanabhīteḥ*).

6. "They have no sense of shame before one another" *anyonyasya na lajjante*: As Ct and Ck explain, they experience no shame, even though they are engaged in cowardly flight that is condemned by all true heroes (*śūragarhite palāyane kriyamāṇe na lajjāṃ prāpnuvantīty arthaḥ*).

"They drag one another out of their way" *viprakarṣanti cānyonyam*: Literally, "they drag one another." We have embellished the phrase in keeping with the comments of Ct and Ck, who supply the phrase "those who obstruct their flight (*palāyana[patana*—Ck] *pratirodhakān*)," and Cg, who adds, "in order to go faster (*drutagamanārtham*)."

7. "hailed" *vardhayāmāsa*: Literally, "he magnified, congratulated." Ct and Ck remark that he hailed him with the words, "Be victorious!" (*vijayī bhaveti vacanenety bhāvaḥ*).

"stared" *niraikṣata*: D6,9–11,T2,3,G3,M5, and the texts and printed editions of Ct and Cr read instead *jayāśiṣā*, "with blessings of victory." With this reading, one must take Rāghava, along with Sugrīva, to be the object of the verb *vardhayāmāsa*. This seems particularly inapposite in light of the fact that Rāma is apparently near death.

8. "Vibhīṣaṇa, who was the cause of the monkeys' terror" *vibhīṣaṇaṃ tam... vānarabhīṣaṇam*: Literally, "Vibhīṣaṇa, the terror of the monkeys." Note the play on Vibhīṣaṇa's name, literally, "the terrifier."

"Jāmbavān... who was close at hand" *samīpasthaṃ jāmbavantam*: D9–11 and the texts and printed editions of Ct and Cr read instead *mahātmānaṃ samīpastham*, "the great [king of the apes], who was close at hand."

9. "fleeing in terror, fearing" *vidravanti paritrastāḥ*: The critical editors mark this *pāda* (c) as doubtful, a rare occurrence in this book. Ñ,V,B,D1,3–7,9,10,T1,G2,3,M5 read instead *dravaṃty āgatasaṃtrāsāḥ*. V1 and the texts and printed editions of Ct read *dravanty āyatasaṃtrāsāḥ*. The meaning is much the same as that of the critical edition.

10. "in all directions" *bahudhā*: Literally, "in many ways."

"as fast as they can" *śīghram*: Literally, swiftly, at once." The adverb might also be construed with the imperative *paryavasthāpaya*, "you must stop."

"only Vibhīṣaṇa" *vibhīṣaṇam*: Literally, "Vibhīṣaṇa."

13. "deeply distraught" *vyathitendriyaḥ*: Literally, "one whose senses were agitated." Ś,Ñ,V,B,D1–4,7–13,T3,G1,2, and the texts and printed editions of Ct and Cr read instead *vyathitas tadā*, "[was] then distraught."

16. "evil and unworthy son" *putreṇa... duṣputreṇa durātmanā*: Literally, "by that son, that evil son, that bad one." We follow Cg, who explains *duṣputreṇa* as "bringing

disgrace to his father through his treacherous fighting (*kapaṭayuddhena pitur avadyāvahena*)."

"has tricked these two" *chalitau*: Literally, "[the two were] deceived." D9–11,M1,2, and the texts and printed editions of Ct and Cr read instead *vañcitau*, "[those two were] tricked." T1,M3, and the texts and printed editions of Cg read instead *cālitau*, literally, "[the two were] caused to move." Cg glosses, "tricked (*vañcitau*)."

"whose valor was untainted by guile" *ṛjuvikramau*: Literally, "[those two] of straightforward valor."

17. "they . . . they" *imau . . . imau*: Cs, alone among the commentators, is disturbed by the apparent redundancy. He proposes to resolve the problem either by taking the two halves of the verse as separate utterances, as we have done, or, in his own idiosyncratic fashion, reading at least one of the pronouns lexically as a compound in the sense of "possessing the beauty of the god of love (*iḥ kāmaḥ tasyāpi mā śobhā yābhyām etau*)." By this he understands that Rāma and Lakṣmaṇa have not lost the beauty associated with Kāmadeva.

"lie sleeping" *suptau*: Literally, "are asleep."

"two hedgehogs" *śalyakau*: The idea here is that the many arrows protruding from the bodies of the heroes make them resemble spiny creatures. Sanskrit does not appear to consistently distinguish between the common Indian porcupine (*Hystrix Leucura*) and such spiny creatures as the collared hedgehog (*Erinaceus Collaris*), both of which range widely over India. Ck and Ct gloss *śvāvidh*, a term generally used to indicate the porcupine but one that appears similarly nonspecific. Cg glosses, *kaṇṭakivarāhaḥ*, "spiny boar *or* pig," which also lacks specificity. At 4.17.34, two animals, *śalyaka* and *śvāvidh*, are named among the five-clawed animals deemed fit for consumption by high-caste Hindus. There the commentators are more copious in their discussion of these animals. (See notes to 4.17.34. Cf. *Mahābhāṣya* [Kielhorn], p. 5, lines 14–17.) At 4.17.34, the two terms were translated as "hedgehog" and "porcupine," respectively, and, for consistency, we use the same terminology here, despite the fact that all translators consulted, with the exception of Dutt and Gorresio, understand the animal to be a porcupine. Dutt (1893, p. 1246) leaves the term untranslated as "Salyakas [*sic*]," noting in a footnote that it refers to "a tree." Dutt is no doubt reading the term as a variant of *sallakī* or *śallakī*, which can refer either to a porcupine or a tree (specifically, the *Shorea Robusta*). The image of a tree, however, does not seem to suit the context. Gorresio (1856, vol. 9, p. 279) takes *śalyaka* in the sense of *śalya*, "stake, staff, dart," translating "*pali*."

18. "upon whose might I had pinned my hopes for royal consecration" *yayor vīryam upāśritya pratiṣṭhā kāṅkṣitā mayā*: Literally, "relying upon the might of whom, I had desired installation." The word *pratiṣṭhā* has many meanings, several of which, including "high station, inauguration, *or* desired goal," would be suitable in the context. We have added the word "royal," following Ct, who glosses, "placement in the kingship (*rājye sthitiḥ*)." See 6.13.9; 6.19.26–27; and 6.100.9 and notes.

"on the point of death" *dehanāśāya*: Literally, "for the destruction of the body." The phrase is ambiguous here, as Cs points out. It can refer either to the death of Rāma and Lakṣmaṇa or the death [at Rāvaṇa's hands] of Vibhīṣaṇa himself. (*svadehanāśāya. yadvā maddehanāśaya.*) Cr, the only other commentator to remark on the expression, glosses, "for the destruction of our advancement (*asmadvṛddhipradhvaṃsanāya*)." Translators are divided. Dutt (1893, p. 1246) and Gita Press (1969, vol. 3, p. 1541) understand as we do. Roussel (1903, vol. 3, p. 143), Pagani (1999, p. 984), and Shastri (1959, vol. 3, p. 122) understand as does Cr. Gorresio's text (6.25.19) reads *mama*, "my," for *deha-*, "body," avoiding the ambiguity of the critical text. We believe it is more likely that Vibhīṣaṇa is referring to what he sees as the impending death of Rāma and Lakṣmaṇa, since he refers to his own probable demise in the following verse.

19. "as good as dead" *vipannaḥ*: Literally, "dead."

"accomplished his vow" *prāptapratijñaḥ*: Ck, Ct, and Cs understand that this refers to Rāvaṇa's vow never to give up Sītā (*nirvṛttasītāparityāgābhāvapratijñaḥ*—so Ct).

"has had his wish fulfilled" *sakāmaḥ... kṛtaḥ*: Literally, "has been made one with a wish." Ck and Ct explain that Rāvaṇa has had his desire fulfilled by his son [Indrajit]. Cr says that this has been accomplished by time or fate (*kālena*). Cs specifies the nature of the wish, saying that it was "to attain unrivaled kingship through the death of me [Vibhīṣaṇa]," and understands that this has been accomplished through the sleep or comatose state of the two heroes. (*mannāśena niṣkaṇṭakarājyaprāptyā kṛtaḥ. anayor evaṃ svāpeneti śeṣaḥ.*)

20. "Vibhīṣaṇa... embraced him" *taṃ pariṣvajya vibhīṣaṇam*: Literally, "him... having embraced Vibhīṣaṇa." Cs thinks that, by effecting a change in the expected word order, i.e., in separating the noun and its pronoun by the gerund, the poet is signaling a change in the expected outcome of Vibhīṣaṇa's lamentation (*padavyatyāsena vilāpa-phalakasya vibhīṣaṇotprekṣitasya vyatyāsaṃ kavir avagamayāmāseti jñeyam*).

21. "Rāvaṇa... will not retain the kingship here" *rāvaṇaḥ... sa rājyaṃ neha lapsyate*: Literally, "He, Rāvaṇa, will not acquire the kingship here." The textual support for the word *rājyam*, "kingship," is quite weak. Only two manuscripts (T2,3) read with the critical edition. Two *devanāgarī* manuscripts (D7,9) read *svarājyam*, "his own kingship," for *sa rājyam*, "he... kingdom." All other manuscripts read either *svakāmam*, "his own desire" (D5,6,10,11,Ct,Ck,Cr), *sa kāmam*, "he [will not obtain] his desire" (T1,G,M,Cg,Cm,Crā,Cv), or *sakāmaḥ* [*na bhaviṣyati*], "he will not be one whose desire is fulfilled" (Ś,Ñ,V,B,D1–4,8,12,13). The reading that probably should have been selected (although marked as doubtful) is *sa kāmam*.

22. "merely pinioned by arrows" *śarasaṃpīḍitau*: Literally, "tormented *or* afflicted by arrows." Our translation attempts to express Sugrīva's reassurance that, despite appearances, Rāma and Lakṣmaṇa are not mortally wounded. Textual support for the reading is strong. However, the texts of the southern commentators, printed editions of their texts, and the translations that follow them show significant variants for this phrase. Thus, D9–11 and the texts and printed editions of Ct, Ck, Cr, and Cs read *garuḍādhiṣṭhitau*, "under the protection of Garuḍa." Ct explains that Rāma and Lakṣmaṇa are *garuḍopāsakatayā vijñātau*, "well known as devotees of Garuḍa," or, as a *bahuvrīhi*, "have Garuḍa as their devotee." Cs regards Ct's gloss of the compound in the first interpretation as "unfounded (*nirmūlam artham*)." Cs himself understands the compound to refer to the fact that Rāma, as Viṣṇu, uses Garuḍa as his vehicle (*garuḍe 'dhiṣṭhitau garuḍavāhano rāmaḥ*). He then generalizes this epithet of Rāma to include Lakṣmaṇa. Cs regards this reading as authentic, since the role of Garuḍa in releasing the serpent-weapons is well known from this passage and from many purāṇic sources. (*ayam eva pāṭho nyāyyaḥ. garuḍāgamanena nāgapāśaviyogasyātrottaratreva bahupurāṇeṣu śravaṇāt.*) Cs further notes Ct's quotation of Cm, saying that Ct, in accepting his own reading in preference to Cm's, suggests that the latter's reading is fanciful (*na rujā*

pīḍitāv iti paṭhitveti tīrthapāṭhasya tadutprekṣitatvaṃ sūcayan nāgojibhaṭṭaḥ svayaṃ pāṅktaṃ garuḍādhiṣṭhitāv iti paṭhitvā garuḍopāsakatayā viditāv iti nirmūlam arthaṃ vadaṃs tādṛśa eveti saṃtoṣṭavyam). See verse 23 below, where Cs continues his attack on Ct.

The reading *garuḍādhiṣṭhitau* raises controversy among the commentators, since it suggests that Sugrīva has some kind of precognition regarding Garuḍa's impending intervention (see verse 33ff. below). Thus, Cr remarks that this phrase makes clear the fact that Sugrīva possesses knowledge of the past, present, and future (*etena sugrīvasya trikālajñatvaṃ vyaktam*). Cv strongly criticizes this reading, however, regarding it as "a lapse on the part of the scribe," since, as he asserts, "Sugrīva has no knowledge of future events." (*garuḍādhiṣṭhitāv iti lekhakapramādāl likhitaḥ. sugrīvasya bhaviṣyad-arthajñānaṃ nāsti.*) Cv further bolsters his argument with reference to Sugrīva's instructions [to Suṣeṇa (see verse 23 below), which make no allusion to any expected help from Garuḍa]. Cv concludes his remarks by noting, as a variant, the reading of the critical edition.

D7,G1,M3, and Cv, Crā, Cg, and Cm read instead *na rujā pīḍitau*, literally, "[those two] are not afflicted by [serious] injury." As Cv, Cg, and Cm [quoted by Ct] explain, the sense of the reading is that the heroes are not fatally wounded, but their injuries are such as to lead to only a temporary loss of consciousness (*iyaṃ rujānayor ātyanti-kahānikarī na bhavati. kiṃtu mohamātrakāriṇīty arthaḥ*—so Cg). All translators of the southern recension follow the reading of Ct, with the exception of Raghunathan (1982, vol. 3, p. 121), who follows Cg.

23. "consoled and reassured" *sāntvayitvā tu samāśvāsya ca*: Commentators differ both as to the exact meanings of these near synonyms and to their objects (see note to 6.2.14). Ct and Ck understand that the first term refers to Sugrīva's reassurance of Vibhīṣaṇa concerning the anticipated grace of Garuḍa (*garuḍānugrahasaṃbhāvanayā*). By the second, Ct understands that Sugrīva's words suggest his own knowledge that Rāma is an *avatāra* of the Lord (*anena sugrīvavākyena rāmaviṣayaṃ svasya bhagavad-avatāratvajñānaṃ sūcitam*). Cs understands the first gerund to have Vibhīṣaṇa as its object and the second to be directed toward Suṣeṇa. This second gerund, he argues, refers to the instructions to Suṣeṇa to go [and take Rāma and Lakṣmaṇa back to Kiṣkindhā] in verse 24 below. Cs then continues his attack on what he views as Ct's muddled theology and confused syntactical skills. He quotes Ct, faulting him for the inadequacy of his syntactical knowledge. He contends that Ct is in error in so frequently construing groups of two or three verses as a single syntactic unit (*nago-jibhaṭṭasya bahusthaleṣu dvitrādīnāṃ ślokānām ekānvayaṃ bruvato 'nvayajñānadāridriyaṃ dyotyate*). He then quotes Ct's remarks about the grace of Garuḍa and Sugrīva's alleged knowledge of Rāma's *avatāra*-hood, recommending that these contradictory statements be utterly disregarded. He claims that it is well known that the devotee (i.e., Garuḍa) would be the receptacle of the grace of the Lord, who is an *avatāra* [rather than the other way around]. (*iti svavacanavyāhatam ity upekṣyam. tena bhagavadavatāra-tvahetor upāsakatvasya tadanugrahapātratvasyaiva ca pratīteḥ.*) See note 22 above, where Cs begins his attack on Ct.

Cr understands *sāntvayitvā* to mean "having informed (*bodhayitvā*)" and *samāśvāsya* as "having dispelled the grief [of] (*tāpaṃ nirasya*)." Both are understood as referring to Vibhīṣaṇa.

24. "once they have regained consciousness" *labdhasaṃjñau*: Ck and Ct understand, "until they will have regained consciousness (*yāval labdhasaṃjñau bhaviṣyataḥ*)." These

commentators, followed by Roussel (1903, vol. 3, p. 143) and Shastri (1959, vol. 3, p. 122), thus understand that the monkeys are to carry the unconscious brothers to Kiṣkindhā and guard them there until they recover. Our interpretation, which accords with that of Cr, is followed by Gita Press (1969, vol. 3, p. 1542), Dutt (1893, p. 1247), and Raghunathan (1982, vol. 3, pp. 121–22). Pagani (1999, p. 984) fails to translate the compound. Gorresio, following his text (6.25.24), which reads *visaṃjñau*, "unconscious," translates, "*che son qui fuor di senso*" (1856, vol. 9, p. 280).

25. "just as Śakra did Śrī when she was lost" *śakro naṣṭām iva śriyam*: Literally, "like Śakra the lost Śrī." The mythological reference is obscure, and the commentators are silent. The allusion, however, appears similar to the one Sītā herself made at 5.36.51. There the commentators provide a variety of mythological references. See notes to 5.36.51.

26–27. "this speech" *etat*: Literally, "this."

"I have heard about" *anubhūtam*: Literally, "experienced." We follow Cg in supplying the pronoun *mayā*, "by me," and in understanding the participle in the sense of "known by me (*mayā jñātam*)." Several of the translators consulted take the term literally to imply that Suṣeṇa had been an actual witness of this mythical contest. See Dutt (1893, p. 1247), Raghunathan (1982, vol. 3, p. 122), and Gita Press (1969, vol. 3, p. 1542). We think, however, that this reading may be too strong. Roussel (1903, vol. 3, p. 143), followed by Shastri (1959, vol. 3, p. 123) and Pagani (1999, p. 984), reads the participle in the rather unusual sense of "took place," thus ignoring the force of the *upasarga*. We think that this reading may be too weak.

"terrible" *sudāruṇam*: D7,9–11, and the texts and printed editions of Ct and Cr read instead *purātanam*, "ancient."

"concealed themselves" *chādayantaḥ*: Literally, "covering, veiling." We follow the interpretation of Ck and Ct, understanding that the *dānavas*, like Indrajit in the present circumstance, concealed themselves from view through their powers of illusion (*māyayendrajidvad ātmānaṃ prachādayantaḥ*).

"who were expert in the use of arrows" *śarasaṃsparśakovidāḥ*: Literally, "[those who were] expert in arrow contact." We follow the reading of the commentators, who understand this unusual use of the term *saṃsparśa-* to refer to "expertise taking the form of striking the target with respect to arrows (*śarasaṃsparśe śaraviṣaye lakṣyavedhanarūpe kovidān*—so Ck, Ct)." Cg glosses *sparśa* with *dānam*, which here he uses in its sense of "cutting, piercing." He glosses, "able to use arrows." (*śaraprayogasamarthāḥ. sparśo dānam iti.*) B2,D4,10,11,13,M1,2, and the texts and printed editions of Ck and Ct read the accusative *-kovidān* for the nominative *-kovidāḥ*. In this reading, the epithet thus applies to the gods rather than to the *asuras*.

28. "Bṛhaspati" *bṛhaspatiḥ*: Bṛhaspati is the *purohita*, or spiritual preceptor, of the gods. He is normally depicted as lacking the life-restorative skills possessed by his arch rival, Uśanas Kāvya or Śukrācārya, the *purohita* of the *asuras*. According to *Mahābhārata* 1.71, Bṛhaspati, whose patrons are suffering from this unequal distribution of knowledge, dispatches his son Kaca to secure the life-restorative spell (*mṛtasaṃjīvanī vidyā*) through the deceitful courtship of Uśanas's daughter, Devayānī. The present passage is one of the few, if not the only one, in which allusion to Bṛhaspati's use of this magical skill is made. Cf. *MatsyaP* 47 and *PadmaP* 5.13.202ff. See R. Goldman 1977 and Sutherland 1979. See 6.7.9–10; 6.11.42; 6.115.51; and notes. Cf. 6.4.42; 6.45.12; and notes.

"with magical spells" *vidyābhiḥ*: Cg and Cm identify these spells as "such spells as the one for bringing the dead back to life (*mṛtasaṃjīvanīprabhṛtibhiḥ*)." Ck and Ct add to this "mental concentration on Garuḍa, etc. (*garuḍādidhyānarūpāmṛtajīvanībhiḥ*—so Ct)." This is in keeping with their reading of verse 22 above, where they seem to prematurely introduce Garuḍa into the narrative. See note to verse 22 above.

29. "the ocean of milk" *kṣīrodam*...*sāgaram*: Literally, "the ocean having milk for water." This is one of the seven oceans of purāṇic cosmology that separate the concentric *dvīpas*, or continents of the earth. The tale of the churning of the ocean for *amṛta*, the nectar or elixir of immortality, is told in the *Bālakāṇḍa* (1.44.14–27 and notes) and many other places in the epic and purāṇic literature (*MBh* 1.15ff.; *BhāgP* 8.6–9; *MatsyaP* 249.51; *ViṣṇuP* 1.9; etc.) See Bedekar 1967, pp. 7–61 and Dange 1969, pp. 239–80. See, too, 6.12.22; 6.41.17; 6.53.23; 6.80.19; 6.105.19; and notes. The mythic association of the ocean of milk with the production of *amṛta*, as noted in verse 32 below, is undoubtedly behind the notion expressed here that that particular ocean is the source of life-restorative healing herbs. See note to verse 30 below. See note to 6.34.17.

30. "Those tawny monkeys" *harayaḥ*: We agree with Cr, Ck, and Ct in understanding the term here to be restricted to Saṃpāti, Panasa, and their party (*saṃpātyādayo harayaḥ*—so Ck, Ct).

"the two powerful healing herbs that grow on the mountains there" *pārvatī te mahauṣadhī*: Literally, "the two great mountain herbs." A number of southern manuscripts (D5–7,T,G1,3,M3) and the texts and printed editions of Cv, Crā, Cm, and Cg read instead the plural, *pārvatīs tā mahauṣadhīḥ*, in place of the dual.

"the divine *saṃjīvakaraṇī*, restorer of life, and the *viśalyā*, healer of arrow wounds" *saṃjīvakaraṇīṃ divyāṃ viśalyām*: Literally, "the divine *saṃjīvakaraṇī* and the *viśalyā*." These are two of the four herbs that Jāmbavān will dispatch Hanumān to procure from the mountain of herbs at 6.61.33 below, where, for a second time, Rāma and Lakṣmaṇa permit themselves to succumb to the power of the weapons Indrajit had received from Brahmā (see 6.36.10 and note).

In the *Rāmopākhyāna* (*MBh* 3.272.5–6), Sugrīva actually employs the *viśalyā* herb along with *mantras* to free Rāma and Lakṣmaṇa from the bonds of Indrajit's arrows. This is in stark contrast to Vālmīki's version in which, in fact, the herbs are neither used nor even fetched at this point since Garuḍa will shortly intervene to make them otiose. In Vālmīki, the herbs will only be secured and employed later on in the narrative as noted above. The abortive reference to the herbs here and the sudden appearance of Garuḍa may suggest that Vālmīki's version of this episode is, in fact, a somewhat clumsy Vaiṣṇava expansion of the narrative. See Brockington 1984, pp. 194–95, 199. See, too, note to verse 32 below.

According to Pagani (1999, p. 1662), the *viśalyā* and *saṃjīvanī* are used on Yudhiṣṭhira to remove Karṇa's arrows in the *Karṇaparvan* (see *MBh* 8.58.21). A plant called *viśalyā* (*Delphinium denudatum*) is mentioned in the medicinal literature. See, for example, *Bhāvaprakāśa* 3.7; *Rajanighaṇṭu* 3.14; 5.158; 6.127; and 24.3; *Aṣṭāṅgahṛdaya* 1.84; 6.38; 15.28; 22.69; etc. It is said to grow in the Himalayas at altitudes between seventeen hundred and twenty-three hundred meters. See 6.61.32–33; 6.89.14–16; and notes.

"created by the gods" *devanirmitām*: The compound is ambiguous, as the prior member can refer to one god or many. Ck and Ct take *deva-* in the singular and see it as a reference to Brahmā (*brahmaṇā nirmitām*). They do this possibly with the thought that it takes a healing herb created by Brahmā to cure a wound inflicted by one of Brahmā's weapons. Cr glosses *paramātmanā*, "by the Supreme Spirit," a term that is itself laden with ambiguity. Roussel (1903, vol. 3, p. 143), Shastri (1959, vol. 3, p. 123), and Pagani (1999, p. 984) all understand the herb to have been produced by a single unnamed divinity. Gita Press (1969, vol. 3, p. 1542) follows Ck and Ct and translates, "Brahmā." Gorresio (1856, vol. 9, p. 281), Dutt (1893, p. 1247), and Raghunathan (1982, vol. 3, p. 122) translate as we do. Our reading seems more in conformance with the plural term *devaiḥ*, "by the gods," in verse 32 below.

31. "two mountains" *parvatau*: D5–7,9–11,T,G1,3,M3, and the texts and printed editions of the southern commentators read instead *kṣīrode*, "in the ocean of milk." Compare 6.61.2–30; 6.89.14–15; and notes, where Hanumān is instructed to go for the medicinal plants to a single mountain of healing herbs (*oṣadhiparvata*), which is there said to be situated between Mount Kailāsa and Mount Ṛṣabha in the Himalayas.

"called Candra and Droṇa" *candraś ca nāma droṇaś ca*: Compare 6.61.29–30 and notes. Both Droṇa and Candra are mentioned in the *Brahmāṇḍapurāṇa* (1.18.76). Mount Droṇa (Droṇācala or Droṇagiri) is well known and mentioned in various *purāṇas* as a source of healing herbs (see, for example, *BhāgP* 5.19.16; *BrahmP* 20.26; *BrahmāṇḍP* 1.19.38; *GaruḍaP* 1.56.6; *KūrmaP* 1.47.14; *Liṅgapurāṇa* 153.6; *Nāradapurāṇa* 1.104.19; and *ViṣṇuP* 2.4.26).

32. "Those two supreme herbs of healing were planted on the mountains there by the gods." *te tatra nihite devaiḥ parvate paramauṣadhī*: We agree with Cg in reading *parvate*, "on the mountain," as a collective singular (*jātyekavacanam*) for the dual. Manuscripts show considerable variation in the first half of the verse. The texts and printed editions of Ct, Cr, and Ck read instead *tau tatra vihitau devaiḥ parvatau tau mahodadhau*, "and those two mountains were placed there near [*or* in] the great ocean by the gods."

"Hanumān" *hanūmān*: The abrupt introduction of Hanumān, hitherto unnamed in this passage, provokes various explanations on the part of the commentators. Ck and Ct note: "Although Panasa and the rest are able to recognize [the herbs], still, Hanumān should go to ensure a speedy return (*yady api panasādayo jānanti tathāpi śīghram āgamanārthaṃ vāyusuto yātu*)." Cr suggests that the reason for sending Hanumān is that a mission of a single individual is more likely to succeed (*ekakartṛkagamanenaiva kāryaṃ setsyatīty abhipretyāha*) and claims that the verse suggests the extraordinary speed of Hanumān (*etena hanūmato vegātiśayaḥ sūcitaḥ*). Cg thinks the idea is that, while Panasa and the rest are to go and bring other herbs, Hanumān is specifically sent to bring the two potent herbs first mentioned in verse 30 above. (*auṣadhyantarānayane panasādayo gacchantu. saṃjīvaviśalyānayane tu hanumān gacchatv iti vijñeyam.*)

Following verse 32, some northern and southern manuscripts (Ś,D1–3,8,12,13,T2,3) insert a lengthy passage of ninety-four lines (App. I, No. 25) in which the divine sage Nārada appears to remind Rāma of his divinity and exhort him to action. Lines 88–94 are known to the entire northern recension (including Ñ,V,B, and Gorresio). In these lines, the wind god, Vāyu, arrives on the scene to whisper a similar exhortation into Rāma's ear and to urge him to call to mind the divinity Garuḍa, enemy of the serpents. In the southern recension and critical edition, no such transitional figures appear. Instead, Garuḍa, unheralded and without any initiative on Rāma's part, suddenly bursts upon the scene, rendering otiose the plan to send Hanumān and the other monkeys to bring the restorative herbs. This mission, however, will be taken up later in the narrative when Rāma, Lakṣmaṇa, and the monkeys are again incapacitated by Indrajit's weapons (see 6.60–61 below). The disruption of the narrative here is curious, especially in light of the *Rāmopākhyāna*, where Sugrīva restores the brothers with the two powerful herbs but without having to send anyone to fetch them. Here, as in the north, it would seem that a Vaiṣṇava hand has expanded and somewhat distorted the narrative. See notes to verse 30 above.

33. "hurling up the water . . . driving away the lightning-streaked clouds" *meghāṃś cāpi savidyutaḥ / paryasyan*: Literally, "tossing the waters and clouds with [their] lightning. D6,7,9–11,T3,G2, and the texts and printed editions of Ct, Ck, and Cr read instead the nominative *meghāḥ*, "clouds," for the critical edition's accusative. This, of course, obliges one to read the adjective *savidyutaḥ*, "with lightning," as a nominative as well. Given this reading, the translation would be, "there arose clouds flashing with lightning and a wind hurling up the waters in the ocean."

"the very mountains" *parvatān*: Literally, "mountains." D5,T1,M3, and the texts and printed editions of Cm and Cg read instead *medinīm*, "the earth."

34. "That powerful wind, driven by a pair of wings, snapped the branches of all the island's great trees and sent them flying, roots and all, into the salt sea." *mahatā pakṣavātena sarve dvīpamahādrumāḥ / nipetur bhagnaviṭapāḥ samūlā lavaṇāmbhasi //*: Literally, "By [means of] of the great wind from wings, all the great trees of the island fell, their branches broken, along with their roots, into the salt sea."

"That . . . wind, driven by a pair of wings" *pakṣavātena*: The blast of wind, of course, is created by Garuḍa's mighty wings, although our text does not introduce Garuḍa explicitly until verse 36 below. Roussel (1903, vol. 3, p. 144) oddly translates, "*coup d'aile de Vāta*," seeming to read the compound in inverted order. In this unhappy choice, he is followed by Shastri (1959, vol. 3, p. 123), "stroke of Vata's wing," and Pagani (1999, p. 985), "*souffle d'aile du vent.*"

"snapped the branches . . . sent them flying" *nipetur bhagnaviṭapāḥ*: Literally, "[their] branches broken, they fell." The text of GPP (6.50.34) shows a typesetting error in which the syllables *petu*[*r*] have been omitted, yielding an erroneous and hypermetric reading: *nirbhagnaviṭapāḥ*, "their branches broken."

"all the island's great trees" *sarve dvīpamahādrumāḥ*: A variety of manuscripts and the printed editions of the southern commentators read instead *sarvadvīpamahādrumāḥ*, which makes it ambiguous as to whether to read the compound as "all the great trees on the island" or "the great trees of all the islands." Among the commentators consulted, only Ct opts for the second reading, referring to the islands in the ocean. In this he is followed by Dutt (1893, p. 1248), Roussel (1903, vol. 3, p. 144), and Pagani (1999, p. 985).

"roots and all" *samūlāḥ*: Literally, "along with [their] roots." D9–11 and the texts and printed editions of Ct and Cr read *salile*, "in the water."

35. "hooded" *bhoginaḥ*: Literally, "possessing hoods [*or* coils]." This term is often used as a kenning for snakes, particularly cobras, but here it must be taken as an adjective modifying *pannagāḥ*, "serpents." The commentators generally understand the term here to mean "having huge bodies (*mahākāyāḥ*—Ct, Cr, Cm; *praśastakāyāḥ*—Cg).

"who dwelt there" *tatravāsinaḥ*: Ck, Ct, and Cr take the reference to be to those snakes living in the nearby Malaya mountains (*tatsamīpamalayanivāsinaḥ*—Cr). Cg understands, "those living on the island of Laṅkā (*laṅkādvīpavāsinaḥ*)." Cm thinks the reference is to "those that live in the ocean (*samudravāsinaḥ*)."

"the great sea serpents" *yādāṃsi*: The term normally refers to any large marine animal. Here, however, the reference is probably to sea snakes, since, like their terrestrial cousins, they would instinctively fear Garuḍa.

"plunged deep into the salt sea" *jagmuś ca lavaṇārṇavam*: Literally, "they went to the salt sea." We agree with Ct, Cg, and Cm, who understand that, in their fear, the sea serpents plunged into the depths (*bhayād antarmagnāni*—Ct). Cr notes that their flight suggests that Garuḍa is aware of Rāma's desire [to have the snakes destroyed] (*etena garuḍasya rāmābhiprāyābhijñatvaṃ sūcitam*).

37. "those two virtuous . . . men" *tau satpuruṣau*: Literally, "those two good men." B1,2,D1,5,7,9–11,T2,3, and the texts and printed editions of Ct and Cr read instead *tu tau puruṣau*, "but those two men."

"immensely powerful" *mahābalau*: Ś,Ñ,V,B,D1–5,7–13,T3,M3, and the texts and printed editions of Ct and Cr read instead the instrumental *mahābalaiḥ*, in which case the adjective applies to the great serpents rather than the two heroes.

38. "Suparṇa" *suparṇaḥ*: This epithet of Garuḍa, meaning "having splendid wings," is frequently used as an alternate name for Garuḍa as well as a generic term for the class of supernatural birds.

"spying" *dṛṣṭvā*: Literally, "having seen." V,D7,9–11,G3, and the texts and printed editions of Ct and Cr read instead *spṛṣṭvā*, "having touched."

"greeted them" *pratyabhinandya*: Literally, "having greeted." Ck, Ct, and Cr understand that Garuḍa greets the brothers with blessings of victory (*vijayāśiṣā*—Ck, Ct). D5,T1,M3, and the texts and printed editions of Cg read instead *pratyabhinanditaḥ*, "greeted, welcomed," which then becomes an adjective modifying Suparṇa.

"with both his hands" *pāṇibhyām*: This term raises the issue as to how we are to visualize Garuḍa. He is sometimes depicted in painting and sculpture as a bird with no human attributes, but also frequently as a sort of bird-man with a human body plus wings and a beaklike nose. Evidently here the poet sees him as somewhat anthropomorphic. See, too, verse 44 below, where the commentators discuss Garuḍa's form.

39. "wounds" *vraṇāḥ*: Ct, Cg, and Ck all take this term in its normal sense of "wounds," presumably those caused by the arrows that had pierced the two heroes. Cr, however, who rejects the idea that these divinities could actually suffer wounds, understands the reference to be to "woundlike indentations caused by the constriction of the *nāgas* (*nāgānāṃ sthityā vraṇavadavabhāsamānāvanatapradeśāḥ*)." See note to 6.35.9.

"lustrous" *suvarṇe*: Cf. note to 6.61.32–33.

40. Ct observes that we are to understand that assistance has been rendered by Garuḍa at the command of the primal form of Lord Rāma, who has incarnated himself here with other divinities (*atrānyair devair avatīrya bhagavato rāmasya mūlamūrter ājñayopakāraḥ saṃpāditaḥ garuḍena tu svarūpata eveti bodhyam*). Ck also elaborates on this theme, bringing out, once more, that, although endowed with divine weapons, Rāma does not kill Indrajit, who is operating under the protection of Brahmā's boon.

Cg and Cm observe that the syllable *-dhi-* in the word *buddhiḥ* of *pāda* c marks the seventeenth syllable of the *Gāyatrīmantra*, which is used as an index of Vālmīki's text. See note to 6.1.1.

"their cardinal virtues" *mahāguṇāḥ . . . tayoḥ*: Our translation agrees with Roussel (1903, vol. 3, p. 144), Shastri (1959, vol. 3, p. 123), and Pagani (1999, p. 985). Raghunathan (1982, vol. 3, p. 122) translates, "priceless."

"courage, prowess, strength, vigor, and fortitude, as well as their insight, intelligence, and memory" *tejo vīryaṃ balaṃ cauja utsāhaś ca . . . / pradarśanaṃ ca buddhiś ca smṛtiś ca*: The qualities enumerated fall into two groups, one dealing with martial virtues and the other with mental abilities. Within each group there is considerable synonymity and overlapping of meaning. Commentators attempt to provide specific differentiated meanings for each of the terms: 1) *tejaḥ*: "the ability to defeat one's enemies (*parābhibhavasāmarthyam*—Ct, Cg, Cm)." Cg gives this and an alternative definition: "intolerance of insult at the hands of one's enemies (*parādhikṣepāsahanam vā*)"; 2) *balam*: "physical [strength] (*śārīram*—Ck, Ct, Cg, Cm)"; 3) *vīryam*: "heroism *or* prowess (*parākramaḥ*—Ct, Cg, Cm)"; 4) *ojaḥ*: "brilliance, luster (*kāntiḥ*—Ct, Cg, Cm)"; 5) *utsāhaḥ*: "unrelenting effort in superhuman [ever-increasing—Cm] undertakings (*lokottarakāryeṣu sthirataraprayatnaḥ*—Cg, Cm)"; 6) *pradarśanam*: "the determination of obscure matters through textual sources and inference (*śabdānumānābhyāṃ parokṣārthaniścayaḥ*—Ct, Ck)"; "knowledge of subtle matters (*sūkṣmārthaparijñānam*—Cg)"; 7) *buddhiḥ*: "determination of mundane matters (*aparokṣaniścayaḥ*—Ct)"; "discrimination (*vivekaḥ*—Cg)"; "perseverance (*adhyavasāyaḥ*)—Cm"; and 8) *smṛtiḥ*: "recollection of things that are experienced (*anubhūtārthāvismaraṇam*—Cg, Cm)." See note to 6.2.14.

41. "Helping the two . . . to their feet" *tāv utthāpya*: Literally, "having caused the two to rise."

"the two . . . heroes" *mahāvīryau*: Literally, "having great strength *or* heroism" D9–11 and the texts and printed editions of Ct and Cr read the singular *mahātejāḥ*, "of great power," which must then be construed with Garuḍa.

"embraced" *sasvaje*: Cr, eager to maintain the appropriate level of deference for Rāma and Lakṣmaṇa, explains, "he grasped their feet (*caraṇānām āliṅganaṃ cakāra*)."

"delighted" *hṛṣṭau*: V3,B1,3,D6,7,10,11,T1,3,G1,3, and the texts and printed editions of Ct and Cr read the nominative singular *hṛṣṭaḥ*. The adjective then would modify Garuḍa.

42. "we . . . here" *āvām iha*: D9–11 and the texts and printed editions of Ct and Cr read instead *upāyena*, "through [some] contrivance." Cr glosses, "by you who understand effort (*yatnajñena tvayā*)," a reference to Garuḍa.

"and . . . swiftly" *śīghraṃ ca*: M1–3 and the texts and printed editions of Cg, Cm, and Crā read instead *pūrvavat*, "as before."

"restored to our full strength" *balinau kṛtau*: Literally, "made strong."

43. "my father, Daśaratha, or my grandfather, Aja" *tātaṃ daśaratham . . . ajaṃ ca pitāmaham*: Literally, "my father, Daśaratha, and my grandfather, Aja." Ct and Ck read a theological interpretation into the verse. Ct notes that "I, who am a portion of the primal being Hiraṇyagarbha [Viṣṇu], have a father, Daśaratha, who is a partial incarnation, or fragment, of Prajāpati Kaśyapa, conformable [to Rāma's own incarnation], and a grandfather, Aja, who is a partial incarnation of four-faced Brahmā (*daśarathaṃ svāvatārocitaṃ kaśyapaprajāpatyaṃśam ajaṃ ca pitāmahaṃ caturmukhabrahmāṃśaṃ me hiraṇyagarbhātmanas tadaṃśasya*)." This latter identification plays on the epithet Pitāmaha, "grandfather," which is often ascribed to Brahmā, as well as the epithet Aja, "unborn," which is often applied to Brahmā and other manifestations of

godhead. As we understand it, Ct's reasoning is that, since Kaśyapa was the father of Viṣṇu in his *vāmanāvatāra*, or dwarf incarnation, and is himself one of the mind-born sons of Brahmā, the human Rāma's father and grandfather must also be incarnations of these divinities. Ck, whose explanation is similar, notes that we should understand that Daśaratha is "a partial incarnation of Virāṭ, Prajāpati, and Viṣṇu (*svāvatārocitavirāṭprajāpativiṣṇvaṃśam iti śeṣaḥ*)." Ck further notes: "Grandfather Aja [lit., the unborn one] is Virāṭ, who is devoid of all conditionality or limits in all three times [past, present, and future] and who is free from any connection with the conditionalities of birth, death, etc. He is the grandfather (*pitāmaha*), the universal ruler, and the four-faced Brahmā, whose innate form is subtle. (*yathājaṃ ca pitāmaham ajaṃ kālatraye 'pi vinā virāḍ upādhyanaṣṭaṃ* [*bha?*] *janimṛtimadupādhisaṃbandharahitaṃ pitāmahaṃ saṃrājaṃ caturmukhabrahmāṇaṃ nijasūkṣmamūrtibhūtam ity arthaḥ.*)"

Cr thinks that the reference to Rāma's forebears suggests that Garuḍa, too, is senior [to Rāma] (*etena garuḍasya vṛddhatvaṃ sūcitam*). See 6.49.1–2; 6.59.7; 6.79.4; 6.87.9–10; 6.105.15; and notes.

44. "spotless garments" *viraje vastre*: Literally, "two garments free from dust." The dual is used to refer to the traditional upper and lower garments.

"Who are you, sir?" *ko bhavān*: Ct and Ck are eager to explain why Rāma appears unable to identify the universally recognizable form of Garuḍa, the great lord of the birds. Their understanding is that Garuḍa retains his natural avian form until he is close enough to the heroes to terrify and drive off the serpent-arrows that have bound them. When he comes close to the fallen heroes, he assumes a human shape in order to stroke and embrace them. Because Rāma and Lakṣmaṇa do not see his avian form, they do not recognize Garuḍa. (*ayaṃ praśno 'pi manuṣyaśarīrocitavyavahāra eva tatsatyatvaprakhyāpanārtho 'tra rāmasamīpāgamanaparyantaṃ pakṣyākāreṇaivāgatya saṃnidhimātreṇa nāgabandhanaṃ ca nirasya rāghavasparśanādyarthaṃ puruṣākāreṇa vyavahṛtavān iti bodhyam.*) See verse 38 above.

45. "his eyes lighting up with joy" *harṣaparyākulekṣaṇaḥ*: Literally, "his eyes filled with joy." Two *devanāgarī* manuscripts (D10,11) and the texts and printed editions of Ct, Ck, and Cr read the accusative *harṣaparyākulekṣaṇam* for the nominative of the critical text. This then makes the description apply to Rāma rather than Garuḍa.

46. "your dear comrade . . . of you both" *sakhā te. . . yuvayoḥ*: Cs feels that the shift from the singular to the dual reflects Garuḍa's embarrassment at having first addressed Rāma with the informal pronoun "*te* (your)." Cs then documents the comradeship of Viṣṇu and Garuḍa, quoting the passage from the *Sauparṇākhyāna* of the *Ādiparvan* of the *Mahābhārata* (1.29.13–16) in which the two exchange boons so that Garuḍa will be placed above Viṣṇu as the insignia on his battle flag and will serve as Viṣṇu's mount. Cs continues, noting that the poet wants us to understand that, although the dual would have been appropriate in accordance with the *chatrinyāya*, or the "maxim of the people with umbrellas" (that is, although Garuḍa is the comrade and servant only of Rāma, Lakṣmaṇa can be included in the general statement), Garuḍa could not have been expected to know that (*evaṃ sati sati ca cchatrinyayāvakāśe na pratyaveyād vainateya iti bhāvo 'pi kaver jñātavyaḥ*). Cg observes that the hidden sense of the word "comrade" here is that of an assistant in the form of a mount (*sakhā vāhanatvena sahāya iti gūḍhoktiḥ*). Cf. 6.47.112 and note.

"your second life breath outside your body" *prāṇo bahiścaraḥ*: Vālmīki is fond of this expression to describe the most intimate comrades and helpers of Rāma. He uses it or a variant at least twice elsewhere to describe Lakṣmaṇa: once at 3.32.13, once at 1.17.17 (*bahiḥ prāṇaḥ*), and again, in reference to all his brothers, at 7.43.12. The sense is similar to the English expressions "a second self" or "alter ego." See, too, notes on 6.19.24; 6.47.123; and 6.89.6 (2026*).

47–48. "the . . . *dānavas*" *dānavāḥ*: D6,10,11, and the texts and printed editions of Ct read instead *vānarāḥ*, "monkeys." This variant might have been motivated by an effort to avoid the seeming redundancy of *asurāḥ* and *dānavāḥ*, terms that are generally used interchangeably.

"with Indra of the hundred sacrifices at their head" *puraskṛtya śatakratum*: Literally, "having placed Śatakratu before [them]."

49. "the sons of Kadrū" *kādraveyāḥ*: Kadrū is the half sister and arch rival of Garuḍa's mother, Vinatā, and the ancestress of all snakes. The story of the rivalry of the sisters and their respective descendants, the snakes and the birds, is well known to the epic and purāṇic literature. The best-known account of the story is at *Mahābhārata* 1.14ff. See note to 6.78.23.

50. "Along with your brother Lakṣmaṇa, a slayer of enemies in battle" *lakṣmaṇena . . . ripughātinā*: Cr appears to understand the epithet as belonging to Indrajit, since he glosses, "these events [see note to verse 51 below] brought about by that slayer of enemies in battle (*ripughātinā samare kṛtam imaṃ vṛttāntam*)."

51. "what had happened" *vṛttāntam*: As Ct and Ck remark, the reference is to the heroes' bondage by the serpent-arrows, which Garuḍa had heard about from the mouths of the gods. (*nāgabandhavṛttāntaṃ śrutvā. devatānāṃ mukhād iti śeṣaḥ.*) D10,11,T3,G3, and the texts and printed editions of Ct (GPP, NSP = 6.50.51) read *vikrāntaḥ*, "valorous," an adjective that here must modify Garuḍa himself. Even though the printed editions of Ct show this variant, his commentary is based on the reading of the critical edition. This has led to mixed results among the translators who follow the text of Ct. Dutt (1893, p. 1249), Roussel (1903, vol. 3, p. 144), and Shastri (1959, vol. 3, p. 124) translate the variant, *vikrāntaḥ*, whereas Pagani (1999, p. 985) and Gita Press (1969, vol. 3, p. 1544) translate the reading found in the critical edition.

52. "be . . . on your guard" *apramādaś ca kartavyaḥ*: Literally, "non-carelessness must be practiced." Cr understands the injunction to refer prospectively to the following verse. Thus, it is because the *rākṣasas* fight unfairly that the brothers must be particularly vigilant (*prakṛtyā svabhāvenaiva rākṣasāḥ kūṭayodhino bhavanty ato yuvābhyām apramādaḥ pramādarāhityaṃ kartavyaḥ*). Cg and Cm understand the phrase in a more restricted and technical sense to mean that Rāma and Lakṣmaṇa must be vigilant with respect to the use of divine weapons that will counteract in each case those of their enemies (*tattadastrānuguṇapratyastraprayogeṣu sāvadhānābhyāṃ bhavitavyam ity arthaḥ*).

53. "the strength . . . lies in the fact that they are honorable" *ārjavaṃ balam*: Literally, "[their] strength is honorableness *or* straightforwardness."

54. "This very example serves to show" *etenaivopamānena*: Literally, "by this very comparison." The example, of course, is Indrajit's defeat of the brothers.

55. "with the affection befitting a friend" *suhṛtsnigdham*: Literally, "with the affection of a friend." Ś,Ñ,V,B3,4,D1–3,7–13,T3,G3, and the texts and printed editions of Ct and Cr read instead *ca susnigdham*, "and very affectionately." We agree with most of the translators, who understand this term (or the variant *susnigdham*) adverbially. Of course, it can also be taken adjectivally to modify *rāmam* in *pāda* a, as Cr suggests, to yield the meaning "Rāma, who showed the affection befitting a friend."

56. "compassionate even to your enemies" *ripūṇām api vatsala*: Rāma's compassion, even for his enemies, is part of the poet's construction of Rāma as the ideal man. Cg, however, understands the epithet here to illuminate the fact that Rāma does not yet know how to accomplish the destruction of Indrajit (*anena indrajidvadhopāyo na jñāta iti dyotyate*).

"just as I came" *yathāgatam*: D9–11,T3, and the texts and printed editions of Ct and Cr read instead *yathāsukham*, "at my pleasure."

Following verse 56, Ñ,V,B,D2,4–7,9–11,13,S insert a passage of two lines [835*]: "And you must not be overly curious regarding our friendship, Rāghava.[1] Once, hero, you have accomplished your purpose on the battlefield, you will know about our friendship."

[1]"Rāghava" *rāghava*: The text of GPP, represented as "B (ed.)" in the critical apparatus, alone among all manuscripts and editions consulted, reads the unattested form *kāṅkṣiṇāḥ* (*kāṅkṣiṇā*—so critical edition), a grammatically incorrect derivative of the verbal root √*kāṅkṣ*, "to wish, desire." This solecism is perhaps a typographical error, as the editors of GPP fail to note Cg's reading (which is the same as the critical reading) as a variant. Only Pagani (1999, p. 986) among the translators consulted has attempted to render this erroneous reading. She translates, without comment, "*Quelque désir que tu en aies.*"

This verse, which is represented in all manuscript traditions except Ś and the northwest (except D2) and the Lahore edition is an attempt to deal with the touchy issue of Rāma's self-awareness as an *avatāra* of Viṣṇu. According to the terms of Rāvaṇa's boon, Rāma must be a man and therefore subject to human limitations. Should he inquire here about the nature of his relationship to Garuḍa, that of a *bhaktin* and a *bhakta* or a *deva* and his *vāhana*, it would, in effect, undermine his self-imposed ignorance as to his true nature (Pollock 1991, pp. 15–54). Cm and Cg observe that Garuḍa, anticipating that Rāma will question him about their friendship, which was mentioned in verse 46 above, urges him not to raise questions on this subject at this point because it is a secret matter. After Rāvaṇa is killed, Rāma will come to realize the nature of their relationship on his own. (*ahaṃ sakhā te kākutsthetyādinoktaṃ sakhitvaṃ katham iti rāmāśayam āśaṅkya rahasyatvād idānīṃ tadviṣayapraśno na kartavyaḥ. rāvaṇavadhānantaraṃ svayam eva jñāsyatīty āha.*) Ct understands that Rāma is not to show excessive interest in this matter in order that he may continue to deceive people [i.e., about his true nature] (*maduktasakhitvaṃ prati lokapratāraṇāyāpi vismayo na kārya ity āha*). See note to 6.28.28–29.

57. "Once you have slaughtered the male population of Laṅkā . . . sparing only the children and the aged" *bālavṛddhāvaśeṣāṃ tu laṅkāṃ kṛtvā*: Literally, "having made Laṅkā such that its remnant consists of children and the aged." The expression is difficult to render literally in English, and we have therefore translated somewhat freely. The idea is that Rāma, chivalrous as ever, will direct his shafts only toward the male *rākṣasas* of fighting age, sparing the noncombatants and thus avoiding collateral damage.

58–59. "Suparṇa . . . Suparṇa" *suparṇaḥ . . . suparṇaḥ*: Since the two verses form a single syntactical unit, several of the commentators are disturbed by the repetition of the name/epithet "Suparṇa." Cr attempts to avoid redundancy by taking one of the occurrences as a descriptive adjective, "characterized by splendid wings (*śobhana-pakṣaviśiṣṭaḥ*)," and the other as a proper noun. Cg, on the other hand, argues that the repetition of the name is acceptable because several different actions are described (*kriyābhedena suparṇapadadvayānvayaḥ*). See note to verse 38 above.

"swift in flight" *śīghravikramaḥ*: We normally render *vikramaḥ* in its sense of "valor, prowess, might." Here, however, the context leads us to agree with Cg, who takes the term in its sense of "stride, pace," glossing, "of swift gait (*śīghragatiḥ*)."

"had healed Rāma of his wounds" *rāmaṃ ca virujaṃ kṛtvā*: Literally, "having made Rāma wound-free."

"reverently circled" *pradakṣiṇam* . . . *kṛtvā*: Ck and Ct believe that, in making this ritual sign of reverence, Garuḍa is demonstrating to the rank and file of the monkeys that Rāma is indeed an incarnation of heavenly divinity (*anena divyadevatāvatāro rāma iti sarvān prākṛtakapīn praty api bodhitam*).

61. This verse provokes Cg to provide a somewhat extensive disquisition on the ironies of Rāma's situation and on the nature and purpose of this *avatāra* of Viṣṇu. His remarks are evidently inspired by, and to a significant extent extracted from, a lengthy discussion triggered by this very same passage on the part of the usually laconic Cv. Both commentators are trying once again to grapple with the apparent irony that Rāma, who is the all-powerful and all-knowing Lord, is subject to the pains, injuries, and indignity of his apparent defeat at the hands of the relatively insignificant Indrajit. Cv explains, in part, that Rāma's near calamity is intended to illustrate that the virtuous and righteous will survive even the most life-threatening disasters, while conversely, the evil and perverse [e.g., Rāvaṇa and Indrajit] will see their plans frustrated, even when success seems within their grasp. Cv then tries, interestingly so, to contextualize the *Rāmāvatāra* within the larger concept of incarnation, arguing that there are several types of *avatāra*, classified according to the types of assistance (*upakāra*) they render in the world. These include not only the familiar *vīrya* (martial) types, such as Matsya, Kūrma, Varāha, and Narasiṃha, but also the *ācārya* ([world] teacher) or *sarva* (universal) types, such as Haṃsa, Hayagrīva, and Kṛṣṇadvaipāyana. Basically, Cv contends that *avatāras* play two roles: one is to physically destroy evil-doers and the other is to teach the ways of righteousness through instruction or example. Cv believes that Rāma represents both functions so that, although he can and does slaughter the evil *rākṣasas* to save the world from their depredations, he also undergoes pain, hardship, and defeat in order to serve the latter function as well.

Cg argues somewhat similarly, saying that, although one of the principal purposes of Rāma's *avatāra* is to kill Rāvaṇa, if that were the only purpose he accomplished, his effort would have been in vain. For, Cg continues, the *avatāra* must also instruct the world in *dharma* but not merely by repeating teachings that are available in the *vedas* and *śāstras* but through his own personal example. It is thus, according to Cg, that Rāma takes on the characteristics of a human being in order to teach *dharma* through his own conduct.

"the *bherī* drums . . . and *mṛdaṅgas*" *bherīḥ* . . . *mṛdaṅgāṃś ca*: On *bherīs*, see 6.17.31–33 and note.

"frolicked about happily" *kṣvelanti*: The verb $\sqrt{}$*kṣviḍ* can mean "to play *or* frolic," on the one hand, or "to roar, whoop, *or* murmur," on the other. Either sense is appropriate here, and both appear in the various translations. The commentators are silent on this matter, but compare note to 5.60.12.

62. "who used trees as their weapons" *nagayodhinaḥ*: Literally, "fighting with immovable objects." The term *naga*, "that which does not [*na*] move [*ga*]," is used as a kenning for trees and mountains, both of which the monkeys employ as weapons.

"clapped their upper arms again and again" *āsphoṭyāsphoṭya*: Literally, "having clapped their upper arms, having clapped their upper arms." This is a common gesture of belligerence in the Indian martial tradition, but it may also be a sign of delight as at 5.8.50. D7,9–11,G2,3,M5, and the texts and printed editions of Ct and Cr read instead *apare sphoṭya*, "others brandishing *or* breaking [trees]." See note to 6.17.13–15.

"they took their stand there by the hundreds of thousands" *tasthuḥ śatasahasraśaḥ*: A number of the translations consulted read the numerical adverb with the gerund *utpāṭya*, "having ripped up," instead of with the finite verb. This reading, proposed by Cr, gives the sense "ripping up trees by the [hundreds of] thousands (*sahasraśo drumān utpāṭya tasthuḥ*)."

64. Ct tells us that there has been a two-day cessation of hostilities at this point, a position he ascribes to the *Āgniveśyarāmāyaṇa*. This break, it seems, is a medical leave to account for the disability of Rāma and Lakṣmaṇa (*atra sthāne dinadvayaṃ yuddhāvahāra ity āgniveśyaḥ*). See note to 6.41.8, where Ct again makes mention of the cessation of hostilities. On the chronology of epic events, see notes to 6.4.4. For additional comments from the *Āgniveśyarāmāyaṇa*, see notes to 6.4.63 and 6.97.33.

The meter is *upajāti*.

Sarga 41

1. "Then Rāvaṇa and the *rākṣasas* heard" *rākṣasaiḥ sārdhaṃ tadā śuśrāva rāvaṇaḥ*: Literally, "Rāvaṇa along with the *rākṣasas* then heard." Our reading of the syntax here accords with that of Cr, Cg, and the majority of the translators consulted. Ct and Cm, however, construe the phrase *rākṣasaiḥ sārdham* with the participle *nardatām*, "of them who were roaring," understanding that the *rākṣasas* Vibhīṣaṇa [and his four companions] are roaring (*rākṣasair vibhīṣaṇādibhiḥ*—so Ct). This reading is followed only by Dutt (1893, p. 1250).

"swift" *tarasvinām*: D7,9–11,T3, and the texts and printed editions of Ct read instead *mahaujasām*, "powerful *or* energetic."

2. "uproar" *ninadam*: Literally, "sound." Cm reads the term as a *bahuvrīhi* compound in the sense of "by which the ocean [i.e., its roar] is overcome *or* drowned out." This would then construe adjectivally with *-nirghoṣam*, "resonance," of *pāda* a. This, according to Cm, is tantamount to saying that the roar was deeper than the ocean [or the ocean's roar]. (*ninadaṃ nirasto nado 'rṇavo yena tam. tad apekṣayā gambhīram iti yāvat.*)

"with its deep and joyous resonance" *snigdhagambhīranirghoṣam*: Literally, "having a smooth and deep sound." The semantic range of *snigdha* does not normally include the sense of "joyous, exuberant." Nonetheless, the context of the passage, including Rāvaṇa's deduction from the sound that the monkeys are now filled with delight, in verse 4 below, lends credence to Ct's explanation that, from the two qualities of the sound, we are to understand that there has been a transformation of the sound of lamentation born from the monkeys' grief [over Rāma's apparent death] (*snigdhagambhīratvena duḥkhamūlarodanādiśabdavyāvṛttiḥ*).

3–4. "it is clear . . . tremendous" *vyaktaṃ sumahatī*: Ñ1,D4,10,11, and the texts and printed editions of Ct read instead *suvyaktaṃ mahatī*, "it is very clear . . . great."

"the ocean itself, abode of Varuṇa" *varuṇālayaḥ*: Literally, "the abode of Varuṇa." D9–11,T3,G1, and the texts and printed editions of Ct, Cr, and Ck read instead *lavaṇārṇavaḥ*, "the salt sea."

6. "who stood at their posts all around him" *samīpaparivartinaḥ*: Literally, "surrounding him nearby."

7. "why . . . rejoicing at a time when they ought to be grieving" *śokakāle samutpanne harṣakāraṇam utthitam*: Literally, "the reason for rejoicing when the time for grieving is at hand."

8. "they climbed the ramparts" *prākāram adhiruhya*: Literally, "having ascended the rampart." That the *rākṣasas* could climb the ramparts suggests to Ct that the cessation of hostilities, which he believes to have followed the disability of Rāma and Lakṣmaṇa, is still in effect (*anenātrāvahāraḥ sūcitaḥ*). See note to 6.40.64 above, where Ct suggests that there has been a two-day cessation (*avahāra*) in the hostilities. See, too, notes to 6.33.2–3; 6.49.33; and 6.62.2.

9. "When those *rākṣasas* saw" *prekṣya rākṣasāḥ*: Literally, "the *rākṣasas* having seen." D9–11 and the texts and printed editions of Ct read instead *sarvarākṣasāḥ*, "all the *rākṣasas*." This poorly attested reading is syntactically defective in that it lacks a verbal element to govern the accusative *rāghavau*, "the two Rāghavas."

"illustrious" *mahābhāgau*: Printed editions of the text of Cg (VSP and KK = 6.51.9) and GPP (6.51.9—Cg's variant) read instead *mahāvegau*, "very swift *or* greatly energetic."

"their hearts sank" *viṣeduḥ*: Literally, "they despaired."

10. "with faces downcast" *viṣaṇṇavadanāḥ*: The textual evidence for this verse is somewhat complicated. A number of manuscripts and the vulgate text of Ct, Cr, and Ck read instead *vivarṇā rākṣasāḥ*, "pale *rākṣasas*." See note 14 below.

"all" *sarve . . . sarve*: The textual evidence does not support the repetition of the term. Northern manuscripts tend to substitute other words for the first, while southern manuscripts tend to substitute other terms for the second. D5–7,T1,2,G3,M3, and the texts and printed editions of the southern commentators substitute *ghorāḥ*, "dreadful." It appears from the critical apparatus that only one manuscript (M4) collated for the critical edition may include both occurrences of the term.

11. "Their dismay evident in their faces" *dīnamukhāḥ*. Literally, "with sad faces."

"the night-roaming *rākṣasas*" *niśācarāḥ*: Literally, "night-roamers." D9–11,T3, and the texts and printed editions of Ct, Cr, and Ck read instead *ca rākṣasāḥ*, "and the *rākṣasas*."

14. "grief" *-śoka-*: Ś,Ñ,V,B1,3,4,D1–5,7–13,T1,3,G1,2,M5, and the texts and printed editions of Ct, Ck, and Cr read instead *-roṣa-*, "anger *or* rage."

"downcast face" *viṣaṇṇavadanaḥ*: Ś,Ñ,V,B2,4,D1–4,7–13,T3, and the texts and printed editions of Ct, Cr, and Ck read instead *vivarṇavadanaḥ*, "with face pale *or* drained of color."

"he said" *abravīt*: D9–11,13,M5, and the texts and printed editions of Ct, Cr, and Ck read instead *abhavat*, "he became [downcast *or* pale-faced]."

15–16. "Indrajit had struck down and bound those two" *baddhau . . . pramathyendrajitā*: Literally, "having been struck down by Indrajit, the two were bound."

"they were given to him as a boon" *dattavaraiḥ*: Literally, "having a given boon." We agree with Cg in reading the compound as a *paranipāta* for *varadattaiḥ*, "granted through a boon." Ct explains, "the meaning is 'acquired through a boon by means of long and arduous penances' (*cirakāladuścaratapasā varaprāptair ity arthaḥ*)." Cr understands that the weapons were acquired as [part of] a grant of immunity, and it is this that makes them unfailing (*prāptābhayapradānair ata evāmoghaiḥ*). It is made clear at 5.46.34 that Indrajit possesses binding weapons that are derived from Brahmā although there they are not associated with serpents. Elsewhere (*Uttarakāṇḍa* 25), Indrajit is said to have received the boon of invisibility along with various weapons as a boon from Śiva for performing various sacrifices. Cf. notes to 6.36.10.

"army" *balam*: The term is ambiguous and can also mean "power *or* strength." Several translators have chosen this latter meaning.

17. "as powerful as the great serpent Vāsuki" *vāsukitejasaḥ*: Literally, "with the energy of Vāsuki." Vāsuki is one of the great mythic *nāgas* of epic and purāṇic tradition. He is, perhaps, most noteworthy for his role as the churning rope in the myth of the churning of the primal ocean for the nectar of immortality. See, for example, 1.44.16,17 and notes. B3,D7,9–11, and the texts and printed editions of Ct and Cr read instead *pāvakatejasaḥ*, "with the brilliance *or* energy of fire." On the story of the churning of the ocean, see 6.12.22; 6.40.29; 6.53.23; 6.80.19; 6.105.19; and notes.

18. "hissing like a serpent" *niśvasann urago yathā*: This is one of the most common tropes in the epic to express the rage of a warrior. It is also used, however, to describe the labored breathing of wounded heroes. See 5.4.11; 5.8.10,26; and 5.13.30–31 and notes. See note to 5.54.10. See, too, 5.36.4–7 and note. See 6.48.22–23; 6.57.81; and 6.76.1. Cf. 6.36.4–7 and note.

19. "Take a large force" *balena mahatā yuktaḥ*: Literally, "joined with a large force."

"fearsome in their deeds" *bhīmakarmaṇām*: D5,6,T,G2,3,M3, and the texts and printed editions of Cg, Cv, and Cr read the vocative *bhīmavikrama*, "O you of fearsome valor." D7,9–11, and the texts and printed editions of Ct and Ck read the nominative *bhīmavikramaḥ*. Both variants would then describe Dhūmrākṣa.

"go forth" *abhiniryāhi*: D6,7,9–11,T3, and the texts and printed editions of Ct and Cr read instead *āśu niryāhi*, "go forth at once."

"to slaughter" *vadhāya*: Cg suggests that the expression "go forth for slaughter" is, in fact, inauspicious [as it might equally suggest the destruction of Dhūmrākṣa and his troops] (*tvaṃ vadhāyābhiniryāhīty amaṅgalasūcakaṃ vacaḥ*).

20. "made his obeisance and, in great excitement" *kṛtvā praṇāmaṃ saṃhṛṣṭaḥ*: D7,9–11, and the texts and printed editions of Ct read instead *parikramya tataḥ śīghram*, "having reverently circumambulated [him] and swiftly."

21. "the palace gates" *taddvāram*: Literally, "the gate of that." We take the reference to be to the gate of the king's residence (*nṛpālaya*) mentioned in the previous verse.

"the officer in charge of the garrison" *balādhyakṣam*: Literally, "supervisor of the army." Ck understands that the officer in question is Prahasta. See 6.43.1 and note, where a number of commentators make the same identification.

"Mobilize" *tvarayasva*: Literally, "cause to hasten."

22. "the leader of his troops" *balānugaḥ*: Literally, "having the army as his followers."

"quickly" *drutam*: D9–11 and the texts and printed editions of Ct and Cr read instead *bhṛśam*, which can be read either adverbially, in the sense of "energetically," or adjectivally with the noun *balam*, in the sense of "large, numerous, powerful."

23. "fastened on their war bells" *baddhaghaṇṭāḥ*: Literally, "those by whom bells are tied on *or* having bells tied on." The commentators and translators differ as to the purpose and location of these bells. Ct, Cr, and Ck all understand that the bells are fastened to the various weapons wielded by the *rākṣasas* (*prāsaśaktyādiṣv iti śeṣaḥ*). In this they are followed by Dutt (1893, p. 1251), who translates, "with bells tied to their arms." Cg understands that the warriors tie the bells around their hips to advertise their valor (*śūratvajñāpanāya kaṭibaddhaghaṇṭā ity arthaḥ*)." In this he may be thinking of the *kaṭitra*, an ornament that consists of a string of small bells worn around the waist or the loins (Apte s.v.). It is not clear whether this is worn by men during combat, as such ornaments are not commonly associated with men. See Sahay 1973, p. 112. However, a dagger belt is known to have been worn at least from the fifth or sixth century CE (Dikshitar 1944, p. 134). Cg's interpretation is followed by Gita Press (1969, vol. 3, p. 1548) and Shastri (1959, vol. 3, p. 126). Roussel (1903, vol. 3, p. 147) and Pagani (1999, p. 988), for some reason, believe that the bells are worn around the neck. Gorresio (1856, vol. 9, p. 286), like us, is uncertain as to the location of the bells and simply translates literally, "*legati lor titinnabuli.*"

24–25. "terrible" *ghorāḥ*: Ś,V1,2,B1–3,D2–6,8,12,13,T1,G1,3,M3, and the texts and printed editions of Cg read instead *digbhyaḥ*, "from [all] directions."

"vigorously" *bhṛśam*: D7,9–11,T3, and the texts and printed editions of Ct and Cr read instead *api*, "as well as."

"armed": The word "armed" has been added.

"short javelins" *bhiṇḍipālaiḥ*: On *bhiṇḍipālas*, see 6.32.30; 6.42.19; 6.53.32; 6.83.25; and notes.

"darts" *prāsaiḥ*: D9–11,T3,G3,M1,2,5, and the texts and printed editions of Ct read *pāśaiḥ*, "nooses."

26–27. "drawn by donkeys" *kharaiḥ*: Literally, "by *or* with donkeys." We follow Cr and Cg, who both understand that the donkeys as well as the banners are attributes of the chariots. This position gains support from the fact that Dhūmrākṣa's chariot is being yoked to donkeys in the following verse. The construction is elliptical, however, and so it is equally possible to understand that the donkeys are yet another mode of transportation, along with the chariots, horses, and elephants. This interpretation is seen in the translations of Gita Press (1969, vol. 3, p. 1548) and Dutt (1893, p. 1252).

"with faces of many different kinds" *vividhānanaiḥ*: The *rākṣasas*' mounts, like the *rākṣasas* themselves, are often represented as having the heads or faces of a variety of animals. Compare verse 28 below and 5.15.4–17. These grotesque variations are also commonly represented in the courtly illustrations of the *Rāmāyaṇa*.

28. "With harsh cries" *kharanisvanaḥ*: The term *khara-*, "harsh," has no doubt been chosen because it echoes the word *kharaiḥ*, "with donkeys," in *pāda* b. Indeed, the compound can be translated as "with the cry *or* braying of a donkey," as several of the translators do. We find this interpretation less persuasive. The commentators are silent.

"wolves" *vṛka-*: B4,D9–11,T3, and the texts and printed editions of Ct substitute *mṛga-*, "deer *or* antelope."

29. "proceeded . . . to the western gate" *niryātaḥ . . . paścimadvāram*: Literally, "went out to the western gate." D6,7,10,11,T2,3,G1,M1,2, and the texts and printed editions of Ck and Cr read instead the ablative *paścimadvārāt*, "from the western gate." Most translators, even those who read with the critical text, understand, "issued from the western gate."

"where the troop leader . . . was stationed" *yatra yūthapaḥ*: Literally, "where the troop leader [was]." D9–11,T2,3, and the texts and printed editions of Ct, Ck, and Cr read *tiṣṭhati*, "he stands [i.e., is stationed]," for the critical edition's *yūthapaḥ*, "troop leader." This reading makes it unnecessary to supply the verb, as we have done.

Following verse 29, D5–7,9–11,S insert a passage of one line [846*]: "Him [Dhūmrākṣa], who with harsh cries, having mounted that excellent chariot yoked to donkeys." This line must be construed with verse 30 below.

30. For similar passages listing inauspicious omens, see 6.26.21–30; 6.31.3–12; 6.45.31–37; 6.53.41–45; 6.65.17–19; 6.94.14–27; and notes.

"fearsome looking" *bhīmadarśanam*: Ñ,V2,3,B,D3,4,T1,G1,M3, and the printed editions of Cg [KK (6.51.29) and VSP (6.51.30)] and Gorresio read instead *bhīmavikramam*, "of fearsome valor." This reading is rendered in the translations of Raghunathan (1982, vol. 3, p. 126) and Gorresio (1856, vol. 9, p. 287).

"birds of ill omen" *śakunāḥ*: The term can refer to birds in general or more specifically to a species of carrion bird, buzzard, or kite. We follow Cg, who glosses, "birds indicative of [evil] omens (*nimittasūcakāḥ pakṣiṇaḥ*)." See notes to 6.4.6 and 6.26.8. See also note to verse 31 below.

"blocking his path" *pratyavārayan*: Literally, "they warded [him] off." D7,9–11,T3,G1,2,M1,2,5, and the texts and printed editions of Ct and Cr read instead *pratyaṣedhayan*, "they obstructed."

31. "long lines of carrion birds perched on the edge of his battle standard" *dhvajāgre grathitāś caiva nipetuḥ kuṇapāśanāḥ*: Literally, "corpse-eaters strung together, perched on the tip of his standard." Compare 6.83.33c and note. See, too, 6.53.43; 6.94.16; and notes.

32. "ghastly pale" *śvetaḥ*: Literally, "white."

"in Dhūmrākṣa's path" *dhūmrākṣasya samīpataḥ*: Literally, "close to Dhūmrākṣa." GPP (6.51. 33b), Gita Press (6.51.33b), and NSP (6.51. 33b) (the critical apparatus for 32d is omitted from the critical edition) read *nipātitaḥ*, "thrown down, hurled down," for *samīpataḥ*, "close to."

33. "It rained blood" *vavarṣa rudhiraṃ devaḥ*: Literally, "The god rained blood." As Cg notes, the god in question is the vedic god Parjanya. This deity's normal and beneficent function is to shower down rain in a timely fashion. For blood raining down, see 6.26.22; 6.31.5; 6.45.926*–36; 6.83.33; 6.94.15; and notes. Cf. note to 6.76.2, inserted passage 1674*, lines 5–7.

"in an unfavorable direction" *pratilomam*: Literally, "inversely *or* against the hair." As in many cultures, a wind blowing from one's back is considered favorable. In this case, the wind was blowing directly in Dhūmrākṣa's face, constituting yet another unfavorable portent. See 6.4.41; 6.43.8; 6.45.35; 6.53.44; 6.65.19; and notes.

"were no longer visible" *na cakāśire*: Literally, "they did not shine."

34. Following verse 34, D5–7,9–11,S insert a passage of one line [850*]: "And all the *rākṣasas* in Dhūmrākṣa's vanguard were stupefied."

35. "that . . . very fearsome *rākṣasa*" *subhīmaḥ*: Literally, "very fearsome one." For some reason Roussel (1903, vol. 3, p. 148), perhaps influenced by the fact that, in verse 34, Dhūmrākṣa had been shaken at the sight of the evil omens described in verses 30–33, erroneously translates, "*terrifié*." In this he has been followed by Shastri (1959, vol. 3, p. 127) and Pagani (1999, p. 988).

"an ocean" *samudra-*: D5,6,10,11,T1,2,G2,3,M, and the texts and printed editions of the southern commentators read instead *mahaugha-*, "a great flood." Cg understands this simply as a kenning for the ocean. Ck, Ct, and Cr understand the reference to be to the [overflowing] ocean at the time of the cosmic dissolution (*pralayasamudraḥ*—Ct). Dutt (1893, p. 1252) and Gita Press (1969, vol. 3, p. 1549) render this interpretation in their translations.

The meter is *vaṃśasthavila*.

Sarga 42

1. "fearsome cries" *bhīmanisvanam*: Manuscript evidence shows a variety of readings in place of this compound. B3,D5,7,9–11,T1,3,M3, and the texts of the southern commentators read instead *bhīmavikramam*, "of fearsome valor."

2. "one another—the former . . . the latter" *anyonyam*: Literally, "one another." We have elaborated the translation somewhat in keeping with the fact that the monkeys fight only with trees, stones, and other found objects, whereas the *rākṣasas* use standard weapons.

"terrifying" *ghoraiḥ*: D5,M3, and the texts and printed editions of Cg and Cm read instead the adverbial *ghoram*, "fiercely, dreadfully," which would then modify the participle *nighnatām*, "slaughtered."

Following verse 2, D5,6,S, and the texts and printed editions of Cg read 6.42.5cd, "with . . . various and dreadful iron clubs, and sharp tridents (*ghoraiś ca parighaiś citrais triśūlaiś cāpi saṃśitaiḥ*)." According to the critical apparatus, these manuscripts repeat the line in its proper place. This repetition, however, does not appear either in KK or VSP. Therefore, only Raghunathan (1982, vol. 3, p. 127), among the translators consulted, translates the line here, but not at its "proper" place. See notes to verses 5–6 below.

3. "smashed . . . to the ground" *bhūmau samīkṛtāḥ*: Literally, "made them level on the ground." Ct understands that the *rākṣasas* have been made equal or level with the ground (*bhūmau samatāṃ prāpitāḥ*). Cr understands that they have been made similar to the earth (*bhūmisādṛśyaṃ prāpitāḥ*). Ck understands that they have been made similar to the earth in that they are no longer moving (*bhūmisamī[pa?]kṛtā bhūmyā samatām aspandatāṃ prāpitāḥ*). Each of these commentators understands the expression as a euphemism for "killed." Thus, Cg and Cm merely gloss, "felled (*pātitāḥ*)."

4. "fletched with heron feathers" *kaṅkapatraiḥ*: See 6.35.12 and note.

5–6. See notes to verse 2 above.

"various" *citraiḥ*: Most translators construe the adjective with *triśūlaiḥ*, "tridents," in *pāda* 5d. We feel, however, that it is best to respect the *pāda* boundary and construe the adjective with *parighaiḥ*, "iron clubs," in *pāda* c.

"sharp" *saṃśitaiḥ*: D9–11,M5 (second time), and the texts and printed editions of Ct read instead the somewhat awkward *saṃśritaiḥ*, "clung to, embraced," which Ct glosses as "grasped (*gṛhītaiḥ*)." Translators who follow the text of Ct generally translate, "held, brandished," etc. G1,3,M3,5 (first time), and the printed editions of Cg read instead *samhataiḥ*, "closely joined, compact." Cg glosses this as *saṃgataiḥ*, "grouped together *or* massed," and takes it as an adjective describing the *rākṣasas* (so Cg, Cm) rather than the weapons. (*saṃhataiḥ saṃgataiḥ. rākṣasaviśeṣaṇam etat.*) Raghunathan (1982, vol. 3, p. 127), who follows the text of Cg, reads the line after verse 2 and follows Cg's interpretation, rendering, "by... Rākshasa bands."

"accomplished great feats" *cakruḥ karmāṇi*: Literally, "they did deeds."

8. "calling out their names" *nāmāni... babhāṣire*: Literally, "they spoke names." We understand, with the commentators, that the monkeys are proclaiming their own names on the battlefield, presumably as part of their challenging of the *rākṣasas* (*svanāmāni*—so Cg).

"the fearsome *rākṣasas*" *rākṣasān bhīmān*: D7,9–11,T3,G1,2, and the printed editions of Ct read *vīrān*, "heroic," for *bhīmān*, "fearsome."

9–10. "With a victorious air" *jitakāśibhiḥ*: The compound is used idiomatically in this sense elsewhere in the literature (cf. *MBh* 2.58.43; 3.21.13; 3.233.6,7; 3.270.17; 3.271.13, etc.; and *Mudrārākṣasa* 2.1.18). See Apte, s.v. Ck, Cm, and Ct gloss, "having conquered fear (*jitabhayaiḥ*)," while Ct and Cm add, as an alternative, "having controlled their breathing (*jitaśvāsaiḥ*)." See 6.44.36. See, too, 6.32.17; 6.42.9–10; 6.43.1, App. I, No. 46, line 32; 6.44.36; 6.49.36 note (1094*); 6.78.38; and notes.

"some of the *rākṣasas*... Other *rākṣasas*" *rākṣasāḥ... kecit... kecit*: Literally, "some *rākṣasas*... some."

"accustomed to drinking blood" *rudhirabhojanāḥ*: Literally, "eating blood." On the bloodthirstiness of *rākṣasas*, see, for example, 3.4.2–8 and 3.65.12–20. See, too, Pollock 1991, pp. 68–75 and S. Goldman 2004b.

11. "were beaten to a shapeless mass" *rāśīkṛtāḥ*: Literally, "were made into piles *or* heaps." We follow the idea of Ck, Ct, and Cm, who seem to understand that the *rākṣasas* are reduced to "heaps" [presumably of flesh] by the blows of the trees (*drumaprahārair hatvā rāśīkṛtā ity arthaḥ*—so Ct). Cr, however, seems to understand that the *rākṣasas*' bodies are piled up in one place (*ekatra sthāpitāḥ*).

12–860*. Verse 12, as it stands in the critical edition, can neither be grammatically construed by itself nor credibly linked syntactically to either of its neighboring verses. It consists, in fact, merely of a string of nouns and adjectives in the instrumental with no appropriate verbal element to make it into a sentence. This situation is unknown to any of the manuscripts collated for the critical edition or the printed editions consulted, all of which have some kind of participle in the nominative that functions as a verb to provide a coherent syntax to the passage. For this reason, we have included 860*, which is found in D5–7, 9–11, and S. This passage adds elephants, horses, and riders to the list of things destroyed by the monkeys and, most critically, adds the phrase, "*kīrṇam... vasudhātalam* (the ground was littered)." See Sutherland 1992.

14. "Their faces pale" *vivarṇavadanāḥ*: V2,3,D9–11,T3, and the texts and printed editions of Ct read instead *viṣaṇṇavadanāḥ*, "with dejected faces."

"the *rākṣasas* fell" *nipetuḥ*: Literally, "they fell."

"fainting" *mūḍhāḥ*: The term normally means "stupefied *or* confused." We follow Cg and Cm, who gloss, "fainting, unconscious (*mūrcchitāḥ*)," and Cr, who glosses, "without consciousness (*saṃjñārahitāḥ*)."

15. "fearsome in their valor" *bhīmavikramāḥ*: D5,T1,2,G3,M3, and the printed editions of Cg read instead *bhīmanisvanāḥ*, "with fearsome cries."

"which struck like thunderbolts" *vajrasparśasamaiḥ*: Literally, "whose touch was equal to the *vajra*." The word *vajra* in this context can refer either to the thunderbolt or the powerful weapon of the god Indra. See note to 6.55.43.

16. "as they rushed swiftly onward" *āpatantaḥ*: Literally, "[those] rushing onward." D9–11 and the texts and printed editions of Ct and Cr read the somewhat awkward *pātayantaḥ*, "felling, knocking down." The participle must take the *rākṣasas* as its subject, thus leading to a problem of interpretation. Translators who follow the texts and printed editions of Ct appear to ignore the term, interpret it as a simplex as in the critical reading, or, in the case of Gita Press (1969, vol. 3, p. 1550) alone, attempt to give its causal meaning. Thus, Gita Press renders, "capable of felling down their adversaries."

Following verse 16, Ñ2,V (V3 after 16ab),B,D13 insert a passage of two lines [862*], while D5,T1,M3, and Cg insert the first line only: "Being slaughtered by the monkeys, the *rākṣasas*, trembling in fear,[1][1] fled in all directions, as they pleased, like deer beset by wolves.[2]"

[1]"trembling in fear" *bhayakātarāḥ*: D5,T1,M3, and the texts and printed editions of Cg (VSP 6.52.17ef; KK 6.52.16ef), as noted, insert the first line [862.1*], substituting the verb *vipradudruvuḥ*, "they [the *rākṣasas*] ran away," for *bhayakātarāḥ*, "trembling in fear."

The verse has probably been inserted to provide a better transition, since the reading of the vulgate and the critical edition makes no mention of the flight of the *rākṣasas* until it has already been completed. The two versions of this passage are translated, respectively, only in Gorresio (1856, vol. 9, p. 289) and Raghunathan (1982, vol. 3, p.127).

19. "with short javelins" *bhiṇḍipālaiḥ*: On *bhiṇḍipālas*, see 6.32.30; 6.41.24–25; 6.53.32; 6.83.25; and notes.

20. "knocked to the ground" *vinihatā bhūmau*: M1–3 and the texts and printed editions of Cg and Cm read *śūlaiḥ*, "with lances," for *bhūmau*, "on the ground." This yields the meaning "struck with lances."

"furious" *saṃkruddhaiḥ*: D5,6,T1,2,G1(first time),M3, and the texts and printed editions of Cg and Cm read instead *sabalaiḥ*, "with their troops." M3 and the texts and printed editions of Cg slightly change the word order. This yields the reading "by the *rākṣasas* and their troops." Raghunathan (1982, vol. 3, p. 128) translates this reading as "by the strong *rākṣasas*."

21. "lay" *śāyitāḥ*: Ñ2,V1,2,B2,D5,G1,2,M3,5, and the texts and printed editions of Cg and Cm read instead *dāritāḥ*, "torn open." Raghunathan (1982, vol. 3, p. 128), the only translator consulted who shares this reading, renders, "others had one flank sheared down." The reading is similar to that of Gorresio (6.28.23cd), who renders, "*lacerato ai fianchi*" (1856, vol. 9, p. 289).

"entrails" *āntraiḥ*: Ck, who is also quoted by Ct, glosses *purītadbhiḥ*. According to Apte (s.v.), the term *purītat* can refer either to entrails in general or to a specific organ that lies close to the heart.

22. "With . . . its abundance of weapons" *śastrabahulam*: D6,T1,2,G1,M1–3, and the texts and printed editions of Cg and Cm read instead *śabdabahulam*, "with its tremendous noise."

23. "With the twanging of bowstrings in place of the sweet sound of the lute" *dhanurjyātantrimadhuram*: Literally, "sweet with bowstrings for stringed instruments." The commentators agree that the term *tantri* (irregular for *tantrī*) here refers to the

vīṇā, or traditional Indian lute. Cr understands the term *madhuram*, "sweet," to mean here, in the context of battle, "a battle delightful to heroes (*śūramanohāri yuddham*)." See Te Nijenhius 1970 and 1974. See, too, note to 1.4.7. Cf. 6.59.36 and note.

"the gasps of the dying for the beating of time" *hikkātālāsamanvitam*: Literally, "with gasps *or* hiccups for the rhythmic clapping of hands." The clapping of hands is the classic way to mark tempo in Indian music. See note to 1.4.7. Our translation follows Cg, who explains the term *hikkā* as "the exiting of breath from the throat after repeated pauses (*viramya viramya kaṇṭhāt pavanodgamaḥ*)." Cs also supports this interpretation, glossing, "a kind of sound produced by the upper or outgoing breath (*ūrdhvavātapravartitaśabdaviśeṣaḥ*)." The idea is probably that of the so-called death rattle. Ck, Ct, and Cr all understand the term to refer to the neighing of the warhorses (*aśvaheṣā*). Cs quotes Ct's opinion but prefers an interpretation closer to Cg's and ours, as indicated above. We believe that the neighing of horses would be less likely to be rhythmic than the stertorous breathing of the gravely wounded. Gorresio (1856, vol. 9, p. 289) interprets similarly to us; he renders, "*i singhiozzi*."

"the faint cries of the wounded in place of singing" *mandrastanitasaṃgītam*: Literally, "with low sounds for singing." Here again we have followed Cg [v.l. *manda-*], who explains, "in which the speech, faint on account of weakness, took the place of excellent singing (*aśaktyā mandabhāṣaṇaṃ tad eva saṃgītaṃ samyaggānaṃ yasmin*)." Ck, Ct, Cr, and Cs take *manda-* [v.l. for *mandra-*] in its sense of a type of elephant and thus understand, "with the trumpeting of *manda* elephants for singing (*mandānāṃ mandākhyagajaviśeṣāṇāṃ stanitaṃ bṛhmitam eva gītaṃ yatra tat*—so Ct)."

"the battle resembled a musical recital" *yuddhagāndharvam ābabhau*: Literally, "it seemed to be a battle-concert." Cv, Cg, and Cm gloss, "battle music (*yuddhasaṃgītam*)," with Cg going on to further gloss *saṃgītam* as "dancing, singing, and instrumental music (*nṛttagītavādyam*)." Gorresio (1856, vol. 9, p. 289) translates, "*ell' era come la danza dei Gandharvi*," following his commentator (Cl), whom he quotes as saying, "the battle resembled a dance of the *gandharvas* (*tat* [*sic*] *yuddhaṃ gāndharvanṛtyam iva* [*sic*] *ābabhau*)." Although Gorresio (1856, vol. 9, pp. 373–74, n. 129) follows this suggestion, he remarks that the notion of the *gandharvas* as celestial musicians is a late, popular one and that the earlier notion of these beings was one of fierce warrior followers of Indra. He thus raises the possibility that the poet's original conception might have been rather different than that suggested by the commentator, that is, the concept of a martial dance, the horrid dance of war. Compare 6.46.25–28, where the battleground is compared to a river. See, too, Introduction, pp. 22–23.

26. "Equal in might to his father" *pitṛtulyaparākramaḥ*: Hanumān's father is, of course, the mighty wind god, Vāyu.

"his eyes now doubly red with rage" *dviguṇatāmrākṣaḥ*: Literally, "his eyes doubly red." See 6.31.72 and notes.

27. "When Dhūmrākṣa . . . took his stand" *vyatiṣṭhata*: Literally, "he stood."

28. "with its wheels, poles, horses" *sacakrakūbaraṃ sāśvam*: D9–11 and the texts and printed editions of Ct read instead *sacakrakūbaramukham*, "with its wheels, poles, and front."

29. "After smashing" *bhaṅktvā*: D10,11, and the texts and printed editions of Ct read instead *tyaktvā*, "leaving aside" (GPP reads *tyatvā* [*sic*] for *tyaktvā*).

"trunks, branches, and all" *saskandhaviṭapaiḥ*: Literally, "with their trunks and branches." Ck, Ct, Cm, and Cr understand *skandha* in its sense of "a large branch (*sthūlaśākhā*)," and understand *viṭapa* in the sense of "a smaller branch (*sūkṣmaśākhā*)." Only Dutt (1893, p. 1255) among the translators consulted follows this interpretation.

30. "Some of the *rākṣasas*" *rākṣasāḥ*...*anye*: A number of the translators (Gita Press 1969, vol. 3, p. 1551; Dutt 1893, p. 1255; and Raghunathan 1982, vol. 3, p. 128) understand that two groups of *rākṣasas* are described in this verse: those whose heads are smashed in *pādas* ab, and those who are felled by trees in *pādas* cd, as if the verse contained the normal *anye*...*anye* construction for this type of expression. Since the *anye* is not repeated, we are inclined to read the verse as a single sentence, as Cr proposes and as it is rendered by the other translators consulted.

33. "Then, in a fury...forcefully" *tataḥ kruddhas tu vegena*: The *pāda* is subject to considerable variation in the various subrecensions and probably should have been marked, in part or whole, as uncertain by the critical editors. Certainly the repetition of the particle *tu* in *pādas* a and d appears suspicious and is found in no version other than the critical edition. See Sutherland 1992. Ñ2,V,B1,2,D6,7,9–11,T2,3,G,M5 read instead *tasya kruddhasya vegena*, "through the force of that angry one." D7,9–11,T3, and the texts and printed editions of Ct, Cr, and Ck read *roṣeṇa*, "in anger," for *vegena*, "forcefully, swiftly." According to Ct's reading, which is rendered in those translations that are based on his text, not only Dhūmrākṣa but Hanumān is described as "enraged." The verse would thus be rendered: "Then, in anger, Dhūmrākṣa brought his mace, with its numerous spikes, down upon the skull of the enraged Hanumān."

34. "fearsome-looking" *bhīmarūpayā*: D9–11,T2,3, and the texts and printed editions of Ct read instead *bhīmavegayā*, "of fearsome impact."

"shrugged off" *acintayan*: Literally, "[he] not thinking *or* caring about."

35. "his every limb buckling" *vihvalitasarvāṅgaḥ*: V3,B2,D7,9–11,M1, and the texts and printed editions of Ct and Cr read *visphārita-*, "quivering, trembling," for *vihvalita-*. Cr glosses, "torn, split open (*vidīrṇāni*)."

36. "surviving" *hataśeṣāḥ*: Literally, "the remnants of the slain."

"They fled back to Laṅkā" *praviviśur laṅkām*: Literally, "They entered Laṅkā."

37. "his enemy" *śatrum*: D5–7,9–11,T3,G1,M5, and the texts and printed editions of Ct and Cr read instead *śatrūn*, "enemies."

"he succumbed to the fatigue born from slaughtering his enemies" *ripuvadhajanitaśramaḥ*: Literally, "he possessed fatigue produced from the slaughter of enemies." Cs understands the internal compound *vadhajanitaśrama*—which we, along with Cr and all translators, read as an instrumental *tatpuruṣa*—as a *dvandva*. This compound, in turn, when read as part of its contextualizing *bahuvrīhi*, yields the sense "he who caused the death and exhaustion of his enemies. (*vadhaś ca janitaśramaś ca tau. ripūṇāṃ vadhajanitaśramau yena sa tathā.*)" Cs explains the distinction between the two actions by noting that Hanumān slaughtered those who stood their ground and exhausted those who fled. (*sthitānāṃ vadhaḥ. vidrutānāṃ ca śrama iti vivekaḥ.*)

The meter is *puṣpitāgrā*.

Cv, Cg, and Cm regard the death of Dhūmrākṣa as a point at which to continue their precise chronology of the epic narrative. Cv claims that the battle between Hanumān and Dhūmrākṣa marks the conclusion of the second day of battle (*dhūmrākṣayuddhena dvitīyam ahaḥ samāptam*). Cm notes that [some] authorities (referring, of course, to Ct's tradition—see note to 6.44.38) claim that Dhūmrākṣa's death occurred on the second day of the bright half of the lunar month Bhādra [August–September] (*dhūmrākṣavadho bhādraśukladvitīyāyām ity āhuḥ*). Cg notes, elliptically, "the killing of

Dhūmrākṣa took place on the second [lunar day (*tithi*) of the lunar fortnight of Phālguna/Caitra] (*dvitīyāyāṃ dhūmrākṣavadhaḥ*)." See notes to 6.4.4 and 6.43.1.

Sarga 43

1. "the officer in charge of the garrison" *balādhyakṣam*: This must be the same officer who was put under the command of Dhūmrākṣa at 6.41.21 above and identified there by Ck as Prahasta. Ct, Cm, and Cg join Ck in making the same identification here. He must now have returned to report the bad news to Rāvaṇa.

Following 1ab, D5–7,9–11,S, and the texts and printed editions of the southern commentators insert a passage of 142 lines, App. I, No. 26 (= GPP 6.53.1cd–6.55.1ab; VSP 6.53.1cd–6.55.1ab; KK 6.53.1cd–6.55.1ab; and Gita Press 6.53.1cd–6.55.1ab). This passage describes the duel between Aṅgada and the *rākṣasa* Vajradaṃṣṭra. This same duel is described by Ñ,V (V2 missing up to line 148),B2–4,D4,13 in App. I, No. 28, which is inserted following verse 6.45.1. The passage closely parallels the duel with Dhūmrākṣa at *sargas* 41 and 42 above.

According to Cv, the death of Vajradaṃṣṭra marks the end of the third day of battle, whereas for Cm and Cg, it falls on the third lunar day (*tithi*) [of the lunar fortnight of Phālguna/Caitra], and for Ct, on the third lunar day (*tithi*) [of the bright half of the month of Bhādra]. See note to 6.4.4. Cf. notes to 6.42.37 and 6.44.38.

[GPP 6.53.1; VSP 6.53.1; KK 6.53.1] When Rāvaṇa, lord of the *rākṣasas*, heard that Dhūmrākṣa had been slain [= 6.43.1ab], he flies into a towering rage and, beside himself with fury, heaves hot sighs like a hissing snake. He then speaks to the mighty heroic *rākṣasa* Vajradaṃṣṭra.[1–3] He orders Vajradaṃṣṭra to sally forth with a complement of *rākṣasas* in order to kill Rāma and Sugrīva along with the monkeys.[4–5] The *rākṣasa* lord Vajradaṃṣṭra, who is described as possessing great powers of illusion, agrees to go and quickly sets out with many troops, elephants, horses, donkeys, camels, chariots, etc.[6–8] Adorning himself and putting on armor, he takes his bow and mounts a grand, gilded chariot. He then sets forth with a vast army of *rākṣasas* bearing every sort of weapon, as well as war-elephants. With its loud roars and flashing weapons, the great army resembles a series of storm clouds in the rainy season with their thunder and lightning.[9–23] Vajradaṃṣṭra's expedition passes through the southern gate of the city, where the troop leader Aṅgada is stationed. There they see inauspicious omens. Meteors fall from the sky, hideous jackals, breathing fire, howl, and fearsome beasts cry out foretelling the destruction of the *rākṣasas*. Moreover, the *rākṣasa* warriors stumble fearfully as they advance. Although he sees these inauspicious omens, mighty Vajradaṃṣṭra summons all his fortitude and pushes onward, eager for battle.[24–31] Seeing the *rākṣasas* issuing forth, the monkeys, with a triumphant air, set up a mighty roar, which fills all quarters. A tumultuous battle between the monkeys and the *rākṣasas* ensues, with the combatants on both sides described as fearsome looking and eager to slaughter one another. The description of the battle follows, with the valiant warriors on both sides cut down with a variety of weapons, fists, rocks, trees, etc.[32–39] The terrifying sound of the clashing weapons, the rumbling chariot wheels, the twanging of bows, and the sounding of conches and drums is heard.[40–43] When the weapons of the *rākṣasas* are lost or destroyed, the battle continues hand to hand, with the monkeys using trees and rocks.

In the course of this battle, many *rākṣasas* are killed.[44–47] At the same time, Vajradaṃṣṭra terrorizes the monkeys with his arrows on the battlefield, just like Yama, himself, ender of all things, armed with his noose at the destruction of the world. Enraged *rākṣasas*, armed with all manner of weapons and expert in the use of divine weapon-spells, continue to slaughter the monkeys.[48–51] Seeing the *rākṣasas* engaged in this slaughter, Vālin's son, Aṅgada, redoubles his fury, like the fire at the destruction of the universe. Seizing a tree, he slaughters the *rākṣasas*, just as a lion might slay lesser beasts.[52–56] The fearsome *rākṣasas* who have confronted Aṅgada now lie like broken trees, their heads smashed in, while the battleground looks terrifying, covered as it is with various chariots, banners, horses, and the blood and bodies of monkeys and *rākṣasas*.[57–60] By the same token, the ground, littered with the jewelry, garments, and parasols of the fallen, is described as resembling an autumn night. The impetuousness of Aṅgada's attack has caused the great army of *rākṣasas* to tremble like a cloud in the wind.[61–64]

[GPP 6.54.1; VSP 6.54.1; KK 6.54.1] Infuriated by Aṅgada's triumphs and the destruction of his forces, mighty Vajradaṃṣṭra twangs the bowstring of his fearsome bow with a sound like that of Indra's thunderbolt, and he begins to shower the monkey army with arrows.[65–68] The *rākṣasa* leaders, too, rally and, mounted on their chariots, continue the battle with various weapons. The heroic monkeys regroup themselves and fight armed with boulders.[69–72] The *rākṣasas* employ thousands of weapons against the principal monkeys, while the heroic monkeys, who resemble rutting elephants, hurl mountains, trees, and huge boulders at the *rākṣasas*.[73–76] The battle continues, and the destruction of the combatants is described. Some have their heads smashed, while others have their arms and feet severed. Their bodies are mangled with weapons and drenched in blood, while carrion birds and jackals swarm about. Headless corpses leap about, terrorizing the faint of heart, while *rākṣasas* and monkeys, with arms, hands, heads, and bodies hacked to pieces, lie fallen everywhere.[77–85] When Vajradaṃṣṭra sees the *rākṣasa* forces being destroyed by the monkeys, he charges into the monkey ranks, bow in hand, cutting them to pieces with his accurate, heron-feathered shafts, five, seven, eight, and nine at a time.[86–93] The terrified hosts of monkeys, their bodies rent by arrows, run to the shelter of Aṅgada as creatures might to the creator, Prajāpati. Seeing the shattered hosts of monkeys, Vālin's son, Aṅgada, is filled with fury and glares at Vajradaṃṣṭra, who returns his gaze. The two warriors, both in a towering rage, at last clash like a lion and a rutting elephant.[94–99] Vajradaṃṣṭra strikes the mighty son of Vālin, Aṅgada, in the vitals with hundreds of thousands of arrows resembling flames of fire. His entire body drenched with blood, mighty Aṅgada, of fearsome valor, hurls a tree at Vajradaṃṣṭra. But the *rākṣasa*, seeing the tree coming, calmly cuts it to pieces so that it falls, shattered, to the ground.[100–105] Observing Vajradaṃṣṭra's prowess, the bull among monkeys seizes a huge boulder and hurls it at him with a roar. But once again the powerful *rākṣasa* sees it coming and calmly leaps from his chariot, mace in hand, to take up his stand on the ground. The boulder hurled by Aṅgada smashes the *rākṣasa*'s chariot, along with its wheels, poles, and horses, in the forefront of the battle.[106–111] The monkey then uproots a huge hill, trees and all, and brings it down upon Vajradaṃṣṭra's head. Vomiting blood, Vajradaṃṣṭra is momentarily dazed and stands grasping his mace, breathing heavily. Recovering, he smashes Aṅgada on the chest in a towering rage.[112–117] Vajradaṃṣṭra drops his mace, and the two, monkey and *rākṣasa*, batter each other with their fists. The two valorous warriors, exhausted from each other's blows and vomiting blood, resemble the planets Mars and Mercury.[118–121] Then immensely powerful Aṅgada, an elephant among monkeys, rips up a tree filled with fruit and flowers, while Vajradaṃṣṭra seizes a huge and shining sword and a shield of oxhide, covered with a network of bells and ornamented with leather.[122–125] Then the monkey and the *rākṣasa* furiously strike at each other without pity, executing various maneuvers in their desire for victory. Fallen to their knees on the ground in their exhaustion, they fight on, glowing with their bleeding wounds, so that they resemble two *kiṃśuka* trees in blossom.[126–129] Finally, in the blink of an eye, the elephant among monkeys Aṅgada, eyes blazing, springs up, like a serpent prodded with a stick. And, with a shining, spotless sword,[1] Aṅgada, mighty son of Vālin, strikes off Vajradaṃṣṭra's enormous head. Struck off by the sword and severed from his blood-drenched body, Vajradaṃṣṭra's beautiful head falls, its eyes still wide with anger.[130–135] When the *rākṣasas* see that Vajradaṃṣṭra has been slain, they are stupefied with fear and dejected, their faces downcast and averted in shame. They flee back to Laṅkā in terror with the leaping monkeys still slaughtering them. But as for mighty Vālin's son, Aṅgada, whose power was equal to that of Indra, bearer of the *vajra*, he rejoices, honored in the midst of the monkey army, like thousand-eyed Indra surrounded by the thirty gods.[136–140]

[1]"with a . . . sword" *khaḍgena*: A number of the commentators, conscious of the fact that the monkeys do not carry formal weapons, observe that, when Aṅgada's tree has been destroyed, he seizes Vajradaṃṣṭra's own sword (*khaḍgenācchidya gṛhītena vajradaṃṣṭrīyeṇa*—so Ct).

Following App. I, No. 26 but before 6.43.1cd, D5–7,9–11,S insert a passage of one line [872*], which provides a transition from the appendix to the present *sarga*: "When Rāvaṇa heard that Vajradaṃṣṭra had been killed by Aṅgada, Vālin's son . . ."

2. "Akampana" *akampanaṃ*: Literally, "unshakeable." A character of this name is known to the southern recension of the *Araṇyakāṇḍa*, where it is he who reports Rāma's slaughter of the *rākṣasas* in Janasthāna to Rāvaṇa. He is the one who first puts into Rāvaṇa's head the idea of abducting Sītā. See *Araṇyakāṇḍa*, App. I, No. 10 (= GPP 3.31). See, too, notes to 3.29.20. See note to verse 5 below. Cf. 6.47.14.

"skilled in the use of every weapon" *sarvaśastraprakovidam*: D9,10,T2,3,G1, and the texts and printed editions of Ct read instead *sarvaśastrāstrakovidam*, "skilled in the use of all weapons and divine weapon-spells."

Following verse 2, Ñ,V,B,D2,5–7,9–11,S insert a passage of two lines [873*]: "He subdues and he defends,[1] and he is esteemed as a leader in battle. He is constantly desirous of my success and is always fond of warfare."

[1]"He subdues and he defends" *eṣa śāstā ca goptā ca*: Literally, "he is a subduer *or* chastiser and a protector." The expression is elliptical, and the commentators explain that he subdues his enemies and protects his own forces (*śāstā śatrūṇāṃ goptā svabalasya*—so Ct).

Following 873*, D2,5–7,9–11,S, and the texts and printed editions of Ct and Cr continue with, while Ñ (Ñ1 after 877*),V,B, and the critical apparatus insert after 5cd, a passage of four lines [878*]: " 'He will defeat the two Kākutsthas and mighty Sugrīva. That scorcher of his foes[1] will slaughter the other fearsome monkeys as well.' When he received that command of Rāvaṇa, that mighty warrior with quick strides made his army hurry."

[1]"That scorcher of his foes" *paraṃtapaḥ*: D7,9–11,G3,M1,2,5, and the texts and printed editions of Ct read instead *na saṃśayaḥ*, "without doubt."

4. "Wearing earrings of burnished gold" *taptakāñcanakuṇḍalaḥ*: Literally, "having earrings of burnished gold." D9–11 and the texts and printed editions of Ct read instead the accusative *taptakāñcanabhūṣaṇam*, "having ornaments of burnished gold." In this reading, the adjective must refer to the chariot rather than Akampana.

Following 4ab, D5–7,9–11,S insert a passage of one line [875*], continuing the description of Akampana: "Looking like a storm cloud, the color of a storm cloud, and with a thunderous sound like the sound of a storm cloud..."

5. "He was incapable of being shaken... Thus he was called Akampana, the unshakeable" *na hi kampayituṃ śakyaḥ... akampanas tataḥ*: Literally, "since he was incapable of being shaken, he was Akampana." The poet here provides an etymological explanation of the *rākṣasa*'s name. See note to verse 2 above.

"in their midst" *teṣām*: Literally, "of them." The pronoun is elliptical in its reference here. We are inclined to agree with Cg, who understands the reference to be to the *rākṣasas* surrounding Akampana (*teṣāṃ rakṣasāṃ madhye tejasāditya iva sthita ity arthaḥ*). The idea is that, in his radiance, Akampana shines among his cohorts. In this interpretation he is followed by Raghunathan (1982, vol. 3, p. 134) and Gita Press (1969, vol. 3, p. 1559). Ct and Cr, on the other hand, understand that Akampana was like a sun among the monkeys, in the sense that they were unable even to gaze upon him because of his radiance (*teṣāṃ vānarāṇāṃ tejasāditya iva duṣprekṣo 'bhūd iti śeṣaḥ*—so Ct). This interpretation is followed in the translations of Dutt (1893, p. 1262), Roussel (1903, vol. 3, p. 158), Shastri (1959, vol. 3, p. 135), and Pagani (1999, p. 995).

Following 5cd, Ñ (Ñ1 continues after 877*),V,B,D4 (continues after 877*) insert a passage of four lines [878*], while D2,5–7,9–11,S insert it following 873* above. See note to verse 2 above for a translation of the passage.

6. "were seized with a lethargy" *dainyam āgacchat*: Literally, "depression *or* lassitude came [to them]." Ck, Ct, Cg, and Cm add the word *manaḥ*, "mind, heart," giving the sense "depression came upon the minds [of the horses]." As Cr notes, this will be the first of the signs indicative of Akampana's impending defeat (*parābhavalakṣaṇāny āha tasyetyādibhiḥ*).

"that had no apparent cause" *akasmāt*: Cr, Ct, and Ck, with whom we agree, understand the adverb in this sense, glossing, "without cause (*nirhetuḥ*—so Ct, Ck)" or "without visible cause (*dṛṣṭakāraṇābhāvāt*—so Cr)." Gorresio (1856, vol. 9, p. 291) and Raghunathan (1982, vol. 3, p. 134) also interpret in this way. The term can also mean "suddenly," and the remaining translators consulted have interpreted it accordingly.

7. "Though normally he delighted in battle" *yuddhābhinandinaḥ*: Literally, "delighting in combat." We have added the words "though normally" to highlight the sudden change in Akampana's demeanor.

"his left eye now began to twitch" *vyasphuran nayanaṃ cāsya savyam*: Literally, "and his left eye twitched." Throbbing or twitching on the left side of the body is an inauspicious omen for a male. See 6.4.6 and note. See, too, 6.53.43 and note.

"his face took on a sickly hue" *vivarṇo mukhavarṇaś ca*: Literally, "the color of his face was devoid of color." Translators of the southern recension understand this somewhat awkward phrase to mean that his face grew pale. We, however, prefer to follow Cg and Cr in understanding the phrase not to mean "devoid of color (*vivarṇaḥ*)" but rather "having an unfavorable *or* adverse color (*viparītavarṇaḥ*)."

"his voice began to crack" *gadgadaś cābhavat svaraḥ*: Literally, "his voice was choked *or* stuttering."

8. "Although the weather had been clear, the sky grew dark and a harsh wind blew." *abhavat sudine cāpi durdinaṃ rūkṣamārutam*: Literally, "and even on a fair day, there arose foul weather with harsh winds." D9–11,T3, and the texts and printed editions of Ct read for *cāpi*, "and even," *kāle*, "at a time [of good weather]." See 6.4.41; 6.41.33; 6.45.35; 6.53.44; 6.65.19; and notes.

"Fierce birds and beasts all uttered fearsome cries." *ūcuḥ khagā mṛgāḥ sarve vācaḥ krūrā bhayāvahāḥ*: The line is somewhat ambiguous, since both the adjectives *krūrāḥ*, "fierce," and *bhayāvahāḥ*, "fearsome," can be taken to modify the birds, the beasts, the birds and the beasts together, or the cries of the birds and beasts. With the exception of Dutt (1893, p. 1262), all translators consulted construe both adjectives with the cries. We, however, prefer the reading of Cr, who applies the first to the creatures and the second to their cries (*krūrāḥ khagamṛgā bhayāvahā vāca ūcuḥ*). See note to 6.26.8.

9. "Akampana" *saḥ*: Literally, "he."

11. " the vast army... armed with trees and boulders, arrayed itself for battle" *mahācamūḥ / drumaśailapraharaṇā yoddhuṃ samavatiṣṭhata*: Literally, "the great army, having trees and boulders for weapons, stood in order to fight." Manuscript evidence shows considerable variation for the verbal form *samavatiṣṭhata*, "it stood." Most variants show a finite verb. However, D9–11,T3,M5, and the texts and printed editions of Ct, Cr, and Ck show the genitive plural of the present participle of the synonymous verb *sam* + *upa* $\sqrt{}$*sthā*, *samupatiṣṭhatām*, which construes with the vulgate reading *drūmaśailaprahārāṇām*, yielding "of them [*teṣām*—verse 11 below] who took up their positions and who struck with trees and boulders." In the vulgate texts, this phrase belongs to a separate verse (=GPP 6.55.15).

12. "who were prepared to lay down their lives" *samabhityaktajīvinām*: Literally, "who had abandoned their lives." The southern commentators show some variation here. Cg reads with the critical edition and glosses, "valuing their bodies [no more highly] than a blade of grass (*tṛṇīkṛtaśarīrāṇām*)." Cm and Cr prefer the variant *samabhityaktadehinām*, "[of them] who [were prepared] to sacrifice their bodies." Cm glosses this reading as "those who had given up their embodied spirits (*samabhityaktā dehina ātmāno yais te teṣām*)." Ck and Ct have the same compound but in the nominative rather than in the genitive plural (*samabhityaktadehinaḥ*), which reading must then construe with the nominative plurals in our 6.43.13 (=GPP 6.55.16cd–17ab). Ck and Ct gloss this reading similarly to Cm, adding that it means that the warriors were "heedless of self-protection (*ātmarakṣānirapekṣāḥ*—so Ct)." Most of the translators

consulted, regardless of the text they follow, translate, "lives." Only Gita Press (1969, vol. 3, p. 1559) and Dutt (1893, p. 1262) follow Ct literally, translating, "souls" and "selves," respectively.

"for the sake of Rāma and Rāvaṇa, respectively" *rāmarāvaṇayor arthe*: Literally, "for the sake of Rāma and Rāvaṇa."

14. "roared . . . bellowed" *vinardatām . . . abhigarjatām*: The two roots √*nard* and √*garj* share the meanings "roar, bellow, etc." Cr attempts to distinguish them, explaining, "*abhigarjatām* means they were challenging one another to battle, and for that very reason they were roaring [*vinardatām*] (*anyonyam abhigarjatāṃ yuddhārtham āhvayatām ata eva vinardatām*)." Cg glosses *vinardatām* as "making leonine roars (*siṃhanādaṃ kurvatām*)" and *abhigarjatām* as "bellowing in [one another's] faces (*abhimukhyena garjanaṃ kurvatām*)."

15. "red" *aruṇavarṇābham*: Literally, "resembling the color red." Several of the commentators are unhappy with this collocation. Ct, Ck, and Cm take the term *aruṇa-*, "reddish color," here as a synonym for smoke, although they offer no lexical support for this. They thus understand the compound to mean "in which there was the appearance of a substance the color of smoke (*dhūmravarṇasya vastuna ābhā yasmiṃs tat*)." Cg understands it as an instrumental *tatpuruṣa* with the sense "that shines with the color of dawn or the color red, that is, with redness (*aruṇavarṇena raktimnābhāti*)."

16. "as pale as floating silk" *kauśeyoddhūtapāṇḍunā*: Literally, "white as raised up silk." D6,9–11,G2, and Ck, Ct, and Cr read *-uddhata-*, which can have a meaning similar to that of the critical reading, *-uddhūta-*, although the commentators and translators render the compound variously. All commentators agree that we are to read the compound as a *paranipāta*, i.e., as *uddhūta* [v.l. *-uddhata-*]*kauśeyapāṇḍunā*. Ct and Ck understand the compound to mean "slightly whitish like *uddhata* silk (*uddhatakauśeyavadīṣatpāṇḍuravarṇena*)." According to Apte (s.v. *uddhata*), who cites this verse, we are to understand the term here to mean "shining, glittering." Cr understands, "of a slightly reddish *or* pale pink color (*īṣadaruṇavarṇenety arthaḥ*)." Cg, who reads with the critical edition, claims that we are to understand that "the dust is both red [as mentioned in verse 15 above] and white, owing to the different types of earth that are stirred up (*rajaso raktatvapāṇḍutve bhūbhedād iti jñeyam*)." Cm, who reads with the critical edition, attractively, but with little lexical support, glosses, "washed, bright, shining *or* white (*-dhauta-*)." Many northern manuscripts, including the text of Gorresio (6.29.19), read *aruṇa-* for *uddhūta-*, yielding the meaning "reddish and whitish like silk."

"the opposing forces" *bhūtāni*: Literally, "creatures, beings." Our translation follows the interpretation of Ct, Ck, Cr, and Cm, who take the term in the nominative to refer to the *rākṣasas* and the monkeys. Cg takes the term in the accusative to refer to objects (*vastūni*) that are shrouded in dust and that the monkeys and the *rākṣasas* (terms he has to supply) therefore cannot see.

17. "armor" *varma*: The manuscript evidence shows considerable variation here, substituting bows, elephants, etc., for armor. Ñ,V,B3,D9–11,T3, and the texts and printed editions of Ct, Ck, and Cr read instead *carma*, "shield."

18. "tumultuous" *tumule*: D7,9–11,G1, and the texts and printed editions of Ct, Ck, and Cr read instead the nominative *tumulaḥ*, which must then be construed with *śabdaḥ*, "din," in *pāda* a.

"though nothing at all could be seen" *na rūpāṇi cakāśire*: Literally, "forms were not visible." Cg understands that these are other things, i.e., articles other than those mentioned in the previous verse (*rūpāṇi padārthāntarāṇi*).

20. "they drenched the earth with blood, making it slick with mud" *rudhirārdrāṃ tadā cakrur mahīṃ paṅkānulepanām*: Literally, "they then made the blood-drenched earth such that it had mud for its ointment."

21. "spattered" *siktam*: Literally, "sprinkled."

"settled" *vyapagatam*: Literally, "vanished *or* went away."

"dead bodies" *śarīraśava-*: Literally, "bodies and corpses." The commentators generally interpret, "bodies in the form of corpses (*śavarūpaiḥ śarīraiḥ*—Ct)."

22. "trees, javelins" *drumaśakti-*: As Cg notes, the trees and boulders would be used by the monkeys, whereas the javelins and other weapons would be used by the *rākṣasas*. (*drumaśailā vānarīyāḥ. śaktyādayo rākṣasīyāḥ.*)

23. "huge as mountains" *parvatopamāḥ*: Literally, "comparable to mountains." Ñ,V1,2,D9–11, and the texts and printed editions of Ct and Cr read the accusative, *parvatopamān*, so that the description is applied to the *rākṣasas* instead of the monkeys.

24. Following verse 24, D5–7,9–11,S (Ñ1,B2,3,D4, after verse 25) insert a passage of two lines [885*]: "Enraged, Akampana, lord of the army of the *rākṣasas*, encouraged all those *rākṣasas* of fearsome valor."

25. "bravely" *vīryataḥ*: This can also be understood in the sense of "forcibly, vigorously" as Dutt (1893, p. 1263), Roussel (1903, vol. 3, p. 159), and Pagani (1999, p. 997) have done.

"seized those weapons from them" *śastrāṇy ācchidya*: Literally, "having seized weapons." We follow the commentators' interpretation in taking the gerund *ācchidya* in the sense of "having seized *or* snatched." The verb *ā* $\sqrt{}$*chid* can also mean "to break up *or* cut," and it has been interpreted—less persuasively in our opinion—in this sense by Roussel (1903, vol. 3, p. 158), followed by Shastri (1959, vol. 3, p. 136) and Pagani (1999, pp. 996–97).

26. "in a towering rage" *paramakruddhāḥ*: B3,D3–5,T1,M1–3, the texts and printed editions of Cg and Cm, and Gorresio's edition read *dvividaḥ*, "Dvivida," for *parama-*, "great." Ś2,Ñ2,V3,B1,2,D2,6–11, and the texts and printed editions of Ct and Cr read instead the nominative singular, *paramakruddhaḥ*, making the adjective modify only the monkey Mainda.

"charged with unparalleled speed" *cakrur vegam anuttamam*: Literally, "they made unsurpassed speed."

27. "immensely swift" *mahāvegāḥ*: D7,9–11, and the texts and printed editions of Cr, Ct, and Ck read instead *mahāvīrāḥ*, "heroic *or* mighty."

"leaders of the troops of tawny monkeys" *hariyūthapāḥ*: Ś,B2,D2,7–12,T3, and the texts and printed editions of Ct and Cr read instead *haripuṃgavāḥ*, "bulls among the tawny monkeys."

Following verse 27, D5,6,9–11,T,G1,2,M (D7,G3, after 889*) insert a passage of one line [890*]: "All the monkeys, troop by troop,[1] powerfully crushed the *rākṣasas*."

[1]"the monkeys, troop by troop" *vānarā gaṇaśaḥ*: D10,11,M1,2, and the texts and printed editions of Cr, Ck, and Ct read instead *nānāpraharaṇaiḥ*, "with various weapons."

Ck believes that [some scribes] pointlessly *or* wrongly make a break, or a *sarga* division, here (i.e., between *sarga* 43 and 44 of the critical edition [= GPP 6.55–56]) (*atra ca mudhā sargam avacchindanti*). Cm and Ct paraphrase Ck's comments, attributing to him the idea that the *sarga* division here is the result of carelessness (*atra sargāvacchedaḥ pramādād iti katakaḥ*).

Sarga 44

3. "at once" *tvaritam*: We read the term adverbially, although it could also be taken adjectivally to modify "chariot," in the sense of "the swift chariot." V,B3,D9–11,T3, and the texts and printed editions of Ct read instead the nominative singular masculine, *tvaritaḥ*, "swift," which would modify an implied *tvam*, "you," i.e., the charioteer.

"where so many monkeys" [*a*]*tra bahavaḥ*: Literally, "here many." A few *devanāgarī* manuscripts (D7,9–11) and the texts and printed editions of Ct read instead *ca balinaḥ*, "and mighty [monkeys]."

4. "with fearsome bodies" *bhīmakāyāḥ*: Ñ2,V,D7,10,11,T3, and the texts and printed editions of Ct read instead *bhīmakopāḥ*, "in a frightening rage."

5. "these boastful warriors" *samaraślāghinaḥ*: Literally, "those who are boastful in battle." The term could also be taken to mean "praiseworthy in battle," although it seems unlikely that Akampana would be in any mood to accord them this tribute. The commentators are silent on this term, and among the translators consulted, only Raghunathan (1982, vol. 3, p. 135), who renders, "foemen worthy of my steel," takes it as a compliment.

6. "whose horses were whipped to a gallop" *prajavitāśvena*: Literally, "with horses that had been urged on." D7,9–11,T3, and the texts and printed editions of Ct and Cr read instead *pracalitāśvena*, "whose horses were running *or* galloping."

"in his fury, assailed" *abhyahanat krodhāt*: Literally, "he struck *or* slew out of anger." D7,9–11, and the texts and printed editions of Ct and Cr read instead *abhyapatad dūrāt*, "he attacked from afar."

7. "to stand before him" *sthātum*: Literally, "to stand."

8. "had come under the power of Akampana" *akampanavaśaṃ gatān*: V3,D7,9–11, and the texts and printed editions of Ct and Cr read instead *akampanaśarānugān*, "pursued by the arrows of Akampana."

"rushed over" *upatasthe*: Literally, "he approached."

9. "the . . . leaders of the troops of leaping monkeys" *plavagayūthapāḥ*: D3,10,11,M1,2, and the texts and printed editions Ct and Cr read instead *te plavagarṣabhāḥ*, "those bulls among the leaping monkeys."

"together" *sahitāḥ*: M1,3, and the texts and printed editions of Cg and Gita Press (6.56.9) read instead *saṃhṛṣṭāḥ*, "excited *or* delighted."

10. "the leaders of the troops of tawny monkeys" *hariyūthapāḥ*: D7,9–11,G1,M5, and the texts and printed editions of Ct and Cr read instead *plavagarṣabhāḥ*, "the bulls among the leaping monkeys."

"they recovered their strength, placing their trust in that powerful warrior" *babhūvur balavanto hi balavantam upāśritāḥ*: Literally, "resorting to that mighty one, they became mighty."

12. "sharp" *śitān*: D9–11,T3, and the texts and printed editions of Ct and Cr read instead *kapiḥ*, "the monkey."

"the mighty monkey" *mahābalaḥ*: Literally, "the one of great strength *or* the mighty one."

13. "Laughing" *prahasya*: D5,6,G2,3, and the texts and printed editions of Cg and Cm read instead *prasahya*, "violently, forcefully." Among the translators consulted, this reading is rendered only by Raghunathan (1982, vol. 3, p. 136), who translates, "with all the force he could summon."

17. "With it": Since the simile provides a weapon, the *vajra*, as the *upamāna*, but none as an *upameya*, we agree with Cg that one needs to understand that Hanumān is using the mountain mentioned in the previous verse as a weapon (*tatra sa śailenety adhyāhāryam*).

"just as" *yathā* . . . *iva*: Literally, "just as . . . like." D7,10,11,G2,M1–3, and the texts and printed editions of the southern commentators read *purā*, "formerly, long ago," for *yathā*, "just as." This may be an attempt to eliminate the redundancy.

"Indra, smasher of citadels, with his *vajra* . . . Namuci" *namucim* . . . *vajreṇeva puraṃdaraḥ*: Literally, "the smasher of citadels with his *vajra* . . . Namuci." See note to 4.22.11. The story of Indra and Namuci is popular and known from the earliest literature, e.g., *ṚV* 1.53.7 and 8.14.13 and *TaiBr* 1.6–7. See, too, Keith 1925, pp. 130–31. The story is also related at *MBh* 9.42.28–31. See also Pagani 1999, p. 1663, n. 2 and Gorresio 1856, vol. 9, p. 374, n. 130. The name Namuci also appears in a list of demons at 7.99*, line 1 (=GPP 7.6.34).

18. "held aloft" *samudyatam*: Ct and Cr understand, probably on the basis of the following verse, that Hanumān has actually hurled the mountain (*hanumatā prakṣiptam*), although the verse does not say so explicitly. Ck wants to have it both ways, glossing, "as if loosed (*muktavat*)."

"with huge half-moon-headed arrows" *mahābāṇair ardhacandraiḥ*: See 6.35.23; 6.55.117; 6.57.57; and notes.

19. "in midair" *ākāśe*: Literally, "in the air." See note to verse 18 above.

"in pieces" *vikīrṇam*: Literally, "scattered."

20. "raced over" *samāsādya*: Literally, "having approached."

21. "with its vast trunk" *mahāskandham*: The term *skandha* can refer equally to the trunk of a tree or its large boughs or branches, and the translators who share this reading are more or less equally divided between the two choices. The exception is Dutt (1893, p. 1265), who idiosyncratically takes the term *skandha* in its sense of "shoulder." Since the poet distinguishes *skandha*, "trunk," from *viṭapa*, "branch," at 6.42.29 above, we believe that he probably intends *skandha* to refer to the trunk here as well.

"Hanumān, blazing with splendor" *mahādyutiḥ*: Literally, "that one of great splendor."

"in battle" *saṃyuge*: D9–11 and the texts and printed editions Ct and Cr read instead *bhūtale*, "on *or* above the ground." This variant is rendered in the translations of Dutt (1893, p. 1265), Roussel (1903, vol. 3, p. 162), and Pagani (1999, p. 998).

"laughing" *prahasya*: V2,3,D9–11,T1,3, and the texts and printed editions of Ct read instead the redundant *pragṛhya*, "having seized."

22. "with tremendous speed" *uruvegena*: Roussel (1903, vol. 3, p. 162), followed by Shastri (1959, vol. 3, p. 137) and Pagani (1999, p. 998), renders, "*à grandes enjambées*."

D1,3,5,12,T,G1,2,M, as well as KK (6.56.22), VSP (6.56.22), Lahore (6.32.22), and the texts of Cg read instead *ūruvegena*, "with the force *or* impact of his thighs." Raghunathan (1982, vol. 3, p. 136), who most probably reads with Cg, as is his practice, attempts to evade the issue by rendering, simply, "by the force of his impact." Only Gorresio (1856, vol. 9, p. 294) among the translators consulted understands the reference to be to Hanumān's thighs, even though his text reads *uruvegena* (6.30.22). He renders, "*con tutta la foga de'suoi femori.*"

"breaking down... tore up" *prabhañjan... dārayat* : We agree with Cg, who understands *dārayat* as an augmentless imperfect (*adārayat*). D4,6,7,9–11,T2,3,G3, and the texts and printed editions of Ct and Cr read the finite verb *babhañja*, "he broke," for the present participle *prabhañjan*, "breaking down."

"with the pounding of his feet" *caraṇaiḥ*: Literally, "with his feet." The odd use of the plural here has prompted Ct, Cg, and Cm—with whom we concur—to gloss, "with his footsteps (*caraṇanyāsaiḥ*)."

23. "Wise" *dhīmān*: D7,10,11, and the texts and printed editions of Ct and Cr read instead the accusative plural *bhīmān*, "fearsome, formidable," which then would most probably modify the *rākṣasa* foot soldiers (*padātikān*) of *pāda* d. Manuscript evidence shows that there are six widely differing variants of the reading in fourteen manuscripts, both northern and southern. The choice of *dhīmān* should be considered doubtful and should be marked as such.

"foot soldiers" *padātikān*: Normally, the term means "a footman *or* peon." Cg and Cr, who read the variant *padātigān*, literally, "going on foot," gloss, "those who go in the state of being pedestrians are *padātigas* (*padātitvena* [so Cr; *padātitayā* Cg] *gacchanti*)." Cr additionally proposes breaking up the term into the elements *padā* and *atigān*. In this reading, *padā*, "with a single foot," becomes the means through which Hanumān destroys the swift-moving (*atiga*) elephants, etc. (*kiṃcātigāñ chīghragamanakartṝn gajādīn padaikacaraṇena jaghāna*).

24. "enraged and wreaking slaughter" *kruddham... prāṇahāriṇam*: Literally, "angry... taking lives." These two adjectives can be taken to refer to Hanumān, as we have done, to Yama (Antaka, "the Ender"), or to both of them. Translators vary in their ascription of the adjectives accordingly.

"on the battlefield" *samare*: Ñ2,V2,3,D9–11, and the texts and printed editions of Ct and Cr read instead *sadrumam*, "[armed] with a tree."

"like Yama himself, the ender of all things" *tam antakam iva*: Literally, "like Antaka (lit., the ender)."

"they fled in all directions" *vipradudruvuḥ*: Literally, "they ran away *or* they scattered."

25. "flew into a rage" *cukrodha*: Literally, "he became angry." B4,D7,9–11, and the texts and printed editions of Ct and Cr read instead *cukṣobha*, "trembled, was agitated."

26. "with fourteen" *caturdaśabhiḥ*: This number has a particular resonance for Vālmīki. Compare the fourteen years of Rāma's exile (2.10.28; 2.16.24; etc.) and the fourteen (3.18.17–25) and then fourteen thousand *rākṣasas* slain by Rāma (3.21.8ff.).

27. "Riddled in this fashion with many volleys of arrows" *sa tathā pratividdhas tu bahvībhiḥ śaravṛṣṭibhiḥ*: The various subrecensions show considerable variation throughout this half verse. The printed texts of Ct, Cr, and Ck read instead *sa tathā viprakīrṇas tu nārācaiḥ śitaśaktibhiḥ*, "covered in this fashion with iron arrows and sharp javelins..."

"densely forested" *prarūḍhaḥ*: Literally, "overgrown." We follow Cv, Cg, Cm, Ck, Cr, and Ct in understanding the term to mean "having trees that are grown (*prarūḍhavṛkṣaḥ*—so Cg, Cm)."

Following verse 27, D5,7,9–11,S insert a passage of two lines [903*–902*, line 2]: "Then the huge, heroic, and very wise[1] Hanumān resembled[2] a flowering *aśoka* tree."

[1]"very wise" *mahāmanāḥ*: Literally, "the very wise one." D9–11,T3, and the texts and printed editions of Ct and Cr read instead *mahābalaḥ*, "of great might."

[2]"Then . . . Hanumān resembled" *prababhau hanūmāṃs tataḥ*: D5–7,9–11,S read instead *vidhūma iva pāvakaḥ*, "like a smokeless fire." The critical editors' choice of *mahāmanāḥ* is difficult to justify. Only Ñ1,B2,3,D2,4 read with the critical edition, whereas the entire south, including the *devanāgarī* manuscripts aligned with the south, read the variant.

30. "lying on the ground" *bhūmau*: Literally, "on the ground."

31. "Terrified" *trastāḥ*: D9–11,T2,3,M5, and texts and printed editions of Ct and Cr read instead *trāsāt*, "out of fear."

32. "running" *sravat-*: B1,D8–11,G3, and the texts and printed editions of Ct and Cr read instead *bhayāt*, "out of fear."

"gasping for breath" *śvasanto* [*vi-*]: Literally, "breathing." D9–11 and the texts and printed editions of Ct and Cr read instead the instrumental participle *prasravadbhiḥ*, "flowing [with sweat]." The adjective then modifies "limbs (*aṅgaiḥ*)."

33. "Trampling" *pramamanthuḥ*: Literally, "they bruised, crushed, *or* injured." Ct and Ck, who read instead *pramathnantaḥ*, "bruising, injuring," take this as a reference to their crushing one another at the gates to the city (*dvāradeśe saṃmardaṃ kurvāṇāḥ*).

35. "endowed with strength" *sattvasampannaḥ*: This can also be translated here—less plausibly in our opinion—as "endowed with goodness *or* virtue."

"in great delight" *prahṛṣṭaḥ*: D9–11,G2, and the texts and printed editions of Ct and Cr read instead the somewhat awkward *pravṛddhaḥ*, "large, great, mature." D7 and the texts of Cr and Cm(?) read the accusative plural *pravṛddhān*, which would make the adjective apply to the monkeys in general. This appears to be the basis for Dutt's rendition, "the seniors" (1893, p. 1266).

"graciously" *anukūlataḥ*: According to Ck and Ct, the adverb refers to Hanumān's friendly glances, words, and embraces (*anukūladarśanavacanāliṅganaiḥ*).

"honored" *saṃpratyapūjayat*: Cg believes that Hanumān is telling the monkeys that he achieved victory only through their assistance (*bhavatsāhāyyenaiva mayā jitam iti*).

36. "With a victorious air" *jitakāśinaḥ*: See 6.32.17; 6.42.9–10; 6.43.1, App. I, No. 26, line 32; 6.49.36; 6.78.38; and notes.

"dragged about" *cakarṣuḥ*: Ck and Ct, who read *cakṛṣuḥ*, note that the monkeys do this in order to kill the surviving *rākṣasas* (*prāṇanāśārtham iti śeṣaḥ*). Cr reads instead *cukruṣuḥ*, "they shouted at, reviled," a variant unnoticed by the critical apparatus.

37. "slaughtering . . . slaying" *nihatya*: Literally, "having killed."

"great . . . and mighty *asura*" *mahāsuram . . . balinam*: In order to maintain the plural parallelism with the many *rākṣasas*, several of the commentators suggest that the term *asura* here is collective for Madhu, Kaiṭabha, and other notorious demons slain by Viṣṇu (*madhukaiṭabhādirūpam*—so Ct). See 7.4.14; 7.22.22; 7.61.27; and 7.94.6. Raghunathan (1982, vol. 3, p. 137) appears to mistake the adjective *balinam*, "mighty," for the accusative of the proper name of the famous demon Bali [Mahābali], who, it should be noted, was not killed by Viṣṇu but merely subdued. See note to 6.105.12.

The meter is *vaṃśasthavila*.

38. Cg and Cm note that the slaying of Akampana takes place on the fourth lunar day [of the lunar fortnight of Phālguna/Caitra] (*caturthyām akampanavadhaḥ*). Ct specifies that this is the fourth lunar day of the bright half of the month of Bhādra (*bhādraśukla-caturthyām akampanavadhaḥ*). Cv understands that the killing of Akampana ends the fourth day [of the battle] (*akampanavadhena ca caturtham ahas samāptam*). See note to 6.4.4.

The meter is *vaṃśasthavila*.

Sarga 45

2. "its military encampments" *gulmān*: See 5.3.27; 6.3.27; 6.27.20; 6.28.31; 6.31.31; 6.62.5; 6.71.1; 6.72.5; 6.84.6; and notes.

Following 2ab, D5–7,9–11,T1,3,G,M, and the texts and printed editions of the southern commentators insert a passage of one line [912*]: "Then, in the morning, Rāvaṇa, overlord of the *rākṣasas* . . ."

Following 2ab, many northern manuscripts insert a passage of three lines [911*]. Following 911* most northern manuscripts (except Ś,B1,D1,2,8) insert a passage of one hundred fifty-eight lines (App. I, No. 28) describing an unsuccessful sortie by Vajradaṃṣṭra, similar to, but not identical with, the southern version in App. I, No. 26. See above under note to 6.43.1.

One wonders what the text-critical status of this incident is. It occurs in all the manuscripts, both northern and southern, except for the six just listed (but, of course, including both Ś manuscripts). That the two accounts differ so much would indicate that they are independent retellings of the same incident. Textual reconstruction seems impossible. It may be necessary simply to understand that the incident may have been, if not original, very early.

3. "Laṅkā" *laṅkām*: D5,7,9–11,T2, and the texts and printed editions of Ct read instead *rājā*, "the king."

4. "angrily" *amarṣitaḥ*: D9–11,T2, the texts and printed editions of Ct, Cr, and Cv, and the text of Gita Press read instead *ātmahitam*, "beneficial to himself." Translators who follow the texts and printed editions of Ct take the term as an adjective modifying Prahasta, with the sense of "loyal, devoted, well-wishing." All printed editions of Cg consulted show the variant *amarṣataḥ*, which must be read adverbially in the sense of "out of anger, angrily." This variant is unattested in the critical apparatus.

"at that critical moment" *kāle*: Literally, "at that time *or* at the proper time." We agree with Cr, who glosses, "even at that time of crisis (*āpatkāle 'pi*)." Cg explains, "at a moment suitable for giving orders (*nideśārhasamaye*)." See note to verse 15 below.

5. "You are skilled in warfare." *yuddhaviśārada*: Literally, "O you who are skilled in warfare." Ñ2,V2,B2,4,D6,9,10,T2,3,G3, and the texts and printed editions of Ct and Cr read instead the vocative plural *yuddhaviśāradāḥ*, "O you [all] who are skilled in warfare," evidently referring to the *rākṣasa* counselors in general.

"means other than war" *anyaṃ yuddhāt*: Literally, "other than war." Printed editions of Ct, as well as Gita Press (6.57.5), read instead the compound *anyayuddhāt*, "through the fighting of another," a reading not reported in the critical apparatus. This reading is, however, rendered in some of the translations that follow the text of Ct and Gita Press. Roussel (1903, vol. 3, p. 164), Shastri (1959, vol. 3, p. 139), and Gita Press (1969, vol. 3, p. 1564) all understand this variant to mean that no warrior other than those listed in verse 6 will be able to lift the siege.

6. "Nikumbha" *nikumbhaḥ*: The monkey Nīla killed a *rākṣasa* warrior named Nikumbha at 6.33.34. But, in all likelihood, this is a reference to a second Nikumbha, one Nikumbha Kaumbhakarṇi, first introduced at 6.8.12. At 6.63.37 this same Nikumbha is apparently identified as the elder brother of Kumbha, who, at 6.63.4, is identified as the son of Kumbhakarṇa. This Nikumbha is slain by Hanumān at *sarga* 64.

7. "placing them under your command" *parigṛhya*: Literally, "having mastered, having taken possession of." We follow the interpretation of Ct, who glosses, "putting them under your control (*svādhīnaṃ kṛtvā*)."

8. "In the face of your sortie... surely" *niryāṇād eva te nūnam*: Literally, "because of your sortie alone... surely." D9–11 and the texts and printed editions of Ct read *tūrṇaṃ ca*, "and quickly," for *te nūnam*, "your... surely."

"irresolute" *capalāḥ*: D9–11 and the texts and printed editions of Ct read instead *calitāḥ*, "agitated, shaken."

10. "fall into your hands" *te... vaśam eṣyati*: Literally, "he will go to your control."

11. "We risk a great calamity, and victory is far from certain in this matter." *āpatsaṃśayitā śreyo nātra niḥsaṃśayīkṛtā*: Literally, "calamity is doubtful [and] benefit is not free from doubt here." The sentence is obscure and elliptical, and it contains at least one grammatical difficulty. The word *śreyaḥ*, "benefit," which is neuter, appears to be modified by the feminine adjective *niḥsaṃśayīkṛtā*, "free from doubt." Our interpretation is supported by the commentators as well as by the northern recension, where the adjective, or its substitute, is found in the neuter. The sentence is subject to a variety of interpretations, and the commentators basically fall into two interpretive camps. Most of them agree that the term *āpat*, "calamity," refers to "death in battle (*yuddha āpan mṛtiḥ*—so Ct)," although Cs offers, as an alternative, "the agony of defeat (*paribhavabhavaṃ duḥkhaṃ vā*)." The commentators similarly agree, for the most part, that the issue in the verse is whether, despite Rāvaṇa's utterance in verse 5 above, the *rākṣasas* should fight. Ct, Ck, Cg, and Cm all quote a verse from the *nītiśāstra*, which has the following sense: "When it is certain that refraining from combat will result in one's death and there is at least a chance of remaining alive if one offers combat, then, according to the learned, that is the appropriate time to fight (*yatrāyuddhe dhruvo mṛtyur yuddhe jīvitasaṃśayaḥ / tam eva kālaṃ yuddhasya pravadanti manīṣiṇaḥ //*)."

It is in the interpretation of the term *śreyaḥ* that the commentators principally differ. For Ct, Ck, Cr, Cs, and Ctr, the word here means "victory (*jayaḥ*)," which they claim Rāvaṇa considers to be assured. Cr continues this line of argument by saying that, even if death cannot be ruled out, still victory, or the highest good, is assured because the *rākṣasas* will attain worldly rewards if they are victorious and otherworldly benefits should they die (*tathāpi śreyaḥ kalyāṇaṃ na saṃśayitaṃ vijaya aihikaphalaprāptir maraṇa āmuṣmikaphalaprāptir iti kalyāṇaṃ niścitam eva*).

Cs regards this explanation as the conventional one but feels that Rāvaṇa would avoid it because it mentions the possibility of death and this is an occasion for encouragement. Cs argues: "The ordinary explanation is 'if you live, you gain the benefits of this world, and if you die, of the next.' But because it is an occasion for encouragement, [Rāvaṇa avoids the allusion to death] (*śreyo 'mṛta aihikaṃ mṛte pāratrikam iti prakṛtānupayuktaṃ vyākhyānaṃ protsāhanasamayatvāt*)."

Cg, Ctr, and Cm understand the term *śreyaḥ* in its somewhat adverbial sense of "better, preferable." Cg and Cm read the passage to mean: "Death in battle itself confers welfare because of the uncertainty of victory and defeat, and the possibility of victory falling to either side (*jayāpajayayor avyavasthitatvena* [*vyavasthitatvena*—so GPP, VSP] *pākṣikajayasyāpi saṃbhavād iti bhāvaḥ*)." Cg then argues that, in the second half of the line, Rāvaṇa rejects an alternative position by stating that, in his [that is, Rāvaṇa's] opinion, "if death is certain, it is better to die fighting than to be killed unresisting by one's enemies (*pakṣāntaraṃ pratikṣipati na tv iti niḥsaṃśayīkṛtā niścitā mṛtis tu yuddhaṃ vinā śatrubhir maraṇaṃ tu na śreya etan mama matam*)." Ctr agrees with the general tenor of these statements. In other words, instead of merely pondering the alternatives, Rāvaṇa is urging battle.

Gorresio's text (6.31.12cd) substitutes, for *pāda* b, *na tu niḥsaṃśayaṃ kṛtam*. This gives the sentence the following meaning: "There is risk of death, but actions that lack certainty are better." Gorresio (1856, vol. 9, p. 297) translates, "*Egli èpur meglio una calamità incerta che l'operar fuor d'incertezza*," and provides a note to this passage (p. 374, n. 131) in which he quotes his commentator, Cl, to the effect that "An action that lacks uncertainty is not the best one. Therefore, one should engage in battle and not turn back from it. (*niḥsaṃśayaṃ niḥsaṃdigdhaṃ kṛtaṃ karma na śreyo 'to yuddhaṃ kāryaṃ na tu tannivartanam*)." Gorresio explains this somewhat obscure comment as follows: "*Per chi é prode, val meglio il travagliarsi in cose il cui successo felice o calamitoso sia incerto, perché quell' incertezza avvalora e stimola il coraggio, che adoperarsi in cose il cui evento sia certo; perché quella certezza allenta ed infiacchisce il vigor dell' animo* (For a hero, it is better to engage in actions in which the outcome, whether happy or calamitous, is uncertain, because this very uncertainty valorizes and stimulates courage, than to engage oneself in matters of which the outcome is certain, because the certainty slackens and weakens the vigor of one's spirit)."

"So tell me what you think is best for us, whether I find it agreeable or not." *pratilomānulomaṃ vā yad vā no manyase hitam*: Literally, "whatever you think beneficial for us, whether it is disagreeable or agreeable." We agree with the majority of the commentators who flesh out this elliptical phrase by adding an imperative form of a verb meaning "to say *or* speak."

12. "Uśanas" *uśanā*: Uśanas Kāvya is everywhere regarded as the *purohita* of the *asuras*. See 6.4.42; and 6.40.28 and notes.

13. "with your . . . counselors" *mantribhiḥ*: The commentators agree that the reference is to the debates involving Vibhīṣaṇa, Mālyavān, and other *rākṣasa* advisers at 6.6–10 (*vibhīṣaṇādibhiḥ saha no 'smābhir idaṃ vakṣyamāṇaṃ mantritapūrvam*—so Cg).

"We debated the matter" *vivādaś cāpi no vṛttaḥ*: Literally, "And our debate transpired." According to Ct, Cr, and Ck, the term *vivāda*, "debate," indicates that, on that earlier occasion, the *rākṣasas* could not reach a unanimous decision as to what was to be done. Cg further comments that it was this debate that caused Vibhīṣaṇa to defect. (*parasparaṃ samavekṣya bahumatitayālocya. no 'smākaṃ vivādaś cāpi vṛttaḥ. yena vibhīṣaṇo niragacchad iti bhāvaḥ*.)

14. "I concluded . . . I foresaw" *vyavasitaṃ mayā . . . dṛṣṭam*: If Prahasta indeed thought that Rāvaṇa should return Sītā to Rāma, he seems to have been curiously

reticent in expressing this view. At any rate, his sage counsel is not recorded. His only part in the council of the *rākṣasas* in *sargas* 8 and 9 was to boast of the slaughter he would wreak among the monkey troops. See 6.8.1–5 and 6.9.1–6.

"war" *yuddham*: Cg believes the word is used figuratively here to mean total extermination [of the *rākṣasas*] (*sarvamaraṇaṃ yuddhaśabdenopacāryate*).

15. "gifts, tokens of respect, and all manner of kind words" *dānaiś ca mānaiś ca . . . sāntvaiś ca*: Cg explains that "gifts" refers to gifts of jewelry, etc., and that "tokens of respect" refers to such flattering remarks as "my life is in your hands" (*dānair bhūṣaṇādipradānair mānais tvadadhīnaṃ jīvitam ityādipriyabhāṣaṇaiḥ*). Ctr notes that servants who are honored with gifts and expressions of esteem are willing to sacrifice their lives for their masters' sake (*anena dānamānādibhiḥ pūjitā bhṛtyāḥ prāṇān api svāmikāryārthe parityajantīti sūcitam*).

"at such a critical moment" *kāle*: Literally, "at that time *or* at the proper time." We agree with Cg in understanding "the time of crisis or calamity (*āpatkāle*)." See note to verse 4 above.

"what pleases you" *priyaṃ tava*: D9–11,G1, and the texts and printed editions of Ct and Cr read instead *hitaṃ tava*, "what is beneficial to you."

16. "I do not care for" *na . . . me . . . rakṣyam*: Literally, "not to be protected by me."

"as I strive to sacrifice" *juhūṣantam*: Literally, "desiring to offer as oblation." Cg notes that the metaphor of one's life as a sacrificial offering carries with it the metaphor of warfare as a fire. He further points out that the verse indicates that the offering of one's life as an oblation brings with it great rewards and that mere involvement in such a battle involves one's own destruction. (*anena jīvitasya haviṣṭvaṃ yuddhasyāgnirūpatvaṃ ca gamyate. tena cātmahaviḥ pradānasya mahāphalatvaṃ yuddhasaṃgatimātreṇa svavināśaś ca dyotyate.*) In addition, he says: "Those who follow conventional wisdom understand '*juhūṣantam*' to mean 'one who desires to abandon.' That is the meaning. (*gatānugatikās tu juhūṣantaṃ tyaktum icchantam ity arthaḥ.*)"

18. "the forest-dwelling monkeys . . . their" *kānanaukasām*: Literally, "of the forest dwellers." Ś1,V3,B2,4,D1,6–13,G,M5, and the texts and printed editions of Ct and Cr read instead the nominative plural, *kānanaukasaḥ*, which makes the adjective modify the birds instead of the monkeys.

"with the crushing force of those thunderbolts that are my arrows" *madbāṇāśanivegena*: Literally, "with the force *or* speed of my arrow-thunderbolts." D9–11 and the texts and printed editions of Ct and Cr read instead *madbāṇānāṃ tu vegena*, "with the force of my arrows." Printed editions of Cg and Cm (VSP 6.57.18; KK 6.57.19) read *madbāṇaśatavegena*, "with the force of hundreds of my arrows," a reading not recorded in the critical apparatus.

"the carrion birds may eat of their flesh to their heart's content" *tṛpyantu māṃsena pakṣiṇaḥ*: Literally, "let the birds be satisfied with flesh." D6,7,9–11,T2,G,M3,5, and the texts and printed editions of the southern commentators read the adjective *māṃsādāḥ*, "flesh eating," in place of *māṃsena*, "with flesh," giving the phrase the sense "flesh-eating birds." See note to 6.26.8.

19. "Addressed in this fashion by Prahasta" *ity uktās te prahastena*: D7,9–11,T2, and the texts and printed editions of Ct and Cr read instead *tasya tad vacanaṃ śrutvā*, "having heard that speech of his."

"making haste" *kṛtatvarāḥ*: D9–11,T2, and the texts and printed editions of Ct and Cr read instead *mahābalāḥ*, "very powerful."

"at the *rākṣasa*'s palace" *rākṣasamandire*: The precise locus of the muster is uncertain. The term *mandira* here can refer to a palace, any large building, an abode, or a camp. The commentators are silent, and the translators render the term variously. It would appear that these events take place after Rāvaṇa has returned from his tour of the city's fortifications at verses 2–4 above, and it is likely that they occur in or just outside his palace.

20. "Within the hour" *muhūrtena*: The term can refer to any short period of time, e.g., a moment or an instant. Vālmīki, indeed, often uses it in this sense (2.11.4; 2.16.14; 2.19.5; etc.), and the majority of the translators consulted have read the term in this way (Shastri 1959, vol. 3, p. 140; Pagani 1999, p. 1000; Roussel 1903, vol. 3, p. 165; Dutt 1893, p. 1268; and Gorresio 1856, vol. 9, p. 297). Given the context, however, we agree with Raghunathan (1982, vol. 3, p. 139) and Gita Press (1969, vol. 3, p. 1565), who evidently take the term in its technical sense of a period of forty-eight minutes, the traditional Indian "hour." Cf., for example, 2.48.9,11; 2.83.21; 4.41.37; and 4.48.20.

"who, armed with every sort of sharp weapon, resembled elephants" *tigmanānāvidhāyudhaiḥ... gajair iva*: The figure is evidently based on the similarity between the large and dark *rākṣasas*, armed with sharp weapons, and elephants with their sharp tusks. D9–11,T2,3, and the texts and printed editions of Ct and Cr read *bhīmaiḥ*, "fearsome," for *tigma-*, "sharp." This adjective then modifies the *rākṣasas*.

21. "clarified butter" *ājya-*: According to Apte (s.v.), *ājya* is the liquid form of clarified butter or ghee, whereas *ghṛta* is the solidified form.

22. "took garlands... and adorned themselves with them" *srajaḥ... jagṛhuḥ... dhārayan*: Literally, "took garlands and wore." Following the commentators, we read *dhārayan* as an augmentless imperfect. We agree with Ct, Ck, Cg, and Cr in understanding that the garlands are to be taken as the object of both verbs. The sequence is somewhat more confusing in the texts and printed editions of Ct, where the verbs belong to separate verses (NSP, Gita Press, and GPP 6.57.22cd and 23ab). Most of the translators consulted follow the commentators as we do. Dutt (1893, p. 1268) and Gita Press (1969, vol. 3, p. 1565), however, take *dhārayan* as part of an entirely separate sentence and supply its object as "armor" and "military accoutrements," respectively.

"had been consecrated with sacred spells" *abhimantritāḥ*: Cg observes that the garlands would have been consecrated with a spell of victory (*vijayamantreṇābhimantritāḥ*).

23. "leapt up" *āplutya*: Literally, "having leapt up." D9–11 and the texts and printed editions of Ct and Cr read instead *utsṛjya*, "having abandoned *or* having set in motion." Ct and Cr, who share this reading, supply, as an object of the gerund, *vāhanāni*, "vehicles." Of the translators who follow Ct's reading, Dutt (1893, p. 1268) renders, "leaving [their vehicles]" and Roussel (1903, vol. 3, p. 165), "*et lançant vivement leur attelages*." In this interpretation Roussel is followed by Shastri (1959, vol. 3, p. 140) and Pagani (1999, p. 1000).

24. "bid them beat the... *bherī* drum" *bherīm āhatya*: Literally, "having beaten the *bherī*." Like many of the translators consulted, we find it unlikely that an aristocratic general like Prahasta would actually beat a drum. Thus, we take the gerund in the sense of the causative. See 6.17.31–33 and note.

"celestial" *divyam*: D9–11 and the texts and printed editions of Ct and Cr read instead *yuktaḥ*, an adjective that would refer to Prahasta himself. This term has a wide range of meanings. Some of the translators who follow the text of Ct understand it to mean "equipped [with weapons]." Gita Press (1969, vol. 3, p. 1566) takes it in its sense of "active."

"well equipped for war" *sajjakalpitam*: Literally, "made ready, equipped." The commentators gloss, "equipped with every weapon (*sarvāyudhayuktam*—so Cr)."

25. This verse and the next consist entirely of adjectives and adjectival phrases in the accusative modifying *ratham*, "chariot," either in verse 24c above or in 27a below.

"driven by a skilled charioteer" *samyaksūtasusaṃyutam*: Literally, "well provided with a proper charioteer." D10,11,T3 read instead *samyaksūtaṃ susaṃyutam*, "having a proper charioteer [and] well furnished." Although D11 is said to be a text of Ct, printed editions of Ct and Cr read instead the variant *saṃyataṃ* [the reading of G1 in the critical apparatus], "well guided, controlled." Despite this, several of the translations that follow Ct appear to translate *saṃyutam*. Printed editions of Cg and Cm read *samyaksūtasusaṃyatam*, "controlled by a proper charioteer."

"blazed with the brilliance of the moon and sun" *sākṣāccandrārkabhāsvaram*: Literally, "having the radiance of the sun and moon themselves." Cg breaks down the figure by arguing that the chariot was like the moon in its quality of delighting and like the sun in brilliance. (*āhlādakatvena candrasāmyam. tejasārkasāmyam.*)

26. "beautiful in every part" *svapaskaram*: Literally, "having good parts." According to *Pā* 6.1.149, *apaskaram* refers to a part of the chariot (*rathāṅgam*). PW (s.v.), followed by Monier-Williams, defines the term as a wheel or any part of a chariot. Apte (s.v.), on the other hand, claims that the term can refer to any part of the chariot except the wheel.

"fretwork of gold" *suvarṇajāla-*: Cg reads *jāla* here as a synonym for *gavākṣa*, "airhole *or* window," although he neglects to do so in his comment on 5.45.3, where the same term is used in a similar context. Compare, however, the note to 5.7.14–15, where *jāla*, there translated as "skylight," does appear to be a kind of opening or window. Cf. 6.50.2 and 6.87.26.

"seemed almost to be laughing with its splendor" *prahasantam iva śriyā*: The figure is based on the common Sanskrit literary convention that laughter is white or bright. The idea is that the chariot is shining brightly. See Ingalls 1965, p. 166, verse 389; p. 226, verse 684; etc.

27. "Prahasta . . . drove . . . out" *niryayau*: Literally, "he went out."

28. Following 28ab, D5–7,9–11,S insert a passage of one line [923*]: "and the blare of musical instruments, which seemed to fill the very earth[1] . . ."

[1]"earth" *medinīm*: D5,T1,G2,M3, and the printed editions of Cg read instead *sāgaram*, "the ocean." This reading is reflected in the translation of Raghunathan (1982, vol. 3, p. 139).

29. Following verse 29, D5–7,9–11,S insert a passage of two lines [924*]: "And closely surrounding him, Prahasta's ministers, Narāntaka, Kumbhahanu, Mahānāda, and Samunnata, marched forth."

30. "in military array" *vyūḍhena*: Perhaps disturbed by the comparison of an orderly group of soldiers to a herd of elephants, Cg insists on glossing the term as "clad in armor (*saṃnaddhakaṅkaṭena*)."

31. "swiftly in anger...he resembled Kāla, the ender of all things" *tūrṇaṃ kruddhaḥ...kālāntakopamaḥ*: Literally, "swiftly, in anger...comparable to Kāla, the ender." Ñ,V1,2,B,D9–11,M3, and the texts and printed editions of the southern commentators read *kālāntakayamopamaḥ*, "like Yama, who brings time [Kāla] itself to an end." The southern commentators compensate for the additional two syllables by dropping either the adverb *tūrṇam*, "swiftly," (Ct, Ck, Cr) or the adjective *kruddhaḥ*, "angry," (Cg, Cm, Cv). These differences are reflected in the various translations. Cr and Cg gloss *kāla*, "Time," as *pralaya*, "the time of universal destruction." Cg thus explains the compound as "that Yama, who is the destroyer at the time of universal destruction (*kāle pralayakāle antako vināśako yo yamaḥ*)." Compare 6.21.26 and note.

32. "As he and the roaring *rākṣasas* set forth, their clamor" *tasya niryāṇaghoṣeṇa rākṣasānāṃ ca nardatām*: Literally, "by the exit sound of him and of the roaring *rākṣasas*." According to Cr, the uproar Prahasta causes consists of the sound of his chariot, etc. (*prayāṇakālikarathādisvanena*), whereas Cg attributes it to his lionlike roar (*nirgamakālikasiṃhanādena*).

"unnatural cries" *vikṛtaiḥ svaraiḥ*: The evil omens described in the following verses (32–38; 41–44) are fairly stereotypical and quite similar to those described below at 6.53.41–44 at the time of the sortie of Kumbhakarṇa. The howling or shrieking of beasts of prey, especially jackals, is a common ill omen. See 6.26.24; 6.31.7; 6.45.34; 6.53.42; 6.83.33; 6.94.22; and notes.

33. "the cloudless sky" *vyabhram ākāśam*: Cg points out that the circling of birds in a cloudless sky is untimely [and thus ominous], since birds normally circle in cloudy weather. (*anena maṇḍalakaraṇasyākālikatvam uktam. sābhrakāle hi pakṣiṇo maṇḍalāny ācaranti.*)

"clockwise" *apasavyāni*: Literally, "not left." Commentators are divided as to whether the birds are circling clockwise or counterclockwise. The normal meaning for the term is "rightward," in this case referring, as several commentators indicate, to *pradakṣiṇa*, or circling something while keeping it always on one's right. The difficulty here is that *pradakṣiṇa* is normally associated with auspiciousness, which in the present context is far from the author's intention. Commentators deal with the issue in one of two ways. In the first, proposed by Ck and followed by Ct, circling in the *pradakṣiṇa*, i.e., clockwise direction, is auspicious only in the case of auspicious birds, such as eagles (*garuḍādīnām*), but it is inauspicious in the case of such inauspicious birds as vultures (*gṛdhrādīnām*). (*garuḍādīnām eva pradakṣiṇaṃ śubhanimittam. gṛdhrādīnāṃ pradakṣiṇaṃ durnimittam*—so Ck.)

Cg, however, proposes that we understand *apasavya* to mean *apradakṣiṇa*, "counterclockwise," thus simplifying the issue of auspiciousness and inauspiciousness. He justifies his reading by quoting *Amarakośa* 3.1.84 (*apasavyaṃ tu dakṣiṇe*). As an alternative, Cg acknowledges the normal lexical meaning of *apasavaya* in the sense of *pradakṣiṇa*, noting, however, in the case of raptors, etc. (*garuḍānām*) [here presumably including the carrion birds], it is the counterclockwise circling that is auspicious. This alternative, in the end, is similar to the position of Ct and Ck. (*apasavyāny apradakṣiṇāni...yadvātra khagā garuḍāḥ. apasavyaṃ pradakṣiṇam. apasavyaṃ tu dakṣiṇam ity amaraḥ. garuḍānāṃ hy apradakṣiṇaṃ śobhanam.*)

The various translations consulted reflect these different opinions. Roussel (1903, vol. 3, p. 166), Shastri (1959, vol. 3, p. 141), and Raghunathan (1982, vol. 3, p. 140) appear to follow Cg's first interpretation, translating, "from left to right." Gita Press

(1969, vol. 3, p. 1567) similarly, but more precisely, renders, "counterclockwise." Pagani (1999, p. 1001), on the other hand, follows Ck's and Ct's interpretation, translating, "*de droite á gauche.*" She provides an explanatory note (p. 1663) in which she identifies the circling of the birds as corresponding to the "*pradakṣiṇā*," which, as she notes, is an auspicious direction in the case of men but ill omened in the case of birds of prey. Dutt (1893, p. 1269) has a somewhat different understanding, translating, "at the right hand of the car." See 6.94.4 and note. See, too, note to 6.4.4 and 6.26.8.

34. "Dreadful" *ghorāḥ*: D12,M3, and the printed editions of Cg read instead the adverb *ghoram*, "dreadfully." This is rendered by Raghunathan (1982, vol. 3, p. 140) as "lugubriously."

"jackals" *śivāḥ*: This feminine noun can be used either for jackals in general or the female of the species. The animal and its howl are associated with inauspicious omens. See 6.26.24; 6.31.7; 6.45.32; 6.53.42; 6.83.33; 6.94.21; and notes. Cf. 6.41.32 and note.

35. "A blazing meteor" *ulkā*: Literally, "meteor." Compare 6.83.36a, where *pāda* a is repeated.

"occluding one another" *anyonyam abhisaṃrabdhāḥ*: Literally, "closely joined to one another." The idea, as we understand it, is that the planets are in close conjunction so that their light is occluded. Cr and Cg both understand that the heavenly bodies are at war with one another (*tatkāle grahayuddham āsīd ity arthaḥ*—so Cg). Translators differ widely in their interpretations. Some, including Dutt (1893, p. 1269), Roussel (1903, vol. 3, p. 166), and Shastri (1959, vol. 3, p. 141), take the adjective in its more common lexical sense of "angered." Pagani (1999, p. 1001) takes the term in a related sense of "excited." Raghunathan (1982, vol. 3, p. 140) translates, "being in combustion," while Gita Press (1969, vol. 3, p. 1567), whose translation is closest to ours, renders, "knitted against [one another]."

"were no longer visible" *na cakāśire*: Literally, "they did not shine."

926*–36. "And over the *rākṣasa*'s chariot, harshly thundering clouds" *meghāś ca kharanirghoṣā rathasyopari rakṣasaḥ*: This line, constituting star passage 926* in the critical apparatus, is found in D5–7, 9–11,S, as well as the texts and all printed editions of the southern commentators. We have inserted it into our translation because, without it, 36ab lacks a subject for its two plural finite verbs other than the improbable *grahāḥ*, "heavenly bodies," of 35d. For 36ab, northern manuscripts read *vavarṣa rudhiraṃ devaḥ prahastasya rathopari*, "The god rained down blood over Prahasta's chariot." Gorresio (1856, vol. 9, p. 299) translates *deva* as "*il terribile Indra*" but notes (p. 375) that his commentator (Cl) points out that, based on the *Amarakośa*, the term could be understood equally well to mean "a cloud." We believe that the restoration of 926* here is justified by the principles for editing (specifically points 2 and 4) laid out by the critical editors (Bhatt 1960, p. xxxiv).

For blood raining down as an omen, see 6.26.22; 6.31.5; 6.41.33; 6.94.15; and notes. Cf. note to 6.76.2, inserted passage 1674*, lines 5–7.

"a vulture, facing to the south . . . on the top of his flagstaff" *ketumūrdhani gṛdhraḥ . . . dakṣiṇāmukhaḥ*: The south is the direction associated with Yama, the god of death.

Following verse 36, D5–7,9–11,S insert a passage of one line [927*], which continues the description of the vulture: "Pecking[1] at itself on both sides, it stole away all his [Prahasta's] luster.[2]"

[1]"Pecking" *tudan*: Literally, "prodding, poking." D10,11, and the texts and printed editions of Ct, Ck, and Cr read instead *nadan*, "shrieking, uttering sounds."

[2]"luster" *prabhām*: Ct and Ck describe this as the "radiance of victory (*jayaśrī*)," whereas Cg understands that Prahasta's face grows pale at the sight of the vulture on his flagstaff (*dhvajāgrārūḍhagṛdhradarśanena prahastamukhaṃ vivarṇam āsīd ity arthaḥ*).

37. "his charioteer was of the *sūta* caste and was a skilled driver of horses" *sāratheḥ . . . sūtasya hayasādinaḥ*: Literally, "of that charioteer who was of the charioteer caste (*sūta*) and a driver of horses." The commentators are clearly disturbed by the seeming redundancy in this passage and evolve several strategies in their effort to minimize or eliminate it. One strategy adopted by all the commentators consulted is to take the term *sūta* not in its direct meaning as charioteer but rather as a name of a person of a mixed caste (that is, the son of a kshatriya man by a brahman woman—*ManuSm* 10.11) whose hereditary occupation is that of a charioteer. We have followed this line of reasoning in our translation. Cs, who, as he so often does, tries to find obscure etymological interpretations for words, proposes, as an alternative, that we break the word up into the components *su* + *ūtaḥ*, in the sense of "well guarded *or* protected (*suṣṭhu ūtaḥ*)," which then becomes an adjective modifying the charioteer's whip (*pratodaḥ*).

The second strategy is to read *hayasādinaḥ*, "driver *or* subduer of horses, charioteer," as a descriptive adjective with an agentive sense. Thus we have "horse trainer (*aśvaśikṣakasya*—Ct, Ck)"; "controller of horses (*hayānāṃ niyantuḥ*—Cr)"; "dispatcher *or* driver of horses (*hayaprasthāpakasya*—Cv, Cg)"; "skilled in teaching the gaits of horses (*aśvagatiśikṣāvicakṣaṇasya*—Cm)"; and "who makes horses go according to his will (*hayān aśvān sādayati gamayati yatheṣṭam*—Cs)." Cs adds a characteristically esoteric alternative explanation in which the term means "one who is accompanied by 'eaters,' i.e., *rākṣasas* (*ādibhiḥ*), who are themselves accompanying the horses (*hayair evānubandhanimittair ādibhī rākṣasaiḥ sahitaḥ sa tathā*—Cs)."

Only Cs has the temerity to deconstruct the word *sārathi* itself, offering the following rather far-fetched etymology: "he who comes into possession of food (*tham annam asyāstīti matvartha ikāraḥ*)." This, in turn, relies on the genuinely esoteric vedic etymology of the *Chāndogya Upaniṣad* (1.3.6) according to which the syllable *tha* of the word *udgītha* [the high chant of the *Sāmaveda*] represents "food" (*annaṃ thaṃ iti hi śrutiḥ*). Cs then breaks down the word *sāra* into *sa* + *ara*, "that which possesses spokes," which thus becomes a kenning for "wheel." The term *sārathi* can then be read to mean "one who earns his bread by the spoked wheel. (*sāreṇārasahitena cakreṇa thiḥ sārathiḥ. tasyeti vā.*)"

"as he plunged into battle" *saṃgrāmam avagāhataḥ*: The texts and printed editions of Ct and Cr read instead *anivartinaḥ*, "not turning back [from battle]."

38. "extraordinary and radiant" *bhāsvarā ca sudurlabhā*: Literally, "shining and hard to attain." Printed editions of the text of Cg read *vasudurlabhā* for *ca sudurlabhā*, "hard to obtain." Cg notes that this is an alternate reading but that it is the one he prefers. He glosses it as "difficult to attain even for the eight Vasus [a class of vedic divinity] (*aṣṭavasudurlabhā*)." Raghunathan (1982, vol. 3, p. 140), the only translator to follow this reading, takes *vasu* in its sense of "wealth," rendering, "which could not be bought by all the wealth in the world." See 6.21.28.

39. "strength" *-bala-*: V,D9–11, and the texts and printed editions of Ct and Cr read instead *-guṇa-*, "virtues, qualities."

"for battle" *yudhi*: Literally, "in battle."

"armed with various weapons" *nānāpraharaṇā*: As Cg points out, the weapons would, of course, be "rocks, trees, etc." (*śilāvṛkṣādinānāpraharaṇā*). Pagani (1999, p. 1001), perhaps unwilling to see the monkeys armed with different kinds of weapons, resorts to the verb, *pra* √*hṛ*, "to strike," translating, "*habile à toutes sortes de coups au combat.*"

40. Following verse 40, D5–7,9–11,S insert a passage of one line [929*]: "[The two armies] of the roaring *rākṣasas* and the bellowing monkeys . . ." This half line construes with 41ab.

41. "in a frenzy of excitement" *pramudite*: Literally, "[both] delighted, excited."

42. "evil-minded" *durmatiḥ*: Cs understands the term in its sense of "foolish, stupid, slow-witted," on the grounds that Prahasta foolishly entertains the illusion of victory even though he has seen and heard for himself the inauspicious omens that surround him. (*apaśakunair iva gatamṛtaiḥ svīyair dṛṣṭaiḥ śrutair api vijayabhramo 'syāstīti. durmatir iti mantavyam.*) This interpretation is similar to that of Raghunathan (1982, vol. 3, p. 140) as well as Roussel (1903, vol. 3, p. 166) and, after him, Shastri (1959, vol. 3, p. 141).

"fast-moving" *vivṛddhavegām*: D9–11,G1,3,M2,3,5, and the texts and printed editions of Ct and Cr read instead the nominative masculine singular *vivṛddhavegaḥ*, in which case the adjective applies to Prahasta rather than the monkey host.

The meter is *vaṃśasthavila*.

Sarga 46

Before verse 1, D5–7,9–11,S insert a passage of nine lines [931*]: "Then seeing Prahasta,[1] whose valor was fearsome,[2] marching forth, Rāma, tamer of his foes, said to Vibhīṣaṇa with a smile:[1–2] 'Who is this enormous creature, who comes so swiftly surrounded by a huge army? What are his strength and valor like?[3–4] Tell me, great-armed hero, about this mighty night-roaming *rākṣasa*.'[5] Upon hearing Rāghava's words, Vibhīṣaṇa said, 'This is the *rākṣasa* Prahasta, the general of the *rākṣasa* lord's army in Laṅkā. He is surrounded by an army of three divisions.[3] He is powerful, skillful with weapons, and renowned for his valor.'[6–9]"

[1]Cg raises an interesting question. Since Prahasta has exited the city through its eastern gate while Rāma is stationed at the northern gate, how, then, is it possible for the latter to see the former, who would be many leagues from his position? Cg's response is that the credible report Rāma would have had of the appearance of some huge warrior would be equivalent to direct observation. (*nanu prahastaḥ pūrvadvārān nirgataḥ. rāmas tūttaradvāri tiṣṭhati sma. katham asyānekayojanasthasākṣātkāraḥ. ucyata āptavacanena pratyakṣatulyena mahākāyaḥ kaścana gacchatīti viditvaiṣa ity āha.*) The question, however, highlights the spuriousness of the insertion.

[2]"whose valor was fearsome" *bhīmaparākramam*: D9–11,G3,M5, and the texts and printed editions of Ct and Cr read instead *raṇakṛtodyamam*, "girded for battle."

[3]"by an army of three divisions" *tribhāgabala-*: We read this is a *bahuvrīhi* compound. Ck and Ct explain: "The meaning is 'He was surrounded by one-third of the *rākṣasa* lord's army that was stationed in Laṅkā' (*rākṣasendrasaṃbandhilaṅkāsthabalasya tṛtīya-bhāgena saṃvṛta ity arthaḥ*—so Ct)." Most of the translators consulted agree with this and understand the reference to be to a third of the army." Raghunathan (1982, vol. 3, p. 140), however, translates, "three quarters of the total strength of the forces."

1–2. "infuriated" *atisaṃjātaroṣāṇām*: Literally, "in whom exceeding rage had arisen." D10,11, and the texts and printed editions of Ct read *-ghoṣāṇām*, "uproar," for *-roṣāṇām*, "rage."

3–4. "the swords... broadswords" *khaḍga-... -ṛṣṭi-*: The text of the critical edition omits the subscript for the vocalic *ṛ*. This typographical error is not noted in the errata. The two types of swords are most likely the single-edged saberlike weapon and the double-edged sword, or broadsword, respectively.

5. "Bounding toward them, the bulls among monkeys" *vānararṣabhāḥ... plavaṅgamāḥ*: Literally, "bulls among monkeys... leaping [monkeys]." D10,11, and the texts and printed editions of Ct and Ck read *tu girīṃs tathā*, "as well as hills," for *vānararṣabhāḥ*, "bulls among monkeys." Cg, the only southern commentator to share the critical reading, is concerned by the apparent redundancy. He offers two possible resolutions. According to the first, the poet uses the term *plavaṅgama*, a kenning for monkey, in order to make clear in the second half of the verse that it is still the monkeys and not the *rākṣasas* who are being described (*vānaraśreṣṭhatve 'py avānara-tvavāraṇāya plavaṅgamā ity uktam*). Cg's second alternative, which we have followed, is to read the term *plavaṅgama* simply as a descriptive adjective and not as a name or designation. His idea is that the monkeys are bounding along in their eagerness to fight (*yadvā plavaṅgamā yuddhotsāhena plavagatyā gacchanto 'saṃjñāyāṃ khaśārṣaḥ*).

6. "the two vast forces" *teṣām... bahūnām*: Literally, "of those many."

"clashed with each other" *anyonyam āsādya*: Literally, "having met each other."

"the one side raining... the other" *varṣatām*: Literally, "of them who were showering." We must, of course, in keeping with the unvarying tenor of the text, understand that the monkeys hurl stones, while the *rākṣasas* shoot arrows.

7. "leaders of the monkey troops" *vānarayūthapān*: B1,D9–11,T1,G1, and the texts and printed editions of Ct, Cr, and Ck read *-puṃgavān*, "bulls [among monkeys]" for *-yuthapan*, "leaders of the troops."

8. "Some of the monkeys" *kecit*: Literally, "some." Even though both monkeys and *rākṣasas* were being slaughtered in the preceding verse, it is evident from the nature of the weapons here, and in verses 9 and 10 below, that the slaughter of the monkeys alone is being described.

"discuses" *paramāyudhaiḥ*: Literally, "excellent *or* supreme weapons." We follow Cv, Cm, Cg, and Ct, who cite either the *Nighaṇṭu* or another, unspecified, lexicon to demonstrate that the term is synonymous with discus (*cakraṃ tu paramāyudham*). Cr glosses *dīvyaśastraiḥ*, "divine weapons." But, as Pagani (1999, p. 1664) points out in her note to the passage, the use of such weapons is not alluded to in the context of these mass battles but is reserved for the use of individual, specially skilled warriors. Translators differ in their renderings. Dutt (1893, p. 1271) gives a more or less literal translation, "(other) powerful weapons." Roussel (1903, vol. 3, p. 168), followed by

Shastri (1959, vol. 3, p. 142), understands "*d'énormes traits*." Pagani (1999, p. 1002), Gita Press (1969, vol. 3, p. 1569), and Raghunathan (1982, vol. 3, p. 141) translate as we do.

9. "robbed of their life breaths" *nirucchvāsāḥ*: Literally, "without breath." This is, of course, a euphemism for "dead." Cr, however, understands that the monkeys have fallen, "breathless in the stupor induced by seeing the approaching *rākṣasas* (*taddarśanajanitamūrcchāhetukapūrvavacchvāsarahitāḥ*)."

"ensnared in the continuous volley of arrows" *iṣusaṃtānasaṃditāḥ*: Literally, "bound in the continuity of arrows." The textual evidence is scattered throughout the various recensions and printed editions, including the texts of the southern commentators. Printed editions of Ct read *iṣusaṃdhānasādhitāḥ*, "overcome by the conjunction of arrows." This reading, however, is not attested in the critical apparatus nor does it appear to be the text on which Ct or Ck comment. These commentaries read instead, as does the text of Gita Press (6.58.13), *iṣusaṃdhānasāditāḥ*, which Ct and Ck gloss as "cut to pieces by that proper release of arrows (*iṣūṇāṃ saṃdhānaṃ samyagvisarjanaṃ tena sāditāḥ khaṇḍitāḥ*)." Ct notes the variant *iṣusaṃdhānasaṃdhitāḥ*, "bound by bonds of arrows." Cg and Cm, on the one hand, and Cv, on the other, show minor variants of this: *iṣusaṃdhānasaṃditāḥ* (Cg, Cm) and *iṣudāmasaṃditāḥ* (Cv). Cv, Ct (glossing *saṃdhitāḥ*), Cg, and Cm, perhaps keeping in mind the incident in which Indrajit strikes down and binds Rāma and Lakṣmaṇa (*sarga* 35), understand, "bound, i.e., stitched, in the bonds of arrows (*iṣava eva saṃdhānāni bandhanarajjavas taiḥ saṃdhitāḥ saṃsyūtāḥ*—so Ct)." Crā reads *iṣusaṃdānasāditāḥ*, which he interprets similarly. Cr reads *-sāditāḥ-*, which he glosses as *vihiṃsitāḥ*, "wounded."

10. "with lances" *śūlaiḥ*: Ñ2,V1,3,B2,D1,3,6,9–11,T3,G3,M5, and the texts and printed editions of Ct read instead *śūraiḥ*, "by heroic [*rākṣasas*]."

12. "the force" *-sparśa-*: Literally, "the touch, contact."

"their teeth and eyes knocked out" *viśīrṇadaśanekṣaṇāḥ*: Literally, "whose teeth and eyes had dropped *or* were shattered." D6,7,10,11,G2, and the texts and printed editions of Ct and Cr read *-vadana-*, "face," for *-daśana-*, "teeth." In recognition of the wide variety of readings, the critical editors have marked the second syllable [*-śī-*] of the participle *viśīrṇa-* as doubtful.

13. "the cries of those screaming in their affliction and the lionlike roars of those who were bellowing" *ārtasvaraṃ ca svanatāṃ siṃhanādaṃ ca nardatām*: Literally, "the cries of distress of the crying and the lion-roar of the roaring."

"in battle" *yudhi*: D9–11 and the texts and printed editions of Ct and Cr read instead *api*, "as well."

14. "Rolling their eyes in rage" *kruddhāḥ . . . vivṛttanayanāḥ*: Literally, "enraged . . . their eyes rolling." The rolling of one's eyes is a common sign of anger in the epic (see note to 6.27.2), and thus we have linked the two adjectives. V1,2,D9–11, and the texts and printed editions of Ct and Cr read instead *vivṛttavadanāḥ*, "their faces rolling about." Translators who follow the text of Ct have struggled with this awkward and inferior reading, rendering such translations as "with their faces moving about" (Dutt 1893, p. 1271), "their mouths distended" (Gita Press 1969, vol. 3, p. 1569), "*les traits bouleversés*" (Roussel 1903, vol. 3, p.168), "their features distorted" (Shastri 1959, vol. 3, p. 142), and "*le visage convulsé*" (Pagani 1999, p. 1003). See notes to 6.27.2 and 6.50.11.

"following the path of heroes" *vīramārgam anuvratāḥ*: Literally, "devoted to the path of heroes." According to Ck and Ct, the *vīramārga*, "the path of heroes," is "characterized by not turning back [in battle] *aparāñmukhatvalakṣaṇaḥ*)." Cg defines it as "skill in battle (*yuddhakauśalam*)." Included in this path are such prescribed behaviors as facing one's enemy, sparing the supplicant, sparing the unarmed, etc. See Hopkins 1889, pp. 227–33.

"great feats" *karmāṇi*: Literally, "deeds, actions."

16. "Narāntaka" *narāntakam*: Another *rākṣasa* of this name is killed by Aṅgada at 6.57.88 below.

17. "nimble-handed" *kṣiprahastaḥ*: D7,9–11,G3, and the texts and printed editions of Ct read instead the accusative *kṣiprahastam*, thus making the adjective refer not to Durmukha but to Samunnata.

"ripped up . . . by the roots" *utpātya*: D6,7,9–11,T2,M3, and the texts and printed editions of the southern commentators read instead *utthāya*, "rising *or* leaping up." This reading obligates one to construe the sequence *sa vipuladrumam*, "he [having uprooted] a huge tree," of *pāda* b as an *avyayībhāva* compound, *savipuladrumam*, "with a big tree," which would then adverbially modify the gerund *utthāya*, "leaping up."

19. "the . . . *rākṣasa* . . . was struck on the head with a tree and so died" *vṛkṣeṇābhihato mūrdhni prāṇāṃs tatyāja rākṣasaḥ*: Literally, "struck on the head with a tree, the *rākṣasa* abandoned life breaths." The line is subject to a number of variations. The texts and printed editions of the southern commentators are divided. The texts and printed editions of Ct, Cr, and Ck read instead *vṛkṣeṇa mahatā sadyaḥ prāṇān saṃtyājayad raṇe*, "by means of a huge tree [he] suddenly caused [his] life breaths to abandon [him] in battle." The texts and printed editions of Cg and Cm read the critical edition's *pāda* c but the vulgate's *pāda* d (*vṛkṣeṇābhihato mūrdhni prāṇān saṃtyājayad raṇe* "struck on the head with a tree, he caused [his] life breaths to abandon [him] in battle"). Commentators and translators struggle somewhat with the awkward reading, especially the causative *saṃtyājayat*. Several of them propose detaching the second half of the verse from the first and supplying the name Tāra in the nominative as the subject of the causative.

20. "this deed" *tat karma*: As Ct and Ck explain, this refers to the virtually instantaneous killing of his four companions (*kṣaṇād eva sacivacatuṣṭayamāraṇakarma*).

21. "Then both armies swirled about like a maelstrom" *āvarta iva saṃjajñe ubhayoḥ senayos tadā*: Literally, "Then it was as if a maelstrom arose in the two armies." The syntax of this verse is problematic and appears to be elliptical. There is no clear *upameya* to stand with the *upamāna*, *āvartaḥ*, "maelstrom," unless one takes *nisvanaḥ*, "sound," from *pāda* d. This is highly problematic, however, and is made all the more unlikely by the presence of the second *iva*, marking *nisvanaḥ* as part of a second simile. Commentators propose two basic solutions. One, which Ct and Cm propose, is to understand that there appears to be a maelstrom in the two armies because of the whirling to and fro of the troops (*itas tato bhramaṇenāvarta iva saṃjajñe*). This is more or less how we understand the passage. Cg takes a completely different approach. He understands *āvartaḥ* to be synonymous with *saṃvartaḥ*, which is a term for the *pralaya*, or universal dissolution at the end of a cosmic cycle. He reads *āvarta iva* as the locative *āvarte* plus *iva* rather than as the nominative *āvartaḥ*, as Ct and others do. Cg (who, with the other southern commentators, reads the synonymous *niḥsvanaḥ* for the critical edition's *nisvanaḥ*) thus understands the verse to mean that the armies emitted a sound like that of the ocean when it is agitated at the time of universal dissolution (*āvarte saṃvarte pralaya iva sthite tasmin yuddhe kṣubhitasya sāgarasya niḥsvana iva senāyā*

niḥsvanaḥ saṃjajñe). Ck interprets similarly. Note the absence of *sandhi* between *saṃjajñe* and *ubhayoḥ*, unnoted in the critical apparatus.

22. "Skilled in combat . . . Prahasta" *prahasto yuddhakovidaḥ*: D9–11 and the texts and printed editions of Ct read instead *rākṣaso raṇadurmadaḥ*, "the *rākṣasa*, intoxicated *or* furious with battle." This variation is rendered by those translators who follow the texts and printed editions of Ct, most of whom understand *durmadaḥ* in the sense of "intoxicated." Gorresio's text (6.32.22) reads a slight variation on this, *prahasto yudhi durmadaḥ*, and he translates it as "*Prahasta furente nella battaglia*" (1856, vol. 9, p. 301).

23. "Heaped up . . . as if covered with fallen mountains, [the earth] looked ghastly" *babhūva nicitā ghorā patitair iva parvataiḥ*: Literally, "heaped up as if with fallen mountains, [the earth] was horrible." Manuscript evidence for *pādas* c and d is scattered. D9,10, and the texts and printed editions of Ct read instead *babhūvāticitā ghoraiḥ parvatair iva saṃvṛtā*, "[the earth] piled very high with the ghastly [corpses] was as if covered with mountains," or "[the earth] piled very high [with corpses] was as if covered with ghastly mountains."

24. "*palāśa* trees" *palāśaiḥ*: This is the "flame-of-the-forest" (*Butea monosperma*), a tree that blooms at the beginning of the hot season (April–May) and has bright orange-red flowers. See note to 6.35.9.

"the month of Mādhava" *mādhave māsi*: Mādhava corresponds to the Gregorian calendar months of April–May; it is also called Vaiśākha and is the second month of the Hindu calendar. Cf. 6.4.46 and note.

25–28. "the battleground resembled a river" *yuddhabhūmimayīṃ nadīm*: Literally, "the river that consisted of the battlefield." The extended and elaborate metaphor expressed in the four verses consists almost entirely of a string of compounds in the accusative case. Syntactically these are to be governed by the verb *teruḥ*, "forded," in verse 29b below. Vālmīki, like Vyāsa, is fond of these elaborate metaphors. See, for example, 5.7.46–48; 6.42.23; and *MBh* 7.13.10–16. Cg and Cm identify the figure of speech as a *sāvayavarūpaka*, "a metaphor with [numerous] elements *or* parts." See Gerow 1971, p. 259. Compare 6.81.9, where a similar figure is employed.

"the ocean to which it flowed was Yama" *yamasāgaragāminīm*: Literally, "going to the ocean of Yama." Since, as far as we know, Yama is not associated in the mythology with the ocean, we agree with Ck and Ct in reading the compound *yamasāgara-* as an appositional *karmadhāraya*, that is, that Yama is, in fact, the ocean, or, in keeping with the tenor of the metaphor, Yama, the god of death, takes the place of the ocean. Cr believes that the word *yama* here stands for the *tāpa*[*sic ma*]*salokaḥ*, i.e., the dark hell, which then takes the place of the ocean. Cg notes that it is well known that Yama frequents battlefields so that he can take away the souls [of the slain], and that he, therefore, stands in place of the ocean. (*yuddhabhūmau yamo jīvagrahaṇāya sannidhatta iti prasiddhiḥ. tadrūpasāgaragāminīm.*)

"Severed heads and trunks made up its fish" *bhinnakāyaśiromīnām*: Cg notes that the equivalence is appropriate because of the twitching or flopping (*sphuritavattvāt*) of the severed body parts.

"pieces of limbs, its grass" *aṅgāvayavaśāḍvalām*: Cg, reading the slight variant *-śādvalām*, understands the reference to be to the digits of the hands and feet, that is, fingers and toes, which would stand in comparison to grass. (*aṅgāvayavāḥ karacaraṇādy aṅgānām avyavā aṅgulaya ity arthaḥ. ta eva śādvalāni śādvalabhūjanyatṛṇāni yasyās tām.*)

"It was crowded with vultures in place of flocks of *haṃsas*, and it was swarming with adjutant storks instead of *sārasa* cranes." *gṛdhrahaṃsagaṇākīrṇāṃ kaṅkasārasasevitām*: The compounds can be read literally, as some translators have done, to mean "crowded with flocks of vultures and *haṃsas* and swarming with adjutant storks and *sārasa* cranes." But this, we believe, goes against the spirit of the metaphor in which the hideous realities of the battlefield, here the carrion birds, i.e., vultures and adjutant storks, take the place of the charming denizens of a real river, i.e., *haṃsas* and *sārasa* cranes.

"adjutant storks" *kaṅka-*: The specific identification of this bird is difficult as the name is used to describe at least four common species: the brahminy kite (*Haliastur indus*), the adjutant stork (*Leptoptilus dubius*), Pallas's fish eagle (*Haliaeetus leucoryphus*), and, as elsewhere in the *Rāmāyaṇa*, the heron (see note to 6.35.12). In the present context, it seems most likely that the hideous carrion-feeding adjutant stork (*Leptoptilus dubius*) is the one intended, as this bird in its height and general configuration would be an appropriate parallel to the graceful *sārasa* crane. See Dave 1984, pp. 392–95. Cg identifies the bird as "a white eagle (*dhavalavarṇaḥ śyenaḥ*)," probably a reference to Pallas's fish eagle. See Grewal 2000, pp. 61, 79. See, too, Fitzgerald 1998.

"the cries of the wounded took the place of its gurgling" *ārtastanitanisvanām*: Literally, "having the roaring of the afflicted for its sound." Cg remarks that the cries of the afflicted would be the sounds produced by their stumbling over the high and low [places] (*nimnonnatapatanajanitasvanaḥ*). Cg goes on to note that, "although the rushing flow of blood would make a sound of its own, the poet uses this expression in order to extend his elaborate metaphor (*yady api rudhirapravāhasyāpi svata eva ghoṣo 'sti tathāpi rūpakatvāyaivam uktam*)." D9 and the texts and printed editions of Ct read instead *āvartasvananiḥsvanām*, "its sound was the sound of a maelstrom."

29. "as might the leaders of elephant herds, a lotus pond covered with lotus pollen" *padmarajodhvastāṃ nalinīṃ gajayūthapāḥ*: Although the main thrust of the figure is to suggest how easily the warriors accomplish the feat, Cg suggests that by the term *-dhvastām*, "covered," we are to understand that the color of the lotus pond has been changed [by the red pollen] so that, like elephants emerging with their bodies reddened from a lotus pond, the warriors, too, would now have their bodies reddened [with blood]. (*padmarajobhir dhvastāṃ varṇāntaraṃ prāptāṃ nalinīṃ sarasīṃ yathā gajayūthapās taranti tīrtvā raktatanavo bhavantīti yāvat. tathāruṇaśarīrā utterur ity arthaḥ*.)

30. "who . . . was rapidly slaughtering" *tarasā . . . vinighnantam*. The adverb *tarasā*, "swiftly," is juxtaposed most closely to the finite verb *dadarśa*, "he spied," with which it shares *pāda* c. Indeed, some translators, including Dutt (1893, p. 1272) and Gorresio (1856, vol. 9, p. 301), construe it in this way. The remaining translators consulted construe the adverb with the participle *vinighnantam* (v.l. *vidhamantam*), translating it variously as "with vehemence" (Gita Press 1969, vol. 3, p. 1570), "*avec vehémence*" (Pagani 1999, p. 1004), "*par sa vaillance*" (Roussel 1903, vol. 3, p. 169), and "with might and main" (Raghunathan 1982, vol. 3, p. 142). D7,9–11, and the texts and printed editions of Ct read instead *vidhamantam*, "scattering, dispersing."

Following verse 30, D5–7,9–11,S insert a passage of eight lines [943*]: "When Prahasta, the general of the army, saw him [Nīla] racing toward him forcefully in battle, he charged at Nīla in his chariot, which had the color of the sun, just as a strong wind in the atmosphere might rush upon a bank of clouds.[1–3] Drawing his bow in that great battle, that foremost of bowmen Prahasta, the general of the army, loosed arrows at Nīla.[4–5] Striking Nīla all at once and piercing him through, those arrows entered the earth with tremendous speed, like angry serpents.[6–7] Struck with those sharp arrows that were like flames of fire, Nīla . . . [struck Prahasta (verse 31c)].[8]"

32. Following verse 32, D6,7,9–11,T,G2,3,M, and the texts and printed editions of the southern commentators insert a passage of one line [944*]: "[Unable to evade] the dreadful swarms of that evil-minded *rākṣasa*'s arrows . . ." Printed editions of the texts of the southern commentators show a number of variants. VSP (6.58.41ab) and KK (6.58.40ab), representing the text of Cg, Cv, and Cm, read instead *tasya bāṇagaṇān ghorān rākṣasasya mahābalaḥ*, "[Unable to evade] the *rākṣasa*'s dreadful swarm of arrows, the immensely powerful [monkey]." GPP (6.58.41ab) and NSP (6.58.41ab) read *tasya bāṇagaṇān eva rākṣasasya durātmanaḥ*, "[Unable to evade] the evil-minded *rākṣasa*'s swarm of arrows."

33–34. "a sudden autumnal squall" *varṣaṃ śāradaṃ śīghram āgatam*: Literally, "an autumnal shower that came quickly." Ct and Ck explain that the bull easily withstands a brief shower in autumn, which is after the season of the serious storms. The figure, they assert, thus suggests that Prahasta's hail of arrows presents no serious threat to Nīla. (*govṛṣasya śaratkāle prābalyaṃ kālasvabhāvād varṣasya tv anyathā tata eva. tena nātikleśakaras tasya śaravarṣa iti sūcitam.*)

"with fortitude" *sahasā*: Literally, "suddenly, forcefully." Most translators have construed the adverb with the noun *śaravarṣam*, "hail of arrows," in the sense of "sudden *or* quick," or with the adjectival compound "his eyes tightly closed (*nimīlitākṣaḥ*)," in the sense of "quickly closing his eyes." Both of these readings seem to us to be grammatically and contextually problematic. We agree with Pagani (1999, p. 1004), who translates, "[*endura*] *avec une grande fermeté*" and Gorresio (1856, vol. 9, p. 302), who translates, "*con gran fermezza sopportò*" in reading the adverb in the sense of "with firmness, fortitude" and construing it with the finite verb *sehe* (v.l. *asahata*—Gorresio 6.32.30b), "he endured."

35. "swift as thought" *manojavān*: D9–11 and the texts and printed editions of Ct read instead *mahābalaḥ*, "mighty," which would then modify Nīla.

Following verse 35, D5–7,9–11,S insert a passage of two lines [945*]: "Then, seizing Prahasta's bow, mighty[1] Nīla quickly broke it and roared again and again."

[1]"Then seizing Prahasta's bow, mighty" *tatas taccāpam udgṛhya prahastasya mahābalaḥ*: D9–11 and the texts and printed editions of Ct substitute *tato roṣaparītātmā dhanus tasya durātmanaḥ*, "Then, beside himself with rage, [he broke] the bow of that evil-minded one," for this line.

36. "Stripped of his bow by Nīla" *vidhanus tu kṛtas tena*: Literally, "rendered bowless by him." The textual transition from verse 35 in the critical edition is rather awkward, as no explanation for Prahasta's loss of his bow is given. In the south, as noted above, Nīla wrests the weapon from Prahasta's grasp and breaks it. In the northern variant [946*], Prahasta drops his bow and arrow of his own accord to seize instead the cudgel of *pāda* c. Here again the critical editors have created a textual sequence that is defective and unknown to any version (see Sutherland 1992).

37. "like two bull-elephants in rut" *prabhinnāv iva kuñjarau*: The basis for the simile, apart from the implicit size and ferocity of the combatants, is the often-described flow

of rut fluid from the temples of bull-elephants. This fluid is supposed to be reddish in color. This would form the basis of the comparison for the blood gushing forth from the wounds of Prahasta and Nīla. See 6.59.81 and note.

38. "razor-sharp fangs" *sutīkṣṇābhir daṃṣṭrābhiḥ*: Ct and Ck note that *rākṣasas* (as well as monkeys) have powerful fangs (*rākṣasānām apy asti daṃṣṭrāprābalyam*).

"they looked like a lion and a tiger and, indeed, moved just like them" *siṃha-śārdūlasadṛśau siṃhaśārdūlaceṣṭitau*: Literally, "they were like a lion and a tiger and had the movements of a lion and a tiger." Cg understands the first compound to express the fact that the two opponents are equal in strength (*siṃhaśārdūlasadṛśāv iti bale sāmyam*).

39. "Seeing victory within their grasp" *vikrāntavijayau*: The compound is obscure and ambiguous, lending itself to a variety of analyses and interpretations. Cg and Ct both appear to read the first member, *vikrānta-*, as an adjective in the sense of "obtained." Thus, Cg explains, "obtaining victory everywhere (*sarvatra prāptavijayau*)," while Ct glosses, "having nearly obtained victory (*prāptaprāyavijayau*)." Cr, in a somewhat similar vein, glosses, "who had brought victory within their grasp, as it were (*vaśīkṛtāv iva vijayau yābhyām*)." We believe that this is the most appropriate rendering in this context and have extended it somewhat in keeping with our view that both warriors are confident of achieving victory. Translators have read the compound variously. Gita Press (1969, vol. 3, p. 1572), apparently following Ct, renders, "well-nigh scored a victory." Raghunathan (1982, vol. 3, p. 143), who translates, "who were victors in every fray," and Pagani (1999, p. 1004), who renders, "*maintes fois victorieux*," seem to follow Cg. Roussel (1903, vol. 3, p. 169) takes *vikrānta-* in its nominal sense of "hero" and reads the compound as a *tatpuruṣa*, in the sense of "*vainqueurs des braves*." In this he is followed by Shastri (1959, vol. 3, p. 144), "vanquishers of other heroes." Dutt (1893, p. 1273) reads the compound as a *bahuvrīhi* based on an underlying *paranipāta karmadhāraya* compound, translating, "endowed with victorious vigor." Most northern manuscripts avoid this awkward compound either by eliminating it completely (e.g., Lahore 6.34.47) or breaking it up as in Gorresio's (6.32.34c) *vikrāntau vijaye*, "courageous in victory."

"were as eager to gain glory as were Vṛtra and Vāsava" *kāñkṣamāṇau yaśaḥ prāptuṃ vṛtravāsavayoḥ samau*: Literally, "equal to Vṛtra and Vāsava, they desired to gain glory." The mythic heroic battle between Indra and the demon Vṛtra, dating from the earliest vedic texts, is a favorite object of comparison for single combats in the epic. See note to 6.75.31.

40. "making a supreme effort" *paramāyastaḥ*: V,B1,4,D2,3,5,9–11,S read instead *paramāyattaḥ*, "with a great effort." Even though the word has a similar meaning to that of the critical edition's reading, the choice of the northern variant over the southern is difficult to understand in light of the principles set forth in the Introduction to the *Bālakāṇḍa* (Bhatt 1960, p. xxxiv).

42. "the mighty *rākṣasa*" *balī*: Literally, "the mighty one." V1,D5,7,9–11,T1,G1,2,M3, and the texts and printed editions of the southern commentators read instead *balāt*, "violently, forcefully."

43. "Prahasta" *tam*: Literally, "him."

45. "by that... that" *sā tena*: Literally," that [boulder]... by that [foremost of monkeys]. D4,9–11, and the texts and printed editions of Ct read instead *nīlena*, "by Nīla."

46. "Prahasta" *saḥ*: Literally, "he."

49. "to hold their lines" *samavasthātum*: Literally, "to stand firm, hold one's ground."

50. "they stood silently, brooding" *dhyānamūkatvam āgatāḥ*: Literally, "they went to the muteness of brooding *or* meditation." Ck, Ct, and Cr liken the speechlessness of the vanquished *rākṣasas* to that of people meditating upon their divinities (*dhyānena devatādhyānena ye mūkā mauninas teṣāṃ bhāvas tattvam*—Ct). Ct explains the phrase to mean that the *rākṣasas* were unable to say a word because of their fear, sorrow, and confusion (*bhayaduḥkhamohaiḥ kimapi vaktuṃ nāśaknuvann ity arthaḥ*). Cg claims that they were devoid of the power of speech because of their brooding (*dhyānena vāgvyāpāraśūnyatvam*).

Following verse 50, D5–7,9–11,S insert a passage of one line [947*]: "Immersed in a terrible ocean of grief, they seemed to be stripped of their senses."

51. The meter is *vaṃśasthavila*; *pāda* c is hypometric.

Cg and Cm note that the death of Prahasta takes place on the fifth lunar day [of the dark half of the lunar fortnight of Phālguna/Caitra] (*pañcamyāṃ prahastavadhaḥ*). Ct understands the reference to be to the fifth lunar day [of the bright half of Bhādrāśvina] (*tatpañcamyāṃ prahastavadhaḥ*). Cv understands that the death of Prahasta takes place on the fifth day [of the battle] (*prahastavadhena pañcamam ahas samāptam*). See 6.4.4.

Following *sarga* 46, KK inserts within brackets two *sargas*, designated as *prakṣiptasarga* 1 and *prakṣiptasarga* 2 (interpolated *sargas* 1 and 2) (= CE 948*; 6.47.4–6, 951*; and App. I, No. 30 [a passage of one hundred forty-eight lines]). These interpolated *sargas* describe Rāvaṇa's dejection over the death of his general Prahasta and his conversation with Mandodarī. Mandodarī rebukes Rāvaṇa for having abducted Sītā and advises him to return her to Rāma with gifts and gestures of submission. Rāvaṇa rejects her advice, vowing to destroy Rāma and the monkey army. He then dispatches additional warriors to the battlefront. These *sargas* correspond to Gorresio 6.33–34. See notes to 6.51.20 and 6.99.13.

Sarga 47

The meter of verses 1–3, 7–25, 32–44, 50, 89–103, 122–123, and 127–135 is *upajāti*. The remaining verses are in *śloka* meter.

1. "Prahasta, the protector of the *rākṣasa* forces, was slain . . . by Nīla, bull among leaping monkeys" *tasmin hate rākṣasasainyapāle plavaṅgamānām ṛṣabheṇa*: Literally, "when the protector of the *rākṣasa* forces was slain by that bull among leaping monkeys."

2. "by Nīla, the son of Agni, the purifier" *pāvakasūnu-*: Literally, "the son of Pāvaka." Like all the monkeys, Nīla is the offspring of one of the vedic divinities. See 1.16.3,13. His affiliation with Agni is made clear at 4.40.2–5.

"No sooner had . . . heard their words than" *tac cāpi teṣāṃ vacanaṃ niśamya*: We understand the particle *ca* with the emphatic *api* in its sense of expressing simultaneity, as noted in Apte (s.v. *ca*). Cg offers two alternative explanations of the significance of the particles *ca* and *api* (*cāpi*). According to the first, they suggest that Rāvaṇa could never have imagined this turn of events [the death of Prahasta] even in his dreams (*tac cāpīty anena rāvaṇena svapne 'pi na tac cintitam iti sūcyate*). According to the second, the particle *api* suggests that, despite the political wisdom that enjoins one to seek clemency when one's enemy is ascendant and one's own power in decline, Rāvaṇa, impelled by his own impending doom, renounces the idea of seeking refuge [with Rāma] and instead gives way to inopportune anger. (*yadvā śatror upacaye svasyāpacaye samāśrayaḥ kārya iti nītiḥ. tathāpi rāvaṇaḥ kālacoditatayā samāśrayaṇaṃ vihāyāsthāne krodhavaśaṃ gata ity apiśabdena sūcyate.*)

3. "he was grief stricken, and his mind was suffused with rage" *śokārditaḥ krodhaparītacetāḥ*: D9–11 and the texts and printed editions of Ct reverse the order of the words *śoka-*, "grief," and *krodha-*, "rage," yielding the sense "he was afflicted with rage, and his mind was suffused with sorrow."

"the principal warriors of the *rākṣasas*, sons of chaos" *nairṛtayodhamukhyān*: D10 and the texts and printed editions of Ct and Cr read instead *rākṣasayūthamukhyān*, "leaders of the *rākṣasa* troops."

"the immortal gods" *amara-*: Literally, "the immortals." D7,10,11, and the texts and printed editions of Ct read *nirjara-*, "ageless."

4. "One ought not underestimate" *nāvajñā . . . kāryā*: Literally, "disregard should not be made." Ct, Cr, and Cm understand the disregard to take the form of the thought, "What can these monkeys do? (*avajñaite kapayaḥ kiṃ kariṣyantīty evaṃrūpā na kāryā*—so Ct, Cm)" or "They are insignificant (*ime tūcchā iti buddhyānādaro na kāryaḥ*—so Cr)." Cg quotes the position taken by Ct and Cm in his alternate explanation of the singular/plural issue noted below.

"an enemy who has" *ripave . . yaiḥ*: The juxtaposition of the singular and plural, as well as of the dative and instrumental, is unusual and awkward. Ct and Cr simply see this as a grammatical irregularity, glossing the plural *ripubhyaḥ* and *ripūṇām*, respectively. Cg acknowledges the position of these commentators, ascribing it to some (*kecit*), but offers his own solution, according to which the dative singular *ripave* refers to Rāma, who is the indirect recipient of the action of disregard, while the instrumental plural *yaiḥ*, "by whom," refers to the monkeys, who are the actual cause of Prahasta's death. (*ripave rāmāya nāvajñā kāryopekṣā na kartavyā kriyāgrahaṇaṃ kartavyam iti caturthī. yaiś ca vānarair hetubhir mama sainyapālaḥ prahastaḥ . . . sūditas tebhyo 'pi nāvajñā kāryety arthaḥ.*)

5. "without further deliberation" *avicārayan*: Literally, "without reflecting *or* hesitating." Ck, Cm, and Ct gloss the participle as "regarding the enemy's army as insignificant (*ripubalaṃ tṛṇīkurvan*)," although why Rāvaṇa would so regard them after explicitly saying in the previous verse that they should not be taken lightly is unclear. Cr's gloss, *ripūṃs tucchatayā gaṇayan*, lends itself to ambiguity, as there are two possible readings of the *sandhi*. If read as it appears in GPP at 6.59.5, with the word breaks as indicated above, it would be a paraphrase of Ct and Ck, "reckoning the enemies as insignificant." One could, however, also read the sequence *tucchatayāgaṇayan* as *tucchatayā + agaṇayan*, giving the sense "not taking my enemies lightly." This appears to us to be more in keeping with the tenor of verse 4 above.

"that extraordinary battlefront" *raṇaśīrṣaṃ tad adbhutam*: Literally, "that wonderful forefront of battle." Ck, Cm, and Ct gloss *raṇaśīrṣam* as "head of the battle (*raṇamūrdhānam*)" and take it as a synonym for battlefield. Cg claims that the battle is extraordinary or miraculous because of the destruction of the strong by the weak (*durbalaiḥ prabalavināśanād āścaryam*).

6. "Rāma and Lakṣmaṇa included" *rāmaṃ ca sahalakṣmaṇam*: Literally, "and Rāma together with Lakṣmaṇa." Cm, perhaps in keeping with the profound Vaiṣṇava tenor

his commentary frequently takes, argues: "Although the apparent meaning of the verse is clear, in reality, we should supply the indeclinable *vinā*, 'without, excluding,' yielding the sense 'I will consume the army of the monkeys, sparing Rāma and Lakṣmaṇa.' (*adyety asya prātītikārthaḥ spaṣṭaḥ. vastutas tu sahalakṣmaṇaṃ rāmaṃ vineti śeṣaḥ . . . vānarānīkaṃ nirdahiṣyāmīti sambandhaḥ.*)" See note to 6.27.4.

Following verse 6, many northern manuscripts and a handful of *devanāgarī* and southern manuscripts insert a passage of four lines [951*], in whole or in part. Of these four lines, the first two appear in brackets in KK (6.59.7) and in VSP (6.59 unnumbered, between verses 6 and 7). Of these two lines, the first appears in brackets as 6.59.6.ef in GPP, which notes in its apparatus that this half verse is additional in the text of Cg. Gita Press includes the line without brackets as 6.59.6ef and is the only translation of the southern text consulted that renders the line. The first two lines read: "This day, I shall gratify the earth with the blood of the monkeys.[1] And I shall send Rāma, together with Lakṣmaṇa, to the abode of Yama.[2]"

7. "a team of superb horses" *turaṅgottamarāji-*: Literally, "a row of superb horses." Ck and Ct understand the sense to be "many horses (*anena bahvaśvayuktatvaṃ rathasyoktam*)." B4,D5–7,9,M3,5, and the texts and printed editions of Cm and Cg read instead *-rāja-*, "king," for *-rāji-*, "line, row." This yields the sense "[yoked to] kings among excellent horses." Cg and Cm understand, "the most excellent horses (*turaṅgaśreṣṭhatamaiḥ*—so Cg)." The only translators consulted who follow this reading, Raghunathan (1982, vol. 3, p. 144) and Pagani (1999, p. 1005), understand the sense to be "royal horses."

"glowed, blazing with splendor" *prakāśamānaṃ vapuṣā jvalantam*: Literally, "shining [and] blazing with beauty." According to Ct, it is because the chariot blazes with beauty that it glows through its own luster (*vapuṣā jvalantam ata eva svabhāsā prakāśamānam*). Cr understands that the vehicle glows of its own accord because it is made of gold and blazes through the splendor of Rāvaṇa's body (*prakāśamānaṃ svarṇamayatvena svataḥ prakāśitaṃ vapuṣā rāvaṇaśarīrakāntyā jvalantam*). Cg feels that the chariot glows because of its ornamentation and blazes because of its own beauty. (*prakāśamānam alaṃkārair bhāsamānam. vapuṣā jvalantaṃ svarūpata eva prakāśamānam.*) Cm understands that the chariot is illuminated both by its splendid horses and its own luster (*turaṅgottamabhāsā svabhāsā ca prakāśamānam ity arthaḥ*).

8. "*bherī* and *paṭaha* drums" *-bherīpaṭaha-*: For *bherī* drums, see 6.17.31–33 and note. *Paṭahas* are a type of drum, commonly a war drum (Vyas 1967, p. 229). See 5.8.36 and note. D5,9–11,T1,G2,M3, and the texts and printed editions of the southern commentators read instead *-paṇava-*, "a type of drum, a war drum." See 5.8.39 and note (Vyas 1967, p. 229).

"to the clapping of arms, war shouts, and lionlike roars" *āsphoṭitakṣveḍitasiṃhanādaiḥ*: The word *āsphoṭita-* refers to the traditional belligerent gesture of Indian warriors of loudly slapping the upper arms with the palms (Alter 1992). Ck, Ct, and Cr understand *-kṣveḍita-* to refer to the shouts of the soldiers, each proclaiming his own valor (*sva[sva]śauryaprakāśikaśabdāḥ*). Cg [v.l. *-kṣvelita-*] understands the term to refer to the sound produced by the clapping of the arms (*kṣvelitaśabdaḥ śabdamātraparaḥ*). In other words, Cg understands that there are only two sounds, the sound of the clapping of the arms and the lionlike roars (*āsphoṭitajanitaśabdaiḥ siṃhanādaiś cety arthaḥ*). Cr interprets *-siṃhanādaiḥ*, "[by] lionlike roars," to mean "loud laughter" (*aṭṭāṭṭahāsāḥ*). Ck understands the term similarly, glossing *ahahāsāḥ*. Cm understands the compound

-kṣvelitasiṃhanādaiḥ not as a *dvandva* but as a compound expressing similitude (*upamitasamāsa*), in the sense of "shouts that were similar to the sounds of the king of beasts (*mṛgendradhvanisadṛśaiḥ kṣvelitaiḥ*)." See notes to 6.4.23–24.

"auspicious hymns of praise" *puṇyaiḥ stavaiḥ*: Several of the translators consulted have taken the adjective *puṇya* in its common meaning of "sacred *or* holy." Roussel (1903, vol. 3, p. 170), followed by Pagani (1999, p. 1006), renders, "*hymnes de triomphe*." Cg, perhaps unwilling to associate sacred or auspicious hymns with Rāvaṇa, glosses, "beautiful (*cārubhiḥ*)." This interpretation appears to have been followed by Gita Press, which renders, "agreeable" (1969, vol. 3, p. 1574). Shastri (1959, vol. 3, pp. 145–46) renders, "hymns of praise," which, if not literal, is textually apposite.

9. "the foremost of the *rākṣasa* lords" *rākṣasarājamukhyaiḥ*: Literally, "the principal *rākṣasa* kings." The expression is somewhat awkward in the plural here and is the subject of considerable textual variation among the different manuscripts. V1,2,D5,6,9–11,T1,2,G1,M3, and the texts and printed editions of the southern commentators read the nominative singular *-mukhyaḥ* for the instrumental plural *-mukhyaiḥ*, thus repeating the epithet used for Rāvaṇa in the previous verse. There, in anticipation of this awkward reading, we have similarly rendered *-rāja-*, "king," as "lord." Many northern manuscripts, as well as the printed editions of Gorresio (6.35.3) and Lahore (6.37.3), retain the instrumental plural but provide a *facilior* by substituting *-yodhamukhyaiḥ*, "foremost of warriors," or *-yodhavīraiḥ*, "warrior-heroes," for *-rājamukhyaiḥ*, "foremost of kings," giving the sense "[surrounded] by the foremost *rākṣasa* warriors *or* warrior-heroes."

"whose bodies resembled mountains or clouds" *śailajīmūtanikāśarūpaiḥ*: Literally, "whose forms resembled mountains and/or clouds." Cg argues that the comparison to mountains is to establish the toughness or hardness of the *rākṣasas*, while the comparison to clouds is an allusion to their ability to contract and expand their bodies. (*kāṭhinyasiddhaye śailaupamyam. saṃkocavikāsārhatvasiddhyai meghaupamyam.*)

"lord of the immortal gods" *amareśaḥ*: M3 and the printed editions of Cg and Cm read instead *asureśaḥ*, "lord of the *asuras*." Cg explains this unexpected epithet for Rudra by alluding to the divinity's dark nature (*tāmasaprakṛtitvāt*). He supports this attribution by quoting a passage that he locates in the "*Upaniṣad* of the Maitrāyaṇīyas, 'He whose portion is darkness, he indeed is Rudra (*yo ha vā asya tāmaso 'ṃśaḥ so 'sau rudra iti*).' " The passage does not appear in the *Maitrāyaṇīyopaniṣad*. This variant is represented only in the translation of Raghunathan (1982, vol. 3, p. 145).

"he resembled Rudra . . . surrounded by his malignant spirits" *bhūtair vṛto rudra iva*: *Bhūtas*, frightening and malignant spirits or ghosts, form a regular part of the terrifying retinue of supernatural beings that surround Lord Śiva, who is, therefore sometimes known by epithets such as Bhūteśa and Bhūtanātha, "lord of ghosts." Notably, Vālmīki uses almost the same simile to describe Rāma when he is beset by the *rākṣasas* under Khara's command in the *Araṇyakāṇḍa* (3.24.10 and note). See verses 23–24 and notes below, where Rāvaṇa is again described in the same way. See 6.59.12; and 6.74.4 and notes. Cf. 6.4.16, where the term is used of Kubera's retinue.

10. "the immensely powerful *rākṣasa*" *mahaujāḥ*: Literally, "the immensely powerful one."

"armed with trees and boulders" *pādapaśailahastam*: Literally, "with trees and boulders in hand."

11. "Closely followed by his army" *senānugataḥ*: Literally, "followed by [his] army." We agree with Cm, Ct, and Ck in reading this as an instrumental *tatpuruṣa*, which places Rāma at the head of his forces. Cr, however, understands an accusative *tatpuruṣa* in the sense of "following his army." Cg explains, "surrounded by his troops, who had assembled on every side in order to protect their master (*svāmisaṃrakṣaṇāya sarvataḥ samavetasenāparivṛtaḥ*)."

"whose arms resembled serpent lords" *bhujagendrabāhuḥ*: The compound must be read as an implicit simile, since serpents, of course, conspicuously lack arms. Cg understands the figure to refer to Rāma's arms having swelled up in his eagerness for battle (*yuddhautsukyena pravardhamānabāhur ity arthaḥ*).

"whose majesty was immense" *pṛthuśrīḥ*: Literally, "of broad *or* extensive majesty *or* splendor." Cg explains that Rāma had acquired a certain splendor as a result of his excitement at the prospect of battle (*yuddhaharṣeṇa saṃjātalakṣmīkaḥ*).

"foremost among those who bear weapons" *śastrabhṛtāṃ variṣṭham*: This is a type of formulaic expression of which the epic poets are fond. Cg explains it here as meaning "cognizant of the relative qualities of the heroic soldiers (*vīrabhaṭatāratamyajñam iti bhāvaḥ*)."

12. "Who is in command of this . . . army" *sainyam . . . kasyedam*: Literally, "Whose is this army?"

"unassailable" *akṣobhyam*: Literally, "unshakeable."

"weapons" *-śastra-*: B2,D10–11,G2, and the texts and printed editions of Ct, Cr, and Ck read instead *-chatra-*, "umbrellas."

"bows" *-āyudha-*: Literally, "weapons." We agree with those commentators who have this reading in understanding *-āyudha-* here to mean "bow." We do so because the compound refers to specific weapons and also in order to avoid redundancy with the word *śastra*, "weapons," in *pāda* a.

"discuses" *-cakra-*: The reading is marked as uncertain by the critical editors. D5,6,10,11,G3,M3, and the texts and printed editions of Ct, Cr, Ck, Cg, and Cm read instead *-śastra-*, "weapon." Commentators who have this reading are distressed by the repetition, as the term also occurs in *pāda* a. They attempt to resolve the redundancy by taking the first occurrence as a generic term for weapons, and the second as a restrictive term for the types of cutting weapons mentioned in the compound in *pāda* b. Crā notes this reading as a variant and suggests that the term be understood to refer to weapons other than those mentioned in the verse (*śastraśabdena paṭhitavyatiriktāny āyudhāny ucyante*).

"its war-elephants as huge as Himalaya, lord of mountains" *nagendropamanāga-*: Literally, "elephants similar to the lord of mountains." D9–11,M1,2,4,5, and the commentaries of Ct, Cr, and Cm (as a variant) read instead *mahendropamanāga-*, "elephants as large as Mount Mahendra." The commentaries and printed editions represented by Cg and M3 read the inferior variant *gajendropamanāga-*, "elephants resembling the lords of elephants." No translators render this variant. See 6.53.24 and note.

13. "for him" *rāmasya*: Literally, "for Rāma." We have dropped the second term, "Rāma," to avoid the awkward repetition in the translation.

14. "that huge *rākṣasa*" *mahātmā*: Literally, "great one." Given the tenor of the verse, we agree with Ct, Ck, and Cg in taking the epithet here, which we normally translate simply as "great," to refer to physical size (*mahādehaḥ*—so Ct; *mahākāyaḥ*—so Cg).

"making its head tremble, is Akampana" *prakampayan nāgaśiraḥ ... akampanam*: Literally, "[who] is making an elephant's head tremble [know him to be] Akampana." Ct, Cg, and Cm carry through the notion of the *rākṣasa*'s great size by saying that it is the weight of his body that causes the elephant's head to shake (*svaśarīrabhārāt svārūḍhanāgasya gajasya śiraḥ saṃkampayann eti*—so Ct). The poet, as he does so often, plays etymologically with his characters' names. Akampana is the name of the great *rākṣasa* warrior who fights with, and is slain by, Hanumān in *sarga* 44 (6.44.29) above. Ct, Cr, and Cm all hasten to inform us that the *rākṣasa* slain here is different from the one killed earlier (*ayam akampanaḥ pūrvahatād anya iti bodhyam*—so Cm). Cg identifies the present Akampana as a son of Rāvaṇa (*enam akampanaṃ rāvaṇaputram avehi*). See note to verse 16 below. See, also, 6.43.2; 6.57.17; and notes.

15. "who brandishes a bow" *dhūnvan dhanuḥ*: Literally, "shaking *or* waving a bow." Cg feels that this phrase expresses the extraordinary strength of Indrajit's arms (*anena bhujabalādhikyam ucyate*).

"that resembles the bow of Śakra" *śakradhanuḥprakāśam*: This can also be interpreted, as some translators have done, as "shining like Śakra's bow, i.e., the rainbow." (Cf. Raghunathan's "gleaming like the rainbow" [1982, vol. 3, p. 145].)

"with his ... protuberant fangs" *-vivṛttadaṃṣṭraḥ*: The sense of the participle *vivṛtta-* in this compound is somewhat obscure. Its normal meaning is "rolling about, turning," but this seems inappropriate in this context. The commentators are silent. Some translators extend the meaning to "round *or* curving," not an implausible choice (Roussel 1903, vol. 3, p. 172; Shastri 1959, vol. 3, p. 146; Gorresio 1856, vol. 9, p. 310; and Dutt 1893, p. 1276). Others, with whom we align ourselves, read the participle as if it were *vivṛta-*, "manifest, displayed" (Gita Press 1969, vol. 3, p. 1575 and Raghunathan 1982, vol. 3, p. 145). Pagani (1999, p. 1006) oddly renders, "*et montre ... ses dants ... étincelants*." Compare 6.55.123 and note.

"who ... resembles an elephant" *karīva bhāti*: Cg notes that this phrase expresses the power of Indrajit's body (*anena kāyabalam*).

"preeminent by virtue of a boon" *varapradhānaḥ*: Literally, "foremost by a boon." We agree with the majority of the commentators and translators in taking the compound as an instrumental *tatpuruṣa*. Cr offers an alternative, that is, to read the compound as a *bahuvrīhi* based on an underlying *karmadhāraya* meaning "for whom his boon is the foremost [thing]." The boon referred to, as several of the commentators note, is the boon of invisibility that Brahmā granted to Indrajit. See notes to 6.36.10 and 7.30.10–13.

16. "immensely powerful" *ativīryaḥ*: Cg (v.l. *ativīraḥ*) understands this term to indicate that, despite Atikāya's lack of powers of illusion, he is even more powerful than Indrajit (*māyābalābhave 'pīndrajito 'tiśayitavīryaḥ*).

"superb chariot-warrior" *atirathaḥ*: This is a term often used in the *Mahābhārata* to indicate elite chariot-warriors (cf. *MBh* 1.2.53; 1.2.150; 1.64.19; 1.108.15; 1.213.61; 3.48.5; 3.84.7; 3.225.26; 7.1–8.41, etc.). Cg claims that Atikāya is called *atirathaḥ* because he possesses an extraordinarily great chariot that is yoked to one thousand horses (*sahasrāśvayuktatvenātiśayitarathaḥ*). Cf. 6.19.18–21.

"the Vindhya mountain, Western mountain, or Mount Mahendra" *vindhyāstamahendrakalpaḥ*: Cg suggests that, by mentioning three separate mountains, the poet is expressing three separate qualities of Atikāya, namely, height, the ability to overcome the energy of his enemies, and immovability (*vindhyāditrayaupamyenonnatatva-*

paratejobhibhāvakatvaniścalatvāny ucyante). Presumably these qualities belong, respectively, to the three mountains named. On the Western mountain (*asta*), see 6.39.15; 6.57.20; 6.78.43; and notes.

"with his gigantic body . . . Atikāya" *atikāyo 'tivivṛddhakāyaḥ*: Literally, "Atikāya [he of the gigantic body], whose body had grown extraordinarily." As elsewhere, the poet plays with and echoes the name of his character, repeating the prefix *ati-*, "very, excessive," three times in the verse in addition to its occurrence in the name of the *rākṣasa*. Devāntaka, Narāntaka, Triśiras, and Atikāya are all said to be the "paternal nephews" of Kumbhakarṇa, and so must also be sons of Rāvaṇa. See 6.56.3 and note. See also note to verse 14 above, where Cg says that Akampana is a son of Rāvaṇa.

17. "his eyes as red as the newly risen sun" *navārkoditatāmracakṣuḥ*: The sequence *-arkodita-* must be read, as Cg suggests, as a *paranipāta* compound whose normal order would be, as in the parallel compound of verse 14, *-uditārka-*.

"who bellows harshly" *kharaṃ garjati*: We read with Cg, Cm, and Ck, who take *kharam* to be an adverb modifying *garjati*, "he bellows" (*kharam iti kriyāviśeṣaṇam*—so Cg). Ct and Cr take *kharam* as an adjective in the sense of "fierce, savage (*krūram*—so Ct)," modifying *gajam*, "elephant." Ct's interpretation is rendered by Roussel (1903, vol. 3, p. 172), who is, in turn, followed by Shastri (1959, vol. 3, p. 146) and Pagani (1999, p. 1006).

"its bells clanging" *ghaṇṭāninadapraṇādam*: Literally, "resounding with the sound of bells." Cg, Cr, and Cm all read the *upasarga pra* in *praṇāda* in the sense of *prakṛṣṭaḥ* or *prabhūtaḥ*, "to a great extent" [here, "loudly"].

18. Several of the commentators are disturbed by the lack of an explicit finite verb in this verse, which undermines its parallelism with others in the passage. Cg proposes bringing down the verb *garjati*, "he [who] bellows" (*garjatīti pūrvaślokād anuṣajyate*). Cv supplies "he goes (*gacchati*)," while Cm supplies "he comes (*āyāti*)."

"which, with its trappings bright with gold, resembles a mountain shrouded in evening clouds" *kāñcanacitrabhāṇḍam . . . saṃdhyābhragiriprakāśam*: We agree with Cg in taking the description of the horse's bright trappings as the basis for the simile of the cloud-shrouded mountain. The idea would be that the huge battle-charger covered with gleaming ornaments resembles the dark mass of a mountain surrounded by a corona of clouds brightly illuminated by the setting [or rising] sun. This linkage, which is explicit in Cg, is implicit, we believe, in Cm, who, with Cg and Cv, shares the reading of the critical edition. Cg and Cm gloss the second compound as a *madhyamapadalopī*, whose meaning is "having a resemblance to a mountain shrouded in evening clouds (*saṃdhyābhrayuktagiriprakāśam*)." D4,9–11, and the texts and printed editions of Ct substitute the nominative ending *-aḥ* for the critical edition's accusative *-am*, which makes the simile refer to Piśāca himself rather than to his horse. Unlike Cg and Cm, Cr reads the compound *saṃdhyābhragiri-* as a *dvandva*, which lends the larger compound the sense "who [Piśāca] resembles an evening [or morning] cloud and a mountain (*saṃdhyābhragiribhyām iva prakāśate*)."

"haloed with light" *marīcinaddham*: Literally, "bound with rays."

19. "a lordly and mountainous bull" *vṛṣendram . . . giriprakāśam*: Literally, "the lord of bulls, resembling a mountain." Ñ1,D1,3,4,6,7,9–11,13,T2,3,G1,3,M5, and the texts and printed editions of Ct and Cr read *śaśi-*, "hare-marked [moon]," for *giri-*, "mountain."

"its power surpassing that of the thunderbolt" *kiṃkaravajravegam*: Literally, "having servant-thunderbolt-power." The compound is obscure and lends itself to a variety of interpretations. We agree basically with Cg, who interprets the compound to mean "that which has a servant in the form of the power of the thunderbolt, that is, which has power greater than even that of the thunderbolt. (*kiṃkaro vajravego yasya tat kiṃkaravajravegam. vajravegād apy adhikavegam ity arthaḥ.*)" Ck and Ct similarly gloss, "to which the power of the *vajra* had become subservient (*kiṃkarabhūto vajravego yasmiṃs tam*—Ct; *kiṃkarabhūto 'nvagbhūto vajravego yasya tat*—Ck)." Cm explains, "for whom the power of the *vajra*, like a servant, did as it was instructed, that is, equal in power to that (*kiṃkaravad yathoktakārivajraṃ tatsamānavegam*)." Cr understands the term *kiṃkara* to mean "doing nothing *or* having no effect (*akiṃcitkaraḥ*)." His idea seems to be that the *vajra* would have no effect upon the lance and that therefore it has the same force as the *vajra*. (*kiṃkaro 'kiṃcitkara ity arthaḥ. vajravad vego yasmiṃs tat.*)

"Triśiras" *triśirāḥ*: Ct and Cm point out that this is "a certain Triśiras (*kaścit triśirāḥ*)," by which they no doubt mean to differentiate the *rākṣasa* described here from the one Rāma killed at *Araṇyakāṇḍa* 26. See, too, note to 3.16.20. See also notes to verse 16 above.

20. "there we see" *bhāti*: Literally, "he appears." Ñ1,V2,3,B1,2,D9–11,13, and the texts and printed editions of Ct, Ck, and Cr read instead *yāti*, "he goes."

"broad, muscular, and splendid" *pṛthuvyūḍhasujāta-*: Literally, "broad, firm, and beautiful." Cr and Cg gloss, "fleshy (*pīnam*)," "wide (*viśālam*)," and "beautiful (*sundaram*)."

"utterly intent" *samāhitaḥ*: We follow Cr in taking this term to describe a state of mental concentration. He glosses, "single-mindedly focused on battle (*yuddha-ikamanāḥ*)." Cg understands, "equipped for battle *or* dressed in armor (*sannaddhaḥ*)."

"brandishing... his bow" *dhanur vidhūnvan*: See note to verse 15 above.

21. "blazing, smoking" *dīptaṃ sadhūmam*: The commentators are in agreement that the weapon appears to blaze because of its gold and gemstones. Since nothing in the verse seems to provide a basis for the image of smoke, Ct, Cr, and Cm argue that it is the dark luster of sapphires that creates the illusion of smoke (*nīlamaṇikāntyā sadhūmam iva*—Ct). Cg, on the other hand, thinks that the mention of smoke has been added simply to complete the fiery imagery of the verse (*abhedanirdeśaḥ sarvathā sādṛśyapratipattaye*).

"*jāmbūnada* gold" *jāmbūnada-*: See note to 6.15.2.

"fearsome" *-ghora-*: Ñ2,B1,D9–11, and the texts and printed editions of Ct read *-vīra-* "valiant, heroic."

22. "huge warrior" *udagraḥ*: Literally, "the tall *or* large one."

"Narāntaka" *narāntakaḥ*: This is one of the four sons of Rāvaṇa mentioned at notes to verse 16 above. Narāntaka is slain by Aṅgada at *Yuddhakāṇḍa* 57.

"who can battle even mountain peaks" *nagaśṛṅgayodhī*: Literally, "mountain peak fighter." The compound is ambiguous; for, just as in the literal English translation, it is not clear whether Narāntaka fights against mountain peaks or uses them as weapons. Both interpretations are plausible and yet problematic in the context. Cg offers the second as his principal explanation, glossing, "he fights with mountain peaks as his instruments (*nagaśṛṅgaiḥ sādhanaiḥ yudhyata iti*)." Cm appears to follow this reading, breaking it down further by reading *nagaśṛṅga-* as a *dvandva* rather than as a *tatpuruṣa*. This gives the sense of "he fights with trees and [mountain] peaks (*nagaiś ca śṛṅgaiś ca yudhyata iti*)." This explanation is plausible in an epic, where the use of trees and mountains as weapons is a commonplace. It is problematic in this context, however, since these weapons are almost exclusively used by the monkeys, but the verse itself indicates that Narāntaka's chariot is crammed with all sorts of conventional weapons. Thus, we have followed the interpretation of Ct and Cr, which is also noted as an alternative explanation by Cg. According to this reading, Narāntaka actually fights against mountain peaks in the absence of any opposing warrior to equal him in order to alleviate the itching of his arms (*pratiyoddhrabhāvād bhūjakaṇḍūnivṛttyartham iti bhāvaḥ*—Ct). Ck has a variant of this interpretation according to which Narāntaka fights against these inanimate objects in his insatiable desire (lit., itching) for combat (*nagaśṛṅgair yudhyata iti tathā raṇakaṇḍv iti śeṣaḥ*). See verse 29 and note below.

23–24. "that . . . white umbrella" *chatraṃ sitam*: The white umbrella is an invariable insignia of royalty in traditional India. See 2.2.5 and 5.8.2 and notes. See 6.115.12–16 and note. See, too, 6.116.25–26 and notes, where these insignia of royalty surround Rāma.

"whose faces are those of tigers, camels, elephant lords, and the king of beasts" *vyāghroṣṭranāgendramṛgendravaktraiḥ*: The compound *-nāgendra-*, "elephant lords," could also be rendered "serpent lords." Ñ2,V1,2,B1,D1,4–6,9–11,13,T1,2,G1,M3,5, and the texts and printed editions of the southern commentators read *-mṛgāśva-*, "deer and horses," for *-mṛgendra-*, "king of beasts." The theriomorphic faces or heads of the *rākṣasas* are a favorite theme of Vālmīki as well as of the later courtly painters. Compare the description of the *rākṣasa* women who guard Sītā at 5.15.9–17 and 5.20.31–33. See, too, 6.41.26–27.

"he resembles Rudra, surrounded by his malignant spirits" *bhūtair vṛto rudra ivāvabhāti*: See notes to verse 9 above.

25. "He wears a crown" *kirīṭī*: Cr takes the possessive suffix *-in* in the sense of "possessing something to an excellent degree." He thus glosses, "possessing an excellent crown (*praśastakirīṭavān*)." Given that Rāvaṇa is represented, especially in his battle guise, as possessing ten heads, one might also translate, "he wears crowns." None of the commentators explicitly suggests this possibility. However, as we see in the next note, it is evident that Cr has this understanding. On Rāvaṇa's variable number of heads, see 5.8.13,19; 5.20.24,26; 5.7.2–14; and notes.

"with his face adorned with swinging earrings" *calakuṇḍalāsyaḥ*: Literally, "having a face that has swinging earrings." As hinted in the previous note, Cr glosses, "of whom the faces are equipped with swinging earrings (*calakuṇḍalair yuktāny āsyāni yasya*)," evidently referring to the ten-headed form of Rāvaṇa.

"an elephant lord" *nāgendra-*: As in the previous verse, the term could equally well mean "serpent lord." Ñ2,D6,10,11,T2,3,G1,2,M, and the texts and printed editions of the southern commentators read instead *nagendra-*, "lord of mountains." The commentators and the translators who follow them are divided as to whether to take the term *nagendra-* in apposition to *-vindhya-* or (so Cg) as a reference to Himalaya. Cg's interpretation seems plausible, as the Himalaya is often regarded as the king or overlord of mountains. Compare *Kumārasambhava* 1.1, where the Himalaya is called *nagādhirājaḥ*.

26. "subduer of his foes" *ariṃdamam*: Ñ2,V,B4,D1,3,4,6,7,9–11,13,G1,3,M1,3, and the texts and printed editions of Ct read the nominative *ariṃdamaḥ*, in which case the epithet applies to Rāma and not Vibhīṣaṇa.

27. "I can clearly make out" *suvyaktaṃ lakṣaye*: Ñ,D6,7,10,T2,G2,M1,2, and the texts and printed editions of Ct, Ck, and Gorresio (6.36.3) read instead *na vyaktaṃ lakṣaye*, "I cannot clearly make out."

28. "Not even . . . like that" *naivaṃvidham*: Literally, "not of such a type." Ñ,V1,2,B2–4,D1–4,11,13,M5, Gorresio's edition (6.36.3), and the commentary of Cr omit the negative particle *na* to read *evaṃvidham*, yielding the sense "of such a type." Among the translators consulted, only Dutt (1893, p. 1277) and Gorresio (1856, vol. 9, p. 312) follow this reading in which the idea is that Rāvaṇa's appearance is like that of the divine and demonic heroes.

"the heroes among the gods and *dānavas*" *devadānavavīrāṇām*: We follow Cr, the only commentator to remark on the compound, in reading it as a *tatpuruṣa* with an introjected *dvandva* (*devadānavayor virāṇām*). The compound can also be read, less plausibly in our opinion, as a complete *dvandva* in the sense of "gods, demons, and heroes." Several of the translators consulted have read the compound in this latter sense.

29. "of that immensely powerful *rākṣasa*" *mahaujasaḥ*: Literally, "of that one of great power." D9–11 and the texts and printed editions of Ct and Cr read instead *mahātmanaḥ*, "of that great one."

"they can all give battle even to mountains" *sarve parvatayodhinaḥ*: Literally, "all [are] mountain fighters." As in the case of the term *nagaśṛṅgayodhī* in verse 22 above, the expression is ambiguous. And, as with the previous expression, it can refer to those who use mountains as weapons or those who actually fight mountains. The commentators are silent here. See note to verse 22 above.

30. "by those blazing warriors" *pradīptaiḥ*: Literally, "by blazing ones."

"fearsome in their valor" *bhīmavikramaiḥ*: D9–11,G1, and the texts and printed editions of Ct read instead *bhīmadarśanaiḥ*, "fearsome in their appearance."

"malignant spirits" *bhūtaiḥ*: Compare verses 9, 23–24 and notes above, where Rudra, similarly surrounded by *bhūtas*, is an object of comparison for Rāvaṇa.

"in bodily form" *dehavadbhiḥ*: Literally, "by those possessing bodies." Ct, Ck, Cg, and Cm appear to take the adjective with the *rākṣasa* warriors and gloss, "having large bodies (*praśastadehaiḥ*)." Cv similarly glosses, "having large bodies (*mahādehaiḥ*)." Cr, who does not gloss the term, clearly also construes it with the warriors surrounding Rāvaṇa.

Following verse 30, D5–7,9–11,S insert a passage of two lines [904*]: "Fortunately, I have caught sight of that evil creature. Now I shall unleash the wrath born of the abduction of Sītā."

32. "at the city gates and the gates of the buildings on the main thoroughfares" *dvāreṣu caryāgṛhagopureṣu*: Literally, "at the gates [and] at the road-house-gateways." Presumably the word *caryā* here refers to the two main roads that would link the four city gates. Commentators differ as to how to understand these references to architectural and defensive structures. They also differ in their analyses of the compound *caryāgṛhagopureṣu*. Cv does not comment on *dvāreṣu* but takes the compound to mean "strong houses [built] on the main roads (*caryāgṛhayuktagopuravat caryāgṛhāṇi ca saṃcāravīthiviśaṅkaṭāni gṛhāṇi*)." Ck understands the compound as follows: "*caryā* refers to main thoroughfares; *gṛha* refers to the [*rākṣasas'*] headquarters; and the *gopuras* are the terraces *or* structures at the outer gates (*caryā mahāmargāḥ, gṛhaṃ mūlāyatanaṃ tasya gopurāṇi bahirdvāraprāsādāḥ*)." Ct agrees with Ck but adds that *dvāreṣu* refers to the

four principal gates of the city of Laṅkā (*laṅkāyāś caturṣv api dvāreṣu*). Cg understands *dvāreṣu* to refer to the inner gates (*antardvāreṣu*) and takes the *caryāgṛhas* to be strongly fortified structures built on either side of the gateways at the city gates, along the roads, to house the soldiers (*caryāyuktāḥ puradvāreṣu gopuraparśvayoḥ bhaṭanivāsārthaṃ nirmitā viśaṅkaṭā gṛhāḥ caryāgṛhāḥ*). Cm explains that the *dvāras* refer to the gates of the inner palisade (*antarāprākāradvāreṣu*). He then reads the compound as a *dvandva* consisting of *caryāgṛhas* and *gopuras*. The former he defines as "houses built at the crossroads" (presumably of the two main thoroughfares). The latter he defines as the main city gates. (*caryāgṛhagopureṣu caryāgṛheṣu gopureṣu ca caryāgṛhāḥ catuṣpathanirmitā gṛhāḥ. gopurāṇi puradvārāṇi.*) Cr understands *dvāreṣu* to refer to all of the gates leading out of Laṅkā. He takes the compound *caryāgṛhagopureṣu* to mean "the outer gates of the houses on the main roads (*caryāṇāṃ mahāmārgāṇāṃ yāni gṛhāṇi teṣāṃ gopureṣu bahirdvāreṣu ca*)." Given the ambiguity of the compound and the diversity of commentarial opinion, it is not surprising that translations vary in their rendering of this passage. See note to 6.48.8 below.

Following verse 32, D5–7,9–11,S insert a passage of four lines in the *upajāti* meter [965*]: "For if the forest-dwelling monkeys should learn that I have come here with you gentlemen, they would take it for an opportunity. Then, all together, they might assault and destroy the empty city, difficult though it may be to conquer."

33. "summarily" *sahasā*: Literally, suddenly, rashly." This reading occurs only in a few, mostly southern, manuscripts (Ś,D5,9,T1,M4,5). With the exception of Ś, the entire north substitutes an entirely different reading for the first half of the verse [966*]. D6,7,10,11,T2,3,M1,2, and the texts and printed editions of Ct and Cr read instead *sacivān*, "his ministers *or* companions." M3 and the texts and printed editions of Cg read instead *sahitān*, which Cg glosses as "all together (*saṃmilitān*)." This reading is rendered as "large bodies of them" in the translation of Raghunathan (1982, vol. 3, p. 147). The critical editors have apparently chosen the slightly awkward reading *sahasā*, as it is the only one represented, however spottily, in both the north and south.

34. "Sugrīva, lord of the tawny monkeys" *harīśaḥ*: Literally, "lord of the tawny monkeys." See verse 37 below, where it is made explicit that the monkey in question is Sugrīva.

"the *rākṣasa* lord . . . he . . . charged at him" *rākṣasendram . . . dudrāva rakṣodhipatim*: Literally, "[he charged] the *rākṣasa* lord . . . the *rākṣasa* overlord."

35. "whose slopes were thick with trees" *bahuvṛkṣasānum*: Literally, "whose slopes had many trees." Alternatively, the compound could be interpreted to mean "with many trees and peaks *or* ridges."

"the latter": The verse provides no pronoun or any other clue to indicate the change of subject. The context, however, makes this clear. Cr tells us that we are "to provide the name 'Rāvaṇa' (*rāvaṇa iti śeṣaḥ*)."

37. "whose force was equal to that of the wind or great Indra's thunderbolt" *anilatulyavegam . . . mahendrāśanitulyavegam*: Literally, "whose force was equal to the wind . . . whose force was equal to the thunderbolt of Mahendra." Cg thinks that Indra is mentioned in order to differentiate his weapon, the *vajra*, from a bolt of portentious [natural] lightning (*autpātikāśanivyāvṛtaye mahendrapadam*). Alternatively, he suggests that the mention of the connection with great Indra, whose long practice enables him to loose the *vajra* with great force, is made in order to illuminate the tremendous

impact of Ravaṇa's weapon (*yadvā mahendrasaṃbandhoktir abhyāsavatā muktatvenātivegadyotanāya*). See note to 6.55.43.

38. "sharp-tipped... appearance" *-prakhyavapuḥ śitāgraḥ*: D9–11 and the printed editions of Ct read instead *-sparśavapuḥ prakāśam*. The meaning of the reading thus presented is somewhat unclear. The first compound, meaning "whose body *or* form had the touch *or* feel [of Indra's thunderbolt]," is clear enough. The word *prakāśam* is, however, problematic. Translators who follow the text of Ct seem to struggle to construe the term. Shastri (1959, vol. 3, p. 148) and Dutt (1893, p. 1278) ignore it entirely. Roussel (1903, vol. 3, p. 174) reads it adverbially in the sense of "*á découvert*." Pagani (1999, p. 1008) translates the term as an adjective in the sense of "*resplendissant*," modifying *sāyakaḥ*, "arrow," which, of course, involves a significant gender disagreement. Gita Press (1969, vol. 3, pp. 1577–78) has *-prakhyavapuḥprakāśam*, a reading shared, apparently, with V2, and translates the entire compound as an adjective modifying Sugrīva, "who shone with his body, which resembled the thunderbolt of Indra."

"just as the fearsome javelin hurled by Guha once pierced Mount Krauñca" *guheritā krauñcam ivograśaktiḥ*: Literally, "like the fierce javelin impelled by Guha [did] Krauñca." As Cg points out, the term "Guha" is an epithet of the divinity Skanda, who, according to legend, pierced Mount Krauñca in order to release a demon of the same name who had been imprisoned there by the *ṛṣi* Agastya. See below 6.51.19; 6.55.12; and notes.

39. "his mind reeling" *viparītacetāḥ*: Literally, "having a perverted *or* contrary mind." We follow Cg, who glosses, "his thoughts whirling (*bhrāntacittaḥ*)." Ct and Cm gloss, "unconscious (*acetāḥ*)."

"*yātudhānas*" *yātudhānāḥ*: Vālmīki uses this term, though not frequently, as a synonym for *rākṣasas*. On a few occasions, he appears to regard *yātudhānas* as a separate class of *rākṣasa*. See 5.3.26 and note. See, too, 6.3.27 and note.

40. "Sudaṃṣṭra" *sudaṃṣṭraḥ*: D6,9–11,T2,3, and the texts and printed editions of Ct and Cr read instead *suṣeṇaḥ*, "Suṣeṇa."

"Jyotimukha" *jyotimukhaḥ*: This unusual name is apparently a version of the name Jyotirmukha lightened for metrical reasons. Cg, apparently in an effort to correct the name, glosses, *jyotirmukhaḥ*. Although this spelling does not appear in the printed editions of Cg, Raghunathan (1982, vol. 3, p. 147) translates, "Jyotirmukha." This "correct form" appears only in the printed text of Gorresio (6.36.16), who translates accordingly (1856, vol. 9, p. 313).

"Nala" *nalaḥ*: As elsewhere in the poem, the list of names varies among recensions and manuscripts. M3 and the texts and printed texts of Cg read instead *nabhaḥ*, "Nabha." This reading appears only in the translation of Raghunathan (1982, vol. 3, p. 147), where, however, it is mistakenly rendered as Nābha.

"took up" *samudyamya*: Ñ2,V1,2,B1–3,D9–11, and the texts and printed editions of Ct and Cr read instead *samutpāṭya*, "uprooting *or* ripping up."

41. "warded off their blows" *teṣāṃ prahārān sa cakāra moghān*: Literally, "he rendered their blows vain."

"with swarms" *-gaṇaiḥ*: Literally, "with groups, hosts." Ñ,V,B,D1–3,9–11,13, and the texts and printed editions of Ct and Cr read instead *-śataiḥ* "with hundreds."

"*jāmbūnada* gold" *jāmbūnada-*: See note to 6.15.2.

42. "fearsome" *bhīmarūpāḥ*: Literally, "of fearsome form." V3,D10,11,M1–3, and the texts and printed editions of the southern commentators read instead *bhīmakāyāḥ*, "of fearsome bodies."

43. "their heroic leaders fallen" *patitāgryavīrāḥ*: Literally, "whose principal heroes had fallen." The reading here shows considerable variation among the manuscripts. D7,9–11,G1, and the texts and printed editions of Ct, Ck, and Cr read instead *patitāś ca vīrāḥ* (*patitāḥ pravīrāḥ*—so Cg, Cm), "those heroes fallen." Unlike the critical reading, these variants do not form a *bahuvrīhi* compound and so function independently in the verse. This leaves open the possibility of taking "heroes" in apposition to *śākhāmṛgāḥ*, "monkeys," in *pāda* c, or as an entirely separate reference, thus distinguishing, as in the critical reading, between the monkey officers and the rank-and-file soldiers. This distinction seems to reflect the situation as described in verse 42 above.

"the dart of fear" *bhayaśalya-*: We follow Ct, Cg, and Cm in reading the compound metaphorically (*bhayam eva śalyaṃ tena viddhāḥ*—so Ct). Cr proposes reading the term *bhaya-*, "fear," adjectivally, thus making the compound mean "by a fearsome arrow (*bhayaṅkaraśareṇa*)."

"the tree-dwelling monkeys" *śākhāmṛgāḥ*: Literally, "branch [dwelling] animals." Cg believes that this particular kenning for the monkeys is used here in connection with the expression "dart of fear," noted above. His argument is that, because the monkeys have dwelt only in the forest, they are unfamiliar with this kind of fear [i.e., the kind presented by Rāvaṇa's weapons] (*vanacāritvenaitādṛśabhayānabhijñāḥ*). See note to 6.15.15.

"the refuge of all" *śaraṇyam*: Literally, "the refuge, the protector." Given the tenor of the epic, which refers to Rāma, from time to time, as the universal savior (5.36.26–29 and notes; 6.13.4 and note), we are inclined to follow Cg's more Śrīvaiṣṇava gloss, "capable of providing refuge to all the world (*sarvalokaśaraṇārham*)." Cg contends that this expression is used here to demonstrate that affliction alone impels one to seek refuge [with the Lord] and not the practice of religious observances, which are authorized for particular times and places with the aim of securing some specific goal (*etenārtir eva śaraṇāgatiprayojikā na tu deśakālādhikāriphalaniyamā ity uktam*). See, too, 6.13.4 and 6.59.8. Cf. 6.31.56; 6.81.14; and notes.

44. "At once" *tataḥ*: Literally, "then." Ct thinks that the adverb is used here to illuminate the instantaneous response on the part of the Lord to those who take refuge with him in affliction. (*atra prapatter ārtaprapattirūpatayā tasyāḥ sadyaḥ phaladyotanāya tata ity uktam. prapattyuttarakṣaṇa ity arthaḥ.*)

"the mighty bowman" *dhanuṣmān*: Literally, "possessing a bow." Ct, Cg, Cm, and Cr all bring out the intensifying character of the possessive suffix *-mant*, glossing, "possessing [*or* master of] a mighty bow (*praśastadhanuṣkaḥ* [*or praśastadhanuḥsvāmī*—so Cr])." Cg notes that the term signifies that Rāma is "skilled at fighting with the bow (*dhanuryuddhasamarthaḥ*)."

"came running" *sahasā jagāma*: Literally, "he went suddenly." Cg understands that, by the adverb *sahasā*, "suddenly," we are to understand that Rāma came speedily, bow in hand, in urgent haste to protect those who had come to him for refuge. This haste, Cg continues, proceeds from Rāma's understanding that Lakṣmaṇa would want to go himself. Thus Rāma wants to intervene before that happens (*sahasety anena lakṣmaṇaḥ svayaṃ gamiṣyāmīti tatpūrvam evāśritatrāṇatvarayā sadhanuḥ san jagāmety uktam*).

"him" *tam*: Cg notes that the reference is to Rāma, who is moving swiftly in order to rescue the afflicted [monkeys]. Lakṣmaṇa, he continues, not wishing to transgress against his lord, shields him [*nigalayati*?]. Cg seems to view Lakṣmaṇa's intervention as an example of the maxim of "dawn at the toll station (*ghaṭṭakuṭīprabhātanyāya*)." This maxim, according to Apte (Appendix E, p. 60), is used to illustrate the failure to accomplish a desired object (*uddeśyāsiddhiḥ*). Here, presumably, the object is Lakṣmaṇa's attempt to prevent Rāma himself from going into battle. (*tathaiva ghaṭṭakuṭyāṃ prabhātam ity āha tam iti. tam ārtatrāṇatvarayā vrajantam. lakṣmaṇaḥ . . . anatikramaṇāya nāthaṃ nigalayati.*)

"accosted" *abhyupetya*: Literally, "having approached." Cg glosses, "having approached on all sides (*abhitaḥ upetya*)." He argues, "We are to understand that Rāma moves about variously on all sides, as if he did not realize that Lakṣmaṇa had come (*anena lakṣmaṇāgamanam ajānann iva nānāpārśveṣu rāmo 'nekadhā jagāmety avagamyate*)."

"these deeply significant words" *vākyaṃ paramārthayuktam*: Cg offers two explanations of this term. In the first, he takes it to mean "truthful," as opposed to "merely polite." In the second, he sees it as meaning "connected to the highest goal," because of its being the instrument of activating the secondary agent [*śeṣabhūta*, i.e., Lakṣmaṇa] in his service to the principal agent [*śeṣiviṣaya*, i.e., Rāma]. (*paramārthayuktaṃ na tūpacārayuktam. yadvā paramārthayuktaṃ paramaprayojanayuktam. śeṣiviṣaye kaiṅkaryasya śeṣabhūtaṃ prati paramaprayojanatvāt.*)" Cg's choice of terminology, contrasting the *śeṣin* (the principal subject) with the *śeṣa* (the subordinate object), also resonates with the well-known Vaiṣṇava mythological and iconographical representation of Lakṣmaṇa as an incarnation of the thousand-headed serpent Śeṣa upon whom Viṣṇu, as Śeṣaśayana or Śeṣaśāyin, rests. D9–11 and the texts and printed editions of Ct and Cr read instead the repetitive *rāmaṃ*, "Rāma." Commentators who share this reading are obliged to add or understand the word *vacanam*, "speech."

*45. "Granted . . . Nonetheless" *kāmam*: Literally, "granted." We agree with Cr and Cg that the word must be read adverbially here.

*"my noble lord" *āryaḥ*: The nominative of the critical reading appears to be supported by only four manuscripts collated for the critical edition (D4,5,M3,4). All remaining manuscripts, both northern and southern, as well as all printed editions consulted, read instead the contextually superior vocative *ārya*. We have emended accordingly.

"you are perfectly capable" *suparyāptaḥ*: Literally, "perfectly capable." We follow Cg, who glosses, "you are perfectly able (*suśakto 'si*)." Ct and Cr, however, think that the missing word should be *aham*, "I," thus lending the following interpretation to the first half of the verse: "Surely, my noble lord, I am perfectly capable of killing this evil-minded *rākṣasa*." Cg allows this as an alternative interpretation. Most northern manuscripts, as well as the printed editions of Lahore (6.37.40) and Gorresio (6.36.21), read *aham*, "I," in place of *kāmam*, "granted." All translations consulted understand Lakṣmaṇa to be referring to himself.

"this evil-minded *rākṣasa*" *durātmanaḥ*: Literally, "of the evil-minded one."

"this despicable creature" *nīcam*: Cg's idea here is that, although Rāma is certainly capable of killing Rāvaṇa, the latter is too lowly a creature to be worthy of engaging in combat with him. (*tathāpi nīcaṃ bhavatā yoddhum anarham ahaṃ vadhiṣyāmi. mahābalena bhavatā nīco 'yaṃ na yoddhum arha iti bhāvaḥ.*)

"Just grant me permission, my lord." *anujānīhi māṃ vibho*: Cg understands that Lakṣmaṇa, as the fragment, or the secondary agent, is requesting permission of the Lord, or the principal agent. He notes that Lakṣmaṇa is suggesting that, without Rāma's permission, his own actions would undermine his true nature. (*prabho śeṣin tvaṃ māṃ śeṣabhūtam anujānīhi. bhavadanujñām antareṇa me kāryakaraṇaṃ svarūpahānikaram iti bhāvaḥ.*)

46. "of true valor" *satyaparākramaḥ*: Cg breaks this common epithet of Rāma into the words *sati* and *aparākramaḥ*. He takes the first word, *sati*, as part of an elliptical absolutive construction, supplying the word *vidheye*. This would mean "a servant being at hand." The second term, *aparākramaḥ*, means "lacking valor." Cg's idea here is that Rāma, having been filled with the fury of battle, now abandons it, seeing that a functionary in the form of Lakṣmaṇa is available. (*sati kasmiṃścid vidheye sati. aparākramo nivṛttaparākramaḥ.*)

"tremendous power" *mahātejāḥ*: Cg glosses, "endowed with the characteristic of tremendous radiance, which bespeaks the extraordinary nature of his excitement on this occasion (*tādātvikaharṣaprakarṣāvedakasuṣamāviśeṣaśālī*)."

47. "astonishingly valorous" *adbhutaparākramaḥ*: Cg understands this to mean that Rāvaṇa appears to be able to draw one missile, fit a second to his bow, and fire a third all at once (*ekam astram ādadāna ivāparaṃ saṃdhatte tatsaṃdadhāna ivāparaṃ mokṣayatīty arthaḥ*).

"for all the three worlds together" *trailokyena*: Literally, "by the triple world." As the various commentators explain, the reference is to the collectivity of the inhabitants of the three worlds, viz., the gods, etc. (*tadvartidevādisamūhair ity arthaḥ*—so Ct).

48. "his weak points and . . . your own" *tasya chidrāṇi . . . svacchidrāṇi ca*: Literally, "his openings and your own openings." Ct, Ck, Cm, and Cr understand the term to mean "openings *or* opportunities for striking (*prahārāvasarān* [*-samayān*—Ct, Ck])." Cg understands Rāvaṇa's weak points to be such things as "carelessness, etc. (*anavadhānādīni*)." He understands [Lakṣmaṇa's] own weak points to be an *upalakṣaṇa*, or a metonymic reference, to any possible weaknesses, just as one might urge someone "to look out for crows." This appears to be an allusion to the maxim of the crow as a destroyer of curds (*kākadadhighātakanyāya*), according to which the warning, "protect the curds from crows (*dadhi kākebhyo rakṣyatām*)," is a metonymic injuction to be aware of all possible threats to the yogurt (*svacchidrāṇi lakṣaya kākān paśyetivat*)." Professor R. K. Sharma reminds us that crows themselves are traditionally regarded as paragons of vigilance, and so the expression might also be read as an instruction to observe (and so emulate) the behavior of these birds. See R. K. Sharma 1964, p. 152.

"defend" *gopaya*: D6,10–11,T3,G1, and the texts and printed editions of the southern commentators read instead *lakṣaya*, "observe."

"strive to protect yourself" *yatnād rakṣātmānam*: Literally, "protect yourself with effort." D9–11 and the texts and printed editions of Ct, Cr, and Ck read instead [*ā*]*tmānaṃ gopāyasva*, "protect yourself."

49. "those words of Rāma Rāghava . . . embraced him" *rāghavasya vacaḥ . . . saṃpariṣvajya . . . rāmam*: Literally, "words of Rāghava . . . embraced Rāma."

"doing him honor" *pūjya*: Cg, who reads the grammatically correct *abhipūjya*, glosses, "respectfully having circled [to the right] (*pradakṣiṇīkṛtya*)."

50. "whose arms resembled the trunks of elephants" *vāraṇahastabāhuḥ*: Literally, "having elephant-trunk arms." Ś1,V3,B1,4,D2,10,11,T3,M1,2, and the texts and

printed editions of Ct and Cr read the accusative *-bāhum* for the critical edition's nominative *-bāhuḥ*, thus making the description apply to Rāvaṇa rather than to Lakṣmaṇa.

"gazed upon" *dadarśa*: Literally, "he saw." Our translation tries to express the fact that, rather than engage Rāvaṇa in battle at this point, Lakṣmaṇa seems merely to stand and watch him attack the monkeys. The sequence of the battle is somewhat odd here, although it is well attested in all recensions. Lakṣmaṇa has rushed off to engage Rāvaṇa in battle, but suddenly, without any introduction, Hanumān intervenes in verse 51. Rāvaṇa then engages in battle with Hanumān and other monkeys for the next thirty-six verses, only turning his attention to Lakṣmaṇa at verse 88, after having first dealt with the monkey warriors.

52. "his right arm" *bhujam... dakṣiṇam*: For some reason, Raghunathan (1982, vol. 3, p. 148) translates, "left arm." No manuscript evidence supports this reading.

"menacing" *trāsayan*: Literally, "frightening."

53. "Because of your invulnerability, you vanquished the gods, *dānavas*, *gandharvas*, and *yakṣas*, along with the *rākṣasas*." *devadānavagandharvā yakṣāś ca saha rākṣasaiḥ / avadhyatvāt tvayā bhagnāḥ*: The syntax is somewhat ambiguous in that the phrase *saha rākṣasaiḥ*, "along with the *rākṣasas*," can be understood to mean either that Rāvaṇa defeated his own race as well as the others mentioned or that, in concert with the *rākṣasas*, he defeated the others. D6,9–11,T2,3,M3, and the texts and printed editions of the southern commentators read instead *devadānavagandharvair yakṣaiś ca saha rākṣasaiḥ / avadhyatvaṃ tvayā prāptam*, "you have obtained invulnerability with respect to gods, *dānavas*, *gandharvas*, and *yakṣas*, along with the *rākṣasas*." This variant avoids the ambiguity of the critical edition.

"But you should fear the monkeys." *vānarebhyas tu te bhayam*: Literally, "but there is fear *or* danger for you from monkeys." Some of the commentators seem disturbed that humans, the other major category excluded from Rāvaṇa's boon, are not mentioned here. Cr takes the term *vānara* to refer to extraordinary people (e.g., Rāma and Lakṣmaṇa) who may resemble ordinary mortals (*vānarebhyaḥ prākṛtanarasadṛśebhyaḥ prākṛtavilakṣaṇajanebhya ity arthaḥ*). Cs argues that humans are to be included because of their similarity to monkeys and that Hanumān naturally mentions his own species first. He also suggests that one could break up the word *vānarebhyaḥ* into two parts, *vā* and *narebhyaḥ*, thus referring more directly to humans (*nara*). (*vānarebhyaḥ kapibhyaḥ. tebhyo 'nṛtatvād narasyeti bhāvaḥ. narebhya ity api kapisāmyād vaktavyam. tathāpi svasyaiva purahsthiteḥ svajāter grahaṇam ity avagantavyam. vānarebhya ity atrāvṛttyā tatrāpi padacchedena vānarebhyo vā tebhya iva narebhyo 'pi bhayam iti.*)

54. "This... hand" *bāhuḥ*: Literally, "arm, forearm, paw."

"with its five fingers" *pañcaśākhaḥ*: Literally, "with its five branches."

"the living spirit" *bhūtātmānam*: The term normally refers to the individual soul and is thus glossed as *jīvātmānam* by Ck and Cm. Cr and Cs gloss, "life breaths (*prāṇān*)" and "life (*prāṇam*)," respectively. See 6.81.20 and note below, where the term is used again but where the context lends it a somewhat different connotation.

"from your body" *dehāt*: D10,11, and the texts and printed editions of Ct read instead *dehe*, "in your body," which then construes with *ciroṣitam*, "where it has long dwelt," to yield the sense "in your body, where it has long dwelt."

56. "acquire eternal fame" *sthirāṃ kīrtim avāpnuhi*: Cg and Cm take the expression to be contemptuous on Rāvaṇa's part (*sopālambhoktiḥ*). Cg understands: "The meaning is

that you will acquire the kind of fame [implicit in the phrase], 'Hanumān crept up on Rāvaṇa and struck him' (*hanumān rāvaṇam upasṛtya prahṛtavān ity etādṛśīṃ kīrtim avāpsyasīty arthaḥ*)."

57. The commentators understand Hanumān's comment in this verse to be a response to Rāvaṇa's taunting remarks. In reminding Rāvaṇa of the death of Akṣa, Ck, Cm, and Ct think that he is demonstrating his valor and therefore that he need not demonstrate it again (*pūrvam eva jñātatvād idānīṃ kimapi madvikramaviṣaye jñātavyaṃ nāstīti bhāvaḥ*—so Ct). Cr understands him to be making a veiled suggestion that he will kill Rāvaṇa (*etena tvām api haniṣyāmīti sūcitam*). Crā argues that Hanumān, recognizing the ironic nature of Rāvaṇa's comments, gives him a fitting reply (*jñātavikrāntam iti vacanaṃ solluṇṭhanaṃ jñātvā taducitam uttaram āha*). See note to verse 56 above.

"struck down" *prahṛtam*: Literally, "struck." Ñ2,V1,2,B4,D2,4–7,9–11,T, and the texts and printed editions of Ct and Cr read instead *prahataṃ*, "slain."

"on an earlier occasion... Akṣa" *pūrvam akṣam*: Hanumān slays Akṣa at *Sundarakāṇḍa* 45.

58. "Addressed in this fashion" *evam uktaḥ*: Cg adds that Rāvaṇa is provoked to rage by Hanumān's revelation of his weak spot (i.e., grief over the loss of his son) (*marmodghāṭanena saṃjātaroṣa ity arthaḥ*).

59. "staggered back and forth" *cacāla... muhur muhuḥ*: Literally, "he moved again and again."

Following 59 ab, D5–7,9–11,S insert a passage of one line [973*]: "Standing still for a moment, the wise and powerful [monkey] steadied himself..."

60. "with the palm of his hand" *talena*: D5,6,9–11,T2,3,G3,M5, and the texts and printed editions of Ct read instead *sa tena*, "he, by that (monkey)," thus eliminating the reference to the palm of the hand.

"like a mountain during an earthquake" *bhūmicale 'calaḥ*: The poet plays on the kenning *acala*, "immovable one," for mountain.

61. "slapped down" *talatāḍitam*: Literally, "struck with the palm of the hand."

"the... gods, and *asuras*" *devāḥ sahāsurāḥ*: Literally, "the gods together with the demons." D10,11, and the texts and printed editions of Cr and Ct read instead *devāḥ surāsuraiḥ*. This reading is redundant in that the terms *deva* and *sura* are, for all practical purposes, fully synonymous. Cr is the only commentator to remark on this reading. He negotiates the difficulty by defining the *devas* as the three great divinities of the Hindu pantheon, the so-called *trimūrti*, Brahmā, etc., thus leaving the term *sura* to refer to the lesser vedic divinities (*devā brahmāditrayaḥ*). On the *asuras*' cheering the discomfiture of Rāvaṇa, see note to verse 110 below.

"cheered" *neduḥ*: We normally translate the verb $\sqrt{}$*nad* as "to roar *or* bellow." However, in the context, as Ct, Cr, and Ck point out, we must understand that the divinities are cheering and applauding Hanumān's feat. Cr says, "They cried, 'Bravo! Bravo!' (*sādhu sādhv ity ūcuḥ*—Cr)." Cf. verse 110 and note below.

64. "why bother praising me?" *kiṃ vikatthase*: Literally, "why are you praising?" The verb *vi* $\sqrt{}$*katth* commonly means "to boast," and most translators take it in this sense. We, however, are inclined to follow Cg, who, citing *Dhātupāṭha* 2.36, takes it in its sense of "[false or ironic] praise." (*kiṃ kimarthaṃ vikatthase ślāghase. katthaślāghāyām iti dhātuḥ.*) This fits the context established in verse 62 above, and, thus far, Rāvaṇa has indulged in no braggadocio.

"Now strike once again" *sakṛt...praharedānīm*: Hanumān appears to have in mind some chivalrous notion of the *code duello* in which the opponents take turns striking at each other. Since he has most recently slapped Rāvaṇa, it is, in his estimation, Rāvaṇa's turn to strike rather than to go on chattering. This appears to be the argument of Cg, who says, " 'When struck by an enemy, strike once again, then again one's own blow leads to *or* provides the means [to demonstrate] valor,' this is Hanumān's intention. By the word 'now,' he means to say, 'Previously, because of my own carelessness, you are still alive,' that is the idea. (*sakṛt tu prahara śatruṇā prahṛte punar ātmanaḥ prahāro vikramaparipāṭīm āṭīkata iti hanumato hṛdayam. idānīm iti pūrvaṃ madanavadhānāj jīvasīti bhāvaḥ.*)"

"fool" *durbuddhe*: This term, of course, can equally mean "evil- *or* perverse-minded one" and is so interpreted by most translators. We, however, along with Raghunathan (1982, vol. 3, p. 149), follow Cg, who glosses, "ignorant of the relative significance of blows (*prahāratāratamyānabhijña*)."

"Rāvaṇa's anger" *krodhas tasya*: Literally, "his anger."

65. "the mighty *rākṣasa*" *vīryavān*: Literally, "the mighty one."

"energetically raised" *yatnāt...udyamya*: Literally, "having raised zealously *or* effortfully." D6,9–11,T2,3,M5, and the texts and printed editions of Ct and Cr read *āvṛtya*, "having turned," for *udyamya*, "having raised."

"Struck once again" *hataḥ punaḥ*: D9–11,M3, and the printed editions of Ct read instead *punaḥ punaḥ*, "again and again," which must then be construed with the verb *saṃcacāla*, "he staggered." Since the line is elliptical without the participle *hataḥ*, "struck," even the commentators and translators who follow the vulgate text tend to add or understand the participle.

66. "stunned" *vihvalam*: Literally, "agitated, perturbed, alarmed." We follow the interpretation of Cg, who glosses, "dazed, stupefied, bewildered (*mūrcchitaḥ*)."

"mighty" *mahābalam*: Cg, evidently disturbed by the fact that Hanumān has been put out of action, uses this epithet to demonstrate that even now he is unconquerable by his enemies (*tadānīm api parair anabhibhavanīyam*).

Following verse 66, D5–7,9–11,S insert a passage of one line [978*]: "Ten-necked Rāvaṇa, the valorous overlord of the *rākṣasas*..."

67. "he tormented" *ādīpayāmāsa*: Literally, "he burned *or* inflamed."

68. "with one hand" *kareṇaikena*: Cr, perhaps in an effort to exaggerate the monkey's strength, suggests adding the gerund *utpāṭya* so that we understand, "having ripped up with one hand and hurled." Cg thinks that the mention of throwing the mountain with one hand would have us understand that Nīla is using the other to ward off Rāvaṇa's arrows (*anenetareṇa śaravāraṇaṃ gamyate*).

69–70. "saw that Rāvaṇa...was engaged in battle...he said" *viprekṣamāṇaḥ... abravīt...saṃyuktaṃ rāvaṇam*: The syntax of verses 69 and 70 is somewhat unclear. It is not entirely certain whether the poet intends the accusative *rāvaṇam* of 70b to be the object of the participle *viprekṣamāṇaḥ*, "seeing," in 69c, the verb *abravīt*, "he spoke," of 69d, or both. Cm, like us, understands that Rāvaṇa is the object only of the participle, "seeing." Ct understands it to be the object of both verbal elements, whereas Cg connects it only with *abravīt*. Our understanding is as follows: Hanumān, having been dazed by Rāvaṇa's blow, has now recovered and, in the normal course of things, would renew his combat with him. Rāvaṇa, however, thinking that Hanumān has been put out of action, turns his attention to a new opponent, Nīla. Seeing this,

Hanumān is angered that he cannot resume the fight because, as he notes, to do so would violate the warrior code of conduct. This interpretation is more or less followed in the translations of Dutt (1893, p. 1281) and Raghunathan (1982, vol. 3, p. 149).

Pagani (1999, p. 1010) and Shastri (1959, vol. 3, p. 150) understand that Hanumān is addressing Rāvaṇa. They believe that he is rebuking Rāvaṇa for engaging in combat with another. Gita Press (1969, vol. 3, p. 1581) shares the view that the remarks are addressed to Rāvaṇa but understands the comment, as we do, i.e., that Hanumān is refraining from continuing his battle with Rāvaṇa because it is not proper to do so under the circumstances. The translation of Roussel (1903, vol. 3, p. 175), like the text itself, is ambiguous in this regard. The notion that Hanumān is angrily rebuking Rāvaṇa for his conduct is supported explicitly only in the northern variant [982* = Gorresio 6.36.51–52].

See 4.17.13, where Vālin rebukes Rāma for attacking him while he was engaged in battle with another. See also *ManuSm* 7.92, where a prohibition on such behavior is given.

72. "Nīla, the lord of the army of tawny monkeys" *haricamūpatiḥ*: Literally, "the lord of the army of tawny monkeys."

"slayer of enemy heroes" *paravīrahā*: The critical apparatus notes a variant found only in GPP (6.59.74d), *varavīrahā*, "slayer of eminent heroes" or "eminent slayer of heroes." We believe that this reading is probably a typographical error, as NSP, an edition of Ct's text, reads with the critical edition, and the editors of GPP have not noted the variant "*para-*." Among the translators consulted, only Pagani (1999, p. 1010) renders this inferior reading, translating, "*éminent destructeur de ces ennemis.*"

"like the fire at the end of time" *kālāgnir iva*: Literally, "like the fire of Kāla." Cf. note to 6.56.8.

73. "*dhavas*" *dhavān*: D9–11 and the texts and printed editions of Ct and Cr read instead *drumān*, "[*aśvakarṇa*] trees."

"in full bloom" *supuṣpitān*: The adjective seems to relate most closely to the mango trees, although it can also be construed with the entire list of trees mentioned. Pagani (1999, p. 1010) and Shastri (1959, vol. 3, p. 150) take the adjective to modify the other, unnamed trees mentioned in *pāda* c.

"various" *vividhān*: Oddly, Roussel (1903, vol. 3, p. 176) translates, "*de toute essence*," which Shastri (1959, vol. 3, p. 151), following Roussel, renders as "of varying fragrance."

74. "as they came toward him" *tān . . . samāsādya*: Literally, "as he approached them." Cg glosses, "having come into [their] proximity (*samīpaṃ prāpya*)."

75. "a great mountain" *mahācalaḥ*: Ñ1,B2,D2–4,6–8,10,11,T2,3,M3,5, the printed editions of Ct (NSP, GPP = 6.59.77), and Gorresio's edition (6.36.56) read instead *mahābalaḥ*, "mighty one," which modifies "he," i.e., Nīla. Roussel (1903, vol. 3, p. 176) renders, "*le colosse*." In this he is followed by Shastri (1959, vol. 3, p. 151).

"shrunk his body" *hrasvaṃ kṛtvā . . . rūpam*: Literally, "having made his form short *or* small." As Hanumān has copiously illustrated in the *Sundarakāṇḍa*, the *vānaras* have a virtually unlimited power to change their size. Nīla appears, however, to be the only monkey other than Hanumān to demonstrate this ability. See 5.1.9,10,144–151; 5.2.43–46; 5.51.7; etc. See Goldman and Goldman 1996, pp. 44–47.

77. "first on the tip of Rāvaṇa's flagstaff, next on the point of his bow, and then on the top of his crown" *dhvajāgre dhanuṣaś cāgre kirīṭāgre ca*: Literally, "on the top of the flagstaff, on the top of the bow, and on the top of the crown." Although the text does not state it, we are to assume that Nīla is swiftly leaping from point to point, as, presumably, Rāvaṇa tries to strike him.

"they were amazed" *vismitāḥ*: Ck, Ct, and Cm indicate that heroes are astonished because of the impossibility of anyone standing on Rāvaṇa's crown in battle (*rāvaṇa-kirīṭe sthiter yuddhe kenāpi duṣkaratvāl lakṣmaṇādayas trayo 'pi vismitāḥ*). Crā notes that Hanumān's astonishment is particularly remarkable, since he is famed for the swiftness of his movements (*na māruter asti gatipramāṇam iti prasiddhagatilāghavo hanumān api saṃjātavismayo 'bhūd ity arthaḥ*).

78. "He . . . invoked . . . the divine weapon-spell of Agni" *astram āhārayāmāsa . . . āgneyam*: Literally, "he invoked the Āgneya *astra*." See note 81 below. See, also, 6.59.83 and note. See, too, note to 6.36.26.

79. "as they watched intently" *labdhalakṣyāḥ*: Literally, "having obtained an object." The term, whose normal sense is "having hit the target," is somewhat obscure here. The commentators generally take it to mean that the monkeys have found an occasion for joy in Nīla having Rāvaṇa humiliated and therefore are delighted. (*labdhaharṣa-viṣayāḥ. ata eva hṛṣṭāḥ*—so Ct.) Cg and Cm, although they share this interpretation, offer, as an alternative, that the monkeys are gazing fixedly at Nīla (*nīlam eva paśyanta iti vārthaḥ*). We believe that this latter interpretation makes more sense in the context and also avoids the redundancy of the previous reading. Raghunathan (1982, vol. 3, p. 150) follows this interpretation. Gorresio (1856, vol. 9, p. 316) renders the compound as "*rinfrancati e baldanzosi.*" Only Ś,D3,12,T2,3 read with the critical edition. Most other manuscripts and editions read *labdhalakṣāḥ*. The reading should probably be emended, although such an emendation would not alter the meaning of the compound.

81. "charged with the divine weapon-spell of Agni" *āgneyena . . . saṃyuktam*: Literally, "conjoined with the Āgneya." We agree with Cg and Cr in understanding the term *āgneya* (literally, "that which belongs to Agni") as an elliptical reference to the *Āgneya-mantra*, or spell for invoking the power of the fire god to charge a weapon. Cf. note to 6.35.5. See 6.55.115; 6.59.83; and notes.

82. "Your swiftness derives from this extraordinary trickery of yours" *lāghavayukto 'si māyayā parayānayā*: Literally, "through this great power of illusion, you are endowed with swiftness." We follow Ct, Ck, Cm, and Cr in taking the word *māyā*, "power of illusion *or* magical power," in the sense of "trickery (*vañcanayā*)." See S. Goldman 2006a.

83–84. "Now try to save your life" *jīvitaṃ khalu rakṣasva*: Literally, "now save your life."

"monkey" *vānara*: Cg, who reads 82cd with 83ab and thus has the synonymous vocatives *kape* and *vānara* in the same verse, tries to spare the poet the accusation of redundancy by taking the former as a kind of adjective in the sense of "having a fickle nature (*cañcalaprakṛte*)."

"You seem to appear in many different forms." *tāni tāny ātmarūpāṇi sṛjase tvam anekaśaḥ*: Literally, "You create many different forms of yourself." Commentators and translators are divided as to how to interpret this phrase. Ct, Ck, Cr, and Cm take the reference to be to the [treacherous] actions, which conform to his nature, that Nīla is performing in self-defense (*ātmayogyāni svaparākramocitāni tāni karmāṇi yady api sṛjasi*). This interpretation has been followed in the translations of Gita Press (1969, vol. 3, p. 1582), Roussel (1903, vol. 3, p. 176), Shastri (1959, vol. 3, p. 151), and, based on a slight variant (Gorresio's edition, 6.36.64), Gorresio (1856, vol. 9, p. 317). Dutt (1893, p. 1282) and Pagani (1999, p. 1011) understand Nīla to be changing himself into many different forms. None of the commentators consulted supports this interpretation. Cg is aware of it, however, and refutes it on the grounds that it contradicts Rāvaṇa's statement in verse 82 above, stressing once again Nīla's extraordinary swiftness. Cg's understanding, and the one we believe is correct, is that, in dashing around Rāvaṇa so swiftly from place to place (as in verse 77 above), Nīla is creating the illusion of multiplying himself. (*lāghavātiśayena sṛjasīva dṛśyasa ity arthaḥ. nanu tāni tānīty anena rāvaṇo nīlaṃ nānātanuparigrahayuktaṃ manyata ity avagamyata iti cen na. kape lāghavayukto 'sīti pūrvoktivirodhāt.*) Crā makes this argument even more explicit in his comments to verse 77.

"loosed" *muktaḥ*: Printed editions of the text of Cg, as well as the apparatus of GPP and Cg's commentary, show the variant *yuktaḥ*, which Cg glosses as *prayuktaḥ*, "employed, deployed." This variant is not recorded in the critical apparatus.

"charged with a divine weapon-spell" *astraprayojitaḥ*: Literally, "employed with an *astra*." We follow Cg, who glosses, "charged with the *mantra* that governs a divine missile (*astramantreṇābhimantritaḥ*)." See note to 6.35.5.

"will rob you of your life, even as you seek to save it" *tvām . . . jīvitaṃ parirakṣantaṃ jīvitād bhraṃśayiṣyati*: Literally, " it will cause you to lapse from your life, [even] as you are guarding your life."

85. "nocked the arrow and, with that divinely charged weapon, struck" *saṃdhāya bāṇam astreṇa . . . atāḍayat*: Cr, the only commentator to discuss this verse, reads the phrase somewhat differently, taking the instrumental *astreṇa* elliptically with *bāṇam* rather than as the *karaṇa*, or instrument, of the finite verb. He glosses, "nocking that arrow, which was charged with the *astra*, that is, the divine weapon-spell (*astreṇāstramantreṇābhimantritaṃ bāṇaṃ saṃdhāya*)." This interpretation is followed by Pagani (1999, p. 1011). Several translators additionally appear to read the gerund *saṃdhāya*, "having nocked," in the sense of "having charged [the arrow with the divine spell]" (Gita Press 1969, vol. 3, p. 1582; Raghunathan 1982, vol. 3, p. 150; and Roussel 1903, vol. 3, p. 176). See note to 6.35.2.

87. "because he was endowed with his father's divine power" *pitṛmāhātmyasaṃyogāt*: Nīla's father is Agni, who will, of course, not permit his son to die as a result of being struck by his own fiery weapon. As Ct puts it, an arrow invested with the divine spell of Agni cannot burn fire itself (*pitur agner māhātmyasaṃyogān na hy agnyastrābhimantrito bāṇo 'gniṃ dagdhum arhati*). Cg comments that this demonstrates Agni's tenderness for his son (*pitṛmāhātmyam agneḥ putratayā dayālutvavaibhavam*). The power of the god of fire to spare certain individuals from the effects of burning is a recurrent theme in Vālmīki. Compare 5.51.8–33 and notes, where fire fails to injure Hanumān when his tail is set alight; and 5.53.18–26, where Sītā is unharmed by the conflagration in Laṅkā. This theme will reemerge most famously later in the *Yuddhakāṇḍa* during the *agniparīkṣā*, or fire ordeal, of Sītā (6.104).

88. Following verse 88, D5–7,9–11,T,G2,3,M, and the texts and printed editions of the southern commentators insert a passage of two lines [987*]: "Confronting him in

the midst of battle and warding the others off,[1] the valorous lord of the *rākṣasas*, blazing, took his stand and twanged his bow."

[1]"Confronting him...and warding the others off" *āsādya...vārayitvā*: Literally, "having met...having warded off." Neither gerund has an explicit object. The commentators, with whom we agree, supply Lakṣmaṇa as the object of the first. They differ, however, regarding the second. Ck and Ct understand that the entire monkey army is the object (*sarvaṃ kapibalam iti śeṣaḥ*). Cr believes that the gerund *vārayitvā* refers to Rāvaṇa's blocking of Lakṣmaṇa's further passage through the battlefield (*taduttaragamanaṃ nivārya*). Cm and Cg, whom we follow, understand the object to be Sugrīva and the other monkey warriors (*sugrīvādīn*).

89. "addressed Rāvaṇa" *tam āha*: Literally, "he addressed him."

"Come after me" *anvehi mām*: D5,6,10,11, and the texts and printed editions of Ct and Cr read *avehi* for *anvehi*. This verb normally has the sense of "to know *or* to understand," and the commentators who share this reading attempt to interpret it in that vein. Ct glosses, "look at (*paśya*)." Cr suggests, "know that I have come (*mām...prāptaṃ jānīhi*)." Printed editions of Cg read instead *abhyehi*, which has much the same sense as the critical reading. Among the translators consulted, Pagani (1999, p. 1011) and Gita Press (1969, vol. 3, p. 1582) follow the interpretation of Ct. Roussel (1903, vol. 3, p. 176) translates, "*Apprends à me connaître maintenant.*"

Pāda d of this *upajāti* verse is hypermetric.

90. "fearsome resonant twanging of his bowstring" *paripūrṇaghoṣaṃ jyāśabdam ugram*: It is unclear whether the adjective *paripūrṇaghoṣam*, literally, "having a full sound," is to be construed with the sound of the bowstring, as we have done, or with Lakṣmaṇa's words (*vākyam*) in *pāda* a. Cr, the only commentator to remark on this adjective, is equally nonspecific. Dutt (1893, p. 1282) and Raghunathan (1982, vol. 3, p. 151) construe the adjective with Lakṣmaṇa's speech, rendering, "uttered in a full voice" and "full-throated," respectively. Gita Press (1969, vol. 3, p. 1583) translates as do we. Roussel (1903, vol. 3, p. 177), Shastri (1959, vol. 3, p. 152), and Pagani (1999, p. 1011) appear to read the sequence *jyāśabdam ugram* as if it were a compound (*jyāśabdogram*). They thus understand the verse to contain a simile in which the resonant words of Lakṣmaṇa are said to be "as fearsome as the sound of a bowstring." Another ambiguity here is that the verse does not make it clear as to whose bowstring is resounding. In the previous verse, Rāvaṇa was described as twanging his bow, and no such action is described in Lakṣmaṇa's case. On the other hand, it is perfectly reasonable to assume that, in the stereotypical manner of ancient Indian warriors, Lakṣmaṇa would be twanging his own bow in response to Rāvaṇa's challenge. Indeed, it is more likely that the sounds of his rival's voice and bowstring would serve to fuel the anger of Rāvaṇa's words.

91. "How fortunate for me" *diṣṭyā*: Cm, acknowledging that the surface meaning of verses 90–93 is clear, lends it an inner, theologically tinged sense in which Rāvaṇa, as a great sinner, feels fortunate to have encountered Lakṣmaṇa (*me pāpiṣṭhasyāpi mama diṣṭyā bhāgyavaśena dṛṣṭimārgaṃ prāpto 'sīti*).

"headed for destruction" *antagāmī*: Literally, "going to [one's] end." Ct glosses, "you will attain destruction (*antaṃ nāśaṃ prāpsyasi*)." Cr offers, "whose characteristic is departure for the next world (*paralokagamanaśīlaḥ*). Cg glosses, "desiring destruction (*vināśecchuḥ*)."

"your wits disordered" *viparītabuddhiḥ*: Ck and Ct gloss, "stupid, foolish (*durbuddhiḥ*)," explaining that this description applies to Lakṣmaṇa because he has come to fight with Rāvaṇa for his own destruction (*mayā saha yuddhāya prāṇanāśārtham āgamanād viparītabuddhir durbuddhiḥ*). Cr explains the term here to mean a person whose mind is perverse in that it is fixed on fighting with someone with whom one ought not do battle (*viparītāyoddhavye yodhanaviṣayā buddhir yasya saḥ*).

"the land of death" *mṛtyudeśam*: Ś,Ñ,V,B,D1–4,8–11, and the texts and printed editions of Ct and Cr read instead *mṛtyulokam*, "the world of Mṛtyu."

92. "As Rāvaṇa was bellowing in this fashion ... replied" *tam āha ... garjantam*: Literally, "he [Lakṣmaṇa] said to him [Rāvaṇa] who was bellowing."

"exposing the white tips of his fangs" *udvṛttasitāgradaṃṣṭram*: Literally, "whose white-tipped fangs were prominent." D5–7,9–11, and the texts and printed editions of Ct and Cr read *-śitāgra-*, "sharp tips," for *-sitāgra-*, "white tips."

93. "your courage ... your strength, your valor, and your prowess" *vīryam ... balaṃ pratāpaṃ ca parākramaṃ ca*: The four terms are closely synonymous and often interchangeable. Cg attempts to restrict the meanings of two of the terms, glossing *pratāpa* as "the ability to intimidate one's enemies (*śatrubhīṣaṇatvam*)" and *parākrama* as "heroism (*śauryam*)." Cg understands, moreover, that here Lakṣmaṇa uses all the terms ironically (*sopahāsoktiḥ*—literally, "mocking speech"). He notes that these are the "heroic" qualities of someone who has taken the guise of an ascetic to abduct Sītā when no one was around (*tava vijane yativeṣeṇa sītām apahṛtavataḥ*). See note to 6.2.14.

96. "released from his bow a ... shower of arrows" *bāṇavarṣam ... vavarṣa ... kārmukasaṃprayuktam*: Literally, "he showered an arrow-shower, which was impelled by his bow." The syntax is somewhat awkward, and the usage of *saṃprayuktam*, "impelled," is unusual. Cr glosses, "released (*tyaktam*)," which is probably the intended sense. Cg, on the other hand, glosses, "fixed to *or* placed on the bow (*saṃhitam*)." Cr, alone among the commentators, attempts to justify the syntax. He argues that the word *saṃprayuktam*, "released," is governed by both the subject, "Rāma's younger brother (*rāmānujaḥ*)," and the apparent instrument, "the bow (*kārmuka-*)," in order to express the identity of the action and the subject (*kriyākriyāvator abhedavivakṣayā saṃprayuktam ity asya viśeṣye 'nvayān nāsaṃbhavaḥ*). Thus, he argues that the syntax is not impossible.

"With these arrows—razor-tipped, half-moon-headed, finely barbed, and crescent-headed" *kṣurārdhacandrottamakarṇibhallaiḥ*: Literally, "with razors, half-moons, excellent barbed ones, and crescent-headed arrows." We share Cg's view that this is a list of four different types of arrows. Cg defines the types as follows: *kṣuras* are those in the form of a barber's cutting tool (i.e., razor) (*nāpitaśastrākāraiḥ*); *ardhacandras* are those whose heads are in the form of the half-moon (*ardhacandrākāramukhaiḥ*); *karṇis* are barbed—literally, "eared"—arrows (*karṇiśaraiḥ*); and *bhallas* are double-edged (*ubhayapārśvadhāraiḥ*) arrows. Raghunathan (1982, vol. 3, p. 151), however, understands that only two types of weapons are described here. He renders, "with razor-sharp half-moon *karnis* and double-edged darts."

"calmly" *na cukṣubhe ca*: Literally, "and he did not tremble." Ct and Ck understand that Lakṣmaṇa did not move from his position (*na svasthānataś cacāla*). Cg says that his heart did not become disturbed (*na kaluṣitahṛdayo 'bhūt*).

"Rāvaṇa's arrows" *śarān*: Literally, "arrows."

Following verse 96, D5–7,9–11,S, and the texts and printed editions of the southern commentators and Gorresio's edition insert a passage of four lines in the *upajāti* meter [989*]: "Seeing his volleys of arrows rendered ineffectual, one after another, the king of the foes of the thirty gods was astonished at Lakṣmaṇa's dexterity. Once more he loosed sharp arrows."

97. "Then, swiftly" *cāśu*: D1,3,7,10,11,T2, and the texts and printed editions of Ct and Cr read instead *cāpi*, "and then."

"sharp-tipped arrows" *śarāñ śitāgrān*: D9,11, and the printed editions of Ct (including Gita Press) read instead *śitāñ śitāgrān*, "sharp with sharp tips." Translators who follow this reading must add a word such as "arrows, shaft."

"whose impact was equal to that of great Indra's *vajra* or the thunderbolt" *mahendravajrāśanitulyavegān*: V3,D9–11, and the printed editions of Ct read instead *mahendratulyo 'śanibhīmavegān*, "[Lakṣmaṇa], who was the equal of great Indra, [fitting arrows], whose impact was as dreadful as that of the thunderbolt." This variant avoids the seeming redundancy of the critical edition's juxtaposition of *vajra* and *aśani*, which are often synonymous. Cf. verse 128 below.

98. "Then, when he had done so" *chittvā ca tān*: Literally, "and having cut them [to pieces]." D9–11 and the texts and printed editions of Ct read instead *śitāñ śarān*, which then construes with *tān praciccheda* of *pāda* a to read, "he cut those sharp arrows to pieces."

"self-existent Brahmā" *svayambhu-*: Literally, "self-existant one."

99. "slackened his grip on his bow" *cāpaṃ śithilaṃ pragṛhya*: Literally, "loosely grasping his bow." We follow the commentators in reading *śithilam* adverbially. One could also take the term adjectivally with *cāpam*, "bow," yielding the sense "grasping his slackened bow." Among the translators, only Raghunathan (1982, vol. 3, p. 151) so renders the term.

"Indra, lord of the thirty gods" *tridaśendra-*: Literally, "the lord of the thirty."

101. "his limbs bathed in sweat" *svedārdragātraḥ*: Ś1,V2,3,D5–7,9–11,T1,2,G,M, and the texts and printed editions of all southern commentators read instead *medārdragātraḥ*, "his limbs moist with fat." The commentators note the irregularity of this form, understanding either that the *sandhi* is irregular (Ct, Ck, Cm) or that the use of the "*a*" stem ending for *medaḥ* is irregular (Cg).

"the immensely powerful . . . seized a javelin" *jagrāha śaktiṃ samudagraśaktiḥ*: The poet plays on the echoing sounds of *śaktim*, "javelin," and *-śaktiḥ*, "power." Ct and Ck understand that Rāvaṇa, facing death, takes up Brahmā's infallible javelin as he sees no other means of saving his life (*atha rāvaṇaḥ prāṇāntāpadaṃ prāptaḥ prakārāntareṇa jīvananirvāham asaṃbhāvya brahmadattām amoghāṃ śaktiṃ jagrāha*).

D7,10,11, and the texts and printed editions of Ct and Cr read *svayam ugraśaktiḥ*, "himself of fierce power," for *samudagraśaktiḥ*, "the immensely powerful one." Translators who follow the text of Ct have either placed the awkward "himself" where they deem it appropriate or have ignored it completely.

"in that battle . . . he had been given by self-existent Brahmā" *svayaṃbhudattāṃ yudhi*: Literally, "in battle . . . [a javelin] given by the self-existent [one]." Some translators construe "in battle (*yudhi*)" with the phrase "given by self-existent Brahmā."

102. "the monkey armies" *vānaravāhinīnām*: Only a few manuscripts (M1–4) read with the critical edition. The textually strongest reading, shared by Ś,B4,D1–6,8,9,

12,13,T,G1,M5, is *vānararākṣasānām*, "[terrifying] the monkeys and the *rākṣasas*." V3,D7,10,11, and the texts and printed editions of Ct and Cr read instead *saṃyati vānarāṇām*, "[terrifying] the monkeys in the battle."

"a smokeless fire" *vidhūmānala-*: Ś,V3,B4,D1,3,5–13,T,G,M1,2,5, and the texts and printed editions of Ct, Ck, and Cr read instead *sadhūmānala-*, "a smoky fire."

103. "Nonetheless" *tathāpi*: Ct and Ck note that [despite being struck by Lakṣmaṇa's arrows] the javelin hits its mark, since, having been infused with the power of Brahmā, it is infallible (*brāhmatvenāmoghatvāt*).

"the younger brother of Bharata . . . with divinely charged weapons" *bharatānujo 'straiḥ*: M3 and the printed editions of Cg read instead *bharatānujograiḥ*. Although the printed editions and printed apparatus fail to show an *avagraha* between *bharatānujo* and [*a*]*graiḥ*, we believe that the only plausible way to make sense of this variant is to understand it as *bharatānujo 'graiḥ*, taking the adjective *agraiḥ* in the sense of "excellent" to modify *bāṇaiḥ*, "arrows," in *pāda* b. Raghunathan (1982, vol. 3, p. 152), the only translator to render this reading, translates, "with arrows fierce as [the fire into which oblations have been made]," thus apparently reading the adjective as *ugra*, "fierce." Such a reading, however, would leave *bharatānuja* in the vocative, which would be entirely inappropriate contextually.

"blazed like sacrificial fires" *hutāgnikalpaiḥ*: Literally, "with [arrows] resembling sacrificial fires." The image derives its force from the fact that the sacrificial fires blaze up brightly when the oblations of ghee, etc., are offered into them.

Following verse 103, D5–7,9–11,S, and all printed editions of the southern commentators insert a passage of four lines in the *upajāti* meter [991*]: "Struck by that javelin, the powerful hero of the Raghus lay burning on the ground. The king swiftly approached him as he lay dazed and seized him with both arms."

104. D5–7,10,11,T,G (G3 after 992*),M, and all printed editions consulted of the southern recension read 6.47.106 before this verse. In this version, Rāvaṇa first attempts and fails to lift Lakṣmaṇa before Lakṣmaṇa calls to mind his Vaiṣṇava nature. Since, according to the principles laid out by the critical editors (Bhatt 1960, p. xxxiv, no. 2), preference should be given to the southern reading, one might question the choice of the northern order here.

"recalled that he himself was an inconceivable portion of Viṣṇu" *viṣṇor acintyaṃ svaṃ bhāgam ātmānaṃ pratyanusmarat*: Literally, "he remembered his own self [as] an unthinkable portion of Viṣṇu." See verse 115 below. The commentators, naturally enough, are deeply concerned about the theological significance of this passage and its implications for the epic's conception of the *avatāra* as, of necessity, not fully cognizant of his own divinity. One must keep in mind here that, in the text of the southern commentators, this verse follows 6.47.106 of the critical edition in which Rāvaṇa is represented as incapable of lifting Lakṣmaṇa's body. Thus, the commentators see the present verse as providing an explanation for Lakṣmaṇa's sudden increase in weight.

The interpretations of the commentators fall into four basic categories. Cv and Cm understand that Lakṣmaṇa is recalling not that he himself is a fragment of Viṣṇu but rather is recalling Lord Viṣṇu himself, who is the root cause of all. For otherwise, they argue [i.e., if Lakṣmaṇa were to remember that he himself is a fragment of Viṣṇu], that would nullify his conception of himself as mere man, which is necessary in order to accomplish the *avatāra*'s purpose, namely, the destruction of Rāvaṇa. Cs takes the same position, understanding *ātman* to refer to the entire root or source [of the universe] (*ātmānaṃ mūlarūpam*). He further argues that, "because of the sufficiency of self-recollection alone for the purpose [of the *avatāra*], one should ignore other interpretations, which have no textual basis (*iti svasmaraṇamātrasyeyatkāryaparyāptatvād itaravyākhyānam amūlatvād upekṣyam*)." In support of this position, Cs cites a verse to the effect that Lakṣmaṇa recalled his own inherent form (*sasmāra rūpaṃ nijam eva lakṣmaṇaḥ*).

Ct and Ck argue essentially that Lakṣmaṇa is recalling that he is a portion of Brahmā in order to save himself from being destroyed by Brahmā's javelin with which he has been struck. This, they argue, illustrates the maxim that one does not injure one's own (*na hi svīyaṃ svaṃ hinasti*). Ck illustrates this by pointing out that the sage Vasiṣṭha, who is himself grounded [as a son] in Brahmā, is not harmed by Brahmā's divinely charged weapon when it is wielded by his arch rival, Viśvāmitra (see 1.55.14–15). Ck further asserts that Lakṣmaṇa's identity with Brahmā can be determined both from his having been rescued by Garuḍa (*Yuddhakāṇḍa* 40) and his having been honored by Agastya and other great *ṛṣis* (*Araṇyakāṇḍa* 11–12). (One must recall here that Ck appears to be a special devotee of Brahmā and elsewhere upholds the supremacy of this divinity over even that of Viṣṇu. See note to 5.1.177.) Ct and Ck, cognizant of the issue of whether the *avatāras* in this epic can know of their divinity, add that Lakṣmaṇa recognizes himself as a portion of the lord's divine energy only momentarily for the purpose of saving himself from destruction by Brahmā's javelin. Ct extends this argument by stating that, in order to maintain the belief of others in the humanity he has adopted in the manner of an actor, Lakṣmaṇa does not sustain the conception of himself as divine at all times. See note below to verse 113.

Cr's position is similar to that of Cv and Cm, in that he understands *ātmānam*, "self," to refer to the controller of the entire universe, that is, Rāma (*sarvaniyantāraṃ rāmam*). He then argues that it is the very recollection of Rāma that brings about the increase in weight that makes it impossible for Rāvaṇa to lift Lakṣmaṇa.

Cg refutes each of these positions, arguing that there is no perceptible logical or causal connection between calling anyone to mind and an increase in bodily weight. He further argues that Lakṣmaṇa cannot be calling Viṣṇu to mind as he himself is essentially the inherent form of Viṣṇu. He also dismisses the argument concerning the necessity of the *avatāra*'s regarding himself as a human, as this has no significant bearing on the question of Lakṣmaṇa's weight. Cg concludes his remarks by stressing the term *acintyam*, "inconceivable," indicating that the mysterious nature of what is transpiring here is beyond rational explanation.

For a discussion of the terms of Rāvaṇa's boon, which require Rāma and Lakṣmaṇa to be, in effect, generally ignorant of their own divinity, see Pollock (1991, pp. 33–43). Pagani (1999, p. 1664) remarks in a note to this passage that, because of the restrictions on Rāma's knowledge of his divine nature, this partial revelation affects only Lakṣmaṇa. See notes to 6.26.31 and 6.28.28–29.

105. "although he grasped" *pīḍayitvā*: Literally, "having pressed *or* crushed."

"unable to budge him" *aprabhur laṅghane 'bhavat*: Literally, "he was not powerful [enough] to jump over *or* get the better of [him]." The term *laṅghana*, normally "leaping *or* passing over," is an odd term in this context, and the commentators differ somewhat as to how to interpret it. We follow Ck and Ct, who gloss, "moving (*cālane*)," noting that Rāvaṇa was unable to budge Lakṣmaṇa, much less lift him (*laṅghane cālane 'pi na prabhur abhavan na samartho 'bhavat kiṃ punar uddharaṇa iti bhāvaḥ*—so Ct). Cr takes the term in its sense of "assaulting, capturing," glossing, "defeating (*parābhave*)." Cv glosses, "weighing (*tolane*)," while Cg understands, "lifting (*uddharaṇe*)." Cm offers, optionally, "lifting (*uddharaṇe*)" or "weighing (*tolane*)."

Cg takes this opportunity to continue his theological discussion, arguing that it is precisely because Lakṣmaṇa is essentially a portion of Viṣṇu that he cannot be lifted. Cg also raises and refutes an objection that would argue against the whole concept that Viṣṇu could possess portions, since the essential nature of Viṣṇu is unitary and has no parts. Cg acknowledges the truth of this proposition but argues that the indivisible quality of the Lord refers only to his essential nature and not, as here, to the varying manifestations of his qualities. (*svarūpeṇa nāṃśatvam ucyate. kiṃtu guṇāvirbhāvatāratamyāt.*)

Cg concludes by remarking that Lakṣmaṇa's human form consists in his having a similar appearance to a human. The issue of the unbearable weight of the divinity resurfaces elsewhere in the Vaiṣṇava literature. Compare *BhāgP* 10.7.26–27, where the child Kṛṣṇa allows himself to be picked up by the whirlwind demon Tṛṇāvarta only to reassume his natural or divine weight to drag the demon down to destruction. See, too, Bhāsa's *Bālacaritam* 1.11. Cf. *MBh* 3.147.15–20.59, where Bhīma is unable to lift Hanumān's tail.

106. "With his two arms" *bhujābhyām*: Cg argues that, by using the dual, the poet, whom he views in any case as mocking Rāvaṇa in this verse, is showing that, although the *rākṣasa* lord could lift the Himalayas, etc., with merely two of his arms, he is unable to budge Lakṣmaṇa, even with all twenty. (*bhujābhyām ity anena himavadādayo dvābhyām evoddhartuṃ śakyam. ayaṃ tu viṃśatibhujair api na śakyata iti sūcyate.*) Cs takes the dual to refer to Rāvaṇa's two sets of ten arms (one on each side). For, Cs argues, if we were to take this simply as a reference to two arms, it would raise the question of why Rāvaṇa, having failed with two, did not use all his arms. (*bhujābhyām ekaikapārśvavṛttidaśakaikatvavivakṣayā bhujābhyām iti uktiḥ. anyathā dvābhyām uddharaṇāśaktas tanuyād eva samagrair bhujair yatnam iti te 'pi vaktavyā bhaveyuḥ.*) On Rāvaṇa's variable number of heads [and arms], see 6.50.11; 6.90.31; 6.92.20; 6.96.20; and notes. See, too, 5.8.13,19; 5.20.24,26; 5.47.2–14; and notes.

"the Himalayas, Mount Mandara, Mount Meru, or even the three worlds along with the immortal gods" *himavān mandaro merus trailokyaṃ vā sahāmaraiḥ*: Only Cg among the commentators feels impelled to specify the significance of each of the mountains mentioned and to document their mobility. Thus, he notes that the Himalaya is the universal standard for steadfastness, citing 1.1.16, where Rāma himself is said to be as unyielding as the Himalayas. Still, he notes that a part of the Himalayan chain, i.e., Mount Kailāsa, was once moved [by Rāvaṇa] (see *Uttarakāṇḍa* 16). Mount Mandara, Cg continues, which was capable of agitating even the incomparably deep ocean of milk, foremost among all oceans, was worn out (*jarjharitatvāt*?) at the time of the churning for the nectar of immortality by the ageless gods, whom he himself [Rāvaṇa] had vanquished (see 1.44.14–17 and notes). As for Meru, the crest-jewel in the circlet of the world's principal mountains, its peak was once hurled into the depths of the ocean off Laṅkā by Vāyu. As for the three worlds themselves, they, too, have had their ups and downs, since they were plunged into the depths of the sea by the demon Hiraṇyākṣa (*BhāgP* 3.17–18; *ŚivaP* [*Rudrasaṃhitā*] 5.42). See 6.18.32–34; 6.48.50; and notes.

"in that battle" *saṃkhye*: Cg believes that this term is included here as a reference to the fact that hostile or evil-hearted creatures, like Rāvaṇa, are unable to lift Lakṣmaṇa, while friendly or devoted ones, like Hanumān (as he is described in verse 112), are able to do so. Thus, he understands that the body of Lakṣmaṇa, when fallen in battle, is heavier than even the Himalayas, etc. (*ripūṇām aprakampyo 'pīty anuvādāt saparikareṇāpi rāvaṇena na śakyam ity api siddham. kathaṃ tarhi hanumatoddhṛta ity atrāha saṃkhya iti. durhṛdayair noddhartuṃ śakya ity arthaḥ. ata eva vakṣyati vāyusūnoḥ suhṛtveneti. anena himavadādibhyo 'pi saṃkhye patitasya lakṣmaṇaśarīrasya garīyastoktā.*)

107. This verse, both in its construction and location, is highly suspect from a text-critical standpoint. According to the critical apparatus, only three manuscripts collated (G1,M4,5) exhibit line cd (When Rāvaṇa saw that Lakṣmaṇa . . . was unconscious, he was astonished [*visaṃjñaṃ lakṣmaṇaṃ dṛṣṭvā rāvaṇo vismito 'bhavat*]). On this basis alone *pādas* cd should have been relegated to the apparatus. A majority of southern manuscripts (D5,7,T,G2,3,M1–3) and several printed editions (KK and VSP) read *pādas* ab following 105, whereas most northern manuscripts (Ñ,V1,2,B1–3) and printed editions (Gorresio and Lahore) read this line (*pādas* ab) or its variant after 105ab. In either case, the half verse would extend the list of adjectives attributed to Lakṣmaṇa as he is being grasped in Rāvaṇa's arms. The translation would yield, "Then grasping Saumitri, humbler of the *dānavas'* pride, who was a portion of Viṣṇu in a human body . . ." The verse is omitted entirely from D6,10,11, and the printed editions of Ct. Because of its textual distribution, the line is rendered in translation only in Gorresio (1856, vol. 9, p. 319) and Raghunathan (1982, vol. 3, p. 152). The critical reading lends itself to an anomalous and improbable scenario in which Rāvaṇa, seeing Lakṣmaṇa unconscious, recognizes him as a portion of Viṣṇu. Even so, the textual evidence once again strongly supports the identification of Lakṣmaṇa and, by extension, Rāma as *avatāras* of Viṣṇu. See verse 104 above.

108. "enraged . . . In his rage" *kruddhaḥ . . . kruddhaḥ*: Ct and Ck note that Hanumān is enraged by the suffering of Lakṣmaṇa (*saumitrikleśanāt kruddhaḥ*). Among the commentators, only Cs remarks on the redundancy, claiming that Hanumān, although angry from his earlier encounter, now becomes exceedingly angry because of the [attempt] to carry off Lakṣmaṇa. (*tataḥ kruddho lakṣmaṇākarṣaṇato 'tikruddhaḥ. kruddhaḥ pūrvam ārabhya kopī.*)

109. "on the floor of his chariot" *bhūmau*: Literally, "on the ground, earth." We follow the suggestion of Cg, who glosses, "on the surface *or* floor of the chariot (*rathabhūmau*)," taking *bhūmi* in its sense of "floor [of a building]." Ct and Ck offer, "the surface that has the form of the back portion of the chariot (*rathapṛṣṭharūpāyāṃ bhūmau*)." We do so against the reading of several of the translators, who understand Rāvaṇa to have been knocked to the ground (Gorresio 1856, vol. 9, p. 319; Dutt 1893, p. 1284; and Roussel 1903, vol. 3, p. 178), because the following text offers no evidence that Rāvaṇa has ever left his vehicle (see verse 118 below). Other translators understand that Rāvaṇa falls *or* falls down, but they do not specify where (Shastri 1959, vol. 3, p. 153; Raghunathan 1982, vol. 3, p. 152; and Pagani 1999, pp. 1012–13). Only Gita Press (1969, vol. 3, p. 1585) translates as we do.

"swayed for a moment and collapsed" *cacāla ca papāta*: Literally, "he moved and fell."

Following verse 109, D5–7,9–11,S insert a passage of three lines [1001*]: "He hemorrhaged blood copiously[1] from his mouths, his eyes, and his ears. After rolling about, he sank down, motionless, on the floor of his chariot. Dazed and half-conscious, he was unable to stand up."

[1]"He hemorrhaged blood copiously" *vavāma rudhiraṃ bahu*: D10,11, and the printed editions of Ct read instead *papāta rudhiraṃ bahu*, "much blood fell [from his mouths] *or* blood fell copiously [from his mouths]."

110. "together with Vāsava" *savāsavāḥ*: Ś,Ñ1,B1,4,D1–4,6,8,10–13,T2,3,G1,3, M1,2,5, and the texts and printed editions of Ct, Ck, and Cr read instead *ca sāsurāḥ*, "and along with the *asuras*." Ct, Ck, and Cm, who notes this as a variant reading, explain that, by harassing the *asuras*, Rāvaṇa has aroused their enmity, just as he has that of the gods (*rāvaṇasya devavad asureṣv api kleśakaratvena teṣām api vairitvāt*).

"cheered" *neduḥ*: Literally, "they roared, shouted." We follow Cg, who adds the words "with joy (*harṣeṇa*)." Ct, Ck, and Cm similarly indicate that the seers, etc., cry out with satisfaction or delight (*saṃtoṣāt*). Cr has them crying out, "Excellent! Excellent!" See verse 64 and note above.

111. "to Rāghava" *rāghavābhyāśam*: Literally, "to the vicinity of Rāghava."

112. "on account of the affection and supreme devotion" *suhṛttvena bhaktyā paramayā ca*: Ct understands *suhṛttva* to refer to Hanumān's companionship with Lakṣmaṇa (*sakhitvena*). Ck extends this definition by referring to the similar companionship of Garuḍa (*garuḍavatsusakhitvena*). See 6.40.46 and note. Cg takes the term in its literal sense of "good-heartedness (*śobhanahṛdayatvam*)," which he takes here to mean a sympathetic or compassionate nature. Cg further insists that this tender or loving nature is all one really needs to exhibit to the Lord and that the particle *ca* here is used in the sense of *anvācaye*, that is, to indicate that *bhakti*, or devotion, is merely a secondary quality in this context. Cs understands the affection, which he glosses as "disinterested assistance (*animittopakartṛtva*)," to be Hanumān's. But he understands the devotion to have Hanumān as its object (*hanumadviṣayiṇyā paramayā bhaktyā ca*).

"Lakṣmaṇa became light" *laghutvam agamat*: Literally, "he went to lightness." According to Ck and Ct, this verse expresses the easy access devotees have to the Lord and his incarnations as a result of the innate nature [of the divine] (*svabhāvasiddham eva*—so Ck). Therefore, this access is not produced by Lakṣmaṇa (*nedaṃ lakṣmaṇena kṛtam*). Ct adds that there is no obstacle to the acquisition of lightness or heaviness on the part of the Lord. On the contrary, Cg feels that Lakṣmaṇa's making himself light for Hanumān alone demonstrates that his lightness is intentional. (*hanumata ekasya laghutvam agamal laghutvam akarot. anena laghutvasya buddhipūrvakatvam uktam.*) Ct and Cm understand the thrust of this verse to be that the evidence of weakness (*aśaktiḥ*) and ignorance (*ajñānam*) on the part of Lakṣmaṇa in this passage is merely for the sake of maintaining his disguise as a mortal (*mūrcchitasyāpi saumitrer jñānaśaktipratipādanena tatra tatra rāmalakṣmaṇayor ajñānāśaktipratyāyakāni vacanāni mānuṣaveṣanirvahaṇa-parāṇīti mantavyāni*—so Cm). In support of this contention, both commentators cite *BhāgP* 5.19.5 in which it is stated that the Lord takes on human birth [as Rāma] not merely to kill a *rākṣasa* [Rāvaṇa] but to serve as an object of instruction for mankind. For, otherwise, why, when the Lord could be enjoying his own inherent nature, would he have subjected himself to the tribulations caused by Sītā. (*tatra śriśuko marttyāvatāras tv iha marttyaśikṣaṇaṃ rakṣovadhāyaiva na kevalaṃ vibhoḥ / kuto 'nyathā syū ramataḥ sva ātman[i—?]aḥ sītākṛtāni vyasanānīśvarasya //*—so Cm.)

"by his enemies" *śatrūṇām*: Cm and Ct understand the plural here to indicate that when Rāvaṇa attempted to lift Lakṣmaṇa, he had the assistance of his followers (*śatrūṇām iti bahuvacanena lakṣmaṇoddharaṇasamaye rāvaṇasyānucarais sahāyyaṃ kṛtam iti gamyate*).

113. "extracted itself" *samutsṛjya*: Literally, "having abandoned *or* been expelled." Ct and Cm think that this is accomplished because of [Lakṣmaṇa's] meditation on his own nature as Brahmā (*brahmatvena dhyānāt tatsamutsargaḥ*). See note to verse 104 above.

"unconquerable" *durjayam*: Cg understands that Lakṣmaṇa's invincibility is the reason for the javelin's departure (*tasya durjayasvarūpatvāc chaktis taṃ tyaktvā gatety bhāvaḥ*). This is reflected in the translation of Raghunathan (1982, vol. 3, p. 153). D9–11 and the texts and printed editions of Ct read instead *nirjitam*, "vanquished, defeated." Cr, disturbed at the thought that Lakṣmaṇa could actually be defeated, glosses, "nearly defeated (*nirjitaprāyam*)." Cf. note to 6.47.126 and Introduction, pp. 100–104.

114. Cg believes that verse 115 should precede this verse. This makes good narrative sense, in that verse 115 continues the discussion of Lakṣmaṇa's recovery upon the removal of Rāvaṇa's weapon, whereas the order of the verses in the critical edition breaks up that sequence with the reference to Rāvaṇa's action. (*etac chlokānantaram āśvasta iti ślokaḥ. tato rāvaṇo 'pīti ślokaḥ paṭhanīyaḥ.*) On the other hand, this order is found nowhere other than in the texts of Cg and Cm (D6,M3) and the printed editions of Cg (VSP 6.5.9.122–123; and KK 6.59.120–121). Raghunathan (1982, vol. 3, p. 153) is the only translator to follow this sequence of verses.

"regaining consciousness" *prāpya saṃjñām*: Cr understands the reference to be to a higher consciousness whose object is the great power of Lakṣmaṇa (*lakṣmaṇaprabhāvaviṣayakātibodham*).

115. "recalling that he himself was an inconceivable portion of Viṣṇu" *viṣṇor bhāgam amīmāṃsyam ātmānaṃ pratyanusmaran*: See verse 104 and notes above.

"freed of that dart" *viśalyaḥ*: We follow Cr, who glosses, "free of darts (*śalyarahitaḥ*)." Ct and Ck understand, "his every limb free from injury (*nīruksarvagātraḥ*—so Ct), while Cg renders, "the openings of his wounds healed over (*prarūḍhavraṇamukhaḥ*)."

"restored to health" *āśvastaḥ*: Ck and Ct gloss, "whose collectivity of senses was restored (*prāptāśvāsendriyagrāmaḥ*—so Ct)," while Cg understands, "having regained consciousness (*labdhasaṃjñaḥ*)."

116. "that the great heroes of that vast host of monkeys had been struck down" *nipātitamahāvīrāṃ vānarāṇāṃ mahācamūm*: Literally, "that great army of monkeys of which the heroes had been felled." M3 and the printed editions of Cg and Cm read *dravantīṃ vānarīṃ camūm*, "the monkey army fleeing," for *pāda* b, *vānarāṇāṃ mahācamūm*, "that great army of monkeys." This reading is rendered only in the translation of Raghunathan (1982, vol. 3, p. 153). Cg notes that the monkeys flee at the sight of Rāvaṇa fixing arrows to his bow (*rāvaṇasya bāṇasaṃdhānadarśanād iti bhāvaḥ*).

117. Following verse 117, D6,7,9–11,T2,3,G1,2,M3,5, (G3,M1,2 insert after 118cd), and the texts and printed editions of the southern commentators insert a passage of one line [1011*]: "Just as did Viṣṇu with concentration [mount the back of] mighty

Garutmān." D7,10,11, and the texts and printed editions of Ct, Ck, and Cr substitute for the second *pāda* of this insert *āruhyāmaravairiṇam*, which yields the sense "as did Viṣṇu upon Garutmān [to punish] the [demon] foe of the immortal gods."

118. "Hanumān, son of Vāyu" *vāyuputreṇa ... hanūmantam*: Literally, "[words uttered] by the son of Vāyu... [climbed up on] Hanumān." D5,7,T1,3,G2,3,M, and the texts and printed editions of Cg and Cm substitute the adjective *balavantam*, "mighty," for the proper noun. Only Raghunathan (1982, vol. 3, p. 153) renders this variant.

"that hero immediately climbed up" *arohat sahasā śūrah*: D9–11 and the texts and printed editions of Ct and Cr read instead *athāruroha sahasā*, "he suddenly climbed up." M3 and the texts and printed editions of Cg read *āruroha mahāśūraḥ*, "the great hero climbed up."

119. "Keeping him in sight" *tam ālokya*: Literally, "having seen him." The phrase is repetitive of *dadarśa*, "gazed upon," in the previous verse (118). Cg notes this and explains that the repetition serves to demonstrate that no interval of time has elapsed [between the actions of the two verses] (*tam ālokyety anuvādo 'vyavahitapūrvakāladyotanārthaḥ*).

"raced " *pradudrāva*: Literally, "he ran." Ct glosses, "he went quickly (*śīghram agamat*)," keeping in mind, no doubt, that Rāma is no longer running but is now riding on Hanumān.

"as did... Viṣṇu... Vairocana" *vairocanam iva ... viṣṇuḥ*: According to Cg, the reference is to the *asura* king Bali Vairocana. The patronymic is, however, somewhat ambiguous, as several of the successive *asura* kings are descendants of Virocana. Moreover, Bali is the one demon rival of the gods whom Viṣṇu does not physically attack, instead famously tricking him out of his sovereignty by adopting the *vāmanāvatāra*, or dwarf incarnation. Cg remarks that the example is chosen simply to indicate how determined or forceful Rāma's approach is (*sāgrahagamanamātre dṛṣṭāntaḥ*). See 6.40.43; 6.49.1–2; 6.53.25; 6.59.7; 6.105.24; and notes. See, too, 1.28.2 and note. Cf. 6.30.22 and note.

120. "with a sound like the crash of a thunderbolt" *vajraniṣpeṣanisvanam*: D4,7,9–11, and the texts and printed editions of Ct and Cr read instead *-niṣṭhuram* for *-nisvanam*, giving the sense "[he made a bowstring sound] as harsh as the crash of a thunderbolt."

121. "Stay where you are!" *tiṣṭha tiṣṭha*: Literally, "Stand! Stand!"

"such an injury" *vipriyam īdṛśam*: Cg understands that the injury in question is either the wounding of Lakṣmaṇa or the abduction of Sītā (*lakṣmaṇaprahārarūpaṃ sītāharaṇarūpaṃ vā*).

"where can you go to escape me" *kva nu ... gato mokṣam avāpsyasi*: Literally, "once gone, where will you obtain freedom?" We follow Cg, who supplies "from me (*mattaḥ*)."

122. "If you were to fly for refuge" *gamiṣyasi*: Literally, "you will go." We follow Ct and Ck, who understand, "you will take refuge with (*śaraṇaṃ gamiṣyasi*)."

"Agni Vaiśvānara" *-vaiśvānara-*: This is a common vedic epithet for Agni. Cr, however, takes it in a general sense, believing that it refers here to Viṣṇu (*atra vaiśvānaraśabdena viṣṇuḥ pūrvottarasāhacaryāt tathā hi sūtraṃ vaiśvānaraḥ sādhāraṇaśabdaviśeṣāt*).

"Śiva, bringer of auspiciousness" *-śaṃkaram*: Literally, "the maker of auspiciousness."

"even ... to the ten directions" *daśa vā diśo vā*: Literally, "or, to the ten directions, or." The ten directions are the four cardinal compass points, the four intermediate points, the zenith, and the nadir. The expression is a common one in the epics to indicate all directions or anywhere in the world. B3,4,D1–3,5,9–11,13,T1,G2,3,M1,2, and the texts and printed editions of Ct and Cr read *daśadhā*, "tenfold," in place of *daśa vā*. Ct and Ck read the adverb with the directions in the sense of the tenfold directions. Cr, as an alternative, breaks the *sandhi* between *daśadhā* and *diśaḥ* to read *daśadhā* + *ādiśaḥ*. He then understands, "through the splitting up of your heads, you, in ten forms, will proceed to the directions (*ādiśaḥ*), that is, to Indra, etc., who are the indicators of the directions (*kiṃca daśadhā śirobhedena daśaprakāras tvam ādiśa upadeśakartṝn indrādīn gamīn gamiṣyasi*). Among the translators consulted, only Dutt (1893, p. 1285) follows this reading, rendering, "or go to the ten cardinal points in ten portions."

"still no matter where you might go, you would not escape me now" *tathāpi me nādya gato vimokṣyase*: Literally, "even so, gone, you will not escape me this day." Cr, however, reads the phrase differently, glossing, "even so, having gone to me, that is, having come within my sight, you will not escape from me, that is, from my arrows (*tathāpi me gato maddṛṣṭipathaṃ prāptas tvaṃ me madbāṇān na vimokṣyase*)." Among the translators consulted, only Raghunathan (1982, vol. 3, p. 153) interprets similarly, rendering, "having come under my eye to-day." For a similar idea, see 6.67.41, where Rāma makes a comparable statement regarding Indrajit.

Pāda d is hypermetric.

123. "will soon return" *sahasābhyupetaḥ*: Literally, "he has suddenly drawn near." We follow the interpretation of Cg, who takes the phrase to mean "having nearly arrived (*abhyupāgataḥ prāyaḥ*)," which he claims should be understood to mean "he will soon come (*acirād āgamiṣyatīty arthaḥ*)." Cg, as an alternative, offers the interesting interpretation that Rāma here makes no distinction between Lakṣmaṇa and himself (*abhedenocyate*). According to this interpretation, Rāma is saying, "He whom you struck with your javelin was, in fact, I, who have now come. So do not feel so proud, thinking, 'I have struck down Lakṣmaṇa.' (*yaḥ śaktyābhihataḥ sa evāham āgatavān asmi. lakṣmaṇaṃ prāharam iti mā gā garvam iti bhāvaḥ*.)" This reading is in keeping with the notion that both brothers are portions of the same divine personality, and it reflects the poet's description of Lakṣmaṇa "as a second life breath outside Rāma's body" (1.17.17 and 3.32.12). See notes to 6.19.24; 6.40.46; and 6.89.6 (2026*).

D5,9–11,T1,3, and the texts and printed editions of Ct and Cr read instead the gerund *abhyupetya*, which Ct glosses as "having vowed (*pratijñāya*)." He then supplies the vow: "I myself, in order to alleviate this pain, will be the death of you, along with your sons and grandsons (wives—Ck), in battle (*sa eṣo 'haṃ tadduḥkhaśāntaye saputrapautrasya te saṃkhye mṛtyur bhaviṣyāmīti śeṣaḥ*)." Ck also quotes this vow. Ck and Ct then read the adverb *sahasā* with *viṣādam* (*gataḥ*), "having suddenly collapsed."

"in his desire to cause you sorrow" *icchan viṣādam*: Literally, "desiring dejection." D7,9–11,T3,G,M1,2,5, and the texts and printed editions of Ct, Ck, and Cr read *gacchan*, "going," for *icchan*, "desiring." This gives an entirely different sense to the *pāda*. In this reading, rather than wishing to bring about the sorrow or despondency of Rāvaṇa, it is Lakṣmaṇa himself who has "gone to despondency," i.e., been knocked temporarily out of combat. This variant is rendered as "swooning, stupefied," etc., in those translations that follow the text of Ct. Ck and Ct read the participle *gacchan* with the word *yuddham*, "battle," which they supply, and then add the participle *gataḥ*, "gone," to construe with *viṣādam*. Thus, they understand, "Lakṣmaṇa, who was going to battle, was reduced to a state of weakness *or* collapse."

"he whom . . . he" *yaś caiṣaḥ . . . sa eṣaḥ*: Literally, "he, who . . . he, this one." Cs sees the pronouns as having three different referents: Lakṣmaṇa, the abduction of Sītā, and the collapse of Lakṣmaṇa. All of these, he argues, will bring about Rāvaṇa's death. (*eṣa lakṣmaṇaḥ. saḥ sītāpahāraḥ. eṣa lakṣmaṇaviṣādaḥ. he rakṣogaṇarāja saputrapautrasya tavādya mṛtyur bhaviṣyati.*)

"to your sons and wives as well" *saputradārasya tava*: Literally, "of you, along with sons and wives." D5,10,11,G2, and the texts and printed editions of Ct and Cr read *-pautrasya* for *-dārasya*, yielding the sense "to your sons and grandsons as well."

Following verse 123, D5–7,9–11,S insert a passage of four lines [1015*]: "And with my arrows, I[1] slaughtered fourteen thousand well-armed and extraordinary-looking *rākṣasas*, who had made their home in Janasthāna."

[1]"I" *etena*: Literally, "by this one." We follow the commentators in taking this as an example of the usage such as, *eṣo 'ham*, "he, that is I," or *ayaṃ janaḥ*, "this person," for the first person. Cg, however, offers two additional alternatives. According to one, the pronoun refers to death (*mṛtyuḥ*), mentioned in the closing *pāda* of the preceding verse, while, according to the second, the reference is to Lakṣmaṇa, between whom and himself Rāma makes no distinction as noted above.

124. "the great monkey" *mahākapim*: D9–11,G3, and the texts and printed editions of Ct and Cr read instead the nominative epithet *mahābalaḥ*, "mighty," which would then refer to Rāvaṇa.

"with sharp arrows" *śarais tīkṣṇaiḥ*: Ś1,B1,D9–11, and the texts and printed editions of Ct read *dīptaiḥ*, "blazing," for *tīkṣṇaiḥ*, "sharp."

Following 124ab, D5–7,9–11,S, and Gorresio's edition insert a passage of one line [1016*, line 1]: "[Rāvaṇa struck] the immensely powerful[1] son of Vāyu, who was carrying Rāghava into battle."

[1]"the immensely powerful" *mahāvīryam*: D9–11 and the texts and printed editions of Ct read instead *mahāvegam*, "very swift *or* very powerful."

D6,7,10,11, and the texts and printed editions of Ct and Cr, as well as Gorresio's edition, insert one additional line [1016*, line 2]: "Filled with tremendous rage and remembering their earlier enmity, [Rāvaṇa struck]." Printed editions of Cg include this line in brackets following line 1016*, line 1 (= VSP 6.59.135cd; KK 6.59.132cd).

125. "since he was endowed with innate blazing energy" *svabhāvatejoyuktasya*: As Cg notes, we must read the noun *svabhāva-*, "inherent nature," adjectivally as *svābhāvika-*, "innate, inherent." Cr also takes *svabhāva-* adjectivally but glosses it as "protected by the innate blazing energy of Rāma (*svābhāvikarāmatejasābhirakṣitasya*)." Cs feels that this term suggests the popular notion that Hanumān derives his energy from the boons [he received from the gods] (4.65.25 and note; *Uttarakāṇḍa* 36). Ct and Ck gloss *tejaḥ*, "blazing energy," as "valor (*śauryam*)."

"in battle" *āhave*: D9,10, and the texts and printed editions of Ct and Cr read instead the awkward *āhate*. This reading, which is rendered by only a few of the translators who follow the text of Ct (Roussel 1903, vol. 3, p. 179; Shastri 1959, vol. 3,

p. 154; and Dutt 1893, p. 1286), is best taken as part of a defective locative absolute construction, "when he was struck by the *rākṣasa*."

126. "wounded" *kṛtavraṇam*: Literally, "him on whom a wound was inflicted." Cr apparently dislikes the idea that Hanumān has actually been wounded. He understands the compound to mean "upon whom an attempt was made to inflict a wound (*vraṇāya kṛtaḥ prayatno yasmiṃs tam*)." Cr undoubtedly is thinking of the boons of invulnerability, etc., that Hanumān received from the gods and of his consequent characterization in Indian tradition as *vajrāṅga*, "he of adamantine body." See notes to verse 125 above. Cf. note to verse 113 above. See, too, Introduction, pp. 63–64; and Goldman and Goldman 1996, p. 55.

"was overwhelmed with rage" *krodhasya vaśam eyivān*: Literally, "he went to the power of anger." Here, as elsewhere, Cr appears to stress the *līlā*, or "play," interpretation of the *avatāra*'s actions, reading the phrase to mean that Rāma merely takes on the appearance of someone who is angry (*ācārakvibantaprakṛtikakartṛkvibantaḥ kiṃca krodhasya krodhavato vaśaṃ kāntiṃ eyivān kopavatsadṛśakāntimān abhavad ity arthaḥ*). Cf. 6.35.19 and note on the similar use of the *kvibanta*.

127. "Advancing toward" *abhisaṃkramya*: The texts and printed editions of Cg (D6,M3) read instead *abhicaṅkramya*, the gerund of the intensive stem of *abhi* √*kram*. Cg glosses it as "approaching repeatedly (*paunaḥ punyena samīpaṃ gatvā*)." This reading is rendered only by Raghunathan (1982, vol. 3, p. 154), who translates, "with repeated attacks."

"Rāvaṇa's chariot" *tasya ... ratham*: Literally, "his chariot."

"well-fletched arrows" *śaraiḥ supuṅkhaiḥ*: D9–11 and the texts and printed editions of Ct read instead *śitaiḥ śarāgraiḥ*, "with sharp arrowheads." Cf. notes to 6.35.12.

"missiles" *-aśani-*: This term, which is commonly used in the epic to denote the thunderbolt or the thunderboltlike weapon of Indra, must be taken here in the generic sense of weapons that are hurled. Pagani (1999, p. 1664), who translates "*foudre,*" in a note on this word says that it refers not to Indra's thunderbolt but to a huge bludgeon that is used as a weapon by certain superhuman characters in the epic. She offers no lexical, textual, or other source in support of this identification, however. Gita Press (1969, vol. 3, p. 1587) takes the term to mean a specific type of missile, "the Aśani". Dutt (1893, p. 1286) understands the term in its primary sense, "thunderbolt." Other translators render it as we do. See note to verse 128 below. See, too, note to 6.55.43.

128. "that resembled Indra's *vajra* or a thunderbolt" *vajrāśanisaṃnibhena*: Literally, "like the *vajra* or the lightning bolt." The terms *vajra* and *aśani* are often synonymous in the sense of "thunderbolt *or* bolt of lightning." Here we take the former to refer to the legendary weapon peculiar to the god Indra. See note to verse 127 above. Cf. verse 97 above. See, too, note to 6.55.43.

"Lord" *bhagavān*: This term is frequently used to describe divinities and great spiritual adepts. Here Cg, citing *Amarakośa* 3.2.26, in which *vīryam*, "strength, heroism," is listed as a synonym of *bhaga*, glosses, "mighty (*vīryavān*)."

"just as ... Indra himself might strike Mount Meru with his *vajra*" *vajreṇa merum ... ivendraḥ*: Cf. 5.1.108–110, where Indra is said to have cut off the wings of the mountains with his *vajra*.

129. "That ... king" *rājā*: Cg believes that the term in this context signifies that Rāvaṇa's royal majesty was undiminished [at the time of being struck by Indra's thunderbolt] (*anyūnarājabhāvaś ca sthitaḥ*).

"the blows of Indra's *vajra* or of thunderbolts" *vajrapātāśanisaṃnipātāt*: Literally, "from the falling of the *vajra* and the fall of the thunderbolt." Ct, Cr, and Ck read the compound as *samāhāradvandva*, or collective dual with a singular ending, meaning "the fall of the *vajra* and the strike of a thunderbolt." Cg understands the compound as a *madhyamapadalopī* compound for which the missing term would be *-yukta-*, i.e., *vajrapātayuktāśanisaṃnipātāt*. This gives the sense of "a lightning strike linked to a blow from the *vajra*."

"dropped his bow" *cāpaṃ ca mumoca*: Cg thinks that Rāvaṇa, even though he is a heroic warrior (*vīraḥ*), drops his bow of his own accord in order to demonstrate that Rāma alone affords protection (*vīro 'pi cāpaṃ mumoca svasya svarakṣyatvāt svayaṃ tyaktavān rāmaikarakṣyatvadyotanāya*).

130. "magnanimous" *mahātmā*: We normally render this as "great." We believe, however, that the context, in which Rāma, seeing that his enemy is incapacitated, refrains from killing him, justifies Cg's gloss: "*mahātmā* means great-minded, that is, compassionate (*mahātmā mahāmanā dayālur ity arthaḥ*)."

"cut off his crown" *kirīṭaṃ ciccheda*: Cg suggests that this was done to humble Rāvaṇa's pride (*mānabhaṅgam akarod ity arthaḥ*).

"which shone like the sun" *arkavarṇam*: Literally, "having the color *or* appearance of the sun."

131. "with the top of his crown severed" *kṛttakirīṭakūṭam*: The commentators understand *-kūṭa* in another of its many senses, viz., "mass (*samūham*)." The idea is that Rāvaṇa, with his ten heads, would have worn multiple crowns.

"resembled a serpent robbed of its venom" *nirviṣāśīviṣasaṃnikāśam*: Cg notes that the simile refers to Rāvaṇa's having lost his bow (verse 129 above) (*taṃ tyaktacāpam ata eva nirviṣāśīviṣasaṃnikāśam*).

132. Cg believes that this verse and the one preceding it express the idea that when it comes to obtaining the Lord's protection, one must cease one's own efforts (*ābhyāṃ ślokābhyāṃ bhagavadrakṣaṇe nimittaṃ svayatnanivṛttir evety uktam*). This idea represents the Tengali school of Śrīvaiṣṇavism, which preaches the total self-surrender (*prapatti*) of the devotee to the Lord. This is sometimes called,"the Cat Doctrine (*mārjāravāda*)." Cs understands that Rāma is suggesting to Rāvaṇa that, by cutting off his crown, the latter should understand that he, Rāma, is quite capable of cutting off his head (*kirīṭatroṭanena tvayāpi [tavāpi?] śiraḥkartanasāmārthyaṃ mamāstīti jñātam eveti bhāvaḥ*).

"You have ... struck down my heroic warriors" *hatapravīraś ca kṛtas tvayāham*: Literally, "By you ... I have been rendered one whose heroes are slain *or* struck down." Cs offers, as an alternative reading, "on your account, I have slaughtered your heroic warriors (*yadvā tvayā nimittabhūtenāhaṃ hatāḥ pravīrās tāvakā yena sa tathā kṛta iti vā*)."

"I shall not bring you under the sway of death" *na tvāṃ ... mṛtyuvaśaṃ nayāmi*: Cg argues that Rāma spares Rāvaṇa here in order to avoid the infamy that would be associated with killing an opponent who was exhausted from a lengthy battle (*cirarаṇapariśrāntakṛntanakṛtāpavādāpanodāya saṃprati bhavataḥ prāṇāpaharaṇakarmaṇo viramāmīty arthaḥ*).

Following verse 132, D5–7,9–11,S insert a passage of four lines in the *upajāti* meter [1019*] in which Rāma's address to Rāvaṇa continues: "Go! Since you are worn out from the battle, you have my leave. Go back to Laṅkā, king of the night-roaming *rākṣasas*, and, when you have recovered, come forth with your chariot and bow. Then, mounted in your chariot, you shall witness my power."

133. "his great crown cut off" *kṛttamahākirīṭaḥ*: D9–11 and the texts and printed editions of Ct and Cr read *bhagna-*, "broken," for the critical edition's *kṛtta-*, "cut off."

134. "had returned to Laṅkā" *praviṣṭe*: Literally, "had entered." We follow Cg and Cr, who supply the word "Laṅkā."

"along with Lakṣmaṇa" *saha lakṣmaṇena*: There is an ambiguity here as to whether we are to understand that Lakṣmaṇa assists Rāma in removing the darts from the monkeys or whether Rāma alone relieves Lakṣmaṇa of his darts at the same time as he relieves the monkeys of theirs. We have chosen the former interpretation, because, at verse 115 above, Lakṣmaṇa has freed himself of Rāvaṇa's weapons through recalling that he was a portion of Viṣṇu. Cg acknowledges this earlier event but understands that Rāma is going through the motions of healing Lakṣmaṇa once again as a token of respect (*saha lakṣmaṇeneti lakṣmaṇasya pūrvam eva viśalyatve 'py ādarāt punaḥkaraṇam*).

"removed those darts" *viśalyān ... cakāra*: Literally, "he made them free from darts." The idea is that Rāma and Lakṣmaṇa remove Rāvaṇa's arrows from the monkeys' bodies. Ck claims that they accomplish this through the use of curative herbs, *mantras*, and meditation (*mantrauṣadhadhyānaiḥ*).

"in the forefront of the great battle" *paramāhavāgre*: Cg claims that Rāma does this right on the battlefield because of the impossibility of conducting the monkeys anywhere else without first removing the arrows (*paramāhavāgra ity anena viśalyakaraṇaṃ vinā sugrīvādīnāṃ harīṇām anyatrānayanāsambhavaḥ sūcyate*).

135. "Indra, lord of the thirty gods" *tridaśendra-*: Literally, "the lord of the thirty."

"the hosts of creatures" *bhūtagaṇāḥ*: The term *bhūta* is highly polysemic. Depending on its context, it may refer to malignant spirits (as at verse 9 above), to the spirits of the departed, i.e., ghosts, or, most generally, to any kind of being whatsoever. Given the breadth implied by the context here, we have taken it in this last, most general sense. Translators have handled the term variously. Some, such as Shastri (1959, vol. 3, p. 155) and Gita Press (1969, vol. 3, p. 1588), appear to omit the term, while others, including Roussel (1903, vol. 3, p. 180), Gorresio (1856, vol. 9, p. 322), and Pagani (1999, p. 1015), leave the term untranslated. Dutt (1893, p. 1287) renders, "ghosts," while Raghunathan (1982, vol. 3, p. 155), apparently referring to the use of the term in its sense of "element," translates, "the hosts of elementals."

"the guardians of the directions, and the denizens of the deep" *diśaś ca / sasāgarāḥ*: Literally, "the directions together with the oceans." Since we do not believe that the poet means us to understand that inanimate objects are rejoicing, we take the terms, as does Cg, to stand, respectively, for the eight *dikpālas*, or divinities that guard the cardinal and intermediary compass points, and the inhabitants of the ocean (*sāgaravāsinaḥ*). Some translators understand that it is the compass points and the oceans themselves that rejoice.

"along with the seers" *sarṣi-*: Ś1,Ñ2,B1,2, D1,5,9–11,M2, and the texts and printed editions of Ct and Cr read instead *sarva-*, "all." This yields the sense of "all the great serpents."

"the creatures of land and water" *bhūmyambucarāś ca*: Literally, "those who roam the land and the water." Cg, who, as noted above, interprets the term *sāgarāḥ* by *lakṣaṇā*, "metonymy," to stand for sea creatures, makes a distinction here between marine animals and those that inhabit other bodies of [presumably fresh] water (*sāgarabhinnāmbucarāḥ*).

According to Cv, the breaking of Rāvaṇa's crown concludes the sixth day [of the battle] (*mukuṭabhaṅgena ṣaṣṭham ahaḥ samāptam*). According to Cm and Cg, this first defeat of Rāvaṇa, including the destruction of his crown, takes place on the sixth day [of the dark half of the month of Phālguna/Caitra] (*ṣaṣṭhyāṃ rāvaṇamukutabhaṅgaḥ*—Cg; *ṣaṣṭhyāṃ rāvaṇasya prathamaparājayaḥ*—Cm). Ct understands that Rāvaṇa's defeat occurs on the evening of the sixth day of the bright half of that same month [of Bhādrāśvina] (*ayaṃ rāvaṇaparābhavas tanmāsīyaśuklaṣaṣṭhyāṃ śāyaṃkāle*). See note to 6.4.4.

Sarga 48

1. "insensible with agitation" *vyathitendriyaḥ*: Literally, "his senses agitated." Cg understands, "his mind filled with misery (*duḥkhitamanaskaḥ*)."

3. "the staff of Brahmā" *brahmadaṇḍa-*: The creator divinity Brahmā is not normally represented as wielding a staff or rod per se. Therefore, the commentators struggle somewhat to precisely identify the object of comparison here. Ct, Cr, and Cm offer as their first, or, in the case of Cr, only, interpretation that the reference is to a particular comet of a fiery color that appears at the end of a *yuga*, or cosmic age (*yugāntasamutthito 'gnivarṇo dhūmaketuḥ*—so Ct). Cg notes that "others (*eke*)" make this identification, although he himself, as we shall see, prefers other interpretations. Cm offers, as his second choice, that the reference is to the *brahmāstra*, or universally destructive divine weapon-spell of Brahmā. Ct also gives this as an alternative, explaining that the basis for the comparison is the infallibility of the *brahmāstra*. Cg offers this as his third alternative. Cg's first choice is "Brahmā's curse (*brahmaśāpaḥ*)." His second is the brahmanical staff (*daṇḍa*) of Vasiṣṭha, which is able to swallow up and neutralize all divine weapons (including the *brahmāstra*, as described at 1.55.15–23 and notes) (*sarvāstranigaraṇakṣamo vasiṣṭhadaṇḍo vā*). One of Rāma's arrows has earlier been compared to the staff of Brahmā (see *Araṇyakāṇḍa* 29.24 and note). The identification of the *brahmadaṇḍa* with the comet presaging universal destruction is followed by Dutt (1893, p. 1287) and Gita Press (1969, vol. 3, p. 1588). Raghunathan (1982, vol. 3, p. 155) and Shastri (1959, vol. 3, p. 156) translate similarly to us. Gorresio (1856, vol. 9, p. 322) renders, "*scettro di Brahma*." Roussel (1903, vol. 3, p. 181) and Pagani (1999, p. 1015) leave the term untranslated. See note to 6.55.120.

"with the brilliance of lightning" *vidyutsadṛśavarcasām*: Literally, "having a luster similar to lightning." D7,9–11,G1, and the texts and printed editions of Ct and Cr read instead *-calita-*, "trembling, flashing," for *-sadṛśa-*, "like," giving the compound the sense of "whose darting splendor was like that of lightning."

5. "by a mere human" *mānuṣeṇa*: Literally, "by a human."

"it is clear" *khalu*: Literally, "certainly, surely."

6. "those frightening words of Brahmā" *tad brahmaṇo ghoraṃ vākyam*: Although Rāvaṇa famously excludes men and other lesser creatures from the list of those who are powerless to harm him (1.15.4–6 and 7.10.17–18), at no point in those passages do we see Brahmā explicitly warning him about men. Ct and Ck are aware of this problem but argue that the warning is implicit in that, as indicated in verse 7 below, Rāvaṇa neglects to request immunity from humans. (*nanu bhagavatā tathā bhayopadeśaḥ kutas tatrāha. devetyādi. yasmān manuṣebhyo na yācitaṃ tasmāt tebhyo bhayaṃ jānīhīty utkam ity anvayaḥ.*)

"Know that you still must fear humans" *mānuṣebhyo vijānīhi bhayaṃ tvam iti*: Literally, "you must know fear *or* danger from men."

"have now come back to haunt me" *mām abhyupasthitam*: Literally, "has come to me."

"for they have proven true" *tat tathā*: Literally, "that [has come about] thus." We follow Ct and Ck in supplying "will come about (*saṃpatsyate*—Ct; *saṃpadyate*—Ck). Cm and Cg understand, "that will not be in vain (*na tu moghaṃ bhaviṣyati*—Cg; *tathā amogham*—Cm)."

7. Ct and Ck use this verse to explain the ascription to Brahmā of the warning in verse 6. See note above.

Following verse 7, D3,5–7,9–11,S insert a passage of nine lines [1026*] in which Rāvaṇa recalls various curses he has incurred that foretell his doom: "I think that Rāma, the son of Daśaratha, is the human of whom long ago Anaraṇya,[1] scion of the Ikṣvāku lineage, had foreknowledge [when he said], 'Most wretched of *rākṣasas*, a man shall be born in my royal lineage who, you evil-minded disgrace to your family, shall destroy you in battle, along with your sons, your ministers, your army, your horses, and your charioteers.'[1–5] And then, too, I was cursed byVedavatī[2] as well, when, long ago, I raped her. She must have been reborn as the fortunate Sītā, delight of Janaka.[6–7] And I am now experiencing what was foretold by Umā, Nandīśvara, Rambhā, and Varuṇa's daughter[3]—for the words of seers never prove false. [8–9]"

[1]"Anaraṇya" *anaraṇyena*: Literally, "by Anaraṇya." Anaraṇya, a king of Ayodhyā (see 1.69.20 and 2.102.8), cursed Rāvaṇa, who in turn killed him (*Uttarakāṇḍa* 19).

[2]"Vedavatī" *vedavatyā*: The story is narrated at *Uttarakāṇḍa* 17.

[3]"Umā, Nandīśvara, Rambhā, and Varuṇa's daughter" *umā nandīṣvaraś cāpi rambhā varuṇakanyakā*: According to Cg, this list names four distinct individuals who either curse Rāvaṇa or foretell his doom (*umādayaś catvāraḥ*). According to Cm, Varuṇa's daughter is Puñjikasthalā, and her mention alludes to a curse Brahmā pronounced on her behalf, a curse that, like some of the others, was intended to bring about Rāvaṇa's death because of his sexual assault on a woman. (*varuṇakanyakā puñjikasthalā. tena ca tannibandhanabrahmaśāpo vivakṣitaḥ. so 'pi strīdharṣaṇanimittavadharūpaḥ.*) Rāvaṇa was cursed once more by Vedavatī, whom he had tried to rape and who immolated herself only to be reborn as Sītā (7.17.23). Rāvaṇa was also cursed by his own daughter-in-law Rambhā, whom he had also raped (7.26.37). However, according to the actual text, it was not Rambhā but Rāvaṇa's nephew Nalakūbara who cursed Rāvaṇa to die if he ever approached another woman who was not his wife (7.26.44). Rāvaṇa had insulted Nandīśvara, who cursed him that he would perish at the hands of monkeys who would be emanations of himself, i.e., of Nandīśvara (7.16.14–16). Dutt (1893) explains the circumstances of the various curses in a footnote on page 1288, although he provides no sources for the episodes. Pagani (1999, pp. 1664–65), too, discusses these incidents in general terms but also gives no sources for the episodes. Puñjikasthalā is mentioned at App. I, No. 3, line 250; see note 4, following 6.9.22. Here Rāvaṇa tells of how, long ago, he spied the woman Puñjikasthalā, who was on her way to Brahmā's abode. Rāvaṇa strips and rapes her, and she arrives at Brahmā's abode in a disheveled state. An *apsaras* named Puñjikasthalā is also identified with Hanumān's mother at 4.65.8. See 4.65.8–9 and S. Goldman 1999. Rambhā is mentioned in the same episode. According to Cm, Rāvaṇa was given a similar curse by the goddess Umā on the

occasion of his shaking Mount Kailāsa (*umāśāpas tu kailāsagiricālanavelāyāṃ rāvaṇa te strīnimittaṃ vadha ity evaṃrūpa iti jñeyam*). The shaking of Mount Kailāsa is described at *Uttarakāṇḍa* 16, although no mention of Umā's curse is made there.

8. "Bearing this in mind" *etad evābhyupāgamya*: Literally, "having approached, having understood." Ct, Ck, and Cr, who read *etad eva samāgamya*, "having approached this, having understood this," as well as Cg and Cm, who read with the critical edition, all gloss, "having known, having understood (*jñātvā*)." Ct, Ck, and Cr understand that what the *rākṣasas* are to keep in mind are Rāvaṇa's words, especially regarding his cause for fear (so Ct) (*madbhayaṃ nimittam*). Cg and Cm take the reference to be to the various curses enumerated by Rāvaṇa in 1026* (see note to verse 7 above).

"on top of the gateways at the main thoroughfares" *caryāgopuramūrdhasu*: See note to 6.47.32 above.

9. "incomparably profound" *apratimagambhīraḥ*: The commentators, some of whom read the variant compound *apratimagāmbhīryaḥ*, which has the same meaning, offer no suggestions as to the sense in which we are to understand Kumbhakarṇa's profundity. The translators consulted offer a variety of interpretations, including "gravity" (Dutt 1893, p. 1288), "grandeur" (Raghunathan 1982, vol. 3, p. 156), "*intrépidité*" (Roussel 1903, vol. 3, p. 181), "*bravoure*" (Pagani 1999, p. 1015), "prowess" (Shastri 1959, vol. 3, p. 156), and "unparalleled in profundity" (Gita Press 1969, vol. 3, p. 1589). Gorresio's edition avoids the phrase, reading instead *apratimasattvaḥ*, "of incomparable strength" (6.37.14). This, in turn, may be a kind of gloss on the southern reading.

"who has been overcome by Brahmā's curse" *brahmaśāpābhibhūtaḥ*: Cr and Cg understand this phrase to mean that Kumbhakarṇa is asleep. They are referring to the episode related at 6.49.22–27 in which, as narrated by Vibhīṣaṇa to Rāma, Brahmā, responding to Indra's frightened pleas, curses Kumbhakarṇa to sleep perpetually like the dead (6.49.23). On Rāvaṇa's plea that he set some limit to this curse, Brahmā modifies it so that Kumbhakarṇa is to sleep for six months at a time, waking only for a single day at the end of each six-month period. This story appears to be at variance with the well-known version at *Uttarakāṇḍa* 10 in which, at the behest of the gods, Kumbhakarṇa is tricked by the god Brahmā and the goddess Sarasvatī into wasting the boon earned through his penances (7.10.2–8) on a request that he sleep for many years (7.10.31–41). Cs gives this matter some attention. With reference to the episode in the *Uttarakāṇḍa*, he concludes that the false boon is, in effect, a curse visited upon Kumbhakarṇa for his continued affliction of creatures. See verse 42 and note below. See 6.49.22–27 and notes.

10. "he . . . defeated" *sa parājitam*: Ś,Ñ,V,B,D1–4,6,8–13, and the texts and printed editions of Ct, Ck, and Cr read instead *samare jitam*, "conquered in battle."

"a fearsome army of *rākṣasas*" *rakṣobalaṃ bhīmam*: Ś,Ñ1,D10,11,T3,G2 read *-bhīmabalam* (so the critical apparatus), "of fearsome strength *or* a fearsome army," for *-balaṃ bhīmam*. Printed editions of the text of Ct (= GPP and NSP 6.60.15) in addition show a space between the words *rakṣaḥ* and *bhīma-*. The commentators who follow this reading (Ct, Ck, and Cr) understand *rakṣaḥ* to be an accusative referring to Kumbhakarṇa and a third object of the gerund *jñātvā*, "realizing." They thus understand, "realizing that the *rākṣasa* [Kumbhakarṇa] was of fearsome strength." Ct and Ck additionally think that the compound *bhīmabalam* can also be taken in the sense of "fearsome army" as the object of the verb *ādideśa*, "he dispatched, he commanded." They argue that this is possible through the rhetorical technique of *āvṛtti* (repetition). This interpretation has perhaps inspired the translation of Pagani (1999, p. 1016), who renders, "*le très puissant Rāvaṇa recourait au rākṣasa à la force redoutable.*"

11. Following verse 11, D5–7,10,11,S insert a passage of one line [1028*]: "[Kumbhakarṇa], who is sleeping comfortably without a care, his mind overcome by his fate.[1]"

[1]"his mind overcome by his fate" *kālo'pahatacetanaḥ*: This is apparently a typographical error for *kālopahatacetanaḥ*. Literally, "his consciousness stricken by Kāla." Although we have normally left the term *kāla* untranslated when it serves as a synonym for Yama, the god of death, we take it here in its sense of "time, destiny, fate."

D6,7,10,11,T2,3, and the texts and printed editions of Ct and Cr read *kāma-*, "desire, lust," for *kāla*, "time, fate."

12. "for six, seven, eight, even nine months at a time" *nava ṣaṭ sapta cāṣṭau ca māsān*: Literally, "for nine, six, seven, and eight months." The duration of Kumbhakarṇa's periods of sleep is difficult to determine with precision because the periods are stated quite differently, seemingly irreconcilably so, at different points in the poem. This provokes the commentators to seek explanations of this passage or its variants that will reconcile the different formulations. In addition to this passage, the statements on this matter are as follows:

1) At 6.49.26, Brahmā, in a modification of his original curse of perpetual sleep, declares that Kumbhakarṇa "will sleep for periods of six months [in between which] he will wake for but a single day (*śayitā hy eṣa ṣaṇmāsān ekāhaṃ jāgariṣyati*)."
2) At 7.10.39, at the urging of Brahmā, Sarasvatī tricks Kumbhakarṇa into requesting a boon "to sleep for many years (*svaptuṃ varṣāṇy anekāni devadeva mamepsitam*)."
3) At 7.13.7, Agastya tells Rāma that Kumbhakarṇa "sleeps without waking for many thousands of years (*bahūny abdasahasrāṇi śayāno nāvabudhyate*)."

Cg is the only commentator to discuss the critical reading. He understands, as we do, that Kumbhakarṇa on different occasions may sleep for nine months or seven months, etc. He relates this to Kumbhakarṇa's nonspecific boon request at 7.10.39. He then refers to the other two formulations, suggesting that the request to sleep for six months at 6.49.26 is either a reference through synecdoche (*upalakṣaṇa*) to the other, longer periods of sleep or represents the minimum time during which Kumbhakarṇa is asleep (*anyūnābhiprāyaṃ vā*) (so, too, Cs). Cg then provides a lengthy quotation from the *Taittirīyasaṃhitā* (7.5.6.1), where, in connection with the *gavāmayana* rite, it is stated that the sacrificial officiants reckon as a month (*māsa*) a period of six days (*ṣaḍahaḥ*). If, Cg argues, we then add up the number of such "months" indicated in the verse, we get a total of thirty "months" (i.e., $6+7+8+9=30$) of 6 days each, or 180 days. This calculation then conforms with the passage at 6.49.26, at which the *rākṣasa* sleeps for six months (based on a thirty-day lunar month).

Ś,Ñ,V1,3,B2,3,D2,4,8,10–12, and the texts and printed editions of Ct, Cr, and Ck, as well as the printed editions of Lahore and Gorresio, read instead *nava sapta daśāṣṭau ca māsān*, "for nine, seven, ten, and eight months." Cg mentions this reading as a variant and comments upon it. Ct attempts to reconcile the three different passages by arguing that the verse does not specify a precise period of time for Kumbhakarṇa to sleep but simply indicates that the period has no upper limit. He further states that the reference at 6.49.26 indicates only that six months is the minimum period for which he must sleep but that, after this, his period of waking is restricted to a single day. In other words, Ct claims "the boon" of Brahmā determines only how long Kumbhakarṇa can be awake, not how long he sleeps. This, he argues, is confirmed by the other two passages mentioned above, where Kumbhakarṇa is said to sleep for many years or for many thousands of years. Cr extends this argument by claiming that, although Brahmā's boon compels Kumbhakarṇa to sleep for six months, nothing prevents him from sleeping naturally beyond that time (*taduttaraṃ svābhāvikanidrāyā niṣedhābhāvāc ca*). Ct then quotes another line of interpretation, which he attributes to others. According to this, the word *aṣṭau* is not to be understood in the sense of the number eight but as the locative of a noun *aṣṭi*, whose meaning here is extended to the sense of "to leave aside (*tyāge*)." According to this reckoning, the compound *daśāṣṭau* has the sense of "leaving out ten." If, then, as Ct suggests, we add up the nine and seven months mentioned in the verse, we arrive at a period of sixteen months, which, with ten months subtracted, leaves the six months of sleep referred to in 6.49.26. Although Ct does not specify his sources, this ingenious interpretation is found in a variety of other commentaries, which differ only in their derivation and lexical identification of *aṣṭau*. Thus Cg, who notes this variant, derives the word from the root √*aś*, in the sense of "eating (*aśanam*)," the meaning of which he extends to "loss *or* destruction (*nāśaḥ*)." Similarly, Cr glosses, "swallowing (*nigaraṇa*)" in the sense of "casting out (*niḥsāraṇe*)" and takes the word in the sense of "eating" (*bhakṣaṇārthakāśadhātuprakṛtikaktinnantaḥ*). Cl, quoted by Gorresio (1856, vol. 9, 377), perhaps deriving the word from the root √*as*, "to throw, toss," glosses, "casting out ten (*daśaprakṣepe sati*)."

Among the translators consulted, only Gorresio (1856, vol. 9, p. 324) is sufficiently persuaded by this line of reasoning to translate the phrase as "*da sei mesi*," arguing his case for doing so on the basis of Cl's interpretation in his explanatory note mentioned above. Other translators consulted understand the duration of the periods of sleep variously. Raghunathan (1982, vol. 3, p. 156), who shares the critical reading, translates as we do. Roussel (1903, vol. 3, p. 182), followed by Pagani (1999, p. 1016), mistakenly understanding *daśāṣṭau* to mean "eighteen," translates, "*neuf, sept et dix-huit mois*." Dutt (1893, p. 1288) renders the vulgate reading literally as "nine, seven, ten, or eight months away." Gita Press (1969, vol. 3, p. 1590) omits the word "seven (*sapta*)," rendering, "nine, ten or eight months." Shastri (1959, vol. 3, p. 157) inexplicably renders, "for periods of two or three or nine days and sometimes for six, seven, or eight months." See note to 6.49.26 below.

Following 12ab, D5–7,10,11,T,G1,2,M, and the texts and printed editions of all southern commentators insert a passage of one line [1029*]: "For, having given his counsel, he fell asleep on the ninth day from now."

This half verse is ambiguous and somewhat controversial in that it raises once again the complex issue of how long Kumbhakarṇa has been asleep, as discussed in the preceding note. Commentators and translators differ considerably over the point from which to count the nine days, over whether one should count backward or forward in time, or about whether the term "day (*ahani*)" here refers, by metonymy (*lakṣaṇā*), to months. Ct quotes the opinion, stated elsewhere by Cg, that Kumbhakarṇa falls asleep on the ninth day before the day on which the battle starts but claims that this is not consistent with the text, since it appears to contradict Rāvaṇa's statement at 6.50.12 that Kumbhakarṇa has been asleep "for a very long time (*sumahān kālaḥ*)." For since, according to the commentators (see note to 6.47.135), we are now at the sixth day of battle, this would mean that Kumbhakarṇa would have only been sleeping for some fifteen days, hardly a very long time by his standards. Moreover, such a reading, one would think, raises the problem of how Kumbhakarṇa, who, through the power of Brahmā's curse, appears to be forced to sleep for a minimum of six months, could be awakened after such a brief span of time. Ct proposes, as an alternative, that we understand the word *ahan*, "day," by *lakṣaṇā*, or secondary meaning, to stand for *māsa*, "month." Thus, according to this interpretation, Kumbhakarṇa would have been asleep for nine months and thus could be awakened. Ct concludes by stating that this will all be made clear later on. Among the translators consulted, only Dutt (1893, p. 1288) follows this line of reasoning, translating, "he hath slept for nine months." This interpretation is, however, difficult to accept, since the counsel to which Rāvaṇa alludes must be the frank advice given to Rāvaṇa in the assembly described in lines 195–229 of App. I, No. 3 (= GPP 6.12.28–40), which follows *sarga* 9 in the critical edition. (See note to 6.9.22.) According to Cg, this assembly would have taken place eleven days before the start of the battle, or seventeen days before the present moment.

Cr takes a completely different approach, claiming that we should understand that, having given his counsel, Kumbhakarṇa fell asleep but will awaken on the ninth day and that he will have reached the limit for the time set for his sleeping on this very day (*jāgariteti śeṣaḥ*).

Cs quotes Ct in full on this point but disagrees with him, finding his argument to be contradicted by the text and claiming that his recourse to *lakṣaṇā* is pointless. As an alternative, Cs proposes that, in stating later on that Kumbhakarṇa has slept for a very long time (6.50.12), Rāvaṇa is merely giving an example of the way in which people who are in misery consider a short period of time as very long (*duḥkhasamayatvenālpakālasyāpi bāhulyoktiḥ*). As another example of this he cites *Bhāgavatapurāṇa* 1.14.7, where Yudhiṣṭhira, in his anxiety over Arjuna's failure to return, claims that he has been gone for seven months. Cs also provides a lexical source for this from the *Nāmamahodadhi* (*ahas tu māsaśabdoktaṃ yatra cintāyutaṃ vrajet / evaṃ saṃvatsarādyaṃ ca viparīte viparyayaḥ //*).

Cs, Cm, and, to a very elaborate extent, Cg take this line as the starting point for a day-by-day chronology of the campaign in Laṅkā. Starting from the day of Rāvaṇa's consultation with his ministers and Vibhīṣaṇa's defection (*sargas* 6–10 including App. I, No. 3, lines 192–229), they attempt to fit the various events and battles into the framework of nine days posited by Rāvaṇa. They justify this chronology by quoting specific verses from the earlier portions of the *Yuddhakāṇḍa* that indicate the passage of time. Cg takes this task particularly seriously, dating the epic's events by the lunar calendar retrospectively from the abduction of Sītā and prospectively until the death of Rāvaṇa. Cg is also concerned with reconciling his chronology (in which the events from Hanumān's meeting with Sītā in Laṅkā and the death of Rāvaṇa span only a little more than a fortnight) with Sītā's statement to Hanumān and Rāvaṇa's to Sītā, in the

Sundarakāṇḍa, concerning the amount of time that remains of Sītā's year of captivity (= the fourteenth year of Rāma's exile). See note at 5.20.8. See also note to 6.4.4. See, too, 6.80.55; 6.96.30; and 6.97.33.

Translators treat the verse variously. Roussel (1903, vol. 3, p. 182) understands that Kumbhakarṇa fell asleep on "*le neuvième jour.*" Pagani (1999, p. 1016) says that he fell asleep "*il y a huit jours.*" Both of these translators avoid the problematic reference to Kumbhakarṇa's counsel by either leaving the word *mantra* untranslated (Roussel) or rendering it as "*incantation*" (Pagani). Shastri (1959, vol. 3, p. 157) renders, "having met in consultation with me nine days ago, he has since fallen asleep." The translations of Gita Press (1969, vol. 3. p. 1590) and Raghunathan (1982, vol. 3, p. 156) are similar to ours.

D4,6,7,10,11,T2,3, and the texts and printed editions of Cr and Ct omit 12cd ("Nonetheless, you must awaken mighty Kumbhakarṇa immediately").

13. "that great-armed warrior" *mahābāhuḥ*: Literally, "the great-armed one."

"will . . . slaughter the monkeys and the two princes" *vānarān rājaputrau ca . . . vadhiṣyati*: Cm, evidently disturbed at the notion that Rāvaṇa could be anticipating the deaths of Rāma and Lakṣmaṇa, insists that we add the adverb *vinā*, "without," so that the phrase would mean "will slaughter just the monkeys but not Rāma and Lakṣmaṇa. This argument evidently derives from Cm's theological reading of the poem. For other examples of this, see notes to 5.18.6,14,16,17, etc. See, too, 6.23.1–3 and notes.

Following verse 13, D5–7,9–11,S insert a passage of one line [1030*]: "Indeed, he is the greatest standard-bearer in battle and the foremost among all the *rākṣasas*."

14. "Addicted to this vulgar pleasure" *grāmyasukhe rataḥ*: According to Cr, the phrase means that Kumbhakarṇa delights in sleep itself (*śayane rataḥ prītimān*).

"my grief at being humiliated . . . will be banished" *abhinirastasya . . . bhaviṣyati na me śokaḥ*: Literally, "the grief of me—who has been defeated—will not exist."

15. "For of what use to me is that hero, whose strength is equal to that of Śakra, if he can be of no assistance to me when I am in such trouble?" *kiṃ kariṣyāmy ahaṃ tena śakratulyabalena hi / īdṛśe vyasane prāpte yo na sāhyāya kalpate //*: Literally, "What will I do with him whose strength is equal to that of Śakra and who is not fit for assistance when such a calamity has arisen?" Ś,Ñ,V,B,D1–4,8–13,G1,3,M1,2,5, and the texts and printed editions of Ct and Cr substitute *ghore*, "dreadful," for the critical edition's *prāpte*, "arisen."

16. "in great agitation" *paramasaṃbhrāntāḥ*: Cg understands that the *rākṣasas*' agitation derives from their concern as to how they will be able to awaken Kumbhakarṇa at the wrong time (*katham enam akāle prabodhayiṣyāma iti vyākulāḥ*).

17. "those eaters of flesh and blood" *māṃsaśoṇitabhojanāḥ*: Although this appears to be simply a general kenning for the carnivorous *rākṣasas*, Cg understands the compound to indicate specifically that the *rākṣasas* fortify themselves for the difficult task of awakening Kumbhakarṇa by first consuming flesh, etc. (*prabodhaśaktivivṛddhyarthaṃ māṃṣādikaṃ bhuktvā*).

"and food" *tathā bhakṣyān*: D9–11 and the texts and printed editions of Ct and Cr read instead *mahad bhakṣyam*, "abundant food." Cg notes that the *rākṣasas* bring garlands, food, etc., in order to appease the pangs of hunger Kumbhakarṇa will experience upon being awakened (*kumbhakarṇasya prabodhakālikakṣuttāpādiśāntaye gandhamālyādikaṃ gṛhītvā yayur ity arthaḥ*).

18–19. "As they passed through the huge gates into . . . cavern" *tāṃ praviśya mahādvārām . . . -guhām*: Literally, "having entered that cavern with its huge gates." According to Ct and Ck, Kumbhakarṇa's residence is a cavity in the ground that was fashioned by the gods and resembled the paradisiacal underworld of Pātāla (*pātālavad devanirmitaṃ bhūbilam ity arthaḥ*). See 7.13.2–6, where Kumbhakarṇa's residence is fashioned by *rākṣasa* architects, who are said to be like Viśvakarman, the architect of the gods.

"which extended a league on every side" *sarvato yojanāyatām*: Literally, "extending one *yojana* all around." Those commentators who note this term understand that the cavern extends for one *yojana* in each of the four cardinal directions. Whether this means that the space is one *yojana* on a side or [measuring from a central point] two *yojanas* on a side is not completely clear. But compare 7.13.4, where Kumbhakarṇa's residence is said to be one *yojana* wide and two long. See notes to 6.18.18–19.

"redolent with every fragrance" *sarvagandhapravāhinīm*: Literally, "streaming forth every fragrance." D7,9–11,M1, and the texts and printed editions of Ct read *puṣpa-*, "flowers," for *sarva-*, "every," yielding the sense "redolent with the fragrance of flowers." Cg, who reads with the critical edition, understands the scent to arise from such things as the sandalpaste smeared on Kumbhakarṇa's body (*kumbhakarṇānuliptacandanādigandhapravāhavatīm*).

"driven back by the force of his breath" *kumbhakarṇasya niśvāsād avadhūtāḥ*: Literally, "[they were] shaken by Kumbhakarṇa's breathing."

"Nonetheless, retaining their footing with difficulty, they managed to enter . . . with effort" *pratiṣṭhamānāḥ kṛcchreṇa yatnāt praviviśuḥ*: Literally, "standing with difficulty, they entered with effort."

20. "splendid" *śubhām*: D9–11,G2,M1,2, and the texts and printed editions of Ct and Cr read instead *ratna-*, "jewels." In this variant, the floors are inlaid with gems as well as gold.

"He was fearsome to behold" *bhīmadarśanam*: Ś,Ñ1,V2,B1,3,4,D1–4,6–12, and the texts and printed editions of Ct and Cr read *-vikramam*, "valor," for *-darśanam*, "appearance," yielding the sense "of fearsome valor."

21. "they began to rouse" *pratyabodhayan*: Literally, "they wakened *or* aroused." The context requires that we read the verb as inceptive.

"grotesque" *vikṛtam*: This word, which can mean "strange, extraordinary, deformed, mutilated, etc.," has been interpreted variously. Cg, the only commentator to remark upon it, understands the term to refer to the transformation of [a person's] appearance during sleep (*nidrākālikavikārayuktam*). Roussel (1903, vol. 3, p. 182), followed by Shastri (1959, vol. 3, p. 157), understands, "*le monstre* ('that monster'—Shastri)." Gita Press (1969, vol. 3, p. 1590) offers, "in an unnatural state." Pagani (1999, p. 1016), evidently following Cg, renders, "[*ils tentèrent de le tirer du profond sommeil*] *qui lui déformait les traits*." Raghunathan (1982, vol. 3, pp. 156–57) and Dutt (1893, p. 1289) appear to ignore the term, while Gorresio's text (6.37.30) reads *vipulam*, "vast," instead.

"in the midst of his long sleep" *mahānidram*: Literally, "[him] whose sleep was great."

"like some crumbled mountain" *vikīrṇam iva parvatam*: Cg glosses the adjective as "slackened (*śithilam*)." The idea, evidently, is that the immensely tall Kumbhakarṇa sprawled in slumber resembles a mountain that has collapsed.

22–23. "immensely powerful" *mahābalam*: D5,9–11, and the texts and printed editions of Ct and Cr read instead *arindamam*, "subduer of foes."

"terrifying them" *trāsayantam*: Literally, "terrifying." D9–11 and the texts and printed editions of Ct read instead *bhrāmayantam*, "causing to spin *or* whirl."

Ct suggests adding the word "people (*janān*)" as the object of the participle. The idea is that, as in verse 19 above, the exhalations of the giant Kumbhakarṇa are powerful enough to knock people off their feet. This reading has provoked Dutt (1893, p. 1289) to compose the following curious note: "An instance of the material sublime unsurpassed in all literature. Kumbhakarṇa himself is the emblem of the material as contrasted with the spiritual typified by Rāma."

"and his huge mouth as wide as the underworld Pātāla: *pātālavipulānanam*: Literally, "having a mouth as wide as Pātāla." Compare verse 50 below and 6.55.28.

"fearsome to behold" *bhīmadarśanam*: D9–11 and the texts and printed editions of Ct read *-vikramam*, "valor," for *-darśanam*, "appearance," yielding the sense "of fearsome valor."

Following 23ab, D5–7,9–11,S insert a passage of two lines [1041*], extending the description of Kumbhakarṇa: "Every limb of that subduer of his foes was sprawled on the bed, and he reeked of blood and marrow. His limbs were clad in golden armlets, and he wore a diadem.[1]"

[1]"that subduer of his foes . . . he wore a diadem" *kirīṭinam arimdamam*" D10,11, and the texts and printed editions of Ct and Cr read instead *kirīṭenārkavarcasam*, "his diadem lent him the brilliance of the sun."

24. "mighty" *mahātmānaḥ*: Literally, "great *or* great-minded." Given the context, we tend to take the term as a physical description, somewhat in the manner of Cr, who glosses, "making a great effort (*atiprayatnāḥ*)." Compare verse 32 below.

"of meats" *māṃsānām*: D9–11 and the texts and printed editions of Ct and Cr read instead *bhūtānām*, "of creatures."

"as huge as Mount Meru" *merusaṃkāśam*: Literally, "resembling Meru."

25. "set down" *cakruḥ*: Literally, "they did *or* made." Cg adds the word "before [him] (*agrataḥ*)," carrying forward the expression from the previous verse.

"deer, buffalo, and boar" *mṛgāṇāṃ mahīṣāṇāṃ ca varāhāṇāṃ ca*: According to Cr, this list constitutes a specification of the creatures (*bhūtānām*) of the vulgate verse above. See note to verse 24 above.

"an astonishing heap of food" *rāśim annasya cādbhutam*: The phrase could equally well be translated, as some translators have done, as "and an astounding heap of rice" (Dutt 1893, p. 1289). Owing, however, to the text's emphasis on the carnivorousness of the *rākṣasas*, we see the phrase as summing up the list of meats rather than supplementing it.

26. "those foes of the thirty gods" *tridaśaśatravaḥ*: Literally, "the foes of the thirty." Cs, who reads a variant, *tridivaśatravaḥ* (= D11), "the foes of the triple heavens," offers two possible interpretations. The first is that the reference is simply to sinners or evildoers, that is, those who are inimical to heaven and are therefore destined for the darkness of hell, etc. (*tridivaśatravaḥ svargadviṣaḥ narakatamaādigāminaḥ pāpina iti yāvat*). Cs's second interpretation is: "The foes of the gods who were present there (*tatsthadevadveṣiṇa iti vā*)."

"strong drink" *madyāni*: D9–11 and the texts and printed editions of Ct and Cr read instead *māṃsāni*, "meats."

27. "they... covered him" *ācchādayāmāsuḥ*: Literally, "they covered." D9–11,G2, and the texts and printed editions of Ct read instead *āśvāsayāmāsuḥ*, "they refreshed *or* revived," which Ct glosses as "they caused to smell *or* inhale (*ghrāpayāmāsuḥ*)." Cr, whose reading is unattested in the critical apparatus, reads *āvāsayāmāsuḥ*, "they perfumed."

28. "*yātudhānas*" *yātudhānāḥ*: See 6.3.27 and note.

"in their thousands" *sahasraśaḥ*: Ś,Ñ,V,B,D1–3,5–13,T,M3, and the texts and printed editions of all southern commentators read instead *tatas tataḥ*, normally, "next" but which Cg glosses as *punaḥ punaḥ*, "again and again." The choice of the critical editors seems questionable here.

29. "tumultuously" *tumulam*: Cg understands, "uninterruptedly (*nirantaraṃ yathā tathā*)."

"in their impatience" *amarṣitāḥ*: Literally, "intolerant, angry, impatient." Cg understands that the *rākṣasas* roar in their anger at Kumbhakarṇa's failure to awaken despite their tremendous efforts (*mahatā prayatenāpy anutthānāj jātakrodhāḥ santo neduḥ*). Cr thinks similarly that they cannot tolerate the delay (*vilambāsahanāḥ*).

30. "Those night-roaming *rākṣasas*" *niśācarāḥ*: Literally, "the night-roaming ones." Unlike the other commentators who, like us, understand that the entire party of *rākṣasas* engages sequentially in the actions listed in the verse, Cr believes that different groups engage in the various actions simultaneously (*kecin niśācarā neduḥ... kecid āsphoṭayāmāsuḥ ... kecic cikṣipuḥ... kecid vipulaṃ svaraṃ cakruḥ*).

"roared" *neduḥ*: Cr understands that the *rākṣasas* are summoning Kumbhakarṇa (*āhvānaṃ cakruḥ*).

"clapped their upper arms" *āsphoṭayāmāsuḥ*: The verb *ā* √*sphuṭ*, "to slap *or* strike," normally refers in the epic to the loud clapping of one's upper arms with the palms of the hands as a sign of delight or as a challenge to battle. Cf. 5.8.50. See, too, 6.40.62; 6.47.8; 6.65.16; and notes. Cr defines it here as "striking the arms, etc. (*bāhvādīnāṃ tāḍanam*)," while Cg appears to understand that the *rākṣasas* are actually striking Kumbhakarṇa (*tāḍayāmāsuḥ*).

"shook him" *cikṣipuḥ*: Literally, "they tossed." We follow Cg, who glosses, "they shook [his] body (*śarīraṃ kampayāmāsuḥ*)." Ck and Ct understand, "they pushed *or* prodded his body with their hands (*hastais taccharīrasya praṇodanaṃ cakruḥ*—so Ct)." Cr thinks that the *rākṣasas* are lifting Kumbhakarṇa's feet and throwing them to the ground [in an effort to get him to stand?] (*tatpādāv utthāpya bhūmau nicikṣipuḥ*).

31. "Upon hearing that din" *śrutvā*. Literally, "having heard."

"*bherī* and *paṭaha* drums" *-bherīpaṭaha-*: For *bherīs*, see 6.17.31–33 and note. B3,4, D6,9–11,G2,M3, and the texts and printed editions of the southern commentators read *-paṇava-* for *-paṭaha-*. According to Apte (s.v.), the *paṭaha* is a small kettledrum. See note to 6.34.12.

"the clapping of the upper arms" *āsphoṭita-*: See note above. Cg, who takes the term in the previous verse to refer to the striking of Kumbhakarṇa, here understands the term as do the other commentators on that verse, glossing, "the sound produced by clapping the [upper] arms (*bāhutāḍanajanyaśabdaḥ*). See notes to 6.4.23–24 and 6.17.13–15.

"the shouting, and the lionlike roars" *-kṣveḍitasiṃhanādam*: The two terms can be synonymous since one of the principal meanings of the root √*kṣveḍ* is "to roar like a lion." (See notes to 5.55.29 and 5.60.12.) The term can also refer to shouting or a war whoop, and we have taken it in this sense to avoid redundancy. Cg argues that we are to take the term *kṣveḍita* here in the general sense of "roaring" and the term *siṃhanāda* in a more specific sense. (*kṣveḍitaśabdena garjitamātram ucyate. siṃhanādam ity ekavadbhāvaḥ.*) See note to 6.4.23–24.

"the birds... came crashing down" *vihaṅgāḥ... nipetuḥ*: Literally, "sky-goers fell." The idea that a loud sound, particularly that of bellowing or shouting, can cause birds to fall from the sky is expressed elsewhere by the poet. Compare 1.16 .16 and 4.14.20.

"flying" *dravantaḥ*: Literally, "running *or* rushing."

"soaring" *kirantaḥ*: Literally, "scattering *or* dispersing." Ct, Ck, and Cr understand, "going *or* flying up (*udgacchantaḥ*—so Ct, Ck; *utpatantaḥ*—so Cr)." Cg simply glosses, "entering (*viśantaḥ*)," while Cm prefers, "filling, pervading (*vyāpnuvantaḥ*)."

The meter is *upajāti*.

32. "huge" *mahātmā*: We follow Cg, who glosses, "having an immense body (*mahāśarīraḥ*)." See note to verse 24 above.

"cacophonous" *bhṛśam*: Literally, "extremely, excessively."

"bludgeons" *musuṇḍī-*: The critical apparatus lists numerous variants for this term. The most popular reading, that is, *bhuśuṇḍīḥ*, is found in Ś1,Ñ2,V1,2,B1–3,D2,4,6,9–11,G1, and the texts and printed editions of Ct and Cr. T1 and the texts and printed editions of Cg and Cm read *musuṇṭhīḥ*. Crā and Ck read *musuṇṭhī-*. According to MW (s.v.) and Apte (s.v.), all are synonymous and appear under the heading of *bhuśuṇḍī*, which is some type of weapon. Ct, Ck, Cr, Cg, and Cm all define their respective variants as types of *mudgaras*, or war hammers. Compare note to 6.60.11, 1336*, n. 1; and 6.78.20, 1726*, n. 3.

The meter is *upajāti*.

33. "with... trees... and their palms" *vṛkṣais talaiḥ*: V3,D9–11, and the texts and printed editions of Ct and Cr read instead *vakṣasthale*, "on his chest."

The meter is *upajāti*.

34. "although powerful, were unable to remain standing before him" *balavanto 'pi sthātuṃ nāśaknuvan puraḥ*: Literally, "although powerful, they were unable to stand before." D6,9–11, and the texts and printed editions of Ct and Cr read instead *kumbhakarṇasya sthātuṃ śekur na cāgrataḥ*, "they were unable to stand before Kumbhakarṇa."

35. The syntax is awkward and causes considerable discomfort to the southern commentators, whose readings, although different, present similar syntactic difficulties. Cv, Cg, and Cm, supported by the printed editions of KK and VSP, argue that *pādas* ab constitute, in fact, a separate elliptical verse whose syntax is to be fleshed out by supplying an appropriate copula (either *babhūvuḥ*, "they were"—Cv, Cm; or *āsan*, "they were"—Cg). This line corresponds to 6.60.42 in KK and VSP. Otherwise, according to Cm and Cv, the three lines (=KK and VSP 6.40.42–43) must still be read as a single sentence, which makes the second occurrence of the word *rākṣasa* in *pāda* e redundant. Ct and Cr, who read the variants *paryavārayat* (so Ct) and *paryavārayan* (so Cr), respectively (=GPP 6.60.43b), "he *or* they surrounded, encircled," for the critical edition's (and Cg's, Cv's, and Cm's) *paryavādayan*, "they sounded," attempt a different resolution. They propose supplying the verb *vādayāmāsuḥ*, "they sounded," after *pāda* d to make a separate syntactic unit out of *pādas* a–d. This unit is equivalent to GPP and NSP 6.60.42, where our *pādas* ef constitute GPP and NSP 6.60.43ab. In our reading, it is necessary, although still somewhat awkward, to read the plural *rākṣasāḥ* of *pāda* b and the singular *daśarākṣasasāhasram*, literally, "ten-*rākṣasa*-thousands," more or less in apposition. We translate, "those *rākṣasas*... ten thousand strong."

"loudly sounded ... right in front of him" *asya purato gāḍham ... paryavādayan*: Given the syntactic difficulties mentioned above, we believe that the adverb *gāḍham*, "intensely," of *pāda* a is best construed with the only finite verb in the sequence, *paryavādayan*, of *pāda* f. Ś,V1,2,B1,D1,3,6–8,10–12,T2,M3, and the texts and printed editions of the southern commentators read *parihitāḥ*, "girt, clothed," for [*a*]*sya purataḥ*, "right in front of him." This yields the sense "[the *rākṣasas*,] who had girded up their loins [literally, 'tightly wrapped *or* clad']." As Cg explains this, it means that the *rākṣasas* were girding themselves for the coming task [of awakening Kumbhakarṇa]. (*parihitā dṛḍhīkṛtaparidhānā āsan. vakṣyamāṇakārye sāvadhānā āsann ity arthaḥ.*) Several southern manuscripts and the texts and printed editions of Ct and Cr read the singular *paryavārayat* for the critical edition's plural *paryavādayan*, which then construes with the singular *daśarākṣasasāhasram* (see below). Translations that follow the text of Ct offer variants of the following: "Then *rākṣasas* of fearsome valor, having girded up their loins, sounded the *mṛdaṅgas*, etc., and all at once ten thousand of them surrounded [Kumbhakarṇa]." Raghunathan (1982, vol. 3, pp. 157–58), the only translator to follow the text of Cg, renders, "Then ten thousand Rākshasas, who ... were men of formidable valour, girding their loins, sounded simultaneously numberless *mṛdangas* ..."

Additionally, Ct argues that the authentic (*pāṅktāḥ*) reading of *pāda* a is *tataḥ prapūritā gāḍhaṃ rākṣasair bhīmavikramaiḥ*. To this he adds the word *guhā*, yielding the sense "the cave was densely filled with *rākṣasas* of fearsome valor."

"those *rākṣasas* ... ten thousand strong" *rākṣasāḥ ... daśarākṣasasāhasram*: Literally, "*rākṣasas* ... ten-*rākṣasa*-thousands." The collocation of the two distantly separated words is awkward. First, it is redundant; and, second, there is no singular verb with which to construe the second term. Cv and Cm, whose reading of the first *pāda* differs from ours, as noted above, propose adding the verb *babhūvuḥ*, "they were," at the end of *pāda* b in an effort to separate the two into different syntactic units. Otherwise, Cm continues, the [second] occurrence of the word *rākṣasa* is otiose (*anyathā rākṣasaśabdo 'pi ricyeta*).

"many conches and jugs" *śaṅkhakumbhagaṇān*: Literally, "hosts of conches and pots." The exact nature of the *kumbha*, "pot *or* jug," as a musical instrument is unclear. It is difficult to determine whether it is a percussion or wind instrument; however, because of its grouping in composition with *śaṅkha*, "conch," we are inclined to understand it as the latter.

36. "they tried to rouse" *pratyabodhayan*: Literally, "they awakened." Given the context, we have followed Cs, who glosses, "they made an effort to awaken (*pratibodhayituṃ kṛtavantaḥ*)."

"as he lay there, like a mass of collyrium" *nīlāñjanacayākāram*: Literally, "who had the form of a heap of collyrium." Ś,Ñ1,V,B,D1–4,8,12,13,G1,M3, the commentaries of Cg and Cm, and the printed editions of KK and VSP (6.60.44) read instead the nominative plural *-ākārāḥ*, in which case the adjective refers to the *rākṣasas* attempting to awaken Kumbhakarṇa. Cg understands this reading to illustrate the fact that the *rākṣasas* form a dark mass around Kumbhakarṇa. Raghunathan (1982, vol. 3, p. 157), the only translator to render this reading, translates, "[then ten thousand Rākshasas] who looked like huge hills of collyrium ..."

"But he was oblivious to it all." *naiva saṃvivide tu saḥ*: Literally, "But he was not at all aware." D9–11 and the texts and printed editions of Ct and Cr read instead *na ca saṃbubudhe tadā*, which can mean either "and he was not then aware [of it]" or "and he did not wake up then."

37. "they resorted to more drastic and more violent efforts" *gurutaraṃ yatnaṃ dāruṇaṃ samupākraman*: Literally, "they commenced an effort that was more weighty and fierce."

38. "drove ... over him" *jaghnuḥ*: Literally, "they beat, struck." We follow the majority of commentators, who understand that the *rākṣasas* beat the animals so as to make them trample Kumbhakarṇa as a means of awakening him (*tasyopari dhāvanāya*—so Cg). Cs, evidently concerned by the use of the bare root √*han*, which usually means "to kill *or* injure," argues that one should take the root √*han* here in the sense of "to go" and read the simplex as a causative, yielding the sense "they caused them to go, drove them." Cs further understands that Kumbhakarṇa is also an implicit object of the verb. (*antarṇītaṇyarthaḥ. etān kumbhakarṇopari gamayāmāsuḥ.*) It is also possible, given the context of the verse, whose second half focuses on noisemaking, that we are to understand that the animals are beaten or prodded in order to make them emit loud noises. This may be further supported by the fact that it is not until verse 47 below that the actual trampling of elephants finally succeeds in awakening Kumbhakarṇa. See notes to 6.27.9; 6.80.29; and 6.81.4.

"with all their might" *sarvaprāṇaiḥ*: Literally, "with all their breaths *or* with all their vital forces."

39. "with great bundles of sticks" *mahākāṣṭhakaṭaṅkaraiḥ*: We can discover no lexical citation for the term *kaṭaṅkara*, which literally would mean "mat maker." Ck, Ct, and Cr, whom we tentatively follow, gloss, "masses *or* bunches (*samūhaiḥ*)." Cv understands, "with twigs located (at the end) of large branches (*mahākāṣṭhasthastambhaiḥ*)." Cg glosses, "with the sticks at the ends of large branches (*mahākāṣṭhāgrastambhaiḥ*)," which he takes to mean "whips mounted at the end of branches (*kāṣṭhāgrasthakāśābhir ity arthaḥ*)." Cm understands the term to refer to a particular type of post (*stambhabhedaḥ*). His interpretation is mentioned by Ct, who ascribes it to him, while Cv (who reads *stambabhedaḥ*, "a type of sheaf of grass,") and Cg ascribe it simply to "some [commentators] (*kecit*)."

"wielded" *-samudyataiḥ*: Literally, "upraised."

40. "filled all of Laṅkā" *laṅkā samabhipūritā ... sarvā*: Literally, "all Laṅkā was filled." D7,9–11, and the texts and printed editions of Ct and Cr read instead *sarvā prapūritā*, "all was filled," for *samabhipūritā*. This weak reading creates an undesirable redundancy through the repetition of the adjective *sarva*, "all," in *pādas* b and c. Cr attempts to eliminate this problem by reading the sequence *sarvā saḥ*, "all of ... he," as a *bahuvrīhi* compound *sarvāsaḥ*, modifying Kumbhakarṇa and meaning "through whom all [the *rākṣasas*] had the hope of victory (*sarveṣāṃ rākṣasānām āsā vijayavañchā yena*)." This interpretation is rather dubious, especially since it is difficult to find any lexical support for a noun *āsā* (as opposed to the normal *āśā*) in the sense of "hope, wish (*vañchā*)."

41. "incessantly" *asaktānām*: Literally, "not obstructed." This adjective, which modifies the *bherī* drums, is best read here as if it were adverbial. Ś,D3,4,6–9,M3, and the texts and printed editions of Crā, Cm, Cg, and Cs (KK 6.60.49; VSP 6.60.49), as well as the commentary of Cr, read instead *āsaktānām*, "attached," which the commentators explain variously. Cr glosses, "suitably placed (*yathāyogyaṃ saṃsthāpitānām*)." Cg explains, "crowded together (*saṃhatānām*)," while Cm understands, "held

by *rākṣasas* (*rākṣasagṛhītānām*)." Cs, who reads *āsaktānām*, glosses the term as if it were *asaktānām*, offering, "not connected by anything whatsoever (*kenāpi padārthenāsaṃbaddhānām*)." Cs further adds that if this is the case, then the drums provide a particular type of sound (*tathā ced eva nādaviśeṣaḥ*).

"with drumsticks of refined gold" *mṛṣṭakāñcanakoṇānām*: The compound actually forms an adjective qualifying the drums. We must in any case assume, however, that these are the instruments with which they are being beaten.

42. "in that profound slumber brought about by the power of the curse" *atinidraḥ ... śāpasya vaśam āpannaḥ*: Literally, "he who possessed excessive sleep and was under the power of a curse." See verse 9 above and note for a discussion of Brahmā's cursing Kumbhakarṇa to perpetual slumber.

"became furious" *kruddhāḥ*: Cr believes that the real meaning here is that the *rākṣasas* temporarily desist from their efforts in frustrated rage (*krodhena nivṛttā iti tātparyam*). Cg, reading ahead to the next verse, understands that, although they are already worked up [by the failure of their efforts], they now become seized with a towering rage. (*kruddhāḥ pūrvam eva kupitāḥ. punar api mahākrodhasamāviṣṭā abhavan.*)

43. "in a towering rage" *mahākrodhasamāviṣṭāḥ*: V3,D6,7,9–11, and the texts and printed editions of Ct and Cr read *tataḥ kopa-*, "then ... in anger," for *mahākrodha-*. See note to previous verse.

"Some of them, in their effort to awaken the *rākṣasa*, actually assaulted him." *tad rakṣo bodhayiṣyantaś cakrur anye parākramam*: Literally, "Some, about to awaken that *rākṣasa*, demonstrated [lit., made] their valor." According to Cg and Cr, whom we follow, the word *parākrama-*, "valor," refers to blows [of the fists, etc.] (*muṣṭiprahārādikam*—so Cg). Other translators tend to read the phrase *parākramaṃ cakruḥ* to mean "they exerted *or* redoubled their efforts *or* energies."

44. Following 44cd, Ñ2,B2,D5–7,9–11,T,G1 (after 1048*),2,3,M insert a passage of one line [1049*]: "Still others poured hundreds of pots of water into his ears." The reference in this line to pouring pots (*kumbha*) into the *rākṣasa*'s ears (*karṇa*) is an obvious play on his name.

45. "powerful *rākṣasas*" *balinaḥ*: Literally, "the powerful ones."

"armed with mallets and war hammers ... brought them down." *kūṭamudgarapāṇayaḥ ... pātayan kūṭamudgarān*: Literally, "having mallets and war hammers in their hands ... brought down mallets and war hammers."

46. "with hundred slayers" *śataghnībhiḥ*. The exact nature of this weapon is unclear, as both defensive and offensive weapons of this name are mentioned in the epics and other texts. In this case, since the weapons appear to be slung by ropes, one has the impression that something like the medieval European flail or chain-mace is intended. Cg, the only commentator to attempt to identify this weapon, says it is a type of mace (*gadāviśeṣaiḥ*). See 6.3.12 and note.

"ropes and straps" *rajjubandhana-*: Literally, "ropes and bindings." Cr understands, "bindings in the form of rope (*rajjurūpabandhanaiḥ*)." Cg, however, whom we follow, reads the compound as a *dvandva* in the sense of "ropes and bindings of leather, etc. (*bandhanāni carmādīni rajjavaś ca bandhanāni ca*)."

47. "they made a thousand elephants trample" *vāraṇānāṃ sahasram ... pradhāvitam*: Literally, "a thousand of elephants was made to run." Compare verse 38 and note above. Shastri (1959, vol. 3, p. 159) inexplicably renders, "titans," for *vāraṇa*, "elephants." The variant *vānarāṇām*, "of monkeys," is cited in the critical apparatus as a

metathesis of *vāraṇānām*, "of elephants," in G1 and G2. Roussel (1903, vol. 3, p. 184) appears to have independently made the same error, translating, "*un millier de Vānaras.*"

"aware of a slight sensation" *buddhaḥ sparśaṃ param*: Literally, "cognizing a mere touch." We follow Cg and Cr, who gloss *param*, normally, "last, final, other," in its adverbial sense of "only (*kevalam*)." Cr understands that Kumbhakarṇa was conscious merely of the touch of the elephants but not of the elephants themselves (*buddhvā paraṃ kevalaṃ sparśam abudhyata gajān nābudhyatety arthaḥ*). Cg has a similar idea, claiming that Kumbhakarṇa woke up (*buddhaḥ viratanidraḥ*) thinking that the trampling of the elephants was merely some insects crawling across his body (*vāraṇapradhāvanaṃ kevalaṃ sparśam abudhyata kīṭādisparśo 'yam iti manyate sma*). Translators vary in their treatment of the word *param*, rendered here as "slight." Gita Press (1969, vol. 3, p. 1593) and Raghunathan (1982, vol. 3, p. 158) translate more or less as we do. Roussel (1903, vol. 3, p. 184) and Pagani (1999, p. 1018) understand the term in the sense of "last *or* final (*dernière*—Roussel; *ultime*—Pagani). Dutt (1893, p. 1291) ignores the term. Shastri (1959, vol. 3, p. 159) appears to render the term as "at last."

48. "Ignoring the tremendous blows of mountaintops and trees that were being hurled down upon him" *sa pātyamānair giriśṛṅgavṛkṣair acintayaṃs tān vipulān prahārān*: Cg understands that, even though Kumbhakarṇa has awakened, the *rākṣasas* continue to rain blows upon him to make him get up (*pātyamānaiḥ prabodhe 'py utthānāya punaḥ kṣipyamāṇaiḥ*). Roussel (1903, vol. 3, p. 184), Pagani (1999, p. 1018), and Shastri (1959, vol. 3, p. 159), interpreting the present participle *acintayan*, "ignoring," in a past sense, understand the reference to be to Kumbhakarṇa's heedlessness of the earlier blows.

"at the violent interruption of his sleep" *nidrākṣayāt*: Literally, "from the destruction of sleep."

"yawning" *vijṛmbhamāṇaḥ*: Cg understands the term to refer to stretching the limbs (*gātrabhaṅgaṃ kurvāṇaḥ*).

"oppressed by fear and hunger" *kṣudbhayapīḍitaḥ*: The compound is somewhat ambiguous, since it can be read, as we have, as a *dvandva* or as a *tatpuruṣa* with the sense of "oppressed by the fear of hunger." Cg mentions both alternatives. In the first, he notes that Kumbhakarṇa's fear is the result of his untimely awakening (*bhayam atrākālabodhanakṛtam*). All translators consulted read the compound as a *tatpuruṣa*, taking it to mean "pangs of hunger" (Raghunathan 1982, vol. 3, p. 158; and Dutt 1893, p. 1291); "severe hunger" (Roussel 1903, vol. 3, p. 184; Pagani 1999, p. 1018; and Shastri 1959, vol. 3, p. 159); or "bugbear of hunger" (Gita Press 1969, vol. 3, p. 1593). Gorresio omits this verse.

The meter is *upajāti*.

49. "which were as strong as mountain peaks" *giriśṛṅgasārau*: D7,10,11, and the texts and printed editions of Ct and Cr read instead *jitavajrasārau*, which can be understood variously. Cr, the only commentator to explain the compound, takes it to mean "[the two arms] by which many warriors, whose strength was, that is, whose bodies were like adamant, had been defeated (*jitā vajrasārā vajrāṅgā bahuyoddhāro yābhyāṃ tau bāhū*). Among the translators consulted, only Gita Press (1969, vol. 3, p. 1593) follows this interpretation. Dutt (1893, p. 1291) renders, "superior in force to the thunder-bolt itself." Roussel (1903, vol. 3, p. 184) offers, "*durs comme des diamants taillés.*" Pagani (1999, p. 1018) translates, "*solides comme des pointes de diamant.*" Shastri (1959, vol. 3, p. 159) understands, "hard as cut diamonds."

"resembled two mountain peaks or great serpents" *nāgabhogācalaśṛṅgakalpau*: Literally, "similar to snake coils and mountain peaks." Cg explains the former simile to refer to the length of Kumbhakarṇa's arms and the second to their hardness. (*dairghye nāgabhogadṛṣṭāntaḥ. kāṭhinye 'calaśṛṅgadṛṣṭāntaḥ*). Alternatively, Cg suggests that the second *upamāna* refers to the thickness or muscularity (*pīnatve*) of the arms.

"grotesquely" *vikṛtam*: We follow Cg in reading the term adverbially (*bhayaṃkaraṃ yathā bhavati tathā*), as does Raghunathan (1982, vol. 3, p. 158), "hideously" and Gorresio (1856, vol. 9, p. 327), "*sformatamente*." The term can also be read as an adjective in the sense of "hideous, monstrous, etc.," modifying *mukham*, "mouth," as has been done by Dutt (1893, p. 1291), Roussel (1903, vol. 3, p. 184), Pagani (1999, p. 1018), Shastri (1959, vol. 3, p. 159), and Gita Press (1969, vol. 3, p. 1593).

"was like the gaping mare's head fire that lies beneath the sea" *vaḍavāmukhābham*: Literally, "like the mouth of the mare." The reference, as Cg notes, is to the mythical submarine mare (*samudramadhyavartiny aśvastrī*). According to Hindu mythology, the mare's mouth, which contains a vast insatiable fire that swallows up the waters of the ocean and is situated at the South Pole, constitutes a gaping portal into the underworld. See O'Flaherty 1971, pp. 9–27. According to *MBh* 1.171.17–22, this fire was formed from the undischarged cataclysmic rage of the sage Aurva. See R. Goldman 1977. Translators have treated the term variously. Gita Press (1969, vol. 3, p. 1593) takes it to refer specifically to the fire. Gorresio (1856, vol. 9, p. 327) renders, "*pari alla bocca del Pâtâla*," while Pagani (1999, p. 1018) translates, "*comme la porte des enfers*." Raghunathan (1982, vol. 3, p. 158) offers, "the abyss of the *Vadavā* fire in the bowels of the sea." Roussel (1903, vol. 3, p. 184), followed by Shastri (1959, vol. 3, p. 159), leaves the term untranslated. See, too, 6.55.118; and 6.61.42 and notes.

The meter is *upajāti*.

50. "as he yawned prodigiously" *jājṛmbhamāṇasya*: Ck, Ct, and Cm read the intensive in the sense of "yawned repeatedly (*punaḥ punar jṛmbhamāṇasya*—so Cm)." This sense has been adopted by those translators who give any force at all to the secondary form.

"his mouth as wide as the underworld Pātāla" *vaktraṃ pātālasaṃnibham*: Literally, "a mouth resembling Pātāla." See verse 23 and note above, as well as 6.55.28 and note.

"the sun, maker of day, risen over the summit of Mount Meru" *meruśṛṅgāgre divākara ivoditaḥ*: Literally, "the maker of day risen on the tip of the summit of Meru." Cg and Ck note the astronomical anomaly of this simile and propose different strategies to resolve it. The issue is that, according to purāṇic cosmology, the great axial mountain Mahāmeru is the central point around which the sun orbits. Therefore, the notion of the sun rising over the summit of Meru becomes impossible. Cg's explanation is that the poet is referring not to the axial Mount Meru but rather to a lesser mountain, which Cg calls Sāvarṇimeru. (*merur atra sāvarṇimeruḥ. tadagrasyaiva sūryasaṃbandhasambhavāt. atra divākarasyoditatvaṃ mahāmeror uttarabhāgasthapuryapekṣayā.*) We are unable to find any other reference to a mountain of this name in the primary or secondary literature. However, a mountain called Sumeru is mentioned at *BrahmāṇḍP* 1.15.42 and *BrahmP* 176.7. Cf., too, *MatsyaP* 9.36, where Merusāvarṇi is named as a son of Brahmā and one of the Manus; and also 11.38, where Manu Sāvarṇya lives on the peak of Meru and performs austerities (cf. *BrahmāṇḍP* 1.1.104). Cg, however, provides another explanation, namely, that one should take the participle *udita*, "risen," in the sense of *dṛṣṭa*, "seen, visible," since one can take a verb of motion (here *udita*) in the sense of awakened. (*yadvodito dṛṣṭa ity arthaḥ. gatyarthānāṃ buddhyarthatvāt.*) Thus, he understands that Kumbhakarṇa awoke just as the sun would awake on Mount Meru. Ck simply identifies the simile as an *abhūtopamā*, i.e., one in which the *upamāna*, or standard of comparison, is not, in fact, real. Ct notes that the basis for the simile is that Kumbhakarṇa's mouth is situated on [the top of] so huge a body (*mahāśarīrasthatvāt*). See 6.18.32–34; 6.47.106; and notes.

51. "was at last fully awake" *pratibuddhaḥ*: We follow Cg, who suggests that what is intended is a full and final awakening (*samyakprabodho 'tra vivakṣitaḥ*).

"like a gale from the mountains" *parvatād iva mārutaḥ*: Literally, "like wind from a mountain."

52. "was like that of a drenching storm cloud crossed by cranes at summer's end" *tapānte sabalākasya meghasyeva vivarṣataḥ*: Literally, "was like that of a showering cloud accompanied by cranes at the end of the hot season." The image of lines of white cranes outlined against black storm clouds is a popular one in Indian literature and painting. Compare, for example, Kālidāsa's *Meghadūta* 1.9. Cg, the only commentator to share this reading, thinks that the simile is based on the appearance of Kumbhakarṇa's bright ornaments against his dark body (*tasya sābharaṇasyety arthaḥ*). This interpretation is supported by, and perhaps derived from, such passages as *RaghuVa* 11.15 and *KumāSaṃ* 7.39, where the poet Kālidāsa describes, respectively, the *rākṣasī* Tāḍakā and the dark goddess Mahākālī with the same simile based upon their wearing white skull ornaments on their dark bodies. Compare the similar description of Kumbhakarṇa at 6.49.3. See, too, Bhāsa's description of Ghaṭotkaca in *Madhyamavyāyoga*, verses 4 and 5. Compare also the similar description of Rāvaṇa at 5.47.2–14 (specifically, verse 8); see notes ad loc.

D6,7,10,11,T2, and the texts and printed editions of Ct, Ck, and Cr substitute, for *pādas* cd, a line with a much more terrifying *upamāna*, "[his appearance] was like that of Kāla, eager to consume all beings at the end of the cosmic age (*yugānte sarvabhūtāni kālasyeva didhakṣataḥ*)."

53. "which resembled blazing fires and whose luster was like that of lightning, looked like two great blazing planets" *dīptāgnisadṛśe vidyutsadṛśavarcasī / dadṛśāte... dīptāv iva mahāgrahau*: Cg attempts to explain the rationale behind each of these fiery images. According to him, the image of lightning is used to express the darting, rolling motions of the demon's eyes when his slumber is interrupted. The image of the planets, which Cg takes to be the baleful Saturn and Mars, shows how oppressive Kumbhakarṇa's gaze would be to others. The image of blazing fire, Cg concludes, expresses Kumbhakarṇa's high degree of cruelty. (*vidyutsadṛśavarcasīti nidrāvirāmakālikacāñcalyoktiḥ. mahāgrahau śanyaṅgārakāv iti parapīḍakatvoktiḥ. dīptāgnisadṛśa iti krauryātiśayoktiḥ.*) Cf. Bhāsa's description of Ghaṭotkaca in his *Madhyamavyāyoga*, verse 5. See, too, 6.49.3 and note.

Following verse 53, D5–7,9–11,S insert a passage of two lines [1063*]: "Then they showed him all the many different kinds of food, and that immensely powerful *rākṣasa* consumed the boars and buffaloes."

54. "drank wine and a pot of marrow" *medaḥkumbhaṃ ca madyaṃ ca papau*: According to Cg, the meat and blood consumed in *pādas* ab were taken to satisfy Kumbhakarṇa's hunger and thirst. (*bubhukṣāśāntyartham māṃsam adann ity arthaḥ... tṛṣṇāśāntyartham śoṇitaṃ pibann ity arthaḥ.*) Cg adds that the additional food and drink mentioned in *pādas* cd is to fatten or strengthen him further (*punar āpyāyanārthaṃ medaḥkumbhān madyaṃ ca papau*).

55. "they approached" *samutpetuḥ*: Normally, the verb has the sense of "to rise *or* spring up." Here, however, we agree with Ct that it has the sense of "coming face to face (*saṃmukham ājagmuḥ*)." Cg explains that up until this point the *rākṣasas* have kept themselves hidden in fear of Kumbhakarṇa. But now, since he is sated and his anger has abated, they dare to approach him openly. (*pūrvaṃ kumbhakarṇabhayād antardhāya sthitāḥ. idānīṃ tṛptatvena śāntakrodhatvāt prakāśam ājagmur ity arthaḥ.*)

Following verse 55, B3,D5–7,9–11,S insert, while Ñ,V,B2,D2,4,13 insert following verse 52, a passage of two lines [1067*]: "His eyes half-closed with sleep, his vision clouded, he cast his glance all around him and addressed[1] those night-roaming *rākṣasas*."

[1]"addresssed" *uvāca*: M1–3 and the printed editions of Cg read instead "he looked at (*dadarśa*)."

56. "astonished at having been awakened" *bodhanād vismitaḥ*: Ct and Cr note that Kumbhakarṇa, whose sleep has no natural termination, is astonished at having been awakened in an untimely fashion (*svabhāvato nidrāpagamābhāvenākālabodhanād iti bhāvaḥ*—so Ct). For "awakening (*bodhanāt*)," Cg glosses, "the awakening of one who is not to be awakened (*aprabodhyabodhanāt*)."

*57. "Why have you gentlemen put so much effort into waking me?" *kim artham aham ādṛtya bhavadbhiḥ pratibodhitaḥ*: Literally, "For what purpose have I been awakened assiduously by you?" The critical edition, evidently as a result of an unnoted typographical error, reads the unattested *āhatya*, "having beaten [me]," instead of *ādṛtya*, which we believe to be correct. The critical apparatus shows Ś,B1,4,D1–3,8,12,13 reading *āgamya*, "having approached [me]," while D5,M5 read *āvṛtya*, "concealing [yourselves]." The critical apparatus shows no other variations. All printed editions of the southern text and all commentators read *ādṛtya*. We have emended accordingly. Commentators understand the verb *ā* $\sqrt{}$*dṛ* in its sense of "to be attentive, effortful, *or* persevering." This interpretation is followed by all translators who have this reading, with the exception of Dutt (1893, p. 1292), who takes the root in its other common sense of "to honor, respect." Compare 6.5010ab and note below, where the same construction is used with the gerund *ādṛtya*.

"and that no danger of any kind presents itself" *bhayaṃ vā neha kiṃcana*: Literally, "or that there is no danger whatever here." M3, as well as the texts and printed editions of Cg, Cv, and Cm, read instead *bhayavān eṣa vā na kim*, "and that he [the king] is not any danger." Among the translators, only Raghunathan (1982, vol. 3, p. 159) renders this variant.

58. "from enemies" *anyebhyaḥ*: Literally, "from others." We agree with Ct, who glosses, "from enemies (*śatrubhyaḥ*)."

"you gentlemen have so urgently awakened me" *tvaritair bhavadbhiḥ pratibodhitaḥ*: Literally, "[I] have been awakened by you hurrying gentlemen."

59. "I shall cast down great Indra or smash Anala, god of fire." *pātayiṣye mahendraṃ vā śātayiṣye tathānalam*: Literally, "I shall cause Mahendra to fall or shatter Anala." B1,3,D7,9–11, and the texts and printed editions of Ct read *dārayiṣye*, "I shall shatter *or* tear to pieces," for *pātayiṣye*, "I shall cast down," while B1,3,D9–11, and the texts and printed editions of Ct read *śītayiṣye*, "I shall cool, quench, *or* freeze," for *śātayiṣe*, "I shall smash."

60. "For no one would have awakened me so violently from my slumber" *na hi . . . suptaṃ bodhayiṣyati māṃ bhṛśam*: Literally, "For he will not violently awaken me who am asleep." One could also plausibly read the adverb *bhṛśam*, "violently," with the adjective *suptam*, "asleep," in the sense of "profoundly," thus yielding "me who was so soundly asleep." Manuscripts show substantial variation in the final two words of *pāda* b, *māṃ bhṛśam*. V3,B2,D9–11, and the texts and printed editions of Ct, Cr, Ck, and Gorresio read instead *mādṛśam*, "someone like me." D4–6,T,G1,M3, and the texts and printed editions of Cg, Cv, and Cm read instead *māṃ* (D6,T3 *me*) *guruḥ*, "[my] elder (i.e., Rāvaṇa) [would not have awakened] me."

61. "Yūpākṣa" *yūpākṣaḥ*: Hanumān kills another *rākṣasa* of this name in the *Sundarakāṇḍa* (5.44.27–30). See Goldman and Goldman 1996, pp. 23–26. See, too, notes to 6.65.1; 6.83.5; and 6.111.7.

"tamer of his foes" *arimdamam*: Ñ1,V,B2,4,D5,T1,M3, and the texts and printed editions of Cg and Cm read instead *mahābalam*, "of great strength."

62. "any . . . such" *hi tādṛśam*: Literally, "indeed such." B3,D9–11, and the texts and printed editions of Ct and Cr read instead *na naḥ kvacit*, "nowhere for us."

"your highness" *rājan*: Literally, "O king." The title used here for Kumbhakarṇa is somewhat unusual, and we understand it in the sense of "prince."

Following 62ab, Ñ1,V,B2,3,D5–7,9–11,13,S insert a passage of one line [1070*]: "A catastrophic danger from a man oppresses us, your highness."

63. "a catastrophic danger . . . confronts us" *nas tumulaṃ bhayam*: Literally, "of us there is a fierce danger."

64. The events mentioned here are among the exploits of Hanumān recounted at *Sundarakāṇḍa* 45. This verse is yet another example of the inaccuracy of Jacobi's argument that the events of the so-called Hanumān episode are not referred to elsewhere in the epic. See Goldman and Goldman 1996, pp. 23–26.

"along with his troops" *sānuyātraḥ*: Literally, "together with his followers *or* retinue."

65. "Rāvaṇa Paulastya" *paulastyaḥ*: Literally, "Paulastya [descendant of Pulastya]."

"was dismissed" *muktaḥ*: Literally, "released." The critical edition's reading *muktā* is evidently a typographical error, which is not noted in the list of errata.

"with the words, 'You are as good as dead.'" *mṛteti*: Given the *sandhi*, the sequence here would normally be interpreted as *mṛta + iti*, that is, the vocative, "O dead man." We are inclined, however, to accept the explanation of Cv, Cg, Cm, and Ck, who understand *mṛta* to stand for the nominative *mṛtaḥ*. According to Cg, who reads the adjective initially as a vocative, what we have here, in fact, is a [nominative] designation missing its case ending (*avibhaktikanirdeśaḥ*), although it may well be only a case of double *sandhi*. These commentators understand the expression to mean that Rāma, regarding Rāvaṇa as practically dead (*mṛtaprāyaḥ*—Cg, Cm) or dead though living (*jīvan mṛtaḥ*—Ck, Ct), let him go. D6,7,9–11,T3,G1,M5, and printed editions of Ct read instead *vrajeti*, "with the words, 'Go!'" Cr, the only commentator to explicitly address this reading, understands that Rāma dismissed Rāvaṇa telling him to go because the latter was already defeated (*parābhūtatvād gaccheti rāmeṇoktvā muktaḥ*). It is somewhat confusing that, although Ct's text reads *vrajeti*, he appears to comment on the critical edition's reading, *mṛteti*.

66. "released him, sparing his life" *vimuktaḥ prāṇasaṃśayāt*: Literally, "released from danger to his life." Cg offers two explanations of the phrase. In the first, he reads the ablative compound *prāṇasaṃśayāt* as if it were a gerund that had lost its characteristic

marker (*lyablope pañcamī*), giving the sense "Rāvaṇa was released after having been brought into peril of his life by Rāma (*sa rāvaṇo rāmeṇa prāṇasaṃśayaṃ nītvādya vimuktaḥ kṛta ity arthaḥ*)." Cm offers this interpretation as well. Cg's second alternative, which is similar to Ct's and Cr's, is the one we have followed.

67. "of Yūpākṣa . . . to him" *yūpākṣa- . . . yūpākṣam*: Literally, "of Yūpākṣa . . . to Yūpākṣa."

68. "I shall . . . slaughter" *hatvā*: Literally, "having slaughtered." D9–11 and the texts and printed editions of Ct read instead *jitvā*, "having conquered."

70. "those . . . words of which the defects were magnified by anger" *tat . . . vākyam . . . roṣavivṛddhadoṣam*: We follow Cr in understanding the adjective to refer to Kumbhakarṇa's words. According to Cr, the defect referred to here is the improper policy (*nītivirodhaḥ*) [implicit in Kumbhakarṇa's plan to take action without consulting with his elders]. Ct, Cm, Cg, and Cs all understand the adjective to be the masculine accusative, modifying an implicit "Kumbhakarṇa." The first three of these commentators understand the defect to refer to bad policy, as does Cr, whereas Cs understands the defect to refer to Kumbhakarṇa's boastful self-praise that has been increased by his anger born of [his learning of Rāvaṇa's] defeat at Rāma's hands (*rāmāt parājayajanyakopena vivṛddho doṣa ātmaślāghanarūpo yasya tam*). Translators vary considerably in what they see as being magnified by Kumbhakarṇa's anger. Thus Dutt (1893, p. 1293) offers, "his spirit of insolence." Roussel (1903, vol. 3, p. 185), followed by Shastri (1959, vol. 3, p. 160), renders, "*la férocité*." Pagani (1999, p. 1019) translates, "*la colère*." Gita Press (1969, vol. 3, p. 1595) renders, "his violence," and Raghunathan (1982, vol. 3, p. 160), "whose judgment was vitiated by anger." Gorresio's text (6.37.98) reads *-ghoṣam*, "sound," for *-doṣam*, "fault," in which case the adjective refers unambiguously to Kumbhakarṇa's speech in the sense of "the volume of which was increased by anger."

The meter is *upajāti*.

71. "Only after you have heard . . . and carefully considered . . . should you attempt to conquer" *śrutvā . . . vimṛśya ca / paścād api . . . vijeṣyasi*: Literally, "having heard . . . and having considered . . . you shall afterward conquer."

"the advantages and disadvantages of any action" *guṇadoṣau*: Literally, "virtue and defect."

72. "prepared to set forth" *saṃpratasthe*: Literally, "he set forth." As Cg notes, we must read this verb proleptically since it is only at verse 79 below that Kumbhakarṇa, having received permission from Rāvaṇa, actually leaves his bed. (*saṃpratasthe prasthātum upacakrame. śayanād utpapāta hety uttaratra vakṣyamāṇatvāt.*) Cm understands similarly.

73. "Once they had awakened Kumbhakarṇa" *taṃ samutthāpya*: Literally, "having made him arise." V3,B3,D6,9–11, and the texts and printed editions of Ct and Cr read instead *suptam utthāpya*, "having made that sleeping one arise."

"fearsome in eye, form, and valor" *bhīmākṣaṃ bhīmarūpaparākramam*: Literally, "of fearsome eyes and fearsome in form and valor."

74. "When they arrived there" *tato gatvā*: Literally, "then, having gone." Ś,Ñ,V1,2,B,D1–4,7–13, and the texts and printed editions of Ct and Cr read instead *te 'bhigamya*, "they, having approached." This reading more or less constrains one to take *daśagrīvam*, "ten-necked [Rāvaṇa]," as the object of the gerund, whereas, in the critical reading, one may either take Rāvaṇa as the object or simply, as we have done,

understand that the palace mentioned in the previous verse is the destination of the *rākṣasas*.

75. "bull among *rākṣasas*" *rākṣasarṣabha*: The final word of the compound, *-ṛṣabha*, is marked as uncertain in the critical edition. The majority of northern and southern manuscripts collated for the critical edition and the texts and printed editions of Ct and Cr read instead *-īśvara* [*rākṣaseśvara*], "lord of the *rākṣasas*."

"How should he proceed?" *katham*: Literally, "How?" We interpret the interrogative adverb as do Cv, Cm, and Cg, who take it as part of an elliptical question, "How should he act (*kathaṃ karotu*)?" Ck and Ct understand it to express the sense of *āhosvit... vā*, a phrase that expresses doubt as to which of a number of options to choose. Cr takes it simply in the sense of the particle *vā*, "or."

"Should he sally forth directly" *tatraiva niryātu*: Literally, "Should he go forth right there?" We follow the commentators, who understand the phrase to mean "Should he proceed straight to the battle [from] where he stands (*tatraiva sthito yuddhāya niryātu*—so Ct)?"

"or will you first see him here" *drakṣyase tam ihāgatam*: Literally, "will you see him when he has come here?"

76. "honored" *pūjitam*: The critical edition marks the participial ending as doubtful. A wide variety of northern and southern manuscripts (B3,4,D6,7,9–11,T1, 2,G1,3,M3) and the texts and printed editons of the southern commentators read instead the imperative *pūjyatām*, "let him be honored."

80. "he rinsed his mouth" *prakṣālya vadanam*: The phrase is ambiguous. It can be rendered equally well as "having washed his face," and, indeed, all translators consulted have done so with the exception of Raghunathan (1982, vol. 3, p. 160), who translates, "he gargled." We believe that Raghunathan is correct, since rinsing the mouth would be part of a normal morning toilet, whereas washing the face could be easily included in Kumbhakarṇa's bath.

"adorned himself splendidly" *paramabhūṣitaḥ*: Literally, "supremely adorned." V3,B3,D7,9–11, and the texts and printed editions of Ct and Cr read instead the redundant *-harṣitaḥ*, "delighted," for *-bhūṣitaḥ*, "adorned."

"he urgently sent for" *tvarayāmāsa*: Literally, "he caused to be hastened." See verse 58 above.

"invigorating drink" *pānaṃ balasamīraṇam*: Literally, "a drink that rouses strength." The commentators agree that this is a strengthening or stimulating drink but offer no hints as to its identity (*balavardhanam*—Cg). See, however, verse 81 below.

81. "on his account" *tasya*: The exact reference of the genitive pronoun is not clear. We have taken it elliptically in the sense of "for his sake, on his account." V3,B1,3,4,D2,7,9–11,M1,2, and the texts and printed editions of Ct and Cr read instead *tatra*, "there," which presumably makes reference to the *rākṣasas* racing back to Kumbhakarṇa's cave.

"intoxicating drink and... food" *madyaṃ bhakṣyāṃś ca*: D5,T1,M3, and the texts and printed texts of Cg dispense with the food, reading *madyakumbhāṃś ca*, "jars of intoxicating drink."

82. "a thousand jars, he" *ghaṭasahasraṃ sa*: D5–7,9–11,S read instead *ghaṭasahasre dve*, "two thousand jars."

83. "exhilarated, and slightly intoxicated" *īṣatsamutkaṭo mattaḥ*: Literally, "somewhat elevated, intoxicated *or* excited." The terms *samutkaṭa* and *matta* form one of those

common pairs of near synonyms, which the commentators often try to distinguish in meaning from each other. Here only Cg attempts to differentiate the two terms. He understands *samutkaṭaḥ* to refer to Kumbhakarṇa's inebriation as a result of the drinking in which he has just indulged, while taking *mattaḥ* to refer to Kumbhakarṇa's innate violence *or* high spirits. (*īṣatsamutkaṭaḥ pāneneṣanmadotkaṭaḥ. mattaḥ svabhāvenonmattaś cety arthaḥ.*) Ct, Cr, and Cm offer no explicit glosses to distinguish between the two terms but appear to suggest a distinction by linking the term *utkaṭaḥ* specifically to the drinking and taking *mattaḥ* separately. See note to 6.2.14.

"in his frenzy" *hṛṣṭaḥ*: Literally, "agitated, excited." D9–11 and the texts and printed editions of Ct and Cr read instead *ruṣṭaḥ*, "angry, furious."

"resembled Yama, who brings time itself to an end" *kālāntakayamopamaḥ*: The compound lends itself to a variety of analyses. Cg understands the first element of the compound, *kāla-*, "time," to mean "at the time of universal destruction (*pralayakāle*)." See note to 6.21.26.

84. "his footsteps shook the very earth" *padanyāsair akampayata medinīm*: Literally, "he caused the earth to shake with his footsteps."

85. "flooded... with light" *prakāśayan*: Literally, "illuminating."

"bodily radiance" *vapuṣā*: Literally, "with his body." We follow Ct and Ck who gloss, "with bodily splendor (*dehakāntyā*)."

"the thousand-rayed sun" *sahasraraśmiḥ*: Literally, "the thousand-rayed one."

"with a garland of hands cupped in reverence" *añjalimālayā*: Literally, "with a garland of *añjalis*." Cr explains that this refers to the people who are making the reverential gesture (*kṛtāñjalijanair ity arthaḥ*), while Cg further specifies that these would be the townsfolk (*añjalimālayā paurajanakṛtayeti śeṣaḥ*).

"Indra of the hundred sacrifices on his way to the abode of self-existent Brahmā" *śatakratur geham iva svayaṃbhuvaḥ*: Literally, "like Śatakratu [on his way to] Svayaṃbhū's house." The image is no doubt chosen to suggest the grandeur of Kumbhakarṇa in procession as well as the reverence accorded him as he passes. It is not clear that the poet has any specific mythological incident in mind. Nonetheless, we do see Indra proceeding to Brahmā's abode in connection with the case of Kumbhakarṇa in the very next *sarga* (6.49.19).

The meter is *vaṃśasthavila*.

Following verse 85, D5–7,9–11,S insert a passage of four lines [1078*]: "When the forest-dwelling monkeys and the guardians of the troops of tawny monkeys,[1] who were stationed outside, suddenly caught sight of that immeasurable slayer of his enemies, who looked like a mountain peak there on the royal highway, they were terrified."

[1]"the guardians of the troops of tawny monkeys" *hariyūthapālāḥ*: D9–11 and the texts and printed editions of Ct and Cr read instead *saha yūthapālaiḥ*, "together with the guardians of the troops."

The meter of lines 1–2 is *vaṃśasthavila*; that of lines 3–4 is *upajāti*.

86–87. The sequence of these two verses in the critical edition is extremely awkward, since we are told of the panic of the monkeys in verse 86 ("Some ran for refuge... on the ground") before we learn that they have even seen Kumbhakarṇa in verse 87 ("Seeing him...fled in all directions"). This situation is not duplicated in either the northern or southern recension of the text. The south avoids the problem by inserting verse 1078* (see note to 6.48.85 above), which anticipates the substance of verse 87 in which the monkeys first catch sight of the giant *rākṣasa*. The vast majority of northern manuscripts and editions reverse the order of the two verses, yielding a more logical narrative sequence, and we have followed this in our translation. The printed text of Gorresio avoids the problem by omitting verses 85–86 entirely.

"as if matching the sun itself with his innate splendor" *spṛśantam ādityam ivātmatejasā*: Literally, "touching Āditya, as it were, with his own splendor." We follow Ct, who understands that Kumbhakarṇa was like the sun. This also suggests, according to Ct, that, like the sun, Kumbhakarṇa is not awake for more than one day at time. (*tatsadṛśam iti yāvat. prāyo dinadvaye nāsya jāgaraḥ.*)

"refuge to Rāma, the refuge of all" *śaraṇyaṃ śaranam*...*rāmaṃ*: Literally, "refuge to Rāma, who is a refuge." The phrase is a common one in the *Yuddhakāṇḍa*. In some occurrences, Rāma's role as the universal refuge is made more explicit. Compare, for example, 6.12.11 and note. See also 6.13.4; 6.47.43; 6.31.56; 6.59.8; 6.81.14; and notes.

The meter of verse 86 is *indravajrā*, while that of verse 87 is *vaṃśasthavila*.

Sarga 49

1–2. The syntax of verses 1–3 is not clearly defined, and commentators and translators alike differ as to where and how to break the sequence into sentences. Translators also disagree as to whether it is Rāma or the monkey army that forms the subject of the gerund *dṛṣṭvā*, "having seen," in 2a. Cg wants to read the first two and a half verses (1–3ab) as a single sentence (*tata ityādi sārdhaślokadvayam ekānvayam*), in which case all the adjectives and figures of speech qualifying Kumbhakarṇa in the first three verses would apply to him as Rāma alone sees him. Cm, whose analysis we follow, suggests as his first alternative that we read verses 1 and 2 as a single sentence (*tato rāma ityādi ślokadvayam ekaṃ vākyam*), in which case the adjectives describing Kumbhakarṇa in 3ab represent him as the monkey army sees him. Cm offers a second alternative, that we read verse 2 as a separate sentence (*yadvā taṃ dṛṣṭveti śloko bhinnaṃ vākyam*). This proposal, however, is weakened by the fact that verse 2 lacks a finite verb. Ct and Cr, however, propose remedying this defect by supplying the words "He [i.e., Rāma] became alert (*yatto babhūveti śeṣaḥ*)." Cv, the earliest of our commentators, offers a more detailed syntactic analysis of the passage. He argues, like Cm, that verse 2 must be syntactically connected with verse 1. The sequence for him is that Rāma, having seen Kumbhakarṇa, took up his bow and watched him. If we do not construe the sequence in this way, Cv continues, and try to link verses 2 and 3, we are confronted with the undesirable repetition of the gerund *dṛṣṭvā* in a single sentence. Or, he argues, we may simply accept the repetition of the action of seeing because of the multitude of visual adjectives in the passage (*dṛśyaviśeṣaṇabāhulyād darśanakriyāvṛttir iti vā parihāraḥ*). Most translators consulted have, against the commentators, read verses 2 and 3 as a single unit. Gita Press (1969, vol. 3, p. 1597), which follows the interpretation of Ct and Cr, is the sole exception, supplying the words "he became alert."

"striding along as did Lord Nārāyaṇa long ago through the heavens" *kramamāṇam ivākāśaṃ purā nārāyaṇaṃ prabhum*: The reference is no doubt to Viṣṇu's *vāmanāvatāra*, or dwarf incarnation, as Cr notes. This popular story is repeated throughout the literature. See, for example, *ŚatBr* 1.2.5.1–9; *VāyuP* 2.36.74–86; and *MBh* 3.270, 3.313, 12.343; etc. See O'Flaherty 1975, pp. 328–29. See 6.40.43; 6.47.119; 6.53.25; 6.59.7; 6.105.24; and notes. See, too, 1.28.2 and note.

3. For a discussion on the syntax, see note to verses 1–2 above.

"who, adorned with his golden armlets, looked like a storm cloud charged with rain" *satoyāmbudasaṃkāśaṃ kāñcanāṅgadabhūṣaṇam*: The simile is no doubt based on the fact that, with the streaks of gold on his huge, dark body, Kumbhakarṇa resembles a thundercloud crossed by streaks of lightning. The image is a common one in the *Rāmāyaṇa*. See verse 5 below. See, too, 6.48.52–53 and notes.

4. "looming above him" *vardhamānam*: Literally, "growing." Cg understands that Kumbhakarṇa is literally increasing in size because of his power of being able to change his shape at will (*kāmarūpatvāt*). Translators consulted either indicate that Kumbhakarṇa is actually growing or that he simply appears to be. Because he is already of gigantic dimensions, we believe that, at this point, he simply appears to grow larger as he draws nearer. Compare, however, 6.53.33–34 and notes, where Kumbhakarṇa does dramatically increase his stature.

"in his amazement" *savismayam*: Cr, referring to the theological notion of Rāma's omniscience, believes that his expression of astonishment, and, indeed, his entire question, is for the purpose eliciting the wonder of his audience (*śrotṛvismayakārakam uvāca sarvajñarāmapraśnena jñātṝṇāṃ vismayo bhavatīti tātparyam*). Pagani (1999, p. 1021), idiosyncratically, takes the term as a reference to Kumbhakarṇa's astonishing characteristic (of being able to grow).

5. "tawny-eyed" *harilocanaḥ*: Most of the commentators gloss, "having tawny or reddish eyes (*kapilanetraḥ*)." Cr, who shares this gloss with the other commentators, also evidently derives the term *hari*, "tawny," from the root $\sqrt{hṛ}$, "to take away," and additionally glosses, "characterized by eyes that rob an enemy of his well-being (*ripusvāsthyāpahārakanetraviśiṣṭaḥ*)." Translators take the term to indicate a variety of colors, including tawny, yellow, and brown. Raghunathan (1982, vol. 3, p. 161) alone takes *hari* in the sense of the noun "monkey," rendering, "with eyes like an ape's." This is not persuasive. Cf. 6.22.33 and 6.39.30 and notes.

"looms over Laṅkā" *laṅkāyāṃ dṛśyate*: Literally, "appears *or* is visible in Laṅkā."

"like a storm cloud laced with lightning" *savidyud iva toyadaḥ*: See note to verse 3 above.

6. "From here he looks like some great and solitary banner raised high above the earth." *pṛthivyāḥ ketubhūto 'sau mahān eko 'tra dṛśyate*: The basis for the figure and thus the identity of the object of comparison are not entirely clear. The critical term here, *ketu*, has two meanings that are relevant in this context. One, which we have hesitantly used, is "flag *or* banner." We have chosen this because it seems as though it is Kumbhakarṇa's enormous height that suggests the image to Rāma. On the other hand, a second meaning of the term, "comet *or* meteor," is also plausible, since Kumbhakarṇa has been described elsewhere as fierce and blazing in appearance, and the epic poet frequently mentions these celestial bodies as terrifying or inauspicious omens. The commentators are surprisingly silent on this point, while the translators are divided. Gorresio (1858, vol. 10, p. 1), Dutt (1893, p. 1295), and Raghunathan

(1982, vol. 3, p. 161) have chosen the former meaning, while Gita Press (1969, vol. 3, p. 1597) and Roussel (1903, vol. 3, p. 187), followed by Shastri (1959, vol. 3, p. 161) and Pagani (1999, p. 1021), have chosen the latter. On omens, see 6.4.6 and note.

8. "by Prince Rāma Kākutstha . . . to him" *rājaputreṇa rāmeṇa . . . kākutstham*: Literally, "by the king's son Rāma . . . [said this] to Kākutstha."

9. "Vāsava" *vāsavaḥ*: Kumbhakarṇa's battle with and defeat of Indra is described below in verses 15–18.

Following verse 9, D5–7,9–11,S insert a passage of one line [1081*]: "There is no other *rākṣasa* to compare with him in size."

10. "flesh-eating demons" *piśitāśanāḥ*: Literally, "flesh-eaters." This class of carnivorous demon is alluded to occasionally in the literature, where the term may also serve as a kenning for "*rākṣasa*." Here, however, the poet presumably means to refer to creatures other than *rākṣasas*, since Kumbhakarṇa would not normally be expected to do battle with his own kind. According to Gorresio (1858, vol. 10, p. 280), the term *piśitāśana* is synonymous with *piśāca*, a class of demons whose origin he traces in purāṇic mythology to the sage Kaśyapa and his consort Piśāca [*sic*], one of the many daughters of Dakṣa.

"*kinnaras*" *-kiṃnarāḥ*: D9–11 and the texts and printed editions of Ct and Cr read instead the redundant *-pannagāḥ*, "great serpents," which is synonymous with *bhujaṃgāḥ* in *pāda* b.

The meter is *upajāti*.

11. "mistakenly thinking that . . . [Kumbhakarṇa] . . . was . . . Kāla himself" *kālo 'yam iti mohitāḥ*: Literally, "deluded [they thought], 'He is Kāla.'" As Cs notes, one might also take *kālaḥ* to refer to Rudra (Śiva), the dark (*kāla*) god, who is frequently represented as armed with a *śūla*, or "lance," and having fearsome eyes.

12. "power . . . derives from the gift of boons" *varadānakṛtaṃ balam*: The "boon" of Kumbhakarṇa is not to enhance his power but rather to prevent the exercise of his grotesque native strength and appetite. For Rāvaṇa's and Indrajit's boons of invulnerability, see 1.14.12–15 and notes; and *Uttarakāṇḍa* 10. On the motif of Rāvaṇa's boon, see Pollock 1991, pp. 15–54. See note to 6.28.28–29.

13. "this" *etena*: D9–11 and the texts and printed editions of Ct and Cr read *bālena*, "as an infant *or* child."

"this huge *rākṣasa*" *mahātmanā*: Literally, "by the great one." See 6.48.32 and note.

15. "the wielder of the sharp *vajra* . . . with it" *vajreṇa śitena vajrī*: Literally, "with the sharp *vajra*, the one possessed of the *vajra*."

"the huge *rākṣasa*" *mahātmā*: Literally, "the great one." See 6.48.32 and note.

The meter is *upendravajrā*.

16. "wise" *dhīmataḥ*: Ñ2,D6,7,9–11,M1,2, and the texts and printed editions of Ct and Cr read instead *rakṣasaḥ*, "of the *rākṣasa*."

"the earth, already terrified, became still more so" *vitrastā bhūyo bhūmir vitatrase*: Literally, "the frightened earth became more frightened." Ś,Ñ,B,V,D1–4,8–13, and the texts and printed editions of Ct and Cr read instead *vitrastāḥ prajā bhūyo vitatrasuḥ* (or minor variants), "the frightened creatures became more frightened." This northern reading seems contextually more apposite than that of the south with its abrupt introduction of the earth.

17. "tore out one of Airāvata's tusks and, with it, struck Vāsava" *vikṛṣyairāvatād dantaṃ jaghāna . . . vāsavam*: Literally, "having extracted a tusk from Airāvata, he struck Vāsava."

18. "Vāsava staggered" *vicacāla sa vāsavaḥ*: D5–7,9–11,T,M3, and the texts and printed editions of the southern commentators read instead *vijajvāla*, "he shone *or* glowed," for *vicacāla*, "he staggered." The commentators struggle somewhat to make sense of this reading. Ct explains, "he seemed to be pervaded by flames on account of the streams of blood (*rudhirapravāhair jvālavyāpta iva babhūva*)." Cr suggests, "he was exceedingly afflicted (*atisaṃtāpaṃ prāpa*)." Cg glosses, "he was infuriated (*cukopeti yāvat*)."

19. "lord of creatures ... they told him ... and his assaulting the gods" *śaśaṃsus te prajāpateḥ ... devānāṃ cāpi dharṣaṇam*: Literally, "they told the lord of creatures about ... and also his assaulting of the gods." The text of Ct, as rendered in GPP (6.61.19) and NSP (6.61.19), reads *śaśaṃsus te divaukasām*, "they reported to the inhabitants of heaven [i.e., the gods]," for *devānāṃ cāpi dharṣaṇam*, "and his assaulting the gods." According to this reading, Indra and the creatures report only the vicious nature of Kumbhakarṇa to the lord of creatures (Prajāpati) and then separately report his devouring of the creatures (but not the assault on the gods) to the gods. This reading has been rendered by Roussel (1903, vol. 3, p. 188), followed by Shastri (1959, vol. 3, p. 162), and by Dutt (1893, p. 1296). Pagani (1999, p. 1022) appears to read *divaukasām* not as an objective genitive governed by *śaśaṃsuḥ* but as an objective genitive construing with *bhakṣaṇam*, "devouring," to yield the dubious translation, "*ils racontèrent aussi qu'il dévorait les créatures et les dieux.*"

Following verse 19, Ñ,B2–4,D2,4–7,9–11,13,S insert a passage of one line [1085*]: "... his destruction of hermitages, and his brutal[1] abduction of other men's wives."

[1]"brutal" *bhṛśam*: Literally, "intense." D5,9–11,G1,M1,2, and the texts and printed editions of Ct and Cr read instead *tathā*, "as well."

20. The transition from indirect discourse to the direct speech of Indra passes uncharacteristically without explicit notice. See note to verse 21 below.

"within no time" *acireṇaiva kālena*: Literally, "in time that is not long."

21. "those words of Vāsava" *vāsavasya vacaḥ*: As noted above, the transition from verse 19 to 20 is awkward. In verse 19, it is Indra, along with the creatures, who all report to Brahmā, and there the poet uses the plural verb form. Here, according to Cg, Indra alone is mentioned because he is the principal member of the delegation (*prādhānyād vāsavagrahaṇam*).

"he sent for" *āvāhayāmāsa*: Ct understands the verb in its religious or ritual sense of "invoking *or* summoning a being through the use of a *mantra*." Here he claims Brahmā invokes or summons the *rākṣasas* by a *mantra* having the characteristics of the *Gāyatrī-mantra* (*gāyatrīlakṣaṇena mantreṇājuhāva*). See note to 6.1.1. Cr simply notes that Brahmā summons the *rākṣasas* into his presence by means of his own power (*sva-śaktyā*).

22. "Fixing him with his glance ... took a deep breath and [said] this" *dṛṣṭvā niśvasya caivedam*: Literally, "having looked and having sighed, [he said] this." This *pāda* (c) shows considerable variation in the manuscripts. D7,10,11,M1,2, and the texts and printed editions of Ct and Cr read instead *kumbhakarṇam athāśvastaḥ*, "regaining his composure, he then [said] to Kumbhakarṇa." Dutt (1893, p. 1296), uniquely, understands the participle *āśvastaḥ*, "composed," in a transitive sense, rendering, "pac-

ifying Kumbhakarṇa." G2,M3, and the texts and printed editions of Cv, Cg, and Cm read *viśvāsya*, "having inspired confidence," for the critical text's *niśvasya*. Cg understands by this that Brahmā is deceptively putting Kumbhakarṇa off his guard. He glosses, "seducing (*pralobhya*)."

23. See 6.48.9 and note. Compare, too, the well-known variant of the story at *Uttarakāṇḍa* 10, where, at the behest of the gods, Kumbhakarṇa is tricked by the god Brahmā and the goddess Sarasvatī into wasting his boon earned through his penances (7.10.2–8) on a request that he sleep for many years (7.10.31–41).

"That very instant" *atha*: Literally, "then."

"of the Lord" *prabhoḥ*: Our assumption is that the term refers to Lord Brahmā. Cg, however, sees it as a reference to Rāvaṇa. Among the translators consulted, only Gita Press (1969, vol. 3, p. 1599) explicitly shares Cg's understanding.

24. "You are cutting down" *nikṛtyate*: Literally, "[a tree] is being cut down."

"a . . . golden tree, just as it is about to bear fruit" *kāñcano vṛkṣaḥ phalakāle*: Literally, "a golden tree at the time of fruit." Commentators are divided as to how to understand this particular metaphor. Ck, Ct, and Cr understand it to refer to "a tree that bears golden fruit (*kāñcanaphalakaḥ*—Ck, Ct)." Cg and Cm take the term "golden (*kāñcanaḥ*)" figuratively, glossing, "as desirable as gold (*kāñcanavat spṛhaṇīyaḥ*)." Cg, however, offers as an alternative that the term "golden tree (*kāñcano vṛkṣaḥ*)" is a kenning for the ornamental *campaka* tree (*campakavṛkṣo vā*) (*Michelia campaka*). Cg further glosses *phalakāle*, "at the time of fruit," as "at the time of blossoming (*puṣpakāle*)," which would be apposite for the *campaka*, a tree noted for its fragrant blossoms but not its fruit. Cs cites a verse from the *Viśvakośa*, according to which the term *kāñcana*, "golden," can refer to a number of trees, including the *kāñcanāra* (*kovidāra*), *campaka*, *nāgakesara* (*Mesua ferrea* [iron wood tree]), *uḍumbara* (*Ficus glomerata* [cluster fig]), or the *puṃnāga* (*Calophyllum Inophyllum* or *Rottlera tinctoria*) (*kāñcanaḥ kāñcanāre syāc campake nāgakesare / uḍumbare ca puṃnāge*). Cs's point is that even such trees, which may not produce edible fruit, ought not to be cut down, if they have been nurtured. In support of this, he cites a verse to the effect that one should not cut down even a poisonous tree if one has nurtured it (*viṣavṛkṣo 'pi saṃvardhya svayaṃ chettum asāmpratam*). Cs further suggests that the reference may actually be to a tree made of gold, in the sense that at the time of bearing fruit it produces gold through its fruit. Elsewhere in the epic the sight or vision of golden trees is a sign that the death of the one who sees them is imminent. Compare 3.45.33; 3.51.17; and 3.64.11; and note to 3.45.33. See also *MBh* 6.94.12.

25. "grandson" *naptāram*: Kumbhakarṇa, like Rāvaṇa, is actually the great-grandson of Brahmā as he is the son of Viśravas, who in turn is the son of Pulastya, the mind-born son of Brahmā (7.9.20–27). See, too, *ManuSm* 1.35.

"you should set some time limit to his sleeping and waking" *kālas tu kriyatām asya śayane jāgare tathā*: Literally, "let a time be fixed with respect to his sleeping and waking." We follow the commentators in understanding *kālaḥ*, "time," in the sense of "restriction of time (*kālaniyamaḥ*—so Ct, Cg)."

26. "for six months" *ṣaṇmāsān*: Several of the commentators, including Ct, Cg, and Cs, note that this constitutes merely the minimum period for Kumbhakarṇa to sleep. Cg explicitly notes that, were this not the case, this verse would contradict verse 6.48.12, where Kumbhakarṇa is said to sleep nine, six, seven, or eight months at a stretch. (*ṣaṇmāsān ity etad arvāṅniṣedhaparam. anyathā nava ṣaṭ sapta cāṣṭau ca māsān iti*

pūrvoktavirodhāt.) For a fuller discussion on the duration of Kumbhakarṇa's sleep, see note to 6.48.12. Cs breaks up the words differently, reading *ṣaṇmāsānekāham* as a compound. He proposes that we read *ṣaṇmāsa-* as the prior member of a modifying compound (*viśeṣaṇasamāsa*), understanding it as a descriptive adjective modifying *anekāham*, in the sense of "six months plus many days." During this period Kumbhakarṇa would not awaken. The extension of sleep by some days is not undesirable, according to Cs, who adds that one should consider that this expansion was already provided for. (*ṣaṇmāsān viśeṣaṇasamāsaḥ. tan madhye na jāgaraṇam. nidrāyāṃ dinādhikyaṃ tu nāniṣṭam. vistaraḥ prāgupapādito 'nusaṃdheyaḥ.*) Cs's second option is to take *ṣaṇmāsān* as a separate word. See, too, notes to 6.9.22 (App. I, No. 3, lines 162–163, and notes). See R. Goldman 2003b and 2006b.

27. "all creatures" *lokān*: Literally, "people *or* worlds."

"raging" *saṃkruddhaḥ*: D9–11 and the texts and printed editions of Ct and Cr read instead *saṃvṛddhaḥ*, "vast."

29. "from his lair" *śibirāt*: Literally, "from the royal camp *or* residence." We follow Ct, who glosses, "from his lair (*nilayāt*)." Ct glosses, "from his own house (*svagṛhāt*)."

"Soon...he will race about, devouring" *bhakṣayan paridhāvati*: Literally, "he is running, while devouring." The commentators, reflecting on the fact that Kumbhakarṇa will actually sally forth against the monkeys at the very end of *sarga* 53 below (6.53.45), note that we are to read the participle *bhakṣayan* in the sense of "for the purpose of eating. (*bhakṣayan. hetau śatā. bhakṣārtham ity arthaḥ*—Ct, Cr.)" Cg, quoting *Pā* 3.2.126, takes the participle in the sense of "for the purpose of" and the present in the sense of the future. (*bhakṣaṇahetoḥ paridhāviṣyati. lakṣaṇahetvoḥ kriyāyā iti śatṛpratyayaḥ. vartamānasāmīpyādinā bhaviṣyadarthe laṭ.*)

30. Ck and Ct believe that Rāma has interjected this question into the midst of Vibhīṣaṇa's speech and that Vibhīṣaṇa responds to it in the following verse. (*punā rāmaḥ pṛcchati. katham enam iti*—so Ct.) It is most unusual, however, for Vālmīki to introduce a new speaker without explicitly indicating this, and we, like other translators consulted, understand the question to show Vibhīṣaṇa thinking out loud, and then, in the following verses, coming up with a solution.

31. Ct and Ck understand this verse to be spoken by Vibhīṣaṇa in response to what they take to be Rāma's question in verse 30 above (*vibhīṣaṇa uttaram āhocyatām iti*—so Ct).

"just some giant mechanical man" *yantram...samucchritam*: Literally, "lofty machine *or* mechanism." The idea seems to be that Vibhīṣaṇa wants to falsely represent the gargantuan Kumbhakarṇa as an animated mannequin, designed merely to frighten the monkeys. Ck and Ct explain that the monkeys are to be told that this was some mere mechanical device created through the power of illusion and erected by Rāvaṇa merely to cause fright. Therefore, Ck and Ct continue, it is really nothing at all. (*samucchritaṃ rāvaṇena. māyayā vibhīṣikārthaṃ nirmitaṃ kiṃcid yantramātram. ato na kiṃcid etad iti.*) Cr understands that Vibhīṣaṇa wants the monkeys to believe that it is a large mechanical *rākṣasa* that loses its power when it comes into his vicinity (*samucchritam atipravṛddham etat pradṛśyamānaṃ rakṣoyantraṃ matsamīpe saṃkucitatejo bhaviṣyatīti śeṣaḥ*). Cg glosses, "a large, that is, tall, device that is a scarecrow. (*yantraṃ bibhīṣikā. samucchritam unnatam.*)" See verse 6.54.5 and note.

32. "encouraging" *sumukhodgatam*: We follow Ct, Ck, and Cr in understanding that Vibhīṣaṇa's words are intended to generate cheerfulness or encouragement on the

part of the frightened monkeys (*vānaralokasya saumukhyasaṃpādanāyodgatam upadiṣṭaṃ vacaḥ*—so Ct). D6,T3,M3, and the texts and printed editions of Cg and Cm read instead *sumukheritam*, "uttered cheerfully."

33. According to Ct, Rāma's order to Nīla and the monkeys to [once again] blockade the city gates suggests that there has been a brief cessation of hostilities following Rāvaṇa's flight. (*yathāpūrvaṃ dvāranirodhe niyuṅkte gaccheti. anena rāvaṇapalāyanottaraṃ madhye 'vahāraḥ sūcitaḥ.*) See notes to 6.33.2–3; 6.41.8; and 6.62.2.

"Nīla Pāvaki" *pāvake*: Literally, "O Pāvaki." The epithet is a patronymic indicating that Nīla is the son of Pāvaka, or Agni, the purifier.

"seize control" *ādāya*: Literally, "having taken." We understand the gerund here in much the same sense of the English verb "to take," i.e., "to seize a military objective." Cr glosses, "having brought under your own control (*svavaśaṃ prāpayya*)."

"the... thoroughfares, and bridges" *caryāś cāpy atha saṃkramān*: The word *caryā* refers to the two main intersecting roads that link the four city gates. See 6.47.32; 6.48.8; and notes. We have taken *saṃkrama* in its sense of "bridge *or* causeway" and understand it to refer to the bridges or drawbridges that span the moats outside the city walls. See 6.3.15,16 and notes. The term could also be taken in the sense of "a narrow *or* difficult passage," and thus be paired with *caryā* to yield the sense "highways and byways." In any case, the idea is that Nīla is to occupy and guard all the exits from the citadel.

34. "Let all the monkeys collect" *upasaṃharan /... vānarāḥ sarve*: We follow Ct in taking the singular participle as an irregular plural (*upasaṃharantaḥ saṃcinvantaḥ*). Cr construes the singular with Nīla, who is therefore to collect the trees, etc., to serve as weapons for his troops (*upasaṃharan san tvaṃ tiṣṭhasva*). The printed editions of Cg and Cm read instead the singular imperative (*upasaṃhara*, "you collect"), presumably also with reference to Nīla. This variant is not noted in the critical apparatus.

"Let... take up their posts" *tiṣṭhantu*: Literally, "let them stay *or* stand." Ñ2, V1,B2,3,D1,9–11,M1,2, and the texts and printed editions of Ct and Cr read the polite second person pronoun *bhavantaḥ*, "you gentlemen." According to this reading, Rāma directs his remarks to the monkey troops themselves. Ct suggests that we then supply the verb *tiṣṭhantu* ("let all you monkeys stay..."). This reading is followed most literally by Dutt (1893, p. 1297) and Gita Press (1969, vol. 3, p. 1600).

"well armed" *sāyudhāḥ*: Literally, "with weapons." Despite the immediate context and the text's uniform assignment of only naturally occurring weapons to the monkeys, Cg understands the adjective to mean "possessing such weapons as swords, etc. (*khaḍgādyāyudhavantaḥ*)."

36. "Nala" *nalaḥ*: D5–7,9–11,T,M3–5, and the texts and printed editions of the southern commentators read instead *tathā*, "as well," thus removing Nala from the group.

"approached" *abhyayuḥ*: Cr glosses, "they blockaded (*rurudhuḥ*)."

Following verse 36, D5–7,9–11,S insert a passage of two lines [1094*]: "When they had heard Rāma's words, the heroic tawny monkeys,[1] with a victorious air, assailed the enemy army with trees."

[1]"the... tawny monkeys" *harayaḥ ...vānarāḥ*: Literally, "tawny monkeys... monmonkeys."

37. "With boulders held aloft and trees in their hands" *śailodyatavṛkṣahastam*: Literally, "with mountain-raised-tree-hands." The compound is somewhat awkward. We follow Ct in reading it as essentially a *dvandva* consisting of two *bahuvrīhis*: *udyataśailam*, "with upraised boulders," and *vṛkṣahastam*, "with trees in hand." Cr sees a slightly different *dvandva*, analyzing the compound as "in the hands of which there were boulders and upraised trees (*śailā udyatavṛkṣāś ca hasteṣu yasya tat*)." Ck reads yet another *dvandva*, this time with *paranipāta*, to yield "with [upraised] boulder, tree, and hand (*śailaṃ vṛkṣaṃ hastaś ca*)." D6,T2,3,G1,3,M3,5, and the texts and printed editions of Cm and Cg read *-dīpta-*, "glowing, glittering," for *-vṛkṣa-*, and the latter is marked as uncertain in the critical edition. This reading can be interpreted to mean "with raised boulders and glittering hands," "their hands glittering with raised boulders," or "with raised boulders in their glittering hands." Raghunathan (1982, vol. 3, p. 163), the only translator to share this reading, renders, "with rocks held aloft in their strong hands."

"resembled a... mass of... clouds, looming up against a mountain" *rarāja .../ gireḥ samīpānugataṃ yathaiva ... -ambhodharajālam*: Literally, "shone just like a mass of clouds that had come near a mountain." Ck and Ct claim that the propriety of the simile lies in the fact that Laṅkā is situated on a mountain (*parvatāgravartilaṅkāyāḥ parito vartamānatvāt tattvam*). This comment is echoed in a footnote by Dutt (1893, p. 1297).

The meter is *upendravajrā*.

Sarga 50

1. "groggy with sleep and drink" *nidrāmadasamākulaḥ*: We follow Cg, the only commentator to analyze this compound, in taking *nidrāmada-*, literally, "sleep intoxication," as a *dvandva*, referring to the effects of Kumbhakarṇa's untimely awakening and indulgence in strong drink immediately afterward (6.48.47–54, 80–83). The compound can also be read as a *tatpuruṣa* in the sense of "the intoxication of sleep." Translators are divided on this issue. Gita Press (1969, vol. 3, p. 1601), Raghunathan (1982, vol. 3, p. 164), and Pagani (1999, p. 1023) translate as we do. Gorresio (1858, vol. 10, p. 4), Dutt (1893, p. 1298), and Roussel (1903, vol. 3, p. 190), followed by Shastri (1959, vol. 3, p. 164), choose the latter interpretation.

2. "that supremely invincible warrior" *paramadurjayaḥ*: Literally, "the supremely invincible one."

"As... continued on his way" *yayau*: Literally, "he went."

"showers of blossoms raining from the houses along his route" *gṛhebhyaḥ puṣpavarṣeṇa*: Literally, "with a shower of flowers from the houses." The commentators suggest adding a participle, either *nirgatena*, "issuing from," (Ct) or *utkṣiptena*, "thrown," (Ck) to modify the compound *puṣpavarṣeṇa*, "shower of flowers." Ck, Ct, and Cs note that the flowers are coming from the hands of the women living in the houses (*tadgṛhavartistrīhastebhyaḥ*—so Ct). Cs offers, as an alternative, that we take the term *gṛha*, "house," metonymically to stand for "housewife." He explains, "Or, 'from the houses' means 'from the wives of other men' according to the saying, 'The housewife is called the house' (*yad vā gṛhebhyaḥ parabhāryābhyo gṛhiṇī gṛham ucyata iti vacanāt*)." As a third alternative, Cs understands the term simply to refer to the houses of the *rākṣasas* (*rākṣasānāṃ gṛhebhyaḥ*).

3. "At length he spied" *saḥ ... dadarśa*: Literally, " he saw."

"covered with a fretwork of gold" *hemajālavitatam*: Cg understands, "covered with louvered windows of gold (*svarṇamayagavākṣavitatam*)," taking *jāla* in the sense of window. Compare note to 5.7.14–15. Among the translators, only Raghunathan (1982, vol. 3, p. 164) follows this interpretation, rendering, "with its golden casements." See 6.45.6 and note. Cf. 6.87.26; and 6.109.1 and note.

"blazed with the radiance of the sun" *bhānubhāsvaradarśanam*: Literally, "with an appearance of sunlight." Ct explains the extraordinary radiance of the palace as deriving from the sun's rays [being reflected] in its jewels (*ratneṣu sūryakīraṇasaṃbandhād adhikatejovattvaṃ gṛhasyeti bhāvaḥ*).

4. "as might the sun a mass of clouds" *sūrya ivābhrajālam*: The expected contrast of light and dark here, that is, the dark *rākṣasa* entering a mansion, which in the previous verse was said to shine with the radiance of the sun, seems to be inverted here. Among the commentators, only Cs takes note of this. He offers two possible explanations. In the first, we are to understand that the palace has a dark watery (i.e., cloudlike) appearance because of its encrustation with dark sapphires. However, in those places where there are no sapphires but diamonds instead, the glittering of the palace justifies the use of this figure (*nidarśanā*), which then does not contradict the solar imagery of verse 3 (*abhrajālaṃ jalasattādaśāyām indranīlakhacanāt tadabhāvadaśāyāṃ vajraiś ca tannidarśanatociteti na bhānubhāsvareti virodhaḥ*). In the second, he proposes wrenching the syntax a bit so as to make the *upamāna*, "mass of clouds (*abhrajālam*)," correspond not to the palace but to the dark *rākṣasa* lord Rāvaṇa (*athavāgrajaṃ rāvaṇam abhrajālam iva dadarśety anvayaḥ*).

"seated on his throne ... seated on his" *āsanastham ... āsanastham*: Literally, "situated on his seat ... situated on his seat."

"from afar" *dūre*: The adverb probably suggests the great depth of Rāvaṇa's hall as he is seen from afar in his inner throne room. Cg, however, relates it to the great height of the Puṣpaka flying palace in which Rāvaṇa is seated (*unnatapuṣpakavattvād iti bhāvaḥ*).

The meter is *upajāti* with a hypermetric *pāda* b.

Following verse 4, D5–7,9–11,S insert a passage of two lines [1095*]: "As Kumbhakarṇa made his way toward his brother's palace, accompanied by hosts of *rākṣasas*,[1] his footsteps shook the very earth." This verse is a repetition, substituting only *-gaṇa-*, "hosts," for *-bala-*, "army," of 6.48.84. Here it seems to be poorly contextualized, as Kumbhakarṇa has already entered the palace in verse 4.

[1] "accompanied by hosts of *rākṣasas*" *rakṣogaṇasamanvitaḥ*: D5,M3, and the texts and printed editions of Cg and Cm read instead the neuter accusative *rakṣogaṇasamanvitam*, which must then modify *bhavanam*, "palace."

5. "the flying palace Puṣpaka" *vimāne puṣpake*: See note to 6.7.5.

6. "he quickly sat up" *tūrṇam utthāya*: Literally, "having stood up." Because of the context of this passage, we do not believe that Rāvaṇa actually leaves his seat at this point. Northern manuscripts substitute *kiṃcit*, "somewhat," for the critical edition's *tūrṇam*, "quickly." See note to verse 7 below.

7. "upon his throne" *paryaṅke*: Literally, "on a couch *or* bed."

"What task must I perform?" *kiṃ kṛtyam iti*: Literally, "What is to be done?"

"Then, springing up... him" *utpatya cainam*: Given the critical reading and the expected protocol of the encounter, we believe this is the first time that Rāvaṇa rises from his throne, and we have therefore rendered *utthāya* in verse 6 above as "sitting up." The idea is that the dejected king was slumped in his seat and sits upright at the sight of his brother. D7,9–11, and the texts and printed editions of Ct and Cr read *punaḥ sa muditotpatya* [irregular *sandhi*—so Ct], "springing up once more, in great delight, he." Among the translators consulted, only Gita Press (1969, vol. 3, p. 1601) explicitly reads this to mean that Rāvaṇa stands up a second time. Roussel (1903, vol. 3, p. 190), followed by Shastri (1959, vol. 3, p. 165), reads the adverb *punaḥ*, "again," with the adjective *muditaḥ*, "in great delight." Dutt (1893, p. 1298) reads *utthāya* in verse 6 as a causal, "raised him [Kumbhakarṇa] up," and then takes *punaḥ* with the verb *pariṣasvaje*, "he embraced." Pagani (1999, p. 1024) interprets as we do (see verse 6 above). Northern manuscripts avoid this issue by reading *kiṃcid utthāya*, "partly rising *or* sitting up," at verse 6 above. This yields a sequence similar to the one we find in the critical text.

9. "his eyes red with rage" *saṃraktanayanaḥ kopāt*: Literally, "with reddened eyes out of anger." One could also construe the ablative *kopāt* with the finite verb *abravīt*, yielding the sense "his eyes reddened, he spoke in anger." Ck and Ct understand that Kumbhakarṇa is angry at having been awakened too early (*akāla udbodhanakopāt*). See note to 6.31.72.

10. "Why have you put such effort into waking me" *kim artham aham ādṛtya tvayā... prabodhitaḥ*: Compare 6.48.57ab, where the same construction occurs. See note to 6.48.57.

"a ghost" *pretaḥ*: Literally, "a departed one." The term is commonly used in India even today to refer to the malevolent spirits of the dead.

All northern manuscripts insert here a passage of fourteen lines [1097*]. Southern manuscripts insert, in whole or in part, the same passage following 6.51.45. See note to 6.51.45 for the translation and a discussion of the critical edition's decision not to include this passage.

11. "His eyes rolling slightly" *īṣat tu parivṛttābhyāṃ netrābhyām*: Literally, "with eyes slightly rolling." The rolling of the eyes is a common indicator of anger in the epic. See 5.20.23; 6.27.2; 6.46.14; etc. Cg notes that the slight rolling of the eyes thus indicates only mild anger (*anenaiṣat kopo lakṣyate*). D7,9–11, and the texts and printed editions of Ct and Cr read *roṣeṇa*, "in anger," for *īṣat tu*, "slightly." Commentators and translators differ as to whether it is Rāvaṇa's or Kumbhakarṇa's eyes that are rolling. Ck and Ct believe that the reference is to Kumbhakarṇa, and in this they are followed by Raghunathan (1982, vol. 3, p. 164), Roussel (1903, vol. 3, p. 190), Shastri (1959, vol. 3, p. 165), and Pagani (1999, p. 1024). Cr believes that the rolling eyes are Rāvaṇa's, and in this he is followed by Dutt (1893, p. 1298), Gorresio (1858, vol. 10, p. 5), Gita Press (1969, vol. 3, p. 1602), and us. Cs quotes Ct on this point but appears to prefer the alternative. Cs argues that, in Ct's interpretation, the word *kruddham*, "angry," that modifies Kumbhakarṇa would be redundant with *roṣeṇa*, "in anger." Cs further notes that the use of the dual number for eyes in the case of the [twenty-eyed] Rāvaṇa is correct, in reference to the two sets of eyes, right and left, on his ten heads. Cs cites a similar use of the dual to refer to Rāvaṇa's arms elsewhere in the text. (*roṣeṇa parivṛttābhyāṃ netrābhyām upalakṣitaṃ kruddhaṃ bhrātaraṃ kumbhakarṇaṃ rāvaṇo 'bravīd iti*

nāgojibhaṭṭaḥ. roṣeṇa parivṛttābhyāṃ netrābhyāṃ pārśvadvayavartinetratvena dvivacanaṃ pūrvaṃ bhujābhyām itivat. tadupalakṣito rāvaṇo [*vānaro* [*sic*]—so KK] *vākyam uvācety anvayo vā. asmin pakṣe kruddhapadaṃ nādhikam.*) See 6.47.106 and note. See, too, 5.8.13,19; 5.20.24,26; 5.47.2–14; and notes. Compare 3.30.8, where Rāvaṇa is said to have twenty arms.

12. "As of today, you have been asleep for a very long time" *adya te sumahān kālaḥ śayānasya*: Literally, "today, a very long time [has passed] while you were sleeping." The phrase *sumahān kālaḥ* galvanizes Ct to revisit the vexed question of the duration of Kumbhakarṇa's slumber, which we have commented upon in detail above in the note to 6.48.12. The problem here, also raised in that earlier context, is that, aside from the various formulations of Kumbhakarṇa's boon/curse, some versions of the text have Kumbhakarṇa participating in Rāvaṇa's recent council of war, which can only have been a few days before Kumbhakarṇa was awakened. Ct reasserts his earlier position that the period specified here must be greater than the six months mandated in Brahmā's curse at 6.49.26. With this in mind, he continues, the vulgate verse [1029* following 6.48.12ab] that indicates that Kumbhakarṇa fell asleep nine days after giving counsel to Rāvaṇa must either be a spurious interpolation or must be using the word "day (*ahan*)" to mean "month." Because of this, Ct goes on, we must understand that the period referred to in this verse must be eight or nine months, from which it follows that the war has been going on for more than six months (*anenāpi yuddhasya ṣaṇmāsādhikakālavyāpitā sūcitā bhavatīti jñāyate*). Cs contests Ct's position. He arues that the battle could not possibly have gone on for six months or more, citing a *Padmapurāṇa* passage that claims that Rāvaṇa was killed on the forty-eighth day of the battle, thus bringing in a new stricture on the duration of Kumbhakarṇa's sleep. See 6.34.2 and note. On the chronology of the *Yuddhakāṇḍa*, see note to 6.4.4.

"resting comfortably" *sukhitaḥ*: Literally, "happy, comfortable." Ś1,D7,9–11, and the texts and printed editions of Ct and Cr read instead *suṣuptaḥ*, "sleeping soundly."

"you do not know of the danger" *na jānīṣe . . . bhayam*: This statement further confirms the spuriousness of verse 1028* mentioned above and the lengthy southern passage that follows *sarga* 9 in the critical edition (App. I, No. 3 = GPP, VSP, KK, Gita Press, NSP 6.10–15), where Kumbhakarṇa is represented as discussing Rāvaṇa's conflict with Rāma (see especially lines 142–229 = *sarga* 12 in GPP, NSP, VSP, Gita Press, and KK). Here the critical edition seems to render moot the energetic debate among the southern commentators to reconcile Kumbhakarṇa's long sleep with his supposed participation in Rāvaṇa's council of war. But see 6.51.2 and note, where the critical edition's evidence appears to support Kumbhakarṇa's participation in the council.

13. "Rāma" *rāmaḥ*: D9–11 and the texts and printed editions of Ct read instead *śrīmān*, "majestic, glorious."

"is cutting us off at the roots" *mūlaṃ naḥ parikṛntati*: Literally, "he is cutting our root." Cg glosses, "afflicting our core forces (*mūlabalam . . . bādhate*)." D9–11,G3, and the texts and printed editions of Ct read *kulam*, "race, family, lineage," for *mūlam*. This yields the sense "he is exterminating our race." Compare note to verse 16 below.

14. "Just look . . . of Laṅkā" *hanta paśyasva laṅkāyāḥ*: We take the particle *hanta* here in its inceptive or asseverative sense, unlike the other translators who render, "Alas," etc. Ñ1,V3,B1,3,D1,2,4,6,7,9–11,13,G,M3, and the texts and printed editions of the southern commentators read the locative *laṅkāyām*, "in Laṅkā," for the genitive *laṅkāyāḥ*, "of Laṅkā." Commentators differ as to how to break up the sequence

paśyasvalaṅkāyāḥ [v.l. *-ām*]. Ct, Cm, Crā, and Cg (second alternative) read the regular *parasmaipada* second person imperative *paśya*, "see, look at," followed by *svalaṅkāyāḥ* [*-ām*], "of [in] my very own Laṅkā," which they gloss as "my own island of Laṅkā (*ātmīyalaṅkādvīpe*—so Cg, Cm, Crā)." Among the translators consulted, only Dutt (1893, p. 1299) clearly follows this reading. Cg (first alternative), whom we follow, reads the irregular *ātmanepada* imperative *paśyasva*, "see, look at," noting the irregularity, plus *laṅkāyāḥ* [*-ām*].

"He has turned them all into one big sea of monkeys after . . . coming" *āgamya vānaraikārṇavaṃ kṛtam*: Literally, "having come, has made [it] a single sea of monkeys." The syntax of the second half of the verse is awkward and elliptical, lacking both a clear subject and a clear object. The commentators are silent. Our assumption is that the poet intends Rāma, the subject of the previous verse, to be the agent of the gerund *āgamya*, "having come," and the passive participle *kṛtam*, "has been made, has been turned into," while the collectivity of the woods and parklands mentioned in *pāda* b constitutes the object of the latter. The north attempts to remedy the difficulty by explicitly making the monkeys the subject of the transformation of the woods, etc. (See Pollock 1984a, pp. 85–86.)

15. "never do I see" *na paśyāmi kadācana*: D6,9–11,G2,M1,2, and the texts and printed editions of Ct and Cr read *kathaṃcana* for *kadācana*. This would lend the passage the sense "in no way can I foresee."

Following verse 15, D5–7,9–11,S (as well as a number of northern manuscripts), in whole or in part and at various points in the *sarga*, insert a passage of three lines [1102*]: "Nor have these monkeys ever been defeated in battle. That is the danger that has arisen. You must save us, mighty warrior.[1] You must destroy them this very day. It is for this purpose, sir, that you have been awakened."

[1]"mighty warrior" *mahābala*: Literally, " O mighty one."

16. "You must understand that I have exhausted all my resources." *sarvakṣapitakośaṃ ca sa tvam abhyavapadya mām*: Literally, "you should know me as one whose resources *or* treasury are all exhausted." The commentators differ somewhat as to the meaning of the word *-kośa-*, "resources." Cg, Cm, Ck, and Ct gloss *aiśyvaryāṇi*, a rather comprehensive term encompassing the notions of wealth, power, and resources in general. Cr suggests, "treasure rooms (*dhanāgārāṇi*)."

"in which only the children and the aged remain" *bālavṛddhāvaśeṣitām*: Cg observes that Rāvaṇa is exaggerating considerably here but that he does so on the basis of the destruction of his core forces (*mūlabala*), which will be discussed later. (*ity atiśayoktiḥ. mūlabalādyutsādanasya vakṣyamāṇatvāt.*) See note to verse 13 above.

17. "Great-armed warrior" *mahābāho*: Literally, "O great-armed one."

"I have never before spoken in this fashion to anyone . . . my brother" *mayaivaṃ noktapūrvo hi kaścid bhrātaḥ*: B1,2,D1,7–13,T3,G3, and the texts and printed editions of Ct and Cr read the nominative *bhrātā*, "brother," for the critical edition's vocative *bhrātaḥ*, "O brother." This reading yields the sense "No brother has ever been addressed by me in this fashion." B4,G2,M3, and the texts and printed editions of Cg and Cm read *kaccit* for the critical edition's *kaścit*. Cg understands the particle as a question marker and thus interprets the phrase to mean "Have I ever spoken to you [in this fashion] before?" Cg, however, notes the variant found in the critical edition. (*kaccid iti praśne. kadācit api noktapūrvo 'sīty arthaḥ. kaścid iti pāṭhe tv anyaḥ kaścid api naivam uktapūrva ity arthaḥ.*)

"and my fullest confidence" *parā saṃbhāvanā ca me*: The term *saṃbhāvanā* has a variety of more or less textually appropriate meanings and has been rendered variously by commentators and translators. Ck and Ct, with whom we tend to agree, gloss, "hope (*āśā*)," understanding, "And there is the hope that this one will accomplish the deed (*ayaṃ kāryaṃ sādhayiṣyatīty āśā cāsti*—so Ct; *kāryasiddhiḥ pratyāśā*—so Ck)." Cg glosses, "respect (*ādaraḥ*)," while Cm offers, "the greatest respect (*atyādaraḥ*)." Dutt (1893, p. 1299) renders, "great is the probability of thy succeeding." Roussel (1903, vol. 3, p. 191) understands, "*ma suprême espérance*." In this he is followed by Shastri (1959, vol. 3, p. 166), who translates "my supreme hopes." Similarly, Gita Press (1969, vol. 3, p. 1602) renders, "my supreme hope." Raghunathan (1982, vol. 3, p. 165) translates, "my supreme confidence in your ability," while Pagani (1999, p. 1024) understands, "*la plus haute estime*."

18. "in our wars with the gods and *asuras*" *devāsuravimardeṣu*: Despite the poet's use of this stereotyped name for the ancient and recurrent war between the gods and *asuras*, that conflict cannot logically be intended here. For, if it were, from what position would the *rākṣasa* Kumbhakārṇa be fighting with both parties to the conflict? Several translators have unreflectingly seen a reference to the *devāsurayuddha* here rather than to the various conflicts between the *rākṣasas* and gods, on the one hand, and between the former and other supernatural beings, on the other. Thus, for example, aside from his numerous conflicts with the *devas*, we see Rāvaṇa, earlier in his career, engaged in battle with the Nivātakavaca *asuras* (*Uttarakāṇḍa* 23) and with the *gandharvas*, *yakṣas*, etc. (*Uttarakāṇḍa* 13–15). This confusion on the part of translators who follow the text of Ct may be a result of the variant reading found in most southern manuscripts. D5,7,9–11,T2,3,G,M5, and the texts and printed editions of the southern commentators read instead *devāsureṣu yuddheṣu*, "in the wars of the gods and *asuras*," which is the most conventional terminology for the classic war between the gods and the *asuras*. See note below on the gods and the *asuras*. See, too, 6.7.7 and note.

"you faced off against" *prativyūhya*: Literally, "having arrayed [an army against an enemy]." This presumably refers to Kumbhakarṇa's generalship of the *rākṣasa* forces in previous battles. Ck and Ct gloss, "having made an opposing force (*prātibhaṭyaṃ kṛtvā*)." Cg offers, "having separated *or* isolated [them] (*vibhajya*)," which Raghunathan (1982, vol. 3, p. 165) renders as "taking them on by turns." Cr understands, "sowing fear (*bhayam utpādya*)." Roussel (1903, vol. 3, p. 191), followed by Shastri (1959, vol. 3, p. 166) and Pagani (1999, p. 1024), construes the gerund somewhat irregularly with the gods and *asuras*, whom he understands to be ranged in battle against Kumbhakarṇa. This also seems to be the interpretation of Gita Press (1969, vol. 3, p. 1602).

"and defeated them" *devāḥ . . . nirjitāś cāsurāḥ*: Literally, "the gods and the *asuras* were defeated." Ś1,V2,3,D4,8–12,T2,3,G3,M5, and the texts and printed editions of Ct and Cr read *amarāḥ*, "immortals," for *asurāḥ*, "*asuras*." This reading, in which Kumbhakarṇa fights and defeats only the immortal gods and not the *asuras*, renders more plausible the understanding that the battle of the gods and *asuras* mentioned earlier in the verse refers to the classic conflict between those two classes of supernatural beings. In this case, Kumbhakarṇa could be seen as fighting on the side of the *asuras*. This reading has been rendered by Roussel (1903, vol. 3, p. 191), Shastri (1959, vol. 3, p. 166), and Dutt (1893, p. 1299).

Following 18cd, Ñ,V,B2–4,D4–7,9–11,S insert a passage of one line [1104*]: "[...defeated them in battle.] So, have recourse to all of your might, warrior of fearsome valor. [For there is...]."

19. "you...must...scatter" *vidhama*: Literally, "you must blow away."

The meter is *rucirā*.

Sarga 51

1. "he laughed and then said these words" *babhāṣe 'tha vacanaṃ prajahāsa ca*: Literally, "he spoke this speech and laughed." Why is Kumbhakarṇa laughing at his brother's misfortune? According to Ck, Ct, and Cs, he does so at the thought that evil-minded Rāvaṇa is now reaping the fruits of his failure to heed the wise counsel of Vibhīṣaṇa, etc. [to release Sītā] (*vibhīṣaṇavaco 'naṅgīkāraphalaṃ prāptaṃ durātmaneti hāsaḥ*—so Ct). We follow Cg, who sensibly proposes that we should invert the order of the actions of speaking and laughing (*atra vyatyayaḥ kāryaḥ*). Ś,V3,B1,D1–3,8–13,M3, and the texts and printed editions of the southern commentators read *babhāṣedam*, "he said this," for the critical edition's *babhāṣe 'tha*, "he then said." This requires either a highly irregular *sandhi* or the citation of the all but invariably *ātmanepada* root $\sqrt{}$*bhāṣ*, "to speak," in the *parasmaipada*. Only Cs takes note of this issue, proposing either that we break the sequence up into *babhāṣe* + *dam*, "he said to that magnanimous one," or accept the variant found in the critical edition. (*daṃ dātāraṃ rāvaṇaṃ praty babhāṣe. babhāṣe 'thety api kvacit pāṭhaḥ.*)

2. "you paid no heed to those who had your welfare at heart" *hiteṣv anabhiyuktena... tvayā*: Literally, "by you who were inattentive to those beneficial [things]." We follow the commentators who understand *hiteṣu* elliptically to refer either to those for whom Rāvaṇa's welfare was paramount (*hitapareṣu*—so Cg) or to those who offered beneficial advice (*hitavādiṣu*—so Ct, Ck). B4,D1,4,6,13,T2,3,G1,M3,5, and the texts and printed editions of Cg and Cm read *anabhiraktena*, "detached from."

"that very calamity" *doṣo hi yaḥ*: Literally, "which flaw *or* which fault." We agree with Cr, who glosses, "the fruits of the evil policy in which you have engaged (*bhavatkṛta-durnayaphalam*)."

"we" *asmābhiḥ*: Literally, "by us." Kumbhakarṇa is probably using the formal first person plural for the singular, but, as Ck and Ct point out, he could also be referring to Vibhīṣaṇa (*mayā vibhīṣaṇena ca*).

"earlier, at the council of ministers" *purā mantravinirṇaye*: Literally, "formerly at the [time of the] determination of counsel." The reference is to the council of Rāvaṇa's ministers at which Vibhīṣaṇa, Kumbhakarṇa, and others offer Rāvaṇa the beneficial advice of returning Sītā. This reference, however, presents textual difficulties. As noted above (see notes to 6.50.12,13 above), the passage in which Kumbhakarṇa and the ministers engage in this debate belongs in its entirety only to the southern text and has been excised from the critical edition and relegated to App. I. No. 3 (see especially lines 200–229), summarized in the notes to *sarga* 9 above. A variety of northern manuscripts include sections of this appendix at various points, but none of them, according to the critical apparatus, includes the section in which Kumbhakarṇa appears (lines 160–163, 200–229). There is also an apparent narrative contradiction in that, at verse 6.50.12 above, Rāvaṇa states that, until the present meeting, Kumbhakarṇa has had no knowledge of Rāma's invasion of Laṅkā. Perhaps the poet has nodded.

3. "You are suffering the immediate consequences of your wicked deed, just as evildoers suffer an instant descent into their respective hells." *śīghraṃ khalv abhyupetaṃ tvāṃ phalaṃ pāpasya karmaṇaḥ / nirayeṣv eva patanaṃ yathā duṣkṛtakarmaṇaḥ*: Literally, "The fruit of wicked action has come to you swiftly indeed, just as the fall into hells [comes] to evildoers." The specific evil deed referred to is, as several of the commentators note, the abduction of Sītā. According to Ck, Ct, and Cg, the immediacy of retribution is in accordance with the maxim, "Through the performance of extreme actions, whether good or evil, one experiences the fruits in this very world (*atyutkaṭaiḥ puṇyapāpair ihaiva phalam aśnute*)."

As Cg points out, the form *duṣkṛtakarmaṇaḥ*, "evildoers," should be read as an accusative plural to maintain the grammatical parallelism of the proposition and the example. This reading, we believe, is further supported by the use of the plural *nirayeṣu*, "into [various] hells." Ct and Cr read the term as a genitive singular, and in this they have been followed by all translators who share this reading.

4. "the consequences" *anubandhaḥ*: Cg, Cm, and Ct all cite *Amarakośa* 3.3.98 in which "the production of evil consequences (*doṣotpādaḥ*)" is given as a meaning of the term. Cr breaks the word *anubandhaḥ* into the adverb *anu*, "in consequence," and the noun *bandhaḥ*, "bond *or* tie," taking the latter term to refer to the bond of love between Rāma and Sītā (*anu bandhaḥ sītārāmayoḥ parasparaṃ prītir na vicāritaḥ*).

5. "what ought to be done first... what ought to be done later" *pūrvakāryāṇi... uttarakāryāṇi*: As Ct, Cg, and Cm note, what should have been done first was reflection (*vicāraḥ*—so Ct) or taking counsel, etc. (*mantraṇādīni*), and only then should the subsequent action itself, i.e., the abduction of Sītā (*sītāharaṇam*—so Ct), have been done. Cg and Cm indicate that Kumbhakarṇa is accusing Rāvaṇa of having proceeded in the reverse order (*viparītaṃ kṛtam*).

"has no comprehension of the distinction between sound and unsound policy" *na sa veda nayānayau*: Literally, "he does not know policy and non-policy."

6. "without reference to the proper time and place" *deśakālavihīnāni*: Literally, "lacking [proper] place and time."

"just as are offerings of food to impious persons" *havīṃṣy aprayateṣv iva*: The precise sense of this illustration is hard to determine because of the multiplicity of meanings of the first term *havīṃṣi* and the elliptical nature of the second, *aprayateṣu*, "unsanctified, impious, unholy." The commentators offer three possible modificands for the adjective *aprayata*. The first, suggested by Ck and Ct, is "fires (*agniṣu*)." Taking *havīṃṣi* in its common sense of "sacrificial oblation," they understand the simile to mean "like oblations offered into unsanctified fires." This interpretation has been followed by all translators of the southern recension. To our mind, however, it is questionable, as the adjective *aprayata*, whose underlying form, *prayata*, refers basically to "pious individuals who have restrained *or* subdued their senses," seems to poorly describe fire. Cr, Cg, and Cm understand the adjective to refer to unworthy people or recipients who are lowly (*atinīceṣu*—so Cr), unfit, or disqualified as recipients (*apātreṣu*—so Cg), or who are heedless, that is, devoid of discrimination (*asāvadhānajaneṣu... arucijaneṣv iti yāvat*—so Cm). This interpretation implies the taking of the noun *haviḥ* in its sense of "a gift," particularly a gift of food to brahmans, and evokes the question of how a brahman becomes an unworthy recipient (*apātra*) as treated in *Manusmṛti* 11.69. This understanding of the figure is adopted and further supported by Ctr (1964, p. 186) in his commentary on the passage, bolstered by Manu's discourse on the futility of gifts to evil or unworthy brahmans at *Manusmṛti* 3.97, 3.142, and 4.192–195. In what is perhaps a glossing of this elliptical phrase, a number of northern manuscripts (Ñ,V1,2,B2,3,D1) and the printed edition of Gorresio (6.40.6) read the instrumental *aprayatair iva*, which yields the sense "[like oblations offered] by impious *or* impure persons." This is rendered by Gorresio (1858, vol. 10, p. 7) as "[*siccome il sacro burro*] *offerto da gente impura*."

7. This is one of those enigmatic epic verses in which groups or categories drawn from various *śāstras* are alluded to only by their numbers, leaving commentators and audiences to determine to the best of their abilities exactly what is being referred to (see 5.33.17–19 and notes). In this case, the subject is clearly *nītiśāstra*, or the science of statecraft. The issue, the propriety of a king's deliberating with his ministers before taking any action, generally parallels some of the discussion in Kauṭilya's *Arthaśāstra*. The reference in the verse is apparently to the issue raised at *Arthaśāstra* 1.4–5 and 1.11 concerning the problem of a king's consultations with his ministers. Kumbhakarṇa seems to decide in favor of a king consulting with several counselors (*ArthŚā* 1.15.34–39) before taking action. See also the discussion of this passage by Friedrich Wilhelm (1960, pp. 11ff.).

Commentators and translators differ considerably in their understanding of what precisely the three types of action and their fivefold application are.

"A king who perceives" *yaḥ prapaśyati*: Literally, "one who perceives." Ñ2,D7,9–11,G1,3, and the texts and printed editions of Ct and Cr read instead *yaḥ prapadyate*, "whoever resorts to."

"the fivefold application" *pañcadhā yogam*: According to Ck, Ct, Cr, Cg, and Cm (second alternative), the application of action is fivefold in reference to the following five categories: 1) the means of undertaking actions (*karmaṇām ārambhopāyaḥ*); 2) the provision of men and material resources (*puruṣadravyasampat*); 3) the divisions of place and time (*deśakālavibhāgaḥ*); 4) the means of avoiding failure (*vipattipratīkāraḥ*); and 5) the success of one's undertaking (*kāryasiddhiḥ*). This list is repeated in the footnotes of Dutt (1893, p. 1300), Gita Press (1969, vol. 3, p. 1603), and Shastri (1959, vol. 3, p. 166), and by Pagani (1999, p. 1665) in her endnote. Cv and Cm (first alternative), however, have a somewhat different list, arguing that the actions are taken with respect to the following five considerations: place, time, self, material resources, and purpose (*deśataḥ kālataś cātmanaś ca dravyataś ca prayojanataś ca*—so Cv). According to Cl, however, as quoted by Gorresio (1858, vol. 10, p. 281) in his endnote to the translation of the passage, the reference is to the five principal modes of royal interaction with neighboring kings, viz., conciliation, gifts or bribery, sowing dissension, punishment, assassination, etc. (*sāmadānabhedadaṇḍavadhādiprayogarūpam*). See 6.9.8; 6.51.11–13; 6.59.28; 6.71.12; and notes. Cf. notes to 6.31.48–49.

"the three types of action" *trayāṇām . . . karmaṇām*: Literally, "of three actions." There is even less unanimity among commentators and translators here than in regard to the fivefold application. According to Ct, Cr, and Ck, the three types of action are conciliation, etc. (*sāmādīnām*), characterized by the three conditions of diminution, increase, and stasis (*kṣayavṛddhisthānalakṣaṇānām*). These terms are used by Kauṭilya at

Arthaśāstra 7.1.28. See, too, the very similar list of *sthāna*, *vṛddhi*, and *hāni* mentioned by Mahodara at 6.52.4 below. This interpretation is followed in Dutt's (1893, p. 1300) footnote to the passage, where he states, "The three kinds of action are treaty, war, etc." Dutt then remarks, "All this is nebulous; and the commentator [Ct] is sadly reticent over this extremely important passage."

Cv, Cg, and Cm understand the three types of action to be classifiable according to a continuum of highest, middlemost, and lowest (*uttamamadhyamādhamakarmaṇām*). The first, and best, of these is applied in situations where a king's own power is in the ascendant and his rival's is on the wane, and consists of invasion and the application of coercive force. The middlemost type of action occurs when one's own and one's rival's power are equal and consists of alliance or conciliation. The third, and lowest, form of action is the seeking of protection or a tributary relationship accompanied by gifts or bribes and is resorted to when the power of one's rival is ascendant over that of one's self. (*tatrātmodayaparajyānisaṃbhavasamaye kriyamāṇaṃ daṇḍopayogi yānam uttamaṃ karma. ātmaparayor balasāmye kriyamāṇaṃ saṃdhānaṃ madhyamaṃ karma. parodayātmajyānisamaye kriyamāṇaṃ dānapūrvasamāśrayaṇam adhamaṃ karma*—so Cg.) This interpretation is followed by Gita Press (1969, vol. 3, p. 1603) in its note to the passage. Compare *Arthaśāstra* 7.1.13–18, where four actions are noted: marching, settling down, compromise, and asylum.

Cl, as quoted in Gorresio's note (1858, vol. 10, pp. 281–82), takes the word *trayāṇām*, "of the three," separately from *karmaṇām*, "of the actions," and sees the former as a reference to the three different types of people to whom action is directed, namely, an enemy (*ripuḥ*), a neutral, that is, someone who offers helpful advice to two disputants, and an object of enmity (*dveṣaviṣayaḥ*—rendered by Gorresio [p. 282] as "*colui che nutre odio*"). (*trayāṇāṃ ripumadhyasthadveṣāṇām. ripur abhighātako madhyastho dvayor vivadamānayor hitāśaṃsī dveṣyo dveṣaviṣayaḥ.*)

Shastri (1959, vol. 3, p. 166), in his footnote to the passage, specifies the three kinds of action as 1) trivial; 2) common or ordinary; and 3) important and urgent. In this he appears to have been followed by Pagani (1999, p. 1664) in her endnote to the passage, where she describes the three types as "*l'action ordinaire, l'action importante et l'action urgente*." Neither translator offers any source or rationale for this classification.

"after coming to a decision" *samayaṃ kṛtvā*: Literally, "having made a pact *or* agreement." We generally agree with the commentators, who understand *samayam* to mean "reflection on the means for effective application (*prayogasādhanavicāram*—so Ct, Cr; *prayogasādhanasaṃpattivicāram*—so Ck)" or "a correct conclusion in the form of a decision (*niścayarūpaṃ siddhāntam*—so Cg; *niścayam*—so Cv, Cm)."

"remains on the proper path" *sabhye vartate pathi*: Literally, "he is on the refined *or* civilized path." Commentators define the path as the path of proper policy (*nītimārge*—Ct, Ck, Cg) or the path of kings (*rājamārge*—Cr). Cg, citing the *Ratnamālā* (*sabhyaḥ sāmājike sādhau*), and Cv gloss *sabhye* as "good *or* proper (*sādhau*)." Cg further notes that the phrase means that one obtains the fruit of proper policy (*samyaññītiphalaṃ prāpnotīty arthaḥ*). Ś,Ñ,V,B,D1–4,7,8,10–13,G2,3, and the texts and printed editions of Ct, Ck, and Cr read *samyak*, "proper," instead of *sabhye*. Ct and Ck advise that we should read the term adverbially, i.e., in the sense of "properly."

8. This verse is obscure and elliptical, and the commentators struggle somewhat to put it all together meaningfully. The vagueness of the allusions provokes Dutt (1893, p. 1300) to make the following remark in a footnote: "One is at sea in the midst of

these formless generalities. The tantalized intellect makes a desperate attempt to grasp the body of the shadow seeming substance, but the empty air mocks his pains. A translator, however, is fast bound to the oar and must pull on, will be, nil be [*sic*]."

"So does" *ca*: Literally, "and." As noted above, the verse is rather elliptical. We agree with Cv, Cg, and Cm in construing this verse also with the phrase, "he remains on the proper path," of verse 7 above.

"who desires to reach a decision" *samayaṃ vicikīrṣati*: Literally, "he desires to make an agreement." We follow Ck, Ct, and Cr in understanding *samaya* here to refer to a decision taken in accordance with the various actions and conditions alluded to in verse 7 above (*kṣayādikālocitasāmādikarmavicāram uktapañcaprakāratatprayogasādhana-saṃpattivicāraṃ ca kartum icchati*—so Ck, Ct). Cv, Cm, and Cg similarly offer, "a decision as to what is to be done (*kāryanirṇayam*)."

"in conformance with the texts on polity" *yathāgamam*: Literally, "in accordance with the *āgamas* (scientific texts)." The reference here, as the commentators point out, is specifically to the science of governance or polity, *nītiśāstra*.

"who pays heed to his ministers" *budhyate sacivān*: D10,11,M1,2, and the texts and printed editions of Ct read instead the instrumental *sacivaiḥ* for the critical text's accusative *sacivān*. Ck, Ct and Cr add the postposition *saha*, "together with," although these commentators tend to differ as to the verb with which the postpositional phrase should be construed. Thus, Ck and Ct read it with *cikīrṣati* (v.l. *vicikīrṣati*), yielding the sense "he desires to reach a decision together with his ministers." Cr, however, reads the phrase with *anupaśyati*, "he recognizes," in *pāda* d, yielding the sense "together with his ministers, he recognizes his true friends." Cg and Cm, who read with the critical edition, nonetheless gloss the instrumental, construing the phrase with *budhyate*, for which they gloss *ālocayati*, yielding the sense "he considers [a resolution as to what is to be done] together with his ministers." Cv is the only commentator to retain the accusative sense in this reading, glossing *sacivāṃś ca buddhyā saṃdhatte*, construing the phrase with the instrumental *buddhyā*, "with his thoughts *or* intelligence," yielding a meaning something like "he reconciles his ministers with his [own] thoughts."

"who recognizes his true friends by virtue of his own intelligence" *buddhyā suhṛdaś cānupaśyati*: Literally, "he sees his friends with his intellect." We tentatively follow the interpretation of Ct and Ck, who understand that the king is making a distinction between a true friend, i.e., one who gives him beneficial advice (*hitavaktā*), and one who offers advice merely to please him (*prabhoḥ sukhamātrajananecchayā vadati*—so Ct; *sukhecchamātrā*[*a*?]*vādī*—so Ck). Cr, somewhat similarly, glosses, "he knows on the basis of various types of investigation that 'these are my [true] friends' (*ime me suhṛda ity anekavidhasvakṛtaparīkṣayā jānāti*)." Cm and Cv, in the same vein, gloss, "he investigates *or* supervises his friends (*suhṛdaś cāvekṣate*—so Cm)." Cm offers as an alternative a rather different gloss: "he deliberates together with his friends (*yadvā suhṛdbhiḥ saha vicārayati*)." The latter is the sole gloss offered by Cg.

9. "A man should pursue" *bhajate puruṣaḥ*: Literally, "a man has recourse to." T2,3, the texts and printed editions of Cg and Cm (VSP 6.63.9 and KK 6.63.9), and the text of Gita Press (6.63.9) read instead the optative *bhajeta*, "one should have recourse to," for the critical edition's *bhajate*. Among the translators consulted, only Gita Press (1969, vol. 3, p. 1604) and Raghunathan (1982, vol. 3, p. 166), who read this variant, translate it as an injunctive. Although this is a minor variant, we, too, have done so, given the didactic nature of the passage.

"all three human ends—righteousness, profit, and pleasure" *dharmam arthaṃ ca kāmaṃ ca sarvān*: Literally, "righteousness, profit, and pleasure—all of them." These constitute the well-known set of the *puruṣārthas*, the three "ends *or* goals of man," that form the armature around which the structure of the social, religious, and political life of traditional India is erected. See 6.52.6; 6.105.13; and notes.

"at their proper times" *kāle*: Literally, "at the time." The commentators and some translators adduce the traditional assignment of each of these modes or spheres of activity to particular portions of the day, viz., *dharma* is chiefly practiced in the morning, *artha* in the afternoon, and *kāma* in the evening or at night. Some of the commentators, including Cg and Cm, elaborate on this idea by stating which combinations of the three are appropriate during the three specified periods. According to Cg, certain of these may be practiced at times other than those strictly prescribed for them in combination with the ones belonging to that particular time. Thus, for example, in the morning *artha* may be pursued along with the prescribed *dharma*, while *dharma* may similarly be practiced with *artha* in the afternoon. *Artha* may be practiced along with *kāma* in the evening, and *dharma* may be practiced together with both at that time. Cg cautions, however, that a person who devotes himself to *kāma*, or pleasure, alone at all three of these times is considered to be the lowest of men (*kevalakāmaṃ sarvakāleṣv api sevāmānaḥ puruṣādhama evety abhisaṃdhiḥ*).

"all at once or two at a time" *trīṇi dvandvāni vā*: Literally, "the three or the pairs *or* or the three pairs." Cv and Cg understand the neuter term *trīṇi* to refer either generically to the three *puruṣārthas* taken individually or to three pairs or combinations (*dvandvāni*) of them. For Cg, the appropriate pairings would be *dharma* and *artha*, *artha* and *dharma*, and *kāma* and *artha*. (*dharmam arthaṃ kāmaṃ ca pratyekaṃ vā. trīṇi dvandvāni vā dharmārthāv arthadharmau kāmārthau vā sarvān vā.*) Cv, on the other hand, lists *dharma* and *artha*, *artha* and *kāma*, and *dharma* and *kāma* (*trīṇi dvandvāni dharmārthāv arthakāmau dharmakāmau vā*). Ck and Ct seem to understand that the number of goals men pursue increases as their status rises. Both of them state that *yuvarājas*, "heirs apparent *or* princes regent" (see note to verse 10 below), and also ministers (*sacivas*—so Ck), practice only the pair consisting of *dharma* and *kāma*, presumably leaving the exercise of the third element, *artha*, statecraft *or* profit, to the king alone (*yuvarājādis tu dvandvāni vā dvandvāny eva dharmakāmadvikāny eva bhajate*—so Ct).

10. "one exercising royal power" *rājamātraḥ*: Literally, "someone of the measure of a king." Ck, Ct, and Cr gloss, "heir apparent *or* prince regent (*yuvarājaḥ*)." It is worth noting that the term *yuvarāja*, literally, "young king," is used by Vālmīki to identify two rather different political posts. One is the designated heir or successor to a reigning king. It is in this sense that Aṅgada is made the *yuvarāja* in the *Kiṣkindhākāṇḍa* (4.25.11,35). The term is also used to designate a prince regent who reigns upon the full or partial retirement of the ruling monarch. This is the position into which Rāma was to have been consecrated prior to his banishment in the *Ayodhyākāṇḍa* (see 2.1.34 and notes). Cf. 6.17.15 and notes; and notes to 6.11.30 and 6.111.14. See, too, 6.116.78–79 and notes, where the term *yuvarāja* appears to be used of someone exercising shared or joint sovereignty. Cg and Cm, however, whom we are inclined to follow, gloss, "one like a king (*rājasadṛśaḥ*)," which we understand to refer to a person in a position to govern. Most northern manuscripts, interpreting with Ck, Ct, and Cr, read instead "a king's son *or* prince (*rājaputraḥ*)," which in itself may be a gloss on this ambiguous term (see Pollock 1984a, pp. 85–86).

"And . . . among these three is foremost" *triṣu caiteṣu yac chreṣṭham*: All the commentators understand, as one of their explanations of this elliptical expression, the reference to be to the three *puruṣārthas* mentioned in verse 9 (*eteṣu triṣu dharmādiṣu sarvamūlatvāt*—so Ct; *dharmārthakāmeṣu*—so Cg). They further argue that it is *dharma*, "righteousness," that is the foremost among them (*yac chreṣṭhaṃ dharmarūpaṃ vastu*—Ct, Cm). Given the context, we believe this is the most plausible interpretation. Cg and Cm, however, offer as an alternative the notion that the "three" refers to the three types of action mentioned in verse 7 above (*eteṣu pūrvokteṣu triṣu bhajaneṣu dharmārthakāmeṣu vā*—so Cg).

"who . . . does not take it to heart" *nāvabudhyate*: Literally, "he does not understand." We follow Cg and Cm, who gloss, "he does not know [how] to put into practice (*ācarituṃ na jānāti*)."

"finds all his great learning to be in vain" *vyarthaṃ tasya bahuśrutam*: Literally, "his great learning has no purpose." Cg understands the verse to be an example of *aprastutapraśaṃsā*, the rhetorical figure of praising that which is not mentioned. What the verse is saying, according to Cg, is that the study of the *śāstras* by a person who abandons *dharma*, the foremost among the *puruṣārthas*, and resorts instead to the least among them, *kāma*, is as meaningless as the roaring of the ocean. By this, Cg indicates, we are to understand that Rāvaṇa's education has been in vain. (*evaṃ sāmānyarūpayāprastutapraśaṃsayā trivargeṣu śreṣṭhaṃ dharmaṃ parityajya jaghanyaṃ kāmam evāśritasya te śāstraśravaṇaṃ samudraghoṣamātram āsīd iti prastuto 'rtho 'vagamyate*.)

11–12. The two verses constitute one very long complex sentence. We have broken it up for the sake of readability.

"self-possessed monarch" *ātmavān*: Literally, "self-possessed one *or* self-controlled one."

"bribery, conciliation, sowing dissension, coercive force" *upapradānaṃ sāntvaṃ vā bhedam . . . ca vikramam*: These are variant names for the standard *nītiśāstra* list of the four modes of interacting with one's rival. They are usually called *sāma*, *dāna*, *bheda*, and *daṇḍa*. See 6.9.8; 6.59.28; 6.71.12; and notes.

"any combination of these means" *yogam*: Literally, "conjunction." The term is somewhat ambiguous here, and commentators and translators differ in the ways in which they understand it. Cv(?), Cg, and Cm, as well as Raghunathan (1982, vol. 3, p. 166) and Gita Press (1969, vol. 3, p. 1604), understand it to refer to the conjunction or combination of the strategies listed in *padas* 11ab (*teṣāṃ yogaṃ samavāyaṃ ca*—so Cg). We follow this interpretation. Ct and Ck, on the other hand, take the term in the sense in which it is used in verse 7 above to refer to the fivefold application, *yoga*, of the four strategic means (*uktapañcavidhaprayogasādhanasaṃpādanam*—so Ct). Gorresio (1858, vol. 10, p. 8) as well as Roussel (1903, vol. 3, p. 192), who is followed by Shastri (1959, vol. 3, p. 167), take *yoga* as a fifth strategic means in the sense of "union [with a rival]." Pagani (1999, p. 1025) renders, "[*celui qui délibère . . . sur les préparatifs*] *d'une entreprise*," apparently taking the term in the sense of *udyoga*, "undertaking."

"the proper and improper ways of applying them" *nayānayau*: Literally, "proper and improper polity."

13. "together with ministers who understand the true nature of things and have his interests at heart" *sahārthatattvajñaiḥ sacivaiḥ saha*: The compound *sahārthatattvajñaiḥ* is ambiguous both because of the polysemy of the term *-artha-* and the different possible ways of analyzing the compound. We understand the compound to be a *dvandva*,

according to which the ministers are both *sahārtha-*, that is, "possessing a common goal [with the king]" and *-tattvajña*, that is, "familiar with the true nature of things." Raghunathan (1982, vol. 3, p. 166), the only translator to follow the text accepted by the critical edition (= the text of Cg, Cm), takes *artha* in its sense of "polity *or* statecraft," rendering, "well versed in polity." His rendering, however, ignores the term *saha-* at the beginning of the compound. The compound could perhaps also be read as a *karmadhāraya* (having a prior member composed of the *bahuvrīhi* compound *sahārtha-*) in the sense of "knowing the true nature of things along with the consequences thereof." Ś,Ñ1,V3,B1,2,D1–3,7–13,M1,2, and the texts and printed editions of Ct, Ck, and Cr read *buddhi-* in place of the postpositional *saha*, "together with," in *pāda* d. This allows Ct, Ck, and Cr and the translators who follow them to read the *saha-* at the beginning of the compound in *pāda* c as a prepositional adverb in the same sense, thus leaving the less complex compound *arthatattvajñaiḥ*, "knowing the essence of polity," to stand on its own.

"over what he ought and ought not do" *kāryākāryam*: Ś,Ñ,D10,11,G2,M1,2, and the texts and printed editions of Ct, Cr, and Ck read instead *kuryāt kāryam*, "he should perform his duty." Cm notes this reading as a variant. With this and the variants noted above, the text of Ct yields a rather different meaning from that found in Cg and the critical edition. Commentators who share this variant reading propose two ways of rendering the verse. Ct and Ck interpret, "whoever, having consulted with ministers who were endowed with the stated virtues and having considered the future auspicious results, performs his own duty, he is a king (*ya ucyamānaguṇaiḥ sacivaiḥ saha hitānubandhaṃ śubham udarkaphalam ālokya vicāryātmanaḥ kāryaṃ kuryāt sa rājā bhavatīty anvayaḥ*—so Ct)." In this they are followed by Roussel (1903, vol. 3, p. 193) and Shastri (1959, vol. 3, p. 167). For Cr's interpretation, see below.

"thrives" *jīvati*: Literally, "he lives." Ñ1,B2,D7,9–11,M1,2, and the texts and printed editions of Ct, Cr, and Ck read [*buddhi*]*jīvibhiḥ* (Ñ1,B2,— [*buddhi*]*jīvanaiḥ*) for the critical edition's [*saha*]*jīvati*. This creates an adjective with the sense "who live by their intelligence *or* wits," which then modifies *sacivaiḥ*, "ministers." Cr thus renders the whole verse as "A king should perform his duty after deliberating over the beneficial consequences for him with ministers who understand the nature of reality and make their living by their intelligence (*buddhir eva jīvo jīvanaṃ tadbuddhir ata evārthatattvajñaiḥ sacivair ātmano hitānubandhaṃ hitapravṛddhim ālokya vicārya rājā kāryaṃ kuryāt*)." This reading is followed by Dutt (1893, p. 1301), Gita Press (1969, vol. 3, p. 1604), and Pagani (1999, p. 1025).

14. The point of the verse, as suggested by Ct and, more elaborately, by Ck, is that a king, e.g., Rāvaṇa, who rejects the salutary advice of good counselors, such as Vibhīṣaṇa (Malyavān—Ck), etc. [who urged the return of Sītā and propitiation of Rāma], in favor of the disastrous advice of bad counselors, such as Prahasta (Ck), etc. [who urged intransigence and belligerence], suffers every calamity (*athottamamantrivibhīṣaṇādimatam apahāya durmantribhir mantraṇamūlaḥ sarvānartha ity āha*—so Ct).

"dumb brutes, in fact" *paśubuddhayaḥ*: Literally, "who have the intelligence of beasts." According to Cg, these are people "who think only about such things as eating and sleeping (*āhāranidrādimātrābhijñāḥ*)."

"the *śāstras*" *śāstra-*: As the commentators point out, the reference is to the treatises on statecraft (*arthaśāstra, nītiśāstra*). Several translators (Shastri 1959, vol. 3, p. 167;

Dutt 1893, p. 1301; Gita Press 1969, vol. 3, p. 1604) render, "scriptures," which we believe is misleading.

"brought into discussions of policy" *mantreṣv abhyantarīkṛtāḥ*: Literally, "made interior to counsel." We follow Cg, who explains, "who have been chosen by a deluded king as counselors in deliberations concerning royal duty (*bhrāntena rājñā mantreṣu rājakāryavicāreṣv abhyantarīkṛtā mantrayitṛtvena vṛtāḥ santaḥ*)." V3,D9–11, and the texts and printed editions of Ct, Ck, and Cr read *mantriṣu*, "among counselors," for the critical text's *mantreṣu*. This gives the phrase the sense "included among [his] counselors."

"out of sheer arrogance" *prāgalbhyāt*: Cg explains, "they desire to speak out of insolence alone without any consideration for the pros and cons. (*ūhāpohau vinā kevaladhārṣṭyāt. vaktum icchanti.*)"

15. "One should not follow the pernicious advice" *na kāryam ahitaṃ vacaḥ*: Literally, "the non-beneficial words should not be acted upon." D9–11 and the texts and printed editions of Ct and Cr read instead *kāryaṃ nābhihitaṃ vacaḥ*, literally, "the words uttered should not be acted upon."

"simply eager to enhance their own positions" *vipulāṃ śriyam icchatām*: Literally, "of those desiring great glory." This can be interpreted, as we have done, to mean "who desire high position *or* state," or, as most other translators have done, to mean "who desire great wealth." We believe that the former is more appropriate, as Kumbhakarṇa seems to be referring to sycophantic ministers who seek to enhance their status at court by offering the king advice that pleases him rather than sound counsel. Raghunathan (1982, vol. 3, p. 166) idiosyncratically understands this phrase, and, indeed, the entire second line of the verse [including "unfamiliar with the treatises on statecraft (*arthaśāstrānabhijñānām*)"], to refer not to counselors but to ignorant and rapacious kings, rendering, "kings who are unacquainted with the teachings of polity but wish for abundant prosperity should not follow the harmful advice of these ignorant men." This rendering strains both the grammar and one's credulity.

16. "And those men who . . . by foolishly uttering . . . pernicious advice that only seems beneficial" *ahitaṃ ca hitākāram . . . jalpanti ye narāḥ*: Literally, "men who prattle what is unbeneficial but has the appearance of benefit."

"undermine all undertakings" *kṛtyadūṣaṇāḥ*: Literally, "spoilers of undertakings." Cm explains, "those who spoil the accomplishment of [any] aim (*siddhārthadūṣakāḥ*)."

"discussions of policy" *mantra* : See note to verse 14 above.

17. "in this world" *iha*: Literally, "here." Although Kumbhakarṇa speaks quite generally, the commentators often attempt to make his remarks refer more specifically to the situation at hand. Thus, Ck glosses, "at the present moment (*idānīm*)." Cr suggests, "here in Laṅkā (*iha laṅkāyām*)," while Cg offers, "with respect to the matter at hand (*prayojanaviṣaye*)."

"some counselors" *mantriṇaḥ*: Literally, "counselors." Ck and Ct understand the verse to refer, in fact, to two different groups of counselors: the bad ones (*durmantriṇaḥ*) and the good ones (*sumantriṇaḥ*). The bad ones, they argue, are the counselors who directly bring about their master's (i.e., Rāvaṇa's) ruin by counseling improper actions. The good ones, perceiving the destruction of their master brought about by the evil counsel of the former group, ally themselves with clever enemies of the king for their own protection. (*kecana durmantriṇo bhartāraṃ tvāṃ nāśayanto hetau śatā tava nāśanimittaṃ viparītāni kṛtyāni kārayanti. kecid sumantriṇo durmantraphalaṃ tava nāśaṃ paśyanto budhaiḥ sarvajñais tava śatrubhiḥ sahitāḥ. svarakṣaṇaṃ kurvantīti śeṣaḥ.*) Cs quotes this position of Ct, ridiculing it as utterly out of keeping with the tenor of the passage and as appealing only to children (*prakaraṇānanukūlatā ca bālānām api bhāsata ity anādaraṇīyaṃ tad iti dik*).

"acting in concert" *sahitāḥ*: Literally, " together with." Cg glosses, "incited by (*preritāḥ*)."

"cunning" *budhaiḥ*: Literally, "wise." Ct and Ck gloss, "omniscient (*sarvajñaiḥ*)"; Cg and Cm gloss, "knowing stratagems (*upāyajñaiḥ*)"; and Cs suggests, "those enemies, that is, those who are inimical to their own king, who know that he has ignorant counselors (*avijñamantrikatvajñānaiḥ śatrubhiḥ svarājavidveṣibhiḥ*)."

"persuade... to engage in self-destructive actions" *viparītāni kṛtyāni kārayanti*: Literally, "[they] cause [him] to perform perverse actions." Cg glosses *viparītāni* as "having perverse results (*viparītaphalakāni*)."

18. "When it comes to evaluating counsel" *mantranirṇaye*: Literally, "in the determination of counsel." Ck and Ct understand that the reference is to the discrimination between good and bad counsel (Ck) or counselors (Ct) (*sumantritvadurmantritvanirṇayaḥ*—so Ct).

"through a full investigation" *vyavahāreṇa*: We take the term in its technical sense of a judicial investigation or legal process. Raghunathan (1982, vol. 3, pp. 166–67), in the same vein, renders, "by skillful questioning." All other translators consulted who share this reading take the term in another of its common senses, "behavior *or* activity." This is more or less the understanding of Cr, who interprets it to refer to the actions of the various ministers (*tadācaraṇena*). Cg thinks the term refers to "equivocal *or* dubious speech (*vyāmiśrabhāṣaṇena*)," which might presumably betray disloyal ministers. Professor R. K. Sharma, in keeping with his interpretation of the term *upasaṃhitān* (see below), suggests that this may refer instead to the devious words of the king's agents who may be seeking to test the ministers' loyalty. (Cf., however, the use of *vyāmiśreṇa* at *BhagGī* 3.6.) Ck and Ct offer, "behavior characterized by the actions and meanings arising from various types of counsel (*tattanmantrajārthakriyālakṣaṇavyavahāreṇa*)," that is, that the quality of counsel [and counselors] is to be judged by the results.

"are, in fact, enemies who are posing as friends" *mitrasaṃkāśān amitrā*: Literally, "enemies who resemble friends."

"although they have actually been suborned" *sacivān upasaṃhitān*: The range of meanings for terms derived from the verb *upa* + *sam* $\sqrt{}$*dhā* normally includes such senses as "connected with, endowed with, accompanied by, referring to, *and* attached *or* devoted to," none of which seems appropriate in the context. Ck attempts to use the standard lexical sense, glossing, "endowed with the state of being ministers (*sacivatvena upasaṃhitān*)." This is far from persuasive. We have followed Cv, Ct, Cm, Cr, and Cg, all of whom understand the term to mean "brought under the influence of one's enemies through the use of bribes, etc. (*utkocādinā śatruvaśīkṛtān*—so Ck)." Roussel (1903, vol. 3, p. 193), followed by Shastri (1959, vol. 3, p. 167) and Pagani (1999, p. 1026), understands the term to mean "*lorsqu'ils sont réunis*." Professor R. K. Sharma offers the interesting suggestion that we disregard, in effect, the *upasarga sam* and take the verb *upa* $\sqrt{}$*dhā* in the technical sense in which it is used at *Arthasāstra* 1.10 and elsewhere in the literature to refer to the series of tests through which a king and his agents seek to ascertain the loyalty or disloyalty of ministers. With this interpretation, we could translate, "once they have been subjected to various tests." Compare, for example, *ArthŚā* 1.10–20, *Amarakośa* 2.8.121, and Hemacandra's *Abhidhānacintāmaṇi* 7.40. See PW, MW, and Apte (s.v. *upadhā*). This reading also determines Professor Sharma's understanding of Cg's gloss on *vyavahāra* as noted above.

19. "his enemies" *anye*: Literally, "others." We follow the commentators, who gloss, "enemies (*śatravaḥ*—so Ct, Cm, Cg)."

"just as birds plunge into the gap in the Krauñca mountain" *krauñcasya kham iva dvijāḥ*: Literally, "as twice-born ones [find] Krauñca's cavity." The Himalayan peak known as Krauñca, or "Crane Mountain," is the subject of two related legends in which it is pierced through by powerful figures, once by the god Skanda and a second time, in rivalry of that piercing, by the legendary brahman warrior Rāma Jāmadagnya (Paraśurāma). These stories are described at *MBh* 3.186.112ff.; 13.166.30ff. (Guha); and *MBh* 9.45.70–73 (Paraśurāma). Cf. *Meghdū* 60; *DevīBhāP* 13.2–36; etc. See 6.47.38 and 6.55.12 below; and 4.42.24–28 and notes. The image of birds flying through one or another of these gaps is fostered not only by the mountain's name but also by the belief that *haṃsas* use this passage in their annual migration from the Indian plains to the Mānasa lake in the Himalayas (cf. *MBh* 7.114.82, where the *haṃsas* are said to fly through the gap on their way to Mount Meru). Compare *Meghdū* 60, where the gap in Mount Krauñca is described as "the gateway of the *haṃsas* (*haṃsadvāram*)," and Mallinātha's commentary ad loc. Interestingly, all commentators who remark on this phrase refer to the fact of the mountain's having been pierced by Skanda's javelin, while none refers to the second piercing by Paraśurāma's arrow. Pagani (1999, p. 1026), who is evidently unfamiliar with the legends of the piercing of the Krauñca mountain, takes the proper name in its ornithological sense of a *saras* crane (*grue cendrée*). She then translates the phrase as "*comme les oiseaux dans un nid de grue cendrée.*" It is not clear what she understands to be the basis of the simile. She has perhaps misunderstood Roussel (1903, vol. 3, p. 193), who renders, "*comme les oiseaux dans une cavité du Kraunca.*" See note following 6.9.22 (App. I, No. 3; lines 209–210, n. 3).

20. "a king who underestimates" *yaḥ . . . avajñāya*: Literally, "one who having ignored *or* disregarded." We agree with Cr, who glosses, "having not taken into account (*aparigaṇayya*)."

"and falls from his lofty state" *sthānāt ca vyavaropyate*: Literally, "he is caused to descend from [his] position." The commentators agree that this means that such a king is deposed (*rājāsanāt . . . pracyāvyate*—so Cg).

Following verse 20, D5,7,10,11,T1,3,G2,3,M3, and the texts and printed editions of the southern commentators insert a passage of two lines [1114*]: "We ought to do[1] what was recommended before by my younger brother.[2] That alone is the beneficial course of action for us.[3] But please do as you wish." The critical edition's reconstruction of this verse (= Cg's) is rendered only by Raghunathan (1982, vol. 3, p. 167).

[1]"We ought to do" *kriyatām*: D6,7,9–11,T3,G3, and the texts and printed editions of Ct and Cr read instead *priyayā*, "by [your] beloved." Ct and Cr explain that this is a reference to Mandodarī. Mandodarī's sage advice to Rāvaṇa is known only to a *prakṣipta*, or interpolated, passage found following *sarga* 46 (App. I, No. 30, lines

1–98 = KK *prakṣiptasarga* 1, following *sarga* 6.48). See, too, 6.99.13 and note, where, in her lament for her slain husband, Mandodarī alludes to the earlier advice she gave him to avoid conflict with Rāma.

[2]"my younger brother" *me 'nujena*: The reference is to Vibhiṣaṇa.

[3]"the . . . course of action" *kāryam*: D7,9–11, and the texts and printed editions of Ct and Cr read instead *vākyam*, "speech, advice."

21. "he knit his brows in anger" *bhrukuṭiṃ caiva saṃcakre*: Literally, "and he made a curving of [his] brows." The knitting of the brows is a conventional sign of anger in Sanskrit literature. See *Nāṭyaśāstra* 7.16,18. Cg understands that Rāvaṇa "raised his eyebrows (*ūrdhvīkṛtabhruvaṃ cakre*)."

22. "How dare you lecture me" *kiṃ māṃ tvam anuśāsasi*: Literally, "Why do you instruct me?" Since the point of Rāvaṇa's remarks is to put Kumbhakarṇa in his place as a junior, and so subordinate, relation, we have tried to capture his implicit rebuke in our rendering.

"like some venerable elder or preceptor" *mānyo gurur ivācāryaḥ*: Commentators and the translators who follow them are divided as how exactly to understand this phrase. We follow the interpretation of Cg, who clearly sees the verse as comparing Kumbhakarṇa to these venerable figures. (*tvaṃ mānyo bahumānarhaḥ. ācārya ācārapravartako gurur iva.*) This interpretation is also followed by Gita Press (1969, vol. 3, p. 1605) and Raghunathan (1982, vol. 3, p. 167). Ct understands that Rāvaṇa is comparing himself to an elder and preceptor. Ck, Ct, and Cr explain the former term as the biological father (*niṣekakartā*—so Ck, Ct; *janakaḥ*—so Cr) and the latter as the one who bestows a second birth (i.e., in the form of the *upanayana* ceremony) or bestows knowledge (*dvitīyajanmadaḥ*—so Ck, Ct; *vidyāpradaḥ*—so Cr). Only the translation of Dutt (1893, p. 1302) follows this interpretation literally. Gorresio (1858, vol. 10, p. 9), Roussel (1903, vol. 3, p. 193), Shastri (1959, vol. 3, p. 168), and Pagani (1999, p. 1026) understand the phrase in a general sense to mean that an elder is to be respected as one's preceptor. This interpretation is in keeping with the reading of Cr.

"Why waste your effort on words like this?" *kim evaṃ vākśramaṃ kṛtvā*: Literally, "Why having made exhaustion through speech in this fashion?" Cg explains the phrase as follows: "Having uttered words whose only result is exhaustion, what fruit can come of it? The meaning is 'It has no purpose.' This is because the time for [discussions of] statecraft has passed. (*prayāsaikaphalāṃ vācam uktvety arthaḥ. kiṃ phalam. kim api prayojanaṃ nāstīty arthaḥ. nītikālasyātītatvād iti bhāvaḥ.*)"

"You must do what suits the present situation." *kāle yuktaṃ vidhīyatām*: Literally, "What is suitable is to be done in [this] time." Cg explains that at the present time, when the opportunity for diplomacy has passed, one must resort to martial valor, which is now appropriate (*kāle nayamārgātītakāle yad yuktaṃ parākramarūpaṃ tad vidhīyatāṃ kriyatām*). D11 and the texts and printed editions of Ct, Ck, and Cr read *yad yuktaṃ tat*, "that which is appropriate," for *kāle yuktam*, "in time . . . [what is] suitable." Since this variant is rather elliptical, commentators who share this reading (Ck, Ct, Cr), in any case, supply the words *atra kāle*, "at this time."

Roussel (1903, vol. 3, p. 193) appears to read the form *vidhīyatām*, the passive imperative of *vi* √*dhā*, "to do, make, *or* bring about," as if it were formed from the verb *vi* √*dhyai*, "to think, consider, *or* contemplate," rendering, "*Ce qui sied* (*présentement*), *qu'on l'examine.*" Of course, such a derivation is not possible. Nonetheless, Roussel appears to have been followed in this by Shastri (1959, vol. 3, p. 168), who renders, "consider what is fitting at the moment," and Pagani (1999, p. 1026), who translates, "*Ce qu'il faut considérer maintenant.*" Compare *pādas* 24ab below, where there is a slight paraphrase of this clause.

23. "It is useless now to keep on repeating what I failed to do then" *nābhipannam idānīṃ yad vyarthās tasya punaḥ kathāḥ*: Literally, "repeated narrations of that which was not accepted are now purposeless."

"error, mental confusion" *vibhramāc cittamohāt*: The commentators differ somewhat in their interpretation of these terms. Cm, Ct, and Cr understand the former term to mean "erroneous *or* perverse knowledge (*viparītajñānam* [*viparyayajñānam*—Cr])." Cg is more specific, taking the term to mean "the consideration of bad policy as good policy (*anītau nītibuddhyā*)." Ct and Cm take the second term to mean "ignorance (*ajñānam*)." Cr understands, "lack of discrimination (*avivekāt*)," while Cg glosses, "the non-arising of knowledge (*jñānānudayāt*)." See note to verse 31 below.

24–25. "if you truly understand what it means to be a brother" *yadi... bhrātṛtvaṃ vāvagacchasi*: Literally, "or, if you understand the state of being a brother." D5–7,10,11,T,G2,M1–3, and the texts and printed editions of the southern commentators read *vikramam*, "valor," for *bhrātṛtvam*, "state of being a brother." In addition, D7,10,11, and the texts and printed editions of Cr and Ct read *adhigacchasi*, "you acquire, possess," for *avagacchasi*. These variants yield "if you truly possess valor." The texts and printed editions of Cg read *avagacchasi* with the critical edition, yielding the sense, as rendered by Raghunathan (1982, vol. 3, p. 167), "If... you really know your own strength."

"then you must immediately do what suits the present situation" *asmin kāle tu yad yuktaṃ tad idānīṃ vidhīyatām*: Compare *pādas* cd of verse 22 above, where a slight variant of this phrase occurs. D9–11 and the texts and printed editions of Ct and Cr read *vicintyatām*, "you must consider," for *vidhīyatām*, "you must do." See notes to verse 22 above.

"this catastrophic result" *doṣam*: Cg makes explicit that the calamity is the attack on the part of Rāvaṇa's enemies. (*doṣaṃ vaiṣamyam. śatrubhir ākramaṇam iti yāvat.*) B3,D9–11, and the texts and printed editions of Ct and Cr read instead *duḥkham*, "sorrow, pain, misery."

Following 24ab, D5–7,T,G2,M3, and the texts and printed editions of Cg and Cm, as well as the text of Gita Press, insert a passage of one line [1115*]: "They do not grieve over[1] what is gone; for what is gone is truly gone."

[1]"They do not grieve over" *nānuśocanti*: There is no expressed subject of the plural verb. One presumes, as does the author of the Gita Press (1969, vol. 3, p. 1605), that the implicit subject is "the wise." Cg and Cm, the only commentators to read this passage, fail to comment on it.

26. "A true friend... A true kinsman" *sa suhṛt... sa bandhuḥ*: Literally, "He is a friend... He is a kinsman." The term *bandhu*, "kinsman," can also mean "friend" and has been rendered in this fashion by some translators. However, given the context and the fact that Rāvaṇa is calling upon Kumbhakarṇa as his brother, we have interpreted the term in the former sense.

"stands by a poor wretch who has lost everything" *vipannārthaṃ dīnam abhyavapadyate*: Literally, "he protects a dejected person whose affairs have failed."

"to those who have gone astray" *apanīteṣu*: Literally, "among those deviating from sound policy." We agree with Ct, who glosses, "[among those who have] set out upon the path of unsound policy (*anītimārgastheṣu*)." Cr offers, "among those who are suffering the miseries arising from unsound policy (*apanītijanitaprāptaduḥkheṣu*)," while Cg glosses, "among men who practice unfavorable policy (*viṣamitanītiṣu puruṣeṣu*)." Cm understands, "among those practicing unsound policy (*apanītimatsu*)."

27. "Rāvaṇa... Kumbhakarṇa... addressed him" *tam... uvāca*: Literally, "[he] addressed him."

"firm and harsh words" *vacanaṃ dhīradāruṇam*: Ct, Cr, and Cg understand, as do we, that the compound is a *dvandva*. Each of these commentators picks out a different pair of statements from Rāvaṇa's speech, one of which is firm (*dhīra*) and the other harsh (*dāruṇa*). Thus, Cg takes Rāvaṇa's words at 25cd ("if... this mission is... [*yadi vā kāryam*...]") to serve as an example of a "firm (*dhīraṃ*)" speech, while the remarks at 26ab ("A true friend is one... [*sa suhṛt*...]") serve as an example of "harsh (*dāruṇa*)" speech. Cs takes the compound to modify not Rāvaṇa's words but Rāvaṇa himself, in the sense that "He remains resolute even now, although he is harsh, that is, cruel, in his words and demeanor. (*dhīram adhunāpi. dāruṇaṃ vacanākaraṇe krūram.*)" This reading would yield the sense "as the firm, but harsh Rāvaṇa was speaking in this fashion..." Cs also acknowledges that the compound can be applied to Rāvaṇa's speech or that it can be read as a locative *tatpuruṣa* referring to Rāvaṇa, in the sense of "harsh in respect to those who are restrained (*dhīreṣu dāruṇam*)."

"thinking, 'He is angry!' " *ruṣṭo 'yam iti vijñāya*: Literally, "having realized, 'He is angry.' " Cg notes that Kumbhakarṇa makes this inference from the fact of Rāvaṇa's having knitted his brows [in verse 21 above] (*bhrukuṭibandhanenānumāyety arthaḥ*).

28. "agitated" *kṣubhitendriyam*: Literally, "of agitated senses."

Ś,Ñ2,V,B2,3,D1–4,8–13,T2,3, and the texts and printed editions of Ct and Cr insert a passage of one line [1117*], either following verse 28 or elsewhere: "Listen attentively to my words, your majesty, subduer of your foes."

29. "Enough of this agonizing" *alam... saṃtāpam upapadya te*: Literally, "enough of you having recourse to agony." See note to verse 37 below.

30. "You need not give way to despondency" *naitan manasi kartavyam*: Literally, "this should not be done in [your] mind." The phrase is elliptical, and we agree with Ct and Cr, who, respectively, take the pronoun *etat*, "this," to refer to "despondency (*dainyam*)" and "suffering (*duḥkham*)." Cg takes the reference to be to Rāvaṇa's remarks in verse 23 concerning his error and mental confusion (see verse 23 above) (*vibhramāc cittamohād vety uktaṃ manasi na kartavyam ity arthaḥ*). We find this less persuasive, however, since, in that passage, he is not so much regretting his own failures as impatiently chiding his brother.

"as long as I am alive" *mayi jīvati*: Cg believes that the phrase is subject to an additional contradictory meaning in which Kumbhakarṇa, in saying that Rāvaṇa should not despair so long as he, Kumbhakarṇa, lives, is really suggesting that he, Kumbhakarṇa, is not going to live very long. Thus, Rāvaṇa should indeed be concerned. (*arthāntaraṃ tu... yady ahaṃ jīviṣyāmi tadaivaṃ na kartavyam. aham eva na jīviṣyāmīty arthaḥ.*)

"I will destroy him on whose account you are so anguished." *tam ahaṃ nāśayiṣyāmi yatkṛte paritapyase*: In keeping with his interpretation of the above phrase *mayi jīvati*, Cg continues to provide an alternative reading of the verse to refer covertly to Kumbhakarṇa's premonition of his own destruction. He therefore interprets this phrase as follows: "On whose account, that is, on my account, you suffer. In other words, you are pained by the thought, 'since he [Kumbhakarṇa] is living so comfortably, he won't carry out the mission for me.' I [Kumbhakarṇa] will cause Rāma to destroy him, that is, me. (*yatkṛte yasya mama kṛte paritapyase 'yaṃ sukhena jīvan matkaryaṃ na karotīti paritapto 'si. taṃ māṃ rāmeṇa nāśayiṣyāmīti.*)" See notes to verse 32 below.

31. "Regardless of your mood" *sarvāvastham*: Literally, "pertaining to all conditions." The compound is somewhat ambiguous, and it is not entirely clear whether one should read it adverbially, as we have done, or adjectivally with "advice (*vācyam*—lit., speech)," in the sense of "advice suitable to all occasions." Cg and Cm, the only commentators to share the critical reading, take the compound adverbially and understand the underlying noun *avasthā*, "condition, state," to refer to Rāvaṇa's emotional states. Cm glosses, "the meaning is 'in all states, such as anger, joy, etc.' (*roṣaharṣādisarvāvasthāsv ity arthaḥ*)." Cg similarly, although somewhat more ambiguously, offers, "[so as to be] situated in all states, such as anger, joy, etc. (*roṣaharṣādisarvāvasthāvasthitam ity arthaḥ*)." The reading is subject to a certain amount of variation in the texts and printed editions of the epic. The texts of Cr and Gorresio read the unambiguous *sarvāvasthāsu*, "under all conditions." Note that this is the gloss Cm suggests. D10 and the texts and printed editions of Ck and Ct read *sarvāvasthāṃ* (*-stha-* —Ck) *gataṃ mayā* for the critical edition's *sarvāvasthaṃ mayā tava*. This then becomes an adjectival phrase modifying an implicit *tvām*, "you [Rāvaṇa]." As Ck and Ct explain it, the expression means "to you who are experiencing every emotional state, such as joy, sorrow, etc. (*sarvāvasthāṃ sukhaduḥkhādisarvāvasthāṃ gataṃ prāptam. tvāṃ pratīti śeṣaḥ.*)" Ct, however, notes that others, whom he does not specify, quote here the passage: "So it is sung, 'The universal condition is the condition of the absence of devotion to Viṣṇu' (*viṣṇor abhaktikāvasthā sarvāvastheti gīyate*)." Presumably this is a theological allusion to Rāvaṇa's lack of devotion to Rāma.

"my bond of kinship and brotherly affection forced me to offer" *avaśyaṃ tu... mayā... bandhubhāvād abhihitaṃ bhrātṛsnehāc ca*: Literally, "because of the bond of kinship and brotherly affection, by me, of necessity... was uttered."

32. "in the present circumstances" *kāle 'smin*: Literally, "at this time." Cg adds, "at this calamitous time (*āpatkāle*)."

"to slaughter your enemies. Now watch, as I do just that in battle." *śatrūṇāṃ kadanaṃ paśya kriyamāṇaṃ mayā raṇe*: Literally, "See the slaughter of enemies being effected in battle by me." Cg, carrying further his alternative inverted reading of Kumbhakarṇa's words begun in verse 30 above, remarks that "the alternative meaning here is the slaughter effected by your enemies (*atra śatrukartṛkaṃ kadanam ity arthāntaram*)." In other words, Cg once more sees Kumbhakarṇa as prophesying his own death.

33. "great-armed warrior" *mahābāho*: Literally, "O great-armed one."

"you shall see" *paśya*: Literally, "see!"

"the hosts of tawny monkeys fleeing, once I have slain Rāma and his brother in the forefront of battle" *mayā samaramūrdhani / hate rāme saha bhrātrā dravantīṃ harivāhinīm*: M3 and the texts and printed editions of Cg (VSP and KK 6.63.34) read *para-*, "enemy," for the critical edition's *hari-*, "tawny monkeys." This is rendered as "the enemy's army" by Raghunathan (1982, vol. 3, p. 168), the only translator to render this reading. This variant, however, enables Cg to continue his alternative interpretation of Kumbhakarṇa's words. In this case, the meaning is "O senior one, that is, O elder brother, this very day you shall see the [*rākṣasa*] army returning on account of Rāma once the front rank of battle has been crushed together with me. (*arthāntaram. he para jyeṣṭha mayā saha samaramūrdhani hate bhagne sati rāme rāmanimittaṃ dravantīm āgacchantīṃ vāhinīṃ paśyeti.*)" Cg does not comment on the word *bhrātrā*, "with the brother," but one would assume that, in this reading, it would have to construe with *mayā*, in the sense of "along with me, your brother."

34. Cg continues his alternative explanation. In this vein, he notes that the alternate meaning of this verse is "You will be happy once you see me and my head tossed far away for the sake of battle, because you will then have given up your anger toward me. Sītā will be desolate [at my death] because she is the mother of the whole world. (*arthāntaram. mayā saha rāmasya raṇād dhetor ānītaṃ dūre kṣiptam. śiro macchiraḥ. dṛṣṭvā sukhī bhava. tadānīṃ mayi roṣatyāgād iti bhāvaḥ. sītā duḥkhitā bhavatu. sarvalokamātṛtvād iti bhāvaḥ.*)"

"great-armed warrior" *mahābāho*: Literally, "O great-armed one."

35. Cg's alternate reading is that we should understand the form *rāmasya*, "of Rāma," as an agentive genitive. This enables us to understand the death to be Kumbhakarṇa's own at the hands of Rāma. The *rākṣasas* whose kinsmen have already been slain will presumably not experience this [Kumbhakarṇa's death] as terribly grievous since, by the maxim, "along with five others, one does not experience misery," they and Kumbhakarṇa will be joining their slain loved ones. (*arthāntaram. rāmasyeti kartari ṣaṣṭhī. rāmakartṛkaṃ mannidhanaṃ ye nihatabāndhavās te rākṣasāḥ paśyantu. na duḥkhaṃ pañcabhiḥ saheti nyāyād iti bhāvaḥ.*) The idea here appears to be similar to that expressed by the English proverb "Misery loves company."

36. "on account of the slaughter of their kinsmen" *svabandhuvadhakāraṇāt*: Ś,Ñ,V1,2,B1,2,4,D1–3,8–12,M1,2, and the texts and printed editions of Ct and Cr read *-śocinām*, "grieving," for *-kāraṇāt*, "on account of." This yields the sense of "grieving for their own kinsmen," which is somewhat redundant in light of the preceding compound, "afflicted with grief (*śokaparītānām*)."

37. "the lord of the leaping monkeys" *plavageśvaram*: D5,T1,G3,M3,5, and the texts and printed editions of Cg (VSP and KK 6.63.38) read instead *plavagottamam*, "best of leaping monkeys."

"like a storm cloud when the sun breaks through" *sasūryam iva toyadam*: Literally, "like a water-giver [rain cloud] together with the sun." The image intended by the poet is not unambiguously clear. In light of the adjective *vikīrṇam*, "torn apart, scattered," we believe that the basis for the simile is the sight of clouds at the end of the rain when shafts of sunlight pierce through them. Cr and Cg, however, understand that the basis for the simile is that Sugrīva's body would be drenched in blood and so would resemble a cloud tinged with red by the [setting?] sun (*rudhirāktatayā sasūryaprakāśaṃ megham iva sthitam ity arthaḥ*—so Cg). Among the translators consulted, the majority simply understand, "lit up by the sun." Only Gita Press (1969, vol. 3, p. 1606) appears to follow the idea expressed by Cg and Cr, rendering, "like a cloud illumined by the (evening) sun." Shastri (1959, vol. 3, p. 169) idiosyncratically reads the simile to refer to the compound simile *parvatasaṃkāśam*, "resembling a mountain," of *pāda* a and completely omits the reference to the cloud. He renders, "who resembles a mountain illumined by the sun." The association of Sugrīva and the sun may perhaps be conditioned by the fact that Sugrīva is the son of the solar divinity Sūrya. Indeed, a few northern manuscripts (Ñ2,V1,2,B2–4), as well as the printed edition of Gorresio, read *sūryaputram*, "son of the sun," for *sasūryam i[va]*.

All northern manuscripts (except Ś,D1–3,5,8,12) and all southern manuscripts insert a passage of five lines [1122*]. The majority of manuscripts have the insert following verse 37, but some northern manuscripts locate the passage elsewhere in the *sarga*: "How can you, blameless one, possibly be afraid, when you are constantly under my protection and that of these *rākṣasas* who are eager to kill Rāma Dāśarathi? Rāghava will kill you this day only if he kills me first.[1] And I for one, overlord of the *rākṣasas*, will never give way to agonizing.[2] Please command me now as you wish, scorcher of your foes."

[1]"only if he kills me first" *pūrvaṃ hate tena mayi*: Literally, "when I have been killed by him before." We agree with Cg in understanding this seemingly grim prediction to be, in fact, a form of reassurance for Rāvaṇa. What Kumbhakarṇa is saying, according to Cg, is that, since he himself cannot be killed by anyone and that impossibility would have to occur before Rāvaṇa could be slain, the latter need have no fear. (*mayi hate sati hi paścāt tvāṃ rāmo hanti haniṣyati. ahaṃ cātmani svasmin saṃtāpaṃ śatruparibhavajaṃ na kadācid api gaccheyaṃ na kenacid dhantuṃ śakya ity arthaḥ. ataḥ kutas te bhayam iti bhāvaḥ.*) D10,11, and the texts and printed editions of Ct read instead *māṃ nihatya kila tvāṃ hi [nihaniṣyati rāghavaḥ]*, "Indeed, only having slain me [will Rāghava kill] you."

[2]"I . . . will never give way to agonizing" *nāham ātmani saṃtāpaṃ gaccheyam*: Literally, "I would not go to [experience] pain in my mind *or* self." We take the term *saṃtāpa* in the same sense in which we read it in verse 29 above. We thus understand that Kumbhakarṇa, unlike Rāvaṇa, would never permit his mental agonizing to dominate his emotions and prevent him from taking effective military action. According to Cg, what Kumbhakarṇa is suggesting is that he would never experience any concern within himself arising from [the fear of] being overcome by an enemy since no one is capable of defeating him (similarly Ck, Ct, Cm, and Cr). (See note 1 above.) Cg, however, in keeping with his exegetical project in this *sarga*, also proposes yet another *arthāntara*, or alternate reading. According to this, Kumbhakarṇa experiences no concern for himself, that is, he does not grieve for his own impending death but grieves only at the thought that, once he himself is slain, Rāma will kill Rāvaṇa. (*ahaṃ atmanı vıṣaye samtāpaṃ na gaccheyaṃ na gacchāmi . . . mannidhanaṃ nānuśocāmīty arthaḥ. kiṃtu mayi hate sati. atha rāgahavas tvāṃ hanti haniṣyatīti saṃtāpaṃ gacchāmīti.*)

38. "You should not send out anyone else" *na paraḥ preṣaṇīyas te*: Ñ2,V,D4,5, 10,11,T,G1,3,M1,2,5, and the texts and printed editions of Ct, Ck, and Cr read *prekṣaṇīyaḥ*, "to be looked at," for the critical edition's *preṣaṇīyaḥ*, "to be sent." The idea of this variant is that Rāvaṇa should not look for any other warrior to go in Kumbhakarṇa's stead. Cr understands that Rāvaṇa should not seek out anyone to assist Kumbhakarṇa (*matsāhāyyārthaṃ nānveṣaṇīyaḥ*).

"warrior of unequaled valor" *atulavikrama*: Literally, "O one of unequaled valor."

"mighty king" *mahābala*: Literally, "O mighty one." D7,9–11, and the texts and printed editions of Ct and Cr read instead the accusative plural *mahābalān*, yielding the sense "[slaughter your] mighty [enemies]."

40. "Indra himself, the smasher of citadels" *puraṃdaraḥ*: Literally, "the smasher of citadels."

41. "cast my weapon aside" *tyaktaśastrasya . . . me*: Literally, "of me, who had abandoned his weapon." The idea, as we understand it, is that, in his contempt for his puny enemies, Kumbhakarṇa will dispense with his lance and rely on his immense size to trample them like so many insects. This interpretation is in keeping with the following verse. Cr, however, believes that Kumbhakarṇa will be forced to fight in this fashion after Rāma and the others have destroyed his weapons (*nanu rāmādibhiḥ śastrāṇi chidyanta iti taiḥ saha kathaṃ tava yuddhaṃ bhaviṣyatīty ata āha*).

"if he valued his life" *jijīviṣuḥ*: Literally, "one wishing to live."

42. "even Indra himself, the wielder of the *vajra*" *api vajriṇam*: Literally, "even the possessor of the *vajra*." D6,7,9–11, and the texts and printed editions of Ct and Cr read instead *savajriṇam*, "along with the wielder of the *vajra*," for [*a*]*pi vajriṇam*. Cr supplies the word *ripum*, "enemy," as a modificand for this otherwise elliptical adjective.

43. "a hail of arrows . . . his blood" *bāṇaughā rudhiram . . . te*: Literally, "those hails of arrows . . . blood." The pronoun *te* is subject to considerable variation throughout the recensions and should probably have been marked as an uncertain reading by the critical editors. Ct, Crā, Cm, and Cr read instead *me*, "my." The enclitic *me* is ambiguous here, in that it may refer either to Kumbhakarṇa's blood (*rudhiram*) or to the hail of arrows (*bāṇaughāḥ*). Ct reads it with blood (*rudhiram*) and understands that only if Rāma is able to survive the blow of Kumbhakarṇa's fist would Rāma's arrows then drink Kumbhakarṇa's blood. But, in Kumbhakarṇa's opinion, this would be impossible. (*me muṣṭivegaṃ rāghavo yadi sahiṣyati tadā rāghavasya bāṇaughā me rudhiraṃ pāsyanti. tatsahanam eva tasyāśakyam iti bhāvaḥ.*) Crā and Cm understand similarly. Cr, on the other hand, understands that, in the event that Rāma should survive the blow of Kumbhakarṇa's fist, then Kumbhakarṇa's arrows will drink his blood (*sa rāghavo yadi me muṣṭivegaṃ sahiṣyati . . . tarhi me bāṇaughā rāghavasya rudhiraṃ pāsyanti*). Cg avoids the issue, reading the pleonastic particle *tu* for *te*. Cg reframes the verse as a rhetorical question, "Rāma will not withstand the initial blow of my fist. How then will he be able to strike me? (*rāmaḥ prathamaṃ me muṣṭiprahāram eva na sahiṣyate. kuto māṃ prahariṣyatīti bhāvaḥ.*)"

"his" *rāghavasya*: Literally, "of Rāghava,"

44. "are you oppressed" *bādhyase*: D7,9–11, and the texts and printed editions of Ct and Cr read instead *tapyase*, "are you burned *or* tormented."

45. "your majesty" *rājan*: D7,9–11, and the texts and printed editions of Ct and Cr read instead *ghoram*, "terrible," an adjective modifying *bhayam*, "fear."

Following 45cd, D5–7,9–11,S insert a passage of two lines [1127*]: "as well as Hanumān, the *rākṣasa*-slayer, who burned Laṅkā. And I shall slaughter those tawny monkeys who stand fast in battle.[1]"

[1]"I shall slaughter . . . who stand fast in battle" *haniṣyāmi saṃyuge samavasthitān*: The printed editions of Ct and Cr read instead *bhakṣayiṣyāmi saṃyuge samupasthite*, "And when the battle is at hand, I shall devour."

Following verse 45, D5–7,9–11,S insert lines 1–9 of 1097* (found following 6.50.10 in the critical edition). The entire star passage is inserted by all northern manuscripts;

most place it following 6.50.10. It is unclear why the critical edition omits this passage as it is known to all manuscripts. Lines 12–14 of 1097* are inserted in all southern manuscripts following line 7 of 1141*, which follows 6.53.11. See note to 6.53.11 for a translation of these lines. There are numerous variants in the text and in the sequence of this passage. The version that appears in the critical edition is found in no major recension or other printed edition. Moreover, the logical sequence of its verses seems confused. Therefore, we render instead the southern version as it appears in printed editions of the southern recension. This corresponds to the following passages in the printed editions: GPP and NSP 6.63.51–54; VSP 6.63.51–55; KK 6.63.52–56; and Gita Press 6.63.52–56. "If you are afraid of Indra, your majesty, or of self-existent Brahmā [GPP 51ab; CE 1097*, line 1],[1] then, once I am roused to fury, even the gods will lie sprawled upon the earth [GPP 51cd; CE 1097(B)*]. I shall slay Yama and devour Agni, the purifier [GPP 52ab; CE 1097*, line 2]. I shall cast Āditya down to earth together with all the heavenly bodies [GPP 52cd; CE 1097*, line 4]. I shall slay Indra of the hundred sacrifices and drink up the ocean, Varuṇa's abode [GPP 53ab; CE 1097*, line 5]. I shall pulverize the mountains and shatter the earth [GPP 53cd; CE 1097*, line 6]. And let all creatures, even as they are being devoured, witness the valor of Kumbhakarṇa, who has slept for so long a time. Not even the triple heavens themselves will make a meal enough to fill me up [GPP 54; CE 1098*, lines 7–9]."

[1]Following line 1, D7,G2,3, and GPP (in brackets following 6.63.51ab) insert a passage of one line [1097(A)*]: "Then I shall destroy [them], as does the many-rayed sun, the darkness of night."

46. "pleasure, the greatest of all pleasures" *sukhāvahaṃ sukham*: Literally, "pleasure that brings pleasure." We follow Ct, who glosses the adjective *sukhāvaham* as "pleasure producing great and ever increasing pleasure (*uttarottaram adhikasukhajanakaṃ sukham*)." Ś,Ñ1,D5,6,8,12,T1,3,M3, and the texts and printed editions of Cm and Cg read *sukhārham* for *sukhāvaham*, "that brings pleasure." The compound *sukhārham* would normally mean "worthy *or* deserving of pleasure." This meaning in the accusative seems impossible in the context, and, in fact, the critical apparatus marks the reading with the notation *sic*. Cg, however, glosses the term with *sukhāvaham*, the same term found in the critical edition and in the text of Ct. It should be noted that since the verse is an *upajāti*, the critical reading creates a hypermetric *pāda* a. Raghunathan (1982, vol. 3, p. 169), the only translator to follow the text of Cg, translates, "[I go forth] to make you happy, who deserve it," despite the syntactical problem that such a reading creates. In keeping with his interpretation of the passage, Cg provides another alternative reading (*arthāntara*), suggesting, "Through your death, Dāśarathi will experience tremendous pleasure (*te vadhena dāśaratheḥ sukhāvaham ity arthāntaram*)."

"through the slaughter of Dāśarathi" *vadhena... dāśaratheḥ*: Cm, in keeping with his larger theological hermeneutic, offers an alternative reading of the passage. He suggests breaking *vadhena*, "through the slaughter," into the locative *vadhe* and the negative particle *na*. This allows him to read as follows: " 'If Rāma Dāśarathi were to be killed, you would not be happy. I, however, am going forth to bring you great happiness.' The poet now says how he will do this, with the passage beginning with the words 'Once I have slain.' 'Once I have slain all the leaders of the troops of tawny monkeys excluding Rāma and Lakṣmaṇa, I will eat them.' That is the syntax. The real meaning is 'Since I am unable to kill Rāma, I will bring you a joy born from the destruction of the leaders of the troops of tawny monkeys.' (*atra vadha iti saptamī. dāśarathe rāmasya vadhe sati tava sukhaṃ na. kiṃtu ahaṃ sukhārhaṃ samāhartuṃ vrajāmi. tat kim ata āha nihatyeti. lakṣmaṇena saha vartamānaṃ rāmaṃ vineti śeṣaḥ. hariyūthamukhyān nihatya sarvān khādāmīti sambandhaḥ. rāmahananasyāśakyatvād dhariyūthamukhyasaṃhāra-janitasukhaṃ tava saṃpādayiṣyāmīti bhāvaḥ.*)"

The meter is *upajāti* with a hypermetric *pāda* a.

47. "to your heart's content" *kāmam*: Literally, "according to [your] desire." D9–11 and the texts and printed editions of Ct and Cr read instead *rājan*, "O king *or* your majesty."

"fine wines" *agryavāruṇīm*: Literally, "fine liquor." Ñ,V1,2,B,D9–11, and the texts and printed editions of Ct and Cr read instead *adya-*, "this day," for *agrya-*, "fine, excellent."

"banish all cares" *vinīyatāṃ jvaraḥ*: Literally, "Let fear *or* anguish be removed." D7,9–11, and the texts and printed editions of Ct and Cr read instead *vinīya duḥkham*, "having banished sorrow." This makes *pāda* b hypometric.

"at long last" *cirāya*: The adverb is ambiguous. In the present context it can mean either "after a long time *or* for a long time." The various translators consulted opt for one or the other of these. We believe the former is more plausible in light of Rāvaṇa's frustration at his inability to break Sītā's will.

"Once I have, this very day, sent Rāma to the abode of Yama, Sītā will at long last submit to your will." *mayādya rāme gamite yamakṣayaṃ cirāya sītā vaśagā bhaviṣyati*: In keeping with their devotional reading of the epic, Cg and Cm propose alternative ways to read this verse. Cg begins by taking the first half of the verse, with its instructions to Rāvaṇa to devote himself to sybaritic pleasures, to be an ironic utterance on the part of Kumbhakarṇa, which would be indicated in speech by tone of voice, etc. (*kākuḥ*). He then proposes breaking *gamite yamakṣayam*, "sent . . . to the abode of Yama," into *gamitā iyam akṣayam*. This yields the alternative meaning (*arthāntara*) "Once Sītā has been sent to her proper lord, Rāma (*rāme viṣaye*), then she will be under his control forever. (*iyam akṣayam iti cchedaḥ. rāme viṣaye gamiteyaṃ sītā cirāya vaśagā bhaviṣyatīty arthāntaram.*)" In a similar fashion, Cm proposes breaking up the sequence *gamite yamakṣayam* into *gamite 'yam akṣayam*. He then argues that Kumbhakarṇa is really saying the following: "Once I have sent Rāma permanently back under the control of Sītā, then, having become a friend, he will, this very day, come to our house. (*rāme gamiteyamakṣayam ity atra gamite 'yam akṣayam iti cchedaḥ. mayā rāme 'kṣayaṃ yathā tathā cirāya sītāvaśaṃ gamite saty ayaṃ rāmo 'dyāgamiṣyati bandhubhūtaḥ sann asmadgṛhaṃ pratīti śeṣaḥ.*)"

The meter is *vaṃśasthavila*.

Sarga 52

1. "with his immense arms" *bāhuśālinaḥ*: Literally, "endowed *or* resplendent with arms." Cg remarks that this and the other descriptions of Kumbhakarṇa's size and physical prowess highlight [in Mahodara's opinion] his unfitness to offer his advice (*prativacanānarhatvadyotanāya viśeṣaṇāni*).

2. "presumptuous" *dhṛṣṭaḥ*: The term can also mean "bold, courageous," and some translators have rendered it in this way. Given the harsh tenor of Mahodara's words, however, this seems less plausible to us.

"you . . . have a vulgar mind" *prākṛtadarśanaḥ*: Literally, "have a common view."

"in any situation" *sarvatra*: Literally, "in all [things]." Some translators have understood this to mean "in every situation" or "in all aspects of a situation." Cm takes the adverb in the sense of "always (*sarvadā*)" and construes it specifically with the adjective "arrogant (*avaliptaḥ*)."

3. "It is not the case that the king does not understand" *na hi rājā na jānīte*: Literally, "For the king does not not know." Cm takes the particle *hi*, "for," to indicate that the statement is an example of *kāku* (*hiśabdaḥ kākvarthaḥ*), which in this case refers to a negative statement used in the sense of affirmation. See note to 6.37.10 for additional examples of double negatives.

"to prattle" *vaktum*: Literally, "to speak."

4. "He is quite familiar with the distinctions of place and time" *deśakālavibhāgavit*: Mahodara is refuting Kumbhakarṇa's implicit charge at 6.51.6 above that Rāvaṇa is ignorant of such distinctions. D10,11,T2,G1,M1,2, and the texts and printed editions of Ct, Ck, and Cr read *-vidhāna-*, "rules, precepts," for the critical reading, *-vibhāga-*, "distinctions." Commentators who follow this reading understand, "knowing the proper actions to be undertaken at various places and times (*deśakālayor ucitakartavyavit*—Ct, Ck)."

"stasis, increase, and diminution" *sthānaṃ vṛddhiṃ ca hāniṃ ca*: See 6.51.7, where the commentators understand the three types of action (*trayāṇām . . . karmaṇām*) to be conciliation, etc. (*sāmādīnām*), as characterized by these three conditions of diminution, increase, and stasis (*kṣayavṛddhisthānalakṣaṇānām*). We follow the majority of the commentators in applying the three states equally to Rāvaṇa and his enemies. Ct alone understands "increase (*vṛddhi*)" to refer only to Rāvaṇa and "diminution (*hāni*)" only to his enemies (*ātmano vṛddhiṃ pareṣāṃ hāniṃ ca*).

"bull among *rākṣasas*" *rākṣasarṣabha*: Ñ1,V1,2,B3,D1,4–6,9–11,13,T1,G3,M2,3,5, and the texts and printed editions of the southern commentators read instead the nominative *rākṣasarṣabhaḥ*, which would then refer to Rāvaṇa rather than Kumbhakarṇa, as in the critical edition.

5. The verse is quite ambiguous in its meaning, and this is only heightened by the variant readings noted in the critical apparatus and by the commentators. The general sense of the verse, as articulated by Cg, who shares the critical reading, is that a discriminating person, such as Rāvaṇa, would not be capable of engaging in the kind of unworthy actions that only a vulgar or inferior person might undertake. For Cg, as for Ct, Ck, Cm, and Cr, this is a rhetorical question, which in asking "What wise man would engage in such actions?" intends to say "None would do so, least of all Rāvaṇa." (*budhaḥ kaḥ kuryāt? na ko 'pi kuryāt. kimuta rāvaṇa iti bhāvaḥ*). Cr takes this verse to suggest that Rāvaṇa's actions have been quite correct (*etena rāvaṇakṛtaṃ samīcīnam eveti sūcitam*). He further understands the verse to be a critique of Kumbhakarṇa's words at 6.51.4, where he rebukes Rāvaṇa for having acted out of the sheer arrogance of his strength. Cv, however, reads the response to the rhetorical question to be "Wise Rāvaṇa would indeed do such a thing (*buddhimān rāvaṇaḥ tādṛśaṃ kuryād ity ayam asyārthaḥ*)."

"wise man" *budhaḥ*: Literally, "wise one." D9–11 and the texts and printed editions of Ck and Cr read instead *naraḥ*, "man." Commentators associated with these texts

(Ck, Ct, and Cr), however, all comment on the critical edition's *budhaḥ*, "wise." Dutt (1893, p. 1305) translates, "person." Roussel (1903, vol. 3, p. 196), Shastri (1959, vol. 3, p. 170), and Pagani (1999, p. 1028) appear to read *naraḥ*. Roussel translates, "*homme (de sens)*"; Shastri, "man of sense"; and Pagani, "*homme sensé*."

"an action such as could only be performed" *śakyam . . . kartum*: Literally, "capable of being performed." Ñ2,V,B1,3,4,D5–7,10,11,M3, and Ct, Ck, Cr, Cs, and Cm, as well as GPP, Gita Press, NNS, and KK, read *aśakyam*, "incapable [of being performed]," for *śakyam*. Cr then glosses the reading *aśakyaṃ kartum* as "improper (*anucitam*)," and Cm, as "unworthy (*anarham*)." For them, then, the sense is "What wise man would perform an act unworthy even of a vulgar-minded man." Ś,Ñ,V,B2–4,D1–4,8–13 read *vaktum*, "to speak *or* say," for the critical edition's *kartum*, "to do." This variant appears in the printed editions of NSP (but not GPP or Gita Press), Lahore, and Gorresio. Dutt (1893, p. 1305), the only translator of the southern text to follow this reading, is perplexed by it. He translates, "But what person ever acteth according to what is proposed feebly," and adds the following notes: "*Vaktum açakyam—incapable of saying*. But what sense can be attached to—'What man acteth according to what is *not* advanced by one having strength...... aged?' I therefore venture to render the passage—*feebly proposed—i.e. proposed with vascillation* [*sic*] *or half-heartedly*."

The second half of the verse in northern texts, such as that of Lahore (6.43.5) and Gorresio (6.43.5), refers to the speech of Kumbhakarṇa rather than the actions of the king, thus rendering the reading *vaktum* easier to construe.

"a . . . man of brute strength" *balavatā*: Literally, "by one possessed of strength." We follow Cg, who glosses, "by one who relies on physical strength alone (*kevalaśauryāvalambinā*)."

"who does not honor his elders" *anupāsitavṛddhena*: Literally, "one by whom elders are not honored." Cs, as ever contrarian in his reading, breaks up the compound and the following interrogative pronoun *kaḥ*, "what . . . man?" so that he reads the vocative *anupāsitavṛddha*, "O you [Kumbhakarṇa] who do not honor your elders," and *inakaḥ*, "lord, master, powerful one [Rāvaṇa]." He then interprets, "our master, who is a wise man, might perform such actions that are suitable for him, even though they would not be undertaken by ordinary people (*budho jñānī tādṛśaṃ prākṛtabuddhibhir ananuṣṭhīyamānaṃ svayogyaṃ kuryāt*)." Alternatively, if one accepts the reading *śakyam* [the critical reading] for *aśakyam* [as discussed above], Cs continues, then we can retain the interrogative pronoun *kaḥ*, "what . . . man," by taking both *anupāsitavṛddha* and *ina*, "powerful one," as vocatives referring to Kumbhakarṇa. Cs claims that Mahodara speaks in this fashion to Kumbhakarṇa either out of anger [at Kumbhakarṇa] in the midst [of the conversation] because he [Kumbhakarṇa] is junior to his master or out of fear of his own destruction in order to make him turn and face him (*svāmyanujatvān madhye kopena svadhvaṃsasādhvasād vā tam abhimukhīkartum evam uktiḥ*). Cs concludes by quoting Ct's and Cm's reading of the term as an instrumental agreeing with *balavatā*. This yields "of brute strength, who does not honor his elders."

6. Mahodara here is refuting Kumbhakarṇa's remarks at verses 6.51.9–12 about separately practicing the three ends of man.

"can be practiced separately" *pṛthagāśrayān*: Literally, "having separate practices." Cg and Cv understand this to mean "having separate causes *or* separate results (*pṛthagkāraṇān bhinnaphalān*)." Cm glosses, "having predetermined results (*vyava-*

sthitaphalān)." All these commentators thus believe that Mahodara is criticizing Kumbhakarṇa's view, since the actual results of various actions are not absolutely fixed. Ck, Ct, and Cr, on the other hand, understand the compound to mean "mutually exclusive and thus not to be practiced simultaneously (*parasparaviruddhā naikānuṣṭheyāḥ*—so Ct)."

"capacity" *lakṣaṇam*: The term normally means "mark, sign, distinguishing characteristic." However, the context forces us to agree with Ct, Cr, and Ck, who gloss, "ability, capacity (*sāmārthyam*)." Cg and Cm understand the term to refer to "that whereby something is discerned" and gloss it here as "a valid means of knowledge" or "reason (so Cm)" (*lakṣyate 'neneti lakṣaṇaṃ pramāṇam* [*kāraṇam* ... *vā*—so Cm]).

"as they truly are" *svabhāvena*: Literally, "through inherent nature." D5–7,T,G1,3,M5, as well as VSP, KK, Crā, and Cg, read instead *svabhāve tān*, "[understand] them with respect to their true nature." The reading of the critical edition is somewhat ambiguous, since it can arguably refer to the inherent nature of Kumbhakarṇa as well as that of the *puruṣārthas*. The commentators who share this reading prefer, as we do, the latter reading, glossing, "correctly, truthfully (*tattvataḥ*)." Cg and Cm, who read *svabhāve*, similarly gloss, "as they truly are (*svarūpataḥ*)." All translators consulted follow suit, with the exception of Dutt (1893, p. 1305), who offers, "[thou art not] naturally [competent]." See 6.51.9; 6.105.13; and notes.

7. "the motivating force" *prayojanam*: Here the term should be taken in its sense of "cause, motive." As suggested by Ct, Ck(?), and Cr, who gloss, "instigating, causing, giving rise to (*prayojakam utpādakam*)," the term must be taken in its sense of "motive." M1,2, and the texts and printed editions of Cm and Cg actually read instead *prayojakam*. They gloss, "effective means toward (*sādhakam*)," which Cg fleshes out by saying, "action alone is the cause of, that is, the means toward, fruits in the form of heaven and hell (*svarganarakarūpāṇāṃ phalānāṃ karmaiva prayojakaṃ sādhakam*)."

"all things" *sarveṣāṃ kāraṇānām*: Literally, "all causes *or* objects."

"in this world" *atra*: Literally, "here."

"even the most wicked actions may bear excellent fruit" *śreyaḥ pāpīyasām* ... *phalaṃ bhavati karmaṇām*: Literally, "the fruit of very evil actions becomes good." As Cg and Cm explain, the argument here derives from the notion that the results of any action are unpredictable (*kiṃtu atra karmajāte pāpīyasām api karmaṇāṃ śreyaḥ phalaṃ bhavati*—so Cg). Ct, Cr, and Ck, however, read the sequence *śreyaḥ pāpīyasām* as a *dvandva* compound, *śreyaḥpāpīyasām*. They then understand, "the fruits of good and evil actions redound upon one and the same agent (*śubhāśubhavyāpārāṇāṃ phalam atraikasminn eva kartari bhavati*)." Dutt (1893, p. 1305) and Gita Press (1969, vol. 3, p. 1609) are the only translators to follow this interpretation. Thus, Gita Press translates, "moreover, the fruit of actions (both) noble and exceedingly sinful, in this world, accrues to the same agent."

8. "Righteousness and sound policy may yield excellent results; but so may their opposites. Still, unrighteousness and unsound policy may also yield results that are calamitous." *niḥśreyasaphalāv eva dharmārthāv itarāv api / adharmānarthayoḥ prāptiḥ phalaṃ ca pratyavāyikam*: Literally, "*Dharma* and *artha* have happiness *or* final beatitude as their fruit, as do the other two. The result of *adharma* and *anartha* is a diminished *or* harmful fruit." Like many of the formulations of the *nītiśāstras* in this passage, this verse is obscure and ambiguous, and is subjected to extensive analysis by the commentators.

"Righteousness and sound policy" *dharmārthau*: Normally, when the three categories of the Hindu *trivarga*—*dharma*, *artha*, and *kāma*—are mentioned as a set, we have rendered the second term as "profit." See verse 6 above. In the present context, however, we believe that the term is better understood as a reference to *arthaśāstra*, with an emphasis on successful political practice. Commentators fall into two basic groups regarding the interpretation of these two critical terms in this verse. Cg, Cv, and Cm, with whom we are in agreement, understand the reference to be to the two kinds of action (*karmaṇī*) that are, respectively, the means to righteousness and sound policy (*dharmārthasādhanabhūte karmaṇī*—so Cg). Ck, Ct, and Cr read the terms in a more soteriological sense. Thus, Ck and Ct understand the terms to refer to two varieties of religious practice, with *dharma* consisting of actions such as prayer, meditation, etc., that do not involve [the expenditure of] wealth. On the other hand, they understand *artha* to refer to those religious practices, such as sacrifice and charitable giving, that can be accomplished only through such expenditure. (*atra dharmaśabdenārthanirapekṣo japadhyānādiḥ. arthaśabdena cārthasādhyo yāgadānādiḥ*—so Ct.) In support of this, they quote *Bhagavadgītā* 18.5 in which Lord Kṛṣṇa declares that sacrifice, charity, and asceticism sanctify the wise (*yajño dānaṃ tapaś caiva pāvanāni manīṣiṇām*). Such activities, Ct and Ck continue, in serving to purify the mind, constitute the means for attaining spiritual liberation (*mokṣa*). The point here, according to Ct and Ck, is that the third member of the *trivarga*, *kāma*, "pleasure," never leads to final beatitude (*niḥśreyasa*). (*teṣāṃ cittaśuddhidvārā mokṣasādhanatvam asti. kāmas tu na kadāpi niḥśreyasaphala iti bhāvaḥ*—so Ct.) Cr has a somewhat different but related interpretation. He, too, understands *niḥśreyasa* to mean "spiritual liberation." However, he understands the respective fruits of *dharma* and *artha* to be the attainment of heaven and earthly rewards, such as kingship (*niḥśreyasaṃ mokṣaḥ phalaṃ yayos tāv api dharmārthāv itarau svargaihikarājyādiphalāv api bhavata iti śeṣaḥ*). Cs interprets similarly.

"but so may their opposites" *itarāv api*: Literally, "the other two as well." The commentators differ broadly in their interpretations, particularly regarding the meaning of the ambiguous pronoun *itarau* "the other two." Ck and Ct understand it to refer to *dharma* and *artha* themselves, which are "other" in the sense that they are distinct from *kāma*, "pleasure *or* desire," and so are conducive to the attainment, respectively, of heaven and worldly prosperity (*abhyudaya*) (*dharmārthau niḥśreyasaphalāv eva santau kāmanāviśeṣeṇetarāv api svargābhyudayaphalāv api bhavataḥ*—so Ct). Cr understands similarly (see note above to *dharmārthau*). These commentators understand that the point of the verse is that, among the three ends attainable through human effort, *dharma* and *artha* are superior to *kāma*.

Cv, Cg, and Cm, whom we follow, understand the verse to be reiterating the idea expressed in the previous verse, that the outcomes of various types of action, righteous and unrighteous, are unpredictable. They understand *itarau* to refer to the opposites of *dharma* and *artha*, specifically to actions that are unrighteous or that reflect unsound policy (*adharmānarthasādhanabhūte karmaṇī*—so Cg).

"unrighteousness and unsound policy" *adharmānarthayoḥ*: In keeping with their interpretation of *dharma* and *artha* discussed above, Ct and Ck continue their soteriological interpretation, arguing that, even when prayer, etc., is practiced, the failure to perform obligatory rites (*nityadharma*) gives rise to *adharma* and *anartha*, which, in turn, produce calamitous results for a person because of the failure to carry out enjoined rites. This situation, they argue, does not hold in the case of optional (*kāmya*) rites. (*japādirūpe kriyāmaye vā nityadharme lupte saty adharmānarthau prāptau bhavataḥ. tayoś ca satoḥ prātyavāyikaṃ vihitākaraṇaprayuktapratyavāyajanyaṃ phalaṃ puṃsaḥ prāptaṃ bhavati. na tu kāmyākaraṇe pratyavāya iti bhāvaḥ*—so Ct.) Cs argues similarly. This line of interpretation strikes us as inappropriate to the context of the passage. It has, however, been followed by translators who base their translations on the text and commentary of Ct.

"results that are calamitous" *pratyavāyikam*: The word is apparently an adjectival derivative of *pratyavāya*, "diminution, danger, contrariety, sin, offense." Ñ1,D5,6, 10,11,T1,M1,2,5, and the texts and printed editions of Ct, Ck, and Cr read instead *prātyavāyikam*. Ct and Ck appear to understand the term as a derivative adjective formed on the base of *pratyavāya* in the sense of "sin [of omission]," in regard to the failure to perform enjoined religious acts (see note to *adharmānarthayoḥ* above). Cr reads the term as a compound, *prātyavayi* plus *kam*, in the sense of "the happiness or beatitude of sinners (*prātyavāyinām aparādhinām kaṃ sukham*)." This beatitude, he argues, is brought about through the cessation of sin that is effected through the practice of *dharma* and *artha* (*yasmāt tat phalam api bhavati pratyavāyasyāpy arthadharmābhyāṃ nivṛttir iti tātparyam*).

9. We understand the point of the verse to be that, since various kinds of action may bear fruit in this world or the next, Rāvaṇa would be justified in pursuing his own desires, which will bring him gratification in the short term. Cr takes the verse as the inspiration to debate the validity of the vedic doctrine of *karma*. He has his objector claim that, since the agent and the action pass away, there are no real karmic consequences. Thus, a sacrificer can no more attain heaven than trees destroyed in a forest fire can still bear fruit, dead people still be nourished by balls of rice, or an extinct lamp be rekindled with oil. Cr refutes Mahodara's fallacious argument, reasserting the inexorable law that action must inevitably bear fruit. Thus, he concludes that it is not incorrect to regard Mahodara's statements as rooted in error, since they contradict the *vedas*. (*nanu karmakartuḥ karmaṇāṃ cehaiva vinaṣṭatvāt pūrvakarmajanitasaṃskārāyattakarmapravṛttir durnivāreti tvaduktir vyāhatāta eva svargaḥ kartṛkriyākarmavināśe 'pi ca yajvanāṃ tadā dāvāgnidagdhānāṃ phalaṃ syād bhūri bhūrūhāṃ mṛtānām api jantūnāṃ piṇḍaś cet tṛptikārako nirvāṇasya ca dīpasya snehaḥ saṃvardhayec chikhām ityādy uktam ity āśaṅkāṃ nivarttayitum āha . . . karmaṇāṃ cāvaśyaṃ phaladātṛtvaṃ sūcitam ata eva vedānāṃ nāprāmāṇyam uktaślokau tu vedaviruddhatvena bhrāntimūlakāv iti na doṣaḥ.*) Cg and Cm understand Mahodara to be refuting the rule that only religiously enjoined action brings auspicious results, while the opposite is true for that which is forbidden (*ato vihitam eva śubhapradaṃ niṣiddhaṃ tu tathā na bhavatīti niyamo nāstīty arthaḥ*—so Cg).

"engage in actions with reference to this world and the next" *aihalaukikapāratryaṃ karma . . . niṣevyate*: Literally, "worldly and otherworldly action is resorted to." The commentators generally understand *karma*, "action," here in the sense of *karmaphala*, "fruits of action." Ct and Ck understand that this is a continuation of the reference to calamitous results mentioned in the previous verse. Thus, for them, the consequences [of *anartha* and *adharma*] in this world would be such things as debt, poverty, etc., while those in the next world would be such things as the torments of hell. (*iharṇadāridryādirūpam. paratra narakayātanādirūpam*—so Ct.) Both commentators understand the verb *niṣevyate*, "is practiced *or* resorted to," in the sense of "is suffered *or* is experienced (*anubhūyate*)." Cg and Cm merely define the two as the fruits of action that are experienced in this and the next word. (*aihalaukikam ihalokopayogi. paratraṃ paralokopayogi ca karma puṃbhir niṣevyate. tatphalaṃ cānubhūyate*—so Cg.)

"a person who indulges in pleasure may still attain excellent consequences" *karmāṇy api tu kalyāni labhate kāmam āsthitaḥ*: Literally, "But one who indulges in desire (*kāma*) obtains good *or* auspicious actions." Here the context compels us to agree with the commentators in taking *karmāṇi* as "the results *or* fruits of actions (*karmaphalāni*—Cg, Cm)." Ct and Ck understand that, even when the pursuit of pleasure runs counter to righteousness, a person may still indulge in it on the basis of one's own asceticism, valor, etc. (*dharmaviruddho yadi kāmas tadā sa svatapovikramādinā samādheyaḥ*—so Ct). They cite a maxim supporting their point, according to which "people do not refrain from setting their cooking vessels on the fire just because there may be beggars around (*na hi bhikṣukāḥ santīti sthālyo nādhiśriyanta iti nyāyād iti bhāvaḥ*)." The idea is that one does not refrain from a necessary activity just because there may be some undesirable consequences. Cg and Cm understand the phrase *kāmam āsthitaḥ* to mean "a person who acts just as he pleases (*yathecchācāraḥ*)." Ct and Ck understand that the verse makes a distinction between *dharma* and *artha*, on the one hand, and *kāma*, on the other, with respect to the immediacy of their results. They understand Mahodara to be arguing that *kāma* brings immediate gratification, unlike *dharma* and *artha*, whose fruits are manifest only after some time or in the next world (*śubhāni tu viśiṣyātrāpi sākṣāl labhate na tu dharmārthavat kālāntare lokāntare vā*—so Ct).

10. Ct and Ck spend considerable energy refuting Cm's and Cg's interpretation of the previous five verses. Ct quotes Cm's comments verbatim, while Ck mockingly rejects the opinions of "Yadvābhaṭṭa" (Cm?). (On the identity and relative dating of "Yadvābhaṭṭa," see Lefeber 1994, p. 24, and n. 77. See notes to 4.33.15,44 and 4.2.56. Cf. 5.1.77 and note. See, too, notes to 6.12.10 and 6.80.1; and Introduction, pp. 99–107). Ct and Ck object to the position that both righteous and unrighteous actions may lead to good or bad results (see verses 8 and 9 above), the position that Cm and Cg ascribe to Mahodara. Cs takes the debate one step further, quoting Ct's refutation of Cm and, in turn, rejecting that refutation. Cs argues that by no means is it universally agreed that only happiness can come of *dharma* and unhappiness of *adharma*, as there are many counter examples in the *purāṇas*, etc., as well as examples from worldly experience. Cs further quotes a verse indicating that even *dharma* becomes *adharma* if it is not practiced by devotees of Viṣṇu, while even sin, when committed by Vaiṣṇava devotees, becomes *dharma* (*dharmo bhavaty adharmo 'pi yo na bhaktaiḥ kṛto hare / pāpaṃ bhavati dharmo 'pi kṛto bhaktais tavācyuta //*). This position, as advanced by Cm, has, in Cs's opinion, been trivialized by Ct.

"The king set his heart on this deed, and we all approved it." *tatra klptam idaṃ rājñā hṛdi kāryaṃ mataṃ ca naḥ*: Literally, "In this matter, the action was conceived by the king in his heart and approved by us." According to Cm and Cg, the deed in question is the abduction of Sītā (*sītāharaṇarūpaṃ kāryaṃ*—so Cg).

12. "in Janasthāna" *janasthāne*: The account of Rāma's slaughter of the *rākṣasās* in Janasthāna is related in the *Araṇyakāṇḍa* (*sargas* 23–29).

13. "You can see . . . those . . . *rākṣasas* whom he . . . defeated . . . still" *ye . . . nirjitās tena . . . / rākṣasāṃs tān . . . api paśyasi*: These *rākṣasa* would probably be the attendants of the *rākṣasa* warrior Khara who are described at 3.26.19 as fleeing the massacre of their master and all his troops (3.24–29). Since they must have been fairly limited in number, and Rāma is generally regarded as having single-handedly slaughtered

Khara's forces down to the last *rākṣasa*, the commentators seem perplexed at the idea that the demons defeated at that time should now be roaming the streets of Laṅkā. Ct deals with the difficulty by glossing *nirjitāḥ*, "defeated," with "put to flight (*vidrāvitāḥ*)." Cg glosses, "those of their kind (*tajjātīyān*)." D5,10,11, and the texts and printed editions of Ct and Cr read *na paśyasi*, "you do not see," for the critical edition's *[a]pi paśyasi*, "you also see." Ct takes the negative as part of an interrogative construction, "don't you see?" Translators who follow the text of Ct also read the sentence as a question. Cr, however, seems to take the negative at face value, thus making moot the question of the *rākṣasa* survivors of Janasthāna.

14. "In your ignorance" *abuddhyā*: This term is subject to variation among the different recensions and texts of the commentators. D9–11 and the texts and printed editions of Ct and Cr read *aho buddhvā*, "Oh, having realized," for the critical edition's *ivābuddhyā*, "in your ignorance ... like." This variant is rendered in the translations of Dutt ("knowing full well [that he resembles]," 1893, p. 1305) and Gita Press ("knowingly," 1969, vol. 3, p. 1610). Roussel (1903, vol. 3, p. 197) appears to mistakenly read the gerund *buddhvā* as a causative, rendering, "*en l'éveillant*," with the sense of "in awakening him [Rāma]." In this he has regrettably been followed by Shastri (1959, vol. 3, p. 171) and Pagani (1999, p. 1029). The texts and printed editions of Cv, Cm, and Cg read instead the irregular negative gerund *abuddhya*, "having not known," for which Cg and Cm gloss the correct form, *abuddhvā*. This variant is rendered only in the translation of Raghunathan (1982, vol. 3, p. 170) as "not realizing." The text of Gorresio (6.43.15) appears to support the negative forms in the critical text and that of Cm, Cv, and Cg, substituting the vocative *abuddhe*, "O you fool," rendered by Gorresio (1858, vol. 10, p. 17) as "*o insensato*."

16. "Our whole army" *idaṃ sarvam*: Literally, "all this." We follow the majority of the commentators, who supply a word for army (*balam, sainyam*).

"your ... there" *tatra ... tava*: D9–11 and the texts and printed editions of Ck, Ct, and Cr read instead *tāta ... bhṛśam*, "my child ... strongly."

17. "lacking all resources ... who possesses a wealth of resources" *hīnārthas tu samṛddhārtham*: Literally, "one with diminished resources ... one with rich resources." Based on the context, we share the view of Ck, Ct, and Cr that these terms refer to the fact that Kumbhakarṇa, without any allies (*sahāyarahitaḥ*—Cr), is proposing to attack Rāma, who has a huge number of allies (*pūrṇasahāyam*—Cr). Cg glosses the former term as "whose strength is diminishing (*hīyamānabalaḥ*)" and the latter as "whose strength is increasing (*vardhamānabalam*)."

"could hope ... to subdue" *vaśam ānetum icchati*: Literally, "he wishes to bring under [his] control."

"like some common fool" *prākṛto yathā*: Literally, "like a common *or* ignorant person." Ñ2,B,D1,3–7,9–11,13,T1,2,M2,3,5, and the texts and printed editions of Ct, Cg, and Cr read instead the accusative *prākṛtam*, in which case the adjective modifies "the enemy (*ripum*)," and has the sense of "as if he were some ordinary [foe]."

"is determined to lay down his life" *niścitaṃ jīvitatyāge*: Literally, "resolved with respect to the abandonment of life." M3 and the texts and printed edtions of Cg and Cm read instead the gerund *niścitya*, "having resolved," which permits the phrase to be construed with the subject of the sentence, *kaḥ*, "who." Only Raghunathan (1982, vol. 3, p. 170) renders this reading, translating, "unless he were bent upon throwing away his life."

18. "who...is...equal to Indra or Vivasvant" *tulyenendravivasvatoḥ*: Literally, "with an equal of Indra and Vivasvant." Cs argues that we must understand that the two gods occupy a single body, thus constituting an unprecedented object of comparison (*abhūtopameyam*). Otherwise, he argues, since Indra and each of the other individual gods have been worsted so many times [by Rāvaṇa], we would have a very unsuitable demonstration of Rāma's power. (*indravivasvator ekadeham āśritayor ity abhūtopameyam. anyathendrādīnām etadādiparābhavasya bahuvāram anubhavann anidarśanārhateti bodhyam.*)

19. "enraged" *saṃrabdham*: Ñ2,V,B1,D1,3,5,7,13,T1,G1,M3, and the texts and printed editions of Cg and Cm read the nominative *saṃrabdhaḥ*, in which case the adjective would apply to Mahodara.

"Rāvaṇa, who caused the world to cry out" *rāvaṇaṃ lokarāvaṇam*: This etymological epithet is a favorite of Vālmīki. See notes to 6.8.12.

20. "you go on talking" *punaḥ...prajalpasi*: D10,11,M1,2, and the texts and printed editions of Ck, Ct, and Cr read *vilambase*, "you delay, hesitate," for *prajalpasi*, "you prattle." D6,9–11,T2,3, and the texts and printed editions of Ct and Cr read *purastāt*, "already," for the critical edition's *punas* [*tām*].

"Sītā will submit to your wishes whenever you desire." *yadecchasi tadā sītā vaśagā te bhaviṣyati*: Cr takes advantage of the *sandhi* to provide a theological reading of the line. Resolving the sequence *tadā sītā*, "then Sītā," as *tādā* + *āsītā*, he understands the latter word to be a *dvandva* compound made up of *āḥ*, which he sees as an epithet of Rāma in his role as "the one who measures out all life breaths," and "Sītā." He interprets the phrase as follows: "By this he says, 'when you desire to solicit Sītā, then both Sītā, together with Ā, that is, with Rāma, the apportioner (?) of all life (*nikhilaprāṇanakarttā*) will be under your control. (*ity ata āha yad yadecchasi sītāprārthanam iti śeṣaḥ. tadaivāsītā—ā nikhilaprāṇanakarttā rāmas tena sahitā sītā te tava vaśagā bhaviṣyati.*)" Compare Cm's reading of verse 31 below.

D5,10,11,T1,M3, and the texts and printed editions of the southern commentators read *yadīcchasi*, "if you desire," for *yadecchasi*, "whenever you desire."

21. "whereby Sītā will come to you" *sītopasthānakārakaḥ*: Literally, "which will cause Sītā's acceptance [of you as a suitor]." Vālmīki uses the term *upasthāna*, "approaching," in the sense of "accepting as a suitor" also at 6.80.43.

"If it appeals to your way of thinking...then hear me out." *rucitaś cet svayā buddhyā...taṃ śṛṇu*: Literally, "If it is pleasing by your own intellect, listen to it." The commentators differ as to how to construe the phrase *svayā buddhyā*, "by your own intellect." Ck and Ct take the half verse as elliptical and flesh it out as follows: "Listen to it. Once you have heard it and reflected upon it with your intellect, you should carry it out if it pleases you. (*taṃ śṛṇu. taṃ śrutvā svayā buddhyā paryālocya rucitaś cet tam anutiṣṭheti śeṣaḥ.*)" Cg construes the phrase more closely with the imperative *śṛṇu*, "listen to," explaining, "Listen with your own opinion, but do not follow the opinion of others (*svayā buddhyā śṛṇu na tu parabuddhim anusarety arthaḥ*)." Cr, whom we follow, construes the phrase more closely with *rucitaḥ*, "pleasing."

22. "Vitardana" *vitardanaḥ*: As noted by Pagani (1999, p. 1666, note 64.1), the name of this *rākṣasa* occurs only in this passage.

23. "we will...engage Rāma in fierce battle" *yuddhaṃ dāsyāmas tasya yatnataḥ*: Literally, "we will give him battle strenuously."

"no further need of such a ruse" *nopāyaiḥ kṛtyam asti naḥ*: Literally, "of us there will be nothing to accomplish through stratagems." The reference, as several commentators point out, is to devices to win over Sītā, such as mentioned in verse 21 above, since, having no further hope with regard to Rāma, she would come to Rāvaṇa of her own accord (*rāmaṃ praty āśānivṛttyā svata eva tadānukūlyasya siddhatvād iti bhāvaḥ*—so Ct).

24. "on the other hand" *atha*: Literally, "then." The logic of the passage, however, forces one to understand a conditional sense.

"then we shall adopt the ruse that I have devised in my mind" *tataḥ samabhipatsyāmo manasā yat samīkṣitam*: Literally, "then we shall adopt what was envisaged with the mind." We follow Cm in supplying the noun "ruse (*upāyajātam*, lit., 'set of stratagems')."

25. "Our bodies rent" *vidārya svatanum*: Literally, "having had our bodies rent." The text is somewhat ambiguous as to the actual agent of the wounding of the *rākṣasas*. Crā, Cg, and Cm understand that the *rākṣasas* see to it that Rāma wounds them (*svatanuṃ vidārya rāmeṇa vidāritāṃ kārayitvā*). Ct and Ck have a similar idea, indicating that the *rākṣasas* have actually put their lives in peril in their battle with Rāma (*svatanum* . . . *vidārya kṛtavidāraṇāṃ saṃpādya yāvat prāṇasaṃkaṭaṃ yuddhvety arthaḥ*). Cs, alone among the commentators, believes that the *rākṣasas*' wounds are self-inflicted (*svatanuṃ bāṇaiḥ svayam eva vidārya*). Among the translators consulted, Raghunathan (1982, vol. 3, p. 171) and Pagani (1999, p. 1030) share this view. Thus, Raghunathan renders, "having inflicted wounds upon ourselves with arrows," while Pagani translates, "*après avoir lacéré nos corps*."

"by sharp arrows" *bāṇaiḥ* . . . *śitaiḥ*: Ñ,V,B1–3,D4–7,9–11,T2,G2,3,M3,5, and Cg, Crā, and Cv, as well as the texts and printed editions of Ct, Cr, and Ck, read *śaraiḥ*, "with arrows," for the adjective *śitaiḥ*, "sharp." However, the printed editions of Cg, i.e., VSP and KK, read with the critical edition, although KK notes the variant. This presents a problem of redundancy, which the commentators attempt to resolve in various ways. Ck and Ct ignore the issue completely. Cr attempts to resolve the problem by reading *śaraiḥ* adjectivally in the sense of "destructive, lethal (*vighātakaiḥ*)." Crā, Cg, and Cm dissociate the two words syntactically. They read the first as the instruments with which the *rākṣasas* cause themselves to be wounded. They then take the second as an instrument of accompaniment, adding the postposition *saha*, "with," so that the word refers separately to the arrows with which the *rākṣasas* will return (i.e., to show to Sītā). Cs faults Cm and Ct for their failure to notice the redundancy and its implications. He believes that the position of Ct and Cm, according to which the *rākṣasas* will actually be wounded in battle by Rāma's arrows and still return alive, is contradicted by the penultimate verse of the *sarga* (verse 34), which Cs claims the other commentators have failed to consider. His argument is as follows: If, according to verse 34, Rāvaṇa himself cannot survive a confrontation with Rāma, how then could his inferiors be wounded by Rāma and still live? Cs believes that Ct and Cm are ascribing too much merit to these lesser *rākṣasas*.

"marked with Rāma's name" *rāmanāmāṅkitaiḥ*: The same adjective is used to describe Rāma's signet ring at 5.34.2 (see note ad loc.). See 4.43.11 and note, where Rāma gives the ring to Hanumān. The phrase used there is *svanāmāṅkopaśobhitam*, "[a ring] engraved with his name." See Sankalia 1973, p. 56. See, too, Salomon 1998 and Pollock 1996.

26. "we shall reverently clasp your feet" *tava pādau grahīṣyāmaḥ*: Literally, "we shall grasp your feet." Touching of the feet is a time-honored gesture of subordination and respect.

"You must then reward us to our heart's content." *tvaṃ naḥ kāmaṃ prapūraya*: Literally, "you must fulfill our desire." Commentators are divided as to whether this sentence forms part of Mahodara's current advice to Rāvaṇa or a part of the false report the *rākṣasas* plan to bring from the battlefield. Cr chooses the latter explanation, whereas Ct, Ck, and Cg choose the former.

27. "from elephant-back" *gajaskandhena*: Literally, "by the shoulder of an elephant." We follow the idea proposed by Cg, Cm, and Cr, who understand that the proclamation is to be made by a man mounted on the back of an elephant (*gajaskandhagatapuruṣeṇa*—so Cg). Among the translators consulted, Dutt (1893, p. 1306) alone understands the term as a proper noun, presumably the name of a *rākṣasa* herald, rendering, "do thou through Gajaskandha publish it all round."

28–29. "feigning the greatest delight" *prīto nāma . . . bhūtvā*: Literally, "having become happy indeed." We follow the commentators who interpret the indeclinable *nāma* as a particle indicating a feigned state or action (*aparamārthe*—so Cm; *alīke*—so Cg).

"heroic warriors" *vīrāṇām*: Literally, "of heroes."

30ab–1138–30cdef. " 'The *rākṣasas* have devoured Rāma along with his companions!' has been heard" *bhakṣitaḥ sasuhṛdrāmo rākṣasair iti viśrute*: The critical edition relegates this line to its apparatus as passage 1138*, despite the fact that it is known to all manuscripts, northern and southern, consulted by the critical editors. No explanation is given for its excision from the critical text. According to the principles on which the critical edition is based (Bhatt 1960, p. xxxiv), there is no reason that the line should be excluded. We have accordingly emended the text. Curiously, although it is not noted in the critical apparatus, the line appears to be missing only from the printed edition of Gorresio (see 6.43.31–32).

"this vicious rumor" *kaulīne*: Normally, this means "scandal *or* evil report." We follow Cg, Cm, Ct, and Ck, who gloss, "popular rumor (*lokavāde; janavāde*—Ct, Ck)." Cg and Cm cite *Amarakośa* 3.3.116 for this definition. Cr alone breaks the sequence into the words *kau*, "earth," which he glosses as "the land of Laṅkā (*laṅkābhūmau*)," and *līne*, which he glosses as "pervaded (*vyāpte*)." For him, then, the sequence means "spread throughout the land of Laṅkā."

31. Cm, in keeping with his Vaiṣṇava theological project, proposes an alternative reading of the verse. By breaking the sequence *naṣṭanāthāgamiṣyati* into *naṣṭa na atha āgamiṣyati* and reading the compound *akāmā*, "unwilling," to mean "desiring only A, i.e., Viṣṇu (= Rāma)," he extracts the following hidden meaning: "Sītā, who loves only Viṣṇu, will not come under your sway, O you who are destroyed! (*naṣṭa na atha āgamiṣyati iti cchedaḥ . . . he naṣṭa rāvaṇa! akāmā viṣṇukāmā sītā. anayopadhayāpi tvadvaśaṃ na gamiṣyatīty arthaḥ.*)" Compare Cr's reading of verse 20 above.

"which will give rise to fear and grief" *bhayaśokānubandhayā*: Ś1,B3,D6,10,11,M1,2, and the texts and printed editions of Ct, Ck, and Cr read *bhūyaḥ*, "once again *or* to a greater extent," for *bhaya-*, "fear."

"believing her husband dead" *naṣṭanāthā*: Literally, "whose husband is dead."

"unwilling though she may be" *akāmā*: Literally, "having no desire."

32. "For . . . and" *hi . . . ca*: Cm continues his alternative reading of the passage (see notes to verse 31 above), here basing his interpretation on his reading of the particle *hi*, "for," in *pāda* a as a marker of the interrogative (*kimiti*). He then interprets the conjunctive particle *ca*, "and," of *pāda* c, in the sense of the particle *api*, "even though."

This yields the alternative sense: " 'Would the famous, supremely devoted wife Sītā come under your sway, even after learning that her husband was dead, even in her despair, even out of feminine frailty? She certainly would not!' That is the construction. (*hīti kim ity arthe. cāpyarthe. sā prasiddhā paramapativratā sītā bhartāraṃ vinaṣṭam avagamyāpi nairāśyād api strīlaghutvāt strīcāpalyād api tvadvaśaṃ pratipatsyate hi? na pratipatsyata eveti yojanā.*)"

"beloved" *rañjanīyam*: D6,7,9–11,T2,3, and the texts and printed editions of Ct and Cr read instead *ramaṇīyam*, "pleasant, charming." Both Ck, who reads with the critical, and Ct, who does not, gloss, "worthy of being followed *or* obeyed (*anuvartituṃ yogyam*)."

"in her despair and feminine frailty" *nairāśyāt strīlaghutvāc ca*: Literally, "out of hopelessness and the weakness of a woman." Cr explains that Sītā, in her fear of being eaten by the *rākṣasas*, will place herself under Rāvaṇa's control in order to protect herself (*rākṣasakartṛkabhakṣaṇabhiyā svarakṣārthaṃ tvadadhīnā bhaviṣyatīty arthaḥ*). Cr goes on to claim that what is suggested here is that, when, at a [later] time, Sītā is told the news that Rāma is actually still alive, by virtue of that [having come under the sway of Rāvaṇa], Rāma also will come under Rāvaṇa's power (*etena tasmin samaye rāmo jīvatīti vṛttāntam uktvā taddvārā rāmo 'pi tvadvaśago bhaviṣyatīti sūcitam*). Cg and Cm gloss, "out of the fickleness of a woman (*strīcāpalāt*—so Cg). See Cr on verse 20 above.

33. "though that is what she deserves" *sukhārhā*: Literally, "deserving comfort."

"she will, by all means, come to you" *sarvathopagamiṣyati*: Literally, "she will approach by all means." The absence of an object of Sītā's approach leaves the door open for Cr and Cm to interpret that she will, in fact, put herself under the power of Rāma. Cm particularly elaborates his previous alternative readings, noting that, even though she had been accustomed to comfort and was subsequently racked with suffering, the supremely devoted wife, Sītā, recognizing that the comfort to be had with Rāvaṇa would bring with it sinfulness, will cleave firmly only to Rāma. (*purā sukhasaṃvṛddhāpīdānīṃ duḥkhakarśitāpi sā paramapativratā sītā tvadadhīnaṃ sukhaṃ jñātvā duritāvāham iti śeṣaḥ. sarvathopagamiṣyati rāmam eveti śeṣaḥ.*)

34. "It would be catastrophic for you to confront Rāma." *rāmaṃ hi dṛṣṭvaiva bhaved anarthaḥ*: Literally, "for, having seen Rāma, a disaster would occur." The disaster, as the commentators note, would be the death of Rāvaṇa. See Cs's anticipatory reference to this verse in notes to verse 25 above.

"Don't be so anxious" *motsuko bhūḥ*: According to Ct, Ck, and Cr, Rāvaṇa should not be so eager to see Rāma (*rāmadarśanārtham*—so Ct). According to Cg and Cm, he should not be eager for battle (*mā raṇotsuko bhūḥ*).

"without fighting" *ayuddhena*: Literally, "by non-battle." Cg takes this to refer to *āsana*, or "stasis," one of the six modes of political policy (*yuddhavyatiriktāsanabalena*). See notes to 6.51.7. Cs understands the term to suggest that, once Rāvaṇa has obtained Sītā and accomplished his purpose, he should then seek refuge with Rāma (*etena sītālābhānantaraṃ kṛtakāryaḥ śaraṇaṃ vrajeti sūcyata iti jñeyam*).

The meter is *upajāti*.

35. "without the loss of one's army" *anaṣṭasainyaḥ*: Ś2,Ñ,V,B1,3,4,D2,6,8,12,13,M3,5, and the texts and printed editions of Cm, Cg, Gorresio, and Lahore read instead *adṛṣṭasainyaḥ*, "whose army is unseen." Cg, the only commentator to comment on this reading, glosses, "without having seen the enemy army (*adṛṣṭaśatrusainyaḥ*)."

Gorresio (1858, vol. 10, p. 19) shares this interpretation. Raghunathan (1982, vol. 3, p. 171) renders, "without employing an army."

"lord of the earth" *mahīpate*: D7,9–11,T1, and the texts and printed editions of Ct and Cr read instead the nominative singular *mahīpatiḥ*, which would serve as the subject in the sense of "a king who is the lord of the earth."

The meter is *vaṃśasthavila*.

Sarga 53

1. "addressed in this fashion" *tathoktaḥ*: Ck and Ct understand the reference to be to Mahodara's advice to avoid combat. Ck expands on this, seeing Mahodara's words as an example of the *bakamantra*, or "the counsel of the crane" (*bakamantraṃ kṛtvā yuddhaṃ na kartavyam ity ukta ity arthaḥ*). The reference is to the crane's habit of remaining immobile and waiting for its prey to come within its grasp.

2. "In killing that evil-minded Rāma" *vadhāt tasya durātmanaḥ / rāmasya*: In keeping with his devotional reading, Cm proposes what he calls the "true meaning (*vāstavārthaḥ*)" of the text: "Although I am a servant of Rāma, whose mind consists of grace even in the midst of suffering, still I belong to that well-known group of *rākṣasas*, headed by Prahasta. From the destruction of it [that group], a terrible danger has presented itself to you. I shall remove that so that you, being free from enmity, shall become happy. (*vāstavārthas tu durātmano duḥkheṣv apy ātmā buddhir anugraharūpā yasya rāmasyāhaṃ rāmadāso 'haṃ yady api tathāpi tasya prasiddhasya prahastamukharākṣasasamūhasyety arthaḥ. vadhāt tava ghoraṃ bhayam upasthitam iti śeṣaḥ. tat pramārjāmy apanayāmi sa tvaṃ nirvairaḥ san sukhī bhaveti sambandhaḥ.*)

"With your enemy out of the way," *nirvairaḥ*: Literally, "lacking an enemy."

3. "True heroes do not boast in vain, like empty clouds thundering." *garjanti na vṛthā śūrā nirjalā iva toyadāḥ*: Literally, "Heroes do not roar *or* thunder in vain like waterless clouds."

"Watch now as my boasts are proven true by my feats in battle." *paśya sampādyamānaṃ tu garjitaṃ yudhi karmaṇā*: Literally, "See the bellowing [boasting] being fulfilled by action in battle."

4. "True heroes" *śūrāḥ*: Literally, "heroes."

"True heroes do not tolerate insult, nor do they indulge in self-praise... they perform" *na marṣayati cātmānaṃ sambhāvayati nātmanā... śūrāḥ... kurvanti*: Literally, "Heroes do not tolerate nor do they honor the self with the self... they perform." Although the subject *śūrāḥ*, "heroes," and the final verb in the verse *kurvanti*, "they perform," are both plural forms, the prior two verbs—*marṣayati*, "he tolerates, abides, forgives," and *sambhāvayati*, "he praises"—are both singular forms. Commentators who share the reading of the critical edition attempt to explain the lack of agreement. Crā and Cg gloss the plural forms and understand the number disagreement to be the result of "transformation *or* inversion (*ubhayatrāpi vyatyayenaikavacanam*)." Cm simply writes it off to "epic irregularity (*ubhayatraikavacanam ārṣam*)." D7,9–11,M1,2, and the texts and printed editions of Ck, Ct, and Cr read instead the plural *facilior marṣayanti*, "they tolerate."

The verb *marṣayati*, "he tolerates," appears to lack a direct object, and those commentators and translators who share this reading propose various strategies for supplying the ellipsis. Cg and Crā, whom we follow, supply, as an object, "the insulting speech rendered by an enemy (*parakṛtām avamānoktim*—Cg; *parakṛtāṃ laghvuktim*—Crā)." This interpretation is incorrectly also ascribed to Cm as well in the critical apparatus. According to VSP, Cm actually takes *ātmānam*, "self," of *pāda* a, by the maxim of the crow's [single but moveable] eyeball (*kākākṣigolikanyāyena*), as the object of both *marṣayati* and *saṃbhāvayati*. Cv and Cm take the phrase *ātmānaṃ na marṣayati* to mean "heroes do not calm themselves once angered without performing an act of valor (*śūrā ātmānaṃ na marṣayati kruddham ātmānaṃ pauruṣam akṛtvā na śamayantīty arthaḥ*)." Raghunathan (1982, vol. 3, p. 172), the only translator to render this reading, translates, "do not spare themselves."

D7,10,11,M1,2, and the texts and printed editions of Ct, Ck, and Cr read the infinitive *saṃbhāvayitum* for the critical edition's finite form, *saṃbhāvayati*. This *facilior* both avoids the apparent number disagreement and eliminates the elliptical quality of the critical reading. Eliminating the second negative particle *na* of the critical reading, the vulgate thus yields the sense "[heroes] cannot bear to indulge in self-praise."

"without swaggering" *adarśayitvā*: Literally, "not having shown." The commentators agree in taking this to mean "not having boasted of their own prowess (*ātmapauruṣam anuktvā*—so Cg)."

"seemingly impossible" *duṣkaram*: Literally, "hard to accomplish."

*5. The text reconstructed by the critical editors appears to be highly defective and cannot be readily construed as a sentence. It reflects the reading of no manuscript collated for the critical edition. See Sutherland 1992. The critical text reads:

viklavānām abuddhīnāṃ rājñāṃ paṇḍitamānīnām /
śṛṇvatām ādita idaṃ tvadvidhānāṃ mahodara //

Literally, "of kings like you, Mahodara, who are cowards, fools, and think themselves wise, and who have heard this from the beginning..."

The verse shows considerable variation across the recensions, and, after careful consideration of the textual evidence, we have concluded that the most appropriate and textually supported available reading is that of the southern manuscripts affiliated with the commentaries of Cv, Cg, Crā, and Cm (the reading is also noted as a variant by Ct), and we have therefore translated accordingly. This text, as it appears at VSP and KK 6.65.5, reads as follows:

viklavānām abuddhīnāṃ rājñā paṇḍitamānīnām /
śṛṇvatā sāditam idaṃ tvadvidhānāṃ mahodara //

"heeding the advice" *śṛṇvatā*: Literally, "by [the king] who was hearing." We follow Cm, who argues that one needs to supply the word *vacaḥ*, "speech, advice." Cv and Cg avoid the necessity of adding the word "advice" by taking all the genitive plural nouns in the sense of ablatives (*pañcamyarthe ṣaṣṭhī*). This yields the sense "by the king hearing from cowards like you..."

"the king has been brought to such a sorry state" *rājñā... sāditam idam*: We follow Cg and Cv, who read the phrase as an abstract construction (*bhāve niṣṭhā*) with the literal sense "it was made despondent by the king." Cv, however, reads the genitive plural *rājñām*, "of kings," for *rājñā*. He thus interprets the verse to mean "kings who listen to cowards such as Mahodara, etc., that is, who are corrupted by bad counsel, experience this sort of calamity (*śṛṇvatāṃ rājñāṃ sādanam idaṃ durmatidūṣitānāṃ rājñāṃ yad vinipātanaṃ tad idam ity arthaḥ*)." Cm appears to read it more strictly as a passive construction, in the sense of "this [situation] was brought to ruin by the king (*rājñā yat sāditam avasādanam asti tad idam iti yojanam*)."

D7,10,11,G2,M1,2, and the texts and printed editions of Ct, Ck, and Cr [noted also as a variant by Cv] and Gorresio [6.44.8] read instead:

viklavānāṃ hy abuddhīnāṃ rājñāṃ paṇḍitamāninām /
rocate tvadvaco nityaṃ kathyamānāṃ mahodara // [=GPP 6.65.5]

This yields the quite different sense "Your [sort of] advice, Mahodara, always pleases kings who are cowardly and foolish but who think themselves wise."

6. "It is people like you" *bhavadbhiḥ*: Literally, "by you gentlemen."

"sycophants of the king" *rājānam anugacchadbhiḥ*: Literally, "by [those] following the king." Cg and Cm gloss, "following the wishes of the king (*rājecchānusāribhiḥ*)."

"saying only what he wants to hear" *priyavādibhiḥ*: Literally, "by [those] saying pleasant things."

"constantly" *nityam*: We read the adverb with the participle *vināśitam*, "destroyed, subverted," taking our cue from Cg, who, as noted below, understands *kṛtyam*, "undertaking," as an ongoing process.

"this undertaking" *kṛtyam etat*: Literally, "this thing that is to be done." Cg understands, "the affair of Sītā's abduction culminating in the battle at hand (*prakṛtayuddhaparyavasāyi sītāharaṇakṛtyaṃ sāditaṃ saṃpāditam*)." D10,11, and the texts and printed editions of Ct, Ck, and Cr read instead *sarvaṃ kṛtyam*, "this entire affair."

7. "in counseling the king ... you have acted ... like an enemy" *rājānam imam āsādya ... amitrakam*: Literally, "having approached the king ... a hostile act." We follow Cr, who glosses *āsādya*, "having approached," with "having approached as a counselor (*mantritvena prāpya*)." We follow Cv, Cm, Ck, and Cg in carrying over the pronoun *bhavadbhiḥ*, "by you gentlemen." The term *amitrakam* has been read in two ways by the commentators. Ct glosses, "a hostile act" and supplies, "has been done" (*amitrakāryaṃ kṛtam iti śeṣaḥ*). Ck similarly offers, "you have done an act that ought not to have been done (*akṛtyaṃ kṛtam*)." Cr glosses, "enemy" and supplies the words "you are an enemy" (*śatrus tvam asīti śeṣaḥ*). Cg and Cm take a quite different tack. They gloss *amitrakam* with the adjective *amitrabhūtam*, "having become an enemy," which then modifies *rājānam*. As Cg explains it, the king has become an enemy to those who failed to prevent him from engaging in improper actions (*akāryapravṛtto rājā yair na nivāryate sa teṣām amitra ity abhiprāyeṇāmitrakam*).

"Laṅkā has been virtually emptied save for the king" *rājaśeṣā kṛtā laṅkā*: Literally, "Laṅkā has been made to have the king as a remainder." Cr interprets this phrase to mean that many of the city's vast armies have been destroyed (*vināśitabahumahābalety arthaḥ*).

"the army decimated" *balaṃ hatam*: Literally, "the army slain." Cr, who has interpreted a previous phrase to refer to the destruction of the armies, takes *bala* here in its other sense of "strength, capability," which, in his view, has been sapped through the destruction of the army and the depletion of the treasury (*kośaḥ kṣīṇaḥ kṣapito 'ta eva balaṃ sāmarthyaṃ hataṃ vināśitam*).

8. "In order to remedy" *samīkartum*: Literally, "to make even."

10. "the idea of battle" *yuddham*: Literally, "battle."

11. "loyalty" *sauhṛdena*: Literally, "by *or* through friendship."

Following verse 11, D5–7,9–11,S insert a passage of nine lines [1141*]; between lines 7 and 8 of which must be inserted an additional three lines [1097*, lines 12–14] (following 6.50.10 of the critical edition) [=GPP 6.65.12–17; KK 6.65.12–18ab; VSP 6.65.12–18ab]: " 'It was for that reason that I had you awakened in order to do away with this danger.[1][1141*, line 1] For now is the hour of the allies of the *rākṣasas*,[2] subduer of your foes.[1141*, line 2] So take your lance and go, like Yama, ender of all things, with his noose in hand.[1141*, line 3] You must devour the monkeys as well as the two princes whose blazing energy is that of the sun.[1141*, line 4] Once they see what you look like, the monkeys will flee, while the hearts of Rāma and Lakṣmaṇa will burst.'[1141*, lines 5–6] When the great king had spoken in this fashion to the immensely powerful Kumbhakarṇa [1141*, line 7], that night-roaming *rākṣasa*[3] [Rāvaṇa] felt as if he had been reborn.[1097*, line 12] Confident of Kumbhakarṇa's strength and knowing his valor, the king was as delighted as the brilliant, hare-marked moon. [1097*, lines 13–14] When he had been addressed in this fashion, the immensely powerful Kumbhakarṇa was delighted. Heeding the king's orders, he made ready.[4][1141*, lines 8–9]"

[1]"It was for that reason ... in order to do away with this danger" *tasmāt tu bhayanāśārtham*: The texts and printed editions of Ct and Cr read instead *śayānaḥ śatrunāśārtham*, "[you] who were sleeping ... for the destruction of the enemy."

[2]"of the allies of the *rākṣasas*" *suhṛdāṃ rākṣasānām*: Literally, "of the friends of the *rākṣasas or* of the friends who are *rākṣasas*." D9–11,G1, and the texts and printed editions of Ct and Cr read instead *sumahān*, "very great," which then modifies *kālaḥ*, lending the phrase the sense "now is the great hour of the *rākṣasas*."

[3]"that night-roaming *rākṣasa*" *rajanīcaraḥ*: D5–7,9–11,S read instead *rākṣasapuṃgavaḥ*, "that bull among *rākṣasas*."

[4]"Kumbhakarṇa ... he made ready: *kumbhakarṇaḥ samudyataḥ*: D9–11 and the texts and printed editions of Ct and Cr read instead *yoddhum udyuktavāṃs tadā*, "he then prepared for battle."

12. "black iron" *-kālāyasam*: See 6.3.12; 6.55.47; and notes. See, too, 5.39.11; 5.51.38; and notes.

13. "equal ... it was fearsome" *-samaṃ bhīmam*: D7,9–11, and the texts and printed editions of Ct and Cr read instead *-samaprakhyam*, "its appearance was equal to [Indra's thunderbolt]." Ct glosses *prakhyā* as "splendor, brilliance (*kāntiḥ*)."

"Indra's thunderbolt ... the *vajra*" *indrāśani- ... vajra-*: It is not clear whether the poet means to distinguish these two terms, which are normally synonymous. See 6.55.43 and note.

"*kinnaras*" *-kiṃnara-*: V,D9–11,G1, and the texts and printed editions of Ct and Cr read instead *-pannaga-*, "great serpents."

14. "adorned with massive garlands of red blossoms" *raktamālyamahādāma*: We follow Ct and Cr in taking the compound as a *bahuvrīhi* with the literal sense of "having red blossoms for its large garlands." This reading is followed by all translators consulted, with the exception of Roussel (1903, vol. 3, p. 200), who reads it as a *dvandva*, rendering, "*Avec ses guirlandes rouges et ses grands liens.*" D6 and the texts and printed editions of Cg and Cm read instead *raktamālyaṃ mahādhāma*, "with red blossoms and of

immense power." Raghunathan (1982, vol. 3, p. 173) is the only translator to read and translate this variant.

"spewed forth its inner fire" *svataś codgatapāvakam*: Literally, "and which emitted fire of *or* by itself." Cg explains that the lance itself emitted sparks because of its [innate] fierceness (*krauryāt svata evotpannāgnikaṇam*).

17. "great" *mahātmānaḥ*: Cg takes *ātman* in its sense of "mind," glossing, "highly intelligent (*mahābuddhayaḥ*)." The translators consulted have rung all the possible changes on this common epithet. Translations include "high-souled" (Dutt 1893, p. 1309); "very intelligent" (Raghunathan 1982, vol. 3, p. 173); "gigantic" (Gita Press 1969, vol. 3, p. 1614); "*puissants*" (Pagani 1999, p. 1031); "*très énergiques*" (Roussel 1903, vol. 3, p. 200); "extremely energetic" (Shastri 1959, vol. 3, p. 173); and "*magnanimi*" (Gorresio 1858, vol. 10, p. 20).

"swift" *śīghrāḥ*: D9–11,T2, and the texts and printed editions of Ct and Cr read instead *śūrāḥ*, "brave, heroic."

"They would . . . kill" *nayeyuḥ . . . kṣayam*: Literally, "they would lead to destruction."

"should you be alone" *ekākinam*: Literally, "one who is alone." We agree with Cr that Rāvaṇa is speaking specifically about a danger to Kumbhakarṇa. Cr adds the word "you (*tvam*)." With the exception of Dutt (1893, p. 1309), who follows this same tack, all other translators consulted take the statement as a general one with the sense of "anyone who is alone."

"caught off guard" *pramattam*: Literally, "incautious, negligent."

18. "by unassailable soldiers" *durdharṣaiḥ sainyaiḥ*: Ś2,Ñ1,V,B1–3,D1–4,7–13, and the texts and printed editions of Ct and Cr read the nominative singular *durdharṣaḥ*, making the adjective "unassailable" refer to Kumbhakarṇa rather than to his troops.

19. "bound upon Kumbhakarṇa's head a chaplet" *srajam . . . ābabandha . . . kumbhakarṇasya*: Literally, "he bound a chaplet *or* garland on [lit., of] Kumbhakarṇa." The precise nature and location of this ornament are difficult to ascertain as the term *sraj* can equally refer to a chaplet bound around the forehead or a garland hung about the neck. In this case, because of the mention of the jewel at the center and because Rāvaṇa will hang a necklace (*hārā*) on Kumbhakarṇa's neck in verse 20 below, we have chosen the former interpretation. Cr, the only commentator to specify the location of the ornament, glosses, "placed around [his] neck (*gale saṃdhārayāmāsa*)." The translators are divided in their choice. See Biswas 1985, p. 102; and 5.42.2 and note, where we translate the term *sragvī* as "he wore a flower chaplet."

The southern commentators, with the exception of Ck, are in agreement that the chaplet or garland is made of gold, and in this they are followed by Gita Press (1969, vol. 3, p. 1614) and Raghunathan (1982, vol. 3, p. 173). Ck glosses only "chaplet *or* garland of jewels (*ratnamālā*)."

"a jewel" *maṇi-*: Roussel (1903, vol. 3, p. 200), followed by Shastri (1959, vol. 3, pp. 173–74) and Pagani (1999, p. 1032), understands that the chaplet is adorned with pearls, rendering, "*un diadème dont l'intérieur était en perles.*"

20. "upon great Kumbhakarṇa" *mahātmanaḥ*: Literally, "of the great one."

"rings" *aṅgulīveṣṭān*: Literally, "finger enclosures." We agree with the commentators in taking this as a kenning for rings. Only Dutt (1893, p. 1309) translates literally, "finger-fences."

"other fine ornaments" *varāṇy ābharaṇāni ca*: Literally, "and fine ornaments."

21. "and placed magnificent earrings on his ears" *śrotre cāsañjayāmāsa śrīmatī cāsya kuṇḍale*: Cm and Crā gloss the appropriate dual *śrotrayoḥ* for the critical edition's singular *śrotre*. This line shows considerable variation among the manuscripts. The texts and printed editions of Ct and Cr read instead *gātreṣu sajjayāmāsa śrotayoś cāsya kuṇḍale* (= GPP 6.65.27cd), "... upon his limbs, and fastened earrings on his ears."

22. "Wearing his golden bracelets and armlets" *kāñcanāṅgadakeyūraḥ*: Literally, "possessing golden bracelets and armlets." The terms *aṅgada* and *keyūra* both refer to ornaments worn around the upper arms. Cg appears to regard the terms as synonymous, taking the second as a corroborative repetition (*anuvāda*) of the first. According to Biswas (1985, p. 105), *aṅgadas* are coiled armlets and *keyūras* are circular armlets with designs, such as crosses, etc., on them. See Biswas 1985, p. 103, figures. 53.4,5; and Vyas 1967, p. 217 and figure 71. See 5.45.12 and note.

"golden necklaces and other ornaments" *niṣkābharaṇa-*: Literally, "*niṣkas* and ornaments." Ct defines *niṣka* as a chest or breast ornament (*urobhūṣaṇam*). *Niṣkas* are necklaces of gold, probably made from coins (Biswas 1985, pp. 101 and 103, figure 3; and Vyas 1967, pp. 217 and 216, figure 70.) See 5.45.12 and note.

"huge-eared" *bṛhatkarṇaḥ*: The epithet is a play on the name Kumbhakarṇa, "having pot[like] ears."

23. "With ... sword belt" *śroṇīsūtreṇa*: Literally, "with a hip-cord." The term frequently refers to an ornamental string or girdle worn around the waist. Here, however, as at 7.108* line 4 [= GPP 7.6.65], the context seems to call for the translation "[sword] belt."

"was as resplendent" *virājitaḥ*: Ñ2,V,B,D1–7,9–11,13,T,G3, and the texts and printed editions of Ct and Cr read instead the instrumental *virājatā*, "shining," which then must modify Kumbhakarṇa's belt. M3 and the texts and printed editions of Cg read instead the finite verb *vyarājata*, "he shone," rendered by Raghunathan (1982, vol. 3, p. 173) as "he looked like."

"Mount Mandara" *mandaraḥ*: Mount Mandara is the mountain used as a churning rod by the gods and demons at the churning of the ocean. On the story of the churning of the ocean, see 6.12.22; 6.40.29; 6.41.17; 6.80.19; 6.105.19; and notes.

"great serpent" *bhujaṃgena*: Literally, "with the serpent." The reference, as noted by Cg, is to the great *nāga* Vāsuki, whom the gods and demons used as their churning rope when the ocean was churned for the *amṛta*.

"when the nectar of immortality was churned forth" *amṛtotpādane*. Literally, "at the production of the *amṛta*." Cg understands the locative to be one of cause (*nimittasaptamī*).

24. "impenetrable ... armor" *nivātam*: Most of the commentators cite a lexical source that defines *nivāta* as "armor that is not to be pierced by any weapon (*śastrābhedyaṃ tu yad varma*)." Cm glosses, "having no holes *or* gaps (*acchidram*)." Cg agrees that the term essentially refers to armor that has no gaps (*nirantaram*) but takes the term in its other sense of "devoid of wind," explaining that the armor prevents the entrance of [even] the wind (*vātapraveśanivārakam*). Among the translators consulted, only Raghunathan (1982, vol. 3, pp. 173–74) follows Cg in this, rendering, "which not even air could penetrate." Cg, however, also cites *Amarakośa* 3.3.84 to justify the meaning "impenetrable armor."

"which could withstand any blow" *bhārasaham*: Literally, "withstanding weight." We follow Ct, Ck, Cr, and the first interpretation of Cg and Cm, according to which the term refers to the ability of the armor to withstand the blows of weapons, such as mountains (*parvatāyudhādiprahārakṣamam*—so Cm). Cv, Cg, and Cm, however, offer a second interpretation, which attempts to render more literally the term *bhāra*, "weight." In this interpretation the adjective refers not so much to the durability of the armor as to its weight. As these commentators put it, when the armor is placed on a scale, it bears up, i.e., balances many *palas* [a unit of weight for measuring gold, etc.]. (*yadvā tulāyāṃ sthāpyamānān bahūn bhārān sahata iti tathā. anekapalabhāranirmitam ity arthaḥ*—so Cm.)

"the king of the mountains" *adrirājaḥ*: The commentators are silent, although the reference is, no doubt, to Himalaya. Cf. *KumāSaṃ* 1.1. See. 6.47.12 and note.

"clouds at sunset" *saṃdhyābhra-*: Literally, "twilight clouds."

The meter is *upajāti*.

25. "His body adorned with every ornament" *sarvābharaṇanaddhāṅgaḥ*: Literally, "his body girded with every ornament." Alternately, this could be translated as "his every limb girded with ornaments." D7,10,11,G2,3,M3, and the texts and printed editions of the southern commentators read *sarvābharaṇasarvāṅgaḥ*, "with his entire body *or* every limb [ornamented] with every ornament."

"Nārāyaṇa when he had resolved to take his three strides" *trivikramakṛtotsāho nārāyaṇaḥ*: The reference is to Viṣṇu's feat of traversing the triple universe in three strides to recapture it for the gods. This is the central act of the *vāmanāvatāra*, or dwarf incarnation, of Viṣṇu. There is a slight difference of opinion as to how precisely to analyze the compound *trivikramaḥ*. The majority of the commentators who comment on the term see it, as do we, as a reference to the three strides (*triṣu vikrameṣu pādanyāseṣu*—so Ct). Cr, however, understands the number *tri*, "three," to refer to the three worlds, glossing, "in order to stride, that is, to set his feet in the three worlds (*triṣu lokeṣu vikramāya padanyāsāya*). See 6.40.43; 6.47.119; 6.49.1–2; 6.59.7; 6.105.24; and notes. See, too, 1.28.2 and note.

26. "bowing his head to him" *praṇamya śirasā tasmai*: Literally, "having bowed with his head to him." We understand the dative *tasmai*, "to him," to serve here as the object of Kumbhakarṇa's bowing, as do the translations consulted. Cr, however, takes it as the indirect object of *pratasthe* (v.l. for *saṃpratasthe*), "he set forth," commenting: "for him, that is, in order to curry favor with him, he set forth (*tasmai tam anukūlayituṃ pratasthe*)."

"the immensely powerful warrior" *mahābalaḥ*: Literally, "one of great strength."

Following 26cd, D5–7,T1,M3, and the texts and printed editions of Cg and Cm insert a passage of one line [1144*], which extends the description of Kumbhakarṇa: "...as he, huge and immensely powerful, was marching forth with a great roar." Of the translators consulted, only Raghunathan (1982, vol. 3, p. 174) renders this line.

27. "that great hero" *mahātmānam*: Literally, "the great one." Ñ2,V1,3,B2,D4,6,7,9–11, and the texts and printed editions of Ct and Cr read instead the nominative plural *mahātmānaḥ*, "great," which then must modify *rathinaḥ*, "chariot-warriors," of *pāda* f.

"to the blare of conches and the beating of war drums" *śaṅkhadundubhinirghoṣaiḥ*: Literally, "together with the sounds of conches and *dundubhis*." See 6.17.31–33 and note.

"by ... soldiers, elephants, horses, and chariots" *sainyaiḥ ... gajaiś ca turaṅgaiś ca syandanaiś ca*: This group would constitute the typical four divisions, *aṅgas*, of the classical Indian army of infantry, cavalry, elephant corps, and chariots. See note to 6.3.24.

28. "serpents" *sarpaiḥ*: Cg, evidently perplexed at the strange array of mounts, remarks: "It is possible for snakes, etc., to serve as mounts, if they are very large (*sarpādīnāṃ mahāśarīrāṇāṃ vāhanatvaṃ saṃbhavatīti bodhyam*)."

"camels" *uṣṭraiḥ*: Roussel (1903, vol. 3, p. 201), followed by Shastri (1959, vol. 3, p. 174), takes the term in its less common sense of "buffalos."

"horses" *aśvaiḥ*: D7,9–11, and the texts and printed editions of Ct read instead *caiva*, "and," thus eliminating the horses from the list.

29. "intoxicated with strong drink" *madotkaṭaḥ*: This could also mean "intoxicated with pride *or* wildly excited." Translators have rendered variations on these two ideas. Our choice was governed by the fact that Kumbhakarṇa had been drinking heavily upon awakening (6.48.54,80–83). Cg glosses, "intoxicated with his natural frenzy (*svābhāvikamadena mattaḥ*)." Cr, however, interprets the term in its sense of "extremely fearsome (*atibhayaṅkaraḥ*)," in which he appears to be followed by Dutt (1893, p. 1310), who renders, "exceedingly terrible."

The meter is *upendravajrā*.

30. "making a huge uproar" *mahānādāḥ*: Literally, "having a huge sound." V1,D9–11, and the texts and printed editions of Ct and Cr read instead *mahāsārāḥ*, "of immense strength," which is redundant in light of *mahābalāḥ*, "immensely powerful," which immediately follows it.

31–32. "With . . . their huge bodies" *sumahākāyāḥ*: D10,11, and the texts and printed editions of Ct, Ck, and Cr read instead *subahuvyāmāḥ*, "many fathoms [in height]," which also must modify the *rākṣasa* soldiers.

"They brandished" *udyamya*: Literally, "having raised." The two verses do not constitute an independent syntactical unit in the original. The gerund here must be subordinated to the finite verb *anvayuḥ*, "behind [him] they came," of verse 30c.

"many fathoms long" *bahuvyāmān*: This adjective is similar to the one used in the vulgate in 31a to describe the *rākṣasas*. The commentators cite *Amarakośa* 2.6.87, which defines a *vyāma* as the distance between the tips of the fingers of a man's outstretched arms, i.e., a fathom. D9–11,T3, and the texts and printed editions of Ct, Ck, and Cr read instead *bhiṇḍi*[*bhindi*—D9]*pālān*, either "short javelins" or "stones to be used with a sling." On *bhiṇḍipālas*, see 6.32.30; 6.42.19; 6.83.25; and notes.

33. "taking on a different form" *anyad vapur ādāya*: Literally, "having taken on a different body." Ck and Ct note that this form is quite different from the handsome, ornamented form mentioned in the preceding verses (*athānyatsālaṅkārasaumyād anyat*). Cr understands similarly.

"hair-raising" *lomaharṣaṇam*: Ñ2,V,B2–4,D6,7,9–11, and the texts and printed editions of Ct and Cr read instead *ghoradarśanam*, "of terrible appearance."

34. "He was now a hundred bow lengths wide and six hundred tall." *dhanuḥśataparīṇāhaḥ sa ṣaṭśatasamucchritaḥ*: Literally, "he, having an expanse *or* circumference of one hundred bows and having a height of six hundred." Our understanding is that Kumbhakarṇa has taken a newly enlarged form for battle. The word "*dhanuḥ* (bow)" is one of the standard units of measurement in early India. It is equal to four *hastas*, or "hands," each of which measures approximately eighteen inches. This would make Kumbhakarṇa approximately 3,600 feet tall and 600 feet wide. Cr reads the pronoun *sa*[*ḥ*], "he," as the first member of the compound in the sense of "together with,"

yielding the sense "a hundred together with six (*ṣaṭsahitaśatasaṅkhyākadhanuṣparimitocchrāyaviśiṣṭaḥ*)." In other words, Cr thinks that Kumbhakarṇa is 106 bow lengths tall (approximately 3,636 feet) [and 100 wide]. These proportions would make him more or less spherical in shape. See 6.84.19 and note.

35. "arranged ... in battle order" *saṃnipatya*: The gerund here, which would normally have the sense "having met together," should probably be read as an unmarked causative. Compare v.l. *saṃnipātya*, "having assembled, convened" (read by Ś2,D8,12,M1, and the text of Ck). We follow Ct and Ck, who gloss, "having arranged in military formation (*vyūhya*)." Cg, the only other commentator to address this form, glosses, "having gone near [the *rākṣasas*] ([*rākṣasānāṃ*] *samīpaṃ gatvā*)."

36. "one after another" *bhāgaśaḥ*: Literally, "in portions *or* part by part."

"so many moths" *śalabhān*: Literally, "moths."

37. "Granted" *kāmam*: We believe the rhetorical context supports our choice of this common sense of the adverb. Cr takes it in another of its senses, "of their own will (*svecchātaḥ*)." Ct and Ck, although they do not gloss *kāmam* in this way, suggest adding the adverb *svataḥ*, "of their own accord." They understand Kumbhakarṇa to be saying that the monkeys in and of themselves have not wronged the *rākṣasas* but are merely under Rāma's control. It is therefore Rāma alone, the root of all the wrongdoing, who should be killed. (*niraparādhās te na hantavyāḥ kiṃtu rāma eva sarvāparādhamūlaṃ hantavya ity āha ... svata iti śeṣaḥ*—so Ct.)

"In fact, their kind" *jātiḥ ... sā*: Literally, "this species."

"of folks like us" *asmadvidhānām*: Cg glosses, "[of us] who are devoted to play (*krīḍāparāṇām*)," to explain the *rākṣasas'* fondness for monkeys. Ck, similarly, describes the species of monkeys as the means of Kumbhakarṇa's amusement (*me krīḍāsādhanabhūtā jātiḥ*).

38. "Once he is killed, all of them will be destroyed" *hate tasmin hataṃ sarvam*: Literally, "when he is killed, all are killed." Cr reasons that, since Rāma is at the root of the whole affair, once he is killed, it will be as if everyone else were killed as well (*tasmin mūlabhūtarāme hate sati sarvaṃ hataṃ nihatam iva bhaviṣyatīti śeṣaḥ*). Cm, acknowledging the manifest meaning of the verse, also offers a true or inner meaning, whereby he suggests that the phrase *sarvaṃ hatam* should be repeated in order to yield the meaning: "I will slay in battle him by whom everything of ours was destroyed. Why? Because once he is slain, everything of his will be destroyed. (*vastutas tu purarodhasya mūlaṃ sahalakṣmaṇo rāghavaḥ khalu sa tu tiṣṭhatu. yena sarvam asmadīyam iti śeṣaḥ. hataṃ saṃyuge vadhiṣyāmi. kutaḥ? tasmin hate tadīyaṃ sarvaṃ hataṃ syād ity āvṛttyā punaryojanīyam.*)" See note to 6.27.4.

39. "the *rākṣasas*" *rākṣasāḥ*: B1,D7,9–11,G,M1,2, and the texts and printed editions of Ct (but not Cg, as mistakenly noted in the critical apparatus) read the genitive singular *rakṣasaḥ*, "as the *rākṣasa* [Kumbhakarṇa was speaking]." Ct reads the construction as a possessive genitive rather than as an absolute and feels obligated to add the words "hearing the words [of the *rākṣasa*]." Lacking an explicit subject, Ct is also forced to add the word "*rākṣasāḥ*." Translators who follow the text of Ct make similar adjustments.

40. For similar passages listing inauspicious omens, see 6.26.21–30; 6.31.3–12; 6.41.30–34; 6.45.31–37; 6.65.17–19; 6.83.32–34; 6.94.14–27; and notes.

"omens" *nimittāni*: The evil omens described in the following verses (41–44) are fairly stereotypical and are quite similar to those described above at 6.45.32–38 on the occasion of Prahasta's sortie. For a discussion of omens, see 6.4.6 and note.

41. "Extremely dreadful" *ca sudāruṇāḥ*: Literally, "and extremely dreadful." The reading is marked as uncertain in the critical edition, as well it should be. Ś,Ñ1,B4,D1,3,4,6–13,T2,3,G1,2,M1–3, and the texts and printed editions of the southern commentators read instead *gardabhāruṇāḥ*, "reddish brown like donkeys." Ñ2,V,B2,3,D2 read *gardabhasvanāḥ*, [V3,B3 *-svarāḥ*], "with the braying sound of donkeys." B1,D5,T1 read *bhṛśa[tatra*—B1]*dāruṇāḥ*, while Gorresio's edition (6.44.42) reads *dāruṇasvarāḥ*. This leaves only G3 and M5 [M4 is not recorded] as reading with the critical edition. The vast majority of northern and southern manuscripts support *gardabha-*, which should have been accepted. The *difficilior* reading would appear to be that of the vulgate, *gardabhāruṇāḥ*. The critical text should probably have read with the vulgate here and been marked as doubtful. See Bhatt 1960, p. xxxiv.

"thundered" *vineduḥ*: Literally, "resounded." This reading, too, is marked as doubtful. D5–7,9–11,T,G2,M1–3, and the texts and printed editions of the southern commentators read instead *babhūvuḥ*, "they were," while Ś,D2,8–12 read *viceruḥ*, "they moved, drifted."

42. The howling or shrieking of beasts of prey, especially jackals, is a common ill omen. See 6.22.24; 6.31.7; 6.45.32,34; 6.83.33; 6.94.22; and notes. Cf. 6.41.32 and note.

"their mouths emitting flames" *sajvālakavalair mukhaiḥ*: Literally, "with mouths that had flaming mouthfuls." The idea is clearly the conventional one that these jackals are belching or vomiting flames. Compare the parallel verse and note at 6.45.34.

"wheeled in clockwise circles" *maṇḍalāny apasavyāni babandhuḥ*: Literally, "they bound non-left circles." Only Cr comments on the expression here, glossing, "moving to the right (*dakṣiṇakramavanti*)." The commentators, however, take considerable pains to explain and analyze the expression when it appears in an identical context at 6.45.33. See notes to that passage. It is curious to note that several of the translators consulted render the identical expression differently in the two passages. Thus Dutt (1893, p. 1269) translates the former occurrence as "at the right hand" but translates it here as "at the left" (p. 1311). Earlier Roussel (1903, vol. 3, p. 166) renders, "*de gauche à droite*," but here he has "*à sa droite*" (p. 201). Earlier Gita Press (1969, vol. 3, p. 1567) renders, "anti-clockwise," but here "right to left" (p. 1616). Pagani (1999, p. 1001) first translates, "*de droite à gauche*," but here she settles for "*vers la gauche*" (p. 1033). See translation and notes to 6.45.33. Gorresio (1858, vol. 10, p. 22) avoids specifying the direction, rendering simply "*in cerchi infausti.*"

43. "a vulture perched upon his lance" *niṣpapāta ca gṛdhro 'sya śūle*. Compare 6.45.36 and note, where a vulture settles on Prahasta's flagstaff. See, too, note to 6.45.33, where the commentators describe vultures as inauspicious birds. M3 and the texts and printed editions of Cg and Cm read *māleva gṛdhro 'sya*, "a vulture like a garland," for the critical edition's *gṛdhro 'sya śūle*, "a vulture . . . on his lance." Raghunathan (1982, vol. 3, p. 175), the only translator to follow this reading, renders, "a vulture plunged down over his head like a garland falling." See note to 6.26.8.

"His left eye throbbed and his left arm trembled." *prāsphuran nayanaṃ cāsya savyo bāhur akampata*: Literally, "his eye throbbed and his left arm trembled." We follow Ct and Cr, who understand that it is the left eye that throbs. This is in keeping with the universal convention of Sanskrit literature that throbbing on the left side of the body is inauspicious for males and auspicious for females. See note to 6.4.6 and 6.43.7.

44. "an ill wind began to blow" *na pravāti sukho 'nilaḥ*: Literally, "a pleasant wind did not blow." Given the all but invariable convention, e.g., at 6.45.35, that makes a harsh

or unpleasant wind along with the crashing of meteors one of the standard ill omens in the repertory of the epic poets, we feel that a literal translation fails to convey the meaning adequately. Most of the translators consulted translate more or less literally. The exceptions are Pagani (1999, p. 1033), who translates similarly to us, "*un vent néfaste se mit à souffler*," and Gorresio. Gorresio's text (6.44.46) reads instead *pravavau na ca mārutaḥ*, "and the wind did not blow." He translates accordingly (1858, vol. 10, p. 22). See 6.4.42; 6.41.33; 6.43.8; 6.45.35; 6.65.19; and notes.

45. "fate" *kṛtānta-*: Literally, "that which makes the end." See note to 6.38.19.

46. "Stepping over the ramparts" *laṅghayitvā prākāraṃ padbhyām*: Literally, "having crossed *or* jumped over the rampart with his two feet. Ck and Ct note that Kumbhakarṇa proceeds on foot because of the absence of any mount capable of carrying him (*tadvahanakṣamavāhanābhāvāt padbhyām iti*—so Ct). Translators have understood either that Kumbhakarṇa leaps over the wall or simply passes through it. Given the extraordinary size that Kumbhakarṇa takes on in verses 33–34 above, it seems likely that the poet visualized him as simply stepping over the walls of the citadel. The majority of northern manuscripts, including the printed editions of Lahore (6.44.48) and Gorresio (6.44.48), read instead *niṣkramya* [*nirgamya*—Gorresio] *puradvārāt*, "going out by the city gate."

47. "who looked like a mountain" *parvatopamam*: Literally, "like a mountain."

48. "like a scattered mass of clouds . . . who resembled a cloud . . . roared thunderously like a cloud" *dravadbhinnam ivābhrajālam . . . nanāda bhūyo ghanavad ghanābhaḥ*: Literally, "[they] fleeing like a scattered mass of clouds . . . he who resembled a cloud roared repeatedly like a cloud." The poet has heavily belabored the cloud similes in this and the preceding two verses, as well as in the following verse. His choice of the word *ghana*, "cloud," which also coveys the sense of "density, solidity, *or* compactness," for Kumbhakarṇa is apparently intended to emphasize the contrast between this great dark, solid figure, and the now dispersed mass of the monkey troops.

The meter is *upajāti*.

49. "a rain-charged cloud" *vāridasya*: Literally, "of a giver of water." This is a common kenning for cloud.

The meter is *upajāti*.

50. "wielding a huge iron club" *vipulaparighavān*: Literally, "possessing a large iron club." The reference to Kumbhakarṇa's weapon is somewhat unclear and has caused concern among the commentators. At verses 12, 14, 29, and 43 above, the poet makes it unambiguously clear that Kumbhakarṇa is armed with a great *śūla*, or lance. A *parigha* or iron club is quite a different type of weapon. (See note to 5.3.30.) Ck and Ct appear to understand that the weapon referred to here is yet another in Kumbhakarṇa's arsenal but is, in fact, very much like a *śūla* (*śūlavad idam apy asyāyudham*). Cr glosses, "equipped with many different kinds of clubs (*anekavidhaparighaviśiṣṭaḥ*)." Cs offers two explanations. According to the first, the weapon Kumbhakarṇa is carrying is none other than his original lance, which Cs sees as being described here as "larger than even an iron club (*vipulaṃ parighād apīti vipulaparighaṃ śūlaṃ tadvān*)." For his second interpretation, Cs cites the *Viśvakośa*, according to which *parigha* is a synonym for "anger." The phrase would thus mean "filled with great anger (*roṣa*)." Cs then goes on to sharply criticize the positions of Ct and Cm on this point. He attacks Ct's claim that Kumbhakarṇa has a second weapon that is like a *śūla*, as this goes against the fact that [Kumbhakarṇa] has only one fixed weapon [here the *daṇḍa*, "club"] that he uses.

Ct then, according to Cs, is glossing something that is nowhere stated. Cs attacks what he takes to be Cm's argument [not clearly stated in Cm] that the adjective *parighavān* modifies not Kumbhakarṇa but the Lord (*prabhuḥ*) of *pāda* d, a position he describes as meaningless. Thus, Cs concludes that both of these commentators' arguments should be ignored. (*idam apy asyāyudham iti nāgojibhaṭṭavyākaraṇaṃ tathā prabhuviśeṣaṇam iti tīrthavyākhyānaṃ cānuktānuvādatvena daṇḍasya niyatāyudhasya pṛthaggrahaṇān nairarthakyāc ca kramād upekṣye.*)

"Lord Yama" *prabhuḥ*: Literally, "the lord." We follow the majority of commentators, who understand the reference to be to the god of death or universal destruction, Yama or Antaka (*prabhuḥ antakaḥ*—so Cg, Cm). Cs takes the term quasi-adjectivally, glossing it as "Yama, who is capable of destruction (*saṃhārasamartho yamaḥ*)." Ct and Ck also take the term in its adjectival sense of " powerful *or* capable. Ct understands that Kumbhakarṇa, in marching forth, is as mighty, that is, as fierce, as the fire at the end of a cosmic age or like Kālāgnirudra (an epithet of Śiva) (*yugānte prabhuḥ kālāgnirudra iva viniḥsṛtaḥ*), while Ck glosses, "angry (*kruddhaḥ*)." See note to 6.56.8.

"with his servants and his rod" *kiṃkaradaṇḍavān*: The compound is somewhat obscure in meaning and has been rendered variously by commentators and translators alike. We follow what appears to be the interpretation of Ck, who takes the underlying compound as a *dvandva* referring to two separate attributes of Yama: his servants (*kiṃkaras*) and his rod of punishment (*daṇḍa*). We believe that this interpretation best fits the context, because, even though it is not referred to in this specific verse, it has been made clear at verses 27–32 above that Kumbhakarṇa is accompanied by a large and fearsome retinue of *rākṣasas*. These troops and the great *śūla* or *parigha* he wields form the basis for the simile in which he is compared to death with his attendants and his rod. Other commentators and translators have attempted to subordinate the term *kiṃkara* in one way or another to *daṇḍa*. Cv, Cm, and Cg base their interpretation on the literal meaning of *kiṃ-kara*, "doing what?" i.e., a servant, and understand the *daṇḍa* to be a sentient or animated being, which keeps on saying, "What must I do? (*kiṃ karomīty avasthāyī sacetano daṇḍaḥ tadvān*)." In other words, the staff itself is the servant of the lord. Ct takes the two terms appositionally, so that the servants who engage in destruction are in effect so many rods of doom (*kiṃkarāḥ saṃhāraparikarāḥ kāladaṇḍā asya santi*).

Translators have treated the compound variously. Roussel (1903, vol. 3, p. 202), in effect inverting the interpretation of Ct, renders "*accompagné des fléaux, ses ministres*." Pagani (1999, p. 1033) understands *daṇḍa* in its other sense of "punishment," offering, "*accompagné des châtiments, ses serviteurs*." Raghunathan (1982, vol. 3, p. 175) seems to follow Cg, Cm, and Cv in rendering, "armed with the rod that works his will." Gita Press (1969, vol. 3, p. 1616) similarly renders, "armed with his rod of punishment waiting upon him (in a living form) like a servant." Dutt (1893, p. 1311) fails to render *kiṃkara*, translating, "armed with the Fatal rod," while Shastri (1959, vol. 3, p. 175) drops the word *daṇḍa*, rendering, "accompanied by his minions."

The meter is *puṣpitāgrā*.

Sarga 54

1. Before verse 1, all southern and northern manuscripts, with the exception of Ś,D1–3,8,12, include a transitional verse of the type normal to the epic in which the

final action of the preceding *sarga* is recapitulated and the principal actor named. The southern variant is found at 1154*, a passage of two lines: "Stepping over the ramparts, enormous and mighty Kumbhakarṇa, resembling a mountain peak, swiftly left the city." The northern variant [1153*] omits the mention of Kumbhakarṇa stepping over the city wall and the comparison of him to a mountain, noting instead that he is followed by many roaring, angry *rākṣasas*.

"Kumbhakarṇa" *saḥ*: Literally, "he."

"shattering" *vidhaman*: Literally, "blowing apart." Cg appears to take the term in its sense of "blowing up [as with breath or bellows one does a fire]," glossing, "burning (*dahan*)."

2. "magnanimous Indra" *maghavatā*: Literally, "the magnanimous one."

3. "Vālin's son" *vāliputraḥ*: Ś,Ñ1,V3,B1,D1–4,6,8–13,T2,3,G3,M2,5, and the texts and printed editions of Ct and Cr read instead *rājaputraḥ*, "the king's son."

4. "in such an access of panic" *bhayatrastāḥ*: Literally, "frightened with fear."

"forgetting who you are" *ātmānam . . . vismṛtya*: Literally, "having forgotten yourself." D7,10,11,G2, and the texts and printed editions of Ct and Cr read the genitive singular *ātmanaḥ*, "your own," for *ātmānam*. This then construes with "heroic deeds (*vīryāṇi*)" and "noble lineage (*abhijanāni*)" of *pāda* b.

5. "gentle friends" *saumyāḥ*: Cs detects a note of irony here, arguing that Añgada is, in fact, spitefully taunting the monkeys for their gentleness [i.e., cowardice] at a moment when they should be displaying their ferocity (*krauryapradarśanakāle 'pi tadaprakāśakā itīrṣyayā saṃbodhanam*).

"Why are you trying to save yourselves?" *kiṃ prāṇān parirakṣatha*: Literally, "Are you protecting your lives?" Cs understands Añgada to be indicating that the monkeys' lives are worthless since they are not carrying out their master's desire (*svāmikāmitākaraṇena jīvanaṃ dhig iti bhāvaḥ*).

"This is no *rākṣasa* capable of fighting." *nālaṃ yuddhāya vai rakṣaḥ*: Most of the translators consulted tend to follow the interpretation of Ct, who glosses, "this *rākṣasa* is not able to fight with us (*etad rakṣo yuddhāyāsmābhir nālaṃ na samartham*)." The context, we believe, supports our interpretation, according to which Añgada is telling the monkeys that the ghastly apparition of Kumbhakarṇa is not, in fact, a real *rākṣasa* warrior. In this vein, Raghunathan (1982, vol. 3, p. 176) renders, "this thing that you dread is not a Rākshasa at all, whom we have to fight . . ."

"It is just some huge scarecrow." *mahatīyaṃ vibhīṣikā*: Literally, "this is a huge 'frightener.' " Añgada is apparently speaking under the influence of the disinformation provided by Vibhīṣaṇa at 6.49.31 above, where the latter stops the panicked flight of the monkeys by having Rāma tell them that Kumbhakarṇa is not a real *rākṣasa* but rather "a mechanical man (*yantram*)." However, at verse 23 below, it appears that Añgada himself is fully aware of Kumbhakarṇa's identity (see note below). Cf. verse 26 below, where the monkeys do not appear to believe Añgada. At 6.49.31, Cg glosses *yantram* as *bibhīṣakā*, virtually the same term we find here. Here, Cg glosses, "an object to inspire fear, in the guise of an artificial man (*bhayajanakaḥ kṛtrimapuruṣaveṣaḥ*)."

6. "scarecrow towering amid the *rākṣasas*" *utthitām . . . rākṣasānāṃ vibhīṣikām*: Literally, "the upraised scarecrow of the *rākṣasas*." We follow the suggestion of Cr, who adds the adverb *madhye*, "in the midst," to construe with the genitive *rākṣasānām*. We take the participle *utthitām*, "towering," adjectivally as we did with the parallel participle *samucchrita* in the same context at 6.49.31. Other translators have rendered the

phrase variously. Roussel (1903, vol. 3, p. 203), followed by Shastri (1959, vol. 3, p. 176) and Pagani (1999, p. 1034), understands the term *vibhīṣikā* in its sense of "terror" rather than a physical object. Roussel translates, "*Cette immense frayeur que 'inspirent les Rākshasas.*" Raghunathan (1982, vol. 3, p. 176) reads the genitive *rākṣasānām* as if it were an instrumental, construing it with the passive participle *utthitām*, and renders, "which the Rākshasas have raised." Dutt (1893, p. 1312) and Gita Press (1969, vol. 3, p. 1617) read *utthitām* as an active participle of an intransitive verb, rendering, respectively, "this fearful phenomenon of the Rākshasas that hath presented itself" and "this nightmare of the ogres, come into being."

7. "When... had been reassured" *samāśvāsya*: Literally, "having reassured." The syntax requires that the causative gerund be read here either as a simplex or as a passive. D5,7,T1,G3, and the texts and printed editions of the southern commentators substitute the simplex *samāśvasya*, "having regained their composure," while some northern texts, including that of Gorresio, substitute the passive participle *samāśvastāḥ*, "comforted, reassured."

"with trees and boulders in hand" *vṛkṣādrihastāḥ*: D9–11 and the texts and printed editions of Ct and Cr read instead *vṛkṣān gṛhītvā*, "having seized trees."

8. "in a rage... wildly enraged" *saṃkruddhāḥ... paramakruddhāḥ*: Cg and Cr propose different strategies for avoiding the apparent redundancy. Cg, whom we follow, specifies that *paramakruddhāḥ*, "wildly enraged," is an adjective modifying the elephants of the simile. Cr, who, along with Ct, reads *saṃrabdhāḥ*, "agitated, inflamed, enraged," for *saṃkruddhāḥ*, "in a rage," takes both adjectives to refer to the monkeys but suggests that the latter were inflamed precisely because they were wildly enraged (*paramakruddhā ata eva saṃrabdhāḥ*).

"immensely powerful" *mahābalāḥ*: The texts and printed editions of Cg and Cm read instead the singular *mahābalaḥ*. This fact is unnoted in the critical apparatus (which notes only T2 reading this variant). Ct and Cr read with the critical text. Cg and Cm, reading the singular, must then construe it with Kumbhakarṇa, the unnamed subject of the verb *kampate*, "he was [not] shaken," in verse 9, *pāda* b. Dutt (1893, p. 1312), who reads the plural with Ct, is evidently disturbed by it and notes, "*Mahavalāh—plu*—evidently a misprint for *mahavalah*—sing."

9. "into hundreds of pieces" *śataśaḥ*: D9–11 and the texts and printed editions of Ct read instead *bahavaḥ*, "many."

10. "that has flared up" *utthitaḥ*: Literally, "sprung up."

11. "like crimson-blossomed trees" *tāmrapuṣpā iva drumāḥ*: Compare 6.55.22 and note.

12. "did not watch where they were going" *nāvalokayan*: Literally, "they did not look." Commentators differ somewhat as to the exact sense of the verb. Ct, whom we more or less follow, glosses, "they did not look before them or behind them (*agrapṛṣṭhadeśaṃ nālokitavantaḥ*)." Cr believes that the monkeys did not even look at their kinsmen and that is why some of them fell into the sea. (*nāvalokayann avālokayan svajanān apīti śeṣaḥ. ata eva kecit samudre patitāḥ.*) Cg believes that the monkeys simply look back (*pṛṣṭhadeśam ity arthaḥ*). Translations vary similarly.

13. "immensely powerful" *balīyasā*: D10,11,G, and the texts and printed editions of Ct and Cr read instead *ca līlayā*, "with ease *or* playfully," referring to the manner with which Kumbhakarṇa is able to decimate the monkey host.

14. "fled down to the shore" *sthalāni tathā nimnam*: Literally, "to places and depression(s)" The phrase is both elliptical, in that it contains no verb, and ambiguous in

its meaning. The commentators, with whom we agree, suggest supplying [or bringing down from 13d] the verb "they fled (*dudruvuḥ*)" or "they had recourse to (*āśritāḥ*—so Cg)." Commentators and translators are divided as to how exactly to understand the terms *sthalāni* and *nimnam*. Cg understands the former term to refer either to regions that are highly suitable for flight (*atidhāvanayogyān deśān*) or elevated places (*unnatadeśān*). The latter construes well with *nimnam*, if we take that in the sense of "low lands *or* hollows." The sense would then be that the monkeys fled high and low. This is slightly problematic because of the lack of number parallelism between *sthalān* in the plural and *nimnam* in the singular.

Another way to read the phrase, proposed by Cr, is to take *nimnam* adverbially so that the fleshed-out phrase would mean "[They ran] downward [to the *sthalas*] (*nimnaṃ yathā bhavati tathā dudruvur iti śeṣaḥ*)." Cr remains silent, however, as to exactly what is meant by *sthalān* here. The term can mean, as Cg proposes, "high ground," but that clearly makes no sense if we read *nimnam* adverbially. The word *sthala* most frequently refers to firm or dry land as opposed to *jala*, "water." Given the context and what we know of the topography of Laṅkā, we believe the term is best taken here in its sense of "shore *or* shoreline." The idea would be that the monkeys, running blindly, would naturally run down from the higher elevations of Mount Trikūṭa, where the city of Laṅkā is located, until they are stopped in any direction by the encircling sea.

Translators struggle with the verse, offering variations on the above possibilities. Thus Dutt (1893, p. 1313) offers, "darted into downs." Roussel (1903, vol. 3, p. 204) appears to take the two terms together in the sense of valley, i.e., low areas, translating, "*par les vallées*." In this he is followed by Shastri (1959, vol. 3, p. 177), who renders, "escaped to the valleys." Pagani (1999, p. 1034) offers, "*couraient sur la terre ferme vers les vallées*." Raghunathan (1982, vol. 3, p. 176) renders, "took refuge in depressions." Gita Press (1969, vol. 3, p. 1618), who understands *nimnam* adverbially as we do, renders, "[they rushed toward] the plains, taking a downward course." Some northern manuscripts, including the printed texts of Gorresio (6.45.23) and Lahore (6.45.22), in what can be taken as an attempt to gloss or rationalize, read *ca nimnāni*, for *tathā nimnam*. This yields a sense similar to that proposed by Cg as one of his alternatives, viz., "to high and low grounds." Gorresio (1858, vol. 10, p. 24) translates, "*forre e balze*."

"Some apes" *ṛkṣāḥ*: Most other translators who share this reading render "bears." The only exception is Roussel (1903, vol. 3, p. 204), who, as usual, leaves such terms untranslated. On the identity of *ṛkṣas*, see 6.4.17 and note. See, too, 1.16.10 and note; and R. Goldman 1989. Cf. 6.55.42 and note.

15. "Some of them plunged into the sea, while others took refuge in caves." *mamajjur arṇave kecid guhāḥ kecit samāśritāḥ*: D1,9–12,T3, and the printed editions of Ct and Cr omit this half verse (15ab).

"sank down" *niṣeduḥ*: Cg understands that the monkeys "remained still on the ground as if fallen (*bhūmau patitā iva tasthuḥ*)." Presumably, he understands that the monkeys are feigning death or unconsciousness. Ñ1,D6,9–11,T2,G2,3,M5, and the texts and printed editions of Ct and Cr read instead *nipetuḥ*, "they fell down." Ct suggests that we supply the words "in order to fight (*yuddhārtham iti śeṣaḥ*)."

Following verse 15, D5–7,9–11,S insert a passage of one line [1161*]: "Some of them fell to the ground, while others lay unconscious [lit., slept] as if dead."

Although the critical editors ascribe this verse to the entire southern recension, the editors of the printed editions of the text of Cg (KK and VSP) seem uncomfortable with it. Therefore, it is bracketed after 6.66.19cd in KK and after 6.66.18cd in VSP.

16. "had broken ranks" *bhagnān*: Literally, "were broken."

17. "I can see no safe place for you" *na paśyāmi . . . sthānam*: Literally, "I do not see a place." We follow Ct and Ck, who gloss, "support, stability (*pratiṣṭhām*)." The idea, as expressed by Ct and Ck, is that, even if the monkeys escape Kumbhakarṇa, Sugrīva will surely execute them for leaving without his orders (*sugrīvājñāṃ vinā gatānāṃ vadha eva sarvatheti bhāvaḥ*—so Ct). Sugrīva's reputation as a harsh ruler is established at 4.52.21–30, where the southern search party chooses suicide rather than face his wrath over their failure to accomplish their mission.

"the earth itself" *mahīm imām*: Literally, "this earth."

18. "Nothing can hinder your progress and your valor." *asaṃgagatipauruṣāḥ*: Literally, "O you whose motion and valor are unobstructed." The commentators (Cr, Ct, Ck, and Cg) generally agree that the term is a vocative referring to the monkeys. However, only Cr and Cg attempt to explain the compound's meaning. The former offers two alternatives. Cr first reads the compound to mean "you whose progress and valor are not to be hindered by your enemies (*na saṅgau ripubhiḥ prāpyau gatipauruṣau yeṣām*)." Cr also proposes a second alternative in which the compound refers to the wives of the monkeys and has the sense "by whom your progress and valor are not recognized (*na saṅgau jñātau gatipauruṣau yaiḥ*)." Cg appears to give no value to the term *-gati-* "motion, progress, gait," glossing, simply, "you whose valor is unobstructed (*apratibaddhapauruṣāḥ*)." Translators vary in their renderings. Dutt (1893, p. 1313) appears to understand the term to mean "cowards," translating, "Ye poltroons." Roussel (1903, vol. 3, p. 204), followed by Shastri (1959, vol. 3, p. 177) and Pagani (1999, p. 1035), construes the compound with the adjective *nirāyudhānām*, "weaponless," understanding that the monkeys drop their weapons so as not to be impeded in their flight, "*Soldats qui fuyez sans armes pour ne pas être gênés dans votre course*." This interpretation is not persuasive, especially in light of 5.49.13, where the compound *asaṃgagatiḥ*, "whose progress is unhindered," serves as a general epithet of the monkeys. Raghunathan (1982, vol. 3, p. 177) follows Cg in omitting the term *-gati-*, rendering, "You, whose prowess knows no check." Gita Press (1969, vol. 3, p. 1618) understands as we do, rendering, "O monkeys! whose movement or valour knows no obstruction."

"weaponless" *nirāyudhānām*: The reference is presumably to the fact that monkeys would have dropped their weapons in their flight. This is the understanding of Ct and Ck, who gloss, "devoid of their weapons, such as stones, trees, etc. (*pāṣāṇavṛkṣādyāyudharahitānām*)." Cs, however, appears to think that the monkeys' dishonor lies in their fleeing unmarked by the weapons loosed by their enemies, glossing, "not marked by the weapons released by their enemies (*ripumuktāyudhānaṅkitānām*)."

"But though you will have survived" *tu jīvatām*: Literally, "But, of [you] who are alive." D10,11,M3, and the texts and printed editions of Ct, Ck, Cs, and Cr read instead *sujīvatām*[*-inām*—M3], "of those who live well." Translators who follow the text of Ct render this as "men of honor, good men *or* those who live an easy life, etc." It should be noted, however, that Ck and Ct, despite the reading of their texts, seem to know only the term *jīvatām*. Only Cs glosses this reading, offering, "possessing good *or* virtuous lives (*sajjīvavatām*)."

19. "you... all" *sarve*: Literally, "all." Cg thinks that Aṅgada wishes to include himself and so adds the pronoun "we (*vayam*)."

"contemptible" *anāryāḥ*: Literally, "ignoble *or* non-*aryan*." Ct and Ck gloss, "rebellious against your master (*svāmidrohiṇaḥ*)."

Following 19 ab, D5–7,9–11,S insert a passage of one line [1165*]: "Where are you going, overcome with fear, like ordinary tawny monkeys?"

20. "great" *mahānti*: Cg, the only commentator to read with the critical edition, glosses, "numerous (*bhūyāṃsi*)." D10,11,G3,M1,2, and the texts and printed editions of Ct, Ck, and Cr read instead *hitāni*, "beneficial." Ck and Ct gloss, "beneficial to your master (*svāmihitakarāṇi*)." Cr understands similarly (*svāmihitakārakatvasūcakāni*). GPP and NSP (6.66.22d) read, perhaps in error, *hatāni*, "destroyed, killed, ruined," a reading attested in the critical apparatus only in Ñ2.

"that we heard... in the public assembly" *janasaṃsadi*: Literally, "in the assembly of the people."

22. Ck, Cs, and Ct note that here Aṅgada is expressing the sentiment, famously stated by Lord Kṛṣṇa at *Bhagavadgītā* 2.37, that a virtuous warrior wins heaven if slain in battle and conquers the earth if he is victorious (*hato vā prāpsyasi svargaṃ jitvā vā bhokṣyase mahīm*).

"our life spans being short" *alpajīvitāḥ*: Raghunathan (1982, vol. 3, p. 177) differs from us and the other translations consulted in understanding this as a general observation. He translates, "life is short in any case."

"we would have died" *nihatāḥ*: Literally, "slain."

"then, since we would have died in battle, we would attain the world of Brahmā, so difficult to reach" *duṣprāpaṃ brahmalokaṃ vā prāpnumo yudhi sūditāḥ*: D10,11, and the texts and printed editions of Cr, Ct and Ck read instead *prāpnuyāmo brahmalokaṃ duṣprāpaṃ ca kuyodhibhiḥ*, "We would attain the world of Brahmā, impossible for cowards to attain."

Following verse 22, D5–7,9–11,S insert a passage of one line [1167*]: "Then, monkeys, we shall enjoy[1] our reward,[2] life[3] in the world of heroes.[4]"

[1]"we shall enjoy" *bhokṣyāmaḥ*: G2,M5, and the texts and printed editions of Cv, Cm, Crā, and Cg read instead the somewhat obscure *mokṣyāmaḥ*, "we shall release *or* set free." Raghunathan (1982, vol. 3, p. 177), the only translator to render this reading, translates, "we shall... earn [the merit] that shall take us to the worlds of bliss when we die." Ct notes that the reading of Cm et al. is both inauthentic and meaningless. (*pāṭho 'pāñktaḥ. nāpi tatrārthasāmañjasyam.*)

[2]"reward" *vasu*: Literally, "wealth." Ct and Ck understand this to be "the bliss arising from Hiraṇyagarbha (*dhanaṃ hiraṇyagarbhabhūm ānandam*)." Cs glosses, "pleasures (*bhogyam*)."

[3]"life" *jīvitam*: D10,11,G1,M1,2, and the texts and printed editions of Ck, Ct, Cs, and Cr read instead *nihatāḥ*, "slain."

[4]"in the world of heroes" *vīralokasya*: Literally, "of the world of heroes." The name conjures up the image of a kind of Indian Elysian fields or Valhalla, and, indeed, Ct and Ck refer to this as a world obtained by heroes who pass through the doorway of the sun. However, in order to avoid contradiction with the preceding verse, all commentators equate this world with the world of Brahmā, a region not normally

attained merely through death in battle (*vīraiḥ sūryadvārā prāpyasya brahmalokasya*—so Ct, Ck). See *Bṛhadāraṇyakopaniṣad* 6.2.15–16, where the path of the sun leads to the immortal world of the gods.

23. "Kumbhakarṇa" *kumbhakarṇaḥ*: There seems to be a contradiction here between Aṅgada's recognition of the *rākṣasa* hero and his assertion at verse 5 above that he is a mere scarecrow. Either the poet has nodded or he wants to represent Aṅgada, like Vibhīṣaṇa at 6.49.31, as lying to the troops in order to prevent their flight.

24. "renowned" *uddiṣṭāḥ*: Literally, "pointed out, held up for illustration." We agree with Ct, Cr, and Cg in understanding the term in its sense of "accounted among great heroes (*mahāvīreṣu gaṇitāḥ*—so Ct)," "known among heroes (*vīreṣu khyātāḥ*—so Cr)," or, "pointed out *or* named (*vyapadiṣṭāḥ*—so Cg)." Cm, however, takes the term in the negative sense of "singled out *or* pointed to by people because of their cowardly flight (*uddiṣṭā ete palāyitā iti janair nirdiṣṭāḥ*). This interpretation is offered as an alternative by Ct.

"by a single warrior" *ekena*: Literally, "by one."

25. "Aṅgada of the golden armlets" *aṅgadaṃ kanakāṅgadam*: This is yet another of Vālmīki's echoing or etymological epithets. Cg attempts to make the epithet more suitable to the narrative context by stating that, in his excess of excitement or energy, Aṅgada is displaying his golden armlets (*utsāhātiśayena prakāśitasvarṇāṅgadam*). Presumably, the idea is that Aṅgada has raised or is waving about his arms. See 6.57.78; 6.116.67; and notes. Cf. 6.52.19 and note.

26. "The *rākṣasa* Kumbhakarṇa" *kumbhakarṇena rakṣasā*: Clearly, the monkeys are not taken in by Aṅgada's claim that the giant *rākṣasa* is merely a scarecrow. See verse 5 and note above; and note to verse 23.

"time to stand our ground" *sthānakālaḥ*: Literally, "time to stand."

"We value our lives; so" *dayitaṃ jīvitaṃ hi naḥ*: Literally, "for life is dear to us."

27. "Having said this much" *etāvad uktvā vacanam*: Literally, "having spoken speech to such an extent."

"the advancing *rākṣasa*" *āyāntam*: Literally, "him who was advancing."

"fled in all directions" *bhejire diśah*: Literally, "they had recourse to the directions."

28. "with . . . respectful words" *bahumānaiḥ*: Literally, "with respects." The reading is subject to considerable variation among the manuscripts and printed editions. Most northern manuscripts, as well as a number of southern manuscripts, including those of the southern commentators, and all printed editions except Gorresio, read instead *anumānaiḥ*, literally, "with inferences, arguments." The southern commentators take this to refer to Aṅgada's adduction of a variety of Rāma's earlier feats of martial valor, which are supposed to inspire confidence in his ability to defeat Kumbhakarṇa. Translations that follow the texts of the southern commentators render this variation. The text of Gorresio (6.45.39) reads instead *abhimānaiḥ*, "with proud words." This reading is not attested in the critical apparatus.

"those . . . wrinkle-faced monkeys" *valīmukhāḥ*: Literally, "the wrinkle-faced ones." Vālmīki occasionally uses this kenning for monkey. Translators either use the generic terms "apes *or* monkeys" or ignore it altogether. See 6.55.2; 6.57.49; 6.83.41; 6.85.2; and notes.

Following verse 28, D5–7,9–11,T,1,2,G,M insert a passage of two lines [1168*]: "Their enthusiasm restored by the wise son of Vālin, all the monkey troop leaders then stood fast, awaiting their orders."

29. This verse is omitted from Ñ1,M5,D9–11, and the texts of Ct, Ck, and Cr, as well as NSP. GPP includes the verse but notes that it is an additional verse in Cg's text. The verse is also omitted from Gorresio's text, although this fact is not noted in the critical apparatus. Ck complains about the impropriety of placing a *sarga* break between 6.54.28 and 6.55.1, arguing that there is no reason to do so since there is no break in the story line and [since his text omits verse 29] no change in meter (*atra ca sargam avacchindantīdam apy ayuktam ekaprakaraṇatvād vṛttabhedarahitatvāc ca*). Ct paraphrases this argument of Ck in his introductory remarks to the next *sarga*.

"Hanumān, the son of Vāyu" *-vāyuputra-*: Literally, "the son of Vāyu." Cm and Cg are quick to defend the honor of the mighty Hanumān, noting that, despite his inclusion in this list of would-be deserters, he was not among those who had actually tried to flee. They argue that we are to understand that Hanumān has merely met up with the returning group of monkey officers and has now turned back with them to fight Kumbhakarṇa. (*atra vāyuputras tu na palāyya nivṛttaḥ. kiṃtv ṛṣabhādibhir militvā kumbhakarṇena saha yuddhārthaṃ nivṛtta iti jñeyam.*)

"turned and headed back to the battlefield" *-abhimukhaṃ raṇaṃ prayātāḥ*: Literally, "facing [they] proceeded to the battlefield." GPP's reading, *gaṇaṃ preyātāḥ*, doubtless is the result of typographical errors.

The meter is *puṣpitāgrā*.

Sarga 55

1. "resigning themselves to death" *naiṣṭhikīṃ buddhim āsthāya*: Literally, "having recourse to a state of mind that was associated with *niṣṭhā*." Commentators and translators differ in their interpretation of this phrase, depending on which of the meanings of the term *niṣṭhā* they find relevant here. Of the several meanings of the term, two are at issue: one is "firmness, fixity, determination" and the other is "finality, death, destruction." Ct and Ck gloss, "firm (*sthirām*)," and Cr, "resolute, unmoving (*acalām*)." Thus, translators who follow the text of Ct understand the phrase to mean "making a firm *or* fixed resolution." Cg and Cm gloss, "destruction, death (*nāśaḥ*)," and understand that the monkeys are resolved to die. (*naiṣṭhikīṃ niṣṭhā nāśas tatsaṃbandhinīm. maraṇavyavasāyinīm ity arthaḥ*—so Cg.) Both interpretations are plausible. We, however, have chosen that of Cg and Cm for two reasons: first, because of the general tenor of this and the preceding *sarga*; and second, specifically because of the references in verse 3 below, where the monkeys are said to be resigned to their death and to have given up their lives (*maraṇe kṛtaniścayāḥ* . . . *tyaktajīvitāḥ*).

2. "the wrinkle-faced monkeys" *valīmukhāḥ*: Literally, "the wrinkle-faced ones." See 6.54.28; 6.57.49; 6.83.41; 6.85.2; and notes. B2,D10,G1, and the texts and printed editions of Ct read instead the adjective *balīyasā*, "powerful, mighty," which then modifies Aṅgada.

"incited to valor" *samudīritavīryāḥ*: Literally, "whose valor was stimulated." Ct, Cm, Cr, and Cg take the adjective *samudīrita* in its sense of "uttered, recited" and understand the compound to mean "those who had proclaimed their own previous feats of valor (*kathitātmīyaprākparākramā ity arthaḥ*—so Cm)."

3. "resigned to death . . . heedless of their lives" *maraṇe kṛtaniścayāḥ* . . . *tyaktajīvitāḥ*: Literally, "who had made a resolution with regard to death . . . who had abandoned

their lives." Cg understands the second adjective to be the cause of the first and glosses, "who were devoid of any hope of living (*jīvanāśārahitāḥ*)." Cr understands the causal relationship to be the other way around. He takes *tyaktajīvitāḥ* in a technical sense, glossing, "having abandoned such activities as eating, etc. (*parityaktabhojanādivyāpārāḥ*)."

5. "struck at" *ardayan*: Literally, "striking, afflicting." D9–11 and the texts and printed editions of Ct and Cr read instead *dharṣayan*, "assailing, being arrogant." Cr glosses, "demonstrating his skill (*svaprāgalbhyaṃ prakaṭayan*)."

"sending . . . flying in all directions" *samantād vyākṣipat*: Literally, "he tossed *or* scattered [them] all around."

6. "Struck down" *pothitāḥ*: The word is subject to numerous variants according to the critical edition. D9–11 and the texts and printed editions of Ct and Cr read instead *tāḍitāḥ*, "struck, struck down."

"in groups of seven and eight hundred, and even in groups of thousands" *śatāni sapta cāṣṭau ca sahasrāṇi ca*: Literally, "seven hundreds and eight and thousands." As is often the case in Sanskrit, the total number of enumerated items can be ambiguous. The sequence of numbers here has been read by various translators as "seven hundred, eight hundred, and thousands" or "eight thousand seven hundred." In light of the way the numbers are used in the following verse to indicate discretely numbered groups of monkeys as well as the repetition of the copulative "and (*ca*)" three times, we are inclined to agree with Cg. He understands that a single blow or action on the part of Kumbhakarṇa has felled the monkeys in groups of a hundred, etc. (*kumbhakarṇasyaikena vyāpareṇa śatādisaṅgharūpeṇa patitā ity arthaḥ*).

7. "sweeping up groups of monkeys—sixteen, eight, ten, twenty, and thirty at a time" *ṣoḍaśāṣṭau ca daśa ca viṃśat triṃśat tathaiva ca / parikṣipya*: Literally, "having embraced *or* having encircled sixteen and eight and ten and twenty and thirty as well." For a discussion of the numbers, see note to verse 6 above.

Following verse 7, D5–7,9–11,S insert a passage of fourteen lines [1175*]: "Rallied with great difficulty, the tawny monkeys regrouped and took their stand once more in the forefront of the battle, with trees and mountains in their hands.[1–2] Then, ripping up a mountain, that bull among leaping monkeys Dvivida hurled himself, like a low-hanging cloud, upon [Kumbhakarṇa], who looked like a mountain peak.[3–4] Having torn it up, the monkey hurled it at Kumbhakarṇa. But, failing to reach that huge [*rākṣasa*], it fell upon his army.[5–6] That huge mountain[1] crushed horses, elephants, and chariots, while yet another mountain peak [crushed] the other *rākṣasas*.[7–8] Struck by the impact of that mountain, the vast battlefield was drenched with the blood of the *rākṣasas*, its horses and chariots destroyed.[9–10] With dreadful cries, the chariot-warriors swiftly struck off the heads of the bellowing monkey leaders with arrows that resembled Kāla, the ender of all things.[11–12] But the great monkeys, for their part, tore up huge trees and crushed chariots, horses, elephants, camels, and *rākṣasas*.[13–14]"

[1]"That huge mountain" *nagottamaḥ*: D9–11 and the texts and printed editions of Ct read instead the accusative plural *gajottamān*, "best *or* most splendid of elephants," which then construes with the list of things and creatures crushed [by the mountain].

8. "many different kinds of trees" *vṛkṣāṃś ca vividhān bahūn*: D9–11 and the texts and printed editions of Ct and Cr read instead *śilāś ca vividhān drumān*, "rocks and various trees."

9. "deflected" *babhañja*: Literally, "he broke, broke up."

10. "directly in the path" *asya . . . purastāt*: Literally, "before him."

The meter is *upajāti*.

11. "the enraged monkey" *kupitaḥ*; Literally, "the angry one."

"the blood-spattered *rākṣasa*" *rudhirāvasiktaḥ*: Literally, "the blood-spattered one."

The meter is *upajāti*.

12. "and resembled a mountain, its highest peak in flames" *giriṃ yathā prajvalitāgra-śṛṅgam*: Ñ,V,B4,T2,G1,2,M1,2,5 read the nominative *girir yathā prajvalitāgraśṛṅgaḥ*, substituting the nominatives for the accusatives of the critical reading. This reading appears to make better rhetorical sense, since it compares the dark mountainous *rākṣasa* Kumbhakarṇa hurling his flaming lance to a volcanic mountain with flames shooting from its summit. GPP and NSP (6.67.19) mix the figure by putting *giriḥ* in the nominative and reading the accusative *prajvalitāgniśṛṅgam*, "with a summit with blazing fire," which would, of course, have to modify the lance. Translations offer various solutions based on these different readings.

"full in the chest" *bāhvantare*: Literally, "between his arms." Cf. verses 44 and 65 below.

"as Guha . . . Mount Krauñca" *guho 'calaṃ krauñcam iva*: The story of how Guha, also known as Skanda, pierced Mount Krauñca, thus liberating the *asura* Krauñca, is narrated at *Mahābhārata* 3.186.112ff. and 13.166.30ff. See, too, 4.42.24. Geese and vultures fly to Mount Meru through the hole made by Guha's javelin (*MBh* 7.114.82). Vālmīki is fond of using this image to describe the wounding of a great warrior by a sharp weapon; see 6.47.38; 6.51.19; and notes.

The meter *is upajāti*.

13. "from his mouth" *mukhāt*: D9–11 and the texts and printed editions of Ct and Cr read instead *ruṣā*, "with anger."

The meter is *vaṃśasthavila*.

14. "in the midst of battle" *saṃyati*: Literally, "in the battle."

The meter is *upajāti*.

Following verse 14, D5–7,9–11,S (except G3) insert a passage of one line [1178*]: "Then mighty Nīla, calming his troops . . ."

15. "Nīla then hurled" *nīlaś cikṣepa*: D5,7,9–11,T1, and the texts and printed editions of Ct, which have already introduced Nīla in their insert 1178*, read instead *pravicikṣepa*, "he hurled."

"but the latter struck it" *tam . . . abhijaghāna*: Literally, "he struck it."

16. "shooting forth sparks and flames" *savisphuliṅgañ sajvālam*: Literally, "with sparks, with flames."

18. "immensely powerful monkeys" *mahābalāḥ*: Literally, "those of great strength."

"battered . . . on all sides" *sarvato 'bhinijaghnire*: D9–11 and the texts and printed editions of Ct and Cr read instead *nijaghnuḥ sarvato yudhi*, "they battered on all sides in battle." T2,G3,M3,5, and the texts and printed editions of Cg and Cm read *[a]bhipra-dudruvuḥ*, "they rushed *or* ran," for the critical text's *[a]bhinijaghnire*, "they battered."

19. "felt to him like mere caresses" *sparśān iva prahārāṃs tān vedayānaḥ*: Literally, "experiencing those blows as if touches." Cr, Ct, and Ck all understand the touches to

be like those of garlands, flowers, etc. (*puṣpamālādisaṃyogān iva*—so Cr). Cg understands that they are like pleasurable contact, that is, like pleasant pressing or massage (*sukhasparśān iva sukhamardanam iva*). According to Dutt's note (1893, p. 1316), Rāmānuja (Crā) understands, "like the feel of wreaths, unguents, etc."

"He crushed . . . with both arms." *bāhubhyāṃ pariṣasvaje*: Literally, "he embraced with his two arms."

20. "blood oozing from his mouth" *pramukhāgataśoṇitaḥ*: Literally, "with blood come to *or* from his mouth." The *upasarga pra* placed at the beginning of the compound is unusual and difficult to construe. Commentators propose two solutions, neither of which seems entirely convincing. Ct, Ck, and Cr read *pra* as an abbreviation of the adverb *prakarṣeṇa*, "to a high degree *or* great extent," and understand that blood is flowing copiously from Ṛṣabha's mouth. M3 and the texts and printed editions of Cg and Cm read instead *pra mukhād vāntaśoṇitaḥ*, "vomiting blood from his mouth." Cg cites *Pā* 1.4.82 *vyavahitāś ca* in support of his contention that here we have a vedic usage in which an *upasarga* may be separated from a verbal form and may precede or follow it. Cg thus construes the *upasarga* with the principal verb in the sentence, *nipapāta*, "he fell down, collapsed." (*preti chedaḥ. mukhād vāntaśoṇitaḥ praṇipapātety anvayaḥ. vyavahitāś cety upasargasya vyavahitaprayogaḥ.*) One problem here is that the resultant form, *praṇipapāta*, normally would have the sense "he bowed down, offered obeisance," which hardly suits the context. See note to 6.75.16.

21. "Kumbhakarṇa, Indra's foe" *indraripuḥ*: Literally, "the foe of Indra."

Following verse 21, M1–3 and the printed texts of Cg and Cm read a passage of one line [1182*]: "And in a rage, he swiftly struck Gandhamādana with his foot."

Despite the statement in the critical apparatus that this line is found in the vulgate, it belongs properly only to the textual tradition of Cg, and thus it appears in KK (6.67.30ab) and VSP (6.67.30ab). The line appears after verse 28 in GPP (=6.67.29ab), with the notation that it is additional in the text of Cg (*idam ardham adhikam go*). In the text of the Gita Press, the verse appears as 6.67.28ef. It is not found in NSP. Because of its peculiar attestation in the printed versions of the southern text, it is rendered in the translations only of Raghunathan (1982, vol. 3, p. 180), Pagani (1999, p. 1037), and Gita Press (1969, vol. 3, p. 1622).

22. "*kiṃśuka* trees" *kiṃśukāḥ*: The red blossoms of the tree make it one of Vālmīki's favorite objects of comparison for a bleeding warrior. See 6.35.9; 6.60.34; 6.62.19; 6.67.33; 6.76.28; and notes. Cf. 6.54.11.

23. "When those . . . had fallen" *patiteṣu*: Ś2,Ñ,V,B2,D3,4,9–13,T2,3,G1,M1,2,5, and the texts and printed editions of Ct and Cr read instead the causative *pātiteṣu*, "among those struck down."

24. "And . . . mighty" *ca mahābalāḥ*: D7,9–11, and the texts and printed editions of Ct and Cr read instead *plavagarṣabhāḥ*, "bulls among leaping monkeys," a repetition of the same epithet that occurs in *pāda* b. Among the commentators who have this reading, only Cr takes note of the redundancy. He explains it by reading the two epithets as belonging to separate clauses, a relative and correlative (*śailābhā ye plavagarṣabhāḥ te plavagarṣabhāḥ śailam iva taṃ kumbhakarṇam samāruhya dadaṃśuḥ*). Most translators who follow this reading drop one of the terms. Dutt (1893, p. 1316) notes the repetition and that he has left out one of the terms from his translation.

25. "gigantic" *mahākāyam*: D6,7,9–11,T2,3, and the texts and printed editions of Ct and Cr read instead *mahābāhum*, "great-armed."

"with ... knees" *jānubhiḥ*: D7,9–11, and the texts and printed editions of Ct and Cr read instead *bāhubhiḥ*, "with their arms."

26. "who already resembled a mountain, now looked like one" *parvatopamaḥ / rarāja ... giriḥ ... iva*: Literally, "who was like a mountain, resembled a mountain."

27. "mighty *rākṣasa*" *mahābalaḥ*: Literally, "the mighty one."

28. "crammed ... until they came out" *prakṣiptāḥ ... nirjagmuḥ*: Literally, "tossed ... they came out." As indicated by our translation, we believe that the idea of the verse is that Kumbhakarṇa has stuffed so many monkeys into his mouth that they overflow through his other orifices.

"into his mouth—as wide as the underworld Pātāla" *vaktre pātālasaṃnibhe*: The phrase is identical to the one at 6.48.50. Compare 6.48.23.

"his nose and ears" *nāsāpuṭābhyām ... karṇābhyāṃ caiva*: Literally, "through two nostrils [lit., nose cavities] and two ears." Pagani (1999, p. 1038), alone among the translators, appears to read *nāsāpuṭābhyām* as a *dvandva* in the sense of "nose and eyelid," rendering, "*par le nez, les paupières, les oreilles*." This is improbable on both syntactic and semantic grounds.

29. "in his towering rage, the furious" *bhṛśasaṃkruddhaḥ ... saṃkruddhaḥ*: Literally, "extremely enraged ... enraged." The commentators ignore the redundancy.

"routed the entire monkey host" *babhañja vānarān sarvān*: Literally, "broke all the monkeys." Cg, the only commentator to address the verb *babhañja*, "he broke," construes it with the participle *bhakṣayan*, "devouring." He then interprets the phrase to mean that Kumbhakarṇa broke up the monkeys in order to eat them (*bhakṣaṇārthaṃ babhañjety arthaḥ*). This interpretation is followed by Raghunathan (1982, vol. 3, p. 180), who renders, "He crumbled up the apes in his hands to eat them." Pagani (1999, p. 1038) understands, "*il les anéantissait*." Gita Press (1969, vol. 3, p. 1623) offers, "mutilated." Others translate, simply, "broke" or "broke down." We believe, however, that the poet uses the verb $\sqrt{}$*bhañj* here in the same sense in which he has used it in the preceding *sarga* (6.54.17,24), that is, "to break up *or* rout [an army]." This reading also seems to us to better suit the syntax of the verse. Cf. note to verse 113 below. See, too, 6.44.7; 6.68.24; 6.84.13–14; 6.87.8; and notes.

30. "frenzied" *mūrcchitaḥ* [*mūrchitaḥ*—so crit. ed.]: Literally, "stupefied, in a daze." Cr, the only commentator to remark on the term, glosses, "augmented, grown great (*pravṛddhaḥ*)." This is followed by Gita Press (1969, vol. 3, p. 1623). Other translators have taken the word in a variety of its senses. Dutt (1893, p. 1317) renders, "transported with passion." Raghunathan (1982, vol. 3, p. 180) has "raging." Gorresio (1858, vol. 10, p. 28) renders, "*insano*." Roussel, followed by Shastri and Pagani, appears to ignore the term.

31. "In that battle" *tasmin*: Literally, "in that." V3,D6,9–11,T2,3, and the texts and the printed editions of Ct and Cr read instead *yuddhe*, "in the battle," while the printed editions of Cg and Cm (KK and VSP) read *saṃkhye*, "in the battle."

33. "their troops decimated and their leaders slain" *hatayūthā vināyakāḥ*: Literally, "their troops slain, their leaders gone." The term *vināyakāḥ* must be read as proposed by Cg, who glosses, "whose leaders are gone (*vigatanāyakāḥ*)," and not in its normal lexical senses of "a remover of obstacles *or* leader." D10,11, and the texts and printed editions of Ct and Cr read *plavaṅgamāḥ*, "leaping monkeys," for *vināyakāḥ*.

"loudly and discordantly" *visvaraṃ bhṛśam*: Ñ1,D10,11, and the texts and printed editions of Ct and Cr read instead *vikṛtaiḥ svaraiḥ*, "with unnatural *or* discordant sounds."

34. "despairing" *khinnacetasaḥ*: Literally, "with dejected minds." Although it is not recorded in the critical apparatus, the printed editions of Ct (GPP and NSP 5.67.41, as well as Gita Press 5.67.41) read *bhinnacetasaḥ*, "broken-hearted."

Following verse 34, D5–7,10,11,T,G1,2,M3, and the texts of the southern commentators insert a passage of eighteen lines [1186*]: "Seeing that the monkeys were routed, [Aṅgada], the son of the son of Indra, wielder of the *vajra*, swiftly charged Kumbhakarṇa in that great battle.[1–2] Seizing a huge mountain peak and roaring again and again, so as to terrify all the *rākṣasa* followers of Kumbhakarṇa, he hurled that mountain peak at Kumbhakarṇa's head.[3–5] Then, struck in the head by that mountain, [Kumbhakarṇa], Indra's foe,[1] blazed up in a towering rage.[6–7] With a mighty roar, terrifying all the monkeys, [Kumbhakarṇa] swiftly charged Vālin's furious son.[8–9] In his fury, the immensely powerful [*rākṣasa*] hurled his lance at Aṅgada.[10] But that mighty bull among monkeys, skilled in the ways of battle, saw it flying toward him and, by means of his agility, dodged it.[11–12] Then, leaping up, he struck [Kumbhakarṇa] on the chest with the palm of his hand. When the latter, who was like a mountain, was struck by him, he was beside himself with rage.[13–14] Regaining his composure, the immensely powerful *rākṣasa* clenched his fist and, with a mocking laugh, let it fly so that [Aṅgada] fell unconscious.[15–16] Once that bull among leaping monkeys had fallen to the ground unconscious, [Kumbhakarṇa] recovered his lance and charged at Sugrīva.[17–18]"

[1]"Then . . . by that mountain, [Kumbhakarṇa], Indra's foe: *śailenendraripus tadā*: D5,T1,M3, and the texts and printed editions of Cg and Cm read instead *giriśṛṅgeṇa mūrdhani*, "with the mountain peak on the head."

36. "the great monkey" *mahākapiḥ*: V3,B4,D9–11, and the texts and printed editions of Ct and Cr read instead *mahābalaḥ*, "immensely powerful."

37. "his every limb unscathed" *vivṛtasarvāṅgaḥ*: The word *vivṛta-* most commonly has the sense "manifested, clear." We understand it in the sense in which it is noted in Apte (s.v. meaning 10), that is, "unhurt, woundless." The reading of the critical edition, although well attested, does not appear in any of the texts that have served as the basis for the translations consulted. Ñ2,V,B1,3,4,D1,6,7,9–11, and the texts and printed editions of Ct, Ck, and Cr read *vivṛtta-*, normally, "turning, whirling," for *vivṛta-*, "unhurt, woundless." Translators who follow the text of Ct have generally rendered the compound as "with stretched *or* braced limbs." Ś,Ñ1,B2,D2,4,5,12,T1,M3, and the texts and printed editions of Cg and Cm read instead *vikṛta-*, "deformed, distorted." Raghunathan (1982, vol. 3, p. 181), the only translator to render this variant, translates, "his body bearing the marks of injuries all over." The critical reading, *vivṛta-*, could also be understood to mean "with all his limbs spread out *or* extended," although to us this seems to make even less sense than the meaning we have offered.

38. "huge monkeys, his body smeared with their blood" *kapiśoṇitadigdhāṅgam . . . mahākapīn*: Literally, "his body smeared with monkey-blood . . . great monkeys."

39. The four actions credited to Kumbhakarṇa are simply listed with no logical or syntactical hierarchy or subordination. Cr, the only commentator to treat this verse, structures it as follows: "You have struck down heroes and devoured troops. Therefore, you have performed an impossibly difficult feat, and for that reason you have gained the highest renown (*tvayā vīrāḥ pātitāḥ sainyāni ca bhakṣitāny ata eva suduṣkaraṃ karma kṛtam ata eva paramaṃ yaśas te tvayā prāptam*)." Translators vary in their structuring of the verse.

"our troops" *sainyāni*: Literally, "troops."

40. "common soldiers" *prākṛtaiḥ*: Literally, "with common *or* ordinary ones."

"Now try to withstand" *sahasva*: Literally, "withstand, endure." Roussel (1903, vol. 3, p. 209) has given the second half of the verse an idiosyncratic rendering that seems impossible to derive from the text. He translates, "*Contente-toi de me tuer, ô Rākshasa, toi qui as l'air d'une montagne.*" In this he has been followed by Pagani (1999, p. 1039) (same wording as Roussel). Shastri (1959, vol. 3, p. 181) appears to have rendered the Sanskrit correctly and then followed his translation with a rendering of Roussel, yielding, "Do thou seek to bear the weight of this rock I am about to hurl on thee, O Titan! Find thy satisfaction in slaying me, O Titan, thou who resemblest a mountain!"

"blow" *nipātam*: Literally, "fall, descent, attack."

41. "that speech . . . a speech" *tad vākyam*: Literally, "that speech."

42. "the grandson of Prajāpati and the son of Ṛkṣarajas" *prajāpates tu pautras tvaṃ tathaivarkṣarajaḥsutaḥ*: Several of the commentators recall the legend according to which Sugrīva is the son of the monkey Ṛkṣasrajas, who was, in turn, born from the mouth of Brahmā [Prajāpati] when he happened to yawn. Cv and Cg retell the legend of the births of Sugrīva and Vālin at some length. Reference to this episode is found at 7.36.35–39. According to Cv's and Cg's account, Ṛkṣarajas had been transformed into an *apsaras* by immersing himself, unwittingly, in a heavenly lake. In this form he aroused the lust of the gods Indra and Sūrya, who, upon touching his/her hand, shed their semen on his/her hair [*vāla*] and neck [*grīva*], respectively. From the semen thus deposited were produced, respectively, the brothers Vālin and Sugrīva. Ṛkṣarajas then regained his male simian form by immersing him/herself on Brahmā's advice in another enchanted pond. For a discussion of this theme, see R. Goldman 1993. Cv and Cg conclude by noting that other authorities derive Sugrīva's lineage differently, making him a son of Vivasvant [i.e., the sun], who was in turn a son of Prajāpati Kāśyapa. The text of Gorresio (6.46.46cd = 1187*) is a variant in which the role of the Sun in the procreation of Sugrīva is mentioned. Gorresio discusses this in his note to the passage (1858, vol. 10, p. 286, n. 17).

Dutt (1893, p. 1318) reads the name "Ṛkṣarajas" to mean "king of bears," as he had done previously, perhaps mistaking *-rajas* for *-rāja*. See note to 6.21.20 above. The same peculiarity is found in Gorresio (1858, vol. 10, p. 29), who translates, "*re degli orsi*." It is not clear why these scholars should think that the king of bears would sire a monkey. Pagani (1999, p. 1039) offers, "*roi des singes*." See R. Goldman 1989. See, too, 1.16.10; and 6.54.14 and note. Cf. note to verse 45 below.

"That is why you boast so" *tasmād garjasi*: Literally, "therefore you roar." It appears, as we have indicated in our translation, that Kumbhakarṇa thinks that Sugrīva is boastful because of his high lineage, etc., and this is how the majority of translators have interpreted the phrase. Raghunathan (1982, vol. 3, p. 181), however, understands the *rākṣasa* to be surprised to hear such boastfulness from so lofty a personage.

He translates, "[Being possessed of learning and valour,] how could you brag thus. . .?"

43. "When Sugrīva had heard" *niśamya*: Literally, "having heard."

"Indra's *vajra* or a thunderbolt" *vajrāśani-*: The terms *vajra* and *aśani* are more or less synonymous in their meanings of "lightning *or* thunderbolt" or the name of Indra's weapon. Our translation attempts to differentiate them. Apte (s.v.) defines the compound simply as "Indra's thunderbolt." The compound is used in both epics to indicate weapons that have tremendous striking force. See notes to 6.42.15; 6.45.17; 6.47.17,127; and 6.53.12. See, too, verse 121 below.

The meter is *upajāti*.

44. "against his . . . chest" *bhujāntare*: Literally, "between the arms." Cf. verses 12 and 65.

"the leaping monkeys" *plavaṅgamāḥ*: The word makes *pāda* c hypermetric. Ñ2,V1,B1–3,D1,3,5,7,9–12,T1,G1,M, and all printed editions read the metrically correct *plavaṅgāḥ*. The irregularity of the meter is not noted in the critical edition. One can only assume that the critical editors have made their choice on the basis of the *lectio difficilior*.

The meter is *upajāti*; *pāda* c is hypermetric.

45. "the apes and tawny monkeys" *haryṛkṣa-*: Most translators understand, "bears and monkeys." See 6.4.17; 6.54.14; and notes. See, too, R. Goldman 1989; and 1.16.10 and note. See note to verse 42 above.

The meter is *upajāti*.

46. "Hanumān, son of Anila" *suto 'nilasya*: Literally, "Anila's son."

"in both hands" *dorbhyām*: Literally, "with both arms."

"gold-corded" *kāñcanadāmajuṣṭam*: Literally, "equipped with golden cords." It is not clear to us exactly how or why cords are affixed to the lance, whether as ornamentation, to enhance the grip, or as a device for throwing it. Some translators render, "with chains of gold" (Gita Press 1969, vol. 3, p. 1625 and Raghunathan 1982, vol. 3, p. 181) or "with golden chains" (Dutt 1893, p. 1319). D7,9–11, and the texts and printed editions of Ct and Cr read instead *kāñcanadāmayaṣṭim*, "with golden cords and pole."

The meter is *upajāti*.

47. Cs provides a variant of this episode, which he claims is to be found in many *purāṇas* etc. (*bahupurāṇādiṣv iyaṃ kathā*). He is provoked, no doubt, by Hanumān's sudden and unheralded intervention in the duel between Sugrīva and Kumbhakarṇa to claim that the episode described here is out of place either because of scribal carelessness or because of the author's excessive eagerness to recount the heroic deeds of Hanumān. (*atra vyatyasya kathanaṃ lekhakapramādataḥ. ślokāś caite 'nantaraṃ paṭhanīyā iti vā kuryuḥ kvacic ca vyatyāsam iti kavikṛta evāyaṃ hanumatparākramakramavarṇanaparāyattacittatayā vyatyāsa iti vā jñeyam.*)

"black iron" *kālāyasam*: See 6.3.12; 6.53.12; and notes. See, too, 5.39.11; 5.51.38; and notes.

"weighing many tons" *bhārasahasrasya*: Literally, "of a thousand *bhāras*." The *bhāra*, like other units of weight in ancient Indian texts, is difficult to translate precisely into a modern unit of measure. Various texts, which do not always agree, give the weights, of course, in terms of other traditional weights. On the basis of the listing of weights in Kane and on a conjecture that the small unit *māṣa*, "black bean," is roughly equivalent to a gram, we calculate that a *bhāra* would be approximately 275 pounds. Thus one thousand of these would come to roughly 137.5 tons, a figure well within the hyperbolic range of Vālmīki and not an unreasonable weight for so gargantuan a figure as Kumbhakarṇa (Kane 1941–1975, vol. 2, p. 880, n. 2352). See Barnett (1913, p. 229), who understands a *bhāra* to be a heavy weight equal to twenty *tulās*.

"bull among leaping monkeys . . . in great excitement" *prahṛṣṭaḥ plavagarṣabhaḥ*: D7,9–11, and the texts and printed editions of Ct and Cr read instead *tadā hṛṣṭaḥ plavaṅgamaḥ*, "then the excited leaping monkey."

Following verse 47, D5–7,9–11,S insert a passage of five lines [1189*]: "When the monkey army saw that lance broken by Hanumān, they roared again and again in great delight and came running from all directions.[1–2] But the *rākṣasa* was frightened and his face downcast. In their delight, the forest-ranging [monkeys] roared like lions.[3–4] Seeing the lance in such a state, they honored Māruti.[5]"

48. "of Laṅkā's Mount Malaya" *laṅkāmalayāt*: The identity of this mountain causes some consternation among the commentators, since the well-known Mount Malaya is located in southern India, and no mountain of this name in Laṅkā has been previously mentioned. Commentators resolve the problem in one of two ways. Crā and Cg understand that there is no contradiction, for even though Kumbhakarṇa is standing on the peak of Mt. Trikūṭa in Laṅkā and Mount Malaya is in another country entirely, his gigantic body is equal to the task of reaching the distant peak (*trikūṭaśikharasthalaṅkādvāre sthitvā yudhyataḥ kumbhakarṇasya pradeśāntarasthalaṅkāmalayaśṛṅgotpāṭanaṃ katham upapadyata iti cet tadanuguṇapramāṇaśarīratvān na doṣaḥ*—so Cg). Cg provides as an alternative explanation that the term "Laṅkā's Malaya" is a metaphorical reference to Mt. Trikūṭa itself (*laṅkāmalayaśabdena trikūṭaṃ vopacaryate*). Ck and Ct understand the reference to be to a Mt. Malaya that is near Laṅkā (*laṅkāmalayāl laṅkāsamīpavartimalayāt*). On this mountain, see also note to 6.61.41.

The meter is *upajāti*.

49. "in battle . . . in battle" *yudhi . . . yudhi*: M3 and the printed editions of Cg read instead *tv atha*, "but then," for the second *yudhi*, "in battle," apparently to avoid the repetition.

"the *yātudhānas*" *yātudhānāḥ*: See 6.3.27 and note.

The meter is *upajāti*.

50. "Seizing . . . carried him off" *jahāra . . . abhipragṛhya*: Ct understands that Kumbhakarṇa places Sugrīva in his armpit and takes him from the midst of the army to another location (*abhigṛhya kakṣapuṭe kṛtvā jahāra sainyamadhyād anyadeśaṃ ināya*)."

The meter is *upendravajrā*.

51. "holding aloft" *utpāṭya*: Literally, "uprooting, tearing up." Vālmīki uses this verb frequently to indicate the uprooting of mountains, trees, etc., as at verse 48 above. In this verse and the next, however, we must understand it, as Cg suggests, in the sense of "holding aloft, raising up (*uddhṛtya*)."

"Sugrīva, who resembled a huge cloud" *mahāmeghanikāśarūpam*: Literally, "he whose form resembled a huge cloud."

"whose form rivaled that of Mount Meru, now resembled Mount Meru with a new, fearsome peak soaring above it" *rarāja merupratimānarūpo merur yathātyucchritaghoraśṛṅgaḥ*: Literally, "he, whose form was similar to Meru, shone like Meru with an extremely high and fearsome peak." Our interpretation is inspired by that of Cg, who understands that the first reference to Mount Meru serves as an object of comparison to Kumbhakarṇa's inherent form, while the second refers to his enhanced appearance as he holds the gigantic Sugrīva above him (*svākārasādṛśyāya prathamaṃ merūpādānam. dvitīyaṃ tu sugrīvadhāraṇakālikasādṛśyāya*)."

The meter is *upajāti*.

52. "The hero Kumbhakarṇa, holding Sugrīva aloft" *samutpāṭya* ... *vīraḥ*: Literally, "the hero, having held aloft." See note on *utpāṭya* at verse 51 above. D10,11,M1,2, and the texts and printed editions of Ct read instead *tam ādāya*, "having taken him," for *samutpāṭya*.

"proceeded on his way" *jagāma*: Literally, "he went." Ct understands that Kumbhakarṇa is heading back to the city and suggests that we add the name "Laṅkā" (*laṅkām iti śeṣaḥ*).

"as the *rākṣasa* lords sang his praises" *saṃstūyamānaḥ* ... *rākṣasendraiḥ*: Literally, "being praised by the *rākṣasa* lords." D9–11,T1,M1,2,5, and the texts and printed editions of Ct, Ck, and Cr read instead the nominative singular *rākṣasendraḥ* for the instrumental plural, yielding the meaning "being praised, the *rākṣasa* lord."

"the cries" *ninādam*: Literally, "the sound." As Ct and Ck note, these are cries of grief (*duḥkhajam*).

"of those who dwelt in heaven, home of the thirty gods" *tridaśālayānām*: Literally, "of those possessing the abode of the thirty." The compound is somewhat elliptical. The reference is clearly to the various denizens of heaven, the gods, seers, etc. Cg glosses, "of those possessing heaven (*svarginām*)," while Cm glosses, "of those who were located in the abode of the thirty (*tridaśālayasthānām*)." The reading *-daśa-* is marked as uncertain in the critical apparatus. Ś,Ñ,V1,B1–3,D2–13,T, and the texts and printed editions of Ck, Ct, and Cr read instead *-diva-*, yielding the compound *tridivālayānām*, "of those whose abode is the triple heaven."

The meter is *upajāti*.

53. "Indra's foe, whose valor was that of Indra ... lord of the tawny monkeys ... the equal of Indra himself" *harīndram indropamam indravīryaḥ* ... *indraśatruḥ*: Literally, "the Indra of tawny monkeys, comparable to Indra, of Indra's valor ... Indra's foe."

"out of the way ... as good as gone" *hṛte* ... *hṛtam*: Literally, "removed ... removed." Ś,Ñ,V1,2,B,D1,2,6–13,T1,M1,2, and the texts and printed editions of Ct and Cr read *hate*, "slain," for *hṛte*, while D5–7,9–11,T1, and the texts and printed editions of Ct and Cr read *hatam*, "slain, destroyed," for *hṛtam*.

The meter is *upajāti*.

56. "By all means" *sarvathā*: D9–11 and the texts and printed editions of Ct and Cr read instead *asaṃśayam*, "without a doubt."

57. The meter is *upendravajrā*.

58. "the king" *pārthivaḥ*: B2,4,D9–11, and the texts and printed editions of Ct, Ck, and Cr read instead *vānaraḥ*, "the monkey."

59. "must not yet have regained consciousness" *na tāvad ātmānaṃ budhyate*: Literally, "he does not yet know himself." Ct and Ck understand that Sugrīva does not know that he has been captured by his enemy because he is dazed (*mohavaśād ātmānaṃ pareṇa gṛhītaṃ na budhyata iti*).

61. "it would incur his most severe displeasure, as his reputation would be forever tarnished" *aprītiś ca bhavet kaṣṭā kīrtināśaś ca śāśvataḥ*: Literally, "[of him] there would be harmful displeasure and eternal destruction of fame." Compare this sentiment with

that expressed by Sītā to Hanumān at 5.35.57, where she argues that Rāma himself must rescue her.

62. "I shall wait... until our king's valor is recouped" *kāṅkṣiṣye vikramaṃ pārthivasya naḥ*: Literally, "I shall await the valor of our king." Ct fleshes out the elliptical phrase by adding the words "[until] I shall witness the valor (*vikramaṃ tu drakṣyāmīti śeṣaḥ*)." V3,D10,11, and the texts and printed editions of Ct read *mokṣitasya*, "once he is freed," for *pārthivasya*, "of [our] king."

63. "halted the flight" *saṃstambhayāmāsa*: Literally, "he immobilized." The idea, as expressed by Cg, is that Hanumān has halted or turned back the army from its flight (*gamanān nivartayāmāsa*).

64. "As he did so, he was strewn" *avakīryamāṇaḥ*: Literally, "being strewn." D7,9–11, and the texts and printed editions of Ct and Cr read instead *abhipūjyamānaḥ*, "being honored." Translations that follow the text of Ct render this variant. Because of the mention of "showers of blossoms," however, most of these translations also add a word like "shower, strewn," etc.

"and at the gates of the buildings on the main thoroughfares" *-caryāgṛhagopura-*: The compound could also be read to mean "on the houses on the main thoroughfares and on gateway towers." See 6.47.32 and note, where the compound and its possible interpretations are discussed in detail.

The meter is *upajāti*.

Following verse 64, D5–7,9–11,S insert a passage of two lines [1192*]: "As he was being sprinkled with showers of parched grain and perfumed water and because of the coolness of the royal highway, the mighty [monkey] gradually regained consciousness."

65. "still held in the arms" *bhujāntarasthaḥ*: Literally, "located within the arms." Cf. notes to verses 12 and 44 above.

"of the much stronger *rākṣasa*" *balīyasaḥ*: Literally, "of the stronger one."

"the great monkey" *mahātmā*: Literally, "the great one."

The meter is *upendravajrā*.

*66. "how in the world can I now strike back" *kathaṃ nu nāma śakyaṃ mayā saṃpratikartum adya*: The sequence *saṃprati* + *kartum* is printed in two ways in the various editions consulted. The critical edition, as well as GPP (6.67.85) and Gita Press (6.67.85), insert a space between *saṃprati* and *kartum*, whereas NSP (6.67.85), KK (6.67.86), VSP (6.67.86), and Gorresio (6.46.71) do not, reading instead *saṃpratikartum*. The former would yield the meaning "How shall I now act?" whereas the latter yields "How shall I strongly retaliate?" The commentators support the latter, and, to our way of thinking, preferable reading, and we have emended and translated accordingly. Cg and Cv, evidently aware of the alternative reading, further observe that, if one accepts it, then the adverb *saṃprati*, "now," becomes redundant in light of the adverb *adya*, "now, today." (*saṃpratikartuṃ samyakpratikartum. anyathādyepi punar uktiḥ syāt*—so Cg.) Manuscripts, of course, do not make a distinction between the two readings. Roussel (1903, vol. 3, p. 210), followed by Shastri (1959, vol. 3, p. 183) and Pagani (1999, p. 1040), translates as if the words were separate.

The meter is *upajāti*.

67. "Suddenly grasping the foe of Indra, lord of the immortal gods, with his fingertips, the king of the tawny monkeys rent his ears with his claws and his nose with his fangs. Then he slashed Kumbhakarṇa along his flanks." *tataḥ karāgraiḥ sahasā*

sametya rājā harīṇām amarendraśatroḥ / nakhaiś ca karṇau daśanaiś ca nāsāṃ dadaṃśa pārśveṣu ca kumbhakarṇam //: The verse is elliptical and somewhat confusing both in the critical text and its variants. A literal rendering would be: "Then, suddenly coming together with his fingertips, the king of the tawny monkeys bit with his nails the ears and with his fangs the nose of the enemy of Indra and [he bit] Kumbhakarṇa on his sides." The critical text presents a number of problems for the translator. The first of these is the seeming redundancy between the terms *karāgraiḥ*, "fingertips," and *nakhaiḥ*, "nails, claws." The second is the difficulty in interpreting the gerund *sametya*, whose normal meaning is "having joined with *or* come together." Finally, the syntax is awkward. The verse contains only one finite verb, *dadaṃśa*, "he bit," which has to serve not only for the act of biting but also for the act of scratching. This verb, then, must serve a dual role, taking as its objects both Kumbhakarṇa, on the one hand, and Kumbhakarṇa's ears and nose, on the other.

The readings of the southern commentators attempt to address some of these difficulties, while the commentators seek to explain away the others. D10,11,M3, and the texts and printed editions of the southern commentators substitute the adjective *kharaiś ca*, "and with sharp [objects]," for *nakhaiś ca*, "and with claws," of *pāda* c. This enables them to take *karāgraiḥ*, "fingertips," in *pāda* a, as a kenning for "claws," reading the two words together as "with his sharp claws." The north substitutes the finite verb *cakarta*, "he cut *or* scratched," for the critical text's *nakhaiś ca*, yielding the sense "he cut *or* tore with his claws."

Ct proposes supplying an additional finite verb *luluñca*, "he tore *or* he tore out," to indicate the action Sugrīva performs with his claws on Kumbhakarṇa's ears. Cr proposes taking, as we have done, *dadaṃśa*, "he bit," generically in the sense of "he tore (*vidārayāmāsa*)." This option is adopted also by northern manuscripts, which substitute *dadāra*, "he tore," for *dadaṃśa*.

D6,7,9–11,T2,3, and the texts and printed editions of Ct and Cr substitute *dadaṃśa pādair vidadāra pārśvau*, "he bit and rent his flanks with his feet," or a close variant for *pāda* d, providing an additional finite verb, *vidadāra*, "he tore," to describe what Sugrīva does to Kumbhakarṇa's flanks. Ct glosses the somewhat awkward plural *pādaiḥ*, "feet," with *pādanakhaiḥ*, "claws of the feet, toenails." Cg and Cm, who do not read with Ct, nonetheless suggest adding the phrase "he tore with his feet (*pādābhyāṃ vidadāreti śeṣaḥ*)." By *pārśveṣu*, Cg, Cm, and Cv (damaged) understand, "the cheeks, the shoulders, and the sides of the abdomen (*pārśveṣu kapolayor aṃsayor udarapārśvayoś ca*)."

We have construed the gerund *sametya*, "having come together," with the instrumental *karāgraiḥ* to indicate that Sugrīva, having lain passive in the grasp of Kumbhakarṇa, now suddenly revives and clutches at his adversary. Commentators have struggled with this word as well. Cr reads it to mean "having reflected in this fashion (*evaṃ vicārya*)," referring to Sugrīva's thoughts in the previous verse. Cg and Cm gloss, "having ruined *or* destroyed (*saṃhṛtya*)," which is what they think Sugrīva has done to Kumbhakarṇa's ears with his claws. The north avoids this problem by substituting *ūrdhvam etya*, "having gone *or* risen up." This is rendered by Gorresio (1858, vol. 10, p. 31) as "*levatosi*." Translators vary in their understanding of the gerund. Dutt (1893, p. 1320) renders, "advancing." Gita Press (1969, vol. 3, p. 1627), following Cr, translates, "Reaching this conclusion." Roussel (1903, vol. 3, p. 211), followed by Shastri (1959, vol. 3, p. 183) and Pagani (1999, p. 1040), renders "*s'attaquant*."

"the foe of Indra, lord of the immortal gods" *amarendraśatroḥ*: Literally, "of the enemy of the lord [Indra] of the immortals." The partitive genitive must construe with the ears and nose (*karṇau ... nāsam*) of *pāda* c. We have modified the syntax somewhat for the sake of clarity. D7,T1,G,M3, and the texts and printed editions of Cg and Cm read instead the accusative *amarendraśatrum*.

The meter is *upajāti*.

68. "bruised" *vimarditaś ca*: D10,11, and the texts and printed editions of Ct and Cr read instead *radair nakhaiś ca*, "[wounded] by fangs and claws."

The meter is *upajāti*.

69. "with terrible force" *bhīmabala-*: An alternate way to take the compound is to read it with Cr as a *bahuvrīhi*, in the sense of "he of fearsome strength," describing Kumbhakarṇa (*bhīmabalena kumbhakarṇena*).

"jumping up, swiftly" *vegavad abhyupetya*: D7,10,11, and the texts and printed editions of Ct and Cr read instead *kandukavaj javena*, "[bouncing up] quickly like a ball."

"by the *rākṣasas*, the foes of the gods" *surāribhiḥ*: Literally, "by the foes of the gods."

The meter is *upendravajrā*.

70. "gushing blood" *śoṇitotsiktaḥ* : Literally, "overflowing with blood."

"covered with waterfalls" *prasravaṇaiḥ*, Literally, "with streams *or* waterfalls."

Following verse 70, D5–7,9–11,S insert a passage of eight lines [1195*]: "The mighty,[1] gigantic, and fearsome-looking *rākṣasa*, drenched with blood, turned back and resolved to do battle once more.[2][1–2] In his rage, Rāvaṇa's younger brother, who was like a mass of black collyrium, resembled, as the blood gushed from him, a storm cloud at sunset.[3][3–4] When Sugrīva had escaped, the enemy of Indra, king of the gods, raced back once more to battle, in a rage. Then that fearsome warrior, reflecting, 'I don't have a weapon,' took up a dreadful war hammer.[4][5–8]"

[1]"mighty" *mahābalaḥ*: D6,9–11,T2,3,G1,3,M5, and the texts and printed editions of Ct and Cr read instead *niśācaraḥ*, "the night-roaming [*rākṣasa*]."

[2]"once more" *bhūyaḥ*: D6,9–11,G2,3, and the texts and printed editions of Ct and Cr read instead *bhīmaḥ*, "fearsome."

[3]D9–11 and the texts and printed editions of Ct read line 2 after line 4.

[4]Lines 5–8 constitute an *upajāti* verse.

71. "great" *mahātmā*: D5,T1,M3, and the texts and printed editions of Cg and Gita Press read instead *mahaujāḥ*, "of immense strength."

"blazing" *pradīptaḥ*: D9–11 and the texts and printed editions of Ct and Cr read instead *pravṛddhaḥ*, "increased, grown great."

Following 71ab, D7,T2,3,G2, and KK (in brackets following 6.67.94ab) insert a passage of two lines [1196*]: "In that form, enraged, he suddenly smashed with his foot and with blows of his fist..."

The meter is *upajāti*.

72. "in his madness" *mohāt*: Literally, "out of delusion." Ct and Ck explain that Kumbhakarṇa has lost all self-control because of his intoxication from drinking blood (*madyādineva raktapānajamadavaivaśyād iti bhāvaḥ*). Cr glosses, "because of a lack of discrimination (i.e., indiscriminately) (*avivekād dhetoḥ*)."

"*piśācas*" *piśacān*: *Piśācas* are yet another class of demons. This appears to be the first mention of their service in Rāvaṇa's ranks. At 5.5.24 there is mention of a *piśāca* named Karāla who has a mansion in Laṅkā, although in the context, it is possible that the term is used as the proper name of a *rākṣasa*. See 6.47.18 and note, where a *rākṣasa* by the name of Piśāca is mentioned. Cf. note to 6.49.10.

"apes" *ṛkṣān*: See note to verses 42 and 45 above.

The meter is *upajāti*.

Following verse 72, D5–7,9–11,S insert a passage of two lines in the *upendrvajrā* meter [1198*]: "He devoured the principal tawny monkeys, just as Death wreaks destruction at the end of a cosmic age."

73. "or more" *bahūn*: Literally, "many."

74. Following verse 74, D5–7,9–11,S insert a passage of three lines [1200*]: "In a towering rage, Kumbhakarṇa raced onward, devouring monkeys. Sweeping them up in his arms, in groups of seven and eight hundred and even in groups of two or three thousand,[1] he ran about devouring them."

[1]"two or three thousand" *śatāni...viṃśat triṃśat tathaiva ca*: Literally, "hundreds...twenty and thirty." In keeping with the general hyperbole of the Kumbhakarṇa episode, we construe the numbers twenty and thirty with hundreds, just as we have done with the numbers seven and eight.

Lines 2 and 3 repeat or closely paraphrase 6a and 7b–d above.

Following 1200*, D7,10,11,G2, and the texts and printed editions of Ct and Cr (Gita Press 6.67.99; KK [in brackets] as 6.67.102; GPP 6.67.99; and NSP 6.67.99) insert an additional passage of four lines [1201*]: "With his sharp fangs, his body smeared with fat, marrow, and blood, and, with garlands of tangled entrails hanging about his ears, Kumbhakarṇa, like Kāla himself, grown powerful at the end of a cosmic era, showered down[1] lances."

[1]"Kumbhakarṇa...showered down" *vavarṣa*: Literally, "he showered down."

The meter is *upajāti*.

76. Following verse 76, D7,10,11,G1, and the texts and printed editions of Ct and Cr (Gita Press 6.67.102–114; KK [in brackets] as 6.67.105–117; KK (1905 edition) [in brackets] 6.67.101–113; GPP 6.67.102–114; and NSP 6.67.102–114) insert a passage of twenty-six lines [App. I, No. 35]: "Although he was stricken, the *rākṣasa* removed that missile.[1] Then the mighty increaser of Sumitrā's joy grew angry.[1–2] With his arrows, he covered Kumbhakarṇa's[2] splendid, shining armor, made of *jāmbūnada* gold, as does Māruta a cloud at twilight.[3][3–4] Enveloped by those arrows with their golden ornamentation, Kumbhakarṇa, who looked like a mass of black collyrium, resembled the many-rayed sun enveloped in clouds.[4][5–6] Then that fearsome *rākṣasa*, his voice like the sound of a mass of thunderclouds, contemptuously addressed these words to the increaser of Sumitrā's joy.[7–8] 'By fearlessly fighting with me in battle, who easily defeated in combat even Yama himself, the ender of all things, you have proven your valor.[9–10] For anyone who could stand before me when I

have a weapon in hand in a great battle, as if before Death himself, is deserving of honor. How much more so someone who could actually offer me combat?[11–12] For not even Lord Śakra himself, mounted on Airāvata and surrounded by all the immortal gods, has ever stood before me.[13–14] I am pleased by the valor you, a mere boy, have shown this day, Saumitri. Letting you go, I wish now to go to Rāghava.[15–16] Since I have been pleased by your valor, strength, and energy in battle, I wish to kill only Rāma. For once he has been slain, all the rest will be slain as well.[5] [17–18] Once I have slain Rāma, I will have my murderous army fight any that remain standing in battle.'[19–20] When the *rākṣasa* had spoken these words mingled with praise, Saumitri, smiling slightly, responded with these fearsome words on the battlefield.[21–22] 'It is true enough that, once you display your valor,[6] you cannot be withstood*[7] by Śakra and the other gods. It is not other than you say, hero, for today we have witnessed your prowess.[23–24] Nonetheless, here stands Rāma Dāśarathi, immovable as a mountain.' But when the night-roaming *rākṣasa* had heard those words, he paid no heed to Lakṣmaṇa.[25–26]"

[1]"removed that missile" *astraṃ tu viśeṣam*: The phrase is elliptical and obscure. It would appear to mean "that peculiar *or* specific missile." We agree with Ct and Cr, who, however, take the adjective *viśeṣa* to mean "whose remainder has departed (*vigataśeṣam*)," fleshing out the phrase with the finite verb *cakāra*, "he made *or* did." This gives the phrase the sense: "He made that weapon such that it had no remainder." The idea is that he removed it completely.

[2]"Kumbhakarṇa's" *asya*: Literally, "his."

[3]"as does Māruta a cloud at twilight" *saṃdhyābhram iva mārutaḥ*: Literally, "like Māruta a twilight-cloud." The simile seems defective in that it is not clear how the wind [Māruta] is supposed to cover or obscure a cloud.

[4]"Enveloped . . . Kumbhakarṇa, who looked like a mass of black collyrium, resembled the many-rayed sun enveloped in clouds" *nīlāñjanacayaprakhyaḥ . . . āpīḍyamānaḥ śuśubhe meghaiḥ sūrya ivāṃśumān*: Literally, "he, being closely pressed *or* garlanded, resembled the many-rayed sun [being garlanded] by clouds." The simile seems inverted, since the dark Kumbhakarṇa, surrounded by the golden arrows, is compared to the brilliant sun surrounded by dark clouds.

[5]"For, once he has been slain, all the rest will be slain as well." *yasmin hate hatam*: Literally, "who when slain . . . it is slain." We follow Cr in fleshing out this elliptical phrase with the words "the whole army (*nikhilaṃ sainyam iti śeṣaḥ*)." This same idea is expressed less elliptically at verse 53c above.

[6]"once you display your valor" *prāpya pauruṣam*: Literally, "having acquired strength *or* valor."

*[7]"cannot be withstood" *asahyam*: The reading of the critical edition, which requires one to construe the adjective with *pauruṣam*, "valor," is probably a typographical error. Printed editions that have this line read the nominative masculine singular *asahyaḥ*, which must then modify *tvam*, "you," a reference to Kumbhakarṇa himself. The only variant (G1) shown in the critical apparatus supports the reading of the printed editions of GPP, NSP, and KK. We have emended accordingly.

77. "seeming as he did so to tear up" *dārayann iva*: Literally, "tearing as it were." Ś,D8–12,T2,3,G3, and the texts and printed editions of Ct and Cr read instead

kampayann iva, "as if making [the earth itself] tremble." The first two syllables of the word *dārayann* are marked as doubtful.

78. "invoking the divine weapon-spell of Rudra" *raudram astraṃ prayojayan*: Literally, "employing the *raudra astra*." The *raudra* appears to be one of the divine weapon-spells or magical weapons of which Rāma is said to be the master. It is not named, however, in the list of divine weapons that Viśvāmitra conferred upon Rāma at *Bālakāṇḍa* 26. Such weapons are invoked mentally, and their power may then be invested in an ordinary arrow or even in such benign-seeming objects as a blade of grass. See, for example, 5.36.26–27 and notes. It is unlikely that, as some translators have understood, the *raudra* weapon is an actual bow. See note to 115 below. See, too, 6.87.33–34; 6.88.2; and notes.

79. "wounded" *viddhasya*: Literally, "pierced, hurt."

Following verse 79, D5–7,9–11,S insert a passage of two lines [1202*]: "Wounded by Rāma's divinely charged weapons, the bull among *rākṣasas* ran about in a towering rage bellowing frightfully and putting the tawny monkeys to flight in the battle."

80. "fletched with peacock feathers" *barhiṇavāsasaḥ*: Literally, "with peacock feathers for clothing." Cf. 6.35.12.

"massive mace . . . fell to the ground" *papātorvyāṃ mahāgadā*: D9–11,T2,3, and the texts and printed editions of Ct and Cr read instead *gadā corvyāṃ papāta ha*, "his mace fell to the ground."

Following verse 80, D5–7,9–11,S insert a passage of one line [1205*]: "And all his weapons were scattered over the ground."

81. "immensely powerful *rākṣasa*" *mahābalaḥ*: Literally, "the immensely powerful one."

"and his feet" *caraṇābhyāṃ ca*: B1,D5,7–11, and the texts and printed editions of Ct and Cr read instead *ca karābhyāṃ ca*, "and with his [open] hands."

82. "as a mountain does its waterfalls" *giriḥ prasravaṇān iva*: D7,G1,2,M3,5, and the texts and printed editions of Ct and Cg read instead *giriḥ prasravaṇaṃ yathā*, "as a mountain does a waterfall"

83. "suffused . . . covered" *mūrcchitaḥ*[*mūrchitaḥ*—so crit. ed.]: The adjective normally means "dazed, stupefied, etc.," and several translators have rendered it in this fashion. It is difficult, however, to read this sense with both "rage (*kopena*)" and "blood (*rudhireṇa*)." We have therefore followed the suggestion of Cg and Cr, who understand the term in its other meaning of "filled, pervaded with (*vyāptaḥ*)."

Following verse 83, D5–7,9–11,S insert a passage of eight lines [1207*]: "Then that mighty *rākṣasa*[1] of fearsome valor, who resembled Yama, the ender of all things, brandished a fearsome mountain peak and hurled it toward Rāma.[1–2] But Rāma nocked seven straight-flying arrows to his bow and, with them, cut that mountain peak to pieces in midair before it ever reached him.[3–4] Righteous Rama, bull among men,[2] cut that immense mountain peak to pieces with arrows whose shafts were variegated with gold.[5–6] Shining with splendor, resembling the peak of Mount Meru,[3] it felled two hundred of the monkey leaders[4] as it fell.[7–8]"

[1]"that mighty *rākṣasa*" *balavān*: Literally, "mighty one."

[2]"bull among men" *puruṣarṣabhaḥ*: D7,9–11, and the texts and printed editions of Ct read instead *bharatāgrajaḥ*, "the older brother of Bharata."

[3]"resembling the peak of Mount Meru" *meruśikharākāram*: Literally, "having the form of the peak of Meru." D10,G3, and the texts and printed editions of Ct read instead the instrumental plural *meruśikharākāraiḥ*, which would make the adjective modify the arrows (*śaraiḥ*) in line 6.

[4]"of the monkey leaders" *vānarendrāṇām*: D9–11 and the texts and printed editions of Ct and Gita Press (6.67.126) read instead *vānarāṇāṃ ca*, "and of the monkeys."

84. "intent" *yuktaḥ*: Literally, "engaged, focused." Cr, the only commentator to remark on this term, glosses, "who had been earlier assigned [this task] by Rāma (*pūrvaṃ rāmeṇa niyuktaḥ*)."

"many methods of doing so" *yogān . . . bahūn*: Literally, "many means."

85. "He cannot distinguish between" *na vijānāti*: Literally, "He does not recognize."

"his allies and his enemies alike" *svān parāṃś caiva*: Literally, "his own and the others as well."

86. "Very well" *sādhu*: We understand the term here as an interjection, a sense in which it is often used in the literature. In the present context, the idea seems to be that, after deliberating over the various possible means of killing Kumbhakarṇa, as indicated in verse 84 above, Lakṣmaṇa has now decided upon this one. The expression here is thus similar to the English expression "I have it!" or "I know!" Most translators, following Cr, have tended to read the term adverbially as a description of how the monkeys should climb upon Kumbhakarṇa. Translations are various, including "straight" (Gita Press 1969, vol. 3, p. 1631), "putting forth their best" (Dutt 1893, p. 1324), and "*bravement*" (Roussel 1903, vol. 3, p. 213). Roussel is followed by Shastri (1959, vol. 3, p. 185), who translates, "courageously," and Pagani (1999, p. 1043), who renders, "*vaillamment*." Raghunathan (1982, vol. 3, p. 186) translates it adjectivally as "[all] able [monkeys]." Gorresio (1858, vol. 10, p. 31) appears to render, "*Or*."

87. "Then" *api*: The particle is used here in verse-initial position as a marker of a change of subject. V3,B2,D2,6,7,9–11,T2,3, and the texts and printed editions of Ct and Cr read instead *adya*, "today."

"falling to the ground" *prapatan . . . bhūmau*: D9–11 and the texts and printed editions of Ct and Cr read instead *pracaran*, "moving about." This yields the sense of "moving about [the battle]ground."

"will not kill any more of the leaping monkeys" *nānyān hanyāt plavaṅgamān*: Literally, "he would not kill other leaping monkeys." For reasons unclear to us, Roussel (1903, vol. 3, p. 213) appears to misread the nominative singular *rākṣasaḥ* (for which the critical apparatus shows no variants) in *pāda* c as an accusative plural (perhaps reading *rakṣasaḥ*). This leads him to the erroneous translation, "*massacrera les Rākshasas, et non plus les autres, les Plavangamas*." In this he has regrettably been followed by Shastri (1959, vol. 3, p. 185), who renders, "will annihilate the titans and not the monkeys" and Pagani (1999, p. 1043), who translates, "*ne pourra . . . tuer que les rākṣasa et non pas les autres, les singes*."

88. "the leaping monkeys" *plavaṅgamāḥ*: B2,3,D9–11,G3, and the texts and printed editions of Ct read instead *mahābalāḥ*, "very powerful ones."

89. "riders mounted on his back" *hastipān*: Literally, "elephant keepers." The term generally applies to elephant drivers or riders (Apte s.v.).

90. "This *rākṣasa* is infuriated" *ruṣṭo 'yam iti rākṣasaḥ*: The placement of the word *rākṣasaḥ* after the quotation marker *iti*, is somewhat irregular, but this practice is not

utterly unknown to Vālmīki. Cv informs us that we should read the *iti* after *rākṣasaḥ* (*ruṣṭo 'yam iti rākṣasa iti. atretiśabda . . . yojyaḥ*). D9–11 and Ct seek to avoid this awkwardness by reading the accusative *rākṣasam* for the nominative *rākṣasaḥ*. In this case the quote becomes "He is infuriated," while *rākṣasa* becomes the explicit object of the verb "sprang toward (*samutpapāta*)" of *pāda* c. D5,9,T1,M3, and the texts and printed editions of Cg read *duṣṭaḥ*, "vicious," for *ruṣṭaḥ*, "infuriated." Raghunathan (1982, vol. 3, p. 186), alone among the translators, appears to follow this reading, rendering, "The Rākshasa runs berserk."

Following verse 90, D5–7,9–11,S insert a passage of three lines [1211*]: "His eyes red with rage, swift and heroic[1] Rāghava rushed swiftly upon the *rākṣasa*, burning him up, as it were, with his gaze. In so doing, he cheered all the troop leaders, who had been battered by the forces of Kumbhakarṇa."

[1]"heroic" *vīraḥ*: D9–11 and the texts and printed editions of Ct read instead *dhīraḥ*, "steadfast."

91. "quiver of arrows" *-tūṇabāṇaḥ*: Given this word order, one would have to take the final members of the compound as a *dvandva* and understand, "with [his splendid] quiver and arrows [fastened on him]." We prefer to follow the suggestion of Cg, who reads the final member as *paranipāta* (*nibaddhottamabāṇatūṇa ity arthaḥ*). This gives the compound the sense of a genitive *tatpuruṣa*, "quiver [full] of arrows."

The meter is *upajāti*.

Following verse 91, Ś,Ñ2,B2,D2,8,9,12,T2,3, and the text of Gita Press (in a footnote following its verse 142 [1969, vol. 3, pp. 1632–33]) insert a passage of twenty-one lines [App. I, No. 36]. According to the critical editors, the passage is known to the second edition of KK (1930) (in brackets following 6.67.145 = crit. ed. 6.55.98), but the passage is not found in the 1913 edition of KK. The translation of this passage appears only in Gita Press (as noted above) and in Raghunathan (1982, vol. 3, pp. 186–87) in brackets. Gita Press notes that this passage is known to only a few manuscripts, while Raghunathan (1982, vol. 3, p. 630), in his note to the *sarga*, remarks that this is one of the two passages in this *sarga* "as to the authenticity of which there is difference of opinion." See verse 76 above for the other passage to which Raghunathan refers. However, both Gita Press and Raghunathan place the passage between verses 98 and 99 of the critical edition. This placement differs from that indicated in the critical apparatus and is not marked as an alternative placement for any manuscript consulted in the collation of the critical apparatus. Since this passage is not part of the standard vulgate text, and is, despite Raghunathan's belief that it is "quite in consonance with what the poet says of Kumbhakarna" (p. 630), seemingly at odds with the tenor of the *rākṣasa*'s characterization, we believe it to be a late Vaiṣṇava interpolation. The following is a summary of the passage: In the midst of the battle between Rāma and Kumbhakarṇa, the latter's brother, Vibhīṣaṇa, appears on the scene, mace in hand, acting on Rāma's behalf. Kumbhakarṇa addresses him, urging him to abandon any tenderness for him, his brother, and to rely on the code of the warrior to strike him down in battle in order to please Rāma.[1–5] Kumbhakarṇa then praises Vibhīṣaṇa, claiming that his actions in defecting to Rāma have served the *rākṣasas*. He states that Vibhīṣaṇa is the only *rākṣasa* in the world who is a protector of truth and righteousness. He further states that no calamity ever befalls those who are devoted to truth and prophesizes that Vibhīṣaṇa alone will survive to carry on the *rākṣasa* dynasty. He then states that, through the grace of Rāma, Vibhīṣaṇa will become king of the *rākṣasas*.[6–10] Kumbhakarṇa warns Vibhīṣaṇa, however, that he should steer clear of him, since, in his own frenzy of battle, he is unable to distinguish between his allies and his enemies. It is his duty, he continues, to protect his younger brother [Vibhīṣaṇa].[11–14] Upon hearing Kumbhakarṇa's words, Vibhīṣaṇa responds, saying that he had spoken earlier in the assembly in order to save the *rākṣasa* race, but, since none of the *rākṣasas* would heed him, he defected to Rāma.[15–18] He begs Kumbhakarṇa to forgive him for his actions, whether they be good or evil. Then, his eyes filled with tears, Vibhīṣaṇa retires to a secluded spot and broods about the coming destruction [of his family].[19–21]

92. "invincible" *paramadurjayaḥ*: D6,9–11,T2,3,G3, and the texts and printed editions of Ct and Cr read the instrumental plural *paramadurjayaiḥ* for the critical edition's nominative singular, thus making the adjective apply to the monkey troops rather than to Rāma.

"Rāma" *rāmaḥ*: D9–11 and the texts and printed editions of Ct and Cr read instead *vīraḥ*, "the hero."

"continued to advance" *sampratasthe*: Literally, "he advanced, set forth."

93–96. These verses consist largely of a string of descriptive adjectives modifying Kumbhakarṇa. They can equally well serve as the objects of *dadarśa*, "he gazed upon," in 93a, as Cg suggests, whom we follow, or as the objects of the gerund *dṛṣṭvā*, "having gazed upon," in 97a, as Cr proposes.

"mighty" *mahābalam*: D7, GPP, and Gita Press read the nominative *mahābalaḥ* for the accusative, thus making the adjective apply to Rāma instead of Kumbhakarṇa. Only Gita Press (1969, vol. 3, p. 1632) translates this variant.

"whose every limb was drenched with blood" *śoṇitāplutasarvāṅgam*: A number of manuscripts, with some variations, and the texts and printed editions of Ct and Cr read instead *śoṇitāvṛtaraktākṣam* [Gita Press = *śoṇitāplutaraktākṣam*], "his eyes reddened and covered [bathed] in blood." The translator of Gita Press and Dutt read the compound as a *dvandva*: "with his body drenched in blood, and with blood-shot eyes" (Dutt 1893, p. 1324), and "bathed in blood, his eyes red (with fury)" (Gita Press 1969, vol. 3, p. 1632).

"He spewed . . . pouring" *sravantam*: Literally, "streaming."

"Drenched with blood, he lapped it up with his tongue." *jihvayā parilihyantaṃ śoṇitaṃ śoṇitokṣitam*: Literally, "licking blood with his tongue [and] drenched with blood." The printed texts of Ct (NSP, GPP, and Gita Press) read instead *sṛkkiṇī śoṇitokṣite*. This gives the half verse the sense "licking with his tongue the blood-drenched corners of his mouth." D5,T1,M3, and the printed editions of Cg and Cm read *śoṇitekṣaṇam*, "with bloody eyes," for *śoṇitokṣitam*, "drenched with blood." This reading is rendered by Raghunathan (1982, vol. 3, p. 186) as "with bloodshot eyes."

"he resembled Yama, who brings time itself to an end" *kālāntakayamopamam*: Literally, "comparable to Yama, Kāla, the ender." The three-member *karmadhāraya* compound is awkward. Normally we leave untranslated the term *kāla*, "Time *or* Doom," when it serves as an epithet or synonym of Yama, but here we render the last two terms as a *tatpuruṣa* because of the additional third term and for the sake of readability. Cg offers as a second alternative that we read *kāla-*, "time," to refer to the time of universal destruction at the end of a cosmic era (*kāle yugāntakāle 'ntako nāśako yama upamā yasya sa tathoktaḥ*), lending the compound the sense "comparable to Yama, who is the ender, that is, the destroyer, at the time of the end of a cosmic era." Cg's first explanation is that, because of the different aspects or conditions of the one individual [Kumbhakarṇa], he is compared to two different aspects of Śiva—that is, as Kāla, or the three-eyed Rudra, and Antaka, that is, the destroyer of Tripura, the triple citidel of the *asuras* (*rudras trinetras tripurāntako vetivat. ekasyaivāvasthābhedāt kālādinā-mabhedaḥ*). Cm and Crā echo this view, and Ct quotes Cm. See 6.21.26 and note. Cf. 6.59.73 and notes for a discussion of Tripura.

98. "at the sound of his bow... it" *cāpanirghoṣāt...ghoṣam*: Literally, "because of the sound of the bow... the sound."

"that bull among *rākṣasas*, sons of chaos" *nairṛtarṣabhaḥ*: Literally, "the bull among *nairṛtas*." Ś,B1,2,D5,7,9–13,T1,M3, and the texts and printed editions of the southern commentators read instead *rākṣasarṣabhaḥ*, "the bull among *rākṣasas*."

99. "his arms like the splendid coils of the king of great serpents" *bhujaṅga-rājottamabhogabāhum*: Ct identifies the king of serpents as Śeṣa. D9–11,T2, and the texts and printed editions of Ct, Ck, and Cr read the nominative *-bāhuḥ* for the critical edition's accusative, *-bāhum*. This reading makes the compound a description of Rāma rather than of Kumbhakarṇa.

"the wind" *vāta-*: D9–11 and the texts and printed editions of Ct and Cr read the somewhat awkward *dhārā-*, "stream, torrent." Translations that follow the text of Ct have, in any case, generally translated "wind *or* storm."

The meter is *upendravajrā*.

100. "Don't lose heart now" *āgaccha... mā viṣādam*: The literal meaning of this phrase would normally be, "Do not come to despondency," i.e., "Do not despair." However, the seeming inappropriateness of this advice in this particular context has inspired the commentators to offer a variety of ingenious interpretations and has led the translators, in many cases, either to ignore the context or force the language. The exact intention of Rāma's words here is not completely clear. We believe that Rāma, fearing that Kumbhakarṇa may have been weakened or worn down by his conflicts with the monkeys, may hesitate to give him battle. Thus he is exhorting him to pluck up his courage to stand and fight. Cv proposes that we break up the sequence *māviṣādam* as *mā aviṣādam* (rather than *mā viṣādam*). This could be taken to lend the phrase the sense of "do not be non-despondent," that is, "don't be too cocky [since you now face me, Rāma]." It is apparent, however, from the remarks of Cm and Cg (first alternative), who tend to follow Cv's interpretation, that we are intended to take *mā* not as the prohibitive particle but rather as the enclitic form of the first person singular accusative pronoun *mām*, and then read *aviṣādam* as a *bahuvrīhi* compound modifying that pronoun. This yields the sense "Come to me, who am free from despondency [i.e., cheerful, confident]." Ck and Ct understand that Rāma is exhorting Kumbhakarṇa not to despair (*mā viṣādam āgaccha*) because it is Rāma that he faces. This appears to lend the verse a soteriological meaning, in that Kumbhakarṇa will attain salvation through death at the hands of Lord Rāma, although neither commentator makes this explicit. Cr offers a similar interpretation, arguing that Rāma is telling Kumbhakarṇa not to be despondent over the destruction of his race, since it is I [Rāma], who stand here, bow in hand (*sa tvaṃ viṣādaṃ svakulavidhvaṃsajanitakhedaṃ mā gaccha prāpnuhi yataḥ pragṛhī-tacāpo 'ham avasthitaḥ*). Cg offers, as his second interpretation, the notion that Rāma is

telling Kumbhakarṇa to give up, through death, the torments of the burden of his body (*yadvā viṣādaṃ mā gaccha maraṇena śarīrabharaṇakleśaṃ tyajety arthaḥ*).

Translators generally offer one of two interpretations. The first is that Kumbhakarṇa should not be afflicted with grief or despair (Dutt 1893, p. 1325; Gita Press 1969, vol. 3, p. 1633; and Raghunathan 1982, vol. 3, p. 187). The second, first given by Roussel (1903, vol. 3, p. 214) and followed by Shastri (1959, vol. 3, p. 186) and Pagani (1999, p. 1044), forces the sense of *viṣāda* to mean "tremble," thus yielding "do not tremble."

"foe of Śakra . . . Rāma" *śakrasapatna rāmam*: D9–11 and the texts and printed editions of Ct and Cr read instead the hypermetric *rākṣasavaṃśanāśanam*, "the destroyer of the *rākṣasa* race."

"You are about to die." *muhūrtād bhavitā vicetāḥ*: Literally, "after a moment you will be deprived of your senses." We agree with the commentators that the adjective *vicetāḥ*, which normally has the sense "unconscious," must be understood here to mean "dead" (*vicetā nirjīvo mṛtaḥ*—so Ct).

The meter is *upajāti*.

101. "When Kumbhakarṇa realized" *vijñāya*: Literally, "having realized."

"caused . . . to sink" *pātayann iva*: Literally, "as if causing to fall." D7,9–11,T2,3, and the texts and printed editions of Ct and Cr read instead *dārayann iva*, "as if rending, breaking." Raghunathan (1982, vol. 3, p. 187) evidently reads the simplex root $\sqrt{pat}$ in its sense of "to leap *or* fly," rendering, "making their hearts jump into their mouths."

Following 101ab, D5–7,9–11,S insert a passage of one line [1213*]: "He ran about in a rage scattering the tawny monkeys in battle."

103. "Virādha, Kabandha, Khara, Vālin, or Mārīca" *nāhaṃ virādhaḥ . . . na kabandhaḥ kharo na ca / na vālī na ca mārīcaḥ*: All the individuals named had previously been killed by Rāma. As Cr notes, Kumbhakarṇa is suggesting the relative weakness of those he names compared to himself (*etena virādhādīnām alpabalavattvaṃ sūcitam*). Virādha was killed by Rāma at *Araṇyakāṇḍa* 3; Kabandha was mortally wounded at 3.66–68; Khara was slain at 3.28.25; Mārīca was shot at 3.42.11–21; and Vālin was mortally wounded at 4.16.25.

104. "war hammer" *mudgaram*: Cg is the only commentator to note the apparent contradiction between this verse and verse 81 above, where Kumbhakarṇa is shown to have lost his last weapon and is thus compelled to fight with his arms and feet. Cg hastens to reassure us that we are to understand that in the interval Kumbhakarṇa has picked up a war hammer (*yady api nirāyudhatvaṃ pūrvam uktam tathāpy adya mudgaraṃ gṛhītavān iti jñeyam*).

"all made of black iron" *sarvakālāyasam*: See 5.39.11; 5.51.38; 6.53.12; and notes.

106. "puny strength" *vīryam . . . laghu*: The term *laghu* is ambiguous here. It can be read, as Cg proposes, adverbially in the sense of "quickly." This sense has been followed by Raghunathan (1982, vol. 3, p. 187), who translates, "without loss of time." Gorresio (1858, vol. 10, p. 33), the only other translator to share this reading, takes the term as an adjective modifying *vīryam*, "strength," rendering, "*l'agile tuo vigore.*" We, too, read the term adjectivally but, in keeping with the contemptuous tenor of Kumbhakarṇa's words, take it in its common sense of "slight, insignificant, puny." V3,B4,D7,9–11, and the texts and printed editions of Ct and Cr read instead [*me*] *'nagha*, "O faultless one."

"against my limbs" *gātreṣu me*: Cr, the only commentator to remark on this phrase, understands, as do we, that Kumbhakarṇa is inviting Rāma to demonstrate his martial prowess against his own huge body. He explains, "Demonstrate your own valor upon my limbs. The meaning is 'shoot your arrows to the best of your ability' (*vīryaṃ svaparākramaṃ me gātreṣu darśaya yāvacchakti śarān prakṣipety arthaḥ*)." This same understanding is shared by Gita Press (1969, vol. 3, p. 1634), Raghunathan (1982, vol. 3, p. 187), and Gorresio (1858, vol. 10, p. 33). Roussel (1903, vol. 3, p. 214), followed by Shastri (1959, vol. 3, p. 186) and Pagani (1999, p. 1044), understands Kumbhakarṇa to be challenging Rāma to demonstrate the strength of his own limbs, rendering, "*Montre-moi . . . la vigueur de tes membres.*" Dutt (1893, p. 1325) appears to read the causative *darśaya* idiosyncratically as some sort of hypothetical simplex, translating, "do thou witness the prowess that is in my frame."

"once I have witnessed your manliness and valor" *dṛṣṭapauruṣavikramam*: Literally, "[you] whose manliness and valor have been seen." The terms *pauruṣa* and *vikrama* as well as the term *vīrya* in *pāda* b are all more or less synonymous in the senses of "strength" and "courage." See note to 6.2.14.

107. "was neither shaken nor harmed" *na cukṣubhe na vyathate*: Literally, "he did not shake; he is not agitated." The two verbs are closely similar in meaning. Cg, the only commentator to take note of this issue, remarks that the action expressed by the root $\sqrt{}$*kṣubh* is mental (*kṣobho 'tra mānasaḥ*), leaving us to assume that the verb $\sqrt{}$*vyath* refers to a physical state.

The meter is *upajāti*.

108. "Those same arrows" *yaiḥ sāyakaiḥ*: Literally, "by which arrows." Both Cg and Cs are disturbed by the use of the plural here, since the text has made it clear at 4.12.2–5 and 4.16.25 that Rāma has employed but a single arrow to accomplish the feats referred to in this verse. Cg explains the plural by stating that it is used because the arrows used earlier are the same kind as those used in the present context (*sālabhedakasya vālināśakasya ca bāṇasyaikatve 'pi bahuvacanaṃ tadvargyāṇām ekatvād upapadyate*). Cs comments that, even though it was stated earlier that Rāma used a single great arrow to split the *tāla* trees [Cs reads the vulgate variant *tāla*, "palmyra tree," for the crit. ed.'s *sāla*], the plural is used here because the description of Kumbhakarṇa's greatness [apparently accentuated by his ability to withstand multiple arrow wounds] serves to enhance the greatness of Rāma (*yady apy ekeṣuṇā bhittvā ca tān sa ityādiṣv eka eva saptatālapāṭako vipāṭa uktaḥ tathāpi kumbhakarṇamahattvavarṇanaṃ rāmamāhātmyopayogīti yair ityādy uktiḥ*).

"pierced the great *sāla* trees" *sālavarā nikṛttāḥ*: See 4.12.2–5.

"slain Vālin" *vālī hataḥ*: See 4.16.25ff.

The meter is *indravajrā*.

109. "absorbed those arrows . . . as one might drink a trickle of water" *sa vāridhārā iva sāyakāṃs tān pibañ śarīreṇa*: Literally, "drinking with his body those arrows like streams of water." The image the poet has in mind is most likely the gentle stream of water poured from a drinking vessel to the mouth or, as Ck and Ct understand, a mountain drinking or absorbing showers of water [rain] (*vāridhārāḥ parvata iva sāyakāñ śarīreṇa pibann iti yojanā*). Hence we have translated "trickle" to indicate how insignificant Kumbhakarṇa finds the blows of Rāma's arrows. The idea, Ck and Ct continue, is that the arrows sink into [Kumbhakarṇa's] body but do not harm him (*etena sarve sāyakāḥ śarīre magnā api na vyathayantīti darśitam*).

"in whirling . . . he had blunted" *jaghāna . . . vyāvidhya*: Literally, "having whirled, he struck." We follow Ck and Ct, who clearly indicate that they understand that Kumbhakarṇa whirls his war hammer in order to slow down or neutralize the arrows (*ugravegaṃ taṃ mudgaraṃ vyāvidhya bhrāmayitvā rāmasya śarapravegaṃ jaghāna*—so Ct). Roussel (1903, vol. 3, p. 214) and Pagani (1999, p. 1044) understand that the action of swinging the war hammer is simultaneous with, but not the cause of, the obstruction of the arrows.

The meter is *upajāti*.

110. "covered with blood, the *rākṣasa*, a terror to the vast hosts of the gods, whirling his war hammer" *rakṣaḥ kṣatajānuliptaṃ vitrāsanaṃ devamahācamūnām / vyāvidhya taṃ mudgaram*: We understand both *vitrāsanam* and *kṣatajānuliptam* to modify the neuter noun *rakṣaḥ*, "*rākṣasa*," since both qualifiers are eminently suited to the description of Kumbhakarṇa. Cr and all translators consulted understand the adjective *vitrāsanam*, "terrifying," to modify *mudgaram*, "war hammer." The translators similarly understand the compound *kṣatajānuliptam*, "covered with blood," to modify the weapon. Both readings are certainly possible.

The meter is *upajāti*.

111. "the excellent divine weapon-spell of Vāyu" *vāyavyam . . . varāstram*: Ñ2,D9–11, and the texts and printed editions of Ct read instead *[a]parāstram*. We believe that the proper interpretation of this reading would be "unsurpassed weapon-spell." However, most of the translators who render the text of Ct translate *apara-* in its other sense of "another." Ś,V1,2,B,D1–3,6,7,12,13,T2,3, and the text of Cr read instead *mahāstram*, "great *or* mighty *astra*." This may be the source of Dutt's rendering, "a mighty *Vāyavya* weapon" (1893, p. 1326). The divine *vāyavya* weapon, associated with the vedic wind god Vāyu, is among those conferred upon Rāma by Viśvāmitra as a reward for the latter's slaying of the *rākṣasī* Tāṭakā at *Bālakāṇḍa* 25. The weapon, there given the proper name "Prathama" (among other variants), is presented to Rāma at 1.26.11. See Jacobi 1893, p. 52, n. 1; cf. R. Goldman 1984, pp. 63ff.

"Kumbhakarṇa" *saḥ*: Literally, "he."

The meter is *upajāti*.

112. "wreaking carnage among the monkey troops" *jaghāna tāṃ vānaravāhinīṃ ca*: Literally, "and it destroyed the monkey army." Cr and some of the translators are concerned at the apparent sense that the entire monkey host has been annihilated here. Cr glosses the term *vānaravāhinīm*, "the monkey army," as "a certain army [i.e., one specific division of the army] (*kāṃcit senām*)." Dutt (1893, p. 1326) translates, as do several other translators, "destroyed that army," but adds a footnote saying, "This, of course, is not to be taken literally." Gita Press (1969, vol. 3, p. 1634), trying to avoid the destruction of the entire army, translates, "and killed a well-known regiment of the monkeys." Gorresio (1858, vol. 10, p. 35) renders, "*e batacchiava a furia i Vānari*." Our solution is similar to that of Raghunathan (1982, vol. 3, p. 188), who renders, simply, "causing great havoc."

The meter is *upendravajrā*.

113. "who had survived that carnage were routed" *bhagnahatāvaśeṣāḥ*: Literally, "the broken, slain remainders." We understand the compound to be a *dvandva* made up of two adjectives describing the monkeys: one is *bhagna*, a term Vālmīki uses widely elsewhere in the sense of "routed" (see verse 29 and note above), and the other is *hatāvaśeṣāḥ*, "remainders of the slain." Commentators and translators propose a variety of alternative interpretations. Ct and Ck gloss, *bhagnasamudgarapatitabāhu hatāvaśiṣṭāḥ*, which could mean either "the routed and the remainder of those slain by the fallen arm with its war hammer," or "the remainder of those slain by the fallen

arm, which was broken and held a war hammer." Cr understands the compound to be a *tatpuruṣa,* glossing, "the remnants of the slain, that is, the slaughter, caused by the breaking, that is, the falling, of Kumbhakarṇa's arm together with the war hammer (*bhagnena samudgarakumbhakarṇabāhupātena hatād hananād avaśeṣāḥ*)." Several of the translators understand that the monkeys are the survivors of those who have been broken, i.e., injured and mutilated, and those who have been slain.

"the edge of the battlefield" *paryantam*: Literally, "to the periphery." Ct and Ck explain, "near the area where the arm and war hammer had fallen (*samudgarabāhupātapradeśasamīpam*)." Cr, on the other hand, understands, "to another place (*deśāntaram*)."

"their bodies trembling" *pravepitāṅgāḥ*: Ś1,D7,9–11, and the texts and printed editions of Ct read instead *prapīḍitāṅgāḥ*, "their bodies crushed *or* wounded."

The meter is *upajāti.*

114. "huge . . . whose peak had been severed" *mahān nikṛttāgraḥ*: D5,7,9–11, and the texts and printed editions of Ct and Cr read instead *mahāsikṛṃttāgraḥ* (D5,9, and Ct and Cr—*kṛttāgraḥ*), "whose peak was severed by a huge sword."

The meter is *upajāti.*

115. "*jāmbūnada* gold" *jāmbūnada-*: See note to 6.15.2.

"charged with the divine weapon-spell of Indra" *aindrāstrayuktena*: Literally, "joined with the *aindra* missile." The idea here, as is explained by Cr and Cg and as seen elsewhere in the epics, is that Rāma has invoked a spell associated with the weapon of Indra to empower an ordinary arrow. See notes to verse 78 above. See, too, 6.47.81 and note. Rāma is given control over Indra's weapon at 1.26.5, although there the weapon is explicitly said to be a *cakra,* or "discus."

"Kumbhakarṇa's" *tasya*: Literally, "of him."

"*sāla* tree" *-sālavṛkṣam*: D6,7,9–11,T2,G2, and the texts and printed editions of Ct and Cr read instead *-tālavṛkṣam*, "palmyra tree." See note to verse 108 above.

The meter is *upajāti.*

116. For some reason, Shastri (1959, vol. 3, p. 187) omits this entire verse from his translation.

"thrashing about" *viveṣṭamānaḥ*: Literally, "winding, twisting." Ś,Ñ,V2,B1–3,D1–4,6–13, and the texts and printed editions of Ct and Cr read instead *viceṣṭamānaḥ*, "moving, writhing, twitching." Cg glosses, "revolving, whirling about (*vivartamānaḥ*)." Dutt (1893, p. 1326) idiosyncratically reads the *upasarga vi* as a privative particle and thus renders the participle as "inert."

The meter is *upajāti.*

117. "Kumbhakarṇa" *tam*: Literally, "him."

"two . . . half-moon-headed arrows" *dvāv ardhacandrau*: Literally, "two half-moon-headed ones." Cg understands that Rāma has fitted both arrows to his bow simultaneously (*yugapat sandhāya*). See 6.44.18. Cf. 6.35.23; 6.57.57; and notes.

The meter is *upajāti.*

Following verse 117, D5–7,9–11,S insert a passage of four lines [1215*]: "His feet fell, making the cardinal and intermediate directions, the hills, the caves,[1] the vast ocean, Laṅkā, and the hosts of monkeys and *rākṣasas* resound."

[1]"the hills, the caves" *girīn guhāḥ*: D9–11,G1, and the texts and printed editions of Ct read instead *girer guhāḥ*, "the caves of the mountain."

The meter is *upajāti.*

118. "Kumbhakarṇa... hurled himself... upon" *dudrāva*: Literally, "he ran toward." Cg raises the otherwise unspoken problem of how Kumbhakarṇa is supposed to move once his arms and feet have been severed. He states that Kumbhakarṇa must have moved on the stumps of his thighs or else both his motion here and his fall as described in the subsequent verses would be impossible. (*ūruśeṣābhyām idam. anyathedaṃ gamanaṃ vakṣyamānaṃ patanaṃ ca na sambhavataḥ*—so Cg.)

"the mare's head fire that lies beneath the sea" *vaḍavāmukha-*: See 6.48.49; 6.61.42; and notes.

"Rāhu, demon of the eclipse" *rāhuḥ*: Literally, "Rāhu."

The meter is *upajāti*.

119. "Kumbhakarṇa's" *tasya*: Literally, "his."

"moaned" *cukūja*: Literally, "he made indistinct sounds."

The meter is *upajāti*.

120. See R. Goldman 1984, pp.101–4, for a comparison of the description of the death of Kumbhakarṇa (verses 120–125) with Homer's description of the death of Pandaros.

"perfect" *ariṣṭam*: Ct, Ck, Cg, and Cm understand the term here to mean "inauspicious to one's enemies (*ripūṇām aśubhapradam*)." Cg and Cm substantiate this interpretation by citing *Amarakośa* 3.3.35.

"resembled the staff of Brahmā or Kāla, the ender of all things" *brahmadaṇḍāntakakālakalpam*: The meaning of the compound is not absolutely clear. The commentators are silent, and translations vary. Raghunathan (1982, vol. 3, p. 189) understands three separate figures, translating, "as invincible as the rod of Brahmā or death or all-destroying time," while Gita Press (1969, vol. 3, p. 1636), understanding, as we do, that *kāla* and *antaka* are more or less synonymous, translates, "resembles the rod of Brahmā (the creator) and the destructive Kāla (Time-Spirit)." Gorresio (1858, vol. 10, p. 36) renders similarly, offering, "*pari allo scettro di Brahma ed alla morte*." Roussel (1903, vol. 3, p. 215) reads the compound in reverse as a kind of *paranipāta*, understanding that the arrow is like the staff of Brahmā at the time of final destruction. He translates, "*pareil au sceptre de Brahmā, à l'époque de la destruction finale*." He is followed in this by Shastri (1959, vol. 3, p. 188). Pagani (1999, p. 1045) has a similar interpretation but makes *kāla* or, "Time," the wielder of Brahmā's staff. She renders, "*pareil à Kāla qui brandit le brahmadaṇḍa à l'heure de la destruction finale*." See note to 6.48.3.

The meter is *upajāti*.

121. *jāmbūnada* gold: *-jāmbūnada-*: See note to 6.15.2.

"Indra's *vajra* or a thunderbolt" *-vajrāśani-*: See verse 43 and note above.

"It shone like the blazing sun or fire" *pradīptasūryajvalanaprakāśam*: The sequence *sūryajvalana-* can be read either as a *dvandva*, as we have done, following the suggestion of Cr, or as a *tatpuruṣa*, which lends the compound the sense of "its luster was like the brilliance of the blazing sun." Translators are divided on this point.

The meter is *upajāti*.

122. "sped on its way... and its power was equal to that of mighty Śakra's thunderbolt" *jagāma śakrāśanitulyavikramaḥ*: D10,11, and the texts and printed editions of Ct and Cr read instead the accusative singular *-bhīmavikramam*, "of fearsome power," for *-tulyavikramaḥ*. This reading slightly changes the meaning of the compound and makes it describe not Rāma's arrow but Kumbhakarṇa himself. It also makes

Kumbhakarṇa the destination of the arrow. The sense thus becomes "[the arrow] sped toward him whose fearsome power was like that of Śakra's thunderbolt."

"as that of Agni Vaiśvānara, undimmed by smoke" *vidhūmavaiśvānara-*: Literally, "smokeless Vaiśvānara." D5,7,T1,G,M, and the texts and printed editions of Cg read instead *sadhūma-*, "smoky," for *vidhūma-*, "smokeless." Only Raghunathan (1982, vol. 3, p. 189) renders this variant.

The meter is *vaṃśasthavila*.

123. "With it, Rāma" *saḥ*: Literally, "he *or* it." The most immediate antecedent is the arrow in verse 122 above. To take it as the subject here, however, would vitiate the force of the simile in *pāda* d, which calls for Rāma himself to be compared to Indra. We therefore follow Cg in taking the pronoun explicitly to refer to Rāma, while we add the phrase "with it" to maintain the narrative consistency.

"its fangs bared" *vivṛttadaṃṣṭram*: The participle *vivṛtta-* would normally have the sense of "turned *or* twisted." Of the two translators consulted who share the critical reading, only Gorresio (1858, vol. 10, p. 37) accepts this, translating, "*con denti ritorti*." We believe that the sense intended is that of *vivṛta*, "opened, bared, uncovered." The doubling of the "t" appears to be *metri causa* to provide the requisite heavy syllable in this position of the *vaṃśasthavila* meter. Raghunathan (1982, vol. 3, p. 189), the other translator to share this reading, agrees, rendering, "with its bared fangs." Compare 6.47.15 and notes.

B2,D6,9–11,T2,3,G1,2, and the texts and printed editions of Ct and Cr read instead *suvṛtta-*, "beautifully rounded, globular." Translations that follow the text of Ct render this variant.

"swinging wildly" *cala-*: Literally, "moving, swinging." Ct understands that the earrings are falling or flying off Kumbhakarṇa's head (*cale gate cāruṇī ramaṇīye kuṇḍale yasmāt*). Dutt (1893, p. 1327), alone among the translators, accepts this interpretation, rendering, "from which the earrings had fallen off."

"Indra, smasher of citadels... of Vṛtra" *vṛtrasya... puraṃdaraḥ*: Literally, "Puraṃdara... of Vṛtra." The legend of Indra slaying Vṛtra is well known throughout the literature far back into the vedic period. See, for example, *AV* 1.32; *TaiS* 6.5.5; *ŚatBr* 1.6.3; *JaimiBr* 2.155; *MBh* 5.9–10; and *Rām* 1.23.17–19. See *BhāgP* 6.12, especially verses 3 and 29. See Bhattacharji 1970, pp. 254ff. and Dikshitar 1951–1955, vol. 1, pp. 189–90. See, too, notes to 5.19.28. See also 6.75.31; 6.97.21; and notes.

The meter is *vaṃśasthavila*.

Following verse 123, D6,7,9–11,T2,3,M3, and the texts and printed editions of the southern commentators insert a passage of two lines [1217*]: "Adorned with its earrings, the enormous head of Kumbhakarṇa resembled the moon in the midst of the sky when the twin stars of Punarvasu have risen at night.[1]"

[1]"the twin stars of Punarvasu have risen at night" *āditye 'bhyudite rātrau*: Literally, "when Āditya has risen at night." The exact meaning of this phrase is unclear, and it is understood variously by the different commentators and translators. The most common sense of the term *āditya* in a context such as this is the sun, but clearly it makes no sense for the sun to be rising at night. Ct, Cs, and Cm (as a variant) propose breaking the sequence *abhyudite rātrau* into *abhyudite 'rātrau* [=*arātrau*], that is, "arisen during the non-night, that is, during the day." Citing *Amarakośa* 3.3.251, they take

alam (from the term *alaṃkṛtam*, "adorned," in line 1) in its sense of "blocking (*vāraṇa*)" and interpret the verse to mean "deprived of its shining earrings, the head of Kumbhakarṇa looked as pallid *or* lusterless as the moon in the sky in the morning when the sun has risen." (*kuṇḍalābhyām alaṃkṛtaṃ vinākṛtam . . . kumbhakarṇasya śiraḥ. arātrau prātaḥkāla āditya udite gaganamadhyasthacandramā iva niṣprabhaṃ bhātīty arthaḥ*—so Ct.) This interpretation has been followed by Dutt (1893, p. 1327), Roussel (1903, vol. 3, p. 215), Pagani (1999, p. 1046), and Shastri (1959, vol. 3, p. 188). Cr, somewhat fancifully, takes *āditye* to mean "two suns." This reading, of course, retains the earrings but now has the moon floating in the sky between two suns. We have followed the interpretation of Cm (first alternative) and Cg, who take the term *āditya* to refer to the *nakṣatra* Punarvasu, which is presided over by the divinity Aditi. According to this rendering, the severed head of Kumbhakarṇa, immobile for a moment through the force of the arrow that severed it and flanked by its glittering earrings, resembles the moon suspended in the sky and flanked by the two twinkling stars that constitute Punarvasu (*kartanavegād gagane sthitaṃ sat kumbhakarṇaśira āditye 'ditidevatāke punarvasunakṣatre rātrāv abhyudite tanmadhyagataś candramā ivābhātīty arthaḥ*—so Cm). Gita Press (1969, vol. 3, p. 1636) and Raghunathan (1982, vol. 3, p. 189) follow this interpretation as well.

Ct and Cs note that many authorities consider this verse to be an interpolation (*ayaṃ ślokaḥ prakṣipta iti bahavaḥ*).

124. Both Ct and Cs note the apparent contradiction between Vālmīki's account of the death of Kumbhakarṇa and that related by Vyāsa in the *Rāmopākhyāna* of the *Mahābhārata* (*MBh* 3.271), where it is Lakṣmaṇa (Saumitri) who kills the *rākṣasa* with the *brahmāstra*. Both commentators offer explanations to rationalize the seeming contradiction. Ct explains that, as our text stated earlier, Rāma had been accompanied by Lakṣmaṇa in his effort to kill Kumbhakarṇa (see verse 92 above). However, because Rāma plays the principal role in this deed, the poet refers to him alone as the killer. On the other hand, Ct continues, Vyāsa speaks of Lakṣmaṇa as the killer because of the latter's assistance to Rāma (*lakṣmaṇasāhityena*). Cs, who typically bitterly rejects any interpretation offered by Ct (or Cm), proposes several alternative explanations, including that Rāma himself is referred to here as "Saumitri" because he was even dearer to Sumitrā than her own son Lakṣmaṇa. It is, Cs contends, thus like the usage of the patronymic Dāśarathi for both Rāma and Lakṣmaṇa. (*sumitrāyā apatyaṃ hi saumitriḥ. tasyāś ca lakṣmaṇād api premapadaṃ rāma iti tadapatyatvenokto vyāsena dāśarathir iti vā.*) Alternatively, Cs proposes that this is a kind of esoteric expression (*guhyabhāṣā*) to refer secretly to Rāma with the term "Saumitri." Finally, Cs argues that the term "Saumitri" might be used for Rāma in the *Mahābhārata* through a substitution of persons (*puṃvyatyāsaḥ*) such as occurs when warriors struck down by the arrows of Bhīma are said to by killed by Dhanañjaya (*śataṃ duryodhanādīṃs te dhanañjayaśarair hatān / darśayiṣyāmīty kṛṣṇena kṛṣṇāṃ pratyudīrite vacasi bhīmasenaśarair hatān iti vaktavye dhanañjaya ity uktivad vā jñeyaḥ*). Cf. note to 6.67.36.

"the gates of the buildings on the main thoroughfares" *caryāgṛhagopurāṇi*: See verse 64 above; and 6.47.32 and note. Here Cg slightly modifies his definition of *caryā*, understanding it now to refer to "areas laid out near the rampart and suitable for the patrolling of soldiers (*caryāḥ prākāropāntaklptabhaṭasaṃcārārhapradeśāḥ*)."

The meter is *upajāti*.

Following verse 124, M3 and texts and the printed editions of Cg (VSP, KK (1905) = 6.67.160; KK = 6.67.174) insert a passage of two lines [1219*]: "Kumbhakarṇa fell, knocking down with his body tens of millions of the leaping monkeys as they fled in all directions." This verse is rendered only in the translation of Raghunathan (1982, vol. 3, p. 189).

125. "who looked like Himalaya" *himavatprakāśam*: D5,7,9–11, and the texts and printed editions of Ct and Cr read instead *hi mahatprakāśam*. Translators who have this reading interpret it generally to mean "of great resplendence."

"crocodiles, shoals of huge fish, and serpents" *grāhān mahāmīnacayān bhujaṅgamān*: The *pāda* is hypermetric, and a number of manuscripts correct this by substituting readings such as *bhujaṅgān* for *bhujaṅgamān*. The printed texts of Ct read instead *grāhān parān mīnavarān bhujaṅgamān*, "great crocodiles, splendid fish, and serpents." Printed texts of Cg read *grāhān varān mīnavarān bhujaṅgān*, "splendid crocodiles, splendid fish, and serpents." See 6.3.14 and note.

"before he entered the earth" *bhūmiṃ ca tathā viveśa*: Literally, "and he entered the earth." Cr understands that it is the tremendous force of Rāma's arrow that drives the body into the seabed (*bāṇavegavaśena . . . ata eva bhūmiṃ samāviveśa*), while Cg thinks that the body simply sinks to the bottom (lit., "it touched the ground") (*bhūmim aspṛśad ity arthaḥ*).

The meter is *upajāti*, with a hypermetric *pāda* c.

126. "the earth shook and all the mountains trembled" *cacāla bhūr bhūmidharāś ca sarve*: Literally, "the earth moved, and all the mountains." We follow Ct and Cs, who supply "they moved (*celuḥ*)" to agree with "mountains (*bhūmidharāḥ*)."

The meter is *upajāti*.

127. "The divine seers, great seers . . . gods" *devarṣimaharṣi- . . . surāḥ*: Roussel (1903, vol. 3, p. 216), followed by Shastri (1959, vol. 3, p. 188) and Pagani (1999, p. 1046), mistakenly reads the compound *devarṣi-* as a *dvandva* in the sense of "gods (*devas*) and *ṛṣis*." Reading the compound in this way creates a redundancy between the synonymous *deva* and *sura*, which might remain unnoticed because of Roussel's practice of leaving the terms untranslated. Dutt (1893, p. 1327) appears to do the same thing, rendering *devas* as "deities," and *suras* as "celestials."

"the spirits of the departed" *bhūtāni*: This term has a variety of meanings in different contexts. It can be used generically to refer to any and all living creatures, and sometimes, more restrictively, to refer, for example, to the malignant spirits that serve as Śiva's attendants. Here, since all the beings listed appear to be hovering in the sky, the generic sense seems to be ruled out. The context also rules out malignant spirits, such as those mentioned at 6.47.9,23 and notes. The reference is probably to the class of departed ancestors, or *pitṛs*. Cs takes the term in another of its senses, that of the five elements that constitute the physical universe. He says that these elements, space, etc., are gratified by the death of Kumbhakarṇa because he had obstructed their natural functions. (*bhūtāny ākāśādīni. svakāryapratibandhakatvāt tadvadhena teṣāṃ toṣaḥ.*) See notes to 6.15.4. Raghunathan (1982, vol. 3, p. 189) comes closest to this idea, rendering, "the elementals." Cf. 6.4.16 and note.

"*guhyakas . . . yakṣas*" *-guhyakāḥ . . . -yakṣa-*: Both are classes of autocthonous semidivine beings associated with Kubera, the god of wealth, and are represented as guardians of his treasure. In some cases, for example, at *Meghadūta* 1 and 5, the terms are interchangeable. Cf. 6.4.16 and note.

The meter is *vaṃśasthavila*, with a hypometric *pāda* d.

Following verse 127, D5–7,9–11,S insert a passage of eight lines [1221*]: "Then upon that great slaying, the wise kinsmen of the king of the *rākṣasas*, sons of chaos, were shaken and wailed loudly, gazing upon the foremost of the Raghus, as might elephants upon a lion.[1][1–4] When he had slain Kumbhakarṇa in battle, Rāma was as resplendent in the midst of the army of tawny monkeys[2] as is the sun when, freed from the mouth of Rāhu, demon of the eclipse, it dispels the darkness of the heavens.[5–8]"

[1]"as might elephants upon a lion" *harim . . . yathā matañgajāḥ*: Literally, "as do the offspring of elephants, the lion." M3 and the printed editions of Cg (VSP, KK 1905 = 6.67.164; KK = 6.67.178) read *surārditāḥ*, "those afflicted by the gods," for *matañgajāḥ*, "elephants." The adjective must refer to the *asuras* or, as Cm contends, the *rākṣasas*. In this reading, the term *hari* must be taken as an epithet of either Indra or Viṣṇu rather than a kenning for "lion." Only Raghunathan (1982, vol. 3, p. 190) renders this reading, translating, "as the Asuras, harried by the gods, did when they looked at Hari."

[2]"in the midst of the army of tawny monkeys" *harisainyamadhye*: G2,3,M, and the printed editions of Cg (VSP, KK 1905 = 6.67.165; KK = 6.67.179) read instead *bhuvi vānaraughe*, "on the ground, in the throng of monkeys." This reading is rendered only by Raghunathan (1982, vol. 3, p. 190), who translates, "[shone] on earth among the apes."

The meter of lines 1–4 is *vaṃśasthavila*.

The meter of lines 5–8 is *upajāti*.

128. "countless" *bahavaḥ*: Literally, "many."

"their faces like blooming lotuses" *prabuddhapadmapratimair ivānanaiḥ*: Literally, "their faces as if having the likeness of awakening lotuses." As most of the commentators point out, the term *pratimā*, which at the end of compounds means "resemblance *or* similitude," must be taken here in the sense of "appearance *or* beauty" because of the force of the particle *iva*, "like." (*pratimāśabdo 'tra rūpavacanaḥ. na tu sadṛśavacana ivaśabdaprayogāt*—so Cg.)

"unassailable" *durāsade*: D9–11 and the texts and printed editions of Ct read instead the accusative *nṛpātmajam*, "son of the king," which then refers to Rāma.

The meter is *vaṃśasthavila*.

129. "whose efforts had never before been thwarted" *aparājitaśramam*: Literally, "of undefeated efforts." The manuscript evidence for this verse is greatly varied. T2,3,M3, and the texts and printed editions of Cg, Cm, and Cv read instead *parājitaśramam*, which must then be rendered as "who had conquered weariness." This reading is rendered only in the translation of Raghunathan (1982, vol. 3, p. 190), who renders, "tirelessly." Ś,Ñ,V,B1,2,4,D1–4,7,8,12,13,G2, and the text of Cr read instead *[a]jitaṃ kadācana*, while D10,11, and the texts and printed editions of Ct reverse the word order to read *kadācanājitam*. Ct explains this reading as "who had never failed to be victorious (*na kadāpy ajayavantam*)."

"Indra, the lord of the immortal gods" *amarādhipaḥ*: Literally, "the lord of the immortals."

The meter is *vaṃśasthavila*.

Cm states that the death of Kumbhakarṇa occurs on the seventh lunar day [of the bright half of the month of Phālguna/Caitra] (*saptamyāṃ kumbhakarṇavadhaḥ*). See 6.4.4 note.

Cv and Cg conclude their comments on this lengthy *sarga* by remarking that scattered throughout it are a number of verses that may not be found in all versions. Cg remarks that he has not commented on those verses. He states his opinion that the [proper] number of verses in the *sarga* is 166 ½. (*atra sarge 'dhikāḥ kecana ślokāḥ kvāpi kvāpi dṛśyante te na vyākhyātāḥ. asmin sarge sārdhaṣaṭṣaṣṭyuttaraśataślokāḥ*.) This count is most closely approximated among the printed editions by VSP and KK (1913), each of which has 167. KK (1930), which includes and numbers several suspect verses including App. I, No. 35, has a total of 181 *ślokas*. Printed editions of Ct show 176 (NSP and GPP) or 177 (Gita Press). The text of Gorresio has 141 and that of Lahore has 155.

Sarga 56

1. "to Rāvaṇa" *rāvaṇāya*: According to Cg and Cm, the syllable "*ya*" in the word *rāvaṇāya*, "to Rāvaṇa," is the eighteenth syllable of the *Gāyatrīmantra* as it is distributed throughout the poem. He notes further that this point marks the completion of seventeen thousand *ślokas* from the beginning of the poem. See note to 6.1.1.

Following verse 1, D5–7,9–11,S insert a passage of eight lines [1222*]: "Your majesty, he, who was like Kāla himself, has now come under Kāla's power.[1] After routing the monkey army and devouring the monkeys, after burning them up for a time, he has been extinguished by the blazing power of Rāma.[1–3] Now, his ears, legs, and arms hacked off, he lies gushing copious blood,[2] his body half-submerged in the fearsome-looking sea.[4–5] Your mountainous brother Kumbhakarṇa, mutilated by Kākutstha's arrows, lies blocking the gates of Laṅkā, like a mangled[3] tree trunk burned by a forest fire and reduced to a shapeless mass.[4][6–8]"

[1]"he, who was like Kāla himself, has now come under Kāla's power" *kālasaṃkāśaḥ saṃyuktaḥ kālakarmaṇā*: Literally, "resembling Kāla, he has been joined to the action of Kāla." Ct and Cr gloss *kālakarmaṇā*, "with the action *or* work of time," as "with death (*mṛtyunā*)." Cg makes this more explicit, explaining that the work of time is the action of death itself (*kālasya mṛtyoḥ karmaṇā maraṇarūpakriyayeti yāvat*). Alternatively, Cg explains the compound as a locative *tatpuruṣa*, glossing, "by action in time, that is, by his own matured *karma* (*yadvā kāle karmaṇā kālakarmaṇā paripakvakarmaṇety arthaḥ*)."

[2]"Now, his ears, legs, and arms hacked off, he lies gushing copious blood" *nikṛttakarṇorubhujo vikṣaran rudhiraṃ bahu*: Literally, "his ears, thighs, and arms cut off, [he is] flowing much blood." D10,11, and the texts and printed editions of Ct and Cr read instead *nikṛttanāsākarṇena vikṣaradrudhireṇa ca*, which would then modify the instrumental *kāyena*, "with a body," in line 4, yielding the sense "with his body gushing blood, its nose and ears cut off." D5,T1,M3, and the texts and printed editions of Cm and Cg read *-kaṇṭha-*, "neck," for the Ct's *-karṇa-*, "ears."

[3]"mangled" *vikṛtaḥ*: Literally, "deformed." D7,9–11,G,M5, and the texts and printed editions of Ct and Ck read instead *vivṛtaḥ*, "exposed." Ct notes that the sense is that Kumbhakarṇa's corpse is exposed because it has lost its clothing. (*vikṛto vivṛtakāyaḥ. avastratvāt.*)

[4]"reduced to a shapeless mass" *lagaṇḍabhūtaḥ*: Cv, Crā, Cm, and Cg refer to two possible meanings of the obscure term *lagaṇḍa*, either "a lump (*piṇḍa*)" or "a python (*ajagara*)." Raghunathan (1982, vol. 3, p. 190), the only translator consulted to share this reading, renders, like us, "a shapeless mass." The texts and printed editions of Ct, Cr, and Ck read instead *agaṇḍabhūtaḥ*. The commentators cite an unnamed lexical source to support their interpretation that the term means "headless, limbless trunk (*aśiraḥpāṇipādas tu kabandho 'gaṇḍa ucyate*)."

3. "Devāntaka, Narāntaka, Triśiras, and Atikāya" *devāntakanarāntakau / triśirāś cātikāyaś ca*: As indicated by the fact that Kumbhakarṇa is their paternal uncle and as explicitly stated by Ct, Ck, and Cr, the four *rākṣasas* named here must be sons of Rāvaṇa. A powerful *rākṣasa* warrior named Triśiras, a lieutenant of Khara, was killed in single combat with Rāma at *Araṇyakāṇḍa* 26. There is, however, no mention there, or in subsequent discussion of these events, that he was a son of Rāvaṇa. It is likely, therefore, that the Triśiras mentioned here is another *rākṣasa* of the same name. The four *rākṣasas* mentioned here will meet their deaths at 6.58.24 (Devāntaka), 6.57.87 (Narāntaka), 6.58.36–42 (Triśiras), and 6.59.104–105 (Atikāya).

4. "Mahodara and Mahāpārśva" *mahodaramahāpārśvau*: According to Ct and Ck, these are half brothers of Kumbhakarṇa (*mahodaramahāpārśvau vimātrajau bhrātarau tasya*). They will be killed in *sarga* 58 below.

5. "Rāvaṇa" *sa rāvaṇaḥ*: D9–11 and the texts and printed editions of Ct and Cr read instead *ākulendriyaḥ*, "his senses disordered."

6. "where have you gone" *kva . . . gacchasi*: Literally, "where are you going?" D5,T1,M3, and the texts and printed editions of Cg read instead *tvam . . . gacchasi*, "you are going." Only Raghunathan (1982, vol. 3, p. 191) renders this variant, translating, "you have deserted [me]."

Following 6ab, D5–7,9–11,S, and the text of Gorresio (line 1 only = 6.47.6cd) insert a passage of two lines [1224*]: "Having abandoned me because of fate, you have gone to the abode of Yama without having first removed this thorn in the side[1] of my kinsmen and me."

[1]"this thorn in the side" *śalyam*: Literally, "dart *or* thorn." A thorn or dart is a common metaphor in Sanskrit literature for a major irritation or affliction. As Cr points out, the reference is to "an arrow in the form of the enemy (*ripurūpaśaram*)." Cg glosses, merely, "grief (*śokam*)."

7. "Now I am truly lost" *idānīṃ khalu ahaṃ nāsmi*: Literally, "Now I do not exist." Ck, Ct, and Cr gloss, "as good as dead (*mṛtaprāyaḥ*)." Although acknowledging this as a possible alternative explanation, Cs ingeniously proposes, as his first alternative, that we read the phrase as *ahaṃ nā nāsmi*, taking *nā* as the nominative singular of *nṛ*, "man," and taking the negative particle *na* from *pāda* d to negate both *asmi*, "I am,"

and *bibhemi*, "I fear." Thus, he understands the phrase to mean "I am not *or* no longer am a man (*ahaṃ nā pumān nāsmi*)." The sense, according to Cs, is that Rāvaṇa now views himself as "virtually castrated." (*ahaṃ nā pumān nāsmi napuṃsakaprāya ity arthaḥ . . . netyāvartate na bibhemi.*)

8. "who was like the fire at the end of time . . . today" *kālāgnipratimo hy adya*: Literally, "like the fire of Kāla . . . today." M3 as well as the printed texts of Cg and Cm read instead *kālāgnirudrapratimaḥ*, which can be interpreted either as "like Rudra in the form of fire at the end of a cosmic age" or, as Raghunathan does, "like the fire at the end of a cosmic age or Rudra." This variant is rendered only in the translation of Raghunathan (1982, vol. 3, p. 191). Cf. note to 6.53.50. See, too, 6.59.52; 6.62.36; 6.83.3; and notes.

"have been slain . . . in battle by Rāghava" *rāghaveṇa raṇe hataḥ*: T3,M3, and the texts and printed editions of Cg and Cm read instead *raṇe rāmeṇa vai hataḥ*, "slain in battle by Rāma." This variant is rendered only in the translation of Raghunathan (1982, vol. 3, p. 191).

9. "Indra's *vajra*" *vajra-*: Literally, "the *vajra*."

11. "will seize the opportunity" *labdhalakṣyāḥ*: Literally, "having obtained an opportunity." An alternative meaning would be "having achieved their objective." Among the translators consulted, only Gorresio (1858, vol. 10, p. 38) understands this latter meaning, rendering, "*ottenuto il loro intento*." The vast majority of northern and southern manuscripts (Ś1,Ñ,V1,2,B,D1,2,6,7,10,13,T1,G,M) as well as all printed editions, except for Gorresio, read instead *labdhalakṣāḥ*. Although the range of meanings would be similar, the critical reading is the weaker and the text should probably be emended to read *labdhalakṣāḥ*. See 6.57.42 and note, where the term is repeated. There, the textual support for the reading *labdhalakṣāḥ* is even stronger. Cf. 6.78.51 and note.

"the unbreachable gates of Laṅkā" *durgāṇi laṅkādvārāṇi*: Like most of the translators consulted, we understand *durgāṇi* to be an adjective in the sense of "impassable, inaccessible, etc.," modifying *dvārāṇi*. The word, however, can also be taken as a noun in the sense of "ramparts, fortifications." This interpretation has been followed by Dutt (1893, p. 1329), who renders, "gateways and fortifications of Laṅkā," and Gorresio (1858, vol. 10, p. 38), who translates "*baluardi ed alle porte di Lanka*." Shastri (1959, vol. 3, p. 190) appears to read the term both ways, rendering, "the gates and fortifications of Lanka . . . which heretofore were impregnable."

12. "what good is Sītā to me now" *kiṃ kariṣyāmi sītayā*: Literally, "what will I do with Sītā?" Cr argues that this expression suggests that Rāvaṇa had desired to win over Sītā for the good of his kingdom, so that now, having lost all interest in rulership, he has similarly become indifferent to Sītā (*etena rājyakalyānārtham eva rāvaṇakartṛkasītāprasādakaraṇecchābhavad iti sūcitam*).

"I can take no pleasure in life" *jīvite nāsti me ratiḥ*: Literally, "there is no pleasure in life for [lit., of] me." D6,9–11,T2,3,G2,M5, and the texts and printed editions of Ct, Ck, and Cr read instead *matiḥ*, "mind, thought, intention," for *ratiḥ*, "pleasure." Translators who follow the text of Ct struggle somewhat with this slightly awkward expression. They tend to follow the suggestion of Ct and Ck, who explain, "there is no intention to remain alive (*saṃjīvatayāvasthāne buddhir nāstīty arthaḥ*)."

13. "surely, death would be better for me than this pointless existence" *nanu me maraṇaṃ śreyo na cedaṃ vyarthajīvitam*: Literally, "surely death [is] better for me; not this pointless existence." Cr suggests that continued existence for Rāvaṇa would be pointless precisely in the event of a failure to avenge Kumbhakarṇa (*yady ahaṃ rāghavaṃ na hanmi tarhi me maraṇaṃ śreya idaṃ bhrātṛvighātakavadharahitaṃ vyarthajīvitaṃ na śreyaḥ*). Cm, after giving a straightforward analysis of the verse, argues that it also contains an inner theological meaning (*vāstavārthaḥ*). According to this reading, the verse means "If I kill Rāghava, the slayer of my brother, then I will not die. But then I will not attain the *summum bonum* [*śreyaḥ*], which consists of the attainment after death of inclusion in the assembly of the Lord. Therefore, this life would be pointless. (*bhrātṛhantāraṃ rāghavaṃ hanmi yadi tadā me mama maraṇaṃ nāsti, ata eva śreyo maraṇānantarabhāvibhagavatpārṣadatāprāptirūpaśreyaś ca nāsti, ata evedaṃ jīvitaṃ vyartham iti sambandhaḥ*.)" See notes to 6.27.4.

GPP (6.68.18) reads the ungrammatical *vyarthajīvitum*, a reading not attested in the critical apparatus or other texts or printed editions of Ct. This does not appear to be a simple misprint, however, as the editors note that Cr and Cg read instead *vyarthajīvitam*, as in the critical edition.

14. "without my brothers" *bhrātṝn samutsṛjya*: Literally, "having let go *or* released brothers." Commentators are divided as to the significance of Rāvaṇa's choice of the plural apparently to refer to Kumbhakarṇa. Cg, Crā, and Cm understand that it is the plural of respect (*bahuvacanaṃ pūjāyām*—Crā, Cm). Ct and Ck understand that Rāvaṇa is regretfully remembering his other slain brothers, Khara, etc. (*kharādayaś cānusmaryante*). Cs proposes three explanations: 1) Rāvaṇa is demonstrating through the use of the plural that he has become weak by equating the passing of one prominent brother with that of many (*ekasya mukhyasya bhrātur gamanenānekaprakāreṇa svadaurbalyam āyātam iti dyotayati bahuvacanena*); 2) equals Ct's explanation; and 3) Rāvaṇa is regretfully remembering his slain brother (Kumbhakarṇa) along with the two he himself has banished, viz., Vibhīṣaṇa and Kubera (*vibhīṣaṇakuberābhyāṃ bahiṣkṛtābhyāṃ saha mṛtam ekaṃ saṃsmṛtya vā bahuvacanam*).

Cs further notes that the natural sense of *ut* $\sqrt{}$*sṛj*, "to release, drive out," evokes the remorse that Rāvaṇa will express at verse 18 below over his banishment of Vibhīṣaṇa (*utsṛjyapadasvārasyād ivottaratra sa nirasto vibhīṣaṇa iti tadanutāpasvārasyāc ca*).

16. This and the following verses mark the only point in the epic where Rāvaṇa exhibits remorse over his treatment of Vibhīṣaṇa.

"This has befallen me, because..." *tad idaṃ mām anuprāptam...yat*: Literally, "since... therefore, this has befallen me." Cr, the only commentator who discusses this verse, understands *idam*, "this," to refer to the misery (*duḥkham*) that has overtaken Rāvaṇa. An alternative way to read the verse would be to take the relative and correlative *yat* and *tat* not adverbially but rather pronominally to refer to the words of Vibhīṣaṇa (*vibhīṣaṇavacaḥ*). This would yield the sense "Those beneficial words of great Vibhīṣaṇa, which in my folly I failed to heed, have now come back to me." This interpretation is offered by Roussel (1903, vol. 3, p. 218), Shastri (1959, vol. 3, p. 190), Pagani (1999, pp. 1047–48), Gorresio (1858, vol. 10, p. 39), Raghunathan (1982, vol. 3, p. 191), and Dutt (1893, p. 1330).

"in my folly" *ajñānāt*: Literally, "out of ignorance."

19. The meter is *puṣpitāgrā*.

Sarga 57

1. "After listening to the lamentations" *śrutvā*: Literally, "having heard." The gerund uncharacteristically lacks a direct object. Ct and Ck suggest that we supply the word *vilāpam*, "lamentation," and we have done so. Cr addresses the issue by taking *vākyam*, "words," of *pāda* d as the object of *śrutvā*, leaving the finite verb *abravīt*, "he said," without an explicit object. In this reading, the sequence would be "upon hearing the words... Triśiras spoke."

"Triśiras" *triśirāḥ*: One of the four sons of Rāvaṇa. See 6.47.16; 6.56.3; and notes.

2. "True enough" *evam eva*: Literally, "in just this fashion." The expression is ambiguous here. We follow the suggestion of Cr, who understands it to be an affirmation or acceptance of the fact of Kumbhakarṇa's death. He glosses it to mean "there is no doubt, whatever, in this matter (*atra saṃśayo nāstīty arthaḥ*)." Ct, Ck, Cm, and Cg understand the phrase to be recapitulating the fact that the mighty Kumbhakarṇa, qualified by all the attributes posited by Rāvaṇa in his lament in *sarga* 56, has indeed been slain because of fate. (*evam eva devadānavadarpahā kālāgnipratima ityādyuktaprakāreṇa mahāvīryo hataḥ. daivād iti śeṣaḥ*—so Ct, Ck.) The phrase could also be taken simply adverbially with the participle *hataḥ*, "slain," in the sense of "that is indeed the fashion in which Kumbhakarṇa was slain."

"dear... uncle, middlemost among you three brothers" *nas tātamadhyamaḥ*: Literally, "the middlemost among our venerable elders." The expression is difficult to convey succinctly in English. The term *tāta* here would refer collectively to Triśiras's father and uncles. Triśiras is referring to the fact that his uncle Kumbhakarṇa is the middlemost of three brothers, born as he was after Rāvaṇa and before Vibhīṣaṇa.

"true men" *satpuruṣāḥ*: Ct glosses, "heroes (*śūrāḥ*)." See 6.59.57 and note.

3. "you are a match for all the three worlds" *tribhuvanasyāpi paryāptas tvam asi*: Literally, "you are sufficient for the three worlds." The idea, as expressed by Ck and Ct, is that Rāvaṇa is capable of conquering the three worlds (*trailokyavijayasamarthaḥ*—so Ck). Cr agrees.

"in this fashion" *īdṛśam*: We follow Cg in taking the term adverbially with the action of grieving or feeling sorry (*śokakriyāviśeṣaṇam*), as opposed to Ct, who reads it adjectivally with *ātmānam*, "self," in the sense of "capable of conquering the three worlds (*trailokyavijayasamartham*)."

4. "Brahmā has given" *brahmadattā*. Cf. the boons that Brahmā gives to Atikāya at 6.59.31.

"rumbling like a thundercloud" *meghasamasvanaḥ*: Literally, "with a sound similar to [that of] a thundercloud." D5,T1,M3, and the texts and printed editions of Cg and Cm read instead *meghasvano mahān*, "huge [and] with the sound of a thundercloud."

5. "even when unarmed" *viśastreṇa*: Literally, "[by you] without a weapon." D5–7,9–11,T,G2,3, and the texts and printed editions of Ct read instead *hi śastreṇa*, literally, "for *or* indeed, [by you] with a weapon." Translations that follow the text of Ct render this variant.

"slain" *viśastāḥ*: D9 and G3 read instead *vitrastāḥ*, "frightened." Ct notes this as a variant reading, explaining it as "the simplex for the appropriate causative, *vitrāsitāḥ*, 'terrified.'" None of the printed editions shows this variant. Dutt (1893, p. 1330), however, appears to read it, rendering, "have... been terrified."

6. "Or rather" *kāmam*: In this context, the adverbial use of this term can also mean "according to desire *or* pleasure." Most of the translators consulted have, in fact, interpreted it in this way. The only exceptions are Raghunathan (1982, vol. 3, p. 192), who reads the term as we do, rendering, "better still," and Gorresio (1858, vol. 10, p. 39), who takes the term in its sense of "surely," rendering, "*pur*."

7. "Rāma shall be laid low" *śayitā rāmaḥ*: Literally, "Rāma will lie down." Cm understands that the true meaning (*vāstavārtha*) of the verse is realized only if we break up the sequence of words here as *śayitā arāmaḥ*, yielding the sense "someone other than Rāma shall lie (*rāmo vyatiriktaḥ kaścana*)." The real meaning of this, then, according to Cm, is that [killing] Rāma is beyond the capacity [of Triśiras] (*rāmasyāsādhyatvād iti bhāvaḥ*). See notes to 6.27.4.

"Śambara by Indra, king of the gods" *śambaro devarājena*: Literally, "Śambara by the king of the gods." The enmity between the *asura* Śambara and Indra, and the latter's destruction of the former, is known to the mythological texts as far back as the *Ṛgveda* (1.51.6; 1.54; 1.112.14; 1.130; 3.47; 7.18; etc.). See 6.63.42 and notes. See, too, 2.9.9–11 and note.

"Naraka by Viṣṇu" *narako viṣṇunā*: A number of the commentators, including Cv, Cm, Cg, and Ct (quoting Cm), identify the demon referred to here as one of the sons of Vipracitti and Siṃhikā. They support this claim by citing a verse from the *Viṣṇupurāṇa* that lists the offspring of this couple. (*ayaṃ narakaḥ siṃhikāyāṃ vipracitter jāteṣu putreṣv anyatamaḥ. tad uktaṃ viṣṇupurāṇe vātāpir namuciś caiva ilvavaḥ sṛmaras tathā / andhako narakas caiva kālanābhas tathaiva ca // iti sa ucyate*—so Cm.) These commentators further assert that this figure is not to be confused with the *asura* of the same name, a son of the goddess earth, who was slain by Kṛṣṇa (*MBh* 5.47.79) (*na tu yadunāyakena hato bhaumaḥ*—so Cm). Cg notes that this must be the case, since the latter Naraka could not have been born at the time of Vālmīki's composition (*tasya vālmīkiprabandhanirmāṇakāla asaṃjātatvāt*).

At 7.27.9 and *Mahābhārata* 3.165.18, Indra is said to have killed [the other?] Naraka and Śambara along with other demons. Elsewhere in the *Mahābhārata* (3.165.18), a demon called Naraka is also said to have been killed by Indra.

8. "impelled as he was by his own impending doom" *kālacoditaḥ*: Literally, "impelled by *kāla* (Time)." Ck and Ct raise the question as to how Rāvaṇa could hope for victory now that he knew that the defeat of Rāma was beyond the capacity of Kumbhakarṇa, one of his most formidable warriors. Their answer is that Rāvaṇa is driven in his actions by Doom or Time (*kāla*). The sense, according to Ct and Ck, is that under the impulsion of the Lord, in the form of Doom (*kāla*), whose motive was to encompass Rāvaṇa's destruction, the latter did not desist from thinking about [further] battle. (*nanu kumbhakarṇāsādhye 'rthe kathaṃ rāvaṇasya tasmāj jayapratyāśayā saṃtoṣas tatrāha kālacodita iti. tannāśapravṛttakālātmakabhagavatpreraṇayā punas tasya yuddhabuddhyanuparama ity arthaḥ*—Ct.)

"he felt . . . that he had obtained a new lease on life" *punarjātam ivātmānaṃ manyate*: Literally, "he thought himself to have been, as it were, reborn."

9. "Devāntaka, Narāntaka . . . Atikāya: *devāntakanarāntakau / atikāyaḥ*: Cg, evidently disturbed that Rāvaṇa has issued no instructions to these warriors, remarks that they react as they do because Triśiras's words apply equally to them (*triśiraso vacanaṃ sveṣām api tulyatvāt*).

10. "cried out, 'I'll go! I'll go!' " *aham aham ity eva garjantaḥ*: Literally, "[they were] bellowing, 'I, I.' " We agree with Cr, who understands that we must add the verbs "I will go, I will go (*gamiṣyāmi gamiṣyāmi*)" and the finite verb "they were (*babhūvuḥ*)."

12. "provided with troops and divinely charged weapons" *astrabalasampannāḥ*: Literally, "endowed with *astras* and troops." The compound could also, less plausibly, be interpreted to mean "endowed with divinely charged weapons *or* weapon-spells and strength" or "endowed with the power of divinely charged weapons *or* weapon-spells." D5,7,9–11,T1,M3, and the texts and printed editions of the southern commentators read instead *subalasampannāḥ*, "endowed with great strength." See note to 6.35.5.

"None had ever been known to suffer defeat in battle" *sarve samaram āsādya na śrūyante sma nirjitāḥ*: Literally, "all of them had not been heard of as defeated once they had encountered battle."

Following verse 12, D5–7,9–11,S insert a passage of one line [1232*]: "even by the gods themselves, together with the *gandharvas*, *kinnaras*, and great serpents."

13. "endowed with higher knowledge" *pravaravijñānāḥ*: It is not entirely clear as to what sort of knowledge the poet is referring, whether it be martial, spiritual, or other. Ct and Ck gloss, "possessing most excellent knowledge (*śreṣṭhajñānavantaḥ*)," while Cg offers, "possessing knowledge of the foremost *śāstras* (*utkṛṣṭaśāstrajñānāḥ*)."

14. "who had crushed the strength of their enemies" *śatrubalapramardanaiḥ*: The compound can also mean "destroyers of enemy armies." D9–11 and the texts and printed editions of Ct and Cr read instead the somewhat irregular *śatrubalaśriyārdanaiḥ*, "destroying the strength and majesty of their enemies."

"magnanimous Indra" *maghavān*: Literally, "the magnanimous one."

The meter is *vaṃśasthavila*.

16. "his two brothers" *bhrātarau*: Literally, "the two brothers." According to Cg, these two are the brothers of Rāvaṇa (*rāvaṇabhrātarau*). At 6.59.1 below, Ck also identifies Mahodara as Rāvaṇa's brother. See, too, 6.58.29 and 6.58.54.

"Mahodara and Mahāpārśva" *mahodaramahāpārśvau*: B1,D3,6,7,9–11,T1,G1,M3,5, and the texts and printed editions of the southern commentators read instead *yuddhonmattaṃ ca mattaṃ ca*, "Yuddhonmatta and Matta." The commentators, anticipating confusion or contradiction when the brothers Mahāpārśva and Mahodara are mentioned in the coming verses (verses 19, 31ff.), indicate that the names in the vulgate are alternative names or nicknames ("Frenzied-in-battle" and "Frenzied") for the names given in the critical edition (*yuddhonmattamattaśabdau mahodaramahāpārśavayoḥ paryāyanāmanī*—so Cm, Ct). Cs shares this view but regards these two warriors as different from the other well-known warriors also called Mahodara and Mahāpārśva, whose battles are described later on (*sargas* 83–86). Mahodara is slain at 6.85.27 and Mahāpārśva, at 6.86.22. Cv, apparently the only southern commentator to read with the critical text, notes the vulgate reading as a variant. All translations consulted, with the exception of Gorresio (1858, vol. 10, p. 40), translate the variant reading. See also Pagani's note on this issue (1999, p. 1666). The Mahodara and Mahāpārśva mentioned are slain below at 6.58.28 and 53, respectively.

17. "Rāvaṇa, who made his enemies cry out" *rāvaṇaṃ ripurāvaṇam*: This is yet another of the etymological epithets of which Vālmīki is so fond. See note to 6.8.12. V3,D7,9–11, and the texts and printed editions of Ct and Cr read instead the more common *lokarāvaṇam*, "who made the worlds cry out." Cf., too, verse 78 and note below.

18. "with all protective herbs and fragrances" *sarvauṣadhībhir gandhaiś ca*: Literally, "with all herbs and with fragrances." According to the commentators, the herbs are intended to ward off the blows of weapons (*āyudhaprahāranivārakauṣadhiviśeṣaiḥ*—so Ct). Cg cites an āyurvedic verse according to which the term *sarvauṣadhī*, "all herbs," refers to a specific set of ten fragrant or healing herbs (*koṣṭhaṃ* [v.l. *koṣṭaṃ*, *kuṣṭhaṃ*, *kuṣṭam*] *māṃsī haridre dve murā śaileyacandane / vacācampakamustāś ca sarvauṣadhyo daśāmṛtāḥ //*). Cf. *Rajananighaṇṭu* 22.61, which specifies eight fragrant healing herbs. The ten plants in question are *koṣṭa* [or *kuṣṭha* v.l. *kuṣṭā*], *Costus speciosus*; *māṃsī*, or musk root, *Nardostachys jatamansi*; two kinds of *haridra*, or turmeric, *Cucuma Longa*; *murā*, an unidentified fragrant plant; *śaileya*, gum benjamin or gum benzoin, *Styrax benzoin*; *candana*, or sandal, *Sirium myrtifolium*; *vacā*, common sweet flag, *Acorus calamus*; *campaka*, or *Michelia campaka*; and *mustā*, the root of nutgrass, *Cyperus rotundus*.

Following verse 18, D5–7,9–11,S (except M5) insert a passage of two lines [1233*]: "Impelled as they were by their own impending doom, Triśiras, Atikāya, Devāntaka, Narāntaka, Mahodara, and Mahāpārśva set forth."

19. "an elephant named Sudarśana" *sudarśanaṃ nāma*: Literally, "named Sudarśana." The critical text lacks a word for elephant, although the kind of creature is evident from the fact that it is a descendant of Indra's great battle-elephant, Airāvata. Ś,Ñ,V,B,D1–4,7–13,G2,M1,2,5, and the texts and printed editions of Ct and Cr read *nāgam*, "elephant," in place of the adverb *nāma*, "by name."

20. "equipped with every weapon and adorned with quivers" *sarvāyudhasamāyuktaṃ tūṇībhiś ca svalaṃkṛtam*: D6,9–11,13,T2,G3,M1,2,5, and the texts and printed editions of Ct read *-samāyuktaḥ* for *-samāyuktam*, making the compound modify Mahodara rather than his elephant. V3,D9–11, and the texts and printed editions of Ct read *[a]py alaṃkṛtaḥ*, "and ornamented," for the critical edition's *svalaṃkṛtam*, making the participle modify Mahodara rather than his elephant.

"Sūrya, impeller of all creatures," *savitā*: Literally, "the impeller." The aspect of the sun as "the impeller of creatures" is celebrated as far back as the *Ṛgveda*, in the famous *Gāyatrīmantra* (*ṚV* 3.62). See note to 6.75.26, 1668*, line 2 and note. Compare notes to 6.93.27, App. I, No. 65, lines 19–20.

"perched on the summit of the western mountain" *astamūrdhani*: Literally, "on the head of Asta." *Asta*, literally, "setting," is the term used to refer to the western mountain range, behind which the sun is perceived to set. See 6.16.47; 6.19.13–15; and notes. Ct and Cg take the simile to suggest Mahodara's imminent demise (*anena śīghraṃ nāśaḥ sūcitaḥ*).

21. "laden with every sort of weapon" *sarvāyudhasamākulam*: Literally, "full of all weapons."

22. "charged with lightning and meteors" *savidyudulkaḥ*: Literally, "with lightning and meteors." It is not clear why a cloud should be accompanied by meteors. Perhaps the reference is to large hailstones.

"flashing fire" *sajvālaḥ*: D5,T1,M3, and the texts and printed editions of Cg read instead *śailāgre*, "[perched] on a mountain peak." This is perhaps an emendation that serves to avoid the seeming redundancy of flames and lightning while at the same time reflecting the comparison of the great chariot to a lofty mountain. Among the translators consulted, only Raghunathan (1982, vol. 3, p. 192) renders this variant.

"traversed by a rainbow" *sendracāpaḥ*: Literally, "with the bow of Indra."

23. "with his three diadems" *tribhiḥ kirīṭaiḥ*: It is evident that we are to take Triśiras's name (i.e., "three-headed") literally.

25. "splendidly yoked" *susaṃyuktam*: According to Cr and Ct, this means "having well-yoked horses (*susaṃyuktāśvam*—so Ct)." Cg, however, glosses, "firm, solid (*sudṛḍham*)."

"It had a fine frame" *sānukarṣam*: Literally, "with an *anukarṣa*." According to Ct, Cr, and Ck, this is a piece or block of wood placed above the axle as a support or receptacle for the yoke pole (*rathākṣopari kūbarādhāratayā sthāpito dāruviśeṣo 'nukarṣaḥ*). These commentators, as well as Cg and Cm, quote *Amarakośa* 2.8.57, which defines *anukarṣa* as "a block of wood placed below (*dārv adhaḥstham*)." Translators take the term variously to mean "axle-tree, bottom, carriage, body (*caisse*)" or leave the term untranslated. The term also occurs at 6.59.18 below. Cf. *MBh* 6.85.34; 6.92.64; 6.102.21; 7.43.17; 7.88.10; 7.97.23; 7.113.17; 7.172.36; 8.24.70; and 9.13.7. Hopkins (1889, pp. 186–87) understands *anukarṣa*, or "the drag," with its various interpretations, as, primarily and most simply, "a piece of additional wood fastened beneath the car for the purpose of quickly repairing damages sustained in battle." He identifies it as "part of the *upaskaras*, or general furnishing, of the war-car." Hopkins goes on to note that the *anukarṣa* may have been used as ballast to prevent the chariot, which, according to him, was very light as it was constructed from bamboo, from tipping over.

26. "Atikāya was as resplendent as . . . illuminated" *saḥ . . . babhau*: Literally, "he shone *or* resembled."

"of the shining sun" *bhāsvataḥ*: Literally, "of the shining one." Textual support for the critical reading is weak. Only four manuscripts (D5,T1,M1,2) read with the critical edition. With the exception of B2, which reads *toyadaḥ*, "a cloud," the remaining northern manuscripts read the nominative *bhāskaraḥ*, "the sun." This reading, in which the sun itself, rather than Mount Meru, becomes the *upamāna*, entails either the elimination of the word "Meru" or its shift to an oblique case. This variant is translated only by Gorresio (1858, vol. 10, p. 41). The remaining southern manuscripts and the texts and printed editions of the southern commentators read the present participle *bhāsayan*, "shining," which must then modify Meru.

27. "Standing in that chariot" *rathe tasmin*: Literally, "in that chariot."

"Indra, *vajra* in hand" *vajrapāṇiḥ*: Literally, "he who has a *vajra* in his hand."

28. "Uccaiḥśravas himself" *uccaiḥśravaḥ-*: Literally, "the one with erect ears." This is the name of Indra's celebrated battle-steed, produced during the churning of the ocean. See 1.44.14–17, esp. notes to verse 14.

29. "Guha" *guhaḥ*: This is one of the several names for the mighty war god, also known as Skanda, Kārttikeya, Subrahmaṇya, Kumāra, etc., who is the son of Lord Śiva.

"amid his enemies in battle" *śatruṣv ivāhave*: D5,7,10,11,T1,M3, and the texts and printed editions of the southern commentators read instead *śikhigato yathā*, "like [Guha] mounted upon his peacock." The peacock is the *vāhana*, or mount, of this divinity.

30. "studded with diamonds" *vajrabhūṣaṇam*: Literally, "adorned with diamonds." D5,7,9–11, and the texts and printed editions of Ct read instead *hemabhūṣaṇam*, "adorned with gold."

"looked like the very image of Viṣṇu" *vapur viṣṇor viḍambayan*: Literally, "imitating the form of Viṣṇu." As the commentators note, we must carry over the finite verb *virarāja*, "resplendent as, resembled," from the previous verse (*virarājety anukarṣaḥ*—so Ct).

"when he had seized the mountain with both arms" *parigṛhya giriṃ dorbhyām*: As the commentators suggest, the reference is to Viṣṇu's having seized Mount Mandara to serve as the churning rod at the time of the churning of the ocean (*samudramathane mandaragiriṃ parigṛhya sthitasya viṣṇoḥ*—so Ct). The story is told at 1.44.14ff. See ad loc. and notes. However, no specific reference is made there to Viṣṇu's having taken hold of the mountain. Northern manuscripts substitute a passage of one line [1240*] in place of 30cd, which states that Viṣṇu uprooted Mount Mandara in battle.

32. "surrounded by incomparable troops . . . were like the gods in Amarāvatī, surrounded by incomparable troops" *balair apratimair vṛtāḥ / surā ivāmarāvatyāṃ balair apratimair vṛtāḥ //*: D10,11, and the texts and printed editions of Ct and Ck read, for the first occurrence of *balair apratimair vṛtāḥ* [*pāda* b], [*a*]*marāvatyāḥ surā iva*, while D5,7,9–11,T,G1,3,M5, and the texts and printed editions of Ct and Ck omit *pādas* cd. The resulting line in the printed text of Ct is thus [*te pratasthur mahātmāno*] *'marāvatyāḥ surā iva*, "As those great warriors set forth [from Laṅkā], like the gods from Amarāvatī." Ct and Ck supply the phrase "from Laṅkā (*laṅkāyāḥ*)."

"those great warriors" *mahātmānaḥ*: Literally, "the great ones."

33. "mounted on elephants and horses and riding on chariots" *gajaiś ca turaṅgaiś ca rathaiś ca*: Literally, "with elephants, horses, and chariots."

35. "The white row of parasols" *chatrāṇām āvaliḥ sitā*: These would be the white parasols, symbols of royalty, that would be held above the princes. The term is subject to variation in the different manuscript traditions. D10,11, and the texts and printed editions of Ct read instead *vastrāṇām āvaliḥ śivā*, "the auspicious line of garments." D5–7,T1,2,G3,M3, and the texts and printed editions of Cg and Cr read *śastrāṇām*, "of weapons," for *chatrāṇām*, "of parasols." This yields the sense "a glittering line of weapons." See 6.47.13–14; 6.60.14; 6.115.13–16; 6.116.25–26; and notes.

"a line of *haṃsas*" *haṃsāvaliḥ*: Although the *haṃsa* is commonly identified as the bar-headed goose, or *Anser indicus*, that cannot be the bird intended here as these birds are not white. More likely the bird represented here is either the Mute swan (*Cygnus olor*) or Whooper swan (*Cygnus cygnus*). See Dave 1985, pp. 422–31. See, too, Thieme 1975, pp. 3–36. See note to 6.110.22.

36. "grimly resolved, for they had determined" *niścitya . . . iti kṛtvā matim*: Literally, "having decided, they made up their mind[s]."

37. "bellowed, roared" *jagarjuś ca praṇeduś ca*: This is another of those pairs of near synonyms of which the poet is so fond. Cg attempts to avoid the redundancy by taking the former term to refer to a thundering sound and the latter to a leonine roar. (*jagarjuḥ meghadhvaniṃ cakruḥ. praṇeduḥ siṃhanādaṃ cakruḥ.*) See note to 6.2.14.

"loosed arrows in their frenzy" *cikṣipuś cāpi sāyakān / jahṛṣuś ca*: Literally, "they threw arrows and were delighted." The critical reading *jahṛṣuḥ* is textually weak, apparently known to only five manuscripts (D2,3,G1,M1,2). According to the critical apparatus, Ś,Ñ2,V1,2,B,D5–13,T,G2,3,M3,5, and the texts and printed editions of all southern commentators read *jagṛhuḥ*, "they grabbed *or* seized." However, unnoted in the critical apparatus is that the printed editions of Gorresio and Lahore read with the critical edition. The few remaining manuscripts (Ñ1,V3,D1,4) read *jahasuḥ*, "they laughed."

Cv, Ct, Cm, and Cg explain their reading *jagṛhuḥ* by taking *cikṣipuḥ* to mean not "they loosed *or* fired" but "they hurled insults." This permits them to take *sāyakān* as the object of the verb *jagṛhuḥ*, "they seized." (*cikṣipuḥ kṣepavacanāny ūcuḥ. sāyakān jagṛhur ity anvayaḥ.*) This interpretation is followed by Raghunathan (1982, vol. 3, p. 194), Roussel (1903, vol. 3, p. 221), and Shastri (1959, vol. 3, p. 193). Dutt (1893, p. 1333), Pagani (1999, p. 1050), and Gita Press (1969, vol. 3, p. 1645) take *sāyakān* as the object of both *cikṣipuḥ* and *jagṛhuḥ*, with the notion that the *rākṣasas* "took up and then loosed their arrows."

38. "the slapping of their arms" *-āsphoṭa-*: See notes to 6.17.13–15.

39. "with its upraised boulders and trees" *samudyataśilānagam*: Literally, "having rocks and immovable objects upraised." The term *naga*, "that which does not go," can refer equally to trees and mountains. We understand with Ct that the reference is to trees (*nagā vṛkṣāḥ*). Dutt (1893, p. 1333), however, alone among the translators consulted, renders, "upraised rocks and stones."

40. "the army of the *rākṣasas*, sons of chaos" *nairṛtaṃ balam*: Literally, "the *nairṛta* army." V2,B3,4,D6,9–11,T2,3,G1, and the texts and printed editions of Ct read *rākṣasam* for *nairṛtam*, yielding "the *rākṣasa* army."

41. "it bristled with huge weapons" *samudyatamahāyudham*: Literally, "its huge weapons raised."

"filled" *vṛtam*: Literally, "surrounded."

42. "perceiving their opportunity" *labdhalakṣyāḥ*: Ś2,Ñ,V,B,D1–3,5–10,12,T1,G,M, and the texts and printed editions of the southern commentators read instead *labdhalakṣāḥ*. See note at 6.56.11. We understand the compound here in more or less the sense proposed by Cr, who understands that the monkeys have now obtained targets for their blows and have therefore raised their weapons (*prāptaprahāraviṣayā ata eva samudyatamahāśailāḥ*). Cg and Cm similarly gloss, "having found scope for their valor (*labdhaparākramaviṣayāḥ*)."

"again and again" *muhur muhuḥ*: T1,M3, and the texts and printed editions of Cm and Cg read instead *mahābalāḥ*, "mighty, powerful."

Following verse 42, D5–7,9–11,S insert a passage of one line [1246*]: "Unable to tolerate the *rākṣasas*, the monkeys roared back at them." The line poses a slight narrative difficulty. Since it was the monkeys themselves who are shown to be bellowing in the preceding verse (42), it seems slightly awkward to have them now roar back at the *rākṣasas*, who have not been described as roaring since verse 37 above. Nonetheless, the difficulty is not insurmountable, as one would understand that the *rākṣasa* army would have continued its vociferation. The problem has persuaded Cr to force the grammar so as to take the nominative *vānarāḥ* of *pāda* b as the object of the verb "they roared back (*pratinardanta* v.l. for *pratinardanti*)" on the somewhat dubious grounds that the fact of the noun's collectivity enables us to read it as an accusative without it being in the second, or objective, case (*samudāyasya karmatvān na dvitīyā*). Cr thus understands that the *rākṣasas* are setting up a counter-roar against the *vānaras*. This interpretation appears to have been followed by Dutt (1893, p. 1333), Roussel (1903, vol. 3, p. 221), and Shastri (1959, vol. 3, p. 193).

43. "the resounding cries" *samudghuṣṭaravam*: Literally, "the sounded cry." Ñ,V,B2–4,D4,6,9–11,T2,3,M5, and the texts and printed editions of Ct and Cr read instead *samutkṛṣṭa-*, "loud."

The meter is *upajāti*.

44. "stormed about" *viceruḥ*: Literally, "they moved about."

"with... boulders" *śailaiḥ*: The word can also refer to mountains, and we have so translated it elsewhere (for example, see verses 46, 48–49 below). Here, however, given the simile, such a translation would be redundant. Cr, the only commentator to deal with this verse, glosses, "with mountain peaks (*śailaśṛṅgaiḥ*)." A number of northern manuscripts, as well as the editions of Gorresio (6.49.32) and Lahore (6.49.30), read instead *śṛṅgaiḥ*, which may similarly be an attempt at a gloss (Pollock 1984a, pp. 85–86).

45. "Armed with trees and boulders... stormed through" *cerur drumaśilāyudhāḥ*: Literally, "they moved about with trees and rocks for weapons." D6,9–11,T2,3, and the texts and printed editions of Ct and Cr read instead *kecit*, "some," in place of *ceruḥ*, "they moved." This restricts the possession of trees and boulders to a third group of monkeys, different from the two mentioned as engaging in aerial and ground assaults. It also deprives the verse of a finite verb, which must then be supplied, as Cr suggests (*vicerur iti śeṣaḥ*). Translations that follow the texts of Ct and Cr tend to construe this third *kecit* with the southern insert [1247*] that follows.

Following verse 45, D5–7,9–11,S insert a passage of two lines [1247*]: "[Some of those] bulls among monkeys [stormed about],[1] having seized trees with huge trunks. Then a fearsome battle took place between the massed *rākṣasas* and monkeys.[2]" All these texts repeat line 2 following 1253* (see notes to verse 56 below).

[1]"[Some of those]... [stormed about]": For the syntax, see note to verse 45 above.

[2]"the massed *rākṣasas* and monkeys" *rakṣovānarasaṃkulam*: Literally, "[battle] crowded with *rākṣasas* and monkeys."

46. "were kept at bay" *vāryamāṇāḥ*: Literally, "being warded off."

"unleashed a stupendous hail" *cakrur vṛṣṭim anuttamām*: Literally, "they made an unsurpassed shower." D7,9–11,T3,G3,M2,3,5, and the texts and printed editions of the southern commentators read instead *anūpamām* [v.l. *anupamām*], "incomparable."

"mountains" *-śailaiḥ*: See note to verse 44 above.

47. "Both the *rākṣasas* and the monkeys... in the battle" *raṇe rākṣasavānarāḥ*: Cr, who evidently wishes to restrict the action to only the monkeys in this verse, breaks up the *sandhi* and this unexceptional *dvandva* compound into the elements *raṇe 'rākṣasāḥ* [=*arākṣasāḥ*], "non-*rākṣasas*," which he glosses as "monkeys inimical to *rākṣasas*," the particle *vā*, "or," and *narāḥ*, "men," which he glosses as "leaping monkeys similar to men" (*arākṣasā rākṣasavirodhino vā narā narasadṛśāḥ plavaṅgamāḥ*).

"the *yātudhānas*" *yātudhānān*: See note to verses 48–49 below.

48–49. "the *yātudhānas*" *yātudhānān*: See 6.3.27 and note.

"by... falling mountain peaks" *śailaśṛṅganipātaiś ca*: Literally, "by the descents of mountain peaks." The critical reading is supported by only a handful of diverse manuscripts (Ś2,D6,8,G1,3). The critical apparatus shows no fewer than fourteen variants, all of which, however, are adjectives in the nominative plural. The critical reading should have been marked as uncertain. The instrumental plural could also be construed as the *karaṇa*, or instrument, of the finite verb *nijaghnuḥ*, "they slaughtered," in *pāda* 49a, yielding the sense "they slaughtered with descents of mountain peaks." It is also possible to take the compound as a *bahuvrīhi* modifying *muṣṭibhiḥ*, "with fists," in the sense of "with fists that had the impact (lit., descent) of mountain peaks." D9,11,M5, and the texts and printed editions of Cg read -[*ā*]*citāṅgāḥ* for *-nipātaiś ca*, yielding the sense "their bodies piled up with mountain peaks." Raghunathan (1982, vol. 3, p. 195) renders this reading, translating, "the bodies of some being buried under mountain crests." D10 and the texts and printed editions of Ct read instead [*a*]*nvitāṅgās te*, which, according to Ct, who glosses, "their bodies covered with mountain peaks (*giriśikharair vyāptadehāḥ*)," has a similar meaning. Cf. note to verse 44 above.

Following verse 49, B3,D5–7,9–11,S, [Ñ,V,B2,4,D4,10 insert line 1 after verse 49; line 2 after 50ab; and lines 3–4 after verse 51] insert a passage of four lines [1248*]: "Meanwhile, the *rākṣasas* cut down those elephants among monkeys with their sharp arrows and slew them with lances, war hammers, swords, darts, and javelins.[1–2] The monkeys and the *rākṣasas*, their bodies drenched with the blood of their foes, struck one another down in their eagerness to conquer one another.[3–4]"

51. The verse, as recorded in the critical edition, appears to us to make only marginal sense. Here a complex set of editorial decisions have resulted in a passage that is actually found in no other manuscript or printed edition of the text. See Sutherland 1992. A comparison of the various versions shows an interpolation of two lines interspersed between and following the lines of the critical edition, and an interpolation of one line into many of the northern manuscripts. In addition, the various versions show different cases for various words so that the same descriptions may apply in one version to the *rākṣasas*, in another to the monkeys, and in yet another to both.

The southern recension—D5–7,9–11,S—inserts two lines, one [1250*] after 51ab, and the other [1251*] after 51cd. The critical text with the two inserts [1250*, 1251*] is most closely represented by the printed editions of Cg (VSP 6.67.56cd–57; KK 6.67.56cd–57). A translation of this passage would be as follows: "Then the earth was filled with *rākṣasas*, crushers of their foes, drunk with battle, like shattered mountains;[51ab–1250*] for they had been thrown down and repulsed, their lances broken by the monkeys.[51cd] Although they were near death,[1] still they put up a wondrous battle with their bare limbs.[1251*]" This version is translated by Raghunathan (1982, vol. 3, p. 195).

[1]"Although they were near death" *āsannāḥ*: Gita Press (1969, vol. 3, p. 1646), which reads a mixed version (see below), takes the participle, less persuasively and somewhat redundantly in our opinion, as "at close quarters." Raghunathan (1982, vol. 3, p. 195) appears to ignore this term.

The printed editions of Ct (GPP, NSP 6.67.55cd–56) show a number of variations from the previous text. This variant would be translated as follows: "Then the earth was filled with shattered *rākṣasas*, who resembled mountains, and who, although drunk with battle, had been battered.[51ab–1250* with variants] They had been thrown down and repulsed by the monkeys with broken rocks.[51cd with variants] Then the monkeys put up a wondrous battle with their bare limbs.[1][1251* with variants]"

[1]"with their bare limbs" *aṅgaiḥ*: Literally, "with limbs." We follow Ct, who glosses, "with hands, feet, etc. (*hastapādādibhiḥ*)," and who, we believe, understands that the monkeys [or *rākṣasas*] are now fighting hand to hand. Roussel (1903, vol. 3, p. 222), followed by Shastri (1959, vol. 3, p. 194) and Pagani (1999, p. 1051), understands that the monkeys are using severed limbs found on the battlefield as weapons.

Gita Press (1969, vol. 3, pp. 1645–46) reads the first line with Ct and the second with Cg. The printed editions of Gorresio and Lahore present still other versions of this passage (Gorresio 6.49.41–42ab; Lahore 6.49.38). Gorresio's edition reads 1250* following 51ab, although this is not noted by the critical apparatus. His version would yield: "Then the earth was filled with shattered *rākṣasas*, who resembled mountains, and who, although drunk with battle, had been battered.[51ab–1250* with variants] Throwing down and being thrown down the *yātudhānas* and the monkeys . . . [1248*, line 8]." Gorresio (1858, vol. 10, p. 43) translates this passage as follows: "*ed era gremito il suolo di Racsasi pari a monti e inebbriati dalla battaglia, quà e là distesi e sgretolati. Rincacciando e i rincacciati, vānari e Racsasi.*"

The Lahore edition (6.49.38) has only two lines (=51 with variants). These would be translated as: "Thrown down and repulsed, their heads broken, the monkeys were battered and shattered, cut down by the *rākṣasas* with their arrows."

52. "Night-roaming *rākṣasas*" *rajanīcarāḥ*: The printed editions of GPP, NSP, and Gita Press (6.69.57) read instead *nairṛtarṣabhāḥ*, "bulls among the sons of chaos (*nairṛtas*)." This variant is not noted in the critical apparatus.

"monkeys with monkeys . . . *rākṣasas* with *rākṣasas*" *vānarān vānaraiḥ* . . . *rākṣasān rākṣaākṣasas*" *vānarān vānaraiḥ* . . . *rākṣasān rākṣasaiḥ*: The commentators are silent on exactly what is happening here. Evidently, we are to understand that the combatants are hurling the bodies [living or dead] of their enemies against other enemies. A majority of the translators consulted understand that it is specifically corpses that are being used as weapons.

53. "the tawny monkeys' . . . them . . . the *rākṣasas*' . . . them" *teṣām* . . . *harīn* . . . *teṣām* . . . *rakṣāṃsi*: Literally, "of them . . . [they slaughtered] tawny monkeys . . . of them . . . [they slaughtered] *rākṣasas*." D9–11 and the texts and printed editions of Ct read *śailān*, "mountains," for the first *teṣām*, and *tadā*, "then," for *harīn*, "tawny monkeys." This lends the first line the sense "seizing stones and mountains, the *rākṣasas* then began to slaughter."

54. "roared like lions" *siṃhanādān vineduḥ*: Literally, "they roared lion roars."

"with boulders, lances, and missiles" *śailaśūlāstraiḥ*: D9–11 and the texts and printed editions of Ct read instead *śailaśṛṅgaiś ca*, "and with mountain peaks." See note to verse 44 above.

55. "their mail and armor pierced" *chinnavarmatanutrāṇāḥ*: The term *tanutrāṇa*, literally, "body protector," is more or less synonymous with *varma*, "armor." Cg, the only commentator to address this issue, glosses, "their body protection, in the form of armor, pierced (*chinnavarmarūpatanutrāṇāḥ*)."

"vital sap" *rasasāram*: The compound is slightly ambiguous, since both *rasa* and *sāra* can refer to tree sap. We take the latter term here in its sense of "most essential portion." Ct, Cg, Cm, and Cr gloss, "tree sap *or* resin (*niryāsam*)."

56. Following verse 56, D5–7,T1,G1,3,M1–3, and the texts and printed editions of Cg insert a passage of two lines [1253*]: "Their minds worked up to a frenzy, all the tawny monkeys, holding huge boulders,[1] slaughtered the *rākṣasas* with many-branched trees."

[1]"huge boulders" *-mahāśilāḥ*: M3, KK, and VSP read instead *-manaḥśilāḥ*, "red arsenic." This variant is rendered only by Raghunathan (1982, vol. 3, p. 195), who translates, "rocks of antimony."

Following 1253*, all these manuscripts repeat line 2 of 1247*. See note to verse 45 above.

57. "horseshoe-headed, half-moon-headed" *kṣuraprair ardhacandraiś ca*: According to Apte (s.v.), *kṣurapra* refers to "an arrow with a sharp horseshoe-shaped head." The critical edition has a small typographical error unnoted in the errata. It mistakenly reads *kṣuraprarairdhacandraiś ca*. Cf. 6.35.23; 6.55.117; and notes. See, too, 6.44.18 and note.

58. "With the monkeys and *rākṣasas* . . . and with all the shattered mountaintops and splintered trees" *vikīrṇaiḥ parvatāgraiś ca drumaiś chinnaiś ca . . . kapirakṣobhiḥ*: Literally, "with shattered mountaintops, split trees, and monkeys and *rākṣasas*." D9–11,M3,5, and the texts and printed editions of Ct read *vikīrṇā*, "littered, scattered," an adjective describing the ground or earth (*vasudhā*), while D9,10, and the texts and printed editions of Ct read *parvatās taiś ca* for the critical edition's *parvatāgraiś ca*. In addition, D9–11,G1, and the texts and printed editions of Ct read *drumacchinnaiś ca* for *drumaiś chinnaiś ca*. Following Ct in reading the latter two compounds as *paranipāta*, the half verse would mean "littered with scattered mountains and splintered trees (*nirastaparvataiḥ . . . chinnadrumaiḥ*)." One can also take the compounds as adjectives meaning "tossed by mountains and shattered by trees," and modifying the compound *kapirakṣobhiḥ*, "with monkeys and *rākṣasas*." The verse would then mean "Littered with monkeys and *rākṣasas*, who had been slain in battle—tossed by mountains and shattered by trees—the ground became impassable." This interpretation has been followed by Roussel (1903, vol. 3, p. 222) and, after him, Shastri (1959, vol. 3, p. 194).

Following verse 58, D5–7,9–11,S insert a passage of four lines [1258*]: "Abandoning their fear, all the monkeys, whose actions reflected their pride and excitement,[1] entered the battlefield, and there, in high spirits and armed with various weapons,[2] they gave battle to the *rākṣasas*."

[1]"whose actions reflected their pride and excitement" *garvitahṛṣṭaceṣṭāḥ*: We follow Cg in reading the first two elements of the compound adverbially. He explains, "they behaved proudly and excitedly (*garvitaṃ hṛṣṭaṃ ca yathā bhavati tathā ceṣṭanta iti*)." Ck, Cr, and Ct read the compound slightly differently to mean "whose pride was aroused and whose actions were excited (*saṃjātagarvā hṛṣṭaceṣṭā yeṣāṃ te*—so Ct)."

[2]"armed with various weapons" *nānāyudhāḥ*: Ct and Ck understand this to refer to the normal weaponry of the monkeys, viz., trees, rocks, teeth, claws, etc. (*drumaśaila-dantanakhādinānāpraharaṇayutāḥ*), while Cg takes it as a reference to weapons seized from the *rākṣasas* (*gṛhītarākṣasāyudhā ity arthaḥ*).

The meter of 1258* is *indravajrā*.

59. "cheered" *neduḥ*: Literally, "they shouted."

The meter is *upajāti*.

60. "the army of the monkey king" *vānararājasainyam*: D9–11 and the texts and printed editions of Ct read instead *vānarasainyam ugram*, "the fierce monkey army."

The meter is *upajāti*.

61. "In an instant... single-handedly" *ekaḥ kṣaṇena*: Literally, "one in an instant." Ś2,Ñ2,V3,B1,4,D8,12,T2,3,G2,M3,5, and the texts and printed editions of Cg, as well as the texts of Gorresio (6.49.55) and Lahore (5.49.50), both unnoted by the critical edition, read instead *ekakṣanena*, "in a single moment *or* instant."

The meter is *upajāti*.

62. "that great warrior" *mahātmānam*: Literally, "the great one."

"rampaged" *carantam*: Literally, "moving, ranging."

63. "One could mark his path" *sa tasya dadṛśe mārgaḥ*: Literally, "His path was seen."

65. B3,D6,7,9–11,T2,3,M5, and the texts and printed editions of Ct read *pāda* ab of verse 65 after verse 66 below.

"in the midst of the battle" *saṃgrāmānte*: Literally, "inside *or* in the interior *or* the end of the battle." Ñ1,V3,B3,4,D4,G1,M3,5, and the texts and printed editions of Cg read instead *saṃgrāmāgre*, "in the forefront *or* vanguard of the battle."

66. See note to verse 65 above for the verse order in printed editions of Ct.

67. "rampaged" *vicacāra*: Literally, "he roamed about."

"everything in his path" *sarvataḥ*: Literally, "on all sides."

68. "to flee" *dhāvitum*: Literally, "to run." D9–11 and the texts and printed editions of Ct and Cr read instead *bhāṣitum*, "to speak." The critical apparatus prints this incorrectly as *bhāvitum*. Translators who follow the text of Ct render *bhāṣitum*, with the exception of Dutt (1893, p. 1336), who mistakenly appears to have read *bhāsitum*, "to appear," and therefore renders, "could not appear prominently."

"in any direction" *kutaḥ*: Literally, "from where." D7,M3, and the texts and printed editions of Cr and Cg read instead *bhayāt*, "out of fear." Raghunathan (1982, vol. 3, p. 196) and Gita Press (1969, vol. 3, p. 1647) render this variant.

"to... stand their ground... stood still" *sthātum... sthitam*: Literally, "to stand... stood."

69. "Pierced" *bhinnāni*: Ś,Ñ2,D2,7–12, and the texts and printed editions of Ct and Cr read instead *bhagnāni*, "broken."

"by that lone warrior, who, with his dart as brilliant as the sun, was like Yama, the ender of all things" *ekenāntakakalpena prāsenādityatejasā*: Literally, "by that one, who resembled Antaka, with the dart that had the splendor of the sun." We share the view of Cr, against the unanimous opinion of the translators consulted, that the first two words of the verse refer to Narāntaka, who is the subject of the participle *bhinnāni*, "pierced," in *pāda* c, and that *prāsena* is the *karaṇa*, or instrument, of the participle (*ekena narāntakena bhagnāni harisainyāni nipetuḥ*). Other translators regard *prāsa* as the subject and regard all the adjectives in *pādas* ab to modify it, yielding the sense "pierced by that single dart, as brilliant as the sun and resembling death, the ender of all things."

70. "of a thunderbolt" *vajra-*: This could also be a reference to Indra's weapon, the *vajra*. Cf. verses 87–88 and notes below.

"wailed loudly" *vinedur mahāsvanam*: Literally, "they roared a loud sound."

*72. "those ... fully recovered" *te 'svasthāḥ*: Literally, "those ... who were unwell." The critical editors have printed the term as if it were the negative by inserting an *avagraha* to mark the elision of the negative prefix "*a*." There is, however, no reason for them to have done so, as manuscripts would not generally mark any such elision. All commentators and printed editions uniformly have the contextually apposite *svasthāḥ*, "healthy, recovered," and this reading has been followed by all translators who share this half verse. The idea, as expressed by Cg, is that the principal monkeys, such as Nīla, etc., who had been knocked unconscious by Kumbhakarṇa, have now recovered, and the poet mentions this to maintain narrative consistency with their later heroic actions (*kumbhakarṇena pātitānāṃ nīlādīnām uttaratra pauruṣakathanasāṅgatyāyaiṣāṃ labdhasaṃjñatvam āha*). None of the commentators acknowledges the possibility of reading *asvasthāḥ*. On the basis of all this, we propose emending the critical text to remove the *avagraha* and have translated accordingly.

73. "in all directions" *itas tataḥ*: Literally, "here and there."

75. "Then" *atha*: D6,7,9–11,T2,3,G,M1,2, and the texts and printed editions of Ct and Cr read instead *dṛṣṭvā*, "having seen."

76. "Hero, you must advance against that *rākṣasa*" *gacchainaṃ rākṣasaṃ vīra*: Literally, "go to that *rākṣasa*, O hero." Ś,Ñ,V,B,D1,4,6,8–12,T2,3,M1,2, and the texts and printed editions of Ct and Cr read the accusative *vīram* for the critical edition's vocative *vīra*, yielding the sense "go to that *rākṣasa* hero."

"terrorizing" *kṣobhayantam*: Literally, "causing to shake *or* tremble." D9–11 and the texts and printed editions of Ct read instead *bhakṣayantam*, "devouring, eating."

"the army of tawny monkeys" *haribalam*: D7,9–11, and the texts and printed editions of Ct read instead *parabalam*, "the army of the enemy."

"you must ... kill him" *prāṇair viyojaya*: Literally, "separate [him] from [his] life breaths."

77. "forth from that host—so like a cloud—as does the many-rayed sun from a host of clouds" *anīkān meghasaṃkāśān meghānīkād ivāṃśumān*: Literally, "from that army, which resembled a cloud, like the one possessing rays from a cloud-army." Cg comments on the basis for the two similes. He notes that the comparison of the monkey army to a mass of clouds is derived from their shared quality of density, whereas the comparison of Aṅgada to the sun is based on their shared quality of emergence from a mass. (*meghasaṃkāśād iti nibiḍatvalakṣaṇasamānadharmaprayukteyam upamā. meghānīkād ity atra tu niṣkramaṇāpādānatvadharmaprayuktety upamādvayasya nirvāhaḥ.*)

V3,D6,7,9–11,T2,3, and the texts and printed editions of Cr, Ck, and Ct read *aṃśumān iva vīryavān* for *meghānīkād ivāṃśumān*. This can be interpreted here either to mean "like the mighty-rayed one" or "that mighty one [Aṅgada], [who was] like the rayed one."

78. "Adorned with his golden armlets ... Aṅgada" *aṅgadaḥ ... aṅgadasaṃnaddhaḥ*: Literally, "Aṅgada girded with *aṅgadas* (armlets)." This is yet another of the etymological epithets of which Vālmīki is so fond. See verse 17 and note above. See 6.54.25; 6.116.67; and notes.

"laced with shining ore" *sadhātuḥ*: Literally, "with minerals *or* metallic ore."

80. "Why bother with" *kim . . . tvaṃ kariṣyasi*: Literally, "what will you do with."

"as hard to the touch as adamant" *vajrasamasparśe*: Ś,Ñ2,V2,B1,4,D2,4–6,8–12, T,G1,2,M3,5, and the texts and printed editions of the southern commentators read instead the accusative *vajrasamasparśam*, which then modifies *prāsam*, "dart."

81. Following verse 81, D5–7,9–11,S insert a passage of one line [1269*]: "Approaching Vālin's son Aṅgada, Narāntaka, in a rage . . ."

82. The meter is *upajāti*.

83. "the coils" *-bhoga-*: Ś1,D5,9–11, and the texts and printed editions of Cr and Ct read instead the awkward *-vīrya-*, "power, strength."

"Narāntaka's" *asya*: Literally, "of him."

The meter is *upajāti*.

84. "the horse" *tasya vājī*: Literally, "his horse."

"its feet driven into the earth" *nimagnapādaḥ*: Literally, "its feet sunken." Ñ2,V3,B1,D2,13,M3, the printed editions of Gorresio and Lahore, and the texts and printed editions of Cg read instead *nimagnatāluḥ*, "its palate sunken in." Of the translators consulted, only Raghunathan (1982, vol. 3, p. 197; "its jaw bashed in") and Gorresio (1858, vol. 10, p. 46; "*col palato schiacciato in bocca*") render this variant.

The meter is *upajāti*.

85. The meter is *upendravajrā*.

86. "great gouts" *tīvram*: We take the term here as an adverb in the sense of "copiously." See 6.59.81 and note.

"he flared up in anger" *vijajvāla*: Literally, "he burned." The verb is somewhat ambiguous here and has lent itself to three different interpretations on the part of the translators. Raghunathan (1982, vol. 3, p. 197) and Shastri (1959, vol. 3, p. 196), like us, understand that Aṅgada flares up in anger at the blow before losing consciousness. Gita Press (1969, vol. 3, p. 1649) and (Dutt 1893, p. 1337) understand that Aṅgada experienced a burning sensation before fainting. Gorresio (1858, vol. 10, p. 46), understands similarly, rendering, "*arse ad ora ad ora come fiamma*." Roussel (1903, vol. 3, p. 224) and Pagani (1999, p. 1053) believe that Aṅgada actually emits flames, "*il projeta des flammes*" (so Roussel).

The meter is *upajāti*.

87. "thunderbolt" *vajra-*: This could also be a reference to Indra's weapon, the *vajra*. However, given the context, it probably refers to a thunderbolt. Cf. verses 70–71 and notes above. Ś,D9–11, and the texts and printed editions of Ct read instead *mṛtyu-*, "death."

The meter is *upajāti*.

88. "His chest shattered by the impact of that fist" *muṣṭiniṣpiṣṭavibhinnavakṣāḥ*: We follow the interpretation of Cr, who takes *-niṣpiṣṭa-* nominally in the sense of "impact (*vega*)" rather than adjectivally in the sense of "crushed" (*muṣṭer niṣpiṣṭena vegena*). D10,11,M1,2, and the texts and printed editions of Ck and Ct read *-nirbhinna-*, "split," for *-niṣpiṣṭa-*, "impact." In addition, D10,11,M5, and the texts and printed editions of Ct and Ck read *-nimagna-*, "sunk in, stove in," for *-vibhinna-*, "shattered." The resulting compound in the text of Ct yields "his chest shattered and stove in by that fist."

The meter is *upajāti*.

89. "that most eminent of heroes" *[a]gryavīre*: Ś,Ñ,V,B,D2–4,6–8,12,13, and the printed editions of Gorresio and Lahore read *ativīrye* [D6—*agra-*], "of extraordinary

power/strength," while D1,5,9–11,T2,3,G,M5, and the texts and printed editions of Ct and Cr read instead *agryavīrye*, "whose valor *or* strength is outstanding." Translators who follow the text of Ct, with the apparent exception of Pagani (1999, p. 1053), render this variant. Given the strength of the textual evidence, the reading *-vīre* should at least have been marked as doubtful.

"hovering in the sky" *antarikṣe*: Literally, "in the sky *or* atmosphere."

The meter is *upendravajrā*.

90. "of extraordinary might and valor" *ativīryavikramaḥ*: D10,11, and the texts and printed editions of Ct read instead the hypometric *atha bhīmakarmā*, "of fearsome deeds."

"he was somewhat astonished" *visiṣmiye so 'pi*: Commentators and translators are divided as to whether this phrase refers to Añgada or Rāma. Ck, Ct, and Cr take the latter position; thus, in their view, the verse's sequence of verbs first has Añgada as the subject, followed by Rāma, and then Añgada again. This interpretation has been followed by Roussel (1903, vol. 3, p. 224), Shastri (1959, vol. 3, p. 197), Gita Press (1969, vol. 3, p. 1650), and Pagani (1999, p. 1053). Cg, whom we have followed, acknowledges that Rāma is astonished at Añgada's feat but believes that the adjective *rāmamanaḥpraharṣaṇam*, "delighting Rāma's heart," must lead us to understand that the word "Rāma" is of secondary importance in this sentence, and that therefore Añgada must be the subject of the verb *visiṣmiye*, "he was astonished." (*visiṣmiye. so 'pīty atra tacchabdena rāmamanaḥpraharṣaṇam ity atra guṇībhūto rāmaśabdaḥ parāmṛśyate.*) We believe that Cg is correct and that it is perfectly plausible that young Añgada might be somewhat surprised at the lethal effect of his heroic blow. This interpretation has also been followed by Dutt (1893, p. 1337) and Raghunathan (1982, vol. 3, pp. 197–98). Gorresio (1858, vol. 10, p. 47) shares the belief that Añgada is the subject of the verb *visiṣmiye*, but he takes it in its other sense of "to be haughty *or* conceited," rendering it (with his variant *nāti*, "not excessively," for the critical edition's *so 'pi*) as "*non superbi fuori di modo*."

"filled once more with energy for battle" *punaś ca yuddhe sa babhūva harṣitaḥ*: Literally, "He became once again excited in battle." Cg understands the phrase somewhat differently from other commentators and translators, glossing, "*harṣita* means 'gratified with praise by the astonished Rāma. He, that is, Añgada, was once again in the battle, that is, he became prepared with respect to battle.' (*harṣito vismitena rāmeṇa ślāghaya toṣitaḥ. sa cāṅgadaś ca punar yuddhe babhūva. yuddhaviṣaye sannaddho babhūvety arthaḥ.*)"

The meter is *vaṃśasthavila*.

Ck, also quoted by Cm, and Ct (at the beginning of GPP 70) note that, in many manuscripts, there is no *sarga* break after verse 90, and that they concur with this division of the text on the grounds that (as Ck noted) the preceding and following sections describe the continuing combat on the part of the same figure (Añgada) (*atra sargāvacchedo bahuṣu pustakeṣu na dṛśyata ity asmābhir api na kṛtaḥ pūrvottaravākyayor ekakartṛkayuddhavarṇanād iti kaṭakaḥ*). According to the critical apparatus, only D10,11 fail to insert a break at this juncture. Among the printed editions consulted, NSP continues to number its verses sequentially in *sarga* 69 after this point to include the following *sarga*, arriving at a total number of 162 *ślokas*. The edition does, however, draw a small line after verse 90 [= NSP 6.69.96] and shifts the *sarga* number of its running header to 70. Among the translations consulted, Dutt (1893, pp. 1330–43) continues *sarga* 69 of his text to include *sarga* 70 but skips a number, moving from *sarga* 69 [LXIX] to *sarga* 71 [LXXI] with no intervening section marker. Roussel (1903, vol. 3, p. 219), too, reads the two *sargas* together for a total of 162 *ślokas* and entitles this extended *sarga* "Sargas LXIX, LXX."

Sarga 58

1. "Devāntaka, Trimūrdhan Paulastya, and Mahodara" *devāntakas trimūrdhā ca paulastyaś ca mahodaraḥ*: It is difficult to determine with precision exactly how many *rākṣasas* are mentioned here and who they are. One would have expected the list to include the remaining five of the six *rākṣasas* who set forth in the previous *sarga* to avenge the death of Kumbhakarṇa, viz., Devāntaka, Triśiras, Atikāya, Mahodara, and Mahāpārśva (see 6.57.9,12). In this verse, however, a maximum of four and, at least arguably, a minimum of two are mentioned. Two of the names or epithets listed here are more or less problematic. The most probable number is three, because in the following verses only Devāntaka, Triśiras, and Mahodara are specifically mentioned as attacking Aṅgada, and because in verse 5 the number is explicitly given as three. The name Trimūrdhan, literally, "three-headed," is almost certainly a variant of Triśiras, but Dutt (1893, p. 1338) takes it as an epithet for the *rākṣasa* Devāntaka. More problematic is the patronymic term *paulastya*, "son *or* descendant of Pulastya." This term is normally used of Rāvaṇa but by normal practice could also refer to any male descendant of the *ṛṣi* Pulastya. Thus, Ck takes it here as an epithet of Rāvaṇa's brother Mahodara (see, too, 6.57.16 and note) (*paulastya iti paulastyo rāvaṇas tadbhrātā mahodaraś ca*). This position is represented in the translations of Roussel (1903, vol. 3, p. 224), Pagani (1999, p. 1054), Shastri (1959, vol. 3, p. 197), and Gorresio (1858, vol. 10, p. 47), all of whom believe that the list consists of Devāntaka, Triśiras (a.k.a. Trimūrdhan), and Mahodara Paulastya. Cg, whom we follow, explicitly rejects Ck's position, claiming that Paulastya here is an epithet of Trimūrdhan (Triśiras) and not of Mahodara. He thus also sees a list of only three *rākṣasas*, viz., Devāntaka, Trimūrdhan Paulastya, and Mahodara. (*paulastya iti trimūrdhaviśeṣaṇam na tu mahodarasya. devāntakādayas trayaś cukruśur iti saṃbandhaḥ.*) Gita Press (1969, vol. 3, p. 1650) represents this position in its translation. Raghunathan (1982, vol. 3, p. 198) also envisions a list of three but wishes to apply the patronymic to both Devāntaka and Trimūrdhan (Triśiras), rendering, "Devāntaka and Triśiras, scions of the Pulasthyas, as well as Mahodara." Dutt (1893, p. 1338), idiosyncratically, sees only two *rākṣasas* in the list and translates, "including the thre[*sic*]-headed Devāntaka and Pulastya's descendant, Mahodara."

2. "magnificent bull elephant" *vāraṇendram*: Literally, "lord *or* best of elephants."

"Aṅgada, Vālin's . . . son" *vāliputram*: Literally, "Vālin's son."

"immensely powerful" *vīryavān*: D6,7,10,11,T1,2,G1,2,M5, and the texts and printed editions of Ct and Cr read instead *vegavān*, "swift."

4. "Triśiras" *triśirāḥ*: In verse 1, this *rākṣasa* is referred to as Trimūrdhan.

5. "those . . . lords of the *rākṣasas*, sons of chaos" *nairṛtendraiḥ*: Literally, "best *or* lords among the *nairṛtas*." D7,10,11, and the texts and printed editions of Ct and Cr read instead *rākṣasendraiḥ*, "lords *or* best among the *rākṣasas*."

7. "leapt up into the sky" *utpapāta*: Literally, "he leapt *or* flew up."

9. "And Surāntaka" *ca surāntakaḥ*: Literally, "and the ender of the gods." The name is clearly a variant of Devāntaka, literally, "ender of gods." D10,11, and the texts and printed editions of Ct, Cr, and Ck read instead *sa mahodaraḥ*, "he, Mahodara."

10. "Mahodara, too" *mahodaraḥ*: Literally, "Mahodara."

"with iron cudgels" *tomaraiḥ*: According to Dikshitar (1944, p. 107), *tomaras* are found in two varieties: *sarvāyasam* and *daṇḍa*. He identifies these as "iron club" and "javelin," respectively. We, along with Gita Press (1969, vol. 3, p. 1651) and Gorresio (1858, vol. 10, p. 48) understand the term here in its former meaning. Other translators consulted either leave the term untranslated or choose the latter meaning (Pagani 1999, p. 1054). Dikshitar (1944, p. 107) cites a commentator on Kauṭilya as identifying the *tomara* as "a rod with an arrowlike edge." See note to 6.59.28; and 6.63.14 and note.

"that struck with the force of thunderbolts" *vajrasaṃnibhaiḥ*: Literally, "[with iron cudgels that were] like the *vajra*." The *vajra* can also refer to Indra's weapon, and some translators take it in this sense. See notes to 6.57.70–71,87–88. See verse 49 below.

11. "Meanwhile" *tadā*: Literally, "then."

12. " immensely powerful and valorous warrior" *mahātejāḥ . . . pratāpavān*: Literally, "powerful and valorous one."

Following verse 12, D5,7,10,11,T1,G3,M3, and the texts and printed editions of the southern commentators insert a passage of one line [1274*]: "That swift and supremely invincible warrior[1] [Aṅgada] putting forth tremendous speed . . ."

[1]"That . . . supremely invincible warrior" *paramadurjayaḥ*: Literally, "the supremely invincible one."

13. "Leaping up, he struck . . . violently" *bhṛśam utpatya jaghāna*: The easiest reading of the syntax would be to construe the adverb *bhṛśam*, "swiftly, violently," with the gerund. And, indeed, the only two translators consulted who share this reading have done so (Raghunathan 1982, vol. 3, p. 198 and Gorresio 1858, vol. 10, p. 48). We, however, believe that the logic of the passage supports construing the adverb with the finite verb, *jaghāna*, "he struck," in *pāda* b. D5–7,9–11,T1,3,G3, and the texts and printed editions of Ct and Cr read instead *samabhidrutya*, "having rushed *or* having raced up," for *bhṛśam utpatya*.

"Mahodara's" *asya*: Literally, "his." Verses 2 and 10 above, as well Ck, Ct, and Cg, support the notion that the elephant is Mahodara's. Perhaps because Aṅgada will attack Devāntaka with the elephant's tusk in verse 14 below, Cr identifies the elephant as belonging to that *rākṣasa* (*devāntakasya mahāgajam*).

"with his open hand" *tālena*: Literally, "with his palm."

"Its eyes knocked out" *petatur locane tasya*: Literally, "its two eyes fell."

"trumpeted loudly" *vinanāda*: D9–11,M3, and the texts and printed editions of Ct and Cr read instead *vinanāśa*, "he was destroyed."

Following 13ab, D5–7,T1,M3, and the texts and printed editions of Cg insert a passage of one line [1275*]: "Through the force of his blow in battle, [the eyes] of that prince of elephants . . ."

14. "rushed upon" *abhidrutya*: T1,2,G1,M, and the texts and printed editions of Cg, Crā, and Cm read instead *abhiplutya*, "having sprung *or* leapt up." Only Raghunathan (1982, vol. 3, p. 198) among the commentators renders this variant.

15. "Swaying with every limb" *vihvalitasarvāṅgaḥ*: D6,7,10,11,M1,2, and the texts and printed editions of Ct and Cr read instead *vihvalas tu tejasvī*, "that powerful one staggered."

"Devāntaka" *saḥ*: Literally, "he."

"lac" *lākṣārasa-*: Literally, "lac juice." Lac is a bright red dye derived from secretions of the insect *Laccifer lacca*, which also yields a resin, the common lacquer. See, too, *Hobson Jobson* 1903, pp. 499–500 (s.v. lac); and note to 4.23.13.

"from his mouth" *mukhāt*: D9–11 and the texts and printed editions of Ct read instead *mahat*, "great, copious."

16. "dreadful" *ghoram*: Ś,Ñ,V,B1,2,4,D (except D6),T1,G3,M1,2,5, and the texts and printed editions of Ct and Cr read instead *vegāt*, "swiftly."

17. "the son of the lord of the monkeys" *vānarendrātmajaḥ*: The reference is to Aṅgada's being the son of the former king of the monkeys, Vālin, not his successor, Sugrīva.

18. "the son of the lord of the tawny monkeys" *haripateḥ putram*: See note to verse 17 above.

"with three ... arrows that resembled venomous serpents" *tribhir āśīviṣopamaiḥ*: Literally, "with three that resembled venomous serpents." In attempting to mediate between the different readings of the two recensions, the critical editors have produced a peculiar version that omits a necessary and expected noun meaning "arrows." Virtually all northern manuscripts as well as the printed editions of Lahore and Gorresio read *śaraiḥ*, "arrows," in place of *tribhiḥ*, "three," yielding the sense "with arrows resembling venomous serpents." The great majority of southern manuscripts (D7,9–11,T2,3,G3,M) and the texts and printed editions of the southern commentators read *bāṇair ajihmagaiḥ*, "with [three] straight-flying arrows." Some manuscripts (Ñ,V2,3,B1,2,4,D4,6,G1,2) substitute the word *bāṇaiḥ*, "with arrows," for *ghoraiḥ*, "dreadful," in *pāda* c. The critical reading is defective and lacks any persuasive textual support. Given the principles on which the critical edition was based, the editors should have probably selected the southern reading and perhaps have marked it as uncertain. See Bhatt 1960, p. xxxiv and Sutherland 1992.

19. "they ran to his aid" *pratasthatuḥ*: Literally, "they set forth."

21. "shooting forth sparks and flames" *savisphuliṅgaṃ sajvālam*: Literally, "with sparks, with flames."

22. "Then" *tataḥ ... tadā*: Literally, "after that ... then." D5,7,9–11,T1,M5, and the texts and printed editions of Ct and Cr read *balī*, "strong, mighty," which modifies Devāntaka, for *tadā*.

"upon witnessing that explosion" *jṛmbhitam ālokya*: Literally, "then having seen that bursting open." D7,10,11,T2,3, and the texts and printed editions of Ct and Cr read the minor variation *sa vijṛmbhitam*. Commentators and translators differ considerably in their understanding of the term *jṛmbhitam* (v.l. *vijṛmbhitam*) here. We believe that Ck and Ct are correct in taking the term in its sense of "manifestation *or* bursting open." They gloss, "that manifestation of Triśiras, which consisted of the shattering of the mountain peak (*triśirasaḥ parvataśikharabhedanarūpaṃ jṛmbhaṇam*)." Cg and Cm understand the term adjectivally in the sense of "broken, smashed (*bhagnam*)," applying it thus to the mountaintop that was shattered in the previous verse. In the absence of any lexical support for such a reading, Cg cites 1.74.17,19 (=GPP 1.75.17,19), where Śiva's bow is said to be *jṛmbhitam*, "disabled, unstrung," through the power of Viṣṇu's uttering of the *mantra* "*hum*." The majority of northern manuscripts seem to support this. B3,D13, and the printed edition of Gorresio substitute, perhaps by way of a gloss, *tat tu bhagnam*, "[seeing] that broken," while the remaining northern manuscripts and the Lahore edition substitute *tat tu cūrṇitam*, "[seeing] that pulverized." We believe that the term at 1.74.17,19 has been correctly understood by Ct and Cr as "slackened *or* unstrung (*śaithilyaṃ prāptam*—so Cr)," but there Cg glosses, "broken (*bhagnam*)." Cr reads the term here adjectivally with *mārutātmajam*, in the sense of "his appearance transformed by his having been suffused with anger (*krodhāveśena pariṇatarūpam*)." Translators have similarly differed. Several of the translators take the term explicitly or implicitly in its sense of "gaping, yawning [with amazement *or* joy]" (Dutt 1893, p. 1339; Roussel 1903, vol. 3, p. 225; Shastri 1959, vol. 3, p. 198; and Pagani 1999, p. 1055). Gita Press (1969, vol. 3, p. 1652) understands as we do.

23. "son of Māruta" *mārutātmajaḥ*: Ś,Ñ,V,B,D1–4,8,10–13, and the texts and printed editions of Ct read instead *kapikuñjaraḥ*, "that elephant among monkeys."

"Devāntaka" *tam*: Literally, "him."

"with . . . which had the force a thunderbolt" *vajravegena*: Literally, "which had the impact of the *vajra*." On *vajra*, see note to verse 10 above. Ñ1,B3,D6,7,9–11,13,T2,3,G2,M1–3, and the texts and printed editions of the southern commentators read instead *vajrakalpena*, "like the *vajra*."

Following verse 23, D5–7,9–11,T,G1,3,M, and the texts and printed editions of the southern commentators insert a passage of two lines [1278*]: "The mighty son of Vāyu then struck him on the head. With a roar, that great monkey made the *rākṣasas* tremble."

24. The meter is *upajāti*.

25. "Trimūrdhan" *trimūrdhā*: D9,10,G2, and the texts and printed editions of Ct read instead yet another synonymous name for Triśiras, *triśīrṣaḥ*, "Triśīrṣa." See note to verse 1 above. Pagani (1999, p. 1055) renders the name and its literal translation, offering, "*Triśiras, le monstre tricéphale*." See, too, her note (1999, p. 1667).

"a fierce shower of sharp-tipped arrows" *niśitāgram ugram . . . bāṇavarṣam*: Literally, "a fierce arrow-shower with sharp tips." D6,7,10,11,T2,G1, and the texts and printed editions of Ct and Cr read *-astram*, "missile *or* divinely charged weapon," for *-agram*, "tip."

The meter is *upajāti*.

Following verse 25, D5–7,9–11,T1,2,G,M, and the texts and printed editions of the southern commentators insert a passage of four lines [1280*]: "But Mahodara, in a towering rage, once again mounted his elephant, which resembled a mountain, just as the many-rayed sun[1] climbs Mount Mandara.[1–2] From there he let fall upon Nīla's chest[2] a shower of arrows, just as a storm cloud, complete with a rainbow and, with a discus in the form of lightning,[3] lets fall a torrent upon a mountain. [3–4]"

[1]"the many-rayed sun" *raśmivān*: Literally, "the many-rayed one."

[2]"Nīla's chest" *nīlasyorasi*: D3,9–11, and the texts and printed editions of Ct read instead *nīlasyopari*, "upon Nīla."

[3]"complete with a rainbow and, with a discus in the form of lightning" *taḍiccakracāpavān*: Literally, "possessing a lightning-discus and a bow." D3,9–11, and the texts and printed editions of Ct read instead *taḍiccakraṃ sa garjan*, "[the cloud] thundering with its discus in the form of lightning." Ct understands the disc, or circle of lightning, to refer to a bow, that is, Indra's bow, or the rainbow (*taḍiccakraṃ cāpam indradhanuś ca yasyāsti saḥ*).

26. "slack limbed" *visṛṣṭagātraḥ*: Literally, "having released limbs." We follow the commentators who understand the compound to mean that Nīla's limbs were loosened or slackened (*śithilagātraḥ*—so Cg on his v.l. *nisṛṣṭagātraḥ*). Cm, however, offers, as an alternative, "whose limbs were under the control of another (*paravaśagātraḥ*)."

"mighty Triśiras" *mahābalena*: Literally, "by the one of great strength."

The meter is *upajāti*.

27. "with its masses of trees" *savṛkṣaṣaṇḍam*: D7,9–11,13, and the texts and printed editions of Ct read instead *savṛkṣakhaṇḍam*, "with its broken pieces of trees."

The meter is *upajāti*.

28. "Crushed together with his elephant by the mountain as it fell" *śailābhinipātabhagnaḥ* ... *tena saha dvipena*: Literally, "[he] broken by the fall of the mountain along with that elephant." See note below.

"mortally wounded" *vipothitaḥ*: We follow Cg, the only commentator to read with the critical edition, who glosses, "injured (*hiṃsitaḥ*)." D10 and the texts and printed editions of Ct read instead *vyāmohitaḥ*, "unconscious." Gita Press (1969, vol. 3, p. 1653) is the only translation to follow the text of Ct here, and it renders this variant. Roussel (1903, vol. 3, p. 226) reads with Ct but has apparently misunderstood the phrase *tena saha dvipena*, taking it as a metaphorical reference to Nīla and as the agent of the participle *vyāmohitaḥ*. He renders, "*que ce grand éléphant* (*des Kapis*) *venait ainsi d'assommer*." In this error he has been followed by Shastri (1959, vol. 3, p. 199) and Pagani (1999, p. 1055).

The meter is *upendravajrā*.

29. Following verse 29, Ñ,B1(line 1 only)–3,D4–7,9–11,S insert a passage of six lines [1283*]: "Furious, the son of Vāyu hurled a mountaintop, but mighty Triśiras shattered it into myriad fragments[1] with his sharp arrows.[1–2] Seeing that his mountain had had no effect, the great monkey[2] released a hail of trees upon the son of Rāvaṇa in battle.[3–4] But with his sharp arrows, valorous Triśiras splintered that hail of trees as it flew toward him in the air, and he roared.[5–6]"

[1]"into myriad fragments" *bibheda bahudhā*: Literally, "he split [it] many ways."

[2]"the great monkey" *mahākapiḥ*: D6,7,9–11,T2,3,M3, and the texts and printed editions of Ct and Cr read instead *tadā kapiḥ*, "then the monkey."

30. "the horses" *hayān*: Ñ1,V3,B3,D9–11,13, and the texts and printed editions of Ct read instead the singular *hayam*, "horse." This seems textually less apt since Triśiras is said to be riding in a chariot, "yoked to splendid horses," at verse 4 above. Perhaps the singular has been chosen to maintain number parallelism with the singular "elephant" of the simile.

"a lion, king of beasts" *mṛgarāṭ*: Literally, "king of beasts." The lion is the proverbial foe of elephants in Sanskrit literature.

31. "just as Yama, ender of all things... Kālarātri, the dark night of universal destruction" *kālarātrim ivāntakaḥ*: Literally, "just as the ender, Kālarātri." See 6.23.15 (where Sītā refers to herself as Kālarātri); and 6.34.15 and notes (v.l. Kālarātrī).

"hurled... unleashes" *cikṣepa*: Literally, "he threw." The simile is an awkward one in that it compares Triśiras's handling of his javelin (*śakti*) with Yama's relationship to Kālarātri. According to the syntax, the common element in the simile would appear to be the act of "having seized, taken up" expressed by the gerund *samādāya* of *pāda* a, and most of the translations consulted read the verse in this way. B1,D6,7,9,10,13, and the texts and printed editions of Ct and Cr read *samāsādya*, which has a similar sense, for *samādāya*. Translations that follow the text of Ct render this in connection with the *upamāna* as "employeth" (Dutt 1893, p. 1340), "take in his service" (Gita Press 1969, vol. 3, p. 1653), "*s'armant*" (Roussel 1903, vol. 3, p. 226; Pagani 1999, p. 1056), and "arming himself" (Shastri 1959, vol. 3, p. 199). We, however, prefer the translations of Gorresio (1858, vol. 10, p. 49, "*spande*") and Raghunathan (1982, vol. 3, p. 200, "lets loose"), who appear to base the comparison of the two actions on the finite verb rather than on the gerund.

32. "blazing meteor" *ulkām*: Literally, "meteor."

"hurtling through the sky" *divi kṣiptām*: Literally, "hurled into the sky." D5–7,9–11,T1,2,M1,3, and the texts and printed editions of the southern commentators read instead the ablative *divaḥ*, "from the sky."

33. "they roared thunderously like storm clouds" *vinedur jaladā iva*: Literally, "they roared like clouds [water-givers]."

34. "in his rage" *roṣāt*: Literally, "from anger." The reading is marked as uncertain by the critical editors and rightly so. D9–11,G2,3,M5, and the texts and printed editions of Ct repeat the word *khaḍgam*, "sword," from *pāda* a in place of *roṣāt*, which yields the meaning "[and he buried] that sword..." D5,6,T1,M3, and the texts and printed editions of Cm and Cg read instead the adjective *vyūḍhe*, "broad," which modifies the word *urasi*, "chest." This variant is found in the translation of Raghunathan (1982, vol. 3, p. 200). Gorresio (1858, vol. 10, p. 50) reads instead the noun *śūraḥ*, "hero," which stands in apposition to Triśiras, rendering "*il prode Trisiras.*" D7 and the text of Cr read instead *ca khaḍgena*, "and with that sword," for *tadā roṣāt*, "then from anger." The instrumental then construes with Cr's finite verb *jaghāna*, as noted below.

"buried it" *nicakhāna*: Literally, "he buried." Ñ2,D6,7,T2,3,G3,M1,3,5, and the texts and printed editions of Cg, Cm, and Cr read instead *nijaghāna*, "he struck [with it]."

35. "Trimūrdhan" *trimūrdhānam*: Ś,Ñ,V,B,D1–4,8,12,13,M3, and the texts and printed editions of Cg read the synonymous variant *triśirasam*, "Triśiras." See note to verse 1 above.

36. "When Hanumān struck him with his open hand" *sa talābhihatas tena*: Literally, "struck by him with his palm, he."

"let his garments slip from his hands" *srastahastāmbaraḥ*: Literally, "having slipped-hand-garments." The sense of this compound is far from clear. It is uncertain as to why Triśiras would be holding garments in the midst of battle. Commentators, who share this reading, are silent as to its meaning. Only three of the translators consulted render this reading. Dutt (1893, p. 1340) takes *hastāmbaraḥ* as a *dvandva* and renders the compound, peculiarly enough, to mean "with his hands and attire dropping off." Roussel (1903, vol. 3, p. 226) takes *hastāmbaraḥ* as a *tatpuruṣa* in the sense of "hand-garment," which he takes to be a kenning for glove or gauntlet, rendering, "*laissa échapper son gantelet.*" In this he is followed by Shastri (1959, vol. 3, p. 199), who renders, "let his gauntlet fall." We have hesitantly read the compound as a *paranipāta* for *hastasrastāmbaraḥ*, "whose garments have slipped from his hands." Ñ2,V1,2,B2–4,D5,T1,G1,M3, and the texts and printed editions of Cg and Gorresio read the more intelligible *-āyudhaḥ*, "weapon," for *-ambaraḥ*, "garment." The remaining northern manuscripts read either *khaḍgahastaḥ*, "sword in hand" (Ś,D2,8,12), or *ślathagātraḥ*, "with slackened limbs" (V3,D4,13).

37. "And as Triśiras fell" *tasya patataḥ*: Literally, "of him who was falling *or* as he was falling."

"grabbed" *samācchidya*: A number of the translations consulted (Dutt 1893, p. 1341; Roussel 1903, vol. 3, p. 226; Shastri 1959, vol. 3, p. 199; and Pagani 1999, p. 1056) take this verb or its variant (D7,9–11, and the texts and printed editions of Ct) [*tam*] *ācchidya* in its sense of "having broken *or* shattered." This, however, makes little sense, as Hanumān will use the weapon effectively in verse 40 below.

"the *rākṣasas*, sons of chaos" *-nairṛtān*: Literally, "the sons of Nirṛti." Ś,Ñ,V,B, D1–4,8–13, and the texts and printed editions of Ct read instead *-rākṣasān*, "the *rākṣasas*."

39. "he seized... by the crown" *nijagrāha kirīṭe*: Literally, "he grasped at the diadem." Ck, Ct, and Cr are evidently skeptical about the ability to capture someone by seizing an easily detachable ornament like a *kirīṭa*. They gloss, "at the place of the diadem (*kirītapradeśe*)." We concur, offering "crown" here to refer to the dome of the skull but also because of its additional meaning as a royal head ornament. This interpretation is shared by Gita Press (1969, vol. 3, p. 1654), who renders, "seized hold of Triśirā by his head covered with a diadem," and by Dutt (1893, p. 1341), who, however, understands *nijagrāha*, "he seized," to mean "he smote," rendering, "smote about his diadem." Other translators read the phrase literally, understanding that Hanumān actually catches hold of the diadem.

40. "with Triśiras's own sharp sword... cut off his heads" *tasya śīrṣāṇy asinā śitena . . . / . . . pracicheda*: Literally, "he cut off his heads with a sharp sword."

"just as did Śakra the heads of Tvaṣṭṛ's son" *tvaṣṭuḥ sutasyeva śirāṃsi śakraḥ*: Literally, "as Śakra, the heads of Tvaṣṭṛ's son." The reference is to Indra's beheading of Viśvarūpa, the three-headed son of Tvaṣṭṛ. The myth is found in numerous places in the vedic corpus. See, for example, *TaiS* 2.5.1ff. Compare also *ŚatBr* 1.6.3.1–5; 5.5.4.2–6; *Maitrāyanī Saṃhitā* 2.4.1; and *JaimiBr* 2.153–157 (Oertel). See Hopkins 1902, p. 130. See 6.70.28 and note.

The meter is *upajāti*.

41. "Like so many stars fallen from the path of the sun" *jyotīṃṣi muktāni yathārkamārgāt*: Literally, "like heavenly luminaries released from the sun's path." The allusion, as Cg points out, is to shooting stars or meteors, which (according to a traditional Indian belief) are souls who, having attained positions in the heavens as a result of meritorious actions, fall to earth upon the exhaustion of their accumulated merit (*muktāny anubhūtapuṇyaphalāni*). See 5.7.39 and note.

The printed editions of Ct (GPP and NSP) read *indramārgāt*, "from the path of Indra," for *arkamārgāt*, "from the path of the sun." Both variants are kennings for the sky or heavens.

"with their gaping orifices and their eyes blazing like Agni Vaiśvānara" *āyatākṣāṇi*... *pradīptavaiśvānaralocanāni*: Literally, "with big *or* extended eyes, with eyes like blazing Vaiśvānara." Ct, Ck, and Cr are disturbed by the apparent redundancy of these two compounds. They avoid it by taking *-akṣa-*, "eye," by a kind of *lakṣaṇā* to stand for "the sense organs in general (*indriyāṇi*)." We agree and understand the reference to be specifically to the apertures of the cranial sense organs, such as nostrils, etc. Gita Press (1969, vol. 3, p. 1654) and Dutt (1893, p. 1341) translate as we do. Roussel (1903, vol. 3, p. 227), followed by Shastri (1959, vol. 3, p. 200) and Pagani (1999, p. 1056), resolves the redundancy by taking *locana* in the sense of "glance," translating, "*regards*." Raghunathan (1982, vol. 3, p. 200) collapses the two expressions, rendering, "with their big eyes that burned like blazing fires."

The meter is *upajāti*.

42. "cheered" *neduḥ*: Literally, "they roared, bellowed."

"the earth trembled" *pracacāla bhūmiḥ*: Cr observes that the earth trembled with joy (*harṣeṇa*).

The meter is *upajāti*.

43–44. "mighty Mahāpārśva" *mahāpārśvo mahābalaḥ*: D9–11,G1,3,M, and the texts and printed editions of Ct, Cg, Cm, Cr, and Ck read instead *matto rākṣasapuṃgavaḥ*, "Matta, bull among *rākṣasas*." As Cg notes, Matta is an alternative name for Mahāpārśva. (*matto mahāpārśvaḥ. matta iti mahāpārśvasya nāmāntaram.*) See note to verse 47 below. See, too, 6.57.16 and note.

"Mahodara" *mahodaram*: D9–11,M1,2, and the texts and printed editions of Ct and Ck read instead *yuddhonmattam*. This is a variant name for Mahodara. Ck merely identifies Yuddhonmatta as "a certain *rākṣasa* (*kaścid rākṣasaḥ*)" (mistakenly noted under verse 47 in the critical apparatus). See note to 6.57.16 above.

"and" *cāpi*: D5,T1,G3,M3, and the texts and printed editions of Cg read instead *ghorām*, "dreadful," which then serves as an additional modifier of *gadām*, "mace."

"splendid" *śubhām*: Ś,Ñ,V,B,D1–4,6,8–13,G1,3,M1,2,5, and the texts and printed editions of Ct read instead *tadā*, "then."

"made of solid iron" *sarvāyasīm*: Literally, "entirely of iron." See 6.59.40. Cf. 6.3.12; 6.53.12; 6.55.47; and notes.

45–46. "It was encircled... it shone... it could terrify" *-parikṣiptām*... *virājamānām*... *-bhayāvahām*: The two verses consist of a series of accusative adjectives and adjectival phrases with no finite verb. Grammatically the verses must be construed with either *jagrāha*, "he seized," in verse 44c, or the gerund *ādāya*, "having grasped," in verse 47a. For the sake of transparent English syntax, we have broken up the sequence into a series of short sentences.

"smeared with flesh and blood" *māṃsaśoṇitalepanām*: Literally, "having flesh and blood for its ointment." D6,9–11,T3,M3, and the texts and printed editions of the southern commentators read instead *-phenilām*, "foaming." Cg distinguishes this description from "reddened with the blood of his enemies (*śatruśoṇitarañjitām*)" in *pāda* 45d, by observing that the former describes the mace's appearance at the time of battle, while the latter describes it prior to battle. (*māṃsaśoṇitaphenilām iti yuddhakālikarūpām. śatruśoṇitarañjitām iti pūrvakālikarūpām.*)

"with splendor" *vapuṣā*: Literally, "with beauty." Ñ,V,B2–4,D9–11,13,M1,2, and the texts and printed editions of Ct read instead *vipulām*, "broad."

"Adorned with red garlands" *raktamālyavibhūṣitām*: Red garlands are associated with a victim about to be slaughtered. This description therefore fits the tone of the passage. See 5.25.19 (cf. 20). Cf. 6.59.21; 6.60.22; and notes.

"the mighty elephants Airāvata, Mahāpadma, and Sārvabhauma" *airāvata-mahāpadmasārvabhauma-*: Literally, "Airāvata, Mahāpadma, and Sārvabhauma." These are three of the great *diggajas*, or elephants that support the earth at its cardinal and intermediate compass points. Airāvata and Sārvabhauma are both named at *Amarakośa* 1.3.3–4, where the *diggajas* are listed. Cg and Cm claim that Mahāpadma ("Great Lotus") is another name for the elephant otherwise known as Puṇḍarīka ("Lotus"), which name is also found in the *Amarakośa* list. Mahāpadma, the guardian of the south, is named among the *diggajas* at 1.39.12,16,17. Airāvata is also the name of Indra's great battle-elephant. Cf. 6.4.5; 6.31.4; and notes.

47. "mighty Mahāpārśva" *mahāpārśvo mahābalaḥ*: The phrase is repeated from 44b. D9–11,G,M, and the texts and printed editions of the southern commentators read instead *matto rākṣasapuṃgavaḥ*, "Matta, that bull among *rākṣasas*," as they do at verse 44 above. See note to verse 44 above.

48. "Mahāpārśva" *mahāpārśvam*: D9–11,G2,M, and the texts and printed editions of the southern commentators read instead *mattānīkam*. This term has the sense of "Matta's army," but Cg and Cr understand this to be yet another alternate name (like Matta) of Mahāpārśva, in which case it would have the sense of "having a frenzied army" (*mattānīka iti ca mahāpārśvasya nāmāntaram*). Translations that follow the texts of the southern commentators accept this latter interpretation, with the exception of Dutt (1893, p. 1341), who renders, "the hosts of Matta." See note to verse 52 below.

49. "Mahāpārśva, in a rage" *kruddhaḥ*: Literally, "the angry one."

"which was like a thunderbolt" *vajrakalpayā*: Literally, "resembling the *vajra*." See notes to verses 10 and 23 above.

50. "gushed forth gouts of blood" *susrāva rudhiraṃ bahu*: Literally, "he poured forth copious blood."

51. "bull among monkeys" *vānarṣabhaḥ*: D9–11 and the texts and printed editions of Ct read instead *vānareśvaraḥ*, "lord among monkeys."

"his lips quivering in his rage, glared at Mahāpārśva" *kruddho visphuramāṇauṣṭho mahāpārśvam udaikṣata*: Literally, "Angry, his lips trembling, he looked at Mahāpārśva." KK places this half verse in brackets (= KK [1913] 6.70.58cd). The half verse is omitted from the translation of Raghunathan (1982, vol. 3, p. 201).

D6,9,T,G1,2,M, VSP, and KK (1905) omit this half verse, replacing it with one line [1290*]: "He ran swiftly and [seizing] the mace of that great one." D7,10,11,G3, as well as the printed editions of Ct (GPP 6.70.63ab and NSP 6.70.159ab) read 1290* following 1289* (see below). The line appears as KK (1913) 6.70.64; VSP 6.70.58cd; and KK (1905) 6.70.58cd. The sequence of verses as it appears in KK is translated only in Raghunathan (1982, vol. 3, p. 201).

Following verse 51, D7,10,11,G3, and the texts and printed editions of Ct (GPP 6.70.58–62 and NSP 6.70.154–158), as well as KK within brackets (6.70.59–63), insert a passage of twenty lines (= five *upajāti* verses) [1289*]: "The swift leader of the monkey heroes, resembling a mountain in form, swiftly approached the *rākṣasa* and, swinging his fist, struck him violently in the chest.[1–4] The latter fell suddenly to the ground, like a tree cut off at the roots, his body drenched with blood.[5–6] Then, swiftly seizing Mahāpārśva's[1] dreadful mace, which resembled the rod of Yama, he roared.[7–8] For a moment that foe of the gods lay as if dead. But then, recovering himself, he, whose color was like that of a cloud at twilight, suddenly leapt up and struck Ṛṣabha, son of Varuṇa, lord of the waters.[2][9–12] The latter fell to the ground unconscious, but, regaining his senses after a while, he sprang up, and, brandishing the *rākṣasa*'s[3] mace, which was like a mountain among the foremost of mountains,[4] struck him with it[5] in battle.[13–16] That terrible mace struck the body of that terrible foe of gods, sacrifices, and brahmans. It split his chest, and he gushed gouts of blood, as Himalaya, the king of mountains,[6] pours forth water stained red with minerals.[7][17–20]"

[1]"Mahāpārśva's" *asya*: Literally, "his."

[2]"Ṛṣabha, son of Varuṇa, lord of the waters" *vārirājātmajam*: Literally, "son of the king of waters."

[3]"the *rākṣasa*'s" *tasya*: Literally, "his."

[4]"which was like a mountain among the foremost of mountains" *adrivarādrikalpām*: This could also be read as "like the foremost mountain among mountains."

[5]"he ... struck him with it" *jaghāna*: Literally, "he struck."

[6]"Himalaya, king of mountains" *adrirājaḥ*: Literally, "the king of mountains."

[7]"water stained red with minerals" *dhātvambhaḥ*: Literally, "mineral-water."

D7,10,11,G3, and the texts and printed editions of Ct (GPP 6.70.63ab and NSP 6.70.159ab) read 1290* following 1289* (see above).

52. "round and round" *punaḥ punaḥ*: Literally, "again and again."

"he struck ... with it" *jaghāna*: Literally, "he struck."

"Mahāpārśva Mattānīka" *mattānīkaṃ mahāpārśvam*: The sequence of these two names for this character appears to be found in none of the manuscripts collated for the critical edition. The entire south shows only the name "Mattānīka," while the north knows only "Mahāpārśva." The reading is thus extremely suspect. D9–11 and the texts and printed editions of Ct read instead *mahātmā saḥ*, "that great one [Ṛṣabha]." Dutt (1893, p. 1342), as he did earlier (see note to verse 48 above), renders *mattānīkam* as "Matta's forces." D5,T1,M3,5, and the texts and printed editions of Cg read *mahātmānam*, "the great [Mattānīka]." Raghunathan (1982, vol. 3, p. 201) renders this as "the mighty Matta." An alternate translation of the critical edition's reading would be to take *mattānīkam* as a descriptive adjective, "whose army was frenzied." See note to verse 48 above. See Sutherland 1992.

53. "Mahāpārśva" *mahāpārśvaḥ*: D9–11,G,M read instead *tadā* (M3 = *tataḥ*] *mattaḥ*, "then Matta."

Following verse 53, D3 (line 1 only),5–7,9–11,S insert a passage of two lines [1292*]: "Once that *rākṣasa* had fallen to the ground—his eyes knocked out, his strength vanished, his life ended—the *rākṣasa* army fled."

Following 1292*, M3, GPP (in brackets unnumbered between 6.70.65 and 66), KK (in brackets as 6.70.68–77), and VSP (as footnote below commentary at bottom of p. 528, marked by an asterisk between verses 6.70.61 and 62) show a passage of twenty-two lines [App. I, No. 37]. In this passage a brother of Mahāpārśva [Matta],

Unmatta, enters the battle only to be slain by the monkey Gavākṣa. No translation consulted renders this passage. Raghunathan (1982, vol. 3, p. 201), however, places an unexplained asterisk at this point in his translation, presumably in reflection of the similar mark in VSP. The footnote in VSP mentions that these verses are found only in late manuscripts (*ete ślokā auttarāhapāṭha evopalabhyante*).

54. "ran for its life" *kevalajīvitārtham*: Literally, "having for its purpose life alone." Cg explains that the *rākṣasas* sought life without glory (*yaśorahitajīvanārtham*)."

"like an ocean scattering in all directions" *bhinnārṇavasaṃnikāśam*: Literally, "resembling a dispersed *or* shattered ocean." The commentators, whom we follow, indicate that the compound is to be read adverbially, although they provide no gloss to illuminate its meaning (*kriyāviśeṣaṇam*—so Ct). Virtually all the translators consulted who share this reading read the compound as if it were a *madhyamapadalopisamāsa*, with a middle term, such as "bank *or* shore (*tīram* or *kūlam*)," omitted. Their idea is that the army is being compared to an ocean that has burst or breached its shores. Such an image is found in the epic (see 6.84.32 and note). However, in the present context, where the image seems to be one of scattering rather than breaching a limit, this sense does not seem as apposite to us. Dutt (1893, p. 1343), alone among the translators consulted, appears to understand the image as we do. He renders, "rushed away, like unto the deep riven (by the winds)."

The meter is *indravajrā*.

Sarga 59

1–3. "his brothers" *bhrātṝn*: The reference is to Triśiras, Devāntaka, and Narāntaka.

"his two paternal uncles, the brothers Mahodara and Mahāpārśva, bulls among *rākṣasas*" *pitṛvyau cāpi . . . mahodaramahāpārśvau bhrātarau rākṣasarṣabhau*: Ct, Cg, and Cr understand that the two brothers are the uncles of Atikāya. (*pitṛvyau kāv ityātrāha. yuddhonmattaṃ cetyādi. bhrātarāv anyonyaṃ bhrātarau*—so Ct.) Ck disagrees, understanding that the brothers are Matta and Yuddhonmatta (variant reading), while the uncles are Kumbhakarṇa and Mahodara (*pitṛvyau kumbhakarṇamahodarau yuddhonmattaṃ ca mattaṃ ca bhrātarāv iti*). (Cf. note to 6.58.43–44.) D5,7,9–11,T1,G1,2,M, and the texts and printed editions of the southern commentators read the variant names *yuddhonmattaṃ ca mattaṃ ca* for *mahodaramahāpārśvau*. See notes to 6.57.16; and 6.58.1,43–44,47. D6,7,9–11, and the texts and printed editions of Ct and Cr read instead *rākṣasottamau*, "foremost among *rākṣasas*."

"granted boons by Brahmā" *brahmadattavaraḥ*: We find out in verses 30 and 31 below that Brahmā had granted Atikāya divine weapon-spells, invulnerability to gods and *asuras*, a suit of celestial armor, and a splendid chariot. Pagani (1999, p. 1667), in a note to this passage, states that, as a consequence of his great asceticism, Atikāya obtained three boons from Brahmā, which were the *brahmāstra* (the divine weapon-spell of Brahmā), a fabulous suit of armor, and the power not to be disturbed by any unwelcome or inopportune desire. The source for Pagani's particular list here is unclear, as it does not agree with her translation of verses 31 and 32 (p. 1059). Citrāv Śāstri, in his *Prācīnacaritrakośa* (1964, s.v. Atikāya), identifies four boons, including a divine weapon-spell, armor, a celestial chariot, and invulnerability to the gods and demons. Cf. 6.80.25, where Rāvaṇa mentions the armor Brahmā gave him for his austerities.

4. "which blazed with the brilliance of a thousand suns" *bhāskarasahasrasya saṃghātam iva bhāsvaram*: Literally, "as radiant as an assemblage of a thousand suns."

5. "great" *mahat*: D7,9–11, and the texts and printed texts of Ct read instead *tadā*, "then."

"Atikāya, adorned with diadem and burnished earrings" *kirīṭī mṛṣṭakuṇḍalaḥ*: Literally, "he who possessed a diadem and who had burnished earrings."

6. Following verse 6, D5–7,9–11,S (G2 after verse 4) insert a passage of two lines [1294*]: "When the monkeys saw the size of his body, they thought,[1] 'It's Kumbhakarṇa arisen once again!' And, stricken with terror, they all huddled together.[2]"

[1]"they thought, 'It's Kumbhakarṇa arisen once again!' " *kumbhakarṇo 'yam utthitaḥ*: We follow Ck, Cr, and Ct in supplying a form of the root $\sqrt{}$*man*, "to think" (*manyamānāḥ*, "thinking"—Ct, Ck; *matvā*, "having thought"—Cr). Like most of the commentators, we understand that one must supply the quotation marker *iti* to indicate that this statement is a direct quote.

[2]"they . . . huddled together" *saṃśrayante parasparam*: Literally, "they took refuge with one another."

7. "his gigantic form . . . like that of Viṣṇu when he traversed the three worlds" *tasya rūpam . . . yathā viṣṇos trivikrame*: Literally, "his form *or* appearance like that in the triple step of Viṣṇu." The reference is to the well-known purāṇic tale of Viṣṇu's *vāmanāvatāra*, or dwarf incarnation, according to which he assumes a gigantic size in order to traverse the universe, thus wresting it from the control of the *asura* king, Bali. See 6.40.43; 6.47.119; 6.49.1–2; 6.53.25; 6.105.24; and notes. See, too, 1.28.2 and note. It will be recalled that Atikāya's name reflects his gargantuan size. See 6.47.16 and note above.

"all the monkeys were stricken with terror" *bhayārtā vānarāḥ sarve*: D6,7,9–11,T2,3,G1,2,M3,5, and the texts and printed editions of the southern commentators read instead *bhayād vānarayūthās te*, "the troops of monkeys out of fear." This variant is represented in the translation of Raghunathan (1982, vol. 3, p. 202). D9–11 and the texts and printed editions of Ct substitute the word *-yodhāḥ*, "warriors," for *-yūthāḥ*, "troops," in this variant.

"in the ten directions" *diśo daśa*: D5–7,9–11,T,G1,2,M3,5, and the texts and printed editions of the southern commentators read instead *tatas tataḥ*, "here and there." Ñ,V,B,D1,4,13,G3, and the printed edition of Gorresio read instead *parasparam*, "to one another." On the basis of the textual evidence presented in the critical edition, the critical reading is weak and should be considered uncertain.

8. "Confronted by Atikāya" *atikāyaṃ samāsādya*: Literally, "having approached Atikāya."

"refuge . . . the refuge of all" *śaraṇyaṃ . . . śaraṇam*: See 6.13.4; 6.47.43; 6.31.56; 6.81.14; and notes. See, too, 5.36.26–29.

9. The critical edition provides no apparatus for this verse. All printed editions consulted read as does the critical edition.

10. "that gigantic warrior" *mahātmānam*: Literally, "the great one." We agree with Cr that the term here refers to the size of Atikāya's body (*mahātmānaṃ bṛhaccharīram*

atikāyam). D6,9–11,T2,3,G1, and the texts and printed editions of Ct read instead *mahākāyam*, "of huge body."

11. "with the gaze of a lion" *harilocanaḥ*: The compound is ambiguous because of the multiple possible meanings of the word *hari*. We agree with the majority of southern commentators, who take it in its common sense of "lion," giving the compound the sense of "with the eyes *or* glance of a lion" (*siṃhadṛṣṭiḥ*—so Ct). Cs takes the reference to be to the eyes either of a lion or a monkey (*siṃhadṛṣṭir markaṭadṛṣṭir vā*). As an alternative, he understands the compound to mean "whose eyes were fixed on the tawny monkeys (*hariṣv eva locanaṃ yasyeti vā*)." The word *hari* also frequently serves as an adjective in the sense of "yellow *or* tawny." Ck understands that Atikāya's eyes are yellow, like those of a lion (*harivat piṅgalanetraḥ*). A number of translators have understood only that the eyes are yellow or another similar color (Gorresio 1858, vol. 10, p. 52; Roussel 1903, vol. 3, p. 229; Shastri 1959, vol. 3, p. 202; and Pagani 1999, p. 1058). Cf. note to 6.60.9.

12. "sharp...formidable" *niśitaiḥ...sutīkṣṇaiḥ*: The adjective *tīkṣṇa* can mean "sharp, pungent, fierce, rough, etc." Unlike most of the other translators consulted, we have rejected its common meaning, "sharp," in an effort to avoid redundancy with the adjective *niśitaiḥ*, "sharp," in *pāda* a.

"Maheśvara surrounded by his malignant spirits" *vṛtaḥ...bhūtair iva maheśvaraḥ*: Literally, "like Maheśvara surrounded by beings." See 6.47.9,23–24; 6.74.4; and notes.

13. "with his glittering chariot-javelins" *rathaśaktībhiḥ*: Literally, "by chariot-javelins." We have carried over the word "glittering (*arciṣmadbhiḥ*)" from verse 12 above to make the simile intelligible. The commentators note the irregular length of the final stem "*ī*." See notes to 6.33.21 and 6.95.9 for discussions of the term *rathaśakti*.

"which resemble the tongues of Kāla" *kālajihvāprakāśābhiḥ*: Kāla, "Time," is used throughout the epics to refer to Yama, the god of death or destruction, or to one of the great deities, Viṣṇu or Śiva, in the guise of the destroyer of the world. Here the image is reminiscent of the representation of Kṛṣṇa as Kāla at *Bhagavadgītā* 11.25–32, where he is said to swallow up all the worlds in his blazing mouths.

14. "well-strung" *sajyāni*: Literally, "with their bowstrings." Ś,Ñ,V,B2–4,D1–11,13,T1,G1,2, and the texts and printed editions of Ct read instead *sajjāni*. Although this term can also refer to a bow that is strung, a more common meaning is "ready, prepared." Several of the translators who follow the text of Ct appear to take it in the latter sense.

"with their golden facing" *hemapṛṣṭhāni*: Literally, "with golden backs."

"the rainbow, Śakra's bow" *śakracāpam*: Literally, "Śakra's bow." This is a standard epic kenning for the rainbow.

15. "Who is this...?" *ka eṣaḥ*: V2,D10,11, and the texts and printed editions of Ct read instead the relative pronoun *yaḥ*, making this verse yet another subordinate clause rather than a question.

16. "with the emblem of Rāhu, demon of the eclipse, waving from his flagstaff" *dhvajaśṛṅgapratiṣṭhena rāhuṇā*: Literally, "with Rāhu situated at the tip of his flagstaff." Principal chariot-warriors in the epics normally fly distinctive banners with some sort of identificatory emblem or device. Here, as some of the commentators indicate, we are to understand that Atikāya's battle flag bears the image of the eclipse demon, Rāhu (*rāhudhvajatvam uktam*—so Ct).

17. “thrice-curved” *triṇatam*: Literally, “triply bent.” The reference is to a recurved bow, which, as Cg mentions, is bent in the middle and at each end (*triṣv ādyantayor madhye ca natam*). See note to 6.35.24.

“as the rainbow, the bow of Indra of the hundred sacrifices” *śatakratudhanuḥprakhyam*: Literally, “resembling the bow of Śatakratu.” See note to verse 14 above.

18. “furnished with flags and banners” *sadhvajaḥ sapatākaś ca*: The terms *dhvajaḥ* and *patākā* form a more or less synonymous pair, as both refer to flags or battle standards. The word *dhvajaḥ* can also refer to a flagstaff, and the redundancy could be mitigated by translating it in that sense. Cg addresses the issue by defining *dhvajaḥ* as “an extraordinary banner (*asādhāraṇaketanam*)” and *patākā* as “the ordinary kind (*sādhāraṇī*).”

“has a fine frame” *sānukarṣaḥ*: See 6.57.25 and note.

“manned by four grooms” *catuḥsādisamāyuktaḥ*: Literally, “equipped with four charioteers.” Cg and Ct understand the term *sādin* in the sense of *sārathiḥ*, “charioteer, driver.” However, since it is difficult to envisage a chariot actually being driven by more than one person at a time, we prefer Cr’s gloss of *aśvavāraiḥ* [*samāyuktaḥ*], “grooms, horse-handlers.” One should keep in mind, however, that, as mentioned in verse 11 above, the chariot is yoked to a thousand horses. This may well account for the additional grooms.

19. “thirty-eight quivers” *viṃśatir daśa cāṣṭau ca tūṇīrāḥ*: Literally, “twenty, ten, and eight quivers.” Gita Press (1969, vol. 3. p. 1658), alone among the translators of the southern text, takes the numbers distributively to refer to the various articles mentioned in the verse, rendering, “twenty quivers, ten . . . bows, and eight bowstrings.”

“bows” *kārmukāṇi*: Cg is concerned that the reference here may be redundant in light of the description of the bows given in verse 14 above. He claims, however, that there is no redundancy, since *kārmuka* refers to a particular type of bow (*kārmukāṇi dhanurbhedā na paunaruktyam*). Raghunathan (1982, vol. 3, p. 203), apparently under the influence of Cg, renders, “crossbows.”

20. “And in his chariot there are two swords, one on each side.” *dvau ca khaḍgau rathagatau pārśvasthau*: D7,9–11, and the texts and printed editions of Ct read *ca pārśvasthau*, “and . . . one on each side,” for *rathagatau*, “in [his] chariot,” and *pradīpau* (*pradīptau*—D11), “lamps (blazing—D11),” for *pārśvasthau*.

“Clearly visible” *vyakta-*: We follow Cg, Cr, and Cm in taking *vyakta* as an adjective modifying *khaḍgau*, “swords.” Cr glosses the term as “characterized by extraordinary splendor *or* beauty (*atikāntiviśiṣṭau eva*).” Ct reads it adverbially as *vyaktam*, in the sense of “clearly, manifestly.” This interpretation has been followed by Roussel (1903, vol. 3, p. 230), Gita Press (1969, vol. 3, p. 1658), and Shastri (1959, vol. 3, p. 202), who take the term in the compound to mean that the swords are certainly of the length described.

“their blades are fifteen feet in length and their hilts, six” *caturhastatsarucitau . . . -hastadaśāyatau*: Literally, “they are ten *hastas* in length and are equipped with four-*hasta* hilts.” The *hasta* is an ancient unit of measurement marking the distance from a man’s elbow to his fingertip. It is more or less equivalent to the ancient western measurement of the cubit and is thus approximately eighteen inches in length. In order to avoid either archaism or obscurantism, we have translated the measurement into modern units. See note to 5.33.18.

Our understanding, shared by Dutt (1893, p. 1344) and Raghunathan (1982, vol. 3, p. 203), is that the total length of each sword is fourteen *hastas*, or twenty-one feet. Some translators appear to believe that the four *hastas* of the hilt are part of the total of ten *hastas* for the entire weapon. We believe that the proportion of blade to hilt thus represented would be implausible. Other translators are ambiguous in their renderings.

"They beautify both sides." *pārśvaśobhinau*: Literally, "beautiful on the sides." D2,5,7,10,11,13,T1,M3, and the texts and printed editions of Cm, Cg, Cr, and Ct read instead *pārśvaśobhitau*. These commentators understand this variant differently. Ct glosses, "beautiful on their own sides (*svapārśvaśobhitau*)." Cr understands that, since the swords are placed on either side of the chariot (or of Atikāya), they therefore beautify both sides (*pārśvasthāv ata eva pārśvayoḥ śobhitaṃ śobhā yābhyāṃ tau*). This is similar to our understanding of the critical reading. Cg and Cm gloss, "beautified by both sides (*pārśvābhyāṃ śobhitau*)."

21. "With a red garland hung about his neck" *raktakaṇṭhaguṇaḥ*: Literally, "having a red neck-thread." We follow the commentators in understanding the reference to be to a garland of red flowers. See 6.58.46 and note.

"his huge mouth like that of Kāla, that dark warrior" *kālaḥ kālamahāvaktraḥ*: We follow Ck, Ct, and Cr in taking the first occurrence of the word *kāla* in its sense of "black, dark" and the second in the sense of "Yama, Time, Death." A literal translation would then be "black with a huge mouth [like that] of Kāla." (*kālaḥ kṛṣṇavarṇaḥ. kālasya mṛtyor iva*—so Ct.)

22. "Himalaya . . . with its . . . twin peaks" *śṛṅgābhyām . . . himavān*: Literally, "Himavat with two peaks."

23. "that . . . of his" *tu yasyaitat*: Literally, "of whom . . . that." The verse, like several of the preceding ones, is actually a relative clause. D9–11 and the texts and printed editions of Ct read instead *ubhābhyāṃ ca*, "and with those two [earrings]."

"radiant" *śubhekṣaṇam*: Literally, "with shining *or* beautiful appearance." This has been rendered by Raghunathan (1982, vol. 3, p. 203) as "serene." The word *īkṣaṇam* can also mean "eye," and Gorresio (1858, vol. 10, p. 53) has rendered the compound accordingly as "[*faccia*] *dai fulgidi occhi*." D7,9–11, and the texts and printed editions of Ct read instead *subhīṣaṇam*, "very fearsome."

"the orb of the full moon passing between the twin stars of the constellation Punarvasu" *punarvasvantaragataṃ pūrṇabimbam ivaindavam*: Literally, "like the full lunar orb situated in the interval of Punarvasu." Punarvasu is generally regarded to be the fifth of twenty-eight *nakṣatras*, or lunar mansions, of ancient Indian astronomy, although according to some sources it is the seventh. Some texts regard it as having two stars, while others represent it has having four. Here, since the simile depends on the image of the bright face of Atikāya between its two golden earrings, the poet would apparently have had the former in mind. See *GaruḍaP* 1.59.2–9. Cf. *AgniP* 130.2–17. See Dange 1986–1990, pp. 298–313; and Kane 1941–1975, vol. 5, pp. 501–4. For a similar use of this constellation in a simile involving earrings, see notes to 6.55.123.

D1,3,6,7,9–11,T2,3,G2,3,M1,2, and the texts and printed editions of the southern commentators read *punarvasvantaragataḥ pari*[*prati*—D6,T2,3,G3]*pūrṇo niśākaraḥ*, literally, "the full moon, bringer of night, situated in the interval of Punarvasu." Note that this variant lacks a *dyotakaśabda*, or specific marker of similitude, a lack that is generally supplied by the translators.

24. "great-armed hero" *mahābāho*: Literally, "O great-armed one!"

"at the sight of whom" *yaṃ dṛṣṭvā*: Literally, "having seen whom." As Cr notes, this verse marks the last of the series of relative clauses that, in effect, make it and the preceding twelve verses a single extended syntactic unit (*dvādaśānām ekatrānvayaḥ*).

"in all directions" *diśaḥ*: Literally, "to the directions."

26. "energetic" *mahotsāhaḥ*: D7,9–11, and the texts and printed editions of Ct read instead *mahātmā hi*, "the great one."

"the younger brother of Kubera Vaiśravaṇa" *vaiśravaṇānujaḥ*: Literally, "born after Vaiśravaṇa."

27. "in battle" *raṇe*: V3,B1,4,D9–11, and the texts and printed editions of Ct read instead *bale*, "in strength."

"deeply learned" *śrutadharaḥ*: Literally, "bearing learning *or* what was heard." Ñ,V,B,D4,5,12,13,M3, and the texts and printed editions of Cg and Cm read instead *śrutidharaḥ*, literally, "holding *śruti or* the *vedas*." This variant is rendered by Raghunathan (1982, vol. 3, p. 203), Gita Press (1969, vol. 3, p. 1658), and Gorresio (1858, vol. 10, p. 53).

28. "highly regarded for his skill" *saṃmataḥ*: Literally, "highly regarded, esteemed."

"chariot, and elephant" *rathe nāge*: D9–11 and the texts and printed editions of Ct read instead *nāgapṛṣṭhe*, "on elephant-back."

"and the noose" *karṣaṇe*: The precise sense of the word here is unclear. However, the context and the parallel passage at 7.32.33 strongly suggest that this is the name of a particular weapon. At that later passage, *karṣaṇa* is unmistakably one of a list of weapons, and Cg, Ck, Cm, and Ct all define the term there as "a type of weapon (*āyudhaviśeṣaḥ*)." We believe that Cm (also quoted by Ct) is correct in understanding the term to refer to weapons such as "the noose *or* lasso, etc." with which one drags an enemy (*kṛṣyate 'neneti karṣaṇaḥ pāśādiḥ*). Cm also suggests an alternative: "a type of iron cudgel [*or* javelin] (*tomarabhedo vā*)." See note to 6.58.10.

Cm further suggests that the three weapons listed—sword, bow, and noose—are used, respectively, from the three platforms indicated, viz., horseback, chariot, and elephant (*aśvarathagajasthānānāṃ krameṇa pratiniyatāyudhāny āha khaḍge dhanuṣi karṣaṇa iti*). Raghunathan (1982, vol. 3, p. 203) follows this suggestion of Cm, translating, "in fighting from horseback with the sword, from the chariot with the bow and from elephant-back with the noose." Other translators consulted attempt to render the term in accordance with various senses of the root √*kṛṣ*, "to draw *or* drag," none of which strikes us as plausible in this context. Dutt (1893, p. 1345) and Gita Press (1969, vol. 3, p. 1658) understand the reference to be to the drawing of the bow or bowstring. Roussel (1903, vol. 3, p. 230), followed by Shastri (1959, vol. 3, p. 203), takes the term in its sense of "destruction, massacre." Pagani (1999, p. 1059) renders, "*de traîner un ennemi á sa merci*." It should be mentioned that, as noted above, these translations do not read "chariot" and therefore cannot make the one-to-one correspondence between platform and weapon that is possible in the texts of Cg and Cm and the critical edition.

"sowing dissension, conciliation, and bribery" *bhede sāntve ca dāne ca*: These are the three nonviolent elements of statecraft referred to frequently in the *nīti* literature and the epics. See 6.9.8; 6.51.11–13; 6.71.12; and notes. Cf. notes to 6.31.48–49.

29. "He is known as" *imaṃ viduḥ*: Literally, "they know him as."

"Dhānyamālinī's" *dhānyamālinyāḥ*: As Cr notes, this is the name of one of Rāvaṇa's junior, literally, alternate, wives (*tadabhidharāvaṇabhāryāntarasya*). Dhānyamālinī is introduced in the *Sundarakāṇḍa*. See 5.20.37 and note; and note to 5.56.68.

"remains secure" *bhavati nirbhayā*: Literally, "[Laṅkā] becomes fearless *or* free from danger."

30. "His mind focused" *bhāvitātmanā*: Literally, "by him whose mind was purified *or* intent." Cr, the only commentator to treat this term, glosses, "he by whom an effort was assiduously made (*bhāvitaḥ pariśīlita ātmā yatno yena tena*)."

31. "self-existent Brahmā granted him ... invulnerability" *avadhyatvaṃ dattam asmai svayaṃbhuvā*: Literally, "the state of being unable to be killed was given to him by Svayaṃbhū." These boons are strikingly similar to those said to have been given to Rāvaṇa at 6.57.4. Most noteworthy here is the gift of invulnerability to supernatural beings, which otherwise seems to be an exclusive property of Rāvaṇa. See verses 1–3 and notes above. See, too, 6.57.4 and notes.

33–34. "stopped ... in its course" *viṣṭambhitam*: Literally, "stopped, obstructed." Cg glosses, "rendered motionless (*niścalīkṛtam*)."

"wise Indra's" *indrasya dhīmataḥ*: D6,7,9–11, and the texts and printed editions of Ct and Cr read the instrumental *dhīmatā* for the genitive *dhīmataḥ*, thus making the adjective apply not to Indra but [redundantly—cf. *dhīmān* in verse 34] to Atikāya.

"of Varuṇa, monarch of the waters" *salilarājasya*: Literally, "of the king of the waters."

36. "twanged his bow" *visphārayāmāsa dhanuḥ*: It is actually the bowstring that is twanged as a warning to one's enemies, and, in most descriptions of this activity, this is expressly stated. See, for example, 6.42.23 and note. Pagani (1999, p. 1667) has a brief note on this practice.

37. "fearsome to behold" *bhīmavapuṣam*: Literally, "of fearsome form *or* appearance."

"the ... leaping monkeys" *plavaṅgamāḥ*: Ś,V3,B1,D1–3,5,7–12,T1,G,M3,5, and the texts and printed editions of the southern commentators read instead *vanaukasaḥ*, literally, "forest dwellers."

38. "Armed with trees and mountain peaks" *pādapair giriśṛṅgaiś ca*: Literally, "with trees and mountain peaks."

39. "among those skilled in the use of divine weapon-spells" *astravidām*: Literally, "of those who know *astras*."

40. "that night-roaming *rākṣasa*" *niśācaraḥ*: Literally, "the night-roaming one." B2,D5,7,9–11,T1,G1,2,M1,2,5, and the texts and printed editions of Ct read instead *viśāradaḥ*, "clever, skillful."

"facing those tawny monkeys" *harīn ... abhimukhaḥ*: Ś,Ñ2,V1,2,B,D1–4,8–12,G1, and the texts and printed editions of Ct and the edition of Gorresio (6.51.39) read instead the accusative plural *abhimukhān*, lending the sequence the meaning "the tawny monkeys facing [him]."

"made of solid iron" *sarvāyasaiḥ*: See notes to 6.58.44. Cf. 6.3.12; 6.53.12; 6.55.47; and notes.

41. "pierced in every limb" *bhinnagātrāḥ*: G3,M3, and the texts and printed editions of Cg and Cm read *bhagnagātrāḥ*, "their limbs broken."

"the leaping monkeys" *plavaṅgamāḥ*: D7,9–11, and the texts and printed editions of Ct and Cr read instead *parājitāḥ*, "defeated."

42. "in the full flush of youth" *yauvanam āsthitaḥ*: Literally, "having reached youth." V3,B1,D1–3,7,9–11,T3,G1,2,M3,5, and the texts and printed editions of the southern commentators read instead *yauvanadarpitaḥ*, "arrogant because of youth." Cs argues that it is not necessary for a lion to be in the full flush of youth to terrorize a

mere herd of deer, and therefore he believes the description should apply to the *rākṣasa* (Atikāya) and not to the lion. (*rākṣasaviśeṣaṇam. na mṛgayūthamathane siṃhasya tāruṇyam apekṣitam.*)

43. "would not strike any that did not resist" *nāyudhyamānaṃ nijaghāna kaṃcit*: Literally, "he did not strike anyone who was not fighting." As Ck and Ct explain, Atikāya refrains from attacking those who are not actually fighting because he is a true hero (*vīratvāt*). Cs sees this quality of Atikāya's to be in keeping with his description as a learned, and therefore highly dharmic, individual in verses 27 and 28 above (*etena śrutadhara ityādīnā sūcitaṃ dharmiṣṭhatvaṃ dhvanitam*).

"armed with bow and quiver" *dhanuḥkalāpī*: Literally, "possessing bow and quiver." The majority of commentators and all translators consulted who share this reading take *kalāpa* in its sense of "quiver." Cg and Cm justify this choice by quoting *Amarakośa* 3.3.128 in which *tūṇīra*, "quiver," is given as one of the meanings of this term (*kalāpo bhūṣaṇe barhe tūṇīre saṃhatāv api*). Cr, alone among the commentators, understands the word in the last of the senses given by *Amara*, "mass, collection (*saṃhati*)," lending the compound the sense "with a collection of bows." It should be noted that *kalāpa* can also mean "arrow," in which case the compound could also mean "with a bow and arrow[s]." This interpretation would seem to be supported by Atikāya's description of himself in the following verse (44) as "having bow and arrow in hand (*śaracāpapāṇiḥ*)."

"approached" *upetya*: Literally, "having approached." Ñ2,V3,B1,D9–11, and the texts and printed editions of Ct read instead *utpatya*, "having jumped up on."

The meter is *upajāti*.

44. "Here I stand, mounted in my chariot" *rathe sthito 'ham*: Literally, "I am standing in my chariot."

"whomever has the ability coupled with resolve" *yasyāsti śaktir vyavasāyayuktā*: Literally, "of whom there is ability linked with resolve." V3,B3,D4,5,9–11,T1,2, and the texts and printed editions of Ct and Cr read the nominative masculine singular *vyavasāyayuktaḥ* for *vyavasāyayuktā*, which lends the compound the sense "he who is resolute."

D5,T1,M3, and the texts and printed editions of Cg and Cm read *kaścit*, "anyone," for *śaktiḥ*, "ability." This variant is rendered only in the translation of Raghunathan (1982, vol. 3, p. 204), who translates, "if anybody dares."

The meter is *upajāti*.

45. "overheard those words of Atikāya as he was speaking" *tat tasya vākyaṃ bruvato niśamya*: Literally, "hearing that speech of him who was speaking." As Ck and Ct remind us, these words were addressed not to Lakṣmaṇa but to Rāma (*tat tasya vākyaṃ rāmaṃ pratyuktam*).

"with a contemptuous smile" *smayitvā*: Literally, "having smiled." The commentators cite *Dhātupāṭha* 32.37 according to which the root $\sqrt{}$*smi*, "to smile," can be used to express contempt or disrespect (*ṣmiṅ anādare iti dhātuḥ*—Cg).

The meter is *upajāti*.

47. "The . . . sound of . . . bowstring could be heard" *jyāśabdaḥ*: Literally, "the sound of the bowstring." The verse lacks a finite verb. We have added the words "could be heard," more or less in keeping with the commentators'suggestion that one supply a verb with the sense of "arose (*udabhūt*)."

"the mountains" *śailān*: D9–11 and the texts and printed editions of Ct read instead *sarvām*, "all, entire." This adjective then construes with *mahīm*, "earth," to yield the sense "the whole earth."

50. "Get out of my way!" *gaccha*: Literally, "Go!"

"Do you really want to provoke me to fight" *kim . . . māṃ yodhayitum icchasi*: Literally, "Do you wish to cause me to fight?" Cr, the only commentator consulted to note the phrase, glosses, " 'Why do you want to make me fight?' The meaning is 'You don't want to [lit., there is no desire]' (*māṃ yodhayituṃ kiṃ kim artham icchasi necchety arthaḥ*)." Translators consulted generally understand, "Why do you wish to fight with me?"

"who am like Kāla himself" *kālasadṛśam*: Literally, "like Kāla."

51. "of the divinely charged weapons" *astrāṇām*: Literally, "of *astras*." D1,6,7,9–11,G1,3, and the texts and printed editions of Ct and Cr read instead *bāṇānām*, "of arrows."

52. "Would you want . . . ?" *icchasi*: Literally, "you wish." We follow the lead of Cr, who adds the words *kim artham*, "why," in taking the sentence as interrogative.

"Don't sacrifice your life by confronting me." *mā prāṇāñjahi madgataḥ*: Literally, "gone to me, do not destroy [your] life breaths." The imperative *jahi* of the root $\sqrt{}$*han*, "to strike *or* kill," is rather awkward in this context. Cg glosses, "do not injure (*mā hiṃsīḥ*)," but still the idiom is strange. Most northern manuscripts and the printed editions of Lahore and Gorresio substitute one or another verb with the sense of "loose, give up, abandon," from the roots $\sqrt{}$*tyaj*, "to abandon," or $\sqrt{}$*muc*, "to release," providing, in effect, a gloss on the slightly difficult southern reading (Pollock 1984a, pp. 85–86). Translations consulted generally take the verb *jahi* as if it had the sense of "give up, forfeit, lose, etc." See 6.67.2 and note.

53. "if you are obstinate" *pratiṣṭabdhaḥ*: Commentators are divided as to the meaning of the term here. Ct and Cr gloss, "egotistical, haughty, obstinate (*ahaṃkāravān*)," and we believe this interpretation best fits the context. Ck, Cg, and Cm take the term to mean "holding your ground *or* remaining facing me (*pratiṣṭhitaḥ*—Ck; *pratimukhaṃ sthitaḥ*—Cg; *abhimukhasthitaḥ*—Cm)." Cm also offers one of his "inner" readings of the verse, according to which Atikāya is really telling Lakṣmaṇa that he should stay if he does not wish to turn back, and that he, Lakṣmaṇa, will depart after gaining victory; that is, that, by a shift in the subject of the verb, it is he, Atikāya himself, who will go [to Yama's abode] after losing his life. (*vastutas tu nivartituṃ necchasi yadi tvaṃ tiṣṭha. gamiṣyasi jayaṃ prāpyeti śeṣaḥ. prāṇān parityajyāhaṃ gamiṣyāmīti kriyāvipariṇāmaḥ.*) See note to 6.27.4.

54. "the weapon of Lord Śiva" *īśvarāyudha-*: Literally, "the weapon of Īśvara." The commentators believe that the term is a reference to Śiva's characteristic weapon, the trident (*triśūla*). This identification has been followed by several of the translators consulted, either in their translations or in their notes. The text of Gorresio (6.51.52) shows a synonymous variant, *aiśvarāyudha-*, unrecorded in the critical apparatus. Gorresio (1858, vol. 10, p. 55) renders, erroneously we believe, "*armi divine*."

55. "This arrow . . . will drink your blood" *eṣa te . . . bāṇaḥ pāsyati śoṇitam*: After showing that he reads the verse in its obvious sense, Cm once again proposes an inverted reading according to which the enclitic pronoun *te*, "your," construes with *bāṇaḥ*, "arrow." Cm then adds the genitive pronoun *mama*, "my," construing with *śoṇitam*, "blood." This yields the sense "your [Lakṣmaṇa's] arrow will drink my [Atikāya's] blood (*vastutas tu te tava bāṇaḥ śoṇitaṃ pāsyati mameti śeṣaḥ*)."

"a ... lion, king of beasts" *mṛgarājaḥ*: Literally, "the king of beasts."

Following verse 55, D5–7,9–11,S insert a passage of one line [1306*]: "Having spoken in this fashion, he fitted an arrow to his bow, in a towering rage."

56. "Prince Lakṣmaṇa" *rājaputraḥ*: Literally, "the son of the king."

"enormously majestic hero ... highly sensible" *bṛhacchrīḥ ... mahārtham*: Literally, "enormously majestic one ... [words] of great sense *or* import." D9–11 and the texts and printed editions of Ct and Cs read *manasvī*, "intelligent," for *bṛhacchrīḥ*, "enormously majestic." These same editions and manuscripts (except for D11) read *bṛhacchrīḥ* (erroneously printed as *manasvī* in the critical apparatus) for *mahārtham*, "highly sensible." Cs explains that these two epithets (*bṛhacchrīḥ* and *manasvī*) show that Lakṣmaṇa is unafraid (*dvābhyām apy abhītatāṃ dyotayati*). It should be noted, however, that Roussel (1903, vol. 3, p. 232), followed by Shastri (1959, vol. 3, p. 204) and Pagani (1999, p. 1061), reads *bṛhacchrīḥ* adverbially. Roussel and Shastri translate the term to mean "*avec une noble fierté*" and "proudly," respectively, while Pagani renders "*majestueusement*."

The meter is *upajāti*.

57. "You cannot attain excellence" *na ... bhavān pradhānaḥ*: Literally, "you, sir, are not the foremost."

"true heroes" *satpuruṣāḥ*: Literally, "virtuous men." We follow the interpretation of Cg, who glosses, "heroic men (*śūrapuruṣāḥ*)." See 6.57.2 and note.

"demonstrate your prowess" *vidarśayasvātmabalam*: Literally, "show your own strength." KK (both editions) and VSP 6.71.58 both break the sequence into *vidarśaya svātmabalam* (instead of *vidarśayasva ātmabalam*), which would yield a sense something like "show the strength of your own [*sva-*] body [*ātmā*]."

"evil-minded wretch" *durātman*: Literally, "O evil-minded one."

The meter is *upendravajrā*.

58. "Show what you are made of through your deeds." *karmaṇā sūcayātmānam*: Literally, "reveal yourself through action."

"truly endowed" *yuktaḥ*: Literally, "endowed, joined."

60. For some reason, this verse has been omitted from the translation of Dutt (1893, p. 1347).

61. "spurting from the gaping holes made in your body by my arrowheads" *gātrād bāṇaśalyāntarotthitam*: Literally, "from the body [blood] arising from the openings of arrow-darts." The term *bāṇaśalya* here can also be taken as a *dvandva* in the sense of "arrows and darts." Of the translators consulted, only Dutt (1893, p. 1347) comes close to this in rendering, "my arrows, resembling darts." Other translators who have this reading take the compound as a *tatpuruṣa* in the sense of "sharp points *or* tips of arrow." Although there is no clear lexical support for such a reading, we are inclined to accept it, as Lakṣmaṇa is not shown to use any weapons other than arrows in the battle that follows. See, too, verse 93 below.

62. "you must know me to be your death" *mṛtyuṃ jānīhi*: Literally, "know death." We follow Cg and Cr in adding the word "me (*mām*)." This interpretation is rendered or paraphrased in most of the translations consulted. Dutt (1893, p. 1347) translates, "death shalt thou know in the conflict," and adds, in a footnote, "The commentator says the passage means—'Thou knowest (me) *for death* itself.' I prefer the sense given." Most northern manuscripts as well as the text of Gorresio make the reading proposed by Cg explicit by including the pronoun *mām* in the second half of the verse. See Pollock 1984a, pp. 85–86.

Following verse 62, D1,2,5–7,9–11,S insert a passage of one line [1311*]: "When Viṣṇu was only a child, he[1] traversed the three worlds in three strides.[2]"

[1]"When Viṣṇu was only a child, he" *bālena viṣṇunā*: Literally, "by the child Viṣṇu."
[2]"in three strides" *tribhiḥ kramaiḥ*: Literally, "with three strides *or* steps." The reference is, of course, to the *vāmanāvatāra*, or dwarf incarnation, of Viṣṇu. See notes to verse 7 above.

63. "splendid" *uttamam*: Literally, "best, excellent."
64. For some reason, Dutt (1893, p. 1347) has, quite jarringly, placed his translation of this verse between *pādas* b and c of verse 63.
"Then . . . watched" *dadṛśus tadā*: T1,M3, the texts and printed editions of Cg and Cm, and Gita Press (6.71.65) read instead *draṣṭum āgaman*, "they came to see."
"spirits of the departed" *bhutāḥ*: See 6.55.127 and note.
"*guhyakas*" *guhyakāḥ*: See 6.55.127 and note.
65. "shrinking, as it were, the space between them" *saṃkṣipann iva cāmbaram*: Literally, "as if compressing the sky." We follow the interpretation of Ct and Cg, who understand, "devouring, as it were, the space between them with the speed of his arrow (*bāṇavegenāntarālasthitam ākāśaṃ grasann iva*—so Ct)." Cr glosses, "as if turning back (*nivartayann iva*)," for *saṃkṣipann iva*. Cv glosses, "as if destroying (*saṃharann iva*)." Most of the translators consulted who read with the critical edition follow the interpretation of Ct and Cg. Pagani (1999, p. 1061) renders, "*parut ébranler l'espace*."
67. "was beside himself with rage" *bhṛśaṃ kruddhaḥ*: Literally, "extremely angry."
"five more" *pañca*: Literally, "five."
70. "drawing the bow" *vicakarṣa*: Literally, "he drew."
"with tremendous force" *vegena*: Literally, "with force *or* speed."
"the arrow" *sāyakam*: D5,7,T1,M3, and the texts and printed editions of Cg and Cm read instead *vīryavān*, "mighty *or* heroic."
71. "straight" *anataparvaṇā*: Literally, "with unbent *or* undepressed joints." The reference is to a bamboo arrow, whose knots or joints are smooth and level with the intermediate portions of the shaft. D2,3,6,7,10,12,T1,G,M, and the texts and printed texts of the southern commentators read instead *nataparvaṇā*, literally, "with depressed [i.e., not protuberant] joints." Despite the fact that the variants would appear to be antonyms, they essentially mean the same thing, since both *nata* and *anata* refer to deviations from the level surface. Cg and Cm, the only commentators to deal with this term in either of its variants, gloss, literally, "with hidden joints (*ni*[*vi*—Cm]*līnaparvaṇā*)." Both commentators agree that the idea is that the arrows are straight (*ṛjuṇeti yāvat*), and we concur. Translators vary considerably in their interpretations. Gita Press (1969, vol. 3, p. 1662), Raghunathan (1982, vol. 3, p. 206), and Gorresio (1858, vol. 10, p. 57) understand the term to refer to smooth, flat, or straight joints of the arrow shaft. Dutt (1893, p. 1348), taking *nata* in its sense of "bent *or* bowed, renders the unlikely "having bent knots." Roussel (1903, vol. 3, p. 233) offers the odd "*aux noeuds adoucis*." Pagani (1999, p. 1061), again idiosyncratically, renders, "*à la pointe effilée*." Shastri (1959, vol. 3, p. 205) ignores the term completely. Compare the note at 6.78.5 to App. I, No. 47, line 10. See 6.114.20 and note.

72. "in battle" *āhave*: The reading is peculiar in the context of the simile. It is not clear why the arrow in Atikāya's head should look like a snake in battle. Given this reading, it is possible perhaps to detach the word from the simile and read it in a general sense: "In that battle... the arrow... resembled a serpent lord." The only translator to share the critical reading, Gorresio (1858, vol. 10, p. 57), renders, "*in una zuffa*." The critical reading, however, does not appear to be a very strong one. Ñ1,D1,5–7,9–11,13,T1,2,G,M, and the texts and printed editions of the southern commentators read instead *acale*, "on *or* in a mountain," while several northern manuscripts read *acalaḥ*, "[like] a mountain." From a rhetorical point of view, this variant is only a modest improvement. It is still not clear why a serpent on a mountain should be red, unless it is through the unexpressed coating by metallic ores. This idea is made explicit in Ñ2,V1,B2–4, which compare the arrow to a mountain reddened with minerals (*dhāturakta ivācalaḥ*). The comparison of the arrow rather than the huge *rākṣasa* to a mountain seems, however, highly suspect. Raghunathan (1982, vol. 3, p. 206), alone among the translators of the southern text, attempts to cope with the simile by shifting the adjectival phrase "smeared with blood (*śoṇitenāktaḥ*)" to the serpent instead of the arrow, rendering, "The arrow... looked like a serpent smeared with blood on a mountain." This too, however, is not very persuasive, since it is not clear why a serpent on a mountain should be smeared with blood.

73. "Tripura" *tripura-*: Literally, "the Triple City." The reference is to the three splendid cities of gold, silver, and iron in the sky, air, and earth, respectively, crafted for the *asuras* by their architect Maya. The cities along with their inhabitants were destroyed by Śiva's fiery arrow. The well-known purāṇic story is found throughout the literature. See 1.73.19; 1.74.12; and notes. Compare *MatsyaP* 128–129; *ŚivaP*, *Rudrasaṃhitā* 5.10; *BhāgP* 7.10, especially verses 66–71; and *MBh* 8.24.1–124. For a translation and discussion of the myth, see O'Flaherty 1975, pp. 125–36, 325. See note to 5.52.13. Tripura is also the personal name of the *asura* king ruling the Three Cities. Ck and Ct understand the term in this sense (*tripurāsurapurasya*). See, too, notes to 6.61.23 and 6.88.2. Cf. notes to 6.55.93–96.

74. "reflecting... thought" *cintayāmāsa* ... *vimṛśya*: Cg and Cm understand the gerund *vimṛśya* to indicate that Atikāya is considering what he ought to do, while the finite verb indicates the content of his thought about Lakṣmaṇa (*karaṇīyaṃ nirdhārya*—so Cg). Cr reverses this (*svakartavyaṃ cintayāmāsa*). Cg and Cm, who gloss the gerund *vidhāya*, which begins the next verse in their text, as "having spoken (*abhidhāya*)," evidently understand the verb *cintayāmāsa*, "he thought," to mean that Atikāya spoke his thought aloud to Lakṣmaṇa. This idea, at any rate, has been adopted by Raghunathan (1982, vol. 3, p. 206) and Dutt (1893, p. 1348), both of whom render, "said." Dutt has a footnote at this point in which he says, "*Chintayāmāsa—thought*, I apprehend, means *said* in this connection." See note to verse below.

75. "Reflecting in this fashion, he lowered his face and both his arms." *vicāryaivaṃ vinamyāsyaṃ vinamya ca bhujāv ubhau*: Literally, "having reflected in this fashion, having lowered his face and having lowered both arms." None of the available printed editions and few, if any, of the manuscripts collated for the critical edition have the same sequence of gerunds as does the critical text. The texts and printed editions of Ct, Ck, and Cr read *vidhāyaivaṃ vidāryāsyaṃ vinamya ca mahābhujau*, literally, "having ascertained thus, having split open his mouth, and having lowered both arms." As noted above, Cg, Cm, and some translators understand *vidhāya*, "having ascertained," in the sense of "having spoken,

having said." Translators who follow the text of Ct render this half verse variously. Dutt (1893, p.1348), ignoring the phrase *vidāryāsyam*, offers, "having spoken thus candidly, he, folding his hands at ease." Gita Press (1969, vol. 3, p. 1662) translates, "Distending his mouth and speaking (to him) as aforesaid, (nay) controlling his mighty arms." Roussel (1903, vol. 3, p. 233), followed by Shastri (1959, vol. 3, p. 205), renders, "*Sur cette considération, il ouvrit la bouche, étira ses grands bras.*" Pagani (1999, p. 1062) similarly translates, "*Sur ce, il ouvrit la bouche, ploya ses grands bras.*" Printed editions of Cg and Cm read instead *vidhāyaivaṃ vinamyāsyaṃ niyamya ca bhujāv ubhau*, literally, "having ascertained in this fashion, having lowered his face, and having restrained both arms." Raghunathan (1982, vol. 3, p. 206), the only translator consulted who renders this variant, translates, "Saying this, he snapped his mouth shut, held his arms close to his side..."

76. "one, three, five, or seven arrows at a time" *ekaṃ trīn pañca sapteti sāyakān*: Literally, "arrows: one, three, five, seven." Translators are divided as to whether the arrows are deployed in groups or if this is a running total of those shot. We are inclined toward the former position on the grounds that, in verses 67–68 above, Atikāya has already shot five arrows at a time.

"nocked them" *saṃdadhe*: Literally, "he joined *or* fitted." This is the normal verb used to express the action of fitting an arrow to a bowstring.

77. "which were like Kāla himself" *kālasaṃkāśāḥ*: Literally, "resembling Kāla."

78. "with many sharp arrows of his own" *niśitair bahubhiḥ śaraiḥ*: Literally, "with many sharp arrows."

79. "yet another sharp arrow" *niśitaṃ śaram*: Literally, "a sharp arrow."

80. "The immensely powerful warrior" *mahātejāḥ*: Literally, "The immensely powerful one."

"with tremendous force" *sahasā*: Literally, "violently, suddenly."

"It then struck" *tataḥ... ājaghāna*: Given the critical reading, we understand the arrow, mentioned in *pāda* b, to be the subject of the verb. Ś,V3,B1,D1–5,7–12,T1,G1,2,M5, and the texts and printed editions of Ct and Cr read *tena*, "with it," for *tataḥ*, "then." In this reading, Atikāya becomes the subject of the verb *ājaghāna*, "he [i.e., Atikāya] struck."

81. "great gouts of blood" *rudhiraṃ tīvram*: See note to 6.57.87.

"as does a rutting elephant rut fluid" *madaṃ matta iva dvipaḥ*: Cr, the only commentator to deal with this verse, notes that the rut fluid of an elephant is reddish in color (*aruṇavarṇam*). He also glosses *mattaḥ*, "rutting," as "maddened in the sense of being characterized by the frenzy of battle (*yuddhotsāhaviśiṣṭaṃ yathā bhavati tathā mattaḥ*)." See 6.46.37 and note.

82. "that mighty man... removed that dart from his body" *sa cakāra... ātmānaṃ viśalyam... vibhuḥ*: Literally, "that powerful one made his body free from darts."

The term *vibhuḥ* here is ambiguous and lends itself to a number of interpretations. One meaning of the term is "lord, prince, *or* king," and some translators, e.g., Dutt ("that lord" [1893, p. 1349]) and Shastri ("that prince" [1959, vol. 3, p. 206]), translate in this sense. Several of the southern commentators, however, see the term as used here in its sense of "supreme divinity," particularly, but not exclusively, in reference to Lakṣmaṇa's status as a partial incarnation of Viṣṇu. Ct thus understands that the reason Lakṣmaṇa is able to rid himself of Atikāya's arrow is because he is the *vibhuḥ*, or "Lord," because of his connection with a portion of Viṣṇu (*viṣṇvaṃśatvānusaṃdhānavān ity arthaḥ*). Cr similarly understands that Atikāya's divinely charged weapon is destroyed by its mere contact with Lakṣmaṇa's [divine] body (*śarīrasaṃbandhamātreṇa śaro dhvasta ity arthaḥ*). The term *vibhuḥ* is equally an epithet of Brahmā, Viṣṇu, or Śiva, and Ck, who has theological interests in Brahmā (Goldman and Goldman 1996, p. 96; and note to 5.1.177), believes that this is the divinity indicated by the term here (*brahmāṃśatvānusaṃdhānavān ity arthaḥ*). Four of the translators consulted follow the interpretation of Ct and Cr, viz., Gita Press ("all-powerful Lakṣmaṇa [who was a part manifestation of Viṣṇu]" [1969, vol. 3, p. 1663]), Roussel ("*Il se guérit . . . lui-même en sa qualité de Vibhu*" [1903, vol. 3, p. 233]), Raghunathan ("Then the all-powerful Lord . . . healed himself [freed himself from pain]" [1982, vol. 3, p. 207]), and Pagani ("*Mais il se débarrassa lui-même . . . de sa flèche, parce qu'il était de nature divine*" [1999, p. 1062]). Pagani (p. 1667) provides a note on the term *vibhuḥ* in which she claims that the term is used here in reference to the divine nature of the sons of Daśaratha.

Although no doubt Vālmīki believes that Lakṣmaṇa, like Rāma, is a partial incarnation of Viṣṇu (see 6.26.31; 6.47.104,115; and notes; and Pollock 1984b and 1991, pp. 15–54), we do not believe it is his intention to allude to that identification in this passage. First, it is unnecessary, because it is quite normal in both Sanskrit epics for outstanding warriors, such as Lakṣmaṇa, to sustain and quickly recover from seemingly life-threatening injuries. Therefore, there is no need to assert the divinity of Lakṣmaṇa as a reason for his rapid recovery. More important, we believe that the occluded nature of divinity in the *Rāmāyaṇa*, which is made necessary by the boons of Rāvaṇa, militates against the idea that Lakṣmaṇa is immune to injury because he is a divinity. Certainly this is not the case elsewhere, where Lakṣmaṇa and Rāma are both injured and represented as near death (see 6.35.8–26 and 6.60.47–49). We have therefore rendered *vibhuḥ* in its most basic sense of "a powerful *or* heroic individual." In this we are in agreement with Gorresio (1858, vol. 10, p. 58), who renders the term as "*il prode Raghuide.*"

"invoking a divine weapon-spell, he nocked it" *astreṇāpi samādadhe*: Literally, "he fitted it with an *astra* as well." Dutt (1893, p. 1349), Raghunathan (1982, vol. 3, p. 207), and Gorresio (1858, vol. 10, p. 58) take the verb *samādadhe* (v.l. *samādade*, *saṃdadhe*) in the sense in which it has been used in the preceding verses (76 and 80), that is, "to nock an arrow." Cr and Cg, however, understand the verb here to refer to Lakṣmaṇa's charging or joining his arrow with the divine weapon-spell. They gloss, respectively, *abhimantrayāmāsa* and *yojayāmāsa*. In this they have been followed by Roussel (1903, vol. 3, p. 233), Shastri (1959, vol. 3, p. 206), Pagani (1999, p. 1062), and Gita Press (1969, vol. 3, p. 1663). We think that both actions are being described in this verse and understand that we need to supply the term *yojayāmāsa*, as in the following verse, to indicate that the arrow is being nocked but also charged with a divine spell.

83. "He charged that arrow with the divine weapon-spell of Agni" *āgneyena tadāstreṇa yojayāmāsa sāyakam*: Literally, "he then connected the arrow with the *āgneya astra*." As Cg, Ct, and Cm note, here the term *astra*, "divine weapon-spell *or* divinely charged weapon," stands, as it does in the previous verse, for the *mantra*, or "spell," that governs any weapon into which it is invoked (*astramantreṇa*). Lakṣmaṇa's access to the divinely charged weapons or divine weapon-spells is noteworthy. At *Bālakāṇḍa* 26–27, Rāma is granted such access as a boon from Viśvāmitra. No such power is ascribed explicitly to Lakṣmaṇa. See note to 6.35.5. Note, however, that in Bhavabhūti's understanding, the *astras* appear to be revealed to most, if not all, of Rāma's male kin. See *UttaRāC* 6.15; 7.9 and 10; etc.

"of that great warrior" *mahātmanaḥ*: Literally, "of that great one." B3,D10,M1,2, and the texts and printed editions of Ct read instead *tadātmanaḥ*, "then, of his own."

"as... his bow" *dhanuś cāsya*: Literally, "and his bow." D4,M3, and the texts and printed editions of Cg and Gita Press read instead *dhanuṣy asya*, "on his bow."

84. "invoked the divine weapon-spell of Sūrya" *sauram astraṃ samādade*: Literally, "he took up *or* called to mind the *saura astra*." The term *sūra* is a less common synonym for *sūrya*. V2,D7,9–11, and the texts and printed editions of Ct and Cr read *raudram*, "belonging to Rudra [Śiva]," in place of *sauram*, "belonging to Sūra." Most of the translators who share this variant understand the sense to be "the weapon of Rudra." Gita Press (1969, vol. 3, p. 1663), however, takes *raudra* in its general adjectival sense of "fearsome." See note to verse 86 below. See, too, 6.55.78; 6.87.33; 6.88.2; and notes.

85. "he had fitted to his bow" *āhitam*: Literally, "placed." We take the term in the sense of *sam* + *ā* √*dhā*, "to nock *or* to fit [to a bow]," which has been used above. See notes to 76 and 80 above. Ct and Ck understand the participle to refer to the conjunction of the arrow with the divine spell, glossing, "in which was placed the power of the divine weapon (*āhitadīvyāstraśaktim*)." Cr appears to have a similar view, glossing, "united, joined (*sandhitam*)." Cg glosses, *saṃhitam*, which could be taken in either the sense of "conjoined" or "placed on a bow."

"just as Kāla, the ender of all things, might his staff of doom" *kāladaṇḍam ivāntakaḥ*: Literally, "as the ender, the staff of Kāla."

86. "charged with the divine weapon-spell of Agni" *āgneyenābhisaṃyuktam*: Literally, "conjoined with the *āgneya*." The phrase is rather elliptical. A number of manuscripts, Ñ,V1,2,B2–4,D7,9–11,13,G1,2, and the texts and printed editions of Ct remedy this by reading instead *āgneyāstrābhisaṃyuktam*, literally, "conjoined with the *āgneya astra*."

"blazing... charged with the divine weapon-spell of Sūrya" *dīptaṃ sūryāstrayojitam*: Literally, "blazing... conjoined with the *sūrya astra*." D7,9–11, and the texts and printed editions of Ct and Cr read *raudram*, "fearsome," for *dīptam*, "blazing." The term is slightly ambiguous, since these same texts read *raudram* in the sense of "belonging to Rudra (Śiva)," in place of *saura*, "belonging to Sūra," in verse 84 above (see note to verse 84 above). Most of the translations that follow the text of Ct and read this variant understand that Atikāya is shooting some combination of the missiles of Rudra and Sūrya, including Dutt (1893, p. 1349), Roussel (1903, vol. 3, p. 233), Shastri (1959, vol. 3, p. 206), and Pagani (1999, p. 1062). Pagani (pp. 1667–68), who understands that the *astra* was consecrated to both Sūrya and Rudra, has a note in which she attempts to justify this association on the basis of an indirect mythological connection they each have with Agni. This, she argues, explains why the two arrows, dedicated, respectively, to Agni and to (Sūrya-) Rudra, cancel each other out.

87. "as they flew through the sky" *ambare*: Literally, "in the sky."

88. "their flames extinguished" *nirarciṣau*: Literally, "flameless."

Following verse 88, D6,7,9–11,T2,G3,M5 insert a passage of one line [1320*], while Ś,V3,B1,D1–3,8,12 substitute it for 88cd. This line appears in printed editions of Ct (GPP, NSP 6.71.88cd), in Lahore (6.52.87), and in brackets in KK (6.71.90ef): "Deprived of their arrows,[1] the two, Lakṣmaṇa and Atikāya,[2] no longer shone in battle.[3]"

[1]"Deprived of their arrows" *śarahīnau*: D7,10,11, and the texts and printed editions of Ct and Cr read instead *dīpyamānau*, "blazing." This variant lends the line the sense "Those two, who had been blazing, [no longer shone]."

[2]"the two, Lakṣmaṇa and Atikāya" *tāv ubhau*: Literally, "those two."

[3]"in battle" *saṃyuge*: D9–11 and the texts and printed editions of Ct read instead *mahītale*, "on the ground."

These variants of the vulgate lend the line the sense "Those two, which *or* who had been blazing, no longer shone on the ground." The reference could be either to the arrows or to the warriors who shot them. Cr and Cs are the only commentators to remark on this line. Cr believes that the reference is to Lakṣmaṇa and Atikāya. His idea is that the reference to the warriors no longer shining suggests that they are suffering regret at the destruction of their prized weapons. (*dīpyamānau tau lakṣmaṇa-rākṣasāv api mahītale na bhrājete. etena bāṇadhvaṃsahetukapaścāttāpas tayor jāta iti dhvanitam.*) Cs agrees with Cr that the reference is to the two archers but feels that their loss of luster is occasioned not only by the failure of their arrows but also by their frustration at the failure of their initial hopes that they had killed their foe. (*tau moktārau lakṣmaṇātikāyāv api dīpyamānau prāk hato 'yam iti parasparaṃ jayaprakāśau na bhrājete sma moghībhūtabāṇāv ity abhrājanaṃ yuktam iti bhāvaḥ.*)

89. "the divinely charged *aiṣīka* missile" *astram aiṣīkam*: Literally, "the *aiṣīka astra*." *Aiṣīka* is the name of one of the divine weapon-spells conferred upon Rāma by Viśvāmitra at *Bālakāṇḍa* 26.6. It is given to him there immediately after the gift of the powerful *brahmaśiras*, or "Brahmā-head weapon." It is not, however, associated in that passage with any specific divinity. The word *aiṣīka* means "reed," and it is Aśvatthāman's investment of an *aiṣīka*, or reed, with the *brahmaśiras astra* at *Mahābhārata* 10.13.17 that lends the whole *Mahābhārata* episode from 10.10 to 10.18 the name *Aiṣīkaparvan*. Note that at *Sundarakāṇḍa* 36.26, Rāma is said to similarly infuse a blade of *darbha* grass with the *brahmāstra*. See, too, note to 5.36.26 (note that the reference to the *Mahābhārata* passage is incorrectly given there as 10.14.17).

D10,11,M1,2, and the texts and printed editions of Ck and Ct read *tvāṣṭram*, "belonging to the divinity Tvaṣṭṛ," instead of *tv astram*, "divine weapon-spell." At 1.26.19, the weapon associated with Tvaṣṭṛ that is given to Rāma is a discus (*cakra*) called Sudāmana and is quite distinct from the *aiṣīka* weapon he is given several verses earlier.

"that divinely charged missile . . . with the divinely charged missile of Indra" *astram aindreṇa*: Literally, "that *astra* with the *aindra*." At 1.26.5, Viśvāmitra gives Rāma a discus (*cakra*) belonging to Indra. V3,B1,3,D1,3,6,T2,3,G1,2,M1,3, and the texts and printed editions of Cg read instead *astreṇaindreṇa*, "with the divine weapon-spell *or* divinely charged missile of Indra." Raghunathan (1982, vol. 3, p. 207), the only translator to render this variant, inexplicably translates "with an arrow united with Rudrā's [*sic*] missile."

90. "prince" *kumāraḥ*: D5,7,T1,G2,M3, and the texts and printed editions of Cg read instead the redundant *ruṣitaḥ*, "angry."

"with the divine weapon-spell of Yama" *yāmyenāstreṇa*: Literally, "with the *yāmya astra*."

91. "that divinely charged missile . . . it" *tad astram . . . tad astraṃ tu*: Literally, "that *astra* . . . but that *astra*." The majority of northern manuscripts and some southern manuscripts, including the printed editions of Cg, read instead some form of the instrumental singular for the second occurrence of the phrase *tad astram* (Ś,B1,D8—*tam astreṇa*; Ñ2,V,B3,D2,3,10,12,M3,5—*tad astreṇa*; B2,D9,11,G3—*tadāstreṇa*), yielding, literally, "with the [*vāyavya*] *astra*."

92. "with volleys of arrows . . . with torrents of rain" *śaradhārābhir dhārābhir*: Literally, "with showers of arrows . . . with showers."

93. "arrowheads" *-agraśalyāḥ*: Literally, "tip darts." Cr glosses, "the tip portion of the dart (*śalyāgrabhāgaḥ*)." See note to verse 61 above.

"with tremendous force" *sahasā*: See note to verse 80 above.

95. "with his impenetrable armor" *avadhyakavacaḥ*: Literally, "whose armor is not to be destroyed."

Following verse 95, Ñ2,V,B2–4,D6,T2,3,M3, and the texts and printed editions of Cg insert a passage of ten lines [1326*]: "He then shot at Lakṣmaṇa an arrow that resembled a venomous serpent.[1] Pierced in a vital spot by that arrow, Lakṣmaṇa Saumitri, tormentor of his foes, lost consciousness for a moment. Then, regaining consciousness, he slew in battle, in that great battle, the horses and charioteer [of Atikāya] with four splendid arrows. That conqueror of his foes then quickly destroyed [Atikāya's] banner.[1] [2–6] Seeing[2] the destruction of his banner, that bull among *rākṣasas* was furious. That powerful subduer of his foes showered[3] [Lakṣmaṇa] with torrents of arrows.[7–8] But Saumitri, unshaken, cut those arrows to pieces with his own arrows.[4] He then released blazing arrows[5] in order to kill that *rākṣasa*.[9–10]"

[1]"That conqueror of his foes then quickly destroyed [Atikāya's] banner." *unmamātha ca vegena dhvajaṃ tasya ripuṃjayaḥ*: D6,T2,3,M3, and the texts and printed editions of Cg omit this line.

[2]"Seeing" *dṛṣṭvā*: Literally, "having seen." D6,M3, and the texts and printed editions of Cg read instead *kṛtvā*, "having done."

[3]"that bull among *rākṣasas* was furious. That powerful . . . showered" *dṛṣṭvā kruddho rākṣasapuṃgavaḥ / abhyavarṣata tejasvī*: D6,T2,3,M3, and the texts and printed editions of Cg omit this line.

[4]"with his own arrows" *śaraiḥ*: Literally, "with arrows."

[5]"then . . . blazing arrows" *ca śarān dīptān*: D6,T2,3,M3, and the texts and printed editions of Cg read instead *lakṣmaṇo bāṇān*, "Lakṣmaṇa [released] arrows."

Among the printed editions consulted, this passage appears as a regular part of the text only in Gita Press (6.71.98–101). KK prints and numbers the passage (6.71.98–100) but encloses it in brackets, adding in a footnote that it is found only in later manuscripts and not in older texts. GPP places these verses, without numbering them, in brackets between its verses 6.71.95 and 96. VSP excludes the passage from its text, placing instead a footnote marker between its 6.71.97cd and ef. It prints the passage in the footnote and notes that it is added [in some manuscripts]. NSP, Gorresio, KK 1905, and Lahore omit the passage entirely. Among the translations consulted, only Gita Press (1969, vol. 3, p. 1664) renders this passage.

96. "that foremost of men" *narottamaḥ*: D6 and the texts and printed editions of Cg and Cm, except for KK 1905, read instead *śarottamaḥ*, "the foremost of arrows." This variant is translated only by Raghunathan (1982, vol. 3, p. 207), who renders, "the most powerful arrow."

"But then" *atha*: Literally, "then."

97. "this *rākṣasa*" *eṣaḥ*: Literally, "this one."

Following verse 97, D5–7,9–11,S insert a passage of one line [1329*]: "For that mighty warrior,[1] encased in his armor, is invulnerable to other divinely charged weapons."

[1]"mighty warrior" *balī*: Literally, "mighty one."

98. "of irresistible force" *amoghavegam*: Literally, "of infallible impact." B2,3,D9–11, and the texts and printed editions of Ct read instead *athogravegam*, "then, [an arrow] of fierce impact."

"charged it with the divine weapon-spell of Brahmā" *brāhmam astram... niyojya*: Literally, "having employed the *brāhma astra*." Cg glosses, "having muttered the spell governing the *brahmāstra* (*brahmāstramantraṃ niyojya japitvā*)."

The meter is *upajāti*.

99. "all the directions, as well as the moon, the sun, the great planets, and the heavens, shook with fear" *diśaḥ sacandrārkamahāgrahāś ca nabhaś ca tatrāsa*: Literally, "the directions, together with the moon, sun, and great planets [trembled *or* were afraid], and the sky trembled *or* was afraid." Cr, perhaps uncomfortable with the notion of the intangible directions trembling, understands the term *diśaḥ*, "directions," to refer to the divinities that govern the quarters (*dikpadena taddevatānāṃ grahaṇān nāsaṃbhavaḥ*).

"groaned" *rarāsa*: Literally, "[the earth] cried out." We understand the reference to be to the rumbling sound that sometimes accompanies earthquakes. Cr glosses, "it shook (*cakampe*)," and most of the translators consulted understand the verb in this sense.

The meter is *upajāti*.

100. "with the divine weapon-spell of Brahmā" *brahmaṇo 'streṇa*: Literally, "with the *astra* of Brahmā."

"charged... fitted it to his bow" *niyujya cāpe*: Literally, "having charged *or* joined... on the bow." The verse is somewhat elliptical since it has only one verbal element to express both the charging of the arrow with the *astra* and the fitting of the arrow to the bow. As it happens, the one verb provided, the gerund *niyujya*, can function in either of these capacities but surely not both. Cr, the only commentator to address this verse, understands the gerund to refer to the fitting of the arrow to the bow and therefore supplies the adjectival participle *yuktam*, "charged with, conjoined with," to construe with the instrumental *astreṇa*, yielding the sense "having fitted to his bow the arrow that had been charged with the *astra*" (*brahmaṇo 'streṇa yuktam ... bāṇaṃ cāpe niyujya*). Since the poet has so regularly used the verb √*yuj* in this passage to refer specifically to the charging of divine weapon-spells (cf. verses 83, 86, 98, etc., above) and has used the verb *sam* √*dhā* to refer to the fitting of an arrow to a bow (cf. verses 76, 80, etc., above), we have taken the gerund in the former sense here and supplied the verb "fitted."

"which was like Indra's *vajra*" *vajrakalpam*: Literally, "like the *vajra*." See 6.58.10 and note.

The meter is *upajāti*.

101. "hurtling toward him" *samāpatantam*: Literally, "as it came flying."

"loosed by Lakṣmaṇa . . . Its force was irresistible" *lakṣmaṇotsṛṣṭam amoghavegam*: For *amoghavegam*, see note to verse 98 above. D7,9–11, and the texts and printed editions of Ct and Cr read instead *lakṣmaṇotsṛṣṭavivṛddhavegam*, literally, "whose force was increased as it was released by Lakṣmaṇa." Translators who follow the text of Ct have understood this compound variously. Dutt (1893, p. 1350) understands a causal relationship between the increased force of the arrow and the fact of Lakṣmaṇa's having released it, translating, "acquiring enhanced vehemence arising from its having been discharged by Lakshmana." Gita Press (1969, vol. 3, p. 1665) and Pagani (1999, p. 1063) posit no causal relationship between the two adjectival phrases (*lakṣmaṇotsṛṣṭa* and *vivṛddhavegam*). Roussel (1903, vol. 3, p. 234), for reasons unclear to us, appears to understand *vivṛddhavegam* as an adjective modifying Lakṣmaṇa and having the sense "*d'un bras vigoureux*." In this impossible reading, he has been followed by Shastri (1959, vol. 3, p. 207), who translates, "[loosed] by the mighty-armed Lakshmana."

"with gold" *suvarṇa-*: V1,2,B3,D10,11,T2,M1–3, and the texts and printed editions of Ct and Cr read instead *suparṇa-*, literally, "beautifully feathered." Among the translators consulted, only Gita Press (1969, vol. 3, p. 1665) and Dutt (1893, p. 1350) render this rather awkward variant. The word is also a name of Garuḍa, and this sense informs Gita Press's rendition: "provided with lovely feathers resembling the wings of Garuḍa (the king of birds)."

"it shone like fire" *jvalanaprakāśam*: Ś,V1,3,B1,3,D2,3,6,8–12,T2,3,G1,3,M1,2,5, and the texts and printed editions of Ct read *śvasana-*, "wind, breath," for *jvalana-*, "fire."

The meter is *upajāti*.

102. "continued to hurtle toward him" *tasya . . . jagāma pārśvam*: Literally, "it went to his side."

"with tremendous speed" *ativegena*: D7,G2,M3, and the texts and printed editions of Cm and Cg read instead *atikāyasya*, "of Atikāya," yielding the sense "to the side of Atikāya."

The meter is *upajāti*.

103. "fiercely blazing" *pradīpta-*: Literally, "blazing, glowing."

"never slackened his efforts" *avipannaceṣṭaḥ*: Literally, "of unfailing actions *or* efforts." D5,T1,G2,M3, and the texts and printed editions of Cg read *-cetāḥ*, "mind," for *ceṣṭaḥ*, "efforts," lending the compound the sense of "his mind undistressed." Among the translators consulted, only Raghunathan (1982, vol. 3, p. 208) renders this variant, translating, "with all his wits about him." The text of Gorresio (6.51.108), however, reads the variant *vinaṣṭacetāḥ*, "his wits scattered *or* destroyed." This reading is unattested in the critical apparatus.

"ploughshares" *halaiḥ*: This appears to be a weapon that resembles the blade of a plough. The *hala*, or "plough," is the characteristic weapon of Balarāma. D6,9–11,T2,3, and the texts and printed editions of Ct and Cr read instead *śaraiḥ*, "with arrows." M1–3 and the texts and printed editions of Cg and Cm read instead *hulaiḥ*, "with knives *or* daggers." Crā and Cg, the latter citing the lexicon of Vaijayantī, understand the term *hula* to refer to a type of double-bladed or double-edged (?) weapon (*dviphalapattrāgram*). See 6.83.23–25 and note.

The meter is *upajāti*.

104. "impervious to those wondrously formed weapons" *tāny āyudhāny adbhutavigrahāṇi moghāni kṛtvā*: Literally, "having rendered ineffective those weapons of wonderful form."

"violently" *prasahya*: Ñ1,V,B1,3,4,D1,3,4,6,9–11,13,T2,3,G1,2,M3,5, and the texts and printed editions of the southern commentators read instead *pragṛhya*, "having seized."

The meter is *upajāti*.

105. "Battered" *-prapīḍitam*: Literally, "pressed, crushed." The critical reading appears weak and is apparently supported only by four southern manuscripts (G3,M1–3). It should at least be marked as doubtful. The majority of manuscripts, including the printed texts of Ct and Cr, read instead *-pramarditam*, "crushed."

Following verse 105, D5–7,9–11,S insert a passage of six lines [1330*]: "Seeing him fallen to the ground, his ornaments scattered,[1] all the surviving night-roaming *rākṣasas* were deeply distressed.[1–2] Despondent, their faces dejected, exhausted from the blows they had received, many of them cried out violently and loudly in discordant voices.[3–4] Then those night-roaming *rākṣasas*, terrified and despairing now that their leader had been slain, turned their faces toward the city and, moving swiftly,[2] fled.[5–6]"

[1]"Seeing . . . his ornaments scattered" *dṛṣṭvā vikṣiptabhūṣaṇam*: D7,9–11, and the texts and printed editions of Ct read instead *vikṣiptāmbarabhūṣaṇam*, "[Seeing him with] his ornaments and clothing scattered."

[2]"swiftly" *tvaritam*: D9–11 and the texts and printed editions of Ct read instead *paritaḥ*, "on all sides."

106. Virtually the entire north (Ś,Ñ,V,B,D1–4,8,12,13) omits this verse, and, according to the principles on which the critical edition is based, the verse should be considered suspect and very likely should have been deleted from the critical text (Bhatt 1960, p. xxxiv).

"who had accomplished their cherished goal" *iṣṭabhāginam*: Literally, "possessing as his portion that which was desired." The commentators, evidently deriving *bhāga*, "share *or* portion," from the sense of the verbal root √*bhaj*, "to obtain for oneself," gloss the compound as "possessing the accomplishment of what was desired (*iṣṭaprāptimantam*—so Cr)." The commentators indicate variously that the cherished object is the death of Atikāya or victory in battle (*iṣṭam atikāyavadhaṃ prāptavantam iti*—so Cv, Cm, Ct; *iṣṭasya jayasya bhāgo prāptiḥ so 'syāstītīṣṭabhāgī tam*—so Cg).

The meter is *vaṃśasthavila*.

According to Ct, the killing of the six *rākṣasa* heroes—Triśiras, Atikāya, Devāntaka, Narāntaka, Mahodara, and Mahāpārśva—was carried out over the six days ending with the sixth [*tithi*] of the dark half of the month Bhādrāśvina (*triśiro 'tikāyadevāntakanarāntakamahodaramahāpārśvānāṃ ṣaḍbhir dinair bhādrāśvinakṛṣṇaṣaṣṭhyantena vadha ityagre spaṣṭam*). See note to 6.4.4.

Following verse 106, T1,M3,5, and the texts and printed editions of Cg and Cm insert a passage of four lines in the *vaṃśasthavila* meter [1331*]. The lines are found in KK (1905 = 6.71.112); KK (1913), in brackets and numbered (6.71.116); VSP, in brackets and numbered (6.71.111); GPP, in brackets, no number, and placed after 109, indicating in a footnote that this verse is an addition in the text of Cg: "Having slain in battle the immensely powerful Atikāya, who resembled a storm cloud, Lakṣmaṇa was delighted. Then, honored by the multitudes of monkeys, he quickly returned to Rāma's side."

Following *sarga* 59, D3,5–7,9–11,T1,2,G,M (Ñ,V1,2,B2–4,D4,13 insert after 6.61; T3 inserts after 6.62) insert a passage of thirty-nine lines [App. I, No. 38]. This passage corresponds to *sarga* 72 in the printed editions of the texts of the southern commentators. "When the king had heard that Atikāya had been slain by great Lakṣmaṇa, he was deeply distressed and he spoke these words [1–2]: 'The supremely hot-tempered bowman[1] Dhūmrākṣa, foremost of those who bear weapons, Akampana, Prahasta, and even Kumbhakarṇa—all of them were immensely powerful *rākṣasa* warriors. They were eager for battle, conquerors of enemy armies, and were never conquered by their foes.[3–6] Those gigantic *rākṣasa* heroes, skilled in the various weapons, were slain together with their troops by Rāma, tireless in action, while many other great heroes were also felled.[7–9] But then, those two heroic[2] brothers were bound by my son, renowned Indrajit, with arrows granted him as a boon.[10–11] I do not understand by what extraordinary powers,[3] illusion, or delusion the brothers Rāma and Lakṣmaṇa escaped the bondage of those arrows, which fearsome bondage neither the gods, the immensely powerful *asuras*, nor the *yakṣas*, *gandharvas*, or *kinnaras*[4] could escape.[12–15] All those heroic *rākṣasa* warriors that sallied forth at my command have been slain in battle by the immensely powerful monkeys. I do not see anyone who, in battle, will slay Rāma, together with Lakṣmaṇa, and their heroic army, together with Sugrīva and Vibhīṣaṇa.[16–19] Oh! How powerful must this Rāma be! How great the power of his divinely charged weapons! For once they encountered his valor, the *rākṣasas* were destroyed.[5] [20–21] It is for fear of him that the citadel of Laṅkā has its doors and gateways shut tight.[6] [22] Let the citadel be guarded at every point by vigilant garrisons.[7] And let all comings and goings in the *aśoka* grove,[8] where Sītā is being guarded, be constantly reported to me.[23–25] And, surrounded by your respective[9] troops, you must take up your positions repeatedly at every point where there is a garrison.[26–27] And, night-roaming *rākṣasas*, you must closely watch the monkeys' every move,[10] whether in the evening, at midnight, or at dawn.[28–29] And you must never underestimate the monkeys. But keep your eyes on[11] the industrious army of our enemies, whether it be stationary or on the move.'[30–31] Then, when they had heard that entire speech of the overlord of Laṅkā, all those immensely powerful *rākṣasas* acted accordingly.[32–33] When Rāvaṇa, overlord of the *rākṣasas*, had given his orders to all of them, he retired to his own dwelling, despondent and pierced with[12] the dart of rage.[34–35] Then, with the fire of rage blazing within him, the immensely powerful overlord of the night-roaming *rākṣasas* sighed over and over again, as he brooded[13] on the death of his son.[14] [36–39]"

[1]"The . . . bowman" *dhanvī*: Ñ1,D3,7,9–11, and the texts and printed editions of Ct and Cr read instead *sarva-*, "all," which yields *sarvaśastrabhṛtāṃ varaḥ*, "foremost of those who bear all weapons."

[2]"heroic" *vīrau*: The printed editions of Ct do not have the term *vīrau* in their line but substitute, in a somewhat different position, the adjective *ghoraiḥ*, "dreadful, feasrsome," which then modifies *śaraiḥ*, yielding the sense "with dreadful arrows."

[3]"extraordinary powers" *prabhāvaiḥ*: Literally, "powers, superhuman faculties." The commentators differ somewhat in their understanding of this ambiguous term. Ct glosses, "powers starting with his own innate strength (*sahajasvabalādivaibhavaiḥ*)." Cr understands, "Rāma's blazing energies (*rāmatejobhiḥ*)." Cg glosses, simply, "power,

capability (*sāmarthyam*)," while Cm understands, "innate divine powers (*sahaja-māhātmyaiḥ*)."

[4]"*kinnaras*" *-kiṃnaraiḥ*: V1,D3,9–11,T2,3, and the texts and printed editions of Ct read instead, *-pannagaiḥ*, "with serpents."

[5]Following line 21, D3,6,7,9,G2,3,M3, and the texts and printed editions of Cg and Cm read an additional line [3*] in which Rāvaṇa appears to be credited with knowledge of Rāma's status as a manifestation of Viṣṇu: "I believe the heroic Rāghava to be the flawless Nārāyaṇa." Only Raghunathan (1982, vol. 3, p. 209) and Gita Press (1969, vol. 3, p. 1667) translate this line.

[6]B2,3,D10,11, and the texts and printed editions of Ct, Ck, and Cr omit line 22. Only Raghunathan (1982, vol. 3, p. 209) and Gita Press (1969, vol. 3, p. 1667) translate this line.

[7]"garrisons" *gulmaiḥ*: M3 and the printed editions of Cg and Cr read instead *guptaiḥ*, "protected." Cg glosses, "by those who effect their own protection (*svayaṃ kṛtarakṣaṇaiḥ*)."

[8]"And . . . in the *aśoka* grove" *aśokavanikāyāṃ ca*: D10,11,M1,2, and the texts and printed editions of Ct and Cr read instead the nominative *aśokavanikā caiva* (*cedam*—M1,2), "and the *aśoka* grove as well." As Ct explains, the *aśoka* grove in this reading is to be listed, along with the citadel of Lañkā mentioned in the previous line, as needing to be guarded.

[9]"respective" *svaiḥ svaiḥ*: D3,7,9–11, and the texts and printed editions of Ct and Cr read instead the seemingly redundant *sainyaiḥ*, "with the troops," which construes with *balaiḥ*, "with the troops." Cr glosses *balaiḥ* with *parākramaiḥ*, which he appears to read adjectivally in the sense of "powerfully."

[10]"every move" *padam*: Literally, "position, place, *or* step." We agree, more or less, with Ct, Ck, and Cr, who gloss, "comings and goings (*gatāgatam*)." Cg glosses, "what is attempted *or* resolved (*vyavasitam*)."

[11]"But keep your eyes on": The phrase has been added. Line 31 lacks a verbal element and is separated by line 30 from the nearest plausible one, the gerundive *draṣṭavyam*, "you must closely watch (lit., it is to be seen [by you])" in line 28. However, we follow Cg, who suggests that we read lines 28 through 31 as a single syntactic unit, thus implying that one should construe *balam*, "army," in line 31, with *draṣṭavyam*.

[12]"pierced with" *vahan*: Literally, "bearing, carrying."

[13]"sighed . . . as he brooded" *vicintayan . . . viniśvasan*: Literally, "thinking . . . sighing." The sentence constituted by lines 36–39 lacks a finite verb.

[14]The meter of lines 36–39 is *vaṃśasthavila* with a hypometric *pāda* a.

Sarga 60

1. The meter is *upajāti*.

2. "When . . . heard" *niśamya*: Since all the southern commentators accept App. I, No. 38, in which Rāvaṇa is apprised of the death of Atikāya, etc. (line 1), as the preceding *sarga* (72) in their texts, they are confronted with a narrative inconsistency. Crā (second alternative), Cg (second alternative), Cm, and Cv understand the present verse to be a repetition of what has gone before (*pūrvoktānuvādaḥ*—so Crā). Crā's first alternative is that Rāvaṇa had previously been informed only of the death of Atikāya

and not of the others (*pūrvaṃ rāvaṇenātikāyavadha eva śruta ity avagamyate*). Cg's first alternative is that Rāvaṇa had previously heard only a general report or rumor of the death of Kumbhakarṇa, etc., but now receives a detailed account from trusted informants (*pūrvaṃ kumbhakarṇādivadhaḥ sāmānyena śrutaḥ saṃpraty āptaiḥ saviśeṣaṃ śruta iti*). See note to 6.59.106.

"The king... the king" *rājā... rājā*: Only Cr among the commentators is concerned about the two occurrences of the term *rājā* in the same verse. He rationalizes it by taking the first occurrence adjectivally in the sense of "endowed with lordly splendor (*aiśvaryadīptyā saṃyutaḥ*)."

"he was stunned and his eyes filled with tears" *mumohāśrupariplutākṣaḥ*: D9–11 and the texts and printed editions of Ct and Cr read instead *mahābāṣpa-* for *mumohāśru*. This yields the sense "his eyes filled with big tears."

The meter is *upajāti*.

3. "Now... that bull-like warrior" *atharṣabhaḥ*: Literally, "now... the bull." Ś,V3,B1,4,D2,3,5,8,10–12,T1,M3, the texts and printed editions of the southern commentators, and the editions of Gorresio and Lahore read instead *ratharṣabhaḥ*, literally, "bull among chariots." The commentators take this compound as a *madhyamapadalopī* in the sense of "foremost of those who ride in chariots, that is, a great chariot-warrior. (*rathasthānām ṛṣabhaḥ. madhyamapadalopī samāsaḥ. mahāratha ity arthaḥ*—so Ck.)" The critical reading seems elliptical and unusual, as it is not common for Vālmīki to use the word *ṛṣabha*, "bull," as a metaphor outside of compounds. See 6.72.33; 6.80.6; 6.81.18; 6.83.8; 6.84.15; and notes. Cf. 6.77.36.

"floundering" *saṃparipupluvānam*: Literally, "floating." The commentators make note of the uncommon use of the middle perfect participle (*kānac*) suffix.

The meter is *upajāti*.

4. "lord of the *rākṣasas*" *rākṣasendra*: D9–11 and the texts and printed editions of Ct read instead *nairṛteśa*, literally, "O lord of the *nairṛtas*."

"despondency" *moham*: Literally, "confusion, delusion *or* affliction, pain."

"Indra's foe" *indrāri-*: Indrajit is referring to himself.

"can escape with his life" *prāṇān samarthaḥ... abhidhartum*: Literally, "is able to maintain the life breaths." D1,5,7,9–11,T1,G,M3,5, and the texts and printed editions of the southern commentators read *abhipātum*, "to protect *or* save," for *abhidhartum*, "to maintain."

The meter is *upajāti* with a hypermetric *pāda* a.

5. "you will surely see" *paśya*: Literally, "see."

"dismembered" *-vikīrṇa-*: Literally, "scattered, strewn."

"my arrows... with... shafts" *-bāṇa-... śaraiḥ*: Literally, "arrows... with arrows."

"bristling" *ācita-*: Literally, "filled, covered, heaped up with."

The meter is *upajāti*.

6. Cm asserts that this verse and the previous one have a hidden inner meaning (*vāstavārtha*) according to which Indrajit is really saying that he is unable actually to kill Rāma since the latter is endowed with strength and valor. Instead, he is able merely to wound him with his arrows. (*atibalaparākramaśālino rāmasya hanane tu nāhaṃ samarthaḥ. athāpy etāvat kariṣyāmi. paśyety āha paśyeti. madbāṇavikīrṇadeham api gatāyuṣaṃ prāptāyuṣaṃ śarair ācitasarvagātraṃ rāmaṃ paśyeti saṃbandhaḥ.*) See notes to 6.27.4.

"Śakra's foe" *śakraśatroḥ*: Indrajit is, once again, referring to himself.

"well founded" *suniścitām*: Literally, "well ascertained." Cr glosses, "truthful (*satyām*)."

"infused with both human and divine power" *pauruṣadaivayuktām*: Literally, "endowed with that which is human and that which is divine." The commentators understand that the term *bala*, "strength, power," is omitted from the compound. Their understanding, as expressed by Ck and Ct, is that Indrajit's vow is effectuated by its being conjoined with human power in the form of his own innate strength and with the divine power granted him by Lord Brahmā (*pauruṣeṇa sahajaśauryabalena daivabalena bhagavadbrahmabalena ca yuktāṃ kriyamāṇām*). The idea is that Indrajit is a fearsome warrior in his own right and is also equipped with the divine weapons conferred upon him by Brahmā. Translators have understood the compound variously. Gita Press (1969, vol. 3, p. 1669), Shastri (1959, vol. 3, p. 209), and Dutt (1893, p. 1353) all understand, more or less, as do we and the commentators. Raghunathan (1982, vol. 3, p. 210), idiosyncratically, understands Indrajit to be swearing by all the gods and his own valor. Gorresio (1858, vol. 10, pp. 60–61), Roussel (1903, vol. 3, p. 238), and Pagani (1999, p. 1065) understand *daiva* nominally in its sense of "fate, destiny." Cf. 6.6.7–8 and notes.

"I shall consume" *saṃtāpayiṣyāmi*: Ś,V2,3,B1,2,4,D2,3,5–12,T1,2,G2,3,M3,5, and the texts and printed editions of the southern commentators and Lahore read instead *saṃtarpayiṣyāmi*, "I shall gratify." The reading should perhaps be marked as doubtful (Bhatt 1960, p. xxxiv). Cv, Cm, and Cg gloss, "I shall fill (*pūrayiṣyāmi*)." Translators who share this reading take the verb metaphorically in the sense of "to overwhelm," with the exception of Raghunathan (1982, vol. 3, p. 210) and Pagani (1999, p. 1065), who read it more literally in the sense of "to sate *or* surfeit."

The meter is *upajāti*.

7. "Mitra" *-mitra-*: Mitra is the vedic divinity of contracts and agreements. V3,D6,7,9–11,T2,G1,2, and the texts and printed editions of Ct and Cr read instead *rudra-*, "Rudra."

"the *sādhyas*, the Aśvins" *-sādhyāśvi-*: Literally, "the perfectible beings and the Aśvins." The *sādhyas* are a class of celestial beings. See *ManuSm* 1.22; 3.195. Ñ,V,B2–4,D3,4,7,9–13,T2, and the texts and printed editions of Ct and Cr read instead *sādhyāś ca*, "and the *sādhyas*," thus eliminating the Aśvins from the list.

"shall witness" *drakṣyanti*: V3,B4,D10,11,T2,3,M3,5, and the texts and printed editions of Cg, Cm, and Ct read instead the future imperative *drakṣyantu*, literally, "they will have to witness."

"of Viṣṇu in Bali's sacrificial enclosure" *viṣṇoḥ . . . baliyajñavāṭe*: This is yet another reference to the *vāmanāvatāra*, or dwarf incarnation, of Lord Viṣṇu. Compare 6.40.43; 6.44.37; 6.49.1–2; 6.47.119; 6.53.25; 6.59.7; 6.105.24; and notes. See 1.28.2 and note.

The meter is *indravajrā*.

8. "Indrajit, the enemy of the lord of the thirty gods" *tridaśendraśatruḥ*: Literally, "the enemy of the lord of the thirty."

"in high spirits" *adīnasattvaḥ*: Literally, "whose spirit was not despondent."

"yoked to . . . donkeys" *khara- . . . yuktam*: Note that, at verse 18 below, a verse that has doubtful textual support, Indrajit's chariot is said to be drawn by horses.

"equipped with the implements of war" *-samādhiyuktam*: Literally, "yoked to a set." We follow the interpretation offered by Ct, Ck, and Cr, in which *samādhi* is defined as anything by which battle is accomplished, i.e., weapons such as a bow, a sword, etc. (*samādhīyate yuddham ebhir iti samādhayo dhanuḥkhaḍgādayas taiś ca yuktam*—so Ck and Ct). This interpretation is followed by most of the translators consulted who share this reading. Cv, Cm, and Cg take *samādhi* in the sense of "a yoke *or* a connection (*saṃbandhaḥ*—so Cm)," lending the compound the sense of "yoked to a brace of splendid donkeys." Among the translators, only Raghunathan (1982, vol. 3, p. 210) appears to follow this interpretation, translating, "to which powerful asses were attached."

The meter is *upajāti*.

9. "the chariot of Indra himself" *hariratha-*: Literally, "the chariot of Hari." Commentators and translators are divided as to how to take the polysemic term *hari*, which, among its many other meanings, can refer to a number of different divinities. Ct and Ck gloss, "Indra's chariot (*indrarathaḥ*)," and, given the context of the chapter in which Indrajit refers to himself several times as "the rival *or* foe of Indra" (see verses 4 and 6 above), we believe that they are probably correct. Raghunathan (1982, vol. 3, p. 210) and Gita Press (1969, vol. 3, p. 1669) translate accordingly. Cg, citing *Amarakośa* 3.3.174, which lists *arka*, "the sun," as one of the meanings of *hari*, glosses, "Sūrya's chariot (*sūryarathaḥ*)." Cr offers no gloss, implying that he understands *hari* in its common use as an epithet of Viṣṇu. This use of the name Hari is followed by all the other translators consulted, except for Gorresio (1858, vol. 10, p. 61), who makes the identification fully explicit by rendering, "*carro di Visnu.*" Even though Pagani (1999, p. 1066) translates, "*ce char... celui de Hari,*" her note follows Cg's interpretation. She there asserts, "*il s'agit de l'immense char du soleil dans lequel les dieux prennent place à tour de rôle chaque mois*" (1999, p. 1668). Cf. note to 6.59.11.

"drove" *jagāma*: Literally, "he went."

"to where the battle raged" *tatra yatra yuddham*: Literally, "there where the battle [was]."

10. "great Indrajit" *mahātmānam*: Literally, "the great one."

"immensely powerful warriors" *mahābalāḥ*: Literally, "immensely powerful ones."

11. "mounted on elephant-back" *gajaskandhagatāḥ*: Literally, "situated on the shoulders of elephants."

"rode splendid chargers" *paramavājibhiḥ*: Literally, "with splendid horses." Because of their acceptance of the southern insert 1335*, discussed below, Roussel (1903, vol. 3, p. 239), Shastri (1959, vol. 3, p. 210), and Pagani (1999, p. 1066) understand the compound to mean "extraordinary mounts [such as the creatures listed in 1335*]."

"They were armed with" *-dharāḥ*: Literally, "bearing."

Following 11ab, D7,10,11,M3,G3 (after11cd), and the texts and printed editions of the southern commentators (KK numbered in brackets 16.73.11cd–12; VSP as a footnote following 6.73.11b) insert a passage of three lines [1335*]: "Those *rākṣasas* of fearsome valor also rode on tigers, scorpions, cats, donkeys, camels,[1] serpents, boars,[2] ferocious[3] lions, jackals huge as mountains, crows,[4] *haṃsas*, and peacocks."

[1]"camels" *-uṣṭraiḥ*: Roussel (1903, vol. 3, p. 239), followed by Shastri (1959, vol. 3, p. 210), takes the term in its sense of "buffalo."

[2]"boars" *varāhaiḥ*: Dutt (1893, p. 1354), presumably as the result of a typographical error, renders, "bears."

[3]"ferocious" *śvāpadaiḥ*: We believe that the adjectival sense of this term, "savage, ferocious," fits the context better than the seemingly redundant sense of "wild beast." Gita Press (1969, vol. 3, p. 1669) and Dutt (1893, p. 1354) render, "beast of prey," although Dutt reads this as a separate member of his list, while Gita Press subordinates

it to lions. Shastri (1959, vol. 3, p. 210) renders, "cheetahs," while Pagani (1999, p. 1066) thinks the reference is to dogs. Roussel (1903, vol. 3, p. 239) leaves the term untranslated.

[4]"crows" *kāka-*: M3 and the texts of VSP and KK read instead *śaśa-*, "rabbits."

Following verse 11, D7,G2, and the printed editions of Gita Press (= 6.73.13cd) and GPP (6.73.12cd) insert a passage of one line [*1336]: "And they were armed with bludgeons,[1] war hammers, *āyaṣṭis* [clubs?], hundred-slayers,[2] and iron clubs." This line is translated only by Gita Press (1969, vol. 3, p. 1669) and Pagani (1999, p. 1066).

[1]"bludgeons" *musṛṇṭhī-*: D7 and the printed texts of GPP and Gita Press read instead *bhṛśuṇḍi-* (*bhuśuṇḍi*—Gita Press). The identification of this weapon is uncertain. See note to 6.48.32 and note to 6.78.20, 1726*, n. 3. Pagani (1999, p. 1066) renders, "*plommées*." Gita Press (1969, vol. 3, p. 1669) leaves the term untranslated and follows it in parentheses with the phrase "probably a kind of fire-arm."

[2]"hundred-slayers" *-śataghnī-*: See note to 6.3.12.

12. "Praised by the night-roaming *rākṣasas*" *stūyamāno niśācaraiḥ*: Literally, "being praised by the *niśācaras*." D9,10, and the texts and printed editions of Ct and Cr read instead *ājiṃ vegena vīryavān*, "That mighty warrior [went forth] swiftly to battle."

"fearsome" *bhīmaiḥ*: Ñ1,V3,B3,D4,5,7–11,13,T1,G,M3,5, and the texts and printed editions of the southern commentators read instead *pūrṇaiḥ*, here, "full-sounding, sonorous."

"the thunderous sound" *mahāsvanaiḥ*: Literally, "with the great sounds." D1,5–7,9–11,T,G2,3,M3,5, and the texts and printed editions of the southern commentators read instead [*cā*]*pi nisvanaiḥ* (*niḥsvanaiḥ*—D1,6,7,10), "with sounds."

13. "illuminated by the full moon" *paripūrṇena . . . candramasā*: Literally, "with the full moon."

14. "with the most splendid, golden yak-tail fly whisks" *haimaiḥ . . . cārucāmaramukhyaiḥ*: Literally, "with the foremost of beautiful chowries, made of gold." Ct, Cr, Cg, and Cm note that the handles of the whisks would be made of gold (*hiranamayadaṇḍaiḥ*—so Ct). This is reasonable, as the whisks themselves would, of course, be yak-tails. See 6.115.13–16 and notes.

"all adorned with gold" *hemavibhūṣitaiḥ*: Literally, "adorned with gold." D9–11,T2,G1, and the texts and printed editions of Ct read instead the nominative *hemavibhūṣaṇaḥ*, "possessing golden ornaments." In this reading the adjective modifies Indrajit.

15. See note to verse 16 below.

"illuminated by Indrajit" *indrajitā*: Literally, "by Indrajit."

16. B4,D4,5,7,9–11,T1,G,M1,2,5, and the texts of the southern commentators omit this verse, as well as verses 17 and 18. Printed editions treat these verses variously. GPP places them unnumbered in brackets between its verses 6.73.15 and 16 (= critical edition 6.60.14 and 15), with a footnote stating that these two and a half verses (critical edition verses 16–18cd) are additional in the text of Cg (*idaṃ sārdhapadyadvayam adhikaṃ go. pāṭhe*). KK places them in brackets numbered as its 6.73.17–18, following critical edition 6.60.14. A footnote indicates that these two verses (five

half verses = critical edition 16–18cd) are found "only in later manuscripts and not in older southern manuscripts (*idaṃ ślokadvayam auttarāhapāṭha eva dṛśyate na tu dākṣiṇātyaprācīnakośeṣu*)." VSP relegates the entire passage to a footnote and makes the same textual observation as does KK. KK 1905 and NSP omit the verses entirely. Lahore (6.53.16–18), Gita Press (6.73.17–19ab), and Gorresio (6.52.16–16) all include and number the verses without comment as part of their texts. Only Gita Press (1969, vol. 3, p. 1670) and Gorresio (1858, vol. 10, pp. 61–62) translate the passage. According to the principles on which the critical edition is based, these verses (verses 16, 17, 18, and possibly 19) should be considered suspect and should have been relegated to the critical apparatus. See Bhatt 1960, p. xxxiv, no. 5.

17. See note to verse 16 above.

"You have conquered even Vāsava in battle" *jitas te yudhi vāsavaḥ*: M3 and the printed editions of GPP, VSP, and KK read instead *tvayā vai vāsavo jitaḥ*, "Vāsava was conquered by you."

"How then would you not more easily slay" *kiṃ punaḥ . . . na vadhiṣyasi*: Literally, "how much more will you not kill." The construction is awkward and unusual, although the sense is clear. D6,T2,3,M3 attempt to improve the syntax by substituting the *upasarga ni* for the awkward negative particle *na*, reading instead *nihaniṣyasi*, "you will slay," for the critical edition's *na vadhiṣyasi*. This variant is seen in all printed editions of the southern texts that read the line, and is the variant rendered in the translation of Gita Press (1969, vol. 3, p. 1670). Similarly, the text of Gorresio (6.52.17) substitutes the pronoun *tvam*, "you," for the negative particle *na*.

18. See note to verse 16 above. Additionally, B3,D13,T2,3,M3, and the texts and printed editions of the southern commentators, including Gita Press, omit *pādas* cd (". . . the hero proceeded swiftly to the shrine of Nikumbhilā in his horse-drawn chariot").

"the shrine of Nikumbhilā" *nikumbhilām*: In the *Sundarakāṇḍa* (5.22.41), Nikumbhilā appears to be the name of a goddess worshiped by the *rākṣasa* women. According to several commentators (ad loc.), this is the name of a manifestation of Bhadrakālī, worshiped at a shrine in western Laṅkā. See 5.22.41 and notes. According to Apte and MW (s.v.), the term may refer to a grove or shrine at the western gate of Laṅkā or generically to any sacrificial ground. Gorresio (1858, vol. 10, p. 62) has adopted this last meaning in his translation. See note to verse 19 below. See 6.69.23; 6.71.13; and notes. See, too, 7.25.2, where Rāvaṇa sees his son Indrajit performing sacrifices in a grove called Nikumbhilā. See S. Goldman 2006b.

"in his horse-drawn chariot" *rathenāśvayujā*: Literally, "with a chariot yoked to horses." Note that, at verse 8 above, Indrajit's chariot is said to be drawn by donkeys. See note to verse 8 above.

19. "the battleground" *yuddhabhūmim*: Although the southern commentators do not know the preceding verse, they understand that Indrajit has, in fact, gone to the place or shrine of Nikumbhilā. Thus, Ck, Ct, and Cr explain, "The term 'battleground' means 'the ground that is conducive to the oblations that bring about victory in battle, that is, the place of Nikumbhilā.' (*yuddhabhūmiṃ yuddhajayasaṃpādakahomasādhanabhūmim. nikumbhilāsthānam ity arthaḥ*—so Ct.)" See note to verse 18 above.

20. "to the accompaniment of sacred *mantras* and in accordance with the ritual prescriptions" *mantravad vidhivat*: Literally, "accompanied by *mantras* and according to the rules." Ct defines the latter term as "the method specified in the *kalpa*, or ritual

texts (*kalpoktaprakārah*)." Cg glosses, "in proper sequence (*kramavat*)." D10–11 and the texts and printed editions of Ct read instead *vidhivan mantrasattamaiḥ*, "according to rule and with excellent *mantras*."

"whose splendor was like that of Agni, eater of oblations... to Agni, eater of oblations" *hutabhoktāraṃ hutabhuksadṛśaprabhaḥ*: Literally, "to the oblation eater... he whose splendor was like that of the oblation eater."

21. "offered oblations to Agni, the purifier, along with ritual offerings of parched grain accompanied by flowers and sandalwood paste" *havir lājasaṃskārair mālyagandhapuraskṛtaiḥ / juhuve pāvakam*: Literally, "he offered oblations to Pāvaka with offerings of parched rice accompanied by flowers and sandalwood paste." Ct, Ck, and Cr, reading the variant *satkāraiḥ*, "with religious observances," for *saṃskāraiḥ*, "with offerings *or* purificatory rites," understand that there are two separate actions in the verse. They supply the gerund *satkṛtya*, "having honored *or* worshiped," which they take to govern the accusative *pāvakam*, "fire." According to this reading, Indrajit first worships the fire god with parched grain, flowers, etc., and then makes his oblation in the form of the goat that will be mentioned in the coming verses (see verse 23 below) (*gandhamālyapuraskṛtair lājasatkārair lājaiḥ pāvakaṃ satkṛtya tatra pāvake vakṣyamāṇasaṃskārasaṃskṛtair havir vakṣyamāṇacchāgarūpaṃ juhāva*—so Ct).

22. Verses 22–25 are identical with or closely parallel verses 6.67.6–9. 6.60.22 = 6.67.6.

"Weapons served as the *śarapatra* grass, myrobalan wood was the kindling." *śastrāṇi śarapatrāṇi samidho 'tha vibhītakāḥ*: Literally, "weapons, *śarapatras*, kindling, and *vibhītakas*." We follow the interpretation of Cg, Cm, Ct, and Cr in understanding that the first and third articles mentioned serve in the roles of the second and fourth, which are necessary elements of any sacrificial performance. The commentators make this judgment on the grounds that these substitutions are mandated in the case of black magical (*abhicāra*) or violent (*raudra*—Cm) rites (*atra tv abhicāraviśeṣe tatsthāne śastrāṇi kṛtānīty bodhyam*—so Cg). This interpretation has similarly been followed by Dutt (1893, p. 1354), Raghunathan (1982, vol. 3, p. 211), and Gita Press (1969, vol. 3, p. 1670). Roussel (1903, vol. 3, p. 239), Shastri (1959, vol. 3, p. 210), and Pagani (1999, p. 1066) read the entire verse as a simple list, either of weapons or sacrificial requisites.

"the *śarapatra* grass" *śarapatrāṇi*: Literally, "arrow-leaves." According to Ct, Cr, Cg, and Cm, this is a type of *kuśa* grass. This grass (*Saccharum spontaneum*) is generally used for mats and roofs and is personified together with *kuśa* grass (*Poa cynosuroides*) as one of Yama's attendants. For some reason, Raghunathan (1982, vol. 3, p. 211) translates "*kuśa* grass." Typically, the sacrificial grass is spread over a stretch of ground to serve as the arena for the sacrifice. This common tall grass is used in other rites, specifically in rituals for the deceased (see *Baudhāyanapitṛmedhasūtra* 1.14:9 as quoted in the *Śrautakośa* 1.II, p. 1096). MW (s.v.) identifies *śarapatra* only as *Tectona grandis* (teak), clearly an unsuitable meaning in this context.

"myrobalan wood" *vibhītakāḥ*: This is the *Terminalia belerica*, one of the myrobalans. The tree is mentioned in the tenth book of the *Ṛgveda* (10.34.1), as its nuts are said to be used as dice for gambling. Pagani (1999, p. 1066) renders "*de graines de vibhītaka*." Cf. 2.85.46 (passim), where the term *vibhītaka* is translated as "beddanut tree," whereas the plant rendered as "myrobalan" is the *āmalaka*. See Brockington 1984, p. 106 and Cowen 1965, pp. 37–38. Cf. MW (s.v.).

"His garments were red" *lohitāni* ... *vāsāṃsi*: The garments of a vedic practitioner would normally be white. The red garments are meant to be associated here with black magic. See 5.25.20, where red garments are tokens of ill omen. See 6.59.21; 6.58.46; 6.67.5; and notes. See, too, *AgniP* 229.14. Cf., however, the comments of Cg on 6.67.5, where he notes that the *vedas* specify red turbans for *ṛtvik* priests. On omens, see 6.4.6.

"his ladle was of black iron" *sruvaṃ kārṣṇāyasam*: See 6.3.12; 6.53.12; 6.55.47; and notes. Black iron, too, is considered inauspicious. See 1.57.9, where Triśaṅku's royal ornaments turn to iron when he is cursed to become a *caṇḍāla*. See *AgniP* 230.1–4. Again, a normal vedic practitioner would use a ladle made of acacia, or cutch, wood (*Acacia catechu*).

23. 6.60.23ab is a close variant of 6.67.7ab.

6.60.23cd = 6.67.7cd.

"the fire altar" *agnim*: All translations consulted take the term mistakenly, we believe, in its most common sense of "fire." Surely, it is the altar that is being spread with weapons and not the fire itself. Compare 1.13.22 for Vālmīki's use of *agni* in this sense, and see Apte (s.v. *agni*). One should note that the *Mānavaśrautasūtra* (5.1.9.17–18) prescribes the use of arrows instead of kindling sticks, *samidh*, in a ritual designed to gain the upper hand in a battle.

"with weapons ... in place of *śarapatra* grass" *śarapatraiḥ*: Literally, "with *śarapatras*." Given the information provided in verse 22 above, we must agree with Ct and Cr, who understand that the reference here is to the weapons that are serving as the surrogate for this grass (*tatpratinidhiśastraiḥ*—so Cr).

"he seized the throat of a ... goat" *chāgasya* ... *galaṃ jagrāha*: As the commentators explain, we are to understand that Indrajit intends the goat to be the offering (*homārtham iti śeṣaḥ*—so Ct). Raghunathan (1982, vol. 3, p. 211) incorporates this into his translation, rendering the verse very strongly as "kindling the fire ... he offered in it the head of a black sheep whose neck he severed." It is not clear why he takes *chāga*, "goat," to mean "sheep."

"pure black" *sarvakṛṣṇasya*: Literally, "entirely black." D9–11,M3, and the texts and printed editions of the southern commentators read instead *kṛṣṇavarṇasya*, "black in color." The significance of a pure black goat is not made clear. However, a female black goat is used in the crematory ritual in the *Āśvalāyana Gṛhyasūtra* (4.2.7); see also *Śrautakośa* 1.II, p. 1071. The color black is associated with things that are inauspicious. See 1.57.9, where the king Triśaṅku, cursed to become a *caṇḍāla*, suddenly finds himself in black clothing, and 5.25.18, where Rāvaṇa is said to be wearing black garments in Trijaṭā's prophetic dream. See, too, 6.4.44; 6.23.19; and notes.

24. 6.60.24a is a close variant of 6.67.8a.

6.60.24bc = 6.67.8bc.

6.60.24d is a close variant of 6.67.8d.

"the smokeless fire with its huge flames displayed signs" *vidhūmasya mahārciṣaḥ / babhūvus tāni liṅgāni*: Literally, "of that smokeless great flamed one there were signs." The propitious signs mentioned are, as Ct, Ck, and Cr note in their comments to verse 25, undoubtedly those described in that verse. Among the translators consulted, only Roussel (1903, vol. 3, p. 239) makes this point explicitly.

"that betokened" *yāny adarśayan*: Literally, "that showed." Ct, Ck, Cr, and Cg understand that these signs had betokened victory for Indrajit [in his battles with the gods (*devādiyuddhe*)—Cr] in the past (*yāni purā svasya vijayam adarśayan*—so Ct). Compare note to 6.67.8.

25. 6.60.25 is virtually identical to 6.67.9.

"his flames swirling in an auspicious clockwise direction" *pradakṣiṇāvartaśikhaḥ*: Compare 5.51.28, where a similar swirling of flames is represented as an auspicious omen.

"himself rose up" *svayam utthitaḥ*: M3 and the texts and printed editions of Cg read instead *svayam āsthitaḥ*, which Cg glosses as "possessing his inherent form (*svayam āsthāvān*)." By this he presumably means that fire is present in its elemental form, for Cg is aware of the critical reading, of which he notes: "If we take the reading *svayam utthitaḥ*, it means that he rose up in the form of a man (*svayam utthita iti pāṭhe puruṣarūpeṇotthita ity arthaḥ*)."

26. "Foremost among those familiar with divine weapon-spells" *astravidāṃ varaḥ*: D5,7,9–11,T1,G, and the texts and printed editions of Ct and Cr read instead *astraviśāradaḥ*, "skilled in divine weapon-spells."

"Indrajit" *saḥ*: Literally, "he."

"the divine weapon-spell of Brahmā" *astram... brāhmam*: Evidently, Indrajit is preparing himself for battle through two separate but simultaneous actions. The first is his oblation to Agni, which, as will be shown in verse 28 below, endows him with the power of invisibility. The second is his invocation of the divine weapon-spell of Brahmā, which provides him with the powerful weapons with which he is able to subdue Rāma and his allies. Since he was already shown to possess the power of invisibility in his earlier encounter with Rāma and Lakṣmaṇa at *sargas* 6.34–35, it appears that he must periodically renew it through repeated performances of this sacrifice. See especially 6.34.39. Perhaps this is all in aid of the narrative necessity of the creation of specific windows of vulnerability on the part of Indrajit that will enable Lakṣmaṇa to finally kill him, when, as Vibhīṣaṇa informs him, he has yet to complete still another of his repeated sacrifices. See 6.71.14; 6.72.10–14; 6.74.2–6; and notes.

"his chariot" *ātmaratham*: Literally, "the chariot of himself." Roussel (1903, vol. 3, p. 239), followed by Pagani (1999, p. 1067), reads this compound as if it were a *dvandva* in the sense of "himself and his chariot." We are not persuaded.

"all of his weaponry" *sarvam*: Literally, "everything [else]."

27. "was being invoked... was being gratified with oblations" *āhūyamāne... hūyamāne*: Literally, "was being invoked... was being oblated." Ct understands that it is the divinity governing the divine weapon-spell, a divinity characterized by the esoteric spell known as "*trimūrtirahasya*," that is, being invoked (*tad astramantradaivate trimūrtirahasyalakṣaṇe kriyamāṇāvāhane*). Ck understands similarly. Ct and Ck further understand that the participle *hūyamāna*, "being oblated," refers not to the offering made to Agni but rather to his being invoked by the *mantra* assigned to that previously mentioned divinity (*taduddeśena tanmantreṇa pāvake hūyamāne ca sati*).

"the heavens shook" *vitatrāsa nabhastalam*: Ct and Ck insist that we are to take the statement literally and not merely as exaggeration (*nāyam arthavādaḥ*).

28. "Indrajit" *saḥ*: Literally, "he."

"he vanished into thin air" *khe 'ntardadhe 'tmānam*: Literally, "he hid himself in the sky." Several of the commentators note that the simplex verb should be read as a causative governing the accusative *ātmānam* and that the elision of the initial *ā* of *ātmānam* is irregular. (*ātmānam antardadhe 'ntardhāpayāmāsa. antarbhāvitaṇyartho 'yam. khe 'ntardadhetmānam ity atrārṣam*—so Cg.)

"charioteer" *-sūtaḥ*: D5–7,9,10,T2,3,G1,3,M5, and the texts and printed editions of Ct and Cr read instead *-śūlaḥ*, "lance."

"his form no longer perceptible" *acintyarūpaḥ*: Literally, "whose form was inconceivable." We understand that the term here refers to the obscurity or invisibility of Indrajit's form. The only commentator to remark on this reading, Cg, glosses, "the power of whose *mantra* was unimaginable (*acintyamantraśaktiḥ*)." Raghunathan (1982, vol. 3, p. 212), the only translator who has this reading, clearly renders Cg's interpretation, offering, "by virtue of the unimaginable powers that he had acquired by his spells." D9–11 and the texts and printed editions of Ct read *-vīryaḥ* for *-rūpaḥ*, yielding the sense "of inconceivable power."

The meter is *upajāti*.

Following verse 28, D1,5–7,9–11,S insert a passage of three lines [1342*]: "Then, roaring in its eagerness to fight, the *rākṣasa* army set out filled with horses and chariots and adorned with flags and banners.[1–2] They slaughtered the monkeys in battle with many shining arrows, ornamented and fierce in their impact, and with iron cudgels and hooks.[1][3]"

[1]"They slaughtered the monkeys in battle . . . with iron cudgels and hooks" *tomarair aṅkuśaiś cāpi vānarāñ jaghnur āhave*: This line is found in the critical apparatus for App. I, No. 39, line 1. Like 1342*, the line is known to D1,5–7,9–11,S, and the texts and printed editions of the southern commentators. Without it, line 3 of 1342* remains a mere sentence fragment. The term "hooks (*aṅkuśaiḥ*)" normally refers to the pointed and hooked goads used by elephant drivers to control their mounts. Here, presumably, it is a type of weapon with a similar form.

Following 1342*, D1,5–7,9–11,S, and the texts and printed editions of all southern commentators insert a passage of forty-six lines (lines 1–34 and 43–54) of a passage of fifty-four lines [App. I, No. 39]. The north (Ś,Ñ,V,B,D2–4,8,12,13) inserts lines 1–42 following 6.83.38. The passage, or at least the forty-two lines common to both the north and the south, should properly have been included in the critical text. The passage reads as follows: "Then, on the battlefield, right before Rāvaṇa's eyes, those fearsome monkeys slaughtered the *rākṣasas* with mountains and trees.[1] [1–2] But then Rāvaṇi, in a rage, turned to the night-roaming *rākṣasas*, saying,[2] 'In your eagerness to slay the monkeys, you gentlemen must fight with your spirits high.'[3–4] Then all those *rākṣasas*, roaring and eager for victory, showered those fearsome monkeys with hails of arrows.[5–6] Meanwhile, Indrajit,[3] surrounded by the *rākṣasas*,[4] tore the monkeys to pieces[5] in battle with broad-tipped arrows,[6] iron arrows, maces, and cudgels.[7–8] Although they were being slaughtered in battle, the monkeys, armed with trees, suddenly rushed at Rāvaṇi, so fearsome to behold.[7] [9–10] Then, in a rage, immensely powerful and vastly energetic Indrajit, son of Rāvaṇa, tore the bodies of the monkeys to pieces.[11–12] Raging in battle, with a single arrow he would pierce nine, five, or seven of the tawny monkeys to the delight of the *rākṣasas*.[13–14] That supremely invincible hero struck down the monkeys in battle with arrows adorned with gold and shining with the splendor of the sun.[15–16] Tormented by those arrows, their limbs severed in battle, the monkeys fell like the great *asuras*, their hopes of victory dashed[8] by the gods.[17–18] In that battle, the enraged bulls among monkeys charged at him who was scorching them like the sun with his fearsome arrows, which resembled burning rays.[19–20] But then, tormented and drenched with blood, all the monkeys fled in all directions, their bodies torn, their wits deserting them.[21–22] But then, exerting their valor on Rāma's behalf, the monkeys, laying down their lives, turned back,[9] roaring in battle, taking up boulders for weapons.[23–24] Making a stand, the leaping monkeys showered Rāvaṇi in battle with trees, mountaintops, and boulders.[25–26] But immensely powerful Rāvaṇi, victorious in battle, parried that great and lethal shower of trees and boulders.[27–28] Then, in turn, that mighty warrior[10] broke the ranks of the monkeys in battle with arrows that shone like fire and resembled venomous serpents.[29–30] Having first pierced Gandhamādana with eighteen sharp arrows, he then, from afar, pierced Nala, who had taken his stand, with nine more.[31–32] Next, that immensely powerful warrior[11] pierced Mainda with seven arrows that tore at his vitals, and he then pierced Gaja in battle with five more.[33–34] Next, he pierced Hanumān with twenty arrows, Nala with ten, Gavākṣa with twenty-five, and Śakrajānu with a hundred. Then, having struck Dvivida with six, he pierced Panasa with ten arrows, Kumuda with fifteen, Jāmbavān with seven, Tāra with three arrows, and Vinata with eight. Then, that immensely powerful archer[12] pierced Vālin's son, Aṅgada, with eighty arrows and struck Śarabha in the chest with a single arrow. He pierced Krathana in the forehead with three arrows.[13] [35–42] He pierced[14] Jāmbavān with ten arrows[15] and Nīla with thirty. Next, he rendered Sugrīva, Ṛṣabha, Aṅgada, and Dvivida unconscious[16] with the sharp and fearsome arrows[17] he had received as a boon.[43–45] Then in a frenzy of violence,[18] like the fire at the end of a cosmic age, he harried in his rage the other[19] monkey leaders with numerous arrows.[46–47] He wrought havoc upon the hosts of the monkeys in that great battle with his swift and well-aimed[20] arrows, shining with the splendor of the sun.[48–49] When Indrajit[21] saw that the monkey army was thrown into chaos, bewildered[22] by the torrents of his arrows and drenched with blood, he was filled with the greatest delight.[23] [50–51] Then, once again, swift and immensely powerful Indrajit,[24] the strong and mighty[25] son of the *rākṣasa* lord, releasing a hail of arrows and a fearsome hail of other weapons, crushed the monkey army.[52–54]"

[1]"Then, on the battlefield, right before Rāvaṇa's eyes, those fearsome monkeys slaughtered the *rākṣasas* with mountains and trees." *tatas te vānarā ghorā rākṣasāṃs tān raṇājire* [1] / *jaghnuḥ śailair drumaiś caiva rāvaṇasyaiva paśyataḥ* [2] //: D1,5–7,9–11,S, and the texts and printed editions of the southern commentators substitute, "They slaughtered the monkeys in battle . . . with iron cudgels and hooks (*tomarair aṅkuśaiś cāpi vānarāñ jaghnur āhave*)." This line has been discussed above in a note to 1342*. These same manuscripts, as well as V3 and the printed editions and texts of the southern commentators, omit line 2.

[2]"saying": Most uncharacteristically the direct quote in line 4 is not preceded by some form of a verb meaning to speak or say. The southern commentators supply such a verb, and we concur.

[3]"Indrajit" *saḥ*: Literally, "he."

[4]"surrounded by the *rākṣasas*" *rakṣobhiḥ saṃvṛtaḥ*: According to several of the commentators, we must understand that Rāvaṇi is hovering closely above the *rākṣasa* army (*rākṣasasainyopari pratyāsannākāśadeśe sthitaḥ*—so Ct); otherwise, as they note, this description contradicts verse 28, where he is said to have vanished into the sky.

[5]"tore . . . to pieces" *vicakarṣa*: D5,G2,M3, and the texts and printed editions of Cg, Cv, and Cm read instead *vicakarta*, "he cut apart *or* slaughtered."

[6]"broad-tipped arrows" *nālīka-*: Lexical sources consulted identify this variously as "an arrow, an iron arrow, a dart, *or* a javelin." We follow Cg, who glosses, "a broad-tipped arrow (*viśālāgraśaraḥ*)."

[7]"suddenly rushed at Rāvaṇi, so fearsome to behold" *abhyadravanta sahasā rāvaṇiṃ ghoradarśanam*: D10,11,M1,2, and the texts and printed editions of Ct and Ck read instead *abhyavarṣanta*, "showered," for *abhyadravanta*, "rushed at," while D10,11,M1,2, and the texts and printed editions of Ct and Ck read *śailapādapaiḥ*, "with mountains and trees," for *ghoradarśanam*, "fearsome to behold." Thus the text of Ct would be rendered as "they suddenly showered Rāvaṇi with mountains and trees." Ñ,V1,2,B,D1–4,6,7,9,T2,3,G1,2,M3, and the texts and printed editions of Cg and Cm read *sahitāḥ*, "all together," for *sahasā*, "suddenly." D5,7,T1,G2,3,M3, and the texts and printed editions of Cg and Cm read *raṇakarkaśam*, "merciless in battle," for *ghoradarśanam*, "fearsome to behold." These variants are translated only by Raghunathan (1982, vol. 3, p. 212), who renders, "[the apes] . . . in a body pursued the son of Rāvaṇa, who was ruthless on the battle-field." Crā and Ck raise the interesting issue of how the monkeys could charge at Indrajit when he had become invisible. Crā explains that they rushed at the spot from which his weapons were being released (*rāvaṇimuktāyudhāgamanapradeśam*). Ck simply says he was perceived merely in terms of his general direction (*kevalaṃ taddiguddeśamātreṇa dṛṣṭaḥ*).

[8]"their hopes of victory dashed" *mathitasaṃkalpāḥ*: Literally, "their desire crushed." Ck, Ct, and Cr understand, "their will to fight taken away (*saṃhṛtayuddhasaṃkalpāḥ*—so Ck, Ct)." We follow Cg and Cm, who gloss, "their fantasies destroyed (*nāśitamanorathāḥ*)."

[9]"turned back" *nivṛttāḥ*: GPP (= 6.73.39) and Gita Press (= 6.73.42) print this term with an *avagraha*, indicating that they read *anivṛttāḥ*, literally, "not turning back." In this case, however, one must understand *nivṛtta* to mean "retreated," and the sense here would be "no longer retreating." NSP (6.73.39) shows no *avagraha*. Cr, who does not read the *avagraha*, understands, "devoid of desire for the pleasures of this world (*iha lokasukhecchārahitāḥ*)." G1,M3, and the texts and printed editions of Cg and Cm read *abhivṛttāḥ*, which Cg glosses as "approaching, facing (*abhimukhaṃ pravṛttāḥ*)."

[10]"in turn, that mighty warrior" *prabhuḥ*: Literally, "lord, mighty one."

[11]"that immensely powerful warrior" *mahāvīryaḥ*: Literally, "immensely powerful one."

[12]"that immensely powerful archer" *mahātejāḥ*: Literally, "immensely powerful one."

[13]"pierced": Lines 35–42 have only three finite verbs: *bibhide*, "he pierced," in line 40; *atāḍayat*, "he struck," in line 41; and *pratyavidhyata*, "he pierced," in line 42. We have repeated the word "pierced" a number of times to enhance readability.

[14]"he pierced": The words have been added for readability.

[15]"with ten arrows" *daśabhiḥ*: Literally, "with ten."

[16]"unconscious" *niṣprāṇān*: Literally, "lifeless, dead." Since the following verses will make it clear that the monkeys named are not, in fact, dead, we understand the term

here in the sense it appears to have at *Mahābhārata* 12.95.12 [Citraśāla edition] (=critical edition 12.96.12c critical apparatus), where a warrior who is *niṣprāṇaḥ* is listed among those who must not be killed in battle. Cr similarly glosses, "as if devoid of life (*prāṇarahitān iva*)."

[17]"arrows": The word has been added for readability.

[18]"in a frenzy of violence" *mūrcchitaḥ* (*mūrchitaḥ*—so crit. ed.): We believe we have selected the most contextually appropriate of the several meanings of this term. Cr and Cg gloss, "increased, grown great (*pravṛddhaḥ*)," an apparent reference to Indrajit's size. This interpretation is followed by Gita Press (1969, vol. 3, p. 1673), who renders, "like the swollen fire of universal destruction." Other translators have offered variations on the meaning "befuddled," such as "transported *or* beside himself with rage, etc."

[19]"other" *anyān*: Printed editions of Ct read instead *vanyān*, "forest creatures."

[20]"well-aimed" *sumuktaiḥ*: Literally, "well-released."

[21]"Indrajit" *saḥ*: Literally, "he."

[22]"bewildered" *mohitām*: D7,9–11,M2, and the texts and printed editions of Ct and Cr read instead *pīḍitām*, "oppressed, afflicted."

[23]"filled with the greatest delight" *hṛṣṭaḥ* ... *parayā prītyā*: Literally, "delighted with supreme pleasure."

[24]"swift ... Indrajit" *indrajit tvaritaḥ*: D10,11, and the texts and printed editions of Ct and Cr read instead *paritas tv indrajit*, "from all sides ... Indrajit."

[25]"strong and mighty" *balī* ... *balī*: Cv, Cm, and Cg remark on the apparent redundancy. As rationalized most fully by the latter two, the first occurrence of the term refers to Indrajit's physical strength (*vīryavattā*), while the second refers to the power he derives from the boons he has received (*varadānavattā*).

D5–7,9–11,S, and the texts and printed editions of the southern commentators omit lines 35–42. Only Gorresio (1858, vol. 10, p. 143) translates these lines.

29. "Emerging from his own army, Indrajit" *sa sainyam utsṛjya*: Literally, "having left the army, he." Ś,Ñ1,D5,7,9–11,T2,G,M2,3, and the texts and printed editions of the southern commentators read *sva-*, "his own," for *saḥ*, "he." Several of the commentators, recalling that Indrajit was said to be hovering above his troops at verse 28, understand that he left the airspace over his own army (*svasainyoparibhāgam utsṛjya*—so Ct).

"torrents of rain" *ambu*: Literally, "water."

The meter is *upendravajrā*.

30. "baffled by his magical illusion" *māyāhatāḥ*: Literally, "struck by illusion." We follow the suggestion of Cr, who glosses, "baffled (*mohitāḥ*)." The reference is to the fact that, although they are being shot by Indrajit, the monkeys are unable to see him and so cannot fight back effectively.

"Śakra's conqueror" *śakrajit*: This is yet another variant of the name Indrajit, "conqueror of Indra."

The meter is *upajāti*.

31. "All they could see ... they could not see" *saṃdadṛśuḥ* ... *na* ... *abhyapaśyan*: Literally, "they saw ... they did not see."

"raining on the monkey troops" *vānaravāhinīṣu*: Literally, "among the monkey armies."

The meter is *upajāti*.

32. "filled all the directions" *sarvā diśaḥ . . . pracchādayāmāsa*: Literally, "he covered all directions." Roussel (1903, vol. 3, p. 241), followed by Shastri (1959, vol. 3, p. 212), incorrectly takes the phrase *sarvā diśaḥ*, "all directions," adverbially in the sense of "in all directions." They then must supply a verb: "*qui décochait*" (Roussel) and "let fly" (Shastri). These two translators understand the verb "he covered (*pracchādayāmāsa*)" to take as its object not the directions but the monkeys.

"with volleys of arrows" *bāṇagaṇaiḥ*: Literally, "with hosts of arrows." D10 and the texts and printed editions of Ct read the somewhat peculiar *bāṇagataiḥ*, literally, "with movements of arrows." Translations that follow the text of Ct ignore this odd compound and render, simply, "arrows."

"further disheartening" *viṣādayāmāsa*: Literally, "he caused [them] to be despondant." Ñ2,V2,B3,D7,9–11,G1,M5, and the texts and printed editions of Ct and Cr read instead *vidārayāmāsa*, "he tore *or* rent."

The meter is *upajāti*.

33. "Brandishing . . . like shining fires" *vyāvidhya dīptānalasaṃnibhāni*: Ñ1,B3,D5, 7,9–11,T1,G1,M5, and the texts and printed editions of Ct and Cr read instead the participle *vyāviddha-*, "whirling," for the critical edition's gerund, *vyāvidhya*, "having brandished *or* whirled." D1,6,9–11,T2,3,G1,M5, and the texts and printed editions of Ct read *-saprabhāṇi*, "with the luster of," for *-saṃnibhāni*, "like." Thus the texts and printed editions of Ct and Cr and those manuscripts that share both variants have the compound *vyāviddhadīptānalasaprabhāṇi*, "having the luster of whirling and blazing fire."

The meter is *upajāti*.

34. "by the sharp arrows" *śitaiḥ . . . -bāṇaiḥ*: D9–11 and the texts and printed editions of Ct read *bāṇaiḥ*, "with arrows," for *śitaiḥ*, "sharp." This yields an obvious redundancy. B3,4,D1,7,G1,M3, and the texts and printed editions of Cg and Cm read instead *śaraiḥ*, "with arrows," yielding a similar redundancy. Cg and Cm, however, are aware of the problem and attempt to resolve it by saying that the word *śaraḥ*, "arrow," must be taken in the sense of "sharp (*tīkṣṇaḥ*)." Roussel (1903, vol. 3, p. 241), followed by Shastri (1959, vol. 3, p. 213), reads both terms nominally, understanding, "arrows and darts."

"like red-blossoming *kiṃśuka* trees" *praphullā iva kiṃśukāḥ*: Literally, "like blossoming *kiṃśukas*." The *kiṃśuka* tree (*Butea frondosa*; "the flame-of-the forest") is noted for its striking bright red-orange blossoms that precede its foliage in the summer. The bright red flowers inspire Vālmīki to use the tree as an object of comparison for bleeding warriors at various points in the poem (see 6.35.9; 6.55.22; 6.67.23; 6.76.28; 6.92.7; and notes). Here, however, the simile seems to be based not so much on the blood of the monkeys as on the flaming arrows that cover their bodies. Cf. 6.62.19 and note.

35. D10,11, and the texts and printed editions of Ct omit verse 35. Most translations that follow the text of Ct therefore also omit it. Gita Press (1969, vol. 3, pp. 1673–74) includes the verse and numbers it as 6.73.60. Pagani (1999, p. 1068), who follows the text of GPP, where the verse occurs unnumbered between verses 6.73.56 and 57 with the notation that it is additional in the texts of Cg and Cr, translates it as well.

36. "with arrows" *śaraiḥ*: Ś1,V2,B3,D7,9–12,G1,M1–3, and the texts and printed editions of Ct read instead *śanaiḥ*, "slowly, gradually," which one would normally construe with the verb "clung (*viviśuḥ*)." Ct, however, insists that the adverb should be

construed with the adjective *tāḍitāḥ*, "struck," yielding the sense "were gradually struck."

"they...clung to one another" *viviśur anyonyam*: Literally, "they entered one another." We follow the interpretation of Ck and Ct, who gloss, "remained clinging to one another's limbs (*anyonyagātraṃ samāśliṣya* [*āśliṣya*—Ck] *tasthuḥ*)." Cg and Cm construe the verb causally with "they fell (*petuḥ*)," glossing, "they fell on top of one another in order to cling *or* huddle (*anyonyoparyālambanārthaṃ petur ity arthaḥ*)."

37–40. "Gaja, Gomukha" *gajagomukhau*: D7,9–11, and the texts and printed editions of Ct read instead *gavayaṃ tathā*, "and Gavaya."

"Jyotimukha" *jyotimukham*: See note to 6.47.40.

41. "fletched with burnished gold" *tapanīyapuṅkhaiḥ*: D9–11 and the texts and printed editions of Ct read instead *-varṇaiḥ*, which lends the compound the sense "of the color of burnished gold."

The meter is *upajāti*.

42. "regarded them no more seriously than showers of rain" *dhārānipātān iva tān vicintya*: Literally, "having considered them as if they were the falling of streams [of water]." B3,D9–11,T1,G,M3, and the texts and printed editions of the southern commentators read *acintya*, "not having thought," for *vicintya*, "having considered." The commentators explain that Rāma pays no heed to them because of their insignificance to him (*tucchatvenāparigaṇayya*—so Cr).

"turned his gaze" *samīkṣamāṇaḥ*: Literally, "gazing, looking." Cg understands that, relying on his own inherent nature, Rāma, significantly, gazes with the appropriate gestures at Lakṣmaṇa, who is preparing to counteract the divine weapon-spell of Brahmā (*svasvabhāvāvalambanena brahmāstrapratikriyāṃ kartum udyuktam iṅgitair abhivīkṣamāṇaḥ san*).

The meter is *upajāti*.

43. "again" *punaḥ*: We understand the adverb here to be an allusion to Indrajit's previous attack on Rāma and Lakṣmaṇa in *sarga* 35. This idea is shared by Shastri (1959, vol. 3, p. 213). Roussel (1903, vol. 3, p. 241) understands it to refer to a renewed attack on the monkey army, while Pagani (1999, p. 1069) and Gorresio (1858, vol. 10, p. 64) take it to refer to Indrajit's renewed recourse to the *mantra* governing the *brahmāstra*. Other translators appear to ignore the term.

"the divine weapon-spell of Brahmā" *brahmāstram*: Cg understands the term to refer to the *mantra* governing the *brahmāstra*. In this he is followed by Pagani (1999, p. 1069). D9–11 and the texts and printed editions of Ct read instead *mahāstram*, "the great *or* powerful divine weapon-spell."

"fierce...us with arrows" *ugram asmañ śaraiḥ*: D9–11 and the texts and printed editions of Ct read instead *asmāñ śitaiḥ śaraiḥ*, "us with sharp arrows."

"constantly" *prasaktam*: We understand the term in its common adverbial sense of "constantly, incessantly." Ck, Ct, and Cr read the term adjectivally in the sense of "obtained (*prāptam*—Ct)," which they see as modifying *-astram*, "missile *or* divine weapon-spell." Among the translators consulted who share this reading, only Pagani (1999, p. 1069) understands the term as we do. The rest follow the commentators. D6,T2,G2,M3,5, and the texts and printed editions of Cg and Cm read instead the nominative adjective *prasaktaḥ*, which, in this context, would mean "intent," describing Indrajit. Raghunathan (1982, vol. 3, p. 214), the only translator who consistently follows the text of Cg, appears to ignore the term.

The meter is *upajāti*.

44. "The great warrior" *mahātmā*: Literally, "the great one."

"by self-existent Brahmā" *svayaṃbhuvā*: Literally, "by the self-existent one."

"is hovering in the sky" *kham āsthitaḥ*: V3,B3,D9–11, and the texts and printed editions of Ct read instead *samāhitaḥ*, "intent, mentally focused."

"How is it possible to kill" *kathaṃ nu śakyaḥ . . . nihantum*: Cr understands Rāma's intention to be that killing a deceitful warrior, like killing a fleeing enemy, brings fault or censure upon the killer. Thus, Cr continues, Rāma is concerned with preserving his reputation as a chivalrous warrior who understands his class duty and is justifying the propriety of the later killing [of Indrajit by Lakṣmaṇa]. (*etena kapaṭayoddhṝṇāṃ hananaṃ palāyanaparahananavad doṣāvaham iti rāmābhiprāyaḥ sūcitaḥ. tena vakṣyamāṇaviśasanasādṛśyaprāptiḥ svadharmajñatvapalāyanāyaiveti dhvanitam.*)

"invisible" *naṣṭadehaḥ*: Literally, "his body destroyed." We follow Ck, Ct, Cg, and Cr, who take the term to mean "having an invisible body (*adṛṣṭadehaḥ*—so Cg)." For a similar use of the root $\sqrt{}$*naś* to refer to invisibility, see 5.11.17 and note.

The meter is *upendravajrā*.

45. "the self-existent . . . Brahmā" *svayaṃbhūḥ*: Literally, "the self-existent one."

"who is the creator of all things . . . And" *prabhavaś ca yo 'sya*: Literally, "and who is the source of this." Commentators and translators vary in their understanding of this reference. Given the tenor of the passage, we are inclined to agree with Ck and Ct, who understand the reference to be to Brahmā's well-known role as the creator of the universe. These commentators further understand the conjunction "and (*ca*)" to indicate that he is also the destroyer of the world. (*yo 'sya sakalasaṃsārasya prabhavaḥ sraṣṭā. cakārāt saṃhartā ca.*—so Ct.) Cr takes Brahmā to be the progenitor of the royal lineage of Manu (*manuvaṃśasya prabhava utpattikāraṇam*). Cg thinks that the reference is to Brahmā's role merely as the creator of the divine weapon-spell (*asyāstrasya prabhava utpattikāraṇam*). Translators consulted which share this reading follow the idea of Cg, with the exception of Gita Press (1969, pp. 1674–75), which represents the view of Ck and Ct.

"inconceivable" *acintyaḥ*: Cg, Ct, and Ck understand the term elliptically in the sense "of inconceivable divine power (*acintyavaibhavaḥ*—so Ck, Ct)."

"wise Lakṣmaṇa" *dhīman*: Literally, "O wise one." Cg takes the term here to refer to the fact that Lakṣmaṇa knows not to be agitated in times of crisis (*āpatsu na calitavyam iti jñānin*). Ck and Ct understand it to refer to Lakṣmaṇa's practice of meditation on Lord Brahmā, which will enable him to endure Indrajit's arrows (*yatas tvam api brahmadhyānasampannas tasmāt sahasva*—so Ct). Both commentators further suggest that only as a result of the grace of the Lord [Brahmā] will Rāma and Lakṣmaṇa attain victory (*evaṃ hi bhagavadanugrahād asmākam api jayo bhaviṣyati nānyathety arthaḥ*—so Ct).

"you must . . . endure with me" *tvam . . . mayā saha . . . sahasva*: As Ct and Ck note, this attitude toward Indrajit's *brāhma* weapons has earlier been adopted by Hanumān (at 5.46.37–41) and by Rāma and Lakṣmaṇa (at 6.35) (*bhagavato brahmaṇa ājñāyā mārutinevāsmābhir api pālanaucityenaitat sahanasyaivaucityād ity āśayenāha*—so Ct). Cs believes that Rāma is saying that he alone is able to withstand Indrajit's weapons but that, through his grace, Lakṣmaṇa will be able to do so as well (*mayā saha sahasvaitena tatsahane mama sāmarthyaṃ madanugrahāt tava sahanam iti dhvanyate*).

The meter is *upajāti*.

46. "is filling all directions" *pracchādayati... sarvā diśaḥ*: Literally, "is covering all directions." Ś1,B2,3,D1,7,9–11, and the texts and printed editions of Ct read the imperative *pracchādayatu*, "let him fill," for the indicative *pracchādayati*. In addition, D9–11 and the texts and printed editions of Ct read *sarvādhikaḥ*, "the greatest of all," for *sarvā diśaḥ*, "all directions." This adjective would then describe Indrajit. See note to verse 32 above.

"presents a sorry sight" *na bhrājate*: Literally, "it does not shine, look splendid."

The meter is *indravajrā*.

47. "and have ceased to fight or show signs either of anger or excitement," *hataroṣaharṣau*: Literally, "whose anger and excitement are destroyed." We follow Ck and Ct, who gloss, "whose signs of excitement and anger (*-harṣaroṣau* by transposition) are not manifested (*aprakāśitaharṣaroṣavikārau*)." D5,T1,M3, and the texts and printed editions of Cg read *gata-*, "gone, departed," for *hata-*, "destroyed."

"will... return to Laṅkā, the abode of the foes of the immortal gods" *pravekṣyaty amarārivāsam*: Literally, "he will enter the abode of the foes of the immortals." Ct and Ck extend Rāma's remarks by adding the clause "after that we will do what we have to do (*paścād yad asmābhir anuṣṭheyaṃ tat kariṣyāva iti śeṣaḥ*)."

"having achieved the greatest glory in battle" *samādāya raṇāgralakṣmīm*: Literally, "having received the foremost success in battle." Cg understands the reference to be to *vijayalakṣmī*, "the glory of victory." Several of the commentators take the term *agra* [v.l. *agrya*], "foremost (lit., tip)," here, to suggest that Indrajit has not achieved the power to effect the complete destruction of his foes (*raṇāgryetyādinā samūlanāśāśaktiḥ sūcitā*—Ct).

The meter is *upajāti*.

48. "At that point... cut down" *tadā viśastau*: Ct and Cg gloss, "oppressed, afflicted (*pīḍitau*)." Cr, however, unwilling to see the divine heroes injured, takes advantage of the *sandhi* with the preceding adverb to read the participle as *aviśastau*, literally, "uninjured," which he glosses as "appearing to be injured (*hiṃsitasadṛśau*)."

"the two brothers" *tau*: Literally, "those two."

"Having laid them low" *viṣādayitvā*: Literally, "having afflicted *or* caused to despair." G1,M3,5, and the texts and printed editions of Cg and Cm read instead *vidarśayitvā*, "having shown (them)." Cg glosses the simplex "having seen (*dṛṣṭvā*)." Only Raghunathan (1982, vol. 3, p. 214) follows this reading, rendering, "and seeing them in that condition."

The meter is *upendravajrā*.

49. "Having thus laid low" *viṣādayitvā*: D9,10, and the texts and printed editions of Ct read instead *niṣūdayitvā*, "having slaughtered" (GPP 6.73.70 *viṣūdayitvā*). Translations that follow the text of Ct render this reading as "worsted, vanquished, defeated, etc."

"the city of Laṅkā, which lay under the protection of the arms of ten-necked Rāvaṇa." *purīṃ daśagrīvabhujābhiguptām*: Literally, "the city protected by the arms of the ten-necked one."

Following verse 49, Ś,V3,B1,D2,3,6,8–12,T2,3, and the texts and printed editions of Ct and Cr insert a passage of two lines in the *indravajrā* meter [1353*]: "Being praised by the *yātudhānas*, he reported everything in great delight to his father."

Sarga 61

1. "Then . . . had been struck down" *tadā sāditayoḥ*: Literally, "then . . . [those two had been] made to sink down." Ct and Ck gloss, "rendered motionless (*niśceṣṭīkṛtayoḥ*)." Cr takes advantage of the possible alternate word division with the preceding adverb *tadā*, "then," to read instead *asāditayoḥ*, literally, "not depressed." He glosses, "[merely] appearing to be pained (*duḥkhitayor iva satoḥ*)."

"the two heroes, Rāma and Lakṣmaṇa" *tayoḥ*: Literally, "the two."

The meter is *upajāti*.

2. "the king of the tree-dwelling monkeys and his heroic warriors" *śākhāmṛgarājavīrān*: Literally, "branch-animal-king-heroes." Cs, alone among the commentators, attempts to analyze this compound and offers two suggestions. The first, which we have followed, is to read it as a *dvandva*. The second is to take it according to the rule *saptamī śauṇḍaiḥ* (*Pā* 2.1.40), in the sense of "those heroes among the kings of the branch-dwelling monkeys." (*śākhāmṛgarājeṣu vīrāś ceti vā. saptamī śauṇḍair iti yogabhāgāt samāsaḥ*.) Translators are divided as to whether to read the compound as a *dvandva* (as we have) referring to both Sugrīva and his warriors or as a *tatpuruṣa* in the sense of "the warriors of the king[s] of the tree-dwelling monkeys." See note to 6.15.15.

"inimitable" *apratimaiḥ*: Literally, "unmatched, unequaled."

The meter is *upajāti*.

3. "Have no fear! . . . this is no time for despondency" *mā bhaiṣṭa nāsty atra viṣādakālaḥ*: The commentators offer a variety of explanations as to why the monkeys should not be afraid on account of the apparent disability of Rāma and Lakṣmaṇa. Ck and Ct offer two alternatives. According to the first, the princes are merely honoring the command of Brahmā (viz., that his weapon must be infallible) and are not, in fact, in any mortal danger (*na tu prāṇapīḍāvantau*). In other words, they need have no fear for Rāma and Lakṣmaṇa. According to Ck's and Ct's second interpretation, the monkeys should not fear any danger at the hands of their enemies, wondering who will protect them now. (*yadvā etāv avaśau viṣaṇṇāv iti yat tatra viṣaye mā bhaiṣṭa. etayor viṣaṇṇayor asmān ko vā rakṣiṣyatīti śatrubhyo bhayaṃ mā bhūt*—so Ct.) Cr suggests that, since the princes only appear to have been struck down, there is no occasion for despondency. In addition, Cr claims that visible despondency and fear on the part of the monkeys over Rāma's and Lakṣmaṇa's apparent fall will only encourage and invite further attack by other enemies. (*avaśāv astravaśasadṛśau sta iti śeṣaḥ. ato viśādakālaḥ khedasamayo naitena yuṣmadaudāsīnyajñāpyarāmalakṣmaṇaudāsīnyajñāne ripūṇāṃ harṣātiśayo bhaviṣyatīti sūcitam. tena ripvantarāṇy apy āgamiṣyantīti dhvanitam*.) Cg and Cm, like Cr, assert that the heroes have fallen merely to show their respect for Brahmā and only appear to be cut down by Indrajit (*sāditāv iva vartamānau*).

The meter is *upajāti*.

Following verse 3, G2 and KK (numbered, in brackets, as 6.74.4) insert an additional *upajāti* verse [1355*]: "There Vibhīṣaṇa, who, by virtue of a boon from the creator, was uninjured[1] by that divine weapon-spell, looked about and, seeing that the army of tawny monkeys had been laid low by the divine weapon-spell of their enemy, said these words to Hanumān, who was similarly unharmed."

[1]"uninjured" *āsāditaḥ*: We render KK's *asāditaḥ* instead of the critical edition's *āsāditaḥ*, "reached, obtained," which is all but impossible to construe in this context and is possibly a typographical error.

4. "of unfailing force" *amoghavegam*: See note to 6.59.89. Ś,Ñ,V,B,D2–5,7–13,M5, and the texts and printed editions of Ct and Cr, as well as the printed editions of Lahore and Gorresio, read *-vīryam*, "power," for *-vegam*, "force."

"to Indrajit" *tasmai*: Literally, "to him."

"why is that an occasion for despondency" *ko 'tra viṣādakālaḥ*: Literally, "What is the occasion for despondency in this [matter]?" Ck and Ct explain that there is, in fact, no occasion for despondency as we should supply: "The two of them [Rāma and Lakṣmaṇa] will get up after a short time (*kṣaṇānantaram utthāsyataḥ*)."

The meter is *upajāti*.

5. "who had already once shown his reverence . . . heard" *mānayitvā . . . śrutvā*: All translations consulted invert the clausal structure of the verse, understanding that Hanumān pays his respects now, only after hearing those words of Vibhīṣaṇa. We believe that the temporal sequence of the original should be maintained and that the reference here is not to some abstract respect for Brahmā's weapon but to Hanumān's very real submission to it when Indrajit deployed the weapon against him at 5.46.34–42 (see translation and notes ad loc.). We believe that this idea is suggested by Cg, who glosses *mānayitvā*, "having shown his reverence," with "having [himself] remained momentarily under the power of the *brahmāstra* (*muhūrtamātraṃ brahmāstraparavaśaḥ sthitvā*)." See note to 5.46.40.

6. "any of those . . . who may still be alive" *yo yo dhārayate prāṇāṃs tam tam*: Literally, "whoever sustains life breaths, him."

"in the decimated army" *etasmin nihate sainye*: Literally, "in this stricken army." Ñ,V,B,D1,4,9–11,13,M5, and the texts and printed editions of Ct read instead *asminn astrahate sainye*, "in this army stricken by that divine weapon-spell."

7. "and that foremost of the *rākṣasas* Vibhīṣaṇa" *-rākṣasottamau*: Literally, "and the foremost of the *rākṣasas*."

"during that night" *rātrau*: Literally, "at night." According to Ct, this reference suggests that Indrajit deployed his *astra* on the seventh night (presumably of the dark half of the month Bhādrāśvina) (*tadā rātrāv ity anena saptamyāṃ rātrāv ayam astraprayoga iti sūcitam*). See note to 6.59.106.

8–9. "that had been dropped . . . fallen" *patitaiḥ . . . patitaiḥ*: Literally, "fallen . . . fallen."

"oozing blood from their limbs" *śravadbhiḥ kṣatajaṃ gātraiḥ*: We take the instrumental *gatraiḥ* here as a *karaṇa*, or means through which the bleeding is accomplished. This reading has been adopted by Gita Press (1969, vol. 3, p. 1677), Dutt (1893, p. 1359), and Raghunathan (1982, vol. 3, p. 215). Roussel (1903, vol. 3, p. 243), followed by Shastri (1959, vol. 3, p. 214), understands *gātraiḥ* here to mean "severed limbs," a third article with which the ground is strewn (in addition to weapons and monkeys). Pagani (1999, p. 1070) takes the term to mean "bodies," and it is to this rather than "monkeys," that she subordinates the long *bahuvrīhi* compound describing the severed limbs. Thus, for her the field is strewn with bodies, weapons, and monkeys.

"and dribbling urine" *praśravadbhiḥ*: Literally, "oozing, flowing." All the commentators who discuss this reading take the term either in its sense of "urinating (*mūtrayadbhiḥ*—so Cv, Cg, and Cm)" or supply the word "urine (*mūtram iti śeṣaḥ*—so Ct)." Gita Press (1969, vol. 3, p. 1677), Dutt (1893, p. 1359), and Raghunathan (1982, vol. 3, p. 215) all follow the commentators as do we. Roussel (1903, vol. 3, p. 243), followed by Shastri (1959, vol. 3, p. 214), appears to ignore the term. Pagani (1999, p. 1070) attempts to subordinate it to the gouts of blood flowing from the monkeys, rendering, "*des flots de sang qui ruisselaient de touts côtés*," an interesting suggestion but grammatically untenable.

10–11. "And there Vibhīṣaṇa and Hanumān" *vibhīṣaṇo hanūmāṃś ca*: Literally, "Vibhīṣaṇa and Hanumān." M3 and the texts and printed editions of Cg and Cm read instead *etāṃś cānyāṃs tato vīrau*, "then the two heroes [saw] these and others."

"Jāmbavān" *jāmbavantam*: D5,T1,M3,5, and the texts and printed editions of Cg and Cm read instead *gavākṣaṃ ca*, "and Gavākṣa."

"Āhuka" *āhukam*: Ñ2,V1,2,B2–4,D1,6,9–11,13, and the texts and printed editions of Ct and Gorresio read instead *eva ca*, "and as well."

"Jyotimukha" *jyotimukham*: See note to 6.47.40.

12. "within the fifth part of a day" *ahnaḥ pañcamaśeṣeṇa*: Literally, "by the fifth remainder of the day." As the commentators note, the reference is to the fifth (and final) portion of the twelve-hour day from sunrise to sunset. The Indian day was traditionally divided into five equal sections each lasting 144 minutes (= 6 *ghaṭikās* of 24 minutes each) named, respectively, *prātaḥ*, "early morning"; *saṃgava*, "late morning"; *madhyāhna*, "early afternoon"; *parāhna*, "late afternoon"; and *sāyāhna*, "early evening." The idea in the verse is that Indrajit's rampage of slaughter takes place during the last period, or the two hours and twenty-four minutes that correspond to "early evening." This is followed by nightfall, after which Hanumān and Vibhīṣaṇa make their grisly search. According to Ct, we are to understand that it took the first four parts of the day for Indrajit to prepare the *brahmāstra* for use (*caturbhir bhāgaiś ca brahmāstrasādhanam ity bodhyam*).

"self-existent Brahmā's favorite" *vallabhena svayaṃbhuvaḥ*: Literally, "by the favorite of the self-existent one." The commentators and translators consulted generally understand this reference to be to the *brahmāstra*, i.e., Brahmā's favorite weapon. Cg notes that the term can refer either to Indrajit or to the *astra*. We are inclined to believe that the former is referred to here but have preserved the ambiguity of the original.

"six hundred and seventy million" *saptaṣaṣṭir... koṭyaḥ*: Literally, "sixty-seven crore." Given the astronomical numbers of monkey warriors described in earlier *sargas*, this number, huge though it is, would represent only a small fraction of Sugrīva's forces. See 6.17.27,30,34,36, etc.; and note to 6.19.32; 411*.

13. "Hanumān and Vibhīṣaṇa sought out" *mārgate... sma hanūmān savibhīṣaṇaḥ*: Literally, "Hanumān along with Vibhīṣaṇa searched, hunted for." Given that Hanumān and Vibhīṣaṇa have already located Jāmbavān among the wounded monkeys in verse 10 above, we agree with Ck and Ct, who gloss, "singling out (*viśiṣyety arthaḥ*—so Ct)." The idea, according to Ck and Ct, is that they seek out Jāmbavān because of his vast knowledge in order to ask him what strategy they should adopt (*tasya bahujñatvād upāyapraśnārtham iti bhāvaḥ* [Ck—*iti śeṣaḥ*]). Cr notes that the seeking out of Jāmbavān suggests that he is endowed with every virtue and that the two seekers have determined that, by meeting him, a good outcome will be achieved. (*etena jāmbavataḥ sarvaguṇasaṃpannatvaṃ sūcitam. tena taddarśanena kalyāṇaṃ bhaviṣyaty eveti tayor niścayaḥ sūcitaḥ.*)

14–15. "wise... showing the signs of advanced age" *svabhāvajarayā yuktaṃ vṛddham*: Literally, "conjoined with natural senescence and aged." We agree with Ck and Ct that the signs of senescence would be the physical signs of age, such as wrinkles, gray hair, etc. (*vayaḥsvabhāvāj jarayā valīpalitādinā yuktam*). Cr, on the other hand, understands the phrase to refer to Jāmbavān's natural virtues, such as fortitude, etc., as well as old age (*svabhāvena svābhāvikadhairyādinā jarayā ca yuktam*). We follow Cr in taking *vṛddha* in its sense of "advanced in knowledge *or* wisdom (*vṛddhaṃ jñānenādhikam*)." This both avoids redundancy with *jarayā* and supplies a motive for his being uniquely sought out for questioning.

"Vibhīṣaṇa Paulastya" *paulastyaḥ*: Literally "Paulastya." This patronymic is rarely used of figures other than Rāvaṇa himself.

"that you have not been mortally wounded" *na prāṇā dhvaṃsitās tava*: Literally, "that your life breaths have not been destroyed."

16. "uttered this speech, articulating the words only with great difficulty" *kṛcchrād abhyudgiran vākyam idam vacanam abravīt*: Literally, "with difficulty uttering speech, he spoke this speech." We agree with the commentators, particularly Cg, in their efforts to avoid the redundancy by taking *vākyam* in the sense of "sounds instrumental to the production of speech (*vākyopayogi svaram*—so Cg)."

"bull among apes" *ṛkṣapuṃgavaḥ*: See 6.4.17 and note.

17. "wounded" *pīḍyamānaḥ*: Literally, "being oppressed." D10 and the texts and printed editions of Ct read instead *viddhagātraḥ*, "[my] limbs pierced."

"I cannot see you" *na tvāṃ paśyāmi cakṣuṣā*: Literally, "I do not see you with my eye *or* sight."

18. "O *rākṣasa*, son of chaos" *nairṛta*: Literally, "O *nairṛta*." D9–11 and the texts and printed editions of Ct read instead *suvrata*, "O one of strict vows, pious one."

"Vāyu Mātariśvan" *mātariśvā*: Literally, "Mātariśvan." Among all his many hundreds of references to the wind and the wind god in the poem, Vālmīki uses this epithet of Vāyu only four times. Cf. 3.65.13; 4.59.19 and note; and 5.56.13.

"does . . . still live" *prāṇān dhārayate kvacit*: Literally, "somewhere or other he supports *or* maintains life breaths." We agree with Cr and Cg, who note that the adverb *kvacit*, normally "somewhere or other," must be read here simply as a marker of interrogation (*kvacid iti praśnārthakam*—so Cr). It seems to function here in the sense of the similar-sounding marker of interrogation, *kaccit*. In fact, most northern manuscripts introduce *kaccit* into the passage. Some rephrase the expression and employ *kaccit* (Ñ2,V1,2,B2,D4), whereas V3,B1,D2,3 substitute an alternative line for 18cd in which the adverb *kaccit* is used.

19. "do you ignore" *atikramya*: Literally, "having skipped over *or* passed over."

"the king's sons Rāma and Lakṣmaṇa" *āryaputrau*: Literally, "the two sons of the noble one." See notes to 6.23.35 and 6.102.35.

"you . . . ask only about Māruti" *pṛcchasi mārutim*: Literally, "you inquire after Māruti."

20. "the . . . extraordinary concern" *snehaḥ . . . paraḥ*: Literally, "supreme affection."

21. "why I inquired only about Māruti" *yasmāt pṛcchāmi mārutim*: Literally, the reason for which I ask about Māruti. See note to verse 19 above.

22. "our army will survive, even if it should be massacred" *hatam apy ahataṃ balam*: Literally, "even though slain, the army would not be slain."

"even though we survive, we are as good as dead" *jīvanto 'pi vayaṃ hatāḥ*: Literally, "even though living, we are slain."

23. "of Agni Vaiśvānara" *vaiśvānara-*: Literally, "of Vaiśvānara." See note to 6.18.37.

24. "wise" *vṛddham*: Literally, "aged." See note to verses 14–15 above.

"Devotedly" *niyamena*: Literally, "with restraint or devotion." Cg takes the term in its sense of a formalized religious observance or gesture of piety, such as crossing the hands to touch the ears (*śrotrahastasaṃsparśavyatyastahastatvādirūpeṇa saha*). Ś,Ñ,V,B, D1–4,7–9,12,13,M1,2, and the texts and printed editions of Ct and Cr read instead *vinayena*, "with humility."

"he respectfully greeted him" *abhyavādayat*: Literally, "he respectfully greeted." Cg understands this to be the formal gesture of deference and respect by a junior to an elder, which includes the announcement of one's own name. This is significant in light of the fact that virtually all manuscripts fail to report any actual speech on Hanumān's part prior to the assertion, in verse 25 below, that Jāmbavān has heard Hanumān's words. Raghunathan (1982, vol. 3, p. 216) incorporates this idea explicitly in his translation, "announcing himself." See *ManuSm* 2.120–126. See 6.115.33 and note. See, too, 5.62.1 and note.

Following verse 24, KK inserts a passage of one line [1373*], bracketed and numbered as 6.73.25ef: "Here I am, foremost of tawny monkeys. Instruct me as to what you want me to do." No translation renders this line.

25. "Although his every organ was in agony" *tathāpi vyathitendriyaḥ*: Literally, "although his senses were pained."

"Jāmbavān, bull among apes" *ṛkṣapuṃgavaḥ*: Literally, "bull among apes." D5,6,9–11,T,G1,3, and the texts and printed editions of Ct and Cr read *plavagottamaḥ*, "best of leaping monkeys."

"Hanumān's words" *hanumato vākyam*: As noted in the previous verse, no actual words of Hanumān are recorded in the text. Cg remarks that the reference would be to the *abhivādana*, or formal greeting, described in the preceding verse, where Hanumān would have said, "It is I, Hanumān" (*hanumān aham asmīty abhivādanavākyam*).

27. "You are the monkeys' greatest friend" *tvam eṣāṃ paramaḥ sakhā*: Literally, "you are their greatest friend."

"Now is the moment for you to show your prowess" *tvatparākramakālo 'yam*: Literally, "This is the time for your prowess."

"for I can see no one else who can accomplish this" *nānyaṃ paśyāmi kaṃcana*: Literally, "I see none other whatsoever." The phrase is elliptical, and we have fleshed it out in keeping with the context.

28. "You must heal the arrow wounds of Rāma and Lakṣmaṇa" *viśalyau kuru cāpy etau . . . rāmalakṣmaṇau*: Literally, "and make these two, Rāma and Lakṣmaṇa, arrow-free." Our translation reflects the fact that the two heroes cannot be healed simply by the removal of Indrajit's arrows but, as will be shown in the following verses, will require applications of specific medicinal herbs to heal them of their injuries.

"and thus restore the spirits" *praharṣaya*: Literally, "restore the spirits, encourage." We follow the interpretation of Cr, who understands that it is the healing of Rāma and Lakṣmaṇa that will restore the monkey's spirits (*sāditau bāṇair ācchāditau rāmalakṣmaṇau viśalyau kurv ata evānīkāni praharṣaya*).

29. "the highest path" *paramam adhvānam*: Cg glosses *dīrgham*, "long," for *paramam*, "highest, supreme." His interpretation has been followed by Raghunathan (1982, vol. 3, p. 217) and Gita Press (1969, vol. 3, p. 1678). Cr glosses, "the path that is best because it is incapable of being traveled by inferior persons (*paramaṃ pāmarair agamyatvena śreṣṭham*)."

"far above the ocean" *upary upari sāgaram*: Cg understands the adverbial phrase *upary upari* in its sense of "slightly above (*sāgarasya samīpoparipradeśe*)," citing *Pā* 8.1.7 (*uparyadhyadhasaḥ sāmīpye*) on the repetition of the term *upari* suggesting proximity. He thus understands that Hanumān will be skimming the waves rather than soaring through the sky. Compare 5.1.65–67, where, when crossing the sea in his quest for Sītā, Hanumān is represented as breaking through the waves with his chest.

"Himalaya" *himavantam*: At 6.40.29–31, Suṣeṇa proposes sending a party of monkeys to the mountains named Candra and Droṇa, which, he says, are situated in the middle of the ocean of milk, in order to secure the medicinal herbs to heal Rāma and Lakṣmaṇa of the wounds inflicted by Indrajit's divinely charged weapons. See 6.40.29–31 and notes. Cf. 6.89.14–15.

30. "You will see . . . Mount Ṛṣabha . . . and the peak of Mount Kailāsa" *ṛṣabham . . . kailāsaśikharaṃ cāpi drakṣyasi*: Cr believes that Hanumān is to go first to Mount Ṛṣabha and that, standing on its peak, he will be able to see Kailāsa (*ṛṣabhaśikhare sthitas tvaṃ kailāsaśikharaṃ drakṣyasi*). Roussel (1903, vol. 3, p. 244), Shastri (1959, vol. 3, p. 216), and Gita Press (1969, vol. 3, p. 1679) all follow Cr's interpretation. This idea is more or less followed by Pagani (1999, p. 1071). Cf. 6.40.29–31 and notes. Mount Ṛṣabha is said to be one of the twenty mountains flanking Mount Meru in the Himalayas. Note that, in his description of the geography of the four directions in the *Kiṣkindhākāṇḍa*, Sugrīva places a Mount Ṛṣabha in the midst of the ocean of milk (4.39.39). The ocean of milk is also the locus of the mountains Candra and Droṇa, which, at 6.40.31, are said to be the sources of healing herbs. D6,T2,3 insert a passage of five lines [1376*] after verse 30 in which Hanumān is instructed to go to Mount Candra and Mount Droṇa, which are located in the ocean of milk (lines 3–5). This insert appears to be an attempt to rationalize the seemingly contradictory identifications of the mountain[s] of healing herbs.

"forbidding" *atyugram*: Literally, "extremely fierce, formidable." We follow Ck and Ct, who understand that the peak is unapproachable because of its lions and other savage animals (*siṃhādibhir duṣpraveśam*). Translators who share this reading have taken the term variously to mean "horrific, inaccessible, steep, etc." V1,B3,4,M, and the texts and printed editions of Cg, Cm, and Cr read instead *atyuccam*, "extremely tall."

31. "Between those two peaks . . . the mountain of healing herbs" *tayoḥ śikharayor madhye . . . auṣadhiparvatam*: The reference, of course, is to Mount Ṛṣabha and Mount Kailāsa mentioned in the previous verse. See, too, 6.89.14–15 and notes.

"covered with every sort of healing herb" *sarvauṣadhiyutam*: Literally, "endowed with all healing herbs."

"glows with unequaled radiance" *pradīptam atulaprabham*: It is a commonplace in the literature that herbs, especially the medicinal herbs of the Himalayas, are luminescent. Cf. *KumāSaṃ* 1.10, where such herbs serve as lamps for the nocturnal lovemaking of the Himalayan forest folk.

32–33. "*mṛtasaṃjīvanī*, 'the restorer of life to the dead,' *viśalyakaraṇī*, 'the healer of arrow wounds,' *sauvarṇakaraṇī*, 'the restorer of a golden glow,' and the great healing herb *saṃdhānī*, 'the joiner of limbs' " *mṛtasaṃjīvanīṃ caiva viśalyakaraṇīm api / sauvarṇakaraṇīṃ caiva saṃdhānīṃ mahauṣadhīm*: The names of the herbs are intended to express their functions. Taken literally, the names would mean, respectively, "reviving the dead," "making arrow-less," "making golden," and "joining." We have rendered the names in keeping with the explanations offered by the various commentators. See 6.89.14–16 and notes.

The first two of these herbs, the *mṛtasaṃjīvanī* and the *viśalyakaraṇī*, are evidently the same as the healing herbs *saṃjīvanī* and *viśalyā* mentioned in a parallel context at 6.40.30 and notes. Cr notes that the first restores the dead to life by its mere touch (*mṛtānāṃ saṃjīvanīṃ sparśamātreṇa saṃjīvanakartrīm*) and the second makes one free from arrows by its mere touch (*sparśamātreṇa bāṇarāhityasaṃpādikām*). *Viśalyā* is identified as *Delphinium denudatum*, which is found in the Himalayas between eight thousand and twelve thousand feet. See note to 6.40.30.

The name *sauvarṇakaraṇī* is one of a series of variants found in the critical apparatus. None of the commentators shows this exact reading. However, Ñ,V1,2,B2–4,D7,11,13,G2,M5, and the texts and printed editions of Cr and Ct come closest, reading *suvarṇakaraṇīm*, literally, "making gold *or* producing a good color." Evidently the idea here is that the herb removes the pallor of the dead or wounded warrior and restores his lustrous golden complexion. Ct explains the name as "producing a color similar to that of gold on the body, etc. (*suvarṇasamānavarṇasya dehādeḥ karaṇīm*)." Cr explains, "producing a splendid color (*śobhanavarṇasaṃpādikām*)." Compare verse 6.40.39, where the bodies of Rāma and Lakṣmaṇa, who there had also been struck down by Indrajit, take on a golden luster (*suvarṇe*) at Garuḍa's touch. V3,B1,D1–4,9,10, and the text of Ck read instead *savarṇakaraṇīm*, literally, "producing the same color." Ck explains this as meaning "producing a color similar to one's previous color, that is, restoring the body's natural glow (*pūrvavarṇasamānavarṇakaraṇīṃ dehakāntikaraṇīm*)." Compare Ct's reading at note to 6.89.16. Ct notes this as a variant reading and provides the first part of Ck's explanation. T2,M3, and the texts and printed editions of Cg and Cm read *sāvarṇyakaraṇīm*, literally, "producing similarity of color," a reading close to that of Ck. Cg explains this to mean that the herb restores the original color to the body except at those places where it has lost color as a result of scarring (*vraṇakṛtavaivarṇyaṃ vihāya pradeśāntarasāvarṇyaṃ karotīti sāvarṇyakaraṇī*). Raghunathan (1982, vol. 3, p. 217), the only translator to read this variant, renders, "restorer-of-the pigment of the skin." The text of Gorresio (6.53.38) reads *svavarṇakaraṇīm*, literally, "producing one's own *or* native color." Gorresio (1858, vol. 10, p. 68) renders, "*raccende altrui . . . il natio colore.*"

The last of the healing herbs, *saṃdhānī*, is explained by Ck and Ct as "reconnecting the blood vessels of even a severed head and trunk to their previous condition (*chinnaśiraḥkabandhayor api yathāpūrvaṃ nāḍīsaṃdhānakaraṇīm*)." Cr explains, "reconnecting severed heads, etc., the way they were before (*chinnaśiraḥprabhṛtīnāṃ yathāpūrvaṃ saṃyojikām*)." Cg understands that the herb heals the skin once arrows have been removed (*viśalye kṛte tvacaḥ saṃdhānaṃ karoti*).

Cg, alone among the commentators, understands that the four healing herbs are to be used in a specific sequence. According to him, once the patient is restored to life by the *mṛtasaṃjīvanī* herb, *viśalyakaraṇī* is applied so that he can move about once more. Next *saṃdhānakaraṇī* is administered so as to heal the wounds in the skin. Finally, *sāvarṇyakaraṇī* is administered to restore the patient's natural complexion. (*jīvanānantaraṃ saṃcārakṣamatayai viśalyaṃ karotīti viśalyakaraṇī. viśalye kṛte tvacaḥ saṃdhānaṃ karotīti saṃdhānakaraṇī. tato vraṇakṛtavaivarṇyaṃ vihāya pradeśāntarasāvarṇyaṃ karotīti sāvarṇyakaraṇī.*)

34. "restore . . . to life" *prāṇair yojya*: Literally, "having caused them to be joined with life breaths."

"son of Vāyu, bearer of scents" *gandhavahātmaja*: Literally, "son of the scent-bearer." This somewhat unusual epithet of Hanumān (and of Vāyu) used here and at verses 64 and 68 below no doubt prefigures the mode in which the herbs are to be employed, for we see, at verse 67 below and again at 6.89.23,24, that these herbs function by the inhalation of their scent, or what might be termed "aromatherapy." See verses 64 and 68 below. See, too, 6.89.23,24 and notes.

35. "bull among tawny monkeys" *haripuṃgavaḥ*: D10 and the texts and printed editions of Ct read instead *mārutātmajaḥ*, "son of Māruta."

"with a great upsurge of strength" *baloddharṣaiḥ*: Literally, "with thrills of strength." We agree with Cg, Ct, Cr, and Ck, whose various glosses all mean "increase, access, *or* upsurge of strength (*balodrekaiḥ*—Ct, Ck)." Pagani (1999, p. 1072) reads the compound as a *dvandva*, despite its plural ending, rendering, "*de courage et de force*."

"with its mighty currents" *toyavegaiḥ*: Literally, "with streams *or* currents of water." D9–11 and the texts and printed editions of Ct read instead *vāyuvegaiḥ*, "with the force of the wind."

36. "the mountain slope . . . that foremost of mountains" *parvatataṭa- . . . parvatottamam*: The commentators generally agree that the reference is to Laṅkā's prominent Mount Trikūṭa (see 6.2.10 and note). Cv alone identifies the mountain as Citrakūṭa. At 5.54.9, Hanumān begins his northward leap from Laṅkā to the Indian subcontinent from the summit of Mount Ariṣṭa, which is possibly a name for one of the three peaks of Trikūṭa. See notes to 5.37.49 and 5.54.9.

"crushing" *pīḍayan*: Hanumān's leap and destruction of the mountain parallels similar descriptions at 5.1.11–51 and 5.54.9–15.

"like a second mountain himself" *dvitīya iva parvataḥ*: In the descriptions of Hanumān's previous transoceanic leaps, he is said to have greatly increased his size (5.1.9–10 and 5.54.16) to make the jumps. Here, however, there is no indication of any change in Hanumān's stature. At 1382*, line 8 (see note to verse 41 below), however, Hanumān is specifically said to increase in size.

37. "caved in" *niṣasāda*: Literally, "it sank down, settled."

"Then . . . it was unable to bear its own weight" *na śaśāka tadātmānam soḍhum*: Literally, "it was then unable to endure itself." We agree with Cr, who takes *ātmānam*, "self, body," to mean "its own body (*svaśarīram*)." One could also read the sequence *tadātmānam*, "then . . . itself," as a compound with the sense "his body," referring to the gigantic body of Hanumān.

38. "The tremendous force of that tawny monkey caused that mountain's trees to fall" *tasya petur nagāḥ . . . harivegāt*: Literally, "its immovable ones fell . . . because of the impact of the tawny one." Ct and Ck explain that it is the force of Hanumān's leap [or preparations for leaping—Ck] that is referred to here (*hanumata utpatana*[*sannāha*—Ck]*vegāt*). Cr glosses, "because of the shaking produced by Hanumān's force (*hanumadvegajanitaprakampanād dhetoḥ*)." Cg calibrates the force applied by Hanumān more precisely, glossing, "through the force of the exertion of power suitable for traveling as far as the mountain of herbs, which is situated in the northern portion of the Himalayas (*himavaduttarapradeśasthauṣadhiparvataparyantagamanocitaśaktyāsthānavegāt*)."

"and burst into flame" *ca jajvaluḥ*: Cg, Ct, and Ck explain that it is the friction resulting from the force with which the trees are knocked about that causes them to ignite (*parasparasaṃgharṣajāgnivaśataḥ*—Ct, Ck). Cr has a similar explanation for the fire but seems to understand that it is the peaks themselves or perhaps both the peaks and the trees that burst into flame (*vṛkṣā harivegād dhanumadvegajanitaprakampanād dhetoḥ bhūmau petuḥ śṛṅgāṇi ca vyakīryantāta eva jajvaluḥ parasparasaṃgharṣajanitavahninā didīpire*).

39. As Ct explains, the battlefield is on Mount Trikūṭa, while Laṅkā is set on one of its peaks (*trikūṭasyaiva yuddhabhūmitvāt tacchikharasyaiva ca laṅkātvāt*).

40. "the gates of her buildings" *-gṛhagopurā*: See 6.47.32; 6.55.64; and notes. The compound can also be read as a *dvandva*, as some translators have done, in the sense of "buildings and gates."

"overcome with panic" *trāsākulā*: Cr, the only commentator to remark on this compound, glosses, "filled with terrified *rākṣasas* (*trāsais trastai rākṣasair ākulā vyāptā*)."

"seemed almost to be dancing" *pranṛttevābhavat*: Vālmīki has used the image of dancing elsewhere to express distress. Compare 2.35.32 and note, where the grief-stricken Daśaratha is said to seem almost to be dancing.

41. "that mountain . . . the mountainous . . . the earth" *pṛthivīdharasaṃkāśaḥ . . . dharaṇīdharam / pṛthivīm*: Literally, "resembling a supporter of the earth . . . that supporter of the earth . . . the earth." The poet attempts to give the verse a kinesthetic effect in his repetition of words signifying "earth." A number of manuscripts, including Ś,Ñ,V,B,D2,3,6–13,T2,3,G1, and the texts and printed editions of Ct, Ck, and Cr, intensify this effect still further by reading the synonymous *pṛthivīdharam* for *dharaṇīdharam*.

Following verse 41, D6,T,G1,M3, and the texts and printed editions of Cg, Cm, and Gita Press include a passage of eight lines [1382*]. This passage appears as KK 6.74.43–46; KK (1905) 6.74.42–45; VSP 6.74.42–45; and Gita Press 6.74.42–45. GPP includes the passage, unnumbered, in brackets between its 6.74.41 and 42. "Then the majestic[1] tawny monkey ascended Mount Malaya,[2] which resembled Mount Meru or Mount Mandara and was filled with all sorts of waterfalls.[1–2] It was covered with every type of tree and creeper and was filled with red and blue lotuses in bloom. Sixty leagues in height, it was frequented by gods and *gandharvas*.[3–4] It was frequented by *vidyādharas*, hosts of sages, and *apsarases*. Adorned with many caves, it was crowded with hosts of various wild animals.[5–6] Terrifying all the *yakṣas*, *gandharvas*, and *kinnaras* there, Hanumān, son of Māruta, increased in size,[3] so that he resembled a great cloud. [7–8]"

[1]"majestic" *śrīmān*: M3 and the texts and printed editions of Cm, Cg, and Gita Press read instead *tasmāt*, "from that [i.e., Mt. Trikūṭa]."

[2]"Mount Malaya" *malayaparvatam*: Cg hastens to inform us that this is the mountain of that name in Laṅkā (as opposed to the well-known Malaya mountain range of southern India) (*malayaparvatam ity atra laṅkāmalaya ucyate*). On the existence of a Mt. Malaya in Laṅkā, see 6.55.48 and note.

[3]"increased in size" *vavṛdhe*: See note to verse 36 above.

Compare this passage to similar descriptions of mountains from which Hanumān leaps at 4.66.34–43; 5.1.4–28; and 5.54.9–24.

42. "fearsome" *ugram*: We follow Ck in taking the term adjectivally to modify *mukham*, "mouth." Ct reads it adverbially with *nanāda*, "roared," in the sense of "horribly, frightfully."

"as the gaping mare's head fire that lies beneath the sea" *vaḍavāmukhavat*: See 6.48.49; 6.55.118; and notes. Ct and Ck understand that Hanumān's mouth is blazing fiercely like the *vaḍavāmukha* fire (*vaḍavāmukhavaj jājvalyamānaṃ mukham*).

"terrifying the *rākṣasas*" *trāsayann iva rākṣasān*: Literally, "as if terrifying the *rākṣasas*." We agree with Cg and Cm, both in taking the participle *trāsayan* in accordance with *Pā* 3.2.126 (*lakṣaṇahetvoḥ kriyāyāḥ*) to indicate that Hanumān roars for the purpose of terrifying and in taking the comparative *iva* here as pleonastic (*vākyālaṃkāre*). As the commentators explain, Hanumān's intention is to keep the *rākṣasas* from making another sortie until he can return from his mission with the healing herbs (*yāvad oṣadhyānayanaṃ tāvad rakṣonirgamo mā bhūd iti teṣāṃ trāsārthaṃ nanādeti bhāvaḥ*—so Ct). This idea appears to be confirmed by the reference to the paralysis of the *rākṣasas* mentioned in the following verse.

D1,9–11,G1, and the texts and printed editions of Ct read *rajanīcarān*, "night-roaming *rākṣasas*," for *iva rākṣasān*, thus avoiding the issue of the particle *iva*.

43. "extraordinary" *adbhutam*: Ś,V,B1,3,D2–4,7–12, and the texts and printed editions of Ct read instead *uttamam*, "great, outstanding."

"fiercely roaring" *nānadyamānasya*: The *yaṅanta* participle can be read either as an intensive, as we have done, or as a frequentative, as in the translation of Dutt (1893, p. 1361), who renders, "as he kept emitting cries."

"all the *rākṣasas*" *rākṣasāḥ sarve*: Ñ,B2–4,D1,6,9–11,T2,3,G1, and the texts and printed editions of Ct read instead *rākṣasavyāghrāḥ*, "the tigers among *rākṣasas*."

"were paralyzed with fear" *na śekuḥ spandituṃ bhayāt*: Literally, "they were not able to stir because of fear." D9–11 and the texts and printed editions of Ct read *kvacit*, "at all, anywhere," for the critical edition's *bhayāt*, "out of fear."

44. "Then . . . to Rāma" *[a]tha rāmāya*: Cg notes that, in order to insure the success of his mission, Hanumān offers obeisance to his chosen divinity (Rāma) (*ayaṃ prārīpsitakarmasamāptaye samyagiṣṭadevatānamaskāraḥ*). Compare 5.1.7, where, prior to undertaking his first transoceanic flight, Hanumān makes gestures of obeisance to Sūrya, Indra, Pavana, Brahmā, and the [great] beings (*bhūtebhyaḥ*). At 5.54.9ff., Hanumān omits any obeisance to the divinities. D10,11,T3,M1,2, and the texts and printed editions of Ct read instead *samudrāya*, "to Samudra."

"turned his thoughts" *samaihata*: Literally, "he wished, longed for." We follow the interpretation of Ct, who glosses, "he thought about (*cintitavān*)." Cr, who reads a variant, *samīhata*, corrects it to our reading and glosses, "he undertook, set about (*akarot*)."

"that vital mission" *paraṃ karma*: Literally, "supreme action *or* task."

45. "Extending his tail, which resembled a serpent, crouching down, laying back his ears, and opening his mouth, which was like the gaping mare's head fire that lies beneath the sea" *puccham udyamya bhujaṃgakalpaṃ vinamya pṛṣṭhaṃ śravaṇe nikuñcya / vivṛtya vaktraṃ vaḍavāmukhābham*: Literally, "having raised his serpentlike tail, having bent his back, having contracted his ears, and having opened his mouth, which was like the mouth of *vaḍavā*." These movements that Hanumān makes in preparation for his leap are also mentioned in connection with his earlier leap at the opening of the *Sundarakāṇḍa* (5.1.30–35). On the basis of the description at 5.1.32, where Hanumān

is said to have "crouched down on his posterior while contracting his legs (*sasāda ca kapiḥ kaṭyāṃ caraṇau saṃcukoca ca*)," we believe that the poet is referring to the same action when he describes the monkey as "bending or curving his back." We have therefore translated, "crouching down." For *vaḍavāmukha-*, see note to verse 42 above.

Cg attempts to explain the purpose or significance of each of Hanumān's actions. The raising of his tail, he says, indicates the excess of his excitement. The bending of his back indicates the holding of his breath in preparation for leaping into the sky. The laying back of his ears is to inflame or enhance his strength, and the opening of his mouth is a sign of determination. (*pucchodyamanenotsāhātireka uktaḥ. pṛṣṭhavinamanenākāśagamanānukūlaprāṇavāyunirodha uktaḥ. śravaṇanikuñcanena baloddīpanam. mukhavyādānenābhiniveśaḥ.*)

"Hanumān . . . with terrifying force" *saḥ . . . sa caṇḍavegaḥ*: Literally, "he . . . he, whose speed *or* impact was fierce." Cv is the only commentator to note the apparent redundancy of the repeated pronoun. He solves the problem by taking the second occurrence as part of the compound, reading *sacaṇḍavegaḥ* and glossing, "with terrifying speed (*caṇḍavegasahitaḥ*)."

The meter is *upajāti*.

46. This verse echoes the elaborate description at 5.1.41–51 and the brief description at 5.54.20, where the blossoming trees of Mount Mahendra and Mount Ariṣṭa, respectively, are swept up in the wake of Hanumān's jump and then fall, respectively, into the sea or onto the ground.

"lesser monkeys" *prākṛtavānarān*: Literally, "ordinary monkeys." The commentators agree that this term refers not to the rank and file of the monkey army but rather to the indigenous species of the region (*trikūṭavane nityavāsān*—Ct). This expression was used earlier by Sītā in differentiating Hanumān from ordinary primates. See 5.34.8.

The meter is *upajāti*.

47. "Garuḍa, foe of serpents" *bhujaṃgāri-*: Literally, "the foe of serpents." The reference, as all commentators agree, is to Garuḍa.

"Mount Meru, the prominent king of the mountains" *meruṃ nagarājam agryam*: Commentators who share this reading are disturbed by the reference to Mount Meru, since Jāmbavān's explicit instructions to Hanumān in verses 29–31 above were to head for the Himalayas and there locate the mountain lying between Mount Kailāsa and Mount Ṛṣabha. The epithet "king of the mountains (*nagarāja*)" is, moreover, most frequently applied to the Himalaya (cf. *KumāSaṃ* 1.1). Cr resolves the seeming contradiction by saying that the Himalaya is intended by the term "Meru," since the former is so much like the latter (*nagarājam ata evāgryaṃ mukhyaṃ meruṃ tatsadṛśaṃ himavantam ity arthaḥ*). Cv, Cg, and Cm explain that Mount Meru is close to Mount Kailāsa (*meruṃ kailāsapārśvavartinam*). All three add that there is another Mount Meru that is adjacent to Himalaya (*asti hy anyo himavadanantaraparvato meruḥ*). Cm and Cg then offer two alternative explanations. One is that Himalaya, the king of the mountains, is called Meru because it is in the direction characterized or defined by Meru (*yadvā merūpalakṣitadiśi sthitaṃ nagarājaṃ himavantam*). The second is that Himalaya is called Meru because it is like Meru and so receives that secondary or metaphorical designation as in the expression "the young man is a lion." (*yadvā merutulyaṃ himavantam. siṃho māṇavaka itivad gauṇaprayogaḥ.*) Cg offers an additional explanation to the effect that Hanumān is heading in the general direction of Mount Meru, in other words, north. (*yadvā merum uddiśya jagāma. uttarāṃ diśam uddiśya jagāmety arthaḥ.*) D9–11 and the texts and printed editions of Ct avoid this entire issue by substituting *śailam*, "mountain," for *merum*.

"drawing, so it seemed, the directions in his wake" *diśaḥ prakarṣann iva*: Literally, "as if dragging the directions." For *prakarṣan*, "drawing," Cr glosses, "as if tossing aside (*prakṣipann iva*)," while Cg understands, "shaking (*kampayan*)."

The meter is *upendravajrā*.

48. The poet does not tell us whether the agitation of the ocean is its natural state, as described, for example, at 6.4.77–88, or is caused by the rush of wind generated by Hanumān's speed, as at 5.1.64–67. Gita Press (1969, vol. 3, p. 1680), the only source to offer an opinion on this, puts in parentheses "by the wind generated by his movement."

"Then ... tossed violently about" *tadā bhṛśaṃ bhrāmita-*: D9–11 and the texts and printed editions of Ct read instead *tadambhasā*, "by its waters," for *tadā bhṛṣam*, "then violently."

The meter is *upajāti*.

49. "forests" *vṛkṣagaṇān*: Literally, "groups of trees." D9–11 and the texts and printed editions of Ct read *pakṣi-*, "birds," for *vṛkṣa-*, "trees," lending the compound the sense "flocks of birds."

"prosperous lands" *sphītañ janān*: Literally, "numerous *or* prosperous people." Since the list otherwise only contains geographical features that are visible from high altitudes, we agree with the commentators, who gloss, "countryside, regions (*janapadān*)." Here, *janapada* should probably be taken in its sense of "countryside," as opposed to "city (*pura-*)," which precedes it. All translators consulted follow the commentators' suggestion here with the exceptions of Gorresio (1858, vol. 10, p. 69), Roussel (1903, vol. 3, p. 246), and Pagani (1999, p. 1072), who take the term to refer to people or populations.

"Hanumān, whose swiftness equaled that of his father" *pitṛtulyavegaḥ*: Literally, "whose speed was equal to his father's."

"flew ... onward" *jagāma*: Literally, "he went."

The meter is *upajāti*.

50. "tirelessly" *gataśramaḥ*: Literally, "whose fatigue had departed." Roussel (1903, vol. 3, p. 246) appears to misunderstand the compound, rendering, "*il se fatiguait.*" Shastri (1959, vol. 3, p. 217) seems to echo this in rendering, "strove."

"Then that foremost of tawny monkeys spied Himalaya, greatest of mountains." *sa dadarśa hariśreṣṭho himavantaṃ nagottamam*: The reading of this line is problematic. Only two of the manuscripts (M1,2) cited in the critical apparatus appear to have this precise reading. The texts and printed editions of Cg, Cm, Ck, and Ct read instead *dadarśa sahasā cāpi himavantaṃ mahākapiḥ*, "suddenly the great monkey spied Himalaya." This reading appears to have the strongest textual support, as it is read by the vast majority of northern and southern manuscripts (Ñ,B2–4,D1,4,6,7,9–11,T,G,M3,5). Ś,Ñ,V,B,D,T1,G,M3,5 all read *mahākapiḥ*, "great monkey." The choice of the critical editors is difficult to understand.

Following 50ab, D5 (line 1),D6,7,9–11,S insert a passage of four lines [1384*]: "Swift and heroic Hanumān, whose valor equaled that of his father, [flew on tirelessly].[1] Endowed with tremendous speed, Hanumān Māruti, tiger among monkeys, flew onward like Māruta himself,[1] making the directions resound with the sound of his passing.[2][2–3] Recalling the words of Jāmbavān,[3] Māruti, endowed with the speed of the wind[4] . . . [4]"

[1]"like Māruta himself" *māruto yathā*: Literally, "like Māruta." D10,11, and the texts and printed editions of Ct read instead *vātaraṃhasā*, "with the speed of the wind."

[2]"with the sound of his passing" *śabdena*: Literally, "with the sound." Although several of the translators consulted see this as a reference to the roaring of Hanumān, we see no reason that this is necessarily correct. The force of the simile seems instead to point to the rushing sound of his rapid flight, which is similar to the howling of the wind.

[3]"Recalling the words of Jāmbavān" *smarañ jāmbavato vākyam*: As several of the commentators note, Hanumān must recall Jāmbavān's instructions in order to prevent himself from overshooting the mountain of herbs in his tremendous speed (*tadvākyaṃ smaranaṃ vegavaśād oṣadhyādiparvatam atītya gamananivṛttyārtham*—so Ct).

[4]"endowed with the speed of the wind" *vātaraṃhasā*: We follow Cg in supplying "characterized by *or* endowed with (*upalakṣita iti śeṣaḥ*)." D7,10–11, and the texts and printed editions of Ct read instead *bhīmavikramaḥ*, "of fearsome valor."

51. "It had . . . It was endowed with": The verse lacks a finite verb. As it stands, *pādas* ab must be construed with the accusative *himavantam* in verse 50d above. We have also added the phrase "It was endowed" to give meaning to the instrumental *śikharaiḥ*, "with peaks," of *pāda* d.

Following verse 51, D5–7,9–11,S insert a passage of one line [1385*] that provides the missing verbal elements: "He reached that foremost of mountains that was beautified with various trees."

52."formidable" *-ghora-*: D6,7,10,11,T2,3,G2, and the texts and printed editions of Ct and Cr read instead *-hema-*, "golden."

"the hosts of the foremost gods and seers" *surarṣisaṃghottama-*: Literally, "the most excellent assembly of gods and seers." We follow Ct and Ck in reading the compound as a *paranipāta* (*uttamasurarṣisaṃghair ity arthaḥ*).

The meter is *upendravajrā*.

53. "the abode of Brahmā" *brahmakośam*: We follow Cg, who cites the *Ratnamālā* in support of his contention that the polysemic term *kośa* should be taken here in the sense of "house, abode (*gṛhe*)." Cg also understands that the divinity referred to here is the classical four-faced creator god, Brahmā. (*brahmaṇaś caturmukhasya kośo gṛham. kośo 'strī kuḍmale 'rthaughe guhyadeśe 'ṇḍaśirṣayoḥ / gṛhe dehe pustakaughe peṭyām asipidhānaka iti ratnamālā.*) Ct, Ck, and Cr understand the term to refer to the place of Lord Hiryaṇyagarbha, another form of Brahmā as a creator divinity. They support this claim by citing *Taittirīyāraṇyaka* 2.19.1 (*prapadye brahma prapadye brahmakośam*—"I resort to Brahmā, I resort to Brahmā's abode"). On that passage, Sāyaṇa glosses, "the world of Brahmā (*brahmalokaḥ*)."

Cm and Cg believe that this and all the sites mentioned in this and the following verse are the names of the ashrams Hanumān sees in verse 52. (*dṛṣṭānām āśramāṇāṃ nāmāny anukrāmati sa brahmakośam ityādinā. brahmakośādīny āśramāṇi*—so Cm.)

"the abode of Hiraṇyagarbha in his silver-naveled form" *rajatālayam*: Literally, "the abode of silver *or* the silver abode." Cg understands this to be a kenning for Mount

Kailāsa, which is sometimes called "Silver *or* White Mountain (*rajatācala*)." This interpretation is perhaps supported by the fact that a significant number of mostly northern manuscripts read either [*a*]*calam* or *girim*, "mountain," for [*ā*]*layam*, "abode." Nonetheless, we believe that because Hanumān is explicitly said to spy Mount Kailāsa first in verse 55, Cg's identification is problematic. Raghunathan (1982, vol. 3, p. 219) is the only translator to follow Cg's interpretation, rendering, "the silver mountain (Kailāsa)." See note to verse 55 below. This leaves us with the perhaps speculative interpretation of Ck, Ct, and Cr, who understand *rajata* to refer to a different form of Hiraṇyagarbha known as *rajatanābhi*, "having a silver navel" (*hiraṇyagarbhāparamūrte rajatanābheḥ sthānam*—so Ct).

"the place where Rudra loosed his arrows" *rudraśarapramokṣam*: Literally, "the loosing of Rudra's arrow[s]." Commentators disagree as to the precise mythological reference. According to Ct, Ck, and Cr, the term refers to the spot from which Rudra shot his arrow[s] in order to destroy Tripura (the Triple City of the *asuras*) (*yatra sthāne sthitvā rudras tripurasaṃhārāya śaraṃ mumoca tat sthānam*—so Ck, Ct). On Tripura, see note to 6.59.73. Cg believes that the reference is to Rudra's archery range, where he shoots his arrows for sport (*rudraśarāḥ pramokṣyante līlārthaṃ yasmiṃs tad rudraśarapramokṣaṃ sthānam*). According to Gorresio (1858, vol. 10, p. 290, footnote 33), Cl, for whom the critical reading is a variant, glosses, "the place in which Rudra loosed his arrows for the destruction of Kāma (*rudrasya kandarpanāśāya śarapramokṣo yasmiṃs tat sthānam*)."

"the abode of Hayānana the horse-faced god" *hayānanam*: Literally, "the horse-faced one." According to the commentators, this is the abode of Hayagrīva, literally, "the horse-necked one," one of the incarnations of Viṣṇu. Cg adds that it is the place at which Hayagrīva was worshiped or propitiated (*hayagrīvārādhanasthānam*).

"the . . . place where Brahmā's head fell" *brahmaśiraḥ*: Literally, "Brahmā's head." Like Raghunathan (1982, vol. 3, p. 219), we have followed the interpretation of Cg, who believes that the reference is to the spot where Brahmā's head fell when it was cut off by Rudra [as a punishment for the creator god's incest with his own daughter] (*rudranikṛttabrahmaśiraḥprakṣepasthānam*). This mythic episode is narrated widely in the vedic and post-vedic literature See, for example, *AitBr* 3.33; *ŚatBr* 1.7.4.1ff., 14.4.2.1ff.; *MatsyaP* 3.32ff.; and *BhāgP* 3.12.28ff. We believe this interpretation best fits the context, with its references to spots made sacred by the dwelling or mythic adventures of significant deities. Ck, Ct, and Cr believe that the reference is to the abode of the divinity who governs Brahmā's weapon (*brahmāstradevatā tatsthānam*).

"the servants of Vaivasvata" *vaivasvatakiṃkarān*: We understand that the reference is to Yama Vaivasvata, the god of death. Cg understands that the *grāmaṇīs* are the servants associated with Vivasvat (*vivasvatsaṃbandhikiṃkarān*). Cg elaborates, "these are the *grāmaṇīs* [*yakṣas*?], etc., who serve [Yama] on the new moon day and stay here in order to rest (*grāmaṇyādīn māsāntaparicārakān viśramārtham atra sthitān*). Cf. note to 6.92.19. Raghunathan (1982, vol. 3, p. 219) takes the patronymic Vaivasvata in the sense of its underlying form Vivasvant, an epithet of the sun. He translates, "he saw too the servents [*sic*] of the sun." Vaivasvata is also the name of the seventh of the fourteen Manus who preside over the cosmic ages known as *manvantaras*.

The meter is *upajāti*.

54. "He saw . . . He also saw" *dadarśa*: Literally, "he saw."

"the place where the *vajra* was presented" *vajrālayam*: Literally, "the place of the *vajra*." Cg, the only commentator to remark on this reading, explains that this is the spot where Brahmā presented the *vajra* to Indra (*indrāya brahmaṇā vajrapradānasthānam*). D10,11, and the texts and printed editions of Ct read instead *vahnyālayam*, "the abode of Vahni, [the god of fire]."

"the abode of Kubera Vaiśravaṇa" *vaiśravaṇālayam*: Literally, "the abode of Vaiśravaṇa."

"the abode of the sun—resplendent as the sun itself" *sūryaprabhaṃ sūryanibandhanam*: In keeping with the tenor of the passage, we take *nibandhanam* in its sense of "abode, residence." Commentators offer other mythological or cosmological explanations. Thus Ct, Ck, and Cr gloss, "the place at which the [seven—Ck] suns meet ([*sapta*]*sūryāṇāṃ yatra sthāne nibandhanaṃ samāveśas tat sthānam*)." Here these commentators understand *nibandhanam* to mean "meeting place (*samāveśaḥ*)." It is because all the suns meet at this one spot that it has such a bright solar radiance according to Ct and Ck (*ata eva tat sūryaprabham*). Cg takes *nibandhanam* in its common sense of "binding, fastening," alluding to an obscure mythological episode in which, according to him, Viśvakarman bound the sun so as to place it upon a touchstone in order to please his wife, Chāyā (*chāyādevīprītaye viśvakarmaṇā śāṇāropaṇāya sūryanibandhanasthānam*). This interpretation is represented in the translation of Gita Press (1969, vol. 3, p. 1681). It is apparently also behind Raghunathan's (1982, vol. 3, p. 219) translation: "the place where the sun had been made to stand still." Because of this interpretation, Cg takes the adjective *sūryaprabham*, "resplendent as the sun itself," with *vaiśravaṇālayam*, "the abode of Vaiśravaṇa" (*sūryaprabham iti vaiśravaṇālayaviśeṣaṇam*). This interpretation is followed by both Gita Press (1969, vol. 3, p. 1681) and Raghunathan (1982, vol. 3, p. 219).

"the throne of Brahmā" *brahmāsanam*: Literally, "Brahmā's seat." We follow the first of Cg's two alternate explanations, understanding the reference to be to the throne created for Brahmā to view and be seen by the hosts of the gods (*devagaṇasaṃdarśanāya kṛtaṃ brahmaṇaḥ siṃhāsanam*). Cg's second alternative is that this is the place or abode of the brahmans, i.e., the seers (*brahmaṇām ṛṣīṇām āsanaṃ sthānaṃ vā*). D6,10,11,M1,2, and the texts and printed editions of Ck and Ct read instead *-ālayam*, "abode," for *-āsanam*, "seat," yielding the sense "the abode of Brahmā." This, however, presents a problem of redundancy in light of the reference to the *brahmakośa*, "the abode of Brahmā," in verse 53. Ck and Ct solve the problem by claiming that the present reference is to the four-faced form of Brahmā (*caturmukhabrahmasthānam*), as opposed to Brahmā in his form of Hiraṇyagarbha.

"the place of Śaṅkara's bow" *śaṅkarakārmukam*: Literally, "Śaṅkara's bow." We follow Cg, who says that the reference is to the place or repository of Śaṅkara's bow (*śaṅkarakārmukaṃ tatsthānam ity arthaḥ*). Ck and Ct name the weapon, noting that this is the place or repository of the king of divine weapons, [Śiva's bow called] Pināka (*pinākāstrarājasthānam*).

"and the very navel of the earth" *nābhiṃ ca vasuṃdharāyāḥ*: Literally, "the navel of the bearer of wealth." This term is not common in the literature, and the commentators differ as to its referent. Ck and Ct understand it to be the abode of Prajāpati, which is known as "the navel of the earth" (*bhūnābhisaṃjñaṃ prājāpatyaṃ sthānam*). Cg, however, understands the reference to be to the fissure [in the earth] that marks the entrance to the underworld Pātāla (*pātālapraveśarandhram*). This interpretation is explicitly followed only by Gita Press (1969, vol. 3, p. 1681). Dutt (1893, p. 1363) in footnote "j" offers the interpretation of Ct and Ck. Raghunathan (1982, vol. 3, p. 219) translates as do we. Roussel (1903, vol. 3, p. 246), followed by Shastri (1959, vol. 3, p. 218) and Pagani (1999, p. 1073), understands, "*le centre de la terre.*"

The meter is *upajāti*.

55. "Then he saw . . . And, at last, he spied" *sa . . . dadarśa*: Literally, "he saw." We have broken the sentence into two syntactic units for the sake of readability.

"the prominent Mount Kailāsa" *kailāsam agryam*: Cg, who had understood *rajatālayam*, literally, "silver abode *or* abode of silver," which we translate as "the abode of Hiraṇyagarbha in his silver-naveled form" (see note to verse 53 above) to refer to Mount Kailāsa, is now confronted with an apparent redundancy. He explains the repetition by saying that "although Kailāsa (i.e., *rajatālaya*) was enumerated in the list of holy places starting with Brahmā's abode, it is mentioned again now in order to point it out in accordance with the way in which Jāmbavān had instructed [Hanumān] (*brahmādisthāneṣu rajatālayam iti pariganitam api jāmbavadupadiṣṭaprakāreṇa darśanāya punar āha*)." Ś,Ñ,V,B1,2,4,D1–4,7–12,G1,2, and the texts and printed editions of Ct and Cr read *ugram*, literally, "fearsome, formidable," for *agryam*, "prominent." Translations that follow the text of Ct generally accept this sense of the word, rendering, "fierce, steep, terrible, etc." Cr, however, takes the term to be a reference to Śiva, i.e., "the fearsome one." In this he is followed by Gita Press (1969, vol. 3, p. 1681), which renders, "Ugra (the mighty Lord Śiva)."

"the rock face of the Himalayas" *himavacchilām*: The exact reference here is unclear. Cv, Cg, and Cm, whom we follow, understand the reference to be to a simple geographical feature, some sort of rocky face or outcropping on the side of Mount Kailāsa (*kailāsapārśve kaścic chilāviśeṣaḥ*). Cv and Cm add that it is well known [from *itihāsa*—so Cm] that this spot is the source of the river Citraśilā. A river of this name is included in the lengthy list of rivers given by Sañjaya at *Mahābhārata* 6.9. The reference to this river is found in the Citraśāla edition of the *Mahābhārata* at 6.9.30. Ck, Ct, and Cr, however, understand the reference to be to the stone seat upon which Śiva practices his ascetic meditations (*bhagavato rudrasya tapaḥsamādhipīṭham*).

"and . . . Ṛṣabha" *tatharṣabham*: This mountain and Kailāsa constitute the two landmarks mentioned by Jāmbavān in verse 30, whereby Hanumān could locate the mountain of healing herbs. D5,7,10,11,T,G2,3,M1,2, and the texts and printed editions of Ct and Cr read instead *taṃ vai vṛṣam*, literally, "and that Vṛṣa *or* that bull." This variant has led to a difference of opinion among the commentators who share it, since the word *vṛṣa*, like *ṛṣabha*, means "bull." Ck and Ct clearly understand this to be a proper name, a variant of Mount Ṛṣabha, since they note that it was mentioned by Jāmbavān (*jāmbavadupadiṣṭam*). Cr, however, in keeping with his reading, noted above, of the adjective *ugra* to refer to Śiva, understands this to be a reference to the bull Nandi, who serves as Śiva's vehicle (*vṛṣaṃ śambhor yānam*). This interpretation is followed in the translation of Gita Press (1969, vol. 3, p. 1681). Dutt (1893, p. 1363) seems to confuse the two interpretations, translating, "and that bull," but noting, "which had been mentioned by Jāmbavān," despite the fact that Jāmbavān, of course, has said nothing about a bull. Shastri (1959, vol. 3, p. 218) also tries to negotiate the two positions, translating, "and Vrisha," but noting, "the name literally means—The Bull of Shiva."

"the . . . golden mountain" *kāñcanaśailam*: This is apparently a description of Mount Ṛṣabha, which was clearly described as golden in verse 30 above. Most translators agree that this refers to Mount Ṛṣabha (or Vṛṣa). Gita Press (1969, vol. 3, p. 1681) follows Cr in taking Vṛṣa as Śiva's bull and clearly understands this as a reference to Mount Ṛṣabha, adding the name. Cr, whose reading and interpretation of *vṛṣam* eliminates Mount Ṛṣabha from the verse, as noted above, takes the term to be a *bahuvrīhi* compound modifying Mount Kailāsa. The sense is "Kailāsa with its mass of golden boulders (*kāñcanaḥ śailaḥ śilāsamūho yasmiṃs taṃ kailāsam*)." Cg notes that the term "golden mountain" was applied earlier to Mount Meru (see Cg on 6.19.13–15), and he therefore appears to understand that the same mountain is intended here. This idea is reflected in the translation of Raghunathan (1982, vol. 3, p. 219), who renders, "the great mountain of gold, Meru."

"all herbs...herbs of healing" *-sarvauṣadhi-...sarvauṣadhi-*: We follow Cg, who distinguishes between merely luminescent herbs, for example, the *tṛṇajyotiḥ* (also known as the *jyotiṣmatī*), and the life-saving medicinal herbs, such as the *mṛtasaṃjīvanī*. (*saṃdīptābhī rātrau jvalantībhiḥ sarvābhir oṣadhībhis tṛṇajyotirbhiḥ saṃpradīptaṃ samyakprakāśamānam. sarvauṣadhiparvatendraṃ mṛtasaṃjīvanyādisarvauṣadhiyuktaparvatendraṃ dadarśa.*)

The meter is *upajāti*.

Following 55ab, D7 (after verse 54) and KK insert a passage of four lines in the *upajāti* meter [1386*] (= KK 6.74.62 bracketed): "And there he saw Vighneśvara together with Nandikeśvara, as well as Skanda, surrounded by the hosts of the gods. And that monkey of outstanding strength also saw Umā with her daughter[1] disporting herself with maidens."

[1]"with her daughter" *sakanyām*: The reference is obscure. The literature does not seem to know of a daughter of Umā. The possible sense "with her maidens" is obviated by the following term *kanyakābhiḥ*, "with her maidens." One might also separate the words *sa* and *kanyām* to yield the sense "he [Hanumān saw] the maiden [Umā]." KK avoids the problem by reading instead *sudurgām*, "the very unapproachable [Umā]."

56. "Hanumān, son of Vāsava's messenger, the wind god" *vāsavadūtasūnuḥ*: Literally, "the son of Vāsava's messenger." There is no agreement among the commentators as to why or under what circumstances Vāyu should be identified as a messenger of Indra. Explanations vary widely. Ck and Ct understand the reference to be to the role of the wind in impelling or driving Indra in the form of clouds (*vāsavasya meghasvarūpiṇo devarājasya dūtaḥ prerakaḥ*). Cr thinks that the reference derives from the antagonism between Indra and Vāyu after the former had struck down the young Hanumān with his *vajra* and, in retaliation, the wind god had inflicted (*tanoti*) suffering (*duḥkham*) on Indra. Cr takes *dūta*, "messenger," to mean "one who inflicts suffering" (*vāsava indro 'pi dūto hanumaduddeśyakavajranipātānantarakāle paritāpito yena kiṃca vāsavasya duḥkhaṃ paritāpaṃ tanoti sa vāyur ity arthaḥ*). See notes to 6.19.13–15. Cm understands that Vāyu acts as a substitute for Vāsava in driving the clouds, etc. (*vāyor vāsavadūtatvaṃ vāsavādeśena meghādiprerakatvāt*). Cg echoes Cm's opinion, adding that it is because of this relationship that Vāyu, acting at the behest of Vāsava, presents a splendid necklace to Rāma at the time of his consecration (6.116.60) (*ata evābhiṣekasamaya indreṇa prerito hāraṃ rāmāyopāharat*). Cs takes the compound *vāsava-*

dūta- as a *bahuvrīhi* in the sense of "the son of him who has Vāsava for his agent, that is, his servant (*vāsavo dūtaḥ proktakārī yasya saḥ tasya sūnuḥ*)" but offers no explanation of the relationship.

"glowing as if with flames of fire" *analaraśmidīptam*: Literally, "blazing with flames of fire." The mountain is not actually on fire but merely illuminated by the phosphorescent glow of the healing herbs. D7,10,11, and the texts and printed editions of Ct and Cr read instead *-rāśi-*, "masses," for *-raśmi-*, "flames, rays."

"began to search" *vicayaṃ cakāra*: Literally, "he made a collection *or* search." The commentators make it clear that we are to take *vicaya* in its sense of "search," since, as the following verses indicate, Hanumān is unable actually to gather any individual herbs.

The meter is *upajāti*.

57. "for thousands of leagues" *yojanasahasrāṇi samatītya*: Literally, "having exceeded thousands of *yojanas*." Ct notes that the word "thousands" here should be taken by secondary meaning to indicate "many" (*sahasraśabdo 'nekopalakṣaṇam*). Cr understands, "many thousands of leagues (*anekasahasrayojanāni*)." Cs specifies, "fifty thousand leagues (*pañcāśatsahasrayojanāni*)." Cg remarks that this reference indicates that Hanumān is tireless (*anena śramarahitatvam uktam*).

58. "recognizing the purpose for which he had come" *vijñāyārthinam āyāntam*: Literally, "having known that a seeker was coming."

"made themselves invisible" *jagmur adarśanam*: Literally, "they went to non-sight."

59. "Losing patience" *amṛṣyamāṇaḥ*: Literally, "not enduring *or* tolerating."

The meter is *upendravajrā*.

60. "What" *kim*: Cr understands *kim* in its pejorative sense, glossing, "despicable (*kutsitam*)." This interpretation is represented in the translation of Gita Press (1969, vol. 3, p. 1682), which renders, "this kind of determination of yours is despicable." Ct understands, "on the strength of what do you show this kind of indifference? (*evaṃprakāram etad audāsīnyaṃ kiṃbalād ity arthaḥ*)."

"in your lack of compassion toward Rāghava" *yad rāghave nāsi kṛtānukampaḥ*: Literally, "in that you are not one who has made any compassion with regard to Rāghava."

The meter is *upajāti*.

61. "began to slide" *calita-*: Literally, "moved." All but two manuscripts (G2,3) collated for the critical edition and all printed editions consulted read instead *jvalita-*, "blazing, flaming." The idea is that, as indicated earlier, the violent wrenching and friction of the rocks and trees cause sparks and fire (see verse 38 above). All translations consulted render this variant. It is astonishing that, given the near unanimity of the recensions, the critical editors should have chosen this extremely weak reading.

The meter is *upendravajrā*.

62. "that hero, whose fearsome power was like that of Garuḍa" *garuḍogravīryaḥ*: Literally, "with Garuḍa's fearsome power." The simile is perhaps an oblique reference to Garuḍa's role in the similar revival of Rāma and Lakṣmaṇa in *sarga* 40.

"the worlds, together with the gods and the lords of the gods" *lokān sasurān surendrān*: The collocation is unusual and awkward. It is also textually weak. Ś,Ñ2,B1,4,D1–5,8–10,12,13,T,G,M3, and the texts and printed editions of Cg, Cm, Cr, Gita Press, Gorresio, and Lahore all read instead *sasurāsurendrān*, "together with the lords of the gods and *asuras*." Among the translators consulted, only Roussel

(1903, vol. 3, p. 246), Shastri (1959, vol. 3, p. 219), and Pagani (1999, p. 1073) render Ct's reading.

"creatures of the air" *khacaraiḥ*: Literally, "going *or* moving in the sky." According to Cr, this refers to the gods, etc. (*devādibhiḥ*).

The meter is *upajāti*.

63. "the sun's path" *bhāskarādhvānam*: Literally, "the path of the maker of light." This is the route by which Hanumān came to the Himalayas in verse 50. Cg takes the term to be a kenning for the sky *or* upper atmosphere (*antarikṣam*). Normally we render the kenning *bhāskara* as "the sun, bringer of light." Since, however, the poet uses the term no fewer than four times in this verse, we have avoided this for brevity.

The meter is *upajāti*.

64. "Holding that mountain" *tena śailena*: Literally, "with that mountain."

"the . . . son of Vāyu, bearer of scents" *gandhavahātmajaḥ*: Literally, "son of the bearer of scents." See verses 34; 68; and notes.

"in the sky" *khe*: In addition to the obvious interpretation shared by all the other commentators and translators consulted, Cs proposes taking *kha* in its sense of "sense organ," which, in this case, he takes to mean Viṣṇu's hand (*khe hastātmaka indriye*).

"holding aloft" *uddhṛtena*: Literally, "held aloft." Only two manuscripts (M1,2) appear to support this reading. The majority of the other manuscripts and all printed editions read instead *arpitena*, "placed." Several of the commentators add "in his hand (*svakare*—so Ct)." It is unclear why the critical editors chose this very weak reading.

"thousand-bladed" *sahasradhāreṇa*: Literally, "of a thousand edges."

The meter is *upajāti*.

65. "Then . . . they roared" *tadā vineduḥ*: Cg is evidently concerned about how the monkeys, who had been described as gravely wounded, are capable of uttering such hearty roars. He explains that we are to understand that they have all been revivified by catching the scent [of the healing herbs] from afar (*anena dūrād eva gandhāghrāṇena sarve jīvitā iti gamyate*). Cs has a similar idea, noting that what is suggested here is that the monkeys recover their bodily consciousness and are made whole by the mere touch of the wind (presumably blowing from the mountain of healing herbs) (*vinedur anena vātamātrasparśena gātrasmṛtir arogatā ca kapīnāṃ jāta iti dhvanyate*). M3 and the texts and printed editions of Cg and Cm read instead *vinedur uccaiḥ*, "they roared loudly."

"the *rākṣasas* in Laṅkā" *laṅkālayāḥ*: Literally, "those whose abode was Laṅkā."

The meter is *upajāti*.

66. "great Hanumān" *mahātmā*: Literally, "the great one."

"on splendid Mount Trikūṭa: *śailottame*: Literally, "on that best of mountains." As Cg reminds us, the reference is to a peak of Mount Trikūṭa (*trikūṭaśikhare*). See notes to verse 39 above.

"bowing his head in respectful salutation" *śirasābhivādya*: Literally, "saluting with his head." See note to verse 26 above.

The meter is *upajāti*.

67. "freed . . . from their arrow wounds" *viśalyau*: Literally, "arrow-free." See note to verse 28 above.

The meter is *upajāti*.

Following verse 67, D1,5–7,9–11,S insert a passage of eight lines [1396*], of which the first four are an *upajāti* verse: "All those heroic tawny monkeys that had been struck down, now healed of their arrow wounds and made whole in an instant by the smell of those wonderful healing herbs, awoke like sleepers when the night is over. [1–4] Ever since the tawny monkeys and *rākṣasas* had begun to fight in Laṅkā, the *rākṣasas* slain in battle by those elephants among monkeys had all been cast into the sea, as soon as they were killed,[1] on the orders of Rāvaṇa for the sake of honor. [2][5–8]"

[1]"slain . . . as soon as they were killed" *hatā hatāḥ*: Literally, "slain, slain." As Ct points out, this is an example of *vīpsā*, "repetition," used to indicate successive or continuous action. As an alternative, several of the commentators take the sequence as a compound, *hatāhatāḥ*, in the sense of "slain and non-slain," to mean those who are mortally wounded. The idea here is that if they are cast into the sea, what then to say of those who are actually dead. (*hatāhatā mumūrṣāvasthāḥ. kiṃ punar mṛtā iti bhāvaḥ*—so Cg.)

[2]"cast into the sea . . . for the sake of honor" *mānārtham . . . kṣipyante . . . sāgare*: The commentators use this passage as an explanation of why the wafting fragrance of the healing herbs does not revive the slain *rākṣasas* along with the fallen monkeys and humans. (*yathā tathā vānarāḥ pratibuddhā evaṃ rākṣasāḥ kimiti na pratibuddhās tatrāha*—so Cm.) To rationalize this, the commentators offer various explanations of the term *mānārtham*. We follow the second explanation of Cm, who understands *māna* in the sense of "pride (*abhimāna*)," arguing that Rāvaṇa disposes of his dead so that his enemies will not think that so many of his troops have been killed (*yadvā māno 'bhimānas tadarthaṃ rākṣasā bahavo hatā iti sarve jñāsyanti tadabhimānād aprakaṭanāyety arthaḥ*). Ct, Cg, and Cm (first alternative) take *māna*, "honor," in its sense of "measure" and *artha*, "for the sake of," in its lexical sense of "prevention." The idea here is that Rāvaṇa, in his desire to retain his sovereignty, has had the dead *rākṣasas* cast into the sea to prevent Rāma's forces from measuring, that is, realizing, the extent of his losses and thus attacking the city, which would now be poorly defended. (*mānārtham. arthaśabdo nivṛttivācī. śatrūṇāṃ hatarākṣaseyattājñānābhāvārtham ity arthaḥ. tatparijñāne tv avaśiṣṭabalasyālpīyastvaṃ jñātvā vānarā laṅkāṃ praviśeyuḥ. te mā pravekṣyann ity etadartho 'yaṃ rāvaṇasyeśvarecchayā vicāraḥ*—so Ct.) See note to 6.108.19, where Ct alludes to this reference as an explanation of why the slain *rākśasas* are not revived at the same time that Indra resurrects the fallen monkeys at the end of the war.

68. "immensely powerful" *udagravīryaḥ*: D9–11,G1,M1,2,5, and the texts and printed editions of Ct read *-vegaḥ*, "speed," for *-vīryaḥ*, lending the compound the sense "immensely swift."

"the son of Vāyu, bearer of scents" *gandhavahātmajaḥ*: Literally, "the son of the bearer of scents." This is the third use in this *sarga* of the relatively rare epithet "bearer of scents" for Vāyu. It seems likely that the poet uses it here because of the context in which the wafting of the scent of the healing herbs is so critical to the narrative. Vāyu's role in supporting his son's mission is thus emphasized. See verses 34; 64; and notes.

The meter is *upendravajrā*.

According to Ct, the revival of Rāma, Lakṣmaṇa, and the monkeys occurs on the eighth day of the dark half of the month Āśvina (*āśvinakṛṣṇāṣṭamyām idam*). See note to 6.4.4.

Sarga 62

1. "sensibly" *arthyam*: Literally, "significant, sensible." We follow the commentators who gloss, "not deviating from sense or sound policy (*arthād anapetam*—so Ct)." We read the term adverbially.

"instructing... as to what should be done next" *vijñāpayan*: Literally, "informing." We follow Ct and Cr, who understand that Sugrīva is informing Hanumān as to what needs to be done next (*agre kartavyam*—so Ct).

2. "the *rākṣasa* princes" *kumārāḥ*: Literally, "the young men, princes." The reference, as indicated by Cr, is to Rāvaṇa's sons who have been slain in the preceding *sargas* (56–59).

"will... be able to launch a sortie against us" *upanirhāram... dātum arhati*: There is wide disagreement among the commentators and translators consulted as to the meaning of the term *upanirhāra*, which apparently does not occur elsewhere in the literature. Our interpretation follows that of Cv and Cm, who understand, "issuing forth to offer battle (*upaniṣkramya yuddhapradānam*—so Cm)." Etymological considerations aside, we believe this interpretation best suits the context. The battle up until now has consisted largely of a series of sorties on the part of a succession of great *rākṣasa* champions. Now that many of these (with the critical exception of Indrajit) have been dispatched, Sugrīva assumes that Rāvaṇa will be unable to launch any more forays against the monkeys. He therefore proposes that the monkeys take the offensive and attack the city.

Cg interprets similarly, although he is uncertain as to whether the term *upanirhāra* refers principally to the setting out or to the fighting. Noting that verbal roots may have many meanings, he offers two interpretations. First, he says that Rāvaṇa will not be able to come out because of his despondency over the killing of his sons. Cg feels that the poet uses the term *nirhāra* in the sense of "the removal *or* disposal of corpses." Perhaps he has in mind the mention in the southern recension (see 1396* following 6.61.67 and notes) of Rāvaṇa's practice of sending out parties to dispose of the *rākṣasa* dead by throwing them into the sea. If so, Cg takes the term to be used in its secondary denotation, or *lakṣaṇā*, which may also refer prospectively to the impending "cremation" of the *rākṣasas* in the conflagration set by the monkeys. His second interpretation is that the word *upanirhāra* refers specifically to a battle offered in the course of a sortie. (*upanirhāram upaniṣkramaṇaṃ yuddhāya nirgamanam iti yāvat. hataputrāditvenānutsāhād rāvaṇo na nirgamiṣyatīti bhāvaḥ. atrāgraheṇa pretaniryāpanarūḍhanirhārapadaprayogaḥ. dātuṃ kartum iti yāvat. dhātūnām anekārthatvāt. upanirhāraśabda upaniṣkramya yuddhaparo vā.*)

Ck understands the term to refer to Rāvaṇa's alleged inability to defend his citadel (*upanirhāraṃ puraraksāṃ dātuṃ saṃpādayituṃ nārhati*). Ct quotes the opinions of both Ck and Cm but believes that the term, in fact, refers to a cessation of hostilities (*yuddhāvahāram*), which, under the circumstances, Rāvaṇa will no longer be able to offer. According to Ct, others believe that by this reference we are to understand that such a cessation has occurred previously. (*upanirhāraṃ yuddhāvahāram asmākaṃ dātuṃ nārhatīty arthaḥ. anenānyadā yuddhāvahāro jāta iti jñāyata ity anye.*) See notes to 6.32.2–3; 6.41.8; and 6.49.33.

Cr offers, as his first explanation, the same interpretation as that of Ck. However, he adds the idea that *upanirhāra* also means the offering of libations of water to [Rāvaṇa's] dead sons. In the absence of his champions, Cr continues, Rāvaṇa will not be able to perform this rite nor should he be given the opportunity to do so. Cr concludes by quoting the interpretation of Cm. (*kiṃca upanirhāraṃ mṛtaputrādyuddeśyakajalaṃ dātuṃ nārhati. avakāśo na dātavya iti tātparyam.*)

Most northern manuscripts and the printed editions of Gorresio (6.53.3) and Lahore (6.54.2), in an apparent effort to gloss the difficult southern reading, substitute *upasaṃhāram*, "attack."

Translations are varied. Gita Press (1969, vol. 3, p. 1684) and Dutt (1893, p. 1365) follow Ck's interpretation. Dutt, however, notes, "*Upanirhāram* is a contested term. Kataka [Ck] gives the sense adopted by me. Tirtha [Cm] says it means 'Rāvana cannot give battle in the open field.' According to others, it means 'He cannot offer truce to us.' " Raghunathan (1982, vol. 3, p. 220) follows Cg, Cm, and Cv, rendering, "will not be able to order a sortie." Roussel (1903, vol. 3, p. 248), followed by Shastri (1959, vol. 3, p. 220), takes the phrase to mean that Rāvaṇa can no longer harm the monkeys. Pagani (1999, p. 1074) thinks that he can no longer defeat them.

3. "Bulls among leaping monkeys! Those leaping monkeys" *plavaṅgamāḥ... plavagarṣabhāḥ*: Literally, "leaping ones... O bulls among leaping ones." We follow Cr in taking the second term as a vocative and the first as the subject of the verbs *santi*, "they are," and *abhyutpatantu* (v.l. *abhipatantu*), "let them leap" (*he plavagarṣabhāḥ ye ye... plavaṅgamāḥ santi te te... abhipatantu*).

"are to... leap into Laṅkā" *laṅkām abhyutpatantu*: Literally, "Let them leap to Laṅkā." Cg explains, "let them leap the rampart and proceed (*prākāram utplutya gacchantu*)."

Following verse 3, KK (6.75.3ef), GPP (unnumbered between 6.75.3 and 4), and VSP (6.75.3ef), all within brackets, and M3 insert a passage of one line [1403*]: "Those tawny monkeys, who resembled Indra [lit., Hari] in order to burn Rāvaṇa's abode..."

4. "when the sun had set and the dread onset of night had come" *astaṃgata āditye raudre tasmin niśāmukhe*: Literally, "when Āditya had gone to the setting mountain at the frightful beginning of the night." There is a difference of opinion among several of the commentators as to the exact chronology of the current assault on Laṅkā. Ck and Ct understand that Vibhīṣaṇa and Hanumān had found Jāmbavān on the battlefield in the waning moments of the previous night (6.61.7–15). Thus, according to them, Hanumān's two round-trip flights first to retrieve and then to replace the mountain of healing herbs have taken exactly thirty *ghaṭikās*, or twelve hours, the length of one tropical day. This, they argue, brings us to the evening of the following day. (*pūrvadivasāpararātriśeṣa ulkāhastābhyāṃ hanūmadvibhīṣaṇābhyāṃ jāmbavadanveṣaṇam. tatas tanniyogata uṣasi parvatāharaṇāya gamanam. athāharaṇaṃ punaś ca tatprāpanaṃ punarāgamanam iti triṃśadghaṭikāmadhye sarvam. tataḥ punaḥ pradoṣe hanumadādīnāṃ laṅkādāhagamanam iti katakādayaḥ*—so Ct.) Cf. notes to 6.59.106 and 6.61.7,12,68 for Ct's chronology. Cg and Cm, on the other hand, believe that the reference to the setting of the sun is not a specific marker of the time of day but merely a way to indicate that it is dark. By "the onset of night," Cg further understands that the first watch (*yāma*) of the night is intended and that the action currently described takes place at the end of that watch, so that it is not twilight but pitch dark. (*nanu pūrvam ulkāhastau tadā rātrāv ity uktam. atrādityāstamayasamaya iti gamyate. ato viruddham iti cen na virodhaḥ. āditye 'staṃgata iti prakāśābhāvoktiḥ. niśāmukha iti rātreḥ prathamayāma ucyate. raudra iti viśeṣaṇād yāmāntatvena gāḍhāndhakāratvam ucyate. hanumāṃś ca mahādbhuta-*

vegaśālitayā muhūrtaṃ mātreṇa prasthāyauṣadhiparvatam ānīya taṃ punas tatra nikṣipyāgatavān iti tasya vegātiśayaś ca pratipādito bhavati—so Cg.) The idea here is that, because of Hanumān's inconceivable speed (*acintyavegātiśayaḥ*—so Cm), he accomplishes the fetching and return of the healing herb mountain in a mere instant. Thus, rather than the twelve hours of day envisaged by Ck and Ct, Cg and Cm believe that virtually no time has elapsed since the discovery of Jāmbavān on the battlefield. Cm acknowledges the position of Ck and Ct as an alternative. Among the translations consulted, only that of Raghunathan (1982, vol. 3, pp. 220–21) represents Cg's thinking, rendering, "at the end of the first watch of the night, when the darkness was intense." The concern for the duration of Hanumān's flight reflects, of course, the commentators' virtual obsession with the chronology of the epic events. It also, naturally, reflects a marked division in the commentators' opinions as to how fast Hanumān actually flies. See note to 6.4.4 and Introduction, p. 17, n. 1 and p. 108. See R. Goldman 2003 and 2006b. Cf. Hopkins 1903.

5. "the sentries at the gates" *ārakṣasthāḥ*: Literally, "stationed at the *ārakṣas*." There is some disagreement among the commentators as to the precise meaning of the term *ārakṣa*, with the different sides citing conflicting lexicons. Ck, Ct, and Cr gloss, "gates (*dvārāṇi*)," and take the *rākṣasas* stationed there to be "the guards posted at the gates (*dvārarakṣiṇaḥ*)." Ct, however, notes that some unspecified commentators understand *ārakṣa* to mean "a garrison *or* army encampment (*gulmam*)." Cg and Cm are apparently the commentators to whom Ct is referring, as they gloss, "posted at the garrisons (*gulmasthāḥ*)." Cg, however, offers two alternatives: "city guards (*nagararakṣiṇaḥ*)" and "guardians of the fortifications (*durgarakṣiṇāṃ sthānaṃ tatrasthā vā*)." He cites the *Ratnamālā*, which defines *ārakṣa* as "watching, guarding (*rakṣaṇam*)." Cs takes *ārakṣa* to refer to any point that needs to be guarded, such as a gate, etc., and considers those posted at such places to be *ārakṣasthas*. He cites the *Viśvakośa*, which defines *ārakṣa* as "that which needs to be guarded (*rakṣaṇīya*)." Cf. 5.3.27; 6.3.27; 6.27.20; 6.28.31; 6.31.31; 6.45.2; 6.71.1; 6.72.5; 6.84.6; and notes.

"with their hideous eyes" *virūpākṣāḥ*: Ct, Ck, Cg, and Cm appear to take this epithet as a kenning for *rākṣasas*. See 6.22.33; 6.27.20; 6.28.31; 6.33.10; and notes.

6. "gateways" *gopura-*: We follow Cg and Cr, who gloss, "city gates (*puradvāram*)." See 6.61.39 and notes.

"towers" *-aṭṭa-*: According to Ct and Cr, this term refers to "a [smaller] house built on top of another house (*gṛhoparitanagṛham*)." Ct cites, as an alternative, *Amarakośa*'s (2.2.12) definition: "a fortified place in front of a guardhouse (*kṣaumam*)." Cg cites the *Amarakośa* in support of his definition and elaborates, quoting an unidentified source, which defines *aṭṭāḥ* as "the places in which warriors inflict harm, that is, guardhouses placed in front of the ramparts (*aṭṭanti hiṃsanti yodhā eṣu sthitvety aṭṭāḥ prākārāgrasthitagṛhāṇi*)." Ck only cites the *Amarakośa*. See note to 6.33.28.

"highways... streets" *pratolīṣu ... cāryāsu*: Ck, Ct, Cr, and Cg define these terms as "main roads and lesser roads (*rathyā ... alparathyā*—so Ct)." See notes to 6.47.32.

"mansions" *prāsādeṣu*: Cr defines *prāsāda* as "a tall house (*uccagṛham*)." See 6.32.2 and note.

7. The two lines that constitute this verse (*pādas* ab and *pādas* cd) are juxtaposed only in the critical edition. As noted below, all southern manuscripts insert a passage of thirteen lines between them, while the northern manuscripts replace *pādas* cd with either *rākṣasānāṃ samādīptaḥ sarveṣāṃ prāṇagardhinām* ("blazing brightly [that fire

burned the houses] of all the *rākṣasas*, who cherished their lives") [1408*] or *rākṣasānāṃ samāsādya sarveṣāṃ dvārarakṣiṇām* ("[that fire] reaching [the houses] of all the *rākṣasa* guardians of the gates [devoured them]") (Ś2,D2–4,8,12, and the Lahore edition). The critical reading seems awkward in any case, as it does not differentiate the terms *gṛham*, "house," and *āvāsaḥ*, "dwelling, residence." Once again, the critical edition has created a passage known to no manuscript tradition. See Sutherland 1992.

"including those who performed the household rites" *gṛhamedhinām*: Literally, "having house-sacrifices." This term, which can be loosely translated as "householder," refers more specifically to brahmans who perform the vedic rites enjoined in the *gṛhyasūtras*. As such, it is an interesting term to apply to the normally antibrahmanical *rākṣasas*. On the other hand, it may refer to an actual priestly class of *rākṣasas*, such as that mentioned at 5.16.2 (see ad loc. and note; and Goldman and Goldman 1996, pp. 65–66). The reading itself is rather weak. According to the critical apparatus, it is attested in only five manuscripts (G1,2,M1,2,5). D5,T1,G3,M3, and the texts and printed editions of Cg, Cv, and Cm read instead *gṛhagardhinām*, "of those who cherish *or* covet their homes." D6,7,10,11,T2,3, and the texts and printed editions of Ct and Cr read the synonymous *gṛhagṛdhnunām*. Cg and Ct gloss their respective variants as "householders (*gṛhasthānām*)." Cr understands, "of those who were particularly covetous of such objects as houses, etc. (*gṛhādiviṣayakaviśeṣecchāvatām*)."

Following 7ab, D1,5–7,9–11,S insert a passage of thirteen lines [1407*]: "Palaces as huge as mountains crashed to the ground. Aloe wood was consumed there, as was the finest sandalwood, along with pearls, shining jewels, diamonds, and coral.[1–3] Fine linens were consumed there, as well as shining silks, along with various woolens and golden utensils and weapons.[4–5] Trappings and ornaments of horses of all different kinds were consumed, along with the neck-chains and girths of elephants and the fine accoutrements of chariots.[6–7] The body armor of warriors and the armor of horses and elephants were burned, along with swords, bows, bowstrings, arrows, iron cudgels, hooks,[1] and javelins.[8–9] The fire there consumed woolen blankets, fly whisks, tiger skins, and abundant musk, together with mansions on every side, all adorned with pearls and jewels.[10–11] And the fire burned heaps of various missiles there. The fire, eater of oblations, consumed the decorations on houses[2] of every kind.[12–13]"

[1]"hooks" *-aṅkuśa-*: See note to 6.60.28, 1342*.

[2]"the decorations on houses" *gṛhacchandān*: Literally, "pleasant things of houses." We follow Cg and Cm, who understand these to be auspicious or apotropaic decorations such as *svastikas* painted on houses (*gṛhacchandān svastikādigṛhavinyāsān*—so Cg). D9–11 and the texts and printed editions of Ct read instead *gṛhāṃś citrān*, "variegated *or* lovely houses."

8–11. Verses 8–11 constitute a single sentence, which comprises a long list of the different attributes and activities of the *rākṣasas* whose houses are destroyed in the fire. In order to make the passage readable in English, we have broken it up into a series of smaller syntactic units, adding words such as "some" and "others" to distinguish the various groups of *rākṣasas* described.

"Fire, the purifier of all things" *pāvakaḥ*: Literally, "the purifier."

"consumed thousands of the houses...As the fire burned their homes: *gṛhasahasrāṇi*...*adahat*: Literally, "it burned thousands of houses." We have repeated the phrase, in keeping with our attempts to make the syntax manageable and the style intelligible in English. D1,2,7,9–11,G2,M3,5, and the texts and printed editions of Ct, Cr, Cg, Cm, and Cv read *śata-*, "one hundred," for *gṛha-*, "homes," yielding the sense "it burned hundreds of thousands [of the residents of Laṅkā]." Ct and Cs supply the word "houses (*gṛhāṇi*)."

"the residents...Some of those residents" *-nivāsinām*: Literally, "of those residents."

"garlands of flowers" *sragdāma-*: Literally, "ties of floral garlands." Our translation follows the interpretation of Cg, who glosses, "flower garlands (*puṣpamālāḥ*)," noting that the word *dāma* here refers to a necklace or a garland (*sragdāmāni puṣpamālā dāmaśabdo hāraparaḥ*). Cg further notes that unnamed masters have indicated that the word *śragdāma* refers to a floral garland made with multiple strands (*sragdāmaśabdenānekasaranirmitapuṣpamālocyata ity ācāryāḥ*). The critical text has an unnoted typographical error, reading *sradgāma-* for *sragdāma-*. D7,10,11, and the texts and printed editions of Ct and Cr read *-bhāṇḍa-*, "ornaments," for *-dāma-*, "tie, strand." See 6.64.2 and note.

"rum" *sīdhu-* : Prakash (1987, vol. 2, pp. 149, 205) understands that this drink is made from distilled sugarcane and *dhātakī* flowers. See *Amarakośa* 3.6.34.

"The garments of some were clutched by their lovers." *kāntālambitavastrāṇām*: Literally, "whose garments were clung to by lovers." Cg interprets this as a *paranipāta* compound, glossing, "whose lovers were clinging to garments (*ālambitavastrakāntānām*)." Cg suggests that this amounts to saying that the *rākṣasas* were given over to sexual pleasure (*ratiparāṇām iti yāvat*).

"went on...drinking" *pibatām*: Literally, "[of those] who were drinking." Cg takes this either as a repetition of the fact that the *rākṣasas* were consuming intoxicants, as indicated by the phrase "their eyes rolling from drinking rum" or as a reference to their consumption of more innocuous beverages such as milk. (*pibatāṃ madyapānaṃ kurvatām. sīdhupānety atra madyapānaṃ kāryam uktam. kṣīrādikaṃ pibatām iti vā.*)

"flared up again and again" *jajvāla ca punaḥ punaḥ*: Cg, the only commentator who understands that it is the *rākṣasas* rather than their houses that are being burned, notes that the fire flares up repeatedly through the infusions of their blood, marrow, and fat (*punaḥ punar ity anena tadrudhiravasāsnehenādhikajvālocyate*).

12–14. Verses 12–14 constitute a single long sentence, most of which consists of adjectives describing the buildings that are being burned. We have broken up the passage into smaller sentences for readability and style.

"firmly built and costly" *sāravanti mahārhāṇi*: Literally, "possessing strength [and] having great value." We follow Ct, Ck, and Cr for the first of these adjectives. They understand the reference to be to the state of being firmly constructed (*sthirasaṃsthānavattvam*—Ck, Ct)." Cg, on the other hand, citing the *Ratnamālā*, takes *sāra* in its sense of "wealth (*artha*)," glossing, "possessing the greatest wealth (*śreṣṭhadhanavanti*)."

"beautiful with their grand upper stories" *gambhīraguṇavanti*: Literally, "possessing profound qualities." We follow Cg here, who takes *gambhīra* in its sense of "a terrace *or* upper story of a building," glossing, "possessing large upper stories or terraces (*mahātalpavanti*)." Cg glosses *-guṇavanti* as "possessing beauty (*saundaryavanti*)." Ct, Ck, and Cr, however, take the compound to mean that the buildings were impenetrable because of their numerous inner enclosures, ramparts, doors, and side doors into inner chambers (*anekakakṣyāprākārāntargehadvāropadvārato durgamatvalakṣaṇagāmbhīryavanti*).

"soaring aloft with their penthouses" *candraśālonnatāni*: Literally, "lofty because of their moon-chambers." We agree with the commentators, who gloss, "penthouse *or* turret (*śirogṛham*)." One is tempted to read the compound as a *paranipāta* in the sense of "having lofty penthouses." D6,10,11,13,M1,2, and the texts and printed editions of Ct read *-uttamāni*, "foremost," for the critical edition's *-unnatāni*, "lofty," yielding the sense of "splendid because of [their] penthouses."

"richly furnished throughout" *sādhiṣṭhānāni sarvaśaḥ*: Literally, "possessing resting places everywhere." We follow the commentators. Cg takes *adhiṣṭhāna* in its sense of "couch seat," glossing, "furnished with beds, chairs, etc. (*śayyāsanādisahitāni*)." Ct similarly glosses, "furnished with couches, etc. (*mañcādisahitāni*)."

"echoed with the cries... the strains... and the tinkling" *nisvanaiḥ... nāditāni*: Literally, "resounding with the sounds."

"of lutes" *-vīṇānām*: V3,D7,9–11, and the texts and printed editions of Ct and Cr read *-varṇānām*, "class, type, *or* sounds." This yields the sense of "[the sounds] of the [different] types *or* the cries of *krauñcas* and peacocks."

15. "at summer's end" *gharmage*: Literally, "in *or* at summer-going." This unusual term, virtually unattested elsewhere, has aroused some disagreement among the commentators and translators. Commentators are divided as to whether to take the term to refer to the hot season proper, the rainy season, which follows it, or the transitional period between the two. Although the term appears to refer to the heat of summer, that idea is seemingly vitiated by the reference to clouds and lightning, which are not a normal feature of that season. Ct and Ck appear to understand the term to refer to the period at the end of the summer when the sun goes away [presumably hidden by the monsoon clouds] (*grīṣmage divākare gate*). Cr seems to understand the reference to be to summer proper when the sun has gone to the condition of [maximum] heat (*grīṣmage savitari satīti śeṣaḥ*). Cv and Cm take the term in the sense of "that from *or* after which heat *or* summer departs, that is, as a kenning for the rainy season (*gharmo 'smād gacchatīti gharmago varṣākālaḥ*)." Cg cites this last position as his opening statement. He then goes on to note that others state that one should add the words "it goes in the summer (*nidāghe gacchatīti śeṣaḥ*)," presumably a reference to the heat. He then states that the word *gharma-* metonymically indicates *gharmānta*, "the end of summer" (*gharmaśabdena gharmānto lakṣyate*). Cg further points out that other commentators understand the term to mean "that which reaches up until the end of summer, that is, the beginning of the rainy season (*taṃ gacchati prāpnotīti gharmago varṣādir ity apare*)." Finally, Cg seems to come around to the idea that the summer is being referred to and that the simile of the blazing gateways viewed against the background of the flaming mansions is based on the superimposition of lightning-laced clouds upon the full blazing heat of summer (*laṅkāyāṃ dahymānāyāṃ saṃtāpe ca samantataḥ prasarati dahymānatoraṇādīni nidāghaprarūḍhasavidyunmeghatulyānīty arthaḥ*). Translators offer one or another of these interpretations, i.e., summer, end of summer, beginning of the rains, or the rainy season.

Following verse 15, D1,6,7,9,11,T2,G1,M1,2,5,D10 (line 1 after 14; line 2 after 15ab),G2,3 (after 15ab), and the texts and printed editions of the southern commentators insert a passage of two lines [1416*]: "Wreathed in flames, the houses looked like the peaks of some great mountain ablaze with a forest fire."

16. "As they were being burned alive" *dahyamānāḥ*: Literally, "being burned."

"in their lofty mansions" *vimāneṣu*: As the commentaries indicate, this term refers specifically to a seven-storied mansion *or* palace (*saptabhūmiprāsādaḥ*—so Ck, Ct). See 5.8.32; 5.10.15; 5.52.11; and notes.

"cast off all their ornaments" *tyaktābharaṇasaṃyogāḥ*: Literally, "who had abandoned the totality of their ornaments." The precise reason for the dying women's abandonment of their ornaments is not clear. Only Cr, among the commentators, touches on this point, claiming that they do so because they are being burned, but still the connection between the two actions is not clear. Perhaps the idea is that the ornaments have grown intolerably hot from the flames. This, at any rate, is the understanding of Gita Press (1969, vol. 3, p. 1685), which translates, "having given up (all) connections with their ornaments (which were melting due to excessive heat)." Roussel (1903, vol. 3, p. 249) understands that the ornaments impeded the women's flight, but there is no evidence to support this view. Apparently interpreting *saṃyoga*, normally, "contact, union," in the unattested sense of "obstruction," he renders, "*Jetant lá les parures qui entravaient* (*leur fuite*)." In this he is followed by Shastri (1959, vol. 3, p. 221) and Pagani (1999, p. 1076). Compare 5.52.12, where Hanumān observed streams of molten metal filled with gemstones when he previously burned the city.

17. "there, engulfed in fire" *tatra cāgniparītāni*: M3 and the texts and printed editions of Cg and Cm read instead *jvalanena parītāni*, "engulfed in flames." They also transpose verses 16 and 17. This variant and order of the verses is reflected only in the translation of Raghunathan (1982, vol. 3, p. 222).

18. "As those mansions" *tāni*: Literally, "those."

"with their thickets of glowing herbs" *dīptauṣadhivanāni ca*: Ś2,Ñ,V,B,D1–4,6–13,T2,G1,M1,2,5, and the texts and printed editions of Ct and Cr read instead *dahyamānāni sarvaśaḥ*, "burning on all sides," or the synonymous *dahyamānāni sarvataḥ*.

19. "with red-blossoming *kiṃśuka* trees" *puṣpitair iva kiṃśukaiḥ*: Literally, "with blossoming *kiṃśukas*." See 6.60.34 and note, where the *kiṃśuka* (*Butea frondosa*) is used in a similar image with fire. See, too, *Sundarakāṇḍa* App. I, No. 13, lines 16–20, at note to 5.52.12. Cf. 6.35.9; 6.55.22; 6.60.34; 6.76.28; and notes.

20. "With its elephants and horses turned loose by their keepers" *hastyadhyakṣair gajair muktair muktaiś ca turagair api*: Literally, "with its elephants freed by the elephant keepers and with horses freed as well." We agree with Cg that we should also supply the words, "and by horse keepers (*muktaiś ca turagair apīty atrāpy aśvādhyakṣair ity adhyāhāryam*)."

"with its huge creatures thrashing about" *bhrāntagrāhaḥ*: Literally, "whose *grāhas* were whirling about." The word *grāha* can refer either to crocodiles or more generally to any large aquatic animal. Cf. note to 5.7.6. See, too, notes to 6.3.14; 6.4.78; 6.14.21; and 6.15.6,7.

"at the end of a cosmic age" *lokānte*: Literally, "at the end of the world." Ct, Cg, and Cm gloss, "at the [universal] destruction (*pralaye*)," i.e., the universal destruction at the end of a *kalpa*, or cosmic age. Cr glosses, "at the time of the destruction of the world (*lokanāśasamaye*). See 6.114.40 and note.

21. "would encounter . . . would encounter" *dṛṣṭvā . . . dṛṣṭvā*: Literally, "having seen . . . having seen."

"roaming free" *muktam*: Literally, "released."

"it, too, would shy away" *nivartate*: Literally, "it turns back."

Following verse 21, D6,7,9–11,S insert a passage of two lines [1422*]: "And as Laṅkā burned, the vast ocean on whose waters its reflection lay looked like a sea of red water."

23. "for a distance of ten leagues" *daśayojanam*: Literally, "for ten *yojanas*." B3,D7,9–11,G2, and the texts and printed editions of Ct and Cr read *śata-*, "a hundred," for *daśa-*, "ten." Cf. note to 5.1.69.

24. "Meanwhile": The word has been added to mark the change of subject.

"rushed forth" *nirgatān bahiḥ*: Literally, "had gone outside."

25. "The shouts . . . the wailing" *udghuṣṭam . . . nisvanaḥ*: Literally, "shouting . . . sound." Given the context, we agree with Cr, who glosses *nisvanaḥ*, "sound," as "sounds of dejection or despair (*dīnaśabdaḥ*)."

26. "the great warriors" *mahātmānau*: Literally, "the two great ones."

27. The great majority of northern manuscripts omit 27cd–28ab ("he produced a thunderous sound that sowed terror among the *rākṣasas*. As he twanged his great bow, Rāma looked as splendid . . ."), making their inclusion in the critical text suspect.

28. See note to verse 27.

"Lord Bhava" *bhagavān . . . bhavaḥ*: The word *bhavaḥ*, literally, "being, source, origin," is a common epithet of Śiva. Ck, however, in keeping with his Brahmaite theology, appears to take the reference here to be to Brahmā in his role as the creator (*bhavaḥ bhavaty asmād eva sargakāla iti bhavaś caturmukharudraḥ*). Ck's explanation is ambiguous, however, since he refers to the divinity as *caturmukharudra*, "four-faced Rudra." Although *caturmukha* is a standard epithet of Brahmā, the name Rudra normally applies to Śiva. Perhaps Ck is representing the four-faced Brahmā manifesting himself as Rudra/Śiva. See note to 6.59.82.

"his bow that consists of the *vedas*" *vedamayaṃ dhanuḥ*: Literally, "the bow that is made of the *vedas*." The precise sense of the expression is unclear. Commentators and translators struggle to make sense of it, while some, chiefly northern, manuscripts evade the issue by substituting more transparent phrases. Ct, Ck, Cm, and Cr understand that the bow has the form of the Absolute Brahman in its audible form (*śabdabrahmātmakam*), or the sound of the recitation of the *vedas*. Although these commentaries are not very detailed, the idea seems to be that the awesome twanging of Rāma's bow recalls the resonant thrumming of the *vedas* or their sacred symbolic syllable *om*. Cf. *Muṇḍakopaniṣad* 2.24, where the syllable *om* is said to be a bow, the *ātman* an arrow, and *brahma* itself the target. Cg offers two interpretations. The first is that the bow's characteristics are mentioned in the *vedas* (*vedoktalakṣaṇaṃ dhanuḥ*). According to his second interpretation, the phrase is a reference to the fact that Śiva's glory is established through vedic passages, such as "he is clothed in an animal skin and holds the bow (or the bow Pināka) (*kṛttivāsāḥ pinākīti śrutyā pratipāditamahimeti vārthaḥ*)." This and similar phrases are well attested in the vedic corpus (see, for example, *Kāṭhaka Saṃhitā* 9.7; *Lāṭyāyana Śrautasūtra* 5.3.12; *Nirukta* 3.21; *Vājasaneyi Saṃhitā* 3.71; *TaitS* 1.8.62; *ŚatBr* 2.6.217; *Āpastambha Śrautasūtra* 8.18.9; *Maitreyi Saṃhitā* 1.10.4; 1.44.15; 1.10.20; and 1.60.16; etc.). Cs, citing a usage from the *Mahābhārata* (critical edition 8.262* line 3 = Citraśāla ed. 8.34.36) (*saṃvatsaro dhanur tad vai*) in which the gods make the year into Śiva's bow, argues that this is a similar, but noncontradictory, conceit (*ity uktis tv ekasyāneke 'bhimānino bhavantīti na viruṇaddhi*).

Among the translators who do not simply render the phrase literally, Dutt (1893, p. 1367) clearly follows the interpretation of Ck, Ct, Cr, and Cm, translating, "his bow having sounds and instinct with Brahma energy." Shastri (1959, vol. 3, p. 222) and

Pagani (1999, p. 1076) translate the phrase literally. However, both of them have notes in which they suggest that the reference is to a bow made in accordance with the prescriptions of the *dhanurveda*, or "science of archery." Pagani (1999, p. 1669) is particularly specific in claiming that the reference here is "undoubtedly" to the bow known as Ajagava, which is made of a combination of goat and cow horn as specified in the *dhanurveda*, a treatise attached to the *Yajurveda*. Neither translator provides any source for this claim, although we believe that in both cases it may derive from Cg's first interpretation (*vedoktalakṣaṇaṃ dhanuḥ*).

Following verse 28, D5–7,9–11,T1,2,G,M, and the texts and printed editions of the southern commentators insert a passage of two lines, the first of which repeats 25ab (reading *nisvanam* for *nisvanaḥ*) and the second of which is [1425]*: "The sound of Rāma's bowstring drowned out[1] both [1425*] the shouts of the monkeys and the wailing of the *rākṣasas*.[25ab]"

[1]"drowned out" *ati . . . śuśruve*: Literally, "it heard over." As the commentators indicate here, the middle form of the perfect must be understood passively (i.e., "it was heard over"). Cr understands, "having exceeded, that is, having surpassed, it became the object of hearing (*atiśuśruve 'tikramyādharīkṛtyety arthaḥ śravaṇaviṣayo babhūva*)."

29. "Those three sounds" *trayam*: Literally, "the triad."

30. "crashed to the ground" *apatad bhuvi*: Literally, "it fell on the ground." Ñ2,V1,2,B2,D9–11, and the texts and printed editions of Ct read instead *abhavad bhuvi*, "it was on the ground."

31. "frantic preparations" *saṃnāhaḥ . . . tumulaḥ*: Literally, "tumultuous preparation." Cr explains, "unbeknownst to one another (*parasparam ajñāyamānaḥ*)." Cg glosses, "great, elaborate (*adhikaḥ*)," for *tumulaḥ*, "tumultuous."

32. "girded themselves for battle" *saṃnahyamānānām*: Literally, "of those who were girding up."

"took on the aspect of the dark night of universal destruction" *raudrīva samapadyata*: Literally, "became like Raudrī." The commentators agree that Raudrī is another name for Kālarātrī or Pralayarātrī (so Cg). See 6.23.15; 6.34.15; 6.58.31; and notes.

33–34. "Creeping near, you must assault the gate" *āsannā dvāram āsādya*: Literally, "[you] being near, having come near *or* attacked the gate." The phrase is awkward and ambiguous with its repetition of forms of the verb *ā* $\sqrt{}$*sad*, "to sit down, approach, attack." According to our understanding, the monkeys are being instructed first to draw near the gate (*āsannāḥ*) and then to assault it (*āsādya*), giving battle to its defenders. No other printed edition or commentator's text shares the critical reading. The southern commentators offer one or another of two synonymous variants, reading either *āsannaṃ dvāram* (Ct, Ck) or *āsannadvāram* (Cg, Cm, Cr) for *āsannā dvāram*. In these readings, the participle *āsannam*, "near," refers to the gate rather than to the monkeys. Ct interprets the phrase to mean "whichever gate is nearest to whichever monkey, having attacked that . . . (*yad yasyāsannaṃ dvāraṃ tat tad āsādya*)." Cr similarly understands that each of the monkeys is to attack the gate that is nearest to himself (*svasvasamīpavartidvāram*). Cg understands the compound *āsannadvāram* to refer to the door to the midmost inner chamber that is nearest to Rāvaṇa's inner apartments (*rāvaṇāntaḥpurāsannamadhyakakṣyādvāram*).

"no matter where he may be posted" *tatra tatra vyavasthitaḥ*: Literally, "positioned *or* assigned there and there."

"should disobey" *vitathaṃ kuryāt*: Literally, "he should make untrue *or* falsify." We agree with Cg and Cm, who indicate that we should "supply the words 'my command' (*macchāsanam iti śeṣaḥ*)." Cr expands a bit, glossing, "your violation of [my] orders, that is, fleeing, etc. (*tavājñāvighātaṃ palāyanādīty arthaḥ*)." Ct glosses, simply, "should flee (*palāyanaṃ kuryāt*)."

35. "had approached ... taken up" *sthiteṣu ... āsādya*:Literally, "when, having approached, they stood."

36. "The violent force of the expansion of his body" *tasya jṛmbhitavikṣepāt*: Literally, "from the agitation *or* shaking of his expansion *or* yawning." The phrase is ambiguous and its meaning less than transparent. We are in agreement with Cg, who understands *jṛmbhita-* in its sense of "enlargement *or* expansion." He glosses the compound with "the expansion of his contracted limbs (*gātravināmavistarāt*)." It may even be that, like other figures in the epic such as Kumbhakarṇa (6.49.4 and 6.53.46) and Hanumān (5.1.8,172; 5.2.13; 5.35.36; 5.37.53; 5.44.24; etc.), Rāvaṇa actually increases his physical proportions as a sign of anger or readiness for action. Among the translators, Raghunathan (1982, vol. 3, p. 223) alone seems influenced by this interpretation, rendering, "The fury with which he shook himself and drew himself to his full height." Other commentators and translators have understood *jṛmbhita* in its other sense of "yawning, gaping," which we find rather inappropriate in this context. Ct, Ck, and Cr understand that a great wind accompanied by a loud roaring proceeds from the force of Rāvaṇa's yawn, which itself is a symptom of his fear and rage (*bhayakrodhajaṃ yajjṛmbhitaṃ vijṛmbhaṇaṃ tadutthavikṣepāt saśabdamahāvāyupravṛttyā*—so Ct, Ck).

"for he looked like an incarnation of the wrath that fills the body of Rudra" *rūpavān iva rudrasya manyur gātreṣv adṛśyata*: Literally, "he looked like the wrath in the limbs of Rudra that has taken a [physical] form." Our interpretation again follows that of Cg, who explains, "Rāvaṇa appeared like wrath itself, which has taken form in the body of Rudra in his aspect as the universal fire at the end of a cosmic age (*rudrasya kālāgnirudrasya gātre yo rūpavān manyuḥ sa iva rāvaṇo 'lakṣyata*)." The phrase also lends itself to the interpretation offered by Ck, Ct, and Cr, that is, "the wrath that appeared in his body was like the incarnate wrath of Rudra (*tasya gātreṣu rūpavān rudrasya manyur iva manyur adṛśyata*—so Cr)." Ct and Ck further indicate that the limbs in which anger physically manifests itself include the furrowed brow, the eyes, the face, etc. (*bhrukuṭicakṣurmukhādiṣv adṛśyata*).

37. Following verse 37, D5–7,9–11,S insert a passage of two lines [1433*]: "And at Rāvaṇa's command, Yūpākṣa, Śoṇitākṣa, Prajaṅgha, and Kampana marched forth with the two sons of Kumbhakarṇa."

38. "Roaring like a lion" *siṃhanādaṃ ca nādayan*: Literally, "causing a lion's roar to sound." Commentators and the translators who follow them are divided as to whether Rāvaṇa is actually roaring or urging his *rākṣasas* to do so as they march forth. The participle is singular, which appears to favor the first of these alternatives advanced by Ck, Ct, and Cr. Ck and Ct indicate that Rāvaṇa roars in order to frighten the monkey troops (*vānarānīkabhayāya svaṃ siṃhanādaṃ nādayan kurvañ śaśāsa*). On the other hand, the verse, both grammatically and contextually, seems awkward if it is the poet's intention to represent the idea put forth by Ct. In the first place, there is no *iti*, or quotation mark, to indicate where Rāvaṇa's direct speech ends. Moreover, it is more

common in the epic for warriors to utter leonine roars when actually marching forth to confront and challenge their enemies (see verse 39 below and 6.57.49, for example). It is for these reasons, perhaps, as well as the fact that in the very next verse the *rākṣasas* march forth "roaring," as if in compliance with their master's order, that Cv, Cm, Cr, and Cg argue that in this verse the singular is used to indicate the plural. Thus, they understand Rāvaṇa to be ordering the *rākṣasas* to roar as they march forth. (*siṃhanādaṃ nādayan nādayantaḥ kurvanto gacchata. nādayann ity atra vyatayo bahulam* [*Pā* 3.1.85] *iti bahuvacanaviṣaya ekavacanam*—so Cg.) This interpretation has been followed only in the translation of Raghunathan (1982, vol. 3, p. 223). The printed texts and editions of Cg, Cm, and Cr read instead *nādayan gacchatātraiva jayadhvaṃ śīghram eva ca*, "[Rāvaṇa] causing [them] to roar and [saying], 'Go, here and now you must quickly conquer.' "

"the lord of the *rākṣasas*" *rākṣaseśvaraḥ*: B1,D2,7,9–11, and the texts and printed editions of Ct and Cr read instead *sa mahābalān*, "he . . . those immensely powerful [*rākṣasas*]." Translations that follow the text of Ct render this variant. G2 and the texts and printed editions of Cg and Cm read instead *sumahābalān*, "those supremely powerful [*rākṣasas*]."

"at once" *atraiva*: Literally, "right here." Cg understands the adverb in its normal sense of location, glossing, "having started from this very house (*asmin gṛha evārabhya*)." B3,D9–11,G1,M3, and the texts and printed editions of Ct and Cr read *adyaiva*, "right now."

39. "at his command" *coditās tena*: Literally, "impelled *or* dispatched by him."

"their weapons glittering" *jvalitāyudhāḥ*: Literally, "having glittering *or* shining weapons." Cg believes that the mention of the glittering of the weapons is to show that the *rākṣasas* engage in some kind of weapons training or drill in the course of their battle marches (*āyudhānāṃ jvalitatvaṃ yuddhāyātrāsu śikṣāviśeṣapradarśanāt*). Evidently, his thinking is that the flashing of the weapons occurs as they are waved around in training or mock combat.

Following verse 39, northern manuscripts (V3,B1,D1–3[after 1435*]) insert lines 1–8, while southern manuscripts (D5–7,9–11,S) insert a passage of nine lines [1436*]: "Then the *rākṣasas*[1] illuminated the sky[2] on every side with the radiance of their ornaments and their own innate splendor as did the tawny monkeys with the fires they had set.[3][1–2] And there the radiance of the moon, lord of the stars, and of the stars, as well as the brilliance of the ornaments of the two armies, illuminated the heavens.[4][3–4] And thus the radiance of the moon, the brilliance of the ornaments, and the blazing light of the heavenly bodies[5] illuminated the armies of the tawny monkeys and the *rākṣasas* on every side.[5–6] And the ocean, with its restless waves, shone more[6] brightly still, illuminated as far as the underworld Pātāla[7] by the glare of the half-burnt[8] houses.[7–8] With its flags and banners and its splendid swords and battle-axes [the *rākṣasa* army . . .].[9]"

[1]"the *rākṣasas* . . . their" *rakṣasām*: Literally, "of the *rākṣasas*." As the verse stands, its only subject is "the tawny monkeys (*harayaḥ*)" in line 2. The context requires that the nominative *rākṣasāḥ*, "the *rākṣasas*," be carried over from the preceding verse.

[2]"the sky . . . the heavens" *vyoma . . . dyām*: The commentators disagree as to the exact referents of these two terms. Cr understands *vyoma* to refer to "space (*ākāśam*)," while

Ct understands, "the space between the two armies (*senāmadhyākāśam*)." Cr, on the other hand, understands *dyām* to refer to "the heavens (*divam*)," while Cg glosses, merely, "space (*ākāśam*)." Ct offers no comment on *vyoma*, presumably understanding it to mean "sky, heavens," while he glosses *dyām* as "the region of space situated between the two armies (*senādvayamadhyagatākāśapradeśam*)."

[3]"with the fires they had set" *agnibhiḥ saha*: Literally, "with the fires."

[4]"as well as [the brilliance] of the ornaments of the two armies, illuminated the heavens" *tayor ābharaṇasthā ca balayor dyām abhāsayat*: Printed editions of the text of Ct read instead *tayor ābharaṇābhā ca jvalitā dyām abhāsayat*, "and the blazing splendor of the ornaments of both of them illuminated the heavens."

[5]"the blazing light of the heavenly bodies" *grahāṇāṃ jvalitā ca bhā*: The texts and printed editions of Cm, Cg, and Cr read instead *gṛhāṇāṃ jvalatāṃ ca bhā*, "and the light of the blazing houses."

[6]"more" *adhikam*: D9–11 and the texts and printed editions of Ct read instead *dhruvam*, "extremely."

[7]"as far as the underworld Pātāla" *saṃsaktapātālaḥ*: Literally, "having Pātāla connected." We follow the interpretation of Cg, the only commentator to share the critical reading, who glosses, "connected with *or* pervaded as far as Pātāla (*pātālaparyantaṃ saṃsaktaḥ*)." Raghunathan (1982, vol. 3, p. 223), the only translator consulted to have this reading, renders, "illumined to its utmost depths in Pātāla." D10,11,M1,2, and the texts and printed editions of Ct and Cr read *-salilaḥ*, "having water that is connected [with the light]."

[8]"And . . . half-burnt" *cārdhapradīptānām*: D7 and the texts and printed editions of Cg and Cm read instead *cordhvapradīptānām*, "and . . . blazing up."

40–41. "various types of foot soldiers" *nānāpatti-*: Cg explains that the various types of foot soldiers are differentiated by their uniforms, weapons, etc. (*veṣāyudhādibhedāt*).

"emerged into view" *dadṛśe*: Literally, "it saw." Verses 40–41 contain only one verbal element, the middle perfect, which, like the similar form *śuśruve* at 1425* (following verse 25 above), must be read as a passive, "it was seen."

"Its darts were flashing" *jvalitaprāsam*: Cg again believes that this is a description of a kind of weapons drill or training practiced during the march. See note to verse 39 above. Cr understands similarly. Our text of Ck understands that the weapons are flashing or blazing because of the friction of the whetstone (*śāṇagharṣaṇāt*). Ct claims to be quoting Ck but understands him to attribute the flashing of the weapons to the hail of arrows (*bāṇavarṣaṇāt*). The critical apparatus cites Ck with the former reading (*śāṇagharṣaṇāt*); it then quotes Ct, who in turn quotes Ck, with the latter reading (*bāṇavarṣaṇāt*). The critical editors then put the former reading in parentheses with a question mark.

42–44. "The soldiers, their arms covered with golden ornaments" *hemajālācitabhujam*: Literally, "its [the army's] arms covered with networks of gold." As Cg points out, the soldiers' arms are bound with masses of golden ornaments (*hemābharaṇajālābaddhabhujam*).

"swung their battle-axes" *vyāveṣṭitaparaśvadham*: The normal sense of *vyāveṣṭita* would be something like "wound around, swathed, wrapped." We follow the commentators (Ct, Cr, Ck) who share this reading and gloss *cālita-*, "moved about." M3 and the texts and printed editions of Cg and Cm read instead *vyāmiśrita-*, which normally means "mixed, intermingled." Cm glosses this reading as "polished, honed (*uttejita-*). Cg, however, reads *vyāveṣṭita-* with Ct and glosses similarly. Raghunathan (1982, vol. 3, p. 224) is the only translator to follow Cm, rendering, "polished."

"They had fixed their arrows to their bows" *bāṇasaṃsaktakārmukam*: Cg is concerned by the apparent redundancy here, since bows were listed among the *rākṣasas'* weapons in verse 40 above. He argues that we should understand that the reference is to spare bows that are worn on the warriors' backs for use in the event of the breakage of the bows mentioned earlier (*yat pūrvoktaṃ kārmukaṃ tadbhaṅge punar ādātuṃ pṛṣṭhe baddham aparam idaṃ kārmukam iti jñeyam*).

"and the honey-wine of their stirrup-cups" *-madhūtseka-*: Literally, "the pouring of honey-wine." We follow the interpretation of Cg, who glosses, "by the imbibing of the heroes' drink (*vīrapāṇasevanena*)." At 4.11.36, the commentators define "the hero's drink" as a drink warriors take before battle to increase their fortitude. See 4.11.36 and note. See 5.59–60; and note to 5.59.8. See Guruge 1960, p. 149.

"Seeing" *dṛṣṭvā*: Literally, "having seen." We have taken all the adjectives describing the army in verses 42–44 as modifying "the army of the *rākṣasas* (*balaṃ* . . . *rākṣasānām*)," the object of the gerund in 44a. Alternatively, one could construe the adjectives in verses 42–43 with the nominative *balam* in 41a, and several of the translators consulted have done so.

"truly terrifying" *sudāruṇam*: D7,9–11, and the texts and printed editions of Ct and Cr read instead *durāsadam*, "unassailable, irresistible."

"leapt forward, roaring" *saṃcacāla* . . . *nanāda ca*: Literally, "moved about and roared." We follow Cg, who glosses, "went toward [them] (*abhimukhaṃ jagāma*)." Ct and Ck understand, "moved about in Laṅkā (*sañcacāla laṅkāyām iti śeṣaḥ*)." Translators are divided in their understanding of the sense of the verb *saṃcacāla*. Dutt (1893, p. 1369), Gita Press (1969, vol. 3, p. 1688), and Raghunathan (1982, vol. 3, p. 224) all understand, as do we, that the monkey army is on the move. Gorresio (1858, vol. 10, p. 74), Roussel (1903, vol. 3, p. 251), Shastri (1959, vol. 3, p. 223), and Pagani (1999, p. 1078) understand the verb in its sense of "to tremble, be agitated."

45. "a moth" *pataṅgaḥ*: V2,3,D1,3,5–12,T1,G1,M3, and the texts and printed editions of the southern commentators read instead the plural, "moths (*pataṅgāḥ*)."

46. "With . . . iron clubs—like bolts of lightning" *-parighāśani*: Literally, "iron club lightning bolts." The precise sense of the compound is not clear. Among the commentators, only Cg gives any hint of an interpretation, glossing, "their iron-club-thunderbolts (*parighavajram*)." The use of the synonym *vajra* for *aśani* suggests here that Cg reads the compound as a metaphor in the sense of iron clubs that were like thunderbolts or like [Indra's] *vajra*. Given the context of the verse, with its emphasis on the radiance of the army, we understand the term to be a compound metaphor, in which the clubs are being compared to bolts of lightning on the basis of the shared characteristic of brilliance. Translators offer three interpretations. Dutt (1893, p. 1369) and Gita Press (1969, vol. 3, p. 1688) understand *aśani* to be a type of weapon and so read the compound as a type of *dvandva*, "iron clubs and *aśanis*." Roussel (1903, vol. 3, p. 251), followed by Shastri (1959, vol. 3, p. 223) and Pagani (1999, p. 1078), understands that the clubs are shooting forth bolts of lightning. In other words, they read the compound presumably as a *tatpuruṣa* in the sense of "the lightning bolts [issuing] from their iron clubs." Raghunathan (1982, vol. 3, p. 224), like us, understands a compound

metaphor but sees it focusing on the force of the clubs rather than on their brilliance. He renders, "iron clubs that could strike like thunder."

"burnished from the rubbing of their arms" *teṣāṃ bhujaparāmarśavyāmṛṣṭa-*: Literally, "wiped by the wiping of arms." Our translation follows the interpretation of Cg (cf. Cm on v.l. *vyāmiśrita* at verse 42–44 above), who glosses, "polished by the constant contact of [their] arms (*santatabhujasparśenottejita-*)." Among the translators consulted, only Raghunathan (1982, vol. 3, p. 224) follows this interpretation, rendering, "polished by constant handling." Ct and Cr understand the adjective *vyāmṛṣṭa* in the same way that they did the adjective *vyāveṣṭita* in verse 42 above, that is, as "brandished, whirled about."

The majority of northern manuscripts, all *devanāgarī* manuscripts, and all southern manuscripts insert, in whole or in part, a passage of six lines [1443*]. D3,5–7,9–11,13,S place 1443* immediately following verse 46. Other manuscripts present a more complicated pattern of inclusion. Since virtually all manuscripts read this passage, its omission from the critical text is curious. See Bhatt 1960, p. xxxiv. "In their eagerness to fight, the tawny monkeys leapt about as if they were crazed, smashing the night-roaming *rākṣasas* with trees, mountains, and fists.[1–2] But as the monkeys rushed about in this fashion, the *rākṣasas*, fearsome to behold,[1] violently hacked off their heads with sharp swords.[2] [3–4] And *rākṣasas*, their ears torn off by fangs, their heads broken with fists, and their bodies smashed by the blows of boulders, staggered about.[5–6]"

[1]"fearsome to behold" *bhīmadarśanāḥ*: Ñ2,V1,2,B2–4,D7,9–11,13,M1,2,5, and the texts and printed editions of Ct and Cr read instead *bhīmavikramāḥ*, "of fearsome valor."

[2]"monkeys . . . violently hacked off . . . with sharp swords" *teṣāṃ kapīnām asibhiḥ śitaiḥ*: Literally, "of the monkeys with sharp swords." D7,9–11,G2, and the texts and printed editions of Ct and Cr read instead *harīṇāṃ niśitaiḥ śaraiḥ*, "of the tawny monkeys with sharp arrows."

47. D9,G1,3,M3,5, and the texts and printed editions of Cg precede this verse with a similar verse in which the subject and object are reversed, so that the monkeys are described as killing the *rākṣasas*. The critical apparatus represents this as a repetition with variations, which leads to a fair amount of confusion. The verse is found at VSP 6.75.64, KK (1905) 6.75.64, and KK 6.75.63 and actually precedes the one found in the critical edition. As the verse occurs in VSP, KK, and KK (1905), it would mean: "Then some of the most distinguished among the monkeys slaughtered the heroes of the swift *rākṣasas* on every side (*tathaivāpy apare teṣāṃ kapīnām abhilakṣitāḥ / pravīrān abhito jaghnū rākṣasānāṃ tarasvinām //*)." It should be noted that, in KK, the second verse does not immediately follow this verse (KK 6.75.63), since that text alone admits a bracketed verse (KK 6.75.64 = 1446*) in which the *rākṣasas*, armed with various weapons, renew their assault on the monkeys. This intervening verse (1446*) is rendered in no translation consulted. GPP prints a bracketed and unnumbered version of what it considers the second verse, between its verses 6.75.64 and 65. In its footnote, GPP identifies this verse as an extra verse found in the text of Cg. The bracketed verse, however, is not an accurate rendering of the "second verse" but rather an error-filled version of the first. It reads the nominative *harivīrāḥ* for the

correct accusative *harivīrān*, "heroes among the tawny monkeys." This verse also reads *sitaiḥ* [sic], "white," for *śitaiḥ*, "sharp." The actual variations that differentiate the second verse from the first are listed in the footnotes to GPP and, when reconstructed, would read similarly to the verse as found in KK and VSP discussed and translated above. This additional verse is rendered only in the translation of Raghunathan (1982, vol. 3, p. 224) as "The more valiant apes attacked and slew the most powerful of the Rākshasa veterans." In keeping with the order of the verses in KK and VSP, this verse precedes Raghunathan's rendition of our verse 47.

"Then . . . began to cut down" *tathaivāpi . . . jaghnuḥ*: Literally, "even so, they slew." This verse follows very poorly from the one that precedes it. It appears to presuppose 1443*, where the give and take of battle has already commenced. As noted above (see notes to verse 46), that passage should probably have been included in the critical text.

48. "The warriors on both sides cursed, bit, struck down, and killed one another." *ghnantam anyaṃ jaghānānyaḥ pātayantam apātayat / garhamāṇaṃ jagarhānyo daśantam aparo 'daśat //*: Literally, "One slew another who was slaying. [Another] knocked down one who was knocking down. Another reviled one who was reviling. Yet another bit one who was biting." A literal translation reads rather awkwardly in English, and we have therefore paraphrased and condensed the verse in translation. The verse does not make it perfectly clear whether the actions describe mutual hostilities between sets of two combatants or whether we see warriors attacking others who are engaged in assaulting third parties. The point, of course, is to show the general chaos and confusion of the melee.

49. "One cried, 'Attack!' 'He's attacking!' said another, while still a third cried, 'I'll attack!' " *dehīty anyo dadāty anyo dadāmīty aparaḥ punaḥ*: Literally, " 'Give,' [said] one. Another gives. Yet another [said], 'I give.' " In keeping, perhaps, with the poet's intention of rendering the chaos and confusion that are the hallmarks of the "fog of war," this verse is elliptical and somewhat obscure, so that it is difficult to be absolutely certain as to what is taking place. It is not clear, for example, whether the combatants are calling out to their opponents, their comrades, or both. We agree with Ct and Ck in supplying the word "battle (*yuddham*)" to flesh out the elliptical phrases containing the verb $\sqrt{}$*dā*, "to give." Cv and Cg similarly supply the word "blow (*praharaṇam*)," so that, according to these two sets of commentators, the verb here means "fight" or "strike." But, again, whether these commands are intended as challenges to a foe or exhortations to a friend is not clear. Translators generally opt for the former interpretation, whereas we incline toward the latter.

Following Cv and Cg, we also understand an implicit quotation mark (*iti*) after *dadāti*, "he gives." This thus becomes one of the things shouted on the battlefield. Most of the translators consulted do not follow this interpretation and thus take this as a reference to someone actually striking or attacking. We tend to understand it as a shouted warning to one's comrade that one of the enemies is about to strike.

" 'Did you wound him?' 'Stand!' " *kiṃ kleśayasi tiṣṭheti*: Literally, "Do you harm *or* torment? Stand!" Again the meaning is obscure. Cv and Cg understand the question to be "Have you fatigued yourself through your exertions? (*ātmānam āyāsena kiṃ kleśayasi.*)" They then understand the imperative *tiṣṭha*, "stop, stay," to be an exhortation to the weary to rest. This interpretation appears to have been followed by most of the translators consulted, with the exception of Raghunathan (1982, vol. 3, p. 224), who seems to take it as a taunting remark addressed to an enemy: "Don't you worry, just wait." It seems somewhat odd and tortured syntactically to us to take the causative of √*kliś*, "to be tormented," reflexively with *ātmānam*, "self," as Cv and Cg have, and we have therefore chosen to understand the question to be directed to an ally concerning whether he has gotten his man, as it were. We also understand an implicit quotation mark (*iti*) after *kleśayasi*, thus separating it from the imperative form *tiṣṭha*, "stay." We understand this latter to be directed either to a friend to hold his place in battle or, as is often the case in the epic, to a foe to challenge him not to stand and fight.

Following verse 49, D9–11,G,M3,5, and the texts and printed editions of the southern commentators insert a passage of one line [1448*], which construes grammatically with verse 50, adding two adjectival phrases describing the battle: "with weapons broken[1] and armor and arms abandoned.[2]"

[1]"with weapons broken" *vipralambhitaśastram*: Literally, "with weapons violated or deceived." The compound is obscure as none of the normal meanings of *vi* + *pra* √*lambh*, "to deceive, violate, trick," seems to apply convincingly to weapons. Translators who follow this reading have offered all sorts of interpretations, including "scattered about" (Dutt 1893, p. 1370), "*souillés*" (Roussel 1903, vol. 3, p. 251), "stained" (Shastri 1959, vol. 3, p. 223), and "dodged" (Gita Press 1969, vol. 3, p. 1689). Pagani (1999, p. 1078) paraphrases, "*Dans ce tourbillon d'épées*."

G3,M3,5, and the texts and printed editions of Cg and Cm read instead *vipralambitavastram*, "with hanging *or* trailing garments." Only Raghunathan (1982, vol. 3, p. 224) renders this reading.

[2]"armor and arms abandoned" *vimuktakavacāyudham*: Literally, "with its released armor and weapons." Cr understands, "in which weapons had been shot into suits of armor (*vimuktāni kavaceṣv āyudhāni yasmin*)." This idea has been followed only by Gita Press (1969, vol. 3, p. 1689).

50. "amid a welter of fists, lances, and swords" *muṣṭiśūlāsisaṃkulam*: Literally, "crowded with fists, lances, and swords." D13,G,M1–3, and the texts and printed editions of Cg, Cm, and Cv read *yaṣṭi-*, "clubs," in place of *muṣṭi-*, "fists." D9–11 and the texts and printed editions of Ct read *-kuntalam* for *-saṃkulam*, "crowded." The word is obscure in this context. Its normal meanings are "the hair of the head," "a drinking cup," and "a plough." The last of these is a possible reading, since *hala*, or "ploughshare," is the name of a weapon mentioned occasionally (e.g., 6.59.103 and note). This is the interpretation Roussel (1903, vol. 3, p. 251) and Shastri (1959, vol. 3, p. 223) follow. We are inclined to understand the term as a variant of *kunta*, "a kind of lance, barbed dart, *or* spear." In this we agree with the translator of Gita Press (1969, vol. 3, p. 1689). See 6.66.4–5 and note.

51. "The *rākṣasas* cut down the monkeys ten and seven at a time" *vānarān daśa sapteti rākṣasā abhyapātayan*: Although the critical apparatus does not clearly indicate this, *pādas* ab do not appear in the text of Ct. GPP reads it in brackets between 6.76.68 and 69. The apparatus merely notes that "B (ed.) [= GPP] reads 51cd [erroneous for bc]."

52. "cut off" *ālambya*: Literally, "having seized *or* overcome."

"whose hair and drawstrings were flying loose" *visrastakeśarasanam*: The critical reading is a peculiar one both textually and contextually. The critical apparatus shows minimal support for the reading *-rasanam* (*rasanā*), "rope, girdle." And its appropriateness in this context is questionable. The vast majority of manuscripts collated for the critical edition, as well as printed editions, read either *-vasanam* or *-vastram*, "clothing," at the end of this compound. The manuscript evidence is complicated. The text of Ct reads instead *vipralambhitavastraṃ ca*. The term *vipralambhita-*, as noted above (note to verse 49, 1448*), is somewhat obscure. Translators who follow the text of Ct generally understand the compound to mean "having their clothing in disorder *or* soiled." The printed texts of Cg and Cm read *visrastakeśavasanam*, "having their hair and garments flying loose."

Sarga 63

1. "In the thick of that fearsome slaughter of heroes" *pravṛtte saṃkule tasmin ghore vīrajanakṣaye*: Literally, "as that dense and fearsome destruction of heroic folk was going on."

"the heroic *rākṣasa* Kampana" *kampanaṃ vīram*: Literally, "the hero Kampana."

2. "struck first, hitting him" *tāḍayāmāsa . . . pūrvam*: Literally, "he struck first."

"Aṅgada staggered" *sa cacāla*: Literally, "he shook *or* moved."

3. "powerful Aṅgada" *saḥ . . . tejasvī*: Literally, "he, the powerful one."

"hurled" *cikṣepa*: Literally, "he threw *or* tossed." Cg understands that we are to supply the words "at Kampana's chest (*kampanorasīti śeṣaḥ*)."

Following verse 3, Ñ,D3–7,9–11,13,S (V1,2,B2,4 after 1456*; B3 after 1457*) insert a passage of sixty-three lines [App. I, No. 43]: "Then, when Śoṇitākṣa saw that Kampana had been slain in battle,[1] he scattered the armies of the swift monkeys and then swiftly pursued them in order to destroy them.[1][2–3] In his chariot, he swiftly and fearlessly bore down upon Aṅgada.[4] He quickly pierced Aṅgada with sharp and fierce arrows, which rent his body and looked like the fire at the end of a cosmic age.[5–6] Valorous Aṅgada, Vālin's son, was riddled with many sharp arrows of every kind.[2] Some were tipped with razors, while others were horseshoe headed. Some were made entirely of iron, while others had heads like calves' teeth or herons' feathers. Some had heads equipped with earlike blades, and others had long heads or heads like the tips of *karavīra* leaves.[3][7–9] Nonetheless, that powerful monkey[4] crushed Śoṇitākṣa's[5] fearsome[6] bow, chariot, and arrows.[10] But then, without hesitation, swift Śoṇitākṣa quickly grabbed his sword and shield, and leapt swiftly into the sky.[7][11–12] Mighty Aṅgada, however, springing up more swiftly still, caught him, and, wresting away his sword with his hand,[8] he roared.[13–14] Then Aṅgada, that elephant among monkeys, brought the sword down forcefully[9] on the flat surface of his shoulder[10] and slashed him diagonally from shoulder to hip.[11][15–16] Clutching that great sword and roaring again and again, Vālin's son pursued other foes in the forefront of battle.[17–18] But then, in a rage, the mighty hero Prajaṅgha, accompanied by Yūpākṣa, charged the immensely powerful son of Vālin in his chariot.[12] [19–20] At the same time, the hero Śoṇitākṣa, with his golden armlets, recovered and, seizing an iron mace, charged him as well.[21–22] Standing between the two of them, Śoṇitākṣa and Prajaṅgha, that greatest of monkeys looked like the full moon between the twin stars of the constellation Viśākhā.[13][23–24] Mainda and Dvivida, who were guarding Aṅgada,[14] stood close by him, eager to watch.[15][25–26] Then, in anger, the huge, enormously powerful *rākṣasas*, making a supreme effort, charged the monkeys, wielding swords, arrows,[16] and maces.[27–28] A great and hair-raising battle took place between the three monkey lords, on the one hand, and the three bulls among *rākṣasas*, on the other, as they engaged one another.[17][29–30] The monkeys[18] tore up trees and hurled them in battle, but immensely powerful Prajaṅgha cut them down[19] with his sword.[31–32] Next, they pelted the chariots and horses[20] of their foes[21] with trees and mountains in battle. But immensely powerful[22] Yūpākṣa cut them down with torrents of arrows.[33–34] Meanwhile, with his mace, the valorous and mighty Śoṇitākṣa broke in half[23] the trees that Mainda and Dvivida had torn up and hurled.[35–36] Then, raising a huge sword that could rend an enemy's vitals, Prajaṅgha ran swiftly toward Vālin's son.[37–38] Seeing him approach, the exceedingly mighty[24] monkey lord struck him with an *aśvakarṇa* tree.[39–40] Then he struck his sword arm with his fist. That blow of Vālin's son caused the sword to fall to the ground.[41–42] When he saw that his sword, which resembled a cudgel,[25] had fallen to the ground, the immensely powerful *rākṣasa*[26] clenched his fist, which was like adamant.[43–44] Then the immensely powerful *rākṣasa*[27] struck the mighty Aṅgada, bull among monkeys, on the forehead, so that he staggered for a moment.[45–46] Coming to his senses, the powerful, valorous, and mighty son of Vālin knocked Prajaṅgha's head from his body.[28] [47–48] When his paternal uncle Prajaṅgha[29] had been slain in battle, Yūpākṣa's eyes filled with tears. His arrows expended, he swiftly descended from his chariot and drew his sword.[49–50] Seeing Yūpākṣa rushing toward him, Dvivida, hastening, struck him on the chest in anger. Then that mighty monkey[30] seized him violently.[51–52] When mighty[31] Śoṇitākṣa saw that his brother had been caught, the immensely powerful[32] *rākṣasa* struck Dvivida on the chest.[53–54] Then[33] the mighty monkey[34] staggered when he was struck by that *rākṣasa*.[35] But when the mace was raised once more, he grabbed it.[55–56] At that moment heroic Mainda, leader of the monkey troops [57] [and powerful, struck Yūpākṣa in the chest with his palm.[15*][36]] Then Śoṇitākṣa and Yūpākṣa, who were faster than the two monkeys, began to drag and throw them about violently in combat.[58–59] But mighty Dvivida ripped open Śoṇitākṣa's face with his claws and then, hurling him swiftly to the ground, crushed him.[60–61] Meanwhile, Mainda, leader of the monkey troops,[37]in a towering rage, crushed Yūpākṣa in his arms so that he fell to the ground, slain.[62 63]"

[1]Ñ2,V1,B4,D3–7,9–11,S omit lines 2–3.

[2]"with . . . arrows of every kind": The phrase has been added to facilitate breaking up the long list of the various types of arrows into manageable syntactical units.

[3]Like many of the translators consulted, we have relied on the commentators for the identification of these various types of arrows. See Glossary of Weapons. See, too, Dutt (1893, p. 1371, notes a–h).

[4]"powerful monkey" *balī*: Literally, "the powerful one."

[5]"Śoṇitākṣa's . . . bow" *dhanuḥ*: Literally, "the bow."

[6]"fearsome" *ugram*: G3,M3, and the texts and printed editions of Cg read instead *agryam*, "splendid, magnificent."

[7]"leapt swiftly into the sky" *utpapāta divaṃ kṣipram*: D7,G1,2,M3, and the texts and printed editions of Cg read *kruddhaḥ*, "in a rage," for *kṣipram*, "swiftly." D3,9–11, and

the texts and printed editions of Ct read *tadā kruddhaḥ*, "then, in a rage," for *divaṃ kṣipram*, "swiftly into the sky."

[8]"caught him, and, wresting away the sword with his hand" *parāmṛśya . . . kareṇa tasya taṃ khaḍgaṃ samācchidya*: There is a slight ambiguity as to whether to construe *kareṇa*, "with his hand," with the gerund *parāmṛśya*, "having caught," or *samācchidya*, "having wrested." Cr, the only commentator to address this issue, takes the former position, understanding that Aṅgada seized Śoṇitākṣa with his hand. Gita Press (1969, vol. 3, p. 1690) and Dutt (1893, p. 1371) read as we do. Raghunathan (1982, vol. 3, p. 225) ignores the words *parāmṛśya*, "having seized," and *kareṇa*, "hand." Roussel (1903, vol. 3, p. 253), followed by Shastri (1959, vol. 3, p. 224), reads the gerunds in senses that seem inappropriate to the context. They understand *parāmṛśya* to mean that Aṅgada withstood the violent impact of Śoṇitākṣa's leap and *kareṇa . . . samācchidya* to mean that he broke the former's sword with his hand. Pagani (1999, p. 1079) follows Roussel in her reading of *parāmṛśya* but understands *kareṇa . . . samācchidya* as we do.

[9]"brought . . . down forcefully" *nijaghāna*: Literally, "he struck."

[10]"on the flat surface of his shoulder" *tasyāṃsaphalake*: The phrase is incorrectly printed in both KK (1905) (6.76.10; *tasyāṃ saphalake*) and GPP (6.76.10; *tasyāṃ sa phalake*). Commentators gloss, "on that flat *or* broad surface that has the form of the shoulder (*aṃsarūpe phalake*—Ct)."

[11]"diagonally from shoulder to hip" *yajñopavītavat*: Literally, "like a sacred thread." The reference is to the braided cord traditionally worn across one shoulder and under the opposing arm by initiated males of the three higher *varṇas* of the vedic brahmanical social system. See note to 6.68.29.

[12]The textual evidence for lines 19–20 is very complicated. The problem lies in the fact that a number of manuscripts and the printed editions of Ct, including GPP, repeat these lines, with some variations, after line 22. The critical apparatus has condensed these four verses into two, creating a version that no text or manuscript knows.

The text of GPP reads as follows:

> *prajaṅghasahito vīro yūpākṣas tu tato balī* / (= line 19 variant)
> *rathenābhiyayau kruddho vāliputraṃ mahābalam* // (= line 20) [= GPP 6.76.12]
>
> Then, in a rage, the mighty hero Yūpākṣa, accompanied by Prajaṅgha, charged the immensely powerful son of Vālin in his chariot.
>
> [lines 21–22 = GPP 6.76.13]
>
> *prajaṅghas tu mahāvīro yūpākṣahito balī* / (= line 19)
> *gadayābhiyayau kruddho vāliputraṃ mahābalam* // [= GPP 6.76.14]
>
> Then, in a rage, the mighty hero Prajaṅgha accompanied by Yūpākṣa charged the immensely powerful son of Vālin with his mace.

KK (1905) and VSP read only the first of these verses (= KK (1905) and VSP 6.76.13) but read it after line 22. KK reads both verses as its verses 6.76.13 and 14, placing verse 14 in brackets, with the notation that it is found in only one of its manuscript sources. Like KK (1905) and VSP, KK reads these verses after line 22. Translations following the text of Ct translate the sequence as indicated in GPP. Raghunathan (1982, vol. 3, p. 225) follows the text of VSP.

[13]"between the twin stars of the constellation Viśākhā" *viśākhayor madhyagataḥ*: Literally, "placed in the middle of the two Viśākhās. Viśākhā is the sixteenth of the lunar mansions, or *nakṣatras*, and consists of two stars. See 6.4.45; 6.90.30; and notes.

[14]"who were guarding Aṅgada" *aṅgadaṃ parirakṣantau*: Cg indicates that their special concern derives from the fact that they are his maternal uncles (*mātulatvād iti bhāvaḥ*).

[15]"eager to watch" *parasparadidṛkṣayā*: Literally, "out of a desire to see one another." The compound is slightly obscure in its meaning. Commentators and translators have offered a variety of interpretations. Ck and Ct, whom we more or less follow, understand, "out of desire to witness the occasion of battle (*yuddhāvasaradidṛkṣayā*). This interpretation is represented in the translation of Dutt (1893, p. 1372). Cg, Cm, and Ct (second interpretation) understand, "out of a desire to know if there are any *rākṣasa* opponents who are a match for themselves (*svānurūpapratibhaṭarākṣasajijñāsayā*)." This interpretation appears to inform Raghunathan's translation (1982, vol. 3, p. 226): "who... were ready to take on any one of the foe who was worthwhile." Roussel (1903, vol. 3, p. 254) and Pagani (1999, p. 1079) understand the compound to mean that the two monkeys were on the alert (Pagani) or prepared for any eventuality (Roussel).

[16]"arrows" *-bāṇa-*: D5,T1,G3,M3, and the texts and printed editions of Cg read instead *-carma-*, "shield."

[17]"A great and hair-raising battle took place between the three monkey lords, on the one hand, and the three bulls among *rākṣasas*, on the other, as they engaged one another." *trayāṇāṃ vānarendrāṇāṃ tribhī rākṣasapuṃgavaiḥ / saṃsaktānāṃ mahadyuddham abhavad romaharṣaṇam //*: Literally, "there was a great hair-raising battle of three monkey lords who were engaged with three bulls among *rākṣasas*."

[18]"The monkeys" *te*: Literally, "they."

[19]"cut them down" *praticiccheda*: D3,10,11, and the texts and printed editions of Ct read instead *praticikṣepa*, "he repulsed, warded off."

[20]"horses" *aśvān*: D3,9–11, and the texts and printed editions of Ct read instead *sarvān*, "all."

[21]"of their foes": The words have been added.

[22]"immensely powerful" *mahābalaḥ*: D5,T1,G1,3,M3,5, and the texts and printed editions of Cg and Cm read instead *niśācaraḥ*, "the night-roaming *rākṣasa*."

[23]"broke in half" *babhañja... madhye*: Literally, "it broke in the middle."

[24]"exceedingly mighty" *mahābalaḥ... atibalaḥ*: Literally, "immensely powerful... exceedingly powerful."

[25]"a cudgel" *musala-*: G,M3, and the texts and printed editions of Cg and Cm read instead *utpala*, "blue lotus."

[26]"the immensely powerful *rākṣasa*" *mahābalaḥ*: Literally, "the immensely powerful one."

[27]"the immensely powerful *rākṣasa*" *mahātejāḥ*: Literally, "the immensely powerful one."

[28]"mighty... knocked... from his body" *kāyāt pātayāmāsa vīryavān*: Literally, "the mighty one caused [it] to fall from the body." Ñ,V1,2,B2–4,D3,4,9–11,13, and the texts and printed editions of Ct read *muṣṭinā*, "with [his] fist," for *vīryavān*, "mighty." D5,T1,G3,M3, and the texts and printed editions of Cg and Cm read instead *khaḍgenāpātayat kṣitau*, "he made it fall to the ground with the sword."

[29]"paternal uncle Prajaṅgha" *pitṛvye*: Literally, "paternal uncle." Ck clarifies by supplying the name.

[30]"that mighty monkey" *balī*: Literally, "the mighty one."

[31]"mighty" *mahābalaḥ*: D9–11 and the texts and printed editions of Ct read instead the accusative *mahābalam*, making the adjective modify Aṅgada.

[32]"immensely powerful" *mahātejāḥ*: D5,T1,G3,M3, and the texts and printed editions of Cg and Cm read instead *gadāgreṇa*, "with the tip of [his] mace."

[33]"Then" *tadā*: D5,T1,G3,M3, and the texts and printed editions of Cg and Cm read instead *gadā-*, "[struck by] the mace."

[34]"the mighty monkey" *mahābalaḥ*: Literally, "the mighty one."

[35]"by that *rākṣasa*" *tena*: Literally, "by that one."

[36]"At that moment heroic Mainda, leader of the monkey troops [57] [and powerful, struck Yūpākṣa in the chest with his palm [15*].]" *etasminn antare vīro maindo vānarayūthapaḥ* / [57] *yūpākṣaṃ tāḍayāmāsa talenorasi vīryavān* // [15*]: The critical edition, as it has reconstructed the passage, presents us with a line [57] that is a mere sentence fragment and that cannot be construed with either the preceding or the following lines. It is found isolated in this fashion in no known version of the text. Manuscript evidence presents three variations:

1) Ñ,V1,2,B2–4,D3,4,6,7,9,13,T2,3,G1,2,M5 omit the line entirely, and this probably should have been the critical editors' choice as well.
2) D10,11, and the texts and printed editions of Ct remedy the fragment by substituting, for the second half of the line, "He [Mainda] came near Dvivida (*dvividābhyāśam āgamat*)."
3) D5,T1,G3,M1–3, and the texts and printed editions of Cg and Cm read an additional line [15*], completing the verse. Both lines (57 and 15*) appear as verse 6.76.32 in KK, and 6.76.31 in KK (1905) and VSP. Both lines also occur in GPP as an unnumbered verse between 6.76.31 and 32. Line 57 occurs as mentioned in 2 above. Line 15* is placed in brackets with the notation that it is an extra line found in the text of Cg. The notes make no mention of the variants found in line 57. Line 57 alone appears in 6.76.32ab in NSP. Gita Press reads a mixed verse, juxtaposing the reading of 2 above with line 15* as its 6.76.32.

Given the confused textual state of the critical edition here, we have opted to include 15* for the sake of readability, although perhaps the best textual choice would be to omit line 57 entirely.

[37]"leader of the monkey troops" *vānarayūthapaḥ*: D3,9–11,G2,M1,2,5, and the texts and printed editions of Ct read *-puṃgavaḥ*, "bull," for *-yūthapaḥ*, "leader."

4. "the *rākṣasa* troops . . . them" *sā . . . camūm*: Literally, "it . . . the army."

"ran headlong" *jagāmābhimukhī*: Literally, "it went facing."

"Kumbha, Kumbhakarṇa's son" *kumbhakarṇasutaḥ*: Literally, "Kumbhakarṇa's son."

Following verse 4, many northern and southern manuscripts insert, in whole or in part, a passage of four lines [1458*]. D6,7,9–11,S insert only lines 2–4: "Having determined to demonstrate his valor, he calmed them with his words.[1] Then, seeing that the army had had its champions slain by the immensely powerful leaping monkeys who had seized their opportunity,[1] the powerful and outstanding *rākṣasa* Kumbha[2] performed all-but-impossible feats in battle.[2–4]"

[1]"who had seized their opportunity" *labdhalakṣaiḥ*: See notes to 6.56.11 and 6.57.42.

[2]"the . . . outstanding *rākṣasa* Kumbha" *utkṛṣṭam . . . rakṣaḥ . . . kumbhaḥ*: We have followed Ct and Cr, who understand the three terms to be in apposition. Cr glosses, "*utkṛṣṭa* means 'great'; the *rākṣasa* is Kumbha (*utkṛṣṭaṃ mahad rakṣaḥ kumbhaḥ*)." Most of the translations consulted construe the adjective similarly. Although this is not completely persuasive, the only plausible alternative, which is to construe the adjective *utkṛṣṭam* with *karma* in line 4, is a bit of a syntactic stretch.

6. "as if it were a second bow of Indra, illumined by the splendor of lightning and a great rainbow" *vidyudairāvatārciṣmad dvitīyendradhanur yathā*: Literally, "like a second bow of Indra, possessed of luster through lightning and *airāvata*." The simile is not transparent. Commentators and translators read the compound *vidyudairāvatārciṣmat* variously. The problem is that several of the terms used are polysemic in their reference to a variety of mythological and/or meteorological phenomena associated with the divinity Indra in his capacity as an atmospheric or storm god. Particularly ambiguous here is the term *airāvata*. In its masculine form, the term is a proper noun referring to Indra's great white battle-elephant. Among the commentators, Ct and Ck refer to this sense of the term, appearing to understand that the name of the elephant derives from its association with Indra's bow, which is, of course, a kenning for the rainbow. The idea here is, as Ct makes clear by quoting the *Vaijayantī* lexicon, that *airāvata* is primarily the name of a long and straight type of rainbow, in other words, a natural phenomenon. (*airāvato 'bhramātaṅgas tasyendradhanuṣā saṃbandhāt. indrāyudhaṃ tv indradhanus tad evarju rohitam. airāvatam ṛjudīrghendradhanus tad yuktaṃ ca. svābhāvikam indradhanur ity arthaḥ*—so Ct.) Ct quotes Cm to the effect that this particular atmospheric phenomenon appears as a portent of calamity (*etac cotpātakāle bhavatīty artha iti tīrthaḥ*).

Cr understands the term *airāvata* to refer specifically to Indra's elephant and reads the simile as follows: "The arrow stands in the place of the lightning and the [large] body of the *rākṣasa*, in the place of Airāvata (*vidyutsthānīyaḥ śara airāvatasthānīyo rākṣasadeha upamānasambandhaḥ*)." This interpretation is cited in Pagani's note to the passage (1999, p. 1669).

Cg and Cm, like Ct and Ck, cite *Vaijayantī* to support their understanding that the term *airāvata* refers to the particular type of rainbow mentioned above. They read the figure as follows: "Lightning stands in the place of the bowstring, while the *airāvata* rainbow is the object of comparison of the bow itself (*jyāsthanīyā vidyud bāṇasthānīyam airāvatam*)." The meaning, according to Cm, is that Kumbha's bow had a radiance similar to that of the *airāvata* rainbow together with lightning (*vidyutsahitairāvatasadṛśadyutimat kumbhadhanuḥ*). Both Cr and Cg indicate that such a combined phenomenon is either a sign of some unusual portent or an imaginary object of comparison (*airāvatādisaṃyoga utpātakāle bhavaty abhūtopamā vā*—so Cg). Cm's comments are quoted by Ct as noted above. We believe that this reading of the figure, which we have followed, is supported by the simpler northern variant seen in the text of Gorresio (6.55.40): *vidyudbhir āvṛtaṃ vyomni śakracāpam ivāparam*, "like a second bow of Śakra, encircled by lightning in the sky."

All translators who read with the critical edition, with the exception of Raghunathan (1982, vol. 3, p. 227), who renders, "the extended rainbow," understand the term *airāvata* to refer to Indra's elephant. See verse 35 and note.

7. "beautifully feathered... arrow" *patriṇā patravāsasā*: Literally, "with a feathered one that had feathers for its garments."

8. "who resembled a mountain peak" *adrikūṭābhaḥ*: Ñ,V1,2,B,D9–11, and the texts and printed editions of Ct read *trikūṭābhaḥ*, "who resembled Mount Trikūṭa."

"lost his footing" *vipramuktapadaḥ*: Literally, "whose feet were released." Ck and Ct understand that Dvivida has splayed *or* stretched his feet (*prasāritaṃ padaṃ yena saḥ*). Cr understands that his feet were stumbling (*praskhalite pade pādau yasya saḥ*). Cg glosses, "with feeble footsteps (*śithilapadavinyāsaḥ*)."

"dazed and twitching" *sphuran... vihvalaḥ*: Literally, "trembling... dazed." D9–11,G1, and the texts and printed editions of Ct read the participle *vihvalan*, "shaking, trembling," for the adjective *vihvalaḥ*, "dazed."

10. "The immensely powerful Mainda" *mahābalaḥ*: Literally, "the immensely powerful one."

11. "tipped with a splendid arrowhead" *sumukham*: Literally, "having a fine tip."

"the immensely powerful *rākṣasa*" *mahātejāḥ*: Literally, "the immensely powerful one."

13. "two... had fallen" *patitau*: D7,9–11,G1, and the texts and printed editions of Ct and Cr read instead *mathitau*, "crushed *or* afflicted."

"who stood with bow drawn" *udyatakārmukam*: Literally, "whose bow was drawn *or* raised."

14. "As Aṅgada rushed upon him... him" *tam āpatantam*: Literally, "him, who was rushing."

"iron shafts" *āyasaiḥ*: Literally, "with things [made] of iron." See 6.3.12; 6.53.12; 6.55.47; and notes. See, too, 5.39.11; 5.51.38; and notes.

"with javelins" *tomaraiḥ*: We normally translate this term as "iron cudgels," but the nature of the trope here requires one to take the term in the second of the senses that Dikshitar (1944, p. 107) assigns to it, i.e., "javelins." See 6.58.10 and note. Cg glosses, "with elephant goads (*aṅkuśaiḥ*)." The context, however, seems to be more of a battle in which warriors attempt to stop a charging elephant with spears rather than one in which an elephant keeper seeks to goad or prompt his mount. Roussel (1903, vol. 3, p. 255), followed by Shastri (1959, vol. 3, p. 226) and Pagani (1999, p. 1081), reads the term outside the simile, understanding that Kumbha throws, in addition to his arrows, three spears at Aṅgada, but this seems an improbable reading.

15. "various" *vividhaiḥ*: Ñ,V1,2,B2,4,D4,7,9–11,G, and the texts and printed editions of Ct and Cr read instead *bahubhiḥ* "many."

"their tips honed to razor sharpness, their cutting edges keen" *akuṇṭhadhārair niśitais tīkṣṇaiḥ*: The sequence of adjectives is somewhat puzzling, since all three mean "sharp." Cg exploits the polysemy that characterizes many Sanskrit lexemes to avoid the apparent redundancy. He glosses *akuṇṭhadhāraiḥ*, literally, "of unblunted edges," with "whose tips were not broken (*abhagnāgraiḥ*)"; *niśitaiḥ*, "honed," with "excellent (*utkṛṣṭaiḥ*)"; and *tīkṣṇaiḥ*, "sharp," with "made of iron (*ayomayaiḥ*)." For this last gloss, he cites the *Ratnamālā*, which lists *loha*, "iron," among the meanings of *tīkṣṇa* (*tīkṣṇaṃ gare mṛdhe loha iti ratnamālā*). See note to 6.2.14.

16. "Kumbha's" *tasya*: Literally, "his."

17. "all those trees" *tān sarvān*: Literally, "all of them." The context and the grammar demand, as Cr and Cg note, that we supply the word "trees (*tarūn*—so Cr)."

"everything that was thrown by Vālin's son" *vāliputrasamīritān*: Literally, "hurled by Vālin's son."

18. Following verse 18, D5–7,9–11,S insert a passage of one line [1464*]: "His blood began to flow and both his eyes were blinded."

19. "with one hand . . . with the other" *pāṇinā . . . ekena . . . pāṇinā*: Literally, "with a hand . . . with one hand."

Following verse 19, D5–7,9–11,S insert a passage of two lines [1466*]: "Pressing it down, trunk and all, with his chest and grasping it firmly with his hand, he bent it down a little way and then tore it up, as might an elephant.[1]"

[1]"as might an elephant" *yathā gajaḥ*: D9–11 and the texts and printed editions of Ct read instead *mahāraṇe*, "in the great battle."

Ct and Cr, probably in anticipation of verse 20, where the tree is compared to Indra's flagstaff, understand that, through the various actions described here, Aṅgada, after bending down the slender trunk, strips the tree of its leaves and smaller branches (*sūkṣmaśākhāṃ kiṃcid avanamyonmamātha niṣpatraṃ kṛtavān*—so Ct). This idea is reflected in a number of translations that follow the commentary of Ct. Ck, however, thinks that the monkey first spreads the tree together with its branches across his chest, then, with one hand, bends its delicate trunk and then releases it (*saskandham enaṃ sālam urasi neveśyaikena kareṇa saṃparkasūkṣmaśākhāṃ kiṃcid avanamyonmamātha taṃ samut[?]sṛjat* [*sic*]).

20–21. "even as he was about to . . . hurl that tree . . . Kumbha cut him down" *tam . . . vṛkṣam . . . samutsṛjantam . . . ciccheda*: Literally, "he cut down him who was releasing the tree." The two verses, as they stand in the critical edition, appear to collapse the normal sequence of actions in this type of encounter. Almost invariably the *rākṣasa* cuts down the weapon flung by a monkey before striking his opponent with his arrows. The use of the present participle *samutsṛjantam*, "releasing," and the lack of any reference to the tree's flying through the air or being struck down have led us to read the verbal adjective inceptively. The context of 21cd and following makes it very clear that it is Aṅgada himself who has been struck down. D10,11, and the texts and printed editions of Ct and Cr read instead the finite *samutsṛjata* (corrected by Ct and Cr to *samudasṛjata*). This variant allows one to read the two verses as separate syntactic units and to supply the expected object *vṛkṣam*, "tree," for the verb *ciccheda*, "he cut," in verse 21, where no explicit object is given. This explanation is given by Ct and Cr. This reading, however, leads to a serious contextual problem, for if only the tree has been hit, why then does Aṅgada collapse in agony and faint? Cr explains as follows: "He, that is Kumbha, with seven arrows cut down the tree [the word being supplied]. It is for that very reason that Aṅgada, his weapon in the form of a tree having been cut down, was agonized. It is for that reason, in turn, that he fell and fainted. (*sa kumbhaḥ saptabhir bāṇaiś ciccheda vṛkṣam iti śeṣaḥ. ata eva sa cheditavṛkṣarūpāyudho 'ṅgado vivyathe. ata eva papāta mumoha ca.*)" As improbable as this explanation, in which so formidable a warrior-hero as Aṅgada collapses and faints at the loss of a tree, may seem, it has been largely adopted by translators who follow the text of Ct and Cr. Ck, who reads with Ct, is evidently disturbed at this improbability and claims that it is instead the endlessly repeated battles that have caused Aṅgada to suffer as described and that we must add words to this effect (*abhīkṣṇaṃ vivyatha iti punaḥ punaḥ kriyamāṇena yuddheneti śeṣaḥ*). This explanation, too, is far from convincing.

"In great agony" *vivyathe 'bhīkṣṇam*: Literally, "he was greatly pained."

22. "in agony" *vyathitam*: Ñ2,V2,B2,3,D9–11,13, and the texts and printed editions of Ct read instead *patitam*, "fallen."

"drowning as it were in the ocean" *sīdantam iva sāgare*: Literally, "as if sinking in the sea." D6,9–11,T2,3,G2, and the texts and printed editions of Ct read instead the accusative *sāgaram* for the critical text's locative *sāgare*, which yields the rather awkward sense of "like a sinking ocean." Translators who follow the text of Ct have generally understood the reference to be to the ebbing tide or the calming of the waves. In either case, the reading is poor and the interpretation unconvincing.

23. "had been gravely wounded" *vyathitam*: Literally, "pained, agonized."

24. "who stood with bow drawn" *udyatakārmukam*: See note to verse 13 above.

27. "as a barrage of trees might stop a rushing stream" *nageneva jalāśayam*: Literally, "like a body of water by something immovable (*naga*)." We agree with Cg and Ct, who gloss *jalāśayam*, normally, "pond, ocean," in the sense of "stream *or* current of water (*jalapravāham*)." The precise sense of the word *naga*, literally, "that which does not move," is uncertain here, since the term serves as a kenning for both "mountain" and "tree." Ct chooses the former alternative and in this is followed by all translators consulted who share this reading. They understand the term to refer to either a mountain or a rock ("a barrage of stones" [Raghunathan 1982, vol. 3, p. 228]). Cr and Cg take the term in the latter sense. Cg, moreover, suggests that the word "tree" here refers to a mass of trees (*vṛkṣaughaparo 'yaṃ śabdaḥ*), and we have followed his suggestion. Perhaps the reference is to a logjam or a wooden dam.

28. "that mass of arrows" *bāṇacayam*: Ś2,Ñ,V,B,D2–5,8–13,T1,G1,3,M3, and all printed editions consulted read *-patham*, "path *or* range," for *-cayam*, "mass."

"get past it" *ativartitum*: D9–11 and the texts and printed editions of Ct read instead the improbable *api vīkṣitum*, "[unable] even to see." Translators who follow the text of Ct struggle with this awkward reading, often adding some verb with the sense of "to transgress *or* get past" in order to make sense of the otherwise opaque simile.

"the ocean, the great reservoir of the waters" *mahodadhiḥ*: Literally, "the great receptacle of waters."

29–30. "he stepped in front of Aṅgada" *aṅgadaṃ pṛṣṭhataḥ kṛtvā*: Literally, "having placed Aṅgada at his back." Translators understand the sense of this phrase variously. Dutt (1893, p. 1375) understands that Sugrīva actually takes Aṅgada on his back, but this seems unreasonable as such a burden would materially impair Sugrīva's ability to fight. Furthermore, for the remainder of the *sarga*, there is no reference to Aṅgada being on Sugrīva's back. Roussel (1903, vol. 3, p. 256) and Pagani (1999, p. 1082) understand the phrase to mean that Sugrīva leaves Aṅgada behind or abandons him. This, too, seems improbable. Our understanding is that Sugrīva, seeing that the monkey troops have failed to rescue Aṅgada and anticipating that Kumbha will now administer the coup de grâce to his fallen nephew, interposes himself between Aṅgada and Kumbha to shield the former as he launches his own attack. This idea is evidently shared by Cg, who, after quoting the phrase, remarks, "the sense is that otherwise he [Kumbha] would kill [Aṅgada] (*anyathā hanyād iti bhāvaḥ*)."

"Sugrīva... he... rushed swiftly upon Kumbha in battle" *abhidudrāva vegena sugrīvaḥ kumbham āhave*: Ś2,Ñ,V,B1–3,D1–4,8–13,G1, and the texts and printed editions of Ct and Cr read instead *abhidudrāva sugrīvaḥ kumbhakarṇātmajaṃ raṇe*, "Sugrīva rushed upon Kumbhakarṇa's son in battle."

"roaming the mountain slopes" *śailasānucaram*: Cg is of the opinion that ranging the mountain slopes makes elephants especially powerful. He supports this claim by citing a verse from Kālidāsa's *Abhijñānaśākuntalam* (2.4) in which an especially powerful character is likened to a mountain-ranging elephant. (*śailasānucaratvenātibalam. giricara iva nāgaḥ prāṇasāraṃ bibhartīti kālidāsokteḥ.*)

31. "The immensely powerful Sugrīva... and" *ca mahābalaḥ*: Literally, "the immensely powerful one... and." D9–11 and the texts and printed editions of Ct read instead *sa mahākapiḥ*, "the great monkey."

"huge mountains" *mahāśailān*: D6,9–11, and the texts and printed editions of Ct read the redundant *mahāvṛkṣān*, "huge trees."

"*aśvakarṇas*, *dhavas*" *aśvakarṇān dhavān*: D9–11 and the texts and printed editions of Ct read instead *aśvakarṇādikān*, "*aśvakarṇas*, etc."

32. "But with his sharp arrows" *niśitaiḥ śaraiḥ*: Literally, "with sharp arrows." D9–11 and the texts and printed editions of Ct read instead *svaśaraiḥ śitaiḥ*, "with his own arrows that were sharp."

"majestic" *śrīmān*: D6,7,T2,3,G2,M3, and the texts and printed editions of Cr, Cm, and Cg read instead *śīghram*, "quickly."

33. "Completely riddled" *ācitāḥ*: Literally, "heaped up." We agree with Cg, who glosses, "completely covered with no gaps (*sarvato nīrandhratayā vyāptāḥ*)." D7,9–11,G2, and the texts and printed editions of Ct and Cr read instead *arditāḥ*, "afflicted, broken."

"with sharp arrows by that fierce and celebrated marksman, Kumbha" *abhilakṣyeṇa tīvreṇa kumbhena niśitaiḥ śaraiḥ*: V3,D5,9–11,T1,3,G1, and the texts and printed editions of Ct, Ck, and Cr omit this line [= 33ab]. Cg, who reads the variant *abhilakṣeṇa*, is the only commentator to have and note this reading. He glosses, "by him whose targets are approached [i.e., hit] (*abhigatalakṣyeṇa*)." See 5.46.28 and note.

"hundred-slayers" *śataghnayaḥ*: Earlier in the epic the commentators have described this as a kind of spiked defensive weapon placed along a city's ramparts. Here Cg, the only commentator to remark on the term, explains, "types of weapons covered with spikes (*śaṅkucitā āyudhaviśeṣāḥ*)." This interpretation is incorporated into the translations of Raghunathan (1982, vol. 3, p. 229) and Gita Press (1969, vol. 3, p. 1695). See notes to 1.5.11 and 6.3.12. Compare 5.2.19; 5.3.30; and 5.41.14, where the *śataghnī* appears to be a hand-held weapon.

35. "snatching away" *sahasā... ākṣipya*: Literally, "having violently seized."

"as lustrous as the bow of Indra" *indradhanuḥprabham*: The bow of Indra, of course, also serves as a kenning for the rainbow, an allusion made explicit in the translation of Gita Press (1969, vol. 3, p. 1695). See verse 6 and note above.

36. "Then... Sugrīva... he... bore down upon" *avaplutya tataḥ*: Literally, "then having leapt down." It is not clear from what position Sugrīva is leaping down, since nothing in the previous passage has shown him leaping upward. The commentators are silent on this point. Gita Press (1969, vol. 3, p. 1695), alone among the translations consulted, attempts to rationalize the expression. The translator, presumably on the basis of his own imagination, indicates that in the preceding verse Sugrīva

had leapt up on Kumbha's chariot to grab his bow and now leaps down from it. He translates, "speedily leaping down from the chariot." Evidently he reads the adverb *tataḥ*, "then," in the sense of "from that." Printed editions of Ct (GPP 6.76.69 and NSP 6.76.69) read *dhanuḥ*, "bow," for *tataḥ*. This variant is not noted in the critical apparatus.

"who now resembled an elephant with broken tusks" *bhagnaśṛṅgam iva dvipam*: Literally, "[who was] like an elephant whose tusks were broken." The simile, no doubt, refers to a breaking of Kumbha's bow in the previous verse.

37. "Your chivalry and your majesty are shared only by Rāvaṇa himself." *saṃnatiś ca prabhāvaś ca tava vā rāvaṇasya vā*: Literally, "modesty and majesty belong either to you or to Rāvaṇa." We follow the commentators in understanding the expression to mean either that Kumbha's virtues are equal to those of Rāvaṇa (Cg) or that, among *rākṣasas*, they belong only to these two individuals (Cr, Ct, Ck). We render *saṃnatiḥ*, "modesty, humility," in keeping with the suggestion of Cm and Cg (first alternative), who gloss, "decorous behavior among the *rākṣasas* (*rākṣaseṣu vinayaḥ*)." Cg amplifies, explaining that the seeming oxymoron "*rākṣasa* decorum" derives here from Kumbha's favorable treatment (i.e., sparing) of the monkeys Aṅgada, Dvivida, and Mainda, even though they have slain his kinsmen—Kampana, Prajaṅgha, Yūpākṣa, and Śoṇitākṣa (*kampanaprajaṅghayūpākṣaśoṇitākṣamārakāṇām aṅgadamaindadvividānāṃ nirākaraṇād rākṣasaprāvaṇyoktiḥ*).

38. "Peer of Prahrāda, Bali, Indra the slayer of Vṛtra, Kubera, and Varuṇa" *prahrādabalivṛtraghnakuberavaruṇopama*: Literally, "O you who are comparable to Prahrāda, Bali, the slayer of Vṛtra, Kubera, and Varuṇa." D4,7,9,11,S read the phonological variant *prahlāda-*, "Prahlāda," for *prahrāda*, "Prahrāda."

Only Cs among the commentators attempts to explain the bases for the choice of these particular mythological figures as objects of flattering comparison. He claims: 1) Prahrāda (v.l. Prahlāda) and Bali are included since, as grandfather and grandson—excluding the representative of the intervening generation, viz., Hiraṇyakaśipu—their mention suggests that Kumbha's fame or glory is greater than that of his father (Kumbhakarṇa); 2) Indra, in his role as the slayer of the demon Vṛtra, is mentioned as an object of comparison for the ability to kill one's enemies; and 3) Kubera and Varuṇa serve as models for wealth and unassailability, respectively. (*pitrapekṣayā kīrtir adhiketi vaktuṃ pitāmahapautrayoḥ prahlādabalyor grahaṇam. vairisaṃhāre vṛtraghnopamā. dhanikatvāpradhṛṣyatvayoḥ kuberavaruṇopamateti jñeyam.*)

"though you are mightier still" *balavattaraḥ*: D7,9–11,T3,G2, and the texts and printed editions of Ct and Cr read instead the accusative *balavattaram*. In this variant, Kumbha's father, Kumbhakarṇa, is the one whose strength is extolled. D5,T1,G3,M3, and the texts and printed editions of Cg and Cm read instead the adverb *balavṛttataḥ*. Cg glosses, "in the exercise of strength (*balavyāpāreṇa*)."

39. "The thirty gods . . . a single-handed" *ekam . . . tridaśāḥ*: Literally, "one . . . thirty." We believe the idea here is that Kumbha is represented as able to single-handedly hold off the massed ranks of the gods. Translators consulted have tended to take the term *ekam* to mean "sole" or "only."

"lance in hand" *śūlahastam*: T1,G3,M3, and the texts and printed editions of Cg and Cm read instead *cāpahastam*, "bow in hand."

"worldly cares" *ādhayaḥ*: Literally, "mental [as opposed to physical] afflictions."

Following verse 39, D5–7,9–11,S insert a passage of one line [1477*]: "Display your valor, wise *rākṣasa*,[1] as I observe your feats.[2]"

[1]"wise *rākṣasa*" *mahābuddhe*: Literally, "O you of great intelligence."
[2]"as I observe your feats" *karmāṇi mama paśyataḥ*: Literally, "as I see actions." D10,11,G1, and the texts and printed editions of Ct read *paśya ca*, "and witness," for *paśyataḥ*, "as [I] see." This yields the sense "witness [my] feats."

40. "Your paternal uncle Rāvaṇa" *pitṛvyas te*: Literally, "your paternal uncle."
"the gift of a boon" *varadānāt*: See note to 6.28.28–29.
"conquered the gods and *dānavas*... while Kumbhakarṇa did so through his own enormous strength" *sahate devadānavān / kumbhakarṇas tu vīryeṇa sahate ca surāsurān*: Literally, "he conquers the *devas* and the *dānavas*... but Kumbhakarṇa conquers the *suras* and *asuras* by strength." Ct indicates that, by mentioning the respective means by which Kumbha's seniors have achieved their conquest, Sugrīva is suggesting that Kumbha conquers by virtue of both of these powers (*tvaṃ tūbhābhyām ity arthaḥ*).
41. "Indrajit's" *indrajitaḥ*: Shastri (1959, vol. 3, p. 228) mistakenly renders "[equal] to Indra."
"archery" *dhanuṣi*: Literally, "in respect to the bow." As Cr notes, we must understand the term to refer to the science of archery (*dhanurvidyāyām*).
42. "all beings" *bhūtāni*: Literally, "beings."
"the great... clash in battle" *mahāvimardaṃ samare*: The words *vimarda* and *samara* overlap in their ranges of meaning in the sense of "war, combat." Some of the commentators have attempted to differentiate the terms. Thus, Cr glosses *vimardam* as "battle (*yuddham*)" and *samare* as "on the battlefield (*saṃgrāmabhūmau*)." Cg glosses *mahāvimarda* as "the great blow[s] (*mahāprahāram*)."
"like that between Śakra and Śambara" *śakraśambarayor iva*: The legendary battle between Indra and the demon Śambara is recorded as early as the *Ṛgveda* (1.54; 1.130; 1.112.14; 1.51.6; 3.47; 7.18; etc.). See 6.57.7 and notes.
43. "missiles" *astra-*: In many contexts, we translate this term as "divinely charged weapons *or* divine weapon-spells." In this case, however, there is no suggestion that Kumbha is using anything other than normal, earthly weapons. See Introduction, p. 112.
45. "Kumbha had first been flattered, but now, at the contemptuous words of Sugrīva" *tena sugrīvavākyena sāvamānena mānitaḥ*: Literally, "honored by that contemptuous speech of Sugrīva." The line is both syntactically and semantically difficult, and the commentators have struggled to rationalize it. Our translation follows the suggestion of Cr, who understands the participle *mānitaḥ*, "flattered, honored," to be part of an emboxed elliptical sentence with the sense "Kumbha had been honored." Cr's reasoning is that Kumbha at first had felt flattered by Sugrīva's words "You have performed an unparalleled [feat]" (verse 43) but now, upon hearing his insulting words "It is only out of fear of incurring censure that I have not killed you thus far" (verse 44), his martial ardor blazes up. (*sāvamānenopālambhān na hato 'sītyādyavamānasahitena sugrīvavākyena kṛtam apratimam ityādinā mānitaḥ satkṛtaḥ kumbho 'bhavad iti śeṣaḥ*.)
Cg and Cs, on the other hand, understand all of Sugrīva's words of praise to be ironic or deceptive. Thus, Cg explains, "the meaning is that he was insulted by the ironic praise (*bahumānena vyājenāvamānita ity arthaḥ*)." Cs understands that Kumbha is being "praised"

with a speech that merely outwardly takes the form of praise while within it lies a core of contempt (*sāvamānenāntaravamānagarbheṇa bahiḥstutirūpeṇa vākyena mānitaḥ*).

Following verse 45, Ñ1,D4–7,9–11,S (Ñ2,V1,2,B,D13 after 1480*) insert a passage of ten lines [1481*]: "Then Kumbha seized Sugrīva with both arms, and the two of them began to breath heavily again and again like elephants covered with rut fluid. Locked in each others limbs, they dragged[1] each other about, releasing, in their exhaustion, smoky flames from their mouths.[1–4] The earth caved in under the blows of their feet, while the ocean, Varuṇa's abode, was agitated, its waves rolling wildly.[5–6] Then Sugrīva, hurling Kumbha upward, made him fall swiftly into the salt sea so that he saw the bottom[2] of that reservoir of waters.[7–8] The fall of Kumbha hurled the mass of water upward so that it rose on every side like the Vindhya mountains or Mount Mandara.[9–10]"

[1]"they dragged" *karṣantau*: Literally, "[those two] dragging." V1,2,D10, and the texts and printed editions of Ct read instead *gharṣantau*, "rubbing, grinding."

[2]"so that he saw the bottom" *darśayan . . . talam*: Literally, "showing [him] the surface." The expression and its variant *darśayan . . . sthalam* (GPP, NSP) are slightly ambiguous. All translators consulted, with the exception of Raghunathan, understand, as do we, that this is a euphemism for sending Kumbha to the bottom of the sea. Raghunathan (1982, vol. 3, p. 230) appears to read the expression in the context of the following verse, where the waters are splashed out of the seabed. He thus renders, "[hurled him into the sea] . . . exposing its floor." Crā (ascribed to Cg in GPP) understands the reference to be not to the bottom of the sea but to dry land, i.e., the seashore. He claims that, in describing Sugrīva's feat of hurling the enormous Kumbha a hundred leagues from the summit of Mount Trikūṭa into the sea at Laṅkā's shore, the passage is intended to illustrate the monkey's immeasurable power (*śatayojanavistīrṇatrikūṭaśikharamadhye yudhyan sugrīvaḥ kumbhaṃ laṅkādvīpatale lavaṇāmbhasi pātayāmāsety abhidhānāt sugrīvasyāparimeyabalavattā dyotyate*).

46. "hurled himself upon" *abhipadya*: Literally, "having attacked." G1 and the texts and printed editions of Ct read instead *abhipātya*, "having thrown down." Ś2,B3,D1,3–5,7–12,T3,G2,3,M5, and the texts and printed editions of Cg read instead *abhipatya*, "having attacked."

"that had the force of a thunderbolt" *vajravegena*: Literally, "having the force *or* speed of the *vajra*." Ñ2,B2,D4,6,7,9–11,T2,3, and the texts and printed editions of Ct and Cr read instead *vajrakalpena*, "like the thunderbolt, adamant, *or* the *vajra*." See 6.64.20 and note.

47. "His skin" *tasya carma*: D7,10,11, and the texts and printed editions of Cr and Ct read instead *tasya varma*, "his armor." In a note, Pagani (1999, p. 1669) has taken this extremely weak reading as a reference to the monkeys' sudden acquisition of military equipment in the second part of the war. See 6.64.17 and note.

"and his blood poured out" *saṃjajñe cāsya śoṇitam*: Literally, "and his blood was produced." Ñ1,D4,M3, and the texts and printed editions of Cg and Cm read *bahu susrāva*, "much [blood] flowed," for *saṃjajñe cāsya*.

"had penetrated to the bone" *pratijaghne 'sthimaṇḍale*: Literally, "it struck in the circle of bones." The reference is probably to the rib cage. Commentators differ in their interpretation of this phrase. Ct, whom we follow, glosses the verb *pratijaghne* as "struck against (*pratihataḥ*)." Cr understands that the fist gains force or momentum within Sugrīva's bony structures (*sugrīvāsthisamūhe pratijaghne vegavattāṃ prāpa*). Cg glosses as does Ct but understands the sense to be that the fist was ineffective against Sugrīva's bones (*mogho babhūvety arthaḥ*). Dutt (1893, p. 1377), perhaps taking his cue from Cr, renders, "and the impetus of that blow broke Sugrīva's bones." On the other hand, Raghunathan (1982, vol. 3, p. 230), following Cg's lead, renders, "the force of the blow was spent when it reached the bones."

48. "briefly" *muhuḥ*: Literally, "for a moment." D9–11,M5, and the texts and printed editions of Ct read instead *mahat*, "great, huge."

"like the flame that arises on Mount Meru when it is struck by lightning" *vajraniṣpeṣasaṃjātajvālā merau yathā girau*: Literally, "like the flame arising from the pounding of the *vajra* on Mount Meru." Cg understands the reference not to be to a forest fire produced by a lightning strike but rather to the mythological incident in which Indra is said to have cut off the wings of the mountains (see 5.1.46,80 and notes; and notes to 5.55.18). The fire, according to Cg, would have arisen at that time from the friction of Indra's weapon, the *vajra* (*vajraniṣpeṣasaṃjātendreṇa pakṣacchedakāle vajrasaṃghaṭṭajanyety arthaḥ*).

Following verse 48, D7,G2 (after 48c), and KK, in brackets (=6.76.88ef and unnoted by the critical apparatus), insert a passage of one line [1483*], which repeats the mention of the flames arising from the force of Kumbha's fist.

49. "Although Sugrīva... had been struck there" *sa tatrābhihataḥ... sugrīvaḥ*: Literally, "struck there, Sugrīva." Ct suggests that the adverb *tatra*, "there," means "on the chest (*urasi*)."

"he clenched his fist" *muṣṭiṃ saṃvartayāmāsa*: We agree with Cg, who takes the verb to mean "he made (*cakāra*)." Most of the translators consulted also take the verb here to mean "to clench *or* double." Cr, on the other hand, takes the verb to mean "whirled about *or* swung (*bhrāmayāmāsa*)." This interpretation appears to have been followed by Roussel (1903, vol. 3, p. 257) and Shastri (1959, vol. 3, p. 229), who understand that the monkey raised his fist. Cr's interpretation, perhaps, informs Pagani's rendition: "*renvoya un coup de poing*" (1999, p. 1083). See 6.64.15 and note.

"as hard as adamant" *vajrakalpam*: Literally, "like the *vajra*." See note to 46 above.

50. "which, radiant with a thousand rays of light, was as brilliant as the sun's orb" *arciḥsahasravikacaṃ ravimaṇḍalasaprabham*. V1,2,D11,G2, and (*pace* the critical apparatus) printed editions of Ct and Cr read the line as a single compound, yielding the translation "as brilliant as [v.l., having the splendor of] the sun's orb, shining with its thousand rays." The critical text's reading, *-saprabham*, "as brilliant as," is marked as uncertain. Ś2,Ñ,V2,3,B1,3,4,D1–4,6–8,12,13,T2,3,G2,M5 read *-saṃnibham*, "resembling," while V1,D9–11,M1,2, and the texts and printed editions of Ct, Ck, and Cr read instead *-varcasam*, "[having] the splendor of." One should recall that Sugrīva is the son of the sun god, Sūrya.

Following verse 50, Ñ,V1,2,B2–4,D4–7,9–11,13,S insert a passage of two lines [1484*]: "Violently struck[1] by that blow, Kumbha was stunned. He then collapsed like fire, the purifier, when its flames have been extinguished."

[1]"struck" *-tāḍitaḥ*: Ñ,V1,2,B2–4,D4,10,13,T1,G1,M5, and the texts and printed editions of Ct read instead *-pīḍitaḥ*, "oppressed, crushed."

51. "the red planet Mars" *lohitāṅgaḥ*: Literally, "the red limbed one." As suggested by Pagani (1999, p. 1669), the choice of the planet Mars here is no doubt intended to suggest the demon's bloody body.

"somehow... from the heavens" *ākāśāt... yadṛcchayā*: Literally, "from the sky by chance." Ck and Ct understand the adverb *yadṛcchayā*, "by chance, accidentally," to mean "because of its subjection to fate (*daivādhīnataḥ*)." This interpretation has been followed by all translations consulted, with the exception of Gorresio (1858, vol. 10, p. 82), who renders, "*spontaneamente*." Ck understands the figure to be an *abhūtopamā*, that is, "a simile with a nonexistent *or* imaginary object of comparison."

52. "the body of Sūrya, lord of cows, when he was vanquished by Rudra" *rudrābhipannasya yathā rūpaṃ gavāṃ pateḥ*: Literally, "like the form of the lord of cows, who was overcome by Rudra." Most of the commentators gloss *gavāṃ pateḥ*, "of the lord of cows," with "of Sūrya (*sūryasya*)." Cv glosses, "of Pūṣan (*pūṣṇaḥ*)." The epithet no doubt derives from Pūṣan's role in the *ṚV* as the guardian of cattle. (See *ṚV* 6.54.7,10; and Keith 1925, vol. 35, p. 107.)

According to a story at *Vāmanapurāṇa* 5.10–18, Sūrya, homologized here with Pūṣan, attempted to stop Rudra, who was on a rampage after being cursed by Brahmā. Rudra seized and whirled Sūrya around by his arms, which became shortened and bloodied in the process. Rudra then threw Sūrya to the ground. The falling of the bloodied and mangled body to the ground is the basis for the simile. See Pagani 1999, p. 1669, who mentions this story but provides no reference.

Since the polysemic term *go*, here rendered as "cow," can also mean, among many other things, "rays of light," one could also understand the kenning to mean "lord of light *or* lord of rays," i.e., the sun.

53. "tremendous" *adhikam*: Normally, the word means "great still, more," and some translators render it in this sense.

The meter is *upajāti*.

Sarga 64

2–3. "That hero" *vīraḥ*: D5,10,11, and the texts and printed editions of Ct read instead *dhīraḥ*, "brave, resolute."

"bound with garlands of flowers" *sragdāmasaṃnaddham*: Literally, "bound with the ties of garlands." Ck understands, "bound with garlands, such as pearl necklaces, etc. (*hārādisragbhiś ca sannadham*)." Cv and Cg render, "bound with masses of garlands (*sragjālanaddham*—so Cv; *sraksamūhanibaddham*—so Cg)." Cr explains, "ornamented with strings of garlands (*srajāṃ dāmabhiḥ sannaddham alaṃkṛtam*)." See 6.64.8–11 and note.

"stamped with the sign of five fingers" *dattapañcāṅgulam*: Literally, "[to which] five fingers are given." The expression is obscure, and the commentators are divided as to its meaning. We follow the interpretation of Cv, Cg, and Cm, who understand, "stamped with a seal in the form of five fingers and colored with sandalwood, saffron, etc. (*candanakuṅkumādinārpitapañcāṅgulamudrāmudritam*—so Cg)." This interpretation is further supported by Cl, as reported in Gorresio (1858, vol. 10, p. 292), who glosses, "having a mark of five fingers placed on top of it (*uparidattapañcāṅgulacihnam*)." Gorresio believes that the meaning of the term is that the club bears an impression of the mark of five fingers by which the *rākṣasa* grasps it. This interpretation is followed in the translations of Raghunathan and Gorresio. Raghunathan (1982, vol. 3, p. 231), however, understands by the term *aṅgula*, "finger," a measure of distance. He renders, "stamped with a seal five finger-breaths [*sic*] in width." Gorresio (1858, vol. 10, p. 82) renders, "*che avea al di sopra un marchio di cinque dita.*" Cg offers a second interpretation, whereby the compound can be read adverbially to modify the verb *ādade*, "he took up," with the sense of "in such a way that he grasped it with five fingers (*dattapañcāṅgulaṃ yathā tathādade*)." This interpretation may have inspired the translation of Roussel (1903, vol. 3, p. 259), who renders, "*prit par la poignée.*" Ct, Ck, and Cr understand quite differently, glossing, "having ligatures of wrought iron measuring five *aṅgulas* (*pañcāṅgulapramāṇā dattāḥ kālāyasapaṭṭabandhā yasmiṃs tam*—so Ct)." An *aṅgula* is a measure of distance equaling eight *yavas*, or "barleycorns," roughly half an inch. This interpretation is followed in the translations of Gita Press (1969, vol. 3, p. 1698) and Dutt (1893, p. 1377). See notes to 6.3.12; 6.53.12; and 6.55.47. Pagani (1999, p. 1084) appears to take the expression simply as an indication of the size of the weapon, rendering, astonishingly, "*longue de cinq pouces.*" Shastri (1959, vol. 3, p. 229) ignores the compound entirely.

"a lordly mountain" *nagendra-*: D3,9–11,G1, and the texts and printed editions of Ct read instead *mahendra-*, "Mount Mahendra."

4. "like . . . in battle" *-samaṃ raṇe*: The word *raṇe*, "in battle," is marked as uncertain in the critical text. D6,T2,3,M3,5, and the texts and printed editions of Cg and Cm read instead *tadā*, "then." D7,9–11,G2, and the texts and printed editions of Ct and Cr read instead [*śakradhavaja*]*samaujasam* for [*śakradhvaja*]*samaṃ raṇe*, yielding, "whose splendor was equal to [that of Śakra's flagstaff]."

"Brandishing it" *tam āvidhya*: Cr glosses, "having firmly grasped (*dṛḍhaṃ gṛhītvā*)."

5–6. "the golden necklace" *niṣkeṇa*: See 6.53.22 and note.

"burnished" *mṛṣṭābhyām*: D1,4,9–11,M3, and the texts and printed editions of Ct read instead *citrābhyām*, "splendid, variegated."

"resembled a storm cloud replete with thunder, lightning, and rainbow" *yathendradhanuṣā meghaḥ savidyutstanayitnumān*: Literally, "like a cloud possessing thunder with lightning and with Indra's bow." Cg explains the basis for the simile in some detail. He argues that Nikumbha's mace plays the role of the rainbow, his ornaments, that of lightning, and his roaring in the previous verse, that of the thunder. Thus, he argues, the *upameya*, or the subject of comparison (i.e., Nikumbha), is in no way defective. (*indradhanuḥsthāne parighaḥ. vidyutsthāne bhūṣaṇāni. vinanādeti pūrvaślokokto vinādaḥ stanayitnusthāna iti nopameyanyūnatā.*) See note to 6.63.35.

7. "The tip of that . . . iron club could smash the lair of the winds in the sky." *parighāgreṇa pusphoṭa vātagranthiḥ*: Literally, "the knot of the winds was burst by the tip of the iron club." The expression is somewhat obscure. We follow the commentators, who generally understand the term *vātagranthiḥ* to refer to the *vātaskandha*, the source of the seven bands of atmospheric winds (*vātagranthir āvahādisaptavātaskandhaḥ*—so Cg). The idea here, as suggested by Ct and noted by Dutt (1893, p. 1378), is that the length of Nikumbha's club (*etena parighasya dairghyam uktam*—Ct) is so great that it can extend into the sky and there destroy the nexus from which the seven named winds (*āvaha*, *pravaha*, etc., see *MBh* 12.229.26–27) emanate (*vātagranthir āvahādisaptamahāvāyūnāṃ saṃdhiḥ*). Cr understands similarly. The nexus of the winds (*vāyuskandha*) is described in the *Bṛhatsaṃhitā* of Varāhamihira at 80.24. In the *Bālakāṇḍa* (1.46.4), Diti

begs of Indra that her shattered fetus should become the *vātaskandhas*, or the seven winds of heaven. (See 1.46.4 and note.) Some translators, including Roussel (1903, vol. 3, p. 259), Gorresio (1858, vol. 10, p. 82), Pagani (1999, p. 1084), and Shastri (1959, vol. 3, p. 230), appear to take the reference to be to an actual incident in which Nikumbha had attacked and smashed the winds. Pagani, in her note to the passage (p. 1670), takes this interpretation so far as to view Hanumān's impending victory over Nikumbha as a kind of revenge for the wrong done to his own father (Vāyu) by Nikumbha with his iron club. The term *vātaskandha* may also refer to the nexus of the internal winds, or breaths, *prāṇa*, etc., so that the whole expression could be seen as a circumlocution for "lethal *or* deadly."

"that huge warrior's" *mahātmanaḥ*: Literally, "of the great one." We agree with the commentators, as well as Gita Press (1969, vol. 3, p. 1698) and Raghunathan (1982, vol. 3, p. 231), in taking the epithet to refer to Nikumbha's enormous size. Gorresio (1858, vol. 10, p. 82) and Pagani (1999, p. 1084) understand the adjective to describe a moral quality in the sense of "noble *or* magnanimous." Shastri (1959, vol. 3, p. 230) and Roussel (1903, vol. 3, p. 259) omit the term.

"It blazed" *prajajvāla*: Commentators understand that the subject of this verb can be either Nikumbha himself or the tip of his iron club (*parigha*). (*prajajvāla nikumbha iti śeṣaḥ. parighāgrabhāga iti vā*—so Ct.)

8–9. "The whirling of... iron club seemed to set the very sky spinning" *-āghūrṇaṃ bhramatīva nabhastalam*: Literally, "whirled... by the iron club, the surface of the sky spins as it were." Cg understands that the word *parigha*, "iron club," is used in a secondary sense to refer to the wind generated by the weapon (*atra parighaśabdena tadvāta upalakṣyate*). Given this reading, Cg understands that the heavens are actually set spinning and that, therefore, the word *iva*, "as if" (translated above as "seemed"), is to be taken as a *vākyālaṃkāra*.

"the heavenly city of Viṭapāvatī" *nagaryā viṭapāvatyā*: Literally, "with the city Viṭapāvatī." The commentators are divided as to the precise reference of this uncommon name. Ct and Ck, in an apparent effort to maintain parallelism between the two cities mentioned and the two kinds of mansions, understand that this is the name of the city of the *gandharvas*. Given the apparent parallelism between the two cities and their respective mansions, we follow this interpretation and understand that the mansions of the *gandharvas* are in Viṭapāvatī. Cg, Cm, and Cr take the reference to be to the city of Alakā, which is normally associated with Kubera and the *yakṣas*. Cm's opinion is quoted by Ct. See 5.3.4 and note.

"the celestial city of Amarāvatī with all its mansions" *saha caivāmarāvatyā sarvaiś ca bhavanaiḥ saha*: *Pādas* 8cd are omitted by B2,D9–11,13, and the printed editions of Ct.

10. "With his iron club and ornaments for his flames" *parighābharaṇaprabhaḥ*: Literally, "whose iron club and ornaments were [his] radiance." Given the tenor of the extended metaphor, we agree with Ct, Ck, and Cg (second alternative) in taking the compound as a *bahuvrīhi*, whose literal meaning would be "having the iron club and ornaments for his radiance." Cg's first explanation, which is not very different, is that Nikumbha shines by virtue of his club and ornaments. (*parighenābharaṇaiś ca prabhātīti parighābharaṇaprabhaḥ. yadvā parighābharaṇāny eva prabhā yasya sa tathā.*)

"his rage for kindling" *krodhendhanah*: D5–7,T,G2,3,M, and the texts and printed editions of Cg and Cm read instead *kapīnāṃ saḥ*, "he... of the monkeys." Cg, the only commentator to remark on this variant, understands that we are to construe the phrase with the adjective *durāsadaḥ*, "unapproachable," in *pāda* a, thus giving the passage the sense "he [Nikumbha] was unapproachable by the monkeys." Raghunathan (1982, vol. 3, p. 231), the only translator consulted to follow this reading, has a seemingly confused rendition, translating, "[the lustre of the club and jewels] seemed to blind the monkeys."

"when it blazes forth" *utthitaḥ*: Literally, "sprung up, arisen."

11. "frozen with fear" *na śekuḥ spanditum bhayāt*: Literally, "they were unable to stir out of fear." Cg, alone among the commentators, attempts to explain why the *rākṣasas* should be afraid of Nikumbha. He reasons that they would be thinking that, since such powerful warriors as Prajaṅgha, etc., had already been slain, what point would there be in so relatively weak a figure as Nikumbha even attempting to fight. Their fear, then, derives from their anticipation of Nikumbha's anger should they express this view (*prabaleṣu prajaṅghādiṣu hateṣu durbalair bhavadbhiḥ kim arthaṃ yuddhāya prayatnaḥ kṛta iti nikumbhaḥ kupyed iti rākṣasānāṃ bhayaṃ veditavyam*).

"thrusting out his chest" *vivṛtyoraḥ*: The verb *vi* √*vṛ* can mean either "to expand, unfold" or "to expose, make manifest." Like Raghunathan (1982, vol. 3, p. 231), we agree with Cg, who glosses *vistārya*, "having expanded," in taking the former meaning, since it is consonant with the situation for Hanumān to thrust out his chest as a sign of courage and defiance. Other commentators gloss, "having made manifest (*prakāśya*—Ct, Ck)." This is followed by most of the translators, who understand that Hanumān is baring his breast. We find this unpersuasive, since, in Vālmīki, at least, the monkeys are not normally shown as wearing clothing.

12. "mighty Nikumbha . . . of mighty Hanumān: *balī balavatas tasya*: Literally, "the mighty one . . . of that mighty one."

13. "adamantine" *sthire*: Literally, "firm, hard, unyielding." This is perhaps an allusion to Hanumān's adamantine body and invulnerability to weapons. See, for example, 4.65.25–26; 5.1.175 and note; and 7.36.11–21. See, too, Goldman and Goldman 1996, pp. 43, 53–57; and 1994.

14. "And . . . staggered" *cacāla ca*: D9–11 and the texts and printed editions of Ct and Ck read instead *na cacāla*, "he did not stagger, was unshaken." Ś2,Ñ,V2,3,B1,2,4,D1–4,7,8,12,G1,2,M1–3, and the texts and printed editions of Cg read the variant *vicacāla* (M1,2, *saṃcacāla*), "staggered," which is rendered in the translation of Raghunathan (1982, vol. 3, p. 231).

15. "by that iron club" *tena*: Literally, "by that." We believe that the reference is to the immediate antecedent, the club, although it could also be interpreted to mean "by him," i.e., by Nikumbha.

"tightly" *balena*: Literally, "strongly, powerfully."

"clenched" *saṃvartayāmāsa*: We understand the verb in the sense in which it is understood by Cg, who glosses, simply, "he made (*cakāra*)." Cr, however, glosses, "he swung (*bhrāmāyāmāsa*)." See note to 6.63.49.

16. "the forceful, immensely powerful, and mighty monkey" *mahātejāḥ . . . vīryavān . . . vegavān*: Literally, "the immensely powerful one, the mighty one, and the forceful one." As is often the case with Vālmīki, the adjectives are roughly synonymous but cumulative in their effect. See note to 6.2.14.

"drove" *abhicikṣepa*: Literally, "he hurled."

17. "skin" *carma*: D1,3,7,10,11, and the texts and printed editions of Ct, Cr, and Ck read instead *varma*, "armor." Cf. 6.63.47 and note.

"That fist sparked flames that resembled lighting bursting forth." *muṣṭinā tena saṃjajñe jvālā vidyud ivotthitā*: Literally, "by that fist, a flame was produced like lightning springing up." D7,9–11,G2,3,M5, and the texts and printed editions of Ct and Cg read *meghe*, "in a cloud," for *jvālā*, "flame."

19. "frighteningly" *bhīmam*: Ck and Ct note that it is the monkeys who are frightened (*kapīnāṃ bhayaṃkaraṃ yathā bhavati tathety arthaḥ*). Cr notes that the sound is a triumphal shout (*vijayaśabdaḥ*). Cg adds that the *rākṣasas* cry out in their delight at the seizure of Hanumān (*hanumadgrahaṇaharṣād iti bhāvaḥ*).

20. "as he was being carried off" *sa . . . hriyamāṇaḥ*: Dutt (1893, p. 1379) mistakenly derives the participle from the root $\sqrt{}$*hrī*, "to be ashamed," rendering, "being thus put to shame."

"by Kumbhakarṇa's son" *kumbhakarṇātmajena hi*: D9–11 and the texts and printed editions of Ct and Ck read instead *hanūmāṃs tena rakṣasā*, "Hanumān . . . by that *rākṣasa*."

"that had the force of a thunderbolt" *vajravegena*: As elsewhere, D7,9–11, 13,T2,G1,2,M3,5, and the texts of the southern commentators read instead *vajrakalpena*. Cf. 6.47.37; 6.57.87; and notes. See 6.63.46 and note.

22. "Exerting all his strength" *paramāyattaḥ*: Literally, "exerting himself supremely."

"that powerful monkey" *vīryavān*: Literally, "the powerful one." D6,9–11,T2,G3, and the texts and printed editions of Ct and Ck read instead *vegavān*, "possessing speed *or* force."

"with tremendous force" *vegena*: Literally, "with force."

23. "Nikumbha's neck . . . Hanumān . . . tore off the huge head of the *rākṣasa*, who was shrieking" *śirodharām . . . utpāṭayāmāsa śiro . . . nadato mahat*: Literally, "[locking] the neck . . . he tore off the huge head of him who was shrieking."

"horribly" *bhairavam*: The term can be read either as an adjective modifying "head (*śiraḥ*)" or, as we have done, as an adverb modifying the participle "shrieking (*nadataḥ*)."

24. "between the . . . armies of Daśaratha's son and the *rākṣasa* lord" *daśarathasutarākṣasendracamvoḥ*: D6,7,11,T2,M3, and the texts and printed editions of Ct, Cr, Cg, and Cm read *-sūnvoḥ*, "sons," in place of *-camvoḥ*, "armies," lending the compound the sense "between the [two] sons of Daśaratha and the *rākṣasa* lord." Commentators understand this reading to refer to the content of the following two *sargas* (65 and 66), which describe the battle between Rāma and the *rākṣasa* Makarākṣa, the son of the *rākṣasa* lord Khara. (*rākṣasendrasūnuḥ kharasuto makarākṣaḥ. anena vakṣyamāṇopakṣepaḥ*—so Ct.) Cs, who reads the variant, offers an idiosyncratic interpretation in opposition to that of Ct and Cm, according to which the term *daśarathasuta-* is made, by lexical manipulation, to stand for the son of the wind, i.e., Hanumān, and the son of the *rākṣasa* lord, Nikumbha. Thus, Cs regards this verse as a summation of the present *sarga* rather than as a foreshadowing of the following two. (*daśarathasutarākṣasendrasūnvor daśasu dikṣu ratho gamanam apratihataṃ yasya tasya vāyoḥ. rathaḥ syāt syandane kāye caraṇe cety viśvaḥ. suto hanumān rākṣasendrasūnur nikumbhaḥ tayoḥ.*)

The meter is *puṣpitāgrā*.

According to Cv, the deaths of Kumbha and Nikumbha conclude the ninth day [of the battle] (*kumbhanikumbhavadhena navamam ahas samāptam*). See note to 6.4.4.

Following verse 24, Ñ1,D5–7,9–11,T,G,M1–3,M5 (following verse 23), and the texts and printed editions of the southern commentators insert a passage of four lines [1491*]: "Once life had departed from Nikumbha, the leaping monkeys bellowed in delight. The directions resounded, the earth seemed to shake, and the heavens seemed to split asunder.[1] But terror entered the host of the *rākṣasas*."

[1]"seemed to split asunder" *paphāleva*: D6,9–11,T, and the texts and printed editions of Ct read instead *papāteva*, "seemed to fall."

The meter is *bhujaṅgaprayāta*.

Sarga 65

1. Cg uses the occasion of the beginning of this *sarga* as the basis for a brief retrospective on the chronology of the battle. He offers two chronologies. According to the first, the action of this *sarga* takes place on the morning of the tenth lunar day [of the dark half of Phālguna/Caitra]. According to the second, we are now in the night of the tenth lunar day, which has been an extremely eventful day. According to Cg, the morning witnessed the deaths of Kampana and Prahasta (6.46), the breaking of Rāvaṇa's crown (6.47), and the awakening and subsequent slaying of Kumbhakarṇa (6.48–55). In the afternoon, Rāma and Lakṣmaṇa were bound by Indrajit's *brahmāstra* (6.60), while the night witnesses Rāma's and Lakṣmaṇa's release from the *brahmāstra* (6.61), the burning of Laṅkā (6.62), and the deaths of Kumbha (6.63), Nikumbha (6.64), Yūpākṣa (6.63.3, App. I, No. 43), Śoṇitākṣa (6.63.3, App. I, No. 43), Prajaṅgha (6.63.3, App. I, No. 43), Kampana (6.63.3), and Makarākṣa (6.66). Why Cg mentions the death of Kampana in both the morning and the evening is not clear. (*prathamapakṣe 'yaṃ daśamyāṃ prātaḥ. dvitīyapakṣe tu daśamyāṃ prātar ārabhya kampanavadhaprahastavadharāvaṇamukuṭabhaṅgakumbhakarṇaprabodhatadvadhāḥ. athāparāhne brahmāstrabandhaḥ rātrau tanmokṣalaṅkādahanakumbhanikumbhayūpākṣaśoṇitākṣaprajaṅghakampanamakarākṣavadhāḥ.*) See note to 6.4.4.

"Nikumbha had been slain and Kumbha struck down" *nikumbhaṃ ca hatam . . . kumbhaṃ ca vinipātitam*: Cs is curious as to why the two events are mentioned at the same time, when Kumbha had been slain previously (in *sarga* 64). He reasons that one should think of Nikumbha in the earlier connection as well, either because he was so powerful or because his death was not much separated from that of Kumbha. (*yady api kumbhavadhaḥ prāg iti kumbhaṃ nikumbhaṃ ceti vaktavyam. tathāpi nikumbho 'tibalavān iti vātyavyavahito nikumbhavadha iti vā nikumbhagrahaṇaṃ prāg iti mantavyam.*)

2. "large-eyed Makarākṣa" *viśālākṣaṃ makarākṣam*: The epithet is no doubt chosen to echo the name *makarākṣa* (literally, "crocodile-eyed"). See notes to 6.14.3; 6.57.17; etc.

4. "the proud . . . hero" *śūro mānī*: Ś2, Ñ2,V1,B1–3,D1–4,8–12,G1,M3, and the texts and printed editions of the southern commentators read instead the compound *śūramānī*, "regarding himself as a hero."

"the . . . night-roaming *rākṣasa*" *niśācaraḥ*: Literally, "the night-roaming one." Printed editions that follow the text of Ct (Gita Press 6.78.4; NSP 6.78.4; and GPP 6.78.4) read instead the accusative *niśācaram*, in which case the sense would be that Makarākṣa replied to the night-roaming *rākṣasa*, i.e., Rāvaṇa.

"courageous" *dhṛṣṭaḥ*: As Cr points out, the *sandhi* makes it impossible to determine whether the intended adjective is *dhṛṣṭaḥ*, "courageous," or *hṛṣṭaḥ*, "happy, excited" (*hṛṣṭo makarākṣaḥ . . . dhṛṣṭa iti chedo vā*). Although we believe the context better suits the former, most of the translations consulted read the latter.

6. "quickly" *tvarāt*: Most commentators gloss the somewhat unusual masculine ablative with the regular feminine instrumental *tvarayā*, "in haste." Cs does the same but offers a characteristically *recherché* alternative explanation, according to which the term is the vocative of a compound epithet with the sense "going quickly." This would be addressed to the commanding officer, "O Speedy One." (*tvarayā atatīti tvarāt. tasya saṃbuddhiḥ.*)

8. "mounted it" *āruroha*: D10,11, and the texts and printed editions of Ct read instead the inferior *samāhūya*, "having summoned, invited." This reading makes little sense contextually. Only Dutt (1893, p. 1380), Roussel (1903, vol. 3, p. 261), and Shastri (1959, vol. 3, p. 230) attempt to render it.

9. "as my vanguard" *purastān mama*: Literally, "before me."

10. Cm, following his normal devotional strategy, understands that the real meaning of the verse is to be ascertained only by supplying the particle *vinā*, "without, excluding," so that the hidden sense is that Makarākṣa has been instructed to kill only the monkeys while sparing Rāma and Lakṣmaṇa. (*ahaṃ rākṣasarājenetyādiślokadvayasya prātītikārthaḥ spaṣṭaḥ. vastutas tu—ahaṃ rāvaneṇa rāmalakṣmaṇau hantum adyājñapto yady api tathāpi lakṣmaṇaṃ rāmaṃ vineti śeṣaḥ. vānarān vadhiṣyāmīti saṃbandhaḥ.*) See note to 6.27.4.

11. "the tree-dwelling monkey" *śākhāmṛgam*: Literally, "the branch [dwelling] animal." See 6.15.15.

12. "hurling my lance" *śūlanipātaiḥ*: Literally, "with casts *or* descents of the lance(s)."

"that has assembled here" *saṃprāptām*" Literally, "arrived." Ñ2,V2,D7,G1,2,M3, and the texts and printed editions of Cg, Cm, Cr, and Gorresio read instead the nominative singular masculine *saṃprāptaḥ*, in which case the adjective modifies Makarākṣa himself, with the sense of "as soon as I get there."

13. "formed themselves into a column" *samāhitāḥ*: Literally, "assembled."

14–15. "with their great fangs" *daṃṣṭriṇaḥ*: Literally, "possessing fangs."

"yellow eyes" *piṅgalekṣaṇāḥ*: The adjective *piṅgala* can also describe a reddish or reddish-brown color. Cf. 6.59.11 and note.

"those heroes" *te . . . śūrāḥ*: D6,9–11,T2,M5, and the texts and printed editions of Ct read *krūrāḥ*, "cruel, fierce," for *śūrāḥ*. M3 and the texts and printed editions of Cg read *sarve*, "all," for *śūrāḥ*.

"roared like bull elephants trumpeting" *mātaṅgā iva nardantaḥ*: Literally, "bellowing *or* roaring like elephants."

"those huge *rākṣasas*" *mahākāyāḥ*: Literally, "having large bodies."

"marched forth" *abhijagmuḥ*: B2,D5,10,11, and the texts and printed editions of Ct read instead *abhijaghnuḥ*, "they beat, slew, *or* attacked." Of the translations that generally follow the text of Ct, only Roussel (1903, vol. 3, p. 262) and, after him, Shastri (1959, vol. 3, p. 232) appear to render this awkward reading. They understand the verb idiosyncratically to mean "to shout," construing it closely with the adjective *hṛṣṭāḥ*, "excited, happy," in 15c, understanding that the *rākṣasas* are shouting with joy.

"the earth" *vasuṃdharām*: D9–11 and the texts and printed editions of Ct read instead *nabhastalam*, "the sky." Among the translations consulted, Roussel (1903, vol. 3, p. 262), and, after him, Shastri (1959, vol. 3, p. 232) render this reading, construing it with their reading of *abhijaghnuḥ* discussed above to represent their understanding that the *rākṣasas* shake the vault of heaven with their joyful cries.

16. "*bherī* drums" *-bherī-* See note to 6.17.31–33.

"clapped their upper arms, and roared out their battle cries" *kṣveḍitāsphoṭitānām*: See note to 6.4.23–24. See, too, 6.47.8; 6.77.16; 6.78.51; and notes.

17. For similar passages listing inauspicious omens, see 6.26.21–30; 6.31.3–12; 6.41.30–34; 6.45.31–37; 6.53.41–45; 6.83.32–34; 6.94.14–27; and notes.

"from the hand of Makarākṣa's charioteer" *karāt tasya... sāratheḥ*: Literally, "from his charioteer's hand." Cg reads the sequence *karāttasya* instead as a *paranipāta* compound (for *āttakarasya*) to which he ascribes the sense "whose hand was under his control (*vaśīkṛtakarasya*)." He further glosses this as "deft-handed (*laghuhastasya*)."

"and" *caiva*: D9–11 and the texts and printed editions of Ct read instead *daivāt*, "because of fate."

18. "robbed of their strength" *vikramavarjitāḥ*: The compound is ambiguous. The word *vikrama-* can refer here either to "strength, valor, energy" or to the "steps, gait, *or* paces" of the horses. The commentators and the translators who follow them (Dutt 1893, p. 1381; Raghunathan 1982, vol. 3, p. 233; Shastri 1959, vol. 3, p. 232; and Gita Press 1969, vol. 3, p. 1701) choose the latter interpretation. According to their understanding, the horses abandon the splendid or various gaits they have previously displayed. Gorresio (1858, vol. 10, p. 85), Roussel (1903, vol. 3, p. 262), and Pagani (1999, p. 1086) choose the former. We tend to agree with the latter group since the reading of the commentators appears to be slightly redundant with the reference to the "halting steps" of the horses in *pāda* c.

"Moving along with halting steps, despondent, they proceeded with tearful faces" *caraṇair ākulair gatvā dīnāḥ sāsramukhā yayuḥ*: These are all common omens predicting the defeat or downfall of a hero. See 6.26.23; 6.83.33; 6.94.26; and notes.

19. "a harsh and fearsome wind, filled with dust" *pravāti pavanaḥ... sapāṃsuḥ kharadāruṇaḥ*: See 6.4.41; 6.41.33; 6.43.8; 6.45.35; 6.53.44; 6.65.19; and notes.

21. "seasoned in combat" *yuddhakauśalāḥ*: Literally, "skilled in battle."

"They raced onward, roaring" *paribabhramur nadantaḥ*: D5,T1,G2,M3, and the texts and printed editions of Cg read instead *paritaḥ samunnadantaḥ*, "roaring on all sides." D10,11, and the texts and printed editions of Ct read instead *muhus te*, "they [raced onward] for a while," for *nadantaḥ*, "roaring."

"crying out, 'Here I am!' 'Here I am!' " *aham aham iti*: Literally, " 'I! I!' " The idea seems to be that the *rākṣasa* warriors are announcing their presence on the battlefield in the hope of engaging their foes.

The meter is *puṣpitāgrā*.

Sarga 66

1. "the bulls among monkeys" *vānarapuṃgavāḥ*: D5,T1,M3, and the texts and printed editions of Cg and Cm read *-yūthapāḥ*, "troop leaders," for *-puṃgavāḥ*, "bulls."

3. "the former with blows of trees and hails of boulders, the latter with volleys of lances and blows of iron clubs" *vṛkṣaśūlanipātaiś ca śilāparighapātanaiḥ*: Literally, "with descents of trees and lances and with descents of boulders and iron clubs." Although neither of the translators who follow this reading—Gorresio (1858, vol. 10, p. 86) and Raghunathan (1982, vol. 3, p. 234)—reflects this, clearly the poet intends to maintain, through the parallel construction, the distinction between the monkeys, who fight

with natural objects, and the *rākṣasas*, who use a full armory of formal weapons. D9–11,T1, and the texts and printed editions of Ct read *gadā-*, "mace," for *śilā-*, "boulders," which tends to break up the parallelism of the construction.

4–5. "the night-roaming *rākṣasas*, who prowl in the darkness" *niśācarāḥ*... *rajanīcarāḥ*: Literally, "night-roamers... night-roamers." Although the translators consulted generally gloss over the apparent redundancy of the two synonymous terms and collapse them, the repetition has not gone unnoticed by some commentators. Our interpretation follows that of Cr, who takes the term *niśācarāḥ* as a descriptive adjective in the sense of "who are fond of feeding at night" and *rajanīcarāḥ* as a kenning or synonym for *rākṣasas* (*niśāyām eva bhojanaśīlā rajanīcarā rākṣasāḥ*). Cg's text reads the nominative plural *apare*, "other [night-roaming *rākṣasas*]," in *pāda* 5b, for the instrumental plural *aparaiḥ*, "with other [weapons]." This enables him to understand that two groups of *rākṣasas* are described, each using a different set of weapons.

"with... lances" *-śūla-*: D5–7,9–11,T,G,M3,5, and the texts and printed editions of the southern commentators read instead *-khaḍga-*, "swords."

"with... swords" *-khaḍgaiḥ*: D5–7,9–11,T,G2,M3,5, and the texts and printed editions of the southern commentators read instead *-kuntaiḥ*, "with barbed darts." See note to 6.62.50.

"with... iron cudgels" *-tomaraiḥ*: See note to 6.58.10.

"with... volleys of arrows" *bāṇapātaiḥ*: M3 and VSP read instead *nirghātaiḥ*. The term is left untranslated in Raghunathan (1982, vol. 3, p. 234). The apparatus of GPP records the variant *nikhātaiḥ*, which it ascribes to Cg. This variant is not attested in the critical apparatus. See below for a discussion of these terms.

"with... *nirghātas*, and other weapons as well" *nirghātaiś cāparais tathā*: Literally, "with *nirghātas* and others as well." This phrase can also be rendered as "and with other *nirghātas* as well." The exact sense of the term *nirghāta*, normally, "hurricane, thunderbolt, calamity," is not clear in this context. Ct and Cr understand the term to refer to a kind of mechanical weapon that makes a loud noise like a thunderbolt (*nirghātās tadvanmahādhvanayo yantrāyudhaviśeṣāḥ*—so Ct). Ck reads *nipātaiḥ* for *nirghātaiḥ* but gives the same gloss as Ct, leaving us to infer that, like Cv, he understands the term *nipāta* in the same sense as *aśani*, "thunderbolt" (*nipātair aśanaiḥ*—so Cv). Cm and Crā note simply that this is the name for a type of weapon (*nirghātasaṃjñakāyudhaviśeṣaiḥ*—so Cm). Cg reads the variant *nikhātaiḥ*, for which he glosses, "a type of weapon (*āyudhaviśeṣaiḥ*)." He does, however, note the critical reading, glossing it as *aśanaiḥ*, "with thunderbolts, *vajras*, *or* missiles." Gorresio, following his commentator Cl, who glosses *prahāraiḥ*, "with blows" (misprinted as *prahāiaiḥ* [1858, vol. 10, p. 292, n. 42]), translates, "*con colpi*," and understands the reference to be to the blows of all weapons listed (p. 87). Gorresio further notes that if one takes the term in its usual and obvious sense (along with his reading *āyasaiḥ*, "iron," for our *aparaiḥ*, "others"), one gets the meaning "with storms of iron (*con bufere de ferro*)."

6. "panicked" *saṃbhrāntamanasaḥ*: Literally, "their minds bewildered."

7. "the *rākṣasas*... The *rākṣasas*" *rākṣasāḥ*... *rākṣasāḥ*: The verse has but a single finite verb and thus appears to be a single sentence. Several of the commentators, however, note that such a sentence would contain the glaring redundancy of repeating the subject, "*rākṣasas*." They propose two solutions to this problem. Cv, Crā, Cm, and Cg

propose supplying an additional finite verb, *babhūvuḥ*, with the sense "they were, they became," of which the second occurrence of the word *rākṣasas* would be the subject and the adjective *jitakāśinaḥ*, "having a victorious air," the predicate. We have followed this suggestion. Cr provides a somewhat forced interpretation whereby the first occurrence of the term must be read as a kind of *lakṣaṇā* with the sense of "possessing many *rākṣasas*." His idea is that the two terms together mean "*rākṣasas* who possess, i.e., command, many *rākṣasas*." The two terms then both refer to the *rākṣasa* officers (*rākṣasāḥ bahurākṣasavanto rākṣasāḥ*). This interpretation has been followed only by Gita Press (1969, vol. 3, p. 1702), which translates, "ogres, who were followed by (many more) ogres." Other translators collapse the two terms.

"in their excitement" *hṛṣṭāḥ*: Literally, "excited." Here, as at 6.65.4, the *sandhi* makes it possible to read either *dhṛṣṭāḥ*, "courageous," as Gorresio (1858, vol. 10, p. 86) has done, or *hṛṣṭāḥ*, as we and other translators have done (Dutt 1893, p. 1382; Raghunathan 1982, vol. 3, p. 234). We have chosen this latter interpretation because of the repeated mention in the text of the characters roaring in excitement. V,B3,D9–11,13, and the texts and printed editions of Ct and Cr read instead *dṛptāḥ*, "proud, arrogant."

"took on an air of victory" *jitakāśinaḥ*: Literally, "having the appearance of victory." See 6.42.9–10 and note.

8. "stopped . . . in their tracks" *vārayāmāsa*: We take the verb in its regular sense of "to check, block, ward off." Cr, however, glosses, "he covered (*ācchādayāmāsa*)."

9. "had been stopped in their tracks" *vāritān*: See note to verse 8 above.

10. "Stay where you are" *tiṣṭha*: Literally, "Stand!"

"I challenge you to single combat" *mayā sārdhaṃ dvandvayuddhaṃ dadāmi te*: Literally, "I give you dual combat with me." D9–11 and the texts and printed editions of Ct read *bhaviṣyati*, "there will be," for *dadāmi te*, "I give to you."

"I shall rob you of your life" *tyājayiṣyāmi te prāṇān*: Literally, "I shall cause you to abandon [your] life breaths."

See note to verse 12 below for a discussion of Cm's devotional reading of this passage.

11. "back then" *tadā*: Literally, "then." The event referred to is described at *Araṇyakāṇḍa* 27–29.

"Therefore, when" *yat*: Literally, "since, wherefore."

"I think" *smṛtvā*: Literally, "having remembered *or* recalled." D6,7,9,T1,2,G,M3,5, and the texts and printed editions of Cg read instead *dṛṣṭvā*, "having seen."

"the author of that foul deed is standing right before me" *madagrataḥ svakarmastham*: D10,11,G3,M1,2,5, and the texts and printed editions of Ct and Ck read *tad-* for *mad-*, "me." Ct and Ck and the translators who follow their text, interpret this to mean "since that day (*taddināditaḥ*)." This variant has some bearing on the interpretation of the compound *svakarmastham*, which is somewhat obscure in its connotation and allows for a variety of readings. Given the critical reading, the adjective must unambiguously refer to Rāma, although its meaning is subject to debate on the part of the commentators. Cr understands that Rāma is described as being engaged in his own proper activity, that is, that he is intent on killing the *rākṣasas* (*svakarmaniratam rākṣasavadhaparāyaṇam ity arthaḥ*). Cv and Cg understand that Rāma should be the appropriate object (*karma*) of the action of killing, that is, he should be killed just as he killed Makarākṣa's father [Khara]. (*svakarmasthaṃ vadhakarmasthaṃ. yathā pitā hatas tathā vadhyam ity arthaḥ.*) Cg offers, as a second alternative, "practicing actions that are in keeping with the code of the kshatriya class (*kṣātradharmakarmānutiṣṭhantam*)." Ct and Ck understand, "you who were the agent of the action that took the form of killing [my] father (*pitṛvadharūpakarmakartāraṃ tvām*)." Cs, reading *tadagrataḥ*, takes, as his first interpretation, the adjective to refer not to Rāma but to Makarākṣa's father, Khara. According to this interpretation, the term would mean "devoted to the law of the *rākṣasas* (*rākṣasadharmaniratam*)." The idea here is that Khara was minding his own business when he was murdered by Rāma. Among the translators consulted, only Gorresio (1858, vol. 10, p. 87), who, however, reads *anāgasam*, "innocent, guiltless," in place of *madagrataḥ*, takes the adjective to refer to Khara, rendering "*che non avea colpa e stava intento al suo ufficio.*" Cf. *ManuSm* 10.1, where the term *svakarma-* is used to refer to the activities proper to the various *varṇas*, or social classes. Crā, Cm, Cg, as a third alternative, Cv, as a second alternative, Cs, as a second alternative, and Ct, quoting Cm and his variant *madagrataḥ*, break up the sequence *svakarma*, normally, "one's own actions," into *su+a+karma*, "extremely improper action." This is the interpretation that we, along with the majority of the translators consulted, have followed. Dutt (1893, p. 1382) ignores the commentators and the *-stham*, rendering, "thy action."

"my rage redoubles" *roṣo 'bhivardhate*: Literally, "anger grows."

See note to verse 12 below for a discussion of Cm's devotional reading of this passage.

12. "My whole body is burning fiercely" *dahyante bhṛśam aṅgāni ... mama*: Literally, "my limbs are burning fiercely." As Cg, Ck, and Ct suggest, Makarākṣa's anguish is caused by his failure to avenge himself on Rāma earlier, for revenge would have eased his anguish (*tadānīm eva dṛṣṭaś cet pratikāreṇa tāpaḥ śāmyed ity arthaḥ*—so Cm, Cg).

"evil-minded" *durātman*: It is perhaps this epithet that inspires Cm to offer an alternative inner devotional meaning for Makarākṣa's words up until this point. According to this interpretation, Makarākṣa's threat to kill Rāma in verse 10 is really an entreaty for Rāma to stay and kill Makarākṣa with his arrows in single combat. In the present verse, Cm offers a heavily forced reading of the epithet, *durātman*, taking it as an epithet of praise in the sense of "one whose heart is essentially compassionate even for evildoers (*duṣṭeṣv apy ātmāntaḥkaraṇaṃ dayāsāraṃ yasya he rāghava*)." Cm reads verses 11 and 12 as a single sentence, the sense of which is that Makarākṣa failed to see Rāma, who, before killing him, killed his father, who was devoted to evil deeds, and that is why Makarākṣa did not die at Rāma's hands at that time. As a result of his failure to be killed at that time, Cm goes on, Makarākṣa's anger, manifested in the burning of his limbs, has grown. (*tasmāt tvaddhastavadhābhāvād iti śeṣaḥ. aṅgāni dahyante roṣaś cābhivardhata iti saṃbandhaḥ.*)

"back then" *tasmin kāle*: Literally, "at that time." As several of the commentators point out, the reference is to the time that Rāma killed Makarākṣa's father, Khara, as described at 3.29.24–28.

13. Cm subjects this verse to his familiar devotional reading. He understands its purport to be that Rāma, who is the Lord of the universe, is sought by all creatures, starting with Brahmā, as eagerly as a deer is by a hungry lion. Thus, Makarākṣa has been desperately longing for the sight of Rāma and cannot describe his good fortune at having found him. (*siṃhasya siṃhasadṛśasya kṣudhārtasya tvaddarśanaṃ kadā bhaviṣyatīti kṣudhayārtasya mṛga iva mṛgyate brahmādibhir iti mṛgaḥ sarveśvaro 'ta evetaraḥ prapañcātīto 'ta eva kāṅkṣitaḥ. brahmādibhir iti śeṣaḥ. etādṛśas tvaṃ diṣṭyā madbhāgyena darśanaṃ prāpto 'si. ato madbhāgyaṃ kiṃ varṇyata iti bhāvaḥ.*)

"I find you here right before my eyes" *darśanam... mama tvaṃ prāptavān iha*: Literally, "you have come here to my sight."

"I have been as desperate to catch you as a famished lion is a deer." *kāṅkṣito 'si kṣudhārtasya siṃhasyevetaro mṛgaḥ*: Literally, "you are desired as is some other animal by a lion oppressed by hunger." Several of the commentators understand that the phrase *itaro mṛgaḥ* means an animal other than a lion (*siṃhetaramṛgamātram*—so Ct).

14. Cm characteristically reverses the sense of this verse. According to his reading, Makarākṣa is saying that he himself will go to the realm of Yama through the force of Rāma's arrows, while Rāma will rejoin those heroes, Sugrīva, etc., who will not have been slain by Makarākṣa. (*tvayā bāṇavegenādya pretarāḍviṣayaṃ gato bhaveyam iti śeṣaḥ. ato man matsakāśād ye śūrāḥ sugrīvādayo 'nihatās taiḥ saha sameṣyasīti sambandhaḥ.*)

"to the realm of Yama, king of the dead" *pretarāḍviṣayam*: Literally, "to the realm of the king of the departed." Cr, the only commentator to treat this term, glosses, "you will enter the range of sight of Yama (*yamasya viṣayaṃ dṛṣṭipathaṃ prāptas tvam*)."

"you shall meet the heroes" *śūrāḥ saha tais tvaṃ sameṣyasi*: Literally, "the heroes... you shall meet with them." V2,3,B1,3,D9–11, and the texts and printed editions of Ct and Cr read *vasiṣyasi*, "you shall dwell [with]," for *sameṣyasi*, "you shall meet."

15. "the two of us" *tvāṃ māṃ caiva*: Literally, "you and me alone."

16. "in the midst of this great conflict" *mahāhave*: Literally, "in the great battle." D3,7,9–11, and the texts and printed editions of Ct read instead *raṇājire*, "on the battlefield."

"give battle" *vartatāṃ yudhi*: Literally, "proceed in battle." Cg and Cm supply the third person polite pronoun *bhavān*, "you sir," to agree with the third person imperative. D10,11, and the texts and printed editions of Ck, Ct, and Cr read the neuter singular nominative or accusative *mṛdham*, "battle," which can then serve as the subject of the verb, with the sense of "let the battle proceed."

"skilled" *abhyastam*: Literally, "practiced."

"even your bare hands" *bāhubhyāṃ vā*: Literally, "or with your two arms."

17. "this speech of the endlessly talkative Makarākṣa" *makarākṣavacaḥ... uttarottaravādinam*: Literally, "[had heard] the words of Makarākṣa... [spoke] to the one who talked on and on."

Following verse 17, B1,2,D5–7,9–11,S insert, while Ś2,Ñ,V,B3,4,D1–3,8,12,13 continue after 1506*, a passage of two lines [1509*]. " 'Why do you boastfully utter all these vain words, *rākṣasa*, which so ill befit you? You cannot be victorious on the field of battle without a fight, merely on the strength of your words.' "

The reasoning of the critical editors in omitting this verse is unclear. It occurs in all manuscripts consulted for the critical edition except for Ś1 and D4.

18. "fourteen thousand *rākṣasas*" *caturdaśa sahasrāṇi rakṣasām*: Rāma kills the fourteen thousand *rākṣasas* at *Araṇyakāṇḍa* 23.

"Triśiras, Dūṣaṇa, and the one who was your father" *pitā ca yaḥ / triśirā dūṣaṇaś cāpi*: Rāma slays Triśiras at 3.26.16–17, Dūṣaṇa at 3.25.7–10, and Khara, Makarākṣa's father, at 3.29.24–28.

19. "their sharp beaks and fangs and their hooked claws" *tīkṣṇatuṇḍanakhāṅkuśāḥ*: Literally, "with sharp beaks and claw-hooks." We have rendered the word *-tuṇḍa-*, "beak, mouth, snout," here as "beaks and fangs," so as to accurately characterize the jackals mentioned in the list of scavengers. Roussel (1903, vol. 3, p. 264), followed by

Pagani (1999, p. 1087), appears to take the metaphorical term *aṅkuśa*, "hook, goad," here to mean "fangs."

Following verse 19, Ś2,Ñ,V,B1,3,4,D1–4,7–9,12,13,G1,2,G3 (after verse 20) insert a passage of two lines [1506*]: "Then, their mouths dripping with blood and their wings bloody, the birds will disperse in great delight by land and air in all directions." The verse appears in the text and translation only of Gorresio (1858, vol. 10, p. 88 = Gorresio's edition 6.58.30). However, Dutt (1893, p. 1382), in a footnote, observes that it is found "in all N.W.P. texts, and in one or two texts published in Bengal." He provides a synopsis of its meaning.

20. "When Rāma had addressed him in this fashion" *evam uktas tu rāmeṇa*: Literally, "but thus addressed by Rāma." D7,9–11,G1–3, and the texts and printed editions of Ct read instead *rāghaveṇaivam uktas tu*, "addressed in this fashion by Rāghava." The critical apparatus mistakenly prints *rāghaveṇaim* for *rāghaveṇaivam*.

"Khara's son, the night-roaming *rākṣasa*" *kharaputro niśācaraḥ*: Ś2,D2,7–12,G1,3, and the texts and printed editions of Ct, Ck, and Cr read *makarākṣaḥ*, "Makarākṣa," for *kharaputraḥ*, "Khara's son," while D7,9–11,13,M1,2, and the texts and printed editions of Ct, Ck, and Cr read *mahābalah*, "of great strength," for *niśācaraḥ*, "night-roaming *rākṣasa*." The resulting vulgate reading would then mean "mighty Makarākṣa."

21. "with a hail of his own arrows" *śaravarṣeṇa*: Literally, "with a shower of arrows."

"the golden-fletched arrows" *rukmapuṅkhāḥ*: Literally, "having golden fletching."

"by the thousand" *sahasraśaḥ*: D9–11 and the texts and printed editions of Ct read instead *suvāsasaḥ*, "well-clothed," that is, "beautifully feathered" (compare 6.63.7). Only Roussel (1903, vol. 3, p. 264) and Shastri (1959, vol. 3, p. 233) render the variant, understanding it to mean that the arrows are richly adorned with jewels.

23. "of their bowstrings striking their armguards" *jyātalayoḥ*: Literally, "of the bowstring and the armguard." The technique of archery, it seems, precludes taking the term *tala* in its sense of either "hand" or "palm," as has been done by some translators (Gita Press 1969, vol. 3, p. 1703 and Raghunathan 1982, vol. 3, p. 235). The term *tala* is also used to indicate the leather armguard used by archers to protect the forearm from the blows of the bowstring. It has been taken in this sense by Gorresio (1858, vol. 10, p. 88), Roussel (1903, vol. 3, p. 264), Shastri (1959, vol. 3, p. 233), and Pagani (1999, p. 1088). The text does not make it clear as to whether an armguard or gauntlet is intended. One should note, however, that, in the *Bālakāṇḍa*, when Rāma and Lakṣmaṇa set out on their journey with Viśvāmitra, they are described as wearing "wrist and finger guards." See 1.21.8 and note. Compare 6.67.25; 6.76.2,24; 6.81.26–27; and notes. See, too, 6.77.30, 1701*, where several of the commentators explicitly take the term in the sense of "armguard (*jyāghātavāraṇam*)." Cf., too, n. 4 to App. I, No. 9, following notes to verse 6.13.5.

"The deafening sound" *svanotkṛṣṭaḥ*: We follow Cg, the only southern commentator to remark on this word. He glosses, "outstanding among sounds (*svaneṣūtkṛṣṭaḥ*)." Cm notes that the sound emitted by the bow is the sound of the bowstring (*dhanurguṇasvanaḥ*). D10,11, and the texts and printed editions of Ct, Ck, and Cr read instead *svano 'nyonyam*. This has been interpreted by Ct and Ck to mean that the sounds of the two bows mingled with each other (*anyonyaṃ dhanurmuktaḥ svano 'nyonyamiśraḥ*—so Ct). Cr understands that the sound was heard mutually, i.e., by Rāma and Makarākṣa (*dhanurmuktaḥ svano 'nyonyaṃ śrūyate*). Roussel (1903, vol. 3, p. 264) and Pagani (1999, p. 1088) follow Ct in understanding that the sounds of the two bows are commingled.

Gita Press (1969, vol. 3, p. 1703) follows Cr, while Dutt (1893, p. 1383) idiosyncratically understands the two references to sound in the verse (*śabdaḥ* and *svanaḥ*) to be to "the outcry of the heroes" and "the twang of the bows," respectively.

"then" *tadā*: B3,D4,9,11, and the texts and printed editions of Ct, Ck, and Cr read instead a second, and therefore redundant, particle *iva*.

24. "assembled in the sky" *antarikṣagatāḥ*: Literally, "[were] located in the sky."

25. "As they pierced each other's bodies" *viddham anyonyagātreṣu*: Literally, "[There was] a piercing in each other's limbs."

28. "the *rākṣasa*'s" *rakṣasaḥ*: Ś2,Ñ,V1,2,B2,4,D1–3,6,8–13,T2,3,G1,M1,2, and the texts and printed editions of Ct read instead *saṃyuge*, "in battle."

"the chariot-horses" *rathāśvān*: The reading is marked as uncertain by the editors of the critical edition. The critical editors provide numerous variants for the reading, most of which have similar meanings. D9 and the texts and printed editions of Ct read instead *hatvā aśvān* [with hiatus], "having slain the horses."

29. "the . . . *rākṣasa* . . . took his stand on the ground" *atiṣṭhad vasudhāṃ rakṣaḥ*: D5,10,11,T1,G3,M3,5, and the texts and printed editions of the southern commentators read instead *tat tiṣṭhad vasudhāṃ rakṣaḥ*, "that *rākṣasa* standing on the ground."

Following verse 29, D7,10,11,G1,M5, and the texts and printed editions of Ct and Cr insert a passage of three lines [1508*]: "That huge and terrifying lance was Rudra's gift, so difficult to obtain.[1] Blazing fiercely in the sky, it seemed like a second weapon of universal destruction.[2] Upon seeing it, all the gods fled, terror stricken, in every direction."

[1]"difficult to obtain" *duravāpam*: Most of the translators consulted understand the term here to mean "hard to grasp, seize, *or* steal."

[2]"a . . . weapon of universal destruction" *saṃhārāstram*: Literally, "divine weapon-spell of destruction." Presumably this is the weapon Rudra uses in his role as universal destroyer.

This passage is absent from most manuscripts of the text of Cg and from VSP. It appears, however, in brackets in KK (6.79.33), with the notation that it is found in seven of the manuscripts collated for that edition.

30. "blazing" *prajvalantam*: Cr understands the participle to have a causative sense, glossing, "burning up enemies (*parān prajvālayat*)."

"in that great battle" *mahāhave*: Ś2,V,B1,2,4,D1–3,5–12,T,G1,3, and the texts and printed editions of Ct, Ck, and Cr read instead *mahātmane*, "at great [Rāghava]."

31. "But . . . with three arrows" *bāṇais tu tribhiḥ*: D1,7,9,11, and the texts and printed editions of Ct, Ck, and Cr read instead *bāṇaiś caturbhiḥ*, "with four arrows."

33. "the great beings, stationed in the sky" *bhūtāni . . . nabhogatāḥ*: Cv and Cg explain the apparent disagreement in gender by citing *Pā* 7.139 (*supāṃ suluk*), which allows for the substitution of declensional endings in certain cases. Cr, however, understands that two classes of beings are mentioned: the terrestrial divinities, such as the goddess Pṛthivī, etc., and the celestial gods (*bhūtāni pṛthivyādidevā nabhogatā devādayaś ca*). No doubt the reference is to the great assemblage of supernatural beings mentioned in verse 24 above.

"of wondrous deeds" *adbhutakarmaṇā*: D7,9–11,G1,3,M, and the texts and printed editions of the southern commentators read instead *akliṣṭakarmaṇā*, "tireless in action."

34. "Halt! Stay right where you are!" *tiṣṭha tiṣṭha*: Literally, "Stand! Stand!"

35. "Seeing Makarākṣa rushing toward him" *taṃ dṛṣṭvā patantam*: Literally, "having seen him rushing *or* flying."

"the divinely charged weapon of Agni, the purifier" *pāvakāstram*: Literally, "the *astra* of Pāvaka." It seems apparent here that Rāma is deploying one of the many divine weapons at his disposal. Some translators, however, understand, simply, "a fiery *or* flaming arrow."

37. "Then, when . . . harried by Rāma's arrows" *rāmabāṇārditās tadā*: D3,7–11,G1, and the texts and printed editions of Ct, Cr, and Ck read instead *rāmabāṇabhayārditāḥ*, "afflicted with the fear of Rāma's arrows."

38. "like" *iva . . . yathā*: Only Cg among the commentators consulted remarks on the redundancy of the two synonymous particles. He notes that they join to yield the same single meaning (*dve apy avyayapade saṃbhūyaikārtham evācakṣāte*).

The meter is *puṣpitāgrā*.

The commentators disagree as to the timing of Makarākṣa's death. Ct, the commentator who is generally most concerned with dating the events of the battle, claims that the event takes place before midnight on the night of the ninth [of the dark half of the month of Āśvina] (*navamyāṃ pūrvarātre 'sya vadhaḥ*). See note to 6.61.7, etc. Cm (and Cg implicitly) understand that Makarākṣa's death takes place on the tenth lunar day [of the dark half of the month of Phālguna/Chaitra] (*daśamyāṃ makarākṣavadhaḥ*). Cg (as alternate opinion) and Cv understand that Makarākṣa's death marks the completion of the tenth day [of battle] (*makarākṣavadhena daśamam ahaḥ samāptam*—so Cv). See note to 6.4.4.

Sarga 67

1. "victorious in battle" *samitiṃjayaḥ*: This stock epithet is perhaps somewhat ironic in the present context. A number of translators render it in the sense of "who had up until now *or* generally been victorious."

Following 1ab, D5–7,9–11,S insert a passage of two lines [1513*]: "Seized with tremendous anger, he gnashed his teeth. Then, furious, he brooded as to what he should do."

2. "you must slay" *jahi*: Literally, "kill." Cm, while acknowledging the manifest meaning (*prātītikārthaḥ*) of the verse, argues, characteristically, that there is an inner meaning. This meaning, he claims, is brought out if we read the imperative of the root √*han*, *jahi*, "kill," as an irregular imperative of the root √*hā*, "to abandon (*jahīhi*)." The idea here is that Rāvaṇa is really telling Indrajit that, although he may have defeated Indra, he has no chance of killing the humans Rāma and Lakṣmaṇa and so had better leave them alone. The sense, he continues, is that, since they are unconquerable, he should abandon all hope of victory. (*balādhikas tvaṃ saṃyuge 'dṛśyo dṛśyamāno vā sarvathendraṃ dṛṣṭvā jayasi tathāpi mānuṣāv api rāmalakṣmaṇau saṃyuge vadhiṣyasi kim. na vadhiṣyasi. atas tau jahi tyaja. ohāk tyāge iti dhātoḥ. tayor asādhyatvāt tajjayaviṣayāśāṃ tyajeti bhāvaḥ.*) Cf. 6.59.52 and note.

4. "the purifying sacrificial fire" *pāvakam*: Literally, "the purifier."

5. "*rākṣasa* women, bearing red turbans" *raktoṣṇīṣadharāḥ striyaḥ*... *rākṣasyaḥ*: According to Ct and Ck, these women are sacrificial attendants (*homaparicārikāḥ*). Cg and Cr note that they bring the turbans for the officiating priests to wear (*ṛtvigdhāraṇārthaṃ raktoṣṇīṣāṇy ānayantya ity arthaḥ*). Cg further substantiates this idea by quoting a vedic passage in which *ṛtvik* priests are described as wearing red turbans (*lohitoṣṇīṣā ṛtvijaḥ pracarantīti śruteḥ*). A number of the translations consulted understand that the women themselves are wearing the turbans. We find this unlikely. Pagani thus renders, "*coiffées de turbans rouges*" (1999, p. 1089). In her note to this passage (p. 1670), she indicates that the commentators understand the *rākṣasa* women to be carrying out the duties of the sacrificers ("*Ces rākṣasī au turban rouge font, d'après les commentaires, office de sacrifiants*"). This, however, as noted above, is not quite correct. See 6.60.22 and notes, where red garments are associated with black magic. Cf. 6.58.45–46; 6.59.21; and notes, where red garlands appear inauspicious. Cf. *AgniP* 229.14, where red garments, garlands, etc., betoken ill when seen in dreams. Cf. 6.15.2; 6.106.2–3 and notes.

6. At 6.60.22–25, Indrajit performs virtually the identical sacrifice before proceeding into combat with the monkey army and Rāma and Lakṣmaṇa.

6.67. 6 = 6.60.22. See notes to that passage.

7. 6.67.7ab is a close variant of 6.60.23ab.

6.67.7cd = 6.60.23cd. See notes to that verse.

8. 6.67.8a is a close variant of 6.60.24a.

6.67.8bc = 6.60.24bc. See notes to that verse.

6.67.8d is a close variant of 6.60.24d.

"When kindled and fed the oblation of rice-gruel" *caruhomasamiddhasya*: Literally, "kindled with the oblation of *caru*." D6,7,9–11,T,G (T1,G3 read *cāru*),M5, and the texts and printed editions of Ct read *śara-* for *caru-*, lending the compound the sense "fed the oblation of *śara* leaves *or* arrows." M3 and the texts and printed editions of Cg read the variant found at 6.60.24.

"betokening victory" *vijayaṃ darśayanti*: Cm argues that the signs point to victory or success with respect only to the oblation and that there will be no victory [for Indrajit] in battle. Therefore, Cm concludes, we are to understand that the only victory for the *rākṣasas* will be for the survivors to make it back to Laṅkā. (*śarahome vijayaṃ darśayanti. anyatra yuddhe vijayo nāsti tathāpi jīvataḥ punar laṅkāpraveśa eva jaya ity avagantavyam.*) Ct echoes this last point. See note to 6.20.24.

9. 6.67.9 is virtually identical to 6.60.25. See notes to that verse.

10. "and thus gratified the gods, *dānavas*, and *rākṣasas*" *tarpayitvātha devadānavarākṣasān*: Ct and Ck are, naturally, disturbed at the idea of offering vedic sacrifices to demonic beings. Ct and Ck understand that the *rākṣasas* are those to whom black magical rites are to be offered (*abhicārayāgīyān iti śeṣaḥ*).

"Indrajit mounted" *āruroha*: Literally, "he mounted."

"which could be rendered invisible" *antardhānagatam*: Literally, "gone to invisibility." Given the description of the chariot in the following verses, we are to understand that the chariot is not yet invisible, but, as the commentators note, it has the capacity to become invisible (*antardhānaśaktiyuktam*—so Cg). Compare note to verse 15 below.

*11. "and a mighty bow fastened in place, that magnificent chariot looked splendid" *āropitamahācāpaḥ śuśubhe syandanottame*: The reading *syandanottame* in *pāda* d, and, indeed, both *pādas* c and d themselves, are poorly attested. The line is not known to Ś,Ñ,V2,3,B1–3,D1–4,8,12,13, or to either of the printed editions that represent the northern recension. Since it is almost entirely lacking in the north, it should have probably been excised from the critical text. Of the southern manuscripts, D5–7,T2,3,G,M, as well as the texts and printed editions of Cr, Cg, Cm, and Cv, read the nominative singular *syandanottamaḥ* for the critical edition's locative *syandanottame*. Only four manuscripts, D9–11,T1, three of them *devanāgarī*, and the texts and printed editions of Ct read with the critical edition. Given this textual situation, we have emended in favor of the former reading, which makes better textual and contextual sense than that of the critical edition. Translations that follow the text of Ct are confronted with a certain awkwardness. They resolve the issue in one of two ways. They may take the compound *āropitamahācāpaḥ* to mean "with a great strung bow" and take the compound to modify Indrajit, who then is described as looking splendid on his magnificent chariot (so Roussel 1903, vol. 3, p. 266; Shastri 1959, vol. 3, p. 235; and Pagani 1999, p. 1089). The idea that the bow is already strung is contextually awkward in light of verse 20 below, where Indrajit is said to first string the bow. Or, like Dutt (1893, p. 1385), they may take the even more farfetched position that the bow itself is the subject of the clause ("and a huge bow, set with sharp arrows, appeared beautiful on that excellent car").

12. "with motifs of arrows, moons, and half-moons." *śaraiś candrārdhacandraiś ca*: Literally, "with arrows and with moons and half-moons." D6,7,9–11,T2,3,G,M, and the texts and printed editions of the southern commentators read *mṛgaiḥ*, "with deer *or* wild animals," for *śaraiḥ*, "with arrows." We agree with the commentators who understand that these are painted or embossed motifs. (*mṛgair mṛgākārapratimābhiḥ. candraiś candrākāraiḥ. ardhacandrai racanāviśeṣaiḥ*—so Cg.)

13. "a . . . conch" *-kambuḥ*: The commentators who remark on this verse are unanimous in understanding the term to refer to a bracelet or circlet (*valayaḥ*) for which meaning they cite *Amarakośa* 3.3.116. All but one of the translations that render this verse follow this interpretation, understanding either that the flag has a golden ring emblazoned on it or is encircled with golden bracelets. The most common meaning of *kambuḥ*, however, is "conch shell." Given the prominence of this article as an auspicious battle trumpet in the epics, we believe it is more probable that it would be represented on a battle flag than would a ring. Pagani is the only translator to share our belief (1999, p. 1089). The term *kambuḥ* can also mean "elephant," which is yet another possibility in this context, as animals are often used as images on such battle standards. Compare, for example, Arjuna's well-known epithet *kapidhvaja*, or Śiva's epithet *ṛṣabhadhvaja*.

"lapis" *vaidūrya-*: This could also be translated as "cat's-eye beryl" or "emerald." Cat's-eye beryl is traditionally said to be found on a mountain in Sri Lanka (Mt. Vidura). *Vaidūrya* is sometimes translated as emerald, which is a green variety of beryl. Lapis lazuli comes largely from the mountains of Afghanistan (in the region of the Kokca River). See Mayrhofer 1956–1980, vol. 3, pp. 267–68 and Apte (s.v.). See, too, notes to 3.30.9; 4.13.5–8; and 5.5.1.2–3. Cf. 6.1.12; 6.3.13; 6.7.45; 6.15.2; 6.17.2; 6.52.12; 6.90.5–7; 6.109.22–27; 6.116.42; and notes.

14. "And protected as he was by the divine weapon-spell of Brahmā, as brilliant as the sun" *tena cādityakalpena brahmāstreṇa ca pālitaḥ*: The appearance of the two occurrences of the conjunctions *ca* and the instrumental pronoun *tena* has led two of the

translators consulted to understand that Indrajit is protected by something in addition to the *brahmāstra*. Raghunathan (1982, vol. 3, p. 236) appears to view the battle standard described in the previous verse as the additional article, rendering, "protected by it and by the possession of the Brahmāstra, which shone like the sun." The translator of Gita Press (1969, vol. 3, p. 1706), however, renders, "protected by that chariot, effulgent as the sun, as well as by the missile presided over by Brahmā." See 6.10.36 and note.

15. "*mantras* peculiar to the *rākṣasas*" *rākṣasair mantraiḥ*: Literally, "with *rākṣasa mantras*." According to Ct, Cg, and Cm, the term refers to magical spells invoking the demoness of chaos, Nirṛti (*nirṛtidevatākaiḥ*—so Cg, Cm). Cr explains, "*mantras* that are well known exclusively to the *rākṣasa* race (*rākṣasakulamātraprasiddhair mantraiḥ*)."

"able to render himself invisible" *antardhānagataḥ*: Literally, "gone to invisibility." We follow Cv, Cg, and Cm, who explain that the reference is merely to Indrajit's capacity to become invisible and that therefore there is no contradiction with verse 17 below, where he actually vanishes. Compare note to verse 10 above.

16. "those two false forest ascetics" *mithyāpravrajitau vane*: Literally, "the two wandering vainly in the forest." Cr, the only commentator to address this phrase, understands, "those two, i.e., Rāma and Lakṣmaṇa, who wandered to, that is, came into, the forest to no purpose (*mithyā nirartham yau vane pravrajitāv āgatau tau rāmalakṣmaṇau*)." He has been followed by most of the translators consulted, with the exception of Raghunathan (1982, vol. 3, p. 237), who, like us, understands the phrase to mean "false *or* fraudulent ascetics." He renders, "those two pseudo-ascetics who roam the forest." Our understanding, we believe, is in keeping with the *rākṣasas*' constant jibe against the heroes as false ascetics and follows the interpretation of Cs, who glosses, "fraudulent renunciants (*kapaṭaviraktācārau*)." See, for example, 5.18.25.

"a great victory in battle" *jayam . . . raṇādhikam*: Literally, "victory, that is battle-great." The adjective presents a slightly unusual syntax. D6,9–11,T2,M1,2,5, and the texts and printed editions of Ct and Cr read instead the *facilior raṇe 'dhikam*, "great [victory] in battle." D7,G3,M3, and the texts and printed editions of Ct and Cm offer an alternative *facilior*, *raṇārjitam*, "earned *or* garnered in battle."

17. "Once I have cleared the earth of monkeys" *kṛtvā nirvānarām urvīm*: Literally, "having made the earth monkey-free. Ñ1,V3,B1,3,D1–4,7,9–11,13,M, and the texts and printed editions of the southern commentators read *adya*, "this very day," for the gerund *kṛtvā*, "having made." This reading presents a syntactic difficulty that the commentators resolve in one of two ways. Cr simply instructs us to supply the gerund *kṛtvā*, "having made (*kṛtveti śeṣaḥ*)." Ct inserts the gerund *kṛtvā* into his gloss. Cg, however, makes *urvīm*, "the earth," the object of the finite verb *kariṣye*, "I will make *or* do," in *pāda* c, yielding the sense "having slain Rāma along with Lakṣmaṇa, I will clear the earth of monkeys." This stratagem, however, leaves the accusative *prītim*, "delight," in *pāda* c, ungoverned by any verb. To remedy this, Cg proposes that we understand an adverbial phrase, "in regard to the pleasure (*prītiṃ prati*), which he then glosses as "with reference to the pleasure (*prītim uddiśya*)."

"and slain Rāma along with Lakṣmaṇa" *hatvā rāmaṃ salakṣmaṇam*: Cm characteristically finds a way to read this verse in the context of the preceding verse by inverting its manifest meaning. As elsewhere, he exploits the lexical option of understanding the root $\sqrt{}$*han*, normally, "to strike *or* kill," in the sense of $\sqrt{}$*gam*, "go *or* approach." He thus can understand the gerund *hatvā* in the sense of "having approached," when it refers to Rāma and Lakṣmaṇa, and as "having slain," when it refers to the monkeys. According to him, the real meaning is that Indrajit plans to kill the monkeys, sparing Rāma and Lakṣmaṇa. (*raṇe salakṣmaṇaṃ rāmaṃ hatvā gatvā vane yau mithyā pravrajitau rāmalakṣmaṇau vineti śeṣaḥ. āhave hatvā vānarān iti śeṣaḥ.*) Ct appears to take umbrage at this explanation. Without mentioning its author, he remarks, "a forced commentary offered out of an intention of praising Rāma is quite false because the poet and the one who recites his composition have no such intention. (*rāmastutiparatayā kleśena vyākhyānaṃ tad vṛthaiva. kaveḥ kavinibaddhavaktuś ca tathā tātparyābhāvād iti.*) See note to 6.27.9.

"I will have given my father the greatest delight." *kariṣye paramāṃ prītim*: Literally, "I will make supreme pleasure." As Cg indicates, we must carry over the word "father" [from verse 16 above] (*pitur ity ādhyāhāraḥ*). Ct similarly supplies the word.

"he became invisible" *antaradhīyata*: Cr notes that the meaning here is that Indrajit desisted from speaking (*vacanād upararāmety arthaḥ*).

18. "fierce... pitiless" *tīkṣṇa-... tīkṣṇaḥ*: Literally, "sharp... sharp."

"Indrajit... foe of Indra" *indraripuḥ*: Literally, "the foe of Indra."

19. "As they prepared to unleash" *sṛjantau*: Literally, "releasing." Ct, Cg, and Cm gloss the future participle *srakṣyantau*, and we believe, given the context, that they are right to read the present participle here inceptively.

"they resembled three-headed cobras" *nāgau triśirasāv iva*: Commentators differ both as to the basis for and the type of this figure. Ck, Ct, and Cr understand that the image is derived from the appearance of the quiver and bow on either side of each hero's head. They all take the figure to be an *utprekṣā* (*tūṇīdhanuḥsambandhāt triśiraso nāgatvotprekṣā*—so Ct). (See Gerow 1971, pp. 131ff.) Cg sees no reference to weapons but rather to the broad and elevated arms and head characteristic of great men (*rāmalakṣmaṇayor mahāpuruṣalakṣaṇapṛthulonnatabhujaśiraskatvaṃ dyotyate*). He understands the figure to be a *dṛṣṭānta*. (See Gerow 1971, p. 199.) Cs understands that the heroes have on one side a quiver and on the other the tip of their bows, with their heads rising between the two. Cs offers an alternative understanding of the figure, taking the term *nāga*, "cobra," in the sense, permitted by the *Viśvakośa*, of "cloud," in which case we are to envisage three-headed storm clouds about to release showers of rain. (*triśirasau ekatra tūṇy aparatra cāpakoṭir madhye śiraś ceti triśirasāv ity arthaḥ. nāgau sarpau. toyaṃ sṛjantau nāgau meghau triśirasau cet tāv iva sṛjantāv iti vā. nāgaḥ krūrācāreṣu toyada iti viśvaḥ.*) This trope is also used to describe Rāma and Lakṣmaṇa at 1.21.7, where the commentators offer a variety of similar but not identical explanations of the image. Some of them suggest that the heroes wear two quivers (see note to 1.21.7). In our opinion, the figure is neither an *utprekṣā* nor a *dṛṣṭānta* but rather what the *alaṃkāraśāstrins* would define as an *utpādyopamā* in which the *upamāna* (in this case the three-headed cobra) does not, in fact, exist (see Gerow 1971, pp. 151–52). Cf. *abhūtopamā*, where the *upamāna* is hypothetical but generalized (Gerow 1971, p. 149).

20. "inundated them" *saṃtatāna*: Literally, "he covered." The verse provides no direct object for the verb. Printed editions of Ct read *saṃtatān iṣudhārābhiḥ*, which is difficult, if not impossible, to construe. The critical apparatus, however, indicates that the text of Ct reads *saṃtatāra*, "he traversed," which also, if it is not simply a misprint, makes little sense here. Ct's explanation is that we are to understand the verb in the sense of "he filled" and then supply the words "all directions." (*saṃtatān* [*sic*] *pūrayāmāsa. sarvā diśa iti śeṣaḥ.*) Among the translations, only Gita Press (1969, vol. 3,

p. 1707), which reads with the critical edition, incorporates this idea, rendering, "covered the quarters."

"as, with a downpour, might a storm cloud charged with rain" *parjanya iva vṛṣṭimān*: Literally, "like a cloud charged with rain." The term *parjanyaḥ*, here rendered as "cloud," can equally well refer to Parjanya, the rain god, and several translators have taken it thus. Given the adjective *vṛṣṭimān*, "charged with rain," however, it seems preferable to understand the term in its generic sense of "cloud *or* storm cloud." See 6.18.9–10; 6.116.9–10; and notes. Cf. 6.94.15 and note.

21. "In his chariot, he flew up into the sky" *sa tu vaihāyasaṃ prāpya sarathaḥ*: Literally, "he, having reached the sky together with his chariot." D9–11 and the texts and printed editions of Ct and Cr read instead *sa tu vaihāyasaratho yudhi*, "possessing an aerial chariot, in battle."

22. "Beset on every side" *parītau*: Literally, "surrounded, overwhelmed."

"invoked a divine weapon-spell" *divyam astraṃ pracakratuḥ*: Literally, "those two made *or* activated a divine weapon-spell." We agree with the interpretation of Cr, who glosses "the invocation of their *mantras* (*divyam astraṃ tanmantrābhimantraṇam*)" for *divyam astram*, "divine *astra*."

23. "who resembled gods" *surasaṃkāśau*: D9,11,M3, and the texts and printed editions of the southern commentators read the instrumental plural *sūryasaṃkāśaiḥ*, "resembling the sun," which would then modify *śaraiḥ*, "with arrows," in *pāda* d.

"did not so much as graze Indrajit" *tam . . . naiva pasparśatuḥ*: Literally, "those two did not touch him."

24. "he had created dense darkness" *dhūmāndhakāram . . . cakre*: Literally, "he made smoky darkness." As several of the commentators note, Indrajit accomplishes this by means of his supernatural powers of illusion (*māyā*). Roussel (1903, vol. 3, p. 267), Shastri (1959, vol. 3, p. 236), and Pagani (1999, p. 1090) all read the compound as a *dvandva*, in the sense of "smoke and darkness."

"so as to obscure the heavens" *pracchādayan nabhaḥ*: Literally, "covering the sky." We agree with Cg and Cm, who understand the present participle here to indicate cause or purpose (*hetau śatṛpratyayaḥ*—so Cg).

"shrouded in a murky fog" *nīhāratamasāvṛtaḥ*: Literally, "enclosed by fog-darkness." D5–7,T, and the texts and printed editions of Cm, Cg, and Cr read instead the plural *-tamasāvṛtāḥ*, in which case the adjective would modify *diśaḥ*, "directions," instead of Indrajit. Only Gita Press (1969, vol. 3, p. 1707) and Raghunathan (1982, vol. 3, p. 237) render this variant.

"make it impossible to see in any direction" *diśaś cāntardadhe*: Literally, "he disappeared the directions." As several of the commentators point out, we must read the simplex here as a causative: "he caused [the directions] to disappear (*antardhāpayām-āsa*—so Ct, Cr)."

25. "the sound of his bowstring striking his armguard" *jyātalanirghoṣaḥ*: See 1.21.8 and note; and notes to 6.66.23; 6.76.2,24; and 6.77.30, 1701*.

"his chariot wheels and horses' hooves: *nemikhurasvanaḥ*: Literally, "the sound of wheel rims and hooves."

"as he darted to and fro" *caratas tasya*: Literally, "of him who was moving."

26. "With his torrent of iron arrows . . . let loose a veritable and prodigious downpour of arrows" *śaravarṣam ivādbhutam . . . vavarṣa . . . nārācaśaravṛṣṭibhiḥ*: Literally, "with a shower of iron arrows, he showered, as it were, a wondrous shower of arrows."

The figure is rather awkward in that it compares a shower of iron arrows to a shower of arrows. Ñ,V3,B2–4,D4,5,9–11,13,T1,G1,2,M1,2,5, and the texts and printed editions of Ct and Cr read *śilāvarṣam ivādbhutam*, "like a prodigious hailstorm *or* like a prodigious shower of stones," for *śaravarṣam ivādbhutam*, "as it were, a wondrous shower of arrows." This reading is not only superior from a rhetorical point of view but is well supported textually.

"the great-armed warrior" *mahābāhuḥ*: Literally, "the great-armed one." The identity of the warrior is not specified. Because there has been no explicit change of subject since verse 24, where Indrajit covers the sky with darkness, and because the weapons mentioned here, *nārācas*, "iron arrows," are the same as those belonging to Indrajit at verse 18, it seems clear to us, as it does to most of the translators consulted, that the warrior described here must be Indrajit. On the other hand, Cr clearly identifies the warrior here as Rāma. In this he is followed only by Pagani (1999, p. 1090).

"dense and blinding darkness" *ghanāndhakāre timire*: The phrase is somewhat redundant, as its literal meaning is "in the dark, dense darkness." The commentators explain in various ways that the intended meaning is "pitch *or* blinding darkness (*ghane nibiḍe 'ndhakāre dṛṣṭyupaghātake timire tamasi*—so Cr)."

27. "who had been granted a boon" *dattavaraḥ*: Ñ,V,B1,2,4,D1–4,6,7,10,11, T2,G1,2,M1,2,5, and the texts and printed editions of Ct read instead the instrumental plural *dattavaraiḥ*, which would then modify the arrows rather than Indrajit. Although in this reading the syntax of the compound is rather muddled, the sense must still be that the arrows were given to Indrajit as a boon. In any case, it is probable that the verse refers to the various boons of weapons, spells, and skill that Indrajit is said to have acquired from Brahmā. See 6.36.10 and note.

29. "arrows" *patagāḥ*: Literally, "flying ones." This noun normally refers to birds, flying insects, or the sun. As Ck suggests, however, here we have to understand the word in the sense of "arrows (*patagā bāṇāḥ*)."

30. "afflicted" *pīḍyamānau*: Literally, "being afflicted." D6,7,9–11, and the texts and printed editions of Ct and Cr read instead *dīpyamānau*, "blazing, burning."

"those shafts" *tān iṣūn*: Literally, "those arrows."

"as they rained down" *patataḥ*: Literally, "falling, flying."

31. "in any direction from which" *yataḥ . . . tatas tataḥ*: Literally, "from which . . . to whichever." The idea here seems to be that, since Rāma and Lakṣmaṇa can neither see nor hear Indrajit, they can retaliate only by aiming along the trajectory of his incoming arrows.

"raining down" *nipatitān*: Literally, "falling *or* flying down."

32. "whose divinely charged weapons flew swiftly" *laghvastraḥ*: Literally, "whose *astras* were light *or* agile." Ñ2,V1,B2,4,D3,6,7,9,10,T2,3,M5, and the texts and printed editions of Ct and Cr read instead the accusative dual *laghvastrau*, which would then describe Rāma and Lakṣmaṇa. Cr, who reads this variant, explains, "whose divinely charged weapons moved great distances in a short time (*laghūny alpakālena bahudūraṃ pracalanaśīlāny astrāṇi yayos tau*)."

33. "with those finely made . . . arrows" *susaṃhitaiḥ*: Literally, "with those well put together [things]." The referent, "arrows," has been supplied. Ñ1,D9–11, and the texts and printed editions of Ct and Cr read instead *susaṃhataiḥ*, "compact, dense."

"like twin *kiṃśuka* trees covered with crimson blossoms" *puṣpitāv iva kiṃśukau*: Literally, "like two blossoming *kiṃśukas*." The *kiṃśuka* tree (*Butea frondosa*), with its red blossoms, is frequently used as an object of comparison for heroes covered with the blood of their own wounds. Cr, however, proposes here that it is the arrows themselves and not the wounded heroes that resemble *kiṃśuka* blossoms, because they are made of gold and smeared with the blood of the many creatures they have previously slain (*suvarṇamayatvena nihatabahujanturudhirāktatvena ca śarāṇāṃ kiṃśukapuṣpopamā*). See 6.35.9; 6.55.22; 6.62.19; 6.76.28; and notes. See, too, note to 6.30.26, App. I, No. 18, lines 27–30, n. 2. Cf. 6.54.11.

34. "No one could follow Indrajit's movements, nor could anyone discern" *nāsya veda gatiṃ kaścin na*: Literally, "no one knew his path nor." Ñ2,V1,B2,D5,10,11,G3, and the texts and printed editions of Ct read *vega[gatiṃ]*, "swift movements," for *veda gatim*.

"Nothing whatever of his could be discerned as if he were the sun hidden behind a dense mass of clouds." *na cānyad viditaṃ kiṃcit sūryasyevābhrasaṃplave*: Literally, "nor was anything else whatever known as of the sun in a mass of clouds." D7,9–11,G2,M1,2, and the texts and printed editions of Ct and Cr read instead *asya*, "of him," for *anyat*, "other," in *pāda* c. GPP (6.80.35) reads *na nāsya*. Although this all-but-meaningless double negative is noted in the critical apparatus as belonging to B (GPP), it is almost certainly a typographical error peculiar to GPP. NSP reads *cāsya* with the critical edition. See 6.37.11; 6.67.36; 6.93.15; 6.95.24; 6.101.36; and notes. See, too, 6.99.24, 3132*, lines 7–8, and n. 4.

35. "robbed of their life breaths" *gatāsavaḥ*: Literally, "their life breaths gone."

36. "the divine weapon-spell of Brahmā" *brāhmam astram*: Nowhere does the poem make clear how or when Lakṣmaṇa acquired the spell governing this ultimate weapon. One may note, however, that Lakṣmaṇa is said to use this divine weapon-spell to kill Kumbhakarṇa at *Mahābhārata* 3.271.16. See note to 6.55.124.

37. "Lakṣmaṇa of auspicious marks" *lakṣmaṇaṃ śubhalakṣaṇam*: This is yet another of the alliterative etymological epithets of which Vālmīki is so fond. See 6.14.3; 6.71.20; 6.73.5; 6.75.16; 6.79.1; 6.89.4; and notes. See also R. Goldman 1984, p.105.

"all the *rākṣasas* of the earth" *rakṣāṃsi pṛthivyām*: Literally, "the *rākṣasas* on the earth." On the issue of the extermination of all the *rākṣasas*, see R. Goldman 2006.

38. Rāma here is exercising his familiar role as a teacher and upholder of the norms of brahmanical civilization in reminding Lakṣmaṇa of the rules of chivalrous combat as laid out in the *nītiśāstras*. The idea, as Ct and Ck explain it, is that the deployment of the *brahmāstra* would be a violation of the rules of chivalry, since it would inevitably destroy the six named categories of *rākṣasas* who had ceased to fight. Moreover, these commentators add, it would result in the (most undesirable) death of Vibhīṣaṇa along with the rest of his race. (*ayudhyamānatvādiṣaṭprakārāṇām api sarvarakṣauddeśena brahmāstrasaṃdhāne vadho bhavati na tu tad yujyata ity arthaḥ. antato vibhīṣaṇasyāpi nāśaprasaṅga ity āśayaḥ*—so Ct.)

"A foe": The referent has been added.

"is fleeing, or is caught off guard" *palāyantaṃ pramattaṃ vā*: Given the context, it is almost certain that we are to understand the adjective *pramatta* in its sense of "careless, negligent, off guard." Ñ2,V1,B2,D9–11, and the texts and printed editions of Ct and Cr read instead *palāyamānaṃ mattaṃ vā*, "is fleeing, or drunk."

39. "mighty warrior" *mahābala*: Literally, "O one of great strength." D7,9–11, and the texts and printed editions of Ct and Cr read instead *mahābhuja*, "O great-armed one."

"let us strive" *yatnaṃ kariṣyāvaḥ*: V1,3,B1,3,D1,2,9–11, and the texts and printed editions of Ct and Cr read instead the first person singular *yatnaṃ kariṣyāmi*, "I will strive," for the first person dual.

"Let us summon" *ādekṣyāvaḥ*: Literally, "we shall instruct *or* command." The verb *ā* √*diś* is used similarly at *Mahābhārata* 3.163.33 in the sense of employing or invoking a divine weapon-spell. Cg and Cm, the only commentators to remark on the term, gloss, "we shall employ (*prayokṣyāvaḥ*)."

40. "if... could but see" *dṛṣṭvā*: Literally, "having seen." Cr explains that the sense here is that Rāma is suggesting his own extraordinary ability to accomplish the unprecedented (*etena svasyāghaṭitaghaṭanāpaṭīyastvaṃ sūcitam*). Ct believes that the reference is an allusion to the episode in the *Rāmopākhyāna* in which, after Rāma and Lakṣmaṇa have been cured of the wounds inflicted by Indrajit, Vibhīṣaṇa presents them with magical water that has been brought by a *yakṣa* from King Kubera himself. This water, when applied to the eyes of Rāma, Lakṣmaṇa, and the monkey warriors, enables them to counteract the illusory power of Indrajit and see him. Ct quotes *Mahābhārata* 3.273.10–12 to support his claim.

"they could then overpower and slay" *balāt... nihaniṣyanti*: Literally, "they will forcibly kill."

41. For a similar idea, see 6.47.122, where Rāma tells Rāvaṇa that there is no place for him to hide.

"no matter where he may hide" *evaṃ nigūḍho 'pi*: Literally, "even though he be hidden in this fashion." Cr raises the question of how Indrajit is to be killed if, after being revealed, he should once again become invisible. He argues that this verse answers this question, in that Rāma's statement suggests his own ability to see everything and the fact that his arrows are both sentient and unstoppable (*etena svasya sarvadarśitvaṃ bāṇānāṃ cetanatvam avyāhatagatitvaṃ ca sūcitam*).

"robbed of his life breaths" *gatāsuḥ*: See note to verse 35 above.

The meter is *upajāti*.

42. "the great hero... the great man" *mahātmā... -pravīraḥ... mahātmā*: No commentator who shares the critical reading remarks on the redundancy of using the word *mahātmā*, "great," twice in a single sentence. We have attempted to soften the redundancy by breaking the verse into two sentences. D9–11,G1, and the texts and printed editions of Ct read *mahārtham*, "of great significance," in place of the first occurrence of the term. This adjective refers not to Rāma but to his speech (*vacanam*).

"urgently began to contemplate how to kill" *vadhāya... tvaritaṃ nirīkṣate*: Literally, "he swiftly seeks in order to kill." The expression is somewhat elliptical. Cg fleshes it out, glossing, "he pondered a means [for killing] (*upāyaṃ cintayati sma*)." Gita Press (1969, vol. 3, p. 1709) appears to incorporate this suggestion, reading the adverb *tvaritam*, "urgently," as an adjective modifying the supplied term *upāyam*, "means." He renders, "began to reflect on the speedy means."

The meter is *vaṃśasthavila* with a hypometric *pāda* a.

Sarga 68

1. According to Cr, this verse suggests that Indrajit is terrified of Rāma and, further, that this then suggests that Rāma is understood to be the Supreme Being (*paramātmā*)

by the vedic passage found at *Taittirīyopaniṣad* 2.8.1 (*Taittirīyāraṇyaka* 8.8.1, etc.), where the vedic gods are said to act in fear of the *ātman*. (*etenendrajito bhītatvaṃ sūcitam. tena rāmasya bhīṣāsmād vātaḥ pavata ityādiśrutigamyatvaṃ sūcitam.*) Cm and Cg remark that the third syllable of the verse, the syllable *ya* of *vijñāya*, represents the nineteenth syllable (*yáḥ*) of the *Gāyatrīmantra* (*ṚV* 3.62.10), which they believe is mapped onto the text of the *Rāmāyaṇa*. Cg adds that this therefore marks the completion of eighteen thousand verses of the text. See note to 6.1.1.

"when Indrajit realized" *vijñāya*: Literally, "having realized." The critical text provides no explicit subject.

"what great Rāghava had in mind" *manas tasya rāghavasya mahātmanaḥ*: Literally, "the mind *or* thoughts of great Rāghava." Ct and Ck suggest that Indrajit is thinking, "He surely intends to kill me with the power of his divine *astras* (*divyāstrabalena sarvathā māṃ jighāṃsatīti jñātvā*)."

2. "that immensely lustrous hero" *mahādyutiḥ*: Literally, "the one of great luster." D6,7,9–11,T2,G1, and the texts and printed editions of Ct and Cr read instead [*a*]*tha rāvaṇiḥ*, "now, Rāvaṇi."

"those courageous *rākṣasas*" *rākṣasānāṃ tarasvinām*: As Ct, Cg, and Cm point out, the reference is to the great fallen *rākṣasa* warriors, such as Kumbhakarṇa, etc.

3. "through the western gate" *paścimena dvāreṇa*: Cg notes that, if Indrajit plans to demoralize Rāma and his forces by displaying the illusory form of Sītā prior to his visiting the Nikumbhilā grove to perform a sacrifice for the sake of invincible weapons, he must display it to Hanumān, the only one among the monkeys who would be able to recognize her. Hanumān is, of course, stationed at the western gate (6.28.27) (*sītāsvarūpābhijñāsyānyasyābhāvād dhanumate māyāṃ darśayituṃ paścimadvāreṇa nirgata ity āha*). Ct, in his comment on the following verse, argues that Indrajit uses the western gate because he is intending to go first to the Nikumbhilā grove, where he performs his black magical rites (6.69.23). Recall that the grove is thought to be on the western side of Laṅkā. Cf. notes to 5.22.41; 6.60.18–19; 6.69.23; and 6.71.13.

4. "perceiving" *dṛṣṭvā*: Literally, "having seen." Cg notes that, since Indrajit has exited by the western gate, he could not possibly see Rāma and Lakṣmaṇa (who are stationed at the northern gate [6.28.30]) (*paścimadvāraniṣkrāntasya rāmalakṣmaṇadarśanāsambhavāt*). He therefore glosses *vicintya*, "having realized [that] *or* having thought." Keeping in mind Cg's caution here, we have rendered, "perceiving," to minimize the visual element.

"his power of magical illusion" *māyām*: We follow Ct and Cg, who gloss, "the power to confuse others (*paravyāmohakarīṃ śaktim*)."

5. "in the midst of his vast host" *balena mahatāvṛtya*: Literally, "having surrounded with a large army." The syntax of the clause is somewhat unclear, as no explicit object of the gerund is indicated. Cg appears to understand the gerund as indirectly linked to the locative *rathe*, "on his chariot," in *pāda* a. He explains, "having surrounded [his chariot] with the army that was present. We are to supply the word *yukte*, 'connected'; the sense being that he placed 'Sītā' in his chariot, which was provided with (*yukte*) [an army]. (*āvṛtya sthitena balena. yukta iti śeṣaḥ. yukte rathe sītāṃ sthāpya.*)"

"he made as if to kill her" *tasyā vadham arocayat*: Literally, "he chose *or* preferred her killing." Our translation is based on the fact that Indrajit does not actually "kill" the illusory Sītā until verses 28–29 below.

6. "that very evil-minded *rākṣasa*" *sudurmatiḥ*: Literally, "that very evil-minded one."

"displaying every intention of killing Sītā" *hantuṃ sītāṃ vyavasitaḥ*: Literally, "resolved to kill Sītā."

7. "from the city" *nagaryāḥ*: V3,D7,9–11, and the texts and printed editions of Ct and Cr read instead *sarve te*, "all those [monkeys]."

9–10. Compare this passage with the elaborate and highly poetic description of Sītā at 5.13.18–36. Pagani (1999, p. 1670), in a footnote to this passage, argues that this description has two purposes: 1) to express Sītā's sorrow through her aspect of mourning; and 2) equally to demonstrate her fidelity to Rāma by maintaining the air of an ascetic that she bore in the forest, thus guaranteeing her chastity. In fact, it merely demonstrates Indrajit's skill in replicating Sītā as she appears in her desolation.

"now much worn" *parikliṣṭa-*: Literally, "fatigued, troubled." Ct and Cr gloss, "soiled (*malinam*)," and most of the translations consulted follow this interpretation. Only Pagani (1999, p. 1092) appears to agree with us that the reference is to the worn or threadbare character of the phantom Sītā's garment. Compare 5.13.20, where Sītā's garment is described as *kliṣṭa-*, "worn."

"unwashed" *amṛjām*: Ck, Ct, and Cr understand the term to mean that Sītā was devoid of the embellishment of such things as unguents, etc. (*udvartanādisaṃskāra-rahitām*—so Ct). Cm takes the reference to be exclusively to the absence of unguents, while Cg sees the term as referring to Sītā's lack of either unguents or ornaments. See 5.13.20 and note, where Sītā is described as lacking ornaments, which may lend some credence to Cg's alternative explanation. Compare, too, 6.102.7 and note. See also S. Goldman 2000.

11. "After observing her closely for a moment and concluding that she was indeed Maithilī" *tāṃ nirīkṣya muhūrtaṃ tu maithilīm adhyavasya ca*: Literally, "having observed her, Maithilī, for a moment, he formed a resolution." Hanumān is able to recognize Sītā because she is in the same desolate state in which he had encountered her in the *Sundarakāṇḍa*. See 5.5.13 and notes.

Following 11ab, Ñ2,V1,B2,4,D5–7,9,T,G2,3,M, and the texts and printed editions of Cg insert, while Ś1,B3,D8,10–12,G1, and the texts and printed editions of Ct substitute for 11cd, a passage of one line [1537*]: "For he had seen Janaka's daughter not long before."

Following either 11ab or 1537*, Ñ2,V,B1,2,4,D1–3,5–7,9,T,G2,3,M, and the texts and printed editions of Cg, Cm, and Gorresio (after 9cd) insert a passage of one line [1538*]: "Having seen Maithilī in the chariot, dejected, her body smeared with dirt..."

12–13. "Sītā" *sītām*: D7,9–11, and the texts and printed editions of Ct and Cr read instead *dīnām*, "dejected."

"in the clutches of the *rākṣasa* lord's son" *rākṣasendrasutāśritām*: Literally, "dependent on the son of the lord of the *rākṣasas*."

"thought, 'What does he mean to do?' Then, after voicing this concern" *abravīt... kiṃ samarthitam asyeti cintayan*: Literally, "he said... thinking, 'What is his intention?' " The syntax of the two verses is rather awkward. The finite verb *abravīt* in 12a appears to float independently of any actual direct address or direct object, which is extremely rare in the epic. Commentators propose two alternative constructions. The first, which we have more or less followed, is that of Ct, Ck, and Cg. Their idea is that we read the quotation marker *iti* to govern both the participle *cintayan*, "thinking," and the finite verb *abravīt*, "he said" (*kim asya samarthitam abhipretam iti svayaṃ cintayan san vānarān praty api kiṃ samarthitam asyety abravīt*—so Ct). In this way, we understand that Hanumān first entertains his thought and then voices it to his monkey companions. Cr resolves the problem by taking the participle *cintayan* not in the sense of "entertaining a specific thought" but in its sense of "brooding, worrying" (*cintayañ cintāṃ prāptaḥ sann asyendrajitaḥ kiṃ samarthitam abhipretam ity abravīd vānarān pratīti śeṣaḥ*). His idea is that Hanumān is worried at the sight of Sītā and then utters his rhetorical question. Neither solution seems ideal to us.

14. "he seized . . . by the head" *mūrdhni . . . parāmṛśat*: Literally, "he grasped *or* touched on the head." As Ct and Cr point out, Indrajit actually seizes Sītā by her hair (*keśapāśe*). This understanding is borne out in verse 16 below. The idea seems to be that Indrajit pulls up the head of the phantom Sītā by the hair in preparation for cutting off her head. Several of the translators consulted understand that Indrajit touches or rubs Sītā's head with his sword or brandishes it over her head, but this seems unlikely in the context. On the theme of seizing someone by the hair in the epics, see Hara 1986. D7,9–11, and the texts and printed editions of Ct and Cr read instead *akarṣayat*, "he dragged," for *parāmṛśat*.

15. "Rāvaṇi" *rāvaṇiḥ*: D7,9–11,G1, and the texts and printed editions of Ct and Cr read instead *rākṣasaḥ*, "the *rākṣasa*."

16. "Sītā seized by her hair" *gṛhītamūrdhajām*: Literally, "her whose hair was seized."

Following 16cd, B4,D5–7,9–11,S, and the texts and printed editions of the southern commentators insert, while Ñ2,B2,3 insert following verse 15, a passage of one line [1541*]: "Seeing Rāma's beloved queen, lovely in every limb . . ."

17. "You have seized her braid" *keśapakṣe parāmṛśaḥ*: Literally, "You have grasped *or* touched on the wing *or* side of the hair." Several of the commentators cite *Amarakośa* 1.6.98, where *pakṣa* is listed among other terms whose meaning is "a bunch *or* tuft [of hair]" (*pāśaḥ pakṣaś ca hastaś ca kalāpārthāḥ kacāt pare*—so Cg). The reference is, no doubt, to the single braid Sītā is said to wear during her captivity. The phantom Sītā would, of course, replicate her appearance. See 5.18.8 and note; and 5.24.32.

"you . . . whose mind has sunk to this" *yasya te matir īdṛśī*: Literally, "you, of whom there is such a thought."

18. "Lowest of the low!" *kṣudra*: Literally, "lowly *or* insignificant one." Cg glosses, "small *or* mean minded (*alpabuddhe*)."

"Criminal!" *pāpaparākrama*: Literally, "O [you] whose valor is evil." We follow Cg, who glosses, "whose valor is evil, that is, unrighteous (*pāpo 'dharmyaḥ parākramo yasya*)." Ct glosses, "O deceitful *or* dirty fighter (*kūṭayodhin*)."

19. "Taken from her home, her country, and the arms of Rāma" *cyutā gṛhāc ca rājyāc ca rāmahastāc ca*: Literally, "fallen from the house and the kingdom and the hand of Rāma." Cg takes the repeated conjunction *ca*, "and," to suggest additional elements associated with the items mentioned. Thus, he takes "home" to include Sītā's servants, "country" to include the army, and "Rāma's hand" to refer to Rāma as Sītā's protector. The idea, he suggests, is that the absence of all these things precludes the possibility of their having offended Indrajit. (*gṛhāt svasadanāt. cakārāt paricārakebhyaś ca. anena bandhumukhād aparādhakaraṇaṃ nāstīty uktam. rājyād rājyopakaraṇāc ca. anena senāmukhena nāparādha ity uktam. rāmahastād rakṣakahastāc ca. tanmukhād apy aparādhaprasaktir nāstīty uktam.*)

"that you should want to kill her" *yad enāṃ hantum icchasi*: D9–11 and the texts and printed editions of Ct read *haṃsi nirdaya* for *hantum icchasi*, yielding the sense "that you strike *or* slay her, O pitiless one."

20. "If you kill" *hatvā*: Literally, "having killed."

"you will certainly die soon" *na ciraṃ jīviṣyasi kathaṃcana*: Literally, "there is no way you will live long."

"through this deed, for which you would deserve to die" *vadhārhakarmaṇānena*: Commentators who analyze this sequence break it into a vocative, *vadhārha*, "O you who deserve to be killed," and *karmaṇā anena*, "by this action." Printed editions, however, do not separate *vadhārha* from *karmaṇā*, as their editors would normally do if they read with the commentators. Translations consulted follow the reading of the commentators, with the exception of Gorresio (1858, vol. 10, p. 93) and Pagani (1999, p. 1093), who read the sequence as we do.

"For . . . you would fall into my clutches" *mama hastagato hy asi*: Literally, "For you are gone into my hands."

21. "once you have lost your life and passed on to the next world" *jīvitam utsṛjya pretya*: Literally, "having given up life, having passed away." Cg and Cm understand that the reference is to the acquisition of the special body in which one suffers the torments of hell (*yātanāśarīraṃ prāpya*—so Cg, Cm). The *yātanāśarīra* is described at *Manusmṛti* 12.16.

"those worlds reserved for those who kill women" *ye ca strīghātināṃ lokāḥ*: Literally, "and the worlds that belong to killers of women." See note to 1.24.11 and R. Goldman 1982.

"that are despised even by others who deserve death at the hands of all men" *lokavadhyaiś ca kutsitāḥ*: Literally, "condemned by those who are to be killed by people." The expression is somewhat ambiguous, and the commentators differ in their interpretations. Ct and Ck understand the term *lokavadhya* to refer to criminals such as thieves, who, although they themselves may merit execution, still shun the worlds reserved for killers of women, which are extremely unpleasant (*ye lokavadhyaiś corādibhir api kutsitā atiduḥkhitayā parihṛtāḥ*). Cr believes that the expression refers to perpetrators of the cardinal sins listed in the *dharmaśāstras*, who are to be executed by all men. His idea is that even such profound evildoers despise the worlds set aside for killers of women and, by extension, the killers of women themselves. (*lokānāṃ sarvajanānāṃ vadhyair mahāpāpibhir apīty arthaḥ. ye kutsitās tair api ye gantuṃ neṣyanta ity arthaḥ.*) This interpretation would seem to be out of keeping with the tenor of the *dharmaśāstras* in which the killing of women is generally regarded as an *upapātaka*, a lesser crime (*ManuSm* 11.66), than those regarded as *mahāpātakas*, or cardinal sins (*ManuSm* 11.54). Perhaps the idea here is similar to what we see in the contemporary penal system, where those who kill especially vulnerable people, such as children, are often held in contempt even by other murderers. See note to 1.24.11 and R. Goldman 1982.

D6,7,M3, and the printed edition of KK (6.81.23) read the locative plural *lokavadhyeṣu*, "among those who deserve to die at the hands of men," for the instrumental plural *lokavadhyaiś ca* of the critical edition, yielding a sense quite similar to that of the critical reading. VSP (6.81.24) and the texts and printed editions of Cv, Cg, and Cm read instead *lokavadhaiṣu*, which these commentators analyze as the vocative *loka-*

vadhya, "O you who deserve death at the hands of people," and *eṣu*, "among these," which they take to be an elliptical reference to the fourteen contemptible worlds [i.e., hells] reserved for killers of women (*he lokavadhya! eṣu caturdaśalokeṣu strīghātināṃ ye kutsitā lokās tān*—so Cg). This variant and interpretation are represented only in the translation of Raghunathan (1982, vol. 3, p. 240), who renders, "O wretch that deserve death at the hands of all the world, you shall die and go to that world, most execrated of all, to which go murderers of women!"

22. "wielding weapons" *sāyudhaiḥ*: Literally, "along with weapons." Cg, evidently concerned lest we think that the monkeys carry military armaments, glosses, "along with means of killing (*sahananasādhanaiḥ*)," letting the generic term suggest the claws, fangs, trees, and stones with which the monkeys typically fight.

23. "Indrajit... drove back" *nyavārayat*: Literally, " he drove back." We agree with Cr, who understands Indrajit to be the subject of the finite verb and who suggests supplying his name. Cm, on the other hand, takes the *rākṣasa* army to be the subject. In this he is followed by Dutt (1893, p. 1389) and Raghunathan (1982, vol. 3, p. 240).

"with his army" *anīkena*: M3 and the texts and printed editions of Cg and Cm read instead *anīkaṃ tu*, which, as Cm notes, makes the *rākṣasa* army the subject of the finite verb (see above).

"fearsomely swift" *bhīmavegānām*: D6,7,9–11,T2,3,G3, and the texts and printed editions of Ct and Cr read instead *bhīmakopānām*, "fearsome in their anger."

"the immensely powerful army... as it rushed onward" *āpatantaṃ mahāvīryaṃ tad anīkam*: Ct, Ck, and Cm understand that the use of the masculine participle *āpatantam* to modify the neuter *anīkam* is the result of an irregularity in the epic language. Our translation follows them in understanding that the monkey army is the sole object of the verb "he drove back." Cg, however, in glossing *anīkaṃ ca*, "and the army," appears to take *mahāvīryam* to be a masculine adjective modifying Hanumān. The sense would thus be "He drove back the immensely powerful one [Hanumān] and his army... as they rushed onward."

26. Cm notes that, while the explicit meaning of the verse is clear, the inner meaning can be extracted by supplying the adjective *āśritām*, "resorted to," to modify *imām*, "her," construing the phrase with Rāma and Lakṣmaṇa. In other words, according to Cm, Indrajit is saying that he will kill Sītā, who has resorted to Rāma and Lakṣmaṇa, as well as Hanumān and Vibhīṣaṇa [but not the heroic brothers]. (*imām ity asya prātītikārthaḥ spaṣṭaḥ. vastutas tu lakṣmaṇaṃ rāmaṃ cāśritām iti śeṣaḥ. imāṃ hatvā tvāṃ cānāryaṃ vibhīṣaṇaṃ ca haniṣyāmīti saṃbandhaḥ.*) See note to 6.27.10.

27. "Now as to what you said... I would respond that" *yad bravīṣi*: Literally, "what you say." We follow Cg and Cr, who understand: "The [elliptical] sentence should be completed in this way: 'In that you say, "She is not to be killed," now hear the response.' (*na hantavyeti yad bravīṣi tatrottaraṃ śṛṇu iti vākyaśeṣaḥ*—so Cg.)"

"one must do whatever causes pain to one's enemies" *pīḍākaram amitrāṇāṃ yat syāt kartavyam eva tat*: Some of the commentators attempt to place Indrajit's extremely Machiavellian view within the boundaries of the discourse of the *dharmaśāstras*. Ct and Ck understand that one is obliged to do even sinful or proscribed things if they harm one's enemies (*śatrūṇāṃ yat pīḍākaraṃ tat pāpam api kartavyam eva*), while Cr argues that Indrajit's statement suggests that the deed he is about to commit does not fall within the definition of the crime of killing a woman (*etena strīvadhadoṣasya nāyaṃ viṣaya iti sūcitam*).

Following verse 27, D7,G1, (and presumably the text of Cr) insert a passage of two lines [1552*]: "Why did Rāma kill Tāṭakā earlier? So, I shall kill Rāma's queen, the daughter of Janaka." Indrajit's effort to justify his actions as recompense for Rāma's having killed a woman has little textual support. It is, however, discussed by Dutt in a footnote (1893, p. 1390).

29. "Hacked in two from her shoulder to her hip" *yajñopavītamārgeṇa chinnā*: Literally, "cut along the path of the sacred thread." The idea, as the commentators suggest in various ways, is that Indrajit cuts the illusory Sītā along the line that would be traced on someone wearing the *yajñopavīta*, or sacrificial thread, which normally is worn by high-caste men over the left shoulder and hanging to the right hip under the right arm (*ManuSm* 2.63). Pagani (1999, p. 1093) understands, "*Coupée en deux... à la manière dont on coupe le cordon du sacrifice*." But surely this is mistaken. See note to 6.63.3, App. I, No. 43, lines 15–16 and n. 11.

30. "that woman" *tām... striyam*: Ś,Ñ2,B,D1,2,7,8,12, and the texts and printed editions of VSP, KK, and Gorresio read *svayam*, "by himself," in place of *striyam*, "woman."

"Rāma's woman, whom I have slaughtered in my wrath" *mayā rāmasya... imāṃ kopena ca niṣūditām*: Literally, "her of Rāma, slain by me through anger." D7, 9–11, and the texts and printed editions of Cr and Ct read instead *priyāṃ śastraniṣūditām* for *kopena ca niṣūditām*, yielding the sense "Rāma's beloved, slain with [my] weapon."

Following verse 30, D5–7,9–11,T2,3,G1,3,M, and the texts and printed editions of the southern commentators insert a passage of one line [1553*], which continues Indrajit's speech: "Vaidehī has been slaughtered. Your efforts have been in vain."

32. "As he withdrew to the safety of his own forces" *tad durgaṃ saṃśritasya tu*: Literally, "of him who had taken recourse to an inaccessible place." The exact sense of the word *durgam*, "inaccessible place, fortress, citadel," is far from certain here. The commentators are of two minds. Ct and Ck understand the reference to be to an inaccessible location in the form of Indrajit's own flying chariot (*khecararatharūpam*). Most of the translators who follow the text of Ct understand some variation of "aerial citadel." Dutt (1893, p. 1390), who translates, "the castle," adds, in a footnote, "the castle built by Indrajit by means of his illusory power in the air." Gita Press (1969, vol. 3, p. 1712) combines both the literal meaning and Ct's interpretation, rendering, "(aerial) chariot, which was actually difficult of access (for others)." Cg and Cm, on the other hand, understand the term *durga* to refer to a protective formation of *rākṣasa* troops that encircle Indrajit (*vyūhīkṛtarākṣasapariveṣṭanarūpam*). Raghunathan (1982, vol. 3, p. 240), alone among the translators consulted, renders this interpretation, translating, "protected as he was on all sides by his forces." Given that no mention is made of Indrajit rising up into the sky in his chariot before the renewed commencement of hostilities in the next *sarga*, we are inclined to agree with this latter interpretation.

33. "thoroughly delighted... in profound dejection" *hṛṣṭarūpaṃ... viṣaṇṇarūpāḥ*: We follow the commentators in taking *-rūpa* in both cases as the suffix *rūpap*, in the sense of "to a great degree" (*praśaṃsāyāṃ rūpap* [*Pā* 5.3.66]—Ck, Ct).

The meter is *vaṃśasthavila*.

Sarga 69

1. "those bulls among monkeys" *vānararṣabhāḥ*: D7,9–11,13, and the texts and printed editions of Ct and Cr read instead *vānarā bhṛśam*, "monkeys... intensely," yielding the sense "the monkeys [ran] as fast as they could."

"glancing back toward Indrajit" *vīkṣamāṇāḥ*: Literally, "looking." We follow Cm and Ct, who supply the phrase "at Indrajit (*tam indrajitam*)." Some translators construe the participle with the phrase *diśaḥ sarvāḥ* in *pāda* c, yielding the sense "glancing about in all directions."

2. "scattered" *vidravataḥ pṛthak*: Literally, "fleeing separately."

"called out to them" *tān uvāca*: Literally, "he said to them."

3. "Where now are all your heroics?" *śūratvaṃ kva nu vo gatam*: Literally, "Where indeed has your heroism gone?"

4. "Follow close behind me" *pṛṣṭhato 'nuvrajadhvaṃ mām*: Ś1,D10,M1,2, and the texts and printed editions of Ct read the negative particle *na*, "not," instead of the *upasarga* [*a*]*nu*-, yielding the peculiar sense "do not go behind me." Ct, the only commentator to have this reading, ignores it. Translators who follow the text of Ct propose a variety of meanings, such as "do not turn your back on me," "do not turn your back on the enemy," etc.

"to run away" *nivartitum*: Literally, "to turn back, withdraw."

5. "wise" *dhīmatā*: D5,M3, and the texts and printed editions of Cg and Cm read instead *vānarāḥ*, "the monkeys."

"the monkeys were highly indignant" *susaṃkruddhāḥ*: Literally, "[they were] enraged." Presumably the monkeys are indignant at Hanumān's taunts about their cowardice. D5,7,G1,2,M3,5, and the texts and printed editions of Cr and Cg read instead the redundant *susaṃhṛṣṭāḥ*, "greatly excited *or* greatly delighted." This reading is rendered only by Raghunathan (1982, vol. 3, p. 241), who translates, "their spirits revived."

7. "wreathed in flames" *arciṣmān*: Literally, "possessing flames." The idea, evidently, is that the monkeys represent flames encircling the fire that is Hanumān.

8. "like Yama, who brings time itself to an end" *kālāntakayamopamaḥ*: See note to 6.21.26.

9. "and... the great monkey" *ca mahākapiḥ*: D7,9–11,13,T2,3, and the texts and printed editions of Ct and Cr read instead *mahatā kapiḥ*, "with tremendous [rage], the monkey."

"hurled... boulder" *pātayac chilām*: The point at which Indrajit and his chariot become visible is not made clear. At 6.67.39–40, Rāma appears to suggest that the use of divine missiles might render Indrajit visible to the monkeys, but there is no indication that this has actually happened. Evidently, we are to understand that Indrajit had made himself and his chariot visible in order to perpetrate the illusion of killing Sītā in *sarga* 68, and there is no indication that he has subsequently returned to invisibility.

10. "the chariot" *rathaḥ*: D7,9, and the texts and printed editions of GPP and NSP read instead the accusative *ratham*, which is impossible to construe in the passive construction of the verse. The critical apparatus marks this reading with the word *sic*. No commentator addresses this reading.

"well out of range" *sudūram*: Literally, "very far away."

11. "Failing in its purpose" *vyartham udyatā*: Literally, "raised up in vain." We follow Ct, who glosses, "deployed in vain (*vyarthaṃ prayuktā*)." Cs, looking ahead to verse 12, notes that there is a difference of opinion as to whether the discharge of the boulder has indeed been totally useless, since, in that verse, its fall wreaks havoc among the ranks of the *rākṣasas*. We agree with him that the futility of Hanumān's act refers only to his failure to achieve its intended purpose, the destruction of Indrajit and his chariot.

"It split open the earth and buried itself." *viveśa dharaṇīṃ bhittvā*: Literally, "having split the earth, it entered [the earth]." Pagani, alone among the translators consulted, reads the gerund *bhittvā* irregularly as intransitive, rendering, "*se brisa*," but this is not persuasive either on grammatical or contextual grounds.

12. "But in falling, it wrought havoc among the *rākṣasa* host." *patitāyāṃ śilāyāṃ tu rakṣasāṃ vyathitā camūḥ*: Literally, "But when the stone had fallen, the army of the *rākṣasas* was afflicted."

"Indrajit" *tam*: Literally, "him." We follow Cr in understanding the reference here to be to Indrajit (*tam indrajitam*). Indrajit, in any case, is the most recent, plausible masculine antecedent for the pronoun. (See verse 11 above.)

Following 12ab, D5–7,9–11,S (except T1) insert a passage of one line [1561*]: "The *rākṣasas* were completely crushed by that stone as it fell."

13. "Arming themselves" *udyatāḥ*: The adjective is somewhat ambiguous in the present context. It can mean "active, diligent, persevering, prepared, etc." We tend to agree with Ct and Cm, who suggest that we supply the gerund "having seized (*gṛhītvā*)," which would then govern the accusatives "trees and mountain peaks (*drumān . . . giriśṛṅgāṇi ca*)." They then understand the line to mean "having seized [trees and mountain peaks], they became ready for battle (*gṛhītvā yuddhārtham udyatā babhūvur ity arthaḥ*)." See note to 6.70.6.

"hurled . . . into the midst of their enemies" *cikṣipur dviṣatāṃ madhye*: D5,T2,3,M3,5, and the texts and printed editions of Cm and Cg read instead *kṣipantīndrajitaḥ saṃkhye*, "they hurled [trees and mountain peaks] at Indrajit in battle." Here we follow Cg, who glosses the genitive *indrajitaḥ* with *indrajitaṃ prati* "toward Indrajit." D9–11,G2, and the texts and printed editions of Ct read instead the accusative *indrajitam*, "at Indrajit."

Following verse 13, Ś,Ñ1,V2,B3,D4–13,T2,3,G,M1–3, and the texts and printed editions of the southern commentators and Lahore insert a passage of two lines [1562*]: "Releasing a great hail of trees and boulders, the leaping monkeys slaughtered their enemies and bellowed forth their various cries."

14. "powerfully . . . by the immensely powerful" *mahāvīryaiḥ . . . vīryāt*: Literally, "by the immensely powerful ones from power." Ñ2,V1,B2,D7,9–11,G1, and the texts and printed editions of Ct read *mahābhīmaiḥ*, "very fearsome," for *mahāvīryaiḥ*.

"writhed" *vyaveṣṭanta*: Literally, "they twisted, turned." Ś1,Ñ,V1,B2–4,D5,7–11, and the texts and printed editions of Ct and Cr read instead *vyaceṣṭanta*, "they rolled."

16–17. "he displayed his valor" *dṛṣṭavikramaḥ*: Literally, "he whose valor was visible *or* apparent." D10,G1, and the texts and printed editions of Ct read instead *dṛḍhavikramaḥ*, "he whose valor was firm *or* unyielding."

"mallets" *kūṭa-*: Ñ2,V1,2,B2,D10,11,T2, and the texts and printed editions of Ct read instead the redundant *śūla-*, "lances."

"The monkeys, in turn, slew his followers in battle." *te cāpy anucarāṃs tasya vānarā jaghnur āhave*: A number of southern and northern manuscripts and the texts and printed editions of Cg, Gorresio, and Lahore read instead *te cāpy anucarās tasya vānarāñ jaghnur ojasā* [Gorresio, Lahore—*āhave* as in the critical edition], "and with their strength [in battle—Gorresio, Lahore], his followers slaughtered the monkeys." This variant is rendered in the translations of Gorresio (1858, vol. 10, p. 95) and Raghunathan (1982, vol. 3, p. 242).

18. "With *sāla* trees, complete with trunks and branches" *saskandhaviṭapaiḥ sālaiḥ*: The *sāla* tree is the *Vatica robusta* or *Shorea robusta*. V3,D10,11, and the texts and printed editions of Ct read instead *suskandhaviṭapaiḥ śailaiḥ*, "with excellent trunks and branches, and with mountains *or* boulders."

19. "There is no point in defeating this army." *na naḥ sādhyam idaṃ balam*: Literally, "This army does not have to be defeated by us."

20. "struggling" *viceṣṭantaḥ*: Literally, "moving about, exerting ourselves."

"sacrificing our lives" *tyaktvā prāṇān*: Literally, "having abandoned *or* sacrificed [our] life breaths."

21. "Let us first report" *vijñāpya*: Literally, "having reported."

22. "calmly and deliberately" *śanaiḥ śanair asaṃtrastaḥ*: Literally, "slowly, slowly, unafraid."

23. "Hanumān was heading back to where Rāghava waited" *hanūmantaṃ vrajantaṃ yatra rāghavaḥ*: Literally, "Hanumān going to where Rāghava [was]."

"to the Nikumbhilā shrine" *nikumbhilām*: According to Ct, the reference is to the shrine, sanctuary, or sacred grove dedicated to the goddess Nikumbhilā. Ct adds, as an alternative, that it may refer to a [sacred] banyan tree (*nikumbhilāṃ caityaṃ tadākhyādevālayaṃ vaṭavṛkṣaṃ vā*). See 6.72.13 and note. According to several commentators, Nikumbhilā is said to be the name of a manifestation of Bhadrakālī worshiped at a shrine in western Laṅkā. See notes to 5.22.41; 6.60.18–19; and 6.71.13. See Rao 1914, vol. 1, pp. 356–58. According to Ct, this visit of Indrajit to Nikumbhilā's shrine takes place on the morning of the tenth day (*daśamyāṃ pūrvāhne nikumbhilāgamanam*). See note to 6.66.38, where Ct identifies the death of Makarākṣa as occurring before midnight on the night of the ninth [of the dark half of the month of Āśvina]. See note to 6.4.4. See, too, S. Goldman 2006b.

"to the sacred fire, purifier of all things" *pāvakam*: Literally, "to the purifier."

Following 23ab, D5–7,9–11,T2,3,G,M, and the texts and printed editions of the southern commentators insert a passage of one line [1568*]: "Eager to offer sacrifice, that evil-minded one went to the Nikumbhilā shrine."

24. "The sacred fire, purifier of all things" *pāvakaḥ*: Literally, "the purifier."

"as . . . the *rākṣasa* poured oblations of blood into it" *rakṣasā . . . hūyamānaḥ . . . homaśoṇitabhuk*: Literally, "the eater of oblation-blood as it was being offered oblations by the *rākṣasa*." We follow Cg in reading the compound *homaśoṇita-* as a *paranipāta* for *śoṇitahoma-*, "oblations of blood," as in verse 25 below. D6,T2,3,G2,3,M3, and the texts and printed editions of Cg and Cm read *māṃsa-*, "flesh," for *homa-*, "oblation," yielding the sense "eater of flesh and blood." The sinister nature of Indrajit's sacrifice is evident from the sanguinary nature of the oblations. Normally blood would never be involved in a vedic sacrifice. Compare the *Bālakāṇḍa* passage (1.18.5), where Viśvāmitra reports to Daśaratha the defiling of his own sacrifices by the blood and flesh poured on the altar by the *rākṣasas* Mārīca and Subāhu.

25. "oblations of blood" *homaśoṇita-*: See note to the previous verse for Cg's reading of the compound.

"that fierce fire" *sa tīvrāgniḥ*: D10,11,G1,M3, and the texts and printed editions of the southern commentators (*pace* critical apparatus) read instead *sutīvro 'gniḥ*, "a very fierce fire." According to Ct, the intensity of the fire is indicative of the impending destruction of the *rākṣasas* (*sutīvro 'gnī rakṣovipatsūcakaḥ*).

26. "in accordance with the sacrificial injunctions" *vidhānavat*: D5,7,9–11,T2,G,M, and the texts and printed editions of the southern commentators read instead *vidhānavit*, "who knew the sacrificial injunctions."

"who knew what was and was not proper conduct, stood around in their vast troops" *vyatiṣṭhanta* . . . *mahāsamūheṣu nayānayajñāḥ*: Our interpretation follows the commentary of Ct, who glosses *nayānayajñāḥ*, "who knew what was and was not proper conduct" with "who knew what was in accordance with the *śāstras* and what was not (*śāstrīyāśāstrīyavidaḥ*)." We understand that the phrase refers to the *rākṣasas'* knowledge of proper ritual performance, which makes them a knowing and appreciative audience for Indrajit's sacrifice. Ct, Ck, and Cr take the term *samūheṣu*, which we have rendered as "in their vast troops," to mean "in battles (*yuddheṣu*)," a sense for which we can find no lexical support. They construe this term with *nayānayajñāḥ*, to yield the sense "who knew what was and was not to be done in battles (*yuddheṣu* . . . *kṛtyākṛtyatattvajñāḥ*—so Ct and Ck)." All translations consulted that have this verse follow the interpretation of Ct, etc., with the exception of Raghunathan (1982, vol. 3, p. 242), who reads the verse as we do, taking, however, *samūha* in its other closely related lexically supported sense of "large numbers."

The meter is *upajāti* with a hypermetric *pāda* b.

Sarga 70

3. "lord of the apes" *ṛkṣapate*: See note to 6.4.17.

4. "With the words, 'So be it' " *tathety uktvā*: Literally, "having said, 'So be it.' " Ś,Ñ2,V1,2,B1,2,D2,3,8,12,13,G3,M3,5, and the texts and printed editions of Cg read instead *tathoktas tu*, "addressed in this fashion."

5. "on the road" *pathi*: D9–11,G1, and the texts and printed editions of Ct read instead *tadā*, "then."

"fresh from battle" *kṛtasaṃgrāmaiḥ*: Literally, "who had given battle."

"breathing hard" *śvasadbhiḥ*: Literally, "breathing, panting, *or* sighing." Ct, Ck, and Cr understand that the monkeys are sighing in their grief born of recalling the murder of Sītā (*sītāvipattismṛtijaduḥkhān niśvasadbhir ity arthaḥ*—so Ct, Ck). We believe it is more probable that the poet wishes to express the exhaustion of the troops coming from the front.

6. "all ready for battle" *udyatam*: Literally, "prepared *or* ready." See note to 6.69.13.

7. "With his army of tawny monkeys" *tena harisainyena*: V2,B1,D2–6,9–11,G1,2,M1,2,5, and the texts and printed editions of Ct, Ck, and Cr read *saha*, "together with," for *hari-*, "tawny monkeys." Ct and Ck take this term to indicate that the army of apes is included. Ck adds, "and with the army of apes as well (*ṛkṣasainyenāpi saha*)." Ct appears to make this same comment. However, in both printed editions of Ct's commentary consulted (GPP and NSP), his gloss reads *rākṣasasainyenāpi saha*, "and with the army of *rākṣasas* as well." This seems to make little sense in

the context and is probably the result of a coincidental typographical error in both editions.

"the illustrious Hanumān" *mahāyaśāḥ*: Literally, "the illustrious one."

9. "When I saw her like that" *tāṃ dṛṣṭvā*: Literally, "having seen her."

"devastated" *udbhrāntacittaḥ*: Literally, "of whirling *or* distracted mind."

12. "unbearable" *asahyaṃ ca*: D5,G2,M3, and the texts and printed editions of Cg read instead *anāsādyam*, "unapproachable." D9–11 and the texts and printed editions of Ct read instead *asaṃhāryam*, "irrepressible, unquenchable."

13. "both rational and meaningful" *hetvarthasaṃhitam*: We agree with the commentators, who gloss *hetu* as "logical argument (*upapatti*)" and *artha* as "purpose *or* meaning (*prayojanam*)," and read the compound as a *dvandva*. Thus, Ct glosses, "replete with logical argument and a particular purpose (*upapattyā viśiṣṭaprayojanena ca sahitam*)." Cg offers, however, an alternative reading of the compound as a *karmadhāraya*, with the sense "having a logical meaning *or* substance" (*heturūpo 'rtho 'bhidheyo hetvārtha iti vā*).

14. "the practice of righteousness . . . it is truly pointless" *dharmo nirarthakaḥ*: Literally, "*dharma* has no purpose." Depending on the precise force of the different aspects of Lakṣmaṇa's argument in this and the following verses, we have translated the terms *dharma* and *adharma*, normally "righteousness" and "unrighteousness," respectively, in a variety of ways. We refer to "righteousness" and "unrighteousness" when the abstract concepts are addressed; "the practice of righteousness" and "the practice of unrighteousness" when the reference appears to be to a mode of conduct; and "the force of righteousness" and "the force of unrighteousness" when the reference is to the power of such practices to affect one's condition and fate in this world and the next.

Not unexpectedly, all the commentators consulted have something to say about Lakṣmaṇa's agnostic views. Ct and Ck understand the thrust of Lakṣmaṇa's argument to be that because *dharma* is unable to protect one from calamities, it is truly pointless. It is, therefore, not one of the principal ends of mankind. Instead, we should rely principally on our own strength. (*tvadāśrito dharmo 'narthebhyas trātuṃ na śaknoti yatas tasmād asau nirarthakaḥ. prādhānyena puruṣārtho na bhavati*—so Ct). Cr remarks that, because the expected effects of *dharma* (i.e., protection) are not evident, *dharma* itself must not exist (*etena kāryābhāvāt talliṅgakānumānāsiddhyā tadgamyadharmasyābhāvaḥ sūcitaḥ*). Cv argues that Lakṣmaṇa's agnostic position derives from his perception of the calamity that has befallen his righteous elder brother and the success of the unrighteous Rāvaṇa (*anena prakāreṇa nityaṃ dharmānusthāyino jyeṣṭhasyānarthadarśanān nityam adharmikasya rāvaṇasyārthadarśanāc ca*). Cg, like Cr, argues that Lakṣmaṇa's position is that the failure of righteousness to protect Rāma is proof that, like the proverbial rabbit's horn, it simply does not exist, a position that, Cg continues, Lakṣmaṇa has been urging on Rāma from the time he acceded to his father's wishes back in the *Ayodhyākāṇḍa*. Unlike Cv, however, Cg extends the argument for nonexistence to include *adharma* as well, since the practice of evil has not kept Rāvaṇa from [accomplishing] his goals. (*nirarthako 'vastubhūtaḥ. apramāṇika iti yāvat. śaśaviṣāṇavat kevalavyavahāramātrāvalambano dharmo 'narthebhyo vyasanebhyas trātuṃ vyasanāni nivārayituṃ na śaknoti . . . adharmo 'pi nirarthakaḥ san rāvaṇam arthebhyo na nivārayituṃ śaknoty ity arthaḥ*.) Cm offers two explanations for Lakṣmaṇa's heresy. His first is that Lakṣmaṇa completely loses his faith in *dharma*, since his mind has been clouded by the enormity of the disaster that has befallen Rāma in the form of Sītā's apparent death (*sītāvadharūpaduḥkhapradarśanāc ca svayaṃ vyasanāsātiśayena kaluṣitāntaḥkaraṇaḥ san dharma eva nāstīty āha*). Cm's second, and more moderate, explanation is that, although Lakṣmaṇa actually understands the validity of *dharma* and *adharma*, he [temporarily] denies it in his overwhelming distress and in his anger at having been prevented from using the *brahmāstra*. (*yadvā lakṣmaṇo dharmādharmayor hitāhitasādhanatvaṃ jānann api sītāhananaśravaṇajaśokākrāntacittaḥ sann anavaratadharmasevinā raghunāthena . . . brahmāstraprayoganivāraṇeṇa krodhāviṣṭaḥ san dharmādharmayor arthānarthahetutvaniyamaṃ nirākaroti.*) In the end, Cm is uncertain whether to understand the term *nirarthaka*, "pointless," to mean that *dharma* is genuinely an empty concept (*anupādeya*) or whether it is merely incapable of being demonstrated (*niṣpramāṇakaḥ*). Cs's explanation is similar to those of the other commentators. However, he does offer an alternative inner meaning (*āntaraṅgikabhāvapakṣaḥ*), whereby Lakṣmaṇa is, in fact, affirming the power of *dharma* to save one from calamity (*tathā hy anarthebhya evaṃvidhebhyo dharmas tvāṃ trātuṃ śaknoti yataḥ sa na nirarthaka iti*). Most of the commentators agree that Rāma's righteous character is demonstrated by his having obeyed his father's instructions, while his control of his senses is proven by the fact that he entertained no evil thoughts toward Kaikeyī and Daśaratha for having deprived him of his rightful inheritance. Several of the commentators document their claims with quotations from various parts of the *Rāmāyaṇa*.

"the path of virtue" *śubhe vartmani*: Literally, "on the good *or* auspicious path." Cm glosses, "the path of righteousness (*dharmamārge*)," while Cs offers, "the path ordained in the *vedas* (*vedavihite . . . mārge*)."

15. "the force of righteousness . . . it does not exist" *dharmaḥ . . . nāsti*: Literally, "*dharma* does not exist." What Lakṣmaṇa means here is not that there is no such thing as a concept or code of *dharma* but that its practice has no real force or effect on the fortunes of those who either submit to it or violate it. Ct paraphrases Lakṣmaṇa's position, saying that only directly perceptible things actually exist. He then steps a bit outside the normal role of the commentator to take issue with this argument, which he equates, oddly enough, with what he terms the "Buddhist" position, that there is no rebirth. Ct's rejection of what is actually Lakṣmaṇa's statement of the *cārvāka*, or materialist, view is that the imperceptibility of an object does not mean that it does not exist, as in the case of such creatures as *piśācas*, etc. (*sthāvarāṇāṃ jāṅgamānāṃ ca paśvādirūpāṇāṃ bhūtānāṃ darśanaṃ sukhāparokṣadarśanaṃ yathāsti tathā dharmo nāsti. asāmarthyād anadhikārāc ca tasmād dharmaḥ sukhasādhanatvavyāpto neti me matiḥ. janmāntarādikaṃ nāsty eveti bauddhamateneyam uktiḥ. na hi taṃ vinā jāyamānasyāpi tatkaraṇakatvam iti bhāvaḥ. yat tu yathā sthāvarādīnāṃ darśanāt tatsattā tathā dharmasya darśanābhāvād dharmo nāstīti vyācakṣate tan na. yogyānupalambhasyaivābhāvasādhakatvāt. dharmasya ca piśācādivad ayogyatvāt.*) Cs quotes Ct, whom he criticizes on the grounds that his argument is derived from the doctrine of the *cārvākas*, an argument he also associates with Cm. Cs then provides an alternate inner interpretation of the verse, according to which Lakṣmaṇa's position is merely a *pūrvapakṣa*, and that, in fact, over time, *dharma* becomes manifest. He does this in part by reading the sequence *dharmas tena nāstīti me matiḥ*—which we translated as "since . . . that force of righteousness . . . it is my opinion that it does not exist"—as *dharmas te na nāstīti me matiḥ*, which he interprets to mean "it is my opinion that with respect to you *dharma* does not not exist (i.e., does exist) (*dharmas te tvadviṣaye na nāstīti me matiḥ*)."

See note to verse 14 above.

16. "This thing called 'righteousness' " *ayam arthaḥ*: Literally, "this matter."

"is not demonstrable in the same way that moving and fixed objects are" *yathaiva sthāvaraṃ vyaktaṃ jaṅgamaṃ ca tathāvidham / na . . . tathā yuktaḥ*: Literally, "is not proven in the way that a fixed object is manifest and a moving one of the same sort." There is a significant difference of opinion between the two groups of southern commentators as to the precise meaning of the terms *vyaktam* and *yuktaḥ*. According to Ck, Ct, and Cr, we are to understand the term *vyaktam* to mean that it is "manifest that animate and inanimate creatures who are not governed by *dharma* and *adharma* are, nonetheless, perfectly happy. (*yathā yasmāt sthāvaraṃ vyaktaṃ dharmaprasaktirahitam api sukhīti vyaktam. tathāvidhaṃ sthāvaravad dharmānadhikṛtaṃ jaṅgamaṃ paśvādy api sukhīti vyaktam*—so Ct.) For these commentators, this statement, therefore, is part of Lakṣmaṇa's logical refutation of the existence of any force of *dharma*, which is accomplished by the refutation of negative concomitance (*vyatireka*) between righteousness (*dharma*) and happiness. These commentators then understand the adjective *yuktaḥ*—which we have rendered as "demonstrable" and view as modifying *arthaḥ*, "matter"—to mean "connected with" and to modify *tvadvidhaḥ*, "[a person] like you [Rāma]." They thus understand the adjective elliptically to mean "wholeheartedly connected with *or* practicing *dharma* (*sarvātmanā dharmayuktaḥ*—Ct, Ck)." According to these commentators, the phrase beginning with "a person like you (*tvadvidhaḥ*)" serves to refute the positive concomitance (*anvaya*) between *dharma* and happiness. Gita Press (1969, vol. 3, p. 1716) and Dutt (1893, pp. 1393–94) follow this interpretation. Our interpretation, along with those of the other translators, is more or less in accordance with that of Cv, Cm, and Cg, for whom *vyaktam* and *yuktaḥ* mean "perceived by direct perception" and "perceptible," respectively (*vyaktaṃ pratyakṣata upalabdham . . . yuktaḥ . . . pratyakṣaḥ*—so Cg)." Cm separates the two halves of the verse more clearly than the other commentators. For him, the first half merely demonstrates the imperceptibility or supersensory quality (*atīndriyaḥ*) of *dharma* but does not prove its nonexistence, since other things that are beyond the range of the senses are known to exist. The second half of the verse, for Cm, serves as a refutation of the existence of *dharma* since, even though it might be imperceptible to the senses, its effect, in the form of happiness, should be demonstrable. (*nanv apratyakṣamātreṇa dharmanirāso nopapadyate. atīndriyasyāpi vastunaḥ sadbhāvād ity āśaṅkya bādhakatarkeṇa nirākaroti tvadvidha iti. atīndriyo 'pi dharmo yadi syāt tarhi tvadvidho na vipadyate. na caivaṃ tasmān nāsti dharma ity arthaḥ.*)

"Otherwise, a person like you would not experience such suffering" *tvadvidho na vipadyate*: Literally, "one such as you does not experience misfortune."

17. "By the same token . . . Rāvaṇa would go" *rāvaṇaḥ . . . vrajet*: Literally, "Rāvaṇa would go."

"real" *bhūtaḥ*: Like most of the commentators, we understand this to mean "really effective, true, etc." Thus, for example, Cr understands, "obtaining its own fruit *or* results (*svaphalaprāpakaḥ*)," while Cm glosses, "real *or* true (*satyaḥ*)."

"hell" *narakam*: Cg, Cr, and Cm do not take the term in its literal sense of a place of punishment in the afterlife, understanding it rather in the sense of hellish suffering in this world, that is, "suffering leading to hell (*narakaprāpakaduḥkham*—so Cr)" or simply "calamity (*vyasanam*—Cm, Cg)." This interpretation makes a certain amount of sense, in that it both maintains the parallelism between Rāma and Rāvaṇa and avoids bringing into the discussion an unseen and unverifiable supernatural consequence of evil that would tend to run against the tenor of Lakṣmaṇa's rationalist argument.

See note to verse 14 above.

18. "can it be true that one obtains felicity through the practice of righteousness and that suffering arises from the practice of unrighteousness" *dharmeṇopalabhed dharmam adharmaṃ cāpy adharmataḥ*: Literally, "One obtains *dharma* through *dharma* and *adharma* from *adharma*." Given the tenor of the passage, one must understand that Lakṣmaṇa is uttering a rhetorical question concerning the normative connection between the practice of *dharma* and happiness, on the one hand, and the practice of *adharma* and suffering, on the other. Certainly Cg, at least, understands that we are to take the verb *upalabhet*, "one obtains," ironically (*kākuḥ*) and instructs us to read the sentence with the sense of "do you really believe that one obtains . . . ? (*upalabheteti manyase kim ity arthaḥ*)." This appears to be the commentators' interpretation. However, none of the printed editions of the texts of the commentators contains the sequence of lines as it appears in the critical edition. Many southern manuscripts insert an additional half verse following 18ab; see below, 1573*. In this textual sequence, the word *yadi*, "if," from line 1574* (see below), is to be construed with 18cd, according to Ct, which makes 18cd a hypothetical statement, "If it were true that one obtained felicity through the force of righteousness, etc." The text of Gorresio apparently tries to rationalize the ambiguity of our reading by substituting the variant: "I obtain unrighteousness through righteousness, and righteousness through unrighteousness (*dharmenopalabhe 'dharmam adharmeṇāpi dharmatām*)." This is rendered by Gorresio (1858, vol. 10, p. 97) as "*io scorgo la virtù confuse col vizio ed il vizio colla virtù*." Gorresio (1858, vol. 10, p. 294) notes, however, that the commentator on his text, Cl, interprets the passage rather differently. Cl's gloss is similar to that of the southern commentators. He glosses, "I see unrighteousness, that is, the misery produced by unrighteousness, arising from righteousness, and righteousness, that is, the happiness arising from righteousness, produced by unrighteousness (*dharmeṇādharmatām adharmajanyaṃ duḥkham adharmeṇa dharmaṃ dharmajanyaṃ sukham upalabhe paśyāmi*)." Gorresio concludes his note with a strange meditation on how Lakṣmaṇa's nihilistic position, which is found in two or three other passages in the epic, is a reflex of the theory of *māyā*, in that it negates the idea of any substantial essence in the concepts of justice and injustice, virtue and vice. These doctrines, which Gorresio characterizes as "sad and deplorable (*tristi e deplorabili dottrine*)," are, he suggests, inherent in the pantheism of brahmanical India.

See note to verse 14 above.

Following 18ab, D6,7,9–11,T2,3,G,M, and the texts and printed editions of all southern commentators insert a passage of one line [1573*]: "Righteousness thus becomes unrighteousness and the two are mutually contradictory."

Following verse 18, D5,7,9–11,T2,3,G,M, and the texts and printed editions of all southern commentators insert a passage of one line [1574*], which, according to Ct, has to be read with 18cd (see above): "If it were true [that one obtained felicity through the practice of righteousness and that suffering arises from the practice of unrighteousness], the suffering associated with unrighteousness would then befall those who link themselves to unrighteousness."

19. "Now, if those people who were averse to unrighteousness would thereby experience the felicity arising from the practice of righteousness, that is, if those who

conducted themselves righteously would experience happiness, then they would receive their just deserts." *yadi dharmeṇa yujyeran nādharmarucayo janāḥ / dharmeṇa caratāṃ dharmas tathā caiṣāṃ phalaṃ bhavet //*: The verse, like many in this passage, is repetitive, elliptical, and ambiguous. Our interpretation borrows substantially from the commentators. A literal, if not entirely lucid, rendering of the verse might be: "If people who did not take pleasure in unrighteousness were to be linked with righteousness and if there were righteousness for those who behaved righteously, then that would be their fruit." See note to verse 14 above.

20. "these two concepts are meaningless" *etau nirarthakau*: Literally, "these two are without purpose."

See note to verse 14 above.

21. This verse, too, is obscure and textually problematic. Lakṣmaṇa's basic argument, as most of the commentators agree, is that *dharma* and, for that matter, *adharma* are transient and cease to have any effect almost instantaneously. They can therefore have no lasting effect in terms of future lives, etc. According to several of the commentators, acts of *dharma*, like other punctual actions, endure only for three instants (presumably of origination, operation, and cessation) and then cease to exist in the fourth. (*pāpakarmāṇaḥ puruṣā yady adharmeṇa kriyāśarīreṇa vadhyante tadā kriyāyās trikṣaṇāvasthāyitvāc caturthakṣaṇe svata eva vadhakarmaṇā nāśakriyayā hato naṣṭo 'dharmaḥ svayaṃ hato 'san bhūtvā kaṃ hantavyaṃ vadhiṣyati*—so Ct.)

The critical reading is particularly awkward in that the first half of the verse speaks of evildoers destroyed by *adharma*, while in the second half it is *dharma* that is destroyed by that act of destruction. With the exception of KK (6.83.22), the printed texts of the southern commentators (GPP, NSP, VSP, and Gita Press) read the sequence *vadhakarmahato dharmaḥ* in *pāda* c, "the force of righteousness would also be destroyed by the very act of destruction," as *vadhakarmahato 'dharmaḥ*, "the force of unrighteousness would also be destroyed by the very act of destruction," (GPP, NSP) or *vadhakarma hato 'dharmaḥ* (VSP and Gita Press), which is understood similarly by the commentators who share it. These variant readings have the advantage of maintaining a more intelligible parallelism between the two halves of the verse. According to the critical apparatus, the reading *adharmaḥ* belongs to the texts of Cr, Cm, Cg, Ck, and Ct, but not to that of Cv, who, they claim, reads with the critical edition. An examination of a transcript of a manuscript of Cv (p. 104) used by the critical editors, however, calls that reading into question. In any case, as several of the commentators note, the mention of either *dharma* or *adharma* should be taken as an *upalakṣaṇa*, or metonomy, to include the other. Cr attempts to improve the parallelism by arguing that, as an alternative, one could read the sequence *vadhyante pāpakarmāṇaḥ*, "evildoers perish," as *vadhyante 'pāpakarmāṇaḥ*, "non-evildoers, i.e., virtuous people, perish." This interpretation parallels the reading of virtually all the northern manuscripts, including the editions of Lahore and Gorresio, which substitute *puṇyakarmāṇaḥ*, "doers of pious deeds," for *pāpakarmāṇaḥ*. Unless we assume, as noted above, that the term *dharma* refers to the whole system of *dharma* and *adharma*, the critical edition's reading of *dharmaḥ* in *pāda* c is awkward at best. Northern manuscripts and printed editions that share this reading avoid the difficulty by substituting *adharmeṇa* for *vadhakarma-* in *pāda* c, yielding the sense "destroyed by *adharma*."

See note to verse 14 above.

22. "Or if we are to understand" *atha vā*: Literally, "or *or* on the other hand." The context requires us to understand that Lakṣmaṇa is advancing a hypothetical argument.

"that it is because of fate . . . fate" *vihitena . . . vidhiḥ*: Literally, "by what is ordained . . . fate." It seems clear to us that the two terms are intended to be synonymous here, and most of the translators consulted undersand them both to mean "destiny" or "the decree of destiny." Ct appears to understand *vihitena* to mean "the superior force, belonging to another, produced from the performance of [a particular part of] an ordained ritual, such as the *śyena*, etc. (*vihitaśyenādyanuṣṭhānajātiśayenānyadīyena*)." Ck understands similarly. This interpretation appears to be the basis upon which Gita Press (1969, vol. 3, p. 1717) renders, "by recourse to a (malevolent) ritual prescribed in the scriptures . . . the destiny (alone) that is engendered by the aforesaid ritual." Cr, similarly, takes the terms to refer to wrongful acts characterized by the superior force created by ordained ritual acts (*vihitena kriyānirmitena kenacid atiśayarūpādiviśiṣṭenādharmeṇa . . . vidhir vihitakarmajanitasvarūpaviśeṣaviśiṣṭa eva pāpena karmaṇā*). Cg understands *vihitena* and *vidhiḥ* to refer to a divinity (*devatā*). Cm, whom we follow, understands the terms to refer to fate (*daivam*).

See note to verse 14 above.

23. "the results . . . are imperceptible" *adṛṣṭapratikāreṇa*: Literally, "having unseen retribution." We follow Cm, who glosses, "the results of which are invisible (*apratyakṣaphalena*)."

"the highest good" *param*: Our interpretation follows that of Cg, Cm, and Cv, all of whom gloss, "the highest good (*śreyaḥ*)." Ct, Ck, and Cr understand the term to refer to the enemy, that is, the object of violence mentioned in the previous verse. Among the translators consulted, this interpretation is followed only by Dutt (1893, p. 1994) and Gita Press (1969, vol. 3, p. 1717).

See note to verse 14 above.

24. "If there really were such a thing as the power of virtue" *yadi sat syāt*: Literally, "if virtue were to exist." We follow Cr in understanding the phrase to mean "if virtuous action existed in such a way as to produce results (*yadi sat satkarma syāt phaladāyakatvena vidyeta*)."

"such a calamity" *īdṛśam*: Literally, "such [a thing]."

"the power of virtue does not exist" *san nopapadyate*: Literally, "virtue is impossible." Cm and Cg understand from the context of *pādas* cd that Lakṣmaṇa is stating that only evil truly exists (*asad eva bhavatīty arthaḥ*—so Cg).

25. "is merely auxiliary to manly effort" *balam . . . anuvartate*: Literally, "follows strength." The idea here, as expressed by the commentators, is that *dharma* may indeed exist but only as a weak force, incapable of producing results on its own. It must therefore rely on the human effort of those it favors. (*ata eva klībaḥ kātaraḥ svataḥ kāryakaraṇāsamarthaḥ. dharmo balam anuvartate kāryotpādane pauruṣam apekṣata ity arthaḥ*—so Cg.) The sentiment is thus similar to that expressed by the proverb "Heaven helps those who help themselves."

"blurs all distinctions" *hṛtamaryādaḥ*: Literally, "whose boundaries have been removed." Although the commentators tend to understand that *dharma* lacks the capacity to produce happiness or other results on its own, we believe that the context supports the idea that *dharma* is inherently unable to distinguish, in terms of its results, between those who practice it and those who do not.

"should... be ignored" *na sevyaḥ*: Literally, "is not to be practiced."

26. "merely auxiliary to manly effort" *balasya... guṇabhūtaḥ*: Literally, "is a subordinate element of strength."

"when it comes to effective action" *parākrame*: Literally, "in valor *or* endeavor." Our interpretation follows that of Cg, who glosses, "with respect to effective means of accomplishing one's object (*kāryasādhane viṣaye*)." D10,11, and the texts and printed editions of Ck, Ct, and Cr read instead the instrumental plural *parākramaiḥ*. Ct and Ck gloss, "with efforts (*prayatnaiḥ*)," and construe it with the phrase *dharmam utsṛjya*, "having abandoned *dharma*," in *pāda* c. This interpretation is followed by Dutt (1893, pp. 1394–95), who renders, "then carefully forsaking virtue." Other translators who follow the text of Ct interpret similarly, although they take the term in its sense of "valorous action." Cr construes the term with *balasya*, "effort," in *pāda* a, understanding, "of effort that is characterized by valorous actions (*parākramair upalakṣitasya balasya*)."

"abandon it" *dharmam utsṛjya*: Literally, "having abandoned *dharma*."

"devote yourself to manly effort, just as you now do to righteousness" *vartasva yathā dharme tathā bale*: Literally, "act with respect to strength as with respect to *dharma*." We flesh out the elliptical statement as the commentators suggest.

See notes to verse 14 above.

27. "then why is it that you would not imprison our father, who acted both untruthfully and cruelly toward you" *anṛtas tvayy akaruṇaḥ kiṃ na baddhas tvayā pitā*: Although several of the commentators shy away from the idea of Lakṣmaṇa talking about imprisoning the old king, this idea is fully in consonance with his angry speech at *Ayodhyākāṇḍa* 18. In fact, southern manuscripts and texts of that passage have him explicitly propose imprisoning and even executing Daśaratha (see note to *Ayodhyākāṇḍa* 18.15.458* = GPP 2.21.12). D10,11, and the texts and printed editions of Ck, Ct, Cr, and Gita Presss (6.83.28cd) read instead *anṛtaṃ tvayy akaraṇe kiṃ na baddhas tvayā vinā*. This reading is awkward and difficult to construe intelligibly. The commentators who share it and the translators who follow them struggle to make sense of it. Ct and Ck understand the passage to mean: "Are you [Rāma] not bound (*baddhaḥ*) by that promise, i.e., Daśaratha's [initial] promise to consecrate his eldest son Rāma despite the king's [subsequent] baseless (*akaraṇe*) falsification (*anṛtam*) [of that promise] through which he [Daśaratha] became separated from you (*tvayā vinā*) i.e., died? (*tvayā satyavacanaṃ pitṛvacanāṅgīkārarūpasatyaparipālanaṃ dharmo 'nuṣṭhīyata iti cet tadā tvayi jyeṣṭha uktasyābhiṣekavacanasyākaraṇe yadanṛtaṃ rājñaḥ prāptaṃ tenānṛtena rājā tvayā vinā bhūtaḥ. mṛta iti śeṣaḥ. atas tena rājño 'bhiṣekakaraṇarūpasatyena tvaṃ baddhaḥ kiṃ na.*)" Some variations of this theme are represented in the translations that follow Ct. Ck defends this reading staunchly against those who read with the critical edition (i.e., Cm, Cg), claiming that they chose the latter *facilior* reading simply to make it easy on themselves (*svayojanasaukāryānusāreṇānyo 'pāṭhīt paraḥ*). Ct quotes Ck's view on the absolute authenticity of his reading (*sarvatra pāṅktaḥ pāṭha iti katakaḥ*). Ct then goes on to quote Cm but rejects his reading (= critical edition) on cultural grounds because of the incompatibility of imprisoning one's own father with the notion of honoring his commands. (*tad ayuktam. pitṛbandhanasya satyavacanaparipālanarūpatvābhāvāt.*) Cr notes the variant reading of Cm but rationalizes it by breaking up the *sandhi* so that we must read three qualifiers of *dharma*—*anṛtaḥ*, "false"; *akaruṇaḥ*, "pitiless"; and *apitā*, "not your father." Cs notes Ct's variant reading and repeats Ct's quotation and critique of

Cm, rejecting that critique as "inconsistent (*asaṃgatam*)" on the basis of the absence of any intention [on Rāma's part] of imprisoning his father (*tasya pitṛbandhana eva tātparyābhāvāt*).

28. "if either righteousness or human effort were to be practiced exclusively" *yadi dharmo bhavet bhūta adharmo vā*: Literally, "if either *dharma* or *adharma* were truly to exist." The commentators suggest that the term *adharma* may be understood here either in its usual sense as the opposite of *dharma*, i.e., "unrighteousness," or as "human effort (*pauruṣam*)" (*adharmo dharmād anyaḥ pauruṣaṃ tad vā*—so Ct). In the context of Lakṣmaṇa's exhortation of Rāma to abandon his passive dependence on *dharma* and to take manly action, we believe the latter alternative is best here. We also follow the commentators in understanding the phrase *bhaved bhūtaḥ* in the sense of "to be principally *or* exclusively practiced (*syāt prādhanyenānuṣṭheyaḥ*—so Ct)." See 6.58.40 and note.

"then the wielder of the *vajra*, Indra of the hundred sacrifices, would not have first slain a sage and then performed a sacrifice" *na sma hatvā muniṃ vajrī kuryād ijyāṃ śatakratuḥ*: Literally, "the wielder of the *vajra*, Śatakratu, having first slain a sage, would not perform a sacrifice." The commentators unanimously understand the reference to be to the story, well known in the *vedas*, epics, and *purāṇas*, in which Indra slays the treacherous *purohita* of the gods, Viśvarūpa Triśiras, son of Tvaṣṭṛ. In most versions of the story, Indra dissipates the sin of *brahmahatyā* he has incurred through this act, not through sacrifice but by distributing his guilt among various willing recipients. The commentators may be conflating this story with its immediate sequel in which Indra kills Vṛtra, who was created by Tvaṣṭṛ to avenge his son's death. In that episode, Indra frees himself of guilt through the performance of a vedic sacrifice, in some versions the *aśvamedha*. See 6.58.40; 6.116.81; and notes.

29. "When either human effort or righteousness is practiced exclusively, it destroys a person" *adharmasaṃśrito dharmo vināśayati*: Literally, "*dharma* relying on *adharma* destroys." We agree with all the commentators in understanding the word *adharma* here once again to refer to *pauruṣa*, "manly *or* human effort." See note to verse 28. The commentators fall into two schools of interpretation with regard to this enigmatic utterance. Cv, Cg, and Cm, whom we follow, understand the statement in the context of the preceding argument, which they see as holding for the practical application of either *dharma* or *pauruṣa* or both as circumstances require. As Cm and Cg put it, "both *dharma* and *adharma* destroy their agent when they are exclusively practiced in isolation from each other (*niyamena pṛthak pṛthag anuṣṭhīyamānau dharmādharmau vināśayataḥ kartāram ity arthaḥ*)." In the following verse, Ct ridicules this position (see note to verse 30 below). Ck and Ct understand the sentence quite differently, taking it to mean "*dharma*, when it is reliant upon *adharma*, that is, combined with human effort, destroys one's enemy (*adharmasaṃśritaḥ pauruṣayukto dharmo ripuṃ vināśayati*—so Ct)." Cr appears to understand the phrase in both of these senses. Translators who render the text of Ct, with the exception of Shastri, follow his interpretation. Shastri (1959, vol. 3, p. 244), idiosyncratically, interprets the sentence to mean "If righteousness gives birth to unrighteousness, it must perish."

30. "Such is righteousness according to my way of thinking" *mama cedaṃ matam . . . dharmo 'yam iti*: Literally, "and this is my opinion, 'this is *dharma*.'" According to the interpretation of Cg and Cm, the reference here is to Lakṣmaṇa's final argument that *dharma* is something to be practiced optionally according to the demands of time and

place (*idaṃ yāthākāmyenobhayacaraṇaṃ yad ayam eva dharma iti mama matam ity arthaḥ*—so Cm). Ct takes violent exception to this interpretation as Cm expressed it in his commentary on the previous verse. Ct paraphrases Cm's position and says, "it is to be ridiculed by scholars (*tat tūpahasanīyam eva vyutpannair ity alam*)."

"my poor brother" *tāta*: Our interpretation follows that of Cg, who cites the *Ratnamālā* for the use of the term *tāta* in the sense of a person deserving of pity *or* in the sense of one's father. (*he tātānukampya. tāto 'nukampye pitarīti ratnamālā.*)

"you cut off righteousness at its root" *dharmamūlaṃ tvayā chinnam*: Literally, "the root of *dharma* was cut by you." As the commentators point out, the root of *dharma* is political power and wealth (*artha*), which Rāma renounced when he relinquished the throne. (*dharmasya mūlaṃ karaṇam artharūpam. tadā prāptakāle rājyam utsṛjatā tvayā chinnam*—so Cg.)

31. This verse is well known and occurs in numerous versions throughout the literature. See, for example, *MBh* 12.8.18. See Sternbach 1965–1967, p. 220 (no. 27), pp. 407–8 (no. 79).

"all righteous actions" *kriyāḥ sarvāḥ*: Literally, "all actions." The force of the context in which *artha*, "wealth, power," is defined as the root of *dharma* (*dharmamūla*) suggests that the phrase here refers only to righteous actions. Ck and Ct understand the actions mentioned here to be of two types: spiritual actions, such as *yoga*, and secular activities that are conducive to pleasure (*yogapradhānā bhogapradhānāś ca*). Ct goes on to note that the former are performed without desire (*niṣkāmatayā kṛtāḥ*), whereas the latter are engaged in out of desire (*sakāmatayā kṛtāḥ*). Cg defines the actions as such virtuous deeds as sacrifice, charity, etc. (*yajñadānādikriyāḥ*). Cm simply understands that the actions are those that are the root or basis of *dharma* (*dharmamūlabhūtakriyāḥ*).

"from wealth" *arthebhyaḥ*: The commentators, with whom we agree, understand the term to refer to the wealth extracted from various sources and various places by a king. Cg is the most specific in describing this wealth as that which is extracted in the form of a tax of one-sixth that is levied in order to protect the people (*prajāpālanāya pradeyaṣaḍbhāgakarapradhānādikāraṇāt*).

"drawn and amassed from different sources" *vivṛddhebhyaḥ saṃvṛddhebhyas tatas tataḥ*: Literally, "increased and augmented from there and there." The two participles are overlapping in their meanings. D7,10,11, and the texts and printed editions of Ct read *pravṛddhebhyaḥ*, "expanded, augmented," for *vivṛddhebhyaḥ*. V2,3,D6,7,10,11, T2,3,G1,3,M3, and the texts and printed editions of the southern commentators read *saṃvṛttebhyaḥ*, "collected, heaped up," for *saṃvṛddhebhyaḥ*. In addition, many northern manuscripts (Ś,Ñ,V1,B2,4,D8,12) read *samṛddhebhyaḥ*, "increased." Given the division of readings, especially among the southern manuscripts, the critical reading of *saṃvṛddhebhyaḥ* should probably be considered doubtful.

"just as rivers flow from the mountains" *parvatebhya ivāpagāḥ*: Literally, "like rivers from mountains." Cg understands the simile to suggest that this means that a king's charitable and other expenditures are to be made out of accumulated interest, without the expenditure of capital (*parvatebhya ity upamānena mūladhanavyayam akṛtvaivārthamūlatayā dānādikriyāḥ kāryā ity uktam*). The idea is that while the rivers flow from the mountains, the mountain itself remains undiminished.

32. "and so becomes powerless" *alpatejasaḥ*: Literally, "of little power or energy." Ś,D9–11,G3, and the texts and printed editions of Ct and Cr read instead *alpacetasaḥ*, "foolish, of little intelligence."

"all his righteous actions" *kriyāḥ sarvāḥ*: See note to verse 31 above.

"cease to flow" *vyucchidyante*: Literally, "they are cut off *or* terminated."

33. "will come to crave them" *sukhakāmaḥ*: Literally, "possessing desire for pleasure."

"dire consequences" *doṣaḥ*: Literally, "fault, disadvantage, evil." Ct, Ck, and Cr understand the reference to be to the harsh punishments, such as beating and imprisonment, [which would be inflicted upon someone who attempts to acquire wealth unlawfully] (*doṣas tāḍanabandhanādirūpaḥ*—so Ct). Most translators consulted understand the term to refer to evil, guilt, crime, etc.

34. This verse, too, is well known and occurs in numerous versions throughout the literature. See, for example, *MBh* 12.8.19. See Sternbach 1965–1967, p. 214 (no. 16), pp. 408–9 (no. 80).

"A rich man has" *yasyārthās tasya*: Literally, "of whom there is wealth, of him [there is]..."

"is considered learned" *sa ca paṇḍitaḥ*: Literally, "and he is a learned man."

35. The verse is well known and occurs in numerous versions throughout the literature. See, for example, *MBh* 12.8.19. See Sternbach 1965–1967, pp. 408–9 (no. 79).

"highly fortunate" *mahābhāgaḥ*: D9–11,G1,2, and the texts and printed editions of Ct read instead the inferior *mahābāhuḥ*, "great-armed."

36. "I cannot imagine... what led you to such a decision" *yena buddhis tvayā kṛtā*: Literally, "on account of which you made your decision." The clause is highly elliptical, and we follow the commentators in supplying the phrase "I cannot imagine." Thus, Ct glosses, "I do not know the expedient (*guṇa*) by which you made up your mind with respect to abandoning wealth. (*tvayā yena guṇena buddhir arthaparityāgaviṣayā kṛtā. taṃ na jāna iti śeṣaḥ.*)"

37. "righteousness, pleasure, and profit" *dharmakāmārthāḥ*: Literally, "*dharma*, *kāma*, and *artha*." Like Cr, we understand the compound to be a *dvandva* referring to the three elements of the *trivarga* that collectively comprise all good things of this world. Ck, Cg, and Ct understand the compound as a *tatpuruṣa* and gloss, "[who possesses] those goals (*arthāḥ*), that is, purposes (*prayojanāni*) that take the form of *dharma* and *kāma* (*dharmakāmarūpā arthāḥ prayojanāni*—so Ct)."

39. The verse is ambiguous and elliptical. Our translation more or less follows the interpretation of Ct, Ck, and Cr, who understand that Lakṣmaṇa is comparing Rāma to the righteous but impoverished ascetics who suffer hardships in this world.

"Those who wander about practicing righteousness" *yeṣām... caratāṃ dharmacāriṇām*: Literally, "of those practitioners of *dharma* who move about *or* practice." The phrase seems both redundant and elliptical, and the commentators have different opinions as to how to deal with the participle *caratām*. Ct and Ck supply the word *dharmam*, "righteousness," as the object of the participle, yielding the redundant sense of "practitioners of *dharma* who practice *dharma*." They attempt to soften the redundancy by glossing "ascetics (*tāpasānām*)" for *dharmacāriṇām*. Cr has a similar interpretation, although he reverses the terms slightly, explaining, "practitioners of *dharma* and so therefore practitioners, that is, people who practice asceticism (*dharmacāriṇām ata eva caratāṃ tapaḥ kurvatāṃ janānām*)." Cg and Cm, who follow Cv, attempt to avoid the redundancy by taking the phrase *yeṣām... caratām* as an *anādare ṣaṣṭhī* and not in apposition with *dharmacāriṇām*. They then understand the participle to construe as an accusative plural (*caratah*). This they gloss as *vidyamānān* and supplement the ellipsis with the word *arthān*. The phrase, then, according to them, refers to those things of value that the practitioners of *dharma* disregard. (*yeṣāṃ caratām ity anādare ṣaṣṭhī. yeṣāṃ caratāṃ yāṃś carato vidyamānān arthān anādṛtya dharmacāriṇām*—so Cg.) Cs cites an unidentified lexical source to the effect that the root √*car* can have the senses of "movement *or* eating (*gatibhakṣaṇayoḥ*)." He then takes *gati*, "movement," in its secondary sense of "knowledge," glossing *caratām* as "of those who possess knowledge (*jñāninām*)," which he construes as an adjective modifying *dharmacāriṇām*. This he then understands to refer to people such as seers. As an alternative, Cs proposes taking the root √*car* in its sense of *bhakṣaṇa*, "eating," in which case he sees the participle as referring to those who eat, that is, the *rākṣasas*. The sense of the passage then, according to him, is that Rāma lacks the resources through which practitioners of righteousness destroy the *rākṣasa* people (*caratāṃ bhakṣayatāṃ rākṣasānām ayaṃ loko jano dharmacāriṇāṃ teṣāṃ yebhyo naśyati te 'rthās tvayi na dṛṣyanta iti vā*).

"lose everything of value in this world" *naśyaty ayaṃ lokaḥ*: Literally, "[their] world is destroyed *or* perishes." We follow the majority of the commentators, who understand *lokaḥ*, "world," to stand for the pleasures of this world (*aihikasukham*—so Cr, Cg, Cm).

"Those things of value" *arthāḥ*: Literally, "wealth."

"the heavenly bodies" *grahāḥ*: Like the commentators, we understand the term in its common sense of the nine planets, including the five planets visible to the naked eye (Mercury, Venus, Mars, Jupiter, and Saturn), the sun, the moon, Rāhu, and Ketu.

40. "when you were living in exile" *tvayi pravrajite*: G2,M2,3, and the texts and printed editions of Cg, Cm, Cv, and Ck read instead *tvayi pravrājite*, "when you were banished."

41. "with feats of valor" *karmaṇā*: Literally, "by an act *or* feat." We agree with Ct, Ck, and Cr, who gloss, "by [my own] heroism *or* valor ([*sva*]*pauruṣeṇa*)."

Following verse 41, Ś,Ñ2,V1,B,D5–12,S insert a passage of two lines [1585*]: "Arise, long-armed tiger among men, firm in your vows! My mighty brother, do you not realize that you are the Supreme Spirit?[1]"

[1]"My mighty brother, do you not realize that you are the Supreme Spirit?" *kim ātmānaṃ mahātmānaṃ mahātman nāvabudhyase*: Literally, "do you not, great one, recognize your soul as the great soul?" D5,10,11,T1,M3, and the texts and printed editions of the southern commentators read a second accusative, *ātmānam*, for the vocative *mahātman*, "great one." The commentators interpret the terms differently from one another. Ct understands *mahātmānam* to mean "the Supreme Spirit (*paramātmānam*)," thus understanding the half verse to mean: "Do you yourself not understand your self to be the Supreme Spirit?" Cg understands similarly but takes *mahātmānam* in the sense of "having a great intellect (*mahābuddhim*)" and the second occurrence of the term *ātmānam* to refer to the Supreme Spirit (*paramātmānam*). His interpretation would then be: "Do you not know yourself to be the wise Ātman, the Supreme Spirit?" Cg further argues that the inner meaning of the half verse is that Rāma has no reason for grief (*tasmād bhavataḥ śokakāraṇaṃ nāstīti hṛdayam*). Cr, the only commentator to read with the critical edition, understands, "O great-souled one! How is it that you do not know yourself, that is, the supreme nature of the self, to be the great spirit that sets all things in motion? By this is suggested that by your will alone all

things come into existence. (*he mahātman mahātmānaṃ sarvapravartakam ātmānaṃ svasvarūpaṃ kuto nāvabudhyase. tavaivecchayā sarvaṃ jātam iti sūcitam.*)"

It is not clear to us why the critical editors have relegated this verse to the apparatus, despite the fact that it is well represented in all recensions. The verse is particularly interesting in that it is one of the few passages in the central books of the epic in which explicit allusion is made to Rāma's status as the supreme divinity. See 6.107.10 and notes.

42. "I have arisen" *ayam . . . uditaḥ*: Literally, "this one is arisen." Ct and Ck gloss, "zealously engaged, ready (*udyuktaḥ*)," while Cg offers either "zealously engaged (*udyuktaḥ*)" or "sprung up, born (*utpannaḥ*)." Cr understands the expression to refer not to Lakṣmaṇa himself but to his entire discourse on the subject of wealth, which he narrated in order to please Rāma and dispel the grief produced by hearing all the various [bad] news (*priyārthaṃ vividhavṛttāntaśravaṇajanitaśokāpanodapūrvakaṃ tava prītyutpattyartham ayam arthābhāvādir udito mayā kathitaḥ*). Cm offers two different explanations of the verse. In the first, he glosses *uditaḥ* as "sprung up, born (*utpannaḥ*)," in the sense that he, Lakṣmaṇa, was born to assist Rāma (*tvanniyojitakāryaṃ kartum evāham utpanna ity arthaḥ*). In the second, he glosses, "I narrated (*uktavān asmi*)," referring to Lakṣmaṇa's recent deconstruction of *dharma* and *adharma* (*ayam ahaṃ dharmādharmakhaṇḍanarūpam artham udita uktavān asmi*).

"to aid you" *tava . . . priyārtham*: Literally, "for the sake of pleasing *or* favoring you." Cm acknowledges this sense but offers an alternative in which he takes the prior member of the compound to be the feminine adjective *priyā*, "beloved," referring to Sītā. In this interpretation, Lakṣmaṇa is offering to act for the sake of Sītā, in the sense that he plans to destroy Laṅkā in order to avenge her murder (*tava priyārthaṃ tava priyā yā sītā tadarthaṃ sītānidhanapratikārārthaṃ laṅkāṃ vinipātayāmīty arthaḥ*).

"I shall . . . completely level" *vinipātayāmi*: Literally, "I shall cause to fall down *or* I shall destroy."

The meter is *puṣpitāgrā*.

Sarga 71

1. "consoling" *āśvāsayāne*: Commentators, some of whom read the widely distributed variant *āśvāsamāne*, note the irregular form and provide the correct form, *āśvāsayamāne*. Cg, who reads with the critical edition, is still disturbed by the tenor of Lakṣmaṇa's remarks and observes that Lakṣmaṇa's words [critiquing *dharma* and *adharma*] were uttered out of affection for his brother and are not an expression of the highest truth. (*anena pūrvoktavādā bhrātṛvātsalyāt tadāśvāsanārthāḥ. na tu paramārthā ity uktam.*)

"after having stationed the troops at their proper posts" *nikṣipya gulmān svasthāne*: As several of the commentators note, the reference is to the detachments of the monkey troops posted at the four gates of Laṅkā (*gulmān svasthāne pūrvāditattaddvāre nikṣipyāvasthāpya*—so Ct). Normally the term *gulma* refers to a military encampment. Cg understands that Vibhīṣaṇa had gone out to make sure that the troops were carrying out their duties (*svakāryakaraṇārtham*). Cf. 6.3.27; 6.27.20; 6.28.31; 6.31.31; 6.45.2; 6.62.5; 6.72.5; 6.84.6; and notes. See, too, 5.3.27 and note.

2. "Surrounded by his four valiant ministers" *vīraiś caturbhiḥ sacivair vṛtaḥ*: D6,7,9–11,T2,3,G1,3,M5, and the texts and printed editions of Ct and Cr read *abhisaṃvṛtaḥ*, "completely surrounded," for *sacivair vṛtaḥ*. According to this reading, the word *vīraiḥ*, "valiant," must be read in its nominal sense of "heroes." See 6.11.3 and note for the four ministers who accompany Vibhīṣaṇa.

"he resembled the leader of a herd surrounded by bull elephants" *mātaṅgair iva yūthapaḥ*: Literally, "like a herd leader by bull elephants." D7,10,11, and the texts and printed editions of Ct and Cr read instead the instrumental plural *yūthapaiḥ* for the nominative singular *yūthapaḥ*. In this reading the term must be read in apposition to *mātaṅgaiḥ*, in the sense of "by elephant herd leaders."

3. "the great Rāghava" *mahātmānaṃ rāghavam*: Cg observes that the patronymic Rāghava here must refer to Lakṣmaṇa, since Vibhīṣaṇa first appears to spy Rāma in the following verse. (*atra rāghavapadaṃ lakṣamaṇaparam. uttaraśloke rāmadarśanasya vakṣyamāṇatvāt.*) We believe that Cg is probably correct since, in any case, Vibhīṣaṇa would likely see the seated Lakṣmaṇa before seeing the supine Rāma, who had collapsed in the previous *sarga* (6.70.10–13). Among the translators consulted, only Gita Press (1969, vol. 3, p. 1720) explicitly follows Cg's suggestion.

"saw...that the monkeys' eyes were awash with tears" *vānarān...dadṛśe bāṣpaparyākulekṣaṇān*: Literally, "he saw the monkeys whose eyes were overwhelmed with tears."

4. "the great Rāma Rāghava" *rāghavam...mahātmānam*: Literally, "the great Rāghava." See note to verse 3 above.

"who lay dazed in Lakṣmaṇa's lap" *moham āpannaṃ lakṣmaṇasyāṅkam āśritam*: Literally, "[him who] had entered a stupor [and] rested in Lakṣmaṇa's lap."

5. "deeply chagrined" *vrīḍitam*: Literally, "embarrassed."

"What's wrong" *kim etat*: Literally, "What [is] this?"

6. "Lakṣmaṇa...said these words" *uvāca lakṣmaṇo vākyam idam*: D5,7,9–11, T1,G1,3,M3, and the texts and printed editions of the southern commentators read instead the somewhat awkward *lakṣmaṇovāca mandārtham*, literally, "Lakṣmaṇa spoke [words] of unhappy import." Commentators note that the *sandhi* is irregular. Commentators and translators struggle with the adjective *mandārtham*. Cr explains, "from which comprehension of meaning is slow (*mandena śainair artho 'rthabodho yasmāt tat*)." Cg glosses, "of little import (*alpārtham*)." Translators who follow the text of the southern commentators differ widely in their renderings of the phrase. Dutt (1893, p. 1397) translates, "pregnant with dire import", Roussel (1903, vol. 3, p. 277), "*peu réfléchi*"; Shastri (1959, vol. 3, p. 245), following Roussel, "impetuous"; Gita Press (1969, vol. 3, p. 1720), "terse"; Raghunathan (1982, vol. 3, p. 246), "briefly"; and Pagani (1999, p. 1098), "*d'une voix faible.*"

7. "Upon hearing Hanumān report" *śrutvā.../ hanūmadvacanāt*: Literally, "having heard from Hanumān's speech."

"on the spot" *iha*: Literally, "here." D9–11 and the texts and printed editions of Ct read *iti* for *iha*. The particle serves as a quotation mark since those versions read the nominative phrase *hatā...sītā*, "Sītā has been slain," for the accusative phrase *hatām... sītām*.

8. "cut Saumitri off even as he was speaking" *kathayantaṃ tu saumitriṃ saṃnivārya*: Literally, "preventing Saumitri, who was speaking." Cg notes that Vibhīṣaṇa interrupts Lakṣmaṇa because he already understands the whole matter for himself (*madhye nivāraṇoktiḥ sarvasya vṛttāntasya svenāvagatatvāt*).

"said these deeply meaningful words to the barely conscious Rāma" *puṣkalārtham idaṃ vākyaṃ visaṃjñaṃ rāmam abravīt*: M3 and the texts of Cv, Cg, and Cm omit this half verse (8cd). Printed editions of Cg include it but note that it is additional. Among the translators, only Raghunathan (1982, vol. 3, p. 246), who follows the text of Cg, omits the half verse. We render *visaṃjñam*, normally, "unconscious," in its other sense of "dazed, confused, semiconscious." It is clear from the context and from the opening verses of the following *sarga* that Rāma is not completely unconscious, although he is in a kind of stupor from the shock of hearing about Sītā's apparent death.

9. "as would be the drying up of the ocean" *sāgarasyeva śoṣaṇam*: Cr and Cs remind us of the well-known epic and purāṇic legend wherein the sage Agastya drinks up the ocean in order to deprive various demons of a hiding place. Cr claims that the reference in the verse indicates that the legend was not well known at the time of the *Rāmāyaṇa* story (*etena tatkāle agastyakartṛkasāgaraśoṣaṇaṃ na prasiddham iti dhvanitam*). Cs, however, understands the simile to imply that the drying up of the ocean is impossible absent the tremendous power of such towering figures as Agastya, etc. (*sāgarasya śoṣaṇam agastyādisamāveśābhāvadaśāyāṃ yathāyuktaṃ tathedam ayuktaṃ manye*). See *MBh* 3.103; *PadmaP*, *Sṛṣṭikhaṇḍa* 19.186; etc.

10. "the plans . . . for Sītā" *abhiprāyam . . . sītāṃ prati*: Literally, "intention with regard to Sītā." Ct, Cr, and Cs indicate that Vibhīṣaṇa is referring to Rāvaṇa's vow never to give up Sītā, even should it cost him his own life (*tadabhiprāyaṃ sarvanāśe 'pi sītā na tyājyety evaṃrūpaṃ jānāmi ca*—so Ct).

"He would never countenance her murder" *na ca ghātaṃ kariṣyati*: Literally, "and he will not effect [her] killing."

12. The precise sense of Vibhīṣaṇa's words is hard to determine. The tenor of his argument is either that Rāvaṇa would have no reason to kill Sītā or that Indrajit would have had no means of doing so. The general idea seems to be that no one can so much as see Sītā, much less kill her. Such is the interpretation of most of the commentators and translators. Ct comments as follows: "Moreover, Sītā is impossible to see by anyone by any means. In any case, why would he kill her after having abducted her? With this idea in mind, he utters the verse beginning, 'Neither by conciliation, etc.' (*kiṃca sītānyena kenāpi kenāpy upāyena draṣṭum evāśakyā, kutas tasyāharaṇapūrvaṃ vadha ity āha naiva sāmneti*)." Cs takes violent exception to Ct's comments here. He quotes his entire statement, claiming that Nāgojibhaṭṭa (Ct) should be satisfied with having brought down the level of discourse here to that of a person who, having heard the entire *Rāmāyaṇa* recited twelve times, wants to know what the relation is between Rāma and Sītā (*nāgojibhaṭṭena samagraṃ rāmāyaṇaṃ dvādaśavāraṃ śrutavataḥ sītāyā rāmasya ca ko 'nubandha iti praśnanītir upārjiteti santoṣṭavyam*)." Cf. Cs's comments to 6.96.12.

"But no one can so much as get a glimpse of her" *sā draṣṭum api śakyeta naiva*: Literally, "she is impossible to see."

"conciliation, sowing dissension, bribery . . . much less through violence" *sāmnā . . . bhedena . . . dānena kuto yudhā*: Following Cg, who glosses "coercive force (*daṇḍena*)" for *yudhā*, "through battle," we have the classic set of the four political expedients (*upāyas*) alluded to earlier in contextually more transparent settings. See 6.9.8; 6.51.11–13; 6.59.28; and notes. Cf. notes to 6.31.48–49.

"any other means" *anyena kenacit*: Literally, "by any other." Cg (implicitly) and Cm (explicitly) break up the expression so that *anyena* refers to "magical *or* delusive means (*māyopāyena*)" and *kenacid* to "another person." Cs refers similarly to means such as deception, etc. (*vañcanādyupāyena*). Cr takes the reference to be to any other person.

13. "After deluding the monkeys" *vānarān mohayitvā*: According to Ct and Ck, this refers to the illusion of cutting Sītā in half (*māyāmayasītācchedaneneti śeṣaḥ*).

"the *rākṣasa* Indrajit" *sa rākṣasaḥ*: Literally, "that *rākṣasa*."

"the shrine known as Nikumbhilā" *caityaṃ nikumbhilāṃ nāma*: This is the sanctuary or sacred grove where Indrajit habitually performs the rites that give rise to his magical powers. Compare 5.22.41; 6.60.18; 6.69.23; and notes.

Following 13ab, D9–11 and the texts and printed editions of Ct and Cr insert a passage of one line [1591*]: "You must know, great-armed warrior, that that daughter of Janaka was illusory." The line appears in all published editions of the southern recension consulted. It appears as 6.84.13cd in NSP, GPP, and Gita Press. In KK it appears in brackets, unnumbered between 6.84.12 and 13, and it is relegated to a footnote in VSP.

15. "dear boy" *tāta*: Ñ,V2,3,B1–3,D1,2,4–6,9–11,13,T1,G1,2,M3, and the texts and printed editions of the southern commentators and all printed editions read instead *tatra*, "there."

"in his desire to undermine the monkeys' valor" *vighnam anvicchatā*... *vānarāṇāṃ parākrame*: Literally, "by him who is seeking an obstacle with respect to the valor of the monkeys." Ct and Ck understand that Indrajit is anticipating the monkeys' exerting their valor to create an obstacle to his sacrifice (*vānarāṇāṃ parākrame sati yāgasya vighnam anvicchatānusaratā saṃbhāvayatā*). This interpretation has been followed by Dutt (1893, p. 1397) and Gita Press (1969, vol. 3, p. 1721). Ct's interpretation is similar to the sense of the northern variant as expressed in the text of Gorresio (6.63.15):

tena havyanimittaṃ tu nūnaṃ māyā pravartitā /
vighnam anicchatā tatra vānarāṇāṃ parākrame //

Gorresio (1858, vol. 10, p. 101) translates: "*Colui di certo per virtù d'un sacrificio produsse sue arti di magìa, non volendo che i Vānari facessero qui ostacolo alla sua forza.*"

"before he completes his sacrifices" *yāvat tan na samāpyate*: Literally, "so long as that is not completed."

16. "this baseless grieving that has overcome you" *imam*... *mithyāsaṃtāpam āgatam*: Literally, "this false grief that has come."

17. "along with us and the leaders of the troops" *asmābhiḥ saha sainyānukarṣibhiḥ*. The phrase is slightly ambiguous. In the first place, it is not perfectly clear whether we are to take the pronoun *asmābhiḥ* in apposition with *sainyānukarṣibhiḥ* in the sense of "with us leaders of the troops." Given the context of this and the following *sarga*, it seems to us that *asmābhiḥ* should be taken separately to refer to Vibhīṣaṇa and his four ministers. The term *anukarṣin* appears to be unattested elsewhere in the sense of "leader," literally, "one who drags *or* attracts." Indeed, the root √*kṛṣ* in a military context normally refers to violent or hostile action, as in the common epithet *śatrukarṣaṇa*, "dragger of foes." The commentators offer slightly different explanations of the term, but all have the basic meaning of "marshals" or "officers." Ct and Ck explain, "those who, having taken the entire army, march (*sarvasenāṃ gṛhītvā gacchadbhiḥ*)," which they then take in apposition with *asmābhiḥ*, glossing, "with us, the leaders (*asmābhiḥ pradhānaiḥ*)." Cr glosses, "those who make the army march (*senāṃ cālayadbhiḥ*)." Cg and Cm gloss, "protectors of the troops, i.e., officers (*sainyapālaiḥ*)."

18. "that *rākṣasa* can be killed" *vadhyo bhaviṣyati*: Literally, "he will be killable."

19. "sharp and pitiless" *niśitās tīkṣṇāḥ*: The two terms overlap in their semantic range in the sense of "sharp, whetted." The word *tīkṣṇa*, here "pitiless," however, has a wider range of meanings, including "harsh, fierce, cruel, etc."

"made swift by the feathers of birds" *patripatrāṅgavājinaḥ*: Literally, "swift through the limbs, that is, the feathers, of feathered ones." The compound is somewhat awkward. We follow Cg and Cm, who explain, "the feathers of the feathered ones are the wings of birds; their limbs are the flight feathers; by means of them [the arrows] are made swift (*patripatrāṇi pakṣipakṣāḥ, teṣām aṅgāṇi barhāṇi, tair vājino vegavantaḥ*)."

"like birds of prey" *patatriṇa ivāsaumyāḥ*: Literally, "like rapacious *or* inauspicious birds." Several of the commentators give the adjutant stork (*kaṅka*) as an example. It should be noted, however, that the term *kaṅka* may also refer to the heron, whose feathers, we believe, are frequently mentioned in the text as those used to fletch arrows. See, for example, 6.35.12; 6.42.4; 6.67.29; and notes.

"Indrajit's blood" *śoṇitam*: Literally, "blood." As Ct notes, we need to understand that it is Indrajit's blood that is to be drunk (*indrajita iti śeṣaḥ*).

20. "you must send forth" *saṃdiśa*: Literally, "instruct *or* command." We follow the suggestion of Ct and Cr, who gloss, *preṣaya*, "dispatch, send."

"Lakṣmaṇa of auspicious marks" *lakṣmaṇaṃ śubhalakṣaṇam*: This is yet another example of the alliterative etymological epithets of which Vālmīki is so fond. See 6.14.3; 6.67.37; 6.73.5; 6.75.16; 6.79.1; 6.89.4; and notes. See also R. Goldman 1984, p. 105.

"just as might Indra, the wielder of the *vajra*, send forth that weapon" *vajraṃ vajradharo yathā*: Literally, "as [does] the *vajra*-bearer, the *vajra*."

21. "So issue your orders" *tvam atisṛja . . . vāṇīm*: Literally, "you must release your speech." D9–11 and the texts and printed editions of Ct and Cr read *vajram*, "the *vajra*," for *vāṇīm*, "speech." To make sense of this reading, Ct and Cr, and the translators who follow them, are compelled to supply, in emulation of the preceding verse, the word "*lakṣmaṇam*," giving the half verse the sense "send forth Lakṣmaṇa . . . as does mighty Indra, the *vajra*."

"for the smashing of the citadels of the *asuras*" *asurapuronmathane*: The texts and printed editions of Ct and Cr read instead *divijaripumathane* (*diviripor*—so Cr), "for the destruction of the enemies of the heaven-born [gods]." D7,G1,M3, and the texts and printed editions of Cg and Cm read the similar *amararipor mathane*, "for the destruction of the enemy of the immortals." Gorresio's edition (6.53.22) reads *asuravaronmathanāya*, "for the destruction of the foremost of the *asuras*."

The meter is *puṣpitāgrā*.

22. "he would become invisible in battle" *bhavaty adṛśyaḥ samare*: Literally, "he becomes invisible in battle." It is not clear why Indrajit, having earlier (6.35.10; 6.38.17; 6.60.29,44; and 6.67.24) been invisible to his enemies in battle, should now need to accomplish yet another ritual to attain the same condition. It would seem that, like the powers attained through ascetic practice, this one diminishes with use and must be periodically renewed.

"grave peril" *saṃśayo mahān*: As Ct and Cs note, we are to understand the term *saṃśayaḥ*, "peril, danger, doubt," in the sense of "mortal danger (*prāṇasaṃśayaḥ*)."

The meter is *vaṃśasthavila* with a hypometric *pāda* a.

Sarga 72

1. "of Vibhīṣaṇa" *tasya*: Literally, "his."

2. "in the presence of the monkeys" *kapisaṃnidhau*: Cr understands the reference to be to a single monkey, viz., Hanumān (*kaper hanumataḥ sannidhau*).

"who sat beside him" *upāsīnam*: Literally, "seated." Ct and Ck gloss, simply, "standing *or* located nearby (*samīpasthitam*)."

3. "Lord of the *rākṣasas*, sons of chaos" *nairṛtādhipate*: Literally, "overlord of the *nairṛtas*." Recall that, despite the fact that Rāvaṇa's regime has yet to be toppled, Rāma has consecrated Vibhīṣaṇa as king of the *rākṣasas* (6.13.7–9 and notes).

"Please repeat what you intended to say." *brūhi yat te vivakṣitam*: Literally, "say what was desired to be said by you."

5. "to station the troops at their proper posts" *gulmaniveśanam*: Literally, "the encampment of the troops." Cf. 5.3.27; 6.3.27; 6.27.20; 6.28.31; 6.31.31; 6.45.2; 6.62.5; 6.71.1; 6.84.6; and notes.

7. Compare verse 6.71.16 and notes.

"illustrious hero" *mahāyaśaḥ*: Literally, "O one of great renown." D7,9,10, and the texts and printed editions of Ct read instead *mahāprabho*, "O great lord."

8. "this baseless grief that has overcome you" *mithyāsaṃtāpam āgatam*: See verse 6.71.16 and notes.

"which serves only to delight your enemies" *śatruharṣavivardhanī*: Literally, "increasing the delight of the enemy."

10. "in order to confront Rāvaṇi... and kill him: *saṃprāpya hantuṃ rāvaṇim*: Literally, "having encountered to kill Rāvaṇi." Ñ1,B3,D4,7,10,11,G2, and the texts and printed editions of Ct and Cr read the participle *saṃprāptam*, "arrived," for the gerund *saṃprāpya*, the subject of which becomes Indrajit instead of Lakṣmaṇa.

11. "full-drawn bow" *dhanurmaṇḍala-*: Literally, "bow-circle."

"shall slay" *hantum*: Literally, "to kill." We are forced to read the infinitive as a finite verb. This awkward reading shows surprisingly few variants in the critical apparatus.

12. "Through the boon of self-existent Brahmā, acquired by virtue of his asceticism" *tapasā varadānāt svayaṃbhuvaḥ*: Literally, "through asceticism from the giving of a boon of the self-existent one." See 6.36.10 and note.

"that hero" *tena vīreṇa*: Literally, "by that hero." D12,G2, and the text of Cm read instead *tena vīryeṇa*, "by that strength *or* heroism."

"will obtain" *prāptam*: Literally, "has obtained." It appears that Ct is correct in asserting that Indrajit is only to receive directly from the sacrificial fire these boons, namely a chariot yoked to horses that can go wherever he wishes as well as the *brahmaśiras* weapon-spell from the propitiated Brahmā upon the completion of his sacrifice at the shrine of the goddess Nikumbhilā in which he is presently engaged (*tena vīreṇendrajitā tapasā prītasya svayaṃbhuvo varadānān nikumbhilāyāṃ devīhome samāpte kāmaturaṅgayukto ratho brahmaśiro 'straṃ cāgneḥ sakāśāl lapsyate*). Ck notes that the *brahmaśiras*, or divine "Brahmā's head" *astra*, is different from the *brahmāstra*, or "the divine weapon-spell of Brahmā" (*brahmaśiro 'straṃ brahmāstrād anyat*). Indrajit had received the latter in the course of his performance of an earlier rite at 6.60.24. Ct further indicates that, by the terms of Brahmā's boon, the possession of this weapon will make Indrajit invulnerable to Lakṣmaṇa but that he will only be able to use it once (*tavāvadhyatvaṃ sakṛtprayogaparyantam iti varadānād brahmaśiro 'straṃ prāptam*). See 5.36.26 and note, where Indrajit is also said to possess the *brahmāstra*. Compare

7.25.7–13, where Indrajit (Meghanāda) receives boons, including the *brahmāstra*, from Paśupati upon the successful completion of seven vedic rites. See 6.36.10 and note. Cf., too, *MBh* 10.14.17, where Aśvatthāman invests a reed with the power of the *brahmaśiras astra*.

"chariot-horses" *turaṅgamāḥ*: Literally, "those who go swiftly." This is a common kenning for horses. Crā, Cm, and Cg understand that here the word "horses" indicates, by metonymy, a chariot as well (*turaṅgamaśabdo rathasyāpy upalakṣaṇam*). Ct understands similarly.

"that can take him wherever he desires" *kāmagāḥ*: Literally, "going according to wish *or* desire."

Following verse 12, D5–7,9–11,T1,2,G,M1,2,5, and the texts and printed editions of the southern commentators insert a passage of two lines [1605*]: "They say that he has already gone to the Nikumbhilā grove together with his army. If he should arise having completed his sacrifice,[1] then you can consider us all as good as dead."

[1]"having completed his sacrifice" *kṛtaṃ karma*: The syntax is defective here. One must supply either the gerund *kṛtvā*, "having performed," as Ck and Ct suggest, or a second finite verb, *syāt*, "it might be." As Cg suggests, this would lend the phrase the sense "if the sacrifice should be completed."

13. "that cunning warrior" *dhīmataḥ*: Literally, "wise one."

"Should an enemy ever strike" *yo ripuḥ . . . hanyāt*: Literally, "which[ever] enemy may strike."

"before you can reach the Nikumbhilā grove and there complete your oblation into the fire" *nikumbhilām asaṃprāptam ahutāgnim . . . tvām*: Literally, "you who have not reached Nikumbhilā and not made oblation to the fire." Ct, Cg, and Cm understand that the reference to Nikumbhilā here is specifically to the roots of a particular banyan tree of that name where Indrajit is to perform his sacrifice (*nikumbhilākhya-nyagrodhamūlasthānam*—so Cg). See 6.69.23 and note. This specification is rendered in the translation of Gita Press (1969, vol. 3, p. 1723), "while you have not (yet) reached (the foot of the banyan tree known by the name of) Nikumbhilā." These commentators make this identification, no doubt, because, as noted by Cg, Indrajit will be shown performing his sacrifice at the foot of a fearsome-looking *nyagrodha* tree (6.74.3,6). Ct and Ck note that this is the sacrificial ground consecrated to the goddess Mahākālī of whom, we are to understand, Nikumbhilā is an epithet (*tadyāgabhūmiṃ mahākālīkṣetraṃ tadākhyanyagrodhamūlarūpam*—so Ct). See 5.22.41 and note. See, too, 6.69.23; 6.74.3,6 and notes. Cr understands the verse to provide for two contingencies: 1) Indrajit fails to reach Nikumbhilā and thus fails to perform his sacrifice, and 2) he reaches it but fails to complete his sacrifice (*nikumbhilām asaṃprāptaṃ tadgamanarahitam akṛtāgniṃ*[v.l. for *ahutāgniṃ*] *tatra gate 'pi kṛtāgnirahitaṃ vā*). Ct explicitly indicates that the intended sacrifice is one associated with sorcery (*abhicārahomam*).

"he shall compass your death" *sa te vadhaḥ*: Literally, "he [will be] your death." The commentators explain the term *vadhaḥ*, "death," here to mean "killer (*mārakaḥ*—so Cg, Cm)." Cm claims that this conditional boon is explained in accordance with the terms under which it was granted to Indrajit in the *Uttarakāṇḍa*. The relevant passage there (7.25.10–12), however, makes no reference to this condition. It also shows

Indrajit receiving his boons from Paśupati, normally an epithet of Śiva, rather than unambiguously from Brahmā.

Following 13cd, D5–7,9–11,S insert a passage of one line [1606*]: "Such was the boon,[1] great-armed warrior, that was granted by the lord of all the worlds.[2]"

[1]"the boon" *varaḥ*: Cg is the only commentator to question the use of the term "boon" in connection with this dire prediction. He explains it by saying, "even though it seems to be a curse, we are to understand it as a boon because of its implication that, if Indrajit is able to reach the Nikumbhilā grove and complete his sacrifice without hindrance, he will become impossible to kill (*yady apy etac chāpavacanam iva pratibhāti tathāpi nikumbhilāprāptihomayor vighnābhāve 'vadhya iti paryavasānād vararūpatvaṃ draṣṭavyam*)." We have found no passage in Vālmīki's *Rāmāyaṇa* where Brahmā actually makes this stipulation. See 6.36.10 and note.

[2]"by the lord of all the worlds" *sarvalokeśvareṇa*: The commentators agree that the reference is to Brahmā, although it should be noted that Indrajit receives the more positive boons from Paśupati as a reward for his sacrifices at 7.25.10–12.

14. "you must depute mighty Lakṣmaṇa" *taṃ diśasva mahābalam*: Literally, "you instruct that one of great strength." D6,7,9–11,G1,2,M, and the texts and printed editions of the southern commentators read the *upasarga sam-* for the masculine accusative pronoun *tam*, "that one." The elimination of the pronoun creates an ambiguity in which the compound *mahābalam* can also be taken in the neuter to mean "a large army." This interpretation has been followed, in fact, by Dutt (1893, p. 1399) and Pagani (1999, p. 1101). D6,7,T2,3,G,M, and the texts and printed editions of Cg and Cm read instead the vocative *mahābala*, "O mighty one," leaving no explicit object at all. Cg and Cm seek to remedy this deficiency by supplying the phrase "someone from among us (*asmāsu kaṃcit*—so Cg)." Raghunathan (1982, vol. 3, p. 248), the only translator to follow this reading, attempts to have it both ways, rendering, "therefore, O Rama of the immense strength, bid Saumitri slay Indrajit."

"you can consider . . . to be as good as dead" *hataṃ viddhi*: Literally, "know as dead."

15. "Well do I know" *jānāmi*: Literally, "I know."

"truly valorous hero" *satyaparākrama*: Literally, "O one whose valor is truth." Cf. 6.26.4.

"that fierce warrior" *raudrasya*: Literally, "of the fierce *or* savage one."

17. "behind a dense mass of clouds" *abhrasaṃplave*: Literally, "in a flood of clouds." Ct and Cm gloss, "in a mass of clouds (*meghasamūhe*)," while Cg glosses, *meghāvaraṇe*, "in a cloud cover."

19–20. "skilled though he may be in the power of illusion" *māyābalaviśāradam*: Literally, "skilled in the power of illusion." D7,9–11, and the texts and printed editions of Ct read *-samanvitam*, "endowed with," for *-viśāradam*, "skilled."

21. "And Vibhīṣaṇa, the great night-roaming *rākṣasa*" *mahātmā rajanīcaraḥ*: Literally, "great roamer of the night."

"who knows this country intimately" *abhijñas tasya deśasya*: Literally, "a recognizer of the region." V3,B3,4,D10,11, and the texts and printed editions of Ct read *abhijñātasya*, while D9–11 and the texts and printed editions of Ct read *māyānām* for *deśasya*. The reading of Ct, *abhijñātasya māyānām*, "of the master of illusion," is both awkward and obscure, since it is difficult to know how to construe the genitive phrase. The three translators who follow this reading are forced to supply the ellipsis. Thus Dutt (1893, p. 1400) renders, "in this engagement with that one skilled in illusion." Roussel (1903, vol. 3, p. 280) offers, "*(pour tomber) sur ce maître en connaissances magiques*." Shastri (1959 vol. 3, p. 248), closely following Roussel, renders, "in order that thou mayest fall upon that master of illusion." D9, the text and commentary of Cr (despite the footnote of GPP, p. 2505), and the text of Gita Press (6.85.23) have a mixed reading, i.e., *abhijñas tasya māyānām*, "the knower (i.e., Vibhīṣaṇa) of his (i.e., Indrajit's) illusion." This is rendered only in the translation of Gita Press (1969, vol. 3, p. 1724).

22. "of fearsome valor . . . extraordinary" *anyad bhīmaparākramaḥ*: Literally, "another [bow] . . . [Lakṣmaṇa] of fearsome valor." We believe the context supports the less common sense of the word *anya*, i.e., "unusual, different, extraordinary." This idea appears to be shared by Roussel (1903, vol. 3, p. 280 ["*spécial*"]) and Shastri (1959, vol. 3, p. 248 ["rare"]). Ck, Ct, and Cr take the term in its more common sense of "other, another." Cr observes that the bow is different from the one Lakṣmaṇa had taken up earlier (*pūrvagṛhītāpekṣayā bhinnam*). Ct and Ck believe that this different bow is one obtained through the grace of the gods (*devānugrahaprāptaṃ param*—so Ct). This use of the term is followed in the translations of Dutt (1893, p. 1400), Gita Press (1969, vol. 3, p. 1724), and Pagani (1999, p. 1101). M3,5, and the texts and printed editions of Cg read *atyadbhutaparākramaḥ*, "[Lakṣmaṇa] of marvelous valor," for the critical edition's reading of *anyad bhīmaparākramaḥ*. This reading, which eliminates the problem of interpreting *anyat*, is rendered only in the translation of Raghunathan (1982, vol. 3, p. 249), who translates,"Lakshmana of the marvelous prowess armed himself with his great bow."

23. "and golden bow" *hemacāpadhṛk*" Literally, "bearing a golden bow." D10,11, and the texts and printed editions of Ct read instead *vāmacāpabhṛt* (v.l. *-dhṛt*). We take the adjective *vāma-* in its common sense of "splendid, beautiful" and thus understand the compound to mean "bearing a beautiful bow." Ct, however, takes the term, somewhat awkwardly in our opinion, in its other sense of "left" and understands the compound to mean "bearing a bow in his left hand (*vāmahastena cāpabhṛt*)." This interpretation has been followed by all translations based on the text of Ct, with the exception of Shastri (1959, vol. 3, p. 248), who ignores the compound entirely.

25. "will strike that fierce warrior and tear his body to pieces" *tasya raudrasya śarīram . . . vidhamiṣyanti hatvā tam*: Literally, "having struck him, [they] will destroy the body of that fierce one." The textual evidence for the critical reading is somewhat weak. Northern manuscripts (Ś,Ñ,V,B,D1–4,8,12,13) substitute a somewhat different verse 1611*, which is similar in meaning and reads the gerund *bhittvā*, "having split," while a number of southern manuscripts (D7,9–11,G3,M3,5), as well as the texts and printed editions of the southern commentators, read *bhittvā*, "having pierced," for the critical edition's *hatvā*, "having struck *or* slain." Gorresio's edition (6.64.26) drops the gerund entirely. A number of translators (Dutt 1893, p. 1400; Raghunathan 1982, vol. 3, p. 249; Roussel 1903, vol. 3, p. 280; and Shastri 1959, vol. 3, p. 248) appear to ignore the fact that the masculine pronoun *tam* cannot be construed with the neuter *śarīram*, "body."

26. "he" *saḥ . . . saḥ*: Literally, "he . . . he." Commentators who share this reading (Cv, Crā, Cg, and Cm) are greatly exercised by the unusual repetition of the pronoun.

They rationalize it by stating that, although there is no distinction of subjects here, there is a distinction between the actions of speaking and going (*asaty api kartṛbhede kriyābhedam āśritya sa iti dviruktiḥ. sa evam uktvā sa yayāv iti nirvāhaḥ*—so Cg). Some southern manuscripts substitute *evam uktvā tu*, "but having spoken in this fashion," for *sa evam uktvā*, thus avoiding the repetition. This is the reading of Ct and Ck, while Cm notes it as the proper (*samyak*) reading. Northern manuscripts and printed editions avoid the problem, reading instead a variant (1612*).

27. "his elder brother's" *guroḥ*: Literally, "of the elder."

28. "his mission blessed" *kṛtasvastyayanaḥ*: Literally, "having had the *svastyayana* performed." The *svastyayana* is a blessing or benediction performed to avert evil at the beginning of a journey or undertaking. Rāma's journeys to the forest in the *Bālakāṇḍa* and *Ayodhyākāṇḍa* are preceded by such blessings by his parents. See 6.83.7 and notes. Compare 1.21.2 and 2.23.2.

29. "Then... followed Lakṣmaṇa" *tadā lakṣmaṇam anvagāt*: D7,9–11,M2, and the texts and printed editions of Ct, Cr, and Ck read instead *lakṣmaṇaṃ tvaritaṃ yayāu*, "went swiftly [after] Lakṣmaṇa." Ct glosses *anuyayāu*,"he followed," for *yayau*, " he went."

30. "Jāmbavān, king of the apes" *ṛkṣarāja-*: Literally, "king of the *ṛkṣas*." This is Vālmīki's most common epithet for Jāmbavān, whose name we add, following Cr. See 6.4.17 and note.

"which was stationed along the way" *pathi viṣṭhitam*: Literally, "situated on the road." As Ct points out, this would be the detachment of Jāmbavān's troops that Hanumān had stationed at the gate of Laṅkā when he departed to report the news of the apparent slaying of Sītā (*hanumatā sītāvadhavṛttāntanivedanārtham āgamanasamaye dvārarakṣārthaṃ pathi sthāpitam ity arthaḥ*). See 6.70.3–6.

31. "Saumitri, delight of his friends" *saumitrir mitranandanaḥ*: This is yet another epithet that plays on the etymology of a character's name. See 6.67.37; 6.71.20; 6.74.7; and notes.

32. "that master of illusion Indrajit" *māyāyogam*: Literally, "he whose mode of practice was illusion." We follow Ct, who understands, "he whose mode of practice was the means to victory in battle through magical illusion alone (*māyāyogaṃ māyayaiva yogo yuddhajayopāyo yasya tam indrajitam*—so Ct). Cr understands similarly.

"according to the decree of Brahmā" *brahmavidhānena*: The reference, as Cg and Cm note, is to Brahmā's boon, whereby Indrajit can only be killed if he fails to reach the Nikumbhilā shrine and there complete his sacrifice (*nikumbhilām asaṃprāptam ityādinoktabrahmavaradānaprakāreṇa*). See verse 13 above. See, too, 6.36.10 and note.

Following verse 32, D5–7,9–11,T1,2 (line 1),3,G,M, and the texts and printed editions of the southern commentators insert a passage of two lines [1620*]: "The valiant son of the king, together with Vibhīṣaṇa, heroic Aṅgada, and the son of Anila..."

33. "as into a vast darkness" *timiram iva*: Literally, "like darkness."

"and abounded in great chariot-warriors" *vipulaṃ mahārathaiś ca*: Ś,Ñ,V1,3,B3, 4,D1,2,9,11,12,M1,2, and the texts and printed editions of Ct and Cr read instead the repeated adjective *gahanam*, "thick," for the critical edition's *vipulam*, "vast, abounding." All the translations consulted that share this verse render *mahārathaiḥ* as "with great chariots." Only Dutt (1893, p. 1401), in a footnote, observes that the term can also refer to "chariot warriors." We believe that this is more likely here, as the term is most commonly used in the epics in this sense. See, for example, 6.60.3; 6.80.6; 6.81.18; 6.83.8; 6.84.15; and notes. Cf. 6.77.36.

The meter is *puṣpitāgrā*.

Sarga 73

1. "Rāvaṇa's younger brother Vibhīṣaṇa" *rāvaṇānujaḥ*: Literally, "Rāvaṇa's younger brother."

"instrumental to the achievement of their own ends" *arthasādhakam*: Literally, "productive of ends." We follow the commentators, who understand that the reference is to Rāma's purposes (*rāmārthaniṣpādakam*—so Cr).

Following verse 1, D5–7,9–11,S insert a passage of two lines [1621*]: "Let the monkeys, armed with trees,[1] at once engage that army of the *rākṣasas*, dark as a storm cloud, which has come into view."

[1]"armed with trees" *pādapāyudhaiḥ*: D7,9–11,G1, and the texts and printed editions of Ct and Cr read instead *ca śilāyudhaiḥ*, "and armed with boulders."

2. "to annihilate... once it has been annihilated" *bhedane... bhinne*: Literally, "in breaking... once broken."

3. "Indra's thunderbolt" *indrāśani-*: See 6.53.13 and note.

4. "so unrighteous and adept in magical illusion" *māyāparam adhārmikam*: We follow the suggestion of Ct in breaking the sequence into *māyāparam*, literally, "devoted to magical illusion," and *adhārmikam*, "unrighteous." Cm breaks the sequence up differently (*māyā-parama-dhārmikam*), understanding the compound to mean "who is perceived as if he were supremely righteous [by virtue of magical illusion] (*paramadhārmikavat pratīyamānam*)." Cs acknowledges Ct's analysis as an alternative but first suggests the somewhat obscure meaning "bearing a superb bow by means of illusion (*māyayā paramadhanurdhāriṇaṃ vā*)."

5. "Lakṣmaṇa, of auspicious marks" *lakṣmaṇaḥ śubhalakṣaṇaḥ*: This is another of Vālmīki's etymological epithets (see 6.71.20; 6.67.37; and notes). Cg takes the epithet here in a contextually relevant sense to mean "endowed with the characteristics of accepting the essence of his friends' advice (*suhṛdvacanasāragrāhitvalakṣaṇayuktaḥ*)." See 6.14.3; 6.67.37; 6.71.20; 6.75.16; 6.79.1; 6.89.4; and notes. See also R. Goldman 1984, p. 105.

"in the direction of the *rākṣasa* lord's son" *rākṣasendrasutaṃ prati*: Literally, "at *or* toward the *rākṣasa* lord's son." Several of the commentators, notably Cv, Cm, Ct, and Ck, attempt to address the question of how Lakṣmaṇa could shoot at Indrajit when the latter is invisible. Their idea is that Lakṣmaṇa showers the *rākṣasa* army with arrows in the hope of striking Indrajit (*tatprāptim uddiśya tatsenāyāṃ vavarṣa ity arthaḥ*—so Ct, Cm). This interpretation is represented in the translations of Raghunathan (1982, vol. 3, p. 250) and Gita Press (1969, vol. 3, p. 1726). Other translators understand that Lakṣmaṇa is simply shooting at Indrajit.

6. "tree-dwelling monkeys" *śākhāmṛgāḥ*: Literally, "branch-animals." See note to 6.15.15.

"armed with huge trees and mountains" *drumādrivarayodhinaḥ*: Literally, "fighting with excellent mountains and trees." D7,10,11, and the texts and printed editions of Ct and Cr read instead *drumapravarayodhinaḥ*, "fighting with excellent (i.e., large) trees." M3 and the texts and printed editions of Cg and Cm substitute *-nakha-*, "claws," for the critical edition's *-vara-*, "excellent," lending the compound the sense "fighting with trees, mountains, and claws."

7. "for their part" *ca*: Literally, "and."

"fought back . . . with upraised" *udyataiḥ samavartanta*: D7,10,11,G1, and the texts and printed editions of Ct read instead *abhyavartanta samare*, "they attacked *or* fought back in battle."

9. "hidden from view" *āvṛtam*: Literally, "covered, enveloped."

10. "at the monkeys, the *rākṣasas*" *te rākṣasā vānareṣu*: Ś2,Ñ,V,B,D2–4,8,10–13,G1,2, and the texts and printed editions of Ct read instead *rākṣasā vānarendreṣu*, "the *rākṣasas*, at the foremost of monkeys."

11. "By the same token, the monkeys struck" *tathaiva . . . vānarāḥ / abhijaghnuḥ*: Literally, "in the very same way, the monkeys struck."

"the bulls among *rākṣasas*" *rākṣasarṣabhān*: D7,10,11, and the texts and printed editions of Ct read instead *sarvarākṣasān*, "all the *rākṣasas*."

12. "as they were being slaughtered" *vadhyamānānām*: B3,D7,10,11,T1,G1, and the texts and printed editions of Ct read instead *yudhyamānānām*, "[of the *rākṣasas*] who were fighting [with the monkeys]" or "[of the *rākṣasas*] who were being fought [by the monkeys]."

13. "unassailable Indrajit" *durdharṣaḥ*: Literally, "the unassailable one."

14. "Emerging from the shadow of the trees" *vṛkṣāndhakārān niṣkramya*: The reference, as several commentators note, is to the [densely forested] Nikumbhilā tract (*nikumbhilākṣetrīyāt*—so Ct). See 6.72.13,14; 6.74.3,6; and notes. Ct, in his effort to keep track of the action of the epic chronologically, observes that Indrajit's emergence from the grove occurs on the evening of the tenth [lunar day of the month] (*idaṃ niḥsaraṇaṃ daśamyāṃ sāyāhne*—so Ct). See note to 6.4.4.

"the *rākṣasa*" *sa rākṣasaḥ*: Cg reads the sequence as *sarākṣasaḥ* and understands it as a *bahuvrīhi* compound in the sense of "along with the *rākṣasas* (*rākṣasasahitaḥ*)." D10 and the texts and printed editions of Ct read *susaṃyatam*, "well-equipped [chariot]," for *rākṣasaḥ*, "*rākṣasa*."

15. "Resembling a mass of black collyrium" *kṛṣṇāñjanacayopamaḥ*: M3 and the texts and printed editions of Cg read instead *kālameghasamaprabhaḥ*, "resembling a black storm cloud."

"his eyes and face an angry red" *raktāsyanayanaḥ*: Literally, "whose face and eyes were red." The reddening of the eyes is a stereotypical sign of anger for the epic poets.

"that cruel *rākṣasa*" *krūraḥ*: Literally, "the cruel one." D10,11,G1, and the texts and printed editions of Ct read instead the variant *bhīmaḥ*, "fearsome." Ś,Ñ,V,B,D1–3,8,12,13,M3, and the texts and printed editions of Cg read instead *kruddhaḥ*, "angry, enraged."

"with his fearsome bow and arrows" *bhīmakārmukaśaraḥ*: Ś,Ñ,V,B,D1–4,8,12,13,M3, and the texts and printed editions of Cg read *-dharaḥ*, "bearing," for *-śaraḥ*, "arrows," lending the compound the sense "bearing a fearsome bow."

16. "Indrajit" *tam*: Literally, "him."

17–18. "But at that moment" *tasmin kāle tu*: The syntax of the passage—wherein Hanumān lifts a tree and then seems to attack the *rākṣasas* with many trees—makes the temporal sequence of events here somewhat unclear. We follow the suggestion of Cg, who understands that Hanumān first uses the single tree to rip through the enemy forces and subsequently uses multiple trees to knock them out (*ādāv ekaṃ vṛkṣam udyamya nirdahan san paścād bahubhir vṛkṣais tad rakṣobalaṃ niḥsaṃjñaṃ cakārety anvayaḥ*).

"took up" *udyamya*: Literally, "having raised." D2,5,10,11,G1,M1,2, and the texts and printed editions of Ct read instead *arujat* (D5,M1,2, *ārujat*), "he broke [off]."

"tore through" *nirdahan*: Literally, "burning, consuming."

19–20. "wreaking . . . destruction upon them" *vidhvaṃsayantam*: Literally, "wreaking havoc, destroying."

"unleashed a hail of weapons" *avākiran*: Literally, "they showered *or* covered." Like most translators, we follow the suggestion of Cr, who glosses, "they hurled weapons (*śastrāṇi prākṣipan*)."

"bearers of sharp lances . . . with their lances, swordsmen with their swords, javelin-wielders with their javelins, and spearmen with their spears" *śitaśūladharāḥ śūlair asibhiś cāsipāṇayaḥ / śaktibhiḥ śaktihastāś ca paṭṭasaiḥ paṭṭasāyudhāḥ*: Literally, "those bearing sharp lances with lances, those with swords in hand with swords, those with javelins in hand with javelins, and those armed with spears with spears." Cg observes that we are to understand that the various warriors, skilled in the various weapons mentioned, showered them down [upon Hanumān] (*śitaśūladharā ityādiviśeṣaṇena yeṣāṃ yeṣv astreṣv atyantapāṭavam asti tais te 'vākirann iti gamyate*).

21–23. "the mountainous monkey . . . Hanumān, in a towering rage" *parvatopamam . . . saṃkruddhaḥ*: Literally, "him who was comparable to a mountain . . . He, who was enraged."

"with . . . barbed darts" *kuntaiḥ*: See note to 6.52.50. Ś2,Ñ,V,B2,4,D4,8,12,M3, and the texts and printed editions of Cg read instead *cakraiḥ*, "with discuses."

"hundred-slayers," *śataghnībhiḥ*: See 6.3.12 and note. Here the weapon is of the type that is thrown.

"short javelins" *bhiṇḍipālaiḥ*: See note to 6.32.30.

24. "destroyer of his enemies" *amitraghnam*: D10,11,G1,2, and the texts and printed editions of Ct read instead *asaṃtrastam*, "undaunted, fearless."

25. "Drive" *yāhi*: Literally, "go."

"if we do not deal with him" *upekṣitaḥ*: Literally, "ignored, neglected."

27. "swords . . . scimitars" *khaḍgān . . . -asi-*: Both terms are normally rendered as "sword." In this case, however, we have used "scimitar" for *asi* to avoid redundancy. D6,M5, and the text of Cg read *paṭṭasāṃś ca* (*paṭṭiśāṃś*—D6), "and spears," for *paṭṭasāsi-*, thus avoiding the possible redundancy. This variant is rendered in the translation of Raghunathan (1982, vol. 3, p. 251). Several other translators drop the second reference to swords.

28. "parrying" *pratigṛhya*: The precise sense of the gerund here is not clear. Unlike Cr and most translators, who understand the verb in its common senses of "to receive *or* seize," we understand the term in its sense of "to resist *or* oppose," since there is no evidence in this passage that the weapons have actually found their mark and wounded Hanumān or that he has taken hold of them. Cr, the only commentator to deal with the issue, glosses, "receiving the weapons on his chest (*śastrāṇi . . . urasi gṛhītvā*)."

29. "Come and fight" *yudhyasva*: Literally, "Fight!"

"you will not escape with your life" *na jīvan pratiyāsyasi*: Literally, "you will not go back living."

30. "If you want to engage me in single combat" *yadi me dvaṃdvam*: Literally, "if single combat of [i.e., with] me." We follow the commentators, who flesh out the elliptical clause by supplying the verb *dadāsi*, "[if] you give."

"with your bare hands" *bāhubhyām*: Literally, "with two arms."

"If you can sustain" *sahasva*: Literally, "Endure!"

"you will prove to be the best of the *rākṣasas*" *tvaṃ rakṣasāṃ varaḥ*: Literally, "you are the best of the *rākṣasas*."

33. "foe-piercing" *śatruvidāraṇaiḥ*: D7,9–11,T1, and the texts and printed editions of Ct and Cr read *-nivāraṇaiḥ*, "turning back, repelling," for *-vidāraṇaiḥ*, "piercing."

"incomparable in their workmanship" *apratimasaṃsthānaiḥ*: Literally, "having incomparable form *or* construction." Ck and Ct gloss, "having incomparable form *or* appearance (*anupamasvarūpaiḥ*)." Cr offers, "characterized by parts that are devoid of comparison (*upamārahitāvayavaviśiṣṭaiḥ*)." Cg glosses, "of incomparable construction, that is, having the shape of *karavīra* leaves, etc. (*anupamasanniveśaiḥ karavīrapatrādyākāraiḥ*)." Compare note to 6.63.3, App. I, No. 43, lines 7–9.

"utterly lethal" *jīvitāntakaraiḥ*: Literally, "life-ending."

34. "by that terror to his foes, Vibhīṣaṇa" *vibhīṣaṇenārivibhīṣaṇena*: Literally, "by foe-terrifying Vibhīṣaṇa." The poet plays on the etymology of Vibhīṣaṇa's name. See note to verse 5 above.

"great Lakṣmaṇa" *mahātmā*: Literally, "the great one."

"unassailable Indrajit" *durāsadam*: Literally, "the unassailable one." Ñ,V,B1,2,4, D4,5,T1,G1,3,M, and the texts and printed editions of Cg read instead *nadantam*, "bellowing, roaring."

The meter is *upajāti*, with a hypermetric *pāda* d. The variant reading of Cg—*nadantam*, for *durāsadam*—mentioned above, was no doubt intended to regularize the meter.

Sarga 74

1. "in great excitement" *jātaharṣaḥ*: Literally, "in whom excitement was generated." The commentators differ slightly as to the cause of Vibhīṣaṇa's excitement. Ct and Ck understand that Vibhīṣaṇa is delighted in the realization that, as a result of the noncompletion of his sacrifice, Indrajit will now surely die in accordance with Brahmā's prophecy (*yāgāsamāptyā brahmavacanād avaśyaṃ mariṣyatīti saṃtuṣṭaḥ*). See notes to 6.72.12,13,32. Cr understands that he is excited at the prospect of Lakṣmaṇa's victory (*lakṣmaṇavijayasamayaprāptyā prāptānando vibhīṣaṇaḥ*).

2. "a vast grove" *mahad vanam*: As the commentators remind us, this is the Nikumbhilā grove, or the grove connected to the Nikumbhilā shrine (*nikumbhilāsambandhivanam*—Cr). See 6.60.18 and note.

"the sacrificial ground" *tat karma*: Literally, "that rite." Since the sacrifice is not actually proceeding at this time, we follow the commentators, who understand the reference to be to the site of the *homa* offering rather than to the rite itself (*homakarmasthānam*—so Ct).

3. "a . . . banyan tree" *nyagrodham*: Cr understands this to be Nikumbhilā's banyan tree (*ficus indicus*) (*nikumbhilāvaṭam*). See notes to 6.69.23; 6.72.13; and verse 6 below.

4. "to malignant spirits" *bhūtānām*: Literally, "of beings." In the context of Indrajit's *abhicāra*, or black magical ritual, we believe the term refers to ghosts or associated malignant spirits or both. Ct and Ck understand that the reference is to the hosts or class of beings or spirits in whom the passionate and turgid qualities, that is, the *rajas* and *tamas guṇas*, predominate (*rajastamaḥpradhānabhūtagaṇānām*). Compare 6.4.14; 6.47.9; 6.59.12; and notes.

5. "is able to bind and slay his enemies in battle with his splendid arrows" *nihanti samare śatrūn badhnāti ca śarottamaiḥ*: Literally, "he slays enemies in battle and binds with excellent arrows." The reference to binding is, no doubt, to Indrajit's ability to ensnare his foes with such weapons as his serpent-arrows. See *sarga* 35.

6. "with your keen arrows" *śarais tīkṣṇaiḥ*: Literally. "with keen arrows." Ñ,V1,B2,4,D9,10,G1, and the texts and printed editions of Ct read *dīptaiḥ*, "blazing, shining," for *tīkṣṇaiḥ*, "keen."

"before he returns to that banyan tree" *tam apraviṣṭaṃ nyagrodham*: Literally, "him, who has not entered the banyan tree." The idea, as several commentators suggest, is that Indrajit, who has come out of the Nikumbhilā grove in response to the attack of Hanumān, must now be stopped before he can return there and complete his sacrifice. According to Cm, once Indrajit reaches the shelter of the banyan's roots, he becomes invincible (*nyagrodhamūlapraveśe duḥsādhyo bhavatīti bhāvaḥ*). The commentators and probably the poet have in mind that a single *nyagrodha* tree often forms a grove of its own through the production of aerial roots that descend from the tree's branches. See notes to 6.69.23; 6.72.13; and verse 3 above.

7. "Saumitri, delight of his friends" *saumitrir mitranandanaḥ*: The epithet is chosen because it echoes the final syllables of Lakṣmaṇa's matronymic. See 6.72.31 and notes.

8. "At that, Indrajit" *sa . . . indrajit*: Literally, "he, Indrajit." We follow the suggestion of Ck and Ct that it is the sound of Lakṣmaṇa's bowstring that attracts Indrajit (*lakṣmaṇadhanuḥśabdaṃ śrutvā tatra pratinivṛtta iti bhāvaḥ*—so Ct).

9. "immensely powerful Lakṣmaṇa" *mahātejāḥ*: Literally, "the immensely powerful one." Although Indrajit's speech will be initially directed to Vibhīṣaṇa, we agree with the unanimous opinion of the commentators that the reference here is to Lakṣmaṇa.

"Give me a fair fight" *samyagyuddhaṃ prayaccha me*: Literally, "Offer me proper battle." We are inclined to agree with Cg's suggestion that Lakṣmaṇa is asking Indrajit to fight him without recourse to illusion or supernatural means (*amāyāyuddham*).

10. "resolute" *manasvī*: The term can also mean "wise, intelligent," and some of the translators consulted render it in this fashion. We, however, follow the interpretation of Cg, who glosses, "firm *or* steady minded (*dṛḍhamanaskaḥ*)."

"challenged in this fashion" *evam uktaḥ*: Literally, "thus addressed."

"turned his gaze" *dṛṣṭvā*: Literally, "having seen."

11. "in our House" *iha*: Literally, "here." Given the context, we are inclined to agree with the reading of Ck, Ct, Cm, and Cr, who understand that the reference is to the *rākṣasa* race or the ruling Paulastyan dynasty (*iha rākṣasīyāsmatkule*—so Ct). Several of the translators consulted also follow this line of interpretation. Cg alone takes the reference to be geographical, glossing, "in Laṅkā (*laṅkāyām*)."

"*rākṣasa*" *rākṣasa*: Cg believes that the term is used ironically here to suggest that Vibhīṣaṇa fails to perceive his kinship with Indrajit (*rākṣasety anena sājātyam api na dṛṣṭavān asīti vyajyate*).

"your son" *putrasya*: Because relationships in traditional India are as much generational as lineal, Indrajit can reasonably regard himself as the "son" of [his uncle] Vibhīṣaṇa. Cf. 6.77.13.

12. "loyalty to your kind" *jātiḥ*: Literally, "race, caste, kind, species." Ck and Ct gloss, "pride in one's kind *or* race (*jātyabhimānaḥ*)." Cs, more specifically, glosses, "the *rākṣasa* race (*rākṣasajātiḥ*)."

"sound judgment" *pramāṇam*: Literally, "valid means of judgment." We follow the commentators, who generally understand that the term refers here to one's judgment as to the boundary between what ought and ought not to be done (*kartavyākartavyamaryādākāraṇam*—so Ct). Cs understands Indrajit to be saying that Vibhīṣaṇa lacks the judgment that should inform him that there is no refuge for someone who opposes or obstructs his elder (*pramāṇaṃ jyeṣṭhavirodhena virodhyāśrayo na sampādya iti pravedayat pramāṇam*).

14. "this glaring difference" *mahad antaram*: Literally, "the great difference *or* distinction."

"How can one even compare" *kva...kva*: Literally, "where [on the one hand] is... [and] where [on the other hand] is...?"

"despicable servitude to one's enemy" *nīcaparāśrayaḥ*: The sequence is somewhat ambiguous and lends itself to at least four interpretations. The first, offered by Ct and Ck, sees the sequence as a kind of *paranipāta* compound having the sense "despicable through having recourse to one who is an enemy by birth, conduct, etc. (*janmakarmādinā yaḥ paras tadāśrayaṃ prāpya nīco nīcaparāśrayaḥ. mayūravyaṃsakāditvāt samāsaḥ*—so Ct.)" The second interpretation reads the sequence as a *karmadhāraya* compound and takes *nīca-*, "lowly," as modifying only the lexeme *para-*, "enemy, stranger." This yields the sense "dependence on despicable enemies." This interpretation has been followed in the translations of Dutt (1893, p. 1405) and Raghunathan (1982, vol. 3, p. 252). A third interpretation is that espoused by Cr, in which the adjective *nīca* is seen not as part of the compound but as a vocative directed to Vibhīṣaṇa, in the sense of "wretched, vile, *or* lowly one." This reading (indicated by a break between the words in Lahore 6.66.14 and Gorresio 6.66.14) is followed by Gorresio (1858, vol. 10, p. 108) and Gita Press (1969, vol. 3, p. 1730). We, however, agree with Roussel (1903, vol. 3, p. 286), Shastri (1959, vol. 3, p. 252), and Pagani (1999, p. 1105) in taking the adjective *nīca*, "despicable," to modify the compound *-parāśrayaḥ*, "recourse *or* servitude to an enemy."

15. Following verse 15, D5–7,9–11,S insert a passage of two lines [1648*]: "Whoever deserts his own side and defects to that of his enemies will, in the end, be killed by the latter, once his own side has been annihilated."

Following 1648*, D7,G2,3,M1,2, and KK (6.87.17–18 in brackets) insert a passage of five lines [1649*] in which Indrajit continues his denunciation of his uncle. These lines are not rendered in any translation consulted.

16. "no kinsman other than you" *svajanena tvayā*: Literally, "by you, a kinsman." We follow the commentators in fleshing out this elliptical phrase. Ct, Cr, Ck, Cg, and Cm all explain, "the meaning is 'by none other' (*nānyenety arthaḥ*)." Cv understands similarly. Cg suggests, as an alternative, that we break the sequence up as *svajane na tvayā* [*śakyam*], yielding the sense "by you [your harshness, etc.] should not have been

demonstrated with respect to your kinsmen, that is, it is inappropriate. (*yadvā svajane viṣaye tvayā na śakyaṃ na kartavyam. anucitaṃ kṛtam iti bhāvaḥ.*)"

"callousness" *paruṣam*: Literally, "harshness." D10,11, and the texts and printed editions of Ct read instead *pauruṣam*, "heroism, manliness, human effort."

17. "why do you disparage me" *kim . . . vikatthase*: Literally, "Why do you disparage?"

"as if you knew nothing" *ajānann iva*: Literally, "as if not knowing."

18. "impudent speech" *pāruṣyam*: Literally, "harshness."

"out of respect for me" *gauravāt*: Literally, "out of gravity *or* seniority." The commentators note that Vibhīṣaṇa is worthy of Indrajit's respect either because he is his elder or because he is a hero. (*pitṛvyatvagauravam āśritya madviṣayaṃ pāruṣyaṃ tyaja. yadvā śūro 'ham iti gauravād dhetor yatpāruṣyaṃ tat tyaja*—so Ct.)

"my nature is not that of the *rākṣasas*. Instead, I share the better nature of virtuous men." *guṇo 'yaṃ prathamo nṛṇāṃ tan me śīlam arākṣasam*: Literally, "this is the foremost quality of men; therefore my conduct is not that of a *rākṣasa*." The phrase is somewhat obscure. Our translation has been influenced somewhat by the commentators, who understand *guṇa* here in the sense in which it is used in Sāṃkhya philosophy. They argue that Vibhīṣaṇa ascribes to himself the pure *sattvaguṇa*, which thus distinguishes him from other *rākṣasas*, who are confined to *rajas* and *tamas*. (*prathamo guṇaḥ sattvam. arākṣasaṃ rajastamaḥprakṛtirakṣakuladurlabham*—so Ct.) Several of the commentators also suggest that by the term *nṛṇām*, "of men," we are to understand "of virtuous men (*sajjanānām*—so Cm)."

19. "Otherwise, how could a brother, even one of radically different character, reject his brother?" *bhrātrā viṣamaśīlena kathaṃ bhrātā nirasyate*: Literally, "How is a brother cast out by a brother with a different character?" The precise sense of this phrase is unclear. At first glance it appears that Vibhīṣaṇa is complaining about his rejection by Rāvaṇa, but the context does not support such an interpretation. Our translation follows the interpretation of Cm, the only commentator to remark on the critical reading, who understands the question to be: "Otherwise, how could a brother, i.e., Rāvaṇa, be rejected, i.e., be injured, by a brother who is different in character from Rāvaṇa (*anyathā viṣamaśīlena rāvaṇaśīlād vilakṣaṇaśīlena bhrātrā katham ayaṃ bhrātā rāvaṇo nirasyate hiṃsyate*)?" This is quoted by Ct. D2,11, and the texts and printed editions of Ct read the nominative *viṣamaśīlo 'pi* for the critical edition's instrumental *viṣamaśīlena*. This yields the sense: "How is a brother of different character rejected by his brother?" Ct justifies his reading by claiming that the reading *viṣamaśīlena*, which he sees as modifying Vibhīṣaṇa, would have the inappropriate sense that Vibhīṣaṇa regards himself as having a perverse character and thus is indeed cruel and intent on unrighteousness (*bhrātā viṣamaśīleneti pāṭhe dāruṇakarmā dharmāratir aham*). He does, however, acknowledge the variant reading and quotes Cm.

Following verse 19, D5–7,9–11,S insert a passage of four lines [1654*]: "One who rejects a person of evil intention, whose conduct has lapsed from righteousness, attains felicity, just as does a person who casts a venomous serpent from his hand.[1] [1–2] And they say that a person of evil conduct—one who engages in the theft of another's property[2] or rapes another man's wife—is to be shunned as is a burning building.[3–4]"

[1] "a person who casts a venomous serpent from his hand" *hastād āśīviṣaṃ yathā*: Literally, "like a venomous serpent from the hand."

[2]"one who engages in the theft of another's property" *parasvaharaṇe yuktam*: D6,T2,3,M3, and the texts and printed editions of Cg and Cm read instead *hiṃsā-parasvaharaṇam* (*-haraṇe*—M3, Cg), "theft of another's property and injury."

21–22. "unremitting hostility" *vairitvam*: Literally, "hostility." We follow the commentators, who understand that Rāvaṇa's hostility is of long duration or constant (*dīrgha*—so Ct, Ck; *baddha*—so Cg, Cm).

"these crimes and defects" *ete doṣāḥ*: Literally, "these flaws *or* faults." See verse 23 below and note.

"perversity" *pratikūlatā*: Ck and Ct take this term as a specific reference to Rāvaṇa's often-demonstrated habit of setting his mind against those who offer him beneficial advice (*hitavaktṛṣu pratikūlabuddhitā*—so Ct). This interpretation is reflected in the translation of Dutt (1893, p. 1406), who renders, "running amuck of counsel." Cm understands, "hostility to the well-being of others (*paraśreyodveṣitvam*)," while Cg and Cr gloss, "engaging in forbidden behavior (*viruddhācaraṇam*)."

23. "because of these crimes and defects" *doṣair etaiḥ*: Literally, "by these flaws *or* faults." See verses 21–22 above and note.

"Neither . . . nor . . . nor . . . shall long endure" *na . . . asti*: Literally, "is not."

24. "whelp" *bālaḥ*: Literally, "boy."

25. "Your death is at hand this very day." *adya te vyasanaṃ prāptam*: Literally, "today your destruction has arrived."

"What can you say to me now" *kim iha tvaṃ tu vakṣyasi*: Literally, "What will you say to that?" B2,D10,11, and the texts and printed editions of Ck, Ct, and Cr read instead *yan māṃ paruṣam uktavān*, "since you have addressed me harshly." Ck, Ct, and Cr take this inferior reading to suggest that Indrajit's impending doom is the direct result of his impertinence toward Vibhīṣaṇa (*yan māṃ paruṣam uktavāṃs tvaṃ purā tasmāt te 'dya vyasanaṃ prāptam*—so Ct).

26. "the two Kākutsthas" *kākutsthau*: Ś,Ñ,V1,2,B,D1–4,8–13, and the texts and printed editions of Ct read instead the singular *kākutstham*, which would then be a reference to Lakṣmaṇa alone.

"you will not escape with your life" *na śakyaṃ jīvituṃ tvayā*: Literally, "you will not be able to live."

"with Prince" *naradevena*: Literally, "with the god among men." The compound is normally a kenning for "king."

"you will accomplish the purpose of the gods" *devatākāryaṃ kariṣyasi*: Literally, "You will do the work of the gods." Commentators are divided as to the precise meaning of the phrase here. Ck, Ct, and Cr, whom we have followed, understand, "you will satisfy *or* please the gods," glossing "satisfaction (*saṃtoṣam*)" for *kāryam*, "work." Cm glosses, "you will do the appointed work of the gods in the form of serving as Yama's messenger (*yamadūtarūpadevatādiṣṭakāryaṃ kariṣyasi*)." What this means, he goes on to say, is that Indrajit will be a servant of Yama's messenger (*yamadūtakiṃkaro bhaviṣyasīti yāvat*). Cg takes Cm's interpretation as his first alternative but offers Cv's as his second, i.e., that Indrajit will suffer the torments of hell (*narakayātanānubhavaṃ vā*).

27. "So demonstrate all the power you can muster." *nidarśaya svātmabalaṃ samudyatam*: Literally, "Cause your own elevated strength to be seen." It is also possible to read the imperative irregularly as the *ātmanepada*, making the sequence *nidarśayasva* + *ātmabalam*. This would avoid the seeming redundancy between *sva-* and

ātma-, both of which mean "one's own." The commentators who share this reading are silent on the division of the words. The critical edition and VSP (6.87.31) do not separate the sequence *nidarśayasvātmabalam* while KK (6.87.33) does so. D9–11 and the texts and printed editions of Ct and Cr read the gerund *nidarśayitvā*, "having demonstrated," in place of the imperative. In this reading, the object can only be *ātmabalam*, thus eliminating the possibility of the redundant *svātma-*.

Cr, the only commentator to remark on the adjective *samudyatam*, which we render as "all... you can muster," glosses, "increased (*pravṛddham*)."

The meter is *vaṃśasthavila*.

Sarga 75

1. "replied" *abravīt*: Literally, "he said." It is unusual in Vālmīki for a speech not to follow immediately upon a verb introducing it. Here, however, the speech begins only in verse 5, after having been introduced a second time with the verb *uvāca*, "he said," in 4a.

"swiftly" *vegena*: B3,D6,7,9–11, and the texts and printed editions of Ct, Ck, and Cr read instead the somewhat redundant *krodhena*, "with rage *or* anger."

2. "ornate" *tu samalaṃkṛte*: Literally, "and well ornamented." D1,2,6,7,9–11,G,M3,5, and the texts and printed editions of the southern commentators read instead *susamalaṃkṛte*, "very well ornamented."

"yoked to black steeds... he resembled Kāla, the ender of all things" *kālāśvayukte... kālāntakopamaḥ*: Literally, "[in the chariot] yoked to black horses... [he who was] like Kāla, the ender." Undoubtedly the poet chooses his words for their echoing effect. Roussel (1903, vol. 3, p. 288), however, appears to understand both occurrences of the term *kāla* to refer to "time *or* the god of death." Thus, he translates the first compound as "*attelé des chevaux de Kāla.*" In this odd interpretation, he is followed by Pagani (1999, p. 1106), who repeats Roussel's phrase verbatim. She then adds a note (1999, p. 1671) in which she argues that the term *kāla* in the sense of Death is repeated in the verse in order to emphasize Indrajit's terrifying and lethal character. In any case, the god of Death (Yama) is normally not associated with horses. If he has any animal for his *vāhana*, it is usually the buffalo. The verse has no expressed finite verb. See 6.21.26 and note.

"with his sword and other weapons raised" *udyatāyudhanistriṃśaḥ*: Ct and Cr note the seeming anomaly in the compound in which a type of weapon, a sword, is mentioned along with the generic term for weapons. They explain this as in the example of the *gobalīvardanyāya*, "the maxim of the cattle and the bull," in which one of a class may be mentioned separately for emphasis, etc. (*udyatāny āyudhāni nistriṃśaḥ khaḍgaś ca yasya gobalīvardanyāyena*—so Cr). Ct ascribes this position to "others (*anye*)." Ck, whom Ct also quotes, tries to avoid redundancy by taking *nistriṃśaḥ*, "sword," in the adjectival sense of "pitiless," thus lending the compound the sense of "pitiless with his upraised weapons (*udyatāyudho nistriṃśo nirghṛṇaś cety arthaḥ*)." Cs, who mentions both interpretations, regards the interpretation of Ct and Cr as an act of desperation (*agatikāgatiḥ*; literally, "recourse of those who have no recourse").

3–4. "fearsome... fingering" *bhīmaṃ parāmṛśya*: Literally, "fearsome... having touched gently." Cf. verse 14 below and note, where the verb is used in its other sense of "drawing a bow." Ś2,Ñ,V1,2,B,D3,4,8–13,M1,2, and the texts and printed editions of Ct and Cr read instead *bhīmabalo bhīmam*, "fearsome [bow] . . . [he] of fearsome power." Translations that follow the text of Ct render this variant. Gorresio (1858, vol. 10, p. 110), who reads this variant, appears to omit the adjective *bhīmabalaḥ* from his translation. Cf. 6.91.9–12 and note.

Virtually all manuscripts collated for the critical edition (with the apparent exception of B1,D1–3,13) insert one or more lines between verses 3 and 4, thus making the transition established in the critical edition suspicious. Ś2,Ñ,V1,2,B2–4,D4,8,12 insert a passage of two lines [1659*], which has Indrajit "gazing (*saṃprekṣya*)" before he speaks, while D5–7,9–11,S insert a passage of three lines [1660*]: "Mounted in his chariot, the mighty and well-adorned bowman, destroyer of his foes,[1] gazed at the adorned younger brother of Rāghava,[2] who, seated on Hanumān's back, was as resplendent as the sun on the mountain where it rises."

[1]"destroyer of his foes" *amitraghnaḥ*: M3 and the texts and printed editions of Cg read instead the accusative *amitraghnam*, making the epithet refer not to Indrajit but to Lakṣmaṇa.

[2]"the . . . younger brother of Rāghava" *rāghavasyānujam*: D6,7,9–11,T2,3, and the texts and printed editions of Ct, Ck, and Cr read instead the nominative *rāvaṇasyātmajaḥ*, "the son of Rāvaṇa."

5. "try to ward off" *vārayiṣyatha*: Literally, "you [all] will ward off *or* oppose." Cg, the only commentator to remark on this reading, understands Indrajit to use the verb ironically or mockingly (*sāpahāsoktiḥ*). Ś,Ñ,V1,2,B2–4,D1–5,7,8,10–13,T2,3,G2,M5, the printed editions of Gorresio and Lahore (6.66.6), and the texts and printed editions of Ct, Ck, and Cr read instead *dhārayiṣyatha*, "you will endure *or* sustain."

6. "will scatter your limbs, as the wind might a heap of straw" *vidhamiṣyanti . . . tūlarāśim ivānalaḥ*: The phrase and the simile are ambiguous in meaning. The primary meaning of *vi* $\sqrt{}$*dhmā* (*dham*) is "to blow, blow away, *or* scatter." The problem is that the most common meaning of *anala* is "fire," and most of the translators, perhaps in accordance with the interpretation of Cg, who glosses, "will burn (*dhakṣyanti*)," give it this sense. However, the word *anala* can also refer to the wind, and, like Roussel (1903, vol. 3, p. 288), followed by Shastri (1959, vol. 3, p. 253), and Gorresio (1858, vol. 10, p. 110), we lean toward the notion that the image is that of straws scattered by a strong wind. The alternate interpretation, however, is entirely possible. A second ambiguity involves the interpretation of the term *tūla-*, which, aside from the meaning we have selected, can also mean "cotton," lending the compound *tūlarāśiḥ* the sense of "a pile *or* bale of cotton." Among the translators consulted, only Pagani interprets the term as we do, rendering, "*une meule de foin*." The text of Gorresio (6.66.7) disambiguates the matter by substituting the term *tṛṇa-*, "grass *or* straw," for *tūla-*.

7. "mangled by sharp arrows, lances, javelins, broadswords, and iron cudgels" *tīkṣṇasāyakanirbhinnāñ śūlaśaktyṛṣṭitomaraiḥ*: The syntax of the line is defective in that the *dvandva* compound in the instrumental either must construe awkwardly with the final member of the *tatpuruṣa* compound (i.e., *-nirbhinnān*, "mangled,") or somehow be made to construe with the subject of the sentence (i.e., the implicit *aham*, "I"). Like Cg and the majority of the translators consulted, we have chosen the first alternative,

as it seems more probable that Indrajit would be attacking with all his weapons rather than carrying some and attacking with others. Ct proposes an alternative, arguing that we should supply the term *upalakṣitaḥ*, "characterized by," so that we understand Indrajit to be describing himself as armed with the various weapons mentioned in the compound. This interpretation has been explicitly followed by Gita Press (1969, vol. 3, p. 1732) and appears also to underlie the translation of Gorresio (1858, vol. 10, p. 110). Ct's suggestion is probably a response to his text, which, as noted below, reads *sāyaka*, "arrows," twice, a reading that, in the first interpretation, would be unquestionably redundant.

"javelins, broadswords, and iron cudgels" *-śaktyṛṣṭitomaraiḥ*: D9,T1,2,G, and the texts and printed editions of Cg read instead *-śaktyaṣṭitomaraiḥ*. Cg explains this as irregular *sandhi* for *śakti-yaṣṭi*, "staves [and] clubs." This variant is rendered only in the translation of Raghunathan (1982, vol. 3, p. 254), who offers, "javelins, shafts, and *tomaras*." As noted above, D9–11 and the texts and printed editions of Ct read the redundant *-sāyakaiḥ*, "arrows," for *-tomaraiḥ*, "iron cudgels."

8. "like a thundering storm cloud" *jīmūtasyeva nadataḥ*: Despite the obvious and repeated basis for the simile in the cloud's sending forth showers of rain or hail, Cg insists that the illustration here is confined to the thundering noise [of the cloud, on the one hand, and of the rumbling chariot or the bellowing Indrajit, on the other] (*jīmūtasyeti nādamātre dṛṣṭāntaḥ*).

"with my deft hands" *kṣiprahastasya me*: Literally, "of me, whose hands are deft."

Following verse 8, D5–7,9–11,S insert a passage of four lines [1661*]: "A while ago, during the night battle,[1] I struck the two of you and your followers unconscious to the ground with my arrows, which are like the thunderbolts of Śakra.[2] [1–2] So I think that you either must have forgotten that, or else, clearly, you are bound for the abode of Yama,[3] since you present yourself to do battle with me, who, in my rage, am like a venomous serpent.[3–4]"

[1]"during the night battle" *rātriyuddhe*: See *sarga* 35.

[2]"like the thunderbolts of Śakra" *śakrāśanisamaiḥ*: D7,9–11,G1,M1–3, and the texts and printed editions of the southern commentators read instead *vajrāśanisamaiḥ*, "like the *vajra* or the thunderbolt." With the exception of Pagani (1999, p. 1106), translators who follow the text of the southern commentators render this variant. In rendering, "*semblables au foudre d'Indra*," Pagani is following the critical text. See 6.55.43 and note.

[3]"clearly, you are bound for the abode of Yama" *vyaktaṃ vā yamasādanam*: Literally, "Yama's abode is manifest." The phrase is elliptical. Commentators who share this reading (Cv, Cg, and Cm) flesh it out in various ways. Cv understands that Yama's abode is now visible [for Lakṣmaṇa] (*prakāśitaṃ dṛṣṭigocaram*). Cm understands *yamasādanam* to mean "attainment of the world Yama, which is manifest in the sense that it is at hand [for Lakṣmaṇa] (*yamasādanaṃ yamalokaprāpanaṃ vyaktaṃ prakāśaṃ sannihitam*)." Cg offers two explanations. The first is similar to that of Cm, while, according to the second, the word *sādanam* should be understood as "abode (*sadanam*)" through its derivation with a suffix that does not alter its meaning. (*yadvā sādanaṃ sadanam. svārthe 'ṇpratyayaḥ.*) D10,11, and the texts and printed editions of Ct, Ck, and Cr read *yāto yamakṣayam*, "[you have] gone to

the abode of Yama." Ct and Ck explain the participle in accordance with *Pā* 3.4.71 as inceptive, the sense being "you are about to depart for Yama's abode." (*ādikarmaṇi ktaḥ. yamakṣayaṃ yamagṛhaṃ prayātum upakrānto 'si*—so Ct and, similarly, Ck.) Cr proposes supplying "you will be [gone to] (*bhaviṣyasi*)." Line 3 is virtually a repetition of 6.76.11.

9. "Lakṣmaṇa" *lakṣmaṇaḥ*: D7,9–11, and the texts and printed editions of Ct and Cr read instead *rāghavaḥ*, "Rāghava."

"his face displayed not the slightest sign of fear" *abhītavadanaḥ*: Literally, "having an unfrightened face." Our interpretation follows that of Cg, who glosses, "whose face was devoid of any alteration due to fear (*bhayavikṛtiśūnyavadanaḥ*)."

10. "The fulfillment of the goals of which you boast is not so easy to accomplish" *uktaś ca durgamaḥ pāraḥ kāryāṇām* ... *tvayā*: Literally, "the far shore of the actions stated by you is difficult to reach."

"He alone is truly wise" *sa buddhimān*: Literally, "he is wise." Cg and Cr understand that the inference to be drawn here is that Indrajit is a fool (*ato durbuddhir asīty arthaḥ*). Cm, evidently trying to move the discourse from the intellectual to the heroic, glosses, "capable, powerful (*samarthaḥ*)."

11. "You are utterly incapable of accomplishing this feat. In fact, no one can accomplish it." *sa tvam arthasya hīnārtho duravāpasya kenacit*: Literally, "You are deficient in purpose with regard to a purpose that is not to be accomplished by anyone."

"Yet after merely boasting about it" *vaco vyāhṛtya*: Literally, "having uttered speech." Ś,Ñ1,V2,B3,D1–3,8,10–13,T3,M1,2, and the texts and printed editions of Ct and Ck read *vācā*, "by [mere] words," for *vacaḥ*, "speech."

12. "on that other occasion" *tadā*: Literally, "then." The allusion is to the battle during which Indrajit earlier incapacitated Rāma and his allies (*sarga* 35).

14. "drew" *parāmṛśya*: Literally, "having drawn." See verses 3–4 above and note, where the verb is used in its sense of "gently stroking *or* fingering."

15. "venomous as serpents" *sarpaviṣopamāḥ*: Literally, "like the venom of serpents." This is an unusual variant of the more common *āśīviṣopamāḥ*, "like venomous serpents." See, for example, 6.58.18 and 6.67.39.

"cascaded upon him" *petuḥ*: Literally, "they fell." Ck and Ct understand the verb to mean that the arrows are thwarted by Lakṣmaṇa's armor and so fall, presumably, harmlessly (*kavacenāhatā iti śeṣaḥ*). Similarly, Cg and Cm propose adding the words "to the ground (*bhūmau*)." This notion appears to inform many of the translations consulted. We, however, find it implausible in light of the following verses where Lakṣmaṇa is unambiguously shown to be wounded by these arrows.

16. "exceedingly powerful in their striking force ... pierced" *atimahāvegaiḥ* ... *vivyādha*: Cg, alone among the commentators, perhaps anticipating the compound *atividdhāṅgaḥ*, "his body riddled [with arrows]," in the following verse, proposes that we take *ati* as an *upasarga* separated from, but construing with, the finite verb, *vivyādha*. This would yield the sense "completely *or* thoroughly pierced." Such a separation (*vyavahitaprayoga*), common in the *vedas*, is permitted by *Pā* 1.4.82 (quoted by Cg) but is extremely rare, to say the least, in epic poetry. See note to 6.55.20.

"Saumitri of auspicious marks" *saumitrim* ... *śubhalakṣaṇam*: The epithet is almost invariably used in conjunction with the name Lakṣmaṇa for its echoing effect. It is rare to see it used otherwise. See 6.14.3; 6.67.37; 6.71.20; 6.73.5; 6.79.1; 6.89.4; and notes.

See also Goldman 1984, p. 105. An epithet of this type used with the epithet Saumitri is *mitranandana* as at 6.74.7; 6.72.31; and notes.

17. "drenched in blood" *rudhireṇa samukṣitaḥ*: Cr has a difficult time accepting the idea that Lakṣmaṇa has been wounded. He understands the verse to be saying, "Struck by those arrows, he was suffused with a red color arising from his anger (*tāḍitaśarīro 'ta eva rudhireṇa krodhahetukāruṇyavarṇena samutthito vyāptaḥ*)." See note to 6.35.9.

18. "what he had done" *ātmanaḥ karma*: Literally, "his own feat *or* action."

"he drew near" *adhigamya*: Literally, "having approached." We understand the gerund here in its sense of "to approach *or* draw near." In this we are at odds with Cg, the only commentator to remark on this reading, who takes it in its other common sense of "having grasped *or* understood." He glosses, "perceiving its effectiveness (*phalavattvena dṛṣṭvā*)." This interpretation appears to be followed only by Raghunathan (1982, vol. 3, p. 255), who collapses the gerunds *prasamīkṣya*, "having seen," and *adhigamya*, to render, "seeing his hits were telling." Ñ2,D5–7,9–11,T1,G1, and the texts and printed editions of Ct and Cr read instead *abhigamya*, which, less ambiguously, means "having approached *or* having faced."

19. In his characteristic fashion, Cm offers a thoroughgoing alternate inner interpretation (*vāstavārthaḥ*) of this and the following three verses, according to which Indrajit is really praising Rāma and Lakṣmaṇa and referring to his own impending doom. See note to 6.27.4.

20. "flocks of kites" *śyenasaṃghāḥ*: See notes to 6.31.11 and 6.87.39–40. Cf. Dave 1985, pp. 242–43.

"as you lie lifeless" *tvāṃ gatāsum*: Literally, "you whose breath is gone."

21. "ever ignoble Rāma, a warrior in name only" *kṣatrabandhuḥ sadānāryaḥ*: Literally, "kinsman of the kshatriyas [and] ever non-*āryan*." The term *bandhu*, "kinsman," at the end of a compound is often used pejoratively to indicate someone who shares the name but not the ideal characteristics of a particular social class. A number of manuscripts (D6,9–11,T2,3,G2,3,M3) and the texts and printed editions of the southern commentators read instead *kṣatrabandhuṃ sadānāryam*, in which case the two adjectives refer to Lakṣmaṇa rather than Rāma.

22. "Yes, he will soon see you" *tvām*: We follow the commentators, who suggest bringing down, as it were, the verb *drakṣyati*, "he will see," from the previous verse.

"sprawled on the ground" *bhūmau*: Literally, "on the ground."

"your armor cut to pieces" *viśastakavacam*: Ñ,V1,B2,3,D5,6,9–11,T1, the printed edition of Gorresio (6.67.24), and the texts and printed editions of Ct read instead *visrastakavacam*, "with armor stripped off *or* slipped away."

23. "perfectly reasonable" *hetumat . . . atyartham*: Literally, "excessively logical." D7,9–11, and the texts and printed editions of Ct read instead *arthajñaḥ*, "who understood the sense *or* meaning [of words]." The variant adjective would then modify Lakṣmaṇa.

Following verse 23, D5–7,9–11,S insert a passage of two lines [1665*]: "Stop boasting of your power,[1] you fool, you *rākṣasa* of cruel deeds.[2] Why go on prattling like this? Prove your valor through valorous action![3]"

[1]"Stop boasting of your power" *vāgbalaṃ tyaja*: Literally, "Give up the power of [mere] words." We agree with Cr, who understands the phrase to mean that Indrajit's words are "without basis (*nirarthakam etat*)."

[2]"of cruel deeds" *krūrakarman hi*: M3 and the texts and printed editions of Cg read instead *krūrakarmāsi*, "you are one of cruel deeds." Ct and Ck understand the compound to refer to Indrajit's use of devious strategies in fighting (*kūṭayuddhavyāpārakartaḥ*).

[3]"Prove your valor through valorous action!" *saṃpādaya sukarmaṇā*: Literally, "Bring [this] about through good action." Cr, whom we follow, glosses, "carry out the accomplishment of your words (*svoktasiddhiṃ kuru*)."

25. "man-eater" *puruṣādana*: V1,B2,D6,T2,3,G1,M3,5, and the texts and printed editions of Cg and Cm read instead *puruṣādhama*, "lowest of men," a reading that is contextually somewhat odd in that Indrajit is, of course, not a man. Raghunathan (1982, vol. 3, p. 255), who translates the text of Cg, evades the issue by rendering, "vile creature." For some reason, Roussel (1903, vol. 3, p. 289), who consistently reads the text of Ct, perhaps misunderstanding the compound or working from a text that shares the reading of Cg, renders, "*le dernier des guerriers*." Shastri (1959, vol. 3, p. 255) once again follows Roussel's lead. Among several other variations on this compound, the text of Gorresio (6.67.28) avoids the problem by reading *rākṣaṣādhama*, "lowest of *rākṣasas*."

26. "sank" *nicakhāna*: Literally, "he dug *or* buried." D7,10,11,G2, and the texts and printed editions of Ct and Cr read instead *vijaghāna*, while D9,T2,3,M3, and the texts and printed editions of Cg read *nijaghāna*. Both verbs have the sense "he struck."

"arrows" *śarān*: Ñ,V1,D6,T,G1,2,M3, and the texts and printed editions of Cg read instead *śitān*, "sharp," which then modifies *nārācān*, "iron arrows," avoiding the redundancy.

Following verse 26, Ñ,V1,2,B,D4–7,9–11,S insert a passage of two lines [1668*]: "Fletched with splendid feathers,[1] those arrows, blazing like serpents, glowed in the chest of the *rākṣasa*, son of chaos, like the rays of Savitṛ.[2]"

[1]"Fletched with splendid feathers" *supatravājitāḥ*: The commentators, perhaps finding the compound redundant, prefer to take *-vājitāḥ* in the sense of "swift." Most of them understand that it is the splendid fletching that lends the shafts their speed (so Ct, Ck, Cg, Cm; *supatraiḥ saṃjātavegāḥ*—so Cg).

[2]"Savitṛ" *savituḥ*: See note to 6.57.20, and compare note to 6.93.27, App. I, No. 65, lines 19–20.

28. "immensely fearsome" *mahābhīmaḥ*: M3 and the texts and printed editions of Cg and Cm read instead *tadā bhīmaḥ*, "then, a fearsome . . ."

"between those two lions—man and *rākṣasa*" *nararākṣasasiṃhayoḥ*: Literally, "of the two man and *rākṣasa* lions."

"each eager to kill the other" *parasparavadhaiṣiṇoḥ*: Ñ2,D6,7,9–11,T3,M3, and the texts and printed editions of the southern commentators read *-jayaiṣiṇoḥ* for *-vadhaiṣiṇoḥ*, lending the compound the meaning "each eager to defeat the other."

29. "For both" *ubhau hi*: D10,11, and the texts and printed editions of Ct read instead *vikrāntau*, "[those two] valorous."

"both were extremely heroic, and both were skilled in every weapon and divine weapon-spell" *ubhāv api suvikrāntau sarvaśastrāstrakovidau*: D9–11 and the texts and printed editions of Ct omit this line.

30. "The two great heroes" *mahāvīrau*: D3,7,9–11,G1,M3,5, and the texts and printed editions of the southern commentators read *tadā*, "then," for *mahā-*, "great."

"like two planets in the heavens" *grahāv iva nabhogatau*: It is a commonplace of traditional Indian astrology to regard two planets visually aligned with each other as in conflict. On the mutual hostility attributed to planets in Indian astrology, see Pingree 1978, p. 230. See, too, 6.78.18 and note.

31. "For . . . the two" *hi tau*: D5,G1,M3, and the texts and printed editions of Cg read instead *[ivā]bhītau*, "fearless *or* undaunted."

"Bala and Vṛtra" *balavṛtrāv iva*: Bala or Vala, like Vṛtra, is a demonic foe whose death at the hands of Indra is recounted in several hymns of the *Ṛgveda* (Bala—2.11.19; 2.12.3; 2.15.8; 3.51.18; 8.14.8; etc.; Vṛtra—1.32; 2.11.18; 2.19.4; 2.20.7; etc.). Several of the commentators are uncomfortable with this identification, since it effectively compares Lakṣmaṇa to a demon. Ct asserts that, by Bala, we are to understand Indra. Cm similarly understands that the word "Bala" refers to Indra in his guise as Purandara, "the smasher of citadels." This epithet is apparently deemed apposite since the demon Bala/Vala in the *Ṛgveda* is represented as inhabiting a fortified cave or citadel (2.12.3 and 8.14.8). Cg attempts to rationalize the identification by arguing that the term "Bala" is a kind of shorthand for Indra's epithet Balaśatru, "foe of Bala." (*balaśabdo balaśatru indraparaḥ. nāmaikadeśe nāmagrahaṇāt.*) Cf. note to 6.46.39. See, too, notes to 6.55.123 and 6.97.21.

32. "the two lions—man and *rākṣasa*" *nararākṣasasiṃhau*: D7,9–11, and the texts and printed editions of Ct and Cr read *-mukhyau*, "foremost of," for *-siṃhau*,"lions [among]." See note to verse 28 above.

33. "the two champions—man and *rākṣasa*" *nararākṣasottamau*: Literally, "the two best of the men and the *rākṣasas*."

"with torrents and hails of arrows" *śaraughavarṣeṇa*: Literally, "with an arrow-flood-shower." Cg thinks we should understand the compound *śaraugha-*, "floods of arrows," also as part of the simile of the storm clouds in the sense of "floods of water." He claims that the word *śara* means "water" in this context, basing his argument on the use of the term in its secondary sense, as in the term *śaradhiḥ*, "receptacle of waters, i.e., ocean." (*śaraugho meghapakṣe jalaughaḥ. śaraśabdo hi jalavācī, śaradhir iti samudraparyāyāt.*) This interpretation is reflected in the translation of Raghunathan (1982, vol. 3, p. 256).

The meter is *vaṃśasthavila*.

Ś,D8,10–12, the texts of Ct, Ck, and Cr, and the editions of NSP and Gita Press omit this verse. This verse and 1669* (see below) do, however, appear unnumbered, in brackets, between verses 6.88.36 and 37 of GPP.

Following verse 33, D5–7,9,S (except G3) insert a passage of four lines [1669*]: "Gaining strength in battle, the two immensely powerful warriors, skilled in battle, fierce with their arrows and swords, and wielding sharp weapons, unceasingly slashed at each other[1] in that great battle, just like Śambara and Vāsava.[2]"

[1]"slashed at each other" *āvivyathatuḥ*: Literally, "those two were pained." Following the printed editions of KK (6.88.40) and VSP (6.88.40), we emend the critical reading to the more contextually apposite *āvivyadhatuḥ*, "those two pierced *or* cut." It appears likely that the critical edition's reading is a typographical error, as its apparatus shows

no variant of *āvivyadhatuḥ*, the reading of all manuscripts consulted for KK. In fact, the critical apparatus shows only one variant (D9), *āvidhya dhanur*, "brandishing the bow." The reading of KK and VSP is also attested in GPP.

[2]"just like Śambara and Vāsava" *śambaravāsavopamau*: See note to 6.63.42.

The meter is *vaṃśasthavila*.

Ck not only omits these two verses (CE 6.75.33 and 1669*) but criticizes them as redundant and interpolated. He notes that they serve to introduce an improper *sarga* break. He claims that the division of *sargas* here, which some manuscripts follow, is incorrect because there is no change of topic, as the battle between Lakṣmaṇa and Indrajit simply continues. (*atra madhye punaruktaṃ ślokadvayaṃ prakṣipya sargam avacchindanti. puraḥ paścād ubhayos tumulaṃ yuddham eva kevalaṃ vartate na kiṃcid arthāntaraṃ prakaraṇāntaram. ato 'yukto 'vacchedaḥ.*) Ct accepts Ck's position and paraphrases his comments, while Cs notes that this is merely one textual tradition (*saṃpradāyaḥ*). This textual issue is a matter of dispute between commentators aligned with Ct and Ck, on the one hand, and those aligned with Cv, Cg, and Cm, on the other. The latter unanimously mark a *sarga* boundary after the critical edition's verse 1669*, and this division is followed in the printed texts of KK and VSP. GPP, NSP, and Gita Press, however, continue with the same *sarga* (6.88 in their calculation) up until the end of *sarga* 76 of the critical edition. Translations are also divided on this issue, although the alignment with the textual traditions is not as obvious. Raghunathan naturally follows the *sarga* break of Cg. Roussel, Gita Press, and Pagani follow that of Ct. Dutt and Shastri, who normally follow Ct, nonetheless show a *sarga* break after the critical edition's verse 32.

Sarga 76

1. See note to 6.75.33 for a discussion of the division of the *sargas* in various editions.

"an arrow" *śaram*: Ñ,V1,2,B1,D1–3,7,9–11,13,G1,2,M, and the texts and printed editions of Ck, Ct, and Cr read instead the plural *śarān*, "arrows."

2. "son of Rāvaṇa" *rāvaṇātmajaḥ*: D7,9–11, and the texts and printed editions of Ct read instead *rākṣasādhipaḥ*, "the *rākṣasa* lord."

"the slapping... against... armguard" *jyātalanirghoṣam*: Literally, "the sound of the bowstring and armguard." We agree with Gorresio (1858, vol. 10, p. 112), who, alone among the translators consulted, understands the term *tala* in its technical sense of the leather armguard worn on the left forearm of an archer to protect it from the blows of the bowstring. Another possible meaning for *tala* is the forearm itself. However, in light of 1.21.8, *Rāmāyaṇa* archers appear to use armguards when shooting (see 6.66.23 and note). Other translators either take the term in its sense of "the palm of the hand" (Gita Press 1969, vol. 3, p. 1735 and Raghunathan 1982, vol. 3, p. 256) or ignore it altogether, believing that the reference is only to the sound or twanging of the bowstring.

3. "observing the downcast face of the *rākṣasa*, son of Rāvaṇa" *taṃ viṣaṇṇamukhaṃ dṛṣṭvā rākṣasaṃ rāvaṇātmajam*: Literally, "having seen that the *rākṣasa*, Rāvaṇa's son, was one whose face was despondent." B1,D2,3,5,13,T1,G1,M1–3, and the texts and printed editions of Cg read instead *vivarṇa*-, "pale," for *viṣaṇṇa*-, "despondent, downcast."

"absorbed in battle" *yuddhasaṃsaktam*: V1,2,B4,D4,9–11,G1,3,M3,5, and the texts and printed editions of the southern commentators read *-saṃyuktam*, "engaged in." Ct, Cm, and Ck explain the compound as meaning "endowed with the frenzy that is conducive to battle (*yuddhajanakaharṣayuktam*—so Ct, Cm)."

4. "unpropitious signs on the person of this son of Rāvaṇa" *nimittāni... asmin rāvaṇātmaje*: Literally, "portents in *or* on this son of Rāvaṇa." Given the context, we must agree with the commentators that this refers to the inauspicious signs, such as the dejected expression, etc., mentioned in the previous verse. On omens, see 6.4.6 and note.

5. "like flames of fire" *agniśikhopamān*: Ñ,V1,2,B2–4,D4,7,9–11,G2, and the texts and printed editions of Ct, Cr, and Ck read instead *āśīviṣopamān*, "like venomous serpents," a reading that is distinctly redundant in light of the simile in the second half of the verse.

"sharp" *niśitān*: B2,3,D9–11, and the texts and printed editions of Ct read instead *viśikhān*, "arrows." This variant is redundant in light of *śarān*, "arrows," in *pāda* b.

"engorged with venom" *viṣolbaṇān*: Literally, "abundant *or* powerful with venom." This may be best seen as a *paranipāta* for *ulbaṇaviṣān*, "with abundant or powerful venom." Ñ,V1,2,B1,2,4,D1–3,5,6,13,T,G3,M, and the texts and printed editions of Cg read instead *mahāviṣān*, "with powerful *or* abundant venom."

6. "Indrajit was... stunned" *abhavan mūḍhaḥ*: Literally, "he was stunned."

7. "But he regained consciousness after a moment. And, his senses fully restored" *upalabhya muhūrtena saṃjñāṃ pratyāgatendriyaḥ*: D10,11,T1, and texts and printed editions of Ct and Ck omit these two *pādas* (ab).

"that hero" *vīraḥ*: Ñ,V1,2,B,D1–4,7,9–11,13,G1,2, the texts and printed editions of Ct, and the printed edition of Gorresio read instead *ājau*, "in battle."

8. "Indrajit" *saḥ*: Literally, "he."

9. "Have you completely forgotten" *kiṃ na smarasi*: Literally, "Do you not remember?"

"in our first encounter" *yuddhe prathame*: Literally, "in the first battle." The reference is to the battle in which Rāma and Lakṣmaṇa were bound with Indrajit's serpent-weapons (6.35).

"in battle" *yudhi*: M3 and the texts and printed editions of Cg read instead *bhuvi*, "on the ground," yielding the sense "[bound, you writhed] on the ground."

"writhed in bondage" *nibaddhaḥ... viceṣṭase*: Literally, "bound, you writhe." Ct understands *viceṣṭase* here in its other sense of "you act." He glosses, "you engage in shooting arrows, etc. (*śarapātādi karoṣi*)." Apparently, Ct's idea is that Indrajit is questioning how Lakṣmaṇa dares to offer him battle now, after having been so easily defeated earlier. Several of the translations (Dutt 1893, pp. 1409–10; Roussel 1903, vol. 3, p. 290; and Shastri 1959, vol. 3, p. 256) follow this interpretation.

10. The verse is closely paraphrased by 1661*, lines 1–2. See notes to 6.75.8.

"like the thunderbolts of Śakra" *śakrāśanisamaiḥ*: Ś,Ñ,V1,2,B2–4,D1–4,7–13,G1,2, and the texts and printed editions of Ct and Cr read instead *vajrāśanisamaiḥ*, "like the *vajra* or the thunderbolt." See 6.55.43 and note.

11. *Pādas* ab virtually repeat line 3 of 1661*. See notes to 6.75.8.

12. "Now stand your ground!" *tiṣṭhedānīṃ vyavasthitaḥ*: Literally, "Now stand resolved, firm." Cr glosses, "your mind resolved, take your stand (*dṛḍhamatiḥ san tvaṃ tiṣṭha*)." Cs similarly glosses "resolved to give battle (*yuddhārthaniścitaḥ*)" for

vyavasthitaḥ, "resolved, firm." Cs goes on to suggest that, by using this expression, Indrajit indicates that he will show himself to Lakṣmaṇa and not resort to the stratagem of invisibility as he did in their first encounter (*anena pūrvavad antardhānaṃ nāstīti sūcyate*). Of course, given that Indrajit's sacrifice has been interrupted, we are, in any case, to understand that he is perhaps no longer given the option of cloaking himself in invisibility.

13. "Hanumān" *hanūmantam*: Recall that it is Hanumān's assault on the *rākṣasas* that first distracts Indrajit from his sacrifice. He begins a battle with the monkey at 6.73.17–30, which is inconclusive and is broken off by the intervention first of Vibhīṣaṇa and then of Lakṣmaṇa.

14. "his frenzy redoubled in his fury" *krodhād dviguṇasaṃrabdhaḥ*: Literally, "doubly furious out of rage." Cg explains that Indrajit feels twice as much anger toward Vibhīṣaṇa as he does toward Lakṣmaṇa and the rest (*lakṣmaṇādiviṣayaroṣāpekṣayā vibhīṣaṇaviṣaye dviguṇaṃ kupita ity arthaḥ*).

15–16. "his face betraying not the slightest sign of fear" *abhītavadanaḥ*: Literally, "whose face is unafraid."

"saying": Unusually, the poet fails to provide a verb introducing a direct quotation. We have supplied one.

17. "inconsequential" *laghavaḥ*: Ck, Cm, and Ct take the adjective to mean "[tender *or* delicate] like garlands of flowers (*puṣpamālāvat*—so Cm, Ct)."

"Indeed, they feel quite pleasant." *sukhā hīme*: Literally, "For, they [are] pleasant." Cm and Ct understand this to mean that they cause no pain (*na tu kleśadā ity arthaḥ*). Cr glosses, "giving pleasure to your enemies (*ripūṇāṃ sukhapradāḥ*)."

18. "if they desire victory in battle" *samare jayakāṅkṣiṇaḥ*: D7,9–11,G1, and the texts and printed editions of Ct and Cr read the redundant *yuddha-*, "battle," for *jaya-*, "victory."

"And, speaking in this fashion, he showered him with hails of arrows." *ity evaṃ taṃ bruvāṇas tu śaravarṣair avākirat*: D7,9–11, and the texts and printed editions of Ct and Cr read instead *ity evaṃ taṃ bruvan dhanvī śarair abhivavarṣa ha*, "and speaking in this fashion, that bowman showered him with arrows."

19. "Indrajit's armor" *kavacam*: Literally, "armor."

"all adorned with gold" *hemabhūṣitam*: Ś,Ñ,V,B,D1–4,7–13,G1,2, and the texts and printed editions of Ct, Lahore (6.68.18), and Gorresio (6.68.19) read instead *kāñcanaṃ mahat*, "golden [and] heavy [armor]."

"like a constellation falling from the sky" *tārājālam ivāmbarāt*: Literally, "like a cluster *or* mass of stars from the sky."

20. "so that he resembled a mountain bristling with trees" *prarūḍha iva sānumān*: Literally, "like an overgrown mountain." Our translation, like that of Raghunathan (1982, vol. 3, p. 257), follows the interpretation of Cg, who glosses, "having full-grown trees (*prarūḍhavṛkṣaḥ*)." The image is suggested by the idea of the mountainous body of Indrajit from which the vast iron arrows of Lakṣmaṇa are protruding. Cm, who shares this reading, glosses, "he was immobilized (*niścalo babhūva*)," evidently taking the participle *prarūḍha* in its sense of "deeply rooted (*prarūḍhamūlaḥ*)." D9–11 and the texts and printed editions of Ct, Ck, and Cr read instead *pratyūṣe bhānumān iva*, "like the bright-rayed sun at dawn." This image, according to Ct, Ck, and Cr, derives from the redness of the blood flowing from Indrajit's wounds (*kṣatajaraktavarṇatvād iti bhāvaḥ*). The image is repeated at verse 31. See 6.76.31 and note.

Following verse 20, D5–7,9–11,S insert a passage of four lines [1672*]: "Then, in a rage, Rāvaṇa's son pierced heroic[1] Lakṣmaṇa, of fearsome valor,[2] with a thousand arrows in combat.[1–2] Thus, Lakṣmaṇa's heavy, celestial[3] armor was cut to pieces. They chased each other all around with constant attack and counterattack.[3–4]"

[1]"heroic" *vīram*: D7,9–11,G1, and the texts and printed editions of Ct read instead the nominative *vīraḥ*, "hero, heroic one," which makes the epithet apply to Indrajit rather than Lakṣmaṇa.

[2]"of fearsome valor" *bhīmavikramam*: D9–11,G1, and the texts and printed editions of the southern commentators read instead the nominative *bhīmavikramaḥ*, which makes the compound describe Indrajit rather than Lakṣmaṇa.

[3]"celestial" *divyam*: Cr claims that the armor was given to Lakṣmaṇa by the gods (*devair dattam ity arthaḥ*). The epic makes no mention of this.

21. Following verse 21, D5–7,9–11,S insert a passage of nine lines [1674*]. Virtually all northern manuscripts insert lines 1, 3–5, and 7 of 1647*, while a number of them add line 6. All editions consulted, with the exception of Lahore, show this insertion in full or in part. Why the editors of the critical edition chose to excise these passages from the critical text is unclear. Lines 8–9 are repeated as verse 33 below. "For a very long time, the two great heroes, both skilled in the arts of war, riddled each other with sharp arrows.[1–2] Fearsome in their valor and striving each for his own victory, they were riddled with masses of arrows, their armor and battle standards cut to pieces.[3–4] Gushing hot blood like two waterfalls gushing water, they released fearsome hails of arrows that made a horrific din, just as two black storm clouds in the sky heralding universal destruction[1] might send forth torrential rains.[5–7] A long time[2] elapsed while they were thus engaged in combat, but neither of them turned his face from combat or felt any weariness.[8–9]"

[1]"just as two black storm clouds . . . heralding universal destruction" *nīlayoḥ kālameghayoḥ*: The term *kāla-* in the compound can also mean "black," and some translators have apparently taken it in this fashion. Such a reading, however, is redundant with the adjective *nīla*, "dark blue, black." We are therefore inclined to agree with Cr, who offers, as his first explanation, "destroying the worlds (*lokavighāṭakayoḥ*)," thus taking *kāla* in its sense of "time *or* doom." Cr notes also that one can understand the reference to be to clouds during the monsoon (*varṣākālikayor vā*). Translators consulted are divided as to whether to take these merely as rain clouds or something more devastating. Dutt (1893, p. 1411) translates, "like . . . black clouds at Doomsday," and notes, "the commentator says the word means 'black clouds'; but I prefer the sense given." It is not clear to which commentator he is referring, as Ct, to whom he normally refers, is silent on this point, while Cr, who does comment, offers both meanings.

[2]"A long time" *mahān kālaḥ*: Ct and Cm understand that the battle rages for many days (*mahān kālo 'nekadinarūpaḥ*).

22. "Deploying" *darśayantau*: Literally, "displaying, manifesting."

"filled the sky with arrows of every size and shape" *śarān uccāvacākārān antarikṣe babandhatuḥ*: Literally, "those two bound arrows of various forms in the sky." The precise sense of the polysemic root √*bandh* here is not certain. Our understanding is that it is used metaphorically to suggest that the warriors shoot their arrows so rapidly that they appear to be bound in chains or webs that cover the sky. Translators render the term variously. Commentators are silent as to the meaning of the verb. Cs explains the compound *uccāvacākārān*, "of every size and shape," as "having forms characterized by numerous varieties (*anekaprabhedaviśiṣṭākārān*)."

23. "flawlessly" *vyapetadoṣam*: Literally, "in such a way that its flaws were gone." We follow Cr in reading the compound adverbially with the participle *asyantau* "[those two] throwing *or* hurling (*vyapetadoṣādi yathā bhavati tathā* [*asyantau*])." Cg believes that the specific flaw alluded to here is that of confusion or delusion (*vyapagatamohatvadoṣam*).

24. "crash of their bowstrings against their armguards" *talanisvanaḥ*: Literally, "the sound of the armguards." Like Gorresio (1858, vol. 10, p. 114), we take the reference here to be an elliptical variant of the compound *jyātalanirghoṣam* at verse 2 above. See note ad loc. Gita Press (1969, vol. 3, p. 1737) translates, "the... sound produced by the impact of the palms... on their bowstrings," while Raghunathan (1982, vol. 3, p. 258) translates, "The thud of bowstring on palm." D7,9–11, and the texts and printed editions of Ct and Cr read instead *tumulaḥ svanaḥ*, "a tumultuous sound."

Following 24ab, Ñ,V1,3 (after line 5 of 1674*),B2–4,D4–7,9–11,S insert a passage of two lines [1675*], "Indeed, that terrible sound of those two, frenzied with battle as they were,[1] burst forth[2] like a fearsome thunderbolt, causing all creatures to tremble in fear.[3]"

[1]"frenzied with battle as they were" *samaramattayoḥ*: Literally, "maddened with battle." V3,D9,10,M1,2, and the texts and printed editions of Ct read instead *samarayattayoḥ*, "exerting [themselves] in battle." D5,T1,G3,M3, and the texts and printed editions of Cg read instead *samarasaktayoḥ*, "engaged *or* locked in battle."

[2]"burst forth" *bhrājate*: Literally, "it shone *or* flashed forth."

[3]"causing all creatures to tremble in fear" *prakampayañ janam*: Literally, "causing people to shake." D9–11 and the texts and printed editions of Ct read instead *sa kampaṃ janayāmāsa*, "that [sound] produced trembling."

Following 24cd, Ś2,V2,D,S insert a passage of two lines [1677*]: "Wounded with golden-fletched iron arrows, the two mighty and illustrious warriors bled copiously, intent on victory."

25. "smeared with blood" *asṛgdigdhāḥ*: In keeping with his interpretation of the star passages quoted above (1674*, line 5; and 1677*), which also refer to Lakṣmaṇa's bleeding wounds, here Cr attempts to deny that the hero is actually wounded. He claims that the arrows are smeared only with the blood of Indrajit and other warriors (*anyayuddhīyaśarīrajenendrajiccharīrajena ca rudhireṇa digdhā vyāptāḥ śarāḥ*). See note to 32 below. See, too, note to 6.35.9.

26. "Meanwhile, some of their arrows" *tayor bāṇāḥ*: Literally, "arrows of those two." The reference is to those missiles that, unlike those in the previous verse, fail to strike their targets.

"were intercepted" *saṃjaghaṭṭire*: Literally, "they clashed with." We follow Ct, who glosses the past passive participle *saṃghaṭṭitāḥ*, "[they were] crashed into."

"by other" *anyaiḥ*: D9–11,T1,M3, and the texts and printed editions of the southern commentators read instead the nominative plural *anye*, "others," which then modifies *bāṇāḥ*, "arrows," making it more explicit that these are arrows other than the ones described in verse 25.

"they smashed and splintered one another" *babhañjuś cicchiduś cāpi*: Literally, "they broke and cut." The syntax here is elliptical, as the verbs lack any explicit direct object. Commentators resolve the issue in various ways. Cr, whom we have followed, supplies the term *parasparam*, "one another," while Cg supplies a direct object, *bānān*, "[other] arrows." According to Gorresio (1858, vol. 10, p. 297), Cl interprets the two verbs as intransitive or reflexive, giving them the sense "they were broken and splintered. (*babhañjur bhagnā babhūvuḥ. cicchiduś ca chinnāś ca.*)" Gorresio, however, feels it is better to interpret the verbs as transitive.

27. "During the struggle, a . . . carpet" *raṇe . . . cayaḥ*: Literally, "in the battle, . . . a pile *or* heap." D7,9, and the texts and printed editions of Cg and Gita Press read instead the nominative *raṇaḥ*, which radically alters the syntax of the entire verse, since now it is the battle that is described as ghastly while the nominative *cayaḥ*, "pile, mass," must be construed as part of a subordinate clause. Raghunathan (1982, vol. 3, p. 258) and Gita Press (1969, vol. 3, p. 1737) struggle to make sense of this reading.

"a carpet of *kuśa* grass" *kuśamayaś cayaḥ*: In some printed texts (Gita Press 6.88.70 and GPP 6.88.70) the second occurrence of the term *cayaḥ* in *pāda* d is broken up into the words *ca* + *yaḥ*, "and which." This leaves the compound *kuśamayaḥ* as an adjective that must modify either "battle" or a supplied term such as "place *or* field." Cr reads the verse in this fashion. See note to 6.60.22.

"two . . . fires" *agnibhyām*: Cg, in an attempt to maintain the precision of the image, informs us that the sacrificial fires in question are the *gārhapatya* and the *āhavanīya*. This suggestion is represented in the translation of Gita Press (1969, vol. 3, p. 1737).

28. "of those two great warriors" *mahātmanoḥ*: Literally, "of the two great ones."

"a *śālmali* and a *kiṃśuka* tree in full bloom . . . before their leaves appear" *supuṣpāv iva niṣpatrau . . . śālmalikiṃśukau*: The comparison with the trees is quite apt, for both the *śālmali*, or silk-cotton (or semul) tree (*Salmalia malabarica* or *Bombax malabaricum*), and the *kiṃśuka*, or "flame-of-the-forest" tree (*Butea frondosa* or *Butea monosperma*), have bright crimson flowers that bloom before their leaves appear. The image draws its force from the comparison of the bleeding wounds of the warriors and the red blossoms of the trees. See notes to 6.30.26, App. I, No. 18, lines 27–30. See, too, note to 6.7.12–13, on the *śālmali* tree. See 6.35.9; 6.55.22; 6.62.19; and notes.

29. "eager to vanquish"*-jayaiṣiṇau*: D5,T1,G1,M3,5, and the texts and printed editions of Cg read instead *-vadhaiṣiṇau*, "eager to kill."

30. "neither of them grew weary" *na śramaṃ pratyapadyatām*: Literally, "the two of them did not attain fatigue."

31. "deeply rooted, yet protruding from their bodies" *śarīrasthair avagāḍhaiḥ*: Literally, "situated in the body and deeply implanted." We agree with Ct and Ck, who gloss *gāḍhamagnaiḥ*, "deeply sunk," for *avagāḍhaiḥ*, as opposed to Cr, who glosses, "dense, firm (*dṛḍhaiḥ*)."

"like twin mountains bristling with trees" *virūḍhāv iva parvatau*: Literally, "like two overgrown mountains." We follow the interpretation of Ck, Ct, Cr, and Cm, who understand, "having full-grown trees (*pravṛddhavṛkṣau*—so Cm, Ct)." Gorresio (1858, vol. 10, p. 115), who translates, "*come due monti vestiti di sprocchi*," indicates in a note (p. 297) that he is following the interpretation of Cl, who glosses, "on which sprouts were growing (*jātāṅkūrau*)." The image is repeated at verse 20 above. See 6.78.20 and note.

32. Here, as earlier (see verse 25 above and note), Cr makes a distinction between Indrajit, whom he sees as actually bloodied, and Lakṣmaṇa, who is merely reddened. He understands two different kinds of redness: one from blood (*rakta*) [i.e., in the case of Indrajit] and the other from reddening (*āruṇya*) [through anger, exertion, etc., in the case of Lakṣmaṇa] (*rudhirābhyām āruṇyaraktābhyām*). See note to 6.35.9.

"resembled blazing fires" *jvalanta iva pāvakāḥ*: The simile is apparently intended to derive its force from the image of a fire glowing red but largely obscured by smoke. Here the blood-smeared bodies suggest flames, while the arrows take the place of smoke.

33. As Cr notes, this verse is a repetition of an earlier one [1674*, lines 8–9]. See notes to verse 21 above.

34. "fray . . . battle . . . combat" *samara- . . . samara- . . . samaram*: The repetition of the same word is perhaps less appealing in English than it is in Sanskrit.

"to aid and comfort" *priyahitam*: Literally, "what was [at once] agreeable and beneficial."

"to give . . . respite from the fatigue of combat" *samarapariśramaṃ nihantum*: Literally, "to counteract *or* destroy battle fatigue." No commentator seems troubled by the apparent contradiction between this verse and the preceding one, where Lakṣmaṇa is said to experience no battle fatigue. Cm, however, understands the compound *samarapariśramaṃ* to be a *bahuvrīhi* in the sense of "experiencing battle fatigue," which he believes modifies Indrajit. Thus, his understanding of the phrase would be "to kill Indrajit, who was suffering from battle fatigue (*samarapariśramaṃ samare pariśramo yasya taṃ indrajitam iti śeṣaḥ*)."

The meter is *vaṃśasthavila*.

Sarga 77

1. "the heroic Vibhīṣaṇa" *śūraḥ saḥ*: Literally, "that hero."

"watching the two of them" *tau dṛṣṭvā*: Literally, "having seen those two." Cg understands that, although Vibhīṣaṇa has entered the battlefield in order to fight, he first stops and stands quietly by in order to see which of the two combatants is more powerful. Once he determines that they are equally matched, he enters the fray to assist Rāma. (*tau lakṣmaṇendrajitau prathamaṃ draṣṭukāmaḥ sa vibhīṣaṇas tau dṛṣṭvā saṃgrāmamūrdhani yoddhuṃ tasthāv ity anvayaḥ. svayaṃ prathamaṃ yuddhaṃ kartum udyukto 'pi tayor balādhikyaṃ draṣṭuṃ tūṣṇīṃ sthitaḥ. tayor balataulye dṛṣṭe svasya rāmaviṣayakiṃcitkārārtham idānīṃ yuddhāya tasthāv ity arthaḥ.*)

"locked in combat" *yudhyamānau . . . prasaktau*: Literally, "fighting . . . intent."

Following 1ab, Ñ,V,B,D5–7,9–11,S insert a passage of two lines [1682*]: "That mighty warrior was eager to watch those two, who, like two rutting elephants, were locked in battle[1] and eager to kill[2] each other."

[1]"That mighty warrior was eager to watch those two, who . . . were locked in battle" *tau draṣṭukāmaḥ saṃgrāme parasparagatau balī* (= line 2): Literally, "The mighty one was

desirous of seeing those two, who were gone to each other in battle." For the first *pāda*, D10,11, and the texts and printed editions of Ct read *tayor yuddhaṃ draṣṭukāmaḥ*, while, for the second *pāda*, Ñ2,V,B1–3,D10,11, and the texts and printed editions of Ct read *varacāpadharo balī*. The resulting line in the text of Ct would thus be rendered as "that mighty warrior, holding his superb bow, was eager to watch their combat."

[2]"eager to kill" *-vadhaiṣiṇau*: B3,D7,9–11,G2, and the texts and printed editions of Ct and Cr read instead *-jayaiṣiṇau*, "eager to vanquish."

2. "his great bow" *mahad dhanuḥ*: Cg notes that the bow must be a temporary attribute of Vibhīṣaṇa, since he is normally described as wielding only a mace. (*dhanus tādātvikaṃ kiṃcit. vibhīṣaṇasya kevalagadāpāṇitvāt.*)

3. "glowing like fire" *śikhisaṃkāśāḥ*: Literally, "resembling the crested one." We agree with Cr, the only commentator to address this term, and with the majority of translators, who understand *śikhin* in its common sense of "fire." Dutt (1893, p. 1412) takes *śikhin* in one of its other common senses, "peacock," and takes the compound to mean "furnished with peacock feathers." This is not a persuasive interpretation. It is remotely possible, however, that Dutt is influenced by a minor northern variant, known to Gorresio, in *pāda* d of verse 2, *barhiṇavāsasaḥ*, "clothed in peacock feathers," which is rendered in the translation of Gorresio (1858, vol. 10, p. 116), who translates, "*guerniti di penne di pavone*." Ś,V2,B1,D3,4,8–12,G1, the printed edition of Gorresio (6.69.4), and the texts and printed editions of Ct read instead *-saṃsparśāḥ*, "having the touch *or* impact [of fire]."

"thick and fast" *samāhitāḥ*: Literally, "compact *or* dense." We share our interpretation of the term with most of the translators. Raghunathan (1982, vol. 3, p. 259) evidently understands the term in its sense of "focused, concentrated," and renders, "squarely hitting their target." This interpretation, we believe, is plausible. Dutt (1893, p. 1412) renders, "powerfully," but this interpretation has little lexical support.

4. "Vibhīṣaṇa's followers" *vibhīṣaṇasyānucarāḥ*: The reference is to the four *rākṣasas*, Vibhīṣaṇa's counselors, who defected with him in *sarga* 10 and are named at 6.28.6. See 6.10.12; 6.11.6; 6.28.6; and notes.

5. "excited" *prahṛṣṭānām*: D10,11, and the texts and printed editions of Ct read instead *pradhṛṣṭānām*, "haughty." Gita Press (1969, vol. 3, p. 1738) plausibly translates, "proud," while Roussel (1903, vol. 3, p. 293), followed by Shastri (1959, vol. 3, p. 258) and Pagani (1999, p. 1111), less convincingly takes the verb *pra* $\sqrt{}$*dhṛṣ* in its sense of "to press close upon, to attack," rendering, "*serrés contre lui*."

6. "who took pleasure in battling the *rākṣasas*" *rakṣoraṇapriyān*: D7,10,11,T1, and the texts and printed editions of Ct read instead *-vadha-*, "slaying," for *-raṇa-*, "battle," giving the compound the sense "fond of killing *rākṣasas*." VSP (6.90.7) inserts a space between *rakṣo* and *raṇapriyān*. Given this, the passage would mean "The *rākṣasa*, foremost of *rākṣasas*, urging on the tawny monkeys, who took pleasure in battle." Among the translators consulted, only Raghunathan (1982, vol. 3, p. 259) appears to render this reading.

7. "Indrajit alone" *eko 'yam*: Literally, "this one."

"is, as it were, the last hope" *parāyaṇam iva sthitaḥ*: Literally, "stands like the last resort." Ñ,V,B,D1–4,7,9–11,13,G1,2, the printed edition of Gorresio, and the texts and printed editions of Cr and Ct read instead *avasthitaḥ*, "taking his stand," for *iva sthitaḥ*.

8. "the enemy forces" *balam*: Literally, "the army *or* forces."

9–11. "the loyal hero Prahasta" *prahasto nihato vīraḥ*: We take the adjective *nihata* here in its sense of "devoted, loyal," as against Cg, who understands the adjective in its more common participial sense of "slain." The meaning then becomes "Prahasta has been slain, as has..." This interpretation has been followed by all translators consulted. The syntax of this reading, however, strikes us as unusual and awkward.

"Cakramālin" *cakramālī*: This *rākṣasa* is not mentioned elsewhere in the critical edition or the vulgate.

"and other mighty foes" *sattvavantaś ca*: Literally, "and those possessed of strength *or* might." Since the term in the critical edition is in the nominative plural, we have taken it as a generic term to include other, unnamed *rākṣasas*. M3, the text of Gorresio (6.69.14), the texts and printed editions of Cg (VSP, KK 6.90.14), and Gita Press (6.89.14) read instead the dual *sattvavantau tau*, in which case the adjective applies only to Devāntaka and Narāntaka. Dutt (1893, p. 1413) renders the epithet as if it were a proper noun, "Satwavanta [*sic*]."

"you have crossed the ocean with your bare hands. You need now only hop across a small puddle." *bāhubhyāṃ sāgaraṃ tīrtvā laṅghyatāṃ goṣpadaṃ laghu*: Literally, "having crossed the ocean with two arms, you must leap an insignificant cow's footprint." The expression, as several commentators suggest, is entirely metaphorical and has nothing to do with the actual crossing of the ocean accomplished by the monkey army. The idea is that, having accomplished a monumental feat in killing the main *rākṣasa* champions, the monkeys have only a relatively small task before them, that of killing Indrajit and mopping up his forces. (*etān rākṣasasattamān nihatya sthitānāṃ bhavatām indrajito hananaṃ bāhubhyāṃ sāgaraṃ tīrtvā sthitasya puṃso goṣpadataraṇam iva sukaram iti nidarśanā. bāhubhyāṃ sāgaraṃ tīrtvevaitān atibalān bahūn rākṣasasattamān nihatya sthitair bhavadbhir goṣpadam iva laghu indrajiddhananarūpaṃ svalpaṃ kāryaṃ laṅghyatām ity anvayaḥ*—so Cg.)

Following verse 9, Ñ,V1,3 (after 9ab),B1 (line 1 only),B2–4,D5–7,9–11,S insert a passage of six lines [1686*] in which the list of slain *rākṣasas* is extended: "Jambumālin, Mahāmālin, Tīkṣṇavega, Aśaniprabha,[1] Suptaghna, Yajñakopa, the *rākṣasa* Vajradaṃṣṭra, Saṃhrādin, Vikaṭa, Nighna,[2] the one called Tapana,[3] Praghāsa, Praghasa, Prajaṅga, Jaṅga, the unassailable Agniketu, mighty Raśmiketu, Vidyujjihva, Dvijihva, and the *rākṣasa* Sūryaśatru."

[1]"Aśaniprabha" *aśaniprabhaḥ*: Dutt (1893, p. 1413) renders, "Hemaprabha," although this variant appears in no printed edition consulted or the critical apparatus.

[2]"Nighna" *nighnaḥ*: D6,7,10,11,M5, and the texts and printed editions of Ct and Cr read instead *arighnaḥ*, which may be taken either as a proper noun, "Arighna," or as an epithet, "foe-slaying." Raghunathan (1982, vol. 3, p. 259), whose text reads with the critical edition, drops the name entirely.

[3]"the one called Tapana" *tapano nāma*: D7,9–11, and the texts and printed editions of Ct and Cr read instead the proper name, *mandaḥ*, "Manda." Translations that follow the text of Ct render this variant. D5,T1,G3,M3, and the texts and printed editions of Cg read instead the proper noun *damaḥ*, "Dama."

12. He is the only one left... for you to conquer" *etāvat... śeṣaṃ vo jetavyam*: Literally, "there is only so much of a remainder to be defeated by you." The context,

especially verses 13 and 14 below, supports Cg's and Cm's claim that the reference is to Indrajit alone (*indrajinmātram eva śeṣam*—so Cm).

"here... here" *iha... iha*: The particle occurs twice in the first half of the critical edition's verse. This awkward repetition apparently occurs in only a few manuscripts (D7,M1,2,5) collated for the critical edition, and in none of the printed editions consulted, which generally read the syntactically preferable *eva... iha* or *eva... iti*. We read the second *iha* of the critical reading as if it were in *pādas* cd.

"All the other *rākṣasas*" *sarve... rākṣasāḥ* Literally, "all the *rākṣasas*."

"joined battle" *samāgamya*: Literally, "having assembled *or* encountered." We follow the interpretation of Ct, who glosses, "having come to war (*yuddhaṃ prāpya*)."

13. "True, it is not right for someone like me, who is like a father to him, to kill one who is like my own son." *ayuktaṃ nidhanaṃ kartuṃ putrasya janitur mama*: Literally, "To encompass the destruction of a son on the part of me, a father, is improper." The phrase can be read in two ways. Taking the term *janitṛ* in its strict lexical meaning, "father," it would mean "the son of my [i.e., Vibhīṣaṇa's] father [i.e., Viśravas]," and this would then refer to Rāvaṇa. This is the interpretation adopted by Roussel (1903, vol. 3, p. 294), who translates, "*le fils de mon père*." In this he has been followed by Shastri (1959, vol. 3, p. 259) and Pagani (1999, p. 1111). These translators evidently understand that Vibhīṣaṇa is saying that, although he could under no circumstances participate in the killing of his brother, he is reluctantly willing to do so in the case of his nephew Indrajit. However, we believe this interpretation is incorrect. As noted above (6.74.11 and note), kinship terms in traditional India are often generational rather than simply lineal, and so Vibhīṣaṇa himself stands in the relationship of a father to his nephew Indrajit, who is thus metaphorically, at least, his "son." The southern commentators reach the same conclusion, although in slightly different ways. Ct and Ck gloss *janituḥ* as "of the brother of one's father (*janayitur bhrātuḥ*), i.e., uncle," which then must be read in apposition with the genitive pronoun *mama*, that is, "of the son of me, his uncle." Cr understands *janituḥ* as "of someone who is born from the same womb, i.e., brother (*samānagarbhe jātasya bhrātur ity arthaḥ*)." Thus, for him, Vibhīṣaṇa is referring to "the son of my brother." Cg and Cm, whom we follow, take the word *janituḥ* metaphorically to refer to someone who stands in the role of a progenitor, in this case, a paternal uncle (*janitur janayituḥ pitṛvyasyety arthaḥ*), again taking the term in apposition to the possessive pronoun. This interpretation is perhaps further supported by the northern variants, which avoid the term *janituḥ* entirely. Thus, the text of Gorresio (6.69.17) substitutes [*nidhane*] *putrasya yatituṃ mayā*, "for me to try [to kill my] son." See 6.74.11 and note.

"I must... compass the death" *nihanyām*: Literally, "I would kill." Since Vibhīṣaṇa will not actually kill Indrajit, we agree with Ct, Ck, and Cr, who, in different ways, make him step back one degree from the act of killing. Ct and Ck add the phrase "through setting up the means of killing (*hananopāyapravartaneneti bhāvaḥ*)." Cr glosses the causative *ghātayeyam*, "I would cause him to be killed." However, as we see in the next verse, Vibhīṣaṇa suggests that he does not kill Indrajit himself only because tears of sorrow cloud his vision.

14. "who will have to finish him off" *śamayiṣyati*: Literally, "he will pacify *or* destroy."

"form up their ranks" *saṃbhūya*: Literally, "having become joined *or* united."

"who have clustered around him" *samīpagān*: Literally, "gone into [his] presence."

15. "beat their tails against the ground" *vivyadhuḥ*: See note to 5.55.30 (=GPP 5.57.43) and 5.40.28 and note, where the term *pravivyadhuḥ* is discussed in a similar context. As in that passage, we understand that this is an aggressive simian gesture of challenge. Cg is silent on the subject here but comments on the *Sundarakāṇḍa* passages. He understands there that the monkeys raise their tails to bring them down forcibly on the ground (*pravivyadhur lāṅgūlān uddhṛtya bhūmāv atāḍayann ity arthaḥ*). This interpretation is also accepted by Raghunathan (1982, vol. 3, p. 260). See 6.78.52 and note.

16. "roaring" *kṣveḍantaḥ*: According to Cg, who comments on the verbal root √*kṣveḍ* at 5.59.29, it refers to lionlike roars. See 5.55.29 and note. See note to 6.4.23–24. See, too, 6.47.8; 6.65.16; 6.78.51; and notes.

"unleashed various screeches, as peacocks do when they see storm clouds" *mumucur vividhān nādān meghān dṛṣṭveva barhiṇaḥ*: The crying of peacocks at the advent of the rainy season is a commonplace in Sanskrit poetry. See, for example, 4.27.18 and *Meghdū* 22.

18. "surrounded" *parivavruḥ*: B4,D9–11, and the texts and printed editions of Ct read instead the gerund *paribhartsya*, "having reviled, abused."

20. "as . . . deafening as the clash" *yathā . . . mahāsvanaḥ*: Literally, "as that great noise *or* as that one that made a great noise." As Cr and Cg remind us, we must supply the term *samprahāraḥ*, "clash, conflict, battle," here once more to render the simile intelligible.

21. "ripped up a *sāla* tree from the mountain" *sālam utpāṭya parvatāt*: The mountain in question must be Mount Trikūṭa. V2,3,D5–7,9–11,T1,M5, and the texts and printed editions of Ct and Cr read *sānum*, "peak, summit," for *sālam*, "*sāla* tree," yielding the sense "he tore a peak from the mountain." B4,D4,7,13,G2,M3, and the texts and printed editions of Cg and Cm read *vīryavān*, "powerful, heroic [Hanumān]," for *parvatāt*, "from the mountain."

"advancing to the attack" *samāsādya*: D10 and the texts and printed editions of Ct read instead the adjective *durāsādaḥ*, "unassailable," which would then modify Hanumān.

Following 21ab, D7,9–11,G1, and the texts and printed editions of Ct, Ck, and Cr insert a passage of one line [1692*]. KK and VSP, both in brackets, insert the line after their 6.90.25ab: "That wise one [Hanumān], after first taking Lakṣmaṇa down from his back . . ."

Ct suggests that, to gain some relief, Hanumān places Lakṣmaṇa, who had been mounted on his shoulders, on the ground (*lakṣmaṇaṃ pṛṣṭhād avaropya viśrāmārthaṃ svārūḍhaṃ lakṣmaṇaṃ bhūmāv avasthāpya*). Cg and Cm, whose texts do not include this line, echo this idea and indicate that we are to understand that the logic of the narrative of Hanumān's impending battle involves this step (*atra hanumato yuddhakathanāt kiṃcid viśramārthaṃ tasya pṛṣṭhād avarūḍho lakṣmaṇa ity avagamyate*—so Cg). The commentarial discussion is striking in that nowhere else in the epic or commentaries have we found a suggestion that Hanumān's endurance has any limit.

22. "having engaged in a . . . struggle with his paternal uncle Vibhīṣaṇa" *sa dattvā . . . yuddhaṃ pitṛvyasya*: Literally, "he, having given battle to his paternal uncle." Cr, alone among the commentators, believes that Indrajit is described here as fighting solely with Lakṣmaṇa but doing so in the presence of Vibhīṣaṇa (*sa indrajit pitṛvyasya samīpe lakṣmaṇaṃ tumulaṃ yuddhaṃ dattvā punar abhyadhāvata*).

"slayer of enemy heroes" *paravīraghnam*: V3,D9–11, and the texts and printed editions of Ct read instead the nominative *paravīraghnaḥ*, thus making the epithet apply not to Lakṣmaṇa but to Indrajit.

23. "those two" *tau*: Cr wants to take the pronoun here in the sense of "well known, celebrated," remarking that it means they were like "the thieves of the elixir of immortality," a reference, no doubt, to the well-known mythological battle between the gods and the demons over this precious substance (*tau prasiddhau tāv amṛtacorarūpau*). See 1.44.14–17 and notes. Gita Press (1969, vol. 3, p. 1740), alone among the translations consulted, appears to follow this interpretation, rendering, "the two celebrated heroes."

24. "The two swift and immensely powerful archers" *mahābalau . . . tarasvinau*: Literally, "the two immensely powerful and swift ones."

"were concealed" *antardadhatuḥ*: Literally, "those two concealed." The verb *antar* √*dhā*, when conjugated in the *parasmaipada*, as in this verse, normally is read transitively, in the sense of "to conceal *or* hide someone *or* something." Indeed, many of the translators consulted have rendered it in this way. To do so, however, breaks the parallelism implicit in the simile, where we are certainly not to understand that the sun and the moon are the ones who conceal each other. We therefore concur with Cv, Ck, and Cm, who read the verb intransitively. Cm, for example, glosses, "they became invisible (*adṛśyau babhūvatuḥ*)."

"summer's end" *uṣṇānte*: The reference is to the onset of the monsoon, or rainy season.

25–26. "one could not perceive" *na . . . na . . . na . . . na . . . na . . . na . . . na . . . adṛśyata*: Literally, "was not visible." The verse individually negates virtually every one of the archery techniques that are listed.

"taking up their arrows" *ādānam*: Literally, "taking." We agree with Cr and Cg in understanding the term to refer to the drawing of an arrow from its quiver (*tūṇīrāc charagrahaṇam*—so Cr).

"nocking them" *saṃdhānam*: Literally, "joining." This is the common term for fitting an arrow to the bowstring. Ck and Ct give this explanation, but Ct offers an alternative: "gripping the bow, that is, seizing it in the left and right hands (*dhanuṣo vā parigrahaḥ savyāpasvayena kārmukagrahaṇam*)."

"drawing back the bowstrings" *vikarṣaḥ*: Literally, "drawing, pulling, bending (as a bow)." Cg, whom we follow, explains, "drawing back to the ear (*ākarṇagrahaṇam*)."

"taking up their stances" *vigrahaḥ*: It is difficult to be certain as to what this polysemic term means in this context. It has no technical meaning specific to archery that we can discover. Most likely, the sense is connected with the term's meanings of "stretching, extension, *or* body." Commentators are both divided and uncertain as to the meaning. We follow the meaning offered by Cm (also the first meaning given by Cg) in which the word is a technical term for one of the various formal positions taken up by archers for shooting. These commentators gloss, "a type of posture, such as the *ālīḍha* [the position wherein the right knee is advanced and the left leg retracted], etc. (*ālīḍhādyavasthānaviśeṣaḥ*)." Several of the commentators quote the *Viśvakośa*, according to which one of the meanings of the term *vigraha* is "separation (*vibhāgaḥ*)." Ct, Cr, and Ck then understand the term to refer to the separation of the arrows (*bāṇānāṃ vibhāgaḥ*), presumably from the bunches in which they are kept in the quivers. Cg, however, offers, as his third alternative, the separation of the bow, the bowstring, etc.

(*dhanurjyādīnāṃ pravibhāgo vā*). Cv's explanation and Cg's second alternative is "a position *or* a stance [for shooting] involving some [external *or* physical?] support (*sāvaṣṭambhāvasthānam*)."

"tightly gripping their weapons" *muṣṭipratisaṃdhānam*: Our translation follows the interpretation of Cv, Ck, Cm, Cr, and Cg, who explain, "clenching the fists around the bow and bowstring (*jyākārmukayor muṣṭibandhanam*—so Cg, Cm, Cv). Ct glosses, merely, "tightly clenching with the fist (*dṛḍhatayā muṣṭisaṃyojanam*)."

27. "nothing could be seen" *na rūpāṇi cakāśire*: Literally, "forms did not shine forth." We agree with Cg and Ct, who take "forms (*rūpāṇi*)" here to refer to visible things (*rūpyanta iti rūpāṇi vastūni*).

"darkness engulfed everything" *tamasā pihitaṃ sarvam āsīt*: Literally, "everything was blocked off by darkness."

Following 27cd, D5–7,9–11,S insert a passage of six lines [1696*]: "Lakṣmaṇa having encountered Rāvaṇi, and Rāvaṇi, Lakṣmaṇa, a terrifying chaos arose[1] from their mutual clash.[1–2] The sky was completely filled with the sharp arrows the two of them swiftly released, so that it became obscured by darkness.[3–4] The cardinal and intermediate directions, too, became crowded with many hundreds of their sharp, flying arrows.[5–6]"

[1]"having encountered . . . a terrifying chaos arose" *prāpya . . . avyavasthā bhavaty ugrā*: Several of the commentators are concerned by the awkward and apparently defective syntax in which the subject[s] of the gerund is [are] not the same as that of the finite verb. Ct, Cr, Cm, and Cg (as a second alternative) propose that we remedy the problem by supplying a finite verb in the dual, meaning "the two fought (*ayudhyatām*—so Ct)." Cv, Cs, and Cg (as a first alternative) supply a phrase to the effect that a mutual conflict arose between the two heroes as they strove to defeat each other. In the course of that conflict, chaos arises (*lakṣmaṇo rāvaṇiṃ rāvaṇiś cāpi lakṣmaṇaṃ prāpya tābhyām anyonyavigrahe 'nyonyābhibhava ugrāvyavasthā bhavati*—so Cg). Commentators are also divided as to the precise meaning of the term *avyavasthā*. Ct understands the term to refer to the slaughter of the noncombatant *vānaras* and *rākṣasas* caused by the [stray] arrows of Lakṣmaṇa and Indrajit (*avyavasthā tattadbāṇair ayudhyadvānararākṣasavadharūpā bhavati*). This may be the first literary reference to what is known in modern military parlance as "collateral damage." This interpretation is interpolated into the translation of Gita Press (1969, vol. 3, p. 1741). Dutt (1893, p. 1414) renders, "critical was the hugger mugger that ensued." Dutt adds a footnote that expresses the interpretation of Ct. Ct goes on to state that we are to understand that the fight is so furious that it is impossible to decide which of the combatants is defeating which. He then adds that the adjective *ugra*, "terrifying, fierce," is meaningless in this context, since it is actually impossible to describe the fearsomeness of the situation. (*yat tu ayam enaṃ nigṛhṇāti sa enaṃ vety aniścayarūpā vyavastheti vyākhyānam. tac cintyam. tasyā avyavasthāyā ugratvasya nirūpayitum aśakyatvāt. ugreti viśeṣaṇavaiyarthyāc ca.*) Cs quotes Ct's interpretation only to refute it as utterly inappropriate (*yan nāgojibhaṭṭenoktaṃ tad asaṅgatam . . . kathanaṃ tu asaṅgatataram iti jñeyam*). Cr glosses the phrase as "the quailing of all hearts (*sarvamanasām asvāsthyaṃ bhavati*)." Cv, Cg, and Cm understand the reference to be to the confusion engendered by the constantly changing fortunes of battle, so that, from moment to moment, it is impossible to determine who is winning and who is

losing (*kṣaṇe kṣaṇe jayaparājayaniyamo nābhūd ity arthaḥ*—so Cg). This interpretation appears to be reflected in the translation of Raghunathan (1982, vol. 3, p. 261).

Following verse 27, D5–7,9–11,S insert a passage of three lines [1697*]: "Everything was shrouded in darkness as when[1] the thousand-rayed sun sets. Thousands of mighty rivers brimming with blood[2] gushed forth. Horrible flesh-eating creatures screeched with terrifying cries.[3]"

[1]"Everything was shrouded in darkness as when" *saṃvṛtaṃ tamaseva*: Literally, "was as if covered with darkness." D10,11 and the texts and printed editions of Ct read instead *saṃvṛte tamasā ca*, in which case there is no simile and the reference is to when the sun, shrouded in darkness, actually set.

[2]"brimming with blood" *rudhiraughā*: Literally, "having blood for its floods."

[3]"screeched with terrifying cries" *vāgbhiś cikṣipur bhīmanisvanam*: Literally, "they threw *or* released a terrifying sound with speech *or* voices."

28. "Heaven help us!" *svasty astu lokebhya iti*: Literally, "May there be well-being for the worlds." We feel that the more idiomatic translation better expresses in English the anxiety that underlies the seers' words. Clearly the ominous signs surrounding the battle are suggestive of the end of the world, and therefore the seers speak as they do.

"came and gathered at that place" *saṃpetuś cātra saṃprāptāḥ*: Our understanding is that, as at many great duels in the epic, celestial beings gather to watch and later cheer the victor. This interpretation appears to be confirmed at 6.78.48, where the gods, *gandharvas*, and *dānavas* gather to celebrate Lakṣmaṇa's triumph over Indrajit. Cg, however, somewhat idiosyncratically, takes the verb *sam* $\sqrt{pat}$, "to assemble, to gather," to mean "to go away." His idea is that the celestial beings are terrified of witnessing this extremely frightening battle and flee. (*saṃpetuḥ. anyatra gatā ity arthaḥ. atighorayuddhadarśanabhayād iti bhāvaḥ.*) This interpretation is explicitly followed in the translation of Raghunathan (1982, vol. 3, p. 261), who renders, "withdrew." Ñ2,V1,B2–4,D9–11, and the texts and printed editions of Ct read instead *saṃtaptāḥ*, "distressed, pained," for the critical edition's *saṃprāptāḥ*, "came, arrived." Although no commentator remarks on this reading, the translations that follow the text of Ct render it and infer from it that the celestial beings actually flee the scene of the battle. For example, Gita Press (1969, vol. 3, p. 1741) renders, "feeling distressed . . . fled away."

30. "as he drove back and forth" *vicariṣyataḥ*: Literally, "who was about to move about." The correct idea is suggested by Ct, who glosses, "as he was about to drive the chariot (*rathasaṃcāraṃ kariṣyataḥ*)."

Note that a previous charioteer of Indrajit was slain at 6.34.27.

Following 30a, D5–7,9–11,S insert a passage of two lines [1700*] (= GPP, NSP, Gita Press 6.89.40b–41a; KK 6.90.39b–40a; VSP 6.90.40b–41a): "[a crescent-headed arrow]. It was yellow[1] and sharp. Radiant and beautifully fletched, when released from the fully stretched bow, it resembled the thunderbolt of great Indra."

[1]"yellow" *pītena*: As Ck, Ct, and Cr note, the color derives from the arrow's gold ornamentation. M1,3, and the texts and printed editions of Cg and Cm read instead the redundant *śitena*, "sharp."

Following 30b, D5–7,9–11,S insert a passage of one line [1701*, line 1]: "with that thunderbolt of an arrow that echoed with the sound of the bowstring striking his armguard.[1]"

[1]"that echoed with the sound of the bowstring striking his armguard" *tala-śabdānunādinā*: Literally, "echoing the sound of the armguard." Curiously enough, the term *tala*, which we have consistently translated in the context of archery as "arm-guard," has been ignored by the commentators up until this point. Here, however, Ck, Cm, Ct, and Cr all gloss *jyāghātavāraṇam*, "bowstring-blow-guard," and explain the sound as that produced by the friction or striking of the bow against the guard (*tasya [talasya] jyāghaṭṭanajo yaḥ śabdas tasyānunādo yasyāsti tena*). See notes to 1.21.8; 6.66.23; 6.67.25; and 6.76.2,24.

Following verse 30, D5–7,9–11,S insert a passage of seven lines [1702*]:
"Now that his charioteer had been slain, the immensely powerful Indrajit, son of Mandodarī,[1] took up the reins himself[2] while still wielding his bow so that those who witnessed this ability[3] in battle thought it a wonder.[4][1–3] But while his hands were busy with the horses, Lakṣmaṇa pierced him with sharp arrows, and while, on the other hand, he was busy with his bow, Lakṣmaṇa loosed[5] his shafts at his horses.[4–5] Thus, during those moments of vulnerability,[6] did the extraordinarily quick[7] Saumitri harry him with torrents of arrows[8] as he drove back and forth fearlessly. [6–7]"

[1]"Indrajit, son of Mandodarī" *mandodarīsutaḥ*: Literally, "the son of Mandodarī."

[2]"took up the reins himself" *svayaṃ sārathyam akarot*: Literally, "he acted the part of the charioteer himself."

[3]"this ability" *sāmarthyam*: D6,7,9–11,T2,3,G1,M5, and the texts and printed editions of Ct, Ck, and Cr read instead *sārathyam*, "his performance as a charioteer."

[4]"thought it a wonder" *tad adbhutam abhūt*: Literally, "that was a wonder [to those who saw it]."

[5]"Lakṣmaṇa loosed" *mumuce*: Literally, "he loosed *or* released."

[6]"during those moments of vulnerability" *chidreṣu teṣu*: Literally, "in those weak points." D7,G1, and the texts and printed editions of Ct read instead *chinneṣu*, "cut down," which must then refer to the horses (*hayeṣu*) in line 5.

[7]"extraordinarily quick" *śīghrakṛttamaḥ*: Literally, "acting most quickly." D6,T2,3, and the texts and printed editions of Cg read instead *śīghravikramaḥ*, "swift in valor *or* swiftly stepping."

[8]"with torrents of arrows" *bāṇaughaiḥ . . . bāṇaughaiḥ*: The compound occurs twice in the critical edition. We have omitted the second occurrence of the compound. D9–11,G1, and the texts and printed editions of Ct read *samare*, "in battle," for *bāṇaughaiḥ* in line 7. M3 and the texts and printed editions of Cg read instead *bāṇeṣu*, which Cg explains as follows: "he [Saumitri], quick in valor in the use of arrows against weak spots (*chidreṣu randhreṣu bāṇeṣu bāṇaprayogeṣu śīghravikrama ity anvayaḥ*)." Raghunathan (1982, vol. 3, p. 261) is the only translator to follow this reading and this interpretation. He renders, "Quick in taking advantage of such opportunities to shoot."

33. "unable to hold themselves back, launched a violent assault" *amṛṣyamāṇāḥ... cakrur vegam*: Literally, "not enduring, they made a violent impulse."

34. "Indrajit's" *asya*: Literally, "his."

35. "Blood gushed visibly" *rudhiraṃ vyaktam... samavartata*: Literally, "blood clearly flowed." D9,M3, and the texts and printed editions of Cg and Cm read instead *raktam*, "blood *or* red," in place of *vyaktam*, "clearly." Cg glosses *raktam* as *śoṇitam*, "blood," in which case the word *rudhiram* must be taken in its adjectival sense of "red."

"of the horses as those monkeys... came crashing down upon them" *teṣām adhiṣṭhitānāṃ tair vānaraiḥ... hayānām*: Literally, "of those horses who were sat upon by those monkeys."

Following verse 35, D5–7,9–11,S insert a passage of one line [1705*]: "Crushed, their bodies broken,[1] the horses fell to the ground, their life breaths gone."

[1]"their bodies broken" *bhagnāḥ*: Literally, "broken." We follow Cr, who glosses, "caused to attain the breaking of limbs (*aṅgabhaṅgaṃ prāpitāḥ*)."

36. "great chariot" *mahāratham*: Only Dutt (1893, p. 1416), among the translators consulted, takes the term as a *bahuvrīhi* in its common sense of "great chariot warrior," although he does note the ambiguity of the compound. Still, nothing in the context indicates that the monkeys have the temerity to directly attack Indrajit. Cf. 6.60.3; 6.72.33; 6.80.6; 6.81.18; 6.83.8; 6.84.15; and notes. Cf. 6.72.33.

37. "its charioteer slaughtered" *mathitasāratheḥ*: Literally, "having a crushed charioteer." Ñ2,V1,2,B3,4,D5,9–11,13, and the texts and printed editions of Ct read the nominative *mathitasārathiḥ* in place of the ablative. In this reading, the compound describes Indrajit, "his charioteer slaughtered," rather than the chariot.

38. "with masses of arrows—and sharp and splendid arrows they were" *niśitaiḥ śarottamaiḥ... bāṇagaṇaiḥ*: The critical reading here is awkward, somewhat redundant, and not particularly strong. A number of northern and southern manuscripts offer variant readings for *niśitaiḥ śarottamaiḥ*, "with sharp and splendid arrows," that refer instead to the death of Indrajit's horses and thus explain why he must now fight on foot. Thus, D7,9–11,G1,M1,2,5, and the texts and printed editions of Ct and Cr read instead *nihatair hayottamaiḥ*, "with [his] excellent horses slain." Ñ,V1,3,B2–4, and the printed edition of Gorresio (6.69.48) read instead *yudhi sūditāśvam*, "his horses slain in battle." Lahore (unnoted by the critical edition) reads instead *nihataiḥ turaṅgaiḥ*, "with horses slain." D6,T2,3 read *nihatāśvasārathim*, "his horses and charioteer slain." Given the distribution and number of the readings, we believe that the idea of Indrajit's horses having been slain is probably original here, although the southern reading may not be.

"was releasing" *sṛjantam*: Ñ2,V1,3,B2,4,D5,11, and the texts and printed editions of Ct read instead *mṛjantam*, literally, "stroking, wiping." The sense of the verbal root √*mṛj* here is not entirely clear. Ct himself is silent, and the translators who follow his text all render some variation on the sense of "loosing, releasing," as in the critical text. Perhaps the idea is similar to the one expressed at 6.75.3 by the gerund *parāmṛśya*, "having stroked *or* having fingered." See notes to 6.75.3 and 14.

"forcefully warded him off" *bhṛśaṃ... nyavārayat*: Ñ2,B2,D7,9–11,G2,M1,2, and the texts and printed editions of Ct and Cr read *vyadārayat*, "he cut up *or* lacerated," for *nyavārayat*, "he warded off."

*"in battle" *ājau*: The critical edition reads the contextually awkward *ādau*, "at the onset *or* at the beginning." Since all printed editions consulted read the contextually appropriate and common *ājau*, "in battle," and no mention of this as a variant is made in the critical apparatus, we can only assume that the critical reading is the result of a typographical error not noted by the compilers of the errata list. We have therefore emended accordingly.

The meter is *vaṃśasthavila*.

Sarga 78

2. "for the sake of victory" *vijayena*: Literally, "by victory." The commentators note the unusual use of the instrumental case, generally indicating that we are to take it in the sense of cause. Cg succinctly remarks that this is an instrumental of purpose, which should be read as a dative. (*vijayeneti prayojane tṛtīyā. vijayāyety arthaḥ.*)

"the two... charged at each other" *abhiniṣkrāntau*: Literally, "the two set out toward." We follow Cm, who glosses, "they ran toward [each other] (*abhimukham adhāvatām*)." Other commentators interpret similarly.

"like two bull elephants" *gajavṛṣāv iva*: Literally, "like two elephant bulls." Cg, alone among the commentators, offers, as a second alternative, that we read the compound as a *dvandva* in the sense of "like a bull and an elephant." Indrajit, as we learned earlier, had been somewhat weakened in the course of battle so that he is compared to a bull, [wheras the stronger Lakṣmaṇa is likened to an elephant] (*yadvā kiṃcid dhīnabalatvād indrajito vṛṣabhatulyatvam*). This reading of the compound is represented only in the translation of Dutt (1893, p. 1416).

3. "their respective masters" *bhartāram*: Literally, "the master."

Following verse 3, Ñ,V1,3,B2–4,D4 (after line 1 of 1710*),5–7,9–11,S insert a passage of thirty-seven lines [App. I, No. 46]: "Then, in great excitement, Rāvaṇa's son urged on all the *rākṣasas*. Praising them, he said these words:[1–2] 'Foremost of the *rākṣasas*! All directions are shrouded in dense darkness[1] so that one cannot distinguish friend from foe.[2] [3–4] Therefore, you gentlemen must continue to fight bravely so as to delude[3] the tawny monkeys. Meanwhile, I shall return to the battle, mounted in another chariot.[4][5–6] So you, gentlemen, must see to it[5] that those evil-minded[6] forest-dwelling monkeys do not attack while I am in the city.'[7–8] When he had spoken in this fashion, that slayer of his foes, Rāvaṇa's son, entered the city of Laṅkā to get another chariot, eluding the notice of[7] the forest-dwelling monkeys.[9–10] He had a splendid chariot, already adorned with gold, fully decked out.[8] It was fully equipped with darts, swords, and arrows, harnessed to magnificent steeds, and driven[9] by a charioteer who was expert with horses and was a trusted adviser.[10] Immensely powerful Rāvaṇi, conqueror in battle, mounted it.[11–14] Then, driven onward by the force of doom, the son of Mandodarī, surrounded by the foremost *rākṣasa* troops, sallied forth swiftly[11] from the city.[15–16] Leaving the city behind, Indrajit, slayer of enemy heroes,[12] charged with his swift steeds toward Lakṣmaṇa and Vibhīṣaṇa.[17–18] Then, seeing the son of Rāvaṇa mounted once more in a chariot, Saumitri, the immensely powerful monkeys, and the *rākṣasa* Vibhīṣaṇa were amazed at that wise hero's[13] speed.[19–21] But, with torrents of arrows, Rāvaṇi, in a rage, cut down the monkey troop leaders in their hundreds and thousands. Bending his bow into a circle,

Rāvaṇi, victorious in battle, relied on his extraordinary quickness to slaughter the tawny monkeys in his rage.[22–25] As they were being massacred by his iron arrows, the tawny monkeys, fearsome in their valor,[14] took refuge with Saumitri, as do all creatures with Brahmā, lord of creatures.[15][26–27] Then the delight of the Raghus, inflamed with the fury of battle, demonstrated his own deftness of hand and split Indrajit's[16] bow.[28–29] But Indrajit[17] took up another bow and swiftly strung it. Yet again Lakṣmaṇa cut it to pieces with three arrows.[30–31] Then, once Rāvaṇi's bow had been cut to pieces, Saumitri pierced him[18] through the chest with five arrows that were like the venom of venomous serpents.[32–33] Loosed from Lakṣmaṇa's mighty bow,[19] those arrows pierced Indrajit's[20] body and then plunged into the earth like huge red serpents.[21] [34–35] His armor pierced,[22] Rāvaṇi spewed blood from his mouth. Nonetheless, he took up a splendid and exceedingly powerful bow with a taut bowstring.[36–37]"

[1]"in dense darkness" *tamasā bahulena*: Ck, Ct, and Cm understand Indrajit to be encouraging the *rākṣasas* by reminding them that night is approaching, the time when the *rākṣasas'* strength is supposed to increase (*evaṃ cāsmākaṃ balakarī rātrir āgatā*—so Ct). See note to 1.25.13. Cf. note to 6.34.1.

[2]"so that one cannot distinguish friend from foe" *neha vijñāyate svo vā paro vā*: Cr wants to add "by the monkeys (*vānarair iti śeṣaḥ*)" to suggest that only the monkeys and not the *rākṣasas* will be blinded in this fashion.

[3]"so as to delude" *mohanāya*: The idea here, according to the commentators, is that by giving battle the *rākṣasas* can conceal from the monkeys the fact that Indrajit has left the field [to secure a new chariot] (*madgamanāparijñānāya*—so Ct).

[4]"another chariot" *ratham*: Literally, "a chariot."

[5]"see to it" *tathā . . . kurvantu yathā*: Literally, "[you] must act in such a way that."

[6]"evil-minded" *durātmānaḥ*: D9–11 and the texts and printed editions of Ct read instead *mahātmānaḥ*, "great ones." Translations that follow the text of Ct treat the epithet in one of two ways. Dutt (1893, p. 1417) and Gita Press (1969, vol. 3, p. 1743) bite the bullet, as it were, and assign the complimentary epithet to the monkeys, as the syntax suggests. Roussel (1903, vol. 3, p. 297), followed by Shastri (1959, vol. 3, p. 261) and Pagani (1999, p. 1114), takes the term in the sense of "courageous" and reads it as a vocative applied by Indrajit to his own *rākṣasa* troops.

[7]"eluding the notice of" *vañcayitvā*: Literally, "having deceived."

[8]"fully decked out" *bhūṣayitvā*: Literally, "having adorned." Cg believes that Indrajit adorns the chariot with his own radiant energy (*svatejasā*).

[9]"driven" *adhiṣṭhitam*: Literally, "mounted, sat in."

[10]"a trusted adviser" *āptopadeśinā*: The commentators understand, "one whose character is to offer beneficial advice (*āptaṃ hitam upadeṣṭuṃ śīlam asty asya*—so Ct, Ck, and Cm)."

[11]"swiftly" *tūrṇam*: Ñ,V1,3,B2–4,D4,9–11,G1, and the texts and printed editions of Ct read instead *vīraḥ*, "that hero."

[12]"slayer of enemy heroes" *paravīrahā*: D9–11 and the texts and printed editions of Ct read instead *paramaujasā*, "with great force *or* energy."

[13]"that wise hero's" *dhīmataḥ*: Literally, "the wise one's."

[14]"fearsome in their valor" *bhīmavikramāḥ*: D6,10,11,M1,2, and the texts and printed editions of Ct read the instrumental plural *bhīmavikramaiḥ* for the nominative,

thus making the epithet apply not to the monkeys but to the iron arrows. Translations that follow the text of Ct generally render this in the sense of "having terrific impetus *or* violence."

[15]"Brahmā, lord of creatures" *prajāpatim*: Literally, "the lord of creatures." This is a common epithet of Brahmā.

[16]"Indrajit's" *tasya*: Literally, "his."

[17]"Indrajit" *saḥ*: Literally, "he."

[18]"once Rāvaṇi's bow had been cut to pieces... him" *chinnadhanvānam ... rāvaṇim:* Literally, "Rāvaṇi, whose bow had been cut."

[19]"Lakṣmaṇa's mighty bow" *mahākārmuka-*: Literally, "the great bow."

[20]"Indrajit's" *tasya*: Literally, "his."

[21]"like huge red serpents" *raktā iva mahoragāḥ*: Ct notes that the arrows, too, are red because they are smeared with blood, implying, it seems, that he understands that the *upamāna* is actually red snakes (*bāṇānām api rudhirasaṃbandhād raktatvam*). We think it more likely, however, that the poet intends an *abhūtopamā*, in which the object of comparison is imaginary. See notes to verse 12 below.

[22]"His armor pierced" *bhinnavarmā*: D9–11,G1, and the texts and printed editions of Ct read instead *chinnadhanvā*, "his bow cut to pieces."

4. "Indrajit" *saḥ*: Literally, "he."

5. "all-but-unstoppable" *sudurāsadam*: Literally, "extremely irresistible." The idea here is conveyed by Cr, who glosses, "impossible for others to ward off (*anyair nivārayitum aśakyam*)."

Following verse 5, Ñ,V1–3,B2–4,D4–7,9–11,S insert a passage of eighteen lines [App. I, No. 47]: "Then the immensely powerful delight of the Raghus calmly showed Rāvaṇi his skill;[1] and a wonderful thing it was.[2][1–2] In a towering rage, he demonstrated his extraordinary swiftness in releasing divinely charged weapons[3] in battle by piercing each of the *rākṣasas* with three arrows.[3–4] Next he struck the son of the *rākṣasa* lord[4] with torrents of arrows.[5] Pierced by his powerful foe-slaying foe, Indrajit[5] nonetheless unceasingly shot many arrows at Lakṣmaṇa.[6–7] But the delight of the Raghus[6] cut them to pieces with his own sharp arrows before they reached him. And then, with a straight[7] crescent-headed arrow, that righteous hero, foremost of chariot-warriors, struck off the head of the chariot-warrior Indrajit's charioteer in battle.[8][8–10] Although they were deprived of their driver, the horses continued to draw the chariot without confusion.[9] They ran in perfect circles;[10] and a wonderful thing it was.[11][11–12] Giving way to rage, Saumitri, firm in his valor, pierced Indrajit's[12] horses with arrows, sowing panic in the battle.[13–14] Unable to endure that act, the powerful[13] son of Rāvaṇa pierced the furious[14] Saumitri with ten arrows.[15–16] But although his arrows had the force of thunderbolts[15] and were as deadly as the venom of serpents,[16] they disintegrated as they struck Lakṣmaṇa's armor,[17] brilliant with gold.[17–18]"

[1]"showed... his skill" *saṃdarśayāmāsa*: Literally, "he showed *or* demonstrated." The commentators supply a variety of contextually apposite objects of the verb, such as "his own valor (*svapauruṣam*—so Ct, Cr)," "his prowess (*parākramam*—so Cg)," and "his deftness of hand (*hastalāghavam*—so Crā)."

[2]"and a wonderful thing it was" *tad adbhutam ivābhavat*: Literally, "that was as if a wonder."

[3]"his extraordinary swiftness in releasing divinely charged weapons" *śīghrāstram*: Literally, "swift *astra*." The compound is puzzling, and the commentators offer a variety of interpretations. Ck and Ct raise the question of how Lakṣmaṇa, while engaged in fighting Indrajit, can possibly manage to shoot all the other *rākṣasas* three times each. They offer two explanations of the term *śīghrāstram*. According to the first, the term refers to a specific type of weapon, which, upon being discharged, somehow pierces all [one's enemies] (*prayogamātreṇa sarvabhedakam astram*—so Ct). As an alternative, they take the term merely as an emotional one, that is, perhaps, hyperbolic (*yadvā bhāvapradhāno nirdeśaḥ*—so Ct). The idea then, in their view, is that Lakṣmaṇa is demonstrating his swiftness in the use of weapons, which takes the form of the capacity to discharge them rapidly (*astraviṣayakaśīghraprayogasāmarthyarūpaṃ śīghrāstratvaṃ sampradarśayann ity arthaḥ*). Most translators, ourselves included, follow this general interpretation. Cg glosses, "the *mantra* of swiftness (*śīghramantram*)," that is, the magical spell that controls and lends velocity to one's divinely charged weapons.

[4]"son of the *rākṣasa* lord" *rākṣasendrasutam*: D5,10,11,T1,G1,3,M5, and the texts and printed editions of Ct read instead *rākṣasendras tu tam*, "but the *rākṣasa* lord [struck] him [Lakṣmaṇa]," thus reversing the sense of the critical reading.

[5]"Indrajit" *saḥ*: Literally, "he." Regardless of who is the subject of the preceding sentence, the pronoun here must refer to Indrajit.

[6]"But the delight of the Raghus" *raghunandanaḥ*: D9–11 and the texts and printed editions of Ct read instead *paravīrahā*, "the slayer of enemy heroes."

[7]"straight" *anataparvaṇā*: See 6.59.71 and note.

[8]"And . . . in battle" *ca raṇe*: Cr, alone among the commentators consulted, suggests, as an alternative, that we read the sequence of words *ca raṇe* together as one word, the dual accusative *caraṇe*, "two feet," in which case Lakṣmaṇa cuts off both the head and the two feet of the charioteer.

[9]"without confusion" *aviklavāḥ*: Literally, "not confused *or* agitated." Cg explains that we are to understand that the composure of the horses is testimony to their extraordinary training (*śikṣāpāṭavātiśayād iti mantavyam*).

[10]"in perfect circles" *maṇḍalāni*: Literally, "circles."

[11]"and a wonderful thing it was" *tad adbhutam ivābhavat*: Literally, "that was as if a wonder."

[12]"Indrajit's" *tasya*: Literally, "his."

[13]"the powerful" *balī*: D10,11, and the texts and printed editions of Ct read instead *raṇe*, "in battle."

[14]" the furious" *tam amarṣaṇam*: D9–11 and the texts and printed editions of Ct read instead *romaharṣaṇam*, "hair-raising, terrifying."

[15]"had the force of thunderbolts" *vajrapratimāḥ*: Literally, "similar to *or* resembling thunderbolts *or vajras*."

[16]"as deadly as the venom of serpents" *sarpaviṣopamāḥ*: Literally, "comparable to snake venom." Ñ2,V1,B2,D6,9, and the texts and printed editions of Ct read instead *sarva-* "all," for *sarpa-*, "serpents," yielding the sense "like all venom."

[17]"Lakṣmaṇa's armor" *kavacam*: Literally, "armor."

6. "Realizing that Lakṣmaṇa's armor was impenetrable" *abhedyakavacaṃ matvā lakṣmaṇam*: Literally, "thinking that Lakṣmaṇa was one whose armor was not to be

pierced." Cv, Cm, and Cg, recalling an earlier passage (known only to the southern recension) in which Indrajit is said to have destroyed Lakṣmaṇa's armor, note that we are to infer that in the interim Lakṣmaṇa has acquired new armor (*abhedyakavacam ity anena pūrvakavacasya bhagnatvāt kavacāntaraṃ dhṛtam iti gamyate*). See 1672*, lines 3–4, following verse 6.76.20 (=NSP and GPP 6.88.57; VSP 6.89.22; and KK 6.89.21).

"him" *lakṣmaṇam*: Literally, "Lakṣmaṇa." In order to avoid repetition the pronoun has been substituted for the proper noun, which also occurs in *pāda* b.

"his extraordinary swiftness in releasing divinely charged weapons" *śīghram astram*: Literally, "a swift *astra*." The similar compound term *śīghrāstram* is used above at App. I, No. 47, line 4. See notes to verse 5 above.

7. "who delighted in battle" *samaraślāghī*: Like most of the translators consulted, we read the compound as do Cg and Cm, who analyze it to mean "he praises battle (*samaraṃ ślāghate*)" and gloss, "fond of battle (*samarapriyaḥ*)." Roussel (1903, vol. 3, p. 299), however, interprets the compound in its other plausible sense of "celebrated in battle," rendering, *l'illustre guerrier*." In this he is followed by Shastri (1959, vol. 3, p. 263) and Pagani (1999, p. 1115).

8. Following verse 8, Ñ,V1,3,B2–4,D5–7,9–11,S insert a passage of one line [1715*]: "[Lakṣmaṇa] drawing back [his bowstring, pierced] in battle Indrajit's face with its splendid earrings."

9. "with sharp arrows" *bāṇair viśikhaiḥ*: The sequence is problematic, and several of the commentators attempt to rationalize it. One explanation is that *viśikha* has "arrow" as one of its more common meanings, but in this sense it would be redundant with *bāṇaiḥ*, "arrows." We follow the suggestion of Cm, who takes *viśikhaiḥ* adjectivally in the sense of "having special tips, that is, sharp (*viśikhaiḥ viśiṣṭaśikhair niśitair iti yāvat*)." Cg, however, takes the *vi-* of *viśikhaiḥ* in the sense of "various (*vividha*)," explaining that the arrowheads had different shapes, such as that of *karavīra* leaves, etc. (*viśikhair vividhaśikhaiḥ. karavīrapatrādyākārāgrair ity arthaḥ*). This interpretation is followed only in the translation of Raghunathan (1982, vol. 3, p. 264), who renders, "with darts having many different kinds of arrow-heads." D10,11, and the texts and printed editions of Ct avoid the problem of the redundancy of *bāṇaiḥ* and *viśikhaiḥ* by reading *vīrau*, "the two heroes," for *bāṇaiḥ*. This, however, merely creates another redundancy with the term *vīrau* in *pāda* a. Ct, although he reads this variant, interprets the term *viśikhaiḥ* in the same way as Cm does.

Following verse 9, D5–7,9–11,S (Ñ,V1,3,B2–4 following 1715*; and V2,B1,D1–4,13 following 1714*) insert a passage of two lines [1717*]: "Then, in that battle, both heroes, Lakṣmaṇa and Indrajit, their limbs drenched with blood, resembled a pair of *kiṃśuka* trees[1] in full bloom."

[1]"resembled a pair of *kiṃśuka* trees" *iva kiṃśukau*: See 6.35.9; 6.55.22; 6.60.34; 6.62.19; 6.76.28; and notes.

10. Following verse 10, D5–7,9–11,S (while Ñ,V,B,D1–4,13 insert lines 1–4) insert a passage of ten lines [1718*]: "Then Rāvaṇa's son, filled with the rage of battle, shot Vibhīṣaṇa in his handsome face with three arrows.[1–2] Once he had pierced the *rākṣasa* lord Vibhīṣaṇa with his three iron-tipped arrows,[1] he shot all the troop leaders of the tawny monkeys with one arrow each.[2][3–4] But the immensely powerful Vibhīṣaṇa,

now still further enraged at him, slew with his mace the horses of that very evil-minded Rāvaṇi.[3][5–6] Then leaping down from his chariot, of which the horses and charioteer had been slain, immensely powerful Indrajit hurled a javelin[4] at his uncle.[7–8] But when Lakṣmaṇa, the increaser of Sumitrā's joy,[5] saw it hurtling toward him, he cut it down with sharp arrows, so that it fell to the ground in ten pieces.[6][9–10]"

[1]"three iron-tipped arrows" *ayomukhais tribhiḥ*: Literally, "with three iron-tipped ones."

[2]"with one arrow each" *ekaikena*: Literally, "one by one."

[3]"of that very evil-minded Rāvaṇi" *rāvaṇeḥ sudurātmanaḥ*: D5,10, and the texts and printed editions of Ct read instead *sa durātmanaḥ*, "he . . . of that evil-minded one," for *sudurātmanaḥ*, "of that very evil-minded one."

[4]"Then . . . a javelin" *atha śaktim*: D6,T1,G1,M, and the texts and printed editions of Cg and Cm read instead *rathaśaktim*, " a chariot-javelin," which Cg glosses as "a javelin mounted in *or* on a chariot (*rathe 'vasthitāṃ śaktim*)." See notes to 6.33.21; 6.59.13; and 6.95.9. This term is rendered only in the translation of Raghunathan (1982, vol. 3, p. 264), who renders, "the javelin that went with the chariot."

[5]"Lakṣmaṇa, the increaser of Sumitrā's joy" *sumitrānandavardhanaḥ*: Literally,"the increaser of Sumitrā's joy."

[6]"so that it fell to the ground in ten pieces" *daśadhā sāpatad bhuvi*: Literally, "it fell tenfold to the ground." D9–11 and the texts and printed editions of Ct read instead the causative [*a*]*pātayat*, "he knocked [it] down," for *sāpatat*, "it fell."

11. "still further enraged at Indrajit" *tasmai dṛḍhataraṃ kruddhaḥ*: Literally, "more firmly angered toward him." Ñ,V,B,D1–3,6,7,10,11,T3,M3,5, Gorresio's edition, and the texts and printed editions of the southern commentators read instead *dṛḍhadhanuḥ*," of firm bow," for *dṛḍhataram*, "more firmly."

12. "those gold-fletched arrows" *te . . . rukmapuṅkhāḥ*: Literally, "those gold-fletched ones."

"resembled huge, red serpents" *raktā iva mahoragāḥ*: Compare the similar figure, following verse 3 above, App. I, No. 46, line 35 and n. 20.

13. "immensely powerful" *mahābalaḥ*: D7,9–11,G2, and the texts and printed editions of Ct and Cr read the accusative *mahābalam* for the critical edition's nominative, thus making the adjective apply not to Indrajit but to his arrow.

14–15. "immeasurable" *amitātmanā*: A number of northern manuscripts as well as M3 and the texts and printed editions of Cg read instead *mahātmanā*, "by the great one." Cg glosses, "of immeasurable intellect (*aprameyabuddhinā*)."

Following verse 15, D5–7,9–12,S insert a passage of two lines [1721*]: "Drawn powerfully by their arms, which resembled iron beams, their two magnificent bows shrieked like a pair of *krauñcas*."

17. "They struck each other head on" *mukhena mukham āhatya*: Literally, "having struck the face with the face,"

Following verse 17, D5–7,9–11,S insert a passage of two lines [1723*]: "There was a collision of those two fearsome-looking arrows and from it arose a terrifying conflagration emitting smoke and sparks."

18. "Colliding with each other . . . like two great planets" *mahāgrahasaṃkāśāv anyonyaṃ saṃnipatya*: The image appears to derive not from a literal collision of planets

but rather from an astronomical observation of planets in apparent conflict when aligned. Cm notes that the planets intended are "like Mars and Saturn, etc. (*aṅgār-akaśanyādiḥ*)." See 6.75.30 and note.

19. "both ... were filled with shame and rage" *vrīḍitau jātaroṣau ca ... ubhau*: Ck, closely paraphrased by both Cm and Ct, is disturbed at the thought that Lakṣmaṇa has anything to be ashamed of. His reasoning is that, although Indrajit has reason to be ashamed (in that he has failed in his purpose of killing Vibhīṣaṇa), Lakṣmaṇa has succeeded in his purpose, which was simply to destroy Indrajit's *astras*. Ck concludes by saying that Lakṣmaṇa is included in the adjective *vrīḍitau*, "ashamed," by the maxim of the men with umbrellas (*chatrinyāya*), according to which one might say that people are carrying umbrellas, when in, fact, only some of them are. (*vrīḍitau svasvaprayuktaśarasya moghatvadarśanena saṃjātalajjau. yady api rāvaṇer eva vrīḍā yuktā lakṣmaṇasya tu tadbāṇa-nivāraṇāya prayoktuḥ sārthakyasattvena vrīḍābhāvas tathāpi tannirākaraṇapūrvakaṃ ripu-vadhaparyantavyāpāreṇopādānāt tadabhāvena tasyāpi lajjeti bodhyam. chatrinyāyena dvi-vacanaprayoga iti kaṭakaḥ*—so Ct and Cm.) Regarding the warriors' rage, Ck, Ct, and Cm understand that Lakṣmaṇa's anger derives from the fact that Indrajit had shot at Vibhīṣaṇa, whom Lakṣmaṇa regards as no different than Rāma himself, while Indrajit is angry merely because Lakṣmaṇa has destroyed his arrow. (*rāmāviśeṣe vibhīṣaṇe bāṇaḥ pramukta iti lakṣmaṇasya roṣaḥ. lakṣmaṇas taṃ parihṛtavān iti rāvaṇe roṣaḥ*—so Ct.) On Cm quoting Ck, see note to the opening of *sarga* 96 and Introduction, p. 105.

20. "the conqueror of great Indra" *mahendrajit*: This is a variant of the warrior's standard epithet, Indrajit.

Following verse 20, D5–7,9–11,S insert a passage of eleven lines [1726*]: "And that [divinely charged weapon] struck down the extremely marvelous weapon of Varuṇa. Then immensely powerful Indrajit, victorious in battle, was enraged, and he nocked the blazing, divinely charged weapon of Agni, which seemed capable of destroying the world.[1][1–3]. But heroic Lakṣmaṇa warded it off with the divinely charged weapon of Sūrya. When Rāvaṇi saw that his divinely charged weapon had been warded off, he was beside himself with rage, and he took up the fearsome, divinely charged weapon of the *asuras* for the destruction of his enemy.[2][4–6] Then from his bow there flew forth blazing mallets and war hammers, as well as lances, bludgeons,[3] maces, swords, and battle-axes.[7–8] But when Lakṣmaṇa there in the battle saw that fearsome, divinely charged weapon of the *asuras*, which was all but impossible to ward off[4] by any creature and capable of destroying every foe,[5] that illustrious hero parried it with the divinely charged weapon of Maheśvara. [9–11]"

[1]"which seemed capable of destroying the world" *lokaṃ saṃkṣipann iva*: Literally, "as if collapsing *or* destroying the world."

[2]"he took up the fearsome, divinely charged weapon of the *asuras* for the destruction of his enemy" *āsuraṃ śatrunāśāya ghoram astraṃ samādade*: D9–11 and the texts and printed editions of Ct read instead *ādade niśitaṃ bāṇam āsuraṃ śatrudāraṇam*, "He took up the sharp, enemy-rending arrow of the *asuras*."

[3]"bludgeons" *bhuśuṇḍyaḥ*: Cg glosses, "types of cudgels (*musulaviśeṣāḥ*)." See notes to 6.48.32 and 6.60.11, 1336*, n. 1.

[4]"But ... that fearsome, divinely charged weapon of the *asuras*, which was all but impossible to ward off" *ghoram astram athāsuram / avāryam*: Literally, "now, the fear-

some *astra* of the *asuras*, not to be warded off." B2,D7,9–11,G1,2, and the texts and printed editions of Cr and Ct read *sudāruṇam*, "very fearsome," for *athāsuram*, "now, of the *asuras*."

[5]"capable of destroying every foe" *sarvaśatruvināśanam*: Literally, "destroying every foe." D9–11 and the texts and printed editions of Ct read instead *sarvaśastravidāraṇam*, "tearing apart *or* destroying all weapons."

21. "Then a tumultuous and wondrous battle took place between the two of them" *tayoḥ sutumulaṃ yuddhaṃ saṃbabhūvādbhutopamam*: Our understanding, shared by other translators consulted, is that the pronoun *tayoḥ*, "of those two," refers to Indrajit and Lakṣmaṇa. Cr, however, understands the pronoun here to refer to the two *astras* (that of the *asuras* and that of Maheśvara, mentioned in lines 9–11 of 1726*). For him, then, the battle between the two would be the fearsome collision of the divine weapons. D9,10, and the texts and printed editions of Ct read instead *tayoḥ samabhavad yuddham adbhutaṃ romaharṣaṇam*, "a wondrous and hair-raising battle arose between those two."

"the supernatural beings surrounded Lakṣmaṇa" *bhūtāni lakṣmaṇaṃ paryavārayan*: Literally, "the creatures surrounded Lakṣmaṇa." The creatures referred to here are doubtless the various types of celestial beings, such as gods, sages, *gandharvas*, *caraṇas*, etc., who stereotypically gather in the heavens to observe major battles. Cr understands that these beings huddle around Lakṣmaṇa not merely to watch but for their own protection (*svasvarakṣārthaṃ tatra tasthuḥ*). This idea is represented in the translations of Raghunathan (1982, vol. 3, p. 266) and Gita Press (1969, vol. 3, p. 1748).

22. "As that . . . battle . . . raged on" *yuddhe*: Literally, "in that battle." One needs to read the first half of the verse as a locative absolute (*sati saptamī*).

23. "with the great birds and the great serpents" *garuḍoragāḥ*: Literally, "with *garuḍa*[*s*] and great serpents." The compound is slightly ambiguous. Given the context in which groups of celestials are mentioned, one would expect the term *garuḍa* to refer to the class of supernatural or semidivine birds, who, along with their half siblings, the great serpents, are descended from the sage Kaśyapa by the sisters (and co-wives of Kaśyapa) Vinatā and Kadrū, respectively. See 4.57.27. See, too, *MBh* 1.19–20. On the other hand, the term *garuḍa*, per se, is rarely, if ever, used in this generic sense, although its synonym, *garutmant*, is so used. The term *garuḍa* chiefly refers to the specific bird-divinity of that name, the mount of Viṣṇu, who had rescued Rāma and Lakṣmaṇa from Indrajit's serpent-weapons at *sarga* 40. The commentators are silent and the translators are divided as to whether to take the term *garuḍa* as a singular or plural. Cf. 6.40.49; 6.90.20; and notes.

"watched over" *rarakṣuḥ*: Literally, "they watched over *or* protected." Cg, evidently thinking that the celestial beings do nothing to actually protect Lakṣmaṇa, sees them mainly as a kind of cheering section, adding the phrase "with words such as, 'Be victorious! Be victorious!' (*jaya jayetyādy uktibhiḥ*)." This interpretation apparently informs the translation of Raghunathan (1982, vol. 3, p. 266), who renders, "were present there, intent on the welfare of Lakshmana." See note to verse 21 above.

24–26. "another arrow, the greatest of all" *anyaṃ mārgaṇaśreṣṭham*: Literally, "another excellent arrow." The context makes it clear that this is not just another arrow that is doomed to failure. Roussel (1903, vol. 3, p. 300), evidently misreading the "*n*" of *anya* for a "*v*," mistakenly understands the *astra* in question to be called "the Avya."

This unfortunate error is replicated by Shastri (1959, vol. 3, p. 265), who translates, "the Avya Weapon." The critical apparatus records no such variant.

"lethal" *śarīrāntakaram*: Literally, "making an end of the body."

"impossible . . . to withstand" *durviṣaham*: D9–11 and the texts and printed editions of Ct read instead *durviṣamam*, "very dangerous *or* fearsome."

"worshiped by the hosts of gods" *devasaṃghaiḥ samarcitam*: Since, as Ck and Ct point out, the *astra* in question is that of Indra, the gods naturally revere it since it belongs to their ruler (*devarājīyatvād eva*—so Ct, Ck). Pagani (1999, p. 1117) understands that the gods worship the arrow because, as indicated in the following verse, it was the means of their victory over the *dānavas*. Cs argues that there is a suggested irony here in that Indrajit, the conqueror of Indra, is to be brought down by the weapon of his conquered foe. In this way, Cs notes, Lakṣmaṇa dispels the infamy that accrued to Indra from his humiliating defeat at the *rākṣasa*'s hands. (*aindram astram anenendrajito hananaṃ tatparājitendradevatākenāstreṇa kurvaṃl lakṣmaṇaḥ svapakṣasthendrāpaprathāṃ vārayāmāseti dhvanyate*.)

27. "This was the very arrow with which" *yena*: Literally, "by which."

"Śakra of the tawny steeds" *śakraḥ . . . harivāhanaḥ*: Literally, "Śakra of the tawny mounts *or* vehicles." This common epithet of Indra has been rendered variously by commentators and translators. We understand the term *hari-* in its sense of "tawny." This is also our understanding of Cg's gloss, "possessing horses of a tawny color (*haritavarṇāśvaḥ*)," and is reflected in those translations that use the word "bay" for *hari*. The terms *hari* and *harita* can also refer to the color green, and both Gita Press (1969, vol. 3, p. 1748) and Raghunathan (1982, vol. 3, p. 266) understand it in this sense. Cr, however, glosses, "mounted on horseback (*aśvārūḍhaḥ*)." This interpretation is followed by Dutt (1893, p. 1421), who translates, "riding the horse," identifying in a note the mount in question as the celestial steed Uccaiḥśravaḥ. Pagani (1999, p. 1117), alone among the translators consulted, understands the term *-vāhana* here in the sense of "driver *or* charioteer," rendering, "*le valeureux aurige*." Cf. 6.90.5–6; 6.95.15 and notes.

28. "foremost of men, placed" *naraśreṣṭho 'bhisaṃdadhe*: D10,11,G3, and the texts and printed editions of Ct omit *pādas* 28b–30a. GPP acknowledges these lines as belonging to the texts of Cg and Cr, and places them unnumbered in brackets between verses 6.90.38 and 39. Gita Press (6.90.68–69) omits the lines altogether. KK [6.91.68cd–70b] and VSP [6.91.690b–71b], reading with the critical edition, include the passage.

29. D10,11,G3 omit this verse. See note to verse 28 above.

"that foe-destroying, divinely charged weapon" *amitradalanam*: Literally, "that enemy-cleaving one." Like Gorresio (1858, vol. 10, p. 122), who reads the variant *amitradamanam*, "foe-taming" (Gorresio 6.70.35), we understand the adjective to refer to the *astra* of Indra described in the preceding verses. Raghunathan (1982, vol. 3, p. 266), the only other translator to read this passage, applies the adjective to Lakṣmaṇa's bow, translating, "the . . . bow, which broke the strength of the foe." We find this interpretation unpersuasive, however, since the verb *sam* $\sqrt{}$*dhā*, "to nock *or* place on the bowstring," in the preceding and following verses, clearly presupposes the arrow [in the accusative] as its object.

"unassailable" *durdharṣaḥ*: D6,T2,3,G2,M3, and the texts and printed editions of Cr and Cg read instead the accusative *durdharṣam*, which then makes the adjective modify Lakṣmaṇa's bow rather than Lakṣmaṇa himself.

"stretching it to its limit" *āyamya*: Literally, "having extended *or* drawn."

30. "Once he had placed the arrow on his splendid bow" *saṃdhāya dhanuṣi śreṣṭhe*: Literally, "having placed on his splendid bow." D10,11,G3, and the texts and printed editions of Ct omit this *pāda*. See note to verse 28 above.

"fortunate Lakṣmaṇa" *lakṣmīvāṃl lakṣmaṇaḥ*: See 6.67.37 and note.

"in order to accomplish his purpose" *arthasādhakam ātmanaḥ*: Literally, "effecting his own purpose." Ck and Ct understand that the words Lakṣmaṇa is about to utter in verse 31 are addressed to the presiding divinity of his divine weapon-spell (*vakṣyamāṇavacanam astrādhiṣṭhātrīṃ devatāṃ praty abravīt*). In this case the divinity is Indra.

31. Lakṣmaṇa's words constitute an example of the kind of "truth act" or "oath by truth" that is common in the literature. See Hopkins 1932. Cs observes that, by Lakṣmaṇa taking an oath based on Rāma's virtues, prior to releasing his divinely charged weapon, we are to understand that the weapon will be unstoppable.

32. "fortunate Lakṣmaṇa" *lakṣmaṇaḥ ... lakṣmaṇaḥ*: As Cv, Cm, and Cg point out, quoting the lexicon of *Amarakośa* (3.1.14), the word *lakṣmaṇaḥ* itself is a synonym of the adjective *lakṣmīvān*, "possessing good fortune." See note above to verse 30. They do so, of course, to absolve the poet of the charge of redundancy.

"charging it with the weapon-spell of Indra" *aindrāstreṇa samāyujya*: Literally, "having conjoined [it] with the *aindra astra*."

33. "It severed ... before falling to the ground" *pramathya ... papāta dharaṇītale*: Literally, "having severed, it fell to the surface of the earth." Ś,Ñ2,V2,B1,D1–4,7,8,10–13,G2,M3, and the texts and printed editions of the southern commentators and Gorresio read instead a causative construction *pātayāmāsa bhūtale*, "made it fall to the surface of the earth."

35. "instantly" *āśu*: V3,D9–11, and the texts and printed editions of Ct read instead *atha*, "now."

"sprawling ... with ... his ... bow" *vidhvastaḥ saśarāsanaḥ*: Cg understands *vidhvastaḥ* here in its sense of "slain (*hataḥ*)." He offers no explanation, however, as to how he understands the term *hataḥ*, "slain," in *pāda* a. Presumably, he would have to read it as "stricken." D9–11 and the texts and printed editions of Ct read instead *vipraviddhaśarāsanaḥ*, "with his bow broken *or* fallen away."

36. "once Indrajit was slain" *nihate tasmin*: Literally, "when he had been slain."

"Vṛtra" *vṛtra-*: See note to 6.75.31.

37. "there arose a mighty shout" *abhijajñe ca saṃnādaḥ*: Literally, "a great sound was produced." Cr understands the sound to be the cry, "Lakṣmaṇa has triumphed (*lakṣmaṇavijayo 'bhūt*)!" D9–11 and the texts and printed editions of Ct read *jajñe 'tha jaya-* for *abhijajñe ca*, yielding the sense "a cry of victory was produced."

"all beings" *bhūtānām*: Literally, "of beings." Ś,D5,7,8,12,T1,G2,3,M3, and the texts and printed editions of Cr, Cg, and Cm read instead *devānām*, "of the gods."

38. "Realizing that their champion had fallen" *patitaṃ samabhijñāya*: Literally, "realizing [him to be] fallen." A number of primarily northern manuscripts show variants that provide a referent: either the pronoun *tam*, "him," or the proper noun *rāvaṇim*, "the son of Rāvaṇa."

"fled in all directions" *diśo bheje*: Literally, "[the ... host] resorted to the directions."

"who now had a victorious air" *jitakāśibhiḥ*: Literally, "having the appearance of victory." See 6.42.9–10; 6.44.36; and note to 6.42.9–10.

39. "all... ran" *sarve...pradhāvitāḥ*: The vast majority of manuscripts, both northern and southern, collated for the critical edition, show a finite verb of motion in place of the critical edition's *sarve*, "all." Thus, Ñ,B1,3,4,D1,2,5,6,9–11,T2,3,G,M1,3,5, the texts and printed editions of all southern commentators, and the edition of Gorresio read *sasruḥ*, "they fled." V1,3 read *petuḥ*, "they took to flight," while Ś,D4,8,12 read *jagmuḥ*, "they went." It is not clear, given the textual evidence, why the critical editors have chosen their reading, which is apparently read by only five manuscripts (V2,B2,D3,T1,M2). The reading forces one to understand the participle *pradhāvitāḥ*, "ran *or* fled," as a finite verb.

"dazed" *naṣṭasaṃjñāḥ*: Literally, "their consciousness destroyed." D10,11, and the texts and printed editions of Ct read *bhraṣṭa-* for *naṣṭa-*, giving the compound the sense of "their heads spinning."

40. "by the hundreds in many directions" *bahudhā... śataśo diśaḥ*: Literally, "in many ways, by the hundreds, to the directions."

41. "threw themselves" *patitāḥ*: Literally, "fell."

"on the mountain" *parvatam*: The reference here is probably to Mount Trikūṭa, unless we are to take the singular in the generic sense of "the mountains," as some translators do. See notes to 6.2.10 and 6.30.18–20.

43. "Once Indrajit had fallen" *tasmin nipatite*: Literally, "when he had fallen."

"vanished in all directions, just as do the solar rays" *yathā... nāvatiṣṭhanti raśmayaḥ / ... gatā diśaḥ*: Literally, "they went to the directions just as the rays do not remain."

"has set behind the western mountain" *astaṃgate*: See notes to 6.39.15; 6.47.16; and 6.57.20.

44. "that warrior" *saḥ*: Literally, "he."

"of immense blazing energy" *mahātejāḥ*: Ñ,V,B,D1–4,7,9–11,13,G1,2, and the texts and printed editions of Ct and Cr read instead *mahābāhuḥ*, "great-armed."

"stripped of life, his limbs sprawling" *vyapāstagatajīvitaḥ*: Commentators and translators are uncertain as to how to interpret this opaque compound. One possible meaning, deriving from the normal sense of *vyapāsta* as "expelled, driven out," would be "whose life was driven out and so departed." But this seems redundant, and no commentator supports it. Cm and Cg, whom we more or less follow, take the compound as a *dvandva*, glossing the first adjective *vyapāsta-* as "whose limbs were tossed about (*vikṣiptāṅgaḥ*)." This interpretation is similar to that of Ck, who understands the reference to be specifically to Indrajit's decapitation, glossing, "whose head and trunk were powerfully driven asunder (*viśeṣaṇopāstaśirahkāyaḥ*)." Ct understands *vyapāsta* to mean "separated from his particular qualities and therefore stripped of life (*vyapāsto viṣeśadharmair ata eva gatajīvitaḥ*)." Cr offers two overlapping explanations of the compound, the first of which is similar to Ct's. He glosses, "whose life has departed because of the abandonment of qualities; moreover, *vyapāsta* means, 'fallen, and therefore stripped of life.' (*vyapāstena dharmatyāgena gataṃ jīvitaṃ yasya saḥ. kiñca vyapāstaḥ patitaḥ sa eva gatajīvito babhūva.*)" Cs, characteristically, offers a unique and somewhat forced explanation, taking *vyapāsta* to be an adjective referring to Lakṣmaṇa, with the sense that that hero was thwarted by Indrajit's previous invisibility. For him, then, the compound should be interpreted to mean "he whose life was made to depart by the thwarted one (*vyapāstena svena pūrvam alakṣyatayā nirastena lakṣmaṇena gataṃ jīvitaṃ yasya sa tathā*)."

45. "its enemy destroyed" *vinaṣṭāriḥ*: Ñ,V1,2,B1,2,4,D2–4,G1,2,M3, and the texts and printed editions of Cm and Cg read instead *naṣṭāriṣṭaḥ*, "its calamities destroyed."

"its oppression nearly at an end" *praśāntapīḍābahulaḥ*: We follow Cm, Cg, Ck, and Ct in reading the compound as a *paranipāta*, with the sense "which has most of its oppressions pacified (*praśāntabahulapīḍaḥ*)."

"filled with joy" *praharṣavān*: B2,M1–3, and the texts and printed editions of Cg and Cm read instead *pratāpavān*, which, as Cg suggests, must be interpreted here to mean "filled with sunlight." Cg remarks that, prior to the death of Indrajit, the sun shone weakly out of fear (*pratāpavān sūryaprakāśavān pūrvaṃ bhayena mandasūryatvāt*). Cf. 1.14.10 and note to 6.99.26, 3127* and n.1, where the sun and other natural phenomena are represented as diminished by fear of Rāvaṇa.

46. "along with ... the bulls among the gods" *saha surarṣabhaiḥ*: D9–11 and the texts and printed editions of Ct read *maharṣibhiḥ*, "with the great seers," for *surarṣabhaiḥ*.

Following verse 46, D5–7,9–11,S insert a passage of four lines [1737*]: "And in the heavens as well was heard the beating of the war drums of the gods along with the sound of dancing *apsarases* and the great *gandharvas*.[1] [1–2] When that *rākṣasa* of cruel deeds had been slain, the heavenly beings uttered words of praise and rained down[2] showers of blossoms. It was a wonder to behold.[3] [3–4]"

[1]"along with the sound of the dancing *apsarases* and of the great *gandharvas*" *nṛtyadbhir apsarobhiś ca gandharvaiś ca mahātmabhiḥ*: Literally, "along with dancing *apsarases* and the great *gandharvas*." The line is elliptical and syntactically awkward. We follow the suggestion of Cv, Cm, and Cg, who add the phrase "the sounds produced by the dancing of the *apsarases* and the singing of the *gandharvas* was heard (*apsarobhir gandharvaiś ca kṛtanartanagānajanyasvanaḥ śuśruva ity arthaḥ*)." This interpretation is also represented in the translation of Raghunathan (1982, vol. 3, p. 267). Note that, despite the renditions of some translators, we should understand that it is the *apsarases* who are dancing while it is implied that the *gandharvas* are engaged in their normal activity, viz., singing. This is so despite the masculine gender of the participle *nṛtyadbhiḥ*, which Cg considers irregular here for the feminine.

[2]"heavenly beings uttered words of praise and rained down" *vavarṣuḥ ... praśaśaṃsuḥ*: Literally, "they rained down and praised." We follow Cv, Cm, and Cg, who understand the gods to be the subject of both verbs. D7,10,11,G1,2,M5, and the texts and printed editions of Ct and Cr read *praśaśāma*, "he calmed *or* suppressed," for *praśaśaṃsuḥ*. Cr and Ct understand this weak reading to be an elliptical reference to the settling of the dust, which presumably had been raised by the battle (*praśaśāma raja iti śeṣaḥ*—so Ct).

[3]"It was a wonder to behold." *tad adbhutam abhūt tadā*: Literally, "that was a wonder."

47. "the heavens" *nabhaḥ*: D5,6,T2,3,G3,M, and the texts and printed editions of Cg and Cm read instead *diśaḥ*, "the directions, quarters."

"the *daityas* and *dānavas*" *daityadānavāḥ*: These two terms, often used as synonyms for the *asuras*, technically refer, respectively, to the demonic descendants of Diti and Danu. Ś,Ñ,V,B,D1–4,7,8,10–12,G2, and the texts and printed editions of Ct, Ck, and Cr read instead *devadānavāḥ*, "the gods and the *dānavas*," which is the stereotypical reading one would expect. Ck and Ct feel it is necessary to explain why the *dānavas*, who are the ancient and implacable foes of the gods, are rejoicing at Indrajit's fall. He notes that he was their enemy as well (*dānavānām api tacchatrutvāt teṣām api harṣaḥ*).

48. "all" *sarve*: Ñ2,V1,2,B2–4,D2,7,9–11,13,G1,2, and the texts and printed editions of Cr, Ck, and Ct read instead *tuṣṭāḥ*, "gratified, pleased."

"their impurities removed" *śāntakaluṣāḥ*: This could also mean "their sins allayed." Commentators are strangely silent as to what is being referred to here. Translators generally understand *kaluṣa*, literally, "dirt, taint," to refer to "sin," or, more generally and more commonly, "troubles, disquiet, etc." Our understanding is that the impurities or sins of the brahmans are those produced by their inability to complete their obligatory vedic rites in the face of the depredations of Indrajit and his followers.

49. "that warrior of unrivaled strength" *tam apratibalam*: Literally, "of him, whose strength was unrivaled."

51. "Their goal obtained" *labdhalakṣāḥ*: Literally, "those by whom a goal is obtained." Ct, Ck, and Cr understand, "having obtained an occasion for joy (*prāptaharṣāvasarāḥ*—Ct, Ck). All three commentators offer an alternative reading based on the interchangeability of the syllables *ra* and *la*. They suggest that if one replaces the *la* of *-lakṣāḥ* with a *ra*, we get the compound *labdharakṣāḥ* with the sense "having obtained protection (*labdharakṣaṇāḥ*)." See 6.56.11 and note.

"that scion of the Raghus" *raghusutam*: Literally, "Raghu's son." Ck, Ct, and Cr indicate that we are to understand, "born in the Raghu dynasty (*raghuvaṃśajam*—so Ct)."

"roaring" *kṣveḍantaḥ*: See 5.55.29 and 5.60.12, but cf. 5.3.25 and note. See, too, 6.48.31; 6.77.16; and notes.

"howling" *nadantaḥ*: D9–11 and the texts and printed editions of Ct read instead *plavantaḥ*, "leaping about."

52. "Beating their tails on the ground" *lāṅgūlāni pravidhyantaḥ*: Literally, "beating *or* lashing their tails." See 5.40.28; 5.55.30; and notes. See, too, 6.77.15 and note.

53. "great and small" *uccāvacaguṇāḥ*: Literally, "of diverse *or* high and low qualities." We agree with Cr, the only commentator to remark on this verse, that this adjective should modify *kapayaḥ* (v.l. *harayaḥ*), "monkeys." The idea seems to be that the monkey troops, regardless of status or station, mingle freely with one another in their exaltation at the destruction of Indrajit. This interpretation is also found in the translations of Gita Press (1969, vol. 3, p. 1751) and Raghunathan (1982, vol. 3, p. 268). Pagani (1999, p. 1118), too, appears to construe the adjective with the monkeys but seems to misread it (as *uccaiḥ*?) to mean "*à voix haute*." Other translators consulted take the term to modify *kathāḥ*, "stories, conversation," in its sense of "varied *or* diverse."

"as they chattered about Rāghava's exploits" *cakruḥ . . . rāghavāśrayajāḥ kathāḥ*: The precise meaning of the compound is uncertain because of the ambiguity of its middle term *āśraya*. The commentators are silent, while most of the translators consulted take the term in its common meanings of "reliance, connection, etc.," so that for them the compound means "arising from reliance on Rāghava." Since to us the term *āśraya* in this sense seems somewhat redundant with the term *-jāḥ*, "produced from," and, since the context is that of praise for Lakṣmaṇa's exploit, we believe that the term *āśraya* should be taken here in its less common sense of "an appropriate act *or* one consistent with character" (see Apte, s.v. meaning 19). This interpretation is apparently shared by Raghunathan (1982, vol. 3, p. 268), who renders, "stories that testified to the qualities of the scion of the Raghus." D9–11 and the texts and printed editions of Ct read instead *rāghavāśrayasatkathāḥ*, "true *or* excellent stories of the exploits of

Rāghava." Translations that follow the text of Ct render this reading variously. Translators also differ somewhat as to whether we should understand the patronymic *rāghava* here to refer to Lakṣmaṇa or Rāma. In our opinion, the context favors the former.

54. "his dear friends . . . Lakṣmaṇa's" *priyasuhṛdaḥ . . . lakṣmaṇasya*: The term *priyasuhṛdaḥ* is ambiguous as it can be read, as we have done, following Ck, as a nominative plural referring to Lakṣmaṇa's allies, Sugrīva, Hanumān, Vibhīṣaṇa, etc.; as an adjective modifying *devāḥ*, "gods," in *pāda* d, as some translators have done; or, following Cg, as a genitive singular agreeing with *lakṣmaṇasya* in the sense of "who is a dear friend" or "who delights his friends." Cg understands the term to mean "dear friend of all (*sarvapriyasuhṛdaḥ*)," basing this interpretation on his alternative reading of the term *asukaram* (see below).

"all-but-impossible" *asukaram*: Literally, "not easy to accomplish." Cr glosses, "impossible for others to accomplish (*anyaiḥ kartum aśakyam*)." Cg, who glosses, "difficult *or* impossible to accomplish (*duṣkaram*)," offers an alternative explanation in which he breaks up the compound not as *a + sukaram* but as *asu + karam*," in the sense of "maintaining *or* saving the lives of all (*sarveṣāṃ prāṇapratiṣṭhāpakam*)." It is on the basis of this alternative, it seems, that Cg understands the term *priyasuhṛdaḥ* as discussed above.

"they were delighted . . . the gods" *hṛṣṭāḥ . . . devāḥ*: Cg understands *hṛṣṭāḥ*, "delighted," to be an optional variant of *hṛṣitāḥ*, which can have the sense of *vismitāḥ*, "astonished *or* amazed." Since Cg understands that the word *devāḥ*, "gods," is the subject of both halves of the verse, he devises a small sequence of their responses to the news of Indrajit's death. According to him, at first the gods are pleased when they learn of the slaying of Indrajit from the mouths of the celestial bards, etc., but then, reflecting upon the virtual impossibility of such a feat, they come to believe that the report is false. When, however, they proceed to the battlefield and witness Lakṣmaṇa's feat for themselves, they become filled with astonishment. (*vismitapratighātayoś ceti vaktavyam iti hṛṣeḥ pākṣika iḍabhāvaḥ. devāś cāraṇādimukhena prathamam indrajiddhananaṃ śrutvā saṃtuṣṭāḥ santaḥ paścāt tasyātyantāśakyatvād atathyaṃ manvānā yuddhabhūmim āgatya tatpratyakṣīkṛtya vismitā āsann iti bhāvaḥ.*)

The meter is *puṣpitāgrā*.

Cv and Cm quote 1754* line 6 (= GPP 6.91.16ab; VSP 6.92.15cd; KK 6.92.15cd) to support their understanding that the battle with Indrajit has occupied three lunar days, namely, the eleventh through the thirteenth day [presumably of the dark half of Phālguna/Caitra]. (*ekādaśyāṃ dvādaśyāṃ trayodaśyāṃ cendrajidyuddham. ahorātrais tribhir vīraḥ kathañcid vinipātita ity uttaratrābhidhānāt*—Cm.) See note to 6.79.7. See, too, note to 6.4.4.

Sarga 79

1. "Lakṣmaṇa of auspicious marks" *lakṣmaṇaḥ śubhalakṣaṇaḥ*: See 6.14.3; 6.67.37; 6.71.20; 6.73.5; 6.75.16; 6.89.4; and notes. See also Goldman 1984, p. 105. Cf. 6.31.1 and note.

"his body drenched with blood" *rudhiraklinnagātraḥ*: Despite Lakṣmaṇa having been wounded several times during his battle with Indrajit (see 6.78), Cr, in keeping with his concern expressed earlier (6.35.9 and note) that Rāma and Lakṣmaṇa as divinities cannot really bleed, argues here that the blood covering Lakṣmaṇa is Indrajit's (*rudhireṇa nihatendrajiccharīrotthitaraktena klinnaṃ gātraṃ yasya saḥ*).

"conqueror of Śakra" *śakrajetāram*: This is a synonym for the epithet "Indrajit." Ś1,Ñ2,V,B2–4,D1,10,11, and the texts and printed editions of Ct read instead *śatrujetāram*, "conqueror of his enemies."

2–3. "taking" *saṃnivartya*: Literally, "having caused [them] to return." D7,9–11,M1,2,5, and the texts and printed editions of Ct and Ck read instead *saṃnipatya*, "having met together *or* assembled." M3 and the texts and printed editions of Cg read instead *saṃnihatya*, which Cg glosses as "having assembled *or* joined up with (*saṃghībhūya*)."

"leaning on" *avaṣṭabhya*: Literally, "having leaned upon." Ck and Ct believe that Lakṣmaṇa requires support because of the pain of his battle wounds (*yuddhavraṇajapīḍāvaśāt*). Cg and Cm ascribe his weakness simply to battle fatigue (*yuddhapāravaśyāt*).

4. "Approaching" *abhikramya*: Literally, "having approached." Ct glosses, "reverentially circling (*pradakṣaṇīkṛtya*)," and this interpretation has been followed by several of the translators.

"Viṣṇu, Indra's younger brother" *indrānujaḥ*: Literally, "the younger brother of Indra." The reference is to Viṣṇu having taken birth in the form of the *vāmanāvatāra* as the child of Aditi and the sage Kaśyapa, who are generally regarded as the parents of the vedic gods, including Indra. This accounts for Viṣṇu's epithet, Upendra "junior Indra." See 6.40.43; 6.49.1–2; 6.59.7; and notes. The simile is slightly awkward, since Viṣṇu, despite his being technically junior to Indra, is, by the period of the epics, regarded as vastly his superior. The figure thus appears to invert the status of Rāma and Lakṣmaṇa. Ñ,V1,3,B2–4,D5–7,9–11,T1,G,M, and the texts and printed editions of Crā, Cm, and Cg read instead [*indrasyeva*] *bṛhaspatiḥ*, which would yield the meaning "like Bṛhaspati [in the presence] of Indra." This figure perhaps is contextually more suitable, as Bṛhaspati, the legendary *purohita* of the gods, is Indra's dependent, although he may still have superior ritual status in that he is a brahman. Cm, Crā, and Cg indicate that the illustration is intended merely to show relative status in terms of dependency (*pāratantryamātre sāmyam*—so Cg; *pradhānopasarjanabhāvenāvasthānamātre dṛṣṭāntaḥ*—so Cm). Ct is aware of the variant and explains it similarly.

Following 4cd, D5–7,9–11,13,T1,G,M, and the texts and printed editions of the southern commentators insert a passage of one line [1744*]: "Moaning softly,[1] he approached and [reported] to great Rāghava."

[1]"Moaning softly" *niṣṭanann iva*: Commentators and translators differ significantly as to the meaning of the participle, the particle *iva*, and even the subject of the phrase. We understand the verb *ni* $\sqrt{}$*stan*, in the sense of "to groan, moan, cry" as it is more or less used in the *Uttarakāṇḍa* (7.404*, line 2 = GPP 7.21.12) and the particle *iva* in its common sense of "slightly, softly." We further understand that the subject here is Lakṣmaṇa, who, in his weakened and wounded condition, is emitting sounds of distress. Cg glosses the participle as "speaking indistinctly (*avyaktākṣaraṃ vadan*)" and understands it to be either merely ornamental (*vākyālaṃkāre*) or to indicate the falsehood of the impression created by Lakṣmaṇa's gestures indicating fatigue [i.e.,

that Indrajit had not been defeated] (*āyāsasyābhinayamātreṇālīkatvadyotanāya vā*). Cr takes the phrase to mean that Lakṣmaṇa, by his pleased facial expressions, is, as it were, already communicating the destruction of Indrajit (*prasādaviśiṣṭamukhadarśanenendrajidvadhaṃ kathayann iva*). Ck and Ct believe that the subject is not Lakṣmaṇa but rather Vibhīṣaṇa, who is referred to in the previous verse, and that the phrase means that the latter is informing Rāma of the death of Indrajit through his own joyful arrival (*vibhīṣaṇaḥ saṃtuṣṭāgamanenaivendrajidvadhaṃ niṣṭanan bodhayann iva*). Translators either follow one these commentators or take the verb *ni* $\sqrt{}$*stan* in its alternative sense of "to cry, to resound." See note to 6.82.37, where we have taken the derivative form *niṣṭānakaḥ* in the sense of "lamentation." See note to 6.89.6.

5. "Vibhīṣaṇa . . . told" *nyavedayata . . . vibhīṣaṇaḥ*: Several of the commentators show some concern over what appears to be a repetition of Lakṣmaṇa's report by Vibhīṣaṇa. They explain this in various ways. Ct and Ck note that Vibhīṣaṇa speaks in anticipation of Rāma's question as to who actually killed Indrajit (*tataḥ kiṃkartṛko vadha ity ākāṅkṣāyām āha*—so Ct). Cg and Cm understand that Lakṣmaṇa is too modest to trumpet his own feats in the presence of his older brother and wants to share the credit for his deed with the others so that Vibhīṣaṇa must relate the story in full (*rāmasannidhau saṃkocavatā lakṣmaṇenāviśeṣeṇendrajidvadhakathanād vibhīṣaṇaḥ spaṣṭatayāha*—so Cg). Cg also proposes an alternative: that, in his excessive excitement, Vibhīṣaṇa repeats the story, even though Lakṣmaṇa has already provided the details (*yadvā lakṣmaṇena sūcanayoktāv api harṣaprakarṣeṇa vibhīṣaṇaḥ punar āha*).

Following verse 5, Ñ,V1,3,B2–4,D5–7,9–11,T1,G,M, and the texts and printed editions of the southern commentators insert a passage of six lines [1747*]: "Now, when the immensely powerful Rāma heard that Lakṣmaṇa had slain Indrajit, he experienced unparalleled delight, and he said these words[1][1–2]: 'Well done, Lakṣmaṇa! I am pleased. You have accomplished an all-but-impossible feat.[2] Know that by the destruction of Rāvaṇi victory is ours![3]'[3–4] Then that mighty hero kissed Lakṣmaṇa, increaser of good fortune,[4] on his head and, in his affection, forcibly took his bashful brother on his lap.[5–6]"

[1]"Rāma . . . these words" *rāmo vākyam*: D9–11,G1, and the texts and printed editions of Ct read instead *vākyaṃ cedam*, "these words."

[2]"accomplished an all-but-impossible feat" *karma cāsukaraṃ kṛtam*: M3 and the texts and printed editions of Cg read instead *karmaṇā sukṛtaṃ kṛtam*, "by [your] action [you have] accomplished a needful action."

[3]"victory is ours" *jitam*: Literally, "[it is] conquered." Ck and Ct think that we should add the words "now by us (*idānīm evāsmābhir iti śeṣaḥ*)." Cr supplies a modificand, "the whole race of *rākṣasas* (*rākṣasajātam iti śeṣaḥ*)."

[4]"increaser of good fortune" *lakṣmivardhanam*: This is yet another of Vālmīki's etymological epithets. See note to verse 1 above. D6,7,9–11, and the texts and printed editions of Cr and Ct read instead *kīrtivardhanam*, "increaser of fame *or* glory." Compare 6.89.9 and note.

6. "The bull among men, Rāma" *puruṣarṣabhaḥ*: Literally, "the bull among men." The transition between verses 5 and 6 is rather abrupt in the critical edition in the

absence of one of the two insert passages 1746* (mainly northern manuscripts) or 1747* (mixed, but largely southern manuscripts). In both of these insert passages, the subject is Rāma rather than Vibhīṣaṇa.

"tightly" *avapīḍitam*: As several of the commentators indicate, the term is ambiguous. It can be read either as we have done, as an adverb modifying the gerund *pariṣvajya*, "having embraced," or as an adjective modifying *tam . . . lakṣmaṇam*, "him, Lakṣmaṇa," in which case it must be understood in the sense of "wounded, pained, oppressed."

"swiftly" *tvaran*: Cg, the only commentator to remark on this participle, believes that Rāma hastens to caress or stroke his brother in order to alleviate the pain of his wounds (*tvarā ca prahāravyathāpanayanāyeti bhāvaḥ*).

Following 6ab, Ñ,V,B2–4,D5–7,9–11,T1,G,M, the texts and printed editions of the southern commentators, and the printed edition of Gorresio (first line only) insert a passage of three lines [1749*]: "And Rāma, distressed with grief,[1] then sighed[2] and gazed tenderly again and again at his brother Lakṣmaṇa, who was pierced with darts, wounded, and breathing hard.[3]"

[1]"distressed with grief" *duḥkhasaṃtaptaḥ*: D7,9–11, and the texts and printed editions of Ct and Cr read instead the accusative *duḥkhasaṃtaptam*, in which case the adjective would modify Lakṣmaṇa and have a sense more like "distressed with pain."

[2]"then sighed" *niśvasitas tadā*: D7,9–11, and the texts and printed editions of Ct and Cr read instead *tadā niḥ[ni—D7,9–11]śvāsapīḍitam*, "then oppressed by sighs," which then modifies Lakṣmaṇa. G2,M3,5, and the texts and printed editions of Cg read instead *tadā niśvasito bhṛśam*, "then sighing deeply."

[3]"was pierced with darts, wounded, and breathing hard" *śalyasampīḍitaṃ śastaṃ niśvasantam*: Continuing his argument from verse 1 above that Lakṣmaṇa has not, in fact, been wounded, Cr interprets all these terms causatively to suggest that Lakṣmaṇa has inflicted these injuries upon Indrajit.

7. "I have been freed from my enemy" *niramitraḥ kṛto 'smi*: Literally, "I have been made one without an enemy." Ct and Ck raise the question of how Rāma can be considered to be freed from his enemies when Rāvaṇa is still alive. They understand that the explanation is implicit in Rāma's immediately following statement that Rāvaṇa will surely now come out to fight with his remaining forces [since Rāma anticipates no difficulty in killing him]. (*kathaṃ rāvaṇe jīvati niramitratvaṃ tatrāha niryāsyatīti. avaśyaṃ niryāsyati*—so Ct, Ck.)

Following 7ab, Ñ,V1,2 (continues),3,B2–4,D5–7,9–11,T1,G,M, the texts and printed editions of the southern commentators, and the printed edition of Gorresio insert a passage of six lines [1754*]: "Now that his son is dead, I reckon that Rāvaṇa is as good as slain in battle. Now that my evil-minded foe has been slain, I am victorious.[1–2] Fortunately, hero, you have cut off cruel Rāvaṇa's right arm in battle. For Indrajit was his main support.[3–4] Vibhīṣaṇa and Hanumān, as well, performed a great deed in battle. And thus was that mighty warrior struck down with great difficulty after three days and nights.[1][5–6]"

[1]"after three days and nights" *ahorātrais tribhiḥ*: Cg and Cm reiterate the idea broached by Cv and Cm at the end of the preceding *sarga* that the duel between

Lakṣmaṇa and Indrajit lasted from the eleventh to the thirteenth [of the dark half of Phālguna/Caitra]. Ct's reckoning is more specific. He goes so far as to specify the exact duration of the battle, claiming that it began in the fourth *prahara* (= late afternoon, between 3 and 6 PM) on the tenth day [of Āśvina] and ended at around the same time on the thirteenth (*daśamyāṃ caturthaprahara ārambhāt trayodaśyāṃ caturthaprahare vadhād iti bhāvaḥ*). See note to 6.4.4.

Following 7cd, D10,11, and the texts and printed editions of Ct insert a passage of one line, which repeats, in reverse order, *pādas* d and e of verse 7 [1755*]: "Surely Rāvaṇa himself will now come forth with a vast array of troops."

8. "surrounded by my own vast army" *balenāvṛtya mahatā*: Literally, "having surrounded with a vast army." The phrase is elliptical and ambiguous. Most translators, like us, understand that Rāma is referring to his own monkey army. Only Raghunathan (1982, vol. 3, p, 269) takes the reference to be to Rāvaṇa's army, with which the *rākṣasa* lord would be surrounded. Among the commentators consulted, only Ct glosses the phrase, taking *bala* in one of its other meanings, "strength," and glosses the gerund *āvṛtya*, "having surrounded," as "having attacked (*ākramya*)." He thus understands the gist of the verse to be "having attacked with my great innate strength, I shall kill him as he marches forth (*niryāntaṃ ca taṃ mahatā balena sahajenāvṛtyākramya nihaniṣyāmi*)."

9. "my guardian" *nāthena*: The most common meanings of this term are "lord, master, husband," and, indeed, Dutt (1893, p. 1425) translates accordingly. But this, of course, is entirely inappropriate contextually. We believe that the term must be taken in its less common but well-attested sense of "guardian, protector" in this context. In this we are in agreement with Gita Press (1969, vol. 3, p. 1753) and Raghunathan (1982, vol. 3, p. 269). Roussel (1903, vol. 3, p. 304), followed by Shastri (1959, vol. 3, p. 267), renders, "*Sous ta direction.*" Pagani (1999, p. 1120) idiosyncratically renders, "*grâce á ton exploit.*" Gorresio (1858, vol. 10, p. 125) offers, "*Coll' ausilio di te.*" Commentators, too, struggle with the seemingly inappropriate term. Ck and Ct take it as a term of endearment (*upalālanārthaṃ nāthaśabdaprayogaḥ*), although they offer no lexical support for this. Cg, deriving the noun from its underlying root $\sqrt{}$*nāth*, in its sense, "to beg," glosses, "begging, pleading (*yācamānena*)," although it is not clear why this interpretation would be appropriate here.

"both Sītā and the earth itself have been placed within my grasp" *sītā ca pṛthivī ca me / na duṣprāpā*: Literally, "Sītā and the earth are not difficult to obtain for me." Pagani (1999, pp. 1622–23), noting the close mythological and etymological associations between Sītā ["furrow"] and the earth, offers a lengthy and highly speculative note on the connections between Sītā and the kingdom as amorous and political objects of contestation between Rāma and Rāvaṇa.

11. "Wise" *mahāprājñaḥ*: Ś,D2,3,5,8,11,12,G2,3,M3, the texts and printed editions of Ct, and the editions of Gorresio (6.71.20) and Gita Press (6.91.21) read instead the vocative, *mahāprājña*, which then must refer to Suṣeṇa.

"Saumitri, so loving of his friends" *saumitrir mitravatsalaḥ*: For other etymological epithets of this type, see note to 6.14.3 and R. Goldman 1984, pp.105–6. See, too, note to verse 1 above.

Ck, Ct, and Cr (on the following verse) note that we are to understand that Suṣeṇa has retained some of the healing herbs from the mountain of medicinal plants that

Hanumān had brought earlier (6.61) (*auṣadhiparvatānayanottaram oṣadhyaḥ suṣeṇena saṃgṛhya sthāpitā ity anena jñāyate*).

"is still riddled with darts" *saśalyaḥ*: Literally, "one with darts." D10,11,T2,3,G1, and the texts and printed editions of Ct read instead *viśalyaḥ*, "free from darts." This reading must then be read in apposition with the adjective *susvasthaḥ*, "restored to health," in *pāda* c.

"and Vibhīṣaṇa" *savibhīṣaṇaḥ*: Literally, "along with Vibhīṣaṇa." D10,11, and the texts and printed editions of Ct instead repeat the epithet *mitravatsalaḥ*, "so loving of his friends," from *pāda* b, which echoes the name Sumitra. See note to verse 1 above.

13. "held... to Lakṣmaṇa's nose" *lakṣmaṇāya dadau nastaḥ*: Literally, "he gave to Lakṣmaṇa nasally." As we see from 6.61.67 above, as well as from the following verse, the mere fragrance of these powerful medicinal herbs effects the cure. Thus, we believe that Raghunathan (1982, vol. 3, p. 269), who renders, "gave... a powder to inhale," is perhaps off the mark. See, too, 6.89.23 and note.

14. "the darts fell away from him" *saḥ... viśalyaḥ samapadyata*: Literally, "he became free from darts."

"his wounds healed over" *saṃrūḍhavraṇaḥ*: Literally, "one whose wounds were healed over." D10,11, and the texts and printed editions of Ct read instead *saṃruddhaprāṇaḥ*, literally, "one whose breaths are obstructed." This term seems hardly to fit the context. Indeed, all translations consulted, with the sole exception of Dutt (1893, p. 1425), who renders, "his outgoing vitality was shut up," and Shastri (1959, vol. 3, p. 268), who appears to ignore the term entirely, render the reading found in the critical edition.

15. "Suṣeṇa" *saḥ*: Literally, "he."

16. "his fever had subsided" *vigatajvaraḥ*: The compound can also mean "free from care *or* anxiety."

"he was free of pain" *gatavyathaḥ*: Ñ,V1,3,B2,3,D6,7,9–11,G2, the texts and printed editions of Ct and Cr, and the printed edition of Gorresio read instead *gataklamaḥ*, "free from fatigue *or* exhaustion."

17. "in good spirits" *mudā*: We follow Cg in taking this as an elliptical reference to Lakṣmaṇa's return to good spirits mentioned in the previous verse. Cg glosses, "we must supply the word[s] 'filled with,' so that the sense is 'Saumitri, who was filled with good spirits' (*mudā yuktam iti śeṣaḥ. mudā yuktaṃ saumitrim...*)." Some translators take the term to refer to Rāma and his allies so that their understanding of the verse is that these figures "rejoiced with joy *or* rejoiced to a great degree."

"Sugrīva, the lord of the leaping monkeys" *plavagādhipaḥ*: Literally, "the lord of the leaping monkeys."

"Jāmbavān" *jāmbavān*: B1,D2,6,7,9–11,13,T1, and the texts and printed editions of Ct and Cr read *vīryavān*, "mighty," in place of the proper noun.

The meter is *vaṃśasthavila*.

18. "while the foremost of the troop leaders were delighted" *hṛṣṭā babhūvuḥ... yūthapendrāḥ*: D7,9–11, and the texts and printed editions of Ct and Cr read instead the singular *babhūva hṛṣṭaḥ... vānarendraḥ*, "while the lord of the monkeys [Sugrīva] was delighted."

The meter is *upajāti* with a hypermetric *pāda* d.

Sarga 80

1. "the ministers of ten-necked Paulastya... to him" *paulastyasacivāḥ... daśagrīvāya*: Literally, "the ministers of Paulastya... [reported] to the ten-necked one."

"confirmed the news for themselves" *abhijñāya*: Literally, "having determined." The meaning and even the form of this word are unclear and a matter of dispute among commentators. They read the word either as a gerund, as we do, or as a dative, in agreement with *daśagrīvāya*, in the sense of "to the ten-necked one who knew." Cm and Cg share the reading of the critical edition. The situation is complicated by the fact that there is a variant, *avajñāya*, which is read only by D10,11, and the texts and printed editions of Ck and Ct but which is acknowledged by a number of commentators. Cm takes the term *abhijñāya* as a gerund, glossing, "having seen (*dṛṣṭvā*)." Ct quotes Cm and adds a further explanation not found in available texts of Cm. He says, "having first heard, they then proceeded to the battlefield, and only after directly observing [that Indrajit had been slain] did they report [to Rāvaṇa] (*pūrvaṃ śrutvā paścād yuddhabhūmiṃ gatvā pratyakṣīkṛtyācacakṣur ity artham āha*)." In a similar vein, Cg glosses, "having known for themselves, that is, having seen with full knowledge (*svayam abhijñāya sābhijñānaṃ dṛṣṭvā*)." This is the interpretation we have followed, as have Gita Press (1969, vol. 3, p. 1756) and Raghunathan (1982, vol. 3, p. 270). Cg provides an alternative explanation for this reading, taking the term as a dative describing Rāvaṇa. Cg then goes on to say, " 'knowing' means that he would have already realized that Indrajit would certainly be slain since his sacrifice had been disrupted. (*athavābhijñāyeti caturthī. pūrvam eva yajñavighnena niścitatadvadhāyety arthaḥ.*)" Ct, Ck, and Cs, who accept the reading *avajñāya*, understand it as a dative, meaning "not knowing" and modifying Rāvaṇa, who does not yet know of his son's death. (*avajñāya avakṣiptā jñā jñānaṃ yasya tasmai. putravadhavṛttāntajñānarahitāyety arthaḥ*—so Ck, Ct.) Translations that follow the text of Ct render this variant. Cr similarly takes the term as a dative but derives it from *ava* $\sqrt{}$*jñā*, in the sense of "to disrespect *or* hold in contempt," arguing that it refers to Rāvaṇa's practice of holding all virtuous people in contempt (*avajñāya sarvasatpuruṣānādarakartre daśagrīvāya*). Cg acknowledges the variant reading and takes it either as a dative in the sense of his second interpretation, that is, "already knowing," or as a gerund meaning "having obtained a sight up to [but not including] direct perception (*sākṣātkāraparyantadarśanaṃ prāpya*)." Ck, in an acerbic comment, criticizes the position held by "Yadvābhaṭṭa" (Cg or Cm?), who reads *avajñāya* as a gerund in the sense of "having seen (*abhijñāya*)" and prattles on incoherently (*atra yadvābhaṭṭas tu avajñāyābhijñāya dṛṣṭveti lyabantam āśrityāsaṅgatam alapat*). See Lefeber 1994, p. 24 and n. 77. See, too, notes to 4.2.56 and 4.33.15. Cf. notes to 5.1.77; 6.12.10; and 6.52.10. See, too, Introduction, pp. 99–107.

"in great distress" *savyathāḥ*: D9–11 and the texts and printed editions of Ct read instead *satvarāḥ*, "in haste."

2. "Great and glorious king!" *mahārāja... mahādyute*: Literally, "O great king! O one of great luster!" B3,D5,9–11,T1,M3, and the texts and printed editions of the southern commentators read the nominative *mahādyutiḥ*, "of great luster," for the vocative *mahādyute*, "O one of great luster!" In this case, the epithet must apply to Indrajit rather than to Rāvaṇa.

"right before our eyes" *miṣatāṃ naḥ*: Literally, "despite the fact that we were watching." As several commentators point out, this phrase should be read as a genitive of disrespect (*anādare ṣaṣṭhī*), and our translation attempts to convey this sense. Ct, aware that the ministers were not actually present at the death of Indrajit, understands the expression to be an example of the maxim of "the people with umbrellas" [i.e., that the actions of a few may be generalized to an entire group]. In other words, the ministers are referring to what the *rākṣasa* combatants saw (*yoddhṛrākṣasair darśanāc chatrinyāyena bodhyam*).

3. "another heroic warrior, that heroic warrior... heroic" *śūraḥ śūreṇa... śūraḥ*: Literally, "the hero, with a hero, the hero." Commentators propose various strategies to minimize the effect of the repetition of the term *śūraḥ*, "hero," to describe Indrajit. Cr proposes reading *pādas* ab as part of the syntax of verse 2 above, while Cg notes that we can account for the repetition by the fact that the two halves of the verse contain separate verbs (*kriyābhedāt*).

"the conqueror of the lord of the all-wise gods" *vibudhendrajit*: Literally, "the conqueror of the lord of the wise ones." Commentators disagree as to how to analyze what appears to be a kenning for Indra, i.e., *vibudhendra*. Our translation follows the interpretation of Cg, who glosses, "conqueror of the lord of the gods (*devendrajit*)." Ct and Ck understand the compound *vibudhendra* to be a *dvandva* with the sense of "the gods and Indra (*vibudhān devān indraṃ ca*)." Cs offers two alternative explanations. In the first, he breaks the compound up into a vocative, *vibudha*, "O wise one," referring to Rāvaṇa, which he glosses as "you who possess the knowledge of what should be done next," and *indrajit*. According to his second alternative, the compound *vibudhendra* is a *madhyamapadalopī*, which must be understood as "Indra accompanied by the gods." (*he vibudha ita uttaraṃ kartavyajñāna. indrajid vibudhaiḥ sahita indras taṃ jayatīti sa tathā vā*.) Finally, Cs addresses Ct's interpretation, criticizing it, since, he argues, if the compound were indeed a *dvandva*, then *indra* should be placed before *vibudha* (*nāgojibhaṭṭavyākhyānaṃ tu sarvathāpīndraśabdasya pūrvanipātasyāvarjanīyatvād upekṣam*).

Following verse 3, Ñ,V1,3,B2–4,D5–7,9–11,S insert a passage of one line [1779*], while V2,B1,D1–4,13 read 1779* for 3cd: "After having ravaged[1] Lakṣmaṇa with his arrows, he [Indrajit] has departed for a higher realm."

[1]"After having ravaged" *saṃtāpya*: Literally, "having pained *or* afflicted." V1,B1,D2–4,6,7,9–11,13, and the texts and printed editions of Ct and Cr read instead *saṃtarpya*, "having gratified."

4. "grievous, terrible, and horrifying" *pratibhayam... dāruṇam / ghoram*: The three terms are more or less synonymous in the sense of "frightful." Several of the commentators try to distinguish them. Thus, Ct says that the death is *dāruṇa*, "grievous," because it gives rise to grief (*śokajanakatvāt*). He glosses *pratibhayam*, "terrible," as "extremely frightening (*atibhayaṃkaram*)" and *ghoram*, "horrible," as "harsh *or* painful (*tīkṣṇam*)." Cr takes *pratibhayam* to mean "frightening (*bhayaṃkaram*)," *dāruṇam* to mean "rending (*dārakam*)," and *ghoram* to mean "unbearable (*asahanīyam*)." Cv, Cm, and Cg take *dāruṇam* to mean "pitiful (*karuṇam*)" and *ghoram* to mean "harsh *or* painful (*tīkṣṇam*)." Cm takes *pratibhayam* to mean "frightening (*bhayaṃkaram*)." See note to 6.2.14.

6. "Great chariot-warrior!" *mahāratha*: Ñ,V1,3,B3,4,D3,9–11, and the texts and printed editions of Ct read instead *mahābala*, "Mighty one!" See 6.60.3; 6.72.33; 6.81.18; 6.83.8; 6.84.15; and notes. Cf. 6.77.36.

7. "even Kāla or Yama, the ender of all things" *kālāntakāv api*: The *dvandva* compound is both unusual and awkward in that the two terms, *kāla*-, "time," and -*antaka*, "the ender [i.e., death]," are often used synonymously in the epic and may even appear together in appositional *karmadhārya* compounds, in the sense of "Kāla, the ender [of all things]" (cf. 6.75.2). Commentators therefore struggle somewhat to differentiate the terms. Ct takes *kāla* to mean "the destroyer of all things (*sarvasaṃhārakaḥ*)" and *antaka* to refer to "his [i.e., Kāla's] officer *or* appointed official (*tadadhikṛtaḥ*)." The idea here appears to be that *kāla*, "time *or* death," is an abstract concept, whereas *antaka* refers to a personified agent, "the god of death." Cr explains somewhat similarly, glossing, "death and Yama (*mṛtyuyamau*)." A further variation on this theme is Crā's and Cm's explanation, whereby *kāla* is "the destroyer of all (*sarvasaṃhārakaḥ*)," while *antaka* is "a person who regards himself as time *or* death (*kālābhimānī puruṣaḥ*)." Cg contents himself in glossing, "two different forms of Yama (*yamasya mūrtibhedau*)." Northern manuscripts tend to avoid the *dvandva* entirely. Cf. 6.21.26 and note.

"What then to speak of Lakṣmaṇa?" *kiṃ punar lakṣmaṇam*: Literally, "how much more [easily] Lakṣmaṇa?"

8. "Today... now" *adya... adya*: The poet lends poignancy to Rāvaṇa's lament by employing *anaphora*, repeating the adverb in initial position several times throughout the passage. Thus, verses 8, 10, 11, and 12 all begin with this word.

"King Vaivasvata" *vaivasvato rājā*: Vaivasvata, son of Vivasvant, is a common patronymic for Yama, the god of death.

"he has... brought you... under the power of time" *yena... tvam... saṃyuktaḥ kāladharmaṇā*: Literally, "by whom you are joined with the rule of time (*kāla*). The compound *kāladharma*, "the rule of time," is a common epic euphemism for death.

"great-armed warrior" *mahābāho*: Literally, "O great-armed one."

9. "who gives up his life" *hanyate*: Literally, "who is slain."

10. "This night" *adya*: Literally, "today." See note to verse 8 above.

"the guardians of the world" *lokapālāḥ*: These are the eight divinities who guard the cardinal and intermediary points of the compass. See note to verse 36 below. See, too, 5.1.8 and note.

"and the seers" *tatharṣayaḥ*: D6,7,9–11,T2,3, and the texts and printed editions of Ct and Cr read instead *maharṣayaḥ*, "the great seers."

"having seen" *dṛṣṭvā*: Ś,V2,B1,D1,2,4,8,12,13,M3, and the texts and printed editions of Cg and Cm read instead *śrutvā*, "having heard."

"will sleep soundly, freed from fear" *sukhaṃ svapsyanti nirbhayāḥ*: Cr, the only commentator to remark on the passage, observes that the suggestion here is that it is the happiness of the gods that causes Rāvaṇa the greatest suffering (*etenedam eva mama mahad duḥkham iti sūcitam*).

11. "through the loss of Indrajit alone" *ekenendrajitā hīnā*: Literally, "diminished by one Indrajit."

"all the three worlds and the... earth" *lokās trayaḥ kṛtsnāḥ pṛthivī ca*: Since the traditional set of the three worlds normally includes the earth, the atmospheric region, and the heavens (*bhūr bhuvaḥ svaḥ*), the commentators are perplexed by the mention of the earth separately from those three regions. They explain it in one of two ways. Cv, Cm, and Ct understand that the reference to the three worlds here includes the underworld known as Pātāla, the atmospheric realm, and heaven (*pātālāntarikṣasvargāḥ*). Thus, for these commentators, the earth is simply a separate, fourth, world. Cg, however, disagrees, arguing that the earth (which he implicitly includes among the three worlds) is mentioned separately because of its primacy. He illustrates this by comparing the utterance to the expression, "the brahmans have come and so has [the brahman] Vasiṣṭha." (*pṛthīvyāḥ pṛthag upādānaṃ prādhānyād yathā brāhmaṇā āgatā vasiṣṭho 'py āgata ity ādau.*) Ñ,V,B,D1–4,7,9–11,13,M3, and the texts and printed editions of the southern commentators read the feminine singular *kṛtsnā*, "all, entire," for the masculine plural *kṛtsnāḥ*, "all, entire," thus making the adjective refer to the earth rather than to the three worlds.

12. "of the daughters of the *rākṣasas*, sons of chaos," *nairṛtakanyānām*: Literally, "of the *nairṛta* maidens." The precise identity of these women is obscured somewhat by the term's possible range of meanings. Although *kanyā* typically refers to a young, unmarried woman, virgin, or daughter, it can also refer to women in general (Apte s.v.).

"shrill trumpeting" *ninādam*: Literally, "sound, roar."

13. "your succession to the throne" *yauvarājyam*: Literally, "the office of heir apparent." See note to 6.51.10.

"all of us" *naḥ*: Literally, "us." We follow Cg, who adds the word "all (*sarvān*)."

"your wife" *bhāryām*: Literally, "a wife." Ñ2,V1,B2,3,D2,3,5,9–11,T1,G1,M5, and the texts and printed editions of Ct read instead the plural *bhāryāḥ*, "wives."

14. "But now you have reversed this" *viparīte hi vartase*: Literally, "for you are in inversion." The idea here, as expressed by Ct, is that now, contrary to the expected and proper order of things, Rāvaṇa must perform the funerary rites for Indrajit (*tvaṃ tu viparīte vartase yatas tvadīyāni [pretakāryāṇi] mayā kartavyāni bhaviṣyanti*). Cm's view is similar to that of Ct. Cr, although taking the finite verb as a causative, similarly understands, "how is it that you have forced me to travel by a reversed path (*viparīte pathi marge tvaṃ hi kathaṃ vartase māṃ pravartayasi*)."

15. Cm, as he does so often, acknowledges that the manifest meaning of the verse is clear, but he suggests an inner meaning to the effect that Rāvaṇa is really saying to Indrajit, "since Rāma and Lakṣmaṇa are still living, what is the point of your existence?" He says this, Cm continues, because of the impossibility of conquering Rāma and Lakṣmaṇa. (*sa tvam ity asya prātītikārthaḥ spaṣṭaḥ. vastutas tu salakṣmaṇe rāme jīvati sati yas tvaṃ jīvitaṃ kasmād vrajasi, tayor asādhyatvād iti bhāvaḥ.*) See note to 6.27.4. All northern *devanāgarī* manuscripts and a few southern manuscripts read the *facilior* variants *kasmād vrajasi putraka*, "son, why have you gone" (V2,B1,D1–4,13), *kva nu yāsyasi putraka*, "son, where will you go" (Ś,D8,12), or *kasmāt tyajasi jīvitam*, "why did you abandon life" (Ñ,V1,3,B2–4,D6,T2,3 [Ñ1—*katham*; B4—*tyakṣyasi*]). D6 is commonly aligned with Cr and sometimes with Cm as well. It is possible that Cm here either read or was familiar with these variants, which would explain his use of the phrase *jīvitaṃ kasmād vrajasi* in his commentary.

"Rāghava, and Lakṣmaṇa: *rāghave ca salākṣmaṇe*: Literally, "And Rāghava along with Lakṣmaṇa." Ñ,V1,B2–4,D5,7,9,11,T1,G3,M3, and the texts and printed editions of the southern commentators read instead *lakṣmaṇe ca sarāghave*, "and Laksmaṇa along with Rāghava." GPP (6.92.15) erroneously prints *lakṣmaṇe na ca rāghave*, "Lakṣmaṇa but not Rāghava."

"this source of all my torment" *mama śalyam*: Literally, "my dart, thorn, splinter, *or* source of pain."

16. Following verse 16, all manuscripts, in whole (southern) or in part (northern), insert a passage of eight lines [1790*]. The text of Ct, however, does not know lines 3–4, a fact unrecorded in the critical apparatus. "His mental anguish over his son further inflamed him, who was already wrathful by nature and blazing with anger, just as, in the hot season, its rays do the sun.[1–2] With his knitted brows[1] conjoined on his forehead, he resembled the ocean, receptacle of waters, at the end of a cosmic age, together with its sharks and mighty waves.[3–4] And as he gaped in his fury, a clearly perceptible and smoky fire shot forth, blazing from his mouth, as if from the mouth of Vṛtra.[2][5–6] Then Rāvaṇa's two eyes, which were red by nature, now grew more so[3] through the fire of his wrath and, blazing, became truly terrible to behold.[4][7–8]"

[1]"With his knitted brows" *bhrukuṭībhiḥ*: Literally, "With the curvings of his brows." The term *bhrukuṭī*, in the sense of "frown," is usually used in the singular. Cg observes that the plural is appropriate here because Rāvaṇa has ten heads (*bahuvacanaṃ daśaśiraskatvāt*). One should note, however, that Cg fails to comment on the fact that, in this and the following verses, reference is made to Rāvaṇa's having only one mouth and two eyes.

[2]Following line 6, D5,7,9–11,T1,G3,M, and the texts and printed editions of the southern commentators read a close variant of the critical edition's verse 6.80.29, repeating it in its proper place.

[3]"which were red by nature, now grew more so" *prakṛtyā rakte ca rakte*: Literally, "red by nature and red."

[4]"truly terrible to behold" *mahāghore*: Literally, "very terrible."

17. "was now transfigured" *-mūrchitam*: Literally, "enhanced, augmented." Although the poet normally uses this adjective in its more common sense of "stunned, insensible, bewildered," here it must be taken in its other sense of "increased, enhanced."

"unbearable" *durāsadam*: Literally, "difficult *or* impossible to approach." D7,9–11, and the texts and printed editions of Ct and Cr read instead *vyavasthitam*, "fixed, settled, determined," which makes little sense in the context. Translations that follow the text of Ct simply ignore the word.

19. "some vast engine being turned by the *dānavas*" *yantrasyāveṣṭyamānasya mahato dānavaiḥ*: The commentators and the translators who follow them, respectively, are divided as to the exact reference here. In our judgment, which we base on the context of the passage with its reference to such notorious demonic warriors as Vṛtra, the poet probably has in mind some great infernal engine of war such as the *dānavas*, the perennial demonic foes of the gods, might employ. Compare 6.3.11 and notes, where some sort of *yantras*, "mechanical devices," for hurling stones (*upalayantrāṇi*) are said to be part of the defensive emplacements of Laṅkā. Compare, too, the use of the term *yantra* at 6.49.11 and note. Ct, Cr, and Ck, however, take the phrase to be an oblique and elliptical reference to the well-known myth of the churning of the ocean [or ocean of milk] in which the gods and the demons use Mount Mandara as a churning rod, which they twirl by using the great serpent lord Vāsuki as the churning rope. In this

interpretation, the *yantra*, or "engine," referred to would be the mountain itself. (*yantrasya mandararūpamathanayantrasya vāsukinā karaṇena dānavaiḥ kṛṣyamāṇasya mathnataḥ kṣīrābdhimathanaṃ kurvato mandarasyeva*—so Ct.) See 1.44.14–27 and notes, especially notes to verse 16. On the story of the churning of the ocean, see 6.12.22; 6.40.29; 6.41.17; 6.53.23; 6.105.19; and notes. This interpretation is no doubt driven by the fact that D10,11, and the texts and printed editions of Ct read *ākṛṣyamāṇasya mathnataḥ*, "[a *yantra*] being dragged [and] churned," for *āveṣṭyamānasya mahataḥ*, "of a great [*yantra*] being turned." Cv and Cg, however, take the *yantra* in question to refer to a press [oil press—Cg] (*tilapīḍanayantrasya*—so Cg). Cg further glosses "powerful [men] (*balavadbhiḥ*)" for *dānavaiḥ*, presumably understanding the term as a metaphor in the sense of "titans, etc." Cm has a different machine in mind, glossing, "a potter's wheel [literally, 'pot-machine,'] (*ghaṭayantrasya*)," which he understands is being spun by *dānavas*. Compare 6.3.11; 6.30.26; 6.49.11; and notes.

20. D10,11, and the texts and printed editions of Ct omit this verse as do translations that follow his text. GPP reads the verse, in brackets and unnumbered, between 6.92.23 and 24.

"petrified with terror" *bhayatrastāḥ*: Literally, "frightened with fear."

"hid themselves" *saṃnililyire*: According to Cg, the only commentator to remark on this verse, the *rākṣasas* hide behind pillars, etc. (*stambhādivyavahitāḥ*).

21. "The *rākṣasas* did not dare come near" *rākṣasā nopacakramuḥ*: Literally, "the *rākṣasas* did not approach."

"intent upon devouring everything in the world" *carācaracikhādiṣum*: Literally, "wishing to eat what moves and what does not move." The compound *carācara-*, "moving and unmoving," is a common epic kenning for the entire contents of the world, which is thus frequently characterized as *sacarācara*, "with its moving and unmoving [contents]." Cg glosses the desiderative adjective *-cikhādiṣum*, "wishing to eat," as "wishing to destroy (*saṃhartum icchum*)."

22. "in their midst" *rakṣasāṃ madhye*: Literally, "in the midst of the *rākṣasas*."

23. "all-but-impossible" *duścaram*: Literally, "hard to practice." D7,9–11, and the texts and printed editions of Ct read instead *paramam*, "supreme, greatest."

"time after time" *teṣu teṣv avakāśeṣu*: Literally, "on occasion after occasion." We follow the interpretation of Cg, Cr, and Ct (first alternative), who understand the reference to be to the moments of completion of Rāvaṇa's courses of austerities (*tattattapaḥsamāptisamayeṣu*). Ck and, following him, Ct (second alternative), however, understand the reference to be to the various places at which Rāvaṇa has propitiated Brahmā (*svāyaṃbhuvasthānaviṣayeṣu*). This interpretation is represented only in the translation of Gorresio (1858, vol. 10, p. 128), who renders, "*or in questo or in quel luogo*."

25. "by *vajra* or javelin" *vajraśaktibhiḥ*: Ñ,V1,2,B,D1–3,6,9–11,13,T2,3, and the texts and printed editions of Ct read instead *vajramuṣṭibhiḥ*. Translations that follow the texts and printed editions of Ct understand this either to mean "by those holding the thunderbolt or *vajra* in their fists" or "by those having adamantine fists." A few of these manuscripts (D2,6,T2,3) and the edition of Gorresio read the singular *-muṣṭinā*. This is rendered by Gorresio (1858, vol. 10, p. 128) as "*colui che impugna il fulmine (Indra)*."

"in any of my battles with the gods and *asuras*" *devāsuravimardeṣu*: The context indicates that we are not to understand the compound in its usual sense of "in the battles between the gods and *asuras*" but rather in reference to Rāvaṇa's conflicts with both of them. This is made explicit by Cr (*mayā saha devāsurayor yuddheṣu*).

26. "even Indra, smasher of citadels himself" *sākṣād api puraṃdaraḥ*: Literally, "even the smasher of citadels in person." Cr takes the compound not in its sense as a standard epithet but, literally, as "even [some]one capable of smashing citadels (*puradāraṇasamārtho 'pi*)."

"equipped with that armor" *tena . . . saṃyuktam*: Literally, "joined with that." We follow Cv, Cg, and Cs in taking the pronoun to refer to the armor mentioned in the previous verse. Cr, on the other hand, reads it more broadly, glossing, "by reason of having attained fearlessness (*abhayaprāptihetunā*)."

"this very day" *adya . . . adya*: Literally, "today . . . today." The commentators are concerned about the apparent redundancy. Ct claims that the redundancy is not a fault, since it is part of an expression of anger (*kruddhoktitvād adyety asya punar uktir na doṣāya*). Other commentaries try to avoid the repetition by supplying a negative particle, thus turning the second half of the verse into a separate sentence.

27–28. With some hesitation we follow the suggestion of Cg in construing the two verses as a single syntactical unit. We do so because verse 27 by itself is technically a relative clause, beginning as it does with the relative pronoun *yat*, "which." Our hesitation stems from the fact that the verses repeat two words (or synonyms), as indicated below.

"for the slaughter of Rāma and Lakṣmaṇa" *rāmalakṣmaṇayor eva vadhāya*: Cm, in keeping with his project of denying any reference to harm or hostility directed toward the *avatāras*, claims that the verse has an inner meaning, so that we should understand that Rāvaṇa is saying that he intends to kill only the monkeys in the battle with Rāma and Lakṣmaṇa (*vastutas tu rāmalakṣmaṇayoḥ saṃbandhyāhave vadhāya vānarāṇām iti śeṣaḥ*).

"trumpets" *tūrya-*: See 6.24.25 and note. Cf. 6.116.34.

"great" *mahat . . . mahat*: We have collapsed the two adjectives for the sake of style. D5–7,9–11,S, and the texts and printed editions of the southern commentators read *mama*, "mine," for the second occurrence of the word in 28b.

"bow and arrows that were given" *saśaraṃ kārmukaṃ . . . dattam . . . dhanuḥ*: Literally, "the bow together with arrows . . . given . . . the bow."

"during my battles with the gods and *asuras*" *devāsuravimardeṣu*: See note to verse 25 above. We follow the suggestion of Cg, who understands that the bow was given to Rāvaṇa at the time of his battles with the gods and *asuras* (*vimardakāle*).

"who was pleased with me" *abhiprasannena*: Literally, "who was pleased."

29. This verse is a close paraphrase of GPP 6.92.12 (= VSP and KK 6.93.20). See note to verse 16 above, 1790*, following line 6: "Tormented by the killing of his son and in the grip of his rage, cruel Rāvaṇa, reflecting in his mind, decided upon the slaughter of Vaidehī."

"heroic" *śūraḥ*: V3,D9–11, and the texts and printed editions of Ct read instead *krūraḥ*, "cruel."

"resolved to kill Sītā" *sītāṃ hantuṃ vyavasyata*: Cm, unwilling as always to contemplate any real hostility toward Sītā on Rāvaṇa's part, claims that the inner meaning of the verse is to be derived from taking the root $\sqrt{}$*han*, normally, "to kill *or* strike," in its lexically sanctioned sense of "to go." Thus, he argues that Rāvaṇa has merely resolved to go and see Sītā. (*vastutas tu sītāṃ hantuṃ gantum. sītādarśanārthaṃ gantuṃ vyavasyatety arthaḥ. hanahiṃsāgatyor iti dhātuḥ.*) Interestingly, the variation in wording, "decided upon the slaughter of Vaidehī (*vaidehyā rocayad vadham*)," of the first occurrence of this verse in the vulgate leads Cm to provide a very different version of its inner meaning. There (at VSP 6.93.20) he explains that Rāvaṇa, having realized in his mind that his own death will be caused by Vaidehī and that Rāma will shortly kill him, resolves upon his own destruction. In his desire to die by Rāma's hand, he then feigns anger so as to conceal from the other *rākṣasas* that he has decided that their entire race is to be annihilated. (*vastutas tu rāvaṇo vaidehyā hetubhūtayā vadhaṃ svavadhaṃ buddhyā samīkṣyetaḥparaṃ rāmo māṃ avaśyaṃ vadhiṣyatīti niścityety arthaḥ. arocayat svavadham ity anuṣaṅgaḥ. rāvaṇakrodhāveśasya sītāhananodyogasya cāyam āśayaḥ svasya rāmahasta-vadhecchayā sakalarākṣasakulanāśaṃ matam itītararākṣasānām aprakaṭanāya krodhāveśādikam ity arthaḥ.*) See notes to 6.27.9; 6.81.4; and 6.91.19. Cf. notes to 6.27.4 and 6.48.38.

30. "The fearsome *rākṣasa*" *sughoraḥ*: Literally, "the fearsome one." Ct and Cg believe, respectively, that it is Rāvaṇa's mind (*cittam*) and nature (*prakṛtiḥ*) that are fearsome.

"fearsome-looking" *ghoradarśanān*: Ñ,B2,3,D9–11,G1,M1–3, and the texts and printed editions of the southern commentators read instead the nominative singular, *ghoradarśanaḥ*, which would then modify Rāvaṇa rather than the *rākṣasas*.

"who were murmuring dejectedly" *dīnasvarān*: Literally, "having dejected sounds *or* voices." We, like Cr and many translators, understand the compound to be a *bahuvrīhi* modifying *niśācarān*, "night-roaming [*rākṣasas*]." Somewhat less plausibly it is possible to take the compound as a simple *karmadhāraya* and read it to mean that Rāvaṇa is uttering (*uvāca*) dejected sounds. This rendering is found in Dutt (1893, p. 1428).

31. "A short time ago" *tatra*: Literally, "there." We follow Ck and Ct, who gloss, "at that time (*tasmin kāle*)."

"my beloved son" *vatsena*: Literally, "by my dear child."

"an apparition of a murdered woman" *kiṃcid eva hatam*: Literally, "something slain." We follow Cg, who glosses, "something false (*kiṃcid alīkam*)." The reference is to Indrajit's illusory slaying of Sītā at *sarga* 68.

32. "I shall murder Vaidehī, so devoted to that false kshatriya!" *vaidehīṃ nāśayiṣyāmi kṣatrabandhum anuvratām*: Literally, "I shall destroy Vaidehī, who is devoted to that relative of the kshatriyas." The term *bandhu*, "a kinsman, relation," is frequently used at the end of compounds in the sense of "in name only." Cm, who typically resists all threats toward and criticism of Rāma and Sītā, offers here one of his "inner readings (*vastutas tu*)." He takes the pejorative term "false kshatriya (*kṣatrabandhum*)" in its literal sense of "a friend *or* kinsman of the kshatriyas," glossing, "Rāma, the best friend of the kshatriyas." He then argues that Rāvaṇa merely wants to upset Sītā slightly, even though he finds doing so distasteful, in order to satisfy the other *rākṣasas* (reading *pāda* b, "just to please myself I shall [*kariṣye priyam ātmanaḥ*]," as "though it displeases me [*kariṣye 'priyam ātmanaḥ*]"). (*ahaṃ kṣatrabandhuṃ kṣatrāṇāṃ bandhuṃ paramāptaṃ rāmam anuvratāṃ vaidehīṃ tathyaṃ* [v.l. for *satyaṃ*] *yathā tathā nāśayiṣyāmi yadi tad idam ātmano 'priyam eva syād ataḥ kariṣya itararākṣasasantoṣārthaṃ tasyāḥ kiṃcid duḥkham iti śeṣaḥ.*)

33–34. "seized his . . . sword . . . and drew it" *uddhṛtya . . . khaḍgam ādāya*: Literally, "having drawn . . . having taken up [his] sword." The syntax of the two verses, which, as Cv notes, must be read together, is somewhat tortured. To render the verse plausibly in English, we have in effect reversed the two gerunds, one of which is in *pāda* a of verse 33 and the other in *pāda* c of verse 34. Ñ2,V,B,D5, and the texts and printed editions of Ct read *utplutya*, "having leapt up," for *uddhṛtya*, "having drawn." No commentator consulted mentions this variant. Among the translators consulted, only Pagani (1999, p. 1123) appears to render it, translating, "*il s'élança d'un bond rapide*."

"magnificent" *guṇasampannam*: Literally, "endowed with virtues *or* qualities." Cg, taking *guṇa* in its sense of "string, cord," understands, "adorned with garlands (*mālyālaṃkṛtam*)."

"which shone like a cloudless sky" *vimalāmbaravarcasam*: Literally, "which had the brilliance of a clear *or* spotless sky." Cr reads the compound as a *bahuvrīhi* in the sense of "possessing a spotless sheath and brilliance (*vimalāmbaraṃ kośo varcas ca yasya tam*)."

"his mind reeling with grief" *bhṛśam ākulacetanaḥ*: Literally, "his mind powerfully agitated."

"from the assembly hall" *sabhāyāḥ*: V2,3,B1,4,D5,7,9–11,T1,G2,3,M, and the texts and printed editions of the southern commentators read instead *sabhāryaḥ*, "with his wife *or* wives."

35. "rushing forth" *vrajantam*: " Literally, "going, proceeding."

"the *rāksasas*" *rākṣasāḥ*: D7,9–11, and the texts and printed editions of Ct read instead the redundant, accusative singular, *rākṣasam*, which then modifies Rāvaṇa.

"roared like lions" *siṃhanādaṃ pracakruśuḥ*: Literally, "they cried a lion's roar." We understand with Ck and Ct that the *rākṣasas*, seeing their lord come forth [apparently to battle], utter a cry that is reminiscent of a lion's roar. Ck further specifies that this cry is appropriate to the time of preparation for battle, etc. (*siṃhanādo nāma yuddhādisajjāhakālinaḥ*). Ct indicates that we should supply the word "ministers" as the subject of the verb (*sacivā iti śeṣaḥ*). Cr, on the other hand, understands *siṃhanādam* to be a *bahuvrīhi* compound modifying the *rākṣasa*, i.e., Rāvaṇa. The idea, then, is that "seeing Rāvaṇa emerge roaring like a lion, the *rākṣasas* cry out."

"they huddled together" *anyonyam āśliṣya*: Literally, "having embraced one another."

36. "Rāvaṇa" *enam*: Literally, "him."

"the four guardians of the world" *lokapālā hi catvāraḥ*: Normally there are eight guardians of the principal and intermediate quarters: Indra, east; Agni, southeast; Yama, south; Nairṛta, southwest; Varuṇa, west; Vāyu, northwest; Kubera, north; and Īśa, northeast. See note to verse 10. The reference here, no doubt, is to the guardians of the four cardinal directions.

Following verse 36, Ñ,V,B2–4,D5–7,9–11,13,S insert a passage of two lines [1796*]: "Rāvaṇa takes and enjoys the finest things in the three worlds. Indeed, he has no equal on earth in valor and might."

37. "went storming toward" *abhidudrāva*: Literally, "he ran toward."

38. "concerned for his welfare" *hitabuddhibhiḥ*: Literally, "having beneficial thoughts *or* thoughts for [his] welfare."

"the angry planet... toward Rohiṇī" *saṃkruddhaḥ ... graho rohiṇīm*: We agree with Ck, Ct, and Cg, who understand the reference to be to the inauspicious planet Mars (*aṅgārika*—Cg; *kuja*—Ct, Ck), which, in this simile, would be entering or occluding the fourth *nakṣatra*, or lunar mansion, Rohiṇī. Gorresio (1858, vol. 10, p. 129), Shastri (1959, vol. 3, p. 271), and Pagani (1999, p. 1123) take the term *graha*, "planet," in its common meaning as a reference to Rāhu, the demon or principle of the eclipse.

However, we think this is less plausible, since eclipses affect the sun and the moon and not *nakṣatras*, such as Rohiṇī. Rohiṇī is one of the lunar mansions, either the ninth (MW s.v.), the fourth (Pingree 1978), or the second (Kirfel 1920). The twenty-seven lunar mansions are personified as the moon's wives, and of these Rohiṇī is his favorite (*MBh* 9.34.40ff.). Compare 5.13.21 and note, where, in a simile involving Sītā, the planet Mars is explicitly said to oppress Rohiṇī. Cf. 5.17.8 and note as well. See note to verses 50–51 below.

40. "not turning back" *anivartinam*: T2,3,M3, and the texts and printed editions of Cg and Cm read instead *anuvartinam*, "continuing onward."

Following verse 40, D5–7,9–11,S insert a passage of one line [1802*]: "Overcome with misery, Sītā, lamenting, said this."

Northern manuscripts insert or substitute 1801*, in part or in whole, a passage of two lines, which similarly provides an introduction to what is represented there as Sītā's thoughts (rather than words) that follow in verse 41. As the critical text stands, it seems out of keeping with the normal style of the epic in which direct speech or thought is generally explicitly introduced. See Sutherland 1992.

41. "From the way he is racing toward me . . . it is clear . . . is going to kill me" *yathā . . . mām . . . samabhidravati . . . / vadhiṣyati . . . mām*: Literally, "in which manner he is running toward me, [in that manner] he will kill me."

"as if I had no one to protect me, although, in fact, I do" *sanāthām . . . mām anāthām iva*: Literally, "me who has a protector, like one who has no protector."

42. "no matter how many times" *bahuśaḥ*: Literally, "many times."

" 'Be my wife, enjoy yourself!' " *bhāryā bhava ramasveti*: Literally, "Be a wife. Enjoy." B1,D1–7,9–12,T2,3,G1,2,M1,2,5, and the texts and printed editions of Cr, Ct, and Ck read instead *bhāryā mama* (*mama bhāryā*—D6,T2,3,5) *bhavasveti*, "be my wife," using the irregular *ātmanepada* form *bhavasva*, "[you] be." Cr, wishing to avoid the sense that Rāvaṇa has made any direct sexual solicitation of Sītā, reads the nominative singular *bhāryā*, "wife," as the accusative plural, *bhāryāḥ* (with loss of *visarga* before a voiced consonant), and takes *bhavasva* in the sense of "[you] obtain." Thus, he understands the line to mean "[you] become an object of reverence to my wives, Mandodarī, etc. (*mama bhāryā mandodarīprabhṛtīr bhavasva prāpnuhi tatpūjyātvena tiṣṭhety arthaḥ*)."

"I rejected him" *pratyākhyāto 'bhavan mayā*: D5,7,9–11,T1,G2,3,M3,5, and the texts and printed editions of the southern commentators read instead *pratyākhyāto dhruvaṃ mayā*, "by me [he] was firmly rejected." In keeping with his interpretation mentioned above, Cr understands that Sītā did not reject Rāvaṇa's advances but rather failed to accept his advice (*pratyākhyātas taduktaṃ nāṅgīkṛtam*).

43. "because I rejected him as a suitor" *anupasthānāt*: Literally, "because of non-acceptance." See 6.52.21 and note for a similar use of the term.

"he has given up all hope of winning me" *mām . . . nairāśyam āgataḥ*: Literally, "he has come to hopelessness [with respect to] me," or so we must read the awkward accusative pronoun *mām* in *pāda* a. A few northern manuscripts and the edition of Gorresio read the *facilior mamānavasthānāt*, "because of my rejection."

"mad passion" *-moha-*: Literally, "confusion, delusion, infatuation." Here the idea seems to be that Rāvaṇa is essentially out of his mind with unfulfilled passion and so becomes homicidal. An alternative reading would be to take the compound *krodhamohasamāviṣṭaḥ* not as "overwhelmed with anger and delusion" but rather as "suffused with delusion because of anger." This idea is apparently rendered in the translations of Roussel (1903, vol. 3, p. 307) and Shastri (1959, vol. 3, p. 271). Pagani (1999, p. 1123) understands, "*son courroux l'égare.*"

44. "the ignoble creature" *anāryeṇa*: Literally, "by the ignoble one."

"Ah! What an evil fate that I should be the cause of the princes' death" *aho dhiṅ mannimitto 'yaṃ vināśo rājaputrayoḥ*: Literally, "Ah! Alas! The destruction of the king's two sons has me for its cause."

Following 44cd, many, primarily northern, manuscripts insert a passage of six lines [1805*] in which Sītā offers further speculations as to the cause of Rāvaṇa's murderous rage. D7,9–11, and the texts and printed editions of Ct, Ck, and Cr insert only lines 1 and 2 of 1805*: "For I just now heard a tumultuous shout from the *rākṣasas* in Laṅkā.[1] It seemed as if many were crying out in great delight."

[1]"For . . . just now . . . a tumultuous shout from the *rākṣasas* in Laṅkā" *sampraty eva hi laṅkāyāṃ rakṣasāṃ tumulaḥ svanaḥ*: D7,9–11, and the texts and printed editions of Ct, Ck, and Cr read instead *bhairavo hi mahān nādo rākṣasānāṃ śruto mayā*, "I heard a great and terrible sound from the *rākṣasas*."

Following verse 44, D5–7,9–11,S insert a passage of two lines [1806*]: "Or, perhaps, having failed to kill Rāma and Lakṣmaṇa, the fierce *rākṣasa*, so evil in his resolve, is going to kill me out of grief for his son."

45. "the advice of Hanumān" *hanūmato . . . tad vākyam*: Literally, "that speech of Hanumān." The context and the commentators make it clear that Sītā is referring to Hanumān's offer, at 5.35.21–29, to carry her to Rāma on his back.

"seated . . . in my husband's lap" *bhartur aṅkagatā satī*: For a possible pregnant ambiguity in the use of the term *satī*, "being," see note to verse 48 below.

"blamelessly" *aninditā*: Literally, "blameless." Apparently Sītā now thinks better of her earlier rejection of Hanumān's offer of rescue on the grounds that she might incur censure for lack of perfect devotion to her husband should she willingly touch the body of another male (see 5.35.62–63 and notes). D9–11,T1, and the texts and printed editions of Ct and Cr read instead *anirjitā*, "not won back." Ct, no doubt thinking of the sentiment expressed by Sītā at 5.35.64 that it would be more appropriate for Rāma to win her back himself in combat with Rāvaṇa than for her to be rescued by Hanumān, adds the phrase "by Rāma (*rāmeṇa*)." Cr understands, "not slain by Rāvaṇa (*rāvaṇenānihatety arthaḥ*)."

47. "she will surely call fondly to mind" *saṃsmariṣyati*: Literally, "she will recall, call to mind, *or* remember."

"righteous deeds, and beauty" *dharmakāryāṇi rūpaṃ ca*: D6,M3, and the texts and printed editions of Cg read instead *dharmakāryānurūpaṃ ca*, literally, "conformable to righteous deeds." Cg, the only commentator to remark on this variant, glosses, "conformability to righteous action (*dharmakāryānurūpatvam*)." Raghunathan (1982, vol. 3, p. 273), the only translator to render this variant, translates, "and his aptness for righteous living (works)."

48. "she will perform his funerary rites" *dattvā śrāddham*: Literally, "having given *śrāddha*." Cr understands the term *śrāddham* adverbially, in the sense of "faithfully offering (*śraddhayā yutaṃ yathā bhavati tathā dattvā*)," although it is not clear what he takes to be the object of the gerund *dattvā*, "having given."

"she will surely mount the funeral pyre or hurl herself into the water" *agnim ārokṣyate nūnam apo vāpi pravekṣyati*: Literally, "she will surely mount the fire *or* fire-altar or enter the water." It is not perfectly clear here whether Sītā is envisaging a kind of maternal *sahagamana*, or ritual death to accompany a beloved person, normally one's husband, or whether she foresees Kausalyā simply committing suicide in her grief and despondency. The use of the verb *ā* √*ruh*, "to mount," rather than the usual √*viś*, "to enter," for entering fire, seems to us to suggest the former. If this is correct, it would appear to be an interesting and unusual variant on the theme of the widow as *satī*. A number of manuscripts, Ñ2,V,B1,2,D7,9–11, and the texts and printed editions of Ct read *āvekṣyate*, "she will enter," for the critical reading's *ārokṣyate*, while T2,3 read the variant *pravekṣyate*, "she will enter." These variants may represent the tradition's discomfort with the idea of a mother attempting to follow her son in death as if she were his wife. Ś,Ñ,V,B,D1–4,8,12,13 (with minor variants), and the editions of Lahore and Gorresio read *prāyaṃ vopagamiṣyati*, "or she will fast unto death," for the critical edition's *apo vāpi pravekṣyati*, thus envisaging another mode of ritual suicide. Note, of course, that unlike the *Mahābhārata*, where the practice of *sahagamana* is not uncommonly referred to, the central narrative of the *Rāmāyaṇa* shows no examples of the practice. Thus, after the death of Daśaratha and at his funeral at *Ayodhyākāṇḍa sargas* 59, 60, and 70, there is not even an allusion to the possibility of the widows' mounting his funeral pyre. Note also how the verse is framed between two perhaps intentional plays on the term *satī*. At verse 45 above, Sītā describes herself as *aninditā*, "blameless," and describes herself further as "sitting on her husband's lap (*bhartur aṅkagatā*)." These adjectives are then followed by the term *satī*. This latter term is ambiguous in this context. It can be read either as a present participle of the root √*as*, "to be," as we have done in verse 45, or in the more highly charged sense of "a virtuous woman, chaste wife." Then in verse 49, in contrast to the virtuous Sītā and Kausalyā, bitter reference is made to the scheming hunchback Mantharā, who is described as *asatī*, literally, "an unchaste woman," a term used in the sense of "depraved woman *or* slut." See S. Goldman 1996.

49. "that . . . slut" *asatīṃ*: Literally, "an unchaste woman" See note to verse 48 above.

"and her wicked scheming" *pāpaniścayām*: Literally, "her of evil intentions."

"such suffering" *idaṃ duḥkham*: Literally, "this suffering." D7,9–11, and the texts and printed editions of Ct read instead *imaṃ śokam*, "this sorrow."

50–51. "the wise *rākṣasa* Supārśva" *supārśvo nāma medhāvī*: Literally, "the wise one named Supārśva." Ct claims that Supārśva is another name for the *rākṣasa* minister Avindhya, supporting this claim by quoting the parallel passage from the *Mahābhārata* (3.273.27–28), where it is said that Avindhya calms the angry Rāvaṇa, who is on the point of slaying Sītā. Compare 5.35.12–13 and notes and *MBh* 3.264.55, where Avindhya, too, is called "wise (*medhāvī*)." At 6.77.9–11, a *rākṣasa* named Supārśva is listed among those already slain. At 6.25.20, a *rākṣasa* named Aviddha is mentioned.

"like the constellation Rohiṇī occluded by a hostile planet and so cut off from the moon, her lord" *rohiṇīm iva candreṇa vinā grahavaśaṃ gatām*: Literally, "like Rohiṇī without the moon, gone to the power of a planet." See note to verse 38 above.

"whose ministers were attempting to restrain him" *nivāryamāṇaṃ sacivaiḥ*: Literally, "who was being held back by ministers." Ñ1,B2,D7,9,10, and the texts and printed editions of Ct and Cr read the nominative *nivāryamāṇaḥ*, "being held back," for the critical edition's accusative *nivāryamāṇam*. According to this reading, as Ct notes, the ministers are trying to prevent Supārśva from speaking inappropriately to Rāvaṇa (*sacivair evaṃ vaktum ayogyam iti nivāryamāṇo 'pi*).

Following verse 50, Ñ,V,B4,D5–7,9–11,S insert a passage of one line [1811*], which fleshes out the somewhat elliptical reference to Supārśva in verse 51a: "At that juncture, his wise and honest minister..."

52. "How can you... even think of killing" *kathaṃ nāma... hantum icchasi*: Literally, "How, indeed, do you wish to kill?"

"ten-necked Rāvaṇa" *daśagrīva*: Literally, "O ten-necked one."

"the younger brother of Kubera Vaiśravaṇa himself" *sākṣād vaiśravaṇānuja*: Literally, "O younger brother of Vaiśravaṇa, in person." Ck and Ct note that, by addressing Rāvaṇa in this way, Supārśva is appealing to the fact that he is born in a noble family (*anena mahākulaprasūtatvam uktam*—so Ct). Cs more explicitly argues that what is suggested here is that unrighteous behavior is improper for someone born in a lineage of seers (*ṛṣivaṃśasaṃbhavasyādharmapravṛttir anucitety anena dhvanyate*). See, too, 6.4.16 and note.

53. "You have completed your discipleship in vedic knowledge" *vedavidyāvratasnātaḥ*: Literally, "[you are one who has] completed the vow of vedic knowledge." As Ct, Ck, and Cr suggest, the idea here is that, after completing the vow of celibacy (*brahmacarya*) that is essential for vedic discipleship, Rāvaṇa was successfully initiated into vedic knowledge and [then] returned home from his *guru*'s house (*vedavidyāgrahāpekṣitābrahmacaryavratapūrvaṃ vidyāṃ gṛhītvā snāto gurukulāt samāvṛttaḥ*—so Ct).

"you are ever devoted to the proper duties of your rank" *svadharmanirataḥ sadā*: The critical reading or a close variant, which is shared by several northern and southern manuscripts (Ñ,V1,B2–4,D4,6,9,M1,2,T2,3), appears to refer to the well-known concept of *svadharma* associated with the ideology of *varṇa*, or class duty, according to which each of the four *varṇas*, or social classes of brahmanical Hinduism, is enjoined to adhere to its own proper occupation. The concept is most famously enunciated at *Bhagavadgītā* 3.35 (see, too, 18.47). Although this concept is essential to the ritual and social order as articulated in the *Rāmāyaṇa*, it is rarely mentioned explicitly in the text. This may, in fact, be the only such reference. V2,D5,7,10,11,T1,G,M3,5, and the texts and printed editions of the southern commentators read instead *svakarmanirataḥ*, "devoted to your own proper rites *or* duties." Ck and Ct explained this reading to mean that, after his studentship, Rāvaṇa, "having completed the marriage rite, is now devoted to the various rituals incumbent on the householder, such as the *agnihotra* and the like (*tadanantaraṃ dāragrahaṇapūrvaṃ nityāgnihotrādisvakarmanirataḥ*)." A number of northern manuscripts (Ś,B1,D1–3,8,12,13) and Gorresio's edition similarly avoid explicit reference to *svadharma* by substituting the pronoun *tvam*, "you," for *sva-*, "one's own." The resulting reading means "you who are devoted to *dharma*."

B1,D9–11, and the texts and printed editions of Ck and Ct read *tathā*, "and *or* thus," instead of *sadā*.

54. "You should spare" *pratyavekṣasva*: Literally, "you should regard, take care of." Ct understands that Rāvaṇa should spare Sītā until he has first killed Rāma (*rāmavadhaparyantam iti śeṣaḥ*). Ck thinks that she should be spared for the duration of the time allotted her by Rāvaṇa (*yāvat pratijñātakālaparyantam iti śeṣaḥ*). Cr, the only commentator to gloss the verb, understands it to mean "look at *or* gaze at continually (*nityaṃ paśya*)."

"You... upon Rāghava" *tvam eva... rāghave*: D7,9–11, and the texts and printed editions of Ct read instead *tasminn eva... āhave*, "upon him, in battle."

55. "your preparations" *abhyutthānam*: Literally, "arrangements for departure." As the commentators indicate, the reference is to preparation for battle (*samarodyogam*—Ct, Cr).

"this very day, the fourteenth of the dark fortnight... tomorrow on the new moon day" *adyaiva kṛṣṇapakṣacaturdaśīm... amāvāsyām*: Cv, Ck, and Cg take this opportunity to provide a day-by-day summary of the war to this point, starting from the reference to sunset on the full-moon day when Rāma's army ascended Mount Suvela. Here the commentators quote 6.29.17. All three commentators give the following identical chronology of events:

Full-moon night—the ascent of Mount Suvela (*sarga* 29).

Day 1 (of the dark half)—the commencement of hostilities; that night Rāma and Lakṣmaṇa are both bound by and released from Indrajit's *nāgapāśas* (*sargas* 31–35).

Day 2—the slaying of Dhūmrākṣa (*sarga* 42).

Day 3—the slaying of Vajradaṃṣṭra (notes to *sarga* 43.1, App. I, No. 26).

Day 4—the slaying of Akampana (*sarga* 43).

Day 5—the slaying of Prahasta (*sarga* 46).

Day 6—the breaking of Rāvaṇa's crown (*sarga* 47).

Day 7—the slaying of Kumbhakarṇa (*sarga* 55).

Day 8—the slaying of Atikāya, etc. (*sarga* 59).

Day 9—the renewed battle with Indrajit; night of the ninth, the slaying of Kumbha, Nikumbha, etc. (*sargas* 63, 64).

Day 10—the slaying of Makarākṣa (*sarga* 66).

Days 11–13—the battle with and slaying of Indrajit (*sargas* 73–78).

Cg adds that the real meaning here is that, since [all] the *rākṣasas* except the core or elite forces of Rāvaṇa and Indrajit have been slaughtered during the two days starting on the ninth and since the killing of Indrajit took the following three days (viz., days 11–13), the advice that Rāvaṇa gird himself up for battle on the fourteenth is appropriate (*vastutas tu navamyāṃ yuddhārambhāt tadārabhya dinadvayena rāvaṇendrajinmūlabalavyatiriktarākṣasanibarhaṇād ekādaśīdvādaśītrayodaśībhir indrajidvadha iti caturdaśyām abhyutthānavacanaṃ yujyata eva*). See note to 6.4.4. See, too, 6.48.12; 6.96.30; and 6.97.33.

56. "equipped with a chariot" *rathī*: Literally, "possessing a chariot." Crā understands the term as a synonym for *mahārathaḥ*, "great chariot-warrior."

"Rāma Dāśarathi" *dāśarathiṃ rāmaṃ*: D10,11, and the texts and printed editions of Ct read the adjective *bhīmam*, "fearsome, formidable," for *rāmam*.

"you, sir... will... win Maithilī" *bhavān prāpsyati maithilīm*: Literally, "you [respectful] will acquire Maithilī." Since Sītā is already in the physical possession of Rāvaṇa, we follow Cr, who explains: "the meaning is that Maithilī will come to be held in high regard as your wife (*bhavadbhāryāpūjyātvena maithilī sthāsyatīty arthaḥ*)." Cm, with his theologian's aversion to verses that speak of harm to Rāma or sexual impropriety toward Sītā, offers an inner meaning of the verse according to which Supārśva is really saying: "Having approached Rāma, you will gain both Dāśarathi and Maithilī, that is, once you have been slain in battle, you will become one of their [heavenly] retinue (*vastutas tu dāśarathiṃ prati gatvā dāśarathiṃ maithilīṃ bhavān prāpsyati raṇe hataḥ saṃs tayoḥ pārṣadatāṃ prāpsyatīty arthaḥ*)."

57. The meter is *vaṃśasthavila*.

Sarga 81

1. "snarling" *śvasan*: Literally, "breathing, panting, *or* sighing."

2. "who stood with their hands cupped in reverence" *prāñjalīn*: The editor's choice of this reading is virtually impossible to justify on textual grounds. All but two of the manuscripts collated for the critical edition as well as the texts of most commentators and printed editions read *prāñjaliḥ*, which makes Rāvaṇa the one cupping his hands in reverence or supplication. Only Ñ2,D1, and the Lahore edition (6.94.2) read with the critical edition. Crā, alone among the commentators, notes the majority reading as a variant, indicating, one assumes, that he reads with the critical edition.

Commentators explain the seeming inversion of hierarchy by remarking either that Rāvaṇa, having been placed in the most desperate situation, shows deference to his surviving officers in order to get them to face battle once again (*paramāpadaḥ prāptyāvaśiṣṭānāṃ yuddhaunmukhyārthaṃ namaskāraṃ karotīty āśayaḥ*—so Ct; Ck similarly) or simply that he wants to supplicate them (*anunayārtham*—so Cg). Perhaps the critical editors have exercised higher criticism in order to avoid having a ruler appear to supplicate his inferiors.

3. "by the entire cavalry and elephant corps" *sarveṇa hastyaśvena*: Ck and Ct understand that the officers are to leave behind not even a single warrior in any of the four divisions of the army (*ekam api hastyaśvarathapādātam atyaktvety arthaḥ*—so Ct). See note to 6.3.24.

"accompanied" *upaśobhitāḥ*: Literally, "adorned, made splendid." Pagani (1999, p. 1125) appears to misread the nominative adjective, taking it in its etymological sense as a modifier of the instrumental "by chariot divisions (*rathasaṃghaiḥ*)." She renders, "*avec vos escadrons de chars éclatants*."

"infantry" *pādātaiḥ*: Literally, "by foot soldiers." D9–11 and the texts and printed editions of Ct read instead the redundant *hastyaśvaiḥ*, "with cavalry and elephant corps." Translations that follow the texts and printed editions of Ct struggle with the redundancy. They tend to omit the second reference to the cavalry and elephant corps. Roussel (1903, vol. 3, p. 309), followed by Shastri (1959, vol. 3, p. 272), attempts a solution by repeating the reference to horses but omitting the second mention of elephants.

4. "Exerting yourselves" *prahṛṣṭāḥ*: Literally, "excited, delighted." D5,6,T1,2,G3, M3, the texts and printed editions of Cg, and the text of Gita Press read instead *varṣantaḥ*, "showering."

"you must isolate Rāma, surround him" *ekaṃ rāmaṃ parikṣipya*: Literally, "having surrounded Rāma alone."

"you must...slay him" *hantum arhatha*: In keeping with his ongoing theological reading of the poem, Cm interprets *pari* √*kṣip*, "to surround," in the sense of "to meet or join"; the adjective *ekam*, "alone," in the sense of "principal, outstanding (*mukhyam*)"; and the verbal root √*han*, "strike, kill," in the sense of "go *or* go to." Thus, for him, the inner meaning (*vāstavārtha*) of this verse and the next is that the *rākṣasa* troops are to meet the leader, Rāma, and go to him in the battle. On the other hand, should Rāma be wounded by arrows in battle, Rāvaṇa himself will go to him the following day as the people look on. (*ekaṃ rāmam ityādi ślokadvayasya vāstavārthas tu śarān varṣanto yūyaṃ parikṣipya militvaikaṃ mukhyaṃ rāmaṃ samare hantuṃ gantum arhatheti sambandhaḥ. atha bhavadbhir vā śarair mahāraṇe bhinnagātraṃ rāmaṃ lokasya paśyato 'haṃ śvo nihantā gantā gamiṣyāmīty arthaḥ.*) See notes to 6.27.4 and 6.80.29. On the use of the root $\sqrt{}$*han* in the sense of $\sqrt{}$*gam*, see 6.27.9. Cf. note to 6.48.38.

5. "Otherwise" *athavā*: The idea here, as the commentators point out, is that Rāvaṇa will act in the event that his warriors are unable to dispatch Rāma (*adya rāmahananāsaṃbhave bhavadbhir adya bhinnagātraṃ śvo nihantāsmi*—so Ct). See the previous note for Cm's alternative reading.

6. "swiftly" *śīghram*: Ñ2,V2,3,B2,D5,7,9–11,T1,G1,3,M, and the texts and printed editions of the southern commentators read instead the adjective *śīghraiḥ* for the critical edition's adverb. In this reading, the adjective must modify *rathaiḥ*, "chariot."

"by . . . and columns of elephants" *nāgānīkaiś ca*: Ñ2,V1,3,D1,6,9–11,M3, the texts and printed editions of the southern commentators, and Gorresio's edition read *nānā-*, "various," for *nāga-*, "elephants," yielding the sense "and with troops of various kinds."

Following verse 6, D5–7,9–11,S insert a passage of three lines [1825*]: "They all hurled lethal iron clubs, spears, arrows, swords, and battle-axes at the monkeys[1–2], and the monkeys hurled trees and boulders at the *rākṣasas*.[3]"

For some reason, Raghunathan (1982, vol. 3, p. 274) does not translate lines 1–2.

7. "at sunrise" *sūryasyodayanaṃ prati*: Ct, apparently followed by Cr, notes that the reference is to daybreak on the fourteenth day of the battle [and of the bright half of Āśvina]. Ct goes on to note that we are to understand that Rāvaṇa makes his abortive attack on Sītā in the closing portion of the night of the thirteenth. (*caturdaśīsūryodayam ārabhyety arthaḥ. trayodaśīrātriśeṣe rāvaṇasya sītāsamīpagamana iti bodhyam.*) See note to 6.4.4.

8. "various types of clubs, darts, swords, and battle-axes" *gadābhir vicitrābhiḥ prāsaiḥ khaḍgaiḥ paraśvadhaiḥ*: Cv, Cg, Cm, Ct, and Cs all note the seeming inconsistency in the apparent ascription of formal weapons to the monkeys, who, it is to be recalled, almost invariably fight only with trees and rocks as well as their teeth, claws, fists, etc. The commentators generally suggest one of two explanations for this departure. According to the first, the monkeys seize these weapons from the hands of their *rākṣasa* foes (*yady api vānarāṇāṃ gadādyāyudhābhāvas tathāpi rākṣasahastebhya ācchidya gṛhītais tais teṣāṃ yuddhasaṃbhava iti bodhyam*—so Ct). Cg offers a second possibility: by metonymy (*upalakṣaṇa*), the names of the weapons given can also designate trees and boulders (*anyonyaṃ jaghnur ity atra śilāvṛkṣāṇām apy upalakṣaṇam*).

Following verse 8, D5,7,9–11,T1,G,M, and the texts and printed editions of the southern commentators insert a passage of two lines [1830*]: "As the battle progressed in this fashion, the huge dust cloud that was raised[1] was made to settle by the torrents of blood gushing from the *rākṣasas* and the monkeys.[2]"

[1]"that was raised" *uddhūtam*: D7,10,11,M2,5, and the texts and printed editions of Ct read instead *hy adbhutam*, "wondrous."

[2]"by the torrents of blood gushing from the *rākṣasas* and the monkeys" *rakṣasāṃ vānarāṇāṃ ca . . . śoṇitaviśravaiḥ*: Literally, "by the blood flows of the *rākṣasas* and the monkeys."

9. This type of epic metaphor is known to the *Mahābhārata* and occurs earlier in the *Yuddhakāṇḍa*. See 6.46.25–28 and notes for a much more elaborate metaphor of battle as a river.

"carrying logjams of corpses" *śarīrasaṃghāṭavahāḥ*: Literally, "bearing clumps of bodies." The commentators understand *saṃghāṭa*, "clumps, multitudes," to refer to logjams (*kāṣṭhasamūhāḥ*—so Ck, Ct) and we are inclined to agree. Cf. 6.33.17 and note.

"war-horses for their fish" *vājimatsyāḥ*: Ñ,V1,2,B2,4,D6,9–11, and the texts and printed editions of Ct and Cr read instead *śaramatsyāḥ*, "arrows for their fish."

Following verse 9, D5–7,9–11,S insert a passage of one line [1832*]: "Then all the monkeys, drenched in torrents of blood..."

10. "those splendid monkeys" *vānarendrāḥ*: Literally, "the Indras among monkeys." M3,5, and the texts and printed editions of Cg read instead *rākṣasānām*, "of the *rākṣasas*."

12. "swarmed about" *abhyadhāvanta*: Literally, "they ran toward."

"laden with fruit" *phalinam*: D9–11 and the texts and printed editions of Ct read instead the contextually inapposite *patitam*, "fallen."

13. "Similarly" *tathā*: D5–7,9–11,T2,3, and the texts and printed editions of Cr and Ct read instead *tadā*, "then."

14. "sought refuge with Daśaratha's son Rāma, the refuge of all" *śaraṇyaṃ śaraṇaṃ yātā rāmaṃ daśarathātmajam*: Cg understands the reference to the monkeys taking refuge with Rāma to indicate that they have no other recourse. The word *śaraṇyam* here, Cg believes, is used to express Rāma's qualities of compassion, etc. He also suggests that Rāma's name and patronymic are used here with a theological intent. The name "Rāma," he argues, is used to express the hero's status as the Supreme Being, while the epithet "son of Daśaratha" suggests that he is, nonetheless, accessible. (*rākṣasair vadhyamānānām ity ākiñcanyānanyagatikatvoktiḥ. śaraṇyaṃ iti dayādyuktiḥ. rāmam iti paratvoktiḥ. daśarathātmajam iti saulabhyoktiḥ.*) See 6.13.4 and 6.59.8; compare 6.31.56; 6.47.43; 6.105.16; and notes. See, too, 5.36.26–29.

16. "fearsome" *mahāghoram*: D9–11 and the texts and printed editions of Ct read instead the nominative plural *mahāghorāḥ*, which makes the adjective modify the implied subject "the *rākṣasas*."

"the *rākṣasas* could no more approach him than can clouds approach the sun in the heavens" *meghāḥ sūryam ivāmbare / nābhijagmuḥ*: Literally, "they did not approach [Rāma] like clouds, the sun in the sky." B1,D5–7,10,11,T1, and the texts and printed editions of Cr and Ct read *adhijagmuḥ* for the critical text's *abhijagmuḥ*. We believe that the context requires that the verb *adhi* $\sqrt{}$*gam* must be taken as a synonym of *abhi* $\sqrt{}$*gam*, "to approach," as does Gita Press (1969, vol. 3, p. 1761) and, similarly, Dutt (1893, p. 1432; "stand before"). Roussel (1903, vol. 3, p. 310), followed by Shastri (1959, vol. 3, p. 273) and Pagani (1999, p. 1125), however, takes the verb in its other sense of "to know, discern." His understanding of the verse is that the warriors could no more perceive Rāma, once he had entered their ranks, than one could perceive the sun obscured by clouds. He renders, "*Lorsqu'il entrait dans leurs rangs comme le soleil dans les nuages, les formidables guerriers ... ne l'apercevaient pas.*" The syntax of the verse can in no way support this interpretation. Roussel and his followers may have been influenced by the following verses in which several references are made to Rāma's being imperceptible to his enemies in battle (verses 18–27 below). Northern manuscripts and the editions of Gorresio and Lahore show a variant that is quite similar to the reading of Roussel, Shastri, and Pagani. Quite possibly Roussel was aware of, and perhaps influenced by, the translation of Gorresio. See note to verse 25 below.

17. "all-but-impossible feats of Rāma... only after he had accomplished them" *kṛtāny eva ... rāmeṇa ... rāmasya ... karmāṇy asukarāṇi*: Literally, "the difficult deeds of Rāma actually accomplished by Rāma." The verse is repetitive and slightly enigmatic. Our translation follows the interpretation of all commentators who treat the verse. They understand that, presumably because of Rāma's blinding speed, the *rākṣasas* can perceive his martial exploits only when they are completed, not while they are actually being performed (*karmāṇi rāmeṇa kṛtāny eva dadṛśur na tu kriyamāṇāni*—so Ck). Roussel (1903, vol. 3, p. 310), followed by Shastri (1959, vol. 3, p. 273) and Pagani (1999, p. 1126), understands the verse to suggest that the *rākṣasas* recognized the feats to be, in fact, those of Rāma. He renders, "*les... exploits... ils les reconnaissaient pour ceux de Rāma.*"

18. "Although he was shaking their vast host and crushing their great chariot-warriors" *cālayantaṃ mahānīkaṃ vidhamantaṃ mahārathān*: Dutt (1893, p. 1432) has completely misread *pādas* ab, rendering the entirely erroneous "Except when guiding the huge army or driving the cars, they [could not see Rāma]." We understand the term *mahārathān*, "great chariot-warriors," as does Gita Press (1969, vol. 3, p. 1761), in its most common usage as a *bahuvrīhi*, describing outstanding chariot-warriors. Other translators understand, "great chariots." See 6.60.3; 6.72.33; 6.80.6; 6.83.8; 6.84.15; and notes. Cf. 6.77.36.

"they could no more see" *dadṛśus te na*: Roussel (1903, vol. 3, p. 310), followed by Shastri (1959, vol. 3, p. 273) and Pagani (1999, p. 1126), understands that the *rākṣasas* did recognize Rāma through his deeds as one might recognize the passage of a violent wind through a forest. Roussel and the others probably have mistakenly read the text's sequence *te na*, "they [did] not," as the instrumental pronoun *tena*, "by reason of that." One should note, however, that the text of GPP (6.93.20) actually reads *tena*, and it is this that may have conditioned Pagani's reading.

19. "through the skill of Rāma... him" *rāmeṇa... rāmam*: Literally, "by Rāma... Rāma."

"cut to pieces, shattered, scorched with arrows, broken, and afflicted by weapons" *chinnaṃ bhinnaṃ śarair dagdhaṃ prabhagnaṃ śastrapīḍitam*: Literally, "cut, split, burned by arrows, broken, and afflicted with weapons." Cg is the only commentator who attempts to differentiate these sometimes seemingly synonymous terms. He defines them as follows: "*chinna* means 'broken into pieces'; *bhinna* means 'torn apart'; *prabhagna* means 'fragmented'; *śastrapīḍita* means 'having darts lodged in their hearts.' (*chinnaṃ khaṇḍitam. bhinnaṃ vidāritam. prabhagnaṃ śakalīkṛtam. śastrapīḍitaṃ hṛdayārpitaśalyam.*)" See note to 6.2.14.

"so swiftly did he move" *śīghrakāriṇam*: Literally, "swift acting."

20. "the inner spirit that resides among the objects of sense" *indriyārtheṣu tiṣṭhantaṃ bhūtātmānam*: The poet appears to use the term *bhūtātmānam* in its common sense of "the individual soul," as opposed to "the universal spirit (*paramātmā*)," although some of the commentators offer this latter meaning as an optional interpretation. Ck and Ct gloss, "soul (*jīva*)," which they understand to be present amid the objects of sense, such as sound, etc., as the one who perceives or experiences them (*indriyārthāḥ śabdādiviṣayās teṣu tiṣṭhantam anubhavitṛtvenāvasthitaṃ bhūtātmānaṃ jīvam*—so Ct). Cr, who calls the figure "an apt illustration (*saddṛṣṭānta*), interprets similarly, glossing, "the

inner spirit *or* individual soul (*antaryāmin*)." Cv understands *bhūtātman* in the sense of "the supreme *or* universal spirit (*paramātman*)," which, through its universal pervasion, is present in subtle form in all sense objects, although it cannot be directly perceived (*indriyārtheṣu śabdādiviṣayeṣu tiṣṭhantaṃ bhūtātmānam iva pratyakṣato 'numīyamāneṣu gandhādiṣu guṇeṣu saukṣmyenānuvṛttaṃ prithivyādisvarūpam iva paramātmanaḥ sarvavyāpitayā candanādiviṣayeṣu tiṣṭhantam*). Cg offers two interpretations, the second of which is essentially that of Cv. Cg's first interpretation is similar to that of Ck and Ct, except that he provides a slightly different etymology for the term *bhūtātman*, according to which "*bhūta* stands for the body, which consists of the five elements (*bhūtas*), so that the compound means 'the animating spirit of the body,' that is, 'the living spirit' (*bhūtātmānaṃ bhūtasya pañcabhūtātmakaśarīrasyātmānaṃ jīvātmānam*)." See notes to 6.15.4. Cm offers three explanations:

1) The first is similar to that of Cv. The term *bhūtātman* refers to the Supreme Spirit, which is present in all bodies as the animating spirit. (*indriyārtheṣu tiṣṭhantam indriyaviṣayeṣu prerakatvena śarīreṣv avatiṣṭhantam. bhūtātmānaṃ paramātmānam.*)
2) The second is similar to that of Ck and Ct. Cm adds only the idea that the *bhūtātman*, or "living spirit," can merely be inferred from the fact of its experiencing the objects of sense (*tenānubhavenānumīyamānam api bhūtātmānaṃ jīvātmānam*).
3) The third is a slight modification of Cv's interpretation. Cm understands *bhūtātman* to be the Supreme Spirit, which, by virtue of its universal pervasion, is present in subtle form as the underlying consciousness with regard to objects of sense, such as sound, etc. (*bhūtātmānaṃ paramātmānaṃ prajā iva paramātmanaḥ sarvavyāpitayā śabdādiviṣayeṣūpādhānacaitanyarūpatayā sūkṣmarūpeṇa tiṣṭhantam*).

According to Gorresio, Cl offers two possible explanations of the term *bhūtātman*, which are found in several of the other commentators. His first gloss is the same as Cr's (*antaryāmin*), while his second is that of Ck and Ct (*jīva*). The term inspires Gorresio (1858, vol. 10, pp. 299–300, n. 59) to provide, in a note, a discussion of the Indian tradition's distinction between the vital principle and the principle of consciousness, which he compares to modern (i.e., mid-nineteenth-century) distinctions between biology and psychology. See 6.47.54 and note, where the term is used but where the context lends it a somewhat different connotation.

21–22. "He is slaughtering . . . He is slaughtering . . . he is slaughtering" *eṣa hanti . . . eṣa hanti . . . eṣa hanti*: Ck and Ct believe that the exclamations or thoughts are articulated, respectively, by the *rākṣasas* in each of the four divisions of the army mentioned; each group believes that Rāma is attacking only their individual force. (*eṣa gajānīkavartī gajānīkam eva hanti nānyam iti gajānīkasthā manyante. evam anye 'pi manyante smety arthaḥ.*) See note to 6.3.24, where the four divisions of the traditional Indian army are discussed.

"great chariot-warriors" *mahārathān*: Here, as elsewhere, some translators take the term to refer to the chariots themselves rather than the warriors. See notes to verse 18 above.

"infantry along with the cavalry" *padātīn vājibhiḥ saha*: Literally, "foot soldiers along with horses."

"because of their seeming similarity to Rāma, all the *rākṣasas* began . . . to slaughter one another in battle, slaying those *rākṣasas* who resembled Rāghava . . ." *te rākṣasāḥ* *sarve rāmasya sadṛśān . . . / anyonyam . . . jaghnuḥ sādṛśyād rāghavasya te*: Literally, "all those *rākṣasas*, because of similarity to Rāghava, killed one another, who resembled Rāma." The verse manages to be both redundant and elliptical at the same time. In and of itself, it is hard to determine what is supposed to be happening here. The following verses, however, make it clear that the *rākṣasas* are under the delusive spell of Rāma's supernatural weapons and thus mistake one another for Rāma. Our translation follows the suggestion of the commentators who flesh out the elliptical adjective *sadṛśān*, "similar," by glossing, "*rākṣasas* appearing to be similar (*sadṛśatvena pratīyamānān rākṣasān*)." Ct refers to a variant reading for the first half of verse 22 that is unattested in the critical apparatus. This reading attempts to avoid the redundancy by making the *rākṣasas* appear in the first instance to be similar to Rāvaṇa rather than Rāma. Some northern manuscripts and the editions of Gorresio (6.73.25–26) and Lahore (6.72.25–26ab) attempt to rationalize the situation by substituting a passage of two lines [1839*], stating that, under the influence of Rāma's divine weapons, the *rākṣasas* see the entire world as consisting of Rāma.

23. "great Rāma . . . him" *rāmam . . . mahātmanā*: Literally, "Rāma . . . by the great one." Like Cr, and apparently Cg, we understand the instrumental *mahātmanā* here as the grammatical subject of the participle *mohitāḥ*, "befuddled," and as referring to Rāma. Cs explicitly indicates that the adjective modifies the weapon. Several of the translations consulted understand in this same way.

"the mighty, divine weapon-spell of the *gandharvas*" *paramāstreṇa gāndharveṇa*: This appears to be one of the weapons given to Rāma by Viśvāmitra at 1.26.14 (see notes to that passage as well), where, however, it appears to be described as a sword (*asi*). There the weapon is also said to "belong to Manu (*mānava*)," although the critical editors mark this reading as doubtful. A number of northern and southern manuscripts, as well as the texts and printed editions of Ct and Cr, read instead *mohanam*, "confusing, befuddling," which would appear to conform better to the present context. One may also note that Rāma is said to use the *mānava* weapon, also called *śīteṣu*, at 1.29.13–17 (see notes to the passage). Interestingly, the weapon there merely stuns or befuddles (*mohayitvā*) the *rākṣasa* Mārīca without killing him. Cg indicates that another two of the weapons, the *prasvāpana* and *praśamana*, also belong to the *gandharvas* (see Cg on GPP 1.27.14; see, too, 1.26.15). See 3.24.28 and note.

"they could not see him" *na te dadṛśire rāmam*: Literally, "they did not see Rāma." See note above for the syntax. Cs believes that, in their befuddlement, the *rākṣasas* in the various sections of the army are unable to see Rāma even when he is fighting right near them (*sainyaikadeśasthā rāmam . . . svasthāne sthitam . . . mohitāḥ santo na dadṛśire*).

"even though . . . the army of his foes" *arivāhinīm*: Literally, "the army of foes." D5,9–11, and the texts and printed editions of Ct read instead *api vāhinīm*, "even though [burning] the army."

24. "saw a thousand Rāmas" *rāmasahasrāṇi . . . paśyanti*: Literally, "they see a thousand Rāmas." Ct and Cr understand that the vision of multiple Rāmas is a result of the confusion caused by Rāma's weapon in the previous verse (*mohakāryam eva*—so Cr). Cg, however, disagrees, saying that the vision of multiplicity, like the inability to see Rāma and the perception of other *rākṣasas* as similar to him, is not caused by the divine weapon-spell but rather by the *rākṣasas*' fear of Rāma. In support of this he cites the statement of the *rākṣasa* Mārīca at 3.37.26 to the effect that, in his terror, he sees a

thousand Rāmas (*adarśanavat sadṛśadarśanavac cānekatvadarśanaṃ nāstrakṛtaṃ kiṃtu bhītikṛtam... mārīcenāpy uktam api rāmasahasrāṇi bhītaḥ paśyāmi rāvaṇeti*).

Cs cites no fewer than three textual sources that support the possibility of Rāma making himself appear first multiple and then single. The first is a quote he attributes to "Bhagavatpāda" (Madhva?) according to which the hero (presumably Rāma) was visible in all directions as he struck [his enemies]. (*uktaṃ ca bhagavatpādaiḥ—sa eva sarvatra ca dṛśyamāno vidikṣu dikṣu prajaghāna sarvaśa iti punaḥ kṣaṇāntara ekam eva paśyanti.*) The second is a passage from the *Saṃgraharāmāyaṇa* of Śrīnārāyaṇapaṇḍitācārya, in which Rāma manifests himself in a single form, although he truly possesses the universal form (*viśvarūpa*). (*uktaṃ ca saṃgraharāmāyaṇe 'pāṅgamātreṇa jaganniyantā nanv ekarūpo 'pi ripūn nihanyāt. svaiśvaryam evaṃ ca nidarśayan hi sa viśvarūpo 'kṛta viśvarūpam. ityādyārabhyaikīcakārātha sa rāmadevo dīpābhimānī hi yathāgnideva ity antena.*) Finally, Cs cites a passage from the *Rāmopākhyāna* (*MBh* 3.274.5–7) in which Rāvaṇa magically makes multiple images of himself and of Rāma and Lakṣmaṇa. Cs notes that this passage does not contradict the present one. (*yat tu bhārate māyāvī cāsṛjan māyāṃ rāvaṇo rākṣasādhipaḥ. atha bhūyo 'pi māyāṃ sa vyadadhād rākṣasādhipa ityādinā rāvaṇamāyayānekarākṣasarāmalakṣmaṇarūpanirmāṇakathanaṃ tadaviruddham ity atrāpi grāhyam.*) The idea here appears to be that, if Rāvaṇa is able to magically re-create himself, so, too, can Rāma.

25. "tip" *koṭim*: As is clear from the syntax, as well as from the comments of Ck, Ct, and Cr, the reference here is to the tip or end of a bow (*dhanuṣkoṭim*—Ct). Three of the translators consulted, however, Gorresio, Roussel, and Shastri, take the term in its sense of a crore, or ten million. They understand that the *rākṣasas* see Rāma's bow as multiple. This reading cannot be sustained on the basis of the grammar. Shastri (1959, vol. 3, p. 274), as usual, simply translates the version of Roussel (1903, vol. 3, p. 310). As noted above, at verse 16, it appears likely that Roussel himself was influenced by Gorresio (1858, vol. 10, p. 134).

"whirling about like a circle of blazing fire" *bhramantīm... alātacakrapratimām*: Literally, "[a tip] that was like the circle of a firebrand whirling about." The commentators are divided in their understanding of the image represented here. Ck and Ct understand that the golden tip of Rāma's bow appears to make a circle because of the rapidity with which it is being drawn back to his ear (*ākarṇavegato 'navasthitam... svarṇamayīm... dhanuṣkoṭiṃ vegavaśād alātacakrapratimāṃ dadṛśuḥ*). Cm, however, understands that the illusion is a result of Rāma's circular movements [in battle] (*rāmasya maṇḍalākāragativiśeṣeṣu bhramantīm ata evālātacakrapratimāṃ kārmukakoṭiṃ dadṛśuḥ*). Cg quotes the opinion of Cm, attributing it to "some [authorities] (*kecit*)," but offers his own opinion that the illusion derives from the incessant drawing of the bowstring. He goes on to argue that the image suggested is that of an apparent circle created by the incessant whirling about of a blazing piece of wood through the phenomenon of the persistence of vision. (*nirantarajyākarṣaṇād iti vayam. alātacakrapratimāṃ nirjvālaṃ kāṣṭhaṃ nirantarabhramaṇenāntarālāgrahaṇāc cakratvena pratīyamānam ivety arthaḥ.*)

26–27. Cg, alone among the commentators, attempts to lend a theological coloring to the metaphor by superimposing Viṣṇu's iconic discus, Sudarśana, upon the common image of the wheel of time (*kālacakra*). He also attempts to provide a rationale for each of the elements of the extended metaphor. (*atha tatra samarasamaye maṇḍalīkṛtakārmukaṃ rāmaṃ sakalaripunighātisudarśanatvena rūpayati.*)

"the sound of his bowstring striking his armguard for its rumbling" *jyāghoṣatalanirghoṣam*: We understand the compound as a *paranipāta* for *jyātalaghoṣanirghoṣam*, "having the sound of bowstring and armguard for its sound." The commentators read it as a *dvandva*, understanding: "The armguard (*tala*) refers to the place where the string strikes the bow. The word 'armguard (*tala*)' indicates the sound of the armguard (*tala*). The bow, then, has for its sound the sounds of both the bowstring and the armguard. (*talaṃ jyāghātasthalam. talaśabdena talaghoṣo lakṣyate. jyāghoṣatalaghoṣau nirghoṣo yasya tat*—so Cm)." See notes to 6.66.23; 6.75.25; 6.76.2,24; 6.77.31 (1701*); and 6.88.58.

"his qualities of blazing energy and mental brilliance for its radiance" *tejobuddhiguṇaprabham*: Commentators differ as to how to interpret and analyze this compound. Ck and Ct understand *tejaḥ*-, "blazing energy," as "courage (*pratāpaḥ*)"; -*buddhi*-, "mental brilliance," as "knowledge (*jñānam*)"; and take the term -*guṇa*- to refer to those two qualities or virtues. Cr reads the compound similarly, without glossing the first two members. Cm understands similarly but glosses *tejaḥ*- as "bodily splendor *or* beauty (*śarīrakāntiḥ*)." Cg reads the compound somewhat differently from the other commentators. He glosses *tejaḥ*- as "courage, valor (*parākramaḥ*)." But through a complex use of metonymy he argues that the term -*buddhi*-, "intellect," actually refers to the axle or pivot point of a wheel (*akṣapradeśaḥ*). He then understands -*guṇa*- to mean "bodily splendor *or* beauty (*śarīrakāntiḥ*)."

"the power of his divine weapon-spell for its sharp edge" *divyāstraguṇaparyantam*: Literally, "having the qualities of a divine *astra* for its limit. We follow the commentators in understanding the term -*guṇa*- here in the sense of "power, greatness, etc." They gloss *vaibhavam* (Ck, Ct), *aiśvaryam* (Cr), and *śaktiḥ* or *māhātmyam* (Cg, Cm). See Introduction, p. 112.

28–30. Several of the commentators, notably Cv, Ck, Cm, Cg, and Ct, spend considerable time attempting to provide the exact and very large numbers of the forces in the *rākṣasa* army, basing their calculations on the definitions of the different military units given in the *Amarakośa* (2.8.81). After attempting to enumerate precisely the various *rākṣasa* forces, Cg suggests that the inclusion of such adjectives as "swift as the wind (*vātaraṃhasām*)" indicates that there are innumerable chariots, elephants, horses, and infantry over and above those whose numbers are specified. (*vātaraṃhasām ityādiviśeṣaṇamahimnā tadbhinnā rathagajaturagapadātayo 'saṃkhyeyā iti bhāvaḥ.*) See, too, Dikshitar 1944, pp. 198–99.

"in the eighth part of a day" *divasasyāṣṭame bhāge*: The period of time referred to here could be one *yāma*, or "watch," that is, a period of three hours, and thus one-eighth of a twenty-four-hour day. On the other hand, some of the commentators offer different interpretations. Ck believes that the reference is to a period of two *muhūrtas*, i.e., ninety-six minutes (*muhūrtadvayena*). Ct concurs but specifies that these are the two closing *muhūrtas* of the fourteenth day of the lunar fortnight (*caturdaśīsaṃbandhyantyamuhūrtadvayena*). Cv similarly notes that, with the destruction of Rāvaṇa's core army, the fourteenth day [of the battle] has been completed (*mūlabalavadhena caturdaśam ahaḥ samāptam*). Cm and Cg understand that the period is two *muhūrtas* (four *ghatikās*—so Cg) decreased by one-quarter [of a *ghaṭikā*], in other words, ninety-six minutes less six (*pādonaghaṭikācatuṣṭaye*). This calculation yields a period of ninety minutes, which corresponds to the eighth part of a twelve-hour tropical day. See note to 6.4.4.

31. "remnants" *hataśeṣāḥ*: See 6.42.36; 6.82.4; and notes.

32. "the playground" *ākrīḍabhūmiḥ*: Cg, who reads the variant *ākrīḍam iva*, understands the term here to refer to the cremation ground, which is, after all, one of the places where Rudra/Śiva disports himself. Cg bases his interpretation on a passage, which he indicates was given earlier, to the effect that "the citadel of Laṅkā will soon resemble a cremation ground (*acireṇa purī laṅkā śmaśānasadṛśī bhaved iti pūrvokteḥ*). See 5.24.24 (GPP 5.26.22). Cf., too, 6.82.20 and note.

"wielder of the Pināka" *pinākinaḥ*: Ś,B1,D1–4,6–12,T2,3,G2,M3,5, and the texts and printed editions of the southern commentators read instead *mahātmanaḥ* (Ś,D8,12,M3—[*su*]*mahātmanaḥ*), "of the [very] great one." Cg, the only commentator to remark on this reading, understands the epithet to refer not to Rudra but to Rāma, in which case the verse would mean that Rāma's battlefield resembled Rudra's playground.

34. "the power of this divine weapon-spell" *etad astrabalaṃ divyam*: Literally, "this divine power of the *astra*." The reference, of course, is to the great *gāndharva* weapon-spell, named in verse 23 above, with which Rāma has accomplished his decimation of the *rākṣasa* army.

"belongs only to me and three-eyed Śiva" *mama vā tryambakasya vā*: Literally, "is mine or Tryambaka's." Cg believes that Rāma makes this assertion to dispel any anticipation that he is employing the kind of magic illusion used by the *rākṣasas*, an anticipation that might arise from his virtually instantaneous destruction of the *rākṣasa* forces (*kṣaṇenānena rakṣaḥpratikṣepajanitāṃ māyāvittvaśaṅkāṃ vārayati*). Cg also indicates that Tryambaka would possess this power at the time of [universal] destruction (*saṃhārakāle 'stīti śeṣaḥ*). Ct believes that, in mentioning that this power belongs to himself and Śiva alone, Rāma is suggesting that he is, in fact, Viṣṇu (*anena svasya viṣṇutvaṃ sūcitam*). See 6.66.6 and note.

Following 34ab, D5–7,9–11,S insert a passage of two lines [1849*], which extends Rāma's audience: "the righteous one [addressed Sugrīva], Vibhīṣaṇa, the monkey Hanumān, the foremost of tawny monkeys Jāmbavān, Mainda, and Dvivida."

35. "the *rākṣasa* host" *rākṣasavāhinīṃ tu*: D7,9–11,G1,2,M1,2,5, and the texts and printed editions of Ct and Cr read the hypermetric *rākṣasarājavāhinīm*, "the host of the *rākṣasa* king."

"who had conquered all fatigue and who was the equal of Śakra in the use of weapons and divine weapon-spells" *śakrasamaḥ . . . astreṣu śastreṣu jitaklamaś ca*: Literally, "the equal of Śakra in the use of weapons and *astras* and who had conquered fatigue." Cr reads the adjective *jitaklamaḥ*, "having conquered fatigue," closely with the locatives referring to the divine weapon-spells and the weapons (*astreṣu* and *śastreṣu*). He therefore seems to understand the verse to mean that Rāma was unwearied in the use of these weapons. This interpretation has been followed by Raghunathan (1982, vol. 3, p. 276) and Gita Press (1969, vol. 3, p. 1763). Roussel (1903, vol. 3, p. 311), followed by Shastri (1959, vol. 3, p. 275) and Pagani (1999, p. 1127), understands that Rāma is simply standing amid the fallen weapons.

"was praised by the . . . hosts of the gods" *saṃstūyate devagaṇaiḥ*: Literally, "is praised by the hosts of the gods." Ct and Ck add the particle *sma* to indicate that the present tense is to be read here as the past. Cg, however, believes that the poet has deliberately used the present to indicate that the uninterrupted praise of Rāma goes on even until today (*saṃstūyata iti vartamānanirdeśena stuter adyāpy avichinnatvam ucyate*).

The meter is *upajāti*.

Sarga 82

1–3. "Thousands of war-elephants and battle-steeds with their riders" *tāni nāgasahasrāṇi sārohāṇāṃ ca vājinām*: Literally, "those thousands of elephants and of horses with their riders." D5,T1,G3,M3, and the texts and printed editions of Cg read *tāni*, "those," for *nāga*-, "elephants," which results in the sequence *tāni tāni*, "those various." This reading makes no explicit reference to the elephants, which are mentioned throughout the preceding *sarga*. Cg seeks to remedy this omission by arguing that the term *vājin*, "battle-steed, horse," whose underlying meaning is "swift *or* feathered one," refers here through *upalakṣaṇa* (metonymy) to the elephants as well.

V3,D6,9–11, and the texts and printed editions of Ct read the nominative/accusative plural *sārohāṇi* for the critical edition's genitive plural *sārohāṇām*. This reading assigns the riders to the elephants rather than the horses.

"sharp" *tīkṣṇaiḥ*: Ñ2,V,B,D1–3,6,9–11, and the texts and printed editions of Ct and Cr read instead, *dīptaiḥ*, "blazing, burning."

4. "When . . . had seen what had happened and . . . had heard about it" *dṛṣṭvā śrutvā ca*: Literally, "having seen and having heard." Several of the commentators suggest that the verse should be construed with the three preceding verses, taking the participle *nihatāni*, "slaughtered" from 3a as the object of the two gerunds. The syntax would thus be "having seen and heard that the [*rākṣasas*, etc.] had been slaughtered . . ." The poet's idea in using the two gerunds is probably to distinguish the survivors of the battle, who had actually witnessed the destruction of the army, from the women who had merely heard about it. Ct and Ck seem to understand that it is the elderly *rakṣasa* males who actually see the troops slaughtered by Rāma while the collectivity of those who are old, have survived the battle, women, and children hear about it (*rāmeṇa hatāni dṛṣṭvā vṛddhās tu śrutvā hataśeṣā bālavṛddhā niśācarā rākṣasyaś ca*).

"the remnants of the night-roaming *rākṣasa* troops" *hataśeṣā niśācarāḥ*: Literally, "night-roamers who were left over from the slain." We have added the word "troops" to make it clear that the reference is to the battle survivors mentioned in 6.81.31 above. Ct and Ck understand the term *hataśeṣāḥ*, "left over from the slain," to refer to those *rākṣasas* who were either too young or too old to have participated in the battle (see note above). Cm, on the other hand, understands that *hataśeṣāḥ* refers to the surviving troops who have returned from the battlefield as well as those who had remained in Laṅkā (*hataśeṣā niśācarā raṇāt pratinivṛttā laṅkāsthāś ca*).

"they huddled together in panic" *saṃbhrāntāḥ . . . samāgamya*: Literally, "[they] agitated, having assembled."

5. "they huddled together" *saha saṃgamya*: Literally, "they assembled together." The phrase seems somewhat redundant. Cr explains the adverb *saha*, "together," as meaning "all at the same time (*ekakālāvacchedena*)." Both he and Cg understand that the women embrace one another (*parasparam āliṅgitā ity arthaḥ*—so Cg).

6. "potbellied" *nirṇatodarī*: We understand the term to refer to Śūrpaṇakhā's pendulous or protuberant stomach. This would tend to be confirmed by the passage at 3.15.8, where Śūrpaṇakhā is said to be "large-bellied (*mahodarī*)" in contrast to Rāma with his "slender waist (*vṛttamadhyama*)." See 3.15.8 and note. See, too, MW (s.v.). Cm appears to share our view. He glosses, "whose belly [hung down] like an elephant's trunk (*karabhodarī*)." Ck, Ct, and Cr, however, ignoring the *upasarga niḥ*, "outward," understand the adjective *nirṇata* to mean "sunken (*nimna*—so Ck, Ct)," and several translators have followed this interpretation.

"snaggletoothed" *karālā*: Cg takes the term in its sense of "hideous, deformed, frightful (*vikaṭā*)." Compare, however, 5.15.8 and note, where the *rākṣasa* women are described.

"that... hag" *vṛddhā*: Literally, "old woman."

"made advances" *āsasāda*: Literally, "she approached."

7–8. Compare the similar yet more elaborate passage at 3.16.8–10 (and note). The two verses constitute a single extended sentence in which the *rākṣasa* woman Śūrpaṇakhā is the subject and Rāma is the object. We have broken it up and restructured it in the interest of English style and readability.

"delicate, yet immensely powerful" *sukumāraṃ mahāsattvam*: Literally, "delicate [and] of immense strength."

"hideous" *hīnarūpā*: Literally, "devoid of beauty."

"Really, someone ought to kill her." *lokavadhyā sā*: Literally, "she ought to be killed by the people." M3 and the texts and printed editions of Cg read *lokanindyā sā*, "she ought to be censured by the people."

"how... could... have possibly hoped to win him" *katham... kāmayāmāsa*: Literally, "How did she desire [Rāma]?"

9–10. "this white-haired crone" *palinī śvetamūrdhajā*: Literally, "the white-haired woman with gray hair." The reading, although fairly well attested textually, appears to be redundant. D7,10,11,T1,M3, and the texts and printed editions of the southern commentators read instead *valinī*, "wrinkled," for *palinī*, "gray-haired." Ñ,V1,2,B,D1–4,6,9,T2,3, and the editions of Lahore and Gorresio read instead *malinā*, "dirty, impure, sinful." Neither Apte nor MW cite *palinī* as an entry; however, both the word *palikī*, "a gray-haired lady," and *palitin*, "gray-haired," are cited.

"so ill suited to Rāghava... advances to him" *apratirūpā sā rāghavasya pradharṣaṇam*: Literally, "she who was not conformable [made] an assault *or* outrage against Rāghava." In the spirit of the *viṣamālaṃkāra* in the preceding passage and at 3.16.8–10, we concur with Cg's interpretation of the term *apratirūpā*. He glosses, "not similar *or* conformable (*ananurūpā*)." Ś1,V,B1,2,D3,8,12,T2,3, and the text of Ck read instead *apratirūpasya*, which makes the adjective modify *rāghavasya*. Ct, noting the variant, explains it as meaning "dissimilar to her in appearance (*tadasadṛśākārasyety arthaḥ*)." Ct glosses the critical reading, which is his as well, as "of deformed appearance (*vikṛtarūpā*)."

"impermissible" *akāryam*: Literally, "not to be done."

"led to the destruction of Dūṣaṇa, Khara, and the *rākṣasas* in general" *rākṣasānāṃ vināśāya dūṣaṇasya kharasya ca*: Literally, "for the destruction of the *rākṣasas*, Dūṣaṇa and Khara" We understand that the *rākṣasa* women are anticipating the extermination of their race and not merely referring to the fourteen thousand *rākṣasa* warriors slain by Rāma in Janasthāna. See 3.19–29.

11. "It was on her account" *tannimittam*: Literally, "because of him, her, *or* it." We agree with Cr in taking the pronoun *tat-* to refer to Śūrpaṇakhā, since the *rākṣasa* women had been speaking so vehemently against her. Ct, Cm, and Cg see the reference to be to the pronoun's closest antecedent, *pradharṣaṇam*, "assault, outrage," in the preceding verse.

"to his own destruction" *vadhāya*: Literally, "for death *or* destruction." Ct and Cr understand the reference to be to the destruction of [all] the *rākṣasas*.

12. "Yet although he has not won over" *na ca... prāpnoti*: Literally, "and he does not acquire." The idea, of course, is that, although Sītā is in Rāvaṇa's possession, she

has never yielded to his advances. Ct adds the words "and he will not acquire (*na prāpsyati ca*)."

"Rāvaṇa has forged . . . enmity" *baddham . . . vairam*: Literally, "enmity was bound." We understand, with Cr, that one needs to supply the subject "Rāvaṇa (*rāvaṇena*)."

13. Virādha's attempted abduction of Sītā is narrated at *Araṇyakāṇḍa* 2–3.

"When he heard" *prekṣya*: Literally, "having seen." We follow the suggestion of Cg, who glosses, "having known (*jñātvā*)." Rāvaṇa was, of course, not a witness to the slaying of Virādha at *Araṇyakāṇḍa* 3.

"who was assaulting" *prārthayānam*: We understand this irregular present participle in its sense of "attacking, assaulting" (Apte s.v.). Translators consulted have taken the verbal root in its more common sense of "solicit, beg, desire," but that sense is far too weak to express Virādha's abortive attempt to carry off Sītā at *Araṇyakāṇḍa* 2.

"by Rāma single-handedly" *ekena rāmeṇa*: Literally, "by Rāma alone." Both Ck and Ct understand *ekena* here to mean "without assistance (*asahāyena*)." But this is at variance with the account of the slaying of Virādha at *Araṇyakāṇḍa* 3, where Lakṣmaṇa actively assists his brother. Cr supplies the word *bāṇena*, lending the verse the sense that Rāma killed Virādha with a single arrow. But this, too, contradicts *Araṇyakāṇḍa* 3.11, where Rāma riddles the *rākṣasa*'s body with seven arrows.

"that should have been a sufficient warning" *paryāptaṃ tan nidarśanam*: Literally, "that was a sufficient demonstration." One could also understand, "[it was] a sufficient demonstration of that" (reading *tannidarśanam* as a *tatpuruṣa* compound). In either case, the idea is that Rāma's earlier heroic deed should have warned Rāvaṇa of the hero's extraordinary power. As Ct and Ck put it, it should have been a demonstration leading to [Rāvaṇa's] understanding that Rāma was superior to the whole world, including the gods and *asuras* (*rāmasya sadevāsurasakalalokātiśayitvāvagamāya paryāptaṃ nidarśanam ity arthaḥ*). The phrase *paryāptaṃ tannidarśanam* is repeated in similar contexts in verses 15–18 below.

14. "Rāma": The proper noun has been added.

Cg argues that one should supply the refrain "that should have been a sufficient warning (*paryāptaṃ tannidarśanam*)." See note to verse 13 above.

15. "Khara, Dūṣaṇa" *kharaḥ . . . dūṣaṇaḥ*: See note to verse 10 above.

"That, too, should have been a sufficient warning" *paryāptaṃ tannidarśanam*: See note to verse 13 above.

16. "Kabandha" *kabandhaḥ*. See *Araṇyakāṇḍa* 65–69.

"who bellowed in a transport of rage" *krodhārto vinadan*: D5,7,9–11,T1,G2,3,M3,5, and the texts and printed editions of the southern commentators read instead *krodhān nādaṃ nadan*, "roaring a roar out of rage."

"That, too, should have been a sufficient warning" *paryāptaṃ tannidarśanam*: See note to verse 13 above.

17. "Vālin" *vālinam*: See 4.16.25.

"who resembled a storm cloud" *meghasaṃkāśam*: Literally, "resembling a cloud." T1,M3, and the texts and printed editions of Cg read *meru-*, "[Mount] Meru," for *megha-*, "cloud," lending the compound the sense "resembling [Mount] Meru."

"That, too, should have been a sufficient warning" *paryāptaṃ tannidarśanam*: See note to verse 13 above.

18. "his dreams shattered" *bhagnamanorathaḥ*: Literally, "whose fantasies were shattered *or* broken." The reference is to the exiled Sugrīva's seemingly vain hopes of

recovering the lordship of the monkeys and Tārā as his queen. Roussel (1903, vol. 3, p. 313), followed by Shastri (1959, vol. 3, p. 276), renders the term *manoratha*, "fantasy, wish," more literally, rendering, "*le char de ces espérances*," while Shastri renders, "the vehicle of his hopes."

"established him in royal sovereignty" *sthāpito rājye*: See 4.25.20–35.

"That, too, should have been a sufficient warning" *paryāptaṃ tannidarśanam*: See note to verse 13 above.

19. "Rāvaṇa paid no heed to the fitting words spoken by Vibhīṣaṇa" *vākyam* . . . / *yuktaṃ vibhīṣaṇenoktam* . . . *tasya na rocate*: Literally, "he does not like the fitting words spoken by Vibhīṣaṇa." For the advice of Vibhīṣaṇa and Rāvaṇa's rejection of it, see 6.9–10.

20. "Rāvaṇa, the younger brother of Kubera" *dhanadānujaḥ*: Literally, "the one born after the giver of wealth."

"this city of Laṅkā would not have become" *neyaṃ laṅkāpurī bhavet*: D10,11, and the texts of Ct read instead *neyaṃ laṅkā bhaviṣyati*, "this Laṅkā will not be . . ." See note to 6.81.32. Cf. 5.24.24.

21. "that . . . Kumbhakarṇa had been slain by Rāghava and that his own beloved son Indrajit had been slain as well" *kumbhakarṇaṃ hatam* . . . *rāghaveṇa* . . . *cendrajitam*: Literally, "Kumbhakarṇa was slain by Rāghava . . . as was Indrajit." We have separated the two references, as Indrajit, in fact, was slain by Lakṣmaṇa at *sarga* 78 above. The correct state of affairs is represented in the southern recension, which includes 1860* translated below. Thus, Lakṣmaṇa is introduced as killing first Atikāya and then Indrajit. See *sarga* 55 for the death of Kumbhakarṇa and *sarga* 59 for the death of Atikāya.

"did not understand" *nāvabudhyate*: Several of the commentators suggest that one should supply an object, "[Rāma's] power *or* valor" (*parākramam iti śeṣaḥ*—so Cg and Cm).

Following 21ab, D4–7,9–11,S insert a passage of one line [1860*]: "and that the unassailable Atikāya had been slain by Lakṣmaṇa." See 6.59 for Atikāya's death.

Following verse 21, D7 (line 1 only) and KK insert a passage of two lines [1862*]: "Even when he saw early on that Hanumān had burned Laṅkā with the fire on his tail and killed Prince Akṣa, he did not understand." See *Sundarakāṇḍa* 45 for Akṣa's death and *Sundarakāṇḍa* 52 for the burning of Laṅkā. This verse appears in brackets as 6.95.22 in KK and is rendered in a footnote by Dutt (1893, p. 1435).

22. " 'My son has been slain in battle! My brother has been slain! My husband has been slain!' " *mama putro mama bhrātā mama bhartā raṇe hataḥ*: Literally, "my son, my brother, my husband has been slain in battle."

"Such are the cries that are heard" *ity evaṃ śrūyate śabdaḥ*: Literally, "thus the sound is heard."

"in household after household of the *rākṣasas*" *rākṣasānāṃ kule kule*: Ñ,V1,2, B3,4,D1–3,7,9–11,M1,2, and the texts and printed editions of Ct and Cr read the feminine *rākṣasīnām*, for the masculine *rākṣasānām*. This lends the passage the sense "[such is the cry] of the *rākṣasa* women in household after household *or* in household after household of the *rākṣasa* women."

23. "has destroyed . . . *rākṣasa* . . . hundreds" *hatāḥ śata-* . . . *rākṣasāś ca*: D9–11 and the texts and printed editions of Ct read instead *tatra tatra* for *hatāḥ śata-* and *hatāś cāpi* for *rākṣasāś ca*, giving the sense "[has] destroyed here and there [by the thousands] . . . and slain [foot soldiers]."

26. "Having been granted his boon... in battle" *dattavaro yudhi*: Literally, "he to whom a boon was given... in battle." The reference, as Cr points out, is to Rāvaṇa's boon of immunity from the gods and other supernatural beings (*devādibhyo mṛtyurāhityarūpam īpsitam yasmai sa daśagrīvaḥ*). Ñ,V1,2,B2,D5–7,9–11,T,G2,3,M3,5, and the texts and printed editions of the southern commentators read instead *dattamahāvaraḥ*, "he to whom a great boon was granted." See notes to 6.28.28–29; 6.31.51–52; and 6.47.104.

"ten-necked Rāvaṇa" *daśagrīvaḥ*: Literally, "the ten-necked one."

"the... danger he faces at Rāma's hands" *rāmahastāt... bhayam... utpannam*: Literally, "the danger that has arisen from Rāma's hand."

27. "not even... or" *na... na... na... na*: Ś,Ñ,V1,2,B,D1–4,6–12,T2,3,G2, and the texts and printed editions of Ct, Cr, and Ck read *taṃ*, "him," for the first negative particle of the critical edition. This makes Rāvaṇa the specific object of the verbal phrase "can save (*paritrātuṃ śaktāḥ*)."

"one who is assailed" *upasṛṣṭam*: The word, whose basic meanings are "joined, troubled, eclipsed, thrown off," seems unusual here. Commentators gloss it variously around the general sense of "engaged in battle (*yuddhāya pravṛttam*—so Cr)," "engaged to be killed (*hantuṃ niyuktam*—so Ck)," or "begun to be killed (*hantum ārabdham*—so Ct, Cm)." We believe that Cv and Cg, who gloss, "assailed, attacked (*upadrutam*)," are closest to the intended meaning.

28. "foretelling" *kathayiṣyanti*: Literally, "they will tell." Cv and Cm gloss, respectively, "they will show (*darśayiṣyanti*)" and "they will indicate (*sūcayiṣyanti*)." Cg, who shares the reading with them, is uncomfortable with the awkward use of the future tense here. He offers two explanations. The first is that there will still be some future portents that, having once appeared, will foretell [Rāvaṇa's doom] (*itaḥ param api kānicin nimittāni prādurbhūya kathayiṣyantīty arthaḥ*). Alternatively, he notes that other authorities suggest that the future is used in the sense of the present (*vartamāne tātparyam ity apy āhuḥ*). Apparently he is referring to Crā, who glosses, "they foretell (*kathayanti*)." D9–11 and the texts and printed editions of Ct and Ck appear to remedy the problem by reading instead *kathayanti hi*, "for they foretell." Ck and Ct are disturbed by the use of the root $\sqrt{}$*kath*, "to tell," with the subject *utpātāḥ*, "portents," and suggest that we must supply the actual subject, which would be Mālyavān and the other *rākṣasa* elders who have foretold the consequences of the portents (*tadutpātaphalaṃ mālyavadādayo vṛddhā iti śeṣaḥ*).

"his death at Rāma's hands" *rāmeṇa rāvaṇasya nibarhaṇam*: Literally, "the destruction of Rāvaṇa by Rāma."

29. On Rāvaṇa's boon, see notes to verse 26 above.

"But Rāvaṇa never requested invulnerability to men" *mānuṣebhyo na yācitam*: Literally, "from men it was not requested."

30. "I believe" *manye*: Literally, "I think." Cg, no doubt recalling that this is the collective lamentation of the *rākṣasa* women, glosses, "we think (*manyāmahe*)."

"that very same dangerous vulnerability" *tad idam... bhayam... ghoram*: Literally, "this [is] that terrible danger."

"to men" *mānuṣāt*: Literally, "from a man." D10,11,G,M3,5, and the texts and printed editions of Ct and Cg read instead the adjective *mānuṣam*, "human, pertaining to men," which would construe with *bhayam*, "danger."

31. "the wise gods" *vibudhāḥ*: Literally, "the wise ones." This is a common kenning for the gods.

"with fierce austerities" *dīptais tapobhiḥ*: Literally, "with blazing austerities."

32. "these grave words" *idam . . . mahad vacaḥ*: Literally, "this great speech."

"the divinities . . . their" *devatānām . . . devatāḥ*: Literally, "of the divinities . . . the divinities."

33. "all the *dānavas* and *rākṣasas*" *sarve dānavarākṣasāḥ*: According to Cg, the reference to the term *dānava* here refers specifically to those *dānavas* who, through their kinship with Mandodarī, Rāvaṇa's chief queen, reside among the *rākṣasas* (*mandodarīsambandhena dānavāś ca kecit rākṣasaiḥ saha tiṣṭhantīti jñeyam*).

"beset by danger" *bhayena prāvṛtāḥ*: Literally, "[they] shrouded *or* covered by fear." The participle is somewhat awkward in this context. The commentators who share this reading (Cv, Cm, Cg) are silent. D10,11, and the texts and printed editions of Cr, Ct, and Ck substitute the equally awkward *prabhṛtāḥ*, "borne *or* supported." Ct and Ck take the passive participle actively, glossing, "they will wander about bearing fear of the gods (*dānavā rākṣasāś ca bhayena prabhṛtā devebhyo bhayaṃ bibhrāṇā eva vicariṣyanti*)." Ct goes on to say, "The meaning is 'they [the *dānavas and rākṣasas*] will be fearful, thinking, "Whether by themselves or through others, the gods will oppress us" ' (*devāḥ svataḥ parato vāsmān pīḍayiṣyantīti bhayayuktā eva bhaviṣyantīty arthaḥ*)." Cr glosses, "supported by fear, that is, nourished [by fear], that is, joined with [fear] (*prabhṛtāḥ poṣitā yuktā ity arthaḥ*)."

34. "the great god, bull-bannered Śiva, destroyer of Tripura" *vṛṣadhvajas tripurahā mahādevaḥ*: Literally, "Mahādeva, whose banner is a bull, the destroyer *or* slayer of Tripura." The term *tripura-* can refer either to the legendary three cities of gold, silver, and iron constructed for the *asuras* by their architect Māyā, or to the *asura* chieftain who rules these cities. Thus, the epithet here is somewhat ambiguous. It can also mean "the slayer of Tripura." See 6.59.73 and note.

35. "a woman shall be born" *utpatsyati . . . nārī*: Śiva's prophecy of the birth of Sītā is not mentioned in the *Uttarakāṇḍa*.

36. "Sītā" *sītā*: Ś,B1,D1–4,8–12, and the texts and printed editions of Ct read instead *sarvān*, "all [of us]."

"just as, long ago, famine was used to devour the *dānavas*" *kṣud yathā dānavān purā*: Literally, "just as famine, long ago, the *dānavas*." The mythological reference here is not clear. Ck, Ct, and Cr note that in an earlier cosmic cycle the gods successfully employed hunger in order to destroy the *dānavas*. (*purā pūrvakalpe. devair dānavanāśārthaṃ prayuktā kṣud yathā dānavān harati sma*—so Ct.) Cg remarks that this event took place immediately after the well-known episode of the bestowing of the *amṛta*, or "nectar of immortality," upon the gods (*devebhyo 'mṛtapradānānantaram iti bodhyam*).

37. "This dreadful lamentation" *ayaṃ niṣṭānako ghoraḥ*: We are inclined to agree with Cl, who, quoted in a note by Gorresio (1858, vol. 10, p. 301), glosses the term *niṣṭānakaḥ* as "that which causes one to roar *or* weep continually (*niṣṭānako nirantaraṃ stānayati rodayatīti*)." For Cl, the term is thus derived from the verb *ni* $\sqrt{}$*stan*, "to roar, make a loud sound, groan." A closely related term, *niṣṭanaḥ*, in the sense of "groan, sigh," is used by Vālmīki at *Uttarakāṇḍa* 404*, line 3 (= GPP 7.21.12a). The term *niṣṭānaka* is also used in the sense of a "loud, sorrowful cry" at *MBh* 7.126.3. Gorresio translates, "*gran pianto*." The southern commentators are virtually unanimous in taking the term to mean "destruction (*nāśaḥ*)." Cv alone glosses, "end (*antaḥ*)." See note to 6.79.4, 1744*, n. 1. Cf. 6.42.23 and note, where the term *stanita* is used in the somewhat similar sense of "faint cries."

38. "Afflicted as we are by Rāghava, we can see no one in the world who can afford us refuge, any more than one could afford refuge to creatures afflicted by Kāla himself at the end of a cosmic age" *taṃ na paśyāmahe loke yo naḥ śaraṇado bhavet / rāghaveṇopasṛṣṭānāṃ kāleneva yugakṣaye //*: Literally, "We do not see him who, in this world, would be a granter of refuge to us who are afflicted by Rāghava, just as by Kāla at the destruction of a cosmic age."

Cg observes that the *rākṣasa* women would have heard this account of Brahmā's boon, etc., from Mandodarī, who, he notes, will be described later on as a "wise woman." (*atra pitāmahādivarapradānavṛttānto rākṣasībhir mandodarīsakāśāc chruta iti jñeyam. sā ca jñānavṛddheti vakṣyate.*)

Following verse 38, D4–7,9–11,S insert a passage of four lines [1869*]: "There is no refuge for us who are placed in such great peril any more than for elephant cows surrounded by a forest fire.[1–2] The great Vibhīṣaṇa Paulastya[1] acted in a timely fashion when he took refuge with him from whom he foresaw this danger.[3–4]"

[1]"Vibhīṣaṇa Paulastya" *paulastyena*: Literally, "the descendant of Pulastya." Cg suggests that this patronymic epithet, which normally refers to Rāvaṇa, is used here to indicate that henceforward Vibhīṣaṇa will be the sustainer of the House of Pulastya (*itaḥ paraṃ tasyaiva paulastyakulapratiṣṭhāpakatvāt tacchabdaprayogaḥ*).

39. "Afflicted and tormented by a terrible fear" *ārtātibhayābhipīḍitāḥ*: Like Cr, the only commentator to remark on this verse, we read the compound as a *dvandva*. In other words, the *rākṣasa* women are both miserable (*ārtāḥ*) and greatly afflicted with terrible fear (*atibhayābhipīditāḥ*). Cr, however, also notes that the junction (*sandhi*) of the words *ārta-* and *-atibhaya-* suggests an alternative reading. In this reading, Cr glosses *ārta* in a lexically unsupported sense as *prāpta*, "arrived, present," lending the compound the sense "afflicted by the terrible present danger." (*ārtātīty atra sandhir ata eva jñāpakād ārtaṃ prāptaṃ yad atibhayaṃ tenābhipīḍitā ity artho vā*). D5,7,T1,G3,M3, and the texts and printed editions of Cg read instead *ārtā bhayabhārapīḍitāḥ*, "miserable [and] oppressed by the weight of fear."

The meter is *vaṃśasthavila*.

Sarga 83

3. "Gnawing at his lip" *saṃdaśya daśanair oṣṭham*: Literally, "having bitten [his] lip with [his] teeth."

"flaring up" *mūrcchitaḥ* (*mūrchitaḥ*—so crit. ed.): Like Cg, who glosses, "increased (*abhivṛddhaḥ*)," we take the term in its sense of "made violent, intensified." Gorresio (1858, vol. 10, p. 139) similarly renders, "*veemente*." D9–11 and the texts and printed editions of Ct read instead *mūrtimān*, "incarnate."

4. "their speech slurred with fear" *bhayāvyaktakathān*: Literally, "having speech that was indistinct with fear." D5–7,T1,G2,3,M3, and the texts and printed editions of the southern commentators read the nominative singular *-kathaḥ* instead of the accusative plural *-kathān*, thus making the phrase apply to Rāvaṇa rather than to his *rākṣasa* attendants. In addition, D10,11, and the texts and printed editions of Ck and Ct

substitute *krodha-*, "rage," for the critical edition's *bhaya-*, "fear." This lends the compound the sense "his speech slurred with anger."

5. "tell Mahodara, Mahāpārśva, and the *rākṣasa* Virūpākṣa" *mahodaraṃ mahāpārśvaṃ virūpākṣaṃ ca rākṣasam / ... vadata*: Several of the translators consulted understand that the named *rākṣasas* are identical with or among the *rākṣasas* addressed by Rāvaṇa in the previous verse. The syntax does not support this reading, however. The idea is that Rāvaṇa instructs his attendants to go and alert Mahodara, etc. Cg notes that Mahodara and Mahāpārśva are ministers (*sacivau*) of Rāvaṇa. The two *rākṣasas* of those names who were killed earlier in the battle at *sarga* 58 were, Cg continues, brothers of Rāvaṇa, whose alternate names were Matta and Pramatta (*pūrvahatau tu mattapramattāparaparyāyau rāvaṇabhrātarau*). A *rākṣasa* named Virūpākṣa is mentioned at 6.27.20, 6.28.14, and 6.33.10, and is killed by Lakṣmaṇa at 6.33.25. Yūpākṣa is said to be crushed by Mainda at an insert to 6.63 following verse 3 (App. I, No. 43, lines 62–63 = GPP 6.76.34), while two *rākṣasas* named Yūpākṣa and Virūpākṣa are said to have been killed by Hanumān at 5.44.30. See Goldman and Goldman 1996, p. 23. See, too, 6.28.31 and note.

"Send forth the troops!" *sainyāni niryāteti*: The syntax is awkward and perhaps elliptical. We believe the best solution is that proposed by Cr, who suggests reading the verb *niryāta*, "[you all] go forth," as an unmarked causative. Alternatively, Cr suggests that if, by the word "troops (*sainyāni*)," we are to understand enemy troops, then we need not read the verb as causative, and the idea would be "go forth to the troops." (*sainyāni yūyaṃ niryāpayata niḥsārayateti mahodarādīñ chīghraṃ vadata. yadi tu sainyaśabdena ripusenā gṛhyeta tadā nāntārbhāvitaṇicūkalpanā.*)

6. "the *rākṣasas* ... the *rākṣasa* warriors" *rākṣasāḥ ... rākṣasān*: Literally, "the *rākṣasas* ... the *rākṣasas*." We agree with Cr, who understands that the first term, in the nominative, refers to Rāvaṇa's *rākṣasa* attendants who are mentioned in 4ab. He understands that the second occurrence of the term, in the accusative, refers to the *rākṣasa* warriors Mahodara, etc., mentioned in 5ab. We have translated accordingly. This distinction is supported, we believe, by the fact that the first group is represented as being terrified, whereas the second, the noble *rākṣasa* champions, are shown as retaining their composure.

"although stricken with fear ... who retained their composure" *bhayārditāḥ / ... avyagrān*: Literally, "afflicted with fear ... not agitated." Cs understands that the *rākṣasas* are caught between two sources of terror. They are fearful of going forth because of Rāma and fearful of not going because of Rāvaṇa (*gamane rāmato bhītir bhītiś cāgamane rāvaṇāt*). Ct understands that the *rākṣasa* warriors have abandoned their fear because of Rāvaṇa's exhortation (*rāvaṇaprotsāhanena tyaktabhayān*). Cs, on the other hand, feels they have simply become undemonstrative since they are resigned to their own death, like a beautiful young woman prepared to accompany her husband [on the funeral pyre] (*sahagāmibhāminīvan nirṇītamaraṇatvenāvyaktān*). Cs goes on, as he often does, to quote and reject the interpretation of Ct. He argues that there is no possibility that Supārśva (presumably a variant for Mahāpārśva) and the other *rākṣasa* warriors will abandon their fear because, first, they had not previously been described as frightened, and, second, because, in any case, they would not lose their fear because of Rāvaṇa's exhortation of the *rākṣasas* under their command. (*yat tu nāgojibhaṭṭena rāvaṇaprotsāhanena tyaktabhayān iti vyākhyātaṃ tat tu supārśavādīnāṃ netṝṇāṃ yadā bhayārditoktāpūrvaṃ tan niyamyānāṃ rākṣasānāṃ rāvaṇaprotsāhanenāvyāgratvoktyasam-*

bhavād upekṣyam.) Cm, however, glosses, "devoid of any enthusiasm for battle (*raṇotsāharahitān*)."

7. "After performing benedictory rites" *kṛtasvastyāyanāḥ*: The *svastyāyana* is a benedictory or propitiatory rite performed to ensure the success of an undertaking, such as a sacrifice or a journey. See 1.21.2 and note, where the term is used to refer to the blessings that Daśaratha and Kausalyā give as Rāma departs on his journey to the forest. See, too, 6.72.28 and notes.

"they all presented themselves before Rāvaṇa" *rāvaṇābhimukhā yayuḥ*: Literally, "they went facing Rāvaṇa." V3,D5,9–11, and the texts and printed editions of Ct read instead *te raṇābhimukhāḥ*, while D4,7,T1,G2,3,M3, and the texts and printed editions of Cr and Cg read *raṇāyābhimukhāḥ*. Both of these variants mean "[they went off] facing battle." Since the following verse shows the *rākṣasas* paying their respects to Rāvaṇa, we cannot understand the variants to mean that the *rākṣasas* proceed directly into combat upon receiving their orders. Nonetheless, several of the translators who follow the texts of the southern commentators do render the variants in this fashion. Cr attempts to avoid the problem. He first reads the sequence *sarve raṇāya*, "all . . . to battle," as the compound *sarveraṇāya*, "for the agitation (*īraṇāya*) of all (*sarveṣām*)," supplying the word "enemies (*ripūṇām*)" and glossing *īraṇāya* as "causing to tremble (*prakampanāya*)." He then glosses *-abhimukhāḥ*, "facing," as "their faces bright (*prakāśitavadanāḥ*)," adding the words "to the presence of Rāvaṇa," after the verb "they went (*yayuḥ*)." His interpretation would then read: "Their faces bright, so as to terrify all their enemies, the *rākṣasas* proceeded into the presence of Rāvaṇa."

8. "those great chariot-warriors" *mahārathāḥ*: D4,5,T1,G3,M3, and the texts and printed editions of Cg read instead *niśācarāḥ*, "night-roaming [*rākṣasas*]." See 6.60.3; 6.72.33; 6.80.6; 6.81.18; 6.84.15; and notes. Cf. 6.77.36.

9. "laughing but beside himself with rage" *prahasya . . . krodhamūrcchitaḥ* (*-mūrchitaḥ*—so crit. ed.): Literally, "having laughed, [he] stupefied with anger." Ct and Ck understand that Rāvaṇa's laughter is a product of his anger (*krodhajo 'tra prahāsaḥ*). Cg, however, sees it as a sign that Rāvaṇa regards his enemies as insignificant (*śatruṣu tṛṇīkārāt*). Cs believes we should understand the term for laughter here as a synonym for weeping (*rodanāparaparyāyo 'yaṃ prahāsaḥ*). Perhaps the idea here is that Rāvaṇa's laughter is forced in order to hide his growing despair from his troops.

10. "I shall lead Rāghava and Lakṣmaṇa" *rāghavaṃ lakṣmaṇaṃ caiva neṣyāmi*: Cm acknowledges the manifest meaning of the verse, but, as is so often the case when he sees hostility directed toward Rāma and Lakṣmaṇa, he adds a second, inner, meaning. Here he argues that we should supply the words "those other than Rāma and Lakṣmaṇa (*rāghavaṃ lakṣmaṇaṃ vinānyān iti śeṣaḥ*)." Cs mockingly criticizes Cm's inner meaning by noting that there is no evidence of Rāvaṇa's killing even a single monkey prior to this or later (*ekasyāpi kaper anāśād atraiva pūrvatrottaratra*). But compare verse 40 below.

"the abode of Yama" *yamasādanam*: Cs notes the obvious meaning but suggests another, which he achieves by breaking up the compound *yamasādanam* into the words *yam* + *asādanam*, which he explains as "him whom, i.e., Rāma, you [i.e., the *rākṣasas* addressed by Rāvaṇa] believe to be indestructible (*yaṃ rāmam asādanam asaṃhāryaṃ manyadhve taṃ rāghavam*)."

11. "I shall avenge Khara, Kumbhakarṇa, Prahasta, and Indrajit" *kharasya kumbhakarṇasya prahastendrajitos tathā / kariṣyāmi pratīkāram*: Literally, "I shall take

counteraction for Khara, Kumbhakarṇa, Prahasta, and Indrajit." Cm and Cg, respectively, suggest inserting the words *vadhasya* and *hananasya*, "[for] the killing [of Khara, etc.]."

12. "the... rivers" *nadyaḥ*: Many manuscripts, including V2,B1,D3,7,10,11, G1,2,M1,2, and the texts and printed editions of Ct and Cr, read instead *ca dyaur*, "and the sky."

"shall disappear from view" *na... na... nāpi... prakāśatvaṃ gamiṣyanti*: Literally, "they shall not go to visibility."

13. "the masses of monkey troops" *vānarayūthānāṃ tāni yūthāni*: The critical reading, which can be read as "troops of monkey troops" or "hosts of monkey hosts," is redundant and poorly supported by the critical apparatus. The great majority of both northern and southern manuscripts collated for the critical edition (Ś2,Ñ2,V,B3,D1–4,6–12,T,G1,2,M1,2,5) and all available commentators and printed editions read *-mukhyānām* for *-yūthānām*, lending the phrase the sense "the hosts *or* troops of principal *or* leading monkeys." All translations render this variant. It is not clear why the critical editors chose their reading.

Following 13ab, D4–7,9–11,S insert a passage of two lines [1877*]: "This very day, with my chariot, powerful as the wind, I shall slaughter the monkey troops with my bow and a mass of feathered arrows.[1]"

[1]"I shall slaughter... a mass of feathered arrows" *śarajālena vadhiṣyāmi patatriṇā*: Literally, "I will slaughter with my feathered arrow-mass." D4,M3,5, and the texts and printed editions of Cg, Crā, Cv, and Cm read instead *vidhamiṣyāmi patriṇā* for *vadhiṣyāmi patatriṇā*. This lends the line the sense "I will smash with my feathered mass of arrows."

14. "I shall wreak havoc upon the lotus ponds that are the monkey troops, their faces like full-blown lotuses, their color that of lotus filaments" *vyākośapadmavaktrāṇi padmakesaravarcasām / ... yūthataṭākāni ... pramathāmy aham*: Literally, "I crush the ponds that are the troops whose faces are full-blown lotuses and whose luster is that of lotus filaments." Following the commentators, we add the word "monkeys" as the substantive to which the adjective *padmakesaravarcasām*, "whose luster is that of lotus filaments," applies. D1,2,G1,M3, and the texts and printed editions of Cv and Cg read instead *ākośa-* for *vyākośa-*, "full-blown." Cv and Cg gloss *ākośa-* as "slightly expanded (*īṣadvikasita-*)."

15. "with their protruding stalks" *sanālaiḥ*: Literally, "with their stalks."

16. "With each of the arrows" *ekeṣuṇā*: Literally, "with one arrow."

"armed with trees" *drumayodhinām*: Literally, "of those tree-fighters."

17. "these women whose husbands, brothers, and sons have been slain" *hato bhartā hato bhrātā yāsāṃ ca tanayā hatāḥ*: Literally, "of whom (fem.) the husband is slain, the brother is slain, and the sons are slain." D9–11 and the texts and printed editions of Ct, Cr, and Ck read instead *hato bhrātā ca yeṣāṃ vai yeṣāṃ ca tanayo hataḥ*, "of whom (masc.) the brother has been slain, and of whom (masc.) the son has been slain." The critical reading, in addition to being far better attested textually, is contextually superior in that it is responsive to the lamentation of the bereaved *rākṣasa* women described at verse 6.82.22, where slain husbands are mentioned in addition to sons

and brothers. Rāvaṇa, it will be recalled, has overheard this lamentation at 6.83.1 above.

18. "robbed of life" *gatacetanaiḥ*: Literally, "whose consciousness is gone." The context, we believe, supports Cg's and Cm's gloss, "with life breaths departed (*gataprāṇaiḥ*)."

"I shall make it so that one will have to strain to see the surface of the earth" *karomi . . . yatnāvekṣyatalāṃ mahīm*: Literally, "I shall make the earth such that its surface is to be seen with effort." The idea, as Cg notes, is that Rāvaṇa intends to strike the monkeys down [so thickly] on the ground that there will be no spaces between their bodies (*nairandhryeṇa bhūmau vānarān pātayiṣyāmīty arthaḥ*).

19. "I shall . . . let . . . gorge" *tarpayiṣyāmi*: Literally, "I shall satisfy *or* sate."

"jackals, vultures" *gomāyavo gṛdhrāḥ*: D10,11, and the texts and printed editions of Ct read instead *kākāś ca gṛdhrāś ca*, "crows and vultures."

"rent by my arrows" *śarārditaiḥ*: Literally, "tormented by arrows." D10,11, and the texts and printed editions of Ct read *-hataiḥ* for *-arditaiḥ*, lending the compound the sense "struck *or* slain by arrows." D7,G2,M3, and the texts and printed editions of Cr and Cg read instead *śarārpitaiḥ*. Here the adjective *-arpita*, normally, "placed, offered, transferred," would have to be taken in the sense in which it is used in the same compound at 3.27.17 (GPP 3.29.19), where it means "pierced *or* wounded," and is so glossed ad loc. by Cg (*saṃkṣata*, "wounded").

20. "Get . . . ready" *kalpyatām*: Cg glosses *ākalpyatām*, which he explains as "ornament, decorate (*alaṃkriyatām*)."

"who remain" *ye 'vaśiṣṭāḥ*: D3,9–11, and the texts of Ct read instead *ye 'tra śiṣṭāḥ*, "who remain here." In the absence of the *upasarga ava*, the participle *śiṣṭāḥ*, "remaining, surviving," can also be construed to mean "trained *or* eminent." Of the translators who share the reading *śiṣṭāḥ*, only Gorresio (1858, vol. 10, p. 140) appears to take cognizance of this set of meanings. He translates, "[*i*] *Racsasi più prestanti*," by which he seems to mean the *rākṣasas* who are most fit [for battle].

21. "Assemble . . . at once" *saṃtvaryatām*: Literally, "hasten together."

22. "in great agitation" *saṃrabdhāḥ*: Cg, the only commentator to share this reading, takes the term in its common sense of "enraged, angry." He argues that the officers are furious because [the *rākṣasa* troops] have not come forth despite their having been repeatedly summoned (*punaḥ punar āhvāne 'py anāgamanāt kupitā ity arthaḥ*). D9–11 and the texts and printed editions of Ct read instead *saṃyuktāḥ*, "engaged, enjoined."

"raced about" *pariyayuḥ*: Literally, "they went around." Cg glosses, "they went by every road (*pratirathyaṃ yayur ity arthaḥ*)."

"rousting" *codayantaḥ*: Literally, "urging, impelling."

23–25. "of fearsome valor" *bhīmavikramāḥ*: Ñ2,B4,D5–7,9–11,T,G,M3,5, and the texts and printed editions of the southern commentators read instead *bhīmadarśanāḥ*, "of fearsome aspect."

"They had mighty arms" *bhujaiḥ*: Literally, "with arms." The syntax here is unclear. We broadly follow Ct, Cg, and Cm, who understand that the instrumental is used to indicate a distinctive feature or mark (*upalakṣaṇe*—so Cg). Some translators ignore the term entirely, while others understand that the *rākṣasas* are holding the listed weapons in their arms.

"They . . . bore all manner of weapons" *nānāpraharaṇaiḥ*: Literally, "with various weapons."

"ploughshares" *halaiḥ*: One assumes that some broad-bladed weapon reminiscent of the agricultural implement is intended. M1,2, and the texts and printed editions of Cg and Cm read instead *hulaiḥ*, "with knives *or* daggers." Cg and Cm cite the lexicon of Vaijayantī in support of their contention that *hula* is a type of double-edged or double-bladed weapon (*dviphalapatrāgrāyudhaviśeṣaiḥ*). Ck appears to show a slight variant, *hulu*, which he defines as a type of weapon (*āyudhaviśeṣaḥ*). See 6.59.103 and note.

"short javelins" *bhiṇḍipālaiḥ*: See 6.32.30; 6.42.19; 6.53.12; and notes.

"hundred-slayers" *śataghnībhiḥ*: See 6.3.12; 6.63.33; and notes.

26. "acting on Rāvaṇa's orders" *rāvaṇājñayā*: Literally, "by the order of Rāvaṇa."

"four commanders of the army" *balādhyakṣāś catvāraḥ*: M3 and the texts and printed editions of Cg read *satvaraḥ*, "in haste," for *catvāraḥ*, "four," and the singular *balādhyakṣaḥ* for the plural *balādhyakṣāḥ*, so that only one officer is involved in bringing the chariot.

Following 21ab, D7 and the printed editions of GPP (6.95.27cd–ab), NSP (6.95.27cd–ab), Gita Press (6.95.27cd–ab), and KK (in brackets = 6.96.27cd–32cd), as well as the text of Ct, insert a passage of thirteen lines [1881*]: "[and they brought up] a full one million chariots, three million[1] war-elephants, and six hundred million horses, donkeys, and camels.[1–2] And innumerable foot soldiers marched up at the king's command. The commanders of the army then arrayed[2] the forces before the king.[3][3–4] At that juncture, the charioteer brought his chariot to a halt. It was covered with celestial garlands and hangings,[4] and adorned with all manner of ornaments.[5–6] It was yoked to celestial steeds and adorned with celestial ornaments.[5] It was filled with every sort of weapon and covered with networks of little bells.[7–8] It was inlayed with all sorts of gems and shone with jeweled pillars. It had thousands of vessels made of *jāmbūnada* gold.[9–10] When the *rākṣasas* saw it, they were all supremely astonished. And Rāvaṇa, lord of the *rākṣasas*, seeing it shining like fire and blazing like ten million suns, leapt to his feet.[11–13]"

[1]"one million . . . three million" *niyutam . . . niyutatrayam*: The term *niyuta* is lexically recorded in the sense both of "one hundred thousand" and "one million" (Apte s.v.). Translators consulted choose one or the other, or, in some cases, leave the term untranslated. Although numerous terms for large numbers occur earlier in the *Yuddhakāṇḍa* (see note to 6.19.32), this term is not among them.

[2]"arrayed" *saṃsthāpya*: Literally, "having placed." The gerund is not resolved by any finite verb.

[3]"before the king" *rājñaḥ . . . puraḥsthitām*: Literally, "standing *or* situated before the king." GPP (6.95.29), KK (6.96.28), and the text of Gita Press (6.95.29) read instead *purasthitām*, "standing in the city." This variant is rendered in Gita Press (1969, vol. 3, p. 1769), Roussel (1903, vol. 3, p. 316), Shastri (1959, vol. 3, p. 279), and Pagani (1999, p. 1131). It is not recorded in the critical apparatus.

[4]"It was covered with celestial garlands and hangings." *divyasragvastrasampannam*: D7, GPP (6.95.30), NSP (6.95.30), KK (6.96.29cd), and Gita Press (6.95.30) all read instead *divyāstravarasaṃpannam*, "endowed with the most excellent of divine missiles." According to the critical apparatus, only D7 and KK (in brackets) read this passage. All translators who render it translate this variant.

[5]"It was yoked to celestial steeds and adorned with celestial ornaments." *divyavāji-samāyuktaṃ divyālaṃkārabhūṣitam*: GPP, NSP, KK, and Gita Press omit this line. The critical apparatus notes that it is omitted only from KK.

27. "that celestial chariot" *rathaṃ divyam*: D9–11 and the texts and printed editions of Ct read instead *tadā bhīmam*, "then [he mounted] that fearsome [chariot]." D7,G2,M3, and the texts and printed editions of Cg read the nominative variant *bhīmaḥ*, "fearsome," in which case the adjective must apply to Rāvaṇa.

"with its own splendor" *svatejasā*: Raghunathan (1982, vol. 3, p. 281) renders, "[the chariot] lit up by his [Rāvaṇa's] splendour."

"In the excess of his power" *sattvagāmbhīryāt*: Literally, "out of the profundity of strength." Here we follow Ct, Cm, and Cr in understanding the term *gāmbhīrya* to refer to excess (*balātiśayāt*—so Ct and Cm). Raghunathan (1982, vol. 3, p. 281) reads the compound as a *dvandva*, rendering, "with his strength and weight," but this is not persuasive. Pagani (1999, p. 1131) idiosyncratically renders, "*du poids énorme de ses troupes*."

"as if he would tear up the earth itself" *dārayann iva medinīm*: Literally, "as if rending the earth." D4,7,9, and the texts and printed editions of Ct read *vārayan*, normally, "covering, warding off, *or* obstructing," for *dārayan*, "rending." None of these meanings makes a great deal of sense here. Of the translators consulted, only Roussel, followed by Shastri, and Pagani attempt to render this variant. Roussel (1903, vol. 3, p. 317) and Shastri (1959, vol. 3, p. 279) understand the participle to mean "*écrasant*" and "bearing down," respectively, while Pagani (1999, vol. 3, p. 1131) understands, "*couvrir*," which leads her to the idiosyncratic translation of *sattvagāmbhīryāt* noted above.

Following 27ab, D5–7,9–11,S insert a passage of one line [1884*]: "He then set forth impetuously, surrounded by many *rākṣasas*."

Following verse 27, D7, the printed editions of GPP (6.95.35–38), NSP (6.95.35–38), Gita Press (6.95.35–38), and KK (in brackets, 6.96.35–38), as well as the text of Ct, insert a passage of nine lines [1885*]: "Then on all sides there arose a tremendous din of trumpets, *mṛdaṅga* and *paṭaha* drums, conches, and the shouts of the *rākṣasas*.[1–2] A tumultuous cry went up, 'Marked by the insignia of the parasol and yak-tail fly whisks, the malevolent king of the *rākṣasas*—the ravisher of Sītā, the murderer of brahmans, and the thorn in the side of the gods—has come to offer battle to the foremost of the Raghus!'[3–5] That mighty roar caused the earth to tremble. And, hearing that sound, the monkeys suddenly fled in terror.[6–7] But great-armed Rāvaṇa, of tremendous blazing power, marched on to battle surrounded by his ministers in order to secure victory.[1] [8–9]"

[1]"marched on to battle . . . in order to secure victory" *ājagāma . . . vijayāya raṇaṃ prati*: Literally, "he came to battle for victory." The texts and printed editions of Ct, KK, and Gita Press read instead the seemingly redundant *jayāya vijayam*, "to victory for victory."

30. "Rāvaṇa marched forth" *niryayau*: Literally, "he went out."

"he resembled Yama, who brings time itself to an end" *kālāntakayamopamaḥ*: Literally, "[he was] similar to Yama, the ender of time." See 6.21.26 and note.

31. "through the gate" *dvāreṇa*: Cg notes that this would be the northern gate (*uttaradvāreṇa*). This is in accord with 6.28.30, where Rāma and Lakṣmaṇa are said to have taken up their positions at the northern gate (see 6.28.30 and note).

32. Verses 32–35 provide a list of inauspicious omens very similar to those that accompany the march of Dhūmrākṣa at 6.41.30–33. For similar passages listing inauspicious omens, see 6.31.3–12; 6.45.31–37; 6.53.41–45; 6.65.17–19; 6.94.14–27; and notes.

"the sun grew dim" *naṣṭaprabhaḥ sūryaḥ*: Literally, "the sun was such that its radiance was destroyed."

"Fierce birds" *dvijāḥ ... ghorāḥ*: All translators consulted who have this reading render the adjective *ghorāḥ* either adverbially or adjectively modifying a supplied term meaning "cries *or* screeches." Although attractive, this reading cannot be easily supported by the grammar. See note to 6.28.8.

33. "It rained blood" *vavarṣa rudhiraṃ devaḥ*: Literally, "the god rained blood." As Cg notes at 6.41.33, the god in question is the vedic rain god Parjanya. See 6.94.15 and note for the identical phrase. For blood raining down, see 6.26.22; 6.31.5; 6.41.33; 6.45.926*–36; 6.94.15; and notes. Cf. note to 6.76.2, 1674*, lines 5–7.

"and the horses stumbled" *caskhaluś ca turaṃgamāḥ*: D5,T1,G,M, and the texts and printed editions of Cg read instead *caskhalus turagāḥ pathi*, "and the horses stumbled on the path." See 6.26.23; 6.65.18; 6.94.26; and notes.

"A vulture alighted on the tip of his flagstaff" *dhvajāgre nyapatad gṛdhraḥ*: Cf. 6.41.31, 6.94.16; and notes.

"jackals ... inauspiciously" *aśivaṃ śivāḥ*: D9–11,M1,2, and the texts and printed editions of Ct read instead *aśivāḥ śivāḥ*, "inauspicious jackals." The phrase contains a play on words, since the term for jackals (*śivāḥ*) can also mean "auspicious." The howling or shrieking of beasts of prey, especially jackals, is a common portent of destruction. See 6.22.24; 6.31.7; 6.45.32,34; 6.53.42; 6.94.21; and notes. Cf. 6.41.32 and note.

36. "A blazing meteor" *ulkā*: Literally, "a meteor." Compare 6.45.35a and note, where the *pāda* is repeated.

"their cries echoed by the crows" *vāyasair anunāditāḥ*: Literally, "echoed by crows." V2,D7,9–11,G2, and the texts and printed editions of Ct read *abhimiśritāḥ*, "mixed with," for *anunāditāḥ*, "echoed."

37. "But heedless" *acintayan*: Literally, "not thinking *or* worrying about."

38. "Hearing the rumbling of the ... chariots" *rathaghoṣeṇa*: Literally, "by the sound of the chariots."

39. "A hugely tumultuous battle then broke out between the monkeys and *rākṣasas*." *teṣāṃ sutumulaṃ yuddhaṃ babhūva kapirakṣasām*: Literally, "There was a very tumultuous battle of monkeys and *rākṣasas*." D10,11, and the texts and printed editions of Ct omit this line (39ab).

40. "ten-necked Rāvaṇa" *daśagrīvaḥ*: Literally, "the ten-necked one."

41. "the wrinkle-faced monkeys" *valīmukhāḥ*: Literally, "the wrinkle-faced ones." Cr glosses, "those whose faces were filled with wrinkles (*valīyuktāni mukhāni yeṣāṃ te*)." See 6.54.28; 6.55.2; 6.57.59; 6.85.3; and notes.

"struck dead, their breathing stopped forever" *nirucchvāsā hatāḥ*: Literally, "struck *or* slain, breathless."

"had their eyes torn out" *cakṣurvivarjitāḥ*: Literally, "ones lacking eyes."

Following 41ab, D5–7,9–11,T1,G1,3,M, and the texts and printed editions of the southern commentators insert a passage of one line [1893*]: "Some were pierced through the heart. Some had their ears cut off."

42. "ten-faced Rāvaṇa" *daśānanaḥ*: Literally, "the ten-faced one."

"the crushing force of his arrows" *śarapravegam*: Literally, "the impact of arrows."

The meter is *upajāti*.

Sarga 84

1. "litter the ground, covering it" *vasudhā tatra prakīrṇā* ... *vṛtā*: Literally, "the ground there was strewn ... covered." B1,D5,7,9–11,T1,G3,M3, and the texts and printed editions of the southern commentators read *tadā*, "then," for *vṛtā*, "covered."

2. "single-handed" *ekataḥ*: Literally, "from one." The exact sense of the adverb here is uncertain. Commentators and translators alike have rendered it variously. We have followed the interpretation of Cg and Cm, who take it as an adjective in the sense of "single," modifying Rāvaṇa (*ekata ekasya rāvaṇasya*). The idea is to emphasize that this massive hail of arrows emanates from the bow of Rāvaṇa alone. This interpretation is followed by Raghunathan (1982, vol. 3, p. 282). Ct and Ck understand, "at every single point (*ekaikasmin pradeśe*)," an interpretation rendered only by Roussel (1903, vol. 3, p. 319). Cr understands, "at a single moment (*ekasminn api kṣaṇe*)," in which he is followed by Gita Press (1969, vol. 3, p. 1771). Pagani (1999, p. 1133) appears to extend somewhat the notions of Ck, Ct, and Cr that the arrows are striking in a single place or at a single time, rendering, "*drue*." Dutt (1893, p. 1440) and Shastri (1959, vol. 3, p. 281) ignore the term entirely.

3. "a forest fire" *pāvaka-*: Literally, "fire."

4. "Rāvaṇa careened" *sa yayau*: Literally, "he went."

"a mighty wind" *mārutaḥ*: Literally, "the wind."

5. "then immediately ... Rāghava" *rāghavaṃ tvaritas tadā*: Literally, "swift [Rāvaṇa] ... then Rāghava." D7,9–11, and the texts and printed editions of Ct read instead *tvaritaṃ rāghavaṃ raṇe*, "swiftly ... Rāghava on the battlefield" or "swift Rāghava on the battlefield."

6. "the encampment" *gulme*: Normally the term *gulma* refers to a military encampment. It can also refer to a particular fighting unit consisting of three *senāmukhas*, for a total of forty-five foot soldiers, twenty-seven cavalry, nine chariots, and nine elephants (Apte s.v.). Cf. note to 6.3.24. See *Amarakośa* 2.8.81. Dutt (1893, p. 1441) leaves the term untranslated and explains it in this latter fashion in a footnote. Other translators render it variously. Gita Press (1969, vol. 3, p. 1172) understands, "division," while Roussel (1903, vol. 3, p. 319) translates, "*son poste d'observation*." Shastri (1959, vol. 3, p. 281) renders, "his division." Pagani (1999, p. 1133) translates, "*son propre post*," while Raghunathan (1982, vol. 3, p. 282) understands, "the investing forces." Gorresio (1858, vol. 10, p. 144) renders, "*esercito*." Cf. 5.3.27; 6.3.27; 6.27.20; 6.28.31; 6.31.31; 6.45.2; 6.62.5; 6.71.1; 6.72.5; and notes.

"and resolved to enter the fight at once" *cakre yuddhe drutaṃ manaḥ*: Literally, "he swiftly made up his mind with regard to battle." D9,M3, and the texts and printed editions of Cg read [*a*]*dbhutam*, "wondrous," for *drutam*, "swiftly." Cg understands the term to be an adverb, which would then lend the phrase the somewhat peculiar sense of "amazingly *or* wonderfully made up his mind." Raghunathan (1982, vol. 3, p. 282), the only translator to render this variant, translates, "resolved to put up a marvelous fight."

7. "Sugrīva turned his face toward the enemy" *sugrīvo 'bhimukhaḥ śatrum*: Literally, "Sugrīva, facing the enemy." Ñ,V,B2–4,D2,10,11,13, and the texts and printed editions of Ct read *abhimukham* for *abhimukhaḥ*. This can be read as either an adjective modifying *śatrum*, "enemy," in the sense of "the enemy who was facing [him]," or as an adverb, with the verb *pratasthe*, "he set forth," in the sense "he set forth toward the enemy."

8. "All the troop leaders . . . voluntarily" *sarve yūthādhipāḥ svayam*: D9–11 and the texts and printed editions of Ct, Ck, and Cr read instead *sarve vānarayūthapāḥ*, "all the troop leaders." Ct and Ck note with regard to the adjective "all (*sarve*)" that we must, of course, exclude Suṣeṇa, who has been left in command of the encampment.

"followed him wielding huge boulders and . . . gigantic trees" *anujahrur mahāśailān . . . mahādrumān*: Literally, "they imitated [him, wielding] great boulders [and] great trees." The syntax is elliptical. If we take the verb *anujahruḥ* to mean "they took up after," governing the accusatives *mahāśailān*, "huge boulders," and *mahādrumān*, "huge trees," then we lack a necessary verb of motion. Cg understands the verb *anujahruḥ* to mean that, in keeping with military protocol, a king's retainers carry his weapons for him. Therefore, the monkeys are carrying Sugrīva's trees and boulders to give to him at the proper moment (*yathā mahārāje yuddhāya gacchati tadāyudhāni bhṛtyā āharanti tathā vānararāje yuddhāya niṣkrāmati tadāyudhabhūtāñ chailavṛkṣādīn samaye dātuṃ vānarā ājahrur iti bhāvaḥ*). Ñ,V,B2–4,D4,6,7,9–11,T2,3,G2,M5, and the texts and printed editions of Ct and Cr read the variant *anujagmuḥ*, "they followed," and propose supplying the gerund *gṛhītvā*, "having seized (*gṛhītveti śeṣaḥ*—so Ct)."

9. "began to slaughter" *jaghāna*: Literally, "he killed." D4,G1,2,M1–3, and the texts and printed editions of Cg read instead *jagāma*, "he went [toward]." D7,9–11, and the texts and printed editions of Ct, Cr, and Ck read instead *mamantha*, "he crushed *or* annihilated."

"felling" *pātayan*: D7,9–11, and the texts and printed editions of Ct read instead *pothayan*, "slaughtering."

10. "the mighty gale at the end of a cosmic age" *yugāntasamaye vāyuḥ*: Literally, "the wind at the time of the end of a *yuga*."

12. "Their heads shattered . . . crumpled" *vikīrṇaśirasaḥ . . . nikṛttāḥ*: Literally, "scattered . . . cut down." GPP and NSP (6.96.12) read *vikarṇaśirasaḥ*, "having heads devoid of ears." This peculiar reading is not recorded in the critical apparatus. It is, however, rendered by Roussel (1903, vol. 3, p. 319) as "*aux têtes sans oreilles*." In this he is followed by Shastri (1959, vol. 3, p. 281), who renders, "their heads shorn of their ears." The texts and printed editions of Ct and Cr, as well as B1,D1–3,7,9–11,13, then read *vikīrṇāḥ*, "scattered," for *nikṛttāḥ*, "crumpled."

13–14. "routed" *prabhagneṣu*: Literally, "broken." See 6.44.7; 6.55.29,113; 6.68.24; 6.87.8; and notes, where the term is used similarly.

"took up his bow" *dhanvī*: Literally, "having a bow."

"the back of a war-elephant" *gajaskandham*: Literally, "the shoulder of an elephant."

15. "the great chariot-warrior" *mahārathaḥ*: Ś,Ñ,V,B,D1–4,7–13,G2, and the texts and printed editions of Ct, Cr, and Ck read instead *mahābalaḥ*, "of great strength." See 6.60.3; 6.72.33; 6.80.6; 6.81.18; 6.83.8 and notes. Cf. 6.77.36.

"unleashing a terrifying roar" *vinadan bhīmanirhrādam*: Literally, "roaring a terrible sound." D7,9–11, and the texts and printed editions of Ct and Cr read the finite verb *nanarda*, "he roared," for the present participle *vinadan*, "[he] roaring."

16. "rallying... he made them hold their lines: *sthāpayāmāsa... saṃpraharṣayan*: Literally, "cheering [them], he made [them] stay."

17. "irascible... flew into a rage" *cukrodha ca mahākrodhaḥ*: Literally, "and the one of great anger became angry." Because of the redundancy, we believe one should take the epithet *mahākrodhaḥ* to refer to a general condition. Sugrīva's notoriously short temper is alluded to by the monkeys in the *Kiṣkindhākāṇḍa* (4.52.22–30), when Aṅgada expresses his fear of being executed by the wrathful Sugrīva should they return unsuccessful from their search for Sītā. Ñ2,V2,B1,2,D9–11, and the texts and printed editions of Ct read *cukrośa*, "he cried out, roared," for *cukrodha*, "he was angry *or* he became angry."

18. "in battle" *saṃpradhane*: D10,11,T1,G3,M5, and the texts and printed editions of Cg, Ck, and Ct read the nominative *saṃpradhanaḥ* in place of the locative. This reading is rather difficult to construe, and the commentators struggle to interpret it. Ct reads the term as a *bahuvrīhi* compound with the sense "whose combat was proper (*samyakpradhanaṃ yuddhaṃ yasya saḥ*)." Ck appears to read the *upasarga sam* in the sense of *samāna*, "equal," glossing, "for whom battle [all battles?] was equal (*samānaṃ pradhanaṃ yuddhaṃ yasya saḥ*)." Cg takes the suffix *ana* as agentive and reads the term to mean "fighter, warrior." (*saṃpradhanaḥ bahulagrahaṇāt kartari lyuṭ. prahartety arthaḥ.*) Crā, who rarely comments on any textual question, believes the appropriate reading should be the locative, explaining that "*saṃpradhane* means 'in battle' (*saṃpradhane yuddhe*)." Translators who read the variant generally take the term in the sense of "valiant, fighting well, etc."

"Virūpākṣa's great war-elephant" *asya... taṃ mahāgajam*: Literally, "that great elephant of his."

"in the face" *pramukhe*: We follow the interpretation of Cg, who glosses, "in the face (*mukhe*)," and those of Ct and Ck, who, perhaps uncertain as to whether an elephant has a face per se, gloss, "in the protuberant region of the face (*prakṛṣṭe mukhapradeśe*)." The locative *pramukhe* can also be read adverbially, in the sense "facing, in front of, opposite to," and several of the translators consulted understand it in this way.

19. "staggered back a bow length" *apāsarpad dhanurmātram*: Literally, "retreated to the measure of a *dhanuḥ*." On the measurement of a *dhanuḥ*, see 6.53.34 and note.

"and collapsed, bellowing" *niṣasāda nanāda ca*: Literally, "he sank down and bellowed."

22. "In his rage at Virūpākṣa... at him" *sa hi tasyābhisaṃkruddhaḥ... virūpākṣāya*: Literally, "enraged at him... at Virūpākṣa" D8,10,11, and the texts and printed editions of Ct read instead *sa hi tasyāpi*[*atha*—D8] *saṃgṛhya*, literally, "taking from him as well," for *sa hi tasyābhisaṃkruddhaḥ*. This weak reading is interpreted by Ct to mean "having received the blow given by him [Virūpākṣa] (*tasyāpi tenāpi dattaṃ prahāraṃ saṃgṛhya gṛhītvā*)."

23. "struck Sugrīva" *prāharat*: Literally, "he struck."

Following verse 23, D6,7,9–11,S insert a passage of five lines [1910*]: "Struck with that sword stroke by the powerful *rākṣasa*, the heroic[1] monkey was rendered unconscious for a moment.[1–2] But then, suddenly springing up, he clenched his fist and brought it down with force upon the *rākṣasa*'s chest in that great battle.[3–4] Struck with the blow of that fist, the night-roaming *rākṣasa* Virūpākṣa . . .[5]"

[1]"heroic" *vīraḥ*: D9–11 and the texts and printed editions of Ct read instead *bhūmau*, "on the ground."

24. "Sugrīva's armor" *sugrīvasya . . . kavacam*: This is one of the extremely rare instances in the poem in which a monkey is said to be equipped for battle with anything other than trees, stones, and other found objects. Cg is struck by this and notes that we must understand by this reference that Sugrīva actually wore armor (*anena sugrīvasyāpi kavacadhāraṇam astīti gamyate*). Pagani (1999, p. 1671) also notes this use of military equipment by monkeys. See 6.63.46 and note.

"Struck with that sword, the monkey" *sa khaḍgābhihataḥ*: Literally, "struck with the sword, he." D9–11,G2,M, and the texts and printed editions of the southern commentators read instead *padbhyām abhihataḥ*, "struck with [his] two feet." Dutt (1893, p. 1442) and Gita Press (1969, vol. 3, p. 1773) appear to follow Cr in taking this variant to mean that Virūpākṣa uses his feet to knock Sugrīva down. The other translators understand it to mean that Sugrīva falls to his knees.

26. "skillfully" *naipuṇyāt*: Literally, "out of dexterity, proficiency."

"the blow" *talaprahāram*: Literally, "the blow of the palm, slap."

"in return struck him" *enam . . . atāḍayat*: Literally, "he struck him."

28. "temple" *śaṅkhadeśe*: The commentators understand, "the region of the bone[s] of the forehead (*lalāṭāsthipradeśe*)." Cm and Cg cite *Amarakośa* 3.3.18 for this meaning (*śaṅkho nidhau lalāṭāsthnīty amaraḥ*). Earlier the commentators understood the term to refer to the temporal bones at the corners of the eyes, and we follow this interpretation here as well. See 6.38.10 and note.

29. "drenched in gore and vomiting blood" *rudhiraklinnaḥ śoṇitaṃ sa samudvaman*: Literally, "he, wet with blood, vomiting blood."

Following verse 29, D5–7,9–11,S insert a passage of one line [1916*]: "Virūpākṣa [vomiting blood] from every orifice, like water from a spring . . ."

30. "Virūpākṣa appeared to the monkeys to have his eyes still more disfigured than before." *dadṛśus te virūpākṣaṃ virūpākṣataraṃ kṛtam*: Literally, "they saw that Virūpākṣa had been made even more *virūpākṣa*." The verse plays on the name Virūpākṣa, "having deformed eyes." Cf. 6.28.31 and note.

31. "as he rolled in convulsions from side to side" *sphurantaṃ parivartantaṃ pārśvena*: Literally, "[he] jerking, rolling on his side." See 6.27.2 and note.

"moaning" *vinardantam*: Literally, "crying."

32. "those . . . vast . . . armies . . . like two great oceans" *balārṇavau . . . mahārṇavau dvāv iva*: Literally, "those army-oceans . . . like two great oceans." The redundant force of the metaphor and simile makes a literal translation awkward. Cr, alone among the commentators, understands the term *balārṇavau* to mean "reservoirs of strength" and to refer not to the armies but to the single combatants Sugrīva and Virūpākṣa, whom he sees as having been dispatched into battle by the monkeys and the *rākṣasas*, respectively (*vānararākṣasānāṃ vānararākṣasaiḥ saṃyati saṃgrāme saṃprayuktau niyojitau balārṇavau parākramasamudrau dvau sugrīvavirūpākṣau bhīmau mahārṇavāv iva sasvanatuḥ*). This reading, which no translator adopts, has a certain appeal in that it follows

the convention of summing up in a longer verse the preceding action and avoids the redundancy of the metaphor and simile mentioned above. On the other hand, it seems contextually awkward in light of the mortal blow delivered to Virūpākṣa at verse 28 and his piteous moaning in verse 31.

"crashed beyond their shorelines" *bhinnavelau*: Literally, "having broken banks *or* shorelines." The idea appears to be that two neighboring bodies of water flood a narrow intervening strip of land to merge tumultuously. D6,9–11,T2,3, and the texts and printed editions of Ct and Cr read *-setū*, "banks *or* bridges," for *-velau*. Cf. 6.58.54 and note.

The meter is *upendravajrā*.

33. "the combined host" *balaṃ samastam*: Literally, " the whole army."

"the . . . *rākṣasa* Virūpākṣa, his eyes disfigured" *virūpanetram*: Literally, "he of disfigured eyes." The term can be taken here either as a variant of Virūpākṣa's name or as a descriptive adjective. See note to verse 30 above. See, too, 6.28.31 and note.

"it became as agitated as the Ganges in raging flood" *unmattagaṅgāpratimaṃ babhūva*: Literally, "[it] was like the wild Gaṅgā." The commentators generally understand the term or its more or less synonymous variant (V1,D10,11, and the texts and printed editions of Ct read instead *udvṛttagaṅgā-*) to mean "like the Gaṅgā when it has risen beyond its banks (*udvelagaṅgā*—so Cg, Ct, Ck, Cm)." The term *unmattagaṅgā* may resonate with the term *unmattagaṅgam*, which is the name of a region where the Gaṅgā flows rapidly and noisily (s.v. Apte). Ct suggests that the agitation of the monkey forces is expressive of their delight whereas that of the *rākṣasas* arises from their grief (*vānarabalam ānandena rākṣasabalaṃ śokeneti śeṣaḥ*).

The meter is *upajāti*.

Sarga 85

3. "by the wrinkle-faced monkeys" *valīmukhaiḥ*: Literally, "by the wrinkle-faced ones." See 6.54.28; 6.55.2; 6.57.59; and 6.83.41.

"he realized that the fortunes of war had turned against him" *yuddhe prekṣya daivaviparyayaṃ*: Literally, "having perceived a reversal of fate in battle."

4. "tamer of his foes" *ariṃdamam*: V3,D9–11, and the texts and printed editions of Ct read instead *anantaram*, "without interval, next." Several of the translators who follow the text of Ct render this as an intensifier of *samīpastham*, "standing near."

"you are my only hope of victory" *jayāśā tvayi me sthitā*: Literally, "my hope of victory rests on you."

5. "Now is the time to repay your obligation to your master." *bhartṛpiṇḍasya kālo 'yaṃ nirveṣṭum*: Literally, "This is the time to repay [your] master's food." The southern commentators agree that the phrase *bhartṛpiṇḍasya* refers to the favors in the form of food, etc., that Mahodara, as a retainer, would have received from his master, Rāvaṇa (*svāmikṛtānnādidānarūpopakārasya*—so Cr). Cl understands slightly differently, glossing, "the favors that one is obliged to perform for one's master (*bhartuḥ kartavyopakārasya*)." Gorresio (1858, vol. 10, p. 302), in a note to the passage, expresses his opinion that the image here is derived from the funerary offerings of *piṇḍas*, or "balls of rice," presented to the departed. However, although the reference to *piṇḍa* might

evoke such an image, the poet probably uses the term in its more general sense of "food." For this idiom, compare *Mālavikāgnimitra* 5.11.4.

6. "to the *rākṣasa* lord" *rākṣasendram*: D5,8–11,G1,M, and the texts and printed editions of Ct and Cg read the nominative *rākṣasendraḥ* for the accusative, which would make the compound modify Mahodara.

7. "urged on by his master's words and his own valor" *bhartṛvākyena* . . . *svena vīryeṇa coditaḥ*: Like some of the translations consulted, we understand that Mahodara is impelled both by Rāvaṇa's order and by his own valor. The commentators, however, propose reordering what they take to be the somewhat scattered syntax of the verse and understand that, although it is his master's command that urges him on, his valor is what enables him to slaughter the monkeys (*bhartṛvākyena coditaḥ san svena vīryeṇa kadanaṃ cakra ity anvayaḥ*—so Cg).

"that immensely powerful *rākṣasa*" *mahābalaḥ*: Literally, "the one of great power."

Following verse 7, D5–7,9–11,S insert a passage of six lines [1923*]: "The immensely powerful monkeys seized huge boulders and, plunging into the fearsome army of their enemies, slaughtered the night-roaming *rākṣasas*.[1] [1–2] But Mahodara, in a rage, with his gold-ornamented arrows, hacked off the monkeys' hands, feet, and thighs in that great battle.[3–4] Then all the monkeys were severely harried by that *rākṣasa*.[2] Some of them fled in the ten directions, while others took refuge with Sugrīva.[5–6]"

[1] "the night-roaming *rākṣasas*" *rajanīcarān*: Literally, "the night-roamers." D9–11 and the texts and printed editions of Ct read instead *sarvarākṣasān*, "all the *rākṣasas*."

[2] "were severely harried by that *rākṣasa*" *rākṣasenārditā bhṛśam*: T2,3,G1,M3,5, and the texts and printed editions of Cm and Cg read *rākṣasair arditā bhṛśam*, "were severely harried by the *rākṣasas*." D9–11 and the texts and printed editions of Ct read instead *rākṣasānāṃ mahāmṛdhe*, "in that great battle with (lit., of) the *rākṣasas*."

8. "who happened to be nearby" *anantaram*: Literally, "without interval." We follow the commentators who understand that Mahodara was near Sugrīva (*anantaraṃ samīpastham*—so Cg). Cf. verse 4 above.

9. "in order to kill Mahodara" *tadvadhāya*: Literally, "for the killing of him."

10. "unstoppable" *durāsadām*: D9–11 and the texts and printed editions of Ct read instead the redundant *tataḥ śilām*, "then the boulder."

11. "fell . . . like a frenzied flock of vultures descending" *nipapāta* . . . *gṛdhracakram ivākulam*: Literally, "it fell like an agitated circle *or* mass of vultures." The commentators observe that the only basis for this rather odd simile is the multiplicity of the stone fragments and the vultures (*śilāyā anekadhā bhagnatvāt tatsādṛśyam*—so Ct). A number of translators render *ākulam* here in its common meaning of "frightened." However, this fits the context poorly, since frightened birds would doubtless fly up and not down. We understand the image to be derived from the once-common sight in India of excited vultures descending en masse on some choice carcass.

12. "at the *rākṣasa* in the forefront of battle" *rakṣase raṇamūrdhani*: Ñ,V2,B2,4,D1–3,9–11,M1,2, the texts and printed editions of Ct and Cr, and the editions of Gorresio (6.77.12) and Lahore (6.76.12—with slight variant) read instead *taṃ sa* (*sa taṃ*—Ñ2,V2,B2,4,D3) *ciccheda naikadhā*, "he cut it into many [pieces]."

"that... conqueror of enemy citadels" *parapuraṃjayaḥ*: D9–11,T2,3, and the texts and printed editions of Ct read instead *parabalārdanaḥ*, "that tormentor of enemy armies."

13. "He brandished... made a display of it before his foe" *āvidhya... tasya darśayan*: Literally, "he having brandished [it], [he] showing [it] to (lit., of) him." The idea apparently is that Sugrīva is brandishing the weapon menacingly in front of Mahodara. Ct, Ck, and Cg suggest supplying terms such as "dexterity *or* deftness of hand (*hastalāghavam*—so Ck, Ct)" as an object of the participle *darśayan*. Their idea is that Sugrīva is showing off his skill with the weapon.

"with its tip... violently" *parighāgreṇa vegena*: Literally, "with the tip of that iron club with force." Ñ,V1,3,B3,4,D3,7,9–11, and the texts and printed editions of Ct and Cr read instead *parigheṇogravegena*, "with that iron club of fierce impact."

15. "With one holding a mace and the other an iron club" *gadāparighahastau*: Literally, "the two with mace and iron club in hand."

Following verse 15, Ñ,V,B3,4,D3,5–7,9–11,S insert a passage of four lines [1929*]: "Then, in a rage, the night-roaming *rākṣasa* Mahodara hurled his mace—blazing with the brilliance of the sun—at Sugrīva.[1–2] Seeing that extremely terrifying mace[1] hurtling toward him, immensely powerful Sugrīva, his eyes red with rage, raised his iron club[2] in that great battle.[3–4]"

[1]"Seeing that... mace" *gadām*: Literally, "the mace." We follow the suggestion of the commentators in supplying an appropriate verbal form (*dṛṣṭveti śeṣaḥ*—so Ct).

[2]"raised his iron club" *samudyamya*: Literally, "having raised." We follow the suggestion of the commentators in supplying the missing object of the gerund (*parigham iti śeṣaḥ*—so Ct).

16. "the *rākṣasa*'s mace" *gadāṃ tasya*: Literally, "his mace."

"shattered by that mace" *sa gadodbhinnaḥ*: D9–11,G1,2, and the texts and printed editions of Ct read instead *tarasā bhinnaḥ* "swiftly *or* forcefully shattered."

18. "just as Mahodara hurled a second mace" *so 'py anyāṃ vyākṣipad gadām*: Literally, "and he, too, threw another mace." D9–11 and the texts and printed editions of Ct read *asya*, "his," for *anyām*, "another."

19. "the two warriors closed in combat with their fists" *muṣṭibhyāṃ tau samīyatuḥ*: Literally, "the two came together with two fists."

"two... fires, eaters of oblations" *hutāśanau*: Literally, "two eaters of oblations."

20. "Slapping each other with their open hands" *talaiś cānyonyam āhatya*: Literally, "having struck each other with [their] palms." B2,D7,9–11, and the texts and printed editions of Ct read instead *talaiś cānyonyam āsādya*, "having attacked each other with [their] palms."

21. "Jumping... to their feet" *utpetatuḥ*: Literally, "those two jumped up."

"The two... flailed at each other with their arms" *bhujaiś cikṣipatuḥ*: Literally, "The two struck with arms."

"yet neither could get the better of the other" *anyonyam aparājitau*: Literally, "the two were mutually undefeated."

Following verse 21, D5–7,9–11,S insert a passage of one line [1933*]: "Then the two heroes, scorchers of their foes, grew exhausted in that hand-to-hand combat."

22. "a sword and a shield that were lying nearby" *khaḍgam adūraparivartinam . . . carmaṇā sārdham*: Literally: "a sword remaining not far away along with a shield."

D9–11 and the text of Ct omit 22cd–23 ("The immensely swift *rākṣasa* Mahodara . . . and a shield"—*rākṣasaś carmaṇā sārdhaṃ mahāvego mahodaraḥ*). GPP includes 22cd–23, unnumbered in brackets, between 6.97.28 and 29. Translations that follow the text of Ct omit this passage and understand the verb "seized," *ājahāra*, in 22a to apply to each of the combatants. In this they follow Ct, who glosses the singular *jahāra*, "he seized," with the dual *jahratuḥ*, "those two seized."

23. D9–11 and the text of Ct omit 22cd–23. See note to verse 22 above.

"a huge sword and shield that had fallen" *mahākhaḍgaṃ carmaṇā patitaṃ saha*: Literally, "a great sword fallen together with a shield."

24. "the two warriors, skilled in the use of weapons" *śastraviśāradau*: Literally, "the two skilled in the use of weapons."

"hurled themselves . . . on the battlefield . . . in the fury of battle" *abhyadhāvatām / . . . raṇe hṛṣṭau yudhi*: Literally, "those two ran toward . . . on the battlefield, excited in battle."

25. "the two" *ubhau tau*: Curiously, Cr wants to read the dual pronoun *ubhau* as a *bahuvrīhi* compound, explaining it to mean "the two whose radiance was like that of Rudra (*oḥ rudrasyeva bhā yayos tāv ubhau*)."

"the two . . . circled . . . to the right and to the left" *dakṣiṇaṃ maṇḍalaṃ ca . . . samparīyatuḥ*: Literally, "the two moved around a rightward circle and." We follow the commentators, who understand the conjunction *ca*, "and," here to suggest that we should supply the phrase "and to the left (*cakārād vāmam ca*—so Ct)" and who gloss "the two circled (*samparīyatuḥ*)" with "the two made (*akurutām*—so Ct)."

26. "Sugrīva's great shield" *mahācarmaṇi*: Literally, "on the great shield." We follow Cr in supplying the proper name. D6,10,11,T2,3,M5, and the texts and printed editions of Ct and Cr read instead *mahāvarmaṇi*, "on the great armor."

27. "The sword lodged in the shield; and as Mahodara struggled to free it . . . the *rākṣasa*'s head: *lagnam utkarṣataḥ khaḍgam . . . śiraḥ*: Literally, "the head of him who was withdrawing the stuck sword."

28. "When they saw that" *tat . . . dṛṣṭvā*: Literally, "that . . . having seen." The syntax of the verse is difficult and seemingly defective. The gerund *dṛṣṭvā*, "having seen," has no clear object. Commentators seek to remedy this by taking the pronoun *tat*, "that," to refer to the severed head of Mahodara (*tac chiraḥ*—so Cg). Cr additionally suggests that we read the genitives in *pādas* a–c as a generic *ṣaṣṭhī* for the accusative (*sambandhasāmānyaṣaṣṭhī*) so that we can then take *rākṣasendrasya*, "of the *rākṣasa* lord," as the object of *dṛṣṭvā*, "having seen." This would yield: "Having seen the *rākṣasa* lord fallen to the ground with his head cut off . . ." We have chosen to read the pronoun *tat* in an abstract sense to refer simply to Mahodara's decapitation.

"fled" *tatra na tiṣṭhati*: Literally, "[it] does not stay there." D10,11, and the texts and printed editions of Ct read instead *na dṛśyate* for *na tiṣṭhati*, yielding the sense "it was not seen there," i.e., it vanished.

29. "Having slain Mahodara" *hatvā tam*: Literally, "having killed him."

"and he and his monkeys roared in unison" *vānaraiḥ sārdhaṃ nanāda*: Literally, "he roared together with the monkeys."

Following verse 29, D5–7,9–11,S insert a passage of ten lines [1940*]: "All the *rākṣasas* had dejected faces and despondent hearts. Their hearts overwhelmed with fear, they all fled.[1–2] Having hurled Mahodara to the earth like the shattered summit[1] of some great mountain, the son of Sūrya was as radiant with splendor as is unassailable Sūrya with his innate radiance.[2] [3–6] Then, having gained the victory, the great lord of the monkeys was praised[3] there, in the forefront of battle, by the joyful hosts of gods, perfected beings, and *yakṣas*, as well as the hosts of creatures who were present on earth.[4][7–10]"

[1]"the . . . summit" *ekadeśam*: Literally, "one part *or* portion." Given that Mahodara has been decapitated, we believe the reference here is to the summit of the mountain that forms the *upamāna*.

[2]Lines 3–6 constitute a verse in the *upajāti* meter.

[3]"the great lord of the monkeys was praised" *vānarendraḥ . . . stuto mahātmā*: D7,10,11, and the texts and printed editions of Ct read the participle *nirīkṣamāṇaḥ* (*nirīkṣyamāṇaḥ*—D7) for *stuto mahātmā*, giving the verse the sense "the great lord of the monkeys was gazed upon."

[4]Lines 6–10 constitute a verse in the *puṣpitāgrā* meter with a hypometric *pāda* d. D10,11, and the texts and printed editions of Ct read the metrically correct but lexically irregular term *haruṣa*[*samākulitaiḥ*], "joyful," for *harṣa*[*samākulitaiḥ*], "joyful." Ct explains: "In the place of the word *harṣa*, there is the reading *haruṣa* to conform to the meter (*harṣapadasthāne haruṣeti pāṭhaś chandonurodhāt*)."

Sarga 86

1. "wrought havoc . . . upon" *kṣobhayāmāsa*: Literally, "he shook *or* agitated."

Following 1ab, D5–7,9–11,S insert a passage of one line [1943*]: "[When Mahodara was struck down] by Sugrīva, [Mahāpārśva], his eyes red with rage, glaring . . ."

2. "On every side" *sarvaśaḥ*: Ś,Ñ,V1,2,B,D2,3,4,7–13, and the texts and printed editions of Ct and Cr read instead *rākṣasaḥ*, "the *rākṣasa*."

3. "the *rākṣasa* . . . cut off . . . shoulders" *skandhāṃś ciccheda rākṣasaḥ*: D1,2,3,8–10, and the texts and printed editions of Ct read instead *cicchedātha sa rākṣasaḥ*, "the *rākṣasa* then cut off," thus omitting the reference to shoulders.

"tore open the sides of others" *pārśvaṃ keṣāṃ vyadārayat*: Literally, "of whom [pl.] he tore the side." Ś,V2,B1,D1–3,7–12, and the texts and printed editions of Ct and Cr read instead *pārśvaṃ* (*pārśve*—Ś,D7) *keṣāṃcid ākṣipat* (*akṣipat*—Ś,D12), "he struck the side of some of those [monkeys]."

4. "stunned" *gatacetasaḥ*: Literally, "those whose consciousness is gone." A number of the translations consulted understand the phrase here to mean "lost heart" (Gita Press 1969, vol. 3, p. 1778) or "lost courage" (Shastri 1959, vol. 3, p. 285). The commentators are silent.

5. "great-armed" *mahābāhuḥ*: Ś,Ñ,V,B,D1–3,6,8–13, and the texts and printed editions of Ct read instead *mahāvegaḥ*, "of great speed *or* force."

"he surged powerfully forward" *vegaṃ cakre*: Literally, "he made a powerful impulse."

"like the ocean on the new- or full-moon day" *parvaṇi*: Literally, "on the *parvan* day." The term is used to designate the four transitional days of the lunar cycle that are days of important observances in the vedic religion. These are the new-moon day, the full-moon day, the first-quarter day (the eighth day), and the third-quarter day (the fourteenth day). Since the spring tides occur on the new- and full-moon days, no doubt it is those two that are specifically intended here. See 5.2.54; 5.5.12; 5.46.15; 5.57.16; and notes. D5,7,9–11,T1,G1,3,M1,2, and the texts and printed editions of Ct substitute the plural *parvasu*.

6. "an iron club" *āyasaṃ parigham*: Since the term *parigha* generally refers to a beam or a club made of or studded with iron, the adjective *āyasa*, "iron," here is somewhat redundant. See verse 12 and note. See, too, 6.3.12; 6.7.2; and notes.

7. "from his chariot... along with his charioteer" *sasūtaḥ syandanāt*: Ś2,Ñ2,V2,3, B1,4,D4,5,10,11,T2,3,G1,3,M, and the texts and printed editions of Ck and Ct read the sequence as a compound, *sasūtasyandanāt*, "from that chariot with its charioteer." Ck and Ct attempt to recuperate this banal reading by understanding the compound elliptically to mean that the charioteer had been slain (*hatasūtasahitarathāt*—Ct) or not slain (*ahata[sūta]sahitarathāt*—Ck) by the same blow. Ct's reading is rendered by Roussel (1903, vol. 3, p. 325) and Shastri (1959, vol. 3, p. 285).

8. "Gavākṣa... accompanied by Jāmbavān, the king of the apes" *sarkṣarājaḥ*: Literally, "one who was accompanied by the king of the apes." Following Cg and Cm, who base their arguments, sensibly enough, on the mention of Gavākṣa starting in verse 11 below, we believe that the reference here is to the warrior Gavākṣa. (*ṛkṣarājo jāmbavān tena sahitaḥ sarkṣarājo gavākṣaḥ. jāmbavantaṃ gavākṣaṃ cety uttaratra vakṣyamāṇatvāt.*) The word *ṛkṣarājaḥ* is, as all commentators and translators agree, an epithet used almost exclusively to designate Jāmbavān. Cr, who shares the critical reading, appears to interpret the sequence *sarkṣarājaḥ* as a case of double *sandhi* for *sa ṛkṣarājaḥ*, that is, "that king of the apes." He thus understands the subject of the verse to be Jāmbavān himself (*ṛkṣarājaḥ sa jāmbavān*). Ñ,V1,3,B2–4,D1–3,9–11,T2,3,G1,2,M2,5, and the texts and printed editions of Ck and Ct read instead *tasyarkṣarājaḥ*, in which the subject again is Jāmbavān rather than his ally Gavākṣa. It is difficult, if not impossible, to construe the genitive pronoun *tasya*, and translators who follow this reading simply drop it. See 6.4.17; 6.39.25; and notes.

9. "Mahāpārśva's horses" *aśvān*: Literally, "horses."

"and smashed his chariot" *syandanaṃ ca babhañja tam*: Literally, "and he broke the chariot." Ck and Ct are at pains to show that the breaking of the chariot occurs only after the slaying of the horses. (*śilāṃ gṛhītvāśvān jaghāna. anantaraṃ syandanaṃ taṃ babhañja*—so Ct.) With this temporal sequence in mind, Ck, evidently thinking that the boulder has been used to kill the horses, suggests that the chariot is destroyed by a mace (*anantaraṃ gadayā syandanaṃ ca babhañja*—so Ck).

10. "after a short while" *muhūrtāt*: Literally, "after a moment."

11. "in the center of his chest" *stanāntare*: Literally, "between the breasts *or* in the interior of the chest."

"with many more" *bahubhiḥ śaraiḥ*: Literally, "with many arrows."

12. "a... iron club" *parigham*: See note to verse 6 above.

13–14. "Enraged" *prakupitaḥ*: D9–11 and the texts and printed editions of Ct read instead *saroṣākṣaḥ*, "with his eyes full of rage."

"powerful" *vegavān*: Literally, "possessing speed *or* great force." B1,D5,10,11, T1,G3,M1,2,5, and the texts and printed editions of Ct read instead the adverb *vegavat*, "forcefully *or* rapidly."

"that iron club" *tam āyasam... parigham*: See notes to verses 6 and 12 above.

15. "by the powerful monkey" *balavatā*: Literally, "by the powerful one."

"struck the bow and arrows from the *rākṣasa*'s hand and knocked off his helmet" *tasya rakṣasaḥ / dhanuś ca saśaraṃ hastāc chirastraṃ cāpy apātayat*: Literally, "[it] caused the *rākṣasa*'s bow with its arrows to fall from the hand and [it knocked down] the head protector." Ct and Ck believe that the iron club not only knocks Mahāpārśva's bow from his hand but takes his hand off with it as well. This, according to Ct, is indicated by the conjunction *ca*, "and," in *pāda* d, and is substantiated by the reference in verse 17 below, where the *rākṣasa* seizes a battle-axe in one hand. (*cād ekaṃ hastaṃ śirastrāṇaṃ cāpātayat. ata evāgre vakṣyaty ekena kareṇeti*—so Ct.)

16. "just below the ear, where his earring hung" *karṇamūle sakuṇḍale*: Literally, "at the root of the ear with its earring."

17. "with one hand" *kareṇaikena*: See note to verse 15 above.

18. "that weapon" *tam*: Literally, "it, that."

"honed with oil" *tailadhautam*: Literally, "washed with oil." Ck, Ct, and Cr note that the process is done for the sake of sharpening the axe (*tailena dhautaṃ taikṣṇyārthaṃ saṃskṛtam*—so Cr). Cg understands that the axe is spotless because of daily applications of oil (*pratidinaṃ tailasecanān niṣkalmaṣam*). Cg evidently believes that the blade is oiled to prevent rust.

"made of the essence of the mountains" *śailasāramayam*: Literally, "made of the essence of stone *or* mountain." Ck, Ct, and Cr take the compound *śailasāra*, "essence of stone *or* mountains," to be a kenning for iron (*śailasāro 'yas tanmayam*—so Ct). Cg does not define *śailasāra* specifically but takes the compound as figurative in the sense of "as hard as that (*tadvat kaṭhinam ity arthaḥ*)." Presumably he understands the reference to be to stone.

19. "Aṅgada's left shoulder blade" *vāmāṃsaphalake*: Literally, "on the flat part of the left shoulder."

20. "clenched" *saṃvartayan*: Literally, "clenching." D1,2,5,10,11,T1,G3,M3,5, and the texts and printed editions of Cr, Cm, Cg, and Ct read instead the irregular finite form, *saṃvartayat*, "he clenched." We follow Ct, who glosses, "he bound (*babandha*)." Cg understands, "he whirled *or* waved about (*bhrāmayāmāsa*)."

21. "Knowing all the body's vital points" *marmajñaḥ*: Literally, "knowing the mortal spots."

22. "By virtue of that blow" *tena . . . nipātena*: Literally, "by that descent."

"dead" *hataḥ*: Literally, "struck *or* slain."

23. "but Rāvaṇa flew into a tremendous rage" *abhavac ca mahān krodhaḥ . . . rāvaṇasya tu*: Literally, "and of Rāvaṇa there arose a great anger."

Following verse 23, D5–7,9–11,S insert a passage of seven lines [1961*]: "Then from the delighted monkeys there arose a mighty lion's roar, shaking, as it were, with its din the city of Laṅkā with its gateways and lofty towers.[1] Indeed, it was like the great and simultaneous roar of the gods along with Indra.[2][1–3] Now, when that enemy of Indra, the lord of the *rākṣasas*, heard the tremendous roar of the heaven-dwelling gods and of the forest-dwelling monkeys in battle, he was enraged, and, turning once more to face the battle, he took up his stand.[3][4–7]"

[1]"Laṅkā with its gateways and lofty towers" *laṅkāṃ sāṭṭāṃ sagopurām*: For *aṭṭa*, "tower," see notes to 6.33.28 and 6.62.6; and for *gopura*, "gateway," see note to 6.61.39.

[2]"like the great and simultaneous roar of the gods along with Indra" *sahendreṇeva devānāṃ nādaḥ . . . mahān*: Literally, "like the great sound of the gods together with Indra." Despite the term *iva*, "like," suggesting that this is merely a simile, it is apparent from the following verse that the gods actually do utter a triumphant roar at the same time as the monkeys do. We have therefore added the word "simultaneous" in an effort to clarify this issue. In this we follow Cv, Cm, and Cg, who make it clear that they understand that both the monkeys and the gods utter shouts of triumph (*mahendreṇa saha devānāṃ nāda iva vānarāṇāṃ ca devānāṃ nādaḥ samabhavad ity arthaḥ*—so Cg). D5,6,9,T1,G1,2,M1,3,5, and the texts and printed editions of Cv, Crā, and Cg read instead *mahendreṇa*, "with great Indra."

[3]The meter of lines 4–7 is *upajāti*.

Sarga 87

1–2. The syntax of the opening verses of this *sarga* in the critical edition, as well as the printed editions of the vulgate, is defective and confused. *Pādas* ab of verse 1 form a relative clause governed by the gerund *dṛṣṭvā*, "having seen," and create an expectation of a finite verb of which Rāvaṇa would be the subject. No such verb is found in the text or recorded in the apparatus. In effect, these *pādas* are grammatically orphaned, as it were. The following lines, beginning with *pādas* cd of verse 1, introduce a new syntactical structure in which a shift is made to a locative absolute construction and the subject of the independent clause becomes Rāvaṇa's anger, *krodhaḥ*, found in *pāda* a of verse 2, while Rāvaṇa himself (*pāda* b of verse 2) becomes the object of the verb *āviveśa*, "it seized hold of, entered," in *pāda* a of verse 2. D9–11 and the texts and printed editions of Ct attempt to address the difficulty by substituting the phrase *sa rāvaṇaḥ*, "he, Rāvaṇa," as a subject of the gerund *dṛṣṭvā* for the critical edition's *tu rākṣasau*, "and now the two *rākṣasas*." Ct then completes the remediation by suggesting that we supply a predicate phrase, "he grew angry (*kruddho jāta iti śeṣaḥ*)." The northern recension avoids the grammatical difficulty either by substituting a consistent locative absolute construction (1962* and Lahore 6.79.1–2) or by providing a correctly structured relative correlative sequence of clauses (1963* and Gorresio 6.79.1–2).

3. "In killing those two, Rāma and Lakṣmaṇa" *hatvā tau rāmalakṣmaṇau*: After noting the manifest meaning of the verse, Cm adds his own "inner meaning (*vastutas tu*)." In keeping with his ongoing project of deflecting any hint of hostility directed toward Rāma, he argues here, as before, that we must understand the gerund *hatvā*, "having slain," in the sense of *gatvā*, "having gone to, approached." See 6.80.29; 6.81.4; and notes. He continues this in the following two verses.

"I shall allay" *apaneṣyāmi*: Cm argues that Rāvaṇa will allay his grief by approaching Rāma but killing only his minions, Sugrīva, etc., who constitute "the branches" of Rāma's "tree" as described in verse 4 below (*śākhārūpasugrīvādīn hatvā duḥkham apaneṣyāmīty arthaḥ*).

4. "the tree that is Rāma" *rāmavṛkṣam*: Cm, continuing his inner reading of the passage from the preceding verse, provides an etymological interpretation of the word *vṛkṣa*. He says, "a *vṛkṣa* is that which 'cuts down,' that is, Rāma is the destroyer of his enemies. (*vṛścayatīti vṛkṣas tam. śatrusaṃhārakaṃ rāmam ity arthaḥ.*)" Compare Śaṅkarācārya's similar etymology for the "world tree (*saṃsāravṛkṣa*)" in his *bhāṣya* to the *Kaṭhopaniṣad* 2.3.1 (or 6.1) (*vṛkṣaś ca vraścanāt*).

"which dispenses fruit and has Sītā for its blossom" *sītāpuṣpaphalapradam*: The compound is somewhat ambiguous in its meaning and lends itself to various interpretations. We follow Cm and Crā in taking it as a *dvandva* in which Rāma's role as a dispenser of fruits is independent of his having Sītā for his flower or blossom (*sītāpuṣpaṃ yasya saḥ sa cāsau phalapradaś ceti sītāpuṣpaphalapradas tam*). Ck and Ct understand similarly but add that Rāma dispenses fruit arising from various actions to all the monkeys by means of that blossom that is Sītā (*sītāpuṣpaṃ yasya saḥ sa cāsau tenaiva puṣpeṇa sarveṣāṃ vānarāṇāṃ tat tat karmajaphalapradas tam*—so Ct). Cr, in a similar vein, notes that the tree that is Rāma dispenses fruit by means of a blossom in the form of Sītā (*sītārūpapuṣpeṇa phalaṃ pradadāti*). The intention of the metaphor, as Ct and Ck suggest, is that, since Rāma is the root of the entire struggle, cutting him off will end Rāvaṇa's difficulties (*mūlocchedaṃ kariṣyāmīty āśayena rāmaṃ sarvāśrayamahāvṛkṣatvena nirūpayati*). This idea is perhaps confirmed by the apparent gloss in the reading [1966*] of most northern manuscripts, as well as the editions of Gorresio (6.79.5–6) and Lahore (6.79.5–6), where Rāvaṇa makes it clear that, in destroying Rāma, all his dependents will be similarly destroyed. On the other hand, it is possible to interpret the critical text to suggest that, with the felling of the tree that is Rāma and the cutting off of its branches in the form of the monkey warriors, the delightful blossom in the form of Sītā will finally fall to Rāvaṇa.

Following verse 4, D5–7,9–11,13,S insert a passage of two lines [1969*]: "and Mainda, Dvivida, Aṅgada, Gandhamādana, Hanumān, Suṣeṇa, and all the troop leaders of the tawny monkeys."

6. "its boar, deer, and elephants" *savarāhamṛgadvipāḥ*: Manuscripts show considerable variation in the construction of this compound. The texts and printed editions of Ct (NSP and GPP 6.99.7d) read instead *trastasiṃhamṛgadvijāḥ*, "with its lions, deer, and birds terrified."

7. "Rāvaṇa then produced" *cakāra*: Literally, "he made."

"the . . . divine weapon-spell, the Tāmasa, bringer of darkness" *tāmasam . . . astram*: Literally, "the *tāmasa astra*." The commentators understand the weapon-spell to be the one whose presiding spirit is Rāhu, the demon of darkness or the eclipse (*tāmasaṃ rāhudevatākam astram*—so Cr). A divine weapon-spell of this name, it should be noted, is among those Viśvāmitra confers upon Rāma at 1.26.17.

"and, with it, he scorched" *nirdadāha*: Literally, "he burned."

"They fled on every side." *prapetuḥ samantataḥ*: The verbal root $\sqrt{pat}$ is ambiguous in that it can mean "to fall" or "to flee." Translators have chosen one or another of these possible meanings. The reading of the Lahore edition (6.78.44), however, clearly has the monkeys fall to the earth (*prapetur mahītale*). The large majority of manuscripts and the remainder of the printed editions clearly understand, in their following verses [1973*], that the monkeys are fleeing.

Following verse 7, Ñ,V1,3,B,D4–7,9–11,T,G1,3,M, and all printed editions consulted except for Lahore insert a passage of two lines [1973*]: "A fearsome cloud of dust[1] arose as the monkeys broke and fled.[2] For they could not withstand that weapon[3] that had been created by Brahmā himself."

[1]"A fearsome cloud of dust" *rajo ghoram*: Literally, "fearsome dust." V3,B1,3,D4,9–11, and the texts and printed editions of Ct read *bhūmau*, "from [lit., on] the earth," for *ghoram*, "fearsome."

[2]"as the monkeys broke and fled" *tair bhagnaiḥ sampradhāvitaiḥ*: Literally, "by those broken, fleeing ones." Cr understands by *bhagnaiḥ* that the monkeys are broken in body (*aṅgabhaṅgaṃ prāptaiḥ*).

[3]"that weapon" *tat*: Literally, "that."

8. "routed" *bhagnāni*: Literally, "broken." See 6.44.7; 6.55.29,113; 6.68.24; 6.84.13–14; and notes, where the term is used similarly.

"he took up his battle stance" *paryavasthitaḥ*: Literally, "[he] stood." We follow Cr, who glosses, "he became ready for battle (*yuddhāyodyukto 'bhavat*)."

Following verse 8, D5–7,9–11,T,G1,3,M, and the texts and printed editions of the southern commentators insert a passage of one line [1974*]: "Since[1] that tiger among *rākṣasas* had put the army of tawny monkeys to flight..."

[1]"Since" *yataḥ*: All printed editions of the text that include this line read instead *tataḥ*, "then." The critical apparatus takes no notice of any such variation.

9–10. Cg offers a theological reading of the passage beginning with 1974* (see note above) and continuing through verse 10. He understands: "[By the fact] of Rāma's being unconquerable, and because of his having abandoned all enmity through his being the repository of limitless graciousness [and] the object to be constantly meditated upon, the stupidity and misfortune of Rāvaṇa, who has failed to immerse himself in the ocean of the nectar of the physical beauty of Śrī Rāma, which is enhanced by that great and splendid bow, which is, as it were, causing to flow the current of nectar, is expressed (*tata ityādi sārdhaślokadvayena rāmasyāparājitatvaṃ niravadhikasaundārya-nidhitvena vairaṃ vihāya nirantarānubhāvyatvaṃ rāvaṇasya durbuddhitvam amṛtapravāham āvarteneva mahatā dhanurvareṇāvartitaṃ śrīrāmadehalāvaṇyāmṛtapūram anavagāhamānasya tasya daurbhāgyaṃ cocyate*)."

"Rāvaṇa" *saḥ*: Literally, "he." Although Rāma himself was the subject of the previous verse, the context obliges us to understand that the pronoun refers to Rāvaṇa.

"like Vāsava with Viṣṇu" *viṣṇunā vāsavaṃ yathā*: The simile derives its logic, as Cr points out, from the fact that Viṣṇu, sometimes called Upendra, "junior Indra," is, since he is born in his dwarf incarnation as the child of Kaśyapa and Aditi, the parents of the vedic gods, considered to be Indra's younger brother. See 6.40.43; 6.47.119; 6.49.1–2; 6.53.26; 6.59.7; 6.105.15,24; and notes. See, too, 1.28.2 and note.

"Holding aloft" *avaṣṭabhya*: We believe that the figure in the verse makes it apparent that we are to understand the verb *ava* √*ṣṭambh* in its sense of "to hold, support" rather than, as several translators consulted have done, in its sense of "to lean on."

Following verse 10, D5–7,9–11,S insert a passage of one line [1976*]: "Then the mighty and immensely powerful Rāma together with Saumitri..."

11. "routed" *bhagnān*: See note to verse 8 above.

"delighted" *hṛṣṭaḥ*: According to Cr, Rāma attains mental delight at the thought, "now I will see a real (lit., great) battle" (*mahāyuddhaṃ drakṣyāmīti buddhyā prāptaharṣa ity arthaḥ*). Cg believes Rāma is gratified that his archenemy has at last appeared (*cirād vairī samāgata iti saṃtuṣṭaḥ*).

12. "he began to twang" *visphārayitum ārebhe*: Cg believes that Rāma's delay in actually shooting arises from his thought: "Will Rāvaṇa now finally submit?" This, Cg

believes, is an indication of Rāma's compassionate nature. (*visphārayitum ārebha ityādi. vilamboktyā kim idānīm api vā nato bhaviṣyati rāvaṇa iti rāmasya dayālutocyate.*)

"powerfully and loudly" *mahāvegaṃ mahānādam*: Literally, "having great force, having great noise." We read the compounds adverbially with the infinitive construction rather than, as do most translations consulted, adjectivally with *dhanuḥ*, "bow," in *pāda* b.

13. Ś,Ñ,V,B,D1–4,6–8,10–12,T2,3,M2,3, and the texts and printed editions of the commentators, as well as the editions of Gorresio and Lahore, transpose verses 13 and 14. This order of the verses has been followed in all translations consulted.

"he looked like Rāhu, the demon of the eclipse" *sa babhūva yathā rāhuḥ*: Literally, "He was just like Rāhu."

"as he bears down upon the sun and the hare-marked moon" *samīpe śaśisūryayoḥ*: Literally, "in the vicinity of the one with the hare and of the sun." Cg and Crā note that the simile is based on the idea of Rāhu approaching the two heavenly bodies on the new-moon day, when they would be in conjunction. Crā is so impressed with the aptness of the figure of the maleficent demon bearing down upon the splendid princes that he notes that the subject and object of comparison are one and the same (*atikrūrasvabhāvasya rāvaṇasya rāmalakṣmaṇayoḥ samīpāgamanam amāvāsyāyāṃ rāhoś candrasūryasamīpāgamanam iveti kṛtvā dṛṣṭāntadārṣṭāntikayor aikarūpyam*—so Crā). It is difficult to conceive of an eclipse of the new moon.

14. On the order of verses 13 and 14, see note 13 above.

"The streams of Rāvaṇa's arrows and the sound of Rāma twanging his bow knocked... down" *rāvaṇasya ca bāṇaughai rāmavisphāritena ca / śabdena... tena petuḥ*: Literally, "they fell because of the floods of Rāvaṇa's arrows and the sound that was Rāma's twanging." No commentators remark on the seeming oddity of Rāvaṇa's appearing to shoot down his own forces. A number of northern manuscripts attempt to correct this situation by substituting Lakṣmaṇa's name for Rāvaṇa's in *pāda* a.

15. "Rāvaṇa" *tam*: Literally, "him."

"with his own sharp arrows" *niśitaiḥ śaraiḥ*: Literally, "with sharp arrows." Cr glosses, "possessing (lit., characterized by) arrows (*śarair upalakṣitaḥ*)."

16. "intercepted" *pratyavārayat*: Literally, "he warded off *or* obstructed."

"with his own arrows" *bāṇaiḥ*: Literally, "with arrows."

17. "one of Lakṣmaṇa's arrows with one of his own" *ekam ekena bāṇena... lakṣmaṇasya*: Literally, "one of Lakṣmaṇa's with one arrow."

18. "Then" *tataḥ*: Ś,B1,D1–3,8–12, and the texts and printed editions of Ct read instead *raṇe*, "in battle."

"leaving... aside" *abhyatikramya*: We agree with Cg, who understands that Rāvaṇa contemptuously breaks off his duel with Lakṣmaṇa since not even one of the latter's arrows has been able to strike him (*ekasyāpi bāṇasya svasminn apatanād anādareṇātikramya*). Cr, more simply, glosses, "leaving aside (*tyaktvā*)." Ct glosses, "having confounded with his arrows (*bāṇair vyākulīkṛtya*)." Translators understand the gerund in a variety of ways: "*sautant par dessus*" (Roussel 1903, vol. 3, p. 328); "leaping over" (Shastri 1959, vol. 3, p. 288); "overpassing" (Gita Press 1969, vol. 3, p. 1782); "bypassing" (Raghunathan 1982, vol. 3, p. 289); and "surpassing" (Dutt 1893, p. 1448).

"as immovable as a mountain" *śailam ivācalam*: The adjective *acala*, "immovable," is also a common kenning for mountain. B3,D4,6,9–11,T2,3,M1,2, and the texts and printed editions of Crā, Cm, and Ct read instead *śailam ivāparam*, "like another *or* unsurpassable mountain." Translations that follow the text of Ct understand the term *apara* to mean either "another" or "unapproachable."

19. "And, as he advanced upon Rāma Rāghava in battle ... upon him" *sa saṃkhye rāmam āsādya ... rāghavopari*: Literally, "he, having approached Rāma in battle ... upon Rāghava." D9–11 and the texts and printed editions of Ct read instead *sa rāghavaṃ samāsādya ... rākṣaseśvaraḥ*, "he, the lord of the *rākṣasas*, having approached Rāghava."

20. "hurtling swiftly toward him" *āpatitāḥ śīghram*: Literally, "flying swiftly."

"loosed" *-cyutāḥ*: Literally, "fallen."

21. "those torrents of immensely powerful arrows" *tāñ śaraughān ... mahāvegān*: Literally, "arrow-streams with tremendous impact." Ś,D1–5,8–12,T1,G1,3,M3, and the texts and printed editions of the southern commentators read instead *mahāghorān*, "immensely fearsome."

"angry" *kruddhān*: D9–11 and the texts and printed editions of Ct read instead the redundant *śarān*, "arrows."

22. "showered ... with ... arrows" *śarair abhivavarṣatuḥ*: D7,9–11,G2, and the texts and printed editions of Ct and Cr read instead *śaravarṣair vavarṣatuḥ*, "those two showered with showers of arrows."

23. "Never yet defeated in battle" *samareṣv aparājitau*: Literally, "unconquered in battles." We take the term to be a general qualification of the two warriors, even though Rāvaṇa was technically defeated by Rāma earlier in *sarga* 47. Ct and Cm, however, gloss, "unimpaired, unrepulsed (*apratihatau*)," apparently understanding the term to refer to the specific battle at hand. The majority of translators understand similarly.

"in an astonishing way" *citram*: All translators consulted understand *citram* to be an adjective modifying *maṇḍalam*, "circle," taking the term to mean either "marvelous" or "various." We, however, have taken the term as an adverb.

"in battle ... keeping his eyes on the trajectory of the other's arrows" *bāṇavegān samudvīkṣya samareṣu*: Literally, "in battles ... having watched the impacts of the arrows." Our understanding of the phrase is that each of the warriors is keeping his eye on the path of the incoming arrows loosed by his adversary and is thus able to avoid being struck. The only translator to read similarly to the critical edition is Gorresio (6.79.54), whose text reads *bāṇavegaṃ samīkṣyantau*, which he translates as "*avendo l'occhio attento all'impeto de'dardi*" (1858, vol. 10, p. 155).

D9–11,G1,3, and the texts and printed editions of Ct read the ablative singular *bāṇavegāt*, "from the impact of [his] arrows," for the accusative plural *bāṇavegān*, "the impacts of the arrows." D5,9–11,T1,G1,3,M1,3, and the texts and printed editions of the southern commentators read *samutkṣiptau*, "[those two] hurled," for *samudvīkṣya*, "having watched." Ś,Ñ,V1,2,B,D1–3,7–12,M3, and the texts and printed editions of the southern commentators read *anyonyam*, "each other, mutually," for *samareṣu*, "in battles." The text of Ct thus reads *bāṇavegāt samutkṣiptāv anyonyam* [*aparājitau*], "with the speed of their arrows, those two [undefeated] shot at each other." Ct glosses, "the two shot at each other forcefully *or* swiftly (*anyonyaṃ vegāt samutkṣiptavantau*)." Cm, who reads *bāṇavegān* with the critical edition, glosses, "they hurled [away] the force of each other's arrows, that is, they fended them off (*anyonyaṃ bāṇavegān samutkṣiptau samutkṣiptavantau nivārayantāv iti yāvat*)." Raghunathan (1982, vol. 3, p. 289), who follows Cm, translates, "rendering nugatory the other's fusillade of arrows." Dutt

(1893, p. 1449) inexplicably renders, "uprooting the earth with the vehemence of their arrows."

24. "all creatures" *bhūtāni*: Literally, "beings."

"those two fierce warriors" *raudrayoḥ*: Literally, "of the two fierce ones."

"like Yama and Death himself, ender of all things" *yamāntakanikāśayoḥ*: The compound is somewhat ambiguous. The epithet *antaka*, "ender," is most commonly used of Yama himself and, for that matter, is a kenning for death. Thus, we normally translate *antaka* as "Yama, the ender of all things." One could, as Dutt (1893, p. 1449) has done, understand the two names to be in apposition so that the compound would mean,"[the two of them were] like Yama, the ender." However, the context would generally require the *upamāna* to consist of two entities, as does the *upameya* (Rāma and Rāvaṇa). The only commentator to propose an interpretation, Cg, understands, "Yama and his ender, i.e., Rudra (*yamatadantakau yamarudrau*)," but we find this unpersuasive. This idea is followed only by Raghunathan (1982, vol. 3, p. 289), who renders, "like Yama (the god of death) and his destroyer (Rudra)." Gita Press (1969, vol. 3, p. 1782) appears to try to separate out two functions associated with Yama, rendering, "the god of retribution and the god of death." Roussel (1903, vol. 3, p. 328), followed by Shastri (1959, vol. 3, p. 288) and Pagani (1999, p. 1140), simply understands the reference to be to two entities, Yama and Antaka, without attempting to differentiate them. Our rendition is closest to that of Gorresio (1858, vol. 10, p. 155), who translates, "*pari a Yama ed alla Morte.*"

26. "fletched with vulture feathers" *gṛdhrapatraiḥ*: Literally, "having vulture feathers." Ct and Cr understand that the arrows are bound with these feathers (*gṛdhrapatrais tadbandhanaiḥ*—so Ct). Cg understands that it is the vulture-feather fletching that makes the arrows so extremely swift and that they have beautiful fletching (*gṛdhrapatair hetubhiḥ suvājitaiḥ saṃjātaśobhanapakṣaiḥ*). Roussel (1903, vol. 3, p. 328), followed by Shastri (1959, vol. 3, p. 288), translates, "*garnies de plumes de hérons.*" Cf. note 6.35.12.

"made the sky appear to be densely covered with latticework" *gavākṣitam ivākāśam*: Literally, "the sky was as if latticed." We agree with Ct, Ck, and Cg, who gloss, "in which latticework was produced (*saṃjātagavākṣam*)." For some reason, the majority of translations consulted take the underlying noun *gavākṣa* in its other common sense of "a hole, airhole, *or* window," but this appears to make little sense in this context. Raghunathan (1982, vol. 3, p. 289) combines the two meanings, rendering, "it seemed to convert it into lattice windows," while Pagani (1999, p. 1140), who renders, "*fut en quelque sorte tissé*," seems to approximate the proper meaning. See 6.109.1. Cf. 6.45.26; 6.50.3; and notes.

27. "With their arrows, the two heroes then created a massive and fearsome darkness" *śarāndhakāraṃ tau bhīmaṃ cakratuḥ paramaṃ tadā*: Literally, "Then the two made a supreme and fearsome arrow-darkness." D5,9–11,T1,G3, and the texts and printed editions of Ct read *ākāśam*, "the sky," in place of *tau bhīmam*, "those two . . . fearsome." In this reading, *śarāndhakāram*, "arrow-darkness," must be read as a *bahuvrīhi* compound modifying *ākāśam*. The phrase would then mean "the two made the sky dark with arrows." D5,9–11, and the texts and printed editions of Ct read *prathamam*, "first of all," for *paramam*, "supreme." M3 and the texts and printed editions of Cg read *samaram*, "battle," for *paramam*, in which case *śarāndhakāram* modifies *samaram*, giving the sense "the two made the battle dark with arrows." This variant is

rendered only in the translation of Raghunathan (1982, vol. 3, p. 289), who renders, "made darkness descend on the battle-ground with their arrows." Cf. 6.92.9 and note for a similar image of arrows darkening the battlefield.

"as might two vast storm clouds arising at sunset" *gate 'staṃ tapane cāpi mahāmeghāv ivotthitau*: Literally, "and like two large clouds arisen when the hot one [i.e., the sun] has gone to the setting [mountain]." The commentators discuss the basis for the simile in terms of the *camatkāra*, or "strikingness," of poetic language. Ct, observing that there is nothing striking about the fact of clouds producing darkness at night, argues that we should understand the indeclinable *api*, "also," to mark an ellipsis that, when supplied, would indicate that the sun, having set, then rises. His idea is that the storm clouds then block out the risen sun during the daytime, which makes the simile more striking. (*apiśabdād astācalaṃ tyaktvodayādriṃ gate 'pīty arthaḥ. divāpīti yāvat. yat tu yathāśrutarītyā rātrāv apīti vyācakṣate tatra na kaścic camatkāraḥ.*) Cs disagrees with Ct. He claims that "the strikingness (*camatkāra*)" of the figure comes from the fact that the clouds create additional darkness during the evening by covering up the moon, etc. He quotes Ct, ridiculing him by saying that his assertion that the figure lacks "strikingness (*camatkāra*)" itself lacks "strikingness (*camatkāra*)." (*candrādikam ācchādya satimirīkaraṇaṃ camatkāra iti "na kaścic camatkāraḥ," iti nāgojibhaṭṭoktir eva niścamatkārā.*) Cs also proposes an alternative reading in which the warriors act like two great clouds in such a way that [with the darkness they create] they make the sun appear to be setting when it is actually shining (*yadvā tapane sūrye saty astaṃ gata iva yathā tathā mahāmeghāv iva cakratuḥ*).

28. "A tumultuous battle... then raged" *babhūva tumulaṃ yuddham*: D9–11,M2, and the texts and printed editions of Ct read instead *tayor abhūn mahā*[*mahad*—M2]-*yuddham*, "there was a great battle between the two."

"like that between Vṛtra and Vāsava" *vṛtravāsavayor iva*: Despite his characterization of the battle as unique, the poet cannot resist the temptation to compare it to the great mythic battle between Indra and Vṛtra that serves as the gold standard of comparison for all great epic duels. See note to 6.75.31.

"unequaled" *anāsādyam*: Literally, "unapproachable, unattainable." Cr glosses, "not to be accomplished by others (*anyaiḥ kartum aśakyam*)." Cg explains, "impossible to accomplish by anyone prior to this (*itaḥ pūrvaṃ kenāpi durlabham*)."

29. "skilled in the use of weapons" *śastraviśāradau*: Ñ,V,B2–4,D4,9–11, and the texts and printed editions of Ct read *yuddha-*, "battle," for *śastra-*, "weapons," lending the compound the sense "skilled in battle."

"and they both hurled themselves at each other in battle" *yuddhe viceratuḥ*: Literally, "those two attacked *or* moved about in battle."

30. "As they maneuvered, waves of arrows preceded them" *ubhau hi yena vrajatas tena tena śarormayaḥ... jagmuḥ*: Literally, "by which [way] the two moved, by that very [way] arrow-waves went." Ct, Ck, Cm, and Cg understand that these are the circular movements (*maṇḍalacāreṇa*) referred to earlier in verse 23 above.

31. "Rāvaṇa, who makes the world cry out" *rāvaṇo lokarāvaṇaḥ*: See note to 6.8.12.

"his hands working swiftly" *saṃsaktahastaḥ*: Literally, "whose hand *or* hands was/were engaged *or* attached." The compound is elliptical and ambiguous. The southern commentators gloss, "whose hand was engaged in deploying his arrows (*bāṇaprayoga āsaktahastaḥ*—so Ct, Ck)." Cl, cited in Gorresio (1858, vol. 10, p. 303, n. 73), understands, "whose hands were firmly fixed to the bow and the bowstring (*dhanuṣi guṇe ca saṃsaktau saṃyuktau hastau yasya saḥ*)."

32. "that chain of iron arrows" *tām*: Literally, "that."

33–34. "divine weapon-spell of Rudra" *raudram astram*: See 6.55.78 and note.

"Allowing no interruption in the stream of his arrows, he...them" *tāñ śarān...acchinnasāyakaḥ*: Literally, "he whose arrows were uninterrupted (lit., uncut)...those arrows." We understand the compound as do Ck and Ct, who gloss, "of uninterrupted arrows, that is, whose hail of arrows was sent forth without gaps. (*avyavacchinnasāyakaḥ. nirantarapravartitabāṇavarṣa iti yāvat.*)" Cs interprets similarly.

D5,7,T1,G,M3,5, and the texts and printed editions of Crā and Cg omit 34cd, "Allowing no interruption in the stream of his arrows, he loosed them toward the lord of the *rākṣasas* (*tāñ śarān rākṣasendrāya cikṣepācchinnasāyakaḥ*)."

35. "harmlessly" *na vyathāṃ janayan*: Literally, "they did not cause harm." The commentators note the irregular absence of the augment in the verbal form.

36. "with a splendid, divinely charged weapon" *paramāstreṇa*: It is normal for Vālmīki to specify the identity of a special *astra*, although the critical text does not do so here. Some northern manuscripts (Ñ,V,B2–4) and the edition of Gorresio (6.79.66) identify the weapon as the *gāndharva astra*. See Introduction, p. 112.

"pierced...through the forehead" *lalāṭe...abhinat*: Ś,B1,D1–5,8,9,12,T,G1,3,M, and the texts and printed editions of Cg, Crā, and Cm read *raṇe*, "in battle," for the verb [*a*]*bhinat*, "he pierced." Since the variant reading provides no finite verb for the sentence, these commentators are obliged to supply a verb, such as *mumoca*, "he loosed, shot." They then must provide an object for this verb in the form of "arrows that are charged with the *paramāstra* (splendid divine weapon-spell)" (*paramāstreṇa śreṣṭhāstramantreṇa yojitān bāṇān mumocety adhyāhartavyam*—so Cm). Crā justifies this interpretation by noting the mention of arrows in the plural in the following verse (*samanantaraśloke bāṇabahutvābhidhānāt*). These commentators additionally take the locative *lalāṭe*, "in the forehead," to mean "toward the forehead" (*lalāṭe lalāṭaviṣaye, lalāṭam uddiśyeti yāvat*—so Crā).

"the *rākṣasa* lord...latter: *rākṣasādhipam*...Literally, "the *rākṣasa* lord."

37. "those arrows...were deflected" *te...-pratikūlitāḥ*: Literally, "they were deflected *or* warded off." These would presumably be the various arrows charged with the divine weapon-spell mentioned in verse 36 above. The passage, as it is constructed in the critical edition and the vulgate, seems to suffer from a problem in its narrative sequence. Rāvaṇa appears to be able to deflect or evade Rāma's weapons, whether singular or plural here, except for the awkward fact that, in verse 36cd, he was shot through the head. This seeming inconsistency may be behind the fact that the subrecension of Crā, Cm, Cv, and Cg replaces the verb *abhinat*, "he pierced," with *raṇe*, "in battle," in 36d as mentioned above, thus making the passage merely state that Rāma shot at Rāvaṇa, not that he hit him. The northern editions of Lahore (cf. 6.78.72–74) and Gorresio (cf. 6.79.64–67) omit any reference to Rāvaṇa's being struck in the forehead. Cv attempts to address the incongruity by proposing that we invert the order of verses 36 and 37, but this does not seem to address the problem adequately.

Crā understands the participle *pratikūlitāḥ*, "warded off," to mean "shattered by Rāvaṇa with his opposing missile (*rāvaṇena pratyastreṇa khaṇḍitāḥ*)." It is difficult, however, to imagine that the broken arrows would then enter the earth.

"the splendid arrows" *bāṇarūpāṇi*: We follow Ck, Ct, and Cr in taking the suffix *rūpa* to suggest the excellence of the thing to which it is appended (*praśaṃsāyāṃ rūpap* [*Pā*

5.3.66]. *praśastā bāṇāh*—so Ct). Cs idiosyncratically takes the noun *bāṇa*, normally, "arrow," in its other sense, "body," and then understands the compound *bāṇarūpāṇi* to mean "beautifying the body." He then argues that Rāma's arrows beautify the body [of Rāvaṇa] by piercing his hands and other limbs before being deflected and entering the earth (*te śarā bāṇarūpāṇi bāṇaṃ kāyaṃ rūpayanti sundarīkurvantīti tāni karādyaṅgāni bhittvā . . . bhūmiṃ viviśuḥ*).

"like five-headed serpents" *pañcaśīrṣā ivoragāḥ*: Vālmīki normally employs this image to refer to people, not arrows. At 5.36.22, Rāma is quoted as comparing himself to a *pañcavaktra* serpent (*pañcavaktreṇa bhoginā*). This is repeated at 5.65.8. We translate the adjective there as "with jaws agape," following the interpretation of Cg, who, deriving the word *pañca* from the root $\sqrt{}$*pac* in the sense of "spread" or "extend," glosses, *vyāttamukhena*, "with mouth wide open." As an alternative explanation, he understands the reference to be to a serpent with five jaws, i.e., heads. It is this second interpretation that has been uniformly adopted by the translations consulted. See 5.65.8; cf. 5.49.21.

At 5.49.21, Sītā is described as *pañcāsyām iva pannagīm*, which we rendered as "like a five-headed cobra" (lit., like a five-mouthed she-cobra). Several of the commentators note that the simile serves to inform Rāvaṇa that Sītā will destroy him and his city with the fire of her grief, just as a cobra would with its fiery venom. The commentator Cs sees the five heads as a reference to the five principal characters who will ultimately bring about Rāvaṇa's downfall, viz., Rāma, Lakṣmaṇa, the king [Sugrīva], Hanumān, and Sītā. However, as an alternative, he reads *pañca* as an adjective, meaning "spread *or* extended," and thus takes the compound to mean "with mouth agape." See 5.36.22; 5.65.8; and notes. Cf. 5.47.2–14 (verse 8). At 5.1.52, Hanumān's outstretched arms are said to resemble "five-headed serpents rearing up from a mountain." See note to verses 39–40 below.

38. "invoked yet another divine weapon-spell" *anyad astraṃ samādade*: Literally, "he took up another *astra*." The editors of the critical edition have marked, quite exceptionally for this volume, the verb *samādade*, "he took up," as uncertain. D5,9–11, T1,G3, and the texts and printed editions of Ct read *cakāra saḥ*, "he made," for *samādade*. Ct glosses, "he produced *or* manifested (*prāduścakāra*)." D7,G2,M3, and the texts and printed edition of Cv(?), Cg, Crā, and Cm read the entire *pāda* somewhat differently: *astraṃ prāduścakāra ha*, "he produced an *astra*."

39–40. "The heads" *-mukhān*: Literally, "faces." The idea, however, appears to be that the arrowheads are shaped like the faces of the various animals mentioned.

"adjutant storks" *kaṅka-*: For a discussion of the identification of this bird in various epic contexts, see note to 6.35.12. Cf. 6.46.28; 6.47.127; 6.55.80; 6.87.26; 6.97.1; and notes.

"crows" *-kāka-*: Ñ2,V,D9–11,T3, and the texts and printed editions of Ct read instead *-koka-*. The term *koka* refers to a variety of animals, including the wolf, the *cakravāka* bird or ruddy goose, the frog, and a kind of lizard. Given the context in which predatory and scavenger animals are mentioned, only the wolf seems a plausible choice. This, in turn, however, creates a problem of apparent redundancy with the term *īhāmṛga-* in *pāda* 40a, and it is perhaps because of this that most of the translators choose to render, "ruddy goose *or* duck." See 5.23.5, where the term is translated as "wolf."

"falcons" *-śyena-*: The term refers to a variety of raptors, including falcons, hawks, eagles, kites, etc. See 4.57.26 and note. Cf. 6.31.11; 6.75.20; and notes.

"wolves" *īhāmṛga-*: See 5.7.12; 5.16.6–9; and notes.

"five-headed serpents with flickering tongues" *pañcāsyāṃl lelihānān*: Literally, "five-faced lickers." The term *lelihāna* is a kenning for snake, derived no doubt from the habit of these animals of flicking their tongues to receive sensory impressions. Ct, Ck, and Cs (first alternative) take the term *pañcāsya* separately from *lelihāna*. Ck takes the term as a kenning for lion, while Ct and Cs gloss, "with the heads of lions (*siṃhamukhān*)." Although neither commentator makes this explicit, it would appear that they are taking the term in the sense "with gaping jaws," as some other commentators do elsewhere in the poem (compare 5.36.22; 5.49.21; 5.65.8; and notes). Only Gita Press (1969, vol. 3, p. 1784) translates accordingly, rendering, "having the heads of terrible lions with their mouths wide open." Cs offers an alternative explanation, whereby the arrows themselves simply have five heads (*pañcamukhāñ charān iti vā*). See note to verse 37 above.

41–42. "employing his powers of illusion" *māyābhiḥ*: Literally, "by means of illusions." D5,T1,G1,3,M3,5, and the texts and printed editions of Cg read instead *māyāvī*, "[he] possessed of the power of illusion." This variant is rendered only Raghunathan (1982, vol. 3, p. 290), who translates, "The master wizard."

"sea monsters" *makara-*: See 6.14.8 and note. See, too, 5.7.6; 5.34.7; and notes.

"venomous serpents" *-āśīviṣa-*: Among the commentators, only Cg seems concerned about the apparent redundancy between this reference and the one- to five-headed serpents in 40c above. He claims that these are different serpents than those mentioned earlier (*atrāśīviṣaśabdaḥ pañcāsyasarpetarasarpaparaḥ*).

43. "Assaulted" *samāviṣṭaḥ*: Literally, "pervaded, overcome."

"invoked" *sasarja*: Literally, "he released." Here, as in the case of Rāvaṇa at verse 38ff. above, the idea is that the warrior employs a *mantra* to invoke the divine weapon-spell, which is then activated in the form of the numerous arrows fired under its influence. Cf. 6.90.15 and note.

"immensely energetic" *mahotsāhaḥ*: D5,7,9–11,T1,G1,3, and the texts and printed editions of Ct and Cr read instead the accusative *mahotsāham*, in which case the adjective must modify Rāma's *astra* and not Rāma himself.

"delight of the Raghus" *raghunandanaḥ*: D7,9–11,G1,M5, and the texts and printed editions of Ct and Cr read instead *raghupuṃgavaḥ*, "bull among the Raghus."

"the divine weapon-spell of Agni, the purifier . . . a weapon-spell" *astram . . . pāvakam*: Literally, "the *pāvaka astra*." Ck and Ct understand that the fiery divine weapon-spell of Rāma is the counter-missile to Rāvaṇa's missile of darkness, the *tāmasa astra* mentioned in verse 7 above (*tamostrasya pratyastraṃ pāvakam iti tat sasarjety āha*—so Ct).

44–45. "Rāma then released" *sasarja*: Literally, "he released."

"Some had heads like the moon or half-moon, while others had heads like comets" *candrārdhacandravaktrāṃś ca dhūmaketumukhān api*: D10,11, and the text of Ct omit this line (44cd). NSP also omits this line, while GPP prints the line, unnumbered, between verses 6.99.45 and 46.

"resembled" *-varṇān*: Literally, "having the appearance *or* color." B2–4,D4,5, T1,G2,3,M3, and the texts and printed editions of Cg and Gorresio read instead *-vaktrān*, "having faces *or* mouths."

46. "Intercepted in the air... disappeared" *-samāhatāḥ / vilayaṃ jagmur ākāśe*: Literally, "struck *or* destroyed in the sky, they went to dissolution." The majority of translators read the locative more closely with the verbal phrase, "they disappeared [in the sky] (*vilayaṃ jagmuḥ*)."

"shattering into thousands of fragments" *jagmuś caiva sahasraśaḥ*: Literally, "and also they went by the thousand." Ñ2,V2,B2,D5,7,9–11, and the texts and printed editions of Ct and Cr read *jaghnuḥ*, "they struck, destroyed," for *jagmuḥ*, "they went." Ct and Cr understand that we should supply the word "monkeys (*vānarān*)" as the object of this verb. According to their reading, Rāvaṇa's arrows vanish only after having slain thousands of monkeys. This interpretation is shared only by Dutt (1893, p. 1450) and Gita Press (1969, vol. 3, p. 1784). Other translators who share this variant read *jaghnuḥ* passively or reflexively, understanding that the arrows themselves were destroyed.

47. "Rāvaṇa's divinely charged weapons" *tadastram*: Literally, "his *astra or* divinely charged weapon" or, reading *tad astram*, "that *astra*."

Following verse 47, Ñ,V,B2–4,D4–7,9–11,S insert a passage of one line [1992*]: "Surrounding Rāghava, those heroes, of whom Sugrīva was the foremost[1]..."

[1]"of whom Sugrīva was the foremost" *sugrīvapramukhāḥ*: Ñ2,V2,3,D9–11,M1,2,5, and the texts and printed editions of Ct read instead *sugrīvābhimukhāḥ*, "facing Sugrīva."

Following 1992*, D5–7,9–11,S continue with a passage of four lines [1993*]: "Then the great[1] Rāghava Dāśarathi, having forcefully destroyed the divinely charged weapon that had been loosed by the arm of Rāvaṇa, was filled with delight.[1–3] The monkey lords were similarly delighted and roared loudly.[4]"

[1]"great" *mahātmā*: M3 and the printed editions of Cg read instead *mahāhave*, "in the great battle."

The meter is *vaṃśasthavila* with a hypometric *pāda* c.

Sarga 88

1. "redoubled his fury... and... invoked... divine weapon-spell" *krodhaṃ ca dviguṇaṃ cakre... astram*: Literally, "made anger double and produced an *astra*." We agree with the commentators that one either must read the verb *cakre*, "he made *or* produced," to govern both the accusatives or repeat the verb *cakre* to govern the accusative *astram*, "divine weapon-spell."

2. "fierce... divine weapon-spell" *raudram... astram*: The adjective *raudra*, which we have rendered here as "fierce," is quite ambiguous in this context. Normally, with reference to a divine weapon-spell, one would understand it to mean "belonging to Rudra, as, for example, at 6.55.78 and 6.87.33–34. Since Rāma has invoked or deployed the *raudra astra* at least twice and Rāvaṇa has thwarted it in its most recent use, we hesitate to assign the use of this particular weapon to Rāvaṇa at this point. Among

the commentators, only Cg addresses this issue. He unambiguously believes that this is the *astra* of the god Rudra (*rudradevatākam*). Ironically, it seems, all translations consulted share Cg's understanding, with the exception of Raghunathan (1982, vol. 3, p. 290), who generally follows Cg closely. He, like us, renders, "fierce." See, too, notes to 6.55.78 and 6.87.33–34.

"by Maya, the craftsman of the *asuras*" *mayena*: Literally, "by Maya." Maya is the well-known artisan and architect of the *asuras*. He has a special relationship with Rāvaṇa, as Mandodarī, Rāvaṇa's chief queen, is said to be his daughter by the *apsaras* Hemā (6.7.2 and note; and *Uttarakāṇḍa* 12.3–18). See verses 30–31 below. This figure is well known in the *Mahābhārata* as the creator of the Pāṇḍavas' marvelous capital of Indraprastha (*MBh* 2.1–3) and in the *purāṇas* as the creator of Tripura, or the Triple City of the *asuras*. See note to 6.59.73. See, too, note to verses 30–31 below.

4. "the mighty gales" *vātāḥ*: Literally, "winds." Cf. 6.84.10 and note.

"and blazing darts" *dīptāś cāśanayaḥ*: The term *aśani* commonly refers to Indra's thunderbolt, but here, as in a number of places in the epic, the reference appears to be to a weapon. See note to verse 19 below. See, too, 5.3.32 and 6.69.16–17.

"various other sharp weapons" *vividhās tīkṣṇāḥ*: Literally, "various sharp [things]."

5. "that divine weapon-spell" *tad astram*: Literally, "that *astra*," or, reading *tadastram*, "his [i.e., Rāvaṇa's] *astra*."

6. "his eyes red with rage" *krodhatāmrākṣaḥ*: See notes to 6.19.22–23 and 6.31.72.

"of Sūrya" *sauram*: Literally, "belonging to the sun." See note to 6.59.84.

7. "discuses flew forth from the bow" *cakrāṇi niṣpetuḥ . . . kārmukāt*: The idea of discuses flying forth from bows is a bit unusual. The term *cakra*, when referring to a weapon, usually indicates a disc and is considered a *mukta*, or "released," weapon (Oppert 1880, p. 15 and Dikshitar 1944, pp. 109, 122). Perhaps what is meant here is an arrow with a discuslike head. The commentators are silent.

8. "on every side" *itas tataḥ*: Literally, "from here and there." D6,7,9–11,T2,M1,2, and the texts and printed editions of Ct read instead *samantataḥ*, "from all around, on every side."

"as the blazing moon, sun, and planets might light up the directions, if they were to fall" *patadbhiś ca diśo dīptaiś candrasūryagrahair iva*: The simile is somewhat ambiguous and perhaps elliptical. We understand it is as a kind of *abhūtopamā*, or simile, in which the object of comparison is nonexistent or hypothetical. An alternative reading is to take the participles *patadbhiḥ*, "falling, descending," and *saṃpatadbhiḥ*, "descending," in *pāda* b, in the senses of "flying" and "falling," respectively, and to construe them both with *taiḥ*, "those [discuses]," in *pāda* a. The translation would then be: "As they flew through the air, they lit up the sky on every side, and, in falling, those blazing [discuses illuminated] the directions as do the moon, sun, and planets." This interpretation is followed by Gita Press (1969, vol. 3, p. 1785), Roussel (1903, vol. 3, p. 331), and Shastri (1959, vol. 3, p. 290). M3 and the texts and printed editions of Cg read the nominative plural *dīptāḥ* for the instrumental plural *dīptaiḥ* in *pāda* c. In this reading we have to understand that the directions are blazing and not the sun, moon, and planets. This is, in fact, the rendition of Raghunathan (1982, vol. 3, p. 291).

11. "Rāghava was not shaken in the least" *na prākampata*: Literally, "he did not tremble."

13. "At this juncture" *etasminn antare*: Cg comments on the apparent impropriety of Lakṣmaṇa's moving to attack Rāvaṇa while the latter is engaged in battle with Rāma. Cg notes that this would normally constitute a grave breach of the warrior code but observes that, in the present case, Rāma, after having struck Rāvaṇa as described in the previous verse, is now resting for a while. Lakṣmaṇa, meanwhile, having earlier set out to do battle with Rāvaṇa (6.87.15–17), has been waiting for a break in Rāma's combat so that he can continue. (*evaṃ rāvaṇaṃ prahṛtya kṣaṇaṃ rāme viśrāmyati satīty arthaḥ. lakṣmaṇaḥ pūrvaṃ yuddhe pravṛtto madhye rāmeṇa yuddhakaraṇād avasarapratīkṣa ity arthaḥ. evam avyākhyāne katham anyena yuddhyamānam anyo yuddhyeteti mahān doṣaḥ syāt.*) Compare notes to verse 17 below.

14. "that immensely lustrous hero" *mahādyutiḥ*: Literally, "the immensely lustrous one."

"shredded" *ciccheda naikadhā*: Literally, "he cut in many ways."

"battle flag with its image of a human head" *dhvajaṃ manuṣyaśīrṣam*: Literally, "a battle standard that had a man's head." The phrase is somewhat ambiguous and can be read in a number of ways. One could, for example, read it to mean "a battle standard that was a human head," assuming that Rāvaṇa adopts this ghastly device of a severed head as a means of terrorizing his enemies or that he has such a head impaled on the top of his flagstaff. It is, perhaps, more likely that, as with other epic heroes, Rāvaṇa has an image emblazoned on his battle flag. Ct offers an unusual interpretation whereby we are to understand that the battle standard has a man on its top (*manuṣyaḥ śīrṣe yasya tam*). But he acknowledges that others understand that the battle standard is merely marked by or connected with a human head (*manuṣyaśīrṣayuktam ity artha ity anye*).

15. "of the charioteer of the *rākṣasa*, son of chaos" *sāratheḥ . . . nairṛtasya*: Literally, "of the charioteer . . . of the *nairṛta*." The collocation is ambiguous. We follow Cr in taking the kenning *nairṛta* to refer to Rāvaṇa. This interpretation is shared by Gita Press (1969, vol. 3, p. 1785) and Dutt (1893, p. 1452). Gorresio's reading (6.80.16), *rathāt tasya mahātmanaḥ*, "from the chariot of that great one," clearly indicates that the reference is to Rāvaṇa and not to the charioteer. In the critical edition's reading, the word *nairṛtasya* could optionally modify *sāratheḥ*, "charioteer," and some have translated accordingly.

16. "sharp arrows . . . his arrows" *tasya bāṇaiḥ . . . niśitaiḥ śaraiḥ*: Literally, "with his arrows . . . with sharp arrows." The critical reading appears redundant but has fairly solid textual support, although the north avoids the redundancy. There are two ways to resolve the problem. The one we have chosen is to understand *bāṇaiḥ* to be an instrumental of accompaniment. The idea is that Lakṣmaṇa uses his arrows to destroy Rāvaṇa's bow and arrows. This solution has also been adopted by Raghunathan (1982, vol. 3, p. 291), the only translator consulted who shares the critical reading. Cg proposes instead that we read the term *śaraiḥ* in its sense of "a type of grass *or* reed" and thus take it as an adjective modifying *bāṇaiḥ*, that is to say that Lakṣmaṇa is shooting "arrows made of reeds" (*śarair ity atra śaraśabdaḥ kāśadaṇḍaviśeṣamayatvaparo bāṇaviśeṣaṇam*). D9–11 and the texts and printed editions of Ct and Ck avoid the problem by reading *tadā*, "then," in place of *śaraiḥ*, "with arrows."

17. "Meanwhile": We add the word in keeping with the idea Cg proposes that there is a brief pause in the action after Rāvaṇa's bow has been destroyed (*evaṃ dhanuṣi chinne kṣaṇaṃ tūṣṇīṃ tiṣṭhati rāvaṇe vibhīṣaṇena kiṃcitkāram āha*). Cg, we believe, is as-

serting that there is a pause here so as to free Vibhīṣaṇa of the criticism that he is attacking someone already engaged in single combat. Compare the note to verse 16 above.

18. "powerful" *vegavān*: D7,9–11, and the texts and printed editions of Ct and Cr read instead *tu tadā*, "but then."

"conceived" *āhārayat*: Literally, "he manifested *or* produced." Cr, the only commentator to remark on this form, glosses, "he made *or* produced (*akarot*)."

19. "immensely powerful . . . javelin" *śaktiṃ mahāśaktiḥ*: Note the play on words. See note to verse 30 below.

"blazing . . . like a blazing bolt of lightning" *dīptāṃ dīptāśanīm iva*: D7,9–11,G2, and the texts and printed editions of Ct and Cr read instead *pradīptām aśanīm iva*, "like a blazing lightning bolt." Cf. verse 4 and note above.

20. "before it reached Vibhīṣaṇa" *aprāptām eva tām*: Literally, "it [the javelin], which had not even reached."

"At that . . . in the battle" *atha . . . tadā raṇe*: Literally, "now, then, in battle." D4,9–11,13, and the texts and printed editions of Ct read *mahāraṇe*, "in the great battle," for *tadā raṇe*, "then, in the battle."

21. "Encircled with gold" *kāñcanamālinī*: Literally, "having a gold garland."

"cut into four pieces" *tridhā chinnā*: Literally, "thrice cut." All translators consulted understand the phrase to mean that the lance fell in three pieces. However, because it was cut by three arrows, technically it would have been split into four pieces.

"in a shower of blazing sparks" *savisphuliṅgā*: Literally, "with sparks."

22. "Then Rāvaṇa took up a . . . javelin" *tataḥ . . . jagrāha . . . śaktim*: Literally, "then he seized a javelin." This is the special javelin, or *śakti*, that Rāvaṇa is given at 7.12.19. See notes to 30–31 below. Cf. notes to verses 2 and 19 above.

"which he prized greatly" *saṃbhāvitatarām*: Literally, "still more esteemed." Commentators are divided as to the precise sense of the term here. Ck, Ct, and Cr understand that the javelin is universally renowned for its infallibility (*amogheti sarvavyākhyātām*—so Ct, Ck). Cm and Cg, however, understand that the weapon was worshiped with sandalwood, etc. (*candanādibhir arcitām*). Translators are also divided. Dutt (1893, p. 1452) and Gita Press (1969, vol. 3, p. 1786) follow Ct. Raghunathan (1982, vol. 3, p. 292) renders, "celebrated for its power." Roussel (1903, vol. 3, p. 332), followed by Shastri (1959, vol. 3, p. 291) and Pagani (1999, p. 1142), understands that the weapon is more reliable or tested [than the previous javelin]. Gorresio (1858, vol. 10, p. 158), with whom we agree, renders, "*da lui tenuta in maggior pregio*." Cf. notes to 6.15.7, 262*, n. 1.

"and even Kāla himself could not withstand it" *kālenāpi durāsadām*: Literally, "irresistible even by Kāla."

23. "Brandished violently" *vegitā*: Literally, "quickened, expedited, *or* agitated." Since Rāvaṇa does not actually throw the weapon at this point, we have to understand that he is shaking or brandishing it violently in preparation for throwing it. Alternatively, one may take the term to be a general description of the javelin, the sense being that, whenever Rāvaṇa would throw it violently, it would blaze up. This is apparently the sense we are to take from Cr's gloss, "thrown with violence (*vegena prakṣiptā*)."

"supremely terrifying" *sumahāghorā*: Ñ,V,B2–4,D7,9–11,13,G1,M5, and the texts and printed editions of Ck, Ct, and Cr read instead *sumahātejāḥ*, "of immense blazing energy."

"with a splendor equal to that of Śakra's thunderbolt" *śakrāśanisamaprabhā*: Literally, "having luster equal to Śakra's *aśani*." D10 and the texts and printed editions of Ct read instead *dīpta-*, "blazing," for *śakra-*. This yields the sense "with a splendor equal to that of a blazing thunderbolt."

24. "ran quickly" *tūrṇam evābhyapadyata*: Literally, "he swiftly approached." The commentators understand, quite correctly in our opinion, that Lakṣmaṇa races to Vibhīṣaṇa's side in order to protect him. Ct understands that Lakṣmaṇa stands in the path of (lit., faces) Rāvaṇa's javelin and so protects Vibhīṣaṇa (*śaktisaṃmukhaṃ svayam āgatya vibhīṣaṇaṃ rakṣitavān ity arthaḥ*). Cg similarly understands that Lakṣmaṇa stands in such a way as to screen Vibhīṣaṇa (*tamācchādya svayam atiṣṭhad ity arthaḥ*).

"was now in mortal danger" *prāṇasaṃśayam āpannam*: Literally, "had come to danger to his life breaths."

26. "by great Lakṣmaṇa" *mahātmanā*: Literally, "by the great one."

"his martial ardor now diverted, decided not to strike his brother" *na prahartuṃ manaś cakre vimukhīkṛtavikramaḥ*: Literally, "his valor made adverse, he made up his mind to not strike *or* did not make up his mind to strike." The half verse is slightly ambiguous. Our interpretation follows that of the commentators, who generally understand that, as a result of Lakṣmaṇa's attack, Rāvaṇa loses his immediate desire to use his javelin to kill Vibhīṣaṇa (*vimukhīkṛtavibhīṣaṇaviṣayaparākramaḥ*—so Cg, Cm; *kuṇṭhitabhrātṛvadhaviṣayotsāhaḥ*—so Ck, Ct). With the exception of Gorresio, translators understand that Lakṣmaṇa's hail of arrows has thwarted or diminished Rāvaṇa's strength or prowess (Gita Press 1969, vol. 3, p. 1786; Dutt 1893, p. 1452; Raghunathan 1982, vol. 3, p. 292; Roussel 1903, vol. 3, p. 332; Shastri 1959, vol. 3, p. 291; and Pagani 1999, p. 1142). Gorresio (1858, vol. 10, p. 159) understands, as we and the commentators do, and similarly adds a referent, the name Vibhīṣaṇa.

Ñ2,B1–3,D5,7,9–11,T2, and the texts and printed editions of Ct read the pronoun *saḥ*, "he," (i.e., Rāvaṇa), in place of the negative particle *na*. In this reading, one would have to understand that Rāvaṇa diverts his attention from Vibhīṣaṇa and resolves to strike Lakṣmaṇa.

28. "so proud of your strength" *balaślāghin*: Literally, "O you who are boastful of strength!" The majority of translators understand the compound as do we. Raghunathan (1982, vol. 3, p. 292), on the other hand, sees it as a term of praise for the adversary rather than a taunt, rendering, "You, whose strength is worthy of all praise."

29. "blood-stained" *lohitalakṣaṇā*: Literally, "characterized by blood *or* redness." The idea, as set forth by the commentators, is that the weapon is stained with the blood of Rāvaṇa's enemies. Cg observes that Rāvaṇa uses this expression to suggest that he has slain his enemies many times in the past (*anena pūrvam api bahudhā ripavo mayā hatā iti vyajyate*).

30–31. "that javelin" *śaktim*: See verse 22 above and note.

"Maya, the craftsman of the *asuras*, had forged it with his magical powers so that it was infallible in slaying one's enemies." *mayena māyāvihitām amoghāṃ śatrughātinīm*: Literally, "made with *māyā* by Maya, unfailing, enemy slaying." One should note that this javelin, which Maya presented to Rāvaṇa on the occasion of the latter's marriage to his daughter, Mandodarī, is said, at *Uttarakāṇḍa* 12.19, to have been acquired by Maya through supreme austerity rather than actually fashioned by him (*pareṇa tapasā labdhām*). See note to verse 2 above.

32. "emitting a roar like that of Śakra's thunderbolt" *śakrāśanisamasvanā*: Literally, "having a sound equal to Śakra's *aśani*." Ś,Ñ,V,B2–4,D1–3,6–13,M1,2, and the texts and printed editions of Ct read *vajra-* for *śakra-*, "Śakra," lending the compound the sense "with a sound equal to that of the *vajra* or the thunderbolt."

"struck" *abhyapatat*: Literally, "it fell upon."

33. "was hurtling toward Lakṣmaṇa" *āpatantīm*: Literally, "flying."

"Rāma Rāghava" *sa rāghavaḥ*: Literally, "that Rāghava." The context makes it clear that Rāma, and not Lakṣmaṇa, is meant.

"addressed it" *tām anuvyāharat*: As several of the commentators point out, Rāma is actually addressing the divinity that presides over the weapon (*śaktyadhiṣṭhātṛdevatām*—so Ct).

"May Lakṣmaṇa be spared!" *svasty astu lakṣmaṇāyeti*: Literally, "May there be well-being for Lakṣmaṇa."

"And may you...be foiled" *moghā bhava*: Literally, "May you be in vain." Ct is evidently disturbed by the fact that, despite Rāma's words, the javelin appears, at least at first, to deliver a mortal blow to Lakṣmaṇa. He argues that Rāma is really saying that the javelin should merely cause pain so that, despite its power of killing by its mere touch, it will thus become foiled by Rāma's utterance. In this way, Ct continues, the truthfulness of Rāma's words is suggested. (*tacchaktis tu pīḍāmātreṇa caritārthāstv iti bhāvaḥ. sparśamātreṇa prāṇāpaharaṇasāmarthyayuktāyāḥ śakter anena svavākyena moghīkaraṇāt svasya satyasaṃkalpatvaṃ sūcitam.*)

Following verse 33, D5,7,9–11,T1,G,M1,3,5 (D6,T2,3,M2 following verse 34) insert a passage of two lines [2006*]: "In a rage, Rāvaṇa hurled that javelin, which was like a venomous serpent. It swiftly buried itself in the breast of fearless Lakṣmaṇa.[1]"

[1]The wording of the verse, particularly that of *pāda* c (*muktāśūrasyabhītasya*... *mamajja* "hurled... It swiftly buried itself in the breast of fearless"), is ambiguous and can be read in at least two ways. The ambiguity is of particular importance to some of the commentators who reject the idea that Lakṣmaṇa could actually be struck or wounded by Rāvaṇa's weapon, especially in light of Rāma's words at verse 33 above. Apart from the sequence of words that we, along with Cg, Ck, and Ct understand, i.e., *muktā āśu urasi abhītasya*, *pāda* c could also be broken up as *muktā śūrasya bhītasya*, which would appear to mean "hurled, [it sunk into] the frightened hero [Lakṣmaṇa]." Ck and Ct, arguing for their analysis of the sequence, note that because the meaning of the verse is not immediately apparent, the poet clarifies it in the following verse (34) (*muktā āśu urasīti chedasya gūḍhatvāt spaṣṭam evāha kavir nyapatad iti*). Cr chooses the second analysis but then has to confront the awkwardness of the resulting term *bhītasya*, "frightened," used in connection with the heroic warrior Lakṣmaṇa. He does this ingeniously by reading the participle as a *bahuvrīhi* compound whose meaning is "from whom fear is constantly removed (*bhītasya bhīr bhayam itā nityaṃ nivṛttā yasmāt tasya lakṣmaṇasya*)." Cr further rejects the notion that Lakṣmaṇa is actually wounded, arguing that we should understand that the javelin merely falls near him. To assert that the weapon actually struck and injured Lakṣmaṇa, Cr argues, would contradict the utterance of Rāma, the Supreme Lord, in verse 33. Thus, Cr continues, his interpretation is in keeping with both *śruti* and *smṛti* (*Śvetāśvatara Upaniṣad* 6.6), where the Supreme Lord is represented as omniscient and omnipotent. (*lakṣmaṇasya san-*

nidhau mamajja papātety arthaḥ. urasi mamajjety arthas tu na yuktaḥ. śaktikarmakarāmakartṛkokter viruddhatvāpatteḥ. ata eva jñaḥ kālakālaḥ kartṛtvaṃ karaṇatvaṃ cetyādiśrutismṛtayaḥ sānukūlāḥ.) Interestingly, Cr is then forced to ascribe Lakṣmaṇa's collapse in the following verses not to any injury but to his extreme delicacy (*mūrcchāvāptis tu tadasparśe 'pi saukumāryātiśayāt*). See note to 6.35.9.

34. "Nonetheless, that immensely brilliant weapon" *sā . . . mahādyutiḥ*: Literally, "that one of great luster."

"like the flickering tongue of a serpent king" *jihvevoragarājasya*: Literally, "like the tongue of a king of serpents."

"fell . . . on Lakṣmaṇa's broad chest" *nyapatat . . . lakṣmaṇasya mahorasi*: Here again, as in his comments to 2006* discussed in note 33 above, Cr denies that Lakṣmaṇa is actually struck. He suggests that we read the particle *iva*, "like *or* as if," from *pāda* c, both with the simile of the serpent's tongue and with the verbal phrase *nyapatat . . . mahorasi*, "[the javelin] fell on the broad chest." Thus, he understands: "It seemed to fall on Lakṣmaṇa's broad chest. The meaning is that it appeared to be situated there because of its extreme proximity. The particle 'like (*iva*)' applies in both contexts. (*lakṣmaṇasya mahorasīva nyapatat. atisānnidhyāt tatsthevālakṣyatety arthaḥ. ivobhayānvayī.*)"

35. "his heart pierced by that javelin, so deeply embedded" *sudūram avagāḍhayā / śaktyā nirbhinnahṛdayaḥ*: D7,9–11, and the texts and printed editions of Cr and Ct read *vibhinna-*, "pierced," for *nirbhinna-*, "pierced." This slight variation permits Cr to exploit the *sandhi* to yield the reading *śaktyā avibhinnahṛdayaḥ*, "his heart not pierced by the javelin." Cr then disposes of the embarrassing adjectival phrase "deeply imbedded (*sudūram avagāḍhayā*) by glossing, "come near (*samāgatayā*)."

37. "He remained lost for a moment in thought" *sa muhūrtam anudhyāya*: Literally, "having thought for a moment." We believe the context suggests that Rāma is brooding *or* grieving for Lakṣmaṇa. Cg, Ck, and Ct, however, believe he is pondering what he should do at this point (*tatkālakartavyaṃ cintayitvā*—so Cg). Ś,B1,D1–3,7–13,M1, and the texts and printed editions of Ck and Ct read instead *muhūrtam iva dhyātvā*, "having thought, as it were, for a moment." Cs appears to understand that, by using the word "like (*iva*)" here, the poet is suggesting that an omniscient being's [i.e., Rāma's] appearance of being lost in thought is merely the *avatāra*'s imitation of worldly [behavior] (*ivena kaviḥ svataḥ sarvavido dhyānaṃ lokānukṛtita iti sūcayati*).

"he flared up in anger" *babhūva saṃrabdhataraḥ*: Literally, "he became very angry *or* excited." We agree with Cr in taking the term *saṃrabdha* in its sense of "furious, angry." Cr suggests that Rāma's anger is feigned. He glosses, "he was as if extremely angry (*atikruddha iva babhūva*)." Ct, however, understands the adjective to mean "filled with increased enthusiasm for battle (*yuddhe 'dhikotsāhavān*)."

38. Following verse 38, D5–7,9–11,S insert a passage of one line [2010*]: "[Reflecting] . . . and[1] seeing Lakṣmaṇa, [Rāghava] with a great and total effort [began . . .]."

[1]"and" *ca*: Cv and Cg take the conjunction to suggest that seeing Lakṣmaṇa in this condition gives Rāma yet another reason—over and above the abduction of Sītā—for wanting Rāvaṇa dead (*na kevalaṃ sītāharaṇāt kiṃtu lakṣmaṇadarśanād apīti caśabdārthaḥ*).

39. "pierced by that javelin... and drenched in blood" *śaktyā bhinnam... rudhirādigdham*: In keeping with his insistence that Lakṣmaṇa is uninjured, Cr reads these two sequences as "not pierced by the javelin (*śaktyā-abhinnam*)" and "not drenched with blood (*rudhira-adigdham*)."

"resembled a mountain with a mighty serpent" *sapannagam ivācalam*: Literally, "like a mountain with a snake." The basis for this odd simile appears to be the image of the large frame of the fallen Lakṣmaṇa, from which protrudes the length of the javelin. Cr, who, as noted above, refuses to entertain the idea that Lakṣmaṇa has been injured by the javelin, thinks instead that the image is based on Lakṣmaṇa's extreme pallor [suggesting perhaps a snowcapped peak?] and his possession of a bow and arrows (*lakṣmaṇasyātigauratvena ca dhanurbāṇaviśiṣṭatvena ceyam upamā*). In many traditional schools of painting, Lakṣmaṇa is represented as very fair in contrast to his dark brother. Some post-Vālmīkian traditions also regard him as an incarnation of the white serpent Śeṣa, or Ananta, who serves as Viṣṇu's couch when the deity sleeps on the cosmic ocean. For a discussion of the color contrast between Rāma and Lakṣmaṇa, as well as other paired *avatāras*, see R. Goldman 1980.

40. "by the swift-handed *rākṣasa*" *kṣiprahastena rakṣasā*: D9–11 and the texts and printed editions of Ct read instead *te pravekeṇa rakṣasām*, "they... by that foremost among the *rākṣasas*."

"they... were unable to extract" *na śekur avamarditum*: Literally, "they were not able to grind [it] down." The commentators offer a variety of reasons for the monkeys' inability to free Lakṣmaṇa from the javelin. Cg understands that the monkeys were still being afflicted by [Rāvaṇa's] arrows (*bāṇārditatvena*), while Cr argues, in addition, that it was because Rāvaṇa had embedded the javelin with such effort (*rāvaṇena yatnataḥ prahitāṃ śaktim avamarditum... na sekuḥ*). Ct and Ck, looking to the next verse, understand that the monkeys were unable to extract the javelin because it had pierced through Lakṣmaṇa's body and was embedded in the earth (*sā śaktiḥ saumitrer dehaṃ nirbhidya dharaṇītalaṃ bhuvaṃ praviṣṭā spṛṣṭavatī*).

41. "which, having transfixed Saumitri, was embedded in the earth" *saumitriṃ sā vinirbhidya praviṣṭā dharaṇītalam*: Cr, of course, reads "not having transfixed (*sā avinirbhidya*)" and understands that the javelin is embedded in the earth near Lakṣmaṇa (*saumitreḥ samīpavarti dharaṇītalaṃ praviṣṭā*).

"Wrenching it out violently" *balavad vicakarṣa ca*: Literally, "and he withdrew powerfully." Ś,B1,D2,6,7,8–12,T2,3,C1,M3, and the texts and printed editions of Ck, Cg, Cr, and Ct read for *balavat*, "violently, powerfully," the adjective *balavān*, "mighty," which then modifies Rāma. Ck and Ct understand that, under normal circumstances, the javelin, after piercing an enemy, would return to Rāvaṇa. In this case, however, its capacity of exiting the body of its victim has been destroyed by the utterance [in verse 33] of Rāma, whose vows are infallible. Thus, it remains lodged [in Lakṣmaṇa] until the Lord extracts and breaks it. (*iyaṃ śaktiḥ sarvadā śatruṃ nirbhidya rāvaṇasamīpam eva prāpnoti. idānīṃ rāmeṇa moghā bhavety uktyā satyasaṃkalpena nāśitaniṣkramaṇaśaktis tatraiva lagnā sā ca bhagavatā vikṛṣya bhagnā*—so Ct.)

43. "Rāghava... and" *caiva rāghavaḥ*: D9–11 and the texts and printed editions of Ct and Cr read instead *ca mahākapim*, "and to the great monkey." Cr understands the epithet to refer to Jāmbavān, who is not named in the verse. Translators who follow the text of Ct, except for Pagani, understand the epithet to refer to Sugrīva.

Pagani (1999, p. 1143), for some reason, translates it as a plural referring to both Hanumān and Sugrīva.

"embraced" *samāśliṣya*: Literally, "having embraced." Ct lends the embrace a theological significance, remarking that, in revealing his own identity [with Lakṣmaṇa], Rāma's embrace leads to the cessation of all pain (*samāśleṣo 'yaṃ sakalapīḍānivṛttiphalakaḥ svatādātmyāvabhāsanarūpaḥ*).

44. "The moment to display my valor is now at hand, a moment" *parākramasya kālo 'yaṃ saṃprāptaḥ*: Literally, "the time of valor has come."

"a thirsty *cātaka*" *kāṅkṣataḥ stokakasya*: Literally, "of a *stokaka*, who is longing." The term *stokaka* is a synonym for the more common name *cātaka* (*Cucculus melanoleucus*), a bird that, according to the Sanskrit poetic convention, lives entirely on raindrops and so, presumably, must remain parched for most of the year, waiting anxiously for the rains. D10,11,T2,3,M1,5, and the texts and printed editions Ck and Ct read instead *kāṅkṣitaṃ cātakasyeva*, "as if desired by (lit., of) the *cātaka*." In this case, the participle modifies *meghadarśanam*, "the sight of rain clouds," rather than the bird itself.

"must die" *vadhyatām*: Literally, "let [him] be slain."

45. "I give you my solemn word here and now . . . that very soon" *asmin muhūrte na cirāt satyaṃ pratiśṛṇomi vaḥ*: Literally, "at this moment, I promise you truthfully, that soon." We follow Cr in understanding the phrase *asmin muhūrte*, "at this moment," to qualify the making of Rāma's promise (*asmin muhūrte vo yuṣmākam agre satyaṃ pratiśṛṇomi pratijñāṃ karomi*) rather than, as Cg suggests, the time frame in which his vow will be accomplished (*asmin muhūrte tatrāpi na cirād drakṣyathety anvayaḥ*). A number of translators have interpreted as does Cg, but we believe that this is inappropriate for two reasons. First, it seems redundant with the phrase *na cirāt*, "soon (lit., not long)," in *pāda* a. Second, it seems to conflict with the fact that Rāma does not kill Rāvaṇa very quickly, because the battle rages on, with various fluctuations and pauses, for another nine chapters until *sarga* 97. On the other hand, it should be noted that, in the following verses, Rāma does vow to kill Rāvaṇa without delay.

46–47. "I will put behind me" *ahaṃ tyakṣye*: Literally, "I shall abandon."

"the terrible suffering and hellish torment" *duḥkham . . . kleśaṃ ca nirayopamam*: Literally, "suffering and distress comparable to hell." Ck and Ct understand that *duḥkha*, "suffering," refers to the mental anguish caused by the loss of the kingdom, etc., whereas *kleśa* refers to physical suffering, similar to the torments of hell. (*rājyanāśādikṛtaṃ ghoraṃ duḥkhaṃ mānasaṃ prāptam. nirayopamo yātanopamaḥ kleśaḥ kāyakleśaś ca prāptaḥ.*)

48–49. "placing . . . on the throne" *kṛto rājye*: Literally, "rendered into kingship."

"on whose account I bridged and crossed the ocean" *yadarthaṃ sāgaraḥ krāntaḥ setur baddhaś ca sāgare*: Literally, "for whose sake the ocean was crossed and the bridge built across the ocean."

"after slaying Vālin in combat" *nihatvā vālinaṃ raṇe*: Rāma's recollection here is interesting. In fact, as Rāma himself points out at *Kiṣkindhākāṇḍa* 18, after striking down Vālin, who was engaged in combat with his brother, the killing of Vālin is to be seen either as the execution of an evildoer or the hunting of an animal, and not as any form of normal combat. See R. Goldman 1997.

50. "a person seen by a serpent whose mere glance is deadly venom" *dṛṣṭiṃ dṛṣṭiviṣasyeva sarpasya*: Literally, "to the sight of a serpent having sight for venom." The *upamāna* is elliptical. We follow Cm, who suggests adding the words "like a person

who comes within the range of sight (*dṛṣṭiviṣayaṃ prāpto jana iva*)." According to Cg, it is well known that certain types of snakes kill people by their mere glance (*kecid dhi sarpāḥ darśanamātreṇa manuṣyān mārayantīti prasiddhiḥ*). The reference puts one in mind of the medieval legend of the basilisk, the mythical beast of European folklore.

Following verse 50, D9–11 and the texts and printed editions of Ct and Cr insert a passage of one line [2017*]: "Or any more than a serpent can, once it comes within the sight of Garuḍa Vainateya.[1]"

[1]"Garuḍa Vainateya" *vainateyasya*" Literally, "of Vainateya." The great celestial bird Garuḍa is the mortal enemy of all snakes. See 6.40.33ff.

52. "along with . . . the gods, the seers, and the celestial bards" *sadevāḥ sarṣicāraṇāḥ*: D9,11, and the texts and printed editions of Ct read instead the partially redundant (since the *gandharvas* are already mentioned in *pāda* c) *siddhagandharvacāraṇāḥ*, "*siddhas*, *gandharvas*, and celestial bards."

"what makes Rāma Rāma" *rāmasya rāmatvam*: Literally, "the Rāma-ness of Rāma." In the context, it is clear that Rāma is talking about his extraordinary martial prowess, which, he suggests, will enable him to defeat the powerful *rākṣasa* lord. This notion is expressed by Cg, who glosses "Rāma-ness (*rāmatvam*)" with "the state of being the one true hero in the world (*jagadekavīratvam*)." Cg does note, however, that the "masters" claim that the reference is to "the purpose of Rāma's *avatāra* (*ācāryās tu rāmāvatāra-prayojanam ity āhuḥ*)." Cm, Ck, Ct, and Cr offer a variety of related explanations, all of which derive from the etymological play on *ramay*, the causative of the root $\sqrt{}$*ram*, "to delight," which the poet so often uses in connection with Rāma's name. Ck and Ct explain that the Rāma-ness of Rāma inheres in the fact that he delights the three worlds, along with the gods and seers, by means of his righteousness, truthfulness, and valor. They go on to add that here Rāma means to say that he will now perform a feat worthy of his nature. (*trīṃl lokān sarṣidevān dharmeṇa satyena śauryeṇa ca ramayatīty anvarthaṃ rāmatvam. taducitaṃ karmādya kariṣyāmīti bhāvaḥ*—so Ct.) Cr glosses, "Rāma-ness is the state of providing delight, etc. (*rāmatvam abhirāmadātṛtvādi*). Cm notes that Rāma-ness derives from the hero's capacity for delighting, which, in turn, can be traced to his valor (*ramayatīti rāma iti vyutpattyā parākrameṇāpi ramayitṛtvam ucyate*). The translators offer several variations on these themes.

53. "as long as the earth shall endure" *yāvad bhūmir dhariṣyati*: Ck and Ct take the verb *dhariṣyati*, "he/she/it will endure," in its transitive sense, "he will sustain, will support," and supply a direct object, "living beings (*prāṇinaḥ*)." This interpretation has been followed in the translations of Dutt (1893, p. 1455) and Gita Press (1969, vol. 3, p. 1789). Cm understands the term *bhūmih*, "earth, ground," here to refer to the battlefield and takes the phrase to mean "so long as the battlefield remains (*yāvad yuddhabhūmir dhariṣyaty avasthāsyate*)."

Following verse 53, D6,7,9,T2,3,G1,2,M, and the texts and printed editions of Cv, Cg, and Cm insert a passage of one line [2020*]: "Having come together, [the worlds will talk] forever about how the battle proceeded."

54. "with great concentration" *samāhitaḥ*: Literally, "composed, concentrated, focused."

55. "And . . . with blazing" *atha pradīptaiḥ*: D7,9–11, and the texts and printed editions of Ct read instead *tathā praviddhaiḥ*, "thus cast away." Cr reads instead *tadā prasiddhaiḥ* (unattested in the critical edition), "then with excellent *or* celebrated [arrows]." Dutt (1893, p. 1455), who renders, "great," may be following this reading.

"with its torrential rains" *dhārābhiḥ*: Literally, "with streams."

56. "And . . . the various arrows" *śarāṇāṃ ca śarāṇāṃ ca*: Literally, "and of arrows and of arrows." D2,10,11, and the texts and printed editions of Ck, Ct, and Cr read the adjective *varāṇām*, "excellent or outstanding," for the first occurrence of *śarāṇām*, yielding the sense "of those excellent arrows." Ct and Cr argue that the conjunction *ca*, "and," implies the inclusion of the cudgels mentioned in verse 55 above (*cān musalānām*—so Ct).

58. "deafening" *mahān*: Literally, "great."

"bowstrings . . . striking against their armguards" *tayor jyātalanirghoṣaḥ*: Literally, "the sound of the bowstrings and forearms of those two." See notes to 6.66.23; 6.75.25; 6.76.2,24; 6.77.31 (1701*); and 6.81.26–27.

"was almost miraculous" *babhūvādbhutopamaḥ*: Literally, "was comparable to a miracle." D7,9–11, and the texts and printed editions of Ct and Cr read instead *babhūvādbhutadarśanaḥ*, "was wonderful to behold," a rather awkward reading in light of the fact that the referent is a sound. Translators who follow the text of Ct struggle to make sense of the reading. Some substitute "to hear" in place of "to behold." Some take the phrase to refer not to the sound but to its terrifying effect on all beings. One, Dutt (1893, p. 1455), translates, "wonderful to behold," but qualifies this somewhat, observing, "*wonderful to witness* is the sense."

59. "covered . . . and thus tormented by the great wielder of the blazing bow" *kīryamāṇaḥ . . . mahātmanā dīptadhanuṣmatārditaḥ*: Literally, "being covered, tormented by that great one, who possesses a blazing bow." Our translation reflects the commentary of Cr, who inserts the phrase *ata eva*, "[and] for that very reason," between the two participles. Pagani (1999, p. 1144) translates the phrase oddly, rendering, "*Criblé des averses de traits . . . dévoré par le feu nourri du resplendissant archer*."

"with dense hails of arrows" *śarajālavṛṣṭibhiḥ*: Literally, "with showers of masses *or* webs of arrows." Ś1 (first time), Ñ2,V (V2 both times), B2,3 (second time), 4, G2, and the printed editions of Ct (GPP and NSP but unattested in the critical apparatus) read the nominative singular hypometric *śarajālavṛṣṭiḥ*. One would expect this to be read as a *bahuvrīhi* compound modifying Rāvaṇa, and so having little semantic difference from the critical reading. Roussel (1903, vol. 3, p. 334), followed by Shastri (1959, vol. 3, p. 293), however, understands the hail of arrows to be the subject of the sentence. This is, of course, not possible grammatically.

"having first joined battle" *sametya*: Literally, "having joined *or* met."

"now fled in terror" *bhayāt pradudrāva*: Literally, "he ran out of fear." Ck and Ct suggest that Rāvaṇa is terrified at the thought that Rāma, in his rage at Rāvaṇa's wounding of his brother Lakṣmaṇa, will now surely kill him (*bhayād bhrātṛpīḍājanitakopena sarvathā māṃ haniṣyaty eva iti bhayād ity arthaḥ*).

"like a great storm cloud driven before the wind" *yathānilenābhihato balāhakaḥ*: Literally, "like a cloud struck by wind."

The meter is *vaṃśasthavila*.

Ct claims that Rāvaṇa's flight takes place in the evening of the new-moon day [of Āśvinā] (*idaṃ palāyanam amāsāyaṃkāle*). See note to 6.4.4.

Sarga 89

Before verse 1, D5,7,10,11,T1,G,M, and the texts and printed editions of the southern commentators insert, while D4,9 insert following verse 1, a passage of two lines [2023*]: "Seeing that heroic Lakṣmaṇa had been struck down in battle with a javelin by mighty Rāvaṇa and was drenched with gouts of blood[1] . . ."

[1]"struck down . . . drenched with gouts of blood" *vinihatam . . . śoṇitaughapariplutam*: As before, Cr maintains his denial of Lakṣmaṇa's injuries. Once again he understands that Rāvaṇa's javelin is merely close to Lakṣmaṇa and that he only appears to be covered with blood as a result of [Rāma's] compassion [toward him] engendered by his anger [at Rāvaṇa] (*śaktyatisānnidhyamātreṇa nipātitaṃ śoṇitaughapariplutaṃ krodhahetukāruṇyena rudhirasamūhavyāptam iva*).

1. "Rāma" *saḥ*: Literally, "he."

"even as he continued to discharge" *visṛjann eva*: Literally, "while still discharging." As Cg explains, the use of the present participle here suggests that, after Rāvaṇa's flight, Rāma wastes no time in arranging for the welfare of Lakṣmaṇa (*visṛjann evetyādivartamānanirdeśena rāvaṇapalāyanānantaraṃ lakṣmaṇayogakṣemānusaṃdhāne 'vilambaḥ sūcitaḥ*).

2. "through the power of Rāvaṇa" *rāvaṇavegena*: Literally, "through the force *or* impact of Rāvaṇa." D4,6,7,9–11,T2,3,M3, and the texts and printed editions of the southern commentators read instead *rāvaṇavīryeṇa*, "through the heroic valor *or* might of Rāvaṇa."

3. "I wonder what power I have left" *mama kā śaktiḥ*: Literally, "What power have I?"

4. "marked with auspicious signs" *śubhalakṣaṇaḥ*: Literally, "of auspicious marks." The epithet used alone here is often used for its alliterative effect with the name Lakṣmaṇa. See 6.14.3; 6.67.37; 6.71.20; 6.73.5; 6.75.16; 6.79.1; and notes. See also R. Goldman 1984, p. 105.

"has truly returned to the elements" *pañcatvam āpannaḥ*: Literally, "attained fiveness." See 6.39.7 and note. See verse 28 below.

5. Compare the similar symptoms of mental distress that afflict Arjuna at *BhagGī* 1.29–31.

"seems to hang its head in shame" *lajjatīva*: Literally, "it is, as it were, ashamed."

"from my grasp" *karāt*: Literally, "from the hand."

"dimmed with tears" *bāṣpavaśaṃ gatā*: Literally, "gone to the influence of tears."

"Dreadful thoughts grow in my mind" *cintā me vardhate tīvrā*: Literally, "my dreadful anxiety grows."

"and I wish now only for death" *mumūrṣā copajāyate*: Literally, "and a desire to die is born."

Following 5cd, D5,7,10,11,T1,G,M1,3,5, and the texts and printed editions of the southern commentators insert a passage of one line [2025*]: "My limbs sink down like those of men walking in a dream.[1]"

[1]"My limbs sink down like those of men walking in a dream." *avasīdanti gātrāṇi svapnayāne nṛṇām iva*: Our interpretation follows that of Cg, who glosses "going in

sleep (*svapnagamane*)" for *svapnayāne* and explains, "men who walk in their sleep drag their feet (*svapne hi gacchatāṃ puruṣāṇāṃ pādāḥ paścād ākṛṣṭā bhavanti*)." Ct and Ck understand the lexeme not as a nominal compound but as an irregular derivative of the root √*svap*, "to sleep," having the same sense as the term *svapna*, "sleep *or* dream." Cr is the only commentator who attempts to clearly distinguish the senses of sleep and dream, explaining, "my limbs sink down like the limbs of men when they experience a nightmare (*svapnasya duḥsvapnakadarśanasya yāne praptau satyāṃ nṝṇāṃ gātrāṇīva me gātrāṇy avasīdanti*).

6. "Thus did Rāma . . . lament" *vilalāpa*: Literally, "he lamented."

Following 6ab, D5–7,10,11,S (D4,9 after 2023*) insert a passage of three lines [2026*]: "When Rāghava had seen his dear brother, who was like another life breath outside his body,[1] deeply wounded in his vitals, wracked with pain, and gasping for breath,[2] he was overcome with enormous grief and gave way to brooding and sorrow."

[1]"another life breath outside his body" *prāṇaṃ bahiścaram*: Literally, "breath moving outside." See 1.17.17; 3.32.12; and notes. See, too, 6.19.24; 6.40.46; 6.47.123; and notes.

[2]"gasping for breath" *viniśvasantam*: Literally, "panting, breathing out." D10,11, and the texts and printed editions of Ct read *niṣṭantaṃ tu*, while M2,3, and the texts and printed editions of Cg read *viniṣṭantam*. Both of these readings would convey the sense of "moaning." See note to 6.79.4, 1744*, n. 1.

7. "I have no further use for battle, for my life, or even for Sītā herself." *na hi yuddhena me kāryaṃ naiva prāṇair na sītayā*: Literally, "there is nothing to be done by [lit. of] me with battle, nor with life breaths, nor with Sītā." V3,D10,11, and the texts and printed editions of Ct omit this line [7ab].

Following verse 7, Ś,D6–12,T2,3, and the texts and printed editions of Ct and Cr insert a passage of two lines [2028*]: "For now, hero, even victory would give me no pleasure. What delight will the moon give in the presence of the blind?[1]"

[1]"in the presence of the blind" *acakṣurviṣayaḥ*: Literally, "in the range of the sightless." We follow Cr, who glosses, "in the presence of blind people (*andhajanasamīpasthaḥ*)." The idea is that victory can give no pleasure to Rāma, who, in his grief for Lakṣmaṇa, has lost the will and faculty to enjoy it, just as the moon can give no pleasure to those who have no faculty to enjoy it. Most translators simply understand that the moon is invisible, but this undermines the point of the simile.

8. "for kingship" *rājyena*: Ś,Ñ2,V,B,D1–3,6,8–12,T2,3, and the texts and printed editions of Ct read instead *yuddhena*, "battle."

"There is now no longer any purpose to this war" *yuddhe kāryaṃ na vidyate*: Literally, "there is nothing to be done in battle."

Following verse 8, manuscripts aligned with the southern recension insert, in whole or in part, a passage of twenty-four lines [2029*]. The full passage, with the exception of lines 7–8, is known to the text of Ct and is best represented in NSP. The texts and printed editions of Cg, Crā, Cm, and Cv know only a small portion of the passage, and this shorter version is best represented in VSP. The equivalencies are provided below:

KK 6.102.12 = 2029* lines 5–6
KK 6.102.13–19 [in brackets] = 2029* lines 9–23
KK 6.102.20 = 2029* lines 7–8

VSP 6.102.13 = 2029* lines 5–6
VSP 6.102.14ab,cd = 2029* lines 7–8
VSP omits the remainder

GPP 6.101.12 = 2029* lines 1–2
GPP 6.101.13 = 2029* lines 3–4
GPP 6.101.14 = 2029* lines 5–6
GPP 6.101 unnumbered between 14 and 15 = 2029* lines 7–8 [as a Cg reading]
GPP 6.101.15–22 = 2029* lines 9–24

NSP 6.101.12 = 2029* lines 1–2
NSP 6.101.13 = 2029* lines 3–4
NSP 6.101.14 = 2029* lines 5–6
[lines 7–8 omitted]
NSP 6.101.15–22 = 2029* lines 9–24

Gita Press P 6.101.13 = 2029* lines 1–2
Gita Press 6.101.14 = 2029* lines 3–4
Gita Press 6.101.15 = 2029* lines 5–6
[lines 7–8 omitted]
Gita Press 6.101.16–23 = 2029* lines 9–24

Approximately one-third of the passage is repeated verbatim from *sarga* 39, where Rāma earlier had experienced the apparent death of Lakṣmaṇa. See notes to 6.39.

" 'Just as that glorious hero followed me as I went to the forest, so will I now follow him to the abode of Yama.[1–2 = 6.39.17] He always cherished his family, and he was ever devoted to me [3 = 6.39.18ab with *ca* for *saḥ*], but now he has been brought to this condition by the *rākṣasas*, who fight deceitfully.[1][4] In country after country there are wives to be found, and in country after country there may be friends.[2] But I do not see any country where I might find a true brother.[3][5–6] As he was lamenting in this fashion, his senses disordered with grief, writhing about and sighing piteously again and again . . .[4][7–8] Unassailable hero, of what use is kingship to me without Lakṣmaṇa? How will I tell his mother, Sumitrā, who doted on her son?[9–10] I shall not be able to endure the reproaches given[5] by Sumitrā.[11 = 6.39.11ab] Whatever shall I tell Kausalyā, and what shall I tell mother Kaikeyī?[6][12 = 6.39.8ab] What shall I say to Bharata and immensely powerful Śatrughna? How would it be if I were to return without him with whom I went to the forest?[7][13–14] Death right here and now would be preferable to the censure of my kinfolk. What evil deed did I perform in some other life as a result of which my righteous brother lies slain before me?[15–17] Alas! My brother! Best of men! Foremost of heroes! Mighty one! How could you leave me and journey alone to the next world? [18–19] Why don't you speak to me, brother, as I lament? Arise! Look around. Why do you lie there? Cast your eyes on me in my sorrow.[20–21] You always used to comfort me, great-armed hero,[8] when I was afflicted with grief, despondent, and distracted in the mountains and forests.'[22–23] As Rāma was speaking in this fashion, his senses disordered with grief... [24]"

[1]"but now he has been brought to this condition by the *rākṣasas*, who fight deceitfully" *imām avasthāṃ gamito rākṣasaiḥ kūṭayodhibhiḥ*: The critical apparatus incorrectly marks these two *pādas* as identical with 6.39.18cd.

[2]"there are wives to be found, and... there may be friends" *kalatrāṇi... ca bāndhavāḥ*: Literally, "there are wives... and friends." Given the tenor of the verse, we have taken the term *bāndhavāḥ* in its sense of "friends, companions" rather than "kinsmen."

[3]"where I might find a true brother" *yatra bhrātā sahodaraḥ*: Literally, "where [there is] a brother born of the same womb." Cr notes that, although Rāma and Lakṣmaṇa have different mothers, they qualify for the term *sahodara* because of their common paternity (*rāmalakṣmaṇayoḥ sahodaratvaṃ tu pitṛhṛdayavarttitvena*). Cs suggests that the term is applicable because Kausalyā shared the impregnating *pāyasam* with Sumitrā. As an alternative, he suggests breaking the sequence *bhrātāsahodaraḥ* into *bhrātā* and *asahodaraḥ*, "non-co-uterine brother." (*pāyasasya kausalyāvibhāgād uddhṛtasya sumitrāyai pradānān nimittād vā lakṣmaṇasya sāhodaryam... asahodaraḥ sann etādṛśo bhrātā yatra... vā.*)

[4]"As he was lamenting in this fashion, his senses disordered with grief, writhing about and sighing piteously again and again" *ity evaṃ vilapantaṃ taṃ śokavihvalitendriyam / viveṣṭamānaṃ karuṇam ucchvasantaṃ punaḥ punaḥ //*: The insertion of these two lines at this juncture in the passage occurs in no known manuscript. For both KK and VSP, the passage occurs at the conclusion of Rāma's words and is followed immediately by the critical edition's verse 9 in which the accusatives describing Rāma mark him clearly as the object of Suṣeṇa's speech. These lines are not known to the manuscripts and editions that follow the text of Ct. GPP includes the verse, indicating that it is additional in Cg's text, and notes that the following eight verses are not found in Cg's text. As the verse stands in GPP, however, it cannot be construed. No manuscript or translation follows the sequence of verses found in the critical edition or GPP. Compare 2029*, line 24.

[5]"given" *dattam*: 6.39.11b reads *bata* "Alas!" for *dattam*.

[6]"Whatever shall I tell Kausalyā, and what shall I tell mother Kaikeyī?" *kiṃ nu vakṣyāmi kausalyāṃ mātaraṃ kiṃ nu kaikeyīm*: See note to 6.39.6.

[7]Compare 6.39.10. The critical edition marks these lines as identical. Although they are very similar, they are not identical.

[8]"You always used to comfort me, great-armed hero" *mahābāho samāśvāsayitā mama*: Literally, "O great-armed one, [you are] a comforter of me."

9. "Then, consoling Rāma, heroic Suṣeṇa spoke these words" *rāmam āśvāsayan vīraḥ suṣeṇo vākyam abravīt*: Ś,B1,D1–4,8–12, and the texts and printed editions of Ct read instead *āśvāsayann uvācedaṃ suṣeṇaḥ paramaṃ vacaḥ*, "Suṣeṇa spoke these excellent words, comforting [him]."

"Great-armed . . . is not dead" *na mṛto 'yaṃ mahābāhuḥ*: Ñ2,D1,9–11, and the texts and printed editions of Ct and Cr read instead *naiva pañcatvam āpannaḥ*, "[Lakṣmaṇa] has not attained fiveness." See notes to verses 5 and 28.

"Lakṣmaṇa, increaser of prosperity" *lakṣmaṇo lakṣmivardhanaḥ*: The epithet is somewhat uncommon in the *Yuddhakāṇḍa*, occurring only in a starred passage at 6.79.5 1747*, lines 5–6. Compare, however, 6.67.37; 6.71.20; 6.73.5; and notes. See note to verse 11, 2032*.

Following 9ab, Ś,V (V3, line 1 only),B1,3,4,D1–4,6,8–12,T2,3, and the texts and printed editions of Ct and Cr insert a passage of two lines [2030*]: "Tiger among men, give up this notion that is causing you such distress, this mournful brooding that causes you as much pain as arrows in the vanguard of the army.[1]"

[1]"this mournful brooding that causes you as much pain as arrows in the vanguard of the army" *śokasaṃjananīṃ cintāṃ tulyāṃ bāṇaiḥ camūmukhe*: Literally, "the [sad] thought producing grief, equal to arrows in the vanguard of the army." Note the critical edition's unnoted misprint of *bāṇaḥ* for *bāṇaiḥ*.

10. Compare Trijaṭā's words to Sītā at 6.38.31–32, where she lists the facial signs indicating that Rāma and Lakṣmaṇa are still alive.

"nor has it darkened or lost its radiance" *nāpi śyāmaṃ na niṣprabham*: V,B2–4,D4,9–11, and the texts and printed editions of Ct, Cr, and Ck read instead *na ca śyāmatvam āgatam*, "has not become dark." M3 and the texts and printed editions of Cg and Cm read *śyāvam*, "dark brown," for the critical reading *śyāmam*, "dark."

"his countenance looks quite radiant and clear" *suprabhaṃ ca prasannaṃ ca mukham asyābhilakṣyate*: Ñ2,V1,2,B,D1–4,9–11, and the texts and printed editions of Ct read *mukham asya nirīkṣyatām* for *mukham asyābhilakṣyate*, lending the line the sense "just look at his clear and radiant face."

11. "The palms of his hands are as red as the lotus" *padmaraktatalau hastau*: Literally, "the two hands have palms that are lotus-red." Ñ2,D4,10,11,M1, and the texts and printed editions of Ck and Ct read *-patra-*, "petal," for *-rakta-*, "red," giving the phrase the sense "whose hands have palms that are like lotus petals."

"people . . . when their life breaths have left them" *gatāsūnām*: Literally, "of those whose life breaths have gone."

"tamer of your foes" *ariṃdama*: Ś,D1,7,8,12,T2,3,M2,3,5, and the texts and printed editions of Cg and Cm read the nominative *ariṃdamaḥ* for the vocative *ariṃdama*, making the epithet refer not to Rāma but to Lakṣmaṇa.

Following 11cd, D5–7,S, and the texts and printed editions of Cg insert a passage of two lines [2032*]: "Such are the faces of long-lived mortals. Surely, Lakṣmaṇa, increaser of prosperity,[1] has not departed this life."

[1]"Lakṣmaṇa, increaser of prosperity" *lakṣmaṇo lakṣmivardhanaḥ*: See note to verse 9 above.

Among the translators consulted, only Raghunathan (1982, vol. 3, p. 295) renders this passage.

12. "unconscious" *prasuptasya*: Literally, "of him who is asleep."

"the rhythmic movement of his chest proclaims that he still lives" *ākhyāsyate... socchvāsaṃ hṛdayam... kampamānaṃ muhur muhuḥ*: Literally, "The chest trembling again and again will proclaim [him] to be one who has breath." Our translation follows the interpretation of Ct, Ck, Cr, Cg, and Cm, who take *socchvāsam*, literally, "with breath, alive," as an adjective modifying the supplied *amum*, "him," that is, Lakṣmaṇa. Some translators (Roussel 1903, vol. 3, p. 336; Shastri 1959, vol. 3, p. 295; and Pagani 1990, p. 1146) understand that it is both the beating of Lakṣmaṇa's heart and his breathing that show he is still alive, but this is redundant and grammatically problematic. Note that the critical edition erroneously prints the meaningless *okhyāsyati* for *ākhyāsyati*, "he will proclaim." The error is not noted in the list of errata.

13. "skilled in speech" *tu vākyajñaḥ*: Ś,Ñ2,V,B,D1–3,8,12, and the texts and printed editions of Ct read instead *mahāprājñaḥ*, "exceedingly wise."

14–15. "the... mountain known as the mountain of healing herbs" *śailam oṣadhiparvatam*: Literally, "the mountain, the mountain of herbs." D4,9–11, and the texts and printed editions of Ct read instead *parvataṃ hi* [*tam*—D4] *mahodayam*, "Mount Mahodaya." A number of other manuscripts similarly name the mountain Mahodaya. It is evident from this verse that the mountain intended here is the same one that Jāmbavān instructed Hanumān to visit and that Hanumān brings back with him in *sarga* 60. There, the mountain is referred to only as the mountain of healing herbs and is precisely located in the Himalayas between Mount Ṛṣabha and Mount Kailāsa (6.61.30). The mountain, we are to understand, is different from the two mountains Candra and Droṇa, described in *sarga* 40, which are said to lie in the midst of the ocean of milk (6.40.29). Those mountains, which the monkeys never actually visit, are said to contain only two of the four healing herbs mentioned in this passage and at 6.61.33.

"splendid... known as the *viśalyakaraṇī*, the healer of arrow wounds" *viśalyakaraṇīṃ nāma viśalyakaraṇīṃ śubhām*: Literally "the splendid arrow remover called *viśalyakaraṇī* ('the arrow remover')." Cv, Cm, and Cg, whom we follow, note that the second occurrence of the term is descriptive [rather than onomastic] (*dvitīyo viśalyakaraṇīśabdo guṇavacanaḥ*). See 6.40.30; 6.61.32–33; and notes. For this line (15cd), the texts and printed editions of Ct read instead *viśalyakaraṇīṃ nāmnā sāvarṇyakaraṇīṃ tathā*, "known as the *viśalyakaraṇī*, the healer of arrow wounds, and the *sāvarṇyakaraṇī*, the restorer of one's original complexion." The variant *sāvarṇyakaraṇī*, literally, "the maker of the same color," is glossed by Ct as "the one that produces a color that is the same as the previous color (*pūrvavarṇasamānavarṇakaraṇīm*)." Compare Ck's variants and comments to 6.61.32–33. See, too, note to verse 24 below.

16. "the *sauvarṇakaraṇī*, the restorer of a golden glow, the *saṃjīvanī*, the restorer of life, and the *saṃdhānakaraṇī*, the joiner of limbs" *sauvarṇakaraṇīm... saṃjīvanīm... saṃdhānakaraṇīm*: Literally, "the *sauvarṇakaraṇī*, the *saṃjīvanī*, and the *saṃdhānakaraṇī*." See note to 6.61.32–33 for an explanation of these names.

"great" *mahātmanaḥ*: Ś,B1,D3,4,8–12,T2,3, and the texts and printed editions of Ct read instead *tvam ānaya*, "you must bring."

D4,9–11, and the texts and printed editions of Ct substitute a passage of one line [2034*, line 1] for 16ab ("the *sauvarṇakaraṇī*, the restorer of a golden glow, the *saṃjīvanī*, the restorer of life"): "And, hero, also the *saṃjīvanī*, the restorer of life, and the powerful herb *saṃdhinī*, the joiner of limbs."

Ś,D2,4,8–12,T2,3, and the texts and printed editions of Ct omit 16cd ("Go swiftly and... bring... the *saṃdhānakaraṇī*, the joiner of limbs").

17. "But, unable to identify those potent herbs" *ajānaṃs tā mahauṣadhīḥ*: Literally, "not knowing those great herbs." One of the numerous problems with this slapdash reprise of Hanumān's fetching of the mountain of herbs (see *sarga* 61) is the awkward fact that, having earlier procured these herbs, he is now unable to recognize them. Other than ascribing this apparent contradiction to the carelessness of the author or redactors, one could perhaps explain Hanumān's failure to identify the herbs by the fact that, during his first mission to the mountain, the herbs had made themselves invisible to him. Indeed, that is why Hanumān finds it necessary to bring back the entire mountain peak (6.61.58–61). Ct, the only commentator who appears to note this problem, explains it in an interesting way. He refers to a lengthy episode commonly interpolated in various places, in whole or in part, into manuscripts and printed editions of the northern recension (App. I, No. 56; Gorresio 6.82; and Lahore 6.82). This is the elaborate story of Hanumān's encounter with the demonic master of illusion Kālanemi, whom Hanumān must overcome and slay before he can continue his quest for the healing herbs. Ct interestingly does not associate this episode with the *Rāmāyaṇa* itself but sees it as belonging to some other, purāṇic, narrative. He argues that we should understand that Hanumān is unable to identify the healing herbs, even though he had seen them before, because his thoughts had been scattered as a result of his elaborate struggle with Kālanemi (*pūrvadṛṣṭānām apy aparicaye purāṇāntaroktakālanemiyuddhakṛtacittacāñcalyaṃ hetur iti bodhyam*).

D1,3,5,T1,M3,5, and the texts and printed editions of Cg read instead the singular *tāṃ mahauṣadhīm*, "that potent herb," for *tā mahauṣadhīḥ*. This variant is rendered only in the text of Raghunathan (1982, vol. 3, p. 295). Compare verses 21 and 22 below.

"majestic monkey" *śrīmān*: Literally, "the majestic one."

18. Following verse 18, Ñ2,V,B,D1,3,5–7,10,11,T1,G,M, and the texts and printed editions of the southern commentators insert a passage of two lines [2038*]: "I gather through reasoning that the comforting herb grows on this very peak, for that is what Suṣeṇa said."

19. "without bringing the *viśalyakaraṇī*, the healer of arrow wounds" *agṛhya... viśalyakaraṇīm*: Literally "not having seized that which makes one free from arrows." For *viśalyakaraṇī*, see note to verse 15 above. The commentators seem concerned that Hanumān mentions only one of the four healing herbs named by Suṣeṇa in verses 15–16 above and offer various explanations. Ct believes that Hanumān specifies the *viśalyakaraṇī* because Lakṣmaṇa, though wounded, is still alive [and so, presumably, is not in need of the *saṃjīvanī*, etc.] (*viśalyakaraṇīṃ lakṣmaṇasya saprāṇatvād avaśyam apekṣitām*). Cs quotes Ct at length and dismisses his interpretation as "impossible (*asambhāvitam*)" on the grounds that Suṣeṇa had clearly instructed Hanumān to bring all four herbs and that, apart from Lakṣmaṇa, there are many wounded and dead monkeys that require the other herbs. Cs proposes instead that we take the term *viśalyakaraṇī* here to refer to the collectivity of all four herbs by means of which Rāma would be freed from "the arrow" in the form of his fear for Lakṣmaṇa's life (*viśalyakaraṇīṃ viśalyo lakṣmaṇaprāṇasaṃśayātmakaśalyarahito rāmaḥ kriyate 'nayā caturvidhayauṣadhyeti sā suṣeṇabhāṣitasarvauṣadhiḥ*).

Cg attempts to avoid the issue by taking the gerund *agṛhya* to mean "not accepting *or* heeding." He then understands that its implied object is Suṣeṇa's speech (*suṣeṇavacanam*).

"the loss of time would lead to dire consequences" *kālātyayena doṣaḥ syāt*: Literally, "there would be a fault through the passage of time." Ct, Ck, and Cg understand that the negative consequence would be the death of Lakṣmaṇa (*lakṣmaṇasya prāṇanāśo doṣaḥ*—so Ct). Cr understands it to be the failure of Hanumān's mission (*doṣaḥ kāryavighātarūpo durguṇaḥ*).

"and there might be a serious calamity" *vaiklavyaṃ ca mahad bhavet*: Cg understands the term to refer to "unmanliness *or* cowardice (*niṣpauruṣatvam*)," which charge would be leveled against Hanumān. This would appear to be the basis of Raghunathan's translation (1982, vol. 3, pp. 295–96), "my reputation would suffer." Ct and Ck understand, "the flaw of incompetence, ignorance, etc. (*acaturājñatvādidoṣaḥ*)."

20. Ct and Ck call attention to the awkward problem of why Hanumān, having once before fetched the mountain with its healing herbs, is obliged to do so again. They explain that the herbs brought on the earlier occasion were used up in treating the dazed monkey troop leaders, and so we must understand that Hanumān needs to be sent once again (*pūrvaṃ saṃgṛhītauṣadhīnāṃ mūrcchitayūthapeṣu vyayāt punar asya preṣaṇam iti bodhyam*—so Ct).

"descended on" *gatvā*: Literally, "having gone."

Following 20ab, D1,3,5–7,10,11,T1,G,M, and the texts and printed editions of the southern commentators insert a passage of four lines, clearly intended to remedy the perceived narrative gap between the information that Hanumān is flying back and his unheralded direct address to Suṣeṇa [2041*]: "Approaching that foremost of mountains, the immensely powerful monkey[1] rocked the mountain peak and uprooted it along with its groves of different flowering trees.[1–2] Then, with both hands, that tiger among tawny monkeys seized that peak, which resembled a black storm cloud charged with rain.[2] He hefted it and [flew off] into the sky.[3][3–4]"

[1]"the immensely powerful monkey" *mahābalaḥ*: Literally, "the immensely powerful one."

[2]"that peak, which resembled a black storm cloud charged with rain" *nīlam iva jīmūtaṃ toyapūrṇam* ... [*śikharam*]: Literally, "[that peak] like a black storm cloud filled with water." For some reason, Roussel (1903, vol. 3, p. 337) understands that Hanumān, and not the mountain, is being compared to a cloud. He translates, "*tel qu'un sombre nuage, chargé de pluie, le Vānara* ..." But this is not possible grammatically, and no attested variant supports such a reading. Roussel is followed in this error by Shastri (1959, vol. 3, p. 296) and Pagani (1999, p. 1147).

[3]"into the sky" *nabhastalāt*: Literally, "from the surface of the sky." The ablative here is rather awkward to construe. A few manuscripts (D6,T1,G,M5), Gita Press (6.101.39), KK (6.102.36), and VSP (6.102.30) substitute *nabhaḥ sthalāt*, "from the ground to the sky." Ct and Ck, who read with the critical edition, gloss, *sthalān nabhaḥ*, "from the ground to the sky," while Cs recognizes *nabhaḥ sthalāt* as a reading known to many manuscripts. However, he criticizes Ct's interpretation and suggests instead that we add the gerund *prāpya*, "having reached," yielding the sense "having gone up into the sky, he flew off (*nabhastalaṃ prāpya utpapātatety anvayaḥ*).

Following verse 20, D5,6,7 (after 2046*),10,11,T1,G1,2 (after 2046*),3 (second line),M, and the texts and printed editions of the southern commentators insert a passage of two lines [2045*]: "Returning, the immensely swift Hanumān set down the mountain peak, and, after resting for a bit, he said this to Suṣeṇa."

21. "those healing herbs" *oṣadhīḥ . . . tāḥ*: D1,3,5–7,T1,G3,M, and the texts and printed editions of Cg read instead the singular *auṣadhīm* (*auṣadhim*—D5,6,G3; *oṣadhim*—VSP) . . . *tām*. See verse 17 and note.

22. "and . . . the healing herbs" *cauṣadhīḥ*: D5,6,T1,G3,M, and the texts and printed editions of Cg read instead the singular *cauṣadhīm* (*cauṣadhim*—D6,T1,G2,M5). See verse 17 and note.

Following verse 22, D1,3,5–7,10,11,T,G,M, and the texts and printed editions of the southern commentators insert, while many northern manuscripts insert after verse 25 or 25ab, a passage of two lines [2054]*: "When the monkeys and the *rākṣasas*[1] saw that feat of Hanumān, impossible even for the gods themselves, they were all[2] amazed."

[1]"the monkeys and the *rākṣasas*" *vānararākṣasāḥ*: D10,11, and the texts and printed editions of Ct read instead *-puṃgavāḥ*, "bulls," for *-rākṣasāḥ*, yielding the sense "the bulls among monkeys."

[2]"all" *sarve*: Ñ1,B3,D5,13,T1,G1,3,M, and the texts and printed editions of Cg read instead *raṇe*, "in battle."

23. "of immense luster" *sumahādyutiḥ*: D5,7,T1,G,M3,5, and the texts and printed editions of Cg read instead the genitive *su*(*tu*—G1)*mahādyuteḥ*, thus making the epithet apply not to Suṣeṇa but to Lakṣmaṇa.

"crushed one of the herbs" *saṃkṣodayitvā tām oṣadhim*: Literally, "having crushed *or* pulverized that herb." Commentators and translators differ as to whether Suṣeṇa merely crushes the herb or actually grinds it into a powder. Thus, Ct glosses, "having crushed (*saṃmardya ity arthaḥ*)," while Cr glosses, "having ground *or* pulverized (*saṃcūrṇīkṛtya*)." We have chosen the former interpretation because we believe that Suṣeṇa simply crushes the plant to release the aroma in which its curative properties are carried. This would be in keeping with verse 6.61.67, where the mere fragrance of the herbs revives Rāma, Lakṣmaṇa, and the stricken monkeys. Although it is not specified, it is apparent from the context provided by verses 19 above and 24 below that the herb in question here is the *viśalyakaraṇī*. See, too, 6.79.13 and note.

"held it to Lakṣmaṇa's nose" *lakṣmaṇasya dadau nastaḥ*: Literally, "he gave it to Lakṣmaṇa nasally." Inhalation therapy is one of the five methods (*pañcakarma*) of administering medications according to the *Āyurveda*. Apte (s.v. *pañcakarma*) quotes a verse to this effect: "The five types of medical treatment are emetics, purgatives, inhalatives or sternutatories, non-oily enemas, and oily enemas. Other types are known, such as vomiting. (*vamanaṃ recanaṃ nasyaṃ nirūhaś cānuvāsanam / pañcakarmedam anyac ca jñeyam utkṣepaṇādikam.*)" See 6.79.13 and note; compare, too, 6.61.67.

24. "No sooner . . . inhaled that aroma than he leapt up" *sa samāghrāya . . . śīghram udatiṣṭhat*: Literally, "having smelled, he rose up quickly."

"who had been pierced by that javelin . . . free from the javelin and the pain it had caused" *saśalyaḥ . . . viśalyo virujaḥ*: Literally, "with a javelin . . . without a javelin, without pain." Note that the word *śalya*, rendered here as "javelin," is also commonly used by the poet to refer to arrows or any other projectile darts. Thus, regardless of the context, we continue to render the name of the herb *viśalyakaraṇī* as "remover of arrow wounds," even though, in the present context, it is employed to remove another type of "*śalya*." See note to verse 15 above. Cr, in keeping with his continuing argument that Lakṣmaṇa has not actually been wounded by Rāvaṇa's javelin, glosses *saśalyaḥ*, "who had been pierced by that javelin," as "filled with the discomfort caused by the javelin having fallen so close to him (*samīpapatitaśalyajanitatāpasahitaḥ*)." He then explains the term *viśalyaḥ*, "free from the javelin," as meaning "free from the agitation caused by his close contact with the javelin (*śalyasaṃsargajavyathārahitaḥ san*)." See note to 6.35.9. See, too, note to 6.88.33 above and passim.

25. "Suṣeṇa" *suṣeṇam*: B3,D10,11,G3, and the texts and printed editions of Ct and Cr read instead *lakṣmaṇam*, "Lakṣmaṇa." In this reading, the word "Lakṣmaṇa" occurs twice. Most translators ignore the second occurrence of the word; however, in an attempt to render both occurrences, Gita Press (1969, vol. 3, p. 1793) translates, "Lakṣmaṇa, who was endowed with auspicious marks."

26. "Come to me, come to me" *ehy ehi*: Literally, "Come, come."

"he embraced him tightly in his affection" *sasvaje snehagāḍham*: Literally, "he embraced [him] tightly and affectionately." D7,10,11,G2, and the texts and printed editions of Ct and Cr read instead the somewhat redundant *sasvaje gāḍham āliṅgya*, "having embraced him tightly, he hugged." Translations that follow the text of Ct struggle to deal with the redundancy.

27. "risen from the dead" *maraṇāt punar āgatam*: Literally, "come again from death."

28. "Sītā, victory, and life itself have no meaning for me" *na hi me jīvitenārthaḥ sītayā ca jayena vā*: Literally, "for there is no purpose for me with life, and Sītā, or victory." Compare 6.39.5–6 and notes.

"victory, and life itself... in living" *jīvitena ... ca jayena vā ... jīvitena*: The critical text is redundant, repeating the term *jīvitena*, "with life," and making the construction of the verse awkward. D5,6,T1,G,M3,5, and the texts and printed editions of Cg modify the reading by substituting *cāpi lakṣmaṇa*, "and, O Lakṣmaṇa," for *ca jayena vā* of *pāda* b, and *vijayena*, "with victory," for the second occurrence in *pāda* c. The reading thus achieved would be: "If you had returned to the elements, Lakṣmaṇa, I would have no use for life or Sītā. Indeed, what purpose would I have for victory?" This reading is followed only in the translation of Raghunathan (1982, vol. 3, p. 296).

"returned to the elements" *pañcatvam āgate*: See 6.39.7 and note; and verse 4 above and note.

29. "distressed at this fainthearted speech" *khinnaḥ śithilayā vācā*: Literally, "distressed by slack speech." The phrase is actually quite ambiguous in this context. Our reading follows that of Ck and Ct, who understand that Lakṣmaṇa is pained to hear Rāma's words that suggest he is wavering in his determination to kill Rāvaṇa and enthrone Vibhīṣaṇa in his place (*ko hi me jīvitenārtha ity evaṃrūpayā rāvaṇavadhavibhīṣaṇarājyadānapratijñāśaithilyakarayā vācā khinna ity arthaḥ*). Cv understands similarly. We believe that this interpretation is amply supported by the tenor of Lakṣmaṇa's words in the following verses. It has also been followed by Dutt (1893, p. 1459), Gita Press (1969, vol. 3, p. 1794), and Pagani (1999, p. 1147). The phrase can also be interpreted to mean that Lakṣmaṇa, weak or pained (*khinnaḥ*), presumably from his earlier injuries, responds in a faint voice (*śithilayā vācā*). This interpretation is

given by Roussel (1903, vol. 3, p. 337), followed by Shastri (1959, vol. 3, p. 297), and by Raghunathan (1982, vol. 3, p. 296). We believe that this is less plausible, especially in light of the miraculous and total curative powers ascribed to the healing herbs used to restore Lakṣmaṇa, evidence of which is given in verse 24 above.

30. "Having... made that vow" *tāṃ pratijñāṃ pratijñāya*: Literally, "having vowed that vow." Several of the commentators explain that the vow is to kill Rāvaṇa (Cr, Cg) and to consecrate Vibhīṣaṇa in his place (Cg). Cm actually quotes Rāma's vow to do both of these things (App. I, No. 9, lines 26–27 = GPP 6.19.19).

"truly valorous warrior" *satyaparākrama*: Literally, " O one of true valor."

31. "blameless hero, the virtuous" *sādhavo 'nagha*: Literally, "the virtuous, O blameless one." D4,9–11,T2,3, and the texts and printed editions of Ct read instead *satyavādinaḥ*, "speakers of truth." This reading yields the tautology that speakers of the truth do not tell lies.

32. "So enough" *tadalam*: D10,11, and the texts and printed editions of Ct and Ck read instead *nālaṃ te*. Here *alam* is glossed by Ck and Ct as *yuktam*, "fitting." The sense of the phrase then becomes "it is not fitting for you to give way to despair."

33. "he comes within range of your arrows" *bāṇapathaṃ gataḥ*: Literally, "gone to the path of [your] arrows." B2,D7,9–11, and the texts and printed editions of Ct read *-vaśam*, "power, sway," for *-patham*, "path, range."

"will no more escape with his life" *na jīvan yāsyate*: Literally, "he will not go, living."

"than would a great bull elephant that comes within the clutches of a... lion" *siṃhasyeva mahāgajaḥ*: Literally, "like a great elephant... of a lion."

34. "I long for" *icchāmi*: Literally, "I desire."

"of that evil-minded wretch" *durātmanaḥ*: Literally, "of the evil-minded one."

"the sun, bringer of day" *divākaraḥ*: Literally, "the day maker."

"before... sets behind the western mountain" *yāvad astaṃ na yāti*: Literally, "so long as it does not go to [Mount] Asta." See note to 6.57.20, etc. Ct observes that here the reference to the setting of the sun leads us to understand that these events take place on the new-moon day of the bright half of the month of Āśvina (*yāvad astaṃ na yātīty anenāśvinaśuklapratipady eṣā vārteti gamyate*). See note to 6.90.1. See note to 6.4.4.

"his day's work done" *kṛtakarmā*: Literally, "whose work is accomplished." Ct explains, "having favored the world in respect to his part of daily duty (*adyatanahartavyāṃśe kṛtalokānugrahaḥ*—Ck similarly)." Cs understands, "the witness of the actions carried out by the people (*kṛtakarmā lokakṛtakarmasākṣī*)," while Cg glosses, "having completed his course (*kṛtasaṃcāraḥ*)."

Following verse 34, D6,7,9–11,G1,2,M1,2 (continues),3,5, and the texts and printed editions of the southern commentators insert a passage of four lines [2071*]: "If you wish the death of Rāvaṇa in battle, if you wish to keep your vow in this matter, and if you wish to recover the king's daughter, then you must, this very day, swiftly heed my advice, noble[1] hero."

[1]"if you wish to recover the king's daughter... noble" *yadi tava rājasutābhilāṣa ārya*: Literally, "if of you there is desire for the daughter of the king... O noble one." M3 and the texts and printed editions of Cg read instead *rājavarātmajābhilāṣaḥ*, "[if there is] desire for the daughter of the best of kings" *or* "[if there is] longing, O son of the

best of kings," for the critical edition's *rājasutābhilāṣa ārya*. Raghunathan (1982, vol. 3, p. 297) renders this as "If... you wish to realize your long-cherished desire, O son of the great King."

The meter is a type of *atijagatī*.

Sarga 90

1. Ct notes that since it has been stated that Rāvaṇa had earlier fled from the battlefield (6.88.59) it is not possible that arrows could be directed at him on that field. From this he concludes that the battle described here took place [earlier] at noon on the new-moon day of [the bright half] of Āśvina. (*pūrvaṃ raṇāt palāyanoktyā rāvaṇoddeśyakaśaravisargasya raṇabhūmāv asambhavād āśvinapratipanmadhyāhna etad yuddhapravṛttiḥ.*) See note to 6.89.34.

Following 1ab, D5–7,10,11,T1,G,M, and the texts and printed editions of the southern commentators insert a passage of one line [2073*]: "That heroic slayer of enemy heroes took up his bow and nocked [fearsome arrows to it]."

Following verse 1, D5–7,10,11,T1,G,M1,3,5, and the texts and printed editions of the southern commentators insert a passage of one line [2076*]: "Then Rāvaṇa, overlord of the *rākṣasas*, mounting another chariot[1] ..."

[1]"another chariot" *anyaṃ ratham*: This phrase is yet another occasion for Cs to disagree with a position Ct takes. The question, of course, is in what way is the chariot referred to here as "other." Ct refers to an episode that he describes as purāṇic in which Rāvaṇa, on the advice of his counselor, Śukrācārya, repairs to the Nikumbhilā grove in order to perform a *homa* ritual that will provide him with a magical war chariot. Cf. 7.25.1–13, where Indrajit carries out similar rituals to gain similar boons. Rāvaṇa's ritual, however, is disrupted by the monkeys, so that his purpose is thwarted. According to Ct, it is in respect to that other, unrealized chariot that the present one is "other." (*athānyaṃ ratham ity anena cātra sthāne rāvaṇena śukrājñayā jayanimittaṃ nikumbhilāyām ārabdhahomakarmaṇo vānaradvārā hiṃsanaṃ purāṇāntaroktam anusaṃdheyam iti sūcitam.*) Cs refutes Ct's position, quoting him in full and ascribing his version to a passage in the *Adhyātmarāmāyaṇa*, whose authority Cs regards as questionable. He expands his refutation by mentioning another "spurious" story in which Aṅgada enters the *antaḥpuram* to drag Mandodarī by her hair into the presence of her husband, Rāvaṇa, in order to pay him back for his treatment of Sītā. This episode is recounted in a number of manuscripts (D4,9,T2,3,D3—App. I, No. 62; Ś,Ñ2, B2,D2,8,12—App. I, No. 63). He thus dismisses Ct's comments, arguing that we are to understand that Rāvaṇa's chariot is "other" only with respect to the one disabled [by Vibhīṣaṇa] in an earlier battle (6.88.17–18). (*atrāpi nāgojibhaṭṭenāthānyaṃ ratham āsthāya tu ... iti vadatā śīghraṃ śukrāntikaṃ yayāv ity ārabhya praviśyāntaḥpure veśmany aṅgado vegavattaraḥ / samānayat keśapāśe dhṛtvā mandodarīṃ śubhām ityādi garbhīkṛtya dṛḍhaṃ syandanam āsthāyety antam adhyātmarāmāyaṇaṃ saṃgṛhītam iti jñāyate. tatprāmāṇye saṃdihate mahānta iti na taduktaṃ jñāpakam. athānyam ity asya pūrve yuddhakāle rathadhvajādīnāṃ śaithilyād anyam ity uktisaṃbhavenoktārthasyāsūcakatvāc ca.*)

Following 2076*, D5–7,10,11,T1,G,M1,2,3,5, and the texts and printed editions of the southern commentators insert a passage of one line [2078*]: "He advanced rapidly upon Kākutstha, as does Rāhu Svarbhānu[1] upon Sūrya, bringer of light."

[1]"Rāhu Svarbhānu" *svarbhānuḥ*: Literally, "the light of heaven." This is a common epithet, known from the *Ṛgveda* (5.40.5,6,8,9) for the demon of the eclipse, who in the later tradition is identified with Rāhu.

2. "in turn pelted" *ājaghāna*: Literally, "he struck."

"enormously fearsome" *mahāghoraiḥ*: D7,10,11,G2, and the texts and printed editions of Ct read instead *mahāśailam*, "a great mountain," which fleshes out the *upamāna* of the simile, giving the sense "as might a storm cloud [pelt] a great mountain with torrents of rain."

"with torrents of rain" *dhārābhiḥ*: Literally, "with streams."

3. "Nonetheless, Rāma" *rāmaḥ*: Literally, "Rāma."

"with great concentration" *samāhitaḥ*: Literally, "focused, concentrated." Printed editions of Cg read instead the accusative *samāhitam*, in which case the adjective modifies Rāvaṇa. This minor reading, which Crā notes as a variant but is unattested in the critical apparatus, is rendered by Raghunathan (1982, vol. 3, p. 297), who translates, "the unshaken Daśagrīva."

"pierced" *nirbibheda*: D3,4,9–11,T2,3, and the texts and printed editions of Ct read instead *abhyavarṣat*, "he showered, pelted."

4. "the ... *dānavas*" *-dānavāḥ*: D9–11 and the texts and printed editions of Ct read instead *-kiṃnarāḥ*, "the *kinnaras*." This is perhaps an emendation to avoid the curious circumstance that the demonic enemies of the gods should seem to be on Rāma's side here. On this issue, see note to verse 25 below.

"This ... is not fair" *na samam*: Literally, "not equal *or* even." Dutt (1893, p. 1460) appears to misunderstand the phrase to mean that the battle is unequaled. He renders, "There had been no other battle like unto the battle of Rāma ... and the Raksha."

Following verse 4, D4 (lines 3–9),6,7,9–11 (7,9–11, lines 1–8),T2,3, and the texts and printed editions of Ct (lines 1–8) insert a passage of nine lines [2082*]: "Upon hearing their nectarlike words,[1] Śakra, the majestic leader of the gods, summoned Mātali and said these words[1–2]: 'You must go at once to great Rāma,[2] foremost of the Raghus, with my chariot. When you reach the earth, you must invite him to mount[3] and so accomplish a great service to the gods.[4]'[3–4] Addressed in this fashion by the king of the gods, Mātali, the god's charioteer, bowed his head to the god and said these words [5–6]: 'I go at once, lord of the gods, and I shall serve as his charioteer.' Then, yoking that splendid chariot to tawny horses,[7–8] he proceeded from heaven for the sake of Rāma's victory.[9]"

[1]"nectarlike words" *vacomṛtam*: Literally, "speech-nectar." Roussel (1903, vol. 3, p. 339) appears to misunderstand the compound, rendering, "*cette parole des Immortels*." In this he is followed by Shastri (1959, vol. 3, p. 297), who renders, "the words of the Immortals," and Pagani (1999, p. 1148), who translates, "*la remarque des Immortels*."

The compound is misprinted in the critical edition as two words, *vaco mṛtam* ("dead speech").

[2]"great Rāma" *bhūyiṣṭham*: Literally, "the greatest one." D9–11,T2, and the texts and printed editions of Ct read instead *bhūmiṣṭham*, "standing on the ground."

[3]"you must invite him to mount" *āhūya*: Literally, "having summoned *or* invited."

[4]"a great service to the gods" *devahitaṃ mahat*: Literally, "great welfare *or* benefit to the gods." Once again Roussel (1903, vol. 3, p. 339) misunderstands, breaking up the compound as the vocative *deva*, "O god," and the accusative *hitam*, "welfare." This leads him to the improbable translation "*rends, ô dieu, ce service important.*"

5–7. "shining like the rising sun" *taruṇādityasaṃkāśaḥ*: Literally, "resembling the young sun."

"its yoke pole made of lapis" *vaidūryamayakūbaraḥ*: A number of translators understand the term *vaidūrya* in its other common sense of "cat's-eye beryl." Roussel (1903, vol. 3, p. 339), followed by Shastri (1959, vol. 3, p. 298) and Pagani (1999, p. 1148), understands, "emerald (*émeraudes*)." The yoke pole is described by Cg and Cm as "a piece of wood that supports the yoke (*yugādhāradāru*)." Both commentators cite *Amarakośa* (2.8.57), whose synonym for *kūbara* is *yugaṃdhara*, "yoke supporter." See 6.57.25 and note. On lapis lazuli, see 5.1.2–3 and notes; and notes to 6.3.13 and 6.67.13.

"its flagstaff made of gold" *rukmaveṇudhvajaḥ*: Literally, "having a golden-staffed flag." Cr, however, reads the compound as a *dvandva*, glossing, "its staff and flag made of gold (*rukmamayau veṇudhvajau yasya saḥ*)."

"from Triviṣṭapa, Indra's heaven" *triviṣṭapāt*: Literally, "from Triviṣṭapa *or* from the triple world." Cg and Cr gloss, "from heaven (*svargāt*)." However, since Triviṣṭapa is sometimes used to refer specifically to the heavenly realm of Indra, that sense seems most apposite in this context.

"splendid tawny horses" *sadaśvaiḥ . . . haribhiḥ*: In this context, the polysemic term *hari* must be understood in its sense of "tawny, yellowish, *or* bay." This meaning is suggested by Cg, who glosses, "of a tawny color (*haritavarṇaiḥ*)." Some translators (Gita Press 1969, vol. 3, pp. 1795–96; Raghunathan 1982, vol. 3, p. 297) take the term *hari* in its sense of "green, greenish." This seems particularly inapposite in light of the comparison of the horses to the sun, not to mention that green is an unlikely color for a horse. See 6.78.27; 6.95.15; 6.116.24; and notes.

"with their golden plumes" *kāñcanāpīḍaiḥ*: Literally, "with golden crest ornaments *or* chaplets." The commentators generally gloss, "with golden ornaments (*svarṇābhāraṇaiḥ*—so Ct, Ck)." Compare 6.33.2–3 and note.

"white tufts" *śvetaprakīrṇakaiḥ*: According to Apte (s.v.), a *prakīrṇaka* is "a tuft of hair used as an ornament for horses." Commentators, citing *Amarakośa* (2.8.31), understand the term in its common sense of "chowrie *or* yak-tail fly whisk." According to MW (s.v.), chowries were also used as ornaments for horses.

Following 7ab, D5–7,9–11,S insert a passage of one line [2084*], which makes Mātali, Indra's charioteer, and not the chariot itself, the subject of the sole principal verb *abhyavartata*, "it drew near," of verses 5–7. "Commanded by the king of the gods, Mātali, mounting the chariot . . ." Southern commentators, all of whom read this line, are obliged to supply the relative and correlative pronouns *yaḥ*, "who," and *tam*, "that," referring to the chariot, in order to make the syntax intelligible.

8. "of thousand-eyed Indra" *sahasrākṣasya*: Literally, "of the thousand-eyed one."

9. "Thousand-eyed Indra" *sahasrākṣeṇa*: Literally, "by the thousand-eyed one."

"this majestic, foe-destroying chariot" *rathaḥ . . . śrīmāñ śatrunibarhaṇaḥ*: D5,6,10,T1,M3, and the texts and printed editions of the southern commentators read instead the vocatives *śrīmāñ śatrunibarhaṇa*, in which case the adjectives modify Rāma rather than the chariot.

10. "sharp" *śitā*: D9–11,T2, and the texts and printed editions of Ct read instead *śivā*, "auspicious."

11. "Rāma" *rāma*: The word is marked as doubtful by the editors of the critical edition. D6,T2,3,G1,M1,3,5, and the texts and printed editions of Cg and Cm read instead *rājan*, "O king." D9–11 and the texts and printed editions of Ct read instead *deva*, "O lord (lit., god)." The edition of Gorresio reads *vīra*, "O hero" (and reads *rāma* for *vīra* in *pāda* a). A number of northern manuscripts, including the printed edition of Lahore, read *yuktam*, "yoked," which then modifies the chariot.

12. "and, after reverentially saluting Mātali" *tam abhivādya ca*: Literally, "and having saluted him *or* it." Commentators are silent as to the object of the gerund *abhivādya*. Translators of the southern texts understand it to be the chariot itself. However, since the action expressed by the causative of the verb *abhi* √*vad* is almost always directed toward a person, and, since it would, we believe, be improper on Rāma's part to take no notice of the divine charioteer, we understand the pronoun *tam* to refer elliptically to Mātali. This idea appears to be supported by the reading of Ñ1,D4,13, and the edition of Gorresio (= 2089* and 2090*), which omit the word *abhivādya* and explicitly have Rāma circumambulate Mātali.

"illuminating the worlds with his splendor as he did so" *lokāṃl lakṣmyā virājayan*: Literally, "making the worlds shine with [his] luster."

13. "chariot duel" *yuddhaṃ dvairatham*: Literally, "a two-chariot battle." Ck and Ct explain the term *dvairatham*, "having two chariots," as "those two who have two chariots are two-chariot warriors; [the battle between] those two is thus called 'belonging to two-chariot warriors' (*dvau rathau yayos tau dvirathau tayor idaṃ dvairatham*)." We, however, follow Cr, who understands the compound slightly differently to mean "in which [battle] there are two chariots that is a two-chariot [battle] (*dvau rathau yasmiṃs tad eva dvairatham*)." D5,T,G1,3,M3,5, and the texts and printed editions of Cg read the adjective *tumulam*, "tumultuous," for *dvairatham*.

14. "Rāghava, who had mastered the most powerful divine weapon-spells, thwarted each divine weapon-spell of the *rākṣasa* king with one of his own—a divine weapon-spell of the *gandharvas* with a divine weapon-spell of the *gandharvas*, a divine weapon-spell of the gods with a divine weapon-spell of the gods." *sa gāndharveṇa gāndharvaṃ daivaṃ daivena rāghavaḥ / astraṃ rākṣasarājasya jaghāna paramāstravit //*: Literally, "Knowing supreme *astras*, Rāghava struck [each] *astra* of the king of the *rākṣasas*: a *gāndharva* with a *gāndharva*, a *daiva* with a *daiva*." See note to 3.24.28.

15. "the lord of the night-roaming *rākṣasas* invoked" *rākṣasādhipaḥ / sasarja . . . niśācaraḥ*: Literally, "the lord of the *rākṣasas*, the night-roaming one, released." See 6.87.43 and note.

16. "the arrows . . . turned into venomous serpents" *te . . . śarāḥ . . . sarpā bhūtvā mahāviṣāḥ*: The idea here is that Rāvaṇa's arrows are infused with the power of the *rākṣasa astra* mentioned in the preceding verse. It is no doubt under the influence of this spell

that they transform themselves into serpents. It will be recalled that serpent-weapons appear to be a part of the *rākṣasa* arsenal. They were used earlier to devastating effect by Indrajit at 6.35.8ff. when he struck down Rāma and Lakṣmaṇa. On that occasion, however, it was the serpents, sons of Kadrū, who turned themselves into arrows for his use rather than, as in the present case, arrows that turn to serpents during flight. See 6.35.8; 6.40.37,49; and notes.

17. "those terrifying serpents" *te ... bhayānakāḥ*: Literally, "those terrifying ones."

18. "by those serpents" *taiḥ*: Literally, "by them."

"with their blazing hoods" *dīptabhogaiḥ*: The term *bhoga* can also refer to the coils of a serpent. Most translators consulted have interpreted in this way. However, given that the serpents are flying straight toward Rāma in the form of arrows, the choice of coils here seems improbable.

"the great serpent Vāsuki" *vāsuki-*: Literally, "Vāsuki." Vāsuki is one of the great mythic *nāgas*, or supernatural serpents, frequently named in mythological texts. It is Vāsuki, for example, who serves as the churning rope in the famous myth of the churning of the cosmic ocean for the nectar of immortality (*amṛta*). See 1.44.14–27 and notes.

19. "he produced" *prāduścakre*: Literally, "he made visible *or* manifest." We follow the gloss given by Ct, Cg, and Cm, "he employed *or* shot (*yuyuje*)." Translators offer a range of interpretations, including "made visible," "summoned," "chose," and "drew forth."

20. "Loosed from Rāghava's bow" *rāghavadhanurmuktāḥ*: D6,T2,3,M3, and the texts and printed editions of Cg and Cm read instead *rāghavaśarā muktāḥ*, "Rāghava's arrows, released."

"the gold-fletched arrows" *te ... rukmapuṅkhāḥ*: Literally, "those gold-fletched ones."

"golden eagles" *suparṇāḥ kāñcanāḥ*: Literally, "golden birds." Suparṇa is a common epithet for the divine bird Garuḍa, who is generally represented as an eagle or other powerful raptor. The idea here is that, under the power of Garuḍa's divine weapon-spell, Rāma's arrows become so many Garuḍas to counter Rāvaṇa's serpents, their ancestral foe. Garuḍa's enmity for and power over serpents is well known in the mythology (*MBh* 1.19–20), and, earlier in the book (*sarga* 40), Garuḍa himself arrives to free Rāma and Lakṣmaṇa from the serpent-weapons of Indrajit. See 6.40.49; 6.78.23; and notes.

"intercepted them" *viceruḥ*: Literally, "they moved about *or* attacked." Given the martial context, we believe that this verb should be taken in its sense of "attack." The idea is that each of the golden bird-arrows intercepts and destroys one of the serpent-arrows.

21. "took the form of eagles" *suparṇarūpāḥ*: Literally, "having the form of birds." See note to verse 20 above.

"those immensely swift arrows" *tān ... mahājavān*: Literally, "those immensely swift ones."

22. "at the thwarting of his divine weapon-spell" *astre pratihate*: Literally, "when the *astra* was counterstruck."

23. "with a veritable torrent of them" *śaraugheṇa*: Literally, "with a torrent of arrows."

Following verse 23, D5–7,9–11,S insert a passage of one line [2097*]: "Taking aim at his battle standard, Rāvaṇa cut it down with a single arrow."

24. "After first knocking the golden battle standard to the floor of the chariot" *pātayitvā rathopasthe rathāt ketuṃ ca kāñcanam*: Literally, "having caused the golden banner to fall from the chariot into the chariot-bottom."

Following verse 24, D7,G1,2,M3, and the texts and printed editions of Cg and Cm insert a passage of one line [2098*]: "Upon witnessing that tremendous feat of evil-minded Rāvaṇa..."

25. "hard pressed" *ārtam*: Literally, "afflicted." Cr, alone among the commentators, expresses disquiet with the notion that Rāma could actually be in trouble. He glosses, "appearing to be that way (*tatvena pratīyamānam*)." See note to verse 4 above. Cf. 6.77.28; 6.78.47–48; and notes.

"the...*dānavas*" *dānavāḥ*: Note how here, too, the demons seem to be on Rāma's side. See note to verse 4 above.

27. "Mercury, the planet baleful to all creatures, stood in occlusion with Rohiṇī" *rohiṇīm...samākramya budhas tasthau...prajānām aśubhāvahaḥ*: Literally, "Budha, the bearer of inauspiciousness to creatures, having transgressed Rohiṇī, stood." Rohiṇī, either the fourth or the ninth lunar asterism (s.v. Apte, MW), is generally regarded as the wife or consort of the moon. Cg notes that, when Mercury crosses or occludes Rohiṇī, oppression of the world occurs (*budhe rohiṇīṃ prāpte jagatpīḍā bhavatīti bhāvaḥ*). Cf. 6.19.34; 6.114.21; and notes. See, too, 4.12.17.

28. "the sun, bringer of day" *divākaram*: Literally, "the maker of day."

29. "The sun, bringer of day" *divākaraḥ*: Literally, "the maker of day."

"its color that of iron" *śastravarṇaḥ*: Literally, "having the color of iron, steel, *or* a weapon." Ct glosses, "its inner circle black (*kṛṣṇāntarmaṇḍalaḥ*)." Cr offers, simply, "black in color (*kṛṣṇavarṇaḥ*)." Cg and Cm gloss, "dark as a sword (*asiśyāmaḥ*)."

"looked ghastly...it seemed" *suparuṣaḥ...adṛśyata*: Literally, "it looked very harsh *or* cruel." We have translated the verb twice for the sake of clarity. Raghunathan (1982, vol. 3, p. 299), however, understands the adjective to refer not to the sun's appearance but to the fierceness of its rays, rendering, "burnt by its touch," but this seems improbable in light of the dimming of the sun's rays.

"In conjunction with a smoke-bannered comet, it seemed to be crossed by a headless trunk." *adṛśyata kabandhāṅkaḥ saṃsakto dhūmaketunā*: Literally, "the one having the mark of Kabandha appeared attached to a smoke-bannered one (i.e., a comet)." We understand *kabandhāṅkaḥ* to be a *bahuvrīhi* compound modifying *divākaraḥ*, "the sun," in *pāda* b, with the sense "having Kabandha for its mark." Ct and Cr analyze the compound as "on whose lap *or* hip (*aṅke*) is Kabandha (*kabandho 'ṅke yasya saḥ*)." Some translators have followed this interpretation. Raghunathan (1982, vol. 3, p. 299), however, alone among the translators, takes *pādas* cd as a separate syntactic unit, rendering, "A headless trunk was seen with the comet trailing from it."

30. In keeping with his ongoing contention that Rāma, as a deity, is never really harmed or afflicted, Ct notes that the evil portents represented in this and the preceding verses are there to suggest that Rāma is acting out the role of a mere human (*eta utpātā rāmasya tathā manuṣyadharmanaṭanasūcakā iti bodhyam*).

"And...of Viśākhā, the constellation of the ruling House of Kosala" *kosalānāṃ ca nakṣatram*: Literally, "And...the constellation of the Kosalas." Normally, Viśākhā refers to twin stars. Cr and Cg explain that the term "the Kosalas" refers to the ruling dynasty of the region, i.e., the Ikṣvākus (*kosalānām ikṣvākūṇām*). Cg further reminds us that Viśākhā is the special constellation of the Ikṣvākus, as indicated earlier in the fourth *sarga* of the *kāṇḍa* (*viśākhāyās tan nakṣatratvam etat kāṇḍacaturthasarge darśitam*). See 6.4.45 and note. In that passage, Lakṣmaṇa assures Rāma of the success of his mission by pointing out that, among other auspicious signs, the Ikṣvāku constellation, Viśākhā, is shining brightly and bodes no ill. See, too, 6.63.3, App. I, No. 43, lines 23–24, and n. 13. Roussel (1903, vol. 3, p. 341), apparently unmindful of this earlier passage, understands, incorrectly, we believe, that Mars is somehow occluding two different asterisms, that of the Kosalas and Viśākhā. In this error he is followed by Shastri (1959, vol. 3, p. 299) and Pagani (1999, pp. 1150, 1672–73). See notes to 6.4.45. See, too, Kirfel 1920, p. 35.

"Mars" *aṅgārakaḥ*: Literally, "Aṅgāraka." Mars, like Mercury (see note to verse 28 above), is a planet whose occlusion of asterisms is considered highly inauspicious.

"This constellation . . . was clearly visible" *vyaktam*: Literally, "was clearly visible." Along with some translators, we understand the term *vyaktam*, "clear, manifest, visible," to be an adjective modifying *nakṣatram*, "constellation." Other translators read the term adverbially with "stood in occlusion of."

31. "With his ten faces and twenty arms, ten-necked Rāvaṇa" *daśāsyo viṃś atibhujaḥ . . . daśagrīvaḥ*: Literally, "with his ten faces and twenty arms, the ten-necked one." Rāvaṇa is represented here in the awesome form he assumes for battle. See notes to 6.47.106; 6.50.11; and 6.92.20 for a discussion of when Rāvaṇa does and does not have multiple heads and arms. See, too, 5.8.13,19; 5.20.24,26; 5.47.2–14; and notes. Cf. 3.30.8.

"like Mount Maināka" *maināka iva parvataḥ*: The simile is no doubt based upon Rāvaṇa's huge size and his protruding limbs and weapon[s], which may recall the peaks and trees of the mountain. This is not one of Vālmīki's most elegant figures, and the propriety of choosing this particular mountain as the *upamāna* is not clear. For a description of Mount Maināka, see 5.1.89–93. See, too, *MBh* 1.19.290*.

32. "Hard pressed" *nirasyamānaḥ*: Literally, "being cast down *or* being defeated." Cr claims that Rāma avoids taking the opposing action of which he is fully capable, entering into the spirit of his role because Rāvaṇa's weapons are products of divine grace. Thus, Cr continues, Rāma's virtue as the protector of the boundaries of proper behavior is made manifest. (*sāmarthyānukūlakṛtiṃ notpādayad vaiyākaraṇamate 'pi kṛter vyāpārakukṣipraviṣṭatvān nāśabdārthatvam etena rāvaṇāstrāṇāṃ devānugrahaviṣayatvaṃ sūcitam. tena rāmasya maryādāpālakatvaguṇo vyaktaḥ.*)

33. "his eyes turning red with fury" *kiṃcitsaṃraktalocanaḥ*: Literally, "his eyes somewhat reddened." See notes to 6.19.22–23 and 6.31.72.

"Rāma flew into a towering rage" *sa . . . jagāma sumahākrodham*: Literally, "he went to very great anger." Cr understands *(su)mahākrodham*, "great anger," to be a *bahuvrīhi* compound modifying Rāvaṇa. He thus understands, "he [Rāma] approached the extremely angry [Rāvaṇa]."

"seeming almost to scorch his foe with his gaze" *nirdahann iva cakṣuṣā*: Literally, "as if burning with his eye." Ñ1,V2,D3,9–11, and the texts and printed editions of Ct and Cr read *rākṣasān*, "the *rākṣasas*," for *cakṣuṣā*, "with his eye." This yields the sense "as if burning the *rākṣasas*."

Following verse 33, D10,11, and the texts and printed editions of Ct continue the *sarga* without a break (GPP and NSP 6.102.39cd, ef).

Sarga 91

D10,11, and the texts and printed editions of Ct continue *sarga* 90. Cs, alone among the commentators, notes that some texts break the *sargas* here, while others, noting the absence of a change in meter that is generally the case at the end of *sargas*, do not. (*uttaragranthena sahaikaḥ khaṇḍa ekonasaptatiślokātmā sarga iti kecid āhuḥ. sargāntima-ślokavṛttādibhedasya prāyikatvāt tasya kruddhasyeti sargaprārambhapadyam iti kecit.*)

2. "The mountain" *śailaḥ*: Unless we are to read this as a generic term for "the mountains," we must assume that the mountain in question is Trikūṭa, upon which the city of Laṅkā is built. This idea is made explicit in the translation of Gita Press (1969, vol. 3, p. 1798). See note to 6.2.10.

"and its deeply rooted trees" *acaladrumaḥ*: Literally, "having immovable trees." V3,D9,11,G1,M, and the texts and printed editions of Ct, Cr, Cg, and Cm read instead *caladrumaḥ*, which, in the context, would be interpreted to mean "its trees shaking." Ck avoids the issue of whether the trees are moveable or immoveable, reading *mahā-drumaḥ*, "with great *or* gigantic trees." This reading is noted by Ct. A number of northern manuscripts, including the edition of Gorresio (6.87.2), similarly avoid this issue by reading *ca sadrumaḥ*, "and together with its trees."

"grew wildly agitated" *babhūva cāpi kṣubhitaḥ*: Literally, "and it became agitated." B1,4,D7,T1,G,M3, and the texts and printed editions of Cg read instead *cātikṣubhitaḥ*, "and [it became] extremely agitated," for *cāpi kṣubhitaḥ*, which we believe is probably the intention of the critical reading as well.

3. "birds with harsh cries" *khagāḥ...paruṣasvanāḥ*: Ś,Ñ,V1,2,B,D1–4,6,8–12,T2,3,M1,2, and the texts and printed editions of Ct, Ck, and Cr, as well as the editions of Gorresio (6.84.3) and Lahore (6.84.3), read instead *kharāḥ*, an ambiguous term here, which has been understood variously by commentators and translators. Ś,Ñ,V1,2,B,D1–4,8–13,T2,3,M2,3,5, and the texts and printed editions of Ct, Ck, Cg, Cr, and Cm, as well as the editions of Gorresio (6.84.3) and Lahore (6.84.3), read *paruṣā ghanāḥ*, "threatening clouds." Cr, the only commentator to discuss the term *kharāḥ*, bases his interpretation on its nominal sense of "asses, donkeys." He understands it to be an adjective, meaning "having the shape of donkeys (*gardabhākṛtayaḥ*)" and modifying "clouds (*ghanāḥ*)." This interpretation is followed only by Gita Press (1969, vol. 3, p. 1798), which translates, "looking like donkeys... clouds." Dutt (1893, p. 1462) takes the term in its adjectival sense of "rough," which he also takes to modify "clouds (*ghanāḥ*)." Gorresio (1858, vol. 10, p. 188) interprets similarly, rendering, "*orride*." Roussel (1903, vol. 3, p. 341) attempts to avoid the issue to some extent. He clearly understands the term to be a noun but leaves it untranslated as "*Des Kharas*." This noun, in turn, he sees as modified by the adjective *kharanirghoṣāḥ*, "braying like asses," which he renders as "*á la voix d' ânes*." Pagani (1999, p. 1150) takes the term in its standard nominal sense of "ass, donkey" but appears to ignore the term *gagane*, "in the sky," of *pāda* b, thus sparing herself the necessity of explaining how these animals can fly. Shastri (1959, vol. 3, p. 300) takes the term in another of its nominal senses to mean "crows." Combining this somewhat awkwardly with the term *ghanāḥ*, which he takes in its sense of "group *or* multitude," he renders, "flocks of crows, braying like donkeys." In this interpretation of *ghanāḥ*, Shastri follows Roussel's "*par troupes*" (1903, vol. 3, p. 341), as does Pagani (1999, p. 1150) with her "*par bandes*." Only the translation of Raghunathan (1982, vol. 3, p. 299), who reads *khagāḥ*, with the critical

edition, and *ghanāḥ*, with the vulgate, etc., represents both birds and clouds as ominous portents.

4. "fear entered Rāvaṇa's heart" *rāvaṇasyāviśad bhayam*: Literally, "fear entered of Rāvaṇa." D5,7,9–11,T1,G,M, and the texts and printed editions of the southern commentators read instead *rāvaṇasyābhavad bhayam*, "Rāvaṇa had fear."

5–6. "The gods, standing in their aerial chariots" *vimānasthāḥ . . . devāḥ*: Some translators understand, as we do, that it is only the gods who are hovering in their flying cars, whereas others understand that the whole list of beings is so situated.

"and the great birds, who soar through the sky" *garutmantaś ca khecarāḥ*: Literally, "and the winged ones, the movers in the sky." A number of translators, like us, take *khecarāḥ*, "moving in the sky," to be an epithet of *garutmantaḥ*, while others understand that these are two separate groups: the great birds and other sky-goers. Cf. notes to 6.113.18 and 6.116.47.

7. "hostile as always to each other" *vigraham āgatāḥ*: Literally, "who had come to hostility." The phrase is ambiguous. We follow Ct, Cr, Cm, and Cg (second interpretation), according to whom it is their partisanship for Rāma and Rāvaṇa, respectively, that arouses the hostility of these two groups of spectators (*rāmarāvaṇapakṣapātāt parasparaṃ kalahāyamānā ity arthaḥ*—so Cg). As is well known, the hostility between the *devas* and the *asuras* is innate, long standing, and legendary. Cg's first interpretation, which some translators have followed, takes the term *vigraham* to refer specifically to the battle at hand. Cg glosses, "They came with reference to the *vigraha*, that is, battle. The meaning is 'they came to watch the battle.' (*vigrahaṃ yuddham uddiśyāgatāḥ. yuddhaṃ draṣṭum āgatā ity arthaḥ.*)"

"shouted words of support" *ūcuḥ . . . vākyaṃ bhaktyā*: Literally, "they spoke words through devotion." The idea, as the following verse makes clear, is that the *asuras* are cheering for Rāvaṇa, and the *devas* for Rāma.

8. "the *asuras* . . . to ten-necked Rāvaṇa" *daśagrīvam . . . asurāḥ*: Literally, "the *asuras* to the ten-necked one." Cg is struck by the fact that the *asuras*, whom Rāvaṇa had also harassed in his career of conquest, nonetheless cheer him on here out of jealousy, lest the gods gain an advantage [through Rāma's victory] (*yady apy asurāṇām api rāvaṇo bādhakas tathāpi devānām atiśayo mā bhūd ity asūyayā rāvaṇaṃ vardhayantīti bodhyam*). Note, too, that the *dānavas* seem to have been siding with Rāma at some points in the preceding *sarga*. Cf. 6.90.4,25; and notes.

9–12. "Rāvaṇa" *sa rāvaṇaḥ . . . rāvaṇaḥ*: Literally, "he Rāvaṇa . . . Rāvaṇa." In keeping with his usual practice in such cases, Cr takes one instance of the name as an epithet, meaning "he who causes the worlds to cry out (*lokānāṃ rāvayitā rāvaṇaḥ*)." See note to 6.52.19.

"fingered his mighty weapons" *spṛśan praharaṇaṃ mahat*: Literally, "touching a great weapon." We tend to agree with Cg here that Rāvaṇa is running his hands over his weaponry while reflecting for a moment as to which one to select at that particular point. (*spṛśan parāmṛśan. kiṃ vedānīṃ grahītum ucitam iti kṣaṇaṃ cintayann ity arthaḥ.*) We render *praharaṇam*, literally, "weapon," as a plural to convey this sense of selection. See 6.75.3–4 and note.

"blazing, as it were, with fury" *pradīpta iva roṣeṇa*: B1,G2,M3, and the printed editions (although not the commentary) of Cg read instead *pradīptam iva roṣeṇa*, which would then modify, along with the other adjectives, *śūlam*, "lance." This minor variant is rendered only in the translation of Raghunathan (1982, vol. 3, p. 300).

"Fitted with barbs ... it was fearsome to look upon" *kūṭaiś citaṃ dṛṣṭibhayāvaham.* Literally, "provided with points, it brought fear to the eye." D6,7,10,11,G2, and the texts and printed editions of Ct and Cr read *citta-*, "mind, heart," in place of *citam,* "provided with." This lends the phrase the meaning: "with its points, it was fearsome to the mind and the gaze." According to Cg, *kūṭas* in this context are iron spikes *or* barbs (*ayaḥśaṅkubhiḥ*).

"Rending and cutting, it was a terror to all beings" *trāsanaṃ sarvabhūtānāṃ dāraṇaṃ bhedanaṃ tathā*: Literally, "frightening, rending, and cutting all beings." Cg attempts to distinguish the types of cutting represented by *dāraṇam* and *bhedanam.* The first he glosses as "cutting like a saw (*krakacavat kṛntanam*)," the second as "slicing in two (*dvidhākaraṇam*)."

13. "by many ... *rākṣasas*" *anekaiḥ ... rākṣasaiḥ*: Ñ2,V1,3,D7,9–11, and the texts and printed editions of Ct and Cr read *anīkaiḥ,* "by troops," for *anekaiḥ,* "by many." Ct, however, glosses, "by large numbers of troops (*anekānīkasaṃkhyaiḥ*)."

"mighty Rāvaṇa" *vīryavān*: Literally, "the heroic *or* mighty one."

"grasped ... in the middle" *madhye jagrāha*: D6,7,9–11,T2,3,G1,2,M2,5, and the texts and printed editions of Ct and Cr read instead *jagrāha yudhi,* "grasped in battle."

14. "the gigantic warrior" *mahākāyaḥ*: Literally, "he of the huge body."

"raised the lance on high" *samudyamya*: Literally, "having taken up *or* raised."

15. "That ... roar" *śabdaḥ*: Literally, "sound."

16. "of the extremely loudly roaring and evil-minded *rākṣasa*" *atinādasya ... tasya durātmanaḥ*: Literally, "of the evil-minded one of exceeding roars." We understand both compounds as *bahuvrīhis* modifying an unexpressed noun, *rāvaṇasya,* "of Rāvaṇa." Raghunathan (1982, vol. 3, p. 300), the only translator consulted whose reading is the same as that of the critical edition, disagrees, rendering, "by that wicked bawling." D7,9–11, and the texts and printed editions of Ct, Ck, and Cr read instead *atikāyasya,* "of him of the huge body."

17. "released a tremendous roar" *vinadya sumahānādam*: Literally, "having roared a very great roar." Cg, alone among the commentators, is at pains to distinguish Rāvaṇa's roar here from the one described previously in verses 14–16 above. According to Cg, the first sound is the result of the effort of lifting the mighty weapon, while the second is uttered in the course of hurling it. (*pūrvaṃ śūlodyamanajanitotsāhakṛtanāda uktaḥ. iha prakṣepajanitotsāhakṛto nāda iti vivekaḥ.*)

18. "instantly" *sadyaḥ*: D9–11,G2, and the texts and printed editions of Ct and Cr read instead *samyak,* "completely, properly."

"though you have your brother as an ally" *bhrātṛsahāyasya*: The compound is slightly ambiguous. Several translators understand it to mean that Rāvaṇa intends to take both Rāma's and Lakṣmaṇa's life with the same blow. We agree with Raghunathan (1982, vol. 3, p. 300), however, who renders, "though you have your brother to aid you." Among the translators consulted, only Gorresio (1858, vol. 10, p. 189) understands the reference to be to Rāvaṇa's brother Vibhīṣaṇa. He adds the pronoun *mio* in italics, rendering, "*che hai per ausilio mio fratello.*"

Cm provides an "inner meaning (*vāstavārtha*)" on this and the following verse. See notes to verse 19 below.

19. "Arrogant in battle though you be" *raṇaślāghin*: Literally, "praising *or* boasting in battle." The term *raṇaślāghin* can be either pejorative, as we understand it to be here, in the sense of a person who vainly boasts of his own prowess, or positive to refer to a

person who is actually worthy of praise in battle. Raghunathan (1982, vol. 3, p. 300) takes it as a term of homage, translating, "you, a foeman worthy of regard." Gorresio (1858, vol. 10, p. 189) understands much as we do. Ñ1,V,B2–4,D4,9–11,13,T2,3, and the texts and printed editions of Ct read instead the nominative *raṇaślāghī* for the critical edition's vocative, making Rāvaṇa apply the term to himself. This reading, of course, makes the term unambiguously positive. See, too, 6.92.1 and note.

"striking you down, I shall quickly reduce you" *tvāṃ nihatya . . . karomi tarasā samam*: Literally, "having struck you down, I shall make [you] equal to." In keeping with his consistent effort to deflect any harm or threat of harm against Rāma, Cm suggests that verses 18 through 20 have an "inner meaning (*vāstavārtha*)," according to which Rāvaṇa means only to approach heroic Rāma and then turn his murderous lance against the monkey hosts, who are Rāma's and Lakṣmaṇa's allies. (*śūlo 'yaṃ vajrasāra ityādisārdhaślokadvayasya vāstavārthas tu mayodyato me śūlas tava bhrātṛsahāyasya bhrātre lakṣmaṇāya sahāyasya vānarasamūhasyety arthaḥ. sadyaḥ prāṇān hariṣyatīti sambandhaḥ. rakṣasām ityādisārdhaślokam ekaṃ vākyam. śūre saty apy eṣo 'haṃ tvāṃ na nihanmy atas tvaṃ tiṣṭha kiṃtu tvāṃ nihatyāgatyety arthaḥ. hanahiṃsāgatyor iti dhātor ayam arthaḥ. nihatānāṃ śūrāṇāṃ rakṣasām. tṛtīyārthe ṣaṣṭhī. samaṃ karomi vānarān iti śeṣaḥ. nihatarākṣasapratikārārthaṃ vānarān haniṣyāmīti bhāvaḥ.*) See note to 6.80.29. See, too, notes to 6.27.9; 6.37.9; 6.80.29; and 6.81.4. Cf. notes to 6.27.4.

20. See note to verse 19 above.

Following verse 20, Ñ1,B2,3,D4–7,9–11,S insert a passage of two lines [3003*]: "Loosed from Rāvaṇa's hand and haloed with garlands of lightning,[1] it looked splendid as it hurtled through the sky, its eight bells making a tremendous clangor."

[1]"with garlands of lighting" *vidyunmālā-*: D6,7,M3, and the texts and printed editions of Cm and Cg read instead *vidyujjvālā-*, "flames *or* flashes of lightning." Cg understands that the lance is wreathed in flames that resemble lightning (*vidyutsadṛśajvālā*).

Following 3003*, Ñ1,B2,3,D4–7,9–11,S (Ñ2,V1,2,B4 after verse 20) insert a passage of two lines [3004*]: "When mighty Rāghava saw that blazing lance, terrible to look upon, he bent his bow and released his arrows."

21. "strove to stop" *vārayāmāsa*: The normal sense of the causal root √*vāray* would be "to arrest, block, *or* turn back." Since, however, the following verses make it clear that Rāma's arrows are unable to stop or deflect the terrible lance, we have translated accordingly. Ck and Ct, unwilling to contemplate the notion that Rāma's arrows should fly in vain, understand that he is using them initially merely to slow the progress of the lance (*prathamaṃ vegabhaṅgam ity arthaḥ*).

"just as Vāsava might" *iva vāsavaḥ*: Literally, "like Vāsava." The simile appears to be a kind of *abhūtopamā* based on the similar inadequacy of rain showers and flights of arrows directed against an unquenchable fiery energy rather than a reference to any specific mythological event.

23. "shattered . . . by the impact of that lance" *śūlasaṃsparśacūrṇitān*: Literally, "pulverized by contact with the lance."

"he was furious" *krodham āharat*: Literally, "he took *or* acquired anger." Ñ2,V1,2,B2–4,D3,10, and the texts and printed editions of Ct read instead *krodhamūrcchitaḥ*, "[he was] beside himself with rage."

24. "crafted for Vāsava" *vāsavanirmitām*: Literally, "crafted for *or* by Vāsava." The compound is ambiguous as it does not make clear whether Indra actually fashioned the weapon or whether it was made for him by one of the smiths of the gods, such as Tvaṣṭṛ or Viśvakarman. On the other hand, Hopkins (1915, p. 122) cites a passage from the *Mahābhārata* according to which Indra does fashion at least some of his weaponry. Raghunathan (1982, vol. 3, p. 301), the only translator to share the critical reading, renders, "fashioned by Vāsava." Ś,Ñ1,B1,D2,3,8,10–12,G1,2,M2, and the texts and printed editions of Ct and Cr read instead *vāsavasaṃmatām*, "esteemed *or* prized by Vāsava."

26. "it collided with the lance" *tasmiñ śūle papāta ha*: Literally, "it fell on that lance."

"its blazing splendor dimmed" *gatadyutiḥ*: Literally, "its radiance gone." M3 and the texts and printed editions of Cg and Cm read the slight variant, *hatadyutiḥ*, "its radiance destroyed."

27. "Rāvaṇa's" *asya*: Literally, "his."

"arrows, arrows that were powerful . . . sharp" *bāṇaiḥ . . . tīkṣṇaiḥ . . . śitaiḥ śaraiḥ*: Literally, "with arrows that were sharp, with sharp arrows." The critical reading is rather redundant, although the broad semantic range of the adjective *tīkṣṇa*, which can mean "sharp, fierce, powerful, pungent, etc.," mitigates somewhat the redundancy of *śita*, "sharp." D10,11, and the texts and printed editions of Ct read *kṣiptaiḥ*, "shot, hurled," for *tīkṣṇaiḥ*, "sharp."

"arrows that were . . . hard as adamant . . . sharp" *vajrakalpaiḥ śitaiḥ śaraiḥ*: D10,11, and the texts and printed editions of Ct and Cr read instead *bāṇavadbhir ajihmagaiḥ*, literally, "possessing *bāṇas* and going straight." The former of these two adjectives is obscure in its meaning and inspires a number of interpretations on the part of the commentators. The normal meaning of *bāṇa* is, of course, "arrow," but such a reading leads to the seemingly tautologous sense "[arrows] possessing arrows." Among the commentators, only Cs is willing to entertain this sense as a possibility. He observes: "It is possible to say that the quality of possessing arrows attributed to the arrows derives from the fact that, through the supernatural power of Rāma, arrows issue forth from some of the primary arrows that are directly loosed from his bowstring (*bāṇavadbhiḥ keṣucit pradhāneṣv sākṣāj jyāvisṛṣṭeṣv iṣuṣu tebhyo 'pi rāmamāhātmyena niḥsaranti bāṇā iti bāṇānāṃ bāṇavattvaṃ sambhavatīti vā tathoktiḥ*)." For the rest, commentators who share this reading, as well as Cg, Cm, and Cs, who note it as a variant, take the term *bāṇa-* in *bāṇavadbhiḥ* in its less common sense of "noise, sound" and thus understand the adjective to mean "resounding (*śabdāyamānaiḥ*—so Ct, Cm)." Cf. 6.92.21 and note.

28. "concentrating his energies" *paramāyattaḥ*: Literally, "exerting himself supremely."

"with . . . feathered shafts" *patribhiḥ*: The word *patrin*, "winged *or* feathered," is a common epic kenning for arrow. Cg argues, however, that there is no redundancy in the verse (between this term and *śaraiḥ*) because of the separate syntax. He notes that some [commentators, e.g., Cm] take the term adjectivally in the sense of "feathered *or* winged." (*patribhis tribhir iti prayogabhedān na punaruktiḥ. patribhiḥ. patravadbhir ity eke.*)

29. "in the midst of that host" *samūhasthaḥ*: The reference is evidently to Rāvaṇa's *rākṣasa* forces that are said to surround him in verse 13 above. Ck and Ct, however, seem to think that the adjective is inspired by the fact that Rāvaṇa has multiple heads and hands. (*samūhasthaḥ samūhatayā sthitaḥ. bahuśiraḥpāṇitvāt tathātvam.*) See notes to verse 30 below.

"like an *aśoka* tree in full bloom" *phullāśoka ivābabhau*: The simile derives from the resemblance of the blood-spattered body of Rāvaṇa to an *aśoka* tree covered with its scarlet blossoms.

30. "grew weary" *jagāma khedam*: Literally, "he went to exhaustion or depression." The term *kheda* can refer either to mental or physical lassitude or distress, and translators understand it variously. We believe the context here best supports an interpretation of physical debility.

"in the midst of his hosts" *samājamadhye*: We believe that this phrase, like the others in the concluding verse, merely echoes the parallel statement in verse 29 above, where Rāvaṇa is described as *samūhasthaḥ*. Cg and Cr, however, understand the term *samāja-* in the sense of "battle *or* battlefield." Cg glosses, "battle (*yuddhe*)," while Cr appears to associate the term with the noun *āji*, "battle *or* battlefield," glossing, "in the middle of the battle *or* battlefield (*ājeḥ saṃgrāmasya madhye*)." This interpretation is followed only by Pagani (1999, p. 1152), who renders, "*au beau milieu du champ de bataille*."

The meter is *upajāti*.

Sarga 92

1. "in battle" *raṇe*: D7,9–11,G2, and the texts and printed editions of Ct read instead *bhṛśam*, "fiercely, severely."

"by Rāma" *tena*: Literally, "by him."

"arrogant in battle" *samaraślāghī*: See 6.91.19 and note.

2. "that mighty warrior" *vīryavān*: Literally, "the mighty *or* powerful one."

"drew back" *āyamya*: Literally, "having stretched *or* bent." Ś,Ñ,V,B2–4,D1–4,6–13,G2, and the texts and printed editions of Ct and Cr read instead *udyamya*, "having taken up."

3. "filled" *pūrayat*: We follow Cv, Cg, and Cm, who share this reading, in taking the form to be an augmentless imperfect. Ñ,V1,B2–4,D1,4,6,9–11,13,T,G3,M, and the texts and printed editions of Ck, Ct, and Cr read instead the present participle *pūrayan*. Commentators who share this reading supplement the participle with a finite verb such as *abhyardayat*, "[filling,] he afflicted" (Ct).

"arrows... with its thousands of arrowlike torrents" *bāṇadhārāsahasraiḥ ... bāṇaiḥ*: The simile appears to be slightly defective, as there is no explicit reference to showers of rain, while the term *bāṇa-* is repeated in *pādas* a and c. Apparently, the poet intends the compound to be a type of compound simile, in the sense of "arrowlike torrents." Indeed, this may be an idiom to express torrential rain, something like "raining cats and dogs" in English.

4. "riddled" *pūritaḥ*: Literally, "filled."

5. "the mighty warrior slowed... so that he received them as if they were no more than rays of sunshine" *vārayan ... gabhastīn iva sūryasya pratijagrāha*: Literally, "blocking, he received [that mass of arrows] as if they were rays of the sun." The precise meaning of the verse is difficult to determine and has caused some confusion among commentators and translators alike. We take our cue here from Ct's and Ck's comments on 6.91.21 above, where they understand the causal root $\sqrt{}$*vāray* to mean "to retard *or* slow down." The idea, as we see it, is that Rāma is neither stopping nor deflecting Rāvaṇa's arrows but rather slowing their momentum so that, even when

they strike him, they are no more harmful than solar rays. Cr, the only commentator to discuss this verse, has a completely different idea. He understands the subject to be Rāvaṇa rather than Rāma. He believes that, in order to stop Rāma's hail of arrows, the *rākṣasa* takes up arrows of his own, which are like rays of the sun [that is, blazing brightly]. (*sa rāvanaḥ śaraiḥ śarajālāni vārayan vārayitum sūryasya gabhastīn kiraṇān iva pratijagrāha śarān iti śeṣaḥ.*) No translator consulted precisely follows Cr's interpretation. However, Dutt (1893, p. 1465) and Raghunathan (1982, vol. 3, p. 301) similarly supply the word "arrows," understanding that Rāma takes up arrows that are like solar rays to counter those of Rāvaṇa.

*6. "sank" *nijaghāna*: Literally, "he struck." Although the reading *nijaghāna* is well supported, the syntax of the verse is awkward, as the only plausible object of *nijaghāna*, *śarasahasrāṇi*, "thousands of arrows," is difficult to construe with this particular verb. Most translators tinker with the syntax to force the sense "struck in the chest with thousands of arrows." The commentators are either unhelpful or silent. A number of primarily northern manuscripts—Ś2,Ñ,V1,2,B1,2,4,D1–5,8,12,13,G3,M1, as well as the editions of Lahore and Gorresio—read instead the apparent *facilior nicakhāna*, "he sunk, buried," which is idiomatic and perhaps serves as a northern gloss. Like Gita Press (1969, vol. 3, p. 1801), we have translated accordingly.

7. "looked like a . . . *kiṃśuka* tree in full bloom" *dṛṣṭaḥ phulla iva . . . kiṃśukadrumaḥ*: See note to 6.60.34.

9. "in the midst of that battle, shrouded as it was in the darkness of their arrows" *śarāndhakāre samare*: Cr explains, "in that battle in which the arrows themselves constituted the darkness (*śara evāndhakāro yasmiṃs tasmin samare*)." Cf. 6.87.27 and note for a similar image of arrows darkening the battlefield.

11. "helpless" *vivaśā*: Cr, apparently unwilling to ascribe powerlessness to the goddess Sītā, glosses, *atikāntimatī*, "exceedingly lovely."

"behind my back" *ajñānāt*: Literally, "because of not knowing *or* ignorance." Commentators are divided as to whether the reference here is to Rāma's ignorance of Sītā's abduction or to Rāvaṇa's ignorance of Rāma's true nature and great prowess. Ck, Ct, and Cr offer the second interpretation, while Cg offers both as alternatives. We believe the former is correct, as it fits well with Rāma's taunting Rāvaṇa for his cowardice. Cg glosses, "because of my ignorance, that is, because I did not see [it] or because of your own lack of discrimination (*mamājñānān mamādarśanāt tvadavivekād iti vā*)." In choosing the latter, Ct is forced to lend a somewhat unusual sense to the term *vīryavān*, "heroic," in *pāda* d. He explains, "Because of ignorance, that is, lack of discrimination and ignorance of my true nature, you are not possessed of heroism. The meaning is: 'You shall soon perish because of this crime that has kindled my rage.' (*ajñānād avivekān matsvarūpājñānāc ca tasmāt tvaṃ vīryavān nāsi ca. matkrodhadīpakena tena pāpena śīghraṃ vinaṅkṣyasīty arthaḥ.*)" Roussel (1903, vol. 3, p. 344), followed by Shastri (1959, vol. 3, p. 302) and Pagani (1999, p. 1152), believes that the reference is to Rāvaṇa's exploitation of Sītā's ignorance. He renders, "*en abusant de son ignorance*."

12. "You . . . abducted . . . And now you think" *hṛtvā . . . manyase*: Literally, "Having abducted, you think."

"when she was alone . . . without me to protect her" *mayā virahitām*: Literally, "deprived of me *or* without me."

"Oh, what a great hero am I!" *śūro 'ham*: Literally, "I [am] a hero."

13. "Molester of other men's wives!" *paradārābhimarśaka*: Ñ,V,B2–4,D9–11,T1,3,G1,M5, and the texts and printed editions of Ct read instead *paradārābhimarśana*[*rṣaṇa*—Ñ1,B2]*m*, "the molestation of other men's wives." In this variant, the abstract noun must be taken as a second object, along with *kāpuruṣaṃ karma*, "contemptible act," of the gerund *kṛtvā*, "having committed," in *pāda* c.

"against defenseless women" *strīṣu* ... *vināthāsu*: Literally, "with regard to women who lack a lord *or* protector."

"Oh, what a great hero am I!" *śūro 'ham*: See note to verse 12 above.

14. "Oh, what a great hero am I!" *śūro 'ham*: See note to verse 12 above.

15. "Kubera, bestower of wealth" *dhanada-*: Literally, "the giver *or* bestower of wealth." See 6.4.16; 6.7.3; 6.22.10; 6.69.26; 6.82.20; 6.98.12–13; 6.110.23; 6.115.24,49; and notes.

"a great ... deed" *karma mahat*: All the commentators are at pains, perhaps unnecessarily, to explain that Rāma is speaking mockingly (*sopahāsoktiḥ*—so Cg).

16. "the truly fitting reward" *sumahat phalam*: Literally, "the very great fruit *or* result."

"evil" *ahitasya*: Ck and Ct focus on the term's sense of "inimical *or* harmful," glossing, "of such a nature as to be harmful both in this world and in the next (*ihāmutrānartharūpasya*)." According to Dutt (1893, p. 1466), this is also Crā's interpretation.

"which you committed in your arrogance" *utsekenābhipannasya*: Literally, "endowed with arrogance *or* pride." We understand with Ct and Cm, who gloss *abhipannasya*, "endowed," with "performed, practiced (*anuṣṭhitasya*)."

17. "evil-minded wretch" *durmate*: Literally, "O evil-minded one."

"as if you were a common thief" *coravat*: Literally, "like a thief."

18. "If you had dared to lay violent hands upon Sītā" *yadi* ... *sītā dharṣitā syāt tvayā balāt*: "If Sītā had been assaulted forcibly by you."

"then and there" *tadā*: We follow Ct, who reads the adverb emphatically, glossing, "that very moment (*tadaiva*)."

"you would have ... joined your brother Khara" *bhrātaraṃ tu kharaṃ paśyeḥ*: Literally, "you would see brother Khara." Rāma is using this circumlocution both to taunt Rāvaṇa over the death of his brother and to indicate that he would have slain him as well had Rāvaṇa only had the courage to assault Sītā in his presence. See 3.28.25. See, too, note to 6.55.103.

19. "evil-minded wretch" *duṣṭātman*: Literally, "O evil-minded one." D7,9–11, and the texts and printed editions of Ct and Cr read instead *mandātman*, "O dull-witted one *or* fool."

"you have come into my presence" *asi mama* ... *cakṣurviṣayam āgataḥ*: Literally, "You have come to the range of my vision."

"the abode of Yama" *yamasādanam*: Cr glosses, "I shall lead you to the place of the Nemins (*yamasādanaṃ nemināṃ sthānaṃ nayāmi*)." The term *nemin* is somewhat obscure and appears to have no lexical basis. It can be interpreted to mean "possessing time (*nema*)." The word *nema* could be understood to be a reference to Yama as Time or Kāla, the destroyer of all. Perhaps Cr is thinking of the *vaivasvatakiṃkaras*, or the servants of death, mentioned at 6.61.53. See 6.61.53 and note.

20. "your head" *śiraḥ*: Cg notes that we are to understand by this reference that now, in his final moments, Rāvaṇa has only a single head (as opposed to the ten heads

that normally characterize his form in battle) (*anena tadānīm antakāle rāvaṇa ekaśiraskaḥ sthita iti gamyate*). See note to 6.47.106.

"as it rolls" *vikīrṇam*: Literally, "scattered."

21. "my arrowheads" *bāṇaśalya-*: The term *śalya* generally refers to a dart, spear, arrow, or other sharp projectile. In this compound, and in the present context, it would appear to be somewhat redundant with *bāṇa-*, normally, "arrow." We understand with Cr, who glosses, "the iron tip portion of an arrow (*ayomayabāṇāgrabhāga-*)." Cf. 6.91.27 and note.

22. "the carrion birds" *patagāḥ*: Literally, "ones who go by flying," i.e., birds. The reference here, however, as Cr notes, must be specifically to carrion birds. He glosses, "vultures and the like (*gṛdhrādayaḥ*)."

24. "the power of his divine weapon-spells . . . redoubled" *dviguṇam . . . astrabalam*: Cm understands that it is Rāma's calling to mind the power of the *astras* (*astrabalaviṣayasmaraṇam*) that has doubled. Ck and Ct believe that it is Rāma's recollection of the wrong that was done to him that causes the redoubling of his energies (*apakārasmaraṇād iti śeṣaḥ*).

25. "All the divine weapon-spells" *astrāṇi sarvāṇi*: Ck and Ct understand that the presiding divinities of the weapon-spells present themselves before Rāma. Ck specifies that these are the sons of Kṛśāśva (*kṛśāśvaputrā astradevatāḥ sannihitā abhuvann ity arthaḥ*). See 1.20.13ff.; 1.27.9; and notes. See, too, *UttaRāC* 1.1.14, lines 7, 8, 9, and verse 15.

"celebrated" *viditātmanaḥ*: See 1.41.7 and note, where both the context and the commentators make it clear that we are to understand the compound as having the sense "well-known, celebrated." There Ct and Cr gloss similarly (*prasiddha or prakhyāta*). Most translators consulted, however, have taken the term in its other sense, "knowing one's self" or "knowing the universal self." See notes to 6.24.7 and 6.31.58.

"And, in his excitement" *praharṣāt*: Ct and Ck understand that Rāma's excitement is a product of the presence of the presiding divinities of the weapon-spells (*astradevatāsaṃnidhijāt*—so Ct). Cr, however, takes it simply to be the joy produced by his zeal for battle (*yuddhotsāhajanitānandāt*).

"that immensely powerful hero" *mahātejāḥ*: Literally, "the immensely powerful one."

26. "within himself" *ātmagatāni*: Literally, "gone to the self." The term is somewhat ambiguous. Like most of the translators consulted, we believe that the term refers to the physical and psychological changes in Rāma mentioned in verse 24 above. Dutt (1893, p. 1466) and Shastri (1959, vol. 3, p. 303), however, understand the term to mean that the signs, including, one presumes, the *astras*, or divine weapon-spells, appear of their own accord. Thus, Dutt translates, "coming of themselves," while Shastri offers, "appearing of themselves." Cf. note to 6.94.29 below.

27. "his heart began to falter" *vighūrṇahṛdayaḥ*: Literally, "whose heart was agitated *or* wavering." Ct, who we believe is correct, glosses, "whose heart is wavering or frightened (*vikalahṛdayaḥ*)." Dutt (1893, pp. 1466–67) takes the term rather literally, rendering, "felt his heart undergoing a revolution." He then alludes to Ct in his note, saying, "*Vighurnahridayah*: had his heart paralysed, according to the commentator. I prefer the sense given as more graphic."

28. "Then" *yadā*: Literally, "when." This verse is technically a subordinate clause that appears to have no resolution until verse 30.

See note to verse 29 below.

29. There is a major difference in the reading of this passage (verses 28–30) on the part of the two schools of southern commentators: those associated with the texts of Ct, Cr, and Ck, on the one hand, and those associated with the texts of Cg, Cm, Crā, and Cv, on the other. The difference hinges on a variant in 29c, where the critical edition and the text of Cg et al. read *na raṇārthāya vartante,* which we have rendered, "proved useless in battle (lit., they did not exist for the purpose of battle)." V2,B1,3,D1–3,5–7,9–11,G3, and the texts and printed editions of Ct, Cr, and Ck read instead *maraṇārthāya,* "for the purpose of [his] death." This variant forces the commentators who share it to understand 28c–29d ["with his heart faltering . . . or counter Rāma's valor in any way. Even those arrows and various other weapons he managed to deploy proved useless in battle—as he now approached the hour of his death (*nāsya pratyakarod vīryaṃ viklavenāntarātmanā // kṣiptāś cāpi śarās tena śastrāṇi vividhāni ca / na raṇārthāya vartante mṛtyukāle 'bhivartataḥ*)] to mean that Rāma desisted from attacking the stunned Rāvaṇa, but that the arrows and other weapons that he, Rāma, had previously unleashed betokened Rāvaṇa's death. (*yāni maraṇārthāya vartante tāni śarāḥ śastrāṇi ca kṣiptā rāmeṇeti śeṣaḥ. ato mṛtyukālo 'bhyavartata rāvaṇasyeti śeṣaḥ*—so Cr.)

D7,10,G2,M2, and the texts and printed editions of Ct additionally read the predicative phrase *mṛtyukālo 'bhyavartata,* "[Rāvaṇa's] hour of death approached," for the critical edition's *mṛtyukāle 'bhivartataḥ* (literally, "of him who was approaching in the hour of [his] death").

30. Following verse 30, D7 and KK (preceding 3024*) add two passages 3025* (three lines) and 3023* (one line), which continue the description of a faltering Rāvaṇa and a retreating chariot. These lines are not rendered in any translation consulted.

Following verse 30, Ś,Ñ,V,B (missing in the text of Gorresio),D1–4,7–13, and the editions of KK [numbered in brackets as 6.105.34, following 3023*], GPP, NSP, and Gita Press [6.103.31] insert a passage of four lines [3024*]: "Perceiving that the lord of the earth was flagging,[1] his strength all gone, the charioteer swiftly turned back that fearsome chariot that rumbled like a storm cloud and quickly[2] fled the battlefield."

[1]"flagging" *patitam*: Literally, "fallen."

[2]"quickly" *śīghram*: D7,9–11, and the texts and printed editions of Ct and Cr read instead *bhītyā,* "out of fear."

The meter is *vaṃśasthavila.*

Sarga 93

1. "in his delusion" *mohāt*: Literally, "out of infatuation *or* confusion." We understand, with Cr, Cg, and Cm, that the term refers to the general lack of discrimination (*avivekāt*—Cg,Cm) that normally afflicts epic warriors in the moments before their death. Cr shares this view, stating explicitly that Rāvaṇa is enraged as a result of the delusion that arises from the fact that the hour of his death is at hand (*āsannamaraṇakāla ity artho 'ta eva mohāt saṃkruddhaḥ*). Ck and Ct, however, believe that the

reference is to the stunned condition of Rāvaṇa that is a result of the assault by Rāma and the monkeys in the closing moments of the previous *sarga*. They understand that Rāvaṇa is only now gradually recovering from his stupor and is therefore able to rebuke his charioteer for removing him from the battlefield. They supply the phrase "gradually freed from his stupor (*śanair mohena mukta iti śeṣaḥ*)."

2–3. The various terms for a weak and powerless person used here naturally overlap considerably in meaning. Commentators and translators render them variously to avoid redundancy. See note to 6.2.14.

"Acting on your own authority" *svayā buddhyā viceṣṭase*: Literally, "you act according to your own idea *or* thought."

5. "utterly undermined" *vināśitaḥ*: Literally, "destroyed."

"over long years" *cirakāla-*: Literally, "for a long time."

"reputation" *pratyayaḥ*: Literally, "confidence, faith, trust." We understand the term, as do the commentators, to refer either to people's belief that Rāvaṇa is a true hero (*pratyayo madviṣayo lokasya śūratvaviśvāsaḥ*—so Ct; Ck and Cr similarly) or to his reputation for never fleeing in battle (*rāvaṇasya yudhi palāyanaṃ nāstīti sarveṣāṃ viśvāsaḥ*—so Cg and Cm; Cv similarly).

6. "you have made me look like a coward in the eyes of an enemy" *śatroḥ ... paśyataḥ ... ahaṃ kṛtaḥ kāpuruṣas tvayā*: Literally, "by you I have been made a coward, although an enemy is watching."

7. "In that you stupidly failed to drive the chariot forward" *yas tvaṃ ratham imaṃ mohān na codvahasi*: Literally, "and you who out of delusion do not drive this chariot away." The phrase is somewhat problematic. We follow Cg, the only commentator who remarks on this reading. Cg explains as follows: "You who do not cause it [the chariot] to go facing but instead drive it away (*yo nodvāhayasy abhimukhaṃ na prāpayasi kiṃtv apavāhayasi sa tvam*)." The texts and printed editions of Ct and Cr read instead *yat tvaṃ katham idaṃ mohān na ced vahasi*. The most probable meaning of this awkward phrase would be: "If somehow you do not drive out of delusion." The idea, then, is that if the charioteer is not acting out of incompetence, it must be because of corruption.

"bribed" *upaskṛtaḥ*: This term, which normally means "embellished, perfected," must be taken here in its less common meaning of "changed, modified." The commentators understand it to mean that the charioteer has been made to turn against his master by bribery (*sa tvaṃ pareṇopaskṛta utkocena vikāraṃ prāpita iti*—so Ct). Ct supports this reading by referring to the grammatical rule according to which the verb $\sqrt{}$*kṛ*, when preceded by the *upasarga upa*, takes the insert *s* (*suṭ*) in the sense of "change *or* cheating (*vaikṛta*)" (*upādvaikṛte 'rthe karoteḥ suṭ*). Compare *Pā* 6.1.139.

8. "Indeed, it is more typical of one's enemies." *ripūṇāṃ sadṛśaṃ caitat*: Literally, "And this is worthy of enemies."

"What you have done is wrong" *na tvayaitat svanuṣṭhitam*: Literally, "This is not properly done by you."

9. "If you are my longtime friend" *yadi vāpy uṣito 'si tvam*: Literally, "or if you have dwelt." The phrase is elliptical and we share the view of the commentators, who gloss, "if you have been by my side for a long time (*cirakālaṃ matsamīpe sthitaḥ*—so Ct)." Cv and Cg, as an alternative, suggest, "a person who has approached deceitfully (*upadhayopasarpitaḥ*—so Cg)."

"or if you recall my many favors" *smaryante yadi vā guṇāḥ*: Literally, "or if virtues are remembered." Although some translators render literally (Raghunathan 1982, vol. 3,

p. 304 ["virtues"]; Dutt 1893, p. 1468 ["merit"]; and Pagani 1999, p. 1154 ["*vertus*"]), we believe the context better supports the commentators' gloss, "favors, honor etc. (*matkṛtopakārah*—so Ct, Ck; *satkārāḥ*—so Cg)" or "the virtues such as helpfulness that are resident in me (*upakartṛtvādimanniṣṭhā guṇāḥ*—so Crā, Cm)." The idea is that the charioteer is expected to show gratitude for his master's past favors, not merely his good qualities.

10. "by that fool" *abuddhinā*: Literally, "by that witless one."

"who wished his master well" *hitabuddhiḥ*: Literally, "of beneficial thoughts."

11. "I am not lacking in my affection for you" *na niḥsnehaḥ*: Literally, "not devoid of affection."

"the favors you have bestowed" *satkriyā*: Literally, "kind favors, respectful treatment."

12. "this favor" *priyam*: D5,7,9–11,M1, and the texts and printed editions of Ct and Cr read instead *hitam*, "benefit."

"out of a desire for your well-being and to preserve your reputation" *mayā tu hitakāmena yaśaś ca parirakṣatā*: Literally, "by me who has a desire for well-being and [by me] protecting reputation *or* fame." Ct and Cr believe that, in saving Rāvaṇa's life, the charioteer is acting to protect both Rāvaṇa's reputation and his own (*jīvanarakṣaṇenātmīyaṃ tvadīyaṃ ca yaśo rakṣatety arthaḥ*—so Ct).

13. "In this matter" *asminn arthe*: As several of the commentators point out, the reference is to the charioteer's having driven Rāvaṇa from the battlefield (*yuddhād apohanarūpe kārye*—so Ct).

"you should not... find fault with me" *na... tvaṃ māṃ... doṣato gantum arhasi*: Literally, "you ought not understand me through fault." One must follow the commentators here in taking the root $\sqrt{}$*gam* in its sense of "to know *or* think." Cm's gloss, "you ought not have a fault-finding eye toward me (*mayi doṣadṛṣṭiṃ kartuṃ nārhasīty arthaḥ*)," is perhaps the clearest rendering. The text of Gorresio (6.89.12), doubtless as a gloss, reads *mantum*, "to think *or* regard," for *gantum*.

"like some lowly and ignoble person" *kaścil laghur ivānāryaḥ*: Literally, "like some trivial, ignoble one." For reasons we cannot determine, several of the translators of the southern text, including Roussel (1903, vol. 3, p. 348), Shastri (1959, vol. 3, p. 304), Raghunathan (1982, vol. 3, p. 304), and Pagani (1999, p. 1154), read the simile as if both terms, *laghuḥ*, "trivial," and *anāryaḥ*, "ignoble," were in the accusative, modifying the charioteer, rather than in the nominative, referring to Rāvaṇa. In this reading, the charioteer is asking Rāvaṇa not to regard him as a lowly and ignoble person. According to the critical apparatus, a number of manuscripts, both southern and northern, read either one or both of the adjectives in the accusative (Ś2,B,D1–3,7–9,12,M2,T2,3—*laghum*; V3,B2–4,D5,9,T1—*anāryam*). However, no southern commentator consulted reads this variant. In addition, the only printed editions to read the accusative here are those of Lahore (6.89.12) and Gorresio (6.89.12), and only Gorresio (1858, vol. 10, p. 194) translates accordingly. It is possible that Roussel, as sometimes appears to be the case, is influenced by Gorresio, while Shastri and, to some extent, Pagani often tend to follow Roussel. Raghunathan's choice, however, remains inexplicable. See Introduction, pp. 114–117, and notes to 6.3.16; 6.98.2; and 6.116.11.

14. "I will tell you" *abhidhāsyāmi*: D9–11 and the texts and printed editions of Ct read instead the elliptical *pratidāsyāmi*, "I will give back." Ct supplies the ellipsis by adding the word *uttaram*, "answer."

"from the battle" *saṃyuge*: Literally, "in battle." Ct corrects the awkward case ending, glossing, "from battle (*saṃyugāt*)." Cg notes the improper case ending of both this term and of his reading *ābhoge* (see the following note). A number of northern manuscripts and the editions of Lahore and Gorresio similarly correct to the ablative.

"as the current of a river is turned back by the rising tide" *nadīvega ivāmbhobhiḥ*: Literally, "as is the force of a river by the waters." Ct and Cm, whom we have followed, understand this to be an elliptical reference to the rising waters of the sea at moonrise, etc. (*candrodayādinā pravṛddhasamudrodakair nadīvega iva*—so Cm). D5,T1,M3,5, and the texts and printed editions of Cg and Cv (Crā and Cm as a variant) read *ābhoge*, "broad expanse," for *ambhobhiḥ*. Cg and Cm understand the term here to mean "higher ground" from which river waters flow back (*ābhoge parvatādyunnatapradeśe nadīvega ivety arthaḥ*—so Cm). Raghunathan (1982, vol. 3, p. 304) translates, "as the force of a stream might be blocked by rising ground." He is, however, cognizant of the critical reading as he places in parentheses "(alt: by the rising tides of the ocean)."

15. "And, heroic warrior, I did not see your wonted enthusiasm and exuberance." *na hi te vīra saumukhyaṃ praharṣaṃ vopadhāraye*: Literally, "For, hero, I do not perceive your cheerfulness or excitement." Ś2,Ñ2,B1,D3,5,8,10–12,T,G,M1,5, and the texts and printed editions of Ck and Ct read *vīrya-*, "heroism, valor," for the vocative *vīra*, "O hero." This yields the compound *vīryasaumukhyam*, which Ct glosses as "cheerfulness or enthusiasm with respect to the acts to be accomplished through valor (*vīryakāryaṃ prati saumukhyam*)." Ck understands similarly. Cr reads the compound as a *bahuvrīhi* modifying the variant reading *prakarṣam*, "superiority." He glosses, "in which there is a manifestation of superior valor (*vīryasyādhikaparākramasya saumukhyaṃ prākaṭyaṃ yasmiṃs tam*)." This would give the line the sense: "I do not see your superiority in which there is a manifestation of your superior valor." D7,10,11,M1, and the texts and printed editions of Ct, Ck, and Cr read *prakarṣam*, "superiority," for the critical edition's *praharṣam*, "exuberance." D6,9–11,G1,M1, and the texts and printed editions of Ct, Ck, and Cr read *na*, "not," for the critical edition's *vā*, "or," yielding a double negative construction. In a footnote, Dutt (1893, p. 1468) says, "Two negatives in this verse amounting [*sic*] to an affirmative. This is the only instance of double negatives in Vālmīki." Despite this assertion, Dutt does not translate affirmatively, and his claim as to the uniqueness of the double negative is dubious at best. See 6.37.11; 6.67.36; 6.95.24; 6.101.36; and notes. See, too, 6.99.24, 3132*, lines 7–8, and n. 4

16. "these" *ta ime*: D9–11 and the texts and printed editions of Ct read instead *bhagnā me*, "my [horses] are broken down."

"as cattle battered by torrential rain" *gāvo varṣahatā iva*: Literally, "like cattle struck by rain." The precise reference of the simile is not entirely clear, and the southern commentators offer little assistance. Perhaps the idea is that the horses, covered with sweat, are likened to drenched cattle. This idea is supported by a few scattered northern variants, such as B3's *-klinnāḥ*, "wet," and Gorresio's *-svinnāḥ*, "sweating." Several of the translators consulted add that the horses are perspiring (Dutt 1893, p. 1468; Raghunathan 1982, vol. 3, p. 304; and Pagani 1999, p. 1155).

17. "all the many" *bhūyiṣṭham*: Literally, "to a large extent." Cr reads the term with *apradakṣiṇam* in *pāda* d, yielding the sense "overwhelmingly inauspicious."

"I foresee no good outcome for us" *lakṣayāmy apradakṣiṇam*: Literally, "I discern that which is inauspicious *or* unfavorable."

18–20. "a good charioteer" *rathakuṭumbinā*: Literally, "a caretaker of the chariot," i.e., charioteer.

"signs" *lakṣaṇāni*: According to Cv, Cg, Cm, and Ct, the reference is to "auspicious and inauspicious omens (*śubhāśubhanimittāni*)." Cm, however, offers, as a first alternative, "such signs as sluggishness in the use of *astras* (divine weapon-spells) and [other] weapons (*astraśastraprayogamāndyādīni*)."

"gestures" *iṅgitāni*: Cm, Cg, and Ct understand that these refer to a pale face (or hands—Cm) and other physical manifestations of emotional distress or well-being (*mukhaprasādavaivarṇyādiceṣṭāś ca*—so Ct).

"the . . . relative strength and weakness" *balābalam*: D9–11 and the texts and printed editions of Ct read instead *mahābala*, "O mighty one."

"of his master" *rathinaḥ*: Literally, "of the chariot owner." The reference is to the warrior who fights from the chariot.

"the elevations and depressions of the terrain" *sthalanimnāni bhumeś ca*: We follow the commentators in taking the term *sthala-*, normally, "firm *or* dry ground," in its sense of "raised ground" (Apte s.v.). Roussel (1903, vol. 3, p. 348) understands the term in its more common sense, translating, "*Les endroits où le terrain est ferme*." In this he is followed by Shastri (1959, vol. 3, p. 304). Pagani (1999, p. 1155) similarly renders, "*le terrain sec*."

"when to retreat" *pratyapasarpaṇam*: The commentators differ slightly on the meaning of this term. Ct, Cm, and Cg understand it to mean "retreating while keeping one's face toward the enemy (*abhimukhasthitasya pṛṣṭhataḥ*)." Cr, on the other hand, understands, "stationing oneself behind one's enemy (*ripupṛṣṭhadeśe sthāpanam*)."

21. "crushing" *raudram*: Literally, "dreadful, fierce." Ct and Ck gloss, "cruel (*krūram*)," while Cg and Cm gloss, "unbearable (*duḥsaham*—so Cg)."

"I acted in this fitting manner" *kṣamaṃ kṛtam idaṃ mayā*: Literally, "this fitting thing was done by me."

22. "on my own account" *svecchayā*: Literally, "through my own inclination *or* desire."

"heroic warrior" *vīra*: Literally, "O hero."

"overwhelmed with love for you, my master" *bhartṛsnehaparītena*: Literally, "overcome with affection for the master."

23. "proper" *yathātattvam*: The phrase is slightly ambiguous. We have translated with the majority of commentators, understanding the word *yathātattvam* adverbially in the sense of "what is fitting *or* proper." Ct appears to break the sequence into *yathā tat tvam*, glossing, "as you shall announce that, which is of the form of my obligation, I will do just that (*yathā tvaṃ tat kāryasvarūpaṃ vakṣyasi tat kariṣyāmi*)."

"With my mind discharged of its obligations" *gatānṛṇyena cetasā*: Literally, "With a mind whose debt is gone." The adjectival compound *gatānṛṇyena* is slightly obscure in its meaning and has been understood in various ways by commentators and translators alike. We believe that the context best supports the interpretation of Cg, who reads the compound as a *paranipāta* in the sense of "a mind that has achieved freedom from debt *or* obligation, that is, has taken a solemn vow to achieve this state (*ānṛṇyaṃ gatena ānṛṇyaṃ kartavyam iti kṛtasaṃkalpena cetasā manasā*)." The closest translation to this interpretation appears to be that of Gorresio (1858, vol. 10, p. 195), who renders, "*con animo intento a sdebitarsi*." Ct understands, "with a mind that has given *or* paid the traditional three debts with which every person is born [that is debts to the *pitṛs*, *devas*, and *ṛṣis*] (*dattarṇatrayeṇa*)." Cr believes that the charioteer's mind has been freed of its obligations to Rāvaṇa through his having saved the latter's life (*gataṃ prāptam ānṛṇyaṃ tava rakṣaṇenarṇābhāvo yasmiṃs tena manasā*). Cm glosses, "with a mind whose freedom from debt is anticipated *or* foreseen (*prekṣitānṛṇyena cetasā*)." Translators vary in their renditions. Dutt (1893, p. 1469) simply renders, "with my whole soul." This interpretation appears also to have been followed by Roussel (1903, vol. 3, p. 348 ["*de tout coeur*"]) and Shastri (1959, vol. 3, p. 305 ["implicitly with all my heart"]). Gita Press (1969, vol. 3, p. 1805) understands, "which feels relieved of all obligations," while Raghunathan (1982, vol. 3, p. 305) offers, "desiring as I do only to do my duty." Pagani (1999, p. 1155) translates, "*avec loyauté*." On the debts with which everyone is born, see *ŚatBr* 1.7.2.1 and *ManuSm* 4.257.

26. "Then . . . pleased" *tatas tuṣṭaḥ*: V2,3,D9–11, and the texts and printed editions of Ct read instead *rathasthasya*, "of [to] him [the charioteer] standing in the chariot."

"ring" *hastābharaṇam*: Literally, "hand ornament." The exact nature of the ornament is not clear. We, along with Roussel (1903, vol. 3, p. 348), Shastri (1959, vol. 3, p. 305), and Pagani (1999, p. 1155), assume that it is a ring. Other translators simply render literally.

27. The meter is *vaṃśasthavila*.

Following *sarga* 93, D5–7,9–11,S insert a passage of sixty-four lines (App. I, No. 65), constituting a separate *sarga* (6.6.105—NSP, GPP, and Gita Press; 6.107—KK and VSP). All translators of the southern recension render this popular passage, which is commonly referred to as the *Ādityahṛdaya*. The passage is regarded as a significant hymn and is incorporated as an integral part of the *Rāmāyaṇa*. Many of the southern commentators consider the piece to be virtually a vedic hymn, assigning to it, in the manner of the *vaidikas*, a principal divinity (either Brahmā [Ct and Ck] or Rāma in the form of the sun [Cr]); a *ṛṣi*, Agastya; a vedic meter, *anuṣṭubh*; and an application (*viniyoga*) that includes the elimination of all obstacles, the acquisition of knowledge of the absolute, and the accomplishment of universal victory. These commentators also suggest that the piece, like the *vedas* themselves, has ancillary texts, variously described as homage to the radiant sun or to *Gayatrī* (cf. note to 6.1.1). In fact, some of the commentators, notably Ck, Ct, Cr, and Cm, invest the text with an almost upaniṣadic quality so that it seems, at times, that they regard its principal divinity merely as the sun, at other times as Lord Viṣṇu, sometimes as Rāma, and at still other times as the upaniṣadic Brahman.

Cg, alone among the commentators who accept this passage, seems less impressed with it. His comments are generally straightforward and avoid the esoteric etymologies and upaniṣadic exegeses of some of his colleagues. In fact, he expresses some disquiet at the way in which the hymn seems at times to exalt Sūrya, a relatively minor divinity in post-vedic India, above even Nārāyaṇa, the central focus of Vaiṣṇava devotion. He makes some effort to rationalize these two tendencies in a set of general comments on the *sarga*'s final verse but indicates that he is also somewhat skeptical regarding the textual authenticity of the piece. He notes that Uḍāli (Cv), whose commentary we believe to be the oldest extant one, does not comment on this *sarga*. Moreover, Cg notes that Uḍāli enumerates 130 *sargas* in the *Yuddhakāṇḍa* and that, if the *Ādityahṛdaya* chapter were to be included, it would raise the total (in Cg's text) to 131. It should be noted, however, that our transcript of Cv's commentary, which includes this passage, numbers it as *sarga* 107 and enumerates the total number of *sargas* in the *kāṇḍa* as 131.

Some of the commentators understand that Agastya has come to bolster the confidence of Rāma, who is anxious about his ability to kill Rāvaṇa (so Cv and Cm). Ct believes that Rāma (as an omnipotent divinity) merely pretends to be afraid, since he wishes to receive the *Ādityahṛdaya* from Agastya for the benefit of the world. Cg understands that Rāma is concerned about how he is to defeat Rāvaṇa without revealing his nature as the supreme divinity.

The passage consists largely of a *stotra*, or hymn of praise, to Āditya, or Sūrya, and, as such, contains numerous names, kennings, and epithets for this celestial deity. Commentators exercise their ingenuity and demonstrate their devotion by providing many multiple interpretations of these names and terms, often giving both the standard mythological reference as well as a more esoteric "functionalist" interpretation based on the etymology of the name. These secondary interpretations tend to refer to the role of the divinity in the creation and maintenance of the world, the dispelling of ignorance and the pains of worldly existence, the salvation of devotees, etc. For the sake of brevity, we have refrained from providing detailed discussions of these interpretive strategies. Readers should be aware, however, that several of the translators consulted tend to interpolate these multiple interpretations of the commentators into their translations.

"Then the blessed Agastya, who, together with the gods, had come to witness the battle, seeing that Rāma was exhausted by combat and overcome with anxiety with regard to the battle and that Rāvaṇa[1] was positioned in the vanguard for further combat, approached Rāma and said [1–4]: 'Rāma, great-armed Rāma,[2] now hear this immemorial secret teaching by means of which, my child, you shall conquer all your enemies.[5–6] One should constantly intone[3] this holy *Ādityahṛdaya*,[4] which destroys all of one's enemies and brings victory. It is eternal, indestructible, supreme, and auspicious.[7–8] It is the auspiciousness of all auspicious things, and it destroys all sins. It calms anxiety and grief, and it is the greatest means for the extension of life.[9–10] So worship Vivasvān, bringer of light,[5] the lord of the worlds, rising with his halo of rays, worshiped by the gods and *asuras*.[11–12] He is the essence of all the gods. Filled with blazing energy, he brings all beings to life with his rays.[6] With his rays he protects the gods, the *asuras*, and all the worlds.[13–14] He is Brahmā,[7] Viṣṇu, Śiva, Skanda, and Prajāpati. He is great Indra, Kubera, the bestower of wealth, Kāla, Yama, Soma, and Varuṇa, lord of the waters.[8][15–16] He is the ancestors, the Vasus, the Sādhyas, the two Aśvins, the Maruts, and Manu. He is Vāyu and Agni. He is all creatures, the breath of life,[9] and the sun, bringer of light and author of the seasons.[10][17–18] He is Āditya, Savitṛ, Sūrya, he who moves through the sky, Pūṣan, and the many-rayed sun. He is the being as radiant as gold, he is the golden seed, the maker of day.[11][19–20] He is the thousand-rayed lord of the tawny steeds, the master of seven horses, and he has myriad rays. He is the dispeller of darkness and he is Śambhu, the auspicious one.[12] He is Tvaṣṭṛ and Mārtaṇḍa of many rays.[21–22] He is Hiraṇyagarbha, the golden embryo, the cooling one, the scorching one, Ravi, and the bringer of light.[13] The son of Aditi, he bears Agni in his womb. He is Śaṅkha.[14] He brings the winter to a close.[23–24] He is the lord of the heavens, the piercer of darkness, and the master of the *Ṛk-*, *Yajur-*, and *Sāmavedas*. Friend of the waters, he is the source of torrential rains. He flies across the path of the Vindhya mountains.[15][25–26] He is the scorching one, the great orb. He is death, the golden one who scorches all beings. A sage, omnipresent, of immense blazing energy, reddish in hue,[16] he is the source of all existence.[27–28] He is lord of the constellations, planets, and stars. He is the giver of life to all, most radiant of all radiant beings. I do homage to you, you of the twelve forms.[17][29–30] Homage to him who rises on the eastern mountain and who sets on the western mountain.[18] Homage to the lord of the hosts of heavenly luminaries. Homage to the lord of day.[31–32] Homage, homage[19] to the victorious one, to him of the tawny horses,[20] who offers victory[21] and auspiciousness. Homage, homage to him of the thousand rays. Homage, homage to Āditya.[33–34] Homage to the fierce warrior. Homage, homage to the swift one.[22] Homage to him who makes the lotus bloom. Homage, homage to Martāṇḍa.[35–36] Homage to radiant Sūrya, who is the lord of Brahmā, Lord Śiva, and the imperishable Viṣṇu,[23] whose radiance is that of Āditya and who, in his fierce form, devours all creatures.[37–38] Homage to the banisher of darkness and the bringer of the thaw,[24] to that immeasurable god who slaughters his enemies and destroys the ungrateful, the lord of heavenly luminaries.[39–40] Homage to Viśvakarman, the maker of all things,[25] to Agni,[26] whose luster is that of burnished gold. Homage to Ravi, the eye of all the worlds,[27] dispeller of darkness.[41–42] He is the lord who destroys the creation and then creates it anew. With his rays, he dries up, scorches, and inundates the world.[28][43–44] Lodged within all beings, he[29] remains awake while they sleep. He is the *agnihotra* sacrifice as well as the reward of those who perform it.[30][45–46] He is all the *vedas*,[31] all sacrifices, and the reward of all sacrifices. He, Lord Ravi, is everything.[32] He is all actions that are done throughout the worlds.[47–48] Even if a man be in distress, difficulty, or danger, or if he be lost in the wilderness,[33] he shall not, Rāghava, so long as he praises the sun,[34] succumb to any harm.[49–50] Therefore, with a focused mind, you should worship that god of gods, the lord of the worlds. For, having intoned this hymn[35] three times,[36] you will be victorious[37] in all your battles.[51–52] This very hour, great-armed warrior,[38] you shall slay[39] Rāvaṇa.' Then, when he had spoken in this fashion, Agastya departed just as he had come.[53–54] When immensely powerful Rāghava had heard that, he became free from care.[40.] Concentrating his mind and greatly pleased, he memorized it.[55–56] Gazing at Āditya and intoning that hymn,[41] he attained supreme happiness. Sipping water three times and having thus become purified, the mighty warrior[42] took up his bow and, his eyes fixed on Rāvaṇa,[43] went forth to battle[44] with a delighted heart.[57–59] Exerting himself to the utmost,[45] he was determined[46] to kill him.[60] Then Ravi himself, surrounded by the hosts of gods, anticipating with a delighted mind the destruction of the lord of the night-roaming *rākṣasas*, gazed upon Rāma and, in great excitement, said, 'Make haste.'[47][61–64]"

[1]"seeing that Rāma was exhausted by combat and overcome with anxiety with regard to the battle and that Rāvaṇa..." *yuddhapariśrāntaṃ samare cintayā sthitam / rāvaṇam ... dṛṣṭvā*: The commentators and translators are divided as to whether Rāma or Rāvaṇa is represented in line 1 as suffering from battle fatigue and anxiety. Although Rāma is not mentioned in any of the first three lines as an explicit object of the gerund *dṛṣṭvā*, "having seen," Ct believes that the referent is Rāma, who, as noted above, he believes to be feigning these disabilities as part of his avatāric plan. Cg similarly understands the reference to be to Rāma, although, as indicated above, for

slightly different reasons. Given the tenor of Agastya's remarks in which he appears to be bolstering Rāma's fortitude, we are inclined to agree with these commentators. Cv, Cm, and Cr, however, understand that the reference is to Rāvaṇa alone since he is exhausted and despondent from his having been worsted in the previous encounter. This view is reflected in the translations of Dutt (1893, p. 1469) and Pagani (1999, p. 1155). The remaining translators understand with Ct and Cg that the reference is to Rāma. See note 40 below.

[2]"Rāma ... Rāma" *rāma rāma*: Cg believes that Agastya's repetition of Rāma's name is caused by three factors: 1) Rāma's being deeply absorbed in anxious thought; 2) Agastya's exceedingly profound respect for Rāma; and 3) Agastya's urgency to carry out his mission (*rāmasya cintāviṣṭatvāt svādarātiśayāt kāryatvarayā*).

[3]"One should ... intone" *japet*: D7,10,11, and the texts and printed editions of Ct and Cm read instead *japam*, "recitation *or* prayer."

[4]"this ... *Ādityahṛdaya*" *ādityahṛdayam*: Literally, "the heart of the sun." In keeping with its quasi-vedic and esoteric nature, the commentators offer a variety of explanations of the name.

[5]"Vivasvān, bringer of light" *vivasvantaṃ bhāskaram*: Literally, "Vivasvān, maker of light." Cr, in keeping with his own theological reading of the *Rāmāyaṇa*, understands that references throughout this passage are both to the sun and to Rāma, who dwells within the sun, since they are both of the same essence (*sūryatadantarvartirāmayos tādātmyāt*).

[6]"he brings all beings to life with his rays" *raśmibhāvanaḥ*: Literally, "causing to exist with rays." According to Ct, Cm, and Ck, the sense here is that the sun brings into being all things through his rays of knowledge (*jñānaraśmibhiḥ sarvaṃ vastujātaṃ bhāvayati sattāsphūrtimat saṃpādayati saḥ*—so Ct). Ct attributes an alternative interpretation to unnamed others, who evidently associate the verb *bhāvayati* with the related term *bhāvanā*, "meditation." He says, "according to others, the meaning is that with his rays he causes *yogins* to meditate, that is, he causes them to attain the world of Brahmā (*raśmibhir yogino bhāvayati brahmalokaṃ prāpayatīty artha ity anye*)."

[7]"Brahmā" *brahmā*: Ct offers dual explanations of each of the names in the verse, referring, in each case, both to the normal mythological figure and also to some etymologically derived feature of the Supreme Being. Cg is chiefly concerned with differentiating those pairs of divinities that seem to be identical. Thus, he distinguishes Prajāpati from Brahmā by stating that the former name is a collective singular here for the nine Prajāpatis of traditional mythology. Similarly, he distinguishes between the normally synonymous Kāla (Time) and Yama by stating that the former term refers specifically to death personified, who is different from Yama, the lord of death. See notes to 6.21.26 and 6.55.93–96.

[8]"Kubera, the bestower of wealth ... and Varuṇa, lord of the waters" *dhanadaḥ ... apāṃpatiḥ*: Literally, "the wealth-giver, the lord of the waters." The latter reference is presumably to Varuṇa, who in post-vedic mythology is normally regarded as the lord of the ocean. On Kubera, see 6.4.16; 6.7.3; 6.22.10; 6.69.26; 6.82.20; 6.92.15; 6.98.12–13; 6.110.23; 6.115.24,49; and notes.

[9]"the Maruts ... He is Vāyu and Agni. He is all creatures, the breath of life" *marutaḥ ... vāyur vahniḥ prajāḥ prāṇaḥ*: Literally, "[He is] the Maruts, Vāyu, fire, creatures, breath." Cg is at pains to differentiate the three terms that refer to air or wind, viz., *marutaḥ*, *vāyuḥ*, and *prāṇaḥ*. He states that the first refers to the seven

atmospheric winds of Hindu cosmology, such as the *āvaha* wind; the second, to the wind that blows on earth; and the third, to the wind *or* breaths located within the body. (*marutaḥ āvahādivāyavaḥ. vāyur bhūlokasaṃcārī. prāṇaḥ śarīrāntaḥstho vāyuḥ.*) See notes to 6.64.7. D7,11,M3, and the texts and printed editions of Cm (= VSP, KK 6.107.9) read the compound *prajāprāṇaḥ*, "life breath of living creatures," for the critical edition's *prajāḥ prāṇaḥ*, "creatures, breath of life."

[10]"and the sun, bringer of light and author of the seasons" *ṛtukartā prabhākaraḥ*: Literally, "maker of seasons, maker of light." We agree with Cg in taking *ṛtukartā* as a modifier of *prabhākaraḥ* (*ṛtukarteti prabhākaraviśeṣaṇam*). Some translators see two distinct entities, while one, Roussel (1903, vol. 3, p. 349), sees three, whom he names "Ṛtu, Kartar, and Prabhākara."

[11]"He is . . . Savitṛ . . . he who moves through the sky . . . and the many-rayed sun. He is the being as radiant as gold, he is the golden seed, the maker of day." *savitā . . . khagaḥ . . . gabhastimān / suvarṇasadṛśo bhānuḥ svarṇaretā divākaraḥ //*: Literally, "Savitṛ, the sky-goer, the rayed-one, like gold, radiant, having golden seed, the day-maker."

[12]"he is Śambhu, the auspicious one" *śambhuḥ*: Literally, "Śambhu." The epithet is most commonly associated with the god Śiva.

[13]"the bringer of light" *bhāskaraḥ*: D10,11, and the texts and printed editions of Ct and Ck read instead, "[*a*]*haskaraḥ*, "maker *or* bringer of day."

[14]"He is Śaṅkha" *śaṅkhaḥ*: Unlike most of the names and epithets in this passage, the term *śaṅkhaḥ*, which most commonly means "conch shell," has no lexically grounded or commonly accepted usage as an epithet for a deity. The commentators break up the term in a variety of ways in an effort to turn it into an intelligible epithet. Thus, for example, Ck and Ct read the term as a kind of *dvandva* compound consisting of *śam*, "supreme bliss," and *kham*, "the sky." (*śaṃ ca khaṃ ca śaṅkhaḥ. paramānandagaganātmety arthaḥ.*) Cm expands upon this etymology by taking *kham* to refer to the space within the heart, understanding the meaning to be "he who possesses unending bliss in the space within the heart" (*śaṅkhaḥ śaṃ sukhaṃ kha ākāśe hṛdayākāśe yasya sa śaṅkho niravadhikānandavān ity arthaḥ*). Cg understands the term to refer to the fact that the sun extinguishes itself in the evening (*śāmyati svayam eva sāyaṃkāla iti śaṅkhaḥ*).

[15]"He flies across the path of the Vindhya mountains." *vindhyavīthīplavaṃgamaḥ*: Literally, "leaping or flying along the *vindhya* path." Commentators differ as to the interpretation of this somewhat obscure reference. We tend to follow the interpretation of Cg, who takes the epithet as a reference to the southern passage of the sun during the winter season, which brings it across this southernmost mountain range of the *madhyadeśa*. This interpretation is explicitly followed in the translation of Raghunathan (1982, vol. 3, p. 306). Cr takes the term *plavaṃgama* in its sense of "leaping monkey," and understands that the sun is the master of the monkeys of the Vindhya region. Pagani (1999, p. 1156), who translates as we do, nonetheless notes that the choice of the term *plavaṃgama* recalls that the sun is the father of the monkey king Sugrīva (p. 1673). Ct, Ck, and Cm (as an alternative) understand *vindhyavīthī* to be a term for the *suṣumnā nāḍī*, or subtle yogic channel of the body.

[16]"the golden one . . . reddish in hue" *piṅgalaḥ . . . raktaḥ*: Literally, "yellow . . . red." We take both terms in the sense of the colors that presumably reflect the appearance of the sun at its rising and setting, respectively. The commentators acknowledge these

meanings but offer additional esoteric senses. Several, including Cg, derive the meaning of the latter term from one sense of its verbal root √*rañj*, "to please," with the idea that the sun pleases or delights all creatures.

[17]"I do homage to you, you of the twelve forms." *dvādaśātman namo 'stu te*: The commentators generally see this as a reference to the sun's passage through the twelve months or the twelve *nakṣatras*, or lunar mansions. Some commentators, such as Cr, add the explanation that the sun is the governor of the twelve Ādityas, or vedic solar divinities. Cg offers only this latter interpretation, listing the Ādityas by name. The epithet in the vocative and the enclitic pronoun *te*, "to you," mark a shift in the passage at which reference to Āditya shifts from the third to the second person. This shift is seen again in the variant of line 36 found in D7 and the texts and printed editions of Ct (= GPP 6.105.18cd). Several of the translators make a shift at earlier points in the passage. However, at line 43 (= GPP 6.105.22), the passage clearly reverts back to the third person. See note 29 below.

[18]"Homage to him who rises on the eastern mountain and who sets on the western mountain." *namaḥ pūrvāya giraye paścime giraye namaḥ*: Literally, "Homage to the eastern mountain, homage to the western mountain." Our translation follows the interpretation of Cg, who understands the references, by a kind of *lakṣaṇā*, to be to the sun, who is situated on the respective mountains at his time of rising and setting (*pūrvāya giraye pūrvabhāgasthagiryupalakṣitāya paścime giraye paścimabhāgasthaparvatopalakṣitāya*). Among the translators consulted, only Raghunathan (1982, vol. 3, p. 307) follows this interpretation. Others render literally. Cg makes no comment on the seemingly irregular dative form *paścime* for the expected *paścimāya*. D7,10,11,T3,M1, and the texts and printed editions of Ct, Ck, and Cr correct the locution, as it were, substituting *paścimāyādraye*, "to the western mountain."

[19]"Homage, homage" *namo namaḥ*: All the commentators agree that the repetition is expressive of a high degree of reverence.

[20]"to him of the tawny horses" *haryaśvāya*: We follow Cg in taking this epithet, normally used of Indra, to refer to the sun's tawny steeds (*śyāmāśvāya*). Interestingly, both Cm and Cr see the reference here to be to Rāma, who has a tawny monkey (*hariḥ*), whom Cm identifies explicitly as Hanumān, as his mount. (*harir hanumān aśvo vāhanaṃ yasya saḥ. anena rāmāvatāraḥ sūcitaḥ*—so Cm.) See 6.78.27; 6.90.5–7; 6.95.15; 6.116.24; and notes.

[21]"to the victorious one . . . who offers victory" *jayāya jayabhadrāya*: Our interpretation of these two terms, like that of Raghunathan (1982, vol. 3, p. 307), follows that of Cg. Cg's second interpretation of the first term, which we have explicitly followed, is that the term *jaya* stands for the one who is victorious (*jayatīti jayo jayī*). According to his first interpretation, the term means "he who offers victory to his worshipers (*upāsakānāṃ jayakarāya*)." Cm's interpretation is similar to this latter one of Cg. Ct and Ck understand the term to mean both "he who grants victory all the way to the Brahmaloka," as well as the name of a celestial gatekeeper of Brahmā (*brahmalokāntasakalajayapradāya jayākhyabrahmadvārapālamūrtaye ca*). Cg glosses the second term as "he who provides both victory and auspiciousness (*jayabhadrayoḥ pradātre*)." Cm suggests, "he who extends auspiciousness and the conquest of disease and sin on the part of his worshipers (*upāsakānāṃ rogapāpādijayaṃ bhadraṃ kalyānāṃ ca prayacchatīti jayabhadraḥ*). Ck and Ct, as their second interpretation, suggest that Jayabhadra is the name of a second gatekeeper of Brahmā. According to them, Jaya and Jayabhadra were forced

by a curse to take lower births in the forms of Rāvaṇa and Kumbhakarṇa, respectively (*jayabhadrākhyadvitīyadvārapālamūrtaye ca . . . imāv eva śāpavaśato 'vatīrṇau rāvaṇakumbhakarṇau*).

[22]"to the swift one" *sāraṅgāya*: The term is highly polysemic, having at least thirty meanings, referring to various animals, plants, deities, instruments, etc. Its basic meaning seems to be "spotted *or* variegated." Commentators vary considerably in their understanding of the term. We follow Cg and the first interpretation of Cm, who, more out of consistency than conviction, take the reference to be to the movement of the sun. Cg bases his interpretation on the purāṇic statement that the sun traverses the distance of two thousand *yojanas* in the space of a half second. (*sāraṃ śīghraṃ gacchatīti sāraṅgas tasmai. ekena nimiṣārdhena dvisahasrayojanaṃ gacchatīti purāṇaprasiddhiḥ.*) This interpretation is also followed by Raghunathan (1982, vol. 3, p. 307). Ct and Cm (fourth alternative) take the term to refer to him who is to be realized by means of the sacred syllable *om* (*sāraṃ praṇavas tatpratipādyāya*—so Ct). This interpretation is followed by Gita Press (1969, vol. 3, p. 1808), Shastri (1959, vol. 3, p. 307), and, in a footnote, Dutt (1893, p. 1472). Pagani (1999, p. 1156), alone among the translators, renders the term literally as "*moucheté*."

[23]"who is the lord of Brahmā, Lord Śiva, and the imperishable Viṣṇu" *brahmeśānācyuteśāya*: Literally, "to the lord of Brahmā, Īśāna, and Acyuta." Commentators agree that, by the mention of the names of the divinities of the *trimūrti*, their stereotypical functions, viz., creation, destruction, and preservation, respectively, are intended.

[24]"the bringer of the thaw" *himaghnāya*: Literally, "the destroyer of the snow."

[25]"to Viśvakarman, the maker of all things" *viśvakarmaṇe*: Literally, "to Viśvakarman."

[26]"to Agni" *vahnaye*: Literally, "to fire (*vahni*)." D9–11 and the texts and printed editions of Ck, Ct, and Cm (as an alternative) read instead *haraye*, "to Hari." Normally, this is an epithet of Viṣṇu, but it also applies to other deities, here, of course, specifically of the sun.

[27]"the eye of all the worlds" *lokasākṣiṇe*: Literally, "to the witness of the worlds."

[28]"and then creates it anew . . . he dries up, scorches, and inundates the world" *sṛjate punaḥ / pāyaty eṣa tapaty eṣa varṣaty eṣa*: Literally, "he creates again . . . he desiccates (lit., causes to drink up), burns, and showers." The reference here is to the common vedic observation that the sun draws up the waters with his rays and returns them in the form of rain. D9–11,M1,3, and the texts and printed editions of the southern commentators read *sṛjati prabhuḥ*, "the lord creates," for *sṛjate punaḥ*, "he creates again."

[29]"he" *eṣaḥ*: Note that the narrative has switched back to the third person. See note 17 above. According to Cg, the previous verse marks the end of the teaching of the *Ādityahṛdaya* per se, but Agastya continues here to praise the divinity who is addressed in that hymn (*evam ādityahṛdayam upadiśya punar api tatpratipādyadevatāṃ stauti*).

[30]"He is the *agnihotra* sacrifice as well as the reward of those who perform it." *eṣa caivāgnihotraṃ ca phalaṃ caivāgnihotriṇām*: Literally, "He is the *agnihotra* and the fruit of the *agnihotrins*." The *agnihotra* is an oblation to *agni* consisting of milk, oil (ghee), and sour gruel. Ct, who also offers an esoteric meaning of this phrase, notes that the reward of the sacrificers consists of the attainment of heaven and that the sense is that Āditya provides it (*svargāpavargarūpaṃ phalaṃ tat pradaś ca*).

[31]"He is all the *vedas*" *vedāś ca*: Literally, "and the *vedas*." D9–11,M1–3, and the texts and printed editions of Ck and Ct read instead *devāś ca*, "[He is all] the gods as well."

[32]"He, Lord Ravi, is everything." *sarva eṣa raviḥ prabhuḥ*: D10,11, and the texts and printed editions of Ck and Ct read instead *sarveṣu paramaprabhuḥ* [D10—*paramaḥ prabhuḥ*], "He is the Supreme Lord in all [worlds]."

[33]"lost in the wilderness" *kāntāreṣu*: Literally, "in the forests."

[34]"so long as he praises the sun" *enam . . . kīrtayan*: Literally, "praising him." The idea, of course, is that one should recite the *Ādityahṛdaya* in times of trouble.

[35]"this hymn" *etat*: Literally, "this."

[36]"three times" *triguṇitam*: We agree with Ck, Ct, and Cr, who understand the term adverbially to mean "thrice" (*saṃjātatriguṇaṃ yathā tathā japtvā*—so Ck and Ct; *trivāram*—so Cr). Dutt (1893, p. 1473), Roussel (1903, vol. 3, p. 350), and Pagani (1999, p. 1157) all take the term adjectivally to indicate that the hymn is replete with the three *guṇas*, or "virtues." We find this interpretation unpersuasive. See note 41 below.

[37]"you will be victorious" *vijayiṣyasi*: D5–7,9–11,G1, and the texts and printed editions of Ct read instead the third person singular *vijayiṣyati*, "he will be victorious."

[38]"great-armed warrior" *mahābāho*: Literally, "O great-armed one."

[39]"you shall slay" *vadhiṣyasi*: D7 and the texts and printed editions of Cr read instead *jayiṣyasi*, "you shall conquer." Dutt (1893, p. 1473), Roussel (1903, vol. 3, p. 350), Shastri (1959, vol. 3, p. 307), and Pagani (1999, p. 1157) all appear to translate this variant, despite the fact that D10,11, and the texts and printed editions of Ct read the variant *jahiṣyasi*, "you shall abandon." However, Cr, who reads the variant *jayiṣyasi*, glosses, *haniṣyasi*, "you shall kill."

[40]"free from care" *naṣṭaśokaḥ*: Literally, "whose grief was destroyed." According to Ct and Ck, Rāma's grief consists of his anxiety with regard to Rāvaṇa (*naṣṭo rāvaṇaviṣayacintārūpaśoko yasya saḥ*). For these two commentators, the reference would be to what they see as Rāma's anxiety or feigned anxiety in line 1. See note 1 above.

[41]"and intoning that hymn" *japtvā tu*: Literally, "but having intoned *or* muttered." D10,11, and the texts and printed editions of Ct read instead *japtvedam*, "having intoned this." D7,G2, and the text of Cr read instead *japtvā triḥ*, "having intoned thrice." See note 36 above.

[42]"the mighty warrior" *vīryavān*: Literally, "the mighty one."

[43]"his eyes fixed on Rāvaṇa" *rāvaṇaṃ prekṣya*: Literally, "having seen Rāvaṇa."

[44]"forth to battle" *yuddhāya*: D10,11, and the texts and printed editions of Ck and Ct read instead *jayārtham*, "for the sake of victory."

[45]"Exerting himself to the utmost" *sarvayatnena mahatā*: Literally, "with great and total effort."

[46]"determined" *dhṛtaḥ*: D9–11 and the texts and printed edition of Ct read instead *vṛtaḥ*. This is apparently translated only by Gita Press (1969, vol. 3, p. 1809), which renders, "He stood vowed to kill."

[47]The meter of the last four lines is *puṣpitāgrā*.

Sarga 94

Before verse 1, D5–7,9–11,S insert a passage of seven lines [3031*]: "Then, in great excitement, Rāvaṇa's charioteer drove Rāvaṇa's chariot swiftly forward. It was a crusher of hostile armies, and, with its lofty banners, it looked like the heavenly city of the *gandharvas*.[1] It was yoked to the finest horses,[2] which were harnessed with trappings of gold. It was filled with instruments of war and garlanded with flags and banners. It brought destruction to the forces of one's enemy and delight to one's own. As the charioteer drove that chariot onward,[3] it made the earth rumble, and it seemed to swallow up the sky.[1–7]"

[1]"the heavenly city of the *gandharvas*" *gandharvanagara-*: Literally, "the city of the *gandharvas*." Several of the commentators note that the comparison is based on the wonderful appearance of the chariot. Cg quotes [Varāha]mihira, who describes the wonders of the celestial city of the *gandharvas*.

[2]"to the finest horses" *paramasampannair vājibhiḥ*: Literally, "with horses endowed with excellence." The compound seems elliptical and the commentators attempt to remedy this by explaining that the horses are endowed with all the best qualities of chariot-horses, such as speed, and so on (*paramai rathavahanocitāśvaguṇair javādibhiḥ saṃpannaiḥ*—so Ct and Ck; Cr similarly).

[3]"Rāvaṇa's charioteer drove Rāvaṇa's chariot... the charioteer drove that chariot onward" *sa rathaṃ sārathiḥ... rāvaṇasya ratham... codayāmāsa sārathiḥ*: Literally, "the charioteer, the chariot... the charioteer urged on Rāvaṇa's chariot." The seven lines (three and one-half *ślokas*) constitute a single sentence in the original. For this reason, the repetition of the words *ratha*, "chariot," and *sārathi*, "charioteer," in lines 1 and 7 has attracted the attention of the commentators. Ct, Cm, and Cg excuse the redundancy on the grounds that so many adjectives (modifying the chariot) intervene between the statement of the subject and object in line 1 and the verb in line 7 that the author has had to repeat the two lines for the sake of recalling the subject and object (*dvitīyarathasārathiśabdāv anekaviśeṣaṇavyavadhānāt pūrvoktāvismaraṇāya tadanuvādakāv eva*—so Ct). Cs, however, understands that the first set of terms refers to Mātali and Indra's chariot, whereas the second refers to Rāvaṇa's charioteer and chariot. In his opinion, the latter drives Rāvaṇa's chariot toward Rāma's. He understands that if one construes the syntax in this fashion, the efforts [of other commentators] to find a rationale for the repetition of the two words are fruitless (*sārathir mātalir yaṃ rathaṃ codayāmāsa taṃ prati rāvaṇasya sārathī rathaṃ pracodāyāmāsety anvayenānayo rathasārathiśabdayoḥ punaruktatābhītyānuvādatāṅgīkaraṇaprayāsa ubhayor aphalaḥ*).

1–2. "with its great flagstaffs" *mahādhvajam*: M3 and the texts and printed editions of Cg read the redundant *mahāsvanam*, "with a loud noise."

"it displayed weapons that were like the weapons of Indra himself" *darśitendrāyudhāyudham*: Literally, "by which Indra-weapon[like] weapons were displayed." G1,M1, and the texts and printed editions of Ck and Ct (unnoted in the critical apparatus) read *āyudhaprabham* for *āyudhāyudham*. The compound would then mean "displaying a radiance like that of Indra's weapons." Cg, who shares the critical reading, offers several additional interpretations. His first is the same as ours. His second is "in which appeared weapons that were like the bows of Indra [rainbows] by virtue of their own extraordinary radiance (*svaprabhāviśeṣaviracitendracāpāny āyudhāni yasmin dṛśyante tādṛśam*)." Cv understands similarly. Cg's third, and final, interpretation, taking *āyudha* in the sense of "bow," is "displaying a bow that was equal to the bow of Indra (*yadvāyudhaṃ dhanur darśitendradhanustulyadhanuṣkam*)."

Following 2ab, Ś2,Ñ,V2,3,B,D1–4,7–13,G1,2, the texts and printed editions of Ck, Ct, and Cr, and the printed editions of KK (in brackets) insert a passage of one line [3032*]: "[the chariot... It glowed with a fearsome radiance.] It seemed like a flying palace being drawn[1] through the sky by water-laden storm clouds."

[1]"being drawn" *uhyamānam*: D9–12 and the texts and printed editions of Ct read instead *dīpyamānam*, "blazing brightly."

3. "of thousand-eyed Indra" *sahasrākṣasya*: Literally, "of the thousand-eyed one."

Following 3cd, V2,3,B3,D5–7,10,11,S insert a passage of one line [3034*]: "who was swiftly twanging his bow, which was bent like the crescent moon." The critical reading of this line seems contextually inapposite, as the accusative of the participle *visphārayantam*, "twanging," forces us to understand that it is Mātali who is engaged in this activity. D6,10,11,T2,3,M, and the texts and printed editions of the southern commentators read instead *visphārayan vai*, in which case the agent of the action is Rāma, which seems far better contextually, if not textually. Ñ1 and B2 insert this line following 4ab, where it makes better sense contextually.

4. "on our right flank... to kill me" *yathāpasavyam ... hantum ātmānam*: Literally, "to the right... to kill [one *or* my]self." The term *apasavyam*, literally, "not left," is somewhat ambiguous as it can mean both "from *or* on the right" and "in a contrary manner." Here, as at 6.45.33, the commentators take the term in two opposite senses. The issue has to do with whether a movement is auspicious or inauspicious for the person undertaking it. Under normal circumstances, an auspicious movement is one that keeps the object toward or around which one is moving on one's right (*pradakṣiṇa*). Moving toward or around something that is on one's left (*apradakṣiṇa*) is normally considered inauspicious. In the present passage, the interpretation depends on how one understands Rāma's reading of Rāvaṇa's movements. We believe that, in this context, the best interpretation is that of Ck and Ct, who take the term in its normal sense of "to the right." The idea is that Rāvaṇa, in keeping Rāma on his right, is proceeding in what he believes to be an auspicious manner and is thus hoping to achieve his goal of killing him. (*apasavyaṃ pradakṣiṇam ... anena rāvaṇena ... ātmānaṃ māṃ hantuṃ matiḥ kṛtā. prathamaprādakṣiṇyena rathasaṃcāralakṣaṇasunimittasaṃpādaneneti śeṣaḥ.*) Cg and Cr, on the other hand, understand *apasavya* to mean *apradakṣiṇa*, or "[a movement] to the left *or* counterclockwise." Cg argues that the sequence *yathāpasavyam* should be broken up to read *yathā* + *ā* + *apasavyam*, that is, "in such a way as to be counter [*ā*] clockwise." Cg then understands that, in proceeding in this fashion, Rāvaṇa is suicidal and therefore determined to kill himself (*ātmānam*) rather than Rāma. Cg further notes that proceeding from the left is a sign of impending destruction (*apasavyatayā gamanaṃ vināśadyotakam ity arthaḥ*). Cr introduces a theological note in an effort to represent both interpretations. He argues that Rāvaṇa is proceeding with an intention to kill the Self (*ātmānam*), that is, the Supreme Spirit (*paramātmānam*), in other words, Rāma. Moreover, Cr continues, in so acting, Rāvaṇa is determined in effect to bring about his own destruction (*apasavyam apradakṣiṇam ... anena rāvaṇenātmānaṃ paramātmānam api ... hantuṃ matiḥ kṛtā kiñcātmānaṃ svam eva*

samare hantuṃ matiḥ kṛtā). Cf. 6.45.33; 6.53.42; and notes. See notes to verses 9 and 15 below.

5. "remain vigilant" *apramādam ātiṣṭha*: Literally, "stand in such a way as not to be negligent." Cg understands that Mātali is to remain vigilant in regard to keeping Rāvaṇa's chariot on his right, since to approach from the left (as Cg believes Rāvaṇa is doing) is to invite disaster. (*tad apasavyagamanasya vināśahetutvād apramādam ātiṣṭhan* (v.l.) *sāvadhānatām avalambamānaḥ. apasavyatāṃ pariharann ity arthaḥ.*) Ct and Ck also understand that Rāma expects Mātali to approach Rāvaṇa from the right (*prādakṣiṇyena*).

6. "with a steady heart and eye" *avyagrahṛdayekṣaṇam*: Ct and Ck believe that Rāma is instructing Mātali to keep his mind and eyes focused on [his own] horses (*avyagram aśvīyahṛdayekṣaṇam*—so Ct).

7. "Indra, the smasher of citadels" *puraṃdara-*: Literally, "the smasher of citadels."

"I am merely reminding you" *smāraye tvām*: Literally, "I would cause you to remember." Ck and Ct understand that Rāma is reminding Mātali of his hereditary occupation as a charioteer (*sahajaṃ sārathyakarma*).

9. "Then, keeping... on his right" *apasavyaṃ tataḥ kurvan*: Literally, "making [the chariot] not left." The commentators, respectively, treat this term as they do at verse 4 above. Cg, in keeping with his earlier interpretation, understands that Mātali is trying to avoid placing his own chariot on [Rāvaṇa's] left, that is, in an inauspicious position or direction (*svarathasyāpasavyatāṃ pariharann ity arthaḥ*). This interpretation is rendered only by Raghunathan (1982, vol. 3, p. 309), who translates, "in a counterclockwise movement." See notes to verse 15 below.

"Mātali discomfited him" *rāvaṇaṃ vyavadhūnayat*: Literally, "he shook *or* agitated Rāvaṇa." Commentators who share the critical reading, including Cm, Ck, Ct, and Cr (who corrects to the expected *vyavādhūnayat*), take the verbal root $\sqrt{}$*dhū* in its basic sense of "to shake, agitate, disturb," glossing, "he shook (*akampayat*—Ct, Cr; *kampayati sma*—Ck; *cālayāmāsa*—Cm)." All the translations consulted that follow the text of Ct understand the verb to mean "to cover *or* envelop." D6,M3, and the texts and printed editions of Cg read *vyavadhānayat*, "he covered." Raghunathan (1982, vol. 3, p. 309), who reads with Cg, understandably renders, "hid." See note to verse 10 below, where the verb used is *avadhūnayat*.

"with the dust raised by his own wheels" *cakrotkṣiptena rajasā*: Literally, "with the dust stirred up by wheels."

10. "red and wide with rage" *tāmravisphāritekṣaṇaḥ*: Literally, "whose eyes are red and dilated." See notes to 6.19.22–23.

"assailed" *avadhūnayat*: Cr, as he did in the previous verse, corrects to the expected *avādhūnayat*. The verb is virtually identical to that used in the previous verse, where translators rendered it variously as "agitated *or* covered." Most translators understand as we do, with the exception of Dutt (1893, p. 1475), who translates, "covered," apparently in an effort to be consistent with his rendering of the previous verse. Cg, having read *avadhānayat* in verse 9, is under no pressure to be consistent and glosses, "he struck (*prāharat*)." See note to verse 9 above.

"who faced him in his chariot" *rathapratimukham*: We understand the compound, as do Ck and Ct, who gloss, "facing with his chariot (*rathena pratimukhaṃ sammukhaṃ rathapratimukham*—so Ct)." Some translators understand the term to mean that Rāma is facing Rāvaṇa's chariot. This interpretation is also plausible.

11. "endowed with great blazing energy" *sumahātejāḥ*: Ś2,Ñ1,B1,D1–4,6–11,13,T3,M2, and the texts and printed editions of Ct and Cr read instead *sumahāvegān*, "of tremendous speed *or* striking force." The variant adjective would refer to the arrows rather than Rāma.

"put patience aside" *dhairyaṃ* ... *laṅghayan*: Literally, "jumping over *or* transgressing patience *or* fortitude." Given the critical reading, one is obliged to take *dhairyam*, normally, "courage, fortitude, firmness," in its sense of "patience, passive endurance." The idea is that Rāma, in his fury at Rāvaṇa's attack, abandons his somewhat detached demeanor and throws himself into the battle. Among the translators consulted, only Gorresio (1858, vol. 10, p. 196) shares this reading, rendering, "*soverchiando* ... *la sua fermezza*." Ñ2,B3,D5,10,11,T1,G,M1,3,5, and the texts and printed editions of the southern commentators read *lambhayan*, "causing to obtain," for the critical edition's *laṅghayan*. Commentators and the translators who follow them understand the verb here in one of two ways. Ck(?) and Ct take the phrase to mean "acquiring courage for battle along with anger (*roṣeṇa saha dhairyaṃ yuddhārabhaṭīṃ lambhayan prāpnuvan*—so Ct)." Cr glosses "joining (*yojayan*)" for *lambhayan*, taking *pāda* b to mean "joining courage [with anger]."

"of Indra" *aindram*: Literally, "belonging to Indra." Ct and Cm offer an alternative explanation. Their interpretation is based on a frequently cited notion that the word "*indra*" is derived from a verbal root $\sqrt{}$*id* and that it can be understood in the sense of "supreme lordship." (Cf., for example, Sāyaṇa on *ṚV* 1.3.4 and Kṛṣṇamitra's commentary to *AmaK* 1.1.41.) The adjectival derivative *aindram* would thus mean "belonging to the supreme deity," that is, Rāma. In other words, they understand that Rāma takes up his own bow. (*kiṃcaindraṃ pārameśvaram idi pāramaiśvarya ity ukteḥ. nijāyudhaṃ jagrāhety arthaḥ*—so Ct.)

14. "Terrifying ... omens" *utpātā dāruṇā*: For similar passages listing inauspicious omens, see 6.26.21–30; 6.31.3–12; 6.41.30–34; 6.45.31–37; 6.53.41–45; 6.94.14–27; and notes. See, too, note to 6.4.6.

"They presaged destruction for Rāvaṇa and victory for Rāghava." *rāvaṇasya vināśāya rāghavasya jayāya ca*: Literally, "[they were] for the destruction of Rāvaṇa and for the victory of Rāghava." V3,D9–11, and the texts and printed editions of Ct read *rāghavasyodayāya*, "for the success *or* prosperity of Rāghava," for *rāghavasya jayāya*.

15. "It rained blood" *vavarṣa rudhiraṃ devaḥ*: Literally, "the god rained blood." The god in question, as Cg notes, is Parjanya, the vedic rain god, and some translators, including Raghunathan (1982, vol. 3, p. 309) and Gita Press (1969, vol. 3, p. 1811), add either the name Parjanya or "the god of rain." A Sanskrit idiom for "it is raining," is *devo varṣati*, and we have translated accordingly. Other translators attempt to cope with the phrase variously. Shastri (1959, vol. 3, p. 309) takes the subject to be "the Gods"; Roussel (1903, vol. 3, p. 353) uses, simply, "*Dieu*"; Dutt (1893, p. 1475) translates literally, "the god"; and Pagani (1999, p. 1158) similarly offers, "*la divinité*." Gorresio (1858, vol. 10, p. 197) avoids the problem by taking a rationalist stance and translating, "*una nube*." See 6.83.33 and note for the identical phrase. For blood raining down, see 6.26.22; 6.31.5; 6.41.33; 6.45.926*–36; 6.83.33; and notes. Cf. note to 6.76.2, 1674*, lines 5–7.

"to the left" *apasavyam*: This verse lends additional complexity to the discussion of the poet's use of the term, since, in this case, unlike those earlier in the *sarga*, the movement is unambiguously inauspicious. It seems as if Cg's earlier gloss, *apradakṣiṇam* (verse 4 above), which he repeats here, must be correct in this context. Ck and Ct, who earlier understood the term to mean *pradakṣiṇa*, evade the apparent trap by reading the ill-attested (D10,11, and the texts and printed editions of Ct and Ck) variant *vyapasavyam*, literally, "non-non-left." Ct and Ck explain that the term means "moving to the left or in such a way that it is opposite of right (*vyapasavyaṃ vigatam apasavyaṃ pradakṣiṇaṃ yathā tathā vāmāvartā ity arthaḥ*)." Although we appreciate Cg's consistency in handling the term throughout the *sarga*, we believe that its inherent ambiguity permits it to be interpreted in opposing senses.

16. "vultures" *-gṛdhra-*: Ct, Cg, and Cm note that the appearance of these carrion eaters is a sure sign of Rāvaṇa's impending death (*anena rāvaṇasyāsannamaraṇatvaṃ sūcitam*—so Cg). Cg and Cm quote a text identified as the *Śakunārṇava* to the effect that vultures circling above someone's house presage his impending demise (*tad uktaṃ śakunārṇava āsannamṛtyor nikaṭe caranti gṛdhrādayo mūrdhni gṛhordhvabhāga iti*). See, for example, 6.41.31; 6.83.33; and notes.

17. "Laṅkā . . . the very ground" *laṅkā . . . vasuṃdharā*: The commentators and the translators who follow them are divided as to whether to understand the term *vasuṃdharā*, "the earth, ground (lit., bearing wealth)," to be a modifier of or in apposition with Laṅkā or, on the other hand, to take the two terms separately, as we have done. The former interpretation is that of Ct and Ck, who regard *vasuṃdharā* as a term modifying Laṅkā (*vasuṃdhareti laṅkāviśeṣaṇam*). Cg and Cm, however, take the term to refer to the territory surrounding Laṅkā (*laṅkāparyantabhūmiḥ*).

"an untimely twilight" *saṃdhyayā*: Literally, "with twilight." We agree with Ck and Ct that one ought to supply the phrase "even though at the inappropriate time (*akāle 'pīti śeṣaḥ*)." We know from *pāda* d that it is daylight and so the sudden twilight is both untimely and eerie.

"as crimson as a *japā* blossom" *japāpuṣpanikāśayā*: Literally, "resembling a *japā* blossoms." Most likely the *japā* is the deep red *Hibiscus rosa-sinensis* (L), a plant commonly found throughout India and used in worship, āyurvedic medicine, etc. Cf. *Meghadūta* 1.36 [*paścād uccair bhujataruvanaṃ maṇḍalenābhilīnaḥ sāṃdhyaṃ tejaḥ pratinavajapāpuṣparaktaṃ dadhānaḥ*], where Kālidāsa, too, compares twilight to the color of *japā* flower. See Brockington 1984, p. 106 and Brandis 1873, p. 28.

18. "flew past" *sampraceruḥ*: Literally, "they moved about together." Ś2,Ñ2,V2,3, B2,4,D1–3,8,10–13,M1,5, and the texts and printed editions of Ct and Ck read instead the *facilior samprapetuḥ*, "they fell together."

"accompanied by violent gusts of wind" *sanirghātāḥ*: The term has various other meanings, several of which could be apposite here. Most translators consulted who share this reading understand the term to refer to the crashing of thunder, but we feel, given the adjective *mahāsvanāḥ*, "with a loud *or* thunderous sound," that this interpretation verges on the redundant.

"Then . . . clearly ominous" *tadāhitāḥ*: Literally, "then not beneficial." Both GPP (6.106.24) and NSP (6.106.24) print *tadā hitāḥ*, "then beneficial," which is clearly incorrect.

"they plunged" *viṣādayantyaḥ*: Literally, "[those meteors] causing [the *rākṣasas*] to despair."

19. "and as the *rākṣasas* prepared to strike, it seemed as if something held back their arms" *rakṣasāṃ ca praharatāṃ gṛhītā iva bāhavaḥ*: Literally, "as the *rākṣasas* were striking, their arms were held back, as it were." Ck and Ct suggest that we supply the phrase "[because they] were paralyzed with fear (*bhayāt stabdhā iti śeṣaḥ*)."

20. "pallid and bright white" *sitāḥ śvetāḥ*: Literally, "white, white." The reading, though well attested, is irredeemably awkward and redundant. Commentators who share the reading ignore it. Translators who share it adopt various strategies to cope with this. The simplest one, adopted by Dutt (1893, p. 1476) and Shastri (1959, vol. 3, p. 309), is simply to collapse the two terms into one, "white," so that there are only three colors of the sunlight. The alternative strategy, which we and Roussel (1903, vol. 3, p. 353) follow, is to attempt to differentiate the two terms. Roussel thus renders, "*pâl, blancs.*" Pagani (1999, p. 1159) in a variant of this appears to take the two terms as different qualities of the two colors yellow and red (*brilliants et clairs*). The text of Cg and printed editions of it (VSP and KK 6.108.26) show a variant unattested in the critical apparatus and unnoted in the apparatus of GPP, viz., *sitāśvetāḥ*, which Cg explains as "white and black *or* dark (*sitā aśvetāś ca*)." This variant is rendered in the translation of Raghunathan (1982, vol. 3, p. 310), who renders, "white and dark." Gita Press (1969, vol. 3, p. 1811), which reads with the critical edition, and Ct nevertheless translate as does Raghunathan.

"played across Rāvaṇa's body" *patitāḥ . . . rāvaṇasyāṅge*: Literally, "fell on Rāvaṇa's body." D9–11,M2, and the texts and printed editions of Ct and Ck read the textually and contextually inferior variant *agre*, "in front of," for *aṅge*, "on the body."

"like veins of variegated ores on a mountainside" *parvatasyeva dhātavaḥ*: Literally, "like the ores of a mountain."

21. "shadowed" *anugatāḥ*: Literally, "followed."

"howled angrily and inauspiciously" *praṇeduḥ . . . saṃrabdham aśivam*: We follow Cr and Cg, who read the two terms *saṃrabdham* and *aśivam* adverbially with the verb *praṇeduḥ*, "they howled." Roussel (1903, vol. 3, p. 353), followed by Shastri (1959, vol. 3, p. 309) and Pagani (1999, p. 1159), reads the two terms less plausibly as adjectives modifying the word *mukham*, "face," in *pāda* c. The howling or shrieking of jackals is a common ill omen in the literature. See 6.22.24; 6.31.7; 6.45.32,34; 6.53.42; 6.83.33; and notes. Cf. 6.41.32 and note.

22. "directly in the face" *pratikūlam*: Literally, "unfavorably, contrarily." We follow Cg, who glosses, "in his face *or* facing him (*abhimukham*)." Cf. 6.4.41 and note.

"blinding him" *kurvan dṛṣṭivilopanam*: Literally, "making a cutting off of sight."

23. "And yet, there was no rumbling of storm clouds." *vinā jaladharasvanam*: Literally, "without the sound of water-bearers [i.e., storm clouds]." The idea here is that the thunderbolts come from a cloudless sky, lending an uncanny quality to the event. The reading, nevertheless, is awkward as it is difficult to conceptualize what the sound of the thunderbolts might be in the absence of thunder. D7,10,11,G2, and the texts and printed editions of Ct, Cr, and Ck read instead *vinā jaladharodayam*, "without the arising [i.e., appearance] of clouds," an evident attempt to improve the text.

24. "dust storm" *pāṃsuvarṣeṇa*: Literally, "by a shower of dust."

25. "In a fearsome assault upon his chariot" *kurvantyaḥ kalahaṃ ghoram . . . tadrathaṃ prati*: Literally, "making a fierce attack *or* assault directed toward his chariot." Unlike most translators, we understand the term *kalaha* in its sense of "battle, warfare" and see the phrase *tadrathaṃ prati*, "toward his chariot," as the locus, or *adhikaraṇa*, of the verbal phrase *kurvantyaḥ kalaham*. Other translators consulted take the term *kalaha* in its more common sense of "quarrel" and understand the participial phrase to mean that the birds are squabbling among themselves. They therefore understand the

phrase *tadratham prati* as the locus of the principal verb *nipetuḥ*, "to descend *or* fall," in *pāda* c.

"*sārika* birds" *sārikāḥ*: Literally, "*sārikas*." This bird is generally identified as a type of mynah (*Acridotheres tristis*). See note to 6.26.29. In a footnote, Shastri (1959, vol. 3, p. 310) identifies the bird as either *Turdas salica* or *gracula religiosa*.

26. "sparks . . . and tears" *sphuliṅgāṃś ca . . . aśrūṇi*: The weeping of horses is a stereotypical portent of calamity for their master. The fact that the horses additionally emit sparks from their hindquarters is, perhaps, suggestive of the magnitude of the occasion. Cf. 2.53.1 and note. On the weeping of horses, either as an evil omen or a sign of grief, see *MBh* 4.37.6; 5.141.1; 6.2.33; and 6.3.42, See, too, *Buddhacarita* 6.53 and *Karṇābhāra* 11. See, too, 6.26.23; 6.65.18; 6.83.33; and notes.

"so that they poured forth both fire and water equally" *mumucuḥ . . . tulyam agniṃ ca vāri ca*: The phrase seems slightly enigmatic. Like several other translators, we understand it more or less as does Cg, who explains that in the act of shedding both tears and sparks, the horses are equally emitting both fire and water (*evam agniṃ ca vāri ca tulyaṃ yathā bhavati tathā mumucuḥ*). Gorresio (1858, vol. 10, p. 198), whose line 6.90.31ab is identical to 25cd, translates similarly. He also, however, provides a footnote (p. 307, n. 86) in which he observes that his commentator (Cl) glosses the phrase *tulyam agniṃ ca vāri ca* as "water that was equal to fire (*agnitulyaṃ vārīty arthaḥ*)." Gorresio then notes that, in conformity with this reading, one might translate, "*Gocciavano i suoi cavalli acqua pari a fuoco o fervente come fuoco*." He further notes that he believes the commentator to be mistaken in this interpretation but that it is grammatically possible. In this case we might understand that the horses are sweating or urinating a fiery fluid.

27. "appeared . . . presaging . . . destruction" *vināśāya . . . saṃprajajñire*: Literally, "they arose for destruction."

28. Following verse 28, D5–7,10,11,S insert a passage of two lines [3040*]: "Upon observing those favorable portents presaging Rāghava's victory, he[1] became immensely happy and thought that Rāvaṇa was as good as dead."

[1]"Rāghava's victory, he" *rāghavasya jayāya*: The verse as represented in the critical edition and in the printed editions of the text of Ct does not specify exactly who the subject of the sentence is. Ct thinks it must be either Lakṣmaṇa or Mātali. His first alternative is followed only in the translation of Dutt (1893, p. 1476). Cr, on the other hand, understands that the subject is the host of gods and other supernatural beings (*devādisamūhaḥ*) who were said, in verse 13 above, to have assembled to watch the battle. Most translators who follow the text of Ct, however, understand the subject to be Rāghava, i.e., Rāma. Printed editions of Cg and Cm read a variant unattested in the critical apparatus, *rāghavaḥ svajayāya*, "Rāghava . . . for his own victory," where Rāma is unambiguously the subject. This reading apparently informs the translation of Raghunathan (1982, vol. 3, p. 310). M1,T1,G1,2 similarly show the variant nominative singular *rāghavaḥ*.

29. "that augured well for him" *ātmagatāni*: Literally, "gone to the self," i.e., referring to him. Cr glosses, "reaching *or* come to him (*ātmānaṃ gatāni prāptāni*)," while Cg explains, "which had appeared for his sake (*ātmārthaṃ prādurbhūtāni*)." Cf. note to 6.92.26 above.

"he redoubled his valor in battle" *cakāra yuddhe 'bhyadhikaṃ ca vikramam*: Literally, "he made increased valor in battle."

The meter is *vaṃśasthavila*.

Sarga 95

1. "great" *sumahat*: According to Ct, the adjective refers not to the intensity but to the length of the battle, which he notes takes many days (*sumahad anekadinavyāpi*). This interpretation is followed only by Gita Press (1969, vol. 3, p. 1812), which renders, "prolonged." On the chronology of the *Yuddhakāṇḍa*, see Introduction, p. 17, note 1 and note to 6.4.4.

"that terrified all the worlds" *sarvalokabhayāvaham*: Cr thinks that the battle is terrifying to all beings because victory [for Rāma] is uncertain (*vijayasyāniścayāt sarveṣāṃ bhayakārakam*).

2. "stood motionless" *niśceṣṭaṃ samatiṣṭhata*: Commentators offer slightly different reasons for the motionlessness of the troops. Ct, Ck, Cg, and Cm all understand that they are absorbed in watching the battle (*tadyuddhadarśanapāravaśyād iti śeṣaḥ*—so Ck, Ct). Cr understands that the troops remain motionless but retain their weapons because of the uncertainty of the victory of either combatant (*vijayasyāniścayād dhetoḥ*).

3. "those two mighty warriors—man and *rākṣasa*" *balavannararākṣasau*: Literally, "the powerful man and *rākṣasa*." Like most commentators and all translators consulted, we understand *balavat*, "mighty," as an adjective in composition with the *dvandva nararākṣasau*, i.e., *balavantau nararākṣasau*. Cg, however, appears to take the word separately, as an adverb in the sense of "exceedingly (*atyantam*)," which, according to him, modifies *vyākṣiptahṛdayāḥ*, yielding "their attention exceedingly riveted."

"their attention was riveted" *vyākṣiptahṛdayāḥ*: Literally, "whose hearts were captivated." We understand the compound as does Cg, who glosses, "their minds focused on watching the battle (*yuddhadarśanasaktacittāḥ*)." Roussel (1903, vol. 3, p. 355), however, followed by Shastri (1959, vol. 3, p. 310), takes the verb *vi* + *ā* $\sqrt{}$*kṣip* in its other sense of "agitated," and understands the compound to mean "*le coeur palpitant*," echoed by Shastri as "their hearts beating rapidly."

4. "Although their hands were filled with all sorts of weapons" *nānāpraharaṇair vyagrair bhujair*: As several of the commentators note, we must read the instrumental *bhujaiḥ*, "with arms *or* hands," as an adjective, "characterized *or* marked by arms *or* hands (*bhujair upalakṣitā iti śeṣaḥ*—so Ct)." The adjective *vyagraiḥ*, "occupied, engaged," has been understood variously by the different translators. Grammatically, however, since it must modify *bhujaiḥ*, there is little scope for interpretation. The most plausible reading, given the semantic range of *vyagraiḥ*, seems to be the one we have offered. A second possibility, one Cr suggests, is to take *nānāpraharaṇaiḥ* as a *bahuvrīhi* modifying *bhujaiḥ*, "having arms in which there are various weapons," and reading *vyagraiḥ*, "eager [for battle]," as an independent adjective. This interpretation is clearly followed by Gita Press (1969, vol. 3, p. 1812), which renders, "impatient for action"; Roussel (1903, vol. 3, p. 355), "*prêts* (*à la lutte*)"; Shastri (1959, vol. 3, p. 310), "ready for combat"; and Dutt (1893, p. 1477), "arms uplifted for a fight." The interpretations of Raghunathan (1982, vol. 3, p. 310), "though their arms had eagerly

snatched their weapons," and Pagani (1999, p. 1160), "*les bras chargés d'armes diverses,*" are similar to ours.

"their minds were filled with astonishment" *vismitabuddhayaḥ*: Literally, "having amazed *or* astonished minds."

"they stood there, gazing at that battle" *tasthuḥ prekṣya ca saṃgrāmam*: D9–11 and the texts and printed editions of Ct read *sarvaṃ te* for *saṃgrāmam*, yielding the awkward sense "they stood there watching everything." No translator consulted renders this literally. The texts and printed editions of Cg and Cm (KK,VSP 6.109.4) read *sarpantaṃ prekṣya saṃgrāmam* for the critical reading, yielding "watching that battle as it moved." This variant is not noted in the critical apparatus. Cm, the only commentator to remark on this reading, glosses, "as it approached (*samīpam āgacchantam*)." Among the translators, only Raghunathan (1982, vol. 3, p. 310) follows this reading, rendering, "that fight, which moved to and fro, and came too close to them."

5. "the *rākṣasas*... the monkeys... both armies, their eyes wide with astonishment" *rakṣasām... cāpi vānarāṇām... vismitākṣāṇāṃ sainyam*: Literally, "the army of the *rākṣasas* and the monkeys, whose eyes were astonished."

"seemed frozen as if in a painting" *citram ivābabhau*: Literally, "looked like a painting." We follow Cm and Ct, who understand the simile to be the stereotypical Sanskrit figure for absorbed or astonished immobility (*citralikhitam iva*). Compare *Abhijñānaśākuntalam* of Kālidāsa 1.4.1. Roussel (1903, vol. 3, p. 355), followed by Shastri (1959, vol. 3, p. 310) and Pagani (1999, p. 1160), takes the term *citram* in its adjectival sense of "strange, wonderful," translating, "*l'aspect des deux armées était étrange,*" but, given the context, this is not persuasive.

6. "grimly determined" *kṛtabuddhī*: Literally, "with their minds made up *or* determined."

"fixed in their enmity" *sthirāmarṣau*: We read the compound as a *bahuvrīhi*, whose literal sense is "whose intolerance *or* indignation was firm." Several of the translators consulted apparently take it as a *dvandva*, offering variants on the idea of "steadfast and indignant."

7. "thought... realized" *iti... iti*: There is no explicit verb, only the quotation markers.

"I must surely die" *martavyam*: We agree with Cg, who glosses, "death is inevitable (*maraṇam avaśyaṃbhāvīti*)." Ct, closely paraphrasing Ck, comments, "one must strike at one's enemy who takes the form of death (*mṛtyurūpaśatrau prahartavyam ity artha iti katakaḥ*)." All translators consulted, with the exception of Pagani, understand that Rāvaṇa, upon observing the ill omens that have attended his return to the battlefield, is grimly resolved to die fighting. Pagani (1999, p. 1160) understands that Rāvaṇa is still determined to slay Rāma and thus is thinking, "*Il faut le tuer.*"

9. "Indra, smasher of citadels" *puraṃdara-*: Literally, "the smasher of citadels."

"the chariot-javelin" *rathaśaktim*: This term, which has bedeviled the minds and exercised the ingenuity of commentators and translators alike on earlier occasions (see 6.33.21; 6.59.13; and notes), continues to present ambiguities here. We have translated in accordance with our understanding of the earlier passages and of the commentaries on them. However, here, apparently because the chariot in question is the great celestial car of the king of the gods, the commentators are more inclined than they were earlier to understand the term *śakti* in its sense of "power" rather than, or in addition to, its sense of "javelin." Thus, Ct glosses, "*rathaśakti* means either the supernatural power of the divine chariot or a particular part of the chariot (*ratha-śaktiṃ divyarathavaibhavaṃ rathāvayavaviśeṣaṃ vā*)." Cm, who notes the critical reading as a variant, glosses it exactly as does Ct. Ck and Cr understand the term only in the first of these two senses. Cg has a similar understanding but avoids any specific reference to "wonderful" or "supernatural power," glossing, merely, "the strength of the chariot (*rathabalam*)." This, in turn, is reminiscent of Cm's principal reading, *ratha-śaktam*, which Cm reads as a *pūrvanipāta* compound, *śaktaratham*, "powerful chariot," glossing, "strong or firm chariot (*dṛḍharatham*)." Although the critical apparatus quotes Cm's variant comments, no manuscript with this reading is attested either there or in the apparatus of KK.

10. "to return blow for blow" *kṛtapratikṛtaṃ kartum*: Literally, "to make a counteraction to the action." Cr understands that Rāma wishes to cut down Rāvaṇa's flagstaff in retaliation (*dhvajacchedanam ity arthaḥ*). Compare verse 26 below and notes.

11. "impossible to withstand" *asahyam*: Literally, "unbearable *or* unendurable." Cg glosses, "impossible to look upon (*durdarśam*)."

Following verse 11, D7,9–11, KK (in brackets), and the texts and printed editions of Ct and Ck insert a passage of one line [3042*]: "Filled with blazing energy, Rāma took aim at the banner and shot his arrow."

12. "came to rest on the ground" *jagāma . . . mahīm*: Literally, "it went to the earth." Some translators (Raghunathan 1982, vol. 3, p. 311; and Gita Press 1969, vol. 3, p. 1813) understand that the arrow actually enters the ground, a common occurrence in the epic, but this is not explicitly stated here.

13. "seemed to blaze up on the battlefield with a fire born of anger" *krodhajenāgninā saṃkhye pradīpta iva cābhavat*: Ñ,V2,3,B2–4,D5,6,9–11,T,G2,3,M1,3,5, and the texts and printed editions of all southern commentators consulted substitute for 13cd, while D7 inserts after 13, a passage of one line [3045*]: "Seeming to blaze with indignation, he became inflamed with wrath." Given the strength of the textual support for 3045*, one wonders at the critical editors' choice.

14. "In an uncontrollable rage" *roṣavaśam āpannaḥ*: Literally, "having gone to the control of anger."

"poured forth" *vaman*: Literally, "vomiting." Cg, the only commentator to remark on the critical reading, takes the verb $\sqrt{}$*vam* in its literal sense but reads the phrase as a figurative usage. He glosses, "seemed to be vomiting [a hail of arrows] (*vamann iva*)." Only Raghunathan (1982, vol. 3, p. 311) renders this reading, translating, "he vomited floods of arrows as it seemed." Ñ2,V1,3,B3,4,D2,3,7,10,11,13,G1, and the texts and printed editions of Ct and Cr read *vavarṣa ha*, "he rained," for [*mahad*] *vaman*.

"celestial" *divyān*: Ñ,V,B2,4,D5,7,9–11,T1,G1,3,M3,5, and the texts and printed editions of the southern commentators read instead *dīptaiḥ*, "blazing," which modifies "arrows (*śaraiḥ*)" in *pāda* d.

15. "Riddled though they were" *te viddhāḥ*: Literally, "they, pierced." D7,10,11, and the texts and printed editions of Ct, Cr, and Ck read instead *te divyāḥ*, "those celestial [horses]." Ct puts forth this adjective as the reason for the horses' ability to avoid stumbling and for their invulnerability to Rāvaṇa's weapons (*skhalanādyabhāve svastha-hṛdayatve ca hetuḥ—divyā iti*).

"the tawny steeds" *harayaḥ*: Cg glosses, "of a tawny *or* bay color," noting that this term is used because these are, in fact, the horses of Indra [who is well known by the epithet Haryaśva, "he of the tawny steeds"] (*harayo haritavarṇā indrāśvatvād iti bhāvaḥ*). See note to 6.78.27.

16–17. "Rāvaṇa... loosed... He also hurled" *rāvaṇaḥ... mumoca*: Literally, "Rāvaṇa released." Verse 17 consists entirely of a list of weapons and other objects hurled by Rāvaṇa. It is therefore necessary, as Cg suggests, to understand that the principal verb of verse 16 also governs these weapons (*mumocety anuṣajyate*). We have rendered the verb with two different English verbs in order to accommodate the different types of weapons. See notes to verse 18 below.

"mountain peaks, and trees" *giriśṛṅgāṇi vṛkṣāṃś ca*: It seems unusual for the well-armed warrior Rāvaṇa to be using the crude weapons normally associated with the monkeys. Perhaps this is a sign of his increasing desperation.

18. "His heart and energies unflagging, he continued to loose his arrows by the thousand" *sahasraśas tato bāṇān aśrāntahṛdayodyamaḥ*: D5,6,T,G3,M3,5, and the texts and printed editions of Cg and Cm read these *pādas* (= cd) after 20cd. This order of the text is represented only in the translation of Raghunathan (1982, vol. 3, p. 311). Ñ2,V1,2,B2,D9–11,T3, and the texts and printed editions of Ct read *abhrānta-*, "not confused *or* not swerving," for the critical reading *aśrānta-*, "unflagging." See notes to verse 19 below.

"he continued to loose... he let fly" *apātayat*: Literally, "he caused to fly *or* fall." As in the previous verse, we have rendered a single verb in two slightly different senses to accommodate the different weapons employed.

"invested with the power of magical illusion" *māyāvihitam*: Literally, "furnished with *māyā*." Cg, Ck, and Ct understand the term to be used here to explain how, apparently, Rāvaṇa is able to shoot such bulky items as maces, mountains, and so forth from his bow (*dhanuṣā katham gadādimocanam ity atrāha māyeti*—so Cg). Cg glosses the term as "performed through the use of his power that can create miracles (*āścaryakaraśaktikṛtam*)."

19. "It was... deafening, and consisted of innumerable weapons" *tumulam... abhavat... naikaśastramayam*: Literally, "it was tumultuous, consisting of many [lit., not one] weapons."

"unendurable" *durdharṣam*: V,B3,4,D4–7,9–11,S, and the texts and printed editions of the southern commentators read instead *tadvarṣam*, "the hail of those [weapons]" or, reading *tad varṣam*, "that hail." This provides an explicit and continuing subject for the verbs at least through 20ab. The critical reading, although lacking this substantive, appears to us to assume it in any case.

"it sowed panic everywhere" *trāsajananam*" Literally, "giving rise to fear."

20. "Missing Rāghava's chariot, it fell upon the monkey host" *vimucya rāghavaratham samantād vānare bale*: Literally, "having released Rāghava's chariot, from all sides on the monkey army." The line is elliptical and lacks any finite verb. We interpret with the commentators, who understand that Rāvaṇa's missiles, diverted from their intended target, i.e., Rāma's chariot, land unintentionally on the monkey troops. Ct and Cm, for example, explain, "'releasing Rāghava's chariot' means that [the hail of weapons], having been discharged with an excess of rage, overshot Rāma's chariot, its intended target, and fell on the monkey army (*rāghavaratham vimucya krodhātiśayena yuktatvāl lakṣyabhūtaṃ rāmaratham atikramya vānare bale 'patat*—so Ct)." Cg interprets similarly but understands that Rāvaṇa's arrows miss their targets not because of his excessive rage but because they are diverted by the arrows Rāma discharges in his own

great fury. (*krodhātiśayena prayuktai rāmaśarair nivāraṇāl lakṣyabhūtaṃ rāghavarathaṃ vimucya vānarabale 'bhavat. tatrāpatad ity arthaḥ.*) This interpretation has been followed by all translators consulted, with the exception of Dutt (1893, p. 1478), who understands that Rāvaṇa intentionally diverts his attention from Rāma's chariot and deliberately fires upon the monkeys.

"with unbroken concentration" *niḥsaṅgenāntarātmanā*: Literally, "with a detached inner mind." We understand the term here with Cg, who glosses, "characterized by an undistracted mind (*avyāsaktena* ... *manasopalakṣitaḥ*)." The idea here is that Rāvaṇa, undeterred by his failure to destroy Rāma's horses and chariot, continues to fight on with great concentration. This interpretation has been followed in the translation of Raghunathan (1982, vol. 3, p. 311). Ct, Ck, Cm, and Cr, however, all take the term *niḥsaṅgena* to mean that Rāvaṇa has given up all hope of life (*prāṇāśāsaṅgarahitena* [*antarātmanā*]—so Ct, Ck, and Cm).

"continued to loose his arrows" *mumoca ca*: Literally, "and he released." No explicit object for the verb is provided, so, like Cg, who adds the word "arrows (*bāṇān*)," we have supplied the ellipsis.

"he quickly filled the entire atmosphere with his shafts" *sāyakair antarikṣaṃ ca cakārāśu nirantaram*: Literally, "and with arrows, he quickly made the atmosphere so that it had no gaps." Ñ2,V1,2,B3,D2,9–11, and the texts and printed editions of Ct read *cakāra sunirantaram* for *cakārāśu nirantaram*, yielding the sense "he made the atmosphere so that it was completely without gaps."

21. "exert himself with such concentration" *vyāyacchamānam* ... *tatparam*: Literally, "striving ... intent on that." We follow Cg's interpretation of these two terms, which, according to this reading, continue the representation, in verse 20, of Rāvaṇa shooting with fierce concentration. This interpretation is also followed by Raghunathan (1982, vol. 3, p. 311). Cg comments, " '*vyāyacchamānam*' means 'making effort,' while '*tatparam*' means 'intent on battle.' (*vyāyacchamānaṃ vyāyacchantaṃ yatnaṃ kurvantaṃ. raṇe tatparaṃ saktam.*)" Ct and Cm understand the participle *vyāyacchamānam* to mean "setting in motion (*pravartayantam*)," no doubt an elliptical reference to the hail of arrows, etc., mentioned in the previous verses. This idea is expressed by Cr, who glosses, "scattering (*vistārayantam*)." He further sees an explicit, if elliptical, object in the form of the sequence *tat param*. For Cr, this is a reference to "that intense *or* unequaled shower [of weapons] (*paraṃ tad varṣaṇam*)." Ck and Ct, however, take the phrase *tatparam* adverbially in the sense of "after that (*tadanantaram*)."

"smiled faintly" *prahasann iva*: Literally, "laughing softly *or* smiling gently." Cg construes the phrase adverbially with the finite verb *saṃdadhe*, "he nocked," and as having the sense "effortlessly (*anāyāsena*)." This, in turn, is rendered by Raghunathan (1982, vol. 3, p. 311) as "playfully."

22. "hundreds of thousands" *śatasahasraśaḥ*: D7–11 and the texts and printed editions of Ct and Cr read instead *śataśo 'tha sahasraśaḥ*, "by the hundred and by the thousand." The critical reading, too, could be rendered similarly. Indeed, Gorresio (1858, vol. 10, p. 200) and Raghunathan (1982, vol. 3, p. 311), both of whom share the critical reading, do so. We, however, prefer our reading in that it appropriately magnifies Rāma's supernatural martial skills, which he deploys in this ultimate battle.

Following verse 22, D7,G1, and KK (in brackets, following 6.109.23) insert a passage of one line [3049*]: "With their torrents of arrows, those two seemed to leave no room for air in the sky." No translation consulted renders this verse. However, the line is a close variant of 25cd. See notes to verse 25 below.

23. "by the two warriors" *tābhyām*: Literally, "by those two."

"it looked as if there were a second shining sky composed entirely of arrows" *śarabaddham ivābhāti dvitīyaṃ bhāsvadambaram*: Literally, "there appeared, as it were, a second shining sky formed by arrows." We agree with Ct and Cm, who gloss the participle *-baddham*, normally, "bound," in its sense of "made, fashioned of (*-racitam*)." The usage is similar to that of the root √*bandh* in such constructions as *setubandha*, "construction of the causeway." The idea here is that the heroes shoot their arrows so thickly and rapidly that they create the illusion of a second glowing sky below the real sky.

24. "failed to hit its precise mark, caused excessive damage, or failed to achieve its intended purpose" *nānimittaḥ . . . nātibhettā na niṣphalaḥ*: Literally, "none was without a target, none pierced excessively, none was fruitless." The precise meanings of and distinctions among these three terms are difficult to ascertain with certainty. If, with Ct, Ck, and Cm and most of the translators consulted, one takes the first term, *animittaḥ*, to mean that an arrow failed to hit its target (*lakṣyam aprāpya vartamānaḥ*—so Ct, Ck), then the other two terms, it would seem, become otiose. In order to maintain a meaningful distinction among the terms, we follow the interpretation of Cg, whose gloss on this first term, *animittaḥ*, is "missing the precise spot on the target (*lakṣyaviśeṣoddeśarahitaḥ*)." He appears to follow Cv, who glosses, "[striking] another part of the target (*lakṣaṇād aparārdhaḥ*)." Cr explains the term as "missing its mark by virtue of excessive excitement in battle (*yuddhotsāhanimittakatvena nimittarahitaḥ*)." Among the commentators, Cv, Cg, Cm, and Cr read the second term, *nātibhettā*, with the critical edition. Cv and Cg understand the reference to be to an arrow that is shot with excessive force and does too much damage. They gloss, "cutting excessively because of a want of measure [of force] (*apekṣitapramāṇād adhikabhettā*—so Cg; Cv similarly). Cm understands, "cutting excessively because of striking (*praharaṇād adhikabhettā*)." Cr similarly glosses, "rending excessively through striking (*tāḍanād adhikavidārakaḥ*)." G2,M2, and the text of Ck read the variant *nātiyatnaḥ*, "none had excessive effort," which appears to be a kind of gloss on the reading *nātibhettā*. Ct notes this variant and quotes Ck's gloss on it: "None had exceeded its effort in order to deflect [an arrow] fired by the enemy. The meaning is that an arrow discharged to deflect [another arrow] did just that. (*nātiyatna iti pāṭhe paraprayuktanivāraṇāya yatnātikrānto na. nirvāraṇāya prayukto nivārayaty evety arthaḥ.*)" Ś2,Ñ2,V,B2,D1–3,5,6,8–13,T3, and the texts and printed editions of Ct read instead *nānirbhettā*, "not not splitting." The double negative is simplified by Ct, who glosses, "fails to pierce (*bhettā na*)." See 6.37.11; 6.67.36; 6.93.15; 6.101.36; and notes. See, too, 6.99.24, 3132*, lines 7–8, and n. 4. For the third term, *niṣphalaḥ*, we follow the gloss of Cv, Cg, and Cm, who understand it to refer to "an arrow that, even though it strikes its target, fails to achieve its purpose (*lakṣye patito 'pi prayojanākārī*)."

Following 24ab, D5,6,7,9–11,S, insert a passage of one line [3050*]: "[Their arrows], striking one another, fell to the earth."

25. "The two heroes" *tau*: Literally, "those two."

"With their torrents of arrows" *śaraughaiḥ*: D9–11,G3, and the texts and printed editions of Ct and Cr read instead *śarair ghoraiḥ*, "with fearsome arrows."

"they seemed to leave no room even for air in the sky" *cakratuḥ* ... *nirucchvāsam ivāmbaram*: Literally, "those two seemed to make the sky airless." The idea is that they filled up the sky with their arrows, leaving no room for air. For *nirucchvāsam*, "airless, breathless," Ct and Cm gloss, "without a space (*nīrandhram*)," while Cg, more specifically, glosses, "without space for air *or* breath (*ucchvāsāvakāśarahitam*)." Cg wants to take the expression literally rather than figuratively, noting that the word *iva*, normally a particle expressing comparison or a figurative usage, is here merely ornamental (*ivaśabdo vākyālaṃkāre*). Compare the similar figure at 3049* (see note 22 above).

Following verse 25, D7,T1,G1, and KK (in brackets, 6.109.27) insert a passage of two lines [3051*]: "Although they stared unblinkingly, neither the monkeys and *rākṣasas*, standing on the ground, nor the gods and *dānavas*, hovering in the air,[1] could perceive the slightest gap."

[1]"hovering in the air" *svasthaiḥ*: Literally, "independent, contented." This reading, found in both the critical edition and KK, makes little sense in this context. Given the fact that the gods, etc., are being contrasted with the monkeys and *rākṣasas*, who are standing on the ground, we believe that both editions have mistaken the correct reading, *khasthaiḥ*, and we have translated accordingly.

26. "Rāvaṇa's horses ... Rāma's" *rāvaṇasya hayān* ... *hayān rāmasya*: Literally, "Rāvaṇa's horses ... Rāma's horses." Cg, evidently reluctant to think of these great warriors simply targeting each other's steeds, takes the term to refer more broadly to the entire equipage, including the charioteers, etc. (*haya ivānyatrāpi sārathyādau jaghnatur ity arthaḥ*).

"trading blow and counterblow" *kṛtānukṛtakāriṇau*: Literally, "effecting action and following action." Compare verse 10 and notes above.

Following verse 26, D5–7,9–11,S insert a passage of six lines [3053*]: "Supremely enraged, the two engaged in an unparalleled battle. Tumultuous and hair-raising, the fight continued for some time.[1][1–2] And so, on the battlefield, those two immensely powerful warriors, Rāvaṇa and the elder brother of Lakṣmaṇa, fought on[2] with their sharp arrows.[3][3–4] For the lord of the *rākṣasas* remained furious with that foremost of the Raghus for having cut down his flagstaff.[4][5–6]"

Southern manuscripts and editions of Cg, Cv, and Cm, who read lines 3053*, end the *sarga* following 3053*, line 6, while the texts and printed editions of Ck and Ct continue the *sarga* with no break following 3053*, line 2. See notes to the opening of *sarga* 96.

[1]"for some time" *muhūrtam*: We believe the term should be taken here in its common sense of an indeterminate period of time. Roussel (1903, vol. 3, p. 356), however, followed by Pagani (1999, p. 1161), understands line 2 to mean that the battle became tumultuous within the space of a moment. He renders, "*En un moment, la lutte devint effroyable* ..."

[2]"fought on" *prayudhymānau*: Literally, "fighting on." The verse has no finite verb, and we have translated the participle as if it were one.

[3]Lines 3–6 are omitted from the printed editions of Ct. GPP, however, in keeping with its effort to represent Cg and Cr as well as Ct, includes the verse in brackets

between verses 6.107.28 and 29, assigning it no number of its own. In a footnote, GPP indicates that the verse is additional in the texts of Cg and Cr. The critical apparatus does not note the absence of the verse from the texts or printed editions of Ct.

[4]The meter of lines 3–6 is *vaṃśasthavila*.

Southern manuscripts and editions of Cg, Cv, and Cm, who read lines 3053*, end the *sarga* following 3053*, line 6, while the texts and printed editions of Ck and Ct continue the *sarga* with no break following 3053*, line 2. See notes to the opening of *sarga* 96

Sarga 96

Like the critical edition, the overwhelming majority of manuscripts mark a *sarga* boundary at or shortly after verse 6.95.26, as various recensions and subrecensions insert one or more verses at that point (3051*, 3052* and/or 3053*). A *sarga* break, however, is not found in the texts and printed editions of Ct, which continue the *sarga* through to the end of the critical edition's *sarga* 96. Translations that follow the text of Ct show no *sarga* break at this point. Dutt (1893, p. 1479), who closely follows the text of Ct and frequently cites him in his notes, however, includes 3053* in his translation and begins a new *sarga* (his section CIX) immediately after it. Compare notes to verse 4 below. Shastri (1959, vol. 3, pp. 311–12) similarly and unexpectedly breaks the *sarga* and inserts 3053*.

With reference to 3053*, lines 3–6 (see notes to 6.95.26), found in manuscripts and printed editions of Cg (= VSP 6.109.28–29 and KK 6.109.29–30), Ck, quoted in the critical edition in the apparatus to 6.96.1, notes that some texts interpolate these verses and then insert a *sarga* break. He argues that this is incorrect, because the topic of the preceding *sarga*, viz., the tumultuous battle, continues unabated. He further notes that one does not see a *sarga* break in a number of manuscripts. (*tumulaṃ romaharṣaṇam ity anantaraṃ prayudhyamānāv ity ādikaṃ ślokaṃ kṛtvātra sargaṃ vicchindanti puraḥ. paścāt tumulayuddhatvaṃ tv ekaprakāra(karaṇa?)tvāc ca nātra yujyate padacchedaḥ. kvacid anavacchedaś ca dṛśyate.*) Cm and Ct paraphrase and expand Ck's comments. Cm's and Ct's comments may be found in the critical edition in the apparatus to 3053*. Cm's remarks are found in VSP in parentheses following his comments after VSP 6.109.29. Ct's remarks are found in GPP and NSP at his comments to 6.107.29. Of particular interest here is that, once again, Cm explicitly quotes Ck. This naturally leads us to seriously question the current, generally accepted scholarly consensus that Cm preceded Ck by at least a century. See Lefeber 1994 (Introduction to the *Kiṣkindhākāṇḍa*), pp. 17–28 and see Introduction, pp. 105–107. See note to 6.78.19, where Cm again quotes Ck.

1. "watched . . . as Rāma and Rāvaṇa" *rāmarāvaṇau . . . dadṛśuḥ*: Literally, "they watched Rāma and Rāvaṇa."

"with amazement in their hearts" *vismitenāntarātmanā*: Literally, "with an astonished inner faculty."

"in this fashion" *tathā*: D6,T2,G,M, and the texts and printed editions of Ct and Cg read instead *tadā*, "then." Cg glosses this reading as "at the time of [the appearance of] the omens (*tadā utpātakāle*)." Cf. 6.4.6 and note.

2. "the two splendid chariot-warriors" *tayos tau syandanottamau*: Literally, "those two splendid chariots of those two." To avoid ascribing, as some translators do, intentionality to the inanimate chariots, we agree with Cg and Cs, who understand the term *syandana*, "chariot," here to refer to chariot-warriors, thus making Rāma and Rāvaṇa the subject of the verse. Cg, referring to passage 3054*, which ascribes anger to the chariots, remarks: "The anger and so on of the chariots is through the instrumentality of the chariot-warriors (*rathayoḥ krodhādikaṃ rathikadvārā*)." Cs proposes two interpretive strategies. The first is to read the verse as containing an implicit relative clause, such that it could be interpreted to mean "The syntax is: The splendid chariots of those two [Rāma and Rāvaṇa], who, enraged with each other and intent on slaying each other, pressed each other hard in battle (*yau parasparam abhikruddhau parasparavadhe yuktau samare 'rdayantau rāmarāvaṇau tayoḥ syandanottamāv ity anvayaḥ*)." Cs proposes, as an alternative, that we understand the term "chariot" here to refer, by secondary usage, to the chariot-warriors. He supports this by citing the well-known example, "the beds are crying," where the word "beds" stands for the children occupying them (*mañcāḥ krośantītivad gauṇo vā prayogaḥ*). A number of northern manuscripts as well as the printed edition of Gorresio (6.92.2b), perhaps in an effort to gloss this awkward reading, substitute *saṃsthitau rathayos tadā*, "then, standing in their chariots," for the critical reading. See note to verse 5 below.

Following 2ab, D5–7,9–11,T,G,M1,3,5, and the texts and printed editions of the southern commentators insert a passage of one line [3054*]: "Enraged at each other and charging toward each other..."

3. "Their charioteers... the movements exemplary of their skill as drivers" *sūtau sārathyajāṃ gatim*: Literally, "the two charioteers... movement produced from charioteership." The commentators gloss the term *sārathyam* with "extraordinary skill (*atinaipuṇyam*—Cr)" or "the work of a charioteer (*sārathikarma*—Cg)." Ct and Cm understand, "arising out of (*or* taking the form of—Cm) the charioteers' art *or* skill (*sūtakarmanaipuṇyajām* [*-rūpām*—Cm])." D6,7,9,T1,G,M1,3,5, and the texts and printed editions of Cg, Cm, and Cr read *sūta-* in place of *sūtau*, which yields the compound *sūtasārathyajām*, whose sense is "arising from the charioteer's art of the charioteers." Since this variant removes the charioteers as the subject of the sentence, translations that follow these texts generally are forced to take Rāma and Rāvaṇa as the subjects.

"driving in circles and in straight lines, advancing and retreating" *maṇḍalāni ca vīthīś ca gatapratyāgatāni ca*: Literally, "circles, lines, goings and comings." These are apparently technical terms associated with the art of chariot warfare. See Hopkins 1889, p. 197. Compare *MBh* 7.18.6, where the terms *maṇḍalāni* and *gatapratyāgatāni* are used similarly.

4. "at tremendous speed" *gativegaṃ samāpannau*: Literally, "attaining speed of movement." Dutt (1893, p. 1479), alone among the translators consulted, fails to render this phrase, substituting instead "and influenced by illusions." This would appear to reflect the readings of B2 and B4, which read, respectively, *māyāvaśasamāpannaiḥ* and *māyābalasamāpannaiḥ*, "endowed with the power of magical illusion." This, in turn, raises an interesting question as to exactly why Dutt, who normally follows the southern recension and the text of Ct, should have included this reading. Compare the opening note above as to Dutt's treatment of the *sarga* break between the critical edition's *sargas* 95 and 96.

5. "their splendid chariots" *tayos tau syandanottamau*: See note to verse 2 above.

6. "Then" *tadā*: Ñ1,D1–3,6,12,13,T3,M, and the texts and printed editions of Cg read instead *tathā*, "in this fashion."

7. "their yoke poles and battle standards brushed each other and their horses stood face to face" *dhuraṃ dhureṇa ... vaktraṃ vaktreṇa vājinām / patākāś ca patākābhiḥ sameyuḥ*: Literally, "yoke came together with yoke, of the horses, face with face, and banners with banners." We agree with Cr's interpretation of the term *dhura* as "yoke pole (*yugandharam*)," since these projecting parts of the chariots would be more likely to touch each other as the vehicles stand head to head.

8. "fiery steeds" *dīptān hayān*: Literally, "glowing *or* blazing horses." The term is, perhaps, a bit odd when applied to horses, but it can mean "excited." Several of the translators who render this reading offer such adjectives as "spirited, ardent, etc." It should be kept in mind, however, that Rāvaṇa's horses were said to be emitting blazing sparks from their hindquarters at 6.94.26 (ad loc. and notes) as one of the evil portents confronting Rāvaṇa. So it is possible that we are meant to take the adjective literally here. Ś2,Ñ2,V1,3,B,D1–3,6,8,12,13,T2,3,M3, and the texts and printed editions of Cg, Gorresio, and Lahore read instead the instrumental plural *dīptaiḥ*, which, more conventionally, modifies Rāma's arrows. Since Raghunathan (1982, vol. 3, p. 312) ignores the adjective entirely, this variant is rendered only in the translation of Gorresio (1858, vol. 10, p. 201).

9. "The night-roaming *rākṣasa*" *niśācaraḥ*: Literally, "the night-roaming one," Ñ1,D4,7,9–11,M2, and the texts and printed editions of Ct and Cr read instead *daśānanaḥ*, "the ten-faced one."

10. "seemed unaffected" *jagāma na vikāram*: Literally, "he did not go to transformation." Cg understands the term *vikāra* in its sense of "a change in facial expression indicating pain (*vedanāsūcakamukhavikāram*)." This interpretation appears to have informed Raghunathan's (1982, vol. 3, p. 312) translation, "he neither lost countenance."

"showed no signs of pain" *na cāpi vyathito 'bhavat*: Literally, "nor was he pained *or* injured."

11. "the night-roaming *rākṣasa*" *niśācaraḥ*: Literally, "the night-roaming one." D7,9–11, and the texts and printed editions of Ct and Cr read instead *daśānanaḥ*, "the ten-faced one."

"of Indra, wielder of the *vajra*" *vajrahastasya*: Literally, "of the one who has the *vajra* in his hand."

"roared with the crash of thunderbolts" *vajrapātasamasvanān*: Literally, "with the sound equal to the fall of the thunderbolt." D10,11, and the texts and printed editions of Ct read instead *vajrasārasamasvanān*, "with a sound that was equal to the best of thunderbolts *or* a powerful thunderbolt."

12. "caused neither ... nor" *na ... pradaduḥ*: Literally, "they did not give." According to Ct, Rāvaṇa's arrows are unable to injure Mātali for two reasons, one supernatural the other physical. Ct notes that Mātali cannot be injured since he is a divinity and therefore possessed of divine powers. He also remarks that arrows fired by Rāvaṇa as his chariot is being drawn away lack the ability to penetrate. (*devatvena divyaśaktimattvāt. apasarpaṇakāle rāvaṇena prakṣiptānām ativedhasāmarthyāyogāc ca.*) Cs claims, however, that Mātali's immunity derives not from any innate supernatural power but from the presence of Rāma (*śrīrāmasānnidhyāt*). Cs first quotes Ct and then goes on, as he often does, to ridicule his argument, saying that, since Rāvaṇa was granted the

wealth of Indra and the other gods, how great could his charioteer (Mātali) be? He regards Ct's interpretation as an example of the popular saying intended to indicate someone's utter stupidity, "Having listened to the entire *Rāmāyaṇa,* one asks, 'Who is Sītā to Rāma?' (*yat tu nāgojibhaṭṭena ... vyākhyātaṃ tad yadendrādīnāṃ daśānanadattā vittā tadā kiyān ayaṃ yanteti vṛtte sati samagrarāmāyaṇaṃ śrutvāpi sītā rāmasya kiṃ bhāvinīty ābhāṇakam anukaroti*)." This is a favorite proverb of Cs. Cf. note to 6.71.12.

"distraction" *saṃmoham*: Literally, "confusion, bewilderment."

13. "at that... as... never" *tayā ... na tathā*: Literally, "by that... not thus." We follow the interpretation of Cg, Cm, and Ct (who reads *yathā*, "in such a way," for *tayā*, "by that"). Cr, alone among the commentators, understands that Rāma is not angered by either the attack on Mātali or himself but, nonetheless, drives back his foe with his weapons (*mātales tayā dharṣaṇayātmanaś ca dharṣaṇayā* [misprinted as *ṣarṣaṇayā* in GPP] *na kruddho 'pi rāghavaḥ śarajālena ripuṃ vimukhaṃ cakāra*). Pagani (1999, p. 1161), alone among the translators, appears to read *ca* for *na*, and thus understands that Rāma is, in fact, outraged by both of the attacks. She translates, "*Furieux de cet outrage fait á Mātali et á lui-même.*"

"made his enemy recoil" *cakāra ... vimukhaṃ ripum*: Literally, "he made his enemy one whose face was averted."

14. Following verse 14, D5–7,9–11,T,G3,M1,3,5, and the texts and printed editions of the southern commentators read 6.96.29 followed by 3071*, line 1, for the first time. See notes to verse 29 below.

15. "by the sounds of maces, cudgels, and iron clubs" *gadānāṃ musalānāṃ ca parighāṇāṃ ca nisvanaiḥ*: Cg remarks that the sounds arise from the great velocity of these weapons (*nisvanair vegajair iti śeṣaḥ*). It should be noted that there has been no mention of these types of weapons in the duel since 6.95.17. This may have some bearing on the vulgate's sequence of verses mentioned in the note to verse 14 above, where Rāvaṇa deploys such weapons. See verse 29 and notes below.

16. "Since the seas were thrown into turmoil" *kṣubdhānāṃ sāgarāṇām*: We agree with Cm and Cg in reading the construction as a genitive absolute (*kṣubdhānāṃ sāgarāṇāṃ satām*—so Cm). Cg glosses the locative absolute for the critical edition's genitive absolute. Ct, however, reads the construction as an elliptical genitive and explains, "the inhabitants of Pātāla, which is the region below the agitated seas, became terrified (*kṣubdhānāṃ sāgarāṇām adhodeśavartipātālavāsino vyathitā jātā iti śeṣaḥ*)." Cr understands a simple possessive genitive in the sense of "the *dānavas* and the great serpents of the agitated oceans became terrified (*kṣubdhānāṃ sāgarāṇāṃ dānavāḥ pannagāś ca vyathitā babhūvur iti śeṣaḥ*)."

18. "were plunged into anxiety, praying" *cintām āpedire*: Literally, "they attained anxiety *or* brooding thought." We have supplied the participle "praying" to make it clear that the following verse is the direct speech of the celestial beings. The exact choice of the word "praying" was influenced by the participle *japantaḥ*, "intoning, muttering, praying," which occurs in 3064*, line 1, immediately following verse 19 in the southern recension. See notes to verse 19 below.

19. Following verse 19, D5–7,9–11,S insert a passage of six lines [3064*]: "Praying in this fashion, the gods, along with the hosts of seers, then watched that extremely terrifying and hair-raising battle between Rāma and Rāvaṇa.[1–2] And the hosts of *gandharvas* and *apsarases* watching that incomparable battle cried, 'Only the sky has the appearance of the sky, the ocean alone is comparable to the ocean, and the battle

between Rāma and Rāvaṇa can be compared only to itself.[1]'[3–5] Speaking in this fashion, they watched the battle between Rāma and Rāvaṇa.[6]"

[1]"Only the sky has the appearance of the sky, the ocean alone is comparable to the ocean, and the battle between Rāma and Rāvaṇa can be compared only to itself." *gaganaṃ gaganākāraṃ sāgaraḥ sāgaropamaḥ / rāmarāvaṇayor yuddhaṃ rāmarāvaṇayor iva //*: As noted by a number of commentators, including those who read the variant (see below), and the author of Gita Press (1969, vol. 3, p. 1816), this is an example of the figure of speech known as *ananvayālaṃkāra*, in which the *upameya*, the subject of comparison, is represented as being unique and therefore having no possible *upamāna*, or standard of comparison, except itself. See Gerow 1971, p. 148. Ct paraphrases Ck, who observes that it is possible to compare the ocean and the sky because they share the qualities of blueness and expansiveness, whereas, in the case of the battle between Rāma and Rāvaṇa, no object of comparison can be stated because of the impossibility of any other such battle. According to Ct, Ck therefore concludes that the figure of speech here is indeed *ananvaya*. Ct also notes that Ck regards the prior half of the verse as an example of *upameyopamā*, i.e., a comparison based on the very thing compared (Gerow 1971, p. 171). This last statement is not to be found in our transcription of Ck or in the critical edition's quotation of his commentary. (*sāgaraṃ nailyavaipulyādināmbaraprakhyam ākāśatulyam iti vaktuṃ śakyam. evam ambaram api sāgaropamam iti śakyam. rāmarāvaṇayor yuddhaṃ tu tadatiriktatādṛśayuddhāsaṃbhavāt svatulyam ity eva vaktuṃ śakyam. tenānupamatvaṃ phalatīty ananvayo 'trālaṃkāraḥ. pūrvārdhe tūpameyopameti katakaḥ.*) D10 and the texts and printed editions of Ct (GPP and NSP 6.107.51cd) read a variant on this popular and often-quoted verse: *sāgaraṃ cāmbaraprakhyam ambaraṃ sāgaropamam*, "The ocean is like the sky and the sky is similar to the ocean." Dutt (1893, p. 1480), Roussel (1903, vol. 3, pp. 357–58), Shastri (1959, vol. 3, p. 313), and Pagani (1999, p. 1162) all render this very poorly attested reading.

20. "razor-tipped arrow" *kṣuram*: See note to 6.33.25. Ś2,Ñ2,V2,3,B1,3,D3, 6–11,13,G1,2,M5, and the texts and printed editions of Cr and Ct read instead *śaram*, "arrow."

"With it, he cut off" *acchindat*: Literally, "he cut." Commentators correct the verbal form to the regular *acchinat*.

"Rāvaṇa's . . . head" *rāvaṇasya śiraḥ*: This verse raises yet again the vexed issue of the number of Rāvaṇa's heads at any given moment. Since, throughout the epic, Rāvaṇa is consistently referred to by epithets such as "ten-headed, ten-necked, etc.," and yet is often described as having only one, commentators have tended to adopt the position that Rāvaṇa shows his terrifying ten-headed form only when engaged in battle. Since here Rāvaṇa is in the greatest and most desperate battle of his life, the use of the singular to describe his head provokes a variety of responses on the part of the commentators. Cg believes firmly that Rāvaṇa has but a single head here, and he bolsters his opinion by quoting a line (App. I, No. 67, line 31 = GPP 6.109.3ab), which represents Rāvaṇa as having only two arms at this particular time. (Rāvaṇa's ten-headed form is normally associated with twenty arms.) (*ekavacanāt tadānīṃ rāvaṇa ekaśirā eva yuddham akarod iti gamyate. ata eva vakṣyati vikṣipya dīrghau niścesṭau bhujāv aṅgadabhūṣitāv ity ādinā.*) Ck, whom Ct also quotes to this effect, comments that the use of the singular suggests that Rāvaṇa's multiple heads are being cut off one after another, and so he proposes that we supply the word *ekaikaśaḥ*, "one at a time." Since the subsequent text will show that Rāvaṇa's severed head(s) keep growing back, Ck supports this argument by indicating that, if all his heads were cut off at once, this regrowth would not occur. (*ekaikaśa iti śeṣaḥ. sakṛddaśaśiraśchede tu na punaḥ prarohaḥ*). Cm and Cs offer a third position. According to them, Rāvaṇa's heads are unambiguously plural. They argue that the singular is used as a collective for a class of similar articles. They support this interpretation by citing a verse that describes Rāvaṇa as having ten faces and twenty arms and, when holding his weapons, is said to resemble Mount Maināka. Cs attempts to reinforce this interpretation by citing a verse he ascribes to "the masters (*ācāryāḥ*)," and one from the *Padmapurāṇa*, both of which clearly refer to Rāvaṇa's multiple heads. (*śira ekavacanaṃ jātāv ekavacanam atrottaratra ca daśāsyo viṃśati bhujaḥ pragṛhītaśarāsanaḥ / adṛsyata daśagrīvo maināka iva parvataḥ // itīva tasyottamāṅgadaśakaṃ yugapan nyakṛntat. kṛttāni tāni punar eva samutthitānīty ācāryair apy ukteḥ. padmapurāṇe ca daśagrīvasya ciccheda śirāṃsi raghunandanaḥ / samutthitāni bahuśo varadānān mamāmbike // iti.*) Cm offers two additional possibilities. The first suggests that the word "head" refers here to multiple heads because Rāvaṇa has those multiple appendages when he is in his battle mode (*daśaśiraḥsahitasya yoddhṛtvābhidhānāc cchira ity atra śirāṃsīty uktam*). As a final option, Cm proposes that the term refers to Rāvaṇa's principal head (*pradhānaśiro vā*). Cr, perhaps wisely, avoids taking a stance on this issue. Translators are similarly divided over the number of Rāvaṇa's heads. Raghunathan (1982, vol. 3, p. 313), no doubt following Cg, translates *śiraḥ*, "head," as a simple singular as does Dutt (1893, p. 1480). Gita Press (1969, vol. 3, p. 1817) understands similarly but adds a footnote, "It seems Rāvaṇa appeared on the battlefield with a single head only during this combat." Gorresio (1858, vol. 10, p. 202) also takes the view that Rāvaṇa has only one head. Roussel (1903, vol. 3, p. 358), followed by Shastri (1959, vol. 3, p. 313) and Pagani (1999, p. 1162), understands that Rāma cuts off only one of Rāvaṇa's many heads. Roussel translates, "*l'une de ces têtes*." For other discussions on the number of Rāvaṇa's heads, see notes to 6.47.106; 6.50.11; 6.90.31; and 6.92.20. See, too, 5.18.13,19; 5.20.24; 5.47.2–14; and notes. Cf. note to 5.20.26 on 518*. Cf., too, 3.30.8.

"majestic" *śrīmat*: The adjective can be taken either as a separate word to modify *śiraḥ*, "head," as we have done, or in composition with the compound "with his [glorious and] shining earrings ([*śrīmaj*]-*jvalitakuṇḍalam*)" to describe Rāvaṇa's earrings. We feel the former is preferable, because it emphasizes once again the majestic appearance of the *rākṣasa* lord as described at such passages as 5.47.2–14.

21. "As the three worlds looked on" *dṛṣṭaṃ lokais tribhis tadā*: Literally, "then [the head] was seen by the three worlds."

"But a new head exactly like it emerged from Rāvaṇa." *tasyaiva sadṛśaṃ cānyad rāvaṇsyotthitaṃ śiraḥ*: Literally, "And another head of Rāvaṇa similar to that arose."

22. "quick-handed . . . acting quickly, quickly" *kṣipraṃ kṣiprahastena . . . kṣiprakāriṇā*: The poet seems to enjoy the effect of the repetition.

23. "yet another appeared in its place" *punar anyat sma dṛśyate*: Literally, "once again, another appeared." D7,9–11, and the texts and printed editions of Cr and Ct read instead *punar eva pradṛśyate*, "once again [one] appeared."

24. "And so in this way" *evam eva*: D3,5,7,G2,M1,3, and the texts and printed editions of Cr, Cm, and Cg read instead *evam eka*[*śatam*]. This yields the meaning,

according to Cg and Cm, "one hundred and one times." Ck provides a devotional interpretation of the scattering of Rāvaṇa's one hundred heads. He claims that, in so doing, Rāma is performing *pūjā* to the hundred feet of Lord Indra of the hundred sacrifices in the form of the one hundred wheels [of his chariot] with [Rāvaṇa's] one hundred lotuslike heads (*śatadhṛticakraśatapadaṃ bhagavataḥ pūjitaṃ rāmeṇa śataśiraḥ-kamalaiḥ*). Ct quotes Ck, although the quotation is somewhat different than the one in our text of Ck. According to Ct, Ck is saying that, with the hundred head-lotuses of Rāvaṇa, Rāma is worshiping the hundred foot-wheels of Sarvatobhadra, the Lord's chariot (*evaṃ ca bhagavataḥ sarvatobhadracakrapadaśatam*). Cg believes, however, that the multiple decapitations are intended to slake the thirst of Rāma's long-thirsting arrows (*punaḥ punaḥ śiraśchedanaṃ ciratṛṣitaśaratṛṣṇānivṛttyartham*).

"all exactly alike" *tulyavarcasām*: We agree with Ck and Ct that the context best supports the meaning of the term *varcaḥ* as "appearance *or* form (*tulyavarcasāṃ tulyākārāṇāṃ* [*śirasām*])" rather than "splendor *or* brilliance," which most translators adopt.

"But still, there seemed to be no way to bring about the end of Rāvaṇa's life" *na caiva rāvaṇasyānto dṛśyate jīvitakṣaye*: Literally, "And yet, no end was visible with respect to the destruction of Rāvaṇa's life." The phrase is somewhat awkward. We follow the interpretation of Ck, Ct, Cg, and Cm, who understand *antaḥ*, "end," in the sense of "final decision, determination, resolution (*niścayaḥ*)." Cr, on the other hand, understands that we should read the genitive plural *śirasām*, "of the heads," from *pāda* b, in this phrase as well, yielding the sense "in the matter of the destruction of life there appeared to be no end to Rāvaṇa's heads (*jīvitakṣaye jīvananivṛt*[*t*]*yarthaṃ rāvaṇasya śirasām anto na dṛśyate śirasām ity ubhayānvayi*)."

26–27. "These are all the very same arrows . . . with which I killed Mārīca and Khara along with Dūṣaṇa. They are the very ones with which I killed Virādha . . . and Kabandha" *mārīco nihato yais tu kharo yais tu sadūṣaṇaḥ / . . . virādhas tu kabandhaḥ . . . / ta ime sāyakāḥ sarve*: Literally, "These are all the arrows with which Mārīca was killed and with which Khara, along with Dūṣaña, and Virādha and Kabandha [were killed]." Mārīca was killed by Rāma at 3.42.11–21; Khara, at 3.28.25; Dūṣaṇa, at 3.25; Virādha, at 3.3; and Kabandha, at 3.66–68.

"upon which I have always relied in battle" *yuddhe pratyayikā mama*: Literally, "trustworthy for (lit., of) me in battle." See 6.97.1–16 and notes, especially note to verse 4.

"so ineffectual" *mandatejasaḥ*: Literally, "whose blazing power is diminished."

Following verse 26, D7,10,11, KK (in brackets), and the texts and printed editions of Ct and Cr insert a passage of one line [3069*]: "with which I pierced the *sāla* trees, the mountains,[1] and Vālin,[2] and [with which] I made the ocean tremble.[3]"

[1]"the *sālā* trees, the mountains" *sālā girayaḥ*: Rāma pierces the *sāla* trees and the mountain[s] at 4.12.3.

[2]"Vālin" *vālī*: Rāma kills Vālin at 4.16.25.

[3]"I made the ocean tremble" *kṣubhito 'mbudhiḥ*: Rāma causes the ocean to tremble at 6.14.

29. A number of southern manuscripts read verse 29 as well as 3071*, line 1, for the first time following verse 14 above. See notes to that passage.

Following verse 29, Ś2,Ñ,B3 (reads twice),4,D5–11,T,G3,M1–3,5, the texts and printed editions of the southern commentators, and the edition of Gorresio (6.92.33) insert a passage of two lines [3071*]: "Then that tremendous and tumultuous hair-raising battle raged on in the air, on the ground, and then on the mountaintop.[1]"

[1]"in the air, on the ground, and then on the mountaintop" *antarikṣe ca bhūmau ca punaś ca girimūrdhani*: The commentators are in agreement that the battle rages in all these locations. Some attribute this to the divine capacity of both chariots to go wherever their masters wish (*rathayoḥ kāmagatvāt tatra tatra kiyatkālaṃ sthiter iti bhāvaḥ*—so Ct). Cg and Cm attribute this to the fierce determination of the combatants (*āgrahāt*). Several of the commentators note that the last phrase refers explicitly to the summit of Mount Trikūṭa. Only Dutt (1893, p. 1481) among the translators consulted understands that these locales are not the places in which the battle takes place but from which the celestial beings mentioned in verse 30 observe it.

30. "all night long" *sarvarātram*: Cg and Cm understand the term *sarvarātram*, literally, "the whole night," to mean "day and night (*ahorātram*)." Ñ,V1,2,B,D2,3,4,9,13,T,2,3,M2, and the texts and printed editions of Cr read *sapta-*, "seven," for *sarva-*, "all," which makes the battle continue for a week. Ct reads with the critical edition, as do Cg and Cm, glossing the term as "day and night," since the singular, as he understands it, is used collectively (*jātāv ekavacanam*). Ct, however, offers a "higher" interpretation, according to which he dissolves the word *sarva-* into its two syllables, the first, "*sa*[*r*]," he notes, is the third consonant of the sibilant class, thus standing for the number 3, while the second syllable "*va*" is the fourth consonant of the class of semivowels, thus representing the number 4. Combining the two numbers, Ct comes up with an esoteric explanation, whereby the word, *sarva-*, "all," really means "seven [i.e., 3 + 4]." Thus, according to Ct, Rāma and Rāvaṇa's chariot duel goes on for seven [days and] nights, a fact he claims is supported by similar references in both the *Padma-* and *Kālikāpurāṇas*. (*jātāv ekavacanam. tenānekāhorātrān ity arthaḥ. vastutaḥ śavarge sakāras tṛtīyas tena traya ucyante. yavarge ca vakāraś caturthas tena catvāra ucyante. militvā saptarātram ity arthaḥ. saptarātram eva ca tayor dvairathaṃ yuddham iti vakṣyamāṇapādmakālikāpurāṇayoḥ spaṣṭam iti dik.*) This argument has proved influential, since most of the translations that follow the text of Ct (and Cr) understand that the battle goes on for seven days and nights. Gorresio (1858, vol. 10, p. 203), whose text reads "*sapta-*," naturally translates similarly.

Cm takes exception to the reading *saptarātra*, which he claims could only meaningfully refer to the duration of the battle prior to the arrival of Agastya (see notes to 6.94.27, App. I, No. 65, esp. line 4). This reading, Cm believes, cannot mean that the duel between Rāma and Rāvaṇa went on for seven days, because that would not be possible and because it is not heard of elsewhere in the *Rāmāyaṇa*. Therefore, Cm concludes that the correct reading is *sarvarātram*, which means "a day and a night." (*saptarātraṃ mahad yuddham avartateti sambandhaḥ. agastyāgamanāt prāg eva siddhasya yuddhasyāyam anuvādaḥ. asmin pāṭhe saptarātrakṛtarāmarāvaṇayuddhasyāsmin rāmāyaṇe 'śrūyamāṇatvenānupapannatvāc ca sarvarātram avartateti pāṭhaḥ samīcīnaḥ. sarvarātram ahorātram ity arthaḥ.*)

Cg expands on Cm's positions. His first alternative is Cm's second, i.e., that the proper reading is *sarvarātram* in the sense of "a day and a night," and that the reading *saptarātram* is thus incorrect (*apapāṭhaḥ*) on the grounds that it would lead to a contradiction of the chronology that will be set forth [at *sarga* 97.33]. As an alternative, Cg expands on Cm's idea that one can accept the reading *saptarātram* and understand *sarvarātram* to be incorrect. Like Cm, he understands that this can only be done if one calculates the number of days in the entire battle. To do this, he then lays out a chronology of the epic story from the time of Hanumān's burning of Laṅkā, which he places on the fourteenth day of the month of Phālguna. He then notes that Rāma reached the shore of the ocean on the full-moon day and lay on his bed of *darbha* grass on the first, second, and third days of the dark half of the month. The ascent of Mount Suvela is placed on the eighth day of the month and the beginning of the battle on the ninth. With this in mind, Cg argues that the entire war [culminating in the duel between Rāma and Rāvaṇa] took seven days. See notes to 6.4.4. For detailed accounts of Cg's chronology, see notes to 6.48.12; 6.80.55; and 6.97.33. (*sarvarātram ahorātram ity arthaḥ. saptarātram ity apapāṭhah. vakṣyamāṇadinasaṃkhyāvirodhāt. yadvā sarvarātram ity apapāṭhaḥ. saptarātram ity eva samyakpāṭhaḥ. phālgunacaturdaśyāṃ hanumatā laṅkādāhaḥ. paurṇamāsyāṃ rāmasya samudratīraprāptiḥ. prathamādvitīyātṛtīyāsu darbhaśayanam. aṣṭamyāṃ suvelārohaṇam. navamyāṃ yuddhārambha iti saptarātraṃ rāmarāvaṇayuddham itīdaṃ cetas tu navame 'hanīty atra vistṛtam.*)

31. "continued night and day without stopping for an hour or even a moment" *naiva rātriṃ na divasaṃ na muhūrtaṃ na ca kṣaṇam / . . . virāmam upagacchati*: Literally, "it did not go to a pause for a night, a day, a *muhūrta*, or an instant."

Following verse 31, D5–7,10,11,T,G1 (after 28),2 (after 28),3,M, and the texts and printed editions of the southern commentators insert a passage of four lines [3074*]: "Then the great driver of the chariot of the foremost of the gods, failing to perceive Rāghava's victory in that battle between those two—the son of Daśaratha and the *rākṣasa* lord—hurriedly spoke these words to Rāma[1] as he stood on the battlefield.[2]"

The meter is *puṣpitāgrā* with a hypermetric *pāda* a.

[1]"great . . . between those two . . . Rāma" *tayoḥ . . . mahātmā . . . rāmam*: D6,T2,3,M2, 3,5, and the texts and printed editions of Cm and Cg omit the word *tayoḥ*. M3 and the texts and printed editions of Cm and Cg likewise substitute the disyllabic word *mahān*, "great," for the trisyllabic *mahātmā*, "great *or* great-minded." D6,T2,3,M3, and the texts and printed editions of Cg read *enam* for *rāmam*. As a result, the verse as it appears in the text of Cg is in a different meter, apparently a type of *ardhasamavṛtta*, where *pādas* a and c have eleven syllables each, and b and d each have thirteen.

[2]"as he stood on the battlefield" *raṇagata-*: Literally, "gone to *or* located on the battle[field]." D10,11, and the texts and printed editions of Ct read *raṇarata-*, "devoted to *or* delighting in battle."

Sarga 97

1. "Why . . . do you merely match him blow for blow" *kim . . . tvam enam anuvartase*: Literally, "why do you follow *or* imitate him?" We follow the interpretation of Cg, who glosses, "you merely use an *astra* to counter an *astra* (*astrasya pratyastrayogamātraṃ karoṣi*)." Ck glosses, "you follow *or* imitate your opponent (*pratibhaṭyam anuruntse*),"

while Ct similarly understands, "you imitate this dangerous [adversary] (*etat pratibhayam anusarasi*)." Cm understands the verb *anuvartase* to mean "you ignore *or* underrate (*upekṣase*)." Most translators consulted follow the suggestions of Ct, Ck, and Cg. Dutt (1893, p. 1482 [misprinted as 1481]), however, who apparently misunderstands Ct, renders, "Why dost thou . . . fear him?"

"as if you knew no better" *ajānann iva*: Literally, "as if not knowing." The phrase is elliptical, and we have chosen to leave it that way in translation. The commentators and some translators offer a variety of suggestions to supply the ellipsis. Cr glosses, "as if not knowing the means to kill [him] (*vadhopāyam abuddhyann iva*)." Cg glosses, "as if not knowing about the *brahmāstra* (*brahmāstram ajānann iva*)." Cs amplifies upon this, supplying the phrase "the fact that Rāvaṇa can be killed by the *brahmāstra* (*rāvaṇasya brahmāstravadhyatām iti śeṣaḥ*)." Cs further notes that the expression " 'as if not knowing' suggests Rāma's omniscience (*ajānann ivety anena rāmasya sarvajñaṃ* [*sic*] *sūcayati*)." Translators offer a variety of presumed objects of the participle *ajānan*, "not knowing." Roussel (1903, vol. 3, p. 359) offers (in parentheses), "*tes resources*," and in this is followed by Shastri (1959, vol. 3, p. 314), "thine own powers." Pagani (1999, p. 1163) similarly translates, "*ton pouvoir*." Raghunathan (1982, vol. 3, p. 314) renders, "what to do." Gita Press (1969, vol. 3, p. 1818), apparently following Cg, adds (in parentheses), "how to dispose of him," and Gorresio (1858, vol. 10, p. 203) adds (in italics), "*l'esser tuo*." Dutt (1893, p. 1482 [misprinted as 1481]), like us, supplies no specific object.

2. "the divinely charged weapon of Grandfather Brahmā" *astraṃ paitāmaham*: Literally, "the *astra* of the grandfather."

3–13. "took up a . . . arrow" *jagrāha . . . śaram*: Verses 3–13 consist of a series of accusative nouns, phrases, and adjectives modifying the arrow. These verses form a single syntactic unit, which we have broken into individual sentences for the sake of readability.

"Presented to him by . . . Agastya, it was a gift of Brahmā" *asmai . . . prādād agastyaḥ . . . brahmadattam*: Literally, "Agastya gave to him . . . given by Brahmā." Ck, Cr, and Ct specify the history of the divine weapon. According to them, Brahmā gave it to Indra, who, in turn, had Agastya confer it upon Rāma (*brahmadattaṃ brahmaṇendrāya dattam. indreṇāgastyadvārā rāmāya dattam*). Agastya had given Rāma the weapon at 3.11.29 (ad loc. and note). This is the same arrow with which Rāma kills Khara at 3.29.23–28 (ad loc. and notes). Even though this is the arrow given by Agastya and fashioned by Brahmā for the purpose of destroying Rāvaṇa, and is among those that Rāma has been using in the previous *sarga* (see 6.96.25–26 and notes), this weapon, fearsome though it is, will not suffice to kill the mighty Rāvaṇa until it is invested with the power of the *brahmāstra* at verse 14 below. Cf. 2.39.11 and note.

"Pavana resided in its feathers. Agni, the purifier, and Sūrya, bringer of light, were in its arrowhead. Its shaft was made of all of space, and the mountains Meru and Mandara lent it their weight." *yasya vājeṣu pavanaḥ phale pāvakabhāskarau / śarīram ākāśamayaṃ gaurave merumandarau //*: Literally, "In whose feathers [there was] Pavana, [in whose] arrowhead [there were] Pāvaka and Bhāskara. [Whose] body was made of space. In [whose] weight [were] Meru and Mandara." The commentators note, in general, that the listing of these various divinities is to show that they are the presiding deities of the various parts of the weapon. Ck and Ct attempt to show how each specific presiding divinity lends his own unique power or property to the arrow. Thus, they argue that the suggestion that space, or *ākāśa*, resides in the arrow's shaft may be interpreted in two different ways. In the first, they derive the term *ākāśa* from its underlying root √*kāś*, "to shine," and then take the term to mean "that which shines everywhere." Alternatively, they understand *ākāśa* to be a kenning for the creator divinity Brahmā, who is "the light of all beings." This latter reference, they argue, suggests the capacity of the weapon to pervade or penetrate everything. These two commentators understand the reference to Pavana to suggest the arrow's capacity for [rapid] motion and take the reference to Pāvaka and the other deities to be to its inability to be withstood. Finally, anticipating the objection that, given the swiftness of the weapon, it must be very light, they refer to the great weight lent to the weapon by the two mighty mountains, Meru and Mandara. (*tatra tatra pavanādīnām adhidevatātvenāvasthānaṃ bodhyam. śarīraṃ madhyabhāga ākāśamayam āsamantāt kāśate prakāśata ity ākāśo brahmā bhagavān bhūtākāśo vā. tena vyāptisāmarthyaṃ pavanatvena gatisāmarthyaṃ pāvakādimattvena duḥsahatvaṃ tarhi laghuḥ syāt tatrāha gaurava iti*—so Ct.) Raghunathan (1982, vol. 3, p. 315), perhaps looking for some parallelism, renders *pāvakabhāskarau* as "the sun and the moon," a rendering supported by no textual, lexical, or commentarial authority.

"the blazing energy of all the elements" *tejasā sarvabhūtānām*: Translators are divided as to whether to understand the term *sarvabhūtānām* as referring to "all creatures," which is the normal interpretation of the sequence *sarvāṇi bhūtāni* or, as Ck, Cr, and Ct suggest, to the five principal elements of the material creation, earth, etc., i.e., the *pañcamahābhūtas*. See notes to 6.15.4. Given the context with its emphasis on the elemental power of the weapon, we are inclined to follow Ct and Ck, who are also followed by Gita Press (1969, vol. 3, p. 1819) and Shastri (1959, vol. 3, p. 314). Other translations consulted understand, "all beings" or "all creatures," except for Dutt (1893, p. 1482 [misprinted as 1481]), who translates, "all objects." To be technically precise, Cg, Cm, Ck, and Ct all gloss *tejasā*, "blazing energy," as "a portion of the strength *or* energy (*sārāṃśena*)."

"chariots" *ratha-*: Ñ2,V1,B2–4,D6,7,9–11, and the texts and printed editions of Cr and Ct read instead *nara-*, "men."

"elephants" *-nāga-*: Dutt (1893, p. 1482 [misprinted as 1481]) chooses the contextually inapposite sense "serpents."

"gateways together with their iron beams" *dvārāṇāṃ parighāṇāṃ ca*: Literally, "doors and iron beams." We agree with the commentators who gloss *dvārāṇām* as "gateways *or* city gates (*gopurāṇām*)." See notes to 6.17.32; 6.61.30; and 6.62.6. In the context of the smashing of defensive installations, we believe that the term *parigha* should be taken in its sense of an iron bar or beam used to bar a gate rather than in its sense of an offensive weapon, "iron club *or* battering ram." Crā, however, takes it in the latter sense, and understands it to be used by metonymy to refer to all weapons (*parighāṇām ity etat sarvāyudhānām apy upalakṣaṇam*). Only Raghunathan (1982, vol. 3, p. 315) understands it in the sense of a weapon, translating, "iron club." See notes to 5.3.30.

"with the blood of many different creatures" *nānārudhira-*: Literally, "with various [kinds of] blood." Cg, alone among the commentators, notes that the blood is "from the piercing of the *asuras* that were to be killed (*vadhyāsurabhedāt*)." Several of the translators understand, somewhat similarly, that the reference is to the number rather than the diversity of the weapon's victims. Cr understands, "the blood connected with the piercing of many bodies (*nidāritānekaśarīrasambandhiśoṇitaiḥ*)."

10. "Hard as adamant" *vajrasāram*: We follow Cg in taking this term as a reference to the hardness of the arrow rather than to its power, which is alluded to in various other ways. Cg glosses, "equal in hardness to adamant (*vajratulyadārḍhyam*)." Some translators understand that the weapon is charged with the power of the thunderbolt. Others agree that *sāra* refers to the arrow's hardness and understand *vajra* in one of its other senses, either "Indra's weapon, the *vajra*," or "diamond."

"it was terrifying in every sort of battle" *nānāsamitidāruṇam*: The term *-samiti-* is ambiguous and lends itself to a variety of interpretations. We partially follow the interpretation of Cg, who takes the term *-samiti-* in its sense of "battle," glossing, "[capable of] ending even a treacherous battle (*kapaṭayuddhasyāpi nivartakam*)." Cr similarly glosses, "of battles (*saṃgrāmāṇām*)." One could also understand *-samiti-* in its sense of "gathering, assembly," and understand then that the weapon "terrorizes various hosts." Roussel (1903, vol. 3, p. 359), followed by Shastri (1959, vol. 3, p. 315), as well as Gita Press (1969, vol. 3, p. 1819) and Dutt (1893, p. 1482 [misprinted as 1481]), all understand the term in this latter sense. D5,G2,M1, and the texts and printed editions of Cg and Ct read *dāraṇam*, "tearing apart," for *dāruṇam*, "terrifying." Ck and Ct understand that the compound is a name or epithet given by the Lord [Brahmā] to Rāma's arrow and expressive of its function (*nānāsamitidāraṇam ity anvartham nāma bhagavatkṛtaṃ rāmabāṇasya*—so Ct).

"to flocks of vultures and adjutant storks" *kaṅkagṛdhrabalānām*: V2,B1,D1,9–11, and the texts and printed editions of Ct read *-bakānām* for *-balānām*, lending the compound the sense "for adjutant storks, vultures, and cranes." Although the critical apparatus claims that Cg reads with the critical edition, both the principal printed editions of Cg's text and commentary, viz., VSP (6.111.11) and KK (6.111.11), show him reading instead *-valānām*, a term that appears to find no lexical support in the sense of "bird." This term is nonetheless glossed by Cg as "a type of vulture (*gṛdhraviśeṣāḥ*)." This variant and interpretation appears to underlie Raghunathan's (1982, vol. 3, p. 315) translation, "kites, vultures, and other birds of prey." On *kaṅka*, see note to 6.35.12 and 6.46.25–28.

14. "in the manner prescribed by the science of archery" *vedaproktena vidhinā*: Literally, "by the injunction set forth in the *veda*." Ck and Ct, with whom we agree, understand the term *veda* here to refer to the *dhanurveda*, the traditional science of weaponry [literally, "the *veda* of the bow"] (*vedo dhanurvedaḥ*). They understand that what is prescribed there are the rules concerning the position of the fist and the eyes, the stance, and the placement of the arrow on the bow (*muṣṭidṛṣṭisthitisaṃdhānādīnāṃ vidhir vidhānaṃ mārgaḥ*). All translators consulted render, "the *veda*," "*vedas*," or "sacred ordinances." Several read the phrase with the gerund *abhimantrya*, "having consecrated with *mantras*," understanding that Rāma has consecrated the arrow with *mantras* as prescribed in the *vedas*. We believe, however, that the context and the syntax offer much stronger support for the interpretation of Ct and Ck. According to Ck and Ct, the *mantra*, or formula, with which Rāma consecrates the arrow is the spell governing the divinely charged weapon of Brahmā (*brahmāstravidyayā*). See, too, note to verse 4 above.

Following verse 14, Ñ,V1,3,B2–4,D4,5,7,9–11,T,G2,3,M, and the texts and printed editions of the southern commentators insert a passage of two lines [3084*]: "As Rāghava was nocking that ultimate arrow, all creatures trembled and the earth shook."

15. "that arrow, which struck at one's vital points" *tam śaraṃ marmaghātinam*: D7,9–11, and the texts and printed editions of Ct read instead *marmavidāraṇam*, "tearing at the vital points."

16. "the *vajra* hurled by Indra, the *vajra* wielder" *vajra iva . . . vajrabāhuvisarjitaḥ*: Literally, "like the *vajra* released by the *vajra*-armed one." The phrase is slightly ambiguous, since the epithet *vajrabāhu-* is susceptible to at least two other interpretations. It could be taken as a simple appositional *karmadhāraya* in the sense of "that arm that was like adamant" or as a *bahuvrīhi* in the sense of "whose arms were like adamant," and so stand as an epithet of Rāma. The situation is further complicated by the ambiguity of the term *vajra*, which can refer to the specific weapon of Indra or to the thunderbolt, both of which can also be viewed as one and the same. An element of the ambiguity is perhaps to be seen in the translation of Pagani (1999, p. 1164), who renders, "*comme la foudre, lancé par ce bras foudroyant.*"

Ñ2,V1,3,B3,D5–7,10,11,T1,G,M1,2,3, and the texts and printed editions of Cg, Ct, and Cr read instead *vajribāhu-*, "the arms of the one possessing the *vajra*," that is, "the arms of Indra, the possessor of the *vajra*." This reading eliminates the ambiguity of the critical reading and is rendered by most translations consulted.

"as inescapable as fate" *kṛtānta iva cāvāryaḥ*: See 6.38.19 and note.

17. "that lethal arrow" *śarīrāntakaraḥ śaraḥ*: Literally, "the arrow that makes the end of bodies." The phrase is awkward to translate literally. D9–11 and the texts and printed editions of Ct read the adjective *paraḥ*, "ultimate, supreme," for *śaraḥ*, "arrow."

18. "lethal" *jīvitāntakaraḥ*: Literally, "making the end of life." D2,7,9–11,M2, and the texts and printed editions of Ct read instead *śarīrāntakaraḥ*, "making the end of bodies."

19. "dutifully" *nibhṛtavat*: Literally, "meekly, humbly, *or* submissively." Cm, Cg, Ct, and Cr, whom we follow, all gloss, "obediently (*vinītavat*)." Ck alone takes the term in its other senses of "motionless (*niścalaḥ*)" or "not agitated *or* disordered (*nirākulaḥ*)."

"returned" *punar āviśat*: Literally, "it entered once more." Dutt (1893, p. 1483) remarks, in a footnote to this verse, "In some texts there is '*napunarāviśat*' i.e., did not enter the quiver." No mention of such a variant appears in the critical apparatus or in those of KK or Lahore.

20. "struck down so suddenly" *hatasyāśu*: Translators differ as to how to construe the adverb *āśu*, "swiftly, suddenly." Most of the translators consulted construe it with the principal finite verb *nipapāta*, "it slipped, fell," in *pāda* c. They understand that the bow and arrows fall immediately from Rāvaṇa's hand. This is grammatically possible but, in our opinion, contextually weak. Raghunathan (1982, vol. 3, p. 316) alone construes the adverb with the present participle *bhraśyamānasya*, "slipping, falling," in *pāda* d, translating, "who . . . had quickly forfeited his life."

"as he lay dying" *bhraśyamānasya jīvitāt*: Literally, "of him who was slipping away from life." B2,3,D10,11,M1, and the texts and printed editions of Ct read instead *bhraśyamānaś ca*, "and who was slipping." This variant, marked "*sic*" in the critical apparatus, is impossible to construe grammatically. Most translations that follow the text of Ct tend to ignore the variant or even the entire word. Roussel (1903, vol. 3, p. 360) attempts to tackle this variant head on. He does so by removing the phrase entirely from the syntax of his verse 21 and using it as a participial phrase, "*Privé de vie*," which, through the use of punctuation, he construes with the nominative singular of *nairṛtendraḥ*, "lord of *nairṛtas*," in the following verse.

21. "once so fearsome in his power and dazzling in his splendor" *bhīmavegaḥ*... *mahādyutiḥ*: Literally, "of terrible force *or* speed... of great splendor."

"like Vṛtra struck down by Indra's *vajra*" *vṛtro vajrahato yathā*: Literally, "like Vṛtra struck *or* slain by the *vajra*." The reference, of course, is to the well-known myth of Indra's slaying of the demon Vṛtra. See notes to 6.55.128 and 6.75.31.

22. "surviving" *hataśeṣāḥ*: Literally, "the ones remaining from those who were slain."

23. "Meanwhile" *ca*: Literally, "and."

"armed with trees" *drumayodhinaḥ*: Literally, "tree-warriors." Readers may recall that the combatants were last mentioned standing wonderstruck, their weapons still in hand (6.95.2).

"that Rāghava was victorious" *vijayaṃ rāghavasya ca*: Literally, "and the victory of Rāghava." GPP (6.108.24), NSP (6.108.24), and Gita Press (6.108.24) read instead *vanarā jitakāśinaḥ*, "the monkeys took on a victorious air."

"roared loudly" *nardantaḥ*: Literally, "roaring." D10,11, and the texts and printed editions of Ct read instead *sarvataḥ*, "from all sides."

"fell upon the *rākṣasas*" *abhipetus tān*: Literally, "they fell upon *or* attacked them."

24. "jubilant... their piteous faces" *hṛṣṭaiḥ*... *karuṇaiḥ*... *mukhaiḥ*: D9–11 and the texts and printed editions of Ct read for *hṛṣṭaiḥ*, "jubilant," *bhraṣṭāḥ*, "fallen," which must refer to the fleeing *rākṣasas*. The treatment of this poorly attested variant seems to vary considerably in the translations that render it. Roussel (1903, vol. 3, p. 360) appears to render it as "*atterrés*." This, in turn, seems to be rendered by Shastri (1959, vol. 3, p. 315) as "in despair." Pagani (1999, p. 1164) seems to straddle the two variants, describing the monkeys as being "*en liesse*," while also describing the *rākṣasas* as "*accablés*." None of these three translations appears to clearly render the phrase *karuṇaiḥ*... *mukhaiḥ*, "with piteous faces," although it is possible, and in Pagani's case likely, that they translate the phrase with the adjectives just quoted.

"the *rākṣasas* fled" *abhyapatan*: Literally, "they fled."

26. "the thirty gods" *tridaśa-*: Literally, "the thirty."

27. "extraordinary" *duravāpā*: Literally, "hard *or* impossible to obtain."

28. "a magnificent shout" *vāg agryā*: Literally, "preeminent speech *or* words."

30. "In slaying... had fulfilled the wishes" *sakāmam*... *cakāra*... *hatvā*: Literally, "having slain, he made [them] so that [they] had their desire." The verse is rather ambiguous and can be read in two somewhat different ways. According to the first, which we and the majority of translators consulted have followed, the sense is that the death of Rāvaṇa is something that Sugrīva, etc., desired as well as Rāma, so that, in accomplishing this, Rāma is, at the same time, fulfilling their desires. Moreover, as several of the commentators note, the monkeys directly benefit from the death of Rāvaṇa. Ck and Ct note that, by Rāma's having accomplished his purpose, viz., the killing of Rāvaṇa, the sovereignty of his allies is solidly and permanently established (*rāvaṇavadhena rāmakārye siddhe kila teṣāṃ rājyaṃ śāśvataṃ pratiṣṭhitaṃ bhavati*). Cg similarly remarks that Aṅgada's desire has been fulfilled, since he, too, sought the death of Rāvaṇa as a recompense [to Rāma] for having made him, like Sugrīva, the heir apparent (*sugrīvavadyuvarājatvena pratyupakārāyāṅgadenāpi rāvaṇavadhasya kāṅkṣitatvāt sakāmatvam*). The other, slightly less plausible reading, is to take the gerund in a temporal sense, understanding that Rāma first kills Rāvaṇa and then separately rewards his allies. To our knowledge, this interpretation has been followed only by the translator of the Gita Press edition (1969, vol. 3, pp. 1820–21), who renders, "on

having dispatched the foremost of the ogres, Śrī Rāma (a scion of Raghu) then fulfilled the desire of Sugrīva, Angada, and Vibhīṣaṇa (by seeing and felicitating them on the fall of Rāvaṇa)."

"immensely powerful" *mahābalam*: Ñ2,B2,D10,11,T2,3,G1,2, and the texts and printed editions of Ct read instead *vibhīṣaṇam*, "[and] Vibhīṣaṇa."

31. "The hosts of the Maruts regained tranquility." *prajagmuḥ praśamaṃ marudgaṇāḥ*: Literally, "The hosts of Maruts went to calmness." Like several other terms for classes of divinities, the term *marut*, which originally refers to a class of vedic storm divinities, often represented as the attendants of Indra, can also refer to the gods in general. Moreover, this term, like the names of various vedic divinities, can also refer to a physical or meteorological phenomenon of which the named divinity is regarded as the personification or superintendent. Cg takes the term here in the second sense, glossing, "the hosts of the gods (*devagaṇāḥ*)." Some translators have followed this interpretation, but since the remainder of the verse refers specifically to natural phenomena, we think that this may not be the best choice. Pagani (1999, p. 1165) alone completely ignores the mythological component, rendering, "*la troupe des vents*." Cr observes that "tranquility" here is meant "freedom from fear (*bhayarāhityam*)."

"the winds blew gently" *mārutā vavuḥ*: Literally, "the winds blew." We follow Cg's and Ct's suggestion on the variant reading *na hi* for *na ca*, in supplying the adverb *sukham*, "softly, pleasantly." Ct's interpretation of the critical reading is that the particle *ca*, "and," should be taken to suggest that the negative particle that precedes it should apply not only to the verb *cakampe*, "[the earth] trembled, shook," but equally to the verb *vavuḥ*, "they blew." In other words, he understands that the winds did not blow. He then argues that we must supply the adjective *krūraḥ*, "fierce." (*mahī na cakampe. māruto na vavau. krūra iti śeṣaḥ.*) D5–7,9–11,T1,G2,3,M1,3, and the texts and printed editions of the southern commentators read the singular *māruto vavau*, "the wind blew," for the critical edition's plural.

"The earth ceased its trembling" *mahī cakampe na*: Literally, "The earth did not shake." Cg reminds us that the earth had been undergoing a continual earthquake up until the death of Rāvaṇa, and that, immediately after his fall, the trembling had ceased (*rāvaṇavadhaparyantaṃ sakampā sthitā mahī tadvadhānantaraṃ niṣkampābhavad iti cāhuḥ*). Cf. 6.94.19 and 6.96.17.

"the sun, the bringer of day, shone with a steady light" *sthiraprabhaś cāpy abhavad divākaraḥ*: Literally, "the maker of day became one whose radiance was fixed." The dimming of the sun was one of the portents accompanying Rāvaṇa's attack. Ct garners from this piece of natural description the information that Rāvaṇa's death takes place three hours before sunset on the ninth day of the bright fortnight of the month of Āśvina (*anenāśvinaśuklanavamyāṃ yāmāvaśeṣadina iti bodhitam*). See note to 6.4.4.

The meter is *vaṃśasthavila*.

32. "Rāghava's closest allies . . . him" *suhṛdviśeṣāḥ . . . rāghavam*: Literally, "the special *or* particular friends *or* allies . . . [around] Rāghava." B3,D7,9–11, and the texts and printed editions of Ct read *suhṛdviśiṣṭāḥ* for *suhṛdviśeṣāḥ*. We understand this variant to be indistinguishable in meaning from the critical reading. However, it can also, if one takes *viśiṣṭa*, "particular, special," in its other sense of "characterized by *or* endowed with," mean "along with [other] allies." This interpretation has been rendered by Gita Press (1969, vol. 3, p. 1821), which translates, "supplemented by their friends." Even

Cg, who reads with the critical edition, glosses the compound as "Jāmbavān and the rest (*jāmbavadādayaḥ*)."

"Sugrīva, Vibhīṣaṇa, and the rest" *sugrīvavibhīṣaṇādayaḥ*: D7,9–11, and the texts and printed editions of Cr and Ct read instead *sugrīvavibhīṣaṇāṅgadāḥ*, "Sugrīva, Vibhīṣaṇa, and Aṅgada."

"who was so magnificent in battle" *raṇe 'bhirāmam*: Literally, "delightful in battle." We follow the lead of Ck and Ct, who gloss, "whose valor in the arena of battle is to be honored by all the world (*raṇaviṣaye sarvajagatpūjanīyaparākramam*)."

"with all due ceremony" *vidhinā*: Literally, "according to rule *or* ceremony." Cg understands that the homage was performed in due order [of precedence] (*krameṇa*).

The meter is *vaṃśasthavila*.

33. "his kinsman and his troops" *svajanabala-*: Strictly speaking, only Lakṣmaṇa can qualify for the term *svajana*, "kinsman," here, and we have translated accordingly. This compound can also be interpreted broadly to mean "the army of his own folk," and this interpretation is represented in the translation of Roussel (1903, vol. 3, p. 361), followed by Shastri (1959, vol. 3, p. 317) and Pagani (1999, p. 1165).

"he looked as resplendent as Indra" *rarāja . . . yathendraḥ*: D10,11,T2, and the texts and printed editions of Ct read *babhūva*, "he was," for *rarāja*, "he shone *or* was resplendent." In addition, these manuscripts (except T2), texts, and editions as well as B2 and B4 read *mahendraḥ*, "great *or* mighty Indra," for *yathendraḥ*, "as *or* like Indra," thus depriving the simile of a *dyotakavācaka*, or word of comparison. Translations that follow the text of Ct and render these variants must, nonetheless, treat the simile as if it were complete.

"the thirty gods" *tridaśa-*: Literally, "the thirty."

The meter is *puṣpitāgrā*.

At the conclusion of the *sarga*, Cg, Cm, and Ct offer further comments on the chronology of the epic events. Cg's and Cm's remarks are very brief and to the point. Cg offers two possible alternative dates for the death of Rāvaṇa, both of which contradict Ct's dating at verse 31 above. Whereas Ct places the event on the ninth day of the bright fortnight of Āśvina, Cg believes that it must be placed either on the new-moon day of Phālguna/Caitra or on the auspicious [or bright?] first day of the lunar fortnight in the month of Caitra at dawn on the waning of the new-moon night. He justifies this second argument by quoting verse 6.96.30 above to the effect that the battle went on day and night. (*phālgunāmāvāsyāyāṃ rāvaṇavadhaḥ. yadvā caitraśuddhapratipadi śiṣṭāmāvāsyāyāṃ prātaḥkāle rāvaṇavadhaḥ. pūrvaṃ sarvarātram avartata ity ukteḥ.*) See, too, 6.48.12; 6.80.55; and 6.96.30. Cm simply notes that Rāvaṇa's death took place on the new-moon day (*amāvāsyāyām*) [presumably of Phālguna, which immediately precedes the first day of the lunar fortnight of Caitra]. Ct, however, launches into an extensive and massively detailed set of arguments concerning the chronology of the epic events. He rejects the dating favored by Cm and Ck (see note to 6.80.55). Ct understands Cm and Ck as placing the beginning of the battle on the first day of the dark half of Caitra (*caitrakṛṣṇapratipadi yuddhārambhaḥ*) and the funeral rites of Rāvaṇa on the first day of the bright half of that same month (*tacchuklapratipadi rāvaṇasaṃskāraḥ*). After a technical discussion of the intercalary days needed to reconcile the solar and lunar calendars, in which Ct alludes to the analogous dating problem of the Pāṇḍavas' exile as discussed in the *Mahābhārata*, he goes on to cite a variety of sources, including the *Vālmīki Rāmāyaṇa*, the *Kālikāpurāṇa*, the *Brahmavaivartapurāṇa*, and the

Āgniveśyarāmāyaṇa, in support of his contention that Rāvaṇa's death takes place on the ninth day of the bright half of the month of Āśvina. Ct rejects the contention raised in some of these texts that differing accounts of the dating, etc., of events in the *Rāmāyaṇa* are to be attributed to the variations in the unfolding of the narrative as it takes place in different cosmic ages. See note to 6.4.4. On Āgniveśya/Agniveśya, see note 6.4.63 and 6.40.64.

Following *sarga* 6.97, V2,B1,3,D5–7,9–11,S insert a passage of sixty-eight lines (App. I, No. 67, lines 27–94; GPP, NSP, Gita Presss = 6.109; VSP, KK = 6.112). Gorresio's text (= 6.93.10–32) knows the passage with some variation and condensation: "Now, when Vibhīṣaṇa saw his brother lying there, vanquished by Rāma,[1] his heart was overwhelmed by a violent access of grief,[2] and he began to lament [27–28]. 'Valorous and renowned hero, well-trained[3] and skilled in statecraft! How is it that you, who deserve a costly bed, now lie slain on the bare ground, your long arms, adorned with bracelets, flung wide[4] and motionless, your diadem, as radiant as the sun, maker of day, askew.[5][29–32] The warning that I had urged upon you[6] earlier has now proven true,[7] hero, for, in your lust and delusion, you did not heed my words.[33–34] That inevitable outcome[8] to which, out of arrogance, Prahasta, Indrajit, and others, such as the great chariot-warrior Kumbhakarṇa, Atikāya, Narāntaka, and you yourself, paid no heed, has come to pass.[35–37] Gone is the boundary marker[9] for the virtuous! Gone the embodiment of righteousness! Gone is the epitome of might! Gone is the object of all praise![10][38–39] The sun has fallen to the earth, the moon is plunged into darkness, the fire has lost its radiance, and manly action itself has lost all vitality[11] now that this hero, foremost of those who bear weapons, has fallen to the ground.[40–42] Now that the tiger among the *rākṣasas* lies sleeping, as it were, in the dust, what now remains in this world, stripped of its sole hero?[12][43–44] The mighty tree that was the *rākṣasa* king—with fortitude for its sprouting leaves, vigorous action[13] for its splendid blooms, asceticism for its strength, and valor for its deep-set roots—has been destroyed in battle by the mighty gale that is Rāghava.[14][45–48] The indomitable bull elephant[15] that was Rāvaṇa—who had blazing energy for his tusks, noble lineage for his backbone, and rage and graciousness for his limbs and trunk—now sleeps on the bare ground, his body ravaged by the lion who is the Ikṣvāku prince.[49–52] The blazing fire that was the *rākṣasa*—with valor and fortitude for its leaping flames, angry breaths for its smoke, and might for its scorching heat—has now been extinguished in battle by the storm cloud that is Rāma.[53–56] That bull in the form of a *rākṣasa*, that bull elephant and conqueror of his enemies, who was so indomitable in their destruction[16]—with his fellow *rākṣasas*[17] for his tail, hump, and horns, and rashness for his ears and eyes[18]—has been slain, struck down by that tiger in the form of the lord of the earth.'[57–60] Rāma then replied to Vibhīṣaṇa, who, overcome with grief, was uttering this speech that was so reasonable and so clear in its sense.[19][61–62] 'This warrior[20] of fierce valor and extraordinarily great energy was not slain in battle without putting up a struggle.[21] He fell fearlessly.[22] [63–64] Those who perish in this fashion, falling on the battlefield in the hopes of success[23] and following the way of the warrior, should not be mourned.[65–66] Now that that wise hero,[24] who had terrified the three worlds and Indra as well in battle, has perished,[25] it is not an occasion for grieving.[67–68] No one has ever been invariably victorious in battle. A hero is either slain by his enemies or slays them in battle.[69–70] For this is the way ordained by the men of old[26] and approved by all warriors: It is certain that a warrior slain in battle is not to be mourned.[71–72] Realizing this certainty and having recourse to the true nature of things, you should, free from anxiety, consider what action is to be taken next.'[73–74] Then Vibhīṣaṇa, consumed with grief, in his concern for his brother's welfare in the next world, replied[27] to the valorous prince, who had spoken those words.[75–76] 'He who had never before been broken in battles with the assembled gods, together with Vāsava, has now been broken in battle upon encountering you, just like the unassailable ocean encountering its shore.[28][77–80] He gave charitably and offered worship appropriately.[29] He enjoyed all pleasures and supported his dependents well. He conferred wealth upon his friends and visited hostility upon his enemies.[81–84] He kindled the sacred fires and practiced profound austerities. He had mastered the *vedas* and was adept in the performance of vedic rituals. Now, therefore, by your grace, I should like to perform the rites for him who has departed this world.'[85–88] Thus properly addressed by Vibhīṣaṇa with these piteous words,[30] the great son of the king, in a lofty spirit, ordered the rite that conveys one to heaven.[89–92] 'Hostilities cease with death. Our purpose[31] has been accomplished. You may now perform his funeral rites, for as he was to you, so he is to me.'[32][93–94]"

Lines 93–94 = 6.99.39 (= GPP 6.109.25; 6.111.100cd–101ab). See note to 6.99.39.

[1]"vanquished by Rāma" *rāmanirjitam*: D9–11 and the texts and printed editions of Ct read instead *nirjitaṃ raṇe*, "vanquished in battle *or* on the battlefield."

[2]"a violent access of grief" *śokavega-*: Literally, "by the force of grief." Cg, alone among the commentators, seeks to explain Vibhīṣaṇa's grieving for the brother who treated him so hatefully. He comments, "Now, seeing that his brother had been slain, Vibhīṣaṇa, unable to endure the violent grief arisen from his natural relationship, laments (*atha bhrātṛvadhadarśanena haṭhāt pravṛttaṃ prakṛtisaṃbandhakṛtaṃ śokaṃ soḍhum aśaknuvan vibhīṣaṇo vilapati*)."

[3]"well-trained" *vinīta*: V3,D10,11,M1, and the texts and printed editions of Ct read instead *pravīṇa*, "competent, able." Ct glosses this as "capable (*samartha*)."

[4]"flung wide" *nikṣipya*: Literally, "having thrown down [your arms]."

[5]"askew" *apavṛttena*: Literally, "reversed, overturned." Ct and Cr understand that Rāvaṇa's diadem has been knocked off by Rāma's arrows (*rāmabāṇais tyājitena*). Cg, whom we follow, understands that the crown has been slightly dislodged by the force of Rāvaṇa's fall (*patanavegād īṣac calitena*).

[6]"The warning that I had urged upon you" *mayā . . . samīritam*: Literally, "uttered by me."

[7]"proven true" *samprāptam*: Literally, "arrived, come about."

[8]"That inevitable outcome" *udarkaḥ*: We follow Ct, Ck, and Cr in taking the term in its common meaning of "future consequence (*uttarakālikavipākaḥ*—so Ct and Ck). Cg understands, "the consequences of the abduction of Sītā (*tasya sītāharaṇarūpasyodarkaḥ phalam*)." Raghunathan (1982, vol. 3, p. 317) follows this interpretation, rendering, "the fruit of that transgression." Other translators consulted take the term to refer to Vibhīṣaṇa's advice or counsel.

[9]"the boundary marker" *setuḥ*: We follow Cg and Cm in taking the term in its sense of "boundary, limit (*maryādā*)." Most translators consulted take the term in its sense of "rampart *or* bridge."

[10]"the object of all praise" *prastāvānāṃ gatiḥ*: Literally, "the goal *or* recourse of praise." We follow Cg, who glosses, "the object of excellent praise (*prakṛṣṭastutīnām ... viśayaḥ*). Cv understands similarly. V1,D10,11,G1, and the texts and printed editions of Ct read *suhastānām*, "those of good hands," for *prastāvānām*. The idea seems to be "the refuge of deft-handed warriors" (so Gita Press 1969, vol. 3, p. 1822).

[11]"and manly action itself has lost all vitality" *vyavasāyo nirudyamaḥ*: Literally, "resolution is without effort." Commentators interpret this variously. Ct, Cm, and Cg understand that, in the absence of a support such as Rāvaṇa, resolution has become inactive (*rāvaṇasadṛśāśrayābhāvād vyavasāya utsāhaśaktir nirvyāpāro 'bhūd ity arthaḥ*—so Cg). Cr understands that exertion has now become purposeless (*utsāhaḥ ... nirarthakaḥ*).

[12]"stripped of its sole hero" *hatavīrasya*: Literally, "whose hero is slain." D10,11,M1, and the texts and printed editions of Ct read instead *gatasattvasya*, "whose essence *or* strength is departed."

[13]"vigorous action" *prasabha-*: D6,7,M3, and the texts and printed editions of Cv, Cg, and Cr read instead *prasaha-*, "fortitude, endurance." Among the translators, only Raghunathan (1982, vol. 3, p. 317) reads this variant. Gita Press (1969, vol. 3, p. 1822) reads with the critical edition but translates, "stubbornness."

[14]The meter of lines 45–60 is *upajāti*.

[15]"The indomitable bull elephant" *gandhahastī*: Literally, "the scent-elephant." See note at 5.8.12. This is a technical term for an elephant whose scent inspires fear in other elephants. See notes to 6.15.33, App. I, No. 16, lines 57–69; and 6.4.14. Cv understands, "the principal [elephant] (*mukhyaḥ*)," while Cg glosses, "rutting elephant (*mattagajaḥ*)," an interpretation that most translators have followed. See note 16 below.

[16]"that bull elephant and conqueror of his enemies, who was so indomitable in their destruction" *parābhijidgandhanagandhahastī*: Literally, "the conquering scent-elephant of destruction." See note 15 above. D10,11,M1, and the texts and printed editions of Ck and Ct read instead *parābhijidgandhanagandhavāhaḥ*, lending to the compound the sense "that conquering wind, bearer of scents." Gorresio (1858, vol. 10, p. 308) provides a somewhat lengthy discussion of the term *gandhahastī* and its use in Buddhist texts.

[17]"his fellow *rākṣasas*" *siṃharkṣa-*: Literally, "lion-*ṛkṣas*." The commentators all quote the *Nighaṇṭu* (Cm, the lexicographer Śāsvata), which cites the term as a synonym for *rākṣasa*. Cv and Cg, however, offer an alternative explanation, according to which the term refers to the nineteenth lunar asterism also known as *Mūlā* (or *Mūla*), which is the *nakṣatra* of the *rākṣasas*. Cg quotes the authority on astronomy Kāśyapa in support of this interpretation. Cf. 6.6.46 and note. Gita Press (1969, vol. 3, p. 1822) provides a note on this word to the same effect. According to Pagani (1999, p. 1674), the term refers to a specific category or type of *rākṣasa*, which has given Rāvaṇa one of his surnames. She defines this name through a literal reading of the term as "bear-lion." She notes, "*Il s'agit d'une catégorie de rākṣasa qui a donné à Rāvaṇa l'un de ses surnoms* (*et dont le nom signifie* '*ours-lion*')." She cites no references and it is difficult to determine the basis on which she makes these claims.

[18]"rashness for his ears and eyes" *cāpalakarṇacakṣuḥ*: Cm, Ct, Ck, and Cr understand *cāpala-*, "rashness," here as "lapsing from righteousness (*dharmebhyaḥ skhalanam*—so Cr)." Cg understands, "excessive lust for sense objects (*viṣayalaulyam*)."

Cs breaks the compound down, understanding Rāvaṇa's auditory rashness as listening to and acting upon things he should not hear, such as Śūrpaṇakhā's complaint. Rāvaṇa's visual transgressions consist in gazing upon things that he should not see, such as the beauty of the wives of others. (*karṇayoś cāpalam aśrāvyaśūrpaṇakhādipralapitaśravaṇena tatra cittapraṇidhānam. cakṣusor anavalokanīyaparadārasaundarya darśanam.*)

[19]"so reasonable and so clear in its sense" *hetumat ... paridṛṣṭārthaniścayam*: Literally, "possessed of reason and having a clear resolution of meaning." Roussel (1903, vol. 3, p. 363), followed by Pagani (1999, p. 1166), understands these terms to apply to the subsequent words of Rāma rather than to the previous speech of Vibhīṣaṇa.

[20]"This warrior" *ayam*: Literally, "this one."

[21]"without putting up a struggle" *niśceṣṭaḥ*: Literally, "motionless *or* inactive." Ck and Ct gloss, "powerless (*aśaktaḥ*)."

[22]"He fell fearlessly." *patito 'yam aśaṅkitaḥ*: Literally, "fearless, he fell." The commentators understand that Rāvaṇa had no fear of death (*mṛtyuśaṅkārahitaḥ*—so Ct, Ck). Cs optionally reads the sequence as *patito yamaśaṅkitaḥ*, that is, "he whom even Yama, the god of death, feared has fallen."

[23]"success" *vṛddhim*: Literally, "increase, prosperity." Ct and Ck take the reference to be to victory, etc. (*jayādikam*), while Cg understands it to be "success in the next world (*paralokavṛddhim*)."

[24]"that wise hero" *yena ... dhīmatā*: Literally, "by that wise one."

[25]"has perished" *asmin kālasamāyukte*: Literally, "in reference to him who is joined with *kāla*," i.e., "in reference to him whose time has come."

[26]"by the men of old" *pūrvaiḥ*: Literally, "by the forefathers." Commentators agree that the reference is to such authorities as Manu.

[27]"in his concern for his brother's welfare in the next world, replied" *uvāca ... bhrātur hitam anantaram*: Literally, "he spoke [with regard to] the subsequent welfare of the brother." Since Vibhīṣaṇa's subsequent words concern the funerary rites of Rāvaṇa, we agree with Raghunathan (1982, vol. 3, p. 318) in taking *anantaram*, "next *or* subsequent," as an adjective modifying *hitam*, "well-being," in the sense of "welfare in the next world." Most translators consulted, however, take the term adverbially with the verb *uvāca*, "he spoke," indicating that Vibhīṣaṇa replies immediately.

[28]Lines 77–92 are in the *upajāti* meter.

[29]"He gave charitably and offered worship appropriately." *anena dattāni supūjitāni*: Literally, "by him [things] were given and were well-worshiped." The commentators flesh out the elliptical line by adding the words "gifts (*dānāni*)" and "*gurus* and gods (*gurudaivatāni*)" to provide respective objects for the participles. D10,11, and the texts and printed editions of Ct read *vanīpakeṣu* "upon beggars *or* mendicants," for *supūjitāni*, "well-worshiped."

[30]"with these piteous words" *vākyaiḥ karuṇaiḥ*: Only Cg among the commentators seems to notice the apparent contradiction between Vibhīṣaṇa's emotional appeal to be permitted to offer the funeral rites in light of his brother's many virtues and the passage at 6.99.32–33 below, where he expresses a disinclination to so honor his vicious brother. Cg explains the discrepancy by noting that Vibhīṣaṇa speaks in this way because, at this moment, he is overwhelmed by an access of grief, although later on he will state that he does not want to perform Rāvaṇa's funeral rites. (*karuṇair ity anena duḥkhātiśayād idānīm evam uktam iti dyotyate. vakṣyati hi nāham asya saṃskāraṃ kariṣyāmīti.*) In light of the critical edition, it is clear that this entire passage is a late

interpolation added in an attempt to smooth over the raw emotions of the original text by promoting the culturally cherished themes of deference of the junior brother and familial harmony.

[31]"Our purpose" *naḥ prayojanam*: According to Cg, Rāma's purpose was the recovery of Sītā (*prayojanaṃ sītālābharūpam*), although later on in the critically established text Rāma will state that his sole purpose was to recover his reputation (6.103.21). In addition, Cg asserts that the syllable of the *Gāyatrīmantra* is represented here by the enclitic pronoun *naḥ* (*atra śloke na iti gāyatryakṣaram*). Cm is more explicit, noting that the twentieth syllable of that *mantra* (*naḥ*) corresponds to the twelfth syllable of this verse (*naḥ*) (*gāyatryāḥ viṃśatitamākṣaraṃ maraṇāntāni vairāṇīty asya ślokasya dvādaśākṣareṇa na iti anena saṃgṛhṇāti*). See note to 6.1.1.

[32]"for as he was to you, so he is to me" *mamāpy eṣa yathā tava*: Literally, "just as he is yours, he is also mine." We agree with the commentators, who understand the reference to be to Rāma's holding the deceased in an affectionate fraternal regard, most likely because, as Cg makes clear, Vibhīṣaṇa is Rāma's "brother" so that Vibhīṣaṇa's brother Rāvaṇa is in a similar relation to Rāma. In any case, as Rāma notes, all hostilities end with death. Roussel (1903, vol. 3, p. 363) and Pagani (1999, p. 1167), on the other hand, understand the pronoun *eṣaḥ*, "he," not to refer to Rāvaṇa but instead to the funeral rite (*saṃskāraḥ*). They thus understand Rāma to be saying that the rite is as much his responsibility as it is Vibhīṣaṇa's.

Sarga 98

1. "when... heard" *śrutvā*: V2,3,B3,D5–7,12,T3,G3, and the texts and printed editions of Ct read instead *dṛṣṭvā*, "having seen."

2. "Although many tried to restrain them, they rolled in the dust of the earth" *vāryamāṇāḥ subahuśo veṣṭantyaḥ kṣitipāṃsuṣu*: Literally, "[they] being very frequently prevented, rolling in the dust of the earth." Roussel (1903, vol. 3, p. 364), followed by Pagani (1999, p. 1167), takes the participle *vāryamāṇāḥ*, "being prevented, held back," in the sense of "covered" and reads the adverb *subahuśaḥ*, "many times," with the participle *veṣṭantyaḥ*, "rolling." These translators thus understand that the women roll about so frequently that they become covered with dust. This seems to be a very unnatural reading of the line, but Roussel, as elsewhere (see note to 6.93.13, and note to verse 21 below; cf. note to verse 23 below), may be influenced by Gorresio's text (6.94.2), which reads, *bahuśaś ceṣṭamānāś ca saṃbaddhāḥ kṣitipāṃsubhiḥ* (cf. 3098*), which he translates as "*e forte dibattendosi e sordidate dalla polvere della terra*" (1858, vol. 10, p. 210). See Introduction, pp. 115–117 and notes to 6.93.13; 6.98.2; and 6.116.11. See, too, verses 21 and 23 below. Cf. 6.3.16.

D4–6,10,11,G2,M1, and the texts and printed editions of Ct and Ck read *raṇa-*, "battlefield," for *kṣiti-*, "earth." This reading seems textually inappropriate, since the *rākṣasa* women do not reach the battlefield until verse 3.

5. "they cried" *vineduḥ*: The verb is somewhat redundant with the participle *nardantyaḥ*, "shrieking," of *pāda* c. Ś2,Ñ,V1,B,D1–4,6,8,12,13,T2,3,G2,M1, the text of Cr, and the printed edition Gorresio avoid the redundancy, reading instead *na rejuḥ*, "they did not shine." V2,3,D10,11, and the texts and printed editions of Ct read instead the redundant *kareṇvaḥ* (GPP *kereṇvaḥ* [*sic*]), "elephant cows."

6. "lying slain" *nihataṃ bhūmau*: Literally, "slain."

9. "Raising her arms" *uddhṛtya ca bhujau*: Literally, "and lifting two arms." Some translators understand that the woman lifts Rāvaṇa's arms, but this seems less plausible to us.

10. "so that his face was bathed with tears, as is a lotus with dewdrops" *snāpayantī mukhaṃ bāṣpais tuṣārair iva paṅkajam*: Literally, "[she] bathing the face with tears, as if a lotus with dew." The simile is slightly awkward, as there is no apparent subject for the phrase expressing the similarity. Gita Press (1969, vol. 3, p. 1825) attempts to complete the simile by adding the subject, translating, "even as nature would cover a lotus with dew-drops." Other translators tend to treat the dewdrops themselves as the subject. One could also understand the verse to indicate that it is the woman's own face that is bathed with tears, but this seems less probable to us.

11. "lying slain" *nihatam*: Literally, "slain."

"they keened . . . then began to lament" *cukruśuḥ . . . paryadevayan*: Literally, "they cried out, they lamented." The two verbs overlap semantically, and Cg attempts to distinguish between the actions they describe. He differentiates two modes of lamentation, which he describes, respectively, as nonverbal and verbal. (*krośo nirakṣaradhvaniḥ. paridevanaṃ sākṣaraśabdaḥ.*)

12–13. "terrorized" *vitrāsitaḥ . . . vitrāsitaḥ*: Literally, "terrorized . . . terrorized."

"he who robbed King Kubera Vaiśravaṇa of his flying palace Puṣpaka" *yena vaiśravaṇo rājā puṣpakeṇa viyojitaḥ*: Literally, "he by whom King Vaiśravaṇa was deprived of the Puṣpaka." See notes to 6.7.5 and 6.37.7.

"tremendous" *mahat*: Literally, "great." Ñ1,D4,7,9–11,13, and the texts and printed editions of Ct and Cr read instead the redundant *raṇe*, "in battle."

14. "He . . . had much to fear from a mere human" *tasyedaṃ mānuṣād bhayam*: Literally, "of him this fear [came] from a man."

15. "by a mere human fighting on foot" *mānuṣeṇa padātinā*: Literally, "by a human foot soldier." The characterization of Rāma as a foot soldier is slightly puzzling, since, in the final duel between Rāma and Rāvaṇa, both combatants fought from their great chariots (see *sarga* 97). The commentators are silent on this matter. Some translators attempt to rationalize the situation by understanding that the *rākṣasīs* are referring to the fact that Rāma traveled to Laṅkā on foot and fought most of the battle without the benefit of Indra's chariot. See, for example, Gita Press (1969, vol. 3, p. 1825), which translates, "by a mortal come walking (all the way from Ayodhyā)."

16. "some feeble creature" *asattvaḥ*: Literally, "one of no strength."

17. "Rāvaṇa's women wept copiously" *bahudhā rurudus tasya tāḥ striyaḥ*: Literally, "those women of his wept copiously." D9–11 and the texts and printed editions of Ct read instead *tasya tā duḥkhitāḥ striyaḥ*, "those sorrowful women of his."

18. "Since you consistently refused to heed the words of your friends, who advised you for your own good" *aśṛṇvatā tu suhṛdāṃ satataṃ hitavādinām*: Literally, "by one not listening to his friends, who speak beneficially." The clause is somewhat elliptical. We follow the advice of the commentators in supplying the term "the words (*vākyam*)" to construe with the genitive *suhṛdām*, "of friends." Cv and Cg, however, offer a second alternative, that we read the genitive *suhṛdām* in the sense of the ablative *suhṛdbhyaḥ*, giving the sense "not hearing from your friends."

"all of us and you yourself have now been ruined all together" *etāḥ samam idānīṃ te vayam ātmā ca pātitāḥ*: Literally, "we, [that is] these (feminine) [and] those (masculine), and you yourself, now together have been caused to fall." The exact referent of the pronoun *te* in *pāda* c is unclear, and the commentators offer various ways to understand it. We follow Cg and Cm in taking it as a nominative masculine plural, referring, elliptically in the critical reading, to the male *rākṣasas* who have been slaughtered. Compare verse 22 below. Ck reads *te* as an instrumental singular, for *tvayā*, construing it idiomatically with the indeclinable *samam* in *pāda* c, yielding the sense of "[we] together *or* along with you." Ct similarly glosses *te* with the instrumental singular *tvayā* but apparently understands it to be the subject of the passive participle *pātitāḥ*, "caused to fall," in *pāda* d. Cr understands *te* as a genitive singular, *tava*, construing with *ātmā*, "self," in *pāda* d, which he understands in its sense of "body (*śarīram*)," yielding the sense "your [i.e., Rāvaṇa's] body."

It should be kept in mind here that no manuscript collated for the critical edition reads exactly as the critical text does. A number of northern manuscripts—Ś2,B2,D1,3,8,12,13, and the printed editions of Gorresio and Lahore—read *aiśvarya-madamattena*, "[by you] intoxicated with the arrogance of power" for *pāda* c, *etāḥ samam idānīṃ te*. According to this reading, the *te* in *pāda* c should be read as suggested by Ct. However, the majority of manuscripts, including the texts of the southern commentators, either substitute for 18cd (Ñ,V,B3,4,D4) or insert after 18ab (B2,D5–7,9–11,T2,3,G,M, and the texts and printed editions of all southern commentators) a passage of one line [3106*] in which an explicit reference is made to the slain *rākṣasa* warriors: "Sītā was abducted [by you] for [your own] death, and the night-roaming *rākṣasas* were caused to be slain."

19. "cruelly" *dhṛṣṭam*: D7,10,11,G3,M5, and the texts and printed editions of Ct and Cr read instead the rather awkward, *dṛṣṭam*, "was seen." Ct and Cr attempt to explain this term by adding the word *phalam*, "fruit, consequences," yielding the sense that Rāvaṇa must have foreseen the dire consequence of his actions.

"desiring, it appears, your own destruction" *ātmavadhakāṅkṣiṇā*: Literally, "[by you] seeking your own death."

20. "this total extermination" *mūlaharam*: Literally, "root destruction." We understand the term, as does Cr, to mean "extirpation of the race [of the *rākṣasas*] (*vaṃśa-vighātakam*)." Cf. 6.36.14–15 and note.

21. "Your brother Vibhīṣaṇa would have had his wish fulfilled" *vṛttakāmo bhaved bhrātā*: Literally, "the brother would be one whose wish was completed." We agree with the commentators that the brother in question is Vibhīṣaṇa. Cm, Ct, and Cg believe that Vibhīṣaṇa's gratification would have derived from Rāvaṇa's acting on his advice (*svavākyakaraṇād iti bhāvaḥ*—so Cg). Cr has a similar idea but indicates more explicitly that the reference is to the fulfillment of Vibhīṣaṇa's desire that Sītā be returned as he had requested (*svaprārthitasītāpradānaviṣayakābhilāṣaprāptaḥ*).

"and Rāma would have become an ally of our House" *rāmo mitrakulaṃ bhavet*: We read the compound *mitrakulam*, literally, "friend-family," as a *paranipāta* compound as suggested by Cm and Cg, that is, as *kulamitram*, "friend of the family." Ct and Cr gloss, "belonging to the party of our friends *or* allies (*mitrapakṣaḥ*)." Gorresio (1858, vol. 10, p. 211), who shares our reading, mistakes the compound for a *dvandva* in the sense of "*la tua famiglia e i tuoi amici*" and understands that the two terms should be taken, along with Vibhīṣaṇa, to make a list of all those who would be gratified had Rāvaṇa returned Sītā. He thus understands the verb *bhavet*, "he would be," to apply to all these groups and individuals. Unfortunately, Gorresio appears to have influenced

Roussel (1903, vol. 3, p. 365) in this misreading. Roussel, however, understands *-kulam* in the sense of "a group," rendering, "*tes nombreux amis*." Roussel, in turn, has been followed by Shastri (1959, vol. 3, p. 319) and Pagani (1999, p. 1168). See note to verse 2 above.

"None of us would have been widowed" *vayaṃ cāvidhavāḥ sarvāḥ*: Literally, "and we all [would be] non-widows."

"enemies" *śatravaḥ*: Since the logic of the women's statement would have precluded the possibility of Rāma and the monkeys becoming his enemies, we agree with Cg, who glosses, "the gods, etc. (*devādayaḥ*)." Pagani (1999, p. 1168), however, seems to ignore the negative particle *na* in *pāda* d, understanding that Rāvaṇa's enemies, presumably Rāma and the monkeys, would be satisfied [by the return of Sītā].

22. "at the same time" *tulyam*: Literally, "equally." We follow Cr and Cg, who understand the term here to mean "simultaneously (*yugapat*—so Cg)."

"cruel Rāvaṇa, you" *tvayā . . . nṛśaṃsena*: Literally, "by you, a cruel one."

23. "Nonetheless, it is true" *kāmam*: We agree with Cv and Cg in reading the term adverbially in its sense of "granted, it is true" rather than, as Cm and most translators have done, in its sense of "according to one's desire." The latter sense would be quite redundant with the term *kāmakāraḥ*, "voluntary action," in *pāda* a. Several of the translators understand the term in its nominal sense of "love, passion," which they believe is being represented as something other than the motive for Rāvaṇa's actions. For example, Roussel (1903, vol. 3, p. 365) translates, "*Ce n'est point toute fois ta passion qui est en cause*." This is both redundant and grammatically impossible. Ct understands the term to mean "sufficient [cause] (*paryāptam*)," an interpretation represented only in the translation of Gita Press (1969, vol. 3, p. 1826). Gorresio (1858, vol. 10, p. 212), whose rendering may have inspired Roussel here, translates, "*Egli è bensi vero . . . che non fu di tanta sciagura cagione efficiente il tuo amore*." See note to verse 2 above.

"fate" *daivam*: This passage renews the poem's debate over the issue of destiny versus free will as the prime mover of events. See Pollock 1986, pp. 33–36. Cs lends a theological interpretation to the passage, understanding that the word "fate (*daivam*)" refers to Hari (i.e., Viṣṇu), the unseen prime mover [of all things] (*adṛṣṭaprerako harir eva*). See 6.6.7–8 and notes; and 6.103.5 and notes.

25. "the relentless march of fate" *daivagatir . . . udyatā*: Literally, "the persevering movement of fate." We understand the adjective *udyatā* here in the sense Ct proposes: "moving toward fruition (*phalonmukhībhūtā*)."

"by . . . act of will" *kāmena*: Literally, "by will *or* desire."

"by imperious command" *ājñayā*: Literally, "by an order."

26. "lament, afflicted with grief . . . shrieking like ospreys" *vilepuḥ . . . kurarya iva duḥkhārtāḥ*: Literally, "they lamented like osprey hens afflicted with grief." The simile is slightly defective, and we have added the word "shrieking" to bring out the force of the common trope in which the wailing of grief-stricken women is likened to the shrill cries of the osprey. Some translations read the adjective "grief-stricken (*duḥkhārtāḥ*)" with "ospreys (*kuraryaḥ*)," yielding the sense "like grief-stricken ospreys." But as ospreys are known for their shrieking and not for their grief, we believe that this is uncalled for. Compare 6.23.1–3 and note. On the *kurara* or *kurarī*, see, Dave 1985, p. 185 and Fitzgerald 1998. Dutt (1893, p. 1488) renders, "like unto so many she-elephants." Perhaps he mistakenly reads *kariṇyaḥ*, although no such variant is attested in the critical apparatus.

Sarga 99

1. "Rāvaṇa's . . . seniormost wife, Mandodarī" *jyeṣṭhā patnī*: Literally, "senior *or* eldest wife."

2. "Mandodarī" *mandodarī*: The critical apparatus notes that here and elsewhere some manuscripts show the variant *maṇḍodarī*. The commentators exert themselves here in an effort to provide an etymology for the queen's name. Their basic argument is that one should understand the name to mean "she whose stomach serves as an ornament, that is, having a slender waist. (*maṇḍanabhūtodarī. kṛśodarīty arthaḥ*—so Ct.)" Cg accepts this etymology but cites an alternative one, according to which the term *maṇḍā* refers to a type of large ant so that the name means "she whose stomach *or* waist is like that of a *maṇḍā* (*maṇḍā pṛthupipīlikā tasyā ivodaraṃ yasyāḥ sā maṇḍodarīty apy āhuḥ*)." The idea is similar to that expressed by the English phrase "wasp-waisted."

"her husband, ten-necked Rāvaṇa" *daśagrīvam . . . patim*: Literally, "the husband, the ten-necked one."

3. "Indra himself, the smasher of citadels" *puraṃdaraḥ*: Literally, "the smasher of citadels."

4. "the gods on earth" *mahīdevāḥ*: The term is ambiguous as it is used in the literature to describe both kings and brahmans. Cg, the only commentator to remark on this reading, glosses, "brahmans (*brāhmaṇāḥ*)." D10,11, and the texts and printed editions of Ct read instead *mahānto 'pi*, "great." This can be interpreted either as a noun in the sense of " the great ones" or as an adjective modifying *ṛṣayaḥ*, "seers." D7,G1,2,M1, and the texts and printed editions of Cr read instead *mahātmānaḥ*, "the great *or* great-souled ones." This variant appears to have been rendered by Raghunathan (1982, vol. 3, p. 321).

5. "How could this be" *kim idam*: Literally, "What [is] this?"

"bull among *rākṣasas*" *rākṣasarṣabha*: Ś2,B1,D1–3,7–11,13, and the texts and printed editions of Ct and Cr read instead *rākṣaseśvara*, "O lord of the *rākṣasas*."

6. "a mere human" *mānuṣaḥ*: Literally, "a human."

"and whom no one could withstand" *aviṣahyam*: Literally, "one not to be endured *or* withstood."

7. "It makes no sense" *nopapadyate*: Literally, "it is not possible *or* it does not stand to reason."

"could have slain you in battle" *vināśas tava . . . saṃyuge*: Literally, "your destruction in battle."

"in realms inaccessible to mere mortals" *mānuṣāṇām aviṣaye*: Literally, "in the non-range of men." Ct and Ck understand the reference to be to the island of Laṅkā itself (*laṅkādvīparūpe deśe*). Cg and Cm simply explain that this is a region that humans cannot reach (*mānuṣāṇām aprāpyadeśe*). The reference, however, may be to Rāvaṇa's ability to travel through the sky, fight the gods in heaven, etc.

8. "that it was, in fact, Rāma who accomplished this feat" *etat karma rāmasya*: Literally, "this deed [was] Rāma's."

"fully equipped for battle" *sarvataḥ samupetasya*: Literally, "equipped *or* endowed in every way." We agree with Cg, Cm, and Cr, who gloss, "you were full of all the instruments of warfare (*sarvayuddhopakaraṇaiḥ pūrṇasya tava*—so Cg)." Ck and Ct understand, "you who were endowed with victory (*jayopetasya tava*)."

Following verse 8, various manuscripts and printed editions diverge from the critical edition and from one another, including or omitting certain verses and varying the order in which some verses appear. Three major textual sequences are represented in the printed editions and translations. These are 1) the texts and printed editions associated with the commentaries of Ct, Ck, and Cr (GPP, NSP, and Gita Press); 2) the texts and printed editions associated with the commentaries of Cv, Crā, Cg, and Cm (VSP and KK); and 3) the northern printed editions as represented by Gorresio and Lahore. Translations align themselves as follows: aligned with the text of Ct are Dutt, Roussel, Shastri, Gita Press, and Pagani; aligned with the text of Cg is Raghunathan; and aligned with the texts of the northern recension is Gorresio, who translates his edition, which is most closely aligned with B. Cv and Crā staunchly defend their sequence of verses, stating that all the others are the result of carelessness on the part of the scribes (*anyathā pāṭhas tu lekhakapramādakṛtaḥ*—so Crā). The order of the verses for Cg (as represented in KK and VSP) is as follows (using the numbering of the critical text): 8, 11, 12, 3113*, 10, 3114* (line 3, omitted from VSP, bracketed in KK), 9, and 13. The order of verses for Ct (as represented in GPP, NSP, and Gita Press) is 8, 10, 3114*, 9, 11, 12, and 13. The order of the verses in Gorresio is 8, 10, 11, 3115*, lines 1–2, 12, 3113*, and 13.

9. "your sensual appetites alone" *indriyaiḥ*: Literally, "by senses *or* sense organs."

"they recalled, as it were" *smaradbhir iva*: Literally, "[by those sense organs] as if remembering." The figure works as a kind of *utprekṣā* in which the quality of memory is ascribed to the sense organs. The trope also serves as a rebuke to Rāvaṇa for his having let his sensual appetites, specifically his lust for Sītā, lead him to his destruction.

"when, long ago . . . you subjugated your senses" *indriyāṇi purā jitvā*: The reference, as several commentators note, is to Rāvaṇa's legendary course of asceticism that earned him the boon of invulnerability through which he was able to conquer the three worlds. See 7.10 for the account of Rāvaṇa's asceticism. Cf. 3.30.17, where Rāvaṇa's austerities are also mentioned.

The textual status of this verse is questionable at best. It is not found in Ñ,V,B3,4,D4, or the editions of Gorresio and Lahore. Thus, according to the principles on which the critical edition is based, it should have been relegated to the critical apparatus (Bhatt 1960, p. xxxiv). In any case, of those manuscripts that do include the verse, none places it at this point in the text.

10. "Vāsava" *vāsavaḥ*: Literally, "Vāsava." D7,10,11,T2,3,M3, and the texts and printed editions of Ct and Cg read instead *kṛtāntaḥ*, "fate." Cf. note to 6.39.19.

"some unimaginable magical illusion" *māyām . . . apratitarkitām*: Our understanding, like that of most of the commentators, is that the illusion is that whereby the divinity has taken on the appearance of Rāma (*apekṣitaśarīragrahaṇahetubhūtāṃ kāñcic chaktim*—so Cm). Cg, however, believes the reference is to the illusory manifestation of Sītā, who is of immeasurable beauty. (*māyāṃ sītārūpām. apratitarkitām aparimeyarūpalāvaṇyām.*) The idea is that the divinities create an irresistibly beautiful woman in the form of Sītā to lure Rāvaṇa to his doom. This interpretation is followed only in the translation of Raghunathan (1982, vol. 3, p. 321), who renders, "[luring you to your doom] with a vision of ineffable loveliness."

Following verse 10, Ś2,Ñ2,B1,D1–3,8,9,12 continue, while Ñ1,D5,6,T,G3,M1,2,5 insert after verse 10; V,B2–4,D7 insert after verse 11; D4 inserts after line 2 of 3115*; and G1,2,M3, and the texts and printed editions of Cg insert after verse 12 a passage of two lines [3113*]: "And when the fearsome monkeys built a bridge over the mighty ocean, then I feared in my heart that Rāma was no mere human." Virtually all available manuscripts and printed editions, with the exception of the texts and printed editions of Ct (NSP omits and GPP brackets), include this verse at some point. Textual evidence would support its inclusion in the critical text.

Following verse 10 or 12, D5,6,7 (only lines 1–2),9–11,S insert a passage of eleven lines [3114*]: "Or perhaps, immensely powerful warrior,[1] you were attacked by Vāsava himself. But then again, what power would Vāsava have even to look upon you in battle, since you were of immense power and tremendous might, and were a terrifying foe of the gods.[2][1–3] Clearly, he is the great *yogin*, the eternal, Supreme Spirit, who has no beginning, middle, or end, who is great and greater than the great.[3][4–5] He is superior to *tamas* and the other elements of nature.[4] He is the creator, who bears the conch, the discus, and the mace. His chest is marked with the *śrīvatsa*. His majesty is eternal. He is unconquerable, everlasting, and enduring.[6–7] He is the truly valorous Viṣṇu, who, taking on a human form, is accompanied by all the gods who have become monkeys.[8–9] He, the immensely radiant, incarnate Lord of all the worlds, out of a desire for the well-being of the worlds, has slain you[5] along with your entourage of *rākṣasas*.[6][10–11]"

[1]"immensely powerful warrior" *mahābala*: Literally, "O immensely powerful one."

[2]"since you were of immense power and tremendous might, and were a terrifying foe of the gods" *mahāvīryaṃ mahāsattvaṃ devaśatruṃ bhayāvaham*: D9–11 and the texts and printed editions of Ct read instead the more or less synonymous *mahābalaṃ mahāvīryaṃ devaśatruṃ mahaujasam*, "[since you were] of immense strength, immense power, and an immensely mighty enemy of the gods." M3 and the texts of Cg, Crā, and Cv omit line 3. It does not appear in VSP, and Ct's variant of it is found in brackets at KK 6.114.13ef. The verse is not rendered in the translation of Raghunathan (1982, vol. 3, p. 321).

[3]"who is great and greater than the great" *mahataḥ paramo mahān*: The phrase *mahataḥ paramaḥ*, "greater than the great," can be understood either in a general sense to allude to the Lord's absolute supremacy or, taking the term *mahat* as it is used in Sāṃkhya philosophy to refer to the second of the primal evolutes of *prakṛti*, to indicate that the Lord is greater than, or prior to, material creation. In either case, the tenor of the verse is distinctly upaniṣadic.

[4]"He is superior to *tamas* and the other elements of nature." *tamasaḥ paramaḥ*: Literally, "greater than *tamas*." We agree with the commentators that *tamas*, the *guṇa*, or quality, of turbidity or darkness, must stand here for the three *guṇas* that qualify *prakṛti*, or the material universe. Cg, for example, glosses *tamasaḥ* as "the circle of material elements (*prākṛtamaṇḍalasya*)." According to Ct, the phrase means that the Lord is the one who sets the material universe in motion (*prakṛteḥ pravartakaḥ*).

[5]"immensely radiant...has slain you" *hatavāṃs tvāṃ mahādyutiḥ*: D10,11, and the texts and printed editions of Ct read instead *devaśatruṃ bhayāvaham*, "[you] a terrifying foe of the gods." In the absence of a verb or a verbal element, Ct is forced, in any case, to supply the form *hatavān*. "he has slain."

[6]As in the case of the *Ādityahṛdaya* section (see note 6.93.27, App. I, No. 65), the commentators exercise themselves to analyze the various theological and scriptural implications of the passage.

11. "he killed your brother Khara" *kharas tava hato bhrātā*: See note to 3.29.23–28.

"it was clear right then that this was no mere human" *tadaivāsau na mānuṣaḥ*: Literally, "right then he [was] not a human." Ś2,Ñ,V3,B1,D1–3,8–13, and the texts and printed editions of Ct read *tadā rāmaḥ*, "then Rāma," for *tadaivāsau*, "right then he."

12. "entered the city of Laṅkā" *laṅkām . . . praviṣṭaḥ*: Hanumān first enters Laṅkā at 5.2.47, but the *rākṣasas* do not become aware of his presence until *sarga* 40.

Following this verse, the text of Cg inserts 3113* (see note to verse 10 above).

13. "You should make peace" *kriyatām avirodhaḥ*: Literally, "non-hostility is to be made." As Cr points out, the hostility with Rāma could have been avoided by the return of Sītā (*sītāsamarpaṇena virodhābhāvaḥ*). The critically established text includes no passage in which Mandodarī actually gives such salutary advice to Rāvaṇa. Her advice to this effect is, however, recorded in a few manuscripts and printed editions (App. I, No. 30, lines 49–98). See notes to 6.51.20, 1114*, n. 1; and 6.46.21, App. I, No. 30.

14. "your life" *dehasya*: Literally, "of [your] body."

15. "who is superior even to Arundhatī and Rohiṇī" *arundhatyā viśiṣṭāṃ tāṃ rohiṇyāś cāpi*: Arundhatī, the wife of the great seer Vasiṣṭha, and Rohiṇī, the wife of the moon god, are often held up as shining examples of wifely devotion. Cg notes here that Sītā is superior to them because, although they are notable only for such devotion, she is also the mother [goddess] (*mānyām ity anena na kevalam arundhatyādivat pātivratyamātraṃ kiṃtu mātṛtvaṃ cety ucyate*).

Following verse 15, D5–7,9–11,S (M2 lines 1–11,12–13 after 15 and 17, respectively) insert a passage of thirteen lines [3116*]: "Sītā is deeply devoted to her husband and flawless in every limb. Though miserable, she is auspicious, more long-suffering even than the earth, bearer of wealth, and more splendid than Śrī.[1] In abducting her in the desolate wilderness by means of a deception, you have brought destruction upon yourself and your race.[2] Now surely, my lord, without even having consummated your desire through union with Maithilī, you have been consumed by the ascetic power of that woman, so devoted to her husband.[3][1–5] In that you were not burnt up at the very moment that you assaulted that slender-waisted woman, it was only because all the gods themselves, including Indra and led by Agni, feared you.[6–7] Inevitably a person[4] reaps the dread[5] consequences of an evil deed when the time comes. Of this there is no doubt.[8–9] A person who does good obtains excellent rewards; one who does evil reaps only misery.[6] Thus, Vibhīṣaṇa has obtained felicity, while you have come to such an evil end.[10–11] You had many other young women more beautiful than she, but still, in your thrall to Kāma, the disembodied god of love,[7] you did not, in your infatuation, realize this.[12–13]"

[1]"more long-suffering even than the earth, bearer of wealth, and more splendid than Śrī" *vasudhāyāś ca vasudhāṃ śriyaḥ śrīm*: Literally, "the bearer of wealth of the bearer of wealth and the *śrī* of Śrī." The idea here, as the commentators point out, is that Sītā is more patient or forbearing than the earth, which is the stereotypical standard for forbearance, and more splendid or venerable than Śrī herself, the exemplar of beauty. Cg takes the reference to the earth, a paragon of forbearance, to suggest that Sītā forbore to burn up Rāvaṇa, which, as a *pativratā*, or perfectly devoted wife, she could easily have done. See 5.20.20.

[2]"you have brought destruction upon yourself and your race" *ātmasvadūṣaṇa*: Literally, "O corrupter of one's self and one's own." We follow the commentators in

taking *-sva-*, "one's own," to refer to Rāvaṇa's family. D7,10,11,M5, and the texts and printed editions of Ck and Ct read instead the nominative *ātmasvadūṣaṇam*. Ct then understands that we need to supply the participle *kṛtam*, "was made [by you]." He thus understands the phrase to mean: "The destruction of your own family was carried out by you (*ātmanaḥ svakulasya nāśanaṃ kṛtam iti śeṣaḥ*)."

[3]The syntax of the first five lines is somewhat awkward. There is no clear finite verb until line 5. We have therefore broken the text's lengthy string of accusatives modifying Sītā into a series of shorter predicative sentences.

[4]"a person" *kartā*: Literally, "an agent."

[5]"dread" *ghoram*: D11 and the texts and printed editions of Ct read instead *bhartaḥ*, "O lord."

[6]"A person who does good obtains excellent rewards; one who does evil reaps only misery." *śubhakṛc chubam āpnoti pāpakṛt pāpam aśnute*: Literally, "A doer of good obtains good; a doer of evil eats evil." We follow the commentators in taking the second occurrence of *pāpam* in the sense of "misery, suffering (*duḥkham*)."

[7]"Kāma, the disembodied god of love" *anaṅga-*: Literally, "the bodiless one." This is a common epithet of the god of love, deriving from the incineration of his body by Śiva. See 1.22.10–14 and notes (especially note to 1.22.10).

16. "you did not realize" *na budhyase*: Cr understands that Mandodarī is indicating by her tone of voice that we are to understand the opposite of her clearly stated negative. In other words, he argues, she is saying that, although Rāvaṇa is fully aware of Mandodarī's superiority to Sītā in all respects, he chose the latter with the intention of worshiping [her]. (*tvaṃ na budhyase kākvā budhyasa evety arthaḥ. etena pūjābuddhyaiva tasyāḥ svīkāras tvayā kṛta iti sūcitam.*) Cf. notes to 5.18.6,16, etc.

17. "has been brought about because of your treatment of Maithilī" *maithilīkṛtalakṣaṇaḥ*: Literally, "having action toward Maithilī as its cause *or* occasion." We understand *kṛta* in the sense of "action," following Cg's and Cr's interpretation. Cg glosses, " 'action toward Maithilī' means 'bringing Maithilī,' that is, having that itself for its occasion *or* cause. (*maithilyāḥ kṛtaṃ maithilīkṛtam, maithilyānayanam ity arthaḥ. tad eva lakṣaṇaṃ nimittaṃ yasya sa tathā.*)" Cr understands, "[caused] by your behavior that was contrary to the wishes of Maithilī (*maithilīpsitaviruddhācaraṇena*)."

Following 17cd, D5–7,9–11,T,G,M2 (following 3116*),3,5, and the texts and printed editions of the southern commentators insert, while Ñ,V,D4,13,M1 substitute, a passage of one line [3118*]: "And you brought this death, the cause of which was Sītā, upon yourself from afar."

19–20. Following verse 20, Ñ,V,B2–4,D4–7,9–11,13,S insert a passage of seventy-five lines [App. I, No. 68]. All translations of the southern recension include the entire passage, while Gorresio inserts only lines 2, 4, 5a, 6b, 7–13, and 50–51: "I seem to have become some other person. Damn the fickle fortune of kings![1] Alas! Your majesty, your youthful face once had a splendid brow, clear complexion, and prominent nose. In loveliness, splendor, and radiance it was the equal, respectively, of the moon, the lotus, and the sun, maker of day. It was rosy,[1] its earrings blazing, and it shone with your lofty diadem.[2–4] In your drinking halls, that face of yours, with its eyes rolling about wildly in intoxication, was so charming with its different garlands and so bright with your lovely smile. How is it, my lord, that it no longer shines so brightly?[5–7] Instead, it is now riddled with Rāma's arrows, red with gouts of blood, spattered with marrow and brains,[2] and soiled with the dust stirred up by the chariots.[3][8–9] Alas, your final state, the bringer of widowhood, has now befallen me, a state[4] that I, foolish as I am, could once never have imagined.[10–11] Thinking, 'My father is the king of the *dānavas*,[5] my husband the lord of the *rākṣasas*, and my son the conqueror of Śakra,' I was immensely arrogant.[12–13] It was my unwavering belief that my protectors, who were crushers of their haughty foes[6] and were heroes[7] famed for their strength and manly valor, had nothing to fear from any quarter.[14–15] How is it, bull among *rākṣasas*,[8] that this unanticipated danger could have come from a mere human to heroes as powerful as all of you?[16–17] Your body, as dark blue as a polished sapphire and as huge as a lofty mountain, once glittered with its bracelets and armlets, garlands, and necklaces of lapis and pearl. It was immensely desirable in the pleasure gardens and fiercely blazing on the battlefields. With the sparkling of its ornaments, it resembled a great storm cloud flashing with lightning. But now this body of yours[9] is covered with innumerable sharp arrows[10] so that it is difficult even to touch and impossible to embrace.[18–23] Indeed, with its arrows deeply lodged in its vital points—severing tendons and ligaments—and set closely together, it looks like a porcupine[11] covered with its quills.[24–25] I see it now, your majesty, fallen on the ground, its complexion the color of blood.[12] Indeed, it looks like a mountain smashed by the blows of a thunderbolt.[26–27] Alas, this dream is, in fact, reality. But how could you have been slain by Rāma? How could you, who were death to even Death himself, have fallen under the power of death?[28–29] My lord was the enjoyer of wealth of all the three worlds and the great bringer of fear to them.[13] He was the conqueror of the world protectors and disturber even of Śaṅkara.[14] Chastiser of the haughty, he manifested great valor. He caused the worlds to tremble and, with his roars, he made all creatures cry out with fear.[15] With his enormous might, he spoke proud words in the presence of his enemies. He was the protector of his troops and dependents and the slayer of warriors of fearsome deeds.[16] He slew *dānava* lords and the *yakṣas* by the thousand. He was the lord and a chastiser and the scourge of the *nivātakavacas*.[17] Destroyer of many sacrifices, he was the guardian of his own people. Breaker of the rules of righteous conduct, he put forth magical illusions in battle. From many different lands,[18] he abducted the daughters of the gods, *asuras*, and men. Bringer of grief to his enemies' wives, he was the leader of his own people. Guardian of the island of Laṅkā, he performed many fearsome deeds. He bestowed upon us many objects of desire, and he was the foremost of chariot-warriors. How hardhearted I am in that, having seen my lord,[19] who was so powerful, struck down by Rāma, I still live[20] though my beloved has been slain.[30–45] Having slept on costly beds, lord of the *rākṣasas*, why do you, all red with dust,[21] now sleep here on the bare ground?[46–47] When my son Indrajit was cut down in battle by Lakṣmaṇa, it was a severe blow to me, but now I am devastated.[48–49] Bereft of all my kinsmen[22] and of my protector in you, and so, bereft of all objects of enjoyment, I shall now forever grieve.[50–51] You have today set forth, your majesty, on a long and arduous road.[23] Please take me with you, afflicted with grief as I am, for I cannot live without you.[52–53] Why did you want to go away, leaving hapless me here, miserable, despondent, and lamenting?[24] Why do you not speak to me?[54–55] Are you not angry, my lord, to see me come forth from the city gate unveiled[25] and on foot?[56–57] And look, you who are so fond of your wives, at your other wives, who have all rushed out dropping their veils of modesty. How can you not be angry at seeing them?[58–59] These women,[26] who were your companions in your amorous sports, are now lamenting bitterly, having lost their protector. Why do you not comfort them? Do you no longer care for them?[60–61] It is because you were cursed by those many women you turned into widows—women of good family, who were consumed by grief, devoted to their husbands, intent upon righteousness, and punctilious in their obedience to their elders—that you have fallen under the power of your enemy, your majesty.[62–64] The curse of those women whom you wronged at that time has now taken effect. It appears likely that the popular saying, 'The tears of women devoted to their husbands never fall to the ground in vain,' has proven true in regard to you, O king.[65–67] How on earth,[27] your majesty, could you, who had conquered all the worlds with your blazing energy and who prided yourself on your valor, have engaged in the contemptible act of abducting a woman?[68–69] That you carried off Rāma's wife after luring him[28] away from his ashram through the use of a fraudulent deer only served as evidence of your cowardice.[29][70–71] I do not recall any cowardice on your part in battle at any time. Therefore, surely, through the reversal of your fortune, this was a sign of your impending doom.[72–73] Knowing the past and the future, wise in regard to the present, [my younger brother-in-law Vibhīṣaṇa,] seeing that Maithilī had been abducted, reflected for a long time and then, sighing[30] . . . [74–75]"

[1]"your youthful face . . . was rosy" *sukumāraṃ te . . . tāmrāsyam*: Literally, "your reddish face [was] youthful *or* tender."

[2]Cs, in his comments to VSP 6.114.38, notes the potential contradiction between this verse and the passage in the *Mahābhārata*'s *Rāmopākhyāna* (3.274.31) in which it is stated that the *brahmāstra* vaporizes Rāvaṇa's body so that not even the ashes are to be seen. Cs manages to resolve the contradiction by a scholastic analysis of some of the terms used and by reference to additional sources of the story. Compare notes to verse 42 below.

[3]"the dust stirred up by the chariots" *syandanareṇubhiḥ*: Literally, "by chariot dusts."

[4]"your final state, the bringer of widowhood, has now befallen me, a state" *paścimā me saṃprāptā daśā vaidhavyakāriṇī*: Literally, "the final state causing widowhood has come to me." We follow Cg in adding the enclitic *te*, "your," to the phrase "final state (*paścimā . . . daśā*)," which Cg glosses as "death (*mṛtyuḥ*)."

[5]"king of the *dānavas*" *dānavarājaḥ*: The reference, as noted by Cg, is to the *asura* Maya. Compare verse 26 and note below. See 7.12.3–18. Cf. notes to 6.88.2,30–31.

[6]"crushers of their haughty foes" *dṛptārimathanāḥ*: The compound could also be interpreted to mean "proud crushers of their foes."

[7]"heroes" *śūrāḥ*: V1,D7,10,11, and the texts and printed editions of Ct and Cr read instead *krūrāḥ*, "fierce, cruel."

[8]"bull among *rākṣasas*" *rākṣasarṣabha*: Ñ2,V1,2,D5,9–11,T1,M2,5, and the texts and printed editions of Ct read instead the plural vocative *rākṣasarṣabhāḥ*, "O bulls among *rākṣasas*."

[9]"Your body . . . this body of yours" *śarīraṃ te*: Literally, "your body." The referent only occurs once; we have repeated it for the sake of readability.

[10]"covered with innumerable sharp arrows" *tīkṣṇair naikaśarais citam*: Ñ2,V,D10, and the printed edition of GPP read instead the somewhat obscure *tīkṣṇair naikacarais citam*, literally, "piled up with many sharp, moveable objects." Among the translators

consulted, only Roussel (1903, vol. 3, p. 368) appears to follow this reading, rendering, somewhat heroically, "*couvert de bandes d'animaux à la dent aiquisée.*" Apparently, he understands the reference to be to carrion beasts.

[11]"porcupine" *śvāvidhaḥ*: See note to 6.40.17.

[12]"I see it... its complexion the color of blood" *paśyāmi rudhiracchavi*: D9–11 and the texts and printed editions of Ct read *śyāmaṃ vai*, "so dark," for *paśyāmi*, "I see." M3 and the texts and printed editions of Cg, Cm, and apparently Cr read instead *śyāvaṃ rudhirasacchavi*, "brownish with a color like that of blood." Among the translators, only Raghunathan (1982, vol. 3, p. 323) renders this variant, translating, "dark with clotted blood."

[13]"the great bringer of fear to them" *trailokyodvegadaṃ mahat*: Literally, "the great bringer of fear to the three worlds."

[14]"the... disturber even of Śaṅkara: *kṣeptāraṃ śaṃkarasya ca*: As Cg notes, the reference here is to the famous incident in which Rāvaṇa, in his arrogance, dares to shake Mount Kailāsa, Śiva's abode. The story is told at *Uttarakāṇḍa* 16.

[15]"with his roars, he made all creatures cry out with fear" *nādair bhūtavirāviṇam*: D9–11 and the texts and printed editions of Ct read instead *sādhubhūtavidāraṇam*, "slaughtering virtuous people."

[16]"He was the protector of his troops and dependents and the slayer of warriors of fearsome deeds." *svayūthabhṛtyagoptāraṃ hantāraṃ bhīmakarmaṇām*: Literally, "the protector of his own troops and dependents, the slayer of those of fearsome deeds." D5,T1,G3,M2,3,5, and the texts and printed editions of Cg read *-vargāṇām*, "hosts," for *-goptāram*, "protector," and *goptāram*, "protector," for *hantāram*, "slayer." This gives the line the meaning: "He was the protector of the hosts of his troops and dependents who committed fearsome deeds." Raghunathan (1982, vol. 3, p. 324) appears to have been influenced by this reading.

[17]"the *nivātakavacas*" *nivātakavacānām*: Literally, "of those who have mail for their armor." This is a name of a class of *asuras*. Rāvaṇa's battles with the *nivātakavacas* are described at *Uttarakāṇḍa* 23. See, too, notes to 6.50.18.

[18]"From many different lands" *tatas tataḥ*: Literally, "from there, from there."

[19]"having seen my lord" *bhartāraṃ dṛṣṭvā*: Lines 30–45 form one syntactical unit, consisting of a series of modifiers for the accusative noun *bhartāram*, "lord." We have broken up the syntax for the sake of readability.

[20]"I still live" *deham imaṃ dhārayāmi*: Literally, "I support this body."

[21]"all red with dust" *reṇupāṭalaḥ*: Ñ2,V1,2,B2–4,D4,9–11, and the texts and printed editions of Ct and Cr read instead *reṇuguṇṭhitaḥ*, "smeared *or* covered with dust."

[22]"Bereft of all my kinsmen" *sāhaṃ bandhujanair hīnā*: Literally, "I, deprived of kinsmen." M3 and the texts and printed editions of Cg read instead *nāham*, "I, not [being]," for *sāham*, "I [am] she." Cg understands the verse to mean that Mandodarī is saying she would not grieve for the loss of her kinsmen, if only Rāvaṇa were still alive. But since she has now lost him, and therefore all her objects of desire, she will grieve. (*bandhujanair hīnāhaṃ na śociṣye, yadi tvaṃ sthitaḥ syāḥ. kiṃtu tvayā hīnāta eva kāmabhogair vihīnā śociṣya iti yojanā.*) This reading and interpretation are followed only in the translation of Raghunathan (1982, vol. 3, p. 324).

[23]"a long... road" *dīrgham adhvānam*: Cg understands this to be the road to heaven reserved for heroes (*vīrasvargam*).

[24]"lamenting" *vilapatīm*: D6,T2,3,G3,M3, and the texts and printed editions of Cg read instead *vilapitaiḥ*, "with lamentations *or* weeping." Raghunathan (1982, vol. 3, p. 324), the only translator consulted who reads with Cg, construes the term with *mandām*, "hapless," rendering the two together as "crazy with wailing."

[25]"unveiled" *anavakuṇṭhitām*: Literally, "not enclosed, not surrounded." Cg, the only commentator to share the critical reading, glosses, "uncovered (*anāvaraṇām*)," i.e., "having no veil." V1,B2–4,D7,10,11, and the texts and printed editions of Ct read instead *anavaguṇṭhitām*, "not veiled." This verse and the next appear to be the first explicit references in the poem to the practice of veiling women of high social standing, although several passages throughout the poem indicate that such women were secluded and protected from the gaze of men who are not their husbands or close relatives. See 2.30.8 and note and 6.102.19–29 and notes.

[26]"These women" *ayam . . . janaḥ*: Literally, "this person." Like most of the translators consulted, we understand the phrase in its common collective meaning of "people," referring specifically here to the junior consorts of Rāvaṇa mentioned in the preceding lines. The phrase could also represent Mandodarī's way of referring to herself, and two translators (Dutt 1893, p. 1493 and Gita Press 1969, vol. 3, p.1831) interpret in this fashion.

[27]"How on earth" *kathaṃ ca nāma*: Literally, "and how, indeed."

[28]"Rāma's wife . . . him" *rāmam . . . rāmapatnī*: Literally, "Rāma . . . Rāma's wife."

[29]"evidence of your cowardice" *te kātaryalakṣaṇam*: Literally, "a sign *or* mark of cowardice." D9–11,G1,2, and the texts and printed editions of Ct read instead *apanīya ca lakṣmaṇam*, "and having lured away Lakṣmaṇa."

[30]The syntax of the final verse is incomplete and is resolved only in verse 21.

21. "illustrious" *mahābhāgaḥ*: Ś2,Ñ1,B1,D1–4,8–12,T1,M3, and the texts and printed editions of Ct read instead the vocative *mahābāho*, "O great-armed one."

"which my . . . brother-in-law Vibhīṣaṇa" *devaro me*: Literally, "my husband's brother."

22. "Through this catastrophe . . . characterized by your obsession, you" *vyasanena prasaṅginā / tvayā*: Literally, " by you through this catastrophe possessing attachment *or* addiction." The syntax of the verse favors reading the adjective *prasaṅginā* as modifying *vyasanena*, "through the catastrophe." Given the critical reading, however, it could also be convincingly taken to modify *tvayā*, "by you," in *pāda* c, giving the sense "by you, in your obsession."

Following 22ab, D5–7,9–11,S insert a passage of one line [3120*], which varies somewhat between the two major textual traditions of the southern commentators. The critical reading as it stands appears in neither the text of Ct, etc., nor that of Cg, etc., and, in fact, makes virtually no sense in the context. Translated literally, it would mean something like "this disaster has ceased on your account, and it is a great and radical cause of destruction (*nivṛttas tvatkṛte 'narthaḥ so 'yaṃ mūlaharo mahān*)." D6,7,9–11,G1,2,M1,5, and the texts and printed editions of Ct and Ck read the first half of this verse as follows: *nivṛttas tvatkṛtenārthaḥ*, "Your action has brought an end to your prosperity." Ct, Ck, and Cr understand this to mean that, by his misdeeds, Rāvaṇa has destroyed his entire sovereignty (*tvatkṛtenārtho 'śeṣaiśvaryalakṣaṇo nivṛttaḥ*). Translations that follow the text of Ct render accordingly. T2,3,M3, and the texts and printed editions of Cg read the first half of the line as *nirvṛttas tvatkṛte 'narthaḥ*, "this disaster has been brought about on your account." This reading is rendered in the translation of Raghunathan (1982, vol. 3, p. 325).

23. "my heart is in a pitiable state" *me buddhiḥ kāruṇye parivartate*: Literally, "my mind falls *or* moves in compassion." We follow Ct and Cg, who gloss *dainye*, "in dejection *or* despondency," for *kāruṇye*, "in compassion."

24. "because of my separation from you" *tvadviyogena*: V2,D5,7,9–11,M2, and the texts and printed editions of Ct and Cr read instead *tvadvināśena*, "because of your destruction *or* loss."

Following verse 24, D5–7,9–11,S insert a passage of six lines [3124*]: "You would not listen to the advice of your friends, who wished you well, and the unanimous and beneficial advice of your brothers,[1] ten-faced *rākṣasa*.[1–2] Nor would you act effectively[2] upon the various[3] logical, sensible, reasonable, beneficial, and friendly words of Vibhīṣaṇa.[3–4] Nor, in your intoxication with your own might, would you listen[4] to the advice offered by Mārīca, Kumbhakarṇa, and my father. And this is the result.[5–6]"

[1]"unanimous . . . of your brothers" *bhrātṝṇām . . . kārtsnyena*: Literally, "by the entirety of brothers."

[2]"effectively" *hetumat*: Literally, "reasonably." We agree with Cg in reading the term adverbially. He glosses, "expediently *or* logically (*yuktimad yathā bhavati tathā*)." The sense, however, seems more in keeping with the glosses of Ct, Cr, and Cm, who take the term as an adjective modifying "words (*abhihitam*, lit., what was spoken)" in the sense of "fruitful, productive (*phalavat*—so Ct, Cm)."

[3]"various" *vividham*: D7,9–11,M1,3, and the texts and printed editions of the southern commentators read instead *vidhivat*, "in accordance with the rules [of the *śāstras*]."

[4]"Nor . . . would you listen" *na śrutam*: Literally, "was not heard [by you]." D7,9–11,T2,3, and the texts and printed editions of Ct read instead *na kṛtam*, "was not done *or* carried out [by you]."

25. "Resembling a black storm cloud, with your yellow garments and bright armlets" *nīlajīmūtasaṃkāśaḥ pītāmbaraśubhāṅgadaḥ*: D5,9–11,T1,M, and the texts and printed editions of the southern commentators read instead three vocatives, *nīlajīmūtasaṃkāśa pītāmbara śubhāṅgada*, "O you who resemble a black storm cloud, O you with yellow garments, O you with bright armlets."

"drenched in blood" *rudhirāplutaḥ*: V2,D7,9–11, and the texts and printed editions of Ct read instead *rudhirāvṛtaḥ*, "covered with blood."

"splaying out all your limbs" *sarvagātrāṇi vikṣipya*: Literally, "having flung wide all limbs." D5,6,10,11,T,G3,M1,3,5, and the texts and printed editions of the southern commentators read instead *svagātrāṇi vinikṣipya*, "having flung out your own limbs."

26. "Why do you not look at me" *kiṃ tvaṃ māṃ nābhyudīkṣase*: V2,D7,9–11,M2, and the texts of Ct and Cr read instead *kiṃ māṃ na pratibhāṣase*, "Why do you not answer me?"

"the granddaughter" *dauhitrīm*: Literally, "the daughter's daughter." D5,6,T,G2,3,M2, and the texts and printed editions of Cg read instead the vocative *dauhitra*, "O grandson," literally, "O daughter's son."

"an . . . skillful *yātudhāna* who never fled in battle" *dakṣasya saṃyugeṣv apalāyinaḥ / yātudhānasya*: Literally, "of the skillful *yātudhāna* who does not run away in battles." According to Ck, Ct, and Cr, the *yātudhāna* in question is Sumāli (v.l. Sumālin). According to Cg, who reads the variant *dauhitra*, the reference is either to Mālyavān or Sumālin. Cg argues that Mandodarī refers to this relationship to make manifest the unobstructed power of (Rāvaṇa's) lineage (*tatsambandhakīrtanam apratihatakula-prabhāvaprakaṭanam*). The reference in either case is to Rāvaṇa's lineage, of which she would have become a member through marriage, and not to Mandodarī's own lineage. Māli, Sumāli, and Mālyavān are the three sons of Sukeśa (7.5). Rāvaṇa is said to be the grandson of Sukeśa at 7.9. See 7.5ff. See, too, note 5 above. On the other hand, Mandodarī is the daughter of Hemā and Maya, son of Diti (7.12). See App. I, No. 68, n. 5, following note to verse 17 above. On *yātudhānas*, see 6.3.27 and note. For some reason, Pagani (1999, p. 1173) treats the genitive adjective *dakṣasya* and the genitive adjectival phrase *saṃyugeṣv apalāyinaḥ* as if they were vocatives referring to Rāvaṇa. The syntax cannot support such a rendering.

Following verse 26, Ñ2,V,B2–4,D5–7,9–11,S insert, while Ñ1,D4 continue following 3130*, a passage of two lines [3127*]: "Arise! Arise! Why do you lie there in the face of this new insult? For today the sun's rays have penetrated Laṅkā without fear.[1]"

[1]"the sun's rays have penetrated Laṅkā without fear" *adya vai nirbhayā laṅkāṃ praviṣṭāḥ sūryaraśmayaḥ*: The reference here is to the fact that the sun and other natural and divine entities had avoided Rāvaṇa during his lifetime out of fear of him. Compare 1.14.10, where the gods complain that the sun, the wind, and the ocean dare not engage in their normal functions in the vicinity of Rāvaṇa. Cf. 6.78.45 and note.

27–28. "as if it were the *vajra* of Indra, the wielder of the *vajra*" *vajro vajradharasyeva*: Literally, "like the *vajra* of the bearer of the *vajra*."

"that smasher of your foes" *śatrupraharaṇaḥ*: Literally, "striking enemies." Ś2,Ñ,V2,D4,8,10,11,13,T3, and the texts and printed editions of Ct read *bahu-*, "many," for *śatru-*, "enemy," lending the compound the sense "striking many."

Following verse 28, D5–7,10,11,13,T,G2,3,M1,3,5, and the texts and printed editions of Ct insert, while Ñ2,B2–4,M2 continue after 3129* and Ñ1,D4 insert after verse 29, a passage of two lines [3130*]: "You lie there embracing the battleground as if it were your beloved. Why then do you not wish to speak to me, as if you were no longer fond of me?[1]"

[1]"as if you were no longer fond of me" *apriyām iva*: Literally, "as if [I were] unloved."

29. "Curse me whose heart" *dhig astu hṛdayaṃ yasyā mama*: Literally, "Damn me whose heart." We agree with Cg, Cm, Cr, and the majority of translators who share this reading in understanding an implicit correlative phrase *tāṃ mām*, "[curse] her, who is me," although it is possible to construe the indeclinable *dhik* with the genitive pronoun *mama* in much the same sense. Among the translators of this reading consulted, only Dutt (1893, p. 1494) construes the indeclinable *dhik* directly with *hṛdayam*, rendering, "Oh fie on this heart of mine." Ñ1,V1,3,B2,D4, and the edition of Gorresio

clearly construe the idiom with the genitive, reading *dhig astu hṛdayasyāsyā mama yat*, which Gorresio renders as "*Onito sia questo mio cuore, che* . . ." Apte (s.v. *dhik*) quotes this phrase as an example of the construction of *dhik* with the genitive.

Following verse 29, B2–4,D5–7,9–11,13,S insert a passage of ten lines [3132*]: "Lamenting in this fashion, her eyes blinded with tears, her heart melting with love, the queen[1] fainted.[1–2] Having collapsed across Rāvaṇa's chest under the force of her swoon, she looked like a blazing streak of lightning across a dark[2] storm cloud reddened at twilight.[3–4] Her co-wives, deeply distressed and weeping, lifted her up, as she had fallen into this state, and comforted her[3] as she wept bitterly.[5–6] 'It is not as if you didn't know,[4] O queen, that the lives of people are transient.[5] This is so even of kings, with their fickle royal fortune[6] through the vicissitudes of life.[7]'[7–8] Addressed in this fashion, she wept loudly, bathing her full breasts with streams of tears.[8][9–10]"

[1]"queen" *devī*: V2,D7,9–11, and the texts and printed editions of Ct and Cr read instead *tadā*, "then."

[2]"dark" *asite*: D7,9–11, and the texts and printed editions of Ct and Cr read instead the redundant *ujjvalā*, "blazing," further modifying lightning.

[3]"lifted her up . . . and comforted her" *samutthāpya . . . tām . . . paryavasthāpayāmāsuḥ*: Roussel (1903, vol. 3, p. 371), followed by Shastri (1959, vol. 3, p. 325), understands the finite verb *paryavasthāpayāmāsuḥ*, "they comforted," to mean "*Et la placèrent au milieu d'elles*." M3 and the texts and printed editions of Cg read *samutpatya*, "having rushed forth *or* having leapt up," for *samutthāpya*, "having lifted up."

[4]"It is not as if you didn't know" *na te na viditā*: Literally, "not by you [it is] not known." The double negative construction as printed in the critical edition is peculiar and is not found in any of the printed editions or texts of the commentators. D7,9–11, and the texts and printed editions of Ct read instead *kiṃ te na viditā*, "do you not know?" M3 and the texts and printed editions of Cm and Cg read *na te suviditā*, literally, "it is not well known by you." Cg understands this to be an example of irony expressed by tone of voice, so that the phrase has the sense "you know perfectly well (*te tvayā suviditā neti kākuḥ suviditaiva*)." Raghunathan (1982, vol. 3, p. 326), the only translator to read with the text of Cg, renders, "Do you not know very well . . . ?" The text of Gorresio (6.95.43a) has the same sequence of syllables as the critical reading but breaks it up differently, reading *na tena viditā*, "it was not known by him," referring presumably to Rāvaṇa. Gorresio (1858, vol. 10, p. 215) renders, "*colui non conobbe*." See 6.37.11; 6.67.36; 6.93.15; 6.95.24; 6.101.36; and notes.

[5]"the lives of people are transient" *lokānāṃ sthitir adhruvā*: Literally, "the state of people is not fixed."

[6]"even of kings, with their fickle royal fortune" *rājñāṃ cañcalayā śriyā*: Compare App. I, No. 68, line 1 (following note to verse 17 above), where Mandodarī curses "the fickle royal fortune of kings (*rājñāṃ cañcalāṃ śriyam*)." Ñ2,D9–11, and the texts and printed editions of Ct read instead *rājñāṃ vai cañcalāḥ śriyaḥ*, "indeed, the royal fortunes of kings are fickle."

[7]"through the vicissitudes of life" *daśāvibhāgaparyāye*: Literally, "in the turning about in the apportionment of conditions." We follow the interpretation of Cg, who understands the term *daśā*, "state *or* condition," to refer to the different stages of a

person's life (*daśānāṃ bālyakaumārayauvanavārdhakādyavasthānāṃ vibhāgasya bhedasya paryāye praptau*). Other commentators and most translators understand more or less similarly, with the startling exception of Pagani (1999, p. 1174), who, apparently confusing the term *daśā*, "state, condition," with *daśa*,"ten," renders, "*Sans que l'on ait le temps de compter jusqu'à dix.*"

[8]"bathing her full breasts with streams of tears" *snāpayantī tv abhimukhau stanāv asrāmbuvisravaiḥ*: We follow Cg and Cm, who gloss *abhimukhau*, literally, "facing," with "high, full, prominent (*unnatau*)." D9–11 and the texts and printed editions of Ct read instead *snāpayantī tadāsreṇa stanau vaktraṃ sunirmalam*, "then bathing her breasts and shining face with tears."

30. "At this juncture" *etasminn antare*: The transition from the middle of Mandodarī's lament, which lacks any concluding verses, to Rāma's speech without the expected transitional verse or verses, is awkward. All printed editions consulted and virtually all manuscripts read either an insert providing the narrative transition [3132*] (see notes to verse 29 above) or begin a new *sarga* with verse 30.

"send these women back" *striyaś caitā nivartaya*: D1,3,7,9–12, and the texts and printed editions of Ct and Cr read instead *strīgaṇaḥ pariśāntvyatām*, "and comfort the women folk."

31. "reflected" *vimṛśya buddhyā*: Literally, "having reflected with his mind." Cg takes this to refer to the vulgate verse (GPP 6.109.23cd) found at App. I, No. 67, lines 87–90 (following *sarga* 97), where Vibhīṣaṇa expresses his desire to perform Rāvaṇa's funeral rites (see note 30 to that passage). At that point, Cg, looking forward to the present passage, notes the apparent contradiction. In light of this, Cg feels that Vibhīṣaṇa is reflecting that, regardless of his own feelings one way or the other, he will perform the rites, if Rāma so permits and not otherwise. (*vimṛśyaitasya yat pretagatasya kṛtyaṃ tat kartum icchāmi tava prasādād ity uktam aṅgīkṛtaṃ vicintyety arthaḥ. rāmasyevānuvṛttyarthaṃ rāmeṇānujñāto 'smi cet tadā kariṣyāmi nānyathety evam anuvṛttyartham.*)

A number of manuscripts, in whole or in part, and the texts and printed editions of Ct show a number of variations on this verse, including the complete omission of *pādas* ef. The verse in the vulgate then reads (=GPP, NSP, Gita Press 6.111.92cd–93ab):

tam uvāca tato dhīmān vibhīṣaṇa idaṃ vacaḥ /
vimṛśya buddhyā praśritaṃ dharmārthasahitaṃ hitam / /

Then, after reflecting, wise Vibhīṣaṇa spoke this speech, which was deferential, replete with righteousness and political sense, and beneficial.

"in order to conform to Rāma's wishes, replied with words that were filled with righteousness and political sense" *rāmasyaivānuvṛttyartham uttaraṃ pratyabhāṣata*: Ś2,Ñ1,B1–3,D1–3,8–13, and the texts and printed editions of Ct omit this line.

34. "Rāma" *rāma*: Ś2,Ñ,B1,4,D1–3,8,9,12,T1,G3,M3, and the texts and printed editions of Cg and Gorresio read instead *kāmam*, "true, granted."

"his qualities" *tasya guṇān*: The term *guṇa* is ambiguous, as it can mean either "virtues" or "qualities" in general. Given this reading, it is possible that Vibhīṣaṇa is using the first meaning ironically. D10,T3, and the texts and printed editions of the southern commentators read instead *tasyāguṇān*, literally, "his non-virtues," i.e., his vices.

35. "greatly pleased" *paramaprītaḥ*: Cg, undoubtedly reflecting upon the fact that Vibhīṣaṇa has expressed his disinclination to follow Rāma's instructions, remarks that we can either understand that Rāma is pleased because of Vibhīṣaṇa's frankness or we can break up the sequence differently (i.e., *param*+*aprītaḥ*) to mean "highly displeased." (*paramaprītaḥ satyavacanakathanād iti bhāvaḥ. aprīta iti vā chedaḥ.*)

"skilled in speech . . . was similarly expert in speech" *vākyajño vākyakovidam*: Literally, "[Rāma] knowing speech, [to Vibhīṣaṇa] expert in speech." A number of manuscripts, including the texts and printed editions of Ct, reverse the case endings of these two synonyms, yielding the reading *vākyajñaṃ vākyakovidaḥ*, "[Vibhīṣaṇa] knowing speech, [to Rāma] expert in speech."

36. "I really ought to do what pleases you" *tavāpi me priyaṃ kāryam*: Ck and Ct understand that Rāma owes Vibhīṣaṇa a favor in the form of royal consecration just as he did in the case of Sugrīva (*sugrīvasyeva tavāpi priyaṃ rājyābhiṣekalakṣaṇaṃ mayā kāryaṃ kartavyam*). Cg capitalizes on the ambiguity of the phrase, arguing that it can be taken to mean that Vibhīṣaṇa ought to gratify Rāma by performing Rāvaṇa's funeral rites or that Rāma should please Vibhīṣaṇa by not performing them. (*tava tvayā me priyam api priyam eva kāryam . . . matpriyatvāt tvaddhitatvāc ca rāvaṇasaṃskāraḥ kriyatām ity arthaḥ. yadvā tavāpi me priyaṃ kāryaṃ madvairiṇo rāvaṇasyāsaṃskaraṇaṃ nāma mama priyaṃ tavāpi kartavyam eva.*)

38. "Rāvaṇa, who made the worlds cry out" *rāvaṇo lokarāvaṇaḥ*: Literally, "Rāvaṇa, who causes the world to cry." This etymological epithet is a favorite of Vālmīki. See note to 6.8.12.

"Indra of the hundred sacrifices" *śatakratu-*: Literally, "he of the hundred sacrifices."

39. Verse 39 = App. I, No. 67, lines 93–94 (following *sarga* 97, with *nivṛttam* for *nirvṛttam*) (= GPP 6.109.25, with *nivṛttam* for *nirvṛttam*; and 6.111.100cd–101ab). See notes 31 and 32 to lines 93–94 ad loc.

"for as he was to you, so he is to me" *mamāpy eṣa yathā tava*: Literally, "just as he is yours, he is also mine." At the previous occurrence of this verse (App. I, No. 67, lines 93–94 = GPP 6.109.25), Ct comments very simply, noting that Rāma is stating that Rāvaṇa is as much an object of affection for him as he is for Vibhīṣaṇa, and that therefore Vibhīṣaṇa should have no hesitation in regard to the performance of Rāvaṇa's funeral rites (*taveva mamāpi snehaviṣayas tataḥ saṃskāraviṣayaṃ śaṅkāṃ mā kuru ity arthaḥ*). Here, however, he subjects the phrase to a more elaborate and more theologically focused interpretation, arguing that, just as Rāvaṇa is to be favored by means of funeral rites, and so on, by Vibhīṣaṇa because he was his brother, so is he to be graced by Rāma himself. He argues, however, that Rāvaṇa was not eligible for any one of the four types of liberation. (*eṣa yathā tava bhrātā saṃskārādinā tavānugrāhyas tathā mamāpy anugrāhya eva. caturvidhamuktiṣv ekāpi nāsya.*) Ct goes on to say that, although Rāvaṇa in his obsessive lust for Sītā did manage to obtain a direct vision of Rāma, he did not have the devotional attitude that Rāma was indeed Viṣṇu, thinking instead that he was a mere human. Ct likens Rāvaṇa's situation to that of the *asura* Hiraṇyakaśipu, who, as described in the *Viṣṇupurāṇa*, was slain by Viṣṇu in the form of the *narasiṃhāvatāra*, without recognizing his killer's divinity. Ct notes that, since Rāvaṇa and Kumbhakarṇa were later [in the *dvāpara yuga*] to be reincarnated as [those great exemplars of *dveṣabhakti*] Śiśupāla and Dantavakra, respectively, they could not have attained liberation or union with the Lord. Ct concludes that it is not possible for one who has obtained the world of the Lord to experience rebirth. Instead, such a person would obtain liberation together with Brahmā. (*tad uktam viṣṇupurāṇe hiraṇyakaśipor viṣṇur ayam ity evaṃ na manasy abhūt. daśānanatve 'py anaṅgaparādhīnatayā jānakīsamāsaktacetaso dāśarathirūpadarśanam evāsīt. nāyam acyuta ity āsaktiḥ. vipadyato 'ntakaraṇasya mānuṣabuddhir eva kevalam abhūd iti. ata eva rāvaṇakumbhakarṇayoḥ śiśupāladantavakrarūpeṇa janma śrūyate. na hi bhagavatsālokyaṃ prāptayor api janma bhavati kiṃtu brahmaṇā saha muktir eva iti siddhāntaḥ.*) See note to 6.105.12.

40. "he deserves a... funeral at your hands" *tvatsakāśāt... saṃskāram.../... arhati*: We understand the unexpressed subject of the verb *arhati*, "he deserves *or* merits," to be Rāvaṇa. Cr appears to take Vibhīṣaṇa as the subject, glossing, " 'You must perform the funeral.' That is what it means (*saṃskāram arhati saṃskāraṃ kuru ity arthaḥ*)." But this seems to force the grammar. This interpretation, however, is followed by Dutt (1893, pp. 1495–96), who renders, "It behoveth thee to perform... his funeral ceremony." Roussel (1903, vol. 3, p. 371) understands the compound *tvatsakāśāt*, "at your hands," literally, "from your presence," to mean "in your presence" and understands the funeral ceremony itself, *saṃskāram* (accusative masculine singular), to be the subject of the verb *arhati*. He renders, "*Il faut qu'en ta présence cette cérémonie s'accomplisse.*" In this interpretation, he is followed by Shastri (1959, vol. 3, p. 326) and Pagani (1999, p. 1175). This interpretation does more violence to the grammar than even that of Cr.

"quick" *kṣipram*: M3 and the texts and printed editions of Cg read instead *prāptum* to complete the verbal phrase *prāptum arhati*, "he deserves to receive."

"proper" *vidhipūrvakam*: Literally, "according to the [śāstraic] rules *or* prescriptions."

"great-armed" *mahābāho*: M3 and the texts and printed editions of Cg attempt to resolve the grammatical problem discussed above by substituting the nominative singular noun *daśagrīvaḥ*, "the ten-necked one," i.e., Rāvaṇa, for *mahābāho*.

"knower of righteousness" *dharmajña*: D7,10,11,G1,2, and the texts and printed editions of Ct read instead *dharmeṇa*, "in accordance with righteousness."

"Thus, you will reap glory" *tvaṃ yaśobhāg bhaviṣyasi*: Literally, "You will be a partaker of glory."

41. "provided Rāvaṇa with a fitting funeral" *saṃskāreṇānurūpeṇa yojayāmāsa rāvaṇam*: Literally, "he conjoined Rāvaṇa with a suitable ceremony." Cv understands that Rāvaṇa's funeral rites take place on the first day of the bright half of the month (*saṃskāreṇa śuklapakṣaprathamā gatā*). See note to 6.4.4.

D9–11 and the texts and printed editions of Ct substitute for *pādas* cd a passage of one line [3142*]: "He began to perform the funeral ceremony for his slain brother Rāvaṇa."

Following verse 41, D7,M2 (preceded by colophon), KK (6.114.103–117ef, lines 1–19 within brackets) insert, while D9–11 insert after 3142*; D5,6,T,G3,M1,3, and VSP (only lines 20–33 = 6.114.104–111) insert after 6.99.41; G1,2 insert lines 1–2 and lines 20–34 after 6.99.41; and Ñ,V,B2,3,4,D4,13, and Gorresio (6.96.7–16) insert lines 19–34 after line 29 of App. I, No. 69, a passage of thirty-four lines [App. I, No. 69]: "Then the lord of the *rākṣasas*, Vibhīṣaṇa, entered the city of Laṅkā and quickly set in motion the *agnihotra*[1] sacrifice for Rāvaṇa.[1–2] And that *rākṣasa* caused to be assembled carts, wooden vessels,[2] the sacred fires, sacrificial priests, sandalwood logs and various other types of logs, fragrant aloe and sweet smelling fragrances, as well as jewels, pearls, and coral.[3–6] Then, after a short while, the *rākṣasa* came forth surrounded by *rākṣasas* and, together with Mālyavān, began to perform the ceremony.[7–8] Then the brahmans, their faces covered with tears, placed Rāvaṇa, overlord of the *rākṣasas*, all clad in linen garments, upon a celestial litter made of gold. Then, lifting that litter, which was made colorful with flowers and varicolored banners, they took up logs of firewood, and, with Vibhīṣaṇa at their head, they faced south and set forth[3] to the accompaniment of the blare of various trumpets and the ceremonious sound of eulogies.[9–14] All the sacred fires were then kindled by the *adhvaryu* priest and placed in vessels.[4] They went forth, preceding the deceased.[5][15–16] Behind them, all the women of the inner apartments swiftly followed, weeping and swaying to and fro[6] on every side.[17–18] Then, in their deep grief, they placed Rāvaṇa on a consecrated[7] spot.[19] To the accompaniment of vedic *mantras*,[8] they built a pyre of sandalwood logs, covered with *padmaka*[9] wood and *uśīra*[10] roots and spread with the skin of a spotted antelope.[11][20–21] The last rites for the king were performed as prescribed in the *vedas*. And then they performed an excellent sacrifice to the ancestors[12] on behalf of the lord of the *rākṣasas*.[22–23] They laid out the altar to the southwest of the pyre and kindled the sacred fires, each in its proper place.[13] Then they all poured out ladles filled with a mixture of curds and clarified butter.[14][24–25] They placed a cart at his feet and a mortar[15] between his thighs.[26] And the learned priests[16] placed[17] all those wooden vessels, the lower and upper fire sticks, and an additional pestle in their proper places according to prescriptions set forth in the *śāstras* and ordained by the great seers.[27–29] Nearby, the *rākṣasas* slaughtered a sacrificial victim[18] and placed the omentum,[19] moistened with clarified butter, over the king.[30–31] Then, with their hearts full of sorrow and their faces drenched with tears, the *rākṣasas*,[20] assisted by Vibhīṣaṇa, adorned Rāvaṇa with fragrances, garlands, and various garments and then sprinkled him with parched grain.[32–34]"

[1]"the *agnihotra*" *agnihotram*: According to Gita Press (1969, vol. 3, p. 1835), this refers to the act of pouring libations on the fire. Dutt (1893, p. 1496) provides a note, according to which this term refers to "a pot for preserving sacred fire." Pagani (1999, p. 1674), in a note, understands that the cremation is the final *agnihotra* for Rāvaṇa. She understands the *agnihotra* to be the twice daily pouring of oblations into the fire required of all brahmans, of whom Rāvaṇa is one. See note to 6.23.24.

[2]"wooden vessels" *dārupātrāṇi*: GPP, KK, and Gita Press all read *-rūpāṇi*, "various types [of wood]," for *-pātrāṇi*, "vessels."

[3]"they . . . set forth" *bhejire*: Literally, "they partook *or* shared." We understand the verb in the sense in which it is read by Ct, who glosses, "they took the road to the cremation grounds (*śmaśānamārgaṃ bhejire*)," and Cr, who glosses, "they went (*jagmuḥ*)."

[4]"placed in vessels" *śaraṇābhigatāḥ*: Literally, "gone to places of refuge." We agree with Ct and Cr, who understand the compound to refer to the placement of the sacred fires in the pots in which they will be carried to the cremation ground (*ādhārasthānakuṇḍasthāḥ*—so Ct). Roussel (1903, vol. 3, p. 372) understands the term in its more familiar sense, translating, "*Tous ceux qui étaient venus se réfugier près de lui.*" In this he is followed by Shastri (1959, vol. 3, p. 326) and Pagani (1999, p. 1175). Dutt (1893, p. 1496) takes the reference to be to "the attendants."

[5]"the deceased" *tasya*: Literally, "of him." The reference is presumably to Rāvaṇa.

[6]"swaying to and fro" *plavamānāni*: We believe that this sense of the root √*plu* best fits the context of the wailing women. Ct takes the root in its more common sense of "to leap," arguing that, in their haste, the women, who would be inexperienced in walking, would appear to be leaping. Evidently his idea is that they are stumbling and recovering themselves (*calanābhyāsābhāvāt tvarayā ca plavamānānīva*). This idea is followed by Dutt (1893, p. 1496), who renders, "speedily leaping (being ever unused to walking)," and by other translators who follow the text of Ct, who understand that the women are "tottering" (for example, see Gita Press 1969, vol. 3, p. 1836).

[7]"consecrated" *prayate*: Literally, "restrained, holy." The term, derived from the verb *pra* √*yam*, "to restrain *or* control one's senses," is properly used of a person, i.e., an ascetic or holy person. While the commentators ignore it, its usage here has occasioned some confusion on the part of translators. We agree with the interpretation of Gita Press (1969, vol. 3, p. 1836). Roussel (1903, vol. 3, p. 372), followed by Shastri (1959, vol. 3, p. 326), understands "*spacieux*." Pagani (1999, p. 1175), somewhat similarly to us, renders, "*préparé*," while Dutt (1893, p. 1496) renders, "the cremation ground."

[8]"vedic *mantras*" *brāhmyā*: Literally, "pertaining to *brahma or* the *vedas*." Commentators differ as to whether the reference is to vedic recitation or ritual.

[9]"*padmaka*" *padmaka-*: A type of tree, the *Prunus cerasoides* (*Cerasus puddum*), or wild Himalayan cherry.

[10]"*uśīra*" *-uśīra-*: The fragrant root of a plant or of a specific type of grass, *Andropogon muricatus* (khus grass).

[11]"with the skin of a spotted antelope" *rāṅkavāstaraṇa-*: Literally, "a cover *or* spread derived from the *raṅku* deer." According to Ck, Ct, and Cr, *raṅku* is a name for the *kṛṣṇasāra*, or spotted antelope. The covering could be either a blanket made from the hair of that animal or, more likely, as Cg and Cm suggest, its skin.

[12]"an . . . sacrifice to the ancestors" *pitṛmedham*: We follow Cg, who clearly understands the *pitṛmedha* to be a separate ritual from the *antyeṣṭi*, or funeral rite itself.

[13]"They laid out the altar to the southwest of the pyre and kindled the sacred fires, each in its proper place." *vediṃ ca dakṣiṇaprācyāṃ yathāsthānaṃ ca pāvakam*: Literally, "and an altar on the southwest and fire according to place." The line is highly elliptical and the two accusatives *vedim*, "altar," and *pāvakam*, "fire," have no verb governing them.

[14]"Then they all poured out ladles filled with a mixture of curds and clarified butter." *pṛṣadājyena saṃpūrṇaṃ sruvaṃ sarve pracikṣipuḥ*: Literally, "they all threw out a ladle filled with speckled butter." D10,11, and the texts and printed editions of Ct and Ck read *skandhe*, "on his shoulder," for *sarve*, "all."

[15]"cart . . . mortar" *śakaṭam . . . ulūkhalam*: As Cg points out, the cart is the one employed to bring King Soma (*somarājānayanaśakaṭam*), while the mortar is the one used for cleansing or threshing the sacrificial rice (*yajñīyavrīhyavahanasādhanam*). Here, as in the case of the other vessels mentioned, we see the practice of sending a sacrificer to the next world with all his sacrificial paraphernalia.

[16]"the learned priests" *vicakṣaṇāḥ*: Literally, "the learned ones." D10,11, and the texts and printed editions of Ct read instead *vicakramuḥ*, "they placed (lit., stepped forward)."

[17]"placed" *dattvā*: Literally, "having given." The three lines 27–29 have no finite verb. Translators and commentators resolve the difficulty in various ways. Some, like us, read the gerund *dattvā* as a finite verb. Others simply supply a verb. A number of commentators and translators construe line 29 with line 30, with which, in all printed

editions of the southern recension, it constitutes a single verse, indicating that the *rākṣasas* kill the *medhyaṃ paśum*, or "sacrificial animal," "according to prescriptions set forth in the *śāstras* and ordained by the great seers."

[18]"a sacrificial victim" *medhyaṃ paśum*: Commentators and translators differ as to which type of animal is sacrificed. Cm, whom Ct quotes, understands that the animal is, in fact, identical with the *paristaraṇikā*, which he takes to be a special royal sacrificial cow (*anustaraṇikāṃ rājagavīm*). Pagani (1999, p. 1175) appears to follow this, rendering, "*la vache du sacrifice*." Cg glosses, "a goat (*chāgam*)," in which opinion he is followed by Shastri (1959, vol. 3, p. 327) and Gita Press (1969, vol. 3, p. 1836). Raghunathan (1982, vol. 3, p. 327) renders, "a sheep." Other commentators and translators, like us, do not specify the species of the victim.

[19]"the omentum" *paristaraṇikām*: We follow Ck, Ct, and Cr, who take the term to refer to the omentum of the sacrificial victim that is placed on the face of the deceased. They cite a *sūtra* supporting this interpretation. (*paristīryate mukham anayeti paristaraṇikā vapā tāṃ rākṣasendrasya mukhe samaveśayan vapāsya mukhaṃ prorṇauti*—so Ck and Ct.) Cg understands the term as a collective singular for a variety of unspecified coverings (*paristaraṇikāṃ paristaraṇāni jātyekavacanam*).

[20]"*rākṣasas*" *te*: Literally, "they."

42. "cremated him" *dadau pāvakaṃ tasya*: Literally, "he gave him fire." It is clear that the critical text is highly elliptical—as evidenced by the hiatus between verses 41 and 42—unless one includes the appendix passage (App. I, No. 69), known to the vast majority of both northern and southern recensions.

Like Cs above, Ct is also aware of the apparent contradiction between this whole passage and the verse in the *Rāmopākhyāna* of the *Mahābhārata* in which it is stated that Rāma's *brahmāstra* had literally vaporized Rāvaṇa's body, leaving no visible trace. Ct, however, rationalizes the seeming contradiction by arguing that the *Mahābhārata* passage is merely an example of hyperbole used to express the extraordinary blazing energy of Rāma's arrow (*rāmabāṇatejovarṇanaviṣaye 'tyuktyalaṃkāraparatvād iti vadanti*). Compare note 2 to App. I, No. 68* (following 6.99.19–20) above. See *MBh* 3.274.31.

"he consoled" *anunayāmāsa*: According to Cg and Cr, Vibhīṣaṇa is gently urging the women to return to the city. This is in keeping with insert 3146*, where that instruction is made explicit, and with the following verse, where we see that the women have indeed returned to Laṅkā. This incident thus shows Vibhīṣaṇa's compliance with Rāma's instructions, at verse 30 above, to send the women back.

Following 42ab, D5–7,10,11 (10 and 11, lines 1–2 only),T,G,M1,3,5, and the texts and printed editions of the southern commentators (Ct, lines 1–2 only) insert a passage of three lines [3145*]: "He bathed and, his garments still wet, offered sesame seeds mixed with water and *dūrva* grass according to the ritual prescriptions. Then, bowing his head to his brother,[1] he offered plain water.[2]"

[1]"his brother" *enam*: Literally, "him."

[2]"he offered plain water" *pradāya codakam*: Literally, "and having offered water." We are inclined to agree with Raghunathan, the only translator consulted to render this line, that the water mentioned here is separate from the water mentioned in line 2. In the absence of a finite verb, we have rendered the gerund *pradāya* as if it were finite.

Following verse 42, D5–7,10,11,S insert a passage of one line [3146*]: "Addressed with the words, 'Please go,'[1] they all then entered the city."

[1]"Addressed with the words, 'Please go'" *gamyatām iti*: Literally, "Please go." The line is elliptical. Cm adds the word *uktāḥ*, "[they were] addressed."

43. "And . . . all the *rākṣasa* women" *ca sarvāsu rākṣasīṣu*: D9–11 and the texts and printed editions of Ct read instead *purīṃ strīṣu rākṣasendraḥ*, yielding the sense "when the women [had entered] the city, the lord of the *rākṣasas* . . ."

"had gone back" *praviṣṭāsu*: Literally, "[when those women] had entered."

As part of his contribution to the ongoing commentarial discussion on the absolute and relative chronology of the epic events, Cg notes here that Vibhīṣaṇa's consecration was performed on the day following Rāvaṇa's funeral, since, as the demon king had fallen in the forefront of battle, Vibhīṣaṇa would experience no period of ritual impurity following his brother's death, which would otherwise have prevented the performance of the ceremony. Cg further notes that Rāma's return to Ayodhyā takes place on the same day as Rāma's consecration of Vibhīṣaṇa. Cg concludes his remarks by saying that the funeral took place on the first [day of the bright half of Caitra]. (*raṇaśirasi hatatvena rāvaṇasyāśaucābhāvād āgata ata evottaradine rājyābhiṣeko 'yodhyāgamanaṃ cānuṣṭhitam. prathamāyāṃ rāvaṇasaṃskāraḥ.*) Cg's remarks are in keeping with Cv's position that the funeral occurred on the first day of the bright half [of Caitra] (*rāvaṇasaṃskāreṇa śuklapakṣaprathamāyām*). As throughout this discussion, Cg's position differs from that of Ct, who, at the conclusion of this *sarga*, places the funeral on the evening of the ninth [of Āśvina] (*ayaṃ saṃskāro navamyām eva sāyaṃkāle*). Compare notes to 6.100.7, where Ct again takes up the issue. See note to 6.4.4.

44. "as did Indra of the hundred sacrifices after slaying Vṛtra" *hatvā yathā vṛtraṃ śatakratuḥ*: Literally, "like the one of one hundred sacrifices having killed Vṛtra." Ś2,B1,D1–3,8–12, and the texts and printed editions of Ct read instead *hatvā vṛtraṃ vajradharo yathā*, literally, "like the *vajra*-bearer having killed Vṛtra." See 6.75.35 and note.

Following verse 44, Ś2,Ñ2,V1,2,B,D1–3,8–13 (D13 after 3141*), and the texts and printed editions of Ct insert a passage of four lines [3147*]: "Then, setting down[1] the bow, arrows, and mighty armor that great Indra had given him and putting aside his wrath now that his enemy had been slain, that slayer of his foes, like the hare-marked moon, resumed his mild demeanor.[2][1–4]"

[1]"setting down" *muktvā*: Literally, "having released."

[2]"like the hare-marked moon . . . his mild demeanor" *śaśīva saumyatvam*: Literally, "like the one possessing a rabbit . . . his mildness." The critical reading presents a mild pun in that the adjective *saumya* means both "gentle, beneficent" and "pertaining to *or* associated with the moon [Soma]." D9–11 and the texts and printed editions of Ct read *rāmaḥ saḥ*, "he, Rāma," for *śaśīva*, "like the moon," thus eliminating both the simile and the pun of the critical edition. Cf. 6.102.35 and note.

The meter is *vaṃśasthavila*.

Sarga 100

1. "proclaiming those auspicious events" *kathayantaḥ śubhāḥ kathāḥ*: Literally, "telling auspicious tales." All translators consulted appear to understand that the supernatural spectators depart, talking among themselves about the stirring events they have witnessed. We believe, however, that the context supports our idea that these great beings depart for their own proper worlds, spreading the good news as it were.

2–3. "the counsel of Sugrīva" *sugrīvasya . . . mantritam*: According to Ct and Ck, the reference here is not merely to Sugrīva's advice during the war but, instead, to his useful and effective counsel in such matters as the mustering of the troops, the search for Sītā, etc. (*senāsaṃmelanasītānveṣaṇādisarvakāryasādhakaṃ mantrasāmarthyam*—so Ct).

"of Lakṣmaṇa Saumitri" *saumitrer lakṣmaṇasya*: Cg, the only commentator to remark on the critical reading, notes the unusual collocation of the name and the matronymic here, observing that the latter is used to show how praiseworthy and fortunate Lakṣmaṇa's mother is (*saumitrer iti tanmātuḥ ślāghanavyañjanāyāsya jananī hi bhāgyavatīti*). V3,D7,10,11,G1,2, and the texts and printed editions of Ct read instead *māruteḥ*, "of Māruti," for *saumitreḥ*, making the verse refer to both Lakṣmaṇa and Hanumān. Ct and Ck, the only commentators to remark on this reading, understand that both qualities, heroism and devotion to Rāma, are shared by both characters (*mārutilakṣmaṇayo rāme 'nurāgaṃ vīryaṃ ca*—so Ct).

Following 3ab, V2,B3,D9–11, and the printed editions of Ct, Gorresio, and KK (in brackets) insert, while Ś2,B1,D1–4,8,12 substitute for 3cd, a passage of one line [3148*]: "[proclaiming] Sītā's devotion to her husband and the valor of Hanumān."

4. "noble" *mahābhāgaḥ*: B1,4,D1–4,7,9–11G1,2, and the texts and printed editions of Ct read instead *mahābāhuḥ*, "the great-armed one."

"he released" *anujñāya*: Literally, "having given permission *or* leave."

"loaned" *-dattam*: Literally, "given." See 6.99.10.

Both Ct and Cs note an inherent narrative contradiction between the present passage and the *Rāmopākhyāna*, where it is said that Rāma retains Indra's chariot until after his reunion with Sītā (*MBh* 3.275.8,49). These commentators, however, downplay the seriousness of this contradiction on the grounds that the *Mahābhārata* story is not as clearly focused on the sequence of events (*yady api bhārate sītāyā āgamanottaraṃ rathād avataraṇaṃ bhagavata uktam tathāpi tatra paurvāparyakrame tātparyābhāvān na kṣatiḥ*—so Ct).

5. "ascended" *āruroha*: D1–3,6,9–11,T2,3, and the texts and printed editions of Ct read instead *utpapāta*, "he flew up."

6. "that foremost of the charioteers of the gods" *surasārathisattame*: D9–11 and the texts and printed editions of Ct read instead *sarathe rathināṃ varaḥ*, "[when he] along with his chariot [had ascended into the sky], [Rāghava] the best of chariot-warriors . . ."

7. "reverently saluted" *abhivāditaḥ*: M3,5, and the texts and printed editions of Cg read instead *pracoditaḥ*, "urged on."

"by the foremost of the tawny monkeys" *hariśreṣṭhaiḥ*: Ś2,V2,B1,D1–3,9–12, and the texts and printed editions of Ct read instead *harigaṇaiḥ*, "by the hosts of tawny monkeys."

Apropos of this verse, Ct raises once again the question of chronology, taking a position reminiscent of that articulated earlier by Cg (at 6.99.43). There, Cg argues that Vibhīṣaṇa's consecration is performed on the day of Rāvaṇa's funeral because Rāvaṇa's death in battle obviates the need for his observing a period of "death impurity," during which the *abhiṣeka* ritual could not be performed. Ct, quoting *Manusmṛti* 5.98, the same verse that must have inspired Cg, argues that it is a mistake to think that there has been a ten-day period of impurity in this case but holds that, in fact, a three-day period of *aśauca* is in force for the tenth, eleventh, and twelfth [of Caitra] so that, according to him, the consecration takes place on the fourth day [after the funeral on the ninth]. (*atha tribhir dinair daśarātraikādaśāhadvādaśāhakartavyakriyāsamāptau. caturthe 'hanīty arthaḥ. nātra daśāham āśaucam iti bhramitavyam.*) It would appear that Ct is alluding to *Manusmṛti* 5.59, which specifies that those in the relationship of a *sapiṇḍa* to the deceased, as is Vibhīṣaṇa to Rāvaṇa, may observe a period of death pollution of one, three, or ten days. Cf. *ManuSm* 5.59. Note, however, that the verse Ct quotes (*ManuSm* 5.98) holds that there is no period of impurity for those who are slain by weapons in battle. See note to 6.99.43 above. On the issue of chronology, see note to 6.4.4.

8. "And then Rāma spoke" *abravīc ca tadā rāmaḥ*: Ś2,B1,D1–3,8–11, and the texts and printed editions of Ct read instead *athovāca sa kākutsthaḥ*, "And then Kākutstha spoke."

"mighty" *sattvasampannam*: Literally, "endowed with strength." V3,D9–11,13, and the texts and printed editions of Ct read instead *mitrasampannam*, "endowed with friends," producing an echoing effect with the matronymic Saumitri. Ñ2,D5,T1,M3, and the texts and printed editions of Cg read instead *satyasampannam*, "endowed with truth."

"of blazing energy" *dīptatejasam*: Ś2,B1,D1–3,8–11, and the texts and printed editions of Ct and Gorresio read instead *śubhalakṣaṇam*, "of auspicious marks," producing an echoing effect with the name Lakṣmaṇa. See 6.67.37; 6.71.20; 6.89.4; and notes.

9. "Gentle brother" *saumya*: Literally, "O gentle one."

"in the kingship of Laṅkā" *laṅkāyām*: Literally, "in Laṅkā." Ct suggests that we should supply the words "on Rāvaṇa's throne itself (*rāvaṇasiṃhāsane sākṣād iti śeṣaḥ*)." Cg reminds us that Rāma had already had Vibhīṣaṇa consecrated on the seashore (6.13.7–9). According to him, the purpose of the repetition of the ceremony is to consecrate Vibhīṣaṇa on Rāvaṇa's actual throne (*samudratīra eva laṅkārājyābhiṣeke kṛte 'pi punarvidhānaṃ rāvaṇasiṃhāsane 'bhiṣekartham*). Perhaps the idea here is that the public consecration would lend greater legitimacy to the new king. Compare notes to 6.19.26 and 27.

"loyal and devoted" *anuraktaṃ ca bhaktaṃ ca*: Cr and Cg attempt to differentiate the two nearly synonymous terms. According to Cr, the former refers to Vibhīṣaṇa's affection for Rāma, while the latter refers to his actions that are in accordance with that affection (*anuraktaṃ madviṣayakānurāgam ata eva bhaktaṃ manniṣṭhaprītyanukūlavyāpāravantam*). Cg understands the former term to refer to Vibhīṣaṇa's performance of the duties of a friend and the latter to his performance of the duties of a servant. (*anuraktam ity anena mitrakṛtyam uktam. bhaktam ity anena dāsyakṛtyam.*)

"and has rendered me great assistance" *caivopakāriṇam*: Literally, "and [is one] possessing assistance." Ś2,B1,D1–3,8–12, and the texts and printed editions of Ct read instead *pūrvopakāriṇam*, "and was formerly helpful."

10. "gentle brother" *saumya*: Literally, "O gentle one."

11. "a golden vessel" *sauvarṇaṃ ghaṭam*: Cr, Cg, Cm, and Ct, in anticipation of their following verses (3153*), where the jar is described as being handed over to a group of monkeys, understand the singular here to be a collective singular (*jātyekavacanam*), representing several vessels.

Following verse 11, D5–7,9–11,T,G,M1,3,5, and the texts and printed editions of the southern commentators insert a passage of five lines [3153*]: "Giving that vessel into the hands[1] of the foremost of monkeys, who were immensely powerful[2] and as swift as thought, he instructed them to fetch water from the ocean.[1–2] Then those immensely powerful[3] monkeys departed with tremendous speed.[3] And when they had fetched water from the ocean, those foremost among the monkeys returned.[4] Then, taking one vessel[4] and placing [Vibhīṣaṇa] on that high throne, [Saumitri]..." [5]

[1]"into the hands" *haste*: Literally, "in the hand." As in the case of the vessel, Cr, Ct, and Cg understand that, because of the plurality of the monkeys, we should take this as a collective singular (*jātyekavacanam*).

[2]"immensely powerful" *mahāsattvān*: D9–11 and the texts and printed editions of Ct read instead the nominative singular *mahāsattvaḥ*, which would then refer to Lakṣmaṇa.

[3]"immensely powerful" *mahābalāḥ*: D9–11 and the texts and printed editions of Ct read instead *manojavāḥ*, "as swift as thought."

[4]"one vessel" *ekaṃ ghaṭam*: This phrase lends credence to the commentators' argument in note 1 above that the previous use of the singular for vessels and hands should be taken as collective.

12. "used that vessel to consecrate" *ghaṭena tena... abhyaṣiñcat*: Literally, "he consecrated with that pot."

Following verse 12, Ñ,V1,2,B2–4,D5–7,9–11,13,T,G,M1,3,5, and the texts and printed editions of the southern commentators insert a passage of one line [3154*]: "According to the prescriptions set forth in the vedic texts, [he consecrated] him who was surrounded by the hosts of his friends.[1]"

[1]"him who was surrounded by the hosts of his friends" *suhṛdgaṇasamāvṛtam*: D9–11,T2,3,M5, and the texts and printed editions of Ct read instead the nominative *suhṛdgaṇasamāvṛtaḥ*, which then modifies Lakṣmaṇa rather than Vibhīṣaṇa.

13. "Thus did that righteous hero consecrate pure-minded Vibhīṣaṇa" *abhyaṣiñcat sa dharmātmā śuddhātmānaṃ vibhīṣaṇam*: Cg understands the term "pure-minded" to mean that Vibhīṣaṇa accepts the consecration only because he was so ordered by Rāma. The higher meaning, according to Cg, is that Vibhīṣaṇa is completely devoted to the service of Rāma. (*śuddhātmānam ity anena rāmājñayābhiṣekam aṅgīkṛtavān. paramārthas tu rāmakaiṅkārya evāsakto 'bhūd ity avagamyate.*) D9–11, KK, and the texts and printed editions of Ct read, for 13ab, *abhyaṣiñcaṃs tadā sarve rākṣasā vānarās tathā* (*tadā*—KK), "and then all the *rākṣasas* and monkeys consecrated [him]."

"the latter's" *tasya*: Literally, "his."

"those *rākṣasas* who were devoted to him" *bhaktā ye cāsya rākṣasāḥ*: We understand the relative clause to be restrictive here and to refer specifically to those *rākṣasas* who, like Vibhīṣaṇa's four loyal ministers, were devoted to his cause. See 6.10.12; 6.11.3,5; 6.28.7; and notes. One might also, perhaps, read the clause to mean that all the *rākṣasas* have now transferred their loyalty to their new king.

Following verse 13ab, Ś2,B1,D1–3,8–12, KK (in brackets), and the texts and printed editions of Ct insert a passage of one line [3157*]: "Experiencing unequaled delight, they praised Rāma."

14. "Rāghava, together with Lakṣmaṇa, experienced the greatest delight." *rāghavaḥ paramāṃ prītiṃ jagāma sahalakṣmaṇah*: Ś2,Ñ,V1,2,B,D1–3,5,7,8,12,13,T1,G1,3,M, and the texts and printed editions of Cg omit 14cd. Based on the principles outlined by the critical editors (Bhatt 1960, p. xxxiv), the line should have been omitted from the critical edition. The critical apparatus provides no rationale for the inclusion of this line. It is not rendered in the translation of Raghunathan (1982, vol. 3, p. 329), leading him to construe lines 14ab with verse 13.

15. "When he had received that great kingdom, which Rāma had conferred upon him, Vibhīṣaṇa" *sa tadrājyaṃ mahat prāpya rāmadattaṃ vibhīṣaṇaḥ*: Literally, "Vibhīṣaṇa, having obtained that great kingdom given by Rāma." D10,11, and the texts and printed editions of Ct omit this line (15ab).

"comforted his people" *prakṛtīḥ sāntvayitvā*: Literally, "having conciliated the elements of state." The term *prakṛti* here is ambiguous. Ct, Ck, Cr, and most of the translators consulted take it in its sense of "subjects, people (*prajā*)," and we tentatively agree with this interpretation. However, equally plausible, in our view, is Cg's interpretation in which the term is taken in its sense of "ministers of state, etc. (*amātya-prabhṛti*)." The idea here would be that Vibhīṣaṇa is attempting to conciliate the ministers and other government officials who would have been loyal to Rāvaṇa. Cg's understanding is, however, that the new king is dispelling the grief of his ministers caused by the loss of their sons, friends, and so forth (*putramitrādivināśajaśokāpa-nodanaṃ kṛtvā*). Raghunathan (1982, vol. 3, p. 329), who follows Cg, renders, "conciliated the estates of the realm." Cf. verse 13 and note above.

16. "unhusked rice, sweetmeats, parched grain, and celestial flowers" *akṣatān moda-kāṃl lājān divyāḥ sumanasas tathā*: Ś2,D1,3,8–11, and the texts and printed editions of Ct read instead *dadhyakṣatān modakāṃś ca lājāḥ sumanasas tathā*, "curds, unhusked rice, sweetmeats, parched grain, and flowers." See 6.116.35 and note.

17. "all those auspicious offerings . . . in an auspicious fashion" *maṅgalyaṃ maṅgalaṃ sarvam*: We follow the interpretation of Cr, according to which the term *maṅgalyam* applies to the entire collection of auspicious materials referred to in the previous verse, while *maṅgalam* is to be read adverbially (*maṅgalyaṃ maṅgalārhaṃ sarvaṃ vastu-jātaṃ maṅgalaṃ yathā bhavati tathā*). Cg, however, believes that the phrase *maṅgalaṃ sarvam* refers to a collection of auspicious substances, such as turmeric, which is different from the assemblage of unhusked rice, etc., mentioned in the previous verse (*maṅgalaṃ haridrādi maṅgaladravyam; sarvam uktākṣatādibhinnam*).

18. "merely out of a desire to please him" *tasyaiva priyakāmyayā*: Cg, the only commentator to share this reading, expands on the expression, adding, "but not out of a desire for his own enjoyment (*na tu svabhogecchayā*)." V3,B2,D10,11,M1, and the texts

and printed editions of Ct read *prati-* for the critical editions's reading of *priya-*, yielding the sense "at his wish."

19. "Rāghava . . . spoke these words" *abravīd rāghavo vākyam*: Ś2,B1,D1–3,8–12, and the texts and printed editions of Ct read instead *uvācedaṃ vaco rāmaḥ*, "Rāma spoke these words."

"who stood beside him" *pārśvataḥ sthitam*: D9–11 and the texts and printed editions of Ct read *praṇatam*, "humble, humbly," for *pārśvataḥ*, "beside," lending the phrase the meaning "who stood [there] humbly."

20–21. "you must enter Rāvaṇa's palace . . . humbly approach" *praviśya rāvaṇagṛhaṃ vinayenopasṛtya ca*: Literally, "having entered the house of Rāvana, having approached with humility." D5–7,M1,3, and the texts and printed editions of Cm and Cg read *vijayenābhinandya ca*, "having gladdened [her] with the victory," for *vinayenopasṛtya ca*, "and having humbly approached." This variant is rendered only by Raghunathan (1982, vol. 3, p. 329), who translates, "and gladden her with the news of my victory." Ś2,Ñ,V,B,D1–4,8–11,13,M2, and the texts and printed editions of Ct substitute, for 20cd, a passage of one line [3165*]: *praviśya nagarīṃ laṅkāṃ kauśalaṃ brūhi maithilīm*, "having entered the city of Laṅkā, ask Sītā about her well-being." KK inserts this line, in brackets, as its 23cd.

"foremost among the victorious" *jayatāṃ śreṣṭha*: Ś2,B1,D1–3,8–11, and the texts and printed editions of Ct read instead *vadatāṃ śreṣṭha*, "O best among speakers, most eloquent one."

"and that I have slain Rāvaṇa" *rāvaṇaṃ ca mayā hatam*: Ś2,D1–3,8–11, and the texts and printed editions of Ct read instead *rāvaṇaṃ ca hataṃ raṇe*, "and that Rāvaṇa has been slain in battle."

Following 20ab, D5–7,T,G,M3,5, and the texts and printed editions (KK after 3165* = KK 6.115.24ab; VSP 6.115.24ab) of Cg and Cr (GPP in brackets, unnumbered between 6.112.22 and 23) insert a passage of one line [3164*]: "Go, gentle friend, to the city of Laṅkā, having taken permission according to the prescribed rules."

22. "once you have related the good news to Maithilī" *priyam etad udāhṛtya maithilyāḥ*: Ñ2,V1,2,B1–3,D3,9–11, and the texts and printed editions of Ct read *ihākhyāhi* for *udāhṛtya*, while Ś2,B1,D1,2,8–12, and the texts and printed editions of Ct read *vaidehyāḥ* for *maithilyāḥ*. This lends to the texts that read both variants, including the printed editions of Ct, the sense "here, you must relate the good news to Vaidehī."

Sarga 101

1. "honored" *pūjyamānaḥ*: Literally, "being honored." Cg notes that Hanumān is being honored by the *rākṣasas* who are pointing out the way [to the palace] (*mārga-pradarśanādibhiḥ pūjyamānatvam*)."

2. "Entering Rāvaṇa's palace, that hero of immense blazing energy" *praviśya tu mahātejā rāvaṇasya niveśanam*: Literally, "and having entered Rāvaṇa's dwelling, that one of great energy." D10,11, and the texts and printed editions of Ct read instead

praviśya ca purīṃ laṅkām anujñāpya vibhīṣaṇam, "and having entered the city of Laṅkā, after taking the permission of Vibhīṣaṇa."

"spied Sītā, who resembled the constellation Rohiṇī cut off from her lord, the hare-marked moon, and occluded by a malevolent planet" *dadarśa śaśinā hīnāṃ sātaṅkām iva rohiṇīm*: Literally, "He saw one who was like an occluded Rohiṇī deprived of the one with the hare *or* rabbit." The reading of the critical edition is both elliptical and ambiguous. The simile is defective in that there is no explicit *upameya*. In order to bring out the sense of the line, therefore, we have added the name "Sītā," the logical object of the verb *dadarśa*, "he saw." The adjective *sātaṅkām* is also ambiguous, perhaps, intentionally so. In reference to a person, it would mean "pained, anguished, afflicted, diseased, ill, *or* afraid." In reference to a celestial body, it would mean, as indicated by Ct, Ck, and Cg, "occluded *or* oppressed by a planet (*grahapīḍāsahitām*—so Ct)." Cr glosses, "filled with dread (*śaṅkāsahitām*)." Rohiṇī, the fourth lunar *nakṣatra*, is stereotypically regarded as the favorite wife of the moon. See 6.80.38; 6.90.27; 6.99.16; and notes. The word *ātaṅkā* is also a name or epithet for the constellation Bharaṇī, which is associated with the eclipse demon Rāhu, perhaps as his source or mother, as indicated by Rāhu's epithet *Bharaṇībhūḥ*. Thus, the intention of the simile may be to compare Sītā to a celestial luminary in the process of being eclipsed. The simile, defective though it is, functions well in two respects. Sītā, like Rohiṇī, is cut off from her beloved lord and is beset by evil attendants in the form of her *rākṣasī* wardresses, although the critical text makes no explicit allusion to these figures here.

Ñ,V1,2,B,D2,4,6,7,10,11,M1,3, and the texts and printed editions of the southern commentators read *mṛjayā hīnām*, "without cleaning *or* bathing," for *śaśinā hīnām*, "cut off from the one possessing a hare." On the issue of Sītā's bathing before seeing Rāma, see 6.102.7,10,13–14, and notes.

Following 2ab, Ś2,Ñ2,B1,3,D1–3,8–12, and the texts and printed editions of Ct insert a passage of two lines [3168*]: "Granted permission, Hanumān then entered[1] that grove of trees. Having entered in the proper fashion, that tawny monkey, who was already known to Sītā..."

[1]"Granted permission, Hanumān then entered" *praviveśābhyanujñāto hanūmān*: Literally, "Hanumān entered, permitted." D9–11 and the texts and printed editions of Ct read instead *tatas tenābhyanujñātaḥ*, "then, permitted by him [Vibhīṣaṇa], [Hanumān]."

Following verse 2, D5–7,10,11,S insert a passage of one line [3169*]: "Joyless, at the foot of a tree, surrounded by *rākṣasa* women..."

3. "Modest, humble, and deferential" *nibhṛtaḥ praṇataḥ prahvaḥ*: The semantic ranges of these three terms overlap in the senses of "modest, deferential, bowing." The commentators explore their wider ranges of meanings in an effort to avoid what they must see as tautology. Cm, Ct, and Cg understand *nibhṛtaḥ* in its sense of "still, motionless (*niścalaḥ*)." Several of the translators consulted interpret the term as either "silent" or "motionless." Cr understands the term to mean "having his mind at ease (*svasthacittaḥ*)." Ct and Cm take the term *prahvaḥ* to mean "humble *or* bowing (*namraḥ*),"

while Cg understands it to mean "with [his] limbs greatly contracted (*prakarṣeṇa saṃkucitagātraḥ*)." Cr, on the other hand, understands, "enunciating words proper to the occasion (*uccāritatātkālikaśabdaḥ san*)." Cr glosses *praṇataḥ* as "bowing his head (*śirasā nataḥ*)," while Cg similarly glosses, "having bowed *or* prostrated himself (*kṛtapraṇāmaḥ san*)."

"greeted her respectfully" *abhivādya*: Cg understands that Hanumān is making a formal greeting by announcing his name (*svanāmasaṃkīrtya*).

Following 3ab, D5–7,9–11,S insert a passage of three lines [3170*]: "When she first saw immensely powerful Hanumān arrive, the queen remained silent. But then, looking more closely,[1] she recognized him and was filled with joy. Seeing her lovely face, Hanumān, foremost of the leaping monkeys . . ."

[1]"When she first saw . . . looking more closely" *dṛṣṭvā . . . dṛṣṭvā*: Literally, "having seen . . . having seen." Several of the commentators attempt to explain the repetition of the gerund *dṛṣṭvā* and the reason why Sītā appears to be unmoved by her initial sight of Hanumān. The general consensus is that she fails to recognize him on first glance either because he is still too distant or because she is glancing about in general and only subsequently focuses her gaze upon him. It is then that, recognizing her old friend, she becomes happy. (*samāgataṃ hanūmantaṃ dṛṣṭvā dūrato 'valokya tattvenājñātvety arthas tūṣṇīm āste dṛṣṭvā samīpato 'valokya smṛtvā hanūmān evāyam iti saṃsmṛtya hṛṣṭābhavat*—so Cr.) Cr further indicates that this recognition suggests that Sītā realizes the success of [Rāma's] mission (*ity anena sītayā kāryasiddhir jñāteti sūcitam*).

4. "that tamer of his enemies" *ariṃdamaḥ*: Ś2,B1,D1–3,8–12, and the texts and printed editions of Ct read instead *amitrajit*, "conqueror of his enemies."

"inquires after your well-being" *kuśalaṃ cāha*: Literally, "and he has spoken [with regard to your] well-being."

Following 4ab, Ñ,D4–7,13,T,G,M3,5, and the texts and printed editions of Cg and Cr insert a passage of one line [3171*]: ". . . along with his ally Vibhīṣaṇa and the troops of tawny monkeys."

5. "through the wise counsel of Lakṣmaṇa" *lakṣmaṇasya nayena ca*: Literally, "and through Lakṣmaṇa's policy *or* statecraft." Ś2,B1,D1–3,9–12, and the texts and printed editions of Ct read instead *lakṣmaṇena ca vīryavān*, "and with Lakṣmaṇa that mighty one [Rāma]."

6. V1,2,B2,4,D10,11,13, and the texts and printed editions of Ct omit this verse.

7. "Thank god, O knower of righteousness, you have survived by virtue of my victory in battle." *diṣṭyā jīvasi dharmajñe jayena mama saṃyuge*: Literally, "Fortunately you live, O knower of *dharma*, through my victory in battle." A number of manuscripts and the texts and printed editions of Ct read instead *tava prabhāvād dharmajñe mahān rāmeṇa saṃyuge*, "through your power, O knower of *dharma*, this great [victory] in battle [has been gained] by Rāma." The reading requires that the first part of verse 8 below be construed with this line. Therefore, we have added in brackets the necessary syntactical elements from 8a. Ct notes that the term "power (*prabhāvāt*)" refers to the extraordinary power deriving from Sītā's absolute devotion to her husband (*pātivratyavaibhavāt*).

According to Cg, the allusion to Sītā's knowledge of righteousness is a specific reference to her adherence to the duties of a faithful wife. He glosses, "you who know the righteous conduct of wifely devotion (*pātivratyadharmajñe*)." The tenor of this and the following verses is in stark contrast to the way Rāma will treat Sītā when they actually meet in *sarga* 103 below.

9. "With grim determination... I" *mayā... dhṛtena*: Literally, "by me [who was] resolved."

"to win you back" *tava nirjaye*: Literally, "with respect to your conquest." Like most translators, we follow the interpretation of Cg and Cm, who gloss, "with respect to your liberation from the hands of my enemy (*śatruhastāt tava vimocane*)." Ct, however, proposes that we supply the word *śatroḥ*, "of the enemy," so that the phrase would mean "in respect to vanquishing your enemy." This interpretation appears to have been followed only by Dutt (1893, p. 1500).

"without pause even for sleep" *alabdhanidreṇa*: Literally, "[by me] not having gotten sleep."

11. "now you are living in your own home, as it were" *svagṛhe parivartase*: Literally, "you live in [your] own home." Because of the reflexive force of the pronoun *sva-*, we believe, as do several other translators, that the usage is metaphorical, indicating that Sītā is now as safe and comfortable in Rāvaṇa's palace as she would be in her own. In this we agree with Ct and Ck. Roussel (1903, vol. 3, p. 377), however, followed by Pagani (1999, p. 1178) and, apparently, by Shastri (1959, vol. 3, p. 330), understands the term *sva-* to mean "his," i.e., Vibhīṣaṇa's house.

"Moreover... he is on his way" *ayaṃ cābhyeti*: Literally, "and he is coming." Ct, Cr, Cm, and Cg all agree that the reference is to Vibhīṣaṇa, and this interpretation is in keeping with the fact that it is indeed Vibhīṣaṇa that Rāma will send to fetch Sītā in *sarga* 102. Shastri (1959, vol. 3, p. 330), alone among translators of the southern recension consulted, mistakenly takes the reference to be to Rāma. The text of Gorresio (6.98.10) reads *ahaṃ cābhyemi*, "I am coming," for the critical reading *ayaṃ cābhyeti*, "he is coming." This, then, must be understood to be the direct speech of Rāma, and Gorresio (1858, vol. 10, p. 222) has translated accordingly.

12. "whose face was like the hare-marked moon" *śaśinibhānanā*: Literally, "with a face like the one possessing a hare."

"sprang to her feet" *samutpatya*: Literally, "having leapt up." D5,9–11, and the texts and printed editions of Ct read instead *tu sā devī*, "but the queen."

"speechless with joy" *praharṣeṇāvaruddhā sā vyājahāra na kiṃcana*: Literally, "obstructed with joy, she did not say anything." Ś2,B1,D1–3,8–12, and the texts and printed editions of Ct read *vyāhartuṃ na śaśāka ha*, "she was unable to speak," for *sā vyājahāra na kiṃcana*, "she did not say anything."

14. "so firmly grounded in righteousness" *dharme vyavasthitā*: Literally, "fixed or established in *dharma*." Ś2,B1,D1–3,8–12, and the texts and printed editions of Ct read instead *dharmapathe sthitā*, "who stood on the path of righteousness."

"choked with joy" *harṣagadgadayā*: Literally, "indistinct *or* stammering with joy." Ś2,D2,3,8–12,M5, and the texts and printed editions of Ct read instead *bāṣpagadgadayā*, "choked with tears."

16. "I can think of no" *na hi paśyāmi*: Literally, "For I do not see."

"response" *pratyabhinandanam*: We tend to follow the interpretation of Cg and Cm, who understand that Sītā is referring to a verbal response, as in words of thanks (*pratipriyavacanam*—so Cg). This interpretation seems reasonable, since, as Cg and Cm note, it provides a rationale for Sītā's hesitation in replying to Hanumān because she was struggling to think of the appropriate words. This is, of course, in addition to her access of joy. (*na kevalaṃ harṣavaśād eva nirvākyāsmi kiṃtu priyākhyātus tava tatsadṛśya-priyavacanasyābhāvād api*—so Cm.) Then, too, this interpretation avoids the redundancy inherent in the explanation of Ck and Ct, who understand that Sītā was trying to think of a suitable material reward or gift (*deyavastu*). For in verses 17 and 18 Sītā will speak in similar terms of the inadequacy of any material reward for Hanumān's service.

"to you who have brought me this wonderful news" *matpriyākhyānakasyeha tava*: Literally, "of you who are telling good news to me here." D9–11 and the texts and printed editions of Ct read the textually inferior *ākhyānakasya bhavato dātum*, "to give to you, a teller."

17. "Nor, gentle monkey, can I think of anything" *na ca paśyāmi tat saumya . . . api vānara*: Literally, "I do not see that, gentle monkey." D9–11 and the texts and printed editions of Ct read the redundant *sadṛśam*, "adequate, suitable," for *tat saumya*, "that, O gentle one," and *tava kiṃcana*, "of you, anything whatsoever," for *api vānara*, "O monkey." This would yield the meaning: "And I do not see anything at all on earth suitable for you." Compare, however, 6.116.69–73, where Sītā gives Hanumān a pearl necklace. See, too, 6.113.40 and notes, where Bharata makes a similar comment to Hanumān.

"for me" *mat-*: Ś2,Ñ1,B4,D2,3,8–13, and the texts and printed editions of Ct read instead the relative pronoun *yat*, "which."

"fitting" *samam*: Literally, "equal, fair." D9–11 and the texts and printed editions of Ct read instead *sukham*, "happiness." Translations that read this variant differ as to whether such a gift would confer happiness on the giver or the receiver.

18. "Neither gold nor silver" *hiraṇyaṃ vā suvarṇaṃ vā . . . na*: Normally, the term *hiraṇya*, like *suvarṇa*, refers to gold. Given the context, however, we agree with Cg, who glosses, "silver (*rajatam*)." Roussel (1903, vol. 3, p. 377) appears to understand the terms to refer to two different types of gold. Nonetheless, he leaves the terms in the original and makes no suggestion as to how they are to be differentiated. Pagani (1999, p. 1178), following him, renders, "*L'or trabaillé ou en pépites*," and notes, on page 1675, that, although both terms originally mean gold, when set in juxtaposition, as here, they refer to worked gold and unrefined gold.

19. D5–7,9–11,S read 19cd twice: once here, and once following 3181* (see note to verse 22 below).

"with these words" *vākyam*: Literally, "speech *or* words." Ñ,Ś2,V1,2,B,D1–12,T,G,M2,3,5, and the texts and printed editions of Ct read instead *harṣāt*, "from joy."

20. "You . . . are capable of speaking" *tvam . . . arhasi bhāṣitum*: Ś2,B1,D1–3,8,12, and the texts and printed editions of Ct read *anindite*, "O blameless one," for *bhāṣitum*, "to speak."

21. "are more precious to me" *viśiṣyate*: Literally, "[this speech] is distinguished from, i.e., better than."

"a heap of all kinds of jewels" *ratnaughād vividhāt*: Literally, "a diverse mass of jewels."

D11 and the texts and printed editions of Ct omit this verse. Among the translators consulted, the verses do not appear in Roussel (1903, vol. 3, p. 377), Shastri (1959, vol. 3, p. 330) or Pagani (1999, p. 1178).

22. D11 and the texts and printed editions of Ct omit this verse. See note to verse 21.

"In that... still standing" *yat sthitam*: The participle *sthitam* seems rather ambiguous here. It can have different meanings in different contexts. In the present context, only two of its possible meanings, however, seem at all plausible. We have taken it in its sense of "living, existing." The idea seems to be that Hanumān is expressing his gratification that Rāma has emerged from the battle not only victorious but unharmed. The term could also be taken in its sense of "having fulfilled a vow *or* agreement," a sense that would accord with Rāma's statement, at verse 9 above, that he had fulfilled his vow. Ct, Ck, and Cr do not accept this verse and therefore do not comment on it. D5,6,T,G1,2,M3,5, and the texts and printed editions of Cg and Cm read *susthitam*, "standing well," for *yat sthitam*, which perhaps supports our interpretation, if we understand the adjective in the sense of "in good health." Cg and Cm do not comment on the term. The reading is known to only three of the translations consulted. Gita Press (1969, vol. 3, p. 1841) renders, "happy," while Raghunathan (1982, vol. 3, p. 331) appears to try to encompass both meanings with his rendering of "happy and well-placed." Gorresio, who reads with the critical edition, either ignores the term or takes it as an implicit copula.

Following verse 22 (D11 and the texts and printed editions of Ct following verse 20), D5–7,9–11,S insert a passage of nine lines [3181*]: "Upon hearing those words of his, Maithilī, the daughter of Janaka, then addressed the son of Pavana in words that were more auspicious still.[1–2] 'Only you are capable of speaking words that are endowed with such superior characteristics, adorned with the virtue of sweetness, and replete with the eight elements of intelligence.[1][3–4] You are the supremely righteous and praiseworthy son of Anila, and there is no doubt that in you alone are found strength, valor, learning, might, courage, supreme competence, blazing energy, forbearance, fortitude, firmness, modesty, and many other excellent virtues.' [5–8] Then, not flustered in the least,[2] he modestly addressed Sītā once again.[9]"

[1]"replete with the eight elements of intelligence" *buddhyā hyaṣṭāṅgayā yuktam*: The commentators quote a verse (*Nītisārakāmandaka* 4.22), which lists the eight capacities of the active mind: "attentiveness, listening, grasping, retention, positive argumentation, negative argumentation, understanding the meaning, and grasping the essential truth (*śuśrūṣā śravaṇaṃ caiva grahaṇaṃ dhāraṇaṃ tathā / ūhāpoho 'rthavijñānaṃ tattvajñānaṃ ca dhīguṇāḥ //*). Gita Press (1969, vol. 3, p. 1842) provides the following note: "(1) Keenness to hear discourses on the Spirit, (2) readiness to hear such discourses, (3) receptivity and (4) retentive power, (5) reasoning for and (6) against a proposition, (7) the faculty of comprehension and (8) realization of truth: these are the eight characteristics of a sound and ripe intelligence." Cg and Cm quote a slightly different list, which reads *smaraṇaṃ* and *pratipādanam*, "memorization and expounding," in place of *grahaṇam* and *dhāraṇam*, "grasping and retention."

[2]"not flustered in the least" *asaṃbhrāntaḥ*: Literally, "not confused *or* agitated."

Following 3181*, D5–7,9–11,S read 19cd for a second time: "...[he] cupped his hands in reverence and, standing before Sītā, replied with these words."

24–25. "dreadful rumors . . . terrifying threats" *ghorarūpasamācārāḥ . . . dāruṇakathāḥ*: Literally, "news of terrible form *or* kind . . . whose conversation was fearsome." We understand the first compound to refer to the cajoling and hectoring of the *rākṣasa* women at 5.21.3ff. and 5.22.21–31, and the latter to refer to the more savage threats to dismember and devour Sītā at 5.22.32–41. Cr takes *samācārāḥ* in its other sense of "conduct, behavior," glossing the compound as "whose actions are of a frightful nature (*bhayaṅkararūpakāriṇyaḥ*)." This interpretation is equally plausible and has been followed by some translators.

Following verse 24, D10,11, and the texts and printed editions of Ct insert a passage of three lines [3180* lines 1, 2, and 4 only = NSP, GPP 6.113.30–31ab; Gita Press 6.113.32–33ab]. Since the critical insert varies significantly in the lines that correspond to those of the texts and printed editions of Ct and cannot be properly construed out of the context of the five verses in which they are embedded in the critical apparatus, we have translated the lines as they are found in the printed editions of Ct: "I heard in this very place, queen, that these *rākṣasa* women—deformed, with deformed bodies, with deformed faces, and with fierce hair and eyes—speaking harsh words repeatedly at Rāvaṇa's command . . ." (*iha śrutā mayā devi rākṣasyo vikṛtānanāḥ / asakṛt paruṣair vākyair vadantyo rāvaṇājñayā // vikṛtā vikṛtākārāḥ krūrāḥ krūrakacekṣaṇāḥ /*).

26–28. The text of these verses, especially in the southern recension, is complex, variable, and perhaps corrupt in some respects. In some cases, commentators and translators alike struggle to make sense of terms and phrases and, on some occasions, simply skip over problematic ones. We have attempted to deal as best as we can with the readings of the available printed editions. To do so, we have made some emendations to the text as indicated below.

"lovely" *śobhane*: Ś2,D1,3,8–12, and the texts and printed editions of Ct read instead *bāhubhiḥ*, "with arms," which construes with *viśālaiś ca* (see below under *caraṇaiś ca*) to yield the meaning "with broad arms."

"with punches, slaps, kicks, fearsome blows of the knees, slashes of my fangs . . . violent clawing, dreadful flying kicks, . . . these kinds of assaults" *muṣṭibhiḥ pāṇibhiś caiva caraṇaiś caiva . . . / ghorair jānuprahāraiś ca daśanānāṃ ca pātanaiḥ // . . . bhṛśaṃ śuṣkamukhībhiś ca dāruṇair laṅghanair hataiḥ / evaṃprakāraiḥ . . . viprakāraiḥ*: Literally, "with fists, hands, and feet . . . with fearsome blows of the knees . . . descents of the teeth, violently with claws, with fearsome leaping blows, with these kinds of assaults."

*"violent clawing" *bhṛśaṃ śuṣkamukhībhiḥ*: Literally, "strongly with [those things] whose faces are parched." We find no persuasive lexical attestation for the term *śuṣkamukhī*, in the absence of which we are left with the two alternatives offered by the commentators. M3 and the texts and printed editions of Cg and Cm read *nakhaiḥ*, "with nails *or* claws," for *bhṛśam*, "violently," and understand the compound *śuṣkamukhībhiḥ* to be a *bahuvrīhi* modifying that noun. The sense, presumably, would then be "with nails whose edges are dry." One problem here is that Cg's reading presents an apparent case of *liṅgabheda*, since the adjective would be feminine while *nakhaiḥ* is masculine. A resolution of the problem may be the intention of the variant found in GPP (in brackets between 6.116.33 and 34), in D5,7,T1,G1,3, and in the text of Cr, which reads the masculine *śuṣkamukhaiś caiva*. Cr, the only commentator to address this particular variant, glosses, "parching *or* scorching [their] faces by throwing fire, etc. (*vahniprakṣepādinā mukhaśoṣaṇaiḥ*)." We have followed the reading and interpretation of Cg, despite its poor attestation and grammatical difficulties, in light of the fact

that at least one northern text, that of Gorresio (6.98.25), in what is perhaps an example of the typical northern strategy of glossing difficult southern readings, reads *bhṛśaṃ śuṣkanakhānāṃ ca* [*tāḍanaiḥ*], "[with] violent [blows] of dried-up nails." This is rendered by Gorresio (1858, vol. 10, p. 223) as "*col batter forte . . . dall' unghie secche.*" This *pāda* (and the next) is omitted by D10,11,M1,2, and the texts and printed editions of Ct.

"with . . . slaps" *pāṇibhiś caiva*" Literally, "and with hands." Ñ2,B1,2,D1,3,9–11, and the texts and printed editions of Ct read *pārṣṇighātaiś ca,* "and with blows of the heels."

"with . . . kicks" *caraṇaiś caiva*: Literally, "with feet." Ś2,D1,3,8–12, and the texts and printed editions of Ct read instead *viśālaiś caiva,* "and with broad," which then construes with *bāhubhiḥ*. See above under "lovely" *śobhane*.

"with . . . fearsome blows of the knees" *ghorair jānuprahāraiś ca*: D9–11 and the texts and printed editions of Ct read instead *jaṅghājānuprahāraiś ca,* "with blows of the thighs and knees."

"with . . . slashes of my fangs" *daśanānāṃ ca pātanaiḥ*: Literally, "with descents of the teeth." Raghunathan (1982, vol. 3, p. 331) renders, "knocking down their teeth." D9–11 and the texts and printed editions of Ct read *dantānāṃ caiva pīḍanaiḥ,* "by crushings with (lit., of) the teeth."

"with . . . these kinds of assaults" *evaṃprakāraiḥ . . . viprakāraiḥ*: D9–11 and the texts and printed editions of Ct read instead *evaṃ prahāraiḥ . . . saṃprahārya,* "having struck . . . thus with blows."

D10,11,M1,2, and the texts and printed editions of Ct omit 27cd ["violently with claws, with fearsome flying kicks (*bhṛśaṃ śuṣkamukhībhiś ca dāruṇair laṅghanair hataiḥ* /)"].

"dreadful" *dāruṇaiḥ*: The text of Cg (and Cm), as it appears in VSP and KK (6.116.36) (unattested in the critical apparatus), reads instead *dāraṇaiḥ,* "tearing." Cg glosses *dāraṇaiḥ* as "with crushing blows or slaps to the cheek (*pīḍanaiḥ kapolatāḍanair vā*)." Among the translators, only Raghunathan (1982, vol. 3, p. 331) knows this variant.

Following verse 27, D7,G1,2, and GPP (in brackets between 6.116.33 and 34) insert a passage of one line [3182*]: "[knocking them down] with their bodies[1] together with their various protuberances, necks, shoulders,[2] and sides." No translation consulted renders this insert.

[1]"with their bodies" *kalevaraiḥ*: Cr construes this noun with *hataiḥ,* "with blows," from 27d, which then must be read as an adjective, "slain." The idea, then, is that Hanumān will strike down some of the *rākṣasa* women with the dead bodies of the ones he has already slain.

[2]"shoulders" *-aṃsa-*: GPP reads instead *-aṃśa-*, "parts."

Following 3182*, D7,G1,2, continue, while D5,6,T,G3,M3,5, and the texts and printed editions of Cg insert following verse 27, and D10,11,M1,2, and the texts and printed editions of Ct insert after 27ab, a passage of one line [3183*]: "Striking them down, I wish to kill those who have harmed you."

For 28cd ("queen, these creatures that have done you such injury. I would like to slaughter them . . ."), Ś2,B2,3,D1–3,8–12, and the texts and printed editions of Ct substitute a passage of one line [3184*]: "I would inflict these calamities[1] upon those who earlier tormented you."

[1]"I would inflict these calamities" *yojayeyam anarthaiś ca*: D9–11 and the texts and printed editions of Ct read instead *ghātaye tīvrarūpābhiḥ*, "I would slaughter [them] those fierce looking creatures by whom..."

29. "Addressed in this fashion by Hanumān... Vaidehī, daughter of Janaka" *evam uktā hanumatā vaidehī janakātmajā*: D9–11 and the texts and printed editions of Ct read instead *ity uktā sā hanumatā kṛpaṇā dīnavatsalā*, "addressed in this fashion by Hanumān, and being long-suffering and tenderhearted toward the downtrodden."

"by Hanumān... to him" *hanumatā... hanūmantam*: Literally, "by Hanumān... to Hanumān."

"illustrious... responded to him in words that were in keeping with righteousness" *uvāca dharmasahitaṃ hanūmantaṃ yaśasvinī*: Ś2,B1,D1–3,8–12, and the texts and printed editions of Ct then substitute for this line (= 29cd) one line [3185*]: "... said this to Hanumān after thinking and reflecting."

31. "It is as a consequence of my evil destiny" *bhāgyavaiṣamyayogena*: Literally, "as a consequence of the unevenness of fate." Ś2,Ñ,V1,2,B,D1–5,8–12, and the texts and printed editions of Ct read *-doṣeṇa*, "through the fault," for *-yogena*, "through the consequence."

"For one always experiences the fruits of one's actions." *svakṛtaṃ hy upabhujyate*: Literally, "for one's own action is experienced *or* enjoyed."

Following verse 31, D9–11 and the texts and printed editions of Ct insert a passage of one line [3189*, line 1]: "You must not speak in this fashion, great-armed warrior,[1] for this was the inevitable course of fate.[2]"

[1]"great-armed warrior" *mahābāho*: Literally, "O great-armed one."

[2]"for this was the inevitable course of fate" *daivī hy eṣā parā gatiḥ*: Literally, "for this is the highest course associated with destiny."

32. "being helpless" *durbalā*: Literally, "weak." One could equally well translate, "being [only] a woman."

"I had to endure all of this here at the hands of... servant women" *dāsīnām... ahaṃ marṣayāmīha*: The expression is elliptical. The literal translation is "I tolerate [of] the servant women here." Several of the commentators supply an object for the verb *marṣayāmī*, "I endure." Thus, Ct, for example, adds the words "this abuse, etc. (*etat tarjanādikam*)."

33. "only on the orders of Rāvaṇa" *ājñaptā rāvaṇena*: Literally, "[they] ordered by Rāvaṇa." V2,D9–11, and the texts and printed editions of Ct read instead *rākṣasena*, "by the *rākṣasa*," for *rāvaṇena*, "by Rāvaṇa."

"foremost of monkeys" *vānarottama*: Ś2,B1,D1–3,8–12, and the texts and printed editions of Ct read instead *mārutātmaja*, "O son of Māruta."

"they will not torment me anymore" *na kuryur hi tarjanam*: Literally, "For they would not make abuse." Ñ,V1,2,B2–4,D7,10,11,13, and the texts and printed editions of Ct and Cr read the present indicative, *na kurvanti*, "they do not," for the optative, *na kuryuḥ*, "they should *or* ought not do."

34. "an ancient verse... that a bear once recited in the presence of a tiger" *vyāghrasamīpe... purāṇaḥ.../ ṛkṣeṇa gītaḥ ślokaḥ*: Cm, Cg, Cr, and Ct (who quotes Cm in part) all tell very similar versions of a fable according to which a hunter who is being pursued by a tiger takes refuge in a tree that a *ṛkṣa* (a bear or ape) had already climbed. Arguing that the hunter is a menace to all forest creatures, the tiger urges the *ṛkṣa* to throw the hunter down to him. The *ṛkṣa*, however, refuses to betray one who has now effectively become his neighbor. He then falls asleep. The tiger then urges the hunter to throw down the *ṛkṣa*, a request with which the hunter promptly complies. But the *ṛkṣa* instinctively catches hold of another branch and so avoids falling into the tiger's clutches. The tiger now once more urges the *ṛkṣa* to throw down the hunter, since the latter has clearly betrayed him. But the *ṛkṣa* refuses to repay evil with evil, promising to protect the hunter, even though he has been wronged by him. See notes to 6.12.12, where the commentators refer to this story. In a note to this verse, Gita Press (1969, vol. 3, p. 1843) paraphrases the tale as it is narrated by Ct.

The identity of the animal is not entirely clear. The term *ṛkṣa* is typically used of a bear, but, in the context of the *Vālmīki Rāmāyaṇa*, it normally refers to a type of primate (see R. Goldman 1989 and notes to 1.1.16). Cg and Cm clearly understand that this is a bear, using the unambiguous term *bhallūka*. Note, however, that, at 6.12.12, Cg clearly identifies the animal in this same story as a *vānara*, or monkey. Cf. note to 6.4.17.

"from me" *me*: D4,7,10,11, and the texts and printed editions of Ct and Cr read instead [*a*]*sti*, "there is [a verse]."

35. "A superior person never requites evil on the part of evildoers with evil." *na paraḥ pāpam ādatte pareṣāṃ pāpakarmaṇām*: Literally, "A high one does not resort to evil with respect to others who have done evil acts *or* the evil acts of others." The commentators gloss *paraḥ*, "other," with either "wise (*prājñaḥ*—Ct, Cm, Cg)" or "righteous (*dharmātmā*—Cr)."

36. "whether people are wicked, virtuous, or even if deserving of death" *pāpānāṃ vā śubhānāṃ vā vadhārhāṇām*: The commentators are divided in their interpretations of this verse. According to Ct and Cm, the simple meaning of the verse is that one should show mercy to the good and wicked alike, since no one is without sin. (*pāpānāṃ vadhārhāṇāṃ vā pāpajaneṣu vadhārheṣu śubhajaneṣu vadhārheṣu satsv api teṣv āryena sajjanena karuṇaṃ kāruṇyaṃ kāryaṃ kartavyam ity arthaḥ*—so Cm). Ct and Cr, however, understand the adjective *vadhārhāṇām*, "worthy of death *or* execution," to refer exclusively to evildoers (*śubheṣv iva pāpeṣu vadhārheṣv api*—so Ct). Cr, alone among the commentators, understands that the verse alludes to the relative seriousness of different offenses. He therefore argues that Sītā is saying that punishment should indeed be inflicted upon those who do wrong but that, in this case, the crimes of the *rākṣasa* women are not so serious as to merit the punishment of death. (*tena yathāparādham eva daṇḍaḥ kārya iti sūcitam. tena rākṣasīnāṃ māraṇayogyo 'parādho nāstīti dhvanitam.*) Cg and Cm understand that the term *vadhārha* applies equally to *śubhānām*, "the virtuous ones," reading the verse on the basis of its final *pāda* to indicate that, in some sense, everyone is guilty (*sarvo 'py aparādhyatīty arthaḥ*). Cg explores the theme of the merciful treatment of sinners rather more elaborately in a theological vein, harking back to the words of Rāma at 6.12.3, where, in the context of his acceptance of Vibhīṣaṇa as a

refugee, he argues that one must accept those who come seeking refuge even if they are guilty. See 6.12.3 and note.

"leaping monkey" *plavaṅgama*: Cg understands Sītā's use of the kenning here to be a pointed one, suggesting that Hanumān [through his flightiness] desires something that he should not. (*plavaṅgama. anabhilaṣitam evābhilaṣitavān khalu bhavān.*) Ś2,B1,D2,3,8–11,M2, and the texts and printed editions of Ct read instead *athāpi vā*, "or even."

"no one is entirely innocent" *na kaścin nāparādhyati*: Literally, "no one does not commit offenses." Cr, however, takes the phrase to mean "not everyone is guilty of the same degree of offense (*kaścin nāparādhyatīti na sarvo 'pi yat kiñcid aparādhyatīty arthaḥ*). This reading supports Cr's interpretation as indicated above. For other examples of double negatives in Vālmīki, see, for example, 6.37.10; 6.95.24; and notes.

37. "One should not harm" *naiva kāryaṃ aśobhanam*: Literally, "inauspiciousness indeed should not be practiced." The commentators generally agree in glossing "punishment (*daṇḍanam*)" for *aśobhanam*.

"the *rākṣasas*, who can take on any form at will" *rakṣasāṃ kāmarūpiṇām*: B1,D1, 2,8,10,11, and the texts and printed editions of Ct read instead *krūrāṇāṃ pāpakarmaṇām*, "those cruel evildoers."

"who... take pleasure in injuring people" *lokahiṃsāvihārāṇām*: The commentators agree that, because injuring others is the natural behavior of the *rākṣasas*, they should not be killed for it (*rākṣasānāṃ parahiṃsaiva svabhāva ity ato 'pi na vadhyā iti*—so Ct).

38. "by Rāma's illustrious wife, Sītā... to her" *sītayā... sītāṃ rāmapatnīṃ yaśasvinīm*: Literally, "by Sītā... to Rāma's wife, illustrious Sītā." D9–11 and the texts and printed editions of Ct read *aninditām*, "blameless, irreproachable," for *yaśasvinīm*, "illustrious."

39. "fitting" *yuktā*: Cg takes the term to have a theological resonance. He sees it as meaning that Sītā is equal in virtues such as providing refuge, etc., to Rāma, who had proclaimed that he was the ultimate refuge of those seeking him. Cg quotes Rāma's earlier comment to Sugrīva to this effect at 6.12.12. Cg goes on to note that we are to understand that this *sarga* expresses Sītā's compassion, her tolerance of wrongs, and her effectiveness. (*kiṃ punar madvidho jana iti svasyottamaśaraṇatvaṃ pratipāditavato rāmasya śaraṇyatvādiguṇavattayā sadṛśīty arthaḥ. anena sargeṇa sītāyā dayālutvam aparādhasahiṣṇutvaṃ ghaṭakatvaṃ coktam iti dhyeyam.*)

"illustrious" *yaśasvinī*: D9–11 and the texts and printed editions of Ct read instead *guṇānvitā*, "endowed with virtues."

40. "Foremost of monkeys" *vānarottama*: B1,D1–3,9–12, and the texts and printed editions of Ct read instead the accusative singular adjective *bhaktavatsalam*, "loving toward his devotees," which would then modify Rāma.

41. "son of Pavana" *pavanātmajaḥ*: D9–11,M3,5, and the texts and printed editions of the southern commentators read instead *mārutātmajaḥ*, "son of Māruta."

"that immensely splendid hero" *mahādyutih*: Literally, "whose radiance *or* splendor is great." D9–11,M2, and the texts and printed editions of Ct read instead *mahāmatiḥ*, "of great intellect, wise."

"lifting Maithilī's spirits" *harṣayan maithilīm*: Literally, "causing Maithilī to rejoice."

42. "Noble lady" *ārye*: Literally, "noble one." D6,9–11,T2,3,M2, and the texts and printed editions of Ct read instead *adya*, "today."

"just as the goddess Śacī gazes upon Indra, lord of the thirty gods" *śacīva tridaśeśvaram*: Literally, "like Śacī [does] the lord of the thirty." Ś2,Ñ,V1,2,B,D1–4,8–13, and the texts and printed editions of Ct read instead *śacīvendraṃ sureśvaram*, "as [does] Śacī, Indra, lord of the gods."

43. "as Śrī incarnate" *sākṣād iva śriyam*: Literally, "like Śrī in visible form."

"immensely swift" *mahāvegaḥ*: Ś2,B1,D1–3,5,7–12,G2, and the texts and printed editions of Ct and Cr read instead *mahātejāḥ*, "of immense blazing energy."

"to where Rāghava waited" *yatra rāghavaḥ*: Literally, "where Rāghava [was]."

Following verse 43, Ś2,Ñ,V1,2,B,D1–4,7–13,M2, and the texts and printed editions of KK (in brackets) read a passage of four lines [3192*]: "Then Hanumān, the minister of the foremost of the tawny monkeys,[1] reported in due sequence the reply that had been uttered by the daughter of the lord of the Janakas to Rāghava, who resembled the foremost of the thirty gods."

[1]"the minister of the foremost of the tawny monkeys" *harivarasacivaḥ*: In the critical reading, the term *harivara-*, "foremost among the tawny monkeys," is a reference to Sugrīva. D7,9–11, and the texts and printed editions of Ct and Cr read instead *sapadi harivaraḥ*, "at once the foremost of the tawny monkeys." In this reading, the epithet *harivara* refers to Hanumān himself.

The meter is *puṣpitāgrā*.

Sarga 102

1. "Approaching" *abhigamya*: Literally, "having approached." Ś2,B1,D8–12, and the texts and printed editions of Ct read instead *so 'bhivādya*, "having respectfully saluted."

"exceedingly wise" *mahāprājñam*: B1,D9–11,13, and the texts and printed editions of Ct read the nominative singular *mahāprājñaḥ*, thus making the adjective modify Hanumān rather than Rāma.

"who understood the matter at hand . . . these words" *vacanam arthajñaḥ*: We understand the term *artha-* in its sense of "matter, business, affair." The idea is that the tactful Hanumān is sensitive to the emotionally fraught situation into which he has been thrust. Raghunathan (1982, vol. 3, p. 333), the only translator consulted to render this reading, appears to take *artha-* in its sense of "meaning," rendering, "who could speak weighing every word of his." Possibly he has mistakenly read the sequence as a compound. The commentators who read this variant are silent. D9–11 and the texts and printed editions of Ct read instead *kamalapatrākṣam*, "whose eyes were [like] lotus petals," which describes Rāma.

2. "Now you really must see" *draṣṭum arhasi*: Literally, "You should see."

"she on whose account we undertook this entire mission and achieved the culmination of our efforts" *yannimitto 'yam ārambhaḥ karmaṇāṃ ca phalodayaḥ*: Literally, "for whose sake [there was] this undertaking and the arising of the fruit of actions." Ct understands the term *karmaṇām* to refer to all the deeds undertaken by Rāma and his allies from the building of the bridge through the slaying of Rāvaṇa. The phrase then refers generically to the success of all these efforts (*karmaṇāṃ setubandha-*

rāvaṇavadhādīnāṃ yaḥ phalodayaḥ phalarūpaḥ). Cr, Cg, and Cm, however, understand the term *karmaṇām* to refer to the various acts leading up to Rāvaṇa's defeat, with that culminating event itself being the fruition of the previous actions (*karmaṇāṃ setubandhanādivyāpārāṇāṃ phalodayo rāvaṇajayaś ca*—so Cm).

3. "was filled with joy... your" *tava harṣam upāgamat*: Literally, "your... went to joy." Ś2,B1,D1–3,8,10–12, and the texts and printed editions of Ct read instead *tvāṃ draṣṭum abhikāṅkṣati* (D10,11, and Ct read *draṣṭuṃ tvām*), "she longs to see you."

4. "Since she trusted me because of the confidence I had earlier inspired in her, she said to me" *pūrvakāt pratyayāc cāham ukto viśvastayā tayā*: Literally, "I was addressed by her who was trusting because of previous confidence." The reference here is to the trust Hanumān inspired in Sītā during their conversations in the *Sundarakāṇḍa* (see 5.29–38, esp., *sarga* 34).

"who, together with Lakṣmaṇa, has accomplished his purpose." *kṛtārthaṃ sahalakṣmaṇam*: Ś2,D1–3,8,10–12, and the texts and printed editions of Ct read instead *iti paryākulekṣaṇā*, "thus [did she speak], her eyes brimming with tears."

5. "was suddenly plunged into gloomy thought" *agacchat sahasā dhyānam*: Cm, Ct, and Cg understand that Rāma is emotionally distraught at the dilemma in which he now finds himself. For if he were to take Sītā back after she had lived in Rāvaṇa's house, he would incur the severe censure of the people, while, if he were to reject his innocent wife, he would thereby commit a grave wrong. (*rāvaṇabhavanoṣitasītāparigrahe mahān lokāpavādo bhavet. nirdoṣāyās tasyāḥ parityāge mahān doṣaḥ syād ity evaṃ kāryadausthyāt kiṃ kartavyam iti cintayāmāsety arthaḥ*—so Cm.) Ct, however, in an evident allusion to the post-Vālmīkian tradition of the *chāyā*, or shadow, Sītā, adds that Rāma is actually plunged into thought as to how he can recover the principal or real Sītā from the fire [in which she was supposed to have been hiding] (*vastuto mukhyasītālābho 'gneḥ kathaṃ syād iti cintātra*). Ct is thus preparing us for the more benign interpretation of Sītā's fire ordeal that is characteristic of such versions of the *Rāmāyaṇa* as the *Ādhyātmarāmāyaṇa* (3.7.1) and the *Rāmcaritmānas* (*Araṇyakāṇḍ doha* 23 *caupais* 1–2; *Laṅkākāṇḍ dohas* 108–109, *caupais* 1–2) that know the *chāyāsītā* tradition. See 5.51.23 and note; and note to 3.43.34. See, too, *KūrmaP* 2.33.112ff. See 6.104.27; 6.106.4; and notes. See Introduction, p. 104.

*"and became somewhat tearful" *āsīd bāṣpapariplutaḥ*: Literally, "he was bathed in tears." It appears that the critical reading, "he was (*āsīt*)," is a misprint, although it is not so indicated in the errata. All available printed editions, north and south, read instead *īṣat*, "slightly, somewhat," and none of them shows any variant on this term in their apparatuses or variant readings. By the same token, the critical apparatus shows no manuscript or edition as reading *īṣat*. We have therefore emended the text accordingly. The word *īṣat* is, however, reflected only in the translations of Gorresio (1858, vol. 10, p. 224), who renders, "*al quanto suffuso di lacrime*"; Roussel (1903, vol. 3, p. 380), "[*une pensée qui lui fit répandre*] *quelques pleurs*"; and Gita Press (1969, vol. 3, p. 1845). The latter, however, reads the adverb not with the term *bāṣpapariplutaḥ* but with the phase *agacchat... dhyānam*, rendering, "became a bit thoughtful."

6. "Heaving long, hot sighs" *dīrgham uṣṇaṃ ca niśvasya*: Literally, "having sighed long and hotly." Cg, the only commentator to remark on this reading, believes that we are to take the length of Rāma's sighs as an indication of the length of his brooding (see verse 5 above). Cg also believes that the warmth of his sighs suggests Rāma's inner torment at the thought: "How can I possibly cause further suffering to Sītā, who has

already suffered so much? (*niḥśvāsadairghyeṇa cintādairghyaṃ gṛhyate. auṣṇyena kathaṃ kliṣṭāṃ tāṃ punaḥ kleṣayiṣyāmīty antastāpo vyajyate.*)" D9–11 and the texts and printed editions of Ct read instead *sa dīrgham abhiniśvasya*, "he, having sighed long."

"staring at the ground" *medinīm avalokayan*: Literally, "looking at the ground *or* earth." Cg understands Rāma's downcast glance to be a gesture indicating that he is lost in brooding thought (*cintāpāravaśyābhinayaḥ*).

"looking like a great storm cloud" *meghasaṃkāśam*: Literally, "resembling a cloud." Raghunathan (1982, vol. 3, p. 333) understands the reference to be specifically to Vibhīṣaṇa's size, while Gita Press (1969, vol. 3, p. 1845) takes it to refer exclusively to his dark complexion. Cg, however, understands the compound to express Vibhīṣaṇa's haste to bring Sītā swiftly (*meghasaṃkāśam ity anena sītānayane kṛtatvaratvam ucyate*).

7. With regard to Rāma's instructions that Sītā be bathed and beautified before meeting him, Cg argues that this is a reference to the forthcoming abuse that Rāma will direct toward her (in *sarga* 103). For, Cg continues, it would not be appropriate for Rāma to direct harsh words toward someone in an obviously miserable condition. Still, Cg goes on, Rāma does not order the adornment of Sītā just so that he can reject her but rather so that he can have her proclaim her loyalty to him in the presence of the gods, Brahmā, etc. (*alaṃkṛtyānayanādeśa uttarakālikaparuṣabhāṣaṇārhatāpratipādanāya. na hi tādṛśadaśāpannāṃ dīnāṃ paruṣaṃ bhāṣituṃ yujyate. tac ca tasyā na parityāgārthaṃ kiṃtu caturmukhādidevatāmukhena tasyāḥ pātivratyaṃ khyāpayitum.*)

"her hair freshly washed" *śiraḥsnātām*: Literally, "having a bathed head." As Pagani (1999, p. 1675) notes, the image of an unbathed and unadorned Sītā is the one conjured up by Indrajit in *sarga* 68, where he seeks to demoralize Rāma's hosts by feigning the murder of Sītā before their very eyes. See 6.68.9–10 and note. A much more elaborate depiction of the disheveled Sītā is found at 5.13.18–35. See, too, S. Goldman 2000. See verse 10 and notes below.

*"Make haste!" *mā ciram*: Literally, "[let there] not [be] a long time." The critical apparatus, presumably in error, writes the two words together, which would yield the sense "[let there be] no short time," i.e., "don't hurry." All other editions consulted print the two words separately, a reading unnoted in the critical apparatus. We have emended accordingly.

8. "had his own wives instruct Sītā in these words" *sītāṃ strībhiḥ svābhir acodayat*: Literally, "with his own women, he urged *or* instructed Sītā *or* he had his own women instruct Sītā." We are inclined to agree with Cg, who reads the verb *acodayat* as a causative so that it is the wives of Vibhīṣaṇa who actually address Sītā in the following verse. Cg glosses, "he urged [her] through the mouth[s] of his own women (*nijastrīmukhenācodayat*)." The idea evidently is that the rules of decorum prevent Vibhīṣaṇa from addressing Sītā directly in the first instance (see 3.54.1; 5.19.2–3; and notes). The form *codayati* can also be understood as the simplex of the tenth *gaṇa* root √*cud*, "to urge, impel." This would be indistinguishable from the causative, and one could therefore also understand the phrase to mean "[Vibhīṣaṇa] in the company of his own women requested Sītā." Roussel (1903, vol. 3, p. 380), followed by Pagani (1999, p. 1181), appears to render in this way, although his phrasing and that of Pagani make it possible or even probable to understand that Sītā is instructed to appear with her own women. The ambiguity of the French phrase "*avec ses femmes*," that is, "with his *or* her women," is, however, absent in Shastri's rendition, "Sita with her attendants" (1959, vol. 3, p. 333). This interpretation is highly deficient from both

the grammatical and contextual points of view. Sītā has, of course, none of her attendants with her.

Following verse 8, D6,7,10,11,T2,3,M1, and the texts and printed editions of Ct and Cr insert a passage of two lines [3199*]: "Then, upon seeing virtuous Sītā, Vibhīṣaṇa, the majestic lord of the *rākṣasas*, cupped his hands to his forehead in reverence and respectfully said."

10. "without having bathed" *asnātā*: See note to verses 7 and 13 above. In the *Mahābhārata* version, Sītā appears in Rāma's presence before she has washed. She is stained with dust, dressed in black, but shines with beauty (*MBh* 3.275.9). Cf. 6.112.4 and notes.

11. "Rāma" *rāmaḥ*: M3 and the texts and printed editions of Cg read instead *rājā*, "the king."

12. "whose vow was devotion to him" *bhartṛbhaktivratā*: Literally, "whose vow was devotion to [her] lord." D5,10,11, and the texts and printed editions of Ct and Ck read instead *bhartṛbhaktyā vṛtā*, "suffused with devotion to her husband."

13–14. Cs notes the passage in the *Rāmopākhyāna* in which Sītā is described as being presented before Rāma with her body covered with dirt, her hair matted, and clad in a black garment (*MBh* 3.275.9). He offers two rationalizations in an attempt to harmonize the seemingly contradictory accounts. According to the first, the *Mahābhārata* describes her as dirty because she has not bathed of her own free will (i.e., she has bathed, but is thus presumably not really clean), while here, too, she makes her toilet only to comply with Rāma's orders. Cs's second interpretation, based on the second half of the *Mahābhārata* verse, is that Rāma, recalling that Hanumān had described her earlier as dirty, continues to see her as such [even though she has, in fact, bathed]. (*nanu mahābhārate tāṃ dṛṣṭvā cārusarvāṅgīṃ yānasthāṃ śokakarṣitām / malopacitasarvāṅgīṃ jaṭilāṃ kṛṣṇavāsasam ity ukteḥ katham atraivaṃ kathanam iti ced ucyate. svacchandenāṅgaśodhanādyabhāvena bhārate malopacitetyādyuktiḥ. atra tu rāmājñayā tasya jātatvena pratikarmaṇā saṃyuktām ityādyuktiḥ. athavā bhāratavacanottarārdhe hanumadvacanena malopacitasarvāṅgīṃ saṃsmarato rāmasya tathaiva darśanam iti pūrvam etādṛśīm iti vārthāṅgīkāreṇa vāvirodhopapatteḥ.*)

"Young women . . . adorned her" *yuvatībhir alaṃkṛtām*: Literally, "adorned by young women." Ś,D8–12, the texts and printed editions of Ct, and the edition of Lahore (6.95.16) read instead *saṃyuktāṃ pratikarmaṇā*, "connected with *or* endowed with personal grooming."

"washed her hair" *śiraḥsnātām*: Literally, "head-washed." See note to verse 7 above.

"shining . . . that was draped in costly fabrics" *dīptāṃ parārghyāmbarasaṃvṛtām*: D9–11 and the texts and printed editions of Ct read instead *sītāṃ rākṣasair vahanocitaiḥ*, which lends the first half of the verse the meaning: "having made Sītā mount a palanquin [borne] by *rākṣasas* accustomed to carrying *or* fit to carry." See 6.106.2–3 and notes.

15. "the great man" *mahātmānam*: Literally, "the great one."

"noting that he was lost in brooding thought" *jñātvābhidhyānam āsthitam*: Literally, "having known [him] to be engaged in meditation *or* thought." B2,D6,7,10,11, T2,3,G1,2,M1,3,5, and the texts and printed editions of the southern commentators read *api* for *abhi-*, lending the sequence the meaning "even though he knew he was lost in brooding thought." The commentators and translators who share this variant reading differ as to who is the subject of the gerund *jñātvā*, "having known." Cr, with whom we agree, understands that Vibhīṣaṇa is the subject of both gerunds: *abhigamya*, "having approached," and *jñātvā*, "having known." Ck, Ct, Cg, and Cm, however, understand Rāma himself to be the subject of the gerund *jñātvā*, and they then supply, as its object, "the arrival of Vibhīṣaṇa (*vibhīṣaṇāgamanam*—so Cg)." In their interpretation, Rāma, although he notes Vibhīṣaṇa's arrival, remains lost in thought. This interpretation is followed by the translations of Dutt (1893, p. 1504) and Raghunathan (1982, vol. 3, p. 333).

16. "Rāghava... three emotions—joy, sorrow, and anger—took hold of him" *harṣo dainyaṃ ca roṣaś ca trayaṃ rāghavam āviśat*: Literally, "a group of three—joy, sorrow, and anger—took possession of Rāghava." D9–11 and the texts and printed editions of Ct read instead *roṣaṃ harṣaṃ ca dainyaṃ ca rāghavaḥ prāpa śatruhā*, "Rāghava, slayer of his enemies, experienced anger, joy, and sorrow."

Commentators differ somewhat on the exact causes of the various emotions that assail Rāma at this moment. Ck and Ct have the most detailed analysis according to which Rāma's anger is produced by the thought that he, his friends, and his brother have experienced so much suffering on account of Sītā, who is therefore viewed as the source of all their troubles. Alternatively, Ct and Ck suggest that Rāma's anger derives from the fact that Sītā had stayed so long in Rāvaṇa's house. This anger will give rise to her forthcoming oath. According to Ck and Ct, Rāma's joy is caused by his seeing Sītā from whom he had been so long separated, while his sorrow is a result of his thought that Sītā had experienced so much suffering while waiting so long for him. (*roṣaṃ sarvānarthamūlayānayā kila sasuhṛdbhrātṛkeṇedaṃ bahuduḥkham anubhūtam iti roṣaḥ. yadvā rāvaṇagṛhe ciroṣitatvanimittaka āropito roṣo bhāviśapathopayogī. ciraviyuktāyādya darśanam iti harṣaḥ. cirakālaṃ matpratīkṣayānayā bahuduḥkham anubhūtam iti dainyam*–so Ct.)

Cr believes that Rāma's sorrow derives from his recollection of Sītā's suffering (*sītākleśasmaraṇajanitadīnatā*). He offers no explanation of the other emotions. Cg and Cm understand that Rāma's joy is produced by Sītā's arrival, which was preceded by the slaying of Rāvaṇa. They attribute both his sorrow and his anger to Sītā's having dwelt in Rāvaṇa's house. Both commentators add a note, in keeping with the alternative explanation of Ck and Ct, that Rāma's anger will give rise to the forthcoming oath. (*rāvaṇavadhapūrvakasītāgamena harṣo rāvaṇabhavanoṣitatvena dainyaṃ roṣaś ca. atra roṣo bhāviśapathopayogitvād āropita iti draṣṭavyam*—so Cg.) Compare verse 35 below, where Sītā similarly experiences three emotions upon seeing Rāma.

17. "Then, perceiving that... now stood beside him... and debating inwardly" *tataḥ pārśvagataṃ dṛṣṭvā savimarśaṃ vicārayan*: Literally, "then having seen [him] who had gone to the side and reflecting with deliberation." We follow Cg and Cm, who gloss *savimarśaṃ vicārayan*, "reflecting with deliberation," with *savitarkaṃ cintayan*, "thinking with ratiocination." Cr interprets similarly. B1,D1–3,9–11, and the texts and printed editions of Ct read instead *tato yānagatāṃ sītām*. This lends the first line of the verse the meaning: "Then, debating inwardly with regard to Sītā, who had arrived in [her] conveyance..." Roussel (1903, vol. 3, p. 381) appears to force the meaning of the verse so that, in his rendition, Rāma is concealing his joy in order to test Sītā, "*Cependant, pour mettre à l'épreuve Sītā qui arrivait en litière... en dissimulant sa joie.*" In this rather forced interpretation, he is followed by Shastri (1959, vol. 3, p. 333) and Pagani (1999, p. 1181).

"miserable" *ahṛṣṭaḥ*: Literally, "unhappy." Ct and Ck explain the term to mean that because he is overwhelmed by the three emotions mentioned in the previous verse, Rāma exhibits no outward signs of happiness (*uktadharmatrayākrāntatvāt prakaṭa-*

harṣarahitaḥ). M3 and the texts and printed editions of Cg and Cm read instead the accusative *ahṛṣṭam*, which, as Cg notes, can be interpreted adverbially with the verb *abravīt* in *pāda* d, yielding the sense "he spoke unhappily," or as an adjective modifying the word "*vibhīṣaṇam*" in *pāda* c. Raghunathan (1982, vol. 3, p. 334), the only translator to render this variant, apparently chooses the former option, translating, "in a toneless voice." Dutt (1893, p. 1504) oddly renders "delighted," while, as noted above, Roussel and his followers understand that Rāma is actually dissimulating.

19. "Heeding those words" *sa tad vacanam ājñāya*: Literally, "having acknowledged *or* received that speech." Ś,B1,D1–3,7–12,G2, and the texts and printed editions of Ct and Cr read instead *tasya tad vacanaṃ śrutvā*, "having heard those words of his."

"made an effort to have the area cleared on every side" *utsāraṇe yatnaṃ kārayāmāsa sarvataḥ*: Literally, "he caused an effort to be made with regard to driving away on every side." As Cg explains in his gloss of the term *utsāraṇe*, "excluding the people (*jananivāraṇe*)," Vibhīṣaṇa is trying to get the assembled crowds to draw back or disperse. The idea, as it will emerge in the following verses, is that he is trying to protect Sītā, a woman of high status, from the gaze of males outside her immediate family. Ś,B1,D1–3,8,10–12, and the texts and printed editions of Ct read instead *utsāraṇaṃ tatra kārayāmāsa dharmavit*, "that knower of righteousness caused a driving away to be done there." Compare the exclamations of the royal guards escorting Padmāvatī at the opening of Bhāsa's *Svapnavāsavadattam*.

20. "Guards" *puruṣāḥ*: Literally, "men." This term, whose most common meaning is "male *or* man" must be taken here in its sense of "functionary, officer, *or* attendant." Ś,D1–3,8–12, and the texts and printed editions of Ct read instead the accusative plural *tān yodhān*, "those warriors," which then serves as the object of the participle *utsārayantaḥ*, "clearing *or* driving away."

"wearing mail and turbans" *kañcukoṣṇīṣiṇaḥ*: Literally, "possessing *kañcukas* and *uṣṇīṣas*." The former term can refer to a suit of armor, a short-fitted jacket, or a corselet. Translators choose one or the other of these meanings. Cg, with whom we agree, glosses *vārabāṇam*, "arrow-proof [vest]." The second term can refer to a variety of headdresses, including turbans, diadems, etc. The point is that these articles of clothing are doubtless intended as insignia or uniforms of guards or court functionaries.

"holding staves and drums in their hands" *vetrajharjharapāṇayaḥ*: Like many of the translators consulted, we understand the compound to be in part a *dvandva* consisting of *vetra-*, "a bamboo cane, staff, *or* lathi," and *jharjhara*, "a drum *or* tambourine." Presumably the former are used to drive back the spectators, while the latter is sounded to get their attention. Ck and Ct, however, understand the second term to be an onomatopoetic word indicating a scraping or jingling sound. They gloss, "whose hands made a sound like '*jharjhara*,' because of their wielding their staves (*vetrair vetragrahaṇair jharjharās tādṛśaśabdavantaḥ pāṇayo yeṣām*)." Among the translators consulted, only Gita Press (1969, vol. 3, p. 1846) follows this interpretation. Gorresio (6.99.23), whose reading is the same as the critical text's, understands the compound as we do, rendering, "*Tenenti in mano tamburi e canne*" (1858, vol. 10, p. 226). In a note, he observes, however, that the commentator (Cl) understands the term *jharjhara* to mean *veṇu*, "bamboo." Gorresio then observes that if he were to have accepted this interpretation, he would have had to translate, "*Tenenti in mano bacchette di bambu e canne*" (p. 312). B1,D1,13, and the texts and printed editions of Cg read *jarjara-*, "old, worn out, wounded," for the critical text's *jharjhara*. Cg extends the meaning of this term to "rough *or* harsh." He glosses the compound as "worn *or* rough because of the staff, that is, those whose hands had a roughness produced by always grasping [staves] (*vetreṇa jarjarāḥ sadāvalambanajanitapāruṣyāḥ pāṇayo yeṣāṃ te*)." This reading and Cg's interpretation are reflected only in the translation of Raghunathan (1982, vol. 3, p. 334), who renders, "Persons... their hands calloused wielding the whip."

"clearing the area" *utsārayantaḥ*: Literally, "clearing *or* driving away." See note to verse 19 above.

21. "apes" *ṛkṣāṇām*: See R. Goldman 1989. See, too, 1.16.10 and note. Cf. 6.4.17; 6.101.34; and notes.

"Then... withdrew to a distance" *dūram utsasṛjus tataḥ*: Literally, "then they escaped to a distance." We follow Cm and Cg, who gloss "they retired *or* fled (*apacakramuḥ*) for *utsasṛjuḥ*, they withdrew." D9–11 and the texts and printed editions of Ct read instead *dūram uttasthur antataḥ*, "they rose up from the inside to a distance." Ct glosses, "having arisen, they departed (*utthāya jagmuḥ*)." Cr takes *antataḥ* in the sense of "from the proximity (*samīpadeśāt*)," reading it with the participle *utsāryamāṇāni*, "being driven off," and then takes the adverb *dūram*, "far," with the finite verb *uttasthuḥ*, "they stood up." This yields, "being driven off from close in, they stood at a distance." This interpretation is rendered by Gita Press (1969, vol. 3, p. 1846).

22. "all... there arose a sound" *sarveṣāṃ dhvanir utthitaḥ*: B1,D3,8–12, and the texts and printed editions of Ct read instead *niḥsvanaḥ sumahān abhūt*, "there was a great sound."

"by a gale" *vāyunā*: Literally, "by the wind."

23. "when... saw them... on all sides" *tān dṛṣṭvā samantāt*: Literally, "having seen them... on all sides." B2,D9–11, and the texts and printed editions of Ct read instead *dṛṣṭvātha jagatyām*, "now having seen on the ground *or* earth." Among the translators who follow the text of Ct, only Roussel (1903, vol. 3, p. 381) attempts to translate this awkward and inferior reading. He renders the term *jagatyām* as "*dans le pays*."

"out of kindness and because he could not abide it" *dākṣiṇyāt tadamarṣāc ca*: The commentators understand the term to refer to Rāma's great tenderness toward the monkey troops who have served him (*svabhaktavānarasenāsu... kṛpāviśeṣāt*—so Ck, Ct). Ct and Ck note that Rāma is angry with Vibhīṣaṇa because he has driven the spectators back without an order to do so (*madājñāṃ vinotsārayatīti vibhīṣaṇe 'marṣaḥ*). The other commentators see Rāma's anger as directed more against the action of driving the monkeys away than against Vibhīṣaṇa personally, although in the following verses it is clear that Rāma is, indeed, angry with Vibhīṣaṇa.

24. "Furious" *saṃrabdhaḥ*: D10,11, and the texts and printed editions of Ct and Ck read instead *saṃrambhāt*, "out of anger *or* agitation."

"seeming almost to burn him up with his eyes" *cakṣuṣā pradahann iva*: Literally, "as if burning with his eye." Burning someone with an angry glance is a common trope in Sanskrit literature. Here, however, Cg seems disturbed at the idea of Rāma's turning such a blazing glance in the direction of Vibhīṣaṇa toward whom he has expressed such gratitude and affection. He attempts to soften the force of the metaphor by suggesting that Rāma is really drinking up Vibhīṣaṇa with his eyes and that his staring hard at a figure who is a fit object of his respect is only caused by Rāma's inability to endure the harsh treatment of his [Rāma's] own people (*cakṣuṣā pradahann iveti locanābhyāṃ pibann ivety uktādarapātrabhūtasya vibhīṣaṇasyaivaṃvidhadarśanaviṣayatākaraṇaṃ svajananigrahāsahiṣṇutvāt*). Cg also proposes, as an alternative, that Rāma is particularly angry because annoyance [toward Vibhīṣaṇa] is superimposed on the anger he feels toward Sītā (as expressed in verse 16 above) (*sītāviṣayasamāropitaroṣaviśeṣād vā*).

25. "with complete disregard for my wishes" *mām anādṛtya*: Literally, "having disrespected *or* dishonored me." The idea, as we have attempted to convey in our translation, is that Rāma feels he has been slighted, since Vibhīṣaṇa has taken it upon himself to drive away the spectators without consulting him. Cr glosses, "without having asked (*apṛṣṭvā*)."

"this business" *udyogam*: Literally, "this undertaking, exertion, *or* industrious activity." B1,D1–3,6,9–11,T2,3,G1,2,M1,2,5, and the texts and printed editions of Ck and Ct read instead *udvegam*, "trouble, agitation."

"These people are like my own kin." *jano 'yaṃ svajano mama*: Literally, "these people are my kinfolk." Since the reference is to the *rākṣasas* and monkeys, we follow Ck, Cr, and Ct, who understand, "like kinfolk, such as my brother, and so forth (*bhrātrādisvajanasadṛśa eva*—so Ck, Ct)." Cm glosses *bandhujana*, in which case we must understand *bandhu* in its sense of "friend" rather than "relative."

26. "curtains" *tiraskriyāḥ*: We follow Cm and Cg in taking the term here as the fourth in a list of specific screening devices designed to protect the modesty of elite women. They gloss, "curtains *or* veils (*tiraskariṇyaḥ*)." Ck, Ct, and Cr, however, take the word to be a generic term for screening devices of which the preceding three are examples (*gṛhāditrayaṃ tiraskriyā āvaraṇam*). Cf. GPP 2.15.20 and *KumāSaṃ* 1.14, where the term is used to indicate a screen or a veil.

"such royal treatment" *īdṛśā rājasatkārāḥ*: Literally, "such royal honors." We understand the adjective *īdṛśāḥ*, "of such a nature," to modify *rājasatkārāḥ*, "royal honors," which, we understand, with Cg, to be a reference to the royal treatment Vibhīṣaṇa accords Sītā by driving the vulgar crowd away from her path. Ck and Ct take the adjective *īdṛśāḥ* to refer elliptically to this treatment, while taking *rājasatkārāḥ* separately to refer to the mere insignia of royalty, such as the parasol and the fly whisk. (*īdṛśā janāpasaraṇādivyāpārā na striyā āvaraṇam, kiṃtu rājasatkārā eva kevalaṃ chatracāmarādivat*—so Ct.) See 6.47.13–14; 6.60.14; 6.115.13–16; 6.116.25–26; and notes.

"that shields a woman; it is her virtuous conduct alone" *vṛttam āvaraṇaṃ striyaḥ*: Literally, "[good] conduct is a covering *or* protection for a woman."

27. "there is nothing wrong with a woman being seen in public" *na . . . darśanaṃ duṣyate striyaḥ*: Literally, "the seeing of a woman is not wrong."

"during emergencies, periods of hardship" *vyasaneṣu . . . kṛcchreṣu*: The commentators attempt to differentiate the nearly synonymous terms. Ct understands the former to mean "a time of death *or* major calamity (*vipattikālaḥ*)," while he glosses the second as "trouble, suffering, pain (*pīḍā*)." Ck understands similarly but is more specific, glossing the former as "the time of the death of one's mother, father, etc. (*mātṛpitrādivipattikālaḥ*)" and the latter as "afflictions such as a serious illness, seizure (by demons?), etc. (*mahārogagrahādipīḍā*)." Cr similarly sees the first term as referring to "distress caused by a major emergency *or* calamity (*āpatkālajanitaḥ khedaḥ*)," while he takes the latter to be "suffering caused by illness, etc. (*rogādijanitaḥ khedaḥ*)." Cg takes the opposite view, understanding the first term to refer to personal distress such as separation from a beloved person (*iṣṭajanaviyogeṣu*), while he takes the second to refer to public upheavals such as the overthrow of the state, etc. (*rājyakṣobhādiṣu*). Cm understands similarly, glossing the first as "suffering caused by the death of a beloved person (*iṣṭajanamaraṇaduḥkham*)" and the second as "major calamities *or* emergencies (*āpatsu*)."

"in time of war" *yuddhe*: Literally, "in battle." Cg, attempting perhaps to find at least one of the conditions in Rāma's list that actually applies to the present circumstance, glosses, "on the battlefield (*yuddhabhūmau*)," presumably on the understanding that Rāma is awaiting Sītā in the area outside the walls of Laṅkā, which had, until recently been a battlefield. D2,4,6,9–11,T2,3,M3, and the texts and printed editions of the southern commentators read instead *yuddheṣu*, "in *or* during battles,"

"at a ceremony of choosing her husband" *svayaṃvare*: Literally, "in a self-choice." Sītā was given to Rāma at *Bālakāṇḍa* 66 as the prize in a contest of strength. The term *svayaṃvara*, "self-choice," is not used there. However, the event is described several times as a *svayaṃvara* during a conversation between Sītā and Anasūyā at *Ayodhyākāṇḍa* 110. See 2.110.23,37,57, and notes. The term is used in the *Bālakāṇḍa* by the daughters of Kuśanābha in their unfortunate encounter with Vāyu, where, refusing his advances, they claim they will never choose their own husband. See 1.31.18 and notes.

28. "She has been through a war" *saiṣā yuddhagatā*: D9–11,T1, and the texts and printed editions of Ct read instead *saiṣā vipadgatā*, "she has been through hardship."

"and has been placed in tremendous hardship" *kṛcchre mahati ca sthitā*: Cg, the only commentator to share and remark on this reading, is similarly alone in taking the term *kṛcchre*, "hardship," here to refer to Sītā's impending ordeal by fire (*vakṣyamāṇāgnipraveśe*). See *sarga* 104. D9–11 and the texts and printed editions of Ct read instead *kṛcchreṇa ca samanvitā*, "[she is] filled with suffering. Cr glosses, "filled with mental suffering (*mānasikaduḥkhena*)."

"there would be nothing wrong in her being seen publicly" *darśane 'syā na doṣaḥ syāt*: Literally, "there would be no fault in the seeing of her." See S. Goldman 1994 and 1996.

29. Ś,Ñ,V,B,D1–4,8–12, and the texts and printed editions of Ck, Ct, and Cr substitute a passage of two lines [3213*]: "Let her therefore leave the palanquin and approach on foot. Let these forest-dwelling monkeys see Vaidehī in my presence."

30. "by Rāma . . . his" *rāmeṇa . . . rāmasya*: Literally, "by Rāma . . . of Rāma."

"reflecting on all of this" *savimarśaḥ*: Literally, "with thought *or* deliberation." The commentators differ as to the content of Vibhīṣaṇa's deliberations. Ck and Ct understand that he is thinking the following: "Since he spoke in this fashion, probably he has no respect for her and has no desire to take her back. If those two things were present, then he would sanction appropriate behavior with respect to the queen. (*evaṃvādād asyāṃ prāyeṇābhimāno nāsti jighṛkṣā ca nāsti. yadi tau syātāṃ tadā rājapatnyucitam upacāram anumanyetaiveti cintāyukta ity arthaḥ.*)"

Cm understands that Vibhīṣaṇa is wondering, "What is the lord's thinking with regard to Sītā? (*sītāviṣaye svāminaś cittaṃ kīdṛśam iti vicāraḥ*)." Cg, in keeping with his interpretation of the term *kṛcchra*, "hardship," in verse 28 above, to refer to Sītā's upcoming fire ordeal, glosses *vimarśa* as "filled with foreboding because of [Rāma's] use of the word 'hardship' (*kṛcchraśabdaprayogāt sāśaṅkaḥ*)."

32. "Because of his demeanor" *iṅgitaiḥ*: Literally, "by the gestures." The term is frequently used to indicate bodily movements or facial expressions that betray inner emotions or hidden intentions.

"seemed to show no regard for his wife" *kalatranirapekṣaiś ca*: Literally, "which had disregard for the wife."

Although the fact is not noted in the critical apparatus, this verse does not belong to the texts of Ct, Ck, and Cr. It is omitted entirely from NSP and placed in parentheses without a number in GPP, which, in a footnote, mentions that it belongs [only] to the text of Cg. It is, however, found in the printed editions of VSP, KK, and Gita Press.

33. "Trying to make her body appear small in her shame" *lajjayā tv avalīyantī sveṣu gātreṣu*: Literally, "through her shame, disappearing into her own limbs." As Ck and Ct explain, Sītā is contracting her limbs because of the shame produced by her having to approach her husband in full view of the people (*janasamakṣabhartṛsamīpasthitijanyalajjayāvalīyantī saṃkocaṃ gacchantī*—so Ct). The idea, as we see it, is that Sītā is attempting to make herself as invisible as possible before the inappropriate gaze of the male spectators. Compare 5.17.3; 5.23.5; 5.56.57; and notes, where, in fear and shame, she similarly shrinks away from the gaze of Rāvaṇa.

34. "there before the assembled people" *janasaṃsadi*: Literally, "in the assembly of the people."

"murmuring" *bhāṣiṇī*: Literally, "saying, speaking."

"My noble husband" *āryaputra*: Literally, "O son of the noble [elder.]" This is the conventional term of address used by a wife to a husband, especially in the Sanskrit dramas. See 2.24.2, where Sītā also uses this term to address Rāma. See 6.23.34 and note. Cf. 6.61.19 and note.

D9–11 and the texts and printed editions of Ct omit this verse.

35. "whose face was more radiant than the moon . . . moonlike face" *mukham . . . saumyaṃ saumyatarānanā*: Literally, "she of the exceedingly lovely face . . . the handsome face." The verse plays on the ambiguity of the term *saumya*, which means both "lovely, gentle," on the one hand, and "moonlike, lunar," on the other. The moon is the literature's virtually universal standard of comparison for facial beauty. Cg notes that the term is used to express the radiance of Sītā's face at the time of her gazing [on Rāma's face] (*udīkṣaṇakālikamukhaprasādam āha saumyeti*). Cf. 3147* following notes to 6.99.44; see, esp., n. 2.

"with amazement, joy, and love" *vismayāc ca praharṣāc ca snehāc ca*: Literally, "out of amazement and out of joy and out of love." The three emotions experienced by Sītā here form a balanced and interesting contrast to those felt by Rāma in verse 16 above. Commentators offer a variety of explanations for the different emotions. Ck and Ct understand that Sītā is astonished at the sight of the abundance of so many friends and followers (*bahumitraparivārasampattidarśanajo vismayaḥ*—so Ct). Cr, on the other hand, thinks that her amazement is produced by the sight of Rāma's anger (*vismayo rāmakopadarśanajanitaḥ*). Cg and Cm think that she is simply amazed to see Rāma once again, something she thought impossible (*aghaṭitarāmapunardarśanād vismayaḥ*—so Cg).

Ck, Cg, Cm, and Ct all agree that Sītā's joy derives from seeing her beloved (*priyadarśanajo harṣaḥ*—so Ct). Only Cg comments on the term *sneha*, "love," which he explains as natural (*svābhāvikaḥ*) to Sītā.

36. "her beloved's face . . . which was as lovely as the full moon rising . . . her face became as radiant as the hare-marked moon" *priyasya / vadanam uditapūrṇacandrakāntaṃ vimalaśaśāṅkanibhānanā tadāsīt*: Literally, "the beloved's face, whose splendor was that of the risen full moon . . . [she] became one whose face resembled

the bright hare-marked one." The poet echoes his lunar imagery from the previous verse. Cg, continuing in his anticipation of the emotionally fraught scenes that are to immediately follow, claims that the comparison of Rāma's face to the newly risen full moon indicates that it was red with rage, while the comparison of Sītā's face to the bright moon suggests its waning in the period that is to follow. (*uditapūrṇacandrety anena koparaktatvam uktam. vimalaśaśāṅkety anenottarakālikakṣayaḥ sūcyate.*)

The meter is *puṣpitāgrā*.

Sarga 103

1. "meekly" *prahvām*: Literally, "humble, meek." Cg, taking his cue from 6.102.33, understands that Sītā is crouching down in shame (*lajjayā namrām*).

"as rage simmered in his heart" *hṛdayāntargatakrodhaḥ*: Literally, "having rage gone into his heart." Ś,B1,D1–4,8–12, and the texts and printed editions of Ct read instead *hṛdayāntargataṃ bhāvam*. This lends the second half of the verse the sense "he began to express the emotion within his heart."

2. "my good woman" *bhadre*: This mode of address is somewhat distant and is clearly meant to foreshadow the harsh words Rāma will now use to address Sītā. Among the commentators consulted, only Cg takes note of this formal mode of address, observing that it is a term used to address someone who is not a close relation (*bhadra ity asaṃbandhanivedakasambodhanam*). Prior to Sītā's abduction, Rāma typically addressed her by her proper name, patronymic, etc., e.g., Sītā, Jānakī, Maithilī (2.23.18,19; 2.21.2,3,4,8; 3.9.2,4; etc.), or with terms of endearment such as *abalā* ("frail lady," 2.25.3,12), *bhīrū* ("timid lady," 3.46.18; 3.53.22), etc. He will do so again after the public demonstration of her faithfulness by a fire ordeal at *sargas* 104–105 as, for example, at 6.111.3,4,5,11, etc. In this context, the use of the formal address is both pointed and striking. Cf. verses 23–25 below, where Rāma again addresses Sītā by name.

"I . . . in battle" *mayā raṇe*: Literally, "by me in battle." D9–11 and the texts and printed editions of Ct read instead *raṇājire*, "on the battlefield."

"Whatever there was to be done through manly valor, I have now accomplished." *pauruṣād yad anuṣṭheyaṃ tad etad upapāditam*: Literally, "What was to be performed out of manliness, that very thing has been done." Cg observes that the real meaning of this statement is that Rāma has acted merely out of the demands of the warrior code and not in an effort to recover Sītā. (*pauruṣād yad anuṣṭheyaṃ tad eva kṛtam. na tu tvallābhāya yatnaḥ kṛta iti bhāvaḥ.*) Ś,D8–12, and the texts and printed editions of Ct read instead *mayaitat*, "by me this [has been done]," for *tad etat*.

3. "my wrath is appeased" *gato 'smy antam amarṣasya*: Literally, "I have gone to the end of [my] anger." Cg, Cm, and Cr all gloss *antam*, "end," with "fruit, result, reward (*phalam*)." This interpretation is explicitly followed by Gita Press (1969, vol. 3, p. 1848), which translates, "I have attained the reward of my indignation."

"eliminated" *uddhṛtau*: Literally, "pulled up, eradicated." Cg glosses, "uprooted (*nirmūlitau*)." Ś,D1–3,8–12, and the texts and printed editions of Ct read instead *nihatau*, "slain, struck down."

4. "witnessed" *dṛṣṭam*: Literally, "seen." Ck and Ct understand the implied subject to be "by the people *or* the worlds (*lokaiḥ*)." Cr suggests adding instead "by you (*tvayā*)."

"I am . . . master of myself" *prabhavāmi . . . cātmanaḥ*: Literally, "and I rule over myself *or* my mind." Along with most translators consulted, we understand, as does Cg, who glosses, "free, independent (*svatantraḥ*)," that Rāma is expressing that he has discharged his obligation to avenge himself on Rāvaṇa. Cr, however, understands, "I have become powerful through my own efforts (*ātmanaḥ svaprayatnāt prabhavāmi prabhāvavān bhavāmi*)." The verb *pra* $\sqrt{}$*bhū* has a spectrum of meanings that include both temporal and supernatural power. Thus, it is possible to understand Cr's comment in a theological sense that Rāma, having through his own human efforts accomplished the destruction of Rāvaṇa, is now free to regard himself once more as the Lord (*prabhu*).

5. "wanton" *calacittena*: Literally, "whose mind is moveable *or* fickle." The term normally refers to someone whose mind is flighty or fickle (compare 6.45.9) and most translators who share this reading render accordingly. This meaning, however, seems a bit weak given the context, where the reference is not to Rāvaṇa's flightiness but rather to his libidinous nature.

"through manly action, I" *mānuṣeṇa mayā*: The phrase can be interpreted in two ways. The word *mānuṣa* can be taken either as a noun, in the sense of "man, mortal," or as an adjective, in the sense of "manly, human," standing elliptically for "manly action *or* effort." In the first interpretation, the two words are in apposition and serve collectively as the *kartṛ*, or subject, of the participle *jitaḥ*, "conquered." Thus the sense would be "[conquered] by me, a man." In the second, *mānuṣeṇa* would be the *karaṇa*, or instrument, lending the phrase the meaning "[conquered] by me through manly action." Cr appears to favor the first interpretation; Ck, Ct, and Cg, the second; while Cm offers both. We believe that the second interpretation is superior in this context, since it is in keeping with the epic's continuing meditation on the opposition between fate (*daiva*) and manly or human effort (*pauruṣa*). See 6.6.7–8; 6.98.23; and notes. See, too, Pollock 1986, pp. 33–36. All translations consulted that share the reading of the critical edition have chosen the first alternative, rendering either "man" or "a mere man." Several northern manuscripts and the edition of Gorresio (6.100.5) appear to gloss the term in favor of the second interpretation, reading instead *pauruṣāt*, "through manly force *or* action." Gorresio (1858, vol. 10, p. 229) translates, "*dalla forza*."

6. "What human purpose can a man serve if his spirit is so feeble" *kas tasya puruṣārtho 'sti puruṣasyālpatejasaḥ*: Literally, "what is the human goal of a man of little energy." The term *puruṣārtha* here is strongly resonant of its common śāstraic use to refer to the four specified goals of human life: *dharma*, *artha*, *kāma*, and *mokṣa*. Here the term may refer, by a kind of metonymy, to life itself. Raghunathan (1982, vol. 3, p. 335), the only translator consulted to render the critical reading, perhaps captures this sense best in translating, "what earthly use is that . . . fellow . . . ?"

A number of manuscripts, the texts and printed editions of Ct and Cr, and the printed editions of Gorresio and Lahore substitute *kas tasya pauruṣeṇārtho mahatāpy alpacetasaḥ*, "of what use is even great manly strength to such a small-minded person?"

9. "of my devoted" *bhaktasya*: Literally, "of the devoted [Vibhīṣaṇa]." Ś,B1,3,D1–3,8–12, and the texts and printed editions of Ct read instead *ca tathā*, "and as well."

"evil" *nirguṇam*: Literally, "devoid of virtues." Cr understands, "characterized by prohibited qualities (*niṣiddhaguṇaviśiṣṭam*)."

10. "As Rāma was saying these words in that fashion" *ity evaṃ bruvatas tasya . . . rāmasya tad vacaḥ*: D10,11,M1,5, and the texts and printed editions of Ct read *śrutvā*,

"having heard," for *tasya*, "of him [Rāma]." This lends the line the meaning: "When Sītā had heard those words of Rāma, who was speaking in this fashion."

Ck and Ct suggest that, by the term *evam*, "in this fashion," we are to understand that Rāma is speaking in such a way as to convey the meaning "I have no use for you" and that it is this punitive attitude that causes Sītā to become tearful through sorrow (*ity evaṃ vadata* [v.l. for *bruvata*] *ity arthāt tvayā me prayojanaṃ nāstīti pratiphalanād duḥkhenāśrupariplutā babhūva*). Cg and Cm indicate that Rāma's words make clear his lack of interest [in Sītā] (*tadvaco nairāśyadyotakaṃ vacaḥ*).

11. "Rāma...his anger...like the raging flame...of a...fire" *rāmasya... krodhaḥ...pāvakasyeva*: Literally, " the anger of Rāma, who was like a fire." The simile is defective in that there is no expressed *upamāna* for Rāma's anger. Cg, the only commentator who reads the line and remarks on it, notes that we are to carry over the word *krodhaḥ*, "anger," to the second half of the verse, understanding that the anger of a fire is its intense blazing (*pāvakasya krodho 'tīva jvalanam*). In something of the same spirit, we supply the phrase "like the raging flame."

"his anger flared up once more" *bhūyaḥ krodho 'bhyavartata*: Ś,B1,3,D1–4,9–12, and the texts and printed editions of Ct read instead *samīpe hṛdayapriyām*, lending the line the meaning: "But as Rāma gazed upon his heart's beloved [who stood] nearby..." This line now construes with 3224*, line 1.

Following 11ab, D9–11 and the texts and printed editions of Ct insert lines 1 and 2 of a passage of three lines [3224*, lines 1 and 3—here following the text of Ct as given at GPP 6.115.11cd–12ab]: "[But as Rāma gazed upon his heart's beloved,] the king's heart was divided within him out of fear of the people's censure.[1] [He then spoke to fair-hipped Sītā,—GPP 6.115.12cd] her eyes like petals of the blue lotus and her hair dark and waving.[2]"

B1,D4, and the texts and printed editions of Ct (NSP and Gita Press omit 11cd, GPP in brackets unnumbered between 6.115.10–11, unnoted in the critical apparatus) omit 11cd.

12. "Knitting his brows on his forehead and glancing at her from the corner of his eye" *sa baddhvā bhrukuṭiṃ vaktre tiryakprekṣitalocanaḥ*: D9–11 and the texts and printed editions of Ct (GPP in brackets for 6.115.11ab) omit this line.

"on his forehead" *vaktre*: Literally, "on the face."

"glancing at her from the corner of his eye" *tiryakprekṣitalocanaḥ*: Literally, "the gaze of whose eyes was oblique." We follow the interpretation of Cm and Cg. Cg understands that Rāma is staring straight ahead of him because he cannot bear the sight of Sītā (*tiryakprekṣaṇaṃ purataḥ sītādarśanāsahiṣṇutvakṛtam*). The only translator to share this reading, Raghunathan (1982, vol. 3, p. 336), renders, "looking askance."

"he spoke harshly to Sītā" *abravīt paruṣaṃ sītām*: D9–11 and the texts and printed editions of Ct read instead *avadad vai varārohām*, "he spoke to that fair-hipped one."

13–14. "Sītā, I have accomplished all that... In my wrath...from the hands of my enemy" *tatkṛtaṃ sakalaṃ sīte śatruhastād amarṣaṇāt*: Ś,B1,D1–3,8–12, and the texts and printed editions of Ct read instead *tatkṛtaṃ rāvaṇaṃ hatvā mayedaṃ mānakāṅkṣiṇā*, "Having killed Rāvaṇa, this was done by me who was desirous [of defending my] honor."

"I have won you back" *nirjitā*: Literally, "[you] are won back *or* conquered [by me]." The pronouns "I (*mayā*)" and "you (*tvam*)" must be supplied, as Cg and Cm suggest.

"just as...Agastya won back the southern lands that had been inaccessible to all living beings" *jīvalokasya.../ agastyena durādharṣā...dakṣiṇeva dik*: Literally, "just as

[was] the southern quarter, unapproachable to the world of the living, by Agastya." The *ṛṣi* Agastya is widely credited in Sanskrit literature for having led the advance of Aryan-brahmanical civilization into peninsular India. See Gorresio 1858, vol. 10, p. 313, n. 103; and Lassen 1858–1874, pp. 582–83. Ck, Ct, Cr, and Cg note that the southern lands were off limits to most beings because of the fear of the demons Ilvala and Vātāpi (Cg, Ilvala only), who infested them. The story of Agastya's destruction of these demons is told at *MBh* 3.94–97.

We follow the reading of Cg, Cr, Ct, and Ck, who argue that we should construe the compound *jīvalokasya*, "the world of the living," with *durādharṣā*, "unassailable, unapproachable," even though the two words are widely separated in the verse. Cm, however, understands the form as a genitive of specification (*nirdhāraṇe ṣaṣṭhī*) and prefers to read it with *nirjitā*, "won back," in 14a, understanding that Agastya won back the southern region in the midst of living creatures. (*jīvalokasyeti nirdhāraṇe ṣaṣṭhī. prāṇijātasya madhye ... agastyena ... nirjiteti.*)

Gita Press (1969, vol. 3, p. 1849) understands the term *durādharṣā*, "unapproachable, unassailable," to refer to Sītā, rendering, "Though difficult to approach for the world of mortals (for fear of Rāvaṇa), you have been won (back)."

15. "it was not on your account" *na tvadartham*: Dutt (1893, p. 1507), perhaps reading a variant (cf. 3226*, where *vā* is read for *na*), translates, "[all my labour, in the battle-field ...] is for thee."

17. "as profoundly disagreeable to me as is a bright lamp to a man afflicted with a disease of the eye" *dīpo netrāturasyeva pratikūlāsi me dṛḍham*: Literally, "as sharply disagreeable to me as a lamp to one with eye disease." Cg, interestingly, observes that, by the use of this comparison, Rāma is really saying that Sītā is without fault. What is suggested, Cg goes on, is that it is through Rāma's own doubts that he has made her disagreeable. (*anenopamānena vastutaḥ sītāyā doṣo nāsti. svasaṃdehenāhaṃ pratikūlīkaromīti vyajyate.*) The idea is that it is not the lamp's fault that it pains the diseased eye.

18. "Here are the ten directions." *etā daśa diśaḥ*: Rāma is suggesting that Sītā is free to go anywhere she pleases.

"I have no further use for you" *kāryam asti na me tvayā*: Literally, "of [by] me there is nothing to be done with you.

"my good woman" *bhadre*: See note to verse 2 above.

19. "powerful" *tejasvī*: Literally, "possessing blazing energy."

"his heart tinged with affection" *suhṛllekhena cetasā*: Literally, "with a mind *or* heart having the tracing *or* coloring of a friend." We follow Cm, Cv, Crā, and Cg, who understand the adjective to mean "conjoined with an excess of longing (*raṇaraṇakātiśayayuktenety arthaḥ*—so Cg). D10,11,T2,3,M1, and the texts and printed editions of Ck and Ct read instead *suhṛllobhena cetasā*, "with a mind *or* heart possessing desire, passion, *or* lust for one's companion."

20. "just risen" *-paribhraṣṭām*: Literally, "fallen from." Ś,Ñ2,V,B,D1–4,7,8,10–12,G2, and the texts and printed editions of Ct, Ck, and Cr read instead *parikliṣṭām* (B1,D4, *parikliṣṭā*) literally, "pained, tormented, pressed." Translations that follow the text of Ct render this word variously with such terms as "pressed, squeezed, soiled, taken, etc."

"by his lustful eye" *duṣṭena cakṣuṣā*: Literally, "with a depraved *or* corrupted eye."

21. "I have recovered my reputation, and that is the purpose for which I won you back." *tadartham nirjitā me tvaṃ yaśaḥ pratyāhṛtaṃ mayā*: Literally, "By me reputation has been taken back. For that purpose you were won back by me." D9–11 and the texts and printed editions of Ct read instead *yad[tad*—D9–11*]arthaṃ nirjitā me tvaṃ so 'yam āsādito mayā*, "I have accomplished the purpose for which I won you back."

"I do not love you anymore." *nāsti me tvayy abhiṣvaṅgaḥ*: Literally, "of me there is not love *or* attachment for [in respect to] you."

"hence" *itaḥ*: Ś,Ñ,V1,2,B2–4,D4–6,8–12,G2,3, and the texts and printed editions of Ct read instead the somewhat contextually awkward quotation marker *iti*.

22. "I have made up my mind in saying this" *iti pravyāhṛtam . . . mayaitat kṛtabuddhinā*: Literally, "[this] has been said in this fashion by me whose mind is made up." D9–11 and the texts and printed editions of Ct read *tad adya* for *iti pra-*, yielding the meaning "so this very day it has been said by me whose mind is made up."

"my good woman" *bhadre*: See note to verse 2 above.

23. "set your mind on" *niveśaya manaḥ*: Literally, "fix *or* focus your heart *or* mind on." Compare the usage at *BhagGī* 12.8b (*mayi buddhiṃ niveśaya*). See note below on "or on whomever you please."

"on Sugrīva, lord of the monkeys, or on the *rākṣasa* lord Vibhīṣaṇa" *sugrīve vānarendre vā rākṣasendre vibhīṣaṇe*: D2,3,9–11,T2,3, and the texts and printed editions of Ct read instead *śatrughne vātha sugrīve rākṣase vā vibhīṣaṇe*. This lends the line the meaning "on Śatrughna, or on Sugrīva, or on the *rākṣasa* Vibhīṣaṇa."

"or on whomever you please" *yathā vā sukham ātmanaḥ*: Literally, "or just as is pleasing to [your] mind *or* yourself." Ct understands that Sītā is being offered the option of returning to her parental home (*svamātṛpitṛkule vā ity arthaḥ*). This phrase could also be construed to be offering Sītā the choice of the specific individuals mentioned in verses 22 and 23. The issue is of significance in keeping with the śāstraic dictum that a woman can never be independent. So, for the commentators at least, Rāma is not giving Sītā away as a wife to the individuals named but rather assigning her to the house of a close relative, who would protect her. Thus, Cm understands that Sītā should pick one of those named individuals who are like sons to her so that she can be supported. (*putrasadṛśeṣu lakṣmaṇādiṣu madhye yatra kutrāpi mano niveśaya. ātmabharaṇārtham iti śeṣaḥ.*) This culturally sensitive issue is addressed most elaborately by Cg, who states that a woman with no protector of her own must get her living in the house of someone and that is why she is supposed to choose from among males such as Lakṣmaṇa, etc. This is because it is enjoined in the *śāstras* that a woman rejected by her husband is to live in the house of a male relative. In this context, Cg refers to the famous quote from *Manusmṛti* 9.3 that a woman must never be independent. Cg concludes by insisting that it would be improper to understand the passage in any other way. (*atra lakṣmaṇādau manaskaraṇaṃ nāmānāthāyā rakṣakatvena tat tadgṛhe vartanam. bhartrā parityaktāyāḥ striyā bandhugṛhe vāsavidhānāt. na strīsvātantryam arhatīti smṛteḥ na tv atrānyathā grahītuṃ yuktam.*) See notes to 6.104.4 on 3229*.

24. "would not long have left you unmolested" *na . . . tvām . . . / marṣayeta ciram*: Literally, "he would not have put up with *or* excused you for long." Ck and Cr, the only commentators to remark on this phrase, understand the adverb *ciram*, "for long," to construe with the participle *parivartinīm*, "residing" (Cr's v.l. *paryavasthitām*), giving the sense "who had long resided." V2,D10,11, and the texts and printed editions of Ct

read the somewhat awkward *na ... tvām ... / marṣyaty aciram*, "he did not spare you for a short time." Ct does not comment on the term *aciram*. Translators who follow the text of Ct either translate as we do, i.e., "for long (*ciram*)," or ignore the term entirely.

25. "Maithilī" *maithilī*: D9–11 and the texts and printed editions of Ct read instead *māninī*, "the self-respecting *or* proud woman." Roussel (1903, vol. 3, p. 384), followed by Shastri (1959, vol. 3, p. 336) and Pagani (1999, p. 1184), understands the variant to mean that Sītā had hitherto long been honored [by her husband].

"and trembled violently" *subhṛśaṃ pravepitā*: Ś,B1,D2,3,8–12, and the texts and printed editions of Ct read instead *rudatī tadā bhṛśam*, "[she] weeping copiously *or* bitterly then [shed tears]."

"a *vallarī* creeper" *vallarī*: The plant is identified by Apte (s.v.) and MW (s.v.) as *Trigonella foenum-graecum* (fenugreek or *methī*). However, the term can also apply to a creeper or any creeping plant. Ś2,D1,5,8,12,T1,M2,3, and the texts and printed editions of Cm and Cg read instead *sallakī* [v.l. *śallakī*]. Cg notes that this is a type of creeper that elephants feed upon (*gajabhakṣyalatāviśeṣaḥ*). Cm understands that the simile depends on the fact that the *sallakī* creeper emits a milky sap when it is broken by the trunks of elephants and that this is the basis of the comparison with Sītā's shedding tears (*gajendrahastābhihatā sallakīlatā yathā kṣīraṃ muñcati tathā bāṣpaṃ mumocety arthaḥ*). According to Apte (s.v.) the *sallakī* is a tree of which elephants are very fond. It is identified by MW (s.v.) as the tree *Boswellia thurifera* (frankincense), which seems inappropriate in the context. Raghunathan (1982, vol. 3, p. 336) renders the variant of Cg and incorporates the comments of Cm. He translates, "like the *sallakī* creeper, crushed by the giant tusker, pouring out its juice."

The meter is *vaṃśasthavila*.

Sarga 104

1. "in this cruel and horrifying manner" *paruṣaṃ lomaharṣaṇam*: Literally, "harshly [and] in a hair-raising manner."

"deeply" *bhṛśam*: Literally, "greatly, intensely." D5,9–12, and the texts and printed editions of Ct read instead *śrutvā*, "having heard *or* having listened." This reading presupposes an unexpressed object such as *vacaḥ*, "speech," which would then be modified by *paruṣam* and *lomaharṣaṇam* as adjectives.

2. "cutting" *rūkṣam*: Literally, "harsh, rough, cruel." Ś,V1,B1,D1,2,8,10–12, and the texts and printed editions of Ct read instead *ghoram*, "terrible, horrible."

"overcome with shame" *lajjayā vrīḍitābhavat*: Literally, "she became ashamed with embarrassment." Cg and Cm, the only commentators to share this reading and remark on it, gloss, "her face completely downcast (*atinamramukhī*)." Ś,B1,D1,2,6–8,10–12,T2,3, and the texts and printed editions of Ct read instead *lajjayāvanatābhavat*, "she was bowed *or* bent down with shame."

3. "Pierced, as it were, by those verbal barbs" *vākśalyais taiḥ saśalyeva*: Literally, "as if [pierced] with darts by those word-darts." Ś,V2,B3,D6,7,9–12,G3, and the texts and printed editions of Cr and Ct read *-śaraiḥ*, "arrows," for the more generic *-śalyaiḥ*, "darts."

4. "tear-stained" *bāṣpaparikliṣṭam*: Ś,Ñ,V1,2,B2–4,D1,2,4,8–12,M1,2,5, and the texts and printed editions of Ct read the slight variant *-klinnam*, "damp, moist," for *-kliṣṭam*, "stained."

Following verse 4, Ñ,V,B,D4,13 add a passage of two lines [3229*]: "I was born in a noble family, and I was given into a noble family. Lord of kings, do you now wish to give me to others as if I were some prostitute?[1]"

[1]"some prostitute" *śailūṣīm*: The term most generally refers to an actress, but, like its male counterpart, *śailūṣa*, it also refers to a person of loose morals. The passage is of particular note as it echoes the words Sītā utters at 2.27.8, where she accuses Rāma of acting like a pimp (*śailūṣa*), eager to hand her over to other men. See R. Goldman 2004. The verse perhaps sheds light on the interpretation of Rāma's instructions in the previous *sarga* (6.103.23) that she should go off with one of his brothers or allies or "whomever you please." In the previous passage, the commentators (Ck, Cm, and Cg) are at pains to assert that she should merely reside as a dependent in the household of these individuals rather than, as the passage seems to suggest, as a consort.

5. "heroic prince" *vīra*: Literally, "O hero."

"improper" *asadṛśam*: Cm, Cg, and Ct understand the term to mean that Rāma's words are improper for him to say and equally improper for Sītā to hear (*tvayā vaktuṃ mayā śrotuṃ cāyogyam*).

"as some vulgar man . . . to his vulgar wife" *prākṛtaḥ prākṛtām iva*: Literally, "like an ordinary [male] . . . to an ordinary [female]."

6. "by my own virtue" *svena cāritreṇa*: Literally, "by my own conduct." The reference, as Cm, Ck, Ct, and Cr point out, is to Sītā's exemplary devotion to her husband (*pātivratyalakṣaṇena*—Ck, Ct).

7. "If you really knew me, you would abandon your suspicion." *parityajemāṃ śaṅkāṃ tu yadi te 'haṃ parīkṣitā*: Literally, "If I were tested by you, you would have to abandon this suspicion." Our translation follows the suggestions of Cg and Cs. Cg glosses *parīkṣitā*, "tested, tried," with "one whose true nature is known (*jñātasvabhāvā*)." Cs explains, "If I were to be tested by you, then you would give up the wrong-headed thought: 'If corruption is found in one [woman], then all [women] must be similar' (*yadi te tvayāhaṃ parīkṣitā syāṃ tademāṃ śaṅkām ekasyā yatra kvāpi duṣṭatve sarvā api tādṛśya iti viparītasambhāvanāṃ tyaja tyakṣyasi*)."

8. "another's body" *gātra-*: Literally, "limbs, body."

"I had no choice in this matter. It is fate that was to blame here." *kāmakāro na me tatra daivaṃ tatrāparādhyati*: Literally, "There was no voluntary action of mine in this; fate offends *or* is to blame in this."

9. "But I could not control my body, which was in the power of another. What could I have done?" *parādhīneṣu gātreṣu kiṃ kariṣyāmy anīśvarā*: "What will I, powerless over my limbs that were under the power of another, do?" One can also construe the line slightly differently to mean: "Since my limbs were under the control of another, what could I, powerless, have done?" See S. Goldman 2001.

10. "my love" *mānada*: Literally, "bestower of pride." This is a common term of endearment for lovers in the literature. See notes to 6.13.7–8; 6.108.5, 3310*, n.1; and 6.110.6.

"despite our long-nurtured love and intimacy" *sahasaṃvṛddhabhāvāc ca saṃsargeṇa ca*: Literally, "because of the emotion that has grown together and contact." We understand the compound *sahasaṃvṛddhabhāvāt* as do Ck and Cr, in the sense of "mutual love that has grown up simultaneously (*saha yugapat saṃvṛddho bhāvaḥ parasparānurāgalakṣaṇaḥ*—so Ct)." Cg, Cm, and Cv put the two terms together as a *dvandva*, which they then explain as "contact and growing together, which has as its cause knowledge of one's true nature (*svabhāvaparijñānahetubhūtasahasaṃvardhanasaṃsargāv api*—so Cg)."

11. "When . . . hero" *yadā vīraḥ*: D9–11,G1,M5, and the texts and printed editions of Ct read instead *mahā-*, "great," for *yadā*. This lends the *pāda* the sense "that great hero was dispatched by you."

"to search for me" *avalokakaḥ*: Literally, "a looker." We follow the commentators, who gloss the infinitive *avalokayitum*, which they further gloss as "to search (*anveṣṭum*)."

"heroic prince" *vīra*: Literally, "O hero." D9–11,M1,2, and the texts and printed editions of Ct read instead *rājan*, "O king."

"while I was still being held in Laṅkā" *laṅkāsthāham*: Literally, "I [was] situated in Laṅkā." Given the syntax of the critical text with its sequence of relative and correlative clauses governed by the adverbs *yadā* and *tadā*, "when" and "then," respectively, we must understand Sītā, who is still in Laṅkā, to be referring to the period of her captivity. As noted above, D9–11,G1,M5, and the texts and printed editions of Ct substitute the adjective *mahā-*, "great," for the relative adverb *yadā*. This substitution permits one to read the verse somewhat differently. According to this reading, Sītā is saying to Rāma, "You sent the great hero Hanumān out to search. Why then did you not [have him] repudiate me in Laṅkā?"

12. "No sooner had I heard your words to that effect" *tvadvākyasamanantaram*: Literally, "immediately after your speech." As Cr explains, the phrase means "at the time following my hearing of those words that informed me of my abandonment (*tyāgabodhakavākyaśravaṇottarakāle*)."

"heroic prince" *vīra*: Literally, "O hero."

"of that monkey lord" *vānarendrasya*: Ś,B1,D1,3,8–12,G1, and the texts and printed editions of Ct read instead *vānarasyāsya*, "of that monkey."

14. "tiger among men" *naraśārdūla*: Ś1,Ñ2,V2,3,B1,D1–3,9–11, and the texts and printed editions of Ct read instead *nṛpaśārdūla*, "O tiger among kings."

"taking into account only that I am a woman" *strītvam eva puraskṛtam*: Literally, "[you] put forward only femaleness (i.e., the fact that I am a woman)." As Cm explains, the phrase means "you have perceived only my womanhood but not my virtuous conduct (*tvayā strītvam eva puraskṛtaṃ dṛṣṭaṃ na tu mama śīlam*)."

15. "Since my name is derived from Janaka, you failed to take into account the fact that I was born from the earth itself . . . given due consideration to my virtuous conduct." *apadeśena janakān notpattir vasudhātalāt / mama vṛttaṃ ca . . . bahu te na puraskṛtam*: Literally, "by the name from Janaka, the birth from the surface of the earth is not, nor is my conduct properly put forward by you." The syntax of the verse as it appears in the critical edition and the texts and printed editions of Cv, Cg, and Cm is awkward and apparently elliptical. Our translation follows the interpretation of Cv and Cm, who understand the participle *puraskṛtam*, "put forward," to also govern the feminine nominative *utpattiḥ* in *pāda* a. Thus, they supply the feminine form *puraskṛtā*. This reading enables them to account for both the instrumental *apadeśena*, "by name," and the negative particle *na* in *pāda* a. One could, perhaps, force the syntax of the instrumental to lend the first half of the verse the sense "Despite my name, my birth was not from Janaka but rather from the surface of the earth." Textual support for the

verse is somewhat suspicious, as Ś (as well as a few other manuscripts) omits this and the following nine verses. At other places in the critical edition, verses with similar textual evidence have been omitted. Compare, for example, the textual evidence for the exclusion of 3261* (following 6.105.27ab), where virtually all manuscripts except Ś and D8 read the line, and yet it is excluded from the critical text. Cf. 6.106.7–13. See Bhatt 1960, p. xxxiv. Cf., too, 6.107.7–13. D6,10,11, and the texts and printed editions of Ck and Ct read the nominative *apadeśo me*, "my name," for the instrumental *apadeśena*. This appears to be a *facilior* reading that irons out, as it were, the syntactical problem of the critical text. This variant yields the meaning: "My name comes from Janaka, not my birth, which is from the surface of the earth." Regardless of the reading, Sītā's point here is that, despite her epithets such as Jānakī, Maithilī, etc., she is not the actual child of the human king Janaka but is rather the daughter of the earth goddess Pṛthivī. As Cr comments, Rāma does not realize that, since Sītā was born from the sacrificial ground and is thus pure from her very birth, she would always be pure (*vasudhātalād yajñabhūmer utpattiś ca na puraskṛtotpattiśuddhyeyaṃ śuddhaiva bhaviṣyatīti matir na kṛtety arthaḥ*). On Sītā's birth, see 1.65.14–17 and notes. See, too, 7.88, where the goddess Pṛthivī fetches Sītā back. See Sutherland 1989 and S. Goldman 2006.

16. Ś,V3,D8,12 omit this verse and, following the principles of the critical edition, its inclusion should be considered doubtful. See note to verse 15 above.

"you do not weigh the fact that, as a boy, you firmly clasped my hand while I was but a child" *na pramāṇīkṛtaḥ pāṇir bālye bālena pīḍitaḥ*: Literally, "the hand that was pressed in childhood by a boy is not taken into account." The reference here, as several commentators point out, is to the act of clasping hands (*pāṇigrahaṇa*), which is the definitive moment in the Hindu wedding ceremony. D6,7,10,11,G2, and the texts and printed editions of Ct and Cr read instead *mama ni-* for *bālena*. This lends the phrase the sense "the hand that was firmly clasped in my childhood."

"you have turned your back on" *te pṛṣṭhataḥ kṛtam*: Literally, "has been placed behind by you."

17. Ś,D8,12 omit this verse and, following the principles of the critical edition, its inclusion should be considered doubtful. See note to verse 15 above.

"who stood there, despondent and brooding" *dīnaṃ dhyānaparaṃ sthitam*: D4,10,11,13, and the text of Ct read instead *dīnaṃ dhyānaparāyaṇam*, "despondent and absorbed in brooding."

18. Ś,D8,12 omit this verse and, following the principles of the critical edition, its inclusion should be considered doubtful. See note to verse 15 above.

"tainted by these false allegations" *mithyāpavādopahatā*: Literally, "afflicted *or* struck by false reproach."

19. Ś,D8,12 omit this verse and, following the principles of the critical edition, its inclusion should be considered doubtful. See note to verse 15 above.

"in this public gathering" *janasaṃsadi*: Literally, "in the assembly of the people."

"the fire, bearer of oblations," *havyavāhanam*: Literally, "the bearer of oblations."

"the only path proper for me" *yā kṣamā me gatiḥ*: Literally, "the path *or* course that is fitting for me." Cg and Cm understand that this path or place (Cm) is suitable for generating trust (*pratyayajananārtham*). This interpretation appears to have influenced the translation of Raghunathan (1982, vol. 3, p. 338), who renders, "How can I vindicate myself? So I will throw myself into the fire."

20. Ś,D8,12 omit this verse and, following the principles of the critical edition, its inclusion should be considered doubtful. See note to verse 15 above.

"he was overcome with anger and closely studied Rāghava's face" *amarṣavaśam āpanno rāghavānanam aikṣata*: Literally, "[having] come under the sway of anger, he looked at Rāghava's face." Commentators and translators differ somewhat in their understanding of the emotion that grips Lakṣmaṇa at this moment. The term *amarṣa* generally refers to "anger, intolerance, indignation," and most of the translators have rendered accordingly. Cg, however, is evidently troubled by the thought that Lakṣmaṇa could display anger toward his older brother and glosses *amarṣavaśam*, "the sway of anger," with *dainyavaśam*, "the sway of sorrow." Regardless of Lakṣmaṇa's inner feelings, it is clear from the following verses that he has no intention of going against his brother's wishes. Our understanding is that Lakṣmaṇa is uncertain as to how to respond to Sītā's dramatic order and is observing Rāma's face closely for signs of how his brother wishes him to proceed. This idea may have inspired the redactors of many of the northern manuscripts and the printed editions of Gorresio (6.101.22) and Lahore (6.97.20), who read instead *vimarṣavaśam*, "the power of hesitation *or* doubt." B1,D1–3,9–11, and the texts and printed editions of Ct read *rāghavaṃ samudaikṣata*, "looked at Rāghava," for the critical reading *rāghavānanam aikṣata*, "looked at Rāghava's face."

21. Ś,D8,12 omit this verse and, following the principles of the critical edition, its inclusion should be considered doubtful. See note to verse 15 above.

"sensing Rāma's intentions" *vijñāya manaśchandaṃ rāmasya*: Literally, "having realized Rāma's mental wish *or* desire." We follow Ct and Cr, who gloss, "intention (*abhiprāyaḥ*)."

"which were betrayed by his facial expression" *ākārasūcitam*: Literally, "indicated *or* inferred by facial expression." As several of the commentators indicate, the expressions in question are the arching of the brow, etc. (*bhrūbhaṅgādyākārasūcitam*—so Ct).

"obedient to Rāma's wishes" *mate rāmaysa*: Literally, "in Rāma's thought *or* purpose." Cg proposes that we supply the participle *sthitaḥ*, giving the sense "firm *or* fixed in Rāma's thoughts."

Following verse 21, B1–3,4,D1–3,9–11, and the texts and printed editions of Ct insert a passage of two lines [3231*]: "And not a single one of his companions dared to appeal to, speak to, or even look at Rāma, who resembled Yama, who brings time itself to an end.[1]"

[1]"Yama, who brings time itself to an end" *kālāntakayama-*: Literally, "Yama, the ender of time." See 6.21.26 and note.

22. Ś,D8,12 omit this verse and, following the principles of the critical edition, its inclusion should be considered doubtful. See note to verse 15 above.

"Then . . . slowly" *tataḥ . . . śanaiḥ*: Cg believes that Sītā walks slowly in order to prolong her last sight (lit., direct cognition *or* perception) of Rāma (*śanaiḥ rāmānubhavena mandaṃ yathā tathā*). B1,D1–3,9–11, and the texts and printed editions of Ct read instead *sthitam . . . tataḥ*, "stood . . . then." This lends the line the sense "then . . . Rāma, who stood [with his face downcast]."

"whose face was downcast" *adhomukham*: Cg attempts a psychological analysis of why Rāma keeps his eyes lowered, suggesting that this gesture is motivated by two factors.

The first is Rāma's shame brought on by the thought: "How can I look upon the guileless trust of a woman so devoted to her husband." Rāma's second thought, according to Cg, is that, if he were to look Sītā in the eye, it might be taken for a gesture of kindness *or* amorous gallantry. (*pativratāyāḥ kathaṃ nirvyājaṃ pratyayaṃ paśyāmīti lajjayā mukhadarśane dākṣiṇyaṃ bhaviṣyatīti buddhyā cāvanatamukham.*)

23. Ś,D8,12 omit this verse and, following the principles of the critical edition, its inclusion should be considered doubtful. See note to verse 15 above.

24. See 5.51.22–28 and notes, where Sītā swears by her fidelity to Rāma to protect Hanumān from the fire and 5.53.17–26, where Hanumān reasons correctly that Sītā's virtue will similarly protect her from the conflagration he has started. Cf. 7.88.10, where Sītā once again swears by her fidelity to her husband. On this type of "truth act," see Hopkins 1932. Cf. 6.106.15 and note.

Ś,D8,12 omit this verse and, following the principles of the critical edition, its inclusion should be considered doubtful. See note to verse 15 above.

"Agni, the purifier" *pāvakaḥ*: Literally, "the purifier."

Following 24cd, D5–7,10,11,T,G1,3,M2,3 and the texts and printed editions of the southern commentators insert a passage of one line [3236*] and then repeat 24cd: "Since Rāghava believes me, whose conduct is pure, to be unchaste, so may Agni, the purifier, witness of all the world, protect me in every way."

Following verse 24, D5–7,T,G1,3,M1,3,5, and the texts and printed editions of Cg insert a passage of two lines [3238*]: "Since I have never, in word, thought, or deed, wronged Rāghava, who knows all righteousness, may Agni, the purifier, protect me."

Following 3238* (D9,M2 continue after 3239*), D5,T1,G3,M3, the texts and printed editions of Cg and Crā, and the edition of Gita Press (6.117.28) insert a passage of three lines [3240*]: "Since the Blessed Lord Āditya, Vāyu, the directions, the moon, the day, the two twilights, the night, the goddess Earth,[1] and whichever others know[2] me to be adorned[3] by my pure conduct, [may Agni, the purifier, protect me]."

[1]"the goddess Earth" *pṛthivī*: Literally, "the earth."

[2]"whichever others know" *ye cānye 'py abhijānanti*: Gita Press, M3, and the texts and printed editions of Cg and Crā read instead *yathānye 'pi vijānanti*, "just as . . . and others know."

[3]"to be adorned" *-bhūṣitām*: M2,3, Gita Press, and the texts and printed editions of Cg and Crā read instead *-saṃyutām*, "endowed with."

25. "the fire, eater of oblations" *hutāśanam*: Literally, "the eater of oblations."

"with complete detachment" *niḥsaṅgenāntarātmanā*: Literally, "with an internal faculty that was without attachment." Cg glosses, "with a mind completely detached with regard to her body (*niḥsaṅgena śarīre nirabhilāṣeṇāntarātmanā manasā*). Ck, who reads with the critical edition, glosses, "[with a mind] devoid of fondness for life (*prāṇaprīti-rahitena*)." Ś,Ñ,V,B,D2–4,8–13,M5, and the texts and printed editions of Ct read instead *niḥśaṅkenāntarātmanā*, "with a fearless *or* courageous heart."

26. "filled with children and the aged" *bālavṛddhasamākulaḥ*: Raghunathan (1982, vol. 3, p. 338) takes -*samākulaḥ* somewhat awkwardly in its other sense of "agitated,

frightened," rendering, "The great concourse of young and old was scared to see . . ." Presumably, we are to understand that most of the able-bodied male *rākṣasas* of Laṅkā have been killed in the war.

"there" *tatra*: D10,11,G1, and the texts and printed editions of Ct read instead *dīptām*, "blazing, glowing," which here refers to Sītā. This reading is rendered only in the translations of Roussel (1903, vol. 3, p. 386), Gita Press (1969, vol. 3, p. 1853), and Pagani (1999, p. 1185). Dutt (1893, p. 1509) mistakenly assigns the adjective to the fire, while Shastri (1959, vol. 3, p. 338) omits it entirely.

Following verse 26, V2 (in scattered order), D5 (lines 6–9 only),6,7,10,11,T1,G, M1,3,5, and the texts and printed editions of the southern commentators insert (while Ś,B1,D1–3,8,9,12,T2,3 continue after 3246*; Ñ1,D4,13 insert after colophon; Ñ2,V1,3,B3,4 insert after 27; B2 continues after 3247*; and M2 further continues after 3248*) a passage of nine lines [3243*]: "Then, in the presence of all those people, Sītā,[1] who, with her ornaments of refined gold, looked herself like newly refined gold, fell into the blazing fire.[1–2] All beings watched as wide-eyed Sītā, resembling a splendid altar of gold,[2] was falling into the fire, bearer of oblations.[3–4] All the three worlds watched as the blessed Sītā, like a pure offering of melted butter,[3] entered the fire. [5–6] When they saw her, who was like a stream of clarified butter sanctified by vedic *mantras* at a sacrifice, falling into the fire, bearer of oblations, all the women began to wail.[7–8] The three worlds, including the gods, *gandharvas*, and *dānavas*, watched her . . . (continuing on to 3244*).[9]"

[1]"Sītā" *sā*: Literally, "she."

[2]"resembling a splendid altar of gold" *rukmavedīm ivottamām*: D10,11,G2,M1, and the texts and printed editions of Ct and Cr read instead *rukmavedinibhāṃ tadā*, "Then, resembling an altar of gold."

[3]"All the three worlds . . . Sītā, like a pure offering of melted butter" *sītāṃ kṛtsnās trayo lokāḥ puṇyām ājyāhutīm iva*: Ś1,B1,3,D1–3,8–11,T2,3, and the texts and printed editions of Ct read instead *ṛṣayo devagandharvā yajñe pūrṇāhutīm iva*, "the seers, gods, and *gandharvas* [watched her,] who was like a complete oblation at a sacrifice."

All printed editions of the southern recension and the translations that follow them include or render this insert. Despite the fact that the critical apparatus shows it, in one place or another, in virtually every manuscript consulted, the printed editions of Gorresio (6.101.35) and Lahore (6.102.7) read only variations of lines 1 and 2. The omission of these lines from the critical text, given the evidence in the critical apparatus, is questionable.

Following 3243*, Ñ,V1,2,B2–4,D5–7,10,11,13,T1,G,M, and the texts and printed editions of the southern commentators insert a passage of one line [3244*, line 3], which must be construed syntactically with line 9 of 3243*: "[her] like a goddess who has been cursed, falling from heaven into hell."

27. "deafening and prodigious cry" *vipulaḥ svanaḥ / . . . adbhutopamaḥ*: Literally, "a loud sound that was like a miracle *or* wonder." Our translation of *adbhutopamaḥ*, "like a miracle," follows Cg and Cm, who gloss, "like a prodigy *or* miracle (*adbhutatulyaḥ*)." This interpretation has been similarly followed by Roussel (1903, vol. 3, p. 387), Pagani (1999, p. 1186), and, with some stretching of the meaning, by Dutt (1893, p.

1510—"unheard of before") and Gita Press (1969, vol. 3, p. 1853—"strange"). Shastri (1959, vol. 3, p. 338) renders, "terrible," while Raghunathan (1982, vol. 3, p. 339) renders, "a great cry from the astounded apes and Rākshasas." Ct and Ck take the term *adbhutopamaḥ* as a *bahuvrīhi* compound modifying *svanaḥ*, "sound *or* cry," and having the sense "in the production of which was the recognition that a miracle was taking place (*āścaryam ity upamā jñānaṃ yat pravṛttau saḥ*)."

At the conclusion of the *sarga*, with its dramatic climatic scene, Cg brings up the subject of Sītā's suffering on the terrestrial plane and the widely known legend, seemingly unknown to Vālmīki, of the real Sītā's having entered the fire at the time of Rāvaṇa's attempted abduction and her replacement by an illusory surrogate (*chāyāsītā* or *māyāsītā*). According to this tradition, the entire *agniparīkṣā*, or fire ordeal, is merely staged as a convenient way to dispose of the false Sītā and recover the real goddess without revealing this divine deception. See 6.102.5; 6.106.4; and notes and Introduction p. 104.

Sarga 105

Before verse 1, V,B2–4,D5–7,10,11,T,G,M1,2 (after 6.104.27),3,5, and the texts and printed editions of the southern commentators insert a passage of two lines [3247*]: "Then righteous Rāma, dejected, hearing the words they were saying, lapsed for a time into gloomy thought, his eyes brimming with tears.[1]

[1]"dejected... lapsed... into gloomy thought, his eyes brimming with tears" *durmanāḥ... dadhyau... bāṣpavyākulalocanaḥ*: Cm, Ck, and Ct understand that Rāma is now depressed at the thought of what he has done to Sītā and at the expressions of grief on the part of the people. Cm feels that Rāma is dejected by the thought that he has brought about a terrible action (*dāruṇakarma kāritam iti cintāparo 'bhūd ity arthaḥ*). Ck and Ct understand that Rāma is thinking, "What have I said? What have I done? What should I do now?" (*kim uktaṃ kiṃ kṛtaṃ kiṃ cātaḥparaṃ kartavyam iti cintāparo babhūva*).

1–3. "King Kubera Vaiśravaṇa: *vaiśravaṇo rājā*: Literally, "King Vaiśravaṇa."

"Yama, dragger of his foes" *yamaś cāmitrakarśaṇaḥ*: Literally, "and Yama, the dragger of non-friends." Yama is known in the literature to drag off his victims with his characteristic weapon, the *pāśa*, or noose. Ś,B1,D1–3,9–11, and the texts and printed editions of Ct read instead *yamaś ca pitṛbhiḥ saha*, "and Yama together with the ancestors."

"great Indra of the thousand eyes" *sahasrākṣo mahendraś ca*: Ś,B1,D1–3,8–12,T2,3, and the texts and printed editions of Ct read instead *ca deveśaḥ*. This lends the phrase the sense "and the thousand-eyed lord of the gods."

"Varuṇa, scorcher of his foes." *varuṇaś ca paraṃtapaḥ*: Ś,B1,D1–3,8,10–12, and the texts and printed editions of Ct read instead *jaleśvaraḥ*, "lord of the waters," for *paraṃtapaḥ*, "scorcher of foes."

"the great god, majestic Śiva, with his half-six eyes" *ṣaḍardhanayanaḥ śrīmān mahādevaḥ*: The unusual epithet *ṣaḍardhanayanaḥ*, "having half of six eyes," is a variant of more common epithets of Śiva such as *trilocanaḥ*, *trinetraḥ*, etc. See note on Brahmā below and notes to verse 12.

"Brahmā" *brahmā*: Cr, alone among the commentators, expresses discomfort at the exclusion of Viṣṇu from the list of deities that assemble in Rāma's presence. He offers two alternative strategies for including his chosen deity. The first is to take the epithet *śrīmān*, "majestic," which appears to refer to Śiva, instead as "he who possesses the goddess Śrī, i.e., Viṣṇu. Alternatively, he proposes that "*aḥ*," a monosyllabic epithet of Viṣṇu, is present in the list after the name of Brahmā but is obscured because of its coalescence with the final "*ā*" of that name. (*brahmā aḥ viṣṇuś ca* . . . *śrīmāñśabdena viṣṇulābho vā bodhyaḥ*). See notes to verse 12 below.

4. "the foremost of the thirty gods" *tridaśaśreṣṭhāḥ*: Literally, "the best among the thirty."

"Rāghava, who stood before them, his hands cupped in reverence" *prāñjaliṃ rāghavaṃ sthitam*: For some reason, Shastri (1959, vol. 3, p. 339) and Dutt (1893, p. 1510) appear to read the adjective *prāñjalim* adverbially, construing it with *abruvan*, "they spoke." Their translations, therefore, have the gods holding their hands in supplication to Rāma. See note to verse 10 below.

5. "the creator of the entire universe" *kartā sarvasya lokasya*: Cg, noticing the seeming contradiction between applying the epithet here to Rāma when it was just applied to Brahmā in verse 2 above, argues that, in fact, there is no contradiction because the earlier reference was to Brahmā's direct or unmediated role as the creator, while here the reference is to Viṣṇu's indirect or mediated role (*pūrvaṃ brahmaṇo 'dvārakaṃ kartṛtvam atra sadvārakaṃ kartṛtvam iti na virodhaḥ*).

"the most ancient one" *śreṣṭhaḥ*: In its most common usage this term, in the sense of "best, foremost," construes with a noun in the genitive plural or is placed at the end of a *tatpuruṣa* compound to mean "the best of *or* foremost among." Since that role is served in the critical reading by the synonymous term *varaḥ*, "best, foremost," we have rendered *śreṣṭhaḥ* in its other sense of "eldest, primal, ancient."

"foremost among those possessing supreme knowledge" *jñānavatāṃ varaḥ*: Literally, "the best of those possessing knowledge." As Ct and Ck point out, the knowledge referred to here must be the ultimate knowledge articulated in the *upaniṣads* (*aupaniṣadajñānavatām*). The word *varaḥ* is marked as doubtful in the critical edition. It has a wide range of manuscript variations, most of which have the sense of "lord." B2,D7,10,11,G1,2,M2, and the texts and printed editions of Ct read instead *jñānavidāṃ vibhūḥ*, "the lord of those who know supreme knowledge."

"How can you . . . stand by and watch . . . How can you not realize" *upekṣase katham* . . . *katham* . . . *nāvabudhyase*: Literally, "How do you ignore *or* overlook, how do you not know?" Cr argues that, in choosing their words in this verse, the gods are saying that Rāma, or Viṣṇu, who is omniscient, must know that Sītā has not the slightest trace of wrongdoing. And therefore, in ascribing guilt to someone he knows to be innocent, he has acted improperly. (*jñānavatāṃ sarvaviṣayakajñānaviśiṣṭānāṃ vibhuḥ svāmī tvaṃ havyavāhane patantīṃ sītāṃ katham upekṣasa etena sītāyā na kiṃcid doṣasaṃsarga iti bhavato jñānam astīti sūcitam. tenādoṣe doṣāropaṇam anucitam iti dhvanitam.*) Compare 6.106.14 and note.

"into the fire, eater of oblations" *havyavāhane*: Literally, "into the eater of oblations."

6. 6cd = 3256*ab. (See note to verse 17 below.)

"Long ago" *pūrvam*: Literally, "earlier." Cm, quoted by Ct, understands the term to refer either to a previous *kalpa*, "a great cosmic age," or to the time before creation itself (*pūrvaṃ pūrvasmin kalpe sṛṣṭeḥ pūrvaṃ vā*).

"the Vasu Ṛtadhāman" *ṛtadhāmā vasuḥ*: Ṛtadhāman, literally, "having truth *or* cosmic order for his abode *or* the resting place *or* abode of truth," is an epithet or name of Viṣṇu, especially in his role as creator.

"the progenitor of the Vasus" *vasūnāṃ ca prajāpatiḥ*: Literally, "and the Prajāpati (lord of progeny *or* creatures) of the Vasus." The term *prajāpati* is commonly used as a proper noun for the creator divinity who generates all creatures at the beginning of each cosmic cycle. See note to verse 25 below. The Vasus are a class of vedic divinities, normally eight in number.

"the untrammeled lord" *svayaṃprabhuḥ*: Literally, "lord in and of himself." We follow the remarks of the commentators who understand the epithet to refer to the lord who is under the control of no other (*itarāniyamyaḥ*—so Ct).

7. "Rudra, the eighth among the Rudras" *rudrāṇām aṣṭamo rudraḥ*: The Rudras are a class of eleven fearsome vedic divinities associated with the god Rudra (*ṚV* 1.85; 1.114; 2.33; etc.). The name "Rudra" in late and post-vedic texts is primarily an epithet of Śiva, as indicated by Ct and Cr, who gloss, "the great god (*mahādevaḥ*)," an epithet of Śiva.

"and . . . fifth among the *sādhyas*" *sādhyānām api pañcamaḥ*: The *sādhyas* are a class of divine beings, known from the *vedas* (see *ṚV* 10.90.7,16, etc.). Ct, Cr, and Cs claim that the fifth of the *sādhyas* is called Vīryavān. See notes to verse 17 below, 3256*, n. 2.

"The twin Aśvins" *aśvinau*: Literally, "the [two] Aśvins." The Aśvins are a well-known pair of vedic divinities, often credited with saving or curing people in distress (*ṚV* 1.116; 5.78, etc.).

8. "You are present before the beginning and after the end of the worlds" *ante cādau ca lokānāṃ dṛśyase tvam*: Literally, "you are visible in the beginning and the end of the worlds." As the various commentators suggest, this is a way to explain that, unlike created beings, Viṣṇu has neither beginning nor end (*anenotpattivināśarāhityam uktam*—so Cg). Ś,B1,D1–3,5,8–12, and the texts and printed editions of Ct read *madhye ca*, "and in the middle," for *lokānām*, "of the worlds."

9. "the lord of the world" *svāmī lokasya*: The phrase is somewhat ambiguous, perhaps intentionally so. It can be interpreted here, as do Ck, Cm, and Ct, to be a reference to Rāma's current kingship of the earth (*bhūlokasyedānīṃ sākṣāt svāmī*). The phrase can also refer to his divine role as the lord of the worlds or universe. Translators are divided.

"the thirty gods" *tridaśa-*: Literally, "the thirty."

10. For a discussion of the implications of this verse for our understanding of the *Vālmīki Rāmāyaṇa*'s position on the divinity of Rāma, see Pollock 1984b and 1991, pp. 15–54. See, too, note to 6.70.40, 1585* and note.

"who I really am, to whom I belong, and why I am here" *yo 'haṃ yasya yataś cāham*: Literally, "who [am] I, whose [am I], and from what [am] I." The commentators generally agree that the first relative pronoun (*yaḥ*) refers to Rāma's true nature (*svarūpapraśnaḥ*—Cg). Cm and Cg take the second relative pronoun (*yasya*) as we have done to refer to Rāma's affiliation (*saṃbandhipraśnaḥ*—so Cg). Cr, however, takes the genitive to be asking whose master Rāma is (*yasya svāmī*). Ck and Ct, who do not read the second pronoun (*yasya*), interpret the third (*yataḥ*) to refer to Rāma's origin or natural state (*yataś ca yatprakṛtikaś ca*—so Ct). Cr takes *yataḥ* to be a question with reference to the world from which Rāma has come (*yato lokād āgato 'ham*). Cg and Cm, whom we have followed, understand the term *yataḥ* to refer to the purpose for which

Rāma has been born (*yata iti prayojanapraśnaḥ*). We believe this is so, because that is the question answered by Brahmā at verse 25 below. D10,11,M1, and the texts and printed editions of Ct read for *yo 'haṃ yasya,* "who [am] I, of whom [am] I," *so 'ham yaś ca,* "and he who I am," thus omitting the critical edition's second question.

11. "Rāma" *rāma*: D10,11,M1, and the texts and printed editions of Ck and Ct read instead *vākyam,* "speech, words."

12. In this and the following verses, as in the *Ādityahṛdaya* passage (App. I, No. 65, following note to 6.93.27), the commentators are at pains to provide etymological and scriptural explanations for most of Viṣṇu's names and epithets. We comment only on those that bear directly on issues of translation.

"majestic" *śrīmān*: Literally "possessed of majesty *or* good fortune." The term can also refer, in a specifically Vaiṣṇava context, to the fact that the Lord has the goddess Śrī or Lakṣmī as his constant companion—so Cg and Cts. (*śrīmān iti nityayoge matup. bhavāñ śrīmān iti sītālakṣmīr bhavān viṣṇur ity uktaśriyaḥ patitvaṃ nityānapāyitvaṃ ca darśitam*—so Cts.) See notes to verse 2 above and verse 19 below.

"Nārāyaṇa" *nārāyaṇaḥ*: The commentators provide two different etymologies for the term. Ck and Ct understand it to mean "he whose residence *or* place is the collectivity of all living creatures," i.e., that he resides in all creatures (*nāraṃ jīvasamūho 'yanaṃ sthānaṃ yasya saḥ*). Cm understands similarly. Cg cites the etymology given at *Manusmṛti* 1.10, where it is said that, because the waters are the sons of men (*nara*), they are called *nārāḥ,* and, since Viṣṇu's resting place (*ayana*) is on the waters, he is therefore called "he who rests on the waters (*nārāyaṇa*)." (*nārā ayanaṃ yasyāsau nārāyaṇaḥ. āpo nārā iti proktā āpo vai narasūnavaḥ / tā yad asyāyanaṃ pūrvaṃ tena nārāyaṇaḥ smṛtaḥ // iti manusmaraṇāt.*) This epithet is used, Cg argues, to indicate that Viṣṇu is the primal cause of the universe (*tena jagatkāraṇatvam uktam*).

"wielder of the discus" *cakrāyudhaḥ*: Literally, "whose weapon is the discus." Ck and Ct argue that the term *cakra,* "discus," is an *upalakṣaṇa* (metonymy) to express the complete set of Viṣṇu's four characteristic *āyudhas*—the discus, mace, conch shell, and lotus (*idaṃ śaṅkhagadāder apy upalakṣaṇam*).

"the single-tusked boar" *ekaśṛṅgo varāhaḥ*: The reference is to Viṣṇu's third incarnation as the *varāhāvatāra,* who raises the earth from the primal seas on his tusk (see *ViṣṇuP* 1.4.3–11,25–29,45–49; *MBh* 3.141; 12.202,339–340; *BhāgP* 3.13–19; and *Varāhapurāṇa* 113–115). Cm cites passages from the *Skandapurāṇa* (2.136 and 5.152) explaining how Viṣṇu came to be called "the single-tusked one." There Viṣṇu in his manifestation as the primal boar is said to have shaken the mountains with one of his tusks. The gods then, pleased, praised him for the accomplishment of this feat with a single tusk. Therefore, henceforth Mādhava (Viṣṇu) came to be called "the single-tusked boar." (*ekaśṛṅgo varāha ādivarāhaḥ. tasyaikaśṛṅgatā skānde darśitā daṃṣṭrayā parvatendrāṇāṃ cālanaṃ kṛtavān mahat / tatas taṃ tuṣṭuvur devā ekaśṛṅgatvasiddhaye // ekaśṛṅgo varāho 'bhūt tadāprabhṛti mādhavaḥ.*)

"the conqueror of your enemies, past and future" *bhūtabhavyasapatnajit*: Commentators are divided as to the meaning of the epithet. Ck and Ct understand that Viṣṇu's enemy is time itself, since it is the cause of birth and death. These commentators believe that the text is alluding to the fact that Viṣṇu is eternal. (*bhūtabhavyakālarūpo yaḥ sapatno janimṛtihetutvāt taṃ jayati saḥ. nitya iti yāvat.*) Cg, however, sees the term as an allusion to Viṣṇu's legendary conquest of such enemies of the past as the demons Madhu and Kaiṭabha (*MBh* 3.194), and to his future killing of the Cedi king Śiśupāla, an event that does not occur until the following *yuga*. The reference to Śiśupāla is to the Cedi monarch who reviles Kṛṣṇa and is slain by him at *MBh* 2.37–42. At *MBh* 2.42.21–24, it is said that blazing energy leaves the body of Śiśupāla when he is slain and enters the body of Kṛṣṇa. Śiśupāla is often held up in Vaiṣṇava theological literature as the archetypal practitioner of *dveṣabhakti*—single-minded concentration on the Lord in the form of obsessional hatred that nonetheless leads to salvation and union. See note to 5.7.68. See, too, 6.44.37; 6.99.39; and notes; and 7.94.5.

13. "the beginning, the middle, and the end" *ca madhye cānte ca*: Literally, "and in the middle, and in the end, and." We follow the commentators in reading the first occurrence of the conjunction *ca*, "and," with an unexpressed third term *ādau*, "in the beginning" (*cakāreṇādāv api*—Cr).

"the four-armed Viṣvaksena" *viṣvaksenaś caturbhujaḥ*: Ct, Cm, and Ck understand the epithet "four-armed (*caturbhujaḥ*)" to refer to the fact that the god possesses four arms that are adept at destroying his enemies (*śatrunirasanadakṣabhujacatuṣṭhayavān*—so Ct). Cg, on the other hand, understands the epithet to refer to Viṣṇu's simultaneously dispensing the four *puruṣārthas*, or "goals of man" (*yugapaccaturvidhapuruṣārthaprada ity arthaḥ*). Commentators offer a variety of interpretations of the epithet Viṣvaksena, literally, "whose army is all pervasive." Ct glosses, "whose hosts that subdue armies are everywhere (*viṣvañcaḥ sarvagatāḥ senāniyāmakagaṇā yasya*)." Ck understands the epithet to mean "whose [armies] are characterized by his own offspring, viz., the gods and *asuras* (*viṣvañcaḥ senāviśeṣāḥ svāpatyadevāsuralakṣaṇaṃ yasya saḥ*)." Cg and Cm understand simply, "whose army is everywhere." According to Cg, this means that Viṣṇu is the lord of everything. (*viṣvadrīcī sarvagatā senā yasya saḥ viṣvaksenaḥ. sarvasvāmīty arthaḥ*—so Cg.) See 6.51.9; 6.52.6; and notes.

14. "You are . . . You are . . . you are": This and the following two verses constitute a list of names and epithets. We have supplied the words "you are" at several points for the sake of readability.

"You are the wielder of the horn bow" *śārṅgadhanvā*: Literally, "possessing the bow made of horn." Ct understands Viṣṇu's bow to be in the form of *kāla*, "time" (*kālarūpaḥ*). This interpretation is rendered in the translation of Dutt (1893, p. 1511) as "thou art the holder of the bow of time."

"you are Hṛṣīkeśa" *hṛṣīkeśaḥ*: Several of the commentators understand this epithet to mean "the master or controller of the senses (*hṛṣīkāṇām indriyāṇām īśo niyantā*—so Ct). This interpretation is rendered by Gita Press (1969, vol. 3, p. 1855), Shastri (1959, vol. 3, p. 339), Raghunathan (1982, vol. 3, p. 340), and Dutt (1893, p. 1511).

"the primal person" *puruṣaḥ*: Literally, "the person, male, man." The commentators, notably Cg, offer multiple etymologies for this term. One of these, "he who lies *or* resides in the lotus *or* innermost space of the heart (*puri hṛdayaguhāyāṃ śeta iti puruṣah*—so Cg)," appears in the translation of Raghunathan (1982, vol. 3, p. 340), who renders, "the Lord That lies in the cave of the heart." Shastri (1959, vol. 3, p. 339) and Dutt (1893, p. 1511) appear to drop the term entirely, while Gita Press (1969, vol. 3, p. 1855) seems to understand it in the sense of *niyantā*, "the controller" (following Cg's and Ct's gloss on *hṛṣīkeśaḥ*; see above), translating, "the Inner Controller" (1969, vol. 3, p. 1855).

"the . . . wielder of the sword" *khaḍgadhṛk*: According to Ct, the reference is to the sword Nandaka, which is known as "knowledge" (*vidyākhyanandakakhaḍgadhṛk*). The proper noun Nandaka appears in Raghunathan (1982, vol. 3, p. 340) and Gita Press

(1969, vol. 3, p. 1855). Dutt (1893, p. 1511) and Shastri (1959, vol. 3, p. 339) understand that Viṣṇu bears a dagger.

"invincible" *ajitaḥ*: Ct glosses, "unconquered by sin and by enemies (*pāpmanāribhiś cājitaḥ*)." This interpretation appears in the translation of Dutt (1893, p. 1511), who renders, "unconquerable by sins."

"and you are Kṛṣṇa of immense strength" *kṛṣṇaś caiva bṛhadbalaḥ*: Roussel (1903, vol. 3, p. 389) and Pagani (1999, p. 1187) understand *bṛhadbalaḥ* as a separate proper name. Dutt (1893, p. 1511) and Shastri (1959, vol. 3, p. 339) render it separately as an adjective. Raghunathan (1982, vol. 3, p. 340) and Gita Press (1969, vol. 3, p. 1855) appear to translate as we do. Most commentators understand the term *bṛhadbalaḥ*, "of immense strength," to refer to the Lord's great power to sustain or uphold (*dharaṇasāmarthyam*—so Cg). Ct and Ck take it to mean that he has the ability to hold up the entire universe as if it were a ball to play with (*aśeṣabrahmāṇḍasya līlākandukavaddhāraṇakṣamaḥ*—so Ct). Cm, however, takes the epithet to be to the *Rāmāvatāra*, understanding *bala* in its sense of "army," and glossing, "he who has great armies of monkeys (*bṛhanti vānarabalāni yasyeti tathā*)." On the name Kṛṣṇa, see note to verse 25 below.

15. "You are the leader of the hosts" *senānīḥ*: Literally, "the army leader, general." Ck and Ct understand this to be a terrestrial reference, "lord of the king's army" (*rājasenāpati*—Ct) (Ck glosses only *rājā*, "king"). Cg understands the reference to be to the heavenly hosts (*devasenānirvāhakaḥ*). Cm continues to interpret in connection with the *Rāmāvatāra*, glossing, "the army leader is he who leads a great army of monkeys; it means a warrior. (*mahatīṃ vānarasenāṃ nayatīti senānīḥ. yodha ity arthaḥ.*)" Gita Press (1969, vol. 3, p. 1855) takes the term as an epithet of the god Kārttikeya, who, according to Śaivite mythology, was born to lead the armies of the gods. See, too, notes to *Bālakāṇḍa* 35 for the birth of Kārttikeya.

"You are the leader of all beings" *grāmaṇīḥ*: Literally, "the leader of the people *or* of the village." We follow Cm, who takes *grāma-* to mean "the class of all living things (*prāṇivargaḥ*)." Cg understands, "the guardian of the heavenly countries, etc. (*divyajanapadādipālakaḥ*)." Ct and Ck understand the term to mean "the counselor (*mantrī*)." Dutt (1893, p. 1511) follows them, rendering "minister," while Gita Press (1969, vol. 3, p. 1855) renders "village headman." Raghunathan (1982, vol. 3, p. 340) translates, "the leader of the world of men."

"You are intelligence, strength" *ca tvaṃ buddhiḥ sattvaṃ*: Literally, "and you [are] intelligence, strength." D10,11, and the texts and printed editions of Ct read instead *sarvaṃ tvaṃ buddhis tvam*, "you [are] all, you [are] intelligence." Ct understands *sarvam*, "all," to refer to "the world, the universe (*jagat*)."

"You are Upendra, Indra's younger brother, and Madhusūdana, slayer of the *asura* Madhu" *tvam upendro madhusūdanaḥ*: Literally, "you are little Indra; [you are] the slayer of Madhu." Since Viṣṇu in his *vāmanāvatāra*, or dwarf incarnation, is born as the son of Kaśyapa and Aditi, the parents of the vedic gods, he earned the epithet Upendra, "Lesser Indra *or* Indra's younger brother." This association is made explicit in the translation of Gita Press (1969, vol. 3, p. 1855). See 6.40.43; 6.49.1–2; 6.59.7; 6.79.4; 6.87.9–10; and notes.

16. "You are the author of Indra's deeds." *indrakarmā*: Literally, "one possessing Indra's work *or* deeds." The various commentators offer three explanations of this ambiguous term. Our translation is inspired by the interpretation of Cg and Ctś, who

gloss the compound as a *bahuvrīhi*, expressing an implied comparison: "whose acts are like those of Indra (*indrasyeva karma yasya saḥ*)." Ctś, however, extends this idea by indicating that, since Viṣṇu is the inner spirit of Indra, he is in reality the agent of Indra's feats, such as the slaying of the demon Vṛtra, etc. (*vṛtrādivadhasyendrāntar-yāmikartṛkatvāt*). Ck and Ct take the word *karma*, "work," in the sense of "creation (*sṛṣṭiḥ*)," lending the compound the sense "having Indra for his creation *or* whose creation is Indra (*indraḥ karma sṛṣṭir yasya sa indrakarmā*)." They support this interpretation with a quote to the effect that Prajāpati (whom they equate here with Viṣṇu) created Indra (*prajāpatir indram asṛjata*). Gita Press (1969, vol. 3, p. 1855) follows this interpretation, rendering, "You are the creator of Indra (in the form of Prajāpati)." Cm takes the term *indra-* in the sense of "lord" and thus reads it to mean "the work of the lord," that is, lordship, which Viṣṇu then possesses (*indrasyeśvarasya karmaiśvaryaṃ tadvān ity arthaḥ*).

"You are the lord of the great gods." *mahendraḥ*: Literally, "great Indra *or* great lord." This epithet is normally used of the god Indra, and the commentators offer various interpretations of its use in this verse. Ct understands, "the lord *or* controller of everything (*sakaleśitā*)." Cg glosses, "endowed with unsurpassed lordship (*niratiśayaiśvaryasaṃpannaḥ*)." Cm, whom we follow, takes the compound as a *tatpuruṣa* rather than a *karmadhāraya*, explaining, "the lord of the great ones, that is, the great gods. The meaning is: 'You are the Lord, the cause of the entire universe.' (*mahatām īśvarāṇām indraḥ. īśitā sakalajagatkāraṇam ity arthaḥ.*)"

"You are the lotus-naveled god" *padmanābhaḥ*: The epithet derives from the version of the creation myth in which a lotus rises from the navel of the sleeping Viṣṇu. From that lotus emerges Brahmā, who proceeds with the actual work of creation. Since Brahmā is the speaker in this passage, Cg notes, "the meaning is that 'you are my progenitor as well' (*mamāpi janaka ity arthaḥ*)."

"You are the destroyer of your enemies in battle." *raṇāntakṛt*: Literally, "the battle-end-maker." We follow the unanimous gloss of the commentators (*raṇe śatrūṇāṃ nāśakartā*—so Ct).

"The divine great seers call you fit for refuge and refuge itself." *śaraṇyaṃ śaraṇaṃ ca tvām āhur divyā maharṣayaḥ*: The terms *śaraṇyam*, "capable of offering refuge *or* protection," and *śaraṇam*, "refuge, protection," overlap somewhat in their semantic fields. Our translation more or less follows the distinction proposed by Ct, who glosses the former as "accessible as a means of refuge (*śaraṇatvena prāpyam*)" and the latter as "protection (*rakṣaṇam*)" itself. See 5.36.26–29; 6.13.4; 6.31.56; 6.47.43; 6.59.8; 6.81.14; and notes.

Cg makes a distinction between the great seers, whom he describes as "capable of the direct perception of supramundane truths (*alaukikatattvasākṣātkārasamarthāḥ*)," and the divine great seers, whom he understands to be Sanaka, etc. (*sanakādayaḥ*). (Sanaka is one of the four mind-born sons of Brahmā created to assist in the creation of the world—*BhāgP* 4.22.39). Ctś gives the same definition of the great seers but indicates that the divine seers are those among them who, like Vālmīki, etc., possess the special knowledge of the secrets of the *avatāras*, etc. (*tatrāpi divyā avatāra-rahasyādiviśeṣajñānavanto vālmīkiprabhṛtayaḥ*). As an alternative, he glosses, "the eternal sages (*nityasūrayaḥ*)."

17. "You are the great bull of a thousand horns and a hundred tongues that is the *veda* itself." *sahasraśṛṅgo vedātmā śatajihvo maharṣabhaḥ*: The commentators are unani-

mous in their understanding that the great thousand-horned, hundred-tongued bull is a metaphor for the *veda* itself, with its thousand *śākhās*, "branches *or* recensional traditions," and its many various ritual injunctions. (*sahasraśṛṅgaḥ sahasraśākhārūpaśṛṅgaḥ. śatajihvo 'nekavidhacodanarūpajihvaḥ*—so Cg.) Cm departs slightly from this interpretation, citing a well-known saying, "the paths of the *Sāmaveda* are a thousand (*sahasraṃ sāmavartmeti prasiddheḥ*)," and Kṛṣṇa's well-known statement in the *Bhagavadgītā* (10.22), "among the *vedas* I am the *Sāmaveda* (*vedānāṃ sāmavedo 'smi*)," to support his contention that the reference here is specifically to the *Sāmaveda*. A number of northern manuscripts, as well as the printed editions of Gorresio (6.102.17) and Lahore (6.98.18), tend to support this interpretation by reading *ṛksāmaśṛṅgaḥ*, "having the *ṛk* and the *sāma* [*vedas*] for its horns," for *sahasraśṛṅgaḥ*.

D10,11,M1, and the texts and printed editions of Ct, Ck, and Cr read *śataśīrṣaḥ*, "having one hundred heads," for the critical edition's *śatajihvaḥ*, "having one hundred tongues." Ct interprets this variant in the same way. Ck, quoted by Ct, understands this as "having the form of *śiśumāraprajāpati*," perhaps a reference to the constellation Śiśumāra, which is thought to be a form of Viṣṇu (see MW and Apte s.v.).

Cg does not take the term *ṛṣabha* in its sense of "bull" but rather derives it from a root √*ṛṣ*, in the sense of "to see *or* perceive." He thus takes it to mean "seer *or* witness," glossing, "the witness *or* seer of actions." He then interprets the compound *maharṣabhaḥ* as a *dvandva* to mean "[You are] great and a seer." (*ṛṣabhaḥ karmaṇām ālocayitā. ṛṣa ālocana iti dhātuḥ. mahāṃś cāsāv ṛṣabhaś ca maharṣabhaḥ. evaṃbhūto vedātmā tvam ity arthaḥ.*) Cm appears to interpret the term *ṛṣabha*, "bull," in its conventional metaphorical sense, "best *or* foremost [of anything]," glossing, "the most supreme (*śreṣṭhatamaḥ*)."

The interpretation that the multiple horns and tongues (or heads) refer, respectively, to the vedic schools and injunctions informs the translations of Raghunathan (1982, vol. 3, p. 340), Gita Press (1969, vol. 3, p. 1855), and Dutt (1893, p. 1511). Roussel (1903, vol. 3, p. 389), followed by Pagani (1999, p. 1187), understands, "(*le dieu*) *aux mille cornes . . . le* (*dieu*) *aux cent têtes*." These two translators understand that *maharṣabha*, "great bull," is a separate attribute. Shastri (1959, vol. 3, p, 339), taking the term *śṛṅga* in its sense of "peak," translates, "Thou art the Himalayas of a hundred [*sic*] peaks . . . the God of a Hundred Tongues, the great bull."

"the sacred utterance *vaṣaṭ*" *vaṣaṭkāraḥ*: This is the sacred exclamation uttered by the *adhvaryu* priest during the vedic sacrifice as the offering to a deity is poured into the *āhavanīya* fire.

"the sacred syllable *oṃ*" *oṃkāraḥ*: The *praṇava*, or sacred syllable *oṃ*, is believed to express the Absolute Brahman in the form of sound. Cg, citing a vedic passage to the effect that *oṃ* is Brahman expressed in a single syllable, glosses, "you are to be expressed by the *praṇava*." (*oṃkāraḥ praṇavavācyaḥ. om ity ekākṣaraṃ brahmeti śruteḥ.*)

"scorcher of your foes" *paraṃtapa*: Cg understands this common martial epithet here in the sense "[You are] supreme austerity (*utkṛṣṭatapaḥ*)." His text reads (as do Ś,Ñ,V,B,D1,2,4,8,9,12,13,T1,G3,M1,5) the compound as a nominative singular, *paraṃtapaḥ*, rather than as a vocative. Cg then understands the compound to mean "[you who are] to be propitiated by supreme austerity. (*paraṃtapa utkṛṣṭatapa ity arthaḥ. utkṛṣṭatapaḥ samārādhyeti yāvat.*)" D7,10,11, and the texts and printed editions of Ct read instead *parāt paraḥ*, "higher than the highest."

Following 17ab, D5–7,10,11,T,G,M1,3,5, and the texts and printed editions of the southern commentators insert a passage of two lines [3256*]: "You are the primal creator of the three worlds, the untrammeled lord.[1] Eldest of all,[2] you are the highest refuge of perfected beings and those striving for perfection.[3]"

[1]line 1 = 6cd above.

[2]"Eldest of all" *pūrvajaḥ*: Literally, "born previously." Ck and Ct cite the vedic utterance, "I am the first born of *ṛta* (cosmic order). (*aham asmi prathamajā ṛtasyeti śruteḥ*—see *Āraṇyasaṃhitā* 1.9a; *TaiBr* 2.8.8.1a; *Taittirīyāraṇyaka* 9.10.6a; *Taittirīyopaniṣad* 3.10.6a; and *Nirukta* 14.2a.) Cg understands the term to mean that Viṣṇu is prior to all those who are dependent on him [e.g., the *siddhas* and the *sādhyas*] and he comes into existence for their protection (*āśritāpekṣāyāḥ pūrvaṃ tadrakṣaṇāya janitaḥ*). Cm glosses, "existing even before creation (*sṛṣṭeḥ pūrvam api sthitaḥ*)."

[3]"the highest refuge of perfected beings and those striving for perfection" *siddhānām api sādhyānām āśrayaḥ*: The *sādhyas*, literally, "those who are to be accomplished or perfected," are a class of divine beings, and, as such, we have left the term untranslated in verse 7 above. In this verse, however, the text is playing on the different derivatives of the root $\sqrt{}$*sidh*, "to be perfected." Our translation follows the gloss of Ct, who understands the first term to mean "those who are ascended *or* who have ascended," and the second to mean "those who desire to ascend." He understands the term *āśrayaḥ* in the sense of "goal." (*siddhānām ārūḍhānāṃ sādhyānām ārurukṣūṇām āśrayaḥ prāpyaḥ*.) Cg understands the *siddhas* to be those who have obtained liberation and the *sādhyas* to be the eternal divinities of that name mentioned in the closing stanza of the *puruṣasūkta* (*ṚV* 10.90.16). Cm agrees with Cg's definition of the *siddhas* but understands the *sādhyas* to be "those to be worshiped *or* propitiated (*sādhyanta ārādhyanta iti sādhyānām*)." Cg then understands the term *sādhya* as an adjective that modifies the *siddhas*. He understands the term *āśraya* to mean "the one who dispenses enjoyments equally." (*siddhānāṃ muktānām. sādhyānāṃ yatra pūrve sādhyāḥ santi devā ity uktānāṃ nityānām āśrayaḥ sāmyabhogapradaḥ*.) Ck understands the *siddhas* to be those beings who have authority to attain Indra's realm and the *sādhyas* to be those who are liberated (*siddhā indrapadādhikārasiddhāḥ sādhyā muktāḥ*).

18. "No one knows" *na viduḥ*: Literally, "they do not know." Cg supplies, as subjects for the verb, "the *vedas* and the vedic scholars (*vedā vaidikāś ca*)." Cr adds the phrase "even those who know the highest truth (*tattvajñā apīti śeṣaḥ*)."

"People wonder, 'Who are you?' " *ko bhavān iti*: Literally, "Who are you?"

"You are manifest" *dṛśyase*: Literally, "You are seen." Since the most characteristic feature of the Supreme Spirit is its interiority and invisibility, several of the commentators feel it necessary to gloss the verb here. Ct glosses, " 'you are seen,' means you are heard of as being the innermost spirit (*dṛśyase 'ntaryāmitayā śrūyase*)." Cg provides a restricted subject, supplying "by *yogis* (*yogibhir iti śeṣaḥ*)."

"in . . . especially brahmans and cows" *brāhmaṇeṣu ca goṣu ca*: Literally, "in brahmans and in cows." This appears to be an example of the *gobalīvardhanyāya*, in which specific members of a group are mentioned along with that group for emphasis. In this case, it is appropriate because cows and brahmans are frequently held up as objects of special sanctity or reverence in the traditional literature. See 1.24.13, where Viśvāmitra urges Rāma to kill Tāṭakā "for the sake of cows and brahmans." Compare 1.25.5. See notes to 6.75.2.

"in . . . the forests" *vaneṣu*: D10,11, and the texts and printed editions of Ct read instead *nadīṣu*, "in the rivers."

19. "majestic" *śrīmān*: Cg sees the term here as referring to both royal fortune or majesty as well as Viṣṇu's association with his twin consorts, Śrī and Lakṣmī. He cites a line from the *Uttaranārāyaṇa*, a supplement to the well-known *puruṣasūkta*, to support this claim. (*śrīmān iti bhūpatitvasyāpy upalakṣaṇam. śrīś* [*hrīś*—so KK, VSP] *ca te lakṣmīś ca patnyāv ity uttaranārāyaṇokteḥ.*) See notes to verses 2 and 12 above.

"a thousand heads" *śataśīrṣaḥ*: Normally, the word *śata* refers to one hundred, but it is also frequently used in the sense of any large number or a myriad. We agree with Cg and Cm that this verse repeats the substance of the opening verse of the *puruṣasūkta* (*ṚV* 10.90), where the primal *puruṣa* is said explicitly to have "a thousand heads, a thousand eyes, and a thousand feet." Therefore, we follow Cg's suggestion that the word *śata* here is intended to express the number one thousand. (*puruṣasūktārtham āha. sahasrety atra śataśabdaḥ sahasravācakaḥ. sahasraśīrṣā puruṣaḥ sahasrākṣaḥ sahasrapād iti śruteḥ.*) Translations variously render "one hundred" or "one thousand."

"You support . . . the earth with all its mountains." *tvaṃ dhārayasi . . . vasudhāṃ ca saparvatām*: Cm sees this as a reference to Viṣṇu's incarnation as the primal tortoise who upheld the great Mount Mandara used by the gods and demons to churn the primal ocean (*saṃpratyādikūrmātmanā stauti*). On the story of the churning of the ocean, see 6.12.22; 6.40.29; 6.41.17; 6.53.23; 6.80.19; and notes. See, too, 1.44.14–27 and notes.

D9–11,M1, and the texts and printed editions of Ct read *pṛthivīṃ sarvaparvatān* for the critical text's *vasudhāṃ ca saparvatām*, yielding the sense "the earth and all the mountains."

20. "At the end of the world" *ante pṛthivyāḥ*: Literally, "At the end of the earth." Commentators differ in their interpretation of this phrase. Ct and Ck do not construe the words together but take the word *ante*, "at the end," separately to mean "at the end of the day." They understand that at the end of the [cosmic] day Viṣṇu appears in the waters that are above the earth. They then argue that what is expressed here is the Lord's inherent power to establish himself both above and below the world. (*tathānte 'harante pṛthivyā uparivartini salile tvam . . . dṛśyase. evaṃ ca pṛthivyā adha upari ca pratiṣṭhitasvaśaktis tvam ity uktam*—so Ct.) These commentators are evidently referring to the second half of the verse, where Viṣṇu is said to support the earth (cf. verse 19). Cg, whom we and virtually all the translators consulted follow, sees the reference to be to Viṣṇu's sleep during the recurrent periods of cosmic night that follow universal destruction. (*dainandinaprayalavṛttāntam āha. anta iti. pṛthivyā ante vināśe.*) Cr glosses *ante* as "in the midst (*madhye*)," understanding that the god manifests himself in the midst of the waters at the end [of the existence] of the earth (*pṛthivyā ante madhye salile*). This reading is reminiscent of the variant *antaḥ*, "within," found in many northern manuscripts and the printed editions of Gorresio (6.102.23) and Lahore (6.98.34).

"you manifest yourself resting on the great serpent" *dṛśyase tvaṃ mahoragaḥ*: Literally, "you appear as the great serpent." We follow Ck, Ct, and Cg in understanding the reference here to be to the fact that, during the periods of dissolution of the ordered universe, Viṣṇu rests on the cosmic serpent Śeṣa. Cg thus reads the term *mahoragaḥ*, "great serpent," as a *bahuvrīhi* compound, "he who has a great serpent, that is, he who lies on Śeṣa (*mahān uragaḥ śeṣo yasya saḥ śeṣaśāyī san*). Because generally no one would be around during periods of dissolution to observe Viṣṇu in his dormant state, Cg adds the phrase "seen by Mārkaṇḍeya, etc." referring to the well-known *Mahābhārata* (3.183–190) and purāṇic legend (*MatsyaP* 167) of the sage Mārkaṇḍeya, whose extreme spiritual advancement enables him to survive the cosmic dissolution and who, wandering across the featureless cosmic ocean, encounters Viṣṇu Nārāyaṇa. Cr appears to understand that Viṣṇu actually manifests himself as the great serpent Śeṣa (*mahoragaḥ śeṣas tvam eva dṛśyase*). Cm shares this view and, in his effort to point out the various allusions to specific *avatāras*, believes that the reference here is to Saṅkarṣaṇa, that is, Balarāma, the elder half brother of Kṛṣṇa, who is understood in many Vaiṣṇava texts to be an incarnation of Śeṣa (see, for example, *MBh* 16.5.12). (*idānīṃ saṅkarṣaṇātmanā stauti—anta iti. mahoragaḥ saṅkarṣaṇa ity arthaḥ.*) See 6.116.90, 3709*, lines 5, 6, n. 16; and notes to 6.4.9 and 6.107.6.

"You support the three worlds" *trīṃl lokān dhārayan*: Literally, "[you] supporting the three worlds." Since Cg understands the entire verse to refer to the period following the dissolution of the material universe, he suggests that we understand that Viṣṇu maintains the world inside him or in his belly (*kukṣau dhārayan*).

21. "I am your heart . . . It is I, Brahmā . . . who made the gods, who are the hairs on your limbs" *ahaṃ te hṛdayam . . . devā gātreṣu lomāni nirmitā brahmaṇā*: Literally, "I am your heart . . . [I] Brahmā made the gods, the hairs on the limbs." Brahmā is the speaker as well as the subject of this verse (see verse 11 above). Several translators render the phrase *devā gātreṣu lomāni nirmitā brahmaṇā* slightly differently, giving the line the sense: "The gods were created in such as way as to be the hairs on your body." (Compare Pagani 1999, p. 1187; Roussel 1903, vol. 3, p. 389; and Shastri 1959, vol. 3, p. 340.) Cr takes *brahmaṇā* in its sense of "the *veda*," and the participle *nirmitāḥ*, "constructed," in the sense of "said, explained." He glosses, "the meaning is 'the *vedas* state that they [the gods] are the hairs on your limbs' (*devā romāṇi . . . te gātreṣu brahmaṇā vedena nirmitāḥ kathitā ity arthaḥ*)." Ck, Ct, and Cs visualize the bodily hair of god [who is the world] as existing in the form of plants, trees, etc. (*oṣadhīvanaspaty-ādineti śeṣaḥ*).

Printed editions of Cg (VSP 6.120.25 and KK 6.120.23) show, as a variant, the genitive or ablative *brahmaṇaḥ*, "of *or* out of Brahmā," for the critical edition's instrumental *brahmaṇā*. This variant is not noted in the critical apparatus. Cg, the only commentator to remark on this reading, glosses, "of *or* from the Supreme Brahman (*parabrahmaṇaḥ*)." He explains, "those gods on your limbs are like the hairs and, like them, inseparable (*brahmaṇaḥ parabrahmaṇaḥ. te devā gātreṣu sthitā romāṇīva sthitās tadvad avinābhūtāḥ.*)" Raghunathan (1982, vol. 3, p. 341), the only translator to render this variant, translates, "the gods are as inseparable from the body of the Supreme Brahmā, O Lord, as is the hair on one's body."

22. "Your ritual practices are the ordinances of the *vedas*." *saṃskārās te 'bhavan vedāḥ*: Literally, "your *saṃskāras* were the *vedas*." The term *saṃskāra* has a broad range of meanings, and some, it seems to us, are more appropriate in the present context than others. Some translators, notably Shastri (1959, vol. 3, p. 340) and Gita Press (1969, vol. 3, p. 1856), understand the term in its sense of "latent mental impressions," but this seems inappropriate in the context. We understand the term in its sense "ritual practices," e.g., the life-cycle rituals that are enjoined in the vedic texts. This view is informed by the interpretation of Ct, Ck, Cr, Cm, Cs, and Cv, who understand the reference to be to those precepts of the *vedas* that instruct (or purify—so Cv) humanity by telling them what they should and should not do. (*saṃskārā bodhakāḥ. pravṛtti-*

nivṛttivyavasthāpakā iti yāvat—so Cm.) Cg cites a vedic passage in support of his contention that the *Ṛgveda* is Viṣṇu's exhalation. (*vedāḥ saṃskārā niḥśvasitabhūtā ity arthaḥ. tasya ha vā etasya mahato bhūtasya niḥśvasitam etad yad ṛgveda ity ādiśruteḥ.*)

"Without you, there is nothing" *na tad asti tvayā vinā*: Literally, "without you, that is not." Cm remarks, "Why go on? Everything that exists, whether sentient or insentient, consists of you alone. (*kiṃ bahunā? sarvaṃ cidacidvastujātaṃ tvadātmakam evety arthaḥ.*)"

23. "your steadfastness, the earth" *sthairyaṃ te vasudhātalam*: Literally, "your stability, the surface of the bearer of wealth." Cf. notes to 6.104.15.

"Soma, your gentleness" *prasādas te somaḥ*: Literally, "Soma *or* the moon is your graciousness." Cf. note to 6.102.35.

"O bearer of the Śrīvatsa mark" *śrīvatsalakṣaṇa*: The Śrīvatsa mark is an auspicious, white, flower-shaped curl on Viṣṇu's chest. Ś1,Ñ2,V1,3,B2,3,D2,3,9–11,T2,3,G2,3,M3, and the texts and printed editions of the southern commentators read instead the nominative singular, *śrīvatsalakṣaṇaḥ*, for the critical edition's vocative, lending the sense "You are the one who bears the Śrīvatsa."

24. The verse is an unmistakable reference to the *vāmanāvatāra*, or dwarf incarnation, of Viṣṇu. The story is widely told in the Vaiṣṇava canon. See 6.40.43; 6.47.119; 6.49.1–2; 6.53.25; 6.59.7; and notes. See, too, 1.28.2 and note.

"you spanned the three worlds with as many strides" *tvayā lokās trayaḥ krāntāḥ . . . vikramais tribhiḥ*: Literally, "by you the three worlds were crossed with three strides."

"After confining" *baddhvā*: Literally, "having bound." According to most standard versions of the story, the overly generous demon king, deprived of his lordship of the three worlds by Viṣṇu's feat, must be bound and confined to the underworld (see, for example, *VāyuP* 2.36.74–86).

"the great *asura*" *mahāsuram*: D9–11 and the texts and printed editions of Ct read instead the adjective *sudāruṇam*, "very dreadful, very fearsome."

25. "You are Kṛṣṇa" *kṛṣṇaḥ*: Literally, "Kṛṣṇa." The commentators generally agree that this term should be taken in its adjectival sense of "black, blue-black, *or* of a dark color (*kṛṣṇavarṇaḥ*)." This is probably because they wish to avoid the apparent anachronism of mentioning an *avatāra* who will not appear until the next cosmic age. Nonetheless, in the context of this thoroughgoing Vaiṣṇava *stotra*, like all translators consulted, with the exception of Raghunathan, we believe that the reference is probably to the name of the other major *avatāra* of Viṣṇu. Raghunathan (1982, vol. 3, p. 341), reading the adjective with *devaḥ*, "the god," renders, "the Lord that has assumed a dark form." See note to verse 14 above.

"You are Prajāpati, the lord of creatures." *prajāpatiḥ*: Literally, "Prajāpati." The epithet is most frequently used of the speaker, Brahmā himself. See note to verse 6 above.

26. "to heaven" *divam*: The commentators differ slightly as to the locus of heaven. Ck and Ct believe that the gods are asking Rāma to return to the Brahmaloka, which is known as the highest vault of heaven, after spending some time pleasurably as king (*mahārājyena kiṃcitkālaṃ prahṛṣṭaḥ san divaṃ paranākākhyaṃ brahmalokam ākrama prāpnuhi*—Ct). Cr understands Rāma's destination to be his eternal playground, Ayodhyā (*nityakrīḍāsthalam ayodhyām ity arthaḥ*).

27. "strength and might" *balavīryam*: The two terms are closely synonymous. Ś,B1,D1–3,8–12, and the texts and printed editions of Ct read the vocative *deva*, "O god," for *bala-*, "strength." This yields the sense "Your strength, O god."

"nor has your valor" *amoghas te parākramaḥ*: Literally, "your valor is not in vain." B3,D7,10,11,G2,M1,5, and the texts and printed editions of Ct read instead the plural *na te moghāḥ parākramāḥ*, "nor have your feats of valor been in vain."

"fail of their purpose" *amoghāḥ*: Literally, "[be] in vain."

Following 27ab, Ñ,V,B,D1–7,9–11,13,S insert a passage of one line [3261*]: "A vision of you, Rāma, is not in vain, nor is your praise."

28. "You are the ancient god and Supreme Spirit . . . to you." *tvāṃ devam . . . purāṇaṃ puruṣottam*: Literally, "to you, the ancient god and supreme person."

"will never fail in any way" *nāsti teṣāṃ parābhavaḥ*: Literally, "of them there is no defeat *or* humiliation."

Following 28ab, D3,5–7,9–11,S insert a passage of two lines [3264* and 3265*]: "They will always attain what they desire in this world and the next.[3264*] [Those are the men who recite[1]] this divine and ancient history, this hymn of praise composed by the seers.[3265*]"

[1]"Those are the men who recite" *ye narāḥ kīrtayiṣyanti*: The phrase is taken from 28c, where we have translated, "those men who praise." However, in the present context, which supplies a direct object, the meaning changes to "they will recite."

Sarga 106

Before verse 1, Ś,B1,D1–3,8,9 (preceded by 3268*),12 insert; while Ñ,V,B2–4 insert line 2 after 1ab; and D5–7,10,11,S insert following verse 9, a passage of two lines [3267*]: "Hearing this, Rāma, foremost among the eloquent, rejoiced at heart. Then that righteous man was absorbed in thought for a while, his eyes clouded with joy." Virtually all manuscripts admit this verse in whole or in part, although in different locations. Its omission from the critical text is questionable.

Following 3267*, D1–3,8,12,N (except V3) continue (either following 3267* or verse 1), while D5–7,10,11,S insert after verse 1 (D9 before 3267*), a passage of two lines [3268*]: "Then, taking Janaka's daughter Vaidehī with him, Agni, the bearer of oblations, in bodily form,[1] swiftly rose up, scattering the pyre."

[1]"in bodily form" *mūrtimān*: We follow Cg, who glosses, "possessed of a human body (*manuṣyavigrahavān*)."

1. "Agni, the shining god of fire" *vibhāvasuḥ*: Literally, "the one whose wealth is light *or* splendor."

"holding Vaidehī at his side" *aṅkenādāya vaidehīm*: Literally, "having taken Vaidehī by [his] hip, flank, *or* lap." Most English translations consulted take the word *aṅka* in its sense of "lap," although this seems to us improbable in light of the verb *utpapāta*, "he leapt *or* stood up." We understand with Cs that the reference is to Agni's right hip or flank, which would be the appropriate place for a male to hold a woman who stands in the relation of a daughter or daughter-in-law to him. (*aṅkena svadakṣiṇotsaṅgenādāya tasya putrībhāgatvāt. yathoktaṃ bhāgo hi dakṣo duhituḥ snuṣāyā iti.*) Cs argues that, since Sītā takes her life, as it were, from Agni, after having fallen into him, it is appropriate for him to regard her as his daughter. Otherwise, it would be inappropriate to say, "on the lap." (*agnipātānantaraṃ jīvane 'gnijātatvaprāptyā tatputrītvasyocitatvāt. anyathāṅkeneti vyartham.*) Other translators apparently share our concern. Gita Press (1969, vol. 3, p. 1857) translates, "taking... in his arms," while both Roussel (1903, vol. 3, p. 391) and Pagani (1999, p. 1188) understand that Agni is holding Sītā "*sur son sein.*"

Following verse 1, D5–7,9(before 3267*)–11,S insert a passage of two lines [3268*], which northern manuscripts insert before verse 1. See above.

2–3. "and clad in a red garment" *raktāmbaradharām*: Sītā, having put off the soiled yellow garments that she wore during her captivity, is now wearing the new clothing given to her at 6.102.13–14. The color of the clothing sends an ambiguous message, since red would suggest both a wedding dress and the draping of a sacrificial victim (6.102.13–14 and notes). Cf. 6.67.5 and note.

"unsinged" *akliṣṭa-*: Literally, "undamaged, unsullied." The idea is, as Cr indicates, that Sītā's adornments have not been damaged even through their contact with the fire (*na kliṣṭāny agnisaṃbandhenāpi vibādhitāni*).

"Her mind was calm" *manasvinīm*: Literally, "high minded *or* proud." We follow Cg, who glosses, "having a calm mind (*prasannamanaskām*)." Ś,V3,D1–3,8–12, and the texts and printed editions of Ct read instead *aninditām*, "blameless."

"she looked unchanged" *tathārūpām*: Literally, "having such an appearance." The idea, as Cg points out, is that Sītā looks exactly as she did the moment she entered the fire, that is, she has suffered no ill effects from its flames (*praveśakālikarūpavatīm*). Cm supports this view.

"holding Vaidehī at his side" *vaidehīm aṅke kṛtvā*: See note to verse 1 above.

"Agni, the shining god of fire" *vibhāvasuḥ*: Literally, "the one whose wealth is light *or* splendor."

4. "the witness of all the world" *sākṣī lokasya*: As Ck and Ct note, Agni, in the form of Vaiśvānara, who resides within the bodies of all living beings, is the witness of all people's actions, both virtuous and sinful, performed mentally, verbally, or physically. (*manovākkāyair lokakṛtapuṇyapāpakarmaṇaḥ sākṣī sākṣād draṣṭā. sarvadehāntarvaiśvānarātmanā nityapratiṣṭhitatvād iti bhāvaḥ.*)

"Here is your Vaidehī" *eṣā te... vaidehī*: Ct, Ck, Cg, and Cs see this phrase as an allusion to the legendary substitution of an illusory Sītā (*māyāsītā* or *chāyāsītā*) for the real one, who is thought to have entered the fire at the time of her abduction by Rāvaṇa. Cs adds the detail that the real Sītā has been living on Mount Kailāsa since the abduction. These commentators thus put a special emphasis on the enclitic pronoun *te*, "your," which they see as referring to Rāma's real wife and not her simulacrum. See 6.102.5; 6.104.27; and notes.

"She has committed no sin." *pāpam asyā na vidyate*: Literally, "Of her there is no sin." Since he subscribes to the *māyāsītā* theory, Ct notes that the real Sītā has no taint of sin even to the extent of having been touched by Rāvaṇa (*pāpaṃ rāvaṇasparśarūpam api*).

5. "of... high moral character" *vṛttaśauṇḍīrā*: Literally, "elevated in *or* by conduct." The compound shows a fair amount of variation on the word *śauṇḍīrā*, "proud, haughty, elevated." The printed editions of Ct (GPP 6.118.6; NSP 6.118.6; and Gita Press 6.118.6) read instead the accusative variant *vṛttaśauṭīryam*, "proud of [his] good conduct *or* heroic in conduct." In this reading, the term agrees with *tvām* and refers to

Rāma. The printed editions of Cg (VSP 6.121.7 and KK 6.121.7) read instead the vocative *vṛttaśauṇḍīra*, "O one of high moral character," which then modifies Rāma.

"She... has never betrayed you" *na tvām aticacāra ha*: Literally, "she has not been unfaithful to you." D10,11, and the texts and printed editions of Ct read instead *na tvām atyacarac chubhā*, "she, the auspicious *or* lovely one, has not been unfaithful to you."

6. "from the deserted forest" *nirjanād vanāt*: D10,11, and the texts and printed editions of Ct read instead *nirjane satī*, "she being in a deserted [place *or* spot]."

Ś,D8,12 omit verses 7–13. Their inclusion in the critical text is questionable. See note to 6.104.15; cf. 3261* (following 6.105.27ab).

7. "by hordes of hideous *rākṣasa* women, dreadful to behold" *rākṣasīsaṃghair vikṛtair ghoradarśanaiḥ*: D1–4,9–11, and the texts and printed editions of Ct read instead *rākṣasībhiś ca ghorābhir ghorabuddhibhiḥ*, "by terrible *rākṣasa* women, with terrible intentions *or* thoughts."

9. "Rāghava" *rāghava*: D1–4,9–11,13, and the texts and printed editions of Ct read instead *maithilīm*, which lends the first line the sense "you must take Maithilī back."

"there is nothing further to be said" *na kiṃcid abhidhātavyam*: Literally, "nothing whatever is to be said." B1,D9–11, and the texts and printed editions of Ct read instead the feminine *abhidhātavyā*, yielding the sense "she is not to be discussed *or* criticized [further]."

Following verse 9, D5–7,10,11,S insert a passage of two lines [3267*]. See the note preceding the notes to verse 1.

10. "firm in his valor" *dṛḍhavikramaḥ*: B1,D1–3,9–11, and the texts and printed editions of Ct read instead *uruvikramaḥ*, "of immense valor." Inexplicably, Pagani (1999, p. 1188) appears to translate this as "*aux longs bras*."

11. "Sītā needed to be proven innocent" *sītā pāvanam arhati*: Literally, "Sītā merits purification." D5,T1,G1,M3, and the texts and printed editions of Cg and Cm read instead *na sītā pāpam arhati*, "Sītā does not deserve [the imputation of] sin." Raghunathan (1982, vol. 3, p. 342), alone among the translators consulted, renders, "Sita is not to be blamed in the least."

"before the three worlds" *triṣu lokeṣu*: B1,3,D1–3,9–11, and the texts and printed editions of Ct read instead *cāpi lokeṣu*, "and before the people." Cr glosses this reading as "in the midst of the people, the *rākṣasas*, and the rest (*rākṣasādijanamadhyeṣu*)."

12. "surely" *khalu*: B1,D1–3,9–11, and the texts and printed editions of Ct read instead *bata*, a particle that can express regret or censure. This value of the particle seems to have been rendered only in the translation of Pagani (1999, p. 1189), who offers, "*Malheur!*"

"the virtuous would have said of me" *vakṣyanti māṃ santaḥ*: Literally, "the virtuous will say about me." B1,D1,2,7,10,11,M1, and the texts and printed editions of Ct and Cr read instead *vakṣyati māṃ lokaḥ*, "people will say of me."

13. "devoted" *bhaktām*: D7,10,11, and the texts and printed editions of Ct and Cr read instead *sītām*, "Sītā."

14. "I... simply stood by" *upekṣe*: Literally, "I ignore *or* I overlook." Compare 6.105.5 and note. D5,10,11, and the texts and printed editions of Ct omit verse 14 (GPP unnumbered, in brackets, between 6.118.16 and 17).

15. "her own blazing energy" *svena tejasā*: Ck and Ct gloss, "by [her] wifely devotion (*pātivratyena*)." See 6.104.24 and note.

17. "auspicious" *śubhā*: B3,D9–11, and the texts and printed editions of Ct read instead *satī*, which, given the context, probably should be read as "virtuous *or* good woman." Cf. Roussel (1903, vol. 3, p. 392), Shastri (1959, vol. 3, p. 342), and Gita Press (1969, vol. 3, p. 1858).

"This . . . woman could never have ruled over" *neyam arhati caiśvaryam*: Literally, "she was incapable of governance." Cg understands the term *aiśvaryam*, literally, "lordship," as an elliptical allusion to the state of having Rāvaṇa as one's lord or husband. He glosses, "she could never have had Rāvaṇa for her lord but could only have me (*rāvaṇaiśvaryaṃ neyam arhati kiṃtu mamaiśvaryam arhatīty arthaḥ*)." D10,11, and the texts and printed editions of Ck and Ct read *vaiklavyam*, "timidity, weakness," for *caiśvaryam*, "and lordship." Ct and Ck gloss, "the oppression of cowardice (*kātarya-pīḍām*)." Cr glosses, "she did not deserve suffering (*vaiklavyaṃ kleśaṃ nārhati*)."

19. "of you . . . respected throughout the worlds" *vaḥ . . . lokamānyānām*: Ś,B2,D2,3, 8–12, and the texts and printed editions of Ct read instead *vaḥ . . . lokanāthānām*, "of [you] lords *or* protectors of the worlds."

20. "When he had uttered these words" *itīdam uktvā vacanam*: Literally, "having spoken that speech." Ś,Ñ,V1,2,B,D1–4,8–11,13,M2, and the texts and printed editions of Ct read instead *ity evam uktvā vijayī*, "having spoken in this fashion, the victorious [Rāma] . . ."

"mighty" *mahābalaḥ*: Literally, "of immense power." Ś,B1,D1,3,8–12,T2,3, and the texts and printed editions of Ct read instead *mahāyaśāḥ*, "glorious, renowned, of great fame."

"by his mighty companions" *mahābalaiḥ*: Literally, "by those immensely powerful ones." Ś,Ñ,V1,2,B,D1–4,8–13,T2,3,G2,M1, and the texts and printed editions of Ct read instead the nominative singular *mahābalaḥ*, "the immensely powerful one," which then becomes a modifier of Rāma.

"Then Rāghava experienced the happiness he so richly deserved." *sukhaṃ sukhārho 'nubabhūva rāghavaḥ*: Literally, "Rāghava, deserving of happiness, experienced happiness."

The meter is *vaṃśasthavila*.

Sarga 107

1. "Maheśvara" *maheśvaraḥ*: Literally, "the great lord." This epithet is most characteristic of Śiva, although it could conceivably apply to any of the great divinities. Since Brahmā appeared to be the spokesman for the gods in the previous *sarga*, the epithet is possibly meant to apply to him. This appears to be the understanding of the majority of northern manuscripts and the printed edition of Gorresio (6.104.1), which read instead *pitāmahaḥ*, "the grandfather," i.e., Brahmā. However, since none of the southern commentators feels called upon to gloss "Brahmā," and since the only other specific reference to the deity in question, *mahādeva-* (at verse 9 below), is also most commonly associated with Śiva, we agree with Cg and Ck, who gloss *rudraḥ*, "Rudra," that the speaker here is probably Śiva. Cf. note to 6.113.8–11.

2. "Foremost of weapon bearers" *śastrabhṛtāṃ vara*: Ñ,V,B2,4,D4,5,7,10,11,13, and the texts and printed editions of Ct and Cr read instead *dharmabhṛtāṃ vara*, "O foremost of those who uphold righteousness."

3. "the vast...darkness...that had engulfed the entire world" *sarvasya lokasya pravṛddham...tamaḥ*: Literally, "the expanded *or* extended darkness of the whole world." Ck, Cr, and Ct gloss *duḥkham*, "pain, misery," for *tamaḥ*, "darkness."

"in the form of the fear of Rāvaṇa" *rāvaṇajaṃ bhayam*: Literally, "[that was the] fear generated by Rāvaṇa."

4–6. "You must now console...see...You must assume...reward...Then...you must establish...At last, once you have offered...and attained...you should give away...and ascend" *āśvāsya...dṛṣṭvā...prāpya...nandayitvā...sthāpayitvā ... iṣṭvā... prāpya...dattvā...gantum arhasi*: Literally, "having consoled, having seen, having attained, having gratified, having established, having sacrificed, having attained, having given, you should go." The entire passage of three verses is a single extended complex sentence, consisting of a string of subordinate clauses governed by eight gerunds that are only resolved in the final *pāda* with the finite construction *gantum arhasi*, "you should go." We have broken the series up into smaller syntactic units and have supplied transitions for the sake of readability. The commentators see this as a recapitulation of Viṣṇu's promise in the *Bālakāṇḍa* (467*, following 1.15.20 = GPP 1.15.29–30). Cf. 1.1.74–76.

"despondent Bharata" *bharataṃ dīnam*: Cs notes that Bharata is despondent over the death of his father and his separation from Rāma (*pitṛnāśena tvadadarśanena ca*).

"illustrious Kausalyā...Kaikeyī" *kausalyāṃ ca yaśasvinīm / kaikeyīṃ ca*: Despite the syntax, which places the adjective in the same *pāda* as Kausalyā, Cg believes that the adjective *yaśasvinīm*, "illustrious," is meant to apply to Kaikeyī, as it is she who is the root cause of the destruction of Rāvaṇa (*yaśasvinīm iti kaikeyīviśeṣaṇaṃ tanmūlatvād rāvaṇavadhasya tasyā yaśasvitvam*). Cg's interpretation, which might appear forced in this context, is, no doubt, inspired by 6.109.19 and 6.115.39. This reading is reflected only in the translation of Raghunathan (1982, vol. 3, p. 342), who renders, "you should bring comfort...to Kausalyā and to Kaikeyī of the great renown." Compare 6.109.17–19; 6.115.39; and notes.

"the Horse Sacrifice" *turagamedhena*: Daśaratha performs an *aśvamedha* in the *Bālakāṇḍa* (1.12–13 and notes), and Rāma performs his *aśvamedha* at 7.83. See S. Goldman 2004. See, too, 6.116.81 and notes.

"the triple heaven" *tridivam*: Commentators differ as to the exact location intended here. Ct and Ck understand the reference to be to the world of Brahmā, which is the third heaven with respect to the two lower realms of earth and atmosphere (*bhūsvaḥpadāpekṣayā tṛtīyaṃ divaṃ brahmalokam*). This interpretation is in keeping with the description at 1.1.76. Cr identifies it as Sāketa, the Vaiṣṇava name for the eternal heavenly city of Ayodhyā. Cs believes it is the shining triple world known as Vaikuṇṭha, which is the abode of Ananta [Śeṣa] in Śvetadvīpa (*śvetadvīpānantāsanavaikuṇṭhākhyaprakāśamānalokatrayam*). Cf. 6.116.90, 3709*, lines 5–6, n. 16. See notes to 6.5.9 and 6.105.20.

7. "here...is" *eṣaḥ*: Literally, "this [one is]." The commentators are virtually unanimous in their opinion that the pronoun here is deictic in that, since Daśaratha will have taken on a divine body, Rāma would not be able to recognize him immediately. Therefore Śiva must point him out with his finger (*eṣa iti puraḥsthasyāpi devadehaparigraheṇājñāyamānatayāṅgulyā nirdeśaḥ*—so Ct). Compare note to verse 30 below.

"your illustrious elder" *gurus tava mahāyaśāḥ*: Cs differs from the other commentators in arguing that we should read the sequence *gurus* + *tava*, "your elder," together as the *bahuvrīhi* compound *gurustava*, "O you who praise [*stava*] your elders [*guru*-]," which is then a vocative epithet of Rāma. As an alternative, he proposes reading all three words together as a *bahuvrīhi* compound with the sense "who is greatly illustrious through the praise of his *gurus*," which would be an epithet of Daśaratha.

8. "Saved by you" *tvayā . . . tāritaḥ*: Literally, "made to cross over by you." It may be that the reference here is to Daśaratha's having been saved from uttering a falsehood by Rāma's willing acceptance of banishment. Gorresio (1858, vol. 10, p. 314), in a note, offers this as one possible explanation. His second is that Rāma would have performed the pious acts and funerary rites obligatory upon the son of a deceased person. Cr, the only commentator to remark on the term *tāritaḥ* here, understands that Daśaratha, who, through his separation from his son Rāma, had gone merely to the world of Indra, has now ascended to the blessed realm of Sāketa, which is characterized by perfect lordship (*putreṇa tvayā tvadviyogena tāritaḥ prasthāpita indralokaṃ sakalaiśvaryaviśiṣṭa sāketaṃ gataḥ*). See note to verse 16 below.

"the majestic king" *śrīmān*: Literally, "the majestic one."

9. "the great god Śiva" *mahādeva*-: Literally, "the great god." See verse 1 above and notes.

"Kākutstha" *kākutsthaḥ*: V3,D7,10,11,G2,M1, and the texts and printed editions of Ct read instead *rāghavaḥ*, "Rāghava."

"who stood atop his flying chariot" *vimānaśikharasthasya*: Literally, "who stood on the top *or* summit of his flying chariot." See 6.115.30 and note.

10. "his own innate splendor" *svayā lakṣmyā*: Literally, "with his own splendor."

13. "I care nothing for heaven and the esteem of the divine seers" *na me svargo bahumataḥ saṃmānaś ca surarṣibhiḥ*: Literally, "heaven is not esteemed by [of] me [nor is] honor by the god-seers." Cg takes the term *surarṣi* as a synonym for the more common term *devarṣi*, "divine seer," and we believe he is probably correct in this. The compound can also be taken as a *dvandva* in the sense of "by the gods and seers." Of the two translators consulted who share this reading, only Gorresio (1858, vol. 10, p. 240), who reads *saṃvāso vā surarṣibhiḥ*, "living together with the *surarṣis*," for *saṃmānaś ca surarṣibhiḥ*, translates in this way, rendering, "*il coabitar coi Devi e coi Risci*." D10,11,G2, and the texts and printed editions of Ct read *samānaś ca surarṣabhaiḥ* for *saṃmānaś ca surarṣibhiḥ*, which gives the line the meaning "Heaven, which is honored by the bulls among the gods, is not esteemed by me."

Following verse 13, M3 and the texts and printed edition of Cg insert a passage of two lines [3285*, lines 3–4]: "Seeing you today, when you have slain your enemy, fulfilled your intention,[1] and completed your sojourn in the wilderness, I have experienced supreme delight."

[1]"fulfilled your intention" *saṃpūrṇamānasam*: Literally, "one by whom one's mental [desire] has been fulfilled."

14. "regarding your banishment" *tava pravrājanārthāni*: Literally, "having your banishment for their object."

"were still rankling in my heart" *sthitāni hṛdraye mama*: Literally, "stand *or* remain in my heart." Cg notes that, in so stating, Daśaratha is suggesting that he has been sorely grieved by the events alluded to (*tena duḥkhito 'bhūvam iti sūcitam*).

"most eloquent of men" *vadatāṃ vara*: Literally, "best among speakers."

15. "safe and sound" *kuśalinam*: Literally, "well, healthy, prosperous."

"like the sun, maker of day, emerging from a dense fog" *nīhārād iva bhāskaraḥ*: Literally, "like the day-maker from fog."

16. "a great man" *mahātmanā*: Literally, "a great one *or* a great-souled one."

"just as a righteous brahman was saved by Aṣṭāvakra" *aṣṭāvakreṇa dharmātmā tārito brāhmaṇo yathā*: As Cg, Cm, and Cs point out, the allusion here is to the *Mahābhārata*'s tale of how the deformed sage Aṣṭāvakra saved his father, Kahola, who had been drowned as punishment for losing a debate. The story is related at *Mahābhārata* 3.134. Other commentators identify this merely as "a purāṇic tale." D7,10,11, and the printed texts of Ct read *kaholaḥ*, "Kahola," for the second occurrence of *tāritaḥ* in *pāda* d. Gorresio (1858, vol. 10, pp. 314–15) notes the story. On the notion that Daśaratha has been saved by the appearance of Rāma, compare notes to 6.115.39, where Ck, Cm, and Ct understand Daśaratha's salvation to have been achieved by the obduracy of Kaikeyī, which is the root cause of the destruction of Rāvaṇa, etc.

17. "my gentle son" *saumya*: Literally, "O gentle one."

"I now realize . . . that you are the Supreme Spirit, who was enjoined" *idānīṃ vijānāmi yathā . . . vihitaṃ puruṣottamam*: Literally, "I know Puruṣottama [to have been] enjoined." Given the context in which this verse is uttered, there is little question but that Cg is correct in understanding the term *puruṣottamam* (v.l. *puruṣottama*) here to be the Vaiṣṇava epithet for the Lord as the Supreme Spirit. He notes, "the use of the term *puruṣottama* expresses the idea, 'You are none other than Viṣṇu, who has taken on a human form in order to slay Rāvaṇa' (*puruṣottamety anena bhavān viṣṇur eva rāvaṇavadhārthaṃ manuṣyatvaṃ gata ity ucyate*)." Despite this, several translators render the epithet in its nontheological sense, "best of men." Printed editions of the text of Cg and Cm (VSP 6.122.18 and KK 6.122.18)—unnoted by the critical edition (p. 788)—read the vocative *puruṣottama* for the critical edition's accusative *puruṣottamam*. Given this reading, the verse has to be understood to mean "O Puruṣottama, I now realize that all this was ordained." Cg fleshes out the ellipsis by supplying the phrase "these events such as the obstruction to your consecration, etc. (*idam abhiṣekavighnādikaṃ karma*)." This idea is reflected in the translation of Raghunathan (1982, vol. 3, p. 344), who renders, "Only now, I know . . . how all this was contrived . . . O best of men." D10,11, and the texts and printed editions of Ct and Ck read *pihitam*, "concealed, covered, disguised," for *vihitam*, "enjoined." Ct and Ck gloss, "The Supreme Spirit was concealed. One must add the phrase 'in the form of my son.' (*pihitaṃ puruṣottamam ācchāditam. matputratveneti śeṣaḥ.*)" Cr adds the accusative pronoun *tvām*, "you," and glosses *pihitam* with *prāptam*, "attained, reached," which we must understand here as "made to come" (*puruṣottamaṃ tvāṃ yathā pihitaṃ prāptam*).

18. "will have achieved her most cherished desire" *siddhārthā*: Literally, "she whose end *or* goal has been achieved."

19. "will the people have achieved their most cherished desire" *siddhārthāḥ . . . narāḥ*: Literally, "men whose end *or* goal has been achieved."

"dripping with water" *jalārdram*: Literally, "moist *or* wet with water." The reference is to the water used in the ritual of royal consecration, which gives that ceremony, the *abhiṣeka*, literally, "the sprinkling," its name. Ś,Ñ2,V,B2–4,D8,10–12, and the texts and printed editions of Ct read instead *rājye caiva*, "in the kingship."

21. "and wise Lakṣmaṇa" *lakṣmaṇena ca dhīmatā*: Ś,Ñ,V1,2,B2,4,D4,8,10,11, the texts and printed editions of Ct, and the printed editions of Gorresio (6.104.27) read instead *matprītyā lakṣmaṇena ca*, "and at my pleasure, with Lakṣmaṇa." This has been more or less correctly rendered by Gorresio (1858, vol. 10, p. 241) as "*per mio amore*," but preferably, we feel, by Gita Press (1969, vol. 3, p. 1861) as "for my pleasure." Roussel (1903, vol. 3, p. 394) incorrectly reads *matprītyā* adjectivally in the sense of "dear," yielding "*avec ma chère Sītā*." In this he has been followed by Shastri (1959, vol. 3, p. 343) and Pagani (1999, p. 1190). Dutt (1893, p. 1516) ignores the phrase entirely.

22. "and have thus fulfilled your vow" *pratijñā saphalā kṛtā*: Literally, "the promise has been made fruitful." Ś1,Ñ2,V1,2,B3,D8,10,11, and the texts and printed editions of Ct read the slight variant *pratijñā pūritā tvayā*, "the vow has been fulfilled by you." The phrase is slightly ambiguous, as it could refer to a vow of Rāma's to carry out his father's order of banishment or to destroy Rāvaṇa. On the other hand, it could also refer to Rāma's having brought about the fulfillment of Daśaratha's promise to Kaikeyī to grant her wishes. Among the commentators, only Cr addresses this question directly, claiming that, in killing Rāvaṇa and thereby satisfying the gods, Rāma has fulfilled his vows (*rāvaṇaṃ hatvā devatāḥ paritoṣitā ata eva pratijñāḥ pūritāḥ*). Among the translations consulted, all, with the exception of Gita Press, understand the reference to be to Rāma's own vow. Raghunathan (1982, vol. 3, p. 344) makes it clear that he believes the reference is to Rāma's vow to spend fourteen years in the forest. He translates: "Having stayed the full term of fourteen years in the forest, you have fulfilled your vow." Dutt (1893, p. 1516) understands similarly. Other translators who see the vow as Rāma's are less clear about what they take that vow to be. Only Gita Press (1969, vol. 3, p. 1861) understands the reference to be to Rāma's dedication to making his father's vow truthful, translating, "my pledge (given to Kaikeyī) has (also) been implemented by you."

23. "You have performed a praiseworthy feat and gained renown" *kṛtaṃ karma yaśaḥ ślāghyaṃ prāptam*: Despite the word order, we agree with Cr in reading the adjective *ślāghyam*, "praiseworthy," to modify only the noun *karma*, "feat, deed." Other commentators are silent on this point, while several translators read the adjective in two different senses with the word *karma*, "feat," and the word *yaśaḥ*, "glory."

25. "may . . . not be visited upon" *na spṛśet*: Literally, "may it not touch."

"I renounce both you and your son" *saputrāṃ tvāṃ tyajāmi*: Daśaratha renounces Kaikeyī and Bharata at *Ayodhyākāṇḍa* 12. See 2.12.11 and note.

26. "he now spoke to him" *punaḥ . . . uvāca*: Literally, "he spoke again."

27. 6.107.27ab = 6.107.32cd.

"In devotedly serving Rāma as well as Sītā Vaidehī, you" *rāmaṃ śuśrūṣatā bhaktyā vaidehyā saha sītayā . . . te*: Literally, "by you who, obeying Rāma with devotion together with Sītā Vaidehī." The syntax of the verse is slightly ambiguous since the phrase *vaidehyā saha sītayā*," together with Sītā Vaidehī," can be read as construing either with *rāmaṃ*, "Rāma," or with *te*, "by you (lit., of you, Lakṣmaṇa)," to indicate either that Lakṣmaṇa served both Rāma and Sītā or that Lakṣmaṇa and Sītā served Rāma. Given the tenor of the narrative and Lakṣmaṇa's role in it, it is far more probable that Lakṣmaṇa is serving both his brother and sister-in-law. Compare Lakṣmaṇa's vow at 2.28.10. See, too, R. Goldman 1980. This is certainly the understanding of Cg, who reorders the words in his gloss to avoid any ambiguity. He glosses, " 'by you serving Rāma along with Sītā,' that is the syntax (*sītayā saha rāmaṃ śuśrūṣatety anvayaḥ*)."

Ñ,V,B2–4,D4,10,11, and the texts and printed editions of Ct omit this verse. Translations that follow the text of Ct omit it as well. Gita Press (1969, vol. 3, p. 1861), however, knows and translates it (6.119.28). The inclusion of the verse in the critical edition is seriously questionable, as it clearly violates the principles set forth by the critical editors in volume 1 (Bhatt 1960, p. xxxiv).

28. "you will attain" *prāpsyasi*: The translation of Gita Press (1969, vol. 3, p. 1861) has apparently accidentally omitted the subject of the verb, "you," resulting in the clearly incorrect reading, "Rama being pleased (with you), will attain."

"and everlasting glory" *mahimānaṃ tathaiva ca*: Literally, "and greatness as well." Since this apparently refers to Lakṣmaṇa's reward in heaven as opposed to his earthly glory mentioned in *pāda* b (*yaśaś ca vipulaṃ bhuvi*), we have added the word "eternal" to emphasize the contrast. Cg makes an interesting remark in this context: that, on the basis of his comments in this verse, it is apparent that Daśaratha is unaware that Lakṣmaṇa, too, is an *avatāra* of Viṣṇu (*lakṣmaṇasyāpi viṣṇvavatāratvaṃ na jānāti daśarathaḥ*).

29. "to the welfare" *śubheṣu*: Literally, "with regard to auspicious *or* propitious things." Ś1,Ñ,V1,2,B2–4,D4,8,10,11,M1, and the texts and printed editions of Ct read instead *hiteṣu*, "welfare *or* benefits." In the context, the difference in meaning appears slight.

30. "All these gods, including Indra, along with the three worlds" *ete sendrās trayo lokāḥ*: Literally, "these with Indra, the three worlds." We follow the suggestion of Cg, who believes that Daśaratha is making a gesture with his hand to include Rudra as well (among the gods present) (*eta iti hastanirdeśena rudro 'py antargataḥ*). Compare note to verse 7 above. All translators consulted subordinate the pronoun and adjective to the phrase *trayo lokāḥ*, understanding, "the three worlds, including Indra." But we believe that the pronoun *ete* makes this problematic and that we should read as Cg suggests.

"have approached" *abhigamya*: Literally, "having approached." Ś,Ñ,V,B2–4,D4,8, 10–13, and the texts and printed editions of Ct read instead *abhivādya*, "having respectfully saluted."

31. "has been revealed by them" *taduktam*: Literally, "is said [to be] by them." We understand the pronoun *tat-* to refer to the gods, divine seers, etc., mentioned in the preceding verse.

"Brahman, the... Supreme Spirit" *brahmanirmitam*: Literally, "consisting of Brahman." The commentators' interpretations differ, however. Cv and Cm gloss, "expounded in the *vedas* (*vedapratipādikam*)." Cg understands, "that is Brahman, who is said to be fashioned in the form of Rāma, that is, incarnated in the form of Rāma (*tad etad brahma rāmo rāmarūpeṇa nirmitaṃ rāmarūpeṇāvatīrṇam ity uktam*)." D10,11,M1, and the texts and printed editions of Ck, Ct, and Cr read instead *brahmasaṃmitam*, "equal to *or* measured out by Brahman." Ct and Ck understand the compound in the same way that Cv and Cm understand the critical reading. They argue that it means "expounded in the vedic passage that states 'all these worlds are within him (*TaiBr* 2.8.8.9a)' (*brahmasaṃmitaṃ brahmaṇāntar asminn ime lokā ityādi śrutyā pratipāditam*)." Cr glosses, simply, "equal to the *vedas* (*vedatulyam*)."

32. 6.107.32cd = 6.107.27ab.

"Devotedly serving Rāma as well as Sītā Vaidehī" *rāmaṃ śuśrūṣatā bhaktyā vaidehyā saha sītayā*: See note to verse 27 above. D10–12 and the texts and printed editions of Ck and Ct read *vyagram*, "intently," for the critical edition's *bhaktyā*, "devotedly." D10–12 and the texts and printed editions of Ck and Ct also read *enam*, "him," for the critical edition's *rāmam*, "Rāma."

"you have attained righteousness" *avāptaṃ dharmacaraṇam . . . tvayā*: Literally, "the practice of *dharma* is attained by you." D7 and the printed editions of Ct read instead the awkward compound *avāptadharmācaraṇam*. Translations that follow this reading are forced to read *avāpta-* as if it were *avāpatam*.

33. For verse 33, Ś,Ñ,V,B,D1–4,8–12,T2,3, and the texts and printed editions of Ct and Ck substitute a passage of two lines [3300*]: "When the king had spoken in this fashion to Lakṣmaṇa, he said, 'My daughter,' and then, sweetly and softly, spoke to his daughter-in-law, who stood with her hands cupped in reverence."

34. "to demonstrate your purity" *tvadviśuddhyartham*: Literally, "for the sake of your purification."

Following verse 34, Ś,Ñ,V,B2–4,D4,8,10–12, and the texts and printed editions of Ct and KK (in brackets, 6.122.36) insert, while B1,D1–3,9 continue following 3301*, a passage of two lines [3302*]: "My daughter, this proof of your virtuous character,[1] so difficult to perform, that you have accomplished, shall outshine[2] the glory of all other women."

[1]"this proof of your virtuous character" *cāritralakṣaṇam*: Literally, "a sign *or* indication of conduct *or* character."

[2]"shall outshine" *abhibhaviṣyati*: Literally, "it will surpass *or* overcome."

35. "Fair-browed woman" *subhru*: Literally, "O one of beautiful brows." Ñ,V1,B2–4,D4,10,11,13,M2, and the texts and printed editions of Ct read instead the adverb *kāmam*, "granted *or* it is true."

"you do not need to be instructed" *na tvam . . . samādheyā*: The verb *sam* + *ā* √*dhā*, normally, "to put together, to concentrate, to take on, to conceive, etc.," does not appear to carry a meaning suitable to the context. Like all translations consulted, we follow the glosses of Ct, Ck, Cm, and Cg, who, in various ways, understand that the verb must be taken in the sense of "to be instructed *or* enjoined (*upadeṣṭavyā*—so Cg)."

36. "and his daughter-in-law" *tathā snuṣām*: Literally, "and the daughter-in-law." Ś,Ñ2,V1,3,B2–4,D8,10–12, and the texts and printed editions of Ct read instead *ca rāghavaḥ*, "and Rāghava." The family dynastic name here refers to Daśaratha.

"radiant" *jvalan*: Literally, "blazing." Ś,Ñ,V,B2–4,D4,8,10–12, and the texts and printed editions of Ct read instead *nṛpaḥ*, "the king."

Following verse 36, Ś,Ñ,V,B,D1–4,8–12,T2,3,M2, the edition of KK (within brackets, 6.122.39), and the texts and printed editions of Ct insert a passage of four lines [3304]: "Mounting his flying chariot, the illustrious and majestic foremost of kings took leave of his two sons and Sītā, and, the hairs of his body bristling with delight,[1] he proceeded to the world of Indra, the foremost of the gods.[2]"

[1]"the hairs of his body bristling with delight" *saṃhṛṣṭatanuḥ*: Literally, "his body thrilled *or* horripilating."

[2]"of Indra, the foremost of the gods" *devapravarasya*: Literally, "of the chief *or* foremost of the gods."

The meter is *upajāti*, with a hypermetric *pāda* b.

Sarga 108

1. "Daśaratha Kākutstha" *kākutsthe*: Literally, "Kākutstha."

"great Indra, the chastiser of Pāka" *mahendraḥ pākaśāsanaḥ*: Ct, Cm, and Cs are disturbed by the fact that both the *Rāmopākhyāna* (*MBh* 2.375.42–43) and the *Padmapurāṇa* (citing the *śloka—pitāmahavarāt tūrṇaṃ jīvayāmāsa tān nṛpaḥ*) ascribe the miracle of the resurrection of the slain monkeys to Brahmā. In an effort to avoid this seeming contradiction, they argue that we are to take the reference to Mahendra here to mean Brahmā, who is accompanied by Indra (*mahendraḥ tatsahito brahmety arthaḥ*—Ct, Cm).

2. "Your seeing us" *darśanam . . . tavāsmākam*: Cg argues that it is the gods who are the agents of the *darśana*, or "vision," here. He acknowledges, however, that others understand that the agent is Rāma (*tavāsmākaṃ darśanam asmatkartṛkaṃ darśanam . . . kecit tu tvatkartṛkam asmadviṣayaṃ darśanam ity artha ity āhuḥ*). This latter position makes better sense to us, as it is the gods who are offering to repay Rāma's service in the form of granting him "the fruit," as it were, of his vision of them.

"I am pleased" *prītiyukto 'smi*: D5,10,11,T2,3,M1,3, and the texts and printed editions of the southern commentators read instead the plural *prītiyuktāḥ smaḥ*, "we are pleased."

"what your heart desires" *yan manasecchasi*: Literally, "what you desire with [your] mind."

3. Ś,Ñ,V1,2,B2,4,D4,8,10–13, and the texts and printed editions of Ct substitute for verse 3 a passage of two lines [3307*]: "Addressed in this fashion by the great god mighty Indra,[1] who was so pleased, Rāghava, delighted and with a very calm mind, spoke these words."

[1]"the great god mighty Indra" *mahendreṇa . . . mahātmanā*: Literally, "by the great one, great Indra."

4. "If you are truly pleased with me" *yadi prītiḥ samutpannā mayi*: Literally, "if pleasure has arisen with respect to me."

"lord of all the gods" *sarvasureśvara*: Ś,Ñ,V1,2,B2–4,D8,10–12, and the texts and printed editions of Ct read instead *te vibudheśvara*, "on your part, O lord of the wise [gods]."

"my words" *me . . . vacanam*: T3,G2,M3, and the texts and printed editions of Cg read *te*, "your," for *me*, "mine," yielding the sense "please make your words come true."

5. "restored to life" *jīvitaṃ prāpya*: Literally, "having obtained life."

Following verse 5, D5–7,9–11,T,G,M1,2,3,5 (M2 inserts 3309* after 3310*, line 2), and the texts and printed editions of the southern commentators (printed editions of Cg read line 1 only) read a passage of two lines [3309*]: "Humbler of pride,[1] I wish to see all of those monkeys who, for my sake, were sundered from their sons and wives now happy once again.[2]"

[1]"Humbler of pride" *mānada*: The term is ambiguous. Its verbal element *-da* can be derived from either the root $\sqrt{}$*do*, "to destroy," as we have done, or from the root $\sqrt{}$*dā*

"to give." In the latter sense the epithet normally means "bestower of pride," and the translations consulted have rendered it in this fashion. See 6.13.7–8; 6.110.6; and notes. Cf. 6.104.10 and note.

[2]"now happy once again" *prītamanasaḥ*: Literally, "their minds *or* hearts pleased *or* delighted."

D7,10,11,G2,M1, and the texts and printed editions of Ct, following 3309*, continue, while Ñ2,V1,2,B2,4,D13,M2 insert after verse 5, a passage of two lines [3310*, lines 1 and 2]: "Bull among the gods, let those valorous heroes who, heedless of death, were slain after making great efforts, live once more.[1] [1–2]"

[1]"Bull among the gods, let . . . live once more" *jīveyuḥ surarṣabha*: Ś,Ñ2,V1,2,B2, 3,D8,10–13, and the texts and printed editions of Ct read instead *jīvayaitān puraṃdara*, 'O destroyer of citadels, bring them to life."

6. "be reunited" *sameyuḥ*: Literally, "let them come together." Ck, Ct, Cm, and Cg understand that the revivified monkeys should be reunited with their sons and wives as mentioned at 3309* (following verse 5 above) (*sameyur ity atra putrair dāraiś cety āvartanīyam*—so Cg). See verse 11 below, where the reunion with relatives is made explicit.

7. "Humbler of pride" *mānada*: See note to 3309* (following verse 5 above).

7ab = 3314*, line 4 (with minor variants). See 3314* following verse 10 below.

8. "choice" *mukhyāni*: Literally, "foremost, principal, best." Ś,Ñ,V1,2,B2–4,D4,8,10–13, and the texts and printed editions of Ct read instead *puṣpāṇi*, "flowers."

9. "words, which manifested his pleasure" *vacanaṃ prītilakṣaṇam*: Literally, "words having signs of pleasure." Cg explains, "*prītilakṣaṇam* means 'that by which pleasure is indicated,' in other words, that which manifests *or* suggests pleasure (*prītir lakṣyate 'neneti prītilakṣaṇaṃ prītivyañjakam*)." Ś,Ñ,V,B3,4,D8,10–13,T1, and the texts and printed editions of Ct read *prītisaṃyutam*, "joined *or* filled with pleasure," for *prītilakṣaṇam*.

10. "This is a major boon" *mahān ayaṃ varaḥ*: Literally, "this is a great boon." As the commentators point out, Indra means that this boon is difficult to accomplish (*duḥsādhyaḥ*—so Cr). As Ct notes, it is difficult to revive even a single dead creature, let alone immeasurable numbers of them, and the feat is thus beyond the capacities of anyone other than Indra. (*ekasyāpi mṛtasya punar ujjīvanaṃ duṣkaram. aparimitamṛtajīvanaṃ tu madatiriktāśakyam.*) Cg goes into some detail as to what is involved here, noting that the greatness of the boon involves bringing about a feat never accomplished before in the form of reassembling in their proper places the scattered hands, feet, tails, etc., of the slain monkeys and bringing them back from the next world (*varasya mahattvam itas tato viprakīrṇakaracaraṇapucchādisvasvasaṃsthānasaṃdhānalokāntaragatānayanādirūpāghaṭitārthaghaṭitatvam*). Cm understands similarly.

"when their sleep is done" *nidrākṣaye*: Literally, "at the end *or* destruction of sleep."

Following 10ab, D5–7,10,11,S, and the texts and printed editions of the southern commentators insert a passage of four lines [3314*]: "Nonetheless, I have never spoken falsely,[1] and therefore this shall come to pass.[1] Those apes and tawny monkeys who have been slain—their heads and arms severed[2] by the *rākṣasas* in battle—shall arise,[3] together with the langurs.[3] Free from their pain and their wounds, they shall be filled once more with strength and vigor.[4][4]"

[1]"I have never spoken falsely" *dvir mayā noktapūrvam*: Literally, "never before by me has it been spoken twice."

[2]"their heads and arms severed" *nikṛttānanabāhavaḥ*: Literally, "whose faces and arms had been cut."

[3]"Those . . . tawny monkeys . . . shall arise" *samutsthāsyanti harayaḥ*: D7,10,11,G2,M1, and the texts and printed editions of Ct read instead *samuttiṣṭhantu te sarve*, "let them all arise."

[4]3314* line 4 = 7ab (with minor variants).

11. "with their friends, their relatives, their kinsmen, and their own people" *suhṛdbhir bāndhavaiś caiva jñātibhiḥ svajanena ca*: The four terms tend to overlap in their semantic fields. It is difficult to find a comparable list of words in English that would convey the specific meanings that each term may carry. Construed more precisely, the terms can have relatively restricted meanings as follows: *suhṛd* refers to friends, companions, or allies; *bāndhava*, to maternal relatives; *jñāti*, to paternal relatives; and *svajana*, generically to all those people, e.g., family, servants, and countrymen, who may be associated with an individual although not necessarily related by blood.

12. Compare 6.4.48; 6.18.32–34; 6.112.17; and notes.

13. "now healed and free of wounds" *saṃvṛtair nirvraṇaiḥ punaḥ*: The critical reading *saṃvṛtaiḥ*, literally, "covered over, knit together, closed up," has to be interpreted here, we believe, in the sense of "healed." No commentator or printed edition shares this reading. G,M1–3, and the texts and printed editions of Cg and Cm, whose reading is closest to the critical text, read instead *saṃvṛttaiḥ*, "became *or* had become." This yields the sense "with limbs *or* bodies that had become free from wounds." Cg explains similarly, "characterized by bodies that had become free from wounds (*nirvraṇaiḥ saṃvṛttair nirvraṇībhūtair gātrair upalakṣitāḥ*)."

Ś,Ñ1,V2,B2–4,D8,10–13, and the texts and printed editions of Ct read instead *idānīṃ nirvraṇaiḥ samaiḥ*, "and [their bodies] now were whole and free from wounds." Translations that follow the text of Ct render this variant, although a number of them understand the term *samaiḥ* in its sense of "equal *or* identical."

Following 13ab, D5–7,10,11,S (M1 after verse 12) insert a passage of one line [3318*]: "Then all those bulls among the tawny monkeys[1] rose up as if they had been sleeping."

[1]"all those bulls among the tawny monkeys" *haripuṃgavāḥ*: D10,11, and the texts and printed editions of Ct read instead *harisattamāḥ*, "the foremost among the tawny monkeys."

Following verse 13, M3 and the texts and printed editions of Cg read a passage of one line [3321*]: "All of the monkeys respectfully saluted Rāghava."

14. "had had his wish fulfilled" *paripūrṇārtham*: Literally, "whose goal had been fulfilled."

"they first praised him, who was so praiseworthy and who was accompanied by Lakṣmaṇa, and then they said" *ūcus te prathamaṃ stutvā stavārhaṃ sahalakṣmaṇam*: Ś2,Ñ,V,B2–4,D8,10–12, and the texts and printed editions of Ct read instead *abruvan paramaprītāḥ stutvā rāmaṃ salakṣmaṇam*, "Having praised Rāma together with Lakṣmaṇa, in the highest delight, they said."

15. "hero" *vīra*: Ñ,D10,11,13, and the texts and printed editions of Ct read instead *rājan*, "O king *or* your majesty."

"long-suffering" *tapasvinīm*: Literally, "wretched *or* miserable [woman]." Ś,Ñ2,V1,2, B,D1–4,8–12,M2, and the texts and printed editions of Ct read instead *yaśasvinīm*, "illustrious, glorious."

Following verse 15, D5,6,T,G1,3,M insert, while V2,D7,10,11,G2, and the texts and printed editions of the southern commentators insert following 16ab, a passage of one line [3323*]: "[You must see,] scorcher of your foes, great Śatrughna and all of your mothers."

16. "once you have gone there" *gatvā*: Literally, "having gone [there]." The idea evidently is that Rāma, after meeting Bharata in Nandigrāma, will proceed to Ayodhyā.

"and so bring joy to the people of the city" *paurān . . . praharṣaya*: Literally, "delight the people."

Following 16ab, V2,D7,10,11,G2, and the texts and printed editions of Ct insert a passage of one line [3323*]. See note to verse 15 above.

17. "When they had spoken in this fashion . . . took their leave of Rāma" *evam uktvā tam āmantrya rāmam*: Literally, "having spoken in this fashion and having taken leave of him, Rāma." Ś,Ñ,V,B2–4,D8,10–12, and the texts and printed editions of Ct read instead *evam uktvā sahasrākṣo rāmam*, "having spoken in this fashion to Rāma, thousand-eyed [Indra]."

"in great delight, they went off to heaven" *hṛṣṭā jagmuḥ surā divam*: Literally, "the happy gods went to heaven." Ś,Ñ2,V1,3,B2,4,D8,10–12, and the texts and printed editions of Ct read instead *yayau hṛṣṭaḥ suraiḥ saha*, "[Indra,] delighted, departed together with the gods."

18. "ordered the army to make camp" *vāsam ājñāpayat*: Literally, "he ordered a dwelling." We follow the commentators, who understand that Rāma orders the monkeys, etc., back to their encampment (*vāsaṃ yathāpūrvaṃ vānarādisthitim ājñāpayat*—so Cr).

19. "radiant with splendor" *śriyā jvalantī*: Literally, "blazing with *śrī*." Cr glosses "the goddess *or* glow of victory (*vijayalakṣmyā*)" for *śriyā*, "with splendor."

"as does the night illumined by the cool-rayed moon" *niśā praṇīteva hi śītaraśminā*: Literally, "like the night led forth by the one of cool rays." Nothing in the normal semantic range of the verb *pra* $\sqrt{}$*nī*, "to lead forth, set, establish," seems entirely appropriate to this simile. Given the context, we follow Cg's gloss, "illuminated (*prakāśitā*)." Roussel (1903, vol. 3, p. 397) translates, "*la nuit à la quelle préside l'astre aux froids rayons*." In this he appears to be followed by Pagani (1999, p. 1193), who renders *praṇītā* as "*sous la conduite de*." Other translators tend to render as we have.

The meter is *vaṃśasthavila*.

Ct concludes his comments on this *sarga* with a discussion of the circumstances under which the slain monkeys have been restored to life. In this discussion he raises several points. The first is that, although Rāma could have easily accomplished this miracle on his own, he effects it through Indra and Brahmā in order to conceal his true divine form, since he remains incarnate in a human body. Next Ct takes up the issue that some authorities appear to believe that Indra has accomplished the resurrection of the monkeys by showering *amṛta* over the battlefield. This, in turn, raises the issue, similar to the one raised earlier in the *kāṇḍa* at the time of Hanumān's revival of the slain monkeys with the fragrance of the life-restoring herb, as to why this wholesale resurrection does not also bring the fallen *rākṣasas* to life. Ct argues that the ashes of the cremated *rākṣasas* would have been thrown into the sea on the day of Rāvaṇa's funeral and so there would be no question of their being restored to life. Moreover, Ct continues, earlier during the battle, it was stated that the bodies of the *rākṣasa* dead were thrown into the ocean. Ct acknowledges that some authorities believe that the verse in which the marine burial of the *rākṣasa* dead is reported is a "modern" interpolation. Still, he sees no contradiction, since he argues that all the slain could not, in fact, be revived by the mere aroma of the healing herbs. Instead, he claims that (as shown in *sarga* 89, where Lakṣmaṇa is revived in this fashion) the restoration can only be accomplished by the individual administration of the crushed or powdered herbs. Ct concludes by noting that, in any case, the dead are unable to smell anything and that nowhere is it stated that Rāvaṇa gave any order to dispose of the dead in the manner described above. (*yady api rāmeṇāpīcchāmātreṇaitat sukaraṃ tathāpi gṛhītamanuṣyadehatvāt tatsvarūpagopanāya sendrabrahmadvārā tathā kṛtam iti dhyeyam. ye 'py amṛtavṛṣṭyendreṇa sarvasamutthānaṃ kṛtam iti vadanti. tatpakṣe 'pi rāvaṇasaṃskāradine sarvarakṣasāṃ dāhādisaṃskārapūrvakaṃ bhasmanaḥ samudre prakṣepān na tadutthānaśaṅkā. pūrvaṃ yuddhakāla eva mṛtānāṃ samudre prakṣepa iti mūla eva pūrvam uktatvāc ca. anye tu sa ślokas tatrādhunikaprakṣiptaḥ. na hy oṣadhigandhamātreṇa sarveṣāṃ viśalyatā. kiṃtu cūrṇīkṛtya tasya dāneneti prāg evoktam. tathā ca tadabhāvān na teṣāṃ viśalyatā. mṛtānāṃ gandhāghrāṇābhāvāc ca. rāvaṇasya tathājñāyā aśravaṇāc cety āhuḥ.*) See note to 6.61.67, 1396* and note. Cf. note to 6.62.2.

Sarga 109

1. "risen at his leisure" *sukhotthitam*: Literally, "who had arisen comfortably." D10,11,M1, and the texts and printed editions of Ct and Cr read instead *sukhoditam*, which, if it is derived from *ud* $\sqrt{i}$ "to arise, get up," would be synonymous with *sukhotthitam*, and, indeed, this is the understanding of Ct, who glosses, "having awakened at leisure (*sukhaprabuddham*—so also Cm, glossing the critical reading)." Cr appears to understand *uditam* to be a participle of $\sqrt{vad}$, "to speak." He then takes the compound as an adverb modifying *uṣitam*, "passed, spent, dwelled," glossing, "who had passed the night in such a way that it was characterized by pleasant conversation (*sukhakathanaviśiṣṭaṃ yathā bhavati tathoṣitam*)."

"wishing him victory" *jayaṃ pṛṣṭvā*: Literally, "having asked about victory." We understand with Ct and Cm that Vibhīṣaṇa is offering the standard auspicious greeting to a king, "*jaya*! [be victorious!] (*jayaśabdaṃ prayujya*)." Pagani (1999, p. 1193) and Raghunathan (1982, vol. 3, p. 347) understand that Vibhīṣaṇa is greeting Rāma as the victor.

2–3. "Here is water for your bath" *snānāni*: Literally, "baths." Our translation, like that of Raghunathan (1982, vol. 3, p. 347), follows the gloss of Cg, who understands, "waters fit for bathing (*snānīyajalāni*)." Cm glosses, "implements for bathing (*snānopa-*

karaṇāni)." Ck, Ct, and Cr gloss, "articles for the bath such as fragrances, oil, etc. (*snānasādhanasugandhatailāni*—so Ck, Ct).

"heavenly sandalpaste, and various kinds of garlands" *candanāni ca divyāni mālyāni vividhāni ca*: D7,10,11, and the texts and printed editions of Cr and Ct transpose the words *divyāni* and *mālyāni*, lending the half verse more the sense of "various kinds of divine sandalpaste and garlands."

"These lotus-eyed women" *imā nāryaḥ padmanibhekṣaṇāḥ*: Literally, "These women whose eyes are like lotuses."

"skilled in the arts of grooming" *alaṃkāravidaḥ*: Literally, "knowing ornamentation."

Following 3ab, T2,3,M3, and the texts and printed editions of Cg insert a passage of one line [3327*, line 1]: "Please accept all of this, out of a desire to grant me your favor."

4. "You should instead invite" *upanimantraya*: Literally, "[you] invite." We have added the word "instead," as Rāma will decline Vibhīṣaṇa's offer to bathe.

5–6. "the... prince" *kumāraḥ*: Ś,Ñ2,V1,3,B2–4,D1–3,8–12,T2,3, and the texts and printed editions of Ct read instead *bharataḥ*, "Bharata."

"who is delicate and accustomed to comforts" *sukhocitaḥ / sukumāraḥ*: Compare the description of Bharata at 3.15.28 and 6.113.26–30.

"is nonetheless true to his vows" *satyasaṃśravaḥ*: Literally, "one of true vows." Cg sees this term as a reference to Bharata's vow to immolate himself should Rāma not return on the very day that his fourteen years of exile are completed (see notes to 2.104.22, 2304*, line 2). See note to verse 20 below. Ñ2,V1,3,B2,3,D5–7,10,11, G1,M1,5, and the texts and printed editions of Ct and Cr read instead *satyasaṃśrayaḥ*, "whose refuge is truth."

"I do not care for" *na me... bahumatam*: Literally, "it is not highly esteemed by me." The idea here is that Rāma does not feel that it would be appropriate for him to give up his ascetic vows when Bharata is still engaged in his while separated from Rāma (*madviyogena bahuvratapare tasmin kathaṃ mayā vratatyāgaḥ kartuṃ yukta iti bhāvaḥ*—so Cg). Compare, however, 3.15.37–39, where Rāma bathes in the Godāvarī River, and 6.112.4 and note, where Cg understands that both Bharata and Rāma have not bathed. See, too, 6.116.13–15 and notes, where the reunited brothers finally bathe in Nandigrāma.

7. "Moreover, we must return... immediately by this very road" *ita eva pathā kṣipraṃ pratigacchāma*: According to Cg, Rāma points with his hand to the road to indicate that it is the same one by which he came. (*ita eveti. anena pathā yenāham āgatas tenety arthaḥ. eṣa iti hastanirdeśapūrvakam ucyate.*) Ś,Ñ,V1,3,B,D2–4,8,10–12, and the texts and printed editions of Ct and Ck read instead *etat paśya yathā* for the critical reading, *ita eva pathā*, lending the line the sense "consider (lit., look at) that whereby we may return to the city immediately."

"is extremely difficult" *paramadurgamaḥ*: Literally, "supremely hard to traverse." Cg understands that the road is difficult because of its extreme length (*atidūratvāt*).

8. "prince" *pārthivātmaja*: Literally, "O son of a king."

9. "which Rāvaṇa took from my brother Kubera by force" *mama bhrātuḥ kuberasya rāvaṇenāhṛtaṃ balāt*: The story of Rāvaṇa's stealing of the Puṣpakavimāna is told at 7.15. See 6.7.5 and notes. Ś,Ñ,V1,B2–4,D4,8,10–13,M2, and the texts and printed editions of Ct read *rāvaṇena balīyasā*, "by Rāvaṇa, who was more powerful," for *rāvaṇenāhṛtaṃ balāt*, "Rāvaṇa took by force." This variant deprives verse 9 of a finite

verbal element and makes it grammatically dependent upon passage 3333*, which follows verse 9 in all southern and most northern manuscripts. See notes to verse 21 below.

Following verse 9, Ś,Ñ2,V1,3,B2–4,D5–8,10–12,S insert a passage of two lines [3333*]: "It is heavenly and superb and moves according to one's desire. It was taken [by Rāvaṇa] after conquering [Kubera] in battle.[1] I have kept it here for your use.[1] Here it is, O hero of unequaled valor.[2]" Given the manuscript support for this verse, its omission from the critical text is highly suspect. See Bhatt 1960, p. xxxiv.

[1]"kept it here for your use" *tvadarthaṃ pālitam*: Literally, "[it was] protected for your sake." Cg sees this phrase as an answer to the potential ethical question as to why Vibhīṣaṇa does not return this stolen vehicle to its rightful owner, Kubera. (*tarhi kuberāya samāgatāya tat kim arthaṃ na dattam ity atrāha. tvadartha iti.*)

10. "which resembles a cloud" *meghasaṃkāśam*: According to Cg, the simile is intended to suggest great speed (*meghasaṃkāśam iti vege dṛṣṭāntaḥ*).

"is kept nearby" *iha tiṣṭhati*: Literally, "it stands *or* is located here." Ct and Cm note that, by "here," Vibhīṣaṇa means "in Laṅkā," but note that, because of its great height, those stationed outside the city in the monkey encampment are able to see it. That is why Vibhīṣaṇa points it out as if it were close at hand. (*laṅkāyāṃ vartamānasyāpi puṣpakasyātyunnatatayā śibirasthair api dṛśyamānatvād idam iti pratyakṣavan nirdeśaḥ.*)

11. "if you are cognizant of" *yadi smarasi*: Literally, "if you remember."

"my wise friend" *prājña*: Literally, "O wise one."

"for a while" *tāvat*: Literally, "so much, just a bit, just a little." Ck and Ct believe we should supply the words "for one day (*ekadivasam iti śeṣaḥ*—so Ct)." Cg understands the period of the requested stay to be two or three days (*dvitradinamātram*).

12. "you can depart" *gamiṣyasi*: Literally, "you will go."

13. "You are very dear to me" *prītiyuktas tu me*: Literally, "but [you are] joined by affection with me." Ś,Ñ,V1,3,B1–3,D1,7,8,10–13,G2,M1,3, and the texts and printed editions of the southern commentators (except Cv) read instead *prītiyuktasya me*, in which case the adjective refers to Vibhīṣaṇa and has the sense "of me who am filled with affection."

14. "But I am not trying to give you orders" *na khalv ājñāpayāmi te*: Literally, "I am certainly not ordering you."

15. "in such a way that all the *rākṣasas* and monkeys could hear him" *rakṣasāṃ vānarāṇāṃ ca sarveṣāṃ copaśṛṇvatām*: Literally, "of all the *rākṣasas* and monkeys who were listening." We understand with Cg that this is an absolutive construction with the sense "while they were listening." Compare 6.110.3 and note.

16. "scorcher of your foes" *paraṃtapa*: Ñ2,V1,3,B2–4,D4,7,10–12, and the texts and printed editions of Ct read instead *pareṇa ca*, "and excellent [counsel]."

"your wholehearted assistance" *sarvātmanā . . . ceṣṭābhiḥ*: Literally, "by those actions [that were done] with the whole self." We agree with Ck, Ct, and Cr in reading these two terms together as one syntactic unit. Ck and Ct gloss, "actions performed in battle with body, speech, and mind (*kāyavāṅmanobhiḥ kṛtayuddhaceṣṭābhiḥ*—so Ct)." Cg, however, believes that *ceṣṭābhiḥ*, for which he glosses, "manly actions (*pauruṣaiḥ*)," should stand alone and that *sarvātmanā* should be construed with the participle "honored (*pūjitaḥ*)" in *pāda* a.

17–19. "But my heart is eager to see...And my heart is eager also to see" *draṣṭum...tvarate manaḥ*: Literally, "[my] heart *or* mind is hastening to see." Verse 18 constitutes a separate series of subordinate clauses. This verse intervenes between *bhrātaram...bharatam*, "[my] brother Bharata," which is the first object of the infinitive *draṣṭum*, "to see," in 17c, and the list of the remaining objects starting with *kausalyām*, "Kausalyā," in *pāda* 19a. We have repeated the verbal phrase in order to make the syntax intelligible.

"he came out to Citrakūṭa" *yo 'sau citrakūṭam upāgataḥ*: The reference is to Bharata's failed mission to persuade Rāma to return to Ayodhyā as king at *Ayodhyākāṇḍa* 76–107.

"he beseeched me, bowing his head to my feet" *śirasā yācataḥ*: Literally, "of him who was begging with his head."

"illustrious Kaikeyī" *kaikeyīṃ ca yaśasvinīm*: Compare 6.107.4–6 and notes, where Cg argues that we should construe the adjective *yaśasvinīm*, "illustrious," with *kaikeyīm*, "Kaikeyī." See, too, 6.116.39 and notes.

"as well as my elders, my friends, and the citizens, together with their children" *gurūṃś ca suhṛdaś caiva paurāṃś ca tanayaiḥ saha*: Ñ2,D10,11, and the texts and printed editions of Ct read instead *guhaṃ ca suhṛdaṃ caiva paurāñ jānapadaiḥ saha*, "and [my] friend Guha, and the people of the city, along with those of the countryside." However, although no available text, printed edition, or manuscript represented in the critical apparatus shows the variant *gṛham*, "house," Roussel (1903, vol. 3, p. 399) appears to have mistakenly read this, as he renders, "*ainsi que ma maison*." In this error he has been followed by Shastri (1959, vol. 3, p. 247), who renders, "as also mine house." Pagani (1999, p. 1194) apparently reads the erroneous representation of the text of Cg and Cr given as a footnote to verse 6.121.20 in GPP, where the singular *gurum* (known only to D3) is mistakenly given for the correct reading of Cg, which is the same as in the critical edition. She therefore renders, "*mon maître et mes amis*."

20. Ś,Ñ1,V1,3,B,D1–4,8–13,M2, and the texts and printed editions of Ct transpose verses 20 and 21.

"For how indeed could I agree to stay here, now that my mission has been accomplished?" *kṛtakāryasya me vāsaḥ kathaṃ svid iha saṃmataḥ*: Literally, "How indeed is dwelling approved of me by whom a mission has been accomplished?" Cg understands that the phrase "now that my mission has been accomplished," means that Rāma has completed his fourteenth year of exile. Cg correctly notes that Rāma's question is rhetorical, noting that, should Rāma delay his return, Bharata would [as he had previously vowed] throw himself into the fire. (*nivartitacaturdaśavarṣapravrājanasya kṛtakāryasya ma iha laṅkāyāṃ vāsaḥ saṃmataḥ kathaṃ svit. na saṃmata ity arthaḥ. anyathā bharatasyāgnipraveśād iti bhāvaḥ.*) See note to verses 5–6 above.

V1,3,B2,4,D4,10,11,M2, and the texts and printed editions of Ct insert a passage of two lines [3335*, = GPP, NSP, and Gita Press 6.121.23]. A number of other northern manuscripts insert 3335* in whole or in part following App. I, No. 71, which they also insert in whole or in part. "Addressed in this fashion by Rāma, Vibhīṣaṇa, lord of the *rākṣasas*, hastening, summoned that flying palace as radiant as the sun."

21. Ś,Ñ1,V1,3,B,D1–4,8–13,M2, and the texts and printed editions of Ct transpose verses 20 and 21.

"my gentle friend" *saumya*: Literally, "gentle one."

"I have already been deeply honored" *pūjito 'smi*: Literally, "I am honored." Cg understands that we should add the phrase "by the gift of the flying palace (*vimānapradāneneti śeṣaḥ*)." Cg then notes that, because this gift now makes the Puṣpaka become Rāma's property, he will later send it back to Kubera, its original owner (*pradattatvena svatvād uttaratra kuberāya preṣayiṣyati*). See 6.115.49, where Rāma sends back the Puṣpakavimāna to Kubera. See notes to 3333* following verse 9 above.

"Please don't be angry" *manyur na khalu kartavyaḥ*: Literally, "anger indeed should not be made." As Cg points out, citing *Amarakośa* 3.3.153, the word *manyuḥ* can mean "sadness, depression (*dainyam*)" as well as "anger." Thus, the phrase could quite plausibly mean "Please don't be sad."

Following verse 21, D7,G2,M3, and the texts and printed editions of Cg insert a passage of two lines [3337* = VSP 6.124.25; KK 6.124.23]: "When he had heard those words of Rāghava, Vibhīṣaṇa, the lord of the *rākṣasas*, departed and quickly returned,[1] bringing that flying palace."

[1]"departed and quickly returned" *tūrṇaṃ pratinivartata*: Literally, "he quickly returned."

This verse is rendered only in the translation of Raghunathan (1982, vol. 3, p. 348). Ct, however, quotes the verse and notes that it is found in some manuscripts.

22–27. Compare the description of the Puṣpa (v.l. *puṣpaka* 5.6.5–14 and notes) and Puṣpaka (5.7.9–15 and notes) in the *Sundarakāṇḍa*. See, too, 6.7.5 and note.

"stood waiting" *tasthau tatra*: Literally, "he stood there."

"its raised platforms were made of lapis" *vaidūryamaṇivedikam*: See notes to 5.3.8–11 and 5.12.35. See, too, notes to 6.3.13 and 6.67.13.

"with penthouses" *kūṭāgāraiḥ*: Cg understands these to be "pavilions (*maṇḍapaiḥ*)," while Ck, Ct, and Cr understand the term to refer to *śālagṛhas*, literally, "chamber houses," which could perhaps refer to either single- or multi-room structures. See note to 5.7.13; cf. 5.10.13–15. See 6.62.12–14 and note.

"white flags and banners" *pāṇḍurābhiḥ patākābhir dhvajaiś ca*: Cg understands that *patākas* are plain banners (*kevaladhvajaiḥ*), while *dhvajas* bear insignia (*sacihnaiḥ*). This distinction appears to be represented in the translation of Gita Press (1969, vol. 3, p. 1867), which renders, "decorated with whitish yellow pennons and flags with armorial bearings." Ck and Ct understand that *patākas* are tiny flags or pennants (*sūkṣmadhvajaiḥ*).

"It was splendid" *śobhitam*: D10,11,M1, and the texts and printed editions of Ct read instead *kāñcanam*, "golden."

"adorned with golden lotuses" *hemapadmavibhūṣitam*: Cg understands that these ornaments are hanging (*lambamānāni*), a suggestion reflected in the translation of Raghunathan (1982, vol. 3, p. 348), who renders, "and it was hung with golden lotuses."

"windows" *-gavākṣitam*: Literally, "windowed." Compare 6.45.26; 6.50.3; 6.87.26; and notes.

"Fashioned by Viśvakarman" *nirmitaṃ viśvakarmaṇā*: See 5.7.10 and note. See, too, 6.111.3; 6.115.23; and notes.

"with many" *bahubhiḥ*: Ñ,V1,B2–4,D4,10,11, and the texts and printed editions of Ct read instead *bṛhadbhiḥ*, "with large, big."

Following verse 27, Ś,Ñ,V1,3,B,D1–4,8–13, and the texts and printed editions of Ct (KK in brackets = 6.124.30) insert a passage of four lines [3341*]: "When Rāma, together with Lakṣmaṇa, saw that the flying palace Puṣpaka of heavenly beauty,[1] which moved according to one's desire, had arrived, he was as delighted as was great Indra long ago at the slaying of Vṛtra.[2]"

[1]"saw...of heavenly beauty" *prekṣya hi divyarūpam*: Ñ1,D4,10,11,13, and the texts and printed editions of Ct read instead *bhūdharasaṃnikāśam*, "resembling a mountain."

[2]"When Rāma, together with Lakṣmaṇa... he was as delighted as was great Indra long ago at the slaying of Vṛtra" *rāmaḥ prahṛṣṭaḥ saha lakṣmaṇena purā yathā vṛtravadhe mahendraḥ*: Ñ,D10,11,13, and the texts and printed editions of Ct read instead *dṛṣṭvā tadā vismayam ājagāma rāmaḥ sasaumitrir udārasattvaḥ*, "then, when noble-spirited Rāma, together with Saumitri, saw [the Puṣpaka], he was wonderstruck."

The meter is *upajāti*.

Sarga 110

1. "When... saw" *dṛṣṭvā*: D6,10,11,T2,3,M1, and the texts and printed editions of Ck and Ct read instead *kṛtvā*, "having made." This lends the phrase the sense "having made the Puṣpaka ready *or* having brought the Puṣpaka near." Cv observes that this is a better reading but acknowledges the critical reading, which he claims should then be read as a causative (so, too, Cm and Cg), i.e., "having shown the Puṣpaka." (*kṛtveti samīcīnaḥ pāṭhaḥ. dṛṣṭveti pāṭhe dṛśir antarbhāvitaṇyartho veditavyaḥ. darśayitvety arthaḥ.*)

"the flying palace Puṣpaka, all adorned with flowers" *puṣpakaṃ puṣpabhūṣitam*: The adjective is doubtless chosen because of the echoing effect of the repeated word *puṣpa*, "flower."

"Rāma, who stood nearby" *avidūre sthitaṃ rāmam*: D5,6,10,11,T1,G1,3,M1,3,5, and the texts and printed editions of the southern commentators read the nominative *sthitaḥ* for the critical edition's accusative *sthitam*. According to this variant, it is Vibhīṣaṇa who is standing nearby.

2. "Cupping his hands in reverence, the humble" *baddhāñjaliḥ prahvaḥ*: Ś2,Ñ,V1,3,B,D1–3,8–12, and the texts and printed editions of Ct read instead *baddhāñjalipuṭaḥ*, "cupping his hands into the hollow of the *añjali* gesture."

"filled with a sense of urgency" *tvarayopetaḥ*: Literally, "accompanied by haste *or* urgency." Cg glosses, "respectfully (*ādaropetaḥ*)."

"What should I do now?" *kiṃ karomi*: Literally, "What do I do." As Cg explains, Vibhīṣaṇa is asking what he must do next (*itaḥ paraṃ kiṃ karavāṇīty arthaḥ*).

3. "in such a way that Lakṣmaṇa could hear them" *lakṣmaṇasyopaśṛṇvataḥ*: We agree with Cg in understanding that Rāma speaks loudly enough for Lakṣmaṇa to hear as a sign of respect for his brother (*lakṣmaṇasaṃmatipūrvakam ity arthaḥ*). Compare 6.109.15 and note.

4. Vibhīṣaṇa, the forest-dwelling monkeys: *vibhīṣaṇa vanaukasaḥ*: Literally, "Vibhīṣaṇa, the forest-dwelling ones." Ś2,Ñ2,V1,3,B2–4,D8,10–12, and the texts and printed editions of Ct read instead *sarva eva vanaukasaḥ*, "all the forest-dwelling monkeys."

"have performed arduous deeds" *kṛtaprayatnakarmāṇaḥ*: Literally, "by whom actions *or* deeds were performed with effort." We follow Cr, who glosses, "those by whom actions, that is, activities, were done with effort, that is, with extreme exertion *or* industry (*kṛtāni prayatnenātyudyogena karmāṇi vyāpārā yais te*). Ct glosses the word *karma* in the compound as "the work of battle (*yuddhakarma*)." Ck understands similarly.

"You must honor them with . . . ornaments" *bhūṣaṇaiś cābhipūjaya*: Literally, "and you must honor with ornaments." Ś2,Ñ2,V1,3,B2–4,D8,10–12, and the texts and printed editions of Ct read instead *sampūjyantāṃ vibhīṣaṇa*, "O Vibhīṣaṇa, they are to be honored."

"and other valuables" *arthaiś ca*: Literally, "and wealth *or* riches." Cr glosses, "things other than those [listed, i.e., gems and ornaments] (*taditaradravyādibhiḥ*)." Ck, Ct, and Cm gloss, "various kinds of food, drink, clothing, etc. (*vicitrānnapānavastrādibhiḥ*)." Cg simply refers to clothing, etc. (*vastrādibhiḥ*). Compare notes to verse 8 below.

5. "besieged . . . with the assistance of these monkeys" *sahaibhir arditā*: Literally, "afflicted *or* tormented [Laṅkā] . . . together with these." Ñ,V1,3,B2–4,D4,10,11, and the texts and printed editions of Ct read instead *sahāmībhis tvayā*, "by you along with these." D5,6,T1,G1,2,M3,5, and the texts and printed editions of Cr, Cv, Cg, and Cm read instead *sahaibhir ajitā*, "unconquered [Laṅkā] together with these." Cg glosses the adjective "unconquered (*ajitā*)" as "previously unconquered even by the gods, etc. (*pūrvaṃ surādibhir apy ajitā*)."

"filled with the excitement of battle" *hṛṣṭaiḥ*: Literally, "delighted, excited." We understand with Ck and Ct that the reference is to the monkeys' being filled with the excitement or frenzy of battle (*yuddhotsāhavadbhiḥ*). Cg, however, understands, "filled with love for me (*mayi prītimadbhir ity arthaḥ*)."

"fear of death" *prāṇabhayam*: Literally, "fear for life breaths."

Following verse 5, Ñ,D4–7,10,11,13,S, and the texts and printed editions of the southern commentators insert a passage of two lines [3347*]: "All these monkeys, who have accomplished their mission, should be honored.[1] You must reward their efforts[2] by bestowing[3] wealth and jewels."

[1]"All these monkeys . . . should be honored" *pūjyantāṃ sarvavānarāḥ*: Ñ2,D10,11, and the texts and printed editions of Ct read instead *sarva eva vanaukasaḥ*, "all the forest-dwelling monkeys."

[2]"You must reward their efforts" *karmaiṣāṃ saphalaṃ kuru*: Literally, "make their work fruitful."

[3]"bestowing" *-pradānena*: Ñ,D4,10,11, and the texts and printed editions of Ct read instead *-pradānaiś ca*, "and with gifts [of]."

6. "by you, bestower of honor . . . who are deserving of honor" *mānārhā mānada tvayā*: Given the context, we believe that the sense of "bestower of honor" as opposed to "humbler of honor" is more apposite for the word *mānada*. Compare 3309* (following 6.108.5) and notes, and 6.108.7 and notes. Cf. 6.13.8; 6.104.10; and notes.

D7,10,11, and the texts and printed editions of Ct read instead *nandyamānā yathā tvayā*, "in such a way that they are gratified by you."

"in your gratitude" *kṛtajñena*: Literally, "[by you who] are grateful."

7. "I am advising you" *saṃbodhayāmi te*: Cg remarks that Rāma uses the verb advisedly to emphasize that he is merely making a suggestion and not issuing an order (*saṃbodhayāmi na tu codayāmīty arthaḥ*).

"so that they may recognize that you" *yatas tvām avagacchanti*: Literally, "such that they know *or* understand you." D7,10,11,G2, and the texts and printed editions of Ct and Cr read instead *sarve tvām abhigacchanti*, which, in the context, would mean much the same as the critical reading, i.e., "all understand *or* recognize you." Roussel (1903, vol. 3, p. 400), however, understands, mistakenly in our opinion, the verb *abhigacchanti* in its sense of "they approach," rendering, "*aussi tous viennent à toi*." In this he has been followed by Pagani (1999, p. 1195), who translates similarly.

"you know both how to acquire wealth and dispense it" *tyāginaṃ saṃgrahītāram ...tvām*: Literally, "you, an abandoner [i.e., giver] and a restrainer [i.e., collector]." Our interpretation follows that of Ck, Ct, and Cm, who gloss, " 'Giver': one should supply the words, 'to suitable recipients.' 'Collector': one who collects according to the proper time and the proper procedure. One should also add the words 'of gems, etc.' (*tyāginam iti. ucitaviṣaya iti śeṣaḥ. saṃgrahītāraṃ yathākālaṃ yathānyāyam. ratnāder iti śeṣaḥ.*)" Cr's understanding of the former term is similar to that of Ck, Ct, and Cm. However, he takes the second term more specifically to refer to a king's role as a collector of taxes, etc., adding the words "in a legitimate fashion from the populace, etc. (*prajādibhyo yathānyāyaṃ grahītāram*)." Cg understands *saṃgrahītāram* somewhat differently, glossing, "the meaning is 'one who gathers, controls, *or* supports his friends or allies by giving wealth' (*dhanapradānena mitrasaṃgrahakāriṇam ity arthaḥ*)." This interpretation is represented in the translation of Raghunathan (1982, vol. 3, p. 349), who renders, "apt for friendship."

"illustrious" *yaśasvinam*: According to Cg, the term here means "possessed of glory achieved through generosity (*tyāgakṛtayaśovantam*)." Ñ,D4,10,11,13, and the texts and printed editions of Ct read instead *jitendriyam*, "who has conquered [his] senses *or* master of the senses."

Following verse 7, Ś2,V1,3,B2,4,D4–8,10–13,S insert, while Ñ,B3 continue after 3348*, a passage of two lines [3349*]: "For, in battle, the troops, being disaffected,[1] will desert a king, a lord of men, who is punitive[2] and lacks all the qualities that would make them love him."

[1]"disaffected" *saṃvignāḥ*: Literally, "agitated, frightened." Several translators believe that the term refers to the troops' fear on the battlefield. We believe, however, that the term refers in this context to the soldiers' lack of loyalty to an abusive ruler.

[2]"in battle... will desert a king, a lord of men, who is punitive" *abhihantāram āhave / tyajanti nṛpatim ... taṃ nareśvaram*: Literally, "[him] striking *or* injuring in battle, they desert the lord of men, him, a lord of men." Our translation follows the commentaries of Cm, Cv, Crā, and Cg, who understand the term *abhihantāram* to refer to a king who is violent and punitive and lacks the quality of graciousness. (*abhihantāraṃ hiṃsanaśīlam. prasādaṃ vinā krodhaikaniratam iti yāvat*—so Cm.) We believe this is correct, as it

provides a stark contrast to the kind of munificent monarch that Rāma is urging Vibhīṣaṇa to be.

For line 2 ("the troops, being disaffected, will desert a king, a lord of men"), D11 and the texts and printed editions of Ck and Ct read instead the close variant, *senā tyajati saṃvignā nṛpatiṃ taṃ nareśvara*. Aside from the slight difference of word order, this reading substitutes the singular *senā* for the plural *sainyāḥ*, "troops," and avoids the redundancy of the critical edition's use of the two synonyms for "king," *nṛpatim*, "lord of men," and *nareśvara*, "lord of men," by placing the second word in the vocative, yielding, "O lord of men," which would then refer to Vibhīṣaṇa. Ck and Ct, and the translators who follow their texts, construe *abhihantāram*, literally, "striking, slaying," with *āhave*, "in battle," understanding that the frightened troops desert a king, even though he slays [the enemy] in battle.

The verse is known to all recensions, all printed editions except Gorresio, the southern commentators, and the vast majority of manuscripts (Ś2,Ñ,V1,3,B2–4,D4–8,10–13,S). As such, its omission from the critical text is questionable.

8. "honored all the monkeys" *vānarāṃs tān ... sarvān evānvapūjayat*: Ct, perhaps concerned about the large number of monkeys to be rewarded, refers to the parallel passage in the *Rāmopākhyāna* (*MBh* 3.275.53), where it states that Rāma camped by the seashore for the night (*uvāsa*) during the distribution to support his argument that it took two days to honor all the monkeys (*sarvavānarapūjārthaṃ dinadvayaṃ vāsaḥ*).

"each according to his share, with gems and other valuables" *ratnārthaiḥ saṃvibhāgena*: Literally, "with jewels and wealth *or* riches, by division *or* sharing." Compare notes to verse 4 above. D7,11,G2,M2, and the texts and printed editions of Cr and Ct read instead the compound *ratnārthasaṃvibhāgena*, which lends a slightly different meaning to *pāda* c, "with a distribution *or* division of gems and wealth." The commentators generally agree that here the term *saṃvibhāga* refers to a distribution of wealth according to the merit of the recipients (*yathārham aṃśakalpanayā*—so Ct). Cg adds that, if the wealth had been distributed in equal shares, it would have been an occasion for anger on the part of those who deserved more [by merit or status] (*samatayā pradāne 'dhikānāṃ kopaprasaṅgād iti bhāvaḥ*).

9–10. "the troop leaders honored with gems and other valuables" *ratnair arthaiś ca yūthapān*: See notes to verses 4 and 5 above. D10,11,M1, and the texts and printed editions of Ct read instead *ratnārthair hariyūthapān*, "the leaders of the troops of tawny monkeys with gems and valuables."

"glorious" *yaśasvinīm*: Ñ,V,D4,10,11, and the texts and printed editions of Ct read instead *manasvinīm*, "wise, virtuous, *or* proud."

"but embarrassed" *lajjamānām*: Literally, "embarrassed." Cr believes that Vaidehī's modesty or embarrassment is natural and appropriate for a woman from a noble family (*svabhāvikamahākulocitalajjāviśiṣṭām*). Cg notes, more incisively, that she is embarrassed to be taken on her husband's lap in the midst of an assembly. He also notes that Rāma helps her onto his lap because of the absence of women to assist her. (*sadasy aṅkārohaṇāya lajjantīm. rāmeṇāṅkāropaṇaṃ ca strīsahāyarahitatvāt.*)

"who was armed with a bow" *dhanuṣmatā*: Although Lakṣmaṇa is normally represented as holding a bow and would probably be represented here as Rāma's bodyguard, Cg believes, probably because Rāma's hands would be full in taking Sītā on his lap, that Lakṣmaṇa is holding Rāma's bow (*rāmadhanurdhāriṇā*).

11. "Kākutstha" *kākutsthaḥ*: D7,10,11,G2,M3, and the texts and printed editions of the southern commentators read instead *pūjayan*, "honoring."

"the *rākṣasa*" *rākṣasam*: V3,D6,7,10,11,T2,3,G1,M3, and the texts and printed editions of the southern commentators read instead *kākutsthaḥ*, "Kākutstha."

12. "you have done all that friends could be expected to do" *mitrakāryaṃ kṛtam*: Literally, "what is to be done by friends has been done." Cf. note to verse 13 below.

13. "scorcher of your foes . . . and ally" *suhṛdā vā paraṃtapa*: Ś,Ñ2,V,B2,4,D8,10–12, and the texts and printed editions of Ct read instead *snigdhena ca hitena ca*, "affectionate and well-disposed," both of which modify "friend (*vayasyena*)."

*"you who fear only unrighteousness" *bhavatādharmabhīruṇā*: Literally, "by you who fear unrighteousness." For some reason, the critical edition (also GPP 6.122.15) breaks the sequence up as *bhavatā dharmabhīruṇā*, yielding the obviously undesirable meaning "by you who fear righteousness." Cg, Cm, and Ct (Cg and Ct quoted in the critical apparatus) explicitly note that we are to break the sequence up as [*bhavatā*] *adharmabhīruṇā*. With the exception of GPP, other printed editions that share this reading break the sequence appropriately.

"have accomplished all that a friend and ally could be expected to do" *yat tu kāryaṃ vayasyena suhṛdā vā . . . / kṛtam . . . tat sarvam*: Literally, "all that which is to be done by a friend or ally has been done." Cf. note to verse 12 above.

14. "you . . . may dwell in . . . your own kingdom" *svarājye vasa*: Cg reads the imperative more pointedly as a subtle warning that Vibhīṣaṇa should not entertain the imperial designs of his late brother. He glosses, "but you must remain in your own kingdom, you should not attack anyone else's [kingdom] as Rāvaṇa did. Therefore, your guards in Janasthāna must be recalled. (*svarājye vasa na tu parakīyaṃ rāvaṇavad ākramitavyam. ato janasthānarakṣiṇaḥ samānetavyā iti bhāvaḥ.*)"

"the heaven-dwelling gods" *divaukasaḥ*: Literally, "those whose dwelling is in heaven."

16. "the immensely powerful monkeys" *vānarās te mahābalāḥ*: Ś2,V,D8,10–12, and the texts and printed editions of Ct read instead *harīndrā harayas tathā*, "the lords of the tawny monkeys and the tawny monkeys."

"him" *rāmam*: Literally, "Rāma." Ś2,Ñ2,V1,2,B2–4,D8,10–12,M2, and the texts and printed editions of Ct read instead *sarve*, "all."

Following verse 16, Ś,Ñ,V1,2,B2–4,D4–8,10–13,T,G,M (M5 after 17 ab) insert a passage of one line [3361*]: "We would energetically[1] roam its groves and towns."

[1]"energetically" *udyuktāḥ*: The term can also mean "diligently," and Cg, evidently recalling the havoc wrought by the celebrating monkeys in Sugrīva's *madhuvana* in the *Sundarakāṇḍa* (5.59–60), understands that the monkeys are reassuring Rāma that they will cause no such disturbance in Ayodhyā. He glosses, " '*udyukta*' means 'carefully.' The meaning is 'without causing any harm to the countryside.' (*udyuktāḥ sāvadhānāḥ. janapadapīḍām akurvanta ity arthaḥ.*)" This interesting interpretation is represented in the translation of Raghunathan (1982, vol. 3, p. 350), who renders, "circumspectly." D10,11, and the texts and printed editions of Ct read instead *mudyuktā vicariṣyāmo vanāny upavanāni ca*, "We will roam its groves and parks in great delight." The textual evidence would support the inclusion of this line into the critical text. See notes to 3348* following verse 7 above.

17. "dripping from your consecration" *abhiṣekārdram*: See 6.13.9; 6.100.12–16; and notes. Cf. 6.107.19. V2,D11, and the texts and printed editions of Ct read instead *abhiṣekārham*, "worthy *or* deserving of consecration."

"O son of the lord of men" *nṛpateḥ suta*: Ñ2,V1,B2,4,D6,10,11,T2,3,M2, and the texts and printed editions of Ct read instead *nṛpasattama*, "O foremost *or* best of kings."

18. "by Vibhīṣaṇa and the monkeys... majestic Rāghava replied to them and to Sugrīva" *vānaraiḥ savibhīṣaṇaiḥ / abravīd rāghavaḥ śrīmān sasugrīvavibhīṣaṇān*: Literally, "by the monkeys with Vibhīṣaṇa... majestic Rāghava said to them, who were accompanied by Sugrīva and Vibhīṣaṇa." Ś,Ñ,V1,2,B2–4,D4,8,10–13,M2, and the texts and printed editions of Ct read *vānarān rāmaḥ* for the critical edition's *rāghavaḥ śrīmān*, lending the line the sense "Rāma said to the monkeys, who were accompanied by Sugrīva and Vibhīṣaṇa."

19. "I would experience a pleasure greater than any other if I could share the joy" *priyāt priyataraṃ labdhaṃ yad aham ... prītiṃ lapsye*: Literally, "in that something dearer than dear [would be] obtained [by me], I would obtain." The syntax of the verse is elliptical and confusing. Commentators attempt to identify exactly what the different sources of Rāma's pleasure might be. Ct indicates that the first pleasure is that of entering Ayodhyā after having accomplished his mission. Beyond that, Ct argues, Rāma would attain pleasure together with his friends [the monkeys, etc.] and with Bharata, etc.—the pleasure being the gratification obtained from his royal consecration. (*prathamataḥ kṛtakṛtyasyāyodhyāpraveśanam eva priyam. tatrāpi suhṛdbhir bhavadbhiḥ sahito bharatādibhiḥ saha. prītiṃ lapsye. rājyābhiṣekasaṃtoṣaṃ lapsya ity arthaḥ.*) Cg understands that the first pleasure is the recovery of Sītā, and that meeting Bharata would be even more pleasurable than that. Finally, he says that entering the city along with his friends would be a pleasure still greater than the preceding one. (*sītālābhaḥ priyam. bharatadarśanaṃ priyāt priyam, bhavadbhiḥ saha purapraveśaḥ priyāt priyataram ity arthaḥ.*)

21. "hastening... quickly ascended... as did" *adhyārohat tvarañ śīghram*: Literally, "hastening, he ascended... quickly." The stanza's only finite verb *adhyārohat*, "he ascended, mounted," is a third person singular but through *kākākṣigolakanyāya* must be understood as taking for its subjects both Sugrīva in *pāda* b and Vibhīṣaṇa in *pāda* d. Ñ,V1,2,B2–4,D4,10,11, and the texts and printed editions of Ct read instead *āruroha mudā yuktaḥ*, "he ascended filled with joy."

"together with his army" *saha senayā*: Ñ,V,B2,3,D4,10,11,M2, and the texts and printed editions of Ct read instead *saha vānaraiḥ*, "together with the monkeys."

22. "vehicle" *-āsanam*: Literally, "seat." The commentators all gloss either *yānam* or *vāhanam*, "vehicle."

"at Rāghava's command" *rāghaveṇābhyanujñātam*: Literally, "permitted by Rāghava."

23. "departed in that... flying palace" *yayau tena vimānena*: Literally, "he went by means of that flying palace." Ñ,V2,D10,11, and the texts and printed editions of Ct read instead *khagatena vimānena*, "the flying palace that had gone into the sky." See 6.7.5; 6.109.22–27; and notes.

"yoked to *haṃsas*" *haṃsayuktena*: The *haṃsa* is usually identified as the bar-headed goose (*Anser indicus*), but the bird intended may well be either the mute swan (*Cygnus olor*) or whooper swan (*Cygnus cygnus*). See Dave 1985, pp. 422–31. See, too, Thieme 1975, pp. 3–36. Cf. note to 6.57.35. The commentators are in agreement that the great flying palace is not actually drawn by these birds. Their general consensus is that some type of depictions of *haṃsas* are part of the décor of the vehicle. Ct notes that other, unnamed commentators, indicate that these artificial *haṃsas* are constructed to look as if they are drawing the vehicle (*haṃsaśabdena vāhakatvākāreṇa nirmitahaṃsa-pratimā ucyata iti vyākhyātāraḥ*—Ck). Cm understands that these *haṃsas* are fashioned to represent the vehicle of Brahmā (*haṃsavadbrahmavāhakatvākāreṇa nirmitā haṃsā ucyate*—Cm). Ck understands that there is no vehicle actually borne by *haṃsas* other than that of Brahmā (*haṃsavāharatho brahmātiriktasya nāsti*). Cs notes that, in reality, it is through the power of the vehicle's inner presiding deity that it appears to move of its own accord and we should understand that it has no need of any other external motive force. (*vastutas tu tadvimānadevasyaiva tādṛśaśaktimattvena svecchayaivānya-nirapekṣeṇa gatir iti jñeyam.*) See 6.111.1. Ś,B1,D1–3,8,12 read *kāmagena*, "moving at will," for *haṃsayuktena*. Although no printed edition shares this reading, it appears to have informed the translation of Dutt (1893, p. 1523), who renders, "coursing at will."

"Delighted in mind and body" *prahṛṣṭaś ca pratītaś ca*: We follow Ct and Cm in taking *pratīta* in its sense of "happy *or* delighted." To avoid redundancy between this term and *prahṛṣṭa*, which also means "delighted," these commentators understand that the former term applies to physical pleasure, such as the bristling of the hairs on the body, while the latter refers to mental delight (*prahṛṣṭo hṛṣṭaromā pratītaḥ prahṛṣṭacittaḥ*). Cg and Cs, however, understand the second term in its sense of "famous, illustrious." Cg glosses, "praised (*ślāghitaḥ*)." This interpretation is represented in the translation of Raghunathan (1982, vol. 3, p. 350), who renders, "receiving the praises of all." Cs glosses, "famous (*prasiddhaḥ*)," an idea similar to that of Gorresio (1858, vol. 10, p. 249), who renders, "*glorioso*."

Following verse 23, D5–7,10,11,S insert a passage of two lines [3369*]: "All those monkeys and apes[1] and the immensely powerful *rākṣasas* seated themselves in that divine vehicle,[2] comfortably and without any crowding."

[1]"those monkeys and apes" *vānararkṣāś ca*: Printed editions of Cg read instead *vānarā hṛṣṭāḥ*, "the delighted monkeys."

[2]"in that divine vehicle" *divye tasmin*: Literally, "in that divine [thing]."

Sarga 111

1. "At Rāma's command" *anujñātaṃ tu rāmeṇa*: See 6.110.22 and note.

"flew onward, like a great cloud driven before the wind" *utpapāta mahāmeghaḥ śvasanenoddhato yathā*: The verb *utpapāta* would properly mean "flew upward," but, given the tenor of the simile, it seems appropriate to understand the motion to be lateral.

D7,10,11,G2, and the texts and printed editions of Ct read instead *haṃsayuktaṃ mahānādam utpapāta vihāyasam*, "yoked to *haṃsas*, it rose into the sky with a mighty roar." See note to 6.110.23.

2. "whose face was like the hare-marked moon" *śaśinibhānanām*: Literally, "whose face was like the one possessing a hare."

3. "fashioned by Viśvakarman" *nirmitāṃ viśvakarmaṇā*: See 5.2.19–22. Cf. 6.109.27 and notes.

4. Following verse 4, Ñ1,D5–7,9–11,13,S insert, while Ś,Ñ2,V,B2–4,D4,8,12 continue after 3382*, a passage of one line [3373*]: "There lies the troublesome lord of the *rākṣasas,* who had been granted a boon." This line appears in all recensions and printed editions consulted as well as in all but a few manuscripts (B1,D1,2,3). Its omission from the critical edition is questionable. The editors may have omitted it on the grounds of higher criticism, since Rāvaṇa has already been cremated (6.99.42). The commentators are not unaware of this issue. Ct understands the reference here to be to Rāvaṇa's cremation ground (*eṣa iti taddāhabhūmidarśanam*). Cg understands that Rāvaṇa lies there in the form of ashes (*śete bhasmasvarūpeṇety arthaḥ*).

5. Following verse 5, D5–7,9–11,S insert a passage of two lines [3376*]: "And here, too, was Dhūmrākṣa slain by the monkey Hanumān, as was Vidyunmālin by the great Suṣeṇa."

6. "slew . . . were also slain" *nihataḥ*: Literally, "[he was] slain."

"impossible to even look upon" *duṣprekṣyaḥ*: Ś2,Ñ,V,B2–4,D4,6,8,12,13,T2,3,M3, and the texts and printed editions of Cg and the edition of Gorresio (6.108.6) read instead *durdharṣaḥ,* "unassailable."

Following 6ab, D5–7,9–11,S insert a passage of one line [3380*]: "Here the *rākṣasa* called Vikaṭa[1] was slain by Aṅgada."

[1]"Vikaṭa" *vikaṭaḥ*: A *rākṣasa* named Vikaṭa is among those listed in an inserted passage (1686* [following 6.77.9–11]) who were slain by Vibhīṣaṇa and his companions. Ct, apparently concerned that only one of the numerous *rākṣasas* listed at 1686* is mentioned here, suggests that we take the name as standing for the entire group (*aṅgadena vikaṭo hata ity anuvādād tad api jātam iti bodhyam*). Cg understands similarly.

7. "as were those other powerful *rākṣasas*" *balino 'nye ca rākṣasāḥ*: We agree with Cr in taking the reference to be to the *rākṣasas'* names in the second half of the verse (*akampano nihatas triśiraḥprabhṛtayo 'nye ca nihatāḥ*).

Following verse 7, D5–7,9–11,T,G,M1,2, and the texts and printed editions of Ct and Cr insert a passage of nine lines [3383*]: "[As were] the two prominent *rākṣasas* Yuddhonmatta and Matta,[1] and also Nikumbha and Kumbha, the two sons of Kumbhakarṇa, [1–2] Vajradaṃṣṭra, Daṃṣṭra,[2] and many *rākṣasas* were slain. And I struck down the unassailable Makarākṣa in battle.[3–4] Akampana, too, was slain as was the mighty Śoṇitākṣa. And it was here in the great battle that Yūpākṣa and Prajaṅgha were killed.[5–6] Here, too, the *rākṣasa* Vidyujjihva, of terrifying appearance, was slain; also slain were Yajñaśatru, the immensely powerful Suptaghna, Sūryaśatru, and the unexcelled Brahmaśatru.[3][7–9]"

[1]"Yuddhonmatta and Matta" *yuddhonmattaś ca mattaś ca*: See note to 6.59.1. Dutt (1893, p. 1524), alone among the translators consulted, takes these names as epithets of Nikumbha and Kumbha, rendering, "mad after conflict."

[2]"Daṃṣṭra" *daṃṣṭraḥ*: Literally, "Fang." No *rākṣasa* of this name is mentioned in the critical text, and there appears to be no other mention of a *rākṣasa* of this name in the texts and printed editions of the southern commentators.

[3]"Brahmaśatru" *brahmaśatruḥ*: No *rākṣasa* of this name appears in the critical text or, apparently, elsewhere in the texts and printed editions of the southern commentators.

8. "Rāvaṇa's wife . . . mourned him" *bhāryā taṃ paryadevayat*: Literally, "the wife mourned him."

"drenched with tears" *sāsreṇa*: Literally, "tearful." Ś,Ñ,V1,B2–4,D1,2,5,7–12,T1,G2,M1,2, and the texts and printed editions of Ck, Ct, and Cr read instead *sāgreṇa*, literally, "with a surplus." This lends the line the sense that Mandodarī's co-wives number more than a thousand.

9. "shore" *tīrtham*: Literally, "crossing spot, ford, bathing spot." This use of the term *tīrtha* is to be distinguished from the usage at 3395*, line 2, where it refers to the holy shrine of Rāmeśvara, a discussion of which will engage the energy and ingenuity of the commentators. Ct and Ck understand, "descent (*avatāra*)." Cr glosses, "a ghat, *or* bathing place (*ghaṭṭaḥ*)." See note 2 to 3395*, line 2, following verse 12 below.

"fair-faced woman" *varānane*: Literally, "having an excellent face."

10. "that bridge is Nala's bridge" *eṣa setuḥ . . . nalasetuḥ*: Several of the commentators offer explanations for the seeming redundancy implicit in the repetition of the term *setuḥ*, "bridge." Cr, whom we follow, understands Rāma to be repeating the term to indicate that this is the very bridge he had Nala build (*mayā baddhaḥ eṣa setur nalasetur bhavati nalenaiva kārita ity arthaḥ*). Ct and Cm understand similarly. Cg takes the second term, *setu*, as a participle derived from the root √*ṣiñ* in the sense of "to build," specifying that the bridge was built by Nala (*eṣa setur nalasetur nalabaddhaḥ ṣiñ bandhana iti dhātuḥ*). He believes that the specification is made here in order to exclude the idea that another bridge was constructed during the previous *kalpa*, for, Cg argues, if an earlier bridge had existed, the building of the newer bridge would have been pointless. (*etena nalasetuḥ setur ity uktyā pūrvakalpakṛtasetvantaraṃ vyāvartyata iti pratyuktam. pūrvam eva setusattve punaḥ setukaraṇavaiyarthyāt.*)

"all-but-impossible" *suduṣkaraḥ*: Literally, "extraordinarily difficult to accomplish." Several of the commentators understand the adjective to mean "impossible for anyone other than Nala to accomplish (*nalabhinnena kartum aśakyam*—so Cr)."

"across the ocean, the reservoir of waters" *sāgare salilārṇave*: Literally, "on the ocean, the ocean of water." The critical reading seems redundant. Of the commentators who share the reading, two of them, Cv and Cg, make efforts to avoid the redundancy. Cv, whom we follow, glosses "collection of water (*salilākare*)" for *salilārṇave*, "ocean of water." Cg takes the term *sāgare* as an elliptical adjective meaning "caused to be dug out by Sagara (*sagarakhānite*)," referring to the legend of Sagara's interrupted sacrifice and the digging of the ocean by his sixty thousand sons as told in the *Bālakāṇḍa* (1.38–43). Cg then notes that the ocean (*arṇava*) is said to be the ocean of water in order to distinguish it from the other oceans well known in purāṇic cosmology, such as the ocean of milk (*salileti kṣīrodādivyāvṛttiḥ*). D7,10,11, and the texts and printed editions of Cr and Ct read *lavaṇārṇave*, "the salt sea," for *salilārṇave*.

11. "boundless and roaring" *apāram abhigarjantam*: Literally, "having no farther shore and roaring." Cg understands the term *apāram*, "having no farther shore," to mean that there are no shores, that is, that there are no islands in the middle [of the ocean] (*apāraṃ madhye dvīpabhūtapārarahitam*). Ś2,Ñ,V,B,D, and the texts and printed editions of Ct read *iva*, "as if," for the critical text's *abhi-*, which lends the passage the sense "seeming to have no farther shore," i.e., "seemingly endless."

12. "And look . . . at the . . . lord of mountains, Mount Maināka, with its golden peak" *hiraṇyanābhaṃ śailendram . . . paśya*: Literally, "Look at the lord of mountains with its golden navel." The compound *hiraṇyanābha* is a common epithet for Mount Maināka. See 5.1.79,89,91–92,123,125, and notes to 5.1.79 and 87 for an explanation of why we interpret the compound to mean "with its golden peak." There appears to be something of a narrative contradiction here in having Rāma point out Mount Maināka to Sītā as they fly across the ocean. At 5.1.129, it is clearly stated that, after his encounter with Hanumān, the mountain once more sank beneath the waves. Note the southern variant of 3394* below, which may be an attempt to silently correct the discrepancy.

"to provide a resting place for Hanumān" *viśramārthaṃ hanumato*: Literally, "for the sake of Hanumān's repose." The incident is described in the *Sundarkāṇḍa* (5.1.79–129). It should be recalled, however, that Hanumān declines the mountain's offer.

Following verse 12, virtually all manuscripts (Ś2,Ñ,V,B,D1–4,8,9,12 read lines 1–3; D5–7,10,11,13,T,G,M1, and the texts and printed editions of the southern commentators read line 3) insert at least line 3 of 3394*: "There on the shore of the ocean was my encampment, Jānakī."

D5–7,9–11,T,G1,3,M1,2,5, and the texts and printed editions of the southern commentators read a slight variation of 3394*, line 3, "[Mount Maināka] is in the middle of the ocean; [and there] is the encampment of the army (*etat kukṣau samudrasya skandhāvāraniveśanam*)." The line is somewhat obscure and our translation follows the interpretation of Ct, who understands that it is Mount Maināka that is situated in the middle of the ocean while the encampment of the army [prior to the crossing] was on its northern shore. (*etan mainākaparvatasvarūpaṃ samudrasya kukṣau vartata iti śeṣaḥ. etad ity āvartate. etad skandhāvaraṇāveśanaṃ senāniveśanam. samudrottaratīrastham iti śeṣaḥ.*) Cg, however, understands that it is the encampment that was located in the middle of the ocean, by which he understands it to have taken place in mid-journey on the bridge itself. (*kukṣau madhye. setūparīti śeṣaḥ.*) Since the original description of the army's crossing at 6.15.31 makes no reference to their making camp while crossing the bridge, we believe that Ct's interpretation is more plausible. It is possible that the term *kukṣau* in the context should be taken in its primary sense of "in the interior" and is intended to address the apparent contradiction mentioned above. The idea would be that Rāma is telling Sītā to observe the golden-peaked mountain shining from beneath the surface of the sea.

Following 3394*, line 3, D5–7,9–11,T,G2,3,M3,5 (while G1,M1 insert differently), and the texts and printed editions of the southern commentators insert a passage of four lines [3395*]: "It was here that, prior to that, the great and lordly god granted his favor.[1][1] And there one can see that sacred spot[2] of great Sāgara, known as Setubandha, 'the Building of the Bridge,' which is worshiped by all the three worlds.[2–3] It is holy, and it is the supreme place for the expiation of great sin.[4]" This passage, and especially its first line, has been the subject of an elaborate and animated debate among the commentators as to its precise significance. There is little doubt that this interpolation alludes to the well-known purāṇic tradition that Rāma propitiated Śiva at the southern tip of the Indian subcontinent and, in his devotion and gratitude to the Lord for his blessing that enabled him to cross the ocean successfully, established there a Śivaliṅga at what is known as the *tīrtha* of Rāmeśvara. Not all the commentators, however, accept this, and those who do, differ as to when the *liṅga* was established.

[1]"It was here that, prior to that, the great and lordly god granted his favor." *atra pūrvaṃ mahādevaḥ prasādam akarod vibhuḥ*: Literally, "Here, formerly, the great god, the Lord, made *prasāda*." For Ct, Ck, Cr, and Cs there is no question that the epithet *mahādevaḥ*, literally, "great god," bears its normal significance as one of the prime epithets of Śiva (*setor nirvighnatā siddhyai samudraprasādānantaraṃ śivasthāpanaṃ rāmeṇa kṛtam iti gamyate*—so Ct). Cm and Cg, however, vigorously reject this position, arguing that here the term refers to the ocean god Sāgara, whose propitiation is fully described at 6.13.22–6.14. Cg argues that no prior mention has been made of any propitiation or other involvement on the part of Śiva in connection with the building of the bridge. Cm offers two explanations as to why the epithet must be understood as referring to the god of the ocean. In the first, he takes the term *mahat* to be a synonym for water, and the god who has the form of that water is *mahādeva*, the god of the waters, i.e., Samudra. In the second, he observes that, even if the term is taken in its normal sense as an epithet of Śiva, we should understand that the reference is to water, one of the eight elemental forms (*aṣṭamūrti*) of that god, and thus still refers to the ocean (*mahādevo mahad iti jalaṃ tadrūpo devo mahādevaḥ samudraḥ . . . yadvā mahādevāṣṭamūrtiṣv anyatamatvān mahādevaśabdena samudra evocyate*).

Ck and Ct understand by the adverb *pūrvam* that the establishment of the Śivaliṅga took place much earlier than the events currently being narrated. Ct understands that the *liṅga* was established at the time the bridge was built, and thus prior to the crossing of the bridge and the war in Laṅkā. Cs quotes Ct but claims that the latter's reading should be rejected, as it is based on an inadequate study of the *purāṇas*, which deal extensively with this topic. Cs himself believes that it is only now, after showing Sītā this spot, that Rāma descends from the flying palace and establishes the Śivaliṅga. To support his view, Cs cites relevant passages from a number of purāṇic sources, including the *Agni-*, *Kūrma-*, and *Skandapurāṇas*. Evidently concerned that the text makes no allusion to Śiva's involvement in the building of the bridge, Ck argues that the term *pūrvam* should be understood to refer to an earlier occurrence of the events in a previous *kalpa*, when the Rāma of that age propitiated Śiva. Cg takes a rationalist and text-based approach to refute these other opinions. He notes that the text has failed to mention any propitiation of Śiva, and therefore the current description cannot be to that divinity. Likewise, he dismisses Ck's argument, noting that, if the bridge had been built in a previous age, there would have been no point in building another one at the present time. Interestingly, Cg also refutes the arguments of those commentators who cite purāṇic sources for the establishment of the Rāmeśvara *tīrtha* by arguing that, although the *purāṇas* may deal effectively with such great cosmological events as the creation and destruction of the universe, they are poor sources for the reconstruction of history, an area in which the epics themselves are far more reliable. He thus argues that one must give credence to the account recorded in the *Rāmāyaṇa* over any found in the *purāṇas*. (*na tv atra rudro mahādevaḥ. tena pūrvaṃ prāsādakaraṇānukteḥ . . . etādṛśapurāṇavacanānusareṇāyaṃ śloko liṅgapratiṣṭhāṃ bodhayatīti. maivam uktadoṣavistārāt. itihāso hi parigrahātiśayāt. granthasauṣṭhavāc ca. itihāsapurāṇaṃ pañcamam ityādāv adhikākṣaratve 'pi pūrvaprayogenābhyarhitatvāc ca purāṇebhyo garīyān iti.*

vedaḥ prācetasād āsīd iti vedamayatoktyā caturmukhavarapradānamūlatayā ca prabalataraḥ. tadvirodhe tāmasapurāṇavacanāni na pramāṇāni. kiṃca purāṇaṃ sargapratisargādiṣv anyaparam iti netihāsavat purāvṛttakathane tātparyavat.) See 6.113.8–11 and note.

It should be noted that, in the textual tradition of Cv, Crā, Cg, and Cm, line 1 of this insert effectively becomes line 4. Several commentators make a point of listing what they believe to be the proper sequence of verses. The sequence reflected in this version is found only in the translation of Raghunathan (1982, vol. 3, p. 351).

[2]"that sacred spot" *tīrtham*: The context of the passage makes it clear that the term must be taken in this sense, in contrast to the way the term must be understood in verse 9 above. Cs and Cm understand the term in its technical sense of a salvific place of pilgrimage. Cm glosses, "a holy place (*puṇyakṣetram*)." Cs alludes to a number of purāṇic references to Rāma's establishing a Śivaliṅga at that spot [Rāmeśvara], since, according to purāṇic legend, it was through Śiva's grace that Rāma was able to build the bridge and kill Rāvaṇa. See notes to verse 9 above; and 6.113.24 and notes.

13. "came over to me" *ājagāma*: Literally, "he came."

14. Following verse 14, D5–7,9–11,S insert a passage of thirty lines [App. I, No. 72]: "Now, when Sītā saw Kiṣkindhā, which had been ruled by Vālin, she humbly spoke these words to Rāma, with the insistence born of love[1][1–2]: 'Your majesty, I should like to go[2] with you to the capital Ayodhyā in the company of Sugrīva's beloved wives, Tārā and the rest, as well as the wives of the other monkey lords.' [3–5] Addressed in this fashion by Vaidehī, Rāghava said, 'So be it.' Then, when they reached Kiṣkindhā, he stopped the flying palace and, looking at Sugrīva, said these words [6–8]: 'Tiger among the monkeys, you must inform all the bulls among monkeys that they are all to go to Ayodhyā with Sītā in the company of their own wives.[9–10] And you, too, immensely powerful Sugrīva, should make haste with all your wives. Let us go, lord of the leaping monkeys!'[11–12] Addressed in this fashion by Rāma of immeasurable blazing energy, Sugrīva, the majestic lord of the monkeys, quickly entered his inner apartments accompanied by everyone.[3] And, looking at Tārā, he said [13–15]: 'My dear, you and the wives of the great monkeys must hasten at Rāma's command. In order to please Maithilī, we must go, taking with us the wives[4] of the monkeys. We will show you Ayodhyā and introduce you to all of Daśaratha's wives.[5]'[16–19] When she had heard those words of Sugrīva, Tārā, who was lovely in every limb, summoned all the wives[4] of the monkeys, saying [20–21], 'Together with all the monkeys, you have been commanded by Sugrīva to go. You must also please me by seeing Ayodhyā. For you are to witness[6] the entrance of Rāma, together with the city folk and country folk, and the splendor of all of Daśaratha's wives.'[22–25] When they had been instructed in this way by Tārā, all the wives[4] of the monkeys attired themselves appropriately, and then, having reverently circumambulated the flying palace,[7] they ascended it[8] in their eagerness to see Sītā.[26–28] Seeing that the flying palace had swiftly risen with all of them, Rāghava spoke once more to Vaidehī as they approached Mount Ṛśyamūka.[9][29–30]"

[1]"with the insistence born of love" *praṇayasādhvasā*: Literally, "with the urgency *or* agitation of love." Ck and Ct understand the term to mean that Sītā is using Rāma's affection in order to get her husband to do what she wants (*praṇayasādhvasaṃ ca bhartuḥ sveṣṭe pravartananimittaṃ yasyāḥ sā*).

[2]"I should like to go" *gantum icche*: Ct notes that, for the purpose of fulfilling Sītā's request, it will be necessary to halt for one day in Kiṣkindhā. He then refers to the *Rāmopākhyāna* (*MBh* 3.275.57) in which it is stated that the day when they must halt is used to perform the consecration of Aṅgada as heir apparent. (*atraitad artham eka-dinavāsah. ata eva bhārate 'ṅgadasya yauvarājyābhiṣeko 'py etad dina uktaḥ.*) Acting on Rāma's instruction (4.25.11), Sugrīva has already consecrated Aṅgada in the *Kiṣ-kindhākāṇḍa* (4.25.35). Ct is probably trying to rationalize the apparent contradiction between the *Yuddhakāṇḍa*'s account and that of the *Rāmopākhyāna*. Further, in light of the redundant consecrations of Vibhīṣaṇa in *sargas* 13 and 100, respectively, Ct may see no internal contradiction in the *Rāmāyaṇa*. See 6.13.9; 6.100.12–16; and notes. See, too, note to 6.51.10.

[3]"by everyone" *taiś ca sarvaiḥ*: Literally, "by all of them." As Cr notes, the reference must be to the monkeys (*vānaraiḥ*).

[4]"the wives" *yoṣitaḥ*: Literally, "the women."

[5]"We will show you Ayodhyā and introduce you to all of Daśaratha's wives." *ayodhyāṃ darśayiṣyāmaḥ sarvā daśarathastriyaḥ*: Literally, "we will cause [you] to see Ayodhyā and all of Daśaratha's women."

[6]"You must also please me by seeing... You must also witness" *mama cāpi priyaṃ kāryam... -darśanena ca*: Literally, "And my favor is to be done by seeing."

[7]"having reverently circumambulated the flying palace" *kṛtvā cāpi pradakṣiṇam*: Literally, "having made a[n auspicious] circle to the right." We agree with the commentators that they are circumambulating the Puṣpakavimāna.

[8]"they ascended it" *adhyārohan vimānaṃ tat*: Literally, "they ascended the flying palace." Cs raises an obscure issue here, which highlights how diligently the commentators attempt to reconcile any possible contradictions in the long and complex epic story. Cs recalls that, earlier in the *Yuddhakāṇḍa*, when Rāma and Lakṣmaṇa had been struck down by the serpent-weapons of Indrajit, Sītā had been forced to fly over the battlefield in the Puṣpakavimāna to witness the apparent death of her husband. In the course of her flight, the *rākṣasī* Trijaṭā, in an effort to reassure Sītā that Rāma was not, in fact, dead, argues that, if he had been killed, the Puṣpakavimāna would not have carried her (6.38.25) because, as noted by Cr at that point, that auspicious vehicle will not carry a widow. This being the case, Cs argues, there is an apparent contradiction in that the flying palace now seems willing to transport Tārā, who was widowed when Rāma killed her husband, Vālin. Cs rebuts this argument first by saying that, because the passage only provides a negative example, the rule stated here cannot be tested since Rāma was not, in fact, dead, and therefore Sītā was not impure. Cs further notes that, even if one were to accept the validity of this rule, it still would not apply, since Tārā has now been remarried to Sugrīva and is therefore no longer a widow. Cs also cites a quotation from *smṛti*, according to which "a woman who has a son [as Tārā does in the form of Aṅgada] cannot be considered a widow (*putriṇy avidhavā iti smṛteḥ*). Interestingly, Cs, who is so meticulous in citing the minor contradiction in this passage, appears to assign, in error, the statements about the Puṣpaka to the *rākṣasī* Saramā. Although Saramā does console Sītā when she is shown the illusory head of her husband, it is, in fact, Trijaṭā who, in all versions of Vālmīki's text of which we are aware, informs her of the *vimāna*'s inability to transport widows.

[9]"as they approached Mount Ṛśyamūka" *ṛśyamūkasamīpe*: Literally, "in the vicinity of Ṛśyamūka."

15. "Laced with... minerals... laced with lightning" *savidyut... dhātubhir vṛtaḥ*: Literally, "with lightning... covered with minerals."

19. "graceful... where, on your account, a great battle took place between cruel Rāvaṇa and great Jaṭāyus" *yatra yuddhaṃ mahad vṛttaṃ tava hetor vilāsini / rāvaṇasya nṛśaṃsasya jaṭāyoś ca mahātmanaḥ*: For 19c–f, D10,11, and the texts and printed editions of Ct substitute a passage of two lines [3402*]: "... where the foremost of birds, mighty Jaṭāyus, of immense blazing energy, was slain on your account by Rāvaṇa, graceful [woman]."

"that... tree, the lord of the forest" *vanaspatiḥ*: Literally, "the forest lord." The term is commonly used for large trees. The reference is to the tree in which the sleeping Jaṭāyus was perched when he was awakened by the cries of Sītā in the clutches of Rāvaṇa (3.48.2).

20. "And it was here, too, that... I slew" *nihataḥ... mayā*: Literally, "was slain by me."

"in battle" *saṃkhye*: D5,M3, and the texts and printed editions of Cg read instead *yatra*, "where," which provides a transition lacking in the critical text.

D10,11, and the texts and printed editions of Ct omit this verse.

Following verse 20 (or 3402*), D5,6,10,11,T,G1,3,M, and the texts and printed editions of the southern commentators insert a passage of one line [3404*]: "And this, lady of the fair complexion, was the site of our ashram."

21. "beautiful" *śubhadarśanā*: Literally, "of beautiful *or* lovely appearance." D5,7,10,11,13,G2,M1, and the texts and printed editions of Cr and Ct read instead the vocative *śubhadarśane*, which then refers to Sītā in the sense "O beautiful woman."

"the... leaf hut" *parṇaśālā*: This is the leaf hut built by Lakṣmaṇa at 3.14.20–21.

Following verse 21, D5,6,T,G1,3,M1,2,5 insert, while D7,G3,M3, and the texts and printed editions of Cg insert following verse 22, a passage of one line [3408*]. For a translation, see notes to verse 22 below.

22. "Look, Maithilī" *paśya maithili*: Ñ,V,B,D1–4,8–12, and the texts and printed editions of Ct read instead *kadalīvṛtaḥ*, "surrounded by plantain trees." This adjective then describes Agastya's ashram.

"the ashram of Agastya" *agastyasyāśramaḥ*: See 3.10.84ff.

Following verse 22, D7,G3,M3, and the texts and printed editions of Cg insert, while D5,6,T,G1,3,M1,2,5 insert following verse 2, a passage of one line [3408*]: "And there is the resplendent ashram of the great Sutīkṣṇa.[1]"

[1]"the... ashram of... Sutīkṣṇa" *āśramaḥ sutīkṣṇasya*: See 3.10.26ff.

23. "the... ashram of Śarabhaṅga" *śarabhaṅgāśramaḥ*: See 3.4.

"Śakra" *śakraḥ*: Literally, "the mighty one." See 3.4.5–21, where Indra visits the ashram of Śarabhaṅga.

24. "the dwellings of the ascetics" *tāpasāvāsāḥ*: Ñ,B1,D4,10,11, and the texts and printed editions of Ct read instead *tāpasā devi*, "the ascetics, O queen."

"where Atri, the ashram elder... dwells" *atriḥ kulapatir yatra*: Literally, "where the *kulapati* Atri [is]." The word *kulapati*, literally, "lord of the family," is a term used to describe the seniormost or chief ascetic in an ashram community. Rāma, Lakṣmaṇa, and Sītā visit Atri's ashram at 2.109.5ff.

"whose radiance is like that of Sūrya or Agni Vaiśvānara" *sūryavaiśvānaraprabhaḥ*: Literally, "whose radiance was that of Sūrya and/or Vaiśvānara." Ś2,Ñ,V1,3,B2–4,D4,8,10–12, and the texts and printed editions of Ct read *-[u]pamaḥ* for *-prabhaḥ*, which lends the compound the meaning "who was like Sūrya or Vaiśvānara."

"It was here, Sītā, that you met the ascetic woman who practiced righteousness." *atra sīte tvayā dṛṣṭā tāpasī dharmacāriṇī*: Commentators understand that the woman in question is Atri's wife, Anasūyā, whom Sītā meets in Atri's ashram (2.109.7ff.).

Ñ,V1,B2–4,D4,6,10,11,13,T2,3,G1,M2, and the texts and printed editions of Ct transpose this line (24ef) and verse 25. M3 and the texts and printed editions of Cg transpose verses 24 and 25.

25. "the giant" *mahākāyaḥ*: Literally, "whose body is large."

"Virādha" *virādhaḥ*: The encounter with Virādha is described at 3.2.4–27.

See notes to verse 24 above on the ordering of the verses in the texts of the southern commentators.

26. "where Kaikeyī's son came to beseech me to return" *yatra māṃ kaikeyīputraḥ prasādayitum āgataḥ*: Literally, "where Kaikeyī's son came to beseech *or* propitiate me."

27. "in the distance" *dūrāt*: Literally, "from afar." Ś,Ñ,V,B3,4,D4,8,10–13, and the texts and printed editions of Ct read instead *ramyā*, "lovely," which describes the river Yamunā.

"where . . . majestic . . . is just coming into view" *yatra śrīmān eṣa prakāśate*: Literally, "where this majestic [ashram] appears." Ś,Ñ,V,B3,D4,8,10–12, and the texts and printed editions of Ct read instead *śrīmān dṛśyate caiṣa maithili*, "and one can see this majestic [ashram], Maithilī."

28. "And over there one can see the Ganges, which flows by three paths, lady of the fair complexion." *eṣā tripathagā gaṅgā dṛśyate varavarṇini*: Ś,Ñ,V,B2–4,D8,10–13, and the texts and printed editions of Ct substitute a passage of one line [3419*]: "And, Sītā, one can see the river Ganges[1] that flows by three paths." The story of the descent of the Gaṅgā is told at *Bālakāṇḍa* 38–43.

[1]"Sītā . . . Ganges": *sīte . . . gaṅgā*: D10,11, and the texts and printed editions of Ct substitute *gaṅgā* for *sīte*, and *puṇyā*, "holy," for *gaṅgā*. This yields the sense "and one can see the holy Ganges, the river that flows by three paths."

"met us" *samāgataḥ*: Literally, "was met." Ś,Ñ,V1,2,B2–4,D8,10–13, and the texts and printed editions of Ck and Ct read instead *sakhā mama*, "my friend." This lends the phrase the sense "where my friend Guha [is]."

Following 28ab, D5–7,T2,3,G,M1,3,5, and the texts and printed editions of Cr and Cg insert a passage of one line [3420*]: "It is crowded with flocks of various birds and its woodlands are filled with blossoms."

Following verse 28, D5–7,T2,3,G,M1,3,5, and the texts and printed editions of Cg and Gita Press (line 1 only) insert a passage of two lines [3424*]: "And there, Sītā, one can see the Sarayū River garlanded with sacrificial posts. It is lined with various trees and creepers[1] and its trees[2] are filled with blossoms."

[1]"creepers" *-latā-*: D5,G3,M3,5, and the texts and printed editions of Cg, Cm, and Gita Press read instead *śata-*, "hundreds."

[2]"trees" *-pādapā*: D5,6,T2,3,G,M, and the texts and printed editions of Cg, Cm, and Gita Press read instead *-kānanā*, "woodlands."

These variants lend the second line the sense: "It is lined with hundreds of various trees and its woodlands are filled with blossoms."

29. "Ayodhyā" *ayodhyā*: Ś,Ñ,V,B,D1–3,7–13,G2, and the texts and printed editions of Cr and Ct read instead *sīte*, "O Sītā," for *'yodhyā*. See 6.113.1 and notes, where the commentators are concerned about whether it would be possible for Rāma to see Ayodhyā from Bharadvāja's ashram.

30. "and the *rākṣasa* Vibhīṣaṇa" *rākṣasaś ca vibhīṣaṇaḥ*: Ś,Ñ,V,B2–4,D6,9–13,T2, 3,M1,2, and the texts and printed editions of Ct read instead *rākṣasāḥ savibhīṣaṇāḥ*, "the *rākṣasas* together with Vibhīṣaṇa."

"gazed at that beautiful city" *dadṛśus tāṃ purīṃ śubhadarśanām*: Ś,Ñ,V,B1,2,D8,10–13, and the texts and printed editions of Ct read instead *saṃhṛṣṭās tāṃ purīṃ dadṛśus tadā*, "then in great delight they gazed upon the city."

31. "Those leaping monkeys gazed upon the city of Ayodhyā" *purīm ayodhyāṃ dadṛśuḥ plavaṅgamāḥ*: Ś,Ñ,V,B2–4,D8,10–13, and the texts and printed editions of Ct read instead *purīm apaśyan plavagāḥ sarākṣasāḥ*, "the leaping monkeys, together with the *rākṣasas*, gazed at the city."

"It had spacious courtyards" *viśālakakṣyām*: Literally, "having broad courtyards *or* enclosures." Ct and Ck gloss, "with its broad avenues (*viśālarathyām*—so Ct)."

The meter is *vaṃśasthavila*.

Sarga 112

1."And so, on the fifth day of the fortnight when the fourteenth year was just complete" *pūrṇe caturdaśe varṣe pañcamyām*: Literally, "when the fourteenth year was completed on the fifth." According to Cv, Cm, and Cg, this would be the fifth day of the bright half of the lunar month of Caitra (March-April), the same date on which Rāma set forth in exile fourteen years earlier. (*pūrṇe caitraśuddhapañcamyām ayodhyāto nirgamanam. tadārabhya caturdaśavarṣe pūrṇe sati pañcamyāṃ caitraśuddhapañcamyām*—so Cg.) Cm and Cv document this with a careful chronology of the battle starting with Rāma's troops' ascent of Mount Suvela. Cg offers a still more elaborate chronology beginning from the day of Rāma's banishment from Ayodhyā and carrying on through his wanderings in the forest, his meeting with Sugrīva, the monkeys' search, the war and its aftermath, and the return journey. Both of these accounts, although they deal with different events, are in close agreement, and these three commentators, especially Cm, are at pains to offer textual citations to demonstrate that the events described take place on the specific days that they assign to them. Cg notices one important contradiction. He observes that, in the *Sundarakāṇḍa*, Sītā mentioned to Hanumān that she had only one month remaining of the year that Rāvaṇa had allowed her before she would either have to submit to him or be eaten (5.35.8 and notes; cf. 5.36.50 and notes), whereas Rāvaṇa himself had told Sītā that she had two months remaining before this grim deadline (3.54.22; 5.20.8). Cg explains the discrepancy by observing that Sītā's calculation is correct, while Rāvaṇa's is a result of his intoxication brought on by drinking too much honey-wine (*avaśiṣṭau dvau māsāv ity uktir madhupānamattatayāvivekakṛtā*).

Several northern manuscripts add that Rāma returned to Ayodhyā on the bright fortnight of Phālguna (February-March) [3430*].

Cg sets out a detailed itinerary of Rāma's adventures:

5th day of *śuddhapakṣa* of Caitra (= *śuklapakṣa)*	camps by Tamasā
6th	Śṛṅgaverapura
7th	at the foot of the *vanaspati*
8th	Bharadvāja's ashram
9th	banks of the Yamunā
10th	Guha tells Rāma to go to Citrakūṭa; Sumantra returns to Ayodhyā
10thnight	death of Daśaratha
11th	Daśaratha embalmed
12th	messengers sent to Bharata
13th	messengers on road
14th (*pūrṇimā*)	messengers arrive in Rājagṛha
kṛṣṇapakṣa pratipad	Bharata sets out for Ayodhyā
1st–8th	Bharata on the road but on the 8th night travels all night
9th sunrise	Bharata arrives in Ayodhyā
9th evening	Daśaratha's funeral
13th day from that = 5th day of *śuddhapakṣa* of Vaiśākhā,	on the early part of that day, Bharata performs *śrāddha* of Daśaratha
6th day of Vaiśākhā	purification of the cremation ground
7th–10th	construction of royal highway
11th	Bharata approaches Rāma
11th night	Bharata camps by the Ganges
12th	Bharata at Bharadvāja's ashram
13th	Bharata meets Rāma
14th (*pūrṇimā*) and *pratipad* (*kṛṣṇapakṣa* of Vaiśākhā)	Bharata at Citrakūṭa
2nd	Bharata departs for Ayodhyā
4th	Bharata enters Ayodhyā
5th	Rāma leaves Citrakūṭa and goes to Atri's ashram
10 years, 1.5 months	Rāma at Atri's ashram
2 years, 10.5 months	Rāma at Pañcavaṭī
14th year of exile	
Caitra	abduction of Sītā
Vaiśākhā	Rāma meets Sugrīva
Āṣāḍha	Rāma slays Vālin
Āśvayuja	dispatch of search parties
Phālguna	fast of Aṅgada's party
14th day of *śuddhapakṣa*	burning of Laṅkā
amāvāsyā	death of Rāvaṇa
1st day of *śuddhapakṣa* of Caitra	funeral of Rāvaṇa
2nd day	consecration of Vibhīṣaṇa, return of Sītā, departure of the gods

3rd	departure from Laṅkā
4th	Rāma in Kiṣkindhā
5th	Rāma at Bharadvāja's ashram

Cm's Chronology:	
Phālguna	
pūrṇimā	climbing of Suvela
1st day of *kṛṣṇapakṣa*	battle begins
1st night	Rāma and Lakṣmaṇa are bound and released
2nd	death of Dhūmrākṣa
3rd	death of Vajradaṃṣtra
4th	death of Makarākṣa [but really dies on the 10th—Cm]
10th	death of Kumbha, Nikumbha, and Makarākṣa
11th–13th	battle with Indrajit
13th	death of Indrajit
Caitra	
1st day of *śuklapakṣa*	funeral of Rāvaṇa
2nd	consecration of Vibhīṣaṇa
3rd	reunion with Sītā
4th	leave Laṅkā, arrive Kiṣkindhā
5th	arrive at Bharadvāja's ashram 14-year period completed
6th	Rāma at Nandigrāma, puts off ascetic garb, enters Ayodhyā
7th (Puṣya *nakṣatra*)	consecration of Rāma

2. "holy sage" *bhagavan*: Literally, "blessed *or* holy one."

"that you hear" *śṛṇoṣi*: Ct and Ck note that we should add the words "from the mouth[s] of your disciple[s], etc. (*śiṣyādimukheneti śeṣaḥ*)."

"that the people of the city are healthy and well fed" *subhikṣānāma yaṃ pure*: Literally, "that there are good alms and an absence of illness in the city." The commentators agree that *subhikṣā-* refers to an abundance of food (*annasamṛddhiḥ*—so Ct).

"intent on his duties" *yuktaḥ*: Literally, "intent, engaged." We agree with the commentators, who understand the reference to be elliptical and offer such glosses as "devoted to protection, etc. (*pālanādau nirataḥ*—Cr)" and "intent upon the protection of the populace (*prajāpālane samāhitaḥ*—so Cg; Ct, Cm similarly)."

3. "smiled" *smitapūrvam*: Literally, "preceded *or* accompanied by a smile." The commentators are in general agreement that Bharadvāja is smiling at the irony of the omniscient Lord Rāma's asking him these questions as if he did not know the answers (*sarvajño 'pi bhagavān ajānann iva māṃ pṛcchati*—so Ct). Cg offers an optional interpretation, according to which Bharadvāja understands that the point of Rāma's questioning is to find out whether Bharata is happy protecting the citizens. The sage smiles, according to Cg, at the thought, "How could he possibly be so [happy], when

he [Bharata] is not a free agent?" (*yadvā kiṃ bharataḥ prajāpālanasaṃtuṣṭo vartata iti praśnasāraṃ matvā paratantre tasmin katham itthaṃ saṃbhavatīti smitakaraṇam.*)

"in great delight" *prahṛṣṭavat*: Cg glosses, "happily (*prahṛṣṭam*)," specifying that the term is to be read adverbially (*kriyāviśeṣaṇam*). Ct reads the indeclinable as if it were an adjective meaning "worthy of happiness (*prahṛṣṭārham*)." Our translation follows the interpretation of Ck and Cm, who take it as if it were an adjective modifying Bharadvāja in the sense of "happy (*prahṛṣṭaḥ san*—so Ck; Cm similarly)."

4. "Smeared with mud and wearing matted locks" *paṅkadigdhaḥ . . . jaṭilaḥ*: Cg, the only commentator to remark on this reading, indicates that Bharata is covered with mud because he has not been bathing. Nonetheless, Cg argues, despite his lack of bathing, he is like someone who has been consecrated for an obligatory ritual performance by means of a symbolic bath. Bharata has failed to bathe, Cg continues, because he is wearing the matted locks of an ascetic, for whom bathing in water is prohibited. Cg then notes the passage at 3.15.27–28, where Lakṣmaṇa imagines that poor, suffering, delicate Bharata is bathing in the cold waters of the Sarayū River. Cg's response to this seeming contradiction is to note that an occasional bath, even for someone in Bharata's situation, is permissible. As an alternative explanation for Bharata's soiled body, Cg suggests that it is because he is sleeping on the bare ground. (*snānābhāvāt paṅkadigdhatvam. snānābhāve 'pi nityānuṣṭhānaṃ dīkṣitavad gauṇasnānena. snānābhāve nimittam āha jaṭila iti. . . . jaṭilānāṃ vāruṇasnānaṃ niṣiddham iti bhāvaḥ. kathaṃ nv apararātreṣu sarayūm avagāhata ityādy uktis tu kādācitkasnānaparatve 'py upapadyate. yadvā sadānāstṛtabhūmiśāyanādinā vā tādṛśatvam.*) The reader will recall that Rāma has declined Vibhīṣaṇa's offer of a luxurious bath on the grounds that he could not indulge in such pleasures when Bharata was depriving himself of them on his account. (See 6.109.5–6 and notes.) See, too, 6.111.26–30 and notes. Compare 6.102.7–14 and notes, where Rāma insists that Sītā bathe before appearing before him.

D10,11, and the texts and printed editions of Ct, Ck, and Cr read instead *ājñāvaśatve*, literally, "under the control of an order," that is, "obedient to your instructions."

"having placed your sandals in a position of honor" *pāduke te puraskṛtya*: Literally, "having put forward your two sandals." The reference is to Bharata's celebrated act of fraternal subordination in which he consecrates Rāma's sandals as a symbol of Rāma's kingship (2.104–105; 2.107.14–22). See, too, 6.113.26–30.

5–7. "When last I saw you . . . At that time: *tvāṃ purā . . . dṛṣṭvā . . . pūrvam*: Literally, "Long ago having seen you . . . long ago." Since the three verses constitute a single, long sentence, the repetition of the synonymous adverbs *purā* and *pūrvam* is redundant. Cg attempts to eliminate the redundancy by suggesting that we read *purā* as an adjective in the sense of *purātana*, "old," and in composition with the following term *cīravasana*, "clad in barkcloth garments." This would create a compound with the sense "clad in old barkcloth garments." (*purācīravasanaṃ purātanacīravasanam. ato na pūrvapadena paunaruktyam.*) We have broken the long sentence into smaller units for the sake of readability.

"with but one lone companion and a woman" *strītṛtīyam*: Literally, "having a woman for a third." The phrase is elliptical, since the second member of Rāma's party, Lakṣmaṇa, is not explicitly mentioned.

"you had been driven from the kingdom" *cyutaṃ rājyāt*: Literally, "fallen from the kingdom *or* the kingship." Cr glosses *rājyāt*, "from the kingdom," with *abhiṣekāt*, "from the consecration."

"to obey your father's instructions and intent on obeying those of Kaikeyī" *pitur vacanakāriṇam . . . kaikeyīvacane yuktam*: Literally, "carrying out father's words . . . intent on Kaikeyī's words."

"an immortal god" *amaram*: Literally, "an immortal *or* deathless one."

"I was deeply saddened" *karuṇā . . . mamāsīt*: Literally, "of me there was pity *or* compassion." We follow the suggestion of Ck, Ct, and Cg in taking the term *karuṇā*, "compassion," here to refer to "sorrow *or* grief (*dainyam*—Ck, Ct; *duḥkham*—Cg)" rather than in its normal sense.

8. "I feel unsurpassed delight" *mama prītir anuttamā*: Literally, "of me there is unsurpassed delight." D7,10,11,G2, and the texts and printed editions of Ct read instead *mamābhūt prītir uttamā*, "of me there was the highest delight."

9–14. And I know . . . There was . . . Then there was . . . I know about . . . I know, too, about how . . . Finally, I know . . . All of that is known to me" *sarvaṃ ca . . . viditaṃ mama . . . yat . . . yathā ca . . . yathā ca . . . yathā . . . sarvaṃ mamaitad viditam*: Literally, "all that is known to me . . . which . . . and how . . . and how . . . how all that is known to me." The six verses constitute a single idea, with the final five verses constituting a single elaborate sentence. We have broken up the syntax for the sake of readability.

"about all the many joys and sorrows you experienced" *sarvaṃ ca sukhaduḥkhaṃ te . . . yat tvayā vipulaṃ prāptam*: Literally, "and all the abundant joy and sorrow obtained by you." As the commentators explain, the joys refer to the pleasures of life in Pañcavaṭī, etc. (*sukhaṃ pañcavaṭīvāsādikṛtam*—so Cg), while the sorrows are those produced by the abduction of Sītā (*duḥkhaṃ sītāharaṇajam*—so Cg) or hardships such as the slaying of Khara (*kharavadhādinā duḥkham*—so Ct, Ck).

"starting with the slaughter in Janasthāna" *janasthānavadhādikam*: D10,11,M1, and the texts and printed editions of Ct, Ck, and Cm read instead *janasthānanivāsinā*, "[by you] who were living in Janasthāna."

"the assault on Sītā" *sītonmathanam eva*: Literally, "the harm *or* injury to Sītā." Given the critical reading, one must assume that the reference is to Sītā's abduction. However, all manuscripts, both northern and southern, refer explicitly to Sītā's abduction. Most northern manuscripts substitute the phrase *sītāyā haraṇaṃ* [Gorresio v.l. *sītāpaharaṇaṃ*] *tathā*, "the abduction of Sītā." Southern manuscripts insert an additional passage. Following 10ab, D1–7,9–11,S insert a passage of one line [3442*]: "and this blameless wife [of yours] was abducted (*hṛtā*)." Southern commentators therefore read both *unmathanam* and *hṛtā*, and are thus confronted with the problem of distinguishing the two events, which would seem to be identical. Ct and Ck handle this by taking the term *unmathanam*, "harm, injury, *or* destruction," to refer to the torments inflicted on Sītā by the *rākṣasa* women in Laṅkā after her abduction (*sītāyā rākṣasībhir laṅkāyāṃ kleśanam*—so Ct). Cg, on the other hand, understands *hṛtā*, "abducted," as an inceptive participle modifying Sītā, "[the object] most desired to be abducted," which, he asserts, avoids redundancy with *unmathanam*. (*hṛtā hartum īpsitā. āśaṃsāyāṃ ktaḥ. ato na sītonmathanam ity anena paunaruktyam.*)

"the feats of the son of the wind god" *karma vātātmajasya*: Literally, "the action *or* deed of the son of the wind." As Ct points out, this term refers collectively to all of Hanumān's heroic deeds, starting with his leap over the ocean and ending with his burning of Laṅkā (*samudralaṅghanādilaṅkādahanāntam*). Ct thus distinguishes Hanumān's burning of Laṅkā from the second burning of the city by the monkey chiefs mentioned in verse 12, *pādas* cd.

"that thorn in the side of the gods" *devakaṇṭakaḥ*: D11 and the texts and printed editions of Ct and Cr read instead *baladarpitaḥ* (v.l. *varadarpitaḥ*), "proud of [his] strength (v.l. proud of his boon)."

"with the thirty gods" *tridaśaiḥ*: Literally, "with the thirty."

"and how they granted you a boon" *yathā dattaś ca te varaḥ*: Literally, "and how a boon was granted to you." As Cg points out, the reference is to Indra's boon through which the slain monkeys were brought back to life, restored to health, and blessed with perpetual forage (6.108.5ff.) (*varo mṛtavānarajīvanādiḥ*).

"through the power of my asceticism" *tapasā*: Literally, "through [my] asceticism." Cr glosses, "through the eye of [supernatural] knowledge (*jñānacakṣuṣā*)."

Following verse 13, D6,7,10,11,G2,M1,2, and the texts and printed editions of Ct and Cr insert a passage of one line [3443*, line 1]: "And how, when Rāvaṇa, that thorn in the side of the gods, had been slain..."

Following verse 14, D6,7,9–11,T2,3,G2,M1, and the texts and printed editions of Ct and Cr insert a passage of one line [3445*]: "My disciples are hastening from here to the city to proclaim the news."

15. "guest-offering" *arghyam*: This is the traditional welcome offering to a respected or venerable visitor, consisting of various articles of food and drink. The full offering consists of water, milk, *kuśa* grass, curds, butter, rice, barley, and white mustard seeds (*āpaḥ kṣīraṃ kuśāgraṃ ca dadhi sarpiḥ sataṇḍulam / yavaḥ siddhārthakaś caivāṣṭāṅgo 'rghaḥ prakīrtitaḥ //* quoted by Apte s.v.).

16. "bowing his head" *śirasā*: Literally, "with his head."

17. "the road I take to Ayodhyā" *mārge ... ayodhyāṃ prati gacchataḥ*: Literally, "on the road of [me] going to Ayodhyā."

"bear fruit out of season and drip with honey" *akālaphalino vṛkṣāḥ ... madhusravāḥ / bhavantu*: Literally, "Let the trees be ones with untimely fruits [and] ones flowing with honey." Ck and Ct note that Rāma makes this request for the sake of the refreshment of the monkeys (*vānarāṇāṃ viśrāmārtham*). Compare Rāma's similar request at 6.108.8–12. See, too, 6.4.48 and note. Note that here, as before, Rāma requests boons only for the benefit of others, not for himself.

Following 17ab, D5–7,9–11,T,G,M1–3, and the texts and printed editions of the southern commentators insert a passage of one line [3446*]: "... and many different kinds of fruits with the fragrance of nectar.[1]"

[1]"the fragrance of nectar" *amṛtagandhīni*: M3 and the texts and printed editions of Cg read *-kalpāni*, "like," for *-gandhīni*, "fragrance." The resulting compound is rendered as "nectar-sweet" in the translation of Raghunathan (1982, vol. 3, p. 355).

Following verse 17, D5–7,10,11,T,G,M1,3,5, and the texts and printed editions of the southern commentators insert a passage of two lines [3448*]: "No sooner had he promised, 'So be it,' then—the moment he had finished speaking—the trees there became just like the trees of heaven."

18. "Then, suddenly": The words have been added to provide a transition, which is missing in the critical text (compare, however, 3448* above, which provides such a transition for the southern recension as does 3449* for the north).

"bare" *śuṣkāḥ*: Literally, "dried, withered."

Following verse 18, D5,6,7,9–11,T,G,M1,3,5, and the texts and printed editions of the southern commentators insert a passage of five lines [3450*]: "Then, as they went along, [the trees] became [filled with fruit, etc.] for a distance of three leagues on every side.[1] Then those delighted bulls among the leaping monkeys, in their thousands, devoured many heavenly fruits to their hearts' desire so that they were as filled with joy as if[1] they had gained heaven.[2][2–5]"

[1]"as . . . as if" *yathaiva*: D7,9–11, and the texts and printed editions of Cr and Ct read instead *mudaiva*, "as if with joy." This lends the last line the sense "filled with joy, as are those who gain heaven."

[2]Lines 2–5 are in the *upajāti* meter.

Sarga 113

1. "had caught sight of Ayodhyā" *ayodhyām . . . samālokya*: Literally, "having looked at Ayodhyā." The commentators are fully aware that it is not possible to see Ayodhyā, at least not from the ground, from Bharadvāja's ashram on the banks of the Ganges. Ck, Ct, and Cm, recalling that Rāma had pointed out the city in the distance to Sītā as they were landing in the ashram (6.111.29 = GPP 6.123.52), note that the sighting took place at the time of the descent of the Puṣpakavimāna (*avataraṇasamaye*—so Ct). Ct had already pointed out, at that earlier occasion, that Ayodhyā was visible from that location only because the high altitude of the Puṣpakavimāna (*gaṅgātīravartibharadvājāśramapradeśage vimāne tasyātyunnatavyomapradeśavṛttitvād ayodhyādidarśanam*—Ct on GPP 6.123.52). Cg, however, takes a different tack, understanding that the action described here is in the present rather than at the time of the landing. He proposes that we understand the gerund *samālokya*, "having seen," in the sense of *samālocya*, "having considered *or* having thought about," since, as he notes, someone situated in the ashram could not possibly see Ayodhyā (*āśramasthasya tadavalokanāsaṃbhavāt*). See notes to verse 2 below.

B2,3,D6,7,10,11,T2,3,G2,M1, and the texts and printed editions of Ck, Ct, and Cr transpose 1cd and 2ab. See notes to verse 2 below.

G1,M3,5, and the texts and printed editions of Cg omit 1cd–2ab. See notes to verse 2 below.

2. "wishing to do a kindness" *priyakāmaḥ*: Given the sequence of the verses of the texts and printed editions of Ct discussed below, Ct understands the adjective here to mean that Rāma wishes to favor Sugrīva and the other monkeys by fulfilling all of their wishes once they reach Ayodhyā (*sugrīvādīnāṃ priyakāmo 'yodhyāyāṃ sarvatatpriyapūraṇakāmaḥ*). Cr, however, understands that Rāma wants to fulfill the wishes of the inhabitants of Ayodhyā (*ayodhyāvāsīnāṃ priyam icchuḥ*).

"spoke kindly" *priyam . . . uvāca*: Again, because of the differing verse order in their texts, Ct and Cr understand the adverb *priyam*, "kindly," to construe with the finite verb *cintayāmāsa* (1b), yielding "he thought kindly" (*priyaṃ yathā bhavati cintayāmāsa*—Ct). Ct then understands the phrase to refer elliptically to Rāma's kindly considering the various actions he should take next (*kartavyajātam iti śeṣaḥ*). Cr understands that Rāma is thinking ahead to prevent Bharata from fulfilling his earlier vow to immolate himself should Rāma not return by the final day of the fourteen-year period of exile (*caturdaśavarṣasamāptidine yadi tvāṃ na paśyāmi tarhi hutāśanaṃ pravekṣyāmīti bharatoktiṃ sasmārety arthaḥ*).

"swift-striding" *tvaritavikramam*: V3,B2,D1,4–7,9–12,T,G2,3,M1, and the texts and printed editions of Ct, Ck, and Cr read instead *tvaritavikramaḥ*, thus making the epithet apply to Rāma instead of Hanumān.

B2,3,D6,7,10,11,T2,3,G2,M1, and the texts and printed editions of Ck, Ct, and Cr transpose 1cd and 2ab. Their texts yield the following sequence: "But when swift-striding Rāma Rāghava had caught sight of Ayodhyā, wishing to do a kindness, he entered into kindly thought. [=GPP 6.125.1] Then, after some reflection, that wise man of blazing energy cast his glance upon the monkeys and then spoke to the leaping monkey Hanumān. [=GPP 6.125.2]"

G1,M3,5, and the texts and printed editions of Cg omit 1cd ["Then after some reflection"]–2ab ["Then Rāma . . . wishing to do a kindness . . . kindly . . . of rapid strides"]. These same texts and manuscripts then read, for 2cd, *cintayitvā hanūmantam uvāca plavagottamam*. The resulting *śloka* [VSP and KK 6.128.1] would be translated as follows: "But when Rāghava had caught sight of Ayodhyā, he was plunged into thought. [And] having reflected, he addressed Hanumān, the foremost of leaping monkeys."

3. M3 and the texts and printed editions of Cg omit 3ab, "Go quickly, best of leaping monkeys. Hastening to Ayodhyā . . ."

5. "my friend and equal" *mamātmasamaḥ sakhā*: Literally, "my friend equal to myself." The commentators differ as to how to interpret Rāma's socially progressive words. Ct does not believe that Rāma is equating the tribal Guha with himself but rather with the *ātman*, or "Supreme Spirit," because of Guha's knowledge of the ultimate truth. (*ātmasamaḥ. tatsadṛśaḥ. tattvajñānitvāt.*) Ck sees the term as a reference to Guha's physical prowess, glossing, "of immense strength (*mahābala ity arthaḥ*)." Cr takes the term to suggest that, [since Rāma and Guha are close and equal friends,] his, Guha's, happiness is Rāma's as well (*tatprītir mamaiva prītir iti dhvanitam*). Cg is the only commentator to address the critical issue of social hierarchy here, arguing that the term *ātmasamaḥ*, "equal to himself," shows that, in the excess of his affection, Rāma ignores Guha's low-caste status and thinks of him as a member of the House of Ikṣvāku (*ātmasamo hīnajātim anavekṣya premātiśayena guham ikṣvākukulīnam amanyata*). Several of the translators consulted understand that Rāma regards Guha as "a second self." See notes to verse 21 below.

"free from anxiety" *vigatajvaram*: Cg alone understands the compound adverbially and takes it to mean "in such a way that he [Guha] will be free from anxiety, that is, from worry caused by his separation from me (*madviśleṣacintājvararahitaṃ yathā tatheti bhaviṣyatīti kriyāviśeṣaṇam*)."

6. "will show you the way to Ayodhyā and will inform you of Bharata's activities" *ayodhyāyāś ca te mārgaṃ pravṛttiṃ bharatasya ca / nivedayiṣyati*: Literally, "he will inform [you] about your path to Ayodhyā and about Bharata's activities."

7. "I have accomplished my purpose" *siddhārtham*: Ct glosses, "that I have successfully completed my purpose in the form of carrying out my father's instructions (*nirvyūḍhapitṛvacanaparipālanarūpaprayojanam*)."

8–11. "Tell him about . . . And tell him about . . . Tell him about": Verses 8–11 consist of a list of actions or events either in the accusative case or belonging to adverbial clauses. The verses contain no finite verb. We understand, with Cv and Cg, that one should carry the imperative *śaṃsa*, "[you] tell, report," from 7c above through the entire sequence.

"the march to the sea" *upayānaṃ samudrasya*: Literally, "the approach of the sea."

"of the great god Śiva" *mahādeva-*: Literally, "the great god *or* Mahādeva." See 3395*, n. 1 (at note to 6.111.12). Cf., too, 6.107.1.

Following verse 11, D5–7,10,11,T,G,M1,3, and the texts and printed editions of the southern commentators insert a passage of two lines [3460*]: "And inform Bharata, gentle friend,[1] that I have come back,[2] together with the king of the *rākṣasas* and the lord of the tawny monkeys."

[1]"gentle friend" *saumya*: Literally, "O gentle one." Cg understands that, by using this epithet, Rāma is telling Hanumān that he must break the news to Bharata gently. Otherwise, he fears that, if Bharata were to learn of his return too suddenly, his joy might be overwhelming. (*anena mandaṃ mandaṃ kathaya. anyathā haṭhān madāgamanaśravaṇe harṣo 'sya unmastako bhaved iti bhāvaḥ.*) See note to verse 17 below.

[2]"that I have come back" *upayātam* ... *mām*: Cg observes that, unless this is done, Bharata will carry out his vow to immolate himself on the fourth day of the half month, since the fourteen years of Rāma's exile would have been exceeded (*anyathā caturthyām eva caturdaśavarṣātikramāt so 'gniṃ praviśed iti bhāvaḥ*). This variant provides a finite verb and syntactical context for the preceding verses (8–11).

12. "Tell him": See notes to verses 8–11 above.

12cd = 35cd, reading the instrumental plural *mahābalaiḥ* for the nominative singular *mahābalaḥ*.

"immensely powerful" *mahābalaḥ*: V3,D5–7,10,11,T,G,M3,5, and texts of the southern commentators read instead the instrumental plural *mahābalaiḥ* for the critical edition's nominative singular, thus making the adjective apply to Rāma's allies.

D2,3,5,9,T2,3,G,M2,3,5, and the texts and printed editions of Cg transpose verses 12 and 13.

13. D2,3,5,9,T2,3,G,M2,3,5, and the texts and printed editions of Cg transpose verses 12 and 13.

14. "you should accurately determine everything about Bharata's state of mind" *jñeyāḥ sarve ca vṛttāntā bharatasya* ... / *tattvena*: Literally, "all Bharata's conditions are to be known according to the truth."

15. "For whose head would not be turned by ... an ... kingdom" *rājyaṃ kasya nāvartayen manaḥ*: Literally, "whose mind would a kingdom not cause to turn around." Ct believes, as do we, that Rāma is informing the people that even one's brothers are not to be trusted (*anena bhrātara evaṃ śaṅkyā iti lokān bodhayati*). Cg sees a more benign view of Bharata, glossing "whose (*kasya*)" as "other than Bharata (*bharatād anyasyaivety arthaḥ*)."

"ancestral" *pitṛpaitāmaham*: Literally, "belonging to one's father and grandfather."

16. "being long accustomed to it" *saṃgatyā*: Literally, "by association." Our translation follows the commentaries of Ck, Cs, Ct (first alternative), and Cm, who gloss, "through long association (*cirakālaparicayena*)." Ck, Ct, and Cs offer an alternative: "or through association with Kaikeyī (*kaikeyīsaṃgatyā vā*)." Ck, Ct, and Cs continue, noting that, should it turn out that Bharata actually does desire to rule, Rāma will go off

somewhere or other and pass his days in ascetic practice (*vayaṃ yatra kvāpi tapasā kālaṃ neṣyāma iti śeṣaḥ*—so Ck, Ct, Cs). In keeping with his position that there is no real likelihood or suspicion of Bharata's coveting the kingship, Cg interprets *saṃgati* here as "association with us, i.e., with Rāma (*asmatsaṃgatyā*)." He wonders if Bharata might be inclined to accept sovereignty at Rāma's insistence because of his joy at seeing Rāma after so long a separation. (*yady api pūrvaṃ sarvātmanā na rājyapālanam aṅgīkaromīty uktam. tathāpi caturdaśavarṣaparyantaṃ madvirahāturatayā maddarśanajaharṣaprakarṣātirekeṇa tvam abhiṣikto bhaveti maduktim aṅgīkariṣyati kim iti bhāvaḥ.*)

"that delight of the Raghus" *raghunandanaḥ*: Cg believes that use of this epithet, with its allusion to the glorious and powerful dynasty of the Raghus, capable of ruling the three worlds, is intended to dispel any doubts as to Bharata's ability to bear the burden of kingship. (*katham asau bharaṇakṣama ity atrāha raghunandana iti. trailokyabharaṇakṣamakulodbhūta ity arthaḥ.*)

"entire... without exception" *sarvām akhilām*: Literally, "entire... entire." The redundant collocation of these two terms is, however, idiomatic, as they often occur together. Only Cg attempts to distinguish them, glossing the second term as "without any gap or exception. The meaning is 'with all its abundant *or* prosperous population.' (*akhilāṃ khilarahitām. samṛddhajanām ity arthaḥ.*)"

17. "his state of mind and his intentions" *buddhiṃ ca... vyavasāyaṃ ca*: Literally, "[his] mind, idea, *or* intention, and [his] resolution." Cr understands *buddhi* in its sense of "resolution *or* determination (*niścayam*)" and *vyavasāya* in its sense of "undertaking, activity, *or* industry (*udyogam*)." Cg believes, however, that the two terms refer to the two possible thoughts on Bharata's part concerning the disposition of the kingdom. According to this interpretation, *buddhi* means the thought that Rāma will take back the kingdom, and *vyavasāya*, that, in the case of Rāma's refusal to do so, he, Bharata himself, will have to rule. (*buddhiṃ matsannidhāne kathaṃcid rājyam aṅgīkariṣyatīti buddhim. vyavasāyaṃ sarvātmanā nāṅgīkariṣyatīti vyavasāyaṃ ca.*) Cg further understands that, in telling Hanumān to return quickly, Rāma is instructing him not to return if it turns out that Bharata wishes to rule. Cg concludes his discussion of this point by noting that some authorities believe that, although Rāma already knows Bharata's intentions (i.e., to defer to Rāma), he enters into this discussion in order to abide by the strictures of *nītiśāstra*, which require a king to investigate everything thoroughly (*loke rājanītipravartanāyaivam atiśaṅkāvacanam uktavān*). Cg understands, however, that, if Rāma himself were to arrive suddenly, the access of Bharata's joy would be overwhelming. Therefore, Cg argues, Rāma sends Hanumān for the sake of [Bharata's] well-being. (*vastutaḥ svasya jhaṭiti gamane bharatasya harṣa unmastako bhaved iti. tasmāt sattvāya hanumantaṃ preṣitavān.*) See 3460*, n. 1, following notes to verse 8 above.

18. "Instructed in this fashion" *iti pratisamādiṣṭaḥ*: Only Cg seeks to give the *upasarga prati* its meaning of "opposition, counter, etc.," here. His understanding is that (probably because of the sensitive nature of the mission) the instructions are not welcome to Hanumān. He glosses, "ordered in an unfavorable way. The meaning is 'instructed against his wishes (lit., his heart).' (*pratikūlaṃ samādiṣṭaḥ. ahṛdayaṃ samādiṣṭa ity arthaḥ.*)" This interpretation finds expression in the translation of Raghunathan (1982, vol. 3, p. 356), who renders, "Thus ordered on an unpleasant errand..."

"took on a human form" *mānuṣaṃ dhārayan rūpam*: Literally, "taking on a human form." The text gives no indication as to why Hanumān feels it necessary to take on a human form. Perhaps the motive is similar to that which leads Sugrīva to instruct him to do so at the time of Hanumān's first meeting with Rāma and Lakṣmaṇa at 4.2.23. See also 4.3.3, where Hanumān actually assumes a human form. There the reason was Hanumān's and Sugrīva's suspicion about who Rāma was and what his intentions might be. Here it may just be that, having left the enchanted demon world of Laṅkā and the monkey-haunted forests of Kiṣkindhā to enter the civilized world of men, Hanumān deems this disguise appropriate. See notes to verses 40–42 below. See 6.115.35, where the other monkeys also take on human form. See, too, notes to 6.114.3.

Following verse 18, D5–7,10,11,S insert, while Ś,D1–4,8,9,12 insert following 18ab, a passage of two lines [3465*]: "Then Hanumān, son of Māruta, flew up swiftly, just as might Garutmān[1] in his desire to seize a mighty serpent."

[1]"Garutmān" *garutmān*: Literally, "the winged one." This is a common variant of the name of Viṣṇu's mount, Garuḍa. Cf. notes to 6.91.6 and 6.116.47.

19–20. "the path of his father" *pitṛpatham*: As the commentators note, the compound refers to the path of the wind, Hanumān's divine father, in other words the atmosphere (*antarikṣam*).

"fearsome" *bhīmam*: M3 and the texts and printed editions of Cg read instead *madhyam*, "[in] the middle."

"the . . . abode of the serpent lords" *bhujagendrālayam*: D6,7,10,11,T2,G2,M1, and the texts and printed editions of Ck, Ct, and Cr read instead *vihagendrālayam*, "abode of the lord *or* lords of the birds." As different commentators indicate, the reference can be taken to refer either to the abode of the great birds or to the lord of the birds, i.e., Garuḍa himself. In either case, the epithet must apply to the *pitṛpatham*, "the path of the father," in *pāda* a, as opposed to *saṃnipātam*, "confluence," in *pāda* d.

21. "informs you that he is safe" *tvāṃ kuśalam abravīt*: We understand that Hanumān is carrying out the instructions that Rāma gave him at verse 5 above to report to Guha that he, Rāma, had returned safe and sound from his sojourn in the forest. See verses 5 and 6, and notes. The phrase can also be understood in its conventional sense of "he inquires after your welfare," as several translators render. The commentators are silent. See verse 33 below.

22. "On the instructions of Bharadvāja, Rāghava spent last night, the night of the fifth, with him. Now, since he has taken his leave of the sage, you shall see him this very day." *pañcamīm adya rajanīm uṣitvā vacanān muneḥ / bharadvājābhyanujñātaṃ drakṣyasy adyaiva rāghavam*: Literally, "This very day you shall see Rāghava, given leave by Bharadvāja, [Rāghava who,] having dwelt the fifth night, today because of the words of the sage . . ." See notes to 6.112.1 for the commentators' opinions on what the phrase "the fifth (*pañcamīm*)" refers to. D9–11 and the texts and printed editions of Ct read *atraiva*, "right here," for *adyaiva*, "this very day."

23. "swift Hanumān . . . swiftly" *mahāvego vegavān*: Literally, "that one of great speed, possessing speed." Our translation follows the distinction Cg proposes, according to which the first epithet refers to Hanumān's innate or natural swiftness, whereas the second describes his movement at this moment. (*mahāvegaḥ svabhāvaḥ. vegavān tādātvikavegavān.*)

"without further hesitation" *avicārayan*: Literally, "not reflecting." The commentators take the participle here to mean "paying no heed to (*agaṇayan*)," although they disagree as to the object to which Hanumān was oblivious. Ct, Ck, Cr, and Cm understand that he was heedless of the fatigue of the journey (*adhvaśramam*). Cg believes that he pays no attention to such things as the beauty of the forests, hills, and rivers along his path (*mārgasthavanagirinadīsaundaryādikam*).

"flew up once more" *utpapāta*: Literally, "he flew up."

"the hairs of his body bristling with excitement" *saṃprahṛṣṭatanūruhaḥ*: Literally, "his body hair excited." The commentators attribute Hanumān's excitement to his getting an opportunity to serve Rāma, who is the delight of the world (*jagadānandarāmasevakatvalābhena*—so Ct), or to his having the privilege of announcing the return of Rāma, who brings delight to all the world (*sakalalokānandakārirāmapratyāgamanaṃ mayā śrāvayitavyaṃ labdham ity asmād dhetoḥ*—Cg).

24. "the spot sacred to Rāma" *rāmatīrtham*: As several commentators point out, the reference here is to the Bhārgava warrior-sage, Rāma (Paraśurāma). See notes to 6.11.9 and 6.111.12, 3395*, n. 2.

"the river Vālukinī" *nadīṃ vālukinīm*: According to Cr, there is a river of this name (*vālukinīṃ tadabhidhāṃ nadīm*). Ct understands similarly. See, too, 6.115.22 and notes. The name appears to be unattested elsewhere.

"And he saw the Gomatī River" *gomatīṃ tāṃ ca so 'paśyat*: B3,D7,10,11, and the texts and printed editions of Ct read instead *varūthīṃ gomatīṃ caiva*, "and [he saw] the rivers Varūthī and Gomatī." See Bhattacharyya 1991 (s.v. *gomatī*). See, too, 2.43.9; 2.65.11; and notes.

Following verse 24, D5–7,10,11,T,G1,2,M1,3, and the texts and printed editions of the southern commentators insert, while G3 and M2 insert after 24ab, a passage of one line [3468*]: "And [he saw] prosperous countries and many thousands of people."

25. Following verse 25, D5–7,10,11,T,G,M2,3,5, and the texts and printed editions of the southern commentators insert a passage of two lines [3470*]. D7,10,11,G2, and the texts and printed editions of Ct reverse the order of the lines: "Adorned with women and old men together with their sons, who were all enjoying themselves, they resembled the trees in Caitraratha, the park of Indra, lord of the gods.[1]"

[1]"Adorned with women and old men together with their sons, who were all enjoying themselves" *strībhiḥ saputrair vṛddhaiś ca ramamāṇaiḥ svalaṃkṛtān*: D7,10,11, and the texts and printed editions of Ct read instead *strībhiḥ saputrair pautraiś ca ramamāṇaiḥ svalaṃkṛtaiḥ*, "with women along with their well-ornamented sons and their grandsons who were enjoying themselves."

26–30. Verses 26–30 consist largely of a series of adjectives and participial phrases modifying Bharata and governed by the finite verb, "he spied (*dadarśa*)," in verse 26c. We have broken up this long sentence for the sake of readability.

"A quarter of a league" *krośamātre*: Literally, "at the measure of a *krośa*." A *krośa* is a traditional Indian measure of distance reckoned to be a quarter of a *yojana*. The actual distance of a *yojana*, which we render as "league," is debatable. MW understands it to be either four to five miles, approximately nine miles, or two and a half miles. (An English league is approximately 5.556 km or 3.45 mi). Given that Hanumān is able to make out the details of Bharata's dress and bodily condition at this distance, it is possible that Vālmīki has the shorter measure of a *krośa* in mind. On the measurement of a *yojana*, see note to 1.5.7.

"he was clad in garments of barkcloth and black antelope skin... was clad in barkcloth and animal skins" *cīrakṛṣṇājināmbaram... valkalājinavāsasam*: Cg claims that the second term (*valkalājinavāsasam*) refers exclusively to Bharata's upper garments and that therefore there is no redundancy, since the first term presumably refers to the lower garments. (*valkalājinavāsasam ity uttarīyoktiḥ. ataś cīrakṛṣṇājināmbaram ity anena na punaruktiḥ.*) Cf. verse 31 below and 6.115.13–16. See Emeneau 1962.

"Wearing matted locks... He had a mass of matted hair piled high" *jaṭilam... samunnatajaṭābhāram*: Cg again attempts to show that two similar terms do not constitute a redundancy, arguing that the first term simply refers to Bharata's having the matted locks of an ascetic, while the second refers specifically to the height of his matted hair. (*pūrvaṃ jaṭāvattvoktiḥ. atra tadbhārasya samunnatatvoktir iti vaiṣamyam.*) See 6.112.4 and notes.

"his body was smeared with dirt" *maladigdhāñgam*: See 6.112.4 and notes, where the commentators take up the issue of Bharata's dirt-smeared body.

"with focused mind" *bhāvitātmānam*: Cg glosses, "who has meditated on the Self (*dhyātātmānam iti*)." According to Cg, the epithet expresses Bharata's control of his mind (*manoniyamoktiḥ*).

"Having placed Rāma's sandals in a position of honor" *pāduke te puraskṛtya*: Literally, "having placed those two sandals forward." See 6.112.4 and note.

"all clad in ochre garments" *kāṣāyāmbaradhāribhiḥ*: Ochre garments are the typical attire of renunciants. Ck, Ct, and Cg note that the court functionaries would be dressed in this fashion according to the maxim, "As is the king, so are the subjects (*yathā rājā tathā prajeti nyāyāt*—so Ct)."

31. "never to abandon" *na... parimoktum*: D6,10,11,T2,3,G1,2,M3,5, and the texts and printed editions of the southern commentators read instead *na... paribhoktum*, "not... to enjoy." The commentators supply a gerund, *parityajya*, "having abandoned," or *parivarjayitvā*, "having avoided," and understand the verse to mean that the citizens were determined never to abandon Bharata and indulge in enjoyments such as fine clothes and ornaments (*rājaputraṃ bharataṃ parivarjayitvā bhoktuṃ samīcīnavastrābharaṇādīny anubhavituṃ na vyavasyanti vyavasāyaṃ na kurvanti*—so Cg). Cg also proposes a reading without supplying a gerund in which he takes the infinitive *paribhoktum*, "to enjoy," in the sense of "to see." According to this reading, the citizens essentially find the king's obsessive mourning for his brother too depressing and try to keep away. (*pari parito vartamānā api paurā bharataṃ bhoktum anubhavitum. draṣṭum iti yāvat... taddarśane nirāśā bhavantīty arthaḥ... caturdaśe varṣe pūrṇe 'pi rāmāgamanādarśanāt prāṇatyāge vyavasitaṃ bharatam ālokayitāṃ paurāṇāṃ khedātiśayo 'nena ślokena sūcyate.*) Translations that follow the texts and printed editions of the southern commentators render this variant and generally translate according to the first interpretation. However, Roussel (1903, vol. 3, p. 410), followed by Shastri (1959, vol. 3, p. 357) and Pagani (1999, p. 1202), understands that the subjects were resolved not to neglect Bharata's maintenance. Roussel translates, "*Ses sujets... étaient résolus de ne point négliger son entretien.*"

32. "who was like a second Dharma, god of righteousness" *dharmam iva... aparam*: Literally, "like another Dharma."

33. "informs you that he is safe" *sa tvā kuśalam abravīt*: See verses 5 and 6 above; and verse 21 and notes above.

34. "I bring you wonderful news" *priyam ākhyāmi te*: Literally, "I tell you good news." Cg, alone among the commentators, expresses disquiet at the way in which Hanumān launches directly into his message without the expected courtesies and formalities of greeting. He offers a number of explanations for Hanumān's abruptness: 1) Hanumān does not praise Bharata because he has never been introduced to him; 2) the mention of his cupping his hands in reverence in verse 32 suggests that he has accompanied this gesture with the appropriate praise; 3) upon seeing Bharata's condition and fearing that he might die if there is even a moment's delay in reporting the good news, Hanumān reports the life-saving news directly. In this he reflects, based on the maxim of the wall [i.e., painting in the absence of a wall (*kuḍyaṃ vinā citrakarmeva*)], that there would be no use of praise if the object of that praise had already withered away; and 4) upon seeing Bharata's condition, Hanumān forgets his true nature (i.e., his manners). (*atrāparicitatvād bharataṃ hanumān nāvandata. yadvā prāñjalir iti padaṃ vandanapūrvakāñjaliparam. athavā bharatadaśādarśanena priyākhyāne kṣaṇavilambe 'pi prāṇahāniśaṅkayā sati kuḍya iti nyāyena vandanoddeśavastuni śīryamāṇe kiṃ vandaneneti tadujjīvakaṃ priyākhyānam evākarot. yadvā taddaśādarśanena svarūpaṃ visasmāra.*)

"you shall put aside your terrible sorrow" *śokaṃ tyakṣyasi dāruṇam*: B2,D10,11, M1,2,5, and the texts and printed editions of Ct read instead *śokaṃ tyaja sudāruṇam*, "you must put aside your very terrible sorrow." This reading obliges the commentators that share it to supply the future form of the verb $\sqrt{}$*bhū*, "to be," *bhaviṣyasi*, "you will be," yielding the sense "[for] you will be reunited."

35. 35cd = 12cd, reading *mahābalaiḥ* for *mahābalaḥ*. See note to verse 12 above.

36. "who is united" *samagrā*: Literally, "whole, entire." The context leads us to agree with Cr, who glosses, "accompanied (*sahitā*)." Cg glosses, "her every wish fulfilled (*sampūrṇamanorathā*)." See 2.34.31 and note; and 3.55.18. Cf. *MBh* 7.50.15, where the term has the sense "safe and sound."

37. "Kaikeyī's son" *kaikayīsutaḥ*: Literally, "the son of Kaikayī." Note the variant of the name Kaikeyī. M1,3, and the texts and printed editions of Cg read instead *bhrātṛvatsalaḥ*, "who loved his brother."

"in a sudden access of delight" *sahasā hṛṣṭaḥ*: Literally, "suddenly delighted."

"and fainted dead away" *moham jagāma ha*: Literally, "he went straight into a swoon." The verse ends with the emphatic particle "*ha*" (here rendered as "[dead] away"), and Cg feels obliged to comment on its meaning here. He takes it as an expletive expressive of amazement and notes: "With respect to Bharata, who was put into such a condition at the mere hearing of the news, the seer [Vālmīki] expresses, through the particle '*ha*,' his wonder at what would have been his condition had Rāma himself suddenly arrived (*hety anena vārtāśravaṇamātreṇaitādṛśāvasthe bharate jhaṭiti rāmāgamane kāvasthā bhaved ity ṛṣir vismayate*)."

39. "with ... teardrops of joy and delight" *aśokajaiḥ prītimayaiḥ ... / ... aśrubindubhiḥ*: Literally, "with drops of tears born from non-sorrow and consisting of delight."

40–42. "Whether you be a god or a man" *devo vā mānuṣo vā*: Cg notes that, even though Hanumān has taken on a human form (at verse 18), the extraordinary degree of his blazing energy gives rise to this doubt (*parigṛhītamanuṣyadehe 'pi hanumati tejo-*

viśeṣāt saṃśayaḥ). See 6.115.35 and notes, where the other monkeys take on human forms. See, too, notes to 6.114.3.

"My gentle friend" *saumya*: Literally, "O gentle one."

"I shall give you, the bearer of this good news who reported it to me" *priyākhyānasya te . . . dadāmi bruvataḥ priyam*: Literally, "I give to you, who are telling good news, [and] who are reporting good news." The commentators propose various interpretations intended, no doubt, to eliminate the apparent redundancy. Ct and Cr understand "good news (*priyam*)" in the sense of "gift, favor, reward." Ct supplies the interrogative pronoun *kim*, lending the passage the sense of a rhetorical question: "What reward shall I give you, who are speaking? I do not see anything to equal this good news (*te kiṃ dadāmy etat priyākhyānasamaṃ na kiṃcit paśyāmīti bhāvaḥ*)." Cr understands *priyam* similarly but takes the genitive participle *bruvataḥ*, "speaking," to refer to Bharata himself, who is asking Hanumān to choose his reward (*te kiṃ dadāmīti bruvato mamāgre priyaṃ svepsitaṃ vadeti śeṣaḥ*). Cr goes on to claim that, since Hanumān does not reply, Bharata lists, in the following verses, the gifts he will confer (*tūṣṇīṃ sthitaṃ taṃ pratyāha gavām iti*). Compare 6.101.17 and notes, where Sītā makes a similar comment to Hanumān.

"a hundred prosperous villages" *grāmāṇāṃ ca śataṃ param*: Literally, "and an excellent hundred [of] villages." Roussel (1903, vol. 3, p. 410) understands the word *param* in its sense of "more than," rendering, "*une centaine de villages en plus*." Raghunathan (1982, vol. 3, pp. 357–58) similarly renders, "more than a hundred villages."

"sixteen maidens . . . to be your wives" *bhāryāḥ kanyāś ca ṣoḍaśa*: Cr understands the term *bhāryā*, "wife," in its etymological sense as "one who is to be supported, i.e., a servant." He glosses, "female workers (*karmakārīḥ*)." Cg, somewhat similarly, glosses, "*bhāryāḥ* means 'worthy of support,' *kanyāḥ* means 'unmarried women.' (*bhāryāḥ bharaṇārhāḥ. kanyā anūḍhastriyaḥ.*)" Cf. notes to 6.116.57–58. See, too, *Adhyātmarāmāyaṇa* 6.14.62. The issue here, no doubt, is the commentators' discomfort with any hint of marriage or sexuality in the case of traditional India's celebrated paragon of celibacy, Hanumān. Of course, in the present context Bharata would have no way of knowing who his visitor really is and would probably not know anything about Hanumān even if he knew he were a monkey. On the celibacy of Hanumān, see the Introduction to the *Sundarakāṇḍa*, pp. 49–52; and Lutgendorf 2007, pp. 299–331 and passim.

43. "seemingly miraculous" *adbhutopamam*: Literally, "comparable to a miracle or a wonder." Cg glosses, "incomparable (*nirupamam*)."

The meter is *vaṃśasthavila*.

Sarga 114

2. "Joy comes to a man even if he has to wait a hundred years" *eti jīvantam ānando naraṃ varṣaśatād api*: Literally, "Joy comes to a man who is living even after (lit., from) a hundred years." We agree with Cg, who suggests that we should supply the word *param*, "after, over," to the compound *varṣaśatāt*, "from one hundred years." The quarter verse *eti jīvantam ānandaḥ* is found twice in the *Mahābhāṣya* (Kielhorn 1962, vol. 1, 277:6; vol. 2, 59:8).

3. "How . . . did Rāghava come to be associated with the tawny monkeys" *rāghavasya harīṇāṃ ca katham āsīt samāgamaḥ*: Literally, "How was there a meeting of Rāghava and the tawny ones." Bharata's question poses a narrative problem. Hanumān has taken the form of a man (see 6.113.18 and note), and, as recently as 6.113.40, it is clear that Bharata thinks that Hanumān must either be a god or a human. Up until this point Hanumān has made no explicit reference to monkeys, at least none that the poet has recorded. The commentators are clearly disturbed by this unusual narrative lacuna and attempt to explain it in a number of ways. Ck and Ct refer back to Hanumān's announcement of Rāma's earlier declaration at 6.113.12 (cf. 6.113.35) to the effect that Rāma has come back with his [immensely powerful] friends. Ck and Ct reason that Bharata has somehow inferred from Hanumān's statement that the reference is to Sugrīva, etc. (*sahamitrair ity asya sugrīvādimitrasahitair ity arthaḥ. tanmukhād avagatya pṛcchati.*) Cg reasons that we have to understand that Bharata had earlier heard the general report of the mustering of a monkey army (*atra vānarasamāgamapraśnena pūrvaṃ bharataḥ sāmānyato vānarasenāsannāhaṃ śrutavān iti gamyate*). Crā and Cm argue that, when Bharata had expressed uncertainty as to whether Hanumān was a man or a god (6.113.40), the latter must have told him that he was the minister of the monkey king Sugrīva (*devo vā mānuṣo veti praśnasyānantaraṃ vānarendrasya sugrīvasya sacivo 'ham iti prativacanaṃ hanumatā dattam ity avagantavyam*).

"and for what reason" *kim āśritya*: Literally, "having depended on what." We agree with the commentators that one should supply the word *prayojanam*, "purpose, reason," here.

4. "Hanumān" *saḥ*: Literally, "he."

5–9. "Great-armed prince" *mahābāho*: Literally, "O great-armed one."

"you already know all about . . . And you know . . . You also know . . . And you know, of course" *sarvam etat . . . yathāvad viditaṃ tava*: Literally, "of [by] you all this is known, just how it was." The passage is made up of a single complex sentence, consisting of a long string of adverbial clauses governed by the adverb *yathā*, "how." We have broken it up into shorter units and repeated the governing verbal phrase for the sake of readability.

"how you . . . declined the kingship" *tvayā . . . yathā rājyaṃ na cepsitam*: Literally, "and how the kingdom was not desired by you."

"the tormentor of his foes" *amitrakarśanaḥ*: D1,G1,M2,3,5, and the texts and printed editions of Cg read the vocative singular *amitrakarśana*, "O tormentor of your foes," for the nominative singular of the critical edition. This then modifies Bharata. Cg, the only commentator to remark on the vocative, argues that we are to understand by this epithet that, although Bharata himself is capable of exercising kingship, he begs his brother to return in keeping with the tradition of primogeniture (*amitrakarśanety anena rājyakaraṇasāmarthye svasya saty api jyeṣṭhānuvṛttyarthaṃ nimantrita iti gamyate*).

"begged him to accept it" *rājyena . . . nimantritas tvayā*: Literally, "[he was] invited by you with the kingship."

"remained faithful to the king's vow" *sthitena rājño vacane*: Literally, "[by him] who was fixed in the word of the king."

10. The exact construction of this verse as it is found in the critical edition is hard to determine with complete accuracy. It would appear that no existing manuscript has its sequence of lines. The southern and *devanāgarī* manuscripts (except for D13), as well Ś and the Lahore edition, separate the two lines of the verse with two additional lines (see 3489* below). The problem here is whether this verse, with or without the insert, is

referring to one or two forests, since the narrative marks the moment of transition when Rāma and his party leave the woodlands of Citrakūṭa and plunge into the wilder interior of the Daṇḍaka Forest (*Ayodhākāṇḍa* 109). The verse in the critical edition appears to refer only to the latter, the wild Daṇḍaka Forest, as do the majority of northern manuscripts and the printed editions and texts unambiguously aligned with them. The problem with the critical reading is that it is difficult to say why, if only the Daṇḍaka Forest is meant, its wildlife is so terrified. Cg, the only commentator to attempt to address this question, suggests that it is because these animals had never before seen humans (*apūrvapuruṣadarśanena*). This seems doubtful, however, especially in light of the insert passage [3489*], where the forest is said to be in a pitiable or lamentable state and trampled by elephants. This would appear to be a reference to 2.109.3, where the forest of Citrakūṭa is said to have been trampled and fouled by Bharata's elephants and horses. It is this, among other things, that persuades Rāma to leave the pleasant groves of Citrakūṭa for the wild Daṇḍaka Forest. Cg, commenting on the adjective *hastimṛditam*, "trampled by elephants," of 3489*, line 2, again tries to shift the focus to the Daṇḍaka Forest, insisting that the elephants in question are wild ones (*vanagajaiḥ*) (rather than the tame elephants of Bharata's army). Cr interprets similarly.

The reconstructed version of the north (similar to Gorresio 6.110.12) substitutes a rather different and less ambiguous verse [3490*]: "Then, when you had departed, Rāghava, together with Lakṣmaṇa [10ab with variant], entered the deserted and dense [v.l. Daṇḍaka] forest infested with snakes" (*apayāte tvayi tadā rāghavaḥ sahalakṣmaṇaḥ / nirjanaṃ vyālasampannaṃ prāviśad gahanaṃ* [(v.l. Gorresio) *daṇḍakaṃ*] *vanam //*).

"Rāma entered" *praviveśa*: Literally, "he entered."

Following 10ab, Ś,D1–12,S, and the Lahore edition insert a passage of two lines [3489*]: "[When you had departed,] that forest was in an extremely lamentable state.[1] It had been trampled by elephants, and, filled as it was with lions, tigers, and other wild beasts, it was fearsome.[2]"

11. "Virādha" *virādhaḥ*: See *Araṇyakāṇḍa* 2.4ff.

12. "Seizing him" *tam utkṣipya*: Literally, "having lifted up, having seized." It would also be possible to understand *utkṣipya* in the sense "having emitted," governing *mahānādam*. This yields the sense "having emitted a loud roar." Compare 3.3.26, where the disposal of the dying Virādha is described in similar terms.

"they hurled" *prakṣipanti sma*: Ck and Ct understand, as is implied in the *Araṇyakāṇḍa* (3.3.26–27), that Rāma and Lakṣmaṇa throw Virādha into a pit (*garte... prakṣiptavantāv ity arthaḥ*). However, Cg understands the plural to indicate that Sītā helped somewhat (*bahuvacanena sītayāpi tatra kiṃcit sāhāyyaṃ kṛtam iti gamyate*).

13. "Śarabhaṅga's lovely ashram" *śarabhaṅgasya ramyam āśramam*: See *Araṇyakāṇḍa* 4.

14. Following verse 14, D7,T2,3,M3, and the texts and printed editions of Cg read verses 16–17b. According to Crā, the proper sequence of the verses should be 16, 17ab, 15, as this follows the narrative. This order is reflected in the translation of Raghunathan (1982, vol. 3, p. 359) and in the text and translation of Gita Press (1969, vol. 3, p. 1884). The order of events as told here does not agree with that of the *Araṇyakāṇḍa*. There the Virādha episode (3.2–3) is followed by the mutilation of Śūrpaṇakhā (3.16–17), after which the battle takes place between Rāma and the fourteen thousand *rākṣasas* under the command of Khara and Dūṣaṇa (3.23–30).

15. For the sequence of verses, see notes to verse 14 above.

"*rākṣasas* of fearsome deeds" *rakṣasāṃ bhīmakarmaṇām*: Ś,Ñ,V,B,D1–4,6–12,T2, 3,G2,M1,2, and the texts and printed editions of Ct, Cr, and Ck read instead *janasthānanivāsinām*, "of the inhabitants of Janasthāna."

Following verse 15, Ś,D5–8,10–13,S insert, in whole or in part, a passage of six lines [3497*]: "Meeting Rāma in battle on the battlefield,[1] those *rākṣasas* were completely wiped out by him, single-handedly in the fourth part of a day.[1–2] Those immensely powerful and valorous inhabitants of the Daṇḍaka Forest, obstructers of asceticism, were slain in battle by Rāghava.[3–4] The *rākṣasas* were crushed, and Khara was slain in battle. Then, after first killing Dūṣaṇa, he subsequently slew Triśiras.[2][5–6]"

[1]"Rāma in battle on the battlefield" *raṇe rāmeṇa saṃyuge*: Literally, "on the battlefield by Rāma in battle." D7,10,11,M1, and the texts and printed editions of Cr and Ct read instead *rāmeṇa raṇamūrdhani*, "by Rāma in the forefront of battle."

[2]"Then, after first killing Dūṣaṇa, he subsequently slew Triśiras" *dūṣaṇaṃ cāgrato hatvā triśirās tadanantaram*: Literally, "[by Rāma] having first slain Dūṣaṇa, following that Triśiras [was slain]."

16–17. For the sequence of verses, see notes to verse 14 above.

"Then, a little later, Śūrpaṇakhā" *tataḥ paścāc chūrpaṇakhā*: Literally, "then, afterward, Śūrpaṇakhā." D7,10,11,G2, and the texts and printed editions of Ct and Cr read instead *paścāc chūrpaṇakhā nāma*, "afterward, the one named Śūrpaṇakhā."

"that foolish creature" *bālā*: The term normally means "girl, young woman," but, given the context, we agree with Cm, Ct, and Cg, who gloss, "foolish *or* stupid [woman] (*mūrkhā*)." Cr similarly glosses, "ignorant [woman] (*ajñā*)."

18. "turned himself into a bejeweled deer" *bhūtvā ratnamayo mṛgaḥ*: Literally, "having become a deer made of jewels."

19. "When she caught sight of it, Vaidehī said to Rāma" *sā rāmam abravīd dṛṣṭvā vaidehī*: Literally, "having seen, she, Vaidehī, said to Rāma." M3 and the texts and printed editions of Cg and Cm read instead *athainam abravīd rāmaṃ vaidehī*, "and Vaidehī said to Rāma.

"beautiful" *kāntaḥ*: Roussel (1903, vol. 3, p. 412) appears to read the adjective *kāntaḥ* as a vocative, *kānta*, "O beloved," rendering, "*ô bien-aimé*." In this he has been followed by Shastri (1959, vol. 3, p. 359) and Pagani (1999, p. 1205). Raghunathan (1982, vol. 3, p. 359) reads similarly. If one is to read the term in this way, one has to understand an irregular hiatus between *kānta* and *āśrame*.

"in our ashram" *āśrame naḥ*: D5–7,10,11,T2,M1,3, and the texts and printed editions of Cm and Ct read instead *āśramo naḥ*, lending the sentence the meaning: "Our ashram would be charming and beautiful."

20. "as he fled and, as he fled" *dhāvantam . . . dhāvantam*: Literally, [him] running . . . [him] running." D7,10,11,M1, and the texts and printed editions of Cr and Ct read *mṛgaṃ tam*, "that deer," for the first *dhāvantam*.

"with a straight arrow" *śareṇānataparvaṇā*: Literally, "with an arrow whose joints were not depressed." See 6.59.71 and note.

21. "when . . . had gone after the deer" *mṛgaṃ yāte tu*: D7,10,11,G2, and the texts and printed editions of Ct and Cr read instead *mṛgayāṃ yāti*, "while [Rāghava] was going hunting."

"violently" *tarasā*: Literally, "suddenly." We follow the gloss of Cg, who understands, "by force (*balātkāreṇa*)."

"just as a baleful planet might seize the constellation Rohiṇī" *jagrāha... grahaḥ...rohiṇīm iva*: Literally, "just as a planet seized Rohiṇī." Cg glosses *graha*, "planet," with "Mars (*aṅgāraka iti yāvat*)." Cf. 6.19.34; 6.90.27; and notes.

22. "who tried to rescue her" *trātukāmam*: Literally, "whose wish was to rescue."

"Rāvaṇa" *rāvaṇaḥ*: D7,10,11,G2, and the texts and printed editions of Cr and Ct read instead *rākṣasaḥ*, "the *rākṣasa*."

23. "some monkeys...who were there on a mountaintop" *parvatamūrdhani... vānarāḥ*: As Ct points out, the reference is to Sugrīva, etc., and Mount Ṛśyamūka. See 3.52.1ff.

"who were there...were astonished to see" *dadṛśur vismitās tatra*: Literally, "there, astonished, they saw." D7,10,11,G2, and the texts and printed editions of Cr and Ct read instead *dadṛśur vismitākārāḥ*, "they, whose forms were astonishing, saw."

Following verse 23, D6,7,10,11,M2, KK (in brackets, unnumbered between 6.129.29 and 30), and the texts and printed editions of Ct insert a passage of two lines [3518*]: "Then, moving with the greatest speed, the immensely powerful *rākṣasa* mounted his flying palace Puṣpaka,[1] swift as thought, together with Vaidehī."

[1]"his flying palace Puṣpaka" *tadvimānam...puṣpakam*: The mention of the Puṣpakavimāna here suggests that this passage is a late interpolation. The epic contains no fewer than five direct or eyewitness accounts of Sītā's abduction, and in none of them is there any reference to Rāvaṇa's use of the Puṣpaka for this purpose. Indeed, the account of the abduction in the *Araṇyakāṇḍa*, given first by the poet and then in Jaṭāyus's report to Rāma, makes it clear that the flying chariot drawn by a team of asses or donkeys in which Rāvaṇa attempts to convey Sītā is utterly destroyed in the battle with Jaṭāyus, its draft animals and charioteer slain. After the destruction of this vehicle, no other is described, and it appears that Rāvaṇa simply flies through the air himself, clutching Sītā to his breast as described by Sugrīva and his companions in the *Kiṣkindhākāṇḍa* and again, in the same *kāṇḍa*, in the accounts of Saṃpāti and Supārśva. Even Ct, who accepts the current passage as genuine, struggles to explain the sudden appearance of the Puṣpaka at this point. He says we are to understand that Rāvaṇa had either parked it in a hidden spot along the road or that it could arrive at his mental summons (*anena mārge kvacit sthāpitaṃ gupte deśa āsīt smṛtimātreṇa vā tad-upasthānaṃ bodhyam*). See 3.49.14; 3.50.8–12; 3.52; 3.63.16–18; 4.6.7; 4.57.11ff.; 4.58.15ff.; and notes.

24. "who made the world cry out" *lokarāvaṇaḥ*: D7,10,11,G2,M1, and the texts and printed editions of Cr and Ct read instead *rākṣaseśvaraḥ*, "lord of the *rākṣasas*." See note to 6.8.12.

25. "covered with gold" *suvarṇaparikrānte*: Literally, "circled *or* sheathed with gold." Cg glosses, "daubed *or* covered in gold (*suvarṇānulipte*)." D5,10,11,T1,M1, and the texts and printed editions of Ct read instead *suvarṇapariṣkāre*, "ornamented with gold." Ct, Ck, and Cr, however, gloss, "having a rampart *or* outer wall made of gold (*suvarṇamayapariṣkāraḥ prākāro yasya*—so Cr)."

"with soothing words" *vākyaiḥ*: Literally, "with words *or* utterances."

Following verse 25, D5–7,10–11,S insert a passage of three lines [3521*]: "But, regarding his words to be as worthless as straw[1] and spurning that bull among the *rākṣasas*, sons of chaos, Vaidehī was placed in an *aśoka* grove. Meanwhile, Rāma returned after killing the deer in the deep forest.[2]"

[1]"But regarding his words to be as worthless as straw" *tṛṇavad bhāṣitaṃ tasya*: Literally, "his words like straw." We follow Cg, who supplies the gerund "having thought *or* regarded (*matvā*)." Ct and Cr understand that both Rāvaṇa and his speech are the objects of the participle *acintayantī*, "not heeding *or* regarding," in line 2. Compare 3.54.1; 5.19.2–3; and notes.

[2]"Meanwhile . . . deep forest" *tataḥ . . . mahāvane*: D7,10,11,G2, and the texts and printed editions of Ct and Cr read instead *tadā . . . tadā vane*, "then . . . then in the forest."

26. "Finding the vulture" *dṛṣṭvā gṛdhram*: Literally, "having seen the vulture." Cg and the printed editions of VSP (6.129.34) and KK (6.129.33) read [*a*]*dṛṣṭvā*, "not having seen." Cg understands that we should add the words *sītāṃ ca*, "and Sītā," to indicate that Rāma is distraught at finding neither Sītā nor Jaṭāyus. This interpretation is reflected in the translation of Gita Press (6.126.33; 1969, vol. 3, pp. 1885–86), which nevertheless reads *dṛṣṭvā*, "having seen," rendering, "Missing Sītā (in the hermitage) as well as the vulture (who was living on the outskirts of the hermitage)." See notes to verse 27 below.

27. "After cremating the . . . vulture" *gṛdhram . . . dagdhvā*: D6,7,10,11,G3,M2,5, and the texts and printed editions of Cr and Ct read *dṛṣṭvā*, "having seen *or* found," for *dagdhvā*, "having burned *or* cremated." This reading makes the line redundant with 26b above, and this, no doubt, has led Gita Press to render the phrase as noted above.

"a dear friend of his father" *priyasakhaṃ pituḥ*: D7,10,11, and the texts and printed editions of Cr and Ct read instead *priyataraṃ pituḥ*, lending the phrase the sense "who was most dear to his father."

*"Rāma wandered along" *rāmaḥ . . . anucaran*: Literally, "Rāma, wandering *or* following." The text of the critical edition is awkward with its singular present participle, *anucaran*, "wandering," which can only be resolved with the dual perfect *āsedatuḥ*, "the two encountered," in *pāda* e. We follow the lead of Cg whose text (as well as B3,D6,T2,3,M2,3) reads the imperfect singular *anvacarat*, "he wandered."

"all in blossom" *puṣpitān*: Literally, "in bloom, blossoming." Cg believes that the mention of blossoms is to suggest the thought: "Who would care for flowers now that Sītā has gone (*puṣpitān ity anena puṣpalobhena kiṃ sītātra gateti matir vyajyate*)?"

"the two princes encountered" *āsedatuḥ*: Literally, "the two encountered, met, *or* attacked." Cr glosses, "the two killed (*jaghnatuḥ*)."

Following 27ab, D5–7,10,11,S insert a passage of one line [3524*]: "Searching for Vaidehī, Rāghava, together with Lakṣmaṇa . . ."

29. "Even before they had met" *pūrvam*: We understand the adverb as do Ct, Cm, and Cg, who believe that the reference here is to the time before the two had actually met (*parasparasānnidhyāt pūrvam*—Ct). Ct explains that their mutual affection could arise prior to their meeting because Rāma had already heard about Sugrīva [from Hanumān], while Sugrīva had seen Rāma from a distance (*rāmasya śravaṇena sugrīvasya dūrād darśanena*).

"an emotional bond" *samāgamaḥ* . . . *hārdaḥ*: Literally, "a union of the heart." Ct and Ck gloss, "mental friendship *or* a friendship of the heart (*mānasaṃ sakhyam*—so Ck). Cm and Cg gloss, "mental or emotional bond (*mānasaḥ saṃbandhaḥ*)."

Following 29ab, D5–7,10,11,T,G1,3,M2,3,5, and the texts and printed editions of the southern commentators insert a passage of one line [3529*]: "Sugrīva had earlier been banished by his enraged brother Vālin.[1]"

[1]"by his . . . brother Vālin" *bhrātrā* . . . *vālinā*: Printed editions of Ct (GPP 6.126.37 and NSP 6.126.37) read the nominative *bhrātā*, "a brother," for the critical edition's *bhrātrā*, "by [his] brother." This variant is not recorded in the critical edition, and Ct's commentary reads *bhrātrā* with the critical edition. However, the editors of GPP mark the form and, in a footnote, provide the reading *bhrātrā*, which they report as belonging to the texts of Cg and Cr. Still, the reading *bhrātā* may be the result of a scribal or printing error. No translation consulted renders the nominative form *bhrātā*.

30. "Once he had slain . . . Vālin . . . in battle" *vālinaṃ samare hatvā*: Note how Hanumān glosses over the rather controversial slaying of Vālin. See Lefeber 1994, pp. 45–50 (esp. p. 49); and 4.16.25ff. and notes.

"Rāma bestowed upon Sugrīva a kingship of his own" *rāmaḥ* . . . *svarājyaṃ pratyapādayat*: Literally, "Rāma [by means of the strength of his own arms] established *or* conferred his own kingship." The syntax here, with the repetition of the word *sva-*, "own" (first found in the compound *svabāhuvīryeṇa*, "through the strength of his own arms" in *pāda* a; and next in *svarājyaṃ*, "his own kingdom"), would normally suggest that Rāma is recovering his own kingship. Only two commentators attempt to deal with this reading. Cr, much as we and other translators have done, finesses the problem simply by glossing *svarājyam*, "his own kingship," with "Sugrīva's lordship (*sugrīvādhipatyam*)." Cs knows the critical reading as a variant. He confronts the problem of *svarājyam* by reading the compound to mean "his own [i.e., Sugrīva's] kingdom, i.e., his [Sugrīva's] kingdom, along with his wealth *or* possessions (*svarājyaṃ svena dravyeṇa sahitaṃ ca tadrājyaṃ ca*)." The idea is that Rāma gave Sugrīva back his kingdom and all his possessions. As an alternative, Cs proposes that we understand *svarājyam* to mean "which belonged rightfully to him [Sugrīva] now that the king [Vālin] had died in battle (*rājñi mṛte samare svasvāmikam iti svarājyam vā*). D5,6,T1,G1,3,M1,3,5, and the texts and printed editions of Cg avoid the issue by reading *rāmasya*, "of Rāma," for *rāmaḥ sva-*. This permits Cg to understand Sugrīva to be the unexpressed subject of the gerund *hatvā*, "having slain," which Cg reads as a causative in which Rāma is the subject of the simplex. Cg explains as follows: "We must supply the name Sugrīva here. The construction thus is that Sugrīva, having caused Vālin to be killed by Rāma's strength of arms, regained his own kingship. (*atra sugrīva iti śeṣaḥ. sugrīvo rāmasya bāhuvīryeṇa vālinaṃ hatvā svarājyaṃ pratyapādayat samapādayad iti sambandhaḥ.*)"

31. "he would search for the princess" *rājaputryās tu mārgaṇam*: Literally, "[he promised] a search for the king's daughter."

33. "lost" *vipranaṣṭānām*: Literally, "destroyed." Ct and Cr explain that the term refers to the time when the monkeys had entered the cave [of Svayaṃprabhā] and did not know the way out (*bilapraveśānantaraṃ nirgamamārgam ajānatām*). The incident is

narrated in the *Kiṣkindhākāṇḍa* (4.49.5–4.52.10). D5,M3, and the texts and printed editions of Cm, Ck, and Cg (Ct as a variant) read instead *viprakṛṣṭānām*, "drawn off *or* delayed." Ck and Ct gloss, "who had exceeded the time (*atītakālānām*)." Cg offers two alternate explanations, glossing, first, "having been delayed for a long time (*bahu-kālavilambitānām*)," and then "having gone far afield because of having entered the cave of Svayaṃprabhā (*svayaṃprabhābile praviṣṭatayā dūraṃ gatānām*)." Cm's gloss on this reading is the same as that of Ct and Cr on the critical reading.

34. "about Sītā's dwelling in the abode of Rāvaṇa" *vasatiṃ sītāyā rāvaṇālaye*: D7,10,11, and the texts and printed editions of Ct and Cr read instead *vasatīṃ sītāṃ rāvaṇamandire*, "that Sītā was living in Rāvaṇa's palace."

35. "Then . . . of my kinsmen" *taj jñātinām*: The identity of the *jñātis*, or relatives, referred to here is difficult to determine if we read the sequence as a compound *tajjñātinām*, which would then have to mean "of his *or* her kinsmen," presumably referring to Sītā's kinsmen, but this is contextually implausible. The *tat* then must be read either as we have done, adverbially in the sense of *tataḥ*, "thus, then, therefore," or pronominally with the preceding noun, *duḥkham*, in the sense of "the *or* that sorrow." Like all translators consulted, we take the term *jñātinām* to be Hanumān's reference to his own kinfolk, that is, the monkeys of the southern search party. The form *jñātinām* has caused some discussion and some disagreement among the commentators. Ct and Cm understand it, as do we, as the genitive plural of the noun *jñāti*. They observe that the absence of the long *ī* that would be expected in this form is an irregularity of epic Sanskrit (*atra dīrghābhāva ārṣaḥ*). Cg, on the other hand, understands the term to have an irregular stem, *jñātin*, which would then account for the short *-i-* of *jñātinām* (*na-kārāntatvam ārṣam*). Cr believes that the other commentators are wrong in understanding the term to refer to kinsmen at all. He takes it to be a regular genitive plural of a stem in *-in*, *jñātin* meaning "one possessed of *jñātam*, 'knowledge.'" He explains that Hanumān is dispelling the dejection caused by the knowledge on the part of the monkeys that they would be unable to find Sītā because they now know, from the words of Saṃpāti, that Sītā is in Laṅkā (*taj jñātināṃ saṃpātivacanena sītāsthitijñānavatām*).

36. Hanumān discovers Sītā in the *aśokavana* at *Sundarakāṇḍa* 13ff.

Following verse 36, D5,T1,G3,M1, insert, while D7,11,G1,2, and the texts and printed editions of Cr and Ct insert after verse 37ab, a passage of one line [3535*]: "And I gave her a splendid ring[1] as a token of recognition."

[1]"a splendid ring" *aṅgulīyam anuttamam*: D7,10,11,G2, and the texts and printed editions of Cr and Ct read instead *rāmanāmāṅgulīyakam*, "a ring with Rāma's name on it."

37. "having thoroughly questioned" *pṛṣṭvā sarvam*: Literally, "having questioned about everything."

"a jewel" *maṇim*: Here, as Ct mentions, the reference is to the *cūḍāmaṇi*, or hair ornament, that Hanumān takes from Sītā as proof that he has indeed found her. The incident is recounted in the *Sundarakāṇḍa* at 5.36.52ff.

Following verse 37, D7,10,11,G2, and the texts and printed editions of Cr and Ct insert, while D5,T1,G3,M1 insert following verse 36, a passage of one line [3535*]. See notes to verse 36 above.

39. “delighted” *hṛṣṭaḥ*: D7,10,11,T1,G2,M1, and the texts and printed editions of Ct and Cr read instead *rāmaḥ*, “Rāma.”

“he . . . regained his will to live” *āśaśaṃse sa jīvitam*: Literally, “he desired life.”

“at the point of death” *jīvitāntam anuprāptaḥ*: Literally, “who has reached the end of life.”

40. “Putting in motion a great undertaking” *udyojayiṣyann udyogam*: Literally, “beginning to undertake an undertaking.” Our interpretation is similar to that of Cg, who glosses, “making an effort (*udyogaṃ kurvan*),” viewing the seemingly redundant phrase as similar to such phrases as “he cooks a cooking of rice (*odanapākaṃ pacatītivat*).” Cr understands similarly. Ct and Cm, on the other hand, understand *udyogam* to mean “setting in motion that by means of which victory is accomplished, that is, an army (*udyujyate jayo 'nenety udyogaṃ balaṃ tad yojayiṣyan protsāhayiṣyan*).” Translations that follow the text of Ct also appear to follow this interpretation. However, Roussel (1903, vol. 3, p. 413) seems to understand *balam*, “army,” in its other sense of “strength *or* energy,” rendering, “*Faisant appel à son énergie* . . .” In this he has been followed by Shastri (1959, vol. 3, p. 360) and Pagani (1999, p. 1206).

“to the destruction of Laṅkā” *laṅkāvadhe*: M3 and the texts and printed editions of Cg read *kāmam*, “willingly,” for *laṅkā-*.

“Agni, the shining god of fire” *vibhāvasuḥ*: Literally, “the one whose wealth is light *or* abounding in light.” See note to 6.106.1.

“at the end of a cosmic age” *lokānte*: Literally, “at the end of the world[s].” Cr glosses, “at the time of the destruction of the worlds (*bhuvananāśasamaye*).” See 6.62.20 and note.

42. “slew . . . killed . . . slew . . . killed” *avadhīt*: Literally, “he killed.” We have repeated the verb several times for the sake of clarity.

“Rāvaṇa's son Indrajit” *rāvaṇasutam*: Literally, “Rāvaṇa's son.”

43. “received boons” *varāṃl lebhe*: The reference is to the boons Rāma receives from Indra in *sarga* 108, whereby the slain monkeys are restored to life and provided with an unending supply of fruits, etc.

Following 43ab, D5–7,10,11,S, insert a passage of two lines [3542*]: “. . . and with Maheśvara, self-existent Brahmā,[1] and Daśaratha. Granted boons by them, the majestic hero[2] met with the seers.[3]”

[1] “with Maheśvara, self-existent Brahmā” *maheśvarasvayaṃbhūbhyām*: Literally, “with Maheśvara and the self-existent one.”

[2] “the majestic hero” *śrīmān*: Literally, “the majestic one.”

[3] “met with the seers” *ṛṣibhiś ca samāgataḥ*: D7,10,11,G2, and the texts and printed editions of Ct and Cr read *samāgataiḥ* for *samāgataḥ*. In this variant, it is the assembled seers who join the gods in granting boons.

44. “And when he had received those boons” *sa tu dattavaraḥ*: The context of the verse, with its reference to Rāma's being reunited with the monkeys, suggests that the boons referred to are those whereby Indra restored all the slaughtered monkeys to life and provided for their nourishment, etc. (6.108). Cr, however, the only commentator to remark on this verse, apparently wishing to avoid redundancy with the term *dattavaraḥ* in his previous verse (3542*), understands the reference to be to

Rāma himself having distributed rewards to Vibhīṣaṇa, etc. (*dattavaraḥ prāpitavibhīṣaṇādimanorathaḥ*).

45. "Nothing can prevent you from seeing" *avighnam... draṣṭum arhasi*: Literally, "you ought to see without obstacle." We follow the commentators who understand *avighnam*, "without obstacle," adverbially. It is also possible to take it as an adjective modifying Rāma, in the sense of "he who has no further obstacles or challenges," and several translators have rendered accordingly.

"on the auspicious day of the moon's conjunction with the constellation Puṣya" *puṣyayogena*: Literally, "with the conjunction of Puṣya." This is the name of the eighth lunar asterism, and the moon's conjunction with it is considered an opportune time to undertake solemn events. See 2.2.10 and note; and 2.3.24. Note that Rāma's original consecration was also to have been held on this day. Cg observes that Rāma is remaining on the banks of the Ganges in order to take advantage of the conjunction (*puṣyayogalābhārtham adya gaṅgātīre sthitaḥ*). Cf. Cm's chronology at note to 6.112.1.

"he is staying there with the sage Bharadvāja" *taṃ vasantaṃ munisaṃnidhau*: Literally, "him who is dwelling in the presence of the sage." D7,10,11,G1,3, and the texts and printed editions of Ct and Cr read the feminine demonstrative pronoun *tām* for the critical editions masculine *tam*, "him." In this variant, the pronoun refers not to Rāma but to the Ganges River.

46. "Then, when Bharata had heard that great and truthful speech of Hanumān, he was delighted." *tataḥ sa satyaṃ hanumadvaco mahan niśamya hṛṣṭo bharataḥ*: Cg raises the issue of how Bharata could possibly know whether Hanumān's extraordinary narrative could be true. He explains: "He knew it to be true by the noncontradictory mode of expression (*aviruddhabhaṅgyā satyatvena jñātam*)."

D7,10,11,G2, and the texts and printed editions of Cr and Ct read instead *tataḥ sa vākyair madhurair hanūmato niśamya hṛṣṭo bharataḥ*, "Then, having heard, Bharata was delighted by the sweet words of Hanumān." This variant lacks an object for the gerund *niśamya*, "having heard," and therefore Cr has provided one in the form of the compound *rāmavṛttāntam*, "the news *or* account of Rāma."

"Cupping his hands in reverence" *kṛtāñjaliḥ*: Literally, "making the *añjali* [gesture]." Since it would apparently be *infra dig* for Prince Bharata to display this sign of obeisance to a mere messenger like Hanumān, Ck and Ct believe we should add the phrase "having remembered Rāma (*rāmaṃ smṛtveti śeṣaḥ*)."

The meter is *vaṃśasthavila*.

Sarga 115

1. "those words that filled him with joy" *paramānandam*: Literally, "supreme joy *or* having supreme joy." The expression is elliptical and the commentators flesh it out by glossing, "causing the greatest joy," and adding the word "speech." (*paramānandakaram. vaca iti śeṣaḥ*—so Cg.)

"who was similarly delighted" *hṛṣṭam*: Literally, "delighted." Like the majority of translators consulted, we read the participle as an adjective modifying *śatrughnam* in *pāda* d. It could also be read adverbially with *ājñāpayāmāsa*, "he gave instructions," in *pāda* c, yielding the sense "he happily *or* delightedly ordered." This may be the interpretation of Dutt (1893, p. 1537), who renders, "delighted," and takes it to modify

Bharata instead of Śatrughna. He may also be under the influence of Gorresio's text, which, with a few manuscripts, reads the nominative singular *hṛṣṭaḥ*. This would unambiguously modify Bharata.

2. "pious" *śucayaḥ*: The adjective could also be rendered as "purified, upright, etc."

"all the divinities and the shrines of the city" *daivatāni ca sarvāṇi caityāni nagarasya ca*: The commentators generally understand the term *daivata* to refer to household divinities (*kuladevatā*) and the city shrines to be the common or public places of worship (*sādhāraṇadevatāyatanāni*—so Ck, Cm, and Ct). Cg glosses, "temples *or* shrines at crossroads (*catuṣpathamaṇḍapān*)." Cf. 6.6.3; 6.7.13; and notes.

Following verse 2, D5–7,10,11,S, and the texts and printed editions of the southern commentators insert, while Ś,Ñ,V1,2,B,D8,9,12,13 continue after 3546*, a passage of two lines [3547*]: "Bards, learned in hymns of praise and the *purāṇas*, all the minstrels,[1] all the skilled musicians, and the courtesans in groups[2] [let them go forth]."

[1]"Bards . . . minstrels" *sūtāḥ . . . vaitālikāḥ*: Cg distinguishes these two groups as "those whose occupation is praising (*stutiśīlāḥ*)" and "panegyrists *or* heralds (*bandinaḥ*)." According to Cm, Ct and Ck, a *sūta* is a special type of bard, while a *vaitālika* is one who recites or praises the royal lineages. (*sūtalakṣaṇarūpaṃ sūtaviśeṣaṇam. vaitālikā vaṃśāvalīkīrtakāḥ.*) Cr agrees with Ct and Ck on the meaning of *vaitālika* but is silent on the term *sūta*. *Sūtas* are the offspring of *vaiśya* fathers by kshatriya wives (*ManuSm* 10.17). Cf. *ManuSm* 10.11, where a child from the daughter of a brahman by a kshatriya is also called *sūta*.

[2]"in groups" *saṃghaśaḥ*: Ś,Ñ,V1,B,D7,8,10–12, and the texts and printed editions of Cr and Ct read instead *sarvaśaḥ*, "all."

All manuscripts, with the exception of V3 and D1–4, collated for the critical edition and all printed editions consulted read these lines with some slight variation. In light of this, it is difficult to say why the critical editors relegated them to the apparatus.

3. "the king's wives" *rājadārāḥ*: The commentators agree that the reference is to the wives of the late king Daśaratha.

"the soldiers" *sainyāḥ*: Ck and Ct gloss, "salaried domestic (lit., inside) guards from the royal palace (*rājabhavanād bhṛtimanto 'bhyantarāḥ*)."

"the army troops and their womenfolk" *senāgaṇāṅganāḥ*: Ck and Ct understand the compound to mean "groups of different types of soldiers, such as foresters, and so on, and groups of women (*āṭavikāntasenābhedās tathāṅganāgaṇāḥ*)."

"the hare-marked moon" *śasi-*: Literally, "the one possessing a hare *or* rabbit."

Following 3ab, D5–7,9–11,S insert a passage of one line [3548*]: "as well as the brahmans, together with the kshatriyas, the leaders of the caste guilds, and the general population.[1]"

[1]"the general population" *gaṇāḥ*: Literally, "hosts, groups, multitudes." It appears that this list is intended to reflect the four *varṇas*, or social classes, of brahmanical India.

M3 and the texts and printed editions of Cg read 3548* following 8cd. See note to verse 8 below.

4. "powerful" *vīryavān*: D10,11, and the texts and printed editions of Ck and Ct read instead *bhāgaśaḥ*, "by divisions."

"conscripted laborers" *viṣṭīḥ*: According to Cg, Crā, and Ck, these are unpaid laborers (*bhṛtiṃ vinā karmakarān*—so Cg). Presumably the reference is to *corvée*, or conscripted labor, rather than slaves, strictly speaking. Cm, Cr, and Ct, however, gloss, "wage laborers (*bhṛtikarān*)." Cv understands, "an army of craftsmen (*śilpasenā*)." Compare *Ayodhyākāṇḍa* 74, where Bharata orders the construction of a royal highway along which he means to escort Rāma back from the forest.

5. "Level the road—depressions, rough places, as well as smooth areas" *samīkuruta nimnāni viṣamāṇi samāni ca*: Literally, "Make even the low ones, the uneven ones, and the even ones." Some commentators understand *viṣamāṇi*, "uneven [places]," to refer to elevations or bumps. The idea, in any case, is that all irregularities of the road are to be smoothed out.

"sparing only the roadside shrines" *sthānāni ca nirasyantām*: Literally, "let those places be rejected." The phrase is rather ambiguous, and we tentatively follow the gloss of Cr, who takes *sthāna* in its sense of "a holy spot *or* shrine," in which case, as Cr further suggests, one must take the verb *nir* $\sqrt{}$*as* in the sense of $\sqrt{}$*tyaj*, "to leave aside, spare." This interpretation has been followed by Gita Press (1969, vol. 3, p. 1889), while the phrase appears to have been largely ignored by most of the other translators consulted. D12 has a minor variant, *sthūlāni*, "bulky, large," for *sthānāni*. This reading is noted as a variant by Cm, who glosses it as "significantly raised spots (*atyunnatapradeśān*)." GPP (1969, vol. 3, p. 2706, n. 4) ascribes this variant to Cg, although it is not recorded in VSP (6.130.5), KK (6.130.5), or the apparatus of the latter. Cg makes no reference to this term or to any of its variants. It appears, however, that this reading has informed the translation of Raghunathan (1982, vol. 3, p. 361), who renders, "and break down the boulders."

"from Nandigrāma onward" *nandigrāmād itaḥ param*: Literally, "further on from Nandigrāma." Several of the commentaries and most of the translators consulted add the phrase, "up to Ayodhyā (*yāvad ayodhyām*)."

6. "some men . . . others" *anye*: Literally, "others."

7. "in our splendid city" *puravarottame*: Literally, "in the foremost of excellent cities." The reference is clearly to Ayodhyā. Cr takes this compound quite literally, glossing, "the city of Ayodhyā, which is superior even to such excellent cities as Vārāṇasī, etc. (*puravarebhyo vārāṇasyādibhyo 'py uttamam ayodhyāpuram*)."

"starting at daybreak" *sūryasyodayanaṃ prati*: Literally, "to the rising of the sun." We understand the expression as does Cg, who glosses, "starting at sunrise (*sūryasyodayanam ārabhya*)." Cg offers, as an alternative gloss, "until sunrise *or* during sunrise (*yāvat sūryasyodayanaṃ vā*)." This second interpretation appears to be followed by Gita Press (1969, vol. 3, p. 1889), which translates, "[decorate the dwellings] . . . till sunrise." We believe it more likely that the houses would be adorned during the daylight hours.

8. "Let hundreds of men strew the broad royal highway with garlands, festoons, and loose blossoms and with fragrant powders in five colors." *sragdāmamuktapuṣpaiś ca sugandhaiḥ pañcavarṇakaiḥ / rājamārgam asaṃbādhaṃ kirantu śataśo narāḥ //*: Our translation is based on the arrangement of verses in the critical edition and in the printed editions of Cg (VSP 6.130.8 and KK 6.130.8). Printed texts of Ct and Cr break up the verses differently so that our 7cd forms a single verse with 8ab (GPP, NSP 6.127.9).

Given that arrangement, Cr understands the flowers and pigments mentioned in 8ab to be the articles with which the houses mentioned in 7c are to be decorated rather than, as in our and Cg's reading, the roads. Since the reading of Ct and Cr leaves no articles of adornment with which to strew the roads, Cr takes the verb *kirantu*, "let them scatter *or* strew," of 8d in the sense of "let them stand (*tiṣṭhantu*)." He then understands our line 8cd to stand alone, with the meaning "let hundreds of men stand there so as to keep the royal highway uncrowded (*śataśo narā rājamārgam asaṃbādhaṃ kartum iti śeṣaḥ kirantu tiṣṭhantv ardhaṃ pṛthak*)." Cr clearly understands that Bharata is ordering security guards to line the road to keep it free for the royal procession. In this he has been followed by translations that render the text of Ct. We take the compound *sragdāmamuktapuṣpaiḥ* as a *dvandva*. Cg, although still understanding a *dvandva*, takes the compound slightly differently, understanding *sragdāma-* as a *tatpuruṣa* in the sense of "lines of garlands," and *muktapuṣpaiḥ* as "red and blue lotuses etc., not strung together (*asūtrabaddhapadmakuvalayādibhiḥ*)." Cg understands this compound to refer to part of the ornamentation of the houses rather than of the roads. We understand with Cg that the phrase *sugandhaiḥ pañcavarṇakaiḥ*, "with fragrant powders in five colors," refers to fragrant powdered substances with which the roads are to be spread (*sugandhaiḥ pañcavarṇakaiḥ pañcavidhavarṇadravyacūrṇai rājamārgaṃ kirantu*). D10,11, and the texts and printed editions of Ct read *suvarṇaiḥ*, "of lovely color *or* gold," for *sugandhaiḥ*, "fragrant."

Following verse 8, M3 and the texts and printed editions of Cg read 3ab followed by 3548*. See notes to verse 3 above. Following 3548*, M3 and the texts and printed editions of Cg read a passage of two lines [3556*]; see below. Among the translators consulted, Raghunathan (1982, vol. 3, p. 362) alone renders this sequence of lines and verses.

Following verse 8, D7,10,11,M1, and the texts and printed editions of Ct and Cr insert a passage of one line [3555*]: "Then, when they had heard the orders of Śatrughna, they were filled with delight."

Following 3555*, D7,10,11,M1 insert; Ś,D1,2,4,8,12,M2 insert after verse 3; B3,D3 continue after 3549*; D5,T,G insert after verse 8; D6,9,M5 insert after second occurrence of 3; and M3 continues after 3548* a passage of two lines [3556*]: "Dhṛṣṭi, Jayanta, Vijaya, Siddhārtha, Arthasādhaka, Aśoka, Mantrapāla, and Sumantra went forth." For the sequence of these verses in Cg, see above. Compare 1.7.2, where an identical list of Daśaratha's ministers is given.

9. "Given their orders . . . swiftly" *tvarayā yuktāḥ*: Literally, "enjoined *or* employed, [they] swiftly." D7,10,11, and the texts and printed editions of Ct and Cr read instead *turagākrāntāḥ*, "riding horses," which would modify *narāḥ*, "men." D5,6,T,G2,3,M3, and the texts and printed editions of Cg and Cm read instead *turagākrāntaiḥ*, "drawn by horses, which modifies *rathaiḥ*, "chariots."

"adorned with gold" *śātakumbhavibhūṣitaiḥ*: D7,10,11,G2, and the texts and printed editions of Ct and Cr read instead *sadhvajaiḥ suvibhūṣitaiḥ*, "well-adorned [and] with flags."

Following verse 9, Ś,Ñ,V,B,D7,8,10–13,M3, and the texts and printed editions of the southern commentators insert a passage of three lines [3557*]: "That very illustrious[1] hero was then surrounded[2] with thousands of foot soldiers bearing flags and holding javelins, broadswords, and nooses[3] in their hands and with thousands of magnificent horses, including some that were truly superb.[4]" V3,D7,10,11,M2,3, and the texts and printed editions of the southern commentators transpose lines 1 and 2. Both Cv and Crā spend considerable effort establishing that this is the correct sequence of verses, ascribing the variant order to scribal error.

[1]"very illustrious" *mahāyaśāḥ*: D1–3,7,10–12,M3, and the texts and printed editions of the southern commentators read instead *patākinām*, "[and those] bearing banners."

[2]"That . . . hero was then surrounded" *vīraḥ parivṛtas tadā*: D7,10,11,M2,3, and the texts and printed editions of the southern commentators read instead *vīrāḥ parivṛtā yayuḥ*, "Those heroes went [forth] surrounded." Presumably the heroes in question are the functionaries listed in 3556*. In the critical edition, the singular *vīraḥ* would presumably refer to Śatrughna or to Bharata himself.

[3]"nooses" *-pāśa-*: M3 and the texts and printed editions of Cg read instead *-prāsa-*, "darts."

[4]"including some that were truly superb" *mukhyatarānvitaiḥ*: Literally, "accompanied by even more outstanding ones." M2(3?) and the texts and printed editions of Cg read *-nara-*, "men," for *-tara-*, "more," lending the compound the sense "accompanied by excellent men."

10. Following verse 10, M2,3, and the texts and printed editions of Cg and Gita Press (6.127.16) insert a passage of one line [3559*]: "together with Kaikeyī, they all reached Nandigrāma." This line is rendered only in the translations of Raghunathan (1982, vol. 3, p. 362) and Gita Press (1969, vol. 3, p. 1889). Cg clearly relegates Kaikeyī to a subordinate position, including her among the lesser consorts of the late king, who follow the principal queens. He claims that Kaikeyī goes forth later [than Kausalyā and Sumitrā], since, in his disdain for her, Bharata had not invited her. Therefore, he argues, she joins the party only when they have all arrived at Nandigrāma (*atra bharatenopekṣayānāhūtatvāt paścān nirgatya kaikeyyā nandigrāmaprāptikāle sāhityam ucyate*). Raghunathan (1982, vol. 3, p. 362) includes her in the position of honor accorded to Kausalyā and Sumitrā. He translates, "with Kausalyā, Sumitrā, and Kaikeyi at their head." Note that the critical text and the text of Ct make no mention of Kaikeyī at this point.

11. D7,10,11, and the texts and printed editions of Cr and Ct read verses 11–12 following verse 16, while M3 and the texts and printed editions of Cg read verse 12 before verse 11.

"The thundering of the horses' hooves" *aśvānāṃ khuraśabdena*: Literally, "by the hoof-sound of the horses."

"seemed to shake the very earth" *saṃcacāleva medinī*: Literally, "the earth shook, as it were."

Following verse 11, D7,10,11, and the texts and printed editions of Cr and Ct insert a passage of one line [3560*]: "And with the trumpeting of the elephants and the din of conches and battle drums . . ."

13–16. "set forth to meet Rāma" *pratyudyayau tadā rāmam*: Literally, "he went forth to Rāma."

"together with his counselors . . . by his ministers" *mantribhiḥ . . . sacivaiḥ saha*: Cg attempts to distinguish these two nearly synonymous terms by defining the former as

Vasiṣṭha, etc. (*vasiṣṭhādibhiḥ*), i.e., *purohitas* and other priests, and the latter as Sumantra, etc. (*sumantrādibhiḥ*), his charioteer and counselors. See note to 6.2.14.

"by panegyrists" *bandibhiḥ*: See note to 3547* above, following verse 2.

"his noble brother's sandals" *āryapādau*: Literally, "the feet of the noble one." The context makes it clear that Cg and Cr are correct in understanding that the reference is to the famous sandals of Rāma, which Bharata had installed on the throne as tokens of Rāma's sovereignty (*rāmapāduke*). See 6.112.4 and notes.

"a white umbrella... and a pair of white yak-tail fly whisks adorned with gold" *pāṇḍuraṃ chatram... śukle ca vālavyajane... hemabhūṣite*: The white umbrella and the yak-tail fly whisk are universal symbols of royalty in India and Indianized southern Asia. Cg notes that the compound *hemabhūṣite*, "adorned with gold," means that the whisks were embellished with golden handles (*hemadaṇḍabhūṣite*). See 6.47.13–14; 6.60.14; and notes. See, too, 6.116.25–26 and notes, where these insignia of royalty are held around Rāma.

17. "Looking about him" *samīkṣya*: We understand with Cg that the gerund indicates that Bharata is looking all around him to spot Rāma's arrival (*samantād rāmāgamanaṃ nirīkṣya*). Cr understands that Bharata is looking at Hanumān (*pavanātmajaṃ samīkṣyovāca*).

"I hope you have not fallen prey to the typical flightiness of monkeys" *kaccin na khalu kāpeyī sevyate calacittatā*: Literally, "Surely, it is not that the simian fickle-mindedness is being resorted to?" The fickle-mindedness of monkeys is a favorite theme of the poet. Compare 4.2.16; 5.8.50; 5.36.31; 5.53.8,12; and 6.45.9.

Following verse 17, D5–7,9–11,T,G,M2,3,5, and the texts and printed editions of the southern commentators insert a passage of one line [3562*]: "Nor are any monkeys, who can take on any form at will, to be seen."

18. "informing him of the reason" *arthaṃ vijñāpayann eva*: We agree with Cg and Cm, who cite the lexicon of Vaijayantī in support of their taking the polysemic term *artha* in its sense of *hetu*, "reason." The idea is that Hanumān is explaining the reason for the delay [in Rāma's arrival] (*vilambahetum*). D10,11,T1, and the texts and printed editions of Ck and Ct read instead *arthyam*, "factual, truthful," which Ck, Ct, and Cr gloss as "not deviating from the [true] matter (*arthānapetam*)," i.e., the truth.

19. "They have reached" *prāpya*: Literally, "having reached." The verse is quite elliptical, lacking both a finite verb and a clear subject. It also appears to construe poorly with the following verse. The idea seems to be that the monkeys have delayed Rāma's arrival as they are reveling in the fruits and honey provided by the overlapping boons of Indra and Bharadvāja (Indra's at 6.108.12; Bharadvāja's at 6.112.15,17–18). Cg suggests that we add both a subject and a finite verb: "the monkeys are taking delight (*vānarāḥ hṛṣyantīti śeṣaḥ*)." Cf. verse 22 below. Ct, Ck, and Cr attempt to construe this verse with the two following verses (see notes below), although these efforts are not, in our opinion, successful.

20. "For such... was the boon granted to Rāma" *tasya caiṣa varo dattaḥ*: Literally, "the boon given of [to] him." The reference is to the boon Indra gave to Rāma on behalf of the monkeys that, wherever they went, the trees would always be in fruit and flower (6.108.12). Ck, Ct, and Cr understand that the pronoun *tasya* refers to Bharadvāja and that the boon was the one given to that sage by Indra, who was pleased with his austerities (Ck, Ct). (*tasya ceti. bharadvājasya cety arthaḥ. vāsaveneti. tattapaḥprasāditenety*

arthaḥ.) Cr understands that Indra's boon is what gives Bharadvāja the power to produce all the desirable things needed to offer hospitality, etc. (*vāsavenaiṣa sarvasāmagrīsampādakaśaktiviśeṣo dattaḥ*). See 6.108.12.

"And this was the hospitality . . . that was offered" *tad ātithyaṃ kṛtam*: Cg understands that the fact that the trees are flowing with honey constitutes the hospitality provided by Bharadvāja. Cg sees this as distinct from the provision of unseasonal fruits, which he regards as the boon of Indra (*sasainyasya rāmasya vāsavenaiṣa varo datto 'kālaphalitvavaro dattas tathā sarvaguṇānvitam ātithyaṃ madhusravatvarūpaṃ bharadvājena kṛtam*). Ck and Ct understand that the hospitality is offered by Bharadvāja to both Rāma and Bharata along with their respective armies (*sasainyasya tava rāmasya ca bharadvājena sarvaguṇānvitam ātithyaṃ kṛtam*). Cr breaks up the sequence *tadātithyam* as *tadā*, "then," + *ātithyam*, "hospitality," and understands the reference to be to the elaborate hospitality afforded by Bharadvāja to Bharata and his host "then" [i.e., fourteen years earlier], when Bharata had passed that way [in his failed effort to bring Rāma back prematurely from exile] (*tadā bhavadgamanasamaye sasainyasya tavātithyaṃ kṛtam*). See *Ayodhyākāṇḍa* 85.

21. "of the . . . forest-dwelling monkeys" *vanaukasām*: Literally, "of those inhabitants of the forest."

"must be crossing" *tarati*: Literally, "it [the army] is crossing."

22. "over toward the Vālukinī River" *vālukinīṃ prati*: Literally, "toward the Vālukinī." See 6.113.24 and notes. D7,10,11,G2,M2, and the texts and printed editions of Cr and Ct read instead *sālavanam*, yielding the sense "over toward the forest of *sāla* trees."

"the leaping monkeys must be crashing" *lolayanti plavaṃgamāḥ*: Literally, "the leaping ones shake *or* agitate."

23. "created by the mind of Brahmā" *manasā brahmanirmitam*: Literally, "fashioned by Brahmā with mind." This phrase has caused some concern among the commentators because it appears to contradict earlier statements (cf. 6.109.25) that the Puṣpaka had been built by Viśvakarman. Ct argues that the flying palace was made by Brahmā, that is, Viśvakarman, who is referred to in this way because of his being equal to Brahmā as a creator (*brahmaṇā sraṣṭṛtvasāmyād viśvakarmaṇā nirmitam*). This interpretation is represented in the translation of Gita Press (1969, vol. 3, p. 1891). Cm, on the other hand, explains that the phrase means that the Puṣpaka was made through the mental effort of Viśvakarman on Brahmā's behalf (*viśvakarmaṇā brahmārthaṃ nirmitam*). Raghunathan (1982, vol. 3, p. 363) appears to be somewhat under the influence of Cm in rendering, "created by an act of will under Brahmā's inspiration."

No specific mention appears to be made of Viśvakarman fashioning the Puṣpakavimāna in the critical text of the *Sundarakaṇḍa* (although *Sundarakāṇḍa* App. I, No. 2, line 6, specifically identifies Viśvakarman as the creator of the vehicle). At 7.15.293*, line 4, we are told that it was fashioned by Brahmā. Cf. 5.7.10. See Jhala's critical note concerning this (1966, p. 479). See 5.6.4 and note; and 5.7.11. See verse 29 and notes below. See, too, 6.109.22–27 and notes, where Viśvakarman is explicitly said to have fashioned the Puṣpakavimāna. *MBh* 3.158.35 attributes the manufacture of the flying palace to Viśvakarman. See Wilson 1864–1877, vol. 3, p. 22. According to *MatsyaP* 160.12, Śiva was the architect of the Puṣpakavimāna.

24. Through the grace of Kubera, bestower of wealth" *dhanadasya prasādena*: Literally, "through the grace of Dhanada." The phrase is awkward here since at no point

does the poem indicate any agency on the part of Kubera in the gift or loan of his flying palace to Rāma. Since, however, the Puṣpaka belongs by rights to Dhanada, perhaps we are simply being reminded here of its true legal ownership, even though the palace was handed over to Rāma by Vibhīṣaṇa (6.109.9–10). See notes to 6.109.9, 3333*; and notes to 6.109.21, where the commentators discuss the issue of the vehicle's ownership. The commentators struggle with the phrase here. According to Ct, the palace belongs to Dhanada through the grace of Brahmā (*etat*... *vimānaṃ prasādena brahmaṇaḥ prasādena dhanadasya bhavatīti śeṣaḥ*). Cg has the same idea, and both of these commentators support their interpretation by citing the *Sundarakāṇḍa* verse in which it is said that, as a result of his extreme austerity, Kubera obtained the Puṣpakavimāna from Grandfather Brahmā (5.7.11). This idea informs the translations of Gita Press (1969, vol. 3, p. 1891), Raghunathan (1982, vol. 3, p. 363), Shastri (1959, vol. 3, p. 363), Roussel (1903, vol. 3, p. 446), and Pagani (1999, p. 1208). Only Gorresio (1858, vol. 10, p. 265) and Dutt (1893, pp. 1538–39) understand the phrase literally. On Kubera, see, too, 6.4.16; 6.7.3; 6.22.10; 6.69.26; 6.82.20; 6.92.15; 6.98.12–13; 6.110.23; 6.115.49; and notes. See notes to verses 49–50 below.

"great Rāma" *mahātmanā*: Literally, "by the great one."

Following 24ab, D6,7,10,11,T2,3,M2,3, and the texts and printed editions of the southern commentators insert a passage of one line [3565*]: "Rāma's vehicle, the flying palace that resembles the newly risen sun..."

25. "the lord of the *rākṣasas*" *rākṣasendraḥ*: D6,7,9–11,T2,3,G1,2,M1,3,5, and the texts and printed editions of the southern commentators read instead *rākṣasaś ca*, "and the *rākṣasa*."

26. "reaching to the heavens" *divam aspṛśat*: Literally, "it touched the sky."

"as the women, children, youths, and elderly cried out, "There's Rāma!" *strībālayuvavṛddhānāṃ rāmo 'yam iti kīrtite*: Literally, "In the saying of the women, children, youths, and elderly, 'that is Rāma!' "

27. "Rāma... in his flying palace" *taṃ vimānastham*: Literally, "him, standing in the flying palace."

28. "with a fitting welcome" *svāgatena yathārthena*: D10,11, and the texts and printed editions of Ct read instead *yathārthenārghyapādyādyaiḥ*, "in the correct fashion with a welcome offering, water to wash [his] feet, etc."

29. "which Brahmā created with his mind" *manasā brahmaṇā sṛṣṭe*: See verse 23 above and notes.

"the elder brother of Lakṣmaṇa" *lakṣmaṇāgrajaḥ*: D7,10,11,G2,M2,3, and the texts and printed editions of the southern commentators read instead *bharatāgrajaḥ*, "the elder brother of Bharata."

"as a second Indra, wielder of the *vajra*" *vajrapāṇir ivāparaḥ*: Literally, "like another one with a *vajra* in [his] hand." D6,7,10,11,T2,3,G1,2, and the texts and printed editions of Ct and Cr read *ivāmaraḥ* for *ivāparaḥ*, lending the phrase the sense "like the immortal wielder of the *vajra*."

30. "humbly" *praṇataḥ*: B3,M3, and the texts and printed editions of Cg read instead *prayataḥ*, "restrained, controlled."

"who stood atop his flying palace" *vimānāgragatam*: Literally, "gone to the top of the *vimāna*." The compound can also be taken to mean "standing in that foremost of *vimānas*." Our translation is influenced by the passage at 6.107.9, where Daśaratha's spirit is described as *vimānaśikharasthasya*, "of [him] standing at the peak *or* summit of a *vimāna*," as well as by the force of the simile. Cf. verse 48 below and note.

"like the sun, maker of day, on the summit of Mount Meru" *merustham iva bhāskaram*: Literally, "like the day maker located on Meru."

Following verse 30, D5–7,9–11,S insert, while Ś,Ñ,B4,D8,12 insert after verse 41, a passage of two lines. The first line = 50ab and the second is recorded as 3571* (= VSP 6.130.39 = KK 6.130.36; Gita Press 6.127.39; GPP 6.127.38; NSP 6.127.38; Gorresio 6.111.47; and Lahore 6.108.47): "Then, with the permission of Rāma, that unexcelled and enormously swift flying palace [50ab], yoked to *haṃsas*,[1] descended to the earth.[3571*]" According to Cv and Crā, this *śloka* (50ab–3571*) belongs here but has been placed elsewhere in some manuscripts through the negligence of scribes. (*meghastham* [v.l. for *merustham*] *iva bhāskaram ity asyānantaraṃ tato rāmābhyanujñātam ityādi śloko draṣṭavyaḥ. anyatra tu lekhakadoṣād upanyastaḥ*—so Cv.)

[1]"yoked to *haṃsas*" *haṃsayuktam*: See 6.110.23 and notes.

31. "Invited on board the flying palace" *āropito vimānam*: Literally, "made to ascend the flying palace." We agree with Cr, who glosses, "caused to mount by Rāma (*rāmeṇārohitaḥ*)."

32. "raising up Bharata . . . him . . . him" *taṃ samutthāpya . . . bharatam*: Literally, "having caused him to stand up . . . Bharata." Since, as part of his obeisance and respectful greeting, Bharata would have prostrated himself or at least stooped to touch Rāma's feet, Rāma bids him to rise.

"whom he had not seen in such a long time" *cirasyākṣipathaṃ gatam*: Literally, "[who was] gone to the range of his sight after a long time."

33. "After warmly greeting Lakṣmaṇa . . . respectfully saluted Vaidehī: *tato lakṣmaṇam āsādya vaidehīṃ ca . . . / . . . abhyavādayata*: Literally, "then having met Lakṣmaṇa and Vaidehī, he made respectful salutation." The syntax of the verse is somewhat ambiguous, as it permits, but does not require, us to take Lakṣmaṇa alone as the object of *āsādya*, "having reached *or* met," and Vaidehī alone as the object of *abhyavādayata*, "he saluted respectfully *or* paid obeisance to." The precise analysis of the syntax is of considerable importance to the commentators, because it brings into sharp focus the critical issues of hierarchy and deference that lie at the core of the social vision of the *Rāmāyaṇa* and the culture of which it forms so important an element. The issue, put most simply, is that the commentators and, we are forced to assume, the poet himself do not want to envisage a scenario in which Bharata would bow or make respectful salutation to his younger brother Lakṣmaṇa. Because the simplest way to read the verse, i.e., that Bharata approaches and respectfully salutes both Lakṣmaṇa and Sītā, would suggest just such an inversion, the commentators go to great lengths either to deny that this is what is happening or to find grounds for rationalizing it. The following are some of the interpretive strategies that they employ. Ck, Ct, and Cm, whom we more or less follow in our translation, take the two verbal forms separately, interpreting *āsādya* in the sense of "honoring Lakṣmaṇa, who was praising him, with an embrace, etc. (*vandamānaṃ lakṣmaṇaṃ pariṣvaṅgādinā saṃbhāvya*—so Ck, Ct)." In this reading, Vaidehī alone is the object of Bharata's obeisance, to which, as the wife of his elder brother Rāma, she is fully entitled. Ct and Cm justify this interpretation on the grounds of the evidence

from the *Rāmāyaṇa* and the *Padmapurāṇa* proving that Bharata is older than Lakṣmana. As an alternative, Cm and Ct propose that one can regard Lakṣmaṇa in some sense as "older" than Bharata and therefore deserving of his obeisance. Two arguments are put forward here. The first, attributed to "others," is that, although Lakṣmaṇa is junior to Bharata in chronological age, he has gained greater stature through his obedience to his own elder [Rāma] and therefore is older, as it were, in virtue (*pare tu yady api lakṣmaṇo bharatāt kaniṣṭho vayasā . . . tathāpi jyeṣṭhānuvartanena svāpekṣayādhikaguṇatvena svavyavahāreṇa jyeṣṭhānuvṛttir evaṃ kartavyeti*). The second argument is that since Lakṣmaṇa is produced from a portion of the divine *pāyasa* that had first been given to Kausalyā, he can be considered Bharata's elder (*kiṃca kausalyāyai prathamaṃ dattapāyasāṃśajatvāl lakṣmaṇasya jyeṣṭhatvam*). On the division of the *pāyasa*, see 1.15.24–27 and notes.

Cv states the case very simply, noting that, although Bharata meets or greets both Sītā and Lakṣmaṇa equally, his gesture of homage (*abhivādanam*) is reserved for Sītā alone. Otherwise, he argues, this passage would represent a contradiction to those in which it was earlier stated that Bharata is the elder of the two. (*āsādanaṃ lakṣmaṇavaidehyoḥ samānam. abhivādanaṃ tu vaidehyā eva veditavyam. anyathā pūrvāparoktaṃ bharatasya jyaiṣṭhyavacanaṃ viruddhaṃ syāt.*)

Cg's understanding is similar to the first interpretation of Ct and Cm. He glosses *lakṣmaṇam āsādya* as "honoring with an embrace Lakṣmaṇa, who had made obeisance [to him] (*lakṣmaṇam āsādya kṛtaṃ namaskāraṃ lakṣmaṇam āliṅganena saṃbhāvya*)." This, he notes, is because Lakṣmaṇa is his junior (*idaṃ ca lakṣmaṇasya kaniṣṭhatvāt*). Cg observes, however, that some authorities believe that, in the presence of Rāma, Bharata would have prohibited Lakṣmaṇa's expected gesture of obeisance (*lakṣmaṇena cikīrṣito namaskāro rāmasannidhau bharatena pratiṣedhita iti cāhuḥ*). Cg makes an additional observation in this connection, noting that the conjunction *ca*, "and," after the name Vaidehī indicates that Bharata's homage to Rāma is included in that which he shows toward Sītā (*cakāro rāmanamaskāraṃ samuccinoti*). Cg offers a strictly chronological order of the births of Bharata and Lakṣmaṇa, dismissing all discussion of the distribution of *pāyasa*, the order of marriage, and so on. Finally, Cg indicates that by the sequential nature of Bharata's greetings, first to Lakṣmaṇa and then to Sītā [against the expected order of precedence], we are to understand that, although Sītā is in Rāma's presence, she is standing somewhat apart from him with Tārā and the other women from Kiṣkindhā (*sītā tārādibhiḥ saha rāmasamīpa eva kiṃcid anyatra sthitety avagamyate*).

Cr offers an ingenious interpretation that is based on his reading of the verb *abhyavādayat* (v.l. for *abhyavādayata*) as both a causative and a simplex, the first taking for its object Lakṣmaṇa and the second Vaidehī. The idea here is that Bharata causes Lakṣmaṇa to honor him, while Bharata himself offers obeisance to Sītā. (*bharato lakṣmaṇam āsādyābhyavādayal lakṣmaṇena praṇāmam akārayat. hetumati ṇic. atha vaidehīm āsādyābhyavādayad avandat. atra svarthe ṇic.*)

Cs also addresses this issue at some length. Contributing a novel solution to the problem, he argues that one can take the verb *abhyavādayat* in its sense of formally declaring one's identity. Thus, according to him, Bharata simply meets or greets Lakṣmaṇa and, upon meeting Sītā, he formally announces his name. (*lakṣmaṇam āsādya prāpya. sītāṃ cāsādya nāma ca bharato 'haṃ bho abhivādayāmīti nāmābravīt.*) Cs then enters into a discussion of the various other commentarial theories mentioned above. He more or less accepts the first argument of Ct and Cm, while noting and rejecting, as overly clever manipulations, those arguments that attempt to prove Lakṣmaṇa's seniority with respect to Bharata. See 6.61.24 and note.

34. Following verse 34, D5–7,10,11,T1,2,G1–3,M, and the texts and printed editions of the southern commentators insert a passage of two lines [3575*]: "And Bharata[1] also embraced Suṣeṇa, Nala, Gavākṣa, Gandhamādana, Śarabha, and Panasa."

[1]"Bharata" *bharataḥ*: D6,7,10,11,G2, and the texts and printed editions of Cr and Ct read instead *paritaḥ*, "[who were] all around him."

35. "took on human forms" *kṛtvā mānuṣaṃ rūpam*: Literally, "having made a human form." Why the monkeys change their form is not made clear, unless it is to put them on the same footing as Hanumān, who had taken on human form earlier at 6.113.18 (see note ad loc.). See, too, 6.113.40–42 and 6.114.3 and notes. Perhaps, as in Hanumān's case, the monkeys feel that a human form is more appropriate for the sophisticated, urbane Kosalan capital. This may be what Cr has in mind when he observes that the monkeys effect this transformation in Ayodhyā with its immortal or divine appearance (*amṛtarūpāyodhyāyām*). Compare 6.116.29, where the monkeys are said to take on human form once again.

Following verse 35, D5–7,10,11,T,G,M1,3,5, and the texts and printed editions of the southern commentators insert; Ś,Ñ,V,B1,3,4,D2,3,8,12,13 continue after 3590*; B2 inserts after 32cd (second occurrence); D1,4,9 further continue after 32cd; and M2 continues after 3591* a passage of four lines [3576*]: "Then Bharata, that prince of immense blazing energy and foremost among those who adhere to righteousness, embraced that bull among monkeys Sugrīva and said, 'Sugrīva, you are a fifth brother to the four of us. A true friend is made by affection, while injury is the hallmark of an enemy.[1]'"

[1]"A true friend is made by affection, while injury is the hallmark of an enemy." *sauhṛdāj jāyate mitram apakāro 'rilakṣaṇam*: Literally, "a friend is produced out of affection, injury is a characteristic of an enemy." For *sauhṛdāt*, "from affection," Ck and Ct gloss, " 'from affection' means 'from assistance preceded by that [affection]' (*sauhṛdāt tatpūrvakopakārāt*)." Cr glosses *sauhṛdāt* as "from assistance free from any deceit (*kāpaṭyarahitopakarāt*)" and glosses *mitram* as "one who is the same as a brother (*bhrātur na bhinnam iti tātparyam*)." Cr defines "the hallmark of an enemy (*arilakṣaṇam*)" as "that which gives rise to enmity (*riputvasaṃpādakam ity arthaḥ*)."

As this passage is known to all manuscripts and printed editions consulted, its omission from the critical text is highly questionable.

36. "graciously spoke these words" *sāntvayan vākyam abravīt*: Literally, "consoling *or* ingratiating, he spoke [this] speech." D7,10,11, and the texts and printed editions of the southern commentators read instead *sāntvavākyam athābravīt*, "[he] now spoke consoling *or* ingratiating words."

"Thank heavens" *diṣṭyā*: Literally, "By fate *or* good fortune." Cr glosses, "through a rise of good fortune (*bhāgyodayena*)."

"through your assistance" *tvayā sahāyena*: Literally, "by you an ally *or* helper."

"has been accomplished" *kṛtam*: Cr hastens to remind us that the credit belongs to Rāma [not Vibhīṣaṇa]. He observes, "We must supply, 'by Rāma' (*rāmeṇeti śeṣaḥ*)."

37. "afterward, humbly worshiped" *paścād vavande vinayānvitaḥ*: Literally, "afterward, filled with humility, he worshiped." D7,10,11,G2, and the texts and printed editions of Cr and Ct read instead *vīro vinayād abhyavādayat*, "the hero respectfully saluted out of humility." In addition, Ś,M2,3, and the texts and printed editions of Cg read *vinayād abhyavādayat* for *vavande vinayānvitaḥ*, "humbly worshiped." This lends the phrase the meaning: "afterward, he respectfully saluted out of humility."

38. "so disconsolate" *viṣaṇṇām*: Ś2, Ñ,V,B,D1–3,7,9–13,M1,2, and the texts and printed editions of Cr and Ct read instead *vivarṇām*, "without color *or* pale."

"soothing her heart" *mano mātuḥ prasādayan*: Literally, "propitiating *or* reconciling [his] mother's heart *or* mind." Cg, the only commentator to remark on this reading, understands that Rāma is begging forgiveness for not having obeyed her instructions [not to go into exile—2.18.18–25] and is urging her now to give up her mental suffering (*mano mātuḥ prasādayann iti pūrvaṃ tvadvākyaṃ nāśrauṣam iti tvayā manastāpo na kārya ity evam prasannām akarod ity arthaḥ*)." Ś,Ñ,V,B1,2,4,D7,8,11–13,T2,M1,2,5, and the texts and printed editions of Cr and Ct read *praharṣayan*, "gladdening," for *prasādayan*, "soothing."

39. "and illustrious Kaikeyī" *kaikeyīṃ ca yaśasvinīm*: Ck, Cm, and Ct believe that Kaikeyī is accorded the epithet "illustrious" here because it was through her obduracy or hardheartedness [in insisting on Rāma's exile] that the king [Daśaratha] obtained salvation from hell, while the gods and the brahman-seers attained supreme felicity and Rāma himself attained glory. (*asyā manodārḍhyena rājā narakāt tāritaḥ. devā brahmarṣayaś ca paramaṃ sukhaṃ prāptāḥ. rāmasya ca yaśo jātam ata eṣa yaśasviny eva*—so Ct.) Cg similarly ascribes her illustriousness, that is, the fact that she is to be universally praised, to her having been the root cause of the conquest of Rāvaṇa (*yaśasvinīm. rāvaṇajayasya tanmūlatvāt sarvaiḥ praśasyamānām ity arthaḥ*). Crā similarly notes that the seer [Vālmīki] uses the adjective *yaśasvinī* of Kaikeyī because she was the cause of the accomplishment of the mission of the gods (*kaikeyyā yaśasvinīm iti viśeṣaṇaṃ devakāryahetubhūtatvād ṛṣiḥ prāyuṅkta*). See, too, 6.107.40; 6.109.17–19; and notes. Cf. notes to 6.107.4–6.

"he approached" *upāgamat*: Cr and Cg remind us that not only did Rāma approach his mothers and household priest but he paid them respectful homage (*gatvābhyavādayat*). Cg reminds us that we must construe the gerund *abhivādya*, "having respectfully saluted," of 39a here as well.

"all his other mothers" *mātṝḥ . . . sarvāḥ*: Literally, "all mothers." In addition to his three named queens, Daśaratha elsewhere in the poem is said to have had "a host of wives (*patnīgaṇa*)" (see 1.17.2 and note) or "350 wives" (see 2.31.10 and 2.34.32).

"the household priest" *purohitam*: The reference here would be to Vasiṣṭha (so Cg). Cv understands the term generically to stand for all the family priests, starting with Vasiṣṭha (*vasiṣṭhādayaḥ*).

41. "full-blown" *ākośāni*: The word is not attested in the available dictionaries, but the context makes it clear that it must be synonymous with the variant reading of the southern commentators, which we have followed. Compare v.l. *akośāni*, "not closed *or* in bud," the reading of Ñ2,B1,D7, and the printed editions of Gorresio (6.111.46) and Lahore (6.108.47). D10,11, and the texts and printed editions of the southern commentators read instead *vyākośāni*, which Ct and Cr gloss as *vikasitāni*, "matured, full-blown."

43. "Here, your majesty, is your well-guarded kingdom, which I have now given back" *etat te rakṣitaṃ rājan rājyaṃ niryātitaṃ mayā*: D7,10,11,G2,M2, and the texts and printed editions of Ct read instead *etat te sakalaṃ rājyaṃ nyāsaṃ niryātitaṃ mayā*, lending the line the following meaning: "Here is your entire kingdom, which I held in trust and have given back."

45. "the granary" *koṣṭhāgāram*: Literally, "the granary chambers." The term can also be taken generically to mean "storehouse."

"the city" *puram*: D7,10,11,G2, and the texts and printed editions of Cr and Ct read instead *gṛham*, "the house, household."

46. "they shed tears" *mumucuḥ...bāṣpam*: Why are they crying? Cg, evidently keeping in mind that both Sugrīva and Vibhīṣaṇa have been responsible for the deaths of their own respective brothers at Rāma's hands, observes: "They wept because they had never seen such brotherly conduct among their own kinsmen (*svakulīneṣv etādṛsabhrātṛvṛttyadarśanād iti bhāvaḥ*)." Cm concentrates on the tears of Vibhīṣaṇa, which he sees as arising both from the *rākṣasa*'s joy at discovering that there are such brothers as these and from grief at the perversity of his own brother (*vibhīṣaṇaś ca bāṣpaṃ mumocedṛśā api bhrātaraḥ santīty ānandena svasya tadvaiparītyajaśokena ca*).

48. "from atop the flying palace" *vimānāgrāt*: Literally, "from the top of the *vimāna*." Compare verse 30 and note.

49. "the god Kubera Vaiśravaṇa" *vaiśravaṇaṃ devam*: Literally, "the god Vaiśravaṇa." See verse 24 and notes above.

50. "the abode of Kubera, bestower of wealth" *dhanadālayam*: Literally, "the abode of the giver of wealth." Kubera is said to reside in the Himalayan city of Alakā (cf. *Meghadūta* 7). See verse 24 and notes above.

Following verse 50, Ś,Ñ1,V,B,D6–8,10–12,T2,3,G2, KK (in brackets = 6.130.59), and the texts and printed editions of Ct insert a passage of two lines [3588*]: "And thus the unsurpassed and heavenly flying palace Puṣpaka, a car for all seasons,[1] swiftly returned to Kubera, bestower of wealth, who was delighted by Rāma's words.[2]"

[1]"unsurpassed...a car for all seasons" *sarvartukam anuttamam*: Literally, "unsurpassed...belonging to all seasons." The connotation of the term *sarvartukam* is not entirely clear to us in the present context, nor do the commentators or translators offer any help as none of them shares this reading. Perhaps the adjective is somehow related to the *vimāna*'s name, Puṣpaka, "Flower." See 6.30.8; 6.108.12; 6.115.20; and notes. D6,7,10,11,T2,3,G2, and the texts and printed editions of Ct read instead *saṃgṛhītaṃ tu rakṣasā*, "which was taken by [that] *rākṣasa*."

[2]"swiftly returned to Kubera, bestower of wealth, who was delighted by Rāma's words" *rāmavākyapramuditaṃ javena dhanadaṃ yayau*: D7,10,11,G2, and the texts and printed editions of Cr and Ct read *agamad dhanadaṃ vegād rāmavākyapracoditam*, "it returned swiftly to the bestower of wealth, urged by Rāma's words," for line 2.

Following 3588* or verse 50, many northern manuscripts, including the printed texts of Gorresio (6.111.48–49 = lines 1–4) and Lahore (6.108.61–63), include a passage [3589*] in which Kubera actually sends the Puṣpakavimāna back to Rāma to serve him, and Rāma receives it with reverence.

51. "Just as Śakra, lord of the immortal gods, might grasp the feet of Bṛhaspati" *bṛhaspateḥ śakra ivāmarādhipaḥ*: Literally, "like Śakra, lord of the immortals, of Bṛhaspati." See 6.7.9–10; 6.11.42; 6.40.28; and notes.

"mighty Rāghava" *rāghavaḥ... vīryavān*: B1,M3, and the texts and printed editions of Cg read the name *rāghavaḥ* twice, yielding an awkward repetition.

"his household priest, who was his equal" *purohitasyātmasamasya*: We concur with Cm and Cr, who identify the *purohita* as Vasiṣṭha, the ancestral *purohita* of the House of Ikṣvāku. Ct, who notes the critical reading as a variant and cites Cm for his interpretation of the alternative reading, explains that the reference is to Vasiṣṭha, who is equal to Lord Rāma because of his knowledge of the supreme truth. (*ātmasamasyeti pāṭhāntaram. brahmajñatvād iti bhāvaḥ vasiṣṭhasyety artha iti tīrthaḥ.*) D10,11,T2,3,M1,5, and the texts and printed editions of Ct and Cr read *-sakhasya*, "friend," for *-samasya*, "equal," yielding the sense "his household priest [and] friend." Ck and Ct, who prefer this variant, are loath to see the venerable seer Vasiṣṭha described as the friend of his junior, Rāma. They understand the reference to be to Vasiṣṭha's son, Suyajña, who would be more of a contemporary to Rāma (*vasiṣṭhaputrasya suyajñasyety arthaḥ*).

"they sat down together, each on a separate, splendid seat" *pṛthag āsane śubhe sahaiva tenopaviveśa*: Literally, "[he] sat together [with him] separately on a splendid seat." We follow Cv, who understands that the two men sit together in the sense of being seated at the same time but on separate seats. (*ekasmin kāla upaveśaḥ. svasmin svasminn āsana ekadaivopaviviśuḥ.*) This idea of separate seats is represented only in the translations of Gita Press (1969, vol. 3, p. 1894) and Raghunathan (1982, vol. 3, p. 365).

The meter is *vaṃśasthavila*.

Sarga 116

1. "Cupping his hands to his forehead in reverence" *śirasy añjalim ādhāya*: Literally, "placing folded hands on the head." Dutt (1893, p. 1541) for some reason understands that Bharata is placing Kaikeyī's palms on his head. He translates, "having placed her palms on his head, Bharata, the enhancer of Kaikeyī's joy..."

"increaser of Kaikeyī's joy" *kaikeyīnandivardhanaḥ*: Cg takes his variant of this epithet, *kaikeyyānandavardhanaḥ*, to indicate that Kaikeyī is now reconciled to Rāma's ascension to the throne. We are to infer this, he continues, from the pleased expression on Kaikeyī's face, etc., when she hears Bharata's words (*kaikeyyānandavardhana ity anena bharatavacane kaikeyīsantoṣo mukhaprasādādināvagamyata iti dyotyate*).

"his elder brother" *jyeṣṭham*: Literally, "the elder one."

2. "You showed my mother respect" *pūjitā māmikā mātā*: Literally, "my mother was honored." As the commentators point out, Kaikeyī was gratified or respected by Rāma's acquiescing to her demands that he abandon the kingship and accept exile to the forest (*taduktavanavāsānuṣṭhānāt*—so Ct).

3. "this... burden" *bhāram*: As Ct points out, the burden Bharata is referring to is that of the kingship (*rājyasya bhāram*).

"set down" *nyastām*: Literally, "deposited." The word has been carefully chosen because of its resonance with the idea that Bharata accepted the kingship of Kosala only as a *nyāsa*, "a deposit *or* a trust." See 2.107.14; 6.115.43; and notes.

"solitary" *ekākinā*: As Ct and Cr indicate, the term refers to a bullock who lacks an equal partner to share the burden of the yoke (*svasamānadhūrvahabalīvardāntara-rahitena*). The figure derives from the fact that draft bullocks in India are generally yoked in pairs and suggests, perhaps, that Bharata would serve as a partner in governance with Rāma.

4. "I think that any threat facing the kingdom, if unaddressed, would be as difficult to remedy as it would be to repair a dike that, breached by a tremendous flood of water, has sprung a leak." *vārivegena mahatā bhinnaḥ setur iva kṣaran / durbandhanam idaṃ manye rājyacchidram asaṃvṛtam //*: The metaphor underlying this verse is a complex one and does not lend itself readily to a translation that is both literal and intelligible. A more or less literal rendering would be as follows: "I regard this uncovered *or* unplugged gap that is the kingdom to be difficult to bind up, just like a leaking dike breached by great water pressure." The idea is that Bharata is once again indicating his incapacity to manage the kingdom. Ct and Cr understand the term *rājyacchidram* as a *tatpuruṣa* in the sense of "the defects *or* liabilities of the kingdom, such as theft (*rājyacchidraṃ corādyupadravaḥ*)." This interpretation finds expression in the translation of Dutt (1893, p. 1541), who renders, "this kingdom infested with thieves." Cg explains the verse as follows: "Just as it is impossible to repair a leaking dike that has been breached by a tremendous force of water without a plug in the form of a mass of branches and clumps of straw to check the flow of water, so is it impossible to govern a kingdom that has many different threats to its integrity in the absence of preventive measures in the form of kingly virtues, such as the king's ability to keep his counsel secret, etc. (*yathā mahatā vārivegena bhinnaḥ kṣaran setur vārivegāhatinirodhakatṛṇa-pūlaśākhāpuñjādisaṃvaraṇaṃ vinā na baddhuṃ śakyate. evaṃ bahuvidhacchidraṃ rājyam api mantragopanādirājaguṇāvaraṇaṃ vinā pālayituṃ* [v.l. *pālituṃ*—so VSP, KK] *na śakyam iti bhāvaḥ*.)" According to this interpretation, Bharata is pleading that he lacks the qualities to be an effective monarch. The translation of Gita Press (1969, vol. 3, p. 1894) appears to read the compound *rājyachidram* as a *samastarūpaka*, or compound metaphor based on an appositional *karmadhāraya*, rendering, "I believe this vulnerable point in the form of administration is difficult to protect, (particularly) when exposed, (even) as a dam that is leaking when breached by a strong onrush of water."

5. "the path you have blazed" *tava mārgam*: Literally, "your path, road." Ct glosses, "skill in protecting that which needs to be protected (*rakṣaṇīyarakṣaṇacāturyam*)."

6–7. As Bharata makes clear in verse 8, the two verses constitute a kind of extended metaphor or parable for Rāma. The commentators attempt to clarify its meaning. The general idea, according to them, is that Rāma, having been sired by Daśaratha for the purpose of ruling the ancestral kingdom and possessing all the qualifications for doing so, would be, should he fail to ascend the throne, like the magnificent but sterile tree described in the parable. Cg goes into some detail in an effort to show how each element in the tree metaphor applies to Rāma. He says that both the tree and Rāma were planted by Daśaratha and stand in the relationship of the subject and object of comparison, respectively. The planting of the tree's seed is comparable to Daśaratha's performance of the *putreṣṭi* sacrifice (*Bālakāṇḍa* 14), and the tree's mighty trunk is analogous to the collectivity of Rāma's brothers. Its many branches stand for the host of Rāma's allies, such as Sugrīva; its blossoms, his auspicious virtues; and its failure to bear fruit, his failure to rule. (*atra vṛkṣarāmayor āropayitṛdaśarathayoś copamānopa-meyabhāvaḥ. bījāvāpasya putreṣṭyādeś ca mahāskandhasya sabhrātṛkatvasya ca praśākha-*

vattvasya sugrīvādimitragaṇasya ca puṣpāṇāṃ kalyāṇaguṇānāṃ ca rājyākaraṇasya phalābhāvasya ca sāmyaṃ dyotyate.)

8. "devoted" *bhaktān*: Ñ1,V,B2–4,D7,10,11,G2, and the texts and printed editions of Cr and Ct read instead *bhartā*, "lord, master."

9. "the whole world" *jagat...sarvataḥ*: Literally, "the world from all sides." D7,10,11,G2, and the texts and printed editions of Cr and Ct read the vocative *rāghava*, "O Rāghava," for *sarvataḥ*, "from all sides."

10. "You should fall asleep and" *śeṣva ca*: B4,T2,3,M3, and the texts and printed editions of Cg read instead the vocative *rāghava*, "O Rāghava." Raghunathan (1982, vol. 3, p. 365) alone renders this variant.

"the sounds of musical ensembles" *tūryasaṃghātanirghoṣaiḥ*: Literally, "with the sounds of groups of musical instruments." Cf. 6.24.25; 6.90.27–28; and notes. See note to verse 34 below.

11. "As long as the wheel of heavenly bodies shall turn and as long as the earth, bearer of wealth, shall endure" *yāvad āvartate cakraṃ yāvatī ca vasuṃdharā*: Literally, "as long as the wheel turns, so long as [is] the bearer of wealth." The commentators generally agree that the term *cakram*, "wheel," refers to the wheel or orb of the celestial bodies (*jyotiścakram*). Roussel (1903, vol. 3, p. 419), followed by Shastri (1959, vol. 3, p. 366), understands the elliptical phrase to refer to the disc of the sun. Gorresio (1858, vol. 10, p. 268) similarly renders, "*la ruota del carro del sole*." See notes to 6.3.16; 6.93.13; and 6.98.2.

The commentators differ, however, in how they interpret the two occurrences of the lexeme *yāvat* (adverb) / *yāvatī* (adjective), taking it variously in its temporal and/or spatial senses, "as long as *or* as far as." Our translation follows the interpretation of Cv, Cg, and Cm, who take both terms in a temporal sense, glossing, for *yāvatī*, "as long as there is stability or endurance (*yāvatkālasthitiḥ*—so Cg)." Ct and Cm take the adverb *yāvat* to express the limit or the end of time (*anena kālāvadhir ucyate*—so Ct). Ct and Cr take the adjective *yāvatī* in a spatial sense as indicating the limits of the land or the earth (*deśāvadhir ucyate*—so Ct). Cr alone takes the adverb *yāvat* in a spatial sense, understanding it to mean "to the extent of the territory over which the circle of heavenly bodies revolves (*jyotiścakraṃ yāvad āvartate yāvad deśaṃ bhramati*)." Translations render variously.

"may you exercise lordship over all in this world" *iha sarvasya svāmitvam abhivartaya*: Literally, "may you carry out *or* set in motion lordship of all here." D6,7,10,11,G1, 2,M1, and the texts of Cr and Ct read *lokasya*, "of the world," for *sarvasya*, "of all."

12. "as he sat on his splendid seat" *niṣasādāsane śubhe*: Literally, "he sat *or* sat down on a splendid seat." We agree with Cr that the subject of the verb "he sat (*niṣasāda*)" is Rāma. However, since Rāma was depicted as sitting down on a splendid seat in the final verse of the preceding *sarga* (6.115.51) and has not had occasion to leave that seat until this point, we have rendered in such a way as to indicate that he remains seated. This issue seems to have troubled Cv and Cg as well. They attempt to solve the problem by arguing that it is Bharata who now takes his seat. Cv and Cg may also be influenced by the fact that it is Bharata and Lakṣmaṇa upon whom the barbers wait first in the following verses. Cv argues that Bharata is the subject of the verb on the grounds that it was already stated that Rāma took his seat earlier (1.115.51) (*atra bharataḥ kartā rāmopaveśasya pūrvam evoktatvāt*). Cg concurs, suggesting that we add the name Bharata.

13. "barbers" *śmaśruvardhakāḥ*: Literally, "beard-cutters."

"with a gentle touch" *sukhahastāḥ*: Literally, "having pleasant hands. "Cr glosses, "those whose hand gives pleasure (*sukhaḥ sukhapradaḥ hasto yeṣām*)."

"quick at their work" *suśīghrāḥ*: Literally, "very fast." Cr glosses, "getting their work done quickly (*śīghraṃ kriyāniṣpādakāḥ*)." Cg takes the adjective to mean that the barbers are capable of working quickly enough so that they finish before the auspicious moment for the consecration (*abhiṣekamuhūrtātilaṅghanaṃ vinā śīghraṃ kartuṃ samarthāḥ*).

"attended upon Rāghava" *rāghavaṃ paryupāsata*: Cg, the only commentator to remark on this reading, understands the verb to mean that the barbers cut or shaved the beards (*śmaśrūṇy avardhanta*). It is not entirely clear exactly which figure or figures are indicated by the epithet *rāghavam*, "Rāghava." Ct, Ck, Cv, Cs, and Cm are silent on the subject, while Cr merely repeats the term from the text. Cg, however, understands that the singular term here designates both Bharata and Lakṣmaṇa (*rāghavam iti bharatalakṣmaṇayoḥ pradarśanātham*). Among the translators consulted, most, like us, use the nonspecific term "Rāghava." Gita Press (1969, vol. 3, p. 1895) and Gorresio (1858, vol. 10, p. 268), however, both render "Rāma." This seems improbable, however, since it appears that Rāma permits himself to be bathed and groomed only after his brothers and allies have been served (see verses 14–15 below). D7,10,11,G2, and the texts and printed editions of Cr and Ct read *paryavārayan*, "they surrounded *or* encircled," for *paryupāsata*, "they attended upon."

14–15. "Bharata . . . Lakṣmaṇa . . . Sugrīva . . . Vibhīṣaṇa had all bathed before him" *pūrvam . . . bharate snāte lakṣmaṇe ca . . . / sugrīve . . . ca . . . vibhīṣaṇe*: Cg explains why each of the figures named must bathe before Rāma. Bharata, he notes, must do so because of Rāma's vow at 6.109.6 that he will not bathe until Bharata does. In the cases of Sugrīva and Vibhīṣaṇa, Cg notes that they have not bathed since they first left their respective cities. Cg gives no explanation for Lakṣmaṇa's priority in bathing. Ct and Cg call our attention to the omission of Śatrughna's name from the list. Ct offers two possible explanations for this. The first is that Śatrughna is too preoccupied with arranging everybody else's bath (to bathe himself). The second is that we are to understand that Śatrughna is included among the group of bathers by *upalakṣaṇa*, or metonymy. (*atra bharatalakṣmaṇayoḥ snānādyabhidhānakāle śatrughnasya tadanabhidhānaṃ tu snānakārayitṛtvāt. upalakṣaṇaṃ vā*.) Cg also offers two explanations, the first of which is similar to Ct's first explanation. His second is somewhat more interesting. He argues, in his characteristically logical way, that [unlike Rāma, Lakṣmaṇa, and Bharata] Śatrughna has nowhere been stated to have taken any sort of ascetic vow [and so would not be in any urgent need of a bath] (*pūrvaṃ vratagrahaṇānukteś ca*). On the other hand, Cg is mindful that other authorities cite the *Saṃkṣiptarāmāyaṇa* verse (1.1.70), which states that, at the end of his period of banishment, Rāma put off the matted locks of an ascetic, together with his brothers, among whom, presumably, Śatrughna would be included.

"Rāma gave up his matted locks and bathed" *viśodhitajaṭaḥ snātaḥ*: Literally, "he whose matted locks were cleansed *or* purified, bathed." Although, as Cg notes, the phrase literally refers to washing of the hair (*jaṭāśodhanaṃ śuddhakeśīkaraṇam*), we must understand that, as indicated at 1.1.70, he is completely removing his matted locks and resuming the groomed hair of an aristocrat. See 1.1.70; 6.109.6; 6.112.4; and notes. All northern manuscripts and the printed editions of Gorresio (6.112.19) and

Lahore (6.109.20) add or substitute a passage of two lines [3602*], which glosses or clarifies the southern reading by making it clear that Rāma actually cuts off his matted locks.

"he stood there, blazing with splendor" *tasthau tatra śriyā jvalan*: Cg notes that the splendor in question is that of Rāma's ornaments (*alaṃkāraśriyā*). He glosses the adverb *tatra*, "there," as *siṃhāsane*, "on a throne (lit., lion's seat)."

16. "mighty and splendid Śatrughna, increaser of the House of Ikṣvāku" *vīryavān* / ... *lakṣmīvān ikṣvākukulavardhanaḥ*: Literally, "the one possessed of valor, the one possessed of Lakṣmī *or* splendor, the increaser of the House of Ikṣvāku." Like all the commentators consulted, except Cr, we take all three adjectives to refer to Śatrughna, since it was he who was put in charge of the bathing and grooming (see verse 13 above). Cr, however, understands the reference to be to Bharata, under whose authority Śatrughna is acting. Most of the translations consulted that actually specify a proper name here agree with us. Roussel (1903, vol. 3, p. 420) understands the adjective *vīryavān*, "mighty, heroic," to refer to Bharata, whom he sees as supervising the toilet of Rāma, while taking the remaining adjectives to refer to Śatrughna, whom he understands to be responsible for Lakṣmaṇa's grooming. In this interesting interpretation, he is followed by Shastri (1959, vol. 3, p. 366).

17. "themselves" *ātmanā*: Literally, "by one's self." As the commentators indicate, the term suggests that the women themselves dressed and ornamented Sītā rather than having it done by maidservants (*ātmanaiva na sairandhrīhastenety arthaḥ*—so Ct, Cm).

18. "all the wives of the Rāghavas" *rāghavapatnīnāṃ sarvāsām*: The precise reference is not clear. It could be either to the wives of Daśaratha, who are mentioned in the previous verse, in which case the translation would be "all the wives of Rāghava (i.e., Daśaratha)." Since these women are widows, however, it would seem inappropriate for them to be adorned and dressed in finery. See *ManuSm* 9.200 and S. Goldman 2000b. We therefore believe that the reference is to the wives of Rāma's three younger brothers, that is, Māṇḍavī, Ūrmilā, and Śrutakīrtī, to whom the brothers are wedded in the *Bālakāṇḍa* (1.70.20; 1.71.5–6; and 1.72.18–20). This understanding is shared by Gorresio (1858, vol. 10, p. 269), the only translator consulted to have this reading. He renders, "*tutte le donne dei Raghuidi*." B1,D1–4,6,7,9–11,S, and the texts and printed editions of the southern commentators read *vānara-*, "monkeys," for "*rāghava-*," giving the phrase the sense "all the wives of the monkeys." The reference is to the female monkeys who serve as Sītā's traveling companions from Kiṣkindhā to Ayodhyā (see note to 6.111.14, App. I, No. 72).

19. "richly adorned throughout" *sarvāṅgaśobhanam*: Literally, "having adornment in every part."

"and brought it up" *abhicakrāma*: Literally, "he came near *or* approached."

20. "that ... chariot standing before him" *rathaṃ sthitam*: Literally, "the chariot [which] stood *or* was located [there]." Ś,Ñ,V1,2,B2,3,D8,12,13,T1,M3, and the texts and printed editions of Cg and Gorresio (6.112.23) and Lahore (6.108.25) read instead *rathottamam*, "that best of chariots *or* that splendid chariot." This reading is rendered in the translations of Gorresio (1858, vol. 10, p. 269) and Raghunathan (1982, vol. 3, p. 366).

"blazing like the orb of the sun" *arkamaṇḍalasaṃkāśam*: D10,11, and the texts and printed editions of Ct read instead *agnyarkāmalasaṃkāśam*: "having a bright *or* spotless appearance like the sun or fire."

"truly valorous" *satyaparākramaḥ*: D7,10,11, and the texts and printed editions of Cr and Ct read instead *parapuraṃjayaḥ*, "the conqueror of enemy citadels."

Following verse 20, Ś,Ñ,V1,2,B,D6–8,10–12,S, and all printed editions of the southern recension insert a passage of four lines [3605*]: "Shining with a splendor like that of great Indra,[1] Sugrīva and Hanumān accompanied him,[2] after having bathed and put on garments that were like those worn in heaven[3] and splendid earrings.[1–2] And Sugrīva's wives and Sītā, eager to see the city, went along as well,[4] covered with splendid ornaments[5] and wearing splendid earrings.[3–4]"

[1]"Shining with a splendor like that of great Indra" *mahendrasadṛśadyutī*: Literally, "having a splendor like that of great Indra (Mahendra)."

[2]"accompanied him" *jagmatuḥ*: Literally, "those two went."

[3]"put on garments that were like those worn in heaven" *divyanibhair vastraiḥ*: Literally, "with garments that were like heavenly ones."

[4]"went along as well" *yayuḥ*: Literally, "they went."

[5]"covered with splendid ornaments" *varābharaṇasampannāḥ*: Literally, "endowed with excellent ornaments." D7,10,11,G2, and the texts and printed editions of Cr and Ct read instead *sarvābharaṇajuṣṭāś ca*, "furnished with every ornament."

21. "Meanwhile ... who had remained in Ayodhyā" *ayodhyāyāṃ tu ... ye*: Literally, "but [those] who [were] in Ayodhyā." There appears to be a slight discontinuity in the narrative here, since, when last we heard of the ministers, they had gone from Nandigrāma to meet Rāma (6.115.13–16). The commentators try to address this gap in various ways. Ct adds the words "at this juncture (*tasminn antara ityādi*), while Cg supplies the gerund "having gone *or* returned (*gatveti śeṣaḥ*)."

D7,10,11, and the texts of Cr and Ct read *ca ... ca*, "and ... and," for *tu ... ye*, "but ... [those] who." These variants lend the line a slightly different sense: "And in Ayodhyā the ministers of King Daśaratha ..."

"placing the household priest at their head" *purohitaṃ puraskṛtya*: The commentators identify the household priest here as Vasiṣṭha, whom we last heard of at the end of *sarga* 115 (see 6.115.51 and notes) seated on a splendid throne next to Rāma in Nandigrāma. Presumably, like the other ministers, he has since returned to the city to plan the consecration.

"purposefully took counsel together" *mantrayāmāsur arthavat*: We understand with Cr that the term *arthavat*, "purposefully," is to be read adverbially (*arthavat yathā bhavati tathā*). Ct amplifies somewhat, glossing, "in such a way that it has an excellent purpose. The meaning is 'they conducted a full deliberation appropriate to the consecration of Rāma.' (*arthavat prayojanottamavat. rāmābhiṣekopayuktam aśeṣavicāraṃ cakrur ity arthaḥ.*)" Cg is most specific, understanding that they conferred with regard to what was necessary for the purpose of putting together the auspicious articles to be used in the consecration (*abhiṣekopayogimaṅgaladravyasampādanārtham evaṃ kartavyam iti mantrayāmāsuḥ*).

Following verse 21, Ś,D6–8,10–13,S insert a passage of one line [3607*]: "And Aśoka, Vijaya, and Sumantra,[1] [who had] met, [took counsel]."

[1]"and Sumantra, [who had] met" *sumantraś caiva saṃgātāḥ*: D7,10,11, and the texts and printed editions of Cr and Ct read instead *siddhārthaś ca samāhitāḥ*, "and

Siddhārtha, [all who were] focused *or* assembled." The substitution of Siddhārtha for Sumantra in this minor variant is explained, perhaps, by the fact that Sumantra, as royal charioteer, has brought the chariot out to Rāma in Nandigrāma. It should be noted, however, that verse 25 below shows Bharata actually taking the reins on the journey back to Ayodhyā. See verses 19 and 26, and notes.

22–23. "with regard to the prosperity of Rāma and the maintenance of the city" *rāmavṛddhyarthaṃ vṛttyarthaṃ nagarasya ca*: Roussel (1903, vol. 3, p. 420), apparently taking the term *vṛtti* in its less common sense of "respectful treatment," somehow construes the two phrases to mean "*sur les honneurs que la ville devait rendre á Rāma.*" In this odd reading he has been followed by Shastri (1959, vol. 3, p. 366) and Pagani (1999, p. 1211). G3,M2,3, and the texts and printed editions of Cg and Cm and Gita Press read *ṛddhyartham*, "for the sake of prosperity," for *vṛttyartham*, "for the sake of maintenance." This variant is rendered in the translation of Gita Press (1969, vol. 3, p. 1896) and Raghunathan (1982, vol. 3, p. 366).

"Preceding all your actions with auspicious rites" *maṅgalapūrvakam*: Literally, "preceded *or* accompanied by auspicious rites *or* benedictions."

"you must do everything necessary" *sarvam... kartum arhatha... yad yat*: Literally, "you must do everything whatever." Since, in the critical edition and the texts and printed editions of Cv, Cg, and Cm, the ministers address their instructions to the *purohita* Vasiṣṭha, Cv, Cg, and Cm are obliged to note that the second person plural *arhatha* is a plural of respect (*pūjāyāṃ bahuvacanam*).

"Having thus instructed the household priest, all the ministers" *iti te mantriṇaḥ sarve saṃdiśya tu purohitam*: B2,D10–12, and the texts and printed editions of Cr and Ct read the nominative singular *ca* (*tu*—D12) *purohitaḥ*, "and the *purohita*," for the accusative singular *tu purohitam*. This adds the *purohita* Vasiṣṭha to the group of ministers who are giving instructions. In this variant, there is no expressed object for the gerund *saṃdiśya*, "having instructed." Ct therefore indicates that the instructions are issued to servants (*kartum arhatheti bhṛtyān pratyuktiḥ*). Translations that follow the texts and printed editions of Ct render this variant, while Gita Press (1969, vol. 3, p. 1896) and Dutt (1893, p. 1542) incorporate Ct's suggestion.

24. "blameless... Indra" *indra ivānaghaḥ*: The syntax and the prosody of the verse seem to favor construing the adjective *anagha*, "without sin *or* blame," with Indra, even though this is not an epithet commonly found in connection with, or even particularly appropriate for, Indra. Nonetheless, it can be read grammatically to refer to Rāma, and some translators have done so.

"mounting... mounted" *āsthāya*: Literally, "having mounted."

"yoked to tawny steeds" *hariyuktam*: The immensely polysemic term *hari* must refer here to the characteristic tawny steeds that draw Indra's chariot and lend him his epithet *harivāhana*, "he whose mounts are tawny steeds." Cg glosses, "yoked to horses characterized by a tawny color (*haritavarṇayuktāśvayuktam*)." See 6.78.27; 6.90.5–7; and 6.95.15 and notes.

25. "the umbrella" *chatram*: This is the white umbrella, the insignia of royalty that Bharata has brought with him. See 6.115.13–16.

"a fan" *vyajanam*: This is merely an article of practical use, used to cool Rāma, and is not to be confused with the ceremonial yak-tail fans mentioned in the following verse. Cg glosses, "made of a palm frond (*tālavṛndamayam*)."

26. "Sugrīva, the lord of the monkeys, held... Vibhīṣaṇa... held" *sugrīvo vānareśvaraḥ... vibhīṣaṇaḥ*: Literally, "Sugrīva, lord of the monkeys... Vibhīṣaṇa." The verse in the critical edition has no verbs whatsoever and, to construe it, one must borrow, as it were, either the verb *jagrāha*, "he held" (from 25a), or *ādade*, "he took up" (from 25b). D10,11, and the texts and printed editions of Ct read *jagṛhe paritaḥ sthitaḥ*, "[he] who stood held toward [Rāma a yak-tail fly whisk]," for *sugrīvo vānareśvaraḥ*, "Sugrīva, the lord of the monkeys." D6,G2,3,M3, and the texts and printed editions of Cr and Cg read *jagrāha purataḥ*, "he, [who stood] before, held [a yak-tail fly whisk]," for *sugrīvo vānareśvaraḥ*, "Sugrīva, the lord of the monkeys." In the absence of the mention of Sugrīva, the texts of the southern commentators assign to Lakṣmaṇa the dual task of fanning Rāma with the *vyajana* (fan) at the same time that he holds the yak-tail fly whisk. Cg explains this by claiming that, in keeping with his earlier vow to do everything for Rāma (GPP 2.30.27 [CE 2.28.10]), Lakṣmaṇa has quickly taken up both objects (*ahaṃ sarvaṃ kariṣyāmīti tvaryobhayagrahaṇam*).

6.116.26 = 6.116.59cd, ef.

28. "the lord of the monkeys" *vānareśvaraḥ*: D7,10,11,13,T1,G,M3,5, and the texts and printed editions of the southern commentators read instead *plavagarṣabhaḥ*, "the bull among leaping monkeys."

29. "who had taken on human form" *mānuṣaṃ vigrahaṃ kṛtvā*: Literally, "having made a human body." See 6.115.35 and note, where all the monkeys are said to have taken on human form.

30. "cheers" *-praṇādaiḥ*: Literally, "sounds." We agree with the commentators who take this term to refer to "the sound made by the people (*manuṣyaśabdaḥ*—so Cr)" and "the people's shouts of joy (*janaharṣapraṇādaiḥ*—so Cg)." Ct, in addition, cites a passage from the *Padmapurāṇa* in which it is said that, as Rāma rode along, a confused uproar (*kālahadhvaniḥ*), consisting of admiring epithets, was heaped upon Rāma by the admiring populace. Cv glosses, "shrill sounds (*tāradhvaniḥ*)."

"the thundering of war drums" *dundubhīnāṃ ca nisvanaiḥ*: Literally, "with the sounds of the *dundubhīs*."

31. "the people" *te*: Literally, "they." Ct and Cr gloss, "the people of the city (*nāgarāḥ*)."

32. "Congratulating Rāma Kākutstha and... by him" *vardhayitvā kākutsthaṃ rāmeṇa*: Literally, "having congratulated Kākutstha... by Rāma." Cf. 2.17.5, where the term *vardhayitvā* is also used in the sense of congratulation.

33. "his subjects" *prakṛtibhiḥ*: In the context, we agree with Cg, who takes the term in its sense of "subjects, citizens, general public (*paurajanaiḥ*)" rather than in its technical sense of "the elements of state."

34. "by musicians" *tūryaiḥ*: Literally, "by musical instruments." Given the context, we are inclined to agree with Ct and Cg, who gloss, "players of musical instruments (*tūryavādakaiḥ*)." This is probably an instance of the type of *upalakṣaṇa* (metonymy) illustrated by the example *śaktayaḥ praviśanti*, that is, "the spears [i.e., spearmen] enter." See note to verse 10 above.

"holding cymbals and *svastikas* in their hands" *tālasvastikapāṇibhiḥ*: Literally, "with cymbals and *svastikas* in their hands." Given the context, we are forced to agree with Ct and Cg in taking the term *svastika* here as a reference to some type of musical instrument, even though there appears to be no lexical support for this interpretation. Ct glosses, "something like a cymbal that can be held in the palm of the hand (*tālavad eva karataladhāryaḥ*)." Cg glosses, simply, "a type of musical instrument (*vādyaviśeṣaḥ*)."

This interpretation is followed in the translations of Gita Press (1969, vol. 3, p. 1897), Raghunathan (1982, vol. 3, p. 367), and, apparently, Dutt (1893, p. 1543). Roussel (1903, vol. 3, p. 421) simply renders, "*de gens qui portaient des Svastikas sur la paume des leurs mains.*" In this he has been followed by Shastri (1959, vol. 3, p. 367) and Pagani (1999, p. 1212). Pagani (p. 1677) has a note to this passage in which she makes it clear that she understands the term *svastika* in its sense of an auspicious sign or symbol. This reading of the compound, however, is forced. Gorresio (1858, vol. 10, p. 270), whose edition reads *tathā svastikapāṇibhiḥ* (6.112.37), understands *svastika* in its sense of "auspicious object," translating, "*oggeti benaugurosi.*"

"by delighted people" *muditaiḥ*: Literally, "by delighted ones."

35. "bearing unhusked, golden rice" *akṣataṃ jātarūpaṃ ca*: Following the commentators, we understand that this auspicious substance is being carried by the people. *Akṣata*, or unhusked rice, is a requisite article of worship in many Hindu ceremonies. We follow Ct and Cg, who take the term *jātarūpa*, which normally means "gold," adjectivally here in the sense of "golden." They suggest that the grain has been colored with turmeric and other coloring agents (*saṃpāditaharidrādivarṇaviśeṣa ity arthaḥ*—so Ct). This interpretation has also been followed by Gita Press (1969, vol. 3, p. 1897) and Raghunathan (1982, vol. 3, p. 367). The other translators understand that gold itself is being carried as well as grain. Roussel (1903, vol. 3, p. 421), however, believes that the road was covered with roasted grains, gold, and cows. See 6.100.16 and note.

36. "of Hanumān, the son of Anila" *anilātmaje*: Literally, "in reference to the son of Anila."

"the people of Ayodhyā" *ayodhyāpuravāsinaḥ*: Literally, "the inhabitants of the city of Ayodhyā."

Following 36c, T1,G3,M3,5, and the texts and printed editions of Cg insert a passage of one line [3617*]: "[the deeds of the monkeys,] the strength of the *rākṣasas*, and the alliance with Vibhīṣaṇa." This line is rendered only in the translation of Raghunathan (1982, vol. 3, p. 367).

Following verse 36, Ś,Ñ,V1,2,B,D6–11,13,T2,3,G1,2,M2, and the texts and printed editions of Ct and Cr insert a passage of one line [3618*]: "the work of the monkeys and the strength of the *rākṣasas* . . ."

Gita Press (1969, vol. 3, p. 1897) reads an additional line (6.128.40), unnoted by the critical apparatus, which appears to be a repetition of 36d followed by 3617* and 3618*.

37. "all of this" *etat*: Literally, "this."

38. "the ancestral home of the Ikṣvākus" *aikṣvākādhyuṣitam*: Literally, "inhabited by Aikṣvākas."

39. D6,7,10,11,T2,3,G2,M3, and the texts and printed editions of the southern commentators transpose verses 39 and 40.

"of his great father, he entered it and respectfully saluted" *pituḥ . . . praviśya ca mahātmanaḥ . . . abhyavādayat*: Literally, "having entered . . . of his great father . . . he respectfully saluted." D6,7,10,11,G1,2, and the texts and printed editions of Ct, as well as the commentaries of Ct, Cr and Cv, read the causative gerund *praveśya*, "having had *or* having made enter," for *praviśya*, "having entered."

T2,3,M3, and the texts and printed editions of Cm and Cg read for *abhyavādayat*, the gerund *cābhivādya ca*, "and having respectfully saluted," while D11 and the texts and printed editions of Ct and Cr read the second person singular imperative *abhivādaya*, "you must respectfully salute," for the critical reading.

The commentators who share the causative variant *praveśya* explain it variously in the absence of any explicit subject of the simplex. Ct understands that we must take the word *mahātmanaḥ*, "great," which in the critical reading must be read as a genitive singular agreeing with *pituḥ*, "father," as an accusative plural referring to Sugrīva, etc., and serving as the object of the causative gerund *praveśya*, yielding the meaning "having caused those great ones [i.e., Sugrīva, etc.] to enter." For Ct, the second person singular imperative *abhivādaya* takes Bharata as its subject. He further understands that we must supply as the object of the causative and the subject of the simplex "the monkeys (*vānarair iti śeṣaḥ*)." In other words, Ct's understanding of the situation is that Rāma instructs Bharata that, once he reaches the palace, he should instruct the important figures, such as Sugrīva, etc., to enter the palace. Bharata should then have the monkeys pay homage to the queens. Ct supports this reading by quoting a *Padmapurāṇa* passage in which Rāma is said to cause Hanumān, Vibhīṣaṇa, and Sugrīva to enter his house in order to purify it, as it were, with the pollen of the lotus feet of his devotees. This interpretation raises the question of why Rāma apparently fails to immediately do homage to his mothers before getting the monkeys to do so. Ct goes on to argue that Rāma had, in fact, done this earlier but in private and not [as in the case of the monkeys] publicly. (*pitur bhavanam āsādya tatra mahātmanaḥ sugrīvādīn mukhyān praveśya kausalyādyā abhivādaya. vānarair iti śeṣaḥ. iti bharatam abravīd iti saṃbandhaḥ. tatra pūrvaṃ sugrīvādipraveśyabījam uktaṃ pādme svaṃ śrīmadbhavanaṃ rāmo bhaktapādābjareṇubhiḥ / śuddhikartumanā rājā hanūmantam akalmaṣam // vibhīṣaṇaṃ ca sugrīvaṃ gṛhaṃ prāveśayat tadā / ity āpātatas tu kausalyādipraṇāmakaraṇaṃ phalam iti bhāti. āntaraṃ mukhyaṃ tu pādmoktaṃ bodhyam. pūrvaṃ tu rāmeṇaikānta eva tadvandanaṃ kṛtam. na tu sarvasamakṣam iti gamyate.*) This reading and interpretation are rendered only in the translations of Roussel (1903, vol. 3, p. 421) and Pagani (1999, p. 1212). Cr's understanding is similar to Ct's. Cv, who reads only *praveśya* in common with Ct, understands that the subject of the simplex and object of the causative is "the queens," while the subject of the causative must be Rāma himself. The idea here is that Rāma makes the queens enter the palace and there respectfully salutes them (*kausalyāṃ ca sumitrāṃ ca kaikeyīṃ ca praveśyābhivādayann uvāceti pūrveṇa saṃbandhaḥ*).

40. D6,7,10,11,T2,3,G2,M3, and the texts and printed editions of the southern commentators transpose verses 39 and 40.

"with these significant words" *arthopahitayā vācā*: Literally, "with speech that was possessed of meaning."

41. "Place at... disposal" *nivedaya*: Literally, "offer, present, entrust to the care of." The idea is that Rāma is making this specific palace available as a guesthouse for Sugrīva.

"the one adjacent to the *aśoka* grove" *sāśokavanikam*: Literally, "the one with the *aśoka* grove." Perhaps Rāma specifies this particular palace in order to appeal to his guest's arboreal proclivities. Cg glosses, "the one that has a park attached to the inner apartments (*antaḥpurodyānasahitam*)." This interpretation is represented in the translation of Raghunathan (1982, vol. 3, p. 367), who renders, "with its inner garden of *aśoka* trees." It is interesting to note here that Rāvaṇa's palace in Laṅkā also had an *aśoka* grove attached to its inner apartments. No doubt Cg has this in mind, but such a grove may, indeed, have been a standard amenity of the women's quarters.

"lapis" *-vaidūrya-*: Literally, "lapis lazuli *or* cat's-eye beryl." See note to 6.67.13.

43. "servants entered... holding" *gṛhītvā viviśuḥ*: Literally, "having taken, they entered." We agree with the commentators in supplying a subject, "servants (*bhṛtyāḥ paricārikāḥ*—so Cr, Cg)" or "guards of the king's palace (*rājabhavanarakṣakāḥ*—so Ct)," for the verb *viviśuḥ*, "they entered."

44. "Rāghava's younger brother" *rāghavānujaḥ*: Although it was Śatrughna who was most recently mentioned (in verse 43), we agree with Cr and Ct that the reference here must be to Bharata, who is in charge of the entire proceedings.

"you must dispatch emissaries in connection with... consecration" *abhiṣekāya... dūtān ājñāpaya*: Literally, "you must order messengers for the consecration."

46. "you are waiting for me" *pratīkṣadhvam*: Literally, "you must wait." We agree with Cm, Cg, and Ct, who take the present imperative in a future sense, "you will be waiting for (*pratīkṣiṣyadhvam*)," and add the word *asmān*, "us."

"these four vessels filled, respectively, with water from each of the four oceans" *caturṇāṃ sāgarāmbhasām / pūrṇair ghaṭaiḥ*: Literally, "with vessels full of the four ocean-waters." The geography suggested here is that in which the Indian subcontinent is understood to be an island surrounded by four oceans that are located, respectively, in the four cardinal directions. This model is different from the classical purāṇic one in which the central continent of Jambudvīpa is surrounded by seven other continents separated from one another by seven oceans, each containing a different fluid. The four oceans are those described by Sugrīva to the monkey search parties in the *Kiṣkindhākāṇḍa* (4.39–42) as lying at the periphery of the known and knowable world. The eastern ocean is mentioned at 4.39.30, the southern ocean at 4.40.21–22, the western ocean at 4.41.8, and the northern ocean at 4.42.53. It should be noted, however, that the description given there of the eastern ocean is a complex one, which mentions several of the purāṇic and other oceans. These are the blood-red Lohita ocean (4.39.33–35), the ocean of milk (4.39.38), and the ocean of fresh water where the submarine mare is located (4.39.42). For a discussion of the *Kiṣkindhākāṇḍa*'s description of the four directions (*digvarṇana*), see Lefeber (1994, pp. 29–35). See also Pagani's note to verse 52 (1999, p. 1677), where she argues that the invention of a northern ocean serves to place India in the center of the world and thus adds legitimacy to Rāma's consecration with water from all four cardinal directions. Cg understands that Sugrīva's instructions for the bringing of the waters of the four oceans includes, by *upalakṣaṇa* (here, metonymy), the waters of the five hundred rivers mentioned in verse 48 below (*sāgarajalānayananiyogo nadījalānayananiyogasyāpy upalakṣakaḥ*).

47. "as huge as elephants" *vāraṇopamāḥ*: Literally, "who were like elephants *or* the equal of elephants."

"like so many Garuḍas, swift in flight" *garuḍā iva śīghragāḥ*: Literally, "like swift-going Garuḍas." Since the term *garuḍa* refers almost exclusively to the great mythical bird-lord who serves as Viṣṇu's mount, we take the figure to be a kind of *abhūtopamā*, a simile in which the object of comparison [in this case multiple Garuḍas] does not exist. This idea appears to be followed by Raghunathan (1982, vol. 3, p. 368), who renders, "who could vie with Garuda in speed," and Roussel (1903, vol. 3, p. 422), who translates, "*on eût dit autant de Garudas au prompt vol.*" Other translators who share this reading understand the term to refer either to birds in general or to one or another species of bird. Cf. note to 6.91.5–6.

48. Verses 48–52 offer a number of problems, owing to apparent inconsistencies and ambiguities in their account of which monkeys bring which water from which sources. The commentators struggle in various ways to rationalize the passage and rid it of its apparent redundancies and contradictions. In the first instance, it would appear from the flow of the narrative that the four monkeys referred to in 48a–c, that is, Jāmbavān, Hanumān, Vegadarśin, and Ṛṣabha, should be the four monkeys instructed by Sugrīva in verses 45–46 above to fetch water, respectively, from each of the four oceans. These would then appear to be the monkeys who, without being further named or numbered, embark on this mission in verse 47. However, some of the monkeys who are stated in verses 49–52 to have carried out Sugrīva's order have different names from those given in verse 48. Moreover, the exact identity of the monkeys who fetch the river water in verse 48ef is not made clear.

"Vegadarśin" *vegadarśī*: This appears to be the name of a monkey. Cr, however, in an effort to harmonize the list of four monkeys in this verse with those specified in the following verses as going to the various oceans, argues that we should take the term here as an epithet of Gavaya, who is said to bring water from the western ocean at verse 51. According to Cr, the epithet means "he whose habit *or* nature is to show off his speed." (*atra vegadarśiśabdena gavayo gṛhyate. vegaṃ darśayati tacchīla iti vyutpatteḥ. ata eva gavayaḥ paścimād iti vakṣyamāṇena na virodhaḥ.*) Among the translators consulted, only Gita Press (1969, vol. 3, pp. 1898–99) follows Cr's interpretation. See 6.4.17; 6.21.23; 6.60.37–40; 6.63.26; and notes.

"fetched . . . they brought" *ānayan . . . upāharan*: In keeping with his argument at verse 46 above, Cg understands that the four monkeys named in this verse bring only river water, leaving to the four monkeys (Suṣeṇa, Ṛṣabha, Gavaya, and Nala [or Anala]) mentioned in verses 49–52 the task of bringing seawater. Cg deals with the repetition of the name Ṛṣabha in 48c and 50a by arguing that there are two different monkeys of the same name. (*evaṃ jāmbavaddhanumadvegadarśyṛṣabhair nadījalānayanam uktvā suṣeṇarṣabhagavaya[ā]nalaiḥ sāgarajalānayanaṃ darśayati . . . ayaṃ carṣabhaḥ pūrvasmād anyaḥ.*) Only Dutt (1893, p. 1544) understands as does Cg. Ct takes the multiple use of the conjunction *ca*, "and," in verse 48 to refer to five hundred additional monkeys, starting with Suṣeṇa, Gavaya, etc. (from verses 49–52), who bring the river water. He claims, however, that this does not suggest a contradiction with the later verses where Suṣeṇa and Gavaya also bring ocean water. (*atra cakāraiḥ suṣeṇagavayādipañcaśatavānaraparigrahaḥ. tad vakṣyati nadīśatānāṃ pañcānāṁ iti. ata eva suṣeṇagavayoḥ samudrajalāhartṛtvena vakṣyamāṇena na virodhaḥ.*) This interpretation is followed in a number of translations, including Roussel (1903, vol. 3, p. 422), Shastri (1959, vol. 3, p. 368), Gita Press (1969, vol. 3, p. 1898), and Pagani (1999, p. 1213).

49. "Suṣeṇa" *suṣeṇaḥ*: Cr, in his effort to harmonize the sets of four monkeys as discussed in the preceding note, argues that the term *suṣeṇaḥ* here is not the proper name of the monkey hero mentioned frequently throughout the *kāṇḍa* but, instead, should be understood as an epithet of Jāmbavān, having the sense of "he who has a splendid army" (*suṣeṇaḥ śobhanasenāvāñ jāmbavān ity arthaḥ*).

Ś2,Ñ,V1,2,3,B,D1,6,8,12,13,T2,3,M1,2,G3 omit this verse and, given the principles adopted by the critical editors, it should not have been admitted to the critical text. See Bhatt 1960, p. xxxiv.

50. "Ṛṣabha" *ṛṣabhaḥ*: It is at this point that Cg makes the comment about the two different Ṛṣabhas noted above. See notes to verse 48 above.

The printed editions of Gorresio (6.112.65), VSP (6.131.56), and KK (6.131.56) all read 50 with 51ab, while GPP (6.128.55), NSP (6.128.55), and Gita Press (6.128.55) read 49cd with 50 (6.128.55). However, the majority of translations of the southern recension consulted render according to the verse alignment of the critical edition in which the golden pot is carried by Gavaya. Gita Press (1969, vol. 3, p. 1899), Gorresio (1858, vol. 10, p. 272), and Lahore (6.109.69) have Ṛṣabha carrying the golden pot. In this they are aligned with the commentary of Cr, who explicitly associates the golden pot with Ṛṣabha, arguing that we should insert the gerund *gṛhītvā*, "having taken" (of which the subject would be Ṛṣabha), after the word *ghaṭam*, "vessel," of 51b.

51. For the sequence and alignment of verses, see note to verse 50 above and notes to 3648* below.

"a golden vessel covered... In it was water" *saṃvṛtaṃ kāñcanaṃ ghaṭam /... toyam*: Literally, "a golden vessel covered... water." The syntax of the verse is awkward as there is no grammatical relationship, not even a conjunction, between the pot and the water. One must assume, of course, that the latter is in the former. Most northern manuscripts and the printed editions of Gorresio (6.112.65) and Lahore (6.109.69) offer a *facilior* reading, substituting the locative *saṃvṛte kāñcane ghaṭe*, "in a golden vessel," for the critical edition's accusative *saṃvṛtaṃ kāñcanaṃ ghaṭam*.

"covered with camphor and red sandalwood paste" *raktacandanakarpūraiḥ saṃvṛtam*: Ś2,Ñ,V,B1–3,D2–4,8,9,12,13,G1,2,M2,3,5, and the texts and printed editions of Cg and Gorresio (6.112.65) read *-śākhābhiḥ* for *-karpūraiḥ*, "camphor," lending the phrase the sense "covered with branches of red sandalwood." Only Gorresio (1858, vol. 10, p. 272) and Raghunathan (1982, vol. 3, p. 368) render this variant.

52. On the verse alignment in the various editions, see notes to verse 50 above and notes to 3648* below.

"He whose power was that of Māruta... and whose pace that of Garuḍa or the wind" *mārutavikramaḥ... garuḍānilavikramaḥ*: Literally, "he whose power is that of Māruta... he whose power *or* pace is that of Garuḍa and/or the wind." The context of the two epithets leads us to render the word *vikrama* in two of its senses, "power" and "pace." The reference is obviously to Hanumān, one of Sugrīva's emissaries named at verse 48 above.

"He... brought": The verse as constituted in the critical edition lacks any verbal element. Given this reading, one is simply forced to supply a verb with the sense of "brought."

"from the northern ocean" *uttarāt*: Literally, "from the northern one."

Following verse 52, D5,7,10,11,T1,G1,2,M3,5, and the texts and printed editions of the southern commentators insert a passage of two lines [3648*]. In the reading of the critical edition, which is shared also by the texts of Cg and Cm, the monkey Nala replaces Hanumān as the emissary who fetches water from the northern ocean. Line 1 of the insert should construe with verse 52, and line 2 with verse 53: "And righteous Nala,[1] endowed with every virtue, [swiftly] brought [frigid water from the northern ocean in a great jeweled urn].[1] Then when he saw that water[2] that had been brought by the foremost of the monkeys, [Śatrughna...].[2]"

[1]"righteous Nala" *dharmātmā nalaḥ*: As noted above, only Raghunathan among the translators consulted follows this reading. D10,11, and the texts and printed editions

of Ct and Cr read instead *dharmātmānilaḥ*, "righteous Ānila [son of Anila]." Both Ct and Cr read *ānilaḥ* and understand the reference to be to Hanumān. The critical apparatus, mistakenly, it appears, breaks up the sequence as *dharmātmā* [*a*]*nilaḥ*, which presumably would introduce yet another monkey, Anila.

[2]"that water" *taj jalam*: As both Ct and Cg point out, the reference is to the same water brought from the oceans and rivers mentioned earlier. (*tat prasiddham. taj jalaṃ teṣāṃ nadīsāgarāṇāṃ jalam*—so Cg.) Cv understands that it is only the seawater (*teṣāṃ sāgarāṇāṃ jalam*).

Note that the adjectives and epithets, which must refer to Hanumān in the critical edition, are applied to Nala or are divided between him and Gavaya. The only translation to follow this interpretation is that of Raghunathan (1982, vol. 3, p. 368). It should be noted, however, that Raghunathan appears to ignore the epithet *māruta-vikramaḥ*, "whose power was that of Māruta." Gita Press (1969, vol. 3, p. 1899) is alone among the translations consulted in construing 52ab with 51cd, and 52cd with 3648* line 1. In this configuration, Gavaya brings frigid water from the western ocean in a jeweled urn. This makes little sense to us, however, as the frigid water should properly come from the northern ocean.

53. "presented that water . . . for the purpose of . . . consecration" *abhiṣekāya . . . nyavedayat*: Literally, "he gave *or* informed for the consecration." The reading of the critical edition is elliptical and perhaps defective, as it lacks an explicit object for the verb *nyavedayat*. If one takes the verb *nyavedayat* in its sense of "he informed," one must then understand that Śatrughna informed the *purohita*, etc., about the consecration, but this is awkward both contextually, since Vasiṣṭha and the other ministers, etc., have already begun the preparations for the consecration (see verse 21), and syntactically, since it is difficult to construe the dative *abhiṣekāya* here. Manuscript traditions of the various recensions present more lucid readings. Several southern manuscripts, as well as the texts and printed editions of the southern commentators, as noted above (see notes to verse 52), include 3648*, whose second line provides a logical object in the form of *taj jalam*, "that water," for the verb. All translations that follow the texts and printed editions of the southern commentators translate accordingly, and, for lack of a better resolution, we have followed suit by adding the words "that water." Many northern manuscripts and the printed editions of Gorresio (6.112.69) and Lahore (6.109.73) provide a direct object, substituting the accusative singular *abhiṣecanikam*, "the materials *or* paraphernalia for consecration," or some similar expression, for the dative singular *abhiṣekāya*, "for the consecration." Gorresio (1858, vol. 10, p. 272) translates, "*annunziò . . . esser pronta ogni cosa per la sacra.*"

"his assistants" *suhṛdbhyaś ca*: Literally, "and to [his] friends." We understand that the reference is to the other officiants who will assist Vasiṣṭha in the consecration ritual. See verse 54 below.

54. "devout" *prayataḥ*: The term normally means "self-controlled, pious, restrained, etc." Ct and Cm gloss *prayatnavān*, "effortful, diligent."

55–56. "Suyajña . . . Vijaya" *suyajñaḥ . . . vijayaḥ*: The list of names in the critical edition and in the texts and printed editions of Ct are similar, except that the order of names is somewhat different and Ct's text omits the name Suyajña. The commentators identify Suyajña as the son of Vasiṣṭha. See note to 6.115.51. It is not clear whether Vijaya, who is named as a minister at 3556* (following notes to 6.115.8), is the same figure as the Vijaya mentioned here.

"just as the Vasus consecrated thousand-eyed Indra Vāsava" *sahasrākṣaṃ vasavo vāsavam yathā*: Literally, "just as the Vasus, [did] thousand-eyed Vāsava."

57–58. Commentators propose two ways of reading the verses with their long lists of instrumentals. Cg, whom we have followed, understands the instrumentals to be those of accompaniment so that the sense is that Vasiṣṭha and the other priest performed the consecration together with the officiating priests, and so forth (*te vasiṣṭhādaya ṛtvigādibhiḥ sahābhyaṣiñcann iti yojanā*) (Cv similarly). Ct and Cr, on the other hand, propose that we take the verb *abhyaṣiñcan*, "they consecrated," as an unmarked causative in the sense "they caused to consecrate," in which case Vasiṣṭha and the other priests are to be understood as the managers of the ceremony in which they cause the other groups to do the actual consecration by sprinkling (*atra vasiṣṭhādayaḥ prayojakakartāraḥ* ... *abhyaṣiñcann abhyaṣecayan*—so Ct).

"in great delight ... they ... with ... merchants" *te saṃprahṛṣṭāḥ sanaigamaiḥ*: The reference here is to Vasiṣṭha, etc., mentioned in verses 55–57 above. D7,10,11,T2,3, and the texts and printed editions of Ct and Cr read the instrumental plural *saṃprahṛṣṭaiḥ*, which can be taken to modify either the general groups who are joining in the consecration or, more specifically, the merchants with whom the adjective is closely juxtaposed.

"with that water and with the extracts of all the different herbs" *sarvauṣadhirasaiś cāpi*: Literally, "and with the juice of every plant *or* herb." Since we understand that the priest and the populace are all sprinkling Rāma more or less simultaneously, we tend to agree with Cg's suggestion that the conjunction *ca*, "and," suggests that we are to include the water mentioned in verse 56 above (*cakārāt salilena ca*).

"with maidens" *kanyābhiḥ*: Ct understands that the maidens are sixteen in number (*kanyābhiḥ ṣoḍaśasaṃkhyābhiḥ*). Roussel (1903, vol. 3, p. 422) and Gita Press (1969, vol. 3, p. 1899) both incorporate this number into their respective translations. Compare verse 35 above.

Following verse 58, D5,7,10,11,T1,G,M3,5, GPP and NSP (6.128.64–67), KK (in brackets, 6.131.65–67) and VSP (unnumbered between 6.131.64 and 65, in brackets), and the texts of the southern commentators insert a passage of eight lines [3662*]: "Then, in a great assembly hall, covered with gold, adorned with precious objects, and beautified by exquisite gems of every kind, great Vasiṣṭha seated Rāma[1] in proper fashion on a throne made of various gems. After that, Vasiṣṭha, together with the officiating priests and seers, consecrated him[2] with the very same bejeweled crown with which, in ancient times, Manu was consecrated and, after him, all the kings in his lineage in succession. It had been fashioned long ago by Brahmā and was dazzling in its splendor.[3]"

[1]"seated Rāma" *kalpayitvā*: Literally, "having settled *or* arranged." We follow Ct, who glosses, "having caused to sit (*upaveśya*)." We understand with Ct and Cr that one must add the name Rāma as an object of the gerund.

[2]"together with the officiating priests and seers, consecrated him" *ṛtvigbhir ṛṣibhiś caiva sahitenābhiṣecitaḥ*: D7,10,11,M3, and the texts and printed editions of Ct and Cg

read instead *ṛtvigbhir bhūṣaṇaiś caiva samayokṣyata rāghavaḥ*, "Rāghava was adorned with jewels [by Vasiṣṭha,] together with the officiating priests."

[3]"dazzling in its splendor" *dīptatejasam*: Ct and Cr suggest that we read this adjective with Rāma, who has to be supplied as the object of *kalpayitvā* (see above). Only Gita Press (1969, vol. 3, p. 1900) among the translators consulted follows this suggestion. Others, like us, take it as a reference to the dazzling splendor of the crown. Shastri (1959, vol. 3, p. 369), however, for some reason, omits the entire passage.

59. 6.116.59cd, ef=6.116.26.

Following 59e, Ś2,Ñ,V1,2,B,D1–4,8,9,12,13,M2,3, and the texts and printed editions of Cg insert a passage of one line [3663*], which expands the description to include Vibhīṣaṇa: "Delighted [Vibhīṣaṇa] held Rāma's magnificent yak-tail fly whisk." Cf. verse 26 above.

60. "on the orders of Vāsava" *vāsavena pracoditaḥ*: Literally, "urged by Vāsava."

"with a hundred lotuses" *śatapuṣkarām*: Presumably, the lotuses are also wrought of gold.

61. "on the orders of Śakra" *śakrapracoditaḥ*: Literally, "urged by Śakra."

"he also gave" *dadau*: Literally, "he gave." No explicit subject is identified. We follow the suggestion of the commentators that one must understand the unidentified subject to be Vāyu, who was the subject of the previous verse.

"a pearl necklace" *muktāhāram*: Since the necklace is said to be interspersed with many other gemstones, Cg glosses, "a necklace mostly of pearl (*muktāpracurahāram*)."

"strung with every sort of jewel" *sarvaratnasamāyuktam*: Literally, "connected *or* provided with all jewels." According to Cg, the reference is to the famous *navaratnas*, or "nine types of gems," classified in the traditional literature (*sarvaratnair navaratnaiḥ*). The list is as follows: pearl, ruby, lapis, *gomeda* (s.v. Apte: a precious or semiprecious stone from the Himalayas that is said to come in four colors), diamond, coral, ruby, emerald, and sapphire (*muktāmāṇikyavaidūryagomedā vajravidrumau / padmarāgo marakataṃ nīlaś ceti yathākramam //* quoted in Apte s.v.).

"an immense gem" *maṇiratna-*: Literally, "a jewel of a gem." We understand with Cg that the reference is to the principal gem (*maṇiśreṣṭhena nāyakena madhye*).

62. "who so richly deserved it" *tadarhasya*: We agree with Ct and the other translators consulted in understanding that what Rāma deserves are the performances of the divine singers and dancers (*tadarhasya devagītanṛttādyarhasya*). One could, perhaps, also understand the phrase to refer to the consecration itself.

63. Crā and Cg remind us that, as Sumantra reports to Daśaratha in the aftermath of Rāma's exile, even the trees, flowers, and animals are drooping and despondent at their separation from the prince (2.53.4–7). Now that he has returned, the land and its living things have revived and blossomed.

"on the festive occasion of Rāghava's consecration" *rāghavotsave*: Literally, "on Rāghava's festival."

64. "First" *pūrvam*: Ct and Cg understand the adverb to refer to the priority of the gifts of livestock to those of precious metals, etc., that will follow (*hiraṇyadānādeḥ pūrvam*—Cg). Cg adds, as an alternative, that it refers to the priority of the brahmans over Sugrīva, etc., as recipients of Rāma's largess (*sugrīvādibhyaḥ pūrvaṃ vā*).

"cows that had newly calved " *dhenūnām . . . gavām*: We follow the commentators who quote the *Amarakośa* (2.9.71), where *dhenu* refers to a cow that has newly calved (*dhenuḥ syān navasūtikā*). We take the term *dhenūnām* with these commentators as a modifier of *gavām*. The idea is that Rāma is giving away demonstrably fertile cows and bulls, which the brahmans can then profitably breed. Roussel (1903, vol. 3, p. 423), followed by Shastri (1959, vol. 3, p. 369) and Pagani (1999, p. 1214), understands the two terms to refer to separate types of cattle, i.e., cows and heifers.

66. "a . . . diadem" *srajam*: Literally, "garland, chaplet, wreath." Translators are divided in their understanding of exactly what this article is in this context.

"encrusted with gems" *maṇivigrahām*: Literally, "having a body *or* expanse of jewels." We follow Cg, who glosses, "consisting mainly of *or* abundant with jewels (*maṇipracuram*)."

67. "greatly pleased" *dhṛtimān*: We are persuaded that, in this context in which Rāma is rewarding his friends and allies with whom he is pleased, Cg is correct in taking the term *dhṛti* in its sense of "pleasure, satisfaction" rather than in its more common meaning, "firmness, fortitude, retention." Thus, he glosses *prītimān*, "pleased." Cg is followed in this interpretation by Gita Press (1969, vol. 3, p. 1901) and Raghunathan (1982, vol. 3, p. 369).

"Rāma gave" *dadau*: Literally, "he gave."

"Aṅgada . . . a pair of armlets" *aṅgadāyāṅgade*: The choice of gift here is clearly governed by the play on Aṅgada's name. See note to 6.14.3.

"adorned with diamonds and gems" *vajraratnavibhūṣite*: D7,10,11, and the texts and printed editions of Ct and Cr read *candraraśmi-*, "rays of the moon," for *vajraratna-*, "diamonds and gems," yielding the rather awkward compound "adorned with the rays of the moon." Translators who follow the text of Ct force the compound to mean "whose luster equals *or* rivals that of the moon."

"variegated with lapis and jewels" *vaidūryamaṇicitre*: D5,10,11,T2,3, and the texts and printed editions of Ct and Cr read instead *vaid[ḍ*—D5,10,11,T2,3*]ūryamayacitre*, another awkward and difficult compound. Cr breaks it up as an appositional *karmadhāraya* compound, yielding the sense "made of lapis, and therefore beautiful (*vaidūryamaye eva citre*)."

68. "presented . . . with" *pradadau*: Since Sītā will give this priceless necklace to Hanumān in verse 72, Cg, perhaps disturbed at the idea that Sītā would so quickly give away her gift, remarks that Rāma gave it to her with the specific intention that she should give it to Hanumān (*sītāyai pradadau hanumate dātavyam ity āśayena dadau*).

69. "keeping her eyes on her husband, Vaidehī" *avekṣamāṇā vaidehī*: Literally, "Vaidehī, looking." Cr understands that Sītā is watching Rāma to determine his intention. Cg addresses this theme more elaborately, saying that we must add the term *bhartāram*, "[her] husband," and noting that the meaning here is that, since women lack independence, Sītā is looking expectantly to get her husband's permission [to present the gifts to Hanumān]. (*avekṣamāṇā bhartāram iti śeṣaḥ. striyāḥ svātantryābhāvād bhartranujñāṃ kāṅkṣitavatīti bhāvaḥ.*) Given the context and what will follow, we believe that Cr and Cg are correct. Ct, however, understands the participle to mean that Sītā is considering or reflecting upon the assistance that he [Hanumān] had rendered her, and so presents him with the gifts. The meaning, he argues, is that she is eager to offer the gifts. (*avekṣamāṇā tatkṛtam upakāraṃ cintayantī pradadau. pradātum iyeṣety arthaḥ.*)

A variant noted by Crā reads instead *avekṣamāṇo* [*avekṣyamāṇo*—D1,2,5,T2,3,G2,3,M5] *vaidehīm*, which makes Rāma the subject and Sītā the object of the verb *ava* $\sqrt{}$*īkṣ*, "to look *or* gaze upon." For some reason, Raghunathan (1982, vol. 3, p. 369) has chosen to render this weak and minor variant. According to this reading, Rāma himself gives the garments and ornaments to Hanumān.

"two spotless and divine garments as well as splendid ornaments" *araje vāsasī divye śubhāny ābhāraṇāni ca*: Because of the differing alignment of verses, some translators understand that these articles are part of Rāma's gift to Sītā, mentioned in the previous verse, rather than Sītā's to Hanumān.

70. "looked back and forth repeatedly" *avaikṣata . . . muhur muhuḥ*: Ct understands that, having taken off her necklace out a of desire to give it away, Sītā looks to her husband for his permission (*ātmanaḥ kaṇṭhād dhāram avamucya ditsayā bhartranumataye bhartāram avaikṣata*). Cg understands that, once she has determined that her husband gave the necklace to her in the assembly in order to have her give it away as a reward to someone, Sītā is looking around with the intention of determining to which of the monkeys she should give it. (*sadasi mahyaṃ hārapradānaṃ kasmaicit pāritoṣikatayā dāpayitum iti niścityāyaṃ hāra eṣu kasmai deya ity āśayenāvaikṣatety arthaḥ.*)

71–72. Our reading of the two verses follows that proposed by Cg in which Rāma, in alluding to the specific virtues of Hanumān, is, in fact, instructing Sītā to give him the necklace. In Cg's reading, each of the named virtues relates to one of the specific feats accomplished by Hanumān in his effort to find Sītā. Thus, his might (*pauruṣa*) is evidenced in his leaping the ocean, his valor (*vikrama*) in his burning of Laṅkā, and his wisdom (*buddhi*) in his penetration of the *aśoka* grove. Cg notes that, if Rāma had not alluded to these specific accomplishments, his words would have constituted an implicit denigration of the other monkeys. (*yasya yasmin. pauruṣaṃ balaṃ samudralaṅghanena. vikramo laṅkādahanena. buddhir aśokavanikāpraveśena. sarvaśaḥ sarvāṇi yasmin santīti yasya saṃtuṣṭāsi tasmai dehīti yojanā. anyathānyeṣāṃ nindoktir eva syāt.*) Cg's reading of the passage is followed by Raghunathan (1982, vol. 3, p. 369). Gorresio's (1858, vol. 10, p. 274) interpretation is similar to Cg's and ours. Cr and the remaining translators of the southern recension understand the passage rather differently. They do not take 72ab to be part of Rāma's instructions to Sītā but see the two verses, 71 and 72, as syntactically independent from each other. According to this reading, Rāma simply tells Sītā to give the necklace to whomever she pleases, and she then, on her own initiative, confers it upon Hanumān, who possesses the virtues enumerated by Rāma.

Following 72cd, D7 (following verse 71),10,11, and the texts and printed editions of Ct read a passage of one line [3677*], extending the list of Hanumān's virtues: "blazing energy, fortitude, glory, skill, capability, humility, and political wisdom."

73. "Wearing that necklace . . . wreathed with a white cloud" *tena hāreṇa . . . / . . . śvetābhreṇa*: Literally, "with the necklace . . . with a cloud."

74. "after some thought" *vīkṣya*: The gerund can mean either "having thought" or "having looked." Ct understands that Rāma turns his gaze to Mainda and the other recipients (*vīkṣya maindadvividanīlān dṛṣṭvā*). Cr believes he is examining the articles that will be given away (*padārthān vīkṣya*).

"every desirable thing" *sarvān kāmaguṇān*: Literally, "all things of desirable qualities." Ct understands this to mean "extremely excellent jewels, etc. (*uttamaratnādīn*)." Cr glosses, "things characterized by desirable qualities (*yathepsitaguṇaviśiṣṭān*)." Cg understands *kāmaguṇān* as a *bahuvrīhi* compound, meaning "having qualities that are to be desired, that is, to be sought after, that is, types of things such as ornaments (*kāmyanta iti kāmāḥ prārthanīyā guṇā yeṣāṃ te tān ābharaṇādivastuviśeṣān*)."

D6,7,10,11,T2,3,G1, and the texts and printed editions of Cr and Ct read verse 74 following verse 76.

75. "the ... monkey lords" *vānareśvarāḥ*: Ś2,D7–12, and the texts and printed editions of Ct and Cr read instead *vānarottamāḥ*, "the foremost among the monkeys."

Ñ2,V,B1,3 continue after 3680*, while Ś2,B2,D5–8,10–12,T2,3,G,M2,3,5 insert after verse 75, and B4 inserts after verse 74, a passage of two lines [3681*]: "Vibhīṣaṇa, Sugrīva, Hanumān, Jāmbavān, and all the principal monkeys [were honored] by Rāma, tireless in action."

Cr, the only commentator to remark on this passage, understands that it should be construed with verse 76. As the passage is known to all recensions and the vast majority of manuscripts, it is questionable why it has been relegated to the critical apparatus. See Bhatt 1960, p. xxxiv.

76. "each one of them ... they all" *sarve ... sarve*: Literally, "they all ... they all."

"returned as they had come" *jagmur eva yathāgatam*: Cr suggests that we add the words "to their respective homes (*svasvaniveśasthānam iti śeṣaḥ*)."

D6,7,10,11,T2,3,G1, and the texts and printed editions of Cr and Ct read verse 74 following verse 76.

Following verse 76, D1–5,9 (after 75),G2,3,M3,5, and the texts and printed editions of Cg insert, while D6,7,10,11,T2,3,G1, and the texts and printed editions of Ct and Cr insert following verse 74, a passage of two lines [3686*, lines 2–3]: "Then, after witnessing [the consecration], those great[1] bulls among monkeys, dismissed by the lord of kings, returned to Kiṣkindhā."

[1]"after witnessing [the consecration], those great" *dṛṣṭvā ... mahātmānaḥ*: Literally, "having seen ... those great [monkeys]." The line is elliptical, lacking as it does any object for the gerund *dṛṣṭvā*, "having seen." Cr, the only commentator to remark upon the passage, glosses, "having seen the consecration (*abhiṣekam avalokya*)." M3 and the texts and printed editions of Cg read instead *natvā ... mahātmānam*, "having prostrated themselves to the great one [Rāma]." This variant is rendered only in the translation of Raghunathan (1982, vol. 3, p. 370).

Following 3686*, line 3, D5–7,9–11,T2,3,G,M3,5, insert a passage of four lines [3688*]: "When mighty[1] Sugrīva, foremost of monkeys, had witnessed Rāma's consecration and had been honored by Rāma, he entered Kiṣkindhā.[1–2] And righteous Vibhīṣaṇa as well, together with those bulls among the *rākṣasas*, sons of chaos,[2][3] having obtained his ancestral inheritance,[3] returned to Laṅkā as King Vibhīṣaṇa.[4][4]"

[1]"mighty" *balī*: D7,10,11,M3, and the texts and printed editions of the southern commentators read instead *purīm*, "the city [of Kiṣkindhā]."

[2]"those bulls among the *rākṣasas*, sons of chaos" *tair nairṛtarṣabhaiḥ*: Literally, "those bulls among the sons of chaos."

[3]"his ancestral inheritance" *kuladhanam*: Literally, "the wealth of the family." The commentators engage in a lengthy discussion of the exact meaning of this term. Ct, Cr, and Cm argue that the ancestral wealth is that of the *rākṣasa* race, i.e., the kingdom of Laṅkā. Cv rejects this argument on the grounds that Vibhīṣaṇa had already received the

kingdom at the time of his consecration and that the reference here is to the treasure of the Ikṣvāku family in the form of its presiding divinity, Jagannātha, identified by the commentators as Śrīraṅganātha, who is given to Vibhīṣaṇa in the form of a flying palace or a palanquin (*vimāna*). This argument is based on references in the *Uttarakāṇḍa* (GPP 7.108.25–28) and the *Padmapurāṇa*, stating that Rāma presents an image of this divinity to Vibhīṣaṇa at the end of his incarnation. Crā cites both positions but seems to favor the latter one. This interpretation is also questioned, however, precisely on the grounds that this gift will not take place until the end of the *Rāmāvatāra*. Cs makes the further suggestion that the treasure of the Ikṣvāku lineage is none other than Rāma himself, whom Vibhīṣaṇa had acquired as a friend and ally. Cs goes on to reject the argument that the *kuladhana* is Śrīraṅganātha on the basis of citations from the *Padma-* and *Skandapurāṇas*. Cs uniquely raises the objection that, since the *Skandapurāṇa* explicitly states that the worship of Śrīraṅga was part of Rāma's daily obligatory religious practice, he could not possibly have given the idol away as this would have prevented him from carrying out his religious obligations for eleven thousand years.

[4]"Vibhīṣaṇa . . . as King Vibhīṣaṇa" *vibhīṣaṇaḥ . . . rājā . . . vibhīṣaṇaḥ*: Literally, "Vibhīṣaṇa, the king Vibhīṣaṇa." To minimize the redundancy, we render the verse as if the *rākṣasa* now returns to his new kingdom, assuming his formal title as King Vibhīṣaṇa. D7,10,11, and the texts and printed editions of Ct and Cr avoid the repetition by reading *mahāyaśāḥ*, "of great luster *or* glory," in place of the second occurrence of the name.

Printed editions of the text of Cg do not include lines 2 and 3 as part of their numbered texts. VSP knows the lines but relegates them to a footnote, commenting that this reading is found only in some manuscripts. KK, noting that line 2 is found in only two of the manuscripts on which its edition is based and that its variant of line 3 occurs only in late manuscripts, includes the lines in brackets at 6.131.87cd and 88ab. Both editions read a variant for line 3 (M3's and Cg's variant: *rāmeṇa sarvakāmaiś ca yathārhaṃ pratipūjitaḥ*, "[Vibhīṣaṇa], honored by Rāma with every desirable thing in keeping with his merit . . .").

Following 3688*, D5–7,10,11,T2,3,G,M3,5, and the texts and printed editions of the southern commentators insert a passage of one line [3694*] following verse 80 in the critical edition. See notes following verse 80 below.

78. "please govern" *ātiṣṭha*: Literally, "you must assume."

"this land of which those kings who came before us took possession with their forces" *gāṃ pūrvarājādhyuṣitāṃ balena*: Literally, "the cow [i.e., earth] settled by *or* inhabited by previous kings with the army." One could also understand the instrumental *balena*, "with the army *or* forces," to mean "by force." As several of the commentators note, the kings of old in question are Manu and his descendants, i.e., the forebears of the Ikṣvāku dynasty.

"as my equal" *tulyaṃ mayā tvam*: Literally, "you equally with me." Cg, the only commentator to remark upon this reading, reminds us that, on the eve of Rāma's earlier, aborted consecration, he had already offered to share power with Lakṣmaṇa. Cg quotes the *Ayodhyākāṇḍa*, where the offer is made (see 2.4.43 and note), and argues that Rāma urges this now because earlier he had done so in the absence of Bharata. Cg perhaps is cognizant here of the irony inherent in the fact that Rāma, who is the tradition's most celebrated victim of the violation of the normative order of succession, should propose that Lakṣmaṇa should take precedence over Bharata, who is, after all, senior to Lakṣmaṇa. Cg bases his argument on Rāma's statement in the *Ayodhyākāṇḍa* (2.16.19) that Rāma never reneges on a promise. In other words, Rāma has essentially no choice but to offer the position of *yuvarāja* to Lakṣmaṇa once again. See 2.16.19 and notes. (*lakṣmaṇemāṃ mayā sārdhaṃ praśādhi tvaṃ vasundharām iti pūrvābhiṣekārambhe bharatāsannidhāne pratijñānāt. rāmo dvir nābhibhāṣata iti niyamāl lakṣmaṇam eva yauvarājye niyuṅkte.*) See note to 6.51.10. D10,11, and the texts and printed editions of Ct and the commentaries of Cm and Cr read *yathā*, "just as," for *mayā*, "with me."

"which was borne" *dhṛtā yā tām*: D10,11, the texts and printed editions of Ct, and the commentaries of Cm and Cr read instead *purastāt taiḥ*, "by those [forefathers] of old." Together with *yathā*, "like," the variant reading noted above, this gives the line the sense "equally, just as was done by those forefathers of old."

The meter is *indravajrā*.

79. "was being offered the position of prince regent of the land" *niyujyamāno bhuvi yauvarājye*: Literally, "[he] being appointed in the prince regency in the land." Cr understands that it is Bharata who is trying to appoint Lakṣmaṇa. G2,M3, and the texts and printed editions of Cg read *[a]pi ca*, "even though," for *bhuvi*, "in the land." See note to 6.51.10.

"was . . . entreated to accept" *paryanunīyamānaḥ*: Literally, "was being entreated." Cr understands that Rāma was doing the entreating while Bharata was offering the position to Lakṣmaṇa. Ct understands that it was Bharata who was urging Lakṣmaṇa to accept the appointment, even though that position should by rights be his own (*nyāyaprāptasvīyayauvarājyena bharatenānunīyamānaḥ*).

"would not do so" *na . . . upaiti yogam*: Literally, "he does not approach *or* go to the occupation, employment, *or* yoke." Unlike the commentators, we take *yoga* in the sense of *niyoga*, "appointment, assignment." Ct and Cr understand the phrase to mean that Lakṣmaṇa did not desire (Ct) or accept (Cr) contact (Ct) or connection (Cr) with the prince regency (*yogaṃ yauvarājyasaṃsargaṃ nopaiti necchati sma*—Ct; *yogaṃ yuvarājatvasaṃbandham . . . nopaity aṅgīcakāra*—Cr). Cg takes *yoga* here to mean "acceptance *or* agreement (*saṃmatim*)." Cg offers two reasons for Lakṣmaṇa's refusal of the prince regency. First, Lakṣmaṇa recognizes the contradiction between his inherent nature as Śeṣanāga and the post of prince regent, and, second, he is aware of the impropriety of his appointment while his elder brother Bharata is present (*sva śeṣatvaviruddhatvajñānāj jyeṣṭhe bharate vidyamāne svasya tadanucitatvajñānāc ceti bhāvaḥ*). Cf. notes to 6.107.4–6.

The meter is *upajāti*.

80. D2–7,9–11,T2,3,G,M2,3,5, and the texts and printed editions of the southern recension read verse 80 following verse 83.

"his friends" *-suhṛd-*: D10,11, and the texts and printed editions of Ct read instead *-suta-*, "sons." This reading raises an interesting chronological question since Rāma will not have sons or become aware of them for many years. On the other hand, in light of the valedictory nature of the passage, which seems to refer generally to the remainder of Rāma's lengthy reign, the reading, although extremely poorly attested, is not utterly absurd.

Following verse 80, Ś,Ñ,V,B1,2,4,D8,12 substitute for 80ab, while B3 continues after 3692* and D2 continues after 3693*, and D5–7,10,11,T2,3,G,M3,5, and the texts and printed editions of the southern commentators insert following 3688* (see notes to verse 76 above) a passage of one line [3694*]: "When that immensely glorious [hero], having slain his foe, and having obtained his entire kingdom . . ."

All subrecensions, editions, as well as the vast majority of both northern and southern manuscripts collated for the critical edition read this line. Its omission from the critical text is questionable. All translations consulted render this verse. See Bhatt 1960, p. xxxiv.

81. "Pauṇḍarīka, Aśvamedha . . . sacrifices" *pauṇḍarīkāśvamedhābhyām*: The Pauṇḍarīka sacrifice is an eleven-day *soma* sacrifice. See *PW* s.v. See, too, Pagani's note (1999, p. 1677), where she provides a detailed description of the rite. On the *aśvamedha* sacrifice, see 1.8.2; 1.11–13; and notes. See, too, 6.107.4–6.

All northern manuscripts and the printed editions of Lahore (6.110.11) and Gorresio (6.113.10) read the minor variant *puṇḍarīka-*. Noteworthy here, however, is the printed text of Gorresio (6.113.10), which reads a further variant, unattested in the critical apparatus or in the apparatus of the Lahore edition, *puṇḍarīkākṣamedhābhyām*, "two sacrifices to Puṇḍarīkākṣa (Viṣṇu)." Gorresio (1858, vol. 10, p. 276) translates, "*due sacrifizi a Pundarīkāksa.*" Gorresio understands *puṇḍarīkākṣa* in its common usage as an epithet of Viṣṇu and notes (p. 317) that Rāma was celebrating two sacrifices to Viṣṇu as Puṇḍarīkākṣa, a name which signifies "lotus-eyed one." In the absence of any other textual support for this reading, we suspect that Gorresio's reading of *akṣa* is for some reason a mistaken transcription of the northern reading.

"Vājapeya" *vājapeyena*: B2,4,D7,10,11, and the texts and printed editions of Ct and Cr read instead *vājimedhena*, "with the Horse Sacrifice." Clearly this reading is redundant in light of the preceding mention of the synonymous *aśvamedha*. Ct rationalizes the repetition by stating that the prior reference is a general statement, whereas the latter is specific (*pauṇḍarīkāśvamedhābhyām iti sāmānyata uktvā tatraiva viśeṣam āha vājimedhena*). Translations that follow the texts and printed editions of Ct render this variant but attempt to avoid the redundancy by leaving the terms untranslated. On the *vājapeya* (lit., drink of strength) sacrifice, see 2.40.20 and note; Kane 1941–1975, vol. 2.ii, p. 1210 and note; Barth 1906, pp. 54–56; and Oldenberg 1894, pp. 44, 57, 192, 225, 250, 264, and 280. Pagani (1999, p. 1215) uses the critical edition's reading of *vājapeya* here and provides a note on the sacrifice (p. 1677).

82. "for ten thousand years" *daśa sahasrāṇi . . . varṣāṇi*: Cr and Cs are disturbed by the apparent contradiction between this verse and the well-known verse in the *Bālakāṇḍa* (1.1.76), where Rāma is said to have ascended to the Brahmaloka after having ruled for eleven thousand years. They each engage in some mathematical manipulation in an effort to show that there is, in fact, no contradiction. Cr, whose reading (see verse 90 below) has Rāma perform ten rather than a hundred Horse Sacrifices, appears to understand that Rāma rules for three periods of ten thousand years, pausing after each to reconsecrate his sovereignty by the performance of *aśvamedhas*. These ritual performances, it seems, may consume three periods of a thousand years each, so that Rāma reigns, in fact, for thirty-three thousand years. Cr's idea, it seems, is that Rāma technically rules for three periods of eleven thousand years each, and thus, he argues, there is no contradiction between this passage and the one at 1.1.76. *rāghavo daśasahasrāṇi daśaguṇitāni sahasrāṇi trisahasrāṇi yeṣu trayastriṃśatsahasravarṣāṇīty arthaḥ. rājyaṃ prāpya daśāśvamedhān ājahve tanmadhya eva yathākālam akarot. kiṃca daśa-*

sahasrāṇi triṃśadvarṣasahasraparyantaṃ rājyaṃ prāpya kṛtvāśvamedhān ājahre trisahasravarṣaparyantaṃ cakāra. ata eva daśavarṣasahasrāṇi daśavarṣaśatāni ceti bālakāṇḍoktena na virodhaḥ. See note to verse 90 below.

"one hundred" *śata-*: Ś,Ñ,V1,2,B,D2–4,7,8,10–12,G1,M2, and the texts and printed editions of Ct and Cr read instead *daśa-*, "ten," thus reducing the number of Rāma's Horse Sacrifices by 90 percent. Compare 1.1.74.

83. "With broad shoulders and his arms extending to his knees" *ājānulambibāhuś ca mahāskandhaḥ*: Rāma is described in similar terms at 1.1.9–10. Compare 2.3.11 and 5.33.15. The peculiar anatomical feature of the arms extending to the knees is a stereotypical characteristic of great personages in the literature.

"ruled the land" *pṛthivīm anvapālayat*: D7,10,11, and the texts and printed editions of Ct and Cr read the slight variant *śaśāsa pṛthivīm imām*, "he ruled this earth *or* land."

"with Lakṣmaṇa at his side" *lakṣmaṇānucaraḥ*: Literally, "having Lakṣmaṇa as his attendant *or* companion."

D2–7,9–11,T2,3,G,M2,3,5, and the texts and printed editions of the southern commentators read verse 80 following verse 83.

84. For a similar description of the Rāmarājya, see *Bālakāṇḍa* (1.1.71–73).

"no widows mourned" *na paryadevan vidhavāḥ*: Literally, "widows did not cry *or* lament." As Cr points out, the meaning is that there were no widows (*vidhavā nābhāvann ity arthaḥ*). Compare 1.1.72, where a similar idea is expressed.

85. "misfortune afflicted no one" *nānarthaḥ kaṃcid aspṛśat*: Literally, "calamity did not touch anyone." Ñ2,V1,2,B2,3,D7,9–11, and the texts and printed editions of Ct and Cr read instead *nānarthaṃ kaścid aspṛśat*, "no one touched (i.e., experienced) misfortune."

86. "Everyone... Everyone" *sarvam... sarvaḥ*: Literally, "all... all." Cr glosses "the collectivity of all people (*sarvajanajātam*)" for the neuter *sarvam*.

"people did not harm" *nābhyahiṃsan*: Literally, "they did not harm *or* cause injury."

87. "people lived for thousands of years and had thousands of sons" *āsan varṣasahasrāṇi tathā putrasahasriṇaḥ*: Literally," they possessed thousands of sons and [of them] there were thousands of years." Like Ct, we understand the implied subject to be "people (*janāḥ*)." Dutt (1893, p. 1547) mistakenly understands that these references are to Rāma rather than to the people in general.

Following verse 87, M3 and the texts and printed editions of Cg and Gita Press (6.128.102ab) insert a passage of two lines [3698*]: "While Rāma ruled the kingdom, all the people could talk about was 'Rāma, Rāma, Rāma.' For, indeed, Rāma was their whole world.[1]"

[1]"For, indeed, Rāma was their whole world." *rāmabhūtaṃ jagad abhūt*: Literally, "The world had become Rāma."

This verse is rendered only in the translations of Raghunathan (1982, vol. 3, p. 371) and Gita Press (1969, vol. 3, p. 1903).

88. "The trees with their spreading boughs were always in flower and filled with fruit." *nityapuṣpā nityaphalās taravaḥ skandhavistṛtāḥ*: Literally, "the trees, broad with their branches, had constant flowers and constant fruit." D10,11, and the texts and printed editions of Ct read instead *nityamūlā nityaphalās taravas tatra puṣpitāḥ*, "the

blossoming trees there were permanently rooted and permanently fruiting." Translations that follow the text of Ct render this reading, although Dutt (1893, p. 1547) and Shastri (1959, vol. 3, p. 371) omit mention of the roots.

"Parjanya brought the rains at the proper time" *kālavarṣī parjanyaḥ*: Literally, "Parjanya possessed timely showers." See 6.18.9–10; 6.67.20; and notes. D10,11, and the texts and printed editions of Ct read *kāma-*, "desire," for *kāla-*, "time," yielding the sense "Parjanya rained according to desire." Cf. 6.94.15 and note.

"the breeze" *mārutaḥ*: Literally, "Māruta." The name of the wind god here refers to the natural phenomenon rather than the deity.

Following verse 88, G3,M3, and the texts and printed editions of Cg insert a passage of one line [3700*]: "The brahmans, the kshatriyas, the *vaiśyas*, and the *śūdras* were all free from grief."

89. "adhered to their own proper occupations and were satisfied with their own duties" *svakarmasu pravartante tuṣṭāḥ svair eva karmabhiḥ*: Literally, "they were occupied in their own activities [and] were satisfied with their own activities." The reference here is to the cultural imperatives inherent in the socioreligious concepts of *varṇāśramadharma* and *svadharma*. Compare 1.1.75 and *BhagGī* 3.35. See R. Goldman 2004.

"they adhered always to the truth" *nānṛtāḥ*: Literally, "[they were] not untruthful."

90. "for ten thousand years" *daśa varṣasahasrāṇi*: As noted at verse 82 above, Cr appears to understand the number of years of Rāma's rule to be thirty-three thousand, although, perhaps as a result of a kind of shorthand or some dropped characters in the GPP, the text of his commentary available to us reads *trayastriṃśadvarṣāni*, or "thirty-three years."

D5,G3,M3,5, and the texts and printed editions of Cg and Gita Press (6.128.106bc) insert a passage of two half *pādas* following 90c [3702* with Cg's variant]: "[And so, for ten thousand years] and ten centuries more, majestic [Rāma ruled his kingdom] together with his brothers."

The majority of northern manuscripts read 3702*, line 1, which, with Cg's variant, is in harmony with 1.1.76, where the length of Rāma's reign is stated in exactly the same words. These *pādas* are rendered in the translations of Raghunathan (1982, vol. 3, p. 371) and Gita Press (1969, vol. 3, p. 1903).

Following verse 90, the final verse of the *Yuddhakāṇḍa* in the critical edition, the vast majority of manuscripts insert one passage or another of similar intent ranging from ten to twenty-five or more lines. Although the evidence shows that most scribes felt the need to include some concluding verses, the textual evidence is disparate and confused as shown by the fact that it has taken the critical editors nearly eight full pages simply to represent the variations. Therefore, even though such additional passages are found in so many manuscripts, we believe that the critical editors were correct in relegating all of them to the apparatus. All of these passages are of the type known in the purāṇic and related literature as *phalaśruti*, that is, passages that set forth the material, moral, and spiritual rewards of those people who hear, read, recite, or copy the holy text to which they are appended. Since such passages normally occur only at the end of texts, their presence here has led some scholars of the epic to argue that the original *Rāmāyaṇa* ended with the *Yuddhakāṇḍa*. This, however, is a dubious proposition as is suggested not only by the universal presence of an *Uttarakāṇḍa* in all known recensions of the *Vālmīki Rāmāyaṇa* but also by the confused nature of these passages themselves. See Introduction, pp. 96–97. What follows is our translation of the *phalaśruti* passage as it appears in the printed text of Ct as represented in the printed editions of NSP and GPP with the additions and variations found in the printed editions of Cg represented in VSP and KK and any relevant or important variations noted in the critical apparatus. This *phalaśruti* is basically represented (in full or in part) in the critical apparatus's passages 3703* [including 3703 F, F3, F7, G, and G5] and 3709*, lines 1–6 [NSP, GPP 6.128.105–122; Gita Press 6.128.107–125; VSP 6.131.103–120; KK 6.131.106–124]: "This, the first poem, was composed long ago[1] by Vālmīki. It is the work of a seer.[2] It leads to good fortune,[3] glory, and long life, and it brings victory to kings.[4] [3703*, lines 1, 2; GPP 6.128.105; VSP 6.131.103] A man who constantly listens to it[5] in this world is freed from sin. A man who desires sons will get them and a man who desires wealth acquires it, if, in this world, they hear about Rāma's consecration. [3703*, lines 3, 4, 5; GPP 6.128.106–107ab; VSP 6.131.103ef–104] A king overpowers his enemies and conquers the earth. Women acquire living sons, just as did his mother in Rāghava, Sumitrā in Lakṣmaṇa, and Kaikeyī in Bharata.[6] [3703 (F)*, lines 8, 3, 4; GPP 6.128.107cd–108; VSP 6.131.105–106ab] He who listens to this *Rāmāyaṇa*, which is the entire tale of the victory of Rāma, tireless in action, obtains a long life. [3703 (F)*, lines 9, 10; GPP 6.128.109; VSP 6.131.107] Whoever listens to this poem, composed by Vālmīki, the work of a seer,[7] faithfully and after subduing his anger, triumphs over all adversities.[8] [3703 (F)*, line 12; 3703 (F7)*; GPP 6.128.110; VSP 6.131.108] And one attains reunion with one's kinsmen at the end of a journey.[9] And they obtain[10] in this world all the boons that they request from Rāghava. [3703*, lines 6, 7; GPP 6.128.111ab, 112ab; VSP 6.131.109] All the gods are pleased with attentive listening on the part of those who hear it. In the house of him who keeps this text malicious spirits are pacified.[11] [3703 (G)*, lines 1, 2; GPP 6.128.112cd–113ab; VSP 6.131.110] A king will conquer the earth; a person journeying far from home will be safe, while marriageable women[12] who hear it will give birth to unsurpassed sons. [3703 (G)*, lines 3, 4; GPP 6.128.113cd–114ab; VSP 6.131.111] Whoever worships and recites this ancient history will be freed from every sin and will live a long life. [3703 (G)*, lines 5, 6; GPP 6.128.114cd–115ab; VSP 6.131.112] Kshatriyas should always listen to it from a brahman with their heads bowed. Then, without a doubt, they will gain lordship and sons. [3703 (G)*, lines 7, 8; GPP 6.128.115cd–116ab; VSP 6.131.113] For Rāma, who is the eternal Viṣṇu, the primal divinity, and the great-armed lord Hari Nārāyaṇa, is always pleased with one who constantly listens to and recites this entire *Rāmāyaṇa*.[13] [3703 (G)*, lines 9–11; GPP 6.128.116cd–117; VSP 6.131.114–115ab] Such is this account of what took place long ago. May you all be blessed. Recite it with confidence, and so may the power of Viṣṇu increase. [3709*, lines 1, 2; GPP 6.128.118; VSP 6.131.118] All the gods are gratified with the hearing and retention[14] of the *Rāmāyaṇa*, and the ancestors are gratified as well on hearing it. [3709*, lines 3, 4; GPP 6.128.119; VSP 6.131.119] Those men who, in this world, copy with devotion this epic[15] of Rāma composed by the seer will gain a place in heaven.[16] [3709*, lines 5, 6; GPP 6.128.120; VSP 6.131.120] After hearing this auspicious and profoundly meaningful poem, a man obtains prosperity for his family, increase of wealth and grain, the finest women, supreme felicity, and the complete accomplishment of his goals on earth.[17] [3703*, lines 8–11; GPP 6.128.121; VSP 6.131.116] Those virtuous people who desire prosperity should religiously listen to this auspicious tale. For it leads to long life, health, glory, brotherly love, wisdom, and vitality.[18] [3703*, lines 12–15; GPP 6.128.122; VSP 6.131.117]"

[1]"long ago" *purā*: Several of the commentators take the term adjectivally in the sense of "old or ancient (*purātanam*)," which would then modify "the first poem (*ādikāvyam*)." The term in either sense presents something of a chronological problem, since the text itself, as Cg points out, was supposed to have been composed by Vālmīki only after Rāma's consecration. In what sense then can the text be said to be ancient? One explanation that no commentator mentions is that the term is, in fact, an indication of the late addition of the *phalaśruti*, whose author[s] would have looked back upon the *Rāmāyaṇa* as an ancient text. Cg proposes a number of interpretations, including that the poem was composed prior to Rāma's incarnation, composed prior to Rāma's sufferings outlined in the *Uttarakāṇḍa*, or, in keeping with the tradition of Vālmīki as the first poet, composed before [the works of] all [other] poets.

[2]"the work of a seer" *ārṣam*: Literally, "belonging to a *ṛṣi*." Ct, Cg, and Cr take *ṛṣi*, "seer," here to mean the *veda* and understand the adjective to mean that the *Rāmāyaṇa* is a supplement to the *vedas* (*vedopabṛṃhaṇam iti yāvat*—so Cg).

[3]"It leads to good fortune" *dhanyam*: Literally, "It is productive of wealth *or* good fortune. G2,3, and the texts and printed editions of Ct read instead *dharmyam*, "It is in keeping with righteousness."

[4]"to kings" *rājñām*: Literally, "of kings." The genitive can construe with either "victory" alone or with all the virtues listed in the verse.

[5]"who constantly listens to it" *yaḥ śṛṇoti sadā*: Literally, "who constantly listens." M3 and the texts and printed editions of Cg read instead *yaḥ paṭhec chṛṇuyāt*, "whoever should recite [or] hear."

[6]Following line 4 (VSP 6.131.106ab), M3 and the texts and printed editions of Cg insert a passage of one line 3703 (F3)*: "And possessed of sons and grandsons, they will be perpetually happy."

[7]"the work of a seer" *ārṣam*: D7,10,11,G2, and the texts and printed editions of Ct and Cr read instead *purā*, "long ago." See notes 2 above and 9 below.

[8]"triumphs over all adversities" *durgāṇy atitarati*: Literally, "he crosses over difficulties."

[9]"And one attains reunion with one's kinsmen at the end of a journey." *samāgamaṃ pravāsānte labhate cāpi bāndhavaiḥ*: Ct and GPP read instead *samāgamya pravāsānte ramante sahabāndhavaiḥ*, "having been reunited at the end of a journey, they rejoice with their kinsmen." Following this line, Ct and the text of GPP repeat 3703 (F)*, line 12, substituting the plural verb *śṛṇvanti*, "they listen," for the singular *śṛṇoti*, and *purā*, "long ago," for *ārṣam* (see note 7 above). This yields the sense: "Those who listen to this poem that was composed long ago by Vālmīki [having been reunited]..."

[10]"they obtain" *prāpnuvanti*: Cg and the printed editions of VSP and GPP read instead the optative singular *prāpnuyāt*, "he would obtain."

[11]"In the house of him who keeps this text malicious spirits are pacified." *vināyakāś ca śāmyanti gṛhe tiṣṭhati yasya vai*: Literally, "In the house of whom it stands, the malicious spirits are pacified." We follow the interpretation of Cr, who takes the subject of *tiṣṭhati*, "it stands *or* exists," to be either the text [of the *Rāmāyaṇa*] itself or one who recites it (*pustakaṃ pāṭhakartā vā*). The printed editions of Cg read the plural *tiṣṭhanti*, "they stand," for the critical edition's and Ct's singular *tiṣṭhati*. In this case, the *vināyakas*, or evil spirits, themselves must be taken as the subject of the verb, lending the line the sense "[Whatever] evil spirits exist in the house of anyone, are pacified."

[12]"marriageable women" *rajasvalāḥ*: The term normally refers to women during their menstrual periods, but, given the context, it probably refers more generally here to women during their reproductive years. Ct, however, takes it in its principal sense, adding that a woman must first take a purifying bath and then [conceive] on the sixteenth day [from her period] (*śuddhasnātānantaraṃ ṣoḍaśadināvadhi*).

[13]Following line 9 in GPP (in brackets, unnumbered, between 116 and 117) and following line 11 in VSP (in brackets = 115cd) and KK (in brackets = 118cd), the texts of the southern commentators insert a passage of one line [3703 (G5)*]: "For Rāma, the foremost of the Raghus, is himself [the primal divinity, etc.], while Lakṣmaṇa is said to be Śeṣa." See notes to 6.5.9; 6.105.20; and 6.107.6.

[14]"with the . . . retention" *grahaṇāt*: Literally, "because of retention." Cr glosses *paṭhanāt*, "with (lit., from) the recitation."

[15]"this epic" *saṃhitām*: The term denotes a sustained composition in verse, such as the text of the *vedas*, etc. Here we take it to refer to the epic poem itself.

[16]"will gain a place in heaven" *teṣāṃ vāsas triviṣṭape*: Literally, "of them [there will be] a residence in Triviṣṭapa." Ct, citing a verse in which it is said that a person who hears any portion of the *Rāmāyaṇa* with devotion goes to Brahmā's world, where he is honored perpetually by Brahmā, glosses "in the world of Brahmā (*brahmaloke*)" for *triviṣṭape*. (*triviṣṭape brahmaloke. śṛṇvan rāmāyaṇaṃ bhaktyā yaḥ pādaṃ padam eva vā / sa yāti brahmaṇaḥ sthānaṃ brahmaṇā pūjyate sadā // iti vacanāt*.) Cr understands the reference to be to Sāketa, the eternal heavenly realm of Ayodhyā, which is the desired destination of all Rāmabhaktas, or devotees of Lord Rāma.

[17]The meter of these fours lines is *upajāti*.

[18]The meter of these fours lines is *indravajrā*.

Glossary of Important Sanskrit Words, Proper Nouns, and Epithets

Agni: god of fire
Airāvata: an elephant; Indra's mount
Akampana: *rākṣasa* warrior slain by Hanumān
Amarāvatī: Indra's heavenly city
Anala; epithet of Agni; god of fire; name of one of Vibhīṣaṇa's advisers
Aṅgada: son of Vālin and Tārā; monkey general; heir apparent to the throne of Kiṣkindhā
Anila: epithet of Vāyu, the wind god
apsarases: celestial maidens or nymphs; known for their beauty
aśoka grove: site of Sītā's confinement in the city of Laṅkā
asuras: class of demons; half brothers of the gods
Aśvins: twin deities of the vedic pantheon; renowned for their beauty
Atikāya: Rāvaṇa's son; *rākṣasa* warrior slain by Lakṣmaṇa
Ayodhyā: capital city of the Ikṣvākus
Bharadvāja: an ascetic sage
Bharata: Daśaratha's second son; son of Kaikeyī
Brahmā: creator divinity of the Hindu "trinity"; "Grandfather" of all living creatures
Brahman: name for the Indian religio-philosophical concept of the impersonal and attributeless absolute principle underlying existence.
Brahmarāśi: name of an asterism
Bṛhaspati: preceptor of the gods
Candra: mountain situated in the midst of the ocean of milk
Candra: the moon god
daityas: class of demons descended from Diti
dānavas: class of demons descended from Danu
Daṇḍaka: forest where Rāma, Sītā, and Lakṣmaṇa spend part of their exile
Daśaratha: Rāma's father; king of Ayodhyā
Dāśarathi: "son of Daśaratha"; epithet of Rāma and Lakṣmaṇa
Devāntaka: *rākṣasa* warrior slain by Hanumān
dharma: righteousness, law; Dharma: god of righteousness
Dhruva: the pole star
Dhūmrākṣa: *rākṣasa* warrior slain by Hanumān
Droṇa: mountain situated in the midst of the ocean of milk
Dūṣaṇa: a general in Khara's army in Janasthāna; slain by Rāṃa
gandharvas: class of semi-divine beings known for their musical abilities; *gandharva* women are noted for their beauty
Ganges: a famous and sacred river; river goddess
Garuḍa: king of birds; Viṣṇu's mount; son of Kaśyapa and Vinatā
Hanumān: Rāma's monkey companion; son of the wind god; counselor to Sugrīva; aids in the finding of Sītā and the destruction of the demon king Rāvaṇa

Himalaya[s]: name of a mountain range; king of the mountains
Ikṣvākus: family name of the royal House of Ayodhyā
Indra: king of the gods; leads their hosts into battle against the *asuras*
Indrajit: epithet of Rāvaṇa's son Meghanāda; slain by Lakṣmaṇa
Jāmbavān: king of the *ṛkṣas*; monkey general; sends Hanumān to bring the mountain of herbs
Janaka: lord of Mithilā; father of Sītā
Jānakī: patronymic of Sītā
Janasthāna: part of the Daṇḍaka Forest; residence of Śūrpaṇakhā and Khara
Kabandha: name of a *rākṣasa* slain by Rāma
Kailāsa: mountain peak in the Himalayas where Śiva and Pārvatī are traditionally said to reside; Kubera, the lord of wealth, is also said to reside there
Kākutstha: "descendant of Kakutstha"; a common patronymic of Rāma and his brothers
Kāla: time incarnate; name of the god of death
Kāma: god of love
Kandarpa: epithet of Kāma, god of love
Kesarin: name of a monkey; father of Hanumān
Khara: brother of Rāvaṇa; slain by Rāma in the Daṇḍaka Forest
kinnaras: mythical creatures with the heads of horses and human bodies; *kinnara* women are famed for their beauty
Kiṣkindhā: capital city of the monkeys
Kubera: god of wealth; son of Viśravas; half brother of Rāvana; king of the *yakṣas* and the *kinnaras*
Kumbha: *rākṣasa* warrior; son of Kumbhakarṇa; slain by Sugrīva
Kumbhakarṇa: gargantuan brother of Rāvaṇa; slain by Rāma
Lakṣmaṇa: son of Daśaratha by Sumitrā; Rāma's constant companion
Lakṣmī: goddess of fortune
Laṅkā: Rāvaṇa's capital city; location of Sītā's confinement
Mandara: mountain used as the churning rod in the churning of the ocean
Mahāpārśva: *rākṣasa* warrior slain by Aṅgada
Maheśvara: epithet of Lord Śiva
Mahodara: *rākṣasa* warrior; Rāvaṇa's brother; slain by Nīla
Maithilī: "woman of Mithilā"; epithet of Sītā
Makarākṣa: *rākṣasa* warrior slain by Rāma
Mālyavān: great-uncle and adviser to Rāvaṇa
Mandodarī: chief queen of Rāvaṇa
Mārīca: a *rākṣasa*; turns himself into a magical deer; slain by Rāma
Māruta: epithet of Vāyu, god of wind; divine father of Hanumān
Māruti: "son of Māruta"; epithet of Hanumān
Maruts: storm gods
Mātali: charioteer of Indra
Maya: architect of the *asuras*; father-in-law of Rāvaṇa
Meru: mythical mountain; the *axis mundi*
Mṛtyu: god of death
Mūla: an asterism
Nala: monkey son of Viśvakarman; designs bridge over the ocean

Nandigrāma: village where Bharata lives during Rāma's exile
Narāntaka: *rākṣasa* warrior slain by Aṅgada
Nikumbha: son of Kumbhakarṇa; adviser to Rāvaṇa; slain by Hanumān
Nikumbhilā: sacred grove where Indrajit sacrifices
Nīla: monkey warrior
Nirṛti: goddess of chaos
Parjanya: god of rain
Pātāla: name of a hell
Pāvaka: "purifier"; epithet of Agni, god of fire
Pavana: epithet of Vāyu, god of wind
piśācas: class of demons
Prahasta: counselor to Rāvaṇa; father of Jambumālin; slain by Nīla
Puṣpa or Puṣpaka: flying palace of Rāvaṇa
Rāghava: "descendant of Raghu"; common patronymic of Rāma and his brothers
Raghu: son of Kakutstha; ancestor of Rāma
Rasātala: name of a hell
Rāvaṇa: main antagonist of the *Rāmāyaṇa*; ten-headed overlord of the *rākṣasas*
Ṛkṣavant: name of a mountain
Rohiṇī: daughter of Dakṣa; favorite consort of the moon
Rudra: epithet of Śiva
Śacī: consort of Indra
Sāgara: god of the ocean
Śakra: "mighty one"; epithet of Indra
Samudra: god of the ocean
Saramā: *rākṣasa* woman; comforts Sītā during her captivity
Sāraṇa: *rākṣasa* spy
Śārdūla: *rākṣasa* spy
Śatrughna: youngest son of Daśaratha by Sumitrā; Bharata's friend and constant companion
Saumitri: "son of Sumitrā"; matronymic of Lakṣmaṇa
Savitṛ: "the impeller"; epithet of Sūrya in his role as the impeller of all creatures
Śiva: one of the three main gods (the "trinity") of the Hindu pantheon along with Brahmā and Viṣṇu
Soma: epithet of Candra, god of the moon
Śrī: goddess of fortune
Sugrīva: king of the monkeys; younger brother of Vālin; friend and ally of Rāma
Śuka: *rākṣasa* spy
Supārśva: *rākṣasa* adviser of Rāvaṇa
Sūrya: sun god; father of Sugrīva
Suṣeṇa: monkey physician; father-in-law of Sugrīva
Suvela: mountain climbed by Rāma and his forces
Trijaṭā: *rākṣasa* woman; comforts Sītā during her captivity
Trikūṭa: mountain on which the city of Laṅkā is located
Tripura: name of the city of the demons; destroyed by Śiva
Triśaṅku: Ikṣvāku king; ancestor of Rāma
Triśiras: *rākṣasa* warrior; slain by Hanumān
Vaidehī: "woman of Videha"; epithet of Sītā

Vajradaṃṣṭra: *rākṣasa* adviser of Rāvaṇa; slain by Aṅgada
Vajrahanu: *rākṣasa* adviser of Rāvaṇa
Vālin: king of the monkeys; husband of Tārā; son of Indra; elder brother of Sugrīva
Varuṇa: god of the ocean
Vāsava: epithet of Indra
Vasiṣṭha: family preceptor of the Ikṣvākus
Vāsuki: name of a great serpent; used as the rope in the churning of the ocean
Vasus: class of deities, normally eight in number
Vāyu: god of wind; divine father of Hanumān
Vegadarśin: monkey warrior
Vibhīṣaṇa: *rākṣasa* lord; brother of Rāvaṇa; ally of Rāma
Vidyujjihva: *rākṣasa* magician
Virādha: *rākṣasa* slain by Rāma
Virūpākṣa: a field marshal of Rāvaṇa; slain by Sugrīva
Viṣṇu: one of the three main gods ("the trinity") of the Hindu pantheon along with Brahmā and Śiva; incarnated on earth in the form of Rāma in order to kill Rāvaṇa
Viśvakarman: god of craft; architect of the gods; father of Nala
Vivavasvān: epithet of Sūrya, the sun god
Vṛtra: demon slain by Indra
yakṣas: semi-divine beings associated with Kubera; the women are known for their beauty
Yama: god of death
yātudhāna: used either as a term for a *rākṣasa* or a specific class of *rākṣasas*

Glossary of Flora and Fauna

āmalaka: myrobalan tree, *Phyllanthus emblica* L.
āmra: mango tree, *Mangifera indica*
aṅkola: type of tree, *Alanguim decapetalum Lam.*
arjuna: white murdah tree, *Terminalia arjuna*
asana: type of tree, *Terminalia tomentosa* Wt.
aśoka: tree with red flowers, *Saraca indica* L., syn. *Jonesia asoka* Roxb.
aśvakarṇa: *sāla* tree, *Vatica robusta* or *Shorea robusta*
bakula: tree with fragrant blossoms, *Mimusops elengi* L.
barhiṇa: peacock, *Pavo cristatus*
bhṛṅgarāja: drongo or fork-tailed shrike, *Dicrurus paradiseus*
bilva: wood-apple tree, *bel*, *Aegle marmelos* (L.) Correa
bimba: plant bearing a bright red gourd, *Momordica monadelpha* Roxb.
cakravāka: a type of sheldrake, also called ruddy shelduck, *Tadorna ferruginea* Pallas (*Anas casarca*)
campaka: tree with fragrant yellow flowers, *Michelia campaka*
cātaka: type of cuckoo, *Cuculus melanoleucus*
ciribilva: (= *karañja*) Indian oilseed plant, *Pongamia glabra*
cūrṇaka: type of tree, *Zizyphus rugosa Lamk.*
cūta: mango tree, *Mangifera indica*
dāḍima: pomegranate tree, *Punica granatum*
darbha: type of grass, *Eragrostis cynosuroides*, syn. *Poa cynosuroides*
dhava: type of tree, *Anogeissus latifolia* Wall. or *Woodfordia floribunda* Salisb., syn. *Grislea tormentosa*
haṃsa: commonly identified as the bar-headed goose, or *Anser indicus*; but can also refer to the Mute swan, *Cygnus olor*, or Whooper swan, *Cygnus cygnus*
hintāla: the marshy date tree, *Phoenix* or *Elate paludosa*
jambū, jambuka: the rose apple tree, *Syzygium cuminii* L., syn. *Eugenia jambos* Linn, Roxb., or the black plum, *Eugenia Jambolana* syn. *Syzugium jambolanum* W.
japā: *Hibiscus rosa-sinensis* L.
kāraṇḍava: generic term for duck; often a goosander or smew, *Mergus merganser* or *Mergus albeus*
karañja: Indian oilseed plant, *Pongamia glabra*
karavīra: oleander, *Nerium odorum*
karṇikāra: fragrant tree with creamy-white flowers, *Pterospermum acerifolium* Willd.
kāśa: type of grass, *Saccharum spontaneum* Mant.
ketaka or *ketakī*: tree with fragrant white flowers, *Pandanus odoratissimus*, syn. *Pandanus tectorius*
khadira: type of tree, *Acacia catechu* Willd. L., syn. *Mimosa catechu* Roxb.
kiṃśuka: type of tree, flame-of-the-forest, *Butea monosperma* (Lam.) Taub., syn. *Butea frondosa*
kokila: Indian cuckoo: *Cuculus indicus*
koṇālaka: possibly a type of wagtail, *Motacilla indica* Gmelin?

kovidāra: tree, *Bauhinia variegata* L.
koyaṣṭibhaka: probably the night heron (*Nycticorax nycticorax*)
krauñca: either the sarus crane, *Grus antigone*, or the eastern common crane, *Grus grus lilfordi*
kṣudratāla: see *tāla*
kuḍaja: =*kuṭaja*: mountain jasmine, *Holarrhena antidysenterica* Wall.
kurabaka: red amaranth, Barleria prionitis
kuśa: type of grass, *Eragrostis cynosuroides*, syn. *Poa cynosuroides*
kuṭaja: tree with white flowers, *Wrightia antidysenterica*
madhūka: mahua tree, *Madhuca latafolia* Roxb., syn. *Madhuca indica* Gmel.
muculinda: tree with yellowish white fragrant flowers, *Pterospermum suberifolium*
nāgavṛkṣa: =*nicula*, type of tree, *Barringtonia acutangula* Gaertn.
nālikera: coconut tree, *Cocos nucifera*
natyūha: =*dātyūha*, a type of bird probably the *cātaka*, *Cuculus melanoleucus*
nimba: neem tree, *Azadirachta indica* A. Juss., *syn. Melia a.* L. and *Melia indica* Brandis
nīpaka: =*nipa/nīpa*, type of tree, *Anthocephalus cadamba* Roxb. Miq.
nyagrodha: banyan tree, *Ficus bengalensis*, syn. *Ficus indica*
padmaka: tree with white, pink, or crimson flowers, probably the *Prunus puddum*
palāśa: type of tree, the flame-of-the-forest, *Butea monosperma*
panasa: jackfruit tree, *Artocarpus integrifolia*
pāṭala: see *pāṭali*
pāṭali: trumpet flower tree, *Bignonia suaveolens* Roxb., syn. *Stereospermum suaveolens* DC
plakṣa: type of tree, *Ficus infectoria* Rox.
puṃnāga: type of tree, a *nāgavṛkṣa*, *Rottleria tinctoria*, or *Calophyllium inophyllum* L.
raṅku: type of deer, perhaps the *kṛṣṇāsara* (spotted antelope)
sāla: type of tree, *Vatica robusta* or *Shorea robusta*
śālmali: silk-cotton tree, *Salmalia malabarica* or *Bombax malabaricum*
saptaparṇa: milkwood tree, *Alstonia scholaris*
śarapatra: type of grass, *Saccharum spontaneum*
sārasa: the Indian sarus crane, *Grus antigone*
sārika/śārika: mynah bird, *Acridotheres tristis*
śiṃśapā: type of tree, *Dalbergia sissoo* or *ougeinensis*
sinduvāra: type of tree, *Vitex negundo*
tāla: palmyra tree or toddy-palm, *Borassus flabellifer*
tamāla: type of tree, *Garcinia xanthochymus* Hook f.
tilaka: type of tree, probably *Clerodendron phlomoides*
timiśa: type of ebony tree, *Dalbergia ougeinensis* Roxb., syn. *Amerimnus ougeinensis* or *Diospyros melanoxylon* Roxb. or *Diospyros embryopteris* Pers.
tinduka: type of ebony tree, *Diospyros embroyopteris Pers.* or D. *melanoxylon Roxb.*
uddālaka: type of tree, probably *Cordia myxa* L.
uśīra: khas-khas grass, *Andropogon muricatus* Retz., syn. *Andropogon squarrosus* L.
vallarī: fenugreek, *Trigonella foenum-graecum*, the term can also apply to a creeper or any creeping plant
varaṇa: type of tree, *Crataeva roxburghii* Kurz., syn. *C. religiosa Forst*
vibhītaka: myrobalan or purple-leaf plum, *Terminalia bellerica*

Glossary of Weapons

(See Introduction, pp. 111–112, and individual notes for discussions on the identifications of specific weapons.)

arrow types
  broad-headed: *nālika*
  calf's-foot-headed: *vatsadanta*
  crescent-headed: *bhalla*
  folded-palm-headed: *añjalika*
  half-iron: *ardhanārāca*
  half-moon-headed: *ardhacandra*
  heads with earlike blades: *karṇi*
  heron-feather-headed: *śilīmukha*
  horseshoe-headed: *kṣurapra*
  iron: *nārāca*
  karavīra leaf-tip-headed: *vipāṭha* (*oleander Nerium odorum*)
  lion-fang-headed: *siṃhadaṃṣṭra*
  long-headed: *śalya*
  razor-tipped: *kṣura*
axe: *paraśu*
barbed dart: *kunta*
battle-axe: *paraśvadha*
bludgeon: *musundī* (v.l. *musṛṇṭhī, bhuśuṇḍi, bhṛśuṇḍi*)
bow: *cāpa, kārmuka, śarāsana, dhanuḥ*, etc.
broad sword, double-edged sword: *ṛṣṭi*
club: *yaṣṭi/yaṣṭī*
cudgel: *musala*
dart: *prāsa*
dart/missile/lance: *āśanī*
discus: *cakra* (small discus: *cakraḥ*; big discus: *cakram*)
hook: *aṅkuśa*
iron club or battering ram: *parigha*
iron cudgel: *tomara*
hundred-slayer: *śataghnī*
javelin: *śakti*
lance: *śūla*
nirghāta: See note to 6.66.4–5
mace: *gadā*
mallet: *kūṭa*
noose: *pāśa*
ploughshare: *hala*
scimitar: *khaḍga* [when used with *asi*]
short javelin: *bhiṇḍipāla/bhindipāla*

sling: *kṣepaṇi/kṣepaṇīyam*
spear: *paṭṭiśa/paṭṭasa*
stave: *daṇḍa*
sword: *asi, khaḍga, nistriṃśa*
trident: *triśūla*
war hammer: *mudgara*

Emendations and Corrections of the Critical Edition

Listed below are the emendations and corrections to the critical text made by the translators. We have inroduced such changes only where we felt it essential for the intelligibility of the text. For a discussion of specific issues concerning the emendations, see the respective notes.

	Critical Text	Emendation
6.2.21	*rāvaṇālayam*	*varuṇālayam*
6.3.8		add *39
6.4.37	*grāhābhyām*	*grahābhyām*
6.4.68	*na*	*naḥ*
6.9.15	*vaidehībhayam*	*vaidehī bhayam*
6.9.15	*kṛte na*	*kṛtena*
6.35.20	*gātram*	*gātre*
6.37.10	*na*	*ca*
6.38.2	*lakṣaṇikāḥ*	*lākṣaṇikāḥ*
6.38.2	*ajñāninaḥ*	*jñāninaḥ*
6.38.3	*ajñāninaḥ*	*jñāninaḥ*
6.38.4	*ajñāninaḥ*	*jñāninaḥ*
6.38.5	*ajñāninaḥ*	*jñāninaḥ*
6.42.12		add 860*
6.45.36		add 926*
6.47.45	*āryaḥ*	*ārya*
6.48.57	*āhatya*	*ādṛtya*
6.52.30		add 1138*
6.53.5	Critical Text *viklavānām abuddhīnāṃ rājñāṃ paṇḍitamānīnām /* *śṛṇvatām ādita idaṃ tvadvidhānāṃ mahodara //* Emendation *viklavānām abuddhīnāṃ rājñā paṇḍitamānīnām /* *śṛṇvatā sāditam idaṃ tvadvidhānāṃ mahodara //*	
6.55.66	*saṃprati kartum*	*saṃpratikartum*
6.55.76, App. 1, No. 35, line 23	*asahyam*	*asahyaḥ*
6.57.72	*te 'svasthāḥ*	*te svasthāḥ*
6.67.11	*-ottame*	*-ottamaḥ*
6.75. 1659*	*āvivyathatuḥ*	*āvivyadhatuḥ*
6.77.38	*ādau*	*ājau*
6.92.6	*nijaghāna*	*nicakhāna*
6.101.26–28	*bhṛśaṃ śuṣkamukhībhiḥ*	*nakhaiḥ śuṣmamukhībhiḥ*

6.102.5	*āsīd*	*īṣad*
6.102.7	*māciram*	*mā ciram*
6.110.13	*bhavatā dharmabhiruṇā*	*bhavatādharmabhiruṇā*
6.114.27	*anucaran*	*anvacarat*

Bibliography of Works Consulted

TEXTS OF THE *VĀLMĪKI RĀMĀYAṆA*

Rāmāyaṇa. (1928–1947). 7 vols. Lahore: D.A.V. College. Northwestern recension critically edited for the first time from original manuscripts by Vishva Bandhu. D.A.V. College Sanskrit Series, nos. 7, 12, 14, 17–20.

Ramayana, poema indiano di Valmici. (1843–1867). Paris: Stamperia Reale. Edited by Gaspare Gorresio.

Rāmāyan of Vālmīki. (1914–1920). 7 vols. Bombay: Gujarati Printing Press. With three commentaries called *Tilaka*, *Shiromani*, and *Bhooshana*. Edited by Shastri Shrinivas Katti Mudholkar.

The Rāmāyaṇa of Vālmīki. (1888). Bombay: Nirṇayasāgar Press. With the commentary (*Tilaka*) of Rāma. Edited by Kāśināth Pāṇdurāng Parab.

The Rāmāyaṇa of Vālmīki. (1930). 4th rev. ed. Bombay: Nirṇayasāgar Press. With the commentary (*Tilaka*) of Rāma. Edited by Wāsudeva Laxmaṇ Śāstrī Paṇśīkar.

Śrīmad Vālmīki-Rāmāyaṇa. (1969). 3 vols. Gorakhpur: Gita Press.

Śrīmadvālmīkirāmāyaṇam. (1911–1913). 7 vols. Bombay: Nirṇayasāgar Press. Also called the Kumbakonam Edition. Edited by T. R. Krishnacharya and T. R. Vyasacharya. Reprint 1930.

Śrīmadvālmīkirāmāyaṇam. (1935). 3 vols. Bombay: Lakṣmīveṅkaṭeśvara Mudraṇālaya. With the commentaries of Govindarāja, Rāmānuja, and Maheśvaratīrtha and the commentary known as *Taniślokī*. Edited by Gaṅgāviṣṇu Śrīkṛṣṇadāsa.

The Vālmīki Rāmāyaṇa: Critical Edition. (1960–1975). 7 vols. Baroda: Oriental Institute. General editors: G. H. Bhatt and U. P. Shah.

TRANSLATIONS OF THE *YUDDHAKĀṆḌA*

Dutt, M. N., trans. (1893). *The Ramayana*. Vol. 6: *Yuddha Kāndam*. Calcutta: Girish Chandra Chackravarti.

Gita Press Edition translation. (1969). See *Śrīmad Vālmīki-Rāmāyaṇa* (1969).

Gorresio, Gaspare, trans. (1856–1858). *Ramayana, poema sanscrito di Valmici*. Vol. 9 (*sargas* 1–37) and vol. 10. Paris: Stamperia Reale.

Pagani, Brigitte. (1999). *Le Rāmāyaṇa de Vālmīki*. Canto 6: La Guerre. Paris: Gallimard. Edited by Madeleine Biardeau.

Raghunathan, N., trans. (1982). *Srimad Vālmīki Ramayana*. Vol. 3. Madras: Vighneswara Publishing House.

Roussel, Alfred, trans. (1903). *Le Rāmāyana de Vālmīki*. Paris: Librairie des cinq parties du monde. Bibliothèque Orientale, no. 8.

Shastri, Hari Prasad, trans. (1959). *The Ramayana of Valmiki*. Vol. 3. London: Shanti Sadan. 2nd ed., 1969.

SANSKRIT TEXTS

Abhidhānavyutpattiprakriyakośaḥ (=*Abhidhānacintāmaṇi*) *of Hemacandra: Classical Dictionary of Sanskrit Synonyms and Antonyms*. (1932). 2 vols. Varanasi: Chowkhamba Sanskrit Series Office. Kashi Sanskrit Series, no. 97. Reprint 1984.

Abhijñānaśākuntalam of Kālidāsa. (1891). 3rd rev. ed. Bombay: Nirṇayasāgar Press. Edited by N. B. Godabole and K. P. Parab.

The Abhijñānaśākuntalam of Kālidāsa. (1957). 8th ed. Bombay: Booksellers' Publishing Co. With the commentary of Rāghavabhaṭṭa. Edited by M. R. Kale.

Adhyātma-Rāmāyaṇa. (1884). Calcutta: Valmiki Press. With the commentary of Ramavarman. Edited by Pandit Jibananda Vidyasagara.

Agnipurāṇam. (1900). Poona: Ānandāśrama Press. Ānandāśrama Sanskrit Series, no. 41. Reprint 1957.

Aitareyabrāhmaṇa. (1931). Poona: Ānandāśrama Press. With the commentary of Śrīmatsāyaṇācārya. Ānandāśrama Sanskrit Series, no. 32.

The Amarakośa. (1940). 11th ed. Bombay: Nirṇayasāgar Press. Edited by Wāsudeva Laxmaṇ Śāstrī Paṇśīkar.

Amarakośa. (1971). Madras: The Adyar Library and Research Centre. The Adyar Library Series, vol. 101. With the unpublished South Indian commentaries *Amarapadavivṛti* of Liṅgayasūrin and the *Amarapadapārijāta* of Mallinātha. Edited by A. A. Ramanathan.

Amarakośa. (2002). Delhi: Eastern Book Linkers. With the commentary of Maheśvara. Edited by Vamanacharya Jhalakikar. Enlarged by Raghunath Shastri Talekar. Revised, enlarged, and improved from Chintamani Shastri Thatte's edition of 1882.

Amarakośa of Amarasimha. (1972). Kuala Lumpur: S. Mishra. With the commentary of Ācārya Kṛṣṇamitra. Edited by Satyadeva Mishra.

Āpastambaśrautasūtra. (1955–1963). 2 vols. Baroda: Oriental Institute. With *Dhūrtasvāmibhāṣya*. Edited by Paṇḍita A. Chinnaswāmī Śāśtrī.

Arthaśāstra. See *Kauṭilīya Arthaśāstra*.

Aṣṭādhyāyī of Pāṇini. (1891). 2 vols. Allahabad: Pāṇini Office. Reprint Delhi: Motilal Banarsidass, 1962. Edited and translated by Śāstrī Chandra Vasu.

Aṣṭādhyāyī of Pāṇini. (1987). Austin: University of Texas Press. Translated by Sumitra M. Katre.

Aṣṭāṅgahṛdayasūtra of Vāgbhaṭṭa. (1997). A machine-readable transcription by R. P. Das and R. E. Emmerick. Göttingen Register of Electronic Texts in Indian Languages (GRETIL), Archive of E-Texts in Unicode (UTF-8), <http://www.sub.uni-goettingen.de/ebene_1/fiindolo/gret_utf.htm#Ayur>.*

Āśvalāyanagṛhyasūtram. (1938). Poona: Ānandāśrama Press. Ānandāśrama Sanskrit Series, no. 105.

Baudhāyana-Dharmasūtra. (1992). Online version based on E. Hultzsch's [1922] and Pandeya's [The Kashi Sanskrit Series 1972] versions. Göttingen Register of Electronic Texts in Indian Languages (GRETIL), Archive of E-Texts in Unicode

*All electronic citations are current as of 12/27/07.

(UTF-8), <http://www.sub.uni-goettingen.de/ebene_1/fiindolo/gret_utf.htm#DhSutra>. Last revised, May 20, 1992.

The Bhagavad-Gita. (1935). Bombay: Gujarati Printing Press. With eleven commentaries. Edited by Shastri Gajanana Shambhu Sadhale.

Bhāgavatapurāṇam. (1965). Nadiyad: Kṛṣṇa Śaṅkar Śāstrī et al. With thirteen commentaries. Edited by Kṛṣṇa Śaṅkar Śāstrī.

Bhāgavatapurāṇam. (1983). Delhi: Motilal Banarsidass. With the commentary *Bhāvārthabodhinī* of Srīdhara Svāmin. Reprint 1988.

Bhāgavatapurāṇam. (2006). Göttingen Register of Electronic Texts in Indian Languages (GRETIL), Archive of E-Texts in Unicode (UTF-8), <http://www.sub.uni-goettingen.de/ebene_1/fiindolo/gret_utf.htm#Pur>. Under revision.

Brahmāṇḍapurāṇa. (2004). Based on Bombay: Venkatesvara Steam Press Edition (or a reprint thereof). Göttingen Register of Electronic Texts in Indian Languages (GRETIL), Archive of E-Texts in Unicode (UTF-8), <http://www.sub.uni-goettingen.de/ebene_1/fiindolo/gret_utf.htm#Pur>.

Brahmāṇḍapurāṇam. (1973). Delhi: Motilal Banarsidass. Edited by J. L. Shastri.

Brahma-Purana. (2004). *Adhyāyas* 1–246 input by Peter Schreiner and Renate Soehnen-Thieme for the Tüebingen Purāṇa Project, University of Zürich, Department for Indology, <http://www.indologie.unizh.ch/text/text.html> or Göttingen Register of Electronic Texts in Indian Languages (GRETIL), Archive of E-Texts in Unicode (UTF-8), <http://www.sub.uni-goettingen.de/ebene_1/fiindolo/gret_utf.htm#Pur>.

Bṛhadaraṇyakopaniṣad. (1958). In *Eighteen Principal Upaniṣads,* Vol. 1. Poona: Vaidika Saṃśodhana Maṇḍala. Edited by V. P. Limaye and R. D. Vadekar.

Bṛhatsaṃhitā of Varāhamihira. (1981–1982). 2 vols. Delhi: Motilal Banarsidass. Translated by M. Ramakrishna Bhat.

Bṛhatsaṃhitā of Varāhamihira. (1996–1997). 2 vols. Varanasi: Varanaseya Sanskrit Vishvavidyalaya. With the commentary of Bhaṭṭopala. Edited by Avadha Vihārī Tripāṭhī. Sarasvatī Bhavan Granthamālā, vols. 20, 97.

Bṛhatsaṃhitā of Varāhamihira. (1998). Digitalized by Michio Yano and Mizue Sugita. Based on the edition of A. V. Tripathi (Sarasvati Bhavan Granthamala Edition), with reference to H. Kern's text and his translation [variants marked by K. & K.'s translation] and Utpala's commentary [marked by U.]. Variants start from *. Version 4.3.

Chāndogya Upaniṣad. (1958). In *Eighteen Principal Upaniṣads,* Vol. 1. Poona: Vaidika Saṃśodhana Maṇḍala. Edited by V. P. Limaye and R. D. Vadekar.

The Devībhāgavatapurāṇam. (1986). Delhi: Nag Publishers.

Dharmākūtam, Yuddhakāṇḍa, by Tryambakarāyamakhī. (1964). Thanjavur: O. A. Narayanaswami. Edited by K. Vasudeva Sastri. Tanjore Saraswathi Mahal Series, no. 111.

Dhātupāṭha. (2004). <http://www.flaez.ch/sanskrit/dhatup.html>.

The Garuḍamahāpurāṇam. (1984). Delhi: Nag Publishers.

Garuḍamahāpurāṇam. (2004). Göttingen Register of Electronic Texts in Indian Languages (GRETIL), Archive of E-Texts in Unicode (UTF-8), <http://www.sub.uni-goettingen.de/ebene_1/fiindolo/gret_utf.htm#Pur>.

Harivaṃśa. See *Mahābhārata: Critical Edition.*

Harivaṃśa. Chitrashala Press Edition. See *Mahābhāratam*—Part VII, *Harivanshaparvan.*

The Hitopadeśa of Narayana. (1967). 6th ed. Delhi: Motilal Banarsidass. Edited by M. R. Kale.

The Hitopadeśa of Narayana Pandit. (1890). Bombay: Nirṇayasāgar Press. Edited by N. B. Godabole and K. P. Parab.

Jaiminīya Brāhmaṇa of the Sāmaveda. (1954). Nagpur: International Academy of Indian Culture. Edited by Raghu Vira and Lokesh Chandra. Sarasvati-vihara Series, Vol. 31.

The Jaiminīya or *Talavakāra Upaniṣad Brāhmaṇa: Text, Translation, and Notes.* (1892–1895). Edited and translated by H. Oertel. *JAOS* 16, pp. 79–260.

Kāmandakīyanītisāra. (1971). Kathamandu: Nepāla Rajakīya Prajña-Pratiṣṭhāna Saṃskṛti Vibhāga. Edited by Devrāja Pauḍela.

Kāṭhakam: Die Saṃhitā der Kāṭha-Śākhā. (1900–1910). 3 vols. Leipzig: F. A. Brochaus. Edited by Leopold von Schroeder. Reprint Weisbaden: Steiner, 1970–1973.

Kaṭha Upaniṣad. (1958). In *Eighteen Principal Upaniṣads,* Vol. 1. Poona: Vaidika Saṃśodhana Maṇḍala. Edited by V. P. Limaye and R. D. Vadekar.

The Kauṣītaka Gṛhyasūtras. (1944). Madras: Anand Press. With the commentary of Bhavatrāta. Edited by Chintamani. Madras University Sanskrit Series, no. 15.

Kauṭilīya Arthaśāstra. (1960–1965). 3 vols. Bombay: University of Bombay. Edited by R. P. Kangle. University of Bombay Studies Sanskrit, Prakrit, and Pali, nos. 1–3.

Kāvyaprakāśa. (1941). Bombay: Karnatak Publishing House. Edited by S. S. Sukthankar.

The Kumārasambhava of Kālidāsa. (1886). Bombay: Nirṇayasāgar Press. With the commentary (the *Sañjīvinī*) of Mallinātha (1–8 *sargas*) and of Sītārāma (8–17 *sargas*). Edited by Nārāyaṇa Bhatta Parvaṇīkara and Kāśīnāth Pāṇḍurang Parab.

Kūrmapurāṇam. (1971). Varanasi: All-India Kashiraj Trust. Edited by Anand Swarup Gupta.

Kūrmapurāṇam. (2004). Göttingen Register of Electronic Texts in Indian Languages (GRETIL), Archive of E-Texts in Unicode (UTF-8), <http://www.sub.uni-goettingen.de/ebene_1/fiindolo/gret_utf.htm#Pur>.

Lāṭyāyana Śrauta Sūtra. (1998). 3 vols. New Delhi: Indira Gandhi National Centre and Motilal Banarsidass. Critically edited and translated by H. G. Ranade.

Liṅgapurāṇam. (2007). Göttingen Register of Electronic Texts in Indian Languages (GRETIL), Archive of E-Texts in Unicode (UTF-8), <http://www.sub.uni-goettingen.de/ebene_1/fiindolo/gret_utf.htm#Pur>.

Mahābhārata. (1929). 6 vols. Poona: Chitrashala Press. With the commentary of Nīlakaṇṭha.

Mahābhārata: Critical Edition. (1933–1970). 24 vols. Poona: Bhandarkar Oriental Research Institute. With *Harivaṃśa* (1969–1971). Critically edited by V. S. Sukthankar et al.

Mahābhāratam—Part VII, *Harivanshaparvan.* (1936). Poona: Chitrashala Press. With the *Bhārata Bhāwadeepa* by Neelakantha. Edited by Pandit Rāmachandrashāstri Kinjawadekar.

Mahābhāṣya. See *The Vyākaraṇa-Mahābhāṣya of Patañjali.*

Maitrāyaṇī Saṃhitā. (1881–1886). 4 vols. Leipzig: F. A. Brochaus. Edited by Leopold von Schroeder. [Part of the *Kṛṣṇayajurveda.*]

Maitrāyaṇī Upaniṣad. (1958). In *Eighteen Principal Upaniṣads,* Vol. 1. Poona: Vaidika Saṃśodhana Maṇḍala. Edited by V. P. Limaye and R. D. Vadekar.

Mālavikāgnimitram of Kālidāsa. (1960). Delhi: Motilal Banarsidass. With the commentary of Kāṭayavema. Edited and translated by M. R. Kale.

Manusmṛti. (1946). 10th ed. Bombay: Nirṇayasāgar Press. With the commentary *Manvarthamuktāvali* of Kullūka. Edited by N. R. Acharya.

Manu-Smṛti. (1972–1982). 5 vols. Bombay: Bharatiya Vidya Bhavan. With nine commentaries by Medhātithi, Sarvajñanārāyaṇa, Kullūka, Rāghavānanda, Nandana, Rāmacandra, Maṇirāma, Govindarāja, and Bhāruci. Edited by Jayantakrishna Harikrishna Dave.

Mārkaṇḍeyapurāṇam. (1967). UP, India: Saṃskṛti-Saṃsthāna. Edited by Śrīrāma Śarmā Ācārya.

Matsyapurāṇam. (1907). Poona: Ānandāśrama Press. Edited by Hari Narayana Apte. Ānandāśrama Sanskrit Series, no. 54.

The Meghadūta of Kālidāsa. (1969). 7th ed. Delhi: Motilal Banarsidass. With the commentary (*Sañjīvinī*) of Mallinātha. Edited with introduction, English translation, critical notes by M. R. Kale.

Mudrārākṣasa of Viśākhadatta. (1940). Poona: Aryabhushan Press. Edited and translated by R. F. Karmarkar.

Muṇḍakopaniṣad. (1958). In *Eighteen Principal Upaniṣads*, Vol. 1. Poona: Vaidika Saṃśodhana Maṇḍala. Edited by V. P. Limaye and R. D. Vadekar.

Nāradapurāṇam. (2004). Göttingen Register of Electronic Texts in Indian Languages (GRETIL), Archive of E-Texts in Unicode (UTF-8), <http://www.sub.uni-goettingen.de/ebene_1/fiindolo/gret_utf.htm#Pur>.

Natyasastra of Bharatamuni. (1971). Varanasi: Banaras Hindu University. With the commentary (*Abhinavabharati*) of Abhinava Guptacharya. Edited with introduction and commentaries *Madhusudani* and *Balakreeda* by Madhusudan Shastri.

The Nighantu and the Nirukta. (1967). Dehli: Motilal Banarsidass. Edited and translated by Lakshman Sarup.

The Nirukta of Yāska. (1993). Vol. 1. 2nd ed. Poona: Bhandarkar Oriental Research Institute. Edited by V. K. Rajavade. Government Oriental Series Class A, no. 7.

The Nirukta of Yāska (with Nighaṇṭu). (1918, 1942). 2 vols. Bombay: Government Central Press. With Durga's commentary. Edited by H. M. Bhadkamkar. Bombay Sanskrit and Prakrit Series, nos. 73 and 85.

Nītisārakāmandaka. (2005). *The Nītisāra or The Elements of Polity by Kāmandaki*. Edited by Rajendralala Mitra. Revised with English translation by Sisir Kumar Mitra. Calcutta: The Asiatic Society, 1982. Bibliotheca Indica. [First edition, based on one recent MS, published in five fascicules, 1849–1884. The revised edition has used other editions and manuscripts of the text and a commentary, which is also published. Nothing is said of the date of the commentary.] Entered by H. Isacson.

Padmapurāṇam. (1893–1894). 4 vols. Poona: Ānandāśrama Press. Edited by Viśvanātha Nārāyaṇa Maṇḍalik. Ānandāśrama Sanskrit Series, no. 131.

Panchatantra. (1869). Vol. 1. Bombay: Oriental Press. Edited by F. Kielhorn. Bombay Sanskrit Series, no. 4.

———. (1868). Vols. 2, 3. Bombay: Oriental Press. Edited by G. Bühler. Bombay Sanskrit Series, no. 3.

———. (1868). Vols. 4, 5. Bombay: Oriental Press. Edited by G. Bühler. Bombay Sanskrit Series, no. 1.

Prācina Caritrakośa. (1964). Written by M. M. Siddheśvar Śāstrī Citrāv. Poona: Bhāratīya Caritrakośa Maṇḍal.

Raghuvaṃśa of Kālidāsa. (1948). Bombay: Nirṇayasāgar Press. With commentary *Sañjīvinī* of Mallinātha; extracts from the commentaries of Vallabhadeva, Hemādri, Dinkara Misra Charitavardhan, Sumativyaya (*Raghuvaṃśasāra*); critical and explanatory notes, various readings, and indexes. With an introduction by H. D. Velankar.

Rājanighantu (=*Nighanturāja* or *Abhidhānacūḍāmaṇi*) *of Narahari Pandita* (alias Nṛsimha). (2004). Based on Calcutta 1933: Siddheshvarayantra. Input by Oliver Hellwig. Göttingen Register of Electronic Texts in Indian Languages (GRETIL), Archive of E-Texts in Unicode (UTF-8), <http://www.sub.uni-goettingen.de/ebene_1/fiindolo/gret_utf.htm#Ayur>.

Rāmcaritmānas of Tulsī Dās. (1938). Gorakhpur: Gita Press. With a commentary by Hanumānprasād Poddār.

Ṛgveda-Samhitā. (1933). 5 vols. Poona: Vaidic Samshodhan Mandal. With the commentary of Sāyaṇāchārya.

Ṛtusaṃhāra of Kālidāsa. (1897). Mumbai: Gopal Nārāyaṇ Company Booksellers.

Śabdakalpadruma by Raja Radha Kanta Deva. (1886). 5 vols. Reprint Varanasi: Chowkhamba Sanskrit Series Office. Chowkhamba Sanskrit Series, no. 93. 3rd ed., 1967.

Sāhityadarpaṇa of Viśvanātha Kavirāja. (1967). Varanasi: Chowkhamba Sanskrit Series Office. Chowkhamba Sanskrit Series, no. 145.

Sāmavediyam Śrautasūtram (with the *Lāṭāyanaśrautasūtra*). (1984). Varanasi: Chowkhamba Sanskrit Series Office.

Śatapatha Brāhmaṇam. (1940). 5 vols. Bombay: Laxmi Venkateshwar Steam Press. With Sāyaṇa's commentary.

The Śiśupālavadha of Māgha. (1902). Bombay: Turkaram Javaji. With the commentary *Sarvāṅkaṣāvya* of Mallinātha. Edited by Wāsudeva Laxmaṇ Śāstrī Paṇśīkar.

———. (1932). Bombay: Gopal Narayan and Co. Edited with introduction, notes, and translation by M. S. Bhandare.

Śivapurāṇam. (1906). Bombay: Veṅkaṭeśvara Press.

Skandapurāṇa Sūtasaṃhitā. (1954). Madras: Balamanorama Press.

Śrautakośa. (1958). 2 vols. Poona: Vaidika Saṃśodhana Maṇḍala. Encyclopedia of vedic ritual comprising the two complementary sections, namely, the Sanskrit section and the English section.

Śvetāśvatara Upaniṣad. (1958). In *Eighteen Principal Upaniṣads*, Vol. 1. Poona: Vaidika Saṃśodhana Maṇḍala. Edited by V. P. Limaye and R. D. Vadekar.

Taittirīyabrāhmaṇam. (1898). Poona: Ānandāśrama Press. Ānandāśrama Sanskrit Series, no. 37.

Taittirīya Saṃhitā. (1871–1872). Leipzig: F. A. Brochaus. Edited by A. Weber.

Taittirīya Upaniṣad. (1958). In *Eighteen Principal Upaniṣads*, Vol. 1. Poona: Vaidika Saṃśodhana Maṇḍala. Edited by V. P. Limaye and R. D. Vadekar.

Uttararāmacarita of Bhavabhūti. (1971). 5th ed. Delhi: Motilal Banarsidass. With the commentary of Ghanśyāma. Notes and translation by P. V. Kane and C. N. Joshi.

Uttararāmacaritam of Bhavabhūti. (1918). Cambridge, Mass.: Harvard University Press. Edited by S. K. Belvalkar. Harvard Oriental Series, Vol. 22.

The Vaijayantī of Yādavaprakāśa. (1893). Madras: Madras Sanskrit and Vernacular Text Publication Society. Edited by Gustav Oppert.

The Vājasaneyi-Sanhitā. (1852). Berlin: Ferd. Dümmler's Verlagsbuchhandlung. In the Mādhyandina and the Kāṇva-Śākha with the commentary of Mahīdhara. Edited by Albrecht Weber. [Part 1 in *The White Yajurveda.*]

Vāmanapurāṇa. (2004). Based on the edition by A. S. Gupta, Varanasi: All India Kashiraj Trust, 1967. Göttingen Register of Electronic Texts in Indian Languages (GRETIL), Archive of E-Texts in Unicode (UTF-8), <http://www.sub.uni-goettingen.de/ebene_1/fiindolo/gret_utf.htm#Pur>.

Vāyupurāṇam. (1959). 2 vols. Calcutta: Gurumandal Press. Gurumandal Series, no. 19.

Viṣṇupurāṇa. (1972). Calcutta: n. p. With the commentary of Śrīdhara. Edited by Sītārāmadāson Kāranātha.

Viṣṇupurāṇa. (2004). Göttingen Register of Electronic Texts in Indian Languages (GRETIL), Archive of E-Texts in Unicode (UTF-8), <http://www.sub.uni-goettingen.de/ebene_1/fiindolo/gret_utf.htm#Pur>.

Viśvākośa. See *Viśvaprakāśa.*

Viśvaprakāśa of Śrī Maheśvara. (1911). Benares: Chowkhamba Sanskrit Book Depot. Edited by Śrī Śīlaskandha Sthavira and Pt. Ratna Gopāla Bhaṭṭa. Chowkhamba Sanskrit Series, no. 37.

The Vyākaraṇa-Mahābhāṣya of Patañjali. (1962). 3rd ed. Poona: Bhandarkar Oriental Research Institute. Edited by F. Kielhorn.

Yājñavalkyasmṛti. (1892). Bombay: Janārdan Mahādev Gurjar. With the commentary of Mitāksharā Vijñāneshvara. Edited by Bapu Shastri Moghe.

Yāska's Nirukta. See *The Nirukta of Yāska.*

Yogasūtram of Maharṣi Patañjali. (1931). Benaras: Jai Krishnadas-Haridas Gupta. With the *Yogapradīpaka* commentary of Pandit Baladewa Miśra. Edited by Pandit Dhundhiraj Śastri.

SECONDARY SOURCES

Ali, Salim, and S. Dillon Ripley. (1968–1974). *Handbook of the Birds of India and Pakistan.* 10 vols. Bombay: Oxford University Press. 2nd ed., 1978–1987.

Alter, Joseph S. (1992). *The Wrestler's Body: Identity and Ideology in North India.* Berkeley and Los Angeles: University of California Press.

Apte, V. S. (1957–1959). *The Practical Sanskrit-English Dictionary.* 3 vols. Poona: Prasad Prakashan.

Arnold, Matthew. (1905). *On Translating Homer.* London: John Murray. New edition with introduction and notes by W.J.D. Rouse.

Barnett, Lionel D. (1914). *Antiquities of India: An Account on the History and Culture of Ancient Hindustan.* New York: G. P. Putnam's Sons. Reprint Calcutta: Punthi Pustak, 1964.

Barth, Auguste. (1906). *Religions of India.* Translated by J. Wood. London: Kegan Paul, Trench, Trübner. 4th ed. Varanasi: Chowkhamba Sanskrit Series Office. Chowkhamba Sanskrit Studies, Vol. 25.

Bedekar, V. M. (1967). "The Legend of the Churning of the Ocean in the Epics and Purāṇas." *Purāṇam* 9.1, pp. 7–61.

Bhatia, H. S., ed. (1984–1986). *Political, Legal and Military History of India*. 10 vols. New Delhi: Deep & Deep.

Bhatt, B. N. (1976). "Estimating the Traditions of the Vālmīki Rāmāyaṇa by the Presence or Absence of the Syllables of Gāyatrī in Them." *JOIB* 26.2, pp. 145–61.

Bhatt, G. H., ed. (1960). *The Bālakāṇḍa: The First Book of the Vālmīki Rāmāyaṇa: The National Epic of India*. Baroda: Oriental Institute.

Bhattacharji, Sukumari. (1970). *The Indian Theogony: A Comparative Study of Indian Mythology from the Vedas to the Purāṇas*. London: Cambridge University Press.

Bhattacharyya, N. N. (1991). *The Geographical Dictionary: Ancient and Early Medieval India*. New Delhi: Munshiram Manoharlal.

Biswas, A. (1985). *Indian Costumes*. New Delhi: Publications Division, Ministry of Information and Broadcasting, Government of India.

Böhtlingk, Otto, and Rudolph Roth. (1855–1875). *Sanskrit-Wörterbuch*. 7 vols. St. Petersburg: Kaiserlichen Akademie der Wissenschaften. Reprint in 7 vols., Osnabrück/Wiesbaden, 1966.

Brandis, Dietrich. (1874). *The Forest Flora of North-West and Central India: A Handbook of the Indigenous Trees and Shrubs of Those Countries*. Reprint Dehra Dun: Bishen Singh Mahendra Pal Singh, 1972.

———. (1906). *Indian Trees: An Account of Trees, Shrubs, Woody Climbers, Bamboos and Palms Indigenous or Commonly Cultivated in the British Indian Empire*. Reprint Dehra Dun: Bishen Singh Mahendra Pal Singh, 1971.

Brockington, John L. (1984). *Righteous Rāma: The Evolution of an Epic*. Delhi: Oxford University Press.

———. (1998). *The Sanskrit Epics*. Leiden: E. J. Brill.

———. (2006). " 'Then in his warlike wrath Rāma bent his bow': Weaponry of the Early *Rāmāyaṇa*." Paper presented at the Eighteenth World Sanskrit Conference, Edinburgh, Scotland, July 10–14, 2006.

Bühler, Georg, trans. (1886). *The Laws of Manu*. Reprint New York: Dover, 1969. Sacred Books of the East, Vol. 25.

Bulcke, Camille. (1959–1960). "The Characterization of Hanumān." *JOIB* 9, pp. 393–402.

———. (1960). "The Rāmāyaṇa: Its History and Character." *PO* 25 (January–October), pp. 36–66.

Cawthon Lang, Kristina A. (2005). "Primate Factsheets: Rhesus macaque (Macaca mulatta) Behavior." <http://pin.primate.wisc.edu/factsheets/entry/rhesus_macaque/behav>. Accessed September 16, 2006.

Chakravarti, P. C. (1941). *Art of War in Ancient India*. Dacca: University of Dacca. Reprint Delhi: Oriental Publishers, 1972.

Chattopadhyay, A. (1966). "Martial Life of Brahamans in Early Medieval India as Known from the Kathasaritsagara." *JOIB* 16.1, pp. 52–59.

Cowen, D. V. (1965). *Flowering Trees and Shrubs in India*. 4th rev. ed. Bombay: Thacker.

Dange, Sadashiv A. (1969). *Legends in the Mahābhārata*. Delhi: Motilal Banarsidass.

———. (1986–1990). *Encyclopaedia of Puranic Beliefs and Practices*. 5 vols. New Delhi: Navrang.

Dave, K. N. (1985). *Birds in Sanskrit Literature*. Delhi: Motilal Banarsidass.
Dey, Nundo Lal. (1927). *The Geographical Dictionary of Ancient and Mediaeval India*. 2nd ed. London: Luzac and Co. Calcutta Oriental Series, no. 21, E. 13.
Dikshitar, V. R. Ramachandra. (1934–1935). "Geographical Data." *Indian Culture*.
———. (1944). *War in Ancient India*. Madras: Macmillan.
———. (1951–1955). *The Purana Index*. 3 vols. Madras: University of Madras.
Doniger, Wendy, and Brian K. Smith, trans. (1991). *The Laws of Manu*. New York: Penguin Books.
Dutt, M. N., trans. (1893). See under Translations of the *Yuddhakāṇḍa*.
Dwyer, Rachel. (2006). *Filming the Gods*. London: Routledge.
Emeneau, Murray B. (1953). "The Composite Bow in India." *Proceedings of the American Philosophical Society* 99, pp. 77–87.
———. (1962). "Barkcloth in India—Sanskrit *valkala*." *JAOS* 82.2, pp. 161–70.
Fitzgerald, James L. (1998). "Some Storks and Eagles Eat Carrion; Herons and Ospreys Do Not: Kaṅkas and Kuraras (and Baḍas) in the *Mahābhārata*." *JAOS* 118.2, pp. 257–61.
Flack, J. C., et al. (2000a). "Being Nice Is Not a Building Block of Morality: Response to Commentary Discussion." *Journal of Consciousness Studies* 7:1–2, pp. 67–77.
———. (2000b). "'Any Animal Whatever': Darwinian Building Blocks of Morality in Monkeys and Apes." *Journal of Consciousness Studies* 7:1–2, pp. 1–29.
———. (2000c). "Patterns of Conflict Intervention and the Control Role in Pigtail Macaque Society." *American Journal of Primatology* 51 (suppl. 1), p. 57.
———. (2000d). "Power, Rank, Dominance Style, and the Silent Bared-Teeth Display in Pigtail Macaque Society." *American Journal of Primatology* 51 (suppl. 1), pp. 57–58.
Gerow, Edwin. (1971). *A Glossary of Indian Figures of Speech*. The Hague: Mouton.
Giteau, Madeleine. (1951). "Le barratage de l'Ocean." *Bulletin de la Société des Études Indochinoises* 26.1, p. 154.
Goldman, Robert P. (1977). *Gods, Priests, and Warriors: The Bhṛgus of the Mahābhārata*. New York: Columbia University Press.
———. (1980). "Rāmaḥ Sahalakṣmaṇaḥ: Psychological and Literary Aspects of the Composite Hero of Vālmīki's *Rāmāyaṇa*." *JIP* 8, pp. 149–89.
———. (1982). "Matricide, Renunciation and Compensation in the Legends of Two Warrior-Heroes of the Sanskrit Epics." In the volume of the Proceedings of the Stockholm Conference Seminar in Indological Studies. *Indologica Taurinensia* 10, pp. 117–31.
———. (1986). "A City of the Heart: Mathurā and the Indian Imagination." *JAOS* 106.3, pp. 471–83.
———. (1989). "Tracking the Elusive *Ṛkṣa:* The Tradition of Bears as Rāma's Allies in Various Versions of the Rāmakathā." *JAOS* 109.4, pp. 545–52.
———. (1993). "Transexualism, Gender, and Anxiety in Traditional India." *JAOS* 113.3, pp. 374–401.
———. (1997). "*Eṣa Dharmaḥ Sanātanaḥ*: Situational Ethics in the Epic Age." In *Relativism, Suffering and Beyond: Essays in Memory of Bimal K. Matilal*. Edited by P. Bilimoria and J. N. Mohanty. New Delhi: Oxford University Press, pp. 187–223.
———. (2000). "Rāvaṇa's Kitchen: A Testimony of Desire and the Other." In *Questioning Ramayanas: A South Asian Tradition*. Edited by Paula Richman. Berkeley

and Los Angeles: University of California Press, pp. 105–16; 374–76. Reprint Delhi: Oxford University Press.

———. (2003). "How Fast Do Monkeys Fly? How Long do Demons Sleep? Reading Commentaries on Sanskrit Epic Poetry as Windows to the Knowledge Systems of Pre-Modern South Asia." Paper presented at the South Asia Seminar, University of Chicago, October 16, 2003.

———. (2004). "Resisting Rāma: Dharmic Debates on Gender and Hierarchy and the Work of the *Vālmīki Rāmāyaṇa*." In *The Rāmāyaṇa Revisited*. Edited by Mandakranta Bose. New York: Oxford University Press, pp. 19–46.

———. (2006a). "The Spirit of the Age: Social Vision and Historical Perspective in the *Mahābhārata* and the *Vālmīkirāmāyaṇa*." In *Shrutimahatī* (R. K. Sharma Felicitation Volume). Delhi: Pratibha Prakashan.

———. (2006b). "How Fast Do Monkeys Fly? How Long Do Demons Sleep?" *Rivista di Studi Sudasiatici*, Rome, no. 1, pp. 185–207.

Goldman, Robert P., ed. and trans. (1984). *The Rāmāyaṇa of Vālmīki: An Epic of Ancient India*. Vol. I, *Bālakāṇḍa*. Introduction by Robert P. Goldman. Annotation by Robert P. Goldman and Sally J. Sutherland. Princeton, N. J.: Princeton University Press.

Goldman, Robert P., and Sally J. Sutherland Goldman. (1994). "Vālmīki's Hanumān: Characterization and Occluded Divinity." *Journal of Vaiṣṇava Studies* 2.4, pp. 31–54.

———. (2004). *Devavāṇīpraveśikā: An Introduction to the Sanskrit Language*. Berkeley: Center for South and Southeast Asian Studies. 3rd rev. ed. 1999, reprint with corrections 2004.

Goldman, Robert P., and Sally J. Sutherland Goldman, eds. and trans. (1996). *The Rāmāyaṇa of Vālmīki: An Epic of Ancient India*. Vol. V, *Sundarakāṇḍa*. Introduction and annotation by Robert P. Goldman and Sally J. Sutherland Goldman. Princeton, N.J.: Princeton University Press.

Goldman, Sally Sutherland (Sally J. Sutherland). (1992). "Suttee, Sati, and Sahagamana: An Epic Misunderstanding." University of Delhi, St. Stephen's College, Delhi, India. (First delivered at the Nineteenth Annual Conference on South Asia, Madison, Wisconsin, November 1990.)

———. (1996). "Soul Food: Eating, Conception, and Gender in the Literature of Premodern India." Paper presented at the annual meeting of the Association of Asian Studies, Honolulu, Hawaii, April 1996. Revised version, Annual Conference on South Asia, Madison, Wisconsin, October 1996.

———. (1999). "A Tale of Two Tales: The Episode of Hanumān's Childhood in the Critical Edition." *Purāṇa* 41.21, pp. 132–53; *JOIB* 48:1–4, pp. 51–57.

———. (2000). "Anklets Away: The Symbolism of Jewelry and Ornamentation in *Vālmīki's Rāmāyaṇa*." In *A Varied Optic: Contemporary Studies in the Ramayana*. Edited by Mandakranta Bose. Vancouver: Institute of Asian Studies, University of British Columbia, pp. 125–53. Reissued as *The Ramayana Culture: Text, Performance and Iconography*. Edited by Mandakranta Bose. New Delhi: D. K. Printworld, 2003.

———. (2001). "The Voice of Sītā in Vālmīki's *Sundarakāṇḍa*." In *Questioning Ramayanas: A South Asian Tradition*. Edited by Paula Richman. Berkeley and Los Angeles: University of California Press, pp. 223–38. Reprint Delhi: Oxford University Press.

———. (2003a). "Re-siting Sītā: Gender and Narrative in Vālmīki's *Sundarakāṇḍa*." *Purāṇa* 45.2, pp. 115–35.

———. (2003b). "Sītā's War: Gender and Narrative in the *Yuddhakāṇḍa* of Vālmīki's *Rāmāyaṇa*." Paper presented at the Twelfth World Sanskrit Conference, Helsinki, Finland, July 2003.

———. (2004a). "Gendered Narratives: Gender, Space, and Narrative Structures in Vālmīki's *Bālakāṇḍa*." In *The Ramayana Revisited*. Edited by Mandakranta Bose. New York: Oxford University Press, pp. 47–85.

———. (2004b). "Who's for Dinner?: Cannibalistic Urges in the *Mahābhārata*." Paper presented at the annual meeting of the American Oriental Society, San Diego, March 2004.

———. (2006a). "Illusory Evidence: *Māyā* in the *Yuddhakāṇḍa* of *Vālmīki's Rāmāyaṇa*." Paper presented at the annual meeting of the American Oriental Society, Seattle, Washington, March 2006.

———. (2006b). "Nikumbhilā's Grove: Rākṣasa Rites in *Vālmīki's Rāmāyaṇa*." Paper presented at the Eighteenth World Sanskrit Conference, Edinburgh, Scotland, July 2006.

———. (2006c). "Rākṣasīs and Other Others: The Archaic Mother in Bhāsa's *Madhyama-vyāyoga*." In *Shrutimahatī* (R. K. Sharma Felicitation Volume). Delhi: Pratibha Prakashan.

González-Reimann, Luis. (2006). "The Divinity of Rāma in the Rāmāyaṇa of Vālmīki." *JIP* 34.3, pp. 203–20.

Gorresio, Gaspare, ed. (1843–1867). See under Texts of the *Vālmīki Rāmāyaṇa*.

Gorresio, Gaspare, trans. (1853–1856). See under Translations of the *Yuddhakāṇḍa*.

Grassmann, Hermann. (1872). *Worterbuch zum Rig-Veda*. Reprint Wiesbaden: Otto Harrassowitz, 1964.

Grewal, Bikram. (2000). *Birds of the Indian Subcontinent*. Hong Kong: Local Color.

Griffith, Ralph T. H. (1870–1874). *The Ramayan of Valmiki, translated into English Verse*. 5 vols. London: Trübner.

Guruge, Ananda. (1960). *The Society of the Rāmāyaṇa*. Maharagama, Ceylon: Saman Press.

Hammer, Niels. (unpublished). "Why Sārus Cranes Epitomize Karuṇarasa in the Rāmāyaṇa."

Hara, Minoru. (1986). "The Holding of the Hair (Keśa grahana)." *Acta Orientalia* 47, pp. 67–92.

Hertel, Johannes, ed. (1908). *Das Pañcatantra: A Collection of Ancient Hindu Tales*. Cambridge, Mass.: Harvard University Press. Harvard Oriental Series, Vol. 12.

Hopkins, Edward Washburn. (1889). "The Social and Military Position of the Ruling Caste in Ancient India, as Represented by the Sanskrit Epic; with an Appendix on the Status of Women." *JAOS* 13, pp. 56–372. Reprint Varanasi: Bharat-Bharati Oriental Publishers and Booksellers, 1972.

———. (1902). "Time and Age in the Sanskrit Epic." *JAOS* 23, pp. 350–57.

———. (1903). "Epic Chronology." *JAOS* 24, pp. 7–56.

———. (1915). *Epic Mythology*. Grundriss der Indo-Arischen Philologie und Altertumskunde, Vol. 3, No. 1B. Strassburg: Karl J. Trübner. Reprint Delhi: Motilal Banarsidass, 1974.

———. (1932). "The Oath in the Hindu Epic." *JAOS* 52, pp. 316–33.

Hora, Sunder Lal. (1952). "Fish in the Rāmāyaṇa." *JAS* 18.2, pp. 63–69.

Ingalls, Daniel H. H. (1965). *An Anthology of Sanskrit Court Poetry: Vidyākara's Subhāṣitaratnakoṣa*. Cambridge, Mass.: Harvard University Press. Harvard Oriental Series, Vol. 44.

Jacob, G. A. (1907). *Laukikanyāyañjali: A Handful of Popular Maxims*. 2 vols. Bombay: Nirṇayasāgar Press. 2nd rev. ed.

Jacobi, Hermann. (1888). *Methods and Tables for Verifying Hindu Dates*. Bombay: Education Society's Press.

———. (1893). *Das Rāmāyaṇa: Geschichte und Inhalt, nebst Concordanz der gedruckten Recensionen*. Bonn: Friedrich Cohen.

Jhala, G. C., ed. (1966). *The Sundarakāṇḍa: The Fifth Book of the Vālmīki Rāmāyaṇa: The National Epic of India*. Baroda: Oriental Institute.

Jones, James. (1962). *The Thin Red Line*. New York: Scribner.

Kane, Pandurang V. (1941–1975). *History of Dharmaśāstra*. 8 vols. Poona: Bhandarkar Oriental Research Institute. Vol. 1, Pt. 1 (1968); Vol. 1, Pt. 2, 2nd ed. (1975); Vol. 2, Pt. 1, 1st ed. (1941), 2nd ed. (1974); Vol. 2, Pt. 2, 2nd ed. (1974); Vol. 3, 2nd ed. (1973); Vol. 4, 2nd ed. (1973); Vol. 5, Pt. 1, 2nd ed. (1974); Vol. 5, Pt. 2 (1962).

Kapadia, B. H. (1967). "Omens, Astrology, etc. in Mṛcchakaṭikam of Śūdraka." *JOIB* 16.3, pp. 233–38.

Keith, Arthur Berriedale. (1914). *The Veda of the Black Yajus School Entitled Taittirīya Sanhitā*. 2 vols. Cambridge, Mass.: Harvard Oriental Series, Vols. 18, 19.

———. (1925). *The Religion and Philosophy of the Veda and Upanishads*. Cambridge, Mass.: Harvard University Press. Harvard Oriental Series, Vols. 31, 32.

Kirfel, Willibald. (1920). *Die Kosmographie der Inder nach Quellen dargestellt*. Bonn-Leipzig: K. Schroeder. Reprint Hildersheim: Georg Olms, 1967.

Lassen, Christian. (1858–1874). *Indische Alterthumskunde*. 4 vols. Leipzig: Kittler, etc. Vol. 1 (1867); Vol. 2 (1874); Vol. 3 (1858); Vol. 4 (1861).

Law, Bimala Churn. (1944). *Mountains of India*. Calcutta: Calcutta Geographical Society.

———. (1954). *Historical Geography of Ancient India*. Paris: Société Asiatique de Paris.

Lee, J. S. (1961). "Archery in India." *Society of Archer-Antiquaries Journal* 4, pp. 19–22.

Lefeber, Rosalind, trans. (1994). *The Rāmāyaṇa of Vālmīki: An Epic of Ancient India*. Vol. IV, *Kiṣkindhākāṇḍa*. Edited by Robert P. Goldman. Princeton, N.J.: Princeton University Press.

Leslie, I. Julia. (1998). "A Bird Bereaved: The Identity and Significance of Vālmīki's Krauñca." *JIP* 26, pp. 455–87.

———. (1999). "The Implications of the Physical Body: Health, Suffering and Karma in Hindu Thought." In *Religion, Health and Suffering*. Edited by John R. Hinnells and R. Porter. London: Kegan Paul, pp. 23–45.

Lüders, Heinrich. (1940). *Philologica Indica*. Gottingen: Vandenhoeck and Ruprecht.

Lutgendorf, Philip. (2007). *Hanuman's Tale: The Messages of a Divine Monkey*. New York: Oxford University Press.

Macdonell, Arthur Anthony. (1897). *Vedic Mythology*. Strassburg: Karl J. Trübner. Edited by Georg Bühler. Grundriss der Indo-Arischen Philologie und Altertumskunde, III Band, 1. Heft A.

Macdonell, Arthur Anthony, and Arthur Berriedale Keith. (1967). *Vedic Index of Names and Subjects*. Delhi: Motilal Banarsidass.

Maestripieri, D. (1999a). "The Biology of Human Parenting: Insights from Nonhuman Primates." *Neuroscience and Biobehavioral Reviews* 23.3, pp. 411–22.

———. (1999b). "Changes in Social Behavior and Their Hormonal Correlates during Pregnancy in Pig-Tailed Macaques." *International Journal of Primatology* 20.5, pp. 707–18.

———. (1999c). "Consistency and Change in the Behavior of Rhesus Macaque Abusive Mothers with Successive Infants." *Developmental Psychobiology* 34.1, pp. 29–35.

———. (1999d). "Fatal Attraction: Interest in Infants and Infant Abuse in Rhesus Macaques." *American Journal of Physical Anthropology* 110.1, pp. 17–25.

———. (1999e). "Formal Dominance: The Emperor's New Clothes?" *Journal of Comparative Psychology* 113.1, pp. 96–98.

———. (1999f). "Primate Social Organization, Gestural Repertoire Size, and Communication Dynamics: A Comparative Study of Macaques." In *The Origins of Language: What Nonhuman Primates Can Tell Us*. Edited by J. B. King. Santa Fe: School of American Research Press, pp. 55–77.

Majumdar, Bimal Kanti. (1955). *The Military System in Ancient India*. Calcutta: World Press.

Mani, Vettam. (1975). *Purāṇic Index*. Delhi: Motilal Banarsidass.

Mayrhofer, Manfred. (1956–1980). *Kurzgefasstes etymologisches Wörterbuch des Altindischen*. 4 vols. Heidelberg: C. Winter.

Meister, Michael, et al. (1988). *Encyclopaedia of Indian Temple Architecture*. Vol. 2, *North India: Foundations of North Indian Style*. New Delhi: American Institute of Indian Studies. Princeton, N.J.: Princeton University Press.

Monier-Williams, Monier. (1899). *A Sanskrit-English Dictionary*. Oxford: Oxford University Press. Reprint 1964.

Morgenstern, Joseph. (2000). "The Thin Red Line." In *Screening Violence*. Edited by Steven Prince. New Brunswick, N.J.: Rutgers University Press, pp. 47–50.

Mumme, Patricia Y. (1991). "*Rāmāyaṇa* Exegesis in *Teṅkalai Śrīvaiṣṇavism*." In *Many Rāmāyaṇas: The Diversity of a Narrative Tradition in South Asia*. Edited by Paula Richman. Berkeley and Los Angeles: University of California Press, pp. 202–16.

Narayan, Pande Syam. (1980). *Geographical Horizon of the Mahābhārata*. Varanasi: Bharata Bharati.

O'Flaherty, Wendy Doniger. (1971). "The Submarine Mare in the Mythology of Śiva." *JRAS* 1, pp. 9–27.

———. (1975). *Hindu Myths*. Middlesex, England: Penguin Books.

Oldenberg, Hermann. (1894). *Die Religion des Veda*. Translated by Shridhar B. Shrotri. Reprint Delhi: Motilal Banarsidass, 1988.

Omprakash. (1961). *Food and Drinks in Ancient India*. Delhi: Munshiram Manoharlal.

———. (1987). *Economy and Food in Ancient India*. 2 vols. Delhi: Bharatiya Vidya Prakashan.

Oppert, Gustav. (1880). *On the Weapons, Army Organisation, and Political Maxims of the Ancient Hindus, with Special Reference to Gunpowder and Firearms*. Madras: Higgenbothem. Reprint Ahmedabad: New Order Book Co., 1967.

Pagani, Brigitte. (1999). See under Translations of the *Yuddhakāṇḍa*.
Pillai, Swamikannu, L. D. (Lewis Dominic). (1922). *An Indian ephemeris, A.D. 700 to A.D. 1799, showing the daily solar and lunar reckoning according to the principal systems current in India, with their English equivalents, also the ending moments of tithis and nakshatras and the years in different eras, A.D., Hijra, Saka, Vikrama, Kaliyuga, Kollam etc., with a perpetual planetary almanac and other auxiliary tables*. Reprint Delhi: Agam 1982.
———. (1922–1923). *An Indian Ephemeris, A.D. 700 to A.D. 1999*. 7 vols. Madras: Government Press.
Pingree, David, ed. and trans. (1978). *The Yavanajātaka of Sphujidhvaja*. 2 vols. Cambridge, Mass.: Harvard University Press. Harvard Oriental Series, Vol. 48.
Pollock, Sheldon. (1984a). "The *Rāmāyaṇa* Text and the Critical Edition." In *The Rāmāyaṇa of Vālmīki: An Epic of Ancient India*. Vol. I, *Bālakāṇḍa*. Introduction by Robert P. Goldman. Annotation by Robert P. Goldman and Sally J. Sutherland. Princeton, N.J.: Princeton University Press, pp. 82–93.
———. (1984b). "The Divine King in the Indian Epic." *JAOS* 104, pp. 505–28.
———. (1996). "The Sanskrit Cosmopolis, 300–1300: Transculturation, Vernacularization and the Question of Ideology." In *The Ideology and Status of Sanskrit*. Edited by Jan E.M. Houben. Leiden: E. J. Brill, pp. 197–247.
———, trans. (1986). *The Rāmāyaṇa of Vālmīki: An Epic of Ancient India*. Vol. II, *Ayodhyākāṇḍa*. Edited by Robert P. Goldman. Introduction and annotation by Sheldon Pollock. Princeton, N.J.: Princeton University Press.
———. (1991). *The Rāmāyaṇa of Vālmīki: An Epic of Ancient India*. Vol. III, *Araṇyakāṇḍa*. Edited by Robert P. Goldman. Introduction and annotation by Sheldon Pollock. Princeton, N.J.: Princeton University Press.
Preuschoft, S., et al. (2000). "Dominance Style or Phylogenetic Affiliation: What Predicts the Social Functions of Affiliative Facial Displays in Pigtailed Macaques." *American Journal of Primatology* 51 (suppl. 1), pp. 82–83.
Prince, Steven. (1998). *Savage Cinema: Sam Peckinpah and the Rise of Ultraviolent Movies*. Austin: University of Texas Press.
———, ed. (2000a). *Screening Violence*. New Brunswick, N.J.: Rutgers University Press.
———. (2000b). "Graphic Violence in the Cinema: Origins, Aesthetic Design, and Social Effects." In *Screening Violence*. Edited by Steven Prince. New Brunswick, N.J.: Rutgers University Press, pp. 1–46.
———. (2000c). "The Aesthetic of Slow-Motion Violence in the Films of Sam Peckinpah." In *Screening Violence*. Edited by Steven Prince. New Brunswick, N.J.: Rutgers University Press, pp. 175–204.
———. (2003). *Classical Film Violence: Designing and Regulating Brutality in Hollywood Cinema, 1930–1968*. New Brunswick, N.J.: Rutgers University Press.
Raghunathan, N., trans. (1982). See under Translations of the *Yuddhakāṇḍa*.
Rao, T. A. Gopinatha. (1914). *Elements of Hindu Iconography*. 2 vols. Madras: The Law Printing House. Reprint Delhi: Motilal Banarsidass, 1985.
Renou, Louis. (1954). *Vocabulaire du Rituel Védique*. Paris: Librairie C. Klincksieck.
Roussel, Alfred, trans. (1903). See under Translations of the *Yuddhakāṇḍa*.
Ruben, Walter. (1936). *Studien zur Textgeschichte des Rāmāyaṇa*. Stuttgart: Verlag W. Kohlhammer.

Sahay, Sachidanand. (1975). *Indian Costume, Coiffure and Ornament*. New Delhi: Munshiram Manoharlal.

Salomon, Richard. (1998). *Indian Epigraphy: A Guide to the Study of Inscriptions in Sanskrit, Prakrit, and the Other Indo-Aryan Languages*. New York: Oxford University Press.

Sankalia, H. D. (1973). *Ramayana: Myth or Reality?* New Delhi: People's Publishing House.

Sarkar, Jagadish Narayan. (1984). *The Art of War in Medieval India*. New Dehli: Munshiram Manoharlal.

Seely, Clinton, trans. (2004). *The Slaying of Meghanada: A Ramayana from Colonial Bengal*. Translation of Michael Madhusudhan Datta's *Meghanadabadha kabya*. New York: Oxford University Press.

Sensarma, P. (1979). *Military Wisdom in the Purāṇas*. Calcutta: Naya Prakash.

Sharma, Ramashraya. (1971). *A Socio-Political Study of the Vālmīki Rāmāyaṇa*. Delhi: Motilal Banarsidass.

Sharma, Ram Karan. (1964). *Elements of Poetry in the Mahābhārata*. Berkeley and Los Angeles: University of California Press.

Sharma, S. K. (1996). "Vidyā, Veda: Their Genesis, Scope, and Illustration." In *Education in Ancient India*. Shri S. B. Velankar Felicitation Volume. Edited by Vijay V. Bedekar. Thane: Itihas Patrika Prakashan, pp. 23–47.

Shastri, Hari Prasad, trans. (1952–1959). See under Translations of the *Yuddhakāṇḍa*.

Shukla, R. K. (2003). *The Geography of the Rāmāyaṇa*. Delhi: Koshal Book Depot.

Singh, Sarva Daman. (1965). *Ancient Indian Warfare, with special reference to the Vedic period*. Leiden: E. J. Brill.

Slatin, Patricia. (2006). "Heroes on an Indo-European Beach? Reflections on Studies by David A. Krooks and Alain Renoir." *Interdisciplinary Journal for Germanic Linguistic and Semiotic Analysis* 11.2, pp. 137–61.

Smith, William. (1988). *Rāmāyaṇa Traditions in Eastern India*. Stockholm: Department of Indology, Stockholm University.

Sobchack, Vivian C. (2000). "The Violent Dance: A Personal Memoir of Death in the Movies." In *Screening Violence*. Edited by Steven Prince. New Brunswick, N. J.: Rutgers University Press, pp. 110–24.

Sternbach, Ludwik. (1965–1967). *The Juridical Studies in Ancient Indian Law*. 2 vols. Delhi: Motilal Banarsidass.

———. (1967). *Cāṇakyanīti Text Tradition*. 2 vols. Hoshiapur: Vishveshvaranand Vedic Research Institute.

Sutherland, Sally J. (Sally J. Sutherland Goldman). (1979). "Śukrācārya the Demons' Priest: Aspects of Character Development in Sanskrit Mythological Literature." Ph.D. dissertation. University of California, Berkeley.

———. (1989). "Draupadi and Sītā: Aggressive Behavior and Female Role-Models." *JAOS* 109.1, pp. 63–67.

———. (1992). "The Text Which Is No Text: Critical Edition as Text." In *Translation East and West: A Cross-Cultural Approach, Selected Conference Papers*. Edited by Cornelia N. Moore and Lucy Lower. Honolulu: East West Center, University of Hawaii at Manoa, pp. 82–92.

Swamikannu Pillai, Lewis Dominic. See Pillai, Swamikannu, L. D. (Lewis Dominic).

Te Nijenhuis, Emmie. (1970). *Dattilam: A Compendium of Ancient Indian Music*. Introduction, translation, and commentary. Leiden: E. J. Brill.

———. (1974). *Indian Music: History and Structure*. Leiden: E. J. Brill.

Thieme, Paul. (1975). "Kranich und Reiher im Sanskrit." In *Studien zur Indologie und Iranistik* 1, pp. 3–36.

Tubb, Gary. (2006). "If You Don't Mind: *bhadraṃ te* in the Sanskrit Epics." Paper presented at the annual meeting of the American Oriental Society, Seattle, Washington, March 2006.

Vaidya, Parashuram Lakshman, ed. (1971). *The Yuddhakāṇḍa: The Sixth Book of the Vālmīki Rāmāyaṇa: The National Epic of India*. Baroda: Oriental Institute.

Vyas, S. N. (1967). *India in the Rāmāyaṇa Age*. Delhi: Atma Ram and Sons.

White, David Gordon. (1996). *The Alchemical Body: Siddha Traditions in Medieval India*. Chicago: University of Chicago Press.

———. (2003). *Kiss of the Yogini: "Tantric Sex" in Its South Asian Contexts*. Chicago: University of Chicago Press.

Whitney, William Dwight. (1889). *A Sanskrit Grammar: Including Both the Classical Language, and the Older Dialects, of Veda and Brahmana*. Cambridge, Mass.: Harvard University Press. Reprint 1967.

Wilhelm, Friedrich. (1960). *Politische Polemiken im Staatslehrbuch des Kauṭalya*. Wiesbaden: O. Harrassowitz.

Wilson, H. H., trans. (1864–1877). *The Vishṇu Purāṇa: A System of Hindu Mythology and Tradition*. 5 vols. Edited by Fitzedward Hall. London: Trübner and Co.

Yule, Henry, and A. C. Burnell. (1903). *Hobson-Jobson: A glossary of colloquial Anglo-Indian words and phrases, and of kindred terms, etymological, historical, geographical and discursive*. London: J. Murray. 2nd ed., edited by William Crooke. Delhi: Munshiram Manoharlal, 1968.

Index

wrist and finger guards, 596–97, 1148. *See also* armguards

Yadvābhaṭṭa: a derisive term for Govindarāja, 590, 966, 1240
Yajñakopa, 139, 1213; fights Rāma, 206; Rāma kills, 208
Yajñaśatru: Rāma shoots, 211
yakṣas, 121; Kubera associated with, 1017–18, 1138, 1158; Kubera ruler of, 127, 522, 1017–18, 1138; Kumbhakarṇa crushes, 269; Kumbhakarṇa's lance kills, 282; Rāvaṇa invulnerable to, 262
Yama, 23; as *antaka*, "ender of all things," 172, 241, 252, 253, 290, 306, 311, 386–87, 396, 522, 668, 843, 851, 975, 1003, 1005, 1034, 1043, 1242, 1293; arrows of, Rāvaṇa likened to, 253; compared to Hanumān, 241; —to Triśiras, 311; Death as, 1198; Kumbhakarṇa compared to, 268; 285; 290; noose of, 843, 975, 1443; Rāvaṇa compared to, 252; Rāvaṇa defeats, 137. See also *antaka*; Death; Mṛtyu
Yamunā, 5, 474, 477, 1488, 1490
yātudhāna, 126, 202, 253, 264, 292, 305, 444, 1032, 1085; Sumāli, name of a, 1397; as synonym for *rākṣasa*, 881; type of *rākṣasa*, 515, 751
Yogamāyā: foretells the destruction of Kaṃsa, 575
yojana(s), 533, 541, 543, 642, 651, 1113; distance of Hanumān's search in, 1103; —of sun from earth in, 649–50; —Sugrīva hurls Kumbha, 1134; length of bridge to Laṅkā in, 619–20; —of Hanumān's jump to capture the sun in, 649–50; measurement of, 1500–1501; —Kumbhakarṇa's residence in, 913; —Laṅkā in, 731; speed of sun in, per half-second 1347
yoke pole. *See* chariots
Yuddhakāṇḍa, 17, 34; action in, 17; annular structure of, 18, 96; characterization in, 43–88; cinematic quality of narrative of, 17, 44, 90–95; chronology of (*see* chronology of the epic); completes circle of story begun in the *Ayodhyākāṇḍa*, 41, 96; complexity of, 43; epithets, patronymics, kennings, and synonyms in, 109–10; extent of, in northern recension, 497, 626; grand scope of, 44; large number of characters in, 44; length of, 3, 43; as mini-epic, 96; narrative consistency of, 663, 942; — *sarga* divisions in, 1327, 1363; oral nature of, 94, 109; *phalaśruti* of, 96–97 (see also *phalaśruti*); political and social impact of, 42; reminiscent of *Ayodhyākāṇḍa*, 28; sequence of text of, 1387–88; setting of, as beyond human habitation, 43; shifting scene of, 44, 94–95; similarity of, to battle books of *Mahābhārata*, 19; style and structure of, 89–98; synopsis of, 7–16; themes of, 17–42, 89; time frame of, 7, 17 (*see also* chronology of the epic); titles of, 18; translations of, 112–18; use of animal names in, 110–11; visual elements in, 89–90, 94; vulgate text of, 114–15; weapons in, 111 (*see also* weapons; *Glossary of Weapons*). *See also* critical edition of *Yuddhakāṇḍa*
yugas (cosmic ages), 285, 334, 397, 754, 906, 1287; blazing meteors at end of, 424, 906; clouds at end of, 289; *dvāpara*, 1400–1401, 1416–47; fire at end of, 23, 153, 294, 312, 317, 342, 347, 367, 387, 397, 414, 424, 437, 482, 983, 1221; immutable progression of, 708; *kali* (*tiṣya*): 33, 186, 708; *kṛta* (golden age), 707–8; relative strength of *dharma* and *adharma* in, 707–8; specific characteristics of, 707–8; sun at end of, 398, 425; winds at end of, 203, 401, 412, 754, 1278. *See also* golden age
Yūpākṣa, 925, 1115, 1122–24, 1126, 1132, 1141, 1270; addresses Kumbhakarṇa, 266–67; minister of